S0-BRQ-046

CONCISE MAJOR 21ST-CENTURY WRITERS

CONCISE MAJOR 21ST-CENTURY WRITERS

A Selection of Sketches from *Contemporary Authors*

Tracey L. Matthews, Project Editor

Volume 4: Mc-Sa

Detroit • New York • San Francisco • New Haven, Conn. • Waterville, Maine • London • Munich

Concise Major 21st-Century Writers

Project Editor
Tracey L. Matthews

Editorial
Michelle Kazensky, Josh Kondek, Lisa Kumar, Julie Mellors, Joyce Nakamura, Mary Ruby

Composition and Electronic Capture
Carolyn A. Roney

Manufacturing
Rita Wimberley

For more information, contact
Thomson Gale
27500 Drake Rd.
Farmington Hills, MI 48331-3535
Or you can visit our internet site at
http://www.gale.com

Library of Congress Control Number: 2006929297

ISBN 0-7876-7539-3 (hardcover : set), ISBN 0-7876-7540-7 (v. 1), ISBN 0-7876-7541-5 (v. 2), ISBN 0-7876-7542-3 (v. 3), ISBN 0-7876-7543-1 (v. 4), ISBN 0-7876-7544-X (v. 5)

Printed in the United States of America
10 9 8 7 6 5 4 3 2 1

Contents

Introduction

Concise Major 21st-Century Writers (*CMTFCW*) is an abridgement of the 2004 eBook-only edition of Thomson Gale's *Major 21st-Century Writers* (*MTFCW*), a set based on Thomson Gale's award-winning *Contemporary Authors* series. *CMTFCW* provides students, educators, librarians, researchers, and general readers with a concise yet comprehensive source of biographical and bibliographical information on 700 of the most influential and studied authors at the turn of the twenty-first century as well as emerging authors whose literary significance is likely to increase in the coming decades.

CMTFCW includes sketches on approximately 700 authors who made writing literature their primary occupation and who have had at least part of their oeuvre published in English. Thus novelists, short story writers, nonfiction writers, poets, dramatists, genre writers, children's writers, and young adult writers of about sixty nationalities and ethnicities are represented. Selected sketches of authors that appeared in the 2004 edition of *MTFCW* are completely updated to include information on their lives and works through 2006. About thirty authors featured in *CMTFCW* are new to this set evidencing Thomson Gale's commitment to identifying emerging writers of recent eras and of many cultures.

How Authors Were Chosen for *CMTFCW*

The preliminary list of authors for *MTFCW* was sent to an advisory board of librarians, teaching professionals, and writers whose input resulted in informal inclusion criteria. In consultation with the editors, the list was narrowed to 700 authors for the concise edition plus criteria were established for adding authors. Criteria our editors used for adding authors not previously published in the last edition of *MTFCW* include:

- Authors who have won major awards
- Authors whose works are bestsellers
- Authors whose works are being incorporated into curricula and studied at the high school and/or college level

Broad Coverage in a Single Source

CMTFCW provides detailed biographical and bibliographical coverage of the most influential writers of our time, including:

- *Contemporary Literary Figures*: Mitch Albom, Sherman Alexie, Maya Angelou, Margaret Atwood, Dan Brown, Michael Chabon, J.M. Coetzee, Don DeLillo, Joan Didion, Dave Eggers, Gabriel Garcia Marquez, Nadine Gordimer, Khaled Hosseini, Toni Morrison, Joyce Carol Oates, Thomas Pynchon, J.K. Rowling, Salman Rushdie, Amy Tan, and John Updike, among many others.

- *Genre Writers*: Ray Bradbury, Tom Clancy, Philip K. Dick, Neil Gaiman, Sue Grafton, Dennis Lehane, Stephen King, Walter Mosley, Christopher Paolini, Anne Rice, Nora Roberts, Art Spiegelman, and Jane Yolen, among many others.

- *Novelists and Short Story Writers*: James Baldwin, Charles Baxter, Peter Carey, Carlos Fuentes, Graham Greene, Sebastian Junger, Sue Monk Kidd, John le Carré, Yann Martel, Rick Moody, Chuck Palahniuk, and Zadie Smith, among many others.

- *Dramatists*: Edward Albee, Samuel Beckett, Athol Fugard, Tony Kushner, David Mamet, Arthur Miller, Neil Simon, Tom Stoppard, Wendy Wasserstein, Alfred Uhry, Paula Vogel, and Tennessee Williams, among many others.

- *Poets*: Gwendolyn Brooks, Allen Ginsburg, Louise Glück, Jorie Graham, Seamus Heaney, Ted Kooser, Mary Oliver, Kenneth Rexroth, Adrienne Rich, Derek Walcott, and C.K. Williams, among many others.

How Entries Are Organized

Each *CMTFCW* biography begins with a series of rubrics that outlines the author's personal history, including information on the author's birth, death, family life, education, career, memberships, and awards. The *Writings* section lists a bibliography of the author's works along with the publisher and year published. The *Sidelights* section provides a biographical portrait of the author's development; information about the critical reception of the author's works; and revealing comments, often by the author, on personal interests, motivations, and thoughts on writing. The *Biographical/Critical Sources* section features a useful list of books, articles, and reviews about the author and his or her work. This section also includes citations for all material quoted in the *Sidelights* essay.

Other helpful sections include *Adaptations*, which lists the author's works that have been adapted by others into various media, including motion pictures, stage plays, and television or radio broadcasts, while the *Work in Progress* section lists titles or descriptions of works that are scheduled for publication by the author.

Using the Indexes

CMTFCW features a Nationality/Ethnicity index as well as a Subject/Genre index. More than sixty nations are represented in the Nationality/Ethnicity index, reflecting the international scope of this set and the multinational status of many authors. The Subject/Genre index covers over fifty genres and subject areas of fiction and nonfiction frequently referenced by educators and students, including social and political literature, environmental issues, and science fiction/science fantasy literature.

Citing *CMTFCW*

Students writing papers who wish to include references to information found in *CMTFCW* may cite sources in their bibliographies using the following format. Teachers adhering to other bibliographic formats may request that their students alter the citation below, which should only serve as a guide:

"Margaret Atwood." *Concise Major 21st-Century Writers.* Ed. Tracey L. Matthews. Detroit: Thomson Gale, 2006, pp. 214-223.

Comments Are Appreciated

CMTFCW is intended to serve as a useful reference tool for a wide audience, so your comments about this work are encouraged. Suggestions for authors to include in future editions of *CMTFCW* are also welcome. Send comments and suggestions to: *Concise Major 21st-Century Writers*, Thomson Gale, 27500 Drake Rd., Farmington Hills, MI 48331-3535; call at 1-248-699-4253; or fax at 1-248-699-8070.

Concise Major 21st-Century Writers Advisory Board

In preparation for the first edition of *Major 20th-Century Writers* (*MTCW*), the editors of *Contemporary Authors* conducted a telephone survey of librarians and mailed a survey to more than 4,000 libraries to help determine the kind of reference resource the libraries wanted. Once it was clear that a comprehensive, yet affordable source of information on twentieth-century writers was needed to serve small and medium-sized libraries, a wide range of resources was consulted: national surveys of books taught in American high schools and universities; British secondary school syllabi; reference works such as the *New York Library Desk Reference, Reading Lists for College-Bound Students: The Books Most Recommended by America's Top Colleges, The List of Books, E.D. Hirsch's Cultural Legacy*, and volumes in Thomson Gale's Literacy Criticism and Dictionary of Literary Biography series. From these resources and with advice of an international advisory board, the author list for the first edition of *MTCW* was finalized, the sketches edited, and the volume published.

For the eBook edition of *Major 21st-Century Writers* (*MTFCW*), the editors compiled a preliminary author list based largely upon a list of authors included in the second print edition of *MTCW* with recommendations based on new inclusion criteria. This list was sent to an advisory board of librarians, authors, and teaching professionals in both the United States and Britain. In addition to vetting the submitted list, the advisors suggested other noteworthy writers. Recommendations made by the advisors ensure that authors from all nations and genres are represented.

Concise Major 21st-Century Writers (*CMTFCW*) is an abridgement of the eBook-only edition of *MTFCW*. The editors built upon the work of past advisors of the eBook edition to create a concise version and added authors who have earned increased recognition since the publication of *MTFCW*. The advisory board for *MTFCW* played a major role in shaping the author list for *CMTFCW*, and the editors wish to thank them for sharing their expertise. The twenty-seven member advisory board includes the following individuals:

- **Carl Antonucci,** Director of Library Services, Capital Community College, Hartford, Connecticut
- **Barbara Bibel,** Reference Librarian, Oakland Public Library, Oakland, California
- **Beverly A. Buciak,** Librarian, Brother Rice High School, Chicago, Illinois
- **Mary Ann Capan,** District Library Media Specialist, Sherrard Jr. Sr. High School, Sherrard, Illinois
- **Linda Carvell,** Head Librarian, Lancaster Country Day School, Lancaster, Pennsylvania
- **Anne Christensen,** Librarian II, Phoenix Public Library, Phoenix, Arizona
- **Peggy Curran,** Adult Services Librarian, Naperville Public Library, Naperville, Illinois
- **Eva M. Davis,** Youth Services Manager, Ann Arbor District Library, Ann Arbor, Michigan
- **Thomas Eertmoed,** Librarian, Illinois Central College, East Peoria, Illinois
- **Lucy K. Gardner,** Director, Howard Community College, Columbia, Maryland

- **Christine C. Godin,** Director of Learning Resources, Northwest Vista College, San Antonio, Texas
- **Francisca Goldsmith,** Senior Librarian, Berkeley Public Library, Berkeley, California
- **Nancy Guidry,** Reference Librarian, Bakersfield College, Bakersfield, California
- **Jack Hicks,** Administrative Librarian, Deerfield Public Library, Deerfield, Illinois
- **Charlie Jones,** School Library Media Specialist, Plymouth High School Library Media Center, Canton, Michigan
- **Carol M. Keeler,** Upper School Media Specialist, Detroit Country Day School, Beverly Hills, Michigan
- **Georgia Lomax,** Managing Librarian, King County Library System, Covington, Washington
- **Mary Jane Marden,** Librarian, M.M. Bennett Library, St. Petersburg College, Pinellas Park, Florida
- **Frances Moffett,** Materials Selector, Fairfax County Public Library, Chantilly, Virginia
- **Ruth Mormon,** Upper School Librarian, The Meadows School, Las Vegas, Nevada
- **Bonnie Morris,** Upper School Media Specialist, Minnehaha Academy, Minneapolis, Minneapolis
- **Nancy Pinkston,** English Teacher, Sherrard Jr. Sr. High School, Sherrard, Illinois
- **Robert Reginald,** Head of Technical Services and Collection Development, California State University, San Bernadino, California
- **Janet P. Sarratt,** Library Media Specialist, John E. Ewing Middle School, Gaffney, South Carolina
- **Brian Stableford,** 0.5 Lecturer in Creative Writing, University College, Winchester (formerly King Alfred's College), Reading, England
- **Stephen Weiner,** Director, Maynard Public Library, Maynard, Massachusetts
- **Hope Yelich,** Reference Librarian, College of William and Mary, Williamsburg, Virginia

Concise Major 21st-Century Writers

VOLUME 1: A-Cl

Abbey, Edward 1927-1989

Abe, Kobo 1924-1993

Achebe, Chinua 1930-

Ackroyd, Peter 1949-

Adams, Alice 1926-1999

Adams, Douglas 1952-2001

Affabee, Eric
See Stine, R.L.

Aghill, Gordon
See Silverberg, Robert

Albee, Edward 1928-

Albom, Mitch 1958-

Aldiss, Brian W. 1925-

Aldrich, Ann
See Meaker, Marijane

Alegría, Claribel 1924-

Alexie, Sherman 1966-

Allan, John B.
See Westlake, Donald E.

Allen, Paula Gunn 1939-

Allen, Roland
See Ayckbourn, Alan

Allende, Isabel 1942-

Allison, Dorothy E. 1949-

Alvarez, A. 1929-

Alvarez, Julia 1950-

Amado, Jorge 1912-2001

Ambrose, Stephen E. 1936-2002

Amichai, Yehuda 1924-2000

Amis, Kingsley 1922-1995

Amis, Martin 1949-

Anand, Mulk Raj 1905-2004

Anaya, Rudolfo A. 1937-

Anderson, Laurie Halse 1961-

Anderson, Poul 1926-2001

Andrews, Elton V.
See Pohl, Frederik

Angelou, Maya 1928-

Anouilh, Jean 1910-1987

Anthony, Peter
See Shaffer, Peter

Anthony, Piers 1934-

Archer, Jeffrey 1940-

Archer, Lee
See Ellison, Harlan

Ard, William
See Jakes, John

Arenas, Reinaldo 1943-1990

Arias, Ron 1941-

Arnette, Robert
See Silverberg, Robert

Aronson, Marc 1948-

Ashbery, John 1927-

Ashbless, William
See Powers, Tim

Asimov, Isaac 1920-1992

Atwood, Margaret 1939-

Axton, David
See Koontz, Dean R.

Ayckbourn, Alan 1939-

Bachman, Richard
See King, Stephen

Bainbridge, Beryl 1934-

Baker, Nicholson 1957-

Baker, Russell 1925-

Baldacci, David 1960-

Baldwin, James 1924-1987

Ballard, J.G. 1930-

Bambara, Toni Cade 1939-1995

Banat, D.R.
See Bradbury, Ray

Banks, Iain M. 1954-

Banks, Russell 1940-

Baraka, Amiri 1934-

Barclay, Bill
See Moorcock, Michael

Barclay, William Ewert
See Moorcock, Michael

Barker, Clive 1952-

Barnes, Julian 1946-

Baron, David
See Pinter, Harold

Barrington, Michael
See Moorcock, Michael

Barthelme, Donald 1931-1989

Bashevis, Isaac
See Singer, Isaac Bashevis

Bass, Kingsley B., Jr.
See Bullins, Ed

Baxter, Charles 1947-

Beagle, Peter S. 1939-

Beattie, Ann 1947-

Beauvoir, Simone de 1908-1986

Beckett, Samuel 1906-1989

Beldone, Phil "Cheech"
See Ellison, Harlan

Bell, Madison Smartt 1957-

Bellow, Saul 1915-2005

Benchley, Peter 1940-2006

Benitez, Sandra 1941-

Berendt, John 1939-

Berger, Thomas 1924-

Berry, Jonas
See Ashbery, John

Berry, Wendell 1934-

Bethlen, T.D.
See Silverberg, Robert

Binchy, Maeve 1940-

Bird, Cordwainer
See Ellison, Harlan

Birdwell, Cleo
See DeLillo, Don

Blade, Alexander
See Silverberg, Robert

Blais, Marie-Claire 1939-

Bliss, Frederick
See Card, Orson Scott

Block, Francesca Lia 1962-

Bloom, Amy 1953-

Blount, Roy, Jr. 1941-

Blue, Zachary
See Stine, R.L.

Blume, Judy 1938-

Bly, Robert 1926-

Boland, Eavan 1944-

Böll, Heinrich 1917-1985

Boot, William
See Stoppard, Tom

Borges, Jorge Luis 1899-1986

Bowles, Paul 1910-1999

Box, Edgar
See Vidal, Gore

Boyle, Mark
See Kienzle, William X.

Boyle, T. Coraghessan 1948-

Brackett, Peter
See Collins, Max Allan

Bradbury, Edward P.
See Moorcock, Michael

Bradbury, Ray 1920-

Bradley, Marion Zimmer 1930-1999

Bragg, Rick 1959-

Brashares, Ann 1967-

Breslin, Jimmy 1930-

Brink, André 1935-

Brodsky, Iosif Alexandrovich 1940-1996

Brodsky, Joseph
See Brodsky, Iosif Alexandrovich

Brodsky, Yosif
See Brodsky, Iosif Alexandrovich

Brookner, Anita 1928-

Brooks, Cleanth 1906-1994

Brooks, Gwendolyn 1917-2000

Brooks, Terry 1944-

Brown, Dan 1964-

Brown, Dee Alexander 1908-2002

Brown, Rita Mae 1944-

Brown, Sterling Allen 1901-1989

Brownmiller, Susan 1935-

Bruchac, Joseph, III 1942-

Bryan, Michael
See Moore, Brian

Buckley, William F., Jr. 1925-

Buechner, Frederick 1926-

Bukowski, Charles 1920-1994

Bullins, Ed 1935-

Burke, Ralph
See Silverberg, Robert

Burns, Tex
See L'Amour, Louis

Busiek, Kurt

Bustos, F.
See Borges, Jorge Luis

Butler, Octavia E. 1947-2006

Butler, Robert Olen 1945-

Byatt, A.S. 1936-

Cabrera Infante, Guillermo 1929-2005

Cade, Toni
See Bambara, Toni Cade

Cain, G.
See Cabrera Infante, Guillermo

Caldwell, Erskine 1903-1987

Calisher, Hortense 1911-

Calvino, Italo 1923-1985

Camp, John 1944-

Campbell, Bebe Moore 1950-

Capote, Truman 1924-1984

Card, Orson Scott 1951-

Carey, Peter 1943-

Carroll, James P. 1943-

Carroll, Jonathan 1949-

Carruth, Hayden 1921-

Carter, Nick
See Smith, Martin Cruz

Carver, Raymond 1938-1988

Cavallo, Evelyn
See Spark, Muriel

Cela, Camilo José 1916-2002

Cela y Trulock, Camilo José
See Cela, Camilo José

Cesaire, Aimé 1913-

Chabon, Michael 1963-

Chang, Iris 1968-2004

Chapman, Lee
See Bradley, Marion Zimmer

Chapman, Walker
See Silverberg, Robert

Charby, Jay
See Ellison, Harlan

Chávez, Denise 1948-

Cheever, John 1912-1982

Chevalier, Tracy 1962-

Childress, Alice 1920-1994

Chomsky, Noam 1928-

Cisneros, Sandra 1954-

Cixous, Hélène 1937-

Clancy, Tom 1947-

Clark, Carol Higgins 1956-

Clark, Curt
See Westlake, Donald E.

Clark, John Pepper
See Clark Bekederemo, J.P.

Clark, Mary Higgins 1929-

Clark Bekederemo, J.P. 1935-

Clarke, Arthur C. 1917-

Clarke, Austin C. 1934-

Clavell, James 1925-1994

Cleary, Beverly 1916-

Clifton, Lucille 1936-

Clinton, Dirk
See Silverberg, Robert

Clowes, Daniel 1961-

VOLUME 2: Co-Gr

Codrescu, Andrei 1946-

Coe, Tucker
See Westlake, Donald E.

Coetzee, J.M. 1940-

Coffey, Brian
See Koontz, Dean R.

Coleman, Emmett
See Reed, Ishmael

Collins, Billy 1941-

Collins, Max Allan 1948-

Colvin, James
See Moorcock, Michael

Condé, Maryse 1937-

Connell, Evan S., Jr. 1924-

Conroy, Pat 1945-

Cook, Roy
See Silverberg, Robert

Cooper, J. California

Cooper, Susan 1935-

Coover, Robert 1932-

Cormier, Robert 1925-2000

Cornwell, Patricia 1956-

Corso, Gregory 1930-2001

Cortázar, Julio 1914-1984

Courtney, Robert
See Ellison, Harlan

Cox, William Trevor
See Trevor, William

Craig, A.A.
See Anderson, Poul

Creeley, Robert 1926-2005

Crews, Harry 1935-

Crichton, Michael 1942-

Crowley, John 1942-

Crutcher, Chris 1946-

Cruz, Victor Hernández 1949-

Culver, Timothy J.
See Westlake, Donald E.

Cunningham, E.V.
See Fast, Howard

Cunningham, J. Morgan
See Westlake, Donald E.

Cunningham, Michael 1952-

Curtis, Price
See Ellison, Harlan

Cussler, Clive 1931-

Cutrate, Joe
See Spiegelman, Art

Dahl, Roald 1916-1990

Dale, George E.
See Asimov, Isaac

Danticat, Edwidge 1969-

Danziger, Paula 1944-2004

Davies, Robertson 1913-1995

Davis, B. Lynch
See Borges, Jorge Luis

Deighton, Len 1929-

Delany, Samuel R. 1942-

DeLillo, Don 1936-

Demijohn, Thom
See Disch, Thomas M.

Denis, Julio
See Cortázar, Julio

Denmark, Harrison
See Zelazny, Roger

dePaola, Tomie 1934-

Derrida, Jacques 1930-

Desai, Anita 1937-

DeWitt, Helen 1957-

Dexter, Colin 1930-

Dexter, John
See Bradley, Marion Zimmer

Dexter, N.C.
See Dexter, Colin

Dexter, Pete 1943-

Diamond, Jared 1937-

Dick, Philip K. 1928-1982

Didion, Joan 1934-

Dillard, Annie 1945-

Disch, Thomas M. 1940-

Disch, Tom
See Disch, Thomas M.

Doctorow, E.L. 1931-

Domecq, H. Bustos
See Borges, Jorge Luis

Domini, Rey
See Lorde, Audre

Dorris, Michael 1945-1997

Douglas, Leonard
See Bradbury, Ray

Douglas, Michael
See Crichton, Michael

Dove, Rita 1952-

Doyle, John
See Graves, Robert

Doyle, Roddy 1958-

Dr. A.
See Asimov, Isaac

Dr. Seuss
See Geisel, Theodor Seuss

Drabble, Margaret 1939-

Drummond, Walter
See Silverberg, Robert

Druse, Eleanor
See King, Stephen

Dubus, Andre, III 1959-

Due, Linnea A. 1948-

Due, Tananarive 1966-

Duke, Raoul
See Thompson, Hunter S.

Duncan, Lois 1934-

Duncan, Robert 1919-1988

Dunn, Katherine 1945-

Durang, Christopher 1949-

Dworkin, Andrea 1946-2005

Dwyer, Deanna
See Koontz, Dean R.

Dwyer, K.R.
See Koontz, Dean R.

Eco, Umberto 1932-

Edelman, Marian Wright 1939-

Edmondson, Wallace
See Ellison, Harlan

Eggers, Dave 1971-

Ehrenreich, Barbara 1941-

Eisner, Will 1917-2005

Eliot, Dan
See Silverberg, Robert

Elkin, Stanley L. 1930-1995

Elliott, Don
See Silverberg, Robert

Elliott, William
See Bradbury, Ray

Ellis, Alice Thomas 1932-

Ellis, Bret Easton 1964-

Ellis, Landon
See Ellison, Harlan

Ellison, Harlan 1934-

Ellison, Ralph 1914-1994

Ellroy, James 1948-

Emecheta, Buchi 1944-

Endo, Shusaku 1923-1996

Enger, L.L.
See Enger, Leif

Enger, Leif 1961-

Epernay, Mark
See Galbraith, John Kenneth

Erdrich, Louise 1954-

Erickson, Steve 1950-

Erickson, Walter
See Fast, Howard

Ericson, Walter
See Fast, Howard

Ernaux, Annie 1940-

Erwin, Will
See Eisner, Will

Esquivel, Laura 1951-

Estleman, Loren D. 1952-

Eugenides, Jeffrey 1960-

Everett, Percival L. 1956-

Fadiman, Anne 1953-

Faludi, Susan 1959-

Farmer, Philip José 1918-

Fast, Howard 1914-2003

Ferlinghetti, Lawrence 1919-

Ferré, Rosario 1938-

Fielding, Helen 1958-

Fitch, John, IV
See Cormier, Robert

Fitzgerald, Penelope 1916-2000

Fleur, Paul
See Pohl, Frederik

Flooglebuckle, Al
See Spiegelman, Art

Fo, Dario 1926-

Foer, Jonathan Safran 1977-

Foote, Horton 1916-

Foote, Shelby 1916-2005

Forché, Carolyn 1950-

Ford, Michael Thomas 1969-

Ford, Richard 1944-

Forsyth, Frederick 1938-

Fowler, Karen Joy 1950-

Fowles, John 1926-2005

Francis, Dick 1920-

Franzen, Jonathan 1959-

Fraser, Antonia 1932-

Frayn, Michael 1933-

Frazier, Charles 1950-

French, Marilyn 1929-

French, Paul
See Asimov, Isaac

Frey, James 1969-

Friedan, Betty 1921-2006

Friedman, Thomas L. 1953-

Frisch, Max 1911-1991

Fry, Christopher 1907-

Fuentes, Carlos 1928-

Fugard, Athol 1932-

Fundi
See Baraka, Amiri

Gaddis, William 1922-1998

Gaiman, Neil 1960-

Gaines, Ernest J. 1933-

Galbraith, John Kenneth 1908-

Gallant, Mavis 1922-

Garcia, Cristina 1958-

Garcia Marquez, Gabriel 1928-

Gardner, John 1933-1982

Gardner, Miriam
See Bradley, Marion Zimmer

Gardons, S.S.
See Snodgrass, W.D.

Garner, Alan 1934-

Gass, William H. 1924-

Gates, Henry Louis, Jr. 1950-

Gee, Maggie 1948-

Geisel, Theodor Seuss 1904-1991

Genet, Jean 1910-1986

Gibbons, Kaye 1960-

Gibson, William 1948-

Gibson, William2 1914-

Gilchrist, Ellen 1935-

Ginsberg, Allen 1926-1997

Ginzburg, Natalia 1916-1991

Giovanni, Nikki 1943-

Glück, Louise 1943-

Godwin, Gail 1937-

Golden, Arthur 1956-

Golding, William 1911-1993

Goodkind, Terry 1948-

Gordimer, Nadine 1923-

Goryan, Sirak
See Saroyan, William

Gottesman, S.D.
See Pohl, Frederik

Gould, Stephen Jay 1941-2002

Goytisolo, Juan 1931-

Grafton, Sue 1940-

Graham, Jorie 1950-

Grant, Skeeter
See Spiegelman, Art

Grass, Günter 1927-

Graves, Robert 1895-1985

Graves, Valerie
See Bradley, Marion Zimmer

Gray, Alasdair 1934-

Gray, Francine du Plessix 1930-

Gray, Spalding 1941-2004

Greeley, Andrew M. 1928-

Green, Brian
See Card, Orson Scott

Greene, Graham 1904-1991

Greer, Richard
See Silverberg, Robert

Gregor, Lee
See Pohl, Frederik

Grisham, John 1955-

Grumbach, Doris 1918-

VOLUME 3: Gu-Ma

Guest, Judith 1936-

Gump, P.Q.
See Card, Orson Scott

Guterson, David 1956-

Haddon, Mark 1962-

Hailey, Arthur 1920-2004

Halberstam, David 1934-

Hall, Donald 1928-

Hall, Radclyffe 1886-1943

Hamilton, Franklin
See Silverberg, Robert

Hamilton, Jane 1957-

Hamilton, Mollie
See Kaye, M.M.

Hamilton, Virginia 1936-2002

Handke, Peter 1942-

Hardwick, Elizabeth 1916-

Hargrave, Leonie
See Disch, Thomas M.

Harjo, Joy 1951-

Harris, E. Lynn 1957-

Harris, Robert 1957-

Harris, Thomas 1940-

Harson, Sley
See Ellison, Harlan

Hart, Ellis
See Ellison, Harlan

Harvey, Jack
See Rankin, Ian

Hass, Robert 1941-

Havel, Vaclav 1936-

Hawkes, John 1925-1998

Hawking, S.W.
See Hawking, Stephen W.

Hawking, Stephen W. 1942-

Haycraft, Anna
See Ellis, Alice Thomas

Hayes, Al
See Grisham, John

Hazzard, Shirley 1931-

Head, Bessie 1937-1986

Heaney, Seamus 1939-

Hébert, Anne 1916-2000

Hegi, Ursula 1946-

Heinlein, Robert A. 1907-1988

Heller, Joseph 1923-1999

Hellman, Lillian 1906-1984

Helprin, Mark 1947-

Hempel, Amy 1951-

Henley, Beth 1952-

Herbert, Frank 1920-1986

Hersey, John 1914-1993

Hiaasen, Carl 1953-

Highsmith, Patricia 1921-1995

Hijuelos, Oscar 1951-

Hill, John
See Koontz, Dean R.

Hillenbrand, Laura 1967-

Hillerman, Tony 1925-

Hinojosa, Rolando 1929-

Hinton, S.E. 1950-

Hoban, Russell 1925-

Hochhuth, Rolf 1931-

Høeg, Peter 1957-

Hoffman, Alice 1952-

Hollander, Paul
See Silverberg, Robert

Homes, A.M. 1961-

hooks, bell 1952-

Hosseini, Khaled 1965-

Houellebecq, Michel 1958-

Houston, Jeanne Wakatsuki 1934-

Howard, Maureen 1930-

Howard, Warren F.
See Pohl, Frederik

Hoyle, Fred 1915-2001

Hubbell, Sue 1935-

Hudson, Jeffrey
See Crichton, Michael

Hughes, Ted 1930-1998

Humes, Edward

Hwang, David Henry 1957-

Ionesco, Eugene 1912-1994

Irving, John 1942-

Isaacs, Susan 1943-

Isherwood, Christopher 1904-1986

Ishiguro, Kazuo 1954-

Ives, Morgan
See Bradley, Marion Zimmer

Jakes, John 1932-

James, Mary
See Meaker, Marijane

James, P.D. 1920-

James, Philip
See Moorcock, Michael

Janowitz, Tama 1957-

Jarvis, E.K.
See Ellison, Harlan

Jarvis, E.K.2
See Silverberg, Robert

Jenkins, Jerry B. 1949-

Jhabvala, Ruth Prawer 1927-

Jiang, Ji-li 1954-

Jimenez, Francisco 1943-

Jin, Ha 1956-

Johnson, Adam 1967-

Johnson, Angela 1961-

Johnson, Charles 1948-

Jones, Diana Wynne 1934-

Jones, Edward P. 1950-

Jones, Gayl 1949-

Jones, LeRoi
See Baraka, Amiri

Jong, Erica 1942-

Jorgensen, Ivar
See Ellison, Harlan

Jorgenson, Ivar2
See Silverberg, Robert

Judd, Cyril
See Pohl, Frederik

Junger, Sebastian 1962-

Karageorge, Michael A.
See Anderson, Poul

Karr, Mary 1955-

Kastel, Warren
See Silverberg, Robert

Kaufman, Moises 1963-

Kavanagh, Dan
See Barnes, Julian

Kaye, M.M. 1908-2004

Kaye, Mollie
See Kaye, M.M.

Keillor, Garrison 1942-

Kelly, Lauren
See Oates, Joyce Carol

Keneally, Thomas 1935-

Kennedy, William 1928-

Kennilworthy Whisp
See Rowling, J.K.

Kerr, M.E.
See Meater, Marijane

Kerry, Lois
See Duncan, Lois

Kesey, Ken 1935-2001

Keyes, Daniel 1927-

Kidd, Sue Monk

Kienzle, William X. 1928-2001

Kincaid, Jamaica 1949-

King, Stephen 1947-

King, Steve
See King, Stephen

Kingsolver, Barbara 1955-

Kingston, Maxine Hong 1940-

Kinnell, Galway 1927-

Kinsella, Thomas 1928-

Kinsella, W.P. 1935-

Kizer, Carolyn 1925-

Knight, Etheridge 1931-1991

Knowles, John 1926-2001

Knox, Calvin M.
See Silverberg, Robert

Knye, Cassandra
See Disch, Thomas M.

Koch, Kenneth 1925-2002

Kogawa, Joy 1935-

Kolb, Edward W. 1951-

Kolb, Rocky
See Kolb, Edward W.

Koontz, Dean R. 1945-

Kooser, Ted 1939-

Kosinski, Jerzy 1933-1991

Kozol, Jonathan 1936-

Krakauer, Jon 1954-

Kumin, Maxine 1925-

Kundera, Milan 1929-

Kunitz, Stanley 1905-

Kushner, Tony 1956-

L'Amour, Louis 1908-1988

L'Engle, Madeleine 1918-

La Guma, Alex 1925-1985

Lahiri, Jhumpa 1967-

Lamb, Wally 1950-

Lange, John
See Crichton, Michael

Laredo, Betty
See Codrescu, Andrei

Laurence, Margaret 1926-1987

Lavond, Paul Dennis
See Pohl, Frederik

Leavitt, David 1961-

le Carré, John 1931-

Lee, Don L.
See Madhubuti, Haki R.

Lee, Harper 1926-

Lee, Stan 1922-

Le Guin, Ursula K. 1929-

Lehane, Dennis 1965-

Leonard, Elmore 1925-

LeSieg, Theo.
See Geisel, Theodor Seuss

Lessing, Doris 1919-

Lester, Julius 1939-

Lethem, Jonathan 1964-

Levi, Primo 1919-1987

Levin, Ira 1929-

Levon, O.U.
See Kesey, Ken

Leyner, Mark 1956-

Lindbergh, Anne Morrow 1906-2001

Lively, Penelope 1933-

Lodge, David 1935-

Logan, Jake
See Smith, Martin Cruz

Long, David 1948-

Loos, Anita 1893-1981

Lorde, Audre 1934-1992

Louise, Heidi
See Erdrich, Louise

Lowry, Lois 1937-

Lucas, Craig 1951-

Ludlum, Robert 1927-2001

Lynch, B. Suarez
See Borges, Jorge Luis

M.T.F.
See Porter, Katherine Anne

Macdonald, Anson
See Heinlein, Robert A.

MacDonald, John D. 1916-1986

Mackay, Shena 1944-

MacKinnon, Catharine A. 1946-

MacLeish, Archibald 1892-1982

MacLeod, Alistair 1936-

Maddern, Al
See Ellison, Harlan

Madhubuti, Haki R.

Maguire, Gregory 1954-

Mahfouz, Naguib 1911-

Mailer, Norman 1923-

Makine, Andreï 1957-

Malabaila, Damiano
See Levi, Primo

Malamud, Bernard 1914-1986

Malcolm, Dan
See Silverberg, Robert

Malouf, David 1934-

Mamet, David 1947-

Mara, Bernard
See Moore, Brian

Marchbanks, Samuel
See Davies, Robertson

Marías, Javier 1951-

Mariner, Scott
See Pohl, Frederik

Markandaya, Kamala 1924-2004

Markham, Robert
See Amis, Kingsley

Marshall, Allen
See Westlake, Donald E.

Marshall, Paule 1929-

Martel, Yann 1963-

Martin, Webber
See Silverberg, Robert

Mason, Bobbie Ann 1940-

Mason, Ernst
See Pohl, Frederik

Mass, William
See Gibson, William2

Massie, Robert K. 1929-

Mathabane, Mark 1960-

Matthiessen, Peter 1927-

Maupin, Armistead 1944-

Mayo, Jim
See L'Amour, Louis

VOLUME 4: Mc-Sa

McBride, James 1957-

McCaffrey, Anne 1926-

McCall Smith, Alexander 1948-

McCann, Edson
See Pohl, Frederik

McCarthy, Cormac 1933-

McCourt, Frank 1930-

McCreigh, James
See Pohl, Frederik

McCullough, Colleen 1937-

McCullough, David 1933-

McDermott, Alice 1953-

McEwan, Ian 1948-

McGuane, Thomas 1939-

McInerney, Jay 1955-

McKie, Robin

McKinley, Robin 1952-

McLandress, Herschel
See Galbraith, John Kenneth

McMillan, Terry 1951-

McMurtry, Larry 1936-

McNally, Terrence 1939-

McPhee, John 1931-

McPherson, James Alan 1943-

Meaker, M.J.
See Meaker, Marijane

Meaker, Marijane 1927-

Mehta, Ved 1934-

Members, Mark
See Powell, Anthony

Méndez, Miguel 1930-

Merchant, Paul
See Ellison, Harlan

Merrill, James 1926-1995

Merriman, Alex
See Silverberg, Robert

Merwin, W.S. 1927-

Michener, James A. 1907-1997

Miéville, China 1973-

Miller, Arthur 1915-

Millett, Kate 1934-

Millhauser, Steven 1943-

Milosz, Czeslaw 1911-2004

Min, Anchee 1957-

Mitchell, Clyde
See Ellison, Harlan

Mitchell, Clyde2
See Silverberg, Robert

Momaday, N. Scott 1934-

Monroe, Lyle
See Heinlein, Robert A.

Moody, Anne 1940-

Moody, Rick 1961-

Moorcock, Michael 1939-

Moore, Alan 1953-

Moore, Brian 1921-1999

Moore, Lorrie
See Moore, Marie Lorena

Moore, Marie Lorena 1957-

Mora, Pat 1942-

Morgan, Claire
See Highsmith, Patricia

Mori, Kyoko 1957-

Morris, Mary McGarry 1943-

Morrison, Chloe Anthony Wofford
See Morrison, Toni

Morrison, Toni 1931-

Morrow, James 1947-

Mortimer, John 1923-

Mosley, Walter 1952-

Motion, Andrew 1952-

Mowat, Farley 1921-

Mukherjee, Bharati 1940-

Munro, Alice 1931-

Murdoch, Iris 1919-1999

Murray, Albert L. 1916-

Myers, Walter Dean 1937-

Myers, Walter M.
See Myers, Walter Dean

Nafisi, Azar 1950-

Naipaul, Shiva 1945-1985

Naipaul, V.S. 1932-

Narayan, R.K. 1906-2001

Naylor, Gloria 1950-

Nemerov, Howard 1920-1991

Newt Scamander
See Rowling, J.K.

Ngugi, James T.
See Ngugi wa Thiong'o

Ngugi wa Thiong'o 1938-

Nichols, John 1940-

Nichols, Leigh
See Koontz, Dean R.

North, Anthony
See Koontz, Dean R.

North, Milou
See Dorris, Michael

North, Milou2
See Erdrich, Louise

Nosille, Nabrah
See Ellison, Harlan

Novak, Joseph
See Kosinski, Jerzy

Nye, Naomi Shihab 1952-

O'Brian, E.G.
See Clarke, Arthur C.

O'Brian, Patrick 1914-2000

O'Brien, Edna 1932-

O'Brien, Tim 1946-

O'Casey, Brenda
See Ellis, Alice Thomas

O'Faolain, Sean 1900-1991

O'Flaherty, Liam 1896-1984

Oates, Joyce Carol 1938-

Oates, Stephen B. 1936-

Oe, Kenzaburo 1935-

Okri, Ben 1959-

Olds, Sharon 1942-

Oliver, Mary 1935-

Olsen, Tillie 1912-

Ondaatje, Michael 1943-

Osborne, David
See Silverberg, Robert

Osborne, George
See Silverberg, Robert

Osborne, John 1929-1994

Oz, Amos 1939-

Ozick, Cynthia 1928-

Packer, Vin
See Meaker, Marijane

Paglia, Camille 1947-

Paige, Richard
See Koontz, Dean R.

Pakenham, Antonia
See Fraser, Antonia

Palahniuk, Chuck 1962-

Paley, Grace 1922-

Paolini, Christopher 1983-

Parfenie, Marie
See Codrescu, Andrei

Park, Jordan
See Pohl, Frederik

Parker, Bert
See Ellison, Harlan

Parker, Robert B. 1932-

Parks, Gordon 1912-2006

Pasternak, Boris 1890-1960

Patchett, Ann 1963-

Paton, Alan 1903-1988

Patterson, James 1947-

Payne, Alan
See Jakes, John

Paz, Octavio 1914-1998

Peretti, Frank E. 1951-

Petroski, Henry 1942-

Phillips, Caryl 1958-

Phillips, Jayne Anne 1952-

Phillips, Richard
See Dick, Philip K.

Picoult, Jodi 1966-

Piercy, Marge 1936-

Piers, Robert
See Anthony, Piers

Pinsky, Robert 1940-

Pinta, Harold
See Pinter, Harold

Pinter, Harold 1930-

Plimpton, George 1927-2003

Pohl, Frederik 1919-

Porter, Katherine Anne 1890-1980

Potok, Chaim 1929-2002

Powell, Anthony 1905-2000

Powers, Richard 1957-

Powers, Tim 1952-

Pratchett, Terry 1948-

Price, Reynolds 1933-

Prose, Francine 1947-

Proulx, E. Annie 1935-

Puig, Manuel 1932-1990

Pullman, Philip 1946-

Pygge, Edward
See Barnes, Julian

Pynchon, Thomas, Jr. 1937-

Quindlen, Anna 1953-

Quinn, Simon
See Smith, Martin Cruz

Rampling, Anne
See Rice, Anne

Rand, Ayn 1905-1982

Randall, Robert
See Silverberg, Robert

Rankin, Ian 1960-

Rao, Raja 1909-

Ravenna, Michael
See Welty, Eudora

Reed, Ishmael 1938-

Reid, Desmond
See Moorcock, Michael

Rendell, Ruth 1930-

Rensie, Willis
See Eisner, Will

Rexroth, Kenneth 1905-1982

Rice, Anne 1941-

Rich, Adrienne 1929-

Rich, Barbara
See Graves, Robert

Richler, Mordecai 1931-2001

Ríos, Alberto 1952-

Rivers, Elfrida
See Bradley, Marion Zimmer

Riverside, John
See Heinlein, Robert A.

Robb, J.D.
See Roberts, Nora

Robbe-Grillet, Alain 1922-

Robbins, Tom 1936-

Roberts, Nora 1950-

Robertson, Ellis
See Ellison, Harlan

Robertson, Ellis2
See Silverberg, Robert

Robinson, Kim Stanley 1952-

Robinson, Lloyd
See Silverberg, Robert

Robinson, Marilynne 1944-

Rodman, Eric
See Silverberg, Robert

Rodríguez, Luis J. 1954-

Rodriguez, Richard 1944-

Roquelaure, A.N.
See Rice, Anne

Roth, Henry 1906-1995

Roth, Philip 1933-

Rowling, J.K. 1965-

Roy, Arundhati 1960-

Rule, Ann 1935-

Rushdie, Salman 1947-

Russo, Richard 1949-

Rybczynski, Witold 1943-

Ryder, Jonathan
See Ludlum, Robert

Sábato, Ernesto 1911-

Sacco, Joe 1960-

Sacks, Oliver 1933-

Sagan, Carl 1934-1996

Salinger, J.D. 1919-

Salzman, Mark 1959-

Sanchez, Sonia 1934-

Sanders, Noah
See Blount, Roy, Jr.

Sanders, Winston P.
See Anderson, Poul

Sandford, John
See Camp, John

Saroyan, William 1908-1981

Sarton, May 1912-1995

Sartre, Jean-Paul 1905-1980

Satterfield, Charles
See Pohl, Frederik

Saunders, Caleb
See Heinlein, Robert A.

VOLUME 5: Sc-Z

Schaeffer, Susan Fromberg 1941-

Schulz, Charles M. 1922-2000

Schwartz, Lynne Sharon 1939-

Scotland, Jay
See Jakes, John

Sebastian, Lee
See Silverberg, Robert

Sebold, Alice 1963-

Sedaris, David 1957-

Sendak, Maurice 1928-

Seth, Vikram 1952-

Shaara, Jeff 1952-

Shaara, Michael 1929-1988

Shackleton, C.C.
See Aldiss, Brian W.

Shaffer, Peter 1926-

Shange, Ntozake 1948-

Shapiro, Karl Jay 1913-2000

Shepard, Sam 1943-

Shepherd, Michael
See Ludlum, Robert

Shields, Carol 1935-2003

Shreve, Anita 1946-

Siddons, Anne Rivers 1936-

Silko, Leslie 1948-

Sillitoe, Alan 1928-

Silverberg, Robert 1935-

Silverstein, Shel 1932-1999

Simic, Charles 1938-

Simon, David 1960-

Simon, Neil 1927-

Simpson, Louis 1923-

Singer, Isaac
See Singer, Isaac Bashevis

Singer, Isaac Bashevis 1904-1991

Škvorecký, Josef 1924-

Smiley, Jane 1949-

Smith, Martin
See Smith, Martin Cruz

Smith, Martin Cruz 1942-

Smith, Rosamond
See Oates, Joyce Carol

Smith, Wilbur 1933-

Smith, Zadie 1976-

Snicket, Lemony 1970-

Snodgrass, W.D. 1926-

Snyder, Gary 1930-

Solo, Jay
See Ellison, Harlan

Solwoska, Mara
See French, Marilyn

Solzhenitsyn, Aleksandr I. 1918-

Somers, Jane
See Lessing, Doris

Sontag, Susan 1933-2004

Soto, Gary 1952-

Soyinka, Wole 1934-

Spark, Muriel 1918-

Sparks, Nicholas 1965-

Spaulding, Douglas
See Bradbury, Ray

Spaulding, Leonard
See Bradbury, Ray

Spencer, Leonard G.
See Silverberg, Robert

Spender, Stephen 1909-1995

Spiegelman, Art 1948-

Spillane, Mickey 1918-

Stack, Andy
See Rule, Ann

Stacy, Donald
See Pohl, Frederik

Stancykowna
See Szymborska, Wislawa

Stark, Richard
See Westlake, Donald E.

Steel, Danielle 1947-

Steig, William 1907-

Steinem, Gloria 1934-

Steiner, George 1929-

Steiner, K. Leslie
See Delany, Samuel R.

Stephenson, Neal 1959-

Sterling, Brett
See Bradbury, Ray

Sterling, Bruce 1954-

Stine, Jovial Bob
See Stine, R.L.

Stine, R.L. 1943-

Stone, Robert 1937-

Stone, Rosetta
See Geisel, Theodor Seuss

Stoppard, Tom 1937-

Straub, Peter 1943-

Styron, William 1925-

Swenson, May 1919-1989

Swift, Graham 1949-

Swithen, John
See King, Stephen

Symmes, Robert
See Duncan, Robert

Syruc, J.
See Milosz, Czeslaw

Szymborska, Wislawa 1923-

Talent Family, The
See Sedaris, David

Talese, Gay 1932-

Tan, Amy 1952-

Tanner, William
See Amis, Kingsley

Tartt, Donna 1964-

Taylor, Mildred D. 1943-

Tenneshaw, S.M.
See Silverberg, Robert

Terkel, Studs 1912-

Theroux, Paul 1941-

Thomas, D.M. 1935-

Thomas, Joyce Carol 1938-

Thompson, Hunter S. 1937-2005

Thornton, Hall
See Silverberg, Robert

Tiger, Derry
See Ellison, Harlan

Tornimparte, Alessandra
See Ginzburg, Natalia

Tremblay, Michel 1942-

Trevor, William 1928-

Trillin, Calvin 1935-

Trout, Kilgore
See Farmer, Philip José

Turow, Scott 1949-

Tyler, Anne 1941-

Tyree, Omar

Uchida, Yoshiko 1921-1992

Uhry, Alfred 1936-

Uncle Shelby
See Silverstein, Shel

Updike, John 1932-

Urban Griot
See Tyree, Omar

Uris, Leon 1924-2003

Urmuz
See Codrescu, Andrei

Vance, Gerald
See Silverberg, Robert

Van Duyn, Mona 1921-2004

Vargas Llosa, Mario 1936-

Verdu, Matilde
See Cela, Camilo José

Vidal, Gore 1925-

Vile, Curt
See Moore, Alan

Vine, Barbara
See Rendell, Ruth

Vizenor, Gerald Robert 1934-

Vogel, Paula A. 1951-

Voigt, Cynthia 1942-

Vollmann, William T. 1959-

Vonnegut, Kurt, Jr. 1922-

Vosce, Trudie
See Ozick, Cynthia

Wakoski, Diane 1937-

Walcott, Derek 1930-

Walker, Alice 1944-

Walker, Margaret 1915-1998

Wallace, David Foster 1962-

Walley, Byron
See Card, Orson Scott

Ware, Chris 1967-

Warren, Robert Penn 1905-1989

Warshofsky, Isaac
See Singer, Isaac Bashevis

Wasserstein, Wendy 1950-2006

Watson, James D. 1928-

Watson, John H.
See Farmer, Philip José

Watson, Larry 1947-

Watson, Richard F.
See Silverberg, Robert

Ways, C.R.
See Blount, Roy, Jr.

Weldon, Fay 1931-

Wells, Rebecca

Welty, Eudora 1909-2001

West, Edwin
See Westlake, Donald E.

West, Owen
See Koontz, Dean R.

West, Paul 1930-

Westlake, Donald E. 1933-

White, Edmund 1940-

Wideman, John Edgar 1941-

Wiesel, Elie 1928-

Wilbur, Richard 1921-

Williams, C.K. 1936-

Williams, Juan 1954-

Williams, Tennessee 1911-1983

Willis, Charles G.
See Clarke, Arthur C.

Wilson, August 1945-2005

Wilson, Dirk
See Pohl, Frederik

Wilson, Edward O. 1929-

Winterson, Jeanette 1959-

Wolf, Naomi 1962-

Wolfe, Gene 1931-

Wolfe, Tom 1931-

Wolff, Tobias 1945-

Woodiwiss, Kathleen E. 1939-

Woodson, Jacqueline 1964-

Wouk, Herman 1915-

Wright, Charles 1935-

Wright, Judith 1915-2000

Xingjian, Gao 1940-

Yolen, Jane 1939-

York, Simon
See Heinlein, Robert A.

Zelazny, Roger 1937-1995

Zindel, Paul 1936-2003

Mc

McBRIDE, James 1957-
(James C. McBride)

PERSONAL: Born 1957; son of Andrew McBride (a minister) and Ruth McBride Jordan (a homemaker; born Rachel Shilsky); married; children: three. *Education:* Attended Oberlin Conservatory of Music; Columbia University, M.A., 1979.

ADDRESSES: *Home*—Bucks County, PA. *Agent*—(music) Cathy Elliott, 463 West 43rd St., Suite 2S, New York, NY 10036; (personal appearances and lectures) American Program Bureau, 36 Crafts Street, Newton, MA 02158. *E-mail*—jamesmcbride@jamesmcbride.com.

CAREER: Journalist; on staff of *Boston Globe, People,* and *Washington Post,* c. 1979-87; jazz saxophonist, composer, and producer, c. 1987-95; currently leader of a twelve-piece jazz R & B band; freelance writer and composer.

AWARDS, HONORS: Anisfield-Wolf Award for Literary Excellence, 1997, and Notable Book of the Year, American Library Association, both for *The Color of Water;* honorary doctorate, Whitman College. Awards for music include Stephen Sondheim Award, American Music Festival, 1993, Richard Rodgers Award, American Arts and Letters, 1996, and Richard Rodgers Horizons Award, ASCAP, 1996; *The Color of Water: A Black Man's Tribute to His White Mother* was chosen as the inaugural selection of "New York City Reads Together," 2003, and the city of Philadelphia's second selection for the city's One Book program, 2004.

WRITINGS:

The Color of Water: A Black Man's Tribute to His White Mother (memoir), Riverhead Books (New York, NY), 1996.

Miracle at St. Anna (novel), Riverhead Books (New York, NY), 2002.

Also author of foreword, *Family: Moments of Intimacy, Laughter and Kinship,* Hodder Headline (London, England). Contributor to periodicals, including *Essence, Rolling Stone,* and *New York Times.* Author, with Ed Shockley, of pop/jazz Broadway musical *Bobos.*

ADAPTATIONS: ABC and Robert Greenwald Productions purchased the rights to produce a TV movie based on *The Color of Water.*

SIDELIGHTS: For Mother's Day in 1981 journalist James McBride penned an essay about his mother for the *Boston Globe.* Readers, moved by the piece, wrote to McBride and encouraged him to write a book. More than a decade after McBride first approached his mother about writing her story, Ruth Jordan finally acquiesced. In 1996 *The Color of Water: A Black Man's Tribute to His White Mother* rolled off the presses. The title of the book reflects Jordan's answer to her son's childhood inquiry about the color of God's skin.

The Color of Water is told in chapters that alternate between the mother's recollections and her son's commentary. Jordan explains how she was born in Poland, the daughter of an Orthodox Jewish rabbi-turned-grocer who immigrated to the American South. She fled the

South to escape sexual abuse by her father, ending up in New York City. There she met and married minister Andrew McBride, helped him establish an all-black Baptist church, and gave birth to eight children. James was the youngest and never met his father, who died shortly before his birth. McBride described how Jordan remarried, had four more children, and raised him and his siblings in lower-income neighborhoods in Brooklyn and Queens. To protect her children from stigma, Ruth led her children to believe that she was a light-skinned black, and until late in his childhood, McBride did not question her. When McBride did ask his mother whether he was white or black, her response was: "You're a human being. Educate yourself or you'll be a nobody." The author explains that during his adolescence, he rebelled against his mother and stepfather's authority and was involved in petty crime. Yet he and his siblings overcame many obstacles, earning college degrees and self-respect. McBride gives much credit for the success of their family to his mother's Orthodox background combined with his father's Christianity.

Some reviewers have compared *The Color of Water* with *Divided to the Vein,* by Scott Minerbrook, another African-American journalist whose mother was white and father was black. Writing in *Booklist,* Alice Joyce called *The Color of Water* and *Divided to the Vein* "remarkably candid," adding "these memoirs reflect earnestly on issues of self stemming from the interracial marriages of their parents." In the *Chicago Tribune,* John Blades wrote: "Though McBride's disillusionment was not so severe as Minerbrook's, his memoir just as forcefully points out how 'divided to the vein' America remains, not just between black and white but also between black and black." He added: "Similar but very different, the two books are both eye-and mind-opening about the eternal convolutions and paradoxes of race in America, as seen from up-close and microcosmic perspectives."

As he delved into his past, McBride came to take pride in his Jewish heritage and became more empathetic to people of all kinds. "The lingering effects of slavery and color consciousness continue to push us in directions we shouldn't go," according to McBride, as reported by Blades. "What I'd like people to come away with is that we have a lot more in common than we think," he told Norman Oder in *Publishers Weekly.* Blades quoted McBride: "I think America is integrating itself kicking and screaming. But it's absolutely essential that we do. We can't survive any other way." According to a reviewer in *Publishers Weekly:* "This moving and unforgettable memoir needs to be read by people of all colors and faiths."

McBride's debut as a novelist came in 2002 with the publication of *Miracle at St. Anna.* Based on an actual incident from World War II, the book is about four soldiers from the segregated 92nd Infantry Division—also known as the Buffalo Soldiers—who find themselves in an isolated part of Italy where a Nazi massacre has just occurred. While caring for a six-year-old boy who was the only survivor of the massacre, the four men join in the Resistance, working with partisans in a tiny Alpine town. Reviewers praised McBride's fresh dialogue—especially that of the corrupt Baptist minister-turned-soldier Bishop Cummings and the exasperated Lieutenant Aubrey Stamps—and his refusal to use stereotypes, even positive ones, when creating his Buffalo Soldiers. Clifford Thompson commented in *Black Issues Book Review* that "McBride weaves his third-person narrative seamlessly among the soldiers and Italian peasants, many of whom emerge as well-rounded characters—no mean feat for a novel that comes in at under 300 pages."

BIOGRAPHICAL AND CRITICAL SOURCES:

PERIODICALS

American Prospect, September 10, 2001, E.J. Graff, review of *The Color of Water,* p. 42.

Black Issues Book Review, March-April, 2002, Clifford Thompson, review of *The Miracle at St. Anna,* pp. 29-30.

Book, January-February, 2002, Stephanie Foote, review of *Miracle at St. Anna,* p. 74.

Booklist, January 1, 1996, p. 782; April 1, 1997, review of *The Color of Water,* p. 1285; February 15, 2002, Margaret Flaganan, review of *Miracle at St. Anna,* p. 1006.

Bulletin with Newsweek, May 15, 2001, Ashley Hay, "Family: A Celebration of Humanity," p. 76.

Chicago Tribune, February 26, 1996, "Tempo" section, p. 1.

Christian Century, November 19, 1997, George Mason, review of *The Color of Water,* p. 1063.

Christianity Today, February 3, 1997, review of *The Color of Water,* p. 61.

Civil Rights Journal, fall, 1998, Kevin R. Johnson, review of *The Color of Water,* p. 44.

Emerge, March, 1996, Lisa Page, review of *The Color of Water: A Black Man's Tribute to His White Mother,* pp. 59-60.

Entertainment Weekly, March 1, 2002, Bruce Fretts, "'Miracle' Worker: *The Color of Water's* James McBride Makes an Impressive Foray into Fiction with a Multi-shaded WWII Tale," p. 72.

Houston Chronicle, March 17, 2002, Fritz Lanham, "McBride's Army," p. 18.
Hungry Mind Review, spring, 1998, review of *The Color of Water,* p. 53.
Jet, April 1, 1996, "Black Journalist Pays Tribute to White Mother in Novel *The Color of Water,*" pp. 62-63.
Kirkus Reviews, December, 2001, review of *Miracle at St. Anna.*
Kliatt Young Adult Paperback Book Guide, March, 1997, review of *The Color of Water,* p. 27; September, 1998, review of *The Color of Water,* p. 6.
Library Journal, January, 1996, p. 110; April 15, 1996, Linda Bredengerd, review of the audio version of *The Color of Water,* p. 144; February 15, 1997, review of the audio version of *The Color of Water,* p. 115; February 15, 2002, Jennifer Baker, review of *Miracle at St. Anna,* p. 178.
Nation, April 22, 1996, Marina Budhos, review of *The Color of Water,* pp. 32-34.
New York Times Book Review, March 2, 1997, review of *The Color of Water,* p. 28; March 3, 2002, Charles Wilson, "An Accidental Truce," p. 16.
Observer (London, England), October 18, 1998, review of *The Color of Water,* p. 16.
People, April 1, 1996, Wayne Kalyn, review of *The Color of Water,* pp. 38-39; February 25, 2002, "Pages," p. 41.
Publishers Weekly, October 30, 1995, Norman Oder, "Black Men, White Relations," pp. 24-25; January 15, 1996, p. 454; February 5, 1996, review of the audio version of *The Color of Water,* pp. 37-38; March 17, 1997, Daisy Maryles, "Behind the Bestsellers," p. 17; August 14, 2000, "James McBride," p. 196; November 26, 2001, review of *The Miracle at St. Anna,* pp. 36-37.
Religious Studies Review, April, 1998, review of *The Color of Water,* p. 214.
St. Louis Post-Dispatch, February 13, 2002, Deborah Peterson, "Soldier's Story of WWII Uses Broad Brush in Painting Blacks," p. E1.
Times Educational Supplement, January 23, 1998, review of *The Color of Water,* p. 10.
Tribune Books (Chicago, IL), February 16, 1997, review of *The Color of Water,* p. 8.
USA Today, January 29, 1996, p. D4.
Voice of Youth Advocates, December, 1997, review of *The Color of Water,* p. 305; April, 1998, review of *The Color of Water,* p. 42.
Wall Street Journal, February 9, 1996, pp. A10, A12.
Washington Post, January 14, 1996, p. 4.

ONLINE

James McBride Web site, http://www.jamesmcbride.com/ (August 25, 2004).

McBRIDE, James C.
See McBRIDE, James

* * *

McCAFFREY, Anne 1926-
(Anne Inez McCaffrey)

PERSONAL: Female. Born April 1, 1926, in Cambridge, MA; daughter of George Herbert (a city administrator and U.S. Army colonel) and Anne Dorothy (a real estate agent; maiden name, McElroy) McCaffrey; married H. Wright Johnson, January 14, 1950 (divorced, 1970); children: Alec Anthony, Todd, Georgeanne. *Education:* Radcliffe College, B.A. (cum laude), 1947; graduate study in meteorology, University of City of Dublin; also studied voice for nine years. *Religion:* Presbyterian. *Hobbies and other interests:* Singing, opera directing, riding and horse care.

ADDRESSES: *Office*—Dragonhold-Underhill, Timmore Lane, Newcastle, County Wicklow, Ireland. *Agent*—Diana Tyler, MBA Literary Agents, 62 Grafton Way, London WIP 5LD, England.

CAREER: Writer. Liberty Music Shops, New York, NY, copywriter and layout designer, 1948-50; Helena Rubinstein, New York, NY, copywriter and secretary, 1950-52. Director of Fin Film Productions, 1979—, and Dragonhold, Ltd. Former professional stage director for several groups in Wilmington, DE.

MEMBER: Science Fiction Writers of America (secretary-treasurer, 1968-70), Mystery Writers of America, Authors Guild, Novelists' Ink, PEN (Ireland).

AWARDS, HONORS: Hugo Award for best novella, World Science Fiction Society, 1968, for "Weyr Search"; Nebula Award for best novella, Science Fiction Writers of America, 1968, for "Dragonrider"; E.E. Smith Award for fantasy, 1975; American Library Association notable book citations, 1976, for *Dragonsong,* and 1977, for *Dragonsinger;* Ditmar Award (Australia), Gandalf Award, and Eurocon/Streso Award, all 1979, all for *The White Dragon;* Balrog citation, 1980, for *Dragondrums;* Golden Pen Award, 1981; Science Fiction Book Club awards, 1986, for *Killashandra,* 1989, for *Dragonsdawn,* 1990, for *The Renegades of Pern* (first place) and *The Rowan* (third place), 1991, for *All the Weyrs of Pern,* 1993, for *Damia's Children,* and 1994, for *The Dolphins of Pern;* John W. Campbell Memorial

Award nomination, 1989, for *Dragonsdawn;* Margaret A. Edwards Lifetime Achievement Award for Outstanding Literature for Young Adults, *School Library Journal,* 1999; Cthulu Award, British Science Fiction Association, 2000.

WRITINGS:

SCIENCE FICTION/FANTASY

Restoree, Ballantine (New York, NY), 1967.

(Editor) *Alchemy and Academe,* Doubleday (New York, NY), 1970.

Get off the Unicorn (short stories), Del Rey (New York, NY), 1977.

The Worlds of Anne McCaffrey (stories), Deutsch (London, England), 1981.

The Coelura, Underwood-Miller (San Francisco, CA), 1983.

Stitch in Snow, Del Rey (New York, NY), 1984.

Three Women, Tor Books (New York, NY), 1992.

(With Elizabeth A. Scarborough) *Powers That Be,* Del Rey (New York, NY), 1993.

(With Elizabeth A. Scarborough) *Power Lines* (sequel to *Powers That Be*), Del Rey (New York, NY), 1994.

An Exchange of Gifts, illustrated by Pat Morrissey, ROC (New York, NY), 1995.

(With Elizabeth A. Scarborough) *Power Play,* Del Rey (New York, NY), 1995.

No One Noticed the Cat, ROC (New York, NY), 1996.

(Editor with Elizabeth A. Scarborough) *Space Opera,* DAW Books (New York, NY), 1996.

If Wishes Were Horses, ROC (New York, NY), 1998.

Nimisha's Ship, Del Rey (New York, NY), 1999.

(With Joe Haldeman and Arthur C. Clarke) *The Best Military Science Fiction of the Twentieth Century,* edited by Harry Turtledove and Martin H. Greenberg, Random House (New York, NY), 2001.

A Gift of Dragons (story collection), illustrated by Tom Kidd, Ballantine Books (New York, NY), 2002.

Freedom's Ransom, Putnam (New York, NY), 2002.

(With Todd McCaffrey) *Dragon's Kin,* Random House (New York, NY), 2003.

(With Mercedes Lackey and Margaret Ball) *Brain Ships,* edited by James Baen, Baen Books (New York, NY), 2003.

(With Jody Lynn Nye) *The Ship Who Saved the Worlds,* Baen Books (New York, NY), 2003.

(With Elizabeth Ann Scarborough) *Changelings,* Del Rey (New York, NY), 2005.

"DRAGONRIDERS OF PERN" SERIES; SCIENCE FICTION

Dragonflight, Ballantine, 1968, hardcover edition, Walker & Co. (New York, NY), 1969, reprinted, Random House (New York, NY), 2002.

Dragonquest: Being the Further Adventures of the Dragonriders of Pern, Ballantine (New York, NY), 1971.

A Time When, Being a Tale of Young Lord Jaxom, His White Dragon, Ruth, and Various Fire-Lizards (short story), NESFA Press (Cambridge, MA), 1975.

The White Dragon, Del Rey (New York, NY), 1978.

The Dragonriders of Pern (contains *Dragonflight, Dragonquest,* and *The White Dragon*), Doubleday (New York, NY), 1978.

Moreta: Dragonlady of Pern (also see below), Del Rey (New York, NY), 1983.

The Girl Who Heard Dragons (story collection), illustrated by Judy King-Rieniets, Cheap Street (New Castle, VA), 1985, illustrated by Michael Whelan, Tor Books (New York, NY), 1994.

Nerilka's Story, Del Rey (New York, NY), 1986.

Dragonsdawn (also see below), Del Rey (New York, NY), 1988, with introduction by James Gunn, illustrated by Michael Whelan, Easton Press (Norwalk, CT), 1988.

The Renegades of Pern, Del Rey (New York, NY), 1989.

All the Weyrs of Pern, Del Rey (New York, NY), 1991.

The Chronicles of Pern: First Fall, Del Rey (New York, NY), 1992.

The Dolphins' Bell: A Tale of Pern, Wildside Press, 1993.

The Dolphins of Pern, Del Rey (New York, NY), 1994.

Dragonseye (also see below), Del Rey (New York, NY), 1997.

The Masterharper of Pern, Del Rey (New York, NY), 1998.

The Skies of Pern, Del Rey (New York, NY), 2001.

On Dragonwings (contains *Dragonsdawn, Dragonseye,* and *Moreta*), Random House (New York, NY), 2003.

"HARPER HALL" SERIES; SCIENCE FICTION

Dragonsong, Atheneum (New York, NY), 1976, reprinted, Simon & Schuster Children's (New York, NY), 2003.

Dragonsinger, Atheneum (New York, NY), 1977, reprinted, Simon & Schuster Children's (New York, NY), 2003.

Dragondrums, Atheneum (New York, NY), 1979, reprinted, Simon & Schuster Children's (New York, NY), 2003.

The Harper Hall of Pern (contains *Dragonsong, Dragonsinger,* and *Dragondrums*), Doubleday (New York, NY), 1979.

"DOONA" SERIES; SCIENCE FICTION

Decision at Doona, Ballantine (New York, NY), 1969.

(With Jody Lynn Nye) *Crisis on Doona,* Ace (New York, NY), 1992.

(With Jody Lynn Nye) *Treaty at Doona,* Ace (New York, NY), 1994.

"SHIP WHO SANG" SERIES; SCIENCE FICTION

The Ship Who Sang, Walker & Co. (New York, NY), 1969.

(With Mercedes Lackey) *The Ship Who Searched,* Baen Books (New York, NY), 1992.

(With Margaret Ball) *PartnerShip,* Baen Books (New York, NY), 1992.

(With S.M. Stirling) *The City Who Fought,* Baen Books (New York, NY), 1993.

(With Jody Lynn Nye) *The Ship Who Won,* Baen Books (New York, NY), 1994.

(With S.M. Stirling) *The Ship Avenged,* Baen Books (New York, NY), 1997.

"DINOSAUR PLANET" SERIES; SCIENCE FICTION

Dinosaur Planet, Futura (London, England), 1977, Del Rey (New York, NY), 1978.

The Dinosaur Planet Survivors, Del Rey (New York, NY), 1984.

The Ireta Adventure (contains *Dinosaur Planet* and *The Dinosaur Planet Survivors*), Doubleday (New York, NY), 1985.

The Mystery of Ireta: Dinosaur Planet, and Dinosaur Planet Survivors, Random House (New York, NY), 2003.

"CRYSTAL SINGER" SERIES; SCIENCE FICTION

Crystal Singer, Del Rey (New York, NY), 1982.

Killashandra, Del Rey (New York, NY), 1985.

Crystal Line, Del Rey (New York, NY), 1992.

Crystal Singer Trilogy (contains *Crystal Singer, Killashandra,* and *Crystal Line*), Del Rey (New York, NY), 1996.

"PLANET PIRATE" SERIES; SCIENCE FICTION

(With Elizabeth Moon) *Sassinak,* Baen Books (New York, NY), 1990.

(With Jody Lynn Nye) *The Death of Sleep,* Baen Books (New York, NY), 1990.

Generation Warriors, Baen Books (New York, NY), 1991.

(With Elizabeth Moon and Jody Lynn Nye) *The Planet Pirates,* Baen Books (New York, NY), 1993.

"ROWAN" SERIES; SCIENCE FICTION

The Rowan, Berkley Publishing (New York, NY), 1990.

Damia, Ace (New York, NY), 1993.

Damia's Children, Putnam (New York, NY), 1993.

Lyon's Pride, Putnam (New York, NY), 1994.

The Tower and the Hive, Putnam (New York, NY), 1999.

"FREEDOM" SERIES; SCIENCE FICTION

Freedom's Landing, Putnam (New York, NY), 1995.

Freedom's Choice, Putnam (New York, NY), 1997.

Freedom's Challenge, Putnam (New York, NY), 1998.

"PEGASUS" SERIES; SCIENCE FICTION

To Ride Pegasus, Ballantine (New York, NY), 1973.

Pegasus in Flight, Del Rey (New York, NY), 1990.

Pegasus in Space, Del Rey (New York, NY), 2000.

"ACORNA" SERIES; SCIENCE FICTION

(With Margaret Ball) *Acorna: The Unicorn Girl,* HarperPrism (New York, NY), 1997.

(With Margaret Ball) *Acorna's Quest,* HarperPrism (New York, NY), 1998.

(With Elizabeth A. Scarborough) *Acorna's People,* HarperPrism (New York, NY), 1999.

(With Elizabeth A. Scarborough) *Acorna's World,* HarperPrism (New York, NY), 2000.

(With Elizabeth A. Scarborough) *Acorna's Search,* HarperCollins (New York, NY), 2001.

(With Elizabeth A. Scarborough) *Acorna's Rebels,* HarperCollins (New York, NY), 2003.

(With Elizabeth A. Scarborough) *Acorna's Triumph,* HarperCollins (New York, NY), 2004.

OTHER

The Mark of Merlin (also see below), Dell (New York, NY), 1971, reprinted, Wildside Press, 2002.

The Ring of Fear (also see below), Dell (New York, NY), 1971.

(Editor) *Cooking out of This World,* Ballantine (New York, NY), 1973.

The Kilternan Legacy (also see below), Dell (New York, NY), 1975, reprinted, Wildside Press, 2002.

Habit Is an Old Horse, Dryad Press (Seattle, WA), 1986.

The Year of the Lucy (novel), Tor Books (New York, NY), 1986.

The Lady (novel), Ballantine (New York, NY), 1987, published as *The Carradyne Touch,* Futura/Macdonald (London, England), 1988.

(Author of text and introduction) Robin Wood, *The People of Pern,* Donning (Norfolk, VA), 1988.

(With Jody Lynn Nye) *The Dragonlover's Guide to Pern,* illustrated by Todd Cameron Hamilton, Del Rey (New York, NY), 1989.

Three Gothic Novels: The Ring of Fear, The Mark of Merlin, The Kilternan Legacy, Underwood-Miller, 1990.

Dragonflight Graphic Novel, HarperCollins (New York, NY), 1993.

Black Horses for the King (juvenile historical fiction), Harcourt (San Diego, CA), 1996.

(Editor with John Betancourt) *Serve It Forth: Cooking with Anne McCaffrey,* Warner Books (New York, NY), 1996.

Dragon, HarperCollins (New York, NY), 1996.

(With Richard Woods) *A Diversity of Dragons,* illustrated by John Howe, HarperPrism (New York, NY), 1997.

Contributor to anthologies, including *Infinity One,* 1970, *Future Love,* 1977, and *Camelot: A Collection of Original Arthurian Tales,* 1995. Contributor to magazines, including *Analog Science Fiction-Science Fact, Galaxy,* and *Magazine of Fantasy and Science Fiction.*

Collections of McCaffrey's manuscripts are housed at Syracuse University, Syracuse, NY, and in the Kerlan Collection, University of Minnesota, Minneapolis.

ADAPTATIONS: *Dragonsong* and *Dragonsinger* were adapted as children's stage plays by Irene Singer and produced in Baltimore, MD; the "Pern" books inspired a cassette of music, *Dragonsongs,* a board game, and two computer games; *The Dragonriders of Pern* was adapted for a television series that premiered in January, 2000; many of McCaffrey's books have been recorded on audiocassette, including *All the Weyrs of Pern, Damia's Children,Dolphins of Pern, The Girl Who Heard Dragons,Dragonquest, The Planet Pirates, The White Dragon,Nerilka's Story,* and *Powers That Be.*

WORK IN PROGRESS: An autobiography.

SIDELIGHTS: Science fiction's much-heralded "Dragon Lady," Anne McCaffrey, resides in Ireland in a home called Dragonhold, where she produces, among her other novels, the fantastic tales of the dragonriders of Pern. A planet protected from deadly spores by fire-breathing dragons and their human partners, Pern is a former colony of Earth that has lost much of its knowledge of science and history. In such novels as *Dragonflight, Dragonquest: Being the Further Adventures of the Dragonriders of Pern,* and *The White Dragon,* McCaffrey presents Pern as a land in which "social structure, tensions, legends, and traditions are all based on the fundamental ecological battle [against the 'Thread' spores] and on the empathetic kinship between dragon and rider," Debra Rae Cohen commented in *Crawdaddy.*

Indeed, that kinship is not taken lightly. As described by *Washington Post* critic Joseph McLellan, "When the dragon eggs are ready to hatch on the planet Pern, it is a major social event with enduring, almost cosmic implications." In a form of permanent selection called "Impression," "each fledgling dragon struggles out of its shell, there is a predestined conjunction of souls; the dragon selects the young human who will be its lifemate, rushing to his or her side and bowling over anyone imprudent enough to stand in the way," the critic added.

Although Pern is inhabited by flying dragons and dominated by a near-feudal society—elements native to fantasy worlds—McCaffrey's creation is based on solid scientific principles. The author in fact took supplementary courses in physics in order to create credible science fiction. The focus of the Dragonrider series—on Pern's society and on the relationship between dragon and rider—puts the science in the background, unlike many science fiction novels. The result, as *New York*

Times Book Review critic Gerald Jonas noted, is that "few are better at mixing elements of high fantasy and hard science in a narrative that disarms skepticism by its open embrace of the joys of wish fulfillment," leading some to call McCaffrey's work "science fantasy." Cohen similarly remarked that, unlike fantasy, there is "no random magic here, no Tolkienesque created language . . . but a meticulously logical civilization, finely crafted." "Despite their fantasy feel, the Dragonrider books have always had a sf premise," Carolyn Cushman stated in *Locus.* While McCaffrey has always hinted at that premise in her books, she explores it fully in 1988's *Dragonsdawn,* the story of how the original colonists of Pern used genetic manipulation to develop Pern's dragons.

It is the fanciful atmosphere of Pern, however, with its never-ending opportunity for adventure, that draws in many fans. Not surprisingly, the dragons are the scene-stealers in McCaffrey's novels; they are described as large, multicolored, flying reptiles "who communicate telepathically with their riders and keep the land free from the vicious Threads, destructive spores that fall from a neighboring planet whenever its irregular orbit brings it close enough," Edra C. Bogle wrote in the *Dictionary of Literary Biography.* Bogle cited *Dragonquest,* the second volume of the "Pern" series, as "full of action and unexpected twists" and indicated that it "may well be the best of these books. The major theme of all the volumes, how to rediscover and preserve the past while maintaining flexibility, is well brought out here."

Behind these magical tales lies a serious social commentary, according to Bogle. "Most of McCaffrey's protagonists are women or children, whom she treats with understanding and sympathy," Bogle said. The injustices these characters suffer, facilitated by an unprogressive social system, "are at the heart of most of McCaffrey's books." In fact, the majority of McCaffrey's novels feature strong heroines: the ruling Weyrwomen of the "Dragonrider" books; the determined young musician of *Crystal Singer* and *Killashandra;* the talented psychics of *To Ride Pegasus* and the "Raven Women" series; and Helva, the independent starship "brain" of *The Ship Who Sang.* Through these works, Bogle indicated, "McCaffrey has brought delineations of active women into prominence in science fiction."

Reviewing *Crystal Singer* for the *New York Times Book Review,* Gerald Jonas described its heroine, Killashandra Ree, as "young, beautiful, intelligent, sexy, and courageous." He also found McCaffrey's language to be "athletic" and contended that the theme of the book is "[o]bsession on a Melvillean scale." In the world McCaffrey creates in the novel, the "living crystal" of the title is an essential element for both space travel and communications. The crystal can only be found on the planet Ballybran, and only be mined by singers who have trained rigorously to produce the right notes with perfect pitch. Most of the narrative is taken up with Killashandra's compulsion to become a crystal singer. Jonas compared McCaffrey's depiction of the crystal singer trade, which includes its "scientific, economic, political and psychological ramifications," to Melville's description of the whaling trade in *Moby Dick.* He went on to note that in McCaffrey's case, this material consumes the book, as if "Moby Dick and Ahab [were] reduced to mere walk-on parts. . . . So what we are left with is a detailed instruction manual for a trade that doesn't exist." However, Jonas concluded that although "[c]rystal singing may not be real . . . Killashandra's obsession comes alive, and readers who get past the first 50 pages will find themselves sharing it."

The "Pern" series, including *Moreta: Dragonlady of Pern, Nerilka's Story, Dragonsdawn, The Renegades of Pern, All the Weyrs of Pern, The Chronicles of Pern: First Fall,* and *The Dolphins of Pern,* explores the history and culture of McCaffrey's created world. *Moreta* and *Nerilka's Story* expand on a legend from the original three books; *Dragonsdawn* and *The Chronicles of Pern: First Fall* tell of the original settlement of Pern, the breeding of dragons, and the early efforts of the settlers to fight Thread. *The Renegades of Pern* and *All the Weyrs of Pern* use their newly recovered technology to find a final solution to the attack of the spores and, in the process, begin to question some of their basic assumptions about their society. McCaffrey has also published "Pern" novels that have little to do with dragons; the "Harper Hall" trilogy draws on the author's experience as a trained vocalist and explain the function of music in Pernese society, while *The Dolphins of Pern* explores human relations with an animal that was just as much an immigrant to Pern as the humans themselves. "There are also three Pern reference books," the author told *Booklist* interviewer Pat Monaghan, "in case you get lost among the many names and places."

McCaffrey's "Dragonriders" series has proved so popular, with each new volume hitting the bestseller lists, "that it has almost transcended genre categorization," Gary K. Reynolds asserted in the *Science Fiction and Fantasy Book Review.* "McCaffrey succeeds so well because she presents a colorful, ideally traditional culture in which each person has his or her place, with corresponding duties and privileges; in which the moral choices are clear; and in which, 'if you try hard enough, and work long enough, you can achieve anything you desire.'" As a result, James and Eugene Sloan concluded in the Chicago *Tribune Books,* McCaffrey's "Dragonriders of Pern" books "must now rank as the most enduring serial in the history of science fantasy."

In 2003 McCaffrey collaborated with her son, Todd McCaffrey, on the "Pern" novel titled *Dragon's Kin,* set in a previously unexplored period in Pern's past. Critics noted that though there are two writers and Anne McCaffrey's style has become familiar to series fans, "Pern" readers would "notice no seams," according to a reviewer for *Publishers Weekly.* Frieda Murray in *Booklist* commented that the collaboration is "a harbinger that Pern, an enduring monument for two generations of sf readers so far, will continue after its originator's departure."

McCaffrey's fiction—and her fans—stretch far beyond the original dragonriders of Pern. Her first published book, *Restoree,* "was ostensibly written 'as a tongue-in-cheek protest' against the cliches of standard space opera," reported Bogle. *Decision at Doona* "lacks a central heroine and a love story," the reviewer stated, and "emphasizes the need for new ways of adapting to new circumstances." *Powers That Be,* a collaboration with Elizabeth A. Scarborough, tells about life and rebellion on a terraformed company planet. "One critic said, 'This is a seamless collaboration,' which we both took very much to heart," McCaffrey told Monaghan; "finally someone is reading us as we should be read!"

Still writing prodigiously in her mid-seventies, McCaffrey added several new volumes to her "Freedom" and "Pegasus" series, concluded the "Rowan" series, launched the "Acorna" series with volumes written in collaboration with Margaret Ball and Scarborough, published *Nimisha's Ship,* a sequel to the 1989 *The Coelura,* and also the non-series volume *If Wishes Were Horses.* Vicky Burkholder in *Voice of Youth Advocates,* characterized *If Wishes Were Horses* as "a short, easily read fairy tale that any McCaffrey fan will enjoy." The book tells the story of teenage Tirza, whose father has gone off to war and whose village has been burnt to the ground. Tirza receives a magical crystal, similar to the ones her mother wears, for her sixteenth birthday. Her first wish with the crystal is for her twin brother, who desperately wants a horse for his birthday. Little does she know that her mother has used her own crystals to wish for the same thing. The two wishes produce results far beyond their expectations. Soon the horse arrives, followed by many more horses, followed in turn by Tirza's father leading his victorious troops home from the war.

While faulting the lack of tension in *Nimisha's Ship,* Joyce Davidson in the *Voice of Youth Advocates* nevertheless dubbed it "a good adventure story" that is "sure to be in high demand wherever there are readers of science fiction." Set in the far future, the novel centers on Nimisha, a dedicated student of engineering. After her father's death she inherits the Rondymense Ship Yards and sets out to design and build a long-range spaceship. It takes more than a dozen years to complete her task. On the ship's first test flight, with Nimisha aboard, it is sucked into a wormhole that transports it to a different space. Here, Nimisha discovers other ships and survivors, both human and alien, who have also been transported to this space by accident. She eventually finds love and motherhood on a new world. Davidson noted: "The book contains open and frank discussions about sex."

In *The Tower and the Hive,* the fifth and final volume in her "Rowan" series, McCaffrey concludes the story of Angharad Gwyn, her husband Jeff Raven, and their offspring, who possess various telekinetic and telepathic powers. Purveyors of interstellar transportation and communication for an alliance of humans and friendly, weasel-like aliens, the Gwyn-Raven family must confront the threat of hostile aliens in the Hivers.

"In Ireland," wrote Jay Kay Klein in *Analog Science Fiction-Science Fact,* "Anne is best known for her champion horses and romantic fiction. There, SF is apt to be confused with children's literature." McCaffrey does admit to an attraction to writing non-SF literature. "I would like to do some [novels] set in Ireland, some romances, just old-fashioned romances, gothic novels as we called them in the seventies," McCaffrey told Monaghan. Her non-science-fiction books include a series of romantic novels written for Dell and also juvenile fiction. *Black Horses for the King,* for instance, is set in post-Roman Britain and draws on McCaffrey's extensive experience with horses to tell about the formation of Arthurian cavalry. "If you tell a good story," the author told Monaghan, "anybody will read it. It doesn't have to be fantasy or science fiction. It could be anything."

BIOGRAPHICAL AND CRITICAL SOURCES:

BOOKS

Arbur, Rosemarie, *Leigh Brackett, Marion Zimmer Bradley, Anne McCaffrey: A Primary and Secondary Bibliography,* G.K. Hall (New York, NY), 1982.

Authors in the News, Volume 2, Thomson Gale (Detroit, MI), 1976.

Bestsellers 89, Issue 2, Thomson Gale (Detroit, MI), 1989.

Brizzi, Mary T., *Anne McCaffrey: A Reader's Guide,* Starmont (West Linn, OR), 1986.

Contemporary Literary Criticism, Volume 17, Thomson Gale (Detroit, MI), 1981.

Dictionary of Literary Biography, Volume 8: *Twentieth-Century American Science-Fiction Writers,* Thomson Gale (Detroit, MI), 1981.

McCaffrey, Todd, *Dragonholder: The Life and Dreams (So Far) of Anne McCaffrey,* Ballantine (New York, NY), 1999.

Roberts, Robin, *Anne McCaffrey: A Critical Companion,* Greenwood Press (Westport, CT), 1996.

St. James Guide to Young Adult Writers, 2nd edition, St. James Press (Detroit, MI), 1999.

Twentieth-Century Children's Writers, 3rd edition, St. James Press (Detroit, MI), 1989.

Twentieth-Century Science-Fiction Writers, 3rd edition, St. James Press (Detroit, MI), 1991.

Twentieth-Century Young Adult Writers, St. James Press (Detroit, MI), 1994.

Walker, Paul, *Speaking of Science Fiction: The Paul Walker Interviews,* Luna (Oradell, NJ), 1978.

PERIODICALS

Analog Science Fiction & Fact, September, 1993, pp. 162-163; April, 1994, pp. 168-169; May, 1994, pp. 163-164; April, 1996, p. 146; October, 1997, Tom Easton, review of *Dragonseye,* pp. 151-152.

Analog Science Fiction/Science Fact, January, 1980, pp. 167-173; August, 1991, p. 77.

Booklist, May 1, 1976, pp. 1266-67; April 1, 1977, p. 1170; September 1, 1978, p. 39; September 1, 1988, p. 4; September 15, 1989, p. 114; March 15, 1994, pp. 1300-01; March 1, 1998, Sally Estes, review of *Freedom's Challenge,* pp. 1044-45; July, 1998, Sally Estes, review of *Acorna's Quest,* p. 1868; March 15, 1999, Sally Estes, review of *The Tower and the Hive,* p. 1260; February 15, 2000, Whitney Scott, review of *The Tower and the Hive,*p. 1128; April 15, 2000, Sally Estes, review of *Pegasus in Space,* p. 1499, and *Black Horses for the King,* p. 1544; June 1, 2000, Sally Estes, review of *Acorna's World,* p. 1866; January 1, 2001, Sally Estes, review of *The Skies of Pern,* p. 870; September 15, 2003, Frieda Murray, review of *Dragon's Kin,* p. 181.

Bulletin of the Center for Children's Books, May, 1996, p. 306.

Crawdaddy, June, 1978.

Curriculum Review, August, 1977, p. 206.

Dallas News, March 25, 1976.

Fantasy Review, April, 1985, p. 29.

Horn Book, July-August, 1996, Ann A. Flowers, review of *Black Horses for the King,* p. 467.

Kirkus Reviews, April 1, 1996, p. 534; April 1, 1998, review of *Freedom's Challenge.*

Library Journal, February 15, 1994, p. 123; May 15, 1998, Jackie Cassada, review of *Freedom's Challenge,* p. 119; February 15, 1999, review of *Nimisha's Ship,* p. 187; April 15, 2000, review of *Pegasus in Space,* p. 128; August, 2000, Jackie Cassada, review of *Acorna's World,* p. 167; October 15, 2003, Jackie Cassada, review of *Dragon's Kin,* p. 101.

Locus, September, 1988; April, 1990, pp. 25, 37; August, 1990, p. 29; April, 1992, p. 35; May, 1993, pp. 33-34.

Los Angeles Times Book Review, September 12, 1982, p. 6; January 29, 1984, p. 8.

Magazine of Fantasy and Science Fiction, February, 1996, p. 36.

New York Times Book Review, August 29, 1982, Gerald Jonas, "Imaginary People," p. 10; January 8, 1984, p. 18; January 8, 1989.

People, March 12, 1984.

Publishers Weekly, October 16, 1995, review of *Camelot,* p. 62; April 22, 1996, p. 73; November 24, 1997, review of *The Masterharper of Pern,* p. 56; March 15, 1999, review of *Nimisha's Ship,* p. 51; April 16, 1999, review of *The Tower and the Hive,* p. 60; August 7, 2000, review of *Acorna's World,* p. 80; February 19, 2001, review of *The Skies of Pern,* p. 74; October 13, 2003, review of *Dragon's Kin,* p. 61.

Quill & Quire, September, 1990, p. 64.

Rigel, winter, 1982.

School Library Journal, September, 1977, p. 132; September, 1994, p. 256; August, 1955, p. 171; June, 1996, p. 153; April, 1998, review of *Freedom's Choice,* p. 161; August, 1998, John Lawson, review of *The Masterharper of Pern,* p. 196; December, 1999, John Lawson, review of *The Tower and the Hive,* p. 164; August, 2000, Christine C. Menefee, review of *Pegasus in Space,* p. 213.

Science Fiction and Fantasy Book Review, July, 1979.

Science Fiction Review, fall, 1982.

Times Literary Supplement, March 14, 1975.

Tribune Books (Chicago, IL), July 13, 1986.

Village Voice Literary Supplement, April, 1984, p. 19.

Voice of Youth Advocates, April, 1992, pp. 17-18; February, 1999, Vicky Burkholder, review of *If Wishes*

Were Horses, pp. 444-445; June, 1999, Joyce Davidson, review of *Nimisha's Ship.*

Washington Post, June 26, 1978.

Wilson Library Bulletin, February, 1991, pp. 90-91; February, 1992, pp. 90-91.

ONLINE

Anne McCaffrey Web site, http://www.annemccaffrey.org/ (September 28, 2004).

Random House Web site, http://www.randomhouse.com/ (June 12, 2000).

* * *

McCAFFREY, Anne Inez
See McCAFFREY, Anne

* * *

McCALL SMITH, Alexander 1948- (Alexander McCall Smith)

PERSONAL: Born 1948, in Southern Rhodesia (now Zimbabwe); married; children: two daughters. *Education:* Studied law in Scotland. *Hobbies and other interests:* Plays bassoon in Really Terrible Orchestra.

ADDRESSES: *Agent*—c/o Publicity Department, Time Warner Book Group UK, Brettenham House, Lancaster Place, London WC2E 7EN, United Kingdom.

CAREER: Professor of medical law at Edinburgh University. Taught law at University of Botswana; helped create a criminal code for Botswana. Human Genetics Commission of the United Kingdom (vice chairman), UNESCO (member, International Bioethics Commission).

WRITINGS:

NONFICTION

(Editor with Tony Carty) *Power and Manoeuvrability,* Q Press (Edinburgh, Scotland), 1978.

(With John Kenyon Mason) *Butterworths Medico-Legal Encyclopedia,* Butterworths (Boston, MA), 1987.

(Editor with Elaine Sutherland) *Family Rights: Family Law and Medical Advances,* Edinburgh University Press (Edinburgh, Scotland), 1990.

(With John Kenyon Mason) *Law and Medical Ethics,* third edition, Butterworths (Austin, TX), 1991.

(With Kwame Frimpong) *The Criminal Law of Botswana,* Juta (Cape Town), 1992.

(Editor with Michael A. Menlowe) *The Duty to Rescue: The Jurisprudence of Aid,* Dartmouth (Brookfield, VT), 1993.

(Editor with Colin Shapiro) *Forensic Aspects of Sleep,* Wiley (New York, NY), 1997.

(With Daniel W. Shuman) *Justice and the Prosecution of Old Crimes: Balancing Legal, Psychological, and Moral Concerns,* American Psychological Association (Washington, DC), 2000.

(With Alan Merry) *Errors, Medicine, and the Law,* Cambridge University Press (New York, NY), 2001.

NO. 1 LADIES' DETECTIVE AGENCY SERIES

The No. 1 Ladies' Detective Agency, D. Philip (Cape Town, South Africa), 1998, Anchor Books (New York, NY), 2005.

Tears of the Giraffe, Polygon (Edinburgh, Scotland), 2000, Anchor Books (New York, NY), 2002.

Morality for Beautiful Girls, Polygon (Edinburgh, Scotland), 2001, Anchor Books (New York, NY), 2002.

The Kalahari Typing School for Men, Polygon (Edinburgh, Scotland), 2002, Pantheon (New York, NY), 2003.

The Full Cupboard of Life, Polygon (Edinburgh, Scotland), 2003, Pantheon (New York, NY), 2004.

In the Company of Cheerful Ladies, Pantheon (New York, NY), 2004.

SUNDAY PHILOSOPHY CLUB SERIES

The Sunday Philosophy Club, Pantheon (New York, NY), 2004.

Friends, Lovers, Chocolate, Pantheon (New York, NY), 2005.

VON IGELFELD SERIES

Portuguese Irregular Verbs, illustrated by Iain McIntosh, Polygon (Edinburgh, Scotland), 2003, Anchor Books (New York, NY), 2005.

The Finer Points of Sausage Dogs, illustrated by Iain McIntosh, Anchor Books (New York, NY), 2005.

At the Villa of Reduced Circumstances, illustrated by Iain McIntosh, Anchor Books (New York, NY), 2005.

SCOTLAND STREET SERIES

44 Scotland Street, illustrated by Iain McIntosh, Anchor Books (New York, NY), 2005.

Espresso Tales: The Latest from 44 Scotland Street, illustrated by Iain McIntosh, Anchor Books (New York, NY), 2006.

CHILDREN'S BOOKS

The Perfect Hamburger, iillustrated by Laszlo Acs, Hamish Hamilton (London, England), 1982.

Film Boy, illustrated by Joanna Carey, Methuen (London, England), 1988.

Mike's Magic Seeds, illustrated by Kate Shannon, Young Corgi (London, England), 1988.

Suzy Magician, Young Corgi (London, England), 1990.

The Five Lost Aunts of Harriet Bean, Blackie (London, England), 1990.

The Muscle Machine, illustrated by Terry McKenna, Hamish Hamilton (London, England), 1995.

The Bubblegum Tree, illustrated by Georgien Overwater, Hippo (London, England), 1996.

Bursting Balloons Mystery, illustrated by Georgien Overwater, Hippo (London, England), 1997.

The Popcorn Pirates, illustrated by Georgien Overwater, Hippo (London, England), 1999.

Akimbo and the Elephants, illustrated by LeUyen Pham, Bloomsbury Children's Books (New York, NY), 2005.

Akimbo and the Lions, illustrated by LeUyen Pham, Bloomsbury Children's Books (New York, NY), 2005.

Akimbo and the Crocodile Man, illustrated by LeUyen Pham, Bloomsbury Children's Books (New York, NY), 2006.

The Cowgirl Aunt of Harriet Bean, illustrated by Laura Rankin, Bloomsbury Children's Books (New York, NY), 2006.

The Five Lost Aunts of Harriet Bean, illustrated by Laura Rankin, Bloomsbury Children's Books (New York, NY), 2006.

Harriet Bean and the League of Cheats, illustrated by Laura Rankin, Bloomsbury Children's Books (New York, NY), 2006.

Author of more than fifty books, including children's books such as *The White Hippo,* Hamish Hamilton; *Marzipan Max,* Blackie; *The Ice-Cream Bicycle,* Viking Read Alone; *The Doughnut Ring,* Hamish Hamilton; *Paddy and the Ratcatcher,* Heinemann; and *The Princess Trick,* Puffin.

OTHER

Children of Wax: African Folk Tales, Interlink Book (New York, NY), 1991.

Heavenly Date and Other Stories, Canongate (Edinburgh, Scotland), 1995.

The Girl Who Married a Lion and Other Tales from Africa, Pantheon (New York, NY), 2004.

Blue Shoes and Happiness, Pantheon (New York, NY), 2006.

ADAPTATIONS: The story "Children of Wax" was made into an animated film; other stories by Smith have been read on BBC Radio. A film adaptation of *The No. 1 Ladies' Detective Agency* will be produced by Richard Sydney Pollack and directed by Anthony Minghella.

SIDELIGHTS: The diverse accomplishments of Alexander McCall Smith, include a distinguished career as a legal scholar and more recent fame as a best-selling novelist. A professor of medical law at Edinburgh University, Smith has published many works on medical ethics and criminal law. For example, he has written about the duty to rescue and the impact of medical advances on parental rights. Smith also had numerous books of fiction for young children and short-story collections in print before he published a series of detective stories set in Botswana. The first installment, *The No. 1 Ladies' Detective Agency,* became a best-selling novel in the United States after it was popularized by word of mouth. Readers and critics have been charmed by the stories, which are more about relationships, customs, and informal justice than sleuthing.

Born and raised in the British colony of Southern Rhodesia (now Zimbabwe), Smith studied law in Edinburgh, Scotland. He then assisted in creating Botswana's first law school, taught law at the University of Botswana, and wrote a criminal code for Botswana. Many years later, in 1992, he would publish *The Criminal Law of Botswana* with Kwame Frimpong. The book interested critics with its discussion of how the country's criminal law is unlike others in southern Africa and how it resembles the Queensland Criminal Code of 1899. Two reviewers regretted that the work is not more detailed: in the *Journal of African Law* Simon Coldham advised that the book is "designed primarily for students," while James S. Read said in the *International and Comparative Law Quarterly,* that the book provides "a short and selective introduction" to the subject.

Most of Smith's legal scholarship treats subjects relating to medical and criminal law issues. He served as co-editor and contributor for *Family Rights: Family Law and Medical Advances,* which contains seven essays about the legal and ethical implications of new medical capabilities that affect the creation of life as well as the extension of life. The essays consider the impact of laws on a family's ability to make their own medical decisions. McCall's contribution, "Is Anything Left of Parental Rights?," addresses the increased autonomy of children.

Reviews of *Family Rights* described the book as an in-depth treatment suitable for specialists and general readers. In the *Sydney Law Review* Belinda Bennett recommended it as "a very readable collection" that avoids jargon and explains the necessary medical and scientific terminology. Jenny L. Urwin said in the *Journal of Medical Ethics* that it provided "interesting and thoughtful analysis" on a previously neglected subject. The book's "interdisciplinary and comparative flavour" was noted in *Family Law* by Andrew Bainham, who also said, "The scholarship in this volume is, for the most part, as original as it is provocative and the two most impressive contributions are by the editors themselves." Writing for *Nature,* Andrew Grubb commented on the context of Smith's essay, saying, "Faced with this largely interventionist judicial attitude, it is left to Sandy McCall Smith to challenge its basis and to sound a note of caution."

In *The Duty to Rescue: The Jurisprudence of Aid* Smith helped compile essays that discuss the moral and sometimes legal duty to provide aid. The writings cover theoretical and philosophical concerns, the possible ways of putting theory into practice, and the state's duty to assist at-risk individuals. Reviewers said the work does a good job of addressing the diverse implications of making rescue a legal obligation. In a review for *Choice,* M.A. Foley called the book "rather comprehensive" and recommended it as a primary reference on the subject. In the *University of British Columbia Law Review* Mitchell McInnes commented that Smith's essay, "The Duty to Rescue and the Common Law," raises an interesting and incomplete point on the subject of how a legal requirement would impact the formation of individual moral intuition. Celia Wells recommended the volume and McCall's contributions in *Criminal Law Review.* She concluded, "This collection sweeps effortlessly across legal, jurisdictional, and philosophical boundaries posing on its way a series of fascinating questions and supplying some clues to the answers."

Smith is also a prolific fiction writer. His books for children reflect both Western and non-Western cultural influences, and are mostly written for new readers. One example showing Smith's African background is *The White Hippo,* a story set in Gambia about the unsuccessful efforts of villagers who want to protect an albino hippo from a white man claiming to be a photographer. In *The Perfect Hamburger,* an old man and a young boy join forces to try to save a family-run hamburger shop from being forced out of business by a chain restaurant.

The twenty-seven stories in *Children of Wax: African Folk Tales* are more suited for older children and storytellers. Smith collected the tales from old and young members of the Ndebele people of Zimbabwe. Featuring shape-changing animals and supernatural powers, they nevertheless contain realistic portrayals of hardship and danger. The stories often serve to condemn bad behaviors such as greed and unfounded trust and show that justice does not always follow wrongdoing. *Library Journal*'s Patricia Dooley warned that this is "emphatically not children's pabulum." In a review for *Choice,* P. Alden was not quite satisfied with the authenticity of Smith's retelling, but said that the stories are "engaging" and that some are notable for their depiction of Zimbabwean women. A *Kirkus Reviews* writer admired the collection for its "evocative, involving narratives that reveal much about the culture from which they spring."

The collection *Heavenly Date and Other Stories* is comprised of original stories by Smith that are international in scope. Among them, "Intimate Accounts" is set in a fictional world, "Bulawayo" happens in Southern Rhodesia, and others take place in Zurich, Lisbon, and Northern Queensland. The dark and funny pieces relate all kinds of strange dates, meetings, and exchanges between men and women. In a review for the *Times Literary Supplement,* Andrew Biswell made note of Smith's inventiveness, stylistic range, and the "remarkable absence of excess baggage" in the collection that he thought showed the influence of African oral storytelling.

Smith's inspiration for *The No. 1 Ladies' Detective Agency* and the protagonist Mma Precious Ramotswe was his admiration for the women of Africa, according to an interviewer in *Publishers Weekly.* The novel and subsequent books in the series— *Tears of the Giraffe, Morality for Beautiful Girls,* and *The Kalahari Typing School for Men*—are mostly about everyday life in Africa. The character of Mma Ramotswe is the dynamic central force behind these stories. A solidly built, divorced woman in her late thirties, she uses a tiny inheritance to start a detective agency. Her work takes place in the city of Gaborone and in cattle country near the Kalahari Desert. She deals mostly with family conflicts, including cheating husbands, and employer-employee troubles. Mma Ramotswe runs a threadbare operation, but she does have an assistant, Mma Makutsi, a secretarial college graduate who has lost better jobs to her prettier classmates. Another key figure is J.L.B. Matekoni, a mechanic who assists them and later becomes engaged to Mma Ramotswe. The bride-to-be is a rather unconventional detective, one who also serves as family counselor, comments on manners and the lack of them, and is less concerned with legally administered justice than with doing right by her clients.

Mma Ramotswe and Smith's novels about her have charmed reviewers, who have found the novels fresh, amusing, and affecting. In a *BookLoons* review, G. Hall described the first installment as "truly unique," explaining that "the best part of the book is, in fact, not the mysteries but the stories of Precious and her father." Mahinder Kingra of the *Baltimore City Paper* judged that in this "deceptively frivolous" novel there is "as honest and sympathetic a portrait of contemporary African life as [Nigerian writer Chinua] Achebe's." Kingra commented that the book is "one of those rare, unassuming novels that seems to contain all of life within its pages, and affirms life in telling its story." Christine Jeffords noted in *Best Reviews* online that Smith "succeeds in giving his story a lilting, lyrical flavor that makes the reader feel almost as if she is listening to a story being spun by a native tale-teller." Comments on the first three novels by Anthony Daniels in the *Spectator* included the assessment "I know nothing else like them." Daniels credited Smith with an admirably simple writing style and the remarkable feat of "creating fictional characters who are decent, goodhearted but not in the least bit dull." And the critic advised that "for all their apparent simplicity, the Precious Ramotswe books are highly sophisticated."

When Alida Becker reviewed the first three books for the *New York Times,* dubbing Mma Ramotswe the "Miss Marple of Botswana," it dramatically increased public awareness of the series. As Becker noted, film rights for the series had already been sold to Anthony Minghella, director of *The English Patient.* In the *Wall Street Journal,* Matthew Gurewitsch found *The No. 1 Ladies' Detective Agency* to be no less than "one of the most entrancing literary treats of many a year." Gurewitsch exulted that Smith planned more stories about Mma Ramotswe and would be publishing a series of academic satires about a professor of Romance philology named Dr. Mortiz-Maria von Igelfeld.

BIOGRAPHICAL AND CRITICAL SOURCES:

PERIODICALS

Choice, February, 1992, P. Alden, review of *Children of Wax,* p. 903; July/August, 1994, M.A. Foley, review of *The Duty to Rescue,* p. 1792.

Criminal Law Review, January, 1996, Celia Wells, review of *The Duty to Rescue,* pp. 71-72.

Family Law, April, 1992, Andrew Bainham, review of *Family Rights,* p. 135.

International and Comparative Law Quarterly, July, 1993, review of *The Criminal Law of Botswana,* pp. 748-749.

Journal of African Law, autumn, 1992, Simon Coldham, review of *The Criminal Law of Botswana,* pp. 193-194.

Journal of Medical Ethics, June, 1992, Jenny L. Urwin, review of *Family Rights,* pp. 108-109.

Kirkus Reviews, June 15, 1991, review of *Children of Wax,* p. 793.

Library Journal, July, 1991, Patricia Dooley, review of *Children of Wax,* p. 106.

Nature, June 27, 1991, Andrew Grubb, review of *Family Rights,* p. 707.

New York Times Book Review, January 27, 2002, Alida Becker, "Miss Marple of Botswana," p. 12.

Publishers Weekly, July 22, 2002, Charlotte Abbott, "From Africa, with Love," p. 75.

Spectator, September 1, 2001, Anthony Daniels, "Something Really New out of Africa," pp. 36-37.

Sydney Law Review, June, 1992, Belinda Bennett, review of *Family Rights,* pp. 253-255.

Times Literary Supplement, November 3, 1995, Andrew Biswell, "Mr Self and Ms Ms," p. 25.

University of British Columbia Law Review, winter, 1994, Mitchell McInnes, review of *The Duty to Rescue,* pp. 201-204.

Wall Street Journal, September 4, 2002, Matthew Gurewitsch, "A Scholarly Scot Writes of African Intrigue," p. D8.

ONLINE

Alexander McCall Smith Home Page, http://www.mccallsmith.com/ (February 15, 2006).

Baltimore City Paper Online, http://citypaper.com/ (September 5-11, 2001), Mahinder Kingra, review of *The No. 1 Ladies' Detective Agency.*

Best Reviews, http://thebestreviews.com/ (October 4, 2002), review of *The No. 1 Ladies' Detective Agency.*

BookLoons, http://bookloons.com/ (December 12, 2002), G. Hall, review of *The No. 1 Ladies' Detective Agency.*

* * *

McCANN, Edson
See POHL, Frederik

* * *

McCARTHY, Charles, Jr.
See McCARTHY, Cormac

* * *

McCARTHY, Cormac 1933-
(Charles McCarthy, Jr.)

PERSONAL: Born July 20, 1933, in Providence, RI; son of Charles Joseph and Gladys (McGrail) McCarthy; married Lee Holleman, 1961 (divorced); married Anne de Lisle, 1967 (divorced); married Jennifer Winkley, 1998; children: (first marriage) Cullen. *Education:* Attended University of Tennessee, four years.

ADDRESSES: Home—El Paso, TX. *Office*—c/o Alfred A. Knopf, 201 East 50th Street, New York, NY 10022. *Agent*—Amanda Urban, International Creative Management, 40 West 57th St., New York, NY 10019.

CAREER: Writer. *Military service:* U.S. Air Force, 1953-56.

AWARDS, HONORS: Ingram-Merrill Foundation grant for creative writing, 1960; American Academy of Arts and Letters traveling fellowship to Europe, 1965-66; William Faulkner Foundation award, 1965, for *The Orchard Keeper;* Rockefeller Foundation grant, 1966; Guggenheim fellowship, 1976; MacArthur Foundation grant, 1981; Jean Stein Award, American Academy and Institution of Arts and Letters, 1991; National Book Award for fiction, 1992, and National Book Critics Award for fiction, both for *All the Pretty Horses;* Lyndhurst Foundation grant; Institute of Arts and Letters award.

WRITINGS:

The Orchard Keeper, Random House (New York, NY), 1965.

Outer Dark, Random House (New York, NY), 1968.

Child of God, Random House (New York, NY), 1974.

The Gardener's Son (teleplay; produced as part of *Visions* series, Public Broadcasting System, 1977), published as *The Gardener's Son: A Screenplay,* Ecco Press (Hopewell, NJ), 1996.

Suttree, Random House (New York, NY), 1979.

Blood Meridian; or, The Evening Redness in the West, Random House (New York, NY), 1985, reprinted with an introduction by Harold Bloom, Modern Library, 2001.

All the Pretty Horses (book one in the *"Border Trilogy"*), Random House (New York, NY), 1992.

The Crossing (book two in the *"Border Trilogy"*), Random House (New York, NY), 1994.

Cities of the Plain (book three in the *"Border Trilogy"*), Random House (New York, NY), 1998.

The Border Trilogy (contains *All the Pretty Horses, The Crossing,* and *Cities of the Plain*), Knopf (New York, NY), 1999.

No Country for Old Men, Knopf (New York, NY), 2005.

Also author of the play *The Stonemason.* Contributor to *Yale Review* and *Sewanee Review.*

SIDELIGHTS: Cormac McCarthy, is frequently compared with such Southern-based writers as William Faulkner, Carson McCullers, and Flannery O'Connor. In a *Dictionary of Literary Biography* essay, Dianne L. Cox stated that McCarthy's work has in common with that of the others "a rustic and sometimes dark humor, intense characters, and violent plots; [he] shares as well their development of universal themes within a highly particularized fictional world, their seriousness of vision, and their vigorous exploration of the English language." "His characters are often outcasts—destitutes or criminals, or both," wrote Richard B. Woodward in the *New York Times.* "Death, which announces itself often, reaches down from the open sky, abruptly, with a slashed throat or a bullet in the face. The abyss opens up at any misstep."

McCarthy's early novels were often set in eastern Tennessee, while his later work focuses on the American Southwest. He has often been singled out for his individual prose style—beautifully lyrical yet spare, eschewing commas and totally stripped of quotation marks. This style has been a source of complaint for some reviewers; in a *New York Times* review of McCarthy's *All the Pretty Horses,* for example, critic Herbert Mitgang lamented: "This reader was put off at first by the author's all too writerly writing. His joined words, without hyphenation, and his unpunctuated, breathless sentences, call too much attention to themselves." Kurt Tidmore contended in the *Washington Post Book World,* however, that "the reader is never confused. Sentences punctuate themselves by the natural rhythm of their words. Everything is perfectly clear. The poetic never overwhelms the realistic." In addition, wrote Madison Smartt Bell in the *New York Times Book Review,* McCarthy's "elaborate and elevated" prose is "used effectively to frame realistic dialogue, for which his ear is deadly accurate." Bell continued: "Difficult as [McCarthy's writing] may sometimes be, it is also overwhelmingly seductive."

Throughout his career, McCarthy has actively avoided public attention, refusing to participate in lecture tours and seldom granting interviews. "Of all the subjects I'm interested in [talking about]," the author commented in the *New York Times,* "writing is way, *way* down at the bottom of the list." "Until very recently," observed Bell, "he shunned publicity so effectively that he wasn't even famous for it." Instead, he has concentrated upon crafting his unique and powerful fictions, unaffected by the critical acclaim that is heaped upon him with each new book. McCarthy has been described by Woodward as "a cult figure with a reputation as a writer's writer" who is, perhaps, "the best unknown novelist in America."

In keeping with McCarthy's reclusive nature, little is known about his early life. He was born Charles McCarthy, Jr., in Providence, Rhode Island, on July 20, 1933, the third of six children in an Irish Catholic family. "Sometime later, he or his family—no one seems to know which—changed his name to Cormac after Cormac MacCarthy, the Irish chieftain who built Blarney Castle," explained *Texas Monthly* contributor Michael Hall. When Cormac was four, he and his family moved to Knoxville, Tennessee, where his father got a job as an attorney for the powerful Tennessee Valley Authority. "After high school, McCarthy studied engineering at the University of Tennessee, then entered the U.S. Air Force. He served in Alaska for a couple of years before returning to Tennessee and reentering the university. He married twice, having a son, Cullen, with his first wife, and living for a period in a renovated barn on a pig farm with his second wife. In 1976, he moved to Texas, the source of much of his inspiration for his most famous works. "In El Paso McCarthy has become a ghost celebrity, an urban legend," Hall wrote. In 1996, the *Texas Monthly* writer continued, several fans spent some time" going through McCarthy's trash and cataloging it . . . to prove that he was not some mythic desert hermit but just as urban as everyone else in the city of more than half a million." "Contrary to popular wisdom, McCarthy is not a recluse," Hall stated. "But he is and always has been an intensely private man and a reluctant public one."

McCarthy's first novel, *The Orchard Keeper,* deals with three people—a young man who is coming of age in the Tennessee mountains, a bootlegger, and an aged orchard keeper—whose lives are intertwined, even though they don't meet until the end of the story. "Through these characters," wrote Cox, "the novel explores the relationship between individual integrity and independence achievable in the remote natural world of the mountains and the social obligations and strictures imposed by the community of men." J.G. Murray, reviewing *The Orchard Keeper* in *America,* felt that the book is interesting "because it does not seem to be autobiographical and [it] rejects the influence, more bad than good, of the Southern mystique." Murray finds McCarthy's view of adulthood "even more precise and sympathetic than his treatment of youth. And, as everyone knows, it is quite exceptional for young writers to be so objective." Writing in *Harper's,* K.G. Jackson called *The Orchard Keeper* "a complicated and evocative exposition of the transiency of life, well worth the concentration it demands."

Outer Dark, McCarthy's next novel, is "so centered on guilt and retribution that it is largely structured around scenes of judgment," according to Cox. *Outer Dark* tells the story of Culla and Rinthy, a brother and sister who suffer the consequences of their incest in very different ways. Many critics, such as Guy Davenport, compared McCarthy's style in this book to that of William Faulkner. In a *New York Times Book Review* article, Davenport wrote that *Outer Dark* "pays its homage to Faulkner," but went on to note that McCarthy's personal writing style "compels admiration, [being] compounded of Appalachian phrases as plain and as functional as an ax. In elegant counterpoint to this barebones English is a second diction taken from that rich store of English which is there in the dictionary to be used by those who can." A *Time* reviewer found that McCarthy's command of local dialect "is surpassed by his poetic descriptions of the land and its people. His is an Irish singing voice imbued with Southern Biblical intonations. The result is an antiphony of speech and verse played against a landscape of penance."

Lester Ballard, the title character of McCarthy's *Child of God,* is a demented backwoodsman, a murderer and necrophiliac. In this 1974 novel the author depicts the spiritual demise of Ballard and at the same time makes him a sympathetic figure. But Richard P. Brickner, writing in the *New York Times Book Review,* described *Child of God* as "an essentially sentimental novel that no matter how sternly it strives to be tragic is never more than morose." Similarly, in a review for *Commonweal,* contributor Robert Leiter called the book "thinner [and] less full-bodied than either *The Orchard Keeper* or *Outer Dark* . . . *Child of God* is a swift exciting read, but we are left with only incisive images strung along a thin plot line, the why and wherefore unexplained." Leiter surmised that the book "will perhaps be looked upon as a bad novel written by a good writer" and concluded that "this would be regrettable, for *Child of God* marks a progression in McCarthy's career. He has learned restraint. The 'old themes' live on in him, but his South is not rendered with the precision of a realist. He has taken realism to the province of folk myth."

Child of God is "a reading experience so impressive, so 'new', so clearly made well that it seems almost to defy the easy esthetic categories and at the same time cause me to thrash about for some help with the necessary description of my enthusiasm," stated Doris Grumbach in *New Republic,* adding, "Cormac McCarthy is a Southerner, a born storyteller, . . . a writer of natural, impeccable dialogue, a literary child of Faulkner." Grumbach went on to say that in McCarthy's style, "the journey from death-in-life to death-in-death, from the hunted to the discovery of the hunting . . . is accomplished in rare, spare, precise yet poetic prose." The reviewer felt the author "has allowed us direct communion with his special kind of chaos; every sentence he writes illuminates, if only for a moment, the great dark of madness and violence and inevitable death that surrounds us all."

In a *New Yorker* review of *Child of God,* Robert Coles compared McCarthy to ancient Greek dramatists, saying that he "simply writes novels that tell us we cannot comprehend the riddles of human idiosyncrasy, the influence of the merely contingent or incidental upon our lives. He is a novelist of religious feeling who appears to subscribe to no creed but who cannot stop wondering in the most passionate and honest way what gives life meaning. . . . From the isolated highlands of Tennessee he sends us original stories that show how mysterious or confusing the world is. Moreover, his mordant wit, his stubborn refusal to bend his writing to the literary and intellectual demands of our era, conspire at times to make him seem mysterious and confusing—a writer whose fate is to be relatively unknown and often misinterpreted. But both Greek playwrights and Christian theologians have been aware that such may be the fate of anyone, of even the most talented and sensitive of human beings."

McCarthy's fourth novel, *Suttree,* again focuses on a misfit character, Cornelius Suttree, and the undesirable society he inhabits. In this book, the author describes Suttree as a man who has spent years in "the company of thieves, derelicts, miscreants, pariahs, poltroons, spalpeens, curmudgeons, clotpolls, murderers, gamblers, bawds, whores, trulls, brigands, topers, tosspots, sots and archsots, lobcocks, smellsmocks, runagates, rakes, and other assorted and felonious debauchees." Reviewing the book in *Spectator,* Frank Rudman called McCarthy "a magnificent writer with a resonant style that moves easily and naturally into a grand register without losing truthfulness. His ear for dialogue is as funny and authentic as that of Mark Twain." Guy Davenport pointed out possible autobiographical elements in the novel and wondered if McCarthy "had asked what part of himself bears the imprint of the world in which he was raised, and answered himself by witnessing what these traits look like exemplified by a gallery of characters ranging from near-idiotic to noble." Writing in *National Review,* Davenport noted further that the reader is "won over . . . to Cormac McCarthy's radically original way with tone and his sense of the aloneness of people in their individuality. At the heart of *Suttree* there is a strange sense of transformation and rebirth in which the protagonist wanders in a forest, sees visions, and emerges as a stranger to all that was before familiar. This is a scene no one else could have written."

Anatole Broyard wrote of the author in a *New York Times* review of *Suttree:* "His people are so vivid that they seem exotic, but this is just another way of saying that we tend to forget the range of human differences. Mr. McCarthy's hyperbole is not Southern rhetoric, but flesh and blood. Every tale is tall, if you look at it closely enough." In the *Washington Post,* Edward Rothstein added another dollop of praise: "It is a measure . . . of McCarthy's skills that the reader becomes engaged with those of [Suttree's] world, even intoxicated by the miasmatic language. For every image that is tiresomely weighty, there is one which illuminates dark crevices. For every horror, there is a sensitive observation. For every violent dislocation, there is a subtly touching dialogue or gesture." Nelson Algren compared *Suttree* with McCarthy's earlier work, noting in the Chicago *Tribune Books:* "There were no telephones, indoor plumbing, electricity, or TV in [his] previous novels. . . . The language of his people was closer to the time of Shakespeare than to our own time. Here he has brought them all to town and into today—without losing the sense of old, old America. And without losing the freshness and the magic of the old wilderness. Although his new wilderness is an industrial wasteland, the magic remains."

In his next novel, 1985's *Blood Meridian; or, The Evening Redness in the West,* McCarthy leaves his home territory of Tennessee for the dusty plains of the Old West, a change possibly the result of the author's own relocation to El Paso, Texas, in 1974. *Blood Meridian* is by far McCarthy's bloodiest novel to date, detailing the adventures of a fourteen-year-old boy referred to only as "the kid" as he travels with a band of bounty hunters, paid by a Mexican governor to collect Indian scalps. The hunters, however, are not picky about their victims, leaving a long, bloody trail behind them as they go. "*Blood Meridian* comes at the reader like a slap in the face," wrote Caryn James in the *New York Times Book Review.* "While [it] is hard to get through, it is harder to ignore."

Though *Blood Meridian* is based loosely upon actual events of the 1840s and 1850s, it bears little resemblance to the historical westerns written by Louis L'Amour and others; instead, Woodward pointed out, it "has distinct echoes of *Moby Dick,* McCarthy's favorite book," for it concentrates on the barren, hellish landscape and near-surreal characters that make up the band of mercenaries. Most prominent among them is a huge, hairless man named Judge Holden. Though he is not the group's leader, "the Judge" commands the respect of the others as he pontificates by the fire each night. It is against the background of Judge Holden that the kid is placed, allowing the reader to evaluate for himself the morality of each character. "*Blood Meridian* stands the world of Louis L'Amour on its head (indeed, heaps hot coals upon it)," claimed *Los Angeles Times Book Review* contributor Tom Nolan, while Tom Pilkington, writing in the *World & I,* labeled it "perhaps the bloodiest book ever penned by an American author."

In defense of the meticulously detailed gore that pervades his novels, McCarthy told Woodward: "There's no such thing as life without bloodshed. . . . I think the notion that the species can be improved in some way, that everyone could live in harmony, is a really dangerous idea. Those who are afflicted with this notion are the first ones to give up their souls, their freedom. Your desire that it be that way will enslave you and make your life vacuous." Most importantly, though, the brutality depicted in McCarthy's writing has not reduced its power; rather, according to James, he "has asked us to witness evil not in order to understand it but to affirm its inexplicable reality; his elaborate language invents a world hinged between the real and surreal, jolting us out of complacency."

"By comparison with the sonority and carnage of *Blood Meridian,*" wrote Woodward, "the world of *All the Pretty Horses* is less risky—repressed but sane." Winner of the National Book Award, *All the Pretty Horses* is the first installment in a three-book epic titled "The Border Trilogy." Set in 1949, it tells the story of John Grady Cole, a sixteen-year-old Texan who, along with his friend, Lacey Rawlins, sets off on horseback for Mexico. It becomes a coming-of-age tale, with Cole learning the skills of survival, facing adversity, and finding romance, all set against the backdrop of a land that has not lost the magic of the old West. "In the hands of some other writer," noted Bell, "this material might make for a combination of *Lonesome Dove* and *Huckleberry Finn,* but Mr. McCarthy's vision is deeper than Larry McMurtry's and, in its own way, darker than Mark Twain's." "What he has given us is a book of remarkable beauty and strength," wrote Tidmore, "the work of a master in perfect command of his medium."

While *All the Pretty Horses* is almost universally considered one of McCarthy's most accessible novels, it did not receive universally favorable reviews. This is due, in part, to the popularity of the novel, which opened it to criticism by reviewers previously unfamiliar with McCarthy's work. While Richard Eder of the *Los Angeles Times Book Review* admitted that "McCarthy's elevated prose does wonders for deserts, mountains, freezing winds, night landscapes and the tangibility of food, a bath and clean clothes," he warned that "loftiness gusts like a capsizing high wind, and the writing can choke on its own ornateness." Still, the strength of *All the Pretty Horses* seems to lie in the integrity of its central character, Cole, who was described by Bruce Allen in the *World & I* as "both a credible and admirable character; he is a perfect vehicle for the expression of the novel's themes." Watching Cole adhere to his values in the face of near-insurmountable adversity gives *All the Pretty Horses* "a sustained innocence and a lucidity new in McCarthy's work," according to Woodward. In addition to winning the National Book Award and garnering its author much greater critical attention, *All the Pretty Horses* also proved to be a tremendous commercial success.

The second installment in McCarthy's "Border Trilogy," 1994's *The Crossing* covers much of the same geographical and emotional terrain as *All the Pretty*

Horses. The Crossing is divided into three sections. In the first, Billy Parham attempts to trap a wolf that has been killing cattle on his family's New Mexico ranch. After he successfully catches the animal, Billy decides to return it to its original territory in Mexico rather than kill it. Billy thus crosses the border with Mexico for the first time in the novel; unfortunately, the wolf is stolen for use in a dog-fighting arena, and Billy has to kill it to end its painful circumstance. After burying the wolf, Billy returns home to find that horse thieves have murdered his parents. The novel's second section finds Billy and his brother, Boyd, again crossing the border into Mexico in search of their parents' killers and their stolen horses. The brothers find and reclaim some of the horses, battle bandits, and have other picaresque adventures. At the close of the section, Boyd falls in love and returns home with a Mexican woman. In the third section, Billy decides after two years to journey back into Mexico to find Boyd. After hearing a song in which Boyd's death is described, Billy locates his brother's body and returns to New Mexico to bury it on his family's ranch.

As happened with *All the Pretty Horses,* critical reaction to *The Crossing* was starkly divided, with some reviewers terming the book an American masterpiece and others criticizing it as overwritten and pretentious. Writing in the Chicago *Tribune Books,* Bruce Allen dubbed it an "ambitious novel" that "offers a masterly display of tonal control and some of the most pitch-perfect rapturous prose being written these days." In particular, Allen praised the "dozens of breathtakingly imaginative descriptive passages" in the book. In contrast, *Los Angeles Times Book Review* contributor Richard Eder echoed his comments about *All the Pretty Horses.* Admitting that "McCarthy is a strong writer and he can be a magical one," Eder admitted: "There are splendid passages in *The Crossing.*" However, the critic also criticized the author's portrayal of Mexico and disapproved of his frequent use of untranslated passages in Spanish. "What is painfully weak," averred Eder, "is much of McCarthy's portrayal and use of Mexico; and it is a very serious weakness." Michiko Kakutani of the *New York Times* also disliked the novel, commenting that "the overall result is not a mythic, post-modernist masterpiece, but a hodge-podge of a book that is derivative, sentimental and pretentious all at once." At the other end of the critical divide, *New York Times Book Review* contributor Robert Hass declared *The Crossing* to be "a miracle in prose, an American original. It deserves to sit on the same shelf certainly with [Toni Morrison's] *Beloved* and [William Faulkner's] *As I Lay Dying.*" Commending the novel's "violent and stunningly beautiful, inconsolable landscapes," Hass called *The Crossing* "a masterwork."

The trilogy concluded with 1998's *Cities of the Plain.* The last installment in the series unites John Grady Cole, the protagonist of *All the Pretty Horses,* with *The Crossing*'s Billy Parham. Set in New Mexico in the 1950s, the novel finds both men working as horse wranglers at the Cross Fours Ranch. Like the previous books in the trilogy, *Cities of the Plain* contains plenty of tight dialogue, cowboy philosophy, extreme violence, and carefully rendered descriptions of the Western landscape. As in *All the Pretty Horses,* the plot comes to focus on romance—in this case, Cole's doomed love for Magdalena, an epileptic Mexican prostitute whose affections are also coveted by her pimp, Eduardo. When Cole's attempt to purchase Magdalena from her boss fails, he plots instead to smuggle her across the Mexican border. After Eduardo learns of the planned escape, however, he arranges to have Magdalena kidnapped and killed. Despite Billy's efforts to keep Cole out of trouble, the younger man returns to the brothel, seeking retribution for Magdalena's death. He enters into a knife fight with Eduardo, a battle which results in the deaths of both men.

Critics responded to the concluding volume of the "Border Trilogy" with mixed reactions. The *Review of Contemporary Fiction*'s Brian Evenson found that despite "some exceptional manipulations of prose," the novel "fails to measure up to either of the two previous volumes." Chilton Williamson, Jr. of *National Review* concurred that "*Cities of the Plain* in some ways makes a less than fitting conclusion to the trilogistic narrative"—although the critic noted that "over three volumes [McCarthy's] writing has lost none of its eloquence nor the description its particularist power." In his assessment of the narrative for *World Literature Today,* William Riggan unfavorably compared its "leisurely, measured, elegiac . . . and dull" pacing and tone with the "action-rich, dialogue-filled, character-driven *Horses*" and *The Crossing.* By contrast, *Time*'s R.Z. Sheppard applauded McCarthy's efforts "to do for cowpunching what Melville did for whaling: describe in documentary detail how the job is done," and called the author "a virtuoso of the lyric description and the free-range sentence."

Despite the groundbreaking success of his "Border Trilogy," McCarthy remains elusive. He is, as Woodward wrote, "a radical conservative who still believes that the novel can, in his words, 'encompass all the various disciplines and interests of humanity.'" Summarizing his work, Cox stressed: "McCarthy is in no way a commercial writer. He is a novelist by profession, and he has not supplemented his income by turning his hand to more lucrative kinds of work such as Hollywood screenwriting. . . . His most perceptive reviewers have consistently predicted more of the same solid work from McCarthy, and he has fulfilled these predictions. He deserves, now, serious attention from students of literature." Woodward concluded, simply, by declaring: "There isn't anyone remotely like him in contemporary American literature."

BIOGRAPHICAL AND CRITICAL SOURCES:

BOOKS

Bell, Vereen, *The Achievement of Cormac McCarthy,* Louisiana State University Press (Baton Rouge, LA), 1988.

Contemporary Literary Criticism, Thomson Gale (Detroit, MI), Volume 4, 1975, Volume 57, 1990, Volume 59, 1990, Volume 101, 1997.

Dictionary of Literary Biography, Thomson Gale (Detroit, MI), Volume 6: *American Novelists since World War II, Second Series,* 1980, Volume 143: *American Novelists since World War II, Third Series,* 1994.

Hall, Wade H., and Rick Wallach, editors, *Sacred Violence: A Reader's Companion to Cormac McCarthy: Selected Essays from the First McCarthy Conference,* University of Texas at El Paso (El Paso, TX), 1995.

McCarthy, Cormac, *Suttree,* Random House (New York, NY), 1979.

PERIODICALS

America, June 12, 1965, J.G. Murray, review of *The Orchard Keeper.*

Booklist, January 1, 1999, review of *Cities of the Plain,* p. 779.

Boston Globe, January 3, 1991; May 3, 1992; July 5, 1992; November 19, 1992.

Chicago Tribune, November 19, 1992; December 6, 1992.

Christian Science Monitor, June 11, 1992.

Commonweal, March 29, 1974; September 25, 1992; November 4, 1994, p. 11; December 2, 1994, p. 29.

English Journal, November, 1995, p. 99.

Esquire, March 27, 1979.

Los Angeles Times Book Review, June 9 1985; May 17, 1992; June 12, 1994, p. 3.

Nation, July 6, 1998, Dagoberto Glib, review of *Cities of the Plain,* p. 38.

National Review, March 16, 1979; March 8, 1985; October 12, 1998, Chilton Williamson, Jr., review of *Cities of the Plain,* p. 61.

New Republic, February 9, 1974; March 10, 1979; May 6, 1985; July 11, 1994, p. 38.

New Statesman, May 2, 1980.

New Statesman & Society, August 19, 1994, p. 38.

Newsweek, January 7, 1974; May 18, 1992; June 13, 1994, p. 54.

New York, May 18, 1992; June 13, 1994, p. 70.

New Yorker, August 26, 1974; August 10, 1992; June 27, 1994, p. 180.

New York Times, January 20, 1979; May 27, 1992; November 19, 1992; June 21, 1994, p. C21.

New York Times Book Review, September 29, 1968; January 13, 1974; February 18, 1979; September 23, 1984; April 28, 1985; December 21, 1986; May 17, 1992; May 31, 1992; August 30, 1992; June 12, 1994, p. 1.

New York Times Magazine, April 19, 1992.

Review of Contemporary Fiction, fall, 1998, Brian Evenson, review of *Cities of the Plain,* p. 250.

Saturday Review, June 12, 1965.

Sewanee Review, October, 1985.

Southern Review, autumn, 1992.

Spectator, May 24, 1980, Frank Rudman, review of *Suttree.*

Texas Monthly, July, 1998, Michael Hall, "Desperately Seeking Cormac," pp. 76-79.

Time, September 17, 1968; January 4, 1993; June 6, 1994, p. 62; May 18, 1998, R.Z. Sheppard, "Thar She Moos," p. 95.

Times Literary Supplement, May 2, 1980; April 21, 1989.

Tribune Books (Chicago, IL), January 28, 1979; May 10, 1992; June 26, 1994, p. 5.

Village Voice, July 15, 1986; May 19, 1992.

Virginia Quarterly Review, autumn, 1986; autumn, 1992.

Washington Post, November 2, 1990; November 19, 1992.

Washington Post Book World, January 13, 1974; March 19, 1979; May 3, 1992; June 28, 1992; June 5, 1994, p. 1.

World & I, September, 1992; October, 1998, Edwin T. Arnold, review of *Cities of the Plain,* p. 258.

World Literature Today, winter, 2000, William Riggan, review of *Cities of the Plain,* p. 173.

* * *

McCOURT, Frank 1930-

PERSONAL: Born August 19, 1930, in Brooklyn, NY; son of Malachy and Angela (a homemaker; maiden name, Sheehan) McCourt; married; wife's name, Alberta (marriage ended); second marriage ended; married

Ellen Frey (a television industry publicist); children (first marriage): Maggie. *Education:* New York University, B.A., M.A.

ADDRESSES: Home—Roxbury, CT. *Agent*—c/o Author Mail, Simon & Schuster, 1230 Avenue of the Americas, New York, NY 10020.

CAREER: Writer. New York Public School system, teacher at various schools, including McKee Vocational and Technical on Staten Island and Peter Stuyvesant High School. Worked in Ireland and New York, NY, as a messenger, houseman, barkeeper, and laborer; costarred (with his brother) in vaudeville act; member of Irish Repertory Theatre; performer in plays, including *A Couple of Blaguards* and *The Irish . . . and How They Got That Way.* Read stories on *Castles of Gold,* a 2002 audio CD involving numerous Irish performers. *Military service:* U.S. Army; served in Germany during the Korean War.

AWARDS, HONORS: Los Angeles Times Book Award, National Book Critics Circle Award in biography/autobiography, *Salon* Book Award, American Library Association Award, and *Boston Book Review*'s Anne Rea Jewell Nonfiction Prize, all 1996, Pulitzer Prize in biography, and American Booksellers Association Book of the Year, both 1997, all for *Angela's Ashes;* named Irish American of the Year, *Irish American Magazine,* 1998.

WRITINGS:

Angela's Ashes: A Memoir, Scribner (New York, NY), 1996.

The Irish . . . and How They Got That Way (play), produced by Irish Repertory Theatre, 1997.

'Tis: A Memoir (sequel to *Angela's Ashes*), Scribner (New York, NY), 1999.

(With others) *Yeats Is Dead: A Mystery by Fifteen Irish Writers,* Knopf (New York, NY), 2001.

(With Malachy McCourt) *Ireland Ever,* photographs by Jill Freedman, Harry N. Abrams (New York, NY), 2003.

Teacher Man, Scribner (New York, NY), 2005.

Also author, with brother, of musical review *A Couple of Blaguards.*

ADAPTATIONS: Angela's Ashes was adapted by Laura Jones and Alan Parker into a film of the same name, directed by Parker, Paramount Pictures, 1999. *'Tis* and *Teacher Man* were recorded as audiobooks.

SIDELIGHTS: Frank McCourt taught writing in the New York Public School system for several years, but waited until he had retired to pen his first book, 1996's award-winning *Angela's Ashes: A Memoir,* which tells the story of McCourt's poverty-stricken childhood in Ireland. The critically acclaimed volume remained on bestseller lists for more than two years, and garnered McCourt both a National Book Critics Circle Award and the Pulitzer Prize. Three years later, McCourt followed up with a sequel, *'Tis: A Memoir.* Robert Sterling Gingher, who described McCourt in *World* as "a consummate storyteller," noted of the author's autobiographical books: "We rarely acknowledge the magical power and mystery of the word, spoken or written, but McCourt's memoirs show that in nearly unimaginable seasons of extreme need, stories can keep us and our very souls alive."

McCourt was born in 1930 in Brooklyn, New York, to parents who had recently immigrated from Ireland. When McCourt was about four years old, his father, Malachy, decided to move the family back to Ireland. As outlined in *Angela's Ashes,* the elder McCourt had experienced difficulties keeping a job in the United States due to a drinking problem. He had even greater difficulties once he returned to his native country. Malachy occasionally found work as a laborer in the economically-depressed Irish town of Limerick, but would often spend an entire Friday night drinking in a pub. As a result, he would be too sick to show up for work on Saturday; ultimately he would be fired.

Between Malachy's sporadic jobs, the family would exist on the scant Irish version of welfare, but Malachy would often spend this meager amount entirely upon alcohol. In his book, McCourt recounts all of this, as well as his mother Angela's efforts to keep the family alive and together by economizing, borrowing from family, and begging from local Catholic parish charity. He describes how his baby sister and two twin brothers died of disease because their family was too poor to ensure proper sanitation and adequate medical care. McCourt himself contracted typhoid as a child and had to be hospitalized for several weeks. There, from the books available in the hospital, he first encountered the works of English playwright William Shakespeare, and he developed a love of literature that would later guide his work.

Several critics reviewing *Angela's Ashes* concluded that McCourt rightfully placed the blame for his family's poverty upon his father. However, McCourt also details his father's sobriety during the work week. "I'm up with him early every morning with the whole world asleep," McCourt recalls in *Angela's Ashes.* "He lights the fire and makes the tea and sings to himself or reads the paper to me in a whisper that won't wake up the rest of the family." Michiko Kakutani of the *New York Times* surmised that "there is not a trace of bitterness or resentment in *Angela's Ashes.*" Devon McNamara reported in the *Christian Science Monitor* that "what has surprised critic and reader alike is how a childhood of poverty, illness, alcoholism, and struggle, in an environment not far removed from the Ireland of [eighteenth-century English writer Jonathan] Swift's 'A Modest Proposal,' came to be told with such a rich mix of hilarity and pathos." McCourt himself told McNamara: "I couldn't have written this book fifteen years ago because I was carrying a lot of baggage around . . . and I had attitudes and these attitudes had to be softened. I had to get rid of them, I had to become, as it says in the Bible, as a child." He explained further: "The child started to speak in this book. And that was the only way to do it, without judging."

Angela's Ashes also discusses McCourt's return to the United States at the age of nineteen, with one of his surviving brothers. The pair made a living with their own vaudeville show for a time, before Frank McCourt turned to teaching. "The reader of this stunning memoir can only hope," declared Kakutani, "that Mr. McCourt will set down the story of his subsequent adventures in America in another book. *Angela's Ashes* is so good it deserves a sequel." Denis Donoghue, discussing the book in the *New York Times Book Review,* asserted: "For the most part, his style is that of an Irish-American raconteur, honorably voluble and engaging. He is aware of his charm but doesn't disgracefully linger upon it. Induced by potent circumstances, he has told his story, and memorable it is." John Elson, in *Time,* wrote favorably of *Angela's Ashes* as well, observing that "like an unpredicted glimmer of midwinter sunshine, cheerfulness keeps breaking into this tale of Celtic woe." Paula Chin, in *People,* hailed it as "a splendid memoir," while McNamara concluded it to be "a book of splendid humanity."

Angela's Ashes ends with McCourt's return to the United States on the boat *Irish Oak.* The last word of the book is nineteen-year-old McCourt's statement "'Tis," a response he made to a crew member remarking on the greatness of America. Thus, *'Tis,* McCourt's 1999 memoir, begins exactly where *Angela's Ashes* leaves off. The book chronicles the author's struggles and successes during his first years in the United States. McCourt describes his first jobs, including cleaning at the Biltmore Hotel, hauling cargo, and cleaning toilets at a diner, gradually moving on to his time in the military during the Korean War and his unconventional education at New York University. Malcolm Jones described *'Tis* in *Newsweek:* "Superficially, *'Tis* is the classic immigrant's tale. . . . [A] melting-pot story where nothing melts. . . . But more than that, it is the story of a man finding two great vocations—teaching and storytelling—and he wins our trust by never touching up his memories."

L. S. Klepp concluded in *Entertainment Weekly* that, although unequal to *Angela's Ashes* in "concentrated power," *'Tis* "has the same clairvoyant eye for quirks of class, character, and fate, and also a distinct picaresque quality. It's a quest for an America of wholesome Hollywood happiness that doesn't exist, and it's about the real America—rendered with comic affection—that McCourt discovers along the way." Similarly, *Library Journal* reviewer Gordon Blackwell asserted, "McCourt's entertaining *'Tis* . . . recounts candidly, and with humor where appropriate, his return to the United States." "In *'Tis,* [McCourt] must live between the tormenting reality of [the American] dream and the sad past of his soul's memory," stated Gingher in *World,* adding: "The book's lyrical power of reclamation has everything to do with its author's ability to live between these worlds, which in some profound way are only vivid and intelligible in terms of each other." John Bemrose related in *Maclean's* that "McCourt ultimately clambers up the ladder of success. But much of *'Tis*'s charm lies in his account of how he almost didn't make it." Mary Ann Gwinn complimented in a *Seattle Times Online* review, "With *Angela's Ashes* and [*'Tis*] McCourt establishes himself a Dickens for our time, a writer who can peel the many layers of society like an onion and reveal the core. . . . *'Tis* seldom loses its woeful tone, but it never loses its mordant humor, and it's struck through with a memory undimmed by the golden forgetfulness of nostalgia."

Following *'Tis,* McCourt turned his talent for memoir writing to *Teacher Man: A Memoir,* an account of his thirty years teaching English to New York City high schoolers. McCourt's "dark humor, lyric voice and gift for dialogue are apparent" in this tale of the ups and downs of his career, observed a *Kirkus Reviews* contributor. With *Teacher Man,* "we get the best self-portrait of a public-school teacher ever written," noted Malcolm Jones in a *Newsweek* review, who suggested that McCourt has "told the tale of that experience so well that when you've finished it, you don't envy him. You envy his students."

In addition to his memoirs, McCourt has written and performed in stage productions. He and one of his brothers created a musical review called *A Couple of*

Blaguards. The duo has also spearheaded *The Irish . . . and How They Got That Way,* a play first produced in September, 1997, at the Irish Repertory Theatre. *Back Stage* contributor Elais Stimac described *The Irish . . . and How They Got That Way* as "a patchwork quilt of songs, stories, and celebration of the history of Irish in America." Its coverage of "all the major events over the past several centuries, as well as anecdotal sidebars . . . are sure to enlighten; and entertain."

BIOGRAPHICAL AND CRITICAL SOURCES:

BOOKS

McCourt, Frank, *Angela's Ashes,* Scribner (New York, NY), 1996.

McCourt, Frank, *'Tis: A Memoir,* Scribner (New York, NY), 1999.

PERIODICALS

Back Stage, January 14, 2000, Elais Stimac, review of *The Irish . . . and How They Got That Way,* p. 37.

Booklist, August, 1999, Donna Seaman, review of *'Tis,* p. 1981; April 1, 2000, Karen Harris, review of *'Tis* (audio recording), p. 1482.

Christian Science Monitor, December 4, 1996, p. 13; March 21, 1997, p. 4.

Commonweal, June 19, 1998, Daniel M. Murtaugh, review of *Angela's Ashes,* p. 28; October 22, 1999, Molly Finn, "Two for Two," p. 24.

Economist, February 27, 1999, review of *'Tis,* p. 83.

Entertainment Weekly, January 22, 1999, Andrew Essex, review of *'Tis,* p. 35; September 24, 1999, L. S. Klepp, "'Tis a Beaut: *Angela's Ashes* Is a Pretty Tough Act to Follow but Frank McCourt Dazzles Us Once Again in *'Tis,* the Enchanting Story of His Adventures—and Misadventures—in America," p. 139.

Irish Literary Supplement, spring, 2000, Vivian Valvano Lynch, "Ashes through a Glass Not Darkly," pp. 23-24.

Kirkus Reviews, July 1, 1996, review of *Angela's Ashes;* September 15, 2005, review of *Teacher Man,* p. 1014.

Library Journal, October 15, 1999, Robert Moore, review of *'Tis,* p. 78; February 1, 2000, Gordon Blackwell, review of *'Tis* (audio recording), p. 132; May 1, 2000, Gloria Maxwell, review of *'Tis* (audio recording), p. 168.

Maclean's, October 18, 1999, John Bemrose, "From Emerald Isle to Green with Envy: A Dreamer Tussles with the American Dream," p. 93.

McCall's, September, 1998, Donna Boetig, "Frank McCourt's Lessons for Parents," p. 110.

Nation, July 27, 1998, Patrick Smith, "What Memoir Forgets," p. 30.

National Review, October 26, 1998, p. 40; September 27, 1999, Pete Hamill, review of *'Tis,* p. 54.

New Criterion, December, 1999, Brooke Allen, review of *Angela's Ashes* and *'Tis,* p. 71.

New Republic, November 1, 1999, R. F. Forester, "'Tisn't the Million-Dollar Blarney of the McCourts," p. 29.

Newsweek, August 30, 1999, review of *'Tis,* p. 58; September 27, 1999, Malcolm Jones, "An Immigrant's Tale: In *'Tis* Frank McCourt Finds America and Himself," p. 66; November 21, 2005, Malcolm Jones, "Among School Children, McCourt Got Schooled; The Author of *Angela's Ashes* Now Looks Back on 30 Years of Ups and Downs in New York City Classrooms," p. 71.

New York, September 27, 1999, Walter Kirn, review of *'Tis,* p. 82.

New York Review of Books, May 25, 2000, Julian Moynahan, "Not-So-Great Expectations," pp. 51-53.

New York Times, September 17, 1996, Michiko Kakutani, review of *Angela's Ashes.*

New York Times Book Review, September 15, 1996, Denis Donoghue, review of *Angela's Ashes,* p. 13; September 14, 1999; Michiko Kakutani, "For an Outsider, It's Mostly Sour Grapes in the Land of Milk and Honey."

People, October 21, 1996, Paula Chin, review of *Angela's Ashes,* p. 42; October 4, 1999, Kim Hubbard, review of *'Tis,* p. 51.

Publishers Weekly, October 4, 1999, review of *'Tis* (audio recording), p. 37; October 4, 1999, Daisy Maryles and Dick Donahue, "McCourt Leads the Court," p. 19; November 1, 1999, review of *'Tis,* p. 51.

Time, September 23, 1996, John Elson, review of *Angela's Ashes,* p. 74; October 4, 1999, Paul Gray, "Frank's Ashes: The Sequel to a Beloved Best Seller Is Glum Going," p. 104.

Wall Street Journal, September 17, 1999, Hugh Kenner, "Alas, 'Taint," p. W11; June 6, 2000, Joseph T. Hallinan, "Whose Life Is It, Anyway? *Angela's Ashes* Suit May Help to Decide; Financial Backers of Old Play by the McCourt Brothers Say They're Due Royalties," p. B1.

World, April, 2000, Robert Sterling Gingher, "Out of the Ashes: The Voice of a Child in Limerick Re-

turns Transformed into That of a Young Man Finding His Place in New York City," pp. 255-261.
World of Hibernia, winter, 1999, John Boland, review of *'Tis,* p. 156.
Writer's Digest, February, 1999, Donna Elizabeth Boetig, "Out of the Ashes," p. 18.

ONLINE

Independent, http://www.independent.co.uk/ (September 18, 1999), Mary Flanagan, "From a Town of Ashes to a City of Gilt."
Newshour Online, http://www.pbs.org/ (March 17, 1999), Terence Smith, interview with McCourt.
Salon.com, http://www.salon.com/ (August 31, 1999), Andrew O'Hehire, "In His Follow-up to Angela's Ashes Frank McCourt Confronts the Indignities of Immigrant Life."
Seattle Times Online, http://www.seattletimes.com/ (September 19, 1999), Mary Ann Gwinn, review of *'Tis.*

* * *

McCREIGH, James
See POHL, Frederik

* * *

McCULLOUGH, Colleen 1937-

PERSONAL: Born June 1, 1937, in Wellington, New South Wales, Australia; married Ric Robinson, April 13, 1984. *Education:* University of Sydney and University of South Wales, B.S. (with honors); Institute of Child Health of London University, M.S. *Hobbies and other interests:* Photography, music, chess, embroidery, painting, cooking, "writing the words side of stage musicals."

ADDRESSES: *Home*—Norfolk Island, Australia. *Office*—c/o Author Mail, Simon & Schuster, 1230 Avenue of the Americas, New York, NY 10020; P.O. Box 333, Norfolk Island, Oceania via Australia.

CAREER: Founder of and worker at the Department of Neurophysiology at the Royal North Shore Hospital of Sydney, 1958-63; Yale University, School of Internal Medicine, New Haven, CT, associate in research neurology department, 1967-77; writer, 1976—. Has also worked as a teacher, a library worker, a bus driver in Australia's Outback, and in journalism.

MEMBER: Gerontology Foundation of Australia, Monash Medical Centre Literary Programme, Macquarie University, Foundation of the Study of Ancient Cultures, American Association for the Advancement of Science (fellow), New York Academy of Science, Board of Visitors of the International Programs Center at the University of Oklahoma.

AWARDS, HONORS: D. Litt., Macquarie University, Sydney, Australia, 1993; honorary founding governor of Prince of Wales Medical Research Institute; designated a "Living National Treasure" in Australia; Scanno Award for Literature, 2000.

WRITINGS:

NOVELS

Tim (also see below), Harper (New York, NY), 1974.
The Thorn Birds, Harper (New York, NY), 1977.
An Indecent Obsession (also see below), Harper (New York, NY), 1981.
A Creed for the Third Millennium, Harper (New York, NY), 1985.
The Ladies of Missalonghi (also see below), Harper (New York, NY), 1987.
The First Man in Rome, Morrow (New York, NY), 1990.
The Grass Crown, Morrow (New York, NY), 1991.
Fortune's Favorites, Morrow (New York, NY), 1993.
Caesar's Women, Morrow (New York, NY), 1996.
Caesar: Let the Dice Fly, Morrow (New York, NY), 1998.
The Song of Troy, Orion (London, England), 1998.
Three Complete Novels (includes *Tim, An Indecent Obsession,* and *The Ladies of Missalonghi*), Wings Books (New York, NY), 1999.
Morgan's Run, Simon & Schuster (New York, NY), 2000.
The October Horse, Simon & Schuster (New York, NY), 2002.
The Touch, Simon & Schuster (New York, NY), 2003.

OTHER

An Australian Cookbook, Harper (New York, NY), 1982.
Roden Cutler, V.C. (biography), Random House Australia (Milson's Point, New South Wales, Australia), 1998.

Contributor to magazines.

ADAPTATIONS: Tim was released as a film, starring Piper Laurie and Mel Gibson, directed and produced by Michael Pate, in 1981. *The Thorn Birds* was broadcast as a ten-hour miniseries on American Broadcasting Companies, Inc. (ABC), in March, 1983, starring Rachel Ward and Richard Chamberlain. Most of McCullough's novels have been adapted as audiobooks, including *The Touch,* Simon & Schuster Audio, 2003.

SIDELIGHTS: "I always write books with peculiar themes: I don't like writing about boy meets girl, boy loses girl, boy gets girl," best-selling author Colleen McCullough told Kay Cassill in a *Publishers Weekly* interview. The plots of McCullough's novels, which include the phonomenally popular *The Thorn Birds, The Ladies of Missalonghi,* and a six-volume history of Caesar's Rome, back her assertion. In her book *Tim,* a middle-aged businesswoman becomes romantically linked with a twenty-five-year-old, mentally retarded man; *The Thorn Birds* turns on a frustrated romance between a young woman and a Roman Catholic cardinal; *An Indecent Obsession*'s heroine, a war nurse to battle-fatigued soldiers, is tacitly engaged to one of her patients and sexually attracted to another. And in the 2003 novel *The Touch,* McCullough weaves a colorful story around Scotsman Alexander Kinross, who travels to California, and thence to Australia during the gold rush of the 1800s. After he pragmatically imports a child bride from the old country, Kinross and his young wife find their lives altered as children are born, lovers are taken, friendships forged, and the family's wealth grows due to the savvy but emotionless Scot's business skills. Such ingenious story lines—combined with a talent for what Christopher Lehmann-Haupt described in a *New York Times* review as "good old-fashioned story telling" and the "requisite happy ending" *Library Journal* reviewer Kathy Piehl reported as central to the author's story mix—have made McCullough's books appeal to millions of readers. "McCullough's characters win sympathy with their spirited striving for love and honor," added a *Publishers Weekly* contributor in reviewing *The Touch,* reflecting another characteristic that has continued to propell the author's epic historical novels up the best-seller charts.

McCullough, a native of Australia, first aspired to a career as a physician but could not afford the necessary tuition for a full medical education. She taught in the Outback, drove a school bus, worked as a librarian, and finally qualified as a medical technician specializing in neurophysiology. It was in this position that she eventually came to work at Yale University. In the evenings, she wrote—but not with an eye toward publication. "I always wrote to please myself," she told Cassill. "I was a little snobby about it—that way I could write entirely as I wished. To write for publication, I thought, was to prostitute myself." Once McCullough decided to approach writing commercially, however, she did so very systematically. "I sat down with six girls who were working for me. They were very dissimilar types, and not especially avid readers. Yet, they were all mad about Erich Segal's *Love Story.* I thought it was bloody awful and couldn't see what girls so basically intelligent could love about it. I asked them what they wanted most out of a book. First, they liked the idea that *Love Story* was about ordinary people. They didn't want to read about what was going on in Hollywood and all that codswallow, and they wanted something with touches of humor. Yet they enjoyed books that made them cry. . . . If you didn't cry the book wasn't worth reading. . . . So, I said, 'That's it, mate. No matter what else you do in a book, don't forget the buckets of tears.'"

McCullough had a story in mind that would conjure "buckets of tears," a grand romance set mostly on a sheep ranch. She knew, however, that this tale—which would eventually be published as *The Thorn Birds*—would be lengthy, and that "no one would publish such a long book as a first novel. So I wrote *Tim.*"

Tim is a "novel of awakenings," according to a *Publishers Weekly* writer, "a lovely and refreshing addition to tales of love." Its two central characters are Mary Horton and Tim Melville. In her climb from an orphanage to success as a mining executive, forty-five-year-old Mary has developed her discipline and self-sufficiency to a high degree but has ignored her emotions. Tim arrives at her home one day to do some yard work. He catches her eye, for he is strikingly handsome. Eventually she learns that this attractive young man is "without the full quid"—that is, he is mentally retarded. First Tim's beauty, then his gentle innocence draw Mary to him, unsettling her rigidly ordered world. This unusual pair experience first love together. When Tim faces being left without a family to care for him, Mary realizes that marriage could be fulfilling and practical for both of them. She must then decide if she has the courage to take such an unconventional step.

Tim was well received by critics. A *New York Times Book Review* contributor praised the story's "delightful freshness," and Margaret Ferrari, writing in *America,* remarked upon McCullough's sensitive treatment of her subject matter: "There are many genuinely touching moments in the novel. . . . Its language is clear and direct, full of colorful Australian slang. McCullough's feeling for character, from major to minor, is compassionate yet concise. They are without exception well-rounded and believable. Her delicacy is perfectly suited to the story. . . . *Tim* is a warm book to read, reassuring about goodness in human nature and about the power of love to overcome worldly obstacles and to make us care more for another person's interests than for our own." A *Publishers Weekly* reviewer called McCullough's telling of the story "accomplished, sensitive, and wise." The author herself was less generous than most reviewers in describing her first novel. "It's an icky book," she told Cassill, "a saccharine-sweet book." In spite of this negative assessment, she was pleased by its success. "I made $50,000 out of *Tim,* which wasn't bad for a first novel, and I thought I'd always be a middle of the road, modest selling, respectable novelist," said McCullough to Phillipa Toomey in the London *Times.*

Having established herself as a good risk in the publishing world, she began to work intensely at getting that long novel she had already "written in her head" down on paper. It was *The Thorn Birds,* a multi-generational saga of the Cleary family and their life on an Australian sheep station named Drogheda. McCullough focuses on three Cleary women: Fiona, her daughter, Meggie, and Meggie's daughter, Justine. Meggie falls in love with Ralph de Bricassart, an ambitious Catholic priest who has known her since her childhood. When he leaves the Outback for the Vatican, Meggie enters into an unhappy marriage that produces one child, Justine. When Father Ralph visits Australia shortly thereafter, he and Meggie consummate their love. Her second child, a son named Dane, is born nine months later. Meggie keeps the knowledge that she has borne Ralph's son her secret, but it makes the boy especially beloved to her. When the child grows up, he, like his father, becomes a priest and leaves Drogheda for Rome; Justine goes to England to become the toast of the London stage.

McCullough was still working full-time at Yale University while drafting this story and so had to confine her writing to the evenings. She spent such long hours sitting at the typewriter that her legs became swollen; she took to wearing elbow-length evening gloves to keep her fingers from blistering and her arms from chafing against her desk. These efforts paid off: she wrote the first two drafts of *The Thorn Birds* in three months, churning out 15,000-word blocks of prose nightly. After working at this pace for a year, the final draft was completed. It was 1,000 pages long and weighed ten pounds. McCullough felt that its hefty size was justified; in her interview with Cassill, she declared: "If an editor had seen *Thorn Birds* in manuscript and 'just loved it,' but suggested it would make a better book if I cut it to a nice 300-page story, I'd have simply said, 'Get stuffed, mate.'"

Her editors made no such suggestion. Sensing that *The Thorn Birds* had the potential to be a major bestseller, they prepared its release carefully and backed it with an extensive publicity campaign. By the time the book became available to the general public, the publishing industry was abuzz with excitement over its prospects; paperback rights had been sold for a then-record price of 1.9 million dollars. This faith and investment in the book were rewarded, for *The Thorn Birds* went on to sell over a half million copies in hardcover and more than seven million copies in paperback.

Some reviewers quickly dismissed the popularity of *The Thorn Birds* as a tribute to marketing rather than a reflection of the book's worth. Amanda Heller denounced McCullough's novel as "awesomely bad" in an *Atlantic* review. "The writing is amateurish, all adjectives and exclamation points. The dialogue is leaden. . . . The characters are mechanical contrivances that permit the plot to grind along without encountering much resistance." And Paul Gray, while admitting in *Time* that "McCullough knows how to stage convincing droughts, floods and fires," declared that she "has not made literature. For a season or so, her book will make commercial history."

Alice K. Turner countered negative assessments of *The Thorn Birds* with praise for the novel's value as entertainment. "To expect *The Thorn Birds* to be a Great Book would be unfair," she suggested in the *Washington Post.* "There are things wrong with it, stock characters, plot contrivances and so forth. But to dismiss it would also be wrong. On its own terms, it is a fine, long, absorbing popular book. It offers the best heartthrob since Rhett Butler, plenty of exotic color, plenty of Tolstoyan unhappiness and a good deal of connivance and action. Of its kind, it's an honest book." Eliot Fremont-Smith further praised McCullough's engaging style in the *Village Voice:* "Her prose, even when stately, owes little to any formula; it is driven by a curiosity of mind, a caring for the subject, and some other great energy within the author that in turn, at one remove, spurs the reader on. *The Thorn Birds* didn't make me laugh and weep, and I could put it down. It is, after all, a romance, and very long. But then I kept picking it up again, more times than can be accounted for by any sense of duty. A fine book."

Both Fremont-Smith and Turner expressed admiration for McCullough's vivid characterizations. "McCullough does make her characters and their concerns come alive," asserted Fremont-Smith. "She gives them (the leads particularly, and Ralph most of all) intelligence and complexity and dimension. Even the minor characters are not dull." Elaborating on the priest's role in the story, Turner wrote, "Very few novels spotlight a Roman Catholic priest as a sex symbol, but Father Ralph's bravura performance in this one rivals the landscape for originality. Father Ralph is simply yummy. . . . And, of course, he is out of the running, which gives the author plenty of opportunity to dangle him as an erotic tease." In her *Publishers Weekly* interview, McCullough said, "Actually, Ralph was supposed to be a minor character. Yet, when I was planning it in my head I was aware I didn't have a dominant male lead. The minute the priest walked into the book I said, 'Ah ha, this is it. This is the male character I've lacked!' But I had to keep him in the story and, logically, he didn't belong in it. The only way I could do it was to involve him emotionally with Meggie, the only woman available. It worked beautifully because again it made more interesting reading to have a love that couldn't be fulfilled. It kept the reader going."

The solid success of *The Thorn Birds* made it almost inevitable that McCullough's next books would be compared with it. "When you produce a book which is well loved—and people do love it—it's a very hard book to bury," noted the author in the London *Times.* Although she believes "a lot of writers keep feeding people the same book," McCullough stated in a *New York Times Book Review* interview with Edwin McDowell that she had "decided long ago . . . to have a bash at different kinds of books." Her third novel, *An Indecent Obsession,* certainly differs from its predecessor in many ways; while *The Thorn Birds* spans three continents and most of a century, *An Indecent Obsession* is set entirely within the confines of a ward of a South Pacific army hospital near the end of World War II. The drama centers on the tension between Honour Langtry, Ward X's nurse, and her group of "troppo" patients—soldiers who have snapped under the strain of tropical jungle fighting. Many reviewers characterized *An Indecent Obsession* as a more serious work than *The Thorn Birds.*

Despite these differences, *Chicago Tribune Book World* reviewer Julia M. Ehresmann found that *An Indecent Obsession* "has McCullough's fingerprints all over it." Comparing the themes of *Tim, The Thorn Birds,* and *An Indecent Obsession,* Ehresmann observed that "in these times when personal gratification is valued so highly, Colleen McCullough is writing about old-time moral dilemmas and largely discarded qualities: self-denial, self-control, and notions of duty, honor, and love as self-displacing virtues." Joanne Greenberg similarly said in the *New York Times Book Review* that *An Indecent Obsession* is "a very old-fashioned novel, with its focus on the conflict between duty and love, a rare concern in contemporary fiction." McCullough's well-drawn characterizations and powerfully evoked setting once again gained praise from many critics, with Greenberg crediting the author's "attention to detail" as the factor that "makes one feel the discomfort of the sweltering tropical nights as well as appreciate the awesome beauty of the sea, the torrential rains and the sunsets." Finally, in his *Washington Post Book World* article, William A. Nolen addressed "the question a lot of potential readers will want answered: Is *An Indecent Obsession* as good as McCullough's *The Thorn Birds?* The question can't be answered. It's like asking if a nice, ripe orange is as tasty as a nice, ripe apple; it depends on your mood and your taste buds. I enjoyed both books, but I thought *An Indecent Obsession* was more intriguing, more thought provoking, than was *The Thorn Birds.*"

Christopher Lehmann-Haupt, however, found fault with the book in the *New York Times.* "We turn the pages," he acknowledged. "I do not mean to make light of Colleen McCullough's already best-selling successor to her gigantically successful *The Thorn Birds.* . . . McCullough is a natural story-teller, more than merely clever at getting up a head of emotional steam. . . . But if [she] expects to be taken seriously as a novelist—and, to judge from the improvement of this book over *The Thorn Birds,* there's no reason why she shouldn't be—she's going to have to write just a little less slickly." McCullough's glibness, continued Lehmann-Haupt, "makes one want to say that *An Indecent Obsession* is merely a gilded version of what I believe teenage readers used to refer to as a nurse book. It isn't really. But far too often, its faults reduce it to medical soap opera."

In 1990, after a decade of research, McCullough embarked on a series of novels set in ancient Rome. The first volume in the series, *The First Man in Rome,* focuses on Gaius Marius and his feud with his brother-in-law, Lucius Cornelius Sulla. The second volume, *The Grass Crown,* deals mainly with handsome and ambitious Sulla as he vies for control over Rome. *Fortune's Favorites,* the third installment, picks up Sulla's story as he grows old and dies; the story then turns to the rise of the younger generation of Roman power-seekers:

Pompey, Crassus, and Julius Caesar. 1996's *Caesar's Women,* the fourth installment, focuses on Caesar's rise to power between 68 and 58 B.C., and *Caesar: Let the Dice Fly* takes the story to 48 B.C. *The October Horse,* which completes McCullough's Roman saga, finds Octavian rising to manhood while Caesar's Rome grows too large for one man to govern. All of the series' volumes feature meticulous details about life in ancient Rome, and portray the timeless traits of men vying for power—lust, deception, and greed—in massive scope, with each volume typically comprising nine hundred pages.

Critics of McCullough's "Roman" series have praised her eye for detail, her research, and her storytelling powers, while noting that the sheer size and scope of the stories sometimes get in the way of character development. For instance, *Washington Post Book World* contributor Judith Tarr remarked that the author's ambition with the series is "laudable" but "a bit too ambitious. The result is often a loss of focus and a failure of Story in the face of History." Reviewing *Fortune's Favorites* in the Chicago *Tribune Books,* Geoffrey Johnson commented: "So intent is McCullough on including every iota of Roman history that occurred during the 14-year span of her novel that she relegates major events to a paragraph, and much of the novel seems to take place in the wings." However, Johnson praised the author for her handling of certain events and characters in the novel, calling it "artfully composed fiction." In his *New York Times Book Review* piece on *Caesar: Let the Dice Fly,* Allen Lincoln described Julius Caesar as "essentially the same character one recalls from his . . . memoirs—brilliant, ambitious, ruthless and fascinating," while *Booklist* reviewer Kathleen Hughes was equally laudatory about McCullough's characterizations in *The October Horse.* Praising the final novel's combination of "political intrigue, romance, drama, and war," Hughes cited the author's "seemingly effortless evocation of the excitement and turmoil" that characterized the wanning Republic under Emperor Octavian.

Centered, like *The Thorn Birds* and *The Touch* on the history of her native Australia, McCullough's husband's family serves as a basis for her 2000 novel *Morgan's Run.* The novel's hero, Richard Morgan, suffers a string of personal tragedies and then becomes the victim of a set-up, culminating in his deportation as one of the first prisoners sent to the Botany Bay penal colony. Though his many misfortunes would defeat a lesser man, Richard rises to the occasion as a leader and a man of principle under the most trying circumstances. Set in the late eighteenth century, the novel reveals how the vicissitudes of war and politics between England, America, and Australia affect one individual. "McCullough's narrative skills are fully displayed in this intricately researched, passionate epic," observed a *Publishers Weekly* reviewer, who added that the book unfolds "a complex, consistently entertaining narrative." In the *New York Times Book Review,* Peter Bricklebank voiced reservations about the "wholly noble" protagonist, feeling that Richard Morgan shows a "lack of compelling emotions." *Library Journal* correspondent Nancy Pearl also felt that Richard is "the major weakness of the novel."

Consistently praised for her strong storytelling skills and with a strong reader following, McCullough responds to the occasional criticism of her work calmly. "Only time tells," she philosophized in her interview with Cassill. "If it lasts, it's good literature. If it dies, it's just another book. Very often the books the critics like today are gone tomorrow." She explained that the greatest change her phenomenal success has wrought in her life has been a feeling of increased security and freedom. The owner of several homes, she spends much of her time on tiny Norfolk Island, located some one thousand miles off the east coast of Australia and inhabited mostly by descendants of the *Bounty* mutineers. Life there suits McCullough perfectly. "It isn't what you are, it's who you are in a place like this," she told Toomey in the London *Times,* "It's incredibly beautiful and peaceful and remote. . . . I get a heck of a lot of work done because there is nothing much else to do."

BIOGRAPHICAL AND CRITICAL SOURCES:

BOOKS

Contemporary Literary Criticism, Volume 27, Thomson Gale (Detroit, MI), 1984.

DeMarr, Mary Jean, *Colleen McCullough: A Critical Companion,* Greenwood Press (Westport, CT), 1996.

Hjerter, Kathleen G., *Doubly Gifted: The Author as Visual Artist,* Harry N. Abrams (New York, NY), 1986.

McCullough, Colleen, *Tim,* Harper (New York, NY), 1974.

PERIODICALS

America, August 10, 1974, Margaret Ferrari, review of *Tim.*

Atlantic, June, 1977, Amanda Heller, review of *The Thorn Birds.*

Best Sellers, May 15, 1974.

Booklist, July, 2000, Diana Tixier Herald, review of *Morgan's Run,* p. 1975; October 15, 2002, Kathleen Hughes, review of *The October Horse,* p. 363; October 15, 2003, Patty Engelmann, review of *The Touch,* p. 357.

Chicago Tribune Book World, October 11, 1981, Julia M. Ehresmann, review of *An Indecent Obsession.*

Christian Century, March 31, 1982.

Entertainment Weekly, November 28, 2003, Rebecca Ascher-Walsh, review of *The Touch,* p. 129.

Kirkus Reviews, September 15, 2003, review of *The Touch,* p. 1149.

Library Journal, August, 2000, Nancy Pearl, review of *Morgan's Run,* p. 154; November 1, 2003, Kathy Piehl, review of *The Touch,* p. 125; April 15, 2004, Barbara Valle, review of *The Touch,* p. 148.

Los Angeles Times Book Review, October 25, 1981.

National Observer, June 20, 1977.

New Leader, July 4, 1977.

Newsweek, April 25, 1977.

New York Times, May 2, 1977; March 25, 1979; September 17, 1981; October 29, 1981; March 26, 1983; March 27, 1983.

New York Times Book Review, April 21, 1974; May 8, 1977; October 25, 1981; November 15, 1981; February 1, 1998, Allen Lincoln, review of *Caesar: Let the Dice Fly,* p. 18; October 22, 2000, Peter Bricklebank, review of *Morgan's Run.*

People, May 7, 1984; November 27, 2000.

Publishers Weekly, March 7, 1977; February 22, 1980; February 18, 1984; October 16, 1995, p. 42; July 24, 2000, review of *Morgan's Run,* p. 67; October 27, 2003, review of *The Touch,* p. 42; November 4, 2003, review of *The October Horse,* p. 62.

Saturday Review, April 16, 1977.

Time, May 9, 1977; May 20, 1985, Paul Gray, review of *The Thorn Birds.*

Times (London, England), November 30, 1981.

Times Literary Supplement, October 7, 1977; December 11, 1981.

Tribune Books (Chicago, IL), October 31, 1993, Geoffrey Johnson, review of *Fortune's Favorites,* p. 3.

Village Voice, March 28, 1977, Eliot Fremont-Smith, review of *The Thorn Birds.*

Washington Post, April 24, 1977; November 26, 1981; March 27, 1983.

Washington Post Book World, October 11, 1981; January 20, 1985; April 28, 1985; November 21, 1993, p. 4.

Writer's Digest, March, 1980.

McCULLOUGH, David 1933-
(David Gaub McCullough)

PERSONAL: Born July 7, 1933, in Pittsburgh, PA; son of Christian Hax (a businessman) and Ruth (Rankin) McCullough; married Rosalee Ingram Barnes, December 18, 1954; children: Melissa, David Jr., William Barnes, Geoffrey Barnes, Doreen Kane. *Education:* Yale University, B.A., 1955. *Hobbies and other interests:* Travel, reading, landscape painting.

ADDRESSES: Agent—Janklow & Nesbit Associates, 445 Park Ave., Ste. 13, New York, NY 10022-2606.

CAREER: Editor and writer for Time, Inc., New York, NY, 1956-61, U.S. Information Agency, Washington, DC, 1961-64, and American Heritage Publishing Co., New York, NY, 1964-70; freelance writer, 1970—. Host of television series *Smithsonian World,* 1984-88, and *The American Experience,* 1988—, for Public Broadcasting Service Television (PBS-TV). Narrator of numerous documentaries, including *The Civil War, Huey Long, The Statue of Liberty, The Shakers,* and *Brooklyn Bridge.* Scholar-in-residence, University of New Mexico, 1979, Wesleyan University Writers Conference, 1982-83; Newman Visiting Professor of American Civilization, Cornell University, 1989. Member, Bennington College Writers Workshop, 1978-79; member of advisory board, Center for the Book, Library of Congress; visiting professor, Dartmouth College and Wesleyan University; member, Harry S Truman Centennial Commission; trustee for Shady Side Academy, Pittsburgh, PA, the National Trust for Historical Preservation, the Harry S Truman Library Institute, the Historical Society of Western Pennsylvania, the Jefferson Memorial Foundation, and the Boston Public Library; honorary trustee, Carnegie Institute. Speaker and lecturer on history.

MEMBER: Society of American Historians (president, 1991—), American Society of Civil Engineers (honorary), American Academy of Arts and Sciences, Protect the History of America (founding member).

AWARDS, HONORS: Special citation for excellence, Society of American Historians, 1973, Diamond Jubilee medal for excellence, City of New York, 1973, and certificate of merit, Municipal Art Society of New York, 1974, all for *The Great Bridge;* National Book Award for history, Francis Parkman Award from Society of American Historians, Samuel Eliot Morison Award, and

Cornelius Ryan Award, all 1978, all for *The Path between the Seas: The Creation of the Panama Canal, 1870-1914;* Civil Engineering History and Heritage award, 1978; *Los Angeles Times* Award for biography, 1981, National Book Award for biography, 1982, and Pulitzer Prize nomination in biography, 1982, all for *Mornings on Horseback;* Emmy Award, for interview with Anne Morrow Lindbergh on *Smithsonian World;* Guggenheim Fellowship, 1987; Pulitzer Prize for Biography, 1993, for *Truman;* Harry S Truman Public Service Award, 1993; St. Louis Literary Award, 1993; Pennsylvania Society Gold Medal Award, 1994; Charles Frankel Prize for contributions to humanities; Distinguished Contribution to American Letters Award; Literary Lion Award, New York Public Library; *The Path between the Seas: The Creation of the Panama Canal, 1870-1914* was a Book-of-the-Month Club selection; Pulitzer Prize in biography category, Christopher Award, finalist for L.L. Winship/PEN New England Award, and Pulitzer Prize for biography, all 2002, all for *John Adams;* Freedom Trail Foundation Patriot Award, 2003. Honorary degrees include H.L.D., Rensselaer Polytechnic Institute, 1983; D.Eng., Villanova University, 1984; Litt.D., Allegheny College, 1984; L.H.D, Wesleyan University, Middletown, CT, 1984; Litt.D., Middlebury College, 1986; Litt.D., Indiana University of Pennsylvania, 1991; H.L.D., University of New Hampshire, 1991; Litt.D., University of South Carolina, 1993; Litt.D., University of Pittsburgh, 1994; Litt.D., Union College, 1994; Litt.D., Washington College, 1994; and L.H.D., Chatham College, 1994.

WRITINGS:

(Editor) C.L. Sulzberger, *The American Heritage Picture History of World War II,* American Heritage Publishing (New York, NY), 1967, revised edition published as *World War II,* McGraw (New York, NY), 1970.

1968–70(Editor) *Smithsonian Library,* six volumes, Smithsonian Institution Press/American Heritage Publishing (Washington, DC).

The Johnstown Flood (Readers Digest Condensed Book), Simon & Schuster (New York, NY), 1968, revised edition 2004.

The Great Bridge: The Epic Story of the Building of the Brooklyn Bridge (Readers Digest Condensed Book), Simon & Schuster (New York, NY), 1972, revised edition with new introduction by the author, 2001.

The Path between the Seas: The Creation of the Panama Canal, 1870-1914, Simon & Schuster (New York, NY), 1977, revised edition, 1999.

Mornings On Horseback: The Story of an Extraordinary Family, a Vanished Way of Life, and the Unique Child Who Became Theodore Roosevelt, (biography), Simon & Schuster (New York, NY), 1981, revised edition with new introduction by the author, 2001.

(And host) *"A Man, a Plan, a Canal—Panama"* (episode of *Nova*), first broadcast on PBS-TV, November 3, 1987.

(Editor with others) *Michael E. Shapiro and Peter H. Frederick, Remington: The Masterworks,* Abrams (New York, NY), 1988.

Brave Companions: Portraits in History, Prentice Hall (New York, NY), 1992.

Truman, Simon & Schuster (New York, NY), 1992.

Why History?, Simon & Schuster (New York, NY), 1996.

John Adams, Simon & Schuster (New York, NY), 2001.

1776, Simon & Schuster (New York, NY), 2005.

Contributor to books, including *A Sense of History: The Best Writing from the Pages of American Heritage,* 1985, and *Extraordinary Lives: The Art and Craft of American Biography,* edited by William Zinsser, 1986. Author of foreword to *Thomas Mellon and His Times,* edited by Mary Louise Briscoe, 1994, *A Bully Father: Theodore Roosevelt's Letters to His Children,* edited by Joan Patterson Kerr, 1995, and *Posterity: Letters of Great Americans to Their Children,* edited by Dorie McCullough Lawson, 2004. Contributor to periodicals, including *Audubon, Architectural Forum, American Heritage, Geo, Smithsonian, New York Times, New Republic, Psychology Today,* and *Washington Post.* Senior contributing editor, *American Heritage;* contributing editor, *Parade.* Narrator of film *Abraham and Mary Lincoln: A House Divided,* 2001. Seminars the author taught at Harvard University's John F. Kennedy School of Government under the Theodore H. White lecture program were published by the Joan Shorenstein Center and Harvard University, 2002.

ADAPTATIONS: John Adams was adapted as an audiobook, read by Edward Herrmann, Simon & Schuster Audio, 2001; *The Great Bridge* was adapted as an audiobook, read by Edward Herrmann, Simon & Schuster Audio, 2004; *The Path between the Seas* was adapted as an audiobook, read by Edward Herrmann, Simon & Schuster Audio, 2004; *1776* was adapted as an audiobook, read by author, Simon & Schuster Audio, 2005.

SIDELIGHTS: David McCullough is known to many Americans as an important disseminator of history not only through his award-winning books, but also through his appearances as host of the PBS television programs *Smithsonian World* and *The American Experience.* Recognition of his abilities includes an Academy Award nomination for a film on the Brooklyn Bridge; best-seller status for *John Adams;* the Pulitzer Prize for his biography of Harry S Truman; and National Book awards for his narrative histories *The Path between the Seas: The Creation of the Panama Canal, 1870-1914* and *Mornings on Horseback: The Story of an Extraordinary Family, a Vanished Way of Life, and the Unique Child Who Became Theodore Roosevelt.* Critic Richard Robbins noted in the Pittsburgh *Tribune-Review* that in these histories, "David McCullough combines a powerful narrative style with an exhaustive concern for the details of a story."

McCullough's first book, *The Johnstown Flood,* grew out of his desire to learn more about the 1889 bursting of a Pennsylvania dam that claimed the lives of more than two thousand people and was one of the most widely reported stories of the late nineteenth century. None of the volumes McCullough consulted proved satisfactory, however, and he finally decided he would have to write the book himself. Upon its publication, several reviewers deemed *The Johnstown Flood* an important addition to the field of social history. For example, Alden Whitman, writing in the *New York Times,* called it "a superb job, scholarly yet vivid, balanced yet incisive."

In 1972 McCullough published *The Great Bridge: The Epic Story of the Building of the Brooklyn Bridge.* Considered by contemporaries and historians to be the greatest engineering feat of America's "Gilded Age," the Brooklyn Bridge was the dream of one man, John Roebling, a wealthy steel cable manufacturer. When he died in 1869, before construction of the bridge actually began, his son Washington A. Roebling became chief engineer, and, over the next thirteen years, saw the bridge completed. McCullough traces the dangers that the younger Roebling faced and the problems he overcame, ranging from corrupt politicians in Boss Tweed's Tammany Hall to cases of the "bends" that afflicted workers and left Roebling himself a semi-invalid for the rest of his life.

The Great Bridge covers both the engineering and social aspects of the bridge's construction. "The whole story is told in David McCullough's admirably written, definitive and highly entertaining book," remarked L.J. Davis in the *Washington Post Book World.* "He is especially adept at weaving in those disparate but relevant details that bring an age to life, from the Cardiff giant to the scandal of Henry Ward Beecher's infidelity. It is hard to see how the story could be better or more thoroughly told." "McCullough does justice to this gamy background," observed Justin Kaplan in *Saturday Review,* "but never allows it to get the better of his subject or his narrative or to turn into that familiar historical stereotype that obscures the fact that the Gilded Age was a period of enormous achievement in virtually every area of activity."

McCullough shifted settings from Brooklyn to Panama for *The Path between the Seas: The Creation of the Panama Canal, 1870-1914.* Once again the author mixes engineering with social, political, and economic history, this time to create a panorama of the canal project from its origins to the day it finally opened. Beginning with the dream of Suez Canal entrepreneur Ferdinand de Lesseps, McCullough describes how political corruption, disease, anti-Semitism, and bankruptcy put an end to French efforts to dig a sea-level canal across the isthmus of Panama. Later, McCullough relates, the Americans under the leadership of Theodore Roosevelt connived to "liberate" Panama from an uncooperative Colombia, conquered the yellow fever and malaria that had plagued the French, and over a ten-year period created the largest and costliest engineering project the world had ever seen.

The Path between the Seas won the 1978 National Book Award as well as several important awards from historical associations. Several reviewers praised the book for its vivid portrayal of the many issues that surrounded the canal's construction. "There are scores of previous volumes on the subject," reported *New York Times Book Review* contributor Gaddis Smith, "but none is so thorough, readable, fair or graceful in the handling of myriad intricately connected elements: French national pride and humiliation, personal courage and corruption, disease and death, medical and engineering genius, political and financial chicanery, and the unsung contribution of tens of thousands of black laborers recruited from the West Indies to do the heavy work." McCullough, commented Walter Clemons in *Newsweek,* "is a storyteller with the capacity to steer readers through political, financial and engineering intricacies without fatigue or muddle. This is grand-scale, expert work." An audiobook of the *The Path between the Seas* was released in 2004.

In his next book, *Mornings on Horseback,* another National Book Award winner in 1982, McCullough examines the early years of the Panama Canal's greatest supporter, Theodore Roosevelt. Unlike many biographies of the Republican Roosevelt, however, McCullough's work encompasses the entire family: Theodore, Sr., philanthropic scion of an old New York Dutch clan; his wife, Martha ("Mittie") Bulloch, a Georgia belle whose family mansion may have been the inspiration for Tara in Margaret Mitchell's *Gone with the Wind;* their daughters, Anna ("Bamie") and Corinne ("Conie"); and sons, Theodore, Jr. and Elliott. Moreover, in its depiction of the Roosevelts, *Mornings on Horseback* affords a glimpse of American society in the years following the Civil War, "a period that has always seemed remote and cartoonlike," explained James Lardner in the *New Republic.* "It introduces us to a collection of fascinating people and makes their society vivid, plausible, and even a tempting destination for anyone planning a trip back in time."

McCullough also breaks new ground by exploring neglected aspects of Theodore, Jr.'s youth, including his bouts of psychosomatic illness and his fascination with killing and preserving animals. As a child "Teddie" suffered from violent attacks of asthma, probably brought on by feelings of inadequacy, that occurred "almost invariably on a Saturday night [in order] to secure a Sunday with his father," reported John Leonard in the *New York Times Book Review.* McCullough notes that the boy's asthma disappeared as soon as he left home to begin studying at Harvard. Roosevelt's enchantment with shooting and the Wild West, the author suggests, stemmed in part from his mother's stories about the Old South and his relatives' exploits in the Confederate Army. McCullough combines these images to create a portrait of a man who, as *Saturday Review* contributor Gary Wills put it, "never felt more alive than when killing something."

McCullough next attempted to write a biography of the painter Pablo Picasso, but after only a few months' work, he developed such a loathing for the artist's personality that he abandoned the project. When an editor suggested that he take on the story of Franklin Delano Roosevelt, McCullough immediately replied, "If I were going to do a twentieth-century President, I would do Harry Truman," according to *New York Times Book Review* contributor Lynn Karpen. Truman was the first president McCullough had ever seen in person. It happened in 1956, in New York City, where McCullough had just begun work as a staff member of the newly created *Sports Illustrated* magazine. "A small crowd had gathered on the sidewalk awaiting the Governor, who was attending a dinner party," McCullough told Karpen. "A limousine pulled up and out stepped. . . Harry Truman. My first thought was, 'My God, he's in color!'" Once McCullough started, *Truman* took ten years to finish. McCullough's dedication to his subject paid off. *Truman,* described by *Time* reviewer Walter Isaacson as a "loving and richly detailed megabiography," earned its author a Pulitzer Prize.

Truman was a plain man who never attended college and might never have left his family's farm if not for World War I. He served in Europe, then returned to his hometown of Independence, Missouri, to marry his longtime sweetheart, Bess Wallace—a woman whose family was convinced that she had married beneath her. Truman was a hard worker, yet he failed both as a farmer and as a haberdasher. He went into politics simply because he needed a job. A tenuous connection with Tom Pendergast, a powerful Democratic leader of the 1920s, led to Truman's appointment as a county judge and, eventually, a place in the U.S. Senate. When he stepped into the presidency upon Franklin Delano Roosevelt's death in 1945, he remarked that there were a million men better qualified for the job than him. Many Americans agreed with him. During his time in office, he was highly unpopular, but his stature has risen in the decades since his presidency. "He was intelligent. He worked hard, read widely, and was always willing to listen to ideas and advice. . . . The same plainness of manner and directness of speech that led so many to dismiss him as a 'little man' helped him win the deep respect, loyalty and affection of such figures as Winston Churchill, George Marshall and Dean Acheson," commented Alan Brinkley in the *New York Times Book Review.* "Perhaps most important, Mr. McCullough argues, he was a decent man with common sense."

McCullough chose to tell Truman's story in a plain, straightforward style that reflected that character of his subject. McCullough's deep admiration for Truman comes through in his book's pages, yet he provides an evenhanded portrait, according to Brinkley: "McCullough manages to keep Truman himself at the center of the story. . . rather than allowing him to become obscured by the complexity of events and institutions that surrounded him. And he deals openly with Truman's many mistakes and weaknesses as a leader."

Isaacson found that "McCullough's main weakness is one he shares with Truman: he occasionally fails to wrestle with the moral complexities of policy." Instead, he provides "a sense of historic sweep" and a "marvelous feel for history" that is based on "an appreciation of colorful tales and an insight into personalities. In this compelling saga of America's greatest common-man President, McCullough adds luster to an old-fashioned historical approach that is regaining respect: the sweeping narrative, filled with telling details and an appreciation of the role individuals play in shaping the world."

John Adams, one of the top-selling nonfiction works of 2001, brought new recognition to another president who had not been highly regarded previously. The first vice president and second president of the United States, Adams was an unpretentious man, yet was often considered conceited and overly ambitious; he also had a fiery temper, which made him some enemies, but so did his honesty and adherence to principle. Adams was overshadowed in his lifetime and after by other founding fathers, particularly the charismatic Thomas Jefferson, and indeed, McCullough considered writing a book about the relationship of Adams and Jefferson, who were alternately friends and adversaries. As he did his research, however, McCullough knew he had to focus on Adams. "I realized that something inside me was saying: Adams is your subject—I had to do a book about John Adams," he told Ronald Kovach, an interviewer for *Writer.* McCullough had a wealth of material on Adams, and the resulting book chronicles Adams's youth in a Massachusetts farming family, his rise as a lawyer, his firm convictions against slavery and for religious freedom, his growth into an activist for American independence, and his key actions as an American statesman—including negotiating a loan from the Netherlands to bolster the finances of the brand-new United States and his move as president to keep the nation out of war with France. The book is also a story of romantic and familial love, some critics observed, sensitively portraying Adams's passionate devotion to his strong-minded wife, Abigail, and the joy he took in being a father.

New York Times reviewer Michiko Kakutani described *John Adams* as "a lucid and compelling work that should do for Adams's reputation what Mr. McCullough's 1992 book, 'Truman,' did for Harry S Truman." She continued, "Like Truman, Adams is portrayed by Mr. McCullough as a scrupulously honest man, dedicated, hard-working and without pretense: a plain-spoken man who steered a remarkably steady course through a particularly turbulent time in the nation's history." Several other critics also saw similarities between Truman and Adams, and in McCullough's treatment of each man. "America's most beloved biographer, David McCullough, has plucked Adams from the historical haze, as he did Harry Truman, and produced another masterwork of storytelling that blends colorful narrative with sweeping insights," reported Walter Isaacson in *Time,* adding, "Though Adams had the same prickliness as Give-'Em-Hell Harry, he's just not quite as colorful." Happily, Isaacson related, McCullough does not try to make Adams something he was not: "Instead he shows how Adams' ability to be sensible and independent made him an important element in the firmament of talents that created a new nation."

Numerous other critics praised McCullough's work as well. Former U.S. defense secretary Caspar W. Weinberger, writing in *Insight on the News,* called the book "a labor of love and skill, assuring McCullough a prime position among our greatest historians. . . . There are few works of history or historical fiction that can match McCullough's descriptions of the daily lives and the all too human motives, quarrels, ambitions and dissension that had to be reconciled and agreed to before our revolution could succeed." *USA Today* commentator Gerald F. Kreyche said of *John Adams,* "It is a masterpiece, a contribution to the literature, and a must read for anyone interested in the birth of our nation." *Book* contributor Don McLeese noted that the biography "combines scholarly research with the readability of historical fiction" and that "McCullough writes of his subject with warmth and respect but not reverence."

Some reviewers found McCullough a bit too admiring of Adams, however. "McCullough's obvious zeal and respect for Adams does limit the depth of his study," maintained Thomas R. Eddlem in the *New American.* He added, "McCullough criticizes Adams only once, taking him to task for signing the tyrannical Alien and Sedition acts. Adams was also widely recognized in his day as vain and ambitious, but McCullough gives the reader little insight into how this reputation came to be. . . . The author leaves the impression that Adams' sense of self-worth was completely justifiable." Pauline Maier, critiquing for the *New York Times Book Review,* thought that "McCullough's reckoning all but ignores the irascibility that undermined Adams's reputation among his contemporaries." Adams emerges, she said, as "admirable but curiously flat," and she concluded that "the wonderfully congenial subject of McCullough's carefully researched, lovingly written biography is more consistently companionable, and also less interesting, than Adams was in his own time."

Commentary reviewer Richard A. Samuelson had a different reservation, remarking that "McCullough tends to gloss over those aspects of Adams's career that do not fit neatly into a personal narrative" and "though McCullough appreciates that Adams was often a profound political thinker and duly notes that he shone as a constitutional architect, the book provides no sustained discussion of Adams's ideas." On the other hand, Samuelson saw "much to recommend in McCullough's vivid portrait of this underappreciated founding father" and called the book "a well-researched and highly readable account, enlivened by the anecdotal style and attention to detail that are the author's trademark." Eddlem, despite criticizing McCullough's admiration for his subject as a bit too keen, added that "generally, Mc-

Cullough's affinity for Adams strengthens this book." And several commentators deemed the biography a well-rounded portrait of Adams and his times. McCullough, observed Kakutani, uses "a fluent narrative style that combines a novelist's sense of drama with a scholar's meticulous attention to the historical record" to provide "a palpable sense of the many perils attending the birth of the American nation" as well as "a sense of Adams's exuberant, conflicted, and thoroughly engaging personality."

In 2005 McCullough published *1776,* a history of George Washington and several other significant generals and soldiers in the year the United States won its independence from Britain. A reviewer for *American Heritage* noted the book is a "splendid reminder of Washington's true stature." In a review of the audiobook, for which the author narrated his own text, a critic from *Publishers Weekly* observed, "McCullough proves that he is as equally adept at reading prose as he is at writing it."

In all his work McCullough emphasizes the value history has for modern Americans. "We're not being quite selfish enough if we don't know history, not that history is likely to repeat itself," McCullough told Robbins. "Besides, there is the matter of commiserating in the agonies and basking in the glories of our fellow human beings from long ago, of not being provincial, of opening our minds and hearts to generations once alive. . . . Why should we deny ourselves the chance to experience life in another time if its available to us? There is a wonderful world called the past, and for heavens sake don't miss it, because if you do you'll be denying yourself a big part of being alive."

BIOGRAPHICAL AND CRITICAL SOURCES:

PERIODICALS

American Heritage, June-July, 2005, review of *1776,* p. 14.

Book, May, 2001, Don McLeese, review of *John Adams,* p. 66.

Commentary, September, 2001, Richard A. Samuelson, review of *John Adams,* p. 75.

Insight on the News, July 23, 2001, Caspar W. Weinberger, review of *John Adams,* p. 27.

Journal of American History, June, 2003, John Howe, review of *John Adams,* p. 210.

Library Journal, June 1, 2004, Don Wismer, review of *The Path between the Seas: The Creation of the Panama Canal, 1870-1914,* p. 197.

New American, September 24, 2001, Thomas R. Eddlem, "Colossus of Independence," p. 27.

New Republic, July 4, 1981, James Lardner, review of *Mornings On Horseback: The Story of an Extraordinary Family, a Vanished Way of Life, and the Unique Child Who Became Theodore Roosevelt;* July 2, 2001, Sean Wilentz, "America Made Easy—McCullough, Adams, and the Decline of Popular History," p. 35.

Newsweek, June 13, 1977, Walter Clemons, review of *The Path between the Seas;* May 21, 2001, David Gates, "John Adams Is in the House: McCullough's Vivid Take on Our Second President," p. 58.

New York Times, April 24, 1968, Alden Whitman, review of *The Johnstown Flood;* May 22, 2001, Michiko Kakutani, "Rediscovering John Adams: The Founder that Time Forgot," p. E1.

New York Times Book Review, June 19, 1977, Gaddis Smith, review of *The Path between the Seas;* July 26, 1981, John Leonard, review of *Mornings On Horseback;* June 21, 1992, Alan Brinkley, review of *Truman,* p. 1; June 21, 1992, Lynn Karpen, interview with McCullough, p. 19; May 27, 2001, Pauline Maier, "Plain Speaking," p. 9.

Publishers Weekly, April 2, 2001, review of *John Adams,* p. 47, and Edward Nawotka, "*PW* Talks with David McCullough," p. 48; July 11, 2005, audiobook review of *1776,* p. 90.

Saturday Review, September 30, 1972, Justin Kaplan, review of *The Great Bridge: The Epic Story of the Building of the Brooklyn Bridge;* June, 1981, Gary Wills, review of *Mornings On Horseback.*

Time, June 29, 1992, Walter Isaacson, review of *Truman,* p. 80; May 28, 2001, Walter Isaacson, "Best Supporting Actor: David McCullough's *John Adams* Shows the Real Drama of Revolutionary Times," p. 88.

Tribune-Review (Pittsburgh, PA), November 11, 1984, Richard Robbins, review of *The Path between the Seas* and *Mornings on Horseback.*

USA Today, November, 2001, Gerald F. Kreyche, review of *John Adams,* p. 81.

Washington Monthly, May, 2001, Michael Waldman, review of *John Adams,* p. 58.

Washington Post Book World, October 1, 1972, L.J. Davis, review of *The Great Bridge.*

Writer, October, 2001, Ronald Kovach, "David McCullough on the Art of Biography," p. 32.

* * *

McCULLOUGH, David Gaub

See McCULLOUGH, David

McDERMOTT, Alice 1953-

PERSONAL: Born June 27, 1953, in Brooklyn, NY; daughter of William J. and Mildred (Lynch) McDermott; married David M. Armstrong (a research neuroscientist), June 16, 1979; children: three. *Education:* State University of New York, B.A., 1975; University of New Hampshire, M.A., 1978.

ADDRESSES: *Home*—Bethesda, MD. *Agent*—Harriet Wasserman Literary Agency, 137 East 36th St., New York, NY 10016.

CAREER: Writer. Lecturer in English at the University of New Hampshire, Durham, 1978-79; fiction reader for *Redbook* and *Esquire,* 1979-80; consulting editor of *Redbook*'s Young Writers Contest; lecturer in writing at the University of California, San Diego; teacher of writing workshops at American University; writer-in-residence, Virginia Center for the Creative Arts, 1995 and 1997; writer-in-residence, Johns Hopkins University, Baltimore, MD.

MEMBER: Writer's Guild, PEN, Associated Writing Programs, Poets and Writers.

AWARDS, HONORS: Whiting Writers Award, 1987; National Book Award nomination, 1987, and PEN/Faulkner Award for fiction nomination, 1988, both for *That Night;* National Book Award, 1998, and American Book Award, Before Columbus Foundation, 1999, both for *Charming Billy.*

WRITINGS:

NOVELS

A Bigamist's Daughter, Random House (New York, NY), 1982.
That Night, Farrar, Straus (New York, NY), 1987.
At Weddings and Wakes, Farrar, Straus (New York, NY), 1991.
Charming Billy, Farrar, Straus (New York, NY), 1998.
Child of My Heart, Farrar, Straus (New York, NY), 2002.

Contributor of short stories to *Redbook, Mademoiselle, Seventeen,* and *Ms.*

ADAPTATIONS: *Child of My Heart* was adapted for audiocassette and CD and released by Audio Renaissance, 2002.

SIDELIGHTS: Award-winning novelist Alice McDermott deals with many aspects of love and family life in her novels, including a love affair between a cynical editor and a novelist, a romance between two teenagers in the early 1960s, and the many nuances of an Irish-American family. She infuses her works with inventiveness and originality and is praised for her storytelling skills, her lyrical writing, and her descriptive detail and imagery. Michael J. Bandler, writing in *Tribune Books,* noted: "McDermott is a spellbinder, adding a cachet of mystery and eloquence to common occurrences."

McDermott's first novel, *A Bigamist's Daughter,* concerns Elizabeth Connelly, a twenty-six-year-old editor at a vanity publisher. Her job consists of reading the summaries of books (instead of the entire manuscript), heaping enthusiasm and praise on the author, extracting payments of $5,000 or more from them, and then trying to explain why the book was never published. Two years of this kind of work at Vista Books has turned Elizabeth into a cynic, and it is at this point in her life that she meets and becomes involved with a southern client still in search of an ending for his novel about a bigamist. Consequently, Connelly ponders her own father's frequent absences from home as she was growing up. As Elizabeth's memories of her father begin to resurface, "she becomes more appealing; she loses the harshness and superficiality that initially alienate the reader," maintained Anne Tyler in the *New York Times Book Review.* LeAnne Schreiber, writing in the *New York Times,* praised the humor in *A Bigamist's Daughter:* "The laughter is wicked but not cruel." And Tyler concluded that the novel "is impressive," adding that at certain moments "McDermott sounds like anything but a first-time novelist. She writes with assurance and skill, and she has created a fascinatingly prismatic story."

A National Book Award finalist, McDermott's second novel, *That Night,* examines love and the loss of innocence through the story of two teenaged lovers and their separation. Set in suburbia during the early 1960s, the novel begins with the story of the night referred to in the title. Rick, one of the neighborhood boys, has been trying to get in touch with his girlfriend, Sheryl, for a number of days, only to be put off by her mother, who will not tell him where she is. His anxiety and rage finally culminate with a visit to Sheryl's house. Accompanied by a bunch of drunk friends, Rick pulls Sheryl's mother from the house, threatening her and demanding to see her daughter. The men in the neighborhood come to her rescue and a battle (in which no one is injured) ensues, with Rick ending up in jail. What Rick does not know is that a few days earlier Sheryl discovered she was pregnant and was whisked away to a cousin's house in a different state. All of this is recalled by a grown woman who was a child of ten during the time of Rick and Sheryl's romance. The incident becomes her initiation (and that of many others in the neighborhood) into the failures of love and the realities and many disappointments of the adult world.

That Night "is concerned not only with . . . [the] loss of innocence but also with the mundane disillusionments that go with adolescence and the rites of growing up," described Michiko Kakutani in the *New York Times.* Bandler maintained that McDermott "has taken as mundane a subject as one can find, a suburban teenage romance and pregnancy, and infused it with the power, the ominousness and the star-crossed romanticism of a contemporary Romeo and Juliet." What separates *That Night* "from the mass of literature that takes on the barely middle-class suburban experience is the almost baroque richness of . . . McDermott's sentences, the intellectual complexity of her moral vision and the explicit emotion of her voice," asserted David Leavitt in the *New York Times Book Review.* Leavitt added, "*That Night* gloriously rejects the notion that this betrayed and bankrupt world can be rendered only in the spare, impersonal prose that has become the standard of so much contemporary fiction, and the result is a slim novel of almost nineteenth-century richness, a novel that celebrates the life of its suburban world at the same moment that it mourns that world's failures and disappointments." Bandler concluded that through her descriptions of "suburban violence" and "loss by separation, McDermott has wrought a miracle, one that is enhanced even more in its telling."

In her 1991 novel *At Weddings and Wakes,* "McDermott's strategy is to use family gatherings to tell the tales of individual family members and the tale of the family as a whole," pointed out Catherine Petroski in *Tribune Books.* The family that McDermott presents is Irish-American and consists of four sisters, only one of whom—Lucy—is married and living with her own family in Long Island. The other three—May, an ex-nun; Agnes, a businesswoman; and Veronica, an introverted alcoholic—still live at home with their stepmother in Brooklyn. The wedding referred to in the title is between May and the mailman Fred, and the wake is also for May, who dies very suddenly just after her wedding. Through her presentation of such a fractured immigrant family, McDermott examines the many tensions that can arise, including the question of how their heritage should be honored. "Many of the Townes' antics are straight out of the prototypical dysfunctional family," observed Petroski. "Its members play their self-destructive and self-limiting roles; they deny the truth and themselves; they are often (usually unwittingly but sometimes not) as cruel to each other as they are tender." Petroski went on to conclude that "it is the actual words of this novel that I will remember—words that bring us a generously imagined, flawlessly realized, extraordinarily complex story of memorable characters whom otherwise we would never have known."

McDermott's fourth novel, *Charming Billy,* was a surprise winner of the 1998 National Book Award. The story is, on the surface, about the life of Billy Lynch, a charming Irish-American who dies from alcoholism at the age of sixty. Yet the novel also probes the whole Irish American culture and what happens to those who break away from it. Running back and forth in time, *Charming Billy* tells of the title character's return from World War II and his romance with a lovely Irish girl. He carefully saves money and sends it to her so that she can join him in America, but she is never heard from again. Billy's cousin tells him that she died of pneumonia, but in fact she simply took the money to open a gas station and marry another man. Brokenhearted, Billy spends the rest of his life mourning his lost love, even though he subsequently marries another woman. At his wake, Billy's friends discuss his life and the tragedy that marred it.

A *Publishers Weekly* reviewer called *Charming Billy* a "poignant and ironic story of a blighted life" and called attention to "dialogue so precise that a word or two conjures a complex relationship." Michiko Kakutani, reviewer for the *New York Times,* stated that "Ms. McDermott's people, unlike so many characters in contemporary American fiction, are defined largely by their relationships to other family members, relationships that are delineated with unusual understanding of how emotional debts and gifts are handed down, generation to generation, and how that legacy creates a sense of continuity and continuance, a hedge against the erasures of time. In *Charming Billy,* Ms. McDermott writes about such matters with wisdom and grace, refusing to sentimentalize her characters, even as she forces us to recognize their decency and goodness. She has written a luminous and affecting novel."

Commonweal writer Rand Richards Cooper pointed out that there is still more to the book than the story of Billy's life or his community. The narrator, though she is a rather ghostly figure, is also a very important one, for she represents the people who have broken free of the claustrophobic Irish-American communities to seek greater freedom and individual identity. In finding these things, Cooper suggested, she has also lost a great deal, for McDermott's book shows that "to shrug off the burdens of group identity is also to shrug off ferocious attachments; and McDermott's novels express doubt about whether, as ties attenuate and the old neighborhood sinks further into the past, anything as vivid and nourishing will take their place. The grand struggle to wrest one's self from the group delivers her protagonists to this deeply American paradox: that getting a life of your own brings a diminished sense of who you are."

In an interview for the *Irish Times* with Jocelyn McClurg, McDermott rejected the idea that her writing shows a preoccupation with death, yet she allowed: "If you're Irish-Catholic—emphasis on Catholic—you're taught to see the world in a certain way, to see life as brief and death as the thing to be prepared for." McClurg commented that "McDermott has developed a style that is completely her own, a multilayered approach to storytelling that effortlessly shifts between points of view, between present and past." McDermott responded: "I don't think our memories work chronologically. . . . Writing fiction is an attempt to make more sense than life makes."

In McDermott's next book, *Child of My Heart,* the author's main character is once again an Irish Catholic, and death—in this case, the death of both pets and humans—remains a seminal part of the story. Nevertheless, the novel is somewhat of a departure from her other books in that it is her first coming-of-age, loss-of-innocence story. "Certainly it's something I challenged myself to do consciously because I hadn't done it before," she told Molly McQuade in a *Booklist* interview. According to McQuade, McDermott called the book "her most heavily plotted fiction, and the most straightforwardly chronological."

The story revolves around the novel's fifteen-year-old narrator, Theresa, a budding Lolita-like beauty whose parents move to the upper-class realm of the Hamptons on Long Island in hopes that she will catch the eye of one of the rich scions and live happily ever after in the lap of luxury. True to at least part of her parents' wishes, Theresa is constantly ogled throughout the book; but the oglers are largely older, married men. When Theresa does decide to succumb and lose her virginity, it's to the advances of a septuagenarian artist already married to a woman much younger than himself. Much of the story focuses on Theresa's other obvious gifts, that is, as a nurturer and caretaker as she spends one summer in the early 1960s babysitting children and pets. In addition, she has invited her cousin Daisy to spend the summer with her. Unknown to anyone at the time, Daisy is dying. To her charges, including Daisy, Theresa is a heaven-sent angel who gives unconditional love to many who will ultimately face tragic loss and sorrow. Much of the novel also revolves around the seemingly mundane day-to-day life of Theresa, such as Theresa changing diapers and visiting the beach. "But McDermott's novel hangs upon that which roils under its surface—disease, adult corruption, the power of art and Theresa's burgeoning sexuality," Tom Deignan pointed out in a review in *America.* In an interview with Dave Weich on Powell's City of Books Web site, McDermott described her novel this way: "The story arises from the voice of a girl who refuses to be reconciled to some simple truths about relationships and how we live and die. The world as Theresa sees it is not acceptable to her. In her own way, she remakes it."

Writing in the *Weekly Standard,* reviewer John Podhoretz said that he had long admired McDermott's novels but concluded, "*Child of My Heart* is a cloying mess." He added, "McDermott tries but fails to infuse the day-to-dayness of ordinary life with mythical beauty." *Chicago Sun-Times* contributor Carolyn See commented that McDermott encounters a problem with her heroine in that she "does not resemble in any way a real adolescent girl." Nevertheless, See remarked, "the quality of the writing, and the exemplary sentiments that that writing expresses, should keep the minds of readers off that persistent problem." Another reviewer, writing in the *Economist,* remarked that McDermott "captures the world of a gorgeous fifteen-year-old girl to an impressive degree," adding that the only thing missing was the "squirm of rebellion" that most teenagers exhibit. Michelle Vellucci, writing in *People,* noted that McDermott "renders with subtlety and restraint an adolescent's blurry view of the adult world. In spare prose she paints deceptively simple pictures and allows the complex truths hidden within to slowly appear."

In her interview with Weich, McDermott remarked that she wrote *Child of My Heart* "very quickly" compared to her usual pace of writing and "without much planning" following the terrorist attacks in the United States on September 11, 2001. She also noted that, when she writes, she doesn't want to just tell a story. "We're bombarded with stories," said McDermott. "Everybody's got a good story. The six o'clock news has a good story just about every night. Oprah has lots of stories. Story is one thing, but that's not what I go to literature for. I go for that line-by-line, felicitous use of language to another end than simply telling me what happened to somebody at some time in their life."

BIOGRAPHICAL AND CRITICAL SOURCES:

BOOKS

Contemporary Literary Criticism, Volume 90, Thomson Gale (Detroit), 1996.

PERIODICALS

America, February 17, 2003, Tom Deignan, review of *Child of My Heart,* pp. 26-27.

Booklist, September 1, 2002, Molly McQuade, "Alice McDermott's Five-Finger Exercise," interview with McDermott, p. 56.

Chicago Sun-Times, Carolyn See, review of *Child of My Heart,* p. 17.

Commonweal, March 27, 1998, Rand Richards Cooper, "Charming Alice: A Unique Voice in American Fiction," p. 10; January 31, 2003, Margaret O'Brien Steinfels, review of *Child of My Heart,* pp. 28-29.

Economist (London, England), January 4, 2003, review of *Child of My Heart,* p. 68.

Irish Times, February 27, 1999, Jocelyn McClurg, interview with McDermott.

Newsweek, November 18, 2002, Malcom Jones, review of *Child of My Heart,* p. 80.

New York Times, February 1, 1982, LeAnne Schreiber, review of *A Bigamist's Daughter,* p. 13; March 28, 1987, Michiko Kakutani, review of *That Night,* p. 10; March 24, 1992, Michiko Kakutani, review of *At Weddings and Wakes,* p. C15; January 13, 1998, Michiko Kakutani, "The Ties That Bind and the Regrets That Strangle," p. E9; February 23, 2003, Ramin Ganeshram, "A Long-Ago Island Inspires Her Fiction," p. 16.

New York Times Book Review, February 21, 1982, Anne Tyler, review of *A Bigamist's Daughter,* pp. 1, 28-29; December 5, 1982, review of *A Bigamist's Daughter,* p. 36; April 19, 1987, David Leavitt, review of *That Night,* pp. 1, 29-31; April 12, 1992, Verlyn Klinkenborg, review of *At Weddings and Wakes,* p. 3; January 11, 1998, Alida Becker, review of *Charming Billy,* p. 8.

People, January 20, 2003, Michelle Vellucci, review of *Child of My Heart,* p. 54.

Publishers Weekly, March 30, 1992, Wendy Smith, "Alice McDermott," interview with McDermott, pp. 85-86; October 6, 1997, review of *Charming Billy,* p. 73; November 23, 1998.

Tribune Books (Chicago), April 30, 1987, Michael J. Bandler, "A Spellbinding Tale of Young Romance," p. 3; March 29, 1992, Catherine Petroski, "Life's Vital, Mysterious Family Rites: Alice Mcdermott Tells an Irish-American Story," pp. 1, 4.

Weekly Standard, December 9, 2002, John Podhoretz, review of *Child of My Heart,* pp. 31-33.

ONLINE

NPR: All Things Considered, http://www.npr.org/ (December 17, 2002), interview with Alice McDermott.

PBS, http://www.pbs.org/ (November 25, 2003), interview with Alice McDermott.

Powell's City of Books, http://www.powells.com/ (November 25, 2003), Dave Weich, "Alice McDermott, Child at Heart."

* * *

McEWAN, Ian 1948-
(Ian Russell McEwan)

PERSONAL: Born June 21, 1948, in Aldershot, England; son of David (an army officer) and Rose Lilian Violet (Moore) McEwan; married Penny Allen, 1982 (divorced, 1995); married Annalena McAfee, 1997; children: two sons, two stepdaughters. *Education:* University of Sussex, B.A. (honors), 1970; University of East Anglia, M.A., 1971. *Hobbies and other interests:* Hiking, tennis.

ADDRESSES: *Agent*—c/o Jonathan Cape, 20 Vauxhall Bridge Rd., London SW1V 2SA, England.

CAREER: Writer, 1970—.

MEMBER: Royal Society of Literature (fellow).

AWARDS, HONORS: Somerset Maugham Award, 1976, for *First Love, Last Rites;* shortlisted for Booker Prize, 1981, for *The Comfort of Strangers,* and 2001, for *Atonement;* Primio Letterario Prato, 1982; London *Evening Standard* award for best screenplay, 1983, for *The Ploughman's Lunch;* Whitbread Award, 1987, for *The Child in Time;* honorary doctorates from University of Sussex, 1989, and University of East Anglia, 1993; Booker Prize, 1998, for *Amsterdam;* shortlisted for Dublin IMPAC Award, 1999, for *Enduring Love;*

Shakespeare Medal, 1999; People's Booker Prize, 2001, Whitbread Novel Award shortlist, and W. H. Smith literary prize, both 2002, and Santiago Prize for European Fiction, National Book Critics Circle Award in fiction, and *Los Angeles Times* Book Award in fiction category, all 2003, all for *Atonement.*

WRITINGS:

SHORT STORIES

First Love, Last Rites (contains "Last Day of Summer" and "Conversations with a Cupboardman"), Random House (New York, NY), 1975.
In between the Sheets, and Other Stories, Simon & Schuster (New York, NY), 1978.
The Short Stories, J. Cape (London, England), 1995.

NOVELS

The Cement Garden, Simon & Schuster (New York, NY), 1978.
The Comfort of Strangers, Simon & Schuster (New York, NY), 1981.
The Child in Time, Houghton Mifflin (Boston, MA), 1987.
The Innocent, Doubleday (Garden City, NY), 1990.
Black Dogs, Doubleday (Garden City, NY), 1992.
Enduring Love, Doubleday (New York, NY), 1998.
Amsterdam, J. Cape (London, England), 1997, Doubleday (New York, NY), 1998.
Atonement, Doubleday (New York, NY), 2002.
Saturday, Nan A. Talese/Doubleday (New York, NY), 2005.

FOR CHILDREN

Rose Blanche, J. Cape (London, England), 1985.
The Daydreamer, illustrated by Anthony Browne, HarperCollins (New York, NY), 1994.

SCREENPLAYS

The Ploughman's Lunch (Greenpoint/Samuel Goldwyn, 1983), Methuen (London, England), 1985.
(With Mike Newell) *Sour Sweet* (adapted from Timothy Mo's novel; British Screen/ Film Four/Zenith, 1989), Faber & Faber (London, England), 1988.
The Innocent (adapted from McEwan's novel), Lakeheart/Miramax/Sievernich, 1993.
The Good Son, Twentieth Century-Fox, 1993.

OTHER

Conversations with a Cupboardman (radio play; based on a story by McEwan), British Broadcasting Corporation (BBC), 1975.
The Imitation Game: Three Plays for Television (contains *Jack Flea's Celebration* [BBC-TV, 1976], *Solid Geometry,* and *The Imitation Game* [BBC-TV, 1980]), J. Cape (London, England), 1981.
Or Shall We Die: An Oratorio (produced at Royal Festival Hall, 1983; produced at Carnegie Hall, 1985), score by Michael Berkeley, J. Cape (London, England), 1983.
Last Day of Summer (adapted from McEwan's short story), 1984.
Strangers (play; adapted from McEwan's novel *The Comfort of Strangers*), produced in London, England, 1989.
A Move Abroad (includes *Or Shall We Die?* and *The Ploughman's Lunch*), Pan (London, England), 1989.

Contributor to periodicals and literary journals, including *Guardian, New American Review, New Review, Radio Times, Sunday Telegraph, Times Literary Supplement, Transatlantic Review,* and *Tri-Quarterly.*

ADAPTATIONS: The Comfort of Strangers was adapted for film by Harold Pinter and directed by Paul Schrader, 1991; *The Cement Garden* was adapted for film by writer-director Andrew Birkin, 1993; *Enduring Love* was adapted for film by Joe Penhall and directed by Roger Michell, 2004; *Atonement* was adapted as an audiobook, Publishing Mills, 2002, and as a film by Christopher Hampton and directed by Sir Richard Eyre, c. 2005.

SIDELIGHTS: British author Ian McEwan is considered by some critics to be the most famous protege of novelist Malcolm Bradbury, a noted professor of creative writing at the University of East Anglia. Within McEwan's fictional worlds—particularly in his early novels—flourishes a haunting perversity: Childhood collides with adult violence, and power manifests itself in aberrant sexuality and political authoritarianism. The element of horror in his works is quickly recognized by the reader; it is the stuff of newspaper headlines, and it pervades human society. McEwan explores such modern horror in a style described by George Stade, writing in the *New York Times Book Review,* as "self-effacing rather than gaudy prose, as cold and transparent as a pane of ice, noticeable only in that things on the other side of it are clearer and brighter than they should be, a touch sinister in their dazzle." Paul Di Filippo, writing in the *St. James Guide to Horror, Ghost, and Gothic Writers,* likewise acknowledged McEwan's "tight prose," and called the novelist "a mask-wearing shaman guiding his readers on the blackest of night-sea journeys."

The collection of stories McEwan wrote at age twenty-two for his master's thesis was published in 1975 as *First Love, Last Rites.* The grotesque characters that inhabit these stories include an incestuous brother and sister, a gentleman who lives in a cupboard, a child-slayer, and a man who keeps the penis of a nineteenth-century criminal preserved in a jar. The stories include "Cocker at the Theatre," in which excessively exuberant stage actors indulge in actual sex during a performance; "Butterflies," wherein a sex criminal recalls his exploits; "Homemade," in which a young man explains the sexual relations he has shared with his sister; and the title story, in which two young lovers destroy a rodent.

Writing in the *New York Review of Books,* Robert Towers praised *First Love, Last Rites* as "possibly the most brilliantly perverse and sinister batch of short stories to come out of England since Angus Wilson's *The Wrong Set.*" Towers described McEwan's England as a "flat, rubble-strewn wasteland, populated by freaks and monsters, most of them articulate enough to tell their own stories with mesmerizing narrative power and an unfaltering instinct for the perfect sickening detail." John Fletcher, meanwhile, wrote in the *Dictionary of Literary Biography,* "Such writing would be merely sensational if it were not, like Kafka's, so pointed, so accurate, so incapable indeed of being appalled. In contemporary writing one has to turn to French literature to encounter a similar contrast between the elegance of the language and the disturbing quality of the material; in writing in English McEwan is wholly unique. No one else combines in quite the same way exactness of notation with a comedy so black that many readers may fail to see the funny side at all."

McEwan's first novel, *The Cement Garden,* has been likened to William Golding's *Lord of the Flies,* in which lost schoolboys degenerate into violent cannibals. *The Cement Garden* depicts four children's regression into a feral state with "suspense and chilling impact but without the philosophy lesson," as William McPherson noted in the *Washington Post Book World.* McEwan's children have been raised in an environment providing isolation similar to that in Golding's novel: a Victorian house standing alone amid the abandoned ruins of a postwar housing subdivision. After their parents die in quick succession, the children cover up the deaths—even hiding one corpse—while the eldest siblings unsuccessfully attempt to assume parental roles. The children eventually lapse into filth and apathy while the house decays until an outsider discovers the orphans' secret and summons the police to the scene.

Towers described *The Cement Garden* as "a shocking book, morbid, full of repellent imagery—and irresistibly readable, . . . the work of a writer in full control of his materials," and called McEwan's approach "magic realism—a transfiguration of the ordinary that has a far stronger retinal and visceral impact than the flabby surrealism of so many 'experimental' novels. The settings and events reinforce one another symbolically, but the symbolism never seems contrived or obtrusive." Fletcher praised the author's "quiet, precise, and sensuous touch" but added that "it is difficult to see how McEwan can develop much further this line in grotesque horror and black comedy, with a strong admixture of eroticism and perversion."

McEwan's second collection of short stories, *In Between the Sheets,* appears, at least initially, to be another consideration of characteristically unsettling characters and activities. The predictably peculiar tales include "Reflections of a Kept Ape," in which a romantic ape laments the end of his affair with a woman writer; "Dead As They Come," wherein a man becomes obsessed with a department store mannequin; "In Between the Sheets," in which a father fantasizes sexual relations with his young daughter; and "Pornography," wherein a misogynistic pornography seller is targeted for revenge by two of his female victims.

Despite the seemingly grotesque nature of its contents, *In Between the Sheets* has been perceived by several critics as evidence of McEwan's more restrained approach to his subject matter. V. S. Pritchett noted in the *New York Review of Books* that "McEwan is experimenting more," but added that the collection contains "two encouraging breaks with 'mean' writing." Reviewing *In Between the Sheets* in the *Washington Post Book World,* Terrence Winch maintained that McEwan's prose "is as clear as a windowpane" and called the author "a gifted story-teller and possibly the best British writer to appear in a decade or more."

In contrast to the eccentric characters of McEwan's earliest works, the prominent figures in his 1981 novel, *The Comfort of Strangers,* are a well-groomed, respectable couple on holiday in Venice. But the author gradually draws these unsuspecting characters into a web of horror that climaxes in sadomasochistic murder. Although continuing his praise for McEwan's gifts as a storyteller, John Leonard found the novel's plot contrived and unbelievable, writing in the *New York Times* that *The Comfort of Strangers,* although penned "by a writer of enormous talent, is definitely diseased." Stephen Koch also faulted the plot while praising McEwan's craftsmanship. "McEwan proceeds through most of this sickly tale with subtlety and promise," Koch stated in the *Washington Post Book World.* "The difficulty is that all this skill is directed toward a climax which, even though it is duly horrific, is sapped by a certain thinness and plain banality at its core. After an impressive send-up, the sadomasochistic fantasy animating *The Comfort of Strangers* is revealed as . . . a sadomasochistic fantasy. And not much more." But Koch went on to praise the novel, adding: "In all his recent fiction, McEwan seems to be reaching toward some new imaginative accommodation to the sexual questions of innocence and adulthood, role and need that have defined, with such special intensity, his generation. . . . I honor him for his effort."

The focus of McEwan's fiction underwent a shift after the birth of his own children. As he told Amanda Smith in an interview for *Publishers Weekly:* "It was both inevitable and desirable that my own range or preoccupation should change and that my emotional range should increase. Having children has been a major experience in my life. . . . It's extended me emotionally, personally, in ways that could never be guessed at. It's inevitable that that change would be reflected in my writing."

McEwan's 1987 novel, *The Child in Time,* confronts a fear universally felt by parents: that a child might become separated from them and be harmed. In the novel a three-year-old girl is abducted from her father while the two are shopping at the grocery store. Despite a massive search, the child is never found and her parents' relationship disintegrates due to guilt, anger, and each parent's isolating grief. The mother retreats to a country house; the father is left to find solace in television, alcohol, and his friendship with a man who, ironically, soon divests himself of adult responsibility and retreats to a childlike state of madness. McEwan's plot is threaded through with political hazards: the threat of nuclear war combines with economic collapse to propel the political state towards authoritarianism.

Some critics felt that the complexity of its subject-matter makes *The Child in Time* uneven. "What McEwan clearly has in mind is to document the . . . timelessness of childhood, to show how the child is never fully dead within us," commented Jonathan Yardley in the *Washington Post Book World.* But, Yardley added, "theme and story never quite connect." Michiko Kakutani agreed in the *New York Times,* noting that "if these motifs were successfully woven together, they might have reinforced McEwan's reverent vision of childhood, endowed it with some sort of symphonic resonance. As it is, they feel like afterthoughts grafted onto [the] story and not fully assimilated into the text." However, R. Z. Sheppard praised *The Child in Time* in *Time,* writing that "McEwan bridges the chasm between private anguish and public policy with a death- defying story, inventive, eventful and affirmative without being sentimental."

McEwan explores the espionage of a past epoch in his fourth novel, *The Innocent,* which critics have compared to the work of such masters of the spy genre as John le Carre and Graham Greene. Set in Berlin during the cold-war 1950s, the book concerns an actual joint effort by the U.S. Central Intelligence Agency (CIA) and the British MI6 to hear Soviet phone conversations by tunneling underground and tapping into East German phone cables. McEwan uses metaphor and symbolism to transform the historic account into a lesson on the dangers of ignoring the Socratic counsel "Know thyself."

In *The Innocent* McEwan sets up the stereotypic rigid Englishman, the brash American, and a sensual German seductress, then proceeds to penetrate their surfaces, flesh them out, and reveal their individuality. A reserved English telephone technician spying on Soviets in cold-war Berlin eventually finds himself outmatched by an American CIA operative. Moreover, the affair he has been conducting with a German woman compels the British agent to murder the woman's husband; the corpse is hacked into pieces and stored in two suitcases.

Comparing *The Innocent* to *The Child in Time, New York Times* critic Kakutani deemed the later work "bone tight: every detail of every event works as a time bomb, waiting to go off, while every image seems to pay off in terms of plot, atmosphere or theme." Richard Eder, writing in the *Los Angeles Times Book Review,* commended the entertaining quality of McEwan's novel but noted that the ending is jarred loose from the work by an interlude of violence Eder dubbed "all but unbearable to read." *The Innocent* "evokes a dark moral world in a highly entertaining fashion," wrote Eder. "Unlike Greene's entertainments, however, McEwan's leaves not even the trace of a feeling behind it." Higgins disagreed. "The reader's reward for all this ambiguity and gore is a book about a spy-tunnel that is not about a tunnel at all," noted the critic, "but about people whom you recognize; you see them every day. . . . This is the function of good novels: They enable us to snoop, undetected, unobserved, into the details of other people's lives."

Black Dogs, published in 1992, is a novel narrated by a man endeavoring to collect the pieces of his family's history and compose a memoir. The black dogs of the book's title refer to a vision that haunts one of the narrator's relatives; they also serve to represent the evil that lurks within every man. "The book richly suggests our human potentialities for mere waste as well as sheer evil, and for a sort of imperilled happiness," noted Caroline Moore in the *Spectator;* "the dogs, which disappear into the foothills of Europe like 'black stains in a grey dawn,' could take any form to reappear." As one of the novel's characters explains: "When the conditions are right, in different countries, at different times, a terrible cruelty, a viciousness against life erupts, and everyone is surprised by the depth of hatred within himself."

The metaphoric canines in *Black Dogs* clearly echo themes more subtly expressed in McEwan's previous fiction. As M. John Harrison noted in the *Times Literary Supplement,* "McEwan's retreat from the cement garden of his earlier books has been exemplary . . . [*Black Dogs* is] an undisguised novel of ideas which is also Ian McEwan's best work."

In McEwan's novel *Enduring Love* a couple's picnic is disrupted by the sight of a hot-air balloon caught in treacherous winds. Efforts to haul the balloon to safety fail, and the balloon crashes to earth. One of the picnickers involved in the rescue attempt rushes to the balloon only to be stopped by another rescuer and urged to pray. The hero soon finds himself stalked by this religious fellow, who nurtures a bizarre obsession. *New York Times* reviewer Christopher Lehmann-Haupt found *Enduring Love* "suspenseful" and "thematically rich."

McEwan followed *Enduring Love* with *Amsterdam,* for which he secured the prestigious Booker Prize in 1998. *Amsterdam* is the story of two longtime friends who form a euthanasia pact only to learn that it ultimately holds regrettable consequences. A *Kirkus Reviews* critic called *Amsterdam* "a smartly written tale that devolves slowly into tricky and soapy vapors," while in the *New York Times* Kakutani deemed it the work of "a writer in complete control of his craft, a writer who has managed to toss off this minor entertainment with such authority and aplomb that it has won him the recognition he has so long deserved."

Critical praise was heaped upon McEwan upon publication of his 2002 novel *Atonement.* The story of a highly imaginative British preteen whose desire to gain dramatic stature within her family results in a false accusation of rape and the destruction of a young man's life, *Atonement* also provokes the reader into questioning the role of the novelist in creating realistic fiction, and what *Commonweal* contributor Edward T. Wheeler called "the relationship between artistic imagination and truth of life." In McEwan's novel, a story is told from the point of view of an impressionable young narrator clearly identified as imaginative and inclined to interpret events to suit her penchant for drama; while the story is narrated by that child grown to adulthood, assertions come into question, facts become clouded, and McEwan's final chapters "undermine the fictional reality of the entire novel," according to *Antioch Review* critic Barbara Beckerman Davis. Davis praised *Atonement* as "McEwan's most intricate book," while in *School Library Journal* Susan H. Woodcock praised it as a "thought- provoking novel" with a story that is "compelling, the characters well drawn and engaging, and the outcome . . . almost always in doubt."

McEwan's 2005 endeavor, the novel *Saturday,* is the story of the Perownes, a seemingly perfect family: neurosurgeon father, attorney mother, and two grown children—a poet daughter and a son who is a skilled musician. The entire novel takes place on one Saturday and centers around Henry, the father, being involved in a car accident and subsequent encounters between the Perownes and Baxter, the ill—both mentally and physically—man in the other car, culminating in Baxter's invasion of the Perownes' home, where he threatens them and is then transformed by the beauty of a poem. In an *America* review, John B. Breslin found that while *Saturday* is "a tightly written story," ultimately it "falls a bit flat." *First Things* contributor Paul J. Griffiths disagreed, however, considering this, McEwan's eighth novel, "perhaps his finest," and noting that it "is an almost-perfect witness to the texture and meaning of a cultured paganism that knows it cannot last."

The Daydreamer constituted a change of pace for McEwan. His first work of fiction for younger readers, the 1994 short-story collection describes the adventures of a gifted ten-year-old named Peter Fortune, who balances his mundane suburban existence with a rich fantasy life. With a heightened sense of imagination, Peter is able to vividly experience what it would be like to trade bodies with his dying cat, make his parents disappear, battle a demonic doll, or abandon his little sister on the bus, all through his daydreams. While *New York Times Book Review* critic David Leavitt noted that McEwan "has an unhappy tendency to talk down to his readers in a way that he could never get away with in an adult novel," the reviewer added that the author "possesses a vivid imagination for the grotesque. Thus he is nowhere more successful in [the book] . . . than when—like his young hero—he lets that imagination get the better of him." Gregory Feeley agreed, writing in the *Washington Post Book World,* "The best scenes . . . combine wit and invention with a sense of the natural order being overturned in a manner that recalls Roald Dahl." Praising McEwan's prose as "vivid and poetic," a *Publishers Weekly* reviewer noted that *The Daydreamer* "reveals a profound understanding of childhood." Also favorable was an assessment by Merritt Moseley, who in a *Dictionary of Literary Biography* entry called *The Daydreamer* a "beautifully written" work.

In addition to his novels, children's books, and short stories, McEwan is the author of several screenplays, including *The Innocent,* based on his novel, and *The Ploughman's Lunch,* derived from his own stage production. *The Ploughman's Lunch* details the behavior of a callously self-serving individual in the equally cold and unfeeling England of the 1980s, when Margaret Thatcher presided as prime minister. Writing in the the *Dictionary of Literary Biography,* Merritt Moseley observed that the film is set in a "coarse, opportunistic, false society" that McEwan indicts for dishonesty. *New York Times* film critic Vincent Canby praised the film as "immensely intelligent."

McEwan has also written several scripts for television, including *Solid Geometry,* notorious in his native Britain for having been banned by the British Broadcasting Corporation in 1979, at an advanced stage of production, due to its "grotesque and bizarre sexual elements." This play, derived from a story in *First Love, Last Rites,* concerns an individual who maintains a pickled penis on his desk. Another television play, *Jack Flea's Birthday Celebration,* features an infantile young man whose mother and girlfriend vie for maternal authority over him. And in *The Imitation Game,* which was broadcast in 1980, a woman's desire to aid in England's war effort is consistently undermined by the country's male-oriented social order. Moseley, in his *Dictionary of Literary Biography* entry on McEwan, proclaimed *The Imitation Game* "a strong play."

Feminist in perspective is *Or Shall We Die?,* an oratorio for which McEwan provided the words to composer Michael Berkeley's music. Moseley noted in the *Dictionary of Literary Biography* that this work "was written at a time of mounting anxiety over the threat of nuclear war," and he acknowledged its notion of "the feminine principle as humanity's potential salvation." Commenting on the violence that some critics perceive as his fictional trademark—and so deem him "Ian Macabre"—McEwan commented to Daniel Johnson in the London *Times,* "I don't think I am particularly obsessed by violence, but at the same time I am very disturbed by it. I suppose many of the things that disturb me find their way into my fiction." Remarking on his preference for the novel over the screenplay or the short story as a fictional means of expressing his concerns, McEwan explained to *Publishers Weekly:* "The reason the novel is such a powerful form is that it allows the examination of the private life better than any other art form. Our common sense gives us such a thin wedge of light on the world, and perhaps one task of the writer is to broaden the wedge."

BIOGRAPHICAL AND CRITICAL SOURCES:

BOOKS

Bestsellers 90, Issue 4, Gale (Detroit, MI), 1991, pp. 50-52.

Burnes, Christina, *Sex and Sexuality in Ian McEwan's Work,* Pauper's Press (Nottingham, England), 1995.

Contemporary Literary Criticism, Gale (Detroit, MI), Volume 13, 1980, Volume 66, 1992.

Contemporary Novelists, 5th edition, St. James Press (Detroit, MI), 1992.

Dictionary of Literary Biography, Gale (Detroit, MI), Volume 14: *British Novelists since 1960,* 1983, pp. 495-500; Volume 194: *British Novelists since 1960, Second Series,* 1998, pp. 207- 215.

Haffenden, John, *Novelists in Interview,* Methuen (London, England), 1985, pp. 526- 527.

McEwan, Ian, *Black Dogs,* J. Cape (London, England), 1992.

Ryan, Kiernan, *Ian McEwan,* Northcote House (Plymouth, England), 1994.

St. James Guide to Horror, Ghost, and Gothic Writers, St. James Press (Detroit, MI), 1998, pp. 400- 402.

Slay, Jack L., Jr., *Ian McEwan,* Twayne (New York, NY), 1996.

Stevenson, Randall, *The British Novel since the Thirties: An Introduction,* University of Georgia Press (Athens, GA), 1986, pp. 185-193.

Taylor, D. J., *A Vain Conceit: British Fiction in the 1980s,* Bloomsbury (London, England), 1989, pp. 55- 59.

PERIODICALS

America, April 30, 1994, p. 22; July 4, 2005, John B. Breslin, "No Ordinary Day," p. 24.
Antioch Review, winter, 2003, Barbara Beckerman Davis, review of *Atonement,* p. 179.
Ariel, April, 1995, pp. 7- 23.
Atlantic, March, 2002, review of *Atonement,* pp. 106-109.
Bomb, fall, 1990, pp. 14- 16.
Booklist, November 1, 2002, Candace Smith, review of *Atonement,* p. 513.
Christian Century, May 22, 2002, Gordon Houser, review of *Atonement,* p. 30.
Commonweal, May 3, 2002, Edward T. Wheeler, review of *Atonement,* p. 26.
Contemporary Review, June, 1995, pp. 320-323.
Critical Quarterly, summer, 1982, pp. 27-31.
Critique, summer, 1994, pp. 205- 218.
Encounter, June, 1975; January, 1979.
English, spring, 1995, pp. 41- 55.
First Things: A Monthly Journal of Religion and Public Life, August-September, 2005, Paul J. Griffiths, "Nor Certitude, Nor Peace," p. 40.
Globe and Mail (Toronto, Ontario, Canada), April 16, 1988; June 2, 1990.
Kirkus Reviews, November 15, 1998.
Listener, April 12, 1979, pp. 526- 527.
London Magazine, August, 1975; February, 1979.
Los Angeles Times Book Review, June 24, 1990, p. 3.
Monthly Film Bulletin, June, 1983.
Nation, October 31, 1987, p. 491.
National Review, January 18, 1993, p. 57.
New Republic, July 23, 1990, p. 37; March 26, 2002, James Wood, review of *Atonement,* p. 26.
New Review, autumn, 1978, pp. 9- 21.
New Statesman, May 11, 1990, pp. 18-19, 35-36.
Newsweek, June 4, 1990, p. 80; October 11, 1993, p. 59A.
Newsweek International, April 8, 2002, interview with McEwan, p. 94.
New Yorker, January 25, 1993, p. 111.
New York Review of Books, March 8, 1979; January 24, 1980; February 4, 1988, p. 18; January 14, 1993, p. 37; April 11, 2002, John Lanchester, review of *Atonement,* p. 24.
New York Times, November 21, 1978; August 14, 1979; June 15, 1981; September 26, 1987; May 29, 1990; January 15, 1998; December 1, 1998.
New York Times Book Review, November 26, 1978; August 26, 1979; July 5, 1981; October 11, 1987, p. 9; June 3, 1990, p. 1; November 8, 1992, p. 7; November 13, 1994, p. 54.
Paris Review, summer, 2002, Adam Begley, interview with McEwan, pp. 30-60.
Publishers Weekly, September 11, 1987, pp. 68-69; July 11, 1994, p. 79; September 2, 2002, review of *Atonement* (audio version), p. 31.
School Library Journal, October, 1994, p. 126; June, 2002, Susan H. Woodcock, review of *Atonement,* p. 172.
Southern Review, March, 1984, pp. 68-80.
Spectator, June 27, 1992, p. 32.
Time, November 17, 1978; September 21, 1987, p. 76; June 25, 1990, p. 69; November 16, 1992, p. 103; September 27, 1993, p. 84.
Times (London, England), February 16, 1981; October 8, 1981; June 27, 1987; May 8, 1990.
Times Literary Supplement, January 20, 1978; September 19, 1978; October 9, 1981; June 19, 1992.
Times Saturday Review, December 8, 1990, pp. 16-17.
Tribune Books (Chicago, IL), November 26, 1978; September 30, 1979; July 19, 1981; June 10, 1990, p. 7.
Village Voice, August 28, 1990, p. 102.
Virginia Quarterly Review, autumn, 1975.
Washington Post Book World, October 29, 1978; August 5, 1979; June 28, 1981; April 30, 1987; June 3, 1990, p. 10; December 4, 1994, p. 19.
World and I, August, 2002, "Atonement: Evolution of Ian Macabre," p. 207.
Yale Review, April, 1993, p. 134; July, 1993, p. 122.

OTHER

Writers Talk: Ideas of Our Time (video), ICA Video, 1989.

* * *

McEWAN, Ian Russell
See McEWAN, Ian

* * *

McGUANE, Thomas 1939-
(Thomas Francis McGuane, III)

PERSONAL: Born December 11, 1939, in Wyandotte, MI; son of Thomas Francis (a manufacturer) and Alice (Torphy) McGuane; married Portia Rebecca Crockett, September 8, 1962 (divorced, 1975); married Margot

Kidder (an actress), August, 1976 (divorced May, 1977); married Laurie Buffett, September 19, 1977; children: (first marriage) Thomas Francis IV; (second marriage) Maggie; (third marriage) Anne Buffett, Heather (stepdaughter). *Education:* Attended University of Michigan and Olivet College; Michigan State University, B.A., 1962; Yale University, M.F.A., 1965; additional study at Stanford University, 1966-67.

ADDRESSES: Home—Box 25, McLeod, MT 59052. *Agent*—Amanda Urban, International Creative Management, 40 West 57th St., New York, New York, 10019.

CAREER: Full-time writer.

MEMBER: Tale Club of New York.

AWARDS, HONORS: Wallace Stegner fellowship, Stanford University, 1966-67; Richard and Hinda Rosenthal Foundation Award in fiction from American Academy, 1971, for *The Bushwacked Piano;* National Book Award fiction nomination, 1974, for *Ninety-two in the Shade;* Montana Governor's Award for the Arts, 1988; Northwestern Bookseller's Award, 1992; Golden Plate Award, American Academy Achievement, 1993; honorary doctorate degrees from Montana State University, 1993, and Rocky Mountain College, 1995.

WRITINGS:

NOVELS

The Sporting Club, Simon & Schuster (New York, NY), 1969.
The Bushwacked Piano (also see below), Simon & Schuster (New York, NY), 1971.
Ninety-two in the Shade (also see below), Farrar, Straus (New York, NY), 1973, reprinted, Vintage (New York, NY), 1995.
Panama, Farrar, Straus (New York, NY), 1977, reprinted, Vintage (New York, NY), 1995.
Nobody's Angel (also see below), Random House (New York, NY), (New York, NY), 1982.
Something to Be Desired, Random House (New York, NY), 1984.
Keep the Change (also see below), Houghton (Boston, MA), 1989.
Nothing but Blue Skies, Houghton (Boston, MA), 1992, reprinted, Vintage (New York, NY), 1994.
Three Complete Novels: Keep the Change, Nobody's Angel, and The Bushwacked Piano, Wings Books (New York, NY), 1993.
The Cadence of Grass, Knopf (New York, NY), 2002.

SCREENPLAYS

Rancho Deluxe, United Artists, 1975.
(Also director) *Ninety-two in the Shade* (adapted from his novel of the same title), United Artists, 1975.
Missouri Breaks (produced by United Artists, 1976), Ballantine (New York, NY), 1976.
(With Bud Shrake) *Tom Horn,* Warner Brothers, 1980.

Also author (with Jim Harrison) of *Cold Feet.*

OTHER

An Outside Chance: Essays on Sport, Farrar, Straus (New York, NY), 1980, reprinted as *An Outside Chance: Classic & New Essays on Sports,* Houghton (Boston, MA), 1990.
In the Crazies: Book and Portfolio, Winn Books (Seattle, WA), 1984.
To Skin a Cat (short stories), Dutton (New York, NY), 1986.
Silent Seasons: Twenty-one Fishing Stories, Clark City Press (Livingston, MT), 1988.
Live Water, with paintings and drawings by John Swan, Meadow Run Press (Stone Harbor, NJ), 1996.
The Longest Silence: A Life of Fishing, Knopf (New York, NY), 1999.
Some Horses, Vintage (New York, NY), 1999.
(With an introduction by Charles Lindsey) *Upstream* (photography), Aperture (New York, NY), 2000.

Special contributor to *Sports Illustrated,* 1969-73.

ADAPTATIONS: The Sporting Club was adapted by Lorenzo Semple, Jr., for a full-length film released by Avco Embassy Pictures in 1971.

SIDELIGHTS: Thomas McGuane has been described in the *New York Times Book Review*as a "highly self-conscious literary grandson of Ernest Hemingway." McGuane's fiction—some of which shares locales and sensibilities with that of Hemingway—brings an ironic twist to the plight of the modern American male. "Thomas McGuane likes dogs, horses, Indians, golf, the road, hawks, rocks, peppery food and outdoor sex," wrote Beverly Lowry in the *New York Times Book Review.* "For characters he has a soft spot for loony old men, hateful, dead or vanished fathers, hot-blooded, sharp-tongued women, struggling protagonists with high-stakes, dangerous male friends. . . . Much more than the *things* of fiction, however, Mr. McGuane is concerned with irony, voice, lingo, dialogue that cries to be read aloud, descriptive passages that are never coy or sloppy. Which is to say that although facts and not literature itself form the backdrop against which he performs, what he's really after is language—fully extended and at serious play." In novels, screenplays and short fiction, McGuane has combined a fascination with language and an affection for macho heroes who—with humor or pathos—retreat from the banality of their middle class backgrounds toward more authentic and self-aware lives.

McGuane's first three novels established his reputation as a flamboyant stylist and satirist. *The Sporting Club, The Bushwacked Piano* and *Ninety-two in the Shade* juxtapose the ugly materialism of modern America against the beauty and power of the natural world. According to *Detroit* magazine writer Gregory Skwira, this trio of books perfectly captures "the hip disillusionment and general disorientation of the late 1960s." Although his early work had earned him high praise from the literary establishment, McGuane temporarily abandoned the novel in the early 1970s for work in the film industry. The personal chaos he experienced during that time is reflected in such later novels as *Panama, Something to Be Desired,* and *Nothing but Blue Skies.* In these books, emotional depth and honesty take precedence over stylistic flamboyance, and many critics regard them as McGuane's finest.

McGuane grew up in an Irish family where storytelling was a natural art. When he announced his intention to become a writer, however, his parents disapproved of his ambition, calling it hopelessly impractical. To counter their skepticism, McGuane devoted himself almost exclusively to his artistic efforts. While his university classmates enjoyed traditional college parties and diversions, McGuane wrote, read voraciously, studied the novel, or engaged in esoteric discussions with fellow students and contemporary novelists Jim Harrison and William Hjortsberg. McGuane's sober disposition earned him the nickname "The White Knight." His singlemindedness paid off: *The Sporting Club* was published when he was nearly thirty, *The Bushwacked Piano*and *Ninety-two in the Shade* followed in quick succession. The plots of these three novels are very different, but they are closely linked in style, theme, and tone. Each is written in what R.T. Smith called in *American Book Review* "amphetamine-paced, acetylene-bright prose." "All present a picture of an America which has evolved into a 'declining snivelization' (from *Bushwacked*), a chrome-plated, chaotic landscape which threatens to lead right-thinking men to extremes of despair or utter frivolity," explained Larry McCaffrey in *Fiction International.* "Each of them presents main characters . . . who have recognized the defiled state of affairs around them, and who are desperately seeking out a set of values which allows them, as Skelton [the protagonist of *Ninety-two in the Shade*] puts it, 'to find a way of going on.'" In McCaffrey's estimation, the most remarkable thing about McGuane's writing is that he is "able to take the elements of this degraded condition and fashion from them shocking, energetic, and often beautiful works of prose—works which both mirror and comment upon our culture and . . . in their eloquence, transcend it."

McGuane's intense approach to his art was altered forever in 1972. Driving at 120 miles per hour on a trip from Montana to Key West, he lost control of his car and was involved in a serious accident. He walked away from it physically unharmed, but so profoundly shaken that he was unable to speak for some time thereafter. After this brush with death, his relentless concentration on writing seemed misguided to him. McCaffrey quoted McGuane in the *Dictionary of Literary Biography Yearbook:* "After the accident, I finally realized I could stop pedaling so intensely, get off the bike and walk around the neighborhood. . . . It was getting unthinkable to spend another year sequestered like that, writing, and I just dropped out." McGuane was also finding it increasingly difficult to support his family on a novelist's income; while his books had received critical acclaim, none had been best-sellers. Accordingly, when movie producer Elliot Kastner asked him if he would be interested in a film project, McGuane eagerly accepted. Over the next few years he wrote several screenplays, and directed the screen version of *Ninety-two in the Shade.*

Changes were not limited to the author's work; his personal life was undergoing a transformation as well. Together with the other members of "Club Mandible"—a loosely-structured group of friends including singer Jimmy Buffett—McGuane began to enjoy a hedonistic lifestyle. He explained to Thomas Carney in *Esquire:* "I had paid my dues. . . . Enough was enough. In 1962 I had changed from a sociopath to a bookworm and now I just changed back. Buffett was in the same shape. We both heard voices telling us to do something." Accordingly, writes Carney, "McGuane the straight arrow who had spent years telling his friends how to live their lives while he lived his like a hermit became McGuane the boogie chieftain, rarely out of full dance regalia. The White Knight began staying out all night, enjoying drugs and drink in quantities. And women other than his wife."

McGuane's name began appearing in tabloids when he became romantically involved with actress Elizabeth Ashley during the shooting of his first film, *Rancho Deluxe.* While still linked with Ashley, McGuane began an affair with Margot Kidder, while both actresses were working on *Ninety-two in the Shade.* When McGuane and his first wife, Becky, divorced, Becky married the male lead of *Ninety-two in the Shade,* Peter Fonda. Tom McGuane subsequently married Margot Kidder, already the mother of his second child. McGuane and Kidder divorced several months later. The unexpected deaths of his father and sister compounded the confusion in McGuane's life. He told Skwira that the media depiction of his activities at that time was "overblown," but admitted, "I had a lot of fun drinking and punching people out for a short period of time."

The turmoil of that interval was clearly reflected in *Panama,* McGuane's first novel in four years. It is a first-person description of the disintegrating life of rock star Chester Hunnicutt Pomeroy, an overnight sensation who is burning out on his excessive lifestyle. In McCaffrey's words, *Panama* "in many ways appears to be a kind of heightened, surreal portrayal of McGuane's own suffering, self-delusion, and eventual self-understanding—a book which moves beyond his earlier novels' satiric and ironic stances." The book drew strong reactions, both favorable and unfavorable. Many reviewers who had unreservedly praised McGuane's earlier work received *Panama* coldly, with some implying that the author's screenwriting stint had ruined him as a novelist. In a *Washington Post Book World* essay, Jonathan Yardley dismissed *Panama* as "a drearily self-indulgent little book, a contemplation of the price of celebrity that was, in point of fact, merely an exploitation of the author's new notoriety." Richard Elman complained in the *New York Times Book Review* that *Panama* "is all written up in a blowsy, first-person prose that goes in all directions and winds up being, basically, a kvetch." He stated that McGuane, "who was once upon a time wacky and droll [and who] is now sloppy and doleful," suffers from an inability to recognize "good" versus "bad" writing. "Everything of craft that must be done right is done wrong. . . . This book isn't written; it is hallucinated. The reader is asked to do the writer's work of imagining."

Other reviewers applauded *Panama* as the novel that finally joins McGuane's stylistic brilliance with an emotional intensity lacking in his earlier efforts. Susan Lardner suggested in a *New Yorker* review that McGuane's work as a director perhaps enriched the subsequent novel: "Maybe as a result of the experience, he has added to his store of apprehensions some dismal views of fame and the idea that life is a circus performance. . . . Whatever risk McGuane may have sensed in attempting a fourth novel with a simultaneous plunge into first person narration, the feat proves successful. The audience is left dazzled by the ingenuity of his turn, somewhat aghast at the swagger, hungry for more." Writing in the *Washington Post Book World-*,Philip Caputo called it McGuane's "most relentlessly honest novel. . . . Although *Panama* is as well written as its predecessors, its first-person point of view endows it with a greater directness; and the book not only gives us a look at the void, it takes us down into it. . . . *Panama* also contains some of the finest writing McGuane has done so far." *Village Voice* contributor Gary L. Fisketjon noted: "*Panama* is more ambitious if less slick than the earlier novels, which were restrained and protected by the net of a hot-wired style and a consummate mockery; the humor here is not as harsh, and the objectivity is informed more by empathy than disdain. . . . Moving beyond satire, McGuane has achieved something difficult and strange, a wonderfully written novel that balances suffering and understanding." And in a Toronto *Globe & Mail* essay, Thad McIlroy deemed *Panama* "one of the best books to have been published in the United States in the last 20 years. It's minimal, mad, disjointed at times, and consistently brilliant, terrifying and exhilarating. McGuane's use of language, and his ever-precise ear for dialogue, raise the novel out of the actual and into the universal, the realm of our finest literature."

McGuane's life stabilized considerably after his 1977 marriage to Laurie Buffett, sister of his friend Jimmy Buffett. Living on his Montana ranch, the author perfected his riding and roping techniques and became a serious rodeo competitor. He commented to Carney in *Esquire,* "I've come to the point where art is no longer as important as life. Dropping six or seven good colts in the spring is just as satisfying as literature." McGuane's new down-to-earth attitude carried over to his prose style, as he explained to a *Detroit* magazine interviewer: "I'm trying to remove the tour de force or superficially flashy side of my writing. I'm trying to write a cleaner, plainer kind of American English. . . . I feel I have considerably better balance than I have ever had in my life and I don't care to show off; I just want to get the job done." Christopher Lehmann-Haupt referred favorably to McGuane's new direction in his *New York Times* review of the novel *Nobody's Angel:* "Both the author's affection for his characters and the strength of his narrative seem to matter even more to him than his compulsion to be stylistically *original.*"

While *Nobody's Angel* echoes the dark tone of *Panama,* McGuane's next novel marks the first time that one of his restless protagonists finds fulfillment. *Something to Be Desired* revolves around Lucien Taylor and his two loves, Emily and Suzanne. When Emily, the more seductive and mysterious of the two, drops Lucien to marry a doctor, Lucien marries the virtuous Suzanne. The newlyweds go to work in Central America, where Lucien finds himself unable to forget Emily. When he hears she has murdered her husband, he deserts his wife and child to bail her out. He moves to Emily's ranch and becomes her lover, but she soon jumps bail, leaving him the ranch. Lucien converts it into a resort and finds happiness in a reconciliation with his family. Ronald Varney commented in the *Wall Street Journal* that "the somewhat bizarre plot twists of Mr. McGuane's story occasionally seem implausible. . . . And yet Mr. McGuane manages to pull this story off rather well, giving it, as in his other novels, such a compressed dramatic style that the reader is constantly entertained and diverted." *New York Times Book Review* critic Robert Roper named McGuane's sixth novel "his best, a remarkable work of honest colors and fresh phrasings that deliver strong, earned emotional effects."

With his 1989 novel *Keep the Change,* McGuane "expanded his emotional territory and deepened his literary and human concerns," to quote *New York Times Book Review* contributor Beverly Lowry. The story centers on Joe Starling, a struggling artist who travels to Montana to take possession of a cattle ranch he is not even sure he wants. During a season of ranching on the family farm, Joe confronts the peculiar characters who have their own ambitions for the land as well as the changing landscape of his hometown of Deadrock. In her review of the work, Lowry concluded: "I don't know of another writer who can walk Thomas McGuane's literary high wire. His vaunted dialogue has not been overpraised; authenticity for him is only the beginning. He can describe the sky, a bird, a rock, the dawn, with such grace that you want to go see for yourself; then he can zip to a scene so funny that it makes you laugh out loud. . . . It's encouraging to see a good writer getting better."

Mid-life crisis is the subject of McGuane's eighth novel, *Nothing but Blue Skies.* The protagonist, Frank Copenhaver, suddenly finds himself separated from his wife and in dire financial straits due to his own wacky behavior. Noting that Frank is "a fully fleshed, believable character," *Bloomsbury Review* correspondent Gregory McNamee added that the book is "a well-considered study of a man confronting midlife crisis and, in the end, overcoming it by sheer force of will." *Time* magazine reviewer John Skow wrote of the work: "McGuane, whose recent novels have seemed a touch broody, enjoys himself with this one. The fine barrelhouse prose of *The Bushwacked Piano* and *Ninety-Two in the Shade* is working again. He waves his arms, he hoots and hollers and thrashes out a rowdy parody of the male psyche under the stress of having to defend itself in the supermarket."

A full decade after publication of *Nothing but Blue Skies* came McGuane's ninth novel, 2002's *The Cadence of Grass.* Here Jim Whitelaw's death leaves his family in a pickle: he has decreed that his daughter, Evelyn, must stay with her husband Paul in order to sell the family business, a bottling franchise. But Evelyn is in the middle of dumping Paul. Soon her entire family is persuading her to stand by her man, if only for the sake of the money. *Library Journal*'s Jim Coan commended the cast of "quirky, humorous, and sometimes downright dangerous characters" in this "absorbing, meaningful, and brilliantly written" novel. Similarly, Daniel Fierman, writing in *Entertainment Weekly,* found the novel a "surprising, affecting mix of bitterness and delicacy." A critic for *Publishers Weekly* felt that *The Cadence of Grass* "has the hip feel of *Panama,* without the drugs and hallucinations." *Esquire*'s Scott Raab, however, dubbed the book a "truncated horse opera . . . [and] pinched of life." Raab further noted, "I dislike it so much—that after finishing it, I immediately reread *The Sporting Club,* [McGuane's] first novel, to see what had gone wrong." Responding to other negative reviews of the novel, Tom Pilkington in *World and I* felt that such a reception "has been unfair." While Pilkington went on to comment that *The Cadence of Grass* is "not a great novel," and "not even McGuane's best," the reviewer still thought that the book "has its rewards." Among these are the book's final pages, which contain "some of the best writing McGuane has ever done." For Pilkington, "The tone is elegiac, and for all the novel's bizarre humor, elegy is precisely the grace note *The Cadence of Grass* should end on."

McGuane's work has drawn comparisons to many famous authors, including William Faulkner, Albert Camus, Thomas Pynchon, F. Scott Fitzgerald, and most especially to Hemingway. Both McGuane and Hemingway portray virile heroes and anti-heroes vibrantly aware of their own masculinity; each author explores themes of men pitted against themselves and other men; each passionately loves game fishing and the outdoors.

Discussing *Ninety-two in the Shade,* Thomas R. Edwards of the *New York Times Book Review* claimed: "Clearly this is Hemingway country. Not just the he-man pleasures of McGuane's men but even the locales of the novels . . . recapitulate Hemingway's western-hemisphere life and works." McCaffrey concurred in a *Fiction International* piece: "If [the set of value-systems of McGuane's protagonists] sounds very familiar to Hemingway's notion of a 'code' devised to help one face up to an empty universe, it should; certainly McGuane's emphasis on male aggressions, his ritualized scenes involving fishing, . . . and even the locales (Key West, the upper Rockies, up in Michigan) suggest something of Papa's influence, though with a distinctly contemporary, darkly humorous flavor."

When asked by Carter in *Fiction International* about the numerous Hemingway comparisons, McGuane replied: "I admire him, of course, and share a lot of similar interests, but I really don't write like him. . . . We have totally different styles. His world view was considerably more austere than mine. His insistence on his metaphysical closed system was fanatical. And he was a fanatic. But it gave him at his best moments a very beautiful prose style. And anyone who says otherwise is either stupid or is a lying sack of snake shit. We have few enough treasures in this twerp-ridden Republic to have to argue over Ernest Hemingway's greatness." To John Dorschner of the *Miami Herald* he speculated, "I can only agree that [my life and Hemingway's] appear to be similar, but that's all. What might be more pertinent is to think how my father was influenced by Hemingway. Places like the Keys and northern Michigan, those were places I was taken by my father."

BIOGRAPHICAL AND CRITICAL SOURCES:

BOOKS

Authors in the News, Volume 2, Thomson Gale (Detroit, MI), 1976.

Contemporary Literary Criticism, Thomson Gale (Detroit, MI), Volume 3, 1975; Volume 7, 1977; Volume 18, 1981; Volume 45, 1987.

Dictionary of Literary Biography, Volume 2: *American Novelists since World War II,* Thomson Gale (Detroit, MI), 1978.

Dictionary of Literary Biography Yearbook: 1980, Thomson Gale (Detroit, MI), 1981.

Klinkowitz, Jerome, *The New American Novel of Manners: The Fiction of Richard Yates, Dan Wakefield, and Thomas McGuane,* University of Georgia Press (Athens, GA), 1986.

Wallace, Jon, *The Politics of Style: Language as Theme in the Fiction of Berger, McGuane, and McPherson,* Hollowbrook (Montrose, CO), 1992.

Westrum, Dexter, *Thomas McGuane,* Twayne (Boston, MA), 1991.

PERIODICALS

America, May 15, 1971.

American Book Review, May-June, 1983.

Antioch Review, spring, 2000, Carolyn Maddux, review of *Some Horses,* p. 244.

Atlantic, September, 1973.

Bloomsbury Review, July-August, 1993, Gregory McNamee, review of *Nothing but Blue Skies.*

Book, May-June, 2002, Josh Karp, "Margaritaville, Inc.," p. 12.

Booklist, September 1, 1999, Dennis Dodge, review of *The Longest Silence,* p. 61; June 1, 1999, Fred Egloff, review of "Some Horses," p. 1760.

Book World, May 2, 1971.

Chicago Tribune, November 5, 1978; April 12, 1985; November 3, 1986.

Chicago Tribune Books, October 14, 1990.

Chicago Tribune Book World, February 15, 1981.

Commonweal, October 26, 1973.

Crawdaddy, February, 1979.

Critique, August, 1975.

Detroit News, April 25, 1982; November 18, 1984.

Detroit News Magazine, August 17, 1980.

Entertainment Weekly, May 10, 2002, Daniel Fierman, review of *The Cadence of Grass,* p. 74.

Esquire, June 6, 1978; July, 2002, Scott Raab, review of *The Cadence of Grass,* p. 22.

Feature, February, 1979.

Fiction International, fall/winter, 1975.

Globe & Mail (Toronto, Ontario, Canada), January 26, 1985; April 4, 1987.

Hudson Review, winter, 1973-74.

Library Journal, May 15, 1999, Deborah Emerson, review of *Some Horse,* p. 122; October 1, 1999, Will Hepfer, review of *The Longest Silence,* p. 103; May 15, 2002, Jim Coan, review of *The Cadence of Grass,* p. 126.

Los Angeles Times Book Review, September 17, 1989.

Miami Herald, October 13, 1974.

Nation, January 31, 1981; March 20, 1982.

New Mexico Humanities Review, fall, 1983.

New Republic, August 18, 1979.

New Statesman, July 26, 1974.

Newsweek, April 19, 1971; July 23, 1973.

New Yorker, September 11, 1971; June 23, 1973; April 19, 1979.

New York Review of Books, December 13, 1973.
New York Times, November 21, 1978; May 23, 1980; March 4, 1982, Christopher Lehmann-Haupt, review of *Nobody's Angel;* December 10, 1984; October 11, 1986; September 14, 1989.
New York Times Book Review, March 14, 1971; July 29, 1973; November 19, 1978, Richard Elman, review of *Panama;* October 19, 1980; February 8, 1981; March 7, 1982; December 16, 1984, Robert Roper, review of *Something to Be Desired;* September 24, 1989, Beverly Lowry, review of *Keep the Change;* September 13, 1992.
Observer, (London, England), January 24, 1993.
Partisan Review, fall, 1972.
People, September 17, 1979; November 3, 1980.
Prairie Schooner, summer, 1993.
Publishers Weekly, May 3, 1999, review of *Some Horses,* p. 59; November 8, 1999, review of *The Longest Silence,* p. 55; May 6, 2002, review of *The Cadence of Grass,* p. 35.
Rapport, January, 1993.
Saturday Review, March 27, 1971.
Spectator, July 13, 1974.
Time, August 6, 1973; June 30, 1980; November 2, 1992, John Skow, review of *Nothing but Blue Skies.*
Times Literary Supplement, May 24, 1985; January 29, 1993.
Village Voice, September 15, 1975; December 11, 1978, Gary L. Fisketjon, review of *Panama.*
Virginia Quarterly Review, spring, 1981.
Wall Street Journal, December 24, 1984, Ronald Varney, review of *Something to Be Desired.*
Washington Post, December 30, 1980; October 2, 1986.
Washington Post Book World, November 19, 1978; February 28, 1982; December 16, 1984.
World and I, September, 2002, Tom Pilkington, review of *The Cadence of Grass.*

ONLINE

Borzoi Reader Online, http://www.randomhouse.com/knopf/ (July 27, 2004), "Thomas McGuane."
IdentityTheory.com Web site, http://www.identitytheory.com/ (July 27, 2004), Robert Birnbaum, "Interview: Thomas McGuane."

* * *

McGUANE, Thomas Francis, III
See McGUANE, Thomas

McINERNEY, Jay 1955-

PERSONAL: Surname is pronounced "*Mac*-in-er-ney"; born January 13, 1955, in Hartford, CT; son of John Barrett (a corporate executive) and Marilyn Jean (Murphy) McInerney; married second wife, Merry Reymond (a student), June 2, 1984 (marriage ended); married third wife, Helen Bransford (a jewelry designer), December 27, 1991; children: two. *Education:* Williams College, B.A., 1976; postgraduate study at Syracuse University. *Hobbies and other interests:* Travel, skiing, tennis, fly-fishing, karate, wine.

ADDRESSES: *Agent*—Amanda Urban, International Creative Management, 40 West 57th St., New York, NY 10019; and Deborah Rogers, Rogers, Coleridge & White Ltd., 20 Powis Mews, London W11 1JN, England.

CAREER: Novelist. *Hunterdon County Democrat,* Flemington, NJ, reporter, 1977; Time-Life, Inc., Osaka, Japan, textbook editor, 1978-79; *New Yorker,* New York, NY, fact checker, 1980; Random House (publishers), New York, NY, member of editorial staff, 1980-81; Syracuse University, Syracuse, NY, instructor in English, 1983; writer, 1983—.

MEMBER: Authors Guild, Authors League of America, PEN, Writers Guild.

AWARDS, HONORS: Princeton in Asia fellowship, 1977.

WRITINGS:

NOVELS

Bright Lights, Big City, Random House (New York, NY), 1984.
Ransom, Random House (New York, NY), 1985.
Story of My Life, Atlantic Monthly Press (New York, NY), 1988.
Brightness Falls, Knopf (New York, NY), 1992.
The Last of the Savages, Knopf (New York, NY), 1996.
Model Behavior: A Novel and Seven Stories, Knopf (New York, NY), 1998.
The Good Life, Knopf (New York, NY), 2006.

OTHER

Bright Lights, Big City (screenplay adaptation of McInerney's novel), Metro-Goldwyn-Mayer/United Artists, 1988.

(Author of introduction) Helen Mitsios, editor, *New Japanese Voices: The Best Contemporary Fiction from Japan,* Grove/Atlantic (New York, NY), 1992.

(Editor) *Cowboys, Indians, and Commuters: The Penguin Book of New American Voices,* Viking (New York, NY), 1994.

Bacchus and Me: Adventures in the Wine Cellar (nonfiction), Lyons (New York, NY), 2000.

How It Ended (short stories), Bloomsbury, 2001.

Contributor to *Look Who's Talking,* edited by Bruce Weber, Washington Square Press, 1986. Wine columnist for *House and Garden.*

ADAPTATIONS: Model Behavior was adapted to audio cassette, 1999.

SIDELIGHTS: Jay McInerney gained critical success and a reputation rarely won by a first-time novelist for his 1984 work *Bright Lights, Big City.* The story concerns an unnamed young man who works as a fact-checker during the day at a stodgy, respectable magazine—some reviewers noticed a resemblance to the *New Yorker,* where McInerney was employed as a fact-checker in 1980—but stays out all night abusing alcohol and cocaine at New York City's popular nightclubs. Disillusioned and trying to cope with the death of his mother and his divorce from a shallow model, the narrator carouses with his friend and devil's advocate, Tad Allagash, who "envies him for his ability to find drugs and girls, to get into hip mischief and yet hold down a job, to do what he pleases without fatigue or remorse," according to Darryl Pinckney in the *New York Review of Books.* The narrator speaks in the second person, present tense, distancing himself from his feelings and describing people and events in, as John Lownsbrough commented in the *Globe and Mail,* an "insinuating" voice. Some critics quoted the novel's first passage as indicative of the tone of the novel: "You are not the kind of guy who would be at a place like this at this time of the morning. But here you are, and you cannot say that the terrain is entirely unfamiliar, although the details are fuzzy. You are at a nightclub talking to a girl with a shaved head. The club is either Heartbreak or the Lizard Lounge. All might come clear if you could just slip into the bathroom and do a little more Bolivian Marching Powder. Then again it might not."

"Bolivian Marching Powder" is a euphemism for cocaine; the frenetic social life of the narrator is analogous to the specious euphoria created by the drug, McInerney explained. As he told interviewer Joyce Wadler for the *Washington Post,* "'Cocaine' is the exact metaphorical equivalent of the idea that tonight, if you go to just one more party, one more place, that's gonna be the one . . . that somehow will fulfill you, and every time you do one more line, you think just one more."

Terence Moran in the *New Republic* applauded the style of *Bright Lights, Big City,* writing that "McInerney employs an unusual and challenging narrative device; he tells the tale through the second person in the historical present tense and fashions a coherent and engaging voice with it, one that is totally believable at almost every moment in the novel." Moran also praised the work as "an accomplished and funny novel, full of clever verbal contraptions and hip social pastiches." A *Publishers Weekly* reviewer also remarked that "The best part of this promising debut is McInerney's humor—it is cynical, deadpan and right on target, delivered with impeccable comic timing." However, while *New York Times* contributor Michiko Kakutani extolled McInerney's "eye for the incongruous detail, his ear for language, his hyperbolic sense of humor, and his ability to conjure up lively characters with a few lines of dialogue and a tart description or two," other critics were not so accepting of the author's approach.

After the release of *Bright Lights, Big City,* McInerney gained attention not only as an author but as a personality, embracing a celebrity lifestyle and socializing with some of his contemporaries at New York night spots. Authors Bret Easton Ellis (*Less than Zero*), Tama Janowitz (*Slaves of New York*), McInerney, and sometimes David Leavitt (*Family Dancing*) were dubbed the "Literary Brat Pack" by the popular press because of their relative youth at the time of their first success, the similar content of their novels, and their self-promotion and demand for high pay. *Los Angeles Times* contributor Nikki Finke said, "They're a new wave of writers soaring to stardom in the '80s at startlingly young ages with innovative writing styles and hip subject matter." Charles Maclean reported in the *Spectator* that the group was "scorned for embracing celebrity, posing for fashion spreads, endorsing products and keeping the gossip columnists busy—all sensible ways of consolidating the appeal these writers have to their mainly young urban professional audience." Remarking on the content of the writing by McInerney, Ellis, and Janowitz, however, Jonathan Yardley opined in the *Washington Post:* "These writers want to have it both ways: to exploit and even glorify indulgence in sex, drugs and luxury on the one hand, and to draw cautionary morals from it on the other."

McInerney's second effort, *Ransom,* centers on Princeton University graduate Christopher Ransom, an American expatriate who lives in Kyoto, Japan, teaching English to Japanese businessmen and studying karate. Events involving friends and family have left him numb: his mother has died; his father, in Ransom's opinion, has sacrificed his integrity by abandoning play writing to write for television; and he has lost his two traveling companions, Annette and Ian, in a drug-related incident at the Khyber Pass. Ron Loewinsohn wrote in the *New York Times Book Review* that the title character "feels guilty about the flabby privilege of his upper-middle-class background, and guilty by association with his father." In addition, blaming himself for the fate of his friends, he tortures himself with regrets and memories. In Japan he hopes to find "a place of austere discipline which would cleanse him and change him," Loewinsohn explained; Ransom's immersion in the martial arts becomes "a form of penance and purification."

Many critics noted that the strength of McInerney's first two novels lies in his humorous delivery and unexpected irreverences. Kakutani attributed "a mastery of [the] idiosyncratic, comic voice" to McInerney and found most of his jokes "amusing and dexterously handled." Together, McInerney's sense of humor and his active interest in human pathos combine to create fiction which, Moran said, "not only jests at our slightly tawdry life, but also celebrates its abiding possibilities."

In *Story of My Life* McInerney returns to the New York club scene, but, as Kakutani reported in the *New York Times,* "Where the young magazine fact checker in *Bright Lights, Big City* merely visited this world, Alison, her roommate Jeannie and their friends are full-time residents here. . . . Cocaine and casual sex are their two obsessions; money to finance their pleasures is a constant preoccupation." Kakutani criticized the author's characterizations, claiming, "Alison and her pals—who dither on endlessly, like adolescent ninnies, about clothes, makeup and their boyfriends' sexual endowments—all seem less like believable women than like a man's paranoid, cartoonlike idea of what such females might be." However, Sarah Sheard, writing for the *Globe and Mail,* applauded McInerney's "fabulous ear for dialogue," adding that he "captures a tortured and articulate spirit trying her hardest to hide inside the IQ of a lawn ornament. . . . [The author] accomplishes this with wit and pacing, impeccable accuracy and, ultimately, compassion."

Brightness Falls is also set in New York in the 1980s—just around the time of the 1987 stock market crash—and comments on drug use, club-going, and greed, but revolves around an older group, "thirtysomethings" in the publishing business. The main characters are Russell Calloway, an editor for a publishing firm; his wife, Corinne, a stockbroker; and their friend Jeff Pierce, a famous author with a drug habit and groupies. John Skow, reviewing the book for *Time,* called it "a funny, self-mocking, sometimes brilliant portrait of Manhattan's young literary and Wall Street crowd, our latest Lost Generation."

Some critics, and even the author himself, compared *Brightness Falls* to Tom Wolfe's *Bonfire of the Vanities.* David Rieff related in the *Washington Post Book World* that McInerney declared in a *Vanity Fair* interview, "'What was going through my mind when I sat down to write this novel was: What if *Bonfire of the Vanities* had real people in it?'" Indeed, in the *Boston Globe,* Matthew Gilbert commented, "While *Brightness Falls* is a sociological critique like *Bonfire,* it's more human than Wolfe's knife-twister." Sven Birkerts, however, reviewing the work for Chicago's *Tribune Books,* noted that the author's gift of farce was still evident, claiming that McInerney is "quite adept at rendering the feel of the publishing milieu. We get bright, satirically edged shots of everything from the lunch-hour confabs over advances and reputations to the rituals of male bonhomie at the urinals." Al J. Sperone in the *Village Voice Literary Supplement* stated that "McInerney has a gift for comic set pieces, and he's generous with snappy repartee, doling out wisecracks for everybody." Birkerts lauded *Brightness Falls* as a "solid and durably plotted book" and added, "Fueled by its images of excess and rendered biographically interesting by its undercurrents of felt remorse, it makes for a quick and compelling reading experience."

McInerney's fifth novel, *The Last of the Savages,* features two characters: the narrator, a New York lawyer named Patrick Keane, and his old college friend Will Savage, now a famous record producer. Patrick, from the vantage point of middle age, recounts his lower-middle-class background and his lifelong desire to be wealthy and aristocratic. While attending college at Yale University, he meets Will, whose privileged southern background is in stark contrast to his own. While Will goes on to achieve fame and even greater fortune as a record producer, Patrick abandons his dreams of a literary career for safe and solid work as a lawyer. Eventually Patrick must come to grips with his homoerotic feelings toward Will.

Many critics were unmoved by McInerney's attempt to encompass a wider historical realm in *The Last of the Savages* than he did with his earlier novels. Noting that the "central concerns" of the novel are "familiar adolescent ones"—youthful rebellion, social climbing, freedom—*New York Times* reviewer Michiko Kakutani remarked that "in order to broaden these coming-of-age quandaries and make 'Savages' seem like a larger novel, Mr. McInerney has tried to turn the story of Will and Patrick into an emblematic saga." However, Kakutani added, "None of these efforts . . . really work." Other reviewers criticized the author for producing a contrived plot and using sloppy prose. *New York Times Book Review* commentator Geoff Dyer, for instance, noted McInerney's tendency "to coast linguistically," while Thomas R. Edwards in the *New York Review of Books* declared that "bad writing here becomes unexpectedly endemic." Edwards added: "Some of the ineptitudes of the novel's prose are just irritating or unintentionally funny. . . . Others flirt with disaster."

The critical drubbing that followed McInerney through much of his early career ultimately prompted a bold move by the author. In 1990, according to a *Publishers Weekly* interview by Lorin Stein, he "struck back." Brandishing a samurai sword on the cover of *Esquire,* McInerney contributed an essay to that magazine that, noted Stein, "lashed out at the country's most prominent critics, claiming that they were prejudiced against young writers. At the same time, he dismissed the latest work of two young writers most closely associated with him," Janowitz and Ellis. But in a 1988 essay coinciding with the publication of *Story of My Life,* James Wolcott revealed in *New Republic* the thinking behind some of the barbs. "So far McInerney hasn't demonstrated the dramatic amplitude or organizational skills to be a novelist," Wolcott wrote. "His specialty is the smart-ass monologue." Acknowledging a character who asks friends what the "three biggest lies are," Wolcott commented that the "third biggest lie is, 'Jay, those critics are just jealous.'" Timing, more than talent, is what brought the author to the fore with *Bright Lights,* added Wolcott: "It caught the last tailwind of the downtown club scene before tired trendies began settling in as sofa spuds in front of their VCRs. . . .And McInerney's fact-checking department [in the novel] came at a time when the New Yorker was still envisioned as a bloodless Henry James arena of sacred hush and elaborate fuss."

In 1998's *Model Behavior,* McInerney retuned to familiar ground, New York City social life. Indeed, this 1998 novel—published with a group of short stories—"can almost be read as a sequel" to *Bright Lights, Big City,* according to *Entertainment Weekly* contributor Benjamin Svetkey. "But different decades, different themes," Svetkey added. "The club-hopping, powder-snorting excesses of the '80s have been replaced with a more '90s-style obsession: the celebrity culture." The title novella revolves around two characters: handsome young novelist Jeremy Green, anxiously awaiting the publication of his first collection; and Jeremy's older—but no wiser—best friend. Connor McKnight is "thirty-two and two-thirds old and not really happy about it," as the book relates. Stuck in a job penning celebrity profiles for the women's magazine *CiaoBella!,* Connor finds his life complicated further when his fashion-model girlfriend Philomena runs off with actor Chip Ralston—the same pretty-boy superstar Connor has been trying to land an interview with. This leaves the dismayed journalist "to lurch around Manhattan dealing with his witchy boss, his boorish but talented best friend and his anorexic sister," as Judith Timson described it in *Maclean's.* Timson admired the way McInerney's writing "comes alive" when depicting Connor's "weird but somehow still warm family." The author configured widely different fates for his two lead characters: Connor remains shallow and bitter but does head-butt a celebrity in a fit of pique, "which could be construed as a good thing," Timson observed. Meanwhile, Jeremy ironically dies in a freak accident as his acclaimed novel is adapted to the big screen.

"*Model Behavior* represents another return to the New York scene, one that mirrored its author's renewed interest in the city," Stein commented. If the book "shows McInerney's disdain for what celebrity is doing to our culture," the critic added, "it also shows a more personal fear of what celebrity does to celebrities. Connor sells out, but Jeremy dies—killed off, one senses, before success can spoil him. He seems too good, or too principled, for the world of McInerney's imagination."

Several favorable notices greeted *Model Behavior,* with critics welcoming the author back to his forte after the overambitious *Last of the Savages. Booklist* contributor Donna Seaman cited the "tightly constructed and viciously funny satire" running through the new collection, adding that "what makes McInerney so likeable is the ingeniousness behind his cynicism." "Sheer delights" is what Sheila Riley called *Model Behavior* in her *Library Journal* assessment. A.O. Scott, writing for the *New York Times Book Review,* praised the author's way with characterization: "It would take a roomful of M.F.A.'s a thousand years to produce a thumbnail sketch as satirically sharp as [McInerney's] . . . precis of his protagonist's family history." And Svetkey, while acknowledging that *Model Behavior* "isn't a perfect book," maintained that the collection explores the era's celebrity-obsessed culture "with more style and wit than it's getting credit for. . . . Frankly, it's a kick having McInerney back in town."

McInerney once told *CA:* "Since college, writing fiction is mainly what I've wanted to do, though I entered college writing poetry; I was convinced that was my metier. I changed, actually, in my senior year when I discovered a number of fiction writers all at once who hit me very hard and in such a way as to make me feel that fiction and narrative prose could be as exciting as lyrical poetry, which was what I was writing—and, ultimately, I came to feel, more exciting. Or I felt rather that my particular ambitions and proclivities were such that I would rather write fiction than poetry." Regarding who and what has influenced the humorous side of his work, McInerney revealed that an author "I read off and on quite a bit and like very much is Evelyn Waugh. I like P.G. Wodehouse, too, and Mark Twain. *Don Quixote* and *Tom Jones* are two novels that I would like to think have something to do with my comic sense. In more contemporary terms, the writer Thomas McGuane, although he's a very serious writer, is also very marvelous with comedy and has influenced me quite a bit, I'd say. J.P. Donleavy's *The Ginger Man* also. . . . And Joyce. The James Joyce of *Ulysses* is one of the funniest writers around, though most people are so daunted by some of his erudition that they forget to laugh."

BIOGRAPHICAL AND CRITICAL SOURCES:

BOOKS

Contemporary Literary Criticism, Thomson Gale (Detroit, MI), Volume 34, 1985, Volume 112, 1999.

Culture in an Age of Money, edited by Nicolaus Mills, Ivan R. Dee, 1990, pp. 216-233.

The Literature of Emigration and Exile, edited by James Whitlark and Wendell Alycock, Texas Tech University Press, 1992, pp. 115-130.

PERIODICALS

Atlantic Monthly, December, 1984, p. 145.

Book, December, 1998, review of *Model Behavior,* p. 77.

Booklist, August, 1998, Donna Seaman, review of *Model Behavior,* p. 1924.

Books, summer, 1998, review of *Model Behavior,* p. R4.

Boston Globe, June 10, 1992, Matthew Gilbert, review of *Brightness Falls,* p. 43.

Chicago Tribune, September 27, 1984; April 1, 1988; April 24, 1988; August 29, 1988.

Chicago Tribune Book World, October 7, 1984; September 15, 1985.

Christian Science Monitor, October 5, 1984, Ruth Doan MacDougall, "Having Fun in New York," p. B5; October 29, 1985; October 29, 1998, review of *Model Behavior,* p. B8.

Commentary, September, 1992, Evelyn Toynton, "High Life," pp. 56-57.

Entertainment Weekly, October 16, 1998, Benjamin Svetkey, "'Bright' Lite," p. 77.

Esquire, May, 1985; September, 1998, review of *Model Behavior,* p. 60.

Globe and Mail (Toronto, Ontario, Canada), November 16, 1985, John Lownsbrough, review of *Bright Lights, Big City;* September 10, 1988, Sarah Sheard, review of *The Story of My Life.*

Harper's, December, 1988.

Interview, June, 1985.

Kirkus Reviews, July 15, 1998, review of *Model Behavior,* p. 991.

Library Journal, September 15, 1998, Sheila Riley, review of *Model Behavior,* p. 112.

Los Angeles Times, September 21, 1984; September 13, 1987.

Los Angeles Times Book Review, October 6, 1985; August 28, 1988, p. 3; June 7, 1992, Richard Eder, "Campfire of the Vanities," p. 3; June 6, 1996, Carter Coleman, "Riding a Ghost Train, Gatsby-Style," p. 10.

Maclean's, November 23, 1998, Judith Timson, review of *Model Behavior,* p. 140.

Ms., August, 1985.

Nation, June 10, 1996, p. 30.

National Review, June 22, 1992, Richard Brookhiser, "And the Moral Is," pp. 54-55.

New Republic, December 3, 1984, Terence Moran, review of *Bright Lights, Big City,* pp. 41-42; October 10, 1988, James Wolcott, "Yada Yada Yada," pp. 38-41.

New Statesman, August 14, 1998, review of *Model Behavior,* p. 47.

Newsweek, October 21, 1985; September 26, 1988, pp. 72-73; June 8, 1992, p. 58.

New Yorker, July 27, 1992.

New York Review of Books, November 8, 1984, Darryl Pinckney, review of *Bright Lights, Big City,* pp. 12-14; May 23, 1996, Thomas R. Edwards, review of *The Last of the Savages,* p. 28; February 18, 1999, review of *Model Behavior,* p. 7.

New York Times, October 30, 1984, Michiko Kakutani, review of *Bright Lights, Big City;* August 24, 1985; August 20, 1988, Kakutani, review of *The Story of My Life;* June 1, 1992, p. 13; April 30, 1996, Kakutani, review of *The Last of the Savages,* p. C17.

New York Times Book Review, November 25, 1984, William Kotzwinkle, "You're Fired, So You Buy a

Ferret," p. 9; September 29, 1985, Ron Loewinsohn, "Land of the Also Rising Sun," p. 42; September 25, 1988, Carolyn Gaiser, "Zonked Again," p. 12; May 31, 1992, Cathleen Schine, review of *Brightness Falls,* p. 7; March 3, 1996, p. 8; May 26, 1996, Geoff Dyer, "Freeing the Slaves," p. 11; September 27, 1998, A.O. Scott, "Babylon Revisited," p. 12.

Observer (London, England), July 12, 1998, review of *Model Behavior,* p. 15; May 2, 1999, review of *Model Behavior,* p. 14.

Publishers Weekly, August 10, 1984, p. 76; July 19, 1985; July 29, 1988, Sybil Steinberg, review of *The Story of My Life,* p. 219; September 14, 1998, Lorin Stein, "Jay McInerney: N.Y. Confidential," p. 39; February 4, 2002, Judith Rosen, "Hip-Lit 101," p. 20.

Saturday Review, November, 1984, p. 88.

Southern Folklore, Volume 8, number 3, 1991, Frank de Caro, "The Three Great Lies," pp. 235-254.

Spectator, December 10, 1988, p. 36; May 30, 1992, p. 32.

Time, October 14, 1985; October 19, 1987; September 19, 1988, p. 95; June 1, 1992, John Skow, "Onward and Yupward," p. 82; May, 20, 1996, p. 76; September 28, 1996, review of *Model Behavior,* p. 84.

Times (London, England), August 26, 1989.

Times Literary Supplement, May 24, 1985, Roz Kaveney, "Solutions to Dissolution," p. 572; April 18, 1986; August 26, 1988, p. 927; May 15, 1992, p. 20; May 27, 1994, p. 20; June 14, 1996, James Campbell, "A Slave to Success," p. 24; July 31, 1998, review of *Model Behavior,* p. 19.

Tribune Books (Chicago, IL), June 7, 1992, Sven Birkerts, review of *Brightness Falls,* p. 3.

Vanity Fair, May, 1992.

Vogue, June, 1992, Graydon Carter, "Vogue Men," pp. 184-185.

Voice Literary Supplement, October 16, 1984, Al J. Sperone, review of *Brightness Falls,* p. 52; October, 1988, p. 42; June, 1992, p. 9.

Wall Street Journal, September 16, 1988, P.J. O'Rourke, review of "The Story of My Life," p. 23; June 12, 1992, Joseph Olshan, "A Golden Couple of the Age of Accretion," p. A12; May 9, 1996, p. A16; September 25, 1998, review of *Model Behavior,* p. W6.

Washington Post, November 6, 1984; December 12, 1984; September 7, 1988.

Washington Post Book World, August 25, 1985; May 24, 1992, David Rieff, review of *Brightness Falls,* p. 1; September 20, 1998, review of *Model Behavior,* p. 4.

ONLINE

Beatrice.com, http://www.beatrice.com/ (June 13, 2002), "Beatrice Interview."

Jay McInerney Web site, http://jaymcinerney.com/ (June 13, 2002).

* * *

McKIE, Robin

PERSONAL: Male. *Education:* Glasgow University, B.S. (math and psychology, with honors). *Hobbies and other interests:* Squash, skiing, walking, photography and traveling.

ADDRESSES: *Office*—Observer, London, England. *Agent*—c/o Henry Holt Co., 115 West 18th St., New York, NY 10011.

CAREER: Writer and editor. *Edinburgh Evening News,* reporter, 1978-78; *Times Higher Educational Supplement,* science correspondent, 1978-82; *Observer,* London, England, science editor, 1984—.

WRITINGS:

Panic: The Story of AIDS, Thorsons, 1986.

(With others) *Chernobyl: The End of the Nuclear Dream,* Vintage Books (New York, NY), 1987.

The Genetic Jigsaw: The Story of the New Genetics, Oxford University Press (New York, NY), 1988.

(With Walter Bodmer) *The Book of Man: The Human Genome Project and the Quest to Discover Our Genetic Heritage,* Little, Brown (London, England), 1994, Scribner (New York, NY), 1995.

(With Christopher Stringer) *African Exodus: The Origins of Modern Humanity,* Holt/John Macrae (New York, NY), 1997.

Dawn of Man: The Story of Human Evolution, Dorling Kindersley Publishing (New York, NY), 2000.

NONFICTION FOR CHILDREN

Lasers, illustrations by Paul Cooper, Elsa Godfrey, and Rob Shone, Franklin Watts (New York, NY), 1983.

Technology: Science at Work, Franklin Watts (New York, NY), 1984.

Nuclear Power, illustrations by Mike Saunders and others, Gloucester Press (New York, NY), 1985.
Solar Power, Gloucester Press (New York, NY), 1985.
Robots, Franklin Watts (New York, NY), 1986.
Energy, Hampstead Press (New York, NY), 1989.

Contributor to periodicals, including *World.*

SIDELIGHTS: Robin McKie, a writer and science editor for the *Observer* in London, England, has published books on subjects ranging from human origin to acquired immune deficiency syndrome (AIDS) and has produced many science volumes for children. Noteworthy among McKie's works is *African Exodus: The Origins of Modern Humanity,* which was written with Christopher Stringer. Scientific advances, many less than a decade old, have transformed researchers' understanding of where and how the human species originated. *African Exodus* challenges the long-held notion that humans evolved in multiple regions approximately two million years ago; rather, it argues that the human race developed in Africa and began migrating throughout the remainder of the world approximately one hundred thousand years ago. In the book, McKie and Stringer contend that the remarkable genetic similarities among various races are of greater importance than the racial differences revealed in other studies. Robert J. Coontz, Jr. commented in *Earth:* "In recounting this 'Out of Africa' scenario, the authors blast away at the rival idea that humans evolved in several parts of the world at the same time. The 'multiregional hypothesis' is dead, Stringer and McKie say; fossil bones and modern DNA both show that things just didn't happen that way."

Despite its unconventional approach to the theory of human evolution, *African Exodus* received widely positive reviews, in particular for its authors' ability to make complex anthropological information comprehendible to readers. A reviewer for *Publishers Weekly* called *African Exodus* "intellectually potent yet eminently accessible."

McKie has also written about genetics in such works as *The Genetic Jigsaw: The Story of the New Genetics* and—with Walter Bodmer—*The Book of Man: The Human Genome Project and the Quest to Discover Our Genetic Heritage.* Ian N.M. Day, reviewing the book for *Lancet,* noted that the authors' "stated aim is to help (lay) readers appreciate the scientific challenges that have been overcome in bringing genetics to this remarkable state of preparedness, and to describe the awkward problems that still lie ahead. Although already familiar with the field, I found this book a fascinating read. . . . The book of man should appeal to professionals for its light overview and to lay readers for the comprehensible journey of self-discovery that it leads them through."

McKie has also produced many science volumes for young readers. These writings for children include *Energy,* which considers alternatives to petroleum and nuclear power; *Lasers; Technology: Science at Work,* which addresses subjects such as energy generation, computer design, and space exploration; *Nuclear Power,* which explains both fission and fusion and provides arguments both for and against nuclear energy; *Solar Power;* and *Robots.* McKie's books for children have been highly praised for their deft handling of the material and inclusion of glossaries, photographs, and diagrams designed to further facilitate children's understanding of complex subjects.

BIOGRAPHICAL AND CRITICAL SOURCES:

PERIODICALS

Appraisal, spring/summer, 1984, pp. 29-30; fall, 1985, pp. 31-32; fall, 1986, pp. 108-109;
Booklist, March 15, 1985, p. 1060; January 1, 1986, p. 683; June 1, 1986, p. 1462; June 1, 1989, p. 1720; December 1, 1994, Donna Seaman, review of *The Book of Man: The Human Genome Project and the Quest to Discover Our Genetic Heritage,* p. 642; July, 1997, Mary Caroll, review of *African Exodus: The Origins of Modern Humanity,* p. 1785.
Earth, February 1998, Robert J. Coontz Jr, review of *African Exodus,* p. 62.
Growing Point, September, 1985, p. 4500.
Humanist, May/June, 1987, p. 46.
Junior Bookshelf, December, 1983, p. 246.
Lancet, May 28, 1994, Ian N.M. Day, review of *The Book of Man,* p. 1348.
Library Journal, June 15, 1997, H. James Birx, review of *African Exodus,* p. 78.
Listener, September 4, 1986, pp. 21-22.
Publishers Weekly, November 21, 1994, review of *The Book of Man,* p. 61; June 9, 1997, review of *African Exodus,* p. 33.
School Library Journal, December, 1983, p. 67; March, 1985, p. 168; November, 1985, p. 80; March, 1986, p. 158; September, 1989, p. 259.

* * *

McKINLEY, Jennifer Carolyn Robin
See McKINLEY, Robin

McKINLEY, Robin 1952-
(Jennifer Carolyn Robin McKinley)

PERSONAL: Born November 16, 1952, in Warren, OH; daughter of William (in the U.S. Navy and Merchant Marines) and Jeanne Carolyn (a teacher; maiden name, Turrell) McKinley; married Peter Dickinson (an author), January 3, 1992. *Education:* Attended Dickinson College, 1970-72; Bowdoin College, B.A. (summa cum laude), 1975. *Politics:* "Few affiliations, although I have strong feelings pro-ERA and pro-freedom—anti-big business and anti-big government. I grow more cynical all the time, and am now more likely to belong to countryside-saving charities." *Religion:* "Lapsed Protestant." *Hobbies and other interests:* Gardening, horses, walking, travel, many kinds of music, and life as an expatriate and the English-American culture chasm.

ADDRESSES: Home—Hampshire, England. *Agent*—Merrilee Heifetz, Writers House, Inc., 21 West 26th St., New York, NY 10010. *E-mail*—nuraddin@aol.com.

CAREER: Writer, 1975—. Ward and Paul (stenographic reporting firm), Washington, DC, editor and transcriber, 1972-73; Research Associates, Brunswick, ME, research assistant, 1976-77; bookstore clerk in Maine, 1978; teacher and counselor at private secondary school in Natick, MA, 1978-79; Little, Brown, Inc. (publisher), Boston, MA, editorial assistant, 1979-81; barn manager on a horse farm, Holliston, MA, 1981-82; Books of Wonder, New York, NY, clerk, 1983; freelance reader, copy, line-editor, and general all-purpose publishing dogsbody, 1983-91.

MEMBER: Many gardening and garden societies.

AWARDS, HONORS: Horn Book Honor List citations, 1978, for *Beauty: A Retelling of the Story of Beauty and the Beast,* 1985, for *The Hero and the Crown,* 1988, for *The Outlaws of Sherwood,* and 1995, for *Knot in the Grain;* Best Books for the Teen Age citation, New York Public Library, 1980, 1981, and 1982, all for *Beauty: A Retelling of the Story of Beauty and the Beast;* Best Young Adult Books citation, American Library Association (ALA), 1982, and Newbery Honor Book, ALA, 1983, both for *The Blue Sword;* Newbery Medal, 1985, for *The Hero and the Crown;* World Fantasy Award for best anthology, 1986, for *Imaginary Lands;* Best Books for the Teen Age and Best Adult Book for the Teen Age, ALA, 1994, for *Deerskin;* Notable Book selection, ALA, for *The Hero and the Crown.* D.H.L., Bowdoin College, 1986, and Wilson College, 1996; World Fantasy Award nomination (with Peter Dickinson) in best collection category, 2003, for *Water: Tales of Elemental Spirits;* Mythopoeic Award for Adult Literature, Mythopoeic Society, 2004, for *Sunshine.*

WRITINGS:

Beauty: A Retelling of the Story of Beauty and the Beast, Harper (New York, NY), 1978.

The Door in the Hedge (short stories), Greenwillow (New York, NY), 1981.

The Blue Sword, Greenwillow (New York, NY), 1982.

The Hero and the Crown, Greenwillow (New York, NY), 1984.

(Editor and contributor) *Imaginary Lands* (short stories; includes "The Stone Fey"), Greenwillow (New York, NY), 1985.

(Adapter) Rudyard Kipling, *Tales from the Jungle Book,* Random House (New York, NY), 1985.

(Adapter) Anna Sewell, *Black Beauty,* illustrated by Susan Jeffers, Random House (New York, NY), 1986.

(Adapter) George MacDonald, *The Light Princess,* illustrated by Katie Thamer Treherne, Harcourt (San Diego, CA), 1988.

The Outlaws of Sherwood, Greenwillow (New York, NY), 1988.

My Father Is in the Navy (picture book), illustrated by Martine Gourbault, Greenwillow (New York, NY), 1992.

Rowan (picture book), illustrated by Donna Ruff, Greenwillow (New York, NY), 1992.

Deerskin (adult fantasy), Putnam (New York, NY), 1993.

A Knot in the Grain and Other Stories, Greenwillow (New York, NY), 1994.

Rose Daughter, Greenwillow (New York, NY), 1997.

The Stone Fey, illustrated by John Clapp, Harcourt (San Diego, CA), 1998.

Spindle's End, Putnam (New York, NY), 2000.

(With Peter Dickinson) *Water: Tales of Elemental Spirits,* Putnam (New York, NY), 2002.

Sunshine, Berkley Books (New York, NY), 2003.

Contributor to anthologies, including *Elsewhere II,* edited by Terri Windling and Mark Arnold, Ace Books, 1982; *Elsewhere III,* edited by Terri Windling and Mark Arnold, Ace Books, 1984; and *Faery,* edited by Terri Windling, Ace Books, 1985. Also contributor of book reviews to numerous periodicals. Author of column, "In the Country," for *New England Monthly,* 1987-88.

ADAPTATIONS: Random House recorded *The Blue Sword* (1994), and *The Hero and the Crown* (1986) on cassette.

SIDELIGHTS: Robin McKinley is the award-winning author of novels, short stories, and picture books that retelling old stories such as "Beauty and the Beast" and "Sleeping Beauty" for a new generation. McKinley's renditions of classic fairy tales have a feminist twist, for they feature empowered girls and young women. No weak-kneed damsels in distress, McKinley's protagonists are females who do things, who are not "waiting limply to be rescued by the hero," as McKinley wrote on her Web site. These self-sufficient heroines "are intelligent, loyal, and courageous—eager and not afraid to cross the physical and psychological barriers that lie between them and the fulfillment of their destinies," wrote Hilary S. Crew in *Twentieth-Century Children's Writers.* In novels such as *Beauty: A Retelling of the Story of Beauty and the Beast,* the Newbery Honor Book *The Blue Sword,* the Newbery Medal-winner *The Hero and the Crown, The Outlaws of Sherwood, Deerskin, Rose Daughter* and *Spindle's End,* McKinley creates fantasy realms filled with realistic detail and powerful characters, elements which attract readers young and old.

Born in 1952, McKinley "grew up a military brat and an only child [who] decided early on that books were much more reliable friends than people," as she wrote on her Web site. Moving every two years, from California to Japan to New York, she found comfort in fictional worlds. "Writing has always been the other side of reading for me," McKinley further commented, "[I]t never occurred to me not to make up stories." However, as a young girl, she also had identity issues. "I despised myself for being a girl," she once explained "and ipso facto being someone who stayed at home and was boring, and started trying to tell myself stories about girls who did things and had adventures."

"Once I got old enough to realize that authorship existed as a thing one might aspire to, I knew it was for me," the author noted on her Web site. "I even majored in English literature in college, a good indication of my fine bold disdain for anything so trivial as earning a living." She saw herself as a writer in the J.R.R. Tolkien or H. Rider Haggard vein, but unlike those authors, she was "going to tell breathtaking stories about *girls* who had adventures." As she further noted on her home page, "I was tired of the boys always getting the best parts in the best books."

Just after graduating summa cum laude from Bowdoin College with a degree in English literature, McKinley began to have adventures of her own, ultimately becoming something of a hero to young women readers in search of strong, honorable role models. Her first publication, written when she was twenty-four, was inspired by viewing an adaptation of "Beauty and the Beast" on television. McKinley was so disappointed with what she saw that she began to write a version of the classic fairy tale herself.

The resulting novel, *Beauty: A Retelling of the Story of Beauty and the Beast,* was immediately published and won praise from readers and critics alike. According to Michael Malone in the *New York Times Book Review,* the novel is "much admired not only for its feminism but for the density of detail in the retelling." "It's simply a filling out of the story, with a few alterations," wrote a *Kirkus Reviews* critic. McKinley's Beauty, or Honour, as she is named in this version, is an awkward child, not a beauty, and her "evil sisters" are caring and kind. Critics have also praised McKinley's handling of fantasy in the medieval setting. "The aura of magic around the Beast and his household comes surprisingly to life," commented a *Choice* critic. The winner of several literary awards, *Beauty* instantly established McKinley as a powerful new voice in young adult literature. Since its publication, *Beauty* has remained one of McKinley's most popular titles, and the author would return to its themes later in her career.

Prior to writing *Beauty,* McKinley had already begun work on books set in a world she created called Damar. She once explained, "I had begun—this would be about 1976—to realize that there was more than one story to tell about Damar, that in fact it seemed to be a whole history, volumes and volumes of the stuff, and this terrified me. I had plots and characters multiplying like mice and running in all directions." The first publication of the "Damar" books was a collection of stories called *The Door in the Hedge,* during the late 1970s. *The Blue Sword,* McKinley's second novel, was published in 1982. The hero in this novel is Harry Crewe, an adolescent woman who must forge her identity and battle an evil force at the same time. The plot takes off when Harry is kidnapped and learns, from her kidnappers, how to ride a horse and battle as a true warrior. While she struggles in the tradition of the legendary female hero of Damar, Aerin, Harry becomes a hero in her own right. Although the story is set in the fantastic world of Damar—characterized as "pseudo-Victorian" by Darrell Schweitzer in *Science Fiction Review*—critics have noted that Harry is a heroine contemporary readers may well understand.

Like *Beauty, The Blue Sword* earned McKinley recognition and praise. *The Blue Sword,* however, provided critics with an understanding of McKinley's ability to create entirely original plots, characters, and fantastic worlds. Moreover, critics and readers alike enjoyed the richness and excitement of the book. *Booklist* contributor Sally Estes, for example, described *The Blue Sword* as "a zesty, romantic heroic fantasy with . . . a grounding in reality that enhances the tale's verve as a fantasy." For *The Blue Sword,* McKinley was awarded the Newbery Honor designation. "Readers," commented Karen Stang Hanley in a *School Library Journal* review, "will cherish the promise that more novels about Damar are forthcoming."

These fans did not have long to wait. In *The Hero and the Crown,* the next "Damar" novel, readers are taken back in time to learn about the legendary warrior woman Harry so revered. McKinley once explained. "I recognized that there were specific connections between Harry and Aerin, and I deliberately wrote their stories in reverse chronological order because one of the things I'm fooling around with is the idea of heroes: real heroes as opposed to the legends that are told of them afterwards. Aerin is one of her country's greatest heroes, and by the time Harry comes along, Harry is expected—or Harry thinks she is—to live up to her. When you go back and find out about Aerin in *Hero,* you discover that she wasn't this mighty invincible figure. . . . She had a very hard and solitary time of her early fate."

At first, Aerin is graceless and clumsy; it takes her a long time to turn herself into a true warrior, and she suffers many traumas. Yet she is clever and courageous, bravely battling and killing the dragons that are threatening Damar. Merri Rosenberg asserted in the *New York Times Book Review* that McKinley "created an utterly engrossing fantasy, replete with a fairly mature romantic subplot as well as adventure." In the opinion of Mary M. Burns in *Horn Book, The Hero and the Crown* is "as richly detailed and elegant as a medieval tapestry. . . . Vibrant, witty, compelling, the story is the stuff of which true dreams are made." Writing in the *New Statesman,* Gillian Wilce praised the book's "completeness, its engaging imagination," while Frances Bradburn of *Wilson Library Bulletin* called the novel a "marvelous tale of excitement and female ingenuity." *The Hero and the Crown* earned McKinley the coveted Newbery Medal in 1985 for the best American children's book of the year. McKinley shared her mixed feelings about winning the award: "The Newbery award is supposed to be the peak of your career as a writer for children or young adults. I was rather young to receive it; and it is a little disconcerting to feel—okay, you've done it; that's it, you should retire now." Fortunately for her fans, McKinley continued to write retellings of traditional favorites as well as original novels and stories.

McKinley's stories include short retellings of classics from Anna Sewell's *Black Beauty* to George MacDonald's *The Light Princess* and Rudyard Kipling's *The Jungle Book.* She has also published a number of short stories and edited *Imaginary Lands,* a collection of fantasies that includes her own "The Stone Fey." In 1998, McKinley republished this story as an illustrated book, with artwork by John Clapp. Set in the world of Damar, *The Stone Fey* relates the story of Maddy, a shepherdess, who falls in love with a Stone Fey, a fairy with skin the color of stone. Entranced by her new love, she drifts away from all the people and things she loves until finally she realizes that the Fey can not return her love. This supernatural romance found praise with reviewers. A contributor for *Publishers Weekly* noted, "While staying true to her penchant for presenting strong female protagonists, Newbery winner McKinley strikes a softer note with this deeply romantic yet ultimately clear-eyed love story." *Booklist*'s Carolyn Phelan felt it was a "haunting story," and Virginia Golodetz, writing in *School Library Journal,* found the writing "passionate."

McKinley has insisted that her work is written for those who want to read it, not just for young people. Yet she has also written some original picture books for children. *Rowan* is a story about a girl selecting and loving a pet dog. *My Father Is in the Navy* portrays a young girl whose father has been away for some time: as he is about to return, she tries to remember what her father looks like. Reviewing *Rowan,* a contributor for *Publishers Weekly* called it an "affable tale of a girl and her pet." And in a *School Library Journal* review of *My Father Is in the Navy,* JoAnn Rees called the picture book a "warm, loving look at a family group."

A return to more familiar ground, *The Outlaws of Sherwood* provides one example of McKinley's penchant for revising and reviving a traditional tale. Instead of concentrating on Robin Hood—or glorifying him—McKinley focuses on other characters in the band of outlaws and provides carefully wrought details about their daily lives: how they get dirty and sick, and how they manage their outlaw affairs. Robin is not portrayed as the bold, handsome marksman and sword handler readers may remember from traditional versions of the "Robin Hood" story. Instead, he is nervous, a poor shot, and even reluctant to form his band of merry men. Not surprisingly, the band of merry men in *The Outlaws of Sherwood* is a band of merry men and *women.* "The young women are allowed to be angry, frankly sexual, self willed—and even to outshoot the men, who don't seem to mind," related *Washington Post Book World* reviewer Michele Landsberg. Maid Marian stands out as a brilliant, beautiful leader and an amazingly talented archer. *The Outlaws of Sherwood* is "romantic and absorbing . . . [and] the perfect adolescent daydream where happiness is found in being young and among friends," concluded Shirley Wilton of *Voice of Youth Advocates.*

McKinley's *Deerskin* also demonstrates her talent for creating new tales out of the foundations of old ones. As Betsy Hearne of *Bulletin of the Center for Children's Books* noted, *Deerskin* is an "adult fantasy" for mature readers; it presents a "darker side of fairy tales." Based on Perrault's "Donkeyskin," a story in which a king assaults his own daughter after his queen dies, McKinley's novel relates how a beautiful princess is raped by her father after the death of her mother. This "is also a dog story," Hearne reminded readers: Princess Lissar survives the brutal attack, and her emotional trauma afterwards, because of her relationship with her dog, Ash. "Written with deep passion and power, *Deerskin* is an almost unbearably intense portrait of a severely damaged young woman. . . . [T]here is also romance, humor, and sheer delight," commented Christy Tyson in *Voice of Youth Advocates.* "*Deerskin* is a riveting and relentless fairy tale, told in ravishing prose," concluded *School Library Journal* critic Cathy Chauvette.

While McKinley has asserted that "Damar has never been a trilogy" and does not want to close off her own mental access to Damar by embedding it completely in text, she has facilitated her readers' access to the mythical kingdom. Some of the stories in *A Knot in the Grain and Other Stories* are set in Damar and include familiar characters. All of these stories, according to Betsy Hearne in *Bulletin of the Center for Children's Books,* bear "McKinley's signature blend of the magical and the mundane in the shape of heroines" who triumph and find love despite the obstacles they face. The stories demonstrate McKinley's "remarkable ability to evoke wonder and belief," asserted *Horn Book* contributor Ann A. Flowers. A reviewer for *Publishers Weekly* called *A Knot in the Grain* a "thrilling, satisfying and thought-provoking collection."

With McKinley's 1992 marriage to British author Peter Dickinson, and her subsequent move to the south of England, the author felt that she could flesh out the "Beauty and the Beast" tale even further than she had done in 1978 with the acclaimed *Beauty.* "I had no intention of ever doing anything with 'Beauty and the Beast' again," McKinley wrote on her Web site. "Absolutely." But upon the suggestion of friends that she work on a short story which could be illustrated, McKinley found time between other projects to hammer out some pages of such a story. The result, six months later, was *Rose Daughter,* a novel over three hundred pages in length, filled with complex narrative elements. Far from being a sequel to *Beauty,* the new novel "is fuller bodied, with richer characterizations and a more mystical, darker edge," according to *Booklist*'s Estes. "Writing *Rose Daughter* was a bit like being possessed," McKinley noted on her Web site. "It was glorious, but it was alarming." In the pages of *Rose Daughter,* readers learn about the early family life and personalities of the three sisters: the acerbic Jeweltongue; Lionheart, a physically daring girl; and the title character Beauty. Unlike the original tale of "Beauty and the Beast," the relationship between the three sisters is loving rather than hostile. Their mother has died, and as the book begins they are living with their wealthy father in a city. When he loses his business, they relocate to a cottage in the countryside, where new hardships bring the family closer together.

One central element to McKinley's *Rose Daughter* is the flower of the title: in their world, roses are extremely difficult to cultivate and need a great deal of actual love; Beauty discovers, in her country garden, that she possesses just such a talent. Yet she is plagued by recurring, disturbing dreams of a dark corridor, a memory of her mother, and the scent of roses. The Beast is a legendary local figure, a tragic hero who is only half-man; Beauty journeys to his castle and begins tending the magic roses in his garden; soon other flora and fauna return to the former wasteland. A romance develops between the two, and her tenderness toward the Beast eventually unlocks the curse that has beset him. "As before, McKinley takes the essentials of the traditional tale and embellishes them with vivid and quirky particulars," declared a contributor for *Publishers Weekly.* Jennifer Fakolt, reviewing the book for *Voice of Youth Advocates,* asserted that "McKinley has captured the timelessness of the traditional tale and breathed into it passion and new life appropriate to the story's own 'universal themes' of love and regeneration." The *Publishers Weekly* reviewer concluded that "this heady mix of fairy tale, magic and romance has the power to exhilarate."

With *Spindle's End,* McKinley once again revamps a fairy tale for modern readers. This time using "Sleeping Beauty" as a template, McKinley created a "novel of complex imagery and characters," according to a critic for *Family Life.* In this tale the infant princess Briar Rose is cursed on her name day by the evil fairy, Pernicia, then—as in the original—taken away to a remote and magical land to be raised, her real identity concealed, in an attempt to escape the wrath of Pernicia. In McKinley's take on the subject, Katriona, a good fairy, takes the young princess away to her village of Foggy Bottom, and there raises her as a village maid named Rosie to await her twenty-first birthday—when she will supposedly prick her finger on a spinning-wheel spindle and fall into an eternal sleep. In order to confound Pernicia, Rosie and her friend Peony exchange places at her birthday. Rosie's kiss awakens the sleeping Peony, who in turn marries the prince, leaving Rosie free to continue the simple life she loves and to marry the village blacksmith.

Critics were generally positive in their evaluations of this reworking. Writing in *School Library Journal,* Connie Tyrrell Burns felt that "McKinley once again lends a fresh perspective to a classic fairy tale, developing the story of 'Sleeping Beauty' into a richly imagined, vividly depicted novel." *Booklist*'s Estes noted that McKinley's reinterpretation of the old fairy tale "takes readers into a credibly developed world." Estes concluded, "Full of humor and romance as well as magic and adventure, and with an ending that has a decided twist, this spellbinding novel is bound to attract McKinley's fans and those who relish the genre." And a critic for *Publishers Weekly* called *Spindle's End* a "luscious, lengthy novel" which is "[d]ense with magical detail and all-too-human feeling."

McKinley continues to create magic and fantasy on the page from her new home in England. The story collection *Water: Tales of Elemental Spirits,* is a collaborative effort with her writer husband. McKinley once explained why she thought such work is important: "As a compulsive reader myself, I believe that you are what you read. . . . My books are also about hope—I hope. Much of modern literature has given up hope and deals with anti-heroes and despair. It seems to me that human beings by their very natures need heroes, real heroes, and are happier with them. I see no point in talking about how life is over and it never mattered anyway. I don't believe it."

In 2003, McKinley created *Sunshine,* a young adult vampire fantasy. A *Kirkus* reviewer described the new book as "an intriguing mix of Buffy the Vampire Slayer and Harry Potter-ish characterization. Mostly for teenagers who don't trip over words like 'eschatology,' and maybe some older fantasy devotees as well." In an interview with *Publishers Weekly,* the author explained the genesis of *Sunshine:* "I've always loved vampires, the old-fashioned creepy frisson kind, not the modern graphic mayhem kind. I've been in a snit for 30 years because most modern horror is too gruesome for me. I reread writers like Stoker, Kipling, Machen, M.R. James, E.E Benson, A. Merritt. Then Buffy the Vampire Slayer happened, with its wry sideways take on vampires and being a girl, and that wonderful business that vampires vaporize when you stake them. Okay, they couldn't have guts on prime time American TV—but it worked."

When not writing, McKinley is busy with a variety of other pastimes, including fencing and gardening. She has added over four hundred rose bushes to the borders of her husband's family home. "I have the scars to prove it," she noted on her Web site. "I think I've discovered reality after all. I'm astonished at how interesting it is. It's giving me more things to write stories about."

BIOGRAPHICAL AND CRITICAL SOURCES:

BOOKS

Authors and Artists for Young Adults, Thomson Gale (Detroit, MI), Volume 4, 1990, Volume 33, 2000.

Children's Literature Review, Volume 10, Thomson Gale (Detroit, MI), 1986.

Dictionary of Literary Biography, Volume 52: *American Writers for Children since 1960: Fiction,* Thomson Gale (Detroit, MI), 1986.

St. James Guide to Fantasy Writers, St. James Press (Detroit, MI), 1996.

St. James Guide to Young Adult Writers, 2nd edition, St. James Press (Detroit, MI), 1999.

Twentieth-Century Children's Writers, 3rd edition, St. James Press (Chicago, IL), 1989.

PERIODICALS

Best Sellers, January, 1985, p. 399.

Booklist, October 1, 1982, Sally Estes, review of *The Blue Sword,* p. 198; April 15, 1992, pp. 1537-1538; April 1, 1993, p. 1416; August, 1994, Frances Bradburn, review of *A Knot in the Grain and Other Stories,* p. 2039; August, 1997, Sally Estes, review of *Rose Daughter,* p. 1898; November 1, 1998, Carolyn Phelan, review of *The Stone Fey,* p. 484;

April, 15, 2000, Sally Estes, review of *Spindle's End,* p. 1543; December 1, 2000, p. 693; April 15, 2001, p. 1561.

Bulletin of the Center for Children's Books, September, 1993, Betsy Hearne, review of *Deerskin,* p. 16; June, 1994, Betsy Hearne, review of *A Knot in the Grain and Other Stories,* p. 327.

Choice, July-August, 1979, review of *Beauty: A Retelling of the Story of Beauty and the Beast,* p. 668.

Family Life, December 1, 2000, review of *Spindle's End,* p. 127.

Horn Book, January-February, 1985, Mary M. Burns, review of *The Hero and the Crown,* pp. 59-60; July-August, 1985, Robin McKinley, "Newbery Medal Acceptance," pp. 395-405 and Terri Windling and Mark Alan Arnold, "Robin McKinley," pp. 406-409; March-April, 1989, p. 218; July-August, 1994, Ann A. Flowers, review of *A Knot in the Grain and Other Stories,* pp. 458-459; September-October, 1997, Lauren Adams, review of *Rose Daughter,* pp. 574-575; May-June, 2000, Anita L. Burkam, review of *Spindle's End,* p. 317.

Junior Bookshelf, June, 1984, pp. 141-142.

Kirkus Reviews, December 1, 1978, review of *Beauty,* p. 1307; August 15, 2003, review of *Sunshine,* p. 1039.

Los Angeles Times Book Review, May 22, 1988, pp. 10-11.

Magazine of Science Fiction and Fantasy, January, 1998, pp. 28-33; April, 1998, pp. 36-37; March, 2001, p. 108.

New Statesman, November 8, 1985, Gillian Wilce, review of *The Hero and the Crown,* p. 28.

New York Times Book Review, January 27, 1985, Merri Rosenberg, review of *The Hero and the Crown,* p. 29; November 13, 1988, Michael Malone, review of *The Outlaws of Sherwood,* p. 54; June 5, 1994, p. 30; January 18, 1998, Kathryn Harrison, review of *Rose Daughter,* p. 18; May 14, 2000, Elizabeth Devereaux, review of *Spindle's End,* p. 27.

Publishers Weekly, April 25, 1986, p. 83; April 29, 1988, p. 73; November 11, 1988, pp. 58-59; August 31, 1992, review of *Rowan,* pp. 78-79; April 25, 1994, review of *A Knot in the Grain and Other Stories,* p. 80; June 16, 1997, review of *Rose Daughter,* p. 60; August 31, 1998, review of *The Stone Fey,* p. 77; March 27, 2000, review of *Spindle's End,* p. 82; Sept 29, 2003, review of *Sunshine,* p. 47.

Resource Links, K.V. Johansen, June 2003, "The Eighties: Diana Wynne Jones, Brian Jacques, John Bellairs, and Robin McKinley," p. 30.

School Library Journal, January, 1983, Karen Stang Hanley, review of *The Blue Sword,* p. 86; May, 1986, p. 106; December, 1986, p. 108; May, 1992, JoAnn Rees, review of *My Father Is in the Navy,* p. 91; October, 1992, p. 93; September, 1993, Cathy Chauvette, review of *Deerskin,* p. 261; May, 1994, p. 128; September, 1997, Julie Cummins, review of *Rose Daughter,* pp. 219-220; January, 1999, Virginia Golodetz, review of *The Stone Fey,* p. 130; June, 2000, Connie Tyrrell Burns, review of *Spindle's End,* p. 150.

Science Fiction Review, August, 1983, Darrell Schweitzer, review of *The Blue Sword,* p. 46.

Voice of Youth Advocates, April, 1989, Shirley Wilton, review of *The Outlaws of Sherwood,* p. 44; August, 1993, Christy Tyson, review of *Deerskin,* p. 168; October, 1994, p. 225.

Washington Post Book World, November 6, 1988, Michele Landsberg, review of *The Outlaws of Sherwood,* p. 15.

Wilson Library Bulletin, January, 1987, Frances Bradburn, review of *The Hero and the Crown,* p. 60.

ONLINE

Robin McKinley's Official Home Page, http://www.robinmckinley.com/ (January 28, 2002).

*   *   *

McLANDRESS, Herschel
See GALBRAITH, John Kenneth

*   *   *

McMILLAN, Terry 1951-
(Terry L. McMillan)

PERSONAL: Born October 18, 1951, in Port Huron, MI; daughter of Edward McMillan and Madeline Washington Tillman; married Jonathan Plummer, September, 1998 (filed for divorce, 2005); children (by Leonard Welch): Solomon Welch. *Ethnicity:* Black *Education:* University of California, Berkeley, B.S., 1979; Columbia University, M.F.A., 1979.

ADDRESSES: Agent—c/o Author Mail, Viking Penguin, 375 Hudson St., New York, NY 10014.

CAREER: Writer. University of Wyoming, Laramie, instructor, 1987-90; University of Arizona, Tucson, professor, 1990-92.

MEMBER: PEN, Author's League.

AWARDS, HONORS: American Book Award, Before Columbus Foundation, 1987, for *Mama;* National Endowment for the Arts fellowship, 1988.

WRITINGS:

Mama, Houghton Mifflin (Boston, MA), 1987.
Disappearing Acts, Viking (New York, NY), 1989.
(Editor) *Breaking Ice: An Anthology of Contemporary African-American Fiction,* Viking (New York, NY), 1990.
(Author of introduction) Spike Lee, with Ralph Wiley, *By Any Means Necessary: The Trials and Tribulations of the Making of Malcolm X . . . including the Screenplay,* Hyperion (New York, NY), 1992.
Waiting to Exhale, Viking (New York, NY), 1992.
How Stella Got Her Groove Back, Viking (New York, NY), 1996.
A Day Late and a Dollar Short, Viking (New York, NY), 2001.
The Interruption of Everything, Viking (New York, NY), 2005.

Contributor to *Five for Five: The Films of Spike Lee,* Stewart, Tabori, 1991. Contributor of short stories to periodicals.

ADAPTATIONS: Waiting to Exhale was adapted for audio cassette, narrated by Terry McMillan, and as a motion picture starring Whitney Houston and Angela Bassett, Twentieth Century-Fox, 1996; *How Stella Got Her Groove Back* was adapted as a film starring Bassett, Whoopi Goldberg, Taye Diggs, and Regina King, Twentieth Century-Fox, 1998; *Disappearing Acts* was adapted for a film by Home Box Office, 2001; *A Day Late and a Dollar Short* was adapted for audio cassette, Penguin Audiobooks, 2001.

SIDELIGHTS: Terry McMillan's character-driven novels, most of them best-sellers, have drawn an audience of all ages, races, and genders. McMillan has a talent for confronting universal themes such as romantic commitment, family obligations, and relationships between parents and children, in ways that resonate in her readers' lives. To quote Anne Bowling in *Writer's Yearbook,* "The women McMillan crafts draw readers by the millions. These characters seem familiar enough to walk through your apartment door, drop a Coach bag on the coffee table and flop down on the couch for a chat." *Booklist* correspondent Vanessa Bush commended McMillan for her "distinctive style of unveiling the trials and mishaps of modern-day life for black folks." Loosely based on her own life experiences, such novels as *Waiting to Exhale* and *How Stella Got Her Groove Back* explore the many lifestyle issues facing educated, dynamic upper-class women as they seek happiness and self-definition through their work and their relationships.

For her portrayal of feisty, tough, black heroines, McMillan has been compared to acclaimed black women writers Alice Walker, Gloria Naylor, and Zora Neale Hurston. McMillan acknowledges the compliment, but asserted in the introduction to the 1990 short-story anthology *Breaking Ice,* which she edited, that her generation of black writers is "a new breed, free to write as we please . . . because of the way life has changed."

"McMillan has the power to be an important contemporary novelist," stated Valerie Sayers in the *New York Times Book Review* in 1989. By that time, McMillan had already garnered attention and critical praise for her first novel, *Mama,* which was published in 1987. Over the next five years predictions about the writer's future began to come true. In 1992 McMillan saw the publication of *Waiting to Exhale,* her third novel. Her publisher sent her on a twenty-city, six-week tour, and McMillan appeared on several popular television programs. As healthy sales of her novels, as well as the purchase of their film rights showed, the author's honest, unaffected writing style clearly struck a chord with the U.S. book-buying public.

McMillan grew up in Port Huron, Michigan, and discovered the pleasure of reading as a teenager while shelving books in a local library. As a student at a community college in Los Angeles, McMillan immersed herself in most of the classics of African-American literature, and at age twenty-five she published her first short story. Eleven years after that, her first novel, *Mama,* was released by Houghton Mifflin.

McMillan was determined not to let her debut novel go unnoticed. Typically, first novels receive little publicity other than the press releases and galleys sent out by the publisher. When McMillan's publisher told her that they could not do more for her, she decided to promote the book on her own. She wrote over 3,000 letters to chain bookstores, independent booksellers, universities, and colleges. By the end of the summer of 1987 she had received several requests to do readings. McMillan then scheduled her own book publicity tour and let her publicist know where she was going.

Mama had started out as a short story. "I really love the short story as a form," explained McMillan in an interview with *Writer's Digest.* "Mama" was just one of several short stories McMillan had tried unsuccessfully to get into print. Then the Harlem Writer's Guild accepted her into their group and advised her that "Mama" really should be a novel and not a short story. After four weeks at the MacDowell artists colony and two weeks at Yaddo, McMillan had expanded her short story into a book of more than 400 pages. When her agent suggested certain revisions, McMillan questioned whether the woman truly understood what the book was about.

Frustrated by this and by other events taking place in her personal life, McMillan took things into her own hands and sent a collection of short stories to Houghton Mifflin, hoping to at least get some free editorial advice. McMillan was surprised when the publisher contacted her, not about the short stories, but about the novel she had mentioned briefly in her cover letter to them. She sent them pages from *Mama* and approximately four days later got word from the publisher that they loved it.

Mama tells the story of the struggle Mildred Peacock has in raising her five children after she throws her drunkard husband out of the house. The novel begins: "Mildred hid the ax beneath the mattress of the cot in the dining room." With those words, McMillan's novel becomes "a runaway narrative pulling a crowded cast of funny, earthy characters," stated Sayers in the *New York Times Book Review.* Because of McMillan's promotional efforts, the novel received numerous reviews—the overwhelming majority of which were positive. Six weeks after *Mama* was published, it went into its third printing. Michael Awkward, reviewing the novel in *Callaloo,* deemed it a "moving, often hilarious and insightful exploration of a slice of black urban life that is rarely seen in contemporary black women's fiction."

Disappearing Acts, McMillan's second novel, tells the story of star-crossed lovers by alternating the narrative between the main characters. Zora Banks and Franklin Swift fall in love "at first sight" when they meet at Zora's new apartment, where Franklin works as part of the renovating crew. Zora is an educated black woman working as a junior high school music teacher; Franklin is a high-school dropout working in construction. In spite of the differences in their backgrounds, the two become involved, move in together, and try to overcome the fear they both feel because of past failures in love.

Writing in the *Washington Post Book World,* David Nicholson pointed out that although this difference in backgrounds is an old literary device, it is one that is particularly relevant to black Americans: "Professional black women complain of an ever-shrinking pool of eligible men, citing statistics that show the number of black men in prison is increasing, while the number of black men in college is decreasing. Articles on alternatives for women, from celibacy to 'man-sharing' to relationships with blue-collar workers like Franklin have long been a staple of black general interest and women's magazines." McMillan expressed her own thoughts on this issue in an article in *Essence.* "Maybe it's just me, but I'm finding it harder and harder to meet men. . . . I grew up and became what my mama prayed out loud I'd become: educated, strong, smart, independent and reliable. . . . Now it seems as if carving a place for myself in the world is backfiring. Never in a million years would I have dreamed that I'd be thirty-eight years old and still single."

Reviewers have commended McMillan for her ability to give such a true voice to the character of Franklin in *Disappearing Acts.* A reviewer for the *Washington Post Book World* called the novel "one of the few . . . to contain rounded, sympathetic portraits of black men and to depict relationships between black men and black women as something more than the relationship between victimizer and victim, oppressor and oppressed." In the *New York Times Book Review* another reviewer stated: "The miracle is that Ms. McMillan takes the reader so deep into this man's head—and makes what goes on there so complicated—that [the] story becomes not only comprehensible but affecting." Not only did McMillan's second novel win critical acclaim, it also was optioned for a film by Home Box Office. Although it also sparked a defamation suit brought by McMillan's former lover, who claimed that McMillan used him as the model for the novel's main male character, the New York State Supreme Court ultimately ruled in McMillan's favor.

Waiting to Exhale tells the stories of four professional black women who have everything except the love of a good man. The overall theme of the book is men's fear of commitment; a sub-theme is the fear of growing old alone. The novel hit a nerve with its readers, both male and female, as many readers seemed to identify with McMillan's characters. According to a *Los Angeles Times* writer, one black male reader proclaimed: "I think I speak for a lot of brothers. I know I'm all over the book. . . . All I can say is, I'm willing to learn. Being defensive is not the answer." That was precisely the response McMillan was hoping to get.

One issue that emerges from reviews of McMillan's books is her use of profanity, and *Waiting to Exhale* sparked the same criticism. One critic referred to the novel's protagonists as male-bashing stand-up comedians who use foul language. For McMillan, reproducing the profane language people actually use is her way of staying close to reality. As she told a *Publishers Weekly* interviewer: "That's the way we talk. And I want to know why I've never read a review where they complain about the language that male writers use!"

"Fans of McMillan's previous novels . . . will recognize McMillan's authentic, unpretentious voice in every page of *How Stella Got Her Groove Back,* " noted Liesl Schillinger in the *Washington Post Book World.* The story of a forty-something businesswoman whose life has been spent raising her son and working her way to success, *How Stella Got Her Groove Back* finds the resourceful, spunky protagonist off to Jamaica to shake up more than just a boring existence. Stella is determined to fill that empty place in her life where a permanent love interest should be, and a twenty-year-old Jamaican named Winston more than fits the bill. She brings Winston back to the United States with her and, almost unbelievably, he is accepted by her eleven-year-old son as well as by her sisters, and life continues happily ever after. Although noting that McMillan's novel "is not deeper or more searching than the average sitcom, no more dramatically powerful than a backyard barbecue," Richard Bernstein cited *How Stella Got Her Groove Back* as "an irreverent, mischievous, diverting novel that at times will make you laugh out loud," in his *New York Times* review. Maxine Chernoff dubbed the novel "not quite serious enough for summer reading" in her review in Chicago's *Tribune Books.* Schillinger praised McMillan for realizing that "women are ready to read about themselves not only as schemers or sufferers, but as the adventurous heroes of their own lives."

A Day Late and a Dollar Short, published in 2001, had its genesis in the early 1990s, but McMillan was sidetracked by the deaths of her mother and her best friend, then by her marriage to Jonathan Plummer. The novel employs six first-person voices to explore the dynamics of one family as the beloved matriarch lies dying in the hospital. "All six voices—male and female, young and old—are fresh and vital, propelling conflict and exposing the strengths and foibles of the good but imperfect people," declared Jewell Parker Rhodes in the *Washington Post Book World.* Rhodes further characterized the novel as a "glorious" work that, "like the best fiction, helped illuminate corners of my own heart. Like a call-and-response chant, [McMillan's] strong characterization and plotting dared me not to laugh, cry and shout upon recognizing this glittering, complicated portrayal of African-American family life."

McMillan does not shy away from portraying the most devastating aspects of modern life in *A Day Late and a Dollar Short.* She tackles infidelity, drug and alcohol abuse, sexual abuse, and sibling rivalry, while allowing her characters to defend—and condemn—themselves through their own commentary. "The story was important to me," the author told a *Publishers Weekly* interviewer. "My hope for my readers is that broken relationships among family members might be looked at again." A *Publishers Weekly* contributor called *A Day Late and a Dollar Short* "a moving and true depiction of an American family, driven apart and bound together by the real stuff of life." In a review for *Book,* Andrea King Collier lauded the work, noting that, "In the hands of McMillan, the master of edgy, ensemble storytelling," the novel "has drama and snap."

With her string of best-sellers, McMillan has proven to be a "crossover" artist who, while writing exclusively about black characters, transcends the bounds of ethnic issues. McMillan's voice belongs to what has been described as "the New Black Aesthetic": one that does not deal with everything from the perspective of race. For example, her novel *The Interruption of Everything* tells the story of Marilyn Grimes, a consummate wife and mother of three grown children who is married to an average Joe. This scenario could aptly describe many women of any race, creed, or nationality. Although her life appears to be a good one, Marilyn has postponed many of her own dreams so long that she can no longer quite remember what they are. Feeling closed in by irrelevant demands, Marilyn sets out to reinvent her life.

As McMillan explained to *Writers Yearbook:* "Everything I write is about empowerment, regardless of what kind it is. It's always about a woman standing up for herself and her rights and her beliefs, and not worrying about what other people think. But one of the things I think fiction should not do is be didactic. I'm not here to preach, I'm not trying to be Gloria Steinem in disguise. I would prefer that you be affected, that by reading something you get a sense of empowerment, and hopefully if it's subtle enough you won't even know it happened."

Commenting on her motivation for writing, McMillan explained to a *Writer* contributor that she has a good reason to keep working. "I write because the world is an imperfect place, and we behave in an imperfect manner. I want to understand why it's so hard to be good, honest, loving, caring, thoughtful and generous. Writing is about the only way (besides praying) that allows me to be compassionate toward folks who, in real life, I'm probably not that sympathetic toward. I want to understand myself and others better, so what better way than to pretend to be them."

BIOGRAPHICAL AND CRITICAL SOURCES:

BOOKS

Authors and Artists for Young Adults, Volume 21, Thomson Gale (Detroit, MI), 1998.

Contemporary Black Biography, Volume 17, Thomson Gale (Detroit, MI), 1998.

Contemporary Literary Criticism, Thomson Gale (Detroit, MI), Volume 50, 1988, Volume 61, 1991.

Patrick, Diane, *Terry McMillan: The Unauthorized Biography,* St. Martin's Press (New York, NY), 1999.

PERIODICALS

Black Issues Book Review, January, 2001, Gwendolyn E. Osborne, review of *A Day Late and a Dollar Short,* p. 15.

Book, January, 2001, Andrea King Collier, review of *A Day Late and a Dollar Short,* p. 71.

Booklist, November 15, 2000, Vanessa Bush, review of *A Day Late and a Dollar Short,* p. 588.

Callaloo, summer, 1988.

Christian Science Monitor, January 11, 2001, "Waiting to Exhale in the Thin Atmosphere of Troubled Siblings," p. 18.

Cosmopolitan, August, 1989.

Detroit News, September 7, 1992.

Emerge, September, 1992; June, 1996.

English Journal, April, 1996, p. 86.

Esquire, July, 1988.

Essence, February, 1990; October, 1992; May, 1995, p. 52; June, 1996, pp. 50, 54.

Library Journal, January 1, 2001, Emily Jones, review of *A Day Late and a Dollar Short,* p. 155.

Los Angeles Times, February 23, 1987; October 29, 1990; June 19, 1992.

Mademoiselle, July, 1996, p. 77.

Newsweek, January 8, 1996, p. 68; April 29, 1996, pp. 76, 79.

New Yorker, April 29, 1996, p. 102.

New York Review of Books, November 4, 1993, p. 33.

New York Times, May 15, 1996, p. B5, C17.

New York Times Book Review, February 22, 1987; August 6, 1989; May 31, 1992; June 2, 1996, p. 21; February 4, 2001, Ruth Coughlin, review of *A Day Late and a Dollar Short,* p. 21.

New York Times Magazine, August 9, 1992.

People, July 20, 1992.

Publishers Weekly, May 11, 1992; July 13, 1992; September 21, 1992; May 6, 1996, p. 30; December 11, 2000, Diane Patrick, "Terry McMillan Is Back," p. 42; December 11, 2000, review of *A Day Late and a Dollar Short,* p. 65.

Time, January 8, 1996, p. 72; May 6, 1996, p. 77.

Tribune Books (Chicago, IL), September 23, 1990; May 31, 1992; May 5, 1996, p. 6.

Village Voice, March 24, 1987.

Wall Street Journal, April 11, 1991.

Washington Post, November 17, 1990; January 25, 2001, Linton Weeks, "Terry McMillan, Encompassing the Family Circle," p. C1.

Washington Post Book World, August 27, 1989; September 16, 1990; May 24, 1992; May 5, 1996, p. 1; February 11, 2001, Jewell Parker Rhodes, "The Price Club," p. 5.

Writer, August, 2001, interview with McMillan, p. 66.

Writer's Digest, October, 1987.

ONLINE

Voices from the Gaps, http://voices.cla.umn.edu/ (April 21, 2004), "Terry McMillan."

Writer's Yearbook, http://www.writersdigest.com/ (March 6, 2001), Anne Bowling, "Terry McMillan: 'Everything I Write Is about Empowerment.'"

* * *

McMILLAN, Terry L.
See McMILLAN, Terry

* * *

McMURTRY, Larry 1936-
(Larry Jeff McMurtry)

PERSONAL: Born June 3, 1936, in Wichita Falls, TX; son of William Jefferson (a rancher) and Hazel Ruth (McIver) McMurtry; married Josephine Ballard, July 15, 1959 (divorced, 1966); children: James Lawrence. *Education:* North Texas State College (now University), B.A., 1958; Rice University, M.A., 1960; additional study at Stanford University, 1960.

ADDRESSES: Home—P.O. Box 552, Archer City, TX 76351.

CAREER: Texas Christian University, Fort Worth, TX, instructor, 1961-62; Rice University, Houston, TX, lecturer in English and creative writing, 1963-69. Visiting professor at George Mason College, 1970, and at American University, 1970-71. Owner of bookshops in Washington, DC, Texas, and Arizona.

MEMBER: PEN American Center (president, 1989-91), Texas Institute of Letters.

AWARDS, HONORS: Wallace Stegner fellowship, 1960; Jesse H. Jones Award, Texas Institute of Letters, 1962, for *Horseman, Pass By;* Guggenheim fellowship, 1964; Academy of Motion Picture Arts and Sciences Award (Oscar) for best screenplay based on material from another medium, 1972, for *The Last Picture Show;* Barbara McCombs/Lon Tinkle Award for continuing excellence in Texas letters, Texas Institute of Letters, 1986; Pulitzer Prize for fiction, Spur Award from Western Writers of America, and Texas Literary Award from Southwestern Booksellers Association, all 1986, all for *Lonesome Dove;* Robert Kirsch Award, *Los Angeles Times,* 2003, for McMurtry's body of work that "grows out of and reflects brilliantly upon the myth and reality of the American West in all of its infinite variety"; Golden Globe award for Best Screenplay, 2005, Academy Award for best adapted screenplay, 2005, and BAFTA award for Best Adapted Screenplay, British Academy of Film and Television Arts, 2006, all for *Brokeback Mountain.*

WRITINGS:

NOVELS

Horseman, Pass By, Harper (New York, NY), 1961, Texas A & M University Press (College Station, TX), 1988, published as *Hud,* Popular Library (New York, NY), 1961.

Leaving Cheyenne, Harper (New York, NY), 1963, Texas A & M University Press (College Station, TX), 1986.

The Last Picture Show (also see below), Dial (New York, NY), 1966, Simon & Schuster (New York, NY), 1989.

Moving On, Simon & Schuster (New York, NY), 1970, Pocket Books (New York, NY), 1988.

All My Friends Are Going to Be Strangers, Simon & Schuster (New York, NY), 1972, published with a preface by the author and afterword by Raymond L. Neinstein, Scribner Paperback Fiction (New York, NY), 2002.

Terms of Endearment, Simon & Schuster (New York, NY), 1975, reprinted with new preface, Scribner (New York, NY), 1999.

Somebody's Darling, Simon & Schuster (New York, NY), 1978.

Cadillac Jack, Simon & Schuster (New York, NY), 1982.

The Desert Rose, Simon & Schuster (New York, NY), 1983.

Lonesome Dove, Simon & Schuster (New York, NY), 1985, reprinted, Simon & Schuster, 2000.

Texasville (sequel to *The Last Picture Show;* also see below), Simon & Schuster (New York, NY), 1987.

Anything for Billy, Simon & Schuster (New York, NY), 1988.

Some Can Whistle (sequel to *All My Friends Are Going to Be Strangers*), Simon & Schuster (New York, NY), 1989.

Buffalo Girls, Simon & Schuster (New York, NY), 1990.

The Evening Star (sequel to *Terms of Endearment*), Simon & Schuster (New York, NY), 1992.

Streets of Laredo (sequel to *Lonesome Dove*), Simon & Schuster (New York, NY), 1993.

(With Diana Ossana) *Pretty Boy Floyd,* Simon & Schuster (New York, NY), 1994.

Three Bestselling Novels (contains *Lonesome Dove, Leaving Cheyenne,* and *The Last Picture Show*) Wings Books (New York, NY), 1994.

Dead Man's Walk (prequel to *Lonesome Dove*), Simon & Schuster (New York, NY), 1995.

The Late Child, Simon & Schuster (New York, NY), 1995.

(With Diana Ossana) *Zeke and Ned,* Simon & Schuster (New York, NY), 1997.

Commanche Moon (prequel to *Lonesome Dove),* Simon & Schuster (New York, NY), 1997.

Duane's Depressed (sequel to *The Last Picture Show*), Simon & Schuster (New York, NY), 1999.

Sin Killer: The Berrybender Narratives, Book 1, Simon & Schuster, 2002.

The Wandering Hill (second book in "The Berrybender Narratives"), Simon & Schuster, 2003.

By Sorrow's River: The Berrybender Narratives, Book 3, Simon & Schuster, 2003.

Loop Group, Simon & Schuster, 2005.

ESSAYS

In a Narrow Grave: Essays on Texas, Encino Press (Austin, TX), 1968, Simon & Schuster (New York, NY), 1989.

It's Always We Rambled: An Essay on Rodeo, Hallman, 1974.

Film Flam: Essays on Hollywood, Simon & Schuster (New York, NY), 1987.

Sacagewea's Nickname: Essays on the American West, New York Review of Books (New York, NY), 2001.

SCRIPTS

(With Peter Bogdanovich) *The Last Picture Show* (screenplay; based on McMurtry's novel of same title; produced by Columbia, 1971), B.B.S. Productions, 1970.

Texasville (screenplay, based on McMurtry's novel of the same title), 1990.

Montana (teleplay), Turner Network Television, 1990.

Falling from Grace (screenplay), Columbia, 1992.

(With Cybill Shepherd) *Memphis* (teleplay; based on a novel by Shelby Foote), Turner Home Entertainment, 1992.

(With Diana Ossana) *Streets of Laredo* (teleplay, based on McMurtry's novel of the same title), CBS, 1995.

(With Diana Ossana) *Dead Man's Walk* (teleplay, based on McMurtry's novel of the same title), ABC, 1996.

OTHER

(Author of foreword) Frederick L. Olmsted, *Journey through Texas: or, A Saddle-Trip on the Southwestern Frontier,* University of Texas Press (Austin, TX), 1978.

(Author of foreword) John R. Erickson, *Panhandle Cowboy,* University of Nebraska Press (Lincoln, NE), 1980.

(Author of introduction) Dan Flores, *Canyon Visions: Photographs and Pastels of the Texas Plains,* Texas Tech University Press (Lubbock, TX), 1989.

(Author of introduction) Donna A. Demac, *Liberty Denied: The Current Rise of Censorship in America,* Rutgers University Press (New Brunswick, NJ), 1990.

(Author of foreword) Clarus Backes, editor, *Growing up Western,* Knopf (New York, NY), 1990.

Crazy Horse (biography), Viking (New York, NY), 1999.

Walter Benjamin at the Dairy Queen: Reflections at Sixty and Beyond (memoir), Simon & Schuster (New York, NY), 1999.

(Editor) *Still Wild: Short Fiction of the American West, 1950 to the Present,* Simon & Schuster (New York, NY), 2000.

Roads, Driving America's Great Highways (memoir), Simon & Schuster (New York, NY), 2000.

Boone's Lick (stories), Simon & Schuster (New York, NY), 2000.

Paradise (memoir), Simon & Schuster (New York, NY), 2001.

Also contributor to *Texas in Transition,* Lyndon Baines Johnson School of Public Affairs, 1986, and *Rodeo: No Guts No Glory,* Aperture (New York, NY), 1994. Contributor of numerous articles, essays, and book reviews for magazines and newspapers, including *Atlantic, Gentleman's Quarterly, New York Times, Saturday Review,* and *Washington Post.* Contributing editor of *American Film,* 1975—.

ADAPTATIONS: Hud, a motion picture starring Paul Newman, Patricia Neal, and Melvyn Douglas and based on *Horseman, Pass By,* was produced by Paramount, 1962; *Lovin' Molly,* based on *Leaving Cheyenne,* was produced by Columbia, 1974; *Terms of Endearment,* based on the novel of the same title, was produced by Paramount, 1983; *Lonesome Dove,* based on the novel of the same title, was produced as a television miniseries, CBS, 1989; *Return to Lonesome Dove,* based on characters from *Lonesome Dove,* was produced as a television miniseries, CBS, 1993; *Desert Rose* was adapted for film by Columbia Pictures from a script by Nora and Delia Ephron.

SIDELIGHTS: In the decades since he published his first novel, Larry McMurtry has emerged as one of Texas's most prominent fiction writers. Though he lived outside Texas for two decades, McMurtry has drawn themes for many of his novels from the uneasy interaction between his native state's mythic past and its problematic, ongoing urbanization during the later decades of the twentieth century. His earliest works, such as the critically acclaimed *Horseman, Pass By* and *The Last Picture Show,* expose the bleak prospects for adolescents on the rural ranches or in the small towns of west Texas, while his novels written in the 1970s, including *Terms of Endearment,* trace Texas characters drawn into the urban milieus of Houston, Hollywood, and Washington, DC. His 1986 Pulitzer Prize-winning novel, *Lonesome Dove,* received high praise for its realistic detailing of a cattle drive from the late nineteenth century, a transformation into fiction of a part of Texas history the author previously approached in his essays on cowboys, ranching, and rodeos. As Si Dunn noted in the *Dallas News,* McMurtry's readers find him "a writer who has made living in Texas a literary experience."

As a spokesman for the status of modern Texas letters, McMurtry has been known to criticize some Texas writers for their tendency to overlook the potentially rich material to be found in Texas's modern, industrialized society and growing urban areas. In *In a Narrow Grave: Essays on Texas,* he concluded: "Texas writers are sometimes so anxious to avoid the accusation of provincialism that they will hardly condescend to render the particularities of their own place, though it ought to be clear that literature thrives on particulars. The material is here, and it has barely been touched. If this is truly the era of the Absurd, then all the better for the Texas writer, for where else except California can one find a richer mixture of absurdities? Literature has coped fairly well with the physical circumstances of life in Texas, but our emotional experience remains largely unexplored, and therein lie the drama, poems, and novels."

In *The Ghost Country: A Study of the Novels of Larry McMurtry,* Raymond L. Neinstein expressed the belief that McMurtry "has journeyed from an old-fashioned regionalism to a kind of 'neo-regionalism,' his characters, and the novels themselves, turning from the land as the locus of their values to an imaginary, fictive 'place.' But they, characters and novels both, are finally not able to manage there, at least not comfortably. McMurtry clearly does not trust 'living in the head'; the pull of the old myth is still strong." McMurtry himself is aware of this dichotomy, as he wrote in *Holiday:* "A part of my generation may keep something of the frontier spirit even though the frontier is lost. What they may keep is a sense of daring and independence, transferred from the life of action to the life of the mind."

In McMurtry's case, this description is particularly apt. The son and grandson of cattle ranchers, he grew up in sparsely populated Archer County in north central Texas. From childhood he was more interested in reading than ranching, but the family stories he heard as a youth exerted an enormous influence on his sense of identity. He wrote in *In a Narrow Grave:* "It is indeed a complex distance from those traildrivers who made my father and my uncles determined to be cowboys to the mechanical horse that helps convince my son that he is a cowboy, as he takes a vertical ride in front of a laundrymat." If he felt pride and nostalgia for the ranching way of life which was vanishing even as he came of age, McMurtry was far less enthusiastic about tiny Archer City, where he attended high school as an honor student. He found little to nourish his imagination within the confines of the town, noting in *In a Narrow Grave:* "I grew up in a bookless town, in a bookless part of the state—when I stepped into a university library, at age eighteen, the whole of the world's literature lay before me unread, a country as vast, as promising, and, so far as I knew, as trackless as the West must have seemed to the first white men who looked upon it."

Interestingly, in creating his own fiction, McMurtry has drawn many of his themes from his bookless, "blood's country" of Texas. His early works portray a fictional town and countryside with a strong resemblance to Archer County. In *Horseman, Pass By,* his first novel, McMurtry introduces the adolescent narrator Lonnie Bannon, who describes a series of tragic events that occur on his grandfather's ranch when an epidemic of hoof-and-mouth disease is discovered. Nearing manhood himself, the orphaned Lonnie is confronted with several role models whose behavior he must evaluate: his step-uncle Hud, an egotistic and ruthless hedonist; his grandfather's hired hand Jesse, a storytelling drifter; and his grandfather, Homer, who, Charles D. Peavy stated in his *Larry McMurtry,* "epitomizes all the rugged virtues of a pioneer ethic." Lonnie's frustration is additionally fanned by the presence of Halmea, the black housekeeper who Peavy suggested is both "love object and mother surrogate" to the young man. John Gerlach noted in the *Dictionary of Literary Biography* that the relationship between Lonnie and Halmea, based on "tenderness, lack of fulfillment, and separation due here to differences in age and race," marks "the beginning of what becomes an essential theme in [McMurtry's] later works—people's needs do not match their circumstances." Peavy sees *Horseman, Pass By* as the first chronicle of another recurring McMurtry theme: "the initiation into manhood and its inevitable corollaries—loneliness and loss of innocence."

Horseman, Pass By was published when its author was twenty-five. While not an immediate commercial success, it established McMurtry's reputation within the Western genre. In an article in *Regional Perspectives: An Examination of America's Literary Heritage,* Larry Goodwyn called McMurtry "one of the most interesting young novelists in the Southwest—and certainly the most embattled in terms of frontier heritage." While McMurtry claimed in *In a Narrow Grave* that "the world quietly overlooked" *Horseman, Pass By,* and that he himself viewed it in retrospect an immature work, the book was not only significant enough to warrant an Academy Award-winning movie adaptation, but also of sufficient literary merit to garner McMurtry a 1964 Guggenheim award for creative writing. Peavy quoted a letter critic John Howard Griffin wrote to McMurtry's agent after reading *Horseman, Pass By:* "This is probably the starkest, most truthful, most terrible and yet beautiful treatment of [ranching country] I've seen. It will offend many, who prefer the glamour treatment—but it is a true portrait of the loneliness and pervading melancholy of cowboying; and of its compensations in nature, in human relationships."

Leaving Cheyenne, McMurtry's second novel, is also set in ranching country. The story revolves around Molly Taylor and the two men she loves throughout her lifetime: Gid, a rancher, and Johnny, a cowboy. Each of the three central characters narrates a section of the book; their intertwined lives are traced from youth to death. "McMurtry is psychologically precise in tracing this three-sided relationship," wrote Walter Clemons in the *New York Times Book Review.* "Odd as the roots of this friendship may seem, there's enduring consideration and feeling in it. The story takes so many years to tell because feelings that last a lifetime are the subject." Gerlach noted that *Leaving Cheyenne* explores a new aspect of the theme of "mismatching and the isolation it brings. . . . The expanded time scheme and number of narrators enrich the themes of the novel." Clemons, who called McMurtry "one of the two best writers to come out of Texas in the [1960s]," claimed that *Leaving Cheyenne* is "a rarity among second novels in its exhilarating ease, assurance and openness of feeling."

When evaluating McMurtry's early works, critics tend to group *Horseman, Pass By* and *Leaving Cheyenne* together due to their similarities of setting and theme. In a discussion of his writings in *New York* magazine, McMurtry himself analyzed the two novels together, with pointed remarks about his attitude concerning them: "It is perhaps worth pointing out that both [*Leaving Cheyenne*] and my first novel were written in the same year—my twenty-third. I revised around on both books for a while, but essentially both incorporate, at best, a 22-year-old's vision. . . . I don't want that vision back, nor am I overjoyed to see the literary results of it applauded." Others praised the young author's efforts, Goodwyn writing: "McMurtry's first two novels . . . were promising efforts to put the materials of frontier culture to serious literary use. . . . [Both books] are in-the-grain novels of people striving to live by the cultural values of the legend. . . . McMurtry speaks through a narrator who is frontiersman enough to move with ease through the tall-in-the-saddle milieu, but sensitive enough to note the ritualized energy and directionless fury surrounding him. . . . Relying . . . on the literary device of the provincial narrator, McMurtry found a voice that seemed to serve well as a strengthening connection between himself and his sources."

The fictional town of Thalia figures peripherally in both *Horseman, Pass By* and *Leaving Cheyenne.* In *The Last Picture Show,* McMurtry's third novel, Thalia becomes the primary setting and the debilitating monotony of small-town life one of the primary themes. Thomas Lask in the *New York Times* described McMurtry's Thalia: "A sorrier place would be hard to find. It is desiccated and shabby physically, mean and small-minded spiritually. Mr. McMurtry is expert in anatomizing its suffocating and dead-end character." The novel's action once again revolves around a group of late adolescents who are struggling to achieve adulthood in the town's confining atmosphere. Peavy wrote of McMurtry: "He examines the town's inhabitants—the oil rich, the roughnecks, the religious fanatics, the high school football stars, the love-starved women—with an eye that is at once sociological and satiric. For the first time he abandons the first-person narrative in his fiction, and the result is a dispassionate, cold look at the sordidness and hypocrisy that characterize the town."

When it was first published in 1966, *The Last Picture Show* raised some controversy in McMurtry's hometown of Archer City and elsewhere for its graphic detailing of teenage sexuality—including exhibitionism, bestiality, petting, masturbation, and homosexuality. "On the surface," Peavy noted, "McMurtry's treatment of small-town sexuality may seem quite sensational; actually, it is accurate. In the cloying confines of Thalia, the only outlet for frustrations, loneliness, boredom, even hatred—for both adolescents and adults—is sex. . . . Some of McMurtry's sexual scenes are highly symbolic, all are important thematically, and none should be taken as sensationalism." W.T. Jack expressed the same opinion in the *New York Times Book Review:* "Offensive? Miraculously, no. McMurtry is an alchemist who converts the basest materials to gold. The sexual encounters are sad, funny, touching, sometimes horrifying, but always honest, always human." Peavy felt, in fact, that "neither Updike nor Salinger has been as successful as McMurtry in describing the gnawing ache that accompanies adolescent sexuality."

Some critics felt that certain characterizations in *The Last Picture Show* approach stereotype. "McMurtry has said that part of the concern of *The Last Picture Show* is to portray how the town is emotionally centered in high school—in adolescence," stated Peavy. "As a result, the protagonist of the book is somewhat inadequately developed." In an essay for *Colonial Times,* McMurtry admitted that his approach to the material in *The Last Picture Show* was "too bitter." Archer City "had not been cruel to me, only honestly indifferent, and my handling of many of the characters in the book represented a failure of generosity for which I blame no one but myself."

According to Peavy, some of the difficulties in McMurtry's novel were surmounted in the film script of *The Last Picture Show* through the added perspective of director and co-writer Peter Bogdanovich. "The film script . . . is a much more sympathetic portrait of McMurtry's hometown than is the novel," Peavy suggested. "The combination of the two young writers [McMurtry and Bogdanovich] was fortunate." Filmed in black and white on location in Archer City, *The Last Picture Show* was a commercial and critical success, winning three Academy Awards including an award for best screenplay based on material from another medium. In an *Atlantic* review, David Denby stated that the movie "reverses many of the sentimental assumptions about small towns that were prevalent in the movies of the forties, but it never becomes a cinematic exposé. It's a tough-minded, humorous, and delicate film—a rare combination in an American movie." Writing for *Newsweek,* Paul D. Zimmerman called the film "a masterpiece" with "a finely tuned screenplay." Zimmerman also claimed that *The Last Picture Show* "is not merely the best American movie of a rather dreary year; it is the most impressive work by a young American director since *Citizen Kane.*"

McMurtry followed *The Last Picture Show* with what is sometimes referred to as his "urban trilogy": *Moving On, All My Friends Are Going to Be Strangers,* and *Terms of Endearment.* These novels represent a radical departure in setting and tone in detailing the lives of Houston urbanites, some of whom travel across the country in various, seemingly aimless pursuits. In her *Western American Literature* study on McMurtry's work, Janis P. Stout wrote of *Moving On* and *All My Friends Are Going to Be Strangers:* "None of the characters in these two novels has any sense of a usable past, and none is purposefully directed toward the future. They inhabit the burgeoning cities of Texas with no apparent means of orienting themselves and nothing to engage them but endless, unsatisfying motion—as the title *Moving On* well indicates." McMurtry uses a revolving set of characters as the cast for all three books. The supporting troupe in one novel may evolve to primary importance in another volume, as is the case with Emma Horton, who appears briefly in *Moving On* and *All My Friends Are Going to Be Strangers* before becoming the protagonist in *Terms of Endearment.* R.C. Reynolds noted in the *Southwest Review:* "Though time sequences often fall out of order in the three novels, key events and characters are repeated often enough to maintain a continuous theme which, not surprisingly, has three parts: sex and its frustrations, academics and its frustrations, and something like culture and its frustrations which McMurtry has branded *Ecch-Texas.*"

Considered as a group, *Moving On, All My Friends Are Going to Be Strangers,* and *Terms of Endearment* did not achieve the favorable critical response that quickly followed McMurtry's earlier books. Stout claimed that "the journey pattern so insistent in McMurtry's first three novels has in [*Moving On* and *All My Friends Are Going to Be Strangers*] become dominant, as the characters drive endlessly and pointlessly around the country chiefly between Texas and California. Not surprisingly, novels so constituted lack cohesive form; or rather, their forms may be described as being imitative to a radical and destructive degree. . . . Unfortunately, this expressive form, by its very nature, is destructive of the overall novelistic structure and renders the work a chronicle of tedium." Goodwyn sensed an ambiguity at work in the novels: "The frontier ethos, removed from the center of [McMurtry's] work, continues to hover around the edges—it surfaces in minor characters who move with purpose through novels that do not."

Reviewers were not unanimously disappointed with the "urban trilogy," however. In a review of *Moving On* for the *New York Times,* John Leonard wrote: "McMurtry has a good ear: [the characters] talk the way people actually talk in Houston, at rodeos, in Hollywood. Mr. McMurtry also has a marvelous eye for locale: the Southwest is superbly evoked. It is a pleasure . . . to escape claustrophobic novels that rely on the excitation of the verbal glands instead of the exploration of social reality." "It is difficult to characterize a talent as outsized as McMurtry's," suggested Jim Harrison in the *New York Times Book Review.* "Often his work seems disproportionately violent, but these qualities in *All My Friends Are Going to Be Strangers* are tempered by his comic genius, his ability to render a sense of landscape and place, and an interior intellectual tension that resembles in intensity that of Saul Bellow's *Mr. Sammler's Planet.* McMurtry . . . has a sense of construction and proper velocity that always saves him." A *Times Literary Supplement* reviewer likewise concluded: "There are few books one remembers with a real sense of affection, but *All My Friends* is indisputably one of them. Mr. McMurtry's talent for characterization and the evocation of place—together with his ability to blend them convincingly, so that they seem almost to interdepend—makes [the protagonist's] near-indefinable yearnings for a past which seems close enough to grab at wholly understandable."

Terms of Endearment, first published in 1975, has since become the most popular segment of the "urban trilogy." The story concerns Aurora Greenway, a New England-born widow who lives in Houston, and her married daughter, Emma. The greater portion of the novel deals with Aurora's relationship with her several "suitors," including a retired armored corps commander and an oil millionaire, but the final chapter follows Emma through a deteriorating marriage to her ultimate death from cancer. *New York Times* critic Christopher Lehmann-Haupt observed that "maybe what keeps one entertained [with the book] is the sympathy with which Mr. McMurtry writes about these people. . . . One laughs at the slapstick, one weeps at the maudlin, and one likes all of Mr. McMurtry's characters, no matter how delicately or broadly they are drawn." Gerlach found Aurora "loveable because she can turn a phrase. . . . Her story has endless permutations but no motion; she is timeless." Though some critics felt that the tragic ending strikes a jarring note following the light comic adventures of Aurora, they nonetheless found the section moving. Robert Towers noted:"The final scenes between the dying Emma and her stricken boys are the most affecting in the book."

Terms of Endearment, according to McMurtry, marked a turning point in his fiction writing. "I was halfway through my sixth Texas novel," he explained in *Atlantic,* "when I suddenly began to notice that where place was concerned, I was sucking air. The book is set in Houston, but none of the characters are Texans." Having himself moved from Houston to Washington, DC, in 1970, McMurtry began to seek new regional settings for his novels. In 1976 he told the *Dallas News:* "I lived in Texas quite a while, and for my own creative purposes had kind of exhausted it. Texas is not an inexhaustible region." He concluded in *Atlantic:* "The move off the land is now virtually completed, and that was the great subject that Texas offered writers of my generation. The one basic subject it offers us now is loneliness, and one can only ring the changes on that so many times."

The three novels McMurtry published between 1978 and 1983 all have primary settings outside of Texas. *Somebody's Darling* centers on the Hollywood career of a young female film director, *Cadillac Jack* follows the cross-country ramblings of an aging antiques dealer, and *The Desert Rose* provides a fictional portrait of a goodhearted Las Vegas showgirl. Critical appraisals of these works concentrate on McMurtry's ability to create appealing characters who are independent of his traditional regional setting. In a *Dictionary of Literary Biography Yearbook* essay, Brooks Landon suggested that *Somebody's Darling* contains "two of [McMurtry's] most mature and most fully realized characters." *Washington Post Book World* contributor Jonathan Yardley similarly stated of *Somebody's Darling:* "Mr. McMurtry's characters are real, believable and touching, his prose has life and immediacy and he is a very funny writer." Less successful, according to reviewers, is *Cadillac Jack,* a novel based in Washington, DC. Peter Prince wrote in *Nation* that the principal character "is the man to squelch everything down to the level of his own deep ordinariness," while Yardley stated in the *Washington Post* that "the city as it emerges in the novel is a mere caricature, like too many of the characters in it." Of the three books, *The Desert Rose* received the most commendation for its sympathetic characterization. Yardley claimed in the *Washington Post Book World:* "In her innocent, plucky, unaffected way [the protagonist] is as courageous a character as one could hope to meet." As Larry McCaffery observed in the *Los Angeles Times Book Review,* McMurtry "flirts with being unbearably cute . . . but his lack of condescension toward characters and situation makes his depictions ring true."

McMurtry's ability to transcend caricature and present his characters as real, living people has earned him a reputation as a mythbreaker. Nowhere is this reputation better supported than in his triptych of historical westerns, *Lonesome Dove, Anything for Billy,* and *Buffalo Girls,* which together successfully debunk the myths of the Old West—with its hardy cowboys, ruthless gunslingers, and savage Indians—recasting them as the sad inhabitants of a dying era.

Lonesome Dove, McMurtry's 800-page, 1985 release, not only returns to the author's native state for its setting—a locale he had consciously avoided for five years—but also concerns the brief cattle drive era that has proven the focus of much of the Western romantic mystique. McMurtry told the *New York Times Book Review* that the novel "grew out of my sense of having heard my uncles talk about the extraordinary days when the range was open," a subject the author had previously addressed only in his nonfiction. According to the reviewers, a strong advantage to the book is the author's objective presentation of frontier life. As George Garrett explained in the *Chicago Tribune Book World, Lonesome Dove* contains "the authority of exact authenticity. You can easily believe that this is how it really was to be there, to live, to suffer and rejoice, then and there. And thus, the reader is most subtly led to see where the literary conventions of the Western came from, how they came to be in the first place, and which are true and which are false." *New York Times Book Review* contributor Nicholas Lemann also wrote of *Lonesome Dove:* "Everything about the book feels true; being anti-mythic is a great aid to accuracy about the lonely, ignorant, violent West." This anti-mythic foundation in the novel, according to Lemann, "works to reinforce the strength of the traditionally mythic parts . . . by making it far more credible than the old familiar horse operas."

Lonesome Dove achieved best-seller status within weeks of its release and was a critical success as well. "McMurtry is a storyteller who works hard to satisfy his audience's yearning for the familiar," stated R.Z. Sheppard in *Time.* "What, after all, are legends made of? The secret of his success is embellishment, the odd detail or colorful phrase that keeps the tale from slipping into a rut." *Newsweek*'s Walter Clemons claimed that the novel "shows, early on, just about every symptom of American Epic except pretentiousness." Clemons concluded: "It's a pleasure . . . to be able to recommend a big popular novel that's amply imagined and crisply, lovingly written. I haven't enjoyed a book more this year." "The aspects of cowboying that we have found stirring for so long are, inevitably, the aspects that are stirring when given full-dress treatment by a first-rate novelist," explained Lemann. *Lonesome Dove* was awarded the Pulitzer Prize for fiction in 1986.

McMurtry's contrasting of the "popular" Old West to the "real" Old West is more heavy-handed in his 1988 novel *Anything for Billy.* Cast in the role of narrator is Benjamin Sippy, a depressed Easterner fascinated by the cowboy adventures he reads and writes about in such dime novels as *Orson Oxx, Man of Iron* and *Solemn Sam, the Sad Man from San Saba.* Fed up with his oppressive wife and his nine horrible daughters, Sippy heads west to live the life of an outlaw. The western plains that await him, though, are not those of his precious dime novels; there are more bugs than buffalo. After a disastrous attempt at train robbery, Sippy meets a buck-toothed simpleton named Billy Bone who, though never having pulled a trigger, has somehow built a reputation as a gunfighter—a reputation he is determined to live up to. With the help of Sippy's writing and a sawed-off shotgun, Billy Bone transforms himself into Billy the Kid.

McMurtry's retelling of the story of Billy the Kid is unique, a portrayal Julian Loose of the *Times Literary Supplement* warned "will certainly upset anyone nostalgic for Hollywood's version of the boy who never grew old." Missing from its pages is the Lincoln County war, mentor-turned-adversary John Chisum, or the traitorous Pat Garrett. The Kid himself is ugly, crude, and ignorant; he is afraid of thunder and lightning; possessing poor vision and bad aim, he compensates by shooting his victims at close range with an oversized gun, often without provocation. "There is nothing heroic or even accomplished about this Billy," lamented Loose, "yet he exudes an irresistible boyish charm" that "attracts followers and lovers who will do 'anything for Billy' but [who] cannot stop him wandering on to his premature and pointless doom."

The theme of *Anything for Billy* is age-old: Don't believe everything you read. Mervyn Rothstein observed in the *New York Times* that, like *Lonesome Dove, Anything for Billy* "is constantly reminding the reader of the disparity between the mythic West of pulp fiction and the considerably less romantic reality of day-to-day life on the frontier." "The book's greatest strength," added *Village Voice*'s M. George Stevenson, "is in Sippy's accounts of how his dime novelist's expectations of the West were either too grand or too mundane." By making Sippy both a writer and reader of pulp fiction, McMurtry points his finger at those who perpetuate the myths of the Old West. Robert Gish, reviewing *Anything for Billy* in the *Los Angeles Times Book Review,* proclaimed the novel "a tall tale that outdoes any previous telling about Billy the *bandito* boy of old New Mexico," and which forces readers to "think again about the real and the imagined West and the rendering of them in words."

As with *Anything for Billy,* 1990's *Buffalo Girls* features a cast of historical characters: Calamity Jane, Wild Bill Hickok, Buffalo Bill Cody, and Sitting Bull. Unlike young Billy Bone, though, the characters in *Buffalo Girls* are depicted at the end of their careers; tired, old and drunk, they travel together in Buffalo Bill's Wild West Show, emulating the adventures that made them into legends. The dwindling lives of McMurtry's characters mirror the approaching demise of the Wild West itself: the once-untamable land is now settled, the animals slaughtered, the bloodthirsty Indians relegated to small parcels of land. "Almost everyone in *Buffalo Girls* knows himself and his world to be on the verge of extinction," Susan Fromberg Schaeffer observed in the *New York Times Book Review.* "They begin to understand that they have outlived their time. The question then becomes whether they can find a new way to live, or at least a new meaning that will justify their lives. That most of them fail to do so should be no surprise, because the Wild West, as Mr. McMurtry seems to conceive it [is] the childhood of our country and, like all childhoods, it must pass."

In his historical Westerns, *New York Times Book Review* critic Jack Butler maintained that McMurtry alternates "the Old Wild West with the West of the present or near-present" in order to counterpoint the overly romanticized myths that permeate American literature. "I'm a critic of the myth of the cowboy," McMurtry explained in the *New York Times.* "I don't feel that it's a myth that pertains, and since it's a part of my heritage I feel it's a legitimate task to criticize it." The reason for the popularity of the cowboy myth—that of the tough-but-fair rogue who adheres to the "code of the West"—is, he believes, rooted in the American psyche. "If you actually read the biography of any of the famous gunfighters . . . they led very drab, mostly very repetitive, not very exciting lives. But people cherish a certain vision, because it fulfills psychological needs. People need to believe that cowboys are simple, strong and free, and not twisted, fascistic and dumb, as many cowboys I've known have been."

Though McMurtry claimed in the *New York Times* that he is "simply having fun reinventing" the myth of the Wild West, critics have found greater significance in his historical novels. Schaeffer described *Buffalo Girls* as "a work of resurrection, a book that rescues an important era of our country's saga both from that taxidermist, the history book, and from that waxwork beautifier, the myth machine." Butler, too, praised McMurtry's efforts as "doing something with the American West that is very much like what William Faulkner did with Mississippi. He is re-(not de-) mythologizing it. . . . None of this would matter if he were not a poet, a resonant scene-setter and a master of voice, but he is; and since the West figures so strongly in our vision of what it means to be American, Mr. McMurtry's labor is, I think, essential literature."

Perhaps because of the success of such films as *The Last Picture Show* and *Terms of Endearment,* as well as the television miniseries *Lonesome Dove,* during the late 1980s McMurtry became known more for his screenplays and the cinematic adaptations of his novels than as a novelist. Reviewers often criticized his books in Hollywood terms, as if they had already been translated to the screen; *The Evening Star,* for example, was panned by Mark Starr of *Newsweek* as "more script than novel," and Robert Plunkett of the *New York Times Book Review* attributed the popularity of the novel's main character, Aurora Greenway, to the performance of Shirley MacLaine in *Terms of Endearment.* "It is damning praise to be termed a 'cinematic' writer," concluded Julia Cameron in the *Los Angeles Times Book Review,* "and McMurtry most certainly is."

A number of McMurtry's more recent novels—including *Texasville, Some Can Whistle, The Evening Star, The Streets of Laredo,* and *The Late Child*—are sequels to earlier novels. McMurtry also penned a sequel to *Texasville,* titled *Duane's Depressed.* "More than any other writer I know of, McMurtry is inclined to return to his earlier books and spin off sequels," observed H.H. Harriman in the *Detroit News.* "It is hard to say exactly what the motivation is here—genuine and fond nostalgia, what could pass for a genuine preoccupation with unfinished business, or more darkly, the less than genuine and never gentle persuasion of a publisher's greed." McMurtry also wrote two prequels to *Lonesome Dove: Dead Man's Walk* and *Comanche Moon.*

Of his sequels, one that weathered the critical storm is *Texasville.* Though it reintroduces the city of Thalia, Texas, and the characters of *The Last Picture Show,* its tone is far different from that of its predecessor. Set thirty years after the events of the first novel, *Texasville* shows Thalia's residents as middle-aged men and women who, having made their fortunes during the oil boom of the 1970s, are now systematically going bankrupt. The town is as stifling and monotonous as ever, but the once-idealistic adolescents of *The Last Picture Show* have ceased to struggle against it. "They have stopped having thoughts," wrote Louise Erdrich in the *New York Times Book Review.* "They simply act out their emotions by destroying things. . . . Waste is celebrated." While the observations of *Texasville*'s main character render the decline of Thalia in a humorous light, it is humor of the darkest, most cynical variety. "If Thalia . . . can stand for modern America," John Clute opined in the *Times Literary Supplement,* "then for Larry McMurtry modern America is terrifyingly like hell."

As the townspeople go rapidly insane, they once again turn to sex—and lots of it—to keep their minds off their moral and financial deterioration. "But there's something sadder and more irrevocable" about the promiscuity in *Texasville,* according to Kakutani. "Everyone is older now, sinking into the disappointments and weariness of middle age, and for most of them, familial security and enduring love are no longer dreamed-of possibilities but lost opportunities, consigned to a receding past." Erdrich, too, noted the difference between the two novels' use of frequent sex: "In *The Last Picture Show,* the quest was not only for sex, but sex linked to tenderness and mystery, to love. In *Texasville,* sex is just sex. It happens everywhere and often."

Though *Texasville* is universally regarded as a very different book from its predecessor, it was still considered by many critics to be a literary success. "While [*Texasville*] lacks the ambition and epic resonance of *Lone-*

some Dove, it shows off the author at his popular storytelling best, and it attests, again, to his sure feeling for people and place," lauded Kakutani. While Yardley described the novel as "a big ol' mess of a book," he ultimately praised *Texasville* as "a novel that transcends its shortcomings . . . [and] is of a piece with all McMurtry's best work."

With *Duane's Depressed,* McMurtry completed his trilogy on the denizens of Thalia, Texas, this time centering on sixty-two-year-old Duane Moore. Oil rich and disillusioned with his life, family, and friends, Duane's dissatisfaction begins to manifest itself in eccentric behavior. He parks his pickup truck and begins walking everywhere. He moves out of his house and chooses to live in a cabin in the woods. Although never of a literary bent, Duane discovers Thoreau and decides to take the philosopher's advice and "live deliberately." Eventually Duane is persuaded to see a psychiatrist, the lesbian Honor Carmichal, with whom he falls hopelessly in love, and who introduces him to Marcel Proust. Discussing the book in the *New York Times Book Review,* Robert Houston observed: "By the book's end, Duane's beginning a fresh, untried kind of trip, one that is both literal and symbolic. He's on a plane to the Pyramids of Egypt, old passions confronted, the unknown ahead." While considering the plot at times forced and the character of Honor Carmichal "a bit too saintly, a bit too wise," Houston nevertheless concluded that "*Duane's Depressed* is a worthwhile end to an important trilogy, one that captures vividly and movingly nearly half a century of life in a great swath of America." A reviewer for *Publishers Weekly* added: "Using barren landscapes and drab interiors to emphasize the subtle, potent drama of Duane's search for himself, McMurtry shines as he examines the issues of alienation, grief and the confrontation with personal mortality."

Receiving mixed reviews were the sequels *Some Can Whistle* and *The Evening Star,* each of which reprises a popular set of characters who, now older, attempt to reconcile with their families and, eventually, themselves. Unlike his sprawling "urban trilogy," McMurtry's sequels are more static, their characters less prone to travel and external relationships. While both novels are rife with dark humor and sudden, jarring tragedy, Kakutani considered the combination "contrived and melodramatic," although adding that it is executed successfully through the author's "fluency and poise as a writer." His penchant for sequels has furthered the criticism of McMurtry as a "cinematic writer," *Time* reviewer Paul Gray noting of *Some Can Whistle:* "Everything and everyone in the tale reeks of Hollywood." Still, his books remain popular among loyal readers. "While utterly satisfying on their own, [these sequels] also give the longtime reader the pleasure of seeing a character mature through the decades," Kakutani explained. "The result is not unlike growing old in the company of a favorite relative or friend."

If *Texasville* has fared the best among McMurtry's sequels, *Streets of Laredo* has probably fared the worst, several critics questioning the wisdom of continuing a tale as well-constructed as *Lonesome Dove.* "Part of the very bittersweet pleasure of finishing reading a great book is that its story and characters are *finite,*" Harriman commented. "In that respect, they 'die,' only to live on in our memories. Sequels then are a kind of exhumation, a dishonor to the memory of the dead." In *Streets of Laredo,* Harriman concluded, "the tried and true caveats about the built-in, inevitable disappointments of sequels have been overlooked, and a Pulitzer Prize-winner has been reduced to pandering."

Not all reviewers disliked *Streets of Laredo. Detroit Free Press* contributor Martin F. Kohn lauded the way McMurtry "depicts the wild West on its last legs—more vicious than ever, as if enraged by its own coming demise at the hands of railroads, growing towns and other constructs of civilization." Kohn called the novel "a delicious, though vividly violent, read," wherein "verbal stands of color are planted at many a turn. . . . relieving the brutal landscape of the main narrative. . . . As a purveyor of time, place, plot and character [McMurtry] remains our novelist laureate of the old West." *New York Times Book Review* critic Noel Perrin suggested that, while on many pages *Streets of Laredo* "is the full equal of *Lonesome Dove,*" "there are also many [pages] on which Mr. McMurtry makes you wish he had left the characters of *Lonesome Dove* in peace."

In *Dead Man's Walk,* a prequel to *Lonesome Dove,* critical opinion was again somewhat mixed. The novel finds teens Gus McCrae and Woodrow Call joining their first mission as Texas Rangers under a self-declared colonel. On the mission they are dogged by merciless Indians, saved by a noblewoman in a leper colony, face death repeatedly, and endure a 200-mile "dead man's walk" across New Mexico. Observed Thomas Flanaghan in the *New York Times Book Review,* "It is a stranger and a more ambitious book than [*Lonesome Dove*], ruthless in its disposition of characters, sparse and vivid in its creation of the inhuman landscapes of New Mexico and the plains." According to some critics, the novel provides no new insight into the development of the central characters, and the plot is preposterous because so many of the facts on which the story is based have been greatly exaggerated. "It's one thing to demystify Rangers and quite another to invent a comic-book past," remarked Noel Perrin in *Washington Post Book World.* "If *Dead Man's Walk* were not a prequel [to *Lonesome Dove*]," wrote John Skow in *Time,* "it would be worth only glancing notice. As things are, it is a satisfactory foothill, with the grand old mountain in view."

In the story chronology of the "Lonesome Dove" series, *Comanche Moon* follows *Dean Man's Walk* and precedes *Lonesome Dove,* filling the twenty-year gap between the end of one book and the beginning of the other. McCrae and Call fight to advance the American frontier in the face of hostile Comanches led first by Buffalo Hump, and later his son Blue Duck. The narrative also explores the love affairs of both men, Gus with a local shopkeeper who marries another, and Woodrow with a prostitute who gives birth to his child. Discussing the novel, a *Kirkus Reviews* critic noted: "While the last third turns workmanlike in its efforts to set up the opening situation for *Lonesome Dove,* McMurtry nevertheless delivers a generally fine tableau of western life, full of imaginative exploits, convincing historical background, and characters who are alive." Barbara Perkins of *Library Journal* wrote: "McMurtry is at his best with a host of characters and painting on this large canvas."

In addition to his many novels, McMurtry has also published the short story collection *Boone's Lick,* memoirs *Walter Benjamin at the Dairy Queen: Reflections at Sixty and Beyond* and *Paradise,* as well as essay collections and a biography of Sioux warrior Crazy Horse, part of the "Penguin Lives" series of short biographies. In *Paradise,* the author ruminates on his parent's difficult marriage before moving forward in time to the period of his mother's death in Archer City, Texas, a period during which McMurtry was traveling the South Sea Islands. The book—part travelogue, part memoir—includes "Some characteristically wonderful passages that only McMurtry could write," maintained *Book* contributor Don McLeese while still expressing disappointment over the brevity of the volume. More enthusiastic, a reviewer for *Publishers Weekly* commented that "Readers of this excellent travelogue, abounding with literary references from Henry James to [Jack] Kerouac, will likely return to the book often to reread . . . favorite passages of McMurtry's meditative prose." Calling McMurtry "such a pro he could make laundry seem interesting," *Booklist* contributor Donna Seaman characterized his approach as "a magnetic blend of irascibility and grace."

Reviewing *Crazy Horse* for *Library Journal,* Stephen H. Peters credited McMurtry with "constructing a thoughtful discussion of Sioux culture around the known facts to show how Crazy Horse was shaped by his society and how he reacted to its destruction as whites spread onto the Great Plains." A reviewer for *Publishers Weekly* remarked: "Deceptively brief and seemingly lightweight, this wonderful work effectively cuts through decades of hyperbole."

In *Walter Benjamin at the Dairy Queen,* McMurtry combines essay with personal reminiscence to demonstrate, as Richard Bernstein of the *New York Times* put it, "how he abandoned the cowboy life in Texas where he grew up, and became . . . a herder of words." The "Walter Benjamin" of the title refers to a German-Jewish literary critic and essayist whom McMurtry first read while at the Dairy Queen in Archer City. The material here is wide ranging, including McMurtry's childhood memories of his parents' ranch, discussion of writers as diverse as Susan Sontag and Miguel Cervantes, a description of McMurtry's 1991 heart attack, and a lament concerning the decline of storytelling in everyday life. For Bernstein, this "memoir is not easy to get a bead on. It meanders: it picks up themes and then picks up other themes, but it often doesn't get to a point. . . . it leaves the reader longing for a stronger theme, great narrative punch." Thomas Mallon voiced a similar sentiment in the *New York Times Book Review* when he stated that the book "reads tantalizingly like the notes toward" an autobiography; "a reader does become frustrated with certain gaps and discontinuities." In contrast, Mike Shea wrote in *Texas Monthly* that McMurtry's "dry and gentle humor makes the essays read like his best fiction," while a *Publishers Weekly* reviewer called *Walter Benjamin at the Dairy Queen* "a thoughtful, elegant retrospective on Texas, his [McMurtry's] work and the meaning of reading by an author who has the range to write with intelligence about both Proust and the bathos of a Holiday Inn marquee."

According to Jeff Kunerth of *Knight-Ridder/Tribune News Service,* "McMurtry proves just how compelling a writer and skilled storyteller he is with *Roads: Driving America's Great Highways.* He confesses to being an avid travel book reader, but he writes a travel book unlike any other." Kunerth referred to the fact that McMurtry does not offer advice to travelers on where to spend the night or where to eat breakfast, but instead "uses the journey to ruminate, to let his mind wander, to think out loud on paper." McMurtry's ruminations include thoughts about his entire life, his books, and the work of other writers, such as Edgar Allan Poe, H.L. Mencken, and John Barth. A writer for *Economist* found McMurtry's musings less compelling, and warned readers unfamiliar with McMurtry's work not to start with

Roads. "Too directionless for travel writing, too ambivalent for a paean, too inconsistent for a diary . . . [McMurtry] offers historical anecdotes, bookwormly musings, autobiographical reminiscences and the occasional pop-culture reference," maintained the *Economist* critic. "But there is little to connect these splintered thoughts save a tangle of blackened highways."

In addition to his writing, McMurtry divides his time between an antiquarian bookstore he founded in Washington, DC, "Archer City," a ranch in Texas that he bought several years ago, and coast-to-coast driving trips behind the wheel of a Cadillac. He explained in *Time:* "Having a bookstore is a good balance to writing. . . . Writing is solitary. Bookselling is social." In 1989 he was chosen president of the PEN American Center, a prestigious writers' organization with affiliates around the world. He was the first non-New Yorker to head the American branch since Indiana's Booth Tarkington, who founded it in 1922.

McMurtry describes his approach to his craft in peculiarly Texan terms. Writing, he claimed in the *Los Angeles Times,* is "the ultimate analogue to my herding tradition. I herd words, I herd them into sentences and then I herd them into paragraphs and then I herd these paragraphs into books." As Raymond Neinstein indicated, the region McMurtry has written about with such success is "a ghost country . . . a country of love and of blood-ties. When those ties break down, when the love is gone, when the inheritance or inheritability of that country is somehow thwarted and its traditions are no longer viable, then the poignancy of the country's neglected beauty, of the tradition's unusable force, and of the human life left to survive without that beauty, that tradition, that center, becomes the subject of McMurtry's powerful and nostalgic novels." These novels, McMurtry told the *Los Angeles Times,* are not based on mere "notes of scandals of the neighborhood," but rather are built by essential flights of imagination. "I am more and more convinced," he declared, "that the essential reward of writing fiction is in the delight of seeing what you can make out of the sole tools of your imagination and your experience."

BIOGRAPHICAL AND CRITICAL SOURCES:

BOOKS

Authors in the News, Volume 2, Thomson Gale (Detroit, MI), 1976.

Bennett, Patrick, *Talking with Texas Writers: Twelve Interviews,* Texas A & M University Press (College Station, TX), 1980.

Bestsellers 89, Issue 2, Thomson Gale (Detroit, MI), 1989.

Burke, John Gordon, editor, *Regional Perspectives: An Examination of America's Literary Heritage,* American Library Association (Chicago, IL), 1971.

Busby, Mark, *Larry McMurtry and the West: An Ambivalent Relationship,* University of North Texas Press, 1995.

Contemporary Literary Criticism, Thomson Gale (Detroit, MI), Volume 2, 1974, Volume 3, 1975, Volume 7, 1977, Volume 11, 1979, Volume 27, 1984, Volume 44, 1987.

Dictionary of Literary Biography, Volume II: *American Novelists since World War II,* Thomson Gale (Detroit, MI), 1978.

Dictionary of Literary Biography Yearbook, Thomson Gale (Detroit, MI), *1979,* 1980, *1980,* 1981, *1986,* 1987, *1987,* 1988, *1993,* 1994.

Jones, Roger Walton, *Larry McMurtry and the Victorian Novel,* Texas University Press, 1994.

Landess, Thomas, *Larry McMurtry,* Steck-Vaughn, 1969.

Lich, Lera Patrick Tyler, *Larry McMurtry's Texas: Evolution of the Myth,* 1987.

McCullough, David W., *People Books and Book People,* Harmony Books (New York, NY), 1981.

McMurtry, Larry, *In a Narrow Grave: Essays on Texas,* Encino Press (Austin, TX), 1968, Simon & Schuster (New York, NY), 1971.

Neinstein, Raymond L., *The Ghost Country: A Study of the Novels of Larry McMurtry,* Creative Arts Book Company (Berkeley, CA), 1976.

Pages: The World of Books, Writers, and Writing, Thomson Gale (Detroit, MI), 1976.

Peavy, Charles D., *Larry McMurtry,* Twayne (Boston, MA), 1977.

Reynolds, Clay, editor, *Taking Stock: A Larry McMurtry Casebook,* 1989.

Schmidt, Dorey, editor, *Larry McMurtry: Unredeemed Dreams,* School of Humanities, Pan American University, 1978.

PERIODICALS

America, March 5, 1983; April 29, 1995, p. 32; November 18, 1995, p. 28.

American Film, November, 1975; December, 1975; January-February, 1976; March, 1976; April, 1976; May, 1976; June, 1976.

Arlington Quarterly, winter, 1969-70.

Atlantic, December, 1971; March, 1975.
Avesta, fall, 1956; fall, 1957.
Best Sellers, July 1, 1970.
Book, July, 2001, Don McLeese, review of *Paradise,* p. 72.
Booklist, April 15, 2001, Donna Seaman, review of *Paradise,* p. 1506; August, 2001, Nancy Spillman, review of *Boone's Lick* (audio version), p. 2143.
Books and Bookmen, November, 1973.
Book Week, October 23, 1966.
Book World, June 21, 1970.
Chicago Tribune, June 9, 1987; November 14, 1989; July 15, 1990, p. 1; October 21, 1990.
Chicago Tribune Book World, October 17, 1982; December 25, 1983; June 9, 1985.
Christian Science Monitor, February 6, 1976.
Coexistence Review, 1958.
Colonial Times, December 21-January 12, 1972.
Commentary, January, 1972.
Commonweal, November 5, 1971; October 20, 1972.
Daily Rag, October, 1972.
Dallas News, January 18, 1976.
Detroit Free Press, November 13, 1988; February 5, 1989; July 25, 1993, p. J6.
Detroit News, February 27, 1972; April 26, 1987; November 13, 1988; July 31, 1993, p. D14.
Economist (US), August 19, 2000, review of *Roads,* p. 75.
Film Quarterly, summer, 1964.
Forum, summer-fall, 1972.
Globe & Mail (Toronto, Ontario, Canada), August 10, 1985; June 20, 1987; January 20, 1990.
Holiday, September, 1965.
Houston Post, October 30, 1966; August 23, 1968.
Kirkus Reviews, September 15, 1997, review of *Comanche Moon.*
Knight-Ridder/Tribune News Service, September 6, 2000, Jeff Kunerth, review of *Roads,* p. K4697.
Library Journal, November 15, 1998, Stephen H. Peters, review of *Crazy Horse,* p. 75; February 1, 2000, Barbara Perkins, review of *Comanche Moon,* p. 133; October 15, 2000, Thomas L. Kilpatrick, review of *Boone's Lick,* p. 102; July, 2001, Cynde Bloom Lahey, review of *Paradise,* p. 90.
Literature/Film Quarterly, April, 1973.
Los Angeles Times, May 27, 1984; January 31, 1989; July 3, 1989; September 28, 1990, p. F1.
Los Angeles Times Book Review, November 14, 1982; September 4, 1983; June 9, 1985; August 16, 1987; October 30, 1988, p. 1; October 22, 1989, p. 2; October 21, 1990, p. 2; June 7, 1992, p. 4; June 4, 1995, p. 3.
Maclean's, December 25, 1978.
Nation, February 3, 1979; November 20, 1982.
National Review, November 26, 1982; November 25, 1983.
New Republic, October 16, 1971; April 1, 1972; November 29, 1975; September 2, 1985.
Newsweek, October 1, 1971; June 3, 1985; September 26, 1988, p. 76; June 8, 1992, p. 58; May 22, 1995, p. 61.
New York, February 5, 1973; April 29, 1974; October 3, 1988, p. 70; November 13, 1995, p. 95.
New Yorker, October 9, 1971; June 14, 1976; August 26, 1985; November 11, 1985.
New York Review of Books, August 13, 1992.
New York Times, December 3, 1966; June 10, 1970; October 22, 1975; December 20, 1978; December 28, 1981; January 23, 1983; June 3, 1985; April 8, 1987; June 27, 1987; February 28, 1988, p. 34; September 28, 1988; November 1, 1988, p. C17; September 5, 1990; October 16, 1990; May 12, 1992, p. C17; August 26, 1994, p. C28; June 28, 1995, p. C19; December 13, 1999, Richard Bernstein, "An Author's Seminal Moment at a Texas Drive-In."
New York Times Book Review, November 13, 1966; July 26, 1970; August 15, 1971; March 19, 1972; October 19, 1975; November 19, 1978; November 21, 1982; October 23, 1983; June 2, 1985; June 9, 1985; September 15, 1985; April 19, 1987, p. 7; May 31, 1987; October 16, 1988, p. 3; October 22, 1989, p. 8; October 7, 1990, p. 3; June 21, 1992, p. 12; May 21, 1995, p. 12; July 25, 1993, p. 9; October 16, 1994, p. 31, May 21, 1995, p. 12; September 10, 1995, p. 33; February 21, 1999, Robert Houston, review of *Duane's Depressed;* November 21, 1999, Thomas Mallon, "Even Cowboys Get the Blues"; November 26, 2000, Karen Karbo, review of *Boone's Lick,* p. 16; June 10, 2001, John Vernon, "Lonesome Son: When Larry McMurtry's Mother Was Dying, He Got as Far Away from the World as Possible," p. 19.
People, May 4, 1987.
Prairie Schooner, summer, 1979.
Publishers Weekly, November 16, 1998, review of *Crazy Horse,* p. 59; December 7, 1998, review of *Duane's Depressed,* p. 51; October 1, 1999, review of *Walter Benjamin at the Dairy Queen,* p. 87; May 21, 2001, review of *Paradise,* p. 92.
Saturday Review, October 17, 1970; October 16, 1971; January 10, 1976.
South Dakota Review, summer, 1966; Vol. 13, no. 2, 1975.
Southwestern American Literature, January, 1971.
Southwestern American Literature: A Bibliography, 1980.
Southwest Review, winter, 1976.

Texas Monthly, November, 1999, Mike Shea, review of *Walter Benjamin at the Dairy Queen,* p. 30.
Texas Observer, February 26, 1971.
Time, October 11, 1971; June 10, 1985; April 20, 1987, p. 71; October 24, 1988, p. 92; October 16, 1989, p. 89; May 25, 1992, p. 73; August 9, 1993; September 19, 1994, p. 82; September 4, 1995, p. 65.
Times (London, England), March 8, 1990.
Times Literary Supplement, March 23, 1973; September 11, 1987; November 3, 1989, p. 1217.
Tribune Books (Chicago, IL), April 5, 1987; October 9, 1988, p. 1; October 15, 1989, p. 4; May 17, 1992, p. 1; September 4, 1994, p. 3; September 10, 1995, p. 6.
Variety, February 14, 1990, p. 58; February 24, 1992, p. 247.
Village Voice, October 30, 1988, p. 63.
Village Voice Literary Supplement, October, 1982.
Vogue, March, 1984.
Washington Post, December 2, 1971; March 4, 1972; June 23, 1974; October 13, 1982; January 13, 1987; February 5, 1989.
Washington Post Book World, November 12, 1978; August 28, 1983; June 9, 1985; April 12, 1987; July 26, 1987; October 9, 1988, p. 1; October 22, 1989, p. 5; October 7, 1990, p. 6; September 4, 1994, p. 9; August 27, 1995, p. 3.
Washington Post Magazine, December 5, 1982.
Western American Literature, fall, 1967; fall, 1969; no. 7, 1972; spring, 1976; November, 1986.
Western Humanities Review, autumn, 1970; winter, 1975.

ONLINE

Los Angeles Times' Calendar Live, http://www.calendarlive.com/printedition/calendar/ (April 27, 2003).

* * *

McMURTRY, Larry Jeff
See McMURTRY, Larry

* * *

McNALLY, Terrence 1939-

PERSONAL: Born November 3, 1939, in St. Petersburg, FL; son of Hubert Arthur and Dorothy Katharine (Rapp) McNally. *Education:* Columbia University, B.A., 1960.

ADDRESSES: Agent—Peter Franklin, Gilbert Parker, William Morris Agency, 1325 Avenue of the Americas, New York, NY 10019-6026.

CAREER: Playwright. Actors Studio, New York, NY, stage manager, 1961, tutor, 1961-62; film critic for *The Seventh Art,* 1963-65; *Columbia College Today,* New York, NY, assistant editor, 1963-65.

MEMBER: American Academy of Arts and Letters, Dramatists Guild (vice president, 1981), Phi Beta Kappa.

AWARDS, HONORS: Henry Evans traveling fellowship, Columbia University, 1960; Stanley Award, 1962, for *This Side of the Door;* Guggenheim fellowship, 1966 and 1969; runner-up, Drama Desk Award for most promising playwright, 1969; Hull Warriner Award, 1973, 1987, and 1989; Obie Award, 1974, for *Bad Habits;* Obie Award for Best Play and Achievement in Playwrighting citations from American Academy of Arts and Letters and National Institute of Arts and Letters, 1975, all for *The Ritz;* Emmy Award, 1990, for *Andre's Mother;* Antoinette Perry (Tony) Award, best book of a musical, 1993, for *Kiss of the Spider Woman;* Pulitzer Prize for drama nomination, 1994, for *A Perfect Ganesh;* Tony Award for best play, and Outer Critics' Circle Award for Best Broadway Play, all 1995, all for *Love! Valour! Compassion!,* and 1996, for *Master Class;* Tony Award, 1998, for *Ragtime;* Tony Award nomination, 2001, for *The Full Monty.*

WRITINGS:

PLAYS

(Adapter) Giles Cooper, *The Lady of the Camellias,* produced on Broadway at Winter Garden Theatre, March 20, 1963.
And Things That Go Bump in the Night (also see below; three-act; first produced in Minneapolis at Tyrone Guthrie Theatre, February 4, 1964; produced on Broadway at Royale Theatre, April 26, 1965), Dramatists Play Service (New York, NY), 1966.
Apple Pie: Three One-Act Plays (includes *Tour,* first produced in Los Angeles at Mark Taper Forum, 1967, as part of *The Scene* [eleven plays by various authors], collection produced as *Collision Course* Off-Broadway (at Café au Go Go, May 8, 1968), published as *Collision Course,* edited by Ed Pa-

rone, Random House (New York, NY), 1968, published under original title, Dramatists Play Service (New York, NY), 1968.

(Author of book) *Here's Where I Belong* (musical; based on novel *East of Eden* by John Steinbeck), music by Robert Waldman, first produced on Broadway at Billy Rose Theatre, February 20, 1968.

Sweet Eros, Next, and Other Plays (contains *Sweet Eros* [one-act], first produced Off-Broadway at Gramercy Arts Theatre, November 21, 1968; *Next,* first produced Off-Broadway at Greenwich Mews Playhouse, February 10, 1969; *Witness* [one-act], first produced Off-Broadway at Gramercy Arts Theatre, November 21, 1968; *Cuba Si!* [also see below; one-act], first produced Off-Broadway at Theatre de Lys, December 9, 1968; and *Botticelli* [also see below]), Random House (New York, NY), 1969.

Noon (one-act; bound with *Morning* by Israel Horovitz and *Night* by Leonard Malfi; first produced on Broadway at Henry Miller's Theatre, November 28, 1968), Random House (New York, NY), 1969.

Botticelli (also see below), Dramatists Play Service (New York, NY), 1969.

Sweet Eros and Witness: Two One-Act Plays (also see below), Dramatists Play Service (New York, NY), 1969.

Cuba Si!, Bringing It All Back Home, Last Gasps: Three Plays(contains *Cuba Si!; Bringing It All Back Home,*[one-act], first produced Off-Broadway at La Mama Experimental Theatre Club, 1969; and *Last Gasps*), Dramatists Play Service (New York, NY), 1970.

Where Has Tommy Flowers Gone?: A Play (also see below; first produced in New Haven, CT, at Yale University Theater, January 7, 1971; produced Off-Broadway at Eastside Playhouse, October 7, 1971), Dramatists Play Service (New York, NY), 1972.

Bad Habits (also see below; two one-acts; contains *Ravenswood* and *Dunelawn;* first produced in East Hampton, NY, at John Drew Theatre, 1971; produced on Broadway at Booth Theatre, May 5, 1974), Dramatists Play Service (New York, NY), 1974.

Let It Bleed, produced as part of *City Stops,* New York, NY, 1972.

Whiskey (also see below; one-act; first produced Off-Broadway at St. Clement's Church, April 29, 1973), Dramatists Play Service (New York, NY), 1973.

The Tubs, first produced in New Haven at Yale University Theater, January, 1974, revised version produced as *The Ritz* (also see below), first produced on Broadway at Longacre Theatre, January 20, 1975.

The Golden Age, produced in New York, NY, 1975.

The Ritz and Other Plays (contains *The Ritz, Where Has Tommy Flowers Gone?, Bad Habits, And Things That Go Bump in the Night, Whiskey,*and *Bringing It All Back Home*), Dodd (New York, NY), 1977.

Broadway, Broadway, produced in East Hampton, NY, 1979.

The Lisbon Traviata (broadcast, 1979; produced in New York, NY, 1985), Dramatists Play Service (New York, NY), 1986.

It's Only a Play: A Comedy (produced in New York, NY, 1982), Dramatists Play Service (New York, NY), 1986.

(Author of book for musical) *The Rink: A New Musical,* music by John Kander (produced in New York, NY, 1984), Samuel French (New York, NY), 1985.

Frankie and Johnny in the Claire de Lune (produced in New York, NY, 1987), Plume (New York, NY), 1990.

Faith, published in *Faith, Hope, and Charity* (produced in New York, NY, 1988), Dramatists Play Service (New York, NY), 1989.

Prelude and Liebstod, produced in New York, NY, 1989.

Up in Saratoga, produced in San Diego, CA, 1989.

(Author of book for musical) *Kiss of the Spider Woman* (adaptation of the novel by Manuel Puig, music by John Kander, lyrics by Fred Ebb, first produced in Purchase, New York, NY, 1990; produced on Broadway, May, 1993), Samuel French (New York, NY), 1997.

Three Plays (contains *The Lisbon Traviata, Frankie and Johnny in the Claire de Lune,* and *It's Only a Play*), New American Library (New York, NY), 1990.

Preludes, Fugues and Rifts, 1991.

Lips Together, Teeth Apart (first produced Off-Broadway at the Manhattan Theatre Club, May 28, 1991), Plume/Penguin (New York, NY), 1992.

A Perfect Ganesh (first produced Off-Broadway at the Manhattan Theatre Club, June 4, 1993), Dramatists Play Service (New York, NY), 1994.

Love! Valour! Compassion! (first produced Off-Broadway at the Manhattan Theatre Club, November 1, 1994; produced on Broadway at the Walter Kerr Theatre, January 20, 1995), Dramatists Play Service (New York, NY), 1995.

Terrence McNally: Fifteen Short Plays, Smith and Kraus (Newbury, VT), 1994.

You and Hugh (a musical for children), music by Robert Kapilow, produced in New York, NY, November 13, 1994.

Love! Valour! Compassion! and A Perfect Ganesh: Two Plays, Plume (New York, NY), 1995.

Andre's Mother and Other Short Plays, Dramatists Play Service (New York, NY), 1995.
Master Class (first produced on Broadway at the Golden Theater, November 5, 1995), Plume (New York, NY), 1996.
Dusk (one-act; produced as part of *By the Sea, by the Sea, by the Beautiful Sea*), Manhattan Theatre Club, June, 1996.
Ragtime, 1997.
Corpus Christi, Grove Press (New York, NY), 1998.
Dead Man Walking (musical adaptation of the book by Sr. Helen Prejean), produced in San Francisco at the War Memorial Opera House, October, 2000.
The Full Monty (stage adaptation of Simon Beaufoy's screenplay), first produced on Broadway at the Eugene O'Neill Theater, October 26, 2000.
The Visit, produced in Chicago at Goodman Theater, October, 2001.
The Stendhal Syndrome, produced in New York, NY at the Elysabeth Kleinhans Theater Center, February, 2004.

SCREENPLAYS

The Ritz (based on play of the same title), Warner Bros., 1977.
(And co-producer) *Earth Girls Are Easy,* Vestron, 1989.
Frankie and Johnny (based on play *Frankie and Johnny in the Claire de Lune*), Paramount, 1991.
Love! Valor! Compassion! (based on play of same title), 1994.

TELEVISION PLAYS

Botticelli, 1968.
Last Gasps, 1969.
(Adapter) John Cheever, *The 5:48,* Public Broadcasting Service (PBS), 1979.
Mama Malone (series), 1983.
Andre's Mother (American Playhouse series), PBS, 1990.

OTHER

Kava: Nature's Answer to Stress, Anxiety, and Insomnia, Prima Health (Rocklin, CA), 1998.
A Man of No Importance (musical; based on film of same title), with new music by Stephen Flaherty, first produced at the Mitzi E. Newhouse Theater at Lincoln Center in New York, October 10, 2002.
At the Statue of Venus (one-woman opera), with composer Jake Heggie, first produced at Opera Colorado in Denver, September 10, 2005.

ADAPTATIONS: Kiss of the Spider Woman was adapted for film in 1985, directed by Hector Babenco, starring William Hurt and Raul Julia.

McNally wrote the book for *Chita Rivera: The Dancer's Life,* a musical expected to open on Broadway at the Schoenfeld Theater, 2005.

SIDELIGHTS: Terrence McNally is known as one of the pillars of contemporary American theater. Discussing McNally with a writer for *Vogue* magazine, playwright William Finn was quoted as saying: "What I think is most extraordinary about him is the way he's made a career. His early things were really entertaining, but he's become an artist, and he's a real role model for playwrights. He's gotten better. Unlike most people, he saved his best for last." The image of McNally as a seasoned veteran of the theater, producing better and better plays while helping along rookie writers through example and mentorship is fitting. McNally wrote his first play, *The Lady of the Camellias,* in 1963, when he was in his early twenties. Since then he has continued to achieve increasing critical and popular success, as well as serving the theater world by serving as vice president of the Dramatists Guild and helping to launch a playwriting department at the Juilliard School. In between, his own work has steadily achieved more and more critical and popular success, including multiple Tony Awards.

Bad Habits, consisting of two one-act skits (*Ravenswood* and *Dunelawn*), each of which takes place in a sanitarium, contains "non-stop hilarity" which is derived from the author's "amused fascination with obsessive behavior," according to *Cue*'s Marilyn Stasio. "Although both plays are casually structured," she noted, "the character satire is dead-on accurate, and for all its zaniness has a niceness of logical clarity that is akin to classical farce."

Bad Habits prompted *Nation* reviewer Harold Clurman to declare that "Terrence McNally is one of the most adept practitioners of the comedy of insult. . . . Both plays [in *Bad Habits*] aim their shafts at institutions for the treatment of psychological disturbances—'encounter groups.' . . . [They] are spoofs and at times quite funny. . . . But there is no real criticism in them: the grotesquerie of the jokes supersedes all. These, in turn, are based on a strain of generalized dislike. . . . We laugh to free ourselves from what is implied."

New Yorker contributor Edith Oliver characterized *Ravenswood*as "virtually plotless. It is a mosaic of edged funny lines that, however far out, always belong to the characters who speak them and to nobody else. The playwright does go overboard from time to time—he is a little too clever, in the British, pejorative sense—but that, I suppose, is the price of his fertile, pell-mell imagination. *Ravenswood* is vintage McNally; *Dunelawn* is not quite . . . but a lot of it is very funny all the same. . . . There are other spots, though, that seem forced or somewhat off-key or just catty."

John Simon of *New York* noted that McNally is one of just a few playwrights who has enough courage to be truly nasty, and felt that "both *Ravenswood* and *Dunelawn* go on a bit too long, and in both McNally succumbs to his chronic weakness, the inability to find the right ending. [Nevertheless, this is McNally] at his sick, mean, absurd yet purposive best, vicious crack topping vicious crack in the most demurely trotted-out fashion. . . . You can call these plays unwholesome, inhuman—whatever you like—but not undazzling or unfunny."

The Ritz, a play *Time* described as "a bedlam of straight-gay confrontations" between visitors to a homosexual bathhouse, is also a fairly typical McNally play. Stasio called it "a classic farce in modern (un)dress. . . . Instead of drawing rooms and ladies' boudoirs, the scene is a male bathhouse; and the inevitable philandering husband . . . dallies with boys instead of dollies. But the structural mechanics are classical—mistaken identity, chase scenes, a network of doors to open and slam." Though she felt that "McNally's humor is genuine and often original," she concluded that "its farce outlets just aren't sufficiently mathematical, subtle, or imaginative to sustain what is still a very bright idea."

Six of McNally's plays reached New York stages in the 1980s. Among them was *The Lisbon Traviata,* a full-length tragic comedy about two gay men obsessed with the opera diva Maria Callas and, more particularly, an obscure pirated recording of the opera *La Traviata* performed by Callas in Lisbon. The first act of the play is comic, and set in the rich, baroque-style apartment of Mendy, an eccentric opera buff, once married, who admits, "Callas was named in my divorce for alienation of affections." The second, more serious, act takes place in the apartment of Stephen, Mendy's Callas cohort, who returns home to find his lover with another, younger, man. The play ends violently.

Critics found the bifurcated structure somewhat troubling, but nevertheless praised McNally's characterization and dialogue. Writing for the *New York Times,* Mel Gussow observed, "In *The Lisbon Traviata* Terrence McNally has written the theatrical equivalent of an operatic double bill—an opera bouffe followed by a tragic denouement." Gussow admired the playwright's grasp of his subject, stating, "One does not have to be a music critic to appreciate Mr. McNally's wit and his encyclopedic knowledge of the art form [opera] under scrutiny." The *Variety* reviewer asked the reader to "imagine a revival of the first act of *The Boys in the Band* and the last of *Who's Afraid of Virginia Woolf?* and you'll have a sense of the dual artistic personality of *The Lisbon Traviata.* Terrence McNally's new play is a sort of chiaroscuro study of gay obsessions and relationships. The funny first half is very funny indeed, but the somber second act doesn't work."

McNally's 1987 romantic comedy, *Frankie and Johnny in the Clair de Lune,* is, according to the *New Yorker*'s Terrence Rafferty, "a long sparring match, a comic clash between sharply opposed attitudes toward romantic love—Johnny's let's-do-it optimism versus Frankie's stubborn, defensive pessimism." Frankie is a waitress in a New York coffee shop where Johnny tends the grill. After a quick date that has ended with the two of them in Frankie's bed, Johnny tries every imaginable ploy to convince her they are meant for one another. Rafferty noted, "He bombards her with charm, jokes, romantic rhetoric, quotations from Shakespeare, autobiographical pathos, beautiful music, and heartfelt (though not terribly rigorous) philosophizing. He's the most eclectic and exhausting suitor imaginable, and he's too much for Frankie, who's determined not to expose herself to the pain and uncertainty of a serious relationship." In the end, Frankie and Johnny's future is left uncertain, though in the final act of brushing their teeth together there rests some hope for domesticity.

Following the popular stage version, McNally helped turn his play into simply *Frankie and Johnny,* a motion picture starring Al Pacino and Michelle Pfeiffer. *Time*'s David Denby found the film to be "no more than a bittersweet valentine to a man who's desperate for love and a woman who's afraid of it, but it's been made with so much sympathy, delicacy, and true intelligence that it's a triumph of sorts—a gallantly hopeful commercial comedy about love in the age of AIDS and the VCR."

The momentum McNally was building through the eighties swung him solidly into the nineties with a string of successes. In 1991 *Lips Together, Teeth Apart* opened at the Manhattan Theatre Club (MTC), home of several of McNally's first-nighters before they headed to Broadway houses. The play concerns two affluent couples spending a Fourth of July weekend at the Fire Island beach house left to one of the women by her brother who died of AIDS. The setting raises many troubling issues for the group, including the potential failure of their marriages, their feelings of homophobia, and the capriciousness of death.

Reviewing the play for the *New York Times,* Frank Rich proclaimed, "The bright wit that has always marked Mr. McNally's writing and the wrenching sorrow that has lately invaded it are blended deftly throughout three concurrently funny and melancholy acts. The evening's moods are as far-ranging as its allusions to *A Star Is Born* and Virginia Woolf and as changeable as its incidental score, which runs from the show-biz cacophony of [the Broadway musical] *Gypsy* to the serenity of [Wolfgang Mozart's opera] *Cosi Fan Tutte.*"

Death looms over McNally's next musical collaboration. In 1992 *Kiss of the Spider Woman,* a musical based on Manuel Puig's novel of the same name, premiered in London to rave reviews. It is the story of two men sharing a prison cell in an unnamed Latin-American country. Molina is a homosexual window dresser arrested for attempting to molest a young man. He is imprisoned with Valentin, a revolutionary jailed for trying to overthrow his country's oppressive regime. Against a backdrop of beating, torture, and murder the men learn to support one another. Molina relies on his fantasies of Aurora, a famous movie actress. He recounts her roles to Valentin in their darkest hours and Aurora, also known as the Spider Woman, joins the men in their cell, dancing and singing and luring them dreamily away from their nightmarish reality.

In *Time,* William A. Henry III called *Kiss of the Spider Woman* "the most rousing and moving musical to reach the West End since *Miss Saigon.*" Edith Oliver admitted in the *New Yorker,* "To burst into tears at a musical just isn't done, but I confess that I did at *Kiss of the Spider Woman,* because of the beautiful performance of Brent Carver, as a homosexual window dresser . . . and because of the distinguished script, by Terrence McNally." For his script, McNally was awarded the Tony Award for best book of a musical in 1993.

The 1993-94 theater season also saw two more McNally premieres at the Manhattan Theatre Club. *A Perfect Ganesh,* the story of two middle-aged Connecticut women touring India under the protectorship of the Hindu god Ganesha, and *Love! Valour! Compassion!,* an account of the lives and relationships of eight gay men who holiday at an upstate New York country house, were each successfully staged. Knowing he has that kind of strong production support affects McNally's writing. In a preface to the published version of these plays, the author confessed, "I wouldn't be a playwright today if it weren't for the regional theater. My regional theater is the Manhattan Theatre Club. I'm a regional theater playwright who just happens to live in New York. Without the unconditional love of MTC . . . these two plays would never have been written. Knowing that they are committed to me as a writer and not as a playwright who is expected to provide them with 'hits' has given me the confidence to write each play as I wanted, not what I think *they* wanted based on expectations from the last play."

Of the two plays, *Love! Valour! Compassion!* met with greater success. It transferred to the Walter Kerr Theatre on Broadway and won the Tony Award for best play in 1995. Still, reviews were mixed. In the *Nation,* David Kaufman lauded the play, saying, "For the ways in which it's told no less than for what it has to say, *Love! Valour! Compassion!* is a remarkably Chekhovian work—which is to say vital and capacious, extremely natural yet poetic and crafted at the same time." John Simon, however, felt the venture was too formulaic. In *New York* magazine he complained, "I am struck . . . by the manipulativeness and meretriciousness of the enterprise, what with its eyedropper-calculated dosage of campy bitchiness, homosexual self-pity, and male nudity in artful rotation. . . . With the obligatory references to AIDS introduced at cannily calibrated distances from one another, and the trusty cliches given each its dollop of McNally wit . . . everything moves forward with the spontaneity of the changing of the guard at Buckingham Palace."

In 1996 McNally achieved a rare feat: *Master Class,* his biographical play about the legendary opera diva Maria Callas, won him a Tony Award for best play for the second year in a row. On the surface *Master Class* depicts a series of master voice classes Callas conducted at Juilliard in the early seventies, at the end of her career. Three students—two sopranos and a tenor—step forward from the audience to learn from the celebrated master. Underneath, however, the play probes the artist's relationship to art—humankind's need for creative expression and the costs and rewards that accompany a lifetime of artistic pursuit.

In *Newsweek,* Jack Kroll announced, "McNally's play is a profile in courage." Vince Canby wrote in the *New*

York Times, "Mr. McNally's achievement has been to take the legendary Callas, the somewhat camp Judy Garland figure of grand opera, and restore to the woman a sense of her passion and intelligence and the singularity of her gifts." However, another *Times* reviewer, Margo Jefferson, felt McNally's depiction of the singer does not rise above caricature. "Mr. McNally wrote expressively and intensely about Callas fans in *The Lisbon Traviata,*" she noted, "Why is he writing so glibly about Callas herself? It seems that he does fans better than he does artists."

McNally had some success with two musicals adapted from films, *Dead Man Walking* and *The Full Monty.* The former is based on the memoir of Sister Helen Prejean, a nun assigned as the spiritual counselor to a murderer on death row in Louisiana. In McNally's musical version, the focus is less on the murderer's journey from denial to repentance than it is on the ways in which Sister Prejean is transformed by her association with Joseph de Rocher, the murderer. According to *Time* reviewer Terry Teachout, "She has grown immeasurably by opera's end through her unflinching acceptance of the implications of De Rocher's monstrous act." *The Full Monty* was a much more light-hearted story, concerning a group of unemployed steelworkers who try to raise money by working as strippers.

McNally stirred up considerable controversy in 2001 with his retelling of the Gospel, set in Corpus Christi, Texas during the 1950s. In *Corpus Christi,* the Christ figure, renamed Joshua, and all his disciples are gay characters in a hostile environment. Joshua dies, ultimately, "for both his sexuality and his message of universal love and tolerance," stated Ed Kaufman in *Hollywood Reporter.* Kaufman termed the musical "brash, bold and thoughtful" and commented on McNally's adept touch at blending "onstage shtick with sentiment, the raunchy with the religious." Other critics were put off by what they perceived as McNally's sermonizing. *Corpus Christi* "is about McNally bending the story of Christ tale to advance his view that homosexuals are endlessly persecuted," claimed Evan Henerson in the Los Angeles *Daily News.* Madeleine Shaner concurred in *Back Stage West* that *Corpus Christi* is "not a very good play; it's a mere in-your-face gay Sunday-school version of the Bible story, with the motivation, the history, the activism, the courageous rebellion of the chosen Messiah left out." A more favorable opinion was expressed by Philip Brandes, who advised in *Los Angeles Time* that those "willing to contemplate the issues raised by the play (and overlook its at times considerable pretensions) will find some powerful depictions of the very real alienation and prejudice endured by social outcasts."

Throughout his decades as a professional playwright McNally has displayed an unwavering commitment to the theater. "The theatre is something to give your life to," McNally related to Richard Alleman in *Vogue.* "It gives your life value and joy. . . . Just stick it out like I did. . . . I don't think we in the theatre can change the world, but I think we can leave it a better and a different place that it was if we hadn't written our plays and acted in them. It's exciting, too—that you have to be there. It's like a good party. You can't hear about a party. You want to be at the party. And the theatre's the party I want to be at."

BIOGRAPHICAL AND CRITICAL SOURCES:

BOOKS

Contemporary American Dramatists, St. James Press (Detroit, MI), 1994.

Contemporary Dramatists, 5th edition, St. James Press (Farmington Hills, MI), 1999.

Contemporary Literary Criticism, Thomson Gale (Detroit, MI), Volume 4, 1975, Volume 7, 1977, Volume 41, 1987.

Dictionary of Literary Biography, Volume 7: *Twentieth-Century American Dramatists,* Thomson Gale (Detroit, MI), 1981.

Gay and Lesbian Literature, St. James Press (Detroit, MI), 1994.

PERIODICALS

American Theatre, March, 1995, pp. 12-17; September, 2001, Rebecca Paller, review of *The Full Monty,* p. 92.

Back Stage, November 10, 2000, Irene Backalenick, review of *The Full Monty,* p. 48; May 18, 2001, Mike Salinas, "Hammerstein Award to McNally," p. 6.

Back Stage West, August 23, 2001, Madeleine Shaner, review of *Corpus Christi,* p. 15.

Chicago Tribune, October 4, 2001, Sid Smith, review of *The Visit.*

Cue, January 14, 1974; February 11, 1974.

Daily News (Los Angeles, CA), August 24, 2001, Evan Henerson, review of *Corpus Christi,* p. L17.

Hollywood Reporter, September 7, 2001, Ed Kaufman, review of *Corpus Christi,* p. 42.

Los Angeles Times, August 24, 2001, Philip Brandes, review of *Corpus Christi,* p. F25.

Nation, March 2, 1974; December 19, 1994, pp. 774-776.

New Republic, March 1, 1975; November 11, 1991, pp. 30-31; August 23, 1993, pp. 31-33; April 3, 1995, pp. 30-32.

Newsweek, February 10, 1975; November 13, 1995, p. 85.

New York, October 25, 1971; February 18, 1974; May 27, 1974; February 3, 1975; October 14, 1991, p. 84; May 17, 1993, p. 103; February 27, 1995, pp. 115-117.

New Yorker, February 18, 1974; February 3, 1975; October 21, 1991, pp. 125-128; May 24, 1993, p. 104; July 12, 1993, p. 95; November 14, 1994, pp. 129-131; November 27, 1995, pp. 109-111.

New York Post, October 17, 2001, "In the Wings," p. 77.

New York Times, January 24, 1971; December 8, 1971; July 6, 1978; October 28, 1987, p. C23; June 2, 1988, p. C23; December 21, 1988, p. C32; June 7, 1989, p. C21; June 26, 1991, pp. C11, C13; November 6, 1995, pp. C11, C13; November 12, 1995, pp. 5, 36; June 1, 1996, p. 12; May 20, 2001, Jerry Tallmer, "A Couple of Regular Guys Bonding, Onstage and Off," p. 11.

New York Times Book Review, August 23, 1998, review of *Almost Home,* p. 16.

Time, October 18, 1971; February 3, 1975; November 30, 1992, p. 78; July 12, 1993, p. 60; August 23, 1993, p. 73; October 23, 2000, Terry Teachout, review of *Dead Man Walking,* p. 84.

Variety, October 20, 1971; October 30, 2000, Charles Isherwood, review of *The Full Monty,* p. 32.

Vogue, May, 1995, pp. 152, 154.

* * *

McPHEE, John 1931-
(John Angus McPhee)

PERSONAL: Born March 8, 1931, in Princeton, NJ; son of Harry Roemer (a physician for Princeton University athletes) and Mary (Ziegler) McPhee; married Pryde Brown, March 16, 1957 (marriage ended); married Yolanda Whitman (a horticulturist), March 8, 1972; children: (first marriage) Laura, Sarah, Jenny, Martha; (stepchildren) Cole, Andrew, Katherine, Vanessa Harrop. *Education:* Princeton University, A.B., 1953; graduate study at Cambridge University, 1953-54.

ADDRESSES: Home—Drake's Corner Rd., Princeton, NJ 08540. *Office*—c/o New Yorker, 25 West 43rd St., New York, NY 10036; c/o Farrar, Straus and Giroux, 19 Union Square West, New York, NY 10003.

CAREER: Author. Playwright for "Robert Montgomery Presents" television show, 1955-57; *Time* magazine, New York, NY, associate editor, 1957-64; *New Yorker* magazine, New York, NY, staff writer, 1964—; Princeton University, Princeton, NJ, Ferris Professor of Journalism, 1975—.

MEMBER: Geological Society of America (fellow).

AWARDS, HONORS: Award in Literature, American Academy and Institute of Arts and Letters, 1977; American Association of Petroleum Geologists Journalism Award, 1982, 1986; Woodrow Wilson Award, Princeton University, 1982; John Wesley Powell Award, United States Geological Survey, 1988; John Burroughs Medal, 1990; Walton Sullivan Award, American Geophysical Union, 1993; Litt.D., Bates College, 1978, Colby College, 1978, Williams College, 1979, University of Alaska, 1980, College of William and Mary, 1988, and Sc.D. Rutgers University, 1988, and Maine Maritime Academy, 1992; Pulitzer Prize, nonfiction, 1999, for *Annals of the Former World.*

WRITINGS:

A Sense of Where You Are: A Profile of William Warren Bradley, Farrar, Straus and Giroux, (New York, NY), 1965.

The Headmaster: Frank L. Boyden of Deerfield, Farrar, Straus and Giroux (New York, NY), 1966.

Oranges, Farrar, Straus and Giroux, (New York, NY), 1967.

The Pine Barrens, Farrar, Straus and Giroux (New York, NY), 1968.

A Roomful of Hovings and Other Profiles (collection), Farrar, Straus and Giroux (New York, NY), 1969.

The Crofter and the Laird, Farrar, Straus and Giroux (New York, NY), 1969.

Levels of the Game, Farrar, Straus and Giroux (New York, NY), 1970.

Encounters with the Archdruid (also see below), Farrar, Straus and Giroux (New York, NY), 1972.

Wimbledon: A Celebration, photographs by Alfred Eisenstaedt, Viking (New York City), 1972.

The Deltoid Pumpkin Seed, Farrar, Straus and Giroux (New York, NY), 1973.

The Curve of Binding Energy, Farrar, Straus and Giroux (New York, NY), 1974.

Pieces of the Frame (collection), Farrar, Straus and Giroux (New York, NY), 1975.

The Survival of the Bark Canoe, Farrar, Straus and Giroux (New York, NY), 1975.

The John McPhee Reader, edited by William Howarth, Farrar, Straus and Giroux (New York, NY), 1977, revised edition published as *The Second John McPhee Reader,* edited by David Remnick and Patricia Strachan, 1996.

Coming into the Country, Farrar, Straus and Giroux (New York, NY), 1977.

Giving Good Weight (collection), Farrar, Straus and Giroux (New York, NY), 1979.

(With Rowell Galen) *Alaska: Images of the Country,* Sierra (California), 1981.

Basin and Range (also see below), Farrar, Straus and Giroux (New York, NY), 1981.

In Suspect Terrain (also see below), Farrar, Straus and Giroux (New York, NY), 1983.

Heirs of General Practice, Farrar, Straus and Giroux (New York, NY), 1984.

Annals of the Former World (contains *Basin and Range* and *In Suspect Terrain*), two volumes, Farrar, Straus and Giroux (New York, NY), 1984.

La Place de la Concorde Suisse, Farrar, Straus and Giroux (New York, NY), 1984.

Table of Contents (collection), Farrar, Straus and Giroux (New York, NY), 1985.

Rising from the Plains (also see below), Farrar, Straus and Giroux (New York, NY), 1986.

Outcroppings (includes portions of *Encounters with the Archdruid, Basin and Range,* and *Rising from the Plains*), photographs by Tom Till, Peregrine Smith (Layton, UT), 1988.

The Control of Nature, Farrar, Straus and Giroux (New York, NY), 1989.

Looking for a Ship, Farrar, Straus and Giroux (New York, NY), 1990.

Assembling California, Farrar, Straus and Giroux (New York, NY), 1993.

The Ransom of Russian Art, Farrar, Straus and Giroux (New York, NY), 1994.

Irons in the Fire, Farrar, Straus and Giroux (New York, NY), 1997.

(Editor, with Carol Rigolot) *The Princeton Anthology of Writing: Favorite Pieces by the Ferris/McGraw Writers at Princeton University,* Princeton University Press (Princeton, NJ), 2001.

The Founding Fish, Farrar, Straus and Giroux (New York, NY), 2002.

SIDELIGHTS: John McPhee is an acclaimed journalist and writer of nonfiction works covering an incredible variety of topics. "Whatever his subject matter, McPhee finds a way to make it interesting and artistic," asserted Norman Sims in *Dictionary of Literary Biography.* Sims further declared that "his beautifully articulated structures, clear prose, and participatory voice have become a model for other literary journalists. . . . [His] work thrives on narrative and characterization. . . . [He] proves the value of what is often considered ordinary life, using writing techniques and a style that are far from ordinary."

Many critics agree that the appeal of McPhee's nonfiction books, mostly collections of his *New Yorker* articles, lies in their offbeat subject matter. "Sometimes it seems that McPhee deliberately chooses unpromising subjects, just to show what he can do with them," remarked *New Republic* reviewer Richard Horwich. Sims called McPhee's range of subjects "unprecedented" in its variety and noted that it includes "basketball and tennis, art and airplanes, the New Jersey Pine Barrens and the wilderness of Alaska, atomic energy and birchbark canoes, oranges and farmers, the Swiss Army and United States Army Corps of Engineers, and the control of nature and the scientific revolution in plate tectonics that created modern geology."

One of the author's early books, *Oranges,* illustrates Horwich's point. The volume delves into the history, growth cycles, and manufacture of that one citrus fruit. Another work, *The Survival of the Bark Canoe,* is "the best book on bark canoes," according to a *Time* critic, who added, "It is part shop manual, part history, and part unforgettable-character sketch." The book introduces canoemaker Henri Vaillencourt, and "by the time we enter [Vaillencourt's] obsession, we are drawn irresistibly to the tapering of thwarts, the laminating of stempieces, the goring of bark," said Christopher Lehmann-Haupt in *New York Times.*

McPhee is regarded by many as a gifted liaison between the specialist and the lay reader. He shows a "pleasantly flexible technique, well-mannered and accommodating," as Michiko Kakutani of *New York Times Book Review* explained it. "Elegant without being elaborate, casual but never flippant, the prose always serves the material at hand, and combined with an obsession for detail . . . it enables [the author] to translate for the layman the mysteries that preoccupy professionals, be they athletes or engineers. He can reveal character in the description of a basketball toss, discover literary metaphors in the movement of subatomic particles," wrote Kakutani.

Many critics believe one of McPhee's strongest works is *Coming into the Country,* in which the author presents an insider's view of one of America's last frontiers—Alaska. The volume consists of "three lengthy bulletins" about Alaska, according to *Time* critic Paul Gray. The first concerns "a canoe trip that McPhee and four companions took down an unspoiled river in the northwestern reaches of the state, well above the Arctic Circle. [In the] second, McPhee tells of a helicopter ride with a committee looking for a site on which to build a new state capital. The last and longest section covers some wintry months spent in Eagle, a tiny settlement on the Yukon river."

Edward Hoagland, who characterized McPhee as no "risk-taker" in his early books, declared in a *New York Times Book Review* of *Coming into the Country* that "he made his will, took the gambit; and in so doing, he introduced a new generosity of tempo to his work, a leisurely artfulness of organization he has not had before." Hoagland further noted that his "main objection to [McPhee's] other books has been that he was too aloof with the reader about himself—almost neurotically so—and not aloof enough about some of the subjects of his pieces, over-admiring them, taking them just at their word."

While *Atlantic* critic Benjamin DeMott enjoyed the author's self-portrait of "his own embarrassments as a city man ravished by the woods but still dependent upon comforts," he saw a greater merit in *Coming into the Country:* "Not the least achievement of [the book] is that, in eschewing formulas, it manages simultaneously to represent fairly the positions of the parties in conflict—developers, conservationists, renegade individualists—and to show forth the implications, for human society, of the loss of the ground on which the dream of 'lighting out for The Territory' has immemorially been based." What the reader gains from this work, concluded DeMott, is a sense that "what is really in view in *Coming into the Country* is a matter not usually met in works of reportage—nothing less than the nature of the human condition."

McPhee has also produced several books on American geology, including *Basin and Range* and *In Suspect Terrain. Basin and Range* begins with McPhee taking "a deceptively simple cross-country trip: Interstate 80," said *Los Angeles Times* critic Carolyn See. The author is accompanied by an accomplished geologist who points out the vast history of various western rock formations, and "the ideas do tumble out—ideas about how ranges and basins were formed, about how silver got deposited in those Nevada bonanzas and how the Great Salt Lakes came to be both salty and great," according to Lehmann-Haupt in another *New York Times* article.

"The descriptions of geologists at work are sympathetic and convincing," wrote C. Vita-Finzi in *Times Literary Supplement.* "The digressions into the language and jargon of the subject should prove chastening to its practitioners." Among the theories discussed in *Basin and Range* is one suggesting that moving segments of the earth, both on land and in the oceans, will eventually cause the west coast of America to break off into the Pacific, making California an island, as Evan Connell explained in a *Washington Post Book World* review. "Metaphorically, of course, many people believe this already has happened." McPhee, Connell continued, "discusses such matters easily. His tone is affable, his meandering appropriate, and the tutorial intent of *Basin and Range* is commendable—for surely nobody could measure the width or depth of our ignorance."

In Suspect Terrain "takes its title from the geologists' phrase for country whose history, as recorded in the rocks, is ambiguous or obscure," Wallace Stegner wrote in a *Los Angeles Times Book Review* piece. McPhee's follow-up to *Basin and Range* explores the geological relationships in urban areas, including a study of the geology of Brooklyn. "A travelogue across country and through time, [*In Suspect Terrain*] is a most instructive book," found Stegner. And while Kakutani of the *New York Times Book Review* felt that "the presence of a shaping, interpretive sensibility . . . 'would have infused [the book with] a measure of welcome warmth," *Detroit News* reviewer Lisa Schwarzbaum maintained that the author's "expertise brings us great chunks of information and explication about subjects not always immediately accessible or even fascinating, in a way that makes them both."

According to T.H. Watkins of *Washington Post Book World,* McPhee's *Basin and Range, In Suspect Terrain, Rising from the Plains,* and *Assembling California* form a "four-volume literary pilgrimage" in which each book is "an exploration of theories, evidences and effects of plate tectonics—[a] science that holds that the surface of the earth is made up of crustal plates that are in constant motion." McPhee's mentor in *Assembling California,* Eldridge Moores, is a world-class tectonicist who "makes an imaginative and articulate guide as McPhee takes a look at California as the definitive expression of plate tectonics." Watkins referred to the book as "vintage McPhee, swift, lucid, authoritative stuff produced with a reporter's sure eye and a writer's love of language."

A chance encounter on a train with Norton Dodge led McPhee to write about the economics professor's unusual art collection. *The Ransom of Russian Art* relates how Dodge came to own 9,000 pieces of art by 600 dissident Soviet artists, describes the Soviet persecution of artists from the mid-1950s to the end of the Communist era, and profiles painter Evgeny Rukhin and other artists. The book includes illustrations of many of the pieces of art. "Unfortunately, Mr. McPhee never alights on any one artist or idea for very long," commented Harlow Robinson in *New York Times Book Review.* "There is a jumpy, almost unfinished quality to the writing here, as though the author could not quite find the key either to Mr. Dodge or to the nonconformist art scene." "McPhee adopts what for him is an unusual stance as an investigative reporter," noted Sims, as he grills Dodge on his association with the CIA, asks about his smuggling activities, and questions where a college professor obtained the millions of dollars required for this enterprise.

From deciphering technological jargon to exploring the surface and depths of the earth, McPhee continues to elucidate his fascination and concern for the environment in *The Control of Nature,* a work comprised of three examples of the battles humans wage against the forces of nature. "What makes such complex, inherently dry subjects fascinating is McPhee himself," reported *Chicago Tribune* critic Kerry Luft. "A tireless researcher, he piles fact upon simile and explains the most intricate detail with metaphor." From a "tragic" Louisiana situation in which attempts are made to divert the Mississippi River, to the "comic opera" of attempts to save an Icelandic town from destruction by a flow of lava, "the narrative emulates the rhythms of the natural flows it describes, each time encountering another monument to human assertion or absurdity," remarked *New York Times Book Review* critic Stephen Pyne. "There is no single persona to represent either side. Almost everyone is implicated, and nearly everything is diffused." Pyne concluded that *The Control of Nature* "is a fascinating, if sometimes disjointed, report from three revealing battlefields in humanity's global war against nature."

McPhee may have won widespread acclaim for his nonfiction, but in a *New York Times Book Review* interview with Stephen Singular, he reveals that his early career interests included a variety of genres. "I wrote poems in college—rank imitations of Pope, Yeats, Housman, Eliot. My senior year I wrote a novel. . . . After college, I sat all day in a captain's chair up on 84th Street trying to write plays for live television." Discussing the inspiration for his articles, McPhee notes that "most of them originate when they strike an echo from my earlier experience, like *The Survival of the Bark Canoe.* When I was quite young, my father took me to a summer camp [where] our canoe trips were a big thing, and I dearly loved them. What you hope is that some subject will interest you and then you will have to deal with it on its own terms."

As for the criticism that his work does not include enough personal material, the author calls the charge "pointless. I'm not going to go out and write *Remembrance of Things Past.* You can't be all things. There are limitations everywhere you look . . . fundamentally, I'm a working journalist and I've got to go out and work." When questioned during a *Los Angeles Times* interview on the absence of moral judgments in his works, McPhee responded, "I want the judgments to be performed by the reader. There are some people who think that one ought to be more forceful in one's judgments and have an ax to grind. I don't want to grind axes in my writing. But I want to have plenty of axes out there for others to do their own grinding on."

In contrast, a critic for *Kirkus Reviews* noted a shift toward a more personal perspective in McPhee's *The Founding Fish.* The critic praised McPhee for first allowing the reader to see things from the fish's perspective, and then from McPhee's, "which is a surprise and a pleasure in a writer known more for his shadowy presence than for stepping into the spotlight." This book's subject matter is the *Alosa sapidissima,* commonly known as the American shad and one of the most primitive of all fish. These fish leave the ocean in hundreds of thousands each year to make their long, arduous journey up river to spawn. McPhee, a long-time angler of the fish (its name means "most savory") traces its history, its place in nature and—of all things—its place in American history: George Washington fed them to his starving soldiers at Valley Forge, and fished them commercially, catching 7,760 in 1771. The fish made a cameo appearance in the life of Henry David Thoreau, played a role in the murder of Lincoln by John Wilkes Booth, and, wrote a reviewer of the book for *Publishers Weekly,* "waylaid Confederate General Pickett in the defense of Richmond and hastened the end of the Civil War."

Donna Seaman wrote in *Booklist,* "McPhee is in great form here, as informative as always but also funny, unusually self-revealing, and quite passionate in his discussions of the dire effects dams have had on shad and rivers alike." *Kirkus Reviews* critic commented, "There isn't a dry patch in this story of a fish and its homewaters," and Bruce Tierney commented for *BookPage,* "It is to McPhee's credit that he can take such an arcane topic and make it interesting, even compelling, to the casual reader. He provides sufficient data to suit the scientists among his readers, while writing an easy conversational style."

Sims concluded, "McPhee's books and articles are regularly included as classics in anthologies of literary journalism. His structural innovation, spare and eloquent style of writing, understated voice, and ability to take on complex subjects and make sense of them for an uninitiated audience have ensured his position in the canon of the genre he has helped to establish."

BIOGRAPHICAL AND CRITICAL SOURCES:

BOOKS

Anderson, Chris, editor, *Literary Nonfiction: Theory, Criticism, Pedagogy,* Southern Illinois University Press (Carbondale, IL), 1989, p. 70.

Anderson, Chris, *Style As Argument: Contemporary American Nonfiction,* Southern Illinois University Press (Carbondale, IL), 1987.

Contemporary Literary Criticism, Volume 36, Thomson Gale (Detroit, MI), 1986.

Dictionary of Literary Biography, Volume 185: *American Literary Journalists, 1945-1995, First Series,* Thomson Gale (Detroit, MI), 1997.

Pearson, Michael, *John McPhee,* Twayne (New York, NY), 1997.

Sims, Norman, and Mark Kramer, editors, *Literary Journalism,* Ballantine (New York, NY), 1995, pp. 3-19.

Sims, Norman, editor, *The Literary Journalists,* Ballantine (New York, NY), 1984, pp. 3-25.

Sims, Norman, editor, *Literary Journalism in the Twentieth Century,* Oxford University Press (New York, NY), 1990, pp. 191-205, 206-227.

Weber, Ronald, editor, *The Literature of Fact: Literary Nonfiction in American Writing,* Ohio University Press (Athens, OH), 1980.

PERIODICALS

Atlantic, January, 1978.

Booklist, October 1, 1994, p. 186; September 1, 2002, Donna Seaman, review of *The Founding Fish,* p. 3.

Bulletin of Bibliography, January, 1981, pp. 45-51.

Chicago Tribune, April 19, 1984; August 27, 1989.

Chicago Tribune Book World, January 6, 1980; August 27, 1989, p. 7; September 16, 1990.

Creative Nonfiction, number 1, 1993, pp. 76-87.

Detroit News, July 12, 1981; March 13, 1983; May 13, 1984.

Kirkus Reviews, September 1, 1994, p. 1195; August 15, 2002, review of *The Founding Fish,* p. 1200.

Los Angeles Times, April 27, 1981; August 6, 1989.

Los Angeles Times Book Review, February 27, 1983; November 9, 1986; July 30, 1989; August 26, 1990.

Maine Times, November 1, 1985, pp. 14-16.

Nation, January 14, 1978.

New Republic, July 11, 1970; September 1, 1973; July 5, 1975; January 7, 1978.

New York Review of Books, March 23, 1978; May 14, 1981; March 2, 1995, pp. 10-13.

New York Times, March 8, 1967; November 2, 1969; July 13, 1973; July 9, 1974; June 18, 1975; November 27, 1975; January 11, 1976, section 11, pp. 20-21; November 25, 1977, section 1, p. 23; November 17, 1979; May 8, 1981; January 24, 1983; April 30, 1984; September 27, 1985.

New York Times Book Review, June 23, 1974; June 22, 1975; November 27, 1977, pp. 1, 48-51; November 18, 1979, pp. 3, 45; May 17, 1981; January 30, 1983; May 6, 1984; October 13, 1985; August 6, 1989, p. 1; December 18, 1994, p. 24.

Publishers Weekly, January 3, 1977, pp. 12-13; July 23, 2001, review of *The Princeton Anthology of Writing,* p. 66; August 26, 2002, review of *The Founding Fish,* p. 57.

Saturday Review, January 22, 1977; April, 1981.

Sewanee Review, fall, 1988, pp. 633-644.

Sierra, October, 1978, pp. 61-63; May-June, 1990, pp. 50-55, 92, 96.

Technical Communication, November, 1987, p. 296.

Time, June 10, 1974; December 15, 1975; December 5, 1977; January 31, 1983.

Times Literary Supplement, February 18, 1983; January 6, 1984; December 7, 1984.

Washington Post, March 19, 1978, pp. L1, L5-6; December 18, 1979.

Washington Post Book World, August 15, 1971; January 22, 1978; April 19, 1981; January 30, 1983; March 13, 1983; April 8, 1984; October 13, 1985; November 9, 1986; September 9, 1990; March 7, 1993; March 12, 1995, p. 13; March 3, 1996, p. 13.

ONLINE

BookPage Web site, http://www.bookpage.com/ (October 7, 2002), Bruce Tierney, "The Allure of an Elusive Fish," review of *The Founding Fish.*

John McPhee Home Page, http://www.johnmcphee.com/ (October 7, 2002).

McPHEE, John Angus
See McPHEE, John

* * *

McPHERSON, James Alan 1943-

PERSONAL: Born September 16, 1943, in Savannah, GA; son of James Allen and Mable (Smalls) McPherson. *Education:* Attended Morgan State University, 1963-64; Morris Brown College, B.A., 1965; Harvard University, LL.B., 1968; University of Iowa, M.F. A., 1969.

ADDRESSES: Office—Department of English, University of Iowa, Iowa City, IA 52242.

CAREER: University of Iowa, Iowa City, instructor in writing at Law School, 1968-69, instructor in Afro-American literature, 1969; University of California, Santa Cruz, faculty member, 1969-70; Morgan State University, Baltimore, MD, faculty member, 1975-76; University of Virginia, Charlottesville, faculty member, 1976-81; University of Iowa, Writers Workshop, Iowa City, professor, 1981—; *Double Take* magazine, editor, 1995—; Stanford University, Palo Alto, CA, behavioral studies fellow, 1997—.

MEMBER: Authors League of America, PEN, American Academy of Arts and Sciences, National Association for the Advancement of Colored People, American Civil Liberties Union.

AWARDS, HONORS: First prize, *Atlantic* short story contest, 1965, for "Gold Coast"; grant from Atlantic Monthly Press and Little, Brown, 1969; National Institute of Arts and Letters award in literature, 1970; Guggenheim fellow, 1972-73; Pulitzer Prize, 1978, for *Elbow Room: Stories;* MacArthur fellowship, 1981; Excellence in Technology award, University of Iowa, 1991; Best American Essays, 1990, 1993, 1994, 1995; Pushcart Prize, 1995.

WRITINGS:

Hue and Cry: Short Stories, Atlantic-Little, Brown (Boston, MA), 1969, reprinted, Ecco Press (New York, NY), 2001.

(Editor, with Miller Williams) *Railroad: Trains and Train People in American Culture,* Random House (New York, NY), 1976.

Elbow Room: Stories, Atlantic-Little, Brown (Boston, MA), 1977.

(Author of foreword) Breece D'J Pancake, *The Stories of Breece D'J Pancake,* Atlantic-Little, Brown (Boston, MA), 1983, reprinted, Little, Brown (Boston, MA), 2002.

Crabcakes: A Memoir, Simon & Schuster (New York, NY), 1998.

(Editor, with DeWitt Henry) *Fathering Daughters: Reflections by Men,* Beacon Press (Boston, MA), 1998.

A Region Not Home: Reflections from Exile, Simon & Schuster (New York, NY), 2000.

Work has been anthologized in books, including *Cutting Edges,* edited by J. Hicks, Holt (New York, NY), 1973; *Black Insights: Significant Literature by Afro-Americans, 1760 to the Present,* edited by Nick A. Ford, Wiley (New York, NY), 1976; *Book for Boston,* edited by Llewellyn Howland and Isabelle Storey, David Godine (Boston, MA), 1980; *Speaking for You,* edited by Kimberly W. Benson, Howard University Press, 1987; *A World Unsuspected,* edited by Alex Harris, Hill, NC], 1987; and *New Black Voices,* New American Library. Contributor to periodicals, including *Atlantic, Esquire, New York Times Magazine, Playboy, Reader's Digest,* and *Callaloo.* Contributing editor, *Atlantic,* beginning 1969; editor of special issue, *Iowa Review,* winter, 1984.

SIDELIGHTS: James Alan McPherson's stories of ordinary, working-class people, though often concerning African-American characters, are noted for their ability to confront universal human problems. "His standpoint," Robie Macauley explained in the *New York Times Book Review,* "[is] that of a writer and a black, but not that of a black writer. [McPherson] refused to let his fiction fall into any color-code or ethnic code." Because of this stance, McPherson's characters are more fully rounded than are those of more racially conscious writers. As Paul Bailey wrote in the *Observer Review* and quoted in *Contemporary Literary Criticism,* "The Negroes and whites [McPherson] describes always remain individual people—he never allows himself the luxury of turning them into Problems." Explaining his approach to the characters in his stories, McPherson was quoted by Patsy B. Perry of the *Dictionary of Literary Biography* as saying: "Certain of these people [my characters] happen to be black, and certain of them happen to be white; but I have tried to keep the color part of most of them far in the background, where these things should rightly be kept." McPherson has published two collections of short stories, *Hue and Cry: Short Stories* and *Elbow Room: Stories.* In 1978 he was awarded the Pulitzer Prize for fiction.

McPherson was born and raised in Savannah, Georgia, a city in which several cultures—including the French, Spanish, and Indian—have been uniquely blended. He cites this rich cultural heritage as a determining factor in his own ability to transcend racial barriers. The McPherson family also influenced his development of values. The author's father, at one time the only licensed black master electrician in Georgia, and his mother, a domestic in a white household, had important contacts in both the white and black communities. Through their efforts, McPherson obtained work as a grocery boy in a local supermarket and as a waiter on a train. These experiences formed the basis for several later stories. McPherson's train employment also allowed him to travel across the country. Perry noted that McPherson "affirms the importance of both white and black communities in his development as an individual and as a writer of humanistic ideas."

McPherson's writing career began in the 1960s while he was still attending law school. His story "Gold Coast" won first prize in a contest sponsored by the *Atlantic* magazine, which has gone on to play a pivotal role in McPherson's career. After earning a bachelor's degree, a law degree, and a master's degree in creative writing, McPherson became a contributing editor of the *Atlantic* in 1969. And the magazine, in conjunction with Little, Brown, also published his two collections of short stories.

McPherson's first collection, *Hue and Cry,* deals with characters whose lives are so desperate that they can only rage impotently against their situations. "The fact that these characters . . . ," wrote Perry, "know nothing else to do except to sink slowly into madness, scream unintelligibly, or seek refuge . . . provides reason enough for McPherson's hue and cry." A *Times Literary Supplement* critic pointed to the book's "mostly desperate, mostly black, mostly lost figures in the urban nightmare of violence, rage and bewilderment that is currently America."

Despite the grim nature of his stories, McPherson manages to depict the lives of his characters with sympathy and grace. Bailey allows that McPherson's "powers of observation and character-drawing are remarkable, displaying a mature novelist's understanding of the vagaries and inconsistencies of human affairs." Writing in *Harper's,* Irving Howe maintained that McPherson "possesses an ability some writers take decades to acquire, the ability to keep the right distance from the creatures of his imagination, not to get murkily involved and blot out his figures with vanity and fuss." Granville Hicks in the *Saturday Review* noted that McPherson "is acutely aware of the misery and injustice in the world, and he sympathizes deeply with the victims whether they are black or white."

Elbow Room, McPherson's second collection, won even more critical praise than its predecessor. Again concerned with characters in desperate situations, the stories of *Elbow Room* are nonetheless more optimistic than McPherson's earlier works, the characters more willing to struggle for some measure of success. They "engage in life's battles with integrity of mind and spirit," as Perry explains. This optimism is noted by several critics. Robert Phillips, reviewing the book for *Commonweal,* found the stories in *Elbow Room* to be "difficult struggles for survival, yet [McPherson's] sense of humor allows him to dwell on moments which otherwise might prove unbearable." Writing in *Newsweek,* Margo Jefferson called McPherson "an astute realist who knows how to turn the conflicts between individual personalities and the surrounding culture into artful and highly serious comedies of manners."

McPherson's ability to create believable characters, and his focus on the underlying humanity of all his characters, has been praised by such critics as Phillips. McPherson's stories, Phillips maintained, "ultimately become not so much about the black condition as the human condition. . . . *Elbow Room* is a book of singular achievement." Macauley explained that McPherson has been able "to look beneath skin color and cliches of attitude into the hearts of his characters. . . . This is a fairly rare ability in American fiction." A *New Yorker* reviewer listed several other characteristics of McPherson's stories that are worthy of attention, calling him "one of those rare writers who can tell a story, describe shadings of character, and make sociological observations with equal subtlety."

McPherson broke a silence of nearly twenty years in 1998 with publication of *Crabcakes: A Memoir,* "a profoundly personal tale of displacement and discovery that is poetic and universal," according to a writer for *Kirkus Reviews.* Roy Hoffman in the *New York Times Book Review* reported that the book, "part lilting memoir, part anxious meditation," deals elliptically with McPherson's long struggle with writer's block, his travels in Japan, and his slow recovery of a sense of connection with his past and present. Hoffman faulted the author for being "far more elusive than the protagonists in his short fiction. . . . When McPherson writes fiction, he insists that his characters reveal whether they've been abandoned by a lover, frozen out by a child. Why should he, as a memoirist, reveal far less?" Conversely, a reviewer for *Black Studies* deemed the book "richly rewarding," and a *Publishers Weekly* reviewer dubbed *Crabcakes* an "intense mosaic" that "combines James Baldwin's moral compulsion to testify and Ishmael Reed's iconoclastic experimentalism."

McPherson followed up *Crabcakes* with *A Region Not Home: Reflections from Exile,* another collection of personal and cultural essays. *Booklist* reviewer Mary Carroll wrote that in this work "McPherson offers flashes of unexpected insight; his path often twists and turns, but his side trips are well worth the time and effort." In *Publishers Weekly* a reviewer added of *A Region Not Home* that, "Throughout, there's an easy kitchentable quality to McPherson's style that invites the reader. . . . these are essays on how to live."

Speaking of the obstacles and opportunities facing black writers in the late twentieth century, McPherson once wrote in the *Atlantic:* "It seems to me much of our writing has been, and continues to be, sociological because black writers have been concerned with protesting black humanity and racial injustice to the larger society in those terms most easily understood by nonblack people. It also seems to me that we can correct this limitation either by defining and affirming the values and cultural institutions of our people for their education or by employing our own sense of reality and our own conception of what human life should be to explore, and perhaps help define, the cultural realities of contemporary American life."

BIOGRAPHICAL AND CRITICAL SOURCES:

BOOKS

Beavers, Herman, *Wrestling Angels into Song: The Fictions of Ernest J. Faines and James Alan McPherson,* University of Pennsylvania Press, 1995.

Contemporary Literary Criticism, Volume 19, Thomson Gale (Detroit, MI), 1981.

Dictionary of Literary Biography, Volume 38: *Afro-American Writers after 1955: Dramatists and Prose Writers,* Thomson Gale (Detroit, MI), 1985.

Wallace, Jon, *The Politics of Style: Language As Theme in the Fiction of Berger, McGuane, and McPherson,* Hollowbrook, 1992.

PERIODICALS

Antioch Review, winter, 1978.

Atlantic, December, 1970; February, 1977, review of *Elbow Room: Stories.*

Black Studies, February 1, 1998.

Booklist, June 1, 1998, review of *Crabcakes: A Memoir,* p. 1682; February 15, 2000, Mary Carroll, review of *A Region Not Home,* p. 1073.

Chicago Tribune Book World, May 25, 1969, review of *Hue and Cry.*

Christian Science Monitor, July 31, 1969, review of *Hue and Cry.*

CLA Journal, June, 1979.

Commonweal, September 19, 1969; September 15, 1978, Robert Phillips, review of *Elbow Room.*

Critique, summer, 1996, p. 314.

Ebony, December, 1981.

Essence, January, 1998, p. 61.

Guardian Weekly, April 16, 1989.

Harper's, December, 1969, Irving Howe, review of *Hue and Cry.*

Kirkus Reviews, November 15, 1997.

Library Journal, January, 1998, p. 100; June 15, 1998, review of *Crabcakes,* p. 96; January, 2000, review of *A Region Not Home,* p. 106.

Nation, December 16, 1978.

Negro Digest, October, 1969; November, 1969.

Newsweek, June 16, 1969; October 17, 1977.

New Yorker, November 21, 1977, review of *Elbow Room.*

New York Review of Books, November 10, 1977.

New York Times Book Review, June 1, 1969, review of *Hue and Cry;* September 25, 1977, review of *Elbow Room;* September 2, 1979; February 13, 1983; May 13, 1984; February 15, 1998, Roy Hoffman, review of *Crabcakes,* p. 15.

People, March 30, 1998, p. 39.

Publishers Weekly, November 17, 1997, p. 44; December 15, 1997, p. 36; May 4, 1998, p. 196; January 24, 2000, review of *A Region Not Home,* p. 302.

Saturday Review, May 24, 1969, review of *Hue and Cry.*

Spectator, November 22, 1969.

Studies in American Fiction, autumn, 1973.

Times Literary Supplement, December 25, 1969.

Washington Post Book World, October 30, 1977; March 6, 1983.

ONLINE

Inertia Online, http://www.inertiamagazine.com/ (August 23, 2004), interview with MacPherson.

* * *

MEAKER, Marijane 1927-
(Ann Aldrich, Mary James, M.E. Kerr, M.J. Meaker, Marijane Agnes Meaker, Vin Packer)

PERSONAL: Born May 27, 1927, in Auburn, NY; daughter of Ellis R. (a mayonnaise manufacturer) and Ida T. Meaker. *Education:* Attended Vermont Junior College; University of Missouri, Columbia, B.A., 1949; attended New School for Social Research.

ADDRESSES: Home—12 Deep Six Dr., East Hampton, NY 11937. *Agent*—Eugene Winick, McIntosh & Otis, Inc., 475 Fifth Ave., New York, NY 10017. *E-mail*—mekerr13@aol.com.

CAREER: Writer. E.P. Dutton (publisher), New York, NY, assistant file clerk, 1949-50; freelance writer, 1949—. Volunteer writing teacher at Commercial Manhattan Central High, 1968. Founding member, Ashawagh Hall Writers' Workshop, Ashawagh, NY, 1982.

MEMBER: PEN, Authors League of America, Society of Children's Book Writers and Illustrators.

AWARDS, HONORS: Maxi Award, *Media and Methods* magazine, 1974, for *Dinky Hocker Shoots Smack!;* Children's Spring Book Festival honor book, *Washington Post Book World,* and Children's Book of the Year designation, Child Study Association, both 1973, both for *If I Love You, Am I Trapped Forever?;* Christopher Award, and Book of the Year Award, *School Library Journal,* both 1978, and named one of the Best Books for the Teen Age, New York Public Library, 1980 and 1981, all for *Gentlehands;* Golden Kite Award, Society of Children's Book Writers, 1981, for *Little Little;* Emphasis on Reading Award, 1985, for *Him She Loves?;* Edgar Allan Poe Award finalist, 1990, for *Fell Back;* California Young Reader Medal, 1992, for *Night Kites;* Margaret A. Edwards Award, American Library Association, 1993, for body of work; National Council of Teachers of English Best Young Adult Novels of the '90s pick, Best Book Honor award, Michigan Library Association, 1994, and *Horn Book* Fanfare Honor book, 1995, all for *Deliver Us from Evie;* Knickerbocker Lifetime Achievement Award, New York State Library Association, 1999; Assembly on Literature for Adolescents Lifetime Achievement Award, 2000; New York Public Library Books for the Teen Age listee, 2002, and Oklahoma Library Association Young Adult Book Award nominee, 2003, both for *Slap Your Sides.* Several books published under the pseudonym M.E. Kerr were named Notable Books of the Year and Best Books for Young Adults by the American Library Association, Outstanding Books of the Year by the *New York Times,* and Best Books of the Year by *School Library Journal.*

WRITINGS:

FOR YOUNG ADULTS; UNDER PSEUDONYM M.E. KERR, EXCEPT AS NOTED

Dinky Hocker Shoots Smack!, Harper (New York, NY), 1972, reprinted, 2002.
If I Love You, Am I Trapped Forever?, Harper (New York, NY), 1973.
The Son of Someone Famous, Harper (New York, NY), 1974.
Is That You, Miss Blue?, Harper (New York, NY), 1975.
Love Is a Missing Person, Harper (New York, NY), 1975.
I'll Love You When You're More like Me, Harper (New York, NY), 1977.
Gentlehands, Harper (New York, NY), 1978.
Little Little, Harper (New York, NY), 1981.
What I Really Think of You, Harper (New York, NY), 1982.
Me, Me, Me, Me, Me: Not a Novel (autobiography), Harper (New York, NY), 1983.
Him She Loves?, Harper (New York, NY), 1984.
I Stay Near You: 1 Story in 3, Harper (New York, NY), 1985.
Night Kites, Harper (New York, NY), 1986.
Fell (also see below), Harper (New York, NY), 1987.
Fell Back (also see below), Harper (New York, NY), 1989.
(Under pseudonym Mary James) *Shoebag,* Scholastic (New York, NY), 1990.
Fell Down (also see below), HarperCollins (New York, NY), 1991.
Linger, HarperCollins (New York, NY), 1993.
Deliver Us from Evie, HarperCollins (New York, NY), 1994.
(Under pseudonym Mary James) *Frankenlouse,* Scholastic (New York, NY), 1994.
"Hello," I Lied, HarperCollins (New York, NY), 1997.

Blood on the Forehead: What I Know about Writing (nonfiction), HarperCollins (New York, NY), 1998.
What Became of Her?, HarperCollins (New York, NY), 2000.
Slap Your Sides, HarperCollins (New York, NY), 2001.
The Book of Fell (contains *Fell, Fell Back,* and *Fell Down*), HarperCollins (New York, NY), 2001.
Snakes Don't Miss Their Mothers, HarperCollins (New York, NY), 2003.
Your Eyes in Stars, HarperCollins (New York, NY), 2006.

Contributor, under pseudonym M.E. Kerr to *Sixteen,* edited by Donald R. Gallo, Delacorte, 1984; *Vissions,* edited by Gallo, 1984; *Connections,* edited by Gallo, 1989; *Scholastic Scope,* 1989, 1995; *Funny You Should Ask,* edited by Gallo, 1992; *Am I Blue?,* edited by Marion Dane Bauer, 1993; *No Easy Answers,* edited by Gallo, 1997; *Bad Behavior,* edited by Mary Higgins Clark; *Family Secrets,* edited by Linda Rowe Fraustino, 1999; *Stay True,* edited by Marilyn Singer, 1999; *I Believe in Water,* edited by Singer, 2000; *On the Fringe,* edited by Gallo, 2001; *Shattered,* edited by Jenifer Armstrong, 2003; and *Hearing Flower,* edited by Singer, 2004.

Meaker's manuscripts as M.E. Kerr are housed at the Kerlan Collection, University of Minnesota.

ADULT FICTION

(Under name M.J. Meaker) *Hometown,* Doubleday (New York, NY), 1967.
Game of Survival, New American Library (New York, NY), 1968.
Shockproof Sydney Skate, Little, Brown (Boston, MA), 1972, reprinted, HarperPerennial (New York, NY), 2002.

ADULT FICTION; UNDER PSEUDONYM VIN PACKER

Dark Intruder, Gold Medal Books (New York, NY), 1952.
Spring Fire, Gold Medal Books (New York, NY), 1952.
Look Back to Love, Gold Medal Books (New York, NY), 1953.
Come Destroy Me, Gold Medal Books (New York, NY), 1954.
Whisper His Sin, Gold Medal Books (New York, NY), 1954.
The Thrill Kids, Gold Medal Books (New York, NY), 1955.
Dark Don't Catch Me, Gold Medal Books (New York, NY), 1956.
The Young and Violent, Gold Medal Books (New York, NY), 1956.
Three-Day Terror, Gold Medal Books (New York, NY), 1957.
The Evil Friendship, Gold Medal Books (New York, NY), 1958.
5:45 to Suburbia, Gold Medal Books (New York, NY), 1958.
The Twisted Ones, Gold Medal Books (New York, NY), 1959.
The Damnation of Adam Blessing, Gold Medal Books (New York, NY), 1961.
The Girl on the Best-seller List, Gold Medal Books (New York, NY), 1961.
Something in the Shadows, Gold Medal Books (New York, NY), 1961.
Intimate Victims, Gold Medal Books (New York, NY), 1962.
Alone at Night, Gold Medal Books (New York, NY), 1963.
The Hare in March, New American Library (New York, NY), 1967.
Don't Rely on Gemini, Delacorte (New York, NY), 1969.

ADULT NONFICTION; UNDER PSEUDONYM ANN ALDRICH, EXCEPT AS NOTED

We Walk Alone, Gold Medal Books (New York, NY), 1955.
We Too Must Love, Gold Medal Books (New York, NY), 1958.
Carol, in a Thousand Cities, Gold Medal Books (New York, NY), 1960.
We Two Won't Last, Gold Medal Books (New York, NY), 1963.
(Under name M.J. Meaker) *Sudden Endings,* Doubleday (New York, NY), 1964, published under pseudonym Vin Packer, Fawcett (New York, NY), 1964.
Take a Lesbian to Lunch, MacFadden-Bartell, 1972.
Highsmith: A Romance of the Fifties, Cleis Press, 2003.

ADAPTATIONS: Dinky Hocker Shoots Smack! was broadcast as a television special by Learning Corporation of America, 1978; and was also optioned for film. *If I Love You, Am I Trapped Forever?* was released as an audio cassette by Random House, 1979; *Fell* was made into a sound recording in 1995 and *Gentlehands* in 1996.

SIDELIGHTS: Marijane Meaker, who writes for young adults almost exclusively as M.E. Kerr, is among the most popular and highly respected authors of American juvenile literature. Called "one of the grand masters of young adult fiction," by Lois Metzger in the *New York Times Book Review,* Meaker is an original writer whose novels *Deliver Us from Evie* and *Dinky Hocker Shoots Smack!* are acknowledged as landmarks of young adult literature. In addition to addressing serious issues, Meaker is known for creating coming-of-age stories and romances in which adolescent protagonists—male and female, straight and gay—face change, deal with the difficulties of relationships, and struggle to take charge of their own lives.

Often celebrated for her understanding of human nature in general and young adults in particular, Meaker is lauded for the color and variety of her characterizations, which often feature offbeat or bizarre figures, as well as for her well-rounded portrayals of adults, a quality considered unusual in books for a teenage audience. Praised as a keen social observer, she often uses a satiric, ironic tone to describe contemporary American morals and mores, which she sees as filled with hypocrisy and corruption. Her books expose inhumanity and injustice in such areas as small-town life and organized religion while encouraging young readers to look beyond racial, cultural, and sexual stereotypes. Addressing such issues as mental illness, physical disability, substance abuse, anti-Semitism, and AIDS as well as the pain of adolescence, Meaker often structures her stories as first-person narratives relayed in a spare, direct prose style; the author also regularly includes quotations from sources such as the Bible, Shakespeare, and contemporary rock songs. Anita Silvey wrote in *Horn Book* that Meaker "is one of the few young adult writers who can take a subject that affects teenagers' lives, can say something important to young readers about it, and can craft what is first and foremost a good story, without preaching and without histrionics." In her *Presenting M.E. Kerr,* Aileen Pace Nilsen described the author as "in a class by herself. Not often does someone come along who is a true teacher and a good writer. M.E. Kerr is both."

Much of Meaker's work as a writer of young adult literature is drawn from her own experience as she wrote in her autobiography *Me, Me, Me, Me, Me: Not a Novel.* "Whenever you find a little smart-mouth, tomboy kid in any of my books, you have found me from long ago." Born in Auburn, New York, a small town near Rochester, the author "grew up always wanting to be a writer," as she related in her essay in *Something about the Author Autobiography Series.* Her father Ellis Meaker, a mayonnaise manufacturer for Ivanhoe Foods, had a wide range of tastes in reading that he passed on to his daughter; Meaker was also influenced by the English teachers who encouraged her as well as the librarians "who," as she noted in *SAAS,* "had to pull me out of the stacks at closing time."

Despite the influences of teachers and librarians, Meaker most often credits her mother, Ida Meaker, for her decision to become a writer. The novelist recalled that her mother, a terrific gossip, "would begin nearly every conversation the same way: 'Wait till you hear this!' Even today, when I'm finished with a book and sifting through ideas for a new one, I ask myself: Is the idea a 'wait till you hear this'?"

As a junior in high school, Meaker started submitting romance stories with a wartime setting to popular women's magazines under the name Eric Ranthram McKay, a pseudonym chosen because her father's initials were E.R.M. Her stories, Meaker recalled in *Me, Me, Me, Me, Me,* "came back like boomerangs, with printed rejection slips attached. Sometimes these rejection slips had a 'sorry' penciled across them, or a 'try again.' These I cherished, and saved and used to buoy my spirits as I began new stories, and kept the old ones circulating."

As an adolescent, Meaker realized that she was a lesbian. As she wrote in her foreword to *Hearing Us Out: Voices from the Gay and Lesbian Community,* she was sent by her parents to ballet class to see if her homosexuality "could be corrected." She was also sent to Stuart Hall, an Episcopal boarding school for girls in Staunton, Virginia. In her foreword to *Hearing Us Out,* Meaker remembered, "When my mother finally did come to terms with me and with terms ('I hate that word *lesbian* and I'll never call you one!'), she asked that there be one promise: 'Never bring any of them to the house! . . . Around here I couldn't hold my head up if it ever got out.'" As Meaker recalled, "My father could never even speak about it. So formed by what others thought, . . . both my parents missed the chance to know my warm and loving friends—as well as to know me better."

At Stuart Hall Meaker became a rebel; in her senior year, she was expelled for throwing darts at pictures of faculty members before her mother arranged her reinstatement with a bishop. In *Me, Me, Me, Me, Me,* she described herself during her Stuart Hall years as "the out-of-line black sheep," but admitted that at the boarding school "there was something stimulating and amusing, and very like life, as I came to know it, in its regulated, intense, dutiful and peculiar ambiance."

After graduation, Meaker went to Vermont Junior College, where she edited the school newspaper, the first publication to print one of her stories. In 1946 she transferred to the University of Missouri, where she initially majored in journalism; Meaker switched to the English program "partly because," as she noted in *SAAS,* "I failed Economics, which one had to pass to get into J-School, and partly because I realized I didn't want anything to do with writing fact. I wanted to make up my own facts."

After graduation in 1949, she moved to New York, NY, and began clerking at the E.P. Dutton publishing company, while also continuing to send out stories. "I wrote anything and everything in an effort to get published," she admitted in *Me, Me, Me, Me, Me.* "I wrote confession stories, articles, 'slick' stories for the women's magazines, poetry, and fillers."

Finally gaining some publicity for her writing and self-promotion efforts, Meaker was offered the chance to write for the Fawcett paperback series Gold Medal Books, and began publishing mysteries and thrillers for adults under the names Vin Packer and Ann Aldrich. While writing adult novels and nonfiction titles, she also began taking classes in psychology, child psychology, sociology, and anthropology at the New School for Social Research in New York, NY. In 1964, she published *Sudden Endings,* a nonfiction book on suicide, as M.J. Meaker; in 1972, she published a successful adult novel titled *Shockproof Sydney Skate,* a story featuring an adolescent protagonist, as Marijane Meaker. At the urging of a friend, she started to consider writing for the young-adult market.

In 1968, Meaker began volunteering as part of an experimental program in New York, NY, where writers went into high schools one day a month in order to interest students in writing. In one of her classes, she met an overweight African-American girl named Tiny who, Meaker recalled in *SAAS,* "wrote some really grotesque stories, about things like a woman going swimming and accidentally swallowing strange eggs in the water, and giving birth to red snakes. . . . One day her mother appeared, complaining that . . . I was encouraging Tiny to write 'weird.'" In their discussion, Meaker learned that Tiny's mother was, the author claimed, "an ardent do-gooder" who left her daughter alone while she went out to do community service. "In other words," Meaker continued, "while Tiny's mom was putting out the fire in the house across the street, her own house was on fire. I was thinking a lot about this." The result was *Dinky Hocker Shoots Smack!,* which Meaker published under the pen name M.E. Kerr, a play on her last name.

Dinky Hocker Shoots Smack! is the story of an obese teenager whose mother is so absorbed in her own work with drug addicts that she fails to notice her daughter; the novel also concerns Dinky's relationship with P. John, a sympathetic classmate who shares a weight problem, and P. John's relationship with his father, whose liberal values have caused the boy to adopt an ultra-conservative view. At the conclusion of the novel, Dinky grabs her mother's attention by inscribing the title legend on the wall of the building in which her mother is receiving the Good Samaritan Award. Meaker's "funny/sad first novel shoots straight from the hip," wrote Pamela D. Pollack in the *School Library Journal,* and dubbed the work "a totally affecting literary experience." Writing in the *New York Times Book Review,* Dale Carlson called the book "a brilliantly funny," "timely, compelling, and entertaining novel."

After this first success the forty-something writer began to rethink the direction of her career. As she wrote in *SAAS,* "As I looked back on my life, things seemed funnier to me than they used to. *I* seemed funnier to me than I used to, and so did a lot of what I 'suffered.' Miraculously, as I sat down to make notes for possible future stories, things that happened to me long ago came back clear as a bell, and ringing, and making me smile and shake my head as I realized I had stories in me about *me.*"

Meaker has since produced a succession of young-adult novels about adolescents who survive their situations while learning about the larger world. In *Is That You, Miss Blue?* she tackles one of her most prominent subjects, religion, in the context of a boarding school story. The title character is a religious mystic who teaches science at an Episcopal boarding school in Virginia; Miss Blue, an inspired teacher, becomes an object of ridicule—and, eventually, a campaign for dismissal—because her intense religious experiences are considered inappropriate by both school authorities and some students. The narrator, fifteen-year-old Flanders Brown, moves from mocking Miss Blue to respecting her former teacher, who suffers a mental breakdown as the result of the pressure. "This is a sophisticated book," wrote Zena Sutherland in *Bulletin of the Center for Children's Books,* "one that demands understanding from its readers and can, at the same time, lead them toward understanding." In *Horn Book,* Mary M. Burns praised the novel as "wryly funny," while in *Best Sellers,* a reviewer wrote that Meaker "can dig deep and scurry around in the loneliest, saddest corners of a reader's soul and always come up with a perceptive thought for teenagers to mull over."

Also focusing on religion, *What I Really Think of You* explores the world of fundamentalist preachers and its effect on the children of these ministers, and also builds on the connection between organized religion and business. The story describes how Opal and Jesse, two teenage PKs, or preacher's kids, deal with the professions of their fathers—one a rich television star and the other a poor Pentecostal minister—and questions of faith while developing a tentative relationship. At the end of the novel, Opal receives the gift of tongues, even after some earlier ambivalence, and finds love with Jesse's religious older brother; her new gift also brings her celebrity status when she is filmed by a television crew in her father's church. *What I Really Think of You* was criticized for making fun of religion, as well as for the inconsistency of Opal's character. However, as Marilyn Kaye wrote in the *New York Times Book Review,* the novel "has integrity. It's hard to believe that a novelist could indulge in such concepts as being 'slain in the spirit,' waiting for 'The Rapture,' faith healing and speaking in tongues without either proselytizing or mocking them—but glory be, M.E. Kerr has done both."

I'll Love You When You're More like Me focuses on Sabra St. Amour, a teenage soap opera star, and Wally Witherspoon, the son of a mortician, who meet while Sabra is vacationing in Wally's Long Island hometown. The teens' common bond is heightened by their shared efforts to deal with dominating parents. During the course of the story, Wally's friend Charlie comes out as a gay teen; at the end of the novel, he agrees to take Wally's place at the funeral home, and all three teenagers begin to break free of parental expectations. A critic in *Kirkus Reviews* noted that the author's "talent for combining the representative and the bizarre has never been so evident as in this inspired cast which seems to write its own story." In *School Library Journal,* Lillian M. Gerhardt praised Meaker for producing "superb serio-comic writing . . . that touches on nothing outside the ken or the conversation of young teens."

Meaker's teen novel *Gentlehands* is considered one of the most controversial books published under her Kerr pseudonym. The story describes the relationship between sixteen-year-old Buddy Boyle, a lower-middle-class boy, and Skye Pennington, a rich and beautiful girl; the larger story concerns Buddy's discovery that his grandfather, the cultured Frank Trenker, is actually a Nazi officer who murdered Jewish prisoners at Auschwitz. Meaker includes pointed social commentary directed at the tiny Long Island village in which the story takes place, as well as strong detail about Trenker's history as an SS officer; consequently, the novel provoked some negative reactions from both Jewish groups and critics of young-adult literature. In an interview with Jim Roginski for *Behind the Covers, Volume II,* Meaker noted that "I wanted to provoke the idea of what if you meet a nice guy, a really nice man, and what if you find out that in his past he wasn't such a nice man? How would you feel?"

Discussing *Gentlehands* in *Interracial Books for Children,* Ruth Charnes noted that, despite the author's intent, it is inappropriate "to give equal weight to the question of morality raised by the Holocaust and to an unrealistic teenage romance." More positive about the novel, Geraldine DeLuca wrote of *Gentlehands* in a review for the *Lion and the Unicorn* that Meaker "has illuminated a painful historical issue, sparing us no detail and yet avoiding sensationalism," although the book suffers because "it depends so much on exaggeration and stereotype." Writing in the *New York Times Book Review,* Richard Bradford cited the book as "important and useful as an introduction to the grotesque character of the Nazi period, as well as to the paradoxes that exist in the heart of man," while in *Publishers Weekly* a reviewer described the book as "a marvel of understatement, diamond insights, irony, and compassion."

In *Little Little* Meaker describes the developing relationship of teens Little Little La Belle, a sophisticated "little person" who is the daughter of her town's leading family, and Sydney Cinnamon, a hunchbacked dwarf abandoned at birth. Little Little's mother wants her to marry the famous but shallow midget evangelist Little Lion, but a party celebrating Little Little's eighteenth birthday exposes Little Lion's true nature as well as the growing romance between Little Little and Sydney. "This is a story about courage and tolerance and growing up without growing bigger," wrote Suzanne Freeman in the *Washington Post Book World.* In the *ALAN Review,* Norma Bagnall called the novel "an outrageously sad-funny book with humor and pathos consistently maintained throughout" that represents "M.E. Kerr at her very best."

With her "Fell" series of young adult novels—*Fell, Fell Back,* and *Fell Down*—Meaker combines her interest in detective fiction with some of her most prominent themes, including betrayal, class conflict, and the politics and prejudices that can be found in prep schools. The series, which combines romance, mystery, and humor, revolves around John Fell, a policeman's son from Seaville, New York. A sensitive, witty gourmet cook who possesses a talent for detection as well as a sharp eye for phoniness, Fell is drawn into the world of privilege when he is asked to impersonate the son of a rich neighbor at the elite Gardner school. After he is asked to join a secret campus society called the Seven, he learns about the intrigue and tyranny underlying the school and discovers that his benefactor has been arrested for selling nuclear secrets. In a review of the novel for *Booklist,* Hazel Rochman claimed, "Not since *Gentlehands* has Kerr so poignantly combined a story of romance, mystery, and wit with serious implications of class conflict and personal betrayal."

In *Fell Back* Fell searches for the cause of the suicide of one of his fellow members in the Sevens club and becomes involved in the drug scene and a love affair as well as with a murder. Reviewers gave the novel a mixed reception, a *Publishers Weekly* critic noting that "the spark that ignited Fell seems to have fizzled out." Marjorie Lewis pointed out in *School Library Journal* that despite the plot's drawbacks, "Fell's charm is considerable, and readers will like him and his insecurities."

Fell Down describes how Fell, who has dropped out of Gardner, returns to the newly coed school to find April, the missing sister of his longtime girlfriend Delia; he soon becomes embroiled in a mystery that spans two generations and involves kidnaping and murder. *Fell Down* is unique among the volumes in the series in that it includes two narrators, Fell and "the Mouth," a ventriloquist who tells his story through the voice of his dummy. Writing in *Booklist,* Hazel Rochman called the novel "a brilliant mystery, one that will have genre fans fitting the pieces together for days," while Christy Tyson wrote in *Voice of Youth Advocates* that Meaker's "mastery at character development is superb, and few can top her for style that can convey both wit and heartache." The "Fell" series was released as a single volume in 2001 under the title *The Books of Fell.*

Linger takes place in the small town of Berryville, Pennsylvania, rather than in Meaker's usual Long Island or upstate New York settings. The book's title refers to a popular restaurant owned by Ned Dunlinger, a powerful pillar of the community. The family of sixteen-year-old Gary Peel, like many of the Berryville residents, considers the Dunlingers akin to royalty; Gary's father manages Linger, his mother does the books, and Gary and his older brother Bobby wait tables. After an argument with Ned Dunlinger over the latter's efforts to shut down a competing Mexican restaurant, Bobby quits Linger, joins the army, and is sent to Saudi Arabia as part of Operation: Desert Storm. The novel includes excerpts from Bobby's Gulf War journal. When Bobby returns home as a hero after being wounded by friendly fire, his happiness quickly fades when injured army buddy Sanchez is openly treated with contempt by the manipulative Ned. *Voice of Youth Advocates* contributor Munat praised *Linger* as "a sensitive and provocative book that reconstructs the emotional climate in the U.S. during the Gulf War," while a *Kirkus Reviews* critic praised the novel as "rich with varied characters and points of view" and with "plenty of thought-provoking parallels."

Another novel that reflects the microcosm of small-town life, *What Became of Her* is narrated by sixteen-year-old E.C. Tobbit. The book focuses on Rosalind Slaymaster, once looked down on due to her job in the local funeral parlor but recently returned to town as a wealthy woman. E.C. and his friend Neal establish a friendship with Slaymaster's adopted daughter, Julie, and through this friendship E.C. discovers the key to Slaymaster's rise in affluence and the past that has driven her need for revenge. Enhanced by the author's "usual witty writing style," *What Became of Her* was praised by *School Library Journal* contributor Susie Paige for its "eerily realistic" portrait of small-town life, "right down to the gossip, cruelty, fear, and insecurity." Frances Bradburn wrote in *Booklist* that Meaker's "unusual, haunting book will hold readers until the final page," while in *Publishers Weekly* a critic wrote that, "with a masterful, invisible hand," the author "quietly adds layers of meaning to a seductive, psychologically riveting story."

Although Meaker includes gay characters in several of her novels, in *Deliver Us from Evie* and *"Hello," I Lied* they become the focus. In *Deliver Us from Evie* a Missouri farm family's eighteen-year-old daughter, Evie Burman, is a talented mechanic who looks like the young Elvis Presley. Problems arise when she falls in love with Patsy Duff, the attractive daughter of the local banker. Narrator Parr, Evie's youngest brother, describes the varied reactions to Evie's coming out—mostly hostile and uncertain with some acceptance—as well as his own romance with Angel Kidder, a religious but hot-blooded teen. The Mississippi floods of 1993 provides a strong symbol; the rising waters are interpreted by some as God's warning to Evie and Patsy, but also as their means of escaping to New York, NY. Writing in the *Wilson Library Bulletin,* Cathi Dunn MacRae noted Meaker's pioneering effort in "tackling the female butch stereotype," while Christine Jenkins described the book in the *Bulletin of the Center for Children's Books* as "vintage Kerr." Writing in the *New York Times Book Review,* Lois Metzger concluded that *Deliver Us from Evie* is "so original, fresh and fiery, you'd think that M.E. Kerr . . . was just now getting started."

"Hello," I Lied also addresses issues of homosexuality and identity. The story is told by seventeen-year-old Lang Penner, a young man who has already come out to his mother but is concerned about how his friends will react. Lang and his mom are living in the Hamptons for the summer, where his mother is working as housekeeper for reclusive rock star Ben Nevada. Lang's lover, Alex, presses him to live openly as a gay man; however, Lang finds himself attracted to Huguette, a young French woman who is visiting Nevada. By summer's end Lang has learned about the complexities of relationships and the fluid nature of identity; in addition, he has acquired sweet memories of "the summer that I loved a girl." Writing in *Horn Book,* Roger Sutton commented that, "Gay themes in young adult literature have been pressing beyond the standard coming-out story. And, as usual, M.E. Kerr is right out in front." According to a *Publishers Weekly* reviewer, *"Hello," I Lied* "successfully challenges readers' assumptions, breaking them down to offer more hopeful, affirming ideas about love and ruth."

In addition to her teen novels, Meaker has also written several books for young readers that focus on less-personal matters. *Snakes Don't Miss Their Mothers* takes place at a Long Island animal shelter run by Mrs. Splinter, and describes life from the point of view of the dogs, cats, and other critters that have taken up residence there. Despite its focus on the animals' hopes of finding a home in a loving adoption, Meaker's book was described by *School Library Journal* contributor Pam Spencer as "light" and "upbeat," and a *Kirkus Reviews* contributor wrote that the goings-on at the busy shelter "should keep young animal lovers happy and occupied." Writing that the author levens "some poignant moments with slapstick comedy," a *Publishers Weekly* reviewer predicted that the animated animal cast of *Snakes Don't Miss Their Mothers* will "wiggle, wag and worm their way into readers' hearts."

In the autobiography *Me, Me, Me, Me, Me: Not a Novel,* Meaker describes her life from the age of fifteen until the publication of her first story in 1951. The result of many letters the author has received from readers, the book presents autobiographical vignettes as well as the author's explanations of the people and experiences that influenced her books. Paul A. Caron, writing in *Best Sellers* stated that Meaker has written a "fascinating, yet timeless look at herself and others, which will not only delight her fans, but will no doubt increase their number." Writing in the *New York Times Book Review,* Joyce Milton noted, "Kerr unveils a deliciously wicked sense of humor," and provides readers with "a satisfying if brief encounter with a humorist whose delight in poking fun at the trappings of authority is unmarred by either self-hatred or pettiness toward others." In *Horn Book,* Nancy C. Hammond explained that Meaker "confesses to being the 'smartmouth' tomboys populating many of her novels. And she is quite as entertaining as they are. Incisive, witty, and immediate, the book is vintage M.E. Kerr."

In addition to her works as M.E. Kerr, Meaker has written for young people under the name Mary James. *Shoebag,* a parody of Franz Kafka's *Metamorphosis* that satirizes both the human and roach worlds, describes a cockroach who turns into a boy. At school, Shoebag, who has been named for the site of his birth, makes friends with Gregor Samson, a boy who also used to be a cockroach. When Gregor decides to remain human, he grants Shoebag his ability to revert back to roach form, and Shoebag is happily reunited with his family. A *Kirkus Reviews* critic called *Shoebag* "a highly original story crammed with clever detail, action, insight, and humor, all combined with impeccable logic and begging to be shared." In *Frankenlouse,* fourteen-year-old Nick, the son of a general who is also his commanding officer in military school, convinces his dad that he is an artist. Throughout the story, Nick creates a cartoon strip featuring a book louse from Mary Shelley's *Frankenstein* who devours a whole collection of classic books—all except for those starting with the letter "m." Elizabeth S. Watson in *Horn Book* commented that in a story that is "not as complicated as it sounds, Meaker "encourage[s] some creative thinking" with this "funny and thought-provoking" read.

Of her career as a young-adult writer, Meaker wrote in *SAAS:* "When I write for young adults I know they're still wrestling with very important problems like winning and losing, not feeling accepted or accepting, prejudice, love—all the things adults ultimately get hardened to, and forgetful of. I know my audience hasn't yet made up their minds about everything, that they're still vulnerable and open to suggestion and able to change their minds. . . . Give me that kind of an audience any day!"

BIOGRAPHICAL AND CRITICAL SOURCES:

BOOKS

Behind the Covers, Volume II, Libraries Unlimited, 1989, pp. 161-176.

Children's Literature Review, Volume 29, Thomson Gale (Detroit, MI), 1993.

Contemporary Literary Criticism, Thomson Gale (Detroit, MI), Volume 12, 1980, Volume 35, 1985.

Donelson, Kenneth L., and Alleen Pace Nilsen, *Literature for Today's Young Adults,* Scott, Foresman, 1980, 2nd edition, 1985.

Kerr, M.E., *Me, Me, Me, Me, Me: Not a Novel,* Harper (New York, NY), 1983.

Nilsen, Alleen Pace, *Presenting M.E. Kerr,* Twayne, 1986.

Rees, David, *Painted Desert, Green Shade: Essays on Contemporary Writers of Fiction for Children and Young Adults,* Horn Book (Boston, MA), 1984.

Something about the Author Autobiography Series, Volume 1, Thomson Gale (Detroit, MI), 1986.

Sutton, Roger, editor, *Hearing Us Out: Voices from the Gay and Lesbian Community,* Little, Brown (Boston, MA), 1994.

Twentieth Century Children's Writers, 3rd edition, St. James Press (Chicago, IL), 1989.

PERIODICALS

ALAN Review, fall, 1981, Norma Bagnall, review of *Little Little,* p. 21; fall, 1997.

Best Sellers, May, 1975, Mrs. John G. Gray, review of *Is That You, Miss Blue?,* p. 49; June, 1983, Paul A. Caron, review of *Me, Me, Me, Me, Me: Not a Novel,* p. 110.

Booklist, June 1, 1987, Hazel Rochman, review of *Fell,* pp. 1515-1516; September 15, 1991, Hazel Rochman, review of *Fell Down,* p. 135; September 15, 1994, p. 125; April 15, 1997, p. 1423; April, 1998, Hazel Rochman, review of *Blood on the Forehead: What I Know about Writing,* p. 1309; June 1, 2000, Stephanie Zvirin, review of *Deliver Us from Evie,* p. 1875, and M.E. Kerr, "A Writer's Life," p. 1878; July, 2000, Frances Bradburn, review of *What Became of Her,* p. 2018; October 1, 2001, Hazel Rochman, review of *Slap Your Sides,* p. 331; September 15, 2003, Ilene Cooper, review of *Snakes Don't Miss Their Mothers,* p. 237.

Bulletin of the Center for Children's Books, July-August, 1975, Zena Sutherland, review of *Is That You, Miss Blue?,* p. 179; November, 1975, Zena Sutherland, review of *Love Is a Missing Person,* p. 48; March, 1990, Robert Strang, review of *Shoebag,* p. 164; September, 1993, Roger Sutton, review of *Linger,* p. 14; December, 1994, Christine Jenkins, review of *Deliver Us from Evie,* pp. 132-133; June, 1998, p. 366; November, 2003, Deborah Stevenson, review of *Snakes Don't Miss Their Mothers,* p. 110.

English Journal, December, 1975, Paul Janeczko, interview with Kerr.

Growing Point, November, 1973, Margery Fisher, review of *Dinky Hocker Shoots Smack!,* p. 2263.

Horn Book, August, 1975, Mary M. Burns, review of *Is That You, Miss Blue?,* p. 365; June, 1977, Mary Kingsbury, "The Why of People: The Novels of M.E. Kerr," pp. 288-295; August, 1983, Nancy A. Hammond, review of *Me, Me, Me, Me, Me,* p. 462; September-October, 1986, Anita Silvey, review of *Night Kites,* p. 597; January-February, 1995, Elizabeth S. Watson, review of *Frankenlouse,* pp. 62-63; July-August, 1997, Roger Sutton, review of *"Hello," I Lied,* pp. 457-458; May, 2000, review of *What Became of Her,* p. 316; November-December, 2001, Lauren Adams, review of *Slap Your Sides,* p. 751.

Interracial Books for Children Bulletin, Volume 9, number 8, 1978, Ruth Charnes, review of *Gentlehands,* p. 18.

Junior Bookshelf, June, 1991, Marcus Crouch, review of *Shoebag,* p. 114.

Kirkus Reviews, July 1, 1977, review of *I'll Love You When You're More like Me,* p. 673; February 15, 1990, review of *Shoebag,* p. 264; July 1, 1993, review of *Linger,* pp. 861-862; November 15, 1994, p. 1533; March 15, 1998, p. 405; October 1, 2003, review of *Snakes Don't Miss Their Mothers,* p. 1225.

Kliatt, March, 2002, Paula Rohrlick, review of *What Became of Her,* p. 16; March, 2003, Claire Rosser, review of *Slap Your Sides,* p. 24.

Lambda Book Report, September, 1997, Nancy Garden, review of *"Hello," I Lied,* p. 37; August-September, 2003, Ann Bannon, interview with Meaker, p. 13.

Lion and the Unicorn, winter, 1979-80, Geraldine DeLuca, "Taking True Risks: Controversial Issues in New Young Adult Novels," pp. 125-148.

New York Times Book Review, February 11, 1973, Dale Carlson, review of *Dinky Hocker Shoots Smack!,* p. 8; October 19, 1975, Alix Nelson, review of *Love Is a Missing Person,* p. 10; April 30, 1978, Richard Bradford, "The Nazi Legacy: Understanding History," p. 30; September 12, 1982, Marilyn Kaye, review of *What I Really Think of You,* pp.

49-50; May 22, 1983, Joyce Milton, review of *Me, Me, Me, Me, Me,* p. 39; April 13, 1986, Audrey B. Eaglen, review of *Night Kites,* p. 30; April 9, 1995, Lois Metzger, review of *Deliver Us from Evie,* P. 25.

Publishers Weekly, June 30, 1975, review of *Love Is a Missing Person,* p. 58; January 9, 1978, review of *Gentlehands,* p. 81; September 29, 1989, review of *Fell Back,* p. 70; March 31, 1997, review of *"Hello," I Lied,* p. 75; May 11, 1998, review of *Blood on the Forehead,* p. 69; April 24, 2000, review of *What Became of Her,* p. 92; November 3, 2003, review of *Snakes Don't Miss Their Mothers,* p. 75.

School Library Journal, December, 1972, Pamela D. Pollack, review of *Dinky Hocker Shoots Smack!,* p. 67; October, 1977, Lillian N. Gerhardt, review of *I'll Love You When You're More like Me,* pp. 124-25; September, 1986, Jennifer FitzGerald, "Challenging the Pressure to Conform: Byars and Kerr," pp. 46-47; September, 1989, Marjorie Lewis, review of *Fell Back,* pp. 272-273; June, 1997, p. 120; May, 1998, pp. 156-157; July, 2000, Susie Paige, review of *What Became of Her,* p. 106; October, 2003, Pam Spencer, review of *Snakes Don't Miss Their Mothers,* p. 169; November, 2003, Carol Fazioli, review of *Me, Me, Me, Me, Me,* p. 82.

Voice of Youth Advocates, October, 1987, Christy Tyson, review of *Fell,* p. 202; December, 1991, Christy Tyson, review of *Fell Down,* pp. 313-314; August, 1993, Florence H. Munat, review of *Linger,* p. 153; October, 1994, Dorothy M. Broderick, review of *Deliver Us from Evie,* p. 208.

Washington Post Book World, May 10, 1981, Susanne Freeman, "Growing up in a Small World," p. 15; June 10, 1990, p. 10.

Wilson Library Bulletin, September, 1994, Cathi Dunn MacRae, review of *Deliver Us from Evie,* pp. 116-117.

ONLINE

M.E. Kerr and Mary James Home Page, http://www.mekerr.com/ (May 3, 2005).

* * *

MEAKER, Marijane Agnes
See MEAKER, Marijane

* * *

MEAKER, M.J.
See MEAKER, Marijane

MEHTA, Ved 1934-
(Ved Parkash Mehta)

PERSONAL: Born March 21, 1934, in Lahore, India; naturalized U.S. citizen, 1975; son of Amolak Ram (a doctor and health official) and Shanti (Mehra) Mehta; married Linn Fenimore Cooper Cary (an assistant program officer at Ford Foundation), December 17, 1983; children: Alexandra Sage, Natasha Cary. *Education:* Pomona College, B.A., 1956; Balliol College, Oxford, B.A. (with honors), 1959; Harvard University, M.A., 1961; Oxford University, M.A., 1962. *Hobbies and other interests:* Indian and Western music, cycling, wine.

ADDRESSES: Home and office—139 East 79th Street, New York, NY 10021-0324. *Agent*—Georges Borchardt, 136 East 57th St., 14th Fl., New York, NY 10022.

CAREER: New Yorker magazine, New York, NY, staff writer, 1961-94; American Heritage Dictionary, member of usage panel, 1982; Yale University, New Haven, CT, Rosenkranz Chair in Writing, 1990-93, lecturer in history, 1990-93, lecturer in English, 1991-93. Case-Western Reserve University, Cleveland, OH, visiting scholar, 1974; Bard College, Annandale-on-Hudson, NY, visiting professor of literature, 1985, 1986; Sarah Lawrence College, Bronxville, NY, Noble Foundation visiting professor of art and cultural history, 1988; Balliol College, Oxford, visiting fellow in literature, 1988-89; New York University, New York, NY, visiting professor of English, 1989-90; Williams College, Williamstown, MA, Arnold Bernhard visiting professor of English and history, 1994; Vassar College, Poughkeepsie, NY, Randolph visiting distinguished professor of English and history, 1994-96. Columbia University Media Studies Center Freedom Forum, senior fellow, 1996-97; Center for Advanced Studies in the Behavioral Sciences, Palo Alto, CA, fellow, 1997-98.

MEMBER: Phi Beta Kappa, Council on Foreign Relations, Century Association (trustee 1972-75), Tarratine Club of Dark Harbor (ME).

AWARDS, HONORS: Hazen fellowship, 1956-59; Secondary Education Board Annual Book Award, 1958, for *Face to Face;* Harvard, Eliot House residential fellowship, 1959-61; Ford Foundation travel and study grants, 1971-76; Guggenheim fellowships, 1971-72, 1977-78; Dupont Columbia Award for excellence in broadcast journalism, 1977-78, for documentary film *Chachaji, My Poor Relation;* Association of Indians in America award, 1978; Ford Foundation public policy grant, 1979-82; John D. and Catherine T. MacArthur Foundation fellowship, 1982-87; Asian/Pacific Americans Library Association distinguished service award, 1986; New York City Mayor's Liberty Medal, 1986; Pomona College centenary Barrows Award, 1987; New York Institute for Humanities fellowship, 1988-92; New York Public Library Literary Lion medal, 1990, and centennial medal, 1996; Asian-American Heritage Month award, New York State, 1991; Balliol College, Oxford, honorary fellow, 1999. Honorary degrees from Pomona College, D.Litt., 1972; Bard College, D.Litt., 1982; Williams College, D.Litt., 1986; Stirling University, Scotland, Doctor of Letters, 1988; and Bowdoin College, L.H.D., 1995.

WRITINGS:

"CONTINENTS OF EXILE" SERIES; AUTOBIOGRAPHICAL

Daddyji (originally published in the *New Yorker*), Farrar, Straus, and Giroux (New York, NY), 1972.

Mamaji (originally published in the *New Yorker*), Oxford University Press (New York, NY), 1979.

Vedi (originally published in the *New Yorker*), Oxford University Press (New York, NY), 1982.

The Ledge between the Streams (originally published in the *New Yorker*), W.W. Norton (New York, NY), 1984.

Sound-Shadows of the New World, W.W. Norton (New York, NY), 1986.

The Stolen Light, W.W. Norton (New York, NY), 1989.

Up at Oxford, W.W. Norton (New York, NY), 1993.

Remembering Mr. Shawn's New Yorker: The Invisible Art of Editing, Overlook Press (New York, NY), 1998.

All for Love, Thunder's Mouth Press (New York, NY), 2001.

Dark Harbor: Building House and Home on an Enchanted Island, Thunder's Mouth Press (New York, NY), 2003.

The Red Letters, Thunder's Mouth Press (New York, NY), 2004.

OTHER

Face to Face: An Autobiography, Atlantic-Little, Brown (Boston, MA), 1957.

Walking the Indian Streets (travel; originally published in the *New Yorker*), Atlantic-Little, Brown (Boston, MA), 1960, revised edition, with new introduction by the author, Weidenfeld and Nicolson (London, England), 1971.

Fly and the Fly-Bottle: Encounters with British Intellectuals (originally published in the *New Yorker*), Atlantic-Little, Brown (Boston, MA), 1963, 2nd edition, with introduction by Professor Jasper Griffin, Columbia University Press (New York, NY), 1983.

The New Theologian (originally published in the *New Yorker*), Harper (New York, NY), 1966.

Delinquent Chacha (originally published in the *New Yorker*), Harper (New York, NY), 1967.

Portrait of India (originally published in the *New Yorker*), Farrar, Straus, and Giroux (New York, NY), 1970, published with new introduction, Yale University Press (New Haven, CT), 1993.

John Is Easy to Please: Encounters with the Written and the Spoken Word (originally published in the *New Yorker*), Farrar, Straus, and Giroux (New York, NY), 1971.

Mahatma Gandhi and His Apostles (originally published in the *New Yorker*), Viking (New York, NY), 1977, 2nd edition, Yale University Press (New Haven, CT), 1993.

The New India (originally published in the *New Yorker*), Viking (New York, NY), 1978.

The Photographs of Chachaji: The Making of a Documentary Film (originally published in the *New Yorker;* also see below), Oxford University Press (New York, NY), 1980.

A Family Affair: India under Three Prime Ministers (sequel to *The New India;* originally published in the *New Yorker*), Oxford University Press (New York, NY), 1982.

Three Stories of the Raj (fiction; originally published in the *New Yorker* and *Atlantic*), Scolar Press (Berkeley, CA), 1986.

Rajiv Gandhi and Rama's Kingdom (sequel to *A Family Affair;* originally published in the *New Yorker* and *Foreign Affairs*), Yale University Press (New Haven, CT), 1994.

A Ved Mehta Reader: The Craft of the Essay (originally published in the *New Yorker*), Yale University Press (New Haven, CT), 1998.

Contributor to anthologies, including: Henry I. Christs and Herbert Potell, editors, *Adventures in Living,* Harcourt (New York, NY), 1962; Leo Kneer, editor, *Perspectives,* Scott Foresman (Chicago, IL), 1963; K.L. Knickerbocker and H.W. Reninger, editors, *Interpreting Literature,* Holt (New York, NY), 1965, 1969; Norman Cousins, editor, *Profiles of Nehru,* Indian Book Company (Delhi, India), 1966; George Arms and others, editors, *Readings for Liberal Education,* Holt (New York, NY), 1967; Walter Havighurst and others, editors, *Exploring Literature,* Houghton Mifflin (Boston, MA),

1968; Nicholas P. Barker, editor, *Purpose and Function in Prose,* Knopf (New York, NY), 1969; Mary V. Gaver, editor, *Background Readings in Building Library Collections,* Scarecrow Press (Metuchen, NJ), 1969; N. Cousins, editor, *Profiles of Gandhi,* Indian Book Company, 1969; Jerome W. Archer and Joseph Schwartz, editors, *A Reader for Writers: A Critical Anthology of Prose Readings,* McGraw-Hill (New York, NY), 1971; Margaret Cormack and Kiki Skagen, editors, *Voices from India,* Praeger Publishers (Westport, CT), 1971; John F. Savage, editor, *Linguistics for Teachers,* Science Research Associates (Chicago, IL), 1973; Albert R. Kitzhaber, editor, *Style and Synthesis,* Holt, 1974; Anne Fremantle, editor, *A Primer of Linguistics,* St. Martin's Press (New York, NY), 1974; Donald J. Johnson and Jean E. Johnson, editors, *Through Indian Eyes,* Praeger Publishers (Westport, CT), 1974; Irving Kenneth Zola, editor, *Ordinary Lives: Voices of Disability and Disease,* Apple-Wood Press (Cambridge, MA), 1983; Dean W. Tuttle, editor, *Self-esteem and Adjusting with Blindness: The Process of Responding to Life's Demands,* C.C. Thomas (Springfield, IL), 1984; Harvey Weiner, editor, *Great Writing,* McGraw Hill, 1987; Helge Rubenstein, editor, *The Oxford Book of Marriage,* Oxford University Press (New York, NY), 1990; George and Barbara Perkins, editors, *Kaleidoscope,* Oxford University Press,1993; Linda Bates, editor, *Transitions: Paragraph to Essay,* St. Martin's Press, 1993; Angela Thirwell, editor, *The Folio Anthology of Autobiography,* Folio Society (London, England), 1994; Roshni Rustomji-Kerns, editor, *Living in America: Poetry and Fiction by South Asian American Writers,* Westview Press (Boulder, CO), 1995; Anne Mazer, editor, *Going Where I'm Coming From: Memoirs of American Youth,* Persea Books (New York, NY), 1995; *Traveller's Literary Companion: The Indian Sub-Continent,* In Print Publishing (Brighton, England), 1996; Chitra B. Divakaruni, editor, *Multitude: Cross-Cultural Readings,* second edition, McGraw-Hill (New York, NY), 1997; Stevan Harrell, editor, *The Human Family,* Westview Press, 1997; Salman Rushdie and Elizabeth West, editors, *Mirrorwork: Fifty Years of Indian Writing 1947-1997,* Holt (New York, NY), 1997; Kennedy Fries, editor, *Staring Back: The Disability Experience from the Inside Out,* Plume (New York, NY), 1997; James A. Banks and others, editors, *Regions: Adventures in Time and Place,* McGraw-Hill, 1999; Eva Hedencrona and others, editors, *Progress: Topics,* Corona, 1999; *Asian American Writers,* McDougal Littel (New York, NY), 2000; *Texts from Other Cultures,* Oxford University Press, 2000; John Biyas and Carol Wershoven, editors, *Along These Lines: Writing Sentences and Paragraphs,* Prentice Hall, 2001; Mary Reath, editor, *Public Lives, Private Prayers,* Sorin Books (Notre Dame, IN), 2001; and Ann Moseley and Jeanette Harris, editors, *Interactions: A Thematic Reader,* Houghton Mifflin (Boston, MA), 2003. Writer and commentator for documentary film *Chachaji, My Poor Relation,* PBS, 1978. Contributor of articles and stories to American, British, and Indian newspapers and magazines, including *Atlantic, Saturday Review, New York Times Book Review, Village Voice, World, Political Science Quarterly, Hindustan Times* (New Delhi), *Asian Post,* and *Debonaire* (Bombay).

Several of Mehta's books have been translated into Dutch, Finnish, French, German, Greek, Gujarati, Hindi, Italian, Japanese, Marathi, Spanish, and Urdu.

SIDELIGHTS: Most well-known for his eleven-volume "Continents of Exile" autobiography series, Ved Mehta was born in India and returns there often in his writings, making this country of contradictions his backdrop, whether his account is political or personal. According to Maureen Dowd in the *New York Times Magazine,* William Shawn, Mehta's editor at the *New Yorker*—where Mehta was a longtime staff writer—has maintained that "more than any other writer Mehta has educated Americans about India, illuminating that country with an insider's sensibility and an outsider's objectivity."

As natives of Lahore, India, which is now Pakistan, Mehta's own parents typified the split in India between West and East, between science and ancient tradition. Mehta's father was educated in medicine in British India and England and became an important figure in India's public health service. Mehta's mother, who had a meager education, was a woman of superstition, confident in the powers of faith healers. When Mehta lost his sight at age four as the result of a bout with meningitis, his mother was convinced his blindness was only a temporary form of punishment and followed a local medicine man's advice, applying antimony to Mehta's eyes and flogging him with twigs, among other things. Mehta's more progressive-minded father believed an education would be the only way for his son to avoid the lot of a blind person in India: alms beggar or chair caner. At age five, Mehta was sent to Bombay's Dadar School for the Blind, an American mission school so lacking in sanitation that the once-healthy boy suffered in succession from numerous infections, including ringworm, typhoid fever, malaria, and bronchitis. At age fifteen, after experiencing the upheaval that accompanied the Partition of India in 1947, he traveled alone to the United States to study at the only American school that would accept him, the Arkansas School for the Blind in Little Rock. From there, Mehta went on to excel at

Pomona College in California, at Balliol College, Oxford, and finally at Harvard University. In 1961, at the age of twenty-six, he became a staff writer for the *New Yorker* magazine. Most of his books have appeared first in installments in the *New Yorker.*

While Mehta's first book, *Face to Face: An Autobiography,* addresses his blindness, many of his subsequent works have avoided this topic. In fact, for a while Mehta demanded that his publishers avoid any reference to his blindness on his book jackets. Writing in the *New York Times Book Review* in 1960, Herbert L. Matthews noted that "Mehta plays an extraordinary trick on his prospective readers and on anyone who does not know about him or has not read his previous book, *Face to Face.* . . . He has written [*Walking the Indian Streets*] about his return to India after ten years' absence as if he had normal vision."

Many of Mehta's books contain elaborate visual imagery, and reviewers have often cited him as the blind man who can see better than can the rest of us. As Carolyn See explained in the *Los Angeles Times:* "When Mehta shows us the building of a dam; hundreds of brightly clad peasants carrying just a few bricks at a time; when in *Mahatma Gandhi and His Apostles,* Mehta conjures up the evenings when the movement was still young, when the fragrance of blossoms was everywhere and Gandhi's followers stayed up late, out of doors, laughing, rubbing each other's backs—a whole world is given to us, and of course the kicker in all this is that . . . Mehta is blind." It was not until *Daddyji,* Mehta's biography of his father, that the author made reference to his blindness once again, and it was not until a later autobiographical work, *Vedi,* that he wrote "from the perspective of total blindness," according to Janet Malcolm in the *New York Review of Books. Vedi* "is entirely without visual descriptions. We follow the blind child into the orphanage, and, like him, we never learn what the place or any of the people in it looked like. We hear, we feel, but we see nothing. . . . As the child misses the familiar persons and things of home, so the reader misses the customary visual clues of literature. . . . Not the least of *Vedi*'s originality is this very stylistic denial, which amounts to an approximation of the experience of blindness."

Although Mehta has written nonfiction, a novel, essays, and even a documentary script, highest critical regard has been for his contributions to the autobiographical genre. *Face to Face,* written when Mehta was in his early twenties, chronicles its author's early life, from his childhood in India to his three-year stay at the Arkansas School for the Blind where, among other things, he first encountered racism—"I wondered how dark I was, how much I looked like a Negro," Peter Ackroyd quoted Mehta in the London *Times.* Commenting on the book for the *New York Herald Tribune Book Review,* Gerald W. Johnson observed, "It is extraordinary when a man at twenty-three has the material for an autobiography that deserves the serious attention of the intelligent, and still more extraordinary when a man so young can present his material in an arresting fashion. . . . Mehta has both material and ability."

Three years after *Face to Face* came *Walking the Indian Streets,* Mehta's memoir of his two-month-long visit to India after a ten-year absence. Maureen Dowd recorded in the *New York Times Magazine* how Mehta idealized his native country during those years by listening to Indian music and dreaming about an arranged marriage to a beautiful Punjabi girl. The India Mehta encountered, however, disturbed him and shattered his idealistic vision. "Everywhere I went, I was assaulted by putrid odors rising from the streets, by flies relentlessly swarming around my face, by the octopus-like hands of a hundred scabrous, deformed beggars clutching at my hands and feet. My time in the West had spoiled me and I could now hardly wait to get back," Mehta wrote of his experience.

While he wrote numerous books on the politics and culture of a changing modern India during the twelve years following the 1960 publication of *Walking the Indian Streets,* Mehta eventually turned once more to the autobiographical form and began disclosing his life in very small chunks, developing the years of his earlier autobiography *Face to Face* into several volumes and then proceeding to cover new ground. The biographical/autobiographical *Daddyji* and *Mamaji* describe his parents' lives before he was born. Both books are noted for their adept presentations of the middle-class family in India. "[*Daddyji*'s] value," commented P.K. Sundara Rajan in the *Saturday Review,* "lies in the fact that . . . Mehta transforms an individual experience into one that is universal." In his *New York Times Book Review* assessment of *Mamaji,* Clark Blaise wrote that "family is the tidiest metaphor for the vastness of India. To understand its compelling and often terrible hold is to possess a special understanding of the culture. . . . Mehta patiently delivers that understanding and courageously presents it without interpretation, limiting even its expected 'warmth' in the service of a sharper clarity." It is also with these two books that "Mehta draws a sharp contrast between his rational, decisive, tough-minded, Western-educated, physician father and his superstitious, backward, uneducated, childish, tender-hearted mother," remarked Malcolm.

The author followed the biographical portraits of his parents with *Vedi,* which begins with Mehta boarding a train for the Bombay school for the blind, located 1,300 miles from his home. Mehta recounts his years at the Dadar School from age five to eight. In a London *Times* article, Philip Howard stated that "without sentimentality or self-pity [Mehta] recreates that vanished and alien world in one of the richest works of memory of our century." Though Mehta was frequently fighting disease, reviewers comment on how effectively this well-to-do boy adapted to his slum-like surroundings. Blaise notes in the *New York Times Book Review* that *Vedi* "is clearly a mature work. . . . Readers of the two earlier volumes of family biography [*Daddyji* and *Mamaji*] will find less of the overt 'India experience' in 'Vedi,' and more of the dreamlike landscape of childhood. The touch and smell of parents, the test of wills, nightmares, pets."

"Now I want to proclaim this autobiography as nothing less than a literary masterpiece," declared *Times Literary Supplement* contributor R.K. Narayan of Mehta's memoir *The Ledge between the Streams.* Howard wrote that in *The Ledge between the Streams* "nothing much happens; except the most important thing in the world, a child growing up to accept life and enjoy the world." *The Ledge between the Streams* encompasses Mehta's years from age nine to fifteen. *New York Times* critic Michiko Kakutani characterized the Mehta described in this memoir as a "clumsy blind boy, plucky but hopelessly gauche when it came to participating in . . . fun and games—flying kites, riding bicycles and ponies, playing hide-and-seek. . . . In any case, having spent the first half of 'The Ledge' documenting the innocent world of his youth, . . . Mehta then goes on to show how that world was destroyed by the 1947 partition of the Indian subcontinent into India and Pakistan," an event that "turned many families, including . . . Mehta's own, into political and religious refugees. It is this depiction of the partition, as filtered through the sensibility of a 12-year-old boy, that distinguishes 'The Ledge' as a memoir." What reviewers also found successful about *The Ledge between the Streams* is the fact that the reader forgets its author is blind, which is precisely Mehta's goal. Mehta moves into his adolescent years with *Sound-Shadows of the New World,* the account of his first three years in the United States at the Arkansas School for the Blind. According to Mary Lutyens in the *Spectator,* "the vivid, detailed descriptions of this homesick boy's gradual adaptation to an alien culture are uplifting and enthralling," while Ackroyd believed "the single most important quality of the young . . . Mehta was his courage; *Sound-Shadows of the New World* is a record of that courage." Ackroyd continued, "Mehta records his life as if his fall into blindness had broken open his perception so that nothing escapes him, and his account has a clarity that is sometimes like clairvoyance . . . he sees the world very clearly; he describes it so carefully, and yet from such an oblique angle, that in parts it is rather like reading some compelling travelogue of an unknown country." This autobiography reveals how the boy who did not know how to eat with a fork and knife when he first arrived in America eventually became president of the student senate and editor of the school newspaper, an experience that convinced him of his desire to become a journalist.

The next installment in the "Continents of Exile" series is *The Stolen Light.* Beginning when the author is eighteen years old, the book chronicles his years at college during the 1950s when he comes of age and launches himself as a writer. Blind and newly emigrated from India, Mehta "poignantly conveys the agony of wanting to fit into the rigidly coded world of a small American college," wrote Susan Allen Toth in the *New York Times Book Review.* Praising the author's "self-deprecating honesty, scrupulous memory and finely honed perceptions," the reviewer found *The Stolen Light* "awe-inspiring" and a "remarkable story of indefatigable energy and determination."

Up at Oxford recounts the author's undergraduate years at Oxford University in England. An outsider on a number of levels, Mehta nevertheless adapted well at Oxford and graduated with honors. He describes his years at the university's Balliol College from his foreign perspective, exploring the gulf between the university's wealthy public-school boys and its less-privileged grammar-school boys; detailing the formal dress and rigid social mannerisms that still prevailed during his period there—1956 to 1959; and remarking on the college's storied past, with its generation after generation of famous graduates. Reviewing the work in *Spectator,* Bevis Hillier noted: "Written with a stripping-the-willows honesty, [*Up at Oxford*] joins the apostolic succession of the best Oxford memoirs."

In 1998 Mehta recalled his experiences writing under William Shawn's editorship in *Remembering Mr. Shawn's* New Yorker: *The Invisible Art of Editing.* Christopher Lehmann-Haupt, reviewing the book in the *New York Times,* found memoir of the author's three-plus decades at the venerable magazine illuminating, concluding that "if [Mehta] is not so comprehensive as Brandon Gill was in *Here at the* New Yorker, he sheds far more light on what the magazine was like to work at."

All for Love breaks the chronological order of the "Continents of Exile" series, returning to Mehta's early twenties, shortly after his arrival in New York. He narrates with brutal honesty the bitter pain and anguish of four loves—Gigi, Vanessa, Lola, and Kilty—and how they ultimately brought him to Freudian psychoanalysis. According to Kathleen Norris of the *New York Times Book Review,* the analyst "helps him understand that the willfulness that had served him so well as 'an Indian in permanent exile, belonging nowhere and everywhere' and had driven him to pursue success against incredible odds, was counterproductive in romance."

Miranda Seymour, writing in the London *Sunday Times,* explained that Mehta required one condition of each of his four loves: they must understand that, and act as though, his blindness is irrelevant and meaningless. Seymour commented on Mehta's "fatal attraction to a type. . . . Beauty is one quality shared by the four deities by whom Mehta is in turn obsessed. Cruelty is the other. It comes in the form of a spectacular indifference to the emotional damage they cause. . . . Love is presented as a trial of endurance, a challenge to his inability to keep up his role as the invincible hero, master of the universe." Seymour found Mehta's approach to relationships intriguing and complex and his confessional tone laudable and found *All for Love* "remarkable. Mehta is a great stylist; combine this with a story of searing honesty and you have a book that demands an intense response."

Dark Harbor: Building House and Home on an Enchanted Island is Mehta's tenth book in the "Continents of Exile" series. Seduced by his dream of finally putting down roots in the New World, he finds himself buying a fifteen-acre lot of land in the rugged terrain of Dark Harbor. To build his house, Mehta hires architect Edward Larrabee Barnes, famous for designing the IBM Building in New York and museums that include the Walker Art Center in Minnesota. Underlying this narrative is an allegorical tale about Mehta's own struggles as a writer and as a man. Even while constructing the house, he finds himself building another edifice—helping to bring into being an enchantment he had thought might elude him. For the house in Dark Harbor is destined to become a home for the woman he falls in love with and marries and, over the years, the children they have together. The eleventh and final book in the series, *The Red Letters,* revolves around a great surprise to Mehta, who is asked to assist his father in writing a novel. Mehta soon realizes that the events his father are describing involve an extramarital affair his father had before Mehta was born. The son must accept a new version of his father and by extension, his mother, who has coped with a close friend of hers becoming involved with her husband.

From 1970 to 1982 Mehta wrote four nonfiction books aimed at sketching the social and political milieu of late-twentieth-century India. According to Dowd, Mehta's "reports include vivid descriptions of Indian politics, dinner parties given by the viceroy, the assault of the industrial revolution, the attempts at birth control. His work explores the conflict between East and West in the Indian culture and its mixture of grace and vulgarity." Dowd further recorded professor of modern Indian literature at Columbia University Robin Lewis's estimation that "in a very quiet way, . . . Mehta is breaking the Western stereotypes and getting America to look at India as something other than a grandiose stage setting. He's taking the raw material of his personal experience and combining it with some of the pains, crises and historical dislocations that India has gone through."

Mehta's *Portrait of India,* published in 1970, "seems as vast as India" to Stephen Spender in the *New York Times Book Review:* "it is immensely readable, and the reader not only has the sense of immersion in the sights, scents and sounds of India, he also meets representative people from high and low walks of life." *New York Times* writer Thomas Lask believed that if the reader can get through the first seventy-five pages, "you will find yourself in a first-class book. . . . It is surprising how, by the end of the book, the Indian continent has managed to assume a knowledgeable shape and how the problems begin to make sense in terms of the people and the land."

Of Mehta's political books, his 1977 work *Mahatma Gandhi and His Apostles* received the most attention, reviewers stressing that of the several hundred biographies written about the "acclaimed father of India," Mehta's is unique. As the author states in the preface to his book, his desire is "both to demythologize Gandhi and to capture something of the nature of his influence on his followers and the nature of the influence of their interpretations of his life on India." To do this, Mehta traveled to India and England to speak directly with a number of the remaining disciples of Gandhi, something no other biographer had thought to do. As *New York Times* contributor Paul Grimes remarked, "the interviews make it clear that Gandhi-ism did not survive with them. Some profess to be still propagating the Mahatma's cause, but it is obvious that over the years their interpretations of it have become warped if they ever were otherwise."

Grimes found Mehta's account of Gandhi "much more than a biography," "a remarkable examination of the life and work of a human being who has been extolled around the world as one of the greatest souls of all time." Other reviewers criticized the writer for concentrating too heavily on Gandhi's personal life. *Times Literary Supplement* reviewer Eric Stokes felt that Mehta, while "busy destroying old myths . . . is silently weaving a new one of his own. . . . The ultimate distortion in Mehta's picture of the Mahatma is . . . that it allows almost no place for the politician." Leonard A. Gordon in the *Nation* likewise sensed that "Mehta has spent so much time with the private Gandhi, fascinated like his subject with food, sex and hygiene, that we learn almost nothing about the man's great appeal and political skills." Nevertheless, Stokes noted, "Mehta's highly readable book may mark the beginning of a phase when Gandhi is eventually rescued from the hagiographers and given a juster appraisal by his countrymen." In Dowd's interview with Mehta, the writer mentioned his hope that Mahatma's idealism be restored in his native country: "Gandhi had the right vision for a poor country. . . . What people in India need basically is fertilizer, clean water, good seed, good storage facilities . . . , and proper sanitation. Those are the priorities. That's what Gandhi taught."

After the 1982 publication of *A Family Affair: India under Three Prime Ministers,* Mehta did not write again about modern India until the 1994 publication of *Rajiv Gandhi and Rama's Kingdom.* Containing essays produced during his visits to India between 1982 and 1993, the book again focuses on the social and political troubles of his native land. In the book, he ponders the assassinations during this period of two Indian leaders, Indira Gandhi and Rajiv Gandhi; explores the continuing government neglect of the hundreds of millions of Indians who live in severe poverty; and describes social and religious issues such as women's rights and Hindu fundamentalism.

Despite his numerous autobiographical works and political tomes, it is as a staff writer on the *New Yorker* that Mehta is best known in the United States and England. And though to some he may be an easy man to classify, as he explained to Dowd: "I don't belong to any single tradition. I am an amalgam of five cultures—Indian, British, American, blind and [the *New Yorker*]." *Publishers Weekly* contributor Stella Dong recorded Mehta's lifelong literary intentions: "I'm not just slavishly following a chronological framework or trying to interpret India or blindness or any of that. All I'm trying to do is to tell a story of not one life, but many lives and through those stories, to try to say something that's universal."

BIOGRAPHICAL AND CRITICAL SOURCES:

BOOKS

Asian American Literature, Thomson Gale (Detroit, MI), 1999.

Contemporary Literary Criticism, Volume 37, Thomson Gale (Detroit, MI), 1986.

Mehta, Ved *Daddyji,* Farrar, Straus, and Giroux (New York, NY), 1972, reprinted, W.W. Norton (New York, NY), 1988.

Mehta, Ved, *Face to Face: An Autobiography,* Atlantic-Little, Brown (Boston, MA), 1957.

Mehta, Ved, *Mahatma Gandhi and His Apostles,* Viking (New York, NY), 1977, reprinted, Yale University Press (New Haven, CT), 1993.

Mehta, Ved, *Mamaji,* Oxford University Press (New York, NY), 1979.

Mehta, Ved, *Sound-Shadows of the New World,* W.W. Norton (New York, NY), 1986.

Mehta, Ved, *Vedi,* Oxford University Press (New York, NY), 1982.

Mehta, Ved, *The Ledge between the Streams,* W.W. Norton (New York, NY), 1984.

Mehta, Ved, *The Stolen Light,* W.W. Norton (New York, NY), 1989.

Mehta, Ved, *Up at Oxford,* W.W. Norton (New York, NY), 1993.

Notable Asian Americans, Thomson Gale (Detroit, MI), 1995.

PERIODICALS

Atlantic, November, 1963; February, 2002, p. 103.

Booklist, August, 2001, Donna Seaman, review of *All for Love,* p. 2061.

Book World, May 10, 1970.

Chicago Tribune Book World, May 10, 1970.

Christian Century, December 14, 1966.

Christian Science Monitor, May 4, 1967; October 17, 1970.

Globe and Mail (Toronto, Ontario, Canada), July 26, 1986.

Guardian Weekly, June 14, 1981.

Journal of Asian Studies, November, 1983.

*Kirkus Reviews,*July 15, 2004.

Library Journal, September 1, 1966; April 1, 1967; August, 2001, Ilse Heidmann, review of *All for Love,* p. 122.

Listener, September 24, 1970; August 18, 1977.

Los Angeles Times, April 16, 1984, Carolyn See, review of *The Ledge between the Streams*, p. 6; March 3, 1989, Garry Abrams, "Ved Mehta Ruminates on Rushdie Furor," p. 1.

Los Angeles Times Book Review, April 2, 1989.

Nation, February 6, 1967; July 2, 1977.

National Review, July 30, 1963.

New Leader, April 10, 1978.

New Republic, May 13, 1967; July 9, 1977.

New Statesman, February 24, 1967; September 25, 1970.

New Statesman & Society, May 19, 1989, p. 26.

Newsweek, December 31, 1962; July 1, 1963; January 17, 1977; January 30, 1978.

New York Herald Tribune Book Review, August 18, 1957, Gerald W. Johnson, review of *Face to Face;* June 16, 1963.

New York Post, January 10, 1962.

New York Review of Books, June 29, 1967; October 7, 1982, Janet Malcolm, review of *Vedi.*

New York Times, April 6, 1967; April 25, 1970, Thomas Lask, review of *Portrait of India;* May 8, 1972; September 3, 1973; March 30, 1977, Paul Grimes, review of *Mahatma Gandhi and His Apostles;* June 11, 1978; October 21, 1979; December 20, 1979; May 1, 1984, Michiko Kakutani, review of *The Ledge between the Streams;* February 27, 1986; May 18, 1998, Christopher Lehmann-Haupt, review of *Remembering Mr. Shawn's "New Yorker,"* p. E8; October 14, 2001, Kathleen Norris, review of *All for Love*, p. 20.

New York Times Book Review, August 21, 1960, Herbert L. Matthews, review of *Face to Face;* August 18, 1963; November 13, 1966; April 5, 1970; January 29, 1978; October 21, 1979, Clark Blaise, review of *Mamaji;* October 17, 1982, Clark Blaise, review of *Vedi;* May 6, 1984; March 9, 1986; August 30, 1987; March 12, 1989, Sharon Toth, review of *The Stolen Light*, p. 12; September 12, 1993, p. 28.

New York Times Magazine, June 10, 1984, Maureen Dowd, review of *The Ledge between the Streams.*

Observer (London, England), March 18, 1962.

Publishers Weekly, January 3, 1986, Stella Dong, interview with Mehta, pp. 57-58; January 27, 1989, Genevieve Stuttaford, review of *The Stolen Light*, p. 461; June 28, 1993, review of *Up at Oxford*, p. 61; November 21, 1994, review of *Rajiv Gandhi and Rama's Kingdom*, p. 60; May 19, 2003, review of *Dark Harbor*, p. 64.

Reporter, May 4, 1967.

Saturday Review, August 17, 1957; November 12, 1966; April 29, 1967; April 25, 1970; May 20, 1972, P.K. Sundara Rajan, review of *Daddyji;* January 22, 1977.

Spectator, May 12, 1961; October 4, 1963; July 28, 1984; May 31, 1986, Mary Lutyens, review of *Sound-Shadows of the New World;* September 25, 1993, Bevis Hillier, review of *Up at Oxford*, p. 27.

Sunday Times (London, England), August 1, 2002, Miranda Seymour, review of *All for Love*, p. 341

Times (London, England), October 19, 1972, review of *Daddyji*, p. E10; June 15, 1977, review of *Mahatma Gandhi and His Apostles*, p. C10; July 5, 1984, Philip Howard, review of *Vedi;* June 8, 1985; May 15, 1986, Peter Ackroyd, "Light Shining in Darkness"; May 20, 1989, Victoria Glendinning, "Vision of Success."

Times Literary Supplement, December 8, 1966; December 4, 1970, review of *Portrait of India;* November 19, 1971; August 5, 1977, Eric Stokes, review of *Mahatma Gandhi and His Apostles;* July 4, 1980; May 29, 1981; July 5, 1984, R.K. Narayan, review of *The Ledge between the Streams;* July 6, 1984, review of *Daddyji, Mammaji;* May 30, 1986.

Washington Post, December 28, 1982.

Washington Post Book World, January 20, 1980; July 25, 1982; March 9, 1986.

World Literature Today, autumn, 1983.

ONLINE

Ved Mehta Home Page, http://www.vedmehta.com/ (July 27, 2004).

* * *

MEHTA, Ved Parkash
See MEHTA, Ved

* * *

MEMBERS, Mark
See POWELL, Anthony

* * *

MÉNDEZ, Miguel 1930-

PERSONAL: Born June 15, 1930, in Bisbee, AZ; son of Francisco Méndez Cardenas (a farmer and miner) and Maria Morales; married Maria Dolores Fontes; children: Miguil Fontes, Isabel Cristina. *Education:* Attended schools in El Claro, Sonora, Mexico, for six years.

ADDRESSES: Office—Department of Spanish and Portuguese, University of Arizona, Modern Languages, Tucson, AZ 85721.

CAREER: Writer. Went to work as an itinerant farm laborer along the Arizona-Sonora border at the age of fifteen; bricklayer and construction worker in Tucson, AZ, 1946-70; Pima Community College, Tucson, AZ, served as instructor in Spanish, Hispanic literature, and creative writing, beginning 1970; University of Arizona, Tuscon, AZ, instructor in Chicano literature, professor emeritus, Spanish and Portuguese.

MEMBER: Association of Teachers of Spanish and Portuguese.

AWARDS, HONORS: Honorary Doctor of Humanities, University of Arizona, 1984; Jose Fuentes Mares National Award of Mexican Literature, Universidad Autonoma de Ciudad Juarez, 1991; Creative Writing fellowship, Arizona Commission on the Arts, 1992.

WRITINGS:

(With others) Octavio I. Romano and Herminio Rios-C., editors, *El Espejo/The Mirror,* Quinto Sol, 1969.

Peregrinos de Aztlan (novel), Editorial Peregrinos, 1974, translation by David W. Foster published as *Pilgrims in Aztlan,* Bilingual Press/ Editorial Bilingue (Tempe, AZ), 1992.

Los criaderos humanos y Sahuaros (poem; title means "The Human Breeding Grounds and Saguaros"), Editorial Peregrinos, 1975.

Cuentos para ninos traviesos: Stories for Mischievous Children (short stories; bilingual edition), translations by Eva Price, Justa (Berkeley, CA), 1979.

Tata Casehua y otros cuentos (short stories; bilingual edition; title means "Tata Casehua and Other Stories"), translations by Eva Price, Leo Barrow, and Marco Portales, Justa (Berkely, CA), 1980.

Critica al poder politico, Ediciones Universal (Miami, FL), 1981.

De la vida y del folclore de la frontera (short stories; title means "From Life and Folklore along the Border"), Mexican-American Studies and Research Center, University of Arizona (Tuscon, AZ), 1986.

El sueno de Santa María de las Piedras (novel), Universidad de Guadalajara, 1986, translation by David W. Foster published as *The Dream of Santa María de las Piedras,* Bilingual Press/Editorial Bilingue (Tempe, AZ), 1989.

Que no mueran los suenos, Era (Mexico), 1991.

Los Muertos También Cuentan, Universidad Autonoma de Ciudad Juarez (Chihuahua, Mexico), 1995.

Entre letras y ladrillos: autobiografia novelada, Bilingual Press/Editorial Bilingue (Tempe, AZ), 1996, translation by David William Foster published as *From Labor to Letters: A Novel Autobiography,* 1997.

Río Santacruz, Ediciones Osuna (Armilla, Granada), 1997.

El Circo que se perdió en el Desierto de Sonora, Fondo de Cultura Económica (Mexico), 2002.

Also author of *El Hombre vibora;Pasen, lectores, pasen. Aqui se hacen imagenes* (poems); *Cuentos para ninos precoces* (short stories); and *Cuentos y ensayos para reir y aprender* (title means "Stories and Essays for Laughing and Learning"), 1988. Contributor to periodicals, including *La Palabra* and *Revista Chicano-Riquena.* The spring-fall, 1981, issue of *La Palabra* is entirely devoted to Méndez' work.

SIDELIGHTS: Miguel Méndez has attracted the admiration of many critics with his richly poetic prose, his erudite language, and his depictions of the poor members of an uprooted society at odds with the Anglo-American culture that threatens their heritage. His first novel, 1974's *Peregrinos de Aztlan* (translated as *Pilgrims in Aztlan* in 1992), is considered a landmark in Chicano literature for its experimental use of Spanglish (a mixture of Spanish and English), its blending of mythology with social realism, and its attention to poor, itinerant farm workers who formed the bulk of early Mexican immigration to the United States.

Much of the author's work uses elements from his Spanish and Yaqui Indian heritages. The name Aztlan in *Peregrinos de Aztlan,* for instance, is taken from the mythic northern homeland of the Aztec Indians of Mexico, and is believed to have been somewhere in the southwestern United States. Loreto Maldonado, the main character of *Peregrinos de Aztlan,* who now wanders the streets of Tijuana, Mexico, making a living by washing cars, was once a revolutionary and served under Pancho Villa. The title character in "Tata Casehua," found in the short-story collection *Tata Casehua y otros cuentos,* is actually the hero warrior Tetabiate, and the story details his search for an heir to whom he can pass on his tribe's history. And Timoteo, a key character in the novel *El sueno de Santa María de las Piedras,* ventures across the United States in search of the earthly god Huachusey, apparently with success, as he is repeatedly told "What you say?" by Americans in answer to his questions about the creator of things he encounters.

Méndez also draws upon his personal past, growing up in a Mexican government farming community and later working in agriculture and construction, for his stories. "During my childhood," he told Juan D. Bruce-Novoa in *Chicano Authors: Inquiry by Interview,* "I heard many stories from those people who came from different places, and, like my family, were newcomers to El Claro. They would tell anecdotes about the [Mexican] Revolution, the Yaqui wars, and innumerable other themes, among which there was no lack of apparitions and superstitions. Those days were extremely dramatic. I learned about tragedy, at times in the flesh." When at the age of fifteen Méndez left Mexico to find work as an agricultural laborer in the United States, he met the exploited people who appear in his fiction—indigent workers, prostitutes, and Hispanics looking for jobs in the North, among others.

Another major component of the author's work is the oral tradition handed down by these poor people; indeed, Méndez sees their plight as one symptom of the loss of that tradition. "Familial, communal, ethnic, and national heritage, which once was preserved by word of mouth, is disappearing into silence," explained Bruce-Novoa. "At the same time, written history represents only the elite classes' vision of the past, ignoring the existence of the poor. Thus, as the poor abandon the oral preservation of their heritage and simultaneously embrace literacy, alienation and a sense of diaspora possess them. Méndez counterattacks through his writing, not only by revealing the threat to the oral tradition, but also by filling his written texts with oral tradition." The author's interest in reclaiming this lost tradition is evidenced in *El sueno de Santa María de las Piedras,* in which he "employs the narrative voice of five old Mexicans . . . in order to unfold the historical fragments of a fictitious, yet universal Mexican town in the Sonora desert between 1830 and 1987," remarked Roland Walter in *Americas Review.*

In 1997, the author's autobiography was published and translated into English as *From Labor to Letters: A Novel Autobiography.* In it Méndez recounts his extraordinary life, going from six years of grade school to manual labor to a university professor and acclaimed writer. Writing in *Melus,* Marco Portales noted, "Presenting himself as the subject of a Cinderella life that he alternately eschews and suggests, Méndez skillfully weaves a narrative from the warp and woof of this consciousness on the experiences he has amassed and imagined, everything in life serving as useful material for the ever-creating Chicano author." In his autobiography, Méndez weavers together passages that read like a diary with other sections that are written in stream-of-consciousness style. He ponders the hardships he experiences and his own doubts about his status as an author. He also talks about his love of life and academia. Portales praised Méndez as a "natural-born writer, an author who has worked and sacrificed to develop the talents with which he is endowed for writing stories and for detailing the seldom recorded and hard lives that Chicanos daily face in the Arizona-Mexico border region of the Mexican-American Southwest." The reviewer also noted that the author's "intuition and legacy is that time will continue to bring out the truth in his writings about the inner feelings and lives of Chicanos, and I believe his book hits the necessary target again."

BIOGRAPHICAL AND CRITICAL SOURCES:

BOOKS

Anaya, Rodolfo A., and Francisco A. Lomeli, editors, *Aztlan: Essays on the Chicano Homeland,* Academia/El Norte (Albuquerque, NM), 1989.

Bruce-Novoa, Juan D., *Chicano Authors: Inquiry by Interview,* University of Texas Press (Austin, TX), 1980.

Martinez, Julio A., *Chicano Scholars and Writers: A Bio-Bibliographical Directory,* Scarecrow Press (Metuchen, NJ), 1979.

Rodriguez del Pino, Salvador, *Interview with Miguel Méndez M.,* Center for Chicano Studies, University of California, Santa Barbara, 1976.

Tatum, Charles M., *Chicano Literature,* Twayne (Boston, MA), 1982.

PERIODICALS

America, July 18, 1992, p. 42.

Americas Review, spring, 1990, Roland Walter, pp. 103-112.

Bloomsbury Review, March-April, 1994, pp. 3, 5.

Booklist, December 15, 1992, p. 719.

Denver Quarterly, fall, 1981, pp. 16-22; spring, 1982, pp. 68-77.

La Palabra, spring-fall, 1981, pp. 3-17, 50-57, 67-76.

Library Journal, March 15, 1993, p. 108.

Melus, spring, 1998, Marco Portales, review of *From Labor to Letters: A Novel Autobiography.*

Publishers Weekly, February 8, 1993, p. 83.

* * *

MERCHANT, Paul

See ELLISON, Harlan

MERRILL, James 1926-1995 (James Ingram Merrill)

PERSONAL: Born March 3, 1926, in New York, NY; died of a heart attack, a complication of AIDS, February 6, 1995, in Tucson, AZ; son of Charles Edward (a stockbroker) and Hellen (Ingram) Merrill; partner of David Jackson. *Education:* Amherst College, B.A., 1947.

CAREER: Poet, novelist, and playwright. *Military service:* U.S. Army, 1944-45.

AWARDS, HONORS: Oscar Blumenthal Prize, 1947; Levinson Prize, *Poetry* magazine, 1949, and Harriet Monroe Memorial Prize, 1951; Morton Dauwen Zabel Memorial Prize, 1965, for "From the Cupola"; National Book Award in poetry, 1967, for *Nights and Days,* and 1979, for *Mirabell: Books of Number;* D.Litt., Amherst College, 1968; Bollingen Prize in Poetry, 1973; Pulitzer Prize, 1976, for *Divine Comedies; Scripts for the Pageant* was nominated for a National Book Critics Circle Award, 1980; *Los Angeles Times* Book Award for Poetry, 1983, and National Books Critics Circle Award, 1989, both for *The Changing Light at Sandover;* Rebekah Johnson Bobbitt National Prize in poetry, 1990.

WRITINGS:

POETRY

Jim's Book: A Collection of Poems and Short Stories, privately printed, 1942.
The Black Swan, Icarus (Athens, Greece), 1946.
First Poems, Knopf (New York, NY), 1951.
Short Stories, Banyan Press (Pawlet, VT), 1954.
The Country of a Thousand Years of Peace, Knopf (New York, NY), 1959, revised edition, Atheneum (New York, NY), 1970.
Selected Poems, Chatto & Windus (London, England), 1961.
Water Street, Atheneum (New York, NY), 1962.
Nights and Days, Atheneum (New York, NY), 1966.
The Fire Screen, Atheneum (New York, NY), 1969.
Braving the Elements, Atheneum (New York, NY), 1972.
Two Poems: From the Cupola and the Summer People, Chatto & Windus (London, England), 1972.
Yannina, Phoenix Book Shop (New York, NY), 1973.
The Yellow Pages: 59 Poems, Temple Bar Bookshop (Cambridge, MA), 1974.
Divine Comedies (includes "The Book of Ephraim"; also see below), Atheneum (New York, NY), 1976.
Metamorphosis of 741, Banyan Press (Chicago, IL), 1977.
Mirabell: Books of Number (published as "Mirabell's Books of Number" in *The Changing Light at Sandover;* also see below), Atheneum (New York, NY), 1978.
Scripts for the Pageant (also see below), Atheneum (New York, NY), 1980.
The Changing Light at Sandover (contains "The Book of Ephraim," "Mirabell's Books of Number," "Scripts for the Pageant," and a new coda), Atheneum (New York, NY), 1982.
From the First Nine: Poems 1946-1976, Atheneum (New York, NY), 1982.
From the Cutting-Room Floor, University of Nebraska Press (Lincoln, NE), 1983.
Late Settings, Atheneum (New York, NY), 1985.
The Inner Room, Knopf (New York, NY), 1988.
Selected Poems, 1946-1985, Knopf (New York, NY), 1992.
A Scattering of Salts, Knopf (New York, NY), 1995.
Self-Portrait in Tyvek Windbreaker and Other Poems, Dedalus Press (Dublin, Ireland), 1995.
Collected Poems, edited by J.D. McClatchy and Stephen Yenser, Knopf (New York, NY), 2001.

PLAYS

The Immortal Husband (produced in New York, NY, 1955), published in *Playbook,* New Directions (New York, NY), 1956.
The Bait (produced in New York, NY, 1953), published in *Artists Theatre,* Grove (New York, NY), 1960.
The Image Maker: A Play in One Act, Sea Cliff Press (New York, NY), 1986.
Collected Novels and Plays, edited by J.D. McClatchy and Stephen Yenser. Knopf (New York, NY), 2002.

OTHER

The Seraglio (novel), Knopf (New York, NY), 1957, reprinted, Atheneum (New York, NY), 1987.
The (Diblos) Notebook (novel), Atheneum (New York, NY), 1965, reprinted, Dalkey Archive Press (Normal, IL), 1994.
Recitative: Prose (nonfiction), North Point Press (San Francisco, CA), 1986.
A Different Person: A Memoir (nonfiction), Knopf (New York, NY), 1993.
Collected Prose, edited by J.D. McClatchy and Stephen Yenser, Knopf (New York, NY), 2004.

Contributor to anthologies, including *Poems on Poetry,* edited by Robert Wallace and J.G. Taaffe, Dutton, 1965, *Poems of Our Moment,* edited by John Hollander, Pegasus, 1968, and *New Yorker Book of Poems,* Viking, 1970. Contributor to periodicals, including *Hudson Review* and *Poetry.* Selections of Merrill's poetry, read by Merrill, was released by Random Audio as part of its "The Voice of the Poet" series, 1999.

Some of Merrill's poetry has been translated into Greek.

SIDELIGHTS: The late James Merrill was recognized as one of the master poets of his generation. Merrill's work was praised for its elegance of style, its moral sensibilities, and its transformation of autobiographical moments into deep and complex poetry. Through a long and productive career, Merrill wrote plays, prose, and fiction, but the bulk of his artistic expression can be found in his poetry. His work won almost every important literary citation from the Pulitzer Prize to the Bollingen Prize and the National Book Award, and he was, according to *New York Times Book Review* essayist Petet Stitt, "one of the most cunning, elusive, thoughtful, challenging and rewarding poets writing." *New York Times* columnist Michiko Kakutani commended Merrill for his "mastery of various verse forms and conventions, his exquisite command of irony and wit . . . his achievement of a wholly distinctive voice—a voice that is cooly elusive as melting sherbet, poised and elaborate as a finely-wrought antique clock." *Washington Post Book World* contributor Joel Conarroe called Merrill "an extravagantly gifted artist . . . America's leading poet."

As soon as he began publishing poetry in 1951, Merrill was recognized as a virtual master of poetic forms. He once explained in the *New York Review of Books* how he took "instinctively . . . to quatrains, to octaves and sestets, when I began to write poems." His earliest works reflect the gentility of his upperclass upbringing as well as his eloquence and wit. But for all their technical virtuosity, his early verses are largely static works, more concerned with objects than people. It was not until his themes became more dramatic and personal that he began to win serious attention and literary acclaim. Merrill received his first National Book Award in 1967 for *Nights and Days,* and his second in 1979 for *Mirabell: Books of Number.* In the interim he won both the Bollingen Prize in Poetry and the Pulitzer Prize, the latter for a book of occult poetry called *Divine Comedies.*

Known in popular circles as "the Ouija poet"—one who composed with assistance from the spirit world—Merrill was always most popular with scholarly audiences. As Brigitte Weeks noted in the *New York Times Book Review,* "Merrill's artistic distinction is for the most part acknowledged, particularly in the academy, where he has already become part of the permanent canon. With his technical virtuosity and his metaphysical broodings, he is, like Wallace Stevens, an ideal seminar poet whose complex work lends itself to exhaustive explication."

Born into a wealthy New York family, Merrill was privately educated in schools that placed a good deal of emphasis on poetry. His interest in language was also fired by his governess—a Prussian-English widow who was fluent in both German and French. She taught young James that English was merely one way of expressing things, while his parents encouraged his early efforts at verse. His first book of poems was privately printed by his father—cofounder of the stockbrokerage firm Merrill-Lynch—during his senior year at Lawrenceville.

When Merrill was twelve, his parents divorced, his governess was discharged, and he was sent to boarding school. The diary he kept during a subsequent vacation in Silver Springs, Florida, included what, in retrospect, would prove to be a revealing entry: "Silver Springs—heavenly colors and swell fish." Years later, in the *New York Review of Books,* Merrill explained how that statement reflected his feelings of loss and foreshadowed a major theme in his poetry. "'Heavenly colors and swell fish.' What is that phrase but an attempt to bring my parents together, to remarry on the page their characteristic inflections—the ladylike gush and the regular-guy terseness? In reality my parents have tones more personal and complex than these, but the time is still far off when I can dream of echoing them."

A fusion of autobiography and archetype would become a hallmark of Merrill's verse, according to Andrew V. Ettin who wrote in *Perspective,* "The transformation of the natural, autobiographical, narrative events and tone into the magical, universal, sonorous, eternal is one of the principal characteristics of Merrill's poetry, perhaps the main source of its splendid and moving qualities." *Dictionary of Literary Biography* contributor William Spiegelman credited Merrill with discovering "what most lyric poets . . . have yet to find: a context for a life, a pattern for presenting autobiography in lyric verse through the mediation of myth and fable."

Influenced not only by events, but also by the act of writing, Merrill, "with increasing awareness, courage and delight, has been developing an autobiography: 'developing' as from a photographic negative which becomes increasingly clear," David Kalstone explained in the *Times Literary Supplement.* "He has not led the kind of outwardly dramatic life which would make external changes the centre of his poetry. Instead, poetry itself has been one of the changes, something which continually happens to him, and Merrill's subject proves to be the subject of the great Romantics: the constant revisions of the self that come through writing verse. Each book seems more specious because of the one which has come before."

While Merrill's verse abounds with details from daily life, Joseph Parisi noted in *Poetry* that it "never reeks of ego." Or, as Helen Vendler observed in the *New York Times Book Review,* the best of Merrill's poems "are autobiographical without being 'confessional': they show none of that urgency to reveal the untellable or unspeakable that we associate with the poetry we call 'confessional'. . . . It is as though a curtain had been drawn aside, and we are permitted a glimpse of . . . a life that goes on unconscious of us, with the narrator so perfectly an actor in his own drama that his presence as narrator is rendered transparent, invisible."

One of the ways Merrill achieved this stance was through the manipulation of meter and rhyme. "His mastery of forms, whether old or new, keeps his self-revelatory poems (and some of them are painful) from the worst lapses of recent poets of the confessional school," X.J. Kennedy observed in the *Atlantic.* "Merrill never sprawls, never flails about, never strikes postures. Intuitively he knows that, as Yeats once pointed out, in poetry, 'all that is personal soon rots; it must be packed in ice or salt.'"

Because they both wrote mystical poems, Yeats and Merrill have often been compared. Like Yeats, whose wife was a medium, Merrill believed he received inspiration from the world beyond. His *Divine Comedies* features an affable ghost named Ephraim who instructs the poet, while Yeats's "A Vision" features the spirit Leo Africanus in a similar role. Critics have found other influences at work in Merrill's poems as well, drawing parallels between his writing and the work of Dante (whose *Divine Comedy* was the inspiration for Merrill's title), W.H. Auden (who, like Merrill, believed that poems are constructed of words, not emotions), and Marcel Proust (who was also dismissed as a mere aesthete early in his career).

In a *Times Literary Supplement* review, David Kalstone further explained how Proust's vision colored Merrill's world. "When he turned to narrative and social comedy, it was always with the sense—Proust's sense—that the world discerned is not quite real, that in its flashing action he might catch glimpses of patterns activated by charged moments of his life." Spiegelman believed that as "an heir to Proust, Merrill achieves a scope in poetry comparable to that of the major novelists: his great themes are the recovery of time (in spite of loss) through willed or automatic memory, and the alternating erosions and bequests of erotic experience. He focuses on what is taken, what abides, in love and time, and considers how to handle them."

In Merrill's early poems these concerns seldom surface. The verse of *First Poems* and *The Country of a Thousand Years of Peace and Other Poems* sometimes struck reviewers as needlessly obscure, devoid of human passion, and removed from actual life. In his *Babel to Byzantium,* James Dickey wrote that to read such poems is "to enter a realm of connoisseurish aesthetic contemplation, where there are no things more serious than gardens (usually formal), dolls, swans, statues, works of art, operas, delightful places in Europe, the ancient gods in tasteful and thought-provoking array, more statues, many birds and public parks, and, always, 'the lovers,' wandering through it all as if they surely lived." Writing of this kind, continued Dickey, "has enough of [Henry] James's insistence upon manners and decorum to evoke a limited admiration for the taste, wit, and eloquence that such an attitude makes possible, and also enough to drive you mad over the needless artificiality, prim finickiness, and determined inconsequence of it all."

In 1959, when Merrill began spending six months of each year in Athens, his poetry took on some of the warmth and intimacy of the old Greek culture. And, as the poems became more personal, they also became more accessible, although their appeal was still limited, as Ian Hamilton explained. "Even though—with *Water Street* in 1962—he had toughened and colloquialized his verse line and eliminated much of the wan artifice that marked his very early work, there was still—in his usual persona—a delicate strain of yearning otherworldliness, a delicate discomfiture which was neither neurotic nor ideological. His was a poetry of, and for, the few—the few kindred spirits," Hamilton wrote in the *Washington Post Book World.*

With each step he took away from rigid formalism, Merrill gained critical ground. Unwilling to restrict his choice and assembly of language, he nevertheless progressed toward a more conversational verse reminiscent of the structure of prose. "The flashes and glimpses of 'plot' in some of the lyrics—especially the longer poems—reminded Merrill's readers that he wanted more than the usual proportion of dailiness and detail in his lyrics, while preserving a language far from the plainness of journalistic poetry, a language full of arabesques, fancifulness, play of wit, and oblique metaphor," wrote Helen Vendler in the *New York Review of Books.* In fact, Merrill tried his hand at both plays and novels and considered writing his epic poem "The Book of Ephraim" as a prose narrative. He abandoned the idea, for reasons that he explains in the poem: "The more I struggled to be plain, the more / Mannerism hobbled me. What for? / Since it had never truly fit, why wear / The shoe of prose? In verse the feet went bare."

It was "The Book of Ephraim"—which appeared in *Divine Comedies*—that prompted many critics to reevaluate the poet. Among them was Harold Bloom, who wrote in the *New Republic,* "James Merrill . . . has convinced many discerning readers of a greatness, or something like it, in his first six volumes of verse, but until this year I remained a stubborn holdout. The publication of *Divine Comedies* . . . converts me, absolutely if belatedly, to Merrill. . . . The book's eight shorter poems surpass nearly all the earlier Merrill, but its apocalypse (a lesser word won't do) is a 100-page verse-tale, 'The Book of Ephraim,' an occult splendor in which Merrill rivals Yeats' 'A Vision,'. . . and even some aspects of Proust."

Spiegelman described *Divine Comedies* as "Merrill's supreme fiction, a self-mythologizing within an epic program. At last Merrill's masters combine with graceful fluency in a confection entirely his own: the reader finds Proust's social world, his analysis of the human heart and the artist's growth; Dante's encyclopedia of a vast universal organization; and Yeats's spiritualism, for which the hints in the earlier volumes gave only small promise. Added to these are the offhand humor of Lord Byron and W.H. Auden, a Neoplatonic theory of reincarnation, a self-reflexiveness about the process of composition, and a virtual handbook of poetic technique. 'The Book of Ephraim,' the volume's long poem, is chapter one of Merrill's central statement."

The two volumes that followed, *Mirabell: Books of Number* and *Scripts for the Pageant,* continue the narrative that "The Book of Ephraim" begins. Together these three poems form a trilogy that was published with a new coda in *The Changing Light at Sandover.* This unprecedented 560-page epic records the Ouija board sessions that Merrill and David Jackson, his companion, conducted with spirits from the other world. Appropriately, Merrill organized each section of the trilogy to reflect a different component of their homemade Ouija board. The twenty-six sections of "The Book of Ephraim" correspond to the board's A to Z alphabet, the ten sections of *Mirabell: Books of Number* correspond to the board's numbering from zero to nine, and the three sections of *Scripts for the Pageant* ("Yes," "&," and "No") correspond to the board's Yes & No. The progression of poems also represents a kind of celestial hierarchy, with each book representing communication with a higher order of spirits than the one before. Humans in the poem are identified by their initials—DJ and JM; spirits speak in all capitals. By the time Merrill transcribed the lessons of the archangels in book three, he offered nothing less than a model of the universe. "Were such information conveyed to us by a carnival 'spiritual adviser,' we could dismiss it as mere nonsense," observed Fred Moramarco in the *Los Angeles Times Book Review,* "but as it comes from a poet of Merrill's extraordinary poetic and intellectual gifts, we sit up and take notice."

In the first book, Merrill's guide is Ephraim, "a Greek Jew / Born AD 8 at XANTHOS," later identified as "Our Familiar Spirit." Over a period of twenty years and in a variety of settings, Ephraim alerts DJ and JM to certain cosmic truths, including the fact that "on Earth / We're each the REPRESENTATIVE of a PATRON" who guides our souls through the nine stages of being until we become patrons for other souls. Witty, refined, full of gossip, Ephraim is "a clear cousin to Merrill's poetic voice," Kalstone wrote in the *Times Literary Supplement.*

Other spirits also appear in the poem, many of them family members or old friends who have died: Merrill's mother and father, the young poet Hans Lodeizen (whose death Merrill addressed in *The Country of a Thousand Years of Peace*), the Athenian Maria Mitsotaki (a green-thumbed gardener who died of cancer), as well as literary figures such as W.H. Auden and Plato. They form a community, according to Ephraim, "WITHIN SIGHT OF ALL CONNECTED TO EACH OTHER DEAD OR ALIVE NOW DO YOU UNDERSTAND WHAT HEAVEN IS IT IS THE SURROUND OF THE LIVING." As Helen Vendler explained in the *New York Review of Books,* "The host receives his visible and invisible guests, convinced that . . . the poet's paradise is nothing other than all those beings whom he has known and has imagined." For this reason, Vendler maintained that "The Book of Ephraim" is "centrally a hymn to history and a meditation on memory—personal history and personal memory, which are, for this poet at least, the muse's materials."

Aware of the incredulity his spiritualism would provoke, Merrill addressed this issue early in book one: "The question / Of who or what we took Ephraim to be / And of what truths (if any) we considered / Him spokesman, had arisen from the start." Indeed, Vendler said, "for rationalists reading the poem, Merrill includes a good deal of self-protective irony, even incorporating in the tale a visit to his ex-shrink, who proclaims the evocation of Ephraim and the other Ouija 'guests' from the other world a *folie a deux* [mutual madness] between Merrill and his friend David Jackson."

In a *Poetry* review, Joseph Parisi suggested that Merrill used "his own doubt and hesitation to undercut and simultaneously to underscore his seriousness in recounting . . . his fabulous . . . message. Anticipating the incredulity of 'sophisticated' and even cynical readers, the poet portrays his own apparent skepticism at these tales from the spirit world to preempt and disarm the attacks, while making the reader feel he is learning the quasi-occult truths . . . along with the poet."

As the experience proceeded, Merrill's skepticism declined. And while the reader's may not, Judith Moffett suggested in *American Poetry Review* that disbelief is not the issue: "Surely any literary work ought to be judged not on its matter but on the way the matter is presented and treated. . . . The critical question, then, should not be, Is this the story he ought to have told? but How well has he told this story?" Moffett, as well as numerous other critics, believed Merrill has told it very well: "'The Book of Ephraim' is a genuinely great poem—a phrase no one should use lightly—and very possibly the most impressive poetic endeavor in English in this century."

In book two, Ephraim is overshadowed by a band of bat-like creatures who "SPEAK FROM WITHIN THE ATOM," demanding "POEMS OF SCIENCE" from JM. These are the fallen angels whose task is now to mind the machinery put in motion by God Biology, whose enemy is Chaos. Their request appears on the board: "FIND US BETTER PHRASES FOR THESE HISTORIES WE POUR FORTH / HOPING AGAINST HOPE THAT MAN WILL LOVE HIS MIND LANGUAGE." As poet, Merrill serves as a vehicle for divine revelation, and, by tapping his "word bank," the bats can combat Chaos. They explain: "THE SCRIBE SHALL / SUPPLANT RELIGION, & THE ENTIRE APPARATUS / DEVELOP THE WAY TO PARADISE." At another point, Merrill learns that he was chosen to receive this vision in part because of his homosexuality: he will devote his energies not to children, but to art.

God Biology's chief messenger is a spirit initially identified as 741, who Merrill names Mirabell. Mirabell warns of the two major threats to human existence: overpopulation and nuclear power. In passages that almost all critics consider elitist, Mirabell explains that there are only two million enlightened souls in the world. The rest are inferior animal souls who reproduce prolifically and into whose hands atomic weaponry now threatens to fall. Too little given to reason and restraint, these souls allow Chaos to gain ground.

While acknowledging that "one can see the intricate rationale of such statements in the context of Mirabell's general themes," Joseph Parisi maintained that readers "may be uncomfortable with the elitism which is implicit, and ultimately counterproductive, if indeed the poem pretends to enlighten and to teach. . . . For all the charm of Mirabell's small circle of friends, some may be put off by their blithe air of superiority, as others may be by the High Tea (not to mention Camp) atmosphere of the Heavenly get-togethers." Stephen Spender pointed out in the *New York Review of Books* that "this reader sometimes feels that Merrill's heaven is a tea party to which he is not likely to be invited because he will not understand the 'in' jokes." Remarked Moffett: "By portraying intelligent poetic and musical gays as the evolutionary *creme de la creme,* Merrill makes himself vulnerable to charges of narcissism; the same could be said of passages in which heaven lavishes praise upon its spokesmen." But, "to be fair," concluded Edmund White in his book, *Loss within Loss: Artists in the Age of AIDS,* "I should point out that the fault lies not in Merrill, but in his bats; they are the ones who portray the hierarchical system. He is merely their scribe."

One of the duties of the bats, Merrill once explained in the *Kenyon Review,* is to prepare David and him for "a seminar with the angels—whose twenty-five lessons are in fact the marrow of the third volume." While the poet here confronts essential questions about the mystery of creation, the structure of the universe, and the fate of man, some critics find the final message of *Scripts for the Pageant* in its organizing principle, "Yes No." Charles Molesworth explained in the *New Republic* that, "taken serially, these three words form irreducible language acts, namely assertion, qualification, and denial. Taken all together, they form the essence of equivocation, which can be seen as either the fullest sort of language act or the very subversion of language." By characterizing his acceptance of the spirits' wisdom in terms of "Yes No," Merrill "transforms the poem into a hymn celebrating, among other things, 'resistance' as 'Nature's gift to man,'" Mary Jo Salter wrote in the *Atlantic*. As the myth is reappraised and corrected by the characters who are themselves a part of it, Salter believed that "'Yes No' becomes an answer to every question: not an equivocation of authorial (or divine) responsibility, but an acknowledgment that 'fact is fable,' that the question of man's future, if any, is one he must answer for himself."

By the time *Scripts for the Pageant* ends, Merrill has made clear his vision of the self as a story that unfolds over time. During one lesson, the angels discuss two previous races of creatures who were destroyed. Afterwards, Merrill, to use Molesworth's words, "advances a set of parallels between the account of the two earlier races and his own childhood, as he was preceded by two siblings and his parents divorced while he was still a child. Autobiography and creation myth: by hinting they're the same Merrill deals with a key modernist, and a key American theme."

Merrill was one of the rare artists who, by virtue of his Merrill Lynch fortune, never needed to concern himself with making a living. His gratitude for that is reflected in his creation of the Ingram Merrill Foundation, a permanent endowment created for writers and painters. Merrill died of a heart attack in February of 1995 while vacationing in Tucson. He continued to write poetry and prose until his death and even published a memoir, *A Different Person,* in 1993. Merrill's final volume of poetry, *A Scattering of Salts,* "provides an elegant closure for his life's work, the kind of bittersweet ending he treasured," remarked Phoebe Pettingell in *The New Leader.* Writing in the *New York Review of Books,* Helen Vendler stated, "In the new volume, Merrill gives on almost every page the impression of looking back over the past, both as he lived it and as he wrote about it. *A Scattering of Salts* is an elegiac book, but one written in an ultimately comic spirit."

Many critics who eulogized Merrill after his death accented the complexity of his style and world-view, but *New York Times Book Review* correspondent Carolyn Kizer commended the poet for another gift entirely. "Mr. Merrill is a great love poet," the critic concluded. "There have been so many breathtaking feats of prestidigitation before our busy eyes that this may have escaped our notice. But it's true. Most of his poems breathe with love. And that is another and even greater gift he has given us."

Collected Poems, edited by J.D. McClatchy and Stephen Yenser, is the first volume in a series compiling all of Merrill's work, including his novels, plays, and collected prose. The 885-page book, which was published on the sixth anniversary of Merrill's death, includes his entire body of poetry from his privately printed *Black Swan* to his posthumous collection *A Scattering of Salts,* the only exceptions being juvenalia and *The Changing Light at Sandover.* In addition, *Collected Poems* brings together for the first time twenty-one of his translations from Apollinaire, Montale, Cavafy, and others and forty-four previously uncollected poems, including elegies to Philip Larkin, Elizabeth Bishop, and others. David Rosen wrote in the *Lambda Book Report* that "this astonishingly beautiful (and blessedly bulky) collection appears at a particularly significant moment in time," as "the necessary angel that enlarges our appreciation of Merrill's poetic achievement and illumines (with a newfound fullness) the creative interplay between his life and oeuvre."

McClatchy told Mel Gussow of the *New York Times,* "Having read him book by book, I was surprised by the sheer bulk of his achievement when it's all put together, and struck too by the sustained brilliance and inventiveness of it, the restless search for new experiences within which to explore old obsessions." Daniel Mendelsohn wrote in the *New York Times Book Review* that "as ravishing as the early work is, you often can't help feeling that in these poems the insights about art and life and death have been learned—book-learned, that is—rather than earned. One of the pleasures of having nearly all of Merrill in one volume is to see how the poet grew into his poetry—how he became willing to grapple with things themselves, rather than the intellectualized or aestheticized symbols of things (black swans, say)." *Advocate* reviewer David Bahr praised Merrill's later poems, which he called "among his best, most inviting and deeply resonant works. . . . His final poems prove that Merrill was not merely a master of measured verse but a profound chronicler of the human condition." *New Republic* contributor Adam Kirsch added: "Reading *Collected Poems* leaves no doubt that Merrill was one of the finest American poets of the last half-century. His achievement was all the more valuable because he was strong in areas where most of his contemporaries were weak. Yet the book also leaves the suspicion that Merrill's major work was left unwritten."

BIOGRAPHICAL AND CRITICAL SOURCES:

BOOKS

Bauer, Mark, *This Composite Voice: The Role of W.B. Yeats in James Merrill's Poetry,:* Routledge (New York, NY), 2003.

Blasing, Mutlu Konuk, *Politics and Form in Postmodern Poetry: O'Hara, Bishop, Ashbery, and Merrill,* Cambridge University Press (New York, NY), 1995.

Bloom, Harold, editor, *James Merrill,* Chelsea House (New York, NY), 1985.

Contemporary Literary Criticism, Thomson Gale (Detroit, MI), Volume 2, 1974, Volume 3, 1975, Volume 6, 1976, Volume 8, 1978, Volume 13, 1980, Volume 18, 1981, Volume 34, 1988, Volume 91, 1996.

Dickey, James, *Babel to Byzantium,* Farrar, Straus (New York, NY), 1968.

Dictionary of Literary Biography, Volume 5: *American Poets since World War II,* Thomson Gale (Detroit, MI), 1980.

Dictionary of Literary Biography Yearbook 1985, Thomson Gale (Detroit, MI), 1986.

Kalstone, David, *Five Temperaments: Elizabeth Bishop, Robert Lowell, James Merrill, Adrienne Rich, John Ashbery,* Oxford University Press (New York, NY), 1977.

Lehman, David, and Charles Berger, editors, *James Merrill: Essays in Criticism,* Cornell University Press (Ithaca, NY), 1982.

Lurie, Alison, *Familiar Spirits: A Memoir of James Merrill and David Jackson,* Viking (New York, NY), 2001.

Materer, Timothy, *James Merrill's Apocalypse,* Cornell University Press, (Ithaca, NY), 2000.

Polito, Robert, *A Reader's Guide to James Merrill's The Changing Light at Sandover,* University of Michigan Press, 1994.

Rotella, Guy L., editor, *Critical Essays on James Merrill,* G.K. Hall (Boston, MA), 1996.

White, Edmund, *Loss within Loss: Artists in the Age of AIDS,* University of Wisconsin Press (Madison, WI), 2001.

Yenser, Stephen, *The Consuming Myth: The Work of James Merrill,* Harvard University Press (Cambridge, MA), 1987.

PERIODICALS

Advocate, May 8, 2001, David Bahr, review of *Collected Poems,* p. 74.

American Poetry Review, September-October, 1979.

American Spectator, January, 1994, p. 64.

Atlantic, March, 1973; October, 1980.

Book, May, 2001, Stephen Whited, review of *Collected Poems,* p. 78.

Booklist, February 1, 2001, Donna Seaman, review of *Collected Poems,* p. 1035.

Chicago Tribune Book World, December 17, 1978; April 24, 1983.

Kenyon Review, winter, 1997, Rachel Hadas, "'We Both Knew This Place': Reflections on the Art of James Merrill," p. 134; spring, 1998, Rachel Hadas, "James Merrill's Early Work: A Revaluation," p. 177.

Kirkus Reviews, July 15, 2004, p. 676, review of *Collected Prose.*

Lambda Book Report, April, 2001, David Rosen, "Necessary Angel," p. 16.

Library Journal, April 15, 2002, p. 90, Barbara Hoffert, review of *Collected Poems;* Oct 1, 2002, p. 94, William Gargan, review of *Collected Novels and Plays.*

Los Angeles Times Book Review, February 13, 1983.

Midwest Quarterly, spring, 2001, Kathryn Jacobs, "How Not to Shed Tears, and What to Do, Instead: James Merrill," p. 334; winter, 2003, p. 236, Richard Holinger, review of *Collected Poems.*

New Criterion, March 2002, p. 24 Daniel Mark Epstein, "Merrill's Progress."

New Leader, December 4, 1978; June 5, 1995, Phoebe Pettingell, review of *A Scattering of Salts,* p. 20.

New Republic, June 5, 1976; November 20, 1976; July 26, 1980; June 5, 1995; p. 38; May 7, 2001, Adam Kirsch, "All That Glitters," p. 40.

Newsweek, February 28, 1983; March 5, 2001, David Gates, "Jimmy of the Spirits," p. 56.

New Yorker, March 27, 1995, p. 49; March 12, 2000, Helen Vendler, "James Merrill: *Collected Poems,*" p. 100.

New York Review of Books, May 6, 1971; September 20, 1973; March 18, 1976; December 21, 1978; May 3, 1979; February 21, 1982; November 4, 1993, p. 31; January 13, 1994, p. 15; May 11, 1995, p. 46.

New York Times, January 29, 1983; May 29, 1985; September 15, 1993; March 14, 2001, Mel Gussow, "An Anthology and Conferences Celebrate James Merrill's Work," p. E1, and "A Year for Reconnecting with the Spirit of a Departed Poet," p. B10.

New York Times Book Review, September 24, 1972; March 21, 1976; April 4, 1976; April 22, 1977, Herbert Mitgang, "Publishing: A Touch of the Pulitzer"; April 29, 1979, Robert B. Shaw, "James Merrill and the Ouija Board"; June 15, 1980, Denis Donoghue, "What the Ouija Board Said"; March 13, 1983; November 12, 1984; September 1, 1985, Petet Stitt, "Poets Witty and Elegiac"; February 15, 1987, Helen Benedict, "In Short"; November 12, 1989, Carolyn Kizer, "Necessities of Life and Death"; December 12, 1993, Brigitte Weeks, "How James Merrill Came of Age"; March 26, 1995,

W.S. Merwin, "The End of More than a Book," p. 3; May 22, 1995; February 22, 2001, Janet Maslin, "Bound by the Spirit World as They Drifted Apart"; March 4, 2001, Daniel Mendelsohn, "A Poet of Love and Loss," p. 16.
Partisan Review, winter, 1967.
Perspective, spring, 1967.
Poetry, June, 1973; October, 1976; December, 1979; September, 1995, p. 354; March, 2002, p. 343, Paul Breslin, "Closet Necessities: James Merrill's Poetics of Reticence."
Publishers Weekly, February 27, 1995, p. 98.
San Francisco Chronicle, March 11, 2001, David Wiegand, "How a Ouija Board Called Forth a Collective Spirit," p. 3.
Saturday Review, December 2, 1972.
Shenandoah, summer, 1976; fall, 1976.
Time, April 26, 1976; June 25, 1979.
Times Literary Supplement, September 29, 1972; October 28, 1977; January 18, 1980; May 22, 1987; December 2, 1988; December 31, 1993, p. 20; January 17, 1997, Stephen Burt, review of *Selected Poems,* p. 22.
Village Voice, December 21, 1993.
Village Voice Literary Supplement, March, 1983.
Wall Street Journal, April 13, 2001, Ben Downing, "Poetry and Parlor Tricks," p. 10.
Washington Post Book World, July 6, 1980; March 27, 1983; July 28, 1985; December 14, 1986.
Yale Review, winter, 1971; spring, 1975; January, 1994, p. 161; October, 1995, p. 144.

ONLINE

Academy of American Poets Web site, http://www.poets.org/ (September 26, 2001), "James Merrill."
Modern American Poetry Web site, http://www.english.uiuc.edu/ (September 26, 2001), Ann T. Keene, "James Merrill's Life," Alan Nadel, "Replacing the Waste Land—James Merrill's Quest for Transcendent Authority," James Merrill, "Merrill: On Puns [1972]," and "Merrill in Correspondence."

OBITUARIES:

PERIODICALS

Los Angeles Times, February 8, 1995, pp. A3, A13.
New Republic, March 6, 1995, p. 46.
Newsweek, February 20, 1995, p. 76.
New York Times, February 7, 1995.
Poetry, September, 1995, p. 311.
Time, February 20, 1995, p. 81.
Times (London), February 15, 1995, p. 19.

* * *

MERRILL, James Ingram
See MERRILL, James

* * *

MERRIMAN, Alex
See SILVERBERG, Robert

* * *

MERWIN, William Stanley
See MERWIN, W.S.

* * *

MERWIN, W.S. 1927-
(William Stanley Merwin)

PERSONAL: Born September 30, 1927, in New York, NY; son of a Presbyterian minister; married Dorothy Jeanne Ferry (divorced); married Dido Milroy (divorced); married Paula Schwartz. *Education:* Princeton University, A.B., 1947; attended one year of graduate study in modern languages.

ADDRESSES: *Home*—Haiku, HI. *Agent*—c/o Author Mail, Atheneum Publishers, 866 3rd Ave., New York, NY 10022-6221.

CAREER: Poet. Tutor in France and Portugal, 1949; tutor of Robert Graves's son in Majorca, 1950; lived in London, England, 1951-54, supporting himself largely by doing translations of Spanish and French classics for British Broadcasting Corporation (BBC) *Third Programme;* playwright for Poets' Theatre, Cambridge, MA, 1956; lived in New York, NY, 1961-63; associated with Roger Planchon's Theatre de la Cite, Lyon, France, ten months during 1964-65; moved to Hawaii in the late 1970s. In 1999, Merwin was named Poetry Consultant to the Library of Congress for a jointly-held position with poets Rita Dove and Louise Glück.

MEMBER: National Institute of Arts and Letters.

AWARDS, HONORS: Kenyon Review fellowship in poetry, 1954; Rockefeller fellowship, 1956; National Institute of Arts and Letters grant, 1957; Arts Council of Great Britain playwriting bursary, 1957; Rabinowitz Foundation grant, 1961; Bess Hokin Prize, *Poetry,* 1962; Ford Foundation grant, 1964-65; fellowship from Chapelbrook Foundation, 1966; Harriet Monroe Memorial Prize, *Poetry,* 1967; Rockefeller Foundation grant, 1969; Pulitzer Prize for poetry, 1971, for *The Carrier of Ladders;* fellowship from the Academy of American Poets, 1973; Guggenheim fellowship, 1973, 1983; Shelley Memorial Award, 1974; Bollingen Prize for poetry, Yale University Library, 1979; Lenore Marshall Poetry Prize, 1994, for *Travels;* Tanning Prize for poetry, 1994; Lila Wallace *Reader's Digest* fellowship, 1994; Lannan Foundation lifetime achievement award,2004; National Book Award for poetry, National Book Foundation, 2005, for *Migration: New and Selected Poems.*

WRITINGS:

POETRY, EXCEPT AS INDICATED

A Mask for Janus (also see below), Yale University Press (New Haven, CT), 1952.

The Dancing Bears (also see below), Yale University Press (New Haven, CT), 1954.

Green with Beasts (also see below), Knopf (New York, NY), 1956.

The Drunk in the Furnace (also see below), Macmillan (New York, NY), 1960.

(Editor) *West Wind: Supplement of American Poetry,* Poetry Book Society (London, England), 1961.

The Moving Target, Atheneum (New York, NY), 1963.

Collected Poems, Atheneum (New York, NY), 1966.

The Lice, Atheneum (New York, NY), 1969.

Animae, Kayak (San Francisco, CA), 1969.

The Miner's Pale Children (prose), Atheneum (New York, NY), 1970, reprinted, Holt (New York, NY), 1994.

The Carrier of Ladders, Atheneum (New York, NY), 1970.

(With A.D. Moore) *Signs,* Stone Wall Press (Iowa City, IA), 1970.

Asian Figures, Atheneum (New York, NY), 1973.

Writings to an Unfinished Accompaniment, Atheneum (New York, NY), 1973.

The First Four Books of Poems (contains *A Mask for Janus, The Dancing Bears, Green with Beasts,* and *The Drunk in the Furnace*), Atheneum (New York, NY), 1975.

The Compass Flower, Atheneum (New York, NY), 1977.

Houses and Travellers (prose), Atheneum (New York, NY), 1977, reprinted, Holt (New York, NY), 1994.

Feathers from the Hill, Windhover (Iowa City, IA), 1978.

Finding the Islands, North Point Press (San Francisco, CA), 1982.

Unframed Originals: Recollections (prose), Atheneum (New York, NY), 1982.

Opening the Hand, Atheneum (New York, NY), 1983.

The Rain in the Trees: Poems, Knopf (New York, NY), 1988.

Selected Poems, Atheneum (New York, NY), 1988.

The Lost Upland (prose), Knopf (New York, NY), 1992.

Travels: Poems, Knopf (New York, NY), 1993.

The Vixen: Poems, Knopf (New York, NY), 1996.

(Compiler) *Lament for the Makers: A Memorial Anthology,* Counterpoint (Washington, DC), 1996.

Flower and Hand: Poems, 1977- 1983, Copper Canyon Press (Port Townsend, WA), 1996.

The Folding Cliffs: A Narrative (prose), Knopf (New York, NY), 1998.

East Window: The Asian Poems, Copper Canyon Press (Port Townsend, WA), 1998.

The River Sound: Poems, Knopf (New York, NY), 1999.

The Pupil, Knopf (New York, NY), 2001.

The Mays of Ventadorn (prose, National Geographic Direction Series), National Geographic (Washington, DC), 2002.

The Ends of the Earth (essays), Shoemaker & Hoard (Washington, DC), 2004.

Migration: New and Selected Poems, Copper Canyon Press (Port Townsend, WA), 2005.

Present Company, Copper Canyon Press (Port Townsend, WA), 2005.

Contributor to numerous anthologies. Merwin's poems have been recorded for the Archive of Recorded Poetry and Literature, 1994.

Contributor to magazines, including *Nation, Harper's, Poetry, New Yorker, Atlantic, Kenyon Review,* and *Evergreen Review.* Poetry editor, *Nation,* 1962.

A reader, with others, on sound recordings, including *Poetry and the American People: Reading, Voice, and Publication in the 19th and 20th Centuries,* Library of Congress Bicentennial Symposium, 2000; *Poetry in America: Favorite Poems: An Evening of Readings and a Special Favorite Poem Audio and Video Presentation,*

Library of Congress (Washington, DC), 2000; *An Evening of Dante in English Translation,* Library of Congress (Washington, DC), 2000.

The W.S. Merwin Archive in the Rare Book Room of the University Library of the University of Illinois at Urbana-Champaign contains notes, drafts, and manuscripts of published and unpublished work by Merwin from the mid-1940s to the early 1980s.

TRANSLATOR

The Poem of the Cid, Dent (London, England), 1959, New American Library (New York, NY), 1962.

(Contributor) Eric Bentley, editor, *The Classic Theatre,* Doubleday (New York, NY), 1961.

The Satires of Persius, Indiana University Press (Bloomington, IN), 1961.

Some Spanish Ballads, Abelard (London, England), 1961, published as *Spanish Ballads,* Doubleday Anchor (New York, NY), 1961.

*The Life of Lazarillo de Tormes: His Fortunes and Adversities,*Doubleday Anchor (New York, NY), 1962.

(Contributor) *Medieval Epics,* Modern Library (New York, NY), 1963.

(With Denise Levertov, William Carlos Williams, and others) Nicanor Parra, *Poems and Antipoems,* New Directions (New York, NY), 1968.

Jean Follain, *Transparence of the World,* Atheneum (New York, NY), 1969, reprinted, Copper Canyon Press (Port Townsend, WA), 2003.

W.S. Merwin: Selected Translations, 1948-1968, Atheneum (New York, NY), 1969.

(And author of introduction) S. Chamfort, *Products of the Perfected Civilization: Selected Writings of Chamfort,* Macmillan (New York, NY), 1969.

Porchia, *Voices: Selected Writings of Antonio Porchia,* Follett (Chicago, IL), 1969, reprinted, Copper Canyon Press (Port Townsend, WA), 2003.

Pablo Neruda, *Twenty Poems and a Song of Despair,* Cape (London, England), 1969, reprinted, with introduction by Christina García, illustrations by Pablo Picasso, Penguin Books (New York, NY), 2004.

(With others) Pablo Neruda, *Selected Poems,* Dell (New York, NY), 1970.

(With Clarence Brown) Osip Mandelstam, *Selected Poems,* Oxford University Press (New York, NY), 1973, reprinted as *The Selected Poems of Osip Mandelstam,* New York Review of Books (New York, NY), 2004.

(With J. Moussaieff Mason) *Sanskrit Love Poetry,* Columbia University Press (New York, NY), 1977, published as *Peacock's Egg: Love Poems from Ancient India,* North Point Press (San Francisco, CA), 1981.

Roberto Juarroz, *Vertical Poems,* Kayak (San Francisco, CA), 1977.

(With George E. Dimock, Jr.) Euripides, *Iphigenia at Aulius,* Oxford University Press (New York, NY), 1978.

Selected Translations, 1968- 78, Atheneum (New York, NY), 1979.

Robert the Devil, Windhover (Iowa City, IA), 1981.

Four French Plays, Atheneum (New York, NY), 1984.

From the Spanish Morning, Atheneum (New York, NY), 1984.

Dante Alighieri, *Purgatorio,* Knopf (New York, NY), 2000.

Gawain and the Green Knight, a New Verse Translation, Knopf (New York, NY), 2002.

Also translator of Lope de Rueda, "Eufemia," in *Tulane Drama Review,* December, 1958; Lesage, "Crispin," in *Tulane Drama Review;* Lope Felix de Vega Carpio, *Punishment without Vengeance,* 1958; Federico García Lorca, "Yerma" and "Blood," 1969.

PLAYS

(With Dido Milroy) *Darkling Child,* produced, 1956.

Favor Island, produced at Poets' Theatre, Cambridge, MA, 1957, and on British Broadcasting Corporation *Third Programme,* 1958.

The Gilded West, produced at Belgrade Theatre, Coventry, England, 1961.

SIDELIGHTS: W.S. Merwin is a major American writer whose poetry, translations, and prose have won praise from literary critics since the publication of his first book. The spare, hard verse comprising the body of Merwin's work has been characterized by many as very difficult reading. However, it is generally agreed that this poetry is worth whatever extra effort may be required to appreciate it. In a *Yale Review* article, Laurence Lieberman stated, "This poetry, at its best—and at our best as readers—is able to meet us and engage our wills as never before in the thresholds between waking and sleeping, past and future, self and anti-self, men and gods, the living and the dead." Although Merwin's writing has undergone many stylistic changes through the course of his career, it is unified by the recurring theme of man's separation from nature. The poet sees the consequences of that alienation as disastrous, both for the human race and for the rest of the world.

Merwin, who feels strongly about ecological issues, once commented: "It makes me angry to feel that the natural world is taken to have so little importance." He gave an example from his own life: "The Pennsylvania that I grew up in and loved as a child isn't there . . . it's been strip-mined: it really is literally not there. This happens to a lot of people, but I don't see why one has to express indifference about it. It matters . . . It's like being told that you can't possibly be mentally healthy." As an illustration of the poet's commitment to environmental concerns, he has lived since the late 1970s on an old pineapple plantation in Hawaii, which he has been painstakingly restoring to its original rainforest state.

Merwin's despair over the desecration of nature is strongly expressed in his collection *The Lice.* Lieberman commented: "To read these poems is an act of self-purification. Every poem in the book pronounces a judgement against modern men—the gravest sentence the poetic imagination can conceive for man's withered and wasted conscience: our sweep of history adds up to one thing only, a moral vacuity that is absolute and irrevocable. This book is a testament of betrayals; we have betrayed all beings that had power to save us: the forest, the animals, the gods, the dead, the spirit in us, the words. Now, in our last moments alive, they return to haunt us." Published in 1969, *The Lice* remains one of Merwin's best-known volumes of poetry. Throughout his subsequent work, Merwin has continued to produce striking poems using nature as a backdrop. *The Vixen,* for instance, is an exploration of the rural forest in southwestern France that Merwin called home for many years. *New Yorker* critic J. D. McClatchy remarked that "the book is suffused with details of country life—solitary walks and garden work, woodsmoke, birdsong, lightfall." In his poem "Leviathan," published in the 1956 collection *Green with Beasts,* Merwin writes of time and nature through the specific examples of the whale as narrated in myth, legend, and observation. In this poem it is nature, represented by sea and whale, that is strong. Conversely, humanity is weak. Chris Semansky in *Poetry for Students* noted: "In his poem 'Leviathan,' W.S. Merwin describes the multiple ways in which the whale has historically served as a symbol to human culture and the ways in which the image of the whale has served as a receptacle for human hopes and fears."

His obsession with the meaning of America and its values makes Merwin like the great nineteenth-century poet Walt Whitman, L. Edwin Folsom noted in *Shenandoah.* "His poetry . . . often implicitly and sometimes explicitly responds to Whitman; his twentieth-century sparsity and soberness—his doubts about the value of America—answer, temper, Whitman's nineteenth-century expansiveness and exuberance—his enthusiasm over the American creation." Folsom summarized his comparison by saying, "Whitman's self sought to contain all, to embody past, present, and future; Merwin's self seeks to contain nothing, to empty itself of a dead past. . . . [Having taken a journey in the past,] Merwin does not return to the present replenished with the native ways: he returns only with an affirmation of man's stupidity and inhumanity, and of an irreplaceable emptiness lying beneath this continent. Having re-taken the Whitmanesque American journey, having relived the creation of the country via the medium of poetry, Merwin finds the American creation to be not a creation at all, but a destruction, an imposed obliteration that he believes will be repaid in kind."

The poetic forms of many eras and societies are the foundation for a great deal of Merwin's poetry. His first books contained many pieces inspired by classical models. According to Vernon Young in the *American Poetry Review,* the poems are traceable to "Biblical tales, Classical myth, love songs from the Age of Chivalry, Renaissance retellings; they comprise carols, roundels, odes, ballads, sestinas, and they contrive golden equivalents of emblematic models: the masque, the Zodiac, the Dance of Death." Merwin's versions are so perfectly rendered, stated Young, that "were you to redistribute these poems, unsigned, among collections of translated material or of English Poetry Down the Ages, any but the most erudite reader would heedlessly accept them as renderings of Theocritus, Catullus, Ronsard. . . . One thing is certain. Before embarking on the narratives published in 1956 and after, Merwin was in secure formal command. Shape and duration, melody, vocal inflection, were under superb control. No stanzaic model was alien to him; no line length was beyond his dexterity." Eric Hartley also commented on the importance of Merwin's background in the *Dictionary of Literary Biography:* "From the first of his career as a poet, Merwin has steeped himself in other cultures and other literary traditions, and he has been praised as a translator. This eclectic background has given him a sense of the presence of the past, of timelessness in time, that comes across emphatically in his poetry. Without some understanding of this background the reader cannot fully appreciate Merwin's poetry. Moreover, without such appreciation one cannot comprehend the thrust of Merwin's poetic and philosophical development."

However, John Vernon pointed out in a *Western Humanities Review* article that Merwin's poems are not difficult in a scholarly sense. The problem is the jaded ear of the modern reader. "These are some of the most unacademic poems I have ever read, in the sense that they could never be discussed in a university classroom, since they have no 'meaning' in any usual sense. . . . I think of what Samuel Beckett said about *Finnegans Wake:* we are too decadent to read this. That is, we are so used to a language that is flattened out and hollowed out, that is slavishly descriptive, that when we encounter a language as delicately modulated and as finely sensual as this, it is like trying to read Braille with boxing gloves on."

Some literary critics have identified Merwin with the group known as the oracular poets, but Merwin himself once commented: "I have not evolved an abstract aesthetic theory and am not aware of belonging to any particular group of writers. I neither read nor write much criticism, and think of its current vast proliferation chiefly as a symptom, inseparable from other technological substitutions. . . . I imagine that a society whose triumphs one after the other emerge as new symbols of death, and that feeds itself by poisoning the earth, may be expected, even while it grows in strength and statistics, to soothe its fears with trumpery hopes, refer to nihilism as progress, dismiss the private authority of the senses as it has cashiered belief, and of course find the arts exploitable but unsatisfying." The essayist for *Contemporary Poets* admitted that "Merwin has been associated with the tradition of contemporary poets known as the oracular poets, and if his surrealistic style has been compared to that of Roethke, Bly, Wright, Dickey, Plath, Olson, and even Lowell, his apocalyptic vision is entirely his own."

Of his development as a writer, Merwin once said, "I started writing hymns for my father almost as soon as I could write at all, illustrating them. I recall some rather stern little pieces addressed, in a manner I was familiar with, to backsliders, but I can remember too wondering whether there might not be some more liberating mode. In Scranton there was an anthology of *Best Loved Poems of the American People* in the house, which seemed for a time to afford some clues. But the first real writers that held me were not poets: Conrad first, and then Tolstoy, and it was not until I had received a scholarship and gone away to the university that I began to read poetry steadily and try incessantly, and with abiding desperation, to write it. I was not a satisfactory student; . . . I spent most of my time either in the university library, or riding in the country: I had discovered that the polo and ROTC stables were full of horses with no one to exercise them. I believe I was not noticeably respectful either of the curriculum and its evident purposes, nor of several of its professors, and I was saved from the thoroughly justified impatience of the administration, as I later learned, by the intercessions of R. P. Blackmur, who thought I needed a few years at the place to pick up what education I might be capable of assimilating, and I did in fact gain a limited but invaluable acquaintance with a few modern languages. While I was there, John Berryman, Herman Broch, and Blackmur himself, helped me, by example as much as by design, to find out some things about writing; of course it was years before I began to realize just what I had learned, and from whom. . . . Writing is something I know little about; less at some times than at others. I think, though, that so far as it is poetry it is a matter of correspondences: one glimpses them, pieces of an order, or thinks one does, and tries to convey the sense of what one has seen to those to whom it may matter, including, if possible, one's self."

The success of Merwin's attempts to convey his vision was summed up by Stephen Spender in the *New York Review of Books:* "These poems communicate a sense of someone watching and waiting, surrounding himself with silence, so that he can see minute particles, listen to infinitesimal sounds, with a passivity of attention, a refusal to disturb with his own observing consciousness the object observed. It is as though things write their own poems through Merwin. At their best they are poems of total attention and as such they protest against our world of total distraction."

Merwin was once asked what social role a poet plays—if any—in America. He commented: "I think there's a kind of desperate hope built into poetry now that one really wants, hopelessly, to save the world. One is trying to say everything that can be said for the things that one loves while there's still time. I think that's a social role, don't you? . . . We keep expressing our anger and our love, and we hope, hopelessly perhaps, that it will have some effect. But I certainly have moved beyond the despair, or the searing, dumb vision that I felt after writing *The Lice;* one can't live only in despair and anger without eventually destroying the thing one is angry in defense of. The world is still here, and there are aspects of human life that are *not* purely destructive, and there is a need to pay attention to the things around us while they are still around us. And you know, in a way, if you don't pay that attention, the anger is just bitterness."

BIOGRAPHICAL AND CRITICAL SOURCES:

BOOKS

Brunner, Edward J., *Poetry As Labor and Privilege: The Writings of W.S. Merwin,* University of Illinois Press (Urbana, IL), 1991.

Christhilf, Mark, *W.S. Merwin the Mythmaker,* University of Missouri Press (Columbia, MO), 1986.

Contemporary Literary Criticism, Thomson Gale (Detroit, MI), Volume 1, 1973, Volume 2, 1974, Volume 3, 1975, Volume 5, 1976, Volume 8, 1978, Volume 13, 1980, Volume 18, 1981.

Contemporary Poets, 6th edition, St. James Press (Detroit, MI), 1996.

Davis, Cheri, *W.S. Merwin,* Twayne (Boston, MA), 1981.

Dickey, James, *Babel to Byzantium,* Farrar, Straus (New York, NY), 1968.

Dictionary of Literary Biography, Volume 5: *American Poets since World War II,* Thomson Gale (Detroit, MI), 1980.

Hix, H. L., *Understanding W.S. Merwin,* University of South Carolina Press (Columbia, SC), 1997.

Hoeppner, Edward Haworth, *Echoes and Moving Fields: Structure and Subjectivity in the Poetry of W.S. Merwin and John Ashbery,* Associated University Presses (Cranberry, NJ), 1994.

Howard, Richard, *Alone with America: Essays on the Art of Poetry in the United States since 1950,* Atheneum (New York, NY), 1969.

Hungerford, Edward, *Poets in Progress,* Northwestern University Press (Evanston, IL), 1962.

Nelson, Cary, and Ed Folsom, editors, *W.S. Merwin: Essays on the Poetry,* University of Illinois Press (Urbana, IL), 1987.

Poetry for Students, Volume 5, Thomson Gale (Detroit, MI), 1999.

Rexroth, Kenneth, *With Eye and Ear,* Herder (New York, NY), 1970.

Rexroth, Kenneth, *American Poetry in the Twentieth Century,* Herder (New York, NY), 1971.

Rosenthal, M. L., *The Modern Poets: A Critical Introduction,* Oxford University Press (New York, NY), 1960.

Shaw, Robert B., editor, *American Poetry since 1960: Some Critical Perspectives,* Dufour (Chester Springs, PA), 1974.

Stepanchev, Stephen, *American Poetry since 1945,* Harper (New York, NY), 1965.

PERIODICALS

American Poetry Review, January- February, 1978;May-June 2004, Margaret Atwood, review of *The Mays of Ventadorn,* p. 29.

Antioch Review, winter, 2006, F.D. Reeve, review of *Migration: New and Selected Poems,* p. 189.

Booklist, November 1, 1996, review of *Lament for the Makers: A Memorial Anthology,* p. 476; January 1, 1999, review of *The Folding Cliffs: A Narrative,* p. 777; March 15, 1999, review of *The Folding Cliffs,* p. 1276; June 1, 2002, Will Hickman, review of *The Mays of Ventadorn,* p. 1668; September 1, 2005, Donna Seaman, review of *Present Company* and *Summer Doorways,* p. 43.

Chicago Tribune Book World, December 26, 1982.

Commonweal, June 18, 1999, review of *The Folding Cliffs,* p. 24.

Concerning Poetry, spring, 1975.

Furioso, spring, 1953.

Hudson Review, winter, 1967-68; summer, 1973; spring, 1999, review of *The Folding Cliffs,* p. 141.

Iowa Review, winter, 1982, Cary Nelson and Ed Folsom, "Fact Has Two Faces: An Interview with W.S. Merwin," pp. 30-66.

Kirkus Reviews, March 15, 2004, review of *The Ends of the Earth: Essays,* p.260; July 1, 2005, review of *Summer Doorways,* p. 721.

Library Journal, January, 1996, p. 104; October 15, 1998, review of *The Folding Cliffs,* p. 74; November 1, 1996, review of *Lament for the Makers,* p. 71; November 15, 2001, Ellen Kaufman, review of *The Pupil: Poems,* p. 71; July, 2004, Maureen J. Delaney-Lehman, review of *The Ends of the Earth,* p. 83; September 1, 2005, Fred Muratori, review of *Present Company,* p. 147.

Los Angeles Times, August 21, 1983.

Los Angeles Times Book Review, August 21, 1983.

Modern Language Quarterly, March, 1983, pp. 65-79; September, 1988, pp. 262-284.

Modern Poetry Studies, winter, 1975.

Nation, December 14, 1970; December 12, 1994, Gerald Stern, "The Lenore Marshall Poetry Prize-1994," p. 733.

New Leader, January 13, 1997, review of *Lament for the Makers,* p. 15; December 14, 1998, review of *The Folding Cliffs,* p. 23.

New Mexico Quarterly, autumn, 1964.

New Republic, March 22, 1999, review of *The River Sound: Poems* and *The Folding Cliffs,* p. 40.

New Yorker, June 3, 1996, J. D. McClatchy, review of *The Vixen: Poems,* p. 92; December, 7, 1998, review of *The Folding Cliffs,* p. 200.
New York Review of Books, May 6, 1971; September 20, 1973; March 27, 1997, review of *The Vixen* and *Lament for the Makers,* p. 18.
New York Times Book Review, October 18, 1970; June 19, 1977; August 1, 1982; October 9, 1983; April 4, 1999, Melanie Rehak, "Poetic Justice"; June 6, 1999, review of *The River Sound,* p. 37; December 5, 1999, review of *The River Sound,* p. 78.
New York Times Magazine, February 19, 1995, p. 39.
Ontario Review, fall-winter, 1977- 78.
Partisan Review, summer, 1958; winter, 1971-72.
Poet and Critic, spring, 1990, pp. 37-40.
Poetry, May, 1953; May, 1961; February, 1963; June, 1964; August, 1974; November, 2005, David Biespiel, "Iron Man," p. 137.
Prairie Schooner, fall, 1957; fall, 1962; winter, 1962-63; fall, 1968; winter, 1971-72.
Publishers Weekly, November, 27, 1995, p. 65; February 24, 1997, review of *Flower and Hand: Poems, 1977-1983,* p. 86; August 15, 2005, review of *Present Company,* p. 35.
Sewanee Review, spring, 1974.
Shenandoah, spring, 1968; winter, 1970; spring, 1978.
Southern Review, April, 1980.
Village Voice, July 4, 1974.
Virginia Quarterly Review, summer, 1973; spring, 1997, review of *Lament for the Makers,* p. 48; spring, 1999, review of *The Folding Cliffs,* p. 67; autumn, 1999, review of *The River Sound,* p. 136.
Voices, January-April, 1953; May- August, 1957; September-December, 1961.
Washington Post Book World, August 31, 1975; September 18, 1977; August 15, 1982; June 3, 1984.
Western Humanities Review, spring, 1970; spring, 1971.
Western Review, spring, 1955.
World Literature Today, autumn, 1996, review of *The Vixen,* p. 964; spring, 1997, review of *Lament for the Makers,* p. 391; autumn, 2000, review of *The River Sound,* p. 820; April-June 2003, John Boening, review of *The Pupil,* p. 104.
Yale Review, summer, 1961; summer, 1968; summer, 1973; July, 1999, review of *The River Sound,* p. 167.

ONLINE

Steven Barclay Agency Web site, http://www.barclayagency.com/ (August 4, 2004), "William S. Merwin."

MICHENER, James A. 1907(?)-1997 (James Albert Michener)

PERSONAL: Born c. February 3, 1907, probably in New York, NY; died of renal failure after choosing to be removed from a kidney dialysis machine, October 16, 1997, in Austin, TX; foster son of Mabel (Haddock) Michener; married Patti Koon, July 27, 1935 (divorced, 1948); married Vange Nord, September 2, 1948 (divorced, 1955); married Mari Yoriko Sabusawa (deceased, 1994), October 23, 1955. *Education:* Swarthmore College, A.B. (summa cum laude), 1929; Colorado State College of Education (now University of Northern Colorado), A.M., 1936; research study at the University of Pennsylvania, University of Virginia, Ohio State University, Harvard University, St. Andrews University, University of Siena. *Politics:* Democrat *Religion:* Society of Friends (Quakers)

CAREER: Writer. Worked variously as an actor in a traveling show and as a sports columnist at the age of fifteen; Hill School, PA, teacher, 1932; George School, PA, teacher, 1933-36; Colorado State College of Education (now University of Northern Colorado), Greeley, associate professor, 1936-41; Macmillan Co., New York City, associate editor, 1941-42, 1946-49; freelance writer, 1949-97. Creator of "Adventures in Paradise" television series, 1959. Visiting professor, Harvard University, 1940-41, and University of Texas at Austin, 1983. Chair, President Kennedy's Food for Peace Program, 1961; congressional candidate from Pennsylvania's Eighth District, 1962; secretary of Pennsylvania Constitutional Convention, 1967-68. Member of U.S. State Department advisory committee on the arts, 1957; U.S. Information Agency advisory committee, 1970-76; U.S. Postal Service advisory committee, 1978-87; National Aeronautics and Space Administration advisory council, 1979-83; U.S International Broadcasting Board, 1983-89. *Military service:* U.S. Naval Reserve, 1942-45; became lieutenant commander; naval historian in the South Pacific.

MEMBER: Phi Beta Kappa.

AWARDS, HONORS: Pulitzer Prize for fiction, 1948, for *Tales of the South Pacific;* D.H.L., Rider College, 1950, and Swarthmore College, 1954; National Association of Independent Schools Award, 1954, 1958; L.L. D., Temple University, 1957; Litt.D., American International College, 1957, Washington University, St. Louis, 1967; Einstein Award, 1967; Bestsellers Paperback of the Year Award, 1968, for *The Source;* George Washington Award, Hungarian Studies Foundation, 1970; U.S. Medal of Freedom, 1977; Franklin Award for distinguished service, Printing Industries of Metropolitan New York, 1980; cited by the President's Committee on the Arts and the Humanities, 1983, for long-standing support of the Iowa Workshop writer's project at the University of Iowa; Lippincott Travelling fellowship, British Museum; U.S. Medal of Freedom; Distinguished Service Medal, NASA; Golden Badge of Order of Merit, 1988.

WRITINGS:

NOVELS

The Fires of Spring, Random House (New York, NY), 1949.

The Bridges at Toko-Ri (first published in *Life,* July 6, 1953), Random House (New York, NY), 1953.

Sayonara, Random House (New York, NY), 1954.

Hawaii (first section originally published in *Life*), Random House (New York, NY), 1959.

Caravans, Random House (New York, NY), 1963.

The Source, illustrated by Richard Sparks, Random House (New York, NY), 1965.

The Drifters, Random House (New York, NY), 1971.

Centennial, Random House (New York, NY), 1974.

Chesapeake, illustrated by Alan Philips, Random House (New York, NY), 1978, illustrated selections published as *The Watermen,* Random House (New York, NY), 1979.

The Quality of Life, Including Presidential Lottery, Transworld (London, England), 1980.

The Covenant, Random House (New York, NY), 1980.

Space, Random House (New York, NY), 1982.

Poland, Random House (New York, NY), 1983.

Texas, Random House (New York, NY), 1985, published in two volumes, University of Texas Press (Austin, TX), 1986; chapter published as *The Eagle and the Raven,* illustrations by Charles Shaw, State House Press (Austin, TX), 1990.

Legacy, Random House (New York, NY), 1987.

Alaska, Random House (New York, NY), 1988.

Journey, Random House (New York, NY), 1989.

Caribbean, Random House (New York, NY), 1989.

The Novel, Random House (New York, NY), 1991.

Mexico, Random House (New York, NY), 1992.

South Pacific (retelling of the musical *South Pacific*), illustrated by Michael Hague, Harcourt, 1992.

Creatures of the Kingdom, Random House (New York, NY), 1993, large print edition, Wheeler, 1994.

Recessional, Random House (New York, NY), 1994.

SHORT STORIES AND SKETCHES

Tales of the South Pacific, Macmillan (New York, NY), 1947.

Return to Paradise, Random House (New York, NY), 1951.

Selected Writings, Modern Library (New York, NY), 1957.

A Michener Miscellany: 1950-1970, Random House (New York, NY), 1973.

(Editor) *Firstfruits: A Harvest of 25 Years of Israeli Writing* (fiction), Jewish Publication Society of America (Philadelphia, PA), 1973.

NONFICTION

(With Harold Long) *The Unit in the Social Studies,* Harvard University Press (Cambridge, MA), 1940.

Voice of Asia, Random House (New York, NY), 1951.

The Floating World, Random House (New York, NY), 1954.

(With A. Grove Day) *Rascals in Paradise* (biographical studies), Random House (New York, NY), 1957.

The Bridge at Andau, Random House (New York, NY), 1957.

Japanese Prints: From the Early Masters to the Modern, Tuttle (Boston, MA), 1959.

Report of the County Chairman, Random House (New York, NY), 1961.

The Modern Japanese Print: An Appreciation, Tuttle (Boston, MA), 1968.

Iberia: Spanish Travels and Reflections, Random House (New York, NY), 1968.

America vs. America: The Revolution in Middle-Class Values, New American Library (New York, NY), 1969.

Presidential Lottery: The Reckless Gamble in Our Electoral System (also see below), Random House (New York, NY), 1969.

The Quality of Life (essays; also see below), Random House (New York, NY), 1969.

Facing East: A Study of the Art of Jack Levine, Random House (New York, NY), 1970.

Kent State: What Happened and Why, Random House (New York, NY), 1971.

About "Centennial": Some Notes on the Novel, Random House (New York, NY), 1974.

Sports in America, Random House (New York, NY), 1976, revised edition published as *Michener on Sport,* Transworld (London, England), 1977, reprinted under original title, Fawcett (New York, NY), 1983.

The Watermen, Random House (New York, NY), 1979.

(With John Kings) *Six Days in Havana,* University of Texas Press (Austin, TX), 1989.

Pilgrimage: A Memoir of Poland and Rome, Rodale (Emmaus, PA),, 1990.

James A. Michener's Writer's Handbook: Explorations in Writing and Publishing, Random House (New York, NY), 1992.

My Lost Mexico, illustrated with photographs by Michener, State House Press (Austin, TX), 1992.

The World Is My Home: A Memoir, Random House (New York, NY), 1992.

Literary Reflections, State House Press (Austin, TX), 1993.

Miracle in Seville, Random House (New York, NY), 1995.

This Noble Land: My Vision for America, Random House (New York, NY), 1996.

A Century of Sonnets, State House Press (Austin, TX), 1997.

OTHER

(Editor) *The Future of the Social Studies,* National Council for the Social Studies (Washington, DC), 1939.

(Editor) *Hokusai Sketchbooks,* Tuttle (Boston, MA), 1958.

(Contributor and author of foreword) Peter Chaitin, editor, *James Michener's U.S.A.,* Crown (New York, NY), 1981.

(Author of preface) John W. Grafton, *America: A History of the First 500 Years,* Crescent Books (New York, NY), 1992.

Many of Michener's works have been translated into foreign languages. Collections of his books and manuscripts are kept at the Swarthmore College and University of Hawaii libraries; the Library of Congress also has a large collection of his papers.

ADAPTATIONS: Tales of the South Pacific was adapted for the stage by Richard Rodgers and Oscar Hammerstein II as the musical *South Pacific;* the play was filmed in 1958. *Return to Paradise, The Bridges of Toko-Ri,* and *Sayonara* were all adapted into motion pictures, as were *Until They Sail* and *Mr. Morgan,* both from *Return to Paradise; Forgotten Heroes of Korea* was adapted into the film *Men of the Fighting Lady,* 1954; *Hawaii* was adapted into the films *Hawaii,* United Artists (UA), 1966, and *The Hawaiians,* UA, 1970; *Centennial* was adapted for television, 1978-79; *Space* was adapted into a television mini-series, 1985.

SIDELIGHTS: The author of over twenty best-selling novels, James Michener was a literary legend, a one-man cottage industry who sold almost one hundred million copies of his books before his 1997 death. Michener penned short stories and almost thirty nonfiction titles, as well, but it is for blockbusters such as *Sayonara, Hawaii, The Source, Centennial, Chesapeake, The Covenant, Space, Poland, Alaska,* and *The Caribbean,* that he is remembered mostly, blending historical research with family sagas to produce works that both entertain and inform. "As a literary craftsman [James] Michener has labored to entertain," said A. Grove Day of the popular novelist in the *Dictionary of Literary Biography.* Arthur Cooper characterized Michener as "the literary world's Cecil B. DeMille" in *Newsweek,* while *Time* reviewer Lance Morrow remarked that "practically entire forests have been felled to produce such trunk-sized novels as *Hawaii* and *The Source.*" Cooper went on to praise Michener as "a popular novelist with an awesome audience for his epic narratives, an unpretentious, solid craftsman." Yet Michener will also be remembered for his works of charity, donating a reputed one hundred million dollars of his income to worthy causes.

Citing *Centennial,* a novel that fictionalizes the history of Colorado from the beginning of time up to 1974, Morrow described a characteristic Michener drama: He "begins with the first faint primordial stirrings on the face of the deep and slogs onward through the ages until he hits the day before yesterday," said Morrow. "He is the Will Durant of novelists, less an artist than a kind of historical compactor." Day added, however, that the author's lengthy novels "also appeal to the thoughtful reader and are laden with details that reveal Michener's academic training and bestow information as well as enlightenment." As Day indicated, "he is a master reporter of his generation, and his wide and frequent travels have given him material for colorful evocation of the lives of many characters in international settings in periods going back to earlier millennia."

Reviewing the breadth of Michener's work, Webster Schott wrote in the *New York Times Book Review* that Michener "has found a formula. It delivers everywhere—Hawaii, Africa, Afghanistan, America, Israel, even outer space. The formula calls for experts, vast research, travel to faraway places and fraternizing with locals. And it calls for good guys and bad guys (both real and imagined) to hold the whole works together. It's a formula millions love. Mr. Michener gratifies their curiosity and is a pleasure to read."

Raised near Doylestown, Pennsylvania, by a foster parent, Michener never knew anything about his actual family background. The Micheners were far from wealthy, and the author had a difficult time of it until he was a teenager and athletics helped to turn his life around. Michener became curious about the world outside of Doylestown at a young age, and he was keenly aware that he would have to make his own way. At the age of fourteen he hitchhiked for several months through forty-five American states. After he returned home, he delivered newspapers, excelled in sports, and wrote a sports column for the local paper. Michener won a sports scholarship to Swarthmore College, and during one summer vacation he traveled with a Chautauqua tent show. (Michener incorporated some of these experiences in his second novel, the semiautobiographical *The Fires of Spring.*) After graduation, he began teaching at a local school and won a Lippincott traveling scholarship to Europe, where he enrolled at St. Andrews University in Scotland, collected folk stories in the Hebrides Islands, studied art history in London and Siena, Italy, toured northern Spain with a troupe of bullfighters, and even worked on a Mediterranean cargo vessel.

After his return to the United States during the Great Depression, Michener taught, earned his master's degree, and served as associate professor at the Colorado State College of Education from 1936 through 1939. He published several scholarly articles on the teaching of social studies, became a visiting professor at Harvard University, and in 1941 was asked to accept an editorship with the Macmillan Company in New York. According to Day in his book *James A. Michener,* the author once told a college group that "no aspirant can avoid an apprenticeship to his literary craft. 'I *did* serve an apprenticeship,' he affirms, 'and a very intense one, and learned what a great many people never learn. I learned how to write a sentence and how to write a paragraph. . . . The English language is so complex, so magnificent in its structure that I have very little patience with people who won't put themselves through an apprenticeship.'"

Michener didn't publish his first work of fiction until around the age of forty, however, a fact he attributes to his disinclination to take risks, particularly during the Depression. And it was not until he volunteered for service in the U.S. Navy in 1942 that he began to collect experiences he could visualize as marketable fiction.

His first assignment as a lieutenant was at a post in the South Pacific, and from 1944 to 1946 he served as a naval historian in that region. During this tour of duty, Michener had the occasion to visit some fifty islands, and "as the war wound down," explained Day, "he retreated to a jungle shack and began writing the stories that were to appear as . . . *Tales of the South Pacific,*" which won the Pulitzer Prize in 1948.

Although *Tales of the South Pacific* is considered a collection of short stories, Michener considered it a novel due to the book's overall theme of America's fight in the South Pacific theatre during World War II. *New York Herald Tribune Weekly Book Review* writer P.J. Searles agreed, stating, "Romantic, nostalgic, tragic—call it what you will—this book seems to me the finest piece of fiction to come out of the South Pacific war." Michener "is a born story teller," *New York Times* writer David Dempsey added, "but, paradoxically, this ability results in the book's only real weakness—the interminable length of some of the tales. Mr. Michener saw so much, and his material is so rich, that he simply could not leave anything out." When the book was published in 1947, Orville Prescott in the *Yale Review* described Michener as "certainly one of the ablest and one of the most original writers to appear on the American literary scene in a long time."

After his discharge, Michener returned to Macmillan as a textbook editor. In 1949, Richard Rodgers and Oscar Hammerstein II adapted *Tales of the South Pacific* into the successful musical *South Pacific;* a share of the royalties from the play—later to become a film—enabled Michener to become a full-time writer. In his book *James A. Michener,* Day reported that the author once told him that "I have only one bit of advice to the beginning writer: be sure your novel is read by Rodgers and Hammerstein." As for the Pulitzer, Michener once commented to Roy Newquist in *Conversations:* "There were editorials that declared it was the least-deserving book in recent years to win the Pulitzer; it was by no means the popular choice. In fact, it was an insulting choice to many. At least two other books had been definitely favored to win. . . . I had no occasion to develop a swelled head."

Throughout the 1950s and early 1960s, Michener continued to set much of his work in the South Pacific and Far East. He was assigned by *Holiday* magazine to write some feature articles about various places in the Pacific, so at the same time he wrote *Return to Paradise,* a collection of short stories and travel sketches. He then wrote some works of nonfiction about the area: *The Voice of Asia* and *The Floating World.* Several novels, including *The Bridges at Toko-Ri, Sayonara, Hawaii,* and *Caravans,* also date from this period in Michener's career.

It was with the novel *Hawaii* that Michener established the format that would see him through several subsequent novels and make him a best-selling author. Although *Tales of the South Pacific* won the Pulitzer Prize, it was not a best-seller, and as *New York Times Magazine* writer Caryn James explained, it was "only when he moved from small stories of people to monolithic tales of places—beginning with the fictionalized history of *Hawaii* in 1959 through Israel in *The Source,* South Africa in *The Covenant, Poland, Chesapeake* and *Space*—did he become the kind of brand-name author whose books hit the best-seller lists before they reach the bookstores."

James noted that "the Michener formula might seem an unlikely one for the media age: big, old-fashioned narratives weaving generations of fictional families through densely documented factual events, celebrating the All-American virtues of common sense, frugality, patriotism. Yet these straitlaced, educational stories are so episodic that they are perfectly suited to the movie and television adaptations that have propelled Michener's success."

In *James A. Michener,* Day described *Hawaii* as "the best novel ever written about Hawaii." It was published a few months after Hawaii was granted statehood in August, 1959. According to Day, the book "is founded on truth but not on fact." Michener drew from his own experiences in the Pacific region to develop *Hawaii* and also consulted a variety of other sources, including missionary accounts. As the author stated in his book *Report of the County Chairman,* his goal was to portray "the enviable manner in which Hawaii had been able to assimilate men and women from many different races."

Writing in the *New York Times Book Review,* Maxwell Geismar praised the book as "a brilliant panoramic novel about Hawaii from its volcanic origins to its recent statehood. It is a complex and fascinating subject, and it is rendered here with a wealth of scholarship, of literary imagination and of narrative skill, so that the large and diverse story is continually interesting." Day reported, "This is not a historical novel in the usual sense, for not one actual name or event is given; rather, it is a pageant of the coming of settlers from many regions; and the main theme might well be: Paradise is not a goal to attain, but a stage to which people of many colors and creeds may bring their traditional cultures to mingle with those of the others and create what may truly be an Eden at the crossroads of a hitherto empty ocean."

Nevertheless, some of the praise was qualified. A *Times Literary Supplement* writer indicated that "Mr. Michener's zestful, knowledgeable progress through the millennia is absorbing. He cannot, of course, with such enormous slabs of raw material to handle and shape, go anywhere deeply below the surface, but there are some splendid sustained passages in his book." William Hogan wrote in the *San Francisco Chronicle* that "as he has adjusted details in Hawaii's history to suit his fiction, the author is forced to adapt characters to fit into the big historical picture. And that is the book's main weakness." Although *Saturday Review* critic Horace Sutton was of a similar opinion, he maintained that *Hawaii* "is still a masterful job of research, an absorbing performance of storytelling, and a monumental account of the islands from geologic birth to sociological emergence as the newest, and perhaps the most interesting of the United States."

After publishing *Hawaii,* Michener became involved in national politics. He actively campaigned for John F. Kennedy and wrote a work of political nonfiction, *Report of the County Chairman,* in which he chronicled that involvement. A later Michener study, *Presidential Lottery,* presented an argument for reform in the method Americans use to select their president. He was also an unsuccessful candidate for the House of Representatives from Pennsylvania's Eighth District.

In 1963, however, Michener returned to fiction with *The Source,* a book researched while he was living in Israel, and described by Day as another best-selling "mammoth volume." In this novel, Michener described the archaeological excavation of Makor Tell, a mound that contains the remnants of various settlements built over the course of many centuries. As Day explained, "artifacts found in the various layers introduce chapters dealing with events in the Holy Land during the period in which the articles were made. . . . Prominent families of several nationalities are followed through the ages; the setting is limited to the invented tell of Makor, the surrounding countryside, and the shores of the Sea of Galilee." Day claimed that *The Source* is "one of the longest of Michener's books, and the best in the opinion of many readers. Although it may lack a clear general theme, its leading topic is certainly the various facets of religion."

Michener's nonfictional account of the Spanish peninsula, *Iberia: Spanish Travels and Reflections* was followed by *The Drifters,* published the same year as his report on the Kent State University shootings. *The Drifters* is a novelistic account that follows the adventures of six young members of the counterculture as they wander through Spain, Portugal, and parts of Africa.

The story is narrated by a sixty-one-year-old man and reflects the author's own interest in modern times and contemporary issues. *Saturday Review* writer David W. McCullough pointed out that *The Drifters* is also "something of a guidebook loosely dressed up as fiction: a guide to quaint and colorful places especially on the Iberian peninsula, and to the life-styles of the rebellious young." According to Peter Sourian in the *New York Times Book Review, The Drifters* "is an interesting trip and Michener is an entertaining as well as a knowledgeable guide. The novel has a more serious purpose, however, which is exhaustively to examine the 'youth revolution.' Michener brings to this task narrative skill and a nicely adequate socio-psychological sophistication." And Thomas Lask of the *New York Times* claimed that "those interested in knowing how a sympathetic member of the older generation views some of the shenanigans of the younger will find *The Drifters* a tolerable interlude, especially as it is spiced with travelogue evocations of foreign climes. Dozens of readers will be making notes of the places they too will want to visit."

Michener returned to his historical panoramas with *Centennial.* The book is narrated by Dr. Lewis Vernor, who is writing a report on the village of Centennial, Colorado. The first part of the book covers the area's early geology, archaeology, and ecology before humans even appear. And then, according to Day, *Centennial* introduces some "seventy named characters . . . not including Indians, fur traders, trappers, cattle drivers, miners, ranchers, dry farmers, real estate salesmen, and assorted townspeople. Again national and ethnic interminglings in a limited region are recorded through many years, and little is omitted from the panorama of the developing American West."

The novel has few all-encompassing themes. As James R. Frakes wrote in the *New York Times Book Review,* "denying himself the luxury of 'flossy conclusions' and dogmatic theorizing, the author allows himself only a very few unqualified extrapolations from the text: the determining endurance of the land, for instance; the interdependence of man, animal, earth, and water; the possibility that white survival in some areas may require a return to the permanent values of the Indian."

In Michener's book, *Chesapeake,* according to Christopher Lehmann-Haupt in the *New York Times,* Michener "does for Maryland's Eastern Shore what he did for Colorado in *Centennial.* By telling the story of dozens of fictional characters who live in a partly imaginary locale, he tries to capture the real history of the area—in the case of the Chesapeake Bay, from the time in the 6th century when Indians and crabs were its chief inhabitants, down to a present when developers and pollutants have taken over."

Michener applied this same pattern to explore the history of South Africa in *The Covenant.* In this book, said William McWhirter in *Time,* the author "manages to cover 15,000 years of African history, from the ritual-haunted tribes of Bushmen to present-day Afrikaners obstinately jeering at appeals for 'human rights.'" Michener's method of combining fiction with nonfiction drew some criticism from reviewers. As Andre Brink noted in the *Washington Post Book World,* "in his portrayal of history the author adapts a curious method also characteristic of his earlier novel, *The Source:* even though well-known historical figures appear in it—the Trek leader Piet Retief, the Boer general De Wet, Prime Minister Daniel Malan and a host of others—many of their major exploits are attributed to fictitious characters appearing alongside of them. Imagine a novel prominently featuring Abraham Lincoln but attributing the Gettysburg Address to a fictitious minor character." However, according to John F. Bums in the *New York Times Book Review,* "the book's accomplishment may be to offer a public inured to stereotypes a sense of the flesh and blood of the Afrikaners, the settlers who grew from harsh beginnings to a white tribe now nearing three million, commanding the most powerful economy and armed forces in Africa."

Writing in the *New York Times,* Stephen Farber described Michener's *Space* as a "fictional rendering of the development of the space program from World War II to the present." Michael L. Smith reported in the *Nation* that "real participants make occasional appearances, but Michener relies primarily on fictional approximations." In fact, said Smith, *Space* "is less a historical novel than a tract. In part, it is a celebration of space exploration as a glorious blend of science, American frontiersmanship and human curiosity. But more than that, it's an impassioned denunciation of what Michener considers one of the gravest dangers facing post-Vietnam America: the proliferation of an 'anti-science movement.'" Ben Bova in the *Washington Post Book World* added that the book "contrasts several varieties of faith, from the simplistic faith of the German rocket engineer who believes that technology can solve any problem, to the faith of the astronauts who believe that flying farther and faster is the greatest good in the world."

Michener began *Poland* in 1977 with the belief that the country would become a focal point within the decade. To write the book, explains Ursula Hegi in the *Los An-*

geles Times Book Review, Michener "visited Poland eight times and traveled throughout the country. He talked to people of different backgrounds and enjoyed the assistance of fifteen Polish scholars." The result was a novelization of the last 700 years of the country's history, including several invasions and partitionings, the Nazi occupation during World War II, and a modern struggle of farmers attempting to form a labor union. As Bill Kurtis reported in the *Chicago Tribune Book World,* "by now, Michener's form is familiar. History is seen through the lives of three fictional families: the nobility of the wealthy Counts Lubonski; the gentry or petty nobility of the Bukowskis; and the peasant heart of Poland, the family Buk. Around them, Michener wraps a detailed historical panorama; he combines fact and fiction to breathe life into nearly 1,000 years of battles, with far more Polish defeats than victories. If recited as dates and incidents, these would otherwise be dry as dust."

Poland received mixed reviews. Hegi claimed that "though Michener captures Poland's struggle and development, he presents the reader with too many names and personal histories, making it difficult to keep track of more than a few characters." Other critics cited omissions, historical inaccuracies, and oversimplifications in Michener's research. And Patricia Blake reported in *Time* that the work glosses over Polish anti-Semitism. However, *Washington Post* reviewer Peter Osnos described *Poland* as "Michener at his best, prodigiously researched, topically relevant and shamelessly intended for readers with neither will nor patience for more scholarly treatments." And, added Hegi, his "descriptions of the country—blooms covering the hillsides, the swift flow of the rivers, splendid groves of beech trees—are as detailed as his depictions of weapons, castles and costumes."

Texas was written when former state governor William Clements invited Michener to create a book that would be timed to appear for the 1986 Texas Sesquicentennial. According to Hughes Rudd in the *New York Times Book Review, Texas,* "at almost 1,000 pages, contains enough paper to cover several New England counties. The novel is so heavy you could probably leave it on a Lubbock, TX, coffee table in a tornado and find it there when everything else was still in the air over Kansas City, KS." The frame for *Texas* concerns a committee appointed by a Texas governor to investigate the state's history and recommend what students should be taught about their state. The story begins early in the sixteenth century when the state was still an unexplored part of Mexico.

Texas received many of the criticisms that are frequently accorded Michener's work. According to Nicholas Lemann in the *Washington Post Book World,* none of the characters "stays in mind as embodying the complexity of real life. The reason is not exactly a lack of art on Michener's part; it's more that the form dictates that everything novelistic must be in the service of delivering history. Nothing ever happens that doesn't embody an important trend." For example, Lemann wrote, "when it's time to recount the story of the battle of the Alamo, [Michener] invents a handful of characters on both sides and has them engaging in dialogue with Jim Bowie, Davy Crockett, and General Santa Anna."

At 149 pages, *Legacy* qualifies as Michener's shortest novel. Prompted by Michener's disgust over events surrounding the Iran Contra scandal during the Reagan administration, the novel centers on the fictional army major, Norman Starr, who has been called to testify at the Senate hearings involving the alleged cover-up of the president's National Security Council. As Starr and his lawyer, Zack McMaster, prepare his defense, Starr thinks about the roles of his ancestors in American history in chapters that discuss the nature of the country's Constitution. As Starr heads for the courthouse he realizes that his moral code and sense of propriety will not allow him to plead the Fifth Amendment as Colonel Oliver North and Admiral John Poindexter have in the novel. Published in 1987, as the U.S. celebrated the bicentennial of its Constitution, *Legacy*'s final pages consist of a complete reprinting of the Constitution. Acknowledging the appeal of the subject matter, critics nevertheless agreed that, in the words of John Ehrlichman, who reviewed it for the *Los Angeles Times Book Review,* "the brevity, research lapses and forced timeliness of [the novel] tarnish Starr's dramatic nobility and in some measure defeat the author's original, worthy objectives."

With *Alaska,* Michener returned to the genre of historical novel. *Alaska* traces the development of the land and its inhabitants from the time of the mastodons to the building of the state's highways. Finding Michener's research thorough and accurate, Chip Brown, in a review for *Book World,* noted further that Michener "is rightfully sympathetic to the native inhabitants of Alaska . . . exploring at length their customs, their shamans, their rituals and trials." In an effort to keep the novel under 1,000 pages, editors convinced Michener to delete a large portion of the *Alaska* manuscript. That portion, a story of a group traveling to the Klondike during the gold rush of 1897, was published the following year as *Journey.*

Discussing Michener's historical epic *Caribbean,* published in 1989, Karen Stabiner wrote in the *Los Angeles Times Book Review,* that Michener "has perfect bestseller pitch: enough intrigue to make life exciting; enough chronological and geographical distance to make the thrills thrilling, not threatening." While finding the characterizations in *Caribbean* "stiff and wooden" and the dialogue unrealistic, reviewer John Hearne, in the *New York Times Book Review,* nevertheless acknowledged that "what cannot be faulted, and what shines from the pages, is a great sympathy on Michener's part for the people who made the events happen."

In the 1990s Michener produced several works unique in his canon. *The Novel* is a work of fiction comprised of four segments, each narrated from a different point of view. It is a portrayal of the publishing world, with sections focusing on a writer named Lukas Yoder, his editor, Yvonne Marmelle, a literary critic, and a friend of Yoder who represents the reading public. Critics generally regarded *The Novel* as a failed experiment focusing on the interior lives of his characters—an area in which Michener's critics have generally found his abilities lacking—unlike the historical narratives at which he excelled. More favorable reviews emerged regarding the autobiographical *The World Is My Home,* which documents Michener's extensive travels and literary endeavors. In the *New York Times Book Review,* Doris Grumbach noted that Michener considers himself a popular storyteller rather than a novelist; she asserted that while Michener's literary talents may be regarded by some as limited, his memoirs indicate that "there is every chance that he will be remembered . . . for being not an ordinary but a highly unusual fellow, almost a Renaissance man, adventurous, inquisitive, energetic, unpretentious and unassuming, with an encyclopedic mind and a generous heart."

Significantly shorter than many of his previous novels, Michener's 1995 work *Miracle in Seville* was classified by some critics as a novella or fable. Set in Spain, the story portrays the quest of Don Cayetano Mota, who faces his last opportunity to prove that his family's ranch can produce great bull-fighting bulls. Allen Joseph of the *New York Times Book Review* praised Michener's vivid evocation of Spanish culture and the suspenseful plot of the narrative: "What emerges most strongly is the real admiration and awe that lovers of bullfighting feel for the *toro bravo.*"

Michener's 1994 novel *Recessional,* concerned with the theme of old age and focusing on the pressures that face the elderly, also represented a departure from his usual fictional output. Reeve Lindbergh of the *Washington Post Book World* emphasized the volume's contrast with Michener's usual technique of depicting broad geographical areas and expansive family sagas in books that are "like going on a field trip with God." *Recessional,* in contrast, depicts the landscape of a human life by portraying Andy Zorn, a doctor who regains his ability to heal through his work at a retirement home. Offering praise for the novel, Mark Jackson of *Books* commented: "Meticulous, incomparable research and vividly drawn characters blend seamlessly within this richly told novel that is concerned with the choices, obstacles and rewards faced by older-but-wiser adults at the Palms retirement center in Florida."

"A Michener novel is a tribute to the industriousness of both author and reader," said James, "and, in addition to the easy-to-swallow data, it contains a morality tale about the heroism of hard work and guts. His thick, fact-filled books seem thoroughly impersonal, but several days in Michener's company show the novels to be perfect expressions of their author's anomalies—moral without being stern, methodical yet digressive, insistently modest yet bursting with ambition, full of social conscience yet grasping at facts as a way to avoid emotion."

Michiko Kakutani commented similarly in the *New York Times* that Michener's books contain many "bits of knowledge," which "served up in the author's utilitarian prose, are part of Mr. Michener's wide popular appeal: readers feel they're learning something, even while they're being entertained, and they're also able to absorb all these facts within a pleasant moral context: a liberal and a humanitarian, Mr. Michener argues for religious and racial tolerance, celebrates the old pioneer ethic of hard work and self-reliance, and offers such incontestable, if obvious, observations as 'war forces men to make moral choices.'"

James quoted literary critic Leslie Fiedler as commenting that Michener "puts a book together in a perfectly lucid, undisturbing way, so that even potentially troublesome issues don't seem so. *Hawaii* is about the problem of imperialism, yet one never senses that. *The Source* is about the Middle East, one of the most troublesome political issues in the world, but he's forgotten all the ambiguities. His approach is that if you knew all the facts, everything would straighten out, so it's soothing and reassuring to read him."

Such an approach has its flaws. *New York Times* critic Thomas Lask explained that Michener "likes to have his characters perform against the background or in accordance with the events of history. The quirks of personality, the oddities of character, the unpredictable Brownian motions of human psychology appear to interest him little. He prefers to represent a history in action." A *Time* reviewer summed up that Michener's "virtue is a powerful sense of place and the ability to convey great sweeps of time. His weakness is an insistence on covering murals with so much background and foreground that he has learned only a few ways of doing faces."

Jonathan Yardley reported in the *New York Times Book Review* that Michener "deserves more respect than he usually gets. Granted that he is not a stylist and that he smothers his stories under layers of historical and ecological trivia, nonetheless he has earned his enormous popularity honorably. Unlike many other authors whose books automatically rise to the upper reaches of the best-seller lists, he does not get there by exploiting the lives of the famous or the notorious; he does not treat sex cynically or pruriently; he does not write trash. His purposes are entirely serious: he wants to instruct, to take his readers through history in an entertaining fashion, to introduce them to lands and peoples they do not know."

Schott concluded that "while the arbiters of letters try to figure out what James A. Michener's fat books are . . . Mr. Michener goes on writing them as if his life depended on it." As Michener once told James, "I don't think the way I write books is the best or even the second-best. The really great writers are people like Emily Bronte who sit in a room and write out of their limited experience and unlimited imagination. But people in my position also do some very good work. I'm not a stylist like Updike or Bellow, and don't aspire to be. I'm not interested in plot or pyrotechnics, but I sure work to get a steady flow. If I try to describe a chair, I can describe it so that a person will read it to the end. The way the words flow, trying to maintain a point of view and a certain persuasiveness—that I can do." And he still has plenty of ideas for future development, he told *Insight* reporter Harvey Hagman in 1986. "I am able to work, and I love it. I have entered a profession which allows you to keep working at top energy. It's a wonderful job I have."

One of Michener's last books was the 1996 *This Noble Land: My Vision for America,* in which he examined the political and social problems besetting his native land and suggested some cures. For Michener, the huge disparity in wealth was destroying America, and he recommended a revised tax system in which the wealthiest are taxed at a higher rate in order to fund more social welfare programs. A critic for *Publishers Weekly* called his analysis "straightforward and congenial" and a "moderate and humane vision." Similarly, Gilbert Taylor, writing in *Booklist,* called the book a "personal declaration of faith in 'legitimate liberalism.'" Michener continued working up to the last in 1997, when he died of kidney failure. *Dictionary of Literary Biography* contributor Day summed up Michener's achievement: "As a scholarly novelist, Michener has won wide popularity without stooping to cheap melodrama. He may best be remembered for his family sagas in which men and women of many heritages intermingle in far-off places." And a contributor for the *Economist* echoed these comments, noting that Michener was less a fine novelist than he was "at heart, an educator and populariser, satisfying readers' demand for information and self-improvement in a palatable, unhectoring way."

BIOGRAPHICAL AND CRITICAL SOURCES:

BOOKS

Authors in the News, Volume 1, Thomson Gale (Detroit, MI), 1976.

Becker, G. J., *James A. Michener,* Ungar (New York, NY), 1983.

Contemporary Literary Criticism, Thomson Gale (Detroit, MI), Volume 1, 1973; Volume 5, 1976; Volume 11, 1979; Volume 29, 1984.

Contemporary Novelists, 6th edition, Thomson Gale (Detroit, MI), 1996.

Conversations with Writers, Thomson Gale (Detroit, MI), 1978.

Day, A. Grove, *James A. Michener,* Twayne (Boston, MA), 1964.

Dictionary of Literary Biography, Volume 6: *American Novelists since World War II,* Second Series, Thomson Gale (Detroit, MI), 1980.

Dybwad, G. L., and Joy V. Bliss, *James A. Michener: The Beginning Teacher and His Textbooks,* The Books Stops Here, 1995.

Groseclose, David A., *James A. Michener: A Bibliography,* State House Press (Austin, TX), 1995.

Hayes, J. P., *James A. Michener,* Bobbs-Merrill (Indianapolis, IN), 1984.

Kings, J., *In Search of Centennial,* Random House (New York, NY), 1978.

Michener, James A., *About "Centennial": Some Notes on the Novel,* Random House (New York, NY), 1974.

Michener, James A., *Iberia: Spanish Travels and Reflections,* Random House (New York, NY), 1968.

Michener, James A., *Report of the County Chairman,* Random House (New York, NY), 1961.

Murrow, Edward Roscoe, *This I Believe,* Volume 2, Simon & Schuster (New York, NY), 1954.

Newquist, Roy, *Conversations,* Rand McNally (Indianapolis, IN), 1967.

Prescott, Orville, *In My Opinion: An Inquiry into the Contemporary Novel,* Bobbs-Merrill (Indianapolis, IN), 1952.

St. James Encyclopedia of Popular Culture, St. James Press (Detroit, MI), 2000.

Severson, Marilyn S., *James A. Michener: A Critical Companion,* Greenwood Press (Westport, CT), 1996.

Stuckey, W. J., *The Pulitzer Prize Novels,* University of Oklahoma Press (Norman, OK), 1966.

Warfel, Harry Redcay, *American Novelists of Today,* American Book (New York, NY), 1951.

PERIODICALS

America, August 31, 1963; September 23, 1978; January 24, 1981.

Antioch Review, fall-winter, 1970-71.

Art America, November, 1969.

Atlantic, March, 1949; July, 1951; September, 1953; April, 1957; October, 1958; September, 1963; May, 1968; June, 1971; November, 1974.

Best Sellers, September 1, 1963; June 15, 1965; July 1, 1968; December 15, 1970; June 15, 1971; November, 1976; September, 1978.

Booklist, December 1, 1993, p. 671; September 1, 1996, Gilbert Taylor, review of *This Noble Land,* p. 3.

Bookmark, June, 1951.

Books, October, 1971; January, 1995, Mark Jackson, review of *Recessional,* p. 12.

Books and Bookmen, December, 1971.

Book Week, May 30, 1965.

Book World, May 5, 1968; June 1, 1969; November 9, 1969; July 4, 1971; July 18, 1971.

Catholic World, June, 1960.

Chicago Sun, February 9, 1949.

Chicago Sunday Tribune, May 6, 1951; November 25, 1951; July 12, 1953; January 31, 1954; December 26, 1954; March 3, 1957; November 22, 1959; May 7, 1961.

Chicago Tribune, January 17, 1982; September 29, 1983, Bill Kurtis, review of *Poland;* June 27, 1985; October 17, 1985; July 2, 1989.

Chicago Tribune Book World, October 3, 1982; September 4, 1983; October 13, 1985.

Children's Book World, November 5, 1967.

Christian Science Monitor, February 5, 1949; May 1, 1951; July 9, 1953; December 23, 1954; February 28, 1957; September 11, 1958; June 3, 1965; May 9, 1968; June 17, 1970; September 18, 1978; November 10, 1980; October 6, 1982.

College English, October, 1952.

Commentary, April, 1981.

Commonweal, April 27, 1951; February 12, 1953; July 31, 1953; April 12, 1957.

Congress Bi-Weekly, June 14, 1965.

Detroit News, October 3, 1982; September 18, 1983; October 27, 1985.

Esquire, December, 1970; June, 1971.

Good Housekeeping, February, 1960.

Guardian, November 10, 1961.

Harper's, January, 1961.

Insight, September 1, 1986.

Kirkus Reviews, August 1, 1995, p. 1051.

Library Journal, October 7, 1970; November 15, 1993, p. 79.

Life, November 7, 1955; June 4, 1971.

Los Angeles Times, November 21, 1985.

Los Angeles Times Book Review, December 7, 1980; October 3, 1982; July 31, 1983; September 4, 1983; September 13, 1987, John Ehrlichman, review of *Legacy;* April 7, 1991.

Nation, February 12, 1949; May 12, 1951; April 20, 1957; January 31, 1959; December 12, 1959; July 19, 1971; March 5, 1983.

National Observer, May 27, 1968; June 7, 1971.

National Review, June 29, 1971; June 29, 1974; November 22, 1974; August 7 and 14, 1976; September 15, 1978; May 27, 1983; November 11, 1983.

New Republic, May 14, 1951; August 17, 1953; May 29, 1961; September 21, 1974; August 7-14, 1976.

New Statesman, June 25, 1960; November 29, 1974.

Newsweek, January 25, 1954; May 14, 1962; August 12, 1963; May 24, 1965; May 6, 1968; September 16, 1974; July 24, 1978; November 24, 1980; January 16, 1984; September 23, 1985.

New Yorker, February 19, 1949; May 3, 1951; January 23, 1954; March 16, 1957; August 14, 1978.

New York Herald Tribune, May 28, 1961.

New York Herald Tribune Book Review, February 2, 1947; February 13, 1949; April 22, 1951; May 20, 1951; October 7, 1951; July 12, 1953; July 19, 1953; January 24, 1954; December 12, 1954; March 3, 1957; August 10, 1958; November 22, 1959; December 20, 1959; August 11, 1963.

New York Magazine, September 2, 1974.

New York Review of Books, December 19, 1968; August 17, 1978.

New York Times, February 2, 1947; February 3, 1947; February 6, 1949; February 7, 1949; April 22, 1951; April 23, 1951; October 30, 1951; July 12, 1953; January 24, 1954; December 12, 1954; March 3, 1957; August 3, 1958; May 1, 1968; June 10, 1971, Thomas Lask, review of *The Drifters;* September 27, 1974; July 1, 1976; August 1, 1978, Christopher Lehmann-Haupt, review of *Chesapeake;* November 14, 1980; September 29, 1982, Stephen Farber, review of *Space;* September 3, 1983; February 20, 1984; September 25, 1984; October 9, 1985; October 31, 1985.

New York Times Book Review, May 16, 1948; May 22, 1949; July 12, 1953; March 3, 1957; November 8, 1959; November 22, 1959; June 18, 1961; August 11, 1963; May 23, 1965; July 24, 1966; May 12, 1968; May 25, 1969; June 6, 1971; June 27, 1971; September 30, 1973; February 10, 1974; September 8, 1974; June 27, 1976; July 23, 1978; November 26, 1978; July 15, 1979; November 23, 1980, John F. Burns, review of *The Covenant;* September 19, 1982; June 12, 1983; September 4, 1983; November 20, 1983; October 13, 1985, Hughes Rudd, review of *Texas;* September 6, 1987; June 26, 1988; July 9, 1989; November 5, 1989; November 12, 1989; September 30, 1990; March 31, 1991; January 19, 1992, Doris Grumbach, review of *The World Is My Home;* November 28, 1993, p. 26; October 16, 1994, p. 20; January 7, 1996, p. 20.

New York Times Magazine, September 8, 1985, Caryn James, "The Michener Phenomenon," pp. 45-52, 56-68.

Palm Springs Life, October, 1974.

Paradise of the Pacific, September-October, 1963.

Philadelphia Bulletin, September 13, 1974.

Publishers Weekly, October 18, 1993, p. 54; August 21, 1995, p. 46; September 2, 1996, review of *This Noble Land,* p. 102.

Reader's Digest, April, 1954.

San Francisco Chronicle, February 4, 1949; May 6, 1951; July 12, 1953; January 29, 1954; December 19, 1954; February 28, 1957; August 17, 1958; November 24, 1959; November 25, 1959; May 3, 1961.

Saturday Evening Post, January, 1976.

Saturday Review, July 1, 1953; February 6, 1954; January 1, 1955; March 2, 1957; November 21, 1959, Horace Sutton, review of *Hawaii;* June 10, 1961; September 7, 1963; May 29, 1965; May 4, 1968; April 12, 1969; May 1, 1971; September 18, 1971, David W. McCullogh, review of *The Drifters;* June 26, 1976; June, 1980; November, 1980.

Saturday Review of Literature, February 12, 1949; April 28, 1951.

School Library Journal, May, 1994, p. 143.

Spectator, June 25, 1954; September 15, 1955; November 10, 1961.

Sports Illustrated, May 12, 1980.

This Week, December 4, 1966.

Time, February 4, 1949; April 23, 1951; July 13, 1953; January 25, 1954; March 4, 1957; November 23, 1959; August 9, 1963; May 28, 1965; May 17, 1968; May 3, 1971; September 23, 1974; June 28, 1976; July 10, 1978; February 9, 1981; October 3, 1983, Patricia Blake, review of *Poland;* October 28, 1985.

Times Literary Supplement, October 26, 1951; July 9, 1954; May 17, 1957; February 19, 1960; June 17, 1960; November 17, 1961; October 14, 1965; November 7, 1968; July 23, 1971; November 22, 1974; July 22, 1977.

U.S. News, February 4, 1980.

U.S. Quarterly Book Review, June, 1947; September, 1951; September, 1955.

Variety, June 22, 1970; November 8, 1972; November 7, 1994.

Vital Speeches, July 15, 1979.

Vogue, November 1, 1966.

Washington Post, September 2, 1983, Peter Osnos, review of *Poland.*

Washington Post Book World, June 4, 1972; September 1, 1974; July 9, 1978; September 30, 1979; November 2, 1980, Andre Brink, review of *The Covenant;* December 6, 1981; September 12, 1982, Ben Bova, review of *Space;* September 29, 1985, Nicholas Lemann, review of *Texas;* July 3, 1988; March 2, 1991; December 8, 1991; October 16, 1994, Reeve Lindbergh, review of *Recessional,* p. 1.

Writer's Digest, April, 1972; May, 1972.

Yale Review, spring, 1947; spring, 1949.

OBITUARIES:

PERIODICALS

Chicago Tribune, October 17, 1997.

Detroit News, October 17, 1997.

Economist, November 1, 1997, "James Michener," p. 92.

Entertainment Weekly, October 31, 1997, Alexandra Jacobs and Gene Lyons, "A Storied Life: James A. Michener 1907-1997," p. 17.

Los Angeles Times, October 17, 1997.

New York Times, October 17, 1997.

People, November 3, 1997, "Epic Journey," p. 67.

USA Today, October 17, 1997.
Washington Post, October 17, 1997.

* * *

MICHENER, James Albert
See MICHENER, James A.

* * *

MIÉVILLE, China 1973(?)-

PERSONAL: Male. Born c. 1973, in London, England. *Education:* Degree from Cambridge University; London School of Economics, master's degree with distinction.

ADDRESSES: *Office*—c/o Del Rey Books, 1540 Broadway, New York, NY 10036.

CAREER: Writer.

AWARDS, HONORS: Nebula Award nomination in novel category, 2002, for *Perdido Street Station;* Philip K. Dick Award special citation, Philadelphia Science Fiction Society, 2002, Hugo Award nomination in best novel category, World Science Fiction Society, Arthur C. Clarke Award shortlist, and World Fantasy Award nomination in best novel category, and British Fantasy Society Award, all 2003, all for *The Scar.*

WRITINGS:

King Rat, Macmillan (New York, NY), 1998.
Perdido Street Station, Del Rey (New York, NY), 2001.
The Scar, Del Rey (New York, NY), 2002.
(With Michael Moorcock, Paul de Fillipo, and Geoff Ryman) *Cities,* Gollancz (London, England), 2003.
Iron Council, Del Rey (New York, NY), 2004.

SIDELIGHTS: China Miéville's debut novel, *King Rat,* was hailed by some critics as an updated take on the urban-gothic fable. In London, after an unknown intruder kills a man, the man's son, Saul, is wrongly convicted of the crime. Put in jail, Saul escapes, helped by a mysterious stranger who claims to be King Rat, a subterranean ruler. What is more, King Rat declares himself the deposed leader of a rodent army and reveals that Saul's mother is also of rat-kind. Now aware of his inborn abilities, Saul discovers he can "eat garbage, move soundlessly and unseen, squeeze through impossibly tiny openings, and climb vertical walls," as a *Kirkus Reviews* contributor described them.

In a variation of the Pied Piper theme, magical hip-hop music also enters into the story, leading to a showdown between King Rat and his young disciple. *King Rat* marks an "auspicious debut," according to a reviewer in *Publishers Weekly,* overcoming a "predictable plot" by pulling "the reader into the story through the kinetic energy" of Miéville's prose. To *Booklist* critic Roland Green, if the book lacks the balance of other works by noted urban-goth authors, those flaws are countered by Miéville's sense of "folkloric expertise . . . his depiction of the grungier side of urban life is vivid and extensive, not to mention well-worded."

Miéville's second book, *Perdido Street Station,* is a fantasy/horror tale set in New Crobuzon, a city full of gangsters, revolutionaries, and assorted human and nonhuman species. Isaac Dan der Crimnebulin and his lover, Lin, an insect-like creature, inadvertently release a flying monster on the city. Isaac and Lin must chase down the monster before the authorities find it, or them. Jackie Cassada, reviewing the novel in *Library Journal,* wrote that Miéville tells a "powerful tale about the power of love and the will to survive." A reviewer for *Publishers Weekly* called the novel "breathtakingly broad" and "an impressive and ultimately pleasing epic."

In Miéville's third book, *The Scar,* published in 2002, fugitives of New Crobuzon find more dangers await them when pirates take them to the floating city of Armada, which is ruled by a devious pair called The Lovers. Some critics have expressed dismay at the plot twists as well as with Miéville's writing style. Others found more to like; Jane Halshall, reviewing *The Scar* for *School Library Journal,* characterized Miéville's writing as "something akin to Lewis Carroll's use of portmanteau."

Iron Council, Miéville's next work, takes readers on a return trip to the city of New Crobuzon, where revolt stirs in the minds of the residents living under a repressive capitalist regime that doles out inhumane reconstructive surgery as punishment. A reviewer for *Publishers Weekly* maintained that "Miéville represents much of what is new and good in contemporary dark fantasy, and his work is must reading for devotees of that genre."

BIOGRAPHICAL AND CRITICAL SOURCES:

PERIODICALS

Booklist, September 15, 1999, review of *King Rat,* p. 239; February 15, 2001, Roland Green, review of *Perdido Street Station,* p. 1122; July, 2002, Regina Schroeder, Jackie Cassada, review of *The Scar,* p. 1833; June 1, 2004, Ray Olson, review of *Iron Council,* pp. 1670-1671.

Bookseller, December 12, 2003, p. 29.

Extrapolation, spring, 2000, Scott Maisano, "Reading Underwater; or, Fantasies of Fluency from Shakespeare to Mieville and Emshwiller," pp. 76-88; fall, 2003, John Reider, "Symposium: Marxism and Fantasy," pp. 375-380; winter, 2003, Carl Freedman, "Toward a Marxist Urban Sublime: Reading China Mieville's *King Rat,*" pp. 395-408.

Kirkus Reviews, August 1, 1999, review of *King Rat,* p. 1181; May 1, 2002, review of Jackie Cassada, review of *The Scar,* p. 625; June 1, 2004, review of *Iron Council,* p. 522.

Library Journal, February 15, 2001, Jackie Cassada, review of *Perdido Street Station,* p. 204; July, 2002, Jackie Cassada, review of *The Scar,* p. 259; July, 2004, Jackie Cassada, review of *Iron Council,* p. 75.

Publishers Weekly, August 23, 1999, review of *King Rat,* p. 53; January 8, 2001, review of *Perdido Street Station,* p. 52; May 20, 2002, review of *The Scar,* p. 51; July 5, 2004, review of *Iron Council,* p. 42.

School Library Journal, March, 2003, Jane Halshall, review of *The Scar,* p. 259.

Spectator, May 6, 2000, Michael Moorcock, review of *Perdido Street Station,* pp. 33-34.

Times Literary Supplement, September 1, 2000, Edward James, review of *Perdido Street Station,* p. 11.

ONLINE

3 am Magazine Online, http://www.3ammagazine.com/ (August 18, 2004), Richard Marshall, "The Road to Perdido: An Interview with China Mieville."

BBC Web site, http://www.bbc.co.uk/ (August 18, 2004), "China Mieville."

Fantastic Fiction Web site, http://www.fantasticfiction.co.uk/ (August 18, 2004), "China Mieville."

Pan Macmillan Web site, http://www.panmacmillan.com/ (August 18, 2004).

Strange Horizon Web Site, http://www.strangehorizon.com/ (August 18, 2004), Cheryl Morgan, interview with Mieville.

* * *

MILLER, Arthur 1915-

PERSONAL: Born October 17, 1915, in New York, NY; son of Isidore (a manufacturer) and Augusta (Barnett) Miller; married Mary Grace Slattery, 1940 (divorced, 1956); married Marilyn Monroe (an actress), June, 1956 (divorced, 1961); married Ingeborg Morath (a photojournalist), 1962; children: (first marriage) Jane Ellen, Robert Arthur; (third marriage) Rebecca Augusta, Daniel. *Education:* University of Michigan, A.B., 1938. *Hobbies and other interests:* Carpentry, farming.

ADDRESSES: *Agent*—International Creative Management, 40 West 57th St., New York, NY 10019.

CAREER: Writer, 1938—. Associate of Federal Theater Project, 1938; author of radio plays, 1939-44; dramatist and essayist, 1944—. Also worked in an automobile parts warehouse, Brooklyn Navy Yard, and a box factory. Resident lecturer, University of Michigan, 1973-74.

MEMBER: Dramatists Guild, Authors League of America, National Institute of Arts and Letters, PEN (international president, 1965-69).

AWARDS, HONORS: Avery Hopwood Awards from the University of Michigan, 1936, for *Honors at Dawn,* and 1937, for *No Villain: They Too Arise;* Bureau of New Plays Prize from Theatre Guild of New York, 1938; Theatre Guild National Prize, 1944, for *The Man Who Had All the Luck;* Drama Critics Circle Awards, 1947, for *All My Sons,* and 1949, for *Death of a Salesman;* Antoinette Perry ("Tony") Awards, 1947, for *All My Sons,* 1949, for *Death of a Salesman,* and 1953, for *The Crucible;* Donaldson Awards, 1947, for *All My Sons,* 1949, for *Death of a Salesman,* and 1953, for *The Crucible;* Pulitzer Prize for drama, 1949, for *Death of a Salesman;* National Association of Independent Schools award, 1954; Obie Award from *Village Voice,* 1958, for *The Crucible;* American Academy of Arts and Letters gold medal, 1959; Anglo-American Award, 1966; Emmy Award, National Academy of Television Arts and Sciences, 1967, for *Death of a Salesman;* Antoinette Perry Award Nominations for best play, 1968, for *The Price,* 1994, for *Broken Glass,* and 2000, for *The Ride down Mt. Morgan;* Brandeis University creative arts award, 1969; George Foster Peabody Award, 1981, for *Playing for Time;* John F. Kennedy Award for Lifetime Achievement, 1984; Algur Meadows Award, 1991; Olivier Award (England), 1996, for *Broken Glass*; Amnesty International Media Spotlight Award, 1997; Dorothy and Lillian Gish Prize, 1999; Tony Lifetime Achievement Award, 1999; Tony Award for Best Play Revival, 1999; National Endowment for the Humanities Lecturer in the Humanities, 2001; National Book Medal for Distinguished Contribution to American Letters, 2001; Japan Art Association Praemium Imperiale International Arts Award, 2001; Tony Award nomination for best play revival, 2002, for *The Crucible;* Principe de Asturias Prize for Literature, 2002; Jerusalem Prize, 2003. Honorary degrees from Oxford University, Harvard University, Brandeis University, University of Michigan, and Carnegie-Mellon University.

WRITINGS:

PLAYS

Honors at Dawn, produced in Ann Arbor, MI, 1936.

No Villain: They Too Arise, produced in Ann Arbor, MI, 1937.

The Man Who Had All the Luck, produced on Broadway at Forest Theatre, November 23, 1944, revived on Broadway, 2002.

All My Sons (three-act; produced on Broadway at Coronet Theatre, January 29, 1947), Reynal (New York, NY), 1947, published with an introduction by Christopher Bigsby, Penguin (New York, NY), 2000.

Death of a Salesman (two acts; produced on Broadway at Morosco Theatre, February 10, 1949), Viking (New York, NY), 1949, published as *Death of a Salesman: Text and Criticism,* edited by Gerald Weales, Penguin (New York, NY), 1977, fiftieth anniversary edition published as *Death of a Salesman: Certain Private Conversations in Two Acts and a Requiem,* with a new preface by Miller, and an afterword by Christopher Bigsby, Penguin (New York, NY), 1999.

(Adaptor) Henrik Ibsen, *An Enemy of the People* (produced on Broadway at Broadhurst Theatre, December 28, 1950), Viking (New York, NY), 1951.

The Crucible (four acts; produced on Broadway at Martin Beck Theatre, January 22, 1953), Viking (New York, NY), 1953, published as *The Crucible: Text and Criticism,* edited by Gerald Weales, Viking (New York, NY), 1977, published as *The Crucible: A Play in Four Acts,* Penguin (New York, NY), 1995.

A View from the Bridge [and] *A Memory of Two Mondays* (produced together on Broadway at Coronet Theatre, September 29, 1955), Viking (New York, NY), 1955, published separately, Dramatists Play Service (New York, NY), 1956, revised version of *A View from the Bridge* (produced off-Broadway at Sheridan Square Playhouse, January 28, 1965), Cresset (London, England), 1956.

After the Fall (produced on Broadway at American National Theatre and Academy, January 23, 1964), Viking (New York, NY), 1964.

Incident at Vichy (produced on Broadway at American National Theatre and Academy, December 3, 1964), Viking (New York, NY), 1965.

The Price (produced on Broadway at Morosco Theatre, February 7, 1968), Viking (New York, NY), 1968.

The Creation of the World and Other Business (produced on Broadway at Shubert Theatre, November 30, 1972), Viking (New York, NY), 1972.

Up from Paradise, with music by Stanley Silverman (musical version of *The Creation of the World and Other Business;* first produced in Ann Arbor, MI, at Trueblood Theatre, directed and narrated by Miller, April, 1974; produced off-Broadway at Jewish Repertory Theater, October 25, 1983), Viking (New York, NY), 1978.

The Archbishop's Ceiling (produced in Washington, DC, at Eisenhower Theatre, Kennedy Center for the Performing Arts, April 30, 1977), Dramatists Play Service (New York, NY), 1976.

The American Clock (first produced in Charleston, SC, at Dock Street Theatre, 1980; produced on Broadway at Harold Clurman Theatre, 1980), Viking (New York, NY), 1980.

Elegy for a Lady [and] *Some Kind of Love Story* (each one act; produced together under title *Two-Way Mirror* in New Haven, CT, at Long Wharf Theatre, 1983), published separately, Dramatists Play Service (New York, NY), 1984.

Playing for Time (stage adaptation of screenplay; produced in England at Netherbow Art Centre, August, 1986), Dramatic Publishing (Chicago, IL), 1985.

Danger: Memory! Two Plays: "I Can't Remember Anything" and "Clara" (each one act; produced on Broadway at Mitzi E. Newhouse Theatre, Lincoln Center for the Performing Arts, February 8, 1987), Grove (New York, NY), 1987.

The Golden Years, Dramatists Play Service (New York, NY), 1990.

The Last Yankee, Dramatists Play Service (New York, NY), 1991.

The Ride down Mt. Morgan, Viking Penguin (New York, NY), 1992, reprinted, 2000.

Broken Glass, Viking Penguin (New York, NY), 1994, Dramatists Play Service (New York, NY), 1994.

Resurrection Blues, produced in Minneapolis, MN, 2002.

Finishing the Picture, produced in New York, NY, 2004.

SCREENPLAYS

(With others) *The Story of G.I. Joe,* United Artists, 1945.

The Crucible (based on the play of the same title; also known as *The Witches of Salem*), Kingsley-International, 1958, published as *The Crucible: Screenplay,* Penguin (New York, NY), 1996.

The Misfits (produced by United Artists, 1961), published as *The Misfits: An Original Screenplay Directed by John Huston,* edited by George P. Garrett, Irvington (New York, NY), 1982.

The Price (based on the play of the same title), United Artists, 1969.

The Hook, MCA, 1975.

Fame (teleplay), National Broadcasting Company (NBC-TV), 1978.

Playing for Time, Columbia Broadcasting System (CBS-TV), 1980.

Everybody Wins, Grove/Atlantic (New York, NY), 1990.

FICTION

Focus (novel), Reynal (New York, NY), 1945, with an introduction by the author, Arbor House (New York, NY), 1984.

The Misfits (novella), Viking (New York, NY), 1961.

Jane's Blanket (juvenile), Collier (New York, NY), 1963.

I Don't Need You Anymore (stories), Viking (New York, NY), 1967.

"The Misfits" and Other Stories, Scribner (New York, NY), 1987.

Homely Girl, a Life, Peter Blum, 1992, reprinted as *Plain Girl: A Life,* Methuen (London, England), 1995.

NONFICTION

Situation Normal, Reynal (New York, NY), 1944.

In Russia, with photographs by wife Inge Morath, Viking (New York, NY), 1969.

In the Country, with photographs by Inge Morath, Viking (New York, NY), 1977.

The Theatre Essays of Arthur Miller, edited by Robert A. Martin, Viking (New York, NY), 1978, revised edition edited by Martin and Steven R. Centola, with foreword by Miller, Da Capo Press (New York, NY), 1996.

Chinese Encounters, with photographs by Inge Morath, Farrar, Straus (New York, NY), 1979.

Salesman in Beijing, with photographs by Inge Morath, Viking (New York, NY), 1984.

Timebends: A Life (autobiography), Grove (New York, NY), 1987.

The Theater Essays of Arthur Miller, Da Capo Press (New York, NY), 1996.

OMNIBUS VOLUMES

(Also author of introduction) *Arthur Miller's Collected Plays* (contains *All My Sons, Death of a Salesman, The Crucible, A Memory of Two Mondays,* and *A View from the Bridge*), Viking (New York, NY), 1957.

Harold Clurman, editor, *The Portable Arthur Miller* (includes *Death of a Salesman, The Crucible, Incident at Vichy, The Price, The Misfits, Fame,* and *In Russia*), Viking (New York, NY), 1971.

Homely Girl: A Life, and Other Stories, Viking (New York, NY), 1995.

(Also author of introduction) *Collected Plays,* Volume II, Viking (New York, NY), 1980.

The Portable Arthur Miller, edited by C. Bigsby, Penguin (New York, NY), 1995.

OTHER

(Author of text with others) *Inge Morath: Portraits,* Otto Muller, 1999.

Mr. Peters' Connections, Penguin (New York, NY), 1999.

(With Serge Toubiana) *The Misfits: Story of a Shoot,* photography by Magnum photographers, Phaidon (New York, NY), 2000.

Echoes down the Corridor: Collected Essays, 1947-1999, edited by S. Centola, Viking (New York, NY), 2000.

On Politics and the Art of Acting, Viking (New York, NY), 2001.

Contributor of essays, commentary, and short stories to periodicals, including *Collier's, New York Times, Theatre Arts, Holiday, Nation, Esquire,* and *Atlantic.*

The University of Michigan at Ann Arbor, the University of Texas at Austin, and the New York Public Library house collections of Miller's papers.

ADAPTATIONS: All My Sons was filmed as a movie by Universal in 1948 and as a television special by the Corporation for Public Broadcasting in 1987; *Death of a Salesman* was filmed as a movie by Columbia in

1951 and as a television special by CBS-TV in 1985; *The Crucible* was filmed in France by Kingsley-International in 1958, adapted for use as an interactive CD-ROM by the University of East Anglia, 1994, and adapted for film again in 1996 by Nicholas Hytner and starring Winona Ryder and Daniel Day-Lewis; *A View from the Bridge* was filmed by Continental in 1962; *After the Fall* was filmed as a television special by NBC-TV in 1969.

SIDELIGHTS: Arthur Miller is widely recognized as a preeminent playwright of twentieth-century American theater. Miller's realistic dramas explore the complex psychological and social issues that plague humankind in the wake of World War II: the dangers of rampant materialism, the struggle for dignity in a dehumanizing world, the erosion of the family structure, and the perils besetting human rights. Several of Miller's best-known plays—*All My Sons, Death of a Salesman,* and *The Crucible*— have been performed for well over forty years, and according to Benjamin Nelson in *Arthur Miller: Portrait of a Playwright,* they "continue to endure, . . . in fact gaining in strength and impact." Nelson described the many plays in the Miller canon as "stunning dramatic achievements." Viewers, he noted, "are jolted by the immediate emotional impact of something real, something vibrantly alive exploding at them with a burst of meaning and a ring of truth. The impact is hardly accidental. Miller's plays are products of a meticulous craftsman with an unerring sense of the theater and the ability to create meaningful people in striking situations."

Although none of Miller's theater work is specifically autobiographical, it has been strongly influenced by his particular life experiences. An early influential event was the Great Depression of the 1930s. Miller was born in New York City in 1915, and until 1929 he lived the comfortable life of an upper-middle-class businessman's son. Then the stock market collapsed, and his father, a coat manufacturer, was forced out of work. First his parents sold their luxury items, one by one, to pay the bills. Later the family had to move from the spacious Harlem apartment of Miller's youth to a tiny house in Brooklyn. Miller told the *New York Times* that the Depression "occurred during a particularly sensitive moment" for him. "I was turning fourteen or fifteen and I was without leaders," he said. "This was symptomatic not just of me but of that whole generation. It made you want to search for ultimate values, for things that would not fall apart under pressure." Like many others at the time, Miller was attracted to the tenets of socialism. In *Arthur Miller: A Collection of Critical Essays,* Harold Clurman suggested that the young man realized "it was not financial stress alone that shook the foundations of American life at that time but a false ideal which the preceding era, the Twenties, had raised to the level of a religious creed: the ideal of Success." Miller saw how his father's fate was shared on all sides by those who had had blind faith in the so-called American Dream, and as a thoughtful man he sought an alternative vision of an ideal society.

In the midst of the Depression, Miller entered the University of Michigan where, to quote Nelson, "the atmosphere was one of challenge rather than despairing finality." An undistinguished high school student, Miller had to prove himself capable of college work in his first year. That accomplished, he matured into a good scholar who spent his spare hours writing for the college newspaper and working as a custodian in a research laboratory that housed several hundred mice. During a mid-semester break in his sophomore year, he turned his hand to playwriting in hopes of winning a prestigious (and lucrative) Avery Hopwood Award from the university. His first play, *Honors at Dawn,* won the award in 1936. The next year he won again with *No Villain: They Too Arise*. Both dramas tackled themes that would later fuel his major works: the sins committed in the name of "free enterprise," sibling rivalry, and moral responsibility to family and community. *Modern American Playwrights* author Jean Gould wrote: "In his plays Arthur Miller was to question and to sit in judgment against the false values of the past and present, as yet a distant outcome of his college years, but already clearly outlined in his early manuscript plays."

All My Sons was Miller's first successful "drama of accountability." In the play, an aging businessman comes to the anguished recognition that his responsibility extends beyond his immediate family to the wider world of humankind. Having sold defective merchandise to the army, and having lied to protect his business when the merchandise caused war planes to crash in battle, the businessman learns that he has in fact caused the death of one of his own sons. His other son, also a war veteran, savagely rebukes him for his warped sense of morality. The son, Chris, has learned from his war experiences that relatedness is not particular but universal; he is shocked by his father's unscrupulous renunciation of that knowledge. Sheila Huftel, in *Arthur Miller: The Burning Glass,* wrote that in *All My Sons,* "Miller is concerned with consciousness, not crime, and with bringing a man face to face with the consequences he has caused, forcing him to share in the results of his creation."

With the box-office proceeds from *All My Sons,* Miller bought a farm in rural Connecticut. There he built himself a studio and began to work on another drama. It was produced in 1949 under the title *Death of a Salesman,* and it received overwhelming critical and public acclaim. The play centers on the emotional deterioration of Willy Loman, an aging and not too successful salesman, who can hardly distinguish between his memories of a brighter past and his setbacks in the dismal present. In the course of the play Willy grapples with the loss of his job and the failure of his two grown sons to achieve wealth, and with it, presumably, happiness. Nelson wrote of Willy: "Shot through with weaknesses and faults, he is almost a personification of self-delusion and waste, the apotheosis of the modern man in an age too vast, demanding and complex for him. . . . He personifies the human being's desire, for all his flaws, to force apart the steel pincers of necessity and partake of magnificence." Willy does aspire to greatness for himself and his sons, but he champions a success ethic that is both shallow and contradictory—the cult of popularity, good looks, and a winning personality. "From the conflicting success images that wander through his troubled brain comes Willy's double ambition—to be rich and to be loved," noted Weales. Facing ruin, Willy still cannot relinquish his skewed values, and he becomes a martyr to them. His sons must come to terms with their father's splintered legacy and determine the essence of his ultimate worth.

Because Willy struggles valiantly for money and recognition, and then fails on both accounts, some critics saw *Death of a Salesman* as an indictment of the American system. In *Newsweek,* Jack Kroll suggested that the drama was "a great public ritualizing of some of our deepest and deadliest contradictions. It is a play about the misplaced energy of the basic human material in American society." The message Miller sends in the work is not so simple, however. Nelson wrote, "One of the strengths of *Death of a Salesman* is its refusal to pin blame exclusively on a person, an institution, or even on an entire society. Although Willy Loman's destruction is partly the fault of his family and the failure of certain values propounded by society, it is no less his own doing." Indeed, while Willy adheres to an adolescent code of values, his son Biff and his neighbor Charley represent alternative reactions to family and society. According to R.H. Gardner in *The Splintered Stage: The Decline of the American Theater,* the play is "an affirmation of the proposition that persistent application of one's talents, small though they may be, pays off. And this, after all, is the substance of the American dream." Willy's tragic decline is given added poignancy by the suggestion that he might have become an expert carpenter had he not pursued the chimeras of wealth and popularity.

On one point most critics agree: *Death of a Salesman* is one of the significant accomplishments of modern American letters. In *The Forties: Fiction, Poetry, Drama,* Lois Gordon called it "the major American drama of the 1940s" and added that it "remains unequalled in its brilliant and original fusion of realistic and poetic techniques, its richness of visual and verbal texture, and its wide range of emotional impact." *New York Times* columnist Frank Rich concluded that *Death of a Salesman* "is one of a handful of American plays that appear destined to outlast the twentieth century. In Willy Loman, that insignificant salesman who has lost the magic touch along with the shine on his shoes after a lifetime on the road, Miller created an enduring image of our unslaked thirst for popularity and success." According to John Gassner in the *Quarterly Journal of Speech,* Miller "has accomplished the feat of writing a drama critical of wrong values that virtually every member of our middle-class can accept as valid. It stabs itself into a playgoer's consciousness to a degree that may well lead him to review his own life and the lives of those who are closest to him. The conviction of the writing is, besides, strengthened by a quality of compassion rarely experienced in our theatre."

Miller rose to prominence during a particularly tense time in American politics. In the early 1950s many national leaders perceived a threat of communist domination even within the borders of the United States, and public figures from all walks of life fell under suspicion of conspiring to overthrow the government. Miller and several of his theater associates became targets for persecution, and in that climate the playwright conceived *The Crucible.* First produced in 1953, *The Crucible* chronicles the hysterical witch-hunt in seventeenth-century Salem, Massachusetts, through the deeds of one courageous dissenter, John Proctor. If Miller began his researches into the Salem witch trials with the communist-hunting trials in mind, he soon uncovered a deeper level for his prospective drama. In his autobiography, *Timebends: A Life,* Miller wrote: "The political question . . . of whether witches and Communists could be equated was no longer to the point. What was manifestly parallel was the guilt, two centuries apart, of holding illicit, suppressed feelings of alienation and hostility toward standard, daylight society as defined by its most orthodox proponents." What Miller reveals in *The Crucible,* to quote *University College Quarterly* essayist John H. Ferres, is the tenet that "life is not worth living when lies must be told to one's self and one's friends to preserve it."

Early reviewers of *The Crucible* saw the play—and often denounced it—as an allegory for the McCarthy hearings on communism. That view has been revised significantly in the wake of the work's continuing popularity. "For a play that was often dismissed as a political tract for the times, *The Crucible* has survived uncommonly well," stated Ferres. Robert A. Martin offered a similar opinion in *Modern Drama.* The play, he wrote, "has endured beyond the immediate events of its own time. . . . As one of the most frequently produced plays in the American theater, *The Crucible* has attained a life of its own; one that both interprets and defines the cultural and historical background of American society." In *Twentieth-Century Interpretations of "The Crucible,"* Phillip G. Hill wrote of the play's pertinence, noting that the work remains "a powerful indictment of bigotry, narrow-mindedness, hypocrisy, and violation of due process of law, from whatever source these evils spring."

The eight-year period following the first production of *The Crucible* was extremely hectic and ultimately dispiriting for Miller. In 1955 he divorced his first wife, Mary Grace Slattery, and the following year married actress Marilyn Monroe. At the same time, his supposed communist sympathies caused his expulsion from a script-writing project based on New York City's Youth Board, and he was denied a passport renewal by the State Department. Shortly after his celebrated second marriage, Miller was subpoenaed to appear before the House Un-American Activities Committee, where he was queried about his political beliefs. Miller admitted to the Committee that he had attended a few informal Communist Party meetings many years earlier, but he refused to name others who had attended the meetings even when the Committee insisted he do so. Helterman wrote, "In a classic case of life imitating art, Miller took the precise position Proctor took before his Puritan judges. Just as Proctor is willing to implicate himself but refuses to name other dabblers with witchcraft, so Miller named himself, but refused to identify any others involved in communist-front activities." Miller was charged with contempt of Congress and was tried and convicted in 1957. His conviction was overturned on appeal the next year.

In 1962 Miller married his third wife, Inge Morath, a professional photographer, and turned his attention to more personal issues. This shift was reflected in his work. *After the Fall, Incident at Vichy,* and other plays from this era introduced a new theme in Miller's work: man's hopeless alienation from himself and others. *Critical Quarterly* contributor Kerry McSweeney maintained that the horrors of World War II as well as his more personal problems caused Miller to reject his vision of possible social harmony among humankind. "His characters now grope alone for values to sustain their dissipating lives and each value, once discovered, slips again into ambiguity," wrote McSweeney. "Most frightening of all is the realization that human corruption, once attributed to conscious deviation from recognizable moral norms, is now seen as an irresistible impulse in the heart of man. The theme of universal guilt becomes increasingly and despairingly affirmed."

In the 1970s, Miller wrote only three plays, *The Creation of the World and Other Business, Up from Paradise,* and *The Archbishop's Calling.* These works, and his 1980 *The American Clock,* did not attract the critical acclaim or popular attention of his earlier works. However, in 1984, his career received a boost with a revival of *Death of a Salesman* in Broadway. The play was an even bigger hit in 1998, and in 1999, it won a Tony Award for Best Revival. In 1996, Miller won an Olivier Award for *Broken Glass,* which was broadcast on the show *Masterpiece Theater* in 1996.

Over the course of his career, Miller has seen his best-known plays produced in such unlikely locales as Moscow and Beijing, where *Death of a Salesman* was one of the first American dramas to be performed. Miller directed the Beijing production of *Salesman* himself, with the help of translators. In *The New Consciousness, 1941-1968,* Helterman wrote, "That [Miller] was able to motivate [Chinese] actors who had survived the cultural revolution and that a play so embedded in American capitalism was able to reach the audience in the capital of communism is testimony that the play's true message is more personal and human than sociological." Miller claimed in *Timebends* that the Chinese reaction to *Death of a Salesman* confirmed "what had become more and more obvious over the decades in the play's hundreds of productions throughout the world: Willy was representative everywhere, in every kind of system, of ourselves in this time . . . not simply as a type but because of what he wanted. Which was to excel, to win out over anonymity and meaninglessness, to love and be loved, and above all, perhaps, to *count.*"

BIOGRAPHICAL AND CRITICAL SOURCES:

BOOKS

Authors and Artists for Young Adults, Volume 15, Thomson Gale (Detroit, MI), 1995.

Bhatia, S. K., *Arthur Miller,* Heinemann (London, England) 1985.

Bigby, Christopher, editor, *The Cambridge Companion to Arthur Miller,* Cambridge University Press (Cambridge, MA), 1997.

Bloom, Harold, *Arthur Miller's "Death of a Salesman,"* Chelsea House (Broomall, PA), 1996.

Bloom, Harold, *Arthur Miller's "The Crucible,"* Chelsea House (Broomall, PA), 1996.

Carson, Neil, *Arthur Miller,* Grove (New York, NY), 1982.

Centola, Steve, *Arthur Miller in Conversation,* Northhouse & Northhouse, 1993.

Centola, Steve, editor, *The Achievement of Arthur Miller: New Essays,* Contemporary Research Press (Dallas, TX), 1995.

Contemporary Dramatists, 6th edition, St. James Press (Detroit, MI), 1999.

Contemporary Literary Criticism, Thomson Gale (Detroit, MI), Volume 1, 1973, Volume 2, 1974, Volume 6, 1976, Volume 10, 1979, Volume 15, 1980, Volume 26, 1983.

Contemporary Theatre, Film, and Television, Volume 31, Thomson Gale (Detroit, MI), 2000.

Corrigan, Robert W., editor, *Arthur Miller: A Collection of Critical Essays,* Prentice-Hall (Englewood, NJ), 1969.

Dictionary of Literary Biography, Volume 7: *Twentieth-Century American Dramatists,* Thomson Gale (Detroit, MI), 1981.

Downer, Alan S., editor, *The American Theatre Today,* Basic Books (New York, NY), 1967.

Evans, Richard, *Psychology and Arthur Miller,* Dutton (New York, NY), 1969, reprinted, Praeger (New York, NY), 1981.

Ferres, John H., editor, *Twentieth-Century Interpretations of "Crucible,"* Prentice-Hall (Englewood Cliffs, NJ), 1972.

French, Warren, editor, *The Forties: Fiction, Poetry, Drama,* Everett/Edwards (Deland, FL), 1969.

Gardner, R. H., *The Splintered Stage: The Decline of the American Theater,* Macmillan (New York, NY), 1965.

Gould, Jean, *Modern American Playwrights,* Dodd (New York, NY), 1966.

Griffin, Alice, *Understanding Arthur Miller,* University of South Carolina Press (Columbia, SC), 1996.

Hayman, Ronald, *Arthur Miller,* Heinemann (London, England), 1972.

Hogan, Robert, *Arthur Miller,* University of Minnesota Press (Minneapolis, MN), 1964.

Huftel, Sheila,*Arthur Miller: The Burning Glass,* Citadel (New York, NY), 1965.

Koon, Helene Wickham, editor, *Twentieth-Century Interpretations of "Death of a Salesman,"* Prentice-Hall (Englewood Cliffs, NJ), 1983.

Martine, James J., editor, *Critical Essays on Arthur Miller,* Hall (Boston, MA), 1979.

Martin, Robert A., editor, *Arthur Miller—New Perspectives,* Prentice Hall (Englewood Cliffs, NJ), 1982.

Martin, Robert, editor, *The Theatre Essays of Arthur Miller,* Methuen (London, England), 1994.

Moss, Leonard, *Arthur Miller,* Twayne (New York, NY), 1967.

Murphy, Brenda, *Miller: Death of a Salesman,* Cambridge University Press (Cambridge, MA), 1995.

Murray, Edward, *Arthur Miller, Dramatist,* Ungar (New York, NY), 1967.

Nelson, Benjamin, *Arthur Miller: Portrait of a Playwright,* McKay (New York, NY), 1970.

Newsmakers 1999, Thomson Gale (Detroit, MI), 1999.

Roudane, Matthew Charles, editor, *Approaches to Teaching Miller's "Death of a Salesman,"* Modern Language Association of America (New York, NY), 1995.

Roudane, Matthew Charles, editor, *Conversations with Arthur Miller,* University Press of Mississippi (Jackson, MS), 1987.

St. James Encyclopedia of Popular Culture, St. James Press (Detroit, MI), 2000.

Welland, Dennis, *Arthur Miller,* Grove (New York, NY), 1961, revised edition published as *Miller: The Playwright,* Methuen (London, England), 1979.

White, Sidney H., *Merrill Guide to Arthur Miller,* Merrill (Columbus, OH), 1970.

PERIODICALS

American Theatre, May, 1986; January, 2002, review of *On Politics and the Art of Acting,* p. 83.

Back Stage West, August 1, 2002, Charles Baldridge, review of *All My Sons,* p. 8.

Book, November, 2000, Jerry Tallmer, review of *Echoes down the Corridor: Collected Essays, 1947-1999,* p. 73.

Booklist, August, 1999, review of *Mr. Peters' Connections,* p. 2012; January 1, 2000, Barbara Baskin, review of *All My Sons,* p. 949; August, 2000, review of *The Misfits,* p. 2096; September 15, 2000, Ray Olson, review of *Echoes down the Corridor,* p. 204; November 1, 2001, Nancy Spillman, review of *The Crucible,* p. 492.

Book Week, March 8, 1964.

Chicago Tribune, September 30, 1980; April 20, 1983; February 17, 1984; April 30, 1985; November 27, 1987.

Daily Telegraph (London, England), May 1, 2000.

Encounter, May, 1957; July, 1959; November, 1971.

Esquire, October, 1959; March, 1961.

Film Quarterly, summer 2002, review of *The Misfits,* p. 28.

Globe & Mail (Toronto, Ontario, Canada), May 19, 1984.
Harper's, November, 1960.
Horizon, December, 1984.
Library Journal, March 1, 1999, review of *Death of a Salesman,* p. 116; September 15, 1999, review of *Mr. Peters' Connections,* p. 83; July, 2000, Nathan Ward, review of *The Misfits,* p. 98; September 15, 2000, Susan L. Peters, review of *Echoes down the Corridor,* p. 80; November 1, 2001, review of *On Politics and the Art of Acting,* p. 120.
Listener, September 27, 1979.
Los Angeles Times, April 10, 1981; November 27, 1982; March 26, 1983; June 10, 1984; June 15, 1984; May 26, 1986; February 14, 1987; November 15, 1987.
Los Angeles Times Book Review, November 8, 1987; October 7, 2001, review of *On Politics and the Art of Acting,* p. 11.
Maclean's, September 16, 1985.
Michigan Quarterly Review, summer, 1967; fall, 1974; spring, 1977; summer, 1985.
Modern Drama, March, 1975; December, 1976; September, 1977; September, 1984.
Nation, July 19, 1975; November 13, 1995, p. 579.
New England Review, fall, 2001, review of *Echoes down the Corridor,* p. 156.
New Leader, November 3, 1980.
New Republic, May 27, 1972; July 19, 1975; May 6, 1978.
New Statesman, February 4, 1966.
Newsweek, February 3, 1964; December 11, 1972; July 7, 1975; November 16, 1987.
New Yorker, July 7, 1975; April 11, 1994, p. 35; December 25, 1995, p. 110; March 18, 2002, John Lahr, review of *The Crucible,* p. 149.
New York Review of Books, March 5, 1964; January 14, 1965; January 9, 1997.
New York Times, February 27, 1949; October 9, 1955; July 6, 1965; June 17, 1979; May 27, 1980; September 30, 1980; November 16, 1980; June 12, 1981; January 30, 1983; February 4, 1983; February 10, 1983; February 13, 1983; October 23, 1983; October 26, 1983; March 30, 1984; May 9, 1984; October 5, 1984; September 15, 1985; February 9, 1986; February 16, 1986; February 1, 1987; February 9, 1987; November 2, 1987.
New York Times Book Review, October 14, 1979; June 24, 1984; November 8, 1987; December 24, 1995, p. 10; December 30, 2001, review of *Echoes down the Corridor,* p. 16.
New York Times Magazine, February 13, 1972.
Paris Review, summer, 1966; summer, 1968.
Premiere, March, 1996, p. 41.
Publishers Weekly, November 6, 1987; August 28, 1995; August 28, 2000, review of *Echoes down the Corridor,* p. 65.
Quarterly Journal of Speech, October, 1949.
Rapport, 2000, review of *Echoes down the Corridor,* p. 37.
Renascence, fall, 1978.
Saturday Review, January 31, 1953; June 4, 1966; July 25, 1970.
Sewanee Review, winter, 1960.
South Carolina Review, spring 1999, review of *Broken Glass,* p. 17.
Studies in Short Fiction, fall, 1976.
Theatre Journal, May, 1980.
Time, December 6, 1976; October 15, 1984; August 18, 1986; May 4, 1987; November 23, 1987.
Times (London, England), April 21, 1983; April 3, 1984; July 4, 1984; July 5, 1984; September 5, 1984; April 19, 1985; August 8, 1986; August 28, 1986; October 31, 1986; December 20, 1986; February 14, 1987; February 19, 1987; March 5, 1987.
Times Literary Supplement, December 25-31, 1987; April 20, 2001, review of *Echoes down the Corridor,* p. 20.
Tribune Books (Chicago, IL), November 15, 1987.
University College Quarterly, May, 1972.
USA Today, May, 1996, p. 80.
Variety, August 30, 1993, p. 26.
Washington Post, October 26, 1969; October 1, 1979; October 16, 1980; October 26, 1980; December 15, 1980; February 13, 1983; February 19, 1984; February 27, 1984; March 2, 1984; February 22, 1987; November 23, 1987; September 13, 2001.

ONLINE

Curtain Up, http://www.curtainup.com/ (May 29, 2003), "Arthur Miller."
PBS Web site, http://www.pbs.org/ (May 29, 2003), "American Masters: Arthur Miller."

OBITUARIES:

PERIODICALS

Chicago Tribune, February 12, 2005, section 1, pp. 1, 7.
New York Times, February 12, 2005, pp. A1, A14-A15.
Times (London, England), February 12, 2005, p. 76.
Washington Post, February 12, 2005, pp. A1, A8.

MILLETT, Kate 1934-

PERSONAL: Born Katherine Murray Millett, September 14, 1934, in St. Paul, MN; daughter of James (an engineer) and Helen (a teacher; maiden name, Feely) Millett; married Fumio Yoshimura (a sculptor), 1965 (divorced, 1985). *Education:* University of Minnesota, B.A. (magna cum laude), 1956; St. Hilda's College, Oxford University, M.A. (first class honors), 1958; Columbia University, Ph.D. (with distinction), 1970. *Politics:* "Left, feminist, liberationist."

ADDRESSES: *Home*—295 Bowery, New York, NY 10003-7104; (summer) Millett Farm, 29 Old Overlook Road, Poughkeepsie, NY 12603. *Agent*—Georges Borchardt, 136 East 57th St., New York, NY 10022.

CAREER: Author and professor. Sculptor, photographer, and painter, 1959—, with numerous exhibitions, including Minami Gallery, Tokyo, Japan, 1963, Judson Gallery, New York, NY, 1967, Los Angeles Womens Building, Los Angeles, CA, 1977, and Courtland Jessup Gallery, Provincetown, MA, 1991-94; writer, 1958—. University of North Carolina at Greensboro, English professor, 1959; New York, NY, kindergarten teacher, 1960-61; Waseda University, Tokyo, English teacher, 1961-63; Barnard College, New York, NY, English and philosophy professor, 1964-69; Bryn Mawr College, Bryn Mawr, PA, sociology professor, 1971; California State University, Sacramento, distinguished visiting professor, 1973; New York University, adjunct professor, 2000—. Founder, Women's Art Colony Farm, Poughkeepsie, NY.

MEMBER: National Organization for Women (education committee chair, 1965-68), Congress of Racial Equality, Phi Beta Kappa.

AWARDS, HONORS: *Library Journal* Best Books of 2001 award for *Mother Millett.*

WRITINGS:

NONFICTION

(Editor) *Token Learning: A Report on the Condition of Higher Education for Women in American Colleges,* National Organization for Women (New York, NY), 1967.

Sexual Politics, Doubleday (Garden City, NY), 1970, Simon & Schuster (New York, NY), 1990, University of Illinois Press (Urbana, IL), 2000.

The Prostitution Papers, Basic Books (New York, NY), 1971.

The Basement: Meditations on Human Sacrifice, Simon & Schuster (New York, NY), 1980.

Going to Iran, Coward (New York, NY), 1981.

The Politics of Cruelty: An Essay on the Literature of Political Imprisonment, Norton (New York, NY), 1994.

AUTOBIOGRAPHY

(Director) *Three Lives* (documentary film), Impact Films, 1971.

Flying, Knopf (New York, NY), 1974, University of Illinois Press (Urbana, IL), 2000.

Sita, Farrar, Straus (New York, NY), 1977, revised with new introduction by Millett, Simon & Schuster (New York, NY), 1992, University of Illinois Press (Urbana, IL), 2000.

(Contributor) *Caterpillars: Journal Entries by 11 Women,* Epona, 1977.

The Loony-Bin Trip, Simon & Schuster (New York, NY), 1990, University of Illinois Press (Urbana, IL), 2000.

A.D.: A Memoir, Norton (New York, NY), 1995.

Kate Millett, Sculptor: The First Thirty-Eight Years, University of Maryland, Baltimore County (Catonsville, MD), 1997.

Mother Millett, Verso (New York, NY), 2001.

Contributor of essays to numerous magazines, including *Ms.*

SIDELIGHTS: Author Kate Millett's *Sexual Politics,* a rare doctoral thesis-turned-bestseller, became a rallying cry for radical feminism in the 1970s. "It attacked the very people credited as authors of sexual liberation—(Sigmund) Freud, D.H. Lawrence, Henry Miller, Jean Genet—and gave emerging 70s feminists the sexual metaphor that went on to define their politics for years to come," Maureen Freely wrote in the *Guardian. Sexual Politics* transformed Millett from anonymous artist to feminist icon; a generation later, she has re-emerged from obscurity with *Mother Millett,* in which she relates her attempts to save her aging mother, Helen, who is institutionalized in their native St. Paul, Minnesota. "In this latest memoir Millett is, as usual, egotistical, prone to paranoia and fascinated by clinical atrocity—but also, as usual, worth reading for her challenges to the less commonly questioned forms of dehumanization," Martha Bridegam wrote in *Gay and Lesbian Review.* "Warts and all, this book belongs in your brain. You'll argue with Kate Millett as you read, but the important part is, you'll think."

Millett's books include *The Loony-Bin Trip, Flying, Sita, The Politics of Cruelty,* and *The Basement: Meditations on Human Sacrifice,* all of which explore the challenges of womanhood in the United States. Though Millett often addresses feminism and homosexuality, "overall social, not just sexual, change is Millett's concern," Susan Paynter wrote in the *Seattle Post-Intelligencer,* "and she uses her teaching, writing and speaking talents to make her contribution."

Millett's *Sexual Politics* had seven printings and sold 80,000 copies in its first publication year. It has been reprinted two times, once in 1990, and again in 2000, the latest edition including a new introduction. Jane Wilson, in the *New York Times Book Review,* called it "an original and useful book . . . that imposed a moratorium on reiterated, dead-end feminist complaint against the male chauvinist pig in the street." Muriel Haynes, in *Saturday Review,* described *Sexual Politics* as "an impressively informed, controlled polemic against the patriarchal order, launched in dead seriousness and high spirits, the expression of a young radical sensibility, nurtured by intellectual and social developments that could barely be glimpsed even twenty years ago."

Her acclaim, however, came at a price, according to Wilson. "In her uncomfortable new spokeswoman status she was urged on by her sisters to do her duty in speaking out on their behalf, while also being browbeaten and harassed for her arrogance and 'elitism in presuming to do so.'"

Millett struggled personally. *Flying* chronicles her attempts to cope with the vast publicity that accompanied *Sexual Politics.* Her devout lesbianism and its effect on family and lovers were central to *Flying,* as well as *Sita* and *A.D.: A Memoir.* "The publicity that has attached to figures such as Kate Millett in America is unimaginable," Emma Tennant wrote in the *Times Literary Supplement.* "Her greatest desire . . . was to reconstruct some sort of personality for herself after the glare of the cameras had begun to fade."

Attempting to give up lithium, she became erratic and her family had her committed to a mental hospital in the early 1980s. Millett based *The Loony-Bin Trip* on her own experiences while in confinement. According to Darby Penny, in a review and interview for *Off Our Backs,* "Millett eloquently traces her horrifying experiences in the mental health system, from her 'involuntary commitment' and electro-shock treatments to the abuse and betrayal endured at the hands of her friends, family, and, ultimately, a legal system that subjected her to incarceration and isolation." Marilyn Yalom, comparing the work to Ken Kesey's bestseller *One Flew over the Cuckoo's Nest,* wrote in the *Washington Post Book World:* "Millett's prose is rich, her passion compelling. . . . [She] takes us into internal landscapes where no one goes by choice." Karen Malpede added in *Women's Review of Books,* "This is a harrowing, hallucinatory, heroic book. . . . It is written in the style of vision and rhapsody, the tongue of a super-agile mind spilling out rivers of image and thought, emotion, sexual desire, fantasy, historical or linguistic fact."

Millett's candor induced a mixed response from many mainstream reviewers. Joy Williams wrote in *Chicago Tribune Books:* "The title tells a great deal about the tone of this book—plucky, breezy, a flip bravado masking a quavery confidence. . . . There is no sense of the mind examining itself, of the judgement of the present upon the past." In Millet's own words about her time in the mental hospital, as told to Darby Penny, "[The] diagnosis does you in; that, and the humiliation of being there. I mean, the indignity you're subjected to."

"Women like [Millett], it was claimed, were acting out at society's expense the unresolved conflicts implicit in their relations with their fathers," Liam Hudson, recalling the backlash to *Sexual Politics,* wrote in the *Times Literary Supplement.* "*The Loony-Bin Trip* reveals that the stock response was uncannily accurate; in fact, it reads at times like a case history made up by a male chauvinist in order to discredit her views. . . . [Millett] describes her realization that, all along, she has been obsessed with her father, and that the nature of her obsession has been incestuous."

Irony had Millett rescuing her mother, who had helped institutionalize her daughter only a few years before. *Mother Millett* features the conflicts and ironies of family, age, institutionalism, and regionalism. "Helen Millett was a feminist before Kate really knew what the word meant and she went on to become a respected business leader later in life. She worked for civil rights, supported gay rights and took to the streets to protest the war in Vietnam," Freely wrote. "But she was also a strict and formidable matriarch. And Kate had always been 'the outlaw of the tribe, the artist, the queer, even the crazy, since in certain ill-advised moments, my sisters and even my mother have seen fit to deliver me over to state psychiatry.'"

"She picked the right daughter," Millett writes in *Mother Millet.* "We are on the lam. It's a movie, and it's the most unlikely American car fantasy. We are Thelma and Louise, this frail old woman beside me, and I some undefined criminal type."

Social ills also interest Millett. *The Basement* is a chilling account of the 1965 torture-death of Indianapolis teenager Sylvia Likens, from her viewpoint as well as that of her killers. In *The Politics of Cruelty: An Essay on the Literature of Political Imprisonment,* Millett, using the Spanish Inquisition as a reference point, rages over what she says is torture as a government policy in nearly half the nations of the world. "The knowledge of torture is itself a political act," she wrote in her conclusion. "To speak of the unspeakable is the beginning of action." Finding *The Politics of Cruelty* alternately engaging and frustrating, Elissa Gelfand wrote in *Women's Review of Books* that "not everyone will share Millett's belief that exposing and condemning the continued global acquiescence in state-sponsored violence constitute political action."

Despite her acclaim for *Sexual Politics,* Millett fell into oblivion for a generation. "How forgotten is Kate Millett?" Leslie Crawford asked in *Salon.com.* "When I stop by my local bookstore to pick up a copy of *Sexual Politics,* it doesn't occur to me that I won't find her seminal work, the one that all but launched the second wave of the women's movement." Crawford recalled an unknowing clerk: "'Let's see . . . Kate Millett,' she taps at the computer and stares at the screen, searching the store's database and, it appears from her puzzled expression, her own. 'Wasn't she a feminist?'"

Someone else was paying attention, though. Upon reading Crawford's review and learning that *Sexual Politics* was out of print, University of Illinois Press (UIP) publicity director Kim Grossmann approached UIP director Willis Regier, who decided to re-publish, not only *Sexual Politics,* but also *Flying, Sita,* and *The Loony-Bin Trip.* On re-issuing these works, Regier stated in a UIP press release, "Had Millett's career fizzled out in 1970, she would have been a romantic episode—the brash and daring Jim Morrison of feminism. But her continued dedication to the things she cared about when she was younger—particularly art and community and movies—makes me inclined to take her early writing even more seriously."

Art is a large part of Millett's life, being a sculptor, photographer, and painter, and founding the Women's Art Colony Farm in Poughkeepsie, New York, for aspiring female writers, visual artists, and musicians. The colony is a self-supporting and economically independent facility, where residents divide their time between their art and working the farm. As Millett stated on her Web site, "We alternate between building and farming. We learn a whole lot from both of them and will use it the rest of our lives, the farm a kind of school of the material reality our educations neglected, giving us skills, know-how, empowerment, even courage."

Staying active in feminist causes, not just nationally, but internationally as well, Millett spoke at a February 2004 conference sponsored by the University of Illinois, *Back to the Future: Generations of Feminism.* Summarized in the *Chicago Journal,* Millett called "the future of feminism" "tonight's evening news gender wars in Iraq and Afghanistan," where prospects for Afghan women have deteriorated. "Where women before would have been flogged, now they're raped for showing an inch of skin at the market." Added the *Chicago Journal,* Millett felt "U.S. women, who should help, are no longer paying attention."

Millett lives in New York, where for a number of years she has been fighting eviction attempts by city officials who want to raze her loft and art studio in lower Manhattan in favor of an urban renewal project. "The day they wreck it, I'll be swinging on the wrecking ball," she told an interviewer for the *New York Times.*

BIOGRAPHICAL AND CRITICAL SOURCES:

BOOKS

Benét's Reader's Encyclopedia of American Literature, 1991, Volume 1, HarperCollins (New York, NY).

PERIODICALS

Art in America, December, 1995, p. 92.
Books and Bookmen, June, 1971.
Book World, November 22, 1970.
Canadian Forum, November-December, 1970.
Gay and Lesbian Review, March 2002, Martha Bridegam, review of *Mother Millett,* pp. 31-32.
Guardian, June 19, 2001, review of *Mother Millett,* p. 8.

Kirkus Reviews, March 1, 1977; June 15, 1995, p. 840.
Library Journal, June 15, 2001, Mirela Roncevic, review of *Mother Millett,* p. 72; January 2002, review of *Mother Millett,* pp. 50-51.
Life, September 4, 1970.
Listener, March 25, 1971.
Los Angeles Times Book Review, September 16, 1979; July 7, 1991, p. 10.
Mademoiselle, February, 1971.
Ms., February, 1981; May, 1988; September-October, 1995, p. 78.
Nation, April 17, 1982; July 23, 2001, Hillary Frey, review of *Mother Millett,* p. 36.
National Review, August 30, 1974.
New Leader, December 14, 1970.
New Republic, August 1, 1970; July 6-13, 1974; July 7-14, 1979; May 16, 1994, pp. 33-38.
New Statesmen & Society, August 5, 1994, p. 38.
Newsweek, July 27, 1970; July 15, 1974.
New Yorker, August 9, 1974.
New York Times, July 20, 1970; August 5, 1970; August 6, 1970; August 27, 1970; September 6, 1970; December 18, 1970; November 5, 1971; May 13, 1977; November 25, 2001, p. 6.
New York Times Book Review, September 6, 1970; June 23, 1974; May 29, 1977; September 9, 1979; May 16, 1982; June 3, 1990, p. 12; June 16, 1991, p. 28; August 13, 1995, p. 17; October 6, 1996, p. 96.
Observer, November 20, 1994, p. 719; August 13, 1995, p. 17.
Off Our Backs, July-August, 2003, Darby Penney interview, "Insist on Your Sanity: An Interview with Kate Millett," p. 40.
People Weekly, April 2, 1979.
Publishers Weekly, April 23, 2001, p. 62.
Saturday Review, August 29, 1970; June 15, 1974; May 28, 1977.
Seattle Post-Intelligencer, March 4, 1973.
Signs, winter, 1996, p. 467.
Time, August 31, 1970; December 14, 1970; July 26, 1971; July 1, 1974; May 9, 1977.
Times Literary Supplement, April 9, 1971; October 7, 1977; November 8, 1991, p. 10; September 2, 1994, p. 32.
Tribune Books (Chicago, IL), June 3, 1990, p. 5.
Washington Post, July 30, 1970.
Washington Post Book World, January 8, 1978; May 13, 1990, p. 7; June 10, 2001, p. TO8, Liza Featherstone, review of *Mother Millett.*
Women's Review of Books, October, 1990, pp. 7-8; June, 1994, pp. 1, 3-4; September, 2001, Meryl Altman, review of *Mother Millett,* pp. 1, 3-4.

ONLINE

Chicago Journal Online http://magazine.uchicago.edu/ (August 5, 2004) "The Future of Feminism," April 2004.
Kate Millett Web site, http://www.katemillett.com/ (August 6, 2004), "Millett Farm."
Salon.com, http://www.salon.com (June 5, 1999), Leslie Crawford, "Kate Millett, the Ambivalent Feminist"; (February 11, 2000) Craig Offman, "Kate Millet Finds a New Home."
University of Chicago, Department of Education Web site, http://www-news.uchicago.edu/ (August 6, 2004), "Back to the Future: Generations of Feminism."
University of Illinois Press Web site, http://www.press.uillinois.edu/ (March 21, 2002).

* * *

MILLHAUSER, Steven 1943-
(Steven Lewis Millhauser)

PERSONAL: Born August 3, 1943, in New York, NY; married Cathy Allis, 1984; children: one son, one daughter. *Education:* Columbia College, B.A., 1965; graduate study at Brown University, 1968-71, 1976-77.

ADDRESSES: *Home*—235 Caroline St., Saratoga Springs, NY 12866. *Office*—Skidmore College, English Department, Palamountain Hall 307, 815 North Broadway, Saratoga Springs, NY 12866. *E-mail*—smillhau@skidmore.edu.

CAREER: Writer and educator. Williams College, visiting associate professor of English, 1986-88; Skidmore College, Saratoga Springs, NY, associate professor, 1988-92, professor of English, 1992—.

AWARDS, HONORS: Prix Médicis Étranger (France), 1975, for *Edwin Mullhouse: The Life and Death of an American Writer, 1943-1954, by Jeffrey Cartwright;* American Academy/Institute of Arts and Letters award for literature, 1987; World Fantasy award, 1990; Lannan literary award for fiction, 1994; Pulitzer Prize for fiction, 1997, for *Martin Dressler: The Tale of an American Dreamer.*

WRITINGS:

NOVELS

Edwin Mullhouse: The Life and Death of an American Writer, 1943-1954, by Jeffrey Cartwright, Alfred A. Knopf (New York, NY), 1972.

Portrait of a Romantic, Alfred A. Knopf (New York, NY), 1977.

From the Realm of Morpheus, William Morrow (New York, NY), 1986.

Martin Dressler: The Tale of an American Dreamer, Crown Publishers (New York, NY), 1996.

SHORT FICTION

In the Penny Arcade (stories and novella), Alfred A. Knopf (New York, NY), 1986.

The Barnum Museum (stories), Poseidon Press (New York, NY), 1990.

Little Kingdoms (three novellas), Poseidon Press (New York, NY), 1993.

The Knife Thrower and Other Stories, Crown Publishers (New York, NY), 1998.

Enchanted Night: A Novella, Crown Publishers (New York, NY), 1999.

The King in the Tree: Three Novellas, Alfred A. Knopf (New York, NY), 2003.

Contributor of short stories to periodicals, including *New Yorker, Tin House, Grand Street, Harper's,* and *Antaeus.* Contributor of story "A Visit" to CD *The New Yorker out Loud,* 1998.

ADAPTATIONS: *Martin Dressler* was released in an audio version by Guidall, 1997; *Enchanted Night* was released in audio versions by Dove Audio, 1999.

SIDELIGHTS: Pulitzer prize-winner Steven Millhauser, hailed by many critics as one of America's finest novelists, made his first entry onto the literary scene with *Edwin Mullhouse: The Life and Death of an American Writer, 1943-54, by Jeffrey Cartwright.* It is the fictitious biography of an eleven-year-old novelist as penned by the novelist's twelve-year-old companion. The young novelist, Edwin Mullhouse, completed only one work, the masterpiece *Cartoons,* prior to his untimely death at age eleven. His biographer records Mullhouse's interest in baseball cards and novelty-shop gifts while unwittingly revealing his own obsessions with Mullhouse and *Cartoons.* As the biographer's self-created rivalry with the late Mullhouse develops, *Edwin Mullhouse* evolves into both a parody of literary biographies and a sardonic portrait of the artist.

Published in 1972, *Edwin Mullhouse* was acclaimed by many reviewers. William Hjortsberg, writing in *New York Times Book Review,* called Millhauser's work "a rare and carefully evoked novel, . . . [that] displays an enviable amount of craft, the harsh discipline that carves through the scar tissue of personality painfully developed during the process known as 'growing up.'" J.D. O'Hara, reviewing the work for *Washington Post Book World,* noted that Millhauser's "characters, like J.D. Salinger's in one way . . . are absurdly precocious children, but their story is for adults." A *New Republic* reviewer was equally impressed with Millhauser's work, calling it "a mature, skillful, intelligent and often very funny novel."

Millhauser continues his depiction of childhood in his second novel, *Portrait of a Romantic.* Arthur Grumm, the twenty-nine-year-old protagonist, gives an account of his life between the ages of twelve and fifteen. He sees himself as a sickly, bored only child who says that "by some accident the children in my neighborhood were older than I and so excluded me from their dusty games." Grumm reveals himself as a vaguely suicidal adolescent divided by the polarized beliefs of his two friends, William Mainwaring, an avowed realist whom Grumm refers to as "my double," and Philip Schoolcraft, an equally vehement romantic referred to by Grumm as "my triple." Schoolcraft introduces Grumm to the romantic life, typified by decay, contemplation, and despair—they pass time pondering Poe and playing Russian roulette. Grumm later forms suicide pacts with the pathetic Eleanor Schumann and eventually with the disillusioned Mainwaring. The bizarre events caused by Grumm's suicide pacts provide an offbeat context for his own internal conflict between realism and romanticism and his weighing of the harsh repercussions inherent in submitting to either attitude.

According to John Calvin Batchelor of *Village Voice,* Millhauser, in his attempts to capture completely every detail, writes "with sometimes suffocating amount of sights and sound." *Times Literary Supplement* critic William Boyd noted that too much effort is lavished on "pages of relentlessly detailed description." Nevertheless, *Portrait of a Romantic* stands as a "remarkable book" by a very talented writer, according to George Stade in *New York Times Book Review.* Stade added: "Once you reread the book the particulars begin to look different. The foreshadowings become luminous with afterglow. What first seemed merely realistic . . . becomes symbolic. What seemed mere fantasy . . . becomes the workings of an iron psychological necessity." William Kennedy, who reviewed the novel for *Washington Post Book World,* also responded with respect and praise, declaring that Millhauser's "achievement is of a high order."

Carl Hausman, the young narrator of Millhauser's 1986 novel *From the Realm of Morpheus,* is watching a baseball game. He chases a foul ball and finds an opening to the underworld, which he immediately investigates, and readers are plunged, *Alice in Wonderland*-style, into the world of Morpheus, the God of Sleep. In what John Crowley in *New York Times Book Review* dubbed "a book, wholly odd yet purposefully unoriginal," Millhauser takes readers on a literary tour that parodies a variety of genres and where characters from history, literature, and legend converse and philosophize in a series of disconnected episodes. While Rob Latham, in the *St. James Guide to Fantasy Writers,* contended that this experiment in mock epic writing falls short of its intended goal, *Washington Post Book World* contributor Michael Dirda praised *From the Realms of Morpheus* as "beautifully composed" and "utterly entrancing."

Millhauser's Pulitzer Prize-winning *Martin Dressler: The Tale of an American Dreamer* tells the story of a quintessential Gilded-Age American entrepreneur, his dreams, and his disappointments. The title character works his way up from his father's cigar shop through a dreamy series of promotions, schemes, and machinations to become the owner and proprietor of a Manhattan hotel, The Grand Cosmo, that is "a leap beyond the hotel" in its fantastical atmosphere and consumerist excess. Janet Burroway, writing for *New York Times Book Review,* described the novel as "a fable and phantasmagoria of the sources of our century," calling Martin "not a parody but a paradigm of the bootstrap capitalist." Critics cited the novel for its imaginative and piercing glimpse into the American psyche and the American dream; *Martin Dressler* explores not only Dressler's business success, but also his personal failures and ultimate unhappiness. A *Booklist* reviewer observed that Millhauser "brings descriptive delicacy to this chronicle of Martin's 'falling upwards' and the forces behind the fall." A *Kirkus Reviews* critic described the novel as "a chronicle of obsession, self-indulgence, and, in a curious way, moral growth, expertly poised between realistic narrative and allegorical fable."

In addition to longer works, Millhauser has also authored many short stories and novellas, most of which have been included in published collections. A writer for *Contemporary Literary Criticism Yearbook 1997* commented that the author "writes of the world of the imagination. The subject of his stories is frequently the artist and the dreamer, the illusionist who creates words to satisfy the needs of others for fantasy. Millhauser's artistic motivation is summarized in a line of his short story, 'Eisenheim the Illusionist' from the collection *The Barnum Museum:* 'Stories, like conjuring tricks, are invented because history is inadequate to our dreams.'"

In his first collection of short stories, *In the Penny Arcade,* Millhauser continues his pursuit of "fiction as a mysterious, magical, enlightening experience" according to Robert Dunn in *New York Times Book Review.* The book is divided into three sections, the first containing the novella *August Eschenburg,* a long story about a German boy who is possessed by the desire to create mechanical devices that approximate life. Creating lifelike models for store windows and for an automaton theater, he dreams about infusing these automatons with life. But when a rival exploits this craft for pornographic purposes, August returns to his home and dreams his dreams in solitude.

The second section of *In the Penny Arcade,* comprised of three stories about real-life characters, contrasts to the artificial-life stories of sections one and three. These stories are more delicate; they are subtle, revealing the "fragility of moods in which nothing much actually happens," according to Al J. Sperone in *Village Voice Literary Supplement.* Similarly Irving Malin, in *Review of Contemporary Fiction* contended, "These stories vary in length and setting and time, [and] they must be read as variations on a theme—the 'perfection' of art. . . . They surprise us because they are less interested in plot, character, and philosophy than in magic, dream, and metaphor." Among the three stories in the final section is the title story, in which a young boy returns to an arcade he has idealized in his mind, seeing it in all its seediness. Robert Dunn noted in *New York Times Book Review* that Millhauser "creates for us this splendid arcade. And he asks us also to be vigilant as we venture with him into the common corners of our ragged world, where the marvelous glows and the true meanings breathe life."

The Barnum Museum collects stories that seek a reconciliation between the worlds of illusion and reality. In "The Sepia Postcard," the narrator buys an old post card and finds that as he examines it more closely the figures on it come alive. In "Rain," a man walks out of a theater and into a storm. As he walks on, he washes away as if he were a watercolor painting. Taken as a whole, this collection addresses the broader issue of imagination, according to Jay Cantor in a review for *New York Times Book Review.* The critic wrote that Millhauser "imagines the imagination as a junk shop with a warren of rooms, one chamber linked to another without any reason except the bewildering reason of the heart." This junk shop is the Barnum Museum, which is "named for the patron saint of charming bunco," P.T. Barnum. Many of the ten stories in the collection engage the reader in what Catherine Maclay in *World and I* dubbed "a playful examination of the imaginary and the real . . . [and the attempt to find] a reconciliation of these opposites." In blurring the lines between these two, Millhauser's postmodern stories help us "find a way to maintain a bridge" between them, according to Maclay.

Other short-story collections include *The Knife Thrower and Other Stories,* which *New York Times Book Review* contributor Patrick McGrath noted showcases Millhauser's "rich, sly sense of humor" and a characteristic "tone of whimsy" that "conceals disturbing subversive energies." In the dozen stories included in this collection the author proves himself to be "American literature's mordantly funny and unfailingly elegant bard of the uncanny," according to a *Publishers Weekly* reviewer, who added that the collection addresses two themes: When does the "pursuit of transcendent pleasure degrade rather than exalt?" and can the pursuit of pleasure be sated "without our becoming jaded or corrupt?" In the tales "Flying Carpets" and "Clair de Lune" he addresses these questions in stories imbued with a fairy tale quality that recalls childhood. "The Sisterhood of Night" and "Balloon Flight, 1879," about a hot-air balloonist during the Franco-Prussian war, in contrast, "suggest new avenues of thought in Millhauser's fiction," according to McGrath. In the title story, according to *Washington Post Book World* reviewer A.S. Byatt, the author "steps beyond the bounds of the comfortable" in describing a virtuoso knife thrower in whose public performances are couched private fantasies. Praising "Paradise Park," Byatt added that the strength of this story lies in "Millhauser's ability to weave detail into detail, the lovingly real and possible into the extravagantly impossible." Commenting on the collection in *Boston Globe,* Margot Livesey concluded that Millhauser's characters are intent upon escape. "Sometimes they go too far . . . ," the critic added, "but in their struggles between the real and surreal, the effable and the ineffable, art and life, these characters and their creator illuminate our struggles to live our daily lives and still keep something larger in mind."

Millhauser's first collection of novellas, *Little Kingdoms,* includes *The Little World of J. Franklin Payne, The Princess, the Dwarf, and the Dungeon,* and *Catalogue of the Exhibition: The Art of Edmund Moorash 1810-1846.* Each of these works continues their author's exploration of the theme of the relationship between the life of the world and the life of imagination, according to Michael Dirda in *Washington Post Book World.* Dirda added that these three stories as grouped "subtly question each other about imagination and its power." In the first, J. Franklin Payne, a newspaper cartoonist, becomes obsessed with the making of an animated cartoon film. In doing so, Nicholas Delbanco, writing for *Chicago Tribune,* noted that he "invents his own reality—not so much in compensation for artistic disappointment as in an effort to improve upon the diurnal world. What seems vivid to him is his own imagination; reality looks dull." In his fixation on the cartoons he is creating, we are reminded of August Eschenburg's fixation on mechanical figures.

The Princess, the Dwarf, and the Dungeon plays with the conventions of the fairy tale genre: a late-medieval time setting, castles, dungeons, evil, dwarves, jealous princes, and virtuous maidens. Frederick Tuten noted in *New York Times Book Review* that "embedded in this story is the narrator's meditation on the art of his time, paintings so lifelike as to cause a dog to lick the portrait of his master." Millhauser's blurring of the lines between reality and imagination is a continuation of the same techniques in his *Barnum Museum* stories. *Catalogue of the Exhibition: The Art of Edmund Moorash 1810-1846* is perhaps the most clever. In a writing style Daniel Green described in *Georgia Review* as "typically energetic," the story is presented as an extended commentary on an exhibition of paintings by the fictional painter Edmund Moorash. Through a close reading of the explanations of the paintings, however, readers see the world of the painter complete with intimations of incest, devil worship, romance, and betrayal. There are four characters in the tale: Moorash, his sister Elizabeth, his friend William Pinney, and William's sister, Sophia. However, as Dirda pointed out, "passion's cross-currents disturb friendship's pallid surface." The result is that these four end up as figures as tragic as the subjects of the paintings at the exhibition. This novella is a work of art about art works and the theme of imagination and reality and the lines between them. Elizabeth keeps a diary in which she writes, "Edmund wants to dissolve forms and reconstruct them so as to release their energy. Art as alchemy." Delbanco noted in *Chicago Tribune* that this is "the credo of the whole" story. But it very well fits as the credo of all Millhauser's works.

Donna Seaman, in her review of Millhauser's 1999 work *Enchanted Night: A Novella* for *Booklist,* noted that the author "has been drifting into fantasy . . . and now he weaves pure magic in this dreamy tale of one fateful summer night." *Enchanted Night,* which is comprised of seventy-four short prose sections with chapters sometimes only one page long, conjures up toys and a mannequin coming to life, an unsuccessful author and his unsuccessful relationship with the mother of a childhood friend, teenage girls breaking into a house leaving cryptic notes, a lonely drunk stumbling home, and a girl waiting for a lover who may be real or may be fantasy.

The three-novella collection published as *The King in the Tree* focuses on the consequences of forbidden amours. In *An Adventure of Don Juan,* based on Gabriel Tellez's sixteenth-century writings about the legendary Spanish lover, the thirty-year-old Don Juan finds his plans to seduce two sisters frustrated when he inadvertently falls in love with one of them. According to *World and I* contributor Edward Hower, Millhauser's protagonist "experiences the sort of conflict shared by many of this author's characters: how to reconcile the sometimes seductive demands of the outer world with the longings that spring from the inner recesses of the soul." The title story also focuses on obsession, retelling the medieval legend of Tristan and Ysolt while also adding psychological depth. As Michael Dirda noted in his *Washington Post Book World* review, in Millhauser's version "all loyalties, strongly felt and believed in—loyalty to one's sovereign, to the marriage vows, to honor, friendship and ones' very self—are ripped apart by the remorseless claims of passionate love." The short novella *Revenge* takes the form of a monologue as a widow gives a tour of her home—and her own life—to a prospective home buyer who, the reader soon discovers, is actually a former rival for the narrator's late husband's affections.

Praising *The King in the Tree* as "rich in verbal dexterity, ambitious romantic imagery, and fascinating insights into the darker regions of the human heart," Hower commented that Millhauser's construction of a "world of artifice" serves to distill from his characters lives "the most intense emotional expression and meaning." In *Los Angeles Times* Jeff Turrentine cited Millhauser's "Gothicism" as well as his love for the nineteenth century that permeates the collection. *The King in the Tree* "is a moving, melancholy book about the unlovely toll exacted by love on those it has abandoned," added Turrentine. A *Kirkus Reviews* writer maintained that "some of the best writing of Millhauser's increasingly brilliant career appears in this collection."

Millhauser's fiction remains widely heralded for its perceptive exploration of the problems and pleasures of youth, and the author continues to be lauded for both his stylistic virtuosity and his capacity to evoke the undercurrents of ordinary life. As Dirda commented in *Washington Post Book World:* "So enchanting is his prose, so delicate his touch, that one surrenders to his plangent word-music as one does to the wistful piano pieces of Ravel and Chopin. Reading Millhauser, there are times when you simply lay the book aside and say to yourself, 'I had not known that sentences could be so simple and so beautiful.'"

BIOGRAPHICAL AND CRITICAL SOURCES:

BOOKS

Contemporary Literary Criticism, Thomson Gale (Detroit, MI), Volume 21, 1982, Volume 54, 1989, Volume 109, 1999.

Contemporary Novelists, 6th edition, St. James Press (Detroit, MI), 1996.

St. James Guide to Fantasy Writers, St. James Press (Detroit, MI), 1996.

PERIODICALS

Booklist, April 1, 1996, review of *Martin Dressler: The Tale of an American Dreamer;* September 15, 1999, Donna Seaman, review of *Enchanted Night: A Novella,* p. 233.

Boston Globe, May 17, 1998, Margot Livesey, review of *The Knife Thrower and Other Stories,* p. D1; March 9, 2003, David Rollow, review of *The King in the Tree.*

Chicago Tribune, October 3, 1993, Nicholas Delbanco, review of *Little Kingdoms,* p. 5.

Entertainment Weekly, May 17, 1996, p. 55; April 10, 1998, review of *Little Kingdoms,* p. 61.

Georgia Review, winter, 1995, Daniel Green, review of *Little Kingdoms,* pp. 960-967.

Kirkus Reviews, March 1, 1996, review of *Martin Dressler;* December 15, 2002, review of *The King in the Tree.*

Los Angeles Times Book Review, October 31, 1999, review of *Enchanted Night,* p. 29; March 16, 2003, Jeff Turrentine, review of *The King in the Tree.*

Nation, September 17, 1977, pp. 250-252; May 6, 1996, p. 68; May 25, 1998, Benjamin Kunkel, review of *The Knife Thrower and Other Stories,* p. 33.

New Republic, September 16, 1972, review of *Edwin Mullhouse: The Life and Death of an American Writer, 1943-1954, by Jeffrey Cartwright.*

New York Times Book Review, September 17, 1972, p. 2; October 2, 1977, pp. 13, 30; January 19, 1986, p. 9; October 12, 1986, Robert Dunn, review of *In the Penny Arcade,* p. 9; June 24, 1990, Jay Cantor, review of *The Barnum Museum,* p. 16; October 3, 1993, p. 9, p. 11; May 12, 1996, p. 8; May 10, 1998, Patrick McGrath, review of *The Knife Thrower and Other Stories,* p. 11; November 14, 1999, Tobin Harshaw, review of *Enchanted Night,* p. 109; March 9, 2003, Laura Miller, review of *The King in the Tree,* p. 1.

Publishers Weekly, August 8, 1986; March 23, 1998, review of *The Knife Thrower and Other Stories,* p. 78; January 20, 2003, review of *The King in the Tree,* p. 55.

Review of Contemporary Fiction, summer, 1986, Irving Malin, review of *In the Penny Arcade,* pp. 146-147; summer, 2000, Brian Evenson, review of *Enchanted Night,* p. 180.

Saturday Review, September 30, 1972; October 1, 1977, p. 28.

Spectator, March 7, 1998, review of *Martin Dressler: The Tale of an American Dreamer,* p. 32.

Time, June 10, 1996, p. 67.

Times Literary Supplement, July 28, 1978, William Boyd, review of *Portrait of a Romantic;* April 3, 1998, review of *Martin Dressler,* p. 23.

Village Voice, March 6, 1978, John Calvin Batchelor, review of *Portrait of a Romantic,* pp. 70-73.

Village Voice Literary Supplement, February, 1986, Al J. Sperone, review of *In the Penny Arcade,* pp. 3-4.

Wall Street Journal, April 24, 1996, p. A12.

Washington Post Book World, September 24, 1972, p. 8; October 9, 1977, p. E5; September 21, 1986, pp. 1, 14; September 5, 1993, p. 5, p. 14; April 28, 1996, p. 3; June 14, 1998, A.S. Byatt, review of *The Knife Thrower and Other Stories,* pp. 1, 10; February 9, 2003, Michael Dirda, review of *The King in the Tree,* p. 1.

World and I, December, 1990, review of *The Barnum Museum,* pp. 406-410; October 1998, review of *The Knife Thrower and Other Stories,* p. 280; June, 2003, Edward Hower, review of *The King in the Tree,* p. 230.

World Literature Today, winter, 1999, review of *The Knife Thrower and Other Stories,* p. 148.

* * *

MILLHAUSER, Steven Lewis

See MILLHAUSER, Steven

* * *

MILOSZ, Czeslaw 1911-2004

(J. Syruc)

PERSONAL: Surname pronounced *Mee*-wosh; born June 30, 1911, in Szetejnie, Lithuania; defected to West, 1951; immigrated to United States, 1960; naturalized U.S. citizen, 1970; died August 14, 2004, in Krakow, Poland; son of Aleksander (a civil engineer) and Weronika (Kunat) Milosz; married Janina Dluska, 1943 (died, 1986); married Carol Tigpen, 1992; children: (first marriage) Antoni, Piotr (sons). *Education:* University of Stephan Batory, M. Juris, 1934. *Religion:* Roman Catholic.

CAREER: Poet, critic, essayist, novelist, and translator. Programmer with Polish National Radio, 1935-39; worked for Polish Resistance during World War II; cultural attache with Polish Embassy in Paris, France, 1946-50; freelance writer in Paris, 1951-60; University of California, Berkeley, visiting lecturer, 1960-61, professor of Slavic languages and literature, 1961-78, professor emeritus, beginning 1978.

MEMBER: American Association for the Advancement of Slavic Studies, American Academy and Institute of Arts and Letters, PEN.

AWARDS, HONORS: Prix Litteraire Européen, 1953, for *La Prise du pouvoir;* Marian Kister Literary Award, 1967; Jurzykowski Foundation award for creative work, 1968; Institute for Creative Arts fellow, 1968; Polish PEN award for poetry translation, 1974; Wandycz Award, 1974; Guggenheim fellow, 1976; Litt. D., University of Michigan, 1977; Neustadt International Literary Prize for Literature, 1978; University Citation, University of California, 1978; Zygmunt Hertz literary award, 1979; Nobel Prize for literature, 1980; honorary doctorate, Catholic University, Lublin, 1981; honorary doctorate, Brandeis University, 1983; Bay Area Book Reviewers Association Poetry Prize, 1986, for *The Separate Notebooks;* Robert Kirsch Award for poetry, 1990; National Medal of Arts, 1990; nominee for National Book Critics Circle Award in poetry category, 2001, for *A Treatise on Poetry*; Gold Medal in poetry, California Book Award, 2001, for *New and Collected Poems, 1931-2001.*

WRITINGS:

Zniewolony umysl (essays), Instytut Literacki (Paris, France), 1953, translation by Jane Zielonko published as *The Captive Mind,* Knopf (New York, NY), 1953, reprinted, Octagon (New York, NY), 1981.

Traktat poetycki (title means "Treatise on Poetry"), Instytut Literacki (Paris, France), 1957, translation by Milosz and Robert Hass published as *A Treatise on Poetry,* Ecco Press (New York, NY), 2001.

Rodzinna Europa (essays), Instytut Literacki (Paris, France), 1959, translation by Catherine S. Leach published as *Native Realm: A Search for Self-Definition,* Doubleday (New York, NY), 1968.

Czlowiek wsrod skorpionow: Studium o Stanislawie Brzozowskim (title means "A Man among Scorpions: A Study of Stanislaw Brzozowski"), Instytut Literacki (Paris, France), 1962.

The History of Polish Literature, Macmillan (New York, NY), 1969, revised edition, University of California Press (Berkeley, CA), 1983.

Widzenia nad Zatoka San Francisco, Instytut Literacki (Paris, France), 1969, translation by Richard Lourie published as *Visions from San Francisco Bay,* Farrar, Straus (New York, NY), 1982.

Prywatne obowiazki (essays; title means "Private Obligations"), Instytut Literacki (Paris, France), 1972.

Moj wiek: Pamietnik nowiony (interview with Alexander Wat; title means "My Century: An Oral Diary"), edited by Lidia Ciolkoszowa, two volumes, Polonia Book Fund (London, England), 1977.

Emperor of the Earth: Modes of Eccentric Vision, University of California Press (Berkeley, CA), 1977.

Ziemia Ulro, Instytut Literacki (Paris, France), 1977, translation by Louis Iribarne published as *The Land of Ulro,* Farrar, Straus (New York, NY), 1984.

Ogrod nauk (title means "The Garden of Knowledge"), Instytut Literacki (Paris, France), 1980.

Dziela zbiorowe (title means "Collected Works"), Instytut Literacki (Paris, France), 1980.

Nobel Lecture, Farrar, Straus (New York, NY), 1981.

The Witness of Poetry (lectures), Harvard University Press (Cambridge, MA), 1983.

The Rising of the Sun, Arion Press (San Francisco, CA), 1985.

Unattainable Earth, translation from the Polish manuscript by Milosz and Robert Hass, Ecco Press (New York, NY), 1986.

Beginning with My Streets: Essays and Recollections (essays), translation by Madeline G. Levine, Farrar, Straus (New York, NY), 1992.

A Year of the Hunter, translation by Madeline G. Levine, Farrar, Straus (New York, NY), 1994.

Legendy nowoczesnosci: Eseje okupacyjne, Literackie (Krakow, Poland), 1996.

Szukanie ojczyzny, Znak (Krakow, Poland), 1996.

Traktat moralny: Traktat poetycki (interviews), Literackie (Krakow, Poland), 1996.

Striving toward Being: The Letters of Thomas Merton and Czeslaw Milosz, edited by Robert Faggen, Farrar, Straus (New York, NY), 1997.

Piesek przydroczny, Znak (Krakow, Poland), 1997, translation published as *Roadside Dog,* Farrar, Straus (New York, NY), 1998.

Zycie na wyspach (essays), Znak (Krakow, Poland), 1997.

Dar = Gabe, Literackie (Krakow, Poland), 1998.

Abecadlo Milosza, Literackie (Krakow, Poland), 1997.

Inne abecadlo, Literackie (Krakow, Poland), 1998.

Zaraz po wojnie: Korespondenczja z pisarzami, 1945-1950 (correspondence), Znak (Krakow, Poland), 1998.

Milosz's ABCs (selections from *Inne Abecadlo* and *Abecadlo Milosza*), translation by Madeline G. Levine, Farrar, Straus (New York, NY), 2001.

To Begin Where I Am: Selected Essays, edited by Bogadana Carpenter and Madeline G. Levine, Farrar, Straus (New York, NY), 2001.

POEMS

Poemat o czasie zastyglym (title means "Poem of the Frozen Time"), [Vilnius, Lithuania], 1933.

Trzy zimy (title means "Three Winters"), Union of Polish Writers, 1936.

(Under pseudonym J. Syruc) *Wiersze* (title means "Poems"), [Warsaw, Poland], 1940.

Ocalenie (title means "Salvage"), Czytelnik (Poland), 1945.

Swiatlo dzienne (title means "Daylight"), Instytut Literacki (Paris, France), 1953.

Kontynenty (title means "Continents"), Instytut Literacki (Paris, France), 1958.

Krol Popiel i inne wiersze (title means "King Popiel and Other Poems"), Instytut Literacki (Paris, France), 1962.

Gucio zaczarowany (title means "Bobo's Metamorphosis"), Instytut Literacki (Paris, France), 1965.

Lied vom Weltende (title means "A Song for the End of the World"), Kiepenheuer & Witsch, 1967.

Wiersze (title means "Poems"), Oficyna Poetow i Malarzy (London, England), 1969.

Miasto bez imienia (title means "City without a Name"), Instytut Literacki (Paris, France), 1969.

Selected Poems, Seabury Press (New York, NY), 1973, revised edition, Ecco Press (New York, NY), 1981.

Gdzie wschodzi slonce i kedy zapada (title means "From Where the Sun Rises to Where It Sets"), Instytut Literacki (Paris, France), 1974.

Utwory poetyckie (title means "Selected Poems"), Michigan Slavic Publications (Ann Arbor, MI), 1976.

The Bells in Winter, translation by Milosz and Lillian Vallee, Ecco Press (New York, NY), 1978.

Poezje, Instytut Literacki (Paris, France), 1981.

Traktat moralny, Krajowa Agencja Wydawnicza (Lublin, Poland), 1981.

Lud da sile swojemu poecie, Spoleczny Komitet Budowy Pomnika (Gdansk, Poland), 1981.

Hymn o Perle (title means "Hymn to the Pearl"), Michigan Slavic Publications (Ann Arbor, MI), 1982.

Ksiega psalmw, Katolicki Uniwersytet Lubelski (Lublin, Poland), 1982.

Swiadectwo poezji, Instytut Literacki (Paris, France), 1983.

The Separate Notebooks, translation by Robert Hass and Robert Pinsky, Ecco Press (New York, NY), 1984.

Ksiegi pieciu megilot, Katolicki Uniwersytet Lubelski (Lublin, Poland), 1984.

The Collected Poems, 1931-1987, Ecco Press (New York, NY), 1988.

Nieobjeta ziemia, Wydawn Literackie (Krakow, Poland), 1988.

(Author of text) Josef Koudelka, *Exiles,* Aperture Foundation (New York, NY), 1988.

Kroniki, Znak (Krakow, Poland), 1988.

The World, translation by Milosz, Arion Press, 1989.

Dalsze okolice, Znak (Krakow, Poland), 1991.

Provinces: Poems, 1987-1991, translation by Milosz and Robert Hass, Ecco Press (New York, NY), 1991.

Haiku, Znak (Krakow, Poland), 1992.

Na brzegu rzeki, Znak (Krakow, Poland), 1994.

Facing the River: New Poems, translation by Milosz and Robert Hass, Ecco Press (New York, NY), 1995.

Jakiegoz to goscia mielismy, Znak (Krakow, Poland), 1996.

Swiat: Poema naiwne (based on a 1943 manuscript), Literackie (Krakow, Poland), 1999.

Poezje, Literackie (Krakow, Poland), 1999.

Wyprawa w dwudziestolecie, Literackie (Krakow, Poland), 1999.

Wypisy z ksiag uzytecznych, Znak (Krakow, Poland), 2000.

New and Collected Poems, 1931-2001, Ecco Press (New York, NY), 2001.

Orfeusz i Eurydyka, Literackie (Krakow, Poland), 2002.

Second Space: New Poems, translated by Robert Hass (with Milosz), Ecco/HarperCollins (New York, NY), 2004.

NOVELS

La Prise du pouvoir, translation by Jeanne Hersch, Gallimard (Paris, France), 1953, original Polish edition published as *Zdobycie wladzy,* Instytut Literacki (Paris, France), 1955, translation by Celina Wieniewska published as *The Seizure of Power,* Criterion (New York, NY), 1955, translation published as *The Usurpers,* Faber (London, England), 1955.

Dolina Issy, Instytut Literacki (Paris, France), 1955, translation by Louis Iribarne published as *The Issa Valley,* Farrar, Straus (New York, NY), 1981.

EDITOR

(With Zbigniew Folejewski) *Antologia poezji spolecznej* (title means "Anthology of Social Poetry"), [Vilnius, Lithuania], 1933.

Piesn niepodlegla (Resistance poetry; title means "Invincible Song"), Oficyna, 1942, Michigan Slavic Publications (Ann Arbor, MI), 1981.

Lettres inedites de O.V. de L. Milosz a Christian Gauss (correspondence), Silvaire, 1976.

(With Drenka Willen) *A Book of Luminous Things: An International Anthology of Poetry,* Harcourt (San Diego, CA), 1996.

TRANSLATOR

(And editor) Jacques Maritain, *Drogami Kleski,* [Warsaw, Poland], 1942.

(And editor) Daniel Bell, *Praca i jej gorycze* (title means "Work and Its Discontents"), Instytut Literacki (Paris, France), 1957.

(And editor) Simone Weil, *Wybor pism* (title means "Selected Works"), Instytut Literacki (Paris, France), 1958.

(And editor) *Kultura masowa* (title means "Mass Culture"), Instytut Literacki (Paris, France), 1959.

(And editor) *Wegry* (title means "Hungary"), Instytut Literacki (Paris, France), 1960.

(And editor) *Postwar Polish Poetry: An Anthology,* Doubleday (New York, NY), 1965, revised edition, University of California Press (Berkeley, CA), 1983.

(With Peter Dale Scott) Zbigniew Herbert, *Selected Poems,* Penguin (New York, NY), 1968.

Alexander Wat, *Mediterranean Poems,* Ardi, 1977.

Ewangelia wedlug sw. Marka (title means "The Gospel according to St. Mark"), Znak (Krakow, Poland), 1978.

Ksiega Hioba (title means "The Book of Job"), Dialogue (Paris, France), 1980.

Anna Swir, *Happy as a Dog's Tail,* Harcourt (San Diego, CA), 1985.

(With Leonard Nathan) Aleksander Wat, *With the Skin: Poems of Aleksander Wat,* Ecco Press (New York, NY), 1989.

Founder and editor, *Zagary* (literary periodical), 1931.

SIDELIGHTS: Czeslaw Milosz ranks among the most respected figures in twentieth-century Polish literature, as well as one of the most respected contemporary poets in the world, being awarded the Nobel Prize for literature in 1980. He was born in Lithuania, where his parents moved temporarily to escape the political upheaval in their native Poland. As an adult, he left Poland due to the oppressive Communist regime that came to power following World War II and lived in the United States since 1960. Milosz's poems, novels, essays, and other works are written in his native Polish and translated by the author and others into English. Having lived under the two great totalitarian systems of modern history, national socialism and communism, Milosz wrote of the past in a tragic, ironic style that nonetheless affirms the value of human life. While the faith of his Roman Catholic upbringing had been severely tested, it remained intact. Terrence Des Pres, writing in the *Nation,* stated that "political catastrophe has defined the nature of our . . . [age], and the result—the collision of personal and public realms—has produced a new kind of writer. Czeslaw Milosz is the perfect example. In exile from a world which no longer exists, a witness to the Nazi devastation of Poland and the Soviet takeover of Eastern Europe, Milosz dealt in his poetry with the central issues of our time: the impact of history upon moral being, the search for ways to survive spiritual ruin in a ruined world."

Born in Lithuania in 1911, Milosz spent much of his childhood in Czarist Russia, where his father worked as a civil engineer. After World War I the family returned to their hometown, which had become a part of the new Polish state, and Milosz attended local Catholic schools. He published his first collection of poems, *Poemat o czasie zastyglym* ("Poem of the Frozen Time"), at the age of twenty-one. Milosz was associated with the catastrophist school of poets during the 1930s. Catastrophism concerns "the inevitable annihilation of the highest values, especially the values essential to a given cultural system. . . . But it proclaims . . . only the annihilation of certain values, not values in general, and the destruction of a certain historical formation, but not of all mankind," Aleksander Fiut explained in *World Literature Today.* The writings of this group of poets ominously foreshadowed World War II.

When the war began in 1939, and Poland was invaded by Nazi Germany and Soviet Russia, Milosz worked with the underground Resistance movement in Warsaw, writing and editing several books published clandestinely during the occupation. One of these books, a collection titled *Wiersze* ("Poems"), was published under the pseudonym J. Syruc. Following the war, Milosz became a member of the new communist government's diplomatic service and was stationed in Paris, France, as a cultural attache. In 1951, he left this post and defected to the West.

The Captive Mind explains Milosz's reasons for defecting and examines the life of the artist under a communist regime. It is, maintained Steve Wasserman in the *Los Angeles Times Book Review,* a "brilliant and original study of the totalitarian mentality." Karl Jaspers, in an article for the *Saturday Review,* described *The Captive Mind* as "a significant historical document and analysis of the highest order. . . . In astonishing gradations Milosz shows what happens to men subjected simultaneously to constant threat of annihilation and to the promptings of faith in a historical necessity which exerts apparently irresistible force and achieves enormous success. We are presented with a vivid picture of the forms of concealment, of inner transformation, of the sudden bolt to conversion, of the cleavage of man into two."

Milosz's defection came about when he was recalled to Poland from his position at the Polish embassy. He refused to leave. Joseph McLellan of the *Washington Post* quoted Milosz explaining: "I knew perfectly well that my country was becoming the province of an empire." In a speech before the Congress for Cultural Freedom, quoted by James Atlas of the *New York Times,* Milosz declared: "I have rejected the new faith because the practice of the lie is one of its principal commandments and socialist realism is nothing more than a different name for a lie." After his defection Milosz lived in Paris, where he worked as a translator and freelance writer. In 1960 he was offered a teaching position at the University of California at Berkeley, which he accepted. He became an American citizen in 1970.

In *The Seizure of Power,* first published in France as *La Prise du pouvoir* in 1953, Milosz rendered as fiction much of the same material found in *The Captive Mind.* The book is an autobiographical novel that begins with the Russian occupation of Warsaw at the close of World War II. As the Russian army approached the Nazi-held city, the Polish Resistance rose against the German occupation troops, having been assured that the Russians would join their fight once the uprising began. But instead, the Russians stood by a few miles outside of the city, allowing the Nazis to crush the revolt unhindered. When the uprising was over, the Russians occupied Warsaw and installed a communist regime. The novel ends with the disillusioned protagonist, a political education officer for the communists, immigrating to the West.

The Seizure of Power "is a novel on how to live when power changes hands," Andrew Sinclair explained in the London *Times.* Granville Hicks, in an article for the

New York Times Book Review, saw a similarity between *The Captive Mind* and *The Seizure of Power.* In both books, "Milosz appeals to the West to try to understand the people of Eastern Europe," maintained Hicks. Told in a series of disjointed scenes meant to suggest the chaos and violence of postwar Poland, *The Seizure of Power* is "a novel of ineffable sadness, and a muffled sob for Poland's fate," wrote Wasserman. Michael Harrington, in a review for *Commonweal,* called *The Seizure of Power* "a sensitive, probing work, far better than most political novels, of somewhat imperfect realization but of significant intention and worth."

After living in the United States for a time, Milosz began to write of his new home. In *Native Realm: A Search for Self-Definition* and *Visions from San Francisco Bay,* Milosz compares and contrasts the West with his native Poland. *Native Realm,* Richard Holmes wrote in the London *Times,* is "a political and social autobiography, shorn of polemic intent, deeply self-questioning, and dominated by the sense that neither historically nor metaphysically are most Westerners in a position to grasp the true nature of the East European experience since the First War." A series of personal essays examining events in Milosz's life, *Native Realm* provides "a set of commentaries upon his improbable career," as Michael Irwin maintained in the *Times Literary Supplement.* Milosz "has written a self-effacing remembrance composed of shards from a shattered life," observed Wasserman. "He tells his story with the humility of a man who has experienced tragedy and who believes in fate and in destiny. It is a work that reflects the stubborn optimism of his heart, even as it dwells on the pessimism of his intellect." Irving Howe, writing in the *New York Times Book Review,* found *Native Realm* "beautifully written." Milosz, Howe continued, "tries to find in the chaos of his life some glimmers of meaning."

In *Visions from San Francisco Bay* Milosz examined his life in contemporary California, a place far removed in distance and temperament from the scenes of his earlier life. His observations are often sardonic, and yet he is also content with his new home. Milosz "sounds like a man who has climbed up, hand over hand, right out of history, and who is both amazed and grateful to find that he can breathe the ahistorical atmosphere of California," Anatole Broyard stated in the *New York Times.* The opening words of the book are "I am here," and from that starting point Milosz describes the society around him. "The intention," noted Julian Symons in the *Times Literary Supplement,* "is to understand himself, to understand the United States, to communicate something singular to Czeslaw Milosz." Broyard takes this idea even further, arguing that Milosz "expresses surprise at 'being here,' taking this phrase in its ordinary sense of being in America and in its other, Heideggerian sense of being-in-the-world."

Although Milosz's comments about life in California are "curiously oblique, deeply shadowed by European experience, allusive, sometimes arch and frequently disillusioned," as Holmes pointed out, he ultimately embraces his adopted home. "Underlying all his meditations," commented Leon Edel in the *New York Times Book Review,* "is his constant 'amazement' that America should exist in this world—and his gratitude that it does exist." "He is fascinated," explained Symons, "by the contradictions of a society with enormous economic power, derived in part from literally nonhuman technical achievement, which also contains a large group that continually and passionately indicts the society by which it is maintained." Milosz, P.J. Kavanagh remarked in the *Spectator,* looked at his adopted country with "a kind of detached glee—at awfulness; an ungloomy recognition that we cannot go on as we are—in any direction. He holds up a mirror and shows us ourselves, without blame and with no suggestions either, and in the mirror he himself is also reflected." Edel believed that Milosz's visions "have authority: the authority of an individual who reminds us that only someone like himself who has known tyranny . . . can truly prize democracy."

The story of Milosz's odyssey from East to West is also recounted in his poetry. Milosz's "entire effort," Jonathan Galassi explained in the *New York Times Book Review,* "is directed toward a confrontation with experience—and not with personal experience alone, but with history in all its paradoxical horror and wonder." Speaking of his poetry in the essay collection *The Witness of Poetry,* Milosz stressed the importance of his nation's cultural heritage and history in shaping his work. "My corner of Europe," he states, "owing to the extraordinary and lethal events that have been occurring there, comparable only to violent earthquakes, affords a peculiar perspective. As a result, all of us who come from those parts appraise poetry slightly differently than do the majority of my audience, for we tend to view it as a witness and participant in one of mankind's major transformations." "For Milosz," Helen Vendler explained in the *New Yorker,* "the person is irrevocably a person in history, and the interchange between external event and the individual life is the matrix of poetry." Writing in *TriQuarterly,* Reginald Gibbons stated that Milosz "seems to wonder how good work can be written, no matter how private its subject matter, without the poet having been aware of the pain and threat of the human predicament."

Milosz saw a fundamental difference in the role of poetry in the capitalist West and the communist East. Western poetry, as Alfred Kazin wrote in the *New York Times Book Review,* is "'alienated' poetry, full of introspective anxiety." But because of the dictatorial nature of communist government, poets in the East cannot afford to be preoccupied with themselves. They are drawn to write of the larger problems of their society. "A peculiar fusion of the individual and the historical took place," Milosz wrote in *The Witness of Poetry,* "which means that events burdening a whole community are perceived by a poet as touching him in a most personal manner. Then poetry is no longer alienated."

For many years Milosz's poetry was little noticed in the United States, though he was highly regarded in Poland. Recognition in Poland came in defiance of official government resistance to Milosz's work. The communist regime refused to publish the books of a defector; for many years only underground editions of his poems were secretly printed and circulated in Poland. But in 1980, when Milosz was awarded the Nobel Prize for Literature, the communist government was forced to relent. A government-authorized edition of Milosz's poems was issued and sold a phenomenal 200,000 copies. One sign of Milosz's widespread popularity in Poland occurred when Polish workers in Gdansk unveiled a monument to their comrades who were shot down by the communist police. Two quotations were inscribed on the monument: one was taken from the Bible; the other was taken from a poem by Milosz.

The Nobel Prize also brought Milosz to the attention of a wider audience in the United States. After 1980 several of his earlier works were translated into English, while his new books received widespread critical attention. The poet's image also graced a postage stamp in Poland. Some of this public attention focused less on Milosz's work as poetry than "as the work of a thinker and political figure; the poems tend to be considered en masse, in relation either to the condition of Poland, or to the suppression of dissident literature under Communist rule, or to the larger topic of European intellectual history," as Vendler maintained. But most reviewers have commented on Milosz's ability to speak in a personal voice that carries with it the echoes of his people's history. Zweig explained that Milosz "offers a modest voice, speaking an old language. But this language contains the resources of centuries. Speaking it, one speaks with a voice more than personal. . . . Milosz's power lies in his ability to speak with this larger voice without diminishing the urgency that drives his words."

Because he lived through some of the great upheavals of twentieth-century Eastern Europe, and because his poetry fuses his own experiences with the larger events in his society, many of Milosz's poems concern loss, destruction, and despair. "There is a very dark vision of the world in my work," he told Lynn Darling of the *Washington Post.* And yet the writer went on to describe himself as "a great partisan of human hope" due to his religious convictions.

Milosz believed that one of the major problems of contemporary society—in both the East and the West—is its lack of a moral foundation. Writing in *The Land of Ulro,* he finds that modern man has only "the starry sky above, and no moral law within." Speaking to Judy Stone of the *New York Times Book Review,* Milosz stated: "I am searching for an answer as to what will result from an internal erosion of religious beliefs." Michiko Kakutani, reviewing *The Land of Ulro* for the *New York Times,* found that "Milosz is eloquent in his call for a literature grounded in moral, as well as esthetic, values. Indeed, when compared with his own poetry, the work of many Westerners—from the neurotic rantings of the Romantics to the cerebral mind games of the avant-gardists—seems unserious and self-indulgent."

Because of his moral vision Milosz's writings make strong statements, some of which are inherently political in their implications. "The act of writing a poem is an act of faith," Milosz claimed in *The History of Polish Literature,* "yet if the screams of the tortured are audible in the poet's room, is not his activity an offense to human suffering?" His awareness of suffering, wrote Joseph C. Thackery in the *Hollins Critic,* makes Milosz a "spokesman of the millions of dead of the Holocaust, the Gulags, the Polish and Czech uprisings, and the added millions of those who will go on dying in an imperfect world."

Milosz also warned of the dangers of political writing. In a PEN Congress talk reprinted in the *Partisan Review,* he stated: "In this century a basic stance of writers . . . seems to be an acute awareness of suffering inflicted upon human beings by unjust structures of society. . . . This awareness of suffering makes a writer open to the idea of radical change, whichever of many recipes he chooses. . . . Innumerable millions of human beings were killed in this century in the name of utopia—either progressive or reactionary, and always there were writers who provided convincing justifications for massacre."

In *The Witness of Poetry* Milosz argued that true poetry is "the passionate pursuit of the Real." He condemned those writers who favor art for art's sake or who think of themselves as alienated, and suggests, as Adam Gussow wrote in the *Saturday Review,* that poets may have "grown afraid of reality, afraid to see it clearly and speak about it in words we can all comprehend." What is needed in "today's unsettled world," Gussow explained, are poets who, "like Homer, Dante, and Shakespeare, will speak for rather than against the enduring values of their communities."

This concern for a poetry that confronts reality was noted by Thackery, who saw Milosz searching "for a poetry that will be at once harsh and mollifying, that will enable men to understand, if not to rationalize, the debasement of the human spirit by warfare and psychic dismemberment, while simultaneously establishing a personal *modus vivendi* and a psychology of aesthetic necessity." Des Pres also noted this unifying quality in Milosz's poetry, a trait he believed Milosz shares with T.S. Eliot. "The aim of both Milosz and Eliot," Des Pres stated, "is identical: to go back and work through the detritus of one's own time on earth, to gather up the worst along with the best, integrate past and present into a culminating moment which transcends both, which embraces pain and joy together, the whole of a life and a world redeemed through memory and art, a final restoration in spirit of that which in historical fact has been forever lost." Vendler wrote that "the work of Milosz reminds us of the great power that poetry gains from bearing within itself an unforced, natural, and long-ranging memory of past customs; a sense of the strata of ancient and modern history; wide visual experience; and a knowledge of many languages and literatures. . . . The living and tormented revoicing of the past makes Milosz a historical poet of bleak illumination."

With the publication in 1986 of *Unattainable Earth,* Milosz continued to show himself as a poet of memory and a poet of witness, for, in the prose footnote to "Poet at Seventy," he wrote of his continued "un-named need for order, for rhythm, for form, which three words are opposed to chaos and nothingness." *Unattainable Earth* uses what Stanislaw Baranczak in *Threepenny Review* called, a "peculiar structure of a modern *silva rerum*" which "consists in including a number of prose fragments, notes, letters, verses of other poets." The book was the first of several lauded collaborative translations between the author and American poet Robert Hass.

A year later, *The Collected Poems, 1931-1987* was published, bringing together *Selected Poems, Bells in Winter, The Separate Notebooks,* and *Unattainable Earth* into one volume. The book contains 180 poems ranging in size from two lines to sixty pages. Forty-five poems appear for the first time in English, of which twenty-six are recently translated older poems and twenty are new poems. Warren W. Werner in *Southern Humanities Review* called the work "a big, varied, and important book . . . a feast of poetry." P.J.M. Robertson in *Queen's Quarterly* lauded the collection as "a gift to cherish, for it contains the song of a man . . . passionately affirming the daily miracle of life and its continuity even now on our battered earth." The critic affirmed that *The Collected Poems* "reveal Milosz's answer to the question of the role of poetry and of art in the twentieth century. . . . a responsibility to see and express beauty: that is, the truth about life in its miraculous complexity." *New York Times Book Review* contributor Edward Hirsch found the volume "one of the monumental splendors of poetry in our age." Baranczak believed that it is a book that can "finally give the English-speaking reader a fairly accurate idea of what [Milosz's] poetry really is, both in the sense of the largeness of its thematic and stylistic range and the uniqueness of his more than half-century-long creative evolution." Don Bogan of the *Nation* stated that "with its clarity, historical awareness and moral vision, *The Collected Poems* is among the best guides we have" to help remind us that "poetry can define and address the concerns of an age."

Milosz followed in 1991 with *Provinces: Poems, 1987-1991.* For Milosz, the life in each individual seems made up of provinces, and one new province which he must now visit is the province of old age. He explored getting older in the thirteen-part sequence titled, 'A New Province,' reporting that "not much is known about that country/ Till we land there ourselves, with no right to return." Hirsch found that these poems about old age have "a penetrating honesty" derived from "a powerful dialectical tension, a metaphysical dispute at work . . . about the conflicting claims of immanence and transcendence, the temporal and the eternal." Ben Howard, in *Poetry,* commented on the inclusion of Milosz's "abiding subjects—the loss of his native Lithuania, the suffering of Eastern Europe, the wrenching upheavals of a long and difficult life," and suggested that the poet through his verse is "asserting his affinity with the common people and his closeness to the soil." *New York Review of Books* contributor Helen Vendler called *Provinces* a collection of "many of Milosz's central themes—including the strangeness of human life (where in the blink of an eye absurdity can turn to bravery, or tranquillity to war), exile, sensuality, memory, Platonic idealism, and iron disbelief." Bill Marx in *Parnassus* described *Provinces* as "an inner landscape of clashing contraries and times. Valleys of sensuous admiration for the earth's delights are broken up by notched peaks of traumatic memory; deserts formed by perceptions of nature's indifference are dotted with oases rooted in intimations of the transcendent."

Beginning with My Streets: Essays and Recollections, published in 1992, is a collection of essays, philosophical meditations, literary criticism, portraits of friends and writers, and a genre that *Observer* reviewer Sally Laird identified as "'chatty narratives' in the Polish tradition." Donald Davie in the *New Republic* deemed the book "more a medley than a collection, with a deceptive air of being 'thrown together,'" made up, as Vendler pointed out, of essays in which Milosz "moves with entire naturalness from Swedenborg to Robinson Jeffers, from Lithuanian scenery to Meister Eckhart, from the Seven Deadly Sins to Polish Marxism." Laird praised in particular the essay "Saligia," in which Milosz took on two multiple perspectives, that of poet and of engaged historian. The book contains accounts of the poet's childhood in Vilnius and closes with his 1980 Nobel lecture. *Washington Post Book World* contributor Alberto Manguel concluded, "Milosz excels in recounting, in finding the happy phrase for a scene or a concept. The invention of the past, the elusiveness of reality, the fluidity of time, the apparent banality or apparent importance of philosophical inquiries are traditional (some would say intrinsic) poetic fodder, and Milosz arranges the questions on the page with economy and elegance."

A Year of the Hunter, published in 1994, is a journal Milosz penned between August of 1987 and August of 1988. John Simon in the *Washington Post Book World* pointed out that these entries were "written on airplanes zooming to lecture engagements, poetry readings, literary congresses and the like." Ian Buruma praised the work in the *Los Angeles Times Book Review* as "a wonderful addition to [Milosz's] other autobiographical writing. The diary form, free-floating, wide-ranging . . . is suited to a poet, especially an intellectual poet, like Milosz," allowing for his entries to range from gardening to translating, from communism to Christianity, from past to present. Indeed, as Michael Ignatieff stated in the *New York Review of Books, A Year of the Hunter* is successful "because Milosz has not cleaned it up too much. Its randomness is a pleasure."

In 1995 Milosz produced the poetry collection *Facing the River: New Poems.* This volume includes verse that deals largely with Milosz's return to Vilnius, the city of his childhood, now the capital of the free republic of Lithuania. In returning, Ignatieff pointed out, Milosz found himself in an ironic circumstance: "Having been a poet of exile, he had now become the poet of the impossible return of the past." The poet recognized many streets, buildings, and steeples in his homeland, but the people from his past were gone. This left Milosz to "bring the absent dead back to life, one by one, in all their aching singularity," as Ignatieff stated. *Facing the River* is not just about Milosz's return to Lithuania and the people that he misses; it also addresses the poet's accomplishments and his views on life. In "At a Certain Age," Milosz declared that old men, who see themselves as handsome and noble, will find: "later in our place an ugly toad/ Half-opens its thick eyelid/ And one sees clearly: 'That's me.'" *Facing the River,* which ends with Milosz wondering, "If only my work were of use to people," left Ignatieff speaking for many readers of Milosz when he wrote: "Those like myself who see the world differently because of him hope he will continue to stand facing the river, and tell us what he sees."

In 1999, at age eighty-eight, Milosz published *Roadside Dog,* a collection "that at first encounter seems an invitation to revisit the remembered landscapes of his life," as Jaroslaw Anders noted in the *New Republic.* In "maxims, anecdotes, meditations, crumbs of worldly wisdom, introspections . . . [and] poems," Milosz took readers on a trip through the sounds and images that have shaped his life as a poet. "Some of these morsels are perfectly finished," Anders found, "others appear sketchy, tentative, even commonplace: assertions in search of proof, thoughts that should become essays, plot lines that need to be tested in a novel. Is this the writer's scrap-book offered generously—but also a little self-indulgently—to his readers, the literary equivalent of a rummage sale?"

David S. Gross saw *Roadside Dog* differently. In his essay, part of a 1999 salute to Milosz published in *World Literature Today,* Gross admitted that it is "hard to say what these little pieces are. Prose poems, I suppose, after Baudelaire and others." Still, the work as a whole "constantly reexamines questions of politics, religion, the nature of poetry, issues of consciousness and meaning, and more, always toward the end of understanding, even reinventing, the self, in order to understand and reinvent the world." Again and again in *Roadside Dog,* said Gross, the poet "tries to get at that which links him with the suffering and the excluded, even though he has not for years had to suffer the same consequences."

Milosz remained active even as he advanced into his nineties. In 2001 he published *Milosz's ABCs,* a brief, alphabetical collection of entries illustrating his experiences and view on life. This may seem an odd approach to a life, but David Kipen stated in the *San Francisco Chronicle* that "in Milosz's hands it illuminates much of twentieth century literature and history and the muddled, tragic no-man's land where they've overlapped." Included are entries on old friends long dead, political movements, historical events, and spiritual matters. The book "derives its coherence from the Nobel Prize-winner's longstanding philosophical preoccupations: the impermanence of life in the face of 'the waters of oblivion,' and the paradox of Christian faith in the context of mass-scale human suffering," mused Kristen Case in the *New Leader.* Case added: "Parallel to the stream of personal recollections, crosscurrents of literary and philosophical thought gradually converge into something like a philosophical system: an understanding of life as a struggle between being and nothingness, creation and destruction. Many of the most compelling entries are those with abstract titles: 'Time,' 'Terror,' 'Curiosity.' Here Milosz granted himself some freedom from the minutiae of memory and engages the intellectual history of his nine decades." Reviewing the book for *Commonweal,* Harold Isbell called it "a remarkable testament to the place of memory in the definition of a conscious self. . . . In this book, the events of history become experience and, finally, art as Milosz turns the memory of experience back to elucidate the event." And John Kennedy recommended in *Antioch Review,* "This is a true 'companion' book; keep it close, for it is as much a gift of luminous moments as poems and parables are." Kennedy valued the book not only for its own sake, but also as a means of understanding its author: "If you want to know the man, if you want to know about the malleability of world consciousness, you must read this book. Milosz's pieces travel the geographies of emotions and tastes. It appears that nothing escapes him: not politics, partisanship, original sin, ethnicity, fear, love, or much else."

Also that year, Milosz published a translation of a work first published in 1957 in his native language: *A Treatise on Poetry.* This lengthy poetic work has four parts which ponder Europe at the turn of the twentieth century, Poland between the two world wars that devastated it, World War II, and the proper place of the poet in the world after the horror of World War II. It also serves as an historical survey of Polish poetry throughout those periods. It is a work that is "gripping, profound and beautiful," according to a writer for the *Economist.* Translated nearly fifty years after it was written, *A Treatise on Poetry* found an audience among a new generation of readers. Nicholas Wroe quoted Milosz in the *Guardian* as commenting: "It has been a great pleasure to see my poem apparently not getting old. . . . It is really a history of Polish poetry in the twentieth century, in connection to history and the problems of so-called historical necessity. And I am proud of having written a poem that deals with historical, political and aesthetic issues even though, of course, I know that for students, the parts of the poem where I deal with Hegelian philosophy and Marxism are, for them, completely exotic. They have such short memories." The year 2001 also saw the publication of another major collection of Milosz's poems, *New and Collected Poems, 1931-2001,* which inspired a *Publishers Weekly* reviewer to predict: "There are few superlatives left for Milosz's work, but this enormous volume, with its portentous valedictory feel, will have reviewers firing up their thesauri nationwide."

Milosz also published a collection of essays in 2001, titled *To Begin Where I Am: Selected Essays.* The subject matter is as varied as the poet's life experiences, and the essays stand as "testaments to a great philosophical mind and astonishing essayist"; they are written with "integrity, humility, and a vast knowledge of the major events and philosophies of Western civilization," advised John Kennedy in the *Antioch Review.* "The truths he extracts are particular, excavated out of the universal human struggles of various political and literary friends." In fact, the essays also form a kind of autobiography, beginning with an account of the poet's life on his grandparents' farm in Lithuania and proceeding on through the tumultuous decades that followed. *America* reviewer John Breslin commended the collection as well, singling out in particular the essay "If Only This Could Be Said," which offers his "fullest and most personal treatment of religion, an indispensable part of the human in his view." Milosz has frequently been pointed out as rather unusual in that he maintained his Catholic faith even through the horrors of two World Wars; many intellectuals who survived that time subsequently suffered crises of faith from which they never recovered. Wroe quoted him as explaining, however, that while he is a Catholic, he will not identify himself as a "Catholic writer," because "if you are branded as a Catholic, you are supposed to testify with every work of yours to following the line of the Church, which is not necessarily my case." Breslin concluded that Milosz's highly individual voice, with its call to faith and hope in the face of darkness, is one "we need to hear in our new and already deeply troubled century."

"Milosz's work is something so extraordinary in our epoch, that it seems to be a phenomenon that he has appeared on the surface of contemporary art from the mysterious depths of reality," declared Krzysztof Dybciak in *World Literature Today.* "At a time when voices of doubt, deadness, and despair are the loudest; when writers are outstripping each other in negation of man, his culture, and nature; when the predominant action is destruction . . . , the world built by the author of 'Daylight' creates a space in which one can breathe freely, where one can find rescue. It renders the world of surfaces transparent and condenses being. It does not promise any final solutions to the unleashed elements of nature and history here on earth, but it enlarges the space in which one can await the Coming with hope. Milosz does not believe in the omnipotence of man, and he has been deprived of the optimistic faith in the self-sufficiency of a world known only through empirical experience. He leads the reader to a place where one can see—to paraphrase the poet's own formula regarding time—Being raised above being through Being."

BIOGRAPHICAL AND CRITICAL SOURCES:

BOOKS

Contemporary Literary Criticism, Thomson Gale (Detroit, MI), Volume 5, 1976, Volume 11, 1979, Volume 22, 1982, Volume 31, 1985, Volume 56, 1989, Volume 82, 1994.

Czarnecka, Ewa, and Alexander Fiut, *Conversations with Czeslaw Milosz,* translation by Richard Lourie, Harcourt (San Diego, CA), 1988.

Czarnecka, Ewa, *Prdrozny swiata: Rosmowy z Czeslawem Miloszem, Komentane,* Bicentennial, 1983.

Czerni, Irena, *Czeslaw Milosz laureat literackiej nagrody Nobla 1980: Katalog wystawy,* Nakl. Uniwersytety Jagiellonskiego (Krakow, Poland), 1993.

Dictionary of Literary Biography, Volume 215: *Twentieth-Century Eastern European Writers, First Series,* Thomson Gale (Detroit, MI), 1999.

Dompkowski, Judith Ann, *Down a Spiral Staircase, Never-ending: Motion As Design in the Writing of Czeslaw Milosz,* P. Lang (New York, NY), 1990.

Dudek, Jolanta, *Gdzie wschodzi slonce i kedy zapada—europejskie korzenie poezji Czeslaw Milosza,* Nakl. Univwersytetu Jagiellonskiego, 1991.

Encyclopedia of World Biography, Thomson Gale (Detroit, MI), 1998.

European Writers, Scribner (New York, NY), 1990.

Fiut, Aleksander, *Rozmowy z Czeslawem Miloszem,* Wydawnictwo Literackie (Krakow, Poland), 1981.

Fiut, Aleksander, *The Eternal Moment: The Poetry of Czeslaw Milosz,* University of California Press (Berkeley, CA), 1990.

Gillon, A., and L. Krzyzanowski, editors, *Introduction to Modern Polish Literature,* Twayne (Boston, MA), 1964.

Goemoeri, G., *Polish and Hungarian Poetry, 1945 to 1956,* Oxford University Press (New York, NY), 1966.

Hass, Robert, *Twentieth-Century Pleasures: Prose on Poetry,* Ecco Press (New York, NY), 1984.

Malinowska, Barbara, *Dynamics of Being, Space, and Time in the Poetry of Czeslaw Milosz and John Ashbery,* P. Lang (New York, NY), 1997.

Milosz, Czeslaw, *The Captive Mind,* Knopf (New York, NY), 1953.

Milosz, Czeslaw, *The History of Polish Literature,* Macmillan (London, England), 1969, revised edition, University of California Press (Berkeley, CA), 1983.

Milosz, Czeslaw, *The Witness of Poetry,* Harvard University Press (Cambridge, MA), 1983.

Milosz, Czeslaw, *The Land of Ulro,* Farrar, Straus (New York, NY), 1984.

Mozejko, Edward, *Between Anxiety and Hope: The Poetry and Writing of Czeslaw Milosz,* University of Alberta Press (Edmonton, Alberta, Canada), 1988.

Nathan, Leonard, and Arthur Quinn, *The Poet's Work: An Introduction to Czeslaw Milosz,* Harvard University Press (Cambridge, MA), 1992.

Nilsson, Nils Ake, editor, *Czeslaw Milosz: A Stockholm Conference, September 9-11, 1991,* Kungl. Vitterhets (Stockholm, Sweden), 1992.

Volynska-Bogert, Rimma, and Wojciech Zaleswski, *Czeslaw Milosz: An International Bibliography 1930-80,* University of Michigan Press (Ann Arbor, MI), 1983.

PERIODICALS

America, December 18, 1982; December 15, 1984, p. 409; May 12, 1990, pp. 472-475; February 1, 1997, Robert Coles, "Secular Days, Sacred Moments," p. 6; January 21, 2002, John Breslin, review of *To Begin Where I Am: Selected Essays,* p. 25.

American Book Review, March, 1985, p. 22.

American Poetry Review, January, 1977.

American Scholar, winter, 2002, Minna Proctor, review of *To Begin Where I Am: Selected Essays,* p. 154.

Antioch Review, summer, 2002, John Kennedy, review of *To Begin Where I Am,* p. 529; winter, 2002, John Kennedy, review of *Milosz's ABCs,* p. 164.

Atlanta Journal-Constitution, April 2, 1989, p. N11; April 12, 1992, p. N11; April 23, 1995, p. M13; April 25, 1995, p. B7; April 26, 1995, p. D1.

Book, November-December, 2001, Stephen Whited, review of *Milosz's ABCs,* p. 64.

Booklist, April 15, 1988, p. 1387; November 1, 1991, p. 497; January 1, 1992, p. 806; March 1, 1992, p. 1191; November 1, 1998, Ray Olson, review of *Roadside Dog,* p. 465; December 15, 2000, Ray Olson, review of *Milosz's ABCs,* p. 780; October 15, 2001, Donna Seaman, review of *To Begin Where I Am,* p. 374.

Book Report, November, 1988, p. 39.

Books Abroad, winter, 1969; spring, 1970; winter, 1973; winter, 1975.

Book Week, May 9, 1965.

Book World, September 29, 1968.

Boston Globe, October 16, 1987, p. 91; August 28, 1994, p. 62.

Canadian Literature, spring, 1989, pp. 183-184.

Chicago Tribune, October 10, 1980; September 6, 1987, p. 6; December 4, 1989, p. 2; March 15, 1992, p. 6; December 18, 1994, p. 5.

Christian Century, December 4, 2002, review of *New and Collected Poems, 1931-2001,* p. 31.

Christian Science Monitor, July 2, 1986, p. 21; October 5, 1990, p. 10; January 17, 1992, p. 14.

Commonweal, July 8, 1955; March 22, 1985, p. 190; November 6, 1992, p. 33-34; February 23, 2001, Harold Isbell, review of *Milosz's ABCs,* p. 20.

Denver Quarterly, summer, 1976.

Eastern European Poetry, April, 1967.

Economist, January 26, 2002, review of *A Treatise on Poetry.*

English Journal, January, 1992, p. 16.

Globe and Mail (Toronto, Ontario, Canada), March 16, 1985.

Guardian Weekly, October 2, 1988, p. 28; November 10, 2001, Nicholas Wroe, "A Century's Witness: Czeslaw Milosz," p. 6.

Harper's Weekly, April, 2002, Helen Vendler, review of *New and Collected Poems, 1931-2001,* p. 72.

Hollins Critic, April, 1982.

Hudson Review, autumn, 1992, p. 509.

Ironwood, number 18, 1981.

Journal of Religion, January, 1987, pp. 141-142.

Library Journal, November 15, 1984, p. 2114; April 15, 1986, p. 84; April 15, 1988, p. 83; January, 1989, p. 45; October 15, 1991, p. 80; September 15, 2001, Gene Shaw, review of *To Begin Where I Am,* p. 80; January, 2002, review of *To Begin Where I Am,* p. 50.

Los Angeles Times, January 14, 1987; September 13, 1987, p. 14.

Los Angeles Times Book Review, May 10, 1981; August 22, 1982; June 5, 1983; August 24, 1984; June 24, 1990, p. 12; November 4, 1990, p. 10; August 15, 1993, pp. 19-20; August 14, 1994, p. 3.

Modern Age, spring, 1986, p. 162.

Nation, December 30, 1978; June 13, 1981; December 22, 1984, p. 686; December 19, 1988, pp. 688-691.

New Leader, October 15, 1984, p. 14; September 19, 1988, p. 19; March 24, 1997, Phoebe Pettingell, review of *Striving toward Being: The Letters of Thomas Merton and Czeslaw Milosz,* p. 13; March, 2001, Kristen Case, review of *Milosz's ABCs,* p. 24.

New Perspectives Quarterly, fall, 1988, p. 55; spring, 1990, p. 44.

New Republic, May 16, 1955; August 1, 1983; October 3, 1988, pp. 26-28; March 16, 1992, pp. 34-37; April 12, 1999, Jaroslaw Anders, "Beauty and Certainty," p. 48.

New Statesman, October 24, 1980; December 17-24, 1982; August 30, 1985, p. 27; August 5, 1988, p. 38.

Newsweek, June 15, 1981; October 4, 1982.

New Yorker, November 7, 1953; March 19, 1984; October 24, 1988, p. 122; July 16, 1990, p. 80; December 24, 2001, John Updike, review of *To Begin Where I Am,* p. 118.

New York Review of Books, April 4, 1974; June 25, 1981; February 27, 1986, p. 31; June 2, 1988, p. 21; August 13, 1992, pp. 44-46; August 11, 1994, p. 41; August 28, 1994, p. 9; May 11, 1995, p. 15; March 23, 1995, pp. 39-42; May 31, 2001, Helen Vendler, review of *A Treatise on Poetry,* p. 27; December 20, 2001, Charles Simic, review of *New and Collected Poems, 1931-2001,* p. 14.

New York Times, June 25, 1968; October 10, 1980; September 4, 1982; August 24, 1984; July 26, 1987; June 2, 1988, p. 21; February 18, 2001, Edward Hirsch, review of *Milosz's ABCs,* p. 10.

New York Times Book Review, April 17, 1955; July 7, 1974; March 11, 1979; February 1, 1981; June 28, 1981; October 17, 1982; May 1, 1983; September 2, 1984; October 20, 1985, p. 60; May 25, 1986, p. 2; July 6, 1986; June 2, 1988, p. 21; June 19, 1988, p. 6; December 8, 1988, p. 26; April 26, 1992, p. 20; May 17, 1992, p. 7; May 31, 1992, p. 22; August 28, 1994, p. 9; June 3, 2001, review of *Milosz's ABCs,* p. 26; December 2, 2001, Harvey Shapiro, review of *New and Collected Poems, 1931-2001,* p. 58; December 9, 2001, review of *New and Collected Poems, 1931-2001,* p. 30; December 16, 2001, review of *New and Collected Poems, 1931-2001,* p. 22; December 23, 2001, review of *New and Collected Poems, 1931-2001,* p. 14; January 27, 2002, Scott Veale, review of *Milosz's ABCs,* p. 24; June 2, 2002, review of *New and Collected Poems, 1931-2001,* p. 23.

New York Times Magazine, January 14, 1990, p. 22.

Observer (London, England), December 2, 1984, p. 19; August 11, 1985, p. 20; July 24, 1988, p. 42; November 22, 1992, p. 64; December 2, 2001, John Kinsella, review of *New and Collected Poems, 1931-2001,* p. 17.

Parnassus, fall, 1983, p. 127; 1989, p. 67; 1992, pp. 100-120.

Partisan Review, November, 1953; spring, 1977; fall, 1985, p. 448; 1986, pp. 177-119; 1990, p. 145.

Poetry, April, 1980; December, 1986, p. 168; January 1993, pp. 223-226; February, 1997, John Taylor, review of *Facing the River,* p. 293; August, 1999, Christian Wiman, review of *Roadside Dog,* p. 286; December, 2001, David Wohajn, review of *A Treatise on Poetry,* p. 161.

Progressive, March, 1985, p. 40.

Publishers Weekly, October 24, 1980; January 31, 1986, p. 362; February 26, 1988, p. 187; January 13, 1992, p. 37; June 6, 1994, p. 49; August 28, 1994, p. 48; September 28, 1998, p. 95; September 28, 1999, review of *Roadside Dog,* p. 95; November 13, 2000, review of *Milosz's ABCs,* p. 92; September 3, 2001, review of *New and Collected Poems, 1931-2001,* p. 82; September 10, 2001, review of *To Begin Where I Am,* p. 73.

Queen's Quarterly, winter, 1989, pp. 954-956.

Reflections, winter, 1985, p. 14.

Review of Contemporary Fiction, spring, 2002, David Seed, review of *Milosz's ABCs,* p. 150.

San Francisco Chronicle, February 4, 2000, p. C1; March 21, 2001, David Kipen, review of *Milosz's ABCs,* p. C1; March 30, 2002, "Milosz, Straight Win California Book Awards," p. D5.

San Francisco Review of Books, spring, 1985, p. 22.

Saturday Review, June 6, 1953; May-June, 1983.

Southern Humanities Review, fall, 1989, pp. 382-386.

Spectator, December 4, 1982.

Stand, summer, 1990, p. 12.

Theology Today, January, 1984.

Threepenny Review, summer, 1989, p. 23.

Times (London, England), July 16, 1981; January 6, 1983; May 19, 1983; February 9, 1985; May 27, 1987.

Times Literary Supplement, December 2, 1977; August 25, 1978; July 24, 1981; December 24, 1982; September 9, 1983; October 3, 1986, p. 1092; February 8, 1988, pp. 955-956; September 2, 1988, p. 955.

Tribune Books (Chicago, IL), May 31, 1981; March 15, 1992, p. 6; December 6, 1992, p. 13; December 18, 1994, p. 5.

TriQuarterly, fall, 1983.

Village Voice, May 2, 1974.

Virginia Quarterly Review, spring, 1975; autumn, 1991, p. 125; summer, 1992, p. 99.

Wall Street Journal, July 24, 1992, p. A10.

Washington Post, October 10, 1980; April 29, 1982; September 20, 1989, p. D1; April 26, 1995, p. C1.

Washington Post Book World, June 14, 1981; August 31, 1986, p. 8; December 22, 1991, p. 15; March 8, 1992, p. 9; October 9, 1994, p. 10.

World Literature Today, winter, 1978; spring, 1978, pp. 372-376; winter, 1985, p. 126; winter, 1987, p. 127; summer, 1987, p. 467; autumn, 1991, p. 735; winter, 1993, p. 210; autumn, 1999 (special Milosz issue), pp. 617-692; spring, 2002, Jerzy R. Krzyzanowski, review of *To Begin Where I Am,* p. 123.

Yale Review, spring, 1990, p. 467.

OBITUARIES:

PERIODICALS

Chicago Tribune, August 16, 2004, section 1, p. 11.

Los Angeles Times, August 15, 2004, p. B14.

New York Times, August 15, 2004, p. A28.

Times (London, England), August 16, 2004, p. 24.

Washington Post, August 15, 2004, p. C9.

ONLINE

New York Times Online, http://www.nytimes.com/ (August 16, 2004).

* * *

MIN, Anchee 1957-

PERSONAL: Born January 14, 1957, in Shanghai, China; immigrated to the United States, 1984; daughter of Naishi (an astronomy instructor) and Dinyun (a teacher; maiden name, Dai) Min; married Qigu Jiang (a painter), 1991 (divorced, 1994); children: Lauryan (daughter). *Education:* Attended the School of the Art Institute of Chicago, 1985-91, received B.F.A., M.F.A. *Hobbies and other interests:* Promoting education in China.

ADDRESSES: Home—CA. *Agent*—Sandra Dijkstra Literary Agency, 1155 Camino del Mar, Ste. 515-C, Del Mar, CA 92014.

CAREER: Writer. Worked in China at Red Fire communal farm, near East China Sea, 1974-76; Shanghai Film Studio, Shanghai, actress, 1976-77, set clerk, 1977-84; worked in the United States as a waitress, messenger, gallery attendant, and babysitter.

AWARDS, HONORS: Carl Sandburg Literary Award, 1993, for *Red Azalea; Red Azalea* was named a Notable Book of the Year, 1994, by the *New York Times.*

WRITINGS:

Red Azalea (memoir), Pantheon (New York, NY), 1994.

Katherine (novel), Riverhead/Putnam (New York, NY), 1995.

Becoming Madame Mao (novel), Houghton Mifflin (Boston, MA), 1999.

Wild Ginger, Houghton Mifflin (Boston, MA), 2002.

Empress Orchid, Houghton Mifflin (Boston, MA), 2004.

SIDELIGHTS: Anchee Min, who grew up in China during the Cultural Revolution, describes her personal experiences in the memoir *Red Azalea,* and also focuses on that period of history in several works of fiction, among them the novels *Becoming Madame Mao* and *Wild Ginger.* The Cultural Revolution, initiated by Chinese Communist Party Chairman Mao Tse-Tung and lasting from 1966 until Mao's death in 1976, was a radical movement intended to revitalize devotion to the original Chinese Revolution. During this time, China's urban youths were organized into cadres of Red Guards and empowered to attack citizens, including party officials, who did not uphold the strict tenets of the Revolution. Recounting her participation in the Little Red Guards, a group of students selected for their fidelity to the Communist Party, Min tells of an attempt to prove her own loyalty to the Party by denouncing Autumn Leaves, a favorite teacher, and accusing her of imperialist activities. Before an assembly of two thousand people, Autumn Leaves was beaten and humiliated and pressured to confess that she was "an American spy." Min then writes, "Autumn Leaves called my name and asked if I really believed that she was an enemy of the country. . . . She asked me with the same exact tone she used when she helped me with my homework. . . . I could not bear looking at her eyes. They had looked at me when the magic of mathematics was explained. . . . When I was ill, they had looked at me with sympathy and love. I had not realized the true value of what all this meant to me until I lost it forever that day at the meeting."

At age seventeen, Min was sent to Red Fire Farm, a collective of some 13,000 workers near the East China Sea. She lived there for three years, enduring hardship, laboring to grow cotton in unyielding soil. Seeking solace from the deprivations, Min engaged in a love affair with a female platoon leader, although both could have easily been betrayed and condemned by other workers. Min eventually escaped Red Fire Farm when picked as a finalist—from a pool of twenty thousand candidates—for a film version of a political opera by Madame Mao, *Red Azalea.* But Min's success was short-lived: in September, 1976, Mao died, Madame Mao fell into disfavor, the political system was thrown into chaos, and the film was abandoned in mid-production. Min worked at the film studio as a set clerk for six years.

With the assistance of actress Joan Chen, a friend from acting school, Min came to the United States in 1984 as a student at the School of the Art Institute of Chicago. She knew virtually no English when she arrived in the United States, and immersed herself in English studies. Min told Penelope Mesic of *Chicago* magazine that she forbade herself to speak any Chinese, "so I would learn the language." In a writing course at the institute, Min wrote about Red Fire Farm. She sent the story to the literary magazine *Granta,* where it was published in the spring of 1992. Based on this story, an agent sold Pantheon the rights to Min's autobiography for a large advance. Min finished writing *Red Azalea* on Christmas Day, 1992. "I was vomiting, my whole body was shaking after a year of living my past life and having to face myself," Min recounted to Mesic. "I was so driven and so glad to be given the opportunity." Min tells *Red Azalea* in uncomplicated declarative sentences, a style that reviewers noted for its effective rendering of the subject matter. According to a *New York* contributor, the writing "suits the brutality of Min's story as well as her own childlike frankness and ferocity." As Min once noted: "I write what I know. I write about what I can't escape from. I don't love writing, but I enjoy the mind battle. I fight with myself to be a winner."

Reviewers also appreciated Min's account of the Cultural Revolution, finding it a significant contribution to Chinese studies. In *Publishers Weekly,* a critic stated that *Red Azalea* "is earthy, frank, filled with stunning beauty and of enormous literary and historical interest." Describing the book as a "roller-coaster ride through Chinese art and politics," *New York Times Book Review* contributor Judith Shapiro remarked that *Red Azalea,* a "memoir of sexual freedom," exists as "a powerful political as well as literary statement."

Katherine, Min's "lyrical" debut novel, according to Bernadine Connelly of the *New York Times Book Review,* recounts the story of Katherine, an American teacher who travels to China to teach English. The novel, declared Connelly, is narrated by one of

Katherine's students, who "uses the clash of their cultures to create a vivid portrait of life in contemporary China." *New Statesman and Society*'s Sarah A. Smith observed, "The romantic sway of Min's language and the perniciously hopeful influence of Katherine wreck the novel's finer points." Smith assessed: "This is a guileless book about a far from guileless time, and a difficult story, too simply told."

Min's 1999 novel *Becoming Madame Mao,* traces the rise to power of Madame Mao in the years 1919 through 1991. *Library Journal* reviewer Shirley N. Quan observed that Min's "characterization of Madame Mao is so strong that one may tend to forget that this work is a novel and not a true biography." A *Publishers Weekly* critic praised Min's "complex psychological portrait of a driven, passionate woman and a period in history which she would suffer, rise and prosper, and then fall victim to her own insatiable thirst for power." The critic commented that "striking metaphors and vivid Chinese proverbs enhance Min's tensile prose." Kristine Huntley, writing in *Booklist,* called the novel "nothing less than brilliant."

Wild Ginger focuses on the later years of the Cultural Revolution in its focus on Maple and Wild Ginger, two teen girls who manage to navigate the difficulties of Mao's regime in different ways. Described as "both a tragic love story and a parable that illustrates the corruption caused by political and moral fanaticism" by *Book* reviewer Susan Tekulve, *Wild Ginger* finds Wild Ginger at first defending her more gentle schoolmate Maple from the attacks of Maoist zealots when both girls are branded suspicious by Maoist officials. While Maple attempts to distance herself from the political fight, the strong-willed Wild Ginger is determined to find acceptance, and she gradually adopts the repressive party line that helps her move up in the ranks of Mao's Red Guard until a love affair causes her to question her priorities. A *Kirkus Reviews* contributor described *Wild Ginger* as "a striking story of love and betrayal [that] recreates the terror and animosities that informed the Cultural Revolution," while in *Library Journal* Edward Cone praised Min for her "lean, expressive prose" and her "talent for mixing irony with humor." "Min continues her extraordinarily acute inquiry into the wounded psyches of martyrs to and survivors of China's horrific Cultural Revolution in her shattering third novel," added Donna Seaman in *Booklist,* writing that the author's "taut and compassionate tale of oppressed teenagers kept in ignorance of the wider world" holds a special relevance for modern teens.

A more historical novel, Min's *Empress Orchid* returns readers to the China of the mid-nineteenth century, and the life of Tsu Hsi, or "Orchid," a seventeen-year-old woman of a poor, rural family who becomes the Chinese emperor's seventh wife, bears the son that will become the "Last Emperor," and, after the emperor's death, rules the country as regent for over four decades. Based on an actual story, the novel follows Orchid's efforts to survive court life and gain the influence needed to ensure that her child will become heir to the dynasty, painting the woman as "a smart politician and demanding mother," according to *People* contributor John Freeman. "Min . . . brilliantly lifts the public mask of a celebrated woman to reveal a contradictory character," noted a *Publishers Weekly* contributor, comparing *Empress Orchid* favorably with *Becoming Madame Mao. Booklist* reviewer Donna Seaman noted that with the novel the author "continues to fulfill her mission to tell the truth about her homeland, particularly China's long tradition of demonizing women," and praised the resulting novel as "insightful, magnetic," and "bewitching."

BIOGRAPHICAL AND CRITICAL SOURCES:

BOOKS

Min, Anchee, *Red Azalea,* Pantheon (New York, NY), 1994.

PERIODICALS

Book, May-June, 2002, Susan Tekulve, review of *Wild Ginger,* p. 81.

Booklist, April 1, 1995, Donna Seaman, review of *Katherine,* p. 1378; March 15, 2000, Kristine Huntley, review of *Becoming Madame Mao,* p. 1293; February 15, 2002, Donna Seaman, review of *Wild Ginger,* p. 971; November 15, 2003, Donna Seaman, review of *Empress Orchid,* p. 548.

Chicago, January, 1994, pp. 55-57, 13-14.

Differences, summer, 2002, Shu-Mei Shih, "Toward and Ethics of Transnational Encounter," p. 90.

Entertainment Weekly, March 25, 1994, p. 50.

Kirkus Reviews, February 15, 2002, review of *Wild Ginger,* p. 214; December 1, 2003, review of *Empress Orchid,* p. 1376.

Kliatt, May, 2004, review of *Wild Ginger,* p. 21.

Library Journal, March 15, 2000, Shirley N. Quan, review of *Becoming Madame Mao,* p. 128; March 1, 2002, Edward Cone, review of *Wild Ginger,* p. 140; December, 2003, Edward Cone, review of *Empress Orchid,* p. 158.

New Statesman & Society, August 25, 1995, Sarah A. Smith, review of *Katherine,* p. 33.
New York, January 31, 1994, p. 63.
New Yorker, February 21, 1994, p. 119.
New York Times, January 26, 1994, p. C19.
New York Times Book Review, February 27, 1994, p. 11; September 10, 1995, Bernadine Connelly, review of *Katherine.*
People, February 16, 2004, review of *Empress Orchid,* p. 43.
Publishers Weekly, December 13, 1993, p. 21; December 20, 1993, p. 57; March 13, 1995, review of *Katherine,* p. 58; April 3, 2000, review of *Becoming Madame Mao,* p. 60; June 5, 2000, Roxane Farmanfarmaian, "After the Revolution," pp. 66-67; March 4, 2002, review of *Wild Ginger,* p. 56; January 19, 2004, review of *Empress Orchid,* p. 53.

ONLINE

Chinese Culture Web site, http://www.chineseculture.net/ (December 2, 1999), "Anchee Min."
USA Today Online, http://www.usatoday.com/ (December 2, 1999), "Anchee Min."

* * *

MITCHELL, Clyde
See ELLISON, Harlan

* * *

MITCHELL, Clyde
See SILVERBERG, Robert

* * *

MOMADAY, Navarre Scott
See MOMADAY, N. Scott

* * *

MOMADAY, N. Scott 1934-
(Navarre Scott Momaday)

PERSONAL: Surname is pronounced "*Ma*-ma-day"; born Navarre Scott Mammedaty, February 27, 1934, in Lawton, OK; son of Alfred Morris (a painter and teacher of art) and Mayme Natachee (a teacher and writer; maiden name, Scott) Mommedaty; married Gaye Mangold, September 5, 1959 (divorced); married Regina Heitzer, July 21, 1978 (divorced); children: (first marriage) Cael, Jill, Brit (all daughters); (second marriage) Lore (daughter). *Education:* Attended Augusta Military Academy; University of New Mexico, A.B., 1958; Stanford University, M.A., 1960, Ph.D., 1963.

ADDRESSES: Office—University of Arizona, 445 Modern Languages Building, P.O. Box 210067, Tucson, AZ 85721. *E-mail*—natachee\@aol.com.

CAREER: Artist, author, and educator. University of California, Santa Barbara, assistant professor, 1963-65, associate professor of English, 1968-69; University of California, Berkeley, associate professor of English and comparative literature, 1969-73; Stanford University, Stanford, CA, professor of English, 1973-82; University of Arizona, Tucson, professor of English and comparative literature, 1982—, regents professor of English; former teacher at New Mexico State University. Has exhibited drawings and paintings in galleries. Museum of American Indian, Heye Foundation, New York, NY, trustee, 1978—. National Endowment for the Humanities, National Endowment for the Arts, consultant, 1970—.

MEMBER: PEN, Modern Language Association of America, American Studies Association, Gourd Dance Society of the Kiowa Tribe.

AWARDS, HONORS: Academy of American Poets prize, 1962, for poem "The Bear"; Guggenheim fellowship, 1966-67; Pulitzer Prize for fiction, 1969, for *House Made of Dawn*; inducted into Kiowa Gourd Clan, 1969; National Institute of Arts and Letters grant, 1970; shared Western Heritage Award with David Muench, 1974, for nonfiction book *Colorado: Summer/Fall/Winter/Spring*; Premio Letterario Internazionale Mondelo (Italy), 1979; inducted into Academy of Achievement, 1993.

WRITINGS:

(Editor) *The Complete Poems of Frederick Goddard Tuckerman,* Oxford University Press (New York, NY), 1965.
(Reteller) *The Journey of Tai-me* (Kiowa Indian folktales), with original etchings by Bruce S. McCurdy, University of California Press (Santa Barbara, CA) 1967, enlarged edition published as *The Way to*

Rainy Mountain, illustrated by father, Alfred Momaday, University of New Mexico Press (Albuquerque, NM), 1969.

House Made of Dawn (novel), Harper (New York, NY), 1968, reprinted, 1989.

Colorado: Summer/Fall/Winter/Spring, illustrated with photographs by David Muench, Rand McNally (Chicago, IL), 1973.

Angle of Geese and Other Poems, David Godine (Boston, MA), 1974.

(And illustrator) *The Gourd Dancer* (poems), Harper (New York, NY), 1976.

The Names: A Memoir, Harper (New York, NY), 1976, reprinted, University of Arizona Press (Tucson, AZ), 1996.

(Author of foreword) An Painter, *A Coyote in the Garden,* Confluence (Lewiston, ID), 1988.

The Ancient Child (novel), Doubleday (New York, NY), 1989.

(Contributor) Charles L. Woodward, *Ancestral Voice: Conversations with N. Scott Momaday,* University of Nebraska Press (Lincoln, NE), 1989.

(Author of introduction) Marcia Keegan, *Enduring Culture: A Century of Photography of the Southwest Indians,* Clear Light (Santa Fe, NM), 1991.

In the Presence of the Sun: A Gathering of Shields, Rydal (Santa Fe, NM), 1992.

In the Presence of the Sun: Stories and Poems, 1961-1991 (poems, stories, art), St. Martin's Press (New York, NY), 1992.

(Author of introduction) Gerald Hausman, *Turtle Island Alphabet: A Lexicon of Native American Symbols and Culture,* St. Martin's Press (New York, NY), 1992.

Circle of Wonder: A Native American Christmas Story, Clear Light (Santa Fe, NM), 1994.

Conversations with N. Scott Momaday, University Press of Mississippi (Jackson, MS), 1997.

The Man Made of Words: Essays, Stories, Passages, St. Martin's Press (New York, NY), 1997.

In the Bear's House, St. Martin's Press (New York, NY), 1999.

Also author of film script of Frank Water's novel, *The Man Who Killed the Deer.* Contributor of articles and poems to periodicals; a frequent reviewer on Indian subjects for the *New York Times Book Review.*

WORK IN PROGRESS: A study of American poetry in the middle period, *The Furrow and the Plow: Science and Literature in America, 1836-1866* (tentative title), for Oxford University Press; a book on storytelling, for Oxford University Press.

SIDELIGHTS: N. Scott Momaday's poetry and prose reflect his Kiowa Indian heritage in structure and theme, as well as in subject matter. "When I was growing up on the reservations of the Southwest," he told Joseph Bruchac in the *American Poetry Review,* "I saw people who were deeply involved in their traditional life, in the memories of their blood. They had, as far as I could see, a certain strength and beauty that I find missing in the modern world at large. I like to celebrate that involvement in my writing." Roger Dickinson-Brown indicated in the *Southern Review* that Momaday has long "maintained a quiet reputation in American Indian affairs and among distinguished *literati*" for his brilliance and range, "his fusion of alien cultures, and his extraordinary experiments in different literary forms."

Momaday is half Kiowa. His mother, Mayme Natachee Scott, is descended from early American pioneers, although her middle name is taken from a Cherokee great-grandmother. Momaday's memoir also includes anecdotes of such Anglo-American ancestors as his grandfather, Theodore Scott, a Kentucky sheriff. His mother, however, preferred to identify with her imagined Indian heritage, adopting the name Little Moon when she was younger and dressing Indian style. She attended Haskell Institute, an Indian school in Kansas, where she met several members of the Kiowa tribe. Eventually she married Momaday's father, also a Kiowa. The author grew up in New Mexico, where his mother, a teacher and writer, and his father, an artist and art teacher, found work among the Jemez Indians in the state's high canyon and mountain country, but he was originally raised among the Kiowas on a family farm in Oklahoma. Although Momaday covers his Anglo-American heritage in the memoir, he prefers, like his mother, "to imagine himself *all* Indian, and to 'imagine himself' back into the life, the emotions, the spirit of his Kiowa forebears," commented Edward Abbey in *Harper's.* He uses English, his mother's language, according to Abbey, to tell "his story in the manner of his father's people; moving freely back and forth in time and space, interweaving legend, myth, and history." In *Modern American Poetry,* Kenneth M. Roemer remarked that Momaday's culturally rich childhood led him to "fall in love with Kiowa, Navajo, Jemez Pueblo, Spanish, and English words."

Momaday's *The Names: A Memoir* explores the author's heritage in autobiographical form. It is composed of tribal tales, boyhood memories, and genealogy, reported *New York Times Book Review* critic Wallace Stegner. Momaday's quest for his roots, wrote Abbey, "takes him back to the hills of Kentucky and north to the high plains of Wyoming, and from there, in memory and imagination, back to the Bering Straits." Stegner described it as "an Indian book, but not a book about wrongs done to Indians. It is a search and a celebration, a book of identities and sources. Momaday is the son of parents who successfully bridged the gulf between Indian and white ways, but remain Indian," he explained. "In boyhood Momaday made the same choice, and in making it gave himself the task of discovering and in some degree inventing the tradition and history in which he finds his most profound sense of himself." *New York Review of Books* critic Diane Johnson agreed that "Momaday does not appear to feel, or does not discuss, any conflict of the Kiowa and white traditions; he is their product, an artist, heir of the experiences of his ancestors and conscious of the benignity of their influence."

Momaday does not actually speak Kiowa, but, in his work, he reveals the language as not only a reflection of the physical environment, but also a means of shaping it. The title of *The Names,* reported Richard Nicholls in *Best Sellers,* refers to all "the names given by Scott Momaday's people, the Kiowa Indians, to the objects, forms, and features of their land, the southwestern plains, and to its animals and birds." When he was less than a year old, Momaday was given the name Tsoaitalee or "Rock-Tree-Boy" by a paternal relative, after the 200-foot volcanic butte in Wyoming, which is sacred to the Kiowas and is known to Anglo-Americans as Devil's Tower. "For the Kiowas it was a place of high significance," Abbey pointed out. "To be named after that mysterious and mythic rock was, for the boy, a high honor and a compelling one. For among the Indians a name was never merely an identifying tag but something much more important, a kind of emblem and ideal, the determining source of a man or woman's character and course of life."

Momaday's first novel, *House Made of Dawn,* tells "the old story of the problem of mixing Indians and Anglos," reported *New York Times Book Review* critic Marshall Sprague. "But there is a quality of revelation here as the author presents the heart-breaking effort of his hero to live in two worlds." In the novel's fractured narrative, the main character, Abel, returns to the prehistoric landscape and culture surrounding his reservation pueblo after his tour of duty in the Army during World War II. Back home, he kills an albino. He serves a prison term and is paroled, unrepentant, to a Los Angeles relocation center. Once in the city, he attempts to adjust to his factory job, like his even-tempered roommate, Ben, a modern Indian, who narrates parts of the novel. During his free time, Abel drinks and attends adulterated religious and peyote-eating ceremonies. He can't cope with his job; and, "because of his contempt," Sprague indicated, he's brutally beaten by a Los Angeles policeman, but returns again to the reservation "in time to carry on tradition for his dying grandfather," Francisco. The novel culminates in Abel's running in the ancient ritual dawn race against evil and death.

According to Kerr, the book is "a creation myth—rife with fabulous imagery, ending with Abel's rebirth in the old ways at the old man's death—but an ironic one, suffused with violence and telling a story of culture loss." The grandfather, he maintained, "heroic, crippled, resonant with the old ways, impotent in the new—acts as a lodestone to the novel's conflicting energies. His incantatory dying delirium in Spanish flexes Momaday's symbolic compass . . . , and around his dying the book shapes its proportions." Francisco is "the alembic that transmutes the novel's confusions," he commented. "His retrospection marks off the book's boundaries, points of reference, and focal themes: the great organic calendar of the black mesa—the house of the sun (which locates the title)—as a central Rosetta stone integrating the ceremonies rendered in Part One, and the source place by which Abel and [his brother] could 'reckon where they were, where all things were, in time.'"

Momaday meets with difficulties in his attempt to convey Indian sensibility in novelistic form, Kerr related. The fractured narrative is open to criticism, in Kerr's opinion, and the "plot of *House Made of Dawn* actually seems propelled by withheld information, that besetting literary error." Of the novel's structure, Dickinson-Brown wrote that the sequence of events "is without fixed order. The parts can be rearranged, no doubt with change of effect, but not always with recognizable difference. The fragments thus presented are the subject. The result is a successful depiction but not an understanding of what is depicted: a reflection, not a novel in the comprehensive sense of the word." Kerr also objected to the author's overuse of "quiet, weak constructions" in the opening paragraph and indicated that "repetition, polysyndeton, and *there* as subject continue to deaden the narrative's force well into the book." *Commonweal* reviewer William James Smith agreed that "Momaday observes and renders accurately, but the material seems to have sunken slightly beneath the surface of the beautiful prose." The critic maintained, however, that the novel should also be regarded as "a return to the sacred art of storytelling and myth-making that is part of Indian oral tradition," as well as an attempt "to push the secular mode of modern fiction into the sacred mode, a faith and recognition in the power of the word." And a *Times Literary Supplement* critic pointed out

Momaday's "considerable descriptive power," citing "a section in which Tosamah [a Los Angeles medicine man/ priest] rehearses the ancient trampled history of the Kiowas in trance—like visionary prose that has moments of splendour."

In a review of *The Way to Rainy Mountain, Southern Review* critic Kenneth Fields observed that Momaday's writing exemplifies a "paradox about language which is often expressed in American Indian literature." Momaday himself has written that "by means of words can a man deal with the world on equal terms. And the word is sacred," commented Fields. "On the other hand . . . the Indians took for their subject matter those elusive perceptions that resist formulation, never entirely apprehensible, but just beyond the ends of the nerves." In a similar vein, Dickinson-Brown maintained that Momaday's poem "Angle of Geese" "presents, better than any other work I know . . . perhaps the most important subject of our age: the tragic conflict between what we have felt in wilderness and what our language means." What Momaday must articulate in *The Way to Rainy Mountain,* Fields argued, is "racial memory," or "the ghostly heritage of [his] Kiowa ancestors," and "what it means to feel himself a Kiowa in the modern American culture that displaced his ancestors."

Described by Fields as "far and away [Momaday's] best book," *The Way to Rainy Mountain* relates the story of the Kiowas journey 300 years ago from Yellowstone down onto the plains, where they acquired horses, and, in the words of John R. Milton in the *Saturday Review,* "they became a lordly society of sun priests, fighters, hunters, and thieves, maintaining this position for 100 years, to the mid-nineteenth century," when they were all but destroyed by the U.S. Cavalry in Oklahoma. And when the sacred buffalo began to disappear, Fields wrote, "the Kiowas lost the sustaining illumination of the sun god," since, as Momaday explains, the buffalo was viewed as "the animal representation of the sun, the essential and sacrificial victim of the Sun Dance." "Momaday's own grandmother, who had actually been present at the last and abortive Kiowa Sun Dance in 1887, is for him the last of the Kiowas," related Fields.

In *The Way to Rainy Mountain,* Momaday uses form to help him convey a reality that has largely been lost. His text is made up of twenty-four numbered sections grouped into three parts, "The Setting Out," "The Going On," and "The Closing In." These parts are in turn divided into three different passages, each of which is set in a different style typeface. The first passage in each part is composed of Kiowa myths and legends, the second is made up of historical accounts of the tribe, and the third passage is a personal autobiographical rendering of Momaday's rediscovery of his Kiowa homeland and roots. Fields explained that in form, the book "resembles those ancient texts with subsequent commentaries which, taken altogether, present strange complexes of intelligence; not only the author's, but with it that of the man in whose mind the author was able to live again."

By the end of the last part, however, wrote Nicholas, the three passages begin to blend with one another, and "the mythic passages are no longer mythic in the traditional sense, that is Momaday is creating myth out of his memories of his ancestors rather than passing on already established and socially sanctioned tales. Nor are the historical passages strictly historical, presumably objective, accounts of the Kiowas and their culture. Instead they are carefully selected and imaginatively rendered memories of his family. And, finally, the personal passages have become prose poems containing symbols which link them thematically to the other two, suggesting that all three journeys are products of the imagination, that all have become interfused in a single memory and reflect a single idea." Dickinson-Brown considered the book's shape a well-controlled "associational structure," distinctively adapted to the author's purpose. The form, according to Fields, forced Momaday "to relate the subjective to the more objective historical sensibility. The writing of the book itself, one feels, enables him to gain both freedom and possession. It is therefore a work of discovery as well as renunciation, of finding but also of letting go."

After *The House Made of Dawn,* Momaday wrote mainly nonfiction and poetry. He did not write another novel for twenty years. "I don't think of myself as a novelist. I'm a poet," he told *Los Angeles Times* interviewer Edward Iwata. Yet, in 1989, the poet completed his second novel, *The Ancient Child.* Building this book around the legend behind his Indian name, Tsoaitalee, Momaday uses the myth to develop the story of a modern Indian artist searching for his identity. A number of reviewers lauded the new novel. Craig Lesley, for one, wrote in the *Washington Post* that *The Ancient Child* "is an intriguing combination of myth, fiction and storytelling that demonstrates the continuing power and range of Momaday's creative vision." A "largely autobiographical novel," according to Iwata, *The Ancient Child* expresses the author's belief that "dreams and visions are pathways to one's blood ancestry and racial memory."

In addition to his poetry and fiction, Momaday is also an accomplished painter. His diverse skill is evident in

In the Presence of the Sun: Stories and Poems, 1961-1991. The collection includes numerous poems from Momaday's early poetic career; twenty new poems; a sequence of poems about the legendary outlaw Billy the Kid; stories about the Kiowas' tribal shields; and sixty drawings by the author. "A slim volume, [*In the Presence of the Sun*] contains the essence of the ancestral voices that speak through him. It is a refined brew of origins, journeys, dreams and the landscape of the deep continental interior," remarked Barbara Bode in the *New York Times Book Review.*

In the Bear's House is a mixture of paintings, poems, dialogues, and prose relating to the bear, an animal of spiritual significance to the Kiowas. "Momaday's blend of biblical and Native American spirituality and language seems almost old-fashioned in light of more separatist studies that have dominated since he first arrived on the scene back in the 60s," remarked a *Kirkus Reviews* contributor. However, the same contributor noted that "Momaday's clean, sharp measures enhance a number of well-made poems that date mostly from recent times." The critic further observed, "The bold brushstrokes of Momaday's paintings echo the power and precision of his poetry and prose."

Momaday views his heritage objectively and in a positive light. He explains much of his perspective as a writer and as a Native American in *Ancestral Voice: Conversations with N. Scott Momaday,* the result of a series of interviews with Charles L. Woodward. *World Literature Today* contributor Robert L. Berner called the volume "an essential tool of scholarship" in analyzing and understanding Momaday and his work. Discussing his heritage with Bruchac, Momaday commented: "The Indian has the advantage of a very rich spiritual experience. As much can be said, certainly, of some non-Indian writers. But the non-Indian writers of today are culturally deprived, I think, in the sense that they don't have the same sense of heritage that the Indian has. I'm told this time and time again by my students, who say, 'Oh, I wish I knew more about my grandparents; I wish I knew more about my ancestors and where they came from and what they did.' I've come to believe them. It seems to me that the Indian writer ought to make use of that advantage. One of his subjects ought certainly to be his cultural investment in the world. It is a unique and complete experience, and it is a great subject in itself."

BIOGRAPHICAL AND CRITICAL SOURCES:

BOOKS

Allen, Paula Gunn, *Recovering the Word: Essays on Native American Literature,* edited by Brian Swann and Arnold Krupat, University of California Press (Berkeley, CA), 1987, pp. 563-579.

Blaeser, Kimberly, *Narrative Chance: Postmodern Discourse on Native American Indian Literatures,* edited by Gerald Vizenor, University of New Mexico Press (Albuquerque, NM), 1989, pp. 39-54.

Brumble, H. David, III, *American Indian Autobiography,* University of California Press (Berkeley, CA), 1988, pp. 165-180.

Contemporary Literary Criticism, Thomson Gale (Detroit, MI), Volume 2, 1974, Volume 19, 1981, Volume 85, 1995, Volume 95, 1997.

Dictionary of Literary Biography, Volume 143: *American Novelists since World War II, Third Series,* Thomson Gale (Detroit, MI), 1994, Volume 175: *Native American Writers of the United States,* Thomson Gale (Detroit, MI), 1997, Volume 256: *Twentieth-Century American Western Writers, Third Series,* 2002, pp. 203-218.

Encyclopedia of World Biography, 2nd edition, Thomson Gale (Detroit, MI), 1998.

Gridley, Marion E., editor, *Indians of Today,* I.C.F.P., 1971.

Gridley, Marion E., *Contemporary American Indian Leaders,* Dodd (New York, NY), 1972.

Hogan, Linda, *Studies in American Indian Literature: Critical Essays and Course Designs,* edited by Paula Gunn Allen, Modern Language Association of America (New York, NY), 1983, pp. 169-177.

Krupat, Arnold, *The Voice in the Margin: Native American Literature and the Canon,* University of California Press (Berkeley, CA), 1989.

Lincoln, Kenneth, *Native American Renaissance,* University of California Press (Berkeley, CA), 1983, pp. 82-121.

Momaday, N. Scott, *The Way to Rainy Mountain,* University of New Mexico Press (Albuquerque, NM), 1969.

Momaday, N. Scott, *The Names: A Memoir,* Harper (New York, NY), 1976.

Native North American Literature, Thomson Gale (Detroit, MI), 1994.

Owens, Louis, *Other Destinies: Understanding the American Indian Novel,* University of Oklahoma Press (Norman, OK), 1992.

Roemer, Kenneth, editor, *Approaches to Teaching Momaday's "The Way to Rainy Mountain,"* Modern Language Association of America (New York, NY), 1988.

St. James Guide to Young Adult Writers, 2nd edition, St. James Press (Detroit, MI), 1999.

Schubnell, Matthias, *N. Scott Momaday: The Cultural and Literary Background,* University of Oklahoma Press (Norman, OK), 1985.

Trimble, Martha Scott, *Fifty Western Writers: A Bio-Bibliographical Sourcebook,* edited by Fred Erisman and Richard W. Etulain, Greenwood Press (Westport, CT), 1982, pp. 313-324.

Velie, Alan R, *Four American Indian Literary Masters: N. Scott Momaday, James Welch, Leslie Marmon Silko, and Gerald Vizenor,* University of Oklahoma Press (Norman, OK), 1982.

PERIODICALS

American Indian Quarterly, May, 1978; winter, 1986, pp. 101-117; summer, 1988, pp. 213-220.

American Literature, January, 1979; October, 1989, p. 520.

American Poetry Review, July-August, 1984.

American West, February, 1988, pp. 12-13.

Atlantic, January, 1977.

Best Sellers, June 15, 1968; April, 1977.

Bloomsbury Review, July-August, 1989, p. 13; July-August, 1993, p. 14; November-December, 1994, p. 25.

Booklist, February 1, 1999, Ray Olson, review of *In the Bear's House,* p. 957.

Canadian Literature, spring, 1990, p. 299.

Commonweal, September 20, 1968.

Denver Quarterly, winter, 1978, pp. 19-31.

Harper's, February, 1977.

Indiana Social Studies Quarterly, Autumn, 1975, Joseph F. Trimmer, "Native Americans and the American Mix: N. Scott Momaday's *House Made of Dawn,*" pp. 75-91.

Journal of Popular Culture, fall, 1999, review of *The Ancient Child,* p. 23.

Kirkus Reviews, March 15, 1999, review of *In the Bear's House,* p. 411.

Listener, May 15, 1969.

Los Angeles Times, November 20, 1989.

Los Angeles Times Book Review, December 27, 1992, p. 6.

Nation, August 5, 1968.

New Yorker, May 17, 1969.

New York Review of Books, February 3, 1977, pp. 19-20, 29.

New York Times, May 16, 1969; June 3, 1970.

New York Times Book Review, June 9, 1968, Marshall Sprague, review of *House Made of Dawn,* p. 5; June 16, 1974; March 6, 1977; December 31, 1989; March 14, 1993, p. 15.

Observer, May 25, 1969.

Publishers Weekly, September 19, 1994, p. 28; February 22, 1999, review of *In the Bear's House,* p. 91.

Saturday Review, June 21, 1969.

Sewanee Review, summer, 1977.

Social Studies, July, 1998, review of *The Man Made of Words,* p. 189.

South Dakota Review, winter, 1975-76, Charles A. Nicholas, review of *The Way to Rainy Mountain,* pp. 149-158.

Southern Review, winter, 1970; January, 1978, Roger Dickinson Brown, review of *House Made of Dawn,* pp. 30-32; April, 1978.

Southwest Review, summer, 1969; spring, 1978, Baine Kerr, review of *House Made of Dawn,* pp. 172-173.

Spectator, May 23, 1969.

Studies in American Fiction, spring, 1983, Michael W. Raymond, review of *House Made of Dawn,* pp. 61-71.

Times Literary Supplement, May 22, 1969.

Tribune Books (Chicago, IL), October 1, 1989; December 4, 1994, p. 9.

Voice of Youth Advocates, October, 1998, review of *The Man Made of Words,* p. 255.

Washington Post, November 21, 1969; November 28, 1989.

Western American Literature, May, 1977, pp. 86-87; November, 1993, Eric Todd Smith, review of *In the Presence of the Sun,* pp. 274-275; spring 1999, review of *The Names* and *House Made of Dawn,* p. 7.

World Literature Today, summer, 1977; winter, 1990, p. 175; summer, 1993, p. 650.

ONLINE

Modern American Poetry, http://www.English.uiuc.edu/maps/poets/ (May 30, 2003), Kenneth Roemer, "N. Scott Momaday: Biographical, Literary, and Multicultural Contexts."

* * *

MONROE, Lyle
See HEINLEIN, Robert A.

* * *

MOODY, Anne 1940-

PERSONAL: Born September 15, 1940, in Wilkerson County, MS; daughter of Fred and Elmire (Williams) Moody; married Austin Stratus, March 9, 1967 (divorced); children: Sascha. *Education:* Attended Natchez Junior College; Tougaloo College, B.S., 1964.

ADDRESSES: Home—New York, NY. *Agent*—c/o Harper & Row, 10 East 53rd St., New York, NY 10022.

CAREER: Congress of Racial Equality (CORE), Washington, DC, organizer, 1961-63, fundraiser, 1964; Cornell University, Ithaca, NY, civil rights project coordinator, 1964-65; artist in residence in Berlin, Germany, 1972; writer. Counsel for New York City's poverty program, 1967.

MEMBER: International PEN.

AWARDS, HONORS: Brotherhood Award from National Council of Christians and Jews, and Best Book of the Year Award from the National Library Association, both 1969, both for *Coming of Age in Mississippi;* silver medal from *Mademoiselle,* 1970, for "New Hopes for the Seventies"; German Academic Exchange Service grant, 1972.

WRITINGS:

Coming of Age in Mississippi (autobiography), Dial (New York, NY), 1968.

Mr. Death: Four Stories, foreword by John Donovan, Harper (New York, NY), 1975.

Contributor to *Ms.* and *Mademoiselle.*

ADAPTATIONS: A sound recording, *Anne Moody Reads Her Mr. Death and Bobo,* was produced by Caedmon in 1980.

WORK IN PROGRESS: Variations on a Dream of Death, short stories; *Black Womans Book; The Clay Gully,* a novel.

SIDELIGHTS: In *Coming of Age in Mississippi,* Anne Moody mined her experiences of racism and discrimination as the oldest of nine children of rural Mississippi sharecroppers. Widely anthologized, Moody's autobiography has become a civil rights era classic. In a profile for the University of Minnesota's Web-based Voices from the Gaps project, researchers noted that the narrative "examines the issues of the awakening civil rights movement, the youth movement and the emergence of her feminist consciousness." They added that the "compelling story" reflects Moody's prose style: "angry, blunt, and incredibly powerful."

As a child, Moody helped her family by cleaning houses. She attended segregated schools, where she excelled, and earned a basketball scholarship to Natchez Junior College. A civil rights activist throughout the 1960s, she participated in the March on Washington and developed a close professional relationship with Reverend Martin Luther King, Jr. But her relationship with the movement soured. As Moody later commented: "In the beginning I never really saw myself as a writer. I was first and foremost an activist in the civil rights movement in Mississippi. When I could no longer see that anything was being accomplished by our work there, I left and went north. I came to see through my writing that no matter how hard we in the Movement worked, nothing seemed to change; that we made a few visible little gains, yet at the root, things always remained the same; and that the Movement was not in control of its destiny—nor did we have any means of gaining control of it. We were like an angry dog on a leash that had turned on its master. It could bark and howl and snap, and sometimes even bite, but the master was always in control."

She continued, "I realized that the universal fight for human rights, dignity, justice, equality, and freedom is not and should not be just the fight of the American Negro or the Indians or the Chicanos, it's the fight of every ethnic and racial minority, every suppressed and exploited person, every one of the millions who daily suffer one or another of the indignities of the powerless and voiceless masses. And this trend of thinking is what finally brought about an end to my involvement in the Civil Rights Movement, especially as it began to splinter and get more narrowly nationalistic in its thinking."

Moody went on to publish essays and a collection of short stories. Rumors abound about her activities since the 1970s, but she grants no interviews and seems to have withdrawn from public life.

BIOGRAPHICAL AND CRITICAL SOURCES:

PERIODICALS

New York Times, December 13, 1968.

New York Times Book Review, January 5, 1969.

Saturday Review, January 11, 1969.

Washington Post Book World, December 1, 1968, January 27, 1969.

ONLINE

Mississippi Writers Page, http://www.olemiss.edu/mwp/ (January 28, 2004), Robert Cummings, profile of Moody.

Voices from the Gaps, http://voices.cla.umn.edu/ (August 7, 2004), "Anne Moody."

MOODY, Hiram F., III
See MOODY, Rick

* * *

MOODY, Rick 1961-
(Hiram F. Moody III)

PERSONAL: Born October 18, 1961, in New York, NY; son of Hiram F. Moody, Jr., and Margaret Maureen (Flynn) Davis. *Education:* Brown University, B.A., 1983; Columbia University, M.F.A., 1986.

ADDRESSES: Home—719 Adams St., Apt. 3R, Hoboken, NJ 07030. *Agent*—Donadio & Ashworth, Inc., 231 W. 22nd St., New York, NY 10011.

CAREER: Farrar, Straus & Giroux, Inc., New York, NY, associate editor, 1988-91; freelance editor, 1991—. Instructor in fiction writing and composition for Riverside Writers Group and Bennington College, 1991—.

Moody and musicians David Grubbs and Hannah Marcus formed the group Wingdale Community Singers and released an album of original songs, 2005.

AWARDS, HONORS: Editors Book Award, Pushcart Press, 1991, for *Garden State: A Novel;* Guggenheim fellowship, 2000; PEN American Center Award for *The Black Veil*, 2003.

WRITINGS:

Garden State: A Novel, Pushcart Press (New York, NY), 1991.

The Ice Storm (novel), Little, Brown (Boston, MA), 1994.

The Ring of Brightest Angels around Heaven (short stories), Warner Books (New York, NY), 1996.

Purple America (novel), Little, Brown (Boston, MA), 1997.

The Ice Storm: The Shooting Script: Screenplay, Introduction, and Notes, preface by Ang Lee, Newmarket Press (New York, NY), 1997.

(Editor, with Darcey Steinke) *Joyful Noise: The New Testament Revisited,* Little, Brown (Boston, MA), 1997.

Hover, photographs by Gregory Crewdson, Artspace Books (San Francisco, CA), 1998.

Demonology (short stories), Little, Brown (Boston, MA), 2000.

The Black Veil: A Memoir with Digressions, Little, Brown (Boston, MA), 2002.

The Diviners (novel), Little, Brown (Boston, MA), 2005.

Contributor of stories and essays to periodicals, including *Paris Review, Antioch Review,* and *Grand Street.* Associate editor, *Fishers Island Gazette,* 1988—.

ADAPTATIONS: The Ice Storm was adapted into a movie and released in 1997.

SIDELIGHTS: Rick Moody, who was born Hiram Moody, is a novelist whose emergence in the 1990s helped herald a new era in American fiction, a turn away from such "mediagenic writers [as] Jay McInerney and Tama Janowitz, [who] once held the limelight with modish novels about fast life in the 1980s," as *Time* reviewer R.Z. Sheppard noted. In contrast, Moody—along with contemporaries like David Foster Wallace, Jonathan Frazen, and Donald Antrim—slants his work by taking "an extra tweak of the commonplace to turn diversion into gnawing unease," according to Sheppard.

Following his debut novel, 1991's *Garden State,* Moody gained national attention with his second published work, *The Ice Storm.* The story is set in upscale New Canaan, Connecticut, in late November of 1973. The Hood family is in crisis, and father Ben copes by drinking and having affairs. Mother Elena is, in the words of a *Time* reviewer, "too obsessed with herself, the *I Ching* and the writings of Masters and Johnson" to recognize the tumult facing her marriage and its effects on her two teenage children. The kids, meanwhile, eagerly turn to drugs and promiscuity in the absence of a guiding force in their lives.

The author "compresses years of estrangement and disillusion into one night of drugs and drinking, seduction and betrayal, felled trees, blackouts, car crashes—enough mayhem to keep the reader cringing in anticipation of the next disaster," commented Dan Begley, writing in the *Chicago Tribune.* "But in fact the damage was done before the rain began to fall . . . when the Hoods formed bonds based on convention, predictable and soulless like the street plan of a subdivision."

Throughout *The Ice Storm,* Moody uses references of the era, providing "layer on layer of contemporary detail—clothes and furniture, television programmes, articles in magazines and comics," wrote Alexander Harrison in his *Times Literary Supplement* review. In doing so, the critic continued, Moody has "done his research, but the result can overwhelm the fact that the book is a retrospective; it exists in the present while it deals with the past." Harrison pointed out that a narrator from today's world ("let me dish you this comedy about a family I know when I was growing up") helps set the scene by establishing that "there are no answering machines. And no call waiting. No compact disc recorders or laser discs" in this story.

But there are "key parties" in which wives draw from a bowl the car keys of their male neighbors to determine with whom to spend the night. "Everyone's confused to begin with and, caught overnight in the weather [the titular storm] and their various liaisons, much more confused by the end," according to Ellen Akins. Her *Los Angeles Times Book Review* piece stated that while the story is "split in perspective among the characters," *The Ice Storm* is "largely uniform in style, rendered in short sentences, many of them not really sentences but bright staccato beats that hammer home a point or ring a few changes on it or take it one step further." And to an *Economist* reviewer, the "built-in transience" of the constant period references is but a small shortcoming in an otherwise "profound" exploration of human frailty. *The Ice Storm* was adapted into a movie released in October 1997, with Kevin Kline starring as Ben Hood.

In 1995 Moody produced a novella and collection of short stories released as *The Ring of Brightest Angels around Heaven.* Called "a spectacular tribute to the banality of degradation" by *Village Voice* critic Clair Messud, *Ring* explores the lives of various denizens of New York City's bohemian East Village. Drugs, rock music, despair, AIDS, and artistic longings intermingle in a way that turns the exotic into the familiar, in Messud's view. "This is a fine but unsettling work," she summed up, "not least because Moody's relation to his material remains unclear. Voyeur and participant, sage and celebrant, he wants to be the man with all the tricks. He captures with piercing clarity the vacuity of his characters' lives but seems, at the same time, to pay tribute to their desperate extremity, in a gesture more social than literary."

Moody returned to the novel with 1997's *Purple America,* which received considerable critical acclaim. A "rapturous" work about love at the end of the twentieth century, according to *Detroit Free Press*reviewer Liesel Litzenburger, *Purple America* shows Moody as "a master at conveying the nuances of a certain sort of stuck, over-reaching, upper-middle-class life—golf courses, scotch- and-sodas, station wagons, tennis socks (with the little colored balls)—as a means of making larger statements." The story concerns Dexter "Hex" Raitliffe, who meets up with a childhood crush as he returns home to care for his invalid mother. In his late thirties, neurotic, alcoholic, and stuttering, Hex is "ill-equipped for this new role as his mother's care giver," as *Lexington Herald-Leader* critic Michael Kelsay noted. After reuniting with Jane Ingersoll, for whom Hex nursed an unrequited crush during high school, he embarks on a spontaneous affair with her—with unhappy results.

Promising that *Purple America* "will stick with you if you stick with it," *Newsweek* critic David Gates noted the challenge the author provides for the reader. At the same time, stated Will Blythe in *Esquire,* Moody "manages to deploy all the standard missiles of postmodernism (parody, list making, the exaltation of language, a geek's love of technology, a multiplicity of voices and forms), but the warheads are tipped—miracles of miracles—with compassion for his characters." To Blythe, Moody "is that rare writer who can make the language do tricks and still suffuse his narrative with soul."

Demonology, released in 2000, is a collection of short stories exploring "love, grief and language, set against the backdrop of modern America," according to Alex Gibbons in a *New Statesman* review. The title entry is a meditation by a man on the death of his sister, a story that may have its impetus in reality; Moody's sister died of a seizure. In another story, "Mansion on the Hill," a deceased sister also figures into the plot. Indeed, wrote reviewer Joe Hartlaub in the online *Bookreporter,* "if there is one unifying theme to the stories in *Demonology* it is the loss of family members," citing not only "Mansion" but also "Hawaiian Night," in which the spectre of a deceased wife casts a pall over a neighborhood party, and "The Double Zero," which deals with a dying boy who comes between two estranged brothers.

One entry that some critics singled out as particularly noteworthy is "Wilkie Ridgway Fahnstock, The Boxed Set." Experimental in form, the story consists of nothing more than a set of liner notes for a collection of cassettes belonging to "a schlemiel who has reached penultimate failure in early adulthood and has nowhere to go," as described by Hartlaub. The cassettes listed are actual songs, and together they paint a picture of their owner. "Absolutely brilliant," decided Hartlaub of this story. Amy Havel of *Review of Contemporary Fiction* was more reserved in her judgment, saying Moody's experimental pieces are "less interesting and more showy" than his traditionally written stories.

Even without its experimental aspects, *Demonology* can be challenging reading. "We are presented situations in which the psyche would be rubbed raw, but we are left to imagine the ramifications, the nuances, the complexities," wrote *New Criterion* critic Max Watman. A *Publishers Weekly* contributor sensed a "low-grade bemusement" in the thirteen *Demonology* pieces, commenting that Moody's prose "strains for hypermodern colloquial detachment, but too often misses its mark." But "to Moody's credit," noted Gibbons, the book, "for all its emotional charge, never becomes mawkish."

Moody unveiled details of his own life in his first nonfiction work, *The Black Veil: A Memoir with Digressions.* The title refers to a legend regarding a Moody ancestor who wore a veil over his face throughout his adult life in penance for causing the accidental death of a childhood friend. The memoir reveals that "circumstances didn't make a sweet spring of youth" for the author, as a *Kirkus Reviews* writer put it. Moody reveals that as a shy, awkward boy he endured his parents' divorce and, for a while, had no fixed address. Solace came in the form of reading and from listening to the tall tales told by his grandfather. In a *New York Times* interview with Bill Goldstein, Moody recalled his grandfather as an archetypical down East Yankee from Maine who "would just tell us ridiculous fibs on occasion, with great delight and enthusiasm. So there was that kind of love for telling stories around."

The Black Veil covers Moody's years as a struggling writer working at publishing houses while coping with personal demons, including a fear of being raped and a bout of alcoholism. Contributors for *Kirkus Reviews* and *Publishers Weekly* both lauded the portrait of a "sympathetic and sensitive" man that emerges from the memoir.

In 2005 Moody released *The Diviners,* his first novel in seven years. The work is the character-driven story of an epic mini-series, the rights to which are being fought over by agents and studio executives. The one problem, of which none of these eager bidders is aware, is that the script has not actually been written yet. Vince Passaro, in a review for *O,* noted that "devastating in its comedy and penetrating in its deep seriousness, *The Diviners* stands now as Moody's best and most ambitious novel." A *Kirkus Reviews* contributor disagreed, however, observing that "it all adds up (or doesn't) to a bloated book about cultural bloat, an empty look at cultural emptiness," and summing up the book as "a novel that might well have been more fun to write than it is to read."

While often compared to twentieth-century writer John Cheever, Moody told an interviewer for *Publishers Weekly* that his main influences included Saul Bellow, Thomas Pynchon, his mentors at Brown University John Hawkes and Angela Carter—"and above all," added the interviewer, "Don DeLillo, the writer whose development Moody's most closely resembles."

Moody worked hard to develop his own literary voice. As a neophyte novelist, "I had this idea that the language had to be pretty restrained or nobody was ever going to publish the books," Moody told Goldstein. "I mean, it was just that simple. But I wasn't yet confident enough about the receptivity of the literary community to really let my voice drift into a more natural albeit slightly more hysterical kind of line length. And then somewhere in the middle of writing [*The Ring of Brightest Angels around Heaven*] I just sort of hit . . . I landed on the vein, in a way. And I suddenly realized that it was okay for me to write these long, torrid sentences and that people would still read the work and many people would be really excited by it." Moody added that his goal as a writer is "to make the language express the great variety of human consciousness and how sort of multifarious consciousness is, but hopefully without ever being too abstract."

BIOGRAPHICAL AND CRITICAL SOURCES:

BOOKS

Contemporary Novelists, 7th edition, St. James Press (Detroit, MI), 2001.

PERIODICALS

Book, January, 2001, Don McLeese, review of *Demonology,* p. 79.

Booklist, April 1, 1994, p. 1424; March 15, 1997, p. 1227; June 1, 2000, Joanne Wilkinson, review of *Purple America,* p. 1850.

Detroit Free Press, May 25, 1997.

Economist, June 18, 1994, p. 98.

Entertainment Weekly, April 25, 1997, p. 64.

Esquire, April, 1997, p. 50; February, 2001, review of *Demonology,* p. 38.

Harper's Bazaar, February, 2001, Melanie Rehak, "Suburban Legend," p. 166.

Kirkus Reviews, March 1, 1994, p. 239; April 1, 2002, review of *The Black Veil: A Memoir with Digressions,* p. 473; July 1, 2005, review of *The Diviners,* p. 705.

Los Angeles Times Book Review, August 7, 1994, p. 15; August 20, 1995, p. 3.

Mother Jones, January, 2001, Ben Ehrenreich, review of *Demonology,* p. 77.

New Criterion, February, 2001, Max Watman, review of *Demonology,* p. 76.

New Jersey Star Ledger, September 26, 1997.

New Statesman, January 21, 2002, Alex Gibbons, review of *Demonology,* p. 56.

New York Times Book Review, August 20, 1995, p. 7.

New Yorker, Septermber 26, 2005, review of *The Diviners,* p. 147.

O, The Oprah Magazine September, 2005, reveiw of *The Diviners,* p. 180.

Observer, July 31, 1994, p. 20.

People, August 22, 1994, p. 24.

Publishers Weekly, March 31, 1997, p. 46; December, 11, 2000, review of *Demonology,* p. 64; March 18, 2002, review of *The Black Veil: A Memoir with Digressions,* p. 86.

Review of Contemporary Fiction, spring, 2001, Amy Havel, review of *Demonology,* p. 189.

San Francisco Review of Books, July/August, 1995, pp. 4-5.

Time, May 30, 1994, p. 65; April 14, 1997, p. 89.

Times Literary Supplement, August 5, 1994, p. 18.

Tribune Books (Chicago, IL), May 29, 1994, p. 5; July 16, 1995, p. 8.

Village Voice, October 17, 1995, p. 75.

ONLINE

Bookreporter.com, http://www.bookreporter.com/ (April 23, 2002), Joe Hartlaub, review of *Demonology.*

New York Times Web site, http://www.nytimes.com/ (April 23, 2002), Bill Goldstein, transcript of interview with Rick Moody.

MOORCOCK, Michael 1939-
(Bill Barclay, William Ewert Barclay, Michael Barrington, Edward P. Bradbury, James Colvin, Philip James, a joint pseudonym, Michael John Moorcock, Desmond Reid, a house pseudonym)

PERSONAL: Born December 18, 1939, in Mitcham, Surrey, England; son of Arthur Edward and June (Taylor) Moorcock; married Hilary Denham Bailey (a writer), October 25, 1962 (divorced, April, 1978); married Jill Riches, May 7, 1978 (divorced, 1983); married Linda Mullens Steele, September 23, 1983; children: (first marriage) Sophie, Katherine, Max. *Education:* Michael Hall, Sussex, Pitman's College, Croydon, Surrey, England.

ADDRESSES: Home—P.O. Box 1230, Bastrop, TX 78602. *Agent*—Howard Morhaim, Howard Morhaim Literary Agency, 841 Broadway, Ste. 604, New York, NY 10003.

CAREER: Writer. Has also worked as a singer-guitarist. *Tarzan Adventures* (juvenile magazine), editor, 1956-58; Amalgamated Press, London, England, editor and writer for the *Sexton Blake Library* and for comic strips and children's annuals, 1959-61; Liberal Party, editor and pamphleteer, 1962; *New Worlds* (science fiction magazine), London, England, editor and publisher, 1964—; worked with rock and roll bands Hawkwind and Blue Oyster Cult; member of rock and roll band Michael Moorcock and the Deep Fix.

MEMBER: Authors Guild, Society of Authors, Royal Overseas League, Amnesty International, Southern Poverty Law Center, Fawcett Society.

AWARDS, HONORS: Nebula Award, Science Fiction Writers of America, 1967, for *Behold the Man;* British Science Fiction Association award and Arts Council of Great Britain award, both 1967, both for *New Worlds;* August Derleth awards, British Fantasy Society (London, England), 1972, for *The Knight of the Swords,* 1973, for *The King of the Swords,* 1974, for *The Jade Man's Eyes,* 1975, for *The Sword and the Stallion,* 1976, for *The Hollow Lands, Legends from the End of Time,* and *The Sailor on the Seas of Fate,* 1977, for *The Weird of the White Wolf,* 1978, for *Gloriana; or, The Unfulfill'd Queen,* 1979, for *The Golden Barge,* 1981, for *The Entropy Tango,* 1985, for *The Chronicles of Castle Brass,* 1986, for *The Dragon in the Sword,* 1987, for *Wizardry and Wild Romance,* and 1988, for *Fan-*

tasy; International Fantasy awards, 1972 and 1973, for fantasy novels; *Guardian* Literary Prize, 1977, for *The Condition of Muzak;* John W. Campbell Memorial Award, 1978, and World Fantasy Award, World Fantasy Convention, 1979, both for *Gloriana; or, The Unfulfill'd Queen;* Bram Stoker Award, Horror Writers Association, 2004, for lifetime achievement.

WRITINGS:

(With James Cawthorn, under house pseudonym Desmond Reid) *Caribbean Crisis,* Sexton Blake Library (London, England), 1962.

The Sundered Worlds, Compact Books (London, England), 1965, published as *The Blood Red Game,* Sphere Books (London, England), 1970.

The Fireclown, Compact Books (London, England), 1965, published as *The Winds of Limbo,* Sphere Books (London, England), 1970.

(Under pseudonym James Colvin) *The Deep Fix,* Compact Books (London, England), 1966.

The Wrecks of Time (bound with *Tramontane* by Emil Petaja), Ace Books (New York, NY), 1966, revised edition published as *The Rituals of Infinity,* Arrow Books (London, England), 1971.

The Twilight Man, Compact Books (London, England), 1966, Berkley Publishing (New York, NY), 1970, published as *The Shores of Death,* Sphere Books (London, England), 1970.

The Ice Schooner, Sphere Books (London, England), 1968, Berkley Publishing (New York, NY), 1969, revised edition, Harrap (London, England), 1985.

Behold the Man, Allison & Busby (London, England), 1969.

(With wife Hilary Bailey) *The Black Corridor,* Ace Books (New York, NY), 1969.

The Time Dweller, Hart-Davis (London, England), 1969, Berkley Publishing (New York, NY), 1971.

(With James Cawthorn, under joint pseudonym Philip James) *The Distant Suns,* Unicorn Bookshop (London, England), 1975.

Moorcock's Book of Martyrs, Quartet Books (London, England), 1976, published as *Dying for Tomorrow,* DAW Books (New York, NY), 1978.

Sojan (juvenile), Savoy Books (Manchester, England), 1977.

Epic Pooh, British Fantasy Society (London, England), 1978.

Gloriana; or The Unfulfill'd Queen, Allison & Busby (London, England), 1978, Avon (New York, NY), 1979.

The Real Life Mr. Newman, A.J. Callow, 1979.

The Golden Barge, DAW Books (New York, NY), 1980.

My Experiences in the Third World War, Savoy Books (Manchester, England), 1980.

The Retreat from Liberty: The Erosion of Democracy in Today's Britain, Zomba Books (London, England), 1983.

(With others) *Exploring Fantasy Worlds: Essays on Fantastic Literature,* edited by Darrell Schweitzer, Borgo, 1985.

Letters from Hollywood, Harrap (London, England), 1986.

(With James Cawthorn) *Fantasy: The One Hundred Best Books,* Carroll & Graf (New York, NY), 1988.

Mother London, Harmony (New York, NY), 1989.

Wizardry and Wild Romance: A Study of Heroic Fantasy, Gollancz (London, England), 1989.

Casablanca, Gollancz (London, England), 1989.

Tales from the Texas Woods, Mojo Press, 1997.

Sailing to Utopia, illustrated by Rick Berry, White Wolf (Stone Mountain, GA), 1997.

King of the City, Scribner (New York, NY), 2000.

(With Storm Constantine) *Silverheart,* Simon & Schuster (London, England), 2000.

London Bone (short stories), Scribner (New York, NY), 2001.

(With China Mieville, Paul de Fillipo, and Geoff Ryman) *Cities,* Gollancz (London, England), 2003.

Contributor, sometimes under pseudonyms William Ewert Barclay and Michael Barrington, among others, to *Guardian, Punch, Ambit,* London *Times,* and other publications. Contributor to anthologies, including *The Road to Science Fiction 5: The British Way* and *Year's Best SF 3.*

Many of Moorcock's novels have provided the story for graphic novels, including *Stormbringer, The Jewell in the Skull,* and *The Crystal and the Amulet,* which were adapted and drawn by James Cawthorn. Writer of comic strips in early 1960s and of the DC comic *Michael Moorcock's Multiverse,* 1-12, 1997—.

"NICK ALLARD/JERRY CORNELL" SERIES

(Under pseudonym Bill Barclay) *Printer's Devil,* Compact Books (London, England), 1966, published under name Michael Moorcock as *The Russian Intelligence,* Savoy Books (Manchester, England), 1980.

(Under pseudonym Bill Barclay) *Somewhere in the Night,* Compact Books (London, England), 1966, revised edition published under name Michael

Moorcock as *The Chinese Agent,* Macmillan (New York, NY), 1970.

(Ghostwriter) Roger Harris, *The LSD Dossier,* Compact Books (London, England), 1966.

"ELRIC" SERIES; "ETERNAL CHAMPION" BOOKS

The Stealer of Souls, and Other Stories (also see below), Neville Spearman (London, England), 1963, Lancer Books (New York, NY), 1967.

Stormbringer, Jenkins (England), 1965, Lancer Books (New York, NY), 1967.

The Singing Citadel (also see below), Berkley Publishing (New York, NY), 1970.

The Sleeping Sorceress, New English Library (London, England), 1971, Lancer Books (New York, NY), 1972, published as *The Vanishing Tower,* DAW Books (New York, NY), 1977.

The Dreaming City, Lancer Books (New York, NY), 1972, revised edition published as *Elric of Melnibone,* Hutchinson (London, England), 1972.

The Jade Man's Eyes, Unicorn Bookshop (London, England), 1973.

Elric: The Return to Melnibone, Unicorn Bookshop (London, England), 1973.

The Sailor on the Seas of Fate, DAW Books (New York, NY), 1976.

The Bane of the Black Sword, DAW Books (New York, NY), 1977.

The Weird of the White Wolf (contains some material from *The Stealer of Souls, and Other Stories* and *The Singing Citadel*), DAW Books (New York, NY), 1977.

Elric at the End of Time, DAW Books (New York, NY), 1985.

The Fortress of the Pearl, Ace Books (New York, NY), 1989.

The Revenge of the Rose, Ace Books (New York, NY), 1991.

"ALBINO" SEQUENCE; "ELRIC" SERIES

The Dreamthief's Daughter: A Tale of the Albino, Warner Books (New York, NY), 2001.

The Skrayling Tree: The Albino in America, Warner Books (New York, NY), 2003.

The White Wolf's Son: The Albino Underground, Warner Books (New York, NY), 2005.

"VON BEK FAMILY" SERIES

The War Hound and the World's Pain, Timescape, 1981.

The Brothel in Rosenstrasse, New English Library (London, England), 1982, Tigerseye Press, 1986.

The City in the Autumn Stars, Ace Books (New York, NY), 1986.

Lunching with the Antichrist: A Family History: 1925-2015 (short stories), Ziesing, 1995.

Von Bek, White Wolf (Stone Mountain, GA), 1995.

"MICHAEL KANE" SERIES; UNDER PSEUDONYM EDWARD P. BRADBURY

Warriors of Mars (also see below), Compact Books (London, England), 1965, published under name Michael Moorcock as *The City of the Beast,* Lancer Books (New York, NY), 1970.

Blades of Mars (also see below), Compact Books (London, England), 1965, published under name Michael Moorcock as *The Lord of the Spiders,* Lancer Books (New York, NY), 1971.

The Barbarians of Mars (also see below), Compact Books (London, England), 1965, published under name Michael Moorcock as *The Masters of the Pit,* Lancer Books (New York, NY), 1971.

Warrior of Mars (contains *Warriors of Mars, Blades of Mars,* and *The Barbarians of Mars*), New English Library (London, England), 1981.

Kane of Old Mars, White Wolf (Stone Mountain, GA), 1998.

"THE HISTORY OF THE RUNESTAFF" SERIES; "ETERNAL CHAMPION" BOOKS

The Jewel in the Skull (also see below), Lancer Books (New York, NY), 1967.

Sorcerer's Amulet (also see below), Lancer Books (New York, NY), 1968, published as *The Mad God's Amulet,* Mayflower Books (London, England), 1969.

Sword of the Dawn (also see below), Lancer Books (New York, NY), 1968.

The Secret of the Runestaff (also see below), Lancer Books (New York, NY), 1969, published as *The Runestaff,* Mayflower Books (London, England), 1969.

The History of the Runestaff (contains *The Jewel in the Skull, Sorcerer's Amulet, Sword of the Dawn,* and *The Secret of the Runestaff*), Granada (London, England), 1979.

Hawkmoon, White Wolf (Stone Mountain, GA), 1995.

"JERRY CORNELIUS" SERIES

The Final Programme (also see below), Avon (New York, NY), 1968, revised edition, Allison & Busby (London, England), 1969.

A Cure for Cancer (also see below), Holt (New York, NY), 1971.
The English Assassin (also see below), Allison & Busby (London, England), 1972.
The Lives and Times of Jerry Cornelius (also see below), Allison & Busby (London, England), 1976.
The Adventures of Una Persson and Catherine Cornelius in the Twentieth Century (also see below), Quartet Books (London, England), 1976.
The Condition of Muzak (also see below), Allison & Busby (London, England), 1977, Gregg (New York, NY), 1978.
The Cornelius Chronicles (contains *The Final Programme, A Cure for Cancer, The English Assassin,* and *The Condition of Muzak*), Avon (New York, NY), 1977.
The Great Rock 'n' Roll Swindle, Virgin Books (London, England), 1980.
The Entropy Tango (also see below), New English Library (London, England), 1981.
The Opium General (also see below), Harrap (London, England), 1985.
The Cornelius Chronicles, Volume 2 (contains *The Lives and Times of Jerry Cornelius* and *The Entropy Tango*), Avon (New York, NY), 1986.
The Cornelius Chronicles, Volume 3 (contains *The Adventures of Una Persson and Catherine Cornelius in the Twentieth Century* and *The Opium General*), Avon (New York, NY), 1987.
The Cornelius Quartet, Phoenix House (London, England), 1993, Four Walls Eight Windows (New York, NY), 2001.
A Cornelius Calendar, Phoenix House (London, England), 1993.
Firing the Cathedral, PS Publishing (Harrogate, England), 2002.

"KARL GLOGAUER" SERIES

Behold the Man, Allison & Busby (London, England), 1969, Avon (New York, NY), 1970.
Breakfast in the Ruins: A Novel of Inhumanity, New English Library (London, England), 1972, Random House (New York, NY), 1974.

"CORUM" SERIES; "ETERNAL CHAMPION" BOOKS

The Knight of the Swords (also see below), Mayflower Books (London, England), 1970, Berkley Publishing (New York, NY), 1971.
The Queen of the Swords (also see below), Berkley Publishing (New York, NY), 1971.
The King of the Swords (also see below), Berkley Publishing (New York, NY), 1971.
The Bull and the Spear (also see below), Berkley Publishing (New York, NY), 1973.
The Oak and the Ram (also see below), Berkley Publishing (New York, NY), 1973.
The Sword and the Stallion (also see below), Berkley Publishing (New York, NY), 1974.
The Swords Trilogy (contains *The Knight of the Swords, The Queen of the Swords,* and *The King of the Swords*), Berkley Publishing (New York, NY), 1977.
The Chronicles of Corum (contains *The Bull and the Spear, The Oak and the Ram,* and *The Sword and the Stallion*), Berkley Publishing (New York, NY), 1978, published as *The Prince with the Silver Hand,* Millennium Books, 1993.

"JOHN DAKER" SERIES; "ETERNAL CHAMPION" BOOKS

The Eternal Champion, Dell (New York, NY), 1970, revised edition, Harper (New York, NY), 1978.
Phoenix in Obsidian, Mayflower Books (London, England), 1970, published as *The Silver Warriors,* Dell (New York, NY), 1973.
The Dragon in the Sword, Granada (London, England), 1986.

"OSWALD BASTABLE" SERIES

The Warlord of the Air (also see below), Ace Books (New York, NY), 1971.
The Land Leviathan (also see below), Quartet Books (London, England), 1974.
The Steel Tsar (also see below), DAW Books (New York, NY), 1983.
The Nomad of Time (contains *The Warlord of the Air, The Land Leviathan,* and *The Steel Tsar*), Granada (London, England), 1984.

"THE DANCERS AT THE END OF TIME" SERIES

An Alien Heat (also see below), Harper (New York, NY), 1972.
The Hollow Lands (also see below), Harper (New York, NY), 1974.
The End of All Songs (also see below), Harper (New York, NY), 1976.
Legends from the End of Time, Harper (New York, NY), 1976.

The Transformations of Miss Mavis Ming, W.H. Allen (London, England), 1977, published as *A Messiah at the End of Time,* DAW Books (New York, NY), 1978.

The Dancers at the End of Time (contains *An Alien Heat, The Hollow Lands,* and *The End of All Songs*), Granada (London, England), 1981.

"COUNT BRASS" SERIES; "ETERNAL CHAMPION" BOOKS

Count Brass (also see below), Mayflower Books (London, England), 1973.

The Champion of Garathorm (also see below), Mayflower Books (London, England), 1973.

The Quest for Tanelorn (also see below), Mayflower Books (London, England), 1975, Dell (New York, NY), 1976.

The Chronicles of Castle Brass (contains *Count Brass, The Champion of Garathorm,* and *The Quest for Tanelorn*), Granada (London, England), 1985.

"BETWEEN THE WARS" SERIES

Byzantium Endures, Secker & Warburg (London, England), 1981, Random House (New York, NY), 1982.

The Laughter of Carthage, Random House (New York, NY), 1984.

Jerusalem Commands, Jonathan Cape (London, England), 1992.

Jerusalem Commands, Jonathan Cape (London, England), 1992.

The Vengeance of Rome, Jonathan Cape (London, England), 2006.

"SECOND ETHER" SERIES

Blood: A Southern Fantasy, William Morrow (New York, NY), 1994.

Fabulous Harbors, Avon (New York, NY), 1995.

The War amongst the Angels, Avon (New York, NY), 1996.

SCREENPLAYS

The Final Programme (based on his novel of the same title; removed name from credits after dispute with director), EMI, 1973.

The Land That Time Forgot, British Lion, 1975.

EDITOR

(And contributor, under name Michael Moorcock and under pseudonym James Colvin) *The Best of "New Worlds,"* Compact Books (London, England), 1965.

Best SF Stories from "New Worlds," Panther Books (London, England), 1967, Berkley Publishing (New York, NY), 1968.

The Traps of Time, Rapp & Whiting (London, England), 1968.

(And contributor, under pseudonym James Colvin) *The Best SF Stories from "New Worlds" 2,* Panther Books (London, England), 1968, Berkley Publishing (New York, NY), 1969.

(And contributor, under pseudonym James Colvin) *The Best SF Stories from "New Worlds" 3,* Panther Books (London, England), 1968, Berkley Publishing (New York, NY), 1969.

The Best SF Stories from "New Worlds" 4, Panther Books (London, England), 1969, Berkley Publishing (New York, NY), 1971.

The Best SF Stories from "New Worlds" 5, Panther Books (London, England), 1969, Berkley Publishing (New York, NY), 1971.

(And contributor) *The Best SF Stories from "New Worlds" 6,* Panther Books (London, England), 1970, Berkley Publishing (New York, NY), 1971.

The Best SF Stories from "New Worlds" 7, Panther Books (London, England), 1971.

New Worlds Quarterly 1, Berkley Publishing (New York, NY), 1971.

New Worlds Quarterly 2, Berkley Publishing (New York, NY), 1971.

New Worlds Quarterly 3, Sphere Books (London, England), 1971.

(With Langdon Jones and contributor) *The Nature of the Catastrophe,* Hutchinson (London, England), 1971.

New Worlds Quarterly 4, Berkley Publishing (New York, NY), 1972.

New Worlds Quarterly 5, Sphere Books (London, England), 1973.

New Worlds Quarterly 6, Avon (New York, NY), 1973.

Before Armageddon: An Anthology of Victorian and Edwardian Imaginative Fiction Published before 1914, W.H. Allen (London, England), 1975.

England Invaded: A Collection of Fantasy Fiction, Ultramarine (Hastings-on-Hudson, NY), 1977.

New Worlds: An Anthology, Fontana (London, England), 1983.

H.G. Wells, *The Time Machine,* Tuttle (Boston, MA), 1993.

(With Michael Butterworth) *Queens of Deliria,* Collector's Guide, 1995.

RECORDINGS; UNDER NAME "MICHAEL MOORCOCK AND THE DEEP FIX"

The New Worlds Fair, United Artists, 1975.
Dodgem Dude/Starcruiser (single), Flicknife, 1980.
The Brothel in Rosenstrasse/Time Centre (single), Flicknife, 1982.
(With others) *Hawkwind Friends and Relations,* Flicknife, 1982.
(With others) *Hawkwind & Co.,* Flicknife, 1983.

Also composer of songs recorded by others, including *Sonic Attack, The Black Corridor, The Wizard Blew His Horn, Standing at the Edge, Warriors, Kings of Speed, Warrior at the End of Time, Psychosonia, Coded Languages, Lost Chances, Choose Your Masks,* and *Arrival in Utopia,* all recorded by Hawkwind; *The Great Sun Jester, Black Blade,* and *Veteran of the Psychic Wars,* all recorded by Blue Oyster Cult.

ADAPTATIONS: The character Elric is featured in role-playing games from the Avalon Hill Game Company and from Chaosium, in comic books published by Pacific Comics, Dark Horse Comics, and by Star Reach Productions, and in miniature figures marketed by Citadel Miniatures; the character Oswald Bastable is featured in a computer game.

WORK IN PROGRESS: Love, a memoir of Mervyn and Maeve Peake; a graphic novel about Elric's early life and training as a sorcerer; a book about Heaven's Gate for the British Film Institute.

SIDELIGHTS: Michael Moorcock was associated with the New Wave, an avant-garde science fiction movement of the 1960s, which introduced a wider range of subject matter and style to the science fiction field. As editor of *New Worlds,* the most prominent of the New Wave publications, Moorcock promotes the movement and provides a showcase for its writing.

The New Wave, wrote Donald A. Wollheim in *The Universe Makers,* was an "effort to merge science fiction into the mainstream of literature . . . The charges brought against old line science fiction were on the basis of both structure and content. Structurally, the charge was made that too much of the writing retained the flavor of the pulps [and] that science fiction writers were not keeping up with the experimental avant-garde. . . . Internally, the charge was made that science fiction actually was dead—because the future was no longer credible. The crises of the twentieth century . . . were obviously insurmountable. We would all never make it into the twenty-first century." In response to Wollheim's comments, Moorcock told *CA* that this conclusion missed the point, for he and his fellow writers "loved the present" and were not, in fact, completely disillusioned with the future. In an interview with Ian Covell of *Science Fiction Review,* Moorcock said of the New Wave: "We were a generation of writers who had no nostalgic love of the pulp magazines, who had come to SF as a possible alternative to mainstream literature and had taken SF seriously. . . . We were trying to find a viable literature for our time. A literature which took account of science, of modern social trends, and which was written not according to genre conventions but according to the personal requirements of the individuals who produced it."

Moorcock has written science fiction adventures in the style of Edgar Rice Burroughs's Mars novels, sword-and-sorcery novels, comic and satirical science fiction, and time-travel science fiction. Some of Moorcock's fantasy novels have earned him major genre awards and an exalted position among fans. Tom Hutchinson in the London *Times,* for example, called Moorcock's sword-and-sorcery novel, *The Chronicles of Castle Brass,* "a masterpiece of modern high fantasy."

Despite their continuing popularity, some of these books, Moorcock admits, were written for the money. *New Worlds* was an influential magazine in the science fiction field, but it was never a financial success. When creditors needed to be paid it was Moorcock, as editor and publisher, who was held responsible. He was often forced to write a quick novel to pay the bills. Charles Platt recounted in his *Dream Makers: The Uncommon People Who Write Science Fiction,* that "it was not unusual for the magazine's staff to be found cowering on the floor with the lights out, pretending not to be home, while some creditor rang the bell and called hopefully through the mail slot in the front door—to no avail."

The genre books that brought Moorcock to critical attention, and those that he considers among his most important, combine standard science fiction trappings with experimental narrative structures. *Breakfast in the Ruins: A Novel of Inhumanity,* for instance, contains a number of historical vignettes featuring the protagonist Karl Glogauer. In each of these, Karl is a different person in a different time, participating in such examples of political violence as the French Revolution, the Paris Commune, a Nazi concentration camp, and a My Lai-style massacre. Interwoven with these vignettes is a homosexual love scene, involving Karl and a black Nigerian, that takes on a mystical connotation as the two lovers seem to merge into each other's identities. Helen Rogan of *Time* described the book as "by turns puzzling, funny, and shocking," and Moorcock as "both bizarrely inventive and highly disciplined." Writing in the *New York Times Book Review,* John Deck called the book "a dazzling historical fantasy."

In the books and stories featuring Jerry Cornelius, Moorcock has experimented with character as well as with narrative structure. Cornelius has no consistent character or appearance. He is, as Nick Totton wrote in *Spectator,* "a nomad of the territories of personality; even his skin color and gender are as labile as his accomplishments." Cornelius's world is just as flexible, containing a multitude of alternative histories, all contradictory, and peopled with characters who die and resurrect as a matter of course. Within this mutable landscape, Cornelius travels from one inconclusive adventure to another, trapped in an endless existence. As Colin Greenland maintained in the *Dictionary of Literary Biography,* Cornelius is "an entirely new kind of fictional character, a dubious hero whose significance is always oblique and rarely stable, equipped to tackle all the challenges of his time yet unable to find a satisfactory solution to any of them."

The Condition of Muzak, completing the initial Jerry Cornelius tetralogy, won the *Guardian* Literary Prize in 1977, bringing Moorcock added praise from the literary world. At the time of the award, W.L. Webb of the *Guardian* wrote, "Michael Moorcock, rejecting the demarcation disputes that have reduced the novel to a muddle of warring sub-genres, recovers in these four books a protean vitality and inclusiveness that one might call Dickensian if their consciousness were not so entirely of our own volatile times." Moorcock, according to Angus Wilson in the *Washington Post Book World,* "is emerging as one of the most serious literary lights of our time. . . . For me his Jerry Cornelius quartet [of novels] assured the durability of his reputation." Ralph Willett, writing in *Science-Fiction Studies,* claimed that during the late 1960s and early 1970s, Moorcock became "that rare phenomenon, the popular novelist whose work has also become a cult among the young and the avant-garde." Willett compared Moorcock to experimental novelist William Burroughs, "especially with respect to the Jerry Cornelius books . . . Moorcock lacks William Burroughs's accurate and devastating satire, and his verbal experiments have been less radical, but in both artists can be observed a basic dissatisfaction with linear methods of representing space and time, a surreal sense of co-existing multiple worlds, and an emphasis on apocalyptic disaster."

After almost a decade-long rest, Moorcock brought back Jerry Cornelius in 2002 in *Firing the Cathedral.* In *Firing the Cathedral,* Cornelius responds to the September, 2001, terrorist attacks on America and their consequences, the realities of global warming, and other apocalyptic events. Patrick Hudson, writing for *The Zone,* stated that the new Cornelius book "finds Moorcock and Cornelius in fine form." He continued, "There's plenty for them to do in the post September 11th world of the war on terrorism, and once more life is cheap and weapons plentiful. Moorcock makes artful use of clippings from the last eighteen months . . . and bits and bobs from the archive throw the broad satirical sweeps into sharp relief."

Moorcock's literary standing was substantially enhanced with the publication of *Byzantium Endures* and *The Laughter of Carthage.* These two novels are the closest Moorcock came to conventional literary fiction, being the purported autobiography of Russian emigré, Colonel Pyat. Pyat was born on January 1, 1900, and the story of his life becomes a history of the twentieth century. Pyat survives the Russian revolution, travels throughout Europe and America, and participates in a number of important historical events. But he is a megalomaniac who imagines himself to be both a great inventor, the equal of Thomas Edison, and a major figure on the stage of world history. He is also an anti-Semite who sees true Christianity, as embodied in the Russian Orthodox Church, as engaged in a battle against the Jews, Orientals, Bolsheviks, and other destroyers of order. He likens Western Christianity to Byzantium, his enemies to Carthage. Naturally, Pyat's account of his life is self-aggrandizing and inaccurate.

Byzantium Endures focuses on the first twenty years of Pyat's life, telling of his opportunistic role in the Russian revolution. Pyat survives the upheaval of the revolution and the subsequent civil war by working first for one side and then another. As Frederic Morton wrote in the *New York Times Book Review,* his mechanical skills are put to good use "repairing the rifles of anarchist guerrillas, fixing the treads of White Army tanks [and] doctoring the engine in one of Trotsky's armed trains." Pyat claims to have invented the laser gun on behalf of Ukrainian nationalists fighting against the Red Army, but when the electrical power failed, so did his gun. "Pyat's self-serving recollections," Bart Mills stated in the *Los Angeles Times Book Review,* "contain a vivid picture of the events of 1917-1920, down to menus, street names and the color of people's moustaches." The novel, wrote Robert Onopa in the *Chicago Tribune Book World,* is "utterly engrossing as narrative, historically pertinent, and told through characters so alive and detail so dense that it puts to shame all but a few writers who have been doing this kind of work all along."

The Laughter of Carthage covers Pyat's life from 1920 to 1924, detailing his escape from Communist Russia and subsequent travels in Europe and America. His activities are sometimes unlawful, requiring him to change his residence and name frequently. He meets everyone from Dylan Thomas to Tom Mix and lives everywhere from Constantinople to Hollywood. Because of the scope of Pyat's adventures, *The Laughter of Carthage* is a sweeping picture of the world during the 1920s. "Moorcock provides an exotic itinerary, a robust cast of opportunists and scoundrels, and a series of dangerous adventures and sexual escapades," noted R.Z. Sheppard of *Time.* "This is epic writing," praised Valentine Cunningham in the *Times Literary Supplement,* adding, "As [D. W.] Griffith stuffed his movies with vast throngs and Promethean matter so Pyat's narration feeds hugely on the numerous people he claims to have met, the history he makes believe he has helped to shape, the many places his traveller's tales take him to."

Pyat's narration, because it is colored by his eccentric, offensive views and his distorted sense of self-importance, gives a fantastic sheen to the familiar historical events he relates. "This is Moorcock's achievement: he has rewritten modern history by seeing it in the distorting mirror of one man's perceptions so that the novel has the imaginative grasp of fantasy while remaining solidly based upon recognizable facts," Peter Ackroyd wrote in the London *Times.* "Moorcock has here created a fiction," Nigel Andrew said in the same paper, "that is seething with detailed life at every level—in the headlong narrative, in the bravura passages of scene-setting description, and, particularly, in the rendering of Pyat's vision of the world." Although Richard Eder of the *Los Angeles Times* found Pyat's narrative to be an "extremely long-winded unpleasantness" because of his political views, the *New York Times Book Review*'s Thaddeus Rutkowski forgave the "sometimes tedious" nature of Pyat's narration. "Most often," he found, "Pyat's tirades are beguiling. They are the pronouncements of a singularly innocent intelligence gone awry."

Moorcock continued Pyat's story with the publication of *Jerusalem Commands.* In it, he recounts Pyat's life between the years of 1924 and 1929, in which he lives as minor celebrity Max Peters in Hollywood. "Moorcock's powers of description—especially when focused on the sights and smells of megalopoli—and his range of references are immense," remarked Mark Sanderson in the *Times Literary Supplement.* However, Sanderson noted, "Like Thomas Pynchon he can simultaneously be highly impressive and deeply boring. But his main achievement in this tetralogy . . . is to force the reader to afford the luckiest bastard in the whole damn universe (Colonel Pyat) a grudging respect. Even a little affection too." Julian Symons, a newcomer to the Colonel Pyat trilogy, found him less than enchanting. Writing for the *London Review of Books,* he said in a commentary on the length of Pyat's memoirs that "Michael Moorcock's purpose, I suppose, was to offer a picaresque view of history in the first half of this century as seen by a man, by no means a hero, shuttled from country to country. It's a pity he chose a narrator suffering from logorrhea."

In *Blood: A Southern Fantasy,* Moorcock returns to the New Wave style of his early writings. Tim Sullivan in the *Washington Post Book World* hailed the return, saying that "the New Wave style is so old it seems new again, adding a certain freshness to the mix." *Blood,* according to David V. Barrett in *New Statesman & Society,* "is both a fantasy and a literary novel" in which the characters (persons of color in a New South where Anglos are in the minority) are gamblers playing games that draw them into other realities. Moorcock borrows previous themes and elements of his earlier stories to create what he terms a "multiverse." In *World Literature Today* Carter Kaplan wrote, "His language is a post-poststructuralist pidgin of Christian humanism, New Age metaphysics, and pulp science fiction that increases in profundity as it becomes more ridiculous. *Blood* translates meaninglessness into epiphany."

Lunching with the Antichrist: A Family History: 1925-2015 is a collection of Moorcock's short stories from his Von Bek family series. The various members of the Von Beks display Moorcock's concept of the "Seeker"—they are characters who spend their time pursuing meaning in their lives. The collection, noted Gerald Jonas in the *New York Times Book Review,* "satisfies the same high standards that [Moorcock] espoused as an editor." Roland Green in *Booklist* hailed Moorcock as "a master of his craft."

Moorcock combines mainstream fiction with a bit of fantasy in *The Brothel of Rosenstrasse,* a novel set in the imaginary city of Mirenburg. The city's brothel is the center of social life, as well as a "microcosm of *fin de siecle* Central Europe; hedonistic, decadent, deluded, and heedless of an inevitable future," as Elaine Kendall wrote in the *Los Angeles Times.* Narrated by an aging hedonist who relates the story of his long and dissipated life, the novel follows a handful of decadent characters to their eventual destruction during the bombardment of Mirenburg. Suffering makes the characters finally come alive in a way they have never been before. "They begin to engage our full attention," Kendall concluded, "and earn not only our sympathy but in some cases, our respect. By then it's too late; Mirenburg and all the good and evil it represented has vanished forever. If there's no parable here, surely there's a moral."

In *Mother London,* Moorcock presents a "complex, layered history of London since the war, seen through the stories of a group of psychiatric patients," explained Brian Applecart in the London *Times.* The novel earned high praise from several critics. Nigel Andrew of the *Listener* called *Mother London* "a prodigious work of imaginative archaeology . . . [in which Moorcock] displays the generosity of spirit, the sweep and sheer gusto of Dickens." Similarly, Gregory Feeler in the *Washington Post Book World* stated that *Mother London* "often indulges its author's crotchets and biases, [but] it also proves warm and humane, often surprisingly funny, and moving in a way Moorcock has never before succeeded in being." "If," wrote Andrew, "this wonderful book does not finally convince the world that [Moorcock] is in fact one of our very best novelists and a national treasure, then there is no justice."

Moorcock composed two more variations of the London theme with *King of the City* and *London Bone. King of the City* follows the life of Denny Dover, from his post-World War II childhood to his exploits as a paparazzo in the '80s and '90s. John Coulthart from *The Edge* wrote, "Art, culture and politics all blend together in a heady, gumbo-like brew. Like the novelists of old, this book has an epic sweep . . . and seeking to encompass all that's worth communicating. . . . While others are concerned with literary games Moorcock's concern is with writing great books." *London Bone* is a collection of nine short stories that pursue ordinary characters whose lives take an extraordinary turn. Some of the stories are about the seedy side of the London tourist trade, Irish-Americans, and brave old ladies. Writing for *The Guardian,* Ian Penman commented that the UFO tales are really about love and family, "Family is the tie that binds these nine pieces together, rather than the nominal city." Penman also wrote that "Moorcock . . . remains a curiously old-fashioned visionary. Which is good, when it includes the 'old-fashioned' virtues of humane interest and the refusal to follow trend for trend's sake."

Moorcock's move from science fiction to mainstream fiction was welcomed by several critics. Observed Gregory Cent in the *Village Voice,* "It's wonderful to see Moorcock grow from a genre writer into, simply, a writer. . . . A mainstream novel gives him far more scope to nourish the obsessions (and also the passion, zaniness, and eye for detail) that made his science fiction both fun and worthwhile." Moorcock, Andrew said, "has had to come the long way to literary recognition. But now, with *The Laughter of Carthage,* he can surely no longer be denied his due; this enormous book—with its forerunner, *Byzantium Endures*—must establish him in the front rank of practising English novelists."

Evaluations of Moorcock's career often emphasize the sheer volume and variety of his work. "It is like trying to evaluate an industry," Philip Oakes noted in the London *Times Magazine.* Throughout his career, Moorcock has shown an impressive ability to write consistently well within a wide range of genres and styles. "I have read about half his prodigious output," Oakes wrote, "and on the strength of that sample Moorcock strikes me as the most prolific, probably the most inventive and without doubt the most egalitarian writer practicing today." Writing in the *Observer* of Moorcock's long career, John Clute described him as "a figure of revolutionary fervour in the British literary world for nearly thirty years." Wilson called Moorcock "one of the most exciting discoveries that I have been able to make in the contemporary English novel during the forty or so years that I have been publishing my own novels and reviewing those of my contemporaries. Exciting for myself and, as is becoming increasingly clear with the appearance of each Moorcock book, for a legion of other readers."

Moorcock moved to Texas in the mid-1990s. Mike Shea covered the 1998 San Antonio Science Fiction Conference, attended by Moorcock, and said that the author "was welcomed with open arms, and his most basic needs—a reasonable number of good bookstores and restaurants—were served. Still, he grumbles that Texas 'is, compared to London, a cultural wasteland. [But] I'm an old whore basically; I can adapt to anything.' He was intrigued by the voices of Texas fiction—literary and speculative—and the attention focused on Austin. He views contemporary Texas writers as myth builders who are 'creating a kind of fiction that is very much going to be characteristic fiction of the twenty-first century.'"

Moorcock brought together his characters Elric of Melnibone and Ulric von Bek in *The Dreamthief's Daughter: A Tale of the Albino,* which begins with the growing power of Hitler. A *Kirkus Reviews* contributor said that "the best arrives early on, during the rise of

Nazi Germany; thereafter, series fans will enjoy the warm familiarity of Elric's bloodthirsty adventures." "Fans of the series should enjoy this addition," wrote a *Publishers Weekly* reviewer. "A topnotch fantasy adventure," was *Library Journal* reviewer Jackie Cassada's comment. *Booklist* contributor Paula Luedtke opened her review of the book with "Moorcock stalwarts, rejoice! The Eternal Champion is back," and concluded by calling *The Dreamthief's Daughter* "quite a romp."

Moorcock talked about his life and work in an article on the *Time Warner Bookmark* Web site, where he said, "I have always been engaged with politics. Tom Paine's my hero. I'd like to help try to make the world a better place. That's why people who know my politics are a little surprised my books have so much to do with kings and princes. I do point out that my heroes, by and large, although doomed to perpetual struggle, tend to triumph over the supernatural and even, sometimes, their aristocratic backgrounds." Moorcock went on to say, "Reality isn't simple. Fiction can be simpler, can offer a relief from that complex world. But no matter how it entertains and distracts us, the best fiction, in my view, whether fantastic or naturalistic, acknowledges those realities. There's an urgent need for such realism. More than at any point in human history our planet's future is now very much in our own hands. I can't help feeling we'd be wise to embrace its complexity rather than pretend it doesn't exist."

Moorcock told *CA:* "Most of my work recently has been in terms of a moral and psychological investigation of Imperialism (Western and Eastern) seen in terms of fiction. Even my fantasy novels are inclined to deal with moral problems rather than magical ones. I'm turning more and more away from SF and fantasy and more towards a form of realism used in the context of what you might call an imaginative framework. Late Dickens would be the model I'd most like to emulate."

Writing in the *Contemporary Authors Autobiography Series,* Moorcock commented of the writing life: "The job of a novelist has its own momentum, its own demands, its own horrible power over the practitioner. When I look back I wonder what I got myself into all those years ago when I realised I had a facility to put words down on paper and have people give me money in return. For ages the whole business seemed ludicrous. I couldn't believe my luck. Frequently, I still can't but it seems an unnatural way of earning a living. Of course, it's no longer easy. It's often a struggle. It spoils my health. . . . I suppose it must be an addiction. I'm pretty sure, though I deny it heartily, that I could now no longer give it up. I'm as possessed as any fool I used to mock."

BIOGRAPHICAL AND CRITICAL SOURCES:

BOOKS

Authors and Artists for Young Adults, Thomson Gale (Detroit, MI), Volume 7, 1992, Volume 26, 1999.

Bilyeu, R., *Tanelorn Archives,* Pandora's Books, 1979.

Callow, A. J., compiler, *The Chronicles of Moorcock,* A.J. Callow, 1978.

Carter, Lin, *Imaginary Worlds,* Ballantine (New York, NY), 1973.

Contemporary Authors Autobiography Series, Volume 5, Thomson Gale (Detroit, MI), 1987.

Contemporary Literary Criticism, Thomson Gale (Detroit, MI), Volume 5, 1976, Volume 27, 1984, Volume 58, 1990.

Dictionary of Literary Biography, Volume 14: *British Novelists since 1960,* Thomson Gale (Detroit, MI), 1983.

Greenland, Colin, *The Entropy Exhibition: Michael Moorcock and the British "New Wave" in Science Fiction,* Routledge & Kegan Paul, 1983.

Harper, Andrew and George McAulay, *Michael Moorcock: A Bibliography,* T-K Graphics, 1976.

Platt, Charles, *Dream Makers: The Uncommon People Who Write Science Fiction,* Berkley Publishing (New York, NY), 1980.

Walker, Paul, editor, *Speaking of Science Fiction: The Paul Walker Interviews,* Luna Publications, 1978.

Wollheim, Donald A., *The Universe Makers,* Harper (New York, NY), 1971.

PERIODICALS

Amazing Stories, May, 1971.

Analog, February, 1970; March, 1990.

Booklist, November 1, 1991, p. 496; February 15, 1995, p. 1064; October 1, 1998, Ray Olson, review of *Behold the Man,* p. 293; March 15, 2001, Paula Luedtke, review of *The Dreamthief's Daughter: A Tale of the Albino,* p. 1361.

Books and Bookmen, June, 1971; September, 1971; October, 1972; May, 1974; August, 1978.

Chicago Tribune Book World, January 31, 1982.

Commonweal, August 1, 1975.

Detroit News, February 24, 1985.

Encounter, November, 1981.

Extrapolation, winter, 1989.

Guardian Weekly, April 10, 1969.

Harper's Bazaar (British edition), December, 1969.

Ink, August, 1971.

Kensington News, April 18, 1969.

Kensington Post, April 4, 1969.
Kirkus Reviews, October 1, 1995, p. 1387.
Library Journal, November 15, 1991, p. 111; April 15, 2001, Jackie Cassada, review of *The Dreamthief's Daughter,* p. 137.
Listener, June 23, 1988; January 18, 1990.
Locus, May, 1989; November, 1989; February, 1990; March, 1990; May, 1993, p. 21.
London Review of Books, September 10, 1992, p. 22.
Los Angeles Times, January 9, 1985; November 10, 1987.
Los Angeles Times Book Review, March 7, 1982; February 7, 1988.
Luna Monthly, November, 1975.
Magazine of Fantasy and Science Fiction, June, 1998, review of *The War amongst the Angels,* p. 39.
New Republic, June 15, 1974.
New Statesman, April 4, 1969; May 18, 1973; June 18, 1976; April 15, 1977.
New Statesman & Society, July 24, 1992, p. 38; January 13, 1995, p. 38.
New Worlds, March, 1969.
New York Times Book Review, April 5, 1970; May 19, 1974; April 25, 1976; February 21, 1982; February 10, 1985; November 23, 1986; March 12, 1995, p. 25.
Observer, April 4, 1976; April 3, 1977.
Publishers Weekly, January 16, 1995, p. 442; June 11, 1995, p. 30; October 30, 1995, p. 49; February 12, 2000, review of *The Dreamthief's Daughter,* p. 188.
Punch, January 16, 1985.
Rapport, Volume 9, number 2, p. 35.
Saturday Review, April 25, 1970.
Science Fiction Chronicle, May, 1998, review of *Kane of Old Mars,* p. 40, review of *The Prince with the Silver Hand,* p. 46.
Science Fiction Monthly, February, 1975.
Science Fiction Review, January, 1971; January, 1979.
Science-Fiction Studies, March, 1976.
Spectator, April 1, 1969; August 10, 1974; November 20, 1976; April 9, 1977; December 24, 1977; June 27, 1981; February 9, 1985.
Speculation, May, 1970; August, 1970.
Texas Monthly, July, 1998, Mike Shea, "Sci-Fi Fo Fum," p. 60.
Time, August 5, 1974; January 28, 1985.
Time Out, September 17, 1971.
Times (London, England), September 6, 1984; November 25, 1984; August 5, 1985; June 18, 1988.
Times Literary Supplement, October 27, 1972; November 9, 1973; May 31, 1974; May 7, 1976; June 30, 1978; July 3, 1981; September 7, 1984; July 1, 1988; February 23, 1990; July 10, 1992, p. 22.
Times Magazine (London, England), November 5, 1978.
Tribune Books (Chicago, IL), March 26, 1989.
Village Voice, March 2, 1982.
Virginia Quarterly Review, spring, 1975.
Washington Post Book World, March 21, 1982; December 23, 1984; September 28, 1986; May 14, 1989; December 31, 1995, p. 9.
World Literature Review, autumn, 1995, p. 796.

ONLINE

Edge, http://www.theedge.abelgratis.co.uk/ (April 28, 2003), John Coulthart, review of *King of the City.*
Guardian Online, http://books.guardian.co.uk/ (April 28, 2003), Ian Penman, "Magical history tours."
Michael Moorcock: Cartographer of the Multiverse, http://www.eclipse.co.uk/sweetdespise/moorcock/ (June 4, 2001).
Multiverse, http://www.multiverse.org/ (April 7, 2003).
PS Publishing, http://www.pspublishing.co.uk/ (April 28, 2003).
Time Warner Bookmark, http://www.twbookmark.com/ (June 4, 2001), "Michael Moorcock Speaks."
Zone, http://www.zone-sf.com/ (April 28, 2003), Patrick Hudson, review of *Firing the Cathedral.*

* * *

MOORCOCK, Michael John
See MOORCOCK, Michael

* * *

MOORE, Alan 1953-
(Curt Vile)

PERSONAL: Born November 18, 1953, in Northampton, England; son of Ernest (a brewery worker) and Sylvia (a printer) Moore; married, 1974; wife's name Phyllis; children: Amber, Leah.

ADDRESSES: *Home*—Northampton, England. *Office*—America's Best Comics, 7910 Ivanhoe St., No. 438, La Jolla, CA 92037.

CAREER: Comics illustrator and writer. Cartoonist for *Sounds* (magazine; under the name Curt Vile), 1979. Founder of Mad Love Publishers, Northampton, MA, 1988, and America's Best Comics, La Jolla, CA, 1999.

AWARDS, HONORS: Eagle Award for Best Comics Writer, 1982 and 1983, for *V for Vendetta,* and for *Swamp Thing;* Jack Kirby Comics Industry Award, for *Swamp Thing;* Jack Kirby Best Writer Award, 1987, Hugo Award, 1988, and *Locus* award, 1988, all for *Watchmen;* Harvey Award for best writer, 1988, for *Watchmen,* 1989, for best story and for best graphic album, both for *The Killing Joke,* 1995 and 1996, both for *From Hell,* 1998, for body of work, 2000, for *League of Extraordinary Gentlemen,* 2001, 2003, and 2004, for *Promethea,* 2003, for best writer for *ABC,* for best continuing series for *League of Extraordinary Gentlemen* Volume 2, and for best single issue or story, for *League of Extraordinary Gentlemen,* Volume 2, number 1; Will Eisner Comic Industry Award, 1988, for best finite series, best graphic album, best writer, and best writer/artist, all for *Watchmen,* 1989, for best graphic album and best writer, both for *The Killing Joke,* 1994, for best new graphic album, for *A Small Killing,* 1995, 1996, and 1997, all for best writer, all for *From Hell,* 2000, for best new series, for *Top Ten,* for best graphic album—reprint, for *From Hell,* and for best writer, for *League of Extraordinary Gentlemen,* 2001, for best single issue, for *Promethea,* number 10, for best continuing series, for *Top Ten,* for best writer, for *League of Extraordinary Gentlemen,* 2003, for best limited series, for *League of Extraordinary Gentlemen* Volume 2, and 2004, for best writer, for *League of Extraordinary Gentlemen, Promethea, Smax, Tom Strong,* and *Tom Strong's Terrific Tales.*

WRITINGS:

GRAPHIC NOVELS; EXCEPT AS NOTED

Shocking Futures, Titan (London, England), 1986.

Twisted Times, Titan (London, England), 1987.

Watchmen, illustrated by Dave Gibbons, DC Comics/Warner (New York, NY), 1987.

(With others) *Swamp Thing,* DC Comics (New York, NY), 1987.

Batman: The Killing Joke, illustrated by Brian Bolland and John Higgins, DC Comics (New York, NY), 1988.

Brought to Light, illustrated by Bill Sienkiewicz, Titan (London, England), 1989.

V for Vendetta, illustrated by David Lloyd, Titan (London, England), 1990.

Miracleman (published in England as *Marvelman*), Eclipse Books (Forestville, CA), 1990–1992.

Big Numbers, illustrated by Bill Sienkiewicz, Mad Love (Northampton, MA), 1990.

The Complete Ballad of Halo Jones, Titan (London, England), 1991.

A Small Killing, illustrated by Oscar Zarate, Victor Gollancz (London, England), 1991.

From Hell, illustrated by Eddie Campbell, Mad Love/Kitchen Sink Press (Northampton, MA), 1991–96.

The Complete Bojefferies Saga, illustrated by Steve Parkhouse, Kitchen Sink Press (Northampton, MA), 1994.

Lost Girls, illustrated by Melinda Gebbie, Kitchen Sink Press (Northampton, MA), 1995.

Voice of the Fire (novel), Victor Gollancz (London, England), 1996.

(With others) *Superman: Whatever Happened to the Man of Tomorrow?,* DC Comics (New York, NY), 1997.

Voodoo, Dancing in the Dark, Wildstorm Productions (La Jolla, CA), 1999.

(With others) *Bloodfeud,* Titan (London, England), 1999.

(With others) *Saga of the Swamp Thing,* DC Comics (New York, NY), 2000.

Top Ten, illustrated by Gene Ha and Zander Cannon, America's Best Comics (La Jolla, CA), 2000.

(With others) *Swamp Thing: The Curse,* DC Comics (New York, NY), 2000.

Love and Death, illustrated by John Totleben, Titan (London, England), 2000.

The League of Extraordinary Gentlemen, illustrated by Kevin O'Neill, America's Best Comics (La Jolla, CA), 2001.

Tom Strong Book 1, illustrated by Chris Sprouse, Titan (London, England), 2001.

Promethea Book 1, illustrated by J.H. Williams III, Titan (London, England), 2001.

Promethea Book 2, illustrated by J.H. Williams, Titan (London, England), 2001.

(With others) *Swamp Thing: A Murder of Crows,* Titan (London, England), 2001.

The Complete D.R. & Quinch, illustrated by Alan Davis, Titan (London, England), 2001.

(With others) *Tom Strong Book 2,* Titan (London, England), 2002.

Captain Britain, illustrated by Alan Davis, Marvel (New York, NY), 2002.

Skizz, illustrated by Jim Baikie, Titan (London, England), 2002.

Tomorrow Stories, America's Best Comics (La Jolla, CA), 2002.

(With others) *Mr. Majestic,* Wildstorm (La Jolla, CA), 2002.

(With others) *Swamp Thing: Earth to Earth,* DC Comics (New York, NY), 2002.

Supreme: The Story of the Year, Checker Book Pub. Group (Centerville, OH), 2002.

Judgement Day, Checker Book Pub. Group (Centerville, OH), 2003.

Supreme: The Return, Checker Book Pub. Group (Centerville, OH), 2003.

The Mirror of Love, illustrated by José Villarubia, Top Shelf Productions (Portland, OR), 2003.

America's Best Comics, America's Best Comics (LA Jolla, CA), 2004.

Also author of *1963.* Contributor to *The Starry Wisdom,* edited by D.M. Mitchell, Creation Books, 1994; and *Doctor Who Weekly;* created comic series, including "The Ballad of Hal Jones," "Skizz," and "D.R. & Quinch" for *2000 A.D.* and "Marvelman" and "V for Vendetta" series for *Warrior* (English anthology magazine). Contributor to comics series, including "Saga of the Swamp Thing" and "Tales of the Green Lantern Corps," DC Comics; to "The League of Extraordinary Gentlemen," "Promethea," "Tom Strong," "Tomorrow Stories," and "Top Ten," for America's Best Comics; and to "Supreme." Also performer on spoken word albums, including *The Birth Caul, Brought to Light, The Moon and Serpent Grand Egyptian Theatre of Marvels, Highbury Working* and *Angel Passage,* as well as the musical albums *The Sinister Ducks* and *The Emperors of Ice Cream.*

ADAPTATIONS: From Hell was adapted for a movie of the same title, starring Johnny Depp, directed by Albert and Allen Hughes, Twentieth Century-Fox, 2002; *The League of Extraordinary Gentlemen* was adapted for a movie of the same title, starring Sean Connery, directed by Stephen Norrington, Twentieth Century-Fox, 2002; *V for Vendetta* was adapted for a movie of the same title by Andy and Larry Wachowski for Warner Brothers, directed by James McTeigue, starring Natalie Portman and Hugo Weaving, 2006.

SIDELIGHTS: Dubbed the "Orson Welles of comics" by Steve Rose in the *Guardian,* Alan Moore is one of a handful of people who transformed the comic book industry in the 1980s, showing that "comic book scripts can have the subtlety of prose fiction, especially when they use their access to the rich potential subject matter of our fascination with heroes," as a contributor to *St. James Guide to Science Fiction Writers* noted. Moore's twelve-part comic-book serial "Watchmen" "changed the genre forever," according to Sridhar Pappu in *Salon.com.* In that series Moore transformed the old superhero model into "rapists, racists and flunkies of Richard Nixon . . . [to be] hunted down in the days before World War III," Pappu wrote. This deconstructing of the comic book hero was hailed a "sci-fi detective masterpiece," as Rose observed, making Moore "the comic industry's de facto leader." According to Rose, for comic fans, Moore is "the undisputed high priest of the medium, whose every word is seized upon like a message from the ether."

Moore has continued to amaze and confound his readers since the mid-1980s, writing series comics as well as graphic novels. For ten years he worked in the murky world of serial killers and madmen, writing his "From Hell" series about Jack the Ripper, the book of which was adapted for a 2002 film starring Johnny Depp. From works such as "V for Vendetta" and "Miracleman," to "The League of Extraordinary Gentlemen," Moore has created a large and significant body of work. As a critic on *Comicon.com* remarked, Moore "was the first modern writer to approach the medium of comics with the same intent and thoughtfulness . . . of any successful novel, screenplay, or theatrical production." Employing both playfulness and deadly earnestness, Moore "created an intoxicating mix of high and low; a nexus where readers could embrace some of the deepest aspirations of humankind while wallowing in the muckiest of trash culture." And writing in *Time,* Andrew D. Arnold declared that Moore "has written the best mainstream books of the last fifteen years while maintaining artistic credibility."

Moore himself is of two minds about his genre-bending "Watchmen," as he confided to Tasha Robinson in an *Onion AV Club* online interview: "In the fifteen years since 'Watchmen,' an awful lot of the comics field [has been] devoted to these very grim, pessimistic, nasty, violent stories which kind of use *Watchmen* to validate what they are, in effect, often just some very nasty stories that don't have a lot to recommend them. . . . It's almost become a genre. The gritty, deconstructivist postmodern superhero comic, as exemplified by *Watchmen,* also became a genre. It was never meant to. It was meant to be one work on its own. I think to that degree, it may have had a deleterious effect upon the medium since then."

Born in Northampton, England, in 1953, Moore grew up in a working-class family. His father was a brewery worker and his mother a printer; their flat was rented from the town council. Indoor plumbing was missing at one grandmother's house while electric lights were absent from the home of his other grandmother. "Looking back on it," Moore told Pappu, "it sounds like I'm describing something out of Dickens. I mean, I'm talking

1955, but 1955 in England. I've seen 'Happy Days' on television. Maybe the American fifties were like that, but that wasn't what the British fifties were like. It was all sort of monochrome, and it was all indoors."

Moore grew up loving imaginative literature, from the Greek and Norse myths to children's books about Robin Hood. The first comics in his youth were British ones, done in black and white, full of school stories. Then he finally got his hands on a "Superman" comic. "I got my morals more from Superman than I ever did from my teachers or peers," Moore told Pappu. "Because Superman wasn't real—he was incorruptible. You were seeing morals in their pure form. You don't see Superman secretly going out behind the back and lying and killing, which, of course, most real-life heroes tend to be doing." At age seventeen Moore was thrown out of his conservative secondary school for dealing drugs, and thereafter took laboring jobs in and around Northampton, working at a sheep-skinning plant and cleaning toilets at a hotel. He finally moved up to an office job at the local gas company, but knew he had to make an effort to do something more creative.

Eventually finding himself married and with a child on the way, Moore quit his job, went on public assistance, and spent a year trying to make a living with his own imagination. One of his ultimately aborted projects during this time was a twenty-part space opera. Eventually he found a cartooning job for the rock weekly *Sounds.* In that magazine he published a comic detective story called "Roscoe Moscow" under the pen name of Curt Vile, but soon decided he was a better writer than artist. Thereafter he contributed works to British magazines such as *Doctor Who Weekly* and *2000 A.D.* In the latter publication, he created several popular comic-strips, including "The Ballad of Halo Jones"—which had one of the first feminist heroes in comics as Halo searches for her proper place in the galaxy—"Skizz," and "D.R. & Quinch," a darkly humorous—some might say deranged—look at college students who take readers through tales of slime wars and psychotic girlfriends.

Moore then began contributing to the British anthology magazine *Warrior,* where he initiated two series which would prove to be breakthroughs for him: "Marvelman"—titled "Miracleman" in the United States—and "V for Vendetta." With these tales, Moore's writing began to take on more of the multi-layered feeling of a novel. "With *Marvelman* there were some bits of cleverness creeping in there but with *V for Vendetta* I think that was where I started to realize that you could get some incredible effects by putting words and pictures together or leaving the words out for a while," Moore told Barry Kavanagh in a *Blather.net* online interview. "I started to realize what you could do with comic storytelling and the . . . layering, the levels of meaning that you could attach to the story. I think that certainly *V for Vendetta* was one of the first real major breakthroughs I made in terms of my own personal style."

With "Marvelman" Moore treats the stereotypical superhero in tights with a new sensitivity, and by the end the hero has become "genuinely godlike," according to the *St. James Guide to Science Fiction Writers* essayist "and graciously offers other humans the chance to join him. He is puzzled by the refusal of some, such as his former wife, to be converted into superhumanity; that failure of imagination, Moore implies, is Marvelman's ultimate limitation." "V for Vendetta," on the other hand, is set in a near-future, fascist Britain, where the only opposition to the government is the Guy Fawkes-masked vigilante known only as "V," a lone vigilante who is killing all the government officials once connected with a concentration camp. Illustrated in black and white by David Lloyd, the series has a gritty, noir feel that attracted readers on both sides of the Atlantic. "V" earned Moore his first awards as well; he received the Eagle Award for Best Writing in both 1982 and 1983.

"When we started to do *V,*" Moore told Kavanagh, "the entirety of the idea was that we would have a dark, romantic, noirish adventurer and then we thought we'd set him in the future and then the details slowly came together and yeah, somewhere out of this we realized we were doing something about the contrast between anarchy and fascism, that there were lots of moral questions being asked and that yes, it was very much centered upon the world of ideas as being in some ways more important than the material world." Moore further told Kavanagh that "V" was also a breakthrough in terms of characters. "I was very pleased with the characterizations in *V.* There's quite a variety of characters in there and they've all got very distinctive characteristics. They've all got different ways of talking, different agendas and I think they're all credible because, well, they felt emotionally credible to me because there's none of them that I absolutely hate."

Moore's work in England did not go unnoticed by American comics publishers and fans, and in 1984 he began working for DC Comics, revamping the character of Swamp Thing for the "Saga of Swamp Thing." Taking over the nearly defunct series at number twenty, he stuck with it through the next forty issues. "It was the first time that I'd got colour and twenty-four pages to play with," Moore related to Kavanagh. "So I was able to kind of splash out and do a few things that I'd only been able to dream about doing with black and white material." Moore appreciated the opportunities as he noted in his introduction to "Saga of the Swamp Thing," the first of the issues he wrote: "The continuity-expert's nightmare of a thousand different super-powered characters co-existing in the same continuum can, with the application of a sensitive and sympathetic eye, become a rich and fertile mythic background with fascinating archetypal characters hanging around, waiting to be picked like grapes on the vine."

Moore depicts the Swamp Thing not as a man who became plantlike, but with all the memories of the man. "Shocked by the discovery that he was not human," explained the reviewer for *St. James Guide to Science Fiction Writers,* "the character first tries to sink into unconsciousness. When he is roused by the need to fight another man-plant being who wants to destroy all humans for their crimes against the vegetable world, Swamp Thing begins to care for some humans." In the end, Swamp Thing becomes able to share his world with them and, in the climax to actually love one human woman.

"Unconventional and serious, [Moore] turned the book into a tool for exploring social issues, using it to discuss everything from racism to environmental affairs," remarked Pappu. Soon Moore had increased monthly circulation of "Swamp Thing" from 17,000 to 100,000 copies by, as Rose commented, transforming the featured creature "from a walking vegetable into a groundbreaking gothic eco-warrior." Also working for DC, Moore penned "Tales of the Green Lantern Corps."

Meanwhile, Moore was also collaborating with Dave Gibbons on an idea for a type of new superhero story with a reconstructed gang of heroes thrown into new situations. Working off characters in the defunct Charlton comics, such as the Question, Mister A, Blue Beetle, and Captain Adam, in "Watchmen" Moore and Gibbons came up with their own super heroes, including Dr. Manhattan with his nuclear powers, Rorschach, Adrian Veit and others. In Moore's take, these superheroes are all plagued by their human emotions and weaknesses. In an alternate America of 1985, super heroes have in fact existed for several decades. They have fought gangsters and then Nazis in World War II, have been purged in the McCarthy era, helped the country win the war in Vietnam, and have become hitmen for the CIA. One such superhero, Comedian, supposedly killed the Watergate journalists Woodward and Bernstein in 1972, thus stabilizing Richard M. Nixon's threatened presidency, and Comedian's own death in October of 1985 becomes the kick-off point for Moore's dark tale. Soon it becomes clear that someone is trying to kill off the second generation of super heroes, and as a nuclear threat becomes more and more urgent, the remaining super heroes know that they must stop this anonymous assassin before time runs out.

The twelve issues of the original "Watchmen" each include notes and end matter, supposedly "documentary" material of the time that is "wittily crafted and weirdly interesting," according to Fredric Paul Smoler in the *Nation.* The series quickly became a cult classic, appealing to adult and teenage readers alike. Rose noted that the series "was a dense, meticulous deconstruction of the whole superhero game that received mainstream 'literary' acclaim," and also became the symbol of a new genre—the graphic novel. *Watchmen* is a "formidably complex work, demanding that readers connect many references in text and art," noted the contributor for *St. James Guide to Science Fiction Writers.*

Before leaving DC Comics to found his imprint Mad Love Publishers, Moore published a Batman story, "The Killing Joke," about the relationship between Batman and Joker, though he came to view this particular venture as a "well-intentioned failure." His more recent projects have often resembled massive, unfinished monoliths. *Brought to Light,* with illustrations by Bill Sienkiewicz, is based on a lawsuit brought against the government for drug-smuggling and arms-dealing. The "1963" series appears to be a fairly genial spoof of early Marvel super heroes, but the series broke off just as Moore was bringing those more-innocent characters into the present, to face contemporary issues in the company of today's scruffier brand of superhero. Only two issues of "Big Numbers" appeared, juxtaposing personal and big-business desires. *A Small Killing,* illustrated by Oscar Zarate, tells the story of Timothy Hole, an advertising man in New York, who is followed by a mysterious little boy.

Far and away Moore's most important project during the 1990s was "From Hell," a fictional account of the 1888 Jack the Ripper crimes, all based on thorough research. A "big, black, monumental work," is how Moore described "From Hell" to Kavanagh. "Victorian. I'm very proud of it." In Moore's version of the Ripper story, Prince Albert, heir to the British throne, has secretly married a woman from the London slums. To save the throne, all evidence of this must be removed, including the other slum women who know. Dr. William Gull, sincere defender of official morality, sets about this task at the request of his sovereign, Queen Victoria. He views himself as a masked vigilante, but history knows him as Jack the Ripper. But Gull is also an enigma: is he a real historical persona or a golem-like creation brought to life by royalty and the Freemasons?

Reviewing the graphic-novel publication of *From Hell* in *Booklist,* Gordon Flagg noted that Moore's "meticulous research . . . helps him evoke Victorian London convincingly, and his . . . storytelling skills make the story grippingly harrowing." Kenneth Turan, reviewing the movie adaptation of the book in the *Los Angeles Times,* noted that Moore's work is "no mere comic book. It's a massive, graphic novel published over the course of a decade and so fiendishly researched and detailed it has more than forty pages of footnotes in small print." And writing in the London *Observer,* Iain Sinclair called *From Hell* a "celebrated graphic novel."

After being imitated for so long as the progenitor of the deconstructed superhero, Moore set out with a new imprint in 1999, America's Best Comics (ABC), to resurrect the old-fashioned super hero. Beginning the practice when in his forties, Moore found a renewed joy in his craft, and his output rose after completion of *From Hell.* One of the turnaround incidents for him was a reclamation project in 1996 of a "very, very, very, very, very lame" superhero, as Moore recalled to Pappu. With Supreme, Moore re-fashions a down-at-heels super hero and had such fun doing it that he figured he could use that model to help breathe new life into a flagging comics industry. His ABC titles include "Promethea," about a mythic warrior woman, "Tom Strong," featuring a very straightforward, moral superhero, and "Top Ten," set in a police precinct where all the officers have superhuman powers.

With "The League of Extraordinary Gentlemen," Moore gathers nineteenth-century fictional personages such as Allan Quatermain from H. Rider Haggard's *King Solomon's Mines,* Captain Nemo from Jules Verne's *20,000 Leagues under the Sea,* Edward Hyde and Dr. Henry Jekyll from Robert Louis Stevenson's novel, Mina Murray from Bram Stoker's *Dracula,* and Hawley Griffin from H.G. Welles's *Invisible Man.* Reviewing the collection *The League of Extraordinary Gentlemen,* a contributor for *Publishers Weekly* called it a "delightful work" that features a "grand collection of signature nineteenth-century fictional characters, covertly brought together to defend the empire." The same reviewer concluded that Moore has created a "Victorian era Fantastic Four, a beautifully illustrated reprise . . . packed with period detail, great humor and rousing adventure."

Moving into his publishing venture, Moore has abandoned his bleak, noirish plot-lines in favor of a lighter touch in his books for ABC. "I feel good about this century," he told Joel Meadows in a *Tripwire* interview. "I feel that we're going somewhere in our minds and our minds are evolving into something. I think that imagination and the world of the imagination are at a premium in these coming times."

In the *Advocate,* Andy Mangels highlighted another passion of Moore's: a poem titled *The Mirror of Love,* which originally appeared in 1988 in a publication called *AARGH!* (Artists against Rampant Government Homophobia). "Moore's *Mirror of Love,*" explained Mangels, "is an epic poem that compresses gay history into a few thousand words, covering the dawn of humanity and ancient Sapphic and Spartan love up through the AIDS crisis and the gay-baiting media of the modern world." Moore, a heterosexual, told Mangels that the poem is "sweeping—melodramatic," and "It's got a very Shakespearean tone to it, but it felt like a big story that deserved to be spoken of in epic tongues. Some of the men and women that we mentioned in it—these are titans. They are the pillars of human culture, let 'alone gay culture.'" Moore and friends published the comic book to benefit the fight against a piece of British legislation that he deemed homophobic. As Moore explained to Mangels: "Whenever any of our countries take these sudden, nasty fascist lunges, then I think it's down to all of us to actually stand up and say something about it."

BIOGRAPHICAL AND CRITICAL SOURCES:

BOOKS

Parkin, Lance, *Alan Moore,* Pocket Essentials, 2001.

St. James Guide to Science Fiction Writers, 4th edition, St. James Press (Detroit, MI), 1996.

PERIODICALS

Advocate, March 16, 2004, Andy Mangels, "From Queer to Eternity: Comic Master Alan Moore Tackles the History of Homosexuality in the Epic Poem *The Mirror of Love,*" p. 52.

Analog: Science Fiction-Science Fact, May, 1988, p. 184; January, 1991, pp. 308-309.

Booklist, June 1, 2000, Gordon Flagg, review of *From Hell,* p. 1830; November 1, 2003, Gordon Flagg, review of *Judgment Day,* p. 487.

Guardian (Manchester, England), February 2, 2002, Steve Rose, "Moore's Murder."

Library Journal, March 15, 1990, pp. 53-55; March 1, 2001, Stephen Weiner, review of *The League of Extraordinary Gentlemen,* p. 82; January, 2004, Steve Raiteri, review of *Across the Universe: The DC Universe Stories of Alan Moore,* p. 79; March 1, 2004, Steve Raiteri, review of *The League of Extraordinary Gentlemen,* Volume 2, p. 62.

Los Angeles Times, October 19, 2001, Kenneth Turan, "Violence Cuts like a Knife in the Jack the Ripper Tale," p. F4.

Nation, October 10, 1987, Fredric Paul Smoler, review of *Watchmen,* pp. 386-387; March 19, 1990, Pagan Kennedy, "P.C. Comics," pp. 386-389.

New Statesman, July 10, 1987, pp. 28-29; December 4, 1987, p. 30; December 18, 1987, p. 41.

Newsweek, January 18, 1988, pp. 70-71.

New York Times, October 19, 2001, Elvis Mitchell, "A Conspiracy Shrouded in London Fog," p. E16.

Observer (London, England), January 27, 2002, Iain Sinclair, "Jack the Rip-Off," p. 8.

Publishers Weekly, February 17, 1989, p. 73; June 14, 1999, p. 62; January 8, 2001, review of *The League of Extraordinary Gentlemen,* p. 49; December 15, 2003, review of *Tom Strong: Book Two,* p. 56; February 9, 2004, review of *The League of Extraordinary Gentlemen,* Volume 2, p. 60.

Rolling Stone, February 11, 1988, pp. 103-108.

Time, December 8, 2000, Andrew W. Arnold, "Best Comics 2000."

ONLINE

Blather.net, http://www.blather.net/ (October 17, 2000), Barry Kavanagh, "The Alan Moore Interview."

Comicon.com, http://www.comicon.com/ (June 2, 2002), "Alan Moore."

Onion AV Club, http://www.theonionavclub.com/ (October 24, 2001), Tasha Robinson, interview with Moore.

Salon.com, http://www.salon.com/ (October 18, 2000), Sridhar Pappu, "We Need Another Hero."

Tripwire, http://www.human-computing.com/Tripwire/ (June 2, 2002), Joel Meadows, interview with Moore.

MOORE, Brian 1921-1999 (Michael Bryan, Bernard Mara)

PERSONAL: Born August 25, 1921, in Belfast, Northern Ireland; died of pulmonary fibrosis, January 10, 1999, in Malibu, CA; immigrated to Canada, 1948; became Canadian citizen; son of James Brian (a surgeon) and Eileen (McFadden) Moore; married Jacqueline Scully (some sources say Sirois), 1951 (marriage ended); married Jean Denney, October, 1967; children: (first marriage) Michael. *Education:* Graduated from St. Malachy's College, 1939.

CAREER: Served with United Nations Relief and Rehabilitation Administration (UNRRA) mission to Poland, 1946-47; *Montreal Gazette,* Montreal, Quebec, Canada, proofreader, reporter, and rewriter, 1948-52; writer, 1952—; University of California, Los Angeles, regents' professor, 1974-75, professor, 1976-89. *Military service:* Served in Belfast Fire Service, 1942-43, and with British Ministry of War Transport in North Africa, Italy, and France, 1943-45.

AWARDS, HONORS: Author's Club first novel award, 1956; Beta Sigma Phi award, 1956; Quebec Literary Prize, 1958; Guggenheim fellowship, 1959; Governor General's Award for Fiction, 1960, for *The Luck of Ginger Coffey,* and 1975, for *The Great Victorian Collection;* U.S. National Institute of Arts and Letters fiction grant, 1961; Canada Council fellowship for travel in Europe, 1962 and 1976; W.H. Smith Prize, 1972, for *Catholics;* James Tait Black Memorial Award, 1975, for *The Great Victorian Collection;* Booker shortlist, 1976, for *The Doctor's Wife;* Scottish Arts Council senior fellowship, and Neill Gunn international fellowship, both 1983; ten best books of 1983 designation, *Newsweek,* 1983, for *Cold Heaven;* Heinemann Award, Royal Society of Literature, 1986, for *Black Robe;* Booker Prize shortlist, 1987, and London *Sunday Express* Book of the Year Prize, 1988, both for *The Color of Blood;* Hughes Irish Fiction award, 1988; Royal Society of Literature fellow; Lifetime Achievement Award, *Los Angeles Times,* 1994. Honorary degrees include D.H.L., Queens University, Belfast, 1989, and National University of Ireland, 1991.

WRITINGS:

NOVELS

Judith Hearne, A. Deutsch (London, England), 1955, published as *The Lonely Passion of Judith Hearne,* Little, Brown (Boston, MA), 1956.

The Feast of Lupercal, Little, Brown (Boston, MA), 1957.
The Luck of Ginger Coffey, Little, Brown (Boston, MA), 1960.
An Answer from Limbo, Little, Brown (Boston, MA), 1962.
The Emperor of Ice-Cream, Viking (New York, NY), 1965.
I Am Mary Dunne, Viking (New York, NY), 1968, with an introduction by Alan Kennedy, McClelland and Stewart (Toronto, Ontario, Canada), 1976.
Fergus, Holt (New York, NY), 1970.
The Revolution Script, Holt (New York, NY), 1971.
Catholics, McClelland and Stewart (Toronto, Ontario, Canada), 1972, Holt (New York, NY), 1973.
The Great Victorian Collection, Farrar, Straus (New York, NY), 1975.
The Doctor's Wife, Farrar, Straus (New York, NY), 1976.
Two Stories, Santa Susana Press (Northridge, CA), 1978.
The Mangan Inheritance, Farrar, Straus (New York, NY), 1979.
The Temptation of Eileen Hughes, Farrar, Straus (New York, NY), 1981.
Cold Heaven, Holt (New York, NY), 1983.
Black Robe, Dutton (New York, NY), 1985.
The Color of Blood, Dutton (New York, NY), 1987.
Lies of Silence, Doubleday (New York, NY), 1990.
No Other Life, Doubleday (New York, NY), 1993.
The Statement, Dutton (New York, NY), 1996.
The Magician's Wife, Bloomsbury (London, England), 1997, Dutton (New York, NY), 1998.

Also author of *Wreath for a Redhead,* 1951, and *The Executioners,* 1951; author, under pseudonym Bernard Mara, of *French for Murder,* 1954, and *A Bullet for My Lady,* 1954.

NOVELS; UNDER PSEUDONYM MICHAEL BRYAN

Intent to Kill, Dell (New York, NY), 1956.
Murder in Majorca, Dell (New York, NY), 1957.

OTHER

(With others) *Canada* (travel book), Time-Life (New York, NY), 1963, third edition, 1968.
The Luck of Ginger Coffey (screenplay; based on Moore's novel), Continental, 1964.
Torn Curtain (screenplay), Universal, 1966.
Catholics (television script; based on Moore's novel), Columbia Broadcasting System, 1973.
Black Robe (screenplay; based on Moore's novel), Alliance Communications, 1987.

Also author of screenplays *The Slave* (based on his novel *An Answer from Limbo*), 1967, *The Blood of Others,* 1984, *Brainwash,* 1985, and *Gabrielle Chanel,* 1988. Contributor of articles and short stories to *Spectator, Holiday, Atlantic,* and other periodicals. *The Lonely Passion of Judith Hearne, Lies of Silence, The Color of Blood,* and *Cold Heaven* have been recorded on audiocassette.

ADAPTATIONS: Catholics was adapted as a play and produced in Edmonton, Alberta, Canada, 1981; *The Lonely Passion of Judith Hearne* was adapted as a feature film, Island Pictures, 1988; *The Temptation of Eileen Hughes* was adapted for television, British Broadcasting Corporation, 1988; *Cold Heaven* was adapted as a feature film, 1991; *The Statement* was adapted for a film directed by Norman Jewison, Sony Pictures Classics, 2003.

SIDELIGHTS: Brian Moore was a Canadian citizen of Northern Irish origin who spent much of his adult life in California. He was also a novelist who "gradually won the recognition his stubborn artistry deserves," to quote Walter Clemons in *Newsweek.* For more than forty years Moore published fiction that reflected his multinational wanderings, his fascination with Catholicism's influence on modern life, and his insight into strained interpersonal relationships. "Book by book," Bruce Cook wrote in *New Republic,* "Brian Moore has been building a body of work that is, in its quietly impressive way, about as good as that of any novelist writing today in English." Cook added: "If Moore lacks the fame he deserves, he nevertheless has an excellent reputation. He is a writer's writer. His special virtues—his deft presentation of his characters, whether they be Irish, Canadian, or American, and the limpid simplicity of his style—are those that other writers most admire."

Moore was one of nine children born to Catholic parents, surgeon James Bernard Moore and Eileen McFadden Moore, her husband's former nurse. He attended St. Malachy's College, Belfast, with the goal of a career in medicine, but abandoned college in 1938. After the outbreak of World War II Moore joined the Belfast Air Raid Precautions Unit and National Fire Service, and later served in the British Ministry of War Transport in

North Africa, Italy, and France, and, after the war, in the United Nations Relief and Rehabilitation Administration in Eastern Europe. Moore returned to Britain only briefly after that, immigrating to Canada in 1948, where he worked for *Montreal Gazette* and attained Canadian citizenship.

According to Christopher Hawtree in *Spectator,* this transatlantic stance "has yielded some sharp views both of his native [Northern] Ireland and of Canada and America." *Time* contributor Patricia Blake felt that Moore's expatriate status produced "a special talent for pungent portraiture of those Irish men and women who are, as James Joyce put it, 'outcast from life's feast:' desperate spinsters, failed priests, drunken poets." Other critics have noted that the very process of moving from place to place fuels Moore's fiction. In *Critique: Studies in Modern Fiction,* John Wilson Foster contended that Moore's novels as a group "trace the growing fortunes in a new continent of one hypothetical immigrant who has escaped Belfast's lower middle-class tedium." London *Times* correspondent Chris Petit also concluded that absence is important to Moore's writing: "The stories have an air of cosmopolitan restlessness, often cross borders, and can be summarized as a series of departures."

Eventually Moore moved to the United States—first to New York and then to Malibu, California. As Kerry McSweeney noted in *Critical Quarterly,* while the author retained Canadian citizenship, and Canada "was the halfway house which mediated his passage from the old world to the new, it has not stimulated his imagination in the way that America has done." Paul Binding elaborated in *Books and Bookmen:* "It is America, with its vigorous non-realistic, especially Gothic literary tradition, which would seem to have supplied Brian Moore with the fictional forms that he needed, that can express—with their violent epiphanies and their distortions and eruptions of the irrational—the anguishes of the uprooted and spiritually homeless, and the baffling diversities of Western society which can contain both puritan, taboo-ridden, pleasure-fearing Belfast and hedonistic, lost, restless California."

Moore published four pulp thrillers between 1951 and 1954, but he first received serious critical attention in 1955 with the publication of *The Lonely Passion of Judith Hearne.* This tale of a lonely, desperate, middle-aged Belfast woman remained in print for the rest of Moore's life. The title character fantasizes about a romance with an unattainable man, questions her faith, and seeks solace in alcohol, all the while being silently stared at by a photograph of her aunt that sits on her nightstand. The story is a "painful, deeply empathetic portrait" that marked "Moore as one of those rare male authors who can write convincingly from a female perspective," John Bemrose commented in *Maclean's. Saturday Review* essayist Granville Hicks was also among the critics who praised *The Lonely Passion of Judith Hearne.* "As a book by a young man about a middle-aged woman," Hicks wrote, "it [is] a remarkable tour de force, but it [is] more than that, for in it one [feels] the terrible pathos of life as it is often led."

Like *The Terrible Passion of Judith Hearne,* Moore's other early novels, including *The Feast of Lupercal, The Luck of Ginger Coffey,* and *The Emperor of Ice-Cream,* are character studies in which the protagonists rebel—sometimes unsuccessfully—against the essentially closed society of Northern Ireland. In *Critical Quarterly,* Kerry McSweeney suggested that the works "are studies of losers, whose fates are determined by the claustrophobic gentility of Belfast and the suffocating weight of Irish Catholicism. [They] illustrate one of the quintessential *donnees* of Moore's fiction: that (in his own words) 'failure is a more interesting condition than success. Success changes people: it makes them something they were not and dehumanizes them in a way, whereas failure leaves you with a more intense distillation of that self you are.'" *Chicago Tribune Book World* reviewer Eugene Kennedy found these novels "a look beneath the aspects of Irish culture that, with a terrible mixture of repression and misuse of its religious heritage, can create pitiable monsters fated to groan eternally beneath the facades of their hypocritical adjustments."

A fascination with Catholicism is central to much of Moore's work. He once told a *Los Angeles Times* interviewer: "I am not a religious person, but I come from a very religious background. Always in the back of my mind, I've wondered what if all this stuff was true and you didn't want it to be true and it was happening in the worst possible way?" According to Paul Gray in *Time,* a refrain common to all of Moore's novels is this: "When beliefs can no longer comfort, they turn destructive." Such is the case in a variety of Moore's works, from *Judith Hearne* to the more recent *Cold Heaven, Black Robe, Catholics,* and *The Color of Blood.* Craig wrote: "Someone who is heading for the moment of apostasy . . . is almost statutory in a Moore novel. . . . A frightening emptiness takes the place of whatever ideology had kept the character going." The opposite may also apply in some of Moore's tales; occasionally non-believing characters are forced to pay heed to the deity through extreme means. "Moore's later novels show the vestigial religious conscience straining to give depth to North American life," observed a *Times Literary Supplement* reviewer. "Faith itself is unacceptable, making unreasonable demands on the behaviour of anyone who is sporadically forced to be honest with himself. Yet bourbon, bedrooms and success do not content the soul: in this, at least, the priests were always right."

Several of Moore's novels—*Fergus, The Great Victorian Collection,* and *Cold Heaven*—make use of miracles and the supernatural to advance the stories. In *The Great Victorian Collection,* for instance, a college professor finds his vivid dream about an exhibit of Victorian memorabilia transformed into reality in a hotel parking lot. Binding suggested that in these works Moore "has tried to explore the complexities of American/Californian life while coming to further terms with the ghosts of his Irish past." These miracles and ghostly visitations do not comfort or sustain; Moore's vision of the supernatural "is terrifying: a brutal energy that mocks our pretensions and transcends our ideas of good and evil," to quote Mark Abley in *Books in Canada.* Peter S. Prescott likewise noted in *Newsweek* that Moore is "concerned with a secular sensibility confronting the more alien aspects of Roman Catholic tradition. . . . He warns us of the ambiguities of miracles in a world that is darker, more dangerous and above all more portentous than we think." Such plot devices can strain verisimilitude, but according to David MacFarlane in *Maclean's,* the author's strength "is his ability to make tangible the unbelievable and the miraculous."

Many of Moore's plots are conventional in their inception, but typically the author brings additional depth of characterization to his stories so that they transcend genre classifications. As Joyce Carol Oates observed in *New York Times Book Review,* Moore has written "a number of novels prized for their storytelling qualities and for a wonderfully graceful synthesis of the funny, the sardonic, and the near tragic; his reputation as a supremely entertaining 'serious' writer is secure." In *Saturday Night,* Christina Newman noted that Moore has a growing readership which has come to expect "what he unfailingly delivers: lucidity, great craftsmanship, and perceptions that evoke our fears, dreams, and shameful absurdities."

"Moore is not only the laureate of Irish drabness but also a psychological writer with some interest in the quirkier aspects of profane love," wrote Taliaferro. "Throughout his career, one has been able to rely on Mr. Moore for narrative competence and psychological interest." Through novels such as *I Am Mary Dunne, The Doctor's Wife,* and *The Temptation of Eileen Hughes,* Moore attained a reputation for uncovering the pitfalls in modern emotional entanglements, especially from the female point of view. In *Nation,* Richard B. Sale commented that the author "has never avoided the silliness, selfishness and sexuality that constitute most people's waking and dreaming thoughts. . . . He can extend the embarrassing scene beyond the point where the ordinary naturalistic novelist would lower the curtain." *Times Literary Supplement* reviewer Paul Bailey noted that it is "typical of Brian Moore's honesty that he should acknowledge that, superficially at least, there are certain liaisons which bear a shocking resemblance to those described in the pages of women's magazines: life, unfortunately, has a nasty habit of imitating pulp fiction." However, *Spectator* correspondent Paul Ableman pointed out that Moore's characters "are not formula figures, whose responses to any situation are predictable, but rather fictional beings that behave like people in the world, generally consistent or revealing a thread of continuity, but always quirky, volatile and sometimes irrational."

Prescott characterized Moore as a novelist who "enjoys playing with his readers' expectations. Aha, he seems to say, you thought I was writing about this; now don't you feel a little foolish to discover that I was really up to something else—something more innocent and yet more terrible—all along?" Moore himself echoed this sentiment in *Los Angeles Times:* "I find it interesting to lull the reader into a sense that he's reading a certain kind of book and then jolt the reader about halfway through to make him realize that it's a different kind of book. That is not a recipe for best sellerdom; it's the opposite." Even the thriller format in such works as *Black Robe* and *The Color of Blood* becomes "a vehicle to explore serious political and theological issues," to quote Anne-Marie Conway in *Times Literary Supplement.* It is this willingness to explore and experiment that contributes to Moore's novelistic originality, according to critics. McSweeney wrote: "One of the most impressive features of Moore's canon has been his ability to keep from repeating himself. Over and over again he has found fresh inventions which have developed his novelistic skills and enabled him to explore his obsessive themes and preoccupations in ways that have made for an increasingly complex continuity between old and new."

Moore's novel *No Other Life* portrays the relationship between Jeannot, a young, black messianic priest who espouses a politically active brand of religious vocation, and Father Paul Michel, the elderly white priest who mentors him. Narrated by Father Michel, the novel is set in a country reminiscent of Haiti, with Jeannot often being compared to the Haitian President Father Jean-Bertrand Aristide, known for his quest to end racism and class conflict in Haiti. Henry Louis Gates Jr. of *New York Times Book Review* saw the novel as "the first fictionalized account of this messianic 40-year-old Catholic priest's rise and fall from power." In a subsequent novel, *The Statement,* Moore again employs a fictional treatment of a historical event, loosely basing his novel (some reviewers argue) on the case of Paul Touvier, a former Nazi who was given a sentence of life imprisonment as punishment for murder in 1994 after decades of successfully evading authorities. Christopher Lehmann-Haupt, writing in *New York Times,* called Moore's novel "an absorbing intellectual thriller that keeps you guessing about its outcome and implications until the final page." Set in France in 1989, *The Statement* focuses on an ex-Nazi named Pierre Brossard who, unlike Touvier, is a devout Roman Catholic who is being hunted by hired assassins. The novel opens with an attempt on Brossard's life and then chronicles his increasingly desperate attempts to escape his own murder or arrest. "Meanwhile," noted Mark Noel Cosgrove of *Quill & Quire,* "issues of culpability, betrayal, and sin and forgiveness are quietly explored."

While Moore enjoyed a substantial critical reputation, he is not extremely well-known to American readers—a state of affairs he welcomed. "I have never had to deal with the problem of a public persona becoming more important than the fiction," he said in *Los Angeles Times.* "I've had a life where I've been able to write without having had some enormous success that I have to live up to." Cook claimed that the author's retiring personality affected the tenor of his work for the better. "In a way," Cook concluded in *Commonweal,* "the sort of writer [Moore] is—private, devoted to writing as an end in itself—is the only sort who could write the intensely felt, personal, and close novels he has. The style, once again, is the man." Bailey wrote: "It isn't fashionable to praise novelists for their tact, but it is that very quality in Brian Moore's writing that deserves to be saluted. It is a measure of his intelligence and his humanity that he refuses to sit in judgment on his characters. It is, as far as I am concerned, an honourable and a considerable measure." Perhaps the best summation of Moore's authorial talents came from *Washington Post Book World* reviewer Jack Beatty, who said of the writer: "Pick him up expecting high talent in the service of a small design, go to him anticipating economy of style, characterization and description, as well as the pleasure of a plot that keeps you reading until the last page, and I can assure that your expectations will get along splendidly with his abilities."

BIOGRAPHICAL AND CRITICAL SOURCES:

BOOKS

Contemporary Literary Criticism, Thomson Gale (Detroit, MI), Volume 1, 1973, Volume 3, 1975, Volume 5, 1976, Volume 7, 1977, Volume 8, 1978, Volume 19, 1981, Volume 32, 1985.

Contemporary Novelists, sixth edition, St. James Press (Detroit, MI), 1996.

Dahlie, Hallvard, *Brian Moore,* Copp, 1969.

Dictionary of Literary Biography, Volume 251: *Canadian Fantasy and Science-Fiction Writers,* Thomson Gale (Detroit, MI), 2001.

Flood, Jeanne, *Brian Moore,* Bucknell University Press, 1974.

McSweeny, Kerry, *Four Contemporary Novelists: Angus Wilson, Brian Moore, John Fowles, V.S. Naipaul,* University of Toronto Press (Toronto, Ontario, Canada), 1983.

O'Donoghue, Jo, *Brian Moore: A Critical Study,* McGill/Queens University Press (Montreal, Quebec, Canada), 1991.

Raban, Jonathan, *The Techniques of Modern Fiction,* Edward Arnold, 1968.

St. James Guide to Fantasy Writers, St. James Press (Detroit, MI), 1996.

Sampson, Denis, *Brian Moore: The Chameleon Novelist,* Doubleday Canada (Toronto, Ontario, Canada), 1998.

PERIODICALS

America, February 27, 1982, Edward J. Curtin, Jr., review of *The Temptation of Eileen Hughes,* pp. 159-160; March 3, 1984, John B. Breslin, review of *Cold Heaven,* pp. 155-157; May 4, 1985, John C. Hawley, review of *Black Robe,* pp. 376-377; December 12, 1987, Kit Reed, review of *The Color of Blood,* p. 460; January 18, 1992, Richard A. Blake, review of *Black Robe,* pp. 38; May 6, 1995, Barbara Roche Rico, review of *No Other Life,* pp. 28-29; February 22, 1997, John C. Hawley, review of *The Statement,* pp. 27-28; May 2, 1998, Sharon Locy, review of *The Magician's Wife,* p. 23.

Atlantic, September, 1981, Phoebe-Lou Adams, review of *The Temptation of Eileen Hughes,* p. 92; October, 1983, Phoebe-Lou Adams, review of *Cold Heaven,* pp. 120-121.

Booklist, October 1, 1993, Mary Carroll, review of *No Other Life,* pp. 251-252; October 15, 1995, Karen Harris, review of *The Doctor's Wife,* p. 421; June 1, 1996, Jim O'Laughlin, review of *The Statement,* p. 1676; November 15, 1997, GraceAnne A. DeCandido, review of *The Magician's Wife,* p. 546; April 15, 1998, Karen Harris, review of *Lies of Silence,* p. 1460; April 1, 2001, Karen Harris, review of *The Magician's Wife* (audiobook), p. 1490.

Books & Bookmen, December, 1968; February, 1980.

Books in Canada, October, 1979; November, 1983.

Canadian Literature, fall, 1986, pp. 150-152; spring, 1989, E. Mozejko, review of *The Color of Blood,* pp. 147-150; spring, 1992, Hallvard Dahlie, review of *Lies of Silence,* pp. 184-186; summer, 2000, Kerry McSweeney, review of *The Magician's Wife,* pp. 155-157.

Chicago Tribune, November 2, 1987.

Chicago Tribune Book World, July 12, 1981; October 30, 1983; May 19, 1985.

Christian Science Monitor, September 24, 1990, Thomas D'Evelyn, review of *Lies of Silence,* p. 15; December 13, 1993, Merle Rubin, review of *No Other Life,* p. 15; July 25, 1996, Michelle Ross, review of *The Statement,* p. B3.

Commentary, October, 1996, Roger Kaplan, review of *The Statement,* pp. 66-67.

Commonweal, August 3, 1956; July 12, 1957; September 27, 1968; August 23, 1974; December 4, 1981, Saul Maloff, review of *The Temptation of Eileen Hughes,* pp. 695-696; May 17, 1985, John R. Breslin, review of *Black Robe,* pp. 313-314; November 6, 1987, J.V. Long, review of *The Color of Blood,* pp. 634-636; October 20, 1989, J.V. Long, "Walking the Tightrope of Mystery: The Lonely Seekers of Brian Moore," pp. 555-558; January 11, 1991, Crystal Gromer, review of *Lies of Silence,* pp. 24-25; November 5, 1993, Paul Elie, review of *No Other Life,* pp. 25-26; October 26, 1996, J.V. Long, review of *The Statement,* pp. 24-25.

Contemporary Review, April, 2001, Liam Heaney, "Brian Moore: Novelist in Search of an Irish Identity," p. 230.

Critical Quarterly, summer, 1976, Kerry McSweeney.

Critique: Studies in Modern Fiction, Volume 9, number 1, 1966; Volume 13, number 1, 1971; winter, 1989, Brian McIlroy, "Naming the Unnamable in Brian Moore's *I Am Mary Dunne,*" pp. 85-94.

Detroit News, October 14, 1979; May 19, 1985.

Economist, March 13, 1993, review of *No Other Life,* p. 102; October 28, 1995, review of *The Statement,* p. 102.

Entertainment Weekly, August 2, 1996, Megan Harlan, review of *The Statement,* pp. 54-55; January 30, 1998, Daneet Steffens, review of *The Magician's Wife,* p. 61.

First Things, January, 1997, John Wilson, review of *The Statement,* pp. 51-52.

Forbes, March 9, 1998, Steve Forbes, review of *The Magician's Wife,* p. 28.

Globe & Mail (Toronto, Ontario, Canada), March 30, 1985; September 5, 1987.

Harper's, October, 1965.

Independent (London, England), September 24, 1997, Jasper Rees, interview with Moore, pp. S2-S3.

Library Journal, May 15, 1981, review of *The Temptation of Eileen Hughes,* p. 1099; April 1, 1985, W. Keith McCoy, review of *Black Robe,* p. 159; September 1, 1990, Lynn Thompson, review of *Lies of Silence,* p. 258; August, 1991, Lisa Blankenship, review of *Lies of Silence,* p. 162; October 1, 1992, Nancy Schaffer, review of *The Lonely Passion of Judith Hearne,* p. 133; August, 1993, Janet Wilson Reit, review of *No Other Life,* p. 154; May 1, 1996, Katherine Holmes, review of *The Statement,* p. 132; November 1, 1997, Judith Kicinski, review of *The Magician's Wife,* p. 117; January, 1999, Joyce Kessel, review of *The Magician's Wife* (audiobook), p. 186.

Life, June 18, 1968; December 3, 1972.

London Review of Books, April 8, 1993, p. 15.

Los Angeles Times, September 11, 1983, Carolyn See, review of *Cold Heaven,* p. 1; September 14, 1983, Garry Abrams, interview with Moore, p. 10; April 7, 1985, Richard Eder, review of *Black Robe,* p. 1; May 26, 1985, Elizabeth Venant, "A Mischevious Leprechaun with Words," p. 3; July 2, 1987; September 15, 1987; December 23, 1987; January 1, 1988; April 10, 1988; March 1, 1992, Tom Christie, "An Irishman in Malibu," p. MAG20; August 7, 1996, Dexter Filkins, interview with Moore, p. E4.

Los Angeles Times Book Review, September 11, 1983; April 7, 1985; September 3, 1990, pp. 3, 9.

Maclean's, September 17, 1979; September 5, 1983, David Macfarlane, review of *Cold Heaven,* p. 49; April 1, 1985, Mark Abley, review of *Black Robe,* p. 54; June 18, 1990, Diane Turbide, review of *Lies of Silence,* p. 66; September 25, 1995, Diane Turbide, review of *The Statement,* pp. 53-54.

Nation, March 15, 1965; June 24, 1968; October 12, 1970; October 3, 1987, Thomas Flanagan, review of *The Color of Blood,* pp. 345-346; November 15, 1993, Amy Wilentz, review of *No Other Life,* pp. 570-573.

National Catholic Reporter, August 27, 1993, J.P. Slavin, review of *No Other Life,* p. 18.

New Leader, September 7, 1981, Mary Gaitskill, review of *The Temptation of Eileen Hughes,* pp. 16-17; August 12, 1996, Tova Reich, review of *The Statement,* pp. 30-31.

New Republic, August 17, 1968; June 9, 1973; October 24, 1983, Bruce Cook, review of *Cold Heaven,* pp. 45-46; November 2, 1987, p. 47; November 2, 1987, Stefan Kanfer, review of *The Color of Blood,* pp. 47-48.

New Statesman, February 18, 1966; October 17, 1975; November 13, 1981, Mary Holland, review of *The Temptation of Eileen Hughes,* p. 26; November 25, 1983, Richard Deveson, review of *Cold Heaven,* p. 28; June 14, 1985, Grace Ingoldby, review of *Black Robe,* pp. 33-34; September 25, 1987, Gillian Wilce, review of *The Color of Blood,* pp. 34-35; February 19, 1993, Boyd Tonkin, review of *No Other Life,* p. 41; September 22, 1995, Boyd Tonkin, review of *The Statement,* p. 34.

New Statesman & Society, April 20, 1990, Boyd Tonkin, review of *Lies of Silence,* p. 36.

Newsweek, June 2, 1975; September 20, 1976; October 15, 1979; July 20, 1981, Peter S. Prescott, review of *The Temptation of Eileen Hughes,* pp. 63-64; September 5, 1983, Peter S. Prescott, review of *Cold Heaven,* pp. 67-68; March 18, 1985, Walter Clemons, review of *Black Robe,* p. 75; September 17, 1990, Peter S. Prescott, review of *Lies of Silence,* p. 59.

New York, August 3, 1981, Abigail McCarthy, review of *The Temptation of Eileen Hughes,* pp. 58-59; February 24, 1992, David Denby, review of *Black Robe* (movie), p. 119.

New Yorker, May 11, 1957; August 4, 1975; August 24, 1981, review of *The Temptation of Eileen Hughes,* p. 100; October 3, 1983, review of *Cold Heaven,* pp. 126-127; July 8, 1985, review of *Black Robe,* pp. 72-73; October 19, 1987, review of *The Color of Blood,* p. 120; September 27, 1993, review of *No Other Life,* p. 105; July 15, 1996, Mary Hawthorne, review of *The Statement,* pp. 78-79.

New York Review of Books, Patricia Craig, review of *The Temptation of Eileen Hughes,* pp. 47-48; December 17, 1987, Neal Acherson, review of *The Color of Blood,* pp. 44-46; December 6, 1990, John Banville, review of *Lies of Silence,* pp. 22-25; October 21, 1993, William Trevor, review of *No Other Life,* pp. 3-4; October 3, 1996, John Gross, review of *The Statement,* pp. 36-37.

New York Times, October 1, 1976; September 12, 1979; July 3, 1981, Christopher Lehmann-Haupt, review of *The Temptation of Eileen Hughes,* pp. 19, C8; September 14, 1983, Christopher Lehmann-Haupt, review of *Cold Heaven,* p. 19, C21; January 15, 1984; February 26, 1984, John J. O'Connor, review of *Catholics* (video), p. H32; March 25, 1985, Christopher Lehmann-Haupt, review of *Black Robe,* pp. 17, C17; September 1, 1987, John Gross, review of *The Color of Blood,* pp. 19, C15; December 23, 1987; December 25, 1987; December 6, 1993, Christopher Lehmann-Haupt, review of *No Other Life,* pp. B2, C18; June 3, 1996, Christopher Lehmann-Haupt, review of *The Statement,* p. B2; August 13, 1996, Mel Gussow, interview with Moore, pp. B1, C11; August 18, 1996, Mel Gussow, review of *The Statement,* p. E2; January 28, 1998, Christopher Lehmann-Haupt, review of *The Magician's Wife,* pp. B10, E10.

New York Times Book Review, October 24, 1965; December 5, 1965; June 23, 1968; September 27, 1970; November 28, 1971; March 18, 1973; June 29, 1975; September 26, 1976; September 9, 1979; November 23, 1980, review of *The Mangan Inheritance,* p. 51; August 2, 1981, Joyce Carol Oates, review of *The Temptation of Eileen Hughes,* p. 3; September 5, 1982, review of *The Temptation of Eileen Hughes,* p. 19; September 18, 1983, Frances Taliaferro, review of *Cold Heaven,* pp. 11-12; September 16, 1984, James Stern, review of *The Lonely Passion of Judith Hearne,* p. 42; March 31, 1985, James Carroll, review of *Black Robe,* p. 7; September 27, 1987, Clancy Sigal, review of *The Color of Blood,* p. 11, Sarah Ferrell, interview with Moore, p. 11; November 6, 1988, p. 34; September 2, 1990, Francine Prose, review of *Lies of Silence,* p. 1, Sharon Shervington, interview with Moore, p. 23; September 12, 1993, Henry Louis Gates Jr., review of *No Other Life,* p. 1, Laurel Graeber, interview with Moore, p. 34; June 30, 1996, Eugen Weber, review of *The Statement,* p. 12; February 1, 1998, Thomas Mallon, review of *The Magician's Wife,* p. 14.

People, August 17, 1981, review of *The Temptation of Eileen Hughes,* p. 12; September 26, 1983, review of *Cold Heaven,* p. 14; April 29, 1985, Campbell Geeslin, review of *Black Robe,* pp. 22-23; October 12, 1987, Campbell Geeslin, review of *The Color of Blood,* pp. 16-17; November 12, 1990, Michael Neill, review of *Lies of Silence,* pp. 32-33; February 9, 1998, Francine Prose, review of *The Magician's Wife,* p. 31.

Publishers Weekly, May 8, 1981, Barbara A. Bannon, review of *The Temptation of Eileen Hughes,* p. 248; February 8, 1985, review of *Black Robe,* p. 67; July 24, 1987, Sybil Steinberg, review of *The Color of Blood,* p. 171; June 22, 1990, Sybil Steinberg, review of *Lies of Silence,* p. 47; June 21, 1993, review of *No Other Life,* p. 82; April 11, 1996, review of *The Statement,* pp. 57-58; October 20, 1997, review of *The Magician's Wife,* p. 53; January 5, 1998, John Blades, interview with Moore, pp. 44-45.

Quill & Quire, April, 1990, review of *Lies of Silence,* p. 28; April, 1993, review of *No Other Life,* p. 22;

September, 1995, p. 66; September, 1997, review of *The Magician's Wife,* p. 68; November, 1998, "Brian Moore: The Chameleon Novelist," p. 34.

Renascence, spring, 1990, J.C. Whitehouse, "Grammars of Assent and Dissent in Graham Greene and Brian Moore," pp. 157-171.

Resource Links, October, 1999, review of *The Magician's Wife,* p. 21.

Review of Contemporary Fiction, spring, 1991, Eamonn Wall, review of *Lies of Silence,* pp. 330-331.

Rolling Stone, November 28, 1991, Peter Travers, review of *Black Robe,* p. 104.

Saturday Night, September, 1968; November, 1970; July-August, 1975; October, 1976; October, 1983, Urjo Kareda, review of *Cold Heaven,* pp. 74-76; August, 1985, Alberto Manguel, review of *Black Robe,* pp. 43-44; May, 1990, Douglas Fetherling, review of *Lies of Silence,* p. 75.

Saturday Review, October 13, 1962; September 18, 1965; June 15, 1968; February 12, 1972; July 26, 1975; September 18, 1976; June, 1981, David Finkle, review of *The Temptation of Eileen Hughes,* p. 56.

Spectator, November 1, 1975; November 10, 1979; October 10, 1981; November 12, 1983; July 13, 1985; February 20, 1993, Dermot Clinch, review of *No Other Life,* p. 37; September 30, 1995, James Simmons, review of *The Statement,* pp. 43-44; September 20, 1997, P.J. Kavanagh, review of *The Magician's Wife,* p. 40.

Time, June 18, 1956; June 21, 1968; October 12, 1970; July 14, 1975; September 6, 1976; September 19, 1983, Patricia Blake, review of *Cold Heaven,* p. 98; March 18, 1985, R.Z. Sheppard, review of *Black Robe,* pp. 82-83; October 5, 1987, Pico Iyer, review of *The Color of Blood,* p. 84; July 1, 1996, Paul Gray, review of *The Statement,* p. 63.

Times (London, England), October 1, 1981; November 3, 1983; June 13, 1985; September 24, 1987; September 25, 1995, Julia Llewellyn Smith, interview with Moore, p. 17.

Times Educational Supplement, April 2, 1993, Liz Heron, review of *No Other Life,* p. S11.

Times Literary Supplement, February 3, 1966; October 24, 1966; April 9, 1971; January 21, 1972; November 10, 1972; October 17, 1975; November 23, 1979; October 9, 1981; October 28, 1983; June 7, 1985; October 2, 1987; April 20, 1990, Seamus Deane, review of *Lies of Silence,* p. 430; February 19, 1993, John Banville, review of *No Other Life,* p. 22; September 22, 1995, Sean O'Brien, review of *The Statement,* p. 22; September 12, 1997, Joyce Carol Oates, review of *The Magician's Wife,* p. 7.

Tribune Books (Chicago, IL), July 24, 1994.

Village Voice, June 30, 1957; October 22, 1979.

Wall Street Journal, July 9, 1981, Raymond Sokolov, review of *The Temptation of Eileen Hughes,* pp. 22, 24; September 19, 1983, Edmund Fuller, review of *Cold Heaven,* pp. 26, 31; November 24, 1987, Lee Lescaze, review of *The Color of Blood,* p. 26; August 31, 1990, Merle Rubin, review of *Lies of Silence,* p. A9; June 4, 1996, Merle Rubin, review of *The Statement,* pp. A15-A16; p. A15; January 13, 1998, Stuart Ferguson, review of *The Magician's Wife,* p. A20.

Washington Post, January 22, 1988.

Washington Post Book World, April 8, 1973; June 1, 1975; October 17, 1976; September 23, 1979; December 9, 1979; June 21, 1981; September 11, 1983; September 2, 1984, review of *Cold Heaven,* p. 12; March 31, 1985, Evan S. Connell, review of *Black Robe,* p. 3; September 6, 1987; February 14, 1988.

ONLINE

Canadian Literary and Art Archives, http:///www.ucalgary.ca/library/ (April 20, 2004), "Moore, Brian, 1921-1999."

OBITUARIES:

PERIODICALS

America, March 20, 1999, John B. Breslin, "In Memoriam: Brian Moore's 'Christ-Haunted' Fiction," p. 27.

Chicago Tribune, January 14, 1999, sec. 3, p. 13.

Los Angeles Times, January 12, 1999, pp. B1, B3.

Maclean's, January 25, 1999, p. 61.

New Yorker, January 25, 1999, p. 29.

New York Times, January 12, 1999, p. C26.

Quill & Quire, March, 1999, p. 17.

Saturday Night, March, 1999, pp. 45-46.

Times (London, England), January 13, 1999.

Times Literary Supplement, January 22, 1999, p. 14.

Washington Post, January 13, 1999, p. B6.

ONLINE

CNN Online, http://www.cnn.com/ (January 12, 1999).

* * *

MOORE, Lorrie

See MOORE, Marie Lorena

MOORE, Marie Lorena 1957-
(Lorrie Moore)

PERSONAL: Born January 13, 1957, Glens Falls, NY; daughter of Henry T., Jr. (an insurance company executive) and Jeanne (Day) Moore. *Education:* St. Lawrence University, B.A. (summa cum laude), 1978; Cornell University, M.F.A., 1982.

ADDRESSES: *Office*—English Department, University of Wisconsin—Madison, 600 North Park St., Madison, WI 53706. *Agent*—Melanie Jackson Agency, 1500 Broadway, Suite 2805, New York, NY 10036.

CAREER: Cornell University, Ithaca, NY, lecturer in English, 1982-84; University of Wisconsin—Madison, assistant professor, 1984-87, associate professor, 1987-91, professor of English, 1991—; writer.

MEMBER: PEN, Associated Writing Programs, Authors Guild, Authors League of America, Phi Beta Kappa.

AWARDS, HONORS: First prize, *Seventeen* magazine short-story contest, 1976, for "Raspberries"; Paul L. Wolfe Memorial Prize for literature, St. Lawrence University, 1978; A.L. Andrews Prize, Cornell University, 1982, for "What Is Seized," "How to Be an Other Woman," and "The Kid's Guide to Divorce"; Associated Writing Programs finalist for short fiction, 1983, for *Self-Help;* Granville Hicks Memorial fellow, 1983; National Endowment for the Arts fellowship and Rockefeller Foundation fellowship, 1989; Jack I. and Lillian L. Poses Creative Arts Citation in Fiction, Brandeis University, 1991; O. Henry Award, 1998, for "People Like That Are the Only People"; John Simon Guggenheim Memorial Foundation fellowship, 1991; 18th Annual PEN/Malamud Award, 2005, for excellence in short fiction.

WRITINGS:

UNDER NAME LORRIE MOORE

Self-Help (short stories), Knopf (New York, NY), 1985.
Anagrams (novel), Knopf (New York, NY), 1986.
The Forgotten Helper (juvenile), Kipling Press (New York, NY), 1987.
Like Life (short stories), Knopf (New York, NY), 1990.
(Editor) *I Know Some Things: Stories about Childhood by Contemporary Writers* (anthology), Faber & Faber (London, England), 1992.
Who Will Run the Frog Hospital? (novel), Random House (New York, NY), 1994.
Birds of America: Stories (short stories), Faber & Faber (London, England), 1998.
(Editor) *The Faber Book of Contemporary Stories about Childhood* (anthology), Faber & Faber (London, England), 1998.
(Coeditor) *The Best American Short Stories* (anthology), Houghton Mifflin (Boston, MA), 2004.

Contributor of short stories to anthologies, including *Best American Short Stories,* edited by Walter Mosley and Katrina Kenison, Houghton Mifflin (Boston, MA), 2003; contributor of stories, essays and book reviews to perodicals and magazines, including *Cosmopolitan, Seventeen, New Yorker, New York Times Book Review, Paris Review,* and *Ms.*

SIDELIGHTS: In a lengthy and comprehensive survey of the American short story for *Harper's,* Vince Passaro placed Marie Lorena Moore among a very short list of "today's best story writers." When collections of stories by Moore, David Foster Wallace, Denis Johnson, and Lydia Davis began to appear in the late 1980s, "a new kind of work stepped out onto the American literary landscape." Passaro added that "Many of her stories are fairly traditional in structure, but there is always that quickness of movement, that slightly skewed narrative perspective that keeps you alert and a little uneasy." In an assessment of Moore's work, June Unjoo Yang wrote in the *Women's Review of Books* that "in the span of several novels and short story collections, she draws attention to our careless use of language, the damage that we inflict upon it and one another by skipping blithely over the underlying significance of our exchanges."

Self-Help, Moore's first book, is a collection of short stories that "examines the idea that lives can be improved like golf swings," according to *New York Times Book Review* critic Jay McInerney. In her book, Moore uses what McInerney called "a distinctive, scalpel-sharp fictional voice" to produce "cohesive and moving" stories. He went on to say that "anyone who doesn't like it should consult a doctor." In the *New York Times,* Michiko Kakutani referred to the stories in *Self-Help* as "fine, funny and very moving pictures of contemporary life among the yuppies that help establish Miss Moore as a writer of enormous talent." She added that Moore, like her characters, "possesses a wry, crackly voice" and "an askew sense of humor."

Moore's sense of humor also won her praise for *Like Life,* her second collection of short stories. "It is [Moore's] laid back sense of humor and the note of alar that lend these accomplished stories their wit and depth," wrote Anna Vaux in the *Times Literary Supplement.* Calling Moore's sense of humor "wry" and "skittish," *Los Angeles Times Book Review* critic Merle Rubin nonetheless found that Moore has "very little ability to create convincing characters or tell stories that invite us to suspend our disbelief as we read them or to brood upon them after they've been read." Other critics found Moore's characters more convincing. *New York Times Book Review* critic Stephen McCauley saw "a new richness and variety of characters" in *Like Life,* while Vaux found that Moore's "women are high-spirited in their disappointments and alarming in their insights; her men are rarely so accomplished in the matter of perception. Their failure to grasp what is going on makes for some of the funnier moments here as well as some of the most surreal."

Birds of America, Moore's third collection of short stories, "is filled with portraits of lost people looking for a place to land," rather like the various birds that appear in each story, according to a reviewer in *Book.* The book was warmly received by critics and readers alike. A *Booklist* critic called it "breathtakingly funny, acutely observant, and slyly poignant," while Irving Malin wrote in the *Review of Contemporary Fiction* that "Moore's latest collection is her best." Passaro noted in *Harper's* that *Birds of America* "shockingly, made it onto *The New York Times Book Review* bestseller list for three brief but, for story fans, glorious weeks shortly after it came out." Moore's characters, mostly women, face insecurity, broken marriages, lost careers, and family tragedies with humor, resignation, honesty, and self-awareness. "Most of the stories explore the ambiguous space between the requirements of adult behaviour and the faulty equipment salvaged from childhood with which we attempt to cope with our lives," wrote James Urquhart in the *New Statesman.* Not all reviewers were so positive in their assessments, however. Writing in *Library Journal,* Joanna M. Burkhardt found the collection to be "dark and depressing," adding that there "is only so much misery a reader can endure." Yang found much to praise about *Bird's of America* in the *Women's Review of Books,* but cautioned that "At her worst . . . Moore can veer into self-indulgence, the abiding love affair with word games deteriorating into something merely clever or gratuitous."

Of her first novel, *Anagrams,* Moore told *Ploughshares* that "It got many bad reviews. . . . I actually had to stop reading them. I just couldn't take it anymore." Even if there was legitimate reason for that observation, the same could not be said for her well-received second novel, *Who Will Run the Frog Hospital?* The book, whose title comes from a painting by Nancy Mladenoff, deals with the innocent dreams of adolescence as portrayed in the memories of a grown woman confronted with a failing marriage. Carole Stabile wrote in *Belles Lettres* that "the beauty of *Who Will Run the Frog Hospital?* lies not in its conjuring up of teenage angst, but in its ability to conjure up much of the headiness and magic . . . that makes growing up bearable and the memory of it so exquisitely sad."

BIOGRAPHICAL AND CRITICAL SOURCES:

PERIODICALS

Belles Lettres, January, 1996, Carole Stabile, review of *Who Will Run the Frog Hospital?,* p. 45.

Book, July, 2001, review of *Birds of America,* p. 84.

Booklist, January 1, 1999, review of *Birds of America,* p. 779.

Harper's, August, 1999, Vince Passaro, review of *Birds of America,* p. 80.

Library Journal, September 1, 1998, Joanna M. Burkhardt, review of *Birds of America,* p. 218.

Los Angeles Times, June 3, 1985.

Los Angeles Times Book Review, June 3, 1990, p. 11.

New Statesman, January 8, 1999, James Urquhart, review of *Birds of America,* p. 58.

New York Times, March 6, 1985.

New York Times Book Review, March 24, 1985; May 20, 1990, p. 7.

Ploughshares, fall, 1998, Don Lee, profile of Lorrie Moore.

Review of Contemporary Fiction, spring, 1999, Irving Malin, review of *Birds of America,* p. 196.

Times Literary Supplement, August 31, 1990, p. 917.

Tribune Books (Chicago, IL), March 24, 1985.

Vanity Fair, September, 1985.

Women's Review of Books, November, 1998, June Unjoo Yang, review of *Birds of America,* p. 15.

* * *

MORA, Pat 1942-
(Patricia Mora)

PERSONAL: Born January 19, 1942, in El Paso, TX; daughter of Raúl Antonio (an optician and business owner) and Estela (a homemaker; maiden name, Delgado) Mora; married William H. Burnside, Jr., July 27,

1963 (divorced, 1981); married Vernon Lee Scarborough (an archaeologist and professor), May 25, 1984; children: (first marriage) William Roy, Elizabeth Anne, Cecilia Anne. *Education:* Texas Western College (now University of Texas—El Paso), B.A., 1963; University of Texas—El Paso, M.A., 1967. *Politics:* Democrat. *Religion:* "Ecumenical." *Hobbies and other interests:* Reading, walking, traveling, visiting with family and friends.

ADDRESSES: Home—3036 Plaza Blanca, Santa Fe, NM 87507; 2925 Sequoia Drive, Edgewood, KY 41017. *Agent*—Elizabeth Harding, Curtis Brown Ltd., Ten Astor Place, New York, NY 10003.

CAREER: Writer, educator, administrator, lecturer, and activist. El Paso Independent School District, El Paso, TX, teacher, 1963-66; El Paso Community College, El Paso, part-time instructor in English and communications, 1971-78; University of Texas—El Paso, part-time lecturer in English, 1979-81, assistant to vice president of academic affairs, 1981-88, director of university museum and assistant to president, 1988-89; full-time writer, 1989—. Host of *Voices: The Mexican-American in Perspective,* broadcast on National Public Radio affiliate KTEP, 1983-84. Member of Ohio Arts Council panel, 1990. W.K. Kellogg Foundation, consultant, 1990-91, and member of advisory committee for Kellogg National Fellowship Program, 1991-94. Distinguished Visiting Professor, Garrey Carruthers Chair in Honors, University of New Mexico, 1999. Advocate to establish El Día de los Niños/El Día de los Libros (Children's Day/Book Day), a national day to celebrate childhood and bilingual literacy held during National Poetry Month, instituted April 30, 1997. Through REFORMA, the National Association to Promote Library Service to the Spanish-Speaking and Latinos, Mora and her siblings established the Estela and Raúl Mora Award. Gives poetry readings and presentations, both nationally and internationally.

MEMBER: Academy of American Poets, International Reading Association, National Association of Bilingual Educators, Society of Children's Book Writers and Illustrators, Texas Institute of Letters, Friends of the Santa Fe Library, Museum of New Mexico Foundation, Spanish Colonial Arts Society, National Council of La Raza.

AWARDS, HONORS: Award for Creative Writing, National Association for Chicano Studies, 1983; Poetry Award, *New America: Women Artists and Writers of the Southwest,* 1984; Harvey L. Johnson Book Award, Southwest Council of Latin American Studies, 1984; Southwest Book Award, Border Regional Library, 1985, for *Chants;* Kellogg National fellowship, 1986-89; Kellogg National Leadership Fellowship, 1986; Leader in Education Award, El Paso Women's Employment and Education, 1987; Chicano/Hispanic Faculty and Professional Staff Association Award, University of Texas—El Paso, 1987, for outstanding contribution to the advancement of Hispanics; Southwest Book Award, 1987, for *Borders;* named to Writers Hall of Fame, *El Paso Herald-Post,* 1988; Poetry Award, Conference of Cincinnati Women, 1990; National Endowment for the Arts fellowship in creative writing, 1994; Southwest Book Award, 1994, for *A Birthday Basket for Tia;* Americas Award commendation, Consortium of Latin Americas Studies Program, "Choices" list designation, Cooperative Children's Book Center, "Children's Books Mean Business" list designation, Children's Book Council, and Notable Books for a Global Society designation, International Reading Association, all 1996, all for *Confetti: Poems for Children;* Premio Aztlan, and Women of Southwest Book Award, both 1997, both for *House of Houses;* nomination, Washington Children's Choice Picture Book Award, 1997, for *Pablo's Tree;* Tomás Rivera Mexican-American Children's Book Award, Southwest Texas State University, 1997, *Skipping Stones* Book Award, 1998, and Apollo Children's Book Award nomination, Apollo Reading Center (Florida), 2002, all for *Tomás and the Library Lady;* Book Publishers of Texas Award, Texas Institute of Letters, 1998, and finalist, PEN Center USA West Literary Award, PEN West, 1999, both for *The Big Sky;* Pellicer-Frost Bi-national Poetry Award, 1999, for a collection of odes; Alice Louis Wood Memorial Ohioana Award for Children's Literature, 2001; Teddy Award, Writers' League of Texas, and Books for the Teen Age selection, New York Public Library, both 2001, both for *My Own True Name.* Mora also has received the Choices Award, Cooperative Book Centers.

WRITINGS:

PICTURE BOOKS; FOR CHILDREN

A Birthday Basket for Tía, illustrated by Cecily Lang, Macmillan (New York, NY), 1992.

Listen to the Desert/Oye al desierto, illustrated by Francesco X. Mora, Clarion Books (New York, NY), 1994.

Agua, Agua, Agua (concept book), illustrated by Jose Ortega, GoodYear Books (Reading, MA), 1994.

Pablo's Tree, illustrated by Cecily Lang, Macmillan (New York, NY), 1994.

(With Charles Ramirez Berg) *The Gift of the Poinsettia,* Piñata Books (Houston, TX), 1995, also produced as a play, *Los Posadas and the Poinsettia,* with text by Pat Mora and Charles Ramirez Berg.

The Race of Toad and Deer (retelling), illustrated by Maya Itzna Brooks, Orchard Books (New York, NY), 1995, revised edition with new text and illustrations, illustrated by Domi, Groundwood/Douglas & McIntyre (Toronto, Ontario, Canada), 2001.

Tomás and the Library Lady (biography), illustrated by Raul Colon, Knopf (New York, NY), 1997, published as *Thomas and the Library Lady,* Dragonfly Books (New York, NY), 1997.

Delicious Hullabaloo/Pachanga deliciosa, illustrated by Francesco X. Mora, Spanish translation by Alba Nora Martinez and Pat Mora, Piñata Books (Houston, TX), 1998.

The Rainbow Tulip, illustrated by Elizabeth Sayles, Viking (New York, NY), 1999.

The Night the Moon Fell (retelling), illustrated by Domi, Groundwood/Douglas & McIntyre (Toronto, Ontario, Canada), 2000.

The Bakery Lady/La señora de la panadería, illustrated by Pablo Torrecilla, translated by Gabriela Baeza Ventura and Pat Mora, Piñata Books (Houston, TX), 2001.

A Library for Juana: The World of Sor Juana Ines (biography), illustrated by Beatriz Vidal, Knopf (New York, NY), 2002.

Maria Paints the Hills, illustrated by Maria Hesch, Museum of New Mexico Press (Santa Fe, NM), 2002.

The Song of Francis and the Animals, illustrated by David Frampton, Eerdman's Books for Young Readers (Grand Rapids, MI), 2005.

POETRY; FOR CHILDREN

The Desert Is My Mother/El desierto es mi madre, art by Daniel Lechon, Piñata Books (Houston, TX), 1994.

Confetti: Poems for Children, illustrated by Enrique O. Sanchez, Lee & Low Books (New York, NY), 1995.

Uno, dos, tres/One, Two, Three, illustrated by Barbara Lavallee, Clarion Books (New York, NY), 1996.

The Big Sky, illustrated by Steve Jenkins, Scholastic (New York, NY), 1998.

My Own True Name: New and Selected Poems for Young Adults, 1984-1999 (anthology), illustrated by Anthony Accardo, Pinata Books (Houston, TX), 2001.

Love to Mama: A Tribute to Mothers (anthology), illustrated by Paula S. Barragán, Lee & Low Books (New York, NY), 2001.

POETRY; FOR ADULTS

Chants, Arte Público Press (Houston, TX), 1984.

Borders, Arte Público Press (Houston, TX), 1986.

Communion, Arte Público Press (Houston, TX), 1991.

Agua Santa/Holy Water, Beacon Press (Boston, MA), 1995.

Aunt Carmen's Book of Practical Saints, Beacon Press (Boston, MA), 1997.

OTHER

Nepantla: Essays from the Land in the Middle, University of New Mexico Press (Albuquerque, NM), 1993.

House of Houses (memoir), Beacon Press (Boston, MA), 1997.

Mora's books have been translated into several languages, including Bengali and Italian. Work represented in anthologies, including *New Worlds of Literature,* Norton (New York, NY), *Revista Chicano-Riqueña: Kikirikí/Children's Literature Anthology,* Arte Público (Houston, TX), 1981, *Tun-Ta-Ca-Tún* (children's literature anthology), Arte Público Press 1986, *The Desert Is No Lady: Southwestern Landscapes in Women's Writing and Art* (also see below), edited by Vera Norwood and Janice Monk, University of Arizona Press (Tucson, AZ), 1997, *Many Voices: A Multicultural Reader,* edited by Linda Watkins-Goffman and others, Prentice-Hall (Englewood Cliffs, NJ), 2001, and *Wachale! Poetry and Prose about Growing up Latino in America,* edited by Ilan Stevens, Cricket Books, 2001. Contributor of poetry and essays to periodicals, including *Best American Poetry, 1996, Calyx; Daughters of the Fifth Sun, Horn Book, Kalliope, Latina, Ms., New Advocate,* and *Prairie Schooner.*

ADAPTATIONS: The text of Mora's poem "Let Us Now Hold Hands" was adapted into a song by Jennifer Stasack for MUSE, a choir at the University of Cincinnati. Mora is among the subjects of *The Desert Is No Lady,* a film by Shelley Williams and Susan Palmer produced by Women Who Make Movies, 1995; the film, which profiles nine contemporary artists and writers from the southwestern United States, prompted a book of the same name (see above).

SIDELIGHTS: Considered among the most distinguished of Hispanic writers, Pat Mora is praised both as an author and an activist for cultural appreciation and conservation. An educator and speaker, she is also a respected advocate for literature and literacy. Mora seeks to establish the recognition and preservation of Mexican-American culture and fostering pride in Latino heritage. She often is called both a regional writer and a feminist. Characteristically, her works are set in the southwestern United States and feature her birthplace of El Paso, Texas, and the surrounding desert as images. In addition, they promote the value of women both nationally and internationally. Considered both specific and universal, Mora's books feature Mexican and Mexican-American protagonists—including herself and her family—and include Hispanic history, legends, customs, and traditions.

Mora is noted for her diversity as a writer as well as for the positive, healing messages with which she underscores her books. As a writer for the young, she has written picture books, a biography, a board book, a counting book, and two retellings of Mayan folktales. She also has written volumes of poetry for children as well as a collection of her poems for young adults, and has edited and contributed to a poetry collection that celebrates motherhood. As a writer for adults, Mora is the author of poetry that characteristically reflects her experience as a person of Mexican heritage—a bilingual, bi-cultural woman who grew up in the southwestern desert. She often addresses the theme of identity, especially that of women, and acknowledges the Hispanic tradition of linking females with the desert. Mora redefines the image by making the desert a strong, independent woman who is both nurturing and sensual, a woman with knowledge to impart to those who will listen. Mora also writes about borders: while recognizing that Mexican Americans live a type of border existence no matter where they live, she sees the border as a powerful image of healing, a place to bridge divisions and to foster mutual understanding. Drawing on her own strength as well as on the women and men who preceded her, the poet attempts to bridge the borders between past and present, between old traditions and new environments, between the sexes, and between Latinos and the world at large. Mora is credited for celebrating the Mexican-American experience while attempting to foster unity among all cultures. In addition to the accolades that she has received as a poet, Mora has been commended as an essayist; she has produced a volume of autobiographical essays, *Nepantla: Essays from the Land in the Middle,* and a memoir in essay form, *House of Houses.*

In her children's books, Mora addresses several of the subjects and themes that constitute her books for adults, such as Mexican-American culture, nature (especially the desert), and the importance of family. Mora often features Hispanic boys and girls who have warm relationships with adults, such as parents, grandparents, teachers, and librarians. Her works often revolve around celebrations, such as parties and holidays, and are filled with food and music. Thematically, Mora promotes the importance of cultural heritage. While acknowledging that being different is often difficult, she proposes that the young Latino—or any child—can become assimilated while still retaining his or her cultural identity. She also stresses the support of family and friends, self-reliance, and the joys of books and reading, among other subjects. As a literary stylist, Mora favors spare but evocative prose that is filled with descriptions and imagery; she also includes basic Spanish phrases in her works, most of which are published in both English and Spanish. Mora's poetry is often anthologized, and her work is studied in elementary schools, high schools, and colleges. Several of her poems, including "1910" and "Illegal Alien," are considered classics. Mora is generally commended as a writer whose contributions to literature, literacy, and cultural awareness have been significant. She also is noted for introducing children to Latino culture in a joyful and entertaining manner. Writing in *Dictionary of Literary Biography,* Nicolás Kanellos stated, "Pat Mora has developed one of the broadest audiences of any Hispanic poet in the United States. . . . Mora's books for children have been acclaimed almost universally for the sensitive and deft portrayals of Mexican Americans and Mexican culture. . . . Mora's writing for children has also helped to bring Hispanic culture to non-Hispanic children." A writer in *Dictionary of Hispanic Biography* concluded, "Mora has been essential to the movement to understand and uphold Mexican-American culture. . . . She provides an excellent model for young Hispanics who are just beginning to understand the past and are about to experience promising futures. . . . As a successful Hispanic writer, and a writer who writes about and for Hispanics, Mora is an exemplary role model for the young people of an increasingly multicultural America."

Mora features her family extensively throughout her works. Born in El Paso, Texas, the author is the daughter of Raúl Mora, an optician, and Estela Delgado Mora, a homemaker; Mora has three siblings, Cecilia, Stella, and Roy (later Anthony). The Mora family is descended from Mexicans and a Spanish sea captain. Mora's paternal grandparents, Lázaro and Natividad, left Chihuahua during the Mexican Revolution (c. 1916) to escape the violent raids of Pancho Villa. The family settled in El Paso, as did her maternal grandparents, Eduardo and

Amelia Delgado, who also had left Mexico during the revolution. Mora's father Raúl was about four years old when he moved to Texas with his family. At seven, he started selling newspapers; by ten, he had the best spots in El Paso. During the Depression, Raúl handled the circulation for the local Spanish newspaper, making a hundred dollars a week in commissions, a princely sum during that time. When the Anglo Americans took over the paper and began to mistreat him, Raúl resigned and went to business college. He then worked at Riggs Optical, a subsidiary of Bausch and Lomb, a company with which he stayed for ten years. During this time, he met and married Estela Delgado. A voracious reader, Estela had excelled as a student in grade school, despite the presence of a racist principal who was prejudiced against Mexicans. As a high school student, she won several speech contests. Estela hoped to go on to college and become a writer, but was unable to continue her education due to the Depression. She met Mora on a blind date when she was seventeen; they were married five years later, in 1939.

As a small child, Mora pointed to a pair of eye glasses and said the word, *antiojos,* which is "glasses" in Spanish. She then began to run around the house, affixing names to everything in it. "Naming things," she wrote in *House of Houses,* "the interest continues." Mora and her siblings were taught both English and Spanish by their parents, so, as the author wrote in *Nepantla: Essays from the Land in the Middle,* "I could derive pleasure from both cultures." Mora often has acknowledged the influence of her maternal grandmother and aunt, who lived with the family. Her grandmother Sotero Amelia Landavazo, called Mamande by the children, was a red-haired orphan who had been taken in and raised by rich relatives. She married Eduardo Delgado, a judge with three grown daughters, one of whom was Mora's mother's half-sister, Ignacia (Nacha) Delgado, whom the Mora children nicknamed Lobo, which is Spanish for wolf. Nacha would come home from work in the evenings and ask affectionately in Spanish, "Where are my little wolves?" Writing in *Nepantla,* Mora recalled, "Gradually, she became our lobo, a spinster aunt who gathered the four of us around her, tying us to her for life by giving us all she had." Nacha would spin tales in Spanish and English for the children and read to them at night. In a quote that she gave to the California State University—Dominguez Hills *NewsRoom,* Mora said, "I learned the power of storytelling from my aunt." Writing in *Nepantla,* Mora called Lobo "a wonderful storyteller" before concluding, "Lobo taught me much about one of our greatest challenges as human beings: loving well." She added, "My tribute to her won't be in annual pilgrimages to a cemetery. I was born in these United States and am very much influenced by this culture. But I do want to polish, polish my writing tools to preserve images of women like Lobo, unsung women whose fierce family love deserves our respect."

Mora attended St. Patrick's School, a Roman Catholic grade school that was run by an order of nuns, the Sisters of Loretto. "Until I'm about seventeen," she noted in *House of Houses,* "I never consider being anything other than a nun, Sister Mary Jude, the name I'd chosen, the patron saint of the impossible." As a young girl, Mora would put on a black lace shawl and play at being a nun, lining up the dining room chairs like pews in a church and lecturing her imaginary class about the things that her teachers had taught her. She also was learning about the power of words. In *House of Houses,* Mora recalled, "Early I sank into stories. Lobo's first, though at the time I'm unaware of her luring, unaware that stories are essential as water. I take books home from school and public libraries, join summer reading clubs, read biographies." The stories and poems in *Childcraft,* a set of books owned by her family, were particular favorites, and Mora devoured the life stories of Clara Barton, Davy Crockett, Amelia Earhart, Betsy Ross, William Penn, Dolly Madison, and Jim Bowie, among others. Mora noted, "I read Nancy Drew books, Bobbsey Twins, Pollyanna, and every book by Laura Ingalls Wilder, whom I discover in the *W's.*" In "Dear Fellow Writer," an introduction that she wrote to her poetry collection *My Own True Name: New and Selected Poems for Young Adults, 1984-1999,* Mora said, "I have always been a reader, which is the best preparation for becoming a writer. When I was in grade school . . . , I read comic books and mysteries and magazines and library books. I was soaking up language." In an interview with Tey Diana Rebolledo in *This Is about Vision: Interviews with Southwestern Writers,* Mora said, "I loved writing in school; it came pretty easily to me." She recalled that, after graduating from eighth grade, she wrote religious poems and typed them on her new typewriter. Mora said in a *Scholastic Authors Online Library* interview. "I had many wonderful teachers who had us memorize poetry. Although, at the time, I probably grumbled and griped about it, it was helpful to me. . . . I always liked poetry. I had lots of books in my house and I would just open them up and read all sorts of poetry." She also liked to listen to soap operas and to the children's show *Let's Pretend* on the radio, to watch cowboy shows on television, to play with dolls, to go to movies and to the local swimming pool, and to build forts from bricks and rocks.

Despite her interest in books and language, Mora did not think of becoming a writer as a child. She related in the *Scholastic Authors Online Library* interview, "I always liked reading, and I always liked writing, but I don't think I thought of being a writer. I say that to students all the time because I never saw a writer like me—who was bilingual. So it's important for kids to realize that writers come in all different shapes and sizes." Although she enjoyed the Mexican traditions at home and often traveled over the border to Mexico, Mora downplayed her ethnicity as a child. She did not want her friends to know that she spoke Spanish to her grandmother and aunt, and she cringed when her father played mariachi music on the radio. At school, Mora found little consolation in being Mexican. "Like many Latinas in this country," she wrote in *Nepantla,* "I was educated with few if any references to my Mexican-American history, to part of my literary and human heritage." When asked by the *Scholastic Authors Online Library* interviewer if she ever felt different from other children because of her Hispanic heritage, Mora stated, "There were times when I wished that my Mexican heritage were a part of my school day. I wished that we had had books that had Spanish in them. And I wished that I had seen things about Mexican culture on the bulletin boards and in the library. One of the reasons that I write children's books is because I want Mexican culture and Mexican-American culture to be a part of our schools and libraries."

In 1949, Raúl Mora opened his own company, United Optical. He worked evenings and weekends to support his family, and he was aided in his business by Estela and the children. "When we aren't in school or doing homework," Mora wrote, "my sisters and I go to the optical and clean the desks or wash finished glasses, but there's always a reward, a stop at the Oasis Drive-In." As a high-school student, Mora attended Loretto Academy, a Catholic school for girls that was run by the same order of nuns who had taught her in grade school; she enjoyed the experience immensely. After graduating from high school, Mora thought about becoming a doctor, then decided to be a teacher. She attended Texas Western College (now the University of Texas—El Paso) and received her bachelor's degree in 1963. Shortly after graduation, she married William H. Burnside, Jr.; the couple had three children: William, Elizabeth, and Cecilia. In the first year of her first marriage, Mora began to teach English and Spanish at grade and high schools in El Paso. When she was twenty-four, Mora was paid a hundred dollars by the Hallmark greeting card company for a children's book that she wrote in rhyme. The book went unpublished, and the fledgling author was not inspired to write again for several years.

Mora received her master's degree from the University of Texas—El Paso in 1967. In 1971, she became a part-time instructor in English and communications at El Paso Community College, a position that she would hold for seven years. In 1981, Mora began her career as an administrator, becoming the assistant to the vice president of academic affairs at the university, and in the same year, was divorced from Burnside. Writing in *Nepantla,* Mora related the beginning of her journey from teacher to writer: "The seemingly endless stacks of essays to read and a growing desire to write finally convinced me to apply for a position that might require a long day, but allow evenings and weekends for my children and my writing. . . . Why are you marking someone else's papers? I would ask myself during the last semesters of teaching freshman English. I thought, You need to be marking your own work." She recalled in *This Is about Vision: Interviews with Southwestern Writers,* "When I went through my divorce and I realized I was edging toward forty, I said to myself, it's now or never. If you're not going to be serious about writing, it's never going to happen." She also became passionate about representing her heritage, sharing the beauty of her culture with others, and affirming the rights of Latinos. Writing in *Nepantla,* Mora stated, "I am a child of the border, that land corridor bordered by the two countries that have most influenced my perception of reality." As she started to write seriously, Mora began to educate herself about her heritage. She bought books about Mexico and Mexican Americans and, as she wrote in *Nepantla,* discovered "images, stories, and rhythms that I wanted to incorporate." She also learned about the political and social difficulties that are encountered by indigenous peoples, knowledge that had a profound effect on her. Mora recalled, "I experienced that not uncommon transformation experienced by many whose pasts have been ignored or diminished: I began to see Mexico, to see its people, hear its echoes, gaze up at its silent and silenced grandeur. My Mexicanness became a source of pride."

Initially, the road to being a writer was a difficult one for Mora. She noted in *This Is about Vision,* "It was hard at the beginning. I have had many more rejections than people would ever think." She acknowledged in *Nepantla,* "Whereas my administrative friends tried discreetly to ignore my vice, the few writers I knew were suspicious of my daytime work. Some of us seem to have a knack for living in *nepantla,* the land in the middle." She added, "There probably isn't a week of my life that I don't have at least one experience when I feel that discomfort, the slight frown from someone that wordlessly asks, What is someone like her doing here?" Nevertheless, Mora persevered. She recalled, "I was persistent, particularly after my first poem was published in 1981. Like Kafka, I hung onto my desk with my teeth. Evenings and weekends, after dishes were washed and homework questions answered, I wrote." In 1981, Mora contributed to *Revista Chicano-Riqueña Kikiriki/Children's Literature Anthology,* a collection published under the editorship of Sylvia Cavazos Pena, and five years later, she contributed to a second anthology, *Tun-Ta-Ca-Tun,* which also was edited by Pena. In 1983, Mora received an award for creative writing from the National Association for Chicano Studies. Her first book, the adult poetry collection *Chants,* was published in 1984. In the same year, Mora married Vernon Lee Scarborough, an archeologist and professor whom she had met at the University of Texas—El Paso. She published her second poetry collection for adults, *Borders,* in 1986, and received a Kellogg national fellowship to study national and international issues of cultural conservation. In 1988, Mora became the director of the museum at the University of Texas—El Paso and also became the assistant to the president of the school.

In 1989, Mora decided to become a full-time writer and speaker. She left El Paso for Cincinnati, Ohio, after her husband, an expert on Mayan culture, was hired to teach anthropology at the University of Cincinnati. In 1991, Mora produced her third adult poetry collection, *Communion,* a work that features the author's reflections about her travels to such places as Cuba, India, Pakistan, and New York City. That same year, Mora's father retired. At the age of seventy-nine, Raúl developed severe depression, then dementia; he died at the age of eighty-one. Mora profiled her father shortly before his death in *House of Houses:* "'How are you doing, honey,' he asks when I visit, fighting tears every minute I'm with him. 'When I get better, I'm going to read your poems.' 'I'm working on my writing,' I say, wondering if my parents were disappointed when I left a safe university title and salary, decided to write and speak full-time. 'We all know our mediums,' my father says. 'What we do best. It's like baseball. One throws this way and one throws that.' With totally open hands, my parents gave me my life."

In 1992, Mora produced her first book for children, *A Birthday Basket for Tía.* A picture book that features an incident taken from the life of her aunt Ignacia Delgado (Lobo), the story describes how young narrator Cecilia, who shares her name with Mora's youngest daughter, finds the perfect present for the ninetieth birthday party that is being held for her beloved great-aunt Tía. With the help—and interference—of her cat Chica, Cecilia fills a basket with reminders of the good times that she and Tía have shared: a mixing bowl that represents their days spent making cookies, a teacup to represent the special brew Tia makes when Cecilia is sick, a book Tia has read to Cecilia, and flowers that represent their times outside. The present is a hit, and Tía puts down her cane to dance with her niece. Written in a repetitive text, *A Birthday Basket for Tia* is both a story and a counting book (it allows children to count to ninety). A *Publishers Weekly* reviewer called the work "poignant" before stating that Mora's text "flows smoothly from one event to the next, and clearly presents the careful planning behind Cecilia's gift-gathering mission." Writing in *School Library Journal,* Julie Corsaro called *A Birthday Basket for Tia* a "warm and joyful story," while *Horn Book*'s Maeve Visser Knoth called Cecilia "an irrepressible child" before concluding that Mora's text "exemplifies the best of recent multicultural publishing. An honest, child-centered story." Mora has stated that Lobo, the inspiration for Tía, really put down her cane and danced at her ninetieth birthday party.

Pablo's Tree is another of the author's popular picture books with a strong intergenerational relationship at its core. The story is set on the fifth birthday of its protagonist, a boy who has been adopted and who lives with his single mother. Pablo is excited because he is going to be with his grandfather, for whom he is named. The elder Pablo—called Lito, short for *abuelito*—has established a tradition for his grandson: every year, he has decorated a special tree in his honor, leaving the decorations as a surprise. In past years, the tree has been festooned with balloons, colored streamers, paper lanterns, and bird cages; this year, Lito has chosen bells and wind chimes as his theme. Pablo and Lito celebrate the day by eating apples and listening to the music coming from the tree; Lito also tells Pablo the story of the tree, which was planted when Pablo's mother adopted him. Writing in *Bulletin of the Center for Children's Books,* Deborah Stevenson commented, "A tale of love and welcome (and neat ornaments), this volume has a celebratory aspect that makes it appealing not just to adoptees but to kids generally.'" Annie Ayres of *Booklist* called *Pablo's Tree* a "lovely and resonant picture book that, like the tree that Pablo discovers . . . rings with happiness and family love." *Horn Book*'s Knoth concluded, "It is a pleasure to read a story which includes adoption and single motherhood without making them central aspects."

The Rainbow Tulip is often considered among Mora's best books. Based on a childhood experience of her mother, Estela, this picture book, which is set in El Paso during the 1920s, features Estelita, a first grader who is caught between two cultures. Estelita realizes that her heritage sets her apart: she sees her mother, who speaks no English and dresses in dark clothes, as old-fashioned. The girls in Estelita's class are dressing as tulips for the upcoming May Day parade, and she wants her costume to be different from the others. When the big day arrives, Estelita comes dressed in all the colors of the rainbow, as opposed to the other children, who are dressed in single hues. Although Estelita is disconcerted at first, she successfully executes a maypole dance and wins her teacher's approval. Her mother, who understands how tough it is to find her place in a new country, tells her that being different is a condition that is both sweet and sour, much like the lime sherbet that is their favorite dessert. Estelita realizes that being different is both hard and exciting, and she recognizes her mother's quiet love for her. Writing in *Children's Literature,* Joan Carris commented, "This is a gentle story, nice for reading at bedtime. And awfully necessary, it seems to me." Carris also called Estelita "an appealing Mexican heroine" before concluding that "the characters come alive in this timely book." *Library Journal*'s Ann Welton wrote, "Mora succeeds in creating a quiet story to which children will respond. . . . This tale of family love and support crosses cultural boundaries and may remind youngsters of times when their families made all the difference."

Tomás and the Library Lady is a work that combines two of Mora's most prevalent themes: the joy of reading and the special quality of intergenerational relationships. Based on an incident in the life of author and educator Tomás Rivera, the first Hispanic to become chancellor of the University of California—Riverside, this slightly fictionalized biographical picture book describes how young Tomás, a member of a family of migrant workers who has traveled from Texas to Iowa for work, is introduced to the world of books by a sympathetic librarian. Tomás' grandfather has told him wonderful stories, but has run out of them; he tells Tomás to go to the library for more. At the library, Tomás meets a kindly librarian, who gives him books in English—signed out on her own card. In return, Tomás teaches Spanish to the librarian. When the season ends, Tomás must return to Texas. The librarian hugs Tomás and gives him a shiny new book to keep, and Tomás gives the librarian a loaf of sweet bread baked by his mother. In an end note, readers learn that the library at the university where Tomás later worked now bears his name. Writing in *Skipping Stones,* Elke Richers commented, "I definitely recommend this book to anyone who likes a good story or who wants to know how reading can make a real difference in someone's life. *Tomás and the Library Lady* is powerful. . . . Don't miss it!" A reviewer in *Publishers Weekly* stated that "young readers and future librarians will find this an inspiring tale." In a review of the Spanish edition (*Tomás y la senora de la biblioteca*) in *Booklist,* Isabel Schon concluded, "Many of us from Hispanic America, who never enjoyed the luxuries of school or public libraries in our countries of origin, will identify with Tomás' story." *Tomás and the Library Lady* actually was the first of Mora's books to be accepted for publication, in 1989. However, it was not published for several years due to the difficulty in finding an appropriate illustrator. Finally, with the addition of the art of Raúl Colón, the book was produced in 1997.

Mora's first collection for a juvenile audience is *Confetti: Poems for Children.* In this work, which is directed to primary graders, narrative poems in free verse describe the American Southwest as seen through the eyes of a young Mexican-American girl. The child, who lives in the desert, views it and its inhabitants through the space of a whole day, from early morning to nightfall. Mora uses the sun, clouds, leaves, and wind as the subjects of several of her poems; in addition, she profiles a wood sculptor, a grandmother, and a baker. A critic in *Kirkus Reviews* noted that the "best of these poems that mix English and Spanish . . . warmly evokes familiar touchstones of Mexican-American life." Writing in *School Library Journal,* Sally R. Dow called *Confetti* a "welcome addition" and stated that the poems "capture the rhythms and uniqueness of the Southwest and its culture." In *The Big Sky,* Mora celebrates the land, people, and creatures of the Southwest in fourteen poems; the volume also includes some poems that are set in the author's home of Ohio. She explores such subjects as the sky, a grandmother, a huge mountain, an old snake, a horned lizard, and coyotes. A *Publishers Weekly* reviewer predicted that the poems in *The Big Sky* "will delight readers of all ages with their playfully evocative imagery." Lisa Falk of *School Library Journal* commented, "This gem is both a lovely poetry book and an evocative look at a magical place." Calling Mora's words "wonderful," Marilyn Courtot of *Children's Literature* commented, "These spare and dramatic poems transport readers to the American Southwest."

Mora's *My Own True Name: New and Selected Poems for Young Adults, 1984-1999* is a collection of sixty poems the author selected from her adult books; she also wrote several new poems for this collection. Mora uses the metaphor of a cactus, which represents human existence, to join the poems thematically. She groups them into three sections: blooms, which represent love and joy; thorns, which represent sorrow and hardship; and roots, which represent family, home, strength, and wisdom. The poems address such subjects as Mora's life as a Latina in the Southwest; her search for identity; and her experience as a mother, especially of teenagers. The author also weaves Mexican phrases, historical figures, and cultural symbols into her poems. Writing in *School Library Journal,* Nina Lindsay stated that Mora "has chosen poems with themes that are accessible to, yet challenging for, teens. . . . This anthology speaks to a young audience, and it should find many readers." Calling the poems "powerful," Gillian Engberg of *Booklist* noted, "The rich, symbolic imagery, raw emotion, and honesty will appeal to mature teens." Delia Culberson of *Voice of Youth Advocates* stated, "The author reaches out to her young adult readers with affection and encouragement. . . . 'Come join the serious and sassy family of writers'—no better advice to the next generation of authors."

After she became a full-time writer and speaker, Mora served as a consultant for the W.K. Kellogg foundation and as a member of the advisory committee for their national fellowship program; she also served as a consultant on the youth exchange program between the United States and Mexico. Mora has taught at the University of New Mexico, where she held the position of Distinguished Visiting Professor. She and her husband have a home in Santa Fe, where they live when they are not in Edgewood, Kentucky, a city near Cincinnati. In 1997, Mora lobbied successfully to establish a national day to celebrate childhood and bilingual literacy. Called El Día de los Niños/El Día de los Libros, the day is part of National Poetry Month. In 2000, Mora and her siblings established the Estela and Raúl Mora Award, a prize named in honor of their parents and coordinated by REFORMA, the National Association to Promote Library Service to Latinos. Mora has become a popular speaker and guest presenter at gatherings of teachers and education professionals. She often speaks at schools, universities, and conferences about such subjects as diversity, heritage, creative writing, cultural conservation, and multicultural education.

In her interview in *This Is about Vision,* Mora stated her philosophy of writing for children: "There is particular pleasure for me in poetry, . . . but I see children's books as very close to that. I have very strong feelings that Chicano kids need good children's books, well illustrated, from big publishing houses, and that is something I would really like to work on." She expounded on this theme in the *New Advocate:* "I want it all—all our complex richness, our diverse cultural experiences and literary traditions, the not-yet-sufficiently-tapped literary wealth, Latino talent. May each of us who cares about literature for children and, by extension, about the lives of children, *all* our children, deepen our commitment to enrich our literature with Latino voices and visions. They are there, ours for the publishing, then AH! Ours for the reading." In an essay in *Horn Book,* Mora explained what has motivated her to write: "I write because I am a reader. I want to give to others what writers have given me, a chance to hear the voices of people I will never meet . . . I enjoy the privateness of writing and reading. I write because I am curious. I am curious about me. Writing is a way of finding out how I feel about anything and everything. . . . Writing is my way of saving my feelings. . . . I write because I believe that Hispanics need to take their rightful place in American literature. I will continue to write and to struggle to say what no other writer can say in quite the same way."

BIOGRAPHICAL AND CRITICAL SOURCES:

BOOKS

Children's Literature Review, Volume 58, Thomson Gale (Detroit, MI), 2000.

Dictionary of Hispanic Biography, Thomson Gale (Detroit, MI), 1996.

Dictionary of Literary Biography, Volume 209: *Chicano Writers, Third Series,* Thomson Gale (Detroit, MI), 1996.

Hispanic Literature Criticism, Thomson Gale (Detroit, MI), 1994.

Ikas, Karen Rosa, *Chicana Ways: Conversations with Ten Chicana Writers,* University of Nevada Press (Reno, NV), 2001.

Mora, Pat, *House of Houses,* Beacon Press (Boston, MA), 1997.

Mora, Pat, *My Own True Name: New and Selected Poems for Young Adults, 1984-1999,* Pinata Books (Houston, TX), 2000.

Mora, Pat, *Nepantla: Essays from the Land in the Middle,* University of New Mexico Press (Albuquerque, NM), 1993.

Notable Hispanic American Women, Thomson Gale (Detroit, MI), 1993.

This Is about Vision: Interviews with Southwestern Writers, edited by William Balassi and others, University of New Mexico Press (Albuquerque, NM), 1990.

PERIODICALS

Booklist, November 1, 1994, Annie Ayres, review of *Pablo's Tree,* p. 507; November 15, 1998, Isabel Schon, review of *Tomás y la señora de la biblioteca,* p. 599; March 15, 2000, Gillian Engberg, review of *My Own True Name: New and Selected*

Poems for Young Adults, 1984-1999, p. 1377; May 1, 2001, Hazel Rochman, review of *Love to Mama: A Tribute to Mothers,* p. 1686; December, 15, 2001, Gillian Engberg, review of *The Race of Toad and Deer,* p. 735; November 15, 2002, Gillian Engberg, review of *A Library for Juana,* p. 605-606; December 15, 2002, Hazel Rochman, review of *Maria Paints the Hills,* p. 760.

Bulletin of the Center for Children's Books, September, 1994, Deborah Stevenson, review of *Pablo's Tree,* p. 20.

Childhood Education, mid-summer, 2002, review of *The Race of Toad and Deer,* p. 34.

Horn Book, July-August, 1990, Pat Mora, "Why I Am a Writer," pp. 436-437; January-February, 1993, Maeve Visser Knoth, review of *A Birthday Basket for Tia,* pp. 76-77; November-December, 1994, Maeve Visser Knoth, review of *Pablo's Tree,* pp. 723-724; July, 2001, D. Beram, review of *Love to Mama: A Tribute to Mothers,* p. 468; November-December, 2002, Mary M. Burns, review of *A Library for Juana,* p. 146.

Journal of Adolescent & Adult Literacy, October, 2002, "An Interview with Pat Mora," p. 183.

Kirkus Reviews, October 1, 1996, review of *Confetti: Poems for Children,* pp. 1476; August 15, 2001, review of *The Race of Toad and Deer,* p. 1218; November 15, 2002, review of *A Library for Juana,* p. 1699-1700.

Kliatt, July, 2002, Patricia A. Moore, *House of Houses.*

Library Journal, 1999, Ann Welton, review of *The Rainbow Tulip.*

MELUS, summer, 2003, Elizabeth Mermann-Jozwiak and Nancy Sullivan, "Interview with Pat Mora," pp. 139-152.

New Advocate, fall, 1998, Pat Mora, "Confessions of a Latina Author," pp. 279-289.

Publishers Weekly, August 31, 1992, review of *A Birthday Basket for Tia,* p. 77; July 21, 1997, review of *Tomás and the Library Lady,* p. 201; March 23, 1998, review of *The Big Sky,* p. 99; April 30, 2001, *Happy Mother's Day,* p. 80; October 28, 2002, review of *A Library for Juana,* p. 71.

Reading Today, October-November, 2002, "Books about the Love of Books," p. 34.

School Library Journal, September 15, 1992, Julie Corsaro, review of *A Birthday Basket for Tia,* p. 156; November, 1996, Sally R. Dow, review of *Confetti: Poems for Children,* p. 100; July, 1998, Lisa Falk, review of *The Big Sky,* p. 90; July, 2000, Nina Lindsay, review of *My Own True Name: New and Selected Poems for Young Adults,* p. 119; April, 2001, Ann Welton, review of *Love to Mama: A Tribute to Mothers,* p. 165; September, 2001, Ann Welton, review of *The Race of Toad and Deer,* p. 219; September, 2001, Lucia M. Gonzalez, review of *Thomas and the Library Lady,* p. S27; January, 2002, Ann Welton, review of *The Bakery Lady/La señora de la panadería,* p. 130; November, 2002, Ann Welton, review of *A Library for Juana,* p. 146.

Skipping Stones, May-June, 1998, Elke Richers, review of *Tomás and the Library Lady,* p. 5.

Voice of Youth Advocates, April, 2001, Delia Culberson, review of *My Own True Name: New and Selected Poems for Young Adults, 1984-1999,* p. 20.

ONLINE

Academy of American Poets, http://www.poets.org/ (August 6, 2004), biography of Pat Mora.

Children's Literature, http://www.childrenslit.com/ (May 21, 2002), Joan Carris, review of *The Rainbow Tulip;* Marilyn Courtot, review of *The Big Sky;* "Meet Authors and Illustrators: Pat Mora."

CSUDH NewsRoom: News from California State University—Dominguez Hills, http://www.csudh.edu/ (March 14, 2002), "Renowned Chicana Educator, Poet Pat Mora, Presents a Reading at California State University, Dominguez Hills."

Ethnopoetics, http://www.reed.edu/ (January 28, 2002), Bea Ogden, "Borderlands."

Houghton Mifflin Web site, http://www.eduplace.com/kids/ (May 19, 2002), "Meet the Author: Pat Mora."

Pat Mora Web site, http://www.patmora.com/ (May 19, 2002).

Scholastic Authors Online Library, http://www.teacher/scholastic.com/ (May 19, 2002), "Pat Mora's Biography" and "Pat Mora Interview Transcript."

Voices from the Gaps: Women Writers of Color, http://voices.cla.umn.edu/ (May 19, 2002), Delia Abreu and others, "Pat Mora."

* * *

MORA, Patricia
See MORA, Pat

* * *

MORGAN, Claire
See HIGHSMITH, Patricia

MORI, Kyoko 1957-

PERSONAL: Born March 9, 1957, in Kobe, Japan; immigrated to the United States, 1977; naturalized U.S. citizen, 1984; daughter of Hiroshi (an engineer) and Takako (a homemaker; maiden name, Nagai) Mori; married Charles Brock (an elementary school teacher), March 17, 1984 (divorced). *Education:* Rockford College, B.A., 1979; University of Wisconsin—Milwaukee, M.A. 1981, Ph.D., 1984. *Politics:* Democrat, feminist. *Hobbies and other interests:* Fiber arts (knitting, spinning, weaving), running, birdwatching.

ADDRESSES: *Home*—Cambridge, MA. *Office*—Department of English, Harvard University, Barker Center, 12 Quincy, Cambridge, MA 02138. *Agent*—Ann Rittenberg, 14 Montgomery Pl., Brooklyn, NY 11215.

CAREER: Saint Norbert College, De Pere, WI, associate professor of English and writer-in-residence, beginning 1984; Harvard University, Cambridge, MA, Briggs-Copeland Lecturer in Creative Writing; writer.

MEMBER: Modern Language Association of America, Associated Writing Programs.

AWARDS, HONORS: Editors' Prize, *Missouri Review,* 1992, for poem "Fallout"; American Library Association Best Book for Young Adults, *New York Times* Notable Book, *Publishers Weekly* Editors' Choice, Council of Wisconsin Writers Best Novel, and Elizabeth Burr award for best children's book of the year, Wisconsin Library Association, all 1993, all for *Shizuko's Daughter;* Paterson Poetry Center Best Books for Young Adults, Council of Wisconsin Writers Best Novel, American Library Association Best Book for Young Adults, and Children's Books of Distinction Award, *Hungry Mind Review,* 1996, all for *One Bird.*

WRITINGS:

Shizuko's Daughter, Holt (New York, NY), 1993.
Fallout (poems), Ti Chucha Press, 1994.
The Dream of Water: A Memoir, Holt (New York, NY), 1995.
One Bird, Holt (New York, NY), 1995.
Polite Lies: On Being a Woman Caught between Cultures (essays), Holt (New York, NY), 1998.
Stone Field, True Arrow, Holt (New York, NY), 2000.

Contributor of short stories to books, including *When I Was Your Age: Original Stories about Growing Up,* edited by Amy Erlich, Candlewick Press (New York, NY), 1999; contributor to periodicals, including *Apalachee Quarterly, Beloit Poetry Journal, Crosscurrents, Kenyon Review—New Series, Prairie Schooner,* and *South-East Review.* Contributor of poems to periodicals, including *Missouri Review, Paterson Review, American Scholar,* and *Denver Quarterly.* Contributor of articles to *Writer.*

WORK IN PROGRESS: A novel; poems.

SIDELIGHTS: In several of her prose works, award-winning novelist and poet Kyoko Mori poignantly describes the devastating pain that haunts a young person who must deal with the death of a beloved parent. After coping with the suicide of her mother when Mori was still a pre-teen, she was then forced to watch her once secure way of life become drastically altered through the tirades of a selfish, patriarchal, and unfeeling father and an insensitive and equally selfish stepmother. This abiding sense of loss, which deprived Mori of both family and community and which has imbued much of her written work, would eventually prompt her to voluntarily give up yet another tie with her youth: her country. Attending an American college on a scholarship program, she felt more in sync with the relaxed, less emotionally inhibited culture of the United States than she did with the strictures in place in Japanese society. Since her college days, Mori has made her home in the United States, where she has written and published several critically acclaimed novels for young adults, the poignant memoir *The Dream of Water,* and *Polite Lies: On Being a Woman Caught between Cultures,* a book of essays.

Mori was born on the main island of Honshu, in the city of Kobe, Japan, in 1957. Located near mountains and water, "Kobe is a very beautiful, sophisticated city," she once noted, "but it is also close to nature." The daughter of an engineer and his wife, she was born with both hips displaced, and spent her first year in leg harnesses to correct her gait. Fortunately, that condition was corrected and Mori was soon able to accompany her mother on walks in the mountains and enjoy the visits to the country home of her grandparents that the family made before she began school. She was inspired with an early love of reading and a love of beauty by her mother. A sensitive and creative woman, Takako Mori made a cultured home for her children, reading to both Kyoko and her younger brother, Jumpei, from the time both children were small. Tragically, Takako committed suicide when Mori was twelve, a victim of depression and, perhaps, the repressive Japanese society that relegated women to a subservient status in relation to their husbands.

While, like most Japanese children, Mori had an early exposure to a few English words and phrases, she began a serious study of the language and its literature when she was twelve. She was immediately struck with the emotional content of much Western writing in comparison with the restraint of its Japanese counterpart; English would be her major in college and she now writes exclusively in her adopted language. "In my teenage years I read a lot of English books in English," she explained in an interview for *Authors and Artists for Young Adults* (*AAYA*). "Before then I don't remember that much what I read, because I don't think that in Japan they really have books written for teenagers. You have to read 'literature'—some 'Great Book' by some guy who died fifty years ago or something. And that was fine; I liked some of that. But to be thirteen and to be a girl and to read that is not necessarily a good experience because [much of Japanese literature] was so male and with such different aesthetics than my everyday life." While she was drawn to the beauty of the language she was exposed to in the books she read in school, Western books such as *Jane Eyre* and *Anne of Green Gables* captured her imagination.

In her junior year of high school, Mori was given the opportunity to study at a school in Mesa, Arizona, for a year as an exchange student. "It was a revelation for me," she once commented. "For the first time in my life I was away from the social constrictions of my society. In Japan there is so much pressure from family. You can't do . . . [certain things] because it will bring shame to your family." After returning to her home, Mori decided to intensify her studies in English; during her first two years of college in Japan she majored in the subject. "After my year in the United States, I began to think of English as my writing language. So much of Japanese aesthetics is involved in not saying what you want to. To talk about yourself in Japanese is considered rude. So English became a much better language for me as a writer." Her focus on writing in English became so intensive that Mori decided to finish her college education in the United States. She earned a scholarship to Rockford College in 1977 and graduated from that school two years later. She went on to complete her master's degree and Ph.D. and establish a career as a writer and educator.

Shizuko's Daughter, Mori's first published book, was released in 1993. Based on a group of short stories that she wrote for her doctoral dissertation, the book tells the story of Yuki, a young girl who returns from a music lesson one day to discover her mother dead by her own hand. "People will tell you that I've done this because I did not love you," reads the suicide note Shizuko leaves for her daughter. "Don't listen to them. When you grow up to be a strong woman, you will know that this is for the best." During the six years that follow, Yuki must learn to deal with the changes in her life that follow her mother's death: the remarriage of her father, the gradual estrangement of grandparents, and her deep feelings of responsibility and guilt over her mother's unhappiness. Calling the book a "jewel," *New York Times Book Review* contributor Liz Rosenberg felt *Shizuko's Daughter* to be "one of those rarities that shine out only a few times in a generation. It begins and ends with a dream, with a death, yet it is not dreamy or tragic."

Shizuko's Daughter wasn't intended to be a young adult novel to begin with. But as Mori began to revise and edit her initial manuscript with the advice of her editor, she realized that conforming it to certain conventions of the genre ultimately made it a better novel: "Because the way I had it before, I time-skipped around a lot. Straightening that out made it a more straightforward book, which is what it needed to be."

One Bird, which Mori published in 1995, is even more concise than the author's first book. In the novel, fifteen-year-old Megumi watches as her mother packs her suitcase and leaves the house of her husband, Megumi's father. Unable to go with her mother because to do so would be neither "appropriate" in Japanese society nor financially possible, Megumi is forced to deal with the vacuum left by her mother's abrupt departure, a vacuum that her distant father avoids filling by staying with an out-of-town mistress for long periods of time. During the course of the novel, her emotions and reactions shift from those of a little girl to those of a young woman through the support of a woman veterinarian whom she meets while attempting to care for a small bird. Ultimately, Megumi is able to creatively find a solution to her problem, a solution whereby she and her mother can spend at least part of the year together. "Kyoko Mori's second novel . . . is so lively and affecting that one imagines its readers will be too engaged by its heroine's situation to notice how much—and how painlessly—they are learning about another culture," according to *New York Times Book Review* critic Francine Prose. Noting that the book is filled with "small, radiant schemes and glints of observation," Prose added that *One Bird* shows that teen feelings and attitudes toward life are universal.

As Mori once noted, writing for teens requires that authors rely more on character and plot than on imagery and style. "Both [*Shizuko's Daughter* and *One Bird*] had to be more straightforward, and in a way I think that this made them better books, because sometimes it is so easy to rely on your ability to write and, when you get to some crucial moment in the narrative, try to get through it through fine writing and strong imagery. And I see this as something that I am tempted to do because I am also a poet."

"But I think what you do well is also your downfall," Mori added. "And I think that when you're a poet as well as a fiction writer, there is always the temptation to do something poetic at a crucial moment. Writing for teens, you're not allowed to do that. You have to be straightforward and direct in developing the characters and manipulating the plot."

One Bird and *Shizuko's Daughter* are essentially the same story, seen from different points of view, according to Mori. "One is a tragic version of the story about an isolated teenager and the other is a more humorous version," the author explained. "In *One Bird,* I think there is an inherent sense of humor and resilience that Megumi doesn't take herself that seriously, not in the way that the teen in *Shizuko's Daughter* has to take herself seriously." Mori characterizes the books as "two flavors of the same thing," admitting that "maybe I needed to do that to grow up. I think that even though I didn't write those books to grow up, it became a process of that. When I first wrote *Shizuko's Daughter,* it was a way of admitting the pain in my life perhaps. And then when I wrote *One Bird,* it was a way of being able to look at that same story with more irreverence. And humor."

In 1990, with the manuscript for *Shizuko's Daughter* circulating among publishers, Mori decided to go to Japan on sabbatical "because it was the only foreign country where I speak the language," she once explained. She planned to keep a journal, out of which poems normally sprang, and then begin work on a new novel. While she was in Japan, visiting parts of the country that she had never seen as a child and spending time with beloved relatives, she thought to herself, "I'm kind of gathering material and waiting for that novel to form." Finding the time to keep a journal record of her thoughts and reflections was not difficult: "I couldn't sleep in Japan because I was jet-lagged," Mori recalled. "I kept waking up; I couldn't fall asleep, . . . but in a way this was good because it gave me a lot of time to write. In the middle of the night I can't sleep; what else am I going to do? I can only read so much."

After returning to her home in Wisconsin and writing several poems based on her experiences in her native country, Mori realized that an autobiography, rather than a novel, was to be the literary outcome of her trip. "I knew in Japan that the trip was so specific to my family that I couldn't see how I could write it as a novel," the writer explained. "I would be translating these facts in an uncreative way rather than transforming them. So I decided that I would do this as a nonfiction, autobiographical narrative." Mori realized from the start of her new project that she had a wealth of literary models, including *The Woman Warrior* by Maxine Hong Kingston, that read like novels but are nonfiction. The result of her creative efforts was *The Dream of Water: A Memoir.*

In *The Dream of Water,* the reader is drawn into the narrator's reality, but that reality is as compelling as a work of fiction due to Mori's ability to imbue her relatives and her setting with qualities that transcend the mundane and everyday. Each person she meets on her trip is linked to past memories, and past and present interweave on both a physical and emotional plain. Her beloved grandfather is dead, and she is left with only memories and the journals a relative saved for Mori after his death. The house where she lived when her mother committed suicide is gone, replaced by a parking lot, and yet the memories that empty space conjures up render it almost ghostlike. Called "deeply private" by *Booklist* contributor Donna Seaman, Mori's memoir unfolds with "dignity and cathartic integrity, chronicling not only her struggle with grief, anger, and guilt" and her growing understanding of the differences between Japanese and U.S. culture, but the author's ability to ultimately "finally feel at home in both worlds."

"I always wanted to be a writer," Mori once said. "When you're a kid, though, you have all these different aspirations, from the firefighter all the way to the great composer, all at the same time. While I had a series of these dreams, being a writer was always on the list. So every year it would be a different list, but the recurring one was that I wanted to be a writer." In grade school she did a lot of writing, but it was actually her mother and grandfather who inspired her to take her writing seriously. "My grandfather wrote journal entries every morning," Mori recalled, looking back at the visits she made to her grandparents' house as a young child. "When I would go and stay with his family, he would get up and write in his diary. And that really inspired me. Writing was a serious thing. It was something my grandfather did every morning." Mori, who now teaches creative writing at Saint Norbert College in De Pere, Wisconsin, considers herself to be a fairly disciplined writer. "I'm not disciplined all the way in my life," she admitted, "but there are three or four things I'm very disciplined about: running is one of them, and writing. Those are things that I don't have a hard time getting to."

A poet as well as a prose writer, Mori's craft follows certain stages, beginning with thoughts jotted down in journal entries, then poetry, and finally into prose. "I don't see the poems as just a process," she explained; "I see them as finished products. But once I do about ten poems, I start thinking, 'There's something I could do with this.' There's a collective thought that kind of forms in that process that leads me to do a longer prose project." Such is the process that Mori has used with each of her longer prose works. "The only time that I really think about audience is in terms of developing the plot as well as the imagery, so it has more to do with technique in the end than with the story itself," the author added.

Until Mori started teaching creative writing, she believed anyone could write, on some level at least. "And that's still true," she admitted. "I think that anyone can write better than he or she is doing *now.* But as I teach more I start thinking that talent really does play a valuable part in this. There are kids who, without trying, write something so much better than the kid who is trying so hard who is a good student. It really has to do with the way they can see."

"But some of the most talented students are not the best disciplined. [While] I think I can motivate them to be disciplined because they have something to work with, they have to put something out there before I can give them direction." She maintains that the better English majors, those who "read and analyze things and write clearly in an expository manner," don't always write the best stories or poems. "They just don't seem to have the 'eye,'" she surmises. "And that, to me, is much more frustrating than working with a talented but undisciplined student whom I have to nag by saying, 'Your rewrite is due in a week,' because I can usually get that student to do it. And if it's two days late, it's okay."

In 1998, Mori published a series of twelve essays wherein she contrasts living in the Midwest and living in Japan, titled *Polite Lies: On Being a Woman Caught between Cultures.* She produced *Stone Field, True Arrow,* her first novel for adults, in 2000. The book tells the story of Maya Ishida, a Japanese-American who left Japan as a child to live with her distant, academic mother in the U.S. Maya, who is married to a schoolteacher and works as a weaver, begins to re-evaluate the events of her past and her present relationships after she learns of her Japanese father's death. While *Library Journal*'s Shirley N. Quan felt that the novel "appears to carry one too many story lines," a *Publishers Weekly* reviewer found Mori's text "graceful in its simplicity of language." Writing in the *New York Times Book Review,* Jeff Waggoner praised *Stone Field, True Arrow* as a "quiet, heartbreaking novel that has as much to say about art as it does about longing."

In addition to an active teaching schedule and a daily schedule given structure by her disciplined attitude towards running and writing, Mori continues to produce books, poems, and short fiction. In 1999, she contributed the autobiographical short story "Learning to Swim" to *When I Was Your Age: Original Stories about Growing Up,* a collection for young adult readers.

BIOGRAPHICAL AND CRITICAL SOURCES:

PERIODICALS

Booklist, January 1, 1995, Donna Seaman, "Poets Remembered," p. 794; December 1, 1997, review of *Polite Lies,* pp. 590-592; June 1, 1998, Stephanie Zvirin, review of *Shizuko's Daughter,* p. 1717; July, 2000, Michelle Kaske, review of *Stone Field, True Arrow,* p. 2008.

Bulletin of the Center for Children's Books, May, 1993, p. 291; January, 1996, p. 161.

English Journal, September, 1994, p. 87.

Horn Book, May, 1993, p. 291.

Kirkus Reviews, November 1, 1997, review of *Polite Lies,* p. 1628.

Library Journal, July, 2000, Shirley N. Quan, review of *Stone Field, True Arrow,* p. 141.

Los Angeles Times Book Review, April 9, 1995, p. 6.

New York Times Book Review, August 22, 1993, Liz Rosenberg, review of *Shizuko's Daughter,* p. 19. February 5, 1995, p. 13; November 12, 1995, Francine Prose, review of *One Bird,* p. 50; March 8, 1998, p. 19; November 5, 2000, Jeff Waggoner, review of *Stone Field, True Arrow.*

Publishers Weekly, January 25, 1993, p. 87; November 7, 1994, p. 54; November 3, 1997, review of *Polite Lies,* p. 71; August 14, 2000, review of *Stone Field, True Arrow,* p. 329.

School Library Journal, September, 1997, Patricia Lothrop-Green, review of *The Dream of Water,* p. 129.

Voice of Youth Advocates, October, 1993, p. 217; February, 1996, p. 374; August, 1997, Hilary S. Crew, review of *One Bird,* pp. 173-176.

Wilson Library Bulletin, January, 1994, p. 117.

MORRIS, Mary Joan McGarry
See MORRIS, Mary McGarry

* * *

MORRIS, Mary McGarry 1943-
(Mary Joan McGarry Morris)

PERSONAL: Born 1943, in Meriden, CT; daughter of John and Margaret (Chiriaco) McGarry; married Michael Morris (an attorney), 1962; children: Mary Margaret, Sarah, Melissa, Michael, Amy. *Education:* Attended University of Vermont, 1960-62, and University of Massachusetts, 1962-63.

ADDRESSES: Home—Andover, MA. *Agent*—Naggar Literary Agency, 216 E. 75th St., New York, NY 10021.

CAREER: Massachusetts Department of Welfare, Lawrence, financial assistance social worker, 1980-86; writer.

AWARDS, HONORS: National Book Award nomination, 1988, and PEN/Faulkner Award nomination, 1989, both for *Vanished.*

WRITINGS:

NOVELS

Vanished, Viking (New York, NY), 1988.
A Dangerous Woman, Viking (New York, NY), 1991.
Songs in Ordinary Time, Viking (New York, NY), 1995.
Fiona Range, Viking (New York, NY), 2000.
A Hole in the Universe, Viking (New York, NY), 2004.
The Lost Mother, Viking (New York, NY), 2005.

Also contributor of book reviews to periodicals, including *New York Times Book Review.*

ADAPTATIONS: A Dangerous Woman was adapted as a feature film starring Deborah Winger.

SIDELIGHTS: As the author of several novels, Mary McGarry Morris has received considerable attention from critics and readers, as well as from prestigious awards panels. Her books are noted for their depictions of mentally and emotionally impaired individuals who have difficulty coping with an inhospitable world. As *New York Times Book Review* contributor Alice McDermott put it, "Morris does not devise plots, but traps: steel-toothed, inescapable traps of circumstance and personality against which her characters struggle . . . and then fail." Ultimately, Morris suggests that these individuals are incapable of surviving their surroundings. Her books typically conclude with violent murders, death apparently being all that is left for characters who have exhausted their other possibilities.

Such grim subjects seem odd coming from Morris, a mother of five children who, following college, went on to live what *Los Angeles Times* writer Elizabeth Mehren described as a "stunningly balanced life." The disorder Morris depicts in her books may stem, in part, from her own childhood. Her parents separated when she was very young and, though her father continued to live separately, he, along with Morris and her mother, moved to Rutland, Vermont, when the author was six years old. It was in Rutland that Morris came to know the small New England communities that she features in her novels. When her mother and stepfather began employing retarded and emotionally disturbed men in their restaurant, she was exposed to another important influence. As she once told *People* magazine writer Kim Hubbard, her mother "believed everyone deserved a chance." The author would later manifest the same concern for society's outsiders by featuring mentally handicapped individuals in her fiction.

After marrying, Morris settled in Andover, Massachusetts, and was soon involved with raising a family and writing. Not surprisingly, her family obligations often took her away from her fiction and poetry. "With five children there couldn't be a set schedule for much," she told *Washington Post* writer Judith Weinraub. "It was always hard to find the time." Morris's writing regimen was also interrupted when she took a job as a social worker in order to help pay the children's college tuition. Consequently, her early attempts at novels remained unfinished, and the work that would eventually prove successful was painfully slow in coming. Her first novel, *Vanished,* took nearly eight years to write, and was then rejected twenty-seven times by publishers and agents. Without a publication to substantiate her abilities, Morris kept her writing a secret from everyone but her family. Despite this isolation, she continued to work on her fiction. "Writing was just *in* me," she told Weinraub. "I even began to think I probably would never be published. And I was accepting of that."

In 1986 Morris finally achieved a partial affirmation of her talents when she placed *Vanished* with noted literary agent Jean V. Naggar; two years later it was published. *Vanished* centers on Aubrey Wallace, a man whose socialization is so severely limited, most consider him retarded. Though he is functional to a certain degree—he has a job, a wife, and children—Aubrey is unquestioning and utterly passive. These qualities lead to trouble when Aubrey crosses paths with Dotty Johnson, a disturbed teenager who has recently killed her sexually abusive father. Dotty attempts to steal Aubrey's pickup, and Aubrey jumps into the cab. Unable to take any action to stop her, Aubrey just rides along, and this beginning is typical of their time together. Whatever Dotty wants, she takes, and whatever Aubrey encounters, he accepts. The next day Dotty kidnaps a baby, and the child becomes part of the roving, maladjusted family, crisscrossing the country from Massachusetts to Florida. They survive by finding work as migrant laborers, by stealing, and by prostitution. Five years after the kidnapping, they move in with a violent ex-convict named Jiggy Huller and his family. When Huller discovers the truth about the kidnaping, he hatches a plan to collect a 25,000 dollar reward for the child that ultimately brings about the novel's bloody conclusion.

Several critics commented that Morris's style and technique in *Vanished* are of an exceptionally high caliber for a first novelist. *New York Times Book Review* contributor Harry Crews noted that "her language is precise, concrete, and sensual. Her eye for telling detail is good, and her ear for the way people talk is tone-perfect." Opinions were divided, however, regarding Morris's handling of the novel's story elements. Some critics suggested that her emotionally charged topics—rape, murder, incest, kidnaping, prostitution, and adultery—run the risk of overwhelming the rest of the book. Richard Eder, writing in the *Los Angeles Times Book Review,* found that the novel, unable to transform its negative subject matter into a meaningful message, "sinks into its chamber of horrors." *New York Times* reviewer Michiko Kakutani also focused on the novel's preoccupation with ugly and sinister elements, but reached a different judgment. "Melodramatic as these events sound," Kakutani wrote, "they are presented with such authority by Ms. Morris that they hum with both the authenticity of real life and the mythic power of fable. This is a startling and powerful debut."

A Dangerous Woman, Morris's second novel, features another emotionally impaired protagonist, Martha Horgan, who is in many ways the counterpart to Aubrey Wallace in *Vanished.* Like Aubrey, Martha Horgan is an outcast, characterized as disturbed by the residents of her Vermont town. She is plagued by physical tics and is unable to interact with others in a mature manner. Sometimes her brutal honesty offends those around her; sometimes she explodes into childish rages. At other times, however, Martha almost becomes a functioning part of her community. Early in the book she gets a job at a dry cleaners and earns a degree of independence. She moves out of her aunt's home and forges a tenuous friendship with a coworker, Birdy. These gains are lost, however, due in part to Martha's insistence on exposing Birdy's lover as a thief. Martha's honesty costs her both the job and the friendship, and she is forced to return to her Aunt Frances's home. There an alcoholic handyman employed by Aunt Frances takes Martha as a temporary lover, then abandons her in favor of Frances. When she is forced to leave her aunt's home, Martha has few options, and tragedy is imminent.

Morris chose to relay much of the novel's action through Martha's disturbed perceptions, and this unconventional approach impressed several reviewers. Richard Eder of the *Los Angeles Times Book Review* wrote that *A Dangerous Woman* "is powerfully and dangerously written. To cast a blinding light on her protagonist, Morris has sacrificed subtleties or shadings. The balance of the outsider as both victim and helpless instigator is difficult to maintain." Jaimy Gordon, writing in the *Washington Post,* maintained that some of the story elements—including Martha's near rape at the age of sixteen—are unnecessary. Gordon also criticized some occasionally clumsy prose in the novel, but praised Morris's "remarkable portrait of a disturbed woman." This judgment was echoed by *Vogue* contributor Michael Upchurch, who emphasized the author's ability to "draw the reader so completely into Martha's world that it becomes impossible not to sympathize with her."

New York Times Book Review contributor Alice McDermott, comparing Morris's two novels, summarized: "*A Dangerous Woman* is not, finally, as convincing or as compelling . . . as was Ms. Morris's first book, nor is the prose quite so striking." Despite these reservations, the critic commended the powerful vision Morris puts forth in both of the novels. "The bleakness of her landscape remains pervasive," McDermott wrote. "This makes all the more remarkable those instants of frail light—a simple man's love for a child, a lost woman's recollection of affection—that she so deftly, so briefly, calls forth from the darkness."

Morris proved with her first two novels that she "can depict society's outsiders—people with bleak presents and no futures—with rare understanding and compassion," noted a *Publishers Weekly* critic. Her third novel,

Songs in Ordinary Time, evidences this as well. The novel revolves around the Fermoyles, a family living in a small town in Vermont in 1960. Marie Fermoyle has struggled for years to support and raise her three children despite the lack of support from her alcoholic ex-husband. Enter Omar Duvall, a con man who convinces Marie to invest in one of his scams. The novel involves numerous subplots involving various friends and neighbors who "each in his or her own way is necessary to the town's ecosystem," commented Vanessa V. Friedman in *Entertainment Weekly.*

Critical reviews of *Songs in Ordinary Time* were mixed. "This novel becomes more powerful as one reads, building to a heart stopping denouement," noted a critic for *Publishers Weekly.* Michiko Kakutani, on the other hand, wrote in the *New York Times Book Review* that the author's protagonists "lack the emotional chiaroscuro that Ms. Morris has lavished on her creations in the past." However, in *USA Today* Susan Kelly argued that *Songs in Ordinary Time* is "beautifully written." Kelly observed, "There is grace and poetry in Morris's prose. She opens the door to these people's souls, showing all their fears and flaws without making them seem ridiculous or unworthy."

In Morris's 2000 novel, *Fiona Range,* the title character is "smart, beautiful, and haunted by a past she cannot live down," according to Carolyn Kubisz in *Booklist.* Abandoned by her unwed mother as a baby, Fiona was raised by her aunt and uncle. Her relationships roll along, disaster after disaster. After her cousin Elizabeth returns from New York City with her fiancé, Fiona ends up sleeping both with him and with one of Elizabeth's former boyfriends. "Fiona knows she needs to reclaim her life, but each step she takes is closer to the abyss," found Harriet Klausner in *BookBrowser.*

Critics were again largely positive in their assessment of *Fiona Range.* "How these characters interact, what they say, and what they hide, makes for entertaining, suspenseful reading," opined Yvette Weller Olson in *Library Journal.* Olson found the work "compelling and satisfying." A *Publishers Weekly* critic's review was mixed, maintaining that the plot tends to "go in circles" and that Fiona's self-destructive nature distances the character from reader sympathy. Nonetheless, the critic went on to praise the "sustained tension in the narrative," and found that "the denouement packs a thriller's excitement." Kubisz found the narrative "slow moving at times," but concluded that Morris's ending, "with its twist of plot and hidden secrets revealed, makes this a worthy read."

In *A Hole in the Universe* Morris tells the story of outcast Gordon Loomis, who comes home after serving a twenty-five-year sentence for a murder he may not have committed. Struggling to cope with life outside prison, the gloomy Gordon just wants to be left alone; instead, he must fend off the intrusive attention of people. He spurns his brother's help in finding him a job, and feels helpless when the spinsterish Delores wants to help him become the "normal" man he wants to be. He tries to avoid the needy teenage daughter of the junkie across the street. Unfortunately, Gordon is unable to keep his life at a safe distance for long. His basic integrity draws him toward the people he seeks to protect, even though he is punished for his good deeds. When new accusations whirl around Gordon for a second crime he did not commit, the tale moves to its fitful conclusion and Gordon emerges as the novel's pathetic but winning hero.

Reviews of *A Hole in the Universe* were predominately enthusiastic. *Booklist* contributor Deborah Donovan found Morris's "empathy for Gordon . . . palpable, leaving the reader in awe of her uncanny ability to capture and convey each personality's unique essence." *New York Times* contributor John Hartl was more reserved in his assessment, writing, "What keeps this borderline potboiler simmering is the sense that the characters really are evolving." On the other hand, *Boston Globe* reviewer Caroline Leavitt applauded the novel's "topnotch suspense" and "expert plotting that make Morris such a superb storyteller," and was especially impressed with the author's inclusion of those "small heroics that resonate and break your heart."

BIOGRAPHICAL AND CRITICAL SOURCES:

PERIODICALS

Booklist, July, 1995, Donna Seaman, review of *Songs in Ordinary Time,* p. 1860; February 15, 2000, Carolyn Kubisz, review of *Fiona Range,* p. 1052; February 1, 2004, Deborah Donovan, review of *A Hole in the Universe,* p. 993.

Chicago Tribune, March 7, 2004, Jessica Treadway, review of *A Hole in the Universe,* p. 4.

Detroit Free Press, February 3, 1991.

Entertainment Weekly, July 28, 1995, Vanessa V. Friedman, review of *Songs in Ordinary Time,* p. 57.

Library Journal, March 15, 2000, Yvette Weller Olson, review of *Fiona Range,* p. 128.

Los Angeles Times, March 7, 1991, pp. E1, E6.

Los Angeles Times Book Review, June 26, 1988, p. 3; January 20, 1991; April 25, 2004, Francie Lin, review of *A Hole in the Universe,* p. 6.

Newsweek, April 8, 1991, David Gates, review of *A Dangerous Woman,* pp. 61, 63.

New York, January 14, 1991, Rhoda Koenig, review of *A Dangerous Woman,* p. 67.

New Yorker, August 8, 1988, pp. 84-85.

New York Times, June 4, 1988, Michiko Kakutani, review of *Vanished,* p. 14.

New York Times Book Review, July 3, 1988, Harry Crews, "On the Lam with Dotty," p. 5; January 13, 1991, Alice McDermott, "The Loneliness of an Ogre," p. 9; August 4, 1995, Michiko Kakutani, review of *Songs in Ordinary Time;* March 21, 2004, John Hartl, review of *A Hole in the Universe,* p. 16.

People, April 15, 1991, Kim Hubbard, review of *A Dangerous Woman,* pp. 93-94.

Publishers Weekly, May 15, 1995, review of *Songs in Ordinary Times,* p. 53; March 13, 2000, review of *Fiona Range,* p. 59; January 26, 2004, review of *A Hole in the Universe,* p. 227.

Time, July 4, 1988, review of *Vanished,* p. 71; January 28, 1991, Mary Carlson, review of *A Dangerous Woman,* pp. 89-90.

USA Today, December 2, 1999, Susan Kelly, "*Songs* No Ordinary Novel"; May 10, 2000, Susan Kelly, "Teen Never Feels at Home in *Range.*"

Vogue, January, 1991, pp. 112-113.

Washington Post, January 8, 1991; March 26, 1991, p. B1, B4; March 7, 2004, Caroline Leavitt, review of *A Hole in the Universe,* p. T6.

ONLINE

BookBrowser.com, http://www.bookbrowser.com/ (May, 2000), Harriet Klausner, review of *Fiona Range.*

* * *

MORRISON, Chloe Anthony Wofford
See MORRISON, Toni

* * *

MORRISON, Toni 1931-
(Chloe Anthony Wofford Morrison)

PERSONAL: Born Chloe Anthony Wofford, February 18, 1931, in Lorain, OH; daughter of George and Ramah (Willis) Wofford; married Harold Morrison, 1958 (divorced, 1964); children: Harold Ford, Slade Kevin. *Ethnicity:* "Black." *Education:* Howard University, B.A., 1953; Cornell University, M.A., 1955.

ADDRESSES: Office—Department of Creative Writing, Princeton University, 185 Nassau St., Princeton, NJ 08544-0001. *Agent*—International Creative Management, 40 W. 57th St., New York, NY 10019.

CAREER: Texas Southern University, Houston, TX, instructor in English, 1955-57; Howard University, Washington, DC, instructor in English, 1957-64; Random House, New York, NY, senior editor, 1965-85; State University of New York—Purchase, associate professor of English, 1971-72; State University of New York—Albany, Schweitzer Professor of the Humanities, 1984-89; Princeton University, Princeton, NJ, Robert F. Goheen Professor of the Humanities, 1989—. Visiting lecturer, Yale University, 1976-77, and Bard College, 1986-88; Clark Lecturer at Trinity College, Cambridge, and Massey Lecturer at Harvard University, both 1990.

MEMBER: American Academy and Institute of Arts and Letters, National Council on the Arts, Authors Guild (council), Authors League of America.

AWARDS, HONORS: National Book Award nomination and Ohioana Book Award, both 1975, both for *Sula;* National Book Critics Circle Award and American Academy and Institute of Arts and Letters Award, both 1977, both for *Song of Solomon;* New York State Governor's Art Award, 1986; National Book Award nomination and National Book Critics Circle Award nomination, both 1987, Pulitzer Prize for Fiction, Robert F. Kennedy Award, and American Book Award, Before Columbus Foundation, 1988, all for *Beloved;* Elizabeth Cady Stanton Award, National Organization of Women; Nobel Prize in Literature, 1993; Pearl Buck Award, Rhegium Julii Prize, Condorcet Medal (Paris, France), and Commander of the Order of Arts and Letters (Paris, France), all 1994; Medal for Distinguished Contribution to American Letters, National Book Foundation, 1996; National Humanities Medal, 2001; subject of Biennial Toni Morrison Society conference in Lorain, Ohio; Coretta Scott King Book Award, 2005, for *Remember: The Journey to School Integration.*

WRITINGS:

FICTION

The Bluest Eye, Holt (New York, NY), 1969, reprinted, Plume (New York, NY), 1994.

Sula, Knopf (New York, NY), 1973.
Song of Solomon, Knopf (New York, NY), 1977.
Tar Baby, Knopf (New York, NY), 1981.
Dreaming Emmett (play), first produced in Albany, NY, January 4, 1986.
Beloved, Knopf (New York, NY), 1987.
Jazz, Knopf (New York, NY), 1992.
Playing in the Dark: Whiteness and the Literary Imagination, Harvard University Press (Cambridge, MA), 1992.
The Dancing Mind (text of Nobel Prize acceptance speech), Knopf (New York, NY), 1996.
Paradise, Knopf (New York, NY), 1998.
Love, Knopf (New York, NY), 2003.

FOR CHILDREN; WITH SON SLADE MORRISON

The Big Box, illustrated by Giselle Potter, Hyperion/Jump at the Sun (New York, NY), 1999.
The Book of Mean People, illustrated by Pascal Lemaître, Hyperion (New York, NY), 2002.
The Book of Mean People Journal, illustrated by Pascal Lemaître, Hyperion (New York, NY), 2002.
The Lion or the Mouse? ("Who's Got Game?" series), illustrated by Pascal Lemaître, Scribner (Mew York, NY), 2003.
The Ant or the Grasshopper? ("Who's Got Game?" series), illustrated by Pascal Lemaître, Scribner (New York, NY), 2003.
The Poppy or the Snake? ("Who's Got Game?" series), illustrated by Pascal Lemaître, Scribner (New York, NY), 2004.
Who's Got Game? Three Fables (contains *The Lion or the Mouse? The Ant or the Grasshopper?* and *The Poppy or the Snake.*), illustrated by Pascal Lemaître, Scribner (Mew York, NY), 2005.

MUSIC

(Author of lyrics) André Previn, *Four Songs for Soprano, Cello, and Piano,* Chester Music (London, England), 1995.
(Author of lyrics) Richard Danielpour, *Spirits in the Well: For Voice and Piano,* Associated Music Publishers (New York, NY), 1998.
(Author of lyrics) Richard Danielpour, *Margaret Garner: Opera in Two Acts,* Associated Music Publishers (New York, NY), 2005.

Also author of lyrics for André Previn's *Honey and Rue,* commissioned by Carnegie Hall, 1992, and Richard Danielpour's *Sweet Talk: Four Songs,* 1996.

EDITOR

The Black Book (anthology), Random House (New York, NY), 1974.
Race-ing Justice, En- Gendering Power: Essays on Anita Hill, Clarence Thomas, and the Construction of Social Reality, Pantheon (New York, NY), 1992.
To Die for the People: The Writings of Huey P. Newton, Writers and Readers (New York, NY), 1995.
Toni Cade Bambara, *Deep Sightings and Rescue Missions: Fiction, Essays, and Conversations,* Pantheon (New York, NY), 1996.
(With Claudia Brodsky Lacour) *Birth of a Nation-'Hood: Gaze, Script, and Spectacle in the O. J. Simpson Case,* Pantheon (New York, NY), 1997.

OTHER

Remember: The Journey to School Integration (for children), Houghton Mifflin (Boston, MA), 2004.

Contributor of essays and reviews to numerous periodicals, including *New York Times Magazine.* Contributor to *Arguing Immigration: The Debate over the Changing Face of America,* edited by Nicolaus Mills, Simon & Schuster (New York, NY), 1994.

ADAPTATIONS: Beloved was adapted to a 1998 film of the same title, starring Oprah Winfrey, Danny Glover, Thandie Newton, and Kimberly Elise, and was directed by Jonathan Demme. *Paradise* was optioned by Harpo Productions for adaptation as a television miniseries. Morrison books, including *Jazz, Beloved, Tar Baby, Paradise, Song of Solomon* and *The Bluest Eye,* have been adapted to audio cassette.

SIDELIGHTS: Nobel laureate Toni Morrison has a central role in the American literary canon, according to many critics, award committees, and readers. Her award-winning novels chronicle small-town African-American life, employing "an artistic vision that encompasses both a private and a national heritage," to quote *Time* magazine contributor Angela Wigan. Through works such as *The Bluest Eye, Song of Solomon,* and *Beloved,* Morrison proves herself to be a gifted storyteller of stories in which troubled characters seek to find themselves and their cultural riches in a society that warps or impedes such essential growth. According to Charles Larson, writing in the *Chicago Tribune Book World,* each of Morrison's novels "is as original as anything that has appeared in our literature in the last twenty years. The contemporaneity that unites them—the troubling persistence of racism in America—is infused with an urgency that only a black writer can have about our society."

Morrison has also proved herself to be an able creator of children's books, working in collaboration with her son Slade Morrison. Together the two writers have produced the rhyming parable *The Big Box* and *The Book of Mean People,* a child's eye view of the world—as seen by a rabbit. They have also collaborated on a series of retellings of the tales from Aesop, titled "Who's Got Game?"

Morrison's artistry has attracted critical acclaim as well as commercial success; *Dictionary of Literary Biography* contributor Susan L. Blake called the author "an anomaly in two respects" because "she is a black writer who has achieved national prominence and popularity, and she is a popular writer who is taken seriously." Indeed, Morrison has won several of modern literature's most prestigious citations, including the 1977 National Book Critics Circle Award for *Song of Solomon,* the 1988 Pulitzer Prize for *Beloved,* and the 1993 Nobel Prize for Literature, the first African American to be named a laureate. *Atlantic* correspondent Wilfrid Sheed noted: "Most black writers are privy, like the rest of us, to bits and pieces of the secret, the dark side of their group experience, but Toni Morrison uniquely seems to have all the keys on her chain, like a house detective. . . . She [uses] the run of the whole place, from ghetto to small town to ramshackle farmhouse, to bring back a panorama of black myth and reality that [dazzles] the senses."

According to Jean Strouse, writing in *Newsweek,* Morrison "comes from a long line of people who did what they had to do to survive. It is their stories she tells in her novels—tales of the suffering and richness, the eloquence and tragedies of the black American experience." Morrison was born Chloe Anthony Wofford in Lorain, Ohio, a small industrial town near the shores of Lake Erie. *New York Review of Books* correspondent Darryl Pinckney described her particular community as "close enough to the Ohio River for the people who lived [there] to feel the torpor of the South, the nostalgia for its folkways, to sense the old Underground Railroad underfoot like a hidden stream."

Two important aspects of Chloe Wofford's childhood—community spirit and the supernatural—inform Toni Morrison's mature writing. In a *Publishers Weekly* interview, Morrison suggested ways in which her community influenced her. "There is this town which is both a support system and a hammer at the same time," she noted. "Approval was not the acquisition of things; approval was given for the maturity and the dignity with which one handled oneself. Most black people in particular were, and still are, very fastidious about manners, very careful about behavior and the rules that operate within the community. The sense of organized activity, what I thought at that time was burdensome, turns out now to have within it a gift—which is, I never had to be taught how to hold a job, how to make it work, how to handle my time."

On several levels the pariah—a unique and sometimes eccentric individual—figures in Morrison's fictional reconstruction of black community life. "There is always an elder there," she noted of her work in *Black Women Writers (1950-1980): A Critical Evaluation.* "And these ancestors are not just parents, they are sort of timeless people whose relationships to the characters are benevolent, instructive, and protective, and they provide a certain kind of wisdom." Sometimes this figure imparts his or her wisdom from beyond the grave; from an early age Morrison absorbed the folklore and beliefs of a culture for which the supernatural holds power and portent. Strouse stated that Morrison's world, both within and outside her fiction, is "filled with signs, visitations, ways of knowing that [reach] beyond the five senses."

As a student, Morrison earned money by cleaning houses; "the normal teenage jobs were not available," she recalled in a *New York Times Magazine* profile by Claudia Dreifus. "Housework always was." Some of her clients were nice; some were "terrible," Morrison added. The work gave her a perspective on black-white relations that touched Morrison's later writing. As she told Dreifus, "In [*The Bluest Eye*] Pauline lived in this dump and hated everything in it. And then she worked for the Fishers, who had this beautiful house, and she loved it. She got a lot of respect as their maid that she didn't get anywhere else." While never explicitly autobiographical, Morrison's fictions draw upon her youthful experiences in Ohio. In an essay for *Black Women Writers at Work* she claimed: "I am from the Midwest so I have a special affection for it. My beginnings are always there. . . . No matter what I write, I begin there. . . . It's the matrix for me. . . . Ohio also offers an escape from stereotyped black settings. It is neither plantation nor ghetto."

After graduating with honors from high school, Morrison attended Howard University, where she earned a degree in English. During this time, she also decided to change her first name to Toni. Morrison then earned a master's degree in English literature from Cornell. During this period, Morrison met and married her husband, an architect with whom she had two sons. In 1955, Morrison became an English instructor at Texas Southern University. Two years later, she returned to Howard University, teaching English until 1964. It was during her stint at Howard that Morrison first began to write. When her marriage ended in 1964, Morrison moved to New York, where she supported herself and her sons by working as a book editor at Random House. Morrison held this position until 1985, during which time she influenced several prominent black writers.

Morrison's own writing career took off in the late 1960s, and several themes and influences were in early evidence. "It seems somehow both constricting and inadequate to describe Toni Morrison as the country's preeminent black novelist, since in both gifts and accomplishments she transcends categorization," wrote Jonathan Yardley in the *Washington Post Book World,* "yet the characterization is inescapable not merely because it is true but because the very nature of Morrison's work dictates it. Not merely has black American life been the central preoccupation of her . . . novels . . . but as she has matured she has concentrated on distilling all of black experience into her books; quite purposefully, it seems, she is striving not for the particular but for the universal." In her work, critics claim, Morrison strives to lay bare the injustice inherent in the black condition and blacks' efforts, individually and collectively, to transcend society's unjust boundaries. Blake noted that Morrison's novels explore "the difference between black humanity and white cultural values. This opposition produces the negative theme of the seduction and betrayal of black people by white culture . . . and the positive theme of the quest for cultural identity." *Newsweek* contributor Strouse observed: "Like all the best stories, [Morrison's] are driven by an abiding moral vision. Implicit in all her characters' grapplings with who they are is a large sense of human nature and love—and a reach for understanding of something larger than the moment."

Quest for self is a motivating and organizing device in Morrison's fiction, as is the role of family and community in nurturing or challenging the individual. In the *Times Literary Supplement,* Jennifer Uglow suggested that Morrison's novels "explore in particular the process of growing up black, female and poor. Avoiding generalities, Toni Morrison concentrates on the relation between the pressures of the community, patterns established within families, . . . and the developing sense of self." According to Dorothy H. Lee in *Black Women Writers (1950-1980),* Morrison is preoccupied "with the effect of the community on the individual's achievement and retention of an integrated, acceptable self. In treating this subject, she draws recurrently on myth and legend for story pattern and characters, returning repeatedly to the theory of *quest.* . . . The goals her characters seek to achieve are similar in their deepest implications, and yet the degree to which they attain them varies radically because each novel is cast in unique human terms." In Morrison's books, blacks must confront the notion that all understanding is accompanied by pain, just as all comprehension of national history must include the humiliations of slavery. She tempers this hard lesson by preserving "the richness of communal life against an outer world that denies its value" and by turning to "a heritage of folklore, not only to disclose patterns of living but also to close wounds," in the words of *Nation* contributor Brina Caplan.

Although Morrison herself told the *Chicago Tribune* that there is "epiphany and triumph" in every book she writes, some critics find her work nihilistic and her vision bleak. "The picture given by . . . Morrison of the plight of the decent, aspiring individual in the black family and community is more painful than the gloomiest impressions encouraged by either stereotype or sociology," observed Diane Johnson in the *New York Review of Books.* Johnson continued, "Undoubtedly white society is the ultimate oppressor, and not just of blacks, but, as Morrison [shows], . . . the black person must first deal with the oppressor in the next room, or in the same bed, or no farther away than across the street."

Morrison is a pioneer in the depiction of the hurt inflicted by blacks on blacks; for instance, her characters rarely achieve harmonious relationships but are instead divided by futurelessness and the anguish of stifled existence. Uglow wrote: "We have become attuned to novels . . . which locate oppression in the conflicts of blacks (usually men) trying to make it in a white world. By concentrating on the sense of violation experienced within black neighborhoods, even within families, Toni Morrison deprives us of stock responses and creates a more demanding and uncomfortable literature." *Village Voice* correspondent Vivian Gornick contended that the world Morrison creates "is thick with an atmosphere through which her characters move slowly, in pain, ignorance, and hunger. And to a very large degree Morrison has the compelling ability to make one believe that all of us (Morrison, the characters, the reader) are penetrating that dark and hurtful terrain—the feel of a human life—simultaneously." Uglow concluded that even the laughter of Morrison's characters "disguises pain, deprivation and violation. It is laughter at a series of bad, cruel jokes. . . . Nothing is what it seems; no appearance, no relationship can be trusted to endure."

Other critics detect a deeper undercurrent to Morrison's work that contains just the sort of epiphany for which she strives. "From book to book, Morrison's larger project grows clear," remarked Ann Snitow in the *Voice Literary Supplement.* "First, she insists that every character bear the weight of responsibility for his or her own life. After she's measured out each one's private pain, she adds on to that the shared burden of what the whites did. Then, at last, she tries to find the place where her stories can lighten her readers' load, lift them up from their own and others' guilt, carry them to glory. . . . Her characters suffer—from their own limitations and the world's—but their inner life miraculously expands beyond the narrow law of cause and effect." *Harvard Advocate* essayist Faith Davis wrote that despite the mundane boundaries of Morrison's characters' lives, the author "illuminates the complexity of their attitudes toward life. Having reached a quiet and extensive understanding of their situation, they can endure life's calamities. . . . Morrison never allows us to become indifferent to these people. . . . Her citizens . . . jump up from the pages vital and strong because she has made us care about the pain in their lives." In *Ms.,* Margo Jefferson concluded that Morrison's books "are filled with loss—lost friendship, lost love, lost customs, lost possibilities. And yet there is so much life in the smallest acts and gestures . . . that they are as much celebrations as elegies."

Morrison sees language as an expression of black experience, and her novels are characterized by vivid narration and dialogue. *Village Voice* essayist Susan Lydon observed that the author "works her magic charm above all with a love of language. Her soaring . . . style carries you like a river, sweeping doubt and disbelief away, and it is only gradually that one realizes her deadly serious intent." In the *Spectator,* Caroline Moorehead likewise noted that Morrison "writes energetically and richly, using words in a way very much her own. The effect is one of exoticism, an exciting curiousness in the language, a balanced sense of the possible that stops, always, short of the absurd."

Although Morrison does not like to be called a poetic writer, critics often comment on the lyrical quality of her prose. "Morrison's style has always moved fluidly between tough-minded realism and lyric descriptiveness," said *Newsweek* contributor Margo Jefferson. "Vivid dialogue, capturing the drama and extravagance of black speech, gives way to an impressionistic evocation of physical pain or an ironic, essay-like analysis of the varieties of religious hypocrisy." Uglow wrote: "The word 'elegant' is often applied to Toni Morrison's writing; it employs sophisticated narrative devices, shifting perspectives and resonant images and displays an obvious delight in the potential of language." *Nation* contributor Earl Frederick concluded that Morrison, "with an ear as sharp as glass . . . has listened to the music of black talk and deftly uses it as the palette knife to create black lives and to provide some of the best fictional dialogue around today."

In the mid-1960s, Morrison completed her first novel, *The Bluest Eye.* Although she had trouble getting the book into print—the manuscript was rejected several times—it was finally published in 1969. At age thirty-eight, Morrison was a published author, and her debut, set in Morrison's hometown of Lorain, Ohio, portrays "in poignant terms the tragic condition of blacks in a racist America," to quote Chikwenye Okonjo Ogunyemi in *Critique.* In *The Bluest Eye,* Morrison depicts the onset of black self-hatred as occasioned by white-American ideals such as "Dick and Jane" primers and Shirley Temple movies. The principal character, Pecola Breedlove, is literally maddened by the disparity between her existence and the pictures of beauty and gentility disseminated by the dominant white culture. As Phyllis R. Klotman noted in the *Black American Literature Forum,* Morrison "uses the contrast between Shirley Temple and Pecola . . . to underscore the irony of black experience. Whether one learns acceptability from the formal educational experience or from cultural symbols, the effect is the same: self- hatred." Darwin T. Turner elaborated on the novel's intentions in *Black Women Writers (1950-1980).* Morrison's fictional milieu, wrote Turner, is "a world of grotesques—individuals whose psyches have been deformed by their efforts to assume false identities, their failures to achieve meaningful identities, or simply their inability to retain and communicate love."

Blake characterized *The Bluest Eye* as a novel of initiation, exploring that common theme in American literature from a minority viewpoint. Ogunyemi contended that, in essence, Morrison presents "old problems in a fresh language and with a fresh perspective. A central force of the work derives from her power to draw vignettes and her ability to portray emotions, seeing the world through the eyes of adolescent girls." Klotman, who called the book "a novel of growing up, of growing up young and black and female in America," concluded her review with the comment that the "rite of passage, initiating the young into womanhood at first tenuous and uncertain, is sensitively depicted. . . . *The Bluest Eye* is an extraordinarily passionate yet gentle work, the language lyrical yet precise—it is a novel for all seasons."

The 1994 reissue of *The Bluest Eye* prompted a new set of appraisals. In an *African American Review* piece, Allen Alexander found that religious references—from both Western and African sources—"abound" in the novel's pages. "And of the many fascinating religious references," Alexander continued, "the most complex . . . are her representations of and allusions to God. In Morrison's fictional world, God's characteristics are not limited to those represented by the traditional Western notion of the Trinity: Father, Son and Holy Ghost." Instead, Morrison presents God as having "a fourth face, one that is an explanation for all those things—the existence of evil, the suffering of the innocent and just—that seem so inexplicable in the face of a religious tradition that preaches the omnipotence of a benevolent God." Cat Moses used the forum of *African American Review* to contribute an essay outlining the blues aesthetic in *The Bluest Eye.* The narrative's structure, Moses wrote, "follows a pattern common to traditional blues lyrics: a movement from an initial emphasis on loss to a concluding suggestion of resolution of grief through motion." In depicting the transition from loss to "movin' on," said the essayist, *The Bluest Eye* "contains an abundance of cultural wisdom."

In 1973's *Sula,* Morrison once again presents a pair of black women who must come to terms with their lives. Set in a Midwestern black community called The Bottom, the story follows two friends, Sula and Nel, from childhood to old age and death. Snitow claimed that through Sula, Morrison discovered "a way to offer her people an insight and sense of recovered self so dignified and glowing that no worldly pain could dull the final light." Indeed, *Sula* is a tale of rebel and conformist in which the conformity is dictated by the solid inhabitants of The Bottom and even the rebellion gains strength from the community's disapproval. *New York Times Book Review* contributor Sara Blackburn contended, however, that the book is "too vital and rich" to be consigned to the category of allegory. Morrison's "extravagantly beautiful, doomed characters are locked in a world where hope for the future is a foreign commodity, yet they are enormously, achingly alive," wrote Blackburn. "And this book about them—and about how their beauty is drained back and frozen—is a howl of love and rage, playful and funny as well as hard and bitter." In the words of *American Literature* essayist Jane S. Bakerman, Morrison "uses the maturation story of Sula and Nel as the core of a host of other stories, but it is the chief unification device for the novel and achieves its own unity, again, through the clever manipulation of the themes of sex, race, and love. Morrison has undertaken a . . . difficult task in *Sula.* Unquestionably, she has succeeded."

Other critics have echoed Bakerman's sentiments about *Sula.* Yardley stated: "What gives this terse, imaginative novel its genuine distinction is the quality of Toni Morrison's prose. *Sula* is admirable enough as a study of its title character, . . . but its real strength lies in Morrison's writing, which at times has the resonance of poetry and is precise, vivid and controlled throughout." Turner also claimed that in *Sula* "Morrison evokes her verbal magic occasionally by lyric descriptions that carry the reader deep into the soul of the character. . . . Equally effective, however, is her art of narrating action in a lean prose that uses adjectives cautiously while creating memorable vivid images." In her review, Davis concluded that a "beautiful and haunting atmosphere emerges out of the wreck of these folks' lives, a quality that is absolutely convincing and absolutely precise." *Sula* was nominated for a National Book Award in 1974.

From the insular lives she depicted in her first two novels, Morrison moved in *Song of Solomon* to a national and historical perspective on black American life. "Here the depths of the younger work are still evident," said Reynolds Price in the *New York Times Book Review,* "but now they thrust outward, into wider fields, for longer intervals, encompassing many more lives. The result is a long prose tale that surveys nearly a century of American history as it impinges upon a single family." With an intermixture of the fantastic and the realistic, *Song of Solomon* relates the journey of a character named Milkman Dead into an understanding of his family heritage and hence, himself. Lee wrote: "Figuratively, [Milkman] travels from innocence to awareness, i.e., from ignorance of origins, heritage, identity, and communal responsibility to knowledge and acceptance. He moves from selfish and materialistic dilettantism to an understanding of brotherhood. With his release of personal ego, he is able to find a place in the whole. There is, then, a universal—indeed mythic—pattern here. He journeys from spiritual death to rebirth, a direction symbolized by his discovery of the secret power of flight. Mythically, liberation and transcendence follow the discovery of self." Blake suggested that the connection Milkman discovers with his family's past helps him to connect meaningfully with his contemporaries; *Song of Solomon,* Blake noted, "dramatizes dialectical approaches to the challenges of black life." According to Anne Z. Mickelson in *Reaching Out: Sensitivity and Order in Recent American Fiction by*

Women, history itself "becomes a choral symphony to Milkman, in which each individual voice has a chance to speak and contribute to his growing sense of well-being."

Mickelson also observed that *Song of Solomon* represents for blacks "a break out of the confining life into the realm of possibility." Charles Larson commented on this theme in a *Washington Post Book World* review. The novel's subject matter, Larson explained, is "the origins of black consciousness in America, and the individual's relationship to that heritage." However, Larson added, "skilled writer that she is, Morrison has transcended this theme so that the reader rarely feels that this is simply another novel about ethnic identity. So marvelously orchestrated is Morrison's narrative that it not only excels on all of its respective levels, not only works for all of its interlocking components, but also—in the end—says something about life (and death) for all of us. Milkman's epic journey . . . is a profound examination of the individual's understanding of, and, perhaps, even transcendence of the inevitable fate of his life." Gornick concluded: "There are so many individual moments of power and beauty in *Song of Solomon* that, ultimately, one closes the book warmed through by the richness of its sympathy, and by its breathtaking feel for the nature of sexual sorrow."

Song of Solomon, which won the National Book Critics Circle Award in 1977, was also the first novel by a black writer to become a Book-of-the-Month Club selection since Richard Wright's *Native Son* was published in 1940. *World Literature Today* reviewer Richard K. Barksdale called the work "a book that will not only withstand the test of time but endure a second and third reading by those conscientious readers who love a well-wrought piece of fiction." Describing the novel as "a stunningly beautiful book" in her *Washington Post Book World* piece, Anne Tyler added: "I would call the book poetry, but that would seem to be denying its considerable power as a story. Whatever name you give it, it's full of magnificent people, each of them complex and multilayered, even the narrowest of them narrow in extravagant ways." Price deemed *Song of Solomon* "a long story, . . . and better than good. Toni Morrison has earned attention and praise. Few Americans know, and can say, more than she has in this wise and spacious novel."

Morrison clearly attained the respect of the literary community, but even in the face of three well-received novels, she did not call herself a writer. "I think, at bottom, I simply was not prepared to do the adult thing, which in those days would be associated with the male thing, which was to say, 'I'm a writer,'" she told Dreifus in 1994. "I said, 'I am a mother who writes,' or 'I am an editor who writes.' The word 'writer' was hard for me to say because that's what you put on your income-tax form. I *do* now say, 'I'm a writer.' But it's the difference between identifying one's work and being the person who does the work. I've always been the latter."

Still, critics and readers had no doubt that Morrison was a writer. Her 1981 book *Tar Baby* remained on bestseller lists for four months. A novel of ideas, the work dramatizes the fact that complexion is a far more subtle issue than the simple polarization of black and white. Set on a lush Caribbean Island, *Tar Baby* explores the passionate love affair of Jadine, a Sorbonne-educated black model, and Son, a handsome knock-about with a strong aversion to white culture. According to Caplan, Morrison's concerns "are race, class, culture and the effects of late capitalism—heavy freight for any narrative. . . . She is attempting to stabilize complex visions of society—that is, to examine competitive ideas. . . . Because the primary function of Morrison's characters is to voice representative opinions, they arrive on stage vocal and highly conscious, their histories symbolically indicated or merely sketched. Her brief sketches, however, are clearly the work of an artist who can, when she chooses, model the mind in depth and detail." In a *Dictionary of Literary Biography Yearbook* essay, Elizabeth B. House outlined *Tar Baby*'s major themes: "the difficulty of settling conflicting claims between one's past and present and the destruction which abuse of power can bring. As Morrison examines these problems in *Tar Baby,* she suggests no easy way to understand what one's link to a heritage should be, nor does she offer infallible methods for dealing with power. Rather, with an astonishing insight and grace, she demonstrates the pervasiveness of such dilemmas and the degree to which they affect human beings, both black and white."

Tar Baby uncovers racial and sexual conflicts without offering solutions, but most critics found that Morrison indicts all of her characters—black and white—for their thoughtless devaluations of others. *New York Times Book Review* correspondent John Irving claimed: "What's so powerful, and subtle, about Miss Morrison's presentation of the tension between blacks and whites is that she conveys it almost entirely through the suspicions and prejudices of her black characters. . . . Miss Morrison uncovers all the stereotypical racial fears felt by whites and blacks alike. Like any ambitious writer, she's unafraid to employ these stereotypes—she embraces the representative qualities of her characters without embarrassment, then proceeds to make them individuals too." *New Yorker* essayist Susan Lardner praised Morrison for her "power to be absolutely persuasive against her own preferences, suspicions, and convictions, implied or plainly expressed," and Strouse likewise contended that the author "has produced that rare commodity, a truly public novel about the condition of society, examining the relations between blacks and whites, men and women, civilization and nature. . . . It wraps its messages in a highly potent love story." Irving suggested that Morrison's greatest accomplishment "is that she has raised her novel above the social realism that too many black novels and women's novels are trapped in. She has succeeded in writing about race and women symbolically."

Reviewers praised *Tar Baby* for its provocative themes and for its evocative narration. *Los Angeles Times* contributor Elaine Kendall called the book "an intricate and sophisticated novel, moving from a realistic and orderly beginning to a mystical and ambiguous end. Morrison has taken classically simple story elements and realigned them so artfully that we perceive the old pattern in a startlingly different way. Although this territory has been explored by dozens of novelists, Morrison depicts it with such vitality that it seems newly discovered." In the *Washington Post Book World,* Webster Schott claimed: "There is so much that is good, sometimes dazzling, about *Tar Baby*—poetic language, . . . arresting images, fierce intelligence—that . . . one becomes entranced by Toni Morrison's story. The settings are so vivid the characters must be alive. The emotions they feel are so intense they must be real people." Maureen Howard stated in *New Republic* that the work "is as carefully patterned as a well-written poem. . . . *Tar Baby* is a good American novel in which we can discern a new lightness and brilliance in Toni Morrison's enchantment with language and in her curiously polyphonic stories that echo life." Schott concluded: "One of fiction's pleasures is to have your mind scratched and your intellectual habits challenged. While *Tar Baby* has shortcomings, lack of provocation isn't one of them. Morrison owns a powerful intelligence. It's run by courage. She calls to account conventional wisdom and accepted attitude at nearly every turn."

In addition to her own writing, Morrison during this period helped to publish the work of other noted black Americans, including Toni Cade Bambara, Gayle Jones, Angela Davis, and Muhammad Ali. Discussing her aims as an editor in a quotation printed in the *Dictionary of Literary Biography,* Morrison said, "I look very hard for black fiction because I want to participate in developing a canon of black work. We've had the first rush of black entertainment, where blacks were writing for whites, and whites were encouraging this kind of self-flagellation. Now we can get down to the craft of writing, where black people are talking to black people." One of Morrison's important projects for Random House was *The Black Book,* an anthology of items that illustrate the history of black Americans. *Ms.* magazine correspondent Dorothy Eugenia Robinson described the work: "*The Black Book* is the pain and pride of rediscovering the collective black experience. It is finding the essence of ourselves and holding on. *The Black Book* is a kind of scrapbook of patiently assembled samplings of black history and culture. What has evolved is a pictorial folk journey of black people, places, events, handcrafts, inventions, songs, and folklore. . . . *The Black Book* informs, disturbs, maybe even shocks. It unsettles complacency and demands confrontation with raw reality. It is by no means an easy book to experience, but it's a necessary one."

While preparing *The Black Book* for publication, Morrison uncovered the true and shocking story of a runaway slave who, at the point of recapture, murdered her infant child so it would not be doomed to a lifetime of servitude. For Morrison, the story encapsulated the fierce psychic cruelty of an institutionalized system that sought to destroy the basic emotional bonds between men and women, and worse, between parent and child. "I certainly thought I knew as much about slavery as anybody," Morrison told an interview for the *Los Angeles Times.* "But it was the interior life I needed to find out about." It is this "interior life" in the throes of slavery that constitutes the theme of Morrison's novel *Beloved.* Set in Reconstruction-era Cincinnati, the book centers on characters who struggle fruitlessly to keep their painful recollections of the past at bay. They are haunted, both physically and spiritually, by the legacies slavery has bequeathed to them. According to Snitow, *Beloved* "staggers under the terror of its material—as so much holocaust writing does and must."

While the book was not unanimously praised—*New Republic* writer Stanley Crouch cited the author for "almost always [losing] control" and of not resisting "the temptation of the trite or the sentimental"—many critics considered *Beloved* to be Morrison's masterpiece. In *People,* V. R. Peterson described the novel as "a brutally powerful, mesmerizing story about the inescapable, excruciating legacy of slavery. Behind each new event and each new character lies another event and another story until finally the reader meets a community of proud, daring people, inextricably bound by culture and experience." Through the lives of ex-slaves Sethe and her would-be lover Paul D, readers "experience American slavery as it was lived by those who were its objects of exchange, both at its best—which wasn't very good—and at its worst, which was as bad as can be imagined," wrote Margaret Atwood in the *New York Times Book Review.* "Above all, it is seen as one of the most viciously antifamily institutions human beings have ever devised. The slaves are motherless, fatherless, deprived of their mates, their children, their kin. It is a world in which people suddenly vanish and are never seen again, not through accident or covert operation or terrorism, but as a matter of everyday legal policy." *New York Times* columnist Michiko Kakutani contended that *Beloved* "possesses the heightened power and resonance of myth—its characters, like those in opera or Greek drama, seem larger than life and their actions, too, tend to strike us as enactments of ancient rituals and passions. To describe *Beloved* only in these terms, however, is to diminish its immediacy, for the novel also remains precisely grounded in American reality—the reality of Black history as experienced in the wake of the Civil War."

Beloved may be an American novel, but its images and influences come from the British Romantic tradition, theorized Martin Bidney in *Papers on Language and Literature.* "Simply to list a few of [the book's] major episodes—ice skating, boat stealing, gigantic shadow, carnival 'freak' show, water-voices sounding the depths—is almost to create a rapidly scrolled plot synopsis of Wordsworth's *Prelude,*" Bidney wrote. "When Baby Suggs declares that the only grace we will receive is the grace we can 'imagine,' or when Sethe tells how Paul D's visionary capacity makes 'windows' suddenly have 'view,' we hear the voice of William Blake." The critic also saw traces of Keats in the scenes of Paul D's musings "on the superiority of imagined love to mere physical sex." But the achievement of the novel ultimately belongs to Morrison, Bidney added: "These few examples are by no means a complete listing of all the Romantic allusive motifs that combined to help make *Beloved* the visionary masterwork it is."

Acclaim for *Beloved* came from both sides of the Atlantic. In his *Chicago Tribune* piece, Larson claimed that the work "is the context out of which all of Morrison's earlier novels were written. In her darkest and most probing novel, Toni Morrison has demonstrated once again the stunning powers that place her in the first ranks of our living novelists." *Los Angeles Times Book Review* contributor John Leonard likewise expressed the opinion that the novel "belongs on the highest shelf of American literature, even if half a dozen canonized white boys have to be elbowed off. . . . Without *Beloved* our imagination of the nation's self has a hole in it big enough to die from." Atwood stated: "Ms. Morrison's versatility and technical and emotional range appear to know no bounds. If there were any doubts about her stature as a pre-eminent American novelist, of her own or any other generation, *Beloved* will put them to rest." London *Times* reviewer Nicholas Shakespeare concluded that *Beloved* "is a novel propelled by the cadences of . . . songs—the first singing of a people hardened by their suffering, people who have been hanged and whipped and mortgaged at the hands of white people—the men without skin. From Toni Morrison's pen it is a sound that breaks the back of words, making *Beloved* a great novel."

But for all its acclaim, *Beloved* became the object of controversy when the novel failed to win either the 1987 National Book Award or the National Book Critics Circle Award. In response, forty-eight prominent African-American authors—including Maya Angelou, Alice Walker, and John Wideman—signed a letter to the editor that appeared in the January 24, 1988, edition of the *New York Times.* The letter expressed the signers' dismay at the "oversight and harmful whimsy" that resulted in the lack of recognition for *Beloved.* The "legitimate need for our own critical voice in relation to our own literature can no longer be denied," declared Morrison's peers. The authors concluded their letter with a tribute to Morrison: "For all of America, for all of American letters, you have advanced the moral and artistic standards by which we must measure the daring and the love of our national imagination and our collective intelligence as a people." The letter sparked fierce debate within the New York literary community, "with some critics accusing the authors of the letter of racist manipulation," according to an entry in *Newsmakers 1988. Beloved* ended up winning the Pulitzer Prize for 1988.

Morrison's subsequent novel, *Jazz,* is "a fictive recreation of two parallel narratives set during major historical events in African-American history—Reconstruction and the Jazz Age," noted *Dictionary of Literary Biography* writer Denise Heinze. Set primarily in New York City during the 1920s, the novel's main narrative involves a love triangle between Violet, a middle-aged woman; Joe, her husband; and Dorcas, Joe's teenage mistress. When Dorcas snubs Joe for a younger lover, Joe shoots and kills Dorcas. Violet seeks to understand the dead girl by befriending Dorcas's aunt, Alice Manfred. Simultaneously, Morrison relates the story of Joe and Violet's parents and grandparents. In telling these stories, Morrison touches on a number of themes: "male/female passion," as Heinze commented; the movement of blacks into large urban areas after Reconstruction; and, as is usually the case with her novels, the effects of racism and history on the African-American community. Morrison also makes use of an unusual storytelling device: an unnamed, intrusive, and unreliable narrator.

"The standard set by the brilliance and intensity of Morrison's previous novel *Beloved* is so high that *Jazz* does not pretend to come close to attaining it," stated *Kenyon Review* contributor Peter Erickson. Nevertheless, many reviewers responded enthusiastically to the provocative themes Morrison presents in *Jazz*. "The unrelenting, destructive influence of racism and oppression on the black family is manifested in *Jazz* by the almost-total absence of the black family," stated Heinze. Writing in the *New York Review of Books,* Michael Wood remarked that "black women in *Jazz* are arming themselves, physically and mentally, and in this they have caught a current of the times, a not always visible indignation that says enough is enough." Several reviewers felt that Morrison's use of an unreliable narrator impeded the story's effectiveness. Erickson, for instance, averred that the narrator "is not inventive enough. Because the narrator displays a lack of imagination at crucial moments, she seems to get in the way, to block rather than to enable access to deeper levels." But Heinze found that Morrison's unreliable narrator allows the author to engage the reader in a way that she has not done in her previous novels: "in *Jazz* Morrison questions her ability to answer the very issues she raises, extending the responsibility of her own novel writing to her readers." Heinze concluded: "Morrison thereby sends an invitation to her readers to become a part of that struggle to comprehend totality that will continue to spur her genius."

Morrison's "genius" was recognized a year after the publication of *Jazz* with a momentous award: the Nobel Prize for Literature. The first black and only the eighth woman to win the award, Morrison told Dreifus that "it was as if the whole category of 'female writer' and 'black writer' had been redeemed. I felt I represented a whole world of women who either were silenced or who had never received the imprimatur of the established literary world." In describing the author after its selection, the Nobel Committee noted, as quoted by Heinze: "She delves into the language itself, a language she wants to liberate from the fetters of race. And she addresses us with the luster of poetry." In 1996, Morrison received another prestigious award, the National Book Foundation Medal for Distinguished Contribution to American Letters; this was followed by the National Humanities Medal in 2001.

In *Paradise,* Morrison's first novel after winning the Nobel Prize, noted *America* contributor Hermine Pinson, "the writer appears to be reinterpreting some of her most familiar themes: the significance of the 'ancestor' in our lives, the importance of community, the concept of 'home,' and the continuing conundrum of race in the United States. The title and intended subject of the text—Paradise—accommodates all of the foregoing themes." Like *Beloved, Paradise* "centers on a catastrophic act of violence that begs to be understood," *National Catholic Reporter* contributor Judith Bromberg explained. "Morrison meticulously peels away layer upon layer of truth so that what we think we know, we don't until she finally confronts us with raw truth." The conflict, and the violence that results from it, comes out of the dedicated self-righteousness of the leading families of the all-black town of Ruby, Oklahoma. "The story begins in Oklahoma in 1976," Pinson said, "when nine men from the still all-black town of Ruby invade the local convent on a mission to keep the town safe from the outright evil and depravity that they believe is embodied in the disparate assembly of religious women who live there." "In a show of force a posse of nine descend on the crumbling mansion in the predawn of a summer morning, killing all four of the troubled, flawed women who have sought refuge there," Bromberg stated.

Many reviewers recognized Morrison's accomplishment in *Paradise.* John Kennedy of *Antioch Review* called Morrison's opening chapter "Faulknerian"; with its "rich, evocative and descriptive passages, it is a haunting introduction to the repressed individuality that stalks 'so clean and blessed a mission.'" The novel "is full of challenges and surprises," wrote *Christian Century* reviewer Reggie Young. "Though it does not quite come up to the standard of Morrison's masterwork, *Beloved,* this is one of the most important novels of the decade." "This is Morrison's first novel since her 1993 *Jazz,*" summed up Emily J. Jones in *Library Journal,* "and it is well worth the wait."

Morrison's 2003 offering, *Love,* is the story of a well-off African American man who runs a hotel for patrons similar to himself. It incorporates elements of bias based on financial status and the strife that money can cause between loved ones. *World Literature Today* contributor Daniel Garrett commented that the book, "which is richer and wilder than most books, reminds me of other entertainments, both within and outside Morrison's oeuvre—and that makes it a surprising disappointment." Nola Theiss disagreed, in a *Kliatt*review, stating that the "language requires careful reading as each sentence is a poem in itself." Theiss concluded that "Raw and ethereal at the same time, *Love* will be read for generations."

In addition to her novels, Morrison has also published in other genres. *Playing in the Dark: Whiteness and the Literary Imagination* is a collection of three lectures that Morrison gave at Harvard University in 1990. Focusing on racism as it has manifested itself in American literature, these essays of literary criticism explore the works of authors such as Willa Cather, Mark Twain, and Ernest Hemingway. In 1992, Morrison edited *Race-ing Justice, En-Gendering Power: Essays on Anita Hill, Clarence Thomas, and the Construction of Social Reality,* eighteen essays about Thomas's nomination to the U.S. Supreme Court.

Turning her attention to younger readers, Morrison collaborated with her son Slade on a 1999 picture book called *The Big Box,* based on a story Slade made up when he was nine. Morrison provided the verse for a tale of three children living in "a big brown box [with] three big locks"; the children have been sent there by their parents, who feel the high-spirited and imaginative youngsters "can't handle their freedom." These children have all done something to upset the parents: Patty is too talkative in the library; Liza Sue allows the chickens to keep their eggs; and Mickey plays when he should not. The adults do not like rebellious children and so put them away, not even bothering to listen to their repeated protest: "I know that you think / You're doing what is best for me. / But if freedom is handled just *your* way / Then it's not my freedom or free."

While the tale ends happily, the generally downbeat tone of the story made some critics wary of the children's book. A contributor for *Publishers Weekly* faulted the picture book for having "little of the childlike perspective that so masterfully informs *The Bluest Eye.* " A *Horn Book* contributor likewise complained of the "heavy-handed irony" that informs much of the book. Hazel Rochman, writing in *Booklist,* decided that *The Big Box* "will appeal most to adults who cherish images of childhood innocence in a fallen world." Ellen Fader, writing in *School Library Journal,* felt the book "will have a hard time finding its audience," as it appears to be for children, but the message "requires more sophistication." A critic for *Kirkus Reviews,* however, noted that the message of the book is "valid" and "strongly made," calling the work "a promising children's book debut." And a reviewer for *Journal of Adolescent and Adult Literacy* also had praise for the title, remarking favorably upon the "haunting message about children who don't fit the accepted definitions of . . . 'normal.'"

Teaming up again with her son Slade, Morrison published another juvenile title in 2002, *The Book of Mean People,* a "bittersweet volume [that] takes meanness in stride and advocates kindness as the antidote," observed a contributor for *Publishers Weekly.* The narrative is a catalog of the things adults do to kids that kids often interpret as being mean. Grownups shout when something is wrong, make children eat things they do not like, and even dictate the time youngsters are to be in bed. These thoughts seemingly come from a bunny featured in the illustrations by Pascal Lemaître. Overall, this second children's title enjoyed a more positive critical reception than the first. A *Kirkus Reviews* critic thought that young readers "who know just what the young narrator is talking about may take to heart the closing advice to smile in the face of frowns." *School Library Journal* contributor Judy Constantinides felt that "the book could be used as a springboard to discuss anger and shouting." Evette Porter, writing in *Black Issues Book Review,* found *The Book of Mean People* "a witty yet candid look at anger from the perspective of a child." The book was published in tandem with an interactive journal so that children can record their responses to situations that make them feel angry and helpless. A reviewer for *Publishers Weekly* thought that the questions supplied as writing prompts in the journal "encourage reflection," while Porter commented that the journal could "serve as a preschool primer in anger-management therapy."

As interesting as such writing projects are, however, it is Morrison's adult fiction that has secured her place among the literary elite. Morrison is an author who labors contentedly under the labels bestowed by pigeonholing critics. She has no objection to being called a black woman writer, because, as she told an interviewer for the *New York Times,* "I really think the range of emotions and perceptions I have had access to as a black person and a female person are greater than those of people who are neither. . . . My world did not shrink because I was a black female writer. It just got bigger." Nor does she strive for that much-vaunted universality that purports to be a hallmark of fine fiction. "I never asked Tolstoy to write for me, a little colored girl in Lorain, Ohio," she told an interviewer for the *New Republic.* "I never asked [James] Joyce not to mention Catholicism or the world of Dublin. Never. And I don't know why I should be asked to explain your life to you. We have splendid writers to do that, but I am not one of them. It is that business of being universal, a word hopelessly stripped of meaning for me. [William] Faulkner wrote what I suppose could be called regional literature and had it published all over the world. That's what I wish to do. If I tried to write a universal novel, it would be water. Behind this question is the suggestion that to write for black people is somehow to diminish the writing. From my perspective there are only black people. When I say 'people,' that's what I mean."

Black woman writer or simply American novelist, Morrison is a prominent and respected figure in modern letters. As testament to her influence, something of a cottage industry has arisen of Morrison assessments. According to a *Time* article, the author "has inspired a generation of black artists, . . . produced seismic effects on publishing . . . [and] affected the course of black-studies programs across the U.S." Several books and dozens of critical essays are devoted to the examination of her fiction. Though popular acceptance of her work has seldom flagged, Morrison found her *Song of Solomon* shooting to the bestseller lists again after being selected by talk-show host Oprah Winfrey as a book-club pick in 1996; in 2002, *Sula* was the novel chosen to close out Winfrey's popular discussion group. The author's hometown of Lorain, Ohio, is the setting for the biennial Toni Morrison Society Conference; a 2000 gathering attracted 130 scholars from around the globe.

In the *Detroit News,* Larson suggested that Morrison's has been "among the most exciting literary careers of the last decade" and that each of her books "has made a quantum jump forward." Ironically, House commended Morrison for the universal nature of her work. "Unquestionably," House wrote, "Toni Morrison is an important novelist who continues to develop her talent. Part of her appeal, of course, lies in her extraordinary ability to create beautiful language and striking characters. However, Morrison's most important gift, the one which gives her a major author's universality, is the insight with which she writes of problems all humans face. . . . At the core of all her novels is a penetrating view of the unyielding, heartbreaking dilemmas which torment people of all races." Snitow noted that the author "wants to tend the imagination, search for an expansion of the possible, nurture a spiritual richness in the black tradition even after 300 years in the white desert." Lee concluded of Morrison's accomplishments: "Though there are unifying aspects in her novels, there is not a dully repetitive sameness. Each casts the problems in specific, imaginative terms, and the exquisite, poetic language awakens our senses as she communicates an often ironic vision with moving imagery. Each novel reveals the acuity of her perception of psychological motivation of the female especially, of the Black particularly, and of the human generally."

"The problem I face as a writer is to make my stories mean something," Morrison stated in an interview in *Black Women Writers at Work.* "You can have wonderful, interesting people, a fascinating story, but it's not about anything. It has no real substance. I want my books to always be about something that is important to me, and the subjects that are important in the world are the same ones that have always been important." In *Black Women Writers (1950-1980),* she elaborated on this idea. Fiction, she wrote, "should be beautiful, and powerful, but it should also work. It should have something in it that enlightens; something in it that opens the door and points the way. Something in it that suggests what the conflicts are, what the problems are. But it need not solve those problems because it is not a case study, it is not a recipe." The author who said that writing to her "is discovery; it's talking deep within myself" told the *New York Times Book Review* that the essential theme in her growing body of fiction is "how and why we learn to live this life intensely and well."

BIOGRAPHICAL AND CRITICAL SOURCES:

BOOKS

American Decades, 1970- 1979, edited by Victor Bondi, Gale (Detroit, MI), 1995.

Awkward, Michael, *Inspiriting Influences: Tradition, Revision, and Afro-American Women's Novels,* Columbia University Press (New York, NY), 1989.

Bell, Roseann P., editor, *Sturdy Black Bridges: Visions of Black Women in Literature,* Doubleday (New York, NY), 1979.

Bjork, Patrick Bryce, *The Novels of Toni Morrison: The Search for Self and Place within the Community,* Peter Lang (New York, NY), 1992.

Black Literature Criticism, Volume 2, Gale (Detroit, MI), 1992.

Bloom, Harold, editor, *Toni Morrison,* Chelsea House (Philadelphia, PA), 1990.

Bruccoli, Matthew J., editor, *Toni Morrison's Fiction,* University of South Carolina Press (Columbia, SC), 1996.

Century, Douglas, *Toni Morrison,* Chelsea House (Philadelphia, PA), 1994.

Christian, Barbara, *Black Women Novelists: The Development of a Tradition, 1892-1976,* Greenwood Press (Westport, CT), 1980.

Contemporary Literary Criticism, Gale (Detroit, MI), Volume 4, 1975, Volume 10, 1979, Volume 22, 1982, Volume 55, 1989, Volume 81, 1994, Volume 87, 1995.

Cooey, Paula M., *Religious Imagination and the Body: A Feminist Analysis,* Oxford University Press (New York, NY), 1994.

Cooper-Clark, Diana, *Interviews with Contemporary Novelists,* St. Martin's Press (New York, NY), 1986.

Coser, Stelamaris, *Bridging the Americas: The Literature of Paule Marshall, Toni Morrison, and Gayl Jones,* Temple University Press (Philadelphia, PA), 1995.

Dictionary of Literary Biography, Gale (Detroit, MI), Volume 6: *American Novelists since World War II,* 1980, Volume 33:*Afro- American Fiction Writers after 1955,* 1984, Volume 143: *American Novelists since World War II, Third Series,* 1994.

Dictionary of Literary Biography Yearbook: 1981, Gale (Detroit, MI), 1982.

Dictionary of Literary Biography Yearbook: 1993, Gale (Detroit, MI), 1994.

Dictionary of Twentieth-Century Culture, Gale (Detroit, MI), Volume 1: *American Culture after World War II,* 1994, Volume 5: *African American Culture,* (Detroit, MI), 1996.

Evans, Mari, editor, *Black Women Writers (1950-1980): A Critical Evaluation,* Doubleday (New York, NY), 1984.

Furman, Jan, *Toni Morrison's Fiction,* University of South Carolina Press (Columbia, SC), 1996.

Gates, Henry Louis, Jr. and K. A. Appiah, editors, *Toni Morrison: Critical Perspectives Past and Present,* Amistad (New York, NY), 1993.

Harding, Wendy, and Jacky Martin, *A World of Difference: An Inter-Cultural Study of Toni Morrison's Novels,* Greenwood Press (Westport, CT), 1994.

Harris, Trudier, *Fiction and Folklore: The Novels of Toni Morrison,* University of Tennessee Press (Knoxville, TN), 1991.

Heinze, Denise, *The Dilemma of "Double-Consciousness": Toni Morrison's Novels,* University of Georgia Press (Athens, GA), 1993.

Holloway, Karla, and Dematrakopoulos, Stephanie, *New Dimensions of Spirituality: A Biracial and Bicultural Reading of the Novels of Toni Morrison,* Greenwood Press (Westport, CT), 1987.

Jones, Bessie W. and Audrey L. Vinson, editors, *The World of Toni Morrison: Explorations in Literary Criticism,* Kendall/Hunt (Dubuque, IA), 1985.

Kramer, Barbara, *Toni Morrison, Nobel Prize-Winning Author,* Enslow (Springfield, NJ), 1996.

Ledbetter, Mark, *Victims and the Postmodern Narrative; or, Doing Violence to the Body: An Ethic of Reading and Writing,* St. Martin's Press (New York, NY), 1996.

McKay, Nellie, editor, *Critical Essays on Toni Morrison,* G. K. Hall (Boston, MA), 1988.

Mekkawi, Mod, *Toni Morrison: A Bibliography,* Howard University Library (Washington, DC), 1986.

Mickelson, Anne Z., *Reaching Out: Sensitivity and Order in Recent American Fiction by Women,* Scarecrow Press (Metuchen, NY), 1979.

Middleton, David L., *Toni Morrison: An Annotated Bibliography,* Garland (New York, NY), 1987.

Modern American Literature, 5th edition, St. James Press (Detroit, MI), 1999.

Morrison, Toni, and Slade Morrison, *The Big Box,* illustrated by Giselle Potter, Hyperion/Jump at the Sun (New York, NY), 1999.

Newsmakers: 1998 Cumulation, Gale (Detroit, MI), 1999.

Notable Black American Women, Book 1, Gale (Detroit, MI), 1992.

Otten, Terry, *The Crime of Innocence in the Fiction of Toni Morrison,* University of Missouri Press (Columbia, MO), 1989.

Page, Philip, *Dangerous Freedom: Fusion and Fragmentation in Toni Morrison's Novels,* University Press of Mississippi (Jackson, MS), 1996.

Peach, Linden, *Toni Morrison,* St. Martin's Press (New York, NY), 1995.

Rainwater, Catherine and William J. Scheick, editors, *Contemporary American Women Writers: Narrative Strategies,* University Press of Kentucky (Lexington, KY), 1985, pp. 205-207.

Rice, Herbert William, *Toni Morrison and the American Tradition: A Rhetorical Reading,* Peter Lang (New York, NY), 1995.

Rigney, Barbara Hill, *The Voices of Toni Morrison,* Ohio State University Press (Columbus, OH), 1991.

Ruas, Charles, *Conversations with American Writers,* Knopf (New York, NY), 1985.

St. James Guide to Young Adult Writers, 2nd edition, St. James Press (Detroit, MI), 1999.

Samuels, Wilfred D. and Clenora Hudson-Weems, *Toni Morrison,* Twayne (Boston, MA), 1990.

Smith, Valerie, editor, *New Essays on Song of Solomon,* Cambridge University Press (New York, NY), 1995.

Tate, Claudia, editor, *Black Women Writers at Work,* Continuum (New York, NY), 1986, pp. 117- 31.

Taylor-Guthrie, Danille, editor, *Conversations with Toni Morrison,* University Press of Mississippi (Jackson, MS), 1994.

Weinstein, Philip M., *What Else but Love?: The Ordeal of Race in Faulkner and Morrison,* Columbia University Press (New York, NY), 1996.

Willis, Susan, *Specifying: Black Women Writing the American Experience,* University of Wisconsin Press (Madison, WI), 1987.

PERIODICALS

African American Review, fall, 1993, Jane Kuenz, "'The Bluest Eye': Notes on History, Community, and Black Female Subjectivity," p. 421; summer, 1994, pp. 189, 223; fall, 1994, p. 423; winter, 1994, pp. 571, 659; spring, 1995, p. 55; winter, 1995, pp. 567, 605; spring, 1996, p. 89; summer, 1998, Allen Alexander, "The Fourth Face: The Image of God in Toni Morrison's *The Bluest Eye,*" p. 293; fall, 1998, review of *Beloved,* p. 415; winter, 1998, review of *Beloved,* p. 563; spring, 1999, review of *Beloved,* p. 105; summer, 1999, review of *Beloved,* p. 325; winter, 1999, Cat Moses, "The Blues Aesthetic in Toni Morrison's *The Bluest Eye,*" p. 623; spring, 2000, Martha Cutter, "The Story Must Go On and On," p. 61, and Cynthia Dobbs, "Circles of Sorrow, Lines of Struggle," p. 362; summer, 2000, E. Shelley Reid, "Beyond Morrison and Walker: Looking Good and Looking Forward in Contemporary Black Women's Stories," p. 313; fall, 2000, Katy Ryan, "Revolutionary Suicide in Toni Morrison's Fiction," p. 389; June 22, 2001, "The One All-Black Town Worth the Pain," "Toni Morrison and the Burden of the Passing Narrative," "Toni Morrison's Jazz and the City," and "Toni Morrison, Oprah Winfrey, and Postmodern Popular Audiences"; December 22, 2001, "Furrowing All the Brows: Interpretation and the Transcendent in Toni Morrison's *Paradise*"; March 22, 2002, "Inscriptions in the Dust," and "Reading and Insight in Toni Morrison's *Paradise.*"

America, August 15, 1998, Hermine Pinson, review of *Paradise,* p. 19.

American Historical Review, February, 1994, p. 327.

American Imago, winter, 1994, p. 421.

American Literature, March, 1980, pp. 87-100; January, 1981; May, 1984; May, 1986; March, 1999, review of *Jazz,* p. 151.

Antioch Review, summer, 2000, John Kennedy, review of *Paradise,* p. 377.

Atlantic, April, 1981.

Black American Literature Forum, summer, 1978; winter, 1979; winter, 1987.

Black Issues Book Review, November-December, 2002, Evette Porter, "The Morrison's Meanies," p. 39; May-June, 2003, Suzanne Rust, review of *The Ant or the Grasshopper,* p. 57.

Black Issues in Higher Education, October 26, 2000, Hilary Hurd, "At Home with Toni Morrison," p. 26.

Black Scholar, March, 1978.

Black World, June, 1974.

Bloomsbury Review, September, 1999, review of *The Big Box,* p. 22.

Booklist, February 15, 1998, review of *Jazz* and *Paradise,* p. 979; June 1, 1999, review of *Paradise,* p. 1797; August, 1999, Hazel Rochman, review of *The Big Box,* p. 2067; May 15, 2003, Francisca Goldsmith, review of *The Ant or the Grasshopper,* p. 1660.

Books and Culture, May, 1998, review of *Paradise,* p. 38.

Callaloo, October- February, 1981; winter, 1999, review of *Song of Solomon,* p. 121; fall, 2000, review of *Sula,* p. 1449.

Centennial Review, winter, 1988, pp. 50-64.

Chicago Tribune, October 27, 1987.

Chicago Tribune Books, August 30, 1988.

Chicago Tribune Book World, March 8, 1981.

Children's Bookwatch, November, 1999, review of *The Big Box,* p. 6.

Christian Century, March 18, 1998, Reggie Young, review of *Paradise,* p. 322.

Christian Science Monitor, October 5, 1987, Merle Rubin, review of *Beloved.*

CLA Journal, June, 1979, pp. 402-414; June, 1981, pp. 419-440; September, 1989, pp. 81- 93.

Classical and Modern Literature, spring, 1998, review of *Jazz,* p. 219.

Commentary, August, 1981.

Commonweal, October 9, 1998, review of *Paradise,* p. 24.

Contemporary Literature, winter, 1983, pp. 413-429; fall, 1987, pp. 364- 377.

Critique, Volume 19, number 1, 1977, Chikwenye Okonjo Ogunyemi, pp. 112-120; spring, 2000, Carl Malmgren, "Texts, Primers, and Voices in Toni Morrison's *The Bluest Eye,*" p. 251.

Detroit News, March 29, 1981.

Economist, June 6, 1998, p. 83.

Entertainment Weekly, January 23, 1998, review of *Paradise,* p. 56.

Essence, July, 1981; June, 1983; October, 1987; May, 1995, p. 222.

Explicator, summer, 1993, John Bishop, review of *The Bluest Eye,* p. 252; fall, 1994, Edmund Napieralski, "Morrison's *The Bluest Eye,*" p. 59.

First World, winter, 1977.

Globe and Mail (Toronto, Ontario, Canada), June 12, 1999, review of *Paradise* and *Song of Solomon,* p. D4.

Harper's Bazaar, March, 1983.

Harvard Advocate, Volume 107, number 4, 1974.

Horn Book, September, 1999, review of *The Big Box,* p. 598.

Hudson Review, spring, 1978; summer, 1998, review of *Paradise,* p. 433.

Hungry Mind Review, spring, 1998, review of *Playing in the Dark: Whiteness and the Literary Imagination,* p. 55; fall, 1999, review of *The Big Box,* p. 33.

Jet, February 12, 1996, p. 4.

Journal of Adolescent and Adult Literacy, review of *The Big Box,* p. 795.

Kenyon Review, summer, 1993, Peter Erickson, review of *Jazz,* p. 197.

Kirkus Reviews, July 15, 1999, review of *The Big Box,* p. 1136; September 1, 2002, review of *The Book of Mean People,* p. 1316.

Kliatt, March, 2005, Nola Theiss, review of *Love,* p. 21.

Knight-Ridder/Tribune News Service, September 19, 2000, Sandy Bauers, "Unabridged Version of Toni Morrison's 'Bluest Eye' Now Available."

Library Journal, February 15, 1998, Emily J. Jones, review of *Paradise,* p. 172; October 15, 1999, review of *Paradise* (audio version), p. 123.

London Review of Books, May 7, 1998, review of *Paradise,* p. 25.

Los Angeles Times, March 31, 1981; October 14, 1987; November 1, 1998, "A Conversation between Michael Silverblatt and Toni Morrison," p. 2.

Los Angeles Times Book Review, August 30, 1987, John Leonard, review of *Beloved;* January 11, 1998, review of *Paradise,* p. 2.

Maclean's, March 30, 1998, review of *Paradise,* p. 65.

Massachusetts Review, autumn, 1977.

MELUS, fall, 1980, pp. 69-82.

Minority Voices, fall, 1980, pp. 51-63; spring-fall, 1981, pp. 59-68.

Modern Fiction Studies, spring, 1988.

Mosaic (Winnipeg, Manitoba, Canada), June, 1996, Laurie Vickroy, "The Politics of Abuse: The Traumatized Child in Toni Morrison and Marguerite Duras," p. 91.

Ms., June, 1974; December, 1974; August, 1987; March, 1998, review of *Paradise,* p. 80.

Nation, July 6, 1974; November 19, 1977; May 2, 1981; January 17, 1994, p. 59; January 26, 1998, review of *Paradise,* p. 25.

National Catholic Reporter, May 22, 1998, Judith Bromberg, review of *Paradise,* p. 35.

New Republic, December 3, 1977; March 21, 1981; October 19, 1987, Stanley Crouch, review of *Beloved;* March 27, 1995, p. 9; March 2, 1998, review of *Paradise,* p. 29.

New Statesman, May 22, 1998, review of *Paradise,* p. 56.

Newsweek, November 30, 1970; January 7, 1974; September 12, 1977; March 30, 1981, "Black Magic" (cover story); September 28, 1987, Walter Clemons, review of *Beloved;* January 12, 1998, review of *Paradise,* p. 62.

New York, April 13, 1981.

New Yorker, November 7, 1977; June 15, 1981; January 12, 1998, review of *Paradise,* p. 78.

New York Post, January 26, 1974.

New York Review of Books, November 10, 1977; April 30, 1981; November 19, 1992, p. 7; February 2, 1995, p. 36; June 11, 1998, review of *Paradise,* p. 64.

New York Times, November 13, 1970; September 6, 1977; March 21, 1981; August 26, 1987; September 2, 1987, Michiko Kakutani, review of *Beloved;* January 24, 1988; January 6, 1998, review of *Paradise,* p. E8.

New York Times Book Review, November 1, 1970; December 30, 1973; June 2, 1974; September 11, 1977; March 29, 1981; September 13, 1987, Margaret Atwood, "Haunted by Their Nightmares," p. 1; October 25, 1992, p. 1; January 11, 1998, review of *Paradise,* p. 6; May 31, 1998, review of *Paradise,* p. 23; May 2, 1999, review of *Paradise,* p. 32.

New York Times Magazine, August 22, 1971; August 11, 1974; July 4, 1976; May 20, 1979; September 11, 1994, Claudia Dreifus, "Chloe Wofford Talks about Toni Morrison," p. 1372.

Observer (London, England), March 29, 1998, review of *Paradise,* p. 15; March 14, 1999, review of *Beloved,* p. 14.

Obsidian, spring/ summer, 1979; winter, 1986, pp. 151-161.

Papers on Language and Literature, summer, 2000, Martin Bidney, "Creating a Feminist- Communitarian Romanticism in Beloved," p. 271.

People, July 29, 1974; November 30, 1987; May 18, 1998, p. 45.

Perspectives on Contemporary Literature, 1982, pp. 10-17.

Philadelphia Inquirer, April 1, 1988.

PR Newswire, February 20, 2003, "Michigan Opera Theatre, Cincinnati Opera, and Opera Company of Philadelphia Announce the Co-commission of *Margaret Gardner* by Composer Richard Danielpour and Librettist Toni Morrison."

Publishers Weekly, July 17, 1987, review of *Beloved;* August 21, 1987; March 2, 1998, p. 29; July 12, 1999, review of *The Big Box,* p. 95; May 1, 2000, Daisy Maryles, "Score: Winfrey 33, Morrison 3," p. 20; April 8, 2002, "Oprah: 46 and Out"; September 9, 2002, review of *The Book of Mean People,* p. 68; November 11, 2002, review of *The Book of Mean People Journal,* pp. 66-67; June 2, 2003, review of *The Ant or the Grasshopper,* p. 50.

Quill and Quire, January, 1998, review of *Paradise* (audio version), p. 33.

Saturday Review, September 17, 1977.

School Library Journal, September, 1999, Ellen Fader, review of *The Big Box,* p. 227; November, 2002, Judith Constantinides, review of *The Book of Mean People,* p. 132.

Southern Review, autumn, 1987.
Spectator, December 9, 1978; February 2, 1980; December 19, 1981.
Studies in American Fiction, spring, 1987; autumn, 1989.
Studies in Black Literature, Volume 6, 1976.
Time, September 12, 1977; March 16, 1981; September 21, 1987; April 27, 1992; October 18, 1993; June 17, 1996, p. 73.
Times (London, England), October 15, 1987, Nicholas Shakespeare, review of *Beloved.*
Times Literary Supplement, October 4, 1974; November 24, 1978; February 8, 1980; December 19, 1980; October 30, 1981; October 16-22, 1987; March 5, 1993; March 27, 1998, review of *Paradise,* p. 22.
U.S. News and World Report, October 19, 1987.
Village Voice, August 29, 1977; July 1-7, 1981.
Vogue, April, 1981; January, 1986.
Voice Literary Supplement, September, 1987; December, 1992, p. 15.
Wall Street Journal, January 20, 1998, review of *Paradise,* p. A16.
Washington Post, February 3, 1974; March 6, 1974; September 30, 1977; April 8, 1981; February 9, 1983; October 5, 1987.
Washington Post Book World, February 3, 1974; September 4, 1977; December 4, 1977; March 22, 1981; September 6, 1987; November 8, 1992, p. 3; January 11, 1998, review of *Paradise,* p. 1.
Women's Journal, April, 1999, review of *Paradise,* p. 20.
Women's Review of Books, December, 1992, p. 1; April, 1998, review of *Paradise,* p. 1.
World Literature Today, summer, 1978; spring, 1993, p. 394; January-April, 2005, Daniel Garrett, review of *Love,* p. 90.

ONLINE

Biography.com, http://www.biography.com/ (February 12, 2003), "Morrison, Tony."
New York Times Online, http://www.nytimes.com/ (January 11, 1998) Brooke Allen, "The Promised Land."
Voices from the Gaps, http://voices.cla.umn.edu/ (February 12, 2003), "Toni Morrison."

* * *

MORROW, James 1947-
(James Kenneth Morrow)

PERSONAL: Born March 17, 1947, in Philadelphia, PA; son of William (a clerk) and Emily (a secretary; maiden name, Develin) Morrow; married Jean Pierce (a teacher), September 11, 1972 (divorced); married Kathryn Ann Smith; children: Kathleen Pierce Morrow and a son. *Education:* University of Pennsylvania, B.A., 1969; Harvard University, M.A.T. (visual studies), 1970. *Politics:* "Thomas Jefferson meets G.B. Shaw." *Religion:* "Pantheist."

ADDRESSES: Home and office—810 North Thomas St., State College, PA 16803. *Agent*—Writers House, 21 West 26th St., New York, NY 10010. *E-mail*—jim.morrow@sff.net.

CAREER: Cambridge Pilot School, Cambridge, MA, English teacher, 1970-71; Chelmsford Public Schools, Chelmsford, MA, instructional materials specialist, 1972-1974; Ordadek Productions, Westford, MA, motion picture writer, director, and editor, 1975-1978; Tufts University, Medford, MA, visiting lecturer in media and communications, 1978-1981; freelance fiction writer, 1980—. Children's book author, Learningways Corporation, Cambridge, 1982-87; visiting lecturer in fiction writing, Pennsylvania State University, University Park, 1990.

MEMBER: National Council of Teachers of English Science Fiction, Fantasy Writers of America, Westford Committee to Halt the Arms Race.

AWARDS, HONORS: Pennsylvania Council of the Arts fellowship, 1988; Nebula Award for best short story, Science Fiction and Fantasy Writers of America, 1988, for "Bible Stories for Adults, No. 17: The Deluge," and for best novella, 1992, for *City of Truth;* World Fantasy Award for best novel, 1991, for *Only Begotten Daughter,* and 1995, for *Towing Jehovah. Blameless in Abaddon* was named a *New York Times* Notable Book of the Year.

WRITINGS:

FICTION

The Wine of Violence, Holt (New York, NY), 1981.
The Adventures of Smoke Baily, (novelization of computer game), Spinnaker, 1983.
The Continent of Lies, Holt (New York, NY), 1984.
This Is the Way the World Ends, Holt (New York, NY), 1986.
Only Begotten Daughter, Morrow (New York, NY), 1990.

Swatting at the Cosmos (short stories), Pulphouse, 1990.
City of Truth (novella), Legend, 1991, St. Martin's (New York, NY), 1992.
Towing Jehovah (first book of the "Godhead Trilogy"), Harcourt (New York, NY), 1994.
Bible Stories for Adults (short stories), Harcourt (New York, NY), 1995.
Blameless in Abbadon (second book of the "Godhead Trilogy"), Harcourt (New York, NY), 1996.
The Eternal Footman (third book of the "Godhead Trilogy"), Harcourt (New York, NY), 1999.
The Last Witchfinder (novel), Morrow (New York, NY), 2006.

CD-ROM; FOR CHILDREN

The Quasar Kids, Collamore, 1987.
What Makes a Dinosaur Sore, Collamore, 1987.
(With Marilyn Segal) *The Lima Bean Dream,* Collamore, 1987.
(With Marilyn Segal) *Not Too Messy, Not Too Neat,* Collamore, 1988.
The Best Bubble-Blower, Collamore, 1988.

OTHER

(With Murray Suid) *Moviemaking Illustrated: The Comicbook Filmbook* (textbook), Hayden, 1973.
(With Joe Adamson) *A Political Cartoon* (screenplay), published in *Scripts I,* Houghton (Boston, MA), 1973.
(With Murray Suid) *Media and the Kids: A Real-World Learning in the Schools* (textbook), Hayden, 1977.
(With Jean Morrow) *The Grammar of Media* (textbook), Hayden, 1978.
(With Murray Suid) *Creativity Catalogue: Comic Book Guide to Creative Projects* (textbook), Fearon, 1981.
(Editor) *Nebula Awards: SFWA's Choices for the Best Science Fiction and Fantasy of the Year,* numbers 26-28, Harcourt (New York, NY), 1992–1994.

Contributing editor, *Media and Methods,* 1978-80; contributing writer to *A Teacher's Guide to NOVA.* Creator of "Suspicion," a board game, for TSR Hobbies, 1977. Freelance fiction reviewer, *Philadelphia Inquirer,* 1986-90. Morrow's books have been translated into many languages, including French, German, Chinese, Czech, and Hungarian.

SIDELIGHTS: "If there is such a thing as an anti-science-fiction writer," declared *New York Times Book Review* contributor David McDonough, "it is James Morrow." "Since the publication of his first novel in 1981," wrote F. Brett Cox in the *St. James Guide to Science Fiction Writers,* Morrow has "produced a substantial body of high-quality work that rates as one of the field's best. While most of his novels and stories are recognizably science fiction, Morrow is not interested in rigid technological and sociological extrapolation; instead, he uses stock science-fictional devices as a means for examining moral and philosophical issues. Morrow's fiction is notable for its rich, often dazzling prose style, as well as for its strongly comic elements. All of these traits place Morrow squarely within a tradition marked variously by such writers as Ray Bradbury, Kurt Vonnegut, Philip K. Dick, and Robert Sheckley."

Morrow's first novel, *The Wine of Violence,* presents a utopian society, Quetzalia, in which violence has been obliterated through ritualized, technologically assisted purging of aggressive fantasies. As the story unfolds, the Quetzalians, despite years of conditioning, engage in a grisly battle of self-defense against a neighboring tribe of cannibals. "Although the plot is driven by a high level of action, culminating with the explorers convincing the Quetzalians to go to war against the Brain-Eaters," Cox explained, "the central concern is more abstract: are the Quetzalians heroes for having conquered the dark side of human nature, or hypocrites whose murderous fantasies belie their professed pacifism? The author's sympathies reveal themselves when one of the Quetzalians realizes that, by fighting the Brain-Eaters, he is acting in the tradition of his Earth ancestors and is now a part of history: 'History, he decided, was a terrible idea.'" The novel, Morrow told *Library Journal,* is "pro-science: the evil comes not from the engineers who built the machine, nor from any inherent flaw in the machines themselves, but from a terrible and arrogant choice regarding their use."

This Is the Way the World Ends offers a satiric attack on the nuclear arms race during the presidency of Ronald Reagan. The unthinkable war occurs, and a group of Americans—each of whom bears some responsibility for the failure of deterrence—awakens on a submarine crewed by the survivors' own ghostly descendants: the "unadmitted" multitudes who will never be born because humanity is extinct. Hauled to Antarctica, the six bewildered men are placed on trial for "crimes against the future." In Cox's view, "Although the novel is, among other things, a scathing critique of the Cold War mentality, Morrow never lets it become a one-sided polemic. The trial is a deliberate presentation of both sides of the deterrence debate, while the 'unadmitted' reveal themselves to be out not for justice, but for revenge." Writing in the *Philadelphia Inquirer,* Jay Neugeboren noted that *This Is the Way the World Ends* "begins where *Dr. Strangelove* ends. . . . [Morrow] deals seriously and intelligently with large issues—moral choice, global survival—within the most unlikely contexts, and in strangely captivating modes."

Often Morrow's satire takes aim at the foibles of organized religion. *Only Begotten Daughter,* which won the World Fantasy Award for best novel in 1991, tells of the immaculate conception and birth of Julie Katz, who is born in New Jersey in 1974 from sperm obtained from an Atlantic City sperm bank. She finds life just as difficult as Jesus had in Judea in the first century: she gets little or no heavenly guidance, and she is opposed by fundamentalist forces rooted in her native New Jersey. "The novel is a savage indictment of the potential evils of organized religion," wrote Cox. "It combines Swiftian satire, black humor, warmly sympathetic characters, with a clear yet eloquent prose style. However one wishes to label it, *Only Begotten Daughter* is one of the most impressive novels of the past decade." Jack Butler of the *New York Times Book Review* likened the novel's form to that of Kurt Vonnegut's works, commending its "dense, hyperkinetic plotting" and "brilliantly funny vignettes."

In *Bible Stories for Adults, Towing Jehovah,* and *Blameless in Abaddon,* Morrow expands his interest in satirizing organized religion. *Bible Stories,* a collection of twelve "dark, funny tales of spirituality," explained McDonough, shows how God interacts with the world he created, often in ways that people misinterpret and misunderstand. The book McDonough concluded, "will be advertised as irreverent," though McDonough himself disagrees, saying that despite Morrow's "biting humor," his writing displays respect for humankind's "place in the great cosmic joke." Gregory Feeley of the *Washington Post Book World* complimented Morrow's stories, saying they are "crisp and readable but they run in the danger of being glib."

In *Towing Jehovah,* God is dead—literally. His corpse has fallen from the heavens, and the Vatican has to contract with an unemployed oil tanker captain, Anthony Van Horne, to tow it to its final resting place in the Arctic. "The bizarre details actually work in context even if . . . they may seem extreme," wrote Joe Mayhew in the *Washington Post Book World.* "It is important, however, to remember that Morrow is writing about the vices of *man.* His novel attacks only the cartoons of religion, not the real thing."

Blameless in Abaddon, the sequel to *Towing Jehovah,* is a modern-dress retelling of the Book of Job. Devastated by a series of personal losses, a small-town magistrate named Martin Candle drags the comatose Corpus Dei before the World Court in The Hague. A *New York Times* notable book of the year, *Blameless in Abaddon* is "diverting and entertaining, sober and demanding, all at once," according to Peter Landry of the *Philadelphia Inquirer.*

The Eternal Footman, the third novel of the "Godhead" trilogy and Morrow's final word on "the post-theistic world," appeared late in 1999. Commenting on the increasingly popular genre of science fiction, Morrow told a reviewer *Library Journal:* "If I could eventually help fuse mainstream fiction's apprehension of human nature with science fiction's comprehension of human knowledge, I wouldn't mind dying one day."

BIOGRAPHICAL AND CRITICAL SOURCES:

BOOKS

St. James Guide to Science Fiction Writers, 4th edition, St. James Press (Detroit, MI), 1996.

PERIODICALS

Christian Science Monitor, July 31, 1992, p. 13.

Denver Post, November 28, 1999, review of *Blameless in Abaddon,* p. F2.

FermiNews, February 15, 2002, Mike Perricone, "Talk of the Lab."

Library Journal, June 15, 1981; April 15, 1992, p. 125.

Locus, June, 1994, pp. 23, 62.

New York Review of Science Fiction, March, 1994, pp. 1, 8-11.

New York Times Book Review, March 18, 1990; March 10, 1996, p. 8; September 15, 1996, p. 40.

Philadelphia Inquirer, August 24, 1986; August 25, 1996.

Pittsburgh Post-Gazette, February 26, 2000, Ken Chiacchia, "Sci-Fi Writers Urged 'To Think Until It Hurts,'" p. B-8.

Publishers Weekly, April 6, 1992, p. 55; March 21, 1994, pp. 69-70; April 4, 1994, p. 61.

San Diego Union Tribune, July 17, 1994; October 10, 1996.

Science Fiction Studies, March, 2003, Fiona Kelleghan, "War of World-Views: A Conversation with James Morrow," p. 1.

Utopian Studies, January 1, 1999, David N. Samuelson, "Overview of Science Fiction Literature in the 1980's and 1990's," p. 198.

Washington Post Book World, October 25, 1981; April 24, 1994, p. 10; March 31, 1996, p. 8.

ONLINE

SF Site, http://www.sfsite.com/ (November, 2000), Nick Gevers, "A Conversation with James Morrow."

* * *

MORROW, James Kenneth
See MORROW, James

* * *

MORTIMER, John 1923-
(John Clifford Mortimer, Sir John Mortimer)

PERSONAL: Born April 21, 1923, in London, England; son of Clifford (a barrister) and Kathleen May (Smith) Mortimer; married Penelope Ruth Fletcher (a writer), 1949 (divorced, 1972); married Penelope Gollop, 1972; children: (first marriage) Sally, Jeremy; (second marriage) Rosamond; stepchildren: Madelon Lee Mortimer Howard, Caroline, Julia Mortimer Mankowitz, Deborah Mortimer Rogers. *Education:* Attended Brasenose College, Oxford. *Hobbies and other interests:* Gardening, opera.

ADDRESSES: *Home*—Turville Heath Cottage, Henley-on-Thames, Oxfordshire RG9 6JY, England. *Agent*—Peters, Fraser & Dunlop, Ltd., 34-43 Russell St., London SW10 0XF, England.

CAREER: Novelist and playwright. Barrister-at-law, London, England, 1948—; master of the bench Inner Temple, 1975. Named to Queen's Council, 1966. Royal Society of Literature and Royal Court Theatre, chairman. Has served as dramatic critic for *New Statesman, Evening Standard,* and *Observer,* all London, England.

MEMBER: Garrick Club.

AWARDS, HONORS: Italia Prize, 1957, for play, *The Dock Brief;* Writers Guild of Great Britain award for best original teleplay, 1969, for *A Voyage round My Father;* Golden Globe award nomination, 1970, for screenplay *John and Mary;* writer of the year, British Film and Television Academy, 1980; Commander of the British Empire, 1986; honorary doctorate in law, Exeter University, 1986; D.Litt., Susquehanna University, Nottingham University, and St. Andrews University; knighted, 1998; British Book Award, *Publishing News,* 2005, for lifetime achievement.

WRITINGS:

Charade (novel), Lane (London, England), 1948.

Rumming Park (novel), Lane (London, England), 1949.

Answers Yes or No (novel), Lane (London, England), 1950, published as *Silver Hook,* Morrow (New York, NY), 1950.

Like Men Betrayed (novel), Collins (London, England), 1953, Lippincott (Philadelphia, PA), 1954.

Three Winters (novel), Collins (London, England), 1956.

Narrowing Stream (novel), Collins (London, England), 1956.

(With first wife, Penelope Ruth Mortimer) *With Love and Lizards* (travel), M. Joseph (London, England), 1957.

Will Shakespeare (stories), Hodder & Stoughton (London, England), 1977.

Rumpole of the Bailey (stories), Penguin, 1978.

Clinging to the Wreakage: A Part of Life (autobiography), Weidenfeld & Nicolson, 1982.

Rumpole's Return (stories), Penguin, 1982.

Trials of Rumpole (stories), Penguin, 1982.

In Character (interviews), Allen Lane, 1983.

Rumpole and the Golden Thread, Penguin, 1984.

Rumpole for the Defence, Penguin, 1984.

A Rumpole Omnibus, Penguin, 1984.

Paradise Postponed (first novel in the "Rapstone Chronicles" series; also see below), Viking, 1985.

The Second Rumpole Omnibus, Viking Penguin, 1988.

Rumpole's Last Case, Viking Penguin, 1988.

Character Parts, Viking Penguin, 1988.

Rumpole and the Age of Miracles, Viking Penguin, 1989.

Rumpole à la Carte, Viking Penguin, 1990.

The Narrowing Stream, Viking Penguin, 1990.

Titmuss Regained (second novel in the "Rapstone Chronicles" series), Viking Penguin, 1991.

Summer's Lease, Viking Penguin, 1991.

Rumpole on Trial, Viking, 1992.

The Rumpole Collection, Viking Penguin, 1993.

The Rapstone Chronicles: Paradise Postponed and Titmuss Regained, Viking Penguin, 1993.

Dunster, Viking Penguin, 1993.

The Best of Rumpole, Viking Penguin, 1993.
Murderers and Other Friends: Another Part of Life, Viking, 1994.
Rumpole and the Angel of Death, Viking, 1995.
Felix in the Underworld, Viking (New York, NY), 1997.
The Third Rumpole Omnibus, Penguin (New York, NY), 1998.
The Sound of Trumpets (third novel in the "Rapstone Chronicles" series), Viking (New York, NY), 1999.
The Summer of a Dormouse: Another Part of Life (memoir), Viking (New York, NY), 2001.
Rumpole Rests His Case, Viking (London, England), 2001.
Rumpole and the Primrose Path, Viking (New York, NY), 2003.
Rumpole and the Penge Bungalow Murders, Viking (New York, NY), 2004.
Where There's a Will, Viking (New York, NY), 2005.

Also author of *Regina vs. Rumpole,* 1981.

PLAYS

Three Plays: The Dock Brief; What Shall We Tell Caroline? [and] *I Spy* (also see below), Elek, 1958, Grove, 1962.
The Wrong Side of the Park (three-act), Heinemann, 1960.
Lunch Hour, and Other Plays (contains *Collect Your Hand Baggage, David and Broccoli,* and *Call Me a Liar*), Methuen, 1960.
Lunch Hour (one-act), Samuel French, 1960.
What Shall We Tell Caroline? (three-act), Heinemann, 1960.
Collect Your Hand Baggage (one-act), Samuel French, 1960.
I Spy, Samuel French, 1960.
Two Stars for Comfort, Methuen, 1962.
(Translator) Georges Feydeau, *A Flea in Her Ear: A Farce* (first produced in London, England, at Old Vic Theatre, February 8, 1966; also see below), Samuel French, 1968.
The Judge (first produced in London, England, at Cambridge Theatre, March 1, 1967), Methuen, 1967.
(Translator) Georges Feydeau, *Cat among the Pigeons* (three-act; first produced in Milwaukee, WI, at Milwaukee Repertory Theatre, November, 1971), Samuel French, 1970.
Five Plays (contains *The Dock Brief, What Shall We Tell Caroline?, I Spy, Lunch Hour,* and *Collect Your Hand Baggage*), Methuen, 1970.
Come as You Are! (contains one-act comedies *Mill Hill, Bermondsey, Gloucester Road,* and *Marble Arch;* first produced, under combined title, in London, England, at New Theatre, January 27, 1970), Methuen, 1971.
A Voyage round My Father (first produced in New York, NY, at Greenwich Theatre, November 24, 1970; also see below), Methuen, 1971.
(Translator) Carl Zuckmayer, *The Captain of Koepenick* (first produced in London, England, at Old Vic Theatre, March 9, 1971), Methuen, 1971.
I, Claudius (two-act; adapted from Robert Graves's novels *I, Claudius* and *Claudius the God*), first produced in London, England, at Queen's Theatre, July 11, 1972.
Knightsbridge, Samuel French, 1973.
Collaborators (two-act), first produced in London, England, at Dutchess Theatre, April 17, 1973.
Heaven and Hell (includes one-act plays *The Fear of Heaven* and *The Prince of Darkness*), first produced in London, England, at Greenwich Theatre, May 27, 1976.
(Translator) Georges Feydeau, *The Lady from Maxim's* (first produced in London, England, at Lyttleton Theatre, October 18, 1977), Heinemann, 1977.
The Bells of Hell (full-length version of *The Prince of Darkness;* first produced in London, England, at Garrick Theatre, July 27, 1977), published as *The Bells of Hell: A Divine Comedy,* Samuel French, 1978.
The Fear of Heaven, Samuel French, 1978.
John Mortimer's Casebook (collected plays, including *The Dock Brief, The Prince of Darkness,* and *Interlude*), first produced in London, England, at Young Vic, January 6, 1982.
When That I Was, first produced in Ottawa, Ontario, Canada, at Arts Centre, February 16, 1982.

Contributor to anthologies, including *English One-Act Plays of Today,* edited by Donald Fitzjohn, Oxford University Press, 1962.

RADIO SCRIPTS

Like Men Betrayed, British Broadcasting Corp. (BBC), 1955.
No Hero, BBC, 1955.
The Dock Brief, BBC, 1957.
Three Winters, BBC, 1958.
Call Me a Liar, BBC, 1958.
Personality Split, BBC, 1964.
Education of an Englishman, BBC, 1964.

A Rare Device, BBC, 1965.
Mr. Luby's Fear of Heaven, BBC, 1976.

TELEVISION PLAYS AND SERIES

David and Broccoli, BBC-TV, 1960.
The Encyclopaedist, BBC-TV, 1961.
The Choice of Kings, Associated Rediffusion, 1966.
The Exploding Azalea, Thames Television, 1966.
The Head Waiter, BBC-TV, 1966.
The Other Side, BBC-TV, 1967.
Desmond, BBC-TV, 1968.
Infidelity Took Place, BBC-TV, 1968.
Married Alive, Columbia Broadcasting System (CBS-TV), January 23, 1970.
Only Three Can Play, Independent Broadcasting Authority, June 6, 1970.
Alcock and Gander, Thames Television, June 5, 1972.
Swiss Cottage, BBC-TV, 1972.
Knightsbridge, BBC-TV, 1972.
Rumpole of the Bailey (two series), BBC-TV, 1975 and 1978.
Will Shakespeare, ATV, 1977.
Unity, BBC-TV, 1978.
A Voyage round my Father, Thames Television, 1980.
(Adapter) *Brideshead Revisited* (based on the novel by Evelyn Waugh), Granada, 1981.
The Ebony Tower, Granada, 1984.
Paradise Postponed, Thames Television, 1986.
Summer's Lease, BBC-TV, 1989.
Die Fledermaus, BBC-TV, 1990.
Cider with Rose, WGBH Boston/Carlton Television, 1998.
Don Quixote, Turner Network Television (TNT), 2000.

Also adapted several Graham Greene stories for television, Thames Television, 1976. Author of *Edwin,* 1984, *Titmus Regained,* 1991, and *Love and War in the Appenines,* 2000.

FILM SCRIPTS

Bunny Lake Is Missing, Columbia Pictures, 1965.
A Flea in Her Ear, Twentieth Century-Fox, 1968.
John and Mary, Twentieth Century-Fox, 1969.
Maschenka, Jorn Donner Productions, 1987.
(With Franco Zeffirelli) *Tea with Mussolini,* G2 Films, 1999.

OTHER

Trees for the New Zealand Countryside: A Planter's Guide, Butterworth-Heinemann, 1987.
(Editor) *The Oxford Book of Villains,* Oxford University Press, 1992.
(Editor) *Great Law and Order Stories,* W.W. Norton, 1992.

Also author of a scenario for ballet, "Home," 1968. Contributor to periodicals.

WORK IN PROGRESS: More scripts for "Rumpole of the Bailey."

SIDELIGHTS: John Mortimer's fiction has been compared to that of Charles Dickens for its eccentric characters, and to that of Evelyn Waugh for its portrayal of class consciousness. Best known in America for his television work, including creating *Rumpole of the Bailey* and adapting Waugh's *Brideshead Revisited* as a television series, Mortimer is renowned in his native England as both a barrister and a playwright/author. The two professions have intermingled in many of Mortimer's writings. From the tippling, cynical Rumpole to Morgenhall, the failed hero of *The Dock Brief,* to the autobiographical young protagonist of *A Voyage round My Father,* writers and lawyers have played major roles in the author's work. He also has a talent for farce as an adapter of Georges Feydeau's plays and as author of his own *Come As You Are!*

The son of a barrister, Mortimer was himself called to the bar in 1948, at about the same time his first novel, *Charade,* was published. He has been viewed as a controversial figure in both fields. In a celebrated 1970 case, Mortimer, as barrister, successfully defended the publishers of a magazine, *Oz,* against charges of pornography; and Mortimer himself has often been criticized for treading past the bounds of propriety in his own work. Mortimer's plays run the gamut of style; as Ronald Hayman wrote in *British Theatre since 1955: A Reassessment,* the author "has oscillated between writing safe plays, catering for the West End audience, and dangerously serious plays, which might have alienated the public [he] had won." Gerald H. Strauss contined in a *Dictionary of Literary Biography* article, "Indicative more of his versatility than of his limitations, this ambivalence is shared by Mortimer with a number of his contemporaries. He can be praised for clever conception and deft management of situations, characters that are believable even when they are largely stereotypes, and dialogue that abounds with witticisms; and all of his plays, not just his ambitious ones . . . are the work of a perceptive social conscience."

To be sure, socially conscious plays thrived during the mid-1950s, when Mortimer's work began receiving serious attention. What separates the author from such peers as John Osborne and Harold Pinter is that Mortimer "applies his exploratory techniques to the middle classes in decline rather than the working classes ascendant," according to John Russell Taylor in his book *Anger and After.* Taylor went on to say, in Mortimer's plays "there are no ready-made villains on whom the blame can be put. . . . instead, the seedy and downtrodden are accepted on their own terms, as human beings, mixtures inevitably of good and bad qualities, and then without glossing over or minimizing the bad qualities, Mortimer gradually unfolds the good for our inspection."

In his book *The Theatre of Protest and Paradox: Developments in the Avant-Garde Drama,* George Wellwarth found another kind of nemesis in Mortimer's stories: "The efficient compromisers are the villains of Mortimer's plays, even though they do not appear in them personally." Wellwarth pointed out that in a typical example of Mortimer drama, the author presents "the glorification of the failure." A failure, Wellwarth added, "is hardly a heroic figure. Mortimer's failures receive their stature by analogy: they are the antithesis of the organization men. . . . [The author] has no use for the survival-of-the-fittest doctrine, since, as he sees it, the terms of the survival are dictated by those who know they will triumph under those terms."

One play that illustrates Wellwarth's theory is *The Dock Brief,* a study of how harsh reality intrudes on pleasant fantasy. Morgenhall is a small-time barrister who gets the chance to defend a murder suspect in a case that could turn his dismal career around. But instead of working diligently on the case, Morgenhall drifts into an elaborate fantasy of success, playing the roles of judge and jury himself, and subsequently ruins his own sense of reality. At the same time, the accused, Fowle, is so caught up in his lawyer's illusions that he too adopts a fantasy perspective on his fate. Thus, even after a mistrial is called because of the barrister's incompetence, the characters exit "with enough illusions to continue living," as Taylor put it. The character of Morgenhall, the author added, "might well have stepped straight from the pages of [Nikolai] Gogol—his seediness and unreliability, his proliferating fantasy life and his impotence in the world of action at once proclaim his kinship with many of the characters in *Dead Souls.*"

While he has been an active and prolific writer for three decades, it is perhaps the late 1970s and early 1980s that saw Mortimer's greatest commercial success. During that period he completed his television series for "Rumpole" and *Brideshead Revisited,* published an autobiography, *Clinging to the Wreakage: A Part of Life,* to accompany his autobiographical play, *A Voyage round My Father,* and produced two versions of *Paradise Postponed,* written concurrently as a novel and a television series. *A Voyage round My Father* was highly regarded by Tom Shales; the *Washington Post* columnist felt that the portrait of a father and son at odds reveals "bonds so deep that words cannot begin to express them, and that is part of what this sublimely lovely play is about." Less impressed was *New York Times* critic Clive Barnes, who felt that the character of Mortimer's blind, disagreeable father "remains a caricature blandly begging for kindness."

While *Voyage* is a fictional telling of the author's early life, *Clinging to the Wreakage* is pure autobiography, a book described by London *Times* critic Michael Ratcliffe as an "exceptionally touching and funny memoir rich in remarkable occasions and disconcerting surprises." Charles Champlin wrote in a *Los Angeles Times* review that, like the play, the book "is a moving but by no means always affectionate account of [Mortimer's] relationship with his father, [who wrote] a standard reference on probate law and who was blind for much of his career. He had an ungovernable temper. . . . and a flair for courtroom dramatics that could make strong men quail." Champlin added that the author "never really doubted [his father's] love; gaining his respect was a difficult, slow process. The autobiography, beautifully written, has the strength and sensitivity of a carefully observed novel." Mortimer followed *Clinging to the Wreakage* with another autobiographical volume, *Murderers and Other Friends,* in which he focuses predominantly on his experiences practicing law as a defense counsel. Critics praised Mortimer's recounting of legal tales, noting that some of the cases later appeared in "Rumpole" episodes. "Mortimer tells us more about the practice of the law than any textbook," remarked David Pannick in *The Times Literary Supplement.*

"A witty chronicle of rural English life as it reflects national fads and preoccupations from 1945 to the present day," is how London *Times* critic Stuart Evans characterized *Paradise Postponed,* the first of three novels in Mortimer's "Rapstone Chronicles" series. The novel and television series concern the Rev. Simeon Simcox, "one of those beaming, affluent, Christian Socialist crusaders," noted Evans. Simcox perplexes his parish by leaving a fortune, not to his family, "but to a maladroit, opportunist local lad who has soared out of the lower middle-class into the rarefied air of the Conservative Cabinet of the present day." The inevitable clash of cultures and politics fuels the tale.

"To a considerable extent the story reflects the prejudices and regrets of the author, and some good times and redeeming optimism, too," found *New York Times* reviewer Francis X. Clines. Mortimer, like Simcox, established himself as a socialist in the classic Bernard Shaw mold, one who maintains that "the idea that you should feel compassion for the less fortunate [should] be your dominant political feeling," as Mortimer stated in Cline's article. And, like his protagonist, the author found himself at a stage in history when Margaret Thatcher's Britain perpetuated "conservatives, class distinctions, unemployment. It's where we started." What he wanted to emphasize in the book, Mortimer told Elizabeth Neuffer in the *Washington Post,* "is that whether [paradise] fails or not, it's better to have believed in it than taken the other view."

In Wellwarth's study, Mortimer is quoted as saying near the beginning of his career: "There may, for all I know, be great and funny plays to be written about successful lawyers, brilliant criminals, wise schoolmasters, or families where the children can grow up without silence and without regret. There are many plays that show that the law is always majestic or that family life is simple and easy to endure. Speaking for myself I am not on the side of such plays and a writer of comedy must choose his side with particular care. He cannot afford to aim at the [defenseless], nor can he, like the more serious writer, treat any character with contempt."

Several short story collections published between 1988 and 1995, including *Rumpole's Last Case, Rumpole and the Age of Miracles, Rumpole à la Carte, Rumpole on Trial,* and *Rumpole and the Angel of Death,* have received critical praise for their entertaining depiction of Rumpole and a colorful cast of supporting characters. Donald E. Westlake observed in the *New York Times Book Review* that while the "Rumpole" stories all conform to a particular formula, they nevertheless remain successful. He describes the formula for "Rumpole" fiction as follows: "A mystery is presented that contains the possibility of a subject to ponder—the workman's right to withhold his labor, say, or the citizen's right to remain silent when charged with an offense." While reviewers have noted this element of redundancy in the Rumpole series, they consistently observe that Mortimer's humor and brilliant characterizations nevertheless continue to attract Rumpole fans to even the weaker stories. "Rumpole, despite his television origins," commented Jon L. Breen in *Armchair Detective,* "is one of the great characters of English literature."

Character Parts is a collection of interviews conducted by Mortimer with a diverse group of people including politicians, writers, actresses, bishops, and criminals. The volume follows the same format as its predecessor, *In Character,* with Mortimer questioning his subjects about various personal and philosophical subjects. Praising Mortimer's interviewing style, Patrick Taylor Martin commented in *Books and Bookmen:* "The interviewees are allowed to reveal themselves; Mortimer passes no judgements and makes only a few carefully neutral observations of his own."

Mortimer's comic novel *Titmuss Regained* focuses on the conflict that ensues between liberals and conservatives when developers plan to create a community named Fallowfield Country Town in the English countryside. "Though the results are frequently as funny as those produced by Evelyn Waugh," asserted Michiko Kakutani in the *New York Times,* "there's none of Waugh's viciousness or malice. It's obvious that Mr. Mortimer sides with the lovers of a pastoral past, but he remains remarkably evenhanded in his satire." Nicci Gerrard in the London *Observer,* however, compared the novel unfavorably to Mortimer's earlier novel, *Paradise Postponed,* complaining that "*Titmuss Regained* is a lazy book which enjoyably passes the time, but relies on neat turns of phrase and fluent comic incident to get through yawns the way a bibulous clubman gestures with his pipe."

In his novel *Summer's Lease* Mortimer satirizes British tourists in Tuscany by targeting what Jonathan Keates called in the *Observer* "our instinctive desire to colonise rather than adapt." The novel also contains a murder mystery as its protagonist, Molly Pargeter, attempts to decode a series of clues to explain the presence of a dead body. While this element of the work generated mixed responses from critics, most praised the novel's satirical message. Critics were less enthusiastic about Mortimer's novel *Dunster,* which focuses on the intense rivalry between a journalist named Dick Dunster and his old college friend, Philip Progmire. When Dunster begins investigating war criminals, he finds himself targeting Progmire's friend and employer, the chairman of Megapolis. "The issues raised are simplistic, so that *Dunster* becomes like a debating chamber that hears one side, then, sensibly, another," commented Gerrard in the *Observer.*

The Sound of Trumpets follows *Titmuss Regained* as the third—and ostensibly the last, according to Mortimer—

volume in the "Rapstone Chronicles" series. The book introduces the young idealistic Labor politician Terry Flitton, who finds himself influenced and then embroiled in scandal by Lord Titmuss in order to win an election. Eventually Terry comes to understand that his liberal views are at odds with his desire for power, and he smears the reputation of his lover's gay friend in order to secure his political standing. In the process, Terry falls in love with a pragmatic older woman and loses his adoring wife. As with his previous novels, Mortimer uses *The Sound of Trumpets* to explore his own political views and criticisms of the British class system. *New York Times Book Review* critic Alison Lurie found much to admire in the novel. Citing Mortimer's "Dickensian range" and an understanding of human nature that echoes the works of Evelyn Waugh and Kingsley Amis, Lurie noted that "Titmuss manipulates everyone around him, just as an author manipulates his characters." Furthermore, wrote Lurie, "Mortimer seems to sympathize with, almost to admire, his most remarkable creation" of Lord Titmuss. Bill Ott of *Booklist* was more ambivalent about the book, calling it a "scathing indictment of sociopolitical tomfoolery . . . but without the tragicomic edge we've come to expect." Nevertheless, Lurie was satisfied with the book's range: "*The Sound of Trumpets* is a wonderful comic novel, but underneath its humor runs a black shadow of pessimism. Politics, it proposes, is always a dirty business."

Mortimer's third volume of autobiography, *The Summer of a Dormouse: Another Part of Life,* focuses on a year in his life as a septuagenarian. Even as he ages "disgracefully," in his words, he manages to write the screenplay for *Tea with Mussolini* (based on cowriter Franco Zeffirelli's childhood), study the Bible, travel, remain active in civic affairs, and live up to his status as a celebrity writer, even though his bad leg confines him to a wheelchair. All the while, wrote E.S. Turner in the *Times Literary Supplement,* he exhibits "his stout Rumpolean common sense." The book is a "short witty entertainment," Turner said, in which "old memories and tall tales . . . jostle with reflections on mortality and mildly dyspeptic judgments on the contemporary scene." With reminiscences ranging from childhood memories of his blind father to sex scandals tried before the House of Lords, *The Summer of a Dormouse* is, according to a *Publishers Weekly* reviewer, "a most civilized and witty book by a most civilized and witty man."

BIOGRAPHICAL AND CRITICAL SOURCES:

BOOKS

Contemporary Literary Criticism, Thomson Gale (Detroit, MI), Volume 28, 1984, Volume 43, 1987.

Contemporary Novelists, seventh edition, St. James (Detroit, MI), 2001.

Contemporary Popular Writers, St. James (Detroit, MI), 1997.

Dictionary of Literary Biography, Volume 13: *British Dramatists since World War II,* Thomson Gale (Detroit, MI), 1982.

Hayman, Ronald, *British Theatre since 1955: A Reassessment,* Oxford University Press, 1979.

Taylor, John Russell, *Anger and After,* Methuen, 1962.

Taylor, John Russell, *The Angry Theatre: New British Drama,* revised edition, Hill & Wang, 1969.

Wellwarth, George, *Theatre of Protest and Paradox: Developments in Avant-Garde Drama,* New York University Press, 1964.

PERIODICALS

Armchair Detective, winter, 1989, p. 107; spring, 1990, p. 240; summer, 1990, p. 364; summer, 1991, p. 357.

Booklist, January 1, 1999, Bill Ott, review of *The Sound of Trumpets,* p. 833.

Books and Bookmen, December, 1986, p. 32.

Chicago Tribune, April 17, 1988; July 24, 1988.

Commonweal, August 10, 1999, p. 465.

Economist, March 24, 1990, p. 97.

Library Journal, May 15, 2001, Stephanie Maher, review of *The Summer of a Dormouse,* p. 124.

Listener, December 17, 1981.

Los Angeles Times, September 28, 1982.

National Catholic Reporter, November 19, 1993, p. 32.

National Review, March 1, 1993, p. 61.

New Statesman & Society, January 1, 1982; March 2, 1990, p. 34.

New Yorker, October 25, 1982; March 20, 1995, p. 78; March 29, 1995, p. 78.

New York Times, November 22, 1961; August 27, 1971; November 20, 1982; October 19, 1986; January 23, 1987; April 10, 1990.

New York Times Book Review, March 28, 1954; May 21, 1989, p. 15; October 15, 1989, p. 37; April 29, 1990, p. 9; December 2, 1990, p. 12; December 27, 1992, p. 6; January 3, 1993, p. 6; March 12, 1995, p. 12; March 17, 1996, p. 20; March 28, 1999, Alison Lurie, "Tantantara!"

Observer (London, England), May 1, 1988; March 18, 1990; April 5, 1992; August 2, 1992.

Publishers Weekly, November 5, 1982; August 25, 1989, p. 51; October 27, 1989, p. 60; December 2, 1990, p. 12; February 2, 1990, p. 76; October 26, 1990, p. 57; September 14, 1992, p. 110; January 9,

1995, p. 50; January 15, 1996, p. 447; January 15, 1996, p. 447; April 30, 2001, review of *The Summer of a Dormouse,* p. 64.
Punch, December 9, 1981.
School Library Journal, March, 1993, p. 242.
Spectator, April 4, 1992, p. 37; October 22, 1994, p. 47.
Time, February 1, 1993, p. 71.
Times (London, England), April 1, 1982; September 19, 1985; September 12, 1986.
Times Literary Supplement, June 23, 1950; July 3, 1953; September 25, 1970; April 3, 1992; October 14, 1994, p. 30; December 29, 2000, E.S. Turner, review of *The Summer of a Dormouse,* p. 29.
Washington Post, February 17, 1981; April 19, 1984; October 19, 1986; July 24, 1988.

* * *

MORTIMER, John Clifford
See MORTIMER, John

* * *

MORTIMER, Sir John
See MORTIMER, John

* * *

MOSLEY, Walter 1952-

PERSONAL: Born 1952, in Los Angeles, CA; married Joy Kellman (a dancer and choreographer). *Education:* Attended Goddard College; received degree from Johnson State College; City College of the City University of New York, M.A., 1991.

ADDRESSES: *Home*—New York, NY. *Agent*—c/o Author Mail, Little, Brown and Company, 1271 Avenue of the Americas, New York, NY 10020.

CAREER: Writer. Founder of publishing degree program at City College of the City University of New York. Associate producer of *Devil in a Blue Dress,* TriStar, 1995, and executive producer of *Always Outnumbered, Always Outgunned,* HBO, 1998. Also worked as a potter and a computer programmer.

MEMBER: Mystery Writers of America (past president), Poetry Society of America (board member), TransAfrica (board member), Full Frame Documentary Film Festival (board member).

AWARDS, HONORS: Shamus Award, Private Eye Writers of America, and Edgar Award nomination for best new mystery, Mystery Writers of America, both 1990, both for *Devil in a Blue Dress;* Grammy Award, best album liner notes, for *Richard Pryor . . . And It's Deep, Too!: The Complete Warner Bros. Recordings (1968-1992),* 2002; Hammett Prize nominee, North American Branch of the International Association of Crime Writers, 2003, for *Bad Boy Brawly Brown;* Risktaker Award, Sundance Institute, 2005; honorary doctorate from City College of the City University of New York.

WRITINGS:

Devil in a Blue Dress, Norton (New York, NY), 1990.
A Red Death, Norton (New York, NY), 1991.
White Butterfly, Norton (New York, NY), 1992.
Black Betty, Norton (New York, NY), 1994.
R.L.'s Dream, Norton (New York, NY), 1995.
A Little Yellow Dog, Norton (New York, NY), 1996.
Gone Fishin', Black Classic Press (Baltimore, MD), 1997.
Always Outnumbered, Always Outgunned: The Socrates Fortlow Stories (also see below), Norton (New York, NY), 1998.
Blue Light, Little, Brown (Boston, MA), 1998.
(Adaptor) *Always Outnumbered, Always Outgunned* (screenplay, based on Mosley's novel), HBO, 1998.
(Editor, with Manthia Diawara, Clyde Taylor, and Regina Austin Norton and author of introduction) *Black Genius: African-American Solutions to African-American Problems,* Norton (New York, NY), 1999.
Walkin' the Dog, Little, Brown (Boston, MA), 1999.
Workin' on the Chain Gang: Contemplating Our Chains at the End of the Millennium, Ballantine (New York, NY), 1999.
Fearless Jones, Little, Brown (Boston, MA), 2001.
Futureland: Nine Stories of an Imminent World, Warner Books (New York, NY), 2001.
Bad Boy Brawley Brown, Little, Brown (Boston, MA), 2002.
What Next: A Memoir toward World Peace, Black Classic Press (Baltimore, MD), 2003.
Six Easy Pieces: Easy Rawlins Stories, Atria (New York, NY), 2003.
Fear Itself: A Mystery, Little, Brown (Boston, MA), 2003.
The Man in My Basement: A Novel, Little, Brown (Boston, MA), 2004.
Little Scarlet, Little, Brown (Boston, MA), 2004.
47, Little, Brown (Boston, MA), 2005.

Cinnamon Kiss, Little, Brown (New York, NY), 2005.
The Wave (science fiction),Warner Books (New York, NY), 2006.
Fortunate Son, Little, Brown and Company (New York, NY), 2006.

Contributor of stories to *New Yorker, GQ, Esquire, USA Weekend, Los Angeles Times Magazine,* and *Savoy.* Contributor of nonfiction to *New York Times Magazine* and *Nation.* Author of album liner notes for *Richard Pryor . . . And It's Deep, Too!: The Complete Warner Bros. Recordings (1968-1992),* 2002.

ADAPTATIONS: Devil in a Blue Dress was adapted by Carl Franklin as a feature film starring Denzel Washington and released by TriStar, 1995.

SIDELIGHTS: "A good private-eye novel . . . is not really about violence; it's about the fallibility of people, about the grotesqueries of modern life, and not least it is about one man, the detective, who defines the moral order." This statement, from *Washington Post* reviewer Arthur Krystal, captures the essence of Walter Mosley's widely praised detective stories. Mosley's novels include a series of hard-boiled detective tales featuring Ezekiel "Easy" Rawlins, who reluctantly gets drawn into investigations that lead him through the tough streets of black Los Angeles. There Easy operates in a kind of gray area, where moral and ethical certainties are hard to decipher. "The Rawlins novels . . . are most remarkable for the ways they transform our expectations of the hard- boiled mystery, taking familiar territory—the gritty urban landscape of post-World War II Los Angeles—and turning it inside out," wrote David L. Ulin in the *Los Angeles Times Book Review.* "Mosley's L.A. is not that of Raymond Chandler, where tycoons and hoodlums cross paths on gambling boats anchored off the Santa Monica coast. Rather, it is a sprawl of black neighborhoods largely hidden from the history books, a shadow community within the larger city, where a unique, street- smart justice prevails."

Ironically, Mosley had ambitions other than writing early in his career. Born in Los Angeles, he made his way to the East Coast, where he began his professional life as a computer programmer. Then one day, as he told D.J.R. Bruckner in the *New York Times,* "I wrote out a sentence about people on a back porch in Louisiana. I don't know where it came from. I liked it. It spoke to me." From that moment, he defined himself as a writer and fulfilled the dream of many would-be authors bound to an office: he quit to devote his full attention to his craft. He continues to write the way he began: "First there is a sentence. Then characters start coming in."

In 1990, readers first met Mosley's Easy Rawlins—and his short- tempered sidekick, Mouse—in *Devil in a Blue Dress.* The novel is set in 1948, when many black World War II veterans, like Easy, found jobs in the area's booming aircraft industry. When Easy loses his job, he grows concerned about the source of his next mortgage payment—until he is introduced to a wealthy white man who offers him a way to make some quick cash: he will pay Easy one hundred dollars to locate a beautiful blonde woman named Daphne Monet, who is known to frequent jazz clubs in the area. Easy takes the job but soon realizes that the task is far more dangerous than he imagined. Reviewing *Devil in a Blue Dress* in *Publishers Weekly,* Sybil Steinberg wrote, "The language is hard-boiled . . . and the portrait of black city life gritty and real."

Mosley followed *Devil in a Blue Dress* with *A Red Death,* set five years later. In the sequel, Easy has used stolen money to buy a couple of apartment buildings and is enjoying the life of a property owner. But he gets into a jam with the Internal Revenue Service, and his only way out is to cooperate with the FBI by spying on a union organizer suspected of being a communist. Again, he gets mired in complications as he tries to make sense out of a dark underworld of extortion and murder. "Mosley's second novel . . . confirms the advent of an extraordinary storyteller," remarked a contributor in *Publishers Weekly.*

Mosley's third novel, *White Butterfly,* fast-forwards to 1956. Easy is married and has a new baby, and his businesses are going well. When three young black women—"good- time girls"—are brutally slain, the crimes are barely reported. But when a white student at the University of California—Los Angeles, meets a similar death, the serial killings finally make headlines. In the meantime Easy is hired by the police to help investigate. His inquiries take him through bars, rib joints, and flophouses until he makes the startling discovery that the latest victim, the daughter of a city official, was a stripper, known by her fans as the "White Butterfly." In fact, nothing in the novel is as it appears, but Easy sorts through the corruption and deception to solve the mystery—at a terrible price to his personal life. *Observer* correspondent Nicci Gerrard commented, "In Mosley's fictional world, there's no such thing as innocence. There's hope (which Mosley calls naivete), and anger (which Mosley calls sense). There's law (white law), cops (the real criminals) and justice (which exists only in a heaven he doesn't believe in). There's love (which he calls heartache), and trying (failure), and then, of course, there's trouble."

By the time Mosley's next Rawlins novel, *Black Betty,* was published in 1994, the author had earned an important endorsement. President Bill Clinton let it be known that Mosley was one of his favorite writers and the "Rawlins" books among his favorite reading. Not surprisingly, *Black Betty* sold 100,000 copies in hardcover and helped to earn Mosley a multi-book contract for further novels in the series. As the action in *Black Betty* commences, Easy is well into mid-life and the 1960s are in full swing. Once again in need of extra money—this time to help support two street children he has taken in—Rawlins agrees to search for a woman he knew back in Houston named Black Betty. The story, to quote Chicago *Tribune Books* reviewer Paul Levine, "is a tale of mendacity and violence told with style and flair from the perspective of the black experience—or rather Mosley's unique version of it." Levine called the book "a sizzling addition to the color-coded series" and added that the author "captures a time and place with dead-on perfect detail and evocative language."

Mosley left his popular detective behind temporarily in 1996 to publish his first non-genre novel, *R. L.'s Dream.* Set in New York City in the late 1980s, the novel explores an unconventional friendship struck in hard times and offers meditations on blues music, especially the unparalleled work of Robert "R. L." Johnson. The story unfolds when Atwater "Soupspoon" Wise, dying of cancer and evicted from his skid row apartment for nonpayment of rent, is taken in by a young white neighbor named Kiki Waters, who has troubles of her own. According to Ulin, *R.L.'s Dream* "is less about life in the modern city than about the interplay between past and present, the way memory and reality intersect. Thus, although Soupspoon and Kiki may share living quarters and a certain fundamental bond, both are essentially lost in their own heads, trying to come to terms with personal history in whatever way they can."

R.L.'s Dream found many fans among critics. *Entertainment Weekly* contributor Tom De Haven called the book a "beautiful little masterpiece, and one probably best read while listening, very late at night, to *Robert Johnson: The Complete Recordings.*" In the *San Francisco Review of Books,* Paula L. Woods dubbed the novel "a mesmerizing and redemptive tale of friendship, love, and forgiveness . . . without doubt, the author's finest achievement to date, a rich literary gumbo with blues-tinged rhythms that make it a joy to read and a book to remember." A *Publishers Weekly* correspondent observed that in *R.L.'s Dream,* Mosley's prose "achieves a constant level of dark poetry" and concluded that the book is "a deeply moving creation of two extraordinary people who achieve a powerful humanity where it would seem almost impossible it should exist."

Mosley returned to the character of Easy Rawlins in *A Little Yellow Dog.* Easy, now working as a school custodian, finds himself the subject of a murder investigation after he discovers a body in the school's garden. *People* contributor Pam Lambert noted that "the vibrant black community is vividly evoked, and [Mosley's] reluctant hero is as ingratiating as ever." *Gone Fishin',* set during the 1930s, examines the lifelong bond that formed between Easy and Mouse as young men. J.D. Reed, in *People,* called *Gone Fishin'* "disturbing, elegant, magical."

Mosley's successful novels incorporate narrative skills that he reportedly learned from his father and from other relatives who, like Easy, moved to Los Angeles in the years following World War II and who passed the time by telling stories. As a result of this oral heritage, Mosley presents "a black world of slang and code words that haven't been delivered with such authority since Chester Himes created his Harlem detective stories," in the opinion of Herbert Mitgang in the *New York Times.* Commenting on Mosley's strength as a writer, *Tribune Books* reviewer Gary Dretzka surmised that the author demonstrates "his ability to tell an interesting period story in an entertaining and suspenseful manner and to create dead-on believable characters whose mouths are filled with snappy dialogue." Clarence Petersen of the *Chicago Tribune* praised "the rhythm of his prose" and the "startling originality of his imagery," presented with an "unselfconscious ease."

Beyond capturing both the music and the nuances of his characters' language, Mosley uses his stories to explore issues of race and class. Some observers have found this exploration too limited; in an essay for *African American Review,* Roger A. Berger contended that detective fiction is "a (white-male) genre rather inimical to a progressive struggle for racial justice, equality, and freedom" and that "Mosley cannot fully disentangle himself from the reactionary politics that are embedded in the genre." A different view was put forth by Digby Diehl, who commented of Mosley's work in the *Los Angeles Times Book Review:* "The insightful scenes of black life . . . provide a sort of social history that doesn't exist in other detective fiction." The critic added, "He re-creates the era convincingly, with all of its racial tensions, evoking the uneasy combination of freedom and disillusion in the post-war black community."

Mosley introduced a new protagonist in *Always Outnumbered, Always Outgunned: The Socrates Fortlow Stories.* Fortlow, after spending twenty-seven years in an Indiana prison for rape and murder, is now a free man living in the largely black Watts section of Los Angeles and trying to lead a moral life. Tough yet philosophical and compassionate, he offers help to a variety of friends and acquaintances—a troubled youth, a cancer patient, an injured dog—and forges relationships with neighbors working for the betterment of their community. The interconnected short stories in *Always Outnumbered, Always Outgunned* form a "not- quite novel," in the words of a *Publishers Weekly* critic, who found the volume's best feature to be "its indelible vision of 'poor men living on the edge of mayhem.'" *Library Journal* contributor Lawrence Rungren thought the book occasionally "a bit contrived or didactic" but added that the main character's appeal made up for these faults. A *People* reviewer also liked Fortlow but deemed the book so "thin on plot and action" that not even such a strong protagonist could make it succeed; the reviewer called Fortlow "a character in search of a novel." *Booklist* commentator Bill Ott, however, lauded *Always Outnumbered, Always Outgunned* as "hard-hitting, unrelenting, poignant short fiction" and remarked that Fortlow, unlike Rawlins, "is a fantasy-free hero." What's more, asserted Sven Birkerts in the *New York Times Book Review,* "Mosley's style suits his subject perfectly. The prose is sandpapery, the sentence rhythms often rough and jabbing. But then—sudden surprise—we come upon moments of undefended lyricism. This, too, belongs to the character portrait."

Fortlow takes center stage again in *Walkin' the Dog,* which also takes the form of related short stories. This book finds the ex-con somewhat materially better off than in *Always Outnumbered, Always Outgunned* but still dealing with moral questions; at one point he launches a protest against police brutality. Some reviewers noted that Mosley manages to avoid the problems sometimes associated with "message" fiction by showing Fortlow's activism as arising naturally from his character. *New York Times Book Review* contributor Adam Goodheart opined that Mosley sometimes veers into sentimentalism, but added, "More often, though, he lets his characters make their own mistakes, and narrates their rough lives in a gentle voice." Goodheart further observed that "like his Athenian namesake, Socrates Fortlow is a streetwise philosopher, always prodding skeptically at others' certainties, offering more questions than answers." The book's concern with social issues also brought its main character comparisons with Tom Joad, hero of John Steinbeck's Depression-era saga *The Grapes of Wrath.* "There is a Steinbeckesque edge to Fortlow's musings on black vs. white and rich vs. poor, and he displays shades of Tom Joad, another convicted killer who desires a better world," commented Michael Rogers in *Library Journal.* Again, Mosley received plaudits for his overall delineation of Fortlow, termed "a uniquely admirable and always unexpected personality" by a *Publishers Weekly* critic, who further praised *Walkin' the Dog* for its "artfully chosen, dead-accurate dialogue."

Mosley ventured into another genre, science fiction, in *Blue Light.* The novel's action takes place in 1965, when numerous people in the San Francisco Bay area are struck by strange rays of blue light that endow them with superhuman powers. These people, dubbed "blues," are then called upon to fight a force of pure evil. The leading character is a man of mixed racial heritage—as is Mosley, the son of a white Jewish mother and a black father—but along the way, racial distinctions blur, as do gender, class, and other differences. Mosley's change of pace drew mixed reviews. *Library Journal* reviewer Michael Rogers, while acknowledging that *Blue Light* represents a departure that might put off Mosley's regular readers, pronounced it "a beautifully written, deeply spiritual novel." In 2001, Mosley published a second work of science fiction titled *Futureland: Nine Stories of an Imminent World.*

With the publication of *Fearless Jones* in 2001, Mosley introduced another mystery series. Set in 1950s Los Angeles, *Fearless Jones* features the duo of Paris Minton, a timid bookstore owner, and his friend Fearless Jones, a World War II veteran. After Minton encounters the seductive but dangerous Elana Love, he calls upon Fearless to help him out of trouble. A *Publishers Weekly* critic called the novel "a violent, heroic, and classic piece of noir fiction." In *Fear Itself,* a 2003 work, Minton and Jones search for a missing man whose disappearance may be linked to a mysterious family diary. According to *Time* contributor Lev Grossman, "*Fear Itself* is a seedy, ever receding labyrinth of petty deceptions, dark desires, and unspeakable deeds."

In 2002 Mosley published *Bad Boy Brawley Brown,* the first "Easy Rawlins" novel in five years. In the work, an old friend asks Easy to locate a young man, Brawley Brown, who has joined an underground political group, the Urban Revolutionary Party. Reluctantly, Easy tackles the job but quickly finds himself in a tangled web of robbery and murder. "As always, Mosley illuminates time and place with a precision few writers can match whatever genre they choose," stated a *Publishers Weekly* contributor. According to *Entertainment Weekly* critic Troy Patterson, "much of the richness of *Bad Boy Brawly Brown* derives from Mosley's skill at connecting the dots between the genre conventions and the particular texture of a life. In Rawlins, the private eye's typical baggy-eyed existentialism—the cynicism and weariness, the spiritual isolation—is married to blue-collar values and a black man's alienation."

The 2004 novel *Little Scarlet* is set in 1965, immediately after the Watts riots. When a black woman is murdered—apparently by a white man—the Los Angeles police employ Rawlins to investigate the case without stirring the flames of racial unrest. As *People* reviewer Champ Clark noted, "*Little Scarlet* focuses on race in a way that gives the book a surprising resonance."

In 2005 Mosley published two books, *47* and *Cinnamon Kiss*. *47* was Mosley's first young adult novel. The narrator is a slave boy, branded simply "47" by his master, who works on a plantation in Georgia. There he meets Tall John, an extraterrestrial masquerading as a runaway slave, who is looking for 47 to help him free the slaves as well as save the world from unearthly creatures. "The sections of 47 that deal with slave life are powerfully described and haunting, . . . I found the [science fiction] plot less compelling," stated Paula Rohrlick in *Kliatt.* However, a *Publishers Weekly* reviewer concluded: "This thought-provoking, genre-bending account of one slave's emancipation . . . makes for harrowing reading."

Mosley then turned his attention back to the Easy Rawlins series with *Cinnamon Kiss.* The novel is set in the 1960's, when the hippie counterculture was on the rise. Easy takes on a job to earn money so he can afford treatment for his daughter who is diagnosed with a rare blood disease. He must travel to San Francisco to search for a missing lawyer and his assistant named Cinnamon Cargill. "The historical moment is less vivid—the hippie encounters are mostly peripheral—but the human drama is more highly charged than ever," commented Ott, again writing in *Booklist.* Berger wrote in *Library Journal,* "Mosley has never been a great literary stylist, but he's a good writer of detective fiction."

The Wave, a novel with science fiction elements, was published in 2006. In the story, Errol Porter starts receiving phone calls that sound like they are from his father, who has been deceased for nine years. Errol meets the caller and learns that it is not his father, but the embodiment of his father's memories, who is part of the "wave" colony created when a meteor crashed to earth over a billion years ago. "Mosley's wandered off turf again, writing imitation Dean Koontz and calling it science fiction," noted Ray Olson in *Booklist.* However, Sara Tompson, reviewing the book for *Library Journal,* called it "taut" and said that it "will hold readers' interest."

In 2006 Mosley also penned the novel *Fortunate Son,* about two boys who, despite their differences, are practically brothers. Eric is white, strong, and lives a life of good fortune. Tommy, born with health problems, is black, impoverished, but eternally optimistic. When they are reunited after years of not seeing each other, the result is "breathtaking," according to a *Publishers Weekly* critic. The same reviewer wrote, "Mosley shows how a certain kind of inarticulate, carnal, involuntary affection transcends just about anything."

Mosley has occasionally produced nonfiction, serving as coeditor of *Black Genius: African-American Solutions to African- American Problems,* in which black intellectuals discuss various social ills, and writing a critique of capitalism in *Workin' on the Chain Gang: Contemplating Our Chains at the End of the Millennium.* But he seeks to explore the problems of modern life in his fiction as well. In his detective stories, his aim is less to create a memorable gumshoe than it is to explore the ethical dilemmas that the character constantly faces. As Mosley told D.J.R. Bruckner of the *New York Times:* "Mysteries, stories about crime, about detectives, are the ones that really ask the existentialist questions such as 'How do I act in an imperfect world when I want to be perfect?' I'm not really into clues and that sort of thing, although I do put them in my stories. I like the moral questions."

BIOGRAPHICAL AND CRITICAL SOURCES:

PERIODICALS

African American Review, summer, 1997, Roger A. Berger, "'The Black Dick': Race, Sexuality, and Discourse in the L.A. Novels of Walter Mosley," pp. 281-295.

Armchair Detective, spring, 1991; winter, 1992.

Bloomsbury Review, November, 1990.

Book, May-June, 2001, "Walter Mosley Meets Colson Whitehead."

Booklist, August, 1997, p. 1848; September 1, 1998, p. 6; February 15, 1999, p. 1006; July, 1999, p. 1896; June 1, 2005, Bill Ott, review of *Cinnamon Kiss,* p. 1712; October 15, 2005, Ray Olson, review of *The Wave,* p. 5.

Boston Book Review, October 1, 1995.
Chicago Tribune, July 1, 1990; June 19, 1991; July 21, 1991; August 24, 1992, p. 1.
Entertainment Weekly, August 18, 1995, pp. 47-48; November 27, 1998, p. 78; July 19, 2002, review of *Bad Boy Brawly Brown,* p. 66; January 9, 2004, Tom Sinclair, review of *The Man in the Basement,* p. 87; July 9, 2004, Tom Sinclair, review of *Little Scarlet,* p. 94.
Esquire, June, 1994, p. 42.
Essence, January, 1991; February, 1997, p. 72.
Forbes, August 11, 1997, Steve Forbes, review of *Gone Fishin',* p. 28.
Globe and Mail (Toronto, Ontario, Canada), July 18, 1992.
Hungry Mind Review, October 1, 1995.
Jet, March 23, 1998, p. 32.
Kliatt, May, 2005, Paula Rohrlick, review of *47,* p. 16.
Library Journal, October 1, 1997, p. 124; October 1, 1998, p. 134; August, 1999, p. 141; June 1, 2001, Roger A. Berger, review of *Fearless Jones,* p. 224; October 1, 2001, Rachel Singer Gordon, review of *Futureland: Nine Stories of an Imminent World,* p. 145; June 1, 2004, Michael Rogers, "Walter Mosley," p. 107; August 1, 2005, Roger A. Berger, review of *Cinnamon Kiss,* p. 60; January 1, 2006, Sara Tompson, review of *The Wave,* p. 105.
Los Angeles Magazine, November, 1998, p. 32; August, 2002, Greil Marcus, "In the Secret Country," pp. 98-103.
Los Angeles Times, May 5, 1992.
Los Angeles Times Book Review, July 29, 1990; July 12, 1992; June 5, 1994, p. 3; August 6, 1995, pp. 3, 8.
Nation, September 18, 1995, pp. 290-291.
Newsweek, July 9, 1990.
New York, September 3, 1990.
New Yorker, September 17, 1990.
New York Times, August 15, 1990; September 4, 1990; August 7, 1991; August 7, 1992; March 20, 2000, Felicia R. Lee, "Walter Mosley: Bracing Views from a Man of Mysteries."
New York Times Book Review, September 6, 1992; June 5, 1994, p. 13; August 13, 1995, pp. 11-12; June 16, 1996, R.W.B. Lewis, review of *A Little Yellow Dog;* November 9, 1997, Sven Birkets, review of *Always Outnumbered, Always Outgunned;* November 7, 1999, Adam Goodheart, review of *Walkin' the Dog;* February 8, 2004, Deborah Solomon, "It's the Money, Stupid"; July 25, 2004, Marilyn Stasio, "Crime," p. 19.
Observer (London, England), October 23, 1994, p. 20.
People, September 7, 1992, p. 105; July 15, 1996, Pam Lambert, review of *A Little Yellow Dog,* pp. 37-38; March 3, 1997, J.D. Reed, review of *Gone Fishin',* p. 43; November 3, 1997, p. 40; January 18, 1999, p. 37; August 9, 1999, p. 338, November 1, 1999, William Plummer, review of *Walkin' the Dog,* p. 551; February 9, 2004, V.R. Peterson, review of *The Man in My Basement,* p. 41; July 26, 2004, Champ Clark, review of *Little Scarlet,* p. 47.
Progressive, April, 2000, Peter Werbe, "Hard-boiled," p. 32.
Publishers Weekly, June 1, 1990, Sybil Steinberg, review of *Devil in a Blue Dress,* p. 46; May 17, 1991, review of *A Red Death,* p. 57; May 29, 1995, p. 65; May 13, 1996, review of *A Little Yellow Dog,* p. 58; October 6, 1997, p. 74; September 14, 1998, p. 44; January 11, 1999, p. 61; November 1, 1999, p. 40; November 15, 1999, p. 46; May 28, 2001, review of *Fearless Jones,* p. 53, and Robert C. Hahn, "PW Talks with Walter Mosley," p. 54; June 17, 2002, review of *Bad Boy Brawly Brown,* p. 45; December 16, 2002, review of *Six Easy Pieces,* p. 49; June 16, 2003, review of *Fear Itself,* p. 54; May 24, 2004, review of *Little Scarlet,* pp. 47-48; May 16, 2005, review of *47,* p. 64; February 13, 2006, review of *Fortunate Son,* p. 62.
Quarterly Black Review, October 1, 1995.
San Francisco Review of Books, February, 1991; September-October, 1995, pp. 12- 13.
Time, August 11, 2003, Lev Grossman, "If You Read Only One Mystery Novel This Summer . . . ," p. 58.
Times (London, England), May 2, 1991.
Tribune Books (Chicago, IL), June 16, 1991; June 28, 1992; June 26, 1994, p. 3.
USA Weekend, June 11, 1993.
Vanity Fair, February, 1993, p. 46.
Village Voice, September 18, 1990.
Wall Street Journal, July 24, 1991.
Washington Post, June 22, 1990.
Washington Post Book World, August 16, 1992; August 20, 1995, p. 7.
West Coast Review of Books, May, 1990.
Writer, December, 1999, Lewis Burke Frumkes, "A Conversation with Walter Mosley," p. 20.

ONLINE

Walter Mosley Web site, http://www.twbookmark.com/authors/61/1447/index.html/ (August 10, 2004).

* * *

MOTION, Andrew 1952- (Andrew Peter Motion)

PERSONAL: Born October 26, 1952, in London, England; son of Andrew Richard (a brewer) and Catherine Gillian (Bakewell) Motion; married Joanna Jane Powell, 1973 (divorced, 1983); married Janet Elisabeth Dalley, 1985; children: two sons, one daughter. *Education:* Oxford University, B.A. (first-class honors), 1974, M.Litt., 1978. *Hobbies and other interests:* Cooking.

ADDRESSES: Agent—Peters Fraser and Dunlop, 5th Floor, The Chambers, Chelsea Harbour, Lots Road, London SW10 OXF, England.

CAREER: Poet, biographer, novelist, editor, and critic. University of Hull, Hull, England, lecturer in English, 1977-81; *Poetry Review,* London, England, editor, 1981-83; Chatto & Windus, London, poetry editor, 1983-89, editorial director, 1985-89; professor of creative writing at the University of East Anglia, 1995-2003; Royal Hollway, London, professor of creative writing, 2003—.

MEMBER: Royal Society of Literature.

AWARDS, HONORS: Newdigate Prize, 1975, for *Inland;* Arvon/*Observer* Poetry Prize, 1981, for *The Letter;* Rhys Memorial Prize, 1984, for *Dangerous Play;* fellow of Royal Society of Literature, 1982; Dylan Thomas Award, 1987, for *Natural Causes;* Somerset Maugham Award, 1987, for *The Lamberts;* Whitbread Award for biography, 1993; appointed poet laureate of England, 1999; Gregory Award; Cholmondeley Award; Cheltenham Prize.

WRITINGS:

Inland (single poem), Cygnet Press (Oxfordshire, England), 1976.

The Pleasure Steamers (single poem), Sycamore Press, 1978.

The Pleasure Steamers (poems; includes "Inland" and "The Pleasure Steamers"), Sycamore Press, 1978, 3rd edition, 1983.

(Editor) *The Poetry of Edward Thomas,* Routledge & Kegan Paul (London, England), 1980.

Independence (single poem), Salamander Press (Edinburgh, Scotland), 1981.

Philip Larkin, Methuen (London, England), 1982.

(Editor, with Blake Morrison) *The New Penguin Book of Contemporary British Poetry,* Penguin (London, England), 1982.

Secret Narratives, Salamander Press (Edinburgh, Scotland), 1983.

Dangerous Play: Poems, 1974-1984, Salamander Press (Edinburgh, Scotland), 1984.

The Lamberts: George, Constant, and Kit (biography), Chatto & Windus (London, England), 1986.

Natural Causes (poems), Chatto & Windus (London, England), 1987.

The Pale Companion (novel), Viking (London, England), 1989.

Famous for the Creatures (novel), Viking (London, England), 1991.

Love in a Life (poems), Faber & Faber (London, England), 1991.

Philip Larkin: A Writer's Life, Farrar, Straus (New York, NY), 1993.

Salt Water (poems), Faber & Faber (London, England), 1997.

Keats (biography), Farrar, Straus (New York, NY), 1998.

Wainewright the Poisoner: The Confessions of Thomas Griffiths Wainewright (nonfiction), Knopf (New York, NY), 2000.

(Editor) *Here to Eternity* (poetry anthology), Faber & Faber (London, England), 2001.

Public Property (poems), Faber & Faber (London, England), 2002.

(Editor) *First World War Poems: The Selected Poems of Isaac Rosenberg,* Faber & Faber (London, England), 2003.

The Invention of Dr. Cake (novel), Faber & Faber (London, England), 2003.

Also author of *The Letter.* Some of Motion's manuscripts are housed at the University of Hull.

SIDELIGHTS: In 1999, British poet Andrew Motion was named poet laureate of England, following in the footsteps of such powerful figures of English literature as Geoffrey Chaucer, Alfred Tennyson, and—most recently—Ted Hughes. Speaking with Mary Riddell in the *New Statesman,* Motion noted that his fondest wish would be to be compared with some of the greats of English poetry. "I know who I'd like to be with when I'm dead—[A. E.] Housman, [Thomas] Hardy and, particularly, Edward Thomas." Motion, the author of several volumes of collected poems as well as biographies and a novel, is considered one of the late twentieth-century's most gifted English poets, winning several major literary prizes and issuing critically acclaimed collections of poetry. Widely recognized for his narrative poetry, Motion fashions fictional characters or portraits of actual figures to give voices to his own feelings on life, love, and loss.

His first collection, *The Pleasure Steamers,* is largely made up of Motion's award-winning poem, "Inland," which depicts its seventeenth-century narrator's forced move to a new village after a flood. Feelings of fear, insecurity, and helplessness are explored as the narrator and other villagers are cast out of their homeland. *Inland,* according to *Times Literary Supplement* critic John Mole, "is a considerable achievement in itself, but it becomes increasingly interesting as one reads and re-reads the poems grouped around it in the collection's first and third sections. It can be seen as an historical paradigm of Andrew Motion's own acute sense of isolation. He too seems to be a stranger in his own land, and poem after poem finds him becoming the ghost of himself."

The other sections of *The Pleasure Steamers* include poems penned after Motion's mother was injured in an accident while horseback riding and left comatose for several years. The accident parallels with the flood in "Inland"; Motion was suddenly thrust into a strange and unsure place with the loss of his mother's vitality and presence. Using the voices of an English family, Motion writes of his "horsey" childhood on an estate, of storing away his mother's clothes, of years of visiting his mother's bedside, and, finally, of dealing with her death. Commenting on Motion's connecting of historical events with present feelings, Mole wrote: "It is the tension between his sense of belonging to, and being refined out of, the world he describes which gives Mr. Motion's work its distinctive strength." Mole concluded that "*Pleasure Steamers* is an impressive book."

Motion further explores the process of grieving a lost love in his lengthy poem "Independence." Set in India, the work is narrated by a man who married in 1947, the year of his country's independence, but lost his young wife and unborn baby after his wife suffered a miscarriage. The poem focuses on public and private independence as the narrator's political freedom is overshadowed by the prison of grief now built around him, but also offers a poignant study of bereavement. "'Independence,'" wrote Mole in a *Times Literary Supplement* review, "is a work of vivid surfaces and considerable depth." Claude Rawson, in the *London Review of Books,* noted that "Motion is very strong at rendering the particularities of grief," and found the poem "a bold as well as a delicately orchestrated success."

As in "Independence," Motion looks through the eyes of others to create storytelling verses in *Secret Narratives,* a collection inspired by secrets: wartime codes, letters, diaries, and whispers. Historical figures, among them Anne Frank and Albert Schweitzer, appear in the poems, which often contain mystical messages. One of the poems inspired *Times Literary Supplement* reviewer Tim Dooley to remark that "Wooding," "a poem of no special intellectual ambition, shows most clearly the strength of feeling Motion can wring from a minimum of technical effects and explains why it is no insult to his predecessors to see this poet as a natural heir to the traditions of Edward Thomas and Ivor Gurney." Dooley found that the poems in *Secret Narratives* "also underline how persistently the subject of mourning has enabled Motion to produce writing of the finest quality."

In addition to his widely read narratives, Motion has edited poetry collections, penned biographies, and issued two critical studies, the first being *The Poetry of Edward Thomas.* Motion's look at Thomas has been praised for its thorough examination of Thomas's work and life. *Times Literary Supplement* reviewer C.H. Sisson commended Motion's work on the widely read Thomas, writing: "One cannot be entirely convinced of the necessity for so much expatiation but, given the existence of the genre, one must say that Andrew Motion has done his work well and that there should be no call for such another study for some time to come."

The second of Motion's critical studies focuses on the work of England's much-loved poet Philip Larkin, about whom Motion also published a biography, *Philip Larkin: A Writer's Life.* Motion's insight on Larkin, who died in 1985, was gained by his friendship with the colorful poet, a rotund, balding character who, in his last years, wrote and spoke prolifically about his unsuccessful attempts at love, his obsession with pornography, and his personal prejudices. In a lengthy *New Yorker* critique of *Philip Larkin: A Writer's Life,* Martin Amis found the biography "confidently managed, and chasteningly thorough; it is also an anthology of the contemporary tendencies toward the literal, the conformist, and the amnesiac. Future historians of taste wishing to study the Larkin fluctuation will not have to look very much further."

Motion earned yet another literary prize with the publication of his biography *The Lamberts: George, Constant, and Kit,* which delves into the destructive ways of a talented family. George Lambert, who died in 1930 at the age of fifty-seven, was Australia's leading painter early in the twentieth century. With his wife, Amy, he moved to Paris, where he took a mistress and subjected his wife and children to abuse. One of his sons, Constant, was a gifted musician and composer of *The Rio Grande* for orchestra and chorus. An alcoholic, Constant died in his forties, as did his son, Kit, manager of the rock group The Who and producer of the rock-opera *Tommy.* At his death, Kit was feeding a twelve-year addiction to heroin.

Infidelity and abuse abound in Motion's portrait of the Lamberts, which London *Times* critic James Wood deemed "a deeply moving chronicle of sheer human waste, balanced by the composed obliquity of Motion's prose." Wood also noted: "Most biographies merely sift the top-soil of history, confirming the already known. Andrew Motion's *The Lamberts* is a biography that mines much deeper, retrieving old truths and creating new realities." A *New York Times* review of *The Lamberts* by Michiko Kakutani also commended Motion's work for being "sympathetic rather than voyeuristic in tone. In fact, in telling this story of talent and loss and missed connections, this story of wayward fathers and damaged sons, Mr. Motion has succeeded in producing both an exemplary family biography and an absorbing social history."

Motion has also written about the life of Romantic poet John Keats in a work described by *America* contributor Nicholas Jones as an "eloquent and strong-minded study." "As the definitive biographer of Keats for the turn of the twenty-first century," Jones continued, "Motion . . . gives us a more intensely human Keats than we have known before—more fiercely masculine, more conflicted about women, more embedded in political liberalism, more anxious about his own powers and his will to create and more subject to a debilitating, near-clinical depression. This Keats is multifaceted and earthy," the *America* contributor concluded, "and Motion rightly places him in a complex and fascinating historical world of personalities and ideologies." "Motion's new biography," declared Phoebe Pettingell in the *New Leader,* "turns out to be a bracing antidote to popular culture's frequently sentimentalized view of Keats. [Motion] . . . knows how to sauce his portraits with postmodern acerbity without obscuring his admiration for his subject." Kim Woodbridge noted in *Library Journal* that "Motion has provided a thorough examination of the social, familial, political, and financial forces that shaped the real man rather than the poet of myth."

The appointment of Motion as poet laureate in 1999 created a stir among literati worldwide. Many critics questioned the appointment for political reasons, debating the wisdom of nominating a relatively pro-establishment figure to follow the well-known, relatively radical Hughes. "Though Ted Hughes's laureate poems were themselves something of an embarrassment in an often brilliant career," wrote Michael Glover in the *New Statesman,* "he gave the job a lift that it hadn't had this century because, unlike so many laureates before him, he had indeed been a good poet. With Hughes as laureate, the image was refurbished." Motion's designation, these critics felt, marks a step away from the "people's poet" they believed Prime Minister Tony Blair's Labour government would search for. They suggested alternatives, including Seamus Heaney, who refused; Nobel Laureate Derek Walcott, who reportedly was interested, but who lives outside Great Britain in the West Indies; and Carol Ann Duffy, a Scottish poet described by Jean Richardson in *Publishers Weekly* as "a feisty lesbian." "The choice of Motion ('minor, obscure, conservative')," wrote *New Statesman* contributor Riddell, "was variously lambasted ('an insult to the country's intelligence,' 'a bag of shite')." However, Riddell concluded, "the issue is not whether he is too tame for his establishment post or too radical. The question is whether such an inward-looking man can square his 'real identity' with the populism required of a punters' poet. . . . We shall see."

Since his appointment as poet laureate, Motion has continued to turn out poetry, to edit anthologies, and to produce two further well-received titles, one, the nonfiction *Wainewright the Poisoner: The Confessions of Thomas Griffiths Wainewright,* and the other the 2003 novel, *The Invention of Dr. Cake.* Motion's 2002 volume of poetry, *Public Property,* includes a half dozen of his poems crafted for official public occasions. Adam Newey, writing in the *New Statesman,* felt that the "key signature [to the collection] is one of loss and grief," and that the "best poems are the evocations of the poet's mother and of a greener England." Newey concluded that Motion has demonstrated "how the laureateship can develop and take its proper place in the life of the nation."

Motion returns again to biography with *Wainewright the Poisoner,* the story of a minor nineteenth-century Romantic painter, critic, and writer, friend of numerous artists, and patron of William Blake. Thomas Wainewright remains best known for his excesses: accused of murdering his uncle for his inheritance, and also his mother-in-law as well as his wife's sister, Helen, he lived in exile from England for nine years. With Helen, death by poisoning seemed to be the diagnosis, and Wainewright had taken out several insurance policies on her life, all of which pointed to his guilt. Motion's account "takes for granted the guilt that Wainewright's contemporaries could not prove," according to *Book*'s Penelope Mesic. The same critic praised Motion's "considerable literary power" with which he is able to forge a "Wainewright empty enough to be plausibly capable of any selfish action." Less favorable was the assessment of *Contemporary Review*'s Richard Whittington-Egan, who felt that despite its "verbal skills, this biographical excursus seems to me to disappoint." However, other critics were more positive in their analysis. *Booklist*'s Michael Spinella found that Motion "has brought to the page a vibrant, fascinating, and nearly undocumented life," and "crafts a . . . tale as complex and compelling as if Wainewright himself had written it." Henry L. Carrigan, Jr., writing in *Library Journal,* called the same work a "fascinating account," while a critic for *Publishers Weekly* felt that Motion "succeeds admirably" in "portraying a man who embodied the Romantic idea that 'good and evil grow on the same tree.'" A contributor to the *Economist* had similar praise for this "remarkable biography." Told in a confessional style, Motion's book has, according to Nicola Upson in the *New Statesman,* "as many faces as its subject."

For his 2003 novel, Motion turns to a subject familiar to him from his own biographies, the poet John Keats. In Motion's telling, Keats does not in fact die of consumption in Rome as the world believes, but instead returns to England where he lives in obscurity, practicing charitable acts. Taking the pseudonym of Dr. Cake, Keats lives anonymously until the end of his life when his secret is discovered by William Tabor, a doctor who is recording health statistics on the poor. Sam Leith, reviewing the novel in the *Spectator,* noted that Motion "uses his story to play with theories of biography, the nature of inspiration, and the character of the Romantic mind."

BIOGRAPHICAL AND CRITICAL SOURCES:

BOOKS

Contemporary Literary Criticism, Volume 47, Thomson Gale (Detroit, MI), 1988.

Contemporary Poets, 6th edition, St. James Press (Detroit, MI), 1996.

Dictionary of Literary Biography, Volume 40: *Poets of Great Britain and Ireland since 1960,* Thomson Gale (Detroit, MI), 1985.

Jones, Peter, and Michael Schmidt, editors, *British Poetry since 1970: A Critical Survey,* Carcanet Press, 1980.

Motion, Andrew, *Pleasure Steamers,* Sycamore Press, 1978.

PERIODICALS

America, September 12, 1998, p. 21, Nicholas Jones, review of *Keats.*

American Spectator, September, 1993, p. 72.

Atlantic, September, 1993, p. 104.

Biography, fall, 2000, Howard Engel, review of *Wainewright the Poisoner: The Confessions of Thomas Griffiths Wainewright,* p. 830.

Book, September, 2000, Penelope Mesic, review of *Wainewright the Poisoner,* p. 80.

Booklist, December 15, 1997, p. 680; June 1, 2000, Michael Spinella, review of *Wainewright the Poisoner,* p. 1836.

Contemporary Review, September, 2000, Richard Whittington-Egan, review of *Wainewright the Poisoner,* p. 183.

Economist, April 10, 1993, p. 99; March 29, 1997, p. 92; November 15, 1997, p. 13; March 18, 2000, review of *Wainewright the Poisoner,* p. 12.

Library Journal, December, 1997, Kim Woodbridge, review of *Keats,* p. 106; June 1, 2000, Henry L. Carrigan, Jr., review of *Wainewright the Poisoner,* p. 126.

London Review of Books, June 17-30, 1982, Claude Rawson, review of *Independence,* pp. 20-21.

National Review, September 6, 1993, p. 65.

New Leader, November 15, 1993, p. 15; December 29, 1997, Phoebe Pettingell, review of *Keats,* p. 20.

New Republic, July 19-26, 1993, pp. 30-37.

New Statesman, May 24, 1999, p. 20; May 31, 1999, p. 44; June 21, 1999, Mary Riddell, "Andrew Motion," p. 18; February 28, 2000, Nicola Upson, review of *Wainewright the Poisoner,* p. 60; October 14, 2002, Adam Newey, review of *Public Property,* p. 53; November 24, 2003, Adam Newey, review of *First World War Poems: The Selected Poems of Isaac Rosenberg,* p. 53.

New Statesman & Society, April 2, 1993, p. 24.

New Yorker, July 12, 1993, Martin Amis, review of *Philip Larkin: A Writer's Life,* pp. 74-80.

New York Times, April 29, 1987, Michiko Kakutani, review of *The Lamberts: George, Constant, and Kit.*

Publishers Weekly, May 24, 1993, p. 73; November 10, 1997, p. 60; July 26, 1999, p. 17; May 22, 2000, review of *Wainewright the Poisoner,* p. 83.

Spectator, October 6, 2001, Grey Gowrie, review of *Here to Eternity,* p. 68; February 22, 2003, Sam Leith, review of *The Invention of Dr. Cake,* p. 39; May 3, 2003, "The Spectator's Notes," p. 12.

Time, September 6, 1993, p. 69.

Times (London, England), October 31, 1987, James Wood, review of *The Lamberts;* May 19, 1999, p. 1.

Times Literary Supplement, August 11, 1978, John Mole, review of *The Pleasure Steamers,* p. 906; January 23, 1981, John Mole, review of *Independence,* p. 80; April 2, 1982, Tim Dooley, review of *Secret Narratives,* p. 392; August 19, 1993, p. 886.

ONLINE

BBC Online, http://www.bbc.co.uk/ (July 26, 2004), "Andrew Motion."
BBC Radio 4 Online, http://www.bbc.co.uk/radio4/ (July 26, 2004), "Andrew Motion."
ContemporayWriters.com, http://www.contemporary writers.com/ (July 26, 2004), "Andrew Motion."
PageWise Web site, http://nc.essortment.com/andrew motion_rcty.htm/ (July 26, 2004), Amanda Hodges, "Biography of Andrew Motion."

* * *

MOTION, Andrew Peter
See MOTION, Andrew

* * *

MOWAT, Farley 1921-
(Farley McGill Mowat)

PERSONAL: Surname rhymes with "poet"; born May 12, 1921, in Belleville, Ontario, Canada; son of Angus McGill (a librarian) and Helen Elizabeth (Thomson) Mowat; married Frances Thornhill, 1947 (marriage ended, 1959); married Claire A. Wheeler (a writer), March, 1964; children: (first marriage) Robert Alexander, David Peter. *Education:* University of Toronto, B.A., 1949.

ADDRESSES: *Home*—Port Hope, Ontario, Canada, and Cape Breton, Nova Scotia. *Agent*—c/o Key Porter Books Ltd., 70 The Esplanade, Toronto, Ontario M5E 1R2, Canada.

CAREER: Author. *Military service:* Canadian Army, Infantry and Intelligence Corps, 1940-46; became captain.

AWARDS, HONORS: President's Medal for best Canadian short story of 1952 from the University of Western Ontario, for "Eskimo Spring"; Anisfield-Wolfe Award for contribution to interracial relations, 1954, for *People of the Deer;* Governor General's Medal for juvenile literature, 1957, for *Lost in the Barrens;* Book of the Year for Children award from the Canadian Association of Children's Librarians, and International Board on Books for Young People Honour List (Canada), both 1958, both for *Lost in the Barrens;* Canadian Women's Clubs award, 1958, for *The Dog Who Wouldn't Be;* Boys' Club Junior Book Award from the Boys' Club of America, 1963, for *Owls in the Family;* National Association of Independent Schools Award, 1963, for juvenile books; Hans Christian Andersen Honour List, 1965, for juvenile books; Canadian Centennial Medal, 1967; Leacock Medal from the Stephen Leacock Foundation, 1970, and L'Etoile de la Mer Honours List, 1972, both for *The Boat Who Wouldn't Float;* D.Litt., Laurentian University, 1970; Vicky Metcalf award from the Canadian Authors' Association, 1971, for his body of work; Doctor of Law from Lethbridge University and University of Toronto, both 1973, and University of Prince Edward Island, 1979; Book of the Year, Canadian Association of Children's Librarians, 1976; Curran Award, 1977, for "contributions to understanding wolves"; Queen Elizabeth II Jubilee Medal, 1978; Knight of Mark Twain, 1980; New York Public Library's Books for the Teen Age, 1980, for *The Great Betrayal: Arctic Canada Now,* and 1981, for *And No Birds Sang;* Officer, Order of Canada, 1981; D.Litt., University of Victoria, 1982, and Lakehead University, 1986; Author's Award, Foundation for the Advancement of Canadian Letters, 1985, for *Sea of Slaughter;* Book of the Year designation, Foundation for the Advancement of Canadian Letters, and named Author of the Year, Canadian Booksellers Association, both 1988, both for *Virunga;* Gemini Award for best documentary script, 1989, for *The New North;* Torgi Talking Book of the Year, Canadian National Institute of the Blind, 1989, for *Virunga;* Canadian Achievers Award, Toshiba, 1990; Award of Excellence, Atlantic Film Festival, for outstanding achievement in narration, Conservation Film of the Year, Wildscreen Film Festival, and finalist, American Cable Entertainment Awards, all 1990, all for *Sea of Slaughter;* Take Back the Nation Award, Council of Canadians, 1991; L.H.D., McMaster University, 1994; L.L.D., Queen's University, 1995; D.Litt., University College of Cape Breton, 1996; Fourth National Prize for Foreign Literature Books, Beiyue Literature and Art Publishing House, 1999, for *Never Cry Wolf, Sea of Slaughter, A Whale for the Killing,* and *People of the Deer.*

WRITINGS:

FOR YOUNG ADULTS

Lost in the Barrens (novel), illustrated by Charles Geer, Atlantic/Little, Brown (Boston, MA), 1956, published as *Two against the North,* illustrated by Alan Daniel, Scholastic-TAB (New York, NY), 1977.

The Dog Who Wouldn't Be (nonfiction), illustrated by Paul Galdone, Atlantic/Little, Brown (Boston, MA), 1957.

Owls in the Family (nonfiction), illustrated by Robert Frankenberg, Atlantic/Little, Brown (Boston, MA), 1961, revised edition, McClelland & Stewart (Toronto, Ontario, Canada), 1973.

The Black Joke (novel), illustrated by D. Johnson, McClelland & Stewart (Toronto, Ontario, Canada), 1962, revised edition, 1973, American edition, illustrated by Victor Mays, Atlantic/Little, Brown (Boston, MA), 1963.

The Curse of the Viking Grave (novel), illustrated by Charles Geer, Atlantic/Little, Brown (Boston, MA), 1966.

NONFICTION FOR ADULTS

People of the Deer, Atlantic/Little, Brown (Boston, MA), 1952, revised edition, McClelland & Stewart (Toronto, Ontario, Canada), 1975.

The Regiment, McClelland & Stewart (Toronto, Ontario, Canada), 1954, revised edition, 1973.

(Editor) Samuel Hearne, *Coppermine Journey: An Account of a Great Adventure,* Atlantic/Little, Brown (Boston, MA), 1958.

The Grey Seas Under: The Perilous Rescue Missions of a North Atlantic Salvage Tug, Atlantic/Little, Brown (Boston, MA), 1958, reprinted, Lyons Press (New York, NY), 2001.

The Desperate People, Atlantic/Little, Brown (Boston, MA), 1959, revised edition, McClelland & Stewart (Toronto, Ontario, Canada), 1975.

(Editor) *Ordeal by Ice: The Search for the Northwest Passage* (also see below), McClelland & Stewart (Toronto, Ontario, Canada), 1960, Atlantic/Little, Brown (Boston, MA), 1961, revised edition, 1973.

The Serpent's Coil: An Incredible Story of Hurricane-Battered Ships and the Heroic Men Who Fought to Save Them, McClelland & Stewart (Toronto, Ontario, Canada), 1961, Atlantic/Little, Brown (Boston, MA), 1962, reprinted, Lyons Press (New York, NY), 2001.

Never Cry Wolf, Atlantic/Little, Brown (Boston, MA), 1963, revised edition, McClelland & Stewart (Toronto, Ontario, Canada), 1973, reprinted, Holt (Austin, TX), 2000.

Westviking: The Ancient Norse in Greenland and North America, illustrated by wife Claire Wheeler, Atlantic/Little, Brown (Boston, MA), 1965.

(Editor) *The Polar Passion: The Quest for the North Pole* (also see below), McClelland & Stewart (Toronto, Ontario, Canada), 1967, revised edition, 1973, Atlantic/Little, Brown (Boston, MA), 1968.

Canada North, Atlantic/Little, Brown (Boston, MA), 1968.

This Rock within the Sea: A Heritage Lost, illustrated with photographs by John de Visser, McClelland & Stewart (Toronto, Ontario, Canada), 1968, Atlantic/Little, Brown (Boston, MA), 1969, new edition, McClelland & Stewart (Toronto, Ontario, Canada), 1976.

The Boat Who Wouldn't Float, McClelland & Stewart (Toronto, Ontario, Canada), 1969, Atlantic/Little, Brown (Boston, MA), 1970.

The Siberians, Atlantic/Little, Brown (Boston, MA), 1970, published in Canada as *Sibir: My Discovery of Siberia,* McClelland & Stewart (Toronto, Ontario, Canada), 1970, revised edition, 1973.

A Whale for the Killing, Atlantic/Little, Brown (Boston, MA), 1972.

Wake of the Great Sealers, illustrated by David Blackwood, Atlantic/Little, Brown (Boston, MA), 1973.

(Editor) *Tundra: Selections from the Great Accounts of Arctic Land Voyages* (also see below), McClelland & Stewart (Toronto, Ontario, Canada), 1973.

The Great Betrayal: Arctic Canada Now (sequel to *Canada North*), 1976, published in Canada as *Canada North Now: The Great Betrayal,* illustrated with photographs by Shin Sugini, McClelland & Stewart (Toronto, Ontario, Canada), 1976.

Top of the World Trilogy (includes *Ordeal by Ice, Polar Passion,* and *Tundra*), McClelland & Stewart (Toronto, Ontario, Canada), 1976.

And No Birds Sang (autobiography), Atlantic/Little, Brown (Boston, MA), 1979.

The World of Farley Mowat: A Selection from His Works, edited by Peter Davison, Atlantic/Little, Brown (Boston, MA), 1980.

Sea of Slaughter, McClelland & Stewart (Toronto, Ontario, Canada), 1984, Atlantic/Little, Brown (Boston, MA), 1985, reprinted, with a new afterword by the author, Chapters (Shelburne, VT), 1996.

My Discovery of America, McClelland & Stewart (Toronto, Ontario, Canada), 1985, Atlantic/Little, Brown (Boston, MA), 1986.

Woman in the Mists: The Story of Dian Fossey and the Mountain Gorillas of Africa, Warner (New York, NY), 1987, published in Canada as *Virunga: The Passion of Dian Fossey,* McClelland & Stewart (Toronto, Ontario, Canada), 1987.

The New Founde Land, McClelland & Stewart (Toronto, Ontario, Canada), 1989.

Rescue the Earth: Conversations with the Green Crusaders, McClelland & Stewart (Toronto, Ontario, Canada), 1990.

My Father's Son: Memories of War and Peace, Houghton Mifflin (Boston, MA), 1992.

Born Naked, Key Porter Books (Toronto, Ontario, Canada), 1993, Houghton Mifflin (Boston, MA), 1994.

Aftermath: Travels in a Post-War World, Key Porter Books (Toronto, Ontario, Canada), 1995, Roberts Rinehart (Boulder, CO), 1996.

A Farley Mowat Reader, Roberts Rinehart (Boulder, CO), 1997.

The Farfarers: Before the Norse, Key Porter Books (Toronto, Ontario, Canada), 1998, Steerforth Press (South Royalton, VT), 2000, published as *The Alban Quest: The Search for a Lost Tribe,* Weidenfeld & Nicolson (London, England), 1999.

Walking on the Land, Key Porter Books (Toronto, Ontario, Canada), 2000, Steerforth Press (South Royalton, VT), 2001.

High Latitudes: A Northern Journey, Key Porter Books (Toronto, Ontario, Canada), 2002, published as *High Latitudes: An Arctic Journey,* Steerforth Press (South Royalton, VT), 2002.

No Man's River, Carroll & Graf (New York, NY), 2004.

OTHER

The Snow Walker (short story collection), Atlantic/Little, Brown (Boston, MA), 1975.

Author of television screenplays *Sea Fare,* 1963, and *Diary of a Boy on Vacation,* 1964. Contributor to *Cricket's Choice,* Open Court, 1974, and to magazines, including *Saturday Evening Post, Argosy, Maclean's,* and *Cricket.* Mowat's books have been translated into more than twenty languages and anthologized in more than 400 works. His manuscripts are held at McMaster University, Hamilton, Ontario, Canada.

ADAPTATIONS: Films include *A Whale for the Killing* (TV movie), American Broadcasting Co. (ABC-TV), 1980; *Never Cry Wolf* (feature film), Disney, 1983; *The New North* (documentary), Norwolf/Noralpha/CTV, 1989; *Sea of Slaughter* (documentary), Canadian Broadcasting Corp. (CBC-TV), 1990; *Lost in the Barrens* (TV movie), Atlantis Films, 1992; and *Curse of the Viking Grave* (TV movie), Atlantis Films, 1992. Audio cassette recordings include *And No Birds Sang,* Books on Tape (Newport Beach, CA), 1991; *Grey Seas Under,* Books on Tape (Newport Beach, CA), 1994; *Lost in the Barrens,* Books on Tape (Newport Beach, CA), 1994; *Never Cry Wolf,* Books on Tape (Newport Beach, CA), 1994; *People of the Deer,* Books on Tape (Newport Beach, CA), 1994; *The Snow Walker,* Books on Tape (Newport Beach, CA), 1994; *A Whale for the Killing,* Books on Tape (Newport Beach, CA), 1994; and *Born Naked,* Books on Tape (Newport Beach, CA), 1995.

SIDELIGHTS: Farley Mowat is one of Canada's best-known authors for adults and children. A writer with vivid powers of observation and the flair of a storyteller, Mowat infuses his work with an affection for the Canadian wilderness and its inhabitants. His books offer tragic glimpses of the extinction of species at the hand of so-called "civilized" humans as well as strong warnings about the future of a human race that devours natural resources unchecked. "Farley Mowat has a remarkably humble view of his place—of man's place in general—in the scheme of things," noted Valerie Wyatt in *Profiles.* "He believes that man is no more and no less important than any of the other animals that inhabit the planet, and he has lived by this philosophy, elaborating on it in his books."

Many of Mowat's works—like *Never Cry Wolf, People of the Deer,* and *A Whale for the Killing*—are written for adult audiences but can also be understood and appreciated by young adult readers. On the other hand, Mowat's children's books—like *The Dog Who Wouldn't Be, Owls in the Family,* and *Lost in the Barrens*—offer stories adults can enjoy. "Mowat is a natural writer for children," claimed Sheila Egoff in *The Republic of Childhood: A Critical Guide to Canadian Children's Literature in English.* "He writes from his own experience, both childhood and adult. With his direct, simple, and lively style he can reveal aspects of life that are necessary in good children's literature if it is to have any enduring value. Qualities such as cruelty, irony, satire—gentled of course—give life and depth to children's literature and they are present in all Mowat's animal stories. They are implied in the style and confronted squarely in the realistic details."

Mowat was born in Belleville, Ontario, the son of a librarian. The author once described himself in an interview as "pretty much an outcast" who spent much of his time reading, wandering in the woods, and writing about nature. While Mowat was still young his family moved frequently. Eventually they found themselves in Saskatoon, Saskatchewan, where his father became head librarian. "It seemed we were always picking up and leaving," Mowat told the interviewer. Still, he made the best of the situation. "I spent monstrous amounts of time in the libraries my father directed," he said. "To his everlasting credit, he never directed my reading. . . . In some of his libraries they kept the 'bad books' under the counter. These I would spirit home by the armful and devour in solitary splendor. My father, of course, knew full well and gave me nothing but encouragement for my writing as well as for my reading."

Another inspirational figure was Mowat's uncle Frank Farley, who was an avid naturalist and tireless traveler. Under his uncle's tutelage, Mowat learned to collect specimens the old-fashioned way: he shot wildlife and stuffed the skins with cotton and took birds' eggs from nests to be sent to museums. "As a lad I felt quite the scientist tromping through the woods murdering things and contemplating corpses in the hallowed halls of museums," Mowat recalled. Time altered his perspective, however, and by fifteen he was banding birds rather than shooting them. In fact, he was the youngest Canadian ever to be issued a permit to band birds.

"It was my uncle Frank Farley who first took me to the far north where I saw the great herds of caribou migrating across the tundra," Mowat remembered. "It would prove momentous in my life." Mowat became more and more entranced by a region of the Canadian Arctic known as "the barrens." His chance to explore was cut short by history, however. Just as he was graduating from high school, World War II broke out, and he joined the same regiment as his father. The regiment, known as the Hastings and Prince Edward, saw brutal fighting during the invasion of Italy. "The war changed my thinking radically," Mowat noted. "I had had no real sense of fear, cruelty, madness, and horror before seeing combat in Italy. . . . I saved myself during the last part of my infantry experience by writing what would eventually become *The Dog Who Wouldn't Be.* Amid the bombs, grenades, strafing, death, and dying, I tried to steep myself in the funny, idyllic world of my childhood." Mowat was discharged in 1946, having advanced to the rank of captain.

"After the war, I deliberately sought out solitude," Mowat said. "I wanted to get away from my own species. I didn't like myself for being one of them." Mowat headed for the Canadian wilderness and spent some years in the company of various Eskimo and Native American tribes, especially the Ihalmiut ("People of the Deer"). The author's first book, *People of the Deer,* chronicles the Ihalmiuts' near extinction as a tribe due to the interference of white traders and the Canadian government. The work was extremely controversial—Mowat condemned his government for its insensitivity to Native American problems. *New York Times Book Review* critic Walter O'Hearn called Mowat "Canada's angriest young man" and added: "If we are at last fumbling toward a grasp of the Eskimo problem, the goading of Farley Mowat is one of the reasons. He has convictions and he can express them in prose that sears the conscience."

Mowat also spent the early postwar years studying wolf behavior in the barrens. He set out to determine what role the wolves were playing in the dwindling numbers of caribou. After months of detailed observation, Mowat discovered that the wolves ate more mice than caribou. In order to convince himself that an animal the size of a wolf could subsist on mice, he began to eat a diet of mice too. When he survived the experiment in good health, he made a report to the government—and was fired.

Mowat's experience among the wolves is chronicled in *Never Cry Wolf,* perhaps his best-known adult work. "Much of what I discovered about wolves flies in the face of our received notions about this species," he told an interviewer. "I learned that wolves mate for life, live in devoted family groups which absorb widowed relations as members of the nuclear family unit, are extremely affectionate and playful, and are far less violent than man. I never saw a wolf commit a wanton act of destruction, cruelty, or maliciousness." *Never Cry Wolf* was published in the Soviet Union as *Wolves, Please Don't Cry!* There it had a significant impact on the treatment of wolves—the government legislated an end to wholesale slaughter of the animals.

Other Mowat titles about man's mistreatment of wildlife followed. *A Whale for the Killing* recounts the slow torture of a marooned whale in a pond in Newfoundland. *Sea of Slaughter* offers a wider view of extinction along the Eastern Seaboard of North America, and *Woman in the Mists: The Story of Dian Fossey and the Mountain Gorillas of Africa* chronicles one field biologist's attempts to save the species she studied. Mowat told *Authors and Artists for Young Adults* that his purpose in these books "was not simply to depress everyone, including myself, but [to warn] that we must change our attitudes toward the species with which we inhabit this earth. We must, in every sense, *share* the planet with them, or we will become its ultimate destroyers. . . . The earth was once *very different and much richer* than it presently is. . . . We have a responsibility to look back in anger and to use that anger to try to salvage the present and ensure the future."

Almost fifty years after the publication of his first book, *People of the Deer,* Mowat returned to its tragic story of the Ihalmiut in *Walking on the Land.* In "this passionate account," as Margaret W. Norton called it in *Library Journal,* he recounts the effects of disease, starvation, and violence on the gentle Inuit band a decade after his first visit. "Mowat presents a multigenerational viewpoint," Norton observed, "through his accounts of Hudson Bay men, missionaries, and other Arctic people as he subtly describes the desolate landscape." Explaining why he chose to revisit the plight of the Ihalmiut, Mowat wrote in the prologue: "My principal reason for doing so is the same as that of writers who continue to tell the story of the Holocaust: to help ensure that man's inhuman acts are not expunged from memory, thereby easing the way for repetitions of such horrors."

In *High Latitudes: An Arctic Journey,* Mowat describes his 1966 trip to northern Canada. Traveling by floatplane "from one isolated settlement to another, Mowat witnesses the devastation being wrought on the native peoples by encroaching white men," stated a critic in *Publisher Weekly.* Reviewing the work in *Booklist,* Gilbert Taylor stated, "Though a thirty-six-year-old event, Mowat's trip touches on continuing environmental and cultural themes." The 2004 work *No Man's River* describes another of Mowat's travels, this time a 1947 journey to the Canadian north. During his stay Mowat befriended a local trapper, and the two men explored the region, often assisting the native peoples who were suffering from disease and famine. A *Publisher Weekly* critic remarked that the author's "vivid descriptions and careful storytelling bring the northern frontier to life as well as any fictional account, yet the characters are real and the adversities loom large."

Mowat's message of responsibility is echoed in his books for children, but in a more lighthearted vein. In his novel *Lost in the Barrens,* for instance, a pair of teenaged boys face a winter alone on the tundra. Their survival depends on a knowledge of the wilderness (on the part of the Indian boy) and an innovative spirit (in the city-bred boy). *Lost in the Barrens* won the prestigious Governor General's Award in Canada and helped to establish Mowat's literary reputation.

Two other books Mowat wrote for juveniles, *The Dog Who Wouldn't Be* and *Owls in the Family,* are memoirs of rather eccentric family pets. Mutt, the dog, has a penchant for climbing fences and trees, while his owl companions, Wol and Weeps, bring dead skunks to the dinner table and feud with cats and crows. In an essay for the *British Columbia Library Quarterly,* Joseph E. Carver contended that Mowat "knows children and what they like and can open doors to adventures both credible and entertaining to his young readers. His stories are credible because Mowat wanted to write them to give permanence to the places, loyalties and experiences of his youth; entertaining because the author enjoys the telling of them. . . . Because almost all of his writing is autobiographical, . . . he relives his experiences so vividly and exuberantly that the action rings with an authenticity the reader cannot help but enjoy."

According to Theo Hersh in *Children's Books and Their Creators,* "Mowat's great gift to children's literature is twofold: He brings his own love of nature to his stories, and he spices it up with his wry sense of humor." Mowat is certainly one of the best-known Canadian writers for children outside the bounds of his own country. His works have been translated into more than fifty languages, and his books have sold in the millions all over the world. In the *Canadian Library Journal,* Mowat stated that "it is an absolute duty" for authors to devote a significant part of their time to writing for youngsters. "It is of absolutely vital importance if basic changes for the good are ever to be initiated in any human culture," he noted. For his own part, he concluded, "the writing of young people's books has been fun—and some of the best and most enduring fun I have ever known."

BIOGRAPHICAL AND CRITICAL SOURCES:

BOOKS

Beacham's Guide to Literature for Young Adults, Volume 2, Beacham Publishing (Osprey, FL), 1990.

Benson, Eugene, and William Toye, editors, *Oxford Companion to Canadian Literature,* 2nd edition, Oxford University Press (Toronto, Ontario, Canada), 1997.

Children's Literature Review, Volume 20, Thomson Gale (Detroit, MI), 1990.

Contemporary Heroes and Heroines, Book III, Thomson Gale (Detroit, MI), 1998.

Contemporary Literary Criticism, Volume 26, Thomson Gale (Detroit, MI), 1983.

Contemporary Popular Writers, St. James Press (Detroit, MI), 1997.

Dictionary of Literary Biography, Volume 68: *Canadian Writers, 1920-1959,* Thomson Gale (Detroit, MI), 1988.

Egoff, Sheila, *The Republic of Childhood: A Critical Guide to Canadian Children's Literature in English,* 2nd edition, Oxford University Press (Don Mills, Ontario, Canada), 1975.

King, James, *Farley: The Life of Farley Mowat,* Steerforth Press (South Royalton, VT), 2003.

Lucas, Alex, *Farley Mowat,* McClelland & Stewart (Toronto, Ontario, Canada), 1976.

Mowat, Farley, *Walking on the Land,* Key Porter Books (Toronto, Ontario, Canada), 2000.

St. James Guide to Young Adult Writers, 2nd edition, St. James Press (Detroit, MI), 1999.

Silvey, Anita, editor, *Children's Books and Their Creators,* Houghton Mifflin (Boston, MA), 1995.

Wyatt, Valerie, *Profiles,* Canadian Library Association (Ottawa, Ontario, Canada), 1975.

PERIODICALS

Atlantic Monthly, April, 2000, review of *Farfarers,* p. 133.

Beaver: Exploring Canada's History, December-January, 1998, Christopher Moore, "Farley's Far-out *Farfarers,*" pp. 54-55; October-November, 2003, John Ayre, "Farley's Version," p. 45-46.

Booklist, February 1, 2000, Julia Glynn, review of *The Farfarers: Before the Norse,* p. 1006; March 15, 2001, Gilbert Taylor, review of *Walking on the Land,* p. 1330; January 1, 2003, Gilbert Taylor, review of *High Latitudes: an Arctic Journey,* pp. 804-805.

British Columbia Library Quarterly, April, 1969, Joseph E. Carver, "Farley Mowat: An Author for All Ages," pp. 10-16.

Canadian Geographic, November-December, 1998, Peter Schledermann, "Is *The Farfarers* simply Far-Fetched?," p. 18; November, 2000, Stephen Smith, "Horror on the Barrens," p. 107.

Canadian Library Journal, September-October, 1973, Farley Mowat, "A Message from the Patron," p. 391.

Canadian Materials, November, 1992, Joe Shepstone, "Farley Mowat on Writing, Nonfiction, and Autobiography."

Chicago Tribune, May 6, 1985.

Kirkus Reviews, July 15, 2004, review of *No Man's River,* p. 677.

Library Journal, January, 2000, Harry Frumerman, review of *The Farfarers,* p. 132; May 1, 2001, Margaret W. Norton, review of *Walking on the Land,* p. 99.

Los Angeles Times, December 13, 1985.

Maclean's, May 20, 1996, "Sticks and Stones. . . " p. 16; November 23, 1998, Christopher Moore, review of *The Farfarers,* p. 139; August 12, 2002, "Latter-Day Prophet: A New Biography Tackles the Passionate Farley Mowat," p. 48.

National Post, October 14, 2000, Noah Richler, "The North, through His Eyes," p. B11.

New York Times, November 8, 1999, "Ha! Taking the Wind out of Leif Ericsson's Sails," p. A4.

New York Times Book Review, November 1, 1959, Walter O'Hearn, review of *People of the Deer.*

People, March 31, 1980.

Publishers Weekly, January 3, 2000, review of *The Farfarers,*p. 63; February 24, 2003, review of *High Latitudes,* p. 65; July 19, 2004, review of *No Man's River,* pp. 154-155.

Time, February 18, 1980; May 6, 1985; October 26, 1987.

Washington Post, October 9, 1983; April 25, 1985; October 25, 1985; November 6, 1998, "Rethinking the Story of North America's First Inhabitants," p. D8.

ONLINE

CBC 4 Kids, http://www.cbc4kids.ca/ (January, 1999), author profile and bibliography.

Farley Mowat, http://www.tceplus.com/mowat.htm/ (December 2, 2001), author biography.

Farley Mowat Web Site (unofficial author home page), http://www.farleymowat.com/ (December 2, 2001).

Independent, http://www.eastnorthumberland.com/news/ (December 8, 1998), Lorraine Dmitrovic, "Under Full Sail: At Thirty-six Books and Counting, Northumberland's Most Famous Author May Have a Few Books in Him Yet."

Salon.com, http://www.salon.com/ (May 11, 1999), Steve Burgess, "Northern Exposure."

OTHER

In Search of Farley Mowat (film), National Film Board of Canada, 1981.

* * *

MOWAT, Farley McGill
See MOWAT, Farley

* * *

M.T.F.
See PORTER, Katherine Anne

MUKHERJEE, Bharati 1940-

PERSONAL: Born July 27, 1940, in Calcutta, India; immigrated to United States, 1961; moved to Canada, 1966, naturalized Canadian citizen, 1972; naturalized U.S. citizen, 1987; daughter of Sudhir Lal (a chemist) and Bina (Banerjee) Mukherjee; married Clark Blaise (a writer and professor), September 19, 1963; children: Bart Anand, Bernard Sudhir. *Ethnicity:* "Indian." *Education:* University of Calcutta, B.A., 1959; University of Baroda, M.A., 1961; University of Iowa, M.F.A., 1963, Ph.D., 1969.

ADDRESSES: *Office*—University of California, Berkeley, English Department, 334 Wheeler Hall, Berkeley, CA 94720-1030. *Agent*—c/o Lynn Nesbit, Janklow & Nesbit, 445 Park Ave., Fl. 13, New York, NY 10022.

CAREER: Writer and educator. Marquette University, Milwaukee, WI, instructor in English, 1964-65; University of Wisconsin-Milwaukee, instructor, 1965; McGill University, Montreal, Quebec, Canada, lecturer, 1966-69, assistant professor, 1969-73, associate professor, 1973-78, professor of English, 1978; Skidmore College, Saratoga Springs, NY, visiting associate professor of English, 1979-80, 1981-82; Emory University, visiting professor of English, 1983; Montclair State College, associate professor of English, 1984; City University of New York, professor of English, 1987-89; University of California, Berkeley, professor of English, 1987—.

MEMBER: PEN.

AWARDS, HONORS: Grants from McGill University, 1968 and 1970, Canada Council, 1973-74 and 1977, Shastri Indo-Canadian Institute, 1976-77, Guggenheim Foundation, 1978-79, and National Endowment for the Arts, 1982; first prize from Periodical Distribution Association, 1980, for short story "Isolated Incidents"; National Magazine Awards second prize, 1981, for essay "An Invisible Woman"; National Book Critics Circle Award for best fiction, 1988, for *The Middleman and Other Stories;* Pushcart Prize, 1999.

WRITINGS:

NOVELS

The Tiger's Daughter, Houghton Mifflin (Boston, MA), 1972.
Wife, Houghton Mifflin (Boston, MA), 1975.
Jasmine, Grove & Weidenfeld, (New York, NY), 1989.
The Holder of the World, Knopf (New York, NY), 1993.
Leave It to Me, Knopf (New York, NY), 1997.
Desirable Daughters, Thea/Hyperion (New York, NY), 2002.
The Tree Bride, Thea/Hyperion (New York, NY), 2004.

SHORT STORIES

Darkness, Penguin (New York, NY), 1985
The Middleman and Other Stories, Grove (New York, NY),1988.

OTHER

(With husband, Clark Blaise) *Days and Nights in Calcutta* (nonfiction), Doubleday (New York, NY), 1977.
(With husband, Clark Blaise) *The Sorrow and the Terror: The Haunting Legacy of the Air India Tragedy*, Viking (New York, NY), 1987.

Contributor to periodicals, including *Mother Jones, New York Times Book Review, Village Voice Literary Supplement, New York Times Sunday Magazine, Des Moines Register, Financial Times, Book Forum, Salmagundi,* and *Saturday Night.*

WORK IN PROGRESS: *Bangalore by the Bay* (third novel in trilogy), for Houghton-Mifflin.

SIDELIGHTS: In a variety of ways, all of Bharati Mukherjee's writings reflect her personal experiences in crossing cultural boundaries. In novels such as *Jasmine, The Tiger's Daughter, The Holder of the World,* and *Desirable Daughters,* as well as in her award-winning short stories, Indian-born Mukherjee supplements her multicultural heritage with "an acute sense of the violence and chaos, however restrained, which can lie beneath the surface of a society, old or new, or of a person," explained Ann Mandel in the *Dictionary of Literary Biography.* A "request for recognition—the desire to be 'visible' . . . to be recognized as person rather than as ethnic stereotype—characterizes much of Mukherjee's writing," Mandel added. "Her characters sometimes cry out to be seen for who they really are; and sometimes, weak or tired, they surrender to taking on the identity of the 'type' that others see them to be." According to an essayist for *Feminist Writers,*

"Mukherjee is perhaps one of the most well-known writers from the Indian diaspora in the United States. Her writing, both fictional and nonfictional, belongs to the growing category of immigrant literature that explores the complex cross-cultural forces which structure the diasporic experience." On the subject of why she writes, Mukherjee told *Feminist Writers,* "I write to discover ideal worlds; I live to repair ruined ones."

Born to wealthy parents in Calcutta, Mukherjee moved to the United States to pursue her studies in English at the University of Iowa. While at the university's writing workshop, she met and married American-born novelist Clark Blaise. Although the couple settled in Canada for several years, they eventually moved back to the United States because of the racism she experienced. As Mukherjee wrote in the introduction to her 1985 short-story collection *Darkness:* "If I may put it in its harshest terms, in Canada, I was frequently taken for a prostitute or shoplifter." Eventually, Mukherjee settled into a teaching career at the University of California at Berkeley.

In *The Tiger's Daughter,* published in 1972, Mukherjee creates a heroine, Tara, who, like herself, returns to India after several years in the West to discover a country quite unlike the one she remembered. Memories of a genteel Brahmin lifestyle are usurped by new impressions of poverty, hungry children, and political unrest. "In other words," a *Times Literary Supplement* reviewer noted, "Tara's westernization has opened her eyes to the gulf between two worlds that still makes India the despair of those who govern it."

"Mukherjee writes entertainingly and with a sort of fluid prose that is very good to read," critic Roger Baker wrote in his review of *The Tiger's Daughter* for *Books and Bookmen.*"She can make her characters spring to life with a word and has what seems to be an acute ear for dialogue." The *Times Literary Supplement* critic added that Mukherjee's "elegant first novel" is skillfully wrought, with lively dialogue and full, descriptive passages. Yet he found the novel's heroine oddly lacking: "Because [Mukherjee] controls her emotions with such a skilled balance of irony and colorful nostalgia her novel is charming and intelligent—and curiously unmoving. . . . Tara herself remains so ineffectual a focus . . . it is hard to care whether or not she will be able to return."

Mukherjee's second novel, *Wife,* is the story of a young Indian woman, Dimple, who attempts to reconcile the Bengali ideal of the perfect passive wife with the demands of real life. Dimple's arranged marriage to an engineer is followed by the couple's immigration to a New York City neighborhood. There she "watches television, sleeps, studies *Better Homes and Gardens,* and timorously meets people," Rosanne Klass detailed in *Ms.*"She is afraid to go out alone, and well she might be, since nobody—on TV or off—seems to talk about anything but murders and muggings." This alien environment, along with Dimple's inherent instability, prompts her to contemplate suicide or murder. "Underneath the passivity lives rage which the heroine is hardly conscious of until it fully extends itself from fantasy to reality," Willa Swanson remarked in the *Antioch Review.*

Swanson found *Wife* a moving study of an individual whom society sees as a trivial object. "There is much wit, a good ear for dialogue, and above all the creation of a character that gives an insight into the sudden, seemingly inexplicable, explosion of a docile, passive person into violence," Swanson related. Yet other reviewers have not been as comfortable with the motive behind Dimple's violent outburst. Klass noted that "possibly Dimple is supposed to be schizophrenic, but . . . it isn't indicated. The book seems to suggest that she goes bonkers from . . . a surfeit of . . . liberated women, Americanized men, and wilting houseplants. I have known a few Indian women in New York. Many had adjustment problems, . . . but none . . . felt that knifing their husbands would really help." Martin Levin, writing in the *New York Times Book Review,* reiterated this sentiment: "The title and the drift of the book imply that the protagonist is in some way a victim of her social status . . . . However oppressed Dimple may be, she is also very crazy, a fact about which the author is amusing but ambiguous. You could raise Dimple's consciousness by ninety degrees and still have a zombie."

The gradual merger of the First and Third worlds is the topic underlying *Jasmine,* Mukherjee's third novel. Jasmine, a poor but independent young Hindu woman, leaves her native country after her husband is killed in a terrorist bombing and gains passage to Florida via ship. Brutally raped by the ship's captain—whom she kills in self-defense—Jasmine travels to New York City to work as an au pair for a Yuppie couple and as a language tutor at Columbia University. After the couple's relationship goes sour, the Indian woman moves to Iowa, where she hopes to escape the flux of modern society. As Eric Larsen noted in the *Los Angeles Times Book Review,* Jasmine "is devastating in Iowa. Her level voice delicately but relentlessly brings out the contradictions of a world trying in vain to resist or ignore the passing of its self-confidence." Reduced to the level of caregiver that she sought to escape in her native India, Jasmine has come full circle; the First and Third worlds travel the same course.

Mukherjee has proven her skill with short stories as well as novels. *Darkness,* published in 1985, contains a dozen tales, most of which were written shortly after the author moved from Canada to the United States. All of the stories feature immigrants—newcomers who attempt to transcend either their cultural past or the unpleasant circumstances of their present. "Mukherjee's characters encounter society in ways that are either marginal or confrontational," explained *Books in Canada* reviewer Neil Bissoondath. "They are challenged by its norms, often fail to understand its mechanics, misinterpret its values; their vision becomes twisted." Particularly in the stories that take place in Canada, racial oppression predominates. In "The World according to Hsu," for example, the title character becomes almost paranoid due to the overt contempt for Indians exhibited by those she seeks to call her fellow countrymen. As Mukherjee writes: "In Toronto, she was not Canadian, not even Indian. She was something called, after the imported idiom of London, a Paki. And for Pakis, Toronto was hell." However, the effect of *Darkness* is not totally bleak; as Patricia Bradbury concluded in *Quill & Quire,* Mukherjee "is showing identities slowly breaking into pieces, cracked open by raw and totally alien dreams. But she always shows this with artistic grace and with the unstated promise that identities, in new and unimaginable moulds, will soon be rebuilt again."

Mukherjee's second story collection, 1988's *The Middleman and Other Stories,* won the National Book Critics Circle Award for best fiction. Focusing on the its author's characteristic theme of Third-World immigrant experiences in North America, *The Middleman and Other Stories* continues to examine the intimate commingling of East and West. Through narrators that include a Smyrnan mercenary, an investment banker based in Atlanta, and, particularly, Indian women attempting to redefine their traditional Hindu upbringing within a far more liberal American culture, Mukherjee's stories remain unsentimental yet affecting in their approach. "The stories in *The Middleman* are streets ahead of those in *Darkness,*" contended *New York Times Book Review* critic Jonathan Raban. "Not only has Ms. Mukherjee vastly enlarged her geographical and social range . . . , but she has greatly sharpened her style. Her writing here is far quicker in tempo, more confident and more sly than it used to be." Joseph Coates maintained in Chicago's *Tribune Books* that in *The Middleman* the author illuminates not only the world of the immigrant to the great melting pot of culture promised by a move to North America, but also the "definitive measure of our collective character" as multigenerational Americans. "By focusing on the most authentic Americans, the ones who just got here," Coates wrote, "Mukherjee makes us see that the reason we persecute and then sentimentalize our newest compatriots is that they too accurately reflect us, the values, priorities and brutalities we'd rather not admit."

After a ten-year sojourn in Canada, Mukherjee returned to her native country in 1973, accompanied by her husband, who was visiting for the first time and eager to embrace his wife's former culture. Together they encountered an India neither anticipated: she found a world far less innocent than the one she remembered, and he met a people more enigmatic than he had imagined. The couple collaborated on *Days and Nights in Calcutta,* a journal of their visit. As James Sloan Allen wrote in the *Saturday Review:* "Blaise, at first blinded by the squalor and the terrors, discovers a magic that enfolds reality in myth and ennobles Bengali life through a love of culture. His journal glows with the enthusiasm of discovery . . . and he turns against 'the whole bloated, dropsical giant called the West.' Mukherjee, by contrast, becomes angry and sad. For her fondly recalled traditions now mask fear and oppression—especially of women." Rather than examine the culture broadly, as her foreign-born husband can, Mukherjee sees individuals, particularly those upper-class women with whom she grew up and whom she would have become. Her visit is filled with love and hate, sympathy and an unwillingness to forgive; she is in exile by choice but, in her words, "while changing citizenship is easy, swapping cultures is not." "It is that sort of honesty, turned by Mukherjee and Blaise upon themselves and their surroundings, that makes this book so distinctive and affecting a chronicle of voyages and discoveries," Margo Jefferson concluded in *Newsweek.*

Mukherjee produced another critically praised novel with *The Holder of the World.* Framed by the narrative of Beigh Masters, a self-styled "asset searcher" on a client-directed quest for a large diamond known as the Emperor's Tear, the novel takes readers three centuries into the past of both the United States and India. The novel's heroine, Hannah Easton, is a rebellious young woman born in Massachusetts in 1670. Mukherjee once told *CA* that, "in literary terms, she is the imagined daughter little 'Pearl Prynne,' the daughter of American literature's first great feminist icon, Hester Prynne of *The Scarlet Letter,*" by Nathaniel Hawthorne. The daughter of a Puritan and her Native-American lover, Hannah is abandoned by her mother, whose defiance of

Western culture serves as an example to her daughter. Hannah's life progresses unconventionally, and she marries an East India Company trader and travels to India. There, after being abandoned by her husband, who has become a pirate, she takes Indian lovers, eventually becoming the wife of a prince. It is "told in Mukherjee's wonderful prose, whose economy allows for lyricism without clutter," noted Kathryn Harrison in Chicago's *Tribune Books.* "Hannah's life is the same sort of cross-cultural fairy tale that captivated" in *Jasmine,* Harrison concluded. Teri Ann Doerksen, a contributor to the *Dictionary of Literary Biography,* found a strong link between *The Holder of the World* and *The Scarlet Letter.* "Reversing the usual binary opposition between occidental and oriental texts, Mukherjee presents Hawthorne's novel as one which has been written out of a knowledge of India," Doerksen noted. "And in doing this Mukherjee has written herself . . . into her text perhaps more effectively even than in the seemingly autobiographical *The Tiger's Daughter.* The novel is also interesting for the way it very subtly parodies the Western construct of India as a nation and the perception of Indians as a homogenous group." The essayist found *The Holder of the World* to be Mukherjee's "most accomplished work to date."

Mukherjee's common themes of identity and dislocation are again a part of *Leave It to Me,* which was published in 1997. As in *Jasmine,* the central character passes through many earthly incarnations. Born in India to an American mother and a Eurasian father, she is abandoned and then placed in a home in Schenectady, New York. Eventually, "Debby" leaves her adopted Italian-American family to look for her birth mother in San Francisco. There, she finds the ex-flower-child who is her birth mother, has sexual intercourse with the man she believes is her biological father, abets her mother's murder, and flees the police when an earthquake diverts their attention from the crime scene. Debby reinvents herself as "Devi Dee," not realizing that this name of an Indian goddess is embedded in the name of the village of Devigaon, where Debby/Devi was born.

This is "Mukherjee's most American work," commented a *Contemporary Novelists* essayist, calling *Leave It to Me* "an enigmatic and alarming meditation on the consequences of America's recent past" in which "Mukherjee's shift from immigrant diasporic writer to multicultural writer is complete." Still, the essayist had some qualms about the book, noting that "few of the characters are as convincing as those who populated her earlier works, and at times the level of coincidence works against this novel." Others held the book in high esteem, including Ellen G. Friedman, who, in the *Review of Contemporary Fiction,* called Debby/Devi "a female, post-Freudian, new-millennium Huckleberry Finn" and "one of a small but growing list of female protagonists who navigate through their plots mostly alone and under their own steam and emerge at the end triumphant to some degree, without parents or men deciding their fates." *Leave It to Me* is, concluded Friedman, "a novel of new realism, postfeminist and postcanonical American narratology." Writing in *Maclean's,* Marni Jackson noted that *Leave It to Me* "mischievously frames the American attitude towards history . . . with the Eastern concept of karma. The novel is a warning that what America sowed in the Sixties, it will eventually have to reap. In Mukherjee's view, this has led to a generation of adults with an inflated sense of entitlement and a shriveled sense of accountability. And it has bred kids like Devi, who have grown up hungry for their own apocalyptic role in history."

In *Desirable Daughters,* the author follows the lives of three Calcutta-born sisters: Tara, Padma, and Parvati. Each takes a different path as they come of age. Born into a family of wealthy, traditional Brahmins, the girls are intelligent, artistic, and doted on by their parents. Yet their opportunities are limited due to their culture. The three girls rebel and wind up on different continents, always struggling to keep their bonds strong. Tara, in California, uncovers a family secret that sets in motion a dangerous plot to kill and kidnap members of her family. Revelation upon revelation forces Tara to "reevaluate everything she ever thought she knew," commented Joanna M. Burkhardt in *Library Journal.* "Artfully conveying the complexities of Indian society, philosophy and religion in India and the United States, Mukherjee's writing is rich, deep, and compelling."

Tara's intelligent, curious character would serve well as a sleuth in a full-fledged mystery novel, in the opinion of *Booklist* reveiwer Donna Seaman, who in appraising *Desirable Daughters* praised the author's "humming power-line sentences," which "carry sparkling commentary on traditional Hindu marriages, caste prejudices, spiritual matters, and the dark side of America's striving Indian immigrant community." Seaman summarized: "Entertaining and intelligent, Mukherjee's graceful novel explores the continuum between tradition and change as it chips away at superficialities to reach the core of human experience." Calling *Desirable Daughters* Mukherjee's very best writing, a *Publishers Weekly* commentator stated, "Only a writer with mature vision, a sense of history and a long-nurtured observation of the Indo-American community could have created this absorbing tale of two rapidly changing cultures and the flash points where they intersect." Irene D'Souza, writing in *Herizons* noted that with *Desireable Daughters* "Mukherjee has established her niche in fiction, writing eloquently of the self-inflicted Indian Diaspora."

Tara Lata's story continues in *The Tree Bride,* the second book of the trilogy that began with *Desirable Daughters.* After a bombing of the home she shares with her ex-husband, Tara becomes obsessed with discovering the truth of her family's history. Through a coincidence—though Tara says, "There are no coincidences, only convergences"—Tara's gynecologist is the granddaughter of a British colonialist named Vertie Treadwell, who knew Tara's great-great- aunt, Tara Lata Gangooly, the woman for whom Tara is named. This aunt, after her betrothed was killed by a snake-bite, was betrothed a second time, in this case to a tree, becoming the "Tree Bride" of the title. With no need now for marriage funds, Tara Lata Gangooly uses her dowry money to support the rising resistance to the British occupation of India. Some reviewers, such as Michiko Kakutani, writing in the *International Herald Tribune,* found *The Tree Bride* to be a "swollen, ungainly novel"; Moni Basu, in the *Atlanta Journal-Constitution* warned that "Mukherjee sets out on uncharted paths, but, unfortunately, gets too tangled in the web of her own plot to make the book the kind of forceful literature she has delivered in the past." Others were impressed by the narrative style: Jyna Scheeren, writing in *Library Journal,* commented that the novel is "expertly written in olden dreamy and silky prose." A critic for *Kirkus Reviews* asserted that "there's almost too much information for a reader to absorb. Still, it's worth the effort." The critic noted that the novel is "filled with absorbing stuff, and really rather brilliantly worked out." In a review for the *Denver Post,* John Freeman commented that the trilogy, when completed, "just might be the Indian-American version of *Roots.*" *Booklist* contributor Donna Seaman praised Mukherjee as "a virtuoso in the crafting of shrewd, hilarious, suspenseful, and significant cross-cultural dramas."

Writing of Mukherjee's contributions to literature, Manju Jaidka stated in *MELUS*: "As a writer who has moved from one geographical and cultural space to another, from India to the American continent . . . her writings speak of the inevitable changes involved in such transitions. There is a re-visioning of ideas and concepts which belong to two different worlds separated by vast oceanic distances. There is also a questioning of biases and prejudices, a deconstruction of social, cultural, and national stereotypes." Another *MELUS* contributor, John K. Hoppe, considered that Mukherjee, while a "postcolonial writer . . . is no multiculturalist . . . . She is plainly disinterested in the preservation of cultures, the hallowing of tradition, obligations of the past." Mukherjee commented on mulitculturalism herself in the *Des Moines Register:* "Multiculturalism emphasizes the difference between racial heritages. This emphasis on the differences has too often led to the dehumanization of the different . . . . Parents express rage or despair at their U.S.-born children's forgetting of, or indifference to, some aspects of Indian culture . . . . I would ask: What is it we have lost if our children are acculturating into the culture in which we are living?"

BIOGRAPHICAL AND CRITICAL SOURCES:

BOOKS

Alam, Fakrul, *Bharati Mukherjee,* Twayne (New York, NY), 1996.

Asian American Literature, Gale (Detroit, MI), 1999.

Contemporary Literary Criticism, Gale (Detroit, MI), Volume 53, 1989, Volume 115, 1999.

Contemporary Novelists, St. James Press (Detroit, MI), 2001.

Dhawan, R.K., *The Fiction of Bharati Mukherjee: A Critical Symposium,* Prestige (New Delhi, India), 1996.

Dictionary of Literary Biography, Gale (Detroit, MI), Volume 60: *Canadian Writers since 1960,* 1986, Volume 218: *American Short Story Writers since World War II, Second Series,* 1999.

Feminist Writers, St. James Press (Detroit, MI), 1996.

Lesser, W., editor, *The Genius of Language,* Pantheon (New York, NY), 2004.

Mukherjee, Bharati, *The Tiger's Daughter,* Houghton Mifflin (Boston, MA), 1972.

Mukherjee, Bharati, *Desirable Daughters,* Thea/Hyperion (New York, NY), 2002.

Nelson, Emmanuel S., editor, *Bharati Mukherjee: Critical Perspectives,* Garland (New York, NY), 1993.

Notable Asian Americans, Gale (Detroit, MI), 1995.

Powell, Anthony, *To Keep the Ball Rolling,* Penguin (London, England), 1983.

PERIODICALS

Amerasia Journal, fall, 1993, p. 103; winter, 1994, p. 188.

American Studies International, June, 1999, S. Krishnamoorthy Aithal, review of *Leave It to Me,* p. 99.

Antioch Review, spring, 1976.

Atlanta Journal-Constitution (Atlanta, GA), Moni Basu, "Rich Writing Overshadowed by Tangled Plot," p. L8.

Bestsellers 89, Issue 2, Gale (Detroit, MI), 1989.

Booklist, April 15, 1997, Hazel Rochman, review of *Leave It to Me,* p. 1365; February 1, 2002, Donna Seaman, review of *Desirable Daughters,* p. 907; June 1, 2004, Donna Seaman, review of *The Tree Bride,* p. 1671.

Books and Bookmen, November, 1973.

Books in Canada, August, 1985, pp. 21-22.

Boston Herald, April 16, 2002, Stephanie Schorow, review of *Desirable Daughters,* p. 43.

Canadian Fiction, May, 1987, Geoff Hancock, interview with Mukherjee, pp. 30-44.

Christian Science Monitor, February 2, 1977.

Connoisseur, August, 1990, p. 84.

Contemporary Literature, spring, 1999, Jennifer Drake, "Looting American Culture: Bharati Mukherjee's Immigrant Narratives," p. 60.

Denver Post, August 22, 2004, John Freeman, "Second in Mukherjee Trilogy Points to Lush Sweep of 'Roots'," p. F11.

Explicator, winter, 1997, pp. 114- 117.

Herizons, spring, 2004, Irene D'Souza, review of *Desirable Daughters,* p. 34.

International Herald Tribune, August 21, 2004, Michiko Kakutani, review of *The Tree Bride,* p. 9.

Kirkus Reviews, June 15, 2004, review of *The Tree Bride,* p. 554.

Library Journal, June 15, 1997, Rebecca A. Stuhr, review of *Leave It to Me,* p. 98; April 1, 2002, Joanna M. Burkhardt, review of *Desirable Daughters,* p. 141; August, 2004, Jyna Scheeren, review of *The Tree Bride,* p. 69.

Los Angeles Times Book Review, September 17, 1989, pp. 3, 10; October 10, 1993, pp. 3, 11.

Maclean's, August 19, 1985, p. 51; October 23, 1989, p. 72; July 21, 1997, Marni Jackson, review of *Leave It to Me,* p. 55.

MELUS, winter, 1995, pp. 91-101; winter, 1999, John K. Hoppe, "The Technological Hybrid as Post-American," pp. 137-155, Manju Jaidka, review of *Leave It to Me,* p. 202.

Mother Jones, December, 1989, p. 43.

Ms., October, 1975.

New Statesman, November 19, 1993, p. 45.

Newsweek, February 7, 1977.

New York, September 25, 1989, p. 132.

New Yorker, November 15, 1993, p. 127.

New York Times, January 25, 1977; November 12, 1993, p. C31.

New York Times Book Review, June 8, 1975; January 12, 1986, p. 14; June 19, 1988, pp. 1, 22; September 10, 1989, p. 9; October 10, 1993, p. 7; January 8, 1995, p. 12; December 3, 1995, p. 49; July 20, 1997, Lorna Sage, review of *Leave It to Me,* p. 33; April 28, 2002, Deborah Mason, review of *Desirable Daughters,* p. 11; May 12, 2002, review of *Desirable Daughters,* p. 26; June 2, 2002, review of *Desirable Daughters,* p. 22; March 23, 2003, Scott Veale, review of *Desirable Daughters,* p. 24.

People, October 25, 1993, p. 51; September 8, 1997, Lan N. Nguyen, review of *Leave It to Me,* p. 36.

Publishers Weekly, January 21, 2002, review of *Desirable Daughters,* p. 62.

Quill & Quire, August, 1985, p. 43.

Review of Contemporary Fiction, fall, 1997, Ellen G. Friedman, review of *Leave It to Me,* p. 232.

San Francisco Chronicle, June 1, 1997, Mary Mackey, review of *Leave It to Me,* p. 1.

Saturday Review, February 5, 1977.

Seattle Times, August 13, 2004, Robert Allen Papinchak, "Past, Present, and Future Intertwine in 'The Tree Bride,'" p. H41.

Time, September 11, 1989, p. 84.

Times Literary Supplement, June 29, 1973.

Tribune Books (Chicago, IL), July 17, 1988, p. 14; October 24, 1993, p. 5.

Washington Post Book World, August 27, 1989, p. 2; October 24, 1993, pp. 1, 11.

World Literature Today, summer, 1986, pp. 520-521.

ONLINE

Beatrice.com, http://www.beatrice.com/ (March 10, 2006), Ron Hogan, interview with Mukherjee.

California Alumni Association at UC Berkeley Web site, http://www.alumni.berkeley.edu/ (March 10, 2006), Russell Schoch, "A Conversation with Bharati Mukherjee."

Jouvert Online, Columbia University, http://152.1.96.5/jouvert/ (March 10, 2006), Tina Chen and S. X. Goudie, "Holders of the Word: An Interview with Bharati Mukherjee."

Powells.com, http://www.powells.com/ (April 4, 2002), Dave Weich, interview with Mukherjee.

* * *

MUNRO, Alice 1931-

PERSONAL: Born July 10, 1931, in Wingham, Ontario, Canada; daughter of Robert Eric (a farmer) and Ann Clarke (Chamney) Laidlaw; married James Armstrong Munro (a bookseller), December 29, 1951 (divorced, 1976); married Gerald Fremlin (a geographer), 1976;

children: (first marriage) Sheila, Jenny, Andrea. *Education:* University of Western Ontario, B.A., 1952. *Politics:* New Democratic Party. *Religion:* Unitarian Universalist.

ADDRESSES: Home—P.O. Box 1133, Clinton, Ontario N0M 1L0, Canada. *Agent*—c/o Writer's Union of Canada, 24 Ryerson St., Toronto, Ontario M5T 2P4.

CAREER: Writer. Artist-in-residence, University of Western Ontario, 1974-75, and University of British Columbia, 1980.

MEMBER: Writers Union of Canada.

AWARDS, HONORS: Governor General's Literary Award, 1969, for *Dance of the Happy Shades,* 1978, for *Who Do You Think You Are: Stories,* 1979, for *The Beggar Maid: Stories of Flo and Rose,* and 1987, for *The Progress of Love;* Canadian Bookseller's Award, 1972, for *Lives of Girls and Women;* Great Lakes Colleges Association award, 1974; Province of Ontario Award, 1974; D. Litt., University of Western Ontario, 1976; Canada-Australia Literary Prize, 1977, and 1994; Marian Engel Award, 1986; Lannan Literary Award, W.H. Smith Award, and Canadian Booksellers' Award, all 1995; finalist, *Los Angeles Times Book Review* Award, 1995; National Book Critics Circle Award for Fiction, 1998, for *The Love of a Good Woman,* and nominee in 2001 in fiction category, for *Hateship, Friendship, Courtship, Loveship, Marriage: Stories;* Rea Award for lifetime achievement, 2001, for significant contributions to the short story genre; lifetime achievement award, Vancouver Public Library, 2005.

WRITINGS:

SHORT STORIES

Dance of the Happy Shades and Other Stories, Ryerson (Toronto, Ontario, Canada), 1968, McGraw-Hill (New York, NY), 1973.
Lives of Girls and Women, McGraw-Hill Ryerson (Toronto, Ontario, Canada), 1971, McGraw-Hill (New York, NY), 1972.
Something I've Been Meaning to Tell You: Thirteen Stories, McGraw-Hill (New York, NY), 1974.
Who Do You Think You Are?: Stories, Macmillan (Toronto, Ontario, Canada), 1978, published as *The Beggar Maid: Stories of Flo and Rose,* Knopf (New York, NY), 1979.
The Moons of Jupiter: Stories, Macmillan (Toronto, Ontario, Canada), 1982, Knopf (New York, NY), 1983.
The Progress of Love, Knopf (New York, NY), 1986.
Friend of My Youth: Stories, Knopf (New York, NY), 1990.
Open Secrets: Stories, Knopf (New York, NY), 1994.
Selected Stories, Knopf (New York, NY), 1996.
The Love of a Good Woman: Stories, Knopf (New York, NY), 1998.
Queenie: A Story, Profile Books/London Review of Books (London, England), 1999.
Hateship, Friendship, Courtship, Loveship, Marriage: Stories, Knopf (New York, NY), 2001.

Contributor to books, including *Canadian Short Stories,* second series, Oxford University Press (New York, NY), 1968; *Sixteen by Twelve: Short Stories by Canadian Writers,* edited by John Metcalf, Ryerson (Toronto, Ontario, Canada), 1970; *The Narrative Voice: Stories and Reflections by Canadian Authors,* edited by David Helwig and Joan Harcourt, Oberon (Ottawa, Ontario, Canada), 1974; *Here and Now,* Oberon (Ottawa, Ontario, Canada), 1977; *Personal Fictions,* Oxford University Press (New York, NY), 1977; *Night Light: Stories of Aging,* Oxford University Press (New York, NY), 1986; and *Best American Short Stories, 1989.* Also contributor to periodicals, including *Atlantic, Canadian Forum, Chatelaine, Grand Street, Queen's Quarterly,* and *New Yorker.*

TELEPLAYS

"A Trip to the Coast," in *To See Ourselves,* Canadian Broadcasting Corp. (CBC), 1973.
"Thanks for the Ride," in *To See Ourselves,* CBC, 1973.
How I Met My Husband (broadcast in *The Plays the Thing,* CBC, 1974), Macmillan (Toronto, Ontario, Canada), 1976.
"1847: The Irish," in *The Newcomers: Inhabiting a New Land,* CBC, 1978.

ADAPTATIONS: "Baptising," in *Lives of Girls and Women,* was adapted and filmed for the CBC *Performance* series, 1975. *Boys and Girls* and *An Ounce of Cure* were adapted for film in 1983 by Atlantis Films in association with the CBC, produced by Janice Platt, Seaton McLean, and Michael Macmillan, directed by Don McBrearty, and distributed by Beacon Films; *Connection* was filmed by the same group in 1986. Munro read her short story "The Progress of Love," produced as a sound recording by American Audio Prose Library (Columbia, MO), 1987. *Friend of My Youth* was produced as a sound recording by Chivers, 2001.

SIDELIGHTS: Alice Munro is considered a master of the short story form. Her work has often drawn comparisons to that of Anton Chekov for its richness of detail. Munro, a Canadian author, is usually concerned with characters living in the small towns of southwestern Ontario, and her stories present "ordinary experiences so that they appear extraordinary, invested with a kind of magic," according to Catherine Sheldrick Ross in *Dictionary of Literary Biography.* Considered one of Canada's major writers, Munro typically refuses to imbue events in her work with moral overtones: her stories offer no resolution, leaving readers to draw their own conclusions regarding the actions of her unpredictable protagonists. "Few people writing today," critic Beverley Slopen claimed in *Publishers Weekly,* "can bring a character, a mood or a scene to life with such economy. And [Munro] has an exhilarating ability to make the readers see the familiar with fresh insight and compassion."

In a review of *Dance of the Happy Shades* in the *New York Times Book Review,* contributor Martin Levin wrote that "the short story is alive and well in Canada. . . . Alice Munro creates a solid habitat for her fiction—southwestern Ontario, a generation or more in the past—and is in sympathetic vibration with the farmers and townspeople who live there." Peter Prince, writing in the *New Statesman,* called the stories in *Dance of the Happy Shades* "beautifully controlled and precise. And always this precision appears unstrained. The proportions so exactly fit the writer's thematic aims that in almost every case it seems that really no other words *could* have been used, certainly no more or less."

Reviewing *Something I've Been Meaning to Tell You* in *Saturday Night,* Kildare Dobbs wrote: "Readers who enjoyed the earlier books because they confirmed the reality of the Canadian small-town experience for a certain generation, or because they seemed to reinforce some of the ideology of the women's movement, will find more of the same. . . . All the stories are told with the skill which the author has perfected over the years, narrated with meticulous precision in a voice that is unmistakably Ontarian in its lack of emphasis, its sly humour and willingness to live with a mystery." Joyce Carol Oates argued that readers will be "most impressed by the feeling behind [Munro's] stories—the evocation of emotions, ranging from bitter hatred to love, from bewilderment and resentment to awe." "In all her work," Oates added in the *Ontario Review,* "there is an effortless, almost conversational tone, and we know we are in the presence of an art that works to conceal itself, in order to celebrate its subject."

Munro "has the ability to isolate the one detail that will evoke the rest of the landscape," wrote Urjo Kareda in *Saturday Night,* calling *Who Do You Think You Are?*—published in the United States as *The Beggar Maid: Stories of Flo and Rose*—a "remarkable, immensely pleasurable collection." A volume of related short stories, *Who Do You Think You Are?* introduces readers to Rose—a wealthy, middle-aged divorcee who grew up in poverty in Hanratty, Ontario—as she fits the pieces of her life together. Julia O'Faolain, writing in the *New York Times Book Review,* added that "Munro captures a kaleidoscope of lights and depths. Through the lens of Rose's eye, she manages to reproduce the vibrant prance of life while scrutinizing the working of her own narrative art. This is an exhilarating collection."

"In *The Progress of Love,* the focus has changed," contended Anne Tyler in the *New Republic.* "The characters in these 11 stories are concerned not so much with the journey as with the journey's hidden meaning—how to view the journey, how to make sense of it. . . . In the most successful of the stories, the end result is a satisfying click as everything settles precisely into place." Munro "is concerned not only with the different configurations of love that occur in the wake of divorces, separations and deaths, but also with the 'progress of love,' the ways in which it endures or changes through time," explained Michiko Kakutani in the *New York Times.* "The results are pictures of life, or relationships, of love, glimpsed from a succession of mirrors and frames—pictures that possess both the pain and immediacy of life and the clear, hard radiance of art." And Oates declared in the *New York Times Book Review* that "Munro writes stories that have the density—moral, emotional, sometimes historical—of other writer's novels"—a claim echoed by several other critics. "*The Progress of Love* is a volume of unflinching audacious honesty," Oates continued, "uncompromisingly downright in its dissection of the ways in which we deceive ourselves in the name of love; the bleakness of its vision is enriched by the author's exquisite eye and ear for detail. Life is heartbreak, but it is also uncharted moments of kindness and reconciliation."

The success of *Friend of My Youth: Stories,* which was published in 1990, won Munro significant critical acclaim. In *Time,* Stefan Kanfer compared her to the great

Russian short story writer and dramatist, Anton Chekhov, while the *New York Times Book Review* included the collection among their "Best Books of 1990." In *Friend of My Youth,* Munro continues her exploration of the movements of relationships and characters with respect to time. "Movement is central to all Munro's stories," wrote Kate Walbert in the *Nation.* "That endings give way to beginnings is the one constant in the lives of these characters." Walbert also asserted that for Munro, "self-identity . . . is a commodity to wage battles for," and for her female protagonists, "self-scrutinization . . . is as habitual as breathing." According to Walbert, the issue for these women is not so much the events of their past—"first marriages, lonely childhoods, severed friendships"—but "who they were in relation to that event." As they trace "their footsteps with . . . How did-I-get-here? wonder," the attempt "to extract the 'I' from a time when who they were was defined *for* them seems a Sisyphean task," since "so many of [their] actions were taken in observance of patriarchal rules."

The 1994 publication of *Open Secrets* prompted Ted Solataroff to call Munro "the mother figure of Canadian fiction" in his review in the *Nation,* placing her writing in the tradition of "the great stylist of 1920's realism, a Katherine Anne Porter brought up to date." Josephine Humphreys, writing in the *New York Times Book Review,* also remarked on Munro's stylistic achievements. She noted that every story in *Open Secrets* contains "a startling leap"—in time, place, or point of view—which "explod[es]—the fictional context," thereby allowing Munro to reach "toward difficult truths." For, as Humphreys claimed, "Ms. Munro's fiction is out to seize—to apprehend—the mystery of existence within time, 'the unforeseen intervention,' the unique quality of a person's fate."

Like her previous collections, *Open Secrets* is largely concerned with the politics of sex. Solataroff found that the stories in *Open Secrets* "develop Munro's master theme from various points in time and from dramatically unexpected angles." Praising "A Wilderness Station"—an epistolary story concerning two brothers, an unsolved murder, and a woman's oppression and descent into madness amid a rough-hewn existence on the Canadian frontier—as "extraordinary writing," he also lauded Munro for her ability to capture what he termed "the male shadow on women's lives." "Carried Away" is a "three-part variation on the theme of being carried away, in its double meaning of love and death"; and "The Albanian Virgin," which first appeared in the *New Yorker,* the critic proclaimed a "masterpiece . . . written with the guts of a burglar."

Munro impressed critics again with her collection *The Love of a Good Woman,* published in 1998. In each story in this collection of tales set in small-town Ontario, murders, affairs, and other dark secrets come to the surface, revealed in the multi-leveled detail for which Munro has become famous. In a sense, one could describe her as "a gossip with a dark twist," mused Tamsin Todd in *New Statesman.* Yet the appeal of her work goes far beyond the lure of hidden secrets or the rich detail of her descriptions. These stories show her talent for pinpointing pivotal instants in her characters' lives, noted Todd. The reviewer added, "Like the teller of medieval morality tales, Munro leads readers along a winding path to those moments when the moral decisions that determine the shape of a life are made."

Hateship, Friendship, Loveship, Courtship, Marriage: Stories shows the author at the height of her powers, with her writing "increasingly intricate and wide-ranging," reported Bruce Allen for *Insight on the News.* Noting that Munro is often called "Canada's Chekhov," Allen went on to say, "That comparison is a reviewer's cliche yet it's unavoidably apt. She has the Russian master's keen eye for detail and his empathy with people of all sorts." The title story of the collection concerns Johanna Parry, a tidy Scottish spinster who has made a life for herself in Canada. When two teenaged girls play a malicious prank on her, she packs up her belongings to move to Saskatchewan, thinking she has received a proposal of marriage. The father of one of the girls lives there, but he knows nothing of the love letters he has supposedly been sending to Johanna. Instead of being crushed by the deception, the woman rises to the occasion and a wedding takes place after all. *Hateship, Friendship, Courtship, Marriage* finds Munro "on top form," advised a reviewer for *Economist,* who added that "she is one of the most accomplished and downright exhilarating writers working today. Her human understanding is acute. From rather unpromising-sounding subject matter she fashions short stories of extraordinary delicacy and resonance."

A compulsive writer for much of her adult life, Munro sees within her work the essence of her ability to transcend aging. "I'm a little panicked at the idea of stopping," she told Jeanne McCulloch and Mona Simpson in *Paris Review,* "as if, if I stopped I could be stopped for good. . . . There are parts of a story where the story fails. . . . The story fails but your faith in the importance of doing the story doesn't fail. That it might is the danger."

BIOGRAPHICAL AND CRITICAL SOURCES:

BOOKS

Besner, Neil K., *Introducing Alice Munro's Lives of Girls and Women: A Reader's Guide,* ECW Press (Toronto, Ontario, Canada), 1990.

Bloom, Harold, editor, *Alice Munro,* Chelsea House (Philadelphia, PA), 1994.

Carrington, Ildikao de Papp, *Controlling the Uncontrollable: The Fiction of Alice Munro,* Northern Illinois University Press (DeKalb, IL), 1989.

Carscallen, James, *The Other Country: Patterns in the Writing of Alice Munro,* ECW Press (Toronto, Ontario, Canada), 1993.

Dahlie, Hallvard, *Alice Munro and Her Works,* ECW Press (Toronto, Ontario, Canada), 1984.

Dictionary of Literary Biography, Volume 53: *Canadian Writers since 1960, First Series,* Thomson Gale (Detroit, MI), 1990.

Encyclopedia of World Literature in the Twentieth Century, St. James Press (Detroit, MI), 1999.

Gibson, Graeme, *Eleven Canadian Novelists: Interviews by Graeme Gibson,* House of Anasi (Toronto, Ontario, Canada), 1973.

Hancock, Geoff, *Canadian Writers at Work: Interviews with Geoff Hancock,* Oxford University Press (Toronto, Ontario, Canada), 1987.

Heble, Ajay, *The Tumble of Reason: Alice Munro's Discourse of Absence,* University of Toronto Press (Toronto, Ontario, Canada), 1994.

MacKendrick, Louis K., editor, *Probable Fictions: Alice Munro's Narrative Acts,* ECW Press (Toronto, Ontario, Canada), 1983.

MacKendrick, Louis K., editor, *Some Other Reality: Alice Munro's Something I've Been Meaning to Tell You,* ECW Press (Toronto, Ontario, Canada), 1993.

Miller, Judith, editor, *The Art of Alice Munro: Saying the Unsayable,* University of Waterloo Press (Waterloo, Ontario, Canada), 1984.

New, W. H., *Dreams of Speech and Violence: The Art of the Short Story in Canada and New Zealand,* University of Toronto Press (Toronto, Ontario, Canada), 1987.

Rasporich, Beverly Jean, *Dance of the Sexes: Art and Gender in the Fiction of Alice Munro,* University of Alberta Press (Edmundton, Alberta, Canada), 1990.

Redekop, Magdalene, *Mothers and Other Clowns: The Stories of Alice Munro,* Routledge (New York, NY), 1992.

Ross, Catherine Sheldick, *Alice Munro: A Double Life,* ECW Press (Toronto, Ontario, Canada), 1997.

Smythe, Karen E., *Figuring Grief: Gallant, Munro, and the Poetics of Elegy,* McGill-Queen's University Press (Montreal, Quebec, Canada), 1992.

Steele, Apollonia, and Jean F. Tener, editors, *The Alice Munro Papers, First Accession: An Inventory of the Archive at the University of Calgary Libraries,* University of Calgary Press (Calgary, Alberta, Canada), 1986.

Steele, Apollonia, and Jean F. Tener, editors, *The Alice Munro Papers, Second Accession,* University of Calgary Press (Calgary, Alberta, Canada), 1987.

Twigg, Alan, *For Openers: Conversations with 24 Canadian Writers,* Harbour Publishing (Madiera Park, British Columbia, Canada), 1981.

York, L., *Other Side of Dailiness: Photography in the Writing of Alice Munro and Timothy Findley,* University of Toronto Press (Toronto, Ontario, Canada), 1987.

PERIODICALS

Belles Lettres, summer, 1990.

Book, July, 2001, review of *Friend of My Youth,* p. 84.

Booklist, August, 1996, p. 1856; August, 2001, Whitney Scott, review of *Friend of My Youth* (sound recording), p. 2143; November 15, 2001, Brad Hooper, review of *Lives of Girls and Women,* p. 555.

Brick, number 40, 1991, Eleanor Wachtel, "An Interview with Alice Munro," pp. 48-53.

Canadian Fiction Magazine, number 43, 1982, pp. 74-114.

Canadian Forum, February, 1969.

Canadian Literature, number 130, 1991, Gerald Lynch, "The One and the Many: English-Canadian Short Story Cycles," pp. 91-104; spring, 1999, review of *Who Do You Think You Are?,* p. 73.

Chatelaine, August, 1975, pp. 42-43; July, 1990, p. 10.

Economist, November 24, 2001, review of *Hateship, Friendship, Courtship, Loveship, Marriage: Stories.*

Entertainment Weekly, November 5, 1999, review of *The Love of a Good Woman,* p. 74; December 10, 1999, review of *The Love of a Good Woman,* p. 102.

Essays on Critical Writing, spring, 1996, p. 71.

Globe & Mail (Toronto, Ontario, Canada), October 30, 1999, review of *The Love of a Good Woman,* p. D28.

Hudson Review, spring, 1999, review of *The Love of a Good Woman,* p. 167.

Insight on the News, February 25, 2002, Bruce Allen, review of *Hateship, Friendship, Loveship, Courtship, Marriage: Stories,* p. 26.

Journal of Canadian Studies, spring, 1991, pp. 5-21; summer, 1991, pp. 156-169; summer, 1994, pp. 184-194.

Listener, June 13, 1974; January 29, 1987, pp. 22-23.

Los Angeles Times Book Review, April 1, 1990, p. 4.

Maclean's, September 22, 1986; May 7, 1990, p. 66; October 17, 1994, pp. 46-49.

Meanjin, Volume 54, number 2, 1995, pp. 222-240.

Ms., November-December, 1996, p. 81.

Nation, May 14, 1990, pp. 678-680; November 28, 1994, pp. 665-668.

New Republic, September 15, 1986; pp. 54-55; May 14, 1990, pp. 50-53; November 31, 1994, pp. 51-53.

New Statesman, May 3, 1974; February 12, 1999, Tamsin Todd, review of *The Love of a Good Woman,* p. 54.

Newsweek, April 2, 1990, pp. 56-57; September 26, 1994, p. 63; October 21, 1996, p. 88.

New Yorker, December 17, 1990, p. 123.

New York Review of Books, May 17, 1990, pp. 38-39; December 22, 1994, pp. 59-60.

New York Times, February 16, 1983; September 3, 1986, p. C22; November 10, 1986; April 17, 1990.

New York Times Book Review, September 23, 1973; September 16, 1979, p. 12; September 14, 1986, pp. 7, 9; March 18, 1990, pp. 1, 31; December 2, 1990, p. 3; September 11, 1994, pp. 1, 36-37; December 10, 1995, p. 44; October 27, 1996, p. 11; December 8, 1996, p. 10; December 14, 1997, p. 36; October 31, 1999, review of *The Love of a Good Woman,* p. 40; December 5, 1999, review of *The Love of a Good Woman,* p. 105; November 25, 2001, William H. Pritchard, review of *Hateship, Friendship, Courtship, Loveship, Marriage: Stories,* p. 9.

Ontario Review, fall, 1974; fall-winter, 1979-80, pp. 87-90.

Paris Review, summer, 1994, pp. 227-264.

Publishers Weekly, August 22, 1986; August 1, 1994, p. 72.

Quill & Quire, June, 1990, p. 29; February, 1999, review of *The Love of a Good Woman,* p. 42.

Resource Links, October, 2001, Ingrid Johnston, review of *The Love of a Good Woman: Stories,* p. 58.

Saturday Night, July, 1974, p. 28; January-February, 1979, pp. 62-63.

Southern Review, summer, 1999, review of *The Love of a Good Woman,* p. 608.

Spectator, October 20, 1990, pp. 37-38; March 13, 1999, review of *The Love of a Good Woman,* p. 36; October 29, 1994, pp. 35-36.

Studies in Canadian Literature, number 5, 1980, Helen Hoy, "'Dull, Simple, Amazing and Unfathomable': Paradox and Double Vision in Alie Munro's Fiction," pp. 100-115.

Time, January 15, 1973; July 2, 1990, pp. 66-67; October 3, 1994, p. 80.

Times Literary Supplement, November 14, 1994, p. 24; November 8, 1996, p. 26; November 29, 1996, p. 13.

Virginia Quarterly Review, spring, 1999, review of *The Love of a Good Woman,* p. 58.

Washington Post Book World, March 18, 1990, pp. 1-2; September 18, 1994, p. 2.

Women's Review of Books, January, 1999, review of *The Love of a Good Woman,* p. 15.

World Literature Today, summer, 1997, p. 589; summer, 1999, review of *The Love of a Good Woman,* p. 526.

Yale Review, April, 1999, review of *The Love of a Good Woman,* p. 157.

ONLINE

Compulsive Reader, http://www.compulsivereader.com/ (April 29, 2002), Bob Williams, review of *Hateship, Friendship, Courtship, Loveship, Marriage: Stories.*

New Republic Online, http://www.powells.com/ (April 29, 2002), Ruth Franklin, review of *Hateship, Friendship, Courtship, Loveship, Marriage: Stories.*

Reading Group Center Web site, www.randomhouse.com/vintage.read/ (April 29, 2002), "A Conversation with Alice Munro."

OTHER

Alice Munro Interview with Kay Bonetti (sound recording), American Audio Prose Library (Columbia, MO), 1987.

* * *

MURDOCH, Iris 1919-1999
(Jean Iris Murdoch)

PERSONAL: Born July 15, 1919, in Dublin, Ireland; died February 8, 1999; daughter of Wills John Hughes (a British civil servant) and Irene Alice (Richardson) Murdoch; married John Oliver Bayley (a professor, novelist, and critic), 1956. *Education:* Somerville College, Oxford, B.A. (first-class honors), 1942; Newnham

College, Cambridge, Sarah Smithson studentship in philosophy, 1947-48. *Religion:* Christian. *Hobbies and other interests:* Learning languages.

CAREER: Writer. British Treasury, London, England, assistant principal, 1942-44; United National Relief and Rehabilitation Administration (UNRRA), administrative officer in London, Belgium, and Austria, 1944-46; St. Anne's College, Oxford University, Oxford, England, fellow and university lecturer in philosophy, 1948-63, honorary fellow, beginning 1963; Royal College of Art, London, lecturer, 1963-67. Member of Formentor Prize Committee.

AWARDS, HONORS: Book of the Year award, *Yorkshire Post,* 1969, for *Bruno's Dream;* Whitehead Literary Award for fiction, 1974, for *The Sacred and Profane Love Machine;* James Tait Black Memorial Prize, 1974, for *The Black Prince;* named commander, 1976, then dame commander, 1986, Order of the British Empire; Booker Prize, 1978, for *The Sea, the Sea;* honorary doctorate, Oxford University, 1987; medal of honor for literature, National Arts Club, 1990; honorary doctorate, Cambridge University, 1993. Chair of psychiatry established in Murdoch's name at Oxford University; scholarship in Murdoch's name established at St. Anne's College, Oxford.

WRITINGS:

NOVELS

Under the Net, Viking (New York, NY), 1954, with an introduction and notes by Dorothy Jones, Longmans, Green (London, England), 1966, Penguin (New York, NY), 1977.

The Flight from the Enchanter, Viking (New York, NY), 1956.

The Sandcastle, Viking (New York, NY), 1957.

The Bell, Viking (New York, NY), 1958, with an introduction by A.S. Byatt, Penguin (New York, NY), 2001.

A Severed Head (also see below), Viking (New York, NY), 1961.

An Unofficial Rose, Viking (New York, NY), 1962.

The Unicorn, Viking (New York, NY), 1963.

The Italian Girl (also see below), Viking (New York, NY), 1964.

The Red and the Green, Viking (New York, NY), 1965.

The Time of the Angels, Viking (New York, NY), 1966.

The Nice and the Good, Viking (New York, NY), 1968.

Bruno's Dream, Viking (New York, NY), 1969.

A Fairly Honorable Defeat, Viking (New York, NY), 1970, with an introduction by Peter J. Reed, Penguin (New York, NY), 2001.

An Accidental Man, Viking (New York, NY), 1971.

The Black Prince (also see below), Viking (New York, NY), 1973, new edition, with an introduction by Martha C. Nussbaum, Penguin (New York, NY), 2003

The Sacred and Profane Love Machine, Viking (New York, NY), 1974.

A Word Child, Viking (New York, NY), 1975.

Henry and Cato, Viking (New York, NY), 1977.

The Sea, the Sea, Viking (New York, NY), 1978, new edition, with an introduction by Mary Kinzie, Penguin (New York, NY), 2001.

Nuns and Soldiers, Viking (New York, NY), 1980, new edition, with an introduction by Karen Armstrong, Penguin (New York, NY), 2002.

The Philosopher's Pupil, Viking (New York, NY), 1983.

The Good Apprentice, Chatto & Windus (London, England), 1985, Penguin (New York, NY), 1987.

The Book and the Brotherhood, Chatto & Windus (London, England), 1987.

The Message to the Planet, Chatto & Windus (London, England), 1989, Viking (New York, NY), 1990.

The Green Knight, Viking (New York, NY), 1994.

Jackson's Dilemma, Viking (New York, NY), 1995.

NONFICTION

Sartre: Romantic Rationalist, Yale University Press (New Haven, CT), 1953, reprinted, Viking (New York, NY), 1987, published as *Sartre: Romantic Realist,* Harvester Press (Sussex, England), 1980.

The Sovereignty of Good over Other Concepts (Leslie Stephen Lecture, 1967; also see below), Cambridge University Press (Cambridge, England), 1967.

The Sovereignty of Good (includes *The Sovereignty of Good over Other Concepts*), Routledge & Kegan Paul (London, England), 1970, Schocken Books (New York, NY), 1971.

The Fire and the Sun: Why Plato Banished the Artists, Clarendon Press (Oxford, England), 1977, Viking (New York, NY), 1990.

Reynolds Stone, Warren Editions (London, England), 1981.

Acastos: Two Platonic Dialogues, Chatto & Windus (London, England), 1986, Viking (New York, NY), 1987.

Metaphysics as a Guide to Morals: Philosophical Reflections, Penguin (New York, NY), 1993.

Existentialists and Mystics: Writings on Philosophy and Literature (essay collection), Penguin (New York, NY), 1998.

PLAYS

(With J.B. Priestley) *A Severed Head* (three-act; based on the author's novel of the same title; first produced in London, England, 1964; produced in New York, NY, 1964), Chatto & Windus (London, England), 1964, Samuel French (New York, NY), 1964.
(With James Saunders) *The Italian Girl* (based on the author's novel of the same title; first produced in Bristol, England, 1967), Samuel French (New York, NY), 1968.
The Servants and the Snow (also see below), first produced in London, England, 1970.
The Three Arrows (also see below), first produced in Cambridge, England, 1972.
The Three Arrows [and] *The Servants and the Snow,* Chatto & Windus (London, England), 1973, Viking (New York, NY), 1974.
Art and Eros, produced in London, England, 1980.
The Servants (opera libretto; adapted from the author's play, *The Servants and the Snow;* produced in Cardiff, Wales, 1980), Oxford University Press (Oxford, England), 1980.
The Black Prince (based on the author's novel of the same title; also see below), produced in London, England, 1989.
The Servants and the Snow, The Three Arrows, The Black Prince: Three Plays, Chatto & Windus (London, England), 1989.
Joanna Joanna, Colophon Press (London, England), 1994.
The One Alone, Colophon Press (London, England), 1995.

OTHER

(Author of foreword) Wendy Campbell-Purdie and Fenner Brockaway, *Woman against the Desert,* Gollancz (London, England), 1964.
A Year of Birds (poems), with engravings by Reynolds Stone, Compton Press (Tisbury, England), 1978.
Something Special: A Story (novella), illustrated by Michael McCurdy, Chatto & Windus (London, England), 1999, Norton (New York, NY), 2000.

Contributor to *The Nature of Metaphysics,* Macmillan, 1957; contributor to periodicals, including *Listener, Yale Review, Chicago Review, Encounter,New Statesman, Nation,* and *Partisan Review.*

ADAPTATIONS: A Severed Head was adapted for film and produced by Columbia Pictures, 1971.

SIDELIGHTS: Iris Murdoch was "one of postwar Britain's greatest novelists," stated Malcolm Bradbury in a remembrance of the author published in *Time* shortly after her death in 1999. Murdoch's novels, the critic explained, are "every one distinctive and different, all displaying that exotic, fantastic imagination that can only be called Murdochian." Described by *Commonweal*'s Linda Kuehl as "a philosopher by trade and temperament," Murdoch developed a reputation for writing novels full of characters embroiled in philosophical turmoil. Though she was originally aligned with the existentialist movement, her philosophy quickly broadened, and critics came to regard her works as "novels of ideas." In addition, Murdoch's plays and nonfiction works encompass similar philosophical debates, thus enhancing her standing as one of her generation's most prolific and important writers. Murdoch's body of work has proved influential in twentieth-century literature and thought. "She draws eclectically on the English tradition" of Charles Dickens, Jane Austen, and William Thackeray "and at the same time extends it in important ways," wrote John Fletcher in the *Concise Dictionary of British Literary Biography.* Jeffrey Meyers, recalling the writer in the *New Criterion,* said "The qualities that made Iris Murdoch a great novelist" include "her technical skill, richness of imagination, philosophical ideas, and moral vision."

Though born an only child of Anglo-Irish parents in Ireland, Murdoch grew up in the suburbs of London and earned a scholarship to a private school when she was thirteen. At Somerville College at Oxford, Murdoch was involved in drama and arts when not immersed in her literature and philosophy studies. Her left-wing politics led her to join the Communist Party for a brief time in the early 1940s, an affiliation that caused the United States to deny her a visa to study in the country after winning a scholarship several years later. Following her distinguished scholastic career, Murdoch worked at the British Treasury during World War II and later for the United Nations Relief and Rehabilitation Administration. While working for the United Nations, she traveled to Belgium, where she met existentialist Jean-Paul Sartre, as well as French writer Raymond Queneau, whose writings greatly influenced her first novel, *Under the Net.* During the 1950s, Murdoch taught philosophy at St. Anne's College at Oxford, and once noted of the experience to Gill Davie and Leigh Crutchley in a *Publishers Weekly* interview: "I love teaching, and if I were not able to teach philosophy I would happily teach something else."

The existentialist movement, a philosophy that became popular in the 1950s in light of the widespread despair caused by World War II, was the impetus for Murdoch's first book. Popularized by such writers as Albert Camus and Sartre, existentialism proposes that because human existence is meaningless, people must act according to their own free will and may never know the difference between right and wrong. Murdoch's *Sartre: Romantic Rationalist* chronicles the thoughts and influences of one of existentialism's most popular writers. Many critics began to view Murdoch as an emerging theorist of the philosophy, but she once told *New York Times* interviewer John Russell, "I was never a Sartrean, or an existentialist." Focusing on Sartre's influential *Being and Nothingness,* Murdoch examines Sartre's philosophy and the events in his personal life that led him to his conclusions. Several critics praised Murdoch's work; in *Commonweal,* Wallace Fowlie called the book "one of the most objective and useful" interpretations of Sartre's works, and Stuart Hampshire of the *New Statesman* termed Murdoch "one who understands the catastrophes of intellectual politics, and who can still take them seriously."

Some reviewers noted similarities between the approach of Sartre and Murdoch. William Van O'Connor wrote in *The New University Wits, and the End of Modernism,* that like Sartre, Murdoch views man as a "lonely creature in an absurd world . . . impelled to make moral decisions, the consequences of which are uncertain." Also like Sartre, said Warner Berthoff in *Fictions and Events: Essays in Criticism and Literary History,* Murdoch believes that writing is "above all else a collaboration of author and reader in an act of freedom." Berthoff continued, "Following Sartre she has spoken pointedly of the making of works of art as not only a 'struggle for freedom' but as a 'task which does not come to an end.'"

Though there are indeed similarities, critics also noted some important differences between the two philosophers. Gail Kmetz wrote in *Ms.* that Murdoch "rejected Sartre's emphasis on the isolation and anguish of the individual in a meaningless world . . . because she felt it resulted in a sterile and futile solipsism. She considers the individual always as a part of society, responsible to others as well as to herself or himself; and insists that freedom means respecting the independent being of others, and that subordinating others' freedom to one's own is a denial of freedom itself. Unlike Sartre, Murdoch saw the claims of freedom and love as identical." Murdoch stated in the *Chicago Review* that "love is the perception of individuals . . . the extremely difficult realisation that something other than oneself is real," and that only when one is capable of love is one free.

One of the major themes in Murdoch's fiction is how best to respect the "reality" of others—how best to live "morally." Together with questions of "love" and "freedom," it is her major concern. Murdoch's "pervasive theme has been the quest for a passion beyond any center of self," explained *New York Times Book Review* critic David Bromwich. "What her characters seek may go by the name of Love or God or the Good: mere physical love is the perilous and always tempting idol that can become destroyer." "The basic idea," said Joyce Carol Oates in the *New Republic,* "seems to be that centuries of humanism have nourished an unrealistic conception of the powers of the will: we have gradually lost the vision of a reality separate from ourselves. . . . Twentieth-century obsessions with the authority of the individual, the 'existential' significance of subjectivity, are surely misguided, for the individual cannot be (as he thinks of himself, proudly) a detached observer, free to invent or reimagine his life." The consequences of trying to do so are repeatedly explored in Murdoch's fiction, beginning with her first published novel, *Under the Net.*

Based on Austrian philosopher Ludwig Wittgenstein's idea that we each build our own "net" or system for structuring our lives, *Under the Net* describes the wanderings of Jake Donaghue as he attempts to structure his. However, "planned ways of life are . . . traps," observed James Gindin in *Postwar British Fiction,* "no matter how carefully or rationally the net is woven, and Jake discovers that none of these narrow paths really works." Only after a series of comic misadventures (which change his attitude rather than his circumstances) is Jake able to accept the contingencies of life and the reality of other people. He throws off the net, an act that takes great courage, in Kmetz's opinion, "for nothing is more terrifying than freedom." *Under the Net* attracted much critical praise; Davie and Crutchley noted that with just one novel to her credit, Murdoch became one of the outstanding English writers of her generation.

Though situations vary from book to book, the protagonists in Murdoch's novels generally fashion a "net" of some kind. It may consist of a set of community mores or a societal role. For Hilary Burde, protagonist of *A Word Child,* the net is a fixed routine. An unloved child born out of wedlock, Hilary becomes a violent juvenile delinquent. When he is befriended by a teacher, he learns that he possesses a remarkable skill with words.

In the rigid structure of grammar he seeks shelter from life's randomness. He wins a scholarship to Oxford and begins what should be a successful career. However, as *New York Times Book Review* critic Bromwich explained, "The structure of things can bear only so much ordering: his university job ends disastrously with an adulterous love affair that is indirectly responsible for two deaths." Twenty years later, Gunnar—the husband of Hilary's former lover—appears in the government office where Hilary holds a menial job. "The novel's subject," related Lynne Sharon Schwartz in the *Nation,* "is what Hilary will do about his humiliation, his tormenting guilt and his need for forgiveness."

What he does, according to Schwartz, is the worst possible thing: "He attempts to order his friends and his days into the kind of strict system he loves in grammar. This rigid life is not only penance but protection as well, against chaos, empty time, and the unpredictable impulses of the self. The novel shows the breakdown of the system: people turn up on unexpected days, they refuse—sometimes comically—to act the roles assigned them, and Hilary's dangerous impulses do come forth and insist on playing themselves out." The tragedy of Hilary's early days is repeated. He falls in love with Gunnar's second wife; they meet in secret and are discovered. Once more, by accident, Hilary commits his original crime.

"At the novel's conclusion," wrote *Saturday Review*'s Bruce Allen, "we must consider which is the illusion: the optimist's belief that we can atone for our crimes and outlive them or the nihilist's certainty (Hilary expresses it) that people are doomed, despite their good intentions, to whirl eternally in a muddle of 'penitence, remorse, resentment, violence, and hate.'" David Bromwich interpreted the moral issue somewhat differently. "Hilary, the artist-figure without an art," he said, "wants to make the world (word) conform to his every design, and is being guided to the awareness that its resistance to him is a lucky thing. . . . Hilary must consent at last to the arbitrariness of an order imposed on him." Learning to accept the chaos of life without the aid of patterns or categories is a constant struggle for Murdoch's characters.

"I believe we live in a fantasy world, a world of illusion. And the great task in life is to find reality," Murdoch once told Rachel Billington in a London *Times* interview. However, the creation of art, she noted to *Publishers Weekly,* should be the novelist's goal. "I don't think a novel should be a committed statement of political and social criticism," she said. "They should aim at being beautiful. . . . Art holds a mirror to nature, and I think it's a very difficult thing to do." The way Murdoch mirrors nature is by creating what she called "real characters." According to Berthoff in *Fictions and Events,* these are "personages who will be 'more than puppets' and at the same time other than oneself." When asked why these characters are usually male, Murdoch once said she had no difficulty in imagining men; while concerned about women's struggle for equality, she did not want to make it a theme of her fiction, and she tended to identify with her male protagonists.

Linda Kuehl, writing in *Modern Fiction Studies,* thought Murdoch had failed in her attempt to create these "real characters." Her propensity for nineteenth-century characters produces many "types" that populate her novels, and "in each successive novel there emerges a pattern of predictable and predetermined types," the critic observed. "These include the enchanter or enchantress—occult, godly, foreign, ancient—who is torn between exhibitionism and introspection, egoism and generosity, cruelty and pity; the observer, trapped between love and fear of the enchanter, who thinks in terms of ghosts, spells, demons and destiny, and imparts an obfuscated view of life; and the accomplice, a peculiar mixture of diabolical intention and bemused charm, who has dealings with the enchanters and power over the observers," Kuehl added. "Though she produces many people," Kuehl continued, "each is tightly controlled in a superimposed design, each is rigidly cast in a classical Murdochian role."

Lawrence Graver, writing in the *New York Times Book Review,* expressed a similar view: "In practice, the more she [talks] about freedom and opaqueness the more over-determined and transparent her novels [seem] to become. . . . Despite the inventiveness of the situations and the brilliance of the design, Miss Murdoch's philosophy has recently seemed to do little more than make her people *theoretically* interesting." Oates mentioned this as well in her *New Republic* article, saying Murdoch's novels are "structures in which ideas, not things, and certainly not human beings flourish." In *The Novel Now: A Guide to Contemporary Fiction,* Anthony Burgess compared Murdoch to a puppeteer who exerts complete control: Murdoch's "characters dress, talk, act like ourselves, but they are caught up in a purely intellectual pattern, a sort of contrived sexual dance in which partners are always changing. They seem to be incapable of free choice."

The Message to the Planet, Murdoch's twenty-fourth novel, published in 1989, contains many of her familiar themes and conflicts. Protagonist Marcus Vallar is a somewhat sinister mathematics genius-turned-philosopher, a man of "'pure thought' who pushes his ideas to the point where they might actually kill him through their sheer intensity," commented Anatole Broyard in the *New York Times Book Review.* A dying man believes Vallar has cursed him. The man sends his friend, Alfred Ludens, in search of Vallar, hoping that Vallar will be able to cure him. Miraculously, Vallar does cure the man, and Ludens is so impressed that he becomes Vallar's disciple. The book's other plot involves Ludens's friend Franca. In her quest for perfect love, Franca tolerates her husband's infidelities while she nurses the dying man. After he recovers, she must deal with her husband's affairs, and eventually she consents to letting one of his lovers move in with them.

Though these creatures of an educated middle class live in a society that Toronto *Globe and Mail* reviewer Phyllis Gottlieb called "hermetic," they "struggle vividly and convincingly to escape the chaos beneath their frail lives," Gottlieb continued. In a *Village Voice* review, Henry Louis Gates, Jr. remarked of *The Message to the Planet,* "The nature of discipleship is a subject Murdoch has made her own, perhaps because it is the most compelling version of one of her great subjects—the character who desperately pursues his fantasy of someone else." Christopher Lehmann-Haupt in the *New York Times* voiced a common perception of Murdoch's writing by stating that the author's "characters are paper thin and as contrived as origami decorations." Despite this, Lehmann-Haupt said, "they burn with such moral passion that we watch them with the utmost fascination." The reviewer also noted that Murdoch's message is "predictably" that "humans are accidental beings with only love to make life bearable in a random universe."

With *Metaphysics as a Guide to Morals,* Murdoch turns to a nonfiction presentation of her philosophical views. *Commonweal* contributor Diogenes Allen characterized the philosophical position presented in the book as consistent with Murdoch's previous writings, "summarized as an update of Plato's allegory of the cave" and asserting the immanence of "the Good." Focusing predominantly on morality, Murdoch recommends that the Christian conception of God be replaced with a neo-Platonic conception of the Good. "Now she applies to her position the expressions 'neo-Christianity' and 'modern Christianity,'" commented Allen. *Metaphysics as a Guide to Morals* brought some negative responses from philosophers; Simon Blackburn, for instance, faulted Murdoch's advocacy of "salvation through Platonized religion" in his review in the *Times Literary Supplement.* Alasdair MacIntyre, however, writing in the *New York Times Book Review,* noted potential critical disagreements with Murdoch's position but remarked that "it is important not to allow such disagreements to distract attention from what is to be learned from this book, both from its central theses and from an impressive range of topics . . . among them the relationship of artistic to moral experience, the relevance of deconstructive arguments and the nature of political morality."

Murdoch was indeed "a philosopher of note," observed John Bemrose, assessing Murdoch's career in *Maclean's,* but he added that "there was no real division" between her fiction and nonfiction work because "her novels are always concerned with the complex interplay of good and evil." Similarly, Jason Cowley maintained in the *New Statesman* that Murdoch's "best novels are intricate moral parables, mini-quests on which her always educated creations embark to answer the question posed by Michael in *The Bell:* 'What is the requirement of the good life?' A moral philosopher, Murdoch was genuinely troubled by this question, and she worried away at it, returning again and again to it, as she sought to refine and animate a secular morality."

Discussing Murdoch's later work, Cowley noted that, "As she grew older, her novels, particularly the sequence of five beginning with *The Philosopher's Pupil* (1983) and ending in *The Green Knight,* became longer, more opaque and mannered: a great continuous symphony, with each work an instrument complementing and commenting on the one that went before." In 1993's *The Green Knight,* Murdoch tries her hand at retelling the powerful tale of Sir Gawain and his unkillable foe, the Green Knight. In the original story, the Green Knight challenges any of King Arthur's knights to chop off his head; Sir Gawain obliges, but the beheaded Green Knight does not die. In Murdoch's tale, the role of Sir Gawain is played by Lucas Graffe, an historian who plots the murder of his brother, Clement. Before he can bludgeon his brother, though, a stranger—possibly a mugger—steps in and takes the blow. Months later, the stranger, Peter Mir, returns, seeking justice from Lucas. "What an outline of the plot . . . fails to convey is the warmth and humour of this book, and the sheer narrative verve," wrote A.N. Wilson in the *Spectator.* "It is hard to put down."

"Reading [Murdoch's] work is like watching an expert needlewoman embroider, with fine silk thread and a dazzling array of stitches, a large, intricate, multicolored piece of fancywork," commented *New York Times Book Review* contributor Linda Simon. "But as the design becomes more complicated and the patterns more repetitious, one senses that the embroiderer may realize more pleasure than the viewer." Tom Shippey, writing in the *Times Literary Supplement,* also found problems with *The Green Knight*—in particular, a lack of plausibility. "It is not a poor grip on reality which strikes one first on reading this novel," he remarked, "rather, its poor grip on *practicality.*" *New Statesman* contributor Kathryn Hughes, however, thought the novel "a thoroughly good suspense" story.

Reviewing Murdoch's 1995 novel, *Jackson's Dilemma,* in the *Spectator,* Caroline Moore made the case that Murdoch's detractors are members of what the author once termed the "journalistic" (or realistic) school of modern fiction, which rejects elements of the romance tradition from which much of Murdoch's fiction is derived. Murdoch's "novels often adapt romantic genres—the love-comedy, the gothic tale," explained Moore. "And they are also romantic in subject and spirit." The premise of *Jackson's Dilemma* is the disaster, mystery, and comedy surrounding the sudden disappearance of Edward Lannion's bride-to-be on the eve of their wedding day. While Lorna Sage, writing in the *Times Literary Supplement,* praised the work as "hilarious and horrible—a mystic farce," Michiko Kakutani in the *New York Times* expressed disappointment with its "highly convoluted plot filled with improbable coincidences and disasters, and a glossy veneer of mythic allusions and philosophical asides."

Something Special, a short story written in the 1950s but not published in full until after Murdoch's death, is a romance between two impoverished young Dubliners and one of the few Murdoch stories that is set in her native Ireland. Yvonne Geary, who works as a sales clerk and lives with her mother and uncle, longs for excitement in her life, but is less than thrilled about Sam Goldman's enthusiastic courtship of her; she finds him rather ordinary, lacking the "something special" she is seeking, but by the end of the story she comes to realize what he has to offer. The story "can be subtle and heartfelt," related Stephen Amidon in the *New York Times Book Review,* but he thought the character of Yvonne underdeveloped and added that "it is hard to see what makes this brief tale special enough to merit a volume of its own." A *Kirkus Reviews* contributor described it as showing Murdoch's style "in embryonic form" but maintained that it "won't add anything to the deservedly high reputation" of the author. *Booklist*'s Donna Seaman, however, praised the story as "standing firmly on its own in spite of its brevity" and "finely nuanced" in its depiction of the characters' tribulations, with the author "at her subtle best." A *Publishers Weekly* reviewer, noting the story's mix of humor and tenderness, called *Something Special* "stunningly affecting."

Murdoch lived for many years in the English countryside and later in the city of Oxford with her husband, John Bayley, a respected literary critic, and she enjoyed gardening when she was not writing. She paid little attention to reviews of her work, even those that were favorable, believing most critiques to be lacking in perception. Her writing was deliberate and well thought out, with a plan of each novel in place before she began writing, which she did in longhand. "I don't see how anyone can think with a typewriter," she once remarked to Davie and Crutchley. Her later novels averaged more than 500 pages each, a length Murdoch insisted was necessary because it enabled them to encompass "more substance, more thoughts," as she once explained to a London *Times* interviewer. The London *Times* also reported that "her enemies are word processors . . . tight, crystalline, first-person novels, existentialism, and analytical philosophy."

Murdoch's work won praise from many scholars and critics over the course of her career. "She wears her formidable intelligence with a careless swagger," Jonathan Raban wrote in *Encounter,* "and her astonishingly fecund, playful imagination looks as fresh and effortless as ever. . . . Part of the joy of reading Iris Murdoch is the implicit assurance that there will be more to come, that the book in hand is an installment in a continuing work which grows more and more important as each new novel is added to it." Added Broyard: "We have to keep revising our expectations of what her books are about—usually we find that we must travel farther and over more difficult terrain than we're accustomed to."

In 1995 Murdoch announced that she was suffering from severe writer's block, an admission that was later altered in 1996 when Bayley informed the London *Daily Telegraph* that she in fact was a victim of Alzheimer's disease. Realizing that her writer's block was attributable to biological forces beyond her control, Murdoch commented, "I'm afraid I am waiting in vain [to write]. Perhaps I had better find some other kind of job." Bradbury remarked in his remembrance for *Time:* "It was a tragic misfortune that, in recent years, this most intellectual of novelists was silenced by Alzheimer's," observing that Murdoch had "one of the most brilliant and engaging of modern minds." He concluded, "The important thing is to return to the moral clarity of that mind" and to her best novels, "for, in a day when fiction has grown more commercial, sensational and morally empty, it is a joy to return to her work—with its sensuous pleasures, fantastic invention, high intelligence and moral dignity."

BIOGRAPHICAL AND CRITICAL SOURCES:

BOOKS

Antonaccio, Maria, and William Schweiker, editors, *Iris Murdoch and the Search for Human Goodness,* University of Chicago Press (Chicago, IL), 1996.

Baldanza, Frank, *Iris Murdoch,* Twayne (New York, NY), 1974.

Bayley, John, *Elegy for Iris,* St. Martin's Press (New York, NY), 1998.

Bayley, John, *Iris and Her Friends: A Memoir of Memory and Desire,* W.W. Norton (New York, NY), 1999.

Berthoff, Warner, *Fictions and Events: Essays in Criticism and Literary History,* Dutton (New York, NY), 1971.

Bradbury, Malcolm, *Possibilities: Essays on the State of the Novel,* Oxford University Press (New York, NY), 1973.

Bradbury, Malcolm, and David Palmer, *The Contemporary English Novel,* Edward Arnold (London, England), 1979, Holmes & Meier (New York, NY), 1980.

Burgess, Anthony, *The Novel Now: A Guide to Contemporary Fiction,* W.W. Norton (New York, NY), 1967.

Byatt, A. S., *Degrees of Freedom: The Novels of Iris Murdoch,* Barnes & Noble (New York, NY), 1965.

Concise Dictionary of British Literary Biography, Volume 8, Thomson Gale (Detroit, MI), 1992.

Conradi, Peter J., *Iris Murdoch: A Life,* Norton (New York, NY), 2001.

Contemporary Literary Criticism, Thomson Gale (Detroit, MI), Volume 1, 1973, Volume 2, 1974, Volume 3, 1975, Volume 4, 1975, Volume 6, 1976, Volume 8, 1978, Volume 11, 1979, Volume 15, 1980, Volume 22, 1982, Volume 31, 1985, Volume 51, 1989.

Dictionary of Literary Biography, Volume 14: *British Novelists since 1960,* Thomson Gale (Detroit, MI), 1982.

Dipple, Elizabeth, *Iris Murdoch: Work for the Spirit,* University of Chicago Press (Chicago, IL), 1982.

Dooley, Gillian, editor, *From a Tiny Corner in the House of Fiction: Conversations with Iris Murdoch,* University of South Carolina Press (Columbia, SC), 2003.

Fletcher, John, *Iris Murdoch: A Descriptive Primary and Annotated Secondary Bibliography,* Garland (New York, NY), 1985.

Gerstenberger, Donna, *Iris Murdoch,* Bucknell University Press (Lewisburg, PA), 1975.

Gindin, James, *Postwar British Fiction,* University of California Press (Berkeley, CA), 1962.

Gordon, David J., *Iris Murdoch's Fables of Unselfing,* University of Missouri Press (Columbia, MO), 1995.

Heusel, Barbara Stevens, *Patterned Aimlessness: Iris Murdoch's Novels of the 1970s and 1980s,* University of Georgia Press (Athens, GA), 1995.

Kellman, Steven G., *The Self-begetting Novel,* Columbia University Press (New York, NY), 1980.

Kermode, Frank, *Modern Essays,* Fontana (London, England), 1971, pp. 261-266.

O'Connor, Patricia J., *To Love the Good: The Moral Philosophy of Iris Murdoch,* P. Lang (New York, NY), 1996.

O'Connor, William Van, *The New University Wits, and the End of Modernism,* Southern Illinois University Press (Carbondale, IL), 1963.

Rabinowitz, Rubin, *Iris Murdoch,* Columbia University Press (New York, NY), 1968.

Spear, Hilda D., *Iris Murdoch,* St. Martin's Press (New York, NY), 1995.

Stade, George, editor, *Six Contemporary British Novelists,* Columbia University Press (New York, NY), 1976.

Thinkers of the Twentieth Century, St. James Press (Chicago, IL), 1987.

Todd, Richard, *Iris Murdoch: The Shakespearean Interest,* Barnes & Noble (New York, NY), 1979.

Todd, Richard, *Iris Murdoch,* Methuen (New York, NY), 1984.

Wolff, Peter, *The Disciplined Heart: Iris Murdoch and Her Novels,* University of Missouri Press (Columbia, MO), 1966.

PERIODICALS

American Scholar, summer, 1993, p. 466.

Atlantic, March, 1988, p. 100; March, 1990, p. 116; March, 1994, p. 130.

Booklist, January 1, 1998, Donna Seaman, review of *Existentialists and Mystics: Writings on Philosophy and Literature,* p. 766; November 15, 2000, Donna Seaman, review of *Something Special,* p. 25.

Chicago Review, autumn, 1959.

Commonweal, November 5, 1953; May 18, 1990, p. 326; June 14, 1991, p. 399; April 23, 1993, p. 24; April 8, 1994, p. 21.

Economist, October 24, 1987, p. 107; October 14, 1989, p. 104; September 25, 1993, p. 99.

Encounter, July, 1974.

Globe and Mail (Toronto, Ontario, Canada), October 28, 1989, Phyllis Gottlieb, review of *The Message to the Planet.*

Interview, November, 1992, p. 80.
Kirkus Reviews, October 1, 2000, review of *Something Special,* pp. 1380-1381.
Listener, April 27, 1978, pp. 533-535.
Modern Fiction Studies (Iris Murdoch issue), autumn, 1959.
Ms., July, 1976, Gail Kmetz, review of *Sartre: Romantic Rationalist.*
Nation, March 29, 1975; October 11, 1975; January 8, 1996, p. 32.
National Review, April 1, 1988, p. 52.
New Criterion, November, 1999, Jeffrey Meyers, "Iris Murdoch: A Memoir," p. 22.
New Leader, April 16, 1990, p. 19.
New Republic, November 18, 1978; June 6, 1988, p. 40; March 5, 1990, p. 40.
New Statesman, January 2, 1954; January 8, 1988, p. 33; September 17, 1993, pp. 39-40.
New Statesman & Society, October 6, 1989, p. 38.
New Yorker, May 18, 1987, p. 113.
New York Review of Books, March 31, 1988, p. 36; March 4, 1993, p. 3.
New York Times, January 6, 1981; February 22, 1990; January 9, 1996, Michiko Kakutani, "A Broken Engagement As Tragic Metaphor," p. 24.
New York Times Book Review, September 13, 1964; February 8, 1970; August 24, 1975; November 20, 1977; December 17, 1978; August 10, 1980; January 4, 1981; March 7, 1982; January 4, 1987, p. 107; January 31, 1988, pp. 1, 26; February 4, 1990, p. 3; January 3, 1993, p. 9; January 9, 1994, p. 7; January 7, 1996, Brad Leithauser, "The Good Servant," p. 6; November 12, 2000, Stephen Amidon, review of *Something Special.*
Observer (London, England), October 25, 1992.
Publishers Weekly, December 13, 1976; November 1, 1993, p. 64; October 23, 1995, p. 57; September 25, 2000, review of *Something Special,* p. 83; November 13, 2000, Bridget Kinsella, "Tribute to a Writer and to Love," p. 25.
Saturday Review, October 5, 1974, Bruce Allen, review of *A Word Child.*
Spectator, September 18, 1993, p. 42; October 7, 1995, Caroline Moore, review of *Jackson's Dilemma.*
Times (London, England), April 25, 1983; January 23, 1988.
Times Literary Supplement, October 23, 1992; September 10, 1993, p. 20; September 29, 1995.
Village Voice, July 17, 1990, p. 73.
Yale Review, April, 1992, p. 207.

OTHER

Iris (film; based on husband John Bayley's biographies), 2001.

OBITUARIES:

PERIODICALS

Maclean's, February 22, 1999, John Bemrose, "Ever Extraordinary: Writer Iris Murdoch Was Admired Worldwide," p. 71.
New Statesman, February 12, 1999, Jason Cowley, "A Divine Literary Intelligence," p. 15.
Time, February 22, 1999, Malcolm Bradbury, "All Kinds of Goodness: Iris Murdoch, 1919-1999," p. 63.

* * *

MURDOCH, Jean Iris
See MURDOCH, Iris

* * *

MURRAY, Albert L. 1916-

PERSONAL: Born June 12, 1916, in Nokomis, AL; son of John Lee and Sudie (Graham) Young; married Mozelle Menefee, May 31, 1941; children: Michele. *Ethnicity:* "Black." *Education:* Tuskegee Institute, B.S., 1939; New York University, M.A., 1948; postgraduate work at University of Michigan, 1940, Northwestern University, 1941, and University of Paris, 1950. *Hobbies and other interests:* Recordings, photography, cookbooks, and gourmet cooking.

ADDRESSES: Home and office—45 West 132nd St., New York, NY 10037.

CAREER: U.S. Air Force, 1943-62, retired as major. Instructor, Tuskegee Institute, 1940-43, 1946-51, director of College Little Theatre; lecturer, Graduate School of Journalism, Columbia University, 1968; Colgate University, O'Connor Professor of Literature, 1970, O'Connor Lecturer, 1973, professor of humanities, 1982; visiting professor of literature, University of Massachusetts, Boston, 1971; Paul Anthony Brick lecturer, University of Missouri, 1972; writer in residence, Emory University, 1978; adjunct associate professor of creative writing, Barnard College, 1981-83; Woodrow Wilson fellow, Drew University, 1983; lecturer and participant in symposia.

MEMBER: International PEN, Authors League of America, Authors Guild, Alpha Phi Alpha.

AWARDS, HONORS: Lillian Smith Award for fiction, 1974, for *Train Whistle Guitar;* Litt.D., Colgate University, 1975; Deems Taylor Award, ASCAP, for music criticism, 1976, for *Stomping the Blues;* Lincoln Center Directors Emeriti Award, 1991.

WRITINGS:

NONFICTION

The Omni-Americans: New Perspectives on Black Experience and American Culture (essays), Outerbridge & Dientsfrey, 1970, published as *The Omni-Americans: Some Alternatives to the Folklore of White Supremacy,* Vintage Book (St. Paul, MN), 1983.
South to a Very Old Place, McGraw (New York, NY), 1972.
The Hero and the Blues, University of Missouri Press (Columbia, MO), 1973.
Stomping the Blues, McGraw (New York, NY), 1976.
(With Count Basie) *Good Morning Blues: The Autobiography of Count Basie,* Random House (New York, NY), 1985.
The Blue Devils of Nada, Pantheon (New York, NY), 1996.
(Editor, with John F. Callahan) *Trading Twelves: The Selected Letters of Ralph Ellison and Albert Murray,* Modern Library (New York, NY), 2000.

NOVELS

Train Whistle Guitar, McGraw (New York, NY), 1974.
The Spyglass Tree, Pantheon (New York, NY), 1991.
The Seven League Boots, Pantheon (New York, NY), 1996.
The Magic Keys, Pantheon (New York, NY), 2005.

SIDELIGHTS: Albert L. Murray's "mythic novels and fresh, discerning artistic and cultural criticism are sheer pleasure to read," states *Booklist* critic Donna Seaman, "but they provide more than a good time: they have helped define the essence of the African American aesthetic." Murray, a retired Air Force major, first gained recognition for his essay collection *The Omni-Americans: New Perspectives on Black Experience and American Culture.* In this book, he argues that black Americans have a distinctive identity of their own, developing a unique culture "which allows them to see themselves 'not as the substandard, abnormal *non-white* people of American social science surveys and the news media, but rather as if they were, so to speak, fundamental *extensions* of contemporary possibilities,'" says *Dictionary of Literary Biography* contributor Elizabeth Schultz. "Like jam session musicians and blues singers, they have learned the skills of improvisation, not only translating white models of excellence into their own terms, but also transforming degrading conditions into culture." Schultz declares that the "abiding concern of [Murray's] writing is the triumph of Afro-American people, who, despite and, indeed, in Murray's view, because of centuries of difficulties, created a courageous, complex, life-sustaining, and life-enhancing culture—apparent in their language, religion, sports, fashions, food, dance, and above all in their music."

Murray has infuriated some people with his unqualified rejection of black nationalism and his preference for terms such as "colored" and "Negro." The writer has repeatedly noted that his skin is brown, not black, and that he knows few people whose skin is truly "white" or "black." Focusing on skin tone only exacerbates prejudice because of it, he believes. In a *Nation* essay, Gene Seymour reports that *The Omni-Americans* "challenged readers to do the hard, honest, necessary work of accepting this complexity. In doing so, the book scolded and ridiculed an assortment of sociologist, ideologues and pundits of all political persuasions who let Marx or Freud frame their views of racial matters."

Murray expresses an interest in blues and jazz in other works, especially in *The Hero and the Blues* and *Stomping the Blues,* which is an attempt to redefine "the music and its connotations for American culture," according to Jason Berry of the *Nation.* S.M. Fry, writing in the *Library Journal,* points out that Murray "views the music not as a primitive musical expression of black suffering but as an antidote to the bad times." Murray, the reviewer says, also emphasizes the importance of the performance, "the performing style and the music itself over the lyrics and social or political connotations." These books have made Murray "one of the foremost literary interpreters of blues, jazz and improvisation," states Brent Staples in the *New York Times Book Review.*

Murray's trilogy of novels—*Train Whistle Guitar, The Spyglass Tree,* and *The Seven League Boots*—are autobiographical in tone. Like the author, their protagonist Scooter grows up in the deep South—fishing and hunting in the bayous, listening to spirituals and blues and folktales. Yet according to Richard M. Ready in *South Atlantic Quarterly, Train Whistle Guitar* is more than a coming-of-age tale; it also reveals the ideas behind

Murray's nonfiction work, because it "works out through a series of improvisatory episodes Murray's commitment to the aesthetic, stylizing dimension of life as a key to the complicated business of making a life for oneself."

Reviewing *The Spyglass Tree,* Charles Monaghan asks in *Washington Post Book World,* "Is Albert Murray America's best black writer? There is certainly a case to be made for it, and his second novel, *The Spyglass Tree* only makes the case stronger." The book followed Scooter from his Alabama home town to college at an unnamed university obviously based on the Tuskegee Institute. Monaghan praises the "nitty-gritty of the book, the marvelous set pieces, . . . Murray's swooping, swerving prose" that add up to "amazing word music."

Murray provided more "invigorating interpretations of music, visual art, and literature dearest to his heart" in the essay collection *The Blue Devils of Nada,* Seaman writes in *Booklist.* A *Publishers Weekly* reviewer calls the contents a set of "elegantly learned essays" that illuminate the theme of "the effort of the engaged artist to document and give shape to the rootlessness and chaos underlying contemporary life in general. . . . Murray writes with passion for, and deep knowledge of, his blues masters."

Murray continued the story of Scooter with *The Seven League Boots,* in which his alter ego becomes a top jazz bassist. It is "Murray's most ambitious novel," in Seaman's opinion, that "affirms Scooter's status as a classical hero. . . . Scooter's story is infused with the elegant energy of jazz, the sonority of history, and the spirituality of art." *Newsweek* critic Malcolm Jones, Jr. calls *The Seven League Boots* "Murray's most singular achievement." Jones notes that Murray gives his protagonist "a splendid career, a movie-star girlfriend and success at every turn. Scooter's problem is that things come to him too easily. Being talented, Murray teaches us, isn't hard. The tough part is living up to what people expect of you and figuring out what to expect of yourself."

BIOGRAPHICAL AND CRITICAL SOURCES:

BOOKS

Bruck, Peter, and Wolfgang Karrer, editors, *The Afro-American Novel since 1960,* B.R. Gruner Publishing (Amsterdam), 1982.

Contemporary Literary Criticism, Volume 73, Thomson Gale (Detroit, MI), 1993.

Dictionary of Literary Biography, Volume 38: *Afro-American Writers after 1955: Dramatists and Prose Writers,* Thomson Gale (Detroit, MI), 1985.

PERIODICALS

American Heritage, September, 1996, p. 68.

American Poetry Review, July-August, 1978, pp. 42-45.

Atlantic Monthly, December, 1974, pp. 118, 120-123.

Black American Literature Forum, fall, 1991, pp. 449-523.

Booklist, February 15, 1996, p. 980; November 1, 1997, p. 448.

Bulletin of Research in the Humanities, summer, 1983, pp. 140-161.

Down Beat, October 20, 1977, pp. 51-52.

Entertainment Weekly, March 8, 1996, p. 60.

Library Journal, February 1, 1977.

Los Angeles Times Book Review, March 26, 1986.

Nation, January 15, 1977; pp. 55-57; March 25, 1996, p. 25.

Newsweek, March 23, 1970, p. 106; January 31, 1972; December 20, 1976; December 9, 1991, p. 71; February 5, 1996, p. 60.

New Yorker, October 17, 1970, pp. 185-186, 189; January 8, 1972; July 22, 1974; April 8, 1996, p. 70.

New York Review of Books, February 24, 1972; June 13, 1974, pp. 37-39; January 16, 1986.

New York Times, April 4, 1972; December 11, 1976; November 22, 1991, p. C29.

New York Times Book Review, May 3, 1970, pp. 6, 34; January 2, 1972; June 4, 1972; December 3, 1972; May 12, 1974, p. 7; December 1, 1974; December 26, 1976; December 26, 1982; February 2, 1986; March 10, 1996, p. 4.

Publishers Weekly, December 18, 1995, pp. 35, 39; February 26, 1996, p. 78.

Rolling Stone, January 13, 1977.

Saturday Review, January 22, 1972, p. 72; May 4, 1974, p. 51.

South Atlantic Quarterly, summer, 1986, pp. 270-282.

Time, January 10, 1972; March 10, 1986.

Times Literary Supplement, July 28, 1978; July 11, 1986.

Tribune Books (Chicago, IL), January 19, 1986.

Voice Literary Supplement, February, 1982.

Washington Post Book World, March 22, 1970; December 26, 1971, p. 11; December 8, 1974; January 8, 1986; November 3, 1991, pp. 7, 11.

MYERS, Walter Dean 1937-
(Walter M. Myers)

PERSONAL: Born Walter Milton Myers, August 12, 1937, in Martinsburg, WV; son of George Ambrose and Mary (Green) Myers; raised by Herbert Julius (a shipping clerk) and Florence (a factory worker) Dean; married second wife, Constance Brendel, June 19, 1973; children: (first marriage) Karen, Michael Dean; (second marriage) Christopher. *Education:* Attended State College of the City University of New York; Empire State College, earned B.A.

ADDRESSES: *Home*—2543 Kennedy Blvd., Jersey City, NJ 07304. *Agent*—c/o Author Mail, HarperCollins Children's Books, 1350 Avenue of the Americas, New York, NY 10019.

CAREER: New York State Department of Labor, Brooklyn, NY, employment supervisor, 1966-69; Bobbs-Merrill Co., Inc. (publisher), New York, NY, senior trade book editor, 1970-77; writer, 1977—. Instructor in creative writing and black history, 1974-75. *Military service:* U.S. Army, 1954-57.

MEMBER: PEN, Harlem Writers Guild.

AWARDS, HONORS: Council on Interracial Books for Children Award, 1968, for *Where Does the Day Go?;* Book of the Year designations, Child Study Association of America, 1972, for *The Dancers,* and 1987, for *Adventure in Granada;* American Library Association (ALA) Notable Children's Books list, 1975, for *Fast Sam, Cool Clyde, and Stuff,* 1978, for *It Ain't All for Nothin',* 1979, for *The Young Landlords,* 1981, for *Legend of Tarik,* 1982, for *Hoops,* 1988, for *Me, Mop, and the Moondance Kid* and *Scorpions,* and 1993, for *Somewhere in the Darkness;* book award from Woodward Park School, 1976, for *Fast Sam, Cool Clyde, and Stuff;* ALA Best Books for Young Adults list, 1978, for *It Ain't All for Nothin',* 1979, for *The Young Landlords,* 1981, for *The Legend of Tarik,* 1982, for *Hoops,* 1988, for *Fallen Angels* and *Scorpion,* 1992, for *Now Is Your Time!: The African-American Struggle for Freedom,* 1993, for *Somewhere in the Darkness,* and 1998, for *Harlem;* Coretta Scott King awards, 1980, for *The Young Landlords,* 1985, for *Motown and Didi: A Love Story;* 1989, for *Fallen Angels,* 1992, for *Now is Your Time!,* 1993, for *Somewhere in the Darkness,* 1994, for *Malcolm X,* 1997, for *Slam!,* and 1998, for *Harlem;* New Jersey State Council for the Arts fellowship, 1981; Notable Children's Trade Book in Social Studies citation, National Council for Social Studies and the Children's Book Council, 1982, for *The Legend of Tarik;* National Endowment for the Arts grant, 1982; Parents' Choice Foundation awards, 1982, for *Won't Know till I Get There,* 1984, for *The Outside Shot,* and 1988, for *Fallen Angels;* author's award, New Jersey Institute of Technology, 1983, for *Tales of a Dead King;* MacDowell fellowship, 1988; Newbery Honor Book designations, 1989, for *Scorpions,* and 1993, for *Somewhere in the Darkness; Boston Globe/Horn Book* award, 1992, for *Somewhere in the Darkness;* ALAN award, 1994; Margaret A. Edwards Award, ALA Young Adult Library Services Association, 1994, for *Hoops, Motown and Didi, Fallen Angels,* and *Scorpion;* Caldecott Honor Book, 1998, for *Harlem;* first annual Virginia Hamilton Literary Award, 1999; first Michael L. Printz Award, 2000, for *Monster; Boston Globe-Horn Book* Award nominee in picture book category, 2003, for *blues journey.*

WRITINGS:

JUVENILE FICTION

(Under name Walter M. Myers) *Where Does the Day Go?,* illustrated by Leo Carty, Parents' Magazine Press (New York, NY), 1969.

The Dragon Takes a Wife, illustrated by Ann Grifalconi, Bobbs-Merrill (Indianapolis, IN), 1972, illustrated by Fiona French, Scholastic (New York, NY), 1995.

The Dancers, illustrated by Anne Rockwell, Parents' Magazine Press (New York, NY), 1972.

Fly, Jimmy, Fly!, illustrated by Moneta Barnett, Putnam (New York, NY), 1974.

The Story of the Three Kingdoms, illustrated by Ashley Bryan, HarperCollins (New York, NY), 1995.

How Mr. Monkey Saw the Whole World, illustrated by Synthia Saint James, Doubleday (New York, NY), 1996.

The Blues of Flats Brown, illustrated by Nina Laden, Holiday House (New York, NY), 2000.

YOUNG ADULT FICTION

Fast Sam, Cool Clyde, and Stuff, Viking Press (New York, NY), 1975.

Brainstorm, photographs by Chuck Freedman, F. Watts (New York, NY), 1977.

Mojo and the Russians, Viking Press (New York, NY), 1977.

Victory for Jamie, illustrated by Norm Walker, Scholastic (New York, NY), 1977.
It Ain't All for Nothin', Viking Press (New York, NY), 1978.
The Young Landlords, Viking Press (New York, NY), 1979.
The Black Pearl and the Ghost; or, One Mystery after Another, illustrated by Robert Quackenbush, Viking Press (New York, NY), 1980.
The Golden Serpent, illustrated by Alice Provensen and Martin Provensen, Viking Press (New York, NY), 1980.
Hoops, Delacorte Press (New York, NY), 1981.
The Legend of Tarik, Viking Press (New York, NY), 1981.
Won't Know till I Get There, Viking Press (New York, NY), 1982.
The Nicholas Factor, Viking Press (New York, NY), 1983.
Tales of a Dead King, Morrow (New York, NY), 1983.
Mr. Monkey and the Gotcha Bird, illustrated by Leslie Morrill, Delacorte Press (New York, NY), 1984.
Motown and Didi: A Love Story, Viking Kestrel (New York, NY), 1984.
The Outside Shot, Delacorte Press (New York, NY), 1984.
Adventure in Granada ("Arrow" series), Viking Kestrel (New York, NY), 1985.
The Hidden Shrine ("Arrow" series), Viking Kestrel (New York, NY), 1985.
Duel in the Desert ("Arrow" series), Viking Kestrel (New York, NY), 1986.
Ambush in the Amazon ("Arrow" series), Penguin (New York, NY), 1986.
Sweet Illusions, Teachers & Writers Collaborative (New York, NY), 1987.
Crystal, Viking Kestrel (New York, NY), 1987, reprinted, 2002.
Shadow of the Red Moon, HarperCollins (New York, NY), 1987.
Fallen Angels, Scholastic (New York, NY), 1988.
Scorpions, HarperCollins (New York, NY), 1988.
Me, Mop, and the Moondance Kid, illustrated by Rodney Pate, Delacorte Press (New York, NY), 1988.
The Mouse Rap, HarperCollins (New York, NY), 1990.
Somewhere in the Darkness, Scholastic (New York, NY), 1992.
The Righteous Revenge of Artemis Bonner, HarperCollins (New York, NY), 1992.
Mop, Moondance, and the Nagasaki Knights, Delacorte Press (New York, NY), 1992.
Darnell Rock Reporting, Delacorte Press (New York, NY), 1994.
The Glory Field, Scholastic (New York, NY), 1994.
Slam!, Scholastic (New York, NY), 1996.
Smiffy Blue: Ace Crime Detective: The Case of the Missing Ruby and Other Stories, Scholastic (New York, NY), 1996.
The Journal of Joshua Loper: A Black Cowboy ("My Name Is America" series), Scholastic (New York, NY), 1999.
The Journal of Scott Pendleton Collins: A World War II Soldier ("My Name Is America" series), Scholastic (New York, NY), 1999.
Monster, illustrated by Christopher Myers, HarperCollins (New York, NY), 1999.
145th Street: Short Stories, Delacorte Press (New York, NY), 2000.
The Journal of Biddy Owens, the Negro Leagues ("My Name Is America" series), Scholastic (New York, NY), 2001.
Patrol, illustrated by Ann Grifalconi, HarperCollins (New York, NY), 2001.
Handbook for Boys, HarperCollins (New York, NY), 2002.
Three Swords for Granada, illustrated by John Speirs, Holiday House (New York, NY), 2002.
The Dream Bearer, HarperCollins (New York, NY), 2003.
Shooter, Amistad (New York, NY), 2004.
Autobiography of My Dead Brother, illustrated by Christopher Myers, Amistad (New York, NY), 2005.
Street Love, Amistad (New York, NY), 2006.

Contributor to short-story anthologies, including *The Color of Absence: Twelve Stories about Loss,* edited by James Howe, Simon & Schuster, 2001.

YOUNG ADULT NONFICTION

The World of Work: A Guide to Choosing a Career, Bobbs-Merrill (Indianapolis, IN), 1975.
Social Welfare, F. Watts (New York, NY), 1976.
Now Is Your Time!: The African American Struggle for Freedom, HarperCollins (New York, NY), 1991.
A Place Called Heartbreak: A Story of Vietnam, illustrated by Frederick Porter, Raintree (Austin, TX), 1992.
Young Martin's Promise, Raintree (Austin, TX), 1992.
Malcolm X: By Any Means Necessary, Scholastic (New York, NY), 1993.
Remember Us Well: An Album of Pictures and Verse, HarperCollins (New York, NY), 1993.
Toussaint L'Ouverture: The Fight for Haiti's Freedom, Simon & Schuster (New York, NY), 1996.

One More River to Cross: An African-American Photograph Album, Harcourt Brace (New York, NY), 1996.

Amistad: A Long Road to Freedom, Dutton (New York, NY), 1998.

At Her Majesty's Request: An African Princess in Victorian England, Scholastic (New York, NY), 1999.

Malcolm X: A Fire Burning Brightly, illustrated by Leonard Jenkins, HarperCollins (New York, NY), 2000.

Bad Boy: A Memoir, HarperCollins (New York, NY), 2001.

The Greatest: Muhammad Ali, Scholastic (New York, NY), 2001.

A Time to Love: Tales from the Old Testament, illustrated by Christopher Myers, Scholastic (New York, NY), 2002.

I've Seen the Promised Land: The Life of Dr. Martin Luther King, Jr., Amistad (New York, NY), 2003.

Antarctica: Journeys to the South Pole, Scholastic (New York, NY), 2004.

USS Constellation, Holiday House (New York, NY), 2004.

(With William Miles) *The Harlem Hellfighters: When Pride Met Courage,* HarperCollins (New York, NY), 2006.

Jazz, illustrated by Christopher Myers, Holiday House (New York, NY), 2006.

POETRY

The Great Migration: An American Story, paintings by Jacob Lawrence, HarperCollins (New York, NY), 1993.

Brown Angels: An Album of Pictures and Verse, HarperCollins (New York, NY), 1993.

Glorious Angels: A Celebration of Children, HarperCollins (New York, NY), 1995.

Harlem: A Poem, illustrated by Christopher Myers, Scholastic (New York, NY), 1997.

Angel to Angel: A Mother's Gift of Love, HarperCollins (New York, NY), 1998.

blues journey, illustrated by Christopher Myers, Holiday House (New York, NY), 2001.

Voices from Harlem, Holiday House (New York, NY), 2004.

Here in Harlem: Poems in Many Voices, Holiday House (New York, NY), 2004.

Contributor to anthologies, including *What We Must SEE: Young Black Storytellers,* edited by Orde Coombs, Dodd, 1971, and *We Be Word Sorcerers: Twenty-five Stories by Black Americans,* edited by Sonia Sanchez, Bantam, 1973. Contributor of articles and fiction to periodicals, including *Black Creation, Black World, McCall's, Espionage, Alfred Hitchcock Mystery Magazine, Essence, Ebony Jr.!,* and *Boy's Life.*

ADAPTATIONS: The Young Landlords was filmed by Topol Productions. Books adapted as audio recordings include *Slam!,* Recorded Books, 2000; *Bad Boy: A Memoir,* Harper Children's Audio, 2001; and *Monster,* Recorded Books, 2001.

SIDELIGHTS: Walter Dean Myers is considered among the premier authors of fiction for young adults, and his books have won dozens of awards, including the prestigious Coretta Scott King Award for multiple books. As Carmen Subryan noted in the *Dictionary of Literary Biography,* "Whether he is writing about the ghettos of New York, the remote countries of Africa, or social institutions, Myers captures the essence of the developing experiences of youth."

While Myers is perhaps best known for his novels that explore the lives of young Harlem blacks, he is equally adept at producing modern fairy tales, ghost stories, and adventure sagas. Subryan found a common theme throughout Myers's far-ranging works. "He is concerned with the development of youths," she wrote, "and his message is always the same: young people must face the reality of growing up and must persevere, knowing that they can succeed despite any odds they face . . . . This positive message enables youths to discover what is important in life and to reject influences which could destroy them."

In *Interracial Books for Children Bulletin,* Myers described his priorities as an author. He tries, he said, to provide good literature for black children, "literature that includes them and the way they live" and that "celebrates their life and their person. It upholds and gives special place to their humanity." He elaborated on this point in an essay for *Something about the Author Autobiography Series* (*SAAS*): "I realized how few resources are available for Black youngsters to open the world to them. I feel the need to show them the possibilities that exist for them that were never revealed to me as a youngster; possibilities that did not even exist for me then."

One possibility Myers never foresaw as a youth was that of supporting himself as a writer. He was born into an impoverished family in Martinsburg, West Virginia, and at age three was adopted by Herbert and Florence Dean, who settled in New York City's Harlem district. Myers had a speech impediment, making it difficult for him to communicate, and at the suggestion of a teacher he began writing down his thoughts in the form of poems and short stories. Although he won awards for his work, his parents did not encourage his literary talents, although his foster father and grandfather were storytellers and his barely literate mother read to him until he was able to read back to her. "From my foster parents, the Deans, I received the love that was ultimately to strengthen me, even when I had forgotten its source," Myers was quoted as saying on the Scholastic Web site. "I was from a family of laborers," Myers remembered in his autobiographical essay, "and the idea of writing stories or essays was far removed from their experience. Writing had no practical value for a Black child. These minor victories [and prizes] did not bolster my ego. Instead, they convinced me that even though I was bright, even though I might have some talent, I was still defined by factors other than my ability." The dawning realization that his possibilities were limited by race and economic status embittered Myers as a teen. "A youngster is not trained to want to be a gasoline station attendant or a clerk in some obscure office," he stated. "We are taught to want to be lawyers and doctors and accountants—these professions that are given value. When the compromise comes, as it does early in Harlem to many children, it comes hard."

Myers admitted he was not ready to accept that compromise. Through high school and a three-year enlistment in the U.S. Army, he read avidly and wrote short stories. After his discharge from the service, he worked in a variety of positions, including mail clerk at the post office, interoffice messenger, and interviewer in a factory. None of these tasks pleased him, and when he began to publish poetry, stories, and articles in magazines, he started to consider a writing profession. "When I entered a contest for picture book writers," he claimed, "it was more because I wanted to write *anything* than because I wanted to write a picture book."

Myers won the contest, sponsored by the Council on Interracial Books for Children, for his text of *Where Does the Day Go?* In that story, a group of children from several ethnic backgrounds discuss their ideas about night and day with a sensitive and wise black father during a long walk. Inspired by the success of his first attempt to write for young people, Myers turned his attention to producing more picture books. Between 1972 and 1975 he published *The Dancers, The Dragon Takes a Wife,* and *Fly, Jimmy, Fly!* Other releases have included *The Golden Serpent,* a fable set in India, and an animal adventure, *Mr. Monkey and the Gotcha Bird.*

Myers accepted an editorial position with the Bobbs-Merrill publishing company in 1970 and worked there until 1977. His seven-year tenure there taught him "the book business from another viewpoint," as he noted in his autobiographical essay. "Publishing is a business," he wrote. "It is not a cultural institution . . . . It is *talked* about as if it were a large cultural organization with several branches. One hears pronouncements like 'anything worthwhile will eventually be published.' Nonsense, of course. Books are published for many reasons, the chief of which is profit." In retrospect, however, Myers felt that he benefited from his experiences at Bobbs-Merrill, even though he was laid off during a restructuring program. "After the initial disillusionment about the artistic aspects of the job, I realized how foolish I had been in not learning, as a writer, more about the business aspects of my craft," he concluded. Armed with the pragmatic knowledge of how the publishing industry works, Myers was thereafter able to support himself by his writing alone.

By the time he left Bobbs-Merrill, Myers had already established a reputation as an able author of fiction geared for African American children, a reputation based largely upon his highly successful novels for teens such as *Fast Sam, Cool Clyde, and Stuff* and *Mojo and the Russians.* Both tales feature, in Subryan's words, adventures depicting "the learning experiences of most youths growing up in a big city where negative influences abound." Central to the stories is the concept of close friendships, portrayed as a positive, nurturing influence. Subryan wrote, "Because of the bonding which occurs among the members of the group, the reader realizes that each individual's potential for survival has increased." Myers followed the two upbeat novels with a serious one, *It Ain't All for Nothin',* that Subryan felt "reflects much of the pain and anguish of ghetto life." The account of a boy caught in a web of parental abuse, conflicting values, and solitary self-assessment, *It Ain't All for Nothin'* "pretties up nothing; not the language, not the circumstances, not the despair," observed Jane Pennington in the *Interracial Books for Children Bulletin.* The story has a positive resolution, however, based on the care and support the central character receives from fellow community members.

Myers strives to present characters for whom urban life is an uplifting experience despite the potentially dangerous influences. In his first Coretta Scott King Award-winner, *The Young Landlords,* several teens learn responsibility when they are given a ghetto apartment building to manage. Lonnie Jackson, the protagonist of *Hoops,* profits from the example of an older friend who has become involved with gamblers. Concerned with stereotyping of a sexual as well as a racial sort, Myers creates plausible female characters and features platonic friendships between the sexes in his works. "The love in *Fast Sam, Cool Clyde, and Stuff* is not between any one couple," wrote Alleen Pace Nilsen in *English Journal.* "Instead it is a sort of a general feeling of good will and concern that exists among a group of inner city kids." Nilsen, among others, also noted that Myers's fiction can appeal to readers of any race. She concluded by saying that he "makes the reader feel so close to the characters that ethnic group identification is secondary." Subryan expressed a similar opinion: "By appealing to the consciousness of young adults, Myers is touching perhaps the most important element of our society. Myers's books demonstrate that writers can not only challenge the minds of black youths but also emphasize the black experience in a nonracist way that benefits all young readers."

With *Scorpions,* Myers tells the story of Jamal, a seventh grader whose life is forever changed when he accepts a gun from an older teen. For this provocative story Myers received the Newbery Honor Book award in 1989. In *Fallen Angels,* a Harlem teenager volunteers for service in the Vietnam War. Mel Watkins in the *New York Times Book Review* wrote, "*Fallen Angels* is a candid young adult novel that engages the Vietnam experience squarely. It deals with violence and death as well as compassion and love, with deception and hypocrisy as well as honesty and virtue. It is a tale that is as thought-provoking as it is entertaining, touching and, on occasion, humorous." Jim Naughton, reviewing *Me, Mop, and the Moondance Kid* in the *Washington Post Book World,* called Myers "one of the best writers of children's and young adult fiction in the country and *Me, Mop, and the Moondance Kid* shows why" in relating the schemes of two recently adopted orphans to find a home for their friend, left behind in the orphanage.

In *Now Is Your Time! The African-American Struggle for Freedom,* a *Washington Post Book World* contributor found that Myers "writes with the vividness of a novelist, the balance of an historian and the passion of an advocate. He tells a familiar story and shocks us with it all over again." Focusing on the black experience in America, Myers relates tales of Malcolm X, Coretta Scott King, Frederick Douglass, businessman James Forten, rebels Nat Turner and John Brown, journalist Ida B. Wells, inventor Lewis Latimer, and sculptor Meta Vaux Warrick, and even the Dandridges of Virginia, the "owners" of Myers's great-grandmother. The *Washington Post Book World* reviewer called *Now Is Your Time!* a "thrilling portrait gallery, expertly delineated . . . . Quite a story, quite a book."

In *The Glory Field,* Myers chronicles five generations of the Lewis family, including years of slavery in the eighteenth century, participation in the U.S. Civil War, years of economic hardship and struggle to maintain control of the family's land, and finally the family's confrontation of the problems that faced many black families in twentieth-century American society. "The story that began with ancestors in leg irons eventually rounds itself out in Harlem," noted Suzanne Curley in the *Los Angeles Times Book Review,* "with a look at the conflict experienced by a contemporary middle-class black teenager who must decide how much of himself he can extend to help a crack-addicted, homeless cousin." Critics have noted the value of Myers's saga, although some have faulted Myers for attempting too broad a scope, given the limited length of his novel. "Maybe what Walter Dean Myers has in *The Glory Field,*" wrote Kenneth C. Davis in the *New York Times Book Review,* "is the seed for several separate novels, or a longer book that would allow more time to know all of the Lewises."

Myers's *Malcolm X: By Any Means Necessary* traces the major events of Malcolm's life in the context of the broader history of the civil rights movement in America. Reviewers praised Myers's depiction of a complex public personality through the use of balanced commentary and language that is both engaging and accessible to young readers. With *Brown Angels, An Album of Pictures and Verse,* Myers offers selections from his collection of antique photographs of African-American children, accompanied by poems for young readers. Reviewers have emphasized the positive, and occasionally sentimental, tone of the book, which some have contrasted with the more grim subject matter of some of Myers's other publications. Commentators praised the sensitivity and beauty of the photographs presented in the book, often stressing the value of images in giving black children a sense of their history. "If *Brown Angels* is just a sampling of the rich treasure Myers has uncovered," stated Michael Patrick Hearn in *Washington Post Book World,* "then he should be locked in the attic until he has produced more volumes." Myers did respond with a second volume of pictures accompanied by poems, titled *Glorious Angels: A Celebration of Children.* While a reviewer for *Publishers Weekly* questioned the "high-flown" tone of Myers's verse, Kathleen Whalin of *School Library Journal* praised the volume as "a glorious feast for the eye and ear."

Slam! is the story of a young basketball player who must adapt to life in a mostly white magnet school. *Toussaint L'Ouverture: The Fight for Haiti's Freedom* is a study of the Haitian activist who led a rebellion against the French planters. *Harlem: A Poem* is a tribute to the music, promise, and dreams of Harlem, in a book illustrated by Myers's son Christopher. A *Publishers Weekly* reviewer called the artwork in *Harlem* "both stark and lyrical . . . . This is by no means an easy book—most of its allusions, if not the poems's significance itself, will need to be explained to children—but its artistic integrity is unmistakable."

Myers, who lost his own mother when he was two, fills *Angel to Angel: A Mother's Gift of Love* with photographs of mothers, grandmothers, and children, accompanied by ten of his poems, which *Booklist* reviewer Ilene Cooper said "will touch a chord both with the children who listen and the mother who reads to them." *One More River to Cross: An African-American Photograph Album* is a collection of photos gathered from archives and family albums, documenting the experience of blacks as they became free and resettled across America. *Amistad: A Long Road to Freedom* is Myers's factual account of the capture of slaves, the voyage to Cuba where they were sold, and the mutiny led by Sengbe as it sailed from Cuba, then landed in Connecticut, as well as the court trials and struggle to return to West Africa.

At Her Majesty's Request: An African Princess in Victorian England is a biography of a young West African princess who is rescued from death by sacrifice by Frederick E. Forbes, a British captain and opponent of slavery. Now named Sarah Forbes Bonetta, the girl returns to England, where she meets Queen Victoria, who takes an interest in her and provides for her education and welfare. Sarah's story is set within the context of the culture and times of England and reflects the unrest in the United States that leads to the Civil War. A *Publishers Weekly* contributor called the book a "moving and very human portrait of a princess."

Myers has contributed several volumes to the "My Name Is America" series. *The Journal of Joshua Loper: A Black Cowboy* is a fictional account of a young black man on the Chisholm Trail in 1871, who becomes a cattle driver, faces up to rustlers and stampedes, and meets historical characters. *Booklist* contributor John Peters called it an "informative, expert peek behind the cowboy mythos." *The Journal of Scott Pendleton Collins: A World War II Soldier* takes a young college student out of the dorm and into D-Day and beyond, and was called "an emotional read" by Randy Meyer in *Booklist. The Journal of Biddy Owens, the Negro Leagues,* set in 1948, is a fictional journal of a boy who does odd jobs and sometimes plays right field for the Birmingham Black Barons. *School Library Journal* reviewer Shawn Brommer wrote that "readers are introduced not only to the last great year of the Negro Leagues, but also to the institutional racism and blatant bigotry that existed in mid-20th-century America." *Booklist* writer Carolyn Phelan felt that Myers's writing "is infused with a love of baseball that is never sappy."

The protagonist of *Monster* is Steve Harmon, a sixteen-year-old accused of felony murder for acting as a lookout during a robbery in which a murder is committed. The novel contains amateur filmmaker Steve's notes in the form of diary entries and a film script, accompanied by black-and-white photographs. A *Horn Book* contributor wrote that Myers "adeptly allows each character to speak for him or herself, leaving readers to judge for themselves the truthfulness of the defendants, witnesses, lawyers, and, most compellingly, Steve himself." Patty Campbell, also writing in *Horn Book,* compared *Monster* to *Catcher in the Rye, The Outsiders,* and *The Chocolate War,* and said that Myers's "stunning new novel . . . joins these landmark books. Looking backward, *Monster* is the peak achievement of a career that has paralleled the growth of the genre."

A *Publishers Weekly* reviewer wrote that with *145th Street: Short Stories,* Myers "creates an overall effect of sitting on the front stoop swapping stories of the neighborhood." The dominant voices are teens, but there are cross-generational stories with a strong sense of history. "Myers has a great natural style," noted a *Horn Book* reviewer, "and is completely at home in a Harlem depicted without adulation but with great affection."

The Blues of Flats Brown is a children's picture book about a dog who flees to Memphis and has a hit record, angering his former owner, the mean A.J. Grubbs, who follows him on to New York. "Myers's shaggy fantasy has the slow-and-easy pacing of a lazy Southern afternoon," wrote a *Publishers Weekly* reviewer. "Myers beautifully conveys the blues' unique roots and the way the music bestows comfort, catharsis, and healing," said Shelle Rosenfeld in *Booklist.*

Myers's second book about Malcolm X, *Malcolm X: A Fire Burning Brightly,* focuses on the stages of Malcolm's life and contains Leonard Jenkins's artwork, "full-color montage illustrations, in acrylic, pastel, and spray paint . . . like mural art, with larger-than-life individual portraits set against the crowded streets and the swirl of politics," wrote Rochman, who noted that nearly every page contains a quote from speeches or writings. "They make us hear his voice." Myers chronicles Malcolm's childhood, time in the Charlestown State Prison, conversion to Islam, leadership of the Black Muslims, break with Elijah Muhammad, and his pilgrimage to Mecca prior to his assassination in 1965.

In *The Greatest: Muhammad Ali,* Myers first documents the life of Cassius Clay, from his childhood in segregated St. Louis, to his Olympic win in 1960, to his life as a professional boxer. Myers then relates Clay's commitment as a Black Muslim and his political activism as a conscientious objector during the Vietnam War. Myers also reports on Ali's major fights against Sonny Liston, Joe Frazier, and George Foreman. *Horn Book* contributor Jack Forman felt the book "is more portrait of Ali's character and cultural impact than a narrative of his life." "This is finally a story about a black man of tremendous courage," wrote Bill Ott in *Booklist,* "the kind of universal story that needs a writer as talented as Myers to retell it for every generation." Khafre K. Abif added in *Black Issues Book Review* that Myers "inspires a new generation of fans by exposing the hazards Ali faced in boxing, the rise of a champion, and now his battle against Parkinson's disease."

In *Bad Boy: A Memoir,* Myers begins with an account of his childhood, then takes the reader through his adolescence—during which he often skipped school and sometimes made deliveries for drug dealers—and to his beginnings as a writer. Rochman said, "The most beautiful writing is about Mama: how she taught him to read, sharing *True Romance* magazines." "The author's growing awareness of racism and of his own identity as a black man make up one of the most interesting threads," wrote Miranda Doyle in *School Library Journal.* "The author's voice and heart are consistently heard and felt throughout," concluded a *Horn Book* contributor.

USS Constellation relates the entire story of the title's ship, from construction to war victories to encounters with slave ships to crew training. The book is complemented by first-person accounts, along with illustrations and charts. Carolyn Phelan of *Booklist* praised this "well-researched" volume, adding that it is a "unique addition to American history collections." In *Publishers Weekly,* a reviewer praised this "meticulously researched, fast-flowing chronicle." The reviewer applauded the book for offering "a larger view of the shaping of America." Betty Carter of *Horn Book,* however, found that although the first-person accounts "lend authenticity while personalizing events," overall the book is "lackluster."

In 2006, Myers coauthored the nonfiction work *The Harlem Hellfighters: When Pride Met Courage* with Bill Miles. The book focuses on the military histories of the United States and Europe that led to the Great War and the formation of the 369th infantry. That regiment, nicknamed the "Harlem Hellfighters," was composed entirely of African American men. A *Kirkus Reviews* contributor found the book to be "marred by uneven storytelling and inadequate documentation." However, a critic for *Publishers Weekly* called the authors' research "impeccable" and pointed out that the book is "a rich history."

The novel *Shooter* focuses on the events leading up to and following a school shooting. Reviewers noted that the similarities to the real-life Columbine tragedy surely reveal Myers's inspiration for the story. *Shooter* is told through a unique narrative approach; the book consists of police reports, news articles, a journal, and other "real-life" documentation of the event. For its dark subject matter and its unique narration, *Shooter* is often compared with *Monster* by critics and followers of Myers's work. Of *Shooter,* Lauren Adams of *Horn Book* wrote that Myers's "exacting look at the many possible players and causes in the events makes for a compelling story." A *Publishers Weekly* reviewer praised Myers's handling of this touchy subject: "Here, no one is completely innocent and no one is entirely to blame." The reviewer concluded, "Readers will find themselves racing through the pages, then turning back to pore over the details once more."

In Myers's next young adult book, *Autobiography of My Dead Brother,* fifteen-year-old Jesse and his best friend Rise are members of long-standing African American social club called the Counts. Things begin to change when Rise slips into a world of drugs and violence and the club reaches gang status. Jesse clings to his artistic talent in order to sustain himself. "Teens . . . will be on edge while . . . Jesse decides if he will allow his environment and peers to dictate the type of man he will become," commented KaaVonia Hinton in *Kliatt.* Francisca Goldsmith, writing for *School Library Journal,* wrote that the novel "paints a vivid and genuine portrait of life that will have a palpable effect on its readers."

"Children and adults," wrote Myers in *SAAS,* "must have role models with which they can identify"; therefore he attempted to "deliver images upon which [they] could build and expand their own worlds." Noting that in his own life he has "acquired the strengths to turn away from disaster," Myers commented: "As a Black writer, I want to talk about my people." In an interview with Roger Sutton in *School Library Journal,* Myers conceded, however, that writing the African-American experience is fraught with complexity and difficulties. "Very often people want more from books than a story," the author explained, "they want books to represent them well. This is where I get the flak." Commenting on the question of writing primarily for a black audience, Myers stated, "I understand that as a black person you are always representing the race, so to speak . . . . So what you have to do is try to write it as well as you can and hope that if you write the story well enough, people won't be offended." Myers perceived an element of racism in the notion that black authors must write about "black subjects" for a primarily black audience. Likewise, he viewed the controversy surrounding the question of whether whites should write about the black experience as "a false issue." He commented, "I think basically you need to write what you believe in."

BIOGRAPHICAL AND CRITICAL SOURCES:

BOOKS

Children's Literature Review, Volume 4, Gale (Detroit, MI), 1982.

Contemporary Black Biography, Volume 8, Gale (Detroit, MI), 1994.

Contemporary Literary Criticism, Volume 35, Gale (Detroit, MI), 1985.

Dictionary of Literary Biography, Volume 33: *Afro-American Fiction Writers after 1955,* Gale (Detroit, MI), 1984.

Myers, Walter Dean, *Bad Boy: A Memoir,* HarperCollins (New York, NY), 2001.

Patrick-Wexler, *Walter Dean Myers,* Raintree Steck-Vaughan (Austin, TX), 1996.

Rush, Theressa G., editor, *Black American Writers: Past and Present,* Scarecrow Press (Metuchen, NJ), 1975.

St. James Guide to Young Adult Writers, 2nd edition, St. James Press (Detroit, MI), 1999.

Something about the Author Autobiography Series, Volume 2, Gale (Detroit, MI), 1986.

PERIODICALS

African-American Review, spring, 1998, R.D. Lane, "'Keepin' It Real': Walter Dean Myers and the Promise of African-American Children's Literature," p. 125.

Black Issues Book Review, November, 1999, review of *Won't Know till I Get There,* p. 75; May, 2001, Khafre K. Abif, review of *The Greatest: Muhammad Ali,* p. 80.

Booklist, October 1, 1992, Stephanie Zvirin, review of *The Righteous Revenge of Artemis Bonner,* p. 321; November 15, 1992, Hazel Rochman, review of *Malcolm X: By Any Means Necessary,* p. 588; September 1, 1995, Ilene Cooper, review of *Glorious Angels: A Celebration of Children,* p. 79; November 15, 1995, Hazel Rochman, review of *Shadow of the Red Moon,* p. 548; April 1, 1996, Susan Dove Lempke, review of *How Mr. Monkey Saw the Whole World,* p. 1373; August, 1996, Jackie Gropman, review of *One More River to Cross: An African-American Photograph Album,* p. 186; September 1, 1996, Hazel Rochman, review of *Toussaint L'Ouverture: The Fight for Haiti's Freedom,* p. 123; November 15, 1996, Bill Ott, review of *Slam!,* p. 579; February 15, 1997, Michael Cart, review of *Harlem: A Poem,* p. 1021; February 15, 1998, Hazel Rochman, review of *Amistad: A Long Road to Freedom,* p. 1003, Ilene Cooper, review of *Angel to Angel: A Mother's Gift of Love,* p. 1006; February 15, 1999, Brad Hooper, review of *One More River to Cross,* p. 1012, Hazel Rochman, review of *Amistad,* p. 1068, John Peters, review of *The Journal of Joshua Loper: A Black Cowboy,* p. 1070; April 1, 1999, Carolyn Phelan, review of *At Her Majesty's Request: An African Princess in Victorian England,* p. 1405; May 1, 1999, Debbie Carton, review of *Monster,* p. 1587; June 1, 1999, Randy Meyer, review of *The Journal of Scott Pendleton Collins: A World War II Soldier,* p. 1830; December 15, 1999, Hazel Rochman, review of *145th Street: Short Stories,* p. 778; February 15, 2000, Hazel Rochman, "The *Booklist* Interview," p. 1101, and review of *Malcolm X: A Fire Burning Brightly,* p. 1103; March 1, 2000, Shelle Rosenfeld, review of *The Blues of Flats Brown,* p. 1242, Stephanie Zvirin, review of *At Her Majesty's Request,* p. 1249; January 1, 2001, Stephanie Zvirin, "The Printz Award Revisited," p. 932, Bill Ott, review of *The Greatest,* p. 952; February 15, 2001, Carolyn Phelan, review of *The Journal of Biddy Owens, the Negro Leagues,* p. 1149, Hazel Rochman, review of *145th Street,* p. 1149; April 15, 2001, Hazel Rochman, review of *Scorpions,* p. 1549; May 1, 2001, Stephanie Zvirin, review of *Monster,* p. 1611, Hazel Rochman, review of *Bad Boy: A Memoir,* p. 1673; January 1, 2002, review of *The Greatest,* p. 766; July, 2004, Carolyn Phelan, review of *USS Constellation,* p. 1841.

Childhood Education, winter, 2001, Marissa McGlone, review of *The Journal of Biddy Owens,* p. 112.

Christian Science Monitor, May 1, 1992, Heather Vogel Frederick, reviews of *Now Is Your Time!: The African-American Struggle for Freedom,* and *Somewhere in the Darkness,* p. 10; February 5, 1993, E. K. Laing, review of *Malcolm X: By Any Means Necessary,* p. 11; December 17, 1993, Karen Williams, review of *Brown Angels: An Album of Pictures and Verse,* p. 12; November 4, 1994, Karen Williams, review of *The Glory Field,* p. 10; May 29, 1997, Karen Williams, review of *Harlem,* p. 1.

English Journal, December, 1993, Alleen Pace Nilsen, review of *Somewhere in the Darkness,* p. 74.

Horn Book, November, 1992, Nancy Vasilakis, review of *Mop, Moondance, and the Nagasaki Knights,* p. 739; March, 1993, Hanna B. Zeiger, review of *The Righteous Revenge of Artemis Bonner,* p. 209; September, 1993, Gail Pettiford Willett, review of *Malcolm X: By Any Means Necessary,* p. 626; January, 1994, Lois F. Anderson, review of *Brown Angels,* p. 82, Mary M. Burns, review of *The Great Migration: An American Story,* p. 88; March, 1995, Ellen Fader, review of *Darnell Rock Reporting,* pp. 194, 200, Peter D. Eieruta, review of *The Glory Field,* p. 200; July, 1996, Ellen Fader, review of *How Mr. Monkey Saw the Whole World,* p. 452; January, 1999, Marilyn Bousquin, review of *At Her Majesty's Request,* p. 82; May, 1999, review of *Monster,* p. 337; November, 1999, Patty Campbell, "The Sand in the Oyster Radical Monster," p. 769; January, 2000, review of *Monster,* p. 42; March, 2000, review of *145th Street,* p. 198; May, 2000, review of *Malcolm X: A Fire Burning Brightly,* p. 336; January, 2001, Jack Forman, review of *The Greatest,* p. 115; July, 2001, review of *Bad Boy,* p. 473; May/June, 2004, Lauren Adams, review of *Shooter,* p. 335; July/August, 2004, Betty Carter, review of *USS Constellation,* p. 469.

Interracial Books for Children Bulletin, Volume 10, Number 4, 1979; Volume 10, Number 6, 1979.

Kirkus, November 15, 2005, review of *The Harlem Hellfighters: When Pride Met Courage,* p. 1235.

Kliatt, July, 2005, KaaVonia Hinton, review of *Autobiography of My Dead Brother,* p. 14.

Los Angeles Times Book Review, January 1, 1995, p. 10; October 15, 1997, Elizabeth Mehren, "Fountain of Stories for Youth; Walter Dean Myers Writes Books for Young People. But Their Realism and Richness Have Adults Reading Them Too," p. E1.

New York Times Book Review, April 9, 1972; May 4, 1975; January 6, 1980, Patricia Lee Gauch, review of *The Young Landlords,* p. 20; November 9, 1980, review of *The Young Landlords,* p. 41; July 12, 1981; June 13, 1982, Diane Gersoni Edelman, review of *Won't Know till I Get There,* p. 26; April 19, 1987, p. 21; September 13, 1987, Jeanne Betancourt, review of *Crystal,* p. 48; January 22, 1989, Mel Watkins, review of *Fallen Angels,* p. 29; May 20, 1990, David Kelly, review of *The Mouse Rap,* p. 44; February 16, 1992, p. 26; November 13, 1994, p. 42; July 20, 1997, Rosemary L. Bray, review of *Harlem,* p. 22; December 5, 1999, review of *Monster,* p. 100; October 21, 2001, Kermit Frazier, review of *Bad Boy,* p. 31.

Publishers Weekly, July 4, 1994, review of *Darnell Rock Reporting,* p. 65; September 5, 1994, review of *The Glory Field,* p. 112; May 8, 1995, review of *The Story of the Three Kingdoms,* p. 296; September 11, 1995, review of *Glorious Angels,* p. 85; February 19, 1996, review of *How Mr. Monkey Saw the Whole World,* p. 215; November 4, 1996, review of *Toussaint L'Ouverture,* p. 76; November 25, 1996, review of *Slam!,* p. 76; January 13, 1997, review of *Harlem,* p. 76; February 8, 1999, review of *At Her Majesty's Request,* p. 215; March 22, 1999, Jennifer M. Brown, "Walter Dean Myers Unites Two Passions," p. 45; April 5, 1999, review of *Monster,* p. 242; January 24, 2000, reviews of *The Blues of Flats Brown,* p. 311, and *145th Street,* p. 312; April 10, 2000, review of *Angel to Angel,* p. 101; February 5, 2001, "Books," p. 90; May 14, 2001, review of *Monster,* p. 85; March 22, 2004, review of *Shooter,* p. 87; June 28, 2004, review of *USS Constellation,* p. 52; January 9, 2006, review of *The Harlem Hellfighters,* p. 55.

School Library Journal, May, 1993, Jean H. Zimmerman, review of *Young Martin's Promise,* p. 100; June, 1993, David A. Linsey, review of *A Place Called Heartbreak: A Story of Vietnam,* p. 120; June, 1994, Roger Sutton, "Threads in Our Cultural Fabric: A Conversation with Walter Dean Myers," p. 24; September, 1994, Tom S. Hurlburt, review of *Darnell Rock Reporting,* p. 220; November, 1994, Carol Jones Collins, review of *The Glory Field,* p. 121; March, 1995, Cheri Estes, review of *The Dragon Takes a Wife,* p. 185; July, 1995, Susan Scheps, review of *The Story of the Three Kingdoms,* p. 67; September, 1995, Kathleen Whalin, review of *Glorious Angels,* p. 196; December, 1995, Tim Rausch, review of *Shadow of the Red Moon,* p. 106; January, 1996, Lynn K. Vanca, review of *Darnell Rock Reporting,* p. 65; May, 1996, Marianne Saccardi, review of *How Mr. Monkey Saw the Whole World,* p. 96; November, 1996, Melissa Hudak, review of *Toussaint L'Ouverture,* p. 116, Tom S. Hurlburt, review of *Slam!,* p. 123; February, 1997, Melissa Hudak, review of *Harlem,* p. 121; May, 1998, Gerry Larson, review of *Amistad,* p. 158; January, 1999, Cindy Darling Codell, review of *At Her Majesty's Request,* p. 149; April, 1999, Gerry Larson, review of *The Journal of Joshua Loper,* p. 140; July, 1999, Coop Renner, review of *The Journal of Scott Pendleton Collins,* p. 98; February, 2000, Eunice Weech, review of *Malcolm X: A Fire Burning Brightly,* p. 114; March, 2000, Karen James, review of *The Blues of Flats Brown,* p. 210; April, 2000, Edward Sullivan, review of *145th Street,* p. 140; January, 2001, Michael McCollough, review of *The Greatest,* p. 152; April, 2001, Shawn Brommer, review of *The Journal of Biddy Owens,* p. 146; May, 2001, Miranda Doyle, review of *Bad Boy,* p. 169; July 9, 2001, review of *Bad Boy,* p. 21; December, 2001, Kathleen Baxter, review of *The Greatest,* p. 39; April, 2005, review of *Here in Harlem: Poems in Many Voices,* p. S56; August, 2005, Francisca Goldsmith, review of *Autobiography of My Dead Brother,* p. 132.

Tribune Books (Chicago), February 26, 1989, p. 8; November 15, 1992, p. 9; September 12, 1993, p. 6; December 10, 1995, p. 5.

Voice of Youth Advocates, April, 2005, Rebecca Hogue Wojahn, review of *Here in Harlem,* p. 14.

Washington Post Book World, July 9, 1989, p. 10; March 8, 1992, p. 11; July 3, 1994, p. 14; May 13, 2001, Karen MacPherson, "Living to Tell," p. 3.

ONLINE

Scholastic Web site, http://teacher.scholastic.com/ (September 26, 2001).

* * *

MYERS, Walter M.

See MYERS, Walter Dean

N

NAFISI, Azar 1950(?)-

PERSONAL: Born c. 1950, in Tehran, Iran; married; children: two. *Education:* Attended University of Oklahoma and Oxford University.

ADDRESSES: *Home*—Washington DC. *Agent*—c/o Author Mail, Random House, 1745 Broadway, New York, NY 10019.

CAREER: Writer and teacher. Johns Hopkins School for Advanced International Studies, professor. Taught literature at three Iranian Universities. Director of the Dialogue Project.

WRITINGS:

Reading "Lolita" in Tehran: A Memoir in Books, Random House (New York, NY), 2003.

Also author of *Anti Terra: A Critical Study of Vladimir Nabokov's Novels,* 1994. Contributor to periodicals, including the *New York Times, Washington Post,* and *Wall Street Journal.*

Reading "Lolita" in Tehran: A Memoir in Books has been translated into more than ten languages.

SIDELIGHTS: When Azar Nafisi was thirteen years old her parents sent her from her home in Iran to Lancaster, England, so that she could finish her schooling. When Nafisi returned to her birthplace things had changed. She returned in 1979 after the revolution of Ayatollah Ruhollah Khomeini. Khomeini had enforced a strict moral code. Women were forced to wear veils and morality police patrolled the streets. According to Michael Harris of the *Los Angeles Times,* Nafisi has said that "in the course of nearly two decades the streets have been turned into a war zone, where young women who disobey the rules are hurled into patrol cars, taken to jail, flogged, fined . . . and sometimes raped or executed." Nafisi was fired from the University of Tehran, where she taught literature, because she refused to wear a veil. From 1995 to 1997 she set up weekly secret meetings with seven female students to discuss literature. *Reading "Lolita" in Tehran: A Memoir in Books* is the story of Nafisi, her students, and the books that they discussed during those meetings. The book has been translated into more than ten languages and is in its fifteenth printing.

As depicted in Nafisi's text, the seven students who meet weekly at the author's home are all very different from each other. Some are married, some are divorced, some are rich, some are poor. Their personalities and passions vary, they have different beliefs, but they are uniquely bonded by the shared experience of reading these novels together and discussing what they mean in their lives. In an article for the *Guardian Unlimited* Paul Allen wrote, "The charismatic passion in the book is not simply for literature itself but for the kind of inspirational teaching of it which helps students to teach themselves by applying their own intelligence and emotions to what they are reading."

"*Reading 'Lolita' in Tehran* is more than a collection of keen perceptions of the nature of literature—though it is certainly and formidably and beautifully that. It is also a portrait of daily life under despotism," noted Charles Matthews in the *Manila Times.* Nafisi divides the book into four sections. Each section discusses a piece of literature: "Lolita," "Gatsby," "James," and "Austen." As readers are taken through the sections they come to know daily life in Iran, the author, and her students and how these great works of literature fit into their lives. Readers also learn how the pieces are relevant and meaningful in their daily operations. In a review for *Library Journal,* Ron Ratliff commented on the lives of Nafisi's students: "Their stories reflect the oppression of the Iranian regime but also the determination not to be crushed by it." He went on to say, "Nafisi's lucid style keeps the reader glued to the page from start to finish." In an article for the *Star Tribune,* Andrea Hoag commented that Nafisi's memoir "is a reminder that a safe, illusory world exists within the imaginary constraints of our great novels, a place where all of us can still take comfort."

In an interview for *Newsweek,* Nafisi claimed that she is grateful to the Islamic Republic regime. "The Islamic Republic took away everything I'd taken for granted. It made me appreciate the feel of the wind on my skin. How lovely the sun feels on your hair. How free you feel when you can lick ice cream in the streets." Nafisi now resides in the United States and teaches literature at Johns Hopkins University.

BIOGRAPHICAL AND CRITICAL SOURCES:

PERIODICALS

Atlantic Monthly, May 27, 2003, Mona Simpson, review of *Reading "Lolita" in Tehran: A Memoir in Books.*

Book, January-February, 2003, Lisa Levy, review of *Reading "Lolita" in Tehran,* pp. 51-52.

Booklist, April 15, 2003, Kristine Huntley, review of *Reading "Lolita" in Tehran,* p. 1443.

Globe & Mail (Toronto, Ontario, Canada), April 19, 2003, Marni Jackson, review of *Reading "Lolita" in Tehran.*

Kirkus Reviews, February 15, 2003, review of *Reading "Lolita" in Tehran,* p. 289.

Library Journal, April 1, 2003, Ron Ratliff, review of *Reading "Lolita" in Tehran,* p. 98.

Los Angeles Times, May 14, 2003, Michael Harris, review of *Reading "Lolita" in Tehran,* p. E-13.

Manila Times, May 14, 2003, Charles Matthews, review of *Reading "Lolita" in Tehran.*

Nation, June 16, 2003, Gloria Emerson, review of *Reading "Lolita" in Tehran,* p. 11.

Newsweek, May 5, 2003, Carla Power, review of *Reading "Lolita" in Tehran,* p. 58.

Publisher's Weekly, March 17, 2003, review of *Reading "Lolita" in Tehran,* p. 62.

Star Tribune, April 6, 2003, Andrea Hoag, review of *Reading "Lolita" in Tehran.*

ONLINE

Atlantic Unbound, http://www.theatlantic.com/ (March 15, 2004), Elizabeth Wasserman, "The Fiction of Life."

BBC News, http://www.newsvote.bbc.co.uk/ (March 15, 2004), "Moving Stories: Azar Nafisi."

Guardian Unlimited, http://books.guardian.co.uk/ (November 3, 2003), Paul Allen, review of *Reading "Lolita" in Tehran.*

Identity Theory, http://identitytheory.com/interviews/ (March 15, 2004), Robert Birnbaum, interview with Azar Nafisi.

* * *

NAIPAUL, Shiva 1945-1985
(Shivadhar Srinivasa Naipaul)

PERSONAL: Born February 25, 1945, in Port of Spain, Trinidad (now Republic of Trinidad and Tobago); died of a heart attack, August 13, 1985, in London, England; son of Seepersad and Dropatie Naipaul; married Virginia Margaret Stuart, 1967; children: one. *Education:* Attended University College, Oxford, 1964-68.

CAREER: Writer. Lecturer at Aarhus University, Aarhus, Denmark, 1972.

MEMBER: Royal Society of Literature (fellow).

AWARDS, HONORS: John Llewelyn Rhys Memorial Prize and Winifred Holtby Memorial Prize, both 1970, and Jock Campbell *New Statesman* Award, 1971, all for *Fireflies;* Whitbread Literary Award, 1973, for *The Chip-Chip Gatherers.*

WRITINGS:

Fireflies (novel), Deutsch (London, England), 1970, Knopf (New York, NY), 1971.

The Chip-Chip Gatherers (novel), Knopf (New York, NY), 1973.

North of South: An African Journey (nonfiction), Simon & Schuster (New York, NY), 1978.

Black and White (nonfiction), Hamish Hamilton (London, England), 1980, published as *Journey to Nowhere: A New World Tragedy,* Simon & Schuster (New York, NY), 1981.

A Hot Country (novel), Hamish Hamilton (London, England), 1983, published as *Love and Death in a Hot Country,* Viking (New York, NY), 1984.

Beyond the Dragon's Mouth (stories), Viking (New York, NY), 1985.

An Unfinished Journey (nonfiction), Viking (New York, NY), 1987.

Contributor of short stories to anthologies, including *Penguin Modern Stories 4,* Penguin, 1970, and *Winter's Tales 20,* Macmillan (London, England), 1974. Contributor of articles to *Times Literary Supplement, London Magazine, New Statesman,* and *Spectator.*

SIDELIGHTS: The younger brother of writer V.S. Naipaul, Shiva Naipaul, an Indian born in Trinidad, established himself as a critically acclaimed author with his first novel, *Fireflies.* Set in a Trinidadian Hindu community, *Fireflies* describes the demise of that community's leaders, the Khoja family, who lose their elevated stature as a result of intrafamily squabbles, arranged and loveless marriages, poor education, and undisciplined and futile attempts to reach goals beyond their grasp. "There is unusually little in Shiva Naipaul's *Fireflies* to lead one to suppose that it is his first novel," wrote Stephen Wall in the London *Observer.* "It is hard to wish any particular episode away once it has been read." In the *New York Times Book Review,* critic Annette Grant deemed *Fireflies* "a remarkable and vivid portrait of an exotic, highly special tribe, the Hindus of Trinidad—who, like most people, are fundamentally unremarkable, but who under examination exhibit a full and rich spectrum of human possibilities." "That the details *do* fascinate," Grant added, "is a tribute both to the author's invention and to his subject."

Like *Fireflies,* Naipaul's second novel, *The Chip-Chip Gatherers,* is set in Trinidad and examines family relationships, this time between two very different families, the affluent Ramsarans and the less prestigious Bholais. Although brought together by marriage, the clans are never able to put aside their differences and work together for their common good. Therefore their association serves no purpose; it is as futile as the work of the village peasants who comb the beach to find the tiny shellfish chip-chip, a bucket of which might provide only a mouthful of meat.

Finding *The Chip-Chip Gatherers* "compelling," A.L. Hendricks in a *Christian Science Monitor* review judged Naipaul to be "a skillful storyteller" who "wastes no words on elaborate descriptions or philosophizing, but lets his characters make his point. He draws them sympathetically and yet never loses his artistic detachment." In his *New Statesman* critique Martin Amis predicted that Naipaul's "next novels will establish him as one of the most accomplished, and most accessible, writers of his generation."

Naipaul's six-month trek through Kenya, Tanzania, and Zambia inspired his next book, *North of South: An African Journey.* In this volume the author recorded his day-to-day observations of Africa in what critic John Darnton in the *New York Times Book Review* dubbed "the genre of travelogue *cum* essay." Naipaul relates his experiences of African life as he viewed it in cafes and buses, schools and homes, and through encounters with merchants, farmers, educators, and others. What impressed him most during his stay in Africa was the extent of European influence on African mores and customs.

Critics found *North of South* to be an interesting and well-written account of African ways, but not necessarily an unbiased and accurate observation. Darnton noted some "striking inaccuracies" and wrote that the citizens Naipaul profiles "are hardly the defining personalities in Africa today." Darnton nevertheless opined that *North of South* is "superbly written." Critic Roland Oliver also found *North of South* lacking in some areas. In his *New Statesman* review Oliver called Naipaul's effort "a witty but not wise book" that "is more informative about touts and tourists, pimps and prostitutes, than about national and international politics of the East African countries. . . . All this is told with a great deal of novelist's sparkle, a power of vivid description and of characterisation through reported dialogue, which will not endear Mr. Naipaul to his many acquaintances when his book comes into their hands."

Further comments about *North of South* came from Lewis Nkosi, who in the *Times Literary Supplement* noted Naipaul's "elegance of style," but concurred with other critics that "it is not that the picture Naipaul paints of Africa is totally unrecognizable; the question is one of perspective and standards used." And Jim Hoagland, writing in the *Washington Post Book World,* deemed *North of South* "ultimately one-dimensional," but judged it a "rare quick good read for the Africa shelf."

Naipaul followed *North of South* with *Journey to Nowhere: A New World Tragedy,* in which he sought to explain and document the bizarre circumstances and events that precipitated the Jonestown Massacre, when more than nine hundred men, women, and children, all members of a cult known as the People's Temple, committed suicide at the command of the sect's leader, Jim Jones. The mass suicide occurred in 1978 in Guyana, where Jones had moved his cult after journalists and concerned family members of the cultists interfered with the group's operation in San Francisco, California. Before instructing his followers to drink the cyanide-laced soft drink he offered them, Jones explained that their suicide was "an act . . . protesting the conditions of an inhuman world." Related deaths included California congressman Leo Ryan and several others who were gunned down on a Guyana airstrip by People's Temple members. Ryan and his entourage were on a mission to investigate the cult and free several members being held against their will.

Naipaul's account of the massacre was applauded by many reviewers, among them D.J. Enright, who wrote in the *Times Literary Supplement* that *Journey to Nowhere* is "a saddening, alarming, depressing book" that is "in part, a tribute to its author's assiduity, fortitude and powers of expression. . . . Only if the author had lived there could he have hoped to be more exhaustive and certain; and then he would not have lived to tell the tale at all." In the *New York Times Book Review* Peter L. Berger regarded Naipaul as "a masterful writer" and found *Journey to Nowhere* a "lively and readable" book. "Naipaul's is a harsh perspective," Berger opined. "It is also a very persuasive one. To be sure, a less idiosyncratic writer would have softened his interpretation, introduced more nuances, perhaps shown more compassion. One strength of the book is that Mr. Naipaul does none of these things, letting the reader make his own modifications if he is so inclined."

Peter Schrag also offered praise for *Journey to Nowhere* in his *Nation* review, calling Naipaul's book "a tough, intelligent, beautifully written account of how Californian and Third World illusions fused to set the stage for the disaster in Guyana." Schrag added that Naipaul "has a flawless ear for the gobbledygook of Third World pretenders, encounter-group gurus, esties [adherents of est, a quasi-religious group], obfuscating politicians and the various other manipulators of rhetoric who populated the world of Pastor Jones." And critic John Coleman, in the *New Statesman,* wrote of *Journey to Nowhere:* "It is one man's view and helps to make hideous sense of that flight to a Guyanan graveyard. Naipaul writes as ever with an ice-tipped pen, elegantly summoning laughter that rings like anger."

Naipaul's third novel, *A Hot Country,* is set in the fictional South African state of Cuyama, a depressed region where politics have become "banditry, cynicism and lies," and where the land has been ravaged, leaving "the foundations of vanished houses," and "archways leading nowhere." Its people, too, are bleak, frustrated, and hopeless as a result of the poverty and hunger that prevail in Cuyama. In a London *Times* review, critic Andrew Sinclair felt Naipaul's "regressive view . . . leaves the readers in the doldrums, with hardly enough energy to turn these pages of fine prose without the least spark of life." And "there is much voluptuous self-surrender to pessimism by the author, who closes off all avenues of hope," wrote Nicholas Rankin in *Times Literary Supplement.* "Yet it does not mask Shiva Naipaul's other considerable talents as a novelist. He deftly captures place, mood and character, and has not lost his eye and ear for embarrassment and discomfiture. . . . *A Hot Country* is a sad book about waste, but a work of art that delights with its craft as it dismays with its vision."

BIOGRAPHICAL AND CRITICAL SOURCES:

BOOKS

Contemporary Literary Criticism, Thomson Gale (Detroit, MI), Volume 32, 1985, Volume 39, 1986.

Dictionary of Literary Biography Yearbook: 1985, Thomson Gale (Detroit, MI), 1986.

PERIODICALS

Choice, January, 1972; October, 1973; October, 1981.

Christian Science Monitor, June 20, 1973.

Nation, May 2, 1981.

National Review, September 28, 1979; October 2, 1981.

New Republic, June 9, 1979; June 16, 1979; May 11, 1987, Geoffrey Wheatcroft, "The Unfinished Journey," p. 26.

New Statesman, April 20, 1973; July 28, 1978; October 31, 1980.

Newsweek, May 21, 1979; June 1, 1979; May 14, 1984.

New Yorker, August 6, 1973; July 2, 1979; May 25, 1981.
New York Times, April 21, 1979; August 16, 1985; March 13, 1987.
New York Times Book Review, February 7, 1971; May 6, 1979; June 29, 1980; July 5, 1981; July 4, 1982; August 12, 1984; March 24, 1985; March 22, 1987.
Observer, November 15, 1970; April 15, 1973; April 25, 1976; July 30, 1978; November 2, 1980.
Spectator, October 30, 1970; April 21, 1973; October 14, 1978; February 7, 1981.
Times (London, England), August 28, 1983.
Times Literary Supplement, December 11, 1970; April 13, 1973; September 29, 1978; October 31, 1980; August 30, 1983; September 12, 1986.
Washington Post Book World, July 1, 1979; April 5, 1981, April 25, 1984, March 24, 1985, April 19, 1987.

OBITUARIES:

PERIODICALS

Detroit Free Press, August 17, 1985.
Los Angeles Times, August 25, 1985.
Newsweek, August 26, 1985.
New York Times, August 16, 1985.
Publishers Weekly, August 30, 1985.
Time, August 26, 1985.
Times (London, England), August 16, 1985; August 21, 1985.
Washington Post, August 17, 1985.

* * *

NAIPAUL, Shivadhar Srinivasa
See NAIPAUL, Shiva

* * *

NAIPAUL, Vidiadhar Surajprasad
See NAIPAUL, V.S.

* * *

NAIPAUL, V.S. 1932-
(Vidiadhar Surajprasad Naipaul)

PERSONAL: Born August 17, 1932, in Chaguanas, Trinidad; son of Seepersad (a journalist and writer) and Dropatie (Capildeo) Naipaul; married Patricia Ann Hale, 1955 (marriage ended); married Nadira Khannum Alvi (a newspaper columnist). *Education:* Attended Queen's Royal College, Trinidad, 1943-48; University College, Oxford, B.A., 1953.

ADDRESSES: Home—Wiltshire, England. *Agent*—c/o Knopf Publicity, 1745 Broadway, New York, NY 10019.

CAREER: Writer. Also worked as a freelance broadcaster for British Broadcasting Corp. (BBC), 1954-56.

MEMBER: British Society of Authors, Royal Society of Literature (fellow).

AWARDS, HONORS: John Llewellyn Rhys Memorial Prize, 1958, for *The Mystic Masseur;* grant from government of Trinidad for travel in Caribbean, 1960-61; Somerset Maugham Award, 1961, for *Miguel Street;* Phoenix Trust Award, 1963; Hawthornden Prize, 1964, for *Mr. Stone and the Knights Companion;* W.H. Smith Award, 1968, for *The Mimic Men;* Booker Prize, 1971, for *In a Free State;* D. Litt, St. Andrew's College, 1979, Columbia University, 1981, Cambridge University, 1983, London University, 1988, and Oxford University, 1992; Bennett Award, *Hudson Review,* 1980; T.S. Eliot Award for Creative Writing, Ingersoll Foundation, 1986; knighted, 1990; David Cohen British Literature Award, 1993; Booker Prize nomination, 2001, for *Half a Life;* Nobel Prize for Literature, Swedish Academy, 2001.

WRITINGS:

The Mystic Masseur (also see below), Deutsch (London, England), 1957, Vanguard (New York, NY), 1959.
The Suffrage of Elvira (also see below), Deutsch (London, England), 1958.
Miguel Street (also see below), Deutsch (London, England), 1959, Vanguard (New York, NY), 1960.
A House for Mr. Biswas, Deutsch (London, England), 1961, McGraw-Hill (New York, NY), 1962, new edition, with an introduction by Ian Buruma, Penguin (New York, NY), 1992.
The Middle Passage: Impressions of Five Societies—British, French, and Dutch in the West Indies and South America (nonfiction), Deutsch (London, England), 1962, Macmillan (New York, NY), 1963.
Mr. Stone and the Knights Companion, Deutsch (London, England), 1963, Macmillan (New York, NY), 1964.

An Area of Darkness (nonfiction), Deutsch (London, England), 1964, Macmillan (New York, NY), 1965.
The Mimic Men, Macmillan (New York, NY), 1967.
A Flag on the Island (short stories), Macmillan (New York, NY), 1967.
The Loss of El Dorado: A History (nonfiction), Deutsch (London, England), 1969, Knopf (New York, NY), 1970, published as *The Loss of El Dorado: A Colonial History,* Vintage (New York, NY), 2003.
In a Free State (short stories), Knopf (New York, NY), 1971.
The Overcrowded Barracoon and Other Articles, Deutsch (London, England), 1972, Knopf (New York, NY), 1973.
Guerrillas, Knopf (New York, NY), 1975.
India: A Wounded Civilization (nonfiction), Knopf (New York, NY), 1977.
The Perfect Tenants and The Mourners, Cambridge University Press (Cambridge, England), 1977.
A Bend in the River, Knopf (New York, NY), 1979, with an introduction by Elizabeth Hardwick, Modern Library (New York, NY), 1997.
The Return of Eva Peron (nonfiction), Knopf (New York, NY), 1980.
A Congo Diary, Sylvester & Orphanos (Los Angeles, CA), 1980.
Among the Believers: An Islamic Journey, Knopf (New York, NY), 1981.
Three Novels (contains *The Mystic Masseur, The Suffrage of Elvira,* and *Miguel Street*), Knopf (New York, NY), 1982.
Finding the Center, Knopf (New York, NY), 1984.
The Enigma of Arrival, Knopf (New York, NY), 1987.
A Turn in the South, Knopf (New York, NY), 1989.
India: A Million Mutinies Now, Heinemann (London, England), 1990, Viking (New York, NY), 1991.
A Way in the World, Knopf (New York, NY), 1994.
(Author of text) Raghubir Singh, *Bombay: Gateway of India* (photographs), Aperture (New York, NY), 1994.
Beyond Belief: Islamic Excursions among the Converted Peoples, Random House (New York, NY), 1998.
Between Father and Son: Selected Correspondence of V.S. Naipaul and His Family, 1949-1953, edited by Gillon Aitken, Knopf (New York, NY), 2000.
Reading and Writing: A Personal Account, New York Review of Books (New York, NY), 2000.
Half a Life (novel), Picador (London, England), 2001, Knopf (New York, NY), 2002.
The Writer and the World, Knopf (New York, NY), 2002.
The Nightwatchman's Occurrence Book: And Other Comic Inventions (contains *The Suffrage of Elvira, Mr. Stones and the Knights Companion,* and *A Flag on the Island*), Vintage (New York, NY), 2002.
Literary Occasions: Essays, Knopf (New York, NY), 2003.
Vintage Naipaul, Vintage (New York, NY), 2004.
Magic Seeds, Knopf (New York, NY), 2004.

Contributor to *Island Voices: Stories from the West Indies,* edited by Andrew Salkey, Liveright (New York, NY), 1970. Contributor of book reviews to periodicals, including *New Statesman* and *New York Review of Books.*

ADAPTATIONS: The Mystic Masseur has been adapted as a film, produced by Ismail Merchant, in 2002.

SIDELIGHTS: V.S. Naipaul, considered one of the world's most gifted novelists, was awarded the 2001 Nobel Prize for literature. As a *New York Times Book Review* critic wrote: "For sheer abundance of talent there can hardly be a writer alive who surpasses V.S. Naipaul. Whatever we may want in a novelist is to be found in his books: an almost Conradian gift for tensing a story, a serious involvement with human issues, a supple English prose, a hard-edged wit, a personal vision of things. Best of all, he is a novelist unafraid of using his brains . . . . His novels are packed with thought, not as lumps of abstraction but as one fictional element among others, fluid in the stream of narrative . . . . [He is] the world's writer, a master of language and perception, our sardonic blessing."

Naipaul is frequently referred to as a writer of the world. He was born in Trinidad to the descendants of Hindu immigrants from northern India, and later educated at England's Oxford University. The idea of Naipaul as "the world's writer" comes largely, as he has pointed out himself, from his rootlessness. Unhappy with the cultural and spiritual poverty of Trinidad, distanced from India, and unable to relate to and share in the heritage of each country's former imperial ruler, Great Britain, Naipaul thought of himself as contentedly existing without ancestors or a heritage. As a result of this nonattachment to region and tradition, most of his work deals with people who, like himself, feel estranged from the societies they are ostensibly part of and who desperately seek ways to belong. The locales Naipaul chooses for his stories represent an extension of this same theme; most take place in emerging Third-World countries in the throes of creating new national identities from the remnants of native and colonial cultures.

Naipaul's early works explore the comic aspects of these themes. Essentially West Indian variations on the comedy of manners, these works present almost farcical accounts of an illiterate and divided society's shift from colonial to independent status, emphasizing the multiracial misunderstandings and rivalries and various ironies resulting from the sudden introduction of such democratic processes as free elections. In *The Mystic Masseur, The Suffrage of Elvira,* and *Miguel Street,* Naipaul exposes the follies and absurdities of Trinidadian society; his tone is detached yet sympathetic, as if he is looking back at a distant past of which he is no longer a part. The tragic aspects of the situation are not examined, nor is there any attempt to involve the reader in the plight of the characters. In his book *V.S. Naipaul,* Michael Thorpe described the prevailing tone of these early books as "that of the ironist who points up the comedy, futility and absurdity that fill the gap between aspiration and achievement, between the public image desired and the individual's inadequacies, to recognize which may be called the education of the narrator: *I had grown up and looked critically at the people around me.*"

A House for Mr. Biswas, published in 1961, marks an important turning point in Naipaul's work, his attention to psychological and social realism foreshadowing the intensive character studies of his later works. In addition, *A House for Mr. Biswas* has the universality of theme his earlier books lacked because of their emphasis on the particularities of Trinidadian society. As a consequence of these developments, many critics regard *A House for Mr. Biswas* as Naipaul's earliest masterpiece. Robert D. Hamner wrote in his biography *V.S. Naipaul* that the novel "is a vital embodiment of authentic West Indian life, but more than that, it transcends national boundaries and evokes universal human experiences. Mr. Biswas' desire to own his own house is essentially a struggle to assert personal identity and to attain security—thoroughly human needs."

A *New York Herald Tribune Books* reviewer noted that "Naipaul has a wry wit and an engaging sense of humor, as well as a delicate understanding of sadness and futility and a profound but unobtrusive sense of the tragi-comedy of ordinary living . . . . His style is precise and assured. In short, he gives every indication of being an important addition to the international literary scene. [*A House for Mr. Biswas*] is funny, it is compassionate. It has more than 500 pages and not one of them is superfluous." Paul Theroux admitted in the *New York Times Book Review* that "it is hard for the reviewer of a wonderful author to keep the obituarist's assured hyperbole in check, but let me say that if the silting-up of the Thames coincided with a freak monsoon, causing massive flooding in all parts of South London, the first book I would rescue from my library would be *A House for Mr. Biswas.*" Thorpe agreed that the novel is "a work of rare distinction," a "'novelist's novel,' a model work." In his *V. S. Naipaul* Thorpe commented that the popularity of *A House for Mr. Biswas* "must be largely due to its universality of subject and theme, the struggle of one ordinary man to climb—or cling on to—the ladder of life." In short, Thorpe concluded, "for West Indian literature *A House for Mr. Biswas* forged [the] connection [between literature and life] with unbreakable strength and set up a model for emulation which no other 'Third World' literature in English has yet equaled."

Since the success of *A House for Mr. Biswas,* Naipaul has increasingly sought broader geographic and social contexts in which to explore his themes. At the same time, his early lighthearted tone gradually has faded as the author examines the more tragic consequences of alienation and rootlessness through the eyes of various "universal wanderers." Noting that "Naipaul's writings about his native Trinidad have often enough been touched with tolerant amusement," Thomas Lask reported in the *New York Times* that the 1971 story collection *In a Free State* deals with the issue: "How does the expatriate fare after he leaves the island?" Noting that Naipaul's stories "focus on the failure of heart, on the animal- like cruelty man exhibits to other men and on the avarice that . . . is the root of all evil," Lask interpreted the fiction to say "that neither customs nor color nor culture seems able to quiet that impulse to destruction, that murderous wantonness that is so much part of our make-up." Characterizing Naipaul's style as "leaner than in the past and much more somber," the critic added: "There is virtually none of the earlier playfulness. He appears to have settled for precision over abundance. Each detail and each incident is made to carry its weight in the narrative. The effect is not small-scaled, for in the title story he has created an entire country. He has not tidied up every loose strand. . . . But there is nothing unfinished in these polished novellas." *In V.S. Naipaul: An Introduction to His Work,* Paul Theroux dubbed *In a Free State* "ambitious . . . a story-sequence brilliant in conception, masterly in execution, and terrifying in effect—the chronicles of a half-a-dozen self-exiled people who have become lost souls. Having abandoned their own countries (countries they were scarcely aware of belonging to), they have found themselves in strange places, without friends, with few loyalties, and with the feeling that they are trespassing. Worse, their lives have been totally altered; for them there is no going back; they have fled, each to his separate limbo, and their existence is like that of souls in a classical underworld." Comparing Naipaul to French author Albert Camus in his focus on "displacement," Theroux noted that "Naipaul is much superior to Camus, and his achievement—a steady advance through eleven volumes—is as disturbing as it is original. *In a Free State* is a masterpiece in the fiction of rootlessness."

The novel *Guerrillas* established Naipaul's reputation in the United States after its publication in 1975. Most reviewers commented on the novelist's somewhat grim outlook, Theroux calling it "a violent book in which little violence is explicit . . . . It is a novel, not of revolt, but of the play-acting that is frequently called revolt, that queer situation of scabrous glamour which Naipaul sees as a throw-back to the days of slavery . . . . *Guerrillas* is one of Naipaul's most complex books; it is certainly his most suspenseful, a series of shocks, like a shroud slowly unwound from a bloody corpse, showing the damaged—and familiar—face last . . . . This is a novel without a villain, and there is not a character for whom the reader does not at some point feel deep sympathy and keen understanding, no matter how villainous or futile he may seem. *Guerrillas* is a brilliant novel in every way, and it shimmers with artistic certainty. It is scarifying in the opposite way from a nightmare. One can shrug at fantasy, but *Guerrillas*—in a phrase Naipaul himself once used—is, like the finest novels, 'indistinguishable from truth.'"

Reviewing the novel in *Time,* Paul Gray contended that "perhaps no one but Naipaul has the inside and outside knowledge to have turned such a dispirited tale into so gripping a book. His island is built entirely of vivid descriptions and offhand dialogue. At the end, it has assumed a political and economic history, a geography and a population of doomed, selfish souls . . . . *Guerrillas* is not a polemic . . . but a Conradian vision of fallibility and frailty. With economy and compassion, Naipaul draws the heart of darkness from a sun-struck land." Noting that Naipaul takes a "hackneyed" theme—"incipient Black Power"—and manages to produce "a more significant treatment of it than most of his contemporaries with similar concerns," Charles R. Larson wrote in the *Nation* that *Guerrillas* "builds so slowly and so skillfully that . . . we are hardly aware of the necessary outcome of the events; it is only in retrospect that we see that the desultory action has in fact been charged with fate . . . . Written in a deliberately flat style, *Guerrillas* is a deeply pessimistic novel, telling us that we have seen about as much political change in the West Indian island republics as we are likely to see."

In *A Bend in the River,* Naipaul returns to the African backdrop of *In a Free State* and confirms his basic pessimism. John Leonard explained in the *New York Times* that the author "despises nostalgia for the colonial past, while at the same time heartlessly parodying . . . the African future." Calling *A Bend in the River* "brilliant and depressing," Leonard added: "It is no secret by now, certainly not since *Guerrillas* . . . that V.S. Naipaul is one of the handful of living writers of whom the English language can be proud, if, still, profoundly uneasy. There is no consolation from him, any more than there is sentiment. His wit has grown hard and fierce; he isn't seeking to amuse, but to scourge."

John Updike, writing in the *New Yorker,* asserted that *A Bend in the River* "proves once more that Naipaul is incomparably well situated and equipped to bring us news of one of the contemporary world's great subjects—the mingling of its peoples . . . . *A Bend in the River* is carved from the same territory [as *In a Free State*]—an Africa of withering colonial vestiges, terrifyingly murky politics, defeated pretensions, omnivorous rot, and the implacable undermining of all that would sustain reason and safety . . . . Rage . . . is perhaps the deepest and darkest fact Naipaul has to report about the Third World, and in this novel his understanding of it goes beyond that shown in *Guerrillas.* . . . Always a master of fictional landscape, Naipaul here shows, in his variety of human examples and in his search for underlying social causes, a Tolstoyan spirit, generous if not genial." In his *Newsweek* review, Walter Clemons described *A Bend in the River* as "a hurtful, claustrophobic novel, very hard on the nerves, played out under a vast African sky in an open space that is made to feel stifling." Noting its political bent, Clemons added, "As an evocation of place, [the novel] succeeds brilliantly" and "confirms Naipaul's position as one of the best writers now at work." Irving Howe was equally laudatory, writing in the *New York Times Book Review* that "Naipaul has mastered the gift of creating an aura of psychic and moral tension."

For his 1987 novel *The Enigma of Arrival* Naipaul selected a new setting: Great Britain. John Thieme explained in the *Dictionary of Literary Biography* that in the years between the publication of *A Bend in the River* and *The Enigma of Arrival* the author "suffered from a serious illness and was deeply moved by the deaths of his younger sister and his brother, Shiva." *The Enigma of Arrival,* Thieme continued, reflects Naipaul's somber personal experience and "is pervaded by a sense of personal loss and fragility." The novel examines the impact of imperialism on a native English estate, slowly decaying along with its reclusive landlord, who is suffering from a degenerative disease. The decay of the manor house and its owner causes the novel's first-person narrator to ponder the inevitability of his own death. Calling *The Enigma of Arrival* "full of intimations of mortality," Thieme added that "ultimately it is as much a generalized lament for human transience and an expression of the writer's all-pervasive sense of vulnerability as an elegy for any particular person or community."

With *A Turn in the South* and *India: A Million Mutinies Now,* Naipaul turned to nonfiction. *A Turn in the South* tells of a journey the author took through the southern United States, ostensibly looking for similarities between his own Trinidadian culture and that of the American South. While the issue of race is "high on his agenda at the outset," Thieme noted that its importance decreases the further into the work the reader explores. Instead, Naipaul finds himself drawn deeper and deeper into a description of the culture of the modern American south, including country western music, strict, conservative Christianity, and the enduring fascination with Elvis Presley. *India: A Million Mutinies Now* represents Naipaul's third consideration of his ancestral homeland. Whereas Naipaul had formerly expressed pessimism about India's ability to overcome centuries of religious and ethnic strife, in this 1990 work he appears to "take . . . heart in what he sees," according to Thomas D'Evelyn in his appraisal of the book for the *Christian Science Monitor.* "As the details accumulate, the reader becomes more deeply involved in a growing appreciation for a life lived under extreme circumstances. Reading Naipaul," D'Evelyn concluded, "one becomes as optimistic about mankind as the author is about India." The author's "cautious optimism represents the primary value of the book," commented Douglas J. Macdonald in *America.* "Pessimism can too easily lead to inertia and Despair . . . . Naipaul's message is that despite the problems, despite the obstacles, the Indians, and by extension the rest of us, must continue to try."

A Way in the World, published in 1994, is a collection of narratives that mix elements of fiction and nonfiction, merging Naipaul's Indian and West Indian heritage with the English history and culture he adopted when he immigrated to England at age eighteen. "His project is simultaneously to construct his own literary inheritance and the legacy he will leave to the world," explained Philip Gourevitch in *Commentary.* "The book . . . combines memoir, historical scholarship, and imaginative writing in a series of nine independent but thematically interlocking narratives. These narratives accumulate to form a dramatic portrait gallery of people—historical and fictionalized—whose lives have been formed and transformed by their encounters with Trinidad. And through the echo chamber of their stories there emerges a portrait of the artist, Naipaul himself, at the apex of his literary consciousness." "Now, near the end of his days," declared *New Republic* contributor Caryl Phillips, "Naipaul is clearly . . . deliberating over the question of whether he ever left home in the first place, for whatever else it is *A Way in the World* is a beautiful lament to the Trinidad he has so often denigrated."

Naipaul labels each of these early narratives "An Unwritten Story." He includes under that title tales about the sixteenth-century sea dog and explorer Sir Walter Raleigh traveling down a branch of the Orinoco River in Guyana in search of gold and not finding it, and an account of nineteenth-century South American revolutionary Francisco Miranda, who plotted a Venezuelan revolution that never materialized. Naipaul also traces the careers of other notables, such as the Trinidadian Marxist revolutionary he dubs "Lebrun," who served as advisor to several independence movements, but was discarded as irrelevant after the regimes were established. "Once in power," declared *Los Angeles Times Book Review* contributor Richard Eder, the nationalists "had no use for him; his ideology was good for building up their strength but they had no intention of actually setting up a Marxist regime." Instead, Lebrun found himself banished to the fringes of society, spending his life in exile, speaking to leftist groups in Great Britain and the United States.

"If there is one thing that unifies the chapters in [*A Way in the World*]," declared *Spectator* reviewer Amit Chaudhuri, "it is its attempt to explore and define the nature of the colonial's memory." Like other reviewers, Chaudhuri contrasted Naipaul's fiction with the work of Conrad, who often looked darkly at the spreading colonialism of Great Britain at the end of the nineteenth and the beginning of the twentieth centuries. The reviewer suggested that Naipaul retraces the colonialism Conrad depicted in his work and shows, in *A Way in the World,* how British imperialism created not just colonies but colonials: men and women with unique sensibilities and memories. "The river, in these 'stories,' no longer remains simply a Conradian image of Western exploration and territorial ambition," Chaudhuri concluded, "but becomes an emblem of the colonial memory attempting to return to its source."

Beyond Belief: Islamic Excursions among the Converted Peoples served as both a return to nonfiction and a sequel to Naipaul's 1981 work *Among the Believers: An Islamic Journey.* Discussing the earlier book with Jeffrey Myers of *American Scholar,* Naipaul described *Among the Believers* as "about people caught at a cultural hinge moment: a whole civilization is on the turn . . . . It seeks to make that change clear, and to make a story of it." *Beyond Belief,* like its predecessor, deals with Islamic countries that are non-Arabic: Indonesia, Iran, Pakistan, and Malaysia. Both books relate stories from individuals Naipaul encountered while traveling extensively through these countries. Comparing the two books, a *Booklist* reviewer observed that in *Beyond Belief* "Naipaul is more dispassionate, letting the people he meets take center stage as they express their struggles with family, religion, and nation." Meyers also observed this dispassionate quality, commenting, "The author of *Guerrillas* and *A Bend in the River* has done what I thought impossible: written a book as boring as its bland gray jacket." Meyers also found Naipaul's central thesis—that "everyone not an Arab who is a Muslim is a convert"—to be "radically flawed." Edward Said agreed, noting in the *Progressive:* "This ridiculous argument would suggest by extension that only a native of Rome can be a good Roman Catholic . . . . In effect, the 400-page *Beyond Belief* is based on nothing more than this rather idiotic and insulting theory . . . . The greater pity is that Naipaul's latest book will be considered a major interpretation of a great religion, and more Muslims will suffer and be insulted."

In support of his thesis, Naipaul points out how Islam came late to these nations and has since remained in conflict with older native traditions. He also shows how the revival of Islamic fundamentalism during the late twentieth century had a negative impact on these "converted" countries. Despite this argument, most critical response to the book expressed disagreement. Noted Jane I. Smith in a review for *Christian Century:* "Naipaul's picture of Islam among the converted peoples is not necessarily inaccurate; it is simply incomplete. And his presupposition that Muslims in the countries he visits have sacrificed their native traditions for a religion in which they can never fully share is a partial truth at best. The whole picture is both broader and considerably more hopeful than this artful but melancholy presentation might have us believe." While also questioning Naipaul's thesis and his generally negative views of Islam, L. Carl Brown in *Foreign Affairs* took a different slant on *Beyond Belief:* "In-depth interviews with a handful of the near-great and the obscure from each country produce brilliant writing and somber stories . . . . *Beyond Belief* is rewarding."

Between Father and Son: Selected Correspondence of V.S. Naipaul and His Family, 1949-1953 presents letters from Naipaul to his father, Seepersad Naipaul, and other members of his family during the time when Naipaul was studying in England on a scholarship. Longtime Naipaul readers will recognize Seepersad, a weary man struggling as a journalist, in the fictional title character in *A House for Mr. Biswas.* During the course of the correspondence, Naipaul's father suffers a heart attack, loses his job at a local newspaper, and dies at the age of forty-seven without having realized his dream of publishing his short stories. "A major theme of the letters is the conflict between devoting oneself to a future career, especially as a writer, and helping others in the family gain an education," noted Bruce King in *World Literature Today.* After his father's death, Vido—as Naipaul was known to his family—contemplates returning to Trinidad, but claims financial hardship in not doing so. Instead, his sister leaves India, where she is studying on scholarship, and returns to Trinidad to take care of family obligations. Naipaul remains in England, convinced that he can best help his family by continuing his studies and working toward his goal of becoming a published writer.

Even as a teenager studying abroad for the first time, Naipaul is concerned with many of the issues for which he will eventually become known. Among the themes familiar to readers of Naipaul's mature writing are "the enigma of arrival, the sadness of separation and exile, neocolonial ambition and the effort to find one's center," according to Abraham Verghese in the *New York Times Book Review.* Nevertheless, continued Verghese, "those who have formed the impression that Naipaul is arrogant and conceited will find little to change their beliefs." Noting that the letters document Naipaul's depression—or what the author himself characterized as a "nervous breakdown"—Joseph Epstein commented in *New Criterion* that Naipaul's literary vision is "hideously complicated"; *Between Father and Son* reminds readers "how little we really know about the workings of first-class literary minds."

In 2001 the Swedish Academy awarded Naipaul the Nobel Prize for Literature, in recognition of what they termed his "incorruptible scrutiny in works that compel us to see the presence of suppressed histories." Critics were nearly unanimous in their approval of the award, although some noted that Naipaul's strong views have been less than decorous throughout the years. "Few writers have offended their readers as regularly as V.S. Naipaul has," wrote Akash Kapur for *Salon.com;* he "has shown a staggering capacity for insensitivity and prejudice." Even while acknowledging Naipaul's hostility toward his native Trinidad, Caryl Phillips commented in the *Guardian* that the author's books "have been written in a sublime English, and with a ferocity of purpose unequaled by any of his contemporaries in the English language. His ability to synthesise, in almost equal part, his fiction and nonfiction—the one genre informing the other both structurally and thematically—has been both original in construction and fascinating to witness."

The Nobel announcement was made barely a month after Islamic fundamentalists seized international attention following the terrorist attacks on New York City and Washington, D.C., on September 11, 2001. Naipaul's often outspoken criticism of fundamentalism cast an air of irony over the Academy's choice. In his *Beyond Belief* Naipaul had dubbed fundamentalist Islam "the most uncompromising kind of imperialism," recalled *Salon.com* reviewer Gavin McNett. While *Los Angeles Times* contributor Tim Rutten cited the Nobel Prize honoree as maintaining, "I don't stand for any country," Rutten went on to note that Naipaul deplores the "calamitous effect" some Islamic sects have had on their countries. Such controversy aside, David Pryce-Jones concluded in the London *Times* that "the Nobel Prize for Literature has gone to someone who deserves it . . . . His use of language is as precise as it is beautiful." Receipt of the Nobel Prize for Literature cemented Naipaul's status as one of the English language's most distinguished and perceptive contemporary writers.

The 2002 publication of *Half a Life* came on the heels of Naipaul's Nobel win. The novel recounts the first forty years of the life of Willie Chandran, the son of a local Hindu ascetic of some renown and his untouchable wife. Willie escapes an unremarkable youth in India to study in England where, confused by his sexual initiation and flustered by both his own heritage and the cultural shifts thrust upon him in 1960s England, he forgoes a budding literary career. Instead, Willie follows Ana, the first woman to express an interest in him, to a Portuguese-ruled African country. Willie remains there for eighteen years, doing nothing much except loathing the native population, enjoying the perks of Ana's wealth, and engaging in a liaison with Ana's best friend.

J.M. Coetzee praised Naipaul's prose in his review for the *New York Review of Books,* calling it "as clean and cold as a knife." While noting the self-righteousness of both Willie and his father—both men "believe they see through other people" but "are incapable of imagining anyone unlike themselves"—Coetzee added that neither character appears to grow during the course of the novel. "Willie's story ends not only without resolution but without any glimpse of what a resolution might look like," the critic commented. Willie's nihilistic tendencies prompted David Kipen to declare in the *San Francisco Chronicle* that "under everything lurks Naipaul's uncharitable treatment of his own characters, robbed of our sympathy through want of his." However, *Booklist* contributor Donna Seaman praised Naipaul for both his language and his "command of both the intimately personal and the sweepingly political," calling *Half a Life* "a psychological complex yet rapidly paced tale of a father and son who fail to fully engage with life." In the *New York Times* contributor Michiko Kakutani continued such praise, complimenting the author for his "uncommon elegance and acerbity," and dubbing the novel "a small masterpiece in its own right and . . . a potent distillation of the author's work to date, a book that recapitulates all his themes of exile, postcolonial confusion, third-world angst, and filial love and rebellion."

In Naipaul's 2002 essay collection *The Writer and the World,* he includes pieces about numerous elections around the world, including the 1984 American presidential campaign; the movement, led by Norman Mailer and Jimmy Breslin, to have New York City named the nation's fifty-first state; the influence of the Peron family on the country of Argentina; and the Black Power movements in America and the Caribbean. The book demonstrates the writer's "tragic view of history," stated Jason Cowley in the London *Observer,* which he has perhaps arrived at because "he has travelled so far and seen so much. He knows something of the world, its pitilessness and struggle, its indifference to human suffering." According to Cowley, after reading *The Writer and the World* one understands why Naipaul was compelled to stop writing in a comic vein. In his travels, the writer has sought to understand history, and his essays combine short biographies, cultural criticism, and historical narrative to arrive at his bleak analysis of the psychology of decolonized people. Sven Birkerts, in the *Washington Times,* similarly remarked that this book emanates an acerbic world view. "Naipaul is merciless and exacting in his fiction as well as his essays and documentary accounts, and many readers have concluded that he is scornful of his subjects, expending upon them a powerful private rage," Birkerts wrote. Yet he found that the essays collected in *The Writer and the World* must correct this misperception. "The more one reads these essays . . . the more clearly one sees that the point of his astringent reportage, his withering portraits of life in various unstable pockets of the Third World, is not to expose the deficits of the people or their culture—though it can certainly look that way—but rather to unmask the grandiose mythologies, the illusions, that flourish where the deeper continuities of civilization are lacking." In 2003 Naipaul published another essay collection, *Literary Occasions: Essays.* Included in this book is his Nobel Prize lecture, as well as essays on other writers of Indian extraction, memories of his childhood, even a foreword from the 1983 edition of his novel *A House for Mr. Biswas.*

Naipaul published his fourteenth work of fiction, *Magic Seeds,* in 2004. He has been quoted as saying it is also his last, but, as Charles Foran wrote in *Globe & Mail,* this is "something he has, admittedly, claimed before." The novel picks up Willie Chandran's life eighteen years after *Half a Life* ended. Willie, who is living with his sister Sarojini in Berlin, decides to travel to India to join a guerrilla group. After seven years with them he is thrown in jail. Willie is released when his book of short stories is republished and he returns to London. James Atlas, writing in the *New York Times Book Review,* noted that the novel "revisits the themes—exile, identity, the precariousness of civilization—that [Naipaul has] been grappling with over the past five decades." Foran added, "the prose is muscular and precise," and "for all his impatience with character, the author possesses rare insights into the hearts of men made desperate by circumstance." A *Publishers Weekly* reviewer called Naipaul "a modern master of the multiple ironies of resentment."

Throughout Naipaul's career he has become increasingly well-accepted as "a writer with a world perspective, whose constantly evolving literary skill has few rivals in contemporary fiction," as an essayist for *Contemporary Novelists* pointed out. Yet his unique viewpoint has drawn critics who have accused him of "racism, chauvinism, and of displaying a nostalgic collaboration with imperialist ideology," reflected Stella Swain in the *Dictionary of Literary Biography.* On the other hand, Swain noted, those enthusiastic about his work generally praise it for its "aesthetic and philosophical considerations or from an appreciation of his honesty. Naipaul is lauded as a sophisticated artist whose refined and subtle prose represents the best of contemporary fiction in English." Swain conjectured that these two opposing views of the writer are difficult to reconcile, "except insofar as it could be said that the confusion he has caused in his reading public is simply an expression of anxieties and conflicts that already exist. In the sense that his work presses such tensions into articulation and dialogue, it is of great value."

BIOGRAPHICAL AND CRITICAL SOURCES:

BOOKS

Contemporary Literary Criticism, Gale (Detroit, MI), Volume 4, 1975, Volume 7, 1977, Volume 9, 1978, Volume 13, 1980, Volume 18, 1981, Volume 37, 1986, Volume 105, 1999.

Contemporary Novelists, 7th edition, St. James Press (Detroit, MI), 2001.

Dictionary of Literary Biography, Gale (Detroit, MI), Volume 125: *Twentieth-Century Caribbean and Black African Writers, Second Series,* 1993, Volume 204:*British Travel Writers, 1940-1997,* 1999, Volume 207: *British Novelists since 1960, Third Series,* 1999.

Dictionary of Literary Biography Yearbook: 1985, Gale (Detroit, MI), 1986.

Dissanayake, Wimal, *Self and Colonial Desire: Travel Writings of V.S. Naipaul,* P. Lang (New York, NY), 1993.

Gorra, Michael Edward, *After Empire: Scott, Naipaul, Rushdie,* University of Chicago Press (Chicago, IL), 1997.

Hamner, Robert D., *V.S. Naipaul,* Twayne (New York, NY), 1973.

Jussawalla, Feroza, editor, *Conversations with V.S. Naipaul,* University Press of Mississippi (Jackson, MI), 1997.

Kamra, Shashi, *The Novels of V. S. Naipaul: A Study in Theme and Form,* Prestige Books/Indian Society for Commonwealth Studies, 1990.

Khan, Akhtar Jamal, *V.S. Naipaul: A Critical Study,* Creative Books, 1998.

King, Bruce, *V.S. Naipaul,* St. Martin's Press (New York, NY), 1993.

Nixon, Rob, *London Calling: V. S. Naipaul, Postcolonial Mandarin,* Oxford University Press (New York, NY), 1992.

Theroux, Paul, *Sir Vidia's Shadow: A Friendship across Five Continents,* Houghton (Boston, MA), 1998.

Theroux, Paul, *V.S. Naipaul: An Introduction to His Work,* Deutsch (London, England), 1972.

Thorpe, Michael, *V.S. Naipaul,* Longmans (London, England), 1976.

Weiss, Timothy, *On the Margins: The Art of Exile in V.S. Naipaul,* University of Massachusetts Press (Amherst, MA), 1992.

PERIODICALS

Africa News Service, December 19, 2001, "Naipaul: The Writer Who Despises His Background."

America, June 15, 1991, pp. 656-657.

American Prospect, January 28, 2002, Amitava Kumar, *The Humor and the Pity,* p. 31.

American Scholar, winter, 1999, Jeffrey Meyers, review of *Beyond Belief,* p. 150.

Américas, March-April, 1998, Sandra Chouthi, "House of Worldly Treasures," p. 4.

Atlantic, May, 1970; January, 1976; July, 1977; June, 1979; February, 2002, Geoffrey Wheatcroft, "A Terrifying Honesty: V.S. Naipaul Is Certainly No Liberal and Herein Lies His Importance," p. 88; November, 2001, review of *Half a Life,* pp. 144-145.

Best Sellers, April 15, 1968.

Book, November- December, 2001, Paul Evans, review of *Half a Life,* p. 62.

Booklist, January 1, 1999, review of *Beyond Belief,* p. 777; August, 2001, Donna Seaman, review of *Half a Life,* p. 2051; May 1, 2002, Donna Seaman, review of *The Writer and the World,* p. 1442.

Books Abroad, winter, 1968; winter, 1969.

Books and Bookmen, October, 1967.

Boston Globe, March 15, 1987; January 22, 1989; December 23, 1990.

Chicago Sunday Tribune, July 12, 1959.

Chicago Tribune, November 14, 2001, Julia Keller, "Why Is V.S. Naipaul So Cranky?"

Choice, June, 1973.

Christian Century, September 9, 1998, Jane I. Smith, review of *Beyond Belief,* p. 835.

Christian Science Monitor, July 19, 1962; March 29, 1968; May 28, 1970; February 28, 1991, p. 11.

Commentary, August, 1994, pp. 27-31.

Commonweal, September 9, 1994, pp. 28-29.

Contemporary Literature, winter, 1968.

Economist (Great Britain), July 16, 1977.

Economist (U.S.), September 12, 1998, review of *Beyond Belief,* p. S7.

Europe Intelligence Wire, October 12, 2002, review of *The Writer and the World.*

Explicator, spring, 2002, Ervin Beck, "Naipaul's B. Wordsworth," p. 175.

Forbes, February 23, 1998, Richard C. Morais, "Tribal Tribulations," p. 149.

Foreign Affairs, September-October, 1998, L. Carl Brown, review of *Beyond Belief,* p. 162.

Globe & Mail (Toronto, Canada), November 20, 2004, Charles Foran, "A Pessimist in Winter," p. D3.

Guardian, September 1, 2001, Paul Theroux, "Into the Lion's Den"; October 12, 2001, Caryl Phillips, "Reluctant Hero."

Illustrated London News, May 20, 1967.

Kenyon Review, November, 1967.

Library Journal, May 15, 1998, James F. DeRoche, review of *Beyond Belief,* p. 91; June 15, 2002, Ravi Shenoy, review of *The Writer and the World,* p. 66; October 1, 2003, Michael Rogers, review of *India: A Wounded Civilization,* p. 123.

Listener, May 25, 1967; September 28, 1967; May 23, 1968.

London, May, 1967.

Los Angeles Times, May 9, 1980; March 15, 1989; October 15, 2001, Tim Rutten, "A Nod to Values We Embrace; People Can Take Heart in V.S. Naipaul's Recent Nobel Prize Win," p. E1.

Los Angeles Times Book Review, June 24, 1979; May 22, 1994, pp. 3, 11.

Modern Fiction Studies, spring, 2002, review of *The Return of Eva Peron,* p. 169.

Nation, October 9, 1967; October 5, 1970; December 13, 1975; July 2, 1977; June 30, 1979; Amitava Kumar, review of *Half a Life,* p. 32.

National Review, October 6, 1970; August 29, 1994, pp. 61-62; February 7, 2000, Francis X. Rocca, review of *Between Father and Son,* p. 48; December 31, 2001, David Pryce-Jones, "Nobility in the Novel"; April 8, 2002, David Pryce-Jones, "Indian War Drums: Rushdie, Naipaul, and the Subcontinent's Challenge."

New Criterion, March, 2000, Joseph Epstein, review of *Between Father and Son,* p. 58.

New Leader, May 4, 1998, Roger Draper, review of *Beyond Belief,* p. 13.

New Republic, July 9, 1977; June 9, 1979; June 10, 1991, pp. 30-34; June 13, 1994, pp. 40-45; July 13, 1998, Fouad Ajami, review of *Beyond Belief,* p. 27; November 5, 2001, James Wood, review of *Half a Life,* p. 31.

New Statesman, May 5, 1967; September 15, 1967; November 7, 1969; October 8, 1971; June 17, 1977; December 17, 2001, Lieve Joris, interview with V.S. Naipaul, p. 54.

Newsweek, December 1, 1975; June 6, 1977; May 21, 1979; June 13, 1994, p. 55.

Newsweek International, August 26, 2002, Ben Moser, review of *The Writer and the World,* p. 57.

New Yorker, August 4, 1962; August 8, 1970; June 6, 1977; May 21, 1979.

New York Herald Tribune Books, June 24, 1962.

New York Review of Books, October 26, 1967; April 11, 1968; December 30, 1971; May 31, 1979; February 14, 1991, pp. 3-5; November 1, 2001, J.M. Coetzee, "The Razor's Edge."

New York Times, December 16, 1967; December 25, 1971; August 17, 1977; May 14, 1979; March 13, 1980; May 17, 1994; October 12, 2001, Sarah Lyall, "Nobel in Literature Goes to Naipaul, an Explorer of Exile," p. A11; October 16, 2001, Michiko Kakutani, "A Young Man in a Strange Place at a Time That Can Never Be Right," p. E1.

New York Times Book Review, October 15, 1967; April 7, 1968; May 24, 1970; October 17, 1971; November 16, 1975; December 28, 1975; May 1, 1977; June 12, 1977; May 13, 1979; May 22, 1994, Brent Staples, "Con Men and Conquerors," pp. 1, 42-43;

June 7, 1998, Michael Ignatieff, "In the Name of the Most Merciful"; January 5, 2000, Mel Gussow, "The Writer-to-Be and His Mentor"; January 16, 2000, Abraham Verghese, "The Family Business"; September 1, 2002, Daphne Merkin, review of *The Writer and the World,* p. 11; November 28, 2004, James Atlas, "A Passage to India," p. 14.

New York Times Magazine, October 28, 2001, Adam Shatz, interview with Naipaul, p. 19.

Observer (London, England), April 30, 1967; September 10, 1967; October 26, 1969; September 22, 2002, Jason Cowley, review of *The Writer and the World,* p. 15.

PMLA, May, 2002, transcript of Naipaul's Nobel lecture, p. 479.

Progressive, November, 1998, Edward W. Said, review of *Beyond Belief,* p. 40.

Publishers Weekly, May 25, 1998, review of *Beyond Belief,* p. 82; November 29, 1999, review of *Between Father and Son,* p. 59; May 13, 2002, review of *The Writer and the World,* p. 58; June 23, 2003, review of *Literary Occasions: Essays,* p. 55; October 18, 2004, review of *Magic Seeds,* p. 49.

Punch, May 10, 1967.

Rocky Mountain News, Ashley Simpson Shires, review of *Literary Occasions,* p. 29D.

St. Louis Post- Dispatch, August 25, 2002, Dale Singer, review of *The Writer and the World,* p. F9.

San Francisco Chronicle, October 17, 2001, David Kipen, "Unsatisfying 'Half' by Naipaul; Novelist Uncharitable to His Characters," p. E1.

Saturday Review, July 2, 1960; October 23, 1971; November 15, 1975.

Seattle Times, August 18, 2002, Michael Upchurch, review of *The Writer and the World,* p. K10.

Smithsonian, December, 2001, Paul Gray, *Any Other Year, Giving Reactionary Author V.S. Naipaul a Nobel Would Have Sparked Debate,* p. 106.

Spectator, September 22, 1967; November 8, 1969; May 14, 1994, p. 36.

Tennessean, October 12, 2003, Brian J. Buchanan, review of *Literary Occasions,* p. D38.

Time, May 25, 1970; December 1, 1975; June 20, 1977; May 21, 1979; May 30, 1994, p. 64; October 22, 2001, Robert Hughes, "Peace and Understanding," p. 84.

Time International, August 3, 1998, "Journey to Islam," p. 39; November 26, 2001, R.Z. Sheppard, review of *Half a Life,* p. 68.

Times (London, England), October 12, 2001, David Pryce-Jones, "Naipaul Is Truly a Nobel Man in a Free State."

Times Literary Supplement, May 31, 1963; April 27, 1967; September 14, 1967; December 25, 1969; July 30, 1971; November 17, 1972.

Transition, December, 1971.

Tribune Books (Chicago, IL), May 13, 1979; April 20, 1980.

Twentieth Century Literature, summer, 2000, Robert M. Greenberg, "Anger and the Alchemy of Literary Method in V.S. Naipaul's Political Fiction: The Case of *The Mimic Men,*" p. 214.

U.S. News & World Report, August 10, 1998, Jonah Blank, "Feuding Literary Titans," p. 39.

Washington Post, October 12, 2001, Linton Weeks, "A Winning Worldview: Globetrotting V.S. Naipaul Collects Nobel Prize for Literature," p. C01; October 26, 2003, Sudip Bose, review of *Literary Occasions,* p. B8.

Washington Post Book World, April 19, 1970; December 5, 1971; November 28, 1976; June 19, 1977; July 1, 1979; May 15, 1994, pp. 1, 14.

Washington Times, August 25, 2002, Sven Birkerts, review of *The Writer and the World,* p. B8.

Weekend Australian, December 28, 2002, Delia Falconer, review of *The Writer and the World,* p. B10.

World Literature Today, summer, 2000, Bruce King, review of *Between Father and Son,* p. 575; spring, 2002, Mervyn Morris, *Sir Vidia and the Prize,* p. 11; April-June, 2003, Bruce King, review of *Half a Life,* p. 90.

World Press Review, July, 1998, L.K. Sharma, "Faith and Neurosis," p. 41.

ONLINE

Salon.com, http://www.salon.com/ (January 18, 2000), Akash Kapur, review of *Between Father and Son;* (October 14, 2001), Gavin McNett, "The Black Sheep."

* * *

NARAYAN, Rasipuram Krishnaswami
See NARAYAN, R.K.

* * *

NARAYAN, R.K. 1906-2001
(Rasipuram Krishnaswami Narayan)

PERSONAL: Born Rasipuram Krishnaswami Narayanaswami, October 10, 1906, in Madras, India; changed surname to Narayan, 1935; died May 13, 2001, in Madras, India; married; wife's name Rajam, 1934 (deceased, 1939); children: Hema (daughter). *Education:*

Maharaja's College (now University of Mysore), received degree, 1930. *Hobbies and other interests:* Music and long walks.

CAREER: Writer. Owner of Indian Thought Publications, Mysore, India.

AWARDS, HONORS: National Prize of the Indian Literary Academy, 1958; Sahitya Academy award, 1961; Padma Bhushan, India, 1964; National Association of Independent Schools award, 1965; D.Litt., University of Leeds, 1967, University of Delhi, Sri Venkateswara University, and University of Mysore; English-speaking Union Book Award, 1975, for *My Days: A Memoir;* Benson Medal and fellow, Royal Society of Literature, 1980; honorary membership and citation, American Academy and Institute of Arts and Letters, 1982; Padma Vibhushan, India, 2000.

WRITINGS:

NOVELS

Swami and Friends: A Novel of Malgudi, Hamish Hamilton (London, England), 1935, Fawcett (New York, NY), 1970, published with *The Bachelor of Arts,* Michigan State College Press (East Lansing, MI), 1957.

The Bachelor of Arts, Nelson (London, England), 1937, published with *Swami and Friends,* Michigan State College Press (East Lansing, MI), 1957.

The Dark Room, Macmillan (London, England), 1938.

The English Teacher, Eyre & Spottiswoode (London, England), 1945, published as *Grateful to Life and Death,* Michigan State College Press (East Lansing, MI), 1953.

Mr. Sampath, Eyre & Spottiswoode (London, England), 1949, published as *The Printer of Malgudi,* Michigan State College Press (East Lansing, MI), 1957.

The Financial Expert, Methuen (London, England), 1952, Michigan State College Press (East Lansing, MI), 1953.

Waiting for the Mahatma, Michigan State College Press (East Lansing, MI), 1955.

The Guide, Viking (New York, NY), 1958.

The Man-Eater of Malgudi, Viking (New York, NY), 1961.

The Vendor of Sweets, Viking (New York, NY), 1967, published as *The Sweet-Vendor,* Bodley Head (London, England), 1967.

The Painter of Signs, Viking (New York, NY), 1976.

A Tiger for Malgudi, Viking (New York, NY), 1983.

Talkative Man, Heinemann (London, England), 1986, Viking (New York, NY), 1987.

The World of Nagaraj, Viking (New York, NY), 1990.

SHORT STORIES

Malgudi Days, Indian Thought (Mysore, India), 1943.

Dodu and Other Stories, Indian Thought (Mysore, India), 1943.

Cyclone and Other Stories, Indian Thought (Mysore, India), 1944.

An Astrologer's Day and Other Stories, Eyre & Spottiswoode (London, England), 1947.

Lawley Road, Indian Thought (Mysore, India), 1956.

Gods, Demons, and Others, Viking (New York, NY), 1964, illustrated by R.K. Laxman, University of Chicago Press (Chicago, IL), 1993.

A Horse and Two Goats and Other Stories, Viking (New York, NY), 1970.

Old and New, Indian Thought (Mysore, India), 1981.

Malgudi Days, Viking (New York, NY), 1982.

Under the Banyan Tree and Other Stories, Viking (New York, NY), 1985.

Malgudi Days II, Viking (New York, NY), 1986.

The Grandmother's Tale, illustrated by R.K. Laxman, Indian Thought (Mysore, India), 1992, published as *The Grandmother's Tale and Selected Stories,* Viking (New York, NY), 1994.

Salt and Sawdust: Stories and Table Talk, Penguin (New Delhi, India), 1993.

A Town Called Malgudi: The Finest Fiction of R.K. Narayan, edited with an introduction by S. Krishnan, Viking (New York, NY), 1999.

Contributor of short stories to periodicals, including *New Yorker.*

OTHER

Mysore, Government Branch Press (Mysore, India), 1939.

Next Sunday: Sketches and Essays, Indian Thought (Mysore, India), 1956, Pearl (Bombay, India), 1960.

My Dateless Diary: A Journal of a Trip to the United States in October 1956, Indian Thought (Mysore, India), 1960, Penguin (New York, NY), 1965.

(Translator) *The Ramayana: A Shortened Modern Prose Version of the Indian Epic,* Viking (New York, NY), 1972.

My Days: A Memoir, Viking (New York, NY), 1974.

Reluctant Guru, Hind Pocket Books (New Delhi, India), 1974.

The Emerald Route (includes play *The Watchman of the Lake*), Government of Karnataka (Bangalore, India), 1977, Ind-US Inc. (Glastonbury, CT), 1980.

(Translator) *The Mahabharata: A Shortened Prose Version of the Indian Epic,* Viking (New York, NY), 1978.

A Writer's Nightmare: Selected Essays, 1958-1988, Penguin (London, England), 1988, Penguin (New York, NY), 1989.

A Story-Teller's World: Stories, Essays, Sketches, Penguin (London, England), 1989, Viking (New York, NY), 1990.

(Editor) *Indian Thought: A Miscellany,* Penguin (London, England), 1997.

The Magic of Malgudi (collection, contains *Swami and Friends, The Bachelor of Arts,* and *The Vendor of Sweets*), edited with an introduction by S. Krishnan, Viking (New York, NY), 2000.

The World of Malgudi (collection, contains *Mr. Sampath, The Financial Expert, The Painter of Signs,* and *A Tiger for Malgudi*), edited with an introduction by S. Krishnan, Viking (New York, NY), 2000.

The Writerly Life: Selected Non-Fiction, Viking (New York, NY), 2001.

Author's manuscript collection is housed at the Mugar Memorial Library, Boston University.

ADAPTATIONS: Narayan's *The Guide* was adapted for the stage by Harvey Breit and Patricia Rinehart and produced Off-Broadway at the Hudson Theatre, 1968. *Mr. Sampath* and *The Guide* were adapted for film.

SIDELIGHTS: R.K. Narayan was perhaps the best-known Indian of his day writing in English. His long and prolific career was marked by well-received novels, novellas, and short stories, almost all of which are set in the fictional backwater town of Malgudi and its environs. Noting that Narayan produced "India's most distinguished literary career of recent times," *New York Times Book Review* correspondent Shashi Tharoor went on to state: "In the West, Mr. Narayan is widely considered the quintessential Indian writer, whose fiction evokes a sensibility and a rhythm older and less familiar to Westerners than that of any other writer in the English language." According to Phil Hogan in the London *Observer,* "Narayan . . . said he was 'a storyteller, nothing more, nothing less.' R.K. Narayan is no more just a storyteller than the Taj Mahal is a large building with a swimming pool. . . . Malgudi may be in the middle of nowhere but all life is here."

In a British Broadcasting Corporation radio interview, Narayan once spoke to William Walsh of his use of the English language in his work: "English has been with us [in India] for over a century and a half. I am particularly fond of the language. I was never aware that I was using a different, a foreign, language when I wrote in English, because it came to me very easily. I can't explain how. English is a very adaptable language. And it's so transparent it can take on the tint of any country." Walsh added in his study *R.K. Narayan* that Narayan's English "is limpid, simple, calm and unaffected, natural in its run and tone, and beautifully measured" in a unique fashion that takes on an Indian flavor by avoiding "the American purr of the combustion engine . . . [and] the thick marmalade quality of British English."

Other critics have noted the rhythms of Narayan's style and the richness of his narrative. Melvin J. Friedman suggested in a comparison with Isaac Bashevis Singer that "both seem part of an oral tradition in which the 'spoken' triumphs over the 'written,'" and theorized that the similarities between Narayan's fiction and the Indian epics echo Singer's prose style and its "rhythm of the Old Testament." Eve Auchincloss noted that the translation-like quality of the language "adds curious, pleasing flavor."

Narayan's fictional setting is Malgudi, a village very similar to his childhood home, Mysore. In Malgudi every sort of human condition indigenous not only to India but to life everywhere is represented. Malgudi has perhaps inevitably drawn comparisons to William Faulkner's Yoknapatawpha County, both because Narayan returns to its setting again and again, and because he uses its eccentric citizens to meditate upon the human condition in a global context. In the *Times Literary Supplement,* Walsh stressed the universal quality of Malgudi: "Whatever happens in India happens in Malgudi, and whatever happens in Malgudi happens everywhere."

The characters in Narayan's novels and short stories often experience some kind of growth or change, or gain knowledge through the experiences they undergo. As Walsh observed, Narayan most often focused on the middle class and its representative occupations, many of which provided the author with titles for his books: *The Bachelor of Arts, The English Teacher, The Financial Expert, The Guide, The Sweet-Vendor.* Walsh explained Narayan's typical structural pattern in terms of concentric circles, whereby the village represents the outer circle, the family is the inner circle, and the hero, the focus of each novel, stands at the hub. "His hero is usually modest, sensitive, ardent, wry about himself," wrote Walsh, "and sufficiently conscious to have an active inner life and to grope towards some existence independent of the family." Walsh further observed that the typical progress of a Narayan hero involves "the rebirth of self and the progress of its pregnancy or education," thereby suggesting the Indian concept of reincarnation.

Closely related to Narayan's gift for characterization is his ability to present his material with sympathy and comic vision. *Los Angeles Times Book Review* contributor Judith Freeman wrote that Narayan "takes a Western reader into the very heart of an Indian village and the family compounds where the little dramas of marriage and money and kinship inevitably result in a tangle of human ties. The foreignness of the setting, rituals and traditions may seem to us exotic, but the underlying humanity of Narayan's dramas can't fail to strike a familiar chord." The critic added: "What is so lovely about Narayan's work, and what makes it so valuable in a world torn by racial misunderstanding, is the gentleness of his vision, the way he makes each of us a member of his wondrous universe." Walsh wrote of Narayan's "forgiving kindness" and labeled his novels "comedies of sadness . . . lighted with the glint of mockery of both self and others."

Addressing the plot structure of Narayan's fictional world, an essayist for the *Encyclopedia of World Biography* explained how the author's stories begin with "realistic settings and everyday happenings in the lives of a cross-section of Indian society. . . . Gradually fate or chance, oversight or blunder, transforms mundane events to preposterous happenings. Unexpected disasters befall the hero as easily as unforeseen good fortune. The characters accept their fates with an equanimity that suggests the faith that things will somehow turn out happily, whatever their own motivations or actions. Progress . . . meets in Malgudi with long-held conventions, beliefs, and ways of doing things. The modern world can never win a clear-cut victory because Malgudi accepts only what it wants, according to its own private logic."

Among Narayan's most well-received short stories have been "An Astrologer's Day" and "A Horse and Two Goats." "An Astrologer's Day" features an encounter between a village astrologer plying his trade in the marketplace and his last client of the day. The exchange begins with the astrologer giving out the usual platitudes until the client grows angry, demanding he be given the truth. The astrologer then tells the client of his past, of how the client was stabbed and thrown into a well many years before, and has been searching for his attacker ever since. The client is impressed by this revelation, then stunned when the astrologer even knows his name. Finally, the astrologer advises him to stop looking for the man who attacked him years ago for the attacker has long since died. After being paid, the astrologer goes home where his wife asks why he is so late returning home. He explains to her that the man he attacked years ago, and believed he had killed, was in fact alive and well. His mind is finally at rest over that violent event in his past. "An Astrologer's Day," as Chelva Kanaganayakam wrote in *Literature of Developing Nations for Students,* "continues to be a heavily anthologized piece. It is of considerable significance that a story which first appeared in 1947 should retain its appeal after more than fifty years."

In "A Horse and Two Goats" Narayan again presents a meeting between two men, this time an elderly Indian who is tending his goats and an American businessman. The story begins with Muni, a poor goatherder, resting in the shade of a statue—a horse made of clay—as his goats graze nearby. An American businessman happens by, interested in purchasing the statue for his house in New York City. Since neither Muni nor the American share a common language, the American assumes that he is negotiating the purchase of the statue while Muni believes he is selling his goats. When the American hands him 100 rupees, a vast sum for the impoverished old man, Muni runs home to tell his wife. The American hires a truck and carts the statue away, the goats wander home by themselves, and a baffled Muni is left to explain to his wife as best he can how he came to have so much money. "The humour and the irony of this tale," wrote Ralph J. Crane in *Reference Guide to Short Fiction,* "lies in the total benign incomprehension that exists between the two, not only in the way neither understands the other's language, but also in the absolute contrast of their cultural and economic backgrounds, emphasized by the way each values the clay horse. Much of this is conveyed through the wonderful double discourse that makes up a significant part of the story, with each of the characters happily developing his own hermetically-sealed interpretation of the other's words and gestures. The story's charm lies in the way Narayan refrains from passing judgment."

Narayan was considered to be the last working writer in a generation that included W.H. Auden, Graham Greene, and Evelyn Waugh. Greene, for one, found much to praise in Narayan's work, once citing his Indian contemporary as "the novelist I most admire in the English language." His talents did not wane with age, according to most critics; in a London *Observer* review of the writer's 1990 novel *The World of Nagaraj,* Hanif Kureishi summarized the author's extensive body of work: "Narayan is a master, in control of all his subtle effects. He is very funny: his use of irony is superb, and there is much going on in the tiny world he describes." "Next time you labour through a long, tediously clever new novel," Kureishi added, "think of the wisdom and humour Narayan gently slips into his small but luminous masterpieces." The book that would ultimately prove to be Narayan's final full-length work of fiction, *The World of Nagaraj* offers a gentle tale of an easygoing townsman whose life is bedeviled by the dual trials of caring for his wayward nephew and trying to write a book about an obscure Indian saint. *New York Times Book Review* essayist Julian Moynahan stated that with his fourteenth novel Narayan offers "the latest building block in a shining edifice . . . [a] subtly variegated and self-authenticating world of fiction in light of certain universal truths." In *Publishers Weekly* a critic enjoyed returning to Narayan's fictional community, noting that, like old friends, "the Malgudi residents are talkative, philosophical and able to confront events with wonder and humor."

Praised by a *Publishers Weekly* contributor as an "exemplary collection from one of India's most distinguished men of letters," *The Grandmother's Tale and Selected Stories* is a collection of nineteen of Narayan's best short fiction. The title story was first published in India in 1992; other stories in the collection span the author's long career. In her *New York Review of Books* essay on the work, Hilary Mantel observed that Narayan makes his world familiar to non-Indian readers. "He can do this because he has such a sharp eye," Mantel explained, adding that "Life surprises him. . . . Any day, any street, any room in an accustomed house, any face known since childhood, can suddenly be fresh and strange and new; one reality peels away, and shows another underneath."

Mantel further expressed that, through his body of work, Narayan proved himself to be "a writer of towering achievement who has cultivated and preserved the lightest of touches." The critic concluded: "Celebrant of both the outer and inner life, he makes us feel the vulnerability of human beings and of their social bonds. Here is the town with its daylight bustle; . . . outside, and within, are the deep forests, where tigers roar in the night."

BIOGRAPHICAL AND CRITICAL SOURCES:

BOOKS

Beatina, Mary, *Narayan: A Study in Transcendence,* P. Lang (New York, NY), 1993.

Contemporary Literary Criticism, Thomson Gale (Detroit, MI), Volume 7, 1977, Volume 28, 1984, Volume 47, 1988, pp. 300-309.

Contemporary Novelists, 7th edition, St. James Press (Detroit, MI), 2001, pp. 752-755.

Encyclopedia of World Biography, 2nd edition, Thomson Gale (Detroit, MI), 1998.

Goyal, Bhagwat S., editor, *R.K. Narayan's India: Myth and Reality,* Sarup & Sons (New Delhi, India), 1993.

Hariprasanna, A., *The World of Malgudi: A Study of R.K. Narayan's Novels,* Prestige Books (New Delhi, India), 1994.

Holstrom, Lakshmi, *The Novels of R.K. Narayan,* Writers Workshop (Calcutta, India), 1973.

Kain, Geoffrey, editor, *R.K. Narayan: Contemporary Critical Essays,* Michigan State University Press (East Lansing, MI), 1993.

Krishnan, S., editor, *Malgudi Landscapes: The Best of R.K. Narayan,* Penguin (New York, NY), 1992.

Literature of Developing Nations for Students, Volume 1, Thomson Gale (Detroit, MI), 2000.

Mohan, Ramesh, editor, *Indian Writing in English,* Orient Longman (Bombay, India), 1978.

Pousse, Michel, *R.K. Narayan: A Painter of Modern India,* P. Lang (New York, NY), 1995.

Ramana, P. S., *Message in Design: A Study of R.K. Narayan's Fiction,* Harmam (New Delhi, India), 1993.

Ram, Atma, editor, *Perspectives on R.K. Narayan,* Humanities Press (Atlantic Highlands, NJ), 1981.

Reference Guide to Short Fiction, St. James Press (Detroit, MI), 1994.

Season of Promise: Spring Fiction, University of Missouri (Columbia, MO), 1967.

Sharan, Nagendra Nath, *A Critical Study of the Novels of R.K. Narayan,* Classical (New Delhi, India), 1993.

Short Stories for Students, Volume 5, Thomson Gale (Detroit, MI), 1999.

Varma, R. M., *Major Themes in the Novels of R.K. Narayan,* Jainsons (New Delhi, India), 1993.

Walsh, William, *R.K. Narayan,* Longman (New York, NY), 1971.

Walsh, William, *R.K. Narayan: A Critical Appreciation,* University of Chicago Press (Chicago, IL), 1982.

PERIODICALS

Ariel, January, 1984.

Atlantic, September, 1983, Phoebe-Lou Adams, review of *A Tiger for Malgudi,* p. 125.

Banasthali Patrika, January 12, 1969; July 13, 1969.

Booklist, September 1, 1994, Donna Seaman, review of *The Grandmother's Tale and Selected Stories,* p. 24.
Books Abroad, summer, 1965; spring, 1971; spring, 1976.
Book World, July 11, 1976; December 5, 1976.
Christian Science Monitor, February 19, 1970.
Daedalus, fall, 1989, p. 232.
Encounter, October, 1964.
Harper's, April, 1965.
Journal of Commonwealth Literature, December, 1966; July, 1968, Perry D. Westbrook, "The Short Stories of R.K. Narayan," p. 41.
Listener, March 1, 1962.
Literary Criterion, winter, 1968.
Literature East and West, winter, 1965, Cynthia vanden Driesen, "The Achievement of R.K. Narayan," pp. 51-64.
London, September, 1970.
London Review of Books, December 4, 1986, pp. 23-24.
Los Angeles Times, May 14, 2001, p. B9.
Los Angeles Times Book Review, October 23, 1994, p. 12; December 11, 1994, p. 9; January 29, 1995, p. 8.
Modern Fiction Studies, spring, 1993, pp. 113-130.
Nation, June 28, 1975.
New Republic, May 13, 1967.
New Statesman, June 2, 1967.
Newsweek, July 4, 1976.
New Yorker, September 15, 1962; October 14, 1967; March 16, 1968; July 5, 1976, p. 82; August 2, 1982, p. 84.
New York Review of Books, June 29, 1967; October 8, 1987, p. 45; February 16, 1995, pp. 9-11; March 21, 1999, review of *The Grandmother's Tale and Selected Stories,* p. 32; February 22, 2001, p. 44.
New York Times, March 23, 1958, p. 5; August 1, 1965; June 20, 1976; August 8, 1983; March 14, 1987, p. 14; May 14, 2001.
New York Times Book Review, May 14, 1967; June 20, 1976; September 4, 1983, p. 4; July 8, 1990, p. 8; July 15, 1990, p. 8; September 11, 1994, p. 40.
Observer (London, England), March 25, 1990, p. 66; July 18, 1993, p. 57; March 21, 1999, review of *The Grandmother's Tale and Selected Stories,* p. 32.
Osmania Journal of English Studies, Volume 7, number 1, 1970.
People, August 29, 1983, review of *A Tiger for Malgudi,* p. 12.
Publishers Weekly, June 20, 1994, review of *The Grandmother's Tale and Selected Stories,* p. 94.
Sewanee Review, winter, 1975.
Studies in Short Fiction, summer, 1994, Tone Sundt Urstad, "Symbolism in R.K. Narayan's 'Naga,'" p. 425.
Times Literary Supplement, May 18, 1967; October 18, 1985, Neville Shack, review of *Under the Banyan Tree and Other Stories,* p. 1168; October 3, 1986, p. 1113; March 23-29, 1990, p. 328; July 23, 1993, p. 20.
Village Voice, November 5, 1985, p. 55.
Wall Street Journal, August 22, 1983, p. 14.
Washington Post, April 14, 1970.
Washington Post Book World, September 4, 1983, pp. 3, 9; July 28, 1985, Frances Taliaferro, review of *Under the Banyan Tree and Other Stories,* p. 7, 13; April 5, 1987, p. 7.
World Literature Today, spring, 1984, p. 325.

OBITUARIES:

PERIODICALS

Economist (U.S.), May 26, 2001, p. 1.
Time International, June 4, 2001, p. 28.

* * *

NAYLOR, Gloria 1950-

PERSONAL: Born January 25, 1950, in New York, NY; daughter of Roosevelt (a transit worker) and Alberta (a telephone operator; maiden name, McAlpin) Naylor; divorced. *Education:* Brooklyn College of the City University of New York, B.A., 1981; Yale University, M.A., 1983.

ADDRESSES: *Office*—One Way Productions, 638 Second St., Brooklyn, NY 11215. *Agent*—Sterling Lord Literistic, 65 Bleecker St., New York, NY 10012-2420.

CAREER: Missionary for Jehovah's Witnesses in New York, North Carolina, and Florida, 1968-75; worked for various hotels in New York, NY, including Sheraton City Squire, as telephone operator, 1975-81; writer, 1981—; One Way Productions, New York, NY, president, 1990—. Writer in residence, Cummington Community of the Arts, 1983; visiting lecturer, George Washington University, 1983-84, and Princeton University, 1986-87; cultural exchange lecturer, United States Information Agency, India, 1985; scholar in residence, University of Pennsylvania, 1986; visiting professor,

New York University, 1986, and Boston University, 1987; Fannie Hurst Visiting Professor, Brandeis University, 1988. Senior fellow, Society for the Humanities, Cornell University, 1988; executive board, Book of the Month Club, 1989-94; producer, One Ways Productions, 1990; visiting scholar, University of Kent, 1992; playwright, Hartford Stage Company, 1994.

MEMBER: PEN, Authors Guild, National Writers Union, Book of the Month Club (executive board member, 1989-94).

AWARDS, HONORS: American Book Award for best first novel, 1983, for *The Women of Brewster Place;* Distinguished Writer Award, Mid-Atlantic Writers Association, 1983; National Endowment for the Arts fellowship, 1985; Candace Award, National Coalition of 100 Black Women, 1986; Guggenheim fellowship, 1988; Lillian Smith Book Award, Southern Regional Council, 1989, for *Mama Day;* New York Foundation for the Arts fellowship, 1991; Brooklyn College President's Medal, 1993; D.H.L., Sacred Heart University, 1994; American Book Award, New Columbus Foundation, 1998, for *The Men of Brewster Place.*

WRITINGS:

The Women of Brewster Place (novel), Viking (New York, NY), 1982.

Linden Hills (novel), Ticknor & Fields (New York, NY), 1985.

Mama Day (novel), Ticknor & Fields (New York, NY), 1988.

Bailey's Cafe (novel), Harcourt (New York, NY), 1992.

Gloria Naylor Reads "The Women of Brewster Place" and "Mama Day" (sound recording), American Audio Prose Library (Columbia, MO), 1988.

(Editor) *Children of the Night: The Best Short Stories by Black Writers, 1967 to the Present,* Little, Brown (Boston, MA), 1995.

The Men of Brewster Place (novel), Hyperion (New York, NY), 1998.

Conversations with Gloria Naylor, edited by Maxine Montgomery, University Press of Mississippi (Jackson, MS), 2004.

Also author of stage adaptation of *Bailey's Cafe,* produced in Hartford, CT, 1994, and of a children's play, *Candy.* Author of unproduced screenplay adaptation of *The Women of Brewster Place,* for American Playhouse, 1984, and of an unproduced original screenplay for Public Broadcasting System's "In Our Own Words," 1985.

Contributor of essays and articles to periodicals, including *Southern Review, Essence, Ms., Life, Ontario Review,* and *People.* Contributing editor, *Callaloo,* 1984—. "Hers" columnist for *New York Times,* 1986.

ADAPTATIONS: The Women of Brewster Place was adapted as a miniseries, produced by Oprah Winfrey and Carole Isenberg, and broadcast by American Broadcasting Co. (ABC-TV) in 1989; it became a weekly ABC series in 1990, produced by Oprah Winfrey, Earl Hamner, and Donald Sipes.

WORK IN PROGRESS: A sequel to *Mama Day,* about Cocoa and Saphira Wade.

SIDELIGHTS: Gloria Naylor won critical and popular acclaim for her first published novel, *The Women of Brewster Place.* In that book, as in her successive novels, including *Linden Hills, Mama Day,* and *The Men of Brewster Place,* Naylor gave an intense and vivid depiction of many social issues, including poverty, racism, homophobia, discrimination against women, and the social stratification of African Americans. Vashti Crutcher Lewis, a contributor to the *Dictionary of Literary Biography,* commented on the "brilliance" of Naylor's first novel, derived from "her rich prose, her lyrical portrayals of African Americans, and her illumination of the meaning of being a black woman in America." In *The Women of Brewster Place* and her other novels, Naylor focuses on "themes of deferred dreams of love (familial and sexual), marriage, respectability, and economic stability, while observing the recurring messages that poverty breeds violence, that true friendship and affection are not dependent on gender, and that women in the black ghettos of America bear their burdens with grace and courage," stated Lewis.

Naylor's parents left Mississippi, where they worked as sharecroppers, to seek new opportunities in New York City. Gloria was born there in 1950. A quiet, precocious child who loved to read, she began writing prodigiously even before her teen years, filling many notebooks with observations, poems, and short stories. After graduating from high school, she worked as a missionary for the Jehovah's Witnesses in the city and in the South. In 1981, she entered Brooklyn College, majoring in English. It was at that time that she read Toni Morrison's novel *The Bluest Eye,* which was a pivotal experience for her. She began to avidly read the work of Zora Neale Hurston, Alice Walker, and other black women novelists, none of which she had been exposed to previously. She went on to earn an M.A. in African-American studies at Yale University; her thesis eventually became her second published novel, *Linden Hills.*

Publication of some short fiction in *Essence* magazine led to her first book contract. *The Women of Brewster Place* is made up of seven interconnected stories, involving seven black women who live in a dreary apartment complex that is isolated from the rest of the city. Though they are from widely varying age groups and social backgrounds, and have very different outlooks and approaches to life, the women become a strong support group for each other as they struggle with the pain and frustration of finding their dreams constantly thwarted by the forces of racism and sexism. Naylor's work won the prestigious American Book Award for the best first novel in 1983.

Reviewing *The Women of Brewster Place* in the *Washington Post,* Deirdre Donahue wrote: "Naylor is not afraid to grapple with life's big subjects: sex, birth, love, death, grief. Her women feel deeply, and she unflinchingly transcribes their emotions. . . . Naylor's potency wells up from her language. With prose as rich as poetry, a passage will suddenly take off and sing like a spiritual. . . . Vibrating with undisguised emotion, *The Women of Brewster Place* springs from the same roots that produced the blues. Like them, her book sings of sorrows proudly borne by black women in America." Lewis described *The Women of Brewster Place* as "a tightly focused novel peopled with well-delineated, realistically portrayed African-American women. Naylor's use of authentic African-American vernacular and precise metaphors are hallmarks."

One of the characters in *Brewster Place* is a refugee from Linden Hills, an exclusive black suburb. Naylor's second novel spotlights that affluent community, revealing the material corruption and moral decay that would prompt an idealistic young woman to abandon her home for a derelict urban neighborhood. Though *Linden Hills,* as the book is called, approaches the Afro-American experience from the upper end of the socioeconomic spectrum, it is also a black microcosm. This book "forms the second panel of that picture of contemporary urban black life which Naylor started with in *Women of Brewster Place,*" wrote *Times Literary Supplement* contributor Roz Kaveney. "Where that book described the faults, passions, and culture of the good poor, this shows the nullity of black lives that are led in imitation of suburban whites."

Naylor was more ambitious in structuring her second novel. *Linden Hills* has been described as a contemporary allegory with gothic overtones, structurally modeled after Dante's *Inferno.* Among its many accomplishments, Dante's Italian masterpiece describes the nine circles of hell, Satan's imprisonment in their depths, and the lost souls condemned to suffer with him. In Naylor's modern version, "souls are damned not because they have offended God or have violated a religious system but because they have offended themselves. In their single-minded pursuit of upward mobility, the inhabitants of Linden Hill, a black, middle-class suburb, have turned away from their past and from their deepest sense of who they are," wrote Catherine C. Ward in *Contemporary Literature.* To correspond to Dante's circles, Naylor uses a series of crescent-shaped drives that ring the suburban development. Her heroes are two young street poets—outsiders from a neighboring community who hire themselves out to do odd jobs so they can earn Christmas money. "As they move down the hill, what they encounter are people who have 'moved up' in American society . . . until eventually they will hit the center of their community and the home of my equivalent of Satan," Naylor told *Publishers Weekly* interviewer William Goldstein. Naylor's Satan is one Luther Nedeed, a combination mortician and real estate tycoon, who preys on the residents' baser ambitions to keep them in his sway.

Naylor's third novel, *Mama Day,* is named for its main character—a wise old woman with magical powers whose name is Miranda Day, but whom everyone refers to as Mama Day. This ninety-year-old conjurer made a walk-on appearance in *Linden Hills* as the illiterate, toothless aunt who hauls about cheap cardboard suitcases and leaky jars of preserves. But it is in *Mama Day* that this "caster of hoodoo spells . . . comes into her own," according to *New York Times Book Review* contributor Bharati Mukherjee. "The portrait of Mama Day is magnificent," Mukherjee wrote. Mama Day lives on Willow Springs, a wondrous island off the coast of Georgia and South Carolina that has been owned by her family since before the Civil War. The fact that slaves are portrayed as property owners demonstrates one of the ways that Naylor turns the world upside down, according to Rita Mae Brown. Another, Brown stated in the *Los Angeles Times Book Review,* is "that the women possess the real power, and are acknowledged as having it." When Mama Day's grandniece Cocoa brings George, her citified new husband, to Willow Springs, he learns the importance of accepting mystery. "George is the linchpin of *Mama Day,*" Brown said. "His rational mind allows the reader to experience the island as George experiences it. Mama Day and Cocoa are of the island and therefore less immediately accessible to the reader." The critical point in the story is the moment when George is asked not only to believe in Mama Day's power, but to act on it. A hurricane has made it impossible to summon a doctor from the mainland, but

Cocoa is critically ill. Mama Day gives George a task to do in order to help save Cocoa's life, but he fails to do it because he only uses his rational thinking. George does ultimately save Cocoa, but doing so demands a great personal sacrifice.

The plot twists and thematic concerns of *Mama Day* have led several reviewers to compare the work to that of Shakespeare. "Whereas *Linden Hills* was Dantesque, *Mama Day* is Shakespearean, with allusions, however oblique and tangential, to *Hamlet, King Lear,* and, especially, *The Tempest,*" wrote Chicago's *Tribune Books* critic John Blades. "Like Shakespeare's fantasy, Naylor's book takes place on an enchanted island. . . . Naylor reinforces her Shakespearean connection by naming her heroine Miranda." Mukherjee also believed that *Mama Day* "has its roots in *The Tempest.* The theme is reconciliation, the title character is Miranda (also the name of Prospero's daughter), and Willow Springs is an isolated island where, as on Prospero's isle, magical and mysterious events come to pass."

Naylor's ambitious attempt to elevate a modern love story to Shakespearean heights "is more bewildering than bewitching," according to Blades. "Naylor has populated her magic kingdom with some appealingly offbeat characters, Mama Day foremost among them. But she's failed to give them anything very original or interesting to do." Mukherjee also acknowledged the shortcomings of Naylor's mythical love story, but added, "I'd rather dwell on *Mama Day*'s strengths. Gloria Naylor has written a big, strong, dense, admirable novel; spacious, sometimes a little drafty like all public monuments, designed to last and intended for many levels of use."

Naylor's fourth novel, *Bailey's Cafe,* also had its inspiration in a literature classic, Edith Wharton's *The House of Mirth.* Like Wharton's novel, *Bailey's Cafe* focuses on women's sexuality and the ways women are defined by society's perceptions of them. With this book, Naylor hoped to deconstruct the Judeo-Christian thinking about women. To achieve this, she took women characters from the Bible and placed them in the twentieth century to relate their stories. Eve runs a boardinghouse and has a reputation for healing troubled women. Eve was banished naked from her father's house, and her place now is suspected by many of being a bordello. Eve's boarders include Sadie, Sweet Esther, Mary, and Jesse Bell, modern women whose stories parallel those in the Bible. "The novel sings the blues of the socially rejected," stated Lewis, "who arrive at Bailey's struggling to find some measure of solace from a brutal American environment filled with racial and sexual stereotypes." The book was a critical success, and was adapted by Naylor as a stage play.

Naylor revisited her first success in 2000 with *The Men of Brewster Place.* Male characters were very marginal in her first novel, functioning mainly as people who wreaked havoc upon the lives of the women of Brewster Place. In *The Men of Brewster Place,* the author fills in the background of those characters, giving insight into their actions. The ten chapters in the book discuss seven individuals known as the sons of Brewster Place: Basil, Eugene, Maxine Lavon Montgomery, Ben, Brother Jerome, Moreland T. Woods, C.C. Baker, and Abshu. Ben, a character who died in the earlier book, is brought back in creative and magical ways. He functions as a sort of Greek chorus, overseeing the events and giving otherworldly perspective.

African American Review writer Maxine Lavon Montgomery called Naylor "a skillful writer adept at creating a range of uniquely individual characters." The author's look at the plight of the black man is rendered "in such a way as to render a compelling fictional expose of his dilemma." *Black Issues in Higher Education* reviewer Jackie Thomas praised *The Men of Brewster Place* as "a profound work that explores the other side of the gender issue." He approved of Naylor's depiction of them as rational beings who "are able to think for themselves and who realize that they have problems they must solve" and concluded: "It is refreshing to see someone address the Black male character and explore him realistically. Certainly, this work should be an inspiration to all who read it, and it should also encourage other writers to explore Black male characters from similar vantage points." But *Booklist* contributor Donna Seaman felt "these characters remain flat, and their stories are cautionary tales, intriguing in terms of the issues they raise yet a touch too facile and melodramatic." Yet, Seaman added, "there are flashes of genuine insight, tragedy, and great warmth." A *Publishers Weekly* writer allowed that the stories "feature the familiar ills of the inner city," but added that "Naylor lends these archetypal situations complexity and depth."

BIOGRAPHICAL AND CRITICAL SOURCES:

BOOKS

African-American Writers, Scribner (New York, NY), 1991.

Black Literature Criticism, Thomson Gale (Detroit, MI), 1992.

Contemporary Literary Criticism, Thomson Gale (Detroit, MI), Volume 28, 1984, Volume 52, 1989.

Contemporary Novelists, 7th edition, St. James Press (Detroit, MI), 2001.

Contemporary Popular Writers, St. James Press (Detroit, MI), 1997.

Dictionary of Literary Biography, Volume 173: *American Novelists since World War II, Fifth Series,* Thomson Gale (Detroit, MI), 1996.

Encyclopedia of World Biography, 2nd edition, Thomson Gale (Detroit, MI), 1998.

Feminist Writers, St. James Press (Detroit, MI), 1996.

Fowler, Virginia C., *Gloria Naylor: In Search of Sanctuary,* Prentice-Hall, 1996.

Hall, Chekita T., *Gloria Naylor's Feminist Blues Aesthetic,* Garland, 1998.

Harris, Trudier, *The Power of the Porch: The Storyteller's Craft in Zora Neale Hurston, Gloria Naylor, and Randall Kenan,* University of Georgia Press (Athens, GA), 1996.

PERIODICALS

Advocate, April 14, 1998, review of *The Men of Brewster Place,* p. 73.

African American Review, summer, 1994, p. 173; spring, 1995, pp. 27, 35; spring, 2000, Maxine Lavon Montgomery, review of *The Men of Brewster Place,* p. 176; spring, 2001, Christopher N. Okonkwo, "Suicide or Messianic Self-Sacrifice?: Exhuming Willa's Body in Gloria Naylor's *Linden Hills,*" p. 117.

American Visions, April, 1996, Dale Edwyna Smith, review of *Children of the Night: The Best Short Stories by Black Writers, 1967 to the Present,* p. 26.

Antioch Review, summer, 1996, Ed Peaco, review of *Children of the Night,* p. 365.

Black Issues in Higher Education, December 10, 1998, Jackie Thomas, review of *The Men of Brewster Place,* p. 31.

Booklist, December 1, 1995; January 1, 1996; March 1, 1998, Donna Seaman, review of *The Men of Brewster Place,* p. 1045; January 1, 1999, Barbara Baskin, review of *The Men of Brewster Place,* p. 900; November 1, 2001, Nancy Spillman, review of *The Men of Brewster Place* (audio version), p. 494.

Boston Herald, April 19, 1998, Judith Wynn, review of *The Men of Brewster Place,* p. 71.

Chicago Tribune Book World, February 23, 1983.

Christian Science Monitor, March 1, 1985.

Commonweal, May 3, 1985.

Contemporary Literature, Volume 28, number 1, 1987.

Detroit News, March 3, 1985; February 21, 1988.

Ebony, May, 1998, p. 14.

Emerge, May, 1998, Valerie Boyd, review of *The Men of Brewster Place,* p. 76.

English Journal, January, 1994, p. 81; March, 1994, p. 95.

Essence, June, 1998, p. 70; August, 2001, review of *Mama Day,* p. 62.

Houston Chronicle, June 9, 1998, Carol Rust, review of *The Men of Brewster Place,* p. 1.

Library Journal, June 1, 1998, p. 187.

London Review of Books, August 1, 1985.

Los Angeles Times, December 2, 1982.

Los Angeles Times Book Review, February 24, 1985; March 6, 1988.

Ms., June, 1985.

New Republic, September 6, 1982.

New York Times, February 9, 1985; May 1, 1990.

New York Times Book Review, August 22, 1982; March 3, 1985; February 21, 1988; April 19, 1998, Roy Hoffman, review of *The Men of Brewster Place,* p. 19.

People, June 22, 1998, p. 39.

Publishers Weekly, September 9, 1983; December 11, 1995, review of *Children of the Night,* p. 56; February 23, 1998, p. 49.

St. Louis Post-Dispatch, July 3, 1998, Andrea M. Wren, review of *The Men of Brewster Place,* p. E7.

San Francisco Review of Books, May, 1985.

Seattle Times, June 2, 1998, review of *The Men of Brewster Place,* p. E1.

Tampa Tribune, May 31, 1998, review of *The Men of Brewster Place,* p. 4.

Times (London, England), April 21, 1983.

Times Literary Supplement, May 24, 1985.

Tribune Books (Chicago, IL), January 31, 1988.

Twentieth Century Literature, fall, 2002, Robin Blyn, "The Ethnographer's Story: Mama Day and the Specter of Relativism," p. 239.

Washington Post, October 21, 1983; May 1, 1990.

Washington Post Book World, March 24, 1985; February 28, 1988.

Women's Review of Books, August, 1985.

Writer, December, 1994, p. 21.

ONLINE

Unofficial Gloria Naylor Web site, http://www.lythastudios.com/gnaylor/ (January 21, 2004).

NEMEROV, Howard 1920-1991
(Howard Stanley Nemerov)

PERSONAL: Born March 1, 1920, in New York, NY; died of cancer of the esophagus, July 5, 1991, in University City, MO; son of David and Gertrude (Russek) Nemerov; married Margaret Russell, January 26, 1944; children: David, Alexander Michael, Jeremy Seth. *Education:* Harvard University, A.B., 1941.

CAREER: Hamilton College, Clinton, NY, instructor, 1946-48; Bennington College, Bennington, VT, member of faculty in literature, 1948-66; Brandeis University, Waltham, MA, professor of English, 1966-69; Washington University, St. Louis, MO, visiting Hurst Professor of English, 1969-70, professor of English, 1970-76, Edward Mallinckrodt Distinguished University Professor of English, 1976-90. Visiting lecturer in English, University of Minnesota, 1958-59; writer-in-residence, Hollins College, 1962-64; consultant in poetry, Library of Congress, 1963-64; chancellor, American Academy of Poets, beginning 1976. *Military service:* Royal Canadian Air Force, 1942-44; became flying officer; U.S. Army Air Forces, 1944-45; became first lieutenant.

AWARDS, HONORS: Bowdoin Prize, Harvard University, 1940; *Kenyon Review* fellowship in fiction, 1955; Oscar Blumenthal Prize, 1958, Harriet Monroe Memorial Prize, 1959, Frank O'Hara Memorial Prize, 1971, Levinson Prize, 1975, all from *Poetry* magazine; second prize, *Virginia Quarterly Review* short story competition, 1958; National Institute of Arts and Letters Grant, 1961; Golden Rose Trophy, New England Poetry Club, 1962; Brandeis Creative Arts Award, 1963; D.L., Lawrence University, 1964, and Tufts University, 1969; National Endowment for the Arts grant, 1966-67; First Theodore Roethke Memorial Award, 1968, for *The Blue Swallows;* St. Botolph's Club (Boston) Prize for Poetry, 1968; Guggenheim fellow, 1968-69; Academy of American Poets fellowship, 1970; O'Hara Prize, 1971; Pulitzer Prize and National Book award, 1978, and Bollingen Prize, Yale University, 1981, all for *The Collected Poems of Howard Nemerov;* National Book Award, Translation, 1978, for *In the Deserts of This Earth;* Aiken Taylor Award for Modern Poetry, *Sewanee Review* and University of the South, 1987; National Medal of the Arts, 1987, for promoting "excellence, growth, support and availability of the arts in the United States"; poet laureate of the United States, 1988-90; honorary degree from Washington and Lee University.

WRITINGS:

The Melodramatists (novel), Random House (New York, NY), 1949.

Federigo; or, The Power of Love (novel), Little, Brown (Boston, MA), 1954.

The Homecoming Game (novel), Simon & Schuster (New York, NY), 1957.

A Commodity of Dreams and Other Stories, Simon & Schuster (New York, NY), 1959.

(Editor and author of introduction) Henry Wadsworth Longfellow, *Selected Poetry,* Dell (New York, NY), 1959.

Poetry and Fiction: Essays, Rutgers University Press (New Brunswick, NJ), 1963.

Journal of the Fictive Life (autobiography), Rutgers University Press (New Brunswick, NJ), 1965, with a new preface, University of Chicago Press (Chicago, IL), 1981.

(Editor and contributor) *Poets on Poetry,* Basic Books (New York, NY), 1965.

(Editor) Marianne Moore, *Poetry and Criticism,* Adams House & Lowell House Printers, 1965.

Stories, Fables, and Other Diversions, David R. Godine (Boston, MA), 1971.

Reflexions on Poetry and Poetics, Rutgers University Press (New Brunswick, NJ), 1972.

Figures of Thought: Speculations on the Meaning of Poetry and Other Essays, David R. Godine (Boston, MA), 1978.

New and Selected Essays, with foreword by Kenneth Burke, Southern Illinois University Press (Carbondale, IL), 1985.

The Oak in the Acorn: On Remembrance of Things Past and on Teaching Proust, Who Will Never Learn, Louisiana State University Press (Baton Rouge, LA), 1987.

A Howard Nemerov Reader, University of Missouri Press (Columbia, MO), 1991.

Contributor to books, including: Ted Hughes and Thom Gunn, editors, *Five American Poets,* Faber (London, England), 1963; Sheldon Norman Grebstein, editor, *Perspectives in Contemporary Criticism,* Harper (New York, NY), 1968; A. Cheuse and R. Koffler, editors, *The Rarer Action: Essays in Honor of Francis Fergusson,* Rutgers University Press, 1971; Shirley Sugarman, editor, *Evolution of Consciousness: Studies in Polarity,* Wesleyan University Press, 1976; and Arthur Edelstein, editor, *Images and Ideas in American Culture: The Functions of Criticism, Essays in Memory of Philip Rahv,* Brandeis University Press, 1979. Contributor of essays, articles and reviews to literary journals, including *Hudson Review, Poetry, Atlantic, Partisan Review,* and *Virginia Quarterly Review.* Contributor of short fiction to *Harvard Advocate, Story, Esquire, Carleton Miscellany, Reporter,* and *Virginia Quarterly Review.* Associate editor of *Furioso,* 1946-51.

POETRY

The Image and the Law, Holt (New York, NY), 1947.

Guide to the Ruins, Random House (New York, NY), 1950.

The Salt Garden, Little, Brown (Boston, MA), 1955.

Small Moment, Ward Ritchie Press, 1957.

Mirrors and Windows, University of Chicago Press (Chicago, IL), 1958.

New and Selected Poems, University of Chicago Press (Chicago, IL), 1960.

Endor: Drama in One Act (verse play; also see below), Abingdon (Nashville, TN), 1961.

The Next Room of the Dream: Poems and Two Plays (includes plays "Endor" and "Cain"), University of Chicago Press (Chicago, IL), 1962.

The Blue Swallows, University of Chicago Press (Chicago, IL), 1967.

A Sequence of Seven with a Drawing by Ron Slaughter, Tinker Press, 1967.

The Winter Lightning: Selected Poems, Rapp & Whiting, 1968.

The Painter Dreaming in the Scholar's House (limited edition), Phoenix Book Shop (New York, NY), 1968.

Gnomes and Occasions, University of Chicago Press (Chicago, IL), 1973.

The Western Approaches: Poems, 1973-75, University of Chicago Press (Chicago, IL), 1975.

The Collected Poems of Howard Nemerov, University of Chicago Press (Chicago, IL), 1977.

Sentences, University of Chicago Press (Chicago, IL), 1980.

Inside the Onion, University of Chicago Press (Chicago, IL), 1984.

Trying Conclusions: New and Selected Poems, 1961-1991, University of Chicago Press (Chicago, IL), 1991.

The Selected Poems of Howard Nemerov, Swallow Press (Athens, OH), 2003.

Also author of *War Stories: Poems about Long Ago and Now,* 1987. Contributor of poems to numerous periodicals, including *Harvard Advocate, Kenyon Review, Poetry, New Yorker, Nation* and *Polemic.*

SOUND RECORDINGS

The Poetry of Howard Nemerov (two audio cassettes), Jeffrey Norton, 1962.

Howard Nemerov, 2 volumes, Tapes for Readers, 1978, 1979.

(Contributor of introduction) *Surly Verses for the Holidays: From D.H. Lawrence to e. e. cummings and Far Beyond,* read by Reed Whittemore, Library of Congress, 1989.

Science and Stories: A Lecture, Library of Congress, 1989.

Language, Nonsense, and Poetry, Library of Congress, 1989.

Prosser Gifford Interviews Howard Nemerov, Library of Congress, 1990.

The Poet and the Poem, Library of Congress, 1990.

Howard Nemerov Reading from His Work, Library of Congress, 1990.

ADAPTATIONS: The Homecoming Game was adapted for film as *Tall Story,* Warner Bros., 1959. "The Junction on a Warm Afternoon" was set to music by William Bolcom, E.B. Marks, 1990.

SIDELIGHTS: Howard Nemerov was a highly acclaimed poet often cited for the range of his capabilities and subject matter, "from the profound to the poignant to the comic," James Billington remarked in his frequently quoted announcement of Nemerov's appointment to the post of United States poet laureate. A distinguished professor at Washington University in St. Louis from 1969 to 1990, Nemerov wrote poetry and fiction that manages to engage the reader's mind without becoming academic, many reviewers reported. Though his works show a consistent emphasis on thought—the process of thinking and ideas themselves—his poems relate a broad spectrum of emotion and a variety of concerns. Writing in the study *Howard Nemerov,* Peter Meinke stated that these contrasting qualities are due to Nemerov's "deeply divided personality." Meinke pointed out that Nemerov himself spoke of a duality in his nature; in the *Journal of the Fictive Life* the poet was quoted as noting that "it has seemed to me that I must attempt to bring together the opposed elements of my character represented by poetry and fiction." Commented Meinke, "These 'opposed elements' in Howard Nemerov's character are reflected in his life and work: in the tensions between his romantic and realistic visions, his belief and unbelief, his heart and mind." If Nemerov harbored impulses toward both poetry and fiction, he expressed them as opposites suspended in balanced co-existence rather than dissonance. A direct expression of this equilibrium is his poem "Because You Asked about the Line between Prose and Poetry."

The Harvard graduate's first book of poems, *The Image and the Law,* characteristically is based on opposed elements, on a duality of vision. Some reviewers have found that this dichotomy leads to a lack of coherence in the verse. *New York Times Book Review* writer Milton Crane, for example, felt that the poems "unfortunately show no unity of conception such as their author attributes to them." The book was also criticized for being derivative of earlier modern poets such as T.S. Eliot, W.H. Auden, W.B. Yeats, and Wallace Stevens. However, Meinke contended that it is Nemerov's "modern awareness of contemporary man's alienation and fragmentation combined with a breadth of wit in the eighteenth century sense of the word" which "sets Nemerov's writing apart from other modern writers."

Like *Image and the Law* and *Guide to the Ruins, The Salt Garden,* when published, drew criticism for being derivative. Years later, when asked if his work had changed in character or style, Nemerov replied in *Poets on Poetry,* "In style, . . . for I began and for a long time remained imitative, and poems in my first books . . . show more than traces of admired modern masters—Eliot, Auden, Stevens, [E. E.] Cummings, Yeats." Meinke, too, maintained that Nemerov in his early work was "writing Eliot, Yeats, and Stevens out of his system." Yet at the same time that some critics faulted Nemerov for his imitation, they were impressed by his growth as a poet.

The Salt Garden, many critics felt, marks the beginning of other changes in Nemerov's work, as well. Meinke observed that in this volume "Nemerov has found his most characteristic voice: a quiet intelligent voice brooding lyrically on the strange beauty and tragic loneliness of life." In a review of *The Collected Poems of Howard Nemerov* included in *The Critical Reception of Howard Nemerov,* Willard Spiegelman, like Meinke, discovered in the poems from *The Salt Garden* "Nemerov's characteristic manner and tone." Spiegelman still found opposed elements, but in balance; he described Nemerov's manner as "genuinely Horatian according to Auden's marvelous definition of looking at 'this world with a happy eye / but from a sober perspective.' Nemerov's *aurea mediocritas* [golden mean] sails between philosophical skepticism . . . and social satire on one side, and, on the other, an open-eyed, child-like appreciation of the world's miracles."

Another change that began with *The Salt Garden* and continued in *Mirrors and Windows, The Next Room of the Dream,* and *The Blue Swallows* was Nemerov's growing concern with nature. He wrote in *Poets on Poetry* of the impact of the natural world on his work: "During the war and since, I have lived in the country, chiefly in Vermont, and while my relation to the landscape has been contemplative rather than practical, the landscape nevertheless has in large part taken over my poetry." This interest in the landscape has led some poets to find echos of the poetry of Robert Frost. The comparison to Frost is also made on the grounds that Nemerov, like Frost, brought philosophical issues into his poetry. As he said in *Poets on Poetry,* he was not so much an observer of nature as its medium, bringing into speech "an unknowably large part of a material world whose independent existence might be likened to that of the human unconscious, a sleep of causes, a chaos of the possible-impossible." Phrasing it differently in the poem "A Spell before Winter," Nemerov wrote, "And I speak to you now with the land's voice, / It is the cold, wild land that says to you / A knowledge glimmers in the sleep of things: / The old hills hunch before the north wind blows."

A feature of the poems more frequently pointed out by critics is a witty, ironic manner and a serious, perhaps pessimistic, philosophy. Not all critics applauded the tragic irony that can be found in Nemerov's poetry. *New York Times* critic Thomas Lask believed that in *The Blue Swallows* the poet's irony has turned bitter, expressing "loathing and contempt for man and his work." In contrast to both these views, Laurence Lieberman, writing in the *Yale Review,* felt that "Nemerov has perfected the poem as an instrument for exercising brilliance of wit. Searching, discursive, clear-sighted, he has learned to make the poem serve his relaxed manner and humane insights so expertly, I can only admire the clean purposefulness of his statements, his thoughtful care, the measure and grace of his lines."

However strong his ironic voice, Nemerov mellowed with age, according to many reviewers. Meinke claimed that "Nemerov has progressed steadily in his poetry to a broader, more tolerant view, less bitter and more sad." Similarly, Spiegelman observed: "Nemerov, growing old, becomes younger as he adopts the manner of an ancient sage. Cynicism barely touches his voice; the occasional sardonic moments are offset by feeling and sympathy. . . . In the 40's and 50's Nemerov was rabbinically fixated on sin and redemption. What was, early on, a source of prophetic despair . . . , becomes in the poems of his middle age the cause of poetic variety and energy, metaphysical delight, and emotional equilibrium." And in her *Part of Nature, Part of Us,* Helen Vendler discerned in a critique of *Collected Poems* that as "the echoes of the *grand maitres* fade, the poems get steadily better. The severity of attitude is itself chastened by a growing humanity, and the forms of the earth grow ever more distinct."

Gnomes and Occasions indulged Nemerov's penchant for short, aphoristic verses in which the images carry the burden of persuasion. In these "gnomes," Nemerov achieves a "Biblical resonance," said Kenneth Burke in his introduction to Nemerov's early poems, which rank with the best postwar American poetry. More than one critic has referred to Nemerov's writings as wisdom literature. For example, Vendler reported in *Part of Nature, Part of Us* that Nemerov's "mind plays with epigram, gnome, riddle, rune, advice, meditation, notes, dialectic, prophecy, reflection, views, knowledge, questions, speculation—all the forms of thought. His wishes go homing to origins and ends." Scholars have linked this stylistic tendency to the poet's Jewish heritage. Meinke described the early Nemerov as a "nonpracticing Jew engaged in a continual dialogue with Christianity . . . testing its relevance in the modern world." In addition to the influence of Dante and St. Augustine, that of W.B. Yeats left its mark on the poems, said *Dictionary of Literary Biography* contributor Robert W. Hill, "not so much in form or style as in subject matter and in a decidedly religious quality of the language." For instance, one of Nemerov's definitions of poetry given in "Thirteen Ways of Looking at a Skylark" stated: "In the highest range the theory of poetry would be the theory of the Incarnation, which seeks to explain how the Word became Flesh."

Nemerov, however, did not reconstruct the world with imagination as other poets have done. Explained Hill, "While Yeats went about his way inventing new religion and culling the cabala for hints and signs, Nemerov's poems show him to be a critic of the secularizers: coming from the Jewish tradition, his sense of the decline of religion is not so easily pacified by new contrivances as Yeats's was. But the connections Nemerov feels with the seers of the past are clearly modern, clearly attached with the threads of the naturalistic modes, the beliefs in touchable things rather than in the untouchable." Thus Nemerov used acts of the imagination not to alter the world but to make it known. To the extent that this process is magical, "Our proper magic is the magic of language," claimed the poet.

Poetry as a link between the material and spiritual worlds emerged as the theme of *Sentences.* In this volume, Nemerov achieved thematic coherence by organizing the poems into three sections, "Beneath," "Above," and "Beyond." Bonnie Costello, writing in *Parnassus,* related that the sections "mark off, respectively, poems of low diction and subject (our social sphere of sex and power), poems of higher diction and subject (metaphysics and poetry), and those of middle diction and subject (our origin and fate)." Critics approved the last two sections more than the first, which they claimed was beneath the level of quality they had come to expect from Nemerov. The section castigated the purveyors of low artistic, social and political values, related Ronald Baughman in the *Dictionary of Literary Biography Yearbook, 1983:* "The reviewers damn the writer for accomplishing the goal which he has set for himself—the portrayal of man acting beneath dignity." Looking over the entire book, Baughman offered, "*Sentences* contains a wide range of poems, extending from the mocking, bitter verse of section one to the interesting but restrained appraisals of section two to the deeply moving contemplations of section three. The volume's theme—the order art gives to the randomness of life—develops with this movement from beginning to end. Nemerov's title is reminiscent of Stephen Spender's poem 'Subject: Object: Sentence,' in which Spender states, 'A sentence is condemned to stay as stated—/ As in *life-sentence, death-sentence,*' for example. As Howard Nemerov dramatizes his life and death sentences, he reveals his attempts to connect, through the power of his art, with the world below, nature above, and the spirit beyond."

The Collected Poems of Howard Nemerov gathers verse from all of the earlier volumes and its publication in 1977 spurred a re-evaluation of Nemerov's work. Phoebe Pettingell noted in the *New Leader* that the book shows "a gradual intensifying of a unified perspective," the poet's obsession with the theme of "man's sometimes tragic, sometimes ludicrous relation to history, death and the universe."

Several reviewers also found much of value in *Trying Conclusions: New and Selected Poems, 1961-1991,* published the year of Nemerov's death. Sidney Burris, writing in the *Southern Review,* found the collection significant because, in addition to containing a dozen new poems, it provided an excellent selection of Nemerov's work beginning with *The Next Room of the Dream,* with *Collected Poems* containing much of the poet's earlier output and therefore functioning as a "companion volume." Burris went on, "The poetry selected for *Trying Conclusions* issues from what Nemerov continually described as a simple respect for an audience who has—or at least ought to have, he always added—more pressing things to do than read his poems. . . . The deepest wish of Nemerov's poetry, particularly of the poems gathered together in *Trying Conclusions,* is that his poems aim ultimately to dignify the world of our recognizably common experience." Pettingell, in the *New Leader,* noted the poet's "mean, satirical wit," and pointed out that the title, *Trying Conclusions,* could be interpreted in many ways, in keeping with the poet's penchant for plays on words. Myers commented that Nemerov "never shied away from trying something new, experimenting with forms and subjects."

Nemerov's prose has also been commended, especially for displaying an irony and wit similar to that of his poems. His novels, as Meinke remarked, "like his poems, . . . are basically pessimistic. The condition of man is not an enviable one: we act foolishly and understand imperfectly. Nemerov's dark viewpoint, which in his poetry is redeemed by beauty, . . . in his fiction is redeemed by humor." Meinke termed *The Melodramatists* "a highly successful first novel," and in the *Nation* Diana Trilling seconded him, commenting that after a slow start, it is "a considerable first novel—literate and entertaining, with a nice satiric barb." *Federigo; or, The Power of Love* and *The Homecoming Game* were also well received, *Atlantic Monthly* reviewer C.J. Rolo noting that the latter novel has "wit, dash, and point." Through the characters in these novels, Nemerov explores "the consequences of the overactive imagination," wrote Carl Rapp in the *Dictionary of Literary Biography.* Characters with romantic expectations of finding meaningful action and self-realization amid the social pressures of their times instead realize that they are the victims of their own fantasies. Thus, the novels, like the poetry, comment on the relationship between imagination and reality.

Nemerov published his last novel, *The Homecoming Game*—about a professor who discovers his limits when faced with opposing groups on campus—in 1957. Rapp suggested, "Nemerov has perhaps come to feel that the novelist himself, with his own incorrigible tendency to fantasize melodramatic scenes and situations, presents a spectacle as ridiculous as that of his own characters. In [later] . . . poems such as 'Novelists' and 'Reflexions of a Novelist,' he observes that it is, of course, the novelist who is preeminently the man with the overactive imagination, the egomaniac." Nemerov once told Robert Boyers in a *Salmagundi* interview that he left off being a novelist when Bennington College chose to retain him as its poet and hired Bernard Malamud to be its novelist.

Though through with the novel form, Nemerov continued to work with prose in short stories and literary criticism. Like his poetry and fiction, his essays won him the respect of many well-known writers and critics. To *Figures of Thought: Speculations on the Meaning of Poetry and Other Essays,* Benjamin DeMott responded in the *New York Times:* "Taken as a whole . . . these 'speculations' are uncommonly stimulating and persuasive. . . . [This book] communicates throughout a vivid sense of the possibility of a richer kind of knowing in all areas than we're in the process of settling for. . . . Like the high art it salutes, it hums with the life of things."

New and Selected Essays, a collection of essays spanning thirty years of Nemerov's criticism, was published in 1985, and prompted critics to give serious attention to the author's prose works. Another collection of Nemerov's essays and works of fiction, along with a smattering of poems, was published in 1991 as *A Howard Nemerov Reader. Southern Review* contributor Sidney Burris found the latter volume important chiefly because of its reprint of *Federigo; or, The Power of Love,* as the rest of its contents could be found in other collections; he added, however, that the book serves as a testament to Nemerov's ability "to provide poetry, criticism, and fiction, all of an extraordinarily high degree of sophistication." Doug Anderson, writing in the *New York Times Book Review,* said the book would be valuable to those who know Nemerov only as a poet, as "his fiction . . . allows him a much wider emotional and imaginative range than do his poems, and his essays . . . reveal Mr. Nemerov as brilliantly incisive, if occasionally curmudgeonly." And in *Poetry,* Robert B. Shaw pronounced, "This volume amply serves its purpose as an introduction to the spectrum of Nemerov's writing in its several forms."

Nemerov's books brought him many major awards for poetry, including the National Book Award and the Pulitzer Prize in 1978, and the Bollingen Prize in 1981, all for *The Collected Poems of Howard Nemerov.*

BIOGRAPHICAL AND CRITICAL SOURCES:

BOOKS

Bartholomay, Julia, *The Shield of Perseus: The Vision and Imagination of Howard Nemerov,* University of Florida Press (Gainesville, FL), 1972.

Dickey, James, *Babel to Byzantium: Poets and Poetry Now,* Farrar, Straus (New York, NY), 1968.

Dictionary of Literary Biography, Thomson Gale (Detroit, MI), Volume 5: *American Poets since World War II, First Series,* 1967, Volume 6: *American Poets since World War II, Second Series,* 1980.

Dictionary of Literary Biography Yearbook: 1983, Thomson Gale (Detroit, MI), 1983.
Duncan, Bowie, editor, *The Critical Reception of Howard Nemerov: A Selection of Essays and a Bibliography,* Scarecrow Press (Metuchen, NJ), 1971.
Labrie, Ross, *Howard Nemerov,* Twayne (Boston, MA), 1980.
Meinke, Peter, *Howard Nemerov,* University of Minnesota Press (Minneapolis, MN), 1968.
Mills, William, *The Stillness in Moving Things: The World of Howard Nemerov,* Memphis State University Press (Memphis, TN), 1975.
Potts, Donna L., *Howard Nemerov and Objective Idealism,* University of Missouri Press (Columbia, MO), 1994.
Vendler, Helen, *Part of Nature, Part of Us: Modern American Poets,* Harvard University Press (Cambridge, MA), 1980.

PERIODICALS

American Poetry Review, May-June, 1975, pp. 4-9.
Atlantic Monthly, June, 1957.
Book World, December 24, 1967, p. 6.
Carleton Miscellany, summer, 1968, pp. 110-114.
Hudson Review, spring, 1968, pp. 207-217.
New Leader, December 30, 1991, p. 27.
New York Times, April 16, 1978, p. 264; December 26, 1978, p. C14.
New York Times Book Review, April 28, 1968, p. 7.
Parnassus, fall-winter, 1973, pp. 153-163; spring-summer, 1975, pp. 27-34; Volume 4, number 2, 1976, pp. 130-138; fall-winter, 1977, pp. 1-57.
Poetry, December, 2003, p. 163.
Poetry Review, spring, 1991, pp. 10-12.
Salmagundi, spring-summer, 1973, pp. 234-257.
Southern Review, Volume 10, 1974, pp. 153-169; autumn, 1976, pp. 891-894.
Trace, January, 1960, pp. 22-25.
Webster Review, Volume 1, number 1, 1974, pp. 34-39.

OTHER

One on One (filmed interview), Kent State University Television Center, 1979.

OBITUARIES:

PERIODICALS

Boston Globe, July 7, 1991, p. 63.
Los Angeles Times, July 8, 1991.
New York Times, July 7, 1991, section 1, p. 18.
Time, July 15, 1991, p. 61.
USA Today, July 8, 1991, p. A2.
Washington Post, July 7, 1991, p. C5.

* * *

NEMEROV, Howard Stanley
See NEMEROV, Howard

* * *

NEWT SCAMANDER
See ROWLING, J.K.

* * *

NGUGI, James T.
See NGUGI wa THIONG'O

* * *

NGUGI wa THIONG'O 1938-
(James T. Ngugi)

PERSONAL: Original name, James Thiong'o Ngugi; born January 5, 1938, in Limuru, Kenya; married; children: five. *Education:* Makerere University, B.A., 1963; University of Leeds, B.A., 1964.

ADDRESSES: Agent—c/o William Heinemann Ltd., 15 Queen St., London W1X 8BE, England.

CAREER: Teacher in East African schools, 1964-70; University of Nairobi, Kenya, lecturer in English literature, 1967-77, became senior lecturer and chair of literature department; New York University, New York, NY, Erich Maria Remarque Professor of Languages, 1992-2002; University of California—Irvine, professor of English and comparative literature and head of International Centre for Writing and Translation, 2002—. Creative writing fellow, Makerere University, 1969-70; visiting lecturer, Northwestern University, 1970-71.

AWARDS, HONORS: Dakar Festival of Negro Arts award, 1965, and the East African Literature Bureau award, both for *Weep Not, Child;* Nonino Prize, 2001, for body of work.

WRITINGS:

Homecoming: Essays on African and Caribbean Literature, Culture, and Politics, Heinemann (London, England), 1972, Lawrence Hill, 1973.

Secret Lives, and Other Stories, Heinemann Educational (London, England), 1974, Lawrence Hill, 1975.

Petals of Blood (novel), Heinemann Educational (London, England), 1977.

(With Micere Githae Mugo) *The Trial of Dedan Kimathi,* Heinemann Educational (London, England), 1977, Swahili translation by the authors published as *Mzalendo kimathi,* c. 1978.

Mtawa Mweusi, Heinemann (London, England), 1978.

Caitaani mutharaba-ini, Heinemann Educational (London, England), 1980, translation by the author published as *Devil on the Cross,* Zimbabwe Publishing, 1983.

Writers in Politics: Essays, Heinemann (London, England), 1981, revised, 1997.

Detained: A Writer's Prison Diary, Heinemann (London, England), 1981.

Njamba Nene na mbaathi i mathagu (juvenile), Heinemann Educational (London, England), 1982.

(Coauthor and translator with Ngugi wa Mirii) *I Will Marry When I Want* (play), Heinemann (London, England), 1982.

Barrel of a Pen: Resistance to Repression in Neo-Colonial Kenya, New Beacon, 1983.

Decolonising the Mind: The Politics of Language in African Literature, Heinemann (London, England), 1986.

Writing against Neocolonialism, Vita, 1986.

Matigari ma Njiruungi, Heinemann (London, England), 1986, translation by Wangui published as *Matigari,* Heinemann (London, England), 1989.

Njambas Nene no Chiubu King'ang'i, Heinemann (London, England), 1986.

Njamba Nene and the Flying Bus (juvenile), translation by Waugui wa Goro, Africa World, 1989.

Njamba Nene's Pistol (juvenile), translation by Waugui, Africa World, 1989.

Moving the Center: The Struggle for Cultural Freedoms, Heinemann (London, England), 1992.

Penpoints, Gunpoints, and Dreams: Towards a Critical Theory of the Arts and the State in Africa, Oxford University Press (New York, NY), 1998.

UNDER NAME JAMES T. NGUGI

The Black Hermit (play; first produced in Nairobi in 1962), Mekerere University Press, 1963, Humanities, 1968.

Weep Not, Child (novel), introduction and notes by Ime Ikeddeh, Heinemann (London, England), 1964, P. Collier, 1969.

The River Between (novel), Humanities, 1965.

A Grain of Wheat (novel), Heinemann, 1967, 2nd edition, Humanities, 1968.

This Time Tomorrow (play; includes *The Reels* and *The Wound in the Heart;* produced and broadcast in 1966, also broadcast on BBC Africa Service in 1967), East African Literature Bureau, 1970.

CONTRIBUTOR TO ANTHOLOGIES

E.A. Komey and Ezekiel Mphahlele, editors, *Modern African Short Stories,* Faber, 1964.

W.H. Whiteley, editor, *A Selection of African Prose,* Oxford University Press, 1964.

Neville Denny, editor, *Pan African Short Stories,* Nelson, 1965.

Oscar Ronald Dathorne and Willfried Feuser, editors, *Africa in Prose,* Penguin (New York, NY), 1969.

OTHER

Contributor of stories to *Transition* and *Kenya Weekly News.* Editor of *Zuka* and *Sunday Nation* (Nairobi).

SIDELIGHTS: Novelist, dramatist, essayist, and literary critic Ngugi wa Thiong'o is East Africa's most prominent writer. Known to many simply as Ngugi, he has been described by Shatto Arthur Gakwandi in *The Novel and Contemporary Experience in Africa* as a "novelist of the people," for his works show his concern for the inhabitants of his native country, Kenya, who have been oppressed and exploited by colonialism, Christianity, and in recent years, by black politicians and businessmen. As *Africa Today* contributor D. Salituma Wamalwa observed: "Ngugi's approach to literature is one firmly rooted in the historical experience of the writer and his or her people, in an understanding of society as it is and a vision of society as it might be."

Throughout his career as a writer and professor, Ngugi has worked to free himself and his compatriots from the effects of colonialism, Christianity, and other non-African influences. In the late 1960s, for example, Ngugi and several colleagues at the University of Nairobi successfully convinced school officials to transform the English Department into the Department of African Languages and Literature. Shortly thereafter Ngugi renounced his Christian name, James, citing Christianity's ties to colonialism. He took in its place his name in Gikuyu (or Kikuyu), the dominant language of Kenya. Ngugi strengthened his commitment to the Kenyan culture in 1977, when he declared his intention to write only in Gikuyu or Swahili, not English. In response to a query posed in an interview for *Journal of Commonwealth Literature* concerning this decision, Ngugi stated "Language is a carrier of a people's culture, culture is a carrier of a people's values; values are the basis of a people's self-definition—the basis of their consciousness. And when you destroy a people's language, you are destroying that very important aspect of their heritage . . . you are in fact destroying that which helps them to define themselves . . . that which embodies their collective memory as a people."

Ngugi's determination to write in Gikuyu, combined with his outspoken criticisms of both British and Kenyan rule, have posed threats to his security. In 1977 Ngugi's home was searched by Kenyan police, who confiscated nearly one hundred books then arrested and imprisoned Ngugi without a trial. At the time of his arrest, Ngugi's play *Ngaahika Ndena* (translated as *I Will Marry When I Want*), coauthored with Ngugi wa Mirii, had recently been banned on the grounds of being "too provocative," according to *American Book Review* contributor Henry Indangasi; in addition, his novel *Petals of Blood,* a searing indictment of the Kenyan government, had just been published in England. Although Ngugi was released from prison a year later, his imprisonment cost him his professorship at the University of Nairobi. When his theatre group was banned by Kenyan officials in 1982, Ngugi, fearing further reprisals, left his country for a self-imposed exile in London.

Ngugi chronicles his prison experience in *Detained: A Writer's Prison Diary,* and expresses his political views in other nonfiction works such as *Barrel of a Pen: Resistance to Repression in Neo-Colonial Kenya.* He has received the most critical attention, however, for his fiction, particularly his novels. Ngugi's first novel *Weep Not, Child* deals with the Mau Mau rebellion against the British administration in the 1950s, and his third novel *A Grain of Wheat* concerns the aftermath of the war and its effects on Kenya's people. Although critics describe the first novel as somewhat stylistically immature, many comment favorably on the universality of its theme of the reactions of people to the stresses and horrors of war and to the inevitable changes brought to bear on their lives.

In contrast, several reviewers believe that *A Grain of Wheat* fulfills the promise of Ngugi's first novel. *A Grain of Wheat* portrays four characters who reflect upon the events of the Mau Mau rebellion and its consequences as they await the day of Kenyan independence, December 12, 1963. G.D. Killam explained in his book *An Introduction to the Writings of Ngugi:* "Uhuru Day, the day when independence from the colonial power is achieved, has been the dream of each of these figures from their schooldays. But there is little joyousness in their lives as they recall over the four days their experiences of the war and its aftermath."

In their book *Ngugi wa Thiong'o: An Exploration of His Writings,* David Cook and Michael Okenimkpe praised the "almost perfectly controlled form and texture" of *A Grain of Wheat.* Killam commented: "*A Grain of Wheat* is the work of a writer more mature than when he wrote his first two books. . . . In *A Grain of Wheat* [Ngugi] takes us into the minds of his characters, sensibilities resonant with ambiguities and contradictions, and causes us to feel what they feel, to share in significant measure their hopes an fears and pain." Shatto Arthur Gakwandi similarly observed in *The Novel an Contemporary Experience in Africa:* "The general tone of *A Grain of Wheat* is one of bitterness and anger. The painful memories of Mau Mau violence still overhang the Kikuyu villages as the attainment of independence fails to bring the cherished social dreams." Gakwandi added: "While the novel speaks against the harshness of colonial oppression, it is equally bitter against the new leaders of Kenya who are neglecting the interests of the peasant masses who were the people who made the greatest sacrifices during the war of liberation. Ngugi speaks on behalf of those who, in his view, have been neglected by the new government."

Petals of Blood, Ngugi's fourth novel, is considered his most ambitious and representative work. Like *A Grain of Wheat, Petals of Blood* describes the disillusionment of the common people in post-independence Kenya. Killam noted, however, that in *Petals of Blood* Ngugi "widens and deepens his treatment of themes which he has narrated and dramatized before—themes related to education, both formal and informal; religion, both Christian and customary; the alienation of the land viewed from the historical point of view and as a process which continues in the present; the struggle for independence and the price paid to achieve it." *Petals of Blood* is also described as Ngugi's most overtly political novel. A *West Africa* contributor noted an ideological shift in the novel "from the earlier emphasis on nationalism and race questions to a class analysis of society." Critics cite in particular the influence of both Karl Marx and Frantz Fanon, the latter of whom, according to Killam, "places the thinking of Marx in the African context." In *World Literature Written in English* Govind Narian Sharma commented: "Whereas traditional religious and moral thought has attributed exploitation and injustice in the world to human wickedness and folly, Ngugi, analyzing the situation in Marxist terms, explains these as 'the effect of laws of social development which make it inevitable that at a certain stage of history one class, pursuing its interests with varying degrees of rationality, should dispossess and exploit another.'"

Petals of Blood concerns four principle characters, all being held on suspicion of murder: Karega, a teacher and labor organizer; Munira, headmaster of a public school in the town of Ilmorog; Abdulla, a half-Indian shopkeeper who was once a guerrilla fighter during the war for independence; and Wanja, a barmaid and former prostitute. "Through these four [characters]," wrote Civia Tamarkin in the *Chicago Tribune Book World,* "Ngugi tells a haunting tale of lost hopes and soured dreams, raising the simple voice of humanity against the perversity of its condition." *American Book Review* contributor Henry Indangasi describes *Petals of Blood* this way: "Through numerous flashbacks, and flashbacks within flashbacks, and lengthy confessions, a psychologically credible picture of the characters, and a vast canvas of Kenya's history is unfolded."

Several reviewers note that Ngugi's emphasis on the economic and political conditions in Kenya at times overshadows his narrative. The *West Africa* contributor explains: "*Petals of Blood* is not so much a novel as an attempt to think aloud about the problems of modern Kenya: the sharp contrast between the city and the countryside, between the 'ill-gotten' wealth of the new African middle-class and the worsening plight of the unemployed workers and peasants." Charles R. Larson expressed a like opinion in *World Literature Today:* "*Petals of Blood* is not so much about these four characters (as fascinating and as skillfully drawn as they are) as it is about political unrest in post-independence Kenya, and what Ngugi considers the failures of the new black elite (politicians and businessmen) to live up to the pre-independence expectations." Foreshadowing Ngugi's 1977 arrest, Larson concludes, "In this sense *Petals of Blood* is a bold venture—perhaps a risky one—since it is obvious that the author's criticisms of his country's new ruling class will not go unnoticed."

Critics also maintain that this emphasis lends a didactic tone to the novel. Larson, for instance, commented in the *New York Times Book Review:* "The weakness of Ngugi's novel as a work of the creative imagination ultimately lies in the author's somewhat dated Marxism: revolt of the masses, elimination of the black bourgeois; capitalism to be replaced with African socialism. The author's didacticism weakens what would otherwise have been his finest work." *New Yorker* contributor John Updike similarly observed that "the characters . . . stagger and sink under the politico-symbolical message they are made to carry." *World Literature Today* contributor Andrew Salkey, on the other hand, offered this view: "It's a willfully diagrammatic and didactic novel which also succeeds artistically because of its resonant characterization and deadly irony. It satisfies both the novelist's political intent and the obligation I know he feels toward his art."

Despite these reservations, the majority of critics concur that *Petals of Blood* is an important literary contribution. Sharma, for example, wrote that "Ngugi's *Petals of Blood* is a complex and powerful work. It is a statement of his social and political philosophy and an embodiment of his prophetic vision. Ngugi provides a masterly analysis of the social and economic situation in modern Kenya, a scene of unprincipled and ruthless exploitation of man by man, and gives us a picture of the social and moral consequences of this exploitation." Cook and Ikenimkpe state that *Petals of Blood* "stands as a rare literary achievement: with all its faults upon it, [it is still] a skillfully articulated work which in no degree compromises the author's fully fledged radical political viewpoint." Indangasis concluded: "In many senses, literary and nonliterary, *Petals of Blood* will remain a major but controversial contribution to African literature, and the literature of colonised peoples."

Controversy was also prevalent following the 1986 publication of Ngugi's second novel in Gikuyu, titled *Matigarima Njiruungi.* Set in an unspecified location, although critics are quick to point out the area's similarities to Kenya, the story centers around the title character, whose name translates as "the patriots who survived the bullets." The tale finds Matigari who once used violence in the fight for his people's liberation, leaving the forest to reclaim his home and reunite his family through peaceful means. After discovering that the heirs of his oppressors have gained control of the house, he is soon arrested. He escapes, embarking on a quest for truth and justice that ends as he is confined to a mental hospital. He again eludes his captors, resolving that "armed power of the people" is needed for justice to prevail. The novel concludes on an ominous note as Matigari burns the house and is attacked by police dogs.

"The publication of *Matigari* in Kenya fired the imagination of peasants and workers in a way that closely paralleled the hero's effect on their fictional counterparts," reported David Maughan-Brown in *Dictionary of Literary Biography: Twentieth-Century Caribbean and Black African Writers.* "Kenya's rulers understood the message only too well," explained *Times Literary Supplement*'s Richard Gibson, adding "at first the police actually searched for the mythical Matigari. Failing to lay hands on him, they seized all the copies they could find of the book." Maughan-Brown concluded: "The 'arrest' of his book effectively consigns Ngugi to a double exile: with Ngugi physically cut off from the peasants and workers in Kenya, who are the source of his inspiration, the banning of his book means that he cannot, through his fiction, communicate with those for whom he writes."

BIOGRAPHICAL AND CRITICAL SOURCES:

BOOKS

Bailey, Diana, *Ngugi wo Thiong'o: "The River Between," a Critical View,* edited by Yolande Cantu, Collins, 1986.

Bjorkman, Ingrid, *Mother, Sing for Me; People's Theatre in Kenya,* Zed Books, 1989.

Black Literature Criticism, Thomson Gale, Volume 3, 1992.

Contemporary Literary Criticism, Thomson Gale, Volume 3, 1975, Volume 7, 1977, Volume 13, 1980, Volume 36, 1986.

Cook, David and Michael Okenimkpe, *Ngugi wa Thiong'o: An Exploration of His Writings,* Heinemann, 1983.

Gakwandi, Shatto Arthur, *The Novel and Contemporary Experience in Africa,* Africana Publishing, 1977.

Killam, G. D., *An Introduction to the Writings of Ngugi,* Heinemann, 1980.

Larson, Charles R., *The Emergence of African Fiction,* Indiana University Press, 1972.

Ngugi wa Thiong'o, *Detained: A Writer's Prison Diary,* Heinemann, 1981.

Palmer, Eustace, *An Introduction to the African Novel,* Africana Publishing, 1972.

Palmer, Eustace, *The Growth of the African Novel,* Heinemann, 1979.

Robson, Clifford B., *Ngugi wa Thiong'o,* Macmillan (London, England), 1979.

Roscoe, Adrian, *Uhuru's Fire: African Literature East to South,* Cambridge University Press, 1977.

Tibble, Ann, *African/English Literature,* Peter Owen (London, England), 1965.

Tucker, Martin, *Africa in Modern Literature: A Survey of Contemporary Writing in English,* Ungar, 1967.

PERIODICALS

African Literature Today, number 5, 1971; Number 10, 1979.

Africa Today, Volume 33, number 1, 1986.

American Book Review, summer, 1979.

Books Abroad, autumn, 1967; spring, 1968.

Books in Canada, October, 1982.

Chicago Tribune Book World, October 22, 1978.

Christian Science Monitor, October 11, 1978; September 5, 1986.

Iowa Review, spring-summer, 1976.

Journal of Commonwealth Literature, September, 1965, number 1, 1986.

Listener, August 26, 1982.

Michigan Quarterly Review, fall, 1970.

New Republic, January 20, 1979.

New Statesman, October 20, 1972; July 24, 1981; June 18, 1982; August 8, 1986.

New Yorker, July 2, 1979.

New York Times, May 10, 1978, November 9, 1986.

New York Times Book Review, February 19, 1978.

Observer (London, England), June 20, 1982.

Times Literary Supplement, January 28, 1965; November 3, 1972; August 12, 197; October 16, 1981; June 18, 1982; May 8, 1987.

Washington Post, October 9, 1978.

West Africa, February 20, 1978.

World Literature Today, spring, 1978; fall, 1978; spring, 1981; autumn, 1982; summer, 1983; winter, 1984; fall, 1987.

World Literature Written in English, November, 1979, autumn, 1982.

* * *

NICHOLS, John 1940-
(John Treadwell Nichols)

PERSONAL: Born July 23, 1940, in Berkeley, CA; son of David G. (a psycho-linguist) and Monique (Robert) Nichols; married Ruth Wetherell Harding, 1965 (divorced); married Juanita Laurene Kusters, 1985 (divorced); married Miel Athena Castagna, 1994 (divorced); children: (first marriage) Luke, Tania. *Education:* Hamilton College, B.A., 1962.

ADDRESSES: Home and office—Box 1165, Taos, NM 87571.

CAREER: Writer, photographer and screenwriter. Has worked as a blues singer in a Greenwich Village cafe, a firefighter in the Chiricahua Mountains of Arizona, and a dishwasher in Hartford, CT; partner and artist in "Jest-No" greeting card business, 1962; English teacher in Barcelona, Spain, for three months. Visiting professor, University of New Mexico, 1992, 1993.

AWARDS, HONORS: New Mexico Governor's Award, 1981; Frank Writers Award, 2003; honorary degrees from Colorado College, Hamilton College, and University of New Mexico; Quality Paperback Book Club selection for *A Ghost in the Music* and *The Magic Journey.*

WRITINGS:

If Mountains Die (nonfiction), photographs by William Davis, Alfred A. Knopf (New York, NY), 1979.
(And photographer) *The Last Beautiful Days of Autumn: A Memoir* (nonfiction photo essay), Holt, Rinehart, & Winston (New York, NY), 1982, reprinted, Ancient City Press (Santa Fe, NM), 2000.
(With Edward Abbey) *In Praise of Mountain Lions,* Albuquerque Sierra Club (Albuquerque, NM), 1984.
On the Mesa, Peregrine Smith (Salt Lake City, UT), 1986.
A Fragile Beauty: John Nichols' Milagro Country, Peregrine Smith (Salt Lake City, UT), 1987.
(And photographer) *The Sky's the Limit: A Defense of the Earth,* W.W. Norton (New York, NY), 1990.
(And photographer) *Keep It Simple: A Defense of the Earth,* W.W. Norton (New York, NY), 1992.
Dancing on the Stones: Selected Essays, University of New Mexico Press (Albuquerque, NM), 2000.
An American Child Supreme: The Education of a Liberation Ecologist, Milkweed Editions (Minneapolis, MN), 2001.

NOVELS

The Sterile Cuckoo, McKay (New York, NY), 1965.
The Wizard of Loneliness, Putnam (New York, NY), 1966.
A Ghost in the Music, Holt (New York, NY), 1979.
American Blood, Holt (New York, NY), 1987.
An Elegy for September, Holt (New York, NY), 1992.
Conjugal Bliss: A Comedy of Marital Arts, Holt (New York, NY), 1994.
The Voice of the Butterfly: A Novel, Chronicle Books (San Francisco, CA), 2001.

NEW MEXICO TRILOGY

The Milagro Beanfield War: A Novel, illustrated by Rini Templeton, Holt (New York, NY), 1974, anniversary edition, 1994.
(And illustrator) *The Magic Journey: A Novel,* Holt (New York, NY), 1978.
The Nirvana Blues: A Novel, Holt (New York, NY), 1981, reprinted, 1999.

OTHER

Sound recordings by the author: *The Milagro Beanfield War,* released by Newman Books-on-Cassette (Albuquerque, NM), 1986; *Landscapes of a Magic Valley,* released by Audio Press (Louisville, CO), 1988; *Readings,* selections from *Magic Journey,* released by American Audio Prose Library (Columbia, MO), 1982; *Interview,* released by American Audio Prose Library (Columbia, MO), 1982. Also contributor of essays and short stories to periodicals.

ADAPTATIONS: The Sterile Cuckoo, directed by Alan J. Pakula and starring Liza Minnelli, was released by Paramount in 1969; *The Milagro Beanfield War,* directed by Robert Redford, was released in 1988; *The Wizard of Loneliness,* directed by Jenny Bowen, was released in 1988.

SIDELIGHTS: Best known for his "New Mexico Trilogy," John Nichols is a novelist, photographer, screenwriter, and environmental nonfiction writer. He was the winner of a 1981 New Mexico Governor's Award and the 2003 Frank Writers Award. Nichols's works are noted for their social and environmental concerns, particularly the cultural conflict between Anglos and Chicanos in New Mexico, social violence, the destruction of natural resources, and economic imbalance. His books are marked by colorful characters and familiar locales, and deal with not only larger social issues, but also focus on the more intimate issues of family and love.

One of Nichols's most highly regarded novels is his first, *The Sterile Cuckoo.* The novel's narrator, Jerry, offers an account of his sophomore year in college, during which time he learned little of academic value, but much of collegiate love. "Square at first sight for its evocation, through half-amused, half-boastful reminiscence, of frat-house drinking revels . . . at second glance, Nichols's book takes on a deeper dimension," Albert Goldman remarked in the *Nation.* "With astuteness and unfailing intuition, the young author has placed at the heart of his college recollections an absolutely unique yet broadly representative character named Pookie Adams. A comedienne, who has adopted the new humor as her personal life style, Pookie is the type of today's funny little old college girl." And, although Jerry is the narrator, this is Pookie's story. "Although Pookie often appears a fragile, childlike moppet encased in a gauzy pink cocoon of Disneyland fantasy . . . her actions and daydreams suggest pathological hatred," observed Goldman. And, the reviewer continued, "Spunky as her efforts are to exorcise fear with farce, their ultimate effect is to make her a 'sterile cuckoo,' cut off from life by the comic persona she originally adopted to protect her deeply damaged personality."

Granville Hicks valued *The Sterile Cuckoo* as "the best of many novels I have recently read about sex and the younger generation. For one thing," he wrote in *Saturday Review,* "it presented a heroine who was both attractive and credible and for the most part unstereotyped. For another, I was impressed by the skill with which the author let the narrator expose himself as a heel." Other reviewers criticized the novel for a lack of realism and for being out of touch with its turbulent times. Richard A. Blessing addressed this issue in an article for the *Journal of Popular Culture.* "Critics of both the novel and the movie have scoffed at its lack of 'realism'. . . . A more discerning reading will show that the nightmare of violence in the atomic age is so pervasive in *The Sterile Cuckoo* that there is scarcely a page on which it is not present." He added, "Let me suggest that Pookie and her friends are as aware of the horror of modern life as are their more recent counterparts at Columbia or Berkeley, but that their response to that horror is different, is more grotesque because the horror is more real and more grotesque to them." Blessing concluded, "Nichols has produced, I think, an important contribution to the popular literature of the '60s."

Nichols's "New Mexico Trilogy" (*The Milagro Beanfield War, The Magic Journey,* and *The Nirvana Blues*) traces the four-decade transformation of a small New Mexico town from a quiet, traditional society to its modern, commercial lifestyle. In the trilogy, Nichols is concerned with the destruction of traditional communities and cultures in the name of progress and, in particular, with the economic system that fosters such destruction.

"At the beginning of the trilogy," John McLellan wrote in the *Washington Post,* "New Mexico was still a relatively unspoiled land, the possession of Indians and Mexicans who lived off the land. It was ripe for spoiling, and the story of that spoiling is a major concern of the trilogy." As Jeffrey Burke of *Harper's* explained the story: "Speculators, developers, politicians—the usual crowd of cashers-in—have weaned the locals away from a land-based economy to the almighty greenback and introduced them to the marvels of installment plans, menial labor, and debt. By the time the older Pueblo get around to actively protesting, they've lost their children, their culture, [and] their farms to the maw of red-blooded, white-skinned capitalism."

In the face of this onslaught by Anglos and their social and economic imperatives, a small act of resistance ignites a clash of cultures. This is the story of *The Milagro Beanfield War.* Hispanic Joe Mondragón, a jack-of-all-trades, decides to tap into an irrigation canal so that he can raise some beans on a plot of his family's land. The only problem is that water is like gold in the West and this water belongs to the forces of Anglo progress. "The beanfield becomes a symbol of the plight of the Chicano in New Mexico—lost water rights, lost lands, and exploitation at the hands of outsiders," wrote Carl R. Shirley in the *Dictionary of Literary Biography Yearbook.* In highlighting this plight, "Nichols draws upon the possibilities inherent in the genre to write a social novel different from most other socially oriented American novels," John E. Loftis maintained in the *Rocky Mountain Review of Language and Literature.* "The central conflict in this novel is between two cultures, two ways of life, two views of reality: the Anglo and the Chicano."

To capture the conflict that swirls around the beanfield, Nichols "creates an original blend of myth and reality in his fictive world," noted Shirley. "The floodgates of the author's imagination are also opened," Shirley added, "and the reader witnesses a phantasmagoria of colorful characters." The result is a novel that suggests to some reviewers a mix of John Steinbeck, William Faulkner, and Gabriel García Márquez. For *National Observer* reviewer Larry L. King, however, *The Milagro Beanfield War* "is a big, gassy, convoluted book that adds up to a disappointment—one somehow failing to equal the sum of its many parts." And, Frederick Busch, writing in the *New York Times Book Review,* found fault with Nichols's many colorful characters. "The characters, first of all, are stereotypes. . . . They don't exist in and of themselves, and they don't act because of inner necessity. . . . They seem instead to act for the sake of yet another amusing tale told by a decent, charming fellow-drinker during an afternoon in a quiet bar."

Loftis, in his review, took account of criticism like that offered by Busch. He commented, "Busch makes several astute observations, but because of the ways in which he applies these observations to the novel, he condemns it for what seem to me wrong reasons." As he pointed out, "Wars, after all, are fought between social groups, not individuals, and Nichols chooses not to focus on an individual protagonist whose personality, values, and consciousness usually provide coherence and continuity to a novel." Instead, continued the critic, "The two cultures, Chicano and Anglo, and the values they represent are the protagonist and antagonist in *The Milagro Beanfield War;* they are forces too powerful to be controlled, too intertwined to be separated into clearly defined and formulated principles, and too random and haphazard in events to be represented by any one character." Loftis concluded, "Nichols's concerns as novelist are primarily social, and he has created an unusual kind of protagonist, and thus novel, to give artistic form to these concerns."

In *The Magic Journey,* the second novel of the trilogy, Nichols again explores the effect of progress on a small Chicano community, Chamisaville. The progress begins with a bang, transforming the sleepy town into a tangled mass of tourist traps. A school bus under repair explodes. The site soon yields hot springs. A shrine is set up to the Dynamite Virgin. Tourists come and spas, hotels, restaurants, and shops spring up to attend to their needs. As with his previous New Mexico novel, Nichols weaves together many elements, making *The Magic Journey* "a plausible history of exploitation, lush with eccentric characters, with myths, legends, ghosts, and revealing shards from the past four decades, all carried by a Dickensian narrative exuberance," Jeffrey Burke wrote in *Harper's.* Jonathan Yardley, writing for the *New York Times Book Review,* found that this "tale of how progress comes to the little Southwestern settlement of Chamisaville—transforming it into the 'playground of the Land of Enchantment' and displacing its true owners in the name of profit—is consistently diverting and occasionally amusing."

According to Burke, Nichols, in mixing humor into this social novel, goes too far, losing the delicate balance necessary for good satire. "Nichols's creative energy runs so often to comic invention, to caricature instead of character . . . that he entertains far more than he instructs," Burke wrote. "The imbalance makes for ambivalence." Shirley saw greater balance in Nichols's storytelling, finding connections between this story and the culture from which it emerges. "*The Magic Journey*'s characters are more in the tradition of Latin America than of the United States," Shirley noted. "In Spanish-speaking countries, personal eccentricity is the norm rather than a deviation; unusual characters or even living caricatures are much more likely to be encountered, not only in literature but also on the streets. Nichols manifests a high degree of understanding of the people about whom he is writing and whose standard he has chosen to carry." In his own way, Nichols hopes to remind readers, in the words he quoted from President Woodrow Wilson, that "we are all caught in a great economic system which is heartless." As Bruce Cook of the *Washington Post* wrote, "Nichols proposes to change that system."

In *The Nirvana Blues,* third in the trilogy, an Anglo garbage man plans a drug deal to earn enough money to buy his own piece of New Mexico from the last Chicano in town. In this way, Nichols "practically shuts the door on any hope he has for the survival of Chicano culture and traditional lifestyle," observed Shirley. Here, as with the previous two novels, "Some of the many comic episodes are truly hilarious," Shirley noted, "but again, as in *The Milagro Beanfield War* and *The Magic Journey,* there is an underlying feeling of sadness and despair at the uncontrollable and inevitable circumstances that lead to the death of Eloy [the last Chicano] and his way of life. Nichols is laughing through his tears and causing his readers to do the same." For Lynn Z. Bloom, writing in *Western American Literature,* "Nichols's cautionary tale makes us yearn for heroes, saviors of the land, preservers of stability, natural beauty, integrity of human relationships." Norbert Blei of the *Chicago Tribune Book World* concluded his evaluation of the "New Mexico Trilogy" with high praise. "It will be," he stated, "one of the most significant contributions to American literature in some time. . . . Nichols has left us with a classic American trilogy."

Published in 1987, *American Blood* is Nichols's investigation of the consequences of the Vietnam war on the American consciousness. Michael P. Smith, a product of and participant in the war's brutal killing fields, finds himself emotionally adrift after the atrocities in which he has participated. He is caught in an on-again, off-again relationship with one of his former platoon members, Tom Carp, who summons him out to New Mexico. There Smith meets Janine Tarr, an older waitress with a teenaged daughter named Cathie. Janine introduces Smith to the process of healing. Together they form a small family, but their nascent peace is ripped apart when Cathie is violently raped and murdered. "It is only in the remains of this fool's paradise," wrote *Washington Post Book World* contributor Kathleen Hirsch, "that the lovers can begin to struggle toward a more authentic framework for survival." "*American Blood* is Nichols's most difficult book to date," stated Paul Pintarich in the *Oregonian,* "filled as it is with violence, evil and a vicious reality that many will interpret as pornography. Readers who endure to the end, however, will find the treatment acceptable." The novel "is a profoundly disturbing book," Ray Mungo concluded in the *San Francisco Examiner-Chronicle.* "Nichols has chosen to mute his engaging sense of humor in favor of the direct hit to the veins. . . . *American Blood* is a painful book to read, yet it leaves us with wisdom and hope."

Nichols returns to the subjects of sex and marriage in *An Elegy for September* and *Conjugal Bliss.* In the former volume an aging writer with a heart problem, in the process of ending his second marriage, begins a relationship by letter with a younger woman. It culminates in an affair lasting a couple of weeks. "From these slight materials, Nichols has constructed a novella," wrote Charles Bowden in the *Los Angeles Times Book Review,* "and in a career studded with wonders, it is one of the finest things he has ever written." In the latter book, Nichols charts the destruction of a marriage in a series of anecdotes and pastiches. "*Conjugal Bliss* is a larger-than-life anti-romance, antic and full of low-jinks," explained *Los Angeles Times Book Review* contributor Ron Carlson; "imagine *Othello* by the writers of *I Love Lucy.*"

Critics have admired the versatility of Nichols's prose. John McLellan noted Nichols's "virtuoso style, the profusion of strange but believable characters, the skill with which small incidents are developed and the curious blend of humor and pathos, which are often found fighting for supremacy in a single phrase." Nichols "has all of Steinbeck's gifts," Norbert Blei stated, "the same overwhelming compassion for people, plus an even finer sense of humor, and the need to celebrate the cause and dignity of man." In her *Book Week* review of *The Sterile Cuckoo,* Patricia MacManus listed "an effervescent wit, a remarkable ear for dialogue, . . . a feeling for off-beat characterizations, and—oh, yes—the saving grace . . . of a rueful sense of the ludicrous" as being some of Nichols's writing assets. "There used to be writers that cared about people," Blei of Chicago's *Tribune Books* noted. "Proletarian writers they were called. . . . Nichols, now, seems almost alone upon this inherited terrain." Blei contended that Nichols's work "reminds us of the love and laughter, the courage it takes to be honest, caring human beings in an age when greed and self-fulfillment seem synonymous." Nichols once commented: "I am a great believer in humor as a weapon and feel that while some of my work may be polemical, it's important that it is also funny and entertaining, and above all compassionate."

Nichols also explained his motivations for writing and how they underwent a change beginning with his third novel: "Basically, my life, my literary focus, my ambitions, changed radically during the mid-1960s when I was active in the anti-Vietnam War movement. I came to view the world, and how it functions, from a mostly Marxist perspective, and most of what I've written since 1966 reflects this perspective. During the 1960s and early-1970s I wrote nearly a dozen novels, motivated by this new point of view, none of which saw the light of publishing day. Yet eventually I began to learn how to create an art that is both polemical and entertaining, and have managed in the past five years to guide a handful of new books into print.

"I am strongly committed, in my life and in my work, to bringing about changes in the nature of our society which I believe absolutely necessary to the well-being of us all. I'm tired of our destruction of human, spiritual, and natural resources, particularly among minorities and working-class and third-world peoples—both in our country and abroad. I hope some day to see a more equal distribution of wealth and opportunity in our nation and around the world, and an end to American imperialism. I have a great faith in the energy of our people, in the vitality of our myriad cultures. I have a tendency to believe that the survival or the destruction of our planet is in the hands of the U.S.A. That makes our nation one of the scariest and most exciting countries on Earth. I just wish that more of our artists and writers would accept social responsibility as an integral part of their credos, instead of wallowing in the cynical, self-centered nihilism that characterizes too much of what is popular and successful nowadays."

In a *Publishers Weekly* review of *The Voice of the Butterfly,* the critic commented on the strong satirical tone of the book, calling it a "completely over-the-top send-up of the mindless ambitions of our shallow, materialistic, upwardly mobile modern-day society." Amy H. Taylor reviewed the novel and conducted an interview of the author for the *Boulder Weekly* Web site. She described *The Voice of the Butterfly* as a "raucous, wild story of a ragtag bunch of activists on a crusade to save an endangered butterfly from a highway bypass." The Butterfly Coalition, a bunch of local misfits, is led by an aging hippie joined by his alcoholic, drug-using ex-wife; their would-be punk rocker son who works at a fast-food burger joint; and a ninety-or-so-year-old chain-smoking woman who owns the last refuge of the endangered insect. During the *Boulder Weekly* interview Nichols commented, "I always hope that you can get political messages across through entertainment and humor . . . and that the body of the work as a whole will encourage people to be hopeful, to sustain themselves with a sense of humor and not to mourn but to organize. What were Joe Hill's famous last words before they shot him, the labor organizer? 'Don't mourn for me boys, organize.' And that's what I hope the literature will ultimately do."

BIOGRAPHICAL AND CRITICAL SOURCES:

BOOKS

Contemporary Authors Autobiography Series, Volume 2, Thomson Gale (Detroit, MI), 1985.

Contemporary Literary Criticism, Volume 38, Thomson Gale (Detroit, MI), 1986.

Dictionary of Literary Biography Yearbook: 1982, Thomson Gale (Detroit, MI), 1983.

Twentieth-Century Western Writers, 2nd edition, St. James Press (Detroit, MI), 1991.

Wild, Peter, *John Nichols,* Boise State University (Boise, ID), 1986.

PERIODICALS

America, February 26, 1966.

Anniston Star (Alabama), May 31, 1987, Barbara Hodge Hall, "*American Blood* Not for Faint of Heart."

Arizona Daily Star, May 31, 1987, Dan Huff, "*American Blood* Is a Brutal War Story That Sticks Like the Most Horrible Dream."

Atlantic Monthly, March, 1965, p. 193.

Best Sellers, January 15, 1965; November, 1979, p. 283; September, 1981, p. 209.

Bloomsbury Review, May-June, 2000, James R. Hepworth, review of *Dancing on the Stones: Selected Essays.*

Booklist, May 1, 1992, review of *An Elegy for September,* p. 1563; April 1, 2001, Kristine Huntley, review of *The Voice of the Butterfly,* p. 1429.

Book Week, January 24, 1965; February 20, 1966.

Chicago Tribune, April 19, 1987, David Guy, "After 'Nam," pp. 3, 9.

Christian Science Monitor, February 4, 1965.

Chronicle Books, June 21-28, 2001, A.D. Amorosi, review of *The Voice of the Butterfly.*

Confluencia, October, 1978.

Denver Post, May 3, 1987, Tom Clark, "Scary Skeleton of Vietnam."

Environment, March 1999, review of *The Milagro Beanfield War,* p. 9.

Harper's, April, 1965; March, 1966; August, 1978, p. 89.

Journal of Popular Culture, summer, 1973, p. 124.

Kirkus Reviews, May 1, 1979, p. 562; April 1, 2001, review of *The Voice of the Butterfly,* p. 448.

Los Angeles Times Book Review, June 28, 1992, Charles Bowden, "Not Just Another Pastel Coyote," pp. 2, 8; April 24, 1994, Ron Carlson, "Love in the Trenches," p. 12.

Nation, February 8, 1965, p. 142.

National Observer, November 16, 1974, p. 27.

New America, spring, 1979.

New Mexican (Santa Fe, NM), May 14, 2000, Antonio Lopez, "Essays of an Adopted Son."

New York Herald Tribune, February 24, 1966, p. 21.

New York Times Book Review, January 17, 1965, p. 46; March 6, 1966, p. 52; October 27, 1974, p. 53; April 16, 1978, p. 15; June 10, 1979, p. 18; October 28, 1979.

Observer, May 15, 1977.

Oregonian, June 7, 1987, Paul Pintarich, "A Postwar Horror Story," p. 24.

Publishers Weekly, June 11, 1982, p. 54; December 13, 1993, review of *Conjugal Bliss: A Comedy of Marital Arts,* p. 62; June 4, 2001, review of *The Voice of the Butterfly,* p. 55.

Rocky Mountain Review of Language and Literature, Volume 38, number 4, 1984, p. 201.

St. Petersburg Times, June 21, 1987, J.A.C. Dunn, "A Smoldering Anger."

San Francisco Chronicle, July 9-15, 2000, Sherry Simpson, "The Writer's Life Knows No Limits."

San Francisco Examiner-Chronicle, April 19, 1987, Ray Mungo, "Terrible Price of War."

Saturday Review, January 30, 1965, p. 26; February 26, 1966, p. 29.

Tribune Books (Chicago, IL), October 7, 1979; August 16, 1981; February 27, 1994, Bryce Milligan, "Welcome to 'A Marriage from Hell.'"

Village Voice, June 30, 1979.

Washington Post, June 17, 1978; August 28, 1981.

Washington Post Book World, September 9, 1979; August 28, 1981; May 11, 1987, Kathleen Hirsch, "A Viet Vet's Unceasing Battle"; July 17, 1992, Ann Hood, "The 30-Day Romance," p. C2.

Weekly Alibi (Albuquerque, NM), June 22-28, 2000, Steven Robert Allen, "Keeping It Simple," pp. 33, 35.

Western American Literature, November, 1975, p. 249; winter, 1982-83, p. 372; spring, 1983, p. 54.

ONLINE

Boulder Weekly, http://www.boulderweekly.com/ (January 28, 2002), Amy H. Taylor, "The Voice of John Nichols," interview with the author of *The Voice of the Butterfly.*

NICHOLS, John Treadwell
See NICHOLS, John

* * *

NICHOLS, Leigh
See KOONTZ, Dean R.

* * *

NORTH, Anthony
See KOONTZ, Dean R.

* * *

NORTH, Milou
See ERDRICH, Louise

* * *

NORTH, Milou
See DORRIS, Michael

* * *

NOSILLE, Nabrah
See ELLISON, Harlan

* * *

NOVAK, Joseph
See KOSINSKI, Jerzy

* * *

NYE, Naomi Shihab 1952-

PERSONAL: Born March 12, 1952, in St. Louis, MO; daughter of Aziz (a journalist) and Miriam Naomi (a Montessori teacher; maiden name, Allwardt) Shihab; married Michael Nye (a lawyer and photographer), September 2, 1978; children: Madison Cloudfeather (son). *Ethnicity:* "Arab-American." *Education:* Trinity University (San Antonio, TX), B.A. (English and world religions; summa cum laude), 1974. *Politics:* Independent. *Religion:* "Ecumenical." *Hobbies and other interests:* Traveling, reading, cooking, gardening, bicycling, watching basketball

ADDRESSES: Home—806 South Main Ave., San Antonio, TX 78204. *E-mail*—nshihab@aol.com.

CAREER: Freelance writer, editor, and speaker, 1974—; Texas Commission on the Arts' Writers in the Schools Project, affilate, 1974-86. Holloway Lecturer, University of California, Berkeley; visiting writer at University of Hawaii, 1991, University of Alaska, Fairbanks, 1994, and University of Texas at Austin, 1995 and 2001; U.S. Information Agency Arts America Program, traveling writer and workshop leader. Poetry editor for *Texas Observer*; translator for Project of Translation from Arabic Literature (PROTA). Member of national council, National Endowment for the Humanities. Featured on eight-part Public Broadcasting Service (PBS) television special *The Language of Life with Bill Moyers,* 1995, on PBS series *The United States of Poetry,* and on National Public Radio.

MEMBER: Poets and Writers, Radius of Arab-American Writers, Texas Institute of Letters, Phi Beta Kappa.

AWARDS, HONORS: Voertman Poetry Prize, Texas Institute of Letters, 1980, for *Different Ways to Pray,* and 1982, for *Hugging the Jukebox; Hugging the Jukebox* named a notable book of 1982, American Library Association (ALA); four Pushcart poetry prizes; I.B. Lavan Award, Academy of American Poets, 1988; Charity Randall Prize for Spoken Poetry (with Galway Kinnell), International Poetry Forum, 1988; Jane Addams Children's Book Award, and Honorary Book designation, National Association for Christians and Jews, both 1992, both for *This Same Sky;* Best Book citation, *School Library Journal,* and Pick of the List citation from American Booksellers Association, both 1994, and Notable Children's Trade Book in the Field of Social Studies citation, National Council for the Social Studies/Children's Book Council, and Jane Addams Children's Book Award, both 1995, all for *Sitti's Secrets;* Judy Lopez Memorial Award for children's literature, and Texas Institute of Letters Best Book for Young Readers, and Dorothy Canfield Fisher Children's Book Award Master List honoree, 1998, all for *Habibi;* Paterson Poetry Prize, for *The Tree Is Older Than You Are;* Guggenheim Fellowship, 1997; Witter Bynner Fellowship, U.S. Library of Congress, 2000; Lee Bennett Hopkins Poetry Award, 2000, for *Come with Me: Poems for a Journey;* National Book Award finalist in young people's literature category, 2002, for *Nineteen Varieties of Gazelle: Poems of the Middle East;* Lannan fellowship, 2003.

WRITINGS:

POETRY, EXCEPT AS NOTED

Different Ways to Pray, Breitenbush (Portland, OR), 1980.

On the Edge of the Sky, Iguana Press (Madison, WI), 1981.
Hugging the Jukebox, Dutton (New York, NY), 1982.
Yellow Glove, Breitenbush (Portland, OR), 1986.
Invisible, Trilobite (Denton, TX), 1987.
Mint (prose; also see below), State Street Press (Brockport, NY), 1991.
Red Suitcase, BOA Editions (Rochester, NY), 1994.
Words under the Words: Selected Poems, Far Corner Books (Portland, OR), 1995.
Fuel, BOA Editions (Rochester, NY), 1998.
Mint Snowball (prose; includes selections previously published in *Mint*), Anhinga Press (Tallahassee, FL), 2001.

POETRY FOR CHILDREN

(Editor) *This Same Sky: A Collection of Poems from around the World,* Four Winds Press (New York, NY), 1992.
(Editor) *The Tree Is Older Than You Are: Poems and Stories from Mexico,* Simon & Schuster (New York, NY), 1995.
(Editor, with Paul Janeczko) *I Feel a Little Jumpy around You: A Book of Her Poems and His Poems Collected in Pairs,* Simon & Schuster (New York, NY), 1996.
(With others) *The Space between Our Footsteps: Poems and Paintings from the Middle East,* Simon & Schuster (New York, NY), 1998, published as *The Flag of Childhood: Poems from the Middle East,* Aladdin (New York, NY), 2002.
(Selector) *What Have You Lost?* (young-adult poetry), with photographs by husband, Michael Nye, Greenwillow Books (New York, NY), 1999.
(Selector) *Salting the Ocean: 100 Poems by Young Poets,* illustrated by Ashley Bryan, Greenwillow Books (New York, NY), 2000.
Come with Me: Poems for a Journey, with images by Dan Yaccarino, Greenwillow Books (New York, NY), 2000.
Nineteen Varieties of Gazelle: Poems of the Middle East, Greenwillow Books (New York, NY), 2002.
Is This Forever, or What? Poems and Paintings from Texas, Greenwillow Books (New York, NY), 2004.
Sweet Sifter in Time: Poems for Girls, illustrated by Terre Maher, Greenwillow Books (New York, NY), 2005.

PICTURE BOOKS

Sitti's Secrets, illustrated by Nancy Carpenter, Macmillan (New York, NY), 1994.
Benito's Dream Bottle, illustrated by Yu Cha Pak, Simon & Schuster (New York, NY), 1995.
Lullaby Raft, illustrated by Vivienne Flesher, Simon & Schuster (New York, NY), 1997.
Baby Radar, illustrated by Nancy Carpenter, Greenwillow Books (New York, NY), 2003.

OTHER

Never in a Hurry (essays; for young adults), University of South Carolina Press (Columbia, SC), 1996.
Habibi (novel; for young adults), Simon & Schuster (New York, NY), 1996.

Also author of chapbooks *Tattooed Feet,* 1977, and *Eye-to-Eye,* 1978. Contributor to *Texas Poets in Concert: A Quartet,* edited by Richard B. Sale, University of North Texas Press, 1990, and *Best American Essays 1991,* edited by Joyce Carol Oates. Contributor of poems, stories, and essays to periodicals, including *Atlantic, Iowa Review, Georgia Review, Ploughshares, Atlanta Review, Indiana Review, Hayden's Ferry Review, Virginia Quarterly Review, Southwest Review, Manoa, Houston Chronicle,* and *Austin Chronicle.*

Recordings include *Rutabaga-Roo* (songs), Flying Cat (San Antonio, TX), 1979; *Lullaby Raft,* Flying Cat (San Antonio, TX), 1981; and *The Spoken Page* (poetry reading), International Poetry Forum (Pittsburgh, PA), 1988.

WORK IN PROGRESS: A novel titled *Florrie Will Do It;* new poems, essays, and picture books.

SIDELIGHTS: Naomi Shihab Nye is known for award-winning poetry that lends a fresh perspective to ordinary events, people, and objects. "For me the primary source of poetry has always been local life, random characters met on the streets, our own ancestry sifting down to us through small essential daily tasks," Nye was quoted by Jane L. Tanner in an essay for the *Dictionary of Literary Biography.* Characterizing Nye's "prolific canon" in *Contemporary Women Poets,* Paul Christensen noted that Nye "is building a reputation . . . as the voice of childhood in America, the voice of the girl at the age of daring exploration." Nye's poetry is also informed by her Palestinian-American background, as well as by other cultures. In her work, according to Tanner, "Nye observes the business of living and the continuity among all the world's inhabitants. . . . She is international in scope and internal in focus."

Nye is also considered one of the leading figures in the poetry of the American Southwest, especially poetry expressing a woman's point of view. A contributor to *Contemporary Poets* wrote that she "brings attention to the female as a humorous, wry creature with brisk, hard intelligence and a sense of personal freedom unheard of" in the trying history of pioneer women.

Nye was born in St. Louis, Missouri, to a Palestinian father and an American mother of German and Swiss descent. As a young girl she read voraciously and listened to her father's stories about his homeland and family. She began writing poems at age six and had them published in a children's magazine at age seven. After spending much of her childhood in St. Louis, Nye moved with her family to Jerusalem, which was then part of Jordan. Nye attended a year of high school in Jordan before her family moved to San Antonio, Texas, where the poet continues to live with her husband and son. "My poems and stories often begin with the voices of our neighbors, mostly Mexican American, always inventive and surprising," Nye wrote in a press release for Four Winds Press. "I never get tired of mixtures." A contributor to *Contemporary Southern Writers* wrote that Nye's poetry "is playfully and imaginatively instructive, borrows from Eastern and Middle Eastern and Native American religions, and resembles the meditative poetry of William Stafford, Wallace Stevens, and Gary Snyder."

Nye's earliest published work includes a 1977 chapbook titled *Tattooed Feet;* another chapbook, *Eye-to-Eye,* followed in 1978. The early poems contained in these books, written in free verse, often reflect the theme of a journey or quest. According to Tanner, "What is remarkable is Nye's ability to draw clear parallels between the ordinary and the sublime."

Nye onced commented: "I have always loved the gaps, the spaces between things, as much as the things. I love staring, pondering, mulling, puttering. I love the times when someone or something is late—there's that rich possibility of noticing more, in the meantime.

"Poetry calls us to pause. There is so much we overlook, while the abundance around us continues to shimmer, on its own."

In her first full-length collection, *Different Ways to Pray,* Nye explores the differences between, and shared experiences of, cultures from California to Texas, from South America to Mexico. In "Grandfather's Heaven," a child declares: "Grandma liked me even though my daddy was a Moslem." As Tanner observed, "with her acceptance of different 'ways to pray' is also Nye's growing awareness that living in the world can sometimes be difficult."

Nye followed *Different Ways to Pray* with *On the Edge of the Sky,* a slim volume printed on handmade paper, and *Hugging the Jukebox,* a full-length collection that also won the Voertman Poetry Prize. In *Hugging the Jukebox,* Nye continues to focus on the ordinary, on connections between diverse peoples, and on the perspectives of those in other lands. She writes: "We move forward, / confident we were born into a large family, / our brothers cover the earth." Nye creates poetry from everyday scenes in "The Trashpickers of San Antonio," where the trashpickers are "murmuring in a language soft as rags." The boy in the title poem "Hugging the Jukebox" is enthusiastic about the jukebox he adopts, singing its songs in a way that "strings a hundred passionate sentences in a single line."

Reviewers generally praised *Hugging the Jukebox,* noting Nye's warmth and celebratory tone. Writing in the *Village Voice,* Mary Logue commented that in Nye's poems about daily life, "sometimes the fabric is thin and the mundaneness of the action shows through. But, in an alchemical process of purification, Nye often pulls gold from the ordinary." According to *Library Journal* contributor David Kirby, the poet "seems to be in good, easy relation with the earth and its peoples." In Christensen's view, Nye "does not avoid the horrors of urban life, but she patches together the vision of simple nature struggling up through the cracks of the city."

Unlike her earlier work, the poems in *Yellow Glove* present a more mature perspective tempered by tragedy and sorrow. In this collection Nye considers the Palestinian-Israeli conflict in "Blood." She describes a café in combat-weary Beirut, bemoans "a world where no one saves anyone," and observes "The Gardener" for whom "everything she planted gave up under the ground." *Georgia Review* contributor Philip Booth declared that Nye brings "home to readers both how variously and how similarly all people live."

In addition to her poetry collections, Nye has produced fiction for children, poetry and song recordings, and poetry translations. She has also produced a book of essays, *Never in a Hurry,* published in 1996, and has edited several books of poems, including the award-winning anthology *This Same Sky.* In her introduction to *This Same Sky,* which represents the work of 129 poets from sixty-eight countries, Nye writes, "Whenever someone suggests 'how much is lost in translation!' I want to say, 'Perhaps—but how much is gained!'" A tremendous amount of work was involved in collecting these poems from around the world but, as Nye told a contributor to the *Children's Literature Review,* that "the poems ended up gathering themselves into sections that felt almost organic—related to family, or words and silences, or losses, or human mysteries. The sky seemed to occur surprisingly often as a universal reference point, which gave us the title."

Reviewers praised *This Same Sky,* which also includes country and poet indices as well as a map. These extras, according to Mary M. Burns in *Horn Book,* give "additional luster to a book which should prove invaluable for intercultural education." Although contributor Lauralyn Persson noted in *School Library Journal* that some of the poems in the collection would be better appreciated by adults, the reviewer added that the book is "brimming with much lovely material." Jim Morgan, in *Voice of Youth Advocates,* found the book's strongest characteristic to be its "sense of real human life behind the words" and a "universality of human concerns across cultures." *Booklist* critic Hazel Rochman called *This Same Sky* "an extraordinary anthology, not only in its global range . . . but also in the quality of the selections and the immediacy of their appeal."

Nye compiled and edited another anthology, *The Tree Is Older Than You Are,* which collects stories and poems from Nye's beloved Mexico, displaying them in both English and Spanish versions. Hazel Rochman, writing in *Booklist,* praised the "dreamy, lyrical writing with sudden leaps from the real to the magical." The 1996 collection *I Feel a Little Jumpy around You* combines 194 "his and her" poems, pairing a poem written by a man with one written by a woman for a lively poetic discussion of the differences between the genders and their perspectives on the world. Anthony Manna, in *Voice of Youth Advocates,* found the most intriguing aspect of the book to be "the degree to which the voices blend and gender boundaries give way to quests, quirks, and needs which signal the ties that bind us." The 1998 anthology *The Space between Our Footsteps* is a collection of the work of 127 contemporary Middle-Eastern poets and artists representing nineteen countries. Angela J. Reynolds in *School Library Journal* noted that "the universality of topics . . . gives insight into a culture and proves that differences are only skin deep."

Sitti's Secrets concerns an Arab-American child's relationship with her *sitti*—Arabic for grandmother—who lives in a Palestinian village. The child, Mona, recalls visiting Sitti in Palestine and how the two of them invented their own sign language to overcome the English-Arabic language barrier. When Mona returns to the United States, she sustains the bond with Sitti through her active imagination. Mona also writes a letter to the president of the United States, asking him for peace and informing him that she knows he would like her sitti a great deal if he were to meet her. Hazel Rochman, in *Booklist,* praised Nye for capturing the emotions of the "child who longs for a distant grandparent" as well as for writing a narrative that deals personally with Arabs and Arab Americans. A contributor to *Kirkus Reviews* asserted that Nye "deftly assembles particulars" of the relationship between grandmother and granddaughter and recounts incidents "with quiet eloquence."

Benito's Dream Bottle, a picture book for very young children, introduces the boy Benito, whose grandmother has stopped dreaming. He helps her fill up her "dream bottle," located between the stomach and the chest, with a world of sights and sounds so that she might dream again. Reviewers for *Publishers Weekly* and *Booklist* found the lists of images a bit overwhelming, but Judy Constantinides, in *School Library Journal,* called the book "inventive" and "lyrical."

In 1997 Nye published *Habibi,* her first young-adult novel. Readers meet Liyana Abboud, an Arab-American teen who moves with her family to her Palestinian father's native country during the 1970s, only to discover that the violence in Jerusalem has not yet abated. As Liyana notes, "in Jerusalem, so much old anger floated around . . . [that] the air felt stacked with weeping and raging and praying to God by all the different names." Autobiographical in its focus, *Habibi* was praised by Karen Leggett, who noted in the *New York Times Book Review* that the novel magnifies through the lens of adolescence "the joys and anxieties of growing up" and that Nye is "meticulously sensitive to this rainbow of emotion." Appraising *Habibi* in *Horn Book,* Jennifer M. Brabander agreed, saying, "The leisurely progression of the narrative matches the slow and stately pace of daily life" in Jerusalem "and the text's poetic turns of phrase accurately reflect Liyana's passion for words and language." As Nye explained to a *Children's Literature Review* contributor: "To counteract negative images conveyed by blazing headlines, writers must steadily transmit simple stories closer to heart and more common to everyday life. Then we will be doing our job."

What Have You Lost? contains 140 contemporary poems for young adults arranged by different themes of loss experienced over a person's lifetime. Written by mostly lesser-known poets, the poems, according to Jessica Roeder in *Riverbank Review,* take "a fresh look at this perennial theme," becoming "an exercise in expanding compassion." Hazel Rochman, in *Booklist,* pointed out that the book would be "a great stimulus for students' personal writing."

Come with Me: Poems for a Journey contains sixteen poems by Nye that are written for grade-school children and focus on journeys, both real and imaginary. A *Publishers Weekly* contributor found it "chock-full of unexpected images," and Shelle Rosenfeld, writing in *Booklist,* described *Come with Me* as ranging from "playful to pensive." Nina Lindsay, in *School Library Journal,* commented, "Each line exerts a pull like gravity."

Salting the Ocean is a collection of poems by children who have attended Nye's writing workshops over a twenty-five-year period. A contributor to *Horn Book* found that while some "occasionally catch fire," for the most part the poems are more imaginative word play than poetry. Linda Zoppa, in *School Library Journal,* said she enjoyed reading Nye's introduction in which the poet explained how she saved the poems over the years and eventually sought permission to print them from the adults who were once her students.

In her book of poetry *Nineteen Varieties of Gazelle,* Nye looks at the Middle East through her Palestinian-American poet's eye, recording the sights, sounds, smells, tastes, and people she encounters, especially in Jerusalem, in a time of terror and struggle. Brabander said that young-adult readers familiar with Nye's *Habibi* and *Sitti's Secrets* will recognize the people and "will feel they are reading the grown-up Liyana's poetry." Nye allows readers a view into the lives of the many innocent people in the Middle East in a post-September 11, 2001, world. A contributor to *Kirkus Reviews* said that reading the poems will "elicit a gasp of surprise, a nod of the head, a pause to reflect," while Hazel Rochman concluded in *Booklist,* that *Nineteen Variations of Gazelle* "will spark discussion and bring readers up close" to what war and vengeance really mean. Nina Lindsay, in *School Library Journal,* observed that Nye's book is "a celebration of her heritage, and a call for peace."

Nye reflected: "As a child I became crucially aware of that sweet sliver of day called *twilight.* I would stand on our little front porch in St. Louis, gazing into the softening light, feeling hugely nostalgic, wanting to hang onto everything. Don't go so soon, something inside me implored. Everything passes before we are ready for it to pass. I'm not done with this day! Please stay.

"Listening to poems read by my mother created a savory, magical atmosphere, suspended in time. Read it again, I would beg her. When I could read for myself, I found my eyes traveling up and down a poem, Langston Hughes, Emily Dickinson, Rabindranath Tagore, William Blake—taking time with each word and phrase, floating peacefully in the beautiful space around the words on the page. Naturally, if one loved to read so much, writing became the automatic 'next activity'—the thank-you letter for all that had been given.

"My advice to anyone who asks for it remains the same for many years: Read, read, then read some more. Find a way to engage in regular daily writing. Consider it parallel to physical fitness. Writing in small blocks of time keeps us flexible, responsive, in tone and tune with muscular, vivid, energetic words.

"Then, find some way to share your work. Become involved in local writing circles, attend readings by writers. Make a system, a notebook, for yourself—where you might send your work, along with a self-addressed stamped envelope, that magical detail. Keep track of what you send where.

"And don't let 'rejections' trouble you too much—they are utterly inevitable, part of the process. Look at your work with a fresh eye when it comes winging home to you. Is there any way you could make it better?

"There is no end to the writing/reading life. It always feels like a beautiful, wildly mysterious beginning. That is the gift we are given, to see again and again."

BIOGRAPHICAL AND CRITICAL SOURCES:

BOOKS

Children's Literature Review, Volume 59, Thomson Gale (Detroit, MI), 2000.

Contemporary Poets, 7th edition, St. James Press (Detroit, MI), 2001.

Contemporary Southern Writers, St. James Press (Detroit, MI), 1999.

Contemporary Women Poets, St. James Press (Detroit, MI), 1997.

Dictionary of Literary Biography, Volume 120: *American Poets since World War II,* Thomson Gale (Detroit, MI), 1992.

PERIODICALS

Book, September-October, 2002, review of *Nineteen Varieties of Gazelle: Poems of the Middle East,* p. 40.

Booklist, October 15, 1992, Hazel Rochman, review of *This Same Sky: A Collection of Poems from around the World,* p. 425; March 15, 1994, Hazel Rochman, review of *Sitti's Secrets,* p. 1374; May 1, 1995, Hazel Rochman, review of *Benito's Dream Bottle,* p. 1580; September 15, 1995, Hazel Rochman, review of *The Tree Is Older than You Are: Poems and Stories from Mexico,* p. 151; September 15, 1997, Hazel Rochman, review of *Habibi,* p. 224; March 15, 1999, review of *The Space between Our Footsteps: Poems and Paintings from the Middle East,* p. 1297; April 1, 1999, Hazel Rochman, review of *What Have You Lost?,* p. 1397; October 15, 2000, Shelle Rosenfeld, review of *Come with Me: Poems for a Journey,* p. 442; December 1, 2000, review of *Come with Me,* p. 693; March 15, 2001, review of *Salting the Ocean: 100 Poems by Young Poets,* p. 1393; April 1, 2002, Hazel Rochman, review of *Nineteen Varieties of Gazelle,* p. 1315.

BookPage, April, 2002, review of *Nineteen Varieties of Gazelle,* p. 26.

Book Report, September, 1999, review of *What Have You Lost?,* p. 75.

Books for Keeps, March, 2002, review of *The Space between Our Footsteps, Habibi,* and *Sitti's Secrets,* p. 4.

Bulletin of the Center for Children's Books, March, 1994, p. 228; March, 1999, review of *What Have You Lost?,* p. 251.

Catholic Library World, September, 1999, review of *Habibi,* p. 19.

Chelsea, June 7, 1999, review of *Fuel,* p. 188.

Children's Book & Play Review, January, 2001, review of *This Same Sky,* p. 4.

Detroit Free Press, April 14, 2002, review of *The Flag of Childhood: Poems from the Middle East,* p. E5.

Five Owls, March, 2001, review of *This Same Sky,* p. 78.

Georgia Review, spring, 1989.

Horn Book, March-April, 1993, Mary M. Burns, review of *This Same Sky,* p. 215; May-June, 1994, Maeve Visser Knoth, review of *Sitti's Secrets,* p. 317-18; November-December, 1996, p. 755; November-December, 1997, Jennifer M. Brabander, review of *Habibi,* pp. 683-684; March, 1999, review of *What Have You Lost?,* p. 218; July, 2000, review of *Salting the Ocean,* p. 472; September-October, 2002, Jennifer M. Brabander, review of *Nineteen Varieties of Gazelle,* p. 591.

Junior Bookshelf, April, 1995, Marcus Crouch, review of *Sitti's Secrets,* p. 65-66.

Kirkus Reviews, February 15, 1994, review of *Sitti's Secrets,* p. 231; April 1, 1998; February 15, 1999, review of *What Have You Lost?,* p. 303; April 15, 2002, review of *Nineteen Varieties of Gazelle,* p. 575.

Kliatt, May, 1999, review of *I Feel a Little Jumpy around You,* p. 31; September, 1999, review of *Habibi,* p. 19.

Library Journal, August, 1982.

MELUS, summer, 2002, Joy Castro, "Nomad, Switchboard, Poet: Naomi Shihab Nye's Multicultural Literature for Young Readers: An Interview," p. 225.

New York Times Book Review, November 16, 1997, Karen Leggett, review of *Habibi,* p. 50; November 23, 1997.

Poetry, March, 1999, review of *Fuel,* p. 357.

Publishers Weekly, April 24, 1995, review of *Benito's Dream Bottle,* p. 71; May 13, 1996, p. 77; September 8, 1997, p. 77; March 8, 1999, review of *What Have You Lost?,* p. 70; September 4, 2000, review of *Come with Me,* p. 108; April 16, 2001, review of *Mint Snowball,* p. 60; February 18, 2002, review of *The Flag of Childhood,* p. 99.

Reading Teacher, February, 1999, review of *Habibi,* p. 504; September, 1999, review of *The Space between Our Footsteps,* p. 85; May, 2001, review of *Come with Me,* p. 824.

Riverbank Review, spring, 1999, Jessica Roeder, review of *What Have You Lost?,* pp. 42-43.

School Library Journal, December, 1992, Lauralyn Persson, review of *This Same Sky,* p. 139; June, 1994, Luann Toth, review of *Sitti's Secrets,* p. 112; June, 1995, Judy Constantinides, review of *Benito's Dream Bottle,* p. 94; September, 1997, Kate McClelland, review of *Habibi,* pp. 223-224; May, 1998, Angela J. Reynolds, review of *The Space between Our Footsteps,* p. 159; April, 1999, review of *What Have You Lost?,* p. 152; July, 2000, Linda Zoppa, review of *Salting the Ocean,* p. 120; September, 2000, Nina Lindsay, review of *Come with Me,* p. 221; May, 2002, Nina Lindsay, review of *Nineteen Varieties of Gazelle,* p. 175.

Teacher Librarian, May, 1999, review of *What Have You Lost?,* p. 45; February, 2001, review of *Salting the Ocean,* p. 26.

Tribune Books (Chicago, IL), March 31, 2002, review of *Nineteen Varieties of Gazelle,* p. 5.

Village Voice, January 18, 1983, p. 37.

Voice of Youth Advocates, April, 1993, Jim Morgan, review of *This Same Sky,* p. 59; August, 1996, Anthony Manna, review of *I Feel a Little Jumpy around You,* p. 178; February, 1999, review of *The Space between Our Footsteps,* p. 413; August, 2001, review of *Salting the Ocean,* p. 171.

Washington Post Book World, May 13, 2001, review of *What Have You Lost?,* p. 5.

ONLINE

Academy of American Poets Web site, http://www.poets.org/ (August 28, 2002), "Naomi Shihab Nye."

Anhinga Press Web site, http://www.anhinga.org/ (February 11, 2003).

Harper/Collins Children's Books, http://www.harperchildrens.com/ (February 11, 2003).

NewPages, http://www.newpages.com/ (February 11, 2003), Denise Bazzett, review of *Mint Snowball.*

Voices from the Gaps Web site, http://voices.cla.umn.edu/ (April 9, 1999), Mindy S. Howie, "Naomi Shihab Nye."

O

O'BRIAN, Patrick 1914-2000

PERSONAL: Born Richard Patrick Russ, December 12, 1914, in Buckinghamshire, England; died January 2, 2000, in Dublin, Ireland; son of Charles (a physician) Russ; married c. 1930s (abandoned marriage); married Mary Wicksteed; children: (first marriage) two.

CAREER: Writer and translator.

WRITINGS:

FICTION

The Last Pool and Other Stories, Secker and Warburg (London, England), 1950.

Testimonies, Harcourt (New York, NY), 1952, reprinted, Norton (New York, NY), 1993, published as *Three Bear Witness,* Secker and Warburg (London, England), 1952.

The Catalans, Harcourt (New York, NY), 1953, published as *The Frozen Flame,* Hart-Davis (London, England), 1953.

The Road to Samarcand, Hart-Davis (London, England), 1954.

The Walker and Other Stories, Harcourt (New York, NY), 1955, published as *Lying in the Sun and Other Stories,* Hart-Davis (London, England), 1956.

The Golden Ocean, Hart-Davis (London, England), 1956, Stein and Day (New York, NY), 1957, revised edition, Macmillan (New York, NY), 1970.

The Unknown Shore, Hart-Davis (London, England), 1959, Norton (New York, NY), 1995.

Richard Temple, Macmillan (New York, NY), 1962.

The Chian Wine and Other Stories, Collins (London, England), 1974.

Collected Short Stories, HarperCollins (London, England), 1994.

The Rendezvous and Other Stories, Norton (New York, NY), 1994.

The Hundred Days, Norton (New York, NY), 1998.

Blue at the Mizzen, Norton (New York, NY), 1999.

Caesar: The Life Story of a Panda Leopard, Norton (New York, NY), 1999.

"AUBREY-MATURIN" SERIES; HISTORICAL FICTION

Master and Commander, Lippincott (Philadelphia, PA), 1969, reprinted, Norton (New York, NY), 1994.

Post Captain, Lippincott (Philadelphia, PA), 1972.

H.M.S. Surprise, Lippincott (Philadelphia, PA), 1973.

The Mauritius Command, Collins (London, England), 1977, Stein and Day (New York, NY), 1978.

Desolation Island, Collins (London, England), 1978, Stein and Day (New York, NY), 1979.

The Fortune of War, Collins (London, England), 1979, Norton (New York, NY), 1991.

The Surgeon's Mate, Collins (London, England), 1980, Norton (New York, NY), 1991.

The Ionian Mission, Collins (London, England), 1981, Norton (New York, NY), 1991.

Treason's Harbour, Collins (London, England), 1983, Norton (New York, NY), 1992.

The Far Side of the World, Collins (London, England), 1984, Norton (New York, NY), 1992.

The Reverse of the Medal, Collins (London, England), 1986, Norton (New York, NY), 1992.

The Letter of Marque, Collins (London, England), 1988, Norton (New York, NY), 1990.

The Thirteen-Gun Salute, Collins (London, England), 1989, Norton (New York, NY), 1991.

The Nutmeg of Consolation, Norton (New York, NY), 1991.

The Truelove, Norton (New York, NY), 1992, published as *Clarissa Oakes,* HarperCollins (London, England), 1992.

The Wine-Dark Sea, Norton (New York, NY), 1993.

The Commodore, Norton (New York, NY), 1995.

The Yellow Admiral, Norton (New York, NY), 1996.

21: The Final Unfinished Voyage of Jack Aubrey: Including Facsimile of the Manuscript, afterword by Richard Snow, Norton (New York, NY), 2004.

The Complete Aubrey/Maturin Novels, Norton (New York, NY), 2004.

TRANSLATOR

Jacques Soustelle, *The Daily Life of the Aztecs on the Eve of the Spanish Conquest,* Weidenfeld and Nicolson (London, England), 1961.

Philippe Erlanger, *St. Bartholemew's Night: The Massacre of Saint Bartholemew,* Pantheon, 1962.

Christine de Rivoyre, *The Wreathed Head,* Hart-Davis (London, England), 1962.

Andre Maurois, *A History of the U.S.A.: From Wilson to Kennedy,* Weidenfeld and Nicolson (London, England), 1964, also published as *From the New Freedom to the New Frontier: A History of the United States from 1912 to the Present,* McKay, 1964.

Louis Aragon, *A History of the USSR: From Lenin to Kruschchev,* McKay, 1964.

Françoise Mallet-Joris, *A Letter to Myself,* Farrar, Straus (New York, NY), 1964.

Haroun Tazieff, *When the Earth Trembles,* Harcourt (New York, NY), 1964.

Henri Nogueres, *Munich: Peace in Our Time,* McGraw-Hill (New York, NY), 1965, published as *Munich: or, The Phoney Peace,* Weidenfeld and Nicolson (London, England), 1965.

Mallet-Jorris, *The Uncompromising Heart: A Life of Marie Mancini, Louis XIV's First Love,* Farrar, Straus (New York, NY), 1966.

Simone de Beauvoir, *A Very Easy Death,* Putnam (New York, NY), 1966.

Maurice Goudeket, *The Delights of Growing Old,* Farrar, Straus (New York, NY), 1966.

Michel Mohrt, *The Italian Campaign,* Viking (New York, NY), 1967.

Clara Malraux, *Memoirs,* Farrar, Straus (New York, NY), 1967.

Lucien Bodard, *The Quicksand War: Prelude to Vietnam,* Little, Brown (Boston, MA), 1967.

Joseph Kessel, *The Horsemen,* Farrar, Straus (New York, NY), 1968.

Simone de Beauvoir, *Les Belles Images,* Putnam (New York, NY), 1968.

Bernard Faae, *Louis XVI; or, The End of a World,* Regnery (Washington, DC), 1968.

Simone de Beauvoir, *The Woman Destroyed,* Putnam (New York, NY), 1969.

Robert Guillian, *The Japanese Challenge,* Lippincott (Philadelphia, PA), 1970.

Andre Martinerie, *A Life's Full Summer,* Harcourt (New York, NY), 1970.

Henri Charriere, *Papillon,* Hart-Davis (London, England), 1970.

Simone de Beauvoir, *The Coming of Age,* Putnam (New York, NY), 1972, published as *Old Age,* Weidenfeld and Nicolson (London, England), 1972.

Miroslav Ivanov, *The Assassination of Heydrich: 27 May 1942,* Hart-Davis (London, England), 1973.

Henri Charriere, *Further Adventures of Papillon,* Morrow (New York, NY), 1973.

Simone de Beauvoir, *All Said and Done,* Putnam (New York, NY), 1974.

Pierre Schoendoerffer, *The Paths of the Sea,* Collins (London, England), 1977.

Yves Berger, *Obsession: An American Love Story,* Putnam (New York, NY), 1978.

Simone de Beauvoir, *When Things of the Spirit Come First: Five Early Tales,* Pantheon (New York, NY), 1982.

Simone de Beauvoir, *Adieux: A Farewell to Sartre,* Pantheon (New York, NY), 1984.

Jean Lacouture, *De Gaulle,* Norton (New York, NY), 1990, published as *De Gaulle: The Rebel, 1890-1944,* Collins (London, England), 1990.

Also translated *Daily Life in the Time of Jesus,* Hawthorn, 1962, published as *Daily Life in Palestine at the Time of Christ,* Weidenfeld and Nicolson (London, England), 1962.

OTHER

(Editor) *A Book of Voyages,* Home and Van Thal, 1947.

Men-of-War, Collins (London, England), 1974, Norton (New York, NY), 1995.

Picasso: A Biography, Putnam (New York, NY), 1976, published as *Pablo Ruiz Picasso: A Biography,* Collins (London, England), 1976.

Joseph Banks: A Life, Harvill (London, England), 1987, D. Godine (Boston, MA), 1993.

ADAPTATIONS: O'Brian's "Aubrey-Maturin" novels were adapted for film as *Master and Commander,* written and directed by Peter Weir, starring Russell Crowe, and released by Twentieth Century-Fox, 2003.

SIDELIGHTS: Although Patrick O'Brian wrote and translated books for more than forty years, it was only in the years shortly before his death in 2000 that the bulk of his fiction became readily available to readers in the United States. O'Brian's work has been favorably reviewed by many American critics, especially his "Aubrey-Maturin" historical fiction series set during the time of the Napoleonic Wars between England and France. Mark Horowitz declared in the *Los Angeles Times Book Review* that "O'Brian is a novelist, pure and simple, one of the best we have." Other professed admirers of O'Brian's work have include writers Eudora Welty, Robertson Davies, and Iris Murdoch. The author's talents, however, extend beyond writing historical thrillers. Besides fiction, he translated the work of several French-language writers, among them Simone de Beauvoir and Henri Lapierre. An accomplished biographer, O'Brian also profiled the lives of painter Pablo Picasso and explorer and naturalist Joseph Banks.

O'Brian's popular historical adventure series, encompassing almost twenty books, follows the exploits of two friends, Jack Aubrey and Stephen Maturin. The protagonists are introduced to the reader, and each other, in 1969's *Master and Commander,* the first book of the series. The two men meet by chance at a musical performance in Spain where Maturin riles Aubrey with a remark about the latter's lack of musical timing. Although this first encounter does not end well, the two encounter one another again the next day, and Aubrey, who has just been offered command of a ship in the British navy, recruits Maturin as the vessel's surgeon. This is the beginning of both the friendship between the men as well as the series of adventures set mainly during the Napoleonic Wars in the early 1800s.

The characters are very different from each other, except for their common interest in music. Aubrey, a robust and cheerful man, is perfectly at home on his ship, which he commands powerfully and fearlessly. In 1989's *The Thirteen-Gun Salute,* O'Brian wrote of Aubrey: "Ordinarily he was not at all aggressive—a cheerful, sanguine, friendly, good-natured creature, severe only in the event of bad seamanship—but when he was on a Frenchman's deck, sword in hand, he felt a wild and savage joy, a fulness of being, like no other; and he remembered every detail of blows given or received . . . with the most vivid clarity." He is, however, unsure of himself and out of his element on land. Maturin is a doctor by profession and is the more serious of the two. Highly prone to skepticism, he is a philosopher and naturalist who collects specimens through the duo's travels. In the same book, O'Brian said that unlike Aubrey, Maturin "disliked violence and . . . took no pleasure in any battle whatsoever." Despite vastly different dispositions and a lack of common interests, the men develop an enduring friendship that lasts through the series.

O'Brian received critical praise for his portrayal of this relationship. However, although the friendship is central to the books, the series is more than an account of the camaraderie between the protagonists. Rather, O'Brian used this liaison as a framework within which he introduced his readers to the world and time these characters inhabit. Richard Snow commented in the *New York Times Book Review* that "on the foundations of this friendship, Mr. O'Brian reconstructs a civilization." Snow, who titled his review of O'Brian's work in the *New York Times Book Review* "An Author I'd Walk the Plank For," called O'Brian's books "the best historical novels ever written." Snow reported similar praise of O'Brian by British critic Peter Wishart, who has claimed that "the relative neglect of Patrick O'Brian by both critics and the book-buying public is one of the literary wonders of the age. It is as baffling as the Inca inability to invent the wheel; or conversely, it is as baffling as the Inca ability to possess an ordered, sophisticated society without the wheel."

Thomas Flanagan asserted in the *New York Times Book Review* that in O'Brian's "strange, agreeable world . . . the central themes are friendship and music, poetry, food, scholarship, astronomy, scientific curiosity and the delights of the natural world." He also expressed appreciation for the realism of O'Brian's imaginary world, the authentic speech of its characters, and the unique turns the novels' action take. In particular, Flanagan referred to O'Brian's treatment of the plot in *Thirteen-Gun Salute.* In this book, Aubrey and Maturin set sail toward the South China Seas to foil a French plot. The reviewer related, however, that the implied urgency of the mission does not detract from O'Brian's detailed narrative. Flanagan illustrated the distinctiveness of O'Brian's writing style by referring to a description of the sunrise observed by Maturin while standing on the deck of his ship: "First there was the sky, high, pure and of a darker blue than he had ever seen. And then there was the sea, a lighter, immensely luminous blue that reflected blue into the air, the shadows and the sails. . . . To these there was added the sun, unseen for so long and unseen even now, since the topsail hid it, but filling the world with an almost tangible light. It flashed on the wings of an albatross that came gliding into the wind so close to the quarterdeck rail that it could very nearly be touched."

John Bayley, writing in the *New York Review of Books,* also commended O'Brian's detailed narratives, citing a chapter from *The Mauritius Command.* In this section of the book, Aubrey's ship is being chased through icebergs and giant waves by a larger vessel. Bayley felt that this episode is akin to Herman Melville's style in the nineteenth-century seafaring novel *Moby Dick,* but he added that "no other writer, not even Melville, has described the whale or the wandering albatross with O'Brian's studious and yet lyrical accuracy."

Nutmeg of Consolation follows the story of Aubrey and Maturin, picking up where the shipwreck of the *Surprise of the South China Sea* at the end of *The Thirteen-Gun Salute* left off. They encounter more adventures on the high seas aboard their new boat, a small Dutch ship named the *Nutmeg.* Aubrey captures an enemy ship then flies off to the Solomon Islands to rescue children from a small-pox-ridden island. Eventually, their wanderings take Aubrey and Maturin to Sydney, Australia, where they find more trouble still. *New York Observer* critic John Gregory Dunne praised O'Brian's language as "elegant, erudite, and dense," while a *Kirkus Reviews* writer found Maturin the most interesting character and assessed the novel as "witty, literate and engaging."

O'Brian's popularity continued to grow, culminating with *The Commodore,* which, as a best-seller, brought its author even greater popular and critical attention. In the 1995 novel, after their ill-fated journey to Peru, Aubrey and Maturin return home to deal with marital problems, then set out again on behalf of the English government to intercept illegal slave-traders off the coast of West Africa and intervene in a French attempt to support anti-British insurgency in Ireland. A *Publishers Weekly* critic commented that "O'Brian writes with clipped efficiency and relies heavily on the arcane and specialized naval and military lexicons." With this novel, several critics theorized about the secret of O'Brian's success. Katherine A. Powers, writing for the *Atlantic Monthly,* made this observation: "The best historical novelists have bridged the gap of time and made a by-gone reality accessible by bringing, without anachronism, the insights of the present to bear upon the past. Patrick O'Brian is *sui generis.* Unlike any other writer of historical novels, he truly belongs to the era in which the majority of his works are set."

The Yellow Admiral was described by several critics as a return to the style of earlier novels in the series. Here Aubrey is a member of Parliament and is embroiled in politics. In contrast to previous novels, O'Brian plots much of the action on dry land. The plot concerns the Aubrey estate and the Aubrey marriage, as naval politics and peacetime threaten to make the captain a "yellowed" admiral—that is, a ranking admiral who is not in command of a ship. However, Maturin ultimately returns from his work with the Chilean independence movement, and Aubrey is finally called to action with the rise of the Napoleonic Wars. A critic for *Publishers Weekly* noted that in *The Yellow Admiral* "O'Brian is at the top of his elegant form." A reviewer for the *Economist* categorized the book as a "thinking man's infonovel," assessing it as "authentic, intelligent, humane, and written wittily and well."

Besides fiction, O'Brian authored biographies of Pablo Picasso and Joseph Banks. James R. Mellow, reviewing *Picasso: A Biography* for the *New York Times Book Review,* called O'Brian's portrayal of the artist "sharply etched." Mellow felt that O'Brian maintains equilibrium between the events in the Spanish painter's life, his art, and social surroundings. The critic also praised the author's research of the history of Spain, noting that it gives the book added authority. O'Brian's volume about Joseph Banks, who traveled with James Cook on an expedition to Tahiti, was lauded by *New York Times Book Review* critic Linda Colley for its "brilliant" descriptions of the voyage. Colley surmised that O'Brian's familiarity with ships and sea journeys due to his historical research for the "Aubrey-Maturin" books contributed to his authoritative work about Banks's travels.

Much to the frustration of his many fans, O'Brian passed away in 2000, having reached eighty-five years of age. According to Dean King in his book *Patrick O'Brian: A Life Revealed,* the novelist actually had a secret past. At age twenty-five O'Brian abandoned his wife and their two children, the younger then dying of spina bifida. At age thirty, he changed his name from Russ to O'Brian, adopting an Anglo-Irish heritage and marrying Mary Wicksteed, an English woman divorced from English barrister Count Dmitri Tolstoy. According to Anthony Day in *Smithsonian,* "When the news broke, Fleet Street turned on [O'Brian]—the Sunday *Times* of London called him a monster, a coward, a hypocrite. But the prevailing sentiment is more likely that of the *Economist* in its fond obituary, which suggested O'Brian's literary persona was a deception 'of the most innocent kind.'" Richard Lacayo noted of the novelist in *Time:* "O'Brian was fascinated with feints and deceptions, with warships that disguise themselves or fly false colors. Was that because he flew false colors himself? . . . What we know for sure is that he was a minor master of 20th century literature. His books will sail on."

BIOGRAPHICAL AND CRITICAL SOURCES:

BOOKS

Cunningham, A.E., *Patrick O'Brian: A Bibliography of First Printings and First British Printings,* Thrommett, 1986.

King, Dean, with John B. Hattendorf, *Harbors and High Seas: An Atlas and Geographical Guide to the Aubrey-Maturin Novels of Patrick O'Brian,* Henry Holt (New York, NY), 1996.

King, Dean, with John B. Hattendorf and J. Worth Estes, *A Sea of Words: A Lexicon and Companion for Patrick O'Brian's Seafaring Tales,* Henry Holt (New York, NY), 1997.

King, Dean, *Patrick O'Brian: A Life Revealed,* Henry Holt (New York, NY), 2000.

PERIODICALS

Atlantic Monthly, July, 1995, p. 92.
Booklist, October 1, 1993; April 1, 2004, p. 1391.
Commentary, January, 2004, p. 47.
Daily Variety, November 5, 2003, p. 2.
Economist, July 19, 1997, p. S16.
Entertainment Weekly, November 21, 2003, p. 89; February 6, 2004, p. 102.
Globe & Mail (Toronto, Ontario, Canada), March 23, 1991, p. C8.
Kirkus Reviews, July 1, 1991; September 1, 1993.
Library Journal, April 15, 2000, p. 140; June 1, 2004, p, 102.
Los Angeles Times Book Review, September 8, 1991, p. 4.
M2 Best Books, December 16, 2003; May 20, 2004.
National Review, January 24, 1994, p. 65.
New Republic, December 15, 2003, p. 26.
New Yorker, November 17, 2003, p. 172.
New York Review of Books, November 7, 1991, pp. 7-8.
New York Times, November 7, 1990.
New York Times Book Review, July 4, 1976, p. 4; January 6, 1991, pp. 1, 37-38; August 4, 1991, p. 9; March 28, 1993, p. 8.
Publishers Weekly, June 5, 1995, p. 34; September 16, 1996, p. 70; November 24, 2003, p. 15.
Rolling Stone, May 14, 1992, p. 83.
Saturday Review, January 23, 1971, pp. 64-66.
Smithsonian, December, 2003, p. 77.
Time, November 10, 2003, p. 84.
Times (London, England), March 28, 1991, p. 20.
Washington Post, August 2, 1992, pp. F1, F4.

OBITUARIES:

PERIODICALS

Los Angeles Times, January 8, 2000, p. A16.
New York Times, January 7, 2000, p. A20.
Times (London, England), January 8, 2000.
Washington Post, January 8, 2000, p. B5.

ONLINE

CNN.com, http://www.cnn.com/ (January 7, 2000).

* * *

O'BRIEN, Edna 1932-

PERSONAL: Born December 15, 1932, in Tuamgraney, County Clare, Ireland; daughter of Michael and Lena (maiden name, Cleary) O'Brien; married Ernest Gébler (an author), 1952 (divorced, 1964); children: Sasha, Carlos (sons). *Education:* Attended Pharmaceutical College of Ireland. *Hobbies and other interests:* Reading, remembering.

ADDRESSES: *Office*—Fraser & Dunlop Scripts Ltd., 91 Regent St., London W1, England. *Agent*—c/o Curtis Brown Group Ltd., Haymarket House, 28-29 Haymarket, London SW1Y 4SP, England.

CAREER: Novelist, short story writer, playwright, and screenwriter. City College, New York, NY, creative writing instructor.

MEMBER: American Academy of Arts and Letters (honorary).

AWARDS, HONORS: Kingsley Amis Award, 1962; *Yorkshire Post* Book of the Year Award, 1970, for *A Pagan Place; Los Angeles Times* Book Award, 1990, for *Lantern Slides,* and 1992, for *Time and Tide.*

WRITINGS:

NOVELS

The Country Girls (also see below), Knopf (New York, NY), 1960.

The Lonely Girl (also see below), Random House (New York, NY), 1962, published as *The Girl with Green Eyes,* Penguin (London, England), 1964.

Girls in Their Married Bliss (also see below), J. Cape (London, England), 1964, reprinted, Plume (New York, NY), 2003.

August Is a Wicked Month (also see below), Simon & Schuster (New York, NY), 1965.

Casualties of Peace (also see below), J. Cape (London, England), 1966.

A Pagan Place, (also see below), Weidenfeld & Nicolson (London, England), 1970, Houghton Mifflin (Boston, MA), 2001.

Zee and Company, (also see below), Weidenfeld & Nicolson (London, England), 1971.

Night: A Novel, Knopf (New York, NY), 1972, reprinted, Houghton Mifflin (Boston, MA), 2001.

Johnny I Hardly Knew You (also see below), Weidenfeld & Nicolson (London, England), 1977, published as *I Hardly Knew You,* Doubleday (New York, NY), 1978.

Seven Novels and Other Short Stories, Collins (London, England), 1978.

The Country Girls Trilogy and Epilogue (contains *The Country Girls, The Lonely Girl,* and *Girls in Their Married Bliss*), Farrar, Straus (New York, NY), 1986, published as *The Country Girls Trilogy: Second Epilogue,* Dutton (New York, NY), 1989.

The High Road (novel), Farrar, Straus (New York, NY), 1988.

Time and Tide, Farrar, Straus (New York, NY), 1992.

House of Splendid Isolation, Farrar, Straus (New York, NY), 1994.

An Edna O'Brien Reader (contains *August Is a Wicked Month, Casualties of Peace,* and *Johnny I Hardly Knew You*), Warner Books (New York, NY), 1994.

Down by the River, Weidenfeld & Nicolson (London, England), 1996.

Wild Decembers, [London, England], 1999, Houghton Mifflin (Boston, MA), 2000.

In the Forest, Houghton Mifflin (Boston, MA), 2002.

SHORT STORIES

The Love Object, J. Cape (London, England), 1968.

A Scandalous Woman, and Other Stories, Harcourt (New York, NY), 1974.

Mrs. Reinhardt, and Other Stories, Weidenfeld & Nicolson (London, England), 1978, published as *A Rose in the Heart,* Doubleday (New York, NY), 1979.

Returning, Weidenfeld & Nicolson (London, England), 1982.

A Fanatic Heart: Selected Stories of Edna O'Brien, foreword by Philip Roth, Farrar, Straus (New York, NY), 1984.

Lantern Slides: Stories, Farrar, Straus (New York, NY), 1990.

Also author of *Stories of Joan of Arc,* 1984.

JUVENILE

The Dazzle, illustrated by Peter Stevenson, Hodder & Stoughton (London, England), 1981.

A Christmas Treat (sequel to *The Dazzle*), illustrated by Stevenson, Hodder & Stoughton (London, England), 1982.

The Expedition, Hodder & Stoughton (London, England), 1982.

The Rescue, illustrated by Stevenson, Hodder & Stoughton (London, England), 1983.

Tales for the Telling: Irish Folk and Fairy Stories, illustrated by Michael Foreman, Atheneum (New York, NY), 1986.

PLAYS

A Cheap Bunch of Nice Flowers (produced in London, England, 1962), Ungar (New York, NY), 1963.

(With others) *Oh! Calcutta!,* produced in New York, 1969), Grove (New York, NY), 1969.

A Pagan Place (produced in the West End, 1972), Knopf (New York, NY), 1970.

The Ladies, produced in London, England, 1975.

The Gathering, produced in Dublin, Ireland, 1974, produced in New York at Manhattan Theatre Club, 1977.

Virginia (produced in Stratford, Ontario, Canada, 1980, produced in London, England, and New York, 1985), Harcourt (New York, NY), 1981, revised edition, 1985.

Flesh and Blood, produced in Bath, England, 1985, produced in New York, 1986.

Madame Bovary (based on the novel by Gustave Flaubert), produced at the Palace, Watford, England, 1987.

Our Father, produced in London, England, 1999.

SCREENPLAYS

The Girl with Green Eyes (based on O'Brien's novel *The Lonely Girl*), Lopert, 1964.
Three into Two Won't Go, Universal, 1969.
X Y and Zee (based on O'Brien's novel *Zee and Company*), Columbia, 1972.

Also author of (with Desmond Davis) *I Was Happy Here,* 1965, revised, 1979; (with others) *The Tempter,* 1975; *A Woman at the Seaside,* 1979; *The Wicked Lady,* 1979; and *The Country Girls,* 1984.

OTHER

Mother Ireland, photographs by Fergus Bourke, Harcourt (New York, NY), 1976.
Arabian Days, photographs by Gerard Klijn, Horizon Press (New York, NY), 1977.
The Collected Edna O'Brien (miscellany), Collins (London, England), 1978.
(Editor) *Some Irish Loving: A Selection,* Harper (New York, NY), 1979.
James and Nora: A Portrait of Joyce's Marriage, Lord John Press (Northridge, CA), 1981.
Vanishing Ireland, photographs by Richard Fitzgerald, J. Cape (London, England), 1986, Potter (New York, NY), 1987.
On the Bone (poetry), Greville Press, 1989.
James Joyce (biography; "Penguin Lives" series), Viking (New York, NY), 1999.

Also contributor to magazines, including *New Yorker, Ladies' Home Journal,* and *Cosmopolitan,* and to various English journals.

Author of television plays, including *The Wedding Dress,* 1963; *The Keys to the Café,* 1965; *Give My Love to the Pilchards,* 1965; *Which of These Two Ladies Is He Married To?,* 1967; *Nothing's Ever Over,* 1968; *Then and Now,* 1973; and *Mrs. Reinhardt, from Her Own Story,* 1981.

ADAPTATIONS: Works adapted for audio include *Wild Decembers* (four cassettes), read by Suzanne Bertish, Houghton Mifflin.

SIDELIGHTS: Irish author Edna O'Brien is "renowned for her anguished female characters, lonely Catholic girls in search of adventure, or single, older women in wretched affairs with married men," wrote Richard B. Woodward in *New York Times Magazine.* "A poet of heartbreak, she writes most tellingly about the hopeless, angry passion that courts self-ruin." Her women are loving, but frustrated, betrayed, lonely, and struggling to escape the role society has assigned them, while her male characters are cruel, cold, drunken, and irresponsible. The divorced mother of two, O'Brien knows about struggle, heartbreak, and pain firsthand. She has used her personal experiences, especially her childhood in Ireland, as sources for many of her works, drawing on her memories to evoke the emotions of her readers. An author of novels, short stories, plays, biographies, and children's books, she is a prolific writer, often considered controversial, who appeals to many types of audiences.

O'Brien was born in Tuamgraney, County Clare, a small, rural, devoutly Catholic village of about 200 people in the west of Ireland. Raised on a farm, she grew up in an area where everyone knew everyone else's secrets, business, and problems. She claims this has helped her in her writing, telling Amanda Smith in *Publishers Weekly,* "I had sort of a limitless access to everyone's life story. For a writer, it's a marvelous chance." Educated first at the local national school and then in a convent, she escaped rural life by attending Pharmaceutical College in Dublin. In 1952, she eloped with Czech-Irish author Ernest Gébler. They moved first to County Wicklow and then to London where O'Brien has remained. They divorced after twelve years, and she raised their two sons alone.

Books were scarce in O'Brien's childhood, and it was not until she was in Dublin that she began to take an interest in them. *Introducing James Joyce* by T.S. Eliot was among her first purchases, and she recalled in *Lear's* that "reading it was the most astonishing literary experience of my life. . . . What I learned from that brief extract from *A Portrait of the Artist as a Young Man* was that as a writer one must take one's material from life, from the simple, indisputable, and often painful world about one, and give it somehow its transfiguration, but at the same time shave all excess and untruth from it, like peeling a willow. What I did not know, although I must have sensed it, was that this would bring me into conflict with parents, friends, and indeed the Irish establishment."

Conflict and writing seemed to go hand in hand for O'Brien throughout her career. The birth of her first published novel, *The Country Girls,* heralded the death of her marriage. Written at the age of twenty-six and published in 1960, *The Country Girls* broke new ground in Irish literature giving a frank speaking voice to women characters. The subject matter and especially the daringly graphic sexual scenes caused this book, and the six that followed, to be banned in Ireland. It was the first novel in what became a trilogy; *The Lonely Girl* and *Girls in Their Married Bliss* completed the set. The three novels were collected in *The Country Girls Trilogy and Epilogue,* published in 1986.

"It's a difficult trip, this coming of age," wrote Mary Rourke in the *Los Angeles Times Book Review* of *The Country Girls Trilogy and Epilogue.* "Two girls set adrift, misdirected, lost at sea. O'Brien tells it with love and outrage, compassion and contempt." The stories revolve around two young women, the "country girls" Kate and Baba, who search for love and sex in a series of tragicomic adventures after being expelled from their convent school. "Miss O'Brien's outlook is intemperate, like Irish weather. She's fond of blarney, but a bleak, literary kind, more in the mood of the later Yeats than of Celtic charm," commented Anatole Broyard, writing in the *New York Times Book Review.* "She has no patience with the ordinary, the soothing monotony of innocent small events." Feelings of loss, conflict, and disappointment in love pervade each novel of the trilogy as the girls try to attain their dreams. *Village Voice* contributor Terrence Rafferty observed that "the psychological insights are sharp, the descriptions graceful and resonant."

O'Brien added the epilogue to the trilogy when the stories were released in one volume. Rafferty explained that it "brings the story full circle, back to earth, in a tragedy that would be unbearable were it not for the exuberance of the writing, the hope engendered by language that goes on and on." The epilogue is presented as Baba's soliloquy, a retrospective view of both women's lives. Broyard, commenting on the entire collection, noted that "everyday scenes . . . are the truest and best parts of Miss O'Brien's work. Reading them, we wonder whether love and sex, for which she has become an ambivalent apologist, are her natural subject after all—or just a burlesque to keep the genuine terrors at bay."

Many of O'Brien's short stories have also been assembled and published as collections, including *A Fanatic Heart: Selected Stories of Edna O'Brien.* Covering two decades of her career, the twenty-nine stories in this collection explore the themes of childhood, love, and loss, all from a woman's perspective. "Most of the stories in *A Fanatic Heart* are set down in languorous, elegiac prose," commented Michiko Kakutani in the *New York Times,* adding that "they're enlivened by Miss O'Brien's earthy humor and her sense of place." She writes of relationships, exile, and betrayal, drawing the reader in by seeming to reveal herself. Tales such as "My Mother's Mother," describing the "ghastly" death of her grandfather one night while saying the Rosary, evoke O'Brien's native Ireland. Others explore the temptations of the flesh in strictly-reared young women, as in "The Connor Girls," or contrast girls with carousing drunks, as in "Irish Revel." Still others concern affairs, mental breakdown, and entrapment in bad marriages. In the *Los Angeles Times Book Review,* Charles Champlin commented, "She writes with a graceful, poetical simplicity, a soft and mesmerizing brogue audible in every cadence." *Washington Post Book World* contributor Jonathan Yardley concluded by saying, "It's all there: the violence, the superstition, the craziness, the drink, the brooding religion, the terrorized women. O'Brien's Ireland is as hard and unremitting a place as O'Connor's South. Yet longings her women feel for love and peace, for a kind connection with another human being, give these stories a tenderness that is both surprising and enriching."

O'Brien presents another side of Ireland in *Tales for the Telling: Irish Folk and Fairy Stories,* a book for children published in 1986. Twelve stories reveal a land of fairy folk, giants, castles, princes and princesses, magic, and heroes. A fierce wolf and a young boy dance to the magic tune of fife music in one tale, and another tells of a giant who betters an opponent with help from his cunning wife. O'Brien writes her stories in standard English, using the characters' conversations to express their Irish descent. "In the dialogue she revels in the glories of local dialect," wrote Elizabeth MacCallum in the Toronto *Globe and Mail,* "and in her descriptive passages she evokes wondrous visions." Another critic, *Times Literary Supplement* contributor Patricia Craig, remarked that O'Brien's stories correspond rather closely to those published in *Donegal Fairy Stories* written by Seumas MacManus, but commented that O'Brien's tales "are notable for their decorativeness and sturdy vocabulary." Diane Roback wrote in *Publishers Weekly* that the "color-rich, vigorous paintings" by Michael Foreman complement "a collection for the entire family [that] fires the imagination."

O'Brien examines more than Ireland in her various writings. In two stage plays, she focuses on Virginia Woolf, and Gustave Flaubert's *Madame Bovary.* "O'Brien . . . knows how to create climax, epiphany and incandescence by compression," observed Jack Kroll in *Newsweek,* discussing the play *Virginia.* In the play, the story of Woolf, one of the Bloomsbury group and a prominent literary figure, encompasses her life from her birth in 1882 to her suicide in 1942. Woolf's "intense subjective style" is echoed throughout the piece, often transcending "chronological narrative," wrote Lawrence Christon in the *Los Angeles Times.* "*Virginia* is virtually a monologue," Christon continued, noting that the play "is top-heavy with talk."

Madame Bovary is similar to *Virginia,* particularly in its use of time and narration. O'Brien claims the title character as her own creation rather than an adaptation of Flaubert's novel. This is a story of love, marriage, boredom, adultery, and death by suicide, and O'Brien's work closely follows Flaubert's piece. The drama takes place in Emma Bovary's mind, even juggling the events as if they were really memories happening in her head, giving the audience clear access to her thoughts and emotions. *Observer* contributor Michael Ratcliffe remarked, "Edna O'Brien has turned Flaubert's novel into a tasteful melodrama whose tragic ironies shine sharp and bright." But, Ratcliffe noted, the "dramatic narrative unfolds in a series of sketches and jerks. . . . Time-leaps and chronology are not always clear." Irving Wardle, writing in the London *Times,* pointed out that "the action unrolls as if by flashes of lightning. . . . the effect is to present an ever-strengthening sequence of hopes and defeats in which grand emotions are brought tumbling down."

While continuing to publish books for children, short stories, and plays, O'Brien waited ten years after *Johnny I Hardly Knew You* before publishing another novel. The long-awaited volume, *The High Road,* concerns Anna, a middle-aged, successful Irish writer recovering from the breakup of an affair. She escapes to an unidentified Spanish island, hoping to take time to write in her diary and repair her broken heart. "This is a disorderly novel about the disorder of human needs and the grotesqueries of appetite, how unsuitable, how inappropriate our longings often are, how difficult it is to find even a moment of pure unspoiled happiness," said Carol Shields in the Toronto *Globe and Mail.* Many critics seemed to share this viewpoint, with *Publishers Weekly* contributor Sybil Steinberg calling *The High Road* "a disappointing narrative." "At its best O'Brien's prose is, as usual, eloquent and passionate, but it cannot disguise the fundamental confusion of this strange little book," wrote Yardley in the *Washington Post.* "There are enough bright moments in it to reward O'Brien's most devoted followers, but few other readers are likely to take any pleasure in trying to make connections between characters that O'Brien herself never makes."

"Raise a jar to Edna O'Brien herself, back among us from foreign parts . . . the black mood of *The High Road* all but dispelled," wrote Elaine Kendall in the *Los Angeles Times* in her discussion of *Lantern Slides: Stories.* "She is at her best again, telling of people and places close to her heart." With *Lantern Slides,* O'Brien returns to the short story. "Though she covers little new ground here, she also digs deeper into the old ground than ever before, unearthing a rich archeology," commented David Leavitt in the *New York Times Book Review.* The title story, "Lantern Slides," was highly praised by many critics, Leavitt labeling it the "collection's masterpiece." Regarding the entire collection, Victoria Glendinning wrote in the London *Times* that "this is good writing; and good thinking." *Times Literary Supplement* contributor Louise Doughty praised *Lantern Slides,* writing that "the same precision with which she portrays landscape is applied to human emotions; there isn't a single character in these stories who is unconvincing. O'Brien continues to display acute powers of observation in a prose that is always neat and often immaculate."

House of Splendid Isolation departed somewhat from the author's usual terrain. The story of an IRA terrorist who takes an elderly woman, Josie, hostage, the novel directly engages the contemporary political struggles in Northern Ireland. Writing in the *New York Times Book Review,* John L'Heureux maintained that the novel's two distinct components are not successfully fused. "Uncomfortable with her story of the terrorist and the lady, Ms. O'Brien seeks refuge in easy symbolism, and her art is swallowed up in rhetoric." Still, noted L'Heureux, O'Brien excels in portraying Josie's world: "The author is comfortable here. She understands the blindness and desperation of these characters and she gets inside them with devastating effects." Focusing on the author's achievement in telling the story of modern Ireland, Chicago *Tribune Books* reviewer Andy Solomon remarked, "Moving beyond her stunningly wrought landscapes of private heartbreak and haunted agony, in this novel O'Brien shows us the land that forged her vision."

O'Brien's confessional tone and use of the first person in many of her novels has led to speculation concerning the distance between her life and her fiction. In the *Dictionary of Literary Biography,* Patricia Boyle Haberstroh quoted an interview between Ludovic Kennedy and O'Brien in which the author said her life and her work are "quite close, but they're not as close as they seem. . . . I think writing, especially semi-autobiographical writing, is the life you might have liked to have had." In an interview with Woodward, O'Brien concluded: "All I know is that I want to write about something that has no fashion and that does not pander to any period or to a journalistic point of view. I want to write about something that would apply to any time because it's a state of the soul." O'Brien also discussed her writing in *Lear's,* noting that "the need to write becomes as intrinsic as the need to breathe. I believe that the hidden reason is to do with time and emotion and the retrieval of both. It is as if the life lived has not been lived until it is set down in this unconscious sequence of words."

O'Brien's novel *Down by the River* is based on the actual case of an Irish girl who became pregnant by a friend of her father, and the theme of the book is the abortion issue in Ireland. In the novel, however, the girl, Mary, becomes pregnant as a result of her father's sexual abuse. The story begins with the father assaulting her for the first time, an act he repeats with more frequency and violence after Mary's mother dies. After returning from London with a neighbor who helps her with the termination of her pregnancy, Mary and the friend are arrested. Her life is torn apart by politicians and anti-abortion advocates who do not know that Mary's father was responsible for the pregnancy. Jose Lanters wrote in *World Literature Today* that *Down by the River* makes the point "about the involvement of church and state in what are often very painful and tragic personal circumstances."

World of Hibernia contributor John McCourt wrote that in *James Joyce,* O'Brien "puts her critical heritage, her vast experience as a novelist and short-story writer, and her dazzling linguistic skills to excellent use in this biography, which will be remembered for its panache, verve, readability, and its humane understanding of Joyce and of the Irish world that formed him." *Booklist* reviewer Mary Carroll noted that O'Brien "also provides thoughtful appreciations of Joyce's major works." *Contemporary Review* contributor John McGurk said that O'Brien reveals "Joyce's love/hate relationship with Dublin and Ireland, with the 'Rock of Rome,' the English Crown, the legal profession: and between home and exile, then his other innermost conflicts between lust and love, order and chaos, family restrictions and the free-booting spirit at odds with the tenacity with which he pursued his life as a writer."

New York Times Book Review contributor Robert Sullivan called *James Joyce* "a hardheaded hagiography in which [O'Brien] spends a lot of time knocking Joyce around, especially the early Joyce, the Joyce who would run into you at the pub, go on about his imminent greatness, pity you, and then hit you up for a couple of quid on his way out. . . . After she's roughed Joyce up," wrote Sullivan, "she raises his hand in the air and proclaims him a genius. . . . Not since Anthony Burgess has anyone so gorgeously sung such praise for a man whose work, let's fact it, can seem incomprehensible to the noninfatuated." Sullivan concluded by saying that "O'Brien's triumph is that while celebrating Joyce and his ecstatic quest to lay image on counterimage . . . she has drawn the desperation and sadness of the man whose name means joy."

BIOGRAPHICAL AND CRITICAL SOURCES:

BOOKS

Concise Dictionary of British Literary Biography, Volume 8: *Contemporary Writers, 1960-Present,* Thomson Gale (Detroit, MI), 1992.

Contemporary Literary Criticism, Thomson Gale (Detroit, MI), Volume 3, 1975, Volume 5, 1976, Volume 8, 1978, Volume 13, 1980, Volume 36, 1986, Volume 65, 1991.

Contemporary Novelists, sixth edition, St. James Press (Detroit, MI), 1996.

Dictionary of Literary Biography, Volume 14: *British Novelists since 1960,* Thomson Gale (Detroit, MI), 1983.

Eckley, Grace, *Edna O'Brien,* Bucknell University Press (Lewisburg, PA), 1974.

Feminist Writers, St. James Press (Detroit, MI), 1996.

Staley, Thomas F., editor, *Twentieth-Century Women Novelists,* Barnes & Noble (Totowa, NJ), 1982.

PERIODICALS

America, April 15, 1995, p. 35.

Atlantic Monthly, July, 1965.

Belles Lettres, fall, 1992, p. 2.

Booklist, January 1, 1998, review of *Down by the River,* p. 731; October 1, 1999, Mary Carroll, review of *James Joyce,* p. 338; February 1, 2000, Grace Fill, review of *Wild Decembers,* p. 996.

Books, June, 1965.

Books and Bookmen, December, 1964.

Chicago Tribune Book World, December 9, 1984, p. 31.

Commonweal, May 5, 2000, Molly Winans, "A Dark Tale, Told in Singing Prose," p. 19.

Contemporary Review, July, 2000, John McGurk, "Edna O'Brien on James Joyce," p. 56.

Entertainment Weekly, April 14, 2000, "The Week," p. 68.

Globe and Mail (Toronto, Ontario, Canada), December 17, 1988; December 31, 1988.
Lear's, July, 1992, pp. 62-65.
Library Journal, October 1, 1999, Shelley Cox, review of *James Joyce,* p. 92.
Los Angeles Times, April 3, 1979; May 1, 1986; December 16, 1988; June 8, 1990.
Los Angeles Times Book Review, June 30, 1985, p. 1; January 19, 1986, p. 4; April 27, 1986, p. 4; September 2, 1990, p. 9; October 31, 1999, review of *James Joyce,* p. 10.
Ms., November, 1988, pp. 76, 78.
National Observer, June 21, 1965.
New Statesman & Society, April 15, 1994, p. 41.
Newsweek, March 18, 1985, p. 72.
New Yorker, June 27, 1994, p. 195.
New York Review of Books, June 3, 1965; August 24, 1967; January 31, 1985, p. 17; December 16, 1999, John Banville, "The Motherless Child," p. 48.
New York Times, November 12, 1984, Michiko Kakutani, review of *A Fanatic Heart: Selected Stories of Edna O'Brien;* March 1, 1985; May 30, 1990.
New York Times Book Review, March 26, 1967; February 9, 1969; September 22, 1974; June 27, 1978; February 11, 1979; November 18, 1984, pp. 1, 38; May 11, 1986, p. 12; March 1, 1987, p. 31; November 20, 1988, p. 11; June 25, 1990, p. 9; June 26, 1994, p. 7; March 22, 1998, review of *Down by the River,* p. 32; January 9, 2000, Robert Sullivan, "Oh Joist, Poor Joist," p. 6; April 9, 2000, Brooke Allen, "The Last of His Kind," p. 7.
New York Times Magazine, March 12, 1989, Richard B. Woodward.
Observer, February 8, 1987.
People Weekly, April 17, 1978; May 1, 2000, Jean Reynolds, review of *Wild Decembers,* p. 41.
Publishers Weekly, November 28, 1986, Diane Roback, review of *Tales for the Telling: Irish Folk and Fairy Stories,* p. 71; December 26, 1986, Amanda Smith, "Edna O'Brien's Magic," p. 30; September 9, 1988, Sybil Steinberg, review of *The High Road,* p. 122; April 25, 1994, review of *House of Splendid Isolation,* p. 56; January 31, 2000, review of *Wild Decembers,* p. 77; June 5, 2000, review of *Wild Decembers,* p. 61.
Saturday Review, June 5, 1965; March 25, 1967.
Spectator, October 9, 1999, review of *Wild Decembers,* p. 42.
Studies in Short Fiction, summer, 1993, Kiera O'Hara, "Love Objects: Love and Obsession in the Short Stories of Edna O'Brien," pp. 317-325; spring 1995, Jeanette Roberts Schumaker, "Sacrificial Women in Short Stories by Mary Lavin and Edna O'Brien," pp. 185-197.
Time, April 17, 2000, Paul Gray, "Perils of the Rustic Life: *Wild Decembers* Portrays a Simmering Irish Feud," p. 82.
Times (London, England), February 6, 1987; October 14, 1988; October 27, 1988; June 7, 1990.
Times Literary Supplement, April 23, 1982, p. 456; January 9, 1987, p. 46; October 28, 1988, p. 1212; June 8, 1990, p. 616; September 18, 1992, p. 23; April 22, 1994, p. 22.
Tribune Books (Chicago, IL), November 20, 1988, p. 6; May 27, 1990, p. 1; July 24, 1994, p. 1.
Variety, December 13, 1999, Matt Wolf, review of *Our Father,* p. 119.
Village Voice, July 1, 1985, Terrence Rafferty, review of *The Country Girls Trilogy and Epilogue,* p. 61.
Vogue, September 1, 1971.
Wall Street Journal, March 31, 2000, Kate Flatley, review of *Wild Decembers,* p. 10.
Washington Post, November 2, 1988.
Washington Post Book World, November 25, 1984, Jonathan Yardley, review of *A Fanatic Heart,* p. 3; August 21, 1994, p. 3.
World Literature Today, winter, 1998, Jose Lanters, review of *Down by the River,* p. 135.
World of Hibernia, fall, 1999, John McCourt, "Edna O'Brien: *James Joyce,*" p. 92.

ONLINE

Salon.com, http://www.salon.com/ (December 2, 1995), "Lit Chat."

* * *

O'BRIEN, Tim 1946-
(William Timothy O'Brien)

PERSONAL: Born October 1, 1946, in Austin, MN; son of William T. (an insurance salesman) and Ava E. (a teacher; maiden name, Schultz) O'Brien; married, 1973; wife's name Ann (a magazine production manager). *Education:* Macalester College, B.A. (summa cum laude), 1968; graduate study at Harvard University.

ADDRESSES: *Home*—Boxford, MA. *Agent*—Lynn Nesbit, International Creative Management, 40 West 57th St., New York, NY 10019.

CAREER: Novelist. *Washington Post,* Washington, DC, national affairs reporter, 1973-74; Breadloaf Writer's Conference, Ripton, VT, teacher. *Military service:* U.S. Army, 1968-70, served in Vietnam; became sergeant; received Purple Heart.

MEMBER: Phi Beta Kappa.

AWARDS, HONORS: O. Henry Memorial Awards, 1976 and 1978, for chapters of *Going after Cacciato;* National Book Award, 1979, for *Going after Cacciato;* Vietnam Veterans of America award, 1987; Heartland Prize, *Chicago Tribune,* 1990, for *The Things They Carried;* has also received awards from National Endowment for the Arts, Massachusetts Arts and Humanities Foundation, and Bread Loaf Writers' Conference; *New York Times Notable Book* designation, American Library Association Notable Book designation, and James Fenimore Cooper Prize for Historical Fiction, all 1995, all for *In the Lake of the Woods.*

WRITINGS:

If I Die in a Combat Zone, Box Me up and Ship Me Home (anecdotes), Delacorte (New York, NY), 1973.

Northern Lights (novel), Delacorte (New York, NY), 1975.

Going after Cacciato (novel), Delacorte (New York, NY), 1978.

The Nuclear Age, Press-22, 1981, Knopf (New York, NY), 1985.

The Things They Carried: A Work of Fiction, Houghton Mifflin (Boston, MA), 1990.

In the Lake of the Woods, Houghton Mifflin (Boston, MA), 1994.

Twinkle, Twinkle, Western Pub. Co. (Racine, WI), 1994.

Tomcat in Love, Broadway Books (New York, NY), 1998.

July, July, Houghton Mifflin (Boston, MA), 2002.

Contributor to magazines, including *Playboy, Esquire,* and *Redbook.*

ADAPTATIONS: July, July was adapted as an audiobook, Houghton Mifflin Audio, 2003.

SIDELIGHTS: Award-winning author Tim O'Brien is perhaps best known for his fictional, yet gripping, portrayals of the Vietnam conflict, especially of its people. Based on his own combat exposure, O'Brien delves into the American psyche and the human experience as he writes not only of what actually happened, but also the emotional and psychological impact of the war. In highly praised novels such as *The Things They Carried, Going after Cacciato,* and *In the Lake of the Woods,* he explores the war and its aftershocks from many vantage points, some intimate and some more distant. "But to label O'Brien a Vietnam author seems limiting, even simplistic," *Library Journal* contributor Mirela Roncevic maintained, "for his work has incessantly challenged his storytelling skills, demonstrating his ability to write both lucidly and succinctly while exploring the arcane relationship between fact and fiction, reality and imagination."

Drafted immediately following his graduation from Macalester College in 1968, O'Brien served two years with the U.S. infantry. In a *Publishers Weekly* interview with Michael Coffey, O'Brien explained his motivation in writing about the war as his need to write with "passion," and commented that to write "good" stories "requires a sense of passion, and my passion as a human being and as a writer intersect in Vietnam, not in the physical stuff but in the issues of Vietnam—of courage, rectitude, enlightenment, holiness, trying to do the right thing in the world."

"Writing fiction is a solitary endeavor," explained O'Brien in an essay quoted in the *Dictionary of Literary Biography Documentary Series.* He elaborated: "You shape your own universe. You practice all the time, then practice some more. You pay attention to craft. You aim for tension and suspense, a sense of drama, displaying in concrete terms the actions and reactions of human beings contesting problems of the heart. You try to make art. You strive for wholeness, seeking continuity and flow, each element performing both as cause and effect, always hoping to create, or to re-create, the great illusions of life."

"It's kind of a semantic game: lying versus truth-telling," described O'Brien, discussing his attitude towards writing in an interview with Ronald Baughman in *Dictionary of Literary Biography Documentary Series.* "But I think it's an important game that writers and readers and anyone interested in art in general should be fully aware of. One doesn't lie for the sake of lying; one does not invent merely for the sake of inventing. One does it for a particular purpose and that purpose always is to arrive at some kind of spiritual truth that one can't discover simply by recording the world-as-it-is. We're inventing and using imagination for sublime reasons—to get at the essence of things, not merely the surface."

O'Brien's first novel, *If I Die in a Combat Zone, Box Me up and Ship Me Home,* is an anecdotal account of an infantryman's year in Vietnam. A semi-fictionalized recounting of his own experiences, O'Brien's book tells the tale of a college educated young man who is drafted, trained for war, and shipped overseas to fight the Vietcong. He relates the story "with as much attention to his own feelings and states of mind as to the details of battle," declared a reviewer in *Times Literary Supplement.* An "interesting and highly readable book," remarked a critic in *New Republic.* Joseph McLellan, writing in *Washington Post Book World,* called *If I Die in a Combat Zone* "powerfully written," and *New York Times Book Review* contributor Annie Gottlieb ended her review with similar praise: "O'Brien writes—without either pomposity or embarrassment—with the care and eloquence of someone for whom communication is still a vital and serious possibility, not a narcissistic vestige. It is a beautiful, painful book, arousing pity and fear for the daily realities of modern disaster."

Northern Lights, O'Brien's next book, creates a progression in the Vietnam tale: the story of the Vietnam soldier coming home to his family. Harvey Perry is the "hero," the soldier who fought for his country, lost an eye in battle, and seems to be all that his father wanted. Paul Perry, on the other hand, is the stay-at-home brother, the "failure" of the family who is married and employed as a farm agent in the family's hometown of Sawmill Landing, Minnesota. *Northern Lights* is about the two brothers' relationship, and the changes that occur during a long and difficult cross-country ski trip. Paul emerges as the real hero after Harvey, upset over the abrupt end of a romance and physically ill, proves to be less adept at survival than his cunning brother. It is Paul who rescues Harvey, much to the surprise of everyone, including himself.

Northern Lights received mixed reviews, with several critics commenting on O'Brien's style. Duncan Fallowell, writing in *Spectator,* called *Northern Lights* "indigestible, as if [the author] is having a crack at raising the great American novel fifty years after it sank." Alasdair Maclean, writing in *Times Literary Supplement,* expressed a similar view, claiming "O'Brien's ambition outreaches his gifts." *New York Times Book Review* contributor John Deck, however, concluded that O'Brien "tells the story modestly and neatly . . . [in] a crafted work of serious intent with themes at least as old as the Old Testament—they still work."

O'Brien takes a new approach to his Vietnam theme in *Going after Cacciato,* winner of the National Book Award in 1979. The chapters read like short stories; several were published seperately before the book's compilation, with two tales winning O. Henry awards. *Cacciato* records the dream journey of Paul Berlin, a U.S. infantryman in Vietnam, and alternates this with the "dreamlike" actualities of war. The story begins in reality when a fellow platoon member, Cacciato—which means "the pursued" in Italian—decides to leave South East Asia and walk to Paris. He never makes it, being found near the Laotian border by a search party that includes Berlin. Berlin later wonders during guard duty one night, what if Cacciato was never found and the group had to track him all the way to Paris? Here Berlin's imagination roams free as fantasies of travel, beautiful women, and, ultimately, Paris, alternate with memories of battle, death, and war. "The fantasy journey is an unworkable idea that nearly sinks the book," claimed a reviewer in *Newsweek.* And Mary Hope, writing in *Spectator,* labeled *Going after Cacciato* a "strained effort." Other critics issued more positive reviews, praising the writing style and the author's abilities. "O'Brien's writing is crisp, authentic and grimly ironic," declared Richard Freedman in *New York Times Book Review. Washington Post Book World* contributor Robert Wilson also commented on the dream elements, calling them "out of place, hard to reconcile with the evocative realism of the rest of the narrative," but closed by writing that "O'Brien knows the soldier as well as anybody, and is able to make us know him in the unique way that the best fiction can."

In *The Nuclear Age,* O'Brien shifts his focus to a civilian's perspective. William Cowling, a Vietnam era antiwar radical, terrorist, and draft dodger, is the protagonist who traded in his radicalism for profits in uranium speculation in the 1990s. A product of the "nuclear age," his childhood fear of nuclear annihilation, a concern rampant during the 1950s, has turned into paranoia in his adulthood. The story opens in 1995, with Cowling digging a bomb shelter in his backyard, but most of the story is told through flashbacks illustrating his childhood and radical young adult years. Eventually, Cowling must accept that the bombs exist and learn to ignore them, ultimately choosing the love of his family over his paranoia. "O'Brien never makes William's hysteria real or convincing," judged Michiko Kakutani in *New York Times.* Richard Lipez, writing in *Washington Post Book World,* called *The Nuclear Age* an "imperfect but very lively novel," an opinion shared by several other reviewers. Lipez praised the "marvelous character" of Cowling, but noted that the impact of O'Brien's "main message" about the craziness of the nuclear age gets lost in the radical actions of another era. *Times Literary Supplement* contributor David Montrose also noted several flaws in the novel, including the characterization of Cowling's friends, but wrote in his conclusion: *The Nuclear Age* "is notable for the lean clarity of O'Brien's prose and the finesse with which, as ever, he evokes states of mind."

O'Brien returns to the subject of Vietnam and the soldier's viewpoint with *The Things They Carried,* a fictional memoir filled with interconnected stories about the conflict and the people involved. The volume is narrated by a character named "Tim O'Brien," whom the author states is not himself, although there are many similarities. One tale records the visit an All-American girl made to her boyfriend in South East Asia, where she eventually becomes so caught up in the war that she wanders off into combat wearing a necklace of human tongues. Another relates the death of a friend whose misstep while playing catch with hand grenades causes him to be blown up by a land mine. The title, *The Things They Carried,* refers to the things a soldier takes into combat with him: not necessarily all physical items, like weapons, but also intangibles such as fear, exhaustion, and memories. Many reviewers praised O'Brien's work, with *New York Times Book Review* contributor Robert R. Harris proclaiming it "a stunning performance. The overall effect of these original tales is devastating." "O'Brien convinces us that such incredible stories are faithful to the reality of Vietnam," declared Julian Loose in *Times Literary Supplement.* Kakutani praised O'Brien's prose, describing it as a style "that combines the sharp, unsentimental rhythms of Hemingway with gentler, more lyrical descriptions . . . [giving] the reader a shockingly visceral sense of what it felt like to tramp through a booby-trapped jungle," and concluded, "With *The Things They Carried,* Mr. O'Brien has written a vital, important book—a book that matters not only to the reader interested in Vietnam, but to anyone interested in the craft of writing as well."

July, July focuses on a group of Darton Hall College students who return to their alma mater for their thirtieth class reunion in July of 1999. In what a *Publishers Weekly* contributor described as "more a group of interwoven short stories or character studies than a traditional novel," O'Brien reveals the disillusionment of a group of middle-agers who look back on their radical, idealistic, free-wheeling, and politically active youth and feel disillusioned with the course of their lives. Describing the characters of *July, July* as "divorced, drunk," and "drifting," *New Statesman* contributor James Hopkin explained that their "reunion reveals old flames, old wounds, and new crises," and noted that O'Brien "shows us how their disenchantment has turned to apathy and political lassitude," a lassitude the author extends to "the nation's body politic." While noting that the novel moves O'Brien away from his characteristic focus on Vietnam, in this tale of disillusioned baby boomers the Vietnam war "hovers in the background like some unfinished business from the past, testing the powers of memory," noted Mirela Roncevic in *Library Journal.*

While the *Publishers Weekly* contributor called *July, July* a "comic tale" in which "sympathy, camaraderie, solidarity and love run deeply throughout," other critics disagreed. John Mort, in a *Booklist* review, maintained that O'Brien's characters, while engaging in "witty" conversation, are fifty-something narcissists lacking a "social conscience," "seem shallow," and "their youthful contempt for any sort of spirituality has not aged well." Hopkin, praising the author's style as "breathless, bitter and designed to give you the jitters," noted that at the novel's core is a "sense of a Middle America gone ideologically idle and paranoid." In contrast, a *Kirkus Reviews* contributor found the novel to be sensitive to its character's strengths and human weaknesses, noting that, "though its parts are of unequal interest and excellence, *July, July* powerfully dramatizes the long, lingering aftermath of what had seemed to those who grew up during it, a veritable year of wonders." For O'Brien's part, he told *Atlantic Unbound* interviewer Josh Karp that the novel represents the sense of unmet expectations that every adult of a certain age must deal with. "I think every generation knows betrayal and loss," the author noted. "No generation is exempt from that. When I wrote the book, I wasn't thinking of Baby Boomers. I was thinking about human beings . . . and to me they could have been part of any generation. I mean, my father's generation—granted they won World War II—but they thought the world would be changed forever, and it wasn't. They know what disappointment and loss is. So, I really thought of it as a more ubiquitous theme that everybody could identify with."

"What can you teach people, just for having been in a war?," O'Brien pondered in response to a question by Larry McCaffery in a *Chicago Review* interview. "By 'teach,' I mean provide insight, philosophy. The mere fact of having witnessed violence and death doesn't make a person a teacher. Insight and wisdom are required, and that means reading and hard thought. I didn't intend *If I Die* to stand as a profound statement, and it's not. Teaching is one thing, and telling stories is another. Instead I wanted to use stories to alert readers to the complexity and ambiguity of a set of moral issues—but without preaching a moral lesson."

BIOGRAPHICAL AND CRITICAL SOURCES:

BOOKS

Contemporary Literary Criticism, Thomson Gale (Detroit, MI), Volume 7, 1977, Volume 19, 1981, Volume 40, 1986.

Dictionary of Literary Biography Documentary Series, Volume 9, Thomson Gale (Detroit, MI), 1991.

Dictionary of Literary Biography Yearbook: 1980, Thomson Gale (Detroit, MI), 1981.

Herzog, T. C., *Tim O'Brien,* Prentice Hall (London, England), 1997.

Kaplan, Steven, *Understanding Tim O'Brien,* University of South Carolina, 1995.

PERIODICALS

America, September 1, 1973; November 17, 1973.

Antioch Review, spring, 1978.

Atlantic, May, 1973; November, 1994, p. 146.

Book, September-October, 2002, Stephanie Foote, review of *July, July,* p. 76.

Booklist, September 1, 2002, John Mort, review of *July, July,* p. 7.

Books and Bookmen, December, 1973.

Chicago Review, number 2, 1982, pp. 129-149.

Chicago Tribune, April 27, 1990; August 23, 1990.

Chicago Tribune Book World, October 6, 1985, p. 39.

Christian Century, May 24, 1995, p. 567.

Christian Science Monitor, March 9, 1978.

College Literature, spring, 2002, Marilyn Wesley, "Truth and Fiction in Tim O'Brien's *If I Die in a Combat Zone* and *The Things They Carried,*" pp. 1-18.

Commonweal, December 5, 1975.

Critique, fall, 1999, Jack Slay Jr., "A Rumor of War," p. 79.

English Journal, January, 1994, p. 82.

Explicator, spring, 2003, Robin Blyn, review of *The Things They Carried,* pp. 109-191.

Guardian, October 20, 1973.

Harper's, March, 1978; August, 1999, Vince Passaro, review of *The Things They Carried,* p. 80.

Kirkus Reviews, July 15, 2002, review of *July, July,* p. 985.

Library Journal, December 18, 1977; September 1, 1998, Marc A. Kloszewski, review of *Tomcat in Love,* p. 216; May 15, 2001, Nancy Pearl, review of *In the Lake of the Woods,* p. 192; July, 2002, Mirela Roncevic, review of *July, July,* pp. 122-123.

Listener, April 1, 1976.

Los Angeles Times, March 22, 1979; March 11, 1990.

Los Angeles Times Book Review, November 3, 1985, p. 16; April 1, 1990, p. 3.

Massachusetts Review, winter, 2002, Pamela Smiley, "The Role of the Ideal (Female) Reader in Tim O'Brien's *The Things They Carried:* Why Should Real Women Play?," pp. 602-613.

Nation, January 29, 1977; March 25, 1978.

New Republic, May 12, 1973, p. 30; February 7, 1976.

New Statesman, January 4, 1974; May 10, 1999, Phil Whitaker, review of *Tomcat in Love,* p. 45; November 11, 2002, James Hopkin, review of *July, July,* p. 40.

Newsweek, February 20, 1978; April 2, 1990, p. 56; October 24, 1994, p. 77.

New Yorker, July 16, 1973; March 27, 1978; October 24, 1994, p. 111.

New York Review of Books, November 13, 1975.

New York Times, February 12, 1978; March 19, 1979; April 24, 1979; September 28, 1985; April 4, 1987; August 4, 1987; March 6, 1990; April 3, 1990.

New York Times Book Review, July 1, 1973, pp. 10, 12; December 2, 1973; October 12, 1975, p. 42; February 12, 1978, pp. 1, 22; November 3, 1985, p. 16; November 17, 1985, p. 7; August 16, 1987, p. 28; March 11, 1990, p. 8; October 9, 1994, pp. 1, 33.

Progressive, December, 1994, p. 40.

Publishers Weekly, August 9, 1985, p. 65; December 15, 1989, p. 35; January 26, 1990, p. 404; February 16, 1990, pp. 60-61; July 11, 1994, p. 61; July 13, 1998, review of *Tomcat in Love,* p. 61; January 6, 2003, review of *July, July,* p. 20.

Saturday Review, February 18, 1978; May 13, 1978.

Spectator, April 3, 1976, p. 22; November 25, 1978, p. 23.

Time, October 24, 1994, p. 74.

Times Literary Supplement, October 19, 1973, p. 1269; April 23, 1976, p. 498; March 28, 1986, p. 342; June 29, 1990, p. 708.

Tribune Books (Chicago, IL), March 11, 1990, p. 5.

Twentieth-Century Literature, spring, 2000, John H. Timmerman, "Tim O'Brien and the Art of the True War Story," p. 100.

Virginia Quarterly Review, summer, 1978; winter, 2003, review of *July, July,* p. 23.

Washington Post, July 31, 1987; April 23, 1990.

Washington Post Book World, May 27, 1973; June 3, 1973, p. 14; June 30, 1974, p. 4; February 19, 1978, p. E4; October 13, 1985, p. 9; April 7, 1991, p. 12.

Whole Earth Review, fall, 1995, p. 58.

ONLINE

Atlantic Unbound, http://www.theatlantic.com/ (October 30, 2002), Josh Karp, interview with O'Brien.

Tim O'Brien Home Page, http://www.illyria.com/tobhp/ (April 7, 2004).

O'FAOLAIN, Sean 1900-1991

PERSONAL: Born John Francis Whelan, February 22, 1900, in Cork, Ireland; changed name to Gaelic variant, 1918; died following a short illness April 20, 1991, in Dublin, Ireland; son of Denis and Bridget (Murphy) Whelan; married Elleen Gould, June, 1928; children: Julia, Stephen. *Education:* University College at Cork of National University of Ireland, B.A., 1921, M.A., 1925; Harvard University, M.A., 1929. *Hobbies and other interests:* Travel and gardening.

CAREER: Fought in Irish Revolution, 1918-21; Irish Republican Army, director of publicity, 1923; Princeton University, Princeton, NJ, and Boston College, Boston, MA, lecturer in English, both 1929; St. Mary's College, Strawberry Hill, England, lecturer in English, 1929-33; full-time author, 1932-91.

MEMBER: Arts Council of Ireland (director, 1957-59), Irish Academy of Letters.

AWARDS, HONORS: John Harvard fellowship, 1928-29; Femina Prize nomination, 1932, for *Midsummer Night Madness and Other Stories;* D.Litt., Trinity College, Dublin, 1957.

WRITINGS:

SHORT STORIES

Midsummer Night Madness and Other Stories, Viking (New York, NY), 1932.
There's a Birdie in the Cage, Grayson, 1935.
The Born Genius: A Short Story, Schuman's, 1936.
A Purse of Coppers: Short Stories, J. Cape (London, England), 1937, Viking (New York, NY), 1938.
Teresa and Other Stories, J. Cape (London, England), 1947, published as *The Man Who Invented Sin and Other Stories,* Devin-Adair, 1948.
The Finest Stories of Sean O'Faolain, Little, Brown (Boston, MA), 1957, published as *The Stories of Sean O'Faolain,* Hart-Davis (London, England), 1958.
I Remember! I Remember! Stories, Little, Brown (Boston, MA), 1962.
The Heat of the Sun: Stories and Tales, Little, Brown (Boston, MA), 1966.
The Talking Trees and Other Stories, Little, Brown (Boston, MA, 1970.
Foreign Affairs and Other Stories, Little, Brown (Boston, MA), 1976.
(With others) *One True Friend and Other Irish Stories,* Structural Readers, 1977.
Selected Stories of Sean O'Faolain, Little, Brown (Boston, MA), 1978.
The Collected Stories of Sean O'Faolain, Constable (London, England), 1980, Little, Brown (Boston, MA), 1983.

NOVELS

A Nest of Simple Folk, J. Cape (London, England), 1933, Viking (New York, NY), 1934, reprinted, Carol Pub. Group (Secaucus, NJ), 1990.
Bird Alone, Viking (New York, NY), 1936, reprinted, Oxford University Press (New York, NY), 1985.
Come Back to Erin, Viking (New York, NY), 1940, reprinted, Greenwood Press (Westport, CT), 1972.
And Again?, Constable (London, England), 1979, Carol Pub. Group (New York, NY), 1989.

BIOGRAPHIES

The Life Story of Eamon De Valera, Penguin (New York, NY), 1934.
Constance Markievicz; or, The Average Revolutionary, J. Cape (London, England), 1934, revised edition published as *Constance Markievicz,* Sphere Books (London, England), 1968, reprinted, Cresset Library (London, England), 1987.
King of the Beggars: A Life of Daniel O'Connell, the Irish Liberator, in a Study of the Rise of the Modern Irish Democracy, 1775-1847, Viking (New York, NY), 1938, abridged edition, Parkside Press (Dublin, Ireland), 1945, Greenwood Press (Westport, CT), 1975.
De Valera, Penguin (New York, NY), 1939.
The Great O'Neill: A Biography of Hugh O'Neill, Earl of Tyrone, 1550-1616, Duell, Sloan & Pearce (New York, NY), 1942, reprinted, Mercier Press, 1970.
Newman's Way: The Odyssey of John Henry Newman, Devin-Adair, 1952, published as *Newman's Way,* Longmans, Green (London, England), 1952.
Vive Moi! (autobiography), Little, Brown (Boston, MA), 1964, published as *Vive Moi! An Autobiography,* Hart-Davis (London, England), 1965.

TRAVEL

An Irish Journey, Longmans, Green (London, England), 1940.

A Summer in Italy, Eyre & Spottiswoode (London, England), 1949, Devin-Adair, 1950.

An Autumn in Italy, Devin-Adair, 1953, published as *South to Sicily,* Collins (London, England), 1953.

OTHER

(Editor) *Lyrics and Satires from Tom Moore,* Cuala Press (Dublin, Ireland), 1929, reprinted, Biblio Distribution Centre, 1971.

(Editor) *The Autobiography of Theobald Wolfe Tone,* Thomas Nelson (London, England), 1937.

She Had to Do Something: A Comedy in Three Acts (first produced in Dublin, 1937), J. Cape (London, England), 1938.

(Compiler) *The Silver Branch: A Collection of the Best Old Irish Lyrics, Variously Translated,* Viking (New York, NY), 1938, reprinted, Books for Libraries, 1968.

The Story of Ireland (history), Collins (London, England), 1943.

(Editor and author of foreword) Samuel Lover, *Adventures of Handy Andy,* Parkside Press, 1945.

(Author of preface) D 83222, *I Did Penal Servitude,* Metropolitan Publishing (Dublin, Ireland), 1945.

The Irish, Penguin (New York, NY), 1947, published as *The Irish: A Character Study,* Devin-Adair, 1949, revised and updated edition, Penguin, 1969, published as *The Story of the Irish People,* Avenel, 1982.

The Short Story (criticism and stories), Collins (London, England), 1948, Devin-Adair, 1951.

The Vanishing Hero: Studies in Novelists of the Twenties, Eyre & Spottiswoode (London, England), 1956, Little, Brown (Boston, MA), 1957, published as *The Vanishing Hero: Studies of the Hero in the Modern Novel,* Grosset (New York, NY), 1957.

(Editor) *Short Stories: A Study in Pleasure,* Little, Brown (Boston, MA), 1961.

Contributor of short stories and articles to numerous magazines, journals, and other periodicals. Editor, *Bell* (Irish periodical), 1940-45.

O'Faolain's letters and manuscripts are collected at the Bancroft Library, University of California—Berkeley.

ADAPTATIONS: Two of O'Faolain's short stories, "Mother Matilda's Book" and "The Man Who Invented Sin," were adapted into plays and broadcast by Granada Television Ltd., 1970.

SIDELIGHTS: "Of all the significant O's in twentieth-century Irish literature," noted Paul A. Doyle in *Best Sellers,* "Sean O'Casey is the most humorous and flamboyant, Liam O'Flaherty the most emotional and unpolished, Frank O'Connor the most satiric and whimsical, and Sean O'Faolain the most versatile and profound." One of modern Ireland's greatest chroniclers, O'Faolain produced many memorable novels, short stories, and nonfiction works during his career, which spanned more than fifty years.

Born John Francis Whelan in County Cork, Ireland, O'Faolain from an early age was inhibited, according to Gordon Henderson's *Dictionary of Literary Biography* article about the author, by "his father's unquestioning respect for authority, his mother's excessive piety, and the preoccupation both had with rising above their peasant-farmer origins." He was also influenced by the plays at the nearby Cork Opera House, and spent much of his time during his youth watching the dramatic presentations of such classics as *The Scarlet Pimpernel* and *The Prisoner of Zenda.* One play in particular had a dramatic effect on O'Faolain; Lennox Robinson's "The Patriot," a story set in an Irish shopkeeper's parlor, elicited a strong reaction from the boy. As O'Faolain related in Henderson's article: "For years I had seen only plays straight from the West End of London. . . . Here was a most moving play about Irish peasants, shopkeeping and farming folk, men and women who could have been any one of my uncles and aunts down the country. It brought me strange and wonderful news—that writers could also write books and plays about the common everyday reality of Irish life."

Perhaps the most important event of O'Faolain's early years, however, was the Easter Rebellion of 1916. Although at first he opposed the uprising, motivated by his father's unwavering loyalty to the crown, O'Faolain soon became outraged at the brutal way the British forces "crushed the rebellion and then systematically executed its leaders," as Henderson put it. "Fired with a new sense of nationalism," he continued, O'Faolain "was soon taking lessons in the Irish language and, at eighteen, joined other young men and women at a summer school for Gaelic speakers in the mountains of West Cork." At the same age, the young man unofficially changed his name from the anglicized John Whelan to the Gaelic Sean O'Faolain. He then joined the Irish Volunteers, an organization that later produced some members of the militant Irish Republican Army (IRA). While O'Faolain eventually became involved with IRA activities—he was the group's publicity director at age twenty-three—the writer avoided the extreme, often violent tactics for which that organization has since become infamous. "To have cast me for the role of a gunman would have been like casting me as a bullfighter," explained O'Faolain in Henderson's piece. It was during this tumultuous period in Irish history that O'Faolain began his writing career.

The author's early works, including the novels *A Nest of Simple Folk* and *Bird Alone,* explore the lives of people caught up in various stages of "The Troubles." Leo O'Donnell, the lead character of *A Nest of Simple Folk,* for example, is seen over a period of sixty-two years, starting in 1854 and ending with the Easter Rebellion. O'Donnell, imprisoned for several years because of his Fenian involvement—the Fenians, an Irish nationalistic group, were established in the nineteenth century—"grows old futilely pursuing patriotic dreams," as Henderson wrote, and passes his strong sense of Gaelic pride on to his nephew, Denis Hussey, a character modeled after O'Faolain himself. As both a political story and a poignant character study, *A Nest of Simple Folk* is "a memorable work, memorable as an instance of the power and passion of memory," according to Donat O'Donnell, reviewing the novel in *Renascence.*

Bird Alone, banned as obscene by Ireland's Censorship Board, opens with the elderly Croney looking back over his life as a builder in Cork. The book focuses on his relationship with his grandfather, a staunch Fenian who helps shape young Crone's political viewpoint. Later, ostracized because of both his Irish activism and a scandal involving a woman who dies while giving birth to his child, Crone becomes a recluse, a "bird alone," living in an attic room.

"This is one of the very few modern novels . . . in which the treatment of character bears the stamp of a complete and subtle mastery," commented V.S. Pritchett about *Bird Alone.* In his *Christian Science Monitor* article, Pritchett continued: "The sympathy is profound to the point of tears—and they are often tears of that convinced laughter which comes when one says, These people are round, whole, real and lovable and yet have that quality of mysteriousness which leaves us . . . in questioning wonder before even those whom we know very well." The reviewer deemed *Bird Alone* "the genre piece of a master." William Troy, on the other hand, had praise not for the characters in the novel, but for its setting. County Cork is presented, Troy declared in *Nation,* as "more real and interesting than any of its inhabitants. This is managed partly through the fluid poetic style and partly through a formal framework which makes possible the rapid transitions and vivid condensations of the memory." Troy did have criticism for *Bird Alone*—he received an impression "of conflicts unresolved, of ambiguities remaining suspended"—but he ultimately cited the book's "flowing current of exquisitely modulated language." This view was shared by *Boston Transcript* critic A.B. Tourtellot, who found that the novel's "major flaw . . . is the inadequate treatment of the story as a story." However, Tourtellot concluded, *Bird Alone* is "a fine and rich book, but fine and rich chiefly because of the craftsmanship of its author and not because of the strength of the story."

O'Faolain's final novel, *And Again?,* published when he was eighty, is a parable about aging, memory, and death. The protagonist, sixty-five-year-old journalist Bob Younger, receives a piece of mail one day from the gods on Mount Olympus. The gods inform Younger that he has been given the chance to relive his life, with a twist: he will have little memory of his early years, and rather than starting as a baby he will start at his present age and grow younger each day. Once Younger accepts the offer, he sets out to learn who he is and where he came from. He gets romantically involved with a number of women through the years, choosing younger women as he himself de-ages. Calling the novel one of "amazing originality and inventiveness," *New York Times Book Review* contributor Carolyn Gaiser noted that *And Again?* "proves to be a charming if erratic tour de force." Writing in the *Los Angeles Times Book Review,* Clare Boylan remarked, "Flawed, luminous and with a matchless understanding of and zest for life, it is reckless, full-blooded, intellectual literature that will delight and invigorate readers malnourished by the Lean Cuisine diet of mannered-modern miniaturists."

Although his novels and books of criticism were well received, O'Faolain eventually earned more acclaim as a short-story writer. In his collections the author examined the many aspects of modern Irish life. "His stories are typically dense, lush, complex, and rich—his is not an art of understatement," noted Gary Davenport in a *Hudson Review* article. O'Faolain "has two major themes: what it means to be Irish, and what it means to be an Irish Catholic. [The author] is a loyal but critical Irishman; he is capable of denouncing Irish provincialism of both the nationalist and religious genres, but unlike [playwright George Bernard] Shaw he denounces it from within: he lives in Ireland and he remains a Catholic. . . . And these stories are full to bursting of life. Landscape provides much of this richness—especially the fecund landscape of his native Cork: low thick clouds, endless rain, sodden earth. And the characters who live in this environment partake of its sense of being outside time."

"In regard to style," commented Paul A. Doyle in his book *Sean O'Faolain,* the author "favors the technique of uniting suggestion and compression. He uses the words 'engrossed' and 'active' in reference to good style. The beginning of the narrative must at once establish the mood of the story and then the writer works carefully word by word, sentence by sentence, toward the total effect—the innermost illumination which is really the story . . . behind the story." Doyle noted: "The superior stories in [O'Faolain's collections] are characterized by subtlety, compassion, understanding, irony, and a perceptive awareness of the complexity of human nature. Themes and insights are suggested and implied rather than flatly stated, and the themes are significant. In these superior stories O'Faolain demonstrates authorial objectivity and detachment; he avoids description for its own sake; and he successfully infuses a poetic mood—subdued and delicate—over the narratives. Overall, then, it may be affirmed that stories such as 'A Broken World,' 'The Man Who Invented Sin,' 'The Silence of the Valley,' 'Up the Bare Stairs'—to mention a few—exemplify considerable artistry and expert control of modern short story techniques."

"Although the tone in his stories is sometimes satiric," offered Henderson, O'Faolain "more often withholds judgement of his characters' actions or adopts the stance of an understanding observer. In this respect O'Faolain says he took Chekhov as his model and acknowledges that he also learned from Chekhov to de-emphasize plot, advance the action indirectly by implication, strive for compression, and suffuse his stories with a poetic mood." O'Faolain's reputation as an important modern author, Henderson concluded, "rests most firmly on his short stories," later efforts which were published in magazines such as *Colliers* and *McCall's.* "Their popular appeal, however, does not reduce his stature as a writer of serious fiction," the critic added. "Like [James] Joyce and [Frank] O'Connor, he took the short story as he received it from [Guy de] Maupassant and [Anton] Chekhov and transformed it into something uniquely his own and uniquely Irish."

O'Faolain continued to write until well into his eighties, and died in 1991. *Dictionary of Literary Biography* contributor Richard J. Thompson noted of the Irish writer that "O'Faolain's place in world letters is guaranteed by his short-story production, which will stand in quality besides the masters of the form from Edgar Allan Poe to Ernest Hemingway. In purely Irish terms he occupies a place of honor not just as a writer but as a literary groundbreaker, a social force, and a kind of national patriarch."

BIOGRAPHICAL AND CRITICAL SOURCES:

BOOKS

Benedict, Keily, *Modern Irish Fiction: A Critique,* Golden Eagle Books (Dublin, Ireland), 1950.

Butler, Pierce, *Sean O'Faolain: A Study of the Short Fiction,* Macmillan (New York, NY), 1993.

Contemporary Literary Criticism, Thomson Gale (Detroit, MI), Volume 1, 1973, Volume 7, 1977, Volume 14, 1980.

Dictionary of Literary Biography, Thomson Gale (Detroit, MI), Volume 15: *British Novelists, 1930-1959,* 1983, Volume 162: *British Short-Fiction Writers, 1915-1945,* 1996.

Doyle, Paul A., *Sean O'Faolain,* Twayne (Boston, MA), 1969.

Harmon, Maurice, *Sean O'Faolain: A Critical Introduction,* University of Notre Dame Press, 1966.

O'Donnell, Donat, *Maria Cross: Imaginative Patterns in a Group of Modern Irish Writers,* Oxford University Press (Oxford, England), 1952.

O'Faolain, Sean, *Vive Moi!* (autobiography), Little, Brown (Boston, MA), 1964.

Rippier, Joseph Storey, *The Short Stories of Sean O'Faolain: A Study in Descriptive Technique,* Barnes & Noble (New York, NY), 1976.

PERIODICALS

Boston Transcript, October 10, 1936.

Chicago Tribune Book World, February 12, 1984.

Christian Science Monitor, August 12, 1936.

Dublin Magazine, April-June, 1955.

Hudson Review, spring, 1979.

Irish Literary Supplement, spring, 1990, p. 19.

Irish University Review, spring, 1976.

London Magazine, June, 1980.

Los Angeles Times, December 28, 1983.

Los Angeles Times Book Review, December 3, 1989, p. 2.

New Republic, February 15, 1939.

New Statesman, April 23, 1976; September 28, 1979.

Newsweek, January 8, 1962.

New Yorker, January 28, 1994, p. 205.

New York Times Book Review, May 12, 1957; January 25, 1976; November 26, 1978; October 11, 1983; September 17, 1989, p. 18.

Renascence, autumn, 1950.

South Atlantic Quarterly, summer, 1976.

Spectator, January 2, 1982, p. 21.

Time, June 26, 1976.

Times Literary Supplement, November 7, 1980; November 20, 1981; December 3, 1982.
Washington Post Book World, October 9, 1983, p. 5; October 29, 1989, p. 9.

OBITUARIES:

PERIODICALS

Chicago Tribune, April 22, 1991.
Los Angeles Times, April 22, 1991.
New York Times, April 22, 1991.
Time, May 6, 1991, p. 73.
Times (London, England), April 22, 1991.
Washington Post, April 22, 1991.

* * *

O'FLAHERTY, Liam 1896-1984

PERSONAL: Born August 28, 1896, on Inishmore in the Aran Islands, Ireland; died September 7, 1984, in Dublin, Ireland; son of Michael and Margaret (Ganly) O'Flaherty; married Margaret Barrington (a writer), February, 1926 (marriage ended, 1932); children: Pegeen O'Flaherty O'Sullivan, Joyce O'Flaherty Rathbone. *Education:* Attended Rockwell College, 1908-12, Blackrock College, 1912-13, and University College, 1913-14.

CAREER: Writer. Founder, Irish Communist Party, 1922. Worked as a miner, lumberjack, hotel porter, and bank clerk in the United States and Canada. *Military service:* Served in Irish Guards during World War I.

AWARDS, HONORS: James Tait Black Memorial Prize, 1926, for *The Informer;* honorary doctorate in literature from National University of Ireland, 1974; Allied Irish Bank—Irish Academy of Letters Award for literature, 1979.

WRITINGS:

NOVELS

Thy Neighbor's Wife, J. Cape (London, England), 1923, Boni & Liveright (New York, NY), 1924, Lythway Press, 1972.
The Black Soul, J. Cape (London, England), 1924, Boni & Liveright (New York, NY), 1925, Wolfhound Press (Dublin, Ireland), 1996.
The Informer, Knopf (New York, NY), 1925, reprinted, Wolfhound Press (Dublin, Ireland), 1999.
Mr. Gilhooley, J. Cape (London, England), 1926, Harcourt (New York, NY), 1927, reprinted, Wolfhound Press (Dublin, Ireland), 1991.
The Assassin, Harcourt (New York, NY), 1928, Dufour, 1983.
The House of Gold, Harcourt (New York, NY), 1929.
The Return of the Brute, Mandrake Press (London, England), 1929, Harcourt (New York, NY), 1930, reprinted, Wolfhound Press (Dublin, Ireland), 1998.
The Puritan, J. Cape (London, England), 1931, Harcourt (New York, NY), 1932, reprinted, Wolfhound Press (Dublin, Ireland), 2001.
Skerrett, Long & Smith, 1932, Dufour (New York, NY), 1988.
The Martyr, Harcourt (New York, NY), 1933.
Hollywood Cemetery, Gollancz (London, England), 1935.
Famine, Random House (New York, NY), 1937, reprinted, David Godine (Boston, MA), 1982.
Land, Random House (New York, NY), 1946.
Insurrection, Gollancz (London, England), 1950, Dufour, 1988.

SHORT STORIES

Spring Sowing, J. Cape (London, England), 1924, Knopf (New York, NY), 1926, reprinted, Books for Libraries Press (Freeport, NY), 1973.
Civil War, Archer (London, England), 1925.
The Child of God, Archer (London, England), 1926.
The Terrorist, Archer (London, England), 1926.
The Tent and Other Stories, J. Cape (London, England), 1926.
The Fairy Goose and Other Stories, Faber & Gwyer (London, England), 1927, Gaige, 1928.
Red Barbara and Other Stories, Faber & Gwyer (London, England), 1928, Gaige, 1928.
The Mountain Tavern and Other Stories, Harcourt (New York, NY), 1929, reprinted, Books for Libraries Press (Freeport, NY), 1971.
The Ecstasy of Angus, Joiner & Steele, 1931, Wolfhound Press (Dublin, Ireland), 1978.
The Wild Swan and Other Stories, Joiner & Steele, 1932.
The Short Stories of Liam O'Flaherty, J. Cape (London, England), 1937, abridged edition, New American Library (New York, NY), 1970.

Two Lovely Beasts and Other Stories, Gollancz (London, England), 1948, Devin-Adair, 1950.
Duil, Sairseal Agus Dill, 1953.
The Stories of Liam O'Flaherty, Devin-Adair, 1956.
Selected Stories, New American Library (New York, NY), 1958.
Short Stories, Brown, Watson, 1961.
Irish Portraits: Fourteen Short Stories, Sphere (London, England), 1970.
More Short Stories of Liam O'Flaherty, New English Library (London, England), 1971.
The Wounded Cormorant and Other Stories, Norton (New York, NY), 1973.
The Pedlar's Revenge and Other Stories, Wolfhound Press (Dublin, Ireland), 1976.
All Things Come of Age: A Rabbit Story, Wolfhound Press (Dublin, Ireland), 1977.
The Wave and Other Stories, Longman (London, England), 1980.
The Collected Short Stories of Liam O'Flaherty, 3 volumes, edited by A.A. Kelly, St. Martin's Press (New York, NY), 1999.

OTHER

Darkness (short story; limited edition), Archer (London, England), 1926.
The Life of Tim Healy, Harcourt (New York, NY), 1927.
A Tourist's Guide to Ireland, Mandrake Press (London, England), 1929, Irish American Book Company (Niwot, CO), 1998.
Joseph Conrad: An Appreciation, E. Lahr (London, England), 1930, Haskell House, 1973.
Two Years (autobiography), Harcourt (New York, NY), 1930.
I Went to Russia (autobiography), Harcourt (New York, NY), 1931.
A Cure for Unemployment, E. Lahr (London, England), 1931.
Shame the Devil (autobiography), Grayson, 1934.
Devil's Playground (screenplay), Columbia, 1937.
Last Desire (screenplay), Lumen Films, 1939.
The Test of Courage, Wolfhound Press (Dublin, Ireland), 1977.
The Wilderness, Wolfhound Press (Dublin, Ireland), 1978, Dodd, 1987.
The Letters of Liam O'Flaherty, selected and edited by A.A. Kelly, Wolfhound Press (Dublin, Ireland), 1996.

Also coauthor of screenplay "The Informer," based on O'Flaherty's novel of the same title, 1935.

ADAPTATIONS: O'Flaherty's novel *The Informer* was filmed three times, most notably in 1935, in an adaptation directed by John Ford and starring Victor McLaglen.

SIDELIGHTS: Criticism of Irish twentieth-century writer Liam O'Flaherty's fiction is marked by a number of paradoxes. He has been both praised and condemned for his "Irishness" and his "anti-Irishness," his naturalism and his expressionism, and his existential awareness and his romantic idealism. While the sheer quantity of his writing could account for such differences in interpretation, the fact that they occur in discussions of the same works implies, rather, that O'Flaherty is a writer of greater complexity than is often acknowledged. In *The English Novel in Transition, 1885-1940,* William C. Frierson suggested that "the author's writings reflect the chaos of his life." And for a writer who has lived as everything from a hotel porter to a revolutionary fighter, wandering to places as far from Ireland as Canada and Rio de Janeiro, the life and the subsequent fiction could be chaotic indeed.

The setting for most of O'Flaherty's novels and short stories is Ireland, and his central characters are often Irish peasants deeply rooted in the land. James H. O'Brien pointed out in his *Liam O'Flaherty* that "collectively O'Flaherty's short stories describe two or three generations of life in the Aran Islands and the west of Ireland; perhaps they reach back even further, so little did life change in those areas until the end of the nineteenth century." Moreover, on the basis of a few of his novels—especially *The Informer*—he is thought of as a novelist of the Irish revolution.

On the other hand, as an early reviewer of *The Informer* was quoted in the *Dictionary of Literary Biography* as commenting, O'Flaherty "never makes the common error . . . of falling into sentiment about Ireland or slipping out of the world of reality into that non-existent world of petulant, half-godlike and utterly fictitious Irishmen that other writers have created out of their false vision and saccharine fancy." Rather, he was part of a second wave of modern Irish writers, along with James Joyce and Sean O'Casey, who rebelled against the Celtic-revivalist ideals of Yeats and Synge. The fact that O'Flaherty was ultimately forced to leave Ireland and take up residence in England further separates him from the Irish literary tradition.

Nevertheless, one aspect of O'Flaherty's fiction grounds him solidly in an Irish tradition, specifically an oral tradition, and this is his ability as a storyteller. As O'Brien explained, "In both novels and short stories, a Gaelic influence is manifest in the directness of narrative, the simplicity of language, and an elemental concern with primary emotions." In a review of *The Tent and Other Stories* reprinted in *Contemporary Literary Criticism,* Edward Shanks saw this influence at work and remarked that O'Flaherty "sees directly and puts down directly what he sees. His best pieces, such as 'The Conger Eel,' have the character of pictures, simple and moving because they mean no more than they say."

A number of critics have taken exception to O'Flaherty's classification as a naturalist. O'Brien believed that the writer's "purpose is not to present a realistic or naturalistic view of the Irish peasant. . . . Instead, O'Flaherty generally uses the simplicity of peasant life to depict elemental reactions and instincts." Frierson similarly wrote: "Although naturalistic in his view of human depravity, in his brutality, and in his insistence upon physical reactions, Mr. O'Flaherty is too forceful to be pessimistic, too violent and too melodramatic to present us with a study of humanity. His distortions are those of the expressionist."

The expressionistic representation of violence and emotion is a characteristic other critics note. Frierson explained it further: "Everywhere there is primitive physical violence, reckless impulse, greed, and cruelty; and the full force of the author's dramatic fervor is exerted by riveting our attention upon physical manifestation of the strongest emotions." H.E. Bates, writing in *The Modern Short Story,* maintained that O'Flaherty, "like [French writer Guy de] Maupassant, saw life in a strong light, dramatically, powerfully. Energy alone is not enough, but the sensuous poetic energy of O'Flaherty was like a flood; the reader was carried away by it and with it, slightly stunned and exalted by the experience."

These different aspects of O'Flaherty's fiction—the Irishman turning away from yet remaining tied to Ireland, the realistic storyteller imbuing his tales with an intense expression of human emotion—are brought together by John Zneimer's interpretation. Comparing O'Flaherty to Dostoevski, Sartre, and Camus, Zneimer, in his *The Literary Vision of Liam O'Flaherty,* placed the Irish writer in an existentialist, as well as Irish, tradition. Because the Ireland in which O'Flaherty lived was an Ireland in which the old values and dreams were being destroyed by twentieth-century reality, O'Flaherty's Irishness and his existential awareness are inextricably tied. As Zneimer maintained, "He speaks in his novels about traditions that have failed in a world that is falling apart, about desperate men seeking meaning through violent acts." Thus Zneimer viewed O'Flaherty's concern both with naturalistic details and the turbulence of human emotions as products of "his increasing awareness of man's mortality and ultimate annihilation in a universe that has no meaning and offers no consolation."

O'Flaherty turned his art, Zneimer concluded, into a religious quest, making his novels "spiritual battlegrounds whereon his characters . . . struggle to find meaning" in a meaningless world. O'Brien perceived this struggle, too, though he expressed it differently: "Beneath O'Flaherty's absorption in the physical, external world lies a belief in the evolutionary process, of men, especially artists, finding fulfillment in the struggle for perfection." In contrast, his short fiction reflected the author's love of Aran life; as *Booklist* contributor Brad Hooper noted of the three-volume *The Collected Stories of Liam O'Flaherty:* "What a great yarn spinner he is, in the best Irish tradition of profiling exuberant characters in a charming style."

BIOGRAPHICAL AND CRITICAL SOURCES:

BOOKS

Bates, H. E., *The Modern Short Story,* T. Nelson, 1945.

Cahalan, James M., *Liam O'Flaherty: A Study of the Short Fiction,* Twayne (Boston, MA), 1991.

Contemporary Literary Criticism, Thomson Gale (Detroit, MI), Volume 5, 1976, Volume 34, 1985.

Costello, Peter, *Liam O'Flaherty's Ireland,* Wolfhound Press, 1996.

Dictionary of Literary Biography, Volume 36: *British Novelists, 1890-1929: Modernists,* Thomson Gale (Detroit, MI), 1985.

Dictionary of Literary Biography Yearbook: 1984, Thomson Gale (Detroit, MI), 1985.

Frierson, William C., *The English Novel in Transition, 1885-1940,* Cooper Square, 1965.

Frigerg, Hedda, *An Old and a New: The Split World of Liam O'Flaherty's Novels,* Uppsala (Stockholm, Sweden), 1996.

Jefferson, George, *Liam O'Flaherty: A Descriptive Bibliography of His Works,* Wolfhound Press (Dublin, Ireland), 1993.

Kelly, A.A., *The Letters of Liam O'Flaherty,* Wolfhound Press (Dublin, Ireland), 1996.

O'Brien, James H., *Liam O'Flaherty,* Bucknell University Press, 1970.

Zneimer, John, *The Literary Vision of Liam O'Flaherty,* Syracuse University Press (Syracuse, NY), 1971.

PERIODICALS

Booklist, February 15, 2000, Brad Hooper, review of *The Collected Stories,* p. 1984.
Library Journal, August, 1998, Michael Rogers, review of *Return of the Brute,* p. 142; August, 2000, Denise J. Stankovics, review of *The Collected Stories,* p. 165.
London Mercury, August, 1926.
New Statesman and Nation, January 21, 1933.
New York Times Book Review, August 30, 1987.
Publishers Weekly, November 29, 1991, p. 46.
Spectator, October 3, 1925.
Time, September 17, 1984, p. 82.
Times Literary Supplement, January 1, 1982.
World of Hibernia, winter, 2000, John Boland, review of *The Collected Stories of Liam O'Flaherty,* p. 19.

OBITUARIES:

PERIODICALS

Chicago Tribune, September 10, 1984.
Los Angeles Times, September 9, 1984.
New York Times, September 9, 1984.
Time, September 17, 1984.

* * *

OATES, Joyce Carol 1938- (Lauren Kelly, Rosamond Smith)

PERSONAL: Born June 16, 1938, in Lockport, NY; daughter of Frederic James (a tool and die designer) and Caroline (Bush) Oates; married Raymond Joseph Smith, January 23, 1961. *Education:* Syracuse University, B.A., 1960; University of Wisconsin, M.A., 1961.

ADDRESSES: Office—Council of the Humanities, 223 185 Nassau St., Princeton University, Princeton, NJ 08544. *Agent*—John Hawkins, 71 W. 23rd St., New York, NY 10010; (for plays) Peter Franklin, c/o William Morris Agency, 1350 Avenue of the Americas, New York, NY 10019. *E-mail*—jcsmith@princeton.edu.

CAREER: Writer. University of Detroit, Detroit, MI, instructor, 1961-65, assistant professor, 1965-67; University of Windsor, Windsor, Ontario, Canada, member of English department faculty, 1967-78; Princeton University, Princeton, NJ, writer-in-residence, 1978-81, professor, 1987—, currently Roger S. Berlind Distinguished Professor in the Humanities.

MEMBER: PEN, American Academy of Arts and Letters, Phi Beta Kappa.

AWARDS, HONORS: Mademoiselle college fiction award, 1959, for "In the Old World"; National Endowment for the Arts grants, 1966, 1968; Guggenheim fellowship, 1967; O. Henry Award, 1967, for "In the Region of Ice," 1973, for "The Dead," and 1983, for "My Warszawa"; Rosenthal Award, National Institute of Arts and Letters, 1968, for *A Garden of Earthly Delights;* National Book Award nomination, 1968, for *A Garden of Earthly Delights,* and 1969, for *Expensive People;* National Book Award for fiction, 1970, for *them;* O. Henry Special Award for Continuing Achievement, 1970 and 1986; Lotos Club Award of Merit, 1975; Pushcart Prize, 1976; *Unholy Loves* selected by the American Library Association as a notable book of 1979; *Bellefleur* nominated for a *Los Angeles Times* Book Prize in fiction, 1980; St. Louis Literary Award, 1988; Rhea Award for the short story, Dungannon Foundation, 1990; Alan Swallow Award for fiction, 1990; co-winner, Heidemann Award for one-act plays, 1990; Bobst Award for Lifetime Achievement in Fiction, 1990; National Book Award nomination, 1990, for *Because It Is Bitter, and Because It Is My Heart;* National Book Critics Circle Award nomination, and Pulitzer Prize finalist, both 1993, both for *Black Water;* Bram Stoker Lifetime Achievement Award for horror fiction, 1994; best new play nomination, American Theatre Critics Association, 1994, for *The Perfectionist;* Pulitzer Prize finalist, 1995, for *What I Lived For;* Bram Stoker Award for Horror, Horror Writers of America, and Fisk Fiction Prize, both 1996, both for *Zombie;* O. Henry Prize Story, 2001, for "The Girl with the Blackened Eye"; National Book Award and Pulitzer Prize finalist, both 2001, both for *Blonde;* Best American Mystery Stories designation, 2002, for "High School Sweetheart"; Peggy V. Helmerich Distinguished Author Award, Tulsa Library Trust, 2002; Common Wealth Literature Award of Distinguished Service, PNC Financial Services Group, 2003; Kenyon Review Award for Literary Achievement, 2003; Fairfax Prize for Lifetime Achievement in the Literary Arts, 2004.

WRITINGS:

NOVELS

With Shuddering Fall, Vanguard Press (New York, NY), 1964.

A Garden of Earthly Delights, Vanguard Press (New York, NY), 1967, revised edition, Random House (New York, NY), 2003.

Expensive People, Vanguard Press (New York, NY), 1967.

them, Vanguard Press (New York, NY), 1969, reprinted with introduction by Greg Johnson and afterword by the author, Modern Library (New York, NY), 2000.

Wonderland, Vanguard Press (New York, NY), 1971, revised, Ontario Review Press (New York, NY), 1992.

Do with Me What You Will, Vanguard Press (New York, NY), 1973.

The Assassins: A Book of Hours, Vanguard Press (New York, NY), 1975.

Triumph of the Spider Monkey: The First-Person Confession of the Maniac Bobby Gotteson As Told to Joyce Carol Oates (novella; also see below), Black Sparrow Press (Santa Barbara, CA), 1976.

Childwold, Vanguard Press (New York, NY), 1976.

Son of the Morning, Vanguard Press (New York, NY), 1978.

Unholy Loves, Vanguard Press (New York, NY), 1979.

Cybele, Black Sparrow Press (Santa Barbara, CA), 1979.

Bellefleur, Dutton (New York, NY), 1980.

Angel of Light, Dutton (New York, NY), 1981.

A Bloodsmoor Romance, Dutton (New York, NY), 1982.

Mysteries of Winterthurn, Dutton (New York, NY), 1984.

Solstice, Dutton (New York, NY), 1985, revised edition, Ontario Review Press (Princeton, NJ), 2000.

Marya: A Life, Dutton (New York, NY), 1986.

You Must Remember This, Dutton (New York, NY), 1987.

American Appetites, Dutton (New York, NY), 1989.

Because It Is Bitter, and Because It Is My Heart, Dutton (New York, NY), 1990.

I Lock My Door upon Myself, Ecco Press (New York, NY), 1990, revised edition, Ontario Review Press (Princeton, NJ), 2002.

The Rise of Life on Earth, New Directions (New York, NY), 1991.

Black Water, Dutton (New York, NY), 1992.

Foxfire: Confessions of a Girl Gang, Dutton (New York, NY), 1993.

What I Lived For, Dutton (New York, NY), 1994.

Zombie, Dutton (New York, NY), 1995.

Tenderness, Ontario Review Press (New York, NY), 1996.

We Were the Mulvaneys, Dutton (New York, NY), 1996.

First Love: A Gothic Tale, Ecco Press (New York, NY), 1996.

Man Crazy, Dutton (New York, NY), 1997.

My Heart Laid Bare, Dutton (New York, NY), 1998.

Broke Heart Blues: A Novel, Dutton (New York, NY), 1999.

Blonde: A Novel, HarperCollins (New York, NY), 2000.

Middle Age: A Romance, Ecco Press (New York, NY), 2001.

Beasts, Carroll & Graf (New York, NY), 2002.

I'll Take You There: A Novel, Ecco (New York, NY), 2002.

The Tattooed Girl: A Novel, Ecco (New York, NY), 2003.

Rape: A Love Story (novella), Carroll & Graf (New York, NY), 2003.

The Falls: A Novel, Ecco (New York, NY), 2004.

Missing Mom, Ecco (New York, NY), 2005.

NOVELS; UNDER PSEUDONYM ROSAMOND SMITH

Lives of the Twins, Simon & Schuster (New York, NY), 1988.

Soul/Mate, Dutton (New York, NY), 1989.

Nemesis, Dutton (New York, NY), 1990.

Snake Eyes, Simon & Schuster (New York, NY), 1992.

You Can't Catch Me, Dutton (New York, NY), 1995.

Double Delight, Dutton (New York, NY), 1997.

Starr Bright Will Be with You Soon, Dutton (New York, NY), 1999.

The Barrens, Carroll & Graf (New York, NY), 2001.

SUSPENSE NOVELS; UNDER PSEUDONYM LAUREN KELLY

Take Me, Take Me with You, Ecco (New York, NY), 2004.

The Stolen Heart, Ecco (New York, NY), 2005.

Blood Mask, Ecco (New York, NY), 2006.

SHORT STORIES

By the North Gate, Vanguard Press (New York, NY), 1963.

Upon the Sweeping Flood and Other Stories, Vanguard Press (New York, NY), 1966.

The Wheel of Love and Other Stories, Vanguard Press (New York, NY), 1970.

Marriages and Infidelities, Vanguard Press (New York, NY), 1972.

The Goddess and Other Women, Vanguard Press (New York, NY), 1974.

Where Are You Going, Where Have You Been?: Stories of Young America, Fawcett (New York, NY), 1974, published as *Where Are You Going, Where Have You Been?: Selected Early Stories,* Ontario Review Press (Princeton, NJ), 1993, expanded edition, edited and with an introduction by Elaine Showalter, Rutgers University Press (New Brunswick, NJ), 1994.

The Hungry Ghosts: Seven Allusive Comedies, Black Sparrow Press (Santa Barbara, CA), 1974.

The Poisoned Kiss and Other Stories from the Portuguese, Vanguard Press (New York, NY), 1975.

The Seduction and Other Stories, Black Sparrow Press (Santa Barbara, CA), 1975.

Crossing the Border: Fifteen Tales, Vanguard Press (New York, NY), 1976.

Night Side: Eighteen Tales, Vanguard Press (New York, NY), 1977.

All the Good People I've Left Behind, Black Sparrow Press (Santa Barbara, CA), 1978.

The Lamb of Abyssalia, Pomegranate (Cambridge, MA), 1980.

A Sentimental Education, Dutton (New York, NY), 1981.

Last Days, Dutton (New York, NY), 1984.

Wild Nights (limited edition), Croissant (Athens, OH), 1985.

Raven's Wing, Dutton (New York, NY), 1986.

The Assignation, Ecco Press (New York, NY), 1988.

Where Is Here?, Ecco Press (New York, NY), 1992.

Heat: And Other Stories, Plume (New York, NY), 1992.

Where Are You Going, Where Have You Been?: Selected Early Stories, Ontario Review Press (New York, NY), 1993.

Haunted: Tales of the Grotesque, Dutton (New York, NY), 1994.

Will You Always Love Me? and Other Stories, Dutton (New York, NY), 1995.

The Collector of Hearts: New Tales of the Grotesque, Dutton (New York, NY), 1999.

Faithless: Tales of Transgression, Ecco Press (New York, NY), 2001.

I Am No One You Know: Stories, Ecco Press (New York, NY), 2004.

The Female of the Species: Tales of Mystery and Suspense, Harcourt (Orlando, FL), 2005.

High Lonesome: New & Selected Stories, 1966-2006, Ecco Press (New York, NY), 2006.

POETRY

Women in Love and Other Poems, Albondacani Press (New York, NY), 1968.

Anonymous Sins and Other Poems (also see below), Louisiana State University Press (Baton Rouge, LA), 1969.

Love and Its Derangements: Poems (also see below), Louisiana State University Press (Baton Rouge, LA), 1970.

Angel Fire (also see below), Louisiana State University Press (Baton Rouge, LA), 1973.

Dreaming America (limited edition), Aloe Editions, 1973.

Love and Its Derangements and Other Poems (includes *Anonymous Sins and Other Poems, Love and Its Derangements,* and *Angel Fire*), Fawcett (New York, NY), 1974.

The Fabulous Beasts, Louisiana State University Press (Baton Rouge, LA), 1975.

Season of Peril, Black Sparrow Press (Santa Barbara, CA), 1977.

Women Whose Lives Are Food, Men Whose Lives Are Money: Poems, illustrated by Elizabeth Hansell, Louisiana State University Press (Baton Rouge, LA), 1978.

The Stepfather (limited edition), Lord John Press (Northridge, CA), 1978.

Celestial Timepiece (limited edition), Pressworks (Dallas, TX), 1981.

Invisible Woman: New and Selected Poems, 1970-1972, Ontario Review Press (New York, NY), 1982.

The Luxury of Sin (limited edition), Lord John Press (Northridge, CA), 1983.

The Time Traveler, Dutton (New York, NY), 1989.

Tenderness: Poems, Ontario Review Press (New York, NY), 1996.

NONFICTION

The Edge of Impossibility: Tragic Forms in Literature, Vanguard Press (New York, NY), 1972.

The Hostile Sun: The Poetry of D. H. Lawrence, Black Sparrow Press (Santa Barbara, CA), 1973.

New Heaven, New Earth: The Visionary Experience in Literature, Vanguard Press (New York, NY), 1974.

Contraries: Essays, Oxford University Press (Oxford, England), 1981.

The Profane Art: Essays and Reviews, Dutton (New York, NY), 1983.

On Boxing, Doubleday (New York, NY), 1987, expanded edition, Ecco Press (New York, NY), 1994.

(With Eileen T. Bender) *Artist in Residence,* Indiana University Press (Bloomington, IN), 1987.

(Woman) Writer: Occasions and Opportunities, Dutton (New York, NY), 1988.

Conversations with Joyce Carol Oates, edited by Lee Milazzo, University Press of Mississippi (Jackson, MS), 1989.

Where I've Been, and Where I'm Going: Essays, Reviews, and Prose, Plume (New York, NY), 1999.

The Faith of a Writer: Life, Craft, Art, Ecco Press (New York, NY), 2003.

FOR YOUNG ADULTS

Big Mouth & Ugly Girl, HarperTempest (New York, NY), 2002.

Small Avalanches and Other Stories, HarperTempest (New York, NY), 2003.

Freaky Green Eyes, HarperTempest (New York, NY), 2003.

Sexy, HarperTempest (New York, NY), 2005.

After the Wreck, I Picked Myself Up, Spread My Wings, and Flew Away, HarperTempest (New York, NY), 2006.

FOR CHILDREN

Come Meet Muffin!, illustrated by Mark Graham, Ecco Press (New York, NY), 1998.

Where Is Little Reynard? (picture book), illustrated by Mark Graham, HarperCollins (New York, NY), 2003.

Naughty Cherie, illustrated by Mark Graham, HarperCollins (New York, NY), 2006.

PLAYS

The Sweet Enemy, produced Off-Broadway, 1965.

Sunday Dinner, produced Off-Broadway, 1970.

Ontological Proof of My Existence (produced Off-Off-Broadway, 1972), published in *Partisan Review,* Volume 37, 1970.

Miracle Play, Black Sparrow Press (Santa Barbara, CA), 1974.

Three Plays, Ontario Review Press (New York, NY), 1980.

Presque Isle, produced in New York City at Theater of the Open Eye, 1984.

Triumph of the Spider Monkey, produced at the Los Angeles Theatre Center, 1985.

American Holiday, produced at the Los Angeles Theatre Academy, 1990.

In Darkest America: Two Plays, Samuel French (New York, NY), 1991.

I Stand before You Naked (produced in New York City at the American Place Theatre; also see below), Samuel French (New York, NY), 1991.

How Do You Like Your Meat? (also see below), produced in New Haven, CT, 1991.

Twelve Plays (contains *Tone Cluster, The Eclipse, How Do You Like Your Meat?, The Ballad of Love Canal, Under/ ground, Greensleeves, The Key, Friday Night, Black* [also see below], *I Stand before You Naked, The Secret Mirror* [also see below], and *American Holiday*), Plume (New York, NY), 1991.

Black, produced at the Williamstown Summer Festival, 1992.

Gulf War, produced by the Ensemble Studio Theatre, 1992.

The Secret Mirror, produced in Philadelphia at the Annenberg Theatre, 1992.

The Rehearsal, produced by the Ensemble Studio Theatre, 1993.

The Perfectionist (also see below; produced in Princeton, NJ, 1993), published in *The Perfectionist and Other Plays,* Ecco Press (New York, NY), 1995.

The Truth- Teller, Circle Rep Play-in-Progress, 1993.

The Perfectionist and Other Plays, Ecco Press (New York, NY), 1995.

HERE SHE IS!, produced in Philadelphia, 1995.

New Plays, Ontario Review Press (New York, NY), 1998.

EDITOR OR COMPILER

Scenes from American Life: Contemporary Short Fiction, Random House (New York, NY), 1973.

(With Shannon Ravenel) *Best American Short Stories of 1979,* Houghton Mifflin (Boston, MA), 1979.

Night Walks, Ontario Review Press (New York, NY), 1982.

First-Person Singular: Writers on Their Craft, Ontario Review Press (New York, NY), 1983.

(With Boyd Litzinger) *Story: Fictions Past and Present* (textbook), Heath (Lexington, MA), 1985.

(With Daniel Halpern) *Reading the Fights: The Best Writing about the Most Controversial of Sports,* Holt (New York, NY), 1988.

The Best American Essays, Ticknor & Fields (New York, NY), 1991.

(With Daniel Halpern) *The Sophisticated Cat: A Gathering of Stories, Poems, and Miscellaneous Writings about Cats,* Dutton (New York, NY), 1992.

The Oxford Book of American Short Stories, Oxford University Press (New York, NY), 1992.

George Bellows: American Artist, Ecco Press (New York, NY), 1995.

The Essential Dickinson, Ecco Press (New York, NY), 1996.

American Gothic Tales, Plume (New York, NY), 1996.

Story: The Art and the Craft of Narrative Fiction, Norton (New York, NY), 1997.

The Best of H.P. Lovecraft, Ecco Press (New York, NY), 1997.

(With R.V. Cassill) *The Norton Anthology of Contemporary Fiction,* Norton (New York, NY), 1997.

(Also author of introduction) *Telling Stories: An Anthology for Writers,* Norton (New York, NY), 1997.

(With Janet Berliner) *Snapshots: Twentieth-Century Mother-Daughter Fiction,* David R. Godine (Boston, MA), 2000.

The Best American Essays of the Century, Houghton (Boston, MA), 2000.

The Best New American Voices 2003, Harvest (San Diego, CA), 2002.

Uncensored: Views and (Re)views (collection of prose pieces), Ecco/HarperCollins (New York, NY), 2005.

(With Otto Penzler) *The Best American Mystery Stories, 2005,* Houghton (Boston, MA), 2005.

Also author of foreword, *Saving Graces: Images of Women in European Cemeteries,* by David Robinson, Norton (New York, NY), 1995. Contributor of fiction, poetry, and nonfiction to periodicals, including *New York Times Book Review, New York Times Magazine, New York Review of Books, New Yorker, Harper's, Times Literary Supplement, Michigan Quarterly Review, Mademoiselle, Vogue, Hudson Review, Paris Review, Grand Street, Atlantic Monthly, Poetry,* and *Esquire.* Editor, with husband, Raymond Smith, of *Ontario Review.*

Most of Oates's manuscripts, including her ongoing journal, are housed in Special Collections, Syracuse University Library.

ADAPTATIONS: Oates's short story "In the Region of Ice" was made into an Academy Award-winning short feature in the 1970s; "Daisy" was adapted for the stage by Victoria Rue and produced Off-Off-Broadway at the Cubiculo, February, 1980; the story "Where Are You Going, Where Have You Been?" was adapted for the screen as *SmoothTalk,* directed by Joyce Chopra and produced by Martin Rosen, Spectrafilm, 1981; the story "Norman and the Killer" was made into a short feature; an opera based on *Black Water* was developed by the American Music Festival Theatre, Philadelphia, with composer John Duffy, 1996; *Foxfire* was adapted as a motion picture, 1996; *Getting to Know You,* a film based on Oates's 1992 short-story collection *Heat,* was released, 2000; *We Were the Mulvaneys* was adapted as a teleplay for the Lifetime network, 2002. Some of Oates's works have been adapted for sound recordings, including the play *Black* by L.A. Theatre Works, "The Woman Who Laughed," by L.A. Theatre Works, 1994, *American Appetites,* by L.A. Theatre Works, 2000, *The Best American Essays of the Century,* 2001, *Middle Age: A Romance, Blonde,* and *Big Mouth & Ugly Girl.*

SIDELIGHTS: For over four decades, Joyce Carol Oates has produced a large body of work consisting of novels, short stories, criticism, plays, and poetry. Few living writers are as prolific as Oates, whose productivity is the cause of much commentary in the world of letters. Not a year has gone by since the mid-1960s in which she has not published at least one book; occasionally as many as three have been released in a single year. Her contributions to the field of poetry alone would be considered a significant output. "Any assessment of Oates's accomplishments should admit that the sheer quantity and range of her writing is impressive," observed a *Contemporary Novelists* essayist. The essayist added: "Oates is a writer who embarks on ambitious projects; her imagination is protean; her energies and curiosity seemingly boundless; and throughout all her writing, the reader detects her sharp intelligence, spirit of inquiry, and her zeal to tell a story."

A prodigious output means nothing if readers do not buy the books. Oates has established a reputation for consistently interesting work, ranging in genre from stories of upper-class domesticity to horror and psychological crime, but everywhere she reveals "an uncanny knack for understanding middle America, suburbia, and the temper of the times," to quote the *Contemporary Novelists* critic. Violence and victimization often feature in Oates's stories and novels, but existential questions of self-discovery abound as well. In an era of postmodernism and deconstruction, she writes in a classic mode of real people in extreme situations. As one *Publishers Weekly* reviewer put it, "Reading an Oates novel is like becoming a peeping tom, staring without guilt into the bright living rooms and dark hearts of America."

In *Book* Oates said, "I am a chronicler of the American experience. We have been historically a nation prone to violence, and it would be unreal to ignore this fact. What intrigues me is the response to violence: its aftermath in the private lives of women and children in particular." Susan Tekulve in *Book* felt that, like nineteenth-century writer Edgar Allan Poe, "Oates merges Gothic conventions with modern social and political concerns, creating stories that feel at once antique and new. But she also shares Poe's love of dark humor and a good hoax." *New York Times Book Review* correspondent Claire Dederer found the author's novels "hypnotically propulsive, written in the key of *What the Hell Is Going to Happen Next?* Oates pairs big ideas with small details in an ideal fictional balancing act, but the nice thing is that you don't really notice. You're too busy rushing on to the next page."

Oates has not limited herself to any particular genre or even to one literary style. She is equally at ease creating realistic short stories—for which she won an O. Henry Special Award for Continuing Achievement—or parodistic epics, such as the popular Gothic novels *Bellefleur, A Bloodsmoor Romance,* and *Mysteries of Winterthurn,* all published in the 1980s. She attracts readers because of her ability to spin suspenseful tales and to infuse the ordinary with terror. As Oates stated in a *Chicago Tribune Book World* discussion of her themes, "I am concerned with only one thing: the moral and social conditions of my generation." Henry Louis Gates, Jr. wrote in the *Nation* that "a future archeologist equipped with only her *oeuvre* could easily piece together the whole of postwar America."

Born into a working-class family, Oates grew up in rural Erie County, New York, spending a great deal of time at her grandparents' farm. She attended a one-room school as a child and developed a love for reading and writing at an early age. By fifteen, she had completed her first novel and submitted it for publication, only to discover that those who read it found it too depressing for younger readers. Oates graduated from Syracuse University in 1960 and earned her master's degree the following year from the University of Wisconsin. It was at Wisconsin that she met and married her husband, Raymond Joseph Smith, with whom she has edited the *Ontario Review.* The newlyweds moved to Detroit, where Oates taught at the University of Detroit between 1961 and 1967. After one of her stories was anthologized in the *Best American Short Stories,* she decided to devote herself to creative writing.

Urban issues are a major theme in Oates's writing, such as her 1969 novel *them,* which earned a National Book Award in 1970. However, her early work also reveals her preoccupation with fictitious Eden County, New York, a setting based on her childhood recollections. Betty De Ramus is quoted in the *Encyclopedia of World Biography* as saying: "Her days in Detroit did more for Joyce Carol Oates than bring her together with new people—it gave her a tradition to write from, the so-called American Gothic tradition of exaggerated horror and gloom and mysterious and violent incidents."

The novel *them* chronicles three decades, beginning in 1937, in the life of the Wendall family. The novel "is partly made up of 'composite' characters and events, clearly influenced by the disturbances of the long hot summer of 1967," Oates acknowledged. Although regarded as a self-contained work, *them* can also be considered the concluding volume in a trilogy that explores different subgroups of U.S. society. The trilogy includes *A Garden of Earthly Delights,* about the migrant poor, and *Expensive People,* about the suburban rich. The goal of all three novels, as Oates explained in the *Saturday Review,* is to present a cross-section of "unusually sensitive—but hopefully representative—young men and women, who confront the puzzle of American life in different ways and come to different ends."

A story of inescapable life cycles, *them* begins with sixteen-year-old Loretta Botsford Wendall preparing for a Saturday night date. "Anything might happen," she muses innocently, unaware of the impending tragedy. After inviting her date to bed with her, Loretta is awakened by the sound of an explosion. Still half asleep, she realizes that her boyfriend has been shot in the head by her brother. Screaming, she flees the house and runs into the street where she encounters an old acquaintance who is a policeman. Forced to become his wife in return for his help, Loretta embarks on a future of degradation and poverty. The early chapters trace Loretta's flight from her past, her move to Detroit, and her erratic relationships with her husband and other men. The rest of the book focuses on two of Loretta's children, Jules and Maureen, and their struggle to escape a second generation of violence and poverty.

New York Times reviewer John Leonard wrote, "*them,* as literature, is a reimagining, a reinventing of the urban American experience of the last thirty years, a complex and powerful novel that begins with James T. Farrell and ends in a gothic dream; of the 'fire that burns and does its duty.'" Leonard added: "*them* is really about all the private selves, accidents and casualties that add up to a public violence." *Christian Science Monitor* contributor Joanne Leedom also noted the symbolic importance that violence assumes and links it to the characters' search for freedom: "The characters live, love, and almost die in an effort to find freedom and to break out of their patterns. They balance on a precipice and peer over its edge. Though they fear they may fall, they either cannot or will not back away, for it is in the imminence of danger that they find life force. The quest in *them* is for rebirth; the means is violence; the end is merely a realignment of patterns."

Throughout the 1970s, Oates continued her exploration of American people and institutions, combining social analysis with vivid psychological portrayals: *Wonderland* probes the pitfalls of the modern medical community; *Do with Me What You Will* focuses upon the legal profession; *The Assassins: A Book of Hours* attacks the political corruption of Washington, DC; *Son of the Morning* traces the rise and fall of a religious zealot who thinks he's Christ; and *Unholy Loves* examines shallowness and hypocrisy within the academic community. In these and all her fiction, the frustrations and imbalance of individuals become emblematic of U.S. society as a whole.

Oates's short stories of this period exhibit similar themes, and many critics judged her stories to be her finest work. "Her style, technique, and subject matter achieve their strongest effects in this concentrated form, for the extended dialogue, minute detail, and violent action which irritate the reader after hundreds of pages are wonderfully appropriate in short fiction," *Dictionary of Literary Biography* contributor Michael Joslin observed. "Her short stories present the same violence, perversion, and mental derangement as her novels, and are set in similar locations: the rural community of Eden County, the chaotic city of Detroit, and the sprawling malls and developments of modern suburbia."

One of Oates's most popular and representative short stories is "Where Are You Going, Where Have You Been?" Frequently anthologized, the story first appeared in 1966 and is considered by many to be a masterpiece of the short form. It relates the sexual awakening of a teenage girl by a mysterious older man through circumstances that assume strange and menacing proportions; it is a study in the peril that lurks beneath the surface of everyday life.

The protagonist, fifteen-year-old Connie, is a typical teenager who argues with her mother over curfews and hair spray, dreams about romantic love with handsome boys, and regards her older, unmarried sister as a casualty. One Sunday afternoon Connie is left home alone. The afternoon begins ordinarily enough with Connie lying in the sun. "At this point," noted Greg Johnson in *Understanding Joyce Carol Oates,* "the story moves from realism into an allegorical dream-vision. Recalling a recent sexual experience as 'sweet, gentle, the way it was in movies and promised in songs,' Connie opens her eyes and 'hardly knew where she was.' Shaking her head 'as if to get awake,' she feels troubled by the sudden unreality of her surroundings, unaware—though the reader is aware—that she has entered a new and fearsome world."

Shortly afterward, a strange man about thirty years old appears in a battered gold convertible. His name is Arnold Friend. Excited by the prospect but also cautious, Connie dawdles about accepting his invitation to take a ride. Friend becomes more insistent until, suddenly, it becomes clear that Friend has no ordinary ride in mind. He makes no attempt to follow Connie as she flees into the house, but he also makes it clear that the flimsy screen door between them is no obstacle. As Mary Allen explains in *The Necessary Blankness: Women in Major American Fiction of the Sixties,* "his promise not to come in the house after her is more disturbing than a blunt demand might be, for we know he will enter when he is ready."

Oates explores another genre with her Gothic novels *Bellefleur, A Bloodsmoor Romance,* and *Mysteries of Winterthurn.* These novels are an homage to old-fashioned Gothics and were written with "great intelligence and wit," according to Jay Parini. Oates told Parini that she considers the novels "parodistic" because "they're not exactly parodies, because they take the forms they imitate quite seriously." The novels feature many of the stock elements of conventional Gothics, including ghosts, haunted mansions, and mysterious deaths. But the plots are also tied to actual events. "I set out originally to create an elaborate, baroque, barbarous metaphor for the unfathomable mysteries of the human imagination, but soon became involved in very literal events," Oates explained in the *New York Times Book Review.* Her incorporation of real history into imaginary lives lends these tales a depth that is absent from many Gothic novels. Though fanciful in form, they are serious in purpose and examine such sensitive issues as crimes against women, children, and the poor, as well as the role of family history in shaping destiny. For these reasons, Johnson believed that "the gothic elements throughout her fiction, like her use of mystical frameworks, serve the larger function of expanding the thematic scope and suggestiveness of her narratives."

Bellefleur is a five-part novel that encompasses thousands of years and explores what it means to be an American. It is the saga of the Bellefleurs, a rich and rapacious family with a "curse," who settle in the Adirondack Mountains. Interwoven with the family's tale are real people from the nineteenth century, including abolitionist John Brown and Abraham Lincoln, the latter who in the novel fakes his own assassination in order to escape the pressures of public life. In his *New York Times Book Review* assessment of the book, John Gardner wrote that its plot defies easy summarization: "It's too complex—an awesome construction, in itself a work of genius," and summarized it as "a story of the world's changeableness, of time and eternity, space and soul, pride and physicality versus love." *Los Angeles*

Times Book Review contributor Stuart Schoffman called the Bellefleurs' story "an allegory for America: America the vain, the venal, the violent." Wrote *New York Times* critic Leonard: "On one level, *Bellefleur* is Gothic pulp fiction, cleverly consuming itself . . . . On another level, *Bellefleur* is fairy tale and myth, distraught literature . . . . America is serious enough for pulp and myth, Miss Oates seems to be saying, because in our greed we never understood that the Civil War really was a struggle for the possession of our soul." Oates herself has acknowledged that the book was partially conceived as a critique of "the American dream," and critics generally agreed that this dimension enhances the story, transforming the Gothic parody into serious art. Among the most generous assessments was Gardner's; he called *Bellefleur* "a symbolic summation of all this novelist has been doing for twenty-some years, a magnificent piece of daring, a tour de force of imagination and intellect."

In 1990 Oates returned to familiar themes of race and violence in *Because It Is Bitter, and Because It Is My Heart.* The story tells of a bond shared between Jinx Fairchild, a black sixteen-year-old living in the small industrial town of Hammond, New York, and Iris Courtney, a fourteen-year-old white girl who seeks help from Jinx when a town bully begins harassing her. During a scuffle, Jinx inadvertently kills the boy, and the story follows Jinx and Iris as their lives are guided by the consequences of this event. Encompassing the years 1956 to 1963, the book explores the issues of racial segregation and downward mobility as the two characters struggle to overcome their past by escaping from the confines of their hometown. "Iris and Jinx are linked by a powerful bond of secrecy, guilt and, ultimately, a kind of fateful love, which makes for a . . . compelling . . . story about the tragedy of American racism," wrote Howard Frank Mosher in the *Washington Post Book World.*

In *American Appetites,* Oates also explores life among the upper- middle class and finds it just as turbulent and destructive beneath the surface as the overtly violent lives of her poorer, urban characters. Ian and Glynnis McCullough live the illusion of a satisfying life in a sprawling suburban house made of glass, surrounded by a full social life and Glynnis's gourmet cooking. When Glynnis discovers her husband's cancelled check to a young woman they once befriended, however, the cracks in their carefully constructed lifestyle are revealed, leading to a fatal incident. *American Appetites* is a departure for Oates in that it is told in large part as a courtroom drama, but critics seem not as impressed by Oates's attempt at conveying the pretentiousness of this group of people as with her grittier tales of poverty and racism. Hermione Lee, writing in the London *Observer,* felt that the theme of Greek tragedy and its "enquiry into the human soul's control over its destiny . . . ought to be interesting, but it feels too ponderous, too insistent." Likewise, Robert Towers in the *New York Times Book Review* praised Oates's "cast of varied characters whom she makes interesting, . . . places them in scrupulously observed settings, and involves them in a complex action that is expertly sustained," but somehow they produce an effect opposite of the one intended. "We're lulled into a dreamy observation of the often dire events and passions that it records," Towers concluded. Bruce Bawer in a *Washington Post Book World* review found the device of conveying ideas "through intrusive remarks by the narrator and *dramatis personae*" ineffective and "contrived." However, Bawer suggested that although *American Appetites* conveys "no sense of tragedy . . . or of the importance of individual moral responsibility," it does "capture something of the small quiet terror of daily existence, the ever-present sense of the possibility of chaos."

Oates reconstructs a familiar scenario in her award-winning *Black Water,* a 1992 account of a tragic encounter between a powerful U.S. senator and a young woman he meets at a party. While driving to a motel, the drunken senator steers the car off a bridge into the dark water of an East Coast river, and although he is able to escape, he leaves the young woman to drown. The events parallel those of Senator Edward Kennedy's fatal plunge at Chappaquiddick in 1969 that left a young campaign worker dead, but Oates updates the story and sets it twenty years later. Told from the point of view of the drowning woman, the story "portrays an individual fate, born out of the protagonist's character and driven forward by the force of events," according to Richard Bausch in the *New York Times Book Review.* Bausch called Oates's effort "taut, powerfully imagined and beautifully written . . . it continues to haunt us." A tale that explores the sexual power inherent in politics, *Black Water* is not only concerned with the historical event it recalls but also with the sexual-political power dynamics that erupted over Clarence Thomas's nomination for Supreme Court Justice in the early 1990s. It is a fusion of "the instincts of political and erotic conquest," wrote Richard Eder in the *Los Angeles Times Book Review.*

Oates's 1993 novel *Foxfire: Confessions of a Girl Gang* recounts in retrospect the destructive sisterhood of a group of teenage girls in the 1950s. The story is pieced together from former Foxfire gang member Maddy Wirtz's memories and journal and once again takes place in the industrial New York town of Hammond. The gang, led by the very charismatic and very angry Legs Sadovsky, chooses their enemy—men—the force that Legs perceives as responsible for the degradation and ruin of their mothers and friends. The girls celebrate their bond to one another by branding each others' shoulders with tattoos. But as they lash out with sex and violence against teachers and father figures, they "become demons themselves—violent and conniving and exuberant in their victories over the opposite sex," wrote *Los Angeles Times Book Review* contributor Cynthia Kadohata. Although Oates acknowledged to *New York Times Book Review* critic Lynn Karpen that *Foxfire* is her most overtly feminist book, she wanted to show that though "the bond of sisterhood can be very deep and emotionally gratifying," it is a fleeting, fragile bond.

In portraying the destructive escapades of these 1950s teenagers, Oates is "articulating the fantasies of a whole generation," remarked *Times Literary Supplement* contributor Lorna Sage, "putting words to what they didn't quite do." Likening the book to a myth, Oates told Karpen that *Foxfire* "is supposed to be a kind of dialectic between romance and realism." Provoking fights, car chases, and acts of vandalism, the Foxfire gang leaves their mark on the gray town—antics that get Legs sent to reform school, "where she learns that women are sometimes the enemy, too," noted Kadohata. *New York Times Book Review* critic John Crowley likened the novel to a Romantic myth whose hero is more compelling than most of the teen-angst figures of the 1950s. Legs, Crowley noted, is "wholly convincing, racing for her tragic consummation impelled by a finer sensibility and a more thoughtful daring than is usually granted to the tragic male outlaws we love and need."

Sexual violence invades another upstate New York family in Oates's *We Were the Mulvaneys,* published in 1996. In sharp contrast to the isolated, emotionally impoverished family introduced in *First Love,* the Mulvaneys are well-known, high-profile members of their community: Michael Mulvaney is a successful roofing contractor and his wife, Corinne, dabbles at an antiques business. As told by Judd, the youngest of the three promising Mulvaney sons, the family comes unraveled after seventeen-year-old Marianne is raped by a fellow high school student. Ashamed of his daughter's "fall from grace," proud and patriarchal Michael banishes her to the home of a relative, an action that drives him to the drunken state that results in the loss of home and job. Meanwhile, other family members succumb to their individual demons. The saga of a family's downfall is uplifted by more positive changes a decade later, which come as a relief to readers who identify with the Mulvaneys as compelling representatives of the contemporary American middle class.

Although, as with much of her fiction, Oates has denied any autobiographical basis for *We Were the Mulvaneys* other than a familiarity with the northern New York setting and once owning a cat answering to the description of the title family's household pet, the creative process involved in creating the novel is almost as evocative as personal experience. "Writing a long novel is very emotionally involving," Oates told Thomas J. Brady in the *Philadelphia Inquirer.* "I'm just emotionally stunned for a long time after writing one." *We Were the Mulvaneys,* which at 454 pages in length qualifies as "long," took many months of note-taking, followed by ten months of writing, according to its author. After being chosen by Oprah Winfrey as one of her book club editions, the novel became the first of Oates's works to top the *New York Times* bestseller list.

Throughout her prolific writing career Oates has distributed her vast creative and emotional energies between several projects at once, simultaneously producing novels, stories, verse, and essays, among other writings. In her 1995 horror novel, *Zombie,* she seductively draws readers into the mind of a serial killer on the order of Jeffrey Dahmer. While straying from fact far enough to avoid the more heinous aspects of Dahmer-like acts, Oates plugs readers directly into the reality of her fictitious protagonist, Quentin P., who "exists in a haze of fantasies blurred by drugs and alcohol and by his inherent mental condition of violent and frenzied desires, thoughts and obsessions," according to *New York Times Book Review* critic Steven Marcus. Through the twisted experimentation on young men (involving, among other things, an ice pick) that Quentin hopes will enable him to create a zombie-like companion who will remain loyal to him forever, Oates "is certain to shock and surely to offend many readers," warned *Tribune Books* critic James Idema, "but there could be no gentler way to tell the story she obviously was compelled to tell."

Within her nonfiction writing, Oates's foray into sports philosophy resulted in the book-length essay *On Boxing,* which led to at least one television appearance as a commentator for the sport. She also submitted a mystery novel to a publisher under a pseudonym and had the thrill of having it accepted before word leaked out that it was Oates's creation. Inspired by her husband's name, in 1988 Oates published the novel *Lives of the Twins* under the name Rosamond Smith. "I wanted a fresh reading; I wanted to escape from my own identity," Linda Wolfe quoted Oates as saying in the *New York Times Book Review.* She would use the Smith pseudonym again for several more mystery novels, including *Soul/Mate,* a story about a lovesick psychokiller, *Nemesis,* another mystery concerning aberrational academics, and *Snake Eyes,* a tale of a tattooed psychopathic artist.

Oates's 1997 novel *Man Crazy* is a reverse image of *Zombie;* it tells the first-person story of a "pathological serial victim," Ingrid Boone, who through a rag-tag childhood, a promiscuous and drugged-out adolescence, and a stint with a satanic motorcycle cult, has her personal identity nearly destroyed. *New York Review of Books* critic A. O. Scott commented that Oates "continually seeks out those places in our social, familial and personal lives where love and cruelty intersect . . . . Oates is clearly interested in exploring the boundary between a world where cruelty lurks below the surface of daily life and one in which daily life consists of overt and constant brutality."

Published in 2000, one of Oates's most successful novels to date is *Blonde,* a fictional re-working of the life of Marilyn Monroe. Oates told a writer at *Publishers Weekly* that, while she was not intent upon producing another historical document on the tragic star, she did want to show "what she was like from the inside." According to some critics, Oates was successful in her endeavor. *Booklist* contributor Donna Seaman commented that the author "liberates the real woman behind the mythological creature called Marilyn Monroe." A *Publishers Weekly* reviewer found the novel "dramatic, provocative and unsettlingly suggestive," adding that Oates "creates a striking and poignant portrait of the mythic star and the society that made and failed her." In *World Literature Today,* Rita D. Jacobs concluded that *Blonde* "makes the reader feel extraordinarily empathetic toward the character Marilyn Monroe and her longing for acceptance and a home of her own."

Oates's first published works were short stories, and she has continued to pen them throughout her career. Her collections of short fiction alone amount to more work than many writers finish in a lifetime. A *Publishers Weekly* reviewer remarked that with her short works Oates has "established herself as the nation's literary Weegee, prowling the mean streets of the American mind and returning with gloriously lurid takes on our midnight obsessions." Whether in macabre horror stories such as those in *The Collector of Hearts: New Tales of the Grotesque* or in realistic works such as those found in *Faithless: Tales of Transgression,* Oates offers "a map of the mind's dark places," wrote *New York Times Book Review* contributor Margot Livesey. *Orlando Sentinel* correspondent Mary Ann Horne stated that in *Faithless,* Oates "does what she does best . . . delving into the dark areas of ordinary consciousness, bringing back startling images from the undercurrent of modern fears and secrets."

Oates uses secrets as a diving board for her exploration of a small town's psyche in *Middle Age: A Romance,* published in 2001. The book opens with the drowning death of sculptor Adam Brandt as he tries to rescue a child. His death becomes a catalyst for the residents of Salthill-on-Hudson, New York. Adam's former lovers begin to investigate his life, dissatisfied husbands become inspired to finally leave, and singles find their soul mates. In *Booklist,* Carol Haggas approved of the title: "Few caught in the throes of middle age would categorize it as 'romantic,' yet what makes Oates's characters romantic is how well they fare on their journeys of personal reinvention and whether they, and the reader, enjoy the trip." While the book received some criticism for lack of a linear plot, *New York Times* critic Claire Dederer viewed that as a strength of Oates's writing. "Naked of a compelling plot, in a strange sense Oates's remarkable ability is clearer than ever. We have time to notice the careful construction of theme, the attention to a cohesive philosophy, the resonant repetition of detail." More than one reviewer noted that the ending of *Middle Age* proves more redemptive than most of Oates's previous fictions. As Beth Kephart summarized in *Book,* "There is light, a lot of it, at the end of this long book." A *Publishers Weekly* contributor concluded it is "reminiscent of her powerful *Black Water,* but equipped with a happy ending, Oates's latest once more confirms her mastery of the form." *St. Louis Post-Dispatch* reviewer Lee Ann Sandweiss likewise noted that *Middle Age* is "Oates's most compassionate and life-affirming work to date . . . . This novel establishes, beyond any doubt, that Joyce Carol Oates is not only [one of] America's most prolific writers but also one of our most gifted."

From the introspection of middle age, Oates moved to the self-discovery of early adulthood in *I'll Take You There.* Called her most autobiographical novel to date, the book deals with an unnamed protagonist as she comes of age at Syracuse University in the early 1960s. Like Oates, "Anellia" (as she calls herself) is raised on a farm in western New York state and is the first in her family to go to college. Anellia cloaks herself in guilt and low self-esteem, bequeathed to her by her brothers and father. They blame her for her mother's death from cancer developed shortly after Anellia was born. Desperate for a mother figure and female companionship, the poor Anellia joins a snobby, bigoted sorority where she seems to be singled out for torment because of her finances and lack of grooming. She feels special pain from the antagonistic relationship she has with the sorority's British housemother, Mrs. Thayer. She uncovers Mrs. Thayer's excessive drinking and both of them are forced to leave the house, humiliated.

Still desperate for love and affection, she starts an affair with African-American philosophy graduate student Vernon Matheius. Vernon is intent on ignoring the civil rights struggles of the times, believing that philosophy is his personal salvation. Their relationship is categorized by discord and Anellia also snoops through his life and uncovers the fact that he has a wife and children he is denying. As Anellia deals with the fallout from her discovery and her separation from Vernon, she receives word that her father, who she thought dead, is dying in Utah. She travels west to be with him at his bedside, hoping to gain a sense of familial kinship. In a twist of irony, she is not allowed to look directly at her father, but steals a glimpse of him through a mirror, which kills him from distress when he sees her.

Critics and fans described *I'll Take You There* as a hallmark of Oates's consistent excellence in style, form, and theme. *Los Angeles Times Book Review* critic Stanley Crouch praised Oates's "masterful strength of the form, the improvisational attitude toward sentence structure and the foreshadowing, as well as the deft use of motifs." Even perceived weaknesses by some critics are regarded by others as quintessential Oatesian mechanics. In Rachel Collins's review for *Library Journal,* she questioned the heavy use of characterization and psychological backgrounding that takes place in about the first 100 pages. A *Publisher's Weekly* reviewer reflected that "Oates's fans will be pleased by the usual care with which she goes about constructing the psychology of Anellia and Vernon." Collins went on to call the book "a bit formulaic," noting that the romance between Anellia and Vernon lacks "the intense sexual energy present in Oates's other works." *Booklist* contributor Donna Seaman wrote that the scenes with Anellia and Vernon are "intense and increasingly psychotic" and Oates's "eroticism verges on the macabre and the masochistic." Vicky Hutchings in the *New Statesman* concluded the book is neither "depressing nor dull, but full of edgy writing as well as mordant wit."

Published in 2003, *The Tattooed Girl* is the story of thirty-nine-year-old writer Joshua Seigl, who has been diagnosed with a debilitating nerve condition. In need of an assistant, he interviews and rejects a number of graduate students, and impulsively hires the vacuous Alma Busch. While it seems like an act of charity, Seigl is increasingly patronizing to Alma, thinking that he has "rescued" her. Alma is described as dim-witted and slow, suffering from a lack of self-esteem and scarred by past sexual trauma, which resulted in the crude tattoo on her face. Seigl, of course, is unaware of Alma's anti-Semitism, which is born of her disfigurement and fueled by her sadistic waiter boyfriend, Dmitri Meatte. As Seigl's health deteriorates, Alma gains psychological strength to sabotage Seigl's health, finances, and mental well-being and eventually hatches a plan to take his life.

While a *Kirkus Reviews* contributor called *The Tattooed Girl* "better- than-average Oates," some reviewers found the characterization of Seigl, Alma, and Dmitri inconsistent. *New York Times* writer Michiko Kakutani said, "The novel gets off to a subtle and interesting start . . . . Oates's keen eye for psychological detail seems to be fully engaged in these pages." Yet she argued that "the attention to emotional detail evinced in the novel's opening pages—in which she limned Seigl's fears of mortality and his anxieties about his family and work—evaporates by the middle of the book, replaced by horror-movie plots and cartoony characters." In the *New York Times Book Review* Sophie Harrison noted that Alma, Seigl, and Dmitri's actions "contradict their given characters, and the irony doesn't always feel intentional." The *Kirkus Reviews* contributor observed that "Oates is onto something with the bruised, malleable figure of Alma," but the secondary figures of Dmitri and Seigl's hypomaniac sister Jet "have nothing like its principal's realness." Even so, Oates continued to receive praise for her style, including a review in *Booklist* which described *The Tattooed Girl* as a "mesmerizing, disturbing tale" told with "her usual cadenced grace."

Also published in 2003 was Oates's second book for young adult readers, *Small Avalanches and Other Stories,* in which she reprises some of her previously published short stories for adults as well as new material. The twelve stories all deal with young people taking risks and dealing with their consequences. As with her adult fiction, Oates maintains her dark tone. *School Library Journal* reviewer Allison Follos observed, "The stories have a slow, deliberate, and unsettling current." James Neal Webb on the *BookPage* Web site echoed that "Oates's trademark is her ability to tap, uncontrived, into the danger that's implicit in everyday life."

In 2004 Oates began publishing suspense novels under a new pseudonym. Writing as Lauren Kelly, Oates has been true to her prolific nature. Indeed, the first three novels published under the moniker were released in less than two years. In the first novel, *Take Me, Take Me with You,* research assistant Lara Quade is mysteriously sent a ticket to a concert. When she redeems the ticket, she finds that her seatmate, Zedrick Dewe is there under identical circumstances. As the story progresses, Lara and Zed's relationship begins to grow, and they eventually discover that their pasts are linked. Reviewing the novel for *Library Journal,* Stacy Alesi called the story "haunting and beautifully written." Interestingly, a *Kirkus Reviews* critic used similar terms to describe the second Kelly novel, *The Stolen Heart.* The critic stated that the novel is "a haunting portrait of grief and psychological fragility." *The Stolen Heart* begins when Merilee Graf is twenty-six years old. When Merilee was ten years old, one of her classmates vanished and was never found. Sixteen years later, Merilee's chance encounter with the missing girl's brother coincides with the death of her own father. Merilee's recollections of the disappearance are then triggered by these events. Although a *Publishers Weekly* contributor thought the story is "overwrought," they also noted that it is "oddly compelling."

In addition to her fiction and poetry, Oates lays claim to a large body of critical essays, ranging in subject matter from literature and politics to sports and quality of life. Although she has said that she does not write quickly, she also has admitted to a driving discipline that keeps her at her desk for long hours. In an era of computers, she continues to write her first drafts in longhand and then to type them on conventional typewriters. She told *Writer:* "Writing to me is very instinctive and natural. It has something to do with my desire to memorialize what I know of the world. The act of writing is a kind of description of an inward or spiritual reality that is otherwise inaccessible. I love transcribing this; there's a kind of passion to it."

BIOGRAPHICAL AND CRITICAL SOURCES:

BOOKS

Allen, Mary, *The Necessary Blankness: Women in Major American Fiction of the Sixties,* University of Illinois Press (Champaign, IL), 1974.

Authors and Artists for Young Adults, Gale (Detroit, MI), Volume 15, 1987, Volume 52, 2003.

Beacham's Guide to Literature for Young Adults, Volume 11, Gale (Detroit, MI).

Bender, Eileen, *Joyce Carol Oates,* Indiana University Press (Bloomington, IN), 1987.

Bloom, Harold, editor, *Modern Critical Views: Joyce Carol Oates,* Chelsea House (New York, NY), 1987.

Concise Dictionary of American Literary Biography: Broadening Views, 1968-1988, Gale (Detroit, MI), 1989.

Contemporary Literary Criticism, Gale (Detroit, MI), Volume 1, 1973, Volume 2, 1974, Volume 3, 1975, Volume 6, 1976, Volume 9, 1978, Volume 11, 1979, Volume 15, 1980, Volume 19, 1981, Volume 33, 1985, Volume 52, 1989, Volume 108, 1998.

Contemporary Novelists, St. James Press (Detroit, MI), 2001.

Contemporary Poets, St. James Press (Detroit, MI), 1996.

Contemporary Popular Writers, St. James Press (Detroit, MI), 1997.

Daly, Brenda O., *Lavish Self- Divisions: The Novels of Joyce Carol Oates,* University Press of Mississippi (Jackson, MS), 1996.

Dictionary of Literary Biography, Gale (Detroit, MI), Volume 2: *American Novelists since World War II,* 1978, Volume 5: *American Poets since World War II,* 1980, Volume 130, *American Short Story Writers since World War II,* 1993.

Dictionary of Literary Biography Yearbook: 1981, Gale (Detroit, MI), 1982.

Encyclopedia of World Biography, 2nd edition, Gale (Detroit, MI), 1998.

Encyclopedia of World Literature in the Twentieth Century, St. James Press (Detroit, MI), 1999.

Feminist Writers, St. James Press (Detroit, MI), 1996.

Johnson, Greg, *Understanding Joyce Carol Oates,* University of South Carolina Press (Columbia, SC), 1987.

Johnson, Greg, *Joyce Carol Oates: A Study of the Short Fiction,* Twayne (Boston, MA), 1994.

Johnson, Greg, *Invisible Writer: A Biography of Joyce Carol Oates,* Dutton (New York, NY), 1998.

Mayer, Sigrid, and Martha Hanscom, *The Reception of Joyce Carol Oates's and Gabriele Wohlmann's Short Fiction,* Camden House (Columbia, SC), 1998.

Modern American Literature, 5th edition, St. James Press (Detroit, MI), 1997.

Reference Guide to American Literature, 4th edition, St. James Press (Detroit, MI), 1999.

Reference Guide to Short Fiction, 2nd edition, St. James Press (Detroit, MI), 1999.

St. James Guide to Horror, Ghost, and Gothic Writers, St. James Press (Detroit, MI), 1998.

Short Story Criticism, Volume 6, Gale (Detroit, MI), 1990.

Twentieth-Century Culture: American Culture after World War II, Gale (Detroit, MI), 1994.

Twentieth-Century Romance and Historical Writers, 2nd edition, St. James Press (Detroit, MI), 1990.

Wagner, Linda W., editor, *Joyce Carol Oates: The Critical Reception,* G.K. Hall (Boston, MA), 1979.

Waller, G.F., *Dreaming America: Obsession and Transcendence in the Fiction of Joyce Carol Oates,* Louisiana State University Press (Baton Rouge, LA), 1979.

Watanabe, Nancy Ann, *Love Eclipsed: Joyce Carol Oates's Faustian Moral Vision,* University Press of America (Lanham, MD), 1997.

PERIODICALS

America, March 16, 1996, p. 18; November 17, 2003, Richard Fusco, review of *A Garden of Earthly Delights,* p. 19.

American Literature, September, 1997, p. 642.

Atlanta Journal- Constitution, December 16, 2001, Michael Upchurch, "*Middle Age* Full of Lingering Expectations," p. C5.

Atlantic Monthly, October, 1969; December, 1973; September, 1997, p. 118.

Book, March, 2001, Susan Tekulve, review of *Faithless: Tales of Transgression,* p. 70; May, 2001, Kristin Kloberdanz, "Joyce Carol Oates," p. 42; November-December, 2001, Beth Kephart, review of *Middle Age: A Romance,* p. 65.

Booklist, April 15, 1998, Brad Hooper, review of *My Heart Laid Bare,* p. 1357; July, 1999, Donna Seaman, review of *Where I've Been, and Where I'm Going: Essays, Reviews, and Prose,* p. 1917; January 1, 2000, Donna Seaman, review of *Blonde,* p. 835; February 1, 2001, Donna Seaman, review of *Faithless,* p. 1020; July, 2001, Carol Haggas, review of *Middle Age,* p. 1952; October 1, 2001, Donna Seaman, review of *Beasts,* p. 300; August, 2002, Donna Seaman, review of *I'll Take You There,* p. 1886; March 1, 2003, Joanne Wilkenson, review of *The Tattooed Girl,* p.1108

Chicago Tribune Book World, September 30, 1979; July 27, 1980; January 11, 1981; August 16, 1981; February 26, 1984; August 12, 1984; January 13, 1985; February 23, 1986.

Choice, March, 1997, p. 1160.

Christian Century, January 13, 2004, p. 7.

Christian Science Monitor, October 30, 1969.

Detroit News, January 15, 1964; May 21, 1972; November 13, 1977; July 27, 1980; October 11, 1981; October 17, 19982; March 11, 1984; February 3, 1985.

Entertainment Weekly, June 20, 2003, review of *The Tattooed Girl,* p. 78; January 9, 2004, Gillian Flynn, review of *Rape: A Love Story,* p. 83.

Globe and Mail (Toronto, Ontario, Canada), February 11, 1984; April 25, 1987.

Kirkus Reviews, December 15, 2002, review of *I'll Take You There,* p.1855; April 1, 2003, review of *The Tattooed Girl,* p. 501; March 15, 2004, review of *Take Me, Take Me with You,* p. 244; May 15, 2005, review of *The Stolen Heart,* p. 559; November 1, 2005, review of *The Female of the Species: Tales of Mystery and Suspense,* p. 1165; February 15, 2006, review of *High Lonesome: New & Selected Stories, 1966-2006,* p. 153.

Library Journal, August 1996, p. 113; August, 1999, Nancy Patterson Shires, review of *Where I've Been, and Where I'm Going,* p. 89; August, 2000, Mary Jones, review of *The Best American Essays of the Century,* p. 102; April 1, 2001, Caroline Mann, review of *The Barrens,* p. 133; July, 2001, Rebecca Bollen, review of *Faithless,* p. 74; August, 2001, Josh Cohen, review of *Middle Age,* p. 164; September 15, 2001, Rochelle Ratner, review of *We Were the Mulvaneys,* p. 130; October 1, 2001, review of *Beasts,* p. 143; September 15, 2002, Rachel Collins, review of *I'll Take You There,* p. 93; March 15, 2004, Stacy Alesi, review of *Take Me, Take Me with You,* p. 106.

Los Angeles Times, April 2, 1981; February 18, 1986; October 13, 1986; November 7, 1986; August 7, 1987; January 31, 1988; July 21, 1988; December 9, 1988; April 16, 1990; April 15, 2003, Josh Cohen, review of *The Tattooed Girl,* p. 126; October 1, 2003, Marianne Orme, review of *The Faith of a Writer: Life, Craft, Art,* p. 75; January, 2004, Josh Cohen, review of *Rape,* p. 159; February 1, 2004, Joshua Cohen, review of *I Am No One You Know,* p. 126; March 1, 2004, Rochelle Ratner, review of *The Tattooed Girl,* p. 126.

Los Angeles Times Book Review, August 12, 1980; September 19, 1982; January 8, 1984; September 30, 1984; January 6, 1985; March 1, 1987; August 16, 1987; January 15, 1989; May 10, 1992; August 22, 1993; October 22, 1995, p. 6; January 26, 2003, Stanley Crouch, "Picking Up Where Faulkner Left Off," p. 3.

Nation, July 2, 1990, pp. 27-29.

New Leader, January-February, 2002, Brooke Allen, review of *Beasts,* p. 28.

Newsmakers, Issue 4, 2000.

New Statesman, January 27, 2003, Vicky Hutchings, review of *I'll Take You There,* p. 55; January 19, 2004, Helena Echlin, review of *The Tattooed Girl,* p. 55.

Newsweek, September 29, 1969; March 23, 1970; August 17, 1981; September 20, 1982; February 6, 1984; January 21, 1985; March 24, 1986; March 9, 1987; August 17, 1987; April 10, 2000, David Gates, "Goodbye, Norma Jeane," p. 76.

New Yorker, December 6, 1969; October 15, 1973; October 5, 1981; September 27, 1982; February 27, 1984.

New York Review of Books, December 17, 1964; January 2, 1969; October 21, 1971; January 24, 1974; October 21, 1982; August 16, 1990; December 21, 1995, p. 32; September 15, 1996, p. 11; September 21, 1997, p. 10.

New York Times, September 5, 1967; December 7, 1968; October 1, 1969; October 16, 1971; June 12, 1972; October 15, 1973; July 20, 1980; August 6, 1981; September 18, 1982; February 10, 1984; January 10, 1985; February 20, 1986; February 10, 1987; March 2, 1987; March 4, 1987; August 10, 1987; April 23, 1988; December 21, 1988; March 30, 1990; August 29, 2003, Michiko Kakutani, "Child of Hell Is Plague on His House."

New York Times Book Review, November 10, 1963; October 25, 1964; September 10, 1967; November 3, 1968; September 28, 1969; October 25, 1970; October 24, 1971; July 9, 1972; April 1, 1973; October 14, 1973; August 31, 1975; November 26, 1978; April 29, 1979; July 15, 1979; October 7, 1979; July 20, 1980; January 4, 1981; March 29, 1981; August 16, 1981; July 11, 1982; September 5, 1982; February 12, 1984; August 5, 1984; January 20, 1985; August 11, 1985; March 2, 1986; October 5, 1986; March 15, 1987; August 16, 1987; January 3, 1988; October 2, 1988; January 1, 1989; January 15, 1989; June 4, 1989, p. 16; May 10, 1992; August 15, 1993; February 13, 1994, p. 34; October 16, 1994, p. 7; October 8, 1995, p. 13; March 10, 1996, p. 7; March 7, 1999, Margot Livesey, "Jellyfish for Dinner Again?," p. 29; September 16, 2001, Claire Dederer, "AARP Recruits," p. 7; January 6, 2002, Amy Benfer, review of *Beasts,* p. 16; May 19, 2002, Lois Metzger, review of *Big Mouth & Ugly Girl,* p. 32; July 13, 2003, Sophie Harrison, "Now I Have Saved Her," p.15.

New York Times Magazine, July 27, 1980; January 3, 1988.

Observer (London, England), August 27, 1989.

Orlando Sentinel, June 27, 2001, Mary Ann Horne, review of *Faithless.*

Philadelphia Inquirer, January 26, 1997.

PR Newswire, April 27, 2003, "PNC Honors Five Giants in the Arts, Science and Public Service."

Publishers Weekly, June 24, 1996, p. 44; August 5, 1996, p. 430; April 20, 1998, review of *My Heart Laid Bare,* p. 45; May 17, 1999, review of *Broke Heart Blues,* p. 55; June 28, 1999, review of *Where I've Been, and Where I'm Going,* p. 68; February 14, 2000, review of *Blonde,* p. 171, "PW Talks with Joyce Carol Oates," p. 172; June 5, 2000, review of *Blonde,* p. 61; January 29, 2001, review of *Faithless,* p. 65; March 26, 2001, review of *The Barrens,* p. 60; August 13, 2001, review of *Middle Age,* p. 284; October 22, 2001, review of *Beasts,* p. 43; April 22, 2002, review of *Big Mouth & Ugly Girl,* p. 71; August 26, 2002, Rachel Collins, review of *I'll Take you There,* p. 93; September 30, 2002, review of *Best New American Voices 2003,* p. 51; February 10, 2003, review of *Small Avalanches and Other Stories,* p. 189; April 21, 2003, review of *The Tattooed Girl,* p. 36; September 15, 2003, Kate Pavao, "PW Talks with Joyce Carol Oates," p. 65, and review of *Freaky Green Eyes,* p. 66; November 24, 2003, review of *Rape,* p. 41; February 2, 2004, review of *I Am No One You Know,* p. 57; May 30, 2005, review of *The Stolen Heart,* p. 40; September 19, 2005, review of *The Female of the Species,* p. 40.

St. Louis Post- Dispatch, September 9, 2001, Lee Ann Sandweiss, "Oates's Latest Is Absorbing, Life-Affirming," p. H10.

Saturday Review, October 26, 1963; November 28, 1964; August 5, 1967; October 26, 1968; November 22, 1969; October 24, 1970; June 10, 1972; November 4, 1972; August, 1981; March-April, 1985.

School Library Journal, July, 2003, Allison Follos, review of *Small Avalanches and Other Stories,* p. 134; April, 2005, Courtney Lewis, review of *Sexy,* p. 138.

Spectator, October 29, 2005, Diana Hendry, review of *Missing Mom,* p. 42.

Time, January 3, 1964; November 1, 1968; October 26, 1970; August 25, 1980; August 17,1981; October 4, 1982; February 23, 1987; August 31, 1987; January 9, 1989; April 17, 2000, Paul Gray, "The Anatomy of an Icon," p. 82.

Times Literary Supplement, June 4, 1970; January 11, 1974; September 12, 1980; March 20, 1981; January 29, 1982; January 28, 1983; July 20, 1984; March 22, 1985; October 18, 1985; January 16, 1987; December 18, 1987; February 14, 1988; September 15, 1989; August 13, 1993, p. 19.

Tribune Books (Chicago, IL), March 1, 1987; July 19, 1987; April 18, 1988; December 18, 1988; April 15, 1990; March 10, 1996; November 5, 1996, pp. 3, 5.

Washington Post Book World, February 22, 1981; August 16, 1981; September 30, 1984; January 6, 1985; February 23, 1986; November 30, 1986; March 8, 1987; January 8, 1989; April 8, 1990.

World Literature Today, autumn, 1996, pp. 959-960; winter, 2001, Rita D. Jacobs, review of *Blonde,* p. 115; summer, 2003, James Knudson, review of *Faithless,* p. 92.

Writer, October, 2001, "Joyce Carol Oates," p. 66; January, 2004, Chuck Leddy, review of *The Faith of a Writer,* p. 45.

Writer's Digest, February, 2001, Katie Struckel, "Find Identity with Joyce Carol Oates," p. 22.

ONLINE

BookPage, http://www.bookpage.com/ (September 1, 2003), James Neal Webb, review of *Small Avalanches and Other Stories.*

* * *

OATES, Stephen B. 1936-
(Stephen Baery Oates)

PERSONAL: Born January 5, 1936, in Pampa, TX; son of Steve Theodore and Florence (Baer) Oates; married Marie Philips; children (from previous marriage): Gregory Allen, Stephanie. *Education:* University of Texas—Austin, B.A. (magna cum laude), 1958, M.A., 1960, Ph.D., 1969.

ADDRESSES: Home—10 Bridle Path, Amherst, MA 01002-1632. *Office*—Department of History, University of Massachusetts, Amherst, MA 01003. *E-mail*—sboates@history.umass.edu.

CAREER: Arlington State College (now University of Texas—Arlington), instructor, 1964-67, assistant professor of history, 1967-68; University of Massachusetts, Amherst, assistant professor, 1968-70, associate professor, 1970-71, professor of history, 1971-80, adjunct professor of English, 1980-85, Paul Murray Kendall Professor of Biography, 1985-98, professor emeritus, 1998—. Guest lecturer at numerous colleges, universities, societies, and associations throughout the United States; has made numerous guest appearances on radio and television programs. Honorary member of board of directors, Abraham Lincoln Association. American history and biography consultant to various commercial and university presses, and consultant to National Endowment for the Humanities for various book, museum, television, and motion-picture projects.

MEMBER: Society of American Historians, American Antiquarian Society, Texas Institute of Letters, Phi Beta Kappa.

AWARDS, HONORS: Texas State Historical Association fellow, 1968; Texas Institute of Letters fellow, 1969; Guggenheim fellow, 1972; Chancellor's Medal for Outstanding Scholarship, University of Massachusetts, 1976; Christopher Award, 1977, and Barondess/Lincoln Award, New York Civil War Round Table, 1978, both for *With Malice toward None: The Life of Abraham Lincoln;* National Endowment for the Humanities senior summer fellow, 1978; Distinguished Teaching Award, University of Massachusetts, 1981; Litt.D., Lincoln College, 1981; graduate faculty fellowship, University of Massachusetts, 1981-82; Christopher Award, 1982, Robert F. Kennedy Memorial Book Award, 1983, and Chancellor's Certificate of Recognition, University of Massachusetts, 1983, all for *Let the Trumpet Sound: The Life of Martin Luther King, Jr.;* Institute for Advanced Studies in the Humanities fellow, 1984; Author's Award for best article of the year, *Civil War Times Illustrated,* 1984, for "Abraham Lincoln: Man and Myth"; University of Massachusetts Presidential Writers Award, 1985; Master Teacher Award, University of Hartford, 1985; Silver Medal winner and semifinalist in national professor of the year competition, Council for Advancement and Support of Education, 1986 and 1987; Kidger Award, New England History Teachers Association, 1992; Nevins-Freeman Award, Chicago Civil War Round Table, 1993.

WRITINGS:

Confederate Cavalry West of the River, University of Texas Press (Austin, TX), 1961.

(Editor and author of introduction and commentary) John Salmon Ford, *Rip Ford's Texas,* University of Texas Press (Austin, TX), 1963, reprinted, 1987.

(General editor and contributor) *The Republic of Texas,* American West Publishing (Palo Alto, CA), 1968.

Visions of Glory: Texas on the Southwestern Frontier, University of Oklahoma Press (Norman, OK), 1970.

To Purge This Land with Blood: A Biography of John Brown, Harper (New York, NY), 1970, revised 2nd edition, University of Massachusetts Press (Amherst, MA), 1984.

(Editor) *Portrait of America,* Volume 1: *From the European Discovery to the End of Reconstruction,* Volume 2: *From Reconstruction to the Present,* Houghton Mifflin (Boston, MA), 1973, 8th edition (with Charles J. Enrico), 2003.

The Fires of Jubilee: Nat Turner's Fierce Rebellion, Harper & Row (New York, NY), 1975.

With Malice toward None: The Life of Abraham Lincoln, Harper & Row (New York, NY), 1977, reprinted, 1994.

Our Fiery Trial: Abraham Lincoln, John Brown, and the Civil War Era, University of Massachusetts Press (Amherst, MA), 1979.

Let the Trumpet Sound: The Life of Martin Luther King, Jr., Harper & Row (New York, NY), 1982.

Abraham Lincoln: The Man behind the Myths, Harper & Row (New York, NY), 1984.

(Editor, author of prologue, and contributor) *Biography as High Adventure: Life-Writers Speak on Their Art,* University of Massachusetts Press (Amherst, MA), 1986.

William Faulkner: The Man and the Artist; A Biography, Harper & Row (New York, NY), 1987.

A Woman of Valor: Clara Barton and the Civil War, Free Press (New York, NY), 1994.

The Approaching Fury: Voices of the Storm, 1820-1861, HarperCollins (New York, NY), 1997.

The Whirlwind of War: Voices of the Storm, 1861-1865, HarperCollins (New York, NY), 1998.

Editor, with Paul Mariani, of "Commonwealth Classics in Biography" series for University of Massachusetts Press, beginning 1986. Contributor to numerous periodicals, including *American Heritage, American History Illustrated, American West, Civil War History, Timeline, Nation, American History Review, Journal of American History,* and *Southwestern Historical Quarterly.*

SIDELIGHTS: Distinguished biographer and educator Stephen B. Oates links his lifelong dual interests in history and literature not only by assuming professorial posts in both disciplines, but by crafting biographies of historical and literary figures as well; and as professor emeritus of history at the University of Massachusetts, he still guides others in that art. "Inevitably," Oates recalled in *Biography as High Adventure: Life—Writers Speak on Their Art,* "biography appealed to me as the form in which I wanted to write about the past, because the best biography—pure biography—was a storytelling art that brought people alive again, eliciting from the coldness of fact 'the warmth of a life being lived,' as Paul Murray Kendall expressed it."

Oates is especially recognized for what he refers to in *Biography as High Adventure* as "a biographical quartet on the Civil War era and its century-old legacies, a quartet that sought to humanize the monstrous moral paradox of slavery and racial oppression in a land based on the ideals of the Declaration of Independence." In these four biographies—*To Purge This Land with Blood: A Biography of John Brown, The Fires of Jubilee: Nat Turner's Fierce Rebellion, With Malice toward None: The Life of Abraham Lincoln,* and *Let the Trumpet Sound: The Life of Martin Luther King, Jr.*—Oates examines the lives of men profoundly committed to the struggle for equality. "All four were driven, visionary men, all were caught up in the issues of slavery and race, and all devised their own solutions to those inflammable problems," writes Oates. "And all perished, too, in the conflicts and hostilities that surrounded the quest for equality in their country." A former civil rights activist himself, Oates considers these men "martyrs of our racial hatred," according to Genevieve Stuttaford in *Publishers Weekly,* "martyrs of what he describes as the hateful thing they hated."

John Brown, the subject of *To Purge This Land with Blood,* the first book in Oates's biographical quartet, was a "white northerner who hated slavery from the outside," explains Oates in *Biography as High Adventure.* Resolved to forcefully abolish slavery by leading an armed insurrection, Brown seized the government arsenal in Harpers Ferry, Virginia, in 1859, but was ultimately captured, tried, and executed. In the *Saturday Review,* T. Harry Williams called the book "a major work, based on research in a wide variety of sources . . . that treats in detail Brown's career before he went to Kansas and his actions in that territory, as well as the blazing climax at Harpers Ferry." Noting in the *New York Times Book Review* that "Brown's activities and motivations . . . have been the subject of heated historiographical debate," Eric Foner observed that unlike previous biographers who have set out "either to vindicate or demolish" Brown's legend as an American folk hero, thereby losing "sight of the man himself," Oates neither indicts nor eulogizes Brown. "Brown's life was filled with drama," noted Foner, "and Oates tells his story in a manner so engrossing that the book reads like a novel, despite the fact that it is extensively documented and researched."

Nat Turner, the subject of Oates's *The Fires of Jubilee,* was a "victim of human bondage, a brilliant and brooding slave preacher blocked from his potential by an impregnable wall," writes Oates in *Biography as High Adventure.* Oates adds that he "tried to narrate Nat's story as graphically and as accurately" as he could, hoping to "convey how the insurrection rocked the South to its foundations and pointed the way to civil war thirty years later." Assessed as "vivid and convincing" by a *Publishers Weekly* contributor, *The Fires of Jubilee* "presents as complete a narrative account of this affair as we are likely to get," remarked Henry Mayer in the *New York Times Book Review.* Oates recreates the violent and doomed 1831 uprising in which more than fifty whites "were murdered by Turner's insurgents, a band that grew from its nucleus of six to more than forty black men," explained Mayer, adding that Oates also devotes much attention to the "indiscriminate reprisals directed by vengeful whites against blacks" in which almost 200 blacks died during "the several weeks' reign of terror that followed Turner's two-day uprising."

Discussing the subject of his third biography, *With Malice toward None,* Oates indicates in *Biography as High Adventure* that "one of the supreme ironies of Lincoln's life—and of my quartet—was that he who spurned violence, he who placed his reverence for the system above his loathing of slavery, ended up smashing the institution in a violent civil war, a war that began because southerners equated Lincoln with John Brown and Nat Turner and seceded from the very system that protected slavery from Lincoln's grasp." Reviewing the work for the *Washington Post Book World,* Bernard Weisberger asserted that "what [Oates] has done in this admirable book is to synthesize basic source materials with an array of new scholarly writing on slavery, Republicanism, the Civil War and Lincoln," a synthesis that Luther Spoehr in *Saturday Review* referred to as "both comprehensive and tightly focused."

Translated into French, Spanish, and Polish, *With Malice toward None* "is an impressive performance," David Herbert Donald commented in the *New York Times Book Review.* "Full, fair and accurate, it does, as its author boasts, cover all significant aspects of Lincoln's life." Oates carefully probes the obfuscatory legends about Lincoln to reveal the man himself. Noting that the Lincoln of *With Malice toward None* is neither Carl Sandburg's "hardscrabble folk-hero, voicing the soul of a lost frontier," nor the "too overrated" figure perceived by the revisionists, Weisberger argued that Oates "has made Lincoln recognizably human instead of homespun saint—moody, unusual, inner-directed, but very successful in the world at large." Donald observed that "what most distinguishes Oates from all previous Lincoln biographers is the fact that he is consistently nonjudgmental."

Let the Trumpet Sound, the last book in Oates's biographical quartet, examines Martin Luther King Jr.'s life "from Montgomery to Memphis," explained Roger Wilkins in the *Washington Post Book World;* Oates traces King's development from the "enormously bright . . . and sensitive" child and the youthful "serious scholar" to his adulthood spent "reshaping and refining against hard experience the moral and intellectual view of the world he had developed in his student days." In the *New York Times Book Review,* Foner found that "King emerges as a charismatic leader, a brilliant tactician of the civil rights struggle, but also a deeply troubled man, subject to periodic bouts of depression and indecisiveness and, like Lincoln, wracked by premonitions of his own death." Calling it "by far the most complete examination of the progression of King's movement and of the crosscurrents that beset it," Harry S. Ashmore noted in a *Chicago Tribune Book World* review that Oates "remained faithful to his conviction that biography is a storytelling art" by capturing "the high drama and moving tragedy of King's brief passage through our time."

Let the Trumpet Sound, which has been translated into French, German, and Arabic, "succeeds very well in describing King's intellect" and represents a "good place to begin for the facts of King's own life," added Wilkins, but it fails to adequately treat the movement's other prominent figures as more than "shadows in King's play." Suspecting that the biography is too uncritical of its subject, Elliott Rudwick similarly suggested in the *American Historical Review* that "Oates pictures King as more heroic than he probably was and greatly overstates the importance of his role in the movement." However, Foner declared that the book "provides more than just a chronicle of King's life; as his story is unfolded, the roles of other prominent personalities of the period become clearer."

A Woman of Valor: Clara Barton and the Civil War evolved from Oates's research into the U.S. Civil War for his other books. He had initially planned to include Barton in his biographical quartet since she was well known for her efforts to aid and save wounded soldiers on the battlefield during the Civil War and for founding the American Red Cross. Once he became fascinated by Barton, however, he decided to devote an entire book to her. Writing in the *New York Times Book Review,* Andrew Delbanco noted of *A Woman of Valor* that though readers "catch glimpses of some of Barton's less attractive features . . . somehow a fully human Clara Barton does not quite come into focus in the book." Delbanco nonetheless found that the biography, "by attempting a close-up view of one woman's efforts to salve the casualties, reveals just how adept Americans became between 1861 and 1865 at killing one another. . . . What Mr. Oates has written is a kind of chronicle of man-made horror, with one appalled but undaunted woman at the center." Suzanne Gordon noted in the *Washington Post Book World* that "for those who are intrigued by battle, this biography will give them what they want and a taste of Clara Barton as well. For those who want to learn more about Barton, they will have to wait for another book, or refer to earlier ones."

Complementing Oates's biographical quartet of historical figures is his *William Faulkner: The Man and the Artist; A Biography,* about one of America's most esteemed literary figures, a voice in the turbulent South for the cause of equality of opportunity and a writer whose fiction frequently concerns the U.S. Civil War and its legacies. Based upon his own native Mississippi, the fictional world Faulkner created spanned generations and microcosmically mirrored the South's changing landscape while exploring the capacity of the human spirit to not only "endure" but "prevail."

Calling *William Faulkner* "romantic and absorbing," *New York Times* contributor Christopher Lehmann-Haupt likened reading it to "racing through a streamlined version" of the more massive, two-volume, fact-filled, scholarly biography by Joseph Blotner: "Suddenly, instead of being the sum of a million particles, Faulkner's life assumes terrific motion. His personality coalesces—the courtliness, the obdurate eyes, the impenetrable silences. There is action to his story." Liberating Faulkner from a "marble block of information," said Lehmann-Haupt, enables him "to live out his life at twice its normal rate and degree of drama." Praising Oates's "streamlined storytelling techniques," John Blades concluded in the *Chicago Tribune Book World* that "with considerable narrative skill, Oates navigates the muddy, turbulent currents of Faulkner's life, so that few readers will come away unmoved by his tragedy and his glory."

Oates refers to books such as *A Woman of Valor* and his *William Faulkner* as "literary" biography, explaining in *Biography as High Adventure* that in his work he tries to "create a life through the magic of language, that seek to illuminate universal truths about humankind through the sufferings and triumphs of a single human being." Oates pointed out in a *Publishers Weekly* interview with William Goldstein that "biography is an exercise in the art of omission," explaining that in *William Faulkner* he tried to suggest the writer's art as well as his life through "the use of telling detail alone." He also expresses to Goldstein why he chose a literary figure as a biographical subject: "I am attracted to figures who have [a profound] sense of history, and Faulkner shares this with the men I have already written about. Faulkner's imagination was fired to incandescence by the history of the South."

Oates's examination of the U.S. Civil War and its legacies continues in the two-part "Voices of the Storm" series, which Oates described as a "biographical history of the antebellum and Civil War era that tries to capture its human experiences, that presents the entire period through the perceptions and feelings of some twenty-three significant figures whose lives and destinies intersected on many levels." Oates noted that his goal in writing the work was to reinfuse that fratricidal war with the passion that he thinks has been wrung out of it through "dry, scholarly analysis." The first volume, 1997's *The Approaching Fury: Voices of the Storm, 1820-1861,* addresses the coming war and demonstrates "in human terms, which is the strength of biography, America's tragic failure to find a peaceful solution to slavery," according to its author. The second part, 1998's *The Whirlwind of War: Voices of the Storm, 1861-1865,* and explores "what it was like, through various individual perceptions, to fight and suffer in that conflict and to make the human decisions that determined the outcome."

In *Biography as High Adventure,* Oates addressed the increasing popularity of biography and offered a possible explanation for why it "may now be the preferred form of reading" in America. Aside from a certain natural curiosity about the lives of others, he argued that in an increasingly complex and technical society, biography's ability to personalize events "demonstrates that the individual does count—which is reassuring to people . . . who often feel caught up in vast impersonal forces beyond their control." Oates indicated that, for him, biography serves not only as "high literary and historical adventure, but deep personal experience as well." Having lived vicariously through the several lives he has documented biographically, Oates believes he has been enriched "beyond measure as a writer and a man," adding that the experience of writing biographies has "reinforced my life-long conviction that the people of the past have never really died. For they enjoy a special immortality in biography, in our efforts to touch and understand them and so to help preserve the human continuum. Perhaps this is what Yeats meant when he said that 'nothing exists but a stream of souls, that all knowledge is biography.'"

BIOGRAPHICAL AND CRITICAL SOURCES:

PERIODICALS

American Historical Review, October, 1983, Elliott Rudwick, review of *Let the Trumpet Sound.*

American History Illustrated, January, 1986; April, 1988, p. 19.

Antioch Review, summer, 1970; fall, 1984, review of *Abraham Lincoln.*

Atlantic, July, 1987, review of *William Faulkner: The Man and the Artist.*
Boston Globe, May 2, 1991, p. 77; May 23, 1992, p. 24; December 18, 1993, p. 13; April 17, 1994, review of *A Woman of Valor,* p. A16.
Chicago Tribune, July 26, 1987, review of *William Faulkner;* December 11, 1990, section 2C, p. 1.
Chicago Tribune Book World, August 8, 1982; September 18, 1983, review of *Let the Trumpet Sound;* April 22, 1984, review of *William Faulkner.*
Christian Science Monitor, February 28, 1977.
Chronicle of Higher Education, November 3, 1982; May 12, 1993, p. A16; June 2, 1993, p. A12; January 5, 1994, p. A17.
Globe and Mail (Toronto, Ontario, Canada), August 23, 1986.
Journal of American History, June, 1987, p. 148.
Library Journal, April 1, 1994, review of *A Woman of Valor,* p. 108.
Los Angeles Times Book Review, August 29, 1982.
Nation, March 29, 1971; May 31, 1975.
National Review, October 23, 1987, review of *William Faulkner,* p. 58.
New Republic, September 13, 1982.
Newsweek, July 6, 1970.
New York Review of Books, December 3, 1970; October 27, 1983, review of *Let the Trumpet Sound.*
New York Times, March 12, 1977, review of *With Malice toward None;* August 25, 1982; August 3, 1987.
New York Times Book Review, November 1, 1970; October 5, 1975; March 13, 1977, review of *With Malice toward None;* September 12, 1982; October 28, 1984, review of *Abraham Lincoln;* September 20, 1987, review of *William Faulkner,* p. 18; June 12, 1994, Andrew Delbanco, review of *A Woman of Valor,* p. 14.
Publishers Weekly, January 13, 1975; August 27, 1982; June 28, 1985; February 21, 1994, William Goldstein, interview with Oates, pp. 240-241.
Saturday Review, August 22, 1970; February 5, 1977, review of *With Malice toward None.*
Spectator, February 25, 1978.
Time, April 26, 1993, pp. 59-60.
Times Literary Supplement, April 28, 1978.
USA Today, July 31, 1987, p. 5D.
Washington Post, January 8, 1994, review of *A Woman of Valor,* p. A12.
Washington Post Book World, March 6, 1977; August 8, 1982; April 29, 1984; August 16, 1987; May 1, 1994, review of *A Woman of Valor,* p. 4.

* * *

OATES, Stephen Baery
See OATES, Stephen B.

O'BRIAN, E.G.
See CLARKE, Arthur C.

* * *

O'BRIEN, William Timothy
See O'BRIEN, Tim

* * *

O'CASEY, Brenda
See ELLIS, Alice Thomas

* * *

OE, Kenzaburo 1935-
(Oe Kenzaburo)

PERSONAL: Surname is pronounced "*Oh*-ey"; born January 31, 1935, in Ehime, Shikoku, Japan; married; wife's name Yukari; children: Hikari Pooh, one other child. *Education:* Tokyo University, earned degree (French literature), 1959.

ADDRESSES: *Home*—585 Seijo-machi, Setagaya-Ku, Tokyo, Japan.

CAREER: Novelist and short story writer, 1952—.

AWARDS, HONORS: Akutagawa prize, Japanese Society for the Promotion of Literature, 1958, for novella *Shiiku;* Shinchosha literary prize, 1964; Tanizaki prize, 1967; Europelia Arts Festival Literary Prize, 1989; Nobel Prize for Literature, 1994; Order of Culture, Japanese government (declined), 1994.

WRITINGS:

IN ENGLISH

Shiiku (novella; title means "The Catch"), [Japan], 1958, translation by John Bester published in *The Shadow of Sunrise,* edited by Saeki Shoichi, [Palo Alto, CA], 1966.

Memushiri kouchi (fiction), [Japan], 1958, translation by Paul St. John Mackintosh and Maki Sugiyama published as *Nip the Buds, Shoot the Kids,* Marion Boyars (New York, NY), 1995.

Kojinteki na taiken (fiction), [Japan], 1964, translation by John Nathan published as *A Personal Matter,* Grove (New York, NY), 1968.

Man'en gannen no futtoboru (fiction), [Japan], 1967, translation by John Bester published as *The Silent Cry,* Kodansha (New York, NY), 1974.

Pinchi ranna chosho (fiction), [Japan], 1976, translation by Michiko N. Wilson and Michael K. Wilson published as *The Pinch Runner Memorandum,* M.E. Sharpe (Armonk, NY), 1995.

Teach Us to Outgrow Our Madness (contains "The Day He Himself Shall Wipe My Tears Away," "Prize Stock," and "Aghwee the Sky Monster"), translation and introduction by John Nathan, Grove (New York, NY), 1977.

Hiroshima Notes (essays), translation by David L. Swain and Toshi Yonezawa, Marion Boyars (New York, NY), 1981, revised edition, 1995.

The Crazy Iris and Other Stories of the Atomic Aftermath, translation by Ivan Morris and others, Grove (New York, NY), 1984.

Jinsei no shinseki, [Japan], 1989, translation by Margaret Mitusani published as *An Echo of Heaven,* Kodansha International (New York, NY), 1996.

Japan, the Ambiguous, and Myself: The Nobel Prize Speech and Other Lectures, translation by Hisaaki Yamanouchi and Kunioki Yanagishita, Kodansha (New York, NY), 1995.

A Healing Family (essays), translation by Stephen Snyder, Kodansha International (New York, NY), 1996.

Shizuka na seikatsu, [Japan], translation by Kunioki Yanagishita and William Wetherall published as *A Quiet Life,* Grove (New York, NY), 1996.

Two Novels: Seventeen, J., translation by Luk Van Haute, introduction by Masao Miyoshi, Blue Moon Books (New York, NY), 1996.

Atarashii hito yo mezameyo, [Japan], 1986, translation by John Nathan published as *Rouse Up, O Young Men of the New Age!,* Grove (New York, NY), 2002.

Kaifuku-suru kazoku, Kodansha (Tokyo, Japan), 1995, translation by Stephen Snyder published as *A Healing Family,* illustrated by Yukari Oe, Kodansha International (New York, NY), 1996.

Chugaeri, [Japan], 1999, translation by Philip Gabriel published as *Somersault: A Novel,* Grove (New York, NY), 2003.

FICTION; IN JAPANESE

Warera no jidai (title means "Our Age"), [Japan], 1959.

Okurete kita seinen (title means "Born Too Late"), [Japan], 1961.

Sakebigoe (title means "Screams"), [Japan], 1962.

Nichijo seikatsu no boken, [Japan], 1971.

Kozui wa waga tamashii ni oyobi, [Japan], 1973.

Seinen no omei, [Japan], 1974.

M/T to mori no fushgi no monogatari (title means "M/T and the Wonders of the Forest"), Iwanami Shoten (Tokyo, Japan), 1990.

Sukuinushi ga nagurareru made (first novel of trilogy "The Flaming Green Tree"; title means "Until the 'Savior' Gets Socked"), Shinchosha (Tokyo, Japan), 1993.

Yureugoku: "vashireshon" (second novel of trilogy "The Flaming Green Tree"; title means "Vacillating"), Shinchosha (Tokyo, Japan), 1994.

Aimaina Nohon no watakushi, Iwanami Shoten (Tokyo, Japan), 1995.

Oinaru hi ni (third novel of trilogy "The Flaming Green Tree"; title means "On the Great Day"), Shinchosha (Tokyo, Japan), 1995.

SHORT STORIES; IN JAPANESE

Oe Kenzaburo shu, [Japan], 1960.

Kodoku na seinen no kyuka, [Japan], 1960.

Seiteki ningen, [Japan], 1968.

Warera no hyoki o ikinobiru michi o oshieyo, [Japan], 1969, enlarged edition, 1975.

Oe Kenzaburo ("Gendai no bungaku" series), [Japan], 1971.

Mizukara waga namida o nugui-tamau hi, [Japan], 1972.

Sora no kaibutsu Agui, [Japan], 1972.

ESSAYS; IN JAPANESE

Jizokusuru kokorozashi, [Japan], 1968.

Kakujidai no sozoryoku, [Japan], 1970.

Kowaremono to shite no ningen, [Japan], 1970.

Okinawa noto, [Japan], 1970.

Kujira no shimetsusuru hi, [Japan], 1972.

Dojidai to shite no sengo, [Japan], 1973.

Jokyo e, [Japan], 1974.

Bungaku noto, [Japan], 1974.

Genshuku na tsunawatari, [Japan], 1974.

Kotoba no yotte, [Japan], 1976.

Sekai no wakamonotachi, [Japan], 1962.

Oe Kenzaburo zensakuhin, [Japan], 1966–67.

Oe Kenzaburo shu ("Shincho Nihon bungaku" series), [Japan], 1969.

(Editor) Mansaku Itami, *Itami Mansaku essei shu,* [Japan], 1971.

OTHER

(With Günter Grass) *Gestern, vor 50 jahren: Ein deutch-japanischer briefwechsel* (title means "Yesterday, 50 Years Ago: A German-Japanese Correspondence"), translation from the Japanese by Otto Putz, Steidl, 1995.

Also author of *The Perverts* (fiction), 1963, and *Adventures in Daily Life* (fiction), 1964.

SIDELIGHTS: Kenzaburo Oe became one of Japan's first authors ever to receive national recognition for his writing while still a university student. When he was awarded the prestigious Akutagawa prize in 1958 for his novella *Shiiku* ("The Catch"), the twenty-three-year-old became one of Japan's most popular writers. Now acclaimed as one of the greatest Japanese writers of the twentieth century, Oe won the 1994 Nobel Prize for Literature.

Oe was born in 1935 in the forested mountain region of Shikoku Island in southern Japan. His father died in 1944. He studied comparative literature at Tokyo University, taking a degree in French literature in 1959. A master of languages, he reads French, Russian, Chinese, English, and Russian, and has been particularly influenced by French and American authors—from Rabelais to Sartre and from Herman Melville and Mark Twain to Norman Mailer. It was from Rabelais, according to translator David Swain in the commentary included his translation of Oe's *Hiroshima Notes,* that Oe learned the image system of grotesque realism, "a mode of literary expression that has enabled Oe to eschew the traditional Japanese literary habits of indirection and suggestive innuendo and to develop instead a more universal style of dealing directly with reality as experienced yet without sacrificing subtlety."

Oe has been politically engaged since his student days when he led demonstrations against the reestablishment of the U.S.-Japan Security Treaty. He has consistently protested war, nuclear weapons, racism, even the nearly sacrosanct "Emperor system." Masao Miyoshi wrote in the *San Francisco Review of Books* that Oe's "passion for the underclass of the earth cannot be challenged." In *Portrait of a Postwar Generation,* Oe wrote movingly of hearing Emperor Hirohito, revered as an unseen and unheard god, announce over the radio on August 15, 1945, that Japan had surrendered: "How could we believe that an August presence of such awful power had become an ordinary human being on a designated summer day?" The cognitive dissonance of hearing that "ordinary" human voice has informed Oe's work: one is never quite sure when the bizarre, the grotesque, or the merely incredible will afflict the comfortable.

Western literature has greatly influenced Oe's writings. At Tokyo University he studied the existentialist philosophy of Jean-Paul Sartre, as well as the works of Blaise Pascal and Albert Camus. His favorite American authors are those whose heroes search for "personal freedom beyond the borders of safety and acceptance"—authors such as Herman Melville, William Faulkner, and Norman Mailer. Oe was most inspired by Mark Twain's character Huckleberry Finn, whom he used as a model for his own fictional hero.

Oe's interest in the political and the absurd are reflected in two of his earlier novels which have been more recently translated into English. *Nip the Buds, Shoot the Kids* is set on the island of Shikoku, Oe's "peripheral" birthplace. It takes place during World War II, as a group of juvenile delinquents are evacuated from a reformatory to a remote village. The boys are mistreated by hostile peasants until the villagers, fearing plague, abandon them. The adolescent narrator tells how the boys band together, caring for each other as well as an abandoned girl and a Korean boy. When the villagers return, they attempt to hush the boys about their abandonment at the hands of those meant to protect them. All but the narrator give in, and he is hounded and chased out of the village "insanely angry, tearful, shivering with cold and hunger." Julian Duplain of the *Times Literary Supplement* wrote: "As a story of misled innocents, Oe's novel draws clear parallels with imperialistic Japanese military policy in the Second World War, as well as providing a rallying cry for antiauthoritarian resistance. To Western readers, the directness of emotion—for example, the boys' honest esteem for one another—sometimes sounds simplistic." A *Kirkus Reviews* writer found *Nip the Buds, Shoot the Kids* to be "more shaded, more graphic, and angrier than *Lord of the Flies,* but the fierce anger is transmuted by Oe's art into literary gold—an anguished plea for tolerance more wrenching than any rant could ever be."

The pivotal event in Oe's life and work was the birth of his brain-damaged son Hikari ("Light") in 1963. As a strong bond developed between Oe and his son, the writer penned several partially autobiographical novels in which the protagonist is the father of a brain-damaged child. The first of these, *A Personal Matter,* is the story of a twenty-seven-year-old man nicknamed Bird, whose wife gives birth to a deformed baby. The boy, looking like a two-headed monster, appears to have a brain hernia, and the doctors tell Bird that the baby will probably die or be a vegetable for life. Bird is so horrified that he chooses to let the baby die rather than face life tied to a retarded son. While his wife and child are in the hospital, Bird runs off to the apartment of a young widow friend, where he escapes into a world of fantasy, sex, and alcohol. He loses his teaching job after being so hung over that he vomits during a lecture. Meanwhile, the baby, being fed only sugar water, refuses to die, so Bird takes him to an abortionist to have him killed. Suddenly, however, he changes his mind and returns the baby to the hospital. Doctors discover that the hernia is only a benign tumor and after successfully operating, they announce that the baby will be normal, though with a low IQ. Bird finds a new job and is reunited once more with his wife and child.

The novel is not as pretty as its ending might suggest. *Washington Post* reviewer Geoffrey Wolff remarked that *A Personal Matter* "reeks of vomit and spilled whisky. Its surreal characters are all vegetables, cut off from history and hope. They define themselves by their despair. They use sex to wound and humiliate one another. They trick themselves with hopeless dreams of a new life, far away." Alan Levensohn surmised that this representation of humanity is Oe's way of suggesting that "the stunted existence Bird's baby will probably have, if Bird allows him to live, comes to seem terribly close to the existence which Bird and the others are making for themselves." John Hearsum similarly commented, "The prose is hard and brittle, the images like tiny nightmares. . . . It communicates the full terror of such a predicament, and confronts the arbitrary horror of the universe without any recourse to fancy techniques."

In his own life, Oe, feeling much like Bird, went off on assignment to report on the international peace meeting in Hiroshima. His *Hiroshima Notes* records his views of the antinuclear movement from 1963 to 1965, focusing on the political bickering of the several factions and lashing out at their failure to recognize the real suffering of the victims of the atomic bombings. Oe drew strength from his encounters with the survivors, and particularly with Dr. Fumio Shigeto, whom Oe saw, according to Yoshio Iwamoto, as "the archetype of the authentic man of Hiroshima, a man who reclaims humanity out of the ashes of dehumanization." Oe's transforming experience in Hiroshima led him to approve the operation that saved Hikari's life, albeit with severe mental limitations. Virtually speechless, Hikari nevertheless later demonstrated a remarkable talent for music composition. Despite continuing health problems and his mental impairment, he released two CDs in Japan that have sold well.

The Pinch Runner Memorandum tells the story of a group of student radicals who construct their own atomic bomb. A brain-damaged boy and his father, a former nuclear physicist, work with Oe and his own son to avert disaster. "The invention of this 'pinch runner' double," Masao Miyoshi wrote in the *Nation,* "suggests the increasing complexity of a writer in positioning himself in his story—and the world." A critic for the *New Yorker* found that "Oe's writing is bold, savage, and often very funny. . . . This complicated book is above all a heartening display of the explosively constructive power of imagination."

Oe's *A Quiet Life,* published in Japan in 1990, is a semifictional account of three nearly adult children, one mentally disabled, who are left to cope alone when their parents move to the United States for eight months. A major theme of the novel is the anxiety of the caregivers over the feelings and needs of the mentally impaired family member, Eeyore, whose communication is rare and often ineffective. They consistently leap to the worst conclusions. When Eeyore writes a musical piece he calls "The Abandoned Child," his brother and sister immediately assume the reference is to Eeyore and his father, which Eeyore is only belatedly able to explain is not the case. "Yet," noted Lindsley Cameron in the *Yale Review,* "the question of the father's guilt is never really resolved. In fact, the novel is in a way a long exploration of that question, and some of its most strongly felt passages condemn the claims of exceptional individuals to exceptional privileges." The book has little plot, but is, said John David Morely, simply an account of the young people's daily life amid "an idiosyncratic set of family and friends, portraits drawn with affection, insight, and that wry humor . . . [that] is one of the defining qualities of [Oe's] talent."

The transformation of suffering is also the theme of Oe's novel *An Echo of Heaven,* which recounts the life of a Japanese woman, Marie Kuraki, whom Oe and the novel's narrator first knew as a teacher of foreign languages and literature in a Tokyo university. Marie marries and has two sons, one severely brain-damaged. As teenagers, the boys commit suicide together, and Marie's estranged husband turns into a drunken wastrel. The novel focuses on Marie's efforts to rise above these tragedies, as she works first with a theater troupe, then with a semi-Christian cult in California, and finally on a peasant commune in Mexico. The commune's leader, in a ploy to hold his project together, plans to transform Marie, a persistent unbeliever now dying of cancer in her late forties, into a saint to be revered by the peasants. Zia Jeffery, writing in the *Nation,* saw the novel as Oe's ironic backward glance at his own career as an artist being transformed from a man "into a martyr, then an image of a martyr and finally into kitsch."

Oe put the capstone on his autobiographical work about his son, Hiraki, with *Rouse Up, O Young Men of the New Age,* in which he traces the boy's development from childhood to young manhood. Employing images from nineteenth-century English poet William Blake, Oe "performs a kind of literary onanism," according to Andrew Irvin in the *Philadelphia Inquirer Online.* As Irvin further noted, with this work Oe "has looked inward and found the seeds of artistic invention in his own books." Again, Oe tells the tale of a famous Japanese author, known only as "K," and his mentally disabled son, nicknamed Eeyore. With his father away on a business trip, Eeyore acts erratically, becomes depressed and even violent. When K returns, he tries to get closer to his son to understand his mood swing; he finds succor and guidance in a strange place: the poetry of Blake. Adam Mars-Jones, writing in the *Guardian Online,* noted that "for most of this book, Oe takes from Blake the marvelous discovery that the most extreme expressions are sometimes the least distorted." Mars-Jones also found Oe's novel "fascinating and even rewarding," though he also noted "it isn't easy to take in." In a *Publishers Weekly* review, a contributor remarked that Oe writes with "depth and passion" about his relationship with his son. The same reviewer felt that Oe's book is "deceptively modest . . . [and] powerful," and that Oe is a "master at the height of his literary powers." Similarly, *Booklist*'s Ray Olson described the novel as "Oe at his best," in both an "intellectual treatise" and a "moving family memoir."

The winning of the Nobel Prize in 1994 marked the beginning of a new artistic era for Oe. His first novel after winning the prize, *Somersault,* "concerns an austere, embattled, and eventually self-destructive religious cult," according to a critic for *Kirkus Reviews.* Inspired by the 1995 events surrounding the Aum Shinrikyo cult, Oe moves away from the autobiographical stance of so many of his works featuring the relationship between him and his disabled son. In this book, artist and art professor Kizo, who is suffering from terminal cancer, falls in love with a boy, Ikuo, whom he met years earlier. Now the professor and his friend are enlisted in the effort to revive a religious cult discredited a decade earlier for terrorist plans. In the course of this work, they become involved with a strange girl, Dancer, who was earlier involved with Ikuo, as well as with a full panoply of characters inside the cult, all jockeying for power. Olson, writing in *Booklist,* called *Somersault* a "thick stew of sexual and more parareligious than religious incidents." Olson also felt that the novel resembles the work of "late Dostoevsky." Shirley N. Quan, reviewing the title for *Library Journal,* thought it "reads like a social/spiritual/religious commentary," and is a "highly literate piece." Commenting on the length of the work—576 pages—a reviewer for *Publishers Weekly* noted that Oe "has attempted to create a sprawling masterpiece, but American readers might decide there's more sprawl than masterpiece here." Similarly, the *Kirkus Reviews* critic found the first half of the novel "tedious." However, according to the same critic, the second half, detailing the reemergence of the thriving cult creates a "series of increasingly complex relationships and tensions." Interestingly, even in this non-autobiographical novel, Oe's son Hikari makes an appearance in the guise of a musical genius who has suffered brain damage.

In his acceptance speech for the Nobel Prize, Oe described how his son had once been "awakened by the voices of birds to the music of Bach and Mozart": "Herein I find the grounds for believing in the exquisite healing power of art. . . . As one with a peripheral, marginal, and off-center existence in the world, I would like to seek how. . . I can be of some use in a cure and reconciliation of mankind."

BIOGRAPHICAL AND CRITICAL SOURCES:

BOOKS

Cameron, Lindsley, *The Music of Light: The Extraordinary Story of Hikari and Kenzaburo Oe,* Free Press (New York, NY), 1998.

Contemporary Literary Criticism, Thomson Gale (Detroit, MI), Volume 10, 1979, Volume 36, 1986, Volume 86, 1995.

Dictionary of Literary Biography, Volume 182: *Japanese Writers since World War II,* Thomson Gale (Detroit, MI), 1997.

Dictionary of Literary Biography Yearbook: 1994, Thomson Gale (Detroit, MI), 1995.

Forest, Philippe, *Oe Kenzaburo: Legendes d'un romancier japonais,* Editions Plein Feux (Paris, France), 2001.

Literature Lover's Companion, Prentice Hall (Englewood, NJ), 2001.

Napier, Susan J., *Escape from the Wasteland: Romanticism and Realism in the Fiction of Mishima Yukio and Oe Kenzaburo,* Harvard University Press (Cambridge, MA), 1991.

Oe, Kenzaburo, *Hiroshima Notes* (essays), translation by David L. Swain and Toshi Yonezawa, Marion Boyars (New York, NY), 1981, revised edition, 1995.

Oe, Kenzaburo, *Japan, the Ambiguous, and Myself: The Nobel Prize Speech and Other Lectures,* translation by Hisaaki Yamanouchi and Kunioki Yanagishita, Kodansha (New York, NY), 1995.

Penguin International Dictionary of Contemporary Biography, Penguin Reference (New York, NY), 2001.

Reference Guide to Short Fiction, St. James Press (Detroit, MI), 1999.

Rubin, Jay, editor, *Modern Japanese Writers,* Scribner (New York, NY), 2000, pp. 277-293.

Short Story Criticism, Volume 20, Thomson Gale (Detroit, MI), 1995.

Wilson, Michiko N., *The Marginal World of Oe Kenzaburo: A Study in Themes and Techniques,* M.E. Sharpe (Armonk, NY), 1986.

PERIODICALS

Best Sellers, July 1, 1968; October, 1977.

Booklist, February 1, 2002, Ray Olson, review of *Rouse Up, O Young Men of the New Age!,* p. 908; March, 2003, Ray Olson, review of *Somersault,* p. 629.

Books Abroad, winter, 1969.

Boundary 2, fall, 1991; summer, 1993.

Christian Century, April 12, 1995, p. 382; December 24, 1997, p. 1226.

Christian Science Monitor, August 8, 1968; October 18, 1994, p. 13.

Critique, Volume 15, number 3, 1974.

Entertainment Weekly, March 22, 2002, review of *Rouse Up, O Young Men of the New Age!,* p. 104.

Hudson Review, autumn, 1968.

Japan Quarterly, July, 1996, p. 90; January, 1997, p. 102; October, 1997, p. 38.

Kirkus Reviews, March 1, 1995, review of *Nip the Buds, Shoot the Kids,* p. 261; February 1, 2002, review of *Rouse Up, O Young Men of the New Age!,* p. 134; February 1, 2003, review of *Somersault,* p. 172.

Library Journal, December, 2002, Shirley N. Quan, review of *Somersault,* p. 180.

Life, August 16, 1968.

Los Angeles Times, October 14, 1994, p. A1; October 19, 1994, p. B7.

Nation, August 5, 1968; May 15, 1995, Masao Miyoshi, review of *The Pinch Runner Memorandum* p. 696; September 30, 1996, Zia Jeffery, review of *An Echo of Heaven,* p. 34.

New Republic, August 17, 1968.

New Yorker, June 8, 1968; November 14, 1994, p. 147; February 6, 1995, p. 38; October 9, 1995, p. 91.

New York Review of Books, October 10, 1968.

New York Times, November 6, 1994, p. 5.

New York Times Book Review, July 7, 1968; September 8, 1985; June 19, 1995, p. 43; July 9, 1995, p.8.

Publishers Weekly, October 17, 1994, p. 17; March 27, 1995, pp. 48, 73; August 7, 1995, p. 438; April 8, 1996, p. 56; January 28, 2002, review of *Rouse Up, O Young Men of the New Age!,* p. 267; January 6, 2003, review of *Somersault,* p. 36.

Rain Taxi, summer, 2001, Jason Picone, review of *Rouse Up, O Young Men of the New Age!*

Review of Contemporary Fiction, fall, 2002, Amy Havel, review of *Rouse Up, O Young Men of the New Age!,* p. 145.

San Francisco Review of Books, March-April, 1995, pp. 8-9.

Studies in Short Fiction, fall, 1974.

Time, October 24, 1994, p. 64.

Times (London, England), May 16, 1995, p. 35.

Times Literary Supplement, October 26, 1984, p. 1227; April 28, 1989; May 12, 1995, Julian Duplain, review of *Nip the Buds, Shoot the Kids,* p. 21; December 27, 1996, p. 32; October 31, 1997.

Voice Literary Supplement, October, 1982.

Washington Post, June 11, 1968, Geoffrey Wolff, review of *A Personal Matter.*

Washington Post Book World, August 25, 1968; September 11, 1977.

World Literature Today, spring, 1978; spring, 1985, p. 318; winter, 1995, pp. 5-16; spring, 1996, p. 475; autumn, 1996, p. 1033; summer, 1997, p. 653; winter, 1997, p. 229.

Yale Review, April, 1997, Lindsley Cameron, review of *A Quiet Life,* p. 150.

ONLINE

Guardian Online, http://www.guardian.co.uk/ (August, 4, 2002), Adam Mars-Jones, review of *Rouse Up, O Young Men of the New Age!*

Nobel e-Museum, http://www.nobel.se/ (1994), "Kenzaburo Oe—Biography."

Philadelphia Inquirer Online, http://www.philly.com/ (May 12, 2002), Andrew Ervin, review of *Rouse Up, O Young Men of the New Age!*

OE KENZABURO
See OE, Kenzaburo

* * *

OKRI, Ben 1959-

PERSONAL: Born March 15, 1959, in Minna, Nigeria. *Education:* Attended Urhobo College (Warri, Nigeria) and University of Essex. *Hobbies and other interests:* Music, art, theater, cinema, martial arts, good conversation, dancing, silence.

ADDRESSES: *Agent*—c/o Author Mail, Orion Publishing Group, Orion House, 5 Upper St. Martin's Lane, London WC2H 9EA, England.

CAREER: Novelist, poet, and author of short fiction. *West Africa* magazine, poetry editor, 1981-87; host of *Network Africa,* BBC World Service, 1984-85. Visiting fellow at Trinity College, Cambridge, 1991-93.

MEMBER: PEN International, Society of Authors.

AWARDS, HONORS: Commonwealth Writers' Prize for Africa, 1987; *Paris Review* Aga Khan prize for fiction, 1987; Booker Prize for fiction, 1991, for *The Famished Road;* Premio Letterario Internazionale Chianti Ruffino-Antico Fattore, 1993; Premio Grinzane Cavour, 1994; Crystal Award, 1995; fellow of the Royal Society of Literature, 1997; Premio Palmi, 2000. Honorary D. Lit., University of Westminster, 1997.

WRITINGS:

Flowers and Shadows (novel), Longman (London, England), 1980.

The Landscapes Within (novel), Longman (London, England), 1981.

Incidents at the Shrine (short stories), Arrow Books (New York, NY), 1986.

Stars of the New Curfew (short stories), Secker & Warburg (London, England), 1988, Viking (New York, NY), 1989.

The Famished Road (novel), Cape (London, England), 1991, Nan A. Talese (New York, NY), 1992.

An African Elegy (poetry), Cape (London, England), 1992.

Songs of Enchantment (novel), Doubleday (New York, NY), 1993.

Astonishing the Gods (novel), Phoenix House (London, England), 1995, Orion, 1998.

Dangerous Love (novel), Phoenix House (London, England), 1996.

A Way of Being Free (novel), Phoenix House (London, England), 1997.

Infinite Riches (novel), Phoenix House (London, England), 1999.

In Arcadia (novel), Phoenix House (London, England), 2002.

Contributor of articles and reviews to periodicals, including *Guardian, Observer,* and *New Statesman.*

SIDELIGHTS: Novelist, poet, and short-story writer Ben Okri continually seeks in his writings to capture the postindependent Nigerian world view, including that country's civil war and its ensuing violence and transformation, no matter how troubling or painful these events may be. In an essay written in 1991, Okri stated that "if the poet begins to speak only . . . of things he can effortlessly digest and recognise, of things that do not disturb, frighten, stir, or annoy us . . . in restricted terms and exclusively with restricted language, then what hope is there for us." As Harry Garuba asserted in the *Dictionary of Literary Biography,* "Even though the manner in which [Okri] explores these issues has sometimes become a matter of contention among his peers, there is . . . little doubt about the importance of his contribution to the development of the contemporary Nigerian novel." With publication of his 1992 novel *The Famished Road,* Okri was praised by Henry Louis Gates, Jr., who wrote in the *New York Times Book Review* that Okri "has ushered the African novel into its own postmodern era through a compelling extension of traditional oral forms that uncover the future in the past. But while *The Famished Road* may signal a new achievement for the African novel in English, it would be a dazzling achievement for any writer in any language."

Okri uses nightmarish imagery and surrealist contortions of reality to portray the bizarre social and political conditions existing inside Nigeria. "Dreams are the currency of Okri's writing," explained Giles Foden in the *Times Literary Supplement,* dreams "made of the stuff of Africa's colossal economic and political problems." An *Economist* reviewer noted of Okri's collective oeuvre, "It has often been hard to tell whether he was describing dream or reality—and it did not seem to matter much anyway." Critics have associated Okri's techniques with those practiced by magic realists, a school of writers who incorporate supernatural elements into otherwise realistic settings. Michiko Kakutani, reviewing *Stars of the New Curfew* for the *New York Times,* commented that Okri's Africa "seems like a continent dreamed up, in tandem, by Hieronymus Bosch and Jorge Luis Borges—a land where history has quite literally become a nightmare." However, Okri insists that the supernatural elements in his works are realistic representations of the Nigerian experience, demonstrating the continuity between the realistic and mystical realms of experience that exists for Nigerians.

Beginning with his first novel, *Flowers and Shadows,* published when Okri was twenty-one years old, he has devoted much of his work to describing the political and social chaos wracking Nigeria, and the pictures he creates are dark and often violent. In his review of *Incidents at the Shrine* for the London *Observer,* Anthony Thwaite called Okri "an obsessive cataloguer of sweat, phlegm, ordure and vomit," while Kakutani noted that the author's characters "live in a state of suspended animation, their private lives overshadowed by political atrocities, whatever ideals they might have had eroded by the demands of day-to-day survival." The narrator of the title story in *Stars of the New Curfew* is a vagabond medicine salesman whose cures often backfire, sending people to violent, grisly deaths. He is constantly on the run from his victims, but cannot outrun his visions. An unnamed character in the story "Worlds That Flourish," also in *Stars of the New Curfew,* flees a hellish city only to find himself in a more literal hell where some people have wings but cannot fly, others have feet that face backward, and an old neighbor appears sporting three eyes. Susan Cronje, who called the book "an important comment on Nigerian society" in her review for the *New Statesman,* said that "Okri's writing is suffused with helpless anger at the alienation of Nigerian society, the corruption not only of the rulers but also of the ruled who seem to connive at their own oppression."

Okri's 1991 novel, *The Famished Road,* which received England's prestigious Booker Prize, further explores the Nigerian dilemma. Charles R. Larson, writing in *World & I,* remarked that "the power of Ben Okri's magnificent novel is that it encapsulates a critical stage in the history of a nation . . . by chronicling one character's quest for freedom and individuation." *The Famished Road*'s main character is Azaro, an *abiku* child torn between the spirit and natural world. Azaro's struggle to free himself from the spirit realm is paralleled by his father's immersion into politics to fight the oppression of the poor. The novel introduces a host of people all of whom "blend together . . . to show us a world which may look to the naked eye like an unattractive ghetto, but which is as spiritually gleaming and beautiful as all the palaces in Heaven—thanks to the everyday, continuing miracle of human love," wrote Carolyn See in the *Los Angeles Times Book Review.*

By novel's end, Azaro recognizes the similarities between the nation and the *abiku;* each is forced to make sacrifices to reach maturity and a new state of being. This affirming ending also "allows rare access to the profuse magic that survives best in the dim forests of their spirit," according to Rob Nixon of the *Village Voice.* Similarly, in her appraisal for the London *Observer,* Linda Grant commented, "Okri's gift is to present a world view from inside a belief system." *Detroit Free Press* contributor John Gallagher deemed the work "a majestically difficult novel that may join the ranks of greatness."

In *Songs of Enchantment,* Okri continues the story and themes raised in *The Famished Road.* However, while the focus in the first book is on the efforts of Azaro's parents to keep him among the living, the second book deals with what Charles R. Larson described in Chicago's *Tribune Books* as "an equally difficult battle to restore the greater community to its earlier harmony and cohesiveness." As Azaro further chronicles the oppression that has hold of his village and his family, the landscape increasingly becomes intermingled with the political and social chaos. At one point, Azaro leaves the village with his father: "It was impossible to determine how long we had been running, or how far we had travelled. But after awhile, it seemed as if Dad had been running in a straight line which paradoxically curved into an enchanted circle. We couldn't break out of the forest." This sequence functions metaphorically, as Azaro comes to realize that the entire nation of Nigeria is undergoing a similarly debilitating series of changes. Because of this, *Songs of Enchantment* more clearly explicates Okri's concerns with the problems visited upon Africa after decolonization. Wrote Larson, "The wonder of *Songs of Enchantment* . . . is that it carries on so richly the saga of nation building implying that countries that have broken the colonial yoke may face an even more difficult struggle."

Okri further makes use of the dreamlike world he is so adept at creating, as well as the world of suspended disbelief inherent to the folktale. For *The Songs of Enchantment* is closer to a collection of folktales than to the novel, and this form further emphasizes Okri's theme of redemption as well as the confusion that is visited upon Azaro and his countrymen. As Judy Cooke pointed out in the *New Statesman,* "Many folk tales are working towards a creation myth, examining causation and identity. . . . Okri's work is perhaps best enjoyed in this context."

After winning the Booker Prize in 1991 for *The Famished Road,* Okri, like many award-winning authors, found himself expected to duplicate this success with his subsequent works. Not surprising, perhaps, his more recent work, penned in different styles and with different intents, has been received more critically. In a *World Literature Today* review, for example, Bruce King noted that while *The Famished Road* is "marvelous," Okri's subsequent books, such as *Songs of Enchantment* have been "repetitious, and endless telling of adventures among the spirits and their influence on society."

As an example of such repetition, like *Songs of Enchantment, Dangerous Love* is a reworking of Okri's second novel, *The Landscapes Within,* published fifteen years earlier. *Dangerous Love* tells the story of Omovo, a young clerk in a chemicals firm who in his spare time paints canvases which depict his bleak ghetto surroundings. Although the "dangerous love" of the title refers to Omovo's love affair with a married woman, the spiritual evil that has consumed Nigeria makes Omovo's art—the belief that he can re-dream his world—just as dangerous.

Dangerous Love is essentially a *künstlerroman*—a novel that traces the evolution of an artist—for Omovo uses his art as a way of finding a spiritual place for himself. Alan Riach wrote in *Contemporary Novelists* of *The Landscapes Within,* "Social and political corruption are the condition and context of Omovo's artistic effort." Indeed, throughout the novel Omovo debates with himself and his friends the role of the Nigerian artist and the art they produce. However, the uncompromising reality of the Nigeria presented by the novelist—the slums, the poverty, the corruption—make it clear that Okri does not hold to this view. As Ruth Pavey wrote in the *New Statesman,* he "conveys a poignant sense of a generation caught between languages and identities. . . . More poignant still is the hindsight we now have: that their fears for the future were better founded than their hopes."

Michael Kerrigan wrote in the *Times Literary Supplement* that in *Dangerous Love* "painter-protagonist, Omovo, is as lost as the reader is in a disturbing slumscape which, though all too oppressively real, seems to clamor for allegorical interpretation." However, it is in *Astonishing the Gods* that Okri truly creates such a landscape; Alev Adil wrote in the *Times Literary Supplement* that in his 1995 novel Okri "has jettisoned reality altogether, preferring to inhabit an allegorical space that bears no scars or traces of modernity whatsoever." The novel's nameless hero, upon learning to read and thus discovering that he and his people are invisible because they are not included in any history books, sets out on a quest to become visible. However, the quest turns into a spiritual journey of understanding for the hero, who achieves perfect invisibility after a series of tests that culminates in his naming of the Invisibles' dream: "creativity and grace." The message of the hero's embracing of his natural state is dual. Wrote Amit Chauduri in the *Spectator,* readers can approach *Astonishing the Gods* "as an affirmation and celebration of the creativity and contributions of those communities which are, to all purposes, 'invisible' to the greater world, and also as an autobiography of an African writer who has 'arrived,' in every sense of that word, in the West."

New Statesman reviewer Guy Mannes-Abbott, who interpreted *Astonishing the Gods* as a work "about language and change," compared Okri's belief, as demonstrated in the novel, in the ability of language to create possibilities for his own language, which he finds "properly worked and exact." Mannes-Abbott concluded that *Astonishing the Gods* is "an impressive, brave and often beautiful little book that is not for the literal-minded." Similarly, Charles R. Larson in the *Nation* called *Astonishing the Gods* "the most remarkable novel" of Okri's career, and welcomed it as "a dazzling and unabashedly spiritual narrative at a time when most writers are afraid to articulate matters of the soul in public."

Okri's 2002 offering, *In Arcadia*—a "variation on *Astonishing Gods,*" to quote King in *World Literature Today*—follows the activities of a film crew as it travels throughout Europe attempting to film a modern-day Arcadia, or paradise. While King found the work unsuccessful as a novel, noting that, "except as a metaphor of life as a journey, the story itself seems purposeless as there are few events and little narrative development," he found it engaging for other reasons. It is "interesting—as the novel becomes art criticism, cultural history, meditation—but the great truths offered appear as cliches," or what *New Statesman*'s William Skidelsky dubbed "Okri's portentous sermonising," which is "often tiresome." Despite *In Arcadia*'s alleged faults, Skidelsky found that the author's "writing has a certain magisterial quality; Okri's disregard for plot and plausibility is perversely charming." "In occasional flashes of humour," the critic added, "he shows that he is not incapable of laughing at his own pretensions. Would that he laughed more often."

Reviewing the short fiction included in *Incidents at the Shrine,* Sara Maitland said of Okri in the *New Statesman* that "sentence by sentence he turns in beautiful, strong prose, dense with lyricism and metaphor, skipping elegantly along the edge of surrealism and never collapsing into it." Okri's descriptions of Nigeria are so finely etched that locale takes on a life of its own, maintained the reviewer. Similar qualities were commended by Maureen Freely in the short stories contained in *Stars of the New Curfew,* prompting her to write in the London *Observer:* "There are many novelists who write as well as Okri, many who share his gift for recreating the texture of everyday life, many who can cut through the surface to expose, as he does, the myths our elders and betters use to keep us in our place. There are very few novelists who can do all three. The fact that Ben Okri has done so in short stories, without ever losing his balance, his humour, or his edge, makes his accomplishment all the more exceptional."

Okri continues to explore the tensions between hope and despair in language critics have consistently praised as graceful, controlled, and spare. "His fiction is full of the thresholds of (im)possibility, of mutability and self-renewal," lauded Mannes-Abbott in the *New Statesman,* "and is rendered in correspondingly unrestricted language: rich, opaque, sometimes rapturous."

BIOGRAPHICAL AND CRITICAL SOURCES:

BOOKS

Adewale, Maja-Pearce, *A Mask Dancing: Nigerian Novelists of the Eighties,* Hans Zell Publishers (London, England), 1992.

Agyeman-Duah, Ivor, *Some African Voices of Our Time,* Anansesem Publications (Accra, Ghana), 1995.

Contemporary Literary Criticism, Volume 87, Thomson Gale (Detroit, MI), 1995.

Contemporary Novelists, 6th edition, St. James Press (Detroit, MI), 1996.

Dictionary of Literary Biography, Volume 157: *Twentieth-Century Caribbean and Black African Writers,* Thomson Gale (Detroit, MI), 1996.

Emenyonu, Ernest, editor, *Literature and Society: Selected Essays on African Literataure,* Zim Pan-African Publishers (Oguta, Nigeria), 1986.

Fraser, Robert, *Ben Okri: Toward the Invisible City,* Northcote House Educational Publishers, 2002.

Gurnah, Abdulrazak, editor, *Essays on African Writing 2,* Heinemann (London, England), 1995.

Moh, Felicia Alu, *Ben Okri: An Introduction to His Early Fiction,* Michigan State University Press (East Lansing, MI), 2002.

Okri, Ben, *Songs of Enchantment,* Doubleday (New York, NY), 1993.

Oxford, J. Currey, *Strategic Transformations in Nigerian Writing: Orality and History in the Work of Rev. Samuel Johnson, Amos Tutuola, Wole Soyinka, and Ben Okri,* Indiana University Press (Bloomington, IN), 1997.

Rutherford, Anna, editor, *From Commonwealth to Post-Colonial,* Dangaroo (Sydney, Australia), 1992.

PERIODICALS

Christian Science Monitor, November 23, 1987; July 10, 1992.

Detroit Free Press, August 30, 1992, p. P9.

Economist, June 15, 1996, p. 3.

Independent (London, England), October 24, 1991, Robert Winder, "The Road to Discovery"; March 3, 1993, Paul Taylor, "Dreams of a Boy on Earth"; March 23, 1993, Hunter Davis, "Ben Okri's Green-Apple, Left-Handed Sort of Day."

Los Angeles Times Book Review, September 24, 1989, pp. 3, 13; June 8, 1992, p. 6.

Nation, May 27, 1996, p. 31.

New Statesman, May 9, 1986, p. 35; July 13, 1986, p. 27; July 25, 1986, p. 30; October 17, 1986, p. 36; July 29, 1988, pp. 43-44; March 26, 1993, p. 41; March 24, 1995, p. 25; April 12, 1996, p. 37; October 7, 2002, William Skidelsky, review of *In Arcadia,* p. 55.

New Statesman & Society, March 22, 1991, p. 44.

New York Times, July 28, 1989.

New York Times Book Review, August 13, 1989, p. 12; June 28, 1992, pp. 3, 20; October 10, 1993.

Observer (London, England), July 10, 1988, p. 42; October 27, 1991, Linda Grant, "The Lonely Road from Twilight to Hard Sun," p. 61.

Spectator (London, England), April 1, 1995, p. 33; August 22, 1998, Andrew Barrow, review of *Infinite Riches,* pp. 34-35; September 28, 2002, Jeremy Treglown, review of *In Arcadia,* pp. 68-69.

Times (London, England), October 24, 1991, Philip Howard, "There Is Wonder Here"; March 13, 1993, Lorraine Griffiths, "Okri: Biography"; March 25, 1993, James Wodall, "In the Land of Fighting Ghosts"; April 7, 1996.

Times Literary Supplement, August 8, 1986, p. 863; August 5-11, 1988, p. 857; April 19, 1991, p. 22; April 17, 1992, p 8; March 10, 1995; April 5, 1996, p. 26; September 11, 1998, review of *Infinite Riches,* p. 23.

Tribune Books (Chicago, IL), July 16, 1989, p. 6; June 14, 1992; October 10, 1993, p. 1.

Village Voice, August 25, 1992, p. 87.
Washington Post, August 7, 1989.
Washington Post Book World, May 24, 1992; October 3, 1993.
World & I, March, 1992, pp. 383-387.
World Literature Today, spring, 1990, p. 349; April-June, 2003, Bruce King, review of *In Arcadia,* pp. 86-67.
World Literature Written in English, fall, 1988, Abioseh Michael Porter, "Ben Okri's *The Landscapes Within:* A Metaphor for Personal and National Development."

* * *

OLDS, Sharon 1942-

PERSONAL: Born November 19, 1942, in San Francisco, CA. *Education:* Stanford University, B.A. (with distinction), 1964; Columbia University, Ph.D., 1972.

ADDRESSES: Home—50 Riverside Drive, New York, NY, 10025-6146. *Office*—New York University, 19 University Pl., Rm. 200, New York, NY, 10003.

CAREER: Poet. Lecturer-in-residence on poetry at Theodor Herzl Institute, 1976-80; visiting teacher of poetry at Manhattan Theater Club, 1982, Nathan Mayhew Seminars of Martha's Vineyard, 1982, Poetry Center, Young Men's Christian Association of New York City, 1982, Poetry Society of America, 1983, New York University, 1983 and 1985, Sarah Lawrence College, 1984, Goldwater Hospital, Roosevelt Island, NY, 1985-90, Columbia University, 1985-86, and State University of New York College—Purchase, 1986; holder of Fanny Hurst Chair, Brandeis University, 1986-87; New York University, New York, NY, associate professor of English, 1992—, acting director of graduate program in creative writing. Founding director, New York University workshop program at Goldwater Hospital, New York.

MEMBER: Poetry Society of America, PEN, Authors Guild.

AWARDS, HONORS: Grants from Creative Artists Public Service, 1978, Guggenheim fellowship, 1981-82, and National Endowment for the Arts fellowship, 1982-83; Madeline Sadin Award, *New York Quarterly,* 1978; younger poets award from *Poetry Miscellany,* 1979; San Francisco Poetry Center Award, 1981, for *Satan Says;* Lamont Poetry Selection of the Academy of American Poets, 1984, and National Book Critics Circle Award, 1985, both for *The Dead and the Living;* T.S. Eliot Prize short list for *The Father,* 1994; Walt Whitman Citation of Merit, New York State Writers Institute, 1998; named New York State Poet, 1998-2000; nominee for National Book Award in poetry category, 2002, for *The Unswept Room;* Academy Fellowship, Academy of American Poets, 2002, for "distinguished poetic achievement at mid-career"; Judge, Griffin Poetry Prize, 2003; Barnes & Noble Writers for Writers Awards, 2004.

WRITINGS:

POETRY

Satan Says, University of Pittsburgh Press (Pittsburgh, PA), 1980.
The Dead and the Living, Knopf (New York, NY), 1984.
The Gold Cell, Knopf (New York, NY), 1987.
The Matter of This World, Slow Dancer Press, 1987.
The Sign of Saturn, Secker & Warburg, 1991.
The Father, Knopf (New York, NY), 1992.
The Wellspring: Poems, Knopf (New York, NY), 1996.
Blood, Tin, Straw, Knopf (New York, NY), 1999.
The Unswept Room, Knopf (New York, NY), 2002.
Strike Sparks: Selected Poems, 1980-2002, Knopf (New York, NY), 2004.

OTHER

(Author of foreword) Tory Dent, *What Silence Equals,* Persea Books (New York, NY) 1993.
(Author of preface) Muriel Rukeyser, *The Orgy: An Irish Journey of Passion and Transformation,* Paris Press (Ashfield, MA) 1997.

CONTRIBUTOR TO ANTHOLOGIES

The Norton Introduction to Poetry, 2nd edition, Norton (New York, NY), 1981.
The Bread Loaf Anthology of Contemporary American Poetry, edited by Robert Pack, Sydney Lea, and Jay Parini, University Press of New England (Hanover, NH), 1985.
Three Genres, The Writing of Poetry, Fiction, and Drama, edited by Stephen Minot, Prentice-Hall (Englewood Cliffs, NJ), 1988.

The Pushcart Prize, VIII: Best of the Small Presses, Wainscott, 1989.

Read to Write, Donald M. Murray, Holt (New York, NY), 1990.

The Longman Anthology of American Poetry: Colonial to Contemporary, edited by Hilary Russell, Longman (New York, NY), 1992.

The Armless Maiden: And Other Tales for Childhood's Survivors, edited by Terri Windling, Tor (New York, NY), 1995.

For a Living: The Poetry of Work, edited by Nicholas Coles and Peter Oresick, University of Illinois Press (Urbana, IL), 1995.

Our Mothers, Our Selves: Writers and Poets Celebrating Motherhood, edited by J.B. Bernstein, Karen J. Donnelly, Bergin & Garvey Trade, 1996.

The House Is Made of Poetry: The Art of Ruth Stone edited by Wendy Barker, Sandra M. Gilbert, Southern Illinois University Press (Carbondale, IL), 1996.

By Herself: Women Reclaim Poetry, edited by Molly McQuade, Graywolf Press (Saint Paul, MN), 2000.

Literature and Its Writers: A Compact Introduction to Fiction, Poetry, and Drama, edited by Ann Charters, Samuel Charters, Bedford/St. Martin's Press (Boston, MA) 2004.

Contributor to literary journals and magazines, including *American Poetry Review, Antioch Review, Atlantic Monthly, Iowa Review, Kayak, Kenyon Review, Massachusetts Review, Mississippi Review, Ms., New Republic, Nation, New Yorker, Paris Review, Pequod, Ploughshares, Poetry, Poetry Northwest, Prairie Schooner,* and *Yale Review.* Olds's works have been translated into Italian, Chinese, French, and Russian.

SIDELIGHTS: Sharon Olds's poetry, which graphically depicts personal family life as well as global political events, has won several prestigious prizes, including the National Book Critics Circle Award. "Sharon Olds is enormously self-aware," wrote David Leavitt in the *Voice Literary Supplement.* "Her poetry is remarkable for its candor, its eroticism, and its power to move." Discussing Olds's work in *Poetry,* Lisel Mueller noted: "By far the greater number of her poems are believable and touching, and their intensity does not interfere with craftsmanship. Listening to Olds, we hear a proud, urgent, human voice."

One of the constant characteristics of Olds's poetry is its accessibility. Her books appeal to a wide audience, and almost all of her work has undergone multiple printings. Her National Book Critics Circle Award-winning volume *The Dead and the Living* alone has sold more than 50,000 copies, ranking her as one of the most profitable of active poets. Her work is viewed in the tradition of Walt Whitman as a celebration of the body, in all its pleasures and pains, and it particularly resonates with women readers. As Charlie Powell put it in a *Salon.com* piece, "Domesticity, death, erotic love—the stark simplicity of Sharon Olds's subjects, and of her plain-spoken language, can sometimes make her seem like the brooding Earth Mother of American poetry."

Born in 1942 in San Francisco, Olds grew up in Berkeley, California. She attended Stanford University and earned her Ph.D. at Columbia in 1972. She was thirty-seven when she published her first book of poems, and she told *Salon.com* that her success was partly due to pure luck. "Anyone who can ever do anything is lucky," she said. "It means that there has been enough education, enough peace, enough time, enough whatever, that somebody can sit down and write. Many lives don't allow that, the good fortune of being able to work at it, and try, and keep trying."

Satan Says, Olds's first collection, explores "the roles in which she experiences herself, 'Daughter,' 'Woman,' and 'Mother,'" according to Mueller. In an article for the *American Book Review,* Joyce Peseroff claimed that throughout *Satan Says,* "the language often does 'turn neatly about.' In Olds's vocabulary ordinary objects, landscapes—even whole planets—are in constant motion. Using verbs which might seem, at first, almost grotesque, she manages to describe a violent, changing universe. . . . In a way, these poems describe a psychic world as turbulent, sensual, and strange as a world seen under water. . . . Sharon Olds convincingly, and with astonishing vigor, presents a world which, if not always hostile, is never clear about which face it will show her."

In a review for the *Nation,* Richard Tillinghast commented on *The Dead and the Living:* "While *Satan Says* was impossible to ignore because of its raw power, *The Dead and the Living* is a considerable step forward. . . . Olds is a keen and accurate observer of people." "I admire Sharon Olds's courage . . . ," declared Elizabeth Gaffney in *America.* "Out of private revelations she makes poems of universal truth, of sex, death, fear, love. Her poems are sometimes jarring, unexpected, bold, but always loving and deeply rewarding." Tillinghast felt, however, that Olds's attempts "to establish political analogies to private brutalization . . . are not very convincing. . . . This becomes a mannerism, representing political thinking only at the superficial level." Nevertheless, Tillinghast conceded that the book "has the chastening impact of a powerful documentary."

Olds's works were described by Sara Plath in *Booklist* as "poems of extreme emotions." Critics have found intense feelings of many sorts—humor, anger, pain, terror, and love. "Her poetry focuses on the primacy of the image rather than the 'issues' which surround it," observed Leavitt, "and her best work exhibits a lyrical acuity which is both purifying and redemptive."

Examples of this "primacy of the image" are displayed in *The Father,* a collection of poems about the death of Olds's father from cancer. While her alcoholic and distant father played a role in many of Olds's earlier poems, here he is the central concern. The author describes his illness, final days, and death in a series of graphic, narrowly focused poems. Writing in *Belles Lettres,* Lee Upton remarked that the collection "amounts to something close to a spiritual ordeal for the reader, for the poems are wrenching in their candor and detail." *American Book Review* contributor Steve Kowit stated: "As a coherent sequence of poems, *The Father* has a most uncommon power—impelling the reader forward with the narrative and dramatic force of a stunning novel." Commenting on the collection's tight focus, Lisa Zeidner in the *New York Times Book Review* noted that "the deliberate tunnel vision is the book's originality and its liability." Clair Willis of the *Times Literary Supplement* came to a similar conclusion about the book, commenting: "The volume as a whole is a risky undertaking, nearly marred simply by offering us too much of the same. Yet finally it works." Upton concluded that *The Father* "is Olds's most important work to date."

Commenting on Olds's achievements in her several volumes of verse, Kowit noted that the poet "has become a central presence in American poetry, her narrative and dramatic power as well as the sheer imagistic panache of her work having won her a large following among that small portion of the general public that still reads verse." That popularity has not met with universal approval from the critics, some of whom have felt that her work lacks depth, revels in graphic images, and is narcissistic. "For a writer whose best poems evince strong powers of observation, Olds spends too much time taking her own emotional temperature," maintained Ken Tucker in the *New York Times Book Review.* "Everything must return to the poet—her needs, her wants, her disappointments with the world and the people around her." In the *New Republic,* Adam Kirsch wrote: "Beneath all the surface agitation, all the vulgar language, the programmatically unfeminine sexual bravado, there is a deadening certainty that makes each poem unsurprising. And therefore ultimately consoling: Olds has a devoted and comparatively large following because no reader will ever be brought by any of her poems to question himself."

Other critics have been eager to champion Olds's work. In a *Seattle Times* review of *Blood, Tin, Straw,* Richard Wakefield noted that Olds writes "poetry more faithful to the felt truth of reality than any prose could be." Wakefield added: "Simply to say that Olds portrays a world suffused with love is to trivialize what these poems indisputably earn." *Poetry Flash* reviewer Richard Silberg commended Olds for "taking on subjects not written before, or not written in these ways . . . and the best of these poems have a density of inspiration line by line." In *Booklist,* Donna Seaman concluded that Olds's work is "blessed by the light that shines on each page from the entranced and grateful eyes of her readers."

"*The Unswept Room* has a maternal slant," Carol Rumens asserted in the *Guardian,* though "never as relentlessly central or focused as the father . . . in previous collections." Rumens added, "Often perceived as a faltering, otherworldly voice, a nymph or dryad crying, singing or softly complaining, mother elicits a more fluttering and uncertain response from her daughter-confessor." The title poem, "The Unswept," describes a depiction of a feast rendered on the mosaic-tiled floor of the Museo Gregoriano Profano. Rumens observed that the poem is "rhythmically clear-cut" and "the shapes of decomposition, 'laid down in tiny tiles by the rhyparographer,' suggest a cooler, more bookish diction, less elevated rhythm, stop-studded glossaries instead of comma-spangled flights."

Kate Daniels, reviewing *The Unswept Room* in the *Women's Review of Books,* noted that "without abandoning her characteristic intensity, [Olds] continues to disquiet and decenter, but in a newly ruminative voice that bespeaks the journey of mid-life." Daniels observed that "as carefully as an archeologist, [Olds] combs through the accoutrements of a life in late middle age," and added that "clearly, the philosophical and spiritual development within so many of the poems in *The Unswept Room* suggests a poet who is preparing herself for the remainder of life rather than mourning her past or bemoaning lost opportunities. . . . Perhaps it is because the room of Olds's life is yet unswept, redolent with the delicious detritus that composes any life."

In an interview with *Salon.com,* Olds addressed the aims of her poetry. "I think that my work is easy to understand because I am not a thinker. I am not a. . . . How can I put it? I write the way I perceive, I guess. It's not really simple, I don't think, but it's about ordinary things—feeling about things, about people. I'm not an intellectual. I'm not an abstract thinker. And I'm interested in ordinary life." She added that she is "not asking a poem to carry a lot of rocks in its pockets. Just being an ordinary observer and liver and feeler and letting the experience get through you onto the notebook with the pen, through the arm, out of the body, onto the page, without distortion."

BIOGRAPHICAL AND CRITICAL SOURCES:

BOOKS

Contemporary Literary Criticism, Thomson Gale (Detroit, MI), Volume 32, 1985, Volume 39, 1986, Volume 85, 1995.

Contemporary Poets, 6th edition, St. James Press (Detroit, MI), 1996.

Contemporary Women Poets, St. James Press (Detroit, MI), 1998.

Contemporary Women's Poetry: Reading/Writing/Practice, edited by Alison Mark and Deryn Rees-Jones, St. Martin's Press (New York, NY), 2000.

Davis, Cortney, *Leopold's Maneuvers,* University of Nebraska Press (Lincoln, NE), 2004.

Dictionary of Literary Biography, Volume 120: *American Poets since World War II,* Thomson Gale (Detroit, MI), 1992.

Gregerson, Linda, *Negative Capability: Contemporary American Poetry,* University of Michigan Press (Ann Arbor, MI) 2001.

Myers, Jack, and David Wojahn, editors, *A Profile of Twentieth-Century American Poetry,* Southern Illinois University Press (Carbondale, IL), 1991.

Oldfield, Sybil, *Women against the Iron Fist: Alternatives to Militarism, 1900 to 1989,* B. Blackwell (Cambridge, MA), 1989.

Ostriker, Alicia, *Dancing at the Devil's Party: Essays on Poetry, Politics, and the Erotic,* University of Michigan Press (Ann Arbor, MI), 2000.

Swiontkowski, Thomson Gale, *Imagining Incest: Sexton, Plath, Rich, and Olds on Life with Daddy,* Susquehanna University Press (Selinsgrove, PA), 2003.

Wolff, Rebecca, *Manderley: Poems,* University of Illinois Press (Urbana, IL), 2001.

PERIODICALS

Albany Times Union, March 30, 1998.

America, June 30, 1984.

American Book Review, February, 1982; April, 1993, p. 24.

American Poetry Review, September, 1984; September-October, 1987, pp. 31-35; November-December, 1989.

Belles Lettres, fall, 1992, p. 30.

Booklist, October 1, 1999, Donna Seaman, review of *Blood, Tin, Straw,* p. 339.

Guardian, April 26, 2003, Carol Rumens, review of *The Unswept Room.*

Nation, October 13, 1984; December, 1992, p. 748.

New Criterion, December, 1999, William Logan, "No Mercy," p. 60.

New Republic, December 27, 1999, Adam Kirsch, "The Exhibitionist," p. 38.

New York Times Book Review, March 18, 1984; March 21, 1993, p. 14; November 14, 1999, Ken Tucker, "Family Ties."

Poetry, June, 1981; January, 1987, p. 231; April, 1994, pp. 39.

Publishers Weekly, November 8, 1993, p. 71; November 27, 1995, p. 65; September 27, 1999, review of *Blood, Tin, Straw,* p. 98.

Seattle Times, January 16, 2000, Richard Wakefield, "Olds' Poems Delve into Depths of Love."

Times Literary Supplement, May 31, 1991, pp. 11-12; July 16, 1993, p. 25.

Voice Literary Supplement, May, 1984.

Women's Review of Books, February, 1984, pp. 16-17; May, 2003, Kate Daniels, "Gritty and Alive," review of *The Unswept Room,* p. 16.

Yale Review, autumn, 1987, p. 140.

ONLINE

Academy of American Poets Web site, http://www.poets.org/ (March 20, 2003).

Gravity: A Journal of Online Writing, Music and Art, http://www.newtonsbaby.com/gravity/ (spring, 2000), Joy Yourcenar, review of *Blood, Tin, Straw.*

New York State Writer's Institute Web site, http://www.albany.edu/writers-inst/ (November 28, 2000), "Sharon Olds: State Poet 1998-2000."

Poetry Flash, http://www.poetryflash.org/ (February-March, 2000), Richard Silberg, review of *Blood, Tin, Straw.*

Salon.com, http://www.salon.com/ (July 1, 1996), Charlie Powell, interview with Olds.

* * *

OLIVER, Mary 1935-

PERSONAL: Born September 10, 1935, in Cleveland, OH; daughter of Edward William (a teacher) and Helen M. (Vlasak) Oliver. *Education:* Attended Ohio State University, 1955-56, and Vassar College, 1956-57.

ADDRESSES: Office—Bennington College, Bennington, VT 05201. *Agent*—c/o Molly Malone Cook Literary Agency, Box 619, Provincetown, MA 02657.

CAREER: Fine Arts Work Center, Provincetown, MA, chair of writing department, 1972-73, member of writing committee, 1984; Case Western Reserve University, Cleveland, OH, Mather Visiting Professor, 1980, 1982; Bucknell University, Lewisburg, PA, poet-in-residence, 1986; University of Cincinnati, Cincinnati, OH, Elliston Visiting Professor, 1986; Sweet Briar College, Sweet Briar, VA, Margaret Banister Writer-in-Residence, 1991-95; Bennington College, Bennington, VT, Catharine Osgood Foster Chair for Distinguished Teaching, 1996—.

MEMBER: PEN.

AWARDS, HONORS: First prize, Poetry Society of America, 1962, for "No Voyage"; Devil's Advocate Award, 1968, for "Christmas, 1966"; Shelley Memorial Award, 1972; National Endowment for the Arts fellow, 1972-73; Alice Fay di Castagnola Award, 1973; Guggenheim fellow, 1980-81; Award in Literature, American Academy and Institution of Arts and Letters, 1983; Pulitzer Prize, 1984, for *American Primitive;* Christopher Award and L.L. Winship Award, both 1991, for *House of Light;* National Book Award for Poetry, 1992, for *New and Selected Poems;* Lannan Literary Award for Poetry, 1998.

WRITINGS:

No Voyage, and Other Poems, Dent (New York, NY), 1963, expanded edition, Houghton Mifflin (Boston, MA), 1965.

The River Styx, Ohio, and Other Poems, Harcourt (New York, NY), 1972.

The Night Traveler, Bits Press, 1978.

Twelve Moons, Little, Brown (Boston, MA), 1978.

Sleeping in the Forest, Ohio Review Chapbook, 1979.

American Primitive, Little, Brown (Boston, MA), 1983.

Dream Work, Atlantic Monthly Press (Boston, MA), 1986.

Provincetown, Appletree Alley, 1987.

(Author of introduction) Frank Gaspar, *Holyoke,* Northeastern University Press, 1988.

House of Light, Beacon Press (Boston, MA), 1990.

New and Selected Poems, Beacon Press (Boston, MA), 1992.

A Poetry Handbook, Harcourt (San Diego, CA), 1994.

White Pine: Poems and Prose Poems, Harcourt (San Diego, CA), 1994.

Blue Pastures, Harcourt (New York, NY), 1995.

West Wind: Poems and Prose Poems, Houghton Mifflin (Boston, MA), 1997.

Rules for the Dance: A Handbook for Writing and Reading Metrical Verse, Houghton Mifflin (Boston, MA), 1998.

Winter Hours: Prose, Prose Poems, and Poems, Houghton Mifflin (Boston, MA), 1999.

The Leaf and the Cloud, Da Capo (Cambridge, MA), 2000.

What Do We Know, Da Capo (Cambridge, MA), 2002.

Why I Wake Early, Beacon (Boston, MA), 2004.

Boston Iris: Poems and Essays, Beacon (Boston, MA), 2004.

Long Life: Essays and Other Writings, Da Capo (Cambridge, MA), 2004.

New and Selected Poems, Volume Two, Beacon (Boston, MA), 2004.

Contributor of poetry and essays to periodicals in England and the United States.

ADAPTATIONS: Oliver's poems have been set to music for mezzo-soprano voice, violin, and piano by composer Augusta Read Thomas in *In Summer,* Theodore Presser (Bryn Mawr, PA), 1994, and for soprano voice and bassoon by composer Ann Kearns in *Six Poems of Mary Oliver,* Casia Publishing Co. (Bryn Mawr, PA), 1997.

SIDELIGHTS: Poet Mary Oliver is an "indefatigable guide to the natural world," wrote Maxine Kumin in *Women's Review of Books,* "particularly to its lesser-known aspects." Oliver's verse focuses on the quiet of occurrences of nature: industrious hummingbirds, egrets, motionless ponds, "lean owls / hunkering with their lamp-eyes." Kumin noted of the poet: "She stands quite comfortably on the margins of things, on the line between earth and sky, the thin membrane that separates human from what we loosely call animal." The power of Oliver's poetry earned her numerous awards, including 1984's Pulitzer Prize for *American Primitive* and the National Book Award in 1992 for *New and Selected Poems.* Reviewing *Dream Work* for the *Nation,* critic Alicia Ostriker numbered Oliver among America's finest poets, as "visionary as [Ralph Waldo] Emerson."

American Primitive, according to *New York Times Book Review*'s Bruce Bennet, "insists on the primacy of the physical." Bennet noted that "recurring images of ingestion" figure throughout the volume, and "as we joyfully devour luscious objects and substances . . . we are continually reminded of our involvement in a process in which what consumes will be consumed." Bennet commended Oliver's "distinctive voice and vision" and asserts that the "collection contains a number of powerful, substantial works." Holly Prado of *Los Angeles Times Book Review* also applauded Oliver's original voice when she wrote that *American Primitive* "touches a vitality in the familiar that invests it with a fresh intensity."

Dream Work continues Oliver's search to "understand both the wonder and pain of nature" according to Prado in a later review for *Los Angeles Times Book Review.* Ostriker sounded this note more specifically when she considered Oliver "among the few American poets who can describe and transmit ecstasy, while retaining a practical awareness of the world as one of predators and prey." Colin Lowndes of the Toronto *Globe & Mail* similarly considered Oliver "a poet of worked-for reconciliations" whose volume deals with thresholds, or the "points at which opposing forces meet." Both Prado and Ostriker praised Oliver's lyrical gift. Ostriker described Oliver's verse as "intensely lyrical, flute-like, slender and swift . . . [riding] on vivid phrases," while Prado called the poetry of *Dream Work* "the best of the real lyrics we have these days." *Dream Work,* for Ostriker, is ultimately a volume in which Oliver moves "from the natural world and its desires, the 'heaven of appetite' . . . into the world of historical and personal suffering. . . . She confronts as well, steadily," Ostriker continued, "what she cannot change."

The transition from engaging the natural world to engaging the more personal is also evident in *New and Selected Poems.* The volume contains poems from eight of Oliver's previous volumes as well as previously unpublished, newer work. Susan Salter Reynolds, in the *Los Angeles Times Book Review,* noticed that Oliver's earliest poems are almost always oriented towards nature, occasionally discuss relatives, but seldom examine her own self. In contrast, she appears constantly in her later works, such as *Long Life: Essays and Other Writings.* This is, as Reynolds noted, a good thing: "This self-consciousness is a rich and graceful addition." Just as the contributor for *Publishers Weekly* called particular attention to the pervasive tone of amazement—also the title of a poem—with regard to things seen in Oliver's work, Reynolds found Oliver's writings to have a "Blake-eyed revelatory quality." Oliver summed up her desire for amazement in her poem "When Death Comes" from *New and Selected Poems:* "When it's over, I want to say: all my life / I was a bride married to amazement. / I was the bridegroom, taking the world into my arms."

Oliver continues her celebration of the natural world in later collections, including *White Pine: Poems and Prose Poems, Blue Pastures, West Wind: Poems and Prose Poems,* and *Winter Hours: Prose, Prose Poems, and Poems.* Critics have compared her work to that of great American lyric poets and celebrators of nature, including Marianne Moore, Elizabeth Bishop, Edna St. Vincent Millay, John Muir, and Walt Whitman. "Oliver's poetry, pure as the cottony seeds of the dandelion," wrote *Poetry* contributor Richard Tillinghast in a review of *White Pine,* "floats above and around the schools and controversies of contemporary American poetry. Her familiarity with the natural world has an uncomplicated, nineteenth-century feeling." *America* reviewer David Sofield, in a critique of the same volume, called Oliver "an Emersonian rhapsode in full flight, but one with something like the canny vulnerability of Elizabeth Bishop when evoking the pathos of creatures great and small." "William Carlos Williams is alive in many of these poems," Sofield explained, as is the "late Wallace Stevens. . . . In putting her own stamp on poems about birds and trees and animals and seasons, and in her unyielding intensity," the *America* contributor concluded, ". . . this Mary Oliver provides serious pleasure."

In *Rules for the Dance: A Handbook for Writing and Reading Metrical Verse* Oliver returns to a subject she visited in *A Poetry Handbook.* Critics had celebrated the earlier volume as the work of "someone who has observed poems and their writing closely and who writes with unassuming authority about the work she and others do," according to a *Publishers Weekly* contributor. Oliver "starts in at poetry's real beginning, discussing the need for patient application: the need, in brief, to write and to do so regularly," explained Pat Monaghan in *Booklist.* "She so deeply knows her craft that she can describe it with perfect simplicity and concision." "Poetry is Oliver's lifeblood," declared *Booklist* contributor Donna Seaman in a review of *Rules for the Dance,* "and she writes about its creation with as much quiet ecstasy, acumen, and artistry as she writes poems themselves."

BIOGRAPHICAL AND CRITICAL SOURCES:

BOOKS

Contemporary Literary Criticism, Thomson Gale (Detroit, MI), Volume 19, 1981, Volume 98, 1998.

Contemporary Literary Criticism Yearbook 1984, Volume 34, Thomson Gale (Detroit, MI), 1985.

Contemporary Poets, 6th edition, St. James Press (Detroit, MI), 1996.
Dictionary of Literary Biography, Volume 5: *American Poets since World War II,* Thomson Gale (Detroit, MI), 1980.
Oliver, Mary, *New and Selected Poems,* Beacon Press, 1992.

PERIODICALS

America, January 13, 1996, David Sofield, review of *White Pine: Poems and Prose Poems.*
Booklist, July, 1994, Pat Monaghan, review of *A Poetry Handbook,* p. 1916; November 15, 1994, Donna Seaman, review of *White Pine,* p. 574; June 1, 1997, Donna Seaman, review of *West Wind: Poems and Prose Poems,* p. 1648; June 1, 1998, Donna Seaman, review of *Rules for the Dance: A Handbook for Writing and Reading Metrical Verse,* p. 1708; March 15, 1999, Donna Seaman, review of *Winter Hours,* p. 1279; September 1, 2000, Donna Seaman, review of *The Leaf and the Cloud,* p. 58; March 15, 2004, Donna Seaman, review of *Long Life: Essays and Other Writings,* p. 1259.
Globe & Mail (Toronto, Ontario, Canada), August 23, 1986.
Library Journal, July, 1997, Ellen Kaufman, review of *West Wind,* p. 87; August, 1998, Lisa J. Cihlar, review of *Rules for the Dance,* p. 104; December, 2000, Louis McKee, review of *The Leaf and the Cloud,* p. 145; December, 2003, Judy Clarence, review of *Owls and Other Fantasies: Poems and Essays,* p. 125; May 1, 2004, Kim Harris, review of *Long Life,* p. 107.
Los Angeles Times Book Review, August 21, 1983, p. 9; February 22, 1987, p. 8; August 30, 1992, p. 6.
Nation, August 30, 1986, pp. 148-150.
New York Times Book Review, July 17, 1983, pp. 10, 22; November 25, 1990, p. 24; December 13, 1992, p. 12.
Poetry, May, 1987, p. 113; September, 1991, p. 342; July, 1993, David Barber, review of *New and Selected Poems,* p. 233; August, 1995, Richard Tillinghast, review of *White Pine,* p. 289; August, 1999, Christian Wiman, review of *Rules for the Dance,* p. 286.
Publishers Weekly, May 4, 1990, p. 62; August 10, 1992, p. 58; June 6, 1994, review of *A Poetry Handbook,* p. 62; October 31, 1994, review of *White Pine,* p. 54; August 7, 1995, review of *Blue Pastures,* p. 457; June 30, 1997, review of *West Wind,* p. 73; March 29, 1999, review of *Winter Hours: Prose, Prose Poems, and Poems,* p. 100; August 28, 2000, review of *The Leaf and the Cloud,* p. 79; July 21, 2003, review of *Owls and Other Fantasies,* p. 188.
Washington Post Book World, February 1, 1987, p. 6.
Whole Earth Review, summer, 1995, Wade Fox, review of *A Poetry Handbook,* p. 30.
Women's Review of Books, April, 1993.

* * *

OLSEN, Tillie 1912(?)-

PERSONAL: Born January 14, 1912 (some sources say 1913), in Omaha, NE; daughter of Samuel (Nebraska state secretary of Socialist Party) and Ida (Beber) Lerner; married Jack Olsen (a printer), 1936; children: Karla Olsen Lutz, Julie Olsen Edwards, Katherine Jo, Laurie. *Education:* High school graduate.

ADDRESSES: Home—1435 Laguna #6, San Francisco, CA 94115. *Agent*—Elaine Markson Literary Agency, 44 Greenwich Ave., New York, NY 10011.

CAREER: Worked in industry and as typist/transcriber. Visiting professor, Amherst College, Amherst, MA, 1969-70, and University of Massachusetts, Amherst, 1974; visiting instructor, Stanford University, 1971; writer-in-residence, Massachusetts Institute of Technology, 1973, and Kenyon College, 1987—; International Visiting Scholar, Norway, 1980; Hill professor, University of Minnesota, 1986. Regents Lecturer, University of California—San Diego, 1978, and University of California—Los Angeles, 1987.

MEMBER: Authors Guild, PEN, Writer's Union.

AWARDS, HONORS: Stanford University creative writing fellowship, 1956-57; Ford Foundation grant in literature, 1959; O. Henry Award for best American short story, 1961, for "Tell Me a Riddle"; fellowship, Radcliffe Institute for Independent Study, 1962-64; National Endowment for the Arts grant, 1968; Guggenheim fellowship, 1975-76; award in literature, American Academy and National Institute of Arts and Letters, 1975; honorary Doctor of Arts and Letters, University of Nebraska, 1979, and Hobart and William Smith College, 1984; Ministry to Women Award, Unitarian Women's Federation, 1980; British Post Office and B.P.W. award, 1980; Tillie Olsen Day designated in San Francisco, 1981; honorary Litt.D., Knox College, 1982, and Albright College, 1986; honorary L.H.D., Clark University, 1985; Bunting Institute fellowship, Radcliffe College, 1985; Litt.D., Wooster College, 1991; Rea Award, 1994; Litt.D., Mills College, 1995.

WRITINGS:

Tell Me a Riddle: A Collection (stories), Lippincott (Philadelphia, PA), 1961, with an introduction by John Leonard, Delta/Seymour Lawrence (New York, NY), 1994, edited with an introduction by Deborah Silverton Rosenfelt, Rutgers University Press (New Brunswick, NJ), 1995.

(Editor and author of biographical interpretation) Rebecca Harding Davis, *Life in the Iron Mills* (nonfiction), Feminist Press (New York, NY), 1972.

Yonnondio: From the Thirties (novel), Delacorte Press (New York, NY), 1974.

Silences (essays), Delacorte Press (New York, NY), 1978.

(Editor) *Mother to Daughter, Daughter to Mother: A Daybook and Reader,* Feminist Press (New York, NY), 1984.

(With Julie Olsen Edwards and Estelle Jussim) *Mothers and Daughters: That Special Quality: An Exploration in Photographs,* Aperture Foundation (New York, NY), 1987.

Short stories appear in more than one hundred anthologies, including *Best American Short Stories,* 1957, 1961, and 1971, *Fifty Best American Stories, 1915-1965, Prize Stories: The O. Henry Awards, 1961, Norton Introduction to Literature,* 1977, *Elements of Literature,* 1978, and *The Modern Tradition,* 1979. Contributor to *Ms., Harper's, College English,* and *Trellis.*

A collection of Olsen's manuscripts is housed in the Berg Collection at the New York Public Library.

SIDELIGHTS: Tillie Olsen writes about those people who, because of their class, sex, or race, have been denied the opportunity to express and develop themselves. In a strongly emotional style, she tells of their dreams and failures, of what she calls "the unnatural thwarting of what struggles to come into being but cannot." Olsen has published relatively little, citing her own life circumstances as the cause. She was forced to delay her writing for some twenty years while working at a number of jobs and raising four children. Her novel *Yonnondio* was begun during the depression but not finished until the early seventies. As Margaret Atwood wrote in the *New York Times Book Review,* "few writers have gained such wide respect on such a small body of published work. . . . Among women writers in the United States, 'respect' is too pale a word: 'reverence' is more like it. This is presumably because women writers, even more than their male counterparts, recognize what a heroic feat it is to have held down a job, raised four children, and still somehow managed to become and to remain a writer."

The daughter of politically active Jewish immigrants, Olsen was influenced by her parents' philosophies about politics and economics, and by the age of eighteen she was a member of the Young Communist League. After leaving high school, Olsen worked various jobs as a laborer, had her first child, and remained politically active. During this time, Olsen was arrested twice for her political activities. In Kansas City, she was jailed for organizing workers at a packinghouse, which induced her to write about the terrible conditions in the slaughterhouses. Around the same time, she was prompted to begin her first book, *Yonnondio: From the Thirties.* She then left the Midwest for California, became involved in the San Francisco Longshoremen's strike of 1934 and was jailed again for her support of unions. In 1936 she married Jack Olsen, also a union organizer. From 1937 onward, Olsen became consumed with her family and did not complete *Yonnondio,* focusing her energy instead on raising her four daughters and working as a waitress and secretary.

Olsen did not take up writing again until 1956, when she received a fellowship from Stanford University after taking a creative writing course at San Francisco State University. In 1959, she received a Ford Foundation grant and completed the O. Henry award-winning short story "Tell Me a Riddle." This novella describes the conflict of a Jewish couple, Eva and David, who have endured thirty-seven years of marriage. The wife, suffering from a terminal disease, also suffers from her husband's insensitivity. Eva has spent her entire life satisfying the needs of her husband and children and continues to do so through her cancerous death. When David's wish to travel supersedes Eva's need for rest and her desire to be in her own home, he sells their house and they travel the United States, visiting their children along the way. Eva finds her only escape from the continuous demands of her husband and children is to hide herself in a closet and relive earlier episodes of her life.

"Tell Me a Riddle" received much critical acclaim. "This novella," commented Margaret B. McDowell in *Contemporary Novelists,* "demonstrates Olsen's artistry in characterization, dialogue, and sensory appeal, and it fully displays, as does all her fiction, her highly rhythmic and metaphorical use of language." *Los Angeles Times Book Review* contributor Elena Brunet praised Olsen's talent for capturing "the modes of speech of characters" regardless of their age. "Tell Me a Riddle," along with several other short stories, was published in a highly praised collection in 1961, also titled *Tell Me a Riddle.* Speaking of the collection, R.M. Elman of *Commonweal* stated that "there are stories in this collection which are perfectly realized works of art."

Teaching positions and grants allowed Olsen to continue to develop her work. Eventually she finished her novel *Yonnondio,* almost forty years after she began it. Hailed by some critics as one of the best novels about the 1930s, *Yonnondio* details the life of a poor family, the Holbrooks, during the Depression. The story is narrated by Mazie Holbrook, the young daughter. Mazie details the family's journey to find work from Wyoming to North Dakota and then Chicago. Initially hopeful and responsive, Mazie gradually becomes absorbed by the futility of their plight when the family moves to the city. Her father becomes increasingly ill-tempered and as he sinks into alcoholism, his physical and verbal abuse towards his wife increases. The narration then shifts to the mother, Anna. Her life is absorbed by those around her—her children and her husband. She endures not only oppression by class, but also by gender. Like Eva in "Tell Me a Riddle," Anna finds her escape in avoiding reality; her solution is to break down mentally rather than confront the pain of reality.

Yonnondio was well received, although some critics found the story too depressing and hopeless. *Yonnondio* "is the story of real people who are visibly shackled by having no money at all and by the daily insults offered by the world to their pride," wrote a contributor to the *New Yorker.* "By the end of the novel . . . pain, rather than building the Holbrook character, has bleached it out" stated Susannah Clapp in her review for the *Times Literary Supplement.* Catherine R. Stimpson, appraising the novel for the *Nation,* noted that although the condition of poverty "seeks to destroy" the characters, "Olsen's compelling gift is her ability to render lyrically the rhythms of consciousness of victims."

"*Yonnondio* is one of the most powerful statements to have emerged from the American 'thirties,'" wrote Peter Ackroyd in the *Spectator,* praising Olsen's work. "A young woman has pulled out of that uneasy time a living document which is full of the wear and tear of the period, and she has done so without doctrinaire blues, and without falling into the trap of a sentimentality which is, at bottom, self-pity." Likewise, *Washington Post Book World* contributor Jack Salzman asserted that "*Yonnondio* clearly must take its place as the best novel to come out of the so-called proletarian movement" of America's Depression era.

Silences, Olsen's subsequent book, is about the difficulties some people have in writing due to economic, social, or familial obligations, as well as from prejudices against color, class, and gender. Because of these difficulties, Olsen argues, some people have written little or nothing; as a result, these voices are never heard, these stories are never told, and they create a void in the world of literature. She supports her viewpoint with examples from her own experience and as well as the struggles of other authors. She includes selections from other writers to illustrate the optimum conditions for writing, then discusses the obstacles that prohibit writers, especially women, from creating. "Olsen's remarkable power comes from having almost never written at all," observed Helen McNeil in a *Times Literary Supplement* review. "First a silent, then a vocal conscience for American women's writing, Olsen writes with an elegance, compassion, and directness rare in any period." Commenting on Olsen's emotional voice, *Antioch Review* contributor Nolan Miller added that *Silences* "bears the stamp of a passionate and reasonably angry voice. What is said here needed to be said."

BIOGRAPHICAL AND CRITICAL SOURCES:

BOOKS

Baker, Christina Looper, and Christina Baker Kline, *The Conversation Begins: Mothers and Daughters Talk about Living Feminism,* Bantam (New York, NY), 1996.

Cardoni, Agnes Toloczko, *Women's Ethical Coming of Age: Adolescent Female Characters in the Prose Fiction of Tillie Olsen,* University Press of America (Lanham, MD), 1997.

Coiner, Constance, *Better Red: The Writing and Resistance of Tillie Olsen and Meridel Le Sueur,* Oxford University Press (New York, NY), 1995.

Contemporary Literary Criticism, Thomson Gale (Detroit, MI), Volume 4, 1975, Volume 13, 1980.

Contemporary Novelists, St. James Press (Detroit, MI), 1986.

Dictionary of Literary Biography, Volume 28: *Twentieth-Century American-Jewish Fiction Writers,* Thomson Gale (Detroit, MI), 1984.

Dictionary of Literary Biography Yearbook: 1980, Thomson Gale (Detroit, MI), 1981.
Faulkner, Mara, *Protest and Possibility in the Writing of Tillie Olsen,* University Press of Virginia (Charlottesville, VA), 1993.
Frye, Joanne S., *Tillie Olsen: A Study of the Short Fiction,* Prentice Hall (Upper Saddle River, NJ), 1995.
Hedges, Elaine, and Shelley Fisher Fishkin, *Listening to Silences,* Oxford University Press (New York, NY), 1994.
Nelson, Kay Hoyle, and Nancy Lyman Huse, *The Critical Response to Tillie Olsen,* Greenwood Press (Westport, CT), 1994.
Orr, Elaine Neil, *Tillie Olsen and a Feminist Spiritual Vision,* University of Mississippi (University, MS), 1987.
Rabinowitz, Paula, *Labor and Desire: Women's Revolutionary Fiction in Depression America,* University of North Carolina Press (Chapel Hill, NC), 1991.
Roberts, Nora Ruth, *Three Radical Women Writers: Class and Gender in Meridel Le Sueur, Tillie Olsen, and Josephine Herbst,* Garland Publisher (New York, NY), 1996.
Short Story Criticism, Volume 11, Thomson Gale (Detroit, MI), 1992.
Van Buren, Jane Silverman, *The Modernist Madonna: Semiotics of the Maternal Metaphor,* Indiana University Press (Bloomington, IN), 1989, pp. 161-167.

PERIODICALS

American Poetry Review, May-June, 1979.
Antioch Review, fall, 1978.
Atlantic Monthly, September, 1978.
Christian Science Monitor, November 9, 1961; September 18, 1978.
Commonweal, December 8, 1961.
Feminist Studies, fall, 1981, pp. 370-406.
Los Angeles Times, May 15, 1980.
Ms., September, 1974.
Nation, April 10, 1972.
New Leader, May 22, 1978.
New Republic, November 13, 1961; March 30, 1974; December 6, 1975; July 29, 1978.
New Yorker, March 25, 1974.
New York Times, July 31, 1978.
New York Times Book Review, November 12, 1961; March 31, 1974; July 30, 1978; June 19, 1983.
Publishers Weekly, November 23, 1984; April 11, 1994, p. 13.
Studies in American Fiction, spring, 1989, pp. 61-69; autumn, 1993, p. 209.
Studies in Short Fiction, fall, 1963; fall, 1986, pp. 401-406; fall, 1994, p. 278.
Time, October 27, 1961.
Times (London, England), October 26, 1985.
Times Literary Supplement, November 14, 1980.
Virginia Quarterly Review, fall, 1974.
Washington Post, September 11, 1978; March 30, 1980.
Women's Studies Quarterly, spring, 1995, p. 219.
Yale Review, winter, 1979.

* * *

ONDAATJE, Michael 1943-
(Philip Michael Ondaatje)

PERSONAL: Born September 12, 1943, in Colombo, Ceylon (now Sri Lanka); immigrated to Canada, 1962; son of Philip Mervyn and Enid Doris (Gratiaen) Ondaatje; married Betty Kimbark, 1963 (marriage ended); married Kim Jones (separated); children: Quintin, Griffin. *Education:* Attended St. Thomas College (Colombo, Ceylon), and Dulwich College (London, England); attended Bishop's University (Lennoxville, Quebec, Canada), 1962-64; University of Toronto, B.A., 1965; Queen's University (Kingston, Ontario, Canada), M.A., 1967. *Hobbies and other interests:* Hound breeding, hog breeding.

ADDRESSES: *Office*—Department of English, Glendon College, York University, 2275 Bayview Ave., Toronto, Ontario M4N 3M6, Canada. *Agent*—c/o Ellen Levine, 15 E. 26th St., Ste. 1801, New York, NY 10010.

CAREER: University of Western Ontario, London, Ontario, Canada, instructor, 1967-71; Glendon College, York University, Toronto, Ontario, Department of English faculty, beginning 1970, became professor; Coach House Press, Toronto, Ontario, editor, 1970-94; *Mongrel Broadsides,* editor; *Brick* (literary journal), editor. Visiting professor, University of Hawaii—Honolulu, 1979, and Brown University, 1990. Director of films, including *Sons of Captain Poetry,* 1970, *Carry on Crime and Punishment,* 1972, *Royal Canadian Hounds,* 1973, *The Clinton Special,* 1974, and *Inventor of Dragland Hog Feeder,* 1975.

AWARDS, HONORS: Ralph Gustafson award, 1965; Epstein award, 1966; E.J. Pratt Medal, 1966; President's Medal, University of Western Ontario, 1967; Canada Council grant, 1968, 1977; Canadian Governor General's Award for Literature, 1971, for *The*

Collected Poems of Billy the Kid, 1980, for *There's a Trick with a Knife I'm Learning to Do,* 1992, for *The English Patient,* and 2000, for *Anil's Ghost;* Books in Canada First Novel Award, 1977, for *Coming through Slaughter;* Canadian Governor General's Award for Poetry, 1979; Canada-Australia Prize, 1980; Toronto Book Award, 1988; Booker Prize, British Book Trust, 1992, for *The English Patient;* Literary Lion Award, New York Public Library, 1993; Giller Prize, and Prix Medicis, both 2000, and *Irish Times* Literature Prize shortlist, 2001, all for *Anil's Ghost;* American Cinema Editors' Robert Wise Award, 2003, for *The Conversations: Walter Murch and the Art of Editing Film.*

WRITINGS:

POETRY

The Dainty Monsters, Coach House Press (Toronto, Ontario, Canada), 1967.

The Man with Seven Toes, Coach House Press (Toronto, Ontario, Canada), 1969.

The Collected Works of Billy the Kid: Left-handed Poems (also see below), Anansi (Toronto, Ontario, Canada), 1970, Berkley (New York, NY), 1975.

Rat Jelly, Coach House Press (Toronto, Ontario, Canada), 1973.

Elimination Dance, Nairn Coldstream (Ilderton, Ontario, Canada), 1978, revised edition, Brick, 1980.

There's a Trick with a Knife I'm Learning to Do: Poems, 1963-1978, W.W. Norton (New York, NY), 1979, published as *Rat Jelly, and Other Poems, 1963-1978,* Marion Boyars (London, England), 1980.

Secular Love, Coach House Press (Toronto, Ontario, Canada), 1984, W.W. Norton (New York, NY), 1985.

All along the Mazinaw: Two Poems (broadside), Woodland Pattern (Milwaukee, WI), 1986.

Two Poems, Woodland Pattern (Milwaukee, WI), 1986.

The Cinnamon Peeler: Selected Poems, Pan (London, England), 1989, Knopf (New York, NY), 1991.

Handwriting, McClelland & Stewart (Toronto, Ontario, Canada), 1998, Knopf (New York, NY), 1999.

NOVELS

Coming through Slaughter (also see below), Anansi (Toronto, Ontario, Canada), 1976, W.W. Norton (New York, NY), 1977.

In the Skin of a Lion (also see below), Knopf (New York, NY), 1987.

The English Patient, Knopf (New York, NY), 1992.

Anil's Ghost, Knopf (New York, NY), 2000.

EDITOR

The Broken Ark (animal verse), illustrated by Tony Urquhart, Oberon (Ottawa, Ontario, Canada), 1971, revised as *A Book of Beasts,* 1979.

Personal Fictions: Stories by Munro, Wiebe, Thomas, and Blaise, Oxford University Press (Toronto, Ontario, Canada), 1977.

The Long Poem Anthology, Coach House (Toronto, Ontario, Canada), 1979.

(With Russell Banks and David Young) *Brushes with Greatness: An Anthology of Chance Encounters with Greatness,* Coach House (Toronto, Ontario, Canada), 1989.

(With Linda Spalding) *The Brick Anthology,* illustrated by David Bolduc, Coach House Press (Toronto, Ontario, Canada), 1989.

From Ink Lake: An Anthology of Canadian Short Stories, Viking (New York, NY), 1990.

The Faber Book of Contemporary Canadian Short Stories, Faber (London, England), 1990.

(With others) *Lost Classics,* Knopf Canada (Toronto, Ontario, Canada), 2000, Anchor (New York, NY), 2001.

(And author of introduction) Mavis Gallant, *Paris Stories,* New York Review Books (New York, NY), 2002.

OTHER

Leonard Cohen (literary criticism), McClelland & Stewart (Toronto, Ontario, Canada), 1970.

The Collected Works of Billy the Kid (play; based on his poetry), produced in Stratford, Ontario, 1973; produced in New York, NY, 1974; produced in London, England, 1984.

Claude Glass (literary criticism), Coach House Press (Toronto, Ontario, Canada), 1979.

Coming through Slaughter (play); first produced in Toronto, Ontario, Canada, 1980.

Tin Roof, Island (British Columbia, Canada), 1982.

Running in the Family, W.W. Norton (New York, NY), 1982.

(With B.P. Nichol and George Bowering) *An H in the Heart: A Reader,* McClelland & Stewart (Toronto, Ontario, Canada), 1994.

(Author of introduction) Anthony Minghella, adaptor, *The English Patient: A Screenplay,* Hyperion Miramax (New York, NY), 1996.

The Conversations: Walter Murch and the Art of Editing Film, Knopf (New York, NY), 2002.

Ondaatje's manuscripts are included in the National Archives, Ottawa, Canada, and the Metropolitan Toronto Library.

ADAPTATIONS: The English Patient was adapted as a motion picture, written and directed by Anthony Minghella, produced by Miramax, 1996; *Anil's Ghost* was adapted as an audiobook read by Alan Cummings, Random House AudioBooks, 2000.

SIDELIGHTS: Canadian poet and novelist Michael Ondaatje dissolves the lines between prose and poetry through the breadth of his works in both genres. "Moving in and out of imagined landscape, portrait and documentary, anecdote or legend, Ondaatje writes for the eye and the ear simultaneously," noted Diane Wakoski in *Contemporary Poets.* Whether reshaping recollections of friends and family from his childhood in old Ceylon in *Running in the Family,* or retelling an American myth in *The Collected Works of Billy the Kid,* Ondaatje "focuses on the internal lives of his multigenerational characters and exhibits a fascination with extraordinary personality types," as observed by a *Contemporary Literary Criticism* essayist, utilizing a writing style that is "whimisical and imaginative . . . marked by vivid detail . . . startling juxtapositions, and a preoccupation with intense experiences." In addition to writing novels, plays, and poetry collections, Ondaatje has edited several books, including *The Faber Book of Contemporary Canadian Short Stories,* praised as a "landmark" by reviewer Christine Bold in *Times Literary Supplement* for its representation of "Canadian voices accented by native, black, French, Caribbean, Indian, Japanese and Anglo-Saxon origins."

Ondaatje's poetry is seen by critics as continually changing, evolving as the author experiments with the shape and sound of words. Although his poetic forms may differ, his works focus on the myths that root deep in common cultural experience. As a poet, he recreates their intellectual expression in depicting the affinity between the art of legend and the world at large. "He cares more about the relationship between art and nature than any other poet since the Romantics," stated Liz Rosenberg in *New York Times Book Review,* "and more than most contemporary poets care about any ideas at all." Some of Ondaatje's verse has approached the fragmentary, as in *Secular Love,* a collection of poems he published in 1985.

New York Times Book Review contributor Adam Kirsch found the poems in *Handwriting* to be "richly sensual images, which are drawn largely from the history, mythology, and landscape of India and China." "*Handwriting* takes one to Ondaatje's Sri Lankan past," wrote Sen Sudeep in *World Literature Today,* "a past that is very much present in his life, one that informs and colors his broader palette, scope, and vision. The fact that he can present Sri Lanka realistically and unexotically lends a believable and even magical edge to his text. His observations are sharp and wry, but at the same time considered, wise, and pragmatic."

Reviewing *Handwriting* in *Poetry,* Henry Taylor wrote that Ondaatje's verses "have sometimes struck me as labored in their seriousness—easier to admire than to like. This new book, in fact, is a deep pleasure to read most of the time, once one has become accustomed to its fragmentary style. This style is singularly appropriate to the themes and subjects of the book, which arise from mixed heritage and the loss of cultural identity." *Library Journal* reviewer Barbara Hoffert called Ondaatje's poetry "deeply evocative and suffused—but never overburdened—with sensuous imagery."

"Concerned always to focus on the human, the private, and the 'real' over the theoretical and the ideological," in his novels and short fiction "Ondaatje examines the internal workings of characters who struggle against and burst through that which renders people passive," noted Diane Watson in *Contemporary Novelists,* "and which renders human experience programmatic and static." The novel *In the Skin of a Lion* focuses on a man raised in rural Canada who, at the age of twenty-one, comes to the growing city of Toronto and lives among the immigrants inhabiting its working-class neighborhoods. Physical actions and inner challenges define Ondaatje's characters as individuals, creators within their own lives, and give both purpose to their existence and redemption to their inner reality. In this work a historical epoch is seen as the struggle of the individual to break free of the confines of his culture rather than simply a collection of social and political goals. As Michael Hulse described *In the Skin of a Lion* in *Times Literary Supplement,* it "maps high society and the sub culture of the underprivileged in Toronto in the 1920s and 1930s. . . . But it is also . . . about communication, about men 'utterly alone' who are waiting (in Ondaatje's terms) to break through a chrysalis."

In *Coming through Slaughter,* a novel well-grounded in the history of early-twentieth-century New Orleans, Ondaatje creates a possible life of the late jazz musician Buddy Bolden, remembered as a brilliant cornetist whose performances were never recorded due to a tragic mental collapse at an early age. Mixing interviews with those who remember Bolden, historical fact, and his richly imagined conception of the musician's inner thoughts on his way to madness, Ondaatje fashions what Watson termed a "fractured narrative . . . [tracing] the personal anarchy of . . . Bolden and the perspectives on him of those who knew him best."

Perhaps Ontaadje's most well-known novel, *The English Patient* tells the story of a Canadian nurse who stays behind in the bombed remains of a villa near the World War II battlefields of northern Italy to tend to an English soldier who has been severely burned. After the couple are joined by two other soldiers, relationships form that parallel, as Cressida Connolly noted in *Spectator,* "those of a small and faded Eden." Ranking the author among such contemporary novelists as Ian McEwan and Martin Amis, Connolly praised the poetic quality of Ondaatje's fiction. "The writing is so heady that you have to keep putting the book down between passages so as not to reel from the sheer force and beauty of it," the reviewer exclaimed, adding that "when I finished the book I felt as dazed as if I'd just awoken from a powerful dream."

Anil's Ghost is a novel set in the present that documents the nearly twenty-year Sri Lankan conflict that began in the 1980s and resulted in the deaths and disappearances of nearly twenty thousand. Anil is a native of Sri Lanka who studied medicine abroad, specializing in forensic pathology, and she has come home as part of a mission to examine the remains of victims to determine possible war crimes. Anil is assisted by Sarath, a government-selected archaeologist, and together they find four skeletons they name Tinker, Tailor, Soldier, and Sailor, the last of which Anil feels will provide the evidence they are seeking. "This narrow examination broadens to involve the wider conflict as Sri Lanka's history and present achieve a simultaneous, terrible maturity," wrote Rebecca J. Davies in *Lancet.* "The earth is oily with wasted blood. Severed heads sit atop stakes. Drivers are crucified on the roadside. Bodies succumb to frail fractures sustained in their dive from helicopters. Even babies and three-year-olds are not immune to the bullets. And yet amid this bloody chaos Ondaatje painstakingly captures the normality of interrupted lives."

New York Times Book Review contributor Janet Maslin compared *Anil's Ghost* to *The English Patient,* writing that it "is a novel more in name than in essence. . . . Ondaatje brings an oblique poetic sensibility to unraveling the mysteries at work here. Layers peel away from both Anil and Sarath, with a past full of ghosts for each of them and assorted vignettes and memories scattered across the book's fertile landscape." Maslin went on to say that "the book's real strengths lie in its profound sense of outrage, the shimmering intensity of its descriptive language and the mysterious beauty of its geography, with so many discrete passages that present the artificer in Mr. Ondaatje so well." *America*'s John Breslin noted that the novel "ends with three pages of acknowledgments to dozens of doctors, lawyers, civil rights workers, Asian scholars, and fellow poets, plus a bibliography that would make any researcher proud. A lot of homework and legwork have gone into this novel."

In addition to poetry and fiction, Ondaatje's interest in filmmaking, fueled perhaps by his involvement in the film adaptation of his novel *The English Patient,* inspired the nonfiction work *The Conversations: Walter Murch and the Art of Film Editing.* Highly praised by reviewers, *The Conversations* examines Murch's life and career as a three-time Oscar winner and collaborator with noted directors Francis Ford Coppola and George Lucas in Zoetrope studios. The creative process is also discussed, as writer and film editor talk about the task of revealing hidden themes and patterns in existing creative works. As Ondaatje noted in an interview with a *Maclean's* contributor, editing—whether of film or one's written work, is "the only place where you're on your own. Where you can be one person and govern it. The only time you control making a movie is in the editing stage." In *Booklist* Carlos Orellana praised *The Conversations* for permitting "readers a peek behind the curtain to reveal a man as mysterious as his art," while in *Publishers Weekly* a reviewer noted: "Through [Murch's] . . . eyes, and Ondaatje's remarkably insightful questions and comments, readers see how intricate the process is, and understand Murch when he says, 'The editor is the only one who has time to deal with the whole jigsaw. The director simply doesn't.'"

Born in Sri Lanka and living in England as a young teen, Ondaatje immigrated to Canada at age eighteen, determined to make a mark as a poet, and gradually moved to fiction. *Running in the Family,* a heartfelt memoir honoring his family and his heritage, blends together family stories with poems, photographs, and personal anecdotes. As his family history follows a path leading from the genteel innocence of the Ceylonese privileged class as the sun set on the British Empire to the harsh glare of the modern age, so Ondaatje's narrative seeks the inner character of his father, a man of whom the author writes, "My loss was that I never spoke to him as an adult." As Anton Mueller in the *Washington Post Book World* wrote, "In reality, this is a mythology exaggerated and edited by the survivors. Seduced by the wealth and luxury of its imaginative reality, Ondaatje enters the myth without disturbing it. With a prose style equal to the voluptuousness of his subject and a sense of humor never too far away, *Running in the Family* is sheer reading pleasure."

BIOGRAPHICAL AND CRITICAL SOURCES:

BOOKS

Contemporary Literary Criticism, Thomson Gale (Detroit, MI), Volume 14, 1980; Volume 29, 1984; Volume 51, 1989; Volume 76, 1993.

Contemporary Novelists, fifth edition, St. James (Detroit, MI), 1991, pp. 710-711.

Contemporary Poets, fifth edition, St. James (Detroit, MI), 1991, pp. 724-725.

Cooke, John, *The Influence of Painting on Five Canadian Writers: Alice Munro, Hugh Hood, Timothy Findley, Margaret Atwood, and Michael Ondaatje,* Edwin Mellen (Lewiston, NY), 1996.

Dictionary of Literary Biography, Volume 60: *Canadian Writers since 1960, Second Series,* Thomson Gale (Detroit, MI), 1987.

Jewinski, Ed, *Michael Ondaatje: Express Yourself Beautifully,* ECW Press, 1994.

Ondaatje, Michael, *Running in the Family* (memoir), W.W. Norton (New York, NY), 1982.

Siemerling, Winfried, *Discoveries of the Other: Alterity in the Work of Leonard Cohn, Hubert Aquin, Michael Ondaatje, and Nicole Brossard,* University of Toronto (Toronto, Ontario, Canada), 1994.

Solecki, Sam, editor, *Spider Blues: Essays on Michael Ondaatje,* Vehicule Press, 1985.

PERIODICALS

America, February 19, 2001, John Breslin, "War on Several Fronts," p. 25.

American Book Review, March, 1999, review of *The Cinnamon Peeler,* p. 23.

Ariel, April, 1997, Josef Pesch, "Post-Apocalyptic War Histories: Michael Ondaatje's *The English Patient,*" p. 117.

Biography, spring, 2000, S. Leigh Matthews, "'The Bright Bone of a Dream': Drama, Performativity, Ritual, and Community in Michael Ondaatje's *Running in the Family,*" p. 352.

Booklist, March 1, 1999, Donna Seaman, review of *Handwriting,* p. 1145; March 15, 2000, Bonnie Smothers, review of *Anil's Ghost,* p. 1294; September 15, 2002, Carlos Orellana, review of *The Conversations: Walter Murch and the Art of Editing Film,* p. 192.

Canadian Forum, January-February, 1993, p. 39.

Canadian Literature, spring, 2002, Douglas Barbour, "Writing through Terror," pp. 187-188.

Christian Science Monitor, May 4, 2000, "An Island Paradise in the Flames of Terror," p. 17.

Economist, June 17, 2000, review of *Anil's Ghost,* p. 14.

English Studies, May, 1996, p. 266.

Essays on Canadian Writing, summer, 1994, pp. 1, 11, 27, 204, 238, 250; fall, 1995, p. 236; winter, 1995, p. 116; spring, 1999, review of *The English Patient,* p. 236; spring, 2002.

Harper's, February, 2003, John Gregory Dunne, review of *The Conversations,* p. 69.

History and Theory, December, 2002, p. 43.

Hudson Review, spring, 2001, Alan Davis, review of *Anil's Ghost,* p. 142.

Journal of Canadian Studies, summer, 2001, Dennis Duffy, "Furnishing the Pictures: Arthur S. Goss, Michael Ondaatje, and the Imag(in)ing of Toronto," p. 106.

Journal of Modern Literature, summer, 2000, William H. New, review of *Anil's Ghost,* p. 565.

Lancet, January 20, 2001, Rebecca J. Davies, "A Tale of the Sri Lankan Civil War," p. 241.

Library Journal, April 15, 1999, Barbara Hoffert, review of *Handwriting,* p. 100; May 15, 2000, Barbara Hoffert, review of *Anil's Ghost,* p. 126; June 1, 2001, Ron Ratliff, review of *Lost Classics,* p. 160.

Los Angeles Times, May 21, 2000, Jonathan Levi, review of *Anil's Ghost,* p. C1.

Maclean's, April 10, 2000, John Bemrose, "Horror in Paradise: Michael Ondaatje Sifts through Sri Lanka's Strife," p. 78; December 18, 2000, p. 66; September 9, 2002, interview with Ondaatje, p. 40.

Modern Language Review, January, 1997, p. 149.

Mosaic, September, 1999, Douglas Malcolm, "Solos and Chorus: Michael Ondaatje's Jazz Politics/Poetics," p. 131.

Nation, January 4, 1993, p. 22; June 19, 2000, Tom LeClair, "The Sri Lankan Patients," p. 31.

National Catholic Reporter, November 19, 1993, p. 30.

New Criterion, May, 2000, Brooke Allen, "Meditations, Good & Bad," p. 63.

New Leader, May, 2000, Tova Reich, review of *Anil's Ghost,* p. 37.

New Republic, March 15, 1993, p. 38.

New Statesman & Society, March 19, 1999, Lavinia Greenlaw, review of *Handwriting,* p. 48.

New Yorker, May 15, 2000, John Updike, review of *Anil's Ghost,* p. 91.

New York Review of Books, January 14, 1993, p. 22; November 2, 2000, John Bayley, review of *Anil's Ghost,* p. 44.

New York Times Book Review, April 24, 1977; December 22, 1985, pp. 22-23; April 11, 1999, Adam Kirsch, "Erotic, Exotic," p. 24; May 11, 2000, Janet Maslin, "Unearthing the Tragedies of Civil War in Sri Lanka"; May 14, 2000, Richard Eder, "A House Divided."

Poetry, May, 2000, Henry Taylor, review of *Handwriting,* p. 96.

Prairie Schooner, spring, 2001, Constance Merritt, review of *Handwriting,* p. 182.

Publishers Weekly, February 22, 1999, review of *Handwriting,* p. 88; March 20, 2000, review of *Anil's Ghost,* p. 70; July 3, 2000, review of *Anil's Ghost,* p. 24; August 12, 2002, review of *The Conversations,* p. 290.

Saturday Night, July, 1968; June, 1997, Valerie Feldner, review of *The English Patient,* p. 12.

School Library Journal, September, 2000, Pam Johnson, review of *Anil's Ghost,* p. 258.

Spectator, September 5, 1992, Cressida Connolly, review of *The English Patient,* p. 32; April 29, 2000, John de Falbe, review of *Anil's Ghost,* p. 29.

Studies in Canadian Literature, 2001 (annual), pp. 71-90.

Time, May 1, 2000, Paul Gray, "Nailed Palms and the Eyes of Gods: Michael Ondaatje's *Anil's Ghost* Is a Stark Successor to *The English Patient,*" p. 75.

Times Higher Education Supplement, July 4, 2003, Roger Crittenden, review of *The Conversations,* p. 27.

Times Literary Supplement, September 4, 1987, p. 948; November 3, 1989, p. 1217; October 19, 1990, p. 1130; September 22, 1992, p. 23; February 5, 1999, Michael O'Neill, review of *Handwriting,* p. 33.

University of Toronto Quarterly, spring, 2001, p. 633; fall, 2001, p. 889.

Virginia Quarterly Review, summer, 1999, review of *Handwriting,* p. 102.

Vogue, May, 2000, John Powers, review of *Anil's Ghost,* p. 201.

Wall Street Journal, April 2, 1999, review of *Handwriting,* p. 6; May 12, 2000, Elizabeth Bukowski, review of *Anil's Ghost,* p. W8.

Washington Post Book World, January 2, 1983, pp. 9, 13; November 1, 1987, p. 4.

World Literature Today, spring, 1999, Sen Sudeep, review of *Handwriting,* p. 333.

ONLINE

BookPage, http://www.bookpage.com/ (October 1, 2001), Ellen Kanner, "New Discoveries from the Author of *The English Patient*" (interview).

* * *

ONDAATJE, Philip Michael
See ONDAATJE, Michael

* * *

OSBORNE, David
See SILVERBERG, Robert

* * *

OSBORNE, George
See SILVERBERG, Robert

* * *

OSBORNE, John 1929-1994
(John James Osborne)

PERSONAL: Born December 12, 1929, in London, England; died of heart failure, December 24, 1994, in Shropshire, England; son of Thomas Godfrey (a commercial artist) and Nellie Beatrice (a barmaid; maiden name, Grove) Osborne; married Pamela Elizabeth Lane (an actress), 1951 (divorced, 1957); married Mary Ure (an actress), November 8, 1957 (divorced, 1963); married Penelope Gilliatt (a drama critic and novelist), May 24, 1963 (divorced, 1967); married Jill Bennett (an actress), April, 1968 (divorced, 1977); married Helen Dawson (a journalist), June 2, 1978; children: (third marriage) Nolan Kate.

CAREER: Dramatist, screenwriter, director, and actor. Worked on trade journals *Gas World* and *Miller* for six months; was a tutor to juvenile actors in a touring group, later the group's assistant stage manager, and finally an actor specializing in characterizations of old men; made first stage appearance at Lyceum, Sheffield, England, in *No Room at the Inn,* 1948; appeared in *The Apollo de Bellac, Don Juan,* and with the English Stage Company at Royal Court: *Death of Satan, Cards of Identity, Good Woman of Setzuan, The Making of Moo,* and *A Cuckoo in the Nest.* Director of stage productions, including *Meals on Wheels,* 1965. Appeared in films and television productions, including *The Parachute,* British Broadcasting Corporation (television), 1967, *First Night of Pygmalion* (television), 1969, as Maidanov in *First Love* (film), 1970, *Get Carter* (film), 1971, *Lady Charlotte* (television), 1977, *Tomorrow Never Comes* (film), 1978, and *Flash Gordon* (film), 1980. Playwright and producer; produced first play at Theatre Royal, Huddersfield, England, 1949, other plays include *Personal Enemy, Opera House,* and *Harrogate,* 1955; comanaged theatrical company at seaside resorts; cofounder-director, with Tony Richardson, of Woodfall Films, 1958-94; Oscar Lewenstein Plays Ltd., London, England, director, 1960-94. Member of council, English Stage Company, 1968-82.

MEMBER: Writers' Guild of Great Britain, Royal Society of Arts, Savile Club, Garrick Club.

AWARDS, HONORS: London *Evening Standard* Drama Award, 1956, for most promising British playwright, 1965, for *A Patriot for Me,* and 1968, for *The Hotel in Amsterdam;* New York Drama Critics Circle Award, 1958, for *Look Back in Anger,* and 1965, for *Luther;* Antoinette Perry ("Tony") Award nominations for best play, 1958, for *Look Back in Anger,* 1959, for *Epitaph for George Dillon* and 1966, for *Inadmissible Evidence;* Tony Award, 1964, for *Luther;* Academy Award for best adapted screenplay, 1963, for *Tom Jones; Plays and Players* best new play award, 1964, for *Inadmissible Evidence,* and 1968, for *The Hotel in Amsterdam;* honorary doctorate, Royal College of Art, 1970; Macallan Award for lifetime achievement, Writers' Guild of Great Britain, 1992.

WRITINGS:

PLAYS

(With Stella Linden) *The Devil inside Him,* produced in Huddersfield, Yorkshire, England, 1950.

(With Anthony Creighton) *Personal Enemy,* produced in Harrogate, Yorkshire, England, 1955.

Look Back in Anger (produced in London, England, at the Royal Court Theatre, 1956; produced on Broadway, 1957), Criterion (New York, NY), 1957, reprinted, Dramatic Publishing (Chicago, IL), 1987.

(With Anthony Creighton) *Epitaph for George Dillon* (produced in Oxford, England, 1957; produced in London, England, 1958; produced in New York, 1958; produced in the West End as *George Dillon,* 1958), Criterion (New York, NY), 1958.

The Entertainer (produced in London, England, 1957; produced in the West End, 1957; produced on Broadway, 1958), Faber (London, England), 1957, Criterion (New York, NY), 1958.

The World of Paul Slickey (produced in London, England, 1959), Faber (London, England), 1959, Criterion (New York, NY), 1961.

Luther (produced in London, England, 1961; produced in the West End, 1961; produced on Broadway, 1963), Faber (London, England), 1961, Criterion (New York, NY), 1962, reprinted, New American Library (New York, NY), 1994.

Plays for England: The Blood of the Bambergs [and] *Under Plain Cover* (both produced in London, England, 1963, and New York, 1965), Faber (London, England), 1963, Criterion (New York, NY), 1964.

Inadmissible Evidence (produced in London, England, 1964; produced in the West End, 1965; produced on Broadway, 1965), Grove (New York, NY), 1965.

A Patriot for Me (produced in London, England, 1965; produced on Broadway, 1969), Faber (London, England), 1966, Random House (New York, NY), 1970, published with *A Sense of Detachment,* Faber, 1983.

A Bond Honoured (adapted from Lope de Vega's *La fianza satisfecha;* produced in London, England, 1966), Faber (London, England), 1966.

Time Present (produced in London, England, then in the West End, 1968), published with *The Hotel in Amsterdam,* Faber (London, England), 1968.

The Hotel in Amsterdam (produced in London, England, then in the West End, 1968), published with *Time Present,* Faber (London, England), 1968.

West of Suez (produced in London, England, 1971), Faber (London, England), 1971.

Hedda Gabler (adapted from Henrik Ibsen's play; produced in London, England, 1972), Faber (London, England), 1972, Dramatic Publishing (New York, NY), 1974.

A Sense of Detachment (produced in London, England, 1972), Faber (London, England), 1973, published with *A Patriot for Me,* Faber, 1983.

A Place Calling Itself Rome (adapted from Shakespeare's *Coriolanus*), Faber (London, England), 1973.

The Picture of Dorian Gray: A Moral Entertainment (adapted from Oscar Wilde's novel; produced in London, England, 1975), Faber (London, England), 1973.

Watch It Come Down (produced in London, England, 1976), Faber (London, England), 1975.

The End of Me Old Cigar (produced in London, England, 1975), published with *Jill and Jack: A Play for Television* (broadcast 1974), Faber (London, England), 1976.

The Father (adapted from August Strindberg's play; produced in London, England, 1988), published as *Strindberg's The Father and Ibsen's Hedda Gabler,* Faber (London, England), 1989.

Dejavu (sequel to *Look Back in Anger;* produced in London, England, 1992), Faber (London, England), 1990, Dramatic Publishing (New York, NY), 1994.

Look Back in Anger and Other Plays (includes *Epitaph for George Dillon, The World of Paul Slickey,* and *Dejavu,*), Faber (London, England), 1993.

Four Plays, Oberon (London, England), 2000.

Contributor to anthologies, including *Modern English Plays,* 1966, and *The Best Short Plays of the World Theatre, 1958-1967,* edited by Stanley Richards, 1968.

TELEVISION PLAYS

A Matter of Scandal and Concern (British Broadcasting Corp. (BBC-TV), 1960, produced for the stage in Nottingham, England, 1962, and New York, 1966), published as *A Subject of Scandal and Concern: A Play for Television,* Faber (London, England), 1961.

The Right Prospectus: A Play for Television (broadcast in 1970), Faber (London, England), 1970.

Very Like a Whale (broadcast in 1970), Faber (London, England), 1971.

The Gift of Friendship (broadcast in 1972), Faber (London, England), 1972.

You're Not Watching Me, Mummy (broadcast in 1980) [and] *Try a Little Tenderness: Two Plays for Television,* Faber (London, England), 1978.

A Better Class of Person: An Extract of Autobiography for Television and "God Rot Tunbridge Wells," Faber (London, England), 1985.

Also author of television plays *Billy Bunter,* 1952, *Robin Hood,* 1953, and *Almost a Vision,* 1976.

SCREENPLAYS

(With Nigel Kneale) *Look Back in Anger* (based on his play), Woodfall Films, 1959.

(With Nigel Kneale) *The Entertainer* (based on his play), Woodfall Films, 1960.

Tom Jones (adapted from the novel by Henry Fielding; produced by Woodfall Films, 1964), published as *Tom Jones: A Film Script,* Faber (London, England), 1964, revised edition, Grove (New York, NY), 1965.

(With Charles Wood) *The Charge of the Light Brigade* (based on the poem by Lord Alfred Tennyson), Woodfall Films, 1968.

Inadmissible Evidence (based on his play), Woodfall Films, 1968.

OTHER

(Translator) Walter Benjamin, *Origins of German Tragic Drama,* Verso (London, England), 1977.

A Better Class of Person: An Autobiography, 1929-1956 (also see below), Dutton (New York, NY), 1981, published as *A Better Class of Person, Volume I: John Osborne, an Autobiography, 1929-1956,* Faber (London, England), 1994.

Too Young to Fight, Too Old to Forget, Faber (London, England), 1985.

The Meiningen Court Theatre, 1866-1890, Cambridge University Press (Cambridge, England), 1988.

Almost a Gentleman, Volume II: An Autobiography, 1955-1966, Faber (London, England), 1991.

Damn You, England (collected prose), Faber (Boston, MA), 1994.

Editor of *Hedda Gabler and Other Plays,* by Henrik Ibsen. Contributor to books, including Tom Maschler, editor, *Declaration,* Dutton (New York, NY), 1958. Contributor to periodicals, including *Encounter, Observer,* and London *Times.*

ADAPTATIONS: Luther was made into a film in 1971; Osborne's screenplay for *Look Back in Anger* was remade for film in 1980 and for television in 1989, as was his screenplay for *The Entertainer,* 1975.

SIDELIGHTS: Prior to John Osborne's arrival on the scene, the British theater consisted mainly of classics, melodramas, and drawing-room comedies. But in 1956, Osborne's third play and first London-produced drama, *Look Back in Anger,* shocked audiences and "wiped the smugness off the frivolous face of English theatre," as John Lahr put it in a *New York Times Book Review* article. "Strangely enough," commented John Mortimer in the *New York Times,* "*Look Back in Anger* was, in shape, a conventional well-made play of the sort that might have been constructed by Noel Coward or Terence Rattigan." Yet, as Mortimer explained, "What made it different was that Jimmy Porter, the play's antihero, was the first young voice to cry out for a new generation that had forgotten the war, mistrusted the welfare state and mocked its established rulers with boredom, anger and disgust." As a result, Mortimer observed, "The age of revivals was over. A new and memorable period in the British theater began."

Look Back in Anger established the struggling actor and playwright as a leading writer for theater, television, and film. And, while his later works may not have created as great a stir as his London debut, as Richard Corliss wrote in *Time,* "The acid tone, at once comic and desperate, sustained Osborne throughout a volatile career." Perhaps more important than its effect on Osborne's personal career, however, was the impact *Look Back in Anger* had on British culture. In Corliss's opinion, the play not only changed British theater, directly influencing playwrights such as Joe Orton and Edward Albee, but it also "stoked a ferment in a then sleepy popular culture." All manner of writers, actors, artists, and musicians (including the Beatles) soon reflected the influence of Osborne's "angry young man."

As *Look Back in Anger* begins, Jimmy Porter is a twenty-five-year-old working-class youth with a provincial university education and bleak hopes for the future. He frequently clashes with his wife, Alison, who comes from a more privileged background. The couple share their tiny flat with Cliff, Jimmy's partner in the sweet-shop business. A triangle forms—Jimmy, Alison, and Alison's friend Helena, who alerts Alison's parents to the squalor their now-pregnant daughter is living in and helps convince Alison to leave Jimmy. Helena, however, stays on and becomes Jimmy's mistress. As time goes on, Alison miscarries and, realizing her love for Jimmy, returns to the flat. Helena decides that she cannot come between Jimmy and his wife any longer and withdraws. Meanwhile, Cliff also leaves the flat in an attempt to better his lot. "And Alison's baby which could have taken Cliff's place in their triangular relationship will never be," Arthur Nicholas Athanason explained in a *Dictionary of Literary Biography* article. "Jimmy and Alison must depend more than ever now on fantasy games to fill this void and to achieve what moments of intimacy and peaceful coexistence they can in their precarious marriage."

With the immediate and controversial success of *Look Back in Anger,* continued Athanason, the author "found himself, overnight, regarded as a critic of society or, more precisely, a reflector of his generation's attitudes toward society. Needless to say, the concern and feeling for intimate personal relationships that are displayed in *Look Back in Anger* may indeed have social and moral implications. But what really moves Osborne in this play seems to be the inability of people to understand and express care for each other better—particularly in their language and their emotional responsiveness. What is new and experimental in British drama about [the play] is the explosive character of Jimmy Porter and his brilliant and dazzling vituperative tirades, in which a renewed delight in a Shavian vigor and vitality of language and ideas is displayed with virtuoso command." Noting a resemblance to Tennessee Williams's play *A Streetcar Named Desire,* Athanason labeled *Look Back in Anger* "an intimate portrait of an extremely troubled working-class marriage (riddled with psychological problems and sexual frustrations), which was, in its way, a theatrical first for British drama."

When *Look Back in Anger* opened in London in 1956, few critics showed enthusiasm for the play. Kenneth Tynan, in a review for the *Observer,* was the most notable exception. He found that Osborne had skillfully captured the character of British youth, "the drift towards anarchy, the instinctive leftishness, the automatic rejection of 'official' attitudes, the surrealist sense of humour." Tynan conceded that because disillusioned youth was at the play's center, it might have been narrowly cast at a youthful audience. "I agree that *Look Back in Anger* is a minority taste," he wrote. "What matters, however, is the size of the minority. I estimate it at roughly 6,733,000, which is the number of people in this country between twenty and thirty."

Most other critics could not see beyond Jimmy's explosive character to examine the themes underlying the fury he directed against the social mores of the day. More recent critics have been able to look back with greater objectivity on the merits and impact of the play. "Osborne, through Jimmy Porter, was voicing the natural uncertainties of the young, their frustrations at being denied power, their eventual expectations of power and their fears of abusing it, either in running a country or a family," noted John Elsom in his book *Post-War British Theatre.* For this reason, Elsom suggested, Osborne was not guilty, as some critics maintained, of simply using Jimmy's anger as a ploy to create shock and sensationalism. Nor was he guilty of portraying the angry young man as cool. "Osborne made no attempt to glamorise the anger," Elsom wrote. "Jimmy was not just the critic of his society, he was also the object for criticism. He was the chief example of the social malaise which he was attacking. Through Jimmy Porter, Osborne had opened up a much wider subject than rebelliousness or youthful anger, that of social alienation, the feeling of being trapped in a world of meaningless codes and customs."

So impressed was Laurence Olivier with *Look Back in Anger* that the actor commissioned Osborne to write a play for him. The result was a drama—*The Entertainer*—which features a leading role that is considered one of the greatest and most challenging parts in late twentieth-century drama. In chronicling the life of wilting, third-rate music-hall comedian Archie Rice, Osborne was acknowledged to be reflecting in *The Entertainer* the fate of postwar Britain, an island suffering recession and unemployment, losing its status as an empire. "Archie is of a piece with the angry Osborne antiheroes of *Look Back in Anger* and [the author's later play] *Inadmissible Evidence,*" noted Frank Rich in a *New York Times* review of a revival of *The Entertainer.* "He's a repulsive, unscrupulous skunk, baiting everyone around him (the audience included); he's also a somewhat tragic victim of both his own self-contempt and of a declining England. If it's impossible to love Archie, we should be electrified or at least antagonized by his pure hostility and his raw instinct for survival. Mr. Osborne has a way of making us give his devils their pitiful due."

The drama's allegory of fading Britain and Olivier's compelling portrayal of Archie made *The Entertainer* a remarkable success in its first production. However, when it was revived on Broadway in 1983 with Nicol Williamson as Archie, *New York Times* reviewer Walter Kerr observed that in the play Osborne "has first shown us, at tedious, now cliché-ridden lengths how dreary the real world has become—what with blacks moving in upstairs, sons being sent off to Suez, and everyone else sitting limply about complaining of it all." Kerr added, "He has then had the drummer hit the rim of the snare as a signal that we're leaping over into music-hall make-believe—only to show us that it is exactly as dreary, exactly as deflated, exactly as dead as the onetime promise in the parlor. There is limpness in the living room and there is limpness before the footlights. . . . There is no transfusion of 'vitality,' no theatrical contrasts."

As Athanason explained, the author "owes a particular indebtedness to the turns and stock-character types of the English music-hall tradition, and, in *The Entertainer* particularly, he set out to capitalize on the dramatic as well as the comic potential of these values. For example, by conceiving each scene of this play as a music-hall turn, Osborne enables the audience to see both the 'public' Archie performing his trite patter before his 'dead behind the eyes' audience and the 'private' Archie performing a different comic role of seeming nonchalance before his own family."

Inadmissible Evidence presents another Osborne type in Bill Maitland, a contemporary London attorney who finds that his lusts for power, money, and women do little to fill the emotional voids in his life. Athanason described the play as opening in a "Kafkaesque dream sequence set in a courtroom that foreshadows the fate of [Maitland,] on trial before his own conscience for 'having unlawfully and wickedly published and made known a wicked, bawdy and scandalous object'—himself." Although he pleads not guilty to the court's indictment of him, his life is presumably the inadmissible evidence that he dares not produce in mitigation.

"Essentially a journey through the static spiritual hell of Maitland's mind, *Inadmissible Evidence* dramatizes a living, mental nightmare that culminates, as Maitland's alienation is pushed to its inevitable end, in a complete nervous breakdown," continued Athanason. "The play is principally a tour de force monologue for one actor, for its secondary characters are mere dream figures and metaphors that externalize the intense conflict going on within Maitland's disintegrating mind." The critic also felt that in this drama Osborne demonstrated his finest writing to date.

Osborne wrote other notable plays, including *A Patriot for Me,* a fictional telling of the trial and last days of Hungary's infamous Captain Redl, who was framed for his homosexuality and pronounced an enemy of the state; and *Luther,* a biography of religious reformist Martin Luther, an antihero in his time. The works that garnered Osborne perhaps the widest notice after the mid-1960s, however, were not plays but autobiographies: *A Better Class of Person: An Autobiography, 1929-1956,* and *Almost a Gentleman, Volume II: An Autobiography, 1955-1966.*

In relating his life story through the age of twenty-six in *A Better Class of Person,* Osborne caught the attention of critics for his caustic, even bitter, descriptions of his home life, especially his relationship with his parents. Osborne's father, who worked intermittently in advertising, was a sickly figure who spent his last years in a sanitarium. His mother, a bartender, seems to be the focal point of the author's harshest remarks. Osborne "looks back, of course, in anger," remarked John Leonard in a *New York Times* article. "In general, he is angry at England's lower middle class, of which he is the vengeful child. In particular, he reviles his mother, who is still alive. Class and mother, in this fascinating yet unpleasant book, sometimes seem to be the same mean thing, a blacking factory." Through his harsh view of family and society, Osborne captured the essence of his time and place. David Hare maintained in the *New Statesman,* "He understands better than any modern writer that emotion repressed in the bricked-up lives of the suburb-dweller does not disappear, but that instead it leaks, distorted, through every pore of the life: in whining, in meanness, in stubbornness, in secrecy."

If Osborne's memories were more bitter than sweet, a number of critics found that the author's hard-bitten style made for an interesting set of memoirs. *Washington Post Book World* reviewer David Richards did not, indicating that "like the male characters in his plays, who fulminate against the sordidness of life, Osborne is probably a romantic *manque.* But it is often difficult to feel the real anguish under the relentless invective of his writing. *A Better Class of Person* is the least likeable of autobiographies, although it should, no doubt, be pointed out that affability has never been one of Osborne's goals." More often, however, critics had praise for the book. Hilary Mantel commented in the *London Review of Books, "A Better Class of Person* is written with the tautness and power of a well-organized novel. It is a ferociously sulky, rancorous book." Hare was impressed by Osborne's style: "His prose is so supple, so enviably clear that you realize how many choices he has always had as a writer."

Other reviewers were taken, as John Russell Taylor put it in *Plays and Players,* by "not the sense of what he is saying, but the sheer force with which he says it." In the words of *Newsweek*'s Ray Sawhill, Osborne "has an explosive gift for denunciation and invective, and what he's written is—deliberately, nakedly—a tantrum. . . . He can blow meanness and pettiness up so large that they acquire a looming quality, like a slow-motion movie scene. His savage relish can be so palpable that you share his enjoyment of the dynamics of rage." Osborne's memoirs constitute "the best piece of writing [the author] has done since *Inadmissible Evidence,*" according to John Lahr in his *New York Times Book Review* piece. "After [that play,] his verbal barrages became grapeshot instead of sharp shooting. He neither revised his scripts nor moderated his cranky outbursts. His plays, like his pronouncements about an England he could no longer fathom, became second-rate and self-indulgent. But *A Better Class of Person* takes its energy from looking backward to the source of his pain before fame softened him. [The work proves that] John Osborne once again is making a gorgeous fuss."

Some readers of *A Better Class of Person* expected more insights into the playwright's writing process; instead, Osborne offered only insights into the playwright. As *Los Angeles Times* critic Charles Champlin pointed out, "There is nothing about stagecraft in *A Better Class of Person,* but everything about the making of the playwright. The [author's *Look Back in Anger*] was abrasive and so is the autobiography. It is also, like the play, savagely well-written, vividly detailed, and corrosively honest, unique as autobiography in its refusal to touch up the author's image. He encourages us to find him impossible and absolutely authentic." The self-portrait that Osborne paints, observed Benedict Nightingale in *Encounter,* "is of a young man of strong likes and (and more often) dislikes, capable of passion but also, as he himself wryly recognizes, of a disconcerting pettiness; a dedicated rebel, though mainly in the sense of not hesitating to make himself objectionable to the dull, drab or conventional. Interestingly, he seems to be without social or political convictions."

Osborne continued his autobiography—his exploration into the people, places, and events that made him the caustic king of the British theater—in *Almost a Gentleman.* In Mantel's view, Osborne's first volume of autobiography "bears witness to the grown man's failure to separate himself emotionally from a woman he despises [his mother]. . . . The consequences of this failure are played out in the second volume: they are a disabling misogyny, a series of failed and painful relationships, a grim determination to spit in the world's eye. He is not lovable, he knows; very well, he'll be hateful then." By the second volume, critics were not surprised by the force of Osborne's hatefulness, so they were able to look beyond it to the writing, its stories and style. As Alan Brien wrote in the *New Statesman,* "Few practitioners provide twin barrels fired at once so often as John Osborne. However, after the initial splutter, there are still a few anecdotes that leave this reader dissatisfied." Brien also found Osborne's writing uneven. "His language comes in two modes. Rather too often his use is slapdash and approximate, at once confusing and surreal." *Times Literary Supplement* contributor Jeremy Treglown faulted the book for disintegrating "into a sad jumble of diary entries, fan-letters, bits of Osborne's journalism and occasional drenching of sentimentality or bile." Yet, Brien admitted, "Almost equally often, he wields his pen like a blow-torch, melting down banalities and clichés into new-minted inventions of his own that sting and sizzle."

In the early 1990s, Osborne looked back on *Look Back in Anger,* writing a sequel titled *Dejavu.* This episode in the life of Jimmy Porter, the angry young man, finds a twice-divorced Jimmy living with his grown daughter Alison in a large country home. His buddy Cliff still spends a lot of time and shares a lot of drinks with Jimmy. The fourth character is a friend of Alison's and Jimmy's soon-to-be lover. "Some of the targets inevitably have changed, and the bile is now more elegantly expressed," observed Jack Pitman in *Variety,* "but otherwise hardly a beat has been missed in the 36 years since 'Anger' rocked the Brits." The biggest change is that Osborne's angry young man has become an angry old man. A reviewer in the *Economist* characterized the result: "For much of the first act Jimmy Porter sounds like an educated Alf Garnett—or, for Americans, an educated Archie Bunker." He rails against his past and how it has brought him to his current station. He failed before and he continues to fail. Suggested the *Economist* review, "He fails in life because he is not willing to make the compromises to his social superiors that are necessary for success in England."

Osborne had a great deal of difficulty having his final play staged, and it was not widely reviewed. The playwright's difficulties at finding success at the end of his career seemed to parallel the difficulties portrayed in this episode of Jimmy Porter's life. *Time* reviewer Richard Corliss called *Dejavu* "a glum sequel to *Anger.* In it [Osborne] described himself as 'a churling, grating note, a spokesman for no one but myself; with deadening effect, cruelly abusive, unable to be coherent about my despair.'" Still, critics found merit in Osborne's ability to turn his critical, mocking eye on himself. Wrote Matt Wolf in the *Chicago Tribune,* "Unendurable as *Dejavu* seems as if it's going to be, it is that rare play which really does improve, and by the last half hour or so, both it—and its superb star, Peter Egan—have long since exerted a rather macabre fascination." Pitman admitted that the play is long and without a coherent plot but acknowledged that "the show takes on an emotional depth as the raging misfit Porter gradually concedes the failure of his life."

Osborne's anger may not have inspired the same following later in his career as it did with the debut of *Look Back in Anger* in 1956. Yet, his impact on the theater remains indisputable. "Few dramatists tried to mimic the Osborne style in the way in which [Harold] Pinter was imitated," Elsom commented. "The success of *Look Back in Anger,* however, destroyed several inhibiting myths about plays: that the theatre had to be genteel, that heroes were stoical and lofty creatures, that audiences needed nice people with whom to identify." John Mortimer maintained that the positive power of Osborne's anger was also beyond dispute. "Osborne's anger was in defense of old values of courage and honor. It was often unreasonable, wonderfully ill considered and always, as he wrote of Tennessee Williams's plays, 'full of private fires and personal visions worth a thousand statements of a thousand politicians.'"

BIOGRAPHICAL AND CRITICAL SOURCES:

BOOKS

Denison, Patricia D., *John Osborne: A Casebook,* Garland (New York, NY), 1997.

PERIODICALS

Boston Globe, January 6, 1992, p. 2.
Cambridge Quarterly, winter, 1965-66, pp. 28-42.
Chicago Tribune, July 19, 1992, sec. 13, p. 20.
Drama Review, Volume VII, number 2, 1962.
Drama: The Quarterly Theatre Review, winter, 1975; autumn, 1978.
Economist, November 23, 1991, p. 100; June 13, 1992, p. 99.
Encounter, May, 1982, pp. 63-70.
Entertainment Weekly, March 20, 1992, p. 72.
Guardian Weekly, November 17, 1991, p. 25; May 15, 1994, p. 28.
Listener, October 15, 1981, p. 441.
Literature and History, autumn, 1988, pp. 194-206.
London Review of Books, November 21, 1991, p. 20.
Los Angeles Times, November 13, 1981; October 18, 1984; February 18, 1985.
Modern Drama, September, 1989, pp. 413-424.
New Republic, November 1, 1969.
New Statesman, December 13, 1974, p. 872; January 24, 1975, p. 118; October 16, 1981, pp. 23-24.
New Statesman and Society, November 15, 1991, p. 47.
Newsweek, December 14, 1981.
New Yorker, March 15, 1982; February 20, 1995, p. 86.
New York Review of Books, January 6, 1966.
New York Times, November 5, 1981; January 21, 1983; January 30, 1983; March 25, 1987, p. C26; January 8, 1995, sec. 2, p. 5.
New York Times Book Review, November 8, 1981, pp. 1, 30, 32.
Observer (London, England), December 15, 1991, p. 49; November 3, 1991, p. 69; September 20, 1992, p. 54; May 1, 1994, p. 24.
Plays and Players, December, 1981, p. 22.
Spectator, November 9, 1991, p. 50; April 23, 1994, p. 39.

Times (London, England), October 15, 1981; May 1, 1983; May 13, 1983; August 10, 1983.
Times Literary Supplement, December 29, 1972, p. 1569; January 4, 1974; October 16, 1981; August 31, 1984; November 15, 1991, p. 21; April 29, 1994, p. 32.
Variety, June 15, 1992, p. 62.
Washington Post Book World, December 27, 1981.

OBITUARIES:

PERIODICALS

Boston Globe, December 27, 1994, p. 59.
Chicago Tribune, December 27, 1994, sec. 2, p. 6.
Los Angeles Times, December 27, 1994, p. A24.
Newsweek, January 9, 1995, p. 66.
New York Times, December 27, 1994, p. A12.
Time, January 9, 1995, p. 75.
Times (London, England), December 27, 1994, p. 15.
Wall Street Journal, December 27, 1994, p. A1.
Washington Post, December 27, 1994, p. D4.

* * *

OSBORNE, John James
See OSBORNE, John

* * *

OZ, Amos 1939-

PERSONAL: Given name Amos Klausner; born May 4, 1939, in Jerusalem, Israel; son of Yehuda Arieh (a writer) and Fania (Mussman) Klausner; married Nily Zuckerman, April 5, 1960; children: Fania, Gallia, Daniel. *Education:* Hebrew University of Jerusalem, B.A., 1963; St. Cross College, Oxford, M.A., 1970.

ADDRESSES: Office—Ben Gurion University Negev, Beer Sheva, Israel. *Agent*—Mrs. D. Owen, 28 Narrow St., London E 14, England.

CAREER: Writer, 1962—. Hulda High School, Givat Brenner, Israel, teacher of literature and philosophy, 1963-86; visiting fellow, St. Cross College, Oxford University, 1969-70; writer-in-residence, Hebrew University of Jerusalem, 1975-76, and 1990, and Colorado College, 1985; University of California—Berkeley, visiting professor, 1980; visiting professor and writer-in-residence, Boston University, and Princeton University, both 1987; Ben Gurion University Negev, Beer Sheva, Israel, professor, 1986—. Has worked as a tractor driver, youth instructor, school teacher, and agricultural worker at Kibbutz Hulda, Israel. *Military service:* Israeli Army, 1957-60; also fought as reserve soldier in the tank corps in Sinai, 1967, and in the Golan Heights, 1973.

MEMBER: PEN, Peace Now, Academy of Hebrew Language, Catalan Academy of the Mediterranean.

AWARDS, HONORS: Holon Prize for Literature, 1965; Israel-American Cultural Foundation award, 1968; B'nai B'rith annual literary award, 1973; Brener Prize, 1978; Officier de l'Ordre des Art et des Lettres, 1984; Bialik Prize, 1986; Prix Femina, 1988; Wingate Prize, 1988; International Peace Prize, German Publishers Association, 1992; Chevalier de la Légion d'Honneur (France), 1997; Israel Prize for Literature, 1998; Goethe Prize, the city of Frankfurt, Germany, 2005, for his "literary output and impressive moral responsibility"; honorary degrees from Hebrew Union College, Western New England College, and Tel Aviv University.

WRITINGS:

Artzot ha' tan (short stories), Massada (Tel Aviv, Israel), 1965, translation by Nicholas de Lange and Philip Simpson published as *Where the Jackals Howl, and Other Stories,* Harcourt (San Diego, CA), 1981.
Makom acher (novel), Sifriat Po'alim (Tel Aviv, Israel), 1966, translation by Nicholas de Lange published as *Elsewhere, Perhaps,* Harcourt (San Diego, CA), 1973.
Michael sheli (novel), Am Oved (Tel Aviv, Israel), 1968, translation with Nicholas de Lange published as *My Michael,* Knopf (New York, NY), 1972.
Ad mavet (two novellas), Sifriat Po'alim (Tel Aviv, Israel), 1971, translation with Nicholas de Lange published as *Unto Death,* Harcourt (San Diego, CA), 1975.
Laga'at ba'mayim, laga'at ba'ruach (novel), Am Oved (Tel Aviv, Israel), 1973, translation with Nicholas de Lange published as *Touch the Water, Touch the Wind,* Harcourt (San Diego, CA), 1974.
Anashim acherim (anthology; title means "Different People"), Ha'Kibbutz Ha'Meuchad (Tel Aviv, Israel), 1974.
Har he'etza ha'raah (three novellas), Am Oved (Tel Aviv, Israel), 1976, translation with Nicholas de Lange published as *The Hill of Evil Counsel,* Harcourt (San Diego, CA), 1978.

Soumchi (juvenile), Am Oved (Tel Aviv, Israel), 1978, translation with Penelope Farmer published as *Soumchi,* Harper (New York, NY), 1980, reprinted, Harcourt (San Diego, CA), 1995.

Be' or ha'tchelet he'azah (essays), Sifriat Po'alim (Tel Aviv, Israel), 1979, translation by Nicholas de Lange published as *Under this Blazing Light: Essays,* Press Syndicate of the University of Cambridge (New York, NY), 1995.

Menucha nechonah (novel), Am Oved (Tel Aviv, Israel), 1982, translation by Hillel Halkin published as *A Perfect Peace,* Harcourt (San Diego, CA), 1985.

Po ve'sham b'eretz Yisra'el bistav 1982 (nonfiction), Am Oved (Tel Aviv, Israel), 1983, translation by Maurie Goldberg-Bartura published as *In the Land of Israel,* Harcourt (San Diego, CA), 1983.

(Editor, with Richard Flantz and author of introduction) *Until Daybreak: Stories from the Kibbutz,* Institute for the Translation of Hebrew Literature (Tel Aviv, Israel), 1984.

Mi-mordot ha-Levanon (essays), Am Oved (Tel Aviv, Israel), 1987, translation by Maurie Goldberg-Bartura published as *The Slopes of Lebanon,* Harcourt (San Diego, CA), 1989.

Black Box (novel), translation by Nicholas de Lange, Harcourt (San Diego, CA), 1988.

La-dat Ishah, Keter (Jerusalem, Israel), 1989.

To Know a Woman, Harcourt (San Diego, CA), 1991.

Ha-Matsav ha-Selishi, Keter (Jerusalem, Israel), 1991.

Fima, Harcourt (San Diego, CA), 1993.

Shetikat ha-Shamayim, Keter (Jerusalem, Israel), 1993.

Al Tagidu Layla, Keter (Jerusalem, Israel), 1994, translation by Nicholas de Lange published as *Don't Call It Night,* Harcourt (San Diego, CA), 1996.

Israel, Palestine, and Peace: Essays, Harcourt (San Diego, CA), 1995.

Panther in the Basement, Harcourt (San Diego, CA), 1997.

Kol ha-tokvot: Mahashavot 'al zehut Yi'sre'elit (title means "All Our Hopes"), Keter (Jerusalem, Israel), 1998.

The Story Begins: Essays on Literature, translated by Maggie Bar-Tura, Harcourt (San Diego, CA), 1999.

The Silence of Heaven: Agnon's Fear of God, translated by Barbara Harshay, Princeton University Press (Princeton, NJ), 2000.

The Same Sea, translated by Nicholas de Lange, Chatto & Windus (London, England), 2001.

Sipur 'al ahavah ve-hoshekh, Keter (Jerusalem, Israel), 2002, translation by Nicholas de Lange published as *A Tale of Love and Darkness,* Harcourt (Orlando, FL), 2004.

Be-'etsem yesh kan shete milhamot, Keter (Jerusalem, Israel), 2002.

(With Izzat Ghazzawi) *Enemies: A Love Affair,* Swiridoff (Künzelsau, Germany), 2002.

Editor of *Siach lochamium* (translated as "The Seventh Day"). Contributor of essays and fiction to Israeli periodicals, including *Davar,* and to journals such as *Encounter, Guardian,* and *Partisan Review.*

Oz's books have been translated into over fifteen languages, including Japanese, Dutch, Norwegian, and Romanian.

ADAPTATIONS: My Michael and *Black Box* were adapted into films in Israel.

SIDELIGHTS: Through fiction and nonfiction alike, Israeli author Amos Oz describes a populace under emotional and physical siege and a society threatened by internal contradictions and contention. According to Judith Chernaik in the *Times Literary Supplement,* Oz writes books that are "indispensable reading for anyone who wishes to understand . . . life in Israel, the ideology that sustains it, and the passions that drive its people." Immensely popular in his own country, Oz has also established an international reputation. In a *New Republic* assessment of the author's talents, Ian Sanders noted: "Oz is an extraordinarily gifted Israeli novelist who delights his readers with both verbal brilliance and the depiction of eternal struggles—between flesh and spirit, fantasy and reality, Jew and Gentile. . . . His carefully reconstructed worlds are invariably transformed into symbolic landscapes, vast arenas where primeval forces clash." *Times Literary Supplement* contributor A.S. Byatt observed that in his works on Israel, Oz "can write with delicate realism about small lives, or tell fables about large issues, but his writing, even in translation, gains vitality simply from his subject matter." *New York Review of Books* correspondent D.J. Enright called Oz Israel's "most persuasive spokesman to the outside world, the literary part of it at least."

"In a sense Amos Oz has no alternative in his novels but to tell us what it means to be an Israeli," wrote John Bayley in the *New York Review of Books.* Oz is a *sabra,* or native-born Israeli who has seen military service in two armed conflicts—the Six Day War and the Yom Kippur War—and has lived most of his adult life as a member of Kibbutz Hulda, one of Israel's collective communities. His fictional themes arise from these experiences and are often considered controversial for their presentations of individuals who rebel against the Israeli society's ideals.

The kibbutz provides Oz with a powerful symbol of the nation's aspirations, as well as serving as a microcosm of the larger Jewish family in Israel, suffocatingly intimate and inescapable, yet united in defense against the hostile forces besieging its borders. *New York Times Book Review* contributor Robert Alter declared that nearly all of Oz's fiction "is informed by the same symbolic world picture: a hemmed-in cluster of fragile human habitations (the kibbutz, the state of Israel itself) surrounded by dark, menacing mountains where jackals howl and hostile aliens lurk." According to *Jewish Quarterly* contributor Jacob Sonntag, the people of Oz's fiction "are part of the landscape, and the landscape is part of the reality from which there is no escape." If the landscape is inescapable, the bonds of family also offer little relief. *New York Times Book Review* correspondent Morris Dickstein wrote, "The core of feeling in Oz's work is always some sort of family, often a family being torn apart." *Los Angeles Times* correspondent Elaine Kendall similarly observed that Oz's fiction "confronts the generational conflicts troubling Israel today; emotional rifts intensified by pressure and privation. In that anguished country, the usual forms of family tension seem reversed; the young coldly realistic; the elders desperately struggling to maintain their belief in a receding ideal."

Alter contended that Oz's work is "symptomatic of the troubled connection Israeli writers increasingly feel with the realities of the Jewish state." Chernaik elaborated on this submerged "interior wilderness" that Oz seems compelled to explore: "The overwhelming impression left by his fiction is of the precariousness of individual and collective human effort, a common truth made especially poignant by a physical landscape thoroughly inhospitable to human settlement, and given tragic dimensions by the modern history of the Jews and its analogues in Biblical history." Oz himself explained in *New Republic* that he tries to tap his own turmoil in order to write. His characters, he said, "actually want two different things: peace and excitement, excitement and peace. These two things don't get along very easily, so when people have peace, they hate it and long for excitement, and when they have excitement, they want peace."

A central concern of Oz's fiction is the conflict between idealistic Zionism and the realities of life in a pluralistic society. As a corollary to this, many of his sabra characters have decidedly ambivalent feelings toward the Arab population, especially Palestinians. *Commentary* essayist Ruth R. Wisse wrote that in book after book, "Oz has taken the great myths with which modern Israel is associated—the noble experiment of the kibbutz, the reclamation of the soil, the wars against the British and the Arabs, the phoenix-like rise of the Jewish spirit out of the ashes of the Holocaust—and shown us their underside: bruised, dazed, and straying characters who move in an atmosphere of almost unalleviated depression." Nehama Aschkenasy offered a similar assessment in *Midstream:* "The collective voice is suspiciously optimistic, over-anxious to ascertain the normalcy and sanity of the community and the therapeutic effect of the collective body on its tormented member. But the voice of the individual is imbued with a bitter sense of entrapment, of existential boredom and nausea, coupled with a destructive surrender to the irrational and the antinomian." Dickstein noted that the author often "takes the viewpoint of the detached participant, the good citizen who does his duty, shares his family's ideals but remains a little apart, wryly skeptical, unable to lose himself in the communal spirit."

"Daytime Israel makes a tremendous effort to create the impression of the determined, tough, simple, uncomplicated society ready to fight back, ready to hit back twice as hard, courageous and so on," Oz told the *Partisan Review.* "Nocturnal Israel is a refugee camp with more nightmares per square mile I guess than any other place in the world. Almost everyone has seen the devil." The obsessions of "nocturnal Israel" fuel Oz's work, as Mark Shechner noted in *Nation.* "In [Oz's] fiction," Shechner wrote, "the great storms that periodically descend on the Jews stir up strange and possessed characters who ride the gusts as if in a dream: raging Zionists, religious fanatics poised to take the future by force, theoreticians of the millennium, strategists of the end game, connoisseurs of bitterness and curators of injustice, artists of prophecy and poets of doctrine."

This is not to suggest, however, that Oz's work is unrelentingly somber or polemical. According to Dickstein, the "glow of Oz's writing comes from the spare and unsentimental warmth of his own voice, his feeling for atmosphere and his gallery of colorful misfits and individualists caught in communal enterprises." Bayley likewise concluded: "One of the admirable things about Oz's novels is the humor in them, a humor which formulates itself in having taken, and accepted, the narrow measure of the Israeli scene. Unlike much ethnic writing his does not seek to masquerade as Weltliterature. It is Jewish literature acquiescing amusedly in its new militantly provincial status."

My Michael, a novel about the psychological disintegration of a young Israeli housewife, was Oz's first work translated and published in English. *New Republic* contributor Lesley Hazleton called the book "a brilliant and evocative portrait of a woman slowly giving way to schizoid withdrawal" and "a superb achievement, . . .

the best novel to come out of Israel to date." In *Modern Fiction Studies,* Hana Wirth-Nesher expressed the view that Oz uses his alienated protagonist "to depict the isolation and fear that many Israelis feel partially as a country in a state of siege and partially as a small enclave of Western culture in a vast area of cultures and landscapes unlike what they have known." Alter praised *My Michael* for managing "to remain so private, so fundamentally apolitical in its concerns, even as it puts to use the most portentous political materials."

Paul Zweig claimed in the *New York Times Book Review* that when *My Michael* was published in Israel, shortly after the Six Day War, it proved "extremely disturbing to Israelis. At a time when their country had asserted control over its destiny as never before, Oz spoke of an interior life which Israel had not had time for, which it had paid no heed to, an interior life that contained a secret bond to the Asiatic world beyond its border." Disturbing though it was, *My Michael* was a best-seller in Israel; it established Oz's reputation among his fellow Israelis and gave him entree into the international world of letters.

Oz's first novel, *Elsewhere, Perhaps,* was his second work to be translated and published abroad. Most critics felt that the book is the best fictional representation of kibbutz life to emerge from Israel. As Sonntag wrote, "I know of no other book that depicts life in the Kibbutz more vividly, more realistically or with greater insight." In *Nation* William Novak noted that the story of sudden, violent events in the lives of three kibbutz families "engages our sympathies because of the compelling sincerity and moral concerns of the characters, and because of the extent to which this is really the story of an entire society." *New York Times Book Review* correspondent A.G. Mojtabai stressed the realistic sense of conflict between military and civilian values portrayed in *Elsewhere, Perhaps.* According to Mojtabai, two perceptions of "elsewhere" are active in the story: "elsewhere, perhaps, the laws of gravity obtain—not here; elsewhere, perhaps in some kingdom by the sea exists the model which our kibbutz imperfectly reflects, a society harmonious, healthful, joyful, loving—not here, not yet." Novak concluded that the novel's publication in the United States "should help to stimulate American appreciation of contemporary Israeli literature and society."

Oz's novel *A Perfect Peace* revolves around two young kibbutzniks—one rebellious after a lifetime in the environment, the other an enthusiastic newcomer—and an aging politician, founder of the collective. According to Alter, the novel is "a hybrid of social realism and metaphysical brooding, and it gains its peculiar power of assertion by setting social institutions and political issues in a larger metaphysical context. There is a vivid, persuasive sense of place here . . . but local place is quietly evoked against a cosmic backdrop." *Times Literary Supplement* reviewer S.S. Prawer observed that the work holds the reader's attention by providing a "variety of boldly drawn characters who reveal themselves to us in and through their speech. . . . Oz's storytelling, with its reliance on journals and inner monologues, is pleasantly old-fashioned." In a *New York Times Book Review* piece, Grace Schulman contended that it is "on a level other than the documentary that this novel succeeds so well. It is concerned with inner wholeness, and with a more profound peace than respect between generations and among countries. . . . The impact of this novel lies in the writer's creation of characters who are outwardly ordinary but inwardly bizarre, and at times fantastic."

Oz began his literary career as an author of short fiction. He has since published several volumes of stories and novellas, including *Where the Jackals Howl and Other Stories, Unto Death,* and *The Hill of Evil Counsel.* "As a seamstress who takes different pieces of cloth and sews them into a quilt, Amos Oz writes short pieces of fiction which together form a quilt in the reader's consciousness," noted J. Justin Gustainis in *Best Sellers.* "Just as the quilt may be of many colors but still one garment, Oz's stories speak of many things but still pay homage to one central idea: universal redemption through suffering."

Aschkenasy suggested that the stories in *Where the Jackals Howl* "are unified by an overall pattern that juxtaposes an individual permeated by a sense of existential estrangement and subterranean chaos with a self-deceiving community collectively intent upon putting up a facade of sanity and buoyancy in order to deny—or perhaps to exorcise—the demons from without and within." Chernaik noted of the same book that the reader coming to Oz for the first time "is likely to find his perception of Israel permanently altered and shaped by these tales."

The novellas in *Unto Death* "take as their theme the hatred that surrounds Jews and that destroys the hated and the haters alike," to quote Joseph McElroy in the *New York Times Book Review. Midstream* contributor Warren Bargad found this theme one manner of expressing "the breakdown of the myth of normalcy which has been at the center of Zionist longing for decades: the envisioned State of Israel, with its promise of autoemancipation, which would make of the Jewish people a nation among nations. For Oz it is still an impossible dream."

Oz revisits similar themes in *Fima,* which portrays the paradoxical futility of the novel's eponymous character. Fima is a despairing divorcee who lives in solitary squalor and has long ago abandoned work as a poet for employment as a receptionist at an abortion clinic. Privately preoccupied with intractable ethical dilemmas and fantasies of running the government, he endures a pathetic, ordinary existence punctuated by public fulminations and interaction with his few friends, ex-wife, and ten-year-old albino son. Fima "is a breathing contradiction, a muddle-headed sage, a gentle buffoon who thinks about life very seriously indeed," wrote Michael Hayward in *Washington Post Book World.* Shechner similarly observed in Chicago *Tribune Books* that "For all his neurosis and ineffectuality, his self-absorption and lassitude, his petulance and his opinions, he is a true-blue peace advocate, like Oz himself." Hayward added, "one always senses that Oz is on the side of his hero's sanity. . . . Fima may not look like one, but he is a survivor."

Fima was well received by critics. According to Patricia Storace in the *New York Review of Books,* the novel's "insistent presentation of trivial daily events, of political discussions that faithfully reproduce recognizable arguments, its vignettes of Jerusalem life, make it seem, read from one angle, a work of talented, experienced and intelligent realism." Storace added that Oz "has made a thoroughly unconventional novel co-exist simultaneously with a work of more conventional realism. This world of whiskey-drinking and divorce, of newspaper-reading and passionate argument, is also the world of good and evil, of life and death."

The novel *Don't Call It Night* centers on the relationship of Theo and Noa, a childless couple who become involved in the establishment of a drug rehabilitation center in their small frontier town. The center is commissioned to honor the memory of one of Noa's former pupils, whose mysterious suicide lends an air of intrigue. Though the enterprise is originally presented to Noa, an idealistic teacher, her reluctance to involve Theo eventually succumbs to necessity. Theo is an experienced city planner and a realist whose expertise proves essential to bringing the task to completion. Despite their differences, as Tony Gould wrote in *Spectator,* "They are more alike than either cares to be, and what they have in common is their need. That is the one constant in a world where everything else is transient—relationships, commitments, even the new town itself, perched on the edge of a desert which is as metaphorical as it is real." Concentrating on atmosphere more than plot, Oz portrays the subtle variations of feeling and temperament that render a seemingly ordinary relationship complex.

Praising the novel in an *Observer* review, Kate Kellaway commented that "*Don't Call It Night* has a meditative confidence that a younger writer could not expect to achieve. It is daringly ambitious; it shows that non-events matter." Though critical of the novel's contrived action and digressions, *Times Literary Supplement* contributor Michael Hofmann believed that *Don't Call It Night* surpasses *Fima* and represents a major contribution to the literary canon of postwar Israel. "At its best," wrote Hofmann, "[the novel] has a kind of Dutch uneventfulness. Elements of nocturne, still life, portrait and landscape are blended to create . . . indelible images in the reader's mind: of the small town at the edge of the desert, of two people at night in their apartment, one asleep, the other musing and pottering by the light of a fridge." Commenting on *Don't Call It Night* in a *New Statesman* interview with Christopher Price, Oz remarked, "Sociology does not interest me. I don't want to know how many people are like Theo and Noa. . . . I want to know what Theo and Noa are really like. This is why I am a storyteller and not a scientist."

In addition to his work as a storyteller, Oz assumes a position of objective detachment as an accomplished political observer and journalist. *In the Land of Israel,* a series of interviews Oz conducted with a wide variety of Israelis, is his best-known work of nonfiction. According to Shechner, the book "provoked an outcry in Israel, where many saw the portraits of Jews as exaggerated and tailored to suit Oz's politics." The study does indeed present a vision of a pluralistic, creatively contentious society, "threatened as much by the xenophobia and self-righteous tribalism within as by enemies without," according to Gene Lyons in *Newsweek.* Christopher Lehmann-Haupt offered a similar opinion in the *New York Times:* "All together, the voices of *In the Land of Israel* serve to elucidate the country's complex ideological cross-currents. And conducted as they are by Mr. Oz, they sing an eloquent defense of what he considers a centrist position, though some of his critics might call it somewhat left-of-center." Lyons felt that the work is most valuable for what it shows the reader about Oz and his belief regarding his country's future. Lyons concluded, "Eloquent, humane, even religious in the deepest sense, [Oz] emerges here—and I can think of no higher praise—as a kind of Zionist Orwell: a complex man obsessed with simple decency and determined above all to tell the truth, regardless of whom it offends."

Under This Blazing Light offers additional commentary on later-twentieth-century Israeli life in essays adapted from interviews and lectures conducted by Oz between 1962 and 1979. His main themes revolve around the necessity of compromise between Israel and the Palestinians and an examination of Hebrew language and literature. Regarding Oz's political analysis, Elizabeth Shostak wrote in *Wilson Library Bulletin,* "the author's principled determination to imagine the other side's point of view without giving up his own loyalty remains both convincing and attractive." On the function of literature in human affairs, Tova Reich wrote in the *New York Times Book Review,* "Oz answers with a refreshingly old-fashioned formulation: it is 'a circle of sorrow—protest—consolation.'" Shostak concluded, "Oz is a direct and lucid essayist."

Israel, Palestine, and Peace is a similar collection of Oz's writings devoted to Middle East politics. "The unusual aspect of Oz's viewpoint," noted Shelley A. Glantz in *Kliatt,* is that he "blames and credits Israeli and Palestinian leaders and citizens equally." Oz reaffirms his belief that peace cannot be achieved without compromise, which inevitably calls for moderation and reciprocal sacrifice. While asserting a two-state solution in which both could coexist without lingering on ceaseless accusation, Oz suggests that the first gesture of conciliation should be to erect "a monument to our mutual stupidity." According to *Washington Post Book World* reviewer Charles Solomon, Oz's essays represent "a compelling vision of tolerance and sanity." A *Kirkus Reviews* contributor similarly praised the volume as "a poignant and powerful collection." "Oz is one of those rare writers who is equally stimulating in fiction and essay," concluded a *Rapport* reviewer. Oz's position did not waver in the face of the escalation of terrorist violence in Israel and elsewhere in the wake of the terrorist attacks on Washington, DC, and New York City on September 11th, 2001. "If we don't stop somewhere, if we don't accept an unhappy compromise, unhappy for both sides, if we don't learn how to unhappily coexist and contain our burned sense of injustice—if we don't learn how to do that, we end up in a doomed state," he explained to *NewsHour* interviewer Elizabeth Farnsworth in a televised discussion of the extension of the Israeli-Palestinian conflict into the twenty-first century.

In an assessment of Oz's nonfiction, Shechner described what he called the "two Amos Ozes." One, Shechner wrote, is "a fiction writer with an international audience, the other an Israeli journalist of more or less hometown credentials. . . . Oz's journalism would seem to have little in common with the crepuscular world of his fiction. A blend of portraits and polemics, it is straightforward advocacy journalism, bristling with editorials and belonging to the world of opinions, ideologies and campaigns." Despite his fiction's sometimes bleak portrayal of Israel, Oz believes in his homeland and expresses strong opinions on how he feels it should be run. Alter noted: "In contrast to the inclination some writers may feel to withdraw into the fastness of language, the Oz articles reflect a strenuous effort to go out into Israeli society and sound its depth." Furthermore, according to Roger Rosenblatt in the *New York Times Book Review,* as a journalist Oz establishes "that he is no ordinary self-effacing reporter on a quest, but a public figure who for years has participated in major national controversies and who regularly gives his views of things to the international press, 'ratting' on his homeland." Schulman suggested in the *Washington Post Book World* that Oz's journalism "may be the way to an esthetic stance in which he can reconcile the conflicting demands of artistic concern and political turbulence."

Critics have found much to praise in Oz's portraits of the struggling nation of Israel. "Oz's words, his sensuous prose and indelible imagery, the people he flings living onto his pages, evoke a cauldron of sentiments at the boil; yet his human vision is capacious enough to contain the destruction and hope for peace," wrote Richard R. Lingeman in the *New York Times.* "He has caught a welter of fears, curses and dreams at a watershed moment in history, when an uneasy, restless waiting gave way to an upsurge of violence, of fearsome consequences. The power of his art fuses historical fact and symbol; he makes the ancient stones of Jerusalem speak, and the desert beyond a place of jackals and miracles." In the *Saturday Review,* Alfred Kazin stated that Oz's effect on him is always to make him realize "how little we know about what goes on inside the Israeli head. . . . To the unusually sensitive and humorous mind of Amos Oz, the real theme of Jewish history—especially in Israel—is unreality. When, and how can a Jew attain reality in the Promised Land, actually touch the water, touch the wind?" Chernaik felt that Oz is "without doubt a voice for sanity, for the powers of imagination and love, and for understanding. He is also a writer of marvelous comic and lyric gifts, which somehow communicate themselves as naturally in English as in Hebrew."

The Same Sea is a lyric novel, written partially in verse, with frequent allusions to the great poetry and prose of the Hebrew tradition. "This is vintage Mr. Oz, arguably his best work ever," Carol Herman observed in the *Washington Times,* although she noted that "those seeking the benefit of his political wisdom will find no explicit comfort here." Reading *The Same Sea* "is like being the guest at a dinner party of a wildly dysfunctional family that is not shy about airing its secrets," as *New York Times* reviewer William M. Hoffman described it. Albert, a recent widower; his son Rico, who is "finding himself" and experimenting with his sexuality in Asia; Dita, Rico's girlfriend, who moves in with Albert after she is cheated out of her money; and Bettine, a down-to-earth woman of Albert's own age who is the only character who consistently speaks in prose, all get to explain themselves. Even Nadia, Albert's dead wife, speaks. "Some rhyme, some don't," Herman said of the characters, but "all breathe." *The Same Sea* "will doubtless be regarded as a defining work from a writer of major significance," Phillip Santo declared in *Library Journal.*

A Tale of Love and Darkness is a "moving, emotionally charged memoir of the renowned author's youth in a newly created Israel," wrote a critic in *Kirkus Reviews.* Focusing on Oz's childhood and adolescence, *A Tale of Love and Darkness* "deals frontally with an upbringing previously inferable only from his stories and novels," according to *Commentary* reviewer Hillel Halkin. The work also follows Oz's development as a writer during a time of great political upheaval. "In this heady, dangerous atmosphere . . . Oz comes of age, blossoming as a man of letters," wrote the *Kirkus Reviews* critic.

Oz is an unusual Israeli writer in that he has chosen to stay at the kibbutz throughout his career, even though the income from his royalties is substantial. Even when he was younger, he said in *Partisan Review,* the kibbutz "evoked and fed my curiosity about the strange phenomenon of flawed, tormented human beings dreaming about perfection, aching for the Messiah, aspiring to change human nature. This perpetual paradox of magnanimous dream and unhappy reality is indeed one of the main threads in my writing." Furthermore, he told the *Washington Post,* his fellow kibbutzniks react to his works in fascinating ways: "It's a great advantage, you know, to have a passionate, immediate milieu and not a literary milieu—a milieu of real people who tell me straight in my face what they think of my writing."

Hebrew is the language in which Oz chooses to write; he calls it a "volcano in action," still evolving rapidly into new forms. Oz likes to call himself the "tribal storyteller," as he explained in the *New York Times:* "I bring up the evil spirits and record the traumas, fantasies, the lunacies of Israeli Jews, natives and those from Central Europe. I deal with their ambitions and the powderbox of self-denial and self-hatred." In a *Washington Post* interview, he maintained that Israel would always be the source from which his inspiration would spring. "I'm fascinated," he said of his homeland. "Yes, indeed, I'm disgusted, appalled, sick and tired sometimes. Even when I'm sick and tired, I'm there. . . . It's my thing, if you will, in the same sense that William Faulkner belonged in the Deep South. It's my thing and my place and my addiction."

Married and the father of three children, Oz speaks and travels frequently, bringing his personal thoughts to television and lecture audiences in Israel and abroad. Describing his creative impulses, Oz told the *New York Times:* "Whenever I find myself in total agreement with myself, then I write an article—usually in rage—telling the government what to do. But when I detect hesitation, more than one inner voice, I discover in me the embryo of characters, the seeds of a novel."

BIOGRAPHICAL AND CRITICAL SOURCES:

BOOKS

Contemporary Literary Criticism, Thomson Gale (Detroit, MI), Volume 5, 1976, Volume 8, 1978, Volume 11, 1979, Volume 27, 1981, Volume 33, 1985, Volume 54, 1989.

Contemporary World Writers, 2nd edition, St. James Press (Detroit, MI), 1993.

Encyclopedia of World Biography, 2nd edition, Thomson Gale (Detroit, MI), 1998.

Encyclopedia of World Literature in the Twentieth Century, 3rd edition, St. James Press (Detroit, MI), 1999.

Hiro, Dilip, *Dictionary of the Middle East,* St. Martin's Press (New York, NY), 1996.

Legends in Their Own Time, Prentice Hall (New York, NY), 1994.

Magill, Frank N., editor, *Cyclopedia of World Authors II,* Salem Press (Pasadena, CA), 1997.

Murphy, Bruce, editor, *Benet's Reader's Encyclopedia,* 4th edition, HarperCollins (New York, NY), 1996.

Oz, Amos, *Israel, Palestine, and Peace: Essays,* Harcourt (San Diego, CA), 1995.

Reference Guide to Short Fiction, 2nd edition, St. James Press (Detroit, MI), 1999.

Short Story Criticism, Volume 66, Thomson Gale (Detroit, MI), 2004.

Wirth-Nesher, Hana, *City Codes: Reading the Modern Urban Novel,* Cambridge University Press (Cambridge, England), 1996.

PERIODICALS

Atlantic, December, 1983; May, 1988.

Best Sellers, October, 1978.

Book, May-June, 2002, Stephen Whited, review of *The Same Sea,* p. 80.

Booklist, February 15, 1999, review of *Kol Ha-Tokvot,* p. 1049; October 15, 2001, Donna Seaman, review of *The Same Sea,* p. 383.

Brick, summer, 2003, Ramona Koval, "An Interview with Amos Oz," pp. 68-80.

Chicago Tribune, December 7, 1989.

Commentary, July, 1974; April, 1984; April, 2004, Hillel Halkin, "Politics and the Israeli Novel," pp. 29-36.

Jewish Quarterly, spring-summer, 1974.

Kirkus Reviews, March 1, 1995, p. 304; July 1, 1995, p. 926; January 1, 1999, review of *The Story Begins,* p. 50; July 15, 2004, review of *A Tale of Love and Darkness,* p. 677.

Kliatt, January, 1996, p. 31; September, 1998, review of *Panther in the Basement,* p. 6; March, 1999, review of *Panther in the Basement,* p. 14.

Library Journal, January, 1999, Gene Shaw, review of *The Story Begins,* p. 97; August, 2001, Philip Santo, review of *The Same Sea,* p. 164; July, 2003, "Amos Oz Unto Death: Two Novellas—Crusade and Late Love"; June 1, 2004, Barbara Hoffert, review of *A Tale of Love and Darkness,* p. 104.

Los Angeles Times, May 21, 1981; June 24, 1985; December 25, 1989.

Los Angeles Times Book Review, December 11, 1983; May 29, 1988, p. 3; May 12, 1991, p. 2; September 3, 1995, p. 9.

Midstream, November, 1976; January, 1985; January, 2002, Leslie Cohen and Elvera Herbstman, review of *The Same Sea,* pp. 44-45.

Modern Fiction Studies, spring, 1978.

Nation, September 7, 1974; June 8, 1985; June 4, 1988, p. 796; November 11, 1996, John Leonard, "What Have We Come Here to Be?," pp. 25-30; January 21, 2002, Morris Dickstein, review of *The Same Sea,* p. 27.

National Review, April 20, 1984.

New Leader, January 6, 1975.

New Republic, November 29, 1975; October 14, 1978; June 27, 1981; July 29, 1985; October 28, 1991, p. 36-40; August 7, 2000, Hillel Halkin, review of *The Disappointments,* p. 39.

New Statesman, October 20, 1995, p. 20.

Newsweek, November 21, 1983; July 29, 1985.

New Yorker, November 18, 1974; August 7, 1978; August 19, 1985; January 31, 1994, p. 89.

New York Review of Books, February 7, 1974; January 23, 1975; July 20, 1978; September 26, 1985; August 18, 1988, p. 30; May 26, 1994, p. 17; June 25, 1995, p. 18; March 5, 1998, review of *Panther in the Basement,* p. 17.

New York Times, May 19, 1978; July 18, 1978; May 22, 1981; October 31, 1983; November 11, 1989; March, 1998, J.M. Coetzee, review of *Panther in the Basement,* pp. 17-18.

New York Times Book Review, May 21, 1972; November 18, 1973; November 24, 1974; October 26, 1975; May 28, 1978; April 26, 1981; March 27, 1983; November 6, 1983; November 25, 1984, p. 44; June 2, 1985; April 24, 1988, p. 7; March 19, 1989, p. 32; February 4, 1990; January 24, 1991, p. 32; June 9, 1991, p. 32; July 26, 1992, p. 24; October 24, 1993, p. 12; June 25, 1995, p. 18; January 11, 1998, review of *Don't Call It Night,* p. 20; December 27, 1998, review of *Panther in the Basement,* p. 20; July 4, 1999, Laurie Adlerstein, review of *The Story Begins,* p. 14; October 28, 2001, William M. Hoffman, "Thou Shalt Not Covet Thy Son's Girlfriend," p. 12.

Observer (London, England), July 7, 1985, p. 21; July 13, 1986, p. 27; June 26, 1988, p. 42; July 17, 1988, p. 42; February 4, 1990, p. 61; February 3, 1991, p. 54; September 12, 1993, p. 53; October 29, 1995, p. 16; May 29, 1999, review of *The Story Begins,* p. 11; February 18, 2001, review of *The Same Sea,* p. 15.

Partisan Review, number 3, 1982; number 3, 1986.

Publishers Weekly, May 21, 1973; September 6, 1993, p. 84; February 27, 1995, p. 92; June 17, 1996, p. 45; February 1, 1999, review of *The Story Begins,* p. 66; September 3, 2001, review of *The Same Sea,* p. 54.

Rapport, Volume 19, number 1, 1995, p. 39.

Saturday Review, June 24, 1972; November 2, 1974; May 13, 1978.

Spectator, January 9, 1982; December 17, 1983; August 10, 1985; April 22, 1995, p. 36; October 7, 1995, p. 54; February 17, 2001, review of *The Same Sea,* p. 39.

Studies in Short Fiction, winter, 1982.

Time, January 27, 1986.

Times (London, England), August 1, 1985.

Times Literary Supplement, July 21, 1972; February 22, 1974; March 21, 1975; October 6, 1978; September 25, 1981; July 27, 1984; August 9, 1985; June 24, 1988, p. 697; December 2, 1988, p. 1342; March 2,

1990; October 13, 1995, p. 24; December 1, 1995, p. 12; December 4, 1998, review of *Panther in the Basement,* p. 12; September 1, 2000, Morris Dickstein, "The Talking Dog of Jerusalem," pp. 12-13; February 9, 2001, review of *The Same Sea,* p. 21.

Tribune Books (Chicago, IL), November 14, 1993, p. 3.

Village Voice, February 14, 1984.

Washington Post, December 1, 1983.

Washington Post Book World, May 28, 1972; May 31, 1981; June 14, 1981; November 13, 1983; July 14, 1985; November 28, 1993, p. 6.

Washington Times, December 9, 2001, Carol Herman, "How Life Goes On in Israel," p. 6.

Whole Earth Review, spring, 1996, p. 77.

Wilson Library Bulletin, June, 1995, p. 104.

World Literature Today, spring, 1982; spring, 1983; summer, 1984; autumn, 1986; autumn, 1995, p. 862; spring, 1998, review of *Panther in the Basement,* p. 449; summer, 1999, review of *The Story Begins,* p. 589; summer-autumn, 2001, Eric Sterling, review of *The Same Sea,* pp. 110-111.

ONLINE

Department for Jewish Zionist Education Web site, http://www.jajz-ed.org.il/ (May 9, 2002), "Amoz Oz, Israeli Novelist."

Online NewsHour, http://www.pbs.org/newshour/ (January 23, 2002), Elizabeth Farnsworth, "Coping with Conflict" (televised interview transcript).

* * *

OZICK, Cynthia 1928-
(Trudie Vosce)

PERSONAL: Born April 17, 1928, in New York, NY; daughter of William (a pharmacist) and Celia (Regelson) Ozick; married Bernard Hallote (a lawyer), September 7, 1952; children: Rachel Sarah. *Education:* New York University, B.A. (cum laude), 1949; Ohio State University, M.A., 1950.

ADDRESSES: Home—34 Soundview St., New Rochelle, NY 10805. *Office*—c/o Alfred A. Knopf Inc., 201 East 50th St., New York, NY 10022. *Agent*—Theron Raines, Raines & Raines, 71 Park Ave., New York, NY 10016.

CAREER: Writer and translator. Filene's Department Store, Boston, MA, advertising copywriter, 1952-53; New York University, New York, NY, instructor in English, 1964-65; City College of the City University of New York, distinguished artist-in-residence, 1981-82. Instructor at fiction workshop, Chautauqua Writers' Conference, July, 1966. Visiting lecturer at numerous colleges and universities.

MEMBER: PEN, Authors League of America, American Academy of Arts and Letters, American Academy of Arts and Sciences, Dramatists Guild, Academie Universelle des Cultures (Paris, France), Phi Beta Kappa.

AWARDS, HONORS: National Endowment for the Arts fellow, 1968; B'nai Brith Jewish Heritage Award, Edward Lewis Wallant Memorial Award, and National Book Award nomination, all 1972, all for *The Pagan Rabbi, and Other Stories;* Epstein Award, Jewish Book Council, 1972, for *The Pagan Rabbi, and Other Stories,* and 1976, for *Bloodshed and Three Novellas;* American Academy of Arts Award for Literature, 1973; Hadassah Myrtle Wreath Award, 1974; O. Henry First Prize Award in fiction, 1975, 1981, and 1984; Pushcart Press Lamport Prize, 1980; Guggenheim fellow, 1982; National Book Critics Circle Award nominations, 1982, 1983, and 1990; Mildred and Harold Strauss Livings grant, American Academy and Institute of Arts and Letters, 1982-87; Distinguished Service in Jewish Letters Award, Jewish Theological Seminary, 1984; Distinguished Alumnus Award, New York University, 1984; PEN/Faulkner Award nomination, 1984; Rea Award for Short Story, Dungannon Foundation, 1986; Lucy Martin Donnelly fellow, Bryn Mawr College, 1992; National Jewish Book Award for Fiction, Jewish Book Council, 1977, for *Bloodshed and Three Novellas;* O. Henry Award, 1992, for "Puttermesser Paired"; PEN/Spiegel-Diamonstein Award for the Art of the Essay, 1997; Harold Washington Literary Award, 1997, from the City of Chicago; John Cheever Award, 1999; National Book Critics' Circle Award nomination for criticism, 2000, for *Quarrel and Quandary.* Honorary degrees from Yeshiva University, 1984, Hebrew Union College, 1984, Williams College, 1986, Hunter College of the City University of New York, 1987, Jewish Theological Seminary, 1988, Adelphi University, 1988, State University of New York, 1989, Brandeis University, 1990, Bard College, 1991, Spertus College, 1991, and Skidmore College, 1992.

WRITINGS:

FICTION

Trust (novel), New American Library (New York, NY), 1966.

The Pagan Rabbi, and Other Stories, Knopf (New York, NY), 1971.

Bloodshed and Three Novellas, Knopf (New York, NY), 1976.

Levitation: Five Fictions, Knopf (New York, NY), 1982.

The Cannibal Galaxy (novel), Knopf (New York, NY), 1983.

The Messiah of Stockholm (novel), Knopf (New York, NY), 1987.

The Shawl (contains the novella *Rosa;* also see below), Knopf (New York, NY), 1989.

Blue Light (play; based on "The Shawl"), produced in Sag Harbor, NY, 1994, produced as *The Shawl* in New York, NY, 1996.

The Puttermesser Papers (novel), Knopf (New York, NY), 1997.

Heir to the Glimmering World (novel), Houghton (New York, NY), 2004.

OTHER

Art and Ardor: Essays, Knopf (New York, NY), 1983.

Metaphor and Memory: Essays, Knopf (New York, NY), 1989.

Epodes: First Poems, with woodcuts by Sidney Chafetz, Logan Elm Press (Columbus, OH), 1992.

What Henry James Knew, and Other Essays on Writers, J. Cape (London, England), 1993.

A Cynthia Ozick Reader, edited by Elaine M. Kauvar, Indiana University Press (Bloomington, IN), 1996.

Fame and Folly: Essays, Knopf (New York, NY), 1996.

Portrait of the Artist as a Bad Character, Pimlico Press (London, England), 1996.

(Author of introduction) Saul Bellow, *Seize the Day,* Penguin (New York, NY), 1996.

(Editor, with Robert Atwan) *The Best American Essays 1998,* Houghton Mifflin (Boston, MA), 1998.

Quarrel and Quandary: Essays, Random House (New York, NY), 2000.

(Editor) *Complete Works of Isaac Bable,* translated by Peter Constantine, Norton (New York, NY), 2001.

(Author of afterword) *Those Who Forget the Past: The Question of Anti-Semitism,* edited with an introduction by Ron Rosenbaum, Random House (New York, NY), 2004.

Contributor of essays, poems, introductions, and translations to numerous anthologies, including Joyce Field and Leslie Field, editors, *Bernard Malamud: A Collection of Critical Essays,* Prentice-Hall (Englewood Cliffs, NJ), 1975; Howard Schwartz and Anthony Rudolf, editors, *Voices within the Ark: The Modern Jewish Poets,* Avon (New York, NY), 1980; and *The Jewish Bible: Thirty-seven American Authors,* Harcourt (New York, NY), 1987. Contributor to "About Books" column in *New York Times Book Review,* 1987. Contributor, under pseudonym Trudie Vocse, of article "Twenty-four Years in the Life of Lyuba Bershadskaya" to *New York Times Magazine.* Contributor of other articles, reviews, poems, and translations to periodicals, including *Commentary, New Republic, Partisan Review, New Leader, New York Times Book Review, Ms., Esquire, New Yorker, American Poetry Review, Harper's,* and *New York Times Magazine.*

SIDELIGHTS: Cynthia Ozick is "an important voice in American fiction, a woman whose intellect . . . is so impressive that it pervades the words she chooses, the stories she elects to tell, and every careful phrase and clause in which they are conveyed," wrote Doris Grumbach in the *Washington Post Book World.* An acclaimed novelist, short story writer, essayist, and critic, Ozick remains best known for her fiction, and in this regard "few contemporary authors have demonstrated her range, knowledge, or passion," added essayist Diane Cole in the *Dictionary of Literary Biography.* Described by Elaine M. Kauvar in *Contemporary Literature* as a "master of the meticulous sentence and champion of the moral sense of art," Ozick writes on a variety of subjects, often mixing such elements as fantasy, mysticism, comedy, satire, and Judaic law and history, in a style that suggests a poet's perfectionism and a philosopher's dialectic. Although many of her works are steeped in Judaic culture and explore the conflict between the sacred and the profane, the epithet "Jewish writer"—as she has been called—is a misnomer according to many critics, including Ozick herself, who claims in *Art and Ardor* that the term is an oxymoron. Rather, to quote Robert R. Harris in *Saturday Review,* she is fundamentally a writer "obsessed with the words she puts on paper, with what it means to imagine a story and to tell it, with what fiction is. The result is a body of work at once as rich as Grace Paley's stories, as deeply rooted in Jewish folklore as Isaac Bashevis Singer's tales, [and] as comically ironic as Franz Kafka's nightmares."

Ozick has attracted the attention of readers and reviewers of serious fiction ever since her first book, *Trust,* was published in 1966. Narrated by an anonymous young woman searching for real and psychological identity, *Trust* is a long, intricately plotted literary novel about personal and political betrayal that, according to *New York Times Book Review* contributor David L. Stevenson, hearkens back to the tradition of Henry James, Joseph Conrad, and D.H. Lawrence. Martin Tucker pointed out in the *New Republic* that Ozick's "style, though shaped by the ancient moderns . . . is not self-consciously imitative. The outstanding achievement of her first novel is its play with words, its love of paradox." Other critics have also praised Ozick's linguistic virtuosity in *Trust,* although several share Tucker's opinion that "sometimes the cleverness of her style is obtrusive." R.Z. Sheppard, for instance, commented in *Book Week* that *Trust* "introduces a novelist of remarkable intelligence, learning, and inventiveness—qualities that make the book an uncommonly rich reading experience, yet qualities so lavishly displayed they frequently hobble . . . Ozick's muse." Nevertheless, Sheppard believed Ozick "still manages a considerable achievement of passion and skill," and Tucker called the novel "brilliant." Stevenson, moreover, hailed the book as "that extraordinary literary entity, a first novel that is a genuine novel, wholly self-contained and produced by a rich, creative imagination."

Following *Trust,* Ozick published three award-winning collections of short fiction—*The Pagan Rabbi, and Other Stories, Bloodshed and Three Novellas,* and *Levitation: Five Fictions*—that firmly established her literary reputation. In a *New York Times Book Review* article on *The Pagan Rabbi* Johanna Kaplan maintained that Ozick proves herself to be "a kind of narrative hypnotist. Her range is extraordinary; there is seemingly nothing she cannot do. Her stories contain passages of intense lyricism and brilliant, hilarious, uncontainable inventiveness—jokes, lists, letters, poems, parodies, satires." Reflecting on the collections, *New York Review of Books* contributor A. Alvarez called Ozick "a stylist in the best and most complete sense: in language, in wit, in her apprehension of reality and her curious, crooked flights of imagination. . . . Although there is nothing stiff or overcompacted about her writing . . . , she . . . has the poet's perfectionist habit of mind and obsession with language, as though one word out of place would undo the whole fabric." Such quality of invention prompted *New York Times* reviewer John Leonard to call the title story of *Levitation* "a masterpiece" and led *New York Times Book Review* contributor Leslie Epstein to regard *The Pagan Rabbi* and *Bloodshed* as "perhaps the finest work in short fiction by a contemporary writer." Ozick's talent furthermore encouraged *Newsweek* contributor Peter S. Prescott to "fearlessly predict that when the chroniclers of our literary age catch up to what has been going on (may Ozick live to see it!), some of her stories will be reckoned among the best written in our time."

Cole provided an indication of Ozick's stylistic virtuosity: "From page to page, Ozick will shift from an elevated Biblical inflection to the stilted Yiddish of the Russian immigrant to a slangy American vernacular; from sharply focused realism to fantastical flights into the supernatural. Magical transformations abound—of women into sea nymphs, trees into dryads, virile young poets into elderly androgynes." Similarly, Ozick's tales defy easy explication, in part because of their "thought-provoking dialectical quality," according to Harris. Carole Horn noted in the *Washington Post Book World:* "You could think about the themes that run through 'Bloodshed,' 'Usurpation' and 'The Mercenary' at great length. . . . The more of the Jewish Idea, as Ozick calls it, you have at your command, the broader the levels of meaning you could explore. But you don't need that to find them interesting reading." Harris pointed out that because Ozick "deals with ideas—many of them steeped in Jewish Law and history—her stories are 'difficult.' But by difficult I mean only that they are not in the least bit fluffy. No word, emotion, or idea is wasted. They are weighty, consequential tales, lightened and at the same time heightened by their visionary aspects. . . . Her stories are elusive, mysterious, and disturbing. They shimmer with intelligence, they glory in language, and they puzzle."

Ozick's works wrestle with theological issues, although the author once described herself as "neither a philosopher nor a theologian, and my focus—as is that of any writer concerned with style—is on writing good sentences." According to Cole, Ozick's work sometimes highlights "characters . . . torn between the opposing claims of two religions. One is always pagan, whether it be the worship of nature or the idolatrous pursuit of art, whereas the other—Judaism—is sacred." Kaplan, among others, viewed this theme in its broadest theological sense as a "variant of the question: what is holy? Is it the extraordinary, that which is beyond possible human experience—dryads ('The Pagan Rabbi') or sea-nymphs ('The Dock-Witch')? Or is the holiness in life to be discovered, to be seen in what is ordinarily, blindly, unthinkingly discounted?" But Eve Ottenberg, in her *New York Times Magazine* profile of Ozick, maintained that this theme has its greatest impact in a specifically Jewish context. "Over and over again . . . ," stated Ottenberg, Ozick's "characters struggle, suffer, perform bizarre feats, even go mad as a result of remaining or finding out what it means to remain—culturally, and above all, religiously—Jewish. . . . Her characters are often tempted into worshiping something other than God—namely, idols. And this struggle marks her characters with a singular aloneness—the aloneness of people who are thinking a great deal about who they are, and for whom thinking, not doing, is the most emotional and engaging aspect of their lives."

Critics have attributed to Ozick's fiction an emphasis on the notion of idolatry. "Idolatry is Cynthia Ozick's great theme," announced Edmund White in a *New York Times Book Review* appraisal of *The Cannibal Galaxy.* "In stories, essays and . . . in her second novel she meditates on this deep concern—the hubris of anyone who dares to rival the Creator by fashioning an idol." Harold Bloom declared in the *New York Times Book Review* that the central point of Ozick's work, culminating in *The Messiah of Stockholm,* is to somehow reconcile her need to create fiction with her desire to remain a follower of the Jewish tradition. "Ozick's vision of literature," wrote Bloom, "is conditioned by her anxiety about idolatry, her fear of making stories into so many idols. And her most profound insight concerns her ambivalence about the act of writing and the condemnation of the religion of art, or the worship of Moloch. This insight comes to the fore when she asks herself the combative question that governs every strong writer: 'Why do we become what we most desire to contend with?'"

Bloom felt that Ozick's response to this question in her early essays and stories "was immensely bitter." The novella *Usurpation,* collected in *Bloodshed and Three Novellas,* is ostensibly "a tale against tale telling," according to Paul Gray in *Time.* "The thoroughly Jewish concern in this work," added Ruth R. Wisse in *Commentary,* "is the writing of fiction itself, in . . . Ozick's view an inheritance from the Gentiles and by nature an idolatrous activity. Art—in the Western tradition of truth to fiction as its own end—is against the Second Commandment, she says, and anti-Jewish in its very impulse. As a Jewish artist, . . . Ozick undertakes to subvert the aesthetic ideal by demonstrating its corrupting and arrogant presumption to truth."

Bloom considered Ozick's "triumph" in *The Messiah of Stockholm* to be "a developed awareness that her earlier view of art as idolatry was too severe. . . . The novel is a complex and fascinating meditation on the nature of writing and the responsibilities of those who choose to create—or judge—tales. Yet on a purely realistic level, it manages to capture the atmosphere of Stockholm and to be, at times, very funny indeed about the daily operations of one of the city's newspapers and . . . [the protagonist's] peculiar detachment from everyday work and life."

In addition to these concerns, *The Messiah of Stockholm* garnered praise for its stylistic vitality. Calling the book "a poetic yet often raucously comic epic" in Chicago's *Tribune Books,* Mona Simpson maintained that "of course, no work of Ozick's can be talked about without first acknowledging the simple brilliance of her prose." John Calvin Batchelor insisted in the *Washington Post Book World* that *The Messiah of Stockholm* "is a superb read, with prose so deft that were it fisticuffs the author would be forbidden by law to combat mortals." But perhaps the finest compliment came from Michiko Kakutani of the *New York Times:* "What distinguishes *The Messiah of Stockholm* and lofts it above your run-of-the-mill philosophical novel is the author's distinctive and utterly original voice. . . . Ozick possesses an ability to mix up the surreal and the realistic, juxtapose Kafkaesque abstractions with Waugh-like comedy. Bizarre images . . . float, like figures in a Chagall painting, above precisely observed, naturalistic tableaux; and seemingly ordinary people suddenly become visionaries capable of madness or magic. The result is fiction that has the power to delight us—and to make us think."

The Shawl, first published in 1989, contains two tales—the short story "The Shawl" and a novella titled *Rosa.* Although both works were published separately—in somewhat different form—in the *New Yorker,* "they take on new resonance and weight from their inclusion here together," wrote Francine Prose in the *New York Times Book Review.* Both stories center on Rosa Lublin, who, in "The Shawl," witnesses the death of her baby daughter, Magda, when the girl is thrown against an electrified fence in a Nazi concentration camp. A linen shawl Rosa had allowed the child to suck on (they had no food) becomes a relic to the bereaved mother, whose story resumes many years later in *Rosa.* Now retired in Miami, mentally unstable, and still unable to accept the fact of her daughter's brutal death, she reveres the shawl because it brings her closer to Magda; it even empowers her to see visions of her daughter as an adolescent or an adult.

In *The Shawl,* commented Prose, "Ozick explores the complex connections among idolatry, maternity and philosophy. . . . Yet *The Shawl* is not a raking-over of familiar ground. Instead, Ms. Ozick goes farther to suggest that history too may be cast in the role of demiurge, that Rosa's idolatrous pantheon includes not only her daughter, but her own past, the war, the 'real life' that, she keeps repeating, has been stolen from her by thieves." Elie Wiesel, writing in Chicago's *Tribune Books,* argued that *The Shawl* "is not a book about the Holocaust, but about men and women who have survived it" and praised Ozick's style: "Rosa's impotent but overwhelming anger, her burning memories, her implacable solicitude, her hallucinations, her shawl—Ozick speaks of them with so much tact and delicacy that we ask ourselves with wonder and admiration what has she done to understand and penetrate Rosa's dark and devastated soul." Irving Halperin, reviewing the book for *Commonweal,* reached a similar conclusion: "It is a testimony to Ms. Ozick's artistry and depth of understanding that Rosa, though given to rage and moments of dementia, is sympathetically drawn."

Ozick has continued to impress critics with her fiction, including *The Puttermesser Papers.* The title character, attorney Rosa Puttermesser, had previously appeared in a few of Ozick's short stories. The novel, however, takes Puttermesser from the age of thirty-four to her death and beyond. Bernard F. Dick in *World Literature Today* commented that "no matter how bizarre the narrative becomes, Ozick moves easily between the poles of verisimilitude and absurdism." *Heir to the Glimmering World* again demonstrates Ozick's art and skill in the novel form by "mixing themes of faith, identify, and art into a crazy salad of a plot set in New York City during the great depression," according to Starr E. Smith in *Library Journal.* Described as a "witty book," *Heir to the Glimmering World* is sure to "will appeal to admirers of the fanciful tales in Ozick's *Puttermesser Papers*" due to its "intellectual depth," added the critic. In the novel Ozick "dramatizes the conflict between theology and science, various modes of mythmaking and survival," Donna Seaman explained in a *Booklist* review.

Ozick's commentaries on fellow writers have been collected in several volumes, among them *What Henry James Knew and Other Essays on Writers, Quarrel and Quandary,* and *Fame and Folly: Essays.* In *What Henry James Knew* Ozick deplores what she considers a cheapening and fragmentation of culture. "Her complaint is the usual one: we are in a deep pit filled with trivia, a hell of baseless chattering, butterfly minds alighting on the ephemeral and flitting away again," wrote Hilary Mantel in the *Spectator.* Mantel praised the style with which Ozick expresses this complaint, finding it "elegant and succinct, and so discriminating and precise that it is difficult to condense or paraphrase her arguments." *Fame and Folly* "is concerned with both the external machinery of fame and the internal mechanisms of self-destruction that shape the lives of artists," according to Kakutani in the *New York Times.* "Ozick presents the reader with a fistful of marvelous essays that live up to her own exacting standards of what an essay should be," the critic continued. "In these pages, Ms. Ozick gives us history, argument and, yes, illumination."

In 2000's *Quarrel and Quandary* Ozick explores topics such as her beloved Henry James, comparisons between a Dostoevsky character and the Unabomber, and what she feels went wrong in the process of adapting Anne Frank's diary to the stage and screen. Dick, in yet another piece for *World Literature Today,* maintained that "one of Cynthia Ozick's great gifts as an essayist is to take the reader on a voyage into a mind." Similarly, Edward Alexander in *Midstream* reported that "her bold formulations come to us with concentrated epigrammatic force and measured cadences that are a music to the inward ear."

Whether critics agree with the sentiments expressed in Ozick's essays or not, they have frequently been impressed by how she mounts her arguments. "She not only constantly illuminates the subjects she deals with, she makes one understand that most answers, most conclusions, most views, are slick and inadequate," observed Gabriel Josipovici in the *Times Literary Supplement.* And in *New Statesman and Society,* Guy Mannes-Abbott concluded: "Ozick has been called the best essayist in America. Better than best, she is the most singular."

BIOGRAPHICAL AND CRITICAL SOURCES:

BOOKS

Alexander, Edward, *The Resonance of Dust: Essays on Holocaust Literature and Jewish Fate,* Ohio State University Press (Columbus, OH), 1979.

Berger, Alan L., *Crisis and Covenant: The Holocaust in American Jewish Fiction,* New York State University Press (Albany, NY), 1985.

Bloom, Harold, editor, *Cynthia Ozick: Modern Critical Views,* Chelsea House (New York, NY), 1986.

Cohen, Sarah Blacher, *Comic Relief: Humor in Contemporary American Literature,* University of Illinois Press (Champaign, IL), 1978.

Cohen, Sarah Blacher, *Cynthia Ozick's Comic Art: From Levity to Liturgy,* Indiana University Press (Bloomington, IN), 1994.

Contemporary Literary Criticism, Thomson Gale (Detroit, MI), Volume 3, 1975, Volume 7, 1977, Volume 28, 1984, Volume 62, 1990.

Dictionary of Literary Biography, Volume 28: *Twentieth-Century American-Jewish Fiction Writers,* Thomson Gale (Detroit, MI), 1984.

Dictionary of Literary Biography Yearbook, Thomson Gale (Detroit, MI), 1982, 1983, 1983, 1984.

Finkelstein, Norman, *The Ritual of New Creation: Jewish Tradition and Contemporary Literature,* State University of New York Press (Albany, NY), 1992.

Friedman, Lawrence S., *Understanding Cynthia Ozick,* University of South Carolina Press (Columbia, SC), 1991.

Kauvar, Elaine M., *Cynthia Ozick's Fiction: Tradition and Invention,* Indiana University Press (Bloomington, IN), 1993.

Kielsky, Vera Emuna, *Inevitable Exiles: Cynthia Ozick's View of the Precariousness of Jewish Existence in a Gentile Society,* Peter Lang (New York, NY), 1989.

Lowin, Joseph, *Cynthia Ozick,* Twayne (Boston, MA), 1988.

Ozick, Cynthia, *Art and Ardor,* Knopf (New York, NY), 1983.

Pinksker, Sanford, *The Uncompromising Fictions of Cynthia Ozick,* University of Missouri Press (Columbia, MO), 1987.

Rainwater, Catherine, and William J. Scheick, editors, *Three Contemporary Women Novelists: Hazzard, Ozick, and Redmon,* University of Texas Press (Austin, TX), 1983.

Rainwater, Catherine, and William J. Scheick, editors, *Contemporary American Women Writers: Narrative Strategies,* University of Kentucky (Lexington, KY), 1985.

Shapiro, Michael, editor, *Divisions between Liberalism and Traditionalism in the American Jewish Community: Cleft or Chasm,* Edwin Mellen (Lewiston, NY), 1991.

Strandberg, Victor H., *Greek Mind/Jewish Soul: The Conflicted Art of Cynthia Ozick,* University of Wisconsin Press (Madison, WI), 1991.

Walden, Daniel, editor, *The World of Cynthia Ozick: Studies in American Jewish Literature,* Kent State University Press (Kent, OH), 1987.

Walden, Daniel, editor, *The Changing Mosaic: From Cahan to Malamud, Roth, and Ozick,* State University of New York Press (Albany, NY), 1993.

PERIODICALS

Booklist, July, 2004, Donna Seaman, review of *Heir to the Glimmering World,* p. 1800.

Book World, June 19, 1966.

Boston Globe, September 13, 1989, p. 41.

Chicago Tribune Book World, February 14, 1982; October 30, 1983.

Christian Century, March 7, 1990, p. 258.

Commentary, June, 1976; March, 1984; May, 1984; July, 1987, p. 52.

Commonweal, December 2, 1966, review of *Trust;* September 3, 1971, review of *The Pagan Rabbi and Other Stories;* December 15, 1989, pp. 711-712.

Contemporary Literature, spring, 1985; winter, 1985.

Critique, Volume IX, number 2, 1967.

Hudson Review, spring, 1984.

Interview, August, 1994, p. 48.

Library Journal, July, 2004, Starr E. Smith, review of *Heir to the Glimmering World.*

London Review of Books, February 4, 1988, p. 17; October 21, 1993, pp. 12-13.

Los Angeles Times, March 11, 1987.

Los Angeles Times Book Review, May 29, 1983, review of *The Cannibal Galaxy;* September 18, 1983; October 8, 1989, p. 2.

Midstream, November, 2000, Edward Alexander, review of *Quarrel and Quandary,* p. 44.

Nation, February 20, 1982; July 23-30, 1983.

New Republic, August 13, 1966, Martin Tucker, review of *Trust;* June 5, 1976; April 6, 1987, review of *The Messiah of Stockholm,* p. 39.

New Statesman, January 8, 1988, p. 32.

New Statesman and Society, June 4, 1993, p. 41.

Newsweek, May 10, 1971, review of *The Pagan Rabbi and Other Stories;* April 12, 1976; February 15, 1982; May 30, 1983, review of *The Cannibal Galaxy;* September 12, 1983.

New Yorker, May 13, 1996, pp. 88-93.

New York Review of Books, April 1, 1976; May 13, 1982; November 30, 1983, review of *The Cannibal Galaxy;* May 28, 1987, review of *The Messiah of Stockholm,* p. 18.

New York Times, July 9, 1966, review of *Trust;* July 5, 1971; January 28, 1982; April 27, 1983; August 29, 1983; March 25, 1987; March 28, 1987, review of *The Messiah of Stockholm;* September 5, 1989, p. C17; October 3, 1989, pp. C15, C21; May 7, 1996, p. B3.

New York Times Book Review, July 17, 1966, David L. Stevenson, review of *Trust;* June 13, 1971, review of *The Pagan Rabbi and Other Stories;* April 11, 1976; January 31, 1982; February 14, 1982; May 22, 1983; September 11, 1983; March 22, 1987, p. 1; April 23, 1989, p. 9; September 10, 1989, pp. 1, 39; December 3, 1989, p. 72; September 15, 1991, p. 34.

New York Times Magazine, April 10, 1983, review of *The Cannibal Galaxy.*

Observer (London, England), November 15, 1987, p. 26; July 7, 1991, p. 57; June 20, 1993, p. 62; September 18, 1994, p. 20.

Publishers Weekly, January 30, 1987, review of *The Messiah of Stockholm,* p. 369; March 27, 1987; February 17, 1989, p. 60; July 28, 1989, p. 204; July 29, 1990, p. 98; August 9, 1991, p. 55; March 22, 2004, p. 70.

Saturday Review, July 9, 1966, review of *Trust;* February, 1982.

Spectator, January 16, 1988, p. 29; May 29, 1993, pp. 25-26.

Time, August 12, 1966, review of *Trust;* April 12, 1976, Paul Gray, review of *Bloodshed and Three Novellas;* February 15, 1982; September 5, 1983.

Times (London, England), April 8, 1982.

Times Literary Supplement, January 26, 1967; April 23, 1982; January 20, 1984; January 25, 1985, p. 102; June 4, 1993, p. 25.

Tribune Books (Chicago, IL), March 1, 1987, review of *The Messiah of Stockholm,* p. 7; April 30, 1989, p. 7; September 17, 1989, p. 6.

USA Today, March 20, 1987, review of *The Messiah of Stockholm,* p. 4D; November 16, 1989, p. D6.

Village Voice, February 10, 1982; April 21, 1987, review of *The Messiah of Stockholm,* p. 45.

Virginia Quarterly Review, summer, 1987, p. 95; winter, 1990, p. 21.

Voice Literary Supplement, March, 1990, p. 11.

Wall Street Journal, June 20, 1997.

Washington Post, February 12, 1990, p. B1.

Washington Post Book World, June 6, 1971, review of *The Pagan Rabbi and Other Stories;* March 13, 1977; February 28, 1982; July 3, 1983; September 25, 1983; March 8, 1987, review of *The Messiah of Stockholm;* November 5, 1989, p. 7.

World Literature Today, winter, 1998, Bernard F. Dick, review of *The Puttermesser Papers,* pp. 135-136; spring, 2001, Bernard F. Dick, review of *Quarrel and Quandary,* p. 339.

P-Q

PACKER, Vin
See MEAKER, Marijane

* * *

PAGLIA, Camille 1947-
(Camille Anna Paglia)

PERSONAL: Born April 2, 1947, in Endicott, NY; daughter of Pasquale (a professor of Romance languages) and Lydia Paglia. *Education:* State University of New York, Binghamton, B.A., 1968; Yale University, M.Phil., 1971, Ph.D., 1974.

ADDRESSES: *Home*—Swarthmore, PA. *Office*—Department of Humanities, University of the Arts, 320 South Broad St., Philadelphia, PA 19102. *Agent*—Lynn Nesbit, Janklow and Nesbit, 598 Madison Ave., New York, NY 10022.

CAREER: Bennington College, Bennington, VT, faculty member in Literature and Languages Division, 1972-80; Wesleyan University, Middletown, CT, visiting lecturer in English, 1980; Yale University, New Haven, CT, fellow of Ezra Stiles College, 1981, visiting lecturer in comparative literature, 1981 and 1984, visiting lecturer in English, 1981-83, fellow of Silliman College, 1984; University of the Arts, Philadelphia, PA, assistant professor, 1984-86, associate professor, 1987-91, professor of humanities, 1991—.

AWARDS, HONORS: National Book Critics Circle Award nomination for criticism, 1991, for *Sexual Personae: Art and Decadence from Nefertiti to Emily Dickinson.*

WRITINGS:

Sexual Personae: Art and Decadence from Nefertiti to Emily Dickinson, Yale University Press (New Haven, CT), 1990.
Sex, Art, and American Culture: Essays, Vintage Books (New York, NY), 1992.
Vamps & Tramps: New Essays, Vintage Books (New York, NY), 1994.
The Birds, BFI Publishing, 1998.
Break, Blow, Burn, Pantheon (New York, NY), 2005.

SIDELIGHTS: Camille Paglia's unorthodox feminist views on the role of sexuality in the development of art and culture in Western civilization became the subject of heated debate with the publication of her first book, *Sexual Personae: Art and Decadence from Nefertiti to Emily Dickinson,* in 1990. In the book, and in her subsequent media statements and campus appearances across the country, Paglia has aroused controversy by accusing the contemporary feminist establishment of suppressing the aesthetics of art and beauty and the dangers of sexuality; she warns that historical reality is being ignored in the push for change. Paglia has in turn been criticized by some for her statements on issues such as date rape, pornography, and educational reform. A selection of her many articles, interviews, and lectures appears in the 1992 publication, *Sex, Art, and American Culture.*

Paglia posits in *Sexual Personae* that "the amorality, aggression, sadism, voyeurism, and pornography in great art have been ignored or glossed over by most academic critics." She highlights the appearances of such themes in order "to demonstrate the unity and continuity of Western culture" and disprove the modernist idea that culture is fragmented and meaningless. Terry Teachout in the *New York Times Book Review* stated that "to this end, *Sexual Personae* serves as an illustrated catalogue of the pagan sexual symbolism that Ms. Paglia believes to be omnipresent in Western art." Paglia outlines a number of sexually- charged figures which she calls "sexual personae," a term that *Nation* contributor Mark Edmundson defined as "erotic archetypes, figures that compel sexual fascination from all perceivers, whatever their professed erotic preferences." These archetypes include the femme fatale, the Great Mother, the vampire, and the hermaphrodite.

Paglia's application of her theory to authors such as the Marquis de Sade, Samuel Taylor Coleridge, and Emily Dickinson proved interesting to many reviewers. "Her fascination with 'perversity' in literature brings her to some startling interpretations," acknowledged Lillian Faderman in the *Washington Post Book World.* The reviewer also observed that Paglia's "discussion of the sexual ambiguities and obsessions that critics have ignored or minimized in major American writers is especially compelling." Walter Kendrick, in his *Voice Literary Supplement* assessment, applauded Paglia's "detailed, subtle readings of [Oscar Wilde's] *The Picture of Dorian Gray* and *The Importance of Being Earnest* and a delicious hatchet job on Emily Dickinson, whom Paglia reads as 'that autocratic sadist,' 'Amherst's Madame de Sade.'"

The author's interest in the sexual element throughout Western history is based on the basic duality or struggle she sees underlying this culture. Using a comparison based on Greek mythology, Paglia comments that the rational, Apollonian force of humanity that creates the order of society is constantly striving to protect itself from the Dionysian, or dark, chaotic forces of nature. She describes the Dionysian element as "the chthonian [earth-bound] realities which Apollo evades, the blind grinding of subterranean force, the long slow suck, the murk and ooze." And despite all the grand scientific and philosophical achievements of Western logic, this irrational pagan force of nature continually wells up, revealing itself in sex, art, and other aspects of popular culture, theorizes Paglia. Sex, especially, reveals these tensions: "Sex is the point of contact between man and nature, where morality and good intentions fall to primitive urges."

This unwieldy instinct unleashes the darker forces that Paglia claims are ignored by mainstream feminists and others who idealize sex as inherently pure, positive, and safe. The perversities that occur in sexual behavior are not caused by social injustice, maintains Paglia, but by natural forces that have not been properly contained by society's defenses. The artifice of society, which is exemplified in the classic works of art, literature, and philosophy of Western culture, is given the highest status by Paglia for this role of protecting and advancing humanity. "Much of western culture is a distortion of reality," she says in *Sexual Personae.* "But reality *should* be distorted; that is, imaginatively amended." Mark Edmundson summarized Paglia's idea that "the glory of art lies in its power to extemporize fictive identities—the personae—that swerve away from biology's literal insistence on what we are . . . . Decadence ritualizes, and thus subdues, erotic violence."

This favorable view of decadence and pornography has set Paglia in direct opposition to the opinions of many in academic and feminist circles. Feminist thought that condemns pornography as the imposition of social prejudice on the inherent goodness of sexuality is decried by Paglia as naive. She accuses feminists with these beliefs of uncritically accepting the ideals of eighteenth-century French philosopher Jean-Jacques Rousseau, who paired nature with freedom and nobility and considered the structures of society oppressive. Paglia's view is that "feminism has exceeded its proper mission of seeking political equality for women and has ended by rejecting contingency, that is, human limitation by nature or fate." Paglia's own brand of feminism, which she outlined in a lecture given at the Massachusetts Institute of Technology, as published in *Sex, Art, and American Culture,* is not based on the Rousseauian idealism which she says was revived in the 1960s, but on the practical realities of sex and culture. She cites as her formative feminist heroes pilot Amelia Earhart, actress Katharine Hepburn, and French theorist Simone de Beauvoir.

Paglia also asserts that "nature's burden falls more heavily on one [the female] sex," that women's natural identity does not create the same type of tension that is found in men. Overwhelmed by the powerful psychological domination of the mother and her relationship with the life and death forces of the earth, men turn to cerebral achievement in an attempt to establish a separate identity from the female and protect themselves from the primal elements, posits Paglia. Statements such as Paglia's widely quoted line, "If civilization had been left in female hands, we would still be living in grass huts," were interpreted by some reviewers to be a rationalization for limiting women's role in society to that of a passive object. Lillian Faderman, in her review of *Sexual Personae* suggested, "Paglia believes that there is indeed a basis for sexual stereotypes that is biological and firmly rooted in the unconscious." Helen Vendler was also concerned that Paglia's theory does not allow for women to participate in cultural achievement equally with men: "To Paglia, women writers remain 'chthonic,' earthbound, and swamp-like, unable to rise to such inventive Apollonian designs," she declared in *New York Review of Books.*

Anticipating such reactions in her introduction to *Sexual Personae,* Paglia asserts that women actually hold a privileged status of power in relation to men: "I reaffirm and celebrate woman's ancient mystery and glamour. I see the mother as an overwhelming force who condemns men to lifelong sexual anxiety, from which they escape through rationalism and physical achievement." In addition, she argues that the power of Apollonian society is, or should be, just as accessible to women as to men. Responding to Vendler, Paglia claimed in the *New York Review of Books* that *Sexual Personae* had been misread and misunderstood by Vendler and others. "From first chapter to last, my thesis is that all writing, all art is Apollonian. Every woman who takes pen or brush in hand is making an Apollonian swerve away from nature, even when nature is her subject."

The untraditional subject and style of the *Sexual Personae,* despite the reservations of some critics, was widely praised. Faderman called *Sexual Personae* "a remarkable book, at once outrageous and compelling, fanatical and brilliant. As infuriating as Paglia often is, one must be awed by her vast energy, erudition and wit." Teachout commented that Paglia "is an exciting (if purple) stylist and an admirably close reader with a hard core of common sense. For all its flaws, her first book is every bit as intellectually stimulating as it is exasperating." Edmundson concluded that in exploring the issue of sexuality and sexual personae in culture Paglia "has found a part of the story that no one is telling. It's a splendid and exhilarating find, and makes for a brilliant book." In *Sexual Personae,* Paglia promised a second volume that will focus on similar themes in popular culture since the turn of the century, particularly Hollywood films and rock music.

In addition to pursuing this work, in 1992 Paglia published *Sex, Art, and American Culture,* a collection of her articles, interviews, and lectures. Included are commentaries on pop-star Madonna, whom Paglia considers "the true feminist" for the street-smart brand of sexuality that fills her rock songs and music videos. "Madonna has taught young women to be fully female and sexual while still exercising control over their lives," Paglia asserts in "Madonna I: Animality and Artifice." In other essays she discusses actress Elizabeth Taylor, artist Robert Mapplethorpe, professor Milton Kessler, and others in the public eye. Also included are Paglia's further indictments of certain academic trends, particularly women's studies and French deconstructionist theory, as found in the essays "Junk Bonds and Corporate Raiders" and "The M.I.T. Lecture."

Two chapters of *Sex, Art, and Modern Culture* are devoted to date rape, which Paglia contends is an ethical violation that contemporary feminists do little to prevent. "Rape is an outrage that cannot be tolerated in civilized society," she posits in "Rape and Modern Sex War." "Yet feminism, which has waged a crusade for rape to be taken more seriously, has put young women in danger by hiding the truth about sex from them." Rather than relying on grievance committees to solve the problem of rape on campuses and elsewhere, Paglia feels the solution lies in informing women about the "what is for men the eroticism or fun element in rape" so that by understanding rape, women can learn to protect themselves from it by using "common sense." In other essays, Paglia, a libertarian, outlines her beliefs that the state should not intrude into the private realm; she is pro-choice and supports decriminalization of prostitution and legalization of drugs. Arguing that Paglia's is an unconventional but important voice, a *Publishers Weekly* reviewer concluded that in *Sex, Art, and Culture* the author presents "an ambitious range of art and ideas, her invocation of primal sexuality adding a missing element to critical debates."

Vamps & Tramps: New Essays is "a hodgepodge of just about everything [Paglia] has written, filmed and said in magazines, newspapers, movies and television" since the publication of *Sex, Art, and Culture* two years earlier, states Suzanne Fields in *Insight on the News.* The book "is paradoxically dazzling and dull, sensuous and senseless, reactive and repetitious," according to Fields. Mary Beard notes in *New Statesman & Society* that the book is "generously subtitled 'new essays.'" Beard explains that there is "nothing remotely new about the ideas" and "very few of the pieces are what most readers would call 'essays' either." Instead, Beard believes the book is "an ill- stitched compilation of book reviews, some (lusty but thin) bits of journalism plus a routine encyclopedia article on the history of love poetry . . . . This is megalomania on a lunatic scale." Beard continues: "Had [Paglia] listened to Carol Gilligan, Marilyn French, Elaine Showalter and the others, she might have learned that she was not the first to wonder about these problems, and that the issues are a good deal more complex than her monomania allows." In a similar vein, *Commentary* writer Elizabeth Kristol writes: "The challenge in reading so melodramatic a writer is figuring out which ideas are genuinely new (and not just unexpected departures from an otherwise predictable ideological platform), which are genuinely original (and not simply designed to shock), and which are sufficiently valuable as to make all the other stuff worth wading through."

Critics noted that *Vamps & Tramps* is a "hodgepodge" in several ways: content, tone, and quality. According to Fields, *Vamps & Tramps* is "a gold mine of theory and intelligent criticism, but be warned. Reading it requires sifting and sorting amid water, dirt and gravel to get to the shining mettle." Steve Sailer remarks in the *National Review:* "Unfortunately *Vamps & Tramps* suffers from the mixing of its author's three discordant personae: scholar, polemicist, and celebrity role model. While never dull, this unabridged compilation can be repetitious. Because Miss Paglia ties every topic into The Theory, most of her op-eds include a rushed recap of the tragicomic world view she elucidated with supreme clarity in *Sexual Personae* 's first chapter." "On the whole, *Vamps & Tramps* is a carnival. We see Paglia here in all her guises, from the highly serious to the completely loopy," writes David Link in *Reason.*

Several critics remarked that a "quieter," less "self-centered" side to Paglia briefly surfaced in *Vamps & Tramps.* "Paglia dispenses her wisdom like Dear Abby on speed," writes Link. "In fact, her prose is consistently among the most colorful and effective today. No one in the chattering classes can match her when it comes to the punishing reproach." However, Link continues, "*Vamps & Tramps* shows a personal side of Paglia that I don't recall having seen before, and it's a welcome departure." As an example of Paglia's softer side, Link cites an essay on four gay men whom Paglia claims have been central to her life. "For once," Link argues, "the writing is not self-centered. In giving the spotlight to others, Paglia demonstrates a grace and generosity few might suspect her of." In *Time,* Richard Corliss comments: "There are also quieter pieces, notably a loving memoir of four homosexual friends who helped her shape her sensibility. But it's silly to ask this brainy pipshriek to calm down; shouting is her form of conversation."

"A book by Paglia is a lot like sex itself," remarks Link, "when it's good, it's very, very good. And when it's bad, it's still pretty good. *Vamps & Tramps* is a step above pretty good." Fields concurs, "*Vamps & Tramps* is not a book for the squeamish or smug, but it's fun to read and watch the author scorch her enemies with the concentrated power of a white-hot mind."

Rather than scorching her enemies in her next books, Paglia offers two close, critical explications instead. *The Birds* is an examination of filmmaker Alfred Hitchcock's masterpiece of the same name, and *Break, Blow, Burn* is a diverse anthology of forty-three poems accompanied by critiques in Paglia's famously irreverent style. The selected poems range in tone, theme, and origin, from sonnets by the sixteenth-century poet and playwright William Shakespeare to lyrics by the twentieth-century singer-songwriter Joni Mitchell. Paglia gives a brief historical context to the poems preceding each essay and composes her analyses using New Criticism, a close-reading method for evaluating and interpreting poetry that was popular in the mid-twentieth century. This approach was met with mixed reviews. "Paglia has here deliberately suppressed much of her own speed, her wit, her wide-ranging intellect, and her fierce energy," lamented *Contemporary* critic Sam Schulman. Yet others disagreed, and Sarah Bramwell, writing in the *National Review,* stated that the essays are "vintage Paglia: bracing, opinionated, and deliciously enjoyable. In her hands, poetry has the seductive scent of forbidden fruit."

BIOGRAPHICAL AND CRITICAL SOURCES:

BOOKS

Contemporary Literary Criticism, Volume 68, Gale, 1991, pp. 303-20.

Paglia, Camille, *Sex, Art, and American Culture: Essays,* Vintage Books, 1992.

Paglia, *Sexual Personae: Art and Decadence from Nefertiti to Emily Dickinson,* Yale University Press, 1990.

PERIODICALS

Cineaste, fall, 1999, Tony Pipolo, review of *The Birds,* p. 59.

Commentary, February 1995, pp. 68-71; July-August, 2005, Sam Schulman, review of *Break, Blow, Burn,* p. 72.

Insight on the News, November 21, 1994, p. 28.

Nation, June 25, 1990, pp. 897-99.

National Review, December 31, 1994, pp. 58-59; May 9, 2005, Sarah Bramwell, review of *Break, Blow, Burn,* p. 43.
New Statesman & Society, April 14, 1995, p. 43.
Newsweek, September 21, 1992, p. 82.
New York, March 4, 1991, pp. 22-30.
New York Review of Books, May 31, 1990, pp. 19-25; August 16, 1990, p. 59.
New York Times Book Review, July 22, 1990, p. 7.
Poetry, October, 2005, Daisy Fried, review of *Break, Blow, Burn,* p. 47.
Publishers Weekly, August 17, 1992.
Reason, February, 1995, pp. 60-63.
Time, January 13, 1992, pp. 62-63, December 12, 1994, p. 90.
Times (London, England), April 13, 1991, pp. 10-11.
Times Literary Supplement, April 20, 1990, p. 414.
Village Voice, September 29, 1992, pp. 92-94.
Voice Literary Supplement, March, 1990, p. 7.
Washington Post Book World, February 18, 1990, p. 5.

* * *

PAGLIA, Camille Anna
See PAGLIA, Camille

* * *

PAIGE, Richard
See KOONTZ, Dean R.

* * *

PAKENHAM, Antonia
See FRASER, Antonia

* * *

PALAHNIUK, Chuck 1962-

PERSONAL: Surname is pronounced "paul-ah-nik"; born February 21, 1962, in Pasco, WA; son of Fred (a railroad brakeman) and Carol (an office manager at a nuclear power plant) Palahniuk. *Education:* University of Oregon, received journalism degree, 1986.

ADDRESSES: Home—Portland, OR. *Agent*—Edward Hibbert, Donadio and Olson, Inc., 121 West 27th St., Ste. 704, New York, NY 10001.

CAREER: Novelist. Briefly worked for a newspaper in Gresham, OR; worked for Freightliner as a service documentation specialist for thirteen years; appeared as rapper "Chucky P." on BBC Radio.

MEMBER: National Cacophony Society.

AWARDS, HONORS: Oregon Book Award, and Pacific Northwest Booksellers Award, both for *Fight Club;* Bram Stoker Award nomination for best novel, Horror Writers Association, 2002, for *Lullaby.*

WRITINGS:

NOVELS

Fight Club, W.W. Norton (New York, NY), 1996.
Invisible Monsters, W.W. Norton (New York, NY), 1999.
Survivor, Norton (New York, NY), 1999.
Choke, Doubleday (New York, NY), 2001.
Lullaby (first in a trilogy), Doubleday (New York, NY), 2002.
Diary, Doubleday (New York, NY), 2003.

NONFICTION

Fugitives and Refugees: A Walk in Portland, Oregon, Crown (New York, NY), 2003.
Stranger Than Fiction, Doubleday (New York, NY), 2004.

Contributor to periodicals, including *Gear, Playboy, Portland Mercury, Independent, L.A. Weekly,* and *Black Book.*

ADAPTATIONS: Fight Club was released as a film in 1999.

WORK IN PROGRESS: Two more novels to complete the trilogy begun with *Lullaby.*

SIDELIGHTS: The author of several unconventional novels as well as a quirky hometown travelogue and a collection of essays on Hollywood cult figures, Chuck Palahniuk began his writing career with the apocalyptic novel *Fight Club,* which became a cult classic and the basis of the 1999 Hollywood film by the same name. It features a secret fight club in which men beat each other bloody and whose members eventually develop into an anarchist army that is funded by selling soap made of liposuctioned human fat. Palahniuk's subsequent works have featured equally shocking and bizarre premises, and are also sustained by the author's black humor and cynical viewpoint. On the heels of the film, Palahniuk quickly published three more novels, *Invisible Monsters, Survivor,* and *Choke.* These works were also reportedly considered to be serious candidates for screen adaptations.

In the wake of *Fight Club,* Palahniuk has repeatedly been called on to tell his own story, in which he once despaired of ever becoming a novelist. His job documenting diesel service procedures left little time for writing. He thought about waiting to write until he retired, but came to the conclusion that he might die before that happened. So Palahniuk snatched moments in waiting rooms, laundromats, and traffic jams, squeezing in the work whenever he could. He sent a manuscript to a publisher and it was rejected, presumably because of its rather shocking content. Instead of feeling discouraged, Palahniuk got mad and decided to send the publisher an even more outrageous story. The novel *Fight Club* was the result.

Palahniuk has also related how life experiences have inspired his novels. *Fight Club* was born of Palahniuk's own fights, and of the lack of response his bruised and bloody face got from coworkers. He told *Salon.com* writer Sarah Tomlinson that he realized "you could really do anything you wanted in your personal life, as long as you looked so bad that people would not want to know the details. I started thinking of a fight club as a really structured, controlled way of just going nuts in a really safe situation." However, in *Fight Club* this "safe" pastime has frightening consequences. The unnamed narrator has a bland, unhappy life, and has been seeking solace, however undeserved, by faking terminal illness at support-group meetings. He befriends Tyler Durden, an unpredictable young man who suggests starting the fight club. It is Durden who starts having an affair with Marla, a woman the narrator met at a meeting where he claimed to have testicular cancer. The fight club inspires countless others and it turns out that Durden has larger, destructive plans for his army of thousands of nihilists. He unveils Project Mayhem, a plan to terrorize corporate America by attacking the world's tallest building.

Critics described *Fight Club* as both disturbing and fascinating. A *Publishers Weekly* writer warned that almost any reader was likely to find something offensive. The reviewer called the book "caustic, outrageous, bleakly funny, violent and always unsettling" as well as "utterly original." In a *Booklist* review, Thomas Gaughan described *Fight Club* as "gen X's most articulate assault yet on baby-boomer sensibilities" and a work sure to disturb young readers' parents. He concluded that it was "powerful, and possibly brilliant."

A *Guardian Unlimited* article by Stuart Jeffries considered the literary and social relevance of *Fight Club.* Jeffries called the novel "the 90s reply to *American Psycho,* Bret Easton Ellis's satire on youthful white-collar greed and banality in Wall Street in the 80s." His interview with Palahniuk revealed that the author has read Kierkegaard, Sartre, and Camus; and Jeffries felt that "it shows in his nihilistic insistence on destroying lifestyles that serve nobody well, and recognizing the importance of mortality." The reviewer also remarked that the book "has proven appealing to men of a certain age. At times it seems to be exclusively about men whose fathers were absent during their childhoods." Moreover, Jeffries surmised that at several points the novel "suggests that all-male clubs are the only way men can reestablish their male potency."

Concern about the impact of *Fight Club* increased with the release of the feature film. The emergence of copycat clubs did not disturb Palahniuk, who believes their members were probably already expressing their violent impulses in other, more dangerous ways. However, a rumor emerged that Twentieth Century-Fox delayed the film's release following the tragic shootings at Columbine High School. In an interview for the *Orlando Weekly Movies,* Palahniuk indirectly commented on the possibility of links between his writing and such acts of violence. He called the fight club experience "an honest, consensual violence. . . . It's not victimizing violence. It's not a chickenshit walking into a crowded place full of helpless people with a gun."

The author's second novel, *Survivor,* is also a violent, darkly comic, bitter picture of American life. Its chapters proceed in reverse chronological order, beginning with forty-seven, and the pages begin with number 289 and end with one. Thus, the reader is introduced to the protagonist Tender Branson moments before his death, as his plane is about to crash into the Australian desert. Branson is telling his story into the jet's black box, explaining how he came to be the last living member of the Creedish Death Cult. His story is outrageous: as a Creedalist, he became an unpaid servant in exchange for donations to the church; slave labor charges and an FBI raid on the Creedish compound resulted in a mass suicide; media interest in Branson turned him into a celebrity and book-selling, self-help guru. But it is also revealed that the cult suicides may in fact be murders, and that Branson's brother Adam may be a survivor and a serial killer.

Reviews of *Survivor* were enthusiastic, although *Fight Club* sometimes cast a shadow over the new novel. A *Kirkus Reviews* writer called the book "brilliant, engrossing, substantial, and fun" and asserted that "Palahniuk carves out credible, moving dramas from situations that seemed simply outlandish and sad on the evening news." In the *Oregonian,* Frank Bures suggested that with *Survivor* Palahniuk "demonstrates his ranges as a writer." Bures compared *Fight Club*'s "twisted carpe diem" to this novel's "ironic laments." The reviewer concluded, "If there is a central theme to *Survivor,* it is . . . disgust at superficiality and sameness. Yet it gets lost among the other questions raised about free will, fate, mindless following, religious hypocrisy, death and other existential, if tangential, matters." *Village Voice* writer Lily Burana was disappointed by what followed a fascinating open: "Problem is, once it is revealed that Tender is the last surviving Creedish, the book becomes predictable. The narrative swerves from the deft, carefully imagined satire of a tiny, workaday life and plunges straight into a 'Toontown-like hyperbolic broadcast of living large before the masses." At the review's end, she also pondered whether "many young-adult readers—hungry kids trapped in suburban and rural America . . . might make a cult hero of Palahniuk."

The original manuscript for Palahniuk's third novel, *Invisible Monsters,* was the story that publishers rejected prior to *Fight Club.* Palahniuk was glad to have had the chance to improve the novel, and rewrote over three-quarters of the book before submitting it. In part a satirical stab at the fashion industry, the novel was conceived after its author sat reading fashion magazines at his local laundromat. Commenting on the novel in the *Village Voice,* Palahniuk called *Invisible Monsters* "a *Valley of the Dolls* book, a summer beach book. . . . Don't take it very seriously." However, he also noted it was inspired by his reading of French philosopher Michael Foucault and Foucault's exploration of identity.

Like *Survivor, Invisible Monsters* begins at its story's end; however, it then reveals episodes in Shannon McFarland's life in a random sequence. Shannon is a former model who lost the lower half of her face in a shooting. She is left without a career and is filled with anger at her ex-boyfriend Manus and her ex-girlfriend Evie, who had an affair after the shooting. Convinced that the pair may be responsible for her wounds, Shannon goes on a cross-country road trip with a new friend, the transgendered Brandy Alexander. Their goal is to confront Evie in Texas, where she is about to be married. In the process, Shannon and Brandy kidnap Manus and start secretly feeding him female hormone pills. In the process, it is revealed that Brandy is Shannon's brother, whom she had believed was dead of AIDS.

The plot's twists and jumps left many reviewers on the fence about *Invisible Monsters.* In the *San Francisco Chronicle,* James Sullivan said, "All this roughhousing will make readers punch-drunk by the book's climax. It's Palahniuk's least successful effort to date, yet there are more than enough moments of insight to recommend" the novel. A *Kirkus Reviews* writer called it "too clever by half: a Chinese box of a novel fascinating in its intricacies but pretty hard to get a grip on whole." A reviewer for *Publishers Weekly* tired of the flashbacks and use of "a fashion photographers commands . . . to signpost the narrator's epiphanies," but acknowledged that the book "does have fun moments when campy banter tops the heroine's flat, whiny bathos." Writing for *Booklist,* George Needham concluded, "By the end, most readers will be both exhausted and exhilarated."

Palahniuk's fourth novel, *Choke,* firmly cemented his reputation as a skilled writer who continues to keep his readers uncomfortable. In this novel, the central character is Victor Mancini, a young man who supplements his paycheck in an unusual way: he fakes choking in a different restaurant every night, confident that someone will volunteer to save him and, upon hearing his hard-luck story, send him cash on a regular basis. Victor is a medical school dropout, works a menial job at a historical village, and is a sex addict who indulges himself mid-flight in airplane bathrooms. Flashbacks show that Victor's mother, now a senile woman in a nursing home, gave him a miserable childhood. However, he still wants to help her. A mysterious doctor at the nursing home reveals that his mother believes he was conceived by her contact with a holy relic, which would make him the son of Jesus.

In a review for the *New York Times* Janet Maslin was both frustrated and impressed by elements in *Choke.* She introduced the story line with the comment that "Palahniuk is hard to beat if you'd like a working definition of the adolescent male state of mind." And she named him among Irvine Welsh and J.G. Ballard as "writers equally devoted to bizarre circumstances and the bleakest of humor." Yet Maslin admired "the sheer, anarchic fierceness of imagination that fuels [the novel's] wildest individual vignettes," and dubbed *Choke* "an uneven but still raw and vital book, punctuated with outrageous, off-the-wall moments that work as often as not."

In the *Oregonian* John Foyston confessed that the novel contains several details he could not openly discuss in "a family newspaper." Foyston came to the conclusion that "With this, his fourth novel, Palahniuk's strengths and weaknesses are plain enough. His most endearing trait—the thing that keeps me reading—is that marvelous quicksilver voice of his. *Choke* also benefits from Palahniuk's taste for obscure and obsessive erudition, which shows up in the ongoing internal monologue of an AWOL med student." The reviewer was left wanting more plot and more agreeable characters, yet he felt that "the exuberance" of the author's "language makes it still worthwhile to brave these often chilly and dark waters."

Another Palahniuk project is a horror trilogy that begins with the novel *Lullaby.* In this bizarre tale, newspaper reporter Carl Streator is writing a story about Sudden Infant Death Syndrome (SIDS) when he discovers a macabre connection with a book of poetry. In each of the five cases of SIDS he investigates he finds the same edition of the book in which an ancient African tribal poem has been reprinted. The poem was originally intended as a way to decrease the tribes' population in desperate times when there was not enough food to go around. Now it has been carelessly reprinted in a book, and the dilemma the reporter faces is that he does not know how many copies of the book are extant and how to get rid of them before it is too late. Teaming up with a real estate agent, Helen Hoover Boyle, who also knows the "culling song," Streator sets out to destroy all known copies of the book. Two more strange characters join in this eerie quest, Mona, Helen's assistant, and her boyfriend, Oyster.

Maslin, writing in the *New York Times,* was again both fascinated and repelled by Palahniuk's "tireless pursuit of the outrageous" in *Lullaby.* Like Kurt Vonnegut, he "juggles nihilism and idealism with fluid, funny ease, and he repeats and rephrases word patterns until they take on an almost mystical aspect." Virginia Heffernan, reviewing *Lullaby* for the *New York Times Book Review,* was less impressed, dubbing the novel a "nauseating picaresque" with "less than zero sacred." A *Kirkus Reviews* contributor saw more to like in the novel, calling it the kind of "outrageous, darkly comic fun . . . you'd expect from Palahniuk." And *Booklist* reviewer John Green felt that what separates *Lullaby* from Palahniuk's earlier work "is its emotional depth, its ability to explore the unbearable pain of losing a child just as richly as it laments our consume-or-die worldview."

Palahniuk's sixth novel, *Diary,* is told in the form of a diary that Misty Marie Kleinman writes for her carpenter husband, Peter Wilmot, who lies in a coma following a suicide attempt. Misty is an artist who prefers the blandly pictorial to edgy modern art; she was attracted to Peter originally because of the picturesque island he took her to live on. However, she wound up working as a waitress to support her daughter and mother-in-law, while Peter's carpentry work became an outlet for his mental instability, as he started engineering hidden rooms in which he plastered obscenities. Misty has now become consumed with her painting, and her friends and acquaintances mysteriously want her to paint more and more; if she stops, she gets excruciating headaches. The force that drives her somehow seems to be controlled by members of her family, whose intentions are unclear.

Typically, reviews of *Diary* were mixed. A *Publishers Weekly* contributor noted that the author "captures the reader hook, line and sinker" from the first page, and then spins a "twisted tale [that is] one of his most memorable works to date." *Booklist*'s John Green similarly found that the book's "fantastically grotesque premise propels the story," but also found fault with the writing, which "lacks the satirical precision" of Palahniuk's other works. In contrast, *Book* contributor James Sullivan praised *Diary* as a "deft meditation on great art and the toll it takes." David Wright, reviewing the novel in *Library Journal,* called *Diary* a "blend of paranoiac horror along the lines of *Rosemary's Baby,*" while Flynn, in *Entertainment Weekly,* dubbed the work "pretty stunning, funky stuff."

BIOGRAPHICAL AND CRITICAL SOURCES:

PERIODICALS

Book, September-October, 2002, Michael Kaplan, interview with Palahniuk, p. 13; September-October, 2003, James Sullivan, review of *Diary,* p. 92.

Booklist, July, 1996, Thomas Gaughan, review of *Fight Club,* p. 1804; September 15, 1999, George Needham, review of *Invisible Monsters,* p. 233; August, 2002, John Green, review of *Lullaby,*

p. 1887; July, 2003, John Green, review of *Diary,* p. 1846; July, 2003, Bill Ott, review of *Fugitives and Refugees,* p. 1858; December 15, 2003, Ted Hipple, review of *Diary,* p. 762.

Entertainment Weekly, May 25, 2001, Troy Patterson, "Hard to Swallow: In *Choke,* the Latest from the Author of *Fight Club,* Chuck Palahniuk's Hip Nihilism Comes to Naught," p. 72; July 18, 2003, Noah Robischon, review of *Fugitives and Refugees,* p. 80; September 5, 2003, Gillian Flynn, review of *Diary,* p. 79; September 26, 2003, Karen Valby, "Chuck Palahniuk Does Not Attend Fight Club," p. 62; September 26, 2003, Noah Robischon, "Joining the Club," p. 67.

Kirkus Reviews, December 15, 1998, review of *Survivor,* p. 1755; August 1, 1999, review of *Invisible Monsters,* p. 1160; June 15, 2002, review of *Lullaby,* p. 834; May 1, 2003, review of *Fugitives and Refugees,* pp. 663.

Kliatt, September, 2003, Jacqueline Edwards, review of *Diary,* pp. 54-55.

Library Journal, March 1, 2001, Heath Madom, review of *Choke,* p. 132; August, 2002, Andrea Kempf, review of *Lullaby,* p. 144; July, 2003, John McCormick, review of *Fugitives and Refugees,* p. 112; July, 2003, David Wright, review of *Diary,* p. 125.

Los Angeles Times, October 15, 1999, review of *Fight Club,* p. 1; October 6, 2002, Susan Salter Reynolds, review of *Lullaby,* p. E1; August 10, 2003, Christopher Reynolds, review of *Fugitives and Refugees,* p. L9.

Newsweek, September 1, 2003, Andrew Phillips, interview with Palahniuk, p. 10.

New York Times, May 24, 2001, Janet Maslin, "An Immature Con Man with a Mom Problem"; September 12, 2002, Janet Maslin, review of *Lullaby,* p. E9; August 31, 2003, Taylor Antrim, review of *Fugitives and Refugees,* and *Diary,* p. 5.

New York Times Book Review, May 27, 2001, Jennifer Reese, review of *Choke,* p. 16; October 20, 2002, Virginia Heffernan, review of *Lullaby,* p. 17.

New York Times Magazine, September 29, 2002, John Glassie, "The Pugilist Novelist" (interview), p. 21.

Oregonian, March 10, 1999, Frank Bures, "*Survivor* Stews over Superficiality of Society"; May 13, 2001, John Foyston, review of *Choke.*

Publishers Weekly, June 3, 1996, review of *Fight Club,* p. 60; July 5, 1999, review of *Invisible Monsters,* p. 56; March 20, 2000, John F. Baker, "*Fight Club* Author to Broadway," p. 15; April 2, 2001, review of *Choke,* p. 37; July 1, 2002, review of *Lullaby,* pp. 46-47; July 8, 2002, John F. Baker, "No D-day Choke for Chuck," p. 12; September 2, 2002, interview with Palahniuk, p. 49; September 30, 2002, Daisy Maryles, "Not a Sleeper," p. 18; May 12, 2003, review of *Fugitives and Refugees,* pp. 51-52; July 7, 2003, review of *Choke,* pp. 26-27; July 7, 2003, review of *Diary,* pp. 50-51; September 8, 2003, Daisy Maryles, "Dear Diary," p. 18; December 1, 2003, review of *Diary,* p. 20.

San Francisco Chronicle, September 12, 1999, James Sullivan, "Model Misbehavior."

Time, September 23, 2002, Richard Lacayo, review of *Lullaby,* p. 76.

Village Voice, February 24-March 2, 1999, Lily Burana, "Cult Club"; October 13-19, 1999, Emily Jenkins, "Extreme Sport."

Washington Post Book World, May 27, 2001, review of *Choke,* p. 6; August 31, 2003, Marc Nesbitt, review of *Diary,* p. p.

Western Journal of Medicine, May, 2002, Shahin Chandrasoma, interview with Palahniuk, pp. 200-202.

ONLINE

Chuck Palahniuk Home Page, http://www.chuckpalahniuk.net/ (March 4, 2004).

Guardian Unlimited, http://www.film.guardian.co.uk/ (May 12, 2000), Stuart Jeffries, "Bruise Control."

Oregonian Online, http://www.oregonlive.com/ (December 12, 2003), Shawn Levy, review of *Postcards from the Future;* (December 19, 2003) "We Barely Saw Ye, Chuck."

Powells.com, http://www.powells.com/ (September 4, 2003), C.P. Farley, "Author Interviews: Chuck Palahniuk."

Salon.com, http://www.salon.com (October 13, 1999), Sarah Tomlinson, "Is It Fistfighting, or Just Multitasking?"

Telegraph Online, http://www.telegraph.co.uk/ (October 21, 2003), William Leith, "A Writer's Life: Chuck Palahniuk."

OTHER

Widmyer, Dennis, Kevin Kolsch, and Josh Chaplinsky, *Postcards from the Future: The Chuck Palahniuk Documentary* (film), ChuckPalahniuk.net, 2003.

* * *

PALEY, Grace 1922-

PERSONAL: Born December 11, 1922, in New York, NY; daughter of Isaac (a doctor) and Mary (Ridnyik) Goodside; married Jess Paley (a motion picture cameraman), June 20, 1942; married second husband, Robert Nichols (a poet and playwright); children: (first marriage) Nora, Dan. *Education:* Attended Hunter College (now Hunter College of the City University of New York), 1938-39, and New York University. *Politics:* "Anarchist, if that's politics." *Religion:* Jewish.

ADDRESSES: Home—126 West 11th St., New York, NY 10011; and Thetford Hill, VT 05074. *Office*—Box 620, Thetford, VT 05074.

CAREER: Writer. Teacher at Columbia University and Syracuse University during the early 1960s; later a member of the literature faculty at Sarah Lawrence College, Bronxville, NY; writer-in-residence, City College of New York; secretary and founding member, Greenwich Village Peace Center, 1961; founding chair, Women's World Organization for Rights, Literature, and Development; former columnist for *Seven Days.*

MEMBER: National Institute of Arts and Letters, American Academy and Institute of Arts and Letters.

AWARDS, HONORS: Guggenheim fellowship in fiction, 1961; National Council on the Arts grant; National Institute of Arts and Letters Award for short story writing, 1970; Edith Wharton Citation of Merit, 1989; named first official New York State Writer by Governor Mario Cuomo, 1989; Rea Award for the Short Story, 1993; Vermont Governor's Award for Excellence in the Arts, 1993; National Book Award nominee and Pulitzer Prize finalist, both 1994, for *The Collected Stories;* Jewish Cultural Achievement Award for Literary Arts, 1994; Lannan Foundation Literary Award for fiction, 1997; named Vermont's 5th State Poet, 2003.

WRITINGS:

The Little Disturbances of Man: Stories of Women and Men at Love (short stories), Doubleday (New York, NY), 1959, published as *The Little Disturbances of Man,* with a new introduction by A.S. Byatt, Virago (London, England), 1980.

Enormous Changes at the Last Minute (short stories), Farrar, Straus (New York, NY), 1974.

Later the Same Day (short stories), Farrar, Straus (New York, NY), 1985.

Leaning Forward (poetry), Granite Press (Penobscot, ME), 1985.

365 Reasons Not to Have Another War, New Society Publications/War Resisters' League (Philadelphia, PA), 1989.

Long Walks and Intimate Talks (stories and poems), paintings by Vera Williams, Feminist Press at The City University of New York (New York, NY), 1991.

New and Collected Poems, Tilbury House (Gardiner, ME), 1992.

The Collected Stories, Farrar, Straus (New York, NY), 1994.

Conversations with Grace Paley, edited by Gerhard Bach and Blaine H. Hall, University Press of Mississippi (Oxford, MS), 1997.

Just As I Thought, Farrar, Straus (New York, NY), 1998.

Begin Again: Collected Poems, Farrar, Straus (New York, NY), 2000.

Contributor of essays to *In the South Bronx of America,* by Mel Rosenthal, Curbstone Press (Willimantic, CT), 1998. Author of forewords to *At His Side: The Last Years of Isaac Babel,* by A.N. Pirozhkova, Steerforth, 1996; *After Sorrow: An American among the Vietnamese,* by Lady Borton, Kodansha, 1996; and *Serious Kissing,* by Barbara Selfridge, Glad Day (Warner, NH), 1999. Author of introduction to *The Author's Dimension: Selected Essays by Christa Wolf,* edited by Alexander Stephen, Farrar, Straus (New York, NY), 1993. Contributor of stories to *Atlantic, Esquire, New Yorker, Ikon, Genesis West, Accent,* and other periodicals.

SIDELIGHTS: With her first two books of short stories, Grace Paley established her niche in the world of letters. Her distinctive voice and verbal gifts have captured the hearts of critics who praise her vision as well as her style. In short and sometimes plotless tales, she plumbs the lives of working-class New Yorkers, mapping out what *New York Review of Books* contributing critic Michael Wood called "a whole small country of damaged, fragile, haunted citizens." Rather than action, Paley relies on conversation to establish character, reproducing Jewish, Black, Irish, and other dialects with startling accuracy. In addition to her story collections, Paly has also produced several volumes of critically acclaimed poetry. According to *Dictionary of Literary Biography* contributor Charlotte Zoë Walker, "Few other fiction writers in late twentieth-century American letters have had so great an influence as Grace Paley on the basis of so few books in a lifetime of work." Walter Clemons's assessment was even more generous; in a *Newsweek* review he proclaimed her "one of the best writers alive."

The daughter of Russian immigrants who arrived in New York around the turn of the century, Paley was raised in the Bronx. At home, her parents spoke Russian and Yiddish, and Paley grew up within two cultures, influenced by the old world as well as the new. From her surroundings, she gleaned the raw material for her short stories, and both her Russian-Jewish heritage and her perceptions of New York street life pervade her work. With the publication of *The Little Disturbances of Man,* Paley began to attract critical attention. Initial sales were modest, but the collection drew a loyal following and good reviews. The *New Yorker* assessed Paley's writing as "fresh and vigorous," noting that "her view of life is her own." The ten stories that comprise the volume focus on the inhabitants of a boisterous city neighborhood where, to use Paley's words, "dumbwaiters boom, doors slam, dishes crash; every window is a mother's mouth bidding the street shut up, go skate somewhere else, come home." Ordinary people in unexceptional circumstances, these characters demonstrate the way man deals with the "little disturbances" of life. In her introduction to the Virago edition of this volume, A.S. Byatt pointed out that "we have had a great many artists, more of them women than not, recording the tragedies of repetition, frequency, weariness and little disturbances. What distinguishes Grace Paley from the mass of these is the interest, and even more, the inventiveness which she brings to her small world."

In "An Interest in Life," the set piece of the collection and the story from which the book's title is drawn, Paley's mode becomes clear. Initially the story of a husband's desertion of his wife and four children, it begins: "My husband gave me a broom one Christmas. This wasn't right. No one can tell me it was meant kindly." In a *Partisan Review* article, Jonathan Baumbach explained how "the matter-of-fact, ironic voice of the protagonist, Ginny, distances the reader from the conventions of her pathos, makes light of easy sentiment, only to bring us, unburdened by melodrama, to an awareness of the character as if someone known to us intimately for a long time. Ginny, in a desperate moment, writes out a list of her troubles to get on the radio show *Strike It Rich.* When she shows the list to John Raftery, a returned former suitor unhappily married to someone else, he points out to her that her troubles are insufficient, merely 'the little disturbances of man.' Paley's comic stories deal in exaggerated understatement, disguise their considerable ambition in the modesty of wit."

Unlike her later fiction, Paley's first book features several conventionally crafted stories that are narrated by a speaker who is not the author and built around a series of incidents that comprise the plot. "The Contest," "Goodbye and Good Luck," "An Irrevocable Diameter," and "A Woman Young and Old" belong to this category. Paley's other approach is more open and fragmentary and can be seen in "An Interest in Life" and "The Used-Boy Raisers," stories narrated respectively by Virginia and Faith, two women not unlike the author. Explained Byatt: "Faith and Virginia both appear elsewhere in Grace Paley's work, with their dependent children, their circumscribed lives, their poverty and resourcefulness, their sexual greed and their consequent continuing openness to exploitation by, and readiness to exploit, men. Their tales have no beginnings and ends, in the sense in which 'An Irrevocable Diameter' has, or, best of the 'well-made tales,' 'In Time Which Made a Monkey of Us All.' But they have beginnings and ends verbally, and they are brilliant, as the choice of the parts that make them is brilliant."

Another six years passed before the appearance of *Enormous Changes at the Last Minute,* Paley's second collection of short stories. During the interim, Paley gave herself to the roles of wife and mother. In addition to her homemaking concerns, Paley submerged herself in political activities—distributing antiwar pamphlets, marching on the Capitol, and traveling overseas to protest American involvement in Vietnam. "I think I could have done more for peace," she told *People,* "if I'd written about the war, but I happen to love being in the streets." Her later commitments were the women's movement and antimilitarist groups, including the Women's World Organization for Rights, Literature, and Development.

Enormous Changes at the Last Minute not only plays off the title of Paley's first volume (*The Little Disturbances of Man*), but also features the same setting and several of the same characters. Faith reappears with her boys Richard and Tonto, and so does Johnny Raftery—his love affair with Ginny recounted this time from his mother's point of view. Plot figures in these stories almost as an afterthought. The tales are open-ended, fragmentary, and sometimes devoid of action. In a story called "A Conversation with My Father," Paley explains why. The piece begins with an ailing father's request to his daughter: "I would like you to write a simple story just once more . . . the kind de Maupassant wrote, or Chekhov, the kind you used to write." Though she would like to please him, the daughter reveals that she has always avoided plot "not for literary reasons, but because it takes all hope away. Everyone real or invented deserves the open destiny of life."

In the eyes of Michele Murray, however, Paley disregards her own requirement. "Even with the glitter of its style, over which Paley skates like some Olympic champion of language, *Enormous Changes* is a book of losses and failures," Murray wrote in the *New Republic*. "It's not tragedy that weighs down these stories, it's no more than despair and repetition. Tragedy suggests depths and alternatives and is built into a world of choices. Paley's world . . . is severely limited, the world as given, without any imagined alternatives, only endless vistas of crumbling buildings, bedrooms opening onto air shafts, and a phalanx of old people's homes."

But Burton Bendow argued that Paley "is right to avoid looking tragedy in the face; she knows where her talent lies. It is, if not for comedy exactly, for virtuoso mimicry. I would guess," he continued in the *Nation*, "that the first thing she has in mind when starting work on one of her better stories is a voice. Definitely not a plot which would keep her to the straight and narrow and cramp her digressions, or a situation or a point of view or even a character, but a voice with a particular ring and particular turns of phrase." Paley herself told *Ms.* interviewer Harriet Shapiro that she "used to start simply from language. . . . I would write a couple of sentences and let them lay there. Not on purpose, but just because I couldn't figure out what was going to come next. I've always worked very blind."

Paley's technique may explain what academics sometimes called the "unevenness" of her writing. As Vivian Gornick wrote in the *Village Voice:* "Her successes are intermittent, unpredictable, often unshapely and without wholeness; there is no progression of revelation, the stories do not build one upon another, they do not—as is abundantly clear in this new collection—create an emotional unity. On the other hand: Paley when she is good is so good that she is worth ninety-nine 'even' writers, and when one hears that unmistakable Paley voice one feels what can be felt only in the presence of a true writer: safe."

Though she acknowledged that Paley's technique of writing is indeed "chancy," *Time*'s Martha Duffy concluded that "the stories—whether two pages or twenty—run their courses as cleanly and surely as arrows flying in air." *Newsweek*'s Walter Clemons summed up his reaction this way: "*Enormous Changes at the Last Minute* was worth the wait."

Several characters from her first two collections, notably Faith, reappear in Paley's third, again much-delayed, collection, *Later the Same Day,* published in 1985. And another decade on, *The Collected Stories* appeared, earning a nomination for the National Book Award. Though the sum of Paley's oeuvre in the short-story genre totaled a mere forty-five stories in 1994, when *Collected Stories* was published, she is nonetheless considered a seminal American short-story writer of the twentieth century. She has also published several volumes of poetry, however, a genre she has favored since her earliest days as a writer, and in which she displays many of the same virtues as those that have made her famous as a short-story writer. Of *Leaning Forward, Long Walks and Intimate Talks, New and Collected Poems,* and *Begin Again,* Carolyn Alessio wrote in *American Writers: A Collection of Literary Biographies,* "Throughout, her poetry has tended to be more baldly political than her fiction and sometimes more limited in scope. Critics, and Paley herself, have downplayed the significance of her poems; she has pronounced them 'mostly about flowers' and 'too literary.' But some of them display the verve and innuendo that energize her fiction."

"What marks Grace Paley's *Begin Again,* . . . apart from its lyricism and close observations of life (human and natural), is the humility and humanity of her voice," remarked Kate Moos in *Ruminator Review. Begin Again* collects work from throughout Paley's writing life, providing a kind of autobiography in poetry, marking her days as peace activist, feminist activist, her years of mothering, and her experience of grandmotherhood, of living in New York City and of Vermont. "This radiant volume is alive with Paley's wise humor and free-flowing empathy," declared Donna Seaman in *Booklist.* A contributor to *Publishers Weekly* compared Paley unfavorably with the poet Adrienne Rich, however, for Paley's failure at the type of well-made poems, finely honed language, and subtle or complex metaphors at which Rich excels. Still, "fans of the fiction will want these unguarded looks at the illimitably appealing Paley persona," this critic added.

Some of Paley's poems are included in her collection *Just As I Thought,* along with essays, reviews, and speeches written over the course of thirty years. Here, more so than in the short-story or poetry collections, Paley's political opinions take center stage, bearing the brunt, occasionally, of critical attention the book was paid. Thus, for example, John Kennedy, reviewing *Just As I Thought* in the *Antioch Review,* called Paley "extremely leftist," and remarked that the author "provokes misunderstanding," and "controversy" by refusing to take into consideration the views of the opposition in some of the pieces collected in the book. But for Iain Finlayson, writing in the London *Times,* the voice displayed throughout this volume "cherishes a flawed world that should be grateful for her tough, passionate love."

In an interview with Eleanor Wachtel, published in *Conversations with Grace Paley,* the author was asked if she was conscious of apportioning time to her political causes. Paley, a founding member of the Greenwich Village Peace Center, replied, "No, I'm just pulled one way or another: writing, politics, house, and family. That's all right. It's an idea of life." Paley continued, "I'm a writer but I'm also a person in the world. I don't feel a terrible obligation to write a lot of books. When I write, I write very seriously and I mean business. I write as well and as truthfully as I possibly can."

BIOGRAPHICAL AND CRITICAL SOURCES:

BOOKS

Arcana, Judith, *Grace Paley's Life Stories: A Literary Biography,* University of Illinois Press (Urbana, IL), 1993.

Bach, Gerhard, and Blaine H. Hall, editors, *Conversations with Grace Paley,* University Press of Mississippi (Oxford, MS), 1997.

Baxter, Charles, "Maps and Legends of Hell: Notes on Melodrama," in *Burning Down the House: Essays on Fiction,* Graywolf Press (St. Paul, MN), 1997.

Benbow-Pfalzgraf, Taryn, editor, *American Women Writers: A Critical Reference Guide from Colonial Times to the Present,* St. James Press (Detroit, MI), 2000, pp. 247-248.

Binder, Wolfgang, and Helmbrecht Breinig, editors, *American Contradictions: Interviews with Nine American Writers,* Wesleyan University Press (Hanover, NH), 1995.

Brown, Rosellen, "You Are Not Here Long," in *Letters to a Fiction Writer,* edited by Frederick Busch, Norton (New York, NY), 1995.

Charters, Ann, editor, "A Conversation with Grace Paley," in *The Story and Its Writer: An Introduction to Short Fiction,* 4th edition, Bedford Books (Boston, MA), 1995.

Contemporary Popular Writers, St. James Press (Detroit, MI), 1997.

Criswell, Jeanne Sallade, "Cynthia Ozick and Grace Paley: Diverse Visions in Jewish and Women's Literature," in *Contemporary American Short Story,* edited by Loren Longsdon and Charles W. Mayer, Western Illinois University Press (Macomb, IL), 1987.

Dictionary of Literary Biography, Thomson Gale (Detroit, MI), Volume 28: *Twentieth-Century American-Jewish Fiction Writers,* 1984, Volume 218: *Short-Story Writers since World War II, Second Series,* 1999.

Gelfant, B. H., "Grace Paley: A Portrait in Collage," in *Women Writing in America,* University Press of New England (Hanover, NH), 1984.

Isaacs, Neil David, *Grace Paley: A Study of the Short Fiction,* Twayne (Boston, MA), 1990.

Klinkowitz, Jerome, editor, *Structuring the Void: The Struggle for Subject in Contemporary American Fiction,* Duke University Press (Durham, NC), 1985.

Mickelson, Anne Z., *Reaching Out: Sensitivity and Order in Recent American Fiction by Women,* Scarecrow Press (Lanham, MD), 1979.

Parini, Jay, *American Writers: A Collection of Literary Biographies,* Charles Scribner's Sons (New York, NY), 2001, pp. 217-233.

Rosen, Norma, *Accidents of Influence: Writing As a Woman and a Jew in America,* State University of New York Press (Albany, NY), 1992.

Short Stories for Students, Volume 3, Thomson Gale (Detroit, MI), 1999.

Taylor, Jacqueline, *Grace Paley: Illuminating the Dark Lives,* University of Texas Press (Austin, TX), 1990.

Todd, Janet, editor, *Women Writers Talking,* Holmes & Meier (New York, NY), 1983, pp. 35-56.

PERIODICALS

American Poetry Review, March, 1994, p. 19.

American Studies International, October, 1997, p. 102.

Antioch Review, winter, 1999, John Kennedy, review of *Just As I Thought,* p. 108.

Booklist, March 1, 1998, p. 1086; February 1, 2000, Donna Seaman, review of *Begin Again,* p. 1005.

Chicago Tribune, April 21, 1985, pp. 54-58.

Commentary, August, 1985.

Commonweal, October 25, 1968; May 20, 1994, p. 33.

Delta, May, 1982, Jerome Klinkowitz, "The Sociology of Metafiction," p. 290.

Entertainment Weekly, July 30, 1999, review of *Just As I Thought,* p. 65.

Esquire, November, 1970.

Forward, April 15, 1994.

Genesis West, fall, 1963.

Guardian (Manchester, England), August 21, 1999, Isobel Montgomery, review of *The Collected Stories,* p. 11; December 4, 2000, James Hopkin, "Genre: Grace x 3," p. 22.

Harper's, June, 1974.

Hudson Review, autumn, 1985, Clara Claiborne Park, "Faith, Grace, and Love," pp. 481-488.

Journal of Ethnic Studies, fall, 1983, Rose Kamel, "To Aggravate the Conscience: Grace Paley's Loud Voice," pp. 29-49.

Library Journal, February 15, 1998, p. 143.

London Review of Books, August 19, 1999, review of *Just As I Thought,* p. 32.

Los Angeles Times, May 22, 1985.

Los Angeles Times Book Review, May 19, 1985.

Massachusetts Review, winter, 1985, Peter Marchant and Earl Ingersoll, "A Conversation with Grace Paley," pp. 606-614.

Melus, spring, 2000, Ethan Goffman, "Grace Paley's Faith," p. 197.

Milwaukee Journal, May 5, 1974.

Ms., May, 1974, Harriet Shapiro, "Grace Paley: 'Art Is on the Side of the Underdog,'" pp. 43-45.

Nation, May 11, 1974, Burton Bendow, "Voices in the Metropolis," pp. 597-598; May 11, 1998, p. 38.

New Criterion, September, 1994.

New Republic, March 16, 1974; April 29, 1985, pp. 38-39; June 29, 1998, p. 35.

New Statesman, March 14, 1980.

Newsweek, March 11, 1974; April 15, 1985; April 25, 1994, p. 64.

New York, April 11, 1994, p. 64.

New Yorker, June 27, 1959.

New York Review of Books, March 21, 1974; August 15, 1985, pp. 26-29; August 11, 1994, p. 23.

New York Times, March 23, 1968, p. 29; February 28, 1974; April 10, 1985, p. C20; November 14, 1986.

New York Times Book Review, April 19, 1959, pp. 28-29; March 17, 1974; April 14, 1985, Robert R. Harris, "Pacifists with Their Dukes Up," p. 7; September 22, 1991; April 19, 1992, p. 10; April 24, 1994, p. 7; May 3, 1994; August 11, 1994; April 19, 1998; June 21, 1998; February 27, 2000, Adam Kirsch, "Lover of Justice, All Kinds," p. 22.

Observer (London, England), January 17, 1993.

Paris Review, fall, 1992, "The Art of Fiction."

Partisan Review, spring, 1975, pp. 303-306; Volume 48, number 2, 1981, Marianne DeKoven, "Mrs. Hegel-Shtein's Tears," pp. 217-223.

People, February 26, 1979, Kristin McMurran, "Even Admiring Peers Worry That Grace Paley Writes Too Little and Protests Too Much."

Poetry, April, 1994, p. 39.

Progressive, November 1, 1997, p. 36; December, 1998, p. 41.

Publishers Weekly, April 5, 1985, pp. 71-72; June 18, 1991; October, 1991, review of *Begin Again,* p. 58.

Regionalism and the Female Imagination, winter, 1979, E.M. Broner, "The Dirty Ladies: Earthy Writings of Contemporary American Women—Paley, Jong, Schor, and Lerman," pp. 34, 41.

Ruminator Review, fall, 2001, Kate Moos, "Forms of Invention," p. 49.

Saturday Review, April 27, 1968, pp. 29-30; March 23, 1974.

Sewanee Review, Volume 81, 1974, William Peden, "The Recent American Short Story," pp. 712-729.

Shenandoah, Volume 27, 1976, Donald Barthelme, William Gass, Grace Paley, and Walker Percy, "A Symposium on Fiction," pp. 3-31; Volume 32, 1981, Joan Lidoff, "Clearing Her Throat: An Interview with Grace Paley," pp. 3-26.

Studies in American Jewish Literature, Volume 2, 1982, Adam J. Sorkin, "'What Are We, Animals?' Grace Paley's World of Talk and Laughter," p. 144; spring, 1988, Minako Baba, "Faith Darwin As Writer-Heroine: A Study of Grace Paley's Short Stories," pp. 40-54.

Studies in Short Fiction, winter, 1994.

Threepenny Review, fall, 1980, pp. 4-6.

Time, April 29, 1974; April 15, 1985; January 27, 1986, pp. 74-77.

Times (London, England), November 7, 1985; September 26, 1987; July 22, 1999, Iain Finlayson, "A Fight for Peace," p. 45.

Times Literary Supplement, February 14, 1975; November 22, 1985.

Vanity Fair, March, 1998, p. 220.

Village Voice, March 14, 1974.

Voice Literary Supplement, June, 1985, pp. 9-10; September, 1992, p. 5.

Washington Post, April 14, 1985, David Remnick, "Grace Paley: Voice from the Village," pp. C1, 14; November 15, 1986.

Washington Post Book World, April 28, 1985, p. C1.

Women and Language, spring, 2000, LaVerne Harrell Clark, "A Matter of Voice: Grace Paley and the Oral Tradition," p. 18.

Writer, November, 2002, Kim Chase, "In Praise of Loose Ends," pp. 21-23.

Yearbook of English Studies, 2001, Judie Newman, "Napalm and After: The Politics of Grace Paley's Short Fiction," p. 2.

ONLINE

New York State Writers Institute Web site, http://www.albany.edu/writers-inst/ (August 10, 2004), "Grace Paley."

Salon.com, http://www.salon.com/ (1996) Wendy Lesser, "Writing with Both Ears," conversation with the author; (October 26, 1998) A.M. Homes, "All My Habits Are Bad," author interview.

Women's World Organization for Rights, Literature, and Development Web site, http://www.wworld.org/about/board/ (August 9, 2004), "Grace Paley."

* * *

PAOLINI, Christopher 1983-

PERSONAL: Born November 17, 1983, in Southern California; son of Kenneth Paolini.

ADDRESSES: *Home*—Paradise Valley, Montana. *Agent*—Simon Lipskar, Writers house, 21 W. 26th St., New York, NY 10010.

CAREER: Writer.

WRITINGS:

Eragon (first volume in "Inheritance Trilogy"), Paolini International (Livingston, MT), 2002, second edition, Alfred A. Knopf (New York, NY), 2003.

Eldest (second volume in "Inheritance Trilogy"), Knopf (New York, NY), 2005.

SIDELIGHTS: Christopher Paolini achieved publishing success while still a teen when his book *Eragon,* the first novel of a projected trilogy, topped the bestseller charts. Paolini, who was home schooled by his parents, began writing *Eragon* at the age of fifteen, after he graduated from an accredited correspondence high school. He wasn't ready to begin college, and so he took the next year to write the first draft of the fantasy. The second draft consumed another year, and his parents, who own a small publishing company, helped with the editing and publishing. Paolini was offered a scholarship to attend Reed College in Portland, Oregon, but instead, he and his parents took the book on the road. Paolini made appearances in schools, libraries, bookstores, and at fairs around the country, where he read from and signed copies of his book while dressed in medieval costume.

The Paolinis also placed some of the books they had printed in Montana book stores, and one of them was purchased by novelist Carl Hiaasen, while the Hiaasen family was in Montana on a fly-fishing trip. Hiaason called his editor at Alfred E. Knopf and suggested that the publisher might want to look at *Eragon.* They did and published a new edition that is approximately 20,000 words shorter. A new cover designed by John Jude Palencar replaced Paolini's own design. After signing with Knopf, Paolini began work on *Eldest,* the second novel in the trilogy.

Paolini's Montana home, located in the scenic Paradise Valley, was an inspiration for his story, described as a "solid, sweeping epic fantasy" by a *Kirkus Reviews* contributor. *Kliatt* contributor Michele Winship reviewed *Eragon,* saying that Paolini "takes a little Tolkien, a little McCaffrey, a coming-of-age quest, and combines them with some wicked good storytelling in this first book."

The fantasy opens to a map of Alagaësia, Eragon's world, where the teen ekes out a living with his uncle and cousin on their farm. The story begins with the fifteen year old discovering a blue gemstone covered with white veins, that is, in fact, an egg. When a beautiful blue dragon emerges from it, Eragon names her Saphira. Over a hundred years, an evil king has destroyed the Dragon Riders, and in bonding with the mythical beast, Eragon becomes such a rider, and is pursued by King Galbatorix, who kills Eragon's family and charges his dark servants with capturing Eragon and Saphira. They become travelers, along with the old storyteller Brom, and Eragon matures over the year during which the story transpires. He gains an understanding of love, loss, and the evil that is present in his world as he is pulled into the struggle between the king and the resistance forces of the Varden. Together, the boy, dragon, and wise old man draw on a combination of magic and traditional methods to protect and defend themselves from humanoid warriors.

In a *Teenreads.com* interview, Paolini said that he had "always been fascinated with the sources of most modern fantasy that lie in Teutonic, Scandinavian, and Old Norse history. This is disregarding a large chunk of writing devoted to the myths from the British Isles. Because of this, I used Old Norse as the basis of my Elven language in *Eragon,* as well as many names. All the Dwarf and Urgal words, however, are my own invention." Paolini provides a glossary of his invented language at the end of the book.

School Library Journal contributor Susan L. Rogers felt that "sometimes the magic solutions are just too convenient for getting out of difficult situations," but felt that fans of the "Lord of the Rings" trilogy will find the characters and plot twists appealing. Writing in the *New York Times Book Review,* Liz Rosenberg cited what she saw as faults, including cliches and "B-movie dialogue." Rosenberg wrote that Paolini's "plot stumbles and jerks along, with gaps in logic and characters dropped, then suddenly remembered, or new ones invented at the last minute. And yet, as Beatrix Potter wrote, 'Genius—like murder will out.' *Eragon,* for all its flaws, is an authentic work of great talent. The story is gripping; it may move awkwardly, but it moves with force. The power of *Eragon* lies in its overall effects—in the sweep of the story and the conviction of the storyteller. Here, Paolini is leagues ahead of most writers, and it is exactly here that his youth is on his side."

Booklist contributor Sally Estes wrote that Paolini's "lush tale is full of recognizable fantasy elements and conventions. But the telling remains constantly fresh and fluid." A *Publishers Weekly* reviewer noted Tolkien's influence on Paolini's writing, including similar naming of geography, the use of landscape as character, and the structure and scale of the story, but noted that, as to language, Paolini "dispenses with the floral, pastoral touch in favor of more direct prose." The reviewer called *Eragon* "an auspicious beginning to both career and series."

The sequel to *Eragon,* titled *Eldest,* is also of epic scope. Eragon and Sasphira continue their battle with the corrupt ruler Galbatorix while Eragon receives more intense Dragon Rider training under the tutelage of the elves. A second story line follows the adventures of Eragon's cousin, who is also battling Galbatorix by organizing an uprising in the small town of Carvahall. As Paolini tells the story, he delves deeper into elf lore and language. Many of the themes touched upon in *Eragon* are further explored in *Eldest.* In an interview with the *New York Times* Paolini stated that the main themes in his work include "the difficulty of deciding how to live honorably and how to deal with violence when it intrudes on someone's life." This did not go unnoticed by critics, and Sarah Couri, writing in the *School Library Journal,* noted that the hero in *Eldest* "thoughtfully examines the question of good at what price."

Many reviewers noted that the plot in *Eldest* effectively advances the overall plot of the trilogy. A *Publishers Weekly* critic stated that "the story leaves off with a promise," while *Booklist* reviewer Estes observed that the book indicates that there is "more cataclysmic battle ahead." In addition, critics commented that the trilogy's characters have continued to develop. "Eragon's journey to maturity is well handled," wrote Couri. "Characters and their relationships continue to develop nicely," added Estes. In a summation of the book for *Horn Book* magazine, contributor Anika L. Burkam wrote: "There's lots of imaginative material . . . the author's enthusiasm for his creation is infectious."

BIOGRAPHICAL AND CRITICAL SOURCES:

PERIODICALS

Booklist, August 15, 2003, Sally Estes, review of *Eragon,* p. 1981; August, 2005, Sally Estes, review of *Eldest,* p. 2016.

Bookseller, September 23, 2005, Patrick J. Eves, "*Eldest* Stays on Top," p. 16.

Christian Science Monitor, August 7, 2003, Yvonne Zipp, "Teen author wins readers book by book."

Horn Book, November-December, 2005, Anika L. Burkam, review of *Eldest,* p. 724.

Kirkus Reviews, July 15, 2003, review of *Eragon,* p. 967.

Kliatt, September, 2003, Michele Winship, review of *Eragon,* p. 10.

New York Times, September 19, 2005, "Q&A: Turning Daydreams Into a Best-Seller," p. 6.

New York Times Book Review, November 16, 2003, Liz Rosenberg, review of *Eragon.*

Publishers Weekly, July 21, 2003, review of *Eragon,* p. 196; July 25, 2005, review of *Eldest,* p. 78.

School Library Journal, September 1, 2003, Susan L. Rogers, review of *Eragon,* p. 218; October, 2005, Sarah Couri, review of *Eldest,* p. 170.

ONLINE

Alagaesia Web site, http://alagaesia.com/ (March 9, 2006), author Home Page.

Teenreads.com, http://www.teenreads.com/ (March 9, 2006), interview with author.

* * *

PARFENIE, Marie
See CODRESCU, Andrei

* * *

PARK, Jordan
See POHL, Frederik

* * *

PARKER, Bert
See ELLISON, Harlan

PARKER, Robert B. 1932-
(Robert Brown Parker)

PERSONAL: Born September 17, 1932, in Springfield, MA; son of Carroll Snow (a telephone company executive) and Mary Pauline (Murphy) Parker; married Joan Hall (an education specialist), August 26, 1956; children: David F., Daniel T. *Education:* Colby College, B.A., 1954; Boston University, M.A., 1957, Ph.D., 1970.

ADDRESSES: *Agent*—Helen Brann Agency, 94 Curtis Rd., Bridgewater, CT 06752.

CAREER: Novelist. Curtiss-Wright Co., Woodridge, NJ, management trainee, 1957; Raytheon, Co., Andover, MA, technical writer, 1957-59; Prudential Insurance Co., Boston, MA, advertising writer, 1959-62; Parker-Farman Co. (advertising agency), Boston, partner, 1960-62; film consultant to Arthur D. Little, 1962-64; Boston University, lecturer in English, 1962-64; Massachusetts State College at Lowell (now University of Lowell), instructor in English, 1964-66; Massachusetts State College at Bridgewater, instructor in English, 1966-68; Northeastern University, Boston, assistant professor, 1968-74, associate professor, 1974-76, professor of English, 1976-79. Lecturer, Suffolk University, 1965-66. *Military service:* U.S. Army, 1954-56.

MEMBER: Writers Guild, Writers League of America.

AWARDS, HONORS: Edgar Allan Poe Award from Mystery Writers of America, 1976, for *Promised Land;* Grand Master Award from Mystery Writers of America, 2002.

WRITINGS:

(With others) *The Personal Response to Literature,* Houghton Mifflin (Boston, MA), 1970.
(With Peter L. Sandberg) *Order and Diversity: The Craft of Prose,* John Wiley (New York, NY), 1973.
(With John R. Marsh) *Sports Illustrated Weight Training: The Athlete's Free-Weight Guide,* Lippincott (Philadelphia, PA), 1974.
(With wife, Joan Parker) *Three Weeks in Spring* (nonfiction), Houghton Mifflin (Boston, MA), 1978.
Wilderness (novel), Delacorte (New York, NY), 1979.
Love and Glory (novel), Delacorte (New York, NY), 1983.
The Private Eye in Hammett and Chandler, Lord John (Northridge, CA), 1984.
Parker on Writing, Lord John (Northridge, CA), 1985.
(With Raymond Chandler) *Poodle Springs,* Putnam (New York, NY), 1989.
(With Joan Parker) *A Year at the Races,* photographs by William Strode, Viking (New York, NY), 1990.
Perchance to Dream: Robert B. Parker's Sequel to Raymond Chandler's "The Big Sleep" (novel), Putnam (New York, NY), 1991.
All Our Yesterdays (novel), Delacorte (New York, NY), 1994.
Spenser's Boston, photographs by Kasho Kumagai, Otto Penzler (New York, NY), 1994.
Boston: History in the Making, Towery Publications (Memphis, TN), 1999.
Gunnman's Rhapsody (novel), Putnam (New York, NY), 2001.
Double Play (novel), Putnam (New York, NY), 2004.

Author, sometimes with wife, Joan Parker, of scripts for television series *Spencer: For Hire* and *B.L. Stryker,* and for television movies based on *Spenser: For Hire* television series for A&E television network. Contributor to *Lock Haven Review* and *Revue des langues vivantes;* contributor of restaurant reviews to *Boston Magazine,* 1976.

"SPENSER" DETECTIVE SERIES

The Godwulf Manuscript (also see below), Houghton Mifflin (Boston, MA), 1974.
God Save the Child (also see below), Houghton Mifflin (Boston, MA), 1974.
Mortal Stakes (also see below), Houghton Mifflin (Boston, MA), 1975, reprinted, ImPress (Pleasantville, NY), 2002.
Promised Land (also see below), Houghton Mifflin (Boston, MA), 1976.
The Judas Goat, Houghton Mifflin (Boston, MA), 1978.
Looking for Rachel Wallace, Delacorte (New York, NY), 1980.
Early Autumn, Delacorte (New York, NY), 1981.
A Savage Place, Delacorte (New York, NY), 1981.
Surrogate: A Spenser Short Story, Lord John (Northridge, CA), 1982.
Ceremony, Delacorte (New York, NY), 1982.
The Widening Gyre, Delacorte (New York, NY), 1983.
Valediction, Delacorte (New York, NY), 1984.
A Catskill Eagle, Delacorte (New York, NY), 1985.
Taming a Sea-Horse, Delacorte (New York, NY), 1986.

Pale Kings and Princes, Delacorte (New York, NY), 1987.
Crimson Joy, Delacorte (New York, NY), 1988.
Playmates, Putnam (New York, NY), 1989.
The Early Spenser: Three Complete Novels (contains *The Godwulf Manuscript, God Save the Child,* and *Mortal Stakes*), Delacorte (New York, NY), 1989.
Stardust, Putnam (New York, NY), 1990.
Pastime, Putnam (New York, NY), 1991.
Double Deuce, Putnam (New York, NY), 1992.
Paper Doll, Putnam (New York, NY), 1993.
Walking Shadow, Putnam (New York, NY), 1994.
Thin Air, Putnam (New York, NY), 1995.
Three Complete Novels (contains *The Godwulf Manuscript, Mortal Stakes,* and *Promised Land*), Wings Books (New York, NY), 1995.
Chance, Putnam (New York, NY), 1996.
Small Vices, Putnam (New York, NY), 1997.
Sudden Mischief, Putnam (New York, NY), 1998.
Hush Money, Putnam (New York, NY), 1999.
Potshot, Putnam (New York, NY), 2001.
Hugger Mugger, Putnam (New York, NY), 2001.
Widow's Walk, Putnam (New York, NY), 2002.
Back Story, Putnam (New York, NY), 2003.
Bad Business, Putnam (New York, NY), 2004.

"JESSE STONE" DETECTIVE SERIES

Night Passage, Putnam (New York, NY), 1997.
Trouble in Paradise, Putnam (New York, NY), 1998.
Death in Paradise, Putnam (New York), 2001.
Stone Cold, Putnam (New York, NY), 2003.
Sea Change, Putnam (New York, NY), 2006.

"SUNNY RANDALL" DETECTIVE SERIES

Family Honor, Putnam (New York, NY), 1999.
Perish Twice, Putnam (New York, NY), 2000.
Shrink Rap, Putnam (New York, NY), 2002.

ADAPTATIONS: The American Broadcasting Corp. (ABC) television series *Spenser: For Hire* was based on Parker's works, 1985-88; film rights were sold to many "Spenser" series novels; *Family Honor* was optioned for a film starring actress Helen Hunt.

SIDELIGHTS: Robert B. Parker's "Spenser" novel series represents "the best American hard-boiled detective fiction since Ross Macdonald and Raymond Chandler," according to *Armchair Detective* writer Anne Ponder. A Boston-based private detective whose first name has never been revealed through more than a quarter century of detective novels, Parker's Spenser has proven to be a popular and enduring sleuth, at once hard-boiled and sensitive, equally able to make wisecracks and literary allusions. "Not for nothing is Parker regarded as the reigning champion of the American toughboy detective novel, heavyweight division," wrote Gene Lyons in *Entertainment Weekly.* "The man has rarely composed a bad sentence or an inert paragraph." Many elements have conspired to assure Spenser's success, among them Parker's writing style, a well-conceived Boston setting, and secondary characters who are far more than ornamentation for the hero. In a *Booklist* review of *Small Vices,* Parker's twenty-fifth "Spenser" novel, Bill Ott asked: "What is it about Spenser and his pals that makes it hard to stay away for long? . . . Spenser lives in the real world and deals with it the way we imagine we would if only we knew how."

Parker's career as a novelist began only after he spent years producing ad copy and technical writing for various companies. At his wife's urging, he completed his Ph.D. and entered the teaching profession to gain more time for his own writing projects. "Being a professor and working are not the same thing," Parker explained to Wayne Warga in the *Los Angeles Times.* In a Toronto *Globe and Mail* interview with Ian Brown, Parker expressed his feelings about the university environment even more frankly: "The academic community is composed largely of nitwits. If I may generalize. People who don't know very much about what matters very much, who view life through literature rather than the other way around. . . . In my fourteen or sixteen years in the profession, I've met more people that I did not admire than at any other point in my life. Including two years in the infantry, where I was the only guy who could read."

It took two and a half years of writing in his spare time for Parker to complete his first fiction manuscript, but only three weeks for it to be accepted for publication. Parker's doctoral thesis examined the classic detective fiction of Raymond Chandler and Dashiell Hammett, and his first novel, *The Godwulf Manuscript,* presents a detective in the tradition of the fictional Philip Marlowe and Sam Spade. A Boston policeman turned private eye after being fired for insubordination, Spenser is "a man's man, all six feet plus of him, a former professional fighter, a man who can take on any opposition," related Newgate Callendar in the *New York Times Book Review.* The character's traditional toughness is balanced by his "honesty and his sensitivity," continued Callendar. "Spenser may be something of a smart aleck but only when he is faced with pomposity and pretension.

Then he reacts, sometimes violently. He is educated and well read, though he never parades his knowledge. His girlfriend is the perfect woman, as smart as he is, and so he never has to chase around. Pushed as he is by his social conscience, he is sometimes dogged enough to seem quixotic."

Parker followed *The Godwulf Manuscript* with *God Save the Child, Mortal Stakes, Promised Land,* and several other "Spenser" novels, and the series' success soon enabled him to quit his teaching post and devote himself to writing full-time. The author has estimated that it takes him three to five months to write a "Spenser" adventure. While some critics find the resulting works thinly plotted, Parker has been widely praised for his evocative descriptions and his sharp, witty dialogue, as well as for introducing a more human, emotional tone to the hard-boiled detective genre. H.R.F. Keating commented in the London *Times* that in the "Spenser" books "there is a concern with human beings that rises at times to compassion and perhaps falls at other times to that commonish complaint among American novelists, 'psychology showing through.' But the seriousness that this indicates is always well-compensated for by Parker's dialogue. Spenser is a wisecracking guy in the firm tradition of the Chandler shamus, and above and beyond this all the conversations in the books are splendidly swift and sharp." In a review of *Pale Kings and Princes, Washington Post Book World* contributor Jean M. White concurred that Parker "writes some of the snappiest and sauciest dialogue in the business . . . lean and taut and crisply told with moments of genuine humor and genuine poignancy." A *Publishers Weekly* correspondent, noting that Spenser "can still punch, sleuth and wisecrack with the best of them," found Parker's prose "as clean as a sea breeze."

One of Parker's most notable departures from his detective novelist predecessors is Spenser's monogamous commitment to his psychologist lover, Susan Silverman. "By all the unwritten rules of private-eye fiction, that [relationship] should have handicapped Spenser's future literary prospects disastrously," declared Derrick Murdoch in the Toronto *Globe and Mail.* "Instead it has allowed him to develop into the most fully rounded characterization of an intelligent human being in the literature—a mixture of idealism, passion, strength, frailty and unselfish tenacity." In his *Sons of Sam Spade, The Private-Eye Novel in the Seventies* David Geherin also stated his belief that the Spenser character has "grown significantly, especially in the area of self-knowledge, thanks in part to the frequent confrontations between his ever-deepening relationship with Susan. Even when she is absent . . . her presence is felt. . . . Parker's handling of Spenser's relationship with Susan effectively disproves Chandler's assertion that the love story and the detective story cannot exist in the same book. Not only do they coexist in Parker's novels, the love story adds an element of tension by serving as a poignant reminder of the vast distance that separates the mean streets from the quiet ones." A *Time* reviewer emphasized, however, that for all the intellectual and romantic dialogue, Parker's novels never lack "slambang action."

Noting Parker's influence on the detective genre, Margaret Cannon explained in the Toronto *Globe and Mail* that "Spenser liberated the PI from California, gave him a whole new line of inquiry, and taught him to love." Furthermore, "with each novel Parker has exhibited growing independence from his predecessors, confidently developing his own themes, characters, and stylistic idiom," wrote Geherin. "However, despite his innovative efforts, he has remained faithful to the conventions of the genre, so effectively laid down by his predecessors," Geherin added. "He has thus earned for himself the right to be designated *the* legitimate heir to the Hammett-Chandler-Macdonald tradition, which, thanks to the efforts of writers like Parker, shows no signs of diminishing."

Parker is so clearly the heir of Chandler in particular that in 1988 the Chandler estate asked him to complete a thirty-page manuscript Chandler left uncompleted at his death. The result is *Poodle Springs,* a novel that carries both authors' names on its title page. Parker has also penned a sequel to Chandler's classic *The Big Sleep,* calling it *Perchance to Dream: Robert B. Parker's Sequel to Raymond Chandler's "The Big Sleep."* In the *New York Times Book Review,* Martin Amis criticized Chandler's portion of *Poodle Springs,* citing the master's stylistic lapses and his homophobia among other flaws, but Amis was even less charitable to the contributions made by Parker. *Perchance to Dream,* the critic wrote, "is a chaos of tawdry shortcuts," and the "character of Marlowe collapses" into an "affable goon." Ed McBain had high praise for the work, however, lamenting the inadequacy of Chandler's original *Poodle Springs* manuscript while lauding Parker's contributions "as a tribute to his enormous skill."

Another departure for Parker—or a harking back to his two mainstream novels, *Wilderness* and *Love and Glory*—is *All Our Yesterdays,* which *New York Times Book Review* contributor Walter Walker felt Parker wrote from a self-conscious desire to be taken seriously by the mainstream literary world. According to Walker, *All Our Yesterdays* "embraces two countries, two families, three generations, love, war, guilt, corruption, and angst." Despite some misgivings, Walker declared the novel to be "a most satisfying reading experience" in the same sense as the Spenser novels—that is, as "entertainment." Wendy Smith voiced similar reservations in the *Washington Post,* finding the novel "thoughtful, though structurally flawed." In his review for the *Times Literary Supplement* Karl Miller concluded that *All Our Yesterdays* "is expertly plotted and tersely written" and that "Spenser fans, and a fair number of professors of English, may be unable to put it down."

Parker took an infrequent side trip away from his usual Boston locale in the 2001 novel *Gunman's Rhapsody,* a retelling of the famous gunfight at the O.K. Corral in Tombstone, Arizona. The shootout involved lawman Wyatt Earp, his brothers Virgil and Morgan, and their friend Doc Holliday, pitting these men against various outlaws roaming the area. Noting that Parker's characterization of Earp is "Spenser with spurs," *Booklist* contributor Wes Lukowsky noted that every "Spenser" novel is in actuality standard Western fare: hard-edged men, prone to violence, in conflict over their code of honor. In *Gunman's Rhapsody* the author may be working familiar ground, but "no one does it better," concluded Lukowsky.

Parker mines the Western vein still further with the "Spenser" novel *Potshot.* In this book the detective and his cohorts travel west to solve the murder of a local man who dared to resist an outlaw group that had terrorized his town for years. The result is "a real treat for fans of the long-running Spenser series: a sort of class reunion in which Spenser and all his favorite fellow tough guys get together to trade quips and bang a few heads," recommended Bill Ott in *Booklist.* He further described the book as "a combination parody of and homage to" the classic western *The Magnificent Seven,* and Parker acknowledged the influence.

Although the characters in a "Spenser" novel do not age as living people do, their creator has allowed them to grow somewhat older during the course of the series. In *Small Vices* Spenser is nearly killed by an assassin, and spends much of the book recovering from the incident, ruminating on mortality and morality during the course of his painful rehabilitation. In her *New York Times Book Review* review, Marilyn Stasio declared that the mythic Spencer "has defied mortality altogether and become like some fertility god who lowers himself into the ground each winter and comes roaring back to life each spring. I say good luck to him." In *Booklist* Lukowsky commented on the longevity of the series in a piece on the novel *Chance,* concluding: "The Spenser series has had its ups and downs over more than twenty years, but this . . . entry finds the quick-witted sleuth and company to be in remarkably good health. Wonderfully entertaining reading."

Reviewers still waxed enthusiastic at Spenser's thirtieth appearance, *Back Story,* published in 2003. Inspired by the promise of a half-dozen Krispy Kreme doughnuts, Spenser takes up the investigation of a very old case involving a murder that took place in the 1970s, during a revolutionary raid on a Boston bank. *Back Story* "showcases the strengths of the series," commented *Booklist* writer Connie Fletcher, noting the novel's "well-developed characters, a deftly constructed plot, dialogue that is witty and crisp without sounding pretentious, evocative settings, and that Parker extra, a clearly defined and beautifully executed moral code." The book's climactic chase scenes and action sequences reveal a writer at the top of his form, decided Stasio in the *New York Times;* "it doesn't get any more immediate than Spenser's nimbly choreographed shootout with three triggermen in Harvard Stadium." *Back Story* is also notable for briefly teaming Spenser with Jesse Stone, the protagonist of another detective series Parker has begun.

Stone is one of two new sleuths introduced by Parker in a novel series; Stone first appears in the book *Night Passage.* Alcoholic, depressed, and recently ditched by his wife, Stone has taken a job as chief of police in a Massachusetts town after being ousted from the Los Angeles police force. He has been hired by corrupt city officials who think he will not be effective, but he soon proves them wrong, uncovering a wealth of criminal activity and setting things right at no small peril to himself. In the *New York Times Book Review,* Stasio observed: "For all the obvious non-Spenserian qualities that determine his character—his relative youth, the drinking thing, his lousy taste in women, an absence of humor, his raw isolation and social insecurities—it is this capacity to change his life and redeem his soul that really distinguishes the appealingly flawed Jesse from Spenser." In *Booklist* Lukowsky contended that the "Stone" series "has a great deal going for it: an empathetic, painfully flawed protagonist; an atmospheric small-town setting rife with corruption; and a whole new set of fascinating secondary characters. Parker is a true craftsman."

Stone continued to get good reactions from reviewers in books that include *Death in Paradise* and *Stone Cold.* In the former, Stone finds the body of a murdered girl near his town's softball field. He must first figure out who she is, then unravel the puzzle of why she was killed. As the mystery plays out, readers also get more insight into Stone's personal life, including an ongoing relationship with his ex-wife. The sleuth's problems are "both interesting and completely believable," wrote Craig Shufelt in *Library Journal,* citing *Death in Paradise* as "another strong effort in what is already an impressive series." A *Publishers Weekly* writer called the novel "beautifully wrought," and added: "As usual with Parker these days . . . the book's ultimate pleasure lies in the words, suffused with a tough compassion won only through years of living, presented in prose whose impeccability speaks of decades of careful writing." Reviewing *Stone Cold* for *Entertainment Weekly,* Bruce Fretts went so far as to say that while Parker was most famous for Spenser, the author's "most rewardingly complicated shamus might be Jesse Stone."

Parker's third fictional PI was created at the request of Academy Award-winning actress Helen Hunt, who asked Parker to write a novel featuring a female investigator Hunt could play in a feature film. Parker obliged, and the result was *Family Honor,* a story in which the heroine, Boston resident Sunny Randall, saves a teenage runaway. *Entertainment Weekly* correspondent Clarissa Cruz described the novel as "a breezy thriller that pits a petite blonde PI against shadowy mobster bruisers and a shady suburban couple. Accompanied by her mini bull terrier and gun-toting gay sidekick, Randall tries to stay a step ahead of the underworld heavies." A *Publishers Weekly* reviewer called Sunny "a female Spenser," adding: "How to live correctly is this novel's theme, as it is in the best Spenser novels." The reviewer concluded that *Family Honor* is "a bravura performance" that "launches what promises to be a series for the ages."

Randall continues her career in the pages of *Perish Twice,* as she sorts through her friends' and relatives' relationship problems while also trying to protect a lesbian activist from a stalker. Tony Marcus, a gangster who challenges Spenser in other books, turns up to complicate the plot, and the novel evolves into "a wholly absorbing puzzle of confused motives and whodunits that Sunny picks at as doggedly as any PI going," advised a *Publishers Weekly* writer. "With its smooth blend of mystery, action and psychological probings," the critic added, *Perish Twice* ranks as "yet another first-rate, though not innovative, offering from a reliable old master." *Booklist* contributor Lukowsky also recommended *Perish Twice* as "vintage Parker: heart-racing action, stilleto-sharp dialogue, menacing tough guys, and very likable narrator/protagonist, and a moving romance." Sunny's third outing, *Shrink Rap,* was heralded as Parker's "strongest mystery in years" by a *Publishers Weekly* reviewer, and Connie Fletcher in *Booklist* described it as "an intriguing look at the psychology of manipulation combined with a knockout plot that builds to a truly creepy, hair-raising climax." Assessing the novelist's achievement as a whole, Jeff Zaleski concluded in *Publishers Weekly:* "Parker's influence on the detective novel is, arguably, nearly as great as Poe's or Conan Doyle's. . . . Parker has modernized the American private-eye novel beyond its pulp roots, bringing to it psychological realism and sociopolitical awareness."

BIOGRAPHICAL AND CRITICAL SOURCES:

BOOKS

Contemporary Popular Writers, St. James Press (Detroit, MI), 1997.

Sons of Sam Spade, The Private-Eye Novel in the Seventies, Ungar Publishing Company (New York, NY), 1980.

St. James Guide to Crime and Mystery Writers, 4th edition, St. James Press (Detroit, MI), 1996.

Tallett, Dennis, *The Spenser Companion: "The Godwulf Manuscript" to "Small Vices": A Reader's Guide,* Companion Books, 1997.

Winks, Robin W., *Mystery and Suspense Writers: The Literature of Crime, Detection, and Espionage,* Scribner (New York, NY), 1998.

PERIODICALS

Armchair Detective, fall, 1984; winter, 1991, p. 113; summer, 1992, p. 343; winter, 1993, p. 112.

Book, September, 2000, Rochelle O'Gorman, review of *Hugger Mugger* (audio review), p. 85; May, 2001, Randy Michael Signor, review of *Potshot,* p. 74; August, 2001, Connie Fletcher, review of *Death in Paradise,* p. 2052; September-October, 2002, "The Many Faces of Robert B. Parker," p. 21.

Booklist, September 1, 1994; March 1, 1996, p. 1077; January 1, 1997, p. 779; July 19, 1997, p. 1776; October 15, 1997, p. 390; January 1, 1998, p. 743; July, 1998, p. 1831; December 15, 1998, p. 707; May 15, 1999, Karen Harris, review of *Night Passage* and *Trouble in Paradise* (audio versions), p. 1712; August 19, 1999, Emily Melton, review of *Family Honor,* p. 1988; February 15, 2000, Bill Ott, review of *Hugger Mugger,* p. 1052; August,

2000, Wes Lukowsky, review of *Perish Twice,* p. 2075; February 15, 2001, Bill Ott, review of *Potshot,* p. 1085; March 15, 2001, Wes Lukowsky, review of *Gunman's Rhapsody,* p. 1333; January 1, 2002, Bill Ott, review of *Widow's Walk,* p. 776; July, 2002, Connie Fletcher, review of *Shrink Rap,* p. 1798; January 1, 2003, review of *Back Story,* p. 807.

Boston Globe, May 20, 1994.

Boston Herald, February 11, 2003, Rosemary Herbert, review of *Back Story,* p. 44.

Chicago Tribune, September 20, 1985; May 29, 1994.

Chicago Tribune Book World, June 28, 1987.

Christian Science Monitor, September 3, 1991, p. 13.

Clues, fall-winter, 1980; spring-summer, 1984.

Critique, fall, 1984.

Entertainment Weekly, October 10, 1997, p. 87; March 26, 1999, p. 80; July 16, 1999, p. 54; September 10, 1999, Clarissa Cruz, "Mad about 'Spenser,'" p. 146; March 31, 2000, "Mass Murder: Juggling Three Book Series, including a New Spenser Novel, Robert B. Parker Is Boston's Peerless Man of Mystery," p. 62; October 3, 2003, Bruce Fretts, review of *Stone Cold,* p. 75.

Forbes, January 12, 1998, p. 28; May 18, 1998, p. 28.

Globe and Mail (Toronto, Ontario, Canada), May 12, 1984; June 6, 1984; June 15, 1985; June 21, 1986.

Kirkus Reviews, August 15, 1994; March 1, 1996; January 15, 1997; July 1, 1997; January 15, 1999.

Library Journal, April 1, 1992; October 1, 1994; November 15, 1998, p. 111; March 15, 2000, Patsy E. Gray, review of *Hugger Mugger,* p. 128; October 1, 2001, Craig Shufelt, review of *Death in Paradise,* p. 143; August, 2002, Ronnie H. Terpening, review of *Shrink Rap,* p. 144; September 15, 2003, Fred M. Gervat, review of *Stone Cold,* p. 96.

Los Angeles Times, January 26, 1981; March 20, 1981; June 21, 1982; January 17, 1984; February 16, 1986; July 3, 1994, p. 10; October 9, 1994, p. 15.

Los Angeles Times Book Review, July 6, 1986; May 10, 1987.

New Republic, March 19, 1977; November 4, 1978.

New Statesman and Society, April 19, 1991, p. 37.

Newsweek, June 7, 1982; June 17, 1985; July 7, 1986; October 4, 1999, p. 66.

New Yorker, July 13, 1987.

New York Times, January 21, 1981; September 20, 1985; July 2, 1987; June 4, 1992; May 11, 1995; August 15, 1996, p. B5; March 9, 2003, Marilyn Stasio, review of *Back Story,* p. 21.

New York Times Book Review, January 13, 1974; December 15, 1974; November 11, 1979; August 2, 1981; May 1, 1983; May 20, 1984; June 30, 1985; June 22, 1986; May 31, 1987; April 23, 1989; October 15, 1989; October 14, 1990, p. 1; January 27, 1991; May 12, 1991, p. 34; July 28, 1991, p. 10; May 31, 1992, p. 34; February 12, 1995, p. 32; May 21, 1995; May 19, 1996, p. 21; April 13, 1997, p. 24; September 21, 1997, p. 36; March 22, 1998, p. 26; September 27, 1998, p. 26; March 21, 1999, p. 26; September 19, 1999, p. 28; May 7, 2000, Marilyn Stasio, review of *Hugger Mugger,* p. 30; October 8, 2000, M. Stasio, review of *Perish Twice,* p. 32; March 25, 2001, M. Stasio, review of *Potshot,* p. 16; October 14, 2001, M. Stasio, review of *Death in Paradise,* p. 26; March 17, 2002, M. Stasio, review of *Widow's Walk,* p. 20; September 22, 2002, M. Stasio, review of *Shrink Rap,* p. 24; March 9, 2003, M. Stasio, review of *Back Story,* p. 21; October 5, 2003, M. Stasio, review of *Stone Cold,* p. 20.

Observer (London, England), March 31, 1991, p. 54; May 19, 1991, p. 59; January 12, 1992, p. 7.

People, May 7, 1984; July 22, 1996, p. 27; September 20, 1999, p. 57; April 1, 2002, Samantha Miller, review of *Widow's Walk,* p. 43.

Plain Dealer (Cleveland, OH), October 14, 2001, Michele Ross, review of *Potshot,* p. J13.

Publishers Weekly, May 4, 1990; November 23, 1990; April 4, 1994; March 20, 1995; March 11, 1996, p. 45; January 27, 1997, p. 80; March 10, 1997, p. 20; August 4, 1997, p. 64; January 12, 1998, p. 46; July 27, 1998, p. 52; February 1, 1999, p. 78; August 16, 1999, review of *Family Honor,* p. 61; September 20, 1999, p. 18; November 1, 1999, review of *Family Honor,* p. 48; March 13, 2000, review of *Hugger Mugger,* p. 65; August 14, 2000, review of *Perish Twice,* p. 331; February 26, 2001, review of *Potshot,* p. 62; July 23, 2001, review of *Death in Paradise,* p. 52; October 8, 2001, Jeff Zaleski, interview with Parker, p. 46; February 4, 2002, review of *Gunman's Rhapsody* (audio version), p. 29; May 6, 2002, review of *Widow's Walk* (audio version), p. 23; August 19, 2002, review of *Shrink Rap,* p. 70; September 30, 2002, Daisy Maryles, "Rap Artistry," p. 18; February 10, 2003, review of *Back Story,* p. 165; September 22, 2003, review of *Stone Cold,* p. 88.

Southwest Review, autumn, 1974.

Time, July 1, 1985; July 7, 1986; July 27, 1987.

Times (London, England), November 4, 1978; May 4, 1987.

Times Literary Supplement, November 30, 1990, p. 1287; November 25, 1994, p. 21.

USA Today, March 20, 1987.

Washington Post, May 17, 1983; March 7, 1984; June 19, 1992; December 20, 1994.

Washington Post Book World, April 15, 1984; June 15, 1986; June 21, 1987; May 24, 1992, p. 6.

Writer's Digest, November, 1997, p. 49; October, 2000, Kelly Nickell, "Robert B. Parker's Boston," p. 16.

PARKER, Robert Brown
See PARKER, Robert B.

* * *

PARKS, Gordon 1912-2006
(Gordon Alexander Buchanan Parks)

PERSONAL: Born November 30, 1912, in Fort Scott, KS; died March 7, 2006, in New York, NY; son of Andrew Jackson and Sarah (Ross) Parks; married Sally Alvis, 1933 (divorced, 1961); married Elizabeth Campbell, December, 1962 (divorced, 1973); married Genevieve Young (a book editor), August 26, 1973; children: (first marriage) Gordon, Jr. (deceased), Toni (Mrs. Jean-Luc Brouillaud), David; (second marriage) Leslie. *Education:* Attended high school in St. Paul, Minnesota. *Politics:* Democrat. *Religion:* Methodist.

CAREER: Photographer, writer, film director, and composer. Worked at various jobs prior to 1937; freelance fashion photographer in Minneapolis, 1937-42; photographer with Farm Security Administration, 1942-43, Office of War Information, 1944, and Standard Oil Company of New Jersey, 1945-48; *Life,* New York, NY, photo-journalist, 1948-72; *Essence* (magazine), New York, NY, editorial director, 1970-73. President of Winger Corp. Director of films, beginning 1968, including *The Learning Tree,* Warner Bros., 1968, *Shaft,* Metro-Goldwyn-Mayer (MGM), 1971, *Shaft's Big Score,* MGM, 1972, *The Super Cops,* MGM, 1974, *Leadbelly,* Paramount, 1975, and several documentaries. Composer of concertos and sonatas performed by symphony orchestras in the United States and Europe. *Exhibitions:* Retrospective exhibitions staged at California African American Museum, Los Angeles, 2000, and George Eastman House, Rochester, NY, 2003.

MEMBER: Authors Guild (member of council, 1973-74), Authors League of America, Black Academy of Arts and Letters (fellow), Directors Guild of America (member of national council, 1973-76), Newspaper Guild, American Society of Magazine Photographers, Association of Composers, and Directors, American Society of Composers, Authors, and Publishers, American Federation of Television and Radio Artists, National Association for the Advancement of Colored People, Directors Guild of New York (member of council), Urban League, Players Club (New York, NY), Kappa Alpha Mu.

AWARDS, HONORS: Rosenwald Foundation fellow, 1942; Photographer of the Year, Association of Magazine Photographers; Frederic W. Brehm Award, 1962; Mass Media Award, National Conference of Christians and Jews, for outstanding contributions to better human relations, 1964; Carr Van Adna Journalism Award, University of Miami, 1964, Ohio University, 1970; voted photographer-writer who had done the most to promote understanding among nations of the world, Nikon, 1967; A.F.D., Maryland Institute of Fine Arts, 1968; Litt.D., University of Connecticut, 1969, and Kansas State University, 1970; Spingarn Medal from National Association for the Advancement of Colored People, 1972; H.H.D., St. Olaf College, 1973, Rutgers University, 1980, and Pratt Institute, 1981; Christopher Award, 1980, for *Flavio;* President's Fellow award, Rhode Island School of Design, 1984; named Kansan of the Year, Native Sons and Daughters of Kansas, 1986; World Press Photo award, 1988; Artist of Merit, Josef Sudek Medal, 1989; inducted into International Photography Hall of Fame and Museum, 2000; Robie Award for humanitarianism, Jackie Robinson Foundation, 2002. Additional awards include honorary degrees from Fairfield University, 1969, Boston University, 1969, Macalaster College, 1974, Colby College, 1974, Lincoln University, 1975, Columbia College, 1977, Suffolk University, 1982, Kansas City Art Institute, 1984, Art Center and College of Design, 1986, Hamline University, 1987, American International College, 1988, Savannah College of Art and Design, 1988, University of Bradford (England), 1989, Rochester Institute of Technology, 1989, Parsons School of Design, 1991, Manhattanville College, 1992, College of New Rochelle, 1992, Skidmore College, 1993, and Montclair State University, 1994, and awards from Syracuse University School of Journalism, 1963, University of Miami, 1964, Philadelphia Museum of Art, 1964, Art Directors Club, 1964, 1968, and International Center of Photography, 1990.

WRITINGS:

Flash Photography, [New York], 1947.

Camera Portraits: The Techniques and Principles of Documentary Portraiture, F. Watts (New York, NY), 1948.

The Learning Tree (novel; also see below), Harper (New York, NY), 1963.

A Choice of Weapons (autobiography), Harper (New York, NY) 1966, reprinted, Minnesota Historical Society, 1986.

A Poet and His Camera (poems), self-illustrated with photographs, Viking (New York, NY), 1968.

Gordon Parks: Whispers of Intimate Things (poems), self-illustrated with photographs, Viking (New York, NY), 1971.

Born Black (essays), self-illustrated with photographs, Lippincott (Philadelphia, PA), 1971.

In Love (poems), self-illustrated with photographs, Lippincott (Philadelphia, PA) 1971.

(Contributor of photographs) Jane Wagner, *J. T.,* Dell (New York, NY), 1972.

Moments without Proper Names (poems), self-illustrated with photographs, Viking (New York, NY), 1975.

Flavio, Norton (New York, NY), 1978.

To Smile in Autumn: A Memoir, Norton (New York, NY), 1979.

Shannon (novel), Little, Brown (Boston, MA), 1981.

Voices in the Mirror: An Autobiography, Doubleday (New York, NY), 1990.

(Author of foreword) Ann Banks, editor, *Harlem: Photographs by Aaron Siskind, 1932-1940,* Smithsonian Institution Press (Washington, DC), 1991.

(Author of introduction) Mandy Vahabzadeh, *Soul Unsold,* Graystone Books (Santa Monica, CA), 1992.

(Author of introduction) Ming Smith, *A Ming Breakfast: Grits and Scrambled Moments,* De Ming Dynasty (New York, NY), 1992.

Arias in Silence, Bulfinch (Boston, MA), 1994.

Glimpses toward Infinity, Little, Brown (Boston, MA), 1996.

(With Eli Reed) *Black in America,* Norton (New York, NY), 1997.

Half Past Autumn: A Retrospective, Bulfinch (Boston, MA), 1997.

(Author of introduction) Archie Givens, editor, *Spirited Minds: African American Books for Our Sons and Our Brothers,* Norton (New York, NY), 1997.

A Star for Noon: An Homage to Women in Images, Poetry, and Music (includes compact disc), Bullfinch (Boston, MA), 2000.

Contributor of articles to *Show, Vogue, Venture,* and other periodicals.

SCREENPLAYS

(And composer of musical score) *The Learning Tree* (based on novel of same title), Warner Brothers-Seven Arts, 1968.

Shaft, Metro-Goldwyn-Mayer, 1971.

Shaft's Big Score, Metro-Goldwyn-Mayer, 1972.

The Super Cops, Metro-Goldwyn-Mayer, 1974.

Leadbelly, Metro-Goldwyn-Mayer, 1976.

Also author of *Martin* (ballet), 1990, and of television documentaries produced by National Educational Television, including *Flavio* and *Mean Streets.*

SIDELIGHTS: Gordon Parks's "life constitutes an American success story of almost mythic proportions," Andy Grundberg once commented in *New York Times.* A high school dropout who had to fend for himself at the age of sixteen, Parks overcame the difficulties of being poor and uneducated to become a *Life* magazine photographer; a writer of fiction, nonfiction, and poetry; a composer; and a film director and producer. The wide scope of Parks's expertise is all the more impressive when viewed in its historical context, for many of the fields he succeeded in formerly had been closed to blacks. Parks was the first black person to work at *Life* magazine, *Vogue,* the Office of War Information, and the Federal Security Administration. He was also the first black to write, direct, produce, and score a film, *The Learning Tree,* based on his 1963 novel. Parks maintained that his drive to succeed in such a variety of professions was motivated by fear. "I was so frightened I might fail that I figured if one thing didn't work out I could fall back on another," Parks stated in the *Detroit News.*

Born and raised in Fort Scott, Kansas, Parks was sent to live with a sister and her husband in Minneapolis after his mother died when he was fifteen. Shortly afterwards, Parks was evicted from the household and had to earn a living. His first professional endeavor was photography, a craft he practiced as a freelance fashion photographer in Minneapolis and later as a Rosenwald Foundation fellow in 1942. In 1948 he was hired as a *Life* magazine photographer, and over his twenty-year affiliation with *Life* photographed world events, celebrities, musicians, artists, and politicians. In addition to his work for *Life,* Parks has exhibited his photography and illustrated his books with photos. In a *New York Times* review of one of Parks's photography exhibitions, Hilton Kramer noted that while Parks is a versatile photographer, "it is in the pictures where his 'black childhood of confusion and poverty' still makes itself felt that he moves us most deeply." Grundberg similarly noted that Parks's "most memorable pictures, and the most vividly felt sections of the exhibition, deal specifically with the conditions and social fabric of black Americans."

Parks found, however, that despite his love of and expertise in photography, he needed to express in words the intense feelings about his childhood. This need resulted in his first novel, *The Learning Tree,* which in some ways parallels Parks's youth. The novel concerns the Wingers, a black family living in a small town in Kansas during the 1920s, and focuses in particular on Newt, the Wingers' adolescent son. A *Time* reviewer commented: "[Parks's] unabashed nostalgia for what was good there, blended with sharp recollections of staggering violence and fear, makes an immensely readable, sometimes unsettling book."

Parks explored his life further in several autobiographical volumes. *A Choice of Weapons* begins when Parks is sixteen and describes how, after his mother's death and an unsuccessful stint living with relatives, Parks found himself out on the street. For a decade, Parks struggled to feed and clothe himself, all the while cultivating his ambition to be a photographer. The book's theme, according to *Washington Post* contributor Christopher Schemering, is that "one's choice of weapons must be dignity and hard work over the self-destructive, if perhaps understandable, emotions of hate and violence." Alluding to the unfortunate circumstances of his youth, Parks expressed a similar view in the *Detroit News.* "I have a right to be bitter, but I would not let bitterness destroy me. As I tell young black people, you can fight back, but do it in a way to help yourself and not destroy yourself." Observing that "what [Parks] has refused to accept is the popular definition of what being black is and the limitations that the definition automatically imposes," Saunders Redding concluded in *New York Times Book Review:* "*A Choice of Weapons* is . . . a perceptive narrative of one man's struggle to realize the values (defined as democratic and especially American) he has been taught to respect."

To Smile in Autumn, Parks's second autobiographical volume, covers the years from 1943 to 1979. Here Parks celebrated "the triumph of achievement, the abundance and glamour of a productive life," wrote *New York Times Book Review* contributor Mel Watkins. Parks also acknowledged, however, that his success was not without a price. Ralph Tyler commented in the *Chicago Tribune Book World:* "Although this third memoir doesn't have the drama inherent in a fight for survival, it has a drama of its own: the conflict confronting a black American who succeeds in the white world." As Parks wrote in *To Smile in Autumn:* "In escaping the mire, I had lost friends along the way. . . . In one world I was a social oddity. In the other world I was almost a stranger."

Schemering noted that the book contains material "recast" from Parks's earlier work, *Born Black,* and is in this respect somewhat disappointing. He wrote: "It's unfortunate to see a major talent and cultural force coast on former successes. Yet, even at half-mast, Parks manages a sporadic eloquence, as in the last few pages when he pays tribute to his son Gordon Parks, Jr., who died in a plane crash." Watkins offered this view: "Gordon Parks emerges here as a Renaissance man who has resolutely pursued success in several fields. His memoir is sustained and enlivened by his urbanity and generosity."

In *Voices in the Mirror: An Autobiography* Parks again recounted his amazing life, from the pain of his mother's death to his later career success as a photographer and filmmaker. Writing in *Washington Post Book World,* Hettie Jones noted that "the book grabs your attention at once and keeps it through the century and across three continents." Similarly, *New York Times Book Review* contributor Michael Eric Dyson remarked that *Voices* is Parks's "most poignant self-portrait" to date and calls the volume "an eloquent missive from the front line of poetry and pain."

In 1997's *Half Past Autumn: A Retrospective,* Parks presented a collection of photos chronicling his career accompanied by occasional narratives describing the time and circumstances associated with the photos. Writing in *Families in Society: The Journal of Contemporary Human Services,* William E. Powell called the book "one that compels me to reflection and to commentary."

BIOGRAPHICAL AND CRITICAL SOURCES:

BOOKS

Authors in the News, Volume 2, Thomson Gale (Detroit, MI), 1976.

Black Literature Criticism, Thomson Gale (Detroit, MI), 1992.

Contemporary Literary Criticism, Thomson Gale (Detroit, MI), Volume 1, 1973, Volume 16, 1981.

Dictionary of Literary Biography, Volume 33: *Afro-American Fiction Writers after 1955,* Thomson Gale (Detroit, MI), 1984.

Harnan, Terry, *Gordon Parks: Black Photographer and Film Maker,* Garrard (Champaign, IL), 1972.

Monaco, James, *American Film Now: The People, the Power, the Money, the Movies,* New American Library (New York, NY), 1979.

Parks, Gordon, *A Choice of Weapons,* Harper (New York, NY), 1966, reprinted, Minnesota Historical Society (St. Paul, MN), 1986.

Parks, Gordon, *The Learning Tree,* Fawcett (Greenwich, CT), 1987.

Parks, Gordon, *To Smile in Autumn: A Memoir,* Norton (New York, NY), 1979.

Parks, Gordon, *Voices in the Mirror: An Autobiography,* Doubleday (New York, NY), 1990.

Rolansky, John D., editor, *Creativity,* North-Holland Publishing (Amsterdam, Holland), 1970.

Turk, Midge, *Gordon Parks,* Crowell (New York, NY), 1971.

PERIODICALS

America, July 24, 1971.

American Photo, September-October, 1991.

American Visions, December, 1989; February, 1991; February-March, 1993, p. 14.

Best Sellers, April 1, 1971.

Black Enterprise, January, 1992.

Black World, August, 1973.

Chicago Tribune Book World, December 30, 1979, Ralph Tyler, review of *To Smile in Autumn.*

Commonweal, September 5, 1969.

Cue, August 9, 1969.

Detroit Free Press, January 9, 1966.

Detroit News, February 1, 1976.

Ebony, July, 1946.

Entertainment Weekly, March 27, 1992.

Families in Society: The Journal of Contemporary Human Services, May, 2000, William E. Powell, review of *Half Past Autumn: A Retrospective,* p. 339.

Films and Filming, April, 1972; October, 1972.

Films in Review, October, 1972.

Focus on Film, October, 1971.

Horn Book, April, 1971; August, 1971.

Jet, August 29, 1988; April 30, 1990; July 31, 1995, p. 21.

Journal of American History, December, 1987.

Library Journal, January, 1992.

Life, October, 1994, p. 26; February, 1996, p. 6.

Modern Maturity, June-July, 1989; October-November, 1990.

Newsweek, April 29, 1968; August 11, 1969; July 17, 1972; April 19, 1976.

New York, June 14, 1976.

New Yorker, November 2, 1963; February 13, 1966.

New York Herald Tribune, August 25, 1963.

New York Times, October 4, 1975; December 3, 1975; March 1, 1986.

New York Times Book Review, September 15, 1963; February 13, 1966; December 23, 1979, Mel Watkins, review of *To Smile in Autumn;* December 9, 1990, Michael Eric Dyson, review of *Voices in the Mirror: An Autobiography,* p. 19; March 1, 1996, p. 16.

PSA (Photographic Society of America) Journal, November, 1992.

Publishers Weekly, October 12, 1990.

Saturday Review, February 12, 1966; August 9, 1969.

School Library Journal, February, 1991.

Show Business, August 2, 1969.

Smithsonian, April, 1989.

Time, September 6, 1963; September 29, 1969; May 24, 1976.

Variety, November 6, 1968; June 25, 1969.

Vogue, October 1, 1968; January, 1976.

Washington Post, October 20, 1978; January 24, 1980.

Washington Post Book World, November 18, 1990, Hettie Jones, review of *Voices in the Mirror,* p. 4.

ONLINE

Online NewsHour, http://www.pbs.org/newshour/ (January 6, 1998), transcript of interview with Parks.

* * *

PARKS, Gordon Alexander Buchanan
See PARKS, Gordon

* * *

PASTERNAK, Boris 1890-1960 (Boris Leonidovich Pasternak)

PERSONAL: Born February 10, 1890, in Moscow, Russia; died of cancer, May 30, 1960, in Peredelkino, U.S.S.R.; buried in Peredelkino; son of Leonid Osipovich (a painter) and Rosa Isidorovna (a pianist; maiden name, Kaufman) Pasternak; married Yevgenia Vladimirovna Lurye Muratova (a painter), 1922 (divorced, 1931); married Zinaida Nikolayevna Neyhaus, 1934; children: (first marriage) Yevgeny; (second marriage) Leonid. *Education:* Attended Marburg University, 1912; received degree from Moscow University, 1913. *Religion:* Russian Orthodox.

CAREER: Writer, translator, and poet. Private tutor in Moscow, Russia, 1908 and 1913-15; clerk in chemical factory in the Urals, 1915-16; librarian in the Library of the Commissariat for Enlightenment and Education.

MEMBER: Writers' Union (C.I.S.), American Academy of Arts and Letters (honorary member).

AWARDS, HONORS: Nobel Prize for literature, 1958 (refused); Bancarella Prize, 1958, for *Doctor Zhivago;* Writers' Union made the author's country home in Peredelkino into a museum and site for annual readings of poetry, 1988.

WRITINGS:

POETRY, EXCEPT AS NOTED

Blitzhetz tucakh (title means "Twin in the Clouds"), [Russia], 1914.

Poverkh barerov (title means "Above the Barriers"), [Moscow, Russia], 1917.

Detstvo Luvers (title means "The Childhood of Luvers"), [Russia], 1919, translation by Robert Payne published as *Childhood,* Straits Times Press, 1941, translation by I. Langnas published as *The Adolescence of Zhenya Luvers,* Philosophical Library (New York, NY), 1961.

Sestra moia zhizn, [Moscow, Russia], 1923, translation by Philip C. Flayderman published as *Sister My Life: Summer, 1917,* Washington Square Press (New York, NY), 1967; also published as *My Sister, Life;* (also see below); reprinted, Northwestern University Press (Evanston, IL), 2001.

Temy i variatsi (title means "Themes and Variations"), [Moscow, Russia], 1923, reprinted, Ardis (New York, NY), 1972.

Vysockaya bolezn (title means "The Lofty Malady"), [C.I.S.], 1924.

Vozdushnye puti (short stories; title means "Aerial Ways"), [C.I.S], 1925, reprinted, Ardis (New York, NY), 1976.

The Year 1905, [C.I.S.], 1926.

Leitenant Shmidt (title means "Lieutenant Schmidt"), [C.I.S], 1927.

Spektorsky (autobiographical), [C.I.S.], 1931.

Okhrannaya gramota (autobiographical prose), [C.I.S.], 1931, translation published as *Safe Conduct: An Autobiography* (also see below).

Vtoroye rozhdenie (title means "Second Birth"), [C.I. S.], 1932.

Stikhotvoreniia v odnom tome (title means "Poetry in One Volume"), Association of Leningrad Writers, 1933.

Poemy (title means "Poems"), [Moscow, Russia], 1933.

Povest (autobiographical prose), [Leningrad, Russia], 1934, translation by George Reavey published as *The Last Summer,* illustrations by V. Konashevich, Avon Books (New York, NY), 1959, revised edition, introduction by Lydia Pasternak Slater, Penguin, 1976.

Stikhotvoreniia, [Moscow, Russia], 1936.

Na rannikh poezdakh (title means "On Early Trains"), [Moscow, Russia], 1943.

Zemnoy proster (title means "Terrestrial Expanse"), [Moscow, Russia], 1945.

Il Dottor Zivago (novel), translation by Pietro Zveteremich, Feltrinelli, 1957, translation by Max Hayward and Manya Harari published as *Doctor Zhivago* (also contains *The Poems of Yurii Zhivago* [see below], translation by Bernard Guilbert Guerney), Pantheon (New York, NY), 1958, reprinted, Harvill P. Collins (London, England), 1982, published in C.I.S. in periodical *Novy Mir* (title means "New World"), January, 1988.

I Remember: Sketch for an Autobiography (autobiographical prose; translation by David Magarshack from the Russian manuscript *Autobiogratichesey ocherk,*) Pantheon (New York, NY), 1959, published in England as *An Essay in Autobiography,* translation by Manya Harari, Harvill P. Collins (London, England), 1959.

Kogda razgulyayetsya (title means "When the Skies Clear"), Harvill P. Collins (London, England), 1959, translation by Michael Harari published as *Poems, 1955-1959,* 1960.

Lettere agli amici georgiani (letters; translation by Clara Coisson from the Russian manuscript *Pis'ma k gursinskim druz'iam,*) Einaudi, 1967, translation with notes and introduction by Magarshack published as *Letters to Georgian Friends,* Harcourt, (New York, NY), 1968.

Slepaia krasavitsa (play), Collins, 1969, reprinted, Izd-vo Alagata, 1981, translation by Hayward and Manya Harari published as *The Blind Beauty,* Harcourt (New York, NY), 1969.

Boris Pasternak: Perepiska s Ol'goi Freidenberg (letters), edited with introduction and notes by Elliott Mossman, Harcourt (New York, NY), 1981, translation by Mossman and Margaret Wettlin published as *The Correspondence of Boris Pasternak and Olga Freidenberg, 1910-1954,* Harcourt, (New York, NY), 1982.

Letters, Summer 1926 (correspondence of Rainer Maria Rilke, Marina Tsvetayeva, and Boris Pasternak), edited by Yevgeny Pasternak, Yelena Pasternak, and Konstantin M. Azadovsky, translated by Wettlin and Walter Arndt, Harcourt (New York, NY), 1985; reprinted, New York Review of Books (New York, NY), 2001.

The Zhivago Poems, translated by Barbara Everest, Aegina Press (Huntington, WV), 1988.

Sobranie Sochineniaei v Peiiati Tomakh, Khudozh. Lit-ra (Moscow, Russia), 1989.

Boris Pasternak ob Iskusstve: "Okrannaeiia Gramota" i Zametki o Khudozhestvennom Tvorchestve, Iskusstvo (Moscow, Russia), 1990.

Second Nature: Forty-six Poems, P. Owen (London, England), 1990.

Sochinenieiia v Dvukh Tomakh, Filin (Tula, Russia), 1993.

So Mnoaei, S Moneaei Svechoeiiu Vroven Miry Rasetisvetchie Viseiiat, BO VFO (Moscow, Russia), 1993.

La Vida es Minuciosa, Ediciones Vigia (Matanzas, Cuba), 1996.

TRANSLATOR; FROM ENGLISH, EXCEPT AS NOTED

(From the Georgian) *Gruzinskie liriki,* [Moscow, Russia], 1935.

William Shakespeare, *Gamlet,* Molodaya Gvardia, 1940.

Shakespeare, *Antonii i Kleopatra,* [Moscow, Russia], 1944.

Shakespeare, *Romeo i Dzhul'etta,* Gos. izd-vo detskoi lit-ry, 1944.

Shakespeare, *Otello,* [C.I.S.], 1945.

(From the Georgian) *Gruzinski Poety,* [Moscow, Russia], 1946.

Shakespeare, *Genrikh IV,* [Moscow, Russia], 1948.

Vil'iam Shekspir (collection), Iskusstvo (St. Petersburg, Russia), 1949.

Shakespeare, *Korol' Lir,* [C.I.S.], 1949, published as *Korol' Lir: Tragediia piati aktakh,* Iskusstvo (St. Petersburg, Russia), 1965.

(With Samuil Marshak) Shakespeare, *Tragedii* (collection), [Moscow, Russia], 1951.

(From the German) Johann Wolfgang von Goethe, *Faust,* [Leningrad, Russia], 1953.

(From the Georgian) *Stikhi o Gruzii,* Izd-vo Soiuza pisateli Gruzii, Zaria vostoki, 1958.

(From the German) Johann Christoph Friedrich von Schiller, *Mariia Stiuart,* Goslitizdat (Moscow, Russia), 1958.

Also translator of German works by Heinrich von Kleist and Rainer Maria Rilke; English works by Ben Jonson, Lord Byron, Percy Bysshe Shelley, and John Keats; Polish works by Juliusz Slowacki; Ukrainian works by Taras Grigorievich Shevchenko; and Hungarian works by Sandor Petofi.

OMNIBUS VOLUMES IN ENGLISH TRANSLATION

Boris Pasternak: The Collected Prose Works (contains *Safe Conduct, Il tratto di Apelle, Aerial Ways, Letters from Tula,* and *The Childhood of Luvers*), edited by Stefan Schimanski, translation by Beatrice Scott and Robert Payne, Lindsay Drummond (London, England), 1945.

Selected Poems, translation by J.M. Cohen, Lindsay Drummond (London, England), 1946.

Selected Writings (contains *Safe Conduct, Aerial Ways, Letters from Tula, The Childhood of Luvers, The Stranger,* and selected poems), New Directions (New York, NY), 1949, published as *Safe Conduct: An Autobiography and Other Writings,* 1958.

Poems, translation by Lydia Pasternak Slater, foreword by Hugh MacDiarmid, P. Russell (Fairwarp, Sussex, England), 1958, revised and enlarged edition, 1958.

Prose and Poems, edited by Schimanski, introduction by Cohen, revised edition, E. Benn (London, England), 1959.

Poems, translation by Eugene M. Kayden, University of Michigan Press (Ann Arbor, MI), 1959, 2nd edition, revised and enlarged, Antioch Press (Yellow Springs, OH), 1964.

In the Interlude: 1945-1960 (includes the poems from *Doctor Zhivago* and *When the Skies Clear*), edited and translated by Henry Kamen, foreword by Maurice Bowra, notes by George Katkov, Oxford University Press (New York, NY), 1962.

Fifty Poems, edited and translated by Slater, Barnes & Noble, (New York, NY), 1963, published as *Poems of Boris Pasternak,* Unwin (London, England), 1984.

The Poems of Doctor Zhivago (contains the poems from *Doctor Zhivago*), translation and commentary by Donald Davie, Barnes & Noble, (New York, NY) 1965.

Seven Poems, translation by George L. Kline, Unicorn Press (Santa Barbara, CA), 1969, 2nd edition, 1972.

My Sister, Life; and Other Poems, edited and texts by Olga Andreyev Carlisle, photographs by Inge Morath, Harcourt (New York, NY), 1976.

Collected Short Prose (contains *Safe Conduct: An Autobiography, The Mark of Apelles,* [translation of *Apellesova cherta*] *Letters from Tula, Without Love, The Childhood of Zhenya Luvers, Aerial Ways,* essays, and articles), edited with introduction by Christopher Barnes, Praeger (New York, NY), 1977.

Selected Poems, translated by Jon Stallworthy and Peter France, Allen Lane (London, England), 1982.

My Sister, Life [and] *A Sublime Malady,* Ardis (New York, NY), 1983.

The Voice of Prose (contains early prose and autobiography), edited by Barnes, Grove Press (New York, NY), 1986.

Selected Writings and Letters, translated by Catherine Judelson, Progress Publishers (Moscow, Russia), 1990.

Works also represented in *The Poetry of Boris Pasternak, 1917-1959,* edited and translated by George

Reavey, 1959, revised edition published as *The Poetry of Boris Pasternak, 1914-1960,* 1960. Pasternak's works have also been collected in *The Collected Prose Works of Boris Pasternak,* 1977.

OMNIBUS VOLUMES IN RUSSIAN

Izbrannye perevody, Sovietskii pisatel, 1940.
Sochineniya, four volumes, edited by G.P. Struve and B.A. Filippov, introduction by Vladimir Veidle, University of Michigan Press (Ann Arbor, MI), 1961, Volume 1: *Stikhi i poemy, 1912-1932,* Volume 2: *Proza, 1915-1958: Povest, rasskazy, avtobiograficheski proizvedeniia,* Volume 3: *Stikhi 1936-1959; Stikhi dlia detei; Stikhi 1912-1957, ne sobrannye v knigi avtora; Atat'i i vystupeniia,* Volume 4: *Doktor Zivago.*
Stikhotvoreniia i poemy, Gos. izd-vo Khudozhestvennoi lit-ry, 1961.
Stikhotvoreniia i poemy, edited by L.A. Ozerov, introduction by A.D. Sinyavsky, Sovietski pisatel, 1965.
Stikhi, edited by Z. Pasternak and E. Pasternak, introduction by Korney Chukovsky, Khudozhestvennaya Literatura, 1966.
Stikhi, Khudozhestvennaya Literatura, 1967.
Izbroe v dvukh tomakh, two volumes, Khudozhestvennaya Literatura, 1985, Volume 1: *Stikhotvoreniia i poemy,* Volume 2: *Stikhotvoreniia.*

OTHER

La Reazione di Wassermann: Saggi e materiali sull'arte (addresses, essays, and lectures; includes translation of Vassermanova reakciia [title means "Wassermann Test" originally published in periodicals in 1914), introduction by Cesare G. De Michelis, Marsilio [Padova, Italy], 1970.
Roger Martin du Gard, Gabriela Mistral, Boris Pasternak (selections from the works of these three Nobel laureates; also contains Nobel Prize announcements, presentation addresses, and acceptance speeches), A. Gregory, 1971.
Pasternak on Art and Creativity (addresses, essays, and lectures), edited by Angela Livingstone, Cambridge University Press (New York, NY), 1985.
Lettres a Mes Amies Francaises: 1956-1960, Gallimard (Paris, France), 1994.
Doktor Zhivago; Avtobiograficheskaia proza; Izbrannye pis`ma, Gudial-Press (Moscow, Russia), 1998.
Boris Pasternak: materialy fonda Gosudarstvennogo muzeia gruzinskoi literatury im. G. Leonidze, "Diogene," (Tbiliski), 1999.
Raskovannyi golos, ESKMO Press (Moscow, Russia), 2000.
Pozhiznennaia priviazannost: perepiska s O.M. Freidenberg (correspondence), ARK-FELKS (Moscow, Russia), 2000.
Boris Pasternak (prose works, selections), Vagrius (Moscow, Russia), 2000.
Marburg Borisa Pasternaka, [Moscow, Russia], 2001.

Composer of "Sonata in B minor for Piano," 1905, and "Prelude in G-sharp minor," 1906; three musical compositions publicly performed in Moscow in 1976.

Pasternak's complete works will be published for the first time in Russia by Slovo in eleven volumes.

ADAPTATIONS: Doctor Zhivago was adapted by Robert Bolt for a film of the same title, directed by David Lean, produced by Carlo Ponti, released by Metro-Goldwyn-Mayer, 1965; the novella *The Last Summer* and the poem "Spektorsky" were adapted by Craig Raine for the libretto to the opera *The Electrification of the Soviet Union,* music by Nigel Osborne, 1986. Several works have been adapted as sound recordings.

SIDELIGHTS: Nobel laureate Boris Pasternak was highly regarded in his native Russia as one of the country's greatest post-revolutionary poets. He did not gain worldwide acclaim, however, until his only novel, *Doctor Zhivago,* was first published in Europe in 1958, just two years before the author's death. Banned in Russia as anti-Soviet, Pasternak's controversial prose work was hailed as a literary masterpiece by both American and European critics, but its publication was suppressed in Russia until 1988. The attention focused on Pasternak and his work as a result of the *Zhivago* affair brought with it a renewed public interest in the author's earlier writings. Consequently, numerous English translations of Pasternak's entire canon, including his poetry, autobiographical prose, and *Doctor Zhivago,* became readily available in the Western world.

Born in 1890 to a cultivated, cosmopolitan Moscow family, Pasternak grew up in an atmosphere that fostered an appreciation of the arts and the pursuit of artistic endeavors. His father, Leonid, was a prominent Russian portrait painter and art teacher, and his mother, Rosa, was a former concert pianist who forfeited a promising musical career in the interest of her husband and children. The Pasternaks were part of an exclusive social circle that consisted of Russia's finest musicians, writers, and painters, including premier novelist Leo

Tolstoy and composers Alexander Scriabin, Sergei Rachmaninov, and Anton Rubinstein. In the rich cultural surroundings of Pasternak's home, observed Gerd Ruge in *Pasternak: A Pictorial Biography,* "art was a normal activity which needed neither explanation nor apology and which could fill out and take possession of a man's whole life."

Pasternak was only four years old when he first met Tolstoy, who attended a concert at the Pasternaks' given by Boris's mother and two professors—a violinist and a cellist—from the Moscow Conservatory. In his 1959 memoir *I Remember: Sketch for an Autobiography,* Pasternak reflected on the impact of the music, especially that of the stringed instruments, played in Tolstoy's honor: "I was awakened . . . by a sweetly poignant pain, more violent than any I had experienced before. I cried out and burst into tears from fear and anguish. . . . My memory became active and my consciousness was set in motion. [From that time I] believed in the existence of a higher heroic world, which must be served rapturously, though it might bring suffering." The family's ongoing contact with Tolstoy—Leonid illustrated the author's novella *Resurrection* in 1898—culminated in "the forlorn station where Tolstoy lay dead in a narrow humble room," related Marc Slonim in the *New York Times Book Review.* According to Slonim, the author's moving recollections, brought to life at Tolstoy's wake and documented in *I Remember,* demonstrate how great a part "the creator of *War and Peace* [played] in the ethical formation of Pasternak, particularly in his developing attitude toward history and nature."

An encounter in 1903 with the celebrated composer Scriabin prompted the fourteen-year-old Pasternak to devote himself entirely to the composition of music. He eagerly embraced the study of music at the Moscow Conservatory and under composer Reinhold Glier but completely renounced his chosen vocation six years later. He attributed the need for this difficult and radical decision to his lack of both technical skill and pitch recognition, explaining in *I Remember,* "I could scarcely play the piano and could not even read music with any fluency. . . . This discrepancy between the . . . musical idea and its lagging technical support transformed nature's gift, which could have served as a source of joy, into an object of constant torment which in the end I could no longer endure." Pasternak not only resented his musical inadequacy but, despising any lack of creativity, perceived it as an omen, "as proof," he wrote in *I Remember,* that his devotion to "music was against the will of fate and heaven."

The author completely disassociated himself from music, cutting all ties to composers and musicians and even vowing to avoid concerts. Still, Pasternak would allow his love of music to color his writings, steeping both the poetry and prose he would later compose in a melodic air of rhythm and harmony. In *Boris Pasternak: His Life and Art,* Guy de Mallac cited Christopher Barnes's assessment of the writer's style: "It is no doubt to Scriabin that Pasternak, and we, are indebted for the poet's initial captivation by music, and for the development of his fine 'composer's ear' which is traceable throughout the strongly 'musical' poetry and prose."

De Mallac suggested that prevailing literary trends in early twentieth-century Russia also exerted a great influence on the impressionable adolescent. The beginnings of the Russian symbolist movement—a romantic reaction to realism that was advocated most notably by writer Alexander Blok—in the 1890s led to a reexamination of accepted artistic concepts. And as World War I approached, Pasternak would, for several years, associate himself with the futurists, a group of writers whose works were marked by a rejection of the past and a search for new forms. De Mallac pointed out that Pasternak was born into a world "of recurrent economic crises and political repression, dissent, and assassination. . . . [Russian czar Nicholas II's] reactionary stance . . . only fed the flames of political and social revolt and exacerbated the critical and hostile attitudes of the intelligentsia. . . . Pasternak . . . soon realized that the society he lived in was doomed to undergo radical upheavals."

Pasternak's early experiences—his development as a youth within a highly cultural milieu, the early associations with Tolstoy and Scriabin, his innate sensitivity and strongly superstitious nature, and the implications of the dawn of the Russian Revolution—combined to profoundly affect his development as a man and as a writer. After studying philosophy at Marburg University in 1912 under neo-Kantian scholar Hermann Cohen, who purported a philosophy of coherence and world order and abjured human intuition or irrationality, Pasternak again made an abrupt and radical change in his life, leaving Marburg that same summer. De Mallac noted that while Pasternak "did not absorb all of Cohen's theories, [the author] was influenced by the philosopher's monotheism and highly ethical standards." In her prologue to the 1976 edition of Pasternak's *My Sister, Life; and Other Poems,* Olga Andrevey Carlisle reaffirmed that although "philosophy was to remain an important element in his life, [after the summer of 1912] it was no longer [his] central concern." The experience of being rejected by a lover was the catalyst that turned Pasternak into a poet.

In 1912 Ida Davidovna, a young woman whom Pasternak had known since childhood, refused the author's proposal of marriage. De Mallac noted that for Pasternak, "creative self-renewal [was] directly induced by a stormy passion." The intensity of the experience with Davidovna, theorized de Mallac, affected Pasternak "so strongly that he soon made another decision: he would not marry a woman; he would divorce a profession. . . . Impelled by [a] new, poetic perception of the world, he began writing poetry." After traveling to Italy, Pasternak returned to Moscow to write.

Through his highly original poetry, Pasternak explored the many moods and faces of nature as well as man's place in the natural world. In his first collection of poems, the 1923 volume *My Sister, Life: Summer 1917,* the author asserted his oneness with nature, a credo which would guide all of his subsequent writings: "It seemed the alpha and omega—/ Life and I are of the same stuff; / And all year round, with snow or snowless, / She was like my alter ego / And 'sister' was the name I called her."

My Sister, Life is marked by the spirit of the revolution. De Mallac suggested that it was Pasternak's "sincere endeavor to apprehend the era's political turmoil, albeit in a peculiar mode of cosmic awareness." The poet evokes the ambience of prerevolutionary Russia in "Summer 1917," a poem that reduces the last weeks of peace before the war to days "Bright with wood sorrel . . . / When the air smelled of wine corks." Another poem from *My Sister, Life,* frequently but loosely translated as "The Racing Stars," captures with startling and unconventional imagery the moment in time when nineteenth-century Russian poet Aleksander Pushkin wrote his passionate poem "The Prophet": "Stars swarmed. Headlands washed in the sea. / Salt sprays blinding. Tears have grown dry. / Darkness brooded in bedrooms. Thoughts swarming, / While the Sphinx listens patiently to the Sahara." Robert Payne commented in *The Three Worlds of Boris Pasternak* that the author's "major achievement in poetry lay . . . in his power to sustain rich and varied moods which had never been explored before."

The 1920s and 1930s were years of transformation for Pasternak. By the end of 1923, he had married painter Yevgenia Vladimirovna and, upon the publication of a second outstanding collection of lyric poetry titled *Themes and Variations,* had established himself as one of Russia's most innovative and significant twentieth-century poets. The author had enjoyed a successful and prolific period through the early 1920s and supported the Russian Revolution at its inception, feeling the movement would be justified if it did not demand the sacrifice of citizens' individuality. But shortly after Joseph Stalin had seized power in the country in 1928, Pasternak wrote only sporadically, feeling stifled by pressure from the Communist government to adhere to the party's ideals in his writings. He chose, instead, to lose himself in the act of translating the works of foreign writers, including William Shakespeare.

Almost simultaneously, the author ended his association with the futurists, considering their concept of new poetry too narrow to accommodate his unique impressions and interpretations. As a consequence of the break, Pasternak lost longtime friend Vladimir Mayakovski, the Russian futurist poet who glorified the Revolution and identified with the Bolshevik party, an extremist wing of the Russian Socialist Democratic party that seized supreme power in Russia through the revolt. Pasternak did not align himself with any other literary movement during his lifetime. Instead, wrote de Mallac, he worked "as an independent, if often isolated, artist, in pursuit of aims he would define for himself."

Several translations of Pasternak's early poetry and prose, including the 1931 autobiographical prose work *Safe Conduct,* began to appear in the United States in the late 1940s. Slonim echoed the majority of the critics when he commented on the inevitable futility of trying to capture the impact of the author's words, especially his poetry, in English translation: "In the case of Pasternak, whose poetry is complex and highly diversified, the perfect marriage of image, music and meaning can be rendered in English only with a certain degree of approximation." Andrey Sinyavsky pointed out in his piece for *Major Soviet Writers: Essays in Criticism* that "authenticity—the truth of image—is for Pasternak the highest criterion of art. In his views on literature and his practice as a poet he is filled with the concern 'not to distort the voice of life that speaks in us.'" Sinyavsky further asserted that the "fullness" of Pasternak's words—at times "light" and "winged," at times "awkward . . . choked and almost sobbing"—was achieved through the freedom with which he wrote in his native language: "In [his] naive, unaffected outpouring of words, which seems at first not to be directed by the poet but to carry him along after it, Pasternak attained the desired naturalness of the living Russian language."

Pasternak's highly metaphorical writing style made his early works somewhat difficult to understand. In *I Remember* the author looked with disapproval at what he termed the "mannerisms" of his youth. In an effort to make his thoughts and images clearer and more accessible to a larger audience, Pasternak worked after 1930 to develop a more direct and classical writing style. Many critics have cited his masterpiece *Doctor Zhivago* and its accompanying poetry as the culmination of these efforts.

De Mallac theorized that *Doctor Zhivago,* the work for which Pasternak is most famous, "was forty years in the making." According to the critic, "Pasternak called 1945 and 1946 his 'years of deep spiritual crisis and change.'" It was during this time that the author began to weave the first draft of his impressions of the war and its effect on his generation with a highly personal love story—in the form of *Doctor Zhivago.*

In the fall of 1946, while married to his second wife, Zinaida Nikolayevna (his marriage to Yevgenia Vladimirovna had ended in divorce in 1931), Pasternak met and fell in love with Olga Ivinskaya, an editorial assistant for the monthly Soviet periodical *Novy Mir.* In her 1978 memoir *A Captive of Time,* Ivinskaya recalled that upon her arrival home from a lecture in which Pasternak read from his translations, she told her mother, "I've just been talking to God." Ivinskaya's admiration for the author was in sharp contrast to Zinaida's coolness, for as de Mallac documented, Pasternak's wife was "little attuned to [her husband's] spiritual and aesthetic pursuits. . . . Her rather brusque and authoritarian manner . . . was ill-oriented to his sensibilities. . . . Pasternak would seek from Ivinskaya the spiritual and emotional solace that his wife had not given him." Many critics have contended that the poems written during Pasternak's affiliation with Ivinskaya are among his best. One such poem was excerpted by Irving Howe in the *New York Times Book Review:* "I have let my family scatter / All my dear ones are dispersed, / And the loneliness always with me / Fills nature and my heart. . . . / You are the good gift of destruction's path, / When life sickens more than disease / And boldness is the root of beauty—/ Which draws us together so close."

The author's affair with Ivinskaya coincided with the Russian Communist Party's renewed attack on deviationist writers. Numerous sources suggested that Stalin showed an unusual tolerance for Pasternak—such special treatment may have stemmed from the author's work as a translator and promoter of Georgian literature, as Stalin was a native of Georgia. Howe reported that "there were rumors in Moscow that the dictator, glancing over a dossier prepared for Pasternak's arrest, had scribbled, 'Do not touch this cloud-dweller.'"

Pasternak's lover, however, was not afforded such consideration. Arrested in 1949 for having engaged in alleged anti-Soviet discourse with the author, Ivinskaya was convicted and sentenced to four years in a labor camp after refusing to denounce her lover as a British spy. As documented in *A Captive of Time,* she suffered systematic psychological torture at the hands of her captors. Pregnant with Pasternak's baby at the time of her imprisonment, Ivinskaya, promised a visit from the author, was instead led through prison corridors to a morgue. Fearing that Pasternak's body lay among the cadavers, she suffered a miscarriage. Although Pasternak remained free, Howe reported that the author "all the while seems to have been haunted by guilt: toward his betrayed wife, toward his lover far off in a camp, toward his colleagues in Russian literature who had been cut down by the regime." Of Ivinskaya, as cited in *A Captive of Time,* Pasternak wrote: "She is all life, all freedom, / A pounding of the heart in the breast, / And the prison dungeons / Have not broken her will." Upon her release, Ivinskaya proclaimed her undying love to Pasternak, and, although he thought it best that they no longer see each other, she eventually won the author back.

Ivinskaya is generally regarded as the model for Lara, the heroine in *Doctor Zhivago.* De Mallac noted that when speaking with certain visitors, Pasternak often "equated" Lara with Ivinskaya. But the critic contended that "Lara is in fact a composite portrait, combining elements of both Zinaida Nikolayevna and Olga Ivinskaya." The novel itself was, de Mallac indicated, "a 'settlement' of sorts" for Pasternak, an attempt to relate in a comprehensive volume of fictional prose the suffering and injustice he had witnessed during the years of the war.

Doctor Zhivago begins with the suicide of young Yuri Zhivago's father. The boy—whose name means "alive"—grows up in Czarist Russia, becomes a doctor, and writes poetry in his spare time. Zhivago marries the daughter of a chemistry professor and is soon drafted as a medical officer in the Revolution. Witnessing the frightening social chaos in Moscow, he leaves with his family upon the completion of his service for refuge in a hamlet beyond the Urals. Zhivago's life soon becomes complicated by the reappearance of Lara, a girl he had known years earlier. Lara has married Strelnikov, a nonpartisan revolutionary who is captured by the Germans and presumed dead. Zhivago is kidnapped by the Red partisans and forced into duty as a frontline physician in Siberia. Returning to the Urals following his release from servitude, he finds that his family has been exiled from Russia. He encounters Lara, whom he has loved since their first meeting, and they have a brief affair. Learning that she is endangered through her union with Strelnikov, who still lives, Zhivago convinces her to seek safety in the Far East with Komarovsky, the wretched lover of Lara's mother; Komarovsky had raped Lara when she was a teenager and then forced her to be his mistress.

Without his one true love, Zhivago goes back to Moscow a broken man. The willing submission of his former intellectual friends to Soviet policies sparks in him a growing contempt for the intelligentsia as a whole. "Men who are not free," he muses, "always idealize their bondage."

Despite the implications of its plot, *Doctor Zhivago* is not ordinarily viewed as a political novel or an attack on the Soviet regime. (Pasternak proclaimed in *My Sister, Life* that he greatly "disliked" writers who "commit themselves to political causes," especially those "who make a career out of being Communists.") Rather, the book is judged by most critics as an affirmation of the virtues of individuality and the human spirit. In a review for *Atlantic Monthly,* Ernest J. Simmons contended that "it is the story of Russians from all walks of life who lived, loved, fought, and died during the momentous events from 1903 to 1929. . . . And the beloved, ineradicable symbol of their existence is Russia."

In an essay for *Major Soviet Writers,* Herbert E. Bowman quoted Pasternak as calling *Doctor Zhivago* "my chief and most important work." Critics have generally considered Zhivago to be an autobiographical character, Pasternak's second self. Slonim commented, "There is no doubt that the basic attitudes of [the] hero do reflect the poet's intimate convictions. [Zhivago] believes that 'every man is born a Faust, with a longing to grasp and experience and express everything in the world.' And he sees history as only part of a larger order."

Like Pasternak, Yuri Zhivago welcomes the Revolution in its infancy as a revitalizing agent with the potential to cleanse his native country of its ills. The character rejects the Soviet philosophy, though, when it becomes incompatible with "the ideal of free personality." Communists always talk of "remaking life," but "people who can talk in this way," claims Zhivago, "have never known life at all, have never felt its spirit, its soul. For them, human existence is a lump of raw material which has not been ennobled by their touch." To Yuri, life "is away out of reach of our stupid theories." Of the higher echelons within the Marxist regime Zhivago declares, "They are so anxious to establish the myth of their infallibility, that they do their utmost to ignore the truth." The truth for Zhivago is that all aspects of the human personality must be acknowledged and expressed, not denied or unduly restrained. In spite of the horrors and trials it depicts, the novel leaves what Slonim referred to as "the impression of strength and faith" existing "underneath the Communist mechanism."

Judged as a work of fiction, *Doctor Zhivago* is, according to many critics, technically flawed. Some reviewers maintained that while Pasternak was a master poet, his inexperience as a novelist is evident in both his flat expository style and his frequent use of coincidence to manipulate the plot of the book. Most reviewers, however, conceded that the book's honest tone superseded any signs of structural awkwardness. David Magarshack commented in *Nation,* "If Pasternak's novel cannot compare as a work of art with the greatest Russian novels of the nineteenth century, it certainly excels them as a social document, as a work of observation of the highest order." Calling *Doctor Zhivago* "one of the great events in man's literary and moral history," Edmund Wilson concluded in the *New Yorker:* "Nobody could have written it in a totalitarian state and turned it loose on the world who did not have the courage of genius. . . . [Pasternak's] book is a great act of faith in art and in the human spirit."

In the summer of 1956 Pasternak submitted his manuscript of *Doctor Zhivago* to *Novy Mir.* The editorial board returned the manuscript to the author with a ten-thousand-word letter of rejection. Excerpted in the *New York Times Book Review,* the letter held that "the spirit of [the] novel [was] that of non-acceptance of the socialist revolution." The board further accused Pasternak of having "written a political novel-sermon par excellence" which was "conceived . . . as a work to be placed unreservedly and sincerely at the service of certain political aims." Although publication of *Doctor Zhivago* was suppressed in Russia, the manuscript was smuggled to the West where it was published, first in Italy by Feltrinelli, in 1957.

Despite the harassment he suffered in his own country, Pasternak enjoyed high acclaim in the West for his novel. In announcing the author's selection as the winner of the Nobel Prize for literature on October 23, 1958, the secretary of the Swedish Academy indirectly focused attention on *Doctor Zhivago* by citing Pasternak's achievements in both poetry and Russia's grand epic tradition. The resulting speculation that the award had, in fact, been given solely for *Doctor Zhivago,* and that the poetry had been mentioned only as a courtesy, immersed the author in a politically charged international controversy that continued even after his death in

1960. While Pasternak initially accepted the award, cabling the message, as quoted in *Time,* that he was "infinitely grateful, touched, proud, surprised, [and] overwhelmed," he officially declined the prize six days later. In *A Captive of Time,* Ivinskaya admitted that she persuaded Pasternak to sign a repudiation "in view of the meaning given the award by the society in which [he] live[d]." Nevertheless, Pasternak was expelled from the Soviet Writers' Union and deemed a traitor. Dusko Doder, writing in the *Los Angeles Times,* related some of the bitter attacks launched against Pasternak after he was named Nobel laureate. A union representative called the writer "a literary whore, hired and kept in America's anti-Soviet brothel." A government official referred to him as "a pig who has fouled the spot where he eats and cast filth on those by whose labor he lives and breathes." Communist propagandists urged that the novelist be banished from Russia. But following Pasternak's refusal of the award and his entreaty to Premier Nikita Khrushchev—in a letter, excerpted in the *New York Times,* he told the Soviet leader, "Leaving the motherland will equal death for me. I am tied to Russia by birth, by life and work"—the author was permitted to remain in his native country. Pasternak died a disillusioned and disgraced man on May 30, 1960. As cited in his obituary in the *New York Times,* one of the poems from *Doctor Zhivago* provides for the author an appropriate epitaph: "The stir is over. . . . / I strain to make the far-off echo yield / A cue to the events that may come in my day. / The order of the acts has been schemed and plotted, / And nothing can avert the final curtain's fall. / I stand alone. . . . / To live life to the end is not a childish task."

In what Philip Taubman, writing in the *New York Times,* termed a "rehabilitation" that "has become perhaps the most visible symbol of the changing cultural climate [in the U.S.S.R.] under [Soviet Communist leader Mikhail] Gorbachev," Pasternak finally earned in death the recognition from his country that was denied him during his lifetime. The author was posthumously reinstated to his place in the Writers' Union on February 19, 1987. And, three decades after its original release, *Doctor Zhivago* was finally published in Russia in 1988 to be freely read and enjoyed as Pasternak had intended.

BIOGRAPHICAL AND CRITICAL SOURCES:

BOOKS

Barnes, Christopher, *Boris Pastermak: A Literary Biography, Volume One: 1890-1928,* Cambridge University Press (New York, NY), 1990.

Brown, Edward J., editor, *Major Soviet Writers: Essays in Criticism,* Oxford University Press (New York, NY), 1973.

Carlisle, Olga Andreyev, *Voices in the Snow: Encounters with Russian Writers,* Random House, 1962, pp. 183-224.

Clowes, Edith W., *Doctor Zhivago: A Critical Companion,* Northwestern University Press (Evanston, I), 1995.

Conquest, Robert, *The Pasternak Affair: Courage of Genius,* Lippincott (Philadelphia, PA), 1969.

Contemporary Literary Criticism, Thomson Gale (Detroit, MI), Volume 7, 1977, Volume 10, 1979, Volume 18, 1981, Volume 63, 1991.

de Mallac, Guy, *Boris Pasternak: His Life and Art,* University of Oklahoma Press (Norman, OK), 1981.

Dyck, J. W., *Boris Pasternak,* Twayne (Boston, MA), 1972.

Erlich, Victor, editor, *Pasternak: A Collection of Critical Essays,* Prentice-Hall (Englewood Cliffs, NJ), 1978.

Evans-Romaine, Karen, *Boris Pasternak and the Tradition of German Romanticism,* O. Sagner (Munich, Germany), 1997.

Fleishman, Lazar, *Boris Pasternak: The Poet and His Politics,* Harvard University Press (Cambridge, MA), 1990.

Gifford, Henry, *Pasternak: A Critical Study,* Cambridge University Press (Cambridge, MA), 1977.

Gladkov, Alexander, *Meetings with Pasternak: A Memoir,* translated and edited with notes and introduction by Max Hayward, Harcourt (New York, NY), 1977.

Hughes, Olga Raevsky, *The Poetic World of Boris Pasternak,* Princeton University Press (Princeton, NJ), 1974.

Ivinskaya, Olga, *A Captive of Time,* translation by Hayward, Doubleday (New York, NY), 1978.

Jennings, Elizabeth, *Seven Men of Vision: An Appreciation,* Vision Press (London, England), 1976, pp. 224-246.

Kostelanetz, Richard, editor, *On Contemporary Literature,* Avon Books (New York, NY), 1964, pp. 486-497.

Mathewson, Rufus W., Jr., *The Positive Hero in Russian Literature,* revised edition, Stanford University Press (Stanford, CA), 1975, pp. 259-278.

Morson, Gary Saul, editor, *Literature and History: Theoretical Problems and Russian Case Studies,* Stanford University Press (Stanford, CA), 1986, pp. 247-262.

Pasternak, Boris, *A Captive of Time,* Doubleday (New York, NY), 1978.

Pasternak, Boris, *Dr. Zhivago,* Pantheon (New York, NY) 1958.
Pasternak, Boris, *I Remember: Sketch for an Autobiography,* Pantheon (New York, NY), 1959.
Pasternak, Boris, *My Sister, Life; and Other Poems,* Harcourt (New York, NY), 1976.
Pasternak, Boris, *Sister My Life, Summer 1917,* Washington Square Press (New York, NY), 1967.
Pasternak, Evgeny, *Boris Pasternak: The Tragic Years 1930-1960,* Harvell Collins (London, England), 1990.
Payne, Robert, *The Three Worlds of Boris Pasternak,* Coward-McCann (New York, NY), 1961.
Poetry Criticism, Thomson Gale (Detroit, MI), Volume 6, 1993.
Rudova, Larissa, *Pasternak's Short Fiction and the Cultural Vanguard,* P. Lang (New York, NY), 1994.
Rudova, Larissa, *Understanding Boris Pasternak,* University of South Carolina Press (Columbia, SC), 1997.
Ruge, Gerd, *Pasternak: A Pictorial Biography,* McGraw-Hill (New York, NY), 1959.
Sendich, Munir, *Boris Pasternak: A Reference Guide,* Macmillian (New York, NY), 1994.
Sutherland, William O. S., Jr., editor, *Six Contemporary Novels,* University of Texas (Austin, TX), 1962, pp. 22-45.

PERIODICALS

Atlantic Monthly, September, 1958, Ernest J. Simmons, review of *Dr. Zhivago.*
British Journal of Aesthetics, spring, 1988, pp. 145-161.
Canadian Forum, December, 1958.
Chicago Tribune, January 25, 1988.
Commonweal, November 14, 1958.
Forum for Modern Language Studies, October, 1990, pp. 315-325.
Los Angeles Times, January 4, 1983, Dusko Doder.
Modern Language Review, October, 1981, pp. 889-903.
Nation, September 13, 1958, David Magarshack, review of *Dr. Zhivago.*
New Republic, September 8, 1958.
New Yorker, November 15, 1958, Edmund Wilson, review of *Dr. Zhivago.*
New York Times, June 23, 1982, John Leonard, review of *The Correspondence of Boris Pasternak and Olga Freidenberg, 1910-1954,* p. C23; February 24, 1987, Philip Taubman, "Reinstatement of Pasternak Approved by Soviet Writers," p. A10.
New York Times Book Review, September 7, 1958; December 7, 1958; April 5, 1959; November 1, 1959; November 12, 1967; February 5, 1978; June 27, 1982, Helen Muchnic, review of *The Correspondence of Boris Pasternak and Olga Freidenberg, 1910-1954,* p. 1.
Philosophy and Literature, October, 1988, pp. 211-231.
Russian Literature, November 15, 1981, pp. 339-358.
Saturday Review, September 6, 1958.
Scottish Slavonic Review, spring, 1986, pp. 69-80.
Soviet Literature, Volume 491, 1989, pp. 137-150.
Spectator, September 5, 1958.
Time, September 15, 1958; October 19, 1959; March 6, 1979; August 18, 1980, Patricia Blake, "The Nobel Prize," p. 64; August 9, 1982, Patricia Blake, review of *The Correspondence of Boris Pasternak and Olga Freidenberg 1910-1954,* p. 72.
Times (London, England), December 12, 1983.
Times Literary Supplement, January 23, 1964.
Washington Post, May 17, 1988.
World Literature Today, autumn, 1977.

OBITUARIES:

PERIODICALS

Harper's, May, 1961.
Nation, June 11, 1960.
Newsweek, June 6, 1960.
New York Times, May 31, 1960, June 1, 1960, June 3, 1960.
Time, June 13, 1960.

* * *

PASTERNAK, Boris Leonidovich
See PASTERNAK, Boris

* * *

PATCHETT, Ann 1963-

PERSONAL: Born December 2, 1963, in Los Angeles, CA; daughter of Frank (a police captain) and Jeanne Ray (a nurse; maiden name, Wilkinson) Patchett. *Education:* Sarah Lawrence College, B.A., 1984; University of Iowa, M.F.A., 1987. *Politics:* "Roosevelt Democrat." *Religion:* Roman Catholic.

ADDRESSES: *Home*—Nashville, TN. *Agent*—Lisa Bankoff, International Creative Management, 40 W. 57th St., New York, NY 10019.

CAREER: Freelance writer. Ecco Press, editorial assistant, 1984; Allegheny College, Meadville, PA, writer-in-residence, 1989-90; Murray State University, Murray, KY, visiting assistant professor, 1992; University of the South, Nashville, TN, Tennessee Williams fellow in Creative Writing, 1997.

AWARDS, HONORS: Award for Fiction, Trans-Atlantic Henfield Foundation, 1984; Editor's Choice Award for Fiction, *Iowa Journal of Literary Studies,* 1986, for "For Rita, Who Is Never Alice"; Editor's Choice Award for Fiction, *Columbia,* 1987, for "The Magician's Assistant's Dream"; residential fellow of Yaddo and Millay Colony for the Arts, both 1989; James A. Michener/Copernicus Award, University of Iowa, 1989, for work on *Patron Saint of Liars;* residential fellow, Fine Arts Work Center, Provincetown, RI, 1990-91; Mary Ingrahm Bunting fellowship, 1993; Janet Heidinger Kafka Prize for best work of fiction, 1994, for *Taft;* Tennessee Writers Award of the Year, *Nashville Banner,* and Guggenheim fellowship, both 1994, both for *The Magician's Assistant;* National Book Critics Circle Award nomination in fiction category, 2001, and PEN/Faulkner Award finalist, and Orange Prize for fiction, both 2002, all for *Bel Canto;* Los Angeles Times Book Award nomination, 2004, for *Truth and Beauty: A Friendship.*

WRITINGS:

NOVELS

The Patron Saint of Liars, Houghton (Boston, MA), 1992.
Taft, Houghton (Boston, MA), 1994.
The Magician's Assistant, Harcourt (New York, NY), 1997.
Bel Canto, HarperCollins (New York, NY), 2001.

OTHER

Truth and Beauty: A Friendship, (memoir), HarperCollins (New York, NY), 2004.

Work represented in anthologies, including *Twenty under Thirty,* edited by Debra Spark, Scribner (New York, NY), 1987; *Twenty for the Nineties,* edited by Monica Wood, J. Weston Walch (Portland, ME), 1992; and *The Anthology of the Fine Arts Work Center,* Sheepshead Press, 1993. Contributor of stories to *Columbia, Seventeen, Southern Review, Paris Review, New Madrid, Epoch,* and *Iowa Review.* Contributor of nonfiction to *GQ, Outside,* and *Vogue.* Editor, *Sarah Lawrence Review,* 1983-84; fiction editor, *Shankpainter,* 1990-91.

ADAPTATIONS: The story "All Little Colored Children Should Learn to Play Harmonica" was adapted as a play; *The Patron Saint of Liars* was filmed for television by CBS, 1997.

SIDELIGHTS: Author of the novels *Taft, The Magician's Assistant,* and *Bel Canto,* Ann Patchett has been hailed one of the most interesting and unconventional writers of her generation. Patchett's power as a writer seems to derive from her unusual ability to make believable the voices of a sweeping array of characters, running the gamut from a Catholic nun to a black blues drummer to a gay magician. In 1984, on her twenty-first birthday, Patchett published her first story, "All Little Colored Children Should Learn to Play Harmonica," a narrative set in the 1940s about a black family with eight children. Patchett, a white woman from Nashville, Tennessee, had actually written the play two years earlier when she was a sophomore at New York's Sarah Lawrence College. "Because I was nineteen, I had the courage and confidence to approach such subject matter with authority," she told Elizabeth Bernstein in an interview for *Publishers Weekly.* Patchett described the origins of her diverse characters as occurring in moments of fantasy. "I never thought it was strange to pick these topics," she recounted to Bernstein. "I just really believe that using your imagination is the one time in your life you can really go anywhere."

The Patron Saint of Liars, Patchett's first novel, shows just such imagination. It tells the story of a young pregnant woman who flees from a dull marriage, driving across the country to find a new, different, and unexpected sense of family at St. Elizabeth's, a Roman Catholic home for unwed mothers in Kentucky. Critics pointed out that the novel may strain belief at times, in particular because it provides no contextual sense of hotly debated social issues surrounding marriage and reproduction in the Catholic Church. However, as Alice McDermott, reviewing the novel in the *New York Times Book Review,* pointed out, Patchett's project is to write "a made up story of an enchanted place." Comparing *The Patron Saint of Liars* to a fairy tale, McDermott explained that "the world of St. Elizabeth's, and of the novel itself, . . . retains some sense of the miraculous, of a genuine, if unanticipated, power to heal."

Patchett's next novel, *Taft,* also received critical praise, though reviewers' opinions differed as to whether or not this work exceeded Patchett's achievement in *The Patron Saint of Liars. Taft*'s action centers around a Memphis blues bar called Muddy's. The black, middle-aged bartender, Nickel, who narrates the story, becomes imaginatively and practically entangled in the life of a white working-class teenager, Fay Taft, and that of her family. Focusing on their relationship, Patchett weaves a multilayered narrative about unconventional kinds of love and improvisational familial ties.

In her critically acclaimed third novel, *The Magician's Assistant,* Patchett continues to explore the themes of unorthodox love, abandonment, and transcendence and the surprising places people go to feel at home. The protagonist and title character, Sabine, has long been in love with the gay magician she assists. As the narrative opens, Parsifal, the magician, who is afflicted with AIDS, dies suddenly from a stroke. Sabine and Parsifal had entered into an unusual marriage, and upon his death, she is embraced by his family, a family she had not known existed. Sabine meets her estranged in-laws, and together they try to put together the pieces of Parsifal's past. As Sabine shares her grief, she finds a hint of redemption and a way to transform herself. Veronica Chambers, reviewing *The Magician's Assistant* for *Newsweek,* called it "a '90s love story wrought with all the grace and classic charm of a 19th-century novel."

By the time her fourth novel was released, Patchett had earned a reputation for quality fiction, and that reputation was sealed with the publication of *Bel Canto.* Loosely based on a real-life 1996 hostage crisis in Lima, Peru, *Bel Canto*—an opera term that means "fine singing"—takes place in an unnamed South American country where the vice-presidential palace is the setting for a birthday reception honoring a prominent businessman, the chairman of a huge Japanese electronics concern. "The poor host country was throwing a birthday party of unreasonable expense, hoping that Hosokawa might help with training, trade, a factory—something that will make it look like the nation is moving away from drug trafficking," according to *Seattle Times* critic Valerie Ryan. One of the star guests at this party is Roxane Cross, a revered American opera soprano who has agreed to perform for her biggest fan, Hosokawa. As the lights dim following her aria, the peace is shattered by the invasion of terrorists. The electronics tycoon, the diva, the vice president and sixty dignitaries are taken hostage. "In a marvelously loopy touch," noted David Kipen in the *San Francisco Chronicle,* "the president has begged off to watch his favorite telenovela." Negotiations reach a stalemate, but inside the mansion, hostages and guerillas are oblivious to the action. Instead, as the siege stretches to four-and-a-half months, hostages and terrorist form bonds of friendship and even love inside the mansion; "pretty soon, nobody wants to kill anybody," in Kipen's words. But some characters are destined not to survive.

Thematically, *Bel Canto* is "similar to my other works in that people are thrown together by circumstance," Patchett told David Podgurski in a *Milwaukee Journal Sentinel* interview. "But I wanted to write a truly omniscient third-person narrative, a 'Russian' novel . . . . I wanted all of the drama as I saw it unfold on television—it seemed so operatic—and to have all that and yet keep it within a narrative that wasn't a potboiler."

Bel Canto received positive notices from many reviewers, among them *Salon.com*'s Laura Miller. "With this scenario, you'd expect [*Bel Canto*] to be populated by the kind of romantic figures found in books and movies like *Chocolat,* cartoonish outlines that invite the reader to stop inside and fancy herself the embodiment of, say, Joyous Sensuality or the Human Spirit. Instead, the characters Patchett has created are just that, characters; they're not empty enough to 'identify' with." *Guardian* contributor Alex Clark applauded Patchett's range. "With bravura confidence and inventiveness she varies her pace to encompass both lightning flashes of brutality and terror and long stretches of incarcerated ennui," he stated. "The novel's sensibilities extend from the sly wit of observational humor to subtle, mournful insights into the nature of yearning and desire."

What was it about the real-life crisis that inspired Patchett's interest in a fictional retelling? In an essay for *First Person Book Page,* she recalled her absorption in the unfolding events of 1996: "Very few disasters happen in slow motion: plane crashes, school shootings, earthquake—by the time we hear about them, they're usually over. But the story in Lima stretched on, one month, two, three . . . ." During that time, she added, "I couldn't stop thinking about these people. There is no such thing as a good kidnapping, but I heard the hostages played chess with their captors. I heard they played soccer. There were rumors of large pizza orders." To Patchett, the story had "all elements I was interested in: the construction of family, the displacement from home, a life that was at once dangerous and completely benign."

Following the death in 2002 of Lucy Grealy, Patchett's long-time friend and author of *Autobiography of a Face,* Patchett wrote the memoir *Truth and Beauty: A Friend-*

ship. In an interview with *Publishers Weekly* contributor Elizabeth Millard, the author explained: "I give talks about my belief in fiction and the importance of the imagination, and I always say that one thing about my novels is that . . . I'm not a character in my books and I like that." Shortly after the death of her emotionally troubled friend, however, in an attempt to deal with her grief, she wrote a piece for *New York* magazine and found herself wanting to write more; *Truth and Beauty* was the result. "When I look back now," she told Millard, "I think it really was a way to sit shiva for a year, to stay on her grave and be unwilling to get up and go on with my life . . . . going over the good times we had together, because things ended on a very bad note, I think it really gave me all the time I needed to feel terrible and to celebrate her. I feel it would be melodramatic to say the book saved my life, but it certainly put me in a better place." Jennifer Reese described *Truth and Beauty* in *Entertainment Weekly* as a "powerful . . . portrait of a fascinating, understandably tormented woman—and of a great friendship . . . . Patchett's voice—perfectly modulated, lucid, and steady—that makes it both true and beautiful." Donna Seaman, writing for *Booklist,* called it "Dazzling in its psychological interpretations, piquant in its wit, candid in its self-portraiture, and gracefully balanced between emotion and reason."

BIOGRAPHICAL AND CRITICAL SOURCES:

BOOKS

American Women Writers, 2nd edition, St. James Press (Detroit, MI), 2000.

PERIODICALS

Atlanta Journal-Constitution, August 26, 2001, Greg Changnon, review of *Bel Canto.*

Booklist, June 12, 2001, Gilbert Taylor, review of *Bel Canto,* p. 1848; March 1, 2004, Donna Seaman, review of *Truth and Beauty: A Friendship,* p. 1098.

BookPage, October, 1997.

Daily News (Los Angeles, CA), July 29, 2001, David Kronke, "Singing Her Praises," p. L16.

Denver Post, June 10, 2001, Glenn Giffin, "Hostage Crisis a Study in Group Dynamics," p. L08.

Entertainment Weekly, July 31, 1992, p. 57; October 10, 1997, p. 87; May 21, 2004, Jennifer Reese, review of *Truth and Beauty,* p. 82.

Library Journal, August, 1997, p. 134.

Milwaukee Journal Sentinel, June 20, 2001, David Podgurski, "Novel Unfolds with the Expansiveness and Drama of Opera" (interview), p. 4.

Newsday, October 18, 1997.

Newsweek, October 13, 1997, Veronica Chambers, review of *The Magician's Assistant,* p. 78.

New York Times, May 31, 2001, Janet Maslin, "Uninvited Guests Wearing You Down? Listen to Opera," p. E7; June 10, 2001, James Polk, "Captive Audience," p. 37.

New York Times Book Review, July 26, 1992, Alice McDermott, review of *The Patron Saint of Liars,* p. 6; October 16, 1994, Diana Postlethwaite, review of *Taft,* p. 11; November 16, 1997, Suzanne Berne, review of *The Magician's Assistant,* p. 17; October 18, 1998, review of *The Magician's Assistant,* p. 36.

Observer (London, England), June 14, 1998, review of *The Magician's Assistant,* p. 18.

Publishers Weekly, July 18, 1994, review of *Taft,* p. 233; July 14, 1997, review of *The Magician's Assistant,* p. 62; October 13, 1997, Elizabeth Bernstein, interview with Patchett, pp. 52-53; April 16, 2001, review of *Bel Canto,* p. 42; March 29, 2004, Elizabeth Millard, review of *Truth and Beauty,* p. 148.

San Francisco Chronicle, June 13, 2001, David Kipen, "Hostage Novel Ropes You In," review of *Bel Cantos,* p. E1.

Seattle Times, June 24, 2001, Valerie Ryan, review of *Bel Canto,* p. J10.

Times Literary Supplement, February 6, 1998, review of *The Magician's Assistant,* p. 21; July 9, 1999, review of *Taft,* p. 21.

Washington Post Book World, January 18, 1998, review of *The Magician's Assistant,* p. 4.

ONLINE

Ann Patchett Home Page, http://www.annpatchett.com/ (August 11, 2004).

BookBrowse.com, http://www.bookbrowse.com/ (August 11, 2004), "A Conversation with Ann Patchett."

BookPage.com http://www.bookpage.com/ (August 11, 2004), Ann Patchett, "Turning a News Story into a Novel"; Laurie Parker, review of *The Magician's Assistant.*

Bookreporter.com, http://www.bookreporter.com/ (August 11, 2004), "On the Road with Ann Patchett, Week 1."

Guardian Unlimited, http://books.guardian.co.uk/ (August 11, 2004), Alex Clark, "Danger Arias."

Salon.com, http://www.salon.com/ (August 11, 2004), Laura Miller, "*Bel Canto* by Ann Patchett."

PATON, Alan 1903-1988
(Alan Stewart Paton)

PERSONAL: Surname rhymes with "Dayton"; born January 11, 1903, in Pietermaritzburg, Natal, South Africa; died of throat cancer, April 12, 1988, in Botha's Hill (near Durban), Natal, South Africa; son of James (a civil servant) and Eunice (James) Paton; married Doris Olive Francis, July 2, 1928 (died October 23, 1967); married Anne Hopkins, 1969; children: (first marriage) David Francis, Jonathan Stewart. *Education:* University of Natal, B.Sc., 1923. *Religion:* Anglican.

CAREER: Writer. Ixopo High School, Ixopo, Natal, South Africa, teacher of mathematics and physics, 1925-28; Maritzburg College, Pietermaritzburg, Natal, teacher of mathematics, physics, and English, 1928-35; Diepkloof Reformatory, near Johannesburg, Gauteng, South Africa, principal, 1935-48; Toc H Southern Africa, Botha's Hill, Natal, honorary commissioner, 1949-58; University of Natal, Durban and Pietermaritzburg, Natal, president of the Convocation, 1951-55 and 1957-59; founder and president, Liberal Party of South Africa (originally the Liberal Association of South Africa before emergence as a political party; declared an illegal organization, 1968), 1958-68. Non-European Boys' Clubs, president of Transvaal association, 1935-48.

MEMBER: Royal Society of Literature (fellow), Free Academy of Arts (Hamburg; honorary member).

AWARDS, HONORS: Anisfield-Wolf *Saturday Review* Award, 1948, Newspaper Guild of New York Page One Award, 1949, London *Sunday Times* Special Award for Literature, 1949, and Oprah Winfrey's Book Club selection, 2003, all for *Cry, the Beloved Country;* Benjamin Franklin Award, 1955; Freedom House Award (U. S.), 1960; Medal for Literature, Free Academy of Arts, 1961; National Conference of Christians and Jews Brotherhood Award, 1962, for *Tales from a Troubled Land;* C.N.A. Literary Award for the year's best book in English in South Africa, 1965, for *Hofmeyr,* and 1973, for *Apartheid and the Archbishop: The Life and Times of Geoffrey Clayton, Archbishop of Cape Town.* L.H.D., Yale University, 1954, Kenyon College, 1962, La Salle University, Philadelphia, 1986; D.Litt., University of Natal, 1968, Trent University, 1971, Harvard University, 1971, Rhodes University, 1972, Williamette University, 1974, University of Michigan—Flint, 1977, University of Durban/Westville, 1986; D.D., University of Edinburgh, 1971; LL.D., Witwatersrand University, 1975.

WRITINGS:

Meditation for a Young Boy Confirmed (poem), S.P.C. K., 1944, Forward Movement, 1954.

Cry, the Beloved Country: A Story of Comfort in Desolation (also see below), illustrated by Sandra Archibald, Scribner (New York, NY), 1948, with an introduction by Lewis Gannett, 1960, illustrated by Howard Rogers, Franklin Library (Franklin Center, PA), 1978, with an introduction by Edward Callan, Collier (New York, NY), 1987.

Cry, the Beloved Country (screenplay; based on his novel of the same title), United Artists, 1951.

South Africa Today, Public Affairs Committee (New York, NY), 1951.

Too Late the Phalarope (Book-of-the-Month Club selection), Scribner (New York, NY), 1953, reprinted, Penguin, 1971, reprinted, Scribner Paperback Fiction (New York, NY), 1995.

The Land and the People of South Africa, Lippincott (Philadelphia, PA), 1955, published as *South Africa and Her People,* Lutterworth (London, England), 1957, revised edition, 1970, revised edition published under original title, Lippincott (Philadelphia, PA), 1972.

South Africa in Transition, Scribner (New York, NY), 1956.

The People Wept, self-published [Kloof, Natal, South Africa], 1957.

Hope for South Africa, Pall Mall Press (London, England), 1958, Praeger (New York, NY), 1959.

Tales from a Troubled Land (stories; also see below), Scribner (New York, NY), 1961, published in England as *Debbie Go Home,* J. Cape (London, England), 1961, new edition, Penguin, 1965.

The Charlestown Story, Liberal Party of South Africa (Pietermaritzburg, Natal, South Africa), 1961.

Hofmeyr (biography), Oxford University Press (London, England), 1964, abridged edition published as *South African Tragedy: The Life and Times of Jan Hofmeyr,* Scribner (New York, NY), 1965, abridged edition published under original title, Oxford University Press (London, England), 1971.

(With Krishna Shah) *Sponono* (play; based on three stories from *Tales from a Troubled Land;* first produced on Broadway, April 2, 1964), Scribner (New York, NY), 1965.

Instrument of Thy Peace: The Prayer of St. Francis, illustrated by Ray Ellis, Seabury (New York, NY), 1968, revised edition, 1982.

The Long View, edited by Edward Callan, Praeger (New York, NY), 1968.

For You Departed, Scribner (New York, NY), 1969, published as *Kontakion for You Departed,* J. Cape (London, England), 1969.

(With others) *Creative Suffering: The Ripple of Hope,* Pilgrim (Boston, MA), 1970.

D.C.S. Oosthuizen Memorial Lectures: Number One, Academic Freedom Committee, Rhodes University (Grahamstown, South Africa), 1970.

Case History of a Pinky, South African Institute of Race Relations (Johannesburg, Gauteng, South Africa), 1972.

Apartheid and the Archbishop: The Life and Times of Geoffrey Clayton, Archbishop of Cape Town, David Philip (Cape Town, Western Cape, South Africa), 1973, Scribner (New York, NY), 1974.

Knocking on the Door (collection of short pieces), edited by Colin Gardner, Scribner (New York, NY), 1975.

Towards the Mountain (autobiography), Scribner (New York, NY), 1980.

Ah, but Your Land Is Beautiful (novel), Scribner (New York, NY), 1981.

Beyond the Present: The Story of Women for Peace, 1976-1986, Brenthurst Press (Houghton, South Africa), 1986.

Diepkloof: Reflections of Diepkloof Reformatory, edited by Clyde Broster, D. Philip (Cape Town, West Cape, South Africa), 1986.

Save the Beloved Country, H. Strydom Publishers (Melville, South Africa), 1987.

Journey Continued (autobiography), Scribner (New York, NY), 1988.

Songs of Africa (collected poems), Gecko Books (Durban, South Africa), 1995.

Author of foreword to *Poppie Nongena,* by Elsa Joubert, Norton (New York, NY), 1985. Paton's manuscripts are housed in the Alan Paton Centre and Archives, University of Natal, Pietermaritzbury, South Africa.

ADAPTATIONS: Lost in the Stars, a musical tragedy adapted for the stage by Maxwell Anderson from *Cry, the Beloved Country,* with music by Kurt Weill, was first produced on Broadway at the Music Box, October 30, 1949; a motion picture, *Lost in the Stars,* based on the musical, was produced by American Film Theatre in 1974; the play *Too Late the Phalarope,* adapted by Robert Yale Libott from Paton's novel of the same title, was first produced on Broadway at the Belasco Theatre, October 11, 1956; the stage and screen rights to *For You Departed* have been sold.

SIDELIGHTS: One of the earliest proponents of racial equality in his native South Africa, Alan Paton first came into the public eye in 1948 with his novel *Cry, the Beloved Country.* This book, which quickly became a classic, would define his reputation for the rest of his life. Almost fifty years later, Carol Iannone wrote in *American Scholar,* "it remains South Africa's most significant novel and a rare example of the successful wedding of literature and social conscience." A landmark publication for its time, the novel follows the fate of a young black African, Absalom Kumalo, the son of a minister, who, having murdered a white citizen who, he later learned, was fighting for racial equality, "cannot be judged justly without taking into account the environment that has partly shaped him," as Edmund Fuller wrote in his book *Man in Modern Fiction: Some Minority Opinions on Contemporary American Writing.* This environment is marked by the hostility and squalid living conditions that faced most of South Africa's nonwhites, victims of South Africa's system of apartheid.

"Three artistic qualities of *Cry, the Beloved Country* combine to make it an original and unique work of art," Edward Callan noted in his study *Alan Paton.* "First, the poetic elements in the language of some of the characters; second, the lyric passages spoken from outside the action, like the well-known opening chapter; and third, the dramatic choral chapters that seem to break the sequence of the story for social commentary, but which in fact widen the horizon of the particular segments of action to embrace the whole land, as well as such universal concerns as fear, hate, and justice."

Paton followed *Cry, the Beloved Country* with another socially conscious novel, *Too Late the Phalarope.* This volume centers on a white Afrikaner, Pieter, whose youthful idealism has tragic consequences. The story hinges on Pieter's love affair with a black girl; according to Alfred Kazin in the *New York Times Book Review,* "Under the 'Immorality Act' of the country, sexual relations between whites and blacks are a legal offense." As Kazin went on to explain, "Pieter is sent to prison, his father strikes [the youth's] name from the great family Bible and dies of shame, and the whole family withdraws from the community in horror at Pieter's crime 'against the race.'"

"Invariably, comparisons [of *Too Late the Phalarope*] with *The Scarlet Letter* and *Crime and Punishment* arise," as Fuller pointed out in another work, *Books with Men behind Them.* "Once Pieter has committed his act, there is no possible release for him but total exposure—a dilemma he shares in part with [*The Scarlet Letter*'s] Arthur Dimmesdale and [*Crime and Punishment*'s] Raskolnikov. Paton gives us a long sequence of superb suspense, arising out of guilty misunderstandings of innocent natural coincidences. But just as the death wish is commonly unconscious, so Pieter suffers an agonized dread of discovery, unconscious of the fact that it is that exposure and its consequences that have motivated him from the start."

A handful of nonfiction works and biographies followed Paton's second novel, but the author received more critical attention for his 1981 book, *Ah, but Your Land Is Beautiful,* which was his first novel in twenty-eight years. The story opens with an act of quiet rebellion. An Indian teenager named Prem enters the Durban Library in Natal, South Africa, and sits down to read. Since she is not white, she is barred from using the facility. However, Prem defies the authorities, and her struggle ignites the embryonic anti-apartheid campaigns of the 1950s. The story goes on to trace the history of such organizations as the Liberal Party (of which Paton was president from 1958 to 1968).

As *Chicago Tribune Book World* reviewer Charles R. Larson saw it, the novel "fairly groans under the weight of human misery and havoc." He also commented that "readers unfamiliar with the horrors of South African politics may be shocked to learn of apartheid legislation against racial mixing at every level of human contact—including funerals and religious services." "Paton's determination to expose injustice is so overwhelming that too often his characters have little life beyond their roles in his morality drama," John Rechy wrote in a *Los Angeles Times Book Review* article. "Emphasizing their admirable hope and courage, he at times denies them the full, defining power of their rage. The unfortunate result is that the evil, too, becomes faceless; a disembodied voice of inquisition barking out injustice." But whatever artistic criticism he had for *Ah, but Your Land Is Beautiful,* Rechy concluded that he "respectfully [envies] Paton's courageous hopefulness, which has allowed him, at age 78 [at the time of publication] to continue to believe that justice may prevail in his beautiful land of entrenched evil."

Newsweek critic Peter S. Prescott saw in Paton's dispassionate style an advantage to the novel's message: the author "offers no diversions, no digressions, no scenes designed to build character, to set a time or place, except as they are shaped by his obsession with this appalling injustice. That in itself would make [*Ah, but Your Land Is Beautiful*] extraordinary; what makes it more so is his ability to keep such a story light and dramatic." In a similar vein, John Romano pointed out in a *New York Times Book Review* piece that in Paton's novel "individual human dilemmas are never swallowed up or diminished by the overarching political context of the story he is telling. Paton is relentless in his faith in the moral meaning of individual human experience." The author's faith, Romano added, "is not a religious one, but a faith in the function, the usefulness of personal sympathy. . . . [Paton's] considerable practical contributions to political life in South Africa aside, his place in the literature of social protest has been secured by his steady devotion to the ideal of the empathetic imagination in fiction."

Originally Paton had hoped to make *Ah, but Your Land Is Beautiful* the first part of a trilogy of novels about South African race relations. Weakened by a heart condition, however, he concentrated on his autobiography. He finished the first volume, *Towards the Mountain,* in 1980, and the second, *Journey Continued,* just before his death in 1988. The books describe Paton's early years as an educator, when he observed the social inequities that prompted *Cry, the Beloved Country,* and his later involvement with the Liberal party, which dissolved in 1968 rather than purge its nonwhite members as the government demanded. In his last years Paton was criticized by many anti-apartheid activists because he opposed their efforts to pressure the government by discouraging foreign investment in South Africa. Such sanctions, Paton argued, would unduly punish South Africa's poorest blacks, and he decried even Nobel Prize-winning clergyman Desmond Tutu for supporting such a strategy. Though controversial, Paton saw his actions as consistent with a lifelong belief in progress through moderation and mutual understanding. As he wrote in *Journey Continued:* "By liberalism I don't mean the creed of any party or any century. I mean a generosity of spirit, a tolerance of others, an attempt to comprehend otherness, a commitment to the rule of law, a high ideal of the worth and dignity of man, a repugnance for authoritarianism and a love of freedom."

BIOGRAPHICAL AND CRITICAL SOURCES:

BOOKS

Alexander, Peter, *Alan Paton: A Biography,* Oxford University Press (New York, NY), 1994.

Callan, Edward, *Alan Paton,* Twayne (New York, NY), 1968, revised edition, 1982.

Contemporary Literary Criticism, Thomson Gale (Detroit, MI), Volume 4, 1975, Volume 10, 1979, Volume 25, 1983, Volume 55, 1989.

Fuller, Edmund, *Man in Modern Fiction: Some Minority Opinions on Contemporary American Writing,* Random House (New York, NY), 1958.

Fuller, Edmund, *Books with Men behind Them,* Random House (New York, NY), 1962.
Paton, Alan, *Towards the Mountain,* Scribner (New York, NY), 1980.
Paton, Alan, *Journey Continued,* Scribner (New York, NY), 1988.

PERIODICALS

American Scholar, summer, 1997, Carol Iannone, "Alan Paton's Tragic Liberalism," pp. 442-451.
Biblio, November, 1998, Rye Armstrong, review of *Cry, the Beloved Country,* pp. 16-18.
Chicago Tribune Book World, February 28, 1982, Charles R. Larson, review of *Ah, but Your Country Is Beautiful;* May 9, 1985.
Christian Century, January 3, 1996, James M. Wall, review of *Cry, the Beloved Country,* p. 3.
Detroit News, March 28, 1982.
Economist, September 10, 1988, review of *Journey Continued,* p. 105.
Globe and Mail (Toronto, Ontario, Canada), May 5, 1984.
Human Rights Quarterly, November, 1992, Roger S. Clark, review of *Cry, the Beloved Country,* pp. 653-656.
London Review of Books, December 3, 1981.
Los Angeles Times, May 22, 1988.
Los Angeles Times Book Review, April 25, 1982, John Rechy, review of *Ah, but Your Country Is Beautiful;* October 30, 1988.
New Republic, March 24, 1982; January 8, 1990, J.M. Coetzee, review of *Save the Beloved Country,* pp. 39-41.
Newsweek, March 15, 1982, Peter S. Prescott, review of *Ah, but Your Land Is Beautiful,* pp. 74-75.
New York Times, July 13, 1981, Joseph Lelyveld, "Alan Paton, at 78, Goads a Still Beloved Country," section A, p. 4; April 2, 1988, John D. Battersby, "Author Reflects on Novel of Apartheid and Hope," pp. 11-12.
New York Times Book Review, August 23, 1953, Alfred Kazin, review of *Too Late the Phalarope;* April 16, 1961; April 4, 1982, John Romano, review of *Ah, but Your Land Is Beautiful,* pp. 7-8; November 20, 1988, William Minter, review of *Journey Continued,* p. 36.
Times (London, England), November 12, 1981, August 26, 1989.
Times Literary Supplement, August 11, 1961, September 23, 1988.
Tribune Books, November 27, 1988.
Washington Post Book World, December 11, 1988.

OBITUARIES:

PERIODICALS

Chicago Tribune, April 13, 1988.
Los Angeles Times, April 12, 1988, p. 1.
National Review, May 13, 1988, p. 22.
New York Times, April 13, 1988.
Times (London, England), April 13, 1988.
U.S. News and World Report, April 25, 1988, p. 15.
Washington Post, April 13, 1988.

* * *

PATON, Alan Stewart
See PATON, Alan

* * *

PATTERSON, James 1947-
(James B. Patterson)

PERSONAL: Born March 22, 1947, in Newburgh, NY; son of Charles (an insurance broker) and Isabelle (a teacher and homemaker; maiden name, Morris) Patterson; married; children: one son. *Education:* Manhattan College, B.A., (summa cum laude) 1969; Vanderbilt University, M.A., 1970.

ADDRESSES: Home—Palm Beach County, FL. *Agent*—Arthur Pine Associates, Inc., 250 W. 57th St., Ste. 417, New York, NY 10019.

CAREER: Writer. J. Walter Thompson Co., New York, NY, 1971-96, junior copywriter, beginning in 1971, vice president and associate creative supervisor of JWT/U.S.A. Co., 1976, senior vice president and creative director of JWT/New York, 1980, executive creative director and member of board of directors, 1984, chair and creative director, 1987, and chief executive officer, 1988, chair of JWT/North America, 1990-96.

AWARDS, HONORS: Edgar Allan Poe Award, Mystery Writers of America, 1977, for *The Thomas Berryman Number.*

WRITINGS:

NOVELS UNLESS OTHERWISE STATED

The Thomas Berryman Number, Little, Brown (New York, NY), 1976.

The Season of the Machete, Ballantine (New York, NY), 1977.

The Jericho Commandment, Crown (New York, NY), 1979.

Virgin, McGraw Hill (New York, NY), 1980.

Black Market, Simon & Schuster (New York, NY), 1986.

The Midnight Club, Little, Brown (New York, NY), 1989.

(With Peter Kim) *The Day America Told the Truth: What People Really Believe about Everything That Matters* (nonfiction), Prentice Hall (Englewood Cliffs, NJ), 1991.

Along Came a Spider, Little, Brown (New York, NY), 1993.

Kiss the Girls, Little, Brown (New York, NY), 1995.

Jack and Jill, Little, Brown (New York, NY), 1996.

(With Peter de Jonge) *Miracle on the 17th Green,* Little, Brown (New York, NY), 1996.

Hide & Seek, Little, Brown (New York, NY), 1996.

See How They Run, Warner Books (New York, NY), 1997.

Cat and Mouse, Little, Brown (New York, NY), 1997.

When the Wind Blows, Little, Brown (New York, NY), 1998.

Pop Goes the Weasel, Little, Brown (New York, NY), 1999.

Cradle and All, Little, Brown (New York, NY), 2000.

Roses Are Red, Little, Brown (New York, NY), 2000.

First to Die, Little, Brown (New York, NY), 2001.

Suzanne's Diary for Nicholas, Little, Brown (New York, NY), 2001.

Violets Are Blue, Little, Brown (New York, NY), 2001.

Second Chance, Little, Brown (New York, NY), 2002.

The Beach House, Little, Brown (New York, NY), 2002.

Black Friday, Warner Books (New York, NY), 2002.

Four Blind Mice, Little, Brown (New York, NY), 2002.

The Lake House, Little, Brown (New York, NY), 2003.

(With Andrew Gross) *Jester,* Little, Brown (New York, NY), 2003.

The Big Bad Wolf, Little, Brown (New York, NY), 2003.

Sam's Letters to Jennifer, Little, Brown (New York, NY), 2004.

(With Andrew Gross) *Third Degree,* Little, Brown (New York, NY), 2004.

London Bridges, Little, Brown (New York, NY), 2004.

SantaKid, illustrated by Michael Garland, Little, Brown (New York, NY), 2004.

Maximum Ride: The Angel Experiment (children's fiction), Little, Brown (New York, NY), 2005.

(With Maxine Paetro) *Fourth of July,* Little, Brown (New York, NY), 2005.

(With Howard Roughan) *Honeymoon,* Little, Brown (New York, NY), 2005.

(With Andrew Gross) *Lifeguard,* Little, Brown (New York, NY), 2005.

Mary, Mary, Little, Brown (New York, NY), 2005.

(With Maxine Paetro) *The Fifth Horseman,* Little, Brown (New York, NY), 2006.

School's Out—Forever, Little, Brown (New York, NY), 2006.

ADAPTATIONS: *Along Came a Spider* was filmed by Paramount in 1997 and released in 2001, starring Morgan Freeman and directed by Lee Tamahori; *Kiss the Girls* was filmed by Paramount in 1997; *Roses Are Red* was adapted for film. *First To Die* was adapted for an NBC television mini-series, and *Along Came a Spider* and *Kiss the Girls* are available on video. All Patterson's mystery novels are available on audio cassette. *Maximum Ride: The Angel Experiment* has been adapted for audiobook.

SIDELIGHTS: Best-selling novelist James Patterson is the former chair of the J. Walter Thompson advertising agency. Writing in *Publishers Weekly,* Andre Bernard and Jeff Zaleski described Patterson as "a novelist who has achieved fame and great fortune through violence-splashed, suspense-pumped crime thrillers."

After writing five novels with modest sales, including the Edgar Allan Poe Award-winning *The Thomas Berryman Number,* Patterson found overnight success with *Along Came a Spider.* The story of a crazed math teacher who kidnaps two of his students, the novel, according to Marilyn Stasio in the *New York Times Book Review,* "does everything but stick our finger in a light socket to give us a buzz."

Along Came a Spider, the first in what has become known as the "nursery rhyme adventures," introduced Alex Cross, a black police psychologist who figures into Patterson's subsequent thrillers. Cross, wrote Cynthia Sanz in *People,* "is known for his obsessive investigations and his ability to get inside the minds of the most deranged killers." Patterson explained to Bernard and Zaleski why a white author chose a black lead character for his mysteries: "It struck me that a black male who does the things that Alex does—who succeeds in a couple of ways, tries to bring up his kids in a good way, who tries to continue to live in his neighborhood and who has enormous problems with evil in the world—he's a hero."

A *Publishers Weekly* reviewer noted that Patterson dedicated his eighth "nursery rhyme" mystery book, *Pop Goes the Weasel,* to "the millions of Alex Cross readers who so frequently ask 'Can't you write faster?'" The next release, *Roses Are Red,* which reveals the identity of the Mastermind—Cross' new enemy—elicited the comment from Rebecca House Stankowski of *Library Journal* that "Patterson's formulaic suspense machine is once again in high gear, and fans of his usual breakneck plotting won't mind that the story is implausible and the surprise ending so surprising that any hint of motivation is sacrificed. They'll be waiting for the next installment." That installment, *Violets Are Blue,* finds Cross following a chain of vampire-like murders across the country as he attempts to find a pattern in the seeming randomness of the bloody killings. At the same time, the Mastermind is closing in on Cross, leading—as Kristine Huntley wrote in her review of the book for *Booklist*—"to the showdown fans have been waiting for."

Between writing *Pop Goes the Weasel* and *Roses Are Red,* Patterson wrote *Cradle and All,* the "reimagined" version of his long-out-of-print *Virgin.* The plot, described by a reviewer for *Publishers Weekly* as "an exciting and moving religious thriller," centers around two pregnant virgins. According to a real-life Third Secret of Fatima carefully guarded by the Catholic Church since 1917, one of these young women may bear the Son of God and the other the Son of the Devil. "While not subtle, this novel tackles issues of faith with admirable gusto," wrote a *Publishers Weekly* critic. Steven Womak, who interviewed Patterson for *BookPage,* noted that this was a "crossover" book, in which the author "ventured into an area few mainstream authors have attempted: spiritual millennial fiction." Another interesting aspect of the book is that Patterson writes through the voice of two different women. When asked if he felt comfortable doing so, he commented to Womak that he "grew up in a house full of women—grandmother, mother, three sisters, two female cats. I cooked for my grandmother's restaurant. . . . I like the way [women] talk, the fact that a lot of subjects weave in and out of conversations. Sometimes men are a little more of a straight line."

During their interview, Womak also asked Patterson about his writing style and whether he made a conscious decision to write in a "decidedly unliterary" style, even although he studied classic literature in the doctoral program at Vanderbilt University. Patterson responded in the affirmative: "I read *Ulysses* and figured I couldn't top that, so I never had any desire to write literary fiction." At about the age of twenty-six, Patterson explained, he read *The Exorcist* and *The Day of the Jackal.* "And I went, Ooh! This is cool. I like these. . . . And I set out to write that kid of book, the kind of book that would make an airplane ride disappear."

While continuing to write his "nursery rhyme" series, Patterson began a new series with *First to Die,* which he followed with *Second Chance.* This series—also written through the female voice and from women's points of view—revolves around a Women's Murder Club consisting of a detective, an assistant district attorney, a reporter, and a medical examiner. Kristine Huntley, reviewing the second book for *Booklist,* commented: "As with Patterson's best novels, the surprises keep coming until the final pages. This novel solidifies the new series and helps guarantee that readers will flock just as eagerly . . . as they do to the Alex Cross novels."

A critic for *Publishers Weekly* called Patterson "always a generous author (lots of plot and intrigue) if not a stylish one." Patterson told Bernard and Zaleski that in his early books "I was writing sentences, and some of the sentences were good. What I've learned over time is telling stories. . . . Ideally, somewhere along the line, I'd like to write sentences that tell a story." In a review for *Violets Are Blue* in the *New York Times,* Janet Maslin commented that much of the popularity Patterson finds among his audience can be attributed to his "shorthand approach. This author likes simple sentences. He keeps his chapters quick and neat. It is very easy to read them. Nobody has to think hard. And the dialogue is uncomplicated, too. 'Martha! There's something behind me!' exclaims one of the . . . victims. 'Oh God! Run! Run, Martha!' It's as if Spot were stalking Dick and Jane."

Patterson's natural and uncomplicated writing style, his fast-moving plots, and his desire—as he remarked to Womak—to make all his books "real page-turners," brought *Violets Are Blue* into the number fifteen spot as an instant best-seller, even while another huge success, *Suzanne's Diary for Nicholas,* was just four months off the presses. "He writes faster than some people read," commented Maslin.

Patterson took a break from his Alex Cross books and delved into the romance genre with *Suzanne's Diary for Nicholas* and a similarly themed novel called *Sam's Letters to Jennifer.* The latter romance concerns the recently widowed Jennifer, a Chicago newspaper columnist whose grief is compounded by the failing health of her beloved grandmother, Sam. When Sam falls into a coma, Jennifer rushes to Lake Geneva, Wisconsin, to care for her. To her surprise, she discovers a stack of letters Sam has written for her, which outline the grandmother's life story. The letters reveal that Sam's marriage was less than ideal and the love of her life was a man with whom she had an affair many years before. Jennifer, still reeling from the loss of her husband, takes comfort in the letters and develops a friendship with Sam's neighbor Brendan, a man who holds even more tragedy in store for her. The novel quickly hit the best-seller list, firmly establishing Patterson as a successful cross-over genre novelist. As a romance novel, it is "cut from the same sentimental cloth" as its predecessor, wrote a reviewer for *Publishers Weekly,* and is "compulsively readable." Though a contributor to *Kirkus Reviews* called it an "epistolary mushfest," Kristine Huntley of *Booklist* appreciated Patterson's trademark surprise ending, which she found "unexpected, touching, and satisfying."

In *London Bridges,* Patterson features two characters from earlier books in the "nursery rhyme" series. The tenth book in the series has appearances by the eponymous villain from 2003's *The Big Bad Wolf* as well as an earlier Cross enemy known as the Weasel. A reviewer for *Publishers Weekly* wrote, "the book is a model of economy, delivering a full package of suspense, emotion and characterization in a minimum number of words."

Ken Bolton introduced his review of *Lifeguard* for *Library Journal* by writing, "Patterson's latest output . . . is the quintessential summer read." The story follows a lifeguard named Ned Kelly, whose idyllic beach life is suddenly transformed when he accepts a job helping some friends commit an art heist. Shortly thereafter, his co-conspirators, as well as his girlfriend, are all found murdered, and Kelly's name gets added to the F.B.I.'s most wanted list. A reviewer for *Publishers Weekly* concluded, "It's a twisty story that will engage the interest of beach-goers everywhere." The author worked with Howard Roughan to write *Honeymoon,* another crime story, this time featuring F.B.I. agent John O'Hara, who is searching for a serial killer named Nora Sinclair. The plot twists and turns as Sinclair manages to seduce her tracker, which a reviewer for *Publishers Weekly* commented, makes "the narrative . . . nearly impossible to stop reading." The reviewer went on to say that the book contains "two of Patterson's most complex characters yet."

The author wrote in a completely new genre during 2005, producing the science-fiction oriented thriller for children titled *Maximum Ride: The Angel Experiment.* The story involves six children who are part human and part bird. The mutants are on a secret mission to save another child, named Angel, from rogue mutants. A *Library Bookwatch* contributor concluded that while the book is a "departure from Patterson's usual formula . . . it shouldn't be missed."

BIOGRAPHICAL AND CRITICAL SOURCES:

PERIODICALS

Booklist, May 15, 2001, Kristine Huntley, review of *Suzanne's Diary for Nicholas,* p. 1708; October 15, 2001, Huntley, review of *Violets Are Blue,* p. 356; January 1, 2002, Huntley, review of *Second Chance,* p. 777; July, 2004, Huntley, review of *Sam's Letters to Jennifer,* p. 1799.

Kirkus Reviews, December 15, 2001, review of *Second Chance,* p. 1712; June 1, 2004, review of *Sam's Letters to Jennifer,* p. 513.

Library Bookwatch, June, 2005, review of *Maximum Ride: The Angel Experiment.*

Library Journal, October 1, 2000, Rebecca House Stankowski, review of *Roses Are Red,* p. 148; July 2001, Margaret Hanes, review of *Suzanne's Diary for Nicholas,* p. 126; July 1, 2005, Ken Bolton, review of *Lifeguard,* p. 70.

New York Times, July 24, 2001, Janet Maslin, "Love Story, or Is That Death Story?," p. 6; November 29, 2001, Maslin, "Bodies Hang in California, and Bullets Fly in Florida," p. 7.

New York Times Book Review, February 7, 1993, Marilyn Stasio, review of *Along Came a Spider,* p. 19.

People, October 7, 1996, Cynthia Sanz, "Jack and Jill," p. 38.

Publishers Weekly, August 2, 1999, review of *Pop Goes the Weasel,* p. 69; March 20, 2000, review of *Cradle and All,* p. 68; February 18, 2002, review of *Second Chance,* p. 75; March 18, 2002, Daisy Maryles and Dick Donahue, "Don't Get Mad, Get Even," p. 19; June 7, 2004, review of *Sam's Letters to Jennifer,* p. 33; July 12, 2004, Maryles, "A Passionate Patterson," p. 12; November 8, 2004, review of *London Bridges,* p. 37; January 31, 2005, review of *Honeymoon,* p. 50; May 16, 2005, review of *Lifeguard,* p. 35.

Reviewer's Bookwatch, March, 2005, Gary Roen, review of *Third Degree.*

ONLINE

BookPage, http://www.bookpage.com/ (April 2, 2002), Steven Womak, "Stretching the Boundaries of the Thriller" (interview).

* * *

PATTERSON, James B.
See PATTERSON, James

PAYNE, Alan
See JAKES, John

* * *

PAZ, Octavio 1914-1998

PERSONAL: Born March 31, 1914, in Mexico City, Mexico; died of cancer, April 19, 1998, in Mexico City, Mexico; son of Octavio Paz (a lawyer) and Josephina Lozano; married Elena Garro (a writer), mid-1930s (marriage ended, mid-1950s); married Marie José Tramini, 1964; children: one daughter. *Education:* Attended National Autonomous University of Mexico, 1932-37. *Politics:* "Disillusioned leftist." *Religion:* Atheist.

CAREER: Writer. Government of Mexico, Mexican Foreign Service, posted to San Francisco, CA, and New York, NY, secretary at Mexican Embassy in Paris, beginning 1945, charge d'affaires at Mexican Embassy in Japan, beginning 1951, posted to Mexican Secretariat for External Affairs, 1953-58, extraordinary and plenipotentiary minister to Mexican Embassy, 1959-62, ambassador to India, 1962-68. Visiting professor of Spanish-American literature, University of Texas—Austin and University of Pittsburgh, 1968-70; Simon Bolivar Professor of Latin American Studies, 1970, and fellow of Churchill College, Cambridge University, 1970-71; Charles Eliot Norton Professor of Poetry, Harvard University, 1971-72; professor of comparative literature, Harvard University, 1973-80. Regent's fellow at University of California—San Diego.

MEMBER: American Academy and Institute of Arts and Letters (honorary).

AWARDS, HONORS: Guggenheim fellowship, 1944; Grand Prix International de Poesie (Belgium), 1963; Jerusalem Prize, Critics Prize (Spain), and National Prize for Letters (Mexico), all 1977; Grand Aigle d'Or (Nice, France), 1979; Premio Ollin Yoliztli (Mexico), 1980; Miguel de Cervantes Prize (Spain), 1982; Neustadt International Prize for Literature, 1982; Wilhelm Heinse Medal (West Germany), 1984; German Book Trade Peace prize, 1984; T.S. Eliot Award for Creative Writing, Ingersoll Foundation, 1987; Tocqueville Prize, 1989; Nobel Prize for Literature, 1990.

WRITINGS:

POETRY

Luna silvestre (title means "Sylvan Moon"), Fabula (Mexico City, Mexico), 1933.

No pasaran!, Simbad (Mexico City, Mexico), 1936.

Raíz del hombre (title means "Root of Man"; also see below), Simbad (Mexico City, Mexico), 1937.

Bajo tu clara sombra y otros poemas sobre España (title means "Under Your Clear Shadow and Other Poems about Spain"; also see below), Españolas (Valencia, Spain), 1937, revised edition, Tierra Nueva (Valencia, Spain), 1941.

Entre la piedra y la flor (title means "Between the Stone and the Flower"), Nueva Voz (Mexico City, Mexico), 1938, 2nd edition, Asociacion Civica Yucatan (Mexico City, Mexico), 1956.

A la orilla del mundo y Primer dia; Bajo tu clara sombra; Raíz del hombre; Noche de resurrecciones, Ars (Mexico City, Mexico), 1942.

Libertad bajo palabra (title means "Freedom on Parole"), Tezontle (Mexico City, Mexico), 1949.

Aguila o sol? (prose poems), Tezontle (Mexico City, Mexico), 1951, 2nd edition, 1973, translation by Eliot Weinberger published as *Aguila o sol?/Eagle or Sun?* (bilingual edition), October House, 1970, revised translation by Eliot Weinberger published under same title, New Directions (New York, NY), 1976.

Semillas para un himno, Tezontle (Mexico City, Mexico), 1954.

Piedra de sol, Tezontle (Mexico City, Mexico), 1957, translation by Muriel Rukeyser published as *Sun Stone/Piedra de sol* (bilingual edition; also see below), New Directions, 1963, translation by Peter Miller published as *Sun-Stone,* Contact (Toronto, Ontario, Canada), 1963, translation by Donald Gardner published as *Sun Stone,* Cosmos (New York, NY), 1969, translation by Eliot Weinberger published as *Sunstone—Piedra de sol,* New Directions (New York, NY), 1991.

La estación violenta, Fondo de Cultura Economica (Mexico City, Mexico), 1958, reprinted, 1978.

Agua y viento, Ediciones Mito (Bogota, Colombia), 1959.

Libertad bajo palabra: Obra poetica, 1935-1958, Fondo de Cultura Economica (Mexico City, Mexico), 1960, revised edition, 1968.

Salamandra (1958-1961) (also see below), J. Mortiz (Mexico City, Mexico), 1962, 3rd edition, 1975.

Selected Poems of Octavio Paz (bilingual edition), translation by Muriel Rukeyser, Indiana University Press, 1963.

Viento entero, Caxton (Delhi, India), 1965.

Blanco (also see below), J. Mortiz (Mexico City, Mexico), 1967, 2nd edition, 1972, translation by Eliot Weinberger published under same title, The Press (New York, NY), 1974.

Disco visuales (four spatial poems), Era (Mexico City, Mexico), 1968.

Ladera este (1962-1968) (title means "Eastern Slope [1962-1968])"; also see below), J. Mortiz (Mexico City, Mexico), 1969, 3rd edition, 1975.

La centena (Poemas: 1935-1968), Seix Barral (Barcelona, Spain), 1969, 2nd edition, 1972.

Topoemas (six spatial poems), Era (Mexico City, Mexico), 1971.

Vuelta (long poem), El Mendrugo (Mexico City, Mexico), 1971.

Configurations (contains *Piedra de sol/Sun Stone, Blanco,* and selections from *Salamandra* and *Ladera este*), translations by G. Aroul and others, New Directions (New York, NY), 1971.

(With Jacques Roubaud, Edoardo Sanguinetti, and Charles Tomlinson; also author of prologue) *Renga* (collective poem written in French, Italian, English, and Spanish), J. Mortiz (Mexico City, Mexico), 1972, translation by Charles Tomlinson published as *Renga: A Chain of Poems,* Braziller, 1972.

Early Poems: 1935-1955, translations by Muriel Rukeyser and others, New Directions (New York, NY), 1973.

3 Notations/3 Rotations (contains fragments of poems by Paz), Carpenter Center for the Visual Arts, Harvard University, 1974.

Pasado en claro (long poem), Fondo de Cultura Economica (Mexico City, Mexico), 1975, revised edition, 1978, translation included in *A Draft of Shadows and Other Poems* (also see below), New Directions (New York, NY), 1979.

Vuelta, Seix Barral (Barcelona, Spain), 1976.

(With Charles Tomlinson) *Air Born/Hijos del aire* (sonnets written in Spanish and English), Pescador (Mexico City, Mexico), 1979.

Poemas (1935-1975), Seix Barral (Mexico City, Mexico), 1979.

A Draft of Shadows and Other Poems, edited and translated by Eliot Weinberger, with additional translations by Elizabeth Bishop and Mark Strand, New Directions, 1979.

Selected Poems (bilingual edition), translations by Charles Tomlinson and others, Penguin (New York, NY), 1979.

Octavio Paz: Poemas recientes, Institucion Cultural de Cantabria de la Diputacion Provincial de Santander, 1981.

Selected Poems, edited by Eliot Weinberger, translations by G. Aroul and others, New Directions (New York, NY), 1984.

Cuatro chopos/The Four Poplars (bilingual edition), translation by Eliot Weinberger, Center for Edition Works (New York, NY), 1985.

The Collected Poems, 1957-1987: Bilingual Edition, New Editions, 1987.

One Word to the Other, Latitudes Press, 1991.

La Casa de la Presencia: Poesía e Historia, Fondo de Cultura Economica (Mexico City, Mexico), 1994.

A Tale of Two Gardens: Poems from India, 1952-1995, edited and translated by Eliot Weinberger, Harcourt (New York, NY), 1997.

Delta de cinco brazos, Galaxia Gutenberg (Barcelona, Spain), 1998.

PROSE

El laberinto de la soledad (also see below), Cuadernos Americanos, 1950, revised edition, Fondo de Cultura Economica (Mexico City, Mexico), 1959, reprinted, 1980, translation by Lysander Kemp published as *The Labyrinth of Solitude: Life and Thought in Mexico,* Grove (New York, NY), 1961.

El arco y la lira: El poema; La revelacion poetica; Poesía e historia, Fondo de Cultura Economica (Mexico City, Mexico), 1956, 2nd edition includes text of *Los signos en rotación* (also see below), 1967, 3rd edition, 1972, translation by Ruth L.C. Simms published as *The Bow and the Lyre: The Poem, the Poetic Revelation, Poetry and History,* University of Texas Press (Austin, TX), 1973, 2nd edition, McGraw-Hill, 1975.

Las peras del olmo, Universidad Nacional Autonoma de Mexico, 1957, revised edition, Seix Barral (Barcelona, Spain), 1971, 3rd edition, 1978.

Tamayo en la pintura mexicana, Universidad Nacional Autonoma de Mexico, 1959.

Cuadrivio: Darío, López Velarde, Pessoa, Cernuda, J. Mortiz (Mexico City, Mexico), 1965.

Los signos en rotación, Sur (Buenos Aires, Argentina), 1965, expanded as *Los signos en rotación y otros ensayos,* edited and with a prologue by Carlos Fuentes, Alianza (Madrid, Spain), 1971.

Puertas al campo (also see below), Universidad Nacional Autonoma de Mexico (Mexico City, Mexico), 1966.

Claude Lévi-Strauss; o, El nuevo festín de Esopo, J. Mortiz (Mexico City, Mexico), 1967, translation by J.S. Bernstein and Maxine Bernstein published as *Claude Levi-Strauss: An Introduction,* Cornell University Press, 1970, published as *On Levi-Strauss,* J. Cape (London, England), 1970.

Corriente alterna, Siglo Veintiuno Editores (Mexico City, Mexico), 1967, translation by Helen R. Lane published as *Alternating Current,* Viking (New York, NY), 1973.

Marcel Duchamp; o, El castillo de la pureza, Era (Mexico City, Mexico), 1968, translation by Donald Gardner published as *Marcel Duchamp; or, The Castle of Purity,* Grossman, 1970.

Conjunciones y disyunciones, J. Mortiz (Mexico City, Mexico), 1969, 2nd edition, 1978, translation by Helen R. Lane published as *Conjunctions and Disjunctions,* Viking (New York, NY), 1974.

México: La última década, Institute of Latin American Studies, University of Texas Press (Austin, TX), 1969.

Posdata (also see below), Siglo Veintiuno, 1970, translation by Lysander Kemp published as *The Other Mexico: Critique of the Pyramid,* Grove (New York, NY), 1972.

(With Juan Marichal) *Las cosas en su sitio: Sobre la literatura española del siglo XX,* Finisterre (Mexico City, Mexico), 1971.

Traducción: Literatura y literalidad, Tusquets (Barcelona, Spain), 1971.

Aparencia desnuda: La obra de Marcel Duchamp, Era (Mexico City, Mexico), 1973, enlarged edition, 1979, translation by Rachel Phillips and Donald Gardner published as *Marcel Duchamp: Appearance Stripped Bare,* Viking (New York, NY), 1978.

El signo y el garabato (contains *Puertas al campo*), J. Mortiz (Mexico City, Mexico), 1973.

(With Julian Rios) *Solo a dos voces,* Lumen (Barcelona, Spain), 1973.

Teatro de signos/Transparencias, selection and montage by Julian Rios, Fundamentos (Madrid, Spain), 1974.

La busqueda del comienzo: Escritos sobre el surrealismo, Fundamentos (Madrid, Spain), 1974, 2nd edition, 1980.

El mono gramático, Seix Barral (Barcelona, Spain), 1974, translation published as *Le singe grammarien,* Skira (Geneva, Switzerland), 1972, translation by Helen R. Lane published as *The Monkey Grammarian,* Seaver, 1981.

Los hijos del limo: Del romanticismo a la vanguardia, Seix Barral (Barcelona, Spain), 1974, translation by Rachel Phillips published as *Children of the Mire: Modern Poetry from Romanticism to the Avant-Garde,* Harvard University Press (Cambridge, MA), 1974.

The Siren and the Seashell, and Other Essays on Poets and Poetry, translations by Lysander Kemp and Margaret Sayers Peden, University of Texas Press (Austin, TX), 1976.

Villaurrutia en persona y en obra, Fondo de Cultura Economica (Mexico City, Mexico), 1978.

El ogro filantrópico: Historia y política, 1971-1978 (also see below), J. Mortiz (Mexico City, Mexico), 1979.

In/mediaciones, Seix Barral (Barcelona, Spain), 1979.

Mexico en la obra de Octavio Paz, edited by Luis Mario Schneider, Promexa (Mexico City, Mexico), 1979.

El laberinto de la soledad; Posdata; Vuelta a el laberinto de la soledad, Fondo de Cultura Economica (Mexico City, Mexico), 1981.

Sor Juana Inés de la Cruz; o, Las trampas de la fe, Seix Barral (Barcelona, Spain), 1982, reprinted, Fondo de Cultura Economica (Mexico City, Mexico), 1994, translation by Margaret Sayers Peden published as *Sor Juana; or, The Traps of Faith,* Harvard University Press (Cambridge, MA), 1988.

(With Jacques Lassaigne) *Rufino Tamayo,* Ediciones Poligrafia (Barcelona, Spain), 1982, translation by Kenneth Lyons published under same title, Rizzoli (New York, NY), 1982, published as *Rufino Tamayo: Tres Ensayos,* Colegio Nacional (México), 1999.

(With John Golding) *Günther Gerzo* (Spanish, English and French texts), Editions du Griffon (Switzerland), 1983.

Sombras de obras: arte y literatura, Seix Barral (Barcelona, Spain), 1983.

Hombres en su siglo y otros ensayos, Seix Barral (Barcelona, Spain), 1984, translation by Michael Schmidt published as *On Poets and Others,* Seaver Books, 1987.

Tiempo nublado, Seix Barral (Barcelona, Spain), 1984, translation by Helen R. Lane with three additional essays published as *On Earth, Four or Five Worlds: Reflections on Contemporary History,* Harcourt (New York, NY), 1985.

The Labyrinth of Solitude, The Other Mexico, Return to the Labyrinth of Solitude, Mexico and the United States, [and] *The Philanthropic Ogre,* translated by Lysander Kemp, Yara Milos, and Rachel Phillips Belash, Grove (New York, NY), 1985.

Arbol adentro, Seix Barral (Barcelona, Spain), 1987, translation published as *A Tree Within,* New Directions (New York, NY), 1988.

Convergences: Essays on Art and Literature, translation by Helen R. Lane, Harcourt (New York, NY), 1987.

The Other Voice: Essays on Modern Poetry, Harcourt (New York, NY), 1991.

Essays on Mexican Art, Harcourt (New York, NY), 1994.

My Life with the Wave, Lothrop (New York, NY), 1994.

Fundación y Disidencia: Dominio Hispánico, Fondo de Cultura Economica (Mexico City, Mexico), 1994.

Generaciones y Semblanzas: Dominio Mexicano, Fondo de Cultura Economica (Mexico City, Mexico), 1994.

Los Privilegios de la Vista, Fondo de Cultura Economica (Mexico City, Mexico), 1994.

Obras Completas, Fondo de Cultura Economica (Mexico City, Mexico), 1994.

An Erotic Beyond: Sade, Harcourt Brace (New York, NY), 1998.

Itinerary: An Intellectual Journey, translated by Jason Wilson, Harcourt (New York, NY), 1999.

EDITOR

Voces de España, Letras de Mexico (Mexico City, Mexico), 1938.

(With others) *Laurel: Antología de la poesía moderna en lengua española,* Seneca, 1941.

Antologie de la poesie mexicaine, Nagel, 1952, translation by Samuel Beckett published as *Anthology of Mexican Poetry,* Indiana University Press (Bloomington, IN), 1958.

Antología poética, Revista Panoramas (Mexico City, Mexico), 1956.

(And translator, with Eikichi Hayashiya) Matsuo Basho, *Sendas de Oku,* Universidad Nacional Autonoma de Mexico (Mexico City, Mexico), 1957, 2nd edition, Seix Barral (Barcelona, Spain), 1970.

Tamayo en la pintura mexicana, Imprenta Universitaria (Mexico City, Mexico), 1958.

Magia de la risa, Universidad Veracruzana, 1962.

Fernando Pessoa, *Antología,* Universidad Nacional Autonoma de Mexico (Mexico City, Mexico), 1962.

(With Pedro Zekeli) *Cuatro poetas contemporaneos de Suecia: Martinson, Lundkvist, Ekeloef, y Lindegren,* Universidad Nacional Autonoma de Mexico (Mexico City, Mexico), 1963.

(With others and author of prologue) *Poesía en movimiento: Mexico, 1915-1966,* Siglo Veintiuno, 1966, translation edited by Mark Strand and published as *New Poetry of Mexico,* Dutton (New York, NY), 1970.

(With Roger Caillois) *Remedios Varo,* Era (Mexico City, Mexico), 1966.

(And author of prologue) Xavier Villaurrutia, *Antología,* Fondo de Cultura Economica (Mexico City, Mexico), 1980.

Mexico: Splendors of Thirty Centuries, Metropolitan Museum of Art, 1990, translated as *Mexico: Esplendores de treinta siglos,* Friends of the Arts of Mexico, 1991.

TRANSLATOR

(And author of introduction) William Carlos Williams, *Veinte Poemas,* Era (Mexico City, Mexico), 1973.

Versiones y diversiones (translations of poems from English, French, Portuguese, Swedish, Chinese, and Japanese), J. Mortiz (Mexico City, Mexico), 1974, reprinted, Galaxia Gutenberg (Barcelona, Spain), 2000.

Apollinaire, *15 Poemas,* Latitudes (Mexico City, Mexico), 1979.

OTHER

La hija de Rappaccini (one-act play; based on a short story by Nathaniel Hawthorne, first produced in Mexico, 1956), translation by Harry Haskell published as *Rappaccini's Daughter* in *Octavio Paz: Homage to the Poet,* Kosmos (San Francisco, CA), 1980.

(Author of introduction) Carlos Fuentes, *Cuerpos y ofrendas,* Alianza (Madrid, Spain), 1972.

(Author of introduction) *Antonio Peláez: Pintor,* Secretaria de Educacion Publica (Mexico), 1975.

(Author of foreword) *A Sor Juana Anthology,* translation by Alan S. Trueblood, Harvard University Press (Cambridge, MA), 1988.

(Author of introduction) James Laughlin, *Random Stories,* Moyer Bell, 1990.

(Author of introduction) Elena Poniatowska, *Massacre in Mexico,* translation by Helen R. Lane, University of Missouri Press (Columbia, MO), 1991.

In Search of the Present, Harcourt (New York, NY), 1991.

Al pasò, Seix Barral (Barcelona, Spain), 1992.

La llama doble: amor y erotisma, Seix Barral (Barcelona, Spain), 1993, translation by Helen R. Lane published as *The Double Flame: Love and Eroticism,* Harcourt (New York, NY), 1995.

(Author of essay) *Nostalgia for Death / Hieroglyphs of Desire: A Critical Study of Villaurrutia,* edited by Eliot Weinberger, Copper Canyon Press (Port Townsend, WA), 1993.

Excursiones/Incursiones: Dominio extranjero, Fondo de Cultura Economica (Mexico City, Mexico), 1994.

Vislumbres de la India, Seix Barral (Barcelona, Spain), 1995, translated by Eliot Weinberger as *In Light of India,* Harcourt Brace (New York, NY), 1997.

Eyes for Consuela, Dramatists Play Service (New York, NY), 1999.

(With others) *Ritual Arts of the New World: Pre-Columbian America,* Abbeville Press (New York, NY), 2000.

El camino de la Pasión, López Velarde, Seix Barral (Mexico), 2001.

Sueño en Libertatd: Escritos políticos, Planeta (Mexico), 2001.

Figures & Figurations, New Directions (New York, NY), 2002.

Octavio Paz: Lettres posthumes à Octavio Pax depuis quelques arcanes majeurs du Tarot, J.M. Place (Paris, France), 2002.

Contributor to *In Praise of Hands: Contemporary Crafts of the World,* New York Graphic Society, 1974; *Avances,* Fundamentos, 1978; *Democracy and Dictatorship in Latin America: A Special Publication Devoted Entirely to the Voices and Opinions of Writers from Latin America,* Foundation for the Independent Study of Social Ideas, 1982; *Instante y revelación,* Fondo Nacional para Actividades Sociales, 1982; *Frustraciones de un destino: La democracia en America Latina,* Libro Libre, 1985; and *Nineteen Ways of Looking at Wang Wei: How a Chinese Poem Is Translated,* edited by Eliot Weinberger, Moyer Bell, 1987. Contributor to numerous anthologies. Founder of literary review, *Barandal,* 1931; member of editorial board and columnist, *El Popular,* late 1930s; cofounder of *Taller,* 1938; cofounder and editor, *El Hijo Prodigo,* 1943-46; editor of *Plural,* 1971-75; founder and editor, *Vuelta,* 1976-98.

SIDELIGHTS: Often nominated for the Nobel Prize in his lifetime, Mexican author Octavio Paz enjoyed a worldwide reputation as a master poet and essayist. Although Mexico figures prominently in Paz's work—one of his best-known books, *The Labyrinth of Solitude,* for example, is a comprehensive portrait of Mexican society—*Los Angeles Times* contributor Jascha Kessler called Paz "truly international." *World Literature Today*'s Manuel Duran felt that Paz's "exploration of Mexican existential values permit[ted] him to open a door to an understanding of other countries and other cultures" and thus appeal to readers of diverse backgrounds. "What began as a slow, almost microscopic examination of self and of a single cultural tradition widens unexpectedly," Duran continued, "becoming universal without sacrificing its unique characteristic." Paz won the Nobel Prize in 1990, and died eight years later at the age of 84. His passing was mourned as the end of an era for Mexico. According to his obituary in *Americas,* "Paz's literary career helped to define modern poetry and the Mexican personality."

Paz was born in 1914 near Mexico City, into a prominent family with ties to Mexico's political, cultural, and military elite. His father served as assistant to Emiliano Zapata, the leader of a popular revolution in 1911. Many Zapatistas were forced into exile when their leader was slain a few years later, and the Paz family relocated to Los Angeles, California, for a time. Back in Mexico City, the family's economic situation declined, but as a teen, Paz found increasing success for his poems and short stories in local publications. His first volume of poetry, *Luna silvestre,* appeared in 1933. While attending law school, however, Paz found himself drawn to leftist politics. When he sent some of his work to famed Chilean poet Pablo Neruda, the senior writer gave it a favorable review and encouraged Paz to attend a congress of leftist-thinking writers in Spain.

In Spain Paz was drawn into the raging Civil War and joined a brigade fighting the armies of fascist dictator Francisco Franco. He returned to Mexico with a mission to popularize the Spanish Republican cause, and spent time in both Berkeley, California, and New York City over the next few years as a graduate student, journalist, and translator. In 1946 he was offered a post as Mexico's cultural attaché to France, and served in his country's diplomatic corps for the next two decades. The work left him enough time to write prodigiously, and during the course of his career he published dozens of volumes of poetry and prose.

One of Paz's best-known works is *El laberinto de la soledad,* which appeared first in 1950 and in English translation as *The Labyrinth of Solitude: Life and Thought in Mexico* eleven years later. "In it Paz argues that Mexicans see themselves as children of the conquering Spanish father who abandoned his offspring and the treacherous Indian mother who turned against her own people," explained an *Americas* essayist. "Because of the wounds that Mexicans suffer as a result of their dual cultural heritage, they have developed a defensive stance, hiding behind masks and taking refuge in a 'labyrinth of solitude.'" The volume became standard reading for students of Latin American history and literature.

One aspect of Paz's work often mentioned by critics is his tendency to maintain elements of prose—most commonly philosophical thought—in his poetry, and poetic elements in his prose. Perhaps the best example to support this claim can be found in Paz's exploration of India, titled *The Monkey Grammarian,* a work which *New York Times Book Review* contributor Keith Botsford called "exceedingly curious" and described as "an extended meditation on the nature of language." In separate *World Literature Today* essays, critics Jaime Alazraki and José Miguel Oviedo discussed the difficulty they would have assigning the book to a literary genre. "It is apparent," Alazraki noted, "that *The Monkey Grammarian* is not an essay. It is also apparent that it is not a poem, at least not in the conventional sense. It is both an essay and a poem, or perhaps neither." Oviedo similarly stated that the book "does not belong to any specific genre—although it has a bit of all of them—because it is deliberately written at the edge of genres."

According to Oviedo, *The Monkey Grammarian* is the product of Paz's long-stated quest "to produce a text which would be an intersection of poetry, narrative and essay." The fusion of opposites found in this work is an important element in nearly all Paz's literary production. In many instances both the work's structure and its content represent a blending of contradictory forces: *Renga,* for example, is written in four languages, while *Air Born/Hijos del aire,* is written in two. According to *World Literature Today* contributor Frances Chiles, Paz strived to create in his writing "a sense of community or communion" which he found lacking in contemporary society. In his Neustadt Prize acceptance speech reprinted in *World Literature Today,* Paz attempted to explain his emphasis on contrasting thoughts: "Plurality is Universality, and Universality is the acknowledging of the admirable diversity of man and his works. . . . To acknowledge the variety of visions and sensibilities is to preserve the richness of life and thus to ensure its continuity."

Through juxtaposition of contrasting thoughts or objects Paz created a more harmonious world, one based on the complementary association of opposites found in the Eastern concept of yin and yang. This aspect of his thinking revealed the influence of his six-year stay in India as Mexican ambassador to that country. Grace Schulman explained Paz's proclivity for Eastern philosophy in a *Hudson Review* essay: "Although he had embraced contraries from the beginning of his writing career . . . [Paz] found in Tantric thought and in Hindu religious life dualities that enforced his conviction that history turns on reciprocal rhythms. In *Alternating Current,* he writes that the Hindu gods, creators or destroyers according to their names and region, manifest contradiction. 'Duality,' he says, 'a basic feature of Tantrism, permeates all Hindu religious life: male and female, pure and impure, left and right. . . . In Eastern thought, these opposites can co-exist; in Western philosophy, they disappear for the worst reasons: far from being resolved into a higher synthesis, they cancel each other out.'"

Critics have pointed to several repeated contrasting images that dramatically capture the essence of Paz's work. Ronald Christ, for example, commented in his *Nation* review of *Aguila o sol?/Eagle or Sun?* (the Spanish portion of which is the equivalent of the English expression "heads or tails?"): "The dual image of the Mexican coin which gives *Eagle or Sun?* its title epitomizes Paz's technique and credo, for we see that there is no question of eagle *or* sun, rather of eagle *and* sun which together in their oppositeness are the same coin." Another of the poet's images which reviewers frequently have mentioned is "burnt water," an ancient Mexican concept which appears in Paz's work in both Spanish and in the Aztec original, "atl tlachinolli." Schulman maintained that "burnt water" is "the dominant image of [Paz's] poetry" and found that the image fulfills a role similar to that of the two sides of the coin in *Eagle and Sun?* She noted: "Paz sees the world burning, and knows with visionary clarity that opposites are resolved in a place beyond contraries, in a moment of pure vision: in that place, there are no frontiers between men and women, life and death." Chiles called the Aztec combination of fire and water "particularly apt in its multiple connotations as a symbol of the union of all warring contraries."

In *Sor Juana; or, The Traps of Faith,* Paz examined the literary achievement of Sor Juana Inés de la Cruz, a seventeenth-century New Spain nun and poetess who produced masterful verse from a convent in Mexico City. *New York Times Book Review* contributor Frederick Luciani wrote, "Her extant works . . . are of such abundance and variety, in such a range of styles, voices and manners, as to be simultaneously seductive and bewildering. With characteristic lucidity, Mr. Paz sorts through this textual morass and arrives at an admiring and sympathetic portrait, but an honest and demythologizing one, too." To understand his subject, Paz addressed the complex and turbulent civilization of colonial Mexico. "It is, after all," according to Jonathan Keates in the London *Observer,* "not only the nun's tale but that of Mexico itself, the kingdom of New Spain, its imposed framework of ideal constructs eroded by mutual resentment between governors and governed and by a chronic fear of change." According to Electa Arenal in *Criticism,* "*Sor Juana; or, The Traps of Faith* is a tour de force—biography, cultural history and ideological criticism all in one. It describes the intellectual, political and religious climate of sixteenth-and seventeenth-century Mexico; comments on the poet as rebel against orthodoxy, then and now; and studies the life, times, and art of a woman with whom Paz identifies and to whom he implicitly compares himself."

With *La llama doble: Amor y erotisma,* translated as *The Double Flame,* Paz provided a social and literary history of love and eroticism, comparing modern manifestations to those of earlier ages, while noting the special relationship between eroticism and poetry. "This book is a product of immense wisdom and patient observation, an approach to passion from the vantage of maturity," wrote Ilan Stavans in the *Washington Post Book World.* "His ultimate thesis is that our society is plagued by erotic permissiveness, placing the stability and continuity of love in jeopardy, and that the difficult encounter between two humans attracted to each other, has lost importance, a development that he believes threatens our psychological and cultural foundations." According to Paz, "Both love and eroticism—the double flame—are fed by the original fire: sexuality."

In *The Other Voice: Essays on Modern Poetry,* Paz offered a critique of twentieth-century poetry, including an analysis of the Romantics and Symbolists and a forceful objection to postmodernism and consumerism. Though noting Paz's conservative New Critic perspective, Raymond Leslie Williams wrote in *American Book Review,* "The breadth of Paz's literary repertoire in this volume, as in all his writing, is impressive. His understanding of Pound, Eliot, Apollinaire, and many other modern poets is vast." Paz emphasized the unifying power of poetry and asserted the importance of a public audience. "The volume's prevailing theme," wrote Ilan Stavans in a *Nation* review, is "poetry as a nonconformist, rebellious force of the modern age." Stavans observed, "Paz argues that while poets are elitists by nature, despite the tiny circulation of their craft it has a profound impact on society." For Paz, as John Butt wrote in the *Times Literary Supplement,* "the poem aspires to be all-encompassing, an image of what a unified theory of life might be, 'a miniature, animated cosmos' which 'unites the ten thousand things' that swirl around us."

Critics have agreed that Paz's great theme of a blended reality situated his work in the forefront of modern literature. As Christ noted: "By contraries then, by polarities and divergences converging in a rhetoric of opposites, Paz established himself as a brilliant stylist balancing the tension of East and West, art and criticism, the many and the one in the figures of his writing. Paz is thus not only a great writer: he is also an indispensable corrective to our cultural tradition and a critic in the highest sense in which he himself uses the word." Enrique Fernandez similarly saw Octavio Paz as a writer of enormous influence. "Not only has he left his mark on world poetry, with a multilingual cortege of acolytes," Fernandez wrote in a *Village Voice* essay, "he is a force to be reckoned with by anyone who chooses that modernist *imitaio Christi,* the Life of the Mind."

Paz ended his diplomatic career in protest in 1968 over Mexico's suppression of student demonstrations in his hometown. The Asian subcontinent, however, continued to hold sway over him creatively. In 1997 his collection *A Tale of Two Gardens: Poems from India, 1952-1995* appeared. A review from Barbara Mujica in *Americas* described the poet as "obsessed with India. Although many American and European writers have been fascinated with the subcontinent, none has studied its culture with the intensity and thoroughness of Paz." Some of the poems in the collection were written in a short Sanskrit form called kayva; the form was also used for some verse that appeared in Paz's prose memoir, *In Light of India,* also published in 1997. As Mujica noted, "In the kavya, Paz evokes exquisite and fleeting erotic images—a young bather emerging from the river, silks slipping off bodies and fluttering in the breeze. . . . These verses are tiny treasures—delicate, suggestive, and profound."

Paz was an active critic of politics for nearly all of his career. Unlike some other leftist Latin-American writers—Gabriel García Marquez, for example—Paz was not a supporter of Communist Cuban leader Fidel Castro. He also criticized Nicaragua's Sandinista guerrilla movement; Mexican demonstrations of solidarity with the Sandinista movement sometimes included the burning of an effigy of Paz. Nor was he a champion of the Zapatista uprising that fomented in a mountainous Mexican state in 1994. The writer, in both his writings and public utterances, defended his views ardently. "Revolution begins as a promise," Paz wrote, according to the *New Republic,* "is squandered in violent agitation, and freezes into bloody dictatorships that are the negation of the fiery impulse that brought it into being. In all revolutionary movements, the sacred time of myth is transformed inexorably into the profane time of history."

Paz died in April of 1998, after suffering from cancer of the spine. His death was announced by no less than the president of Mexico, Ernesto Zedillo. "This is an irreplaceable loss for contemporary thought and culture—not just for Latin America but for the entire world," Notimex, the government news agency, quoted Zedillo as saying. Gabriel Zaid, who cofounded the literary journal *Vuelta* with Paz, recalled the writer's last public appearance, in December of 1997, in a piece for *Time International.* "The day was overcast and gray," Zaid wrote. "Octavio spoke of the sun, of gratitude and of grace. And the sun, as if engaged in conversation, peered down on him through the clouds."

BIOGRAPHICAL AND CRITICAL SOURCES:

BOOKS

Contemporary Literature Criticism, Thomson Gale (Detroit, MI), Volume 3, 1975, Volume 4, 1975, Vol-

ume 6, 1976, Volume 10, 1979, Volume 19, 1981, Volume 51, 1989, Volume 65, 1989.
Encyclopedia of World Biography, second edition, Thomson Gale (Detroit, MI), 1998.
Hispanic Literature Criticism, Thomson Gale (Detroit, MI), 1989.
Ivask, Ivar, *The Perpetual Present: The Poetry and Prose of Octavio Paz,* University of Oklahoma Press, 1973.
Poetry Criticism, Thomson Gale (Detroit, MI), Volume 1, 1989.
Roman, Joseph, *Octavio Paz,* Chelsea House, 1994.
Wilson, Jason, *Octavio Paz,* Twayne, 1986.

PERIODICALS

American Book Review, August-September, 1992, p. 3.
Americas, August, 1998, Barbara Mujica, review of "A Tale of Two Gardens," p. 60.
Booklist, November 15, 1991, p. 595.
Commonweal, January 27, 1989, p. 50.
Comparative Literature, fall, 1989, p. 397.
Criticism, Volume XXXI, number 4, p. 463.
Hudson Review, autumn, 1974.
Interview, October, 1989.
Journal of Youth Services in Libraries, summer, 1990, p. 311.
Kirkus Reviews, January 1, 1995, p. 62.
Library Journal, January, 1995, p. 79.
London Review of Books, May 18, 1989, p. 20.
Los Angeles Times, November 28, 1971.
Los Angeles Times Book Review, September 18, 1988, p. 3; April 30, 1995, p. 6.
Nation, August 2, 1975; February 17, 1992, p. 205.
New Republic, October 9, 1995, p. 40.
New Yorker, May 15, 1995, p. 93.
New York Times Book Review, December 27, 1981; December 25, 1988, p. 12; April 19, 1998, Laura Jamison, review of *An Erotic Beyond;* June 7, 1998, Edward Hirsch, "Octavio Paz: In Defense of Poetry."
Observer (London, England), January 15, 1989, p. 49.
Publishers Weekly, January 16, 1995, p. 444.
Small Press, winter, 1994, p. 89.
Times (London, England), June 8, 1989.
Times Literary Supplement, December 30, 1988-January 5, 1989, p. 1435; July 24, 1992, p. 6; August 2, 1996, p. 7.
Tribune Books (Chicago, IL), September 11, 1988, p. 24.
Village Voice, March 19, 1985.
Washington Post Book World, July 23, 1995, p. 11.
World Literature Today, autumn, 1982; autumn, 1994, p. 795; winter, 1995, p. 111.

OBITUARIES:

PERIODICALS

Americas, August, 1998, "Octavio Paz," p. 62.
Chicago Tribune, April 21, 1998, sec. 1, p. 1.
Los Angeles Times, April 20, 1998, p. A18; April 21, 1998, p. A1.
New Republic, May 11, 1998, "A Poet Passes," p. 10.
New York Times, April 21, 1998, p. A1.
Time, May 4, 1998, "Died. Octavio Paz," p. 27.
Time International, May 4, 1998, "Global Conversationalist Octavio Paz: 1914-1998," p. 52.
Washington Post, April 21, 1998, p. B6.

* * *

PERETTI, Frank E. 1951-

PERSONAL: Born January 13, 1951, in Lethbridge, Alberta, Canada; son of Gene E. (a minister) and Joyce E. (a homemaker; maiden name, Schneider) Peretti; married Barbara Jean Ammon (a homemaker), June 24, 1972. *Education:* Attended University of California—Los Angeles, 1976-78. *Politics:* Conservative. *Religion:* Christian. *Hobbies and other interests:* Carpentry, sculpturing, bicycling, hiking, music, aviation.

ADDRESSES: Home—ID. *Agent*—c/o Blanton/Harrell, Inc., 2910 Poston Ave., Nashville, TN 37203.

CAREER: Licensed minister; associate pastor of community church in Washington state, 1978-84; K-2 Ski Factory, Washington state, production worker (ski maker), 1985-88; writer and public speaker, 1986—. Has worked as a musician and storyteller.

AWARDS, HONORS: Gold Medallion Award, Evangelical Christian Publishers Association, and Readers' and Editors' Choice awards, *Christianity Today,* all for *Piercing the Darkness.*

WRITINGS:

"COOPER KIDS ADVENTURES" SERIES

The Door in the Dragon's Throat, Crossway (Westchester, IL), 1986.

Escape from the Island of Aquarius, Crossway (Westchester, IL), 1986.
The Tombs of Anak, Crossway (Westchester, IL), 1987.
Trapped at the Bottom of the Sea, Crossway (Westchester, IL), 1988.
The Secret of the Desert Stone, Word Publications (Nashville, TN), 1996.
The Legend of Annie Murphy, Word Publications (Nashville, TN), 1997.
The Deadly Curse of Toco-Rey, Word Publications (Nashville, TN), 1996.
Flying Blind, Tommy Nelson (Nashville, TN), 1997.

THE VERITAS PROJECT

Hangman's Curse, Tommy Nelson (Nashville, TN), 2001.
Nightmare Academy, Tommy Nelson (Nashville, TN), 2002.

OTHER

This Present Darkness (novel), Crossway (Westchester, IL), 1986.
Tilly (novel; based on his radio play), Crossway (Westchester, IL), 1988.
Piercing the Darkness (also see below), Crossway Books (Westchester, IL), 1989.
All Is Well, illustrated by Robert Sauber, Word (Dallas, TX), 1991.
Prophet, Crossway Books (Westchester, IL), 1992.
The Oath, Word Publications (Nashville, TN), 1995.
The Visitation, Word Publications (Nashville, TN), 1999.
This Present Darkness and *Piercing the Darkness,* Crossway Books (Westchester, IL), 2000.
The Wounded Spirit (memoir), Word Publications (Nashville, TN), 2000.
No More Victims, Word Publications (Nashville, TN), 2001.
(Reteller, with Sharon Lamson, Cheryl McKay, and Bill Ross) *Wild & Wacky Totally True Bible Stories: All About Obedience,* Tommy Nelson (Nashville, TN), 2002.
(Reteller, with Bill Ross) *Wild & Wacky Totally True Bible Stories: All About Faith,* Tommy Nelson (Nashville, TN), 2002.
(Reteller, with Bill Ross) *Wild & Wacky Totally True Bible Stories: All About Courage,* Tommy Nelson (Nashville, TN), 2002.
(Reteller, with Bill Ross) *Wild & Wacky Totally True Bible Stories: All About Helping Others,* Tommy Nelson (Nashville, TN), 2002.
No More Bullies: For Those Who Wound or Are Wounded, Word Publications (Nashville, TN), 2003.

Author of the radio drama *Tilly.* The *Wild & Wacky Totally True Bible Stories* series has been produced on videocassette and DVD. Contributor to Christian periodicals.

SIDELIGHTS: Frank E. Peretti is a bestselling author of Christian fiction, with over nine million copies of his books sold. "Mr. Peretti's publisher acclaims him the successor to C.S. Lewis; the *Darkness* novels have sold millions. Yet the author's name is virtually unknown outside the Christian community," wrote Jared Lobdell in the *National Review.* Writing in *Christianity Today,* Michael G. Maudlin called Peretti the "great fundamentalist novelist, the father of the blockbuster Christian fiction."

Hailed in *Time* and *Newsweek* as the creator of the crossover Christian thriller, Peretti is the son of a minister and an ordained minister himself, and writes evangelical stories that celebrate the divine power of God and prayer. In his writing, inspired by conservative Christian theology, angels vanquish demons and good always prevails over evil. "The battle against the demonic has always been Peretti's principal theme," wrote Etta Wilson in *BookPage.* With novels such as *This Present Darkness, Piercing the Darkness, Prophet, The Oath,* and *The Visitation,* Peretti almost single-handedly created the genre of Christian thrillers for adult readers. His books for young readers, including the titles in the "Cooper Kids Adventure" series and the "Veritas Project" series have done the same for middle-grade and young adult readers.

Born in 1951, in Canada, Peretti had, as Jeremy Lott noted in *Christianity Today,* "a hellish childhood." A glandular birth defect known as cystic hygroma led to infected and swollen lymph nodes in his neck as a baby, a condition that caused a baseball-sized lump on his throat. When his father's Pentecostal ministry led the family from Canada to Seattle, Washington, the infant Peretti had the first of seven operations. However, once the cyst was removed, his tongue became affected, swelling and elongating, turning black, and oozing blood. "I was having trouble eating—imagine trying to swallow, even to chew, without the help of your tongue," Peretti told Lott. More operations followed, but the child's tongue—affected by toxins sent by the lymph glands—continued to protrude from his mouth, making speaking another trying event in his life. Even the faith healer Oral Roberts could do nothing for the symptoms the child showed.

When Peretti was at home, people did not stare or torment him for his differences. At school, however, he was embarrassed not only by his long, black tongue, but also by his diminutive size. As he told Jana Riess in *Publishers Weekly,* he looked like a "small, frail freak" as a kid. He began to retreat from public life of any sort, feeling safe only at home with his loving parents and siblings, and tucked away in his room with comic books, trading cards, and an active imagination that created stories starring various movie monsters. As Peretti noted in his memoir, *The Wounded Spirit,* "I think part of me wanted to be one, at least a monster who wins. I wouldn't have minded being Frankenstein. At least monsters could do something about their pain." He began to write monster stories, and he and his brother even built their own monsters, one of them called Xenarthex.

Peretti's condition slowly improved, aided in part by a speech therapist who trained Peretti at age twelve to be able to talk with his tongue inside his mouth. His Christian background also helped him through these difficult years, as he has commented. By the time he was in high school in Seattle, his storytelling skills had attracted a group of neighborhood kids. After graduating, he began playing banjo with a local bluegrass group. Married in 1972, he left the band and started a Christian music ministry, then studied English and film at UCLA for a time before he assisted in pastoring a small Assembly of God church on Vashon Island, Washington, with his father.

Peretti gave up the ministry in 1983, however, working in a ski factory, and began writing short stories and his first adult novel, *This Present Darkness.* Once the novel was finished, Peretti tried unsuccessfully to get his manuscript published with mainstream publishers. Finally Crossway Books, a Christian publishing house in Illinois, bought the book. *This Present Darkness* features protagonist Pastor Hank Busche and his heroic efforts to save a small college town from the Legions of Hell. The demons, in the guise of the Universal Consciousness Society, conspire to purchase the college and then subjugate humankind with the help of a Satanist professor, a New Age minister, a corrupt multinational corporation, and a police chief. Pastor Busche is aided in his efforts by a skeptical reporter who begins to see that this nefarious plot means to subjugate not only the townspeople, but the entire human race. The conspiracy is dramatically defeated when Pastor Busche summons an army of angels to repel the demons.

Published in 1986, this debut novel sold poorly for a year, suffering from poor distribution and a lack of promotion. Then the Christian singer Amy Grant began to praise the book to her audience, and word of mouth picked up. By 1988, the novel was selling 40,000 copies a month and Peretti was deep into a sequel, *The Piercing Darkness.* Peretti had a succession of blockbuster novels thereafter, including *Prophet, The Oath,* and *The Visitation.*

Peretti's first nonfiction book, *The Wounded Spirit,* was inspired by the 1999 shootings at Columbine High School that left thirteen people dead. Peretti explores the causes of youth violence and suggests some possible solutions by relating experiences from his own childhood and young adult years. In the book he details his painful youth and the cystic hygroma which caused him to be branded as an outsider, suffering the jibes and taunts of fellow students. Peretti compares this to the condition of Eric Harris and Dylan Klebold, the perpetrators of the Columbine tragedy, who had been teased and ostracized for their differences. It was a high school gym teacher who finally came to Peretti's aid, merely by being someone with whom a troubled young man could speak about his problems. Peretti urges those who hurt others to be kinder and more aware of the effects of their actions. He also encourages those who are injured by the pettiness and insensitivity of others to speak out about their pain, rather than letting resentments build. Reviewing *The Wounded Spirit* in *Publishers Weekly,* a critic stated: "This book is full of painful stories, but also memorable moments of hope, as Peretti recounts instances when a peer or a teacher stood up for him. This remarkable memoir will inspire readers to undertake similar acts of courageous compassion."

Peretti has also written a number of books specifically for young readers. In 1990, he created the first in a series of exotic adventure stories featuring Christian archaeologist Dr. Jake Cooper and his children, Jay and Lila. The first, *The Door in the Dragon's Throat,* involves a treasure hunt in the Middle East, while the second, *Escape from the Island of Aquarius,* tells of a manhunt for a missionary missing amongst a satanic cult in the South Pacific. In eight books, Peretti takes readers into cave tombs with a mysterious religion, and even into a battle between Soviet and CIA agents. In *The Secret of the Desert Stone,* the children and their father investigate a bizarre two-mile-high stone that appears overnight in Togwana. *The Deadly Curse of Toco-Rey* finds the trio in the jungles of Central America fighting the eponymous curse. *The Legend of Annie Murphy* has them dealing with a hundred-year-old ghost. And in *Flying Blind,* the importance of faith is emphasized when Jay must try to land his uncle's Cessna after suffering a head injury that has left him temporarily blind.

In "The Veritas Project" series, inaugurated in 2000 with *Hangman's Curse,* Peretti has developed books targeted at both teens and "tweens." Again using a family as the center of action, the author posits a secret government project, the Veritas Project, which is meant to aid the FBI in breaking drug rings and solving other crimes. *School Library Journal*'s Elaine Fort Weischedel called the series an "evangelical Christian X-Files." Featured in each title are Nate and Sarah Springfield, and their twin children, Elijah and Elisha. In the debut title in the series, *Hangman's Curse,* the family goes undercover in a small town high school to try and solve a baffling crime. A mysterious curse has struck several of the football players, leaving them raving and crazed, tied to their hospital beds. In their delirium, they all mutter the name Abel Frye. Elijah and Elisha befriend many of the kids at school in an attempt to get the bottom of this Abel Frye mystery. Soon it becomes clear that the deadly madness is connected to a spider breeding in the walls of the school, and Elisha is put into mortal danger.

Weischedel felt that Peretti "develops the plot nicely," and that the religiosity of the Springfield family "does not interrupt the flow of the story, nor does anyone get preachy." Weischedel concluded, "Young teens should enjoy this fast-paced and atmospheric novel." A contributor for *Publishers Weekly* similarly praised *Hangman's Curse,* noting that Peretti's "comfortably paced, compelling performance consistently draws readers along." The same reviewer concluded, "Peretti has an obvious knack . . . for emphasizing his beliefs without preaching."

Peretti returns to the "Veritas Project" with the 2002 title, *Nightmare Academy,* in which the project team has a new assignment—to find out what really happened to two runaways. The Springfield twins go undercover again, posing as runaways themselves, ending up in an academy where there is no such thing as absolute truth.

Peretti has also coauthored, with Bill Ross, a series of books about the Bible, "Wild & Wacky Bible Stories," humorous retellings of stories that deal with themes including courage, helping others, obedience, and faith. A character named Mr. Henry relates the experiences of various biblical figures as they pertain to the topic at hand and how they connect to today's world. The books have also been adapted for videocassette and DVD, with Peretti himself playing the "absent-minded professor-type host," according to Kirsten Martindale in *School Library Journal.* Martindale further noted that the series "embraces biblical philosophy and religious values" and will have viewers "smiling their way through some traditionally serious subjects."

Commenting on the appeal of Peretti's novels, Lobdell wrote, "Whatever their genre may be, it is not 'fantasy.' . . . Still, Mr. Peretti deserves his sales, and many readers will get exactly what they want from his books."

BIOGRAPHICAL AND CRITICAL SOURCES:

BOOKS

Peretti, Frank E., *The Wounded Spirit* (memoir), Word Publications (Nashville, TN), 2000.

PERIODICALS

Booklist, September 1, 1995, John Mort, review of *The Oath,* p. 6; June, 1999, John Mort, review of *The Visitation,* p. 1743.

Bookstore Journal, January, 1988, p. 163.

Christianity Today, April 29, 1996, Michael G. Maudlin, review of *The Oath,* p. 24; August 9, 1999, Susan Wise Bauer, review of *The Visitation,* p. 70; March 4, 2001, Jeremy Lott, review of *The Wounded Spirit,* p. 99.

Dallas Morning News, December 2, 2000, Berta Delgado, "Author Tells All to Help Heal Others," p. 1G.

Harper's, September, 1996, Vince Passaro, review of *The Oath,* pp. 64-70.

Journal of Popular Culture, winter, 1994, Jay R. Howard, "Vilifying the Enemy: The Christian Right and the Novels of Frank Peretti," pp. 193-206.

Library Journal, August, 1989, p. 165; October 15, 1989, p. 50; November 1, 1991, p. 68; September 1, 1995, p. 158.

Nation, February 19, 1996, Donna Minkowitz, review of *The Oath,* pp. 25-28.

National Review, August 20, 1990, Jared Lobdell, review of *This Present Darkness,* pp. 45-47.

People, June 18, 1990, Andrew Abrahams, "Moved by the Spirit of the Lord, Frank Peretti Writes Theological Thrillers That Sell to Heaven," pp. 62-63.

Publishers Weekly, May 15, 1995, p. 15; August 17, 1998, Carol Chapman Stertzer, "Frank Peretti," p. S28; July 31, 2000, Marcia Nelson, "Post-Columbine Reflections," p. 44; October 30, 2000, review of *The Wounded Spirit,* p. 68, Jana Riess, "PW Talks with Frank Peretti," p. 69; May 14, 2001, review of *Hangman's Curse,* p. 40.

School Library Journal, February, 1986, p. 89; May, 1986, p. 96; July, 2001, Elaine Fort Weischedel, review of *Hangman's Curse,* p. 112; Kirsten Martindale, review of *Mr. Henry's Wild & Wacky World* (videocassettes), p. 64.

Seattle Times, September 1, 1999, Sally Macdonald, "'Christian Thrillers' Convert Readers," p. B1; June, 2002.

Time, November 13, 1995, Martha Duffy, review of *The Oath,* p. 105.

Voice Literary Supplement, July, 1990, p. 15.

ONLINE

BookPage, http://www.bookpage.com/ (January 6, 2001), Etta Wilson, "Maturity Marks Frank Peretti's *The Visitation.*"

Frank Peretti Home Page, http://thewoundedspirit.com/ (June 11, 2002).

Steeling the Mind of America, http://www.steelingthemind.com/ (January 6, 2001), "Steeling Speaker, Frank Peretti Page."

* * *

PETROSKI, Henry 1942-

PERSONAL: Born February 6, 1942, in New York, NY; son of Henry Frank (a trucking company clerk) and Victoria (Rose) Petroski; married July 15, 1966; wife's name Catherine (a writer); children: Karen, Stephen. *Education:* Manhattan College, B.M.E, 1963; University of Illinois, M.S., 1964, Ph.D., 1968.

ADDRESSES: Office—Department of Civil and Environmental Engineering, P.O. Box 90287, Duke University, Durham, NC 27708-0287.

CAREER: University of Texas, Austin, assistant professor of engineering mechanics, 1968-74; Argonne National Laboratory, IL, began as mechanical engineer and failure analyst, became group leader, 1975-80; Duke University, Durham, NC, began as associate professor, 1980, director of graduate studies, 1981-86, professor of civil and environmental engineering, 1987-93, Aleksandar S. Vesic Professor of Civil Engineering and chair, department of civil and environmental engineering, 1992—, professor of history, 1995—, chair, 1991-2000.

MEMBER: Institution of Engineers of Ireland, National Academy of Engineering, American Society for Engineering Education, American Society of Mechanical Engineers, American Society of Civil Engineers, American Academy of Mechanics, Society for National Philosophy, Society for the History of Technology.

AWARDS, HONORS: National Science Foundation grant, 1973-75, 1982-84, 1989-95; Illinois Arts Council Literary Award, 1976; National Endowment for the Humanities fellow, 1987-88; National Humanities Center fellow; Guggenheim fellow, 1990-91; Ralph Coats Roe Medal, American Society of Mechanical Engineers, 1991; Civil Engineering History and Heritage Award, American Society of Civil Engineers, 1993; Clarkson University, honorary doctor of science, 1990; distinguished alumnus award, Manhattan College, 1992, and University of Illinois, 1994; honorary doctor of humane letters degree, Trinity College, 1997; honorary doctor of science degree, Valparaiso University, 1999.

WRITINGS:

To Engineer Is Human: The Role of Failure in Successful Design, St. Martin's Press (New York, NY), 1985.

Beyond Engineering: Essays and Other Attempts to Figure without Equations, illustrations by Karen Petroski, St. Martin's Press (New York, NY), 1986.

The Pencil: A History of Design and Circumstance, Knopf (New York, NY), 1990.

The Evolution of Useful Things, Knopf (New York, NY), 1992.

Design Paradigms: Case Histories of Error and Judgment in Engineering, Cambridge University Press (New York, NY), 1994.

Engineers of Dreams: Great Bridge Builders and the Spanning of America, Knopf (New York, NY), 1995.

Invention by Design: How Engineers Get from Thought to Thing, Harvard University Press (Cambridge, MA), 1996.

Remaking the World: Adventures in Engineering, Knopf (New York, NY), 1997.

The Book on the Bookshelf, Knopf (New York, NY), 1999.

Paperboy: Confessions of a Future Engineer, Knopf (New York, NY), 2002.

Small Things Considered: Why There Is No Perfect Design, Knopf (New York, NY), 2003.

Pushing the Limits: More Adventures in Engineering, Knopf (New York, NY), 2004.

Contributor to numerous professional journals; columnist for *American Scientist* and *ASEE Prism.*

SIDELIGHTS: For Henry Petroski, a professor of civil and environmental engineering at Duke University, the civil, mechanical, electrical, chemical, and structural engineers of this world are unsung heroes of history. He has written several acclaimed nonfiction books—including *Pushing the Limits: More Adventures in Engineering, Remaking the World: Adventures in Engineering,* and *Small Things Considered: Why There Is No Perfect Design*—that discuss the ways in which innovations designed by often-neglected engineers have tremendously impacted life on this planet—from the obvious achievements like bridges, which connect communities, to more mundane objects like the pencil and the Post-it Note. As he told Jennifer Howard in an interview for *Publishers Weekly,* "In this country at least, architects get most of the glory; engineers, meanwhile, tend to labor in obscurity." Petroski's books joined others that captured the reading public during the 1980s and 1990s, but *MIT's Technology Review* critic Samuel C. Florman praised Petroski as a standout in the genre, since he is also an engineer himself. "Only a practicing engineer can 'feel' what it is to do engineering and 'know' engineering with heart and soul," Florman pointed out.

Born in 1942, Petroski grew up in Brooklyn and Queens, two boroughs of New York City that owe much of their development to bridges of historic significance and enduring grace. The first in his family to attend college, Petroski graduated with an engineering degree from Manhattan College, and earned advanced degrees from the University of Illinois. He began his academic career at the University of Texas—Austin as an assistant professor of engineering mechanics in 1968, and then spent the latter part of the 1970s as a failure analyst at Argonne National Laboratory, a government research and development institute affiliated with the University of Chicago. He joined the faculty of Duke University in North Carolina in 1980, and rose to become chair of the department of civil and environmental engineering.

As an engineer, Petroski specialized in fracture mechanics, or how and why things break. Of particularly crucial interest to this field are the flaws that cause concrete dams to crack and suspension bridges to collapse. Yet Petroski had been a lifelong avid reader, and wrote poetry for some time before finding his metier in essays on technology for newspapers and magazines. He had always wanted to explore the division between the liberal arts and scientific achievement, an intellectual gulf he began to notice as an undergraduate, as he explained to Howard in *Publishers Weekly.* "Liberal arts [students] sometimes gave the impression that they were superior because they were studying intellectual stuff and engineering was just technical stuff and we didn't know anything about culture and tradition," Petroski said.

The sinking of an oil rig in the North Sea in 1980, followed the next year by the ruinous collapse of elevated walkways inside the Kansas City Hyatt Regency hotel, spurred Petroski to investigate some of the more notable failures of engineering. The result was his first book, *To Engineer Is Human: The Role of Failure in Successful Design,* published in 1985.

A *New York Times Book Review* assessment of *To Engineer Is Human* by Michael Markow asserted that its author "explains relevant engineering principles and how engineers deal with such risks in a way that nonprofessionals will understand." The book became the basis for a television documentary produced by the British Broadcasting Corporation.

In Petroski's next book, *Beyond Engineering: Essays and Other Attempts to Figure without Equations,* illustrated by his daughter Karen, the engineering expert attempts to show how the process of engineering changes daily life in innumerable ways, and along with it, history itself. The 1986 volume contains thirty essays that discuss, among other fields, computer technology, and in one section he makes a tongue-in-cheek argument for converting sports statistics to metric measurement. A *Publishers Weekly* reviewer declared it to be "written with savvy and wit," and termed it a volume that "will delight engineers and lay people alike."

Petroski earned a great deal of critical attention for his 1990 book, a handsome volume that could legitimately claim to be the first of a genre. *The Pencil: A History of Design and Circumstance* aimed to be more than just the chronological story of a humble object; as Petroski asserted, the pencil and its development is symbolic for all technological advance. Though its creation was borne of the accidental discovery of graphite, the perfection of the pencil as an artifact evolved by deliberate inventiveness, and what resulted was an object that nearly every literate person on the planet has used. "The story of a single object told in depth can reveal more about the whole of technology and its practitioners than a sweeping survey of all the triumphant works of civil, mechanical, electrical, and every other kind of engineering," Petroski wrote.

As a book, *The Pencil*'s origins arose when Petroski, new to Duke, developed a dislike for the standard-issue pencils at the university. They were blue, not the traditional yellow, and wrote poorly. He wrote a technical article about breakage of pencil points, which tied in with his specialty in fracture mechanics. "It sounds frivolous, but if you can't understand how a pencil point breaks, you can't understand how an airplane wing breaks," he explained to Richard Wolkomir in the *Smithsonian.* In the pencil article, he wanted to include something about the evolution of pencil design, but found source material on the matter lacking.

As Petroski explains, the history of the pencil began in the classical era, when Romans used lead to write on wax. The instrument employed, however, was called a stylus, and had a point so sharp that it could also be used as a weapon; one leader even stabbed another in front of the Roman Senate in a notorious incident. But it was not until a violent storm in Keswick, England yielded a toppled tree with roots encased in an unusual black substance, which produced a superb line on paper, that the modern history of the pencil began. The odd discovery led to the unearthing of a large mine in England's Lake District, and for the next several generations, Britain was the leading manufacturer of pencils in the world. The pure graphite from the Borrowdale mine was encased in a cedar sheath for writing, and use of the writing instrument soared along with literacy rates. A 1790s war, however, cut off France from British pencil imports, and French manufacturers raced to make their own. In the process they discovered that a heat-fused mixture of refined graphite and clay yielded an equally good writing material.

Throughout *The Pencil* Petroski provides arcane and significant trivia alike, such as why yellow became the standard color. The American writer Henry David Thoreau came from a family that owned the most respected pencil-making business in the United States during the early nineteenth century; Petroski also offers anecdotes about and quotes from famous pencil abusers in literary history. Even in modern times, billions of pencils are sold annually. "The very commonness of the pencil, the characteristic of it that renders it all but invisible and seemingly valueless, is really the first feature of successful engineering," he notes. "Good engineering blends into the environment, becomes a part of society and culture so naturally that a special effort is required to notice it."

The Pencil received mostly positive reviews. *Smithsonian* writer Dennis Drabelle observed wryly that the book "is not without its, well, leaden moments. Professorially, Petroski tends to bog down his information in directions, transitions and summaries." But Jeffrey L. Meikle, critiquing the book for *Business History Review,* found that such digressions only add to the book's charm. "Exhaustively researched and engagingly written, *The Pencil* provides a definitive history of a common artifact organized around the theme that pencil-making became more efficient and useful as it evolved from an activity of secretive, tradition-bound craftsmen to one directed by scientific method in the service of business," Meikle wrote. "In addition to a recognition and ample demonstration of the mutual dependence of invention and business, the book's strong points include admirably clear descriptions of mechanical processes, an eclectic array of literary and popular references to the pencil, and a strong expressive prose as simple—and complex—as the pencil itself."

Petroski's next work explores similar themes, but assesses a variety of commonplace objects. Published in 1992, *The Evolution of Useful Things* contained essays on the evolution of the paper clip, the Post-it Note, the zipper, fast-food packaging, masking tape, and even the safety pin. This last object, as the author explains, also originated in ancient Rome, but only the invention of a protective sheath with an integral spring designed into it in 1849 made its popularity and myriad uses soar. Petroski explains why women's clothes are buttoned on a different side than men's—at one time, women usually had maids to help them dress, while men did it themselves—and he sketches the decades-long quest to perfect the zipper. It was only in 1921, he notes, that galoshes with the device, made by the rubber company, B.F. Goodrich, helped the patented slide fastener find its niche. Post-it Notes, he writes elsewhere in the volume, were created in the 1980s when an engineer at the 3M company grew impatient with the slips of paper that he used to mark pages in books, because they constantly fell out. He exploited a new adhesive that left no mark on the page.

In his book Petroski discusses other notable achievements in the development of everyday objects. "No matter what you're designing, it always means compromise, which is why nothing is ever perfect," he told Wolkomir in the *Smithsonian.* "You're always dealing with competing objectives, like make it strong but make it cheap."

Around the time of the 1994 publication of his fifth book, *Design Paradigms: Case Histories of Error and Judgment in Engineering,* Petroski became a professor of history at Duke as well. His next book, *Engineers of Dreams: Great Bridge Builders and the Spanning of America,* was published the following year. "Bridges have become symbols and souls of cities," he declares in his book, but goes on to bemoan the fact that the engineers who helped make them safe for human traffic seemed to have been forgotten by history. He explores the careers of five famous American bridge builders, and describes their achievements. Along the way, he writes of the evolution of materials in bridge-building, and some deadly failures to take the physics of weather into account in design—providing accounts of a few spans that collapsed or proved dangerous in high wind. He also explains the contentious conflicts between bridge engineers and their architect colleagues.

Among the men that *Engineers of Dreams* profiles are Gustav Lindenthal, the first commissioner of bridges for New York City; James Buchanan Eads, the creator of St. Louis's historic road and railroad span over the Mississippi River; and David B. Steinman, the engineer behind the Mackinac Bridge, erected in 1953 to link Michigan's upper and lower peninsulas. As Petroski told Howard in the interview for *Publishers Weekly,* "here the people play a much larger role" in design than in more anonymous, ubiquitous objects like the pencil. "[I like to see] how they interact, their personal failings, their feuds with each other, their rivalries, their jealousies. I also just like the stories of how these things came to be."

A *New York Times Book Review* assessment from M.R. Montgomery praised the interesting biographical sketches in *Engineers of Dreams,* but stated that "Petroski's seamlessly linked biographies illustrate a greater theme: engineers will push a technology beyond its limits when they forget the lessons of history. When there is hubris at the drafting table, it is as fatal as it is at a general's map table."

Petroski's next book was designed as a text for introductory college courses as well as a book for the general reader, with a greater degree of technical illustrations and diagrams. *Invention by Design: How Engineers Get from Thought to Thing* appeared in 1996, and provides case histories within nine categories of objects. Among them are the paper clip, the pencil, the pop-top for aluminum cans—designed by its inventors as a technical failure, because it breaks, but not completely—and the fax machine. This revolutionary telecommunications device, as Petroski notes, appeared on the market long before it came into widespread use; its story allows the author to explain how technology requires an infrastructure to become both successful and ubiquitous. The Boeing 777 airplane and the Bay Bridge in San Francisco are among the other case histories discussed. "Petroski's mosaic approach provides a wonderfully comprehensive synthesis of what it is that engineers actually do," opined Florman in *MIT's Technology Review.* "He maintains a light touch that is sadly lacking in most works about engineering. . . . Happily, an encounter with any one of Petroski's books should lead readers to explore his others."

Petroski's *Remaking the World: Adventures in Engineering* contains eighteen essays originally published in *American Scientist,* an engineering journal. Here the author discusses the ways in which engineers sometimes inadvertently alter the course of history. He writes of the long history behind the creation of the Chunnel, the English Channel tunnel between Britain and France, the North Sea disaster, and the Hyatt hotel tragedy. Scattered throughout *Remaking the World* are literary quotes and interesting anecdotes, such as the story of Henry Robert, author of *Robert's Rules of Order*—still the standard procedural manual on conducting official meetings—who was a military engineer by profession. Here, he also writes of some famous slow technological starters. Radio, for instance, was dismissed as irrelevant in its early years because it was created as a method of person-to-person communication; only the realization that radio signals from a single source had a wide range of broadcast caused others to take note of its potential.

Other memorable projects and how they came into existence critiqued in *Remaking the World* are the Eiffel Tower, the Ferris Wheel, and the Petronas Twin Towers—the world's tallest building—in Kuala Lampur, Malaysia. Petroski writes of the individual engineers behind the works, and the creative processes that brought them to fruition, but also notes that for some, far more prosaic elements affected the final design. The designers of the Concorde supersonic airliner, for instance, were forced to take noise-reduction laws in New York State into account in the planning stages. The need to reduce air resistance required flying at very high altitudes and this affected the design of its fuselage, which in turn restricted passenger area and made the Concorde's airfare available only to the affluent.

Petroski uses *Remaking the World* to discuss the failure to establish a Nobel Prize in engineering, though its namesake had wanted to recognize achievements in the field. A contributor for *Kirkus Reviews* called the tome "a disappointingly flat collection of musings on engineering history," and faulted the author for failing to give proper emphasis to the actual marvel itself and how it was developed from a technical standpoint. *Forbes* reviewer Christine Larson offered a more positive appraisal, however. "Petroski's plain-English summaries of engineering fundamentals make this a rewarding read for both working engineers and armchair inventors," Larson asserted. Though she did criticize Petroski for straying from the subject matter at times, Larson concluded that "the book's real charm lies in the countless anecdotes and bits of historic and engineering trivia that pepper each essay, rich details guaranteed to stay with you."

Petroski's voracious reading appetite led him to write yet another book that was the singular work of its kind. *The Book on the Bookshelf,* published in 1999, tracks the history of book storage and display throughout the centuries. Petroski begins by describing the ways in which scholars in ancient Greece and Rome stored precious scrolls, and then moves on to explain the systems developed to house bound manuscripts during the early medieval era. Book cabinets, locking chests, the turning lecterns of Renaissance Italy, and the rotating cases from Victorian times are also discussed.

Moving into the modern era, Petroski evaluates the history of library shelving, including the innovative sliding shelf developed by the British Museum in the 1880s. Behind this recitation of technical data, however, is the story of the evolution of the accessibility of the principal objects themselves. Books were once so valuable that they were locked up for safety. "The images of chained books are among the most haunting in *The Book on the Bookshelf,*" wrote John Updike in the *New Yorker* in a review of Petroski's book, "since we do not instinctively recognize them as marking a forward stage in the liberation and dissemination of the written word."

The invention of the printing press revolutionized the Western world, and resulted in an explosion of printed matter and the accompanying need to find new storage and classification methods, as Petroski recounts. Imprinted spines identifying title and author, for instance, did not emerge until the sixteenth century. Throughout the text are quotes from famous writers, and concluding it is Petroski's appendix of light-hearted suggestions for arranging books in a collection. Alphabetically by author, or by subject, are two of the more prosaic ones, but he also notes that volumes can be shelved by appearance or even according to their opening sentence. "The charm of Petroski's book, however, lies not in this rigorous chronology but in the marginalia . . . to be asked to wonder how and when readers first thought of arranging books vertically on a shelf; to learn that the ideal length of a shelf is 40 inches, so that it won't sag in the center—these are trivial and happy details in which any true book lover will rejoice," declared Alberto Manguel in a *New York Times Book Review* critique.

BIOGRAPHICAL AND CRITICAL SOURCES:

PERIODICALS

ASEE Prism, February, 2000, Viva Hardigg, "The Poet Laureate of Technology," pp. 24-26.

Booklist, April 15, 1986, Mary Ellen Sullivan, review of *Beyond Engineering,* pp. 1169-1170; September 1, 1995, Gilbert Taylor, review of *Engineers of Dreams,* p. 24; October 15, 1996, Bryce Christensen, review of *Invention by Design,* p. 390; December 1, 1997, Gilbert Taylor, review of *Remaking the World,* p. 602; August, 1999, Gilbert Taylor, review of *The Book on the Bookshelf,* p. 1990; August, 2004, Gilbert Taylor, review of *Pushing the Limits: More Adventures in Engineering,* p. 1885.

Business History Review, summer, 1990, Jeffrey L. Meikle, review of *The Pencil,* p. 334.

Chicago Tribune, May 17, 1992, review of *To Engineer Is Human,* sec. 8, p. 14.

Economist, February 10, 1990, review of *The Pencil,* p. 93.

Entertainment Weekly, September 26, 2003, Wook Kim, review of *Small Things Considered: Why There Is No Perfect Design,* p. 99.

Forbes, March 9, 1998, Christine Larson, review of *Remaking the World,* p. S163.

Insight on the News, December 18, 1995, Matthys Levy, review of *Engineers of Dreams,* p. 25.

Journal of the American Medical Association, May 28, 1997, Dwight K. Oxley, review of *Design Paradigms,* p. 1651.

Kirkus Reviews, November 15, 1997, review of *Remaking the World,* p. 1694; July 1, 2004, review of *Pushing the Limits: More Adventures in Engineering,* p. 621.

Library Journal, December, 1997, Mark L. Shelton, review of *Remaking the World,* p. 144.

Los Angeles Times Book Review, June 4, 1986, Peter DeLeon, review of *Beyond Engineering,* p. 4.

MIT's Technology Review, August-September, 1997, Samuel C. Florman, review of *Invention by Design,* p. 64.

New Statesman and Society, September 3, 1993, Carl Gardner, review of *The Evolution of Useful Things,* p. 40.

New Yorker, October 4, 1999, John Updike, "Groaning Shelves," pp. 106-110.

New York Times Book Review, December 1, 1985, Michael Markow, review of *To Engineer Is Human,* p. 25; October 15, 1995, M.R. Montgomery, "To Get to the Other Side," p. 22; September 26, 1999, Alberto Manguel, "Up Against the Wall," p. 9.

Publishers Weekly, March 7, 1986, review of *Beyond Engineering,* p. 86; July 31, 1995, review of *Engineers of Dreams,* p. 63; September 4, 1995, Jennifer Howard, "Henry Petroski: Bridges as Archetypal Structures," p. 43; September 30, 1996, review of *Invention by Design,* p. 69; November 10, 1997, review of *Remaking the World,* p. 67; July 5, 1999, review of *The Book on the Bookshelf,* p. 46; July 21, 2003, review of *Small Things Considered: Why There Is No Perfect Design,* p. 183; July 12, 2004, review of *Pushing the Limits: More Adventures in Engineering,* p. 56.

Science, May 18, 1990, Robert Friedel, review of *The Pencil,* p. 894; May 21, 1993, Steven Lubar, review of *The Evolution of Useful Things,* p. 1166; October 7, 1994, Robert Mark, review of *Design Paradigms,* p. 146.

Science News, November 1, 2003, review of *Small Things Considered: Why There Is No Perfect Design,* p. 287.

Smithsonian, October, 1990, Dennis Drabelle, review of *The Pencil,* p. 202; October, 1993, Richard Wolkomir, "A Chronicler of Thingamabobs and Doohickeys," p. 133.

Time, December 21, 1992, review of *The Evolution of Useful Things,* p. 79.

U.S. News & World Report, January 22, 1990, Lewis J. Lord, "The Little Artifact That Could," p. 63.

Washington Post Book World, December 29, 1986, Curt Suplee, review of *Invention by Design,* p. 8.

* * *

PHILLIPS, Caryl 1958-

PERSONAL: Born March 13, 1958, in St. Kitts, West Indies; immigrated to England, 1958. *Education:* Queen's College, Oxford, B.A. (honours), 1979.

ADDRESSES: *Home*—New York, NY. *Office*—Department of English, Barnard College, New York, NY 10027-6598. *Agent*—(literary) Georgia Garrett, A.P. Watt Ltd., 20 John St., London WC1N 2DR, England; (dramatic) Judy Daish, Judy Daish Associates, 2 St. Charles Place, London W10 6EQ, England.

CAREER: Writer. *Observer* Festival of Theatre, Oxford, founding chairman, 1978, artistic director, 1979; writer-in-residence, Factory Arts Center (Arts Council of Great Britain), London, England, 1980-82, University of Mysore, Mysore, India, 1987, University of Stockholm, Stockholm, Sweden, 1989, and National Institute of Education, Singapore, summer, 1994; Arvon Foundation, England, writing instructor, summers, 1983—; visiting lecturer, University of Ghana, 1990, and University of Poznan, Poland, 1991; Amherst College, Amherst, MA, visiting writer, 1990-92, co-director of Creative Writing Center, 1992-97, writer-in-residence, 1992-97, professor of English, 1997-98; Humber College, Toronto, Ontario, Canada, visiting writer, August 1992 and 1993; New York University, visiting professor of English, fall, 1993; Barnard College, Columbia University, New York, NY, professor of English, Henry R. Luce Professor of Migration and Social Order, 1998—, director of Initiatives in the Humanities, 2003—, director of Barnard Forum on Migration. Heartland Productions, director, 1994-2000; University of West Indies, Barbados, visiting professor of humanities, summer 1999-2000. Faber & Faber, Boston, MA, consultant editor, 1992-94, London, England, series editor, 1996-2000. British Council, senior advisor for literature, 2002—; visiting writer at schools, including Yale University, 2004. Coordinator, speaker, and participant of international conferences, seminars and festivals, 1986—. Member, Arts Council of Great Britain drama panel, 1982-85; British Film Institute Production Board, 1985-88; Bush Theater board, 1985-89; and "The Caribbean Writer" board, United States Virgin Islands, 1989—; University of Kent, honorary senior member, beginning 1988; *World Literature Written in English,* member of advisory board, beginning 1998; British Council, member of arts advisory committee; *Belgian Journal of English Language and Literatures,* member of advisory board, 2003—.

AWARDS, HONORS: British Arts Council bursary, 1984; fiftieth anniversary fellowship, British Council, 1984; Giles Cooper Award, British Broadcasting Corp. (BBC), 1984, for *The Wasted Years;* Malcolm X Prize for Literature, 1985, for *The Final Passage;* Martin Luther King Memorial Prize, 1987, for *The European Tribe;* Young Writer of the Year Award, London *Sunday Times,* 1992; Guggenheim fellowship, 1992; Booker

Prize nomination, 1993, and James Tait Black Memorial Prize, 1994, both for *Crossing the River;* included on *Granta* list of Best Young British Writers, 1993; Lannan Literary Award for fiction, 1994, for oeuvre; Rockefeller Foundation Bellagio residency, 1994; A.M. Hon., Amherst College, 1995; Hon. D., Leeds Metropolitan University, 1997; University of West Indies Humanities Scholar of the Year, 1999; fellow, Royal Society of Literature, 2000; Silver Ombu award for best screenplay, Mar del Plata Film Festival (Argentina), 2002, for *The Mystic Masseur;* Mel and Lois Tukman Fellow, New York Public Library's Dorothy and Lewis B. Cullman Center for Scholars and Writers, 2002-03; Hon.D., University of York, 2003; Hon.D. Letters, University of Leeds, 2003; National Book Critics Circle Award finalist for fiction, 2003, and PEN/Faulkner Award for Fiction nomination, and Commonwealth Writers Prize for Best Book, both 2004, all for *A Distant Shore.*

WRITINGS:

FICTION

The Final Passage, Penguin (New York, NY), 1985.
A State of Independence, Farrar, Straus (New York, NY), 1986.
Higher Ground, Viking (London, England), 1989, Viking (New York, NY), 1990.
Cambridge, Bloomsbury (London, England), 1991, Knopf (New York, NY), 1992.
Crossing the River, Bloomsbury (London, England), 1993, Knopf (New York, NY), 1994.
The Nature of Blood, Knopf (New York, NY), 1997.
A Distant Shore, Knopf (New York, NY), 2003.

PLAYS

Strange Fruit (first produced at Crucible Theatre, Sheffield, England, 1980), Amber Lane Press, 1981.
Where There Is Darkness (produced at Lyric Hammersmith Theatre, London, England, 1982), Amber Lane Press, 1982.
The Shelter (first produced at Lyric Hammersmith Theatre, 1983), Amber Lane Press, 1984.

Also author of *The Hotel Cristobel.*

SCREENPLAYS

Welcome to Birmingham (documentary), Central TV, 1983.
"The Hope and Glory," aired on *Play for Today,* British Broadcasting Corporation (BBC), 1984.
"Lost in Music," aired on *Global Report,* BBC, 1984.
The Record, Channel 4, 1985.
Playing Away (aired on *Film on 4,* Channel 4, 1986), Faber & Faber (London, England), 1987.
(And coproducer) *The Final Passage,* Channel 4, 1996.
The Mystic Masseur, Merchant Ivory Productions, 2001.

RADIO PLAYS

The Wasted Years (produced for BBC Radio 4, 1984), Methuen (London, England), 1985.
Crossing the River, BBC Radio 3, 1985.
The Prince of Africa, BBC Radio 3, 1987.
Writing Fiction, BBC Radio 4, 1991.
A Kind of Home: James Baldwin in Paris, BBC Radio 4, 2004.

RADIO DOCUMENTARIES

St. Kitts Independence (Pride of Place), BBC Radio 4, 1983.
Sport and the Black Community, BBC Radio 4, 1984.
No Complaints: James Baldwin at Sixty, BBC Radio 4, 1985.
The Spirit of America, BBC Radio 4, 1995.
These Islands Now: Transformations in British Culture, BBC Radio 3, 1995.
(Editor) *Extravagant Strangers: The "Other" Voice in English Literature* (produced for BBC Radio 3, 1997), published as *Extravagant Strangers: A Literature of Belonging,* Vintage (New York, NY), 1997.
"I Too Am America," aired on *Archive Hour,* BBC Radio 4, 2004.

OTHER

The European Tribe (nonfiction), Farrar, Straus (New York, NY), 1987.
(Editor) *The Right Set: A Tennis Anthology,* Vintage (New York, NY), 1999.
The Atlantic Sound (nonfiction), Knopf (New York, NY), 2000.
A New World Order, Secker & Warburg (London, England), 2001, Vintage (New York, NY), 2002.

Contributor of articles to periodicals, including London *Times* and *Sunday Times, Caribbean Review of Books, Guardian, Financial Times, New York Times, New Re-*

public, New York Times Book Review, Washington Post Book World, Daily Telegraph, Los Angeles Times Book Review, Race Today Review, and *Bomb.* Contributor of articles to anthologies, including *Lost Classics,* edited by Michael Ondaatje and others, Knopf Canada (Toronto, Ontario, Canada), 2000; and *How Novelists Work,* edited by Maura Dooley, Seren Press, 2000. *Bomb* magazine, New York, NY, contributing editor, 1993—; Graywolf Press, Minneapolis, MN, consulting editor, 1994—; *Wasifiri* magazine, London, England, advisory editor, 1995—.

Some of the author's works have been translated into French, Swedish, Dutch, German, Portuguese, Spanish, Polish, Greek, Finnish, Japanese, and Turkish.

Phillips's manuscripts are housed at the Beinecke Library, Yale University, New Haven, CT.

SIDELIGHTS: The compromised identity of the black West Indian, their African roots, and their displacement to other reaches is the common thread that links the writings of author and educator Caryl Phillips. A prolific writer of novels, television and movie scripts, radio dramas, and nonfiction pieces, Phillips focuses on "migration, belonging, discovery and hope," as quoted in a Barnard College Web site summary. As Phillips added on the online site, "It is the same story rewritten in many ways. I feel it is my duty to tell the story and I can't stop telling it. As long as I feel I have something to say I have the obligation of saying it and I will keep on writing."

Phillips's work is a reflection of his own roots and multinational existence in three cultures: Caribbean, British, and American. He was born in the West Indies, on the Island of St. Kitts, although his family migrated to Leeds, England, when he was only a few months old. He was raised in a working-class neighborhood where his parents instilled in him the importance of education. Teaching by example, both parents eventually earned college degrees. Although participating in sports gave him self-confidence, Phillips took academics to heart and was the first person from his school to be accepted into Oxford University. First studying theater and directing a number of plays, Phillips switched to studying English literature and language and graduated after three years with honors.

In addition to writing, Phillips has traveled the globe teaching and participating in seminars. Since graduating from college in 1979, Phillips has been a visiting professor, lecturer, and writer-in-residence at a dozen universities on almost every continent and has participated in over sixty seminars in over twenty countries, serving as the keynote speaker at many events. In the introduction to his book of essays, *The European Tribe,* Phillips acknowledges that early in his career he "felt like a transplanted tree that had failed to take root in foreign soil." *The European Tribe* is the result of Phillips's journeys throughout the world to examine racism and define his own place in a white-dominated society. This book won the Martin Luther King Memorial Prize.

In novels such as *The Final Passage* and *A State of Independence,* Phillips's main characters wander without firm roots between their native West Indies and England. *Higher Ground,* a trilogy of stories that encompasses a period of 200 years, examines, through multiple points of view, the lingering consequences of being uprooted from one's homeland. Each story concerns the survival of individuals adrift in a hostile culture, but the author extends his outlook to include the perspective of a white European female. Phillips again uses contrasting points of view in his historical novels *Cambridge* and *Crossing the River.*

In *The Final Passage,* Phillips's first novel and winner of the Malcom X Prize for Literature, protagonist Leila Preston intends to emigrate with her baby from their Caribbean island home to England. Although Leila is fleeing from the emotional pain of a bad marriage to Michael, a lazy and unfaithful drunk, she ends up traveling with him after a last-minute reconciliation. Not surprisingly, "the new start proves to be a resumption of the old pain," wrote David Montrose in the *Times Literary Supplement.* Despite Michael's promise to reform, he backslides into his old habits. Also, Leila's mother, who had already immigrated to England, is dying in a hospital. "England itself administers further hurts," Montrose pointed out. "Walls carry racist slogans, landlords' signs stipulate 'no coloureds.'" After five months, Leila leaves Michael for good and returns home to the West Indies. "Her prospects of serenity remain uncertain, but the outlook at least seems promising," Montrose commented in the *Times Literary Supplement,* adding later that Phillips's writing "sustains an atmosphere of emotional adversity." Calvin Forbes, a critic for the *Washington Post Book World,* noticed that Phillips "is one of the few black writers considering the cross-Atlantic relationship."

John Sutherland summed up Phillips's second novel, *A State of Independence,* in the *London Review of Books* as a work that thematically "deals with the contradictions inherent in being a 'British West Indian.'" The narrative takes place on an island modeled closely after St. Kitts; Bertram Francis, the main character, arrives home after twenty years spent in England as a scholarship student who failed to reach many of his goals. The island is about to become an independent nation, and, like his homeland, Bertram would like to cast off the last vestiges of his Britishness. However, he soon discovers that his brother has died, his mother bitterly resents his long absence, and an old friend who has risen to the position of deputy prime minister of the new regime thinks little of his scheme to start up a local business. This highly placed friend reminds Bertram that this "is no longer the island he left," observed a reviewer in *Best Sellers,* who commented further that "Bertram's own independence has estranged him from the people and the island he once knew." Perceiving the book as a discussion on "the national tensions of post-imperialism," Sutherland stated in the *London Review of Books* that *A State of Independence* "is both a promising and an accomplished work."

The opening story of Phillips's novella trilogy, *Higher Ground,* is titled "Heartland" and is, in the words of Charles Johnson of the *Los Angeles Times Book Review,* "a chilling, Kafkaesque parable about the slave trade." The narrator, a shepherd on the West African coast, is taken captive by British traders and sold to one of their associates, who teaches him English as well as the fundamentals of slave trading. Eventually, this nameless narrator cooperates with the British, betraying his fellow Africans. "He is half-slave and half-free, poised in a nightmarish limbo between two cultures," Johnson remarked. When the narrator does finally defy his captors—unable to tolerate the abuse of a black teenage girl he himself helped to enslave—his dubious freedom is ended for good and he is sold on the auction block. Critic Adam Lively, in a review for the *Times Literary Supplement,* singled out "Heartland" as being "a particularly impressive single sweep of narrative," and commented that it "owes its immediacy to [the] strength of visual imagination."

The second story in *Higher Ground* is "The Cargo Rap," which is told by convict Rudi Williams in letters he writes from prison during the late 1960s. A self-proclaimed Marxist-Leninist and an adherent of the Black Power movement, Rudi sends home letters full of politics and polemic. "Ironically, Rudi's black nationalist tirades to his family against 'race-mixing' and integration are at odds with his uncritical acceptance of (white) Marx and Lenin," Johnson remarked in the *Los Angeles Times Book Review,* complimenting Phillips for "a fine job of showing the contradictions in Rudi's character."

Higher Ground closes with the title novella, a story about Irina, a Jewish refugee from Poland, who encounters England in much the same way as do Phillips's black Caribbean characters. The story is set in the 1950s when, according to Penelope Lively in the *Times Literary Supplement,* "the backlash against postwar immigration is beginning to be felt." Irina marries, but attempts to commit suicide after the marriage deteriorates, and is sent to a hospital, where she develops an aversion to further emotional attachments. Upon her release from the hospital, Irina meets a West Indian named Louis, and they share a sexual encounter, although "their friendship across the gulf of cultures falters," according to Johnson in the *Los Angeles Times Book Review.* Johnson appreciated that the author's "ever growing skill . . . does allow us to know Irina and the suffering of the dispossessed, the forgotten."

In *Cambridge,* Phillips not only employs another white woman as a major character, he also writes from her perspective. The diary of Emily Cartwright, the British daughter of a West Indies plantation owner, comprises the bulk of the novel and provides a feminine perspective on the institution of slavery. Although she might be considered as liberal for her era because she is revolted by conditions on the plantation, Emily nonetheless believes that Africans—an inferior race in her opinion—were intended by God to work for whites. "Unable to comprehend the negative effects of slavery on both slave and slaveholder, she is convinced it is [the slaveholder's] contact with the slaves that causes the otherwise good Christian white man to behave in repulsive ways," summed up Clarence Major in the *Washington Post Book World.*

Emily's commentary is countered by the journal of an elderly slave known as Cambridge, who has been thrown in jail for defying his captors. As a teenager, he had been Olumide, an African kidnapped by slave traders and intended for sale in America. The captain, however, "renames him Tom, like a pet, and keeps him," according to Major in the *Washington Post Book World.* Tom becomes an educated Christian, renames himself David Henderson, and marries. When his wife dies, he decides to embark on a journey to Africa as a Christian proselytizer, but is kidnapped by the ship's captain and again enslaved, at a plantation in the West Indies. Olumide ultimately receives the name Cambridge—a reference to his fluency in English—from the slave overseer at the plantation. Cambridge has spent many years in hard servitude by the time Emily makes her visit. When she encounters Cambridge, she resents his attitude and is "offended by his speaking the King's English with much flourish, his arrogance in addressing her without permission in terms that suggest an equal standing," stated Calvin Forbes in the Chicago *Tribune Books.*

In his devotion to Christianity, Cambridge resembles other characters from Phillips's fiction—for example, the shepherd in "Heartland," and Bertram in *A State of Independence*—whose identities are split between two irreconcilable worlds. He "is enslaved twice—first in England . . . and secondly upon his return as a 'free man of color' to Africa," Forbes commented. The author's deft handling of his characters elicited praise from reviewers, including Forbes, who remarked that "One of the marvels of . . . *Cambridge* is how artfully [Phillips] manages to convey in a relatively few pages the frailties of many of the people caught in slavery's web." Major, writing in the *Washington Post Book World,* was particularly impressed with the character of Emily, declaring that "her nineteenth-century white racist mentality becomes a black author's allegorical and ironic means of making one of the subtlest, but most insistent, statements ever about the troubled and urgent relationships between a particular past and the present, Africa and Europe, justice and injustice."

"*Crossing the River* consists of four separate stories bound together by a central theme—slavery and its legacy," commented Lucasta Miller in a review of the novel for the *New Statesman & Society.* In "The Pagan Coast," Phillips offers the story of a freed slave, Nash, and his liberal, well-meaning former owner, Edward. Nash travels to Africa as a missionary, but when his correspondence home to Edward abruptly ceases, Edward himself travels to Africa in search of Nash. Once in Liberia, Edward discovers that Nash has died. "West" features Martha Randolph, an elderly black woman longing to reach California in the late nineteenth century, as well as other black pioneers who ventured west during this period. "Crossing the River" features journal entries by a slave-ship owner in the mid-1700s. The final piece, "Somewhere in England," is set in Yorkshire during World War II and concerns a white English woman's affair with a black soldier. The four narrative pieces are framed by the words of an anonymous African father who despairs at having sold his children into slavery after his crops failed. "Gradually, as the stories in the main text unfold, we realize that this father has taken on the mythic proportions of the continent of Africa, that his abandonment represents the irreversible history of entire peoples," noted Janet Burroway in the *New York Times Book Review.*

Critics responded enthusiastically to *Crossing the River,* and the book was awarded several prizes. Commenting on the author's use of myriad historical sources in fashioning the novel, *Times Literary Supplement* reviewer Oliver Reynolds averred, "One of Phillips's gifts is his ability to transform his sources into the felt life of fiction." In her review of the work, Miller also praised Phillips's use of historical elements: "His deep awareness of the historical process is combined with an exceptionally intelligent prose style—clear, unencumbered, and compassionate." Nicholas Lezard, writing in the *London Review of Books,* commended the author's ability to evoke the language and tone of previous eras and places. Lezard contended, "Phillips's talent has developed along the lines of accomplished ventriloquism." Burroway concluded in her review of the work that it "presents a brilliantly coherent vision of two and half centuries of the African diaspora." The novel was a finalist for Britain's prestigious Booker Prize for literature.

The dichotomies Major mentioned in reviewing *Cambridge*—"Africa and Europe, justice and injustice"—are discussed by Phillips as present-day concerns in *The European Tribe.* As Ashok Bery explained in a review of the work for the *Times Literary Supplement,* Phillips "travelled around Europe for nearly a year in an attempt to understand the forces that had helped to shape him; [*The European Tribe*] comes out of that period." Phillips attempts to reconcile "his divided Afro-British self by examining the Europeans as a Pan-Africanist anthropologist might, treating the French, British, Soviets, and Spanish as a single white tribe determined to keep people of color . . . down," Charles R. Johnson remarked in the *Los Angeles Times Book Review.* From visits to countries around the world, Phillips records incidents of racism and intolerance, including the actions of France's National Front party to put a halt on African immigration. In Oslo he was detained by suspicious customs officials; in Detroit he was harassed by police. *The European Tribe,* Johnson concluded, "comprised partly of personal odyssey, partly of political indictment, is too important a book to be ignored."

Phillips examines the slave trade again in *The Atlantic Sound,* a narrative tracing the busy slave trading route from Liverpool, England, to Accra, Ghana, to Charleston, South Carolina. In three stories featuring historical characters, Phillips contrasts his own observations of the three cities with a character whose life was bound up in the slave trade. He writes of John Ocansey, a nineteenth-century trader based in Liverpool, Philip Quaque, an African priest of the eighteenth century who lived in Ghana, and J. Waites Waring, a Charleston judge of the 1940s. "The book's central theme," Edward G. McCormack remarked in *Library Journal,* "is the exploitation of blacks by the Western world since

1553." A critic for *Publishers Weekly* praised Phillips for his "keen intelligence, careful research and well-expressed truths," while Victoria Bond and Kelly Ellis, wrote in the *Black Issues Book Review* that the author possesses "penetrating, proactive insight and a historian's careful and acute eye."

Phillips's seventh novel, the widely acclaimed *A Distant Shore,* won the Commonwealth Writers Prize for Best Book of 2004, was a finalist for the National Book Critics Circle Award for Fiction, and was nominated for the PEN/Faulkner Award for Fiction. Like other novels by the author, *A Distant Shore* brings to life the struggles of two displaced people of conflicting races and cultures. Unlike Phillips's other works, however, this book takes place in the present. One main character is Dorothy, a white teacher in her fifties who, amidst scandal, was forced to retire early and then relocated to the town where her family has roots. The other main character is Gabrial, a black African who fled the violence of his country and the pain of his lost life there, starting a new one in the same British town as Dorothy. The story tells, sometimes in reverse chronology, of an anxious relationship between the two that is scrutinized by the local, somewhat mistrustful townspeople. Discussing his decision to address the present in his fiction, Phillips told Morrison: "It seems odd that it's taken me until now to set a novel in the present. The rest have been historical. I had to describe my own roots before I could deal with contemporary events."

Many reviews of *A Distant Shore* were positive. As a *Publishers Weekly* review noted, Phillips depicts his protagonists "with a faithful eye that reveals their inner beauty as clearly as their defects. A true master of form, he manipulates narrative time . . . and perspective to create a disjointed sense of place that mirrors the tortured, fractured inner lives of his characters." In the *Black Issues Book Review,* Denolyn Carroll remarked, "The author's clever pacing of the novel, through sudden shifts in thought and time sequences, keeps the story intriguing. His use of descriptive detail and subtle symbolism is achingly on point." And Morrison commented that *A Distant Shore* "neatly dissects what [Dorothy] . . . sees as a decline in civility and standards in modern Britain—a situation her less punctilious neighbors blame on immigration." Writing in *Library Journal,* Kellie Gillespie added that "Phillips has created a poignant and quietly powerful portrait of contemporary alienation," while in *Entertainment Weekly* Lori L. Tharps summarized *A Distant Shore* as a "Greek tragedy set in modern England" that, "while critiquing Britain's current racial climate, offers storytelling both raw and heartbreaking."

Although he has found success as a novelist, Phillips was initially known as a playwright. In plays such as *Strange Fruit* and *A Kind of Home: James Baldwin in Paris,* his characters struggle with the same doubts over identity and rootlessness that define the protagonists in his novels. The two brothers in *Strange Fruit,* living in England, typify this crisis—one "rejects all non-black values," the other is "torn between 'white' and 'black' values," according to Diana Devlin in *Drama.* However, as the novelist/playwright remains aware, a simple rejection of "white values" will not resolve the conflict of identity that concerns his protagonist. In the radio play *A Kind of Home* Phillips tells the story of a man he knew personally and views as another displaced soul, creating a work that follows Baldwin from Harlem to exile in Paris and his development as a major twentieth-century writer.

Phillips noted of his work, as quoted in the *Africa News Service:* "Why do I write? Because it is a way of organizing my feelings about myself and the world around me. . . . Writing provides a means by which I can sit in judgement upon myself and reach conclusions (however temporary) that enable me to shuffle towards the next day and another crisis. And then, of course, there is the technical challenge of writing. To say what I have to say, and to hope to say it in the most incisive manner. To strive towards this goal, and fail honestly, yet continue to strive. To aspire to purify the language; to desire to sharpen the blade of narrative clarity, and then strike quick unseen blows. For me, writing is all of this."

Capturing the essence of Phillips's contribution to contemporary literature, Ledent remarked that the writer's "compassionate engagement with lonely, marginalized characters helps us to transgress such artificial boundaries as race, gender, and nation, and calls into question the myths of homogeneity that all too often underlie conquistadorial impulses, both personal and collective. This is why Phillips's work affords an uncompromising, yet eminently humane, reflection on the composite societies in which we live." And Morrison summarized, "Not only is [Phillips] one of the most accomplished black novelists writing in English, but he is fast becoming known as one of the most productive all-around men of letters anywhere."

BIOGRAPHICAL AND CRITICAL SOURCES:

BOOKS

Contemporary Dramatists, 6th edition, St. James Press (Detroit, MI), 1999.

Contemporary Novelists, 7th edition, St. James Press (Detroit, MI), 2001.

Dictionary of Literary Biography, Volume 157: *Twentieth-Century Caribbean and Black African Writers, Third Series,* Thomson Gale (Detroit, MI), 1995.

Phillips, Caryl, *The European Tribe* (nonfiction), Farrar, Straus (New York, NY), 1987.

PERIODICALS

Africa News Service, January 22, 2004, "Caryl Phillips 'Crossing Borders' at British Council."

Best Sellers, October, 1986, p. 252.

Black Issues Book Review, November, 2000, Victoria Bond and Kelly Ellis, review of *The Atlantic Sound,* p. 49; March-April, 2004, Donolyn Carroll, review of *A Distant Shore,* p. 51.

Booklist, February 15, 1998, Brad Hooper, reviews of *Crossing the River* and *Cambridge,* p. 979; December 15, 1998, Vanessa Bush, review of *Extravagant Strangers: A Literature of Belonging,* p. 721; September 1, 2003, Donna Seaman, review of *A Distant Shore,* p. 7.

Drama, summer, 1982, p. 52.

Economist, June 17, 2000, "Ethnic Identity: A Novel Eye," p. 12.

Entertainment Weekly, October 24, 2003, Lori L. Tharps, review of *A Distant Shore,* p. 112.

Essence, December, 1987, p. 26; November, 1989, p. 32.

Kirkus Reviews, August 15, 2003, review of *A Distant Shore,* p. 1041.

Library Journal, December, 1998, Mary Paumier Jones, review of *Extravagant Strangers,* p. 105; October 1, 2000, Edward G. McCormack, review of *The Atlantic Sound,* p. 122; October 15, 2003, Kellie Gillespie, review of *A Distant Shore,* p. 99.

London Review of Books, April 3, 1986, p. 5; September 23, 1993, p. 21.

Los Angeles Times Book Review, July 19, 1987, pp. 3, 11; October 1, 1989, pp. 2, 11.

M2 Best Books, May 18, 2004, "2004 Commonwealth Writers Prize Winners Announced."

New Republic, June 13, 1994, p. 40; October 24, 1994, p. 34.

New Statesman & Society, May 23, 1993, p. 34; March 17, 2003, Benjamin Markovits, review of *A Distant Shore,* p. 54.

Newsweek International, May 10, 1999, Rana Dogar, "A Citizen of the World," p. 63.

New Yorker, August 10, 1992, p. 76.

New York Review of Books, April 26, 2001, Pankaj Mishra, review of *The Atlantic Sound,* p. 49.

New York Times Book Review, August 9, 1987, p. 7; September 24, 1989, p. 27; April 29, 1990, p. 38; February 16, 1992, p. 1; January 30, 1994, p. 10; October 29, 2000, Geoffrey Moorhouse, "African Connection," p. 12.

Publishers Weekly, May 22, 1987, p. 62; June 23, 1989, p. 50; January 19, 1990, p. 103; December 13, 1991, p. 44; November 22, 1993, p. 49; November 16, 1998, review of *Extravagant Strangers,* p. 55; September 18, 2000, review of *The Atlantic Sound,* p. 95; September 29, 2003, review of *A Distant Shore,* p. 44.

Time International, May 19, 2003, Donald Morrison, "A Writer of Wrongs: British Novelist Caryl Phillips Takes on History's Worst Injustices, and Still Has Time for Golf," p. 62.

Times Literary Supplement, March 8, 1985, p. 266; April 10, 1987, p. 396; June 2, 1989, p. 619; May 14, 1993, p. 22.

Tribune Books (Chicago, IL), March 1, 1992, section 14, p. 6.

Washington Post Book World, March 4, 1990, p. 8; February 9, 1992, pp. 4, 10.

ONLINE

Caryl Phillips Web site, http://www.carylphillips.com/ (August 6, 2004).

Contemporary Writers in the UK Web site, http://www.contemporarywriters.com/authors/ (August 6, 2004).

Guardian Online, http://books.guardian.co.uk/ (May 15, 2004), "The Silenced Minority"; (July 17, 2004) "Kingdom of the Blind."

University of Liège English Department Web site, http://www.ulg.ac.be/facphl/ (August 6, 2004) "Caryl Phillips."

Yale Daily News Online, http://www.yaledailynews.com/ (February 10, 2004), Dan Adler, "Novelist Emphasizes Human Aspect of Books."

* * *

PHILLIPS, Jayne Anne 1952-

PERSONAL: Born July 19, 1952, in Buckhannon, WV; daughter of Russell R. (a contractor) and Martha Jane (a teacher) Phillips; married; children: one son, two stepsons. *Education:* West Virginia University, B.A. (magna cum laude), 1974; University of Iowa, M.F.A., 1978.

ADDRESSES: Home—17 Hawthorn Rd., Brookline, MA 02146; fax: 617-739-5188. *Office*—Brandeis University, Department of English and American Literature, Rabb 249, Waltham, MA, 02454-9110. *Agent*—Lynn Nesbit, Janklow & Nesbit, 445 Park Ave., 13th Floor, New York, NY 10022-2606. *E-mail*—jphillip@brandeis.edu.

CAREER: Writer, professor, essayist. Boston University, Boston, MA, adjunct associate professor of English, 1982-1999; Brandeis University, Waltham, MA, Fanny Howe Chair of Letters, 1986-87, and fiction writer in residence, 1999—. Has also taught at Harvard University, Humboldt State University, New York University, Williams College, and writers conferences throughout the United States.

MEMBER: Authors League of America, Authors Guild, PEN.

AWARDS, HONORS: Pushcart Prize, Pushcart Press, 1977, for *Sweethearts,* 1979, for short stories "Home" and "Lechery," and 1983, for short story "How Mickey Made It"; Fels Award in fiction, Coordinating Council of Literary Magazines, 1978, for *Sweethearts;* National Endowment for the Arts fellowship, 1978 and 1985; St. Lawrence Award for fiction, 1979, for *Counting;* Sue Kaufman Award for first fiction, American Academy and Institute of Arts and Letters, 1980, for *Black Tickets;* O. Henry Award, Doubleday & Co., 1980, for short story "Snow"; Bunting Institute fellowship, Radcliffe College, 1981, for body of work; National Book Critics Circle Award nomination, American Library Association Notable Book citation, and *New York Times* Best Books of 1984 citation, all 1984, all for *Machine Dreams;* Guggenheim fellowship, 1988; Academy Award in Literature, American Academy of Arts and Letters, 1997.

WRITINGS:

FICTION

Sweethearts (stories), Truck Press (Durham, NC), 1976.
Counting (stories), Vehicle Editions (New York, NY), 1978.
Black Tickets (stories), Delacorte (New York, NY), 1979.
How Mickey Made It (story), Bookslinger Editions (St. Paul, MN), 1981.
The Secret Country (story), Palaemon Press (Chapel Hill, NC), 1983.
Machine Dreams (novel), Dutton (New York, NY), 1984.
Fast Lanes (stories), Vehicle Editions (New York, NY), 1984.
Shelter (novel), Houghton (Boston, MA), 1994.
MotherKind (novel), Knopf (New York, NY), 2000.

Contributor of essay to Jock Sturges, *The Last Day of Summer: Photographs,* Aperture (New York, NY), 1991.

RECORDINGS

Jayne Anne Phillips Interview with Kay Bonetti, American Audio Prose Library (Columbia, MO), 1991.
Jayne Anne Phillips Reads Souvenir and Machine Dreams, American Audio Prose Library (Columbia, MO), 1991.

OTHER

Contributor of writings to anthologies, including *Best American Short Stories,* 1979; *The O. Henry Awards,* 1980; *The Pushcart Prize Anthology,* vols. I, II, IV; *Norton Anthology of Short Fiction; American Short Story Masterpieces; The Eleventh Draft,* 1999; and *Why I Write,* 1999. Contributor of short stories to magazines, including *Atlantic Monthly, Canto, Doubletake, Epoch, Esquire, Fiction, Granta, Grand Street, Harper's, Iowa Review, North American Review, Paris Review, Persea, Ploughshares, Redbook,* and *Rolling Stone.* Phillips's works have been translated into twelve foreign languages.

SIDELIGHTS: Jayne Anne Phillips "stepped out of the ranks of her generation as one of its most gifted writers," wrote Michiko Kakutani in the *New York Times.* "Her quick, piercing tales of love and loss [demonstrate] a keen love of language, and a rare talent of illuminating the secret core of ordinary lives with clear-sighted unsentimentality," Kakutani continued.

The short stories in *Black Tickets,* Phillips' first effort for a commercial press, fall into three basic categories: very short stories, interior monologues by damaged misfits from the fringes of society, and longer stories about family life. In these stories, noted Michael Adams in the *Dictionary of Literary Biography Yearbook: 1980,* "Phillips explores the banality of horror and the horror of the banal through her examination of sex, violence, innocence, loneliness, illness, madness, various forms of love and lovelessness," and lack of communication. These stories were drawn, observed James N. Baker of *Newsweek,* "from observations she made in her rootless days on the road," in the mid-1970s when she wandered from West Virginia to California and back again, "then developed in her imagination."

"Most of the stories in *Black Tickets,*" stated Thomas R. Edwards in the *New York Review of Books,* "examine the lives of people who are desperately poor, morally deadened, in some way denied comfort, beauty, and love." While some of these stories deal with alienation within families, others are "edgy, almost hallucinatory portraits of disaffected, drugged out survivors of the 60s," according to Kakutani. Stories of this genre in the collection include "Gemcrack," the monologue of a murderer driven by a voice in his head that he calls "Uncle," and "Lechery," the story of a disturbed teenaged girl who propositions adolescents. These are "brittle episodes of despair, violence and sex," declared *Harper's* reviewer Jeffrey Burke, characterized by "economy and fierceness [and] startling sexuality," to quote Walter Clemons of *Newsweek.*

Other stories focus on less unique individuals. They are about "more or less ordinary people, in families, who are trying to love each other across a gap," according to Edwards. Stories such as "Home," "The Heavenly Animal," and "Souvenir" all deal with the problems of grown-up children and their aging parents: a young woman's return home forces her divorced mother to come to terms with both her daughter's and her own sexuality; a father attempts to share his life—Catholic senior citizens meals, car repairs—with his daughter and fails; a mother slowly dying of cancer still has the courage to comfort her daughter. In them, Edwards stated, "Phillips wonderfully captures the tones and gestures in which familial love unexpectedly persists even after altered circumstances have made [that love] impossible to express directly."

While some reviewers—like Carol Rumens in the *Times Literary Supplement,* who called the dramatic monologues in *Black Tickets* "dazzling"—enjoyed Phillips' richly sensuous language, others contended that the author's best work is found in the more narrative stories concerning the sense of alienation felt by young people returning home. Stone called these stories "the most direct and honest of the longer works in the collection" and stated that "the language in these stories serves character and plot rather than the other way around." "The strength in these stories," said Mary Peterson in the *North American Review,*"is that even narrative gives way to necessity: honesty gets more time than forced technique; language is simple and essential, not flashy; and even the hard truth, the cruel one, gets telling."

Machine Dreams, Phillips' fifth book, was her first novel. According to John Irving, writing in the *New York Times Book Review,* the novel is the prose format in which Phillips excels. He stated that Phillips is at her best "when she sustains a narrative, manipulates a plot, and develops characters through more than one phase of their lives or behaviors." In *Machine Dreams,* the author used the family in much the same way she had in some of the stories in *Black Tickets.* The sprawling novel tells the story of the Hampson family—Mitch, Jean, their daughter Danner and son Billy—focusing on the years between World War II and the Vietnam War, although it does show glimpses of an earlier, quieter time in Jean's and Mitch's reminiscences. It is the story of the family's collapse, told from the viewpoints of each family member.

In a larger sense, however, *Machine Dreams* is about disorientation in modern life, tracing, in the words of Allen H. Peacock in Chicago's *Tribune Books,* "not only [the Hampsons'] uneasy truce with contemporary America but contemporary America's unending war with itself." Mitch and Jean were raised in the days of the Depression, hard times, "but characterized by community, stability and even optimism. You could tell the good guys from the bad ones in the war Mitch fought," said Jonathan Yardley in the *Washington Post Book World. Machine Dreams* is, he concluded, "a story of possibility gradually turning into disappointment and disillusion," in which the Hampson family's dissolution mirrors "the simultaneous dissolution of the nation." Peacock echoed this analysis, declaring, "This is the stuff of tragedy: disintegration of a family, disintegration by association of a society." Toronto *Globe and Mail* contributor Catherine Bush pointed out that the machine dreams of the title, "the belief in technology as perpetual onward-and-upward progress; the car as quintessential symbol of prosperity; the glamour of flight . . . become nightmares. Literally, the dream comes crashing down when Billy leaps out of a flaming helicopter in Vietnam." Bush noted that the Vietnam conflict itself, however, is not the cause of the dissolution; appropriately, she observes, Phillips "embeds the war in a larger process of breakdown."

Part of this tragedy lies in the characters' inability to understand or control what is happening to them. Kakutani explained: "Everywhere in this book there are signs that the old certainties, which Miss Phillips's characters long for, have vanished or drifted out of reach. Looking for love, they end up in dissonant marriages and improvised relationships; wanting safety, they settle for the consolation of familiar habits." For them, there are no answers, there is no understanding. "This fundamental inexplicability to things," stated Nicholas Spice in the *London Review of Books,* "is compounded for Phillips's characters by their uncertainty about what it is exactly that needs explaining. Emerson's dictum 'Dream delivers us to dream, and there is no end to illusion' might aptly stand as the motto of the book."

Many reviewers recognized the strength and power of Phillips' prose in *Machine Dreams.* Novelist Anne Tyler wrote in the *New York Times Book Review* that "the novel's shocks arise from small, ordinary moments, patiently developed, that suddenly burst out with far more meaning than we had expected. And each of these moments owes its impact to an assured and gifted writer." Phillips also rises to the technical challenge of using more than one point of view. As John Skow of *Time* magazine declared, "Phillips . . . expresses herself in all four [character] voices with clarity and grace." Geoffrey Stokes wrote in the *Voice Literary Supplement,* "That *Machine Dreams* would be among the year's best written novels was easy to predict," and Yardley called the novel "an elegiac, wistful, rueful book."

Like *Machine Dreams,* Phillips' next work—another collection of short stories—concerns itself with discontinuity and isolation from the past. *Fast Lanes* begins with "stories of youthful drift and confusion and gradually moves, with increasing authority, into the past and what we might call home," commented Jay McInerney in the *New York Times Book Review.* Many of the characters "are joined more by circumstances than by relationships"; they "lack purpose and authority," said Pico Iyer of *Time* magazine. "Their world is fluid, but they do not quite go under. They simply float." These are people, added Kakutani, for whom "rootlessness has become the price of freedom, alienation the cost of self-fulfillment."

In some reviewers' opinions, *Fast Lanes* suffers in comparison with *Machine Dreams.* For instance, Kakutani stated that although "these [first] pieces remain shiny tributes to [the author's] skills, they rarely open out in ways that might move us or shed light on history the way that . . . *Machine Dreams* did." David Remnick, writing for the *Washington Post Book World,* found that the last two stories in the book—the ones most reminiscent of the novel—are "such strong stories that they erase any disappointment one might have felt in the other five. They are among the best work of one of our most fascinating and gritty writers, and there can be little disappointment in that." Chicago *Tribune Books* contributor Alan Cheuse similarly said that in these stories "you can see [Phillips'] talent grow and flex its muscles and open its throat to reach notes in practice that few of us get to hit when trying our hardest at the height of our powers."

Some of Phillips' best writing, concluded Marianne Wiggins of the *Times Literary Supplement,* concerns "the near-distant, fugitive past—life in the great USA fifteen years ago," reflecting the unsettledness of that period in American life. In some ways Phillips' writing returns to themes first expounded by the poets and novelists of the Beat generation; *Los Angeles Times Book Review* contributor Richard Eder called *Fast Lanes* "the closing of a cycle that began over three decades ago with Kerouac's 'On the Road,'" the novel about the post-World War II generation's journey in search of the ultimate experience. "It is the return trip," Eder concluded, "and Phillips gives it a full measure of pain, laced with tenderness." McInerney echoed this assessment, calling Phillips "a feminized Kerouac."

Unlike her expansive *Machine Dreams,* Phillips' second novel is "a tighter, smaller book, limited to a few voices and a few days; but what it lacks in scope, it gains in intensity," according to Andrew Delbanco in the *New Republic.* In this novel Phillips once again examined human loss, this time the loss of childhood innocence. Set in 1963 in a West Virginia summer camp for girls, *Shelter,* like Phillips' earlier fiction, renders a full range of voices. As Delbanco noted, Phillips "writes in the idiom of the trailer-park Mama as comfortably as in that of the bookish dreamer." He added, "In *Shelter,* where each chapter amounts to an interior monologue belonging to a different consciousness, [Phillips'] virtuosity is on full display. The result is a novel that has the quality of an extended eavesdrop."

Shelter tells the connected stories of four of the campers—fifteen-year-old Lenny Swenson, her eleven-year-old sister Alma, Lenny's friend Cap Briarley, and Alma's friend Delia Campbell—as well as those of Buddy, the eight-year-old son of the camp's cook, and Carmody, his ex-con stepfather. But as Gail Caldwell stated in the *Boston Globe,* "it is [the character of] Parson, a holy madman living on the fringes of the camp, who is Phillips' great creation." Parson has come to the camp ostensibly to lay pipe with a road crew, but actually in pursuit of Carmody, whom he met in prison. "I wanted to think about evil," Phillips told Delbanco in explaining her motivation for writing *Shelter,* "about whether evil really exists or if it is just a function of damage, the fact that when people are damaged, they damage others."

The children in *Shelter,* Deb Schwartz explained in the *Nation,* are "confused, lonely, struggling to temper a barrage of information and emotions with only the crudest of skills. They are slightly grotesque, clumsily chasing their half-formed desires and attempting to outrun their fears." The four young girls have more than summer camp in common: Lenny's and Alma's mother was in the midst of a love affair with Delia's father at the time he committed suicide. "Phillips," Schwartz wrote, "goes straight and true into their hearts and illuminates how children make sense of what they can."

Kakutani also commended Phillips' characterization: "In delineating the girls' relationships to one another and to their families, Ms. Phillips manages to conjure up the humid realm of adolescence: its inchoate yearnings, its alternately languid and hectic moods of expectation." Kakutani pointed out, too, the skillful way in which child molestation and incest are alluded to and "covered over with layers of emotional embroidery that transform the event even while setting it down in memory."

Though most reviews contain accolades for *Shelter,* R.Z. Sheppard's review in *Time* found fault. Describing the novel as "overwritten and trendy," Sheppard noted that its treatment of sexual abuse will undoubtedly prove "a hot selling point." By contrast, Ann Hulbert wrote in the *New York Times Book Review:* "To be sure, Ms. Phillips plays skillfully with the rich metaphoric implications of violated children—the religious overtones of creatures being cast out, the mythic dimensions of generational rivalry and decay." Hulbert concluded that Phillips is "an astute chronicler of American preoccupations."

In Phillips' 2000 novel, *MotherKind,* the author returned briefly to the Appalachian sites of *Machine Dreams* and *Shelter,* but placed most of the action in the Boston suburbs where Kate, the book's protagonist, now makes her home. Kate was born in West Virginia, and returns there to tell her mother, ill with cancer, that she is pregnant; her mother, whose death is expected within the year, agrees to move in with Kate in Boston. Katherine, Kate's mother, sacrifices all in order to be able to meet her new grandchild, and to live her last days close to a daughter with whom she has an extremely strong bond.

The novel, told from a third-person omniscient viewpoint that allows readers to hear the thoughts of all the major characters, dwells mostly with Kate's experience of new motherhood, and with her mother's decline into death. About the early weeks with her son Tatie, Kate reflects:

"The days and nights were fluid, beautiful and discolored; everything in her was available to her, as though she'd become someone else, someone with a similar past history in whom that history was acknowledged rather than felt, someone who didn't need to make amends or understand, someone beyond language. She was shattered. Something new had come of her. Moments in which she crossed from consciousness to sleep, from sleep to awareness, there was a lag of an instant in which she couldn't remember her name, and she didn't care. She remembered him."

At the same time Kate celebrates this new life with her whole being, she must bear witness to her beloved mother's weakening state. But a new baby and a dying mother are not Kate's only challenges: her son's father is also the father of two boys from a marriage he is still trying to dissolve, and the older boys are not eager to join a reconstituted family with a new "mom" and half-brother. Kate must find a way to make a connection with these boys that does not threaten their tie to their own mother, or their burgeoning sense of identity and independence.

The book's title comes from the agency Kate calls to help her care for her mother toward the end. At her Web site, Phillips herself described the relationship between the title and the novel in these words: "'MotherKind' is a term that refers to the human family women enter when they become mothers—a term that should be common usage. They enter a territory that is the other side of childhood and move from being someone's daughter, someone's lover, into the sudden fruition of passion and attachment that is labor, birth, and caring for an infant. . . . In *MotherKind,* birth and death happen as concurrent transformations, and the amazing strength of that relationship courses through and beyond both."

Critics' reactions to *MotherKind* were mixed. While a *Publishers Weekly* reviewer called the novel Phillips' "best so far," and applauded it as a "deeply felt, profoundly affecting" work, Richard Eder of the *New York Times* complained that "there are many pages that the writing fails to bring to life." Like Eder, Michiko Kakutani, who also reviewed the book for the *New York Times,* compared the writing unfavorably to the domestic evocations of John Updike and Anne Tyler, stating that "the mundane routines of daily life do not fully engage her imagination." While the reviews of both Eder and Kakutani were lengthy and respectful of Phillips's gifts as a writer, both evinced disappointment in *MotherKind.* Other reviewers, however, found much to commend in the novel. *Chicago Tribune* reviewer Alan Cheuse likened the novel to a Mary Cassatt portrait of mother and child, "beautifully composed and emotionally wrenching." "Even the most commonplace care, . . . becomes lyrical—but never, never sentimental—in the enlivening embrace of Phillips' wonderful prose," he added. In *Booklist* Brad Hooper remarked, "The story brims with vivid details of day-to-day family life, revealed largely through dialogue, which Phillips unerringly captures with consummate authenticity," an opinion that was also voiced by Judy Goldman in *Washington Post Book World,* "Her lastest novel is further proof of an extraordinary ability to reflect the texture of real life." Moreover, in a lengthy review for the *Knight-Ridder/Tribune News Service* Marta Salij concluded, "Too few books touch on the ferocity of women's lives, the intense will it takes to shepherd births and deaths without shrinking. *MotherKind* is the rare one that tells that truth." *MotherKind* is "both technically impressive and deeply moving," asserted a *Sunday Telegraph* reviewer, who added that the novel "deserves to be widely read by both men and women."

BIOGRAPHICAL AND CRITICAL SOURCES:

BOOKS

Contemporary Literary Criticism, Thomson Gale (Detroit, MI), Volume 15, 1980, Volume 33, 1985.
Dictionary of Literary Biography Yearbook: 1980, Thomson Gale (Detroit, MI), 1981.
Short Story Criticism, Volume 16, Thomson Gale (Detroit, MI), 1994.

PERIODICALS

Afterimage, October, 1985, p. 20.
Booklist, April 5, 2000, Brad Hooper, review of *MotherKind,* p. 1525.
Books and Arts, November 23, 1979.
Books and Bookmen, December, 1984, p. 25.
Boston Globe, April 5, 1987, p. 100; September 4, 1994, p. A12.
Boston Magazine, September, 1994, p. 70.
Boston Review, August, 1984; June, 1987, p. 25.
Chicago Tribune, September 30, 1979; May 14, 2000, Alan Cheuse, review of *MotherKind.*
Christian Science Monitor, June 7, 1985, p. B7.
Commonweal, October 19, 1984.
Detroit News, January 27, 1980; December 13, 1984.
Elle, April, 1987.
Encounter, February, 1985, p. 45.
Entertainment Weekly, December 2, 1994, p. 66.
Esquire, December, 1985.
Globe and Mail (Toronto, Canada), July 28, 1984.
Harper's, September, 1979.
Harper's Bazaar, September, 1994, p. 306.
Horizon, October, 1987, p. 63.
Irish Times, February 29, 2000, Eileen Battersby, "Fraught for Her Comfort."
Kirkus Reviews, February 15, 1987.
Knight-Ridder/Tribune News Service, May 24, 2000, Marta Salij, review of *MotherKind.*
Listener, December 13, 1984, p. 30.
London Review of Books, February 7, 1985, p. 20; October 1, 1987, p. 23.
Los Angeles Times, April 24, 1986.
Los Angeles Times Book Review, July 9, 1984; April 19, 1987, p. 3; September 4, 1994.
Ms., June, 1984; June, 1987, p. 18.
Nation, November 14, 1994, pp. 585-588.
New Leader, December 3, 1979.
New Republic, December 24, 1984; September 2, 1985; December 26, 1994, pp. 39-40.
New Statesman and Society, November 9, 1984; February 10, 1995, p. 45; September 2, 2000; October 9, 2000, Justine Ettler, review of *Motherkind.*
Newsweek, October 22, 1979; July 16, 1984.
New Yorker, October 24, 1994, p. 111.
New York Review of Books, March 6, 1980.
New York Times, June 12, 1984; June 28, 1984; January 6, 1985; April 4, 1987; April 11, 1987, p. 11; June 19, 1988; January 12, 1992; August 30, 1994, p. C19; May 12, 2000, Michiko Kakutani, "Caretaker for Both Son and Mother"; May 28, 2000, Richard Eder, "The Ties That Bind."
New York Times Book Review, September 30, 1979; July 1, 1984; March 17, 1985; May 5, 1985; May 3, 1987, p. 7; March 6, 1988, p. 32; September 18, 1994, p. 7.
North American Review, winter, 1979.
Observer (London, England), October 28, 1984; September 6, 1987, p. 25; October 30, 1988, p. 44.
Publishers Weekly, May 9, 1980; June 8, 1984; March 1, 1985; February 27, 1987, p. 152; December 4, 1987, p. 68; March 20, 2000, review of *MotherKind,* p. 72.

Quill and Quire, September, 1984.
San Francisco Chronicle, July 22, 1984; April 5, 1987.
Spectator, November 3, 1984.
Sunday Telegraph (London, England), October 1, 2000.
Threepenny Review, spring, 1981.
Tikkun, January-February, 1990, p. 68.
Time, July 16, 1984; June 1, 1987, p. 70; September 19, 1994, p. 82; May 15, 2000, Paul Gray, "Matters of Life and Death: Jayne Anne Phillips' *MotherKind* Tells a Moving Tale of Birth and Illness without Easy Ironies or Pathos," p. 84.
Times Literary Supplement, November 14, 1980; November 23, 1984; September 11, 1987, p. 978; September 22, 2000, Annmarie S. Drury, "West Virginians."
Tribune Books (Chicago, IL), June 24, 1984; July 22, 1984; April 19, 1987, p. 6.
USA Today, April 10, 1987, p. D8.
Village Voice, October 29, 1979.
Virginia Quarterly Review, winter, 1985, p. 23.
Voice Literary Supplement, June, 1984; February, 1986.
Wall Street Journal, July 25, 1984.
Washington Monthly, March, 1985, p. 42.
Washington Post, September 4, 1994, p. 5.
Washington Post Book World, December 21, 1979; June 24, 1984; April 26, 1987; May 14, 2000, Judy Goldman, review of *MotherKind.*
West Coast Review of Books, November, 1984.
Women's Review of Books, July, 1987, p. 24.

ONLINE

Jayne Anne Phillips Web site, http://www.JayneAnne Phillips.com/ (August 17, 2004).

* * *

PHILLIPS, Richard
See DICK, Philip K.

* * *

PICOULT, Jodi 1966-

PERSONAL: Surname is pronounced "*pee*-koe"; born May 19, 1966, in NY; daughter of Myron Michel (a securities analyst) and Jane Ellen (a nursery school director; maiden name, Friend) Picoult; married Timothy Warren van Leer (a technical sales representative), November 18, 1989; children: Kyle Cameron, Jacob Matthew, Samantha Grace. *Education:* Princeton University, B.A., 1987; Harvard University, M.Ed., 1990.

ADDRESSES: Home—P.O. Box 508, Etna, NH 03750. *E-mail*—c/o agent Laura Gross, lglitag@aol.com.

CAREER: Allyn & Bacon, Inc., Newton, MA, developmental editor, 1987-88; junior high school teacher of English and creative writing in Concord and Natick, MA, 1989-91; writer, 1991—.

AWARDS, HONORS: New England Book Award Winner for Fiction, New England Booksellers Association, 2003, for her entire body of work; Best Mainstream Fiction Novel designation, Romance Writers of America, 2003, for *Second Glance.*

WRITINGS:

NOVELS

Songs of the Humpback Whale, Faber & Faber (London, England), 1992.
Harvesting the Heart, Viking (New York, NY), 1994.
Picture Perfect, Putnam (New York, NY), 1995.
Mercy, Putnam (New York, NY), 1996.
The Pact: A Love Story, Morrow (New York, NY), 1998.
Keeping Faith, Morrow (New York, NY), 1999.
Plain Truth, Pocket Books (New York, NY), 2000.
Salem Falls, Pocket Books (New York, NY), 2001.
Perfect Match, Atria Books (New York, NY), 2002.
Second Glance, Atria Books (New York, NY), 2003.
My Sister's Keeper, Atria Books (New York, NY), 2004.
Vanishing Acts, Atria Books (New York, NY), 2005.
The Tenth Circle, Atria Books (New York, NY), 2006.

ADAPTATIONS: Picoult's novels *The Pact* and *Plain Truth* were adapted for television and aired on the Lifetime network, 2002 and 2004. *My Sister's Keeper* was optioned by Fine Line Films for theatrical release.

SIDELIGHTS: Since her first success with *Songs of the Humpback Whale* in 1992, novelist Jodi Picoult has produced several other books in quick succession, often working on two books simultaneously. While she did tell an interviewer for the *Allen-Unwin* Web site that "I moonlight as a writer. My daylight hours are spent with my three children," her writing time has become more constant since her husband chose to be a stay-at-home dad. Picoult's themes center on women's issues, family, and relationships. According to Donna Seaman in *Booklist,* the author is "a writer of high energy and conviction."

Picoult's second work, *Harvesting the Heart,* concerns Paige O'Toole, an Irish Catholic with some artistic talent. The product of an unhappy childhood and adolescence, Paige leaves home after high school and lands a job at a diner where she sketches customers. There she meets her future husband, the egocentric Nicholas Prescott, whom she eventually puts through medical school after his parents disown him. After their first child is born, Paige becomes frustrated with the pressures of motherhood and increasingly estranged from the busy Nicholas. At the end of her patience, she decides to leave her family and seek her own mother, who left her when Paige was only five. Paige's heartwrenching decision leads her to deal with her own identity as she discovers she is not like her irresponsible mother. A happy ending ensues, with Paige returning to her family and Nicholas learning to take on more family responsibilities. A *Kirkus Reviews* critic found that the book had "some good writing, but not enough to sustain a concept-driven and rather old-fashioned story."

After producing *Harvesting the Heart,* Picoult published *Picture Perfect,* a study of wife abuse, and *Mercy,* a story dealing with euthanasia. In 1998 she published *The Pact: A Love Story,* a legal thriller set in a New Hampshire town. The novel concerns the Hartes and the Golds, neighbors and close friends. Their teenaged children, Chris and Emily, who grew up almost as brother and sister, become romantically involved and enter into a suicide pact. However, Chris survives and is charged with murder. After an investigation, he is jailed, and the friendship between the two families dissolves. According to a *Kirkus Reviews* critic, the trial scenes in *The Pact* are "powerful," and the novel itself is "an affecting study of obsession, loss, and some of the more wrenching varieties of guilt." Seaman, writing in *Booklist,* dubbed Picoult's book "a finely honed, commanding, and cathartic drama."

The author's 1999 novel, *Keeping Faith,* also concerns characters in a small town struggling to maintain their concepts of honesty and faith. The protagonist, Mariah White, discovers that her husband has been unfaithful and subsequently sinks into depression. Her seven-year-old daughter, Faith, is upset by her mother's behavior and begins conversing with an imaginary friend, as well as acting as if she has newfound religious powers. Their lives enter a state of increasing upheaval as more and more of the faithful and the curious come to partake of Faith's supposed healing powers. Faith's father sues for custody of the girl, and an emotional court scene ensues. Margaret Flanagan, in *Booklist,* called the novel "a mesmerizing morality play."

Picoult's novel *Plain Truth* is set in the Pennsylvania Amish country. When a dead infant is discovered in the barn of an Amish farmer, a police investigation suggests that the mother is an eighteen-year-old Amish girl and that the baby did not die of natural causes. Although the teen denies responsibility, she is arrested and charged with murder. She is defended by a Philadelphia attorney, Ellie Hathaway, who soon clashes both with the will of her client and with the cultural values of Amish society. In the process of building her client's difficult defense, Ellie discovers more and more about her own inner life and personal values, while also learning to appreciate the values of the "plain people." Many reviewers praised the novel's suspenseful plot, its characterization, and its skillful portrait of Amish culture. *Knight-Ridder/Tribune News Service* contributor Linda DuVal said that in *Plain Truth* Picoult writes with "clarity" and "depicts a simple, yet deceptively complex, society of people who share a sense of compassion and the unshakable belief in the goodness of their fellow men and women."

In *My Sister's Keeper,* Picoult uses her characters to explore the ramifiications of cloning and gene replacement therapy, asking whether birthing one child to save the life of another child makes one a good mother—or a very bad one. A *Kirkus Reviews* critic declared that in *My Sister's Keeper* the novelist "vividly evokes the physical and psychic toll a desperately sick child imposes on a family, even a close and loving one." Noting that there are "no easy outcomes in a tale about individual autonomy clashing with a sibling's right to life," the reviewer explained that "Picoult thwarts our expectations in unexpected ways" and dubbed *My Sister's Keeper* "a telling portrait" of a modern American family under stress.

Picoult once noted of her work: "I am particularly concerned with what constitutes the truth—how well we think we know the people we love and the lives we live. I also write about the intricacies of family ties and connections, which often unearth questions that have no easy answers."

BIOGRAPHICAL AND CRITICAL SOURCES:

PERIODICALS

Booklist, April 1, 1998, Donna Seaman, review of *The Pact: A Love Story;* May 15, 1999, Margaret Flanagan, review of *Keeping Faith;* December 15, 2002, Kristine Huntley, review of *Second Glance;* January 1, 2004, Kristine Huntley, review of *My Sister's Keeper.*

Kirkus Reviews, August 15, 1993, review of *Harvesting the Heart;* March 15, 1998, review of *The Pact;* April 15, 2002, review of *Perfect Match;* January 1, 2003, review of *Second Glance;* January 15, 2004, review of *My Sister's Keeper.*

Knight-Ridder/Tribune News Service, June 15, 2000, Linda DuVal, review of *Plain Truth,* p. K239.

Library Journal, May 1, 2002, Nancy Pear, review of *Perfect Match;* February 15, 2003, Diana McRae, review of *Second Glance;* March 15, 2004, Kim Uden Rutter, review of *My Sister's Keeper.*

Publishers Weekly, May 6, 2002, review of *Perfect Match;* February 16, 2004, review of *My Sister's Keeper.*

ONLINE

Allen-Unwin Web site, http://www.allen-unwin.com/ (October 2, 2000), interview with Picoult.

Jodi Picoult Web site, http://www.jodipicoult.com/ (August 23, 2004).

* * *

PIERCY, Marge 1936-

PERSONAL: Born March 31, 1936, Detroit, MI; daughter of Robert Douglas and Bert Bedoyna (Bunnin) Piercy; married Michel Schiff (a physicist), 1958 (divorced, 1959); married Robert Shapiro (a computer scientist), 1962 (divorced, 1980); married Ira Wood (a writer and publisher), June 2, 1982. *Education:* University of Michigan, A.B., 1957; Northwestern University, M.A., 1958. *Politics:* Democrat. *Religion:* Jewish.

ADDRESSES: *Office*—Leapfrog Press, P.O. Box 1495, Wellfleet, MA 02667. *Agent*—Lois Wallace, Wallace Literary Agency, Inc., 177 E. 70th St., New York, NY. *E-mail*—leapfrog@c4.net.

CAREER: Writer. Indiana University, instructor, 1960-62; University of Kansas, poet-in-residence, 1971; Thomas Jefferson College and Grand Valley State College, distinguished visiting lecturer, 1975, 1978, and 1980; Holy Cross University, fiction writer-in-residence, 1976; Fine Arts Work Center, Provincetown, MA, staff member, 1976-77; women's writers conference, Cazenovia, NY, visiting faculty, 1976, 1978, 1980; University of Indiana, writers conference, poetry and fiction workshops, 1977, 1980; State University of New York—Buffalo, Butler Chair of Letters, 1977; Purdue University, summer write-in, 1977; Hartwick College, women's writers conference, visiting faculty, 1979, 1981, 1984; Vanderbilt University, Nashville, writers conference, 1981; Ohio State University, fiction writer-in-residence, 1985; University of California—San Jose, poetry and fiction, 1985; University of Cincinnati, poet-in-residence, 1986; University of Michigan, DeRoy distinguished visiting professor, 1992; Center for the Book, Fort Lauderdale, FL, resident poet, 2000. Also active in political and civic organizations, including Students for a Democratic Society, 1965-69, and North American Congress on Latin America, 1966-67. Consultant, New York State Council on the Arts, 1971, Lower Cape Women's Center, 1973-76, Massachusetts Council on the Arts Poetry Board, 1974, Massachusetts Foundation for Humanities and Council on the Arts, 1974, Wesleyan University Press Poetry Program, 1982-92, Massachusetts Arts Lottery Council, 1988-89, and Roots of Choice, 1995—. Member of boards of directors, Transition House, 1976, *Contemporary Novelists,* St. James Press, London, England, 1985—, Massachusetts Council on the Arts and Humanities, 1986-91, Israeli Center for the Creative Arts (HILAI), 1989-1995; artistic advisory board, American Poetry Center, 1988—; governor's appointee to the Massachusetts Cultural Council, 1990-91. Member, Writers Board, 1985-86, International Board, Aleph: Alliance for Jewish Renewal, 1993—, PEN New England, 1996—, *FEMSPEC: An Interdisciplinary Feminist Journal,* 1998—, Eastern Massachusetts Abortion Fund, 1999—, and American Story Project, 2000. Advisory editor, APHRA, 1975-77; advisor, Poetry on the Buses, 1979-81, Siddur Project, P'nai Or, 1986-91, and Am-Ha-Yam, 1988-98; literary advisory poetry panel, National Endowment for the Arts, 1989; served on the panels of *Harper Dictionary of Contemporary Usage,* 1982-83, and Massachusetts Council on Arts and Humanities, literature, 1985-86; Radcliffe Bunting Institute Selection Committee, 1987. Judge, Scholastic Awards, 1981, Avery Hopwood Contest, University of Michigan, 1983, 1988, *Negative Capability,* poetry contest, 1987, 1994, Alice Fay Di Castagnola Award, Poetry Society of America, 1993, and Ann Stanford Poetry Prize, University of Southern California, 1995. Poetry editor, *Tikkun,* 1988-96; editor, Leapfrog Press, 1997—; poetry editor, *Lilith,* 1999—.

MEMBER: PEN, National Organization for Women, Authors Guild, Authors League, National Writers Union, Poetry Society of America, National Audubon Society, Massachusetts Audubon Society, New England Poetry Club.

AWARDS, HONORS: Hopwood Award, University of Michigan, for poetry and fiction, 1956, and for poetry, 1957; Borestone Mountain Poetry Award, 1968 and 1974; literary award, Massachusetts Governor Communication on the Status of Women, 1974; National Endowment for the Arts award, 1978; Faculty Association medal, Rhode Island School of Design, 1985; Carolyn Kizer Poetry Prize, 1986 and 1990; Sheaffer Eaton-PEN New England Award for Literary Excellence, 1989; Golden Rose Poetry Prize, New England Poetry Club (NEPC), 1990; May Sarton Award, NEPC, 1991; Brit ha-Darot Award, Shalom Center, 1992; Barbara Bradley Award, NEPC, 1992; Arthur C. Clarke Award for best science fiction novel in the United Kingdom, 1992; named James B. Angell and Lucinda Goodrich Downs Scholar; Orion Scott Award in Humanities; Arthur C. Clarke Award, 1993, for *Body of Glass;* American Library Association Notable Book Award, 1997, for *What Are Big Girls Made Of?;* Litt.D., Lesley College, 1997, Bridgewater State College; Paterson Poetry Prize, 2000, for *The Art of Blessing the Day: Poems with a Jewish Theme.*

WRITINGS:

POETRY

Breaking Camp, Wesleyan University Press (Middletown, CT), 1968.
Hard Loving, Wesleyan University Press (Middletown, CT), 1969.
(With Bob Hershon, Emmet Jarrett, and Dick Lourie) *4-Telling,* Crossing Press (Freedom, CA), 1971.
To Be of Use, Doubleday (Garden City, NY), 1973.
Living in the Open, Knopf (New York, NY), 1976.
The Twelve-spoked Wheel Flashing, Knopf (New York, NY), 1978.
The Moon Is Always Female, Knopf (New York, NY), 1980.
Circles on the Water: Selected Poems of Marge Piercy, Knopf (New York, NY), 1982.
Stone, Paper, Knife, Knopf (New York, NY), 1983.
My Mother's Body, edited by Nancy Nicholas, Knopf (New York, NY), 1985.
Available Light, Knopf (New York, NY), 1988.
Mars and Her Children, Knopf (New York, NY), 1992.
What Are Big Girls Made Of?, Knopf (New York, NY), 1997.
Early Grrrl: The Early Poems of Marge Piercy, Leapfrog Press (Wellfleet, MA), 1999.
The Art of Blessing the Day: Poems with a Jewish Theme, Knopf (New York, NY), 1999.
Colors Passing through Us, Knopf (New York, NY), 2003.

NOVELS

Going down Fast, Trident (Roseville, MN), 1969.
Dance the Eagle to Sleep, Doubleday (Garden City, NY), 1970.
Small Changes, Doubleday (Garden City, NY), 1973.
Woman on the Edge of Time, Knopf (New York, NY), 1976.
The High Cost of Living, Harper (New York, NY), 1978.
Vida, Summit (New York, NY), 1980.
Braided Lives, Summit (New York, NY), 1982.
Fly Away Home, Summit (New York, NY), 1984.
Gone to Soldiers, Summit (New York, NY), 1987.
Summer People, Summit (New York, NY), 1989.
He, She & It, Knopf (New York, NY), 1991, published as *Body of Glass,* Michael Joseph (London, England), 1992.
The Longings of Women, Fawcett Columbine (New York, NY), 1994.
City of Darkness, City of Light: A Novel, Fawcett Columbine (New York, NY), 1996.
(With husband Ira Wood) *Storm Tide,* Fawcett Columbine (New York, NY), 1998.
Three Women, Morrow (New York, NY), 1999.
The Third Child, Morrow (New York, NY), 2003.

RECORDINGS

Marge Piercy: Poems, Radio Free People (New York, NY), 1969.
Laying down the Tower, Black Box (New York, NY), 1973.
Reclaiming Ourselves, Radio Free People (New York, NY), 1974.
Reading and Thoughts, Everett/Edwards (Deland, FL), 1976.
At the Core, Watershed Tapes (Washington, DC), 1976.

Has made several sound recordings or contributed to recordings, including a reading on cassette of excerpts from *Braided Lives, Woman on the Edge of Time,* and poetry, American Audio Prose Library (Columbia, MO), 1986; New Letters on the Air, interview and poetry reading, University of Missouri-Kansas City (Kansas City, MO), 1989; audiobook, *The Longings of Women,* Time Warner (New York, NY), 1994; BBC Radio Drama, broadcast of *Body of Glass,* 1995; excerpt from *Mars and Her Children* included in oratorio *Women of Valor,* by Andrea Clearfield, 1999.

OTHER

The Grand Coolie Damn, New England Free Press (Somerville, MA), 1970.

(With husband Ira Wood) *The Last White Class: A Play about Neighborhood Terror* (produced in Northampton, MA, 1978), Crossing Press (Freedom, CA), 1979.

Parti-Colored Blocks for a Quilt: Poets on Poetry (essays), University of Michigan Press (Ann Arbor, MI), 1982.

(Editor) *Early Ripening: American Women Poets Now,* Unwin Hyman (Cambridge, MA), 1988.

(With Nell Blaine) *The Earth Shines Secretly: A Book of Days,* Zoland Books (Cambridge, MA), 1990.

(With husband Ira Wood) *So You Want to Write: How to Master the Craft of Fiction and the Personal Narrative,* Leapfrog Press (Wellfleet, MA), 2001.

Sleeping with Cats: A Memoir, Morrow (New York, NY), 2002.

Work represented in over one hundred anthologies, including *Best Poems of 1967,* Pacific Books (Kailua, HI), 1968; *New Women,* edited by Robin Morgan, Joanne Cooke, and Charlotte Bunch-Weeks, Bobbs-Merrill (Indianapolis, IN), 1970; *The Fact of Fiction,* edited by Cyril Gilassa, Canfield Press (San Francisco, CA), 1972; *Psyche: The Feminine Poetic Consciousness,* Dial (New York, NY), 1973; *The Norton Introduction to Poetry,* third edition, edited by J. Paul Hunter, Norton (New York, NY), 1986; *Half the Human Experience: The Psychology of Women,* fourth edition, Janet Shibley Hyde, Heath (Lexington, KY), 1991; *The Book of Eros: Arts and Letters from Yellow Silk,* edited by Lily Pond and Richard Russo, Harmony Books (New York, NY), 1995; *The Oy of Sex: Jewish Women Write Erotica,* edited by Marcy Sheiner, Cleis Press (San Francisco, CA), 1999; and *Bearing Life: Women's Writings on Childlessness,* edited by Rochelle Ratner, Feminist Press (New York, NY), 2000. Contributor of poetry, fiction, essays, and reviews to periodicals, including *Paris Review, American Poetry Review, New York Times Book Review, Transatlantic Review, Mother Jones, New Republic, Ms., Woman's Day, Lilith, Michigan Quarterly Review, Village Voice,* and *Prairie Schooner.* Interviewed in anthology *Fooling with Words: A Celebration of Poets and Their Craft,* edited by Bill Moyers, Morrow (New York, NY), 1999.

Piercy's books have been translated into many foreign languages, including French, Danish, Dutch, German, Hebrew, Italian, Japanese, Norwegian, Swedish, and Turkish. Piercy's manuscript collection and archives are housed at the University of Michigan Harlan Hatcher Graduate Library.

ADAPTATIONS: Gone to Soldiers has been designed for Macintosh Power Books, Voyager Co., 1992; television mini-series rights to *The Longings of Women* were attained by Granada Television, 1995.

SIDELIGHTS: Feminist poet/novelist Marge Piercy writes about the oppression of individuals she sees in society, infusing her works with political statements, autobiographical elements, and realist and utopian perspectives. "Almost alone among her American contemporaries, Marge Piercy is radical and writer simultaneously, her literary identity so indivisible that it is difficult to say where one leaves off and the other begins," wrote Elinor Langer in the *New York Times Book Review.* A prominent and sometimes controversial writer, Piercy first became politically active in the 1960s, when she joined the civil rights movement and became an organizer for Students for a Democratic Society (SDS). After a few years, she concluded that the male power structure associated with the mainstream capitalist society was also operating in the anti-war movement and that women were being relegated to subservient work. In 1969 Piercy shifted her allegiance to the fledgling women's movement, where her sympathies have remained.

Piercy openly acknowledges that she wants her writing—particularly some of her poems—to be "useful." "What I mean by useful," she explained in the introduction to *Circles on the Water,* "is simply that readers will find poems that speak to and for them, will take those poems into their lives and say them to each other and put them up on the bathroom wall and remember bits and pieces of them in stressful or quiet moments. That the poems may give voice to something in the experience of a life has been my intention. To find ourselves spoken for in art gives dignity to our pain, our anger, our lust, our losses. We can hear what we hope for and what we most fear in the small release of cadenced utterance."

Piercy's moralistic stance, more typical of nineteenth- than twentieth-century writers, has alienated some critics, producing charges that she is more committed to her politics than to her craft. The notion makes Piercy bristle. "As a known feminist I find critics often naively imagine I am putting my politics directly into the mouth of my protagonist," she told Michael Luzzi in an interview collected in *Parti-Colored Blocks for a Quilt.* "That I could not possibly be amused, ironic, interested in the consonances and dissonances. . . . They notice what I have created and assume I have done so blindly, instead of artfully, and I ask again and again, why? I think reviewers and academics have the fond and foolish notion that they are smarter than writers. They also assume if you are political, you are simpler in your mental apparatus than they are; whereas you may well have the same background in English and American literature they have, but add to it a better grounding in other European and Asian and South American literatures, and a reasonable degree of study of philosophy and political theory."

Fellow feminist and poet Erica Jong sympathized with Piercy's dilemma, writing in the *New York Times Book Review* that Piercy is "an immensely gifted poet and novelist whose range and versatility have made it hard for her talents to be adequately appreciated critically." Piercy's sense of politics is deep-rooted. She grew up poor and white in a predominantly black section of Detroit. Her mother was a homemaker with a tenth-grade education and her father a millwright who repaired and installed machinery. From her surroundings, Piercy learned about the inequities of the capitalist system: "You see class so clearly there," she told Celia Betsky in the *New York Times Book Review.* "The indifference of the rich, racism, the strength of different groups, the working-class pitted against itself."

Piercy wrote candidly about those early years in her 2002 memoir, *Sleeping with Cats.* One of the title felines is Fluffy, the author's childhood pet, and the two would spend hours curled up together on the creaking porch swing. While inquisitive and intelligent, Piercy found that school was no haven from her hardscrabble home life; she recounts "the stench of urine and the yellow dirty halls" of her elementary school, the "old books, old desks, and the contempt of the teachers for us and themselves." Her parents, taking a disinterested stand in the girl's education, made it clear that they would have preferred their daughter to be a "healthy flirtatious little girl, a sort of minor-league Shirley Temple," as Pierce wrote in *Sleeping with Cats.* Rebelling, Piercy became a shoplifter and sexual adventurist instead. But the young girl's academic success overshadowed the negative images; she went on to win a scholarship to the University of Michigan and became the first in her family to attend college.

An enthusiastic undergraduate, Piercy was encouraged in her writing by winning several Hopwood awards. Still, professional success did not come easily. Ten years elapsed before Piercy was able to give up a series of odd jobs and support herself by writing. Her first six novels were rejected, and she suspects that *Going down Fast* found a publisher largely because of its lack of women's consciousness and its male protagonist. The narrative features a Jewish teacher, Anna Levinowitz, who sees issues of class and sexual politics while watching her childhood home being razed: "The outer wall and circle of windows were gone to dust. The pale blue walls were nude to the passerby. She felt a dart of shame." In an essay for *Dictionary of Literary Biography,* Sue Walker saw *Going down Fast* as a book that "confronts the questions, 'what have I done with my life? where am I going?'" Anna's role as a sexual object for her lover is depicted in a kitchen scene, where the man pinches Anna as she prepares his meal. "Piercy finds that men often see their relations to women as taming and dominating," noted Walker.

Piercy kept writing political novels featuring female characters, often with backgrounds similar to her own. In 1973, she published *Small Changes,* a novel that *New Republic* contributing critic Diane Schulder labeled "one of the first to explore the variety of lifestyles that women . . . are adopting in order to give meaning to their personal and political lives." Addressing women's issues head on, this book conveys what *New York Times Book Review* contributing critic Sara Blackburn called "that particular quality of lost identity and desperation, which, once recognized as common experience, has sparked the rage and solidarity of the women's liberation movement." In an essay she wrote for *Women's Culture: The Women's Renaissance of the Seventies,* Piercy described the book as "an attempt to produce in fiction the equivalent of a full experience in a consciousness-raising group for many women who would never go through that experience."

To demonstrate the way female subjugation cuts across social strata, Piercy included both a working-class woman, Beth, and a middle-class intellectual, Miriam, as main characters in *Small Changes.* In her depiction of these women, Piercy concentrated on what Catharine R. Stimpson of the *Nation* called "the creation of a new sexuality and a new psychology, which will permeate and bind a broad genuine equality. So doing, [Piercy] shifts the meaning of small change." Stimpson continued: "The phrase no longer refers to something petty and cheap but to the way in which a New Woman, a New Man, will be generated: one halting step after another. The process of transformation will be as painstaking as the dismantling of electrified barbed wire."

Widely reviewed, *Small Changes* received qualified praise. No critics dismissed the novel as unimportant, and most commended Piercy's energy and intelligence, but many objected to the rhetoric of the book. "There is not a good, even tolerable man in the whole lot of characters," observed Margaret Ferrari in her *America* review. "While the women in the novel are in search of themselves, the men are mostly out to destroy themselves and anyone who crosses their paths. The three main ones in the novel are, without exception, stereotyped monsters." For this reason, Ferrari described her reaction to the novel as "ambivalent. The realistic Boston and New York locales are enjoyable. The poetry is alluring and the characters' lives are orchestrated so that shrillness is always relieved. . . . In short, the novel is absorbing despite its political rhetoric." After praising Piercy's "acute" social reportage and her compelling story line, Richard Todd raised a similar objection. "What is absent in this novel is an adequate sense of the oppressor," he wrote in the *Atlantic*. "And beyond that a recognition that there are limits to a world view that is organized around sexual warfare. It's hard not to think that Piercy feels this, knows that much of the multiplicity and mystery of life is getting squeezed out of her prose, but her polemical urge wins out."

Piercy challenges the validity of such criticisms. "People tend to define 'political' or 'polemical' in terms of what is not congruent with their ideas," she told Karla Hammond in an interview collected in *Parti-Colored Blocks for a Quilt*. "In other words, your typical white affluent male reviewer does not review a novel by Norman Mailer as if it were political the same way he would review a novel by Kate Millet. Yet both are equally political. The defense of the status quo is as political as an attack on it. A novel which makes assumptions about men and women is just as political if they're patriarchal assumptions as if they're feminist assumptions. Both have a political dimension." And a few reviewers conceded their biases. William Archer, for instance, speculated in his *Best Sellers* review that "the special dimension of this book becomes apparent only through a determined suspension of one's preconceptions and a reexamination of their validity."

If *Small Changes* delineates the oppression of women, *Woman on the Edge of Time* affords a glimpse of a better world. The story of a woman committed to a mental hospital and her periodic time travels into the future, the novel juxtaposes the flawed present against a utopian future. "My first intent was to create an image of a good society," notes Piercy in *Women's Culture: The Women's Renaissance of the Seventies,* "one that was not sexist, racist, or imperialist: one that was cooperative, respectful of all living beings, gentle, responsible, loving, and playful. The result of a full feminist revolution." Despite a cool reception by critics, *Woman on the Edge of Time* remains one of Piercy's personal favorites. "It's the best I've done so far," she wrote in 1981.

With *Vida,* her sixth novel, Piercy returned to the real world of the sixties and seventies, cataloging the breakdown of the anti-war movement and focusing on a political fugitive who will not give up the cause. Named for its main character, Davida Asch, the novel cuts back and forth from past to present, tracing Vida's evolution from liberal to activist to a member of a radical group called the Network. Still on the run for her participation in a ten-year-old bombing, Vida must contend with a splintered group that has lost its popular appeal as well as the nagging temptation to slip back into society and resume normal life. "The main action is set in the autumn of 1979," explained Jennifer Uglow in *Times Literary Supplement,* "as Vida faces divorce from her husband (turned media liberal and family man), her mother's final illness, her sister's imprisonment and the capture of an old colleague and lover. The pain of these separations is balanced against the hope offered by a new lover, Joel." At the story's close, Joel, a draft dodger, is captured by the Federal Bureau of Investigation and Vida, for whom the loss is acute, is not certain she can continue. But she does. "What swept through us and cast us forward is a force that will gather and rise again," she reflects, hunching her shoulders and disappearing into the night.

A former political organizer, Piercy writes from an insider's point of view, and critics contended that this affects the novel. "There is no perspective, there are not even any explanations," said Langer in *New York Times Book Review.* "Why we are against the war, who the enemy is, what measures are justified against the state—all these are simply taken for granted." And while a state of "war" may well exist between American capitalists and American radicals, the 1960s revolutionaries are not of the same caliber as the French Resistance workers or the Yugoslav partisans, according to *Village Voice* contributing reviewer Vivian Gornick. "Vida Asch and her comrades are a parody of the Old Left when the Old Left was already a parody of itself," she stated.

Politics aside, reviewers found much that was praiseworthy in the novel. "The real strength of the book lies not in its historical analysis but in the power with which the loneliness and desolation of the central characters are portrayed," noted Uglow. Lore Dickstein called it "an extraordinarily poignant statement on what has happened to some of the middle-class children of the Sixties," in *Saturday Review.* And Langer commended *Vida* as "a fully controlled, tightly structured dramatic narrative of such artful intensity that it leads the reader on at almost every page."

In Piercy's following novel, *Braided Lives,* she "reminds us, growing up female in the 1950s hurt," wrote Brina Caplan in a review for the *Nation.* Jill Stuart, the protagonist, relates how difficult it was for women to survive this time period with esteem and independence intact. Jill describes the obstacles and events that challenged young girls coming of age in the 1950s, including attitudes toward sex, career, marriage, rape, abortion, lesbianism, verbal and physical abuse, sexual harassment, and women in general. "*Braided Lives* affects us by contrast—by distinctions made between then and now, between those who have and have not survived and, most important, between the subtleties of individual development and the more general movement of history," stated Caplan.

In the novel, Jill finds life at home almost unbearable; her father is indifferent and her mother is manipulative. Her parents expect that she will follow traditional ways and get married after high school, have children, and be a homemaker. Jill manages to escape this prescribed female role when she receives a scholarship to college. At college she and her friends vow never to end up as their mothers. "I don't know a girl who does not say, 'I don't want to live like my mother,'" Jill asserts in *Braided Lives.* Jill and her female friends enjoy their initial independence at college; they discuss philosophy and politics and engage in sexual experimentation. But these women are ambivalent and unsure of what they really want out of life. "One moment they are declaiming the need for total honesty with men and vowing that they will never end up possessive and dependent like their mothers. The next, they will do something 'castrating' to their boyfriends, in whom they wouldn't dream of confiding their frequent pregnancy scares," pointed out the *New York Time*'s Katha Pollitt.

"Is it our mothers, ourselves, or our men who mold us?" Jill wonders as she watches some of her friends succumb to cultural pressures and follow the path of their mothers. Many of Jill's friends fare poorly under traditional female roles. Donna, her best friend and cousin, is "haunted by a despair that she believes only marriage can alleviate," according to Caplan. She marries a man who later secretly punctures her diaphragm because he thinks she should get pregnant; when Donna does become pregnant, she gets an illegal abortion and bleeds to death. Another friend, Julie, marries and exists discontentedly in domesticity, while Theo is committed to an institution, first by her psychiatrist who raped her and, again, when she is expelled from college for sleeping with another girl. Out of her circle of friends, Jill alone survives with independence and esteem intact, despite the cultural pressures.

Piercy considers *Braided Lives* one of her best and most original works. In general, critics liked the writing too, but some noted that the novel deals too excessively with the problems of women. Caplan pointed out that *Braided Lives* seems "to accommodate almost every humiliation to which women are liable." Similarly, Pollitt found that Piercy "makes Jill & Company victims of every possible social cruelty and male treachery, usually more than once." Pollitt commended, however, Piercy's representation of female characters as fighters by noting that even those who did not survive the cultural oppression fought against the attitudes of the day. Pollitt concluded that the book "is a tribute to Piercy's strengths" and "by virtue of her sheer force of conviction, plus a flair for scene writing, she writes thought-provoking, persuasive novels, fiction that is both political and aimed at a popular audience but that is never just a polemic or just a potboiler."

A strong protagonist and an engaging plot are also the components of *Fly Away Home,* Piercy's eighth novel. Thanks to these strengths, this oft-told tale of a woman's coming to awareness because of divorce becomes "something new and appealing: a romance with a vision of domestic life that only a feminist could imagine," said *Ms.* reviewer Ellen Sweet. Though Daria Walker, the main heroine, is a traditional wife in a conventional role, Alane Rollings deems her "a true heroine. Not a liberated woman in the current terms of career-aggressiveness," Rollins continued in Chicago *Tribune Books,* "she is a person of 'daily strengths' and big feelings. When we first meet her, she is a success almost in spite of herself, a Julia Child-type TV chef and food writer, but more important to her, a loving wife and mother in a lovely home." Sweet concurred, calling Daria a "Piercy masterpiece."

Not everyone agreed with this assessment. Because Daria's self-awakening is tied to her growing awareness of her husband's villainy, and because Ross, the husband, is a sexist profiteer who exemplifies the inequities of the capitalist system, some critics suggested that "politics sometimes takes precedence over characterization," as Jeanne McManus put it in the *Washington Post Book World.* "Daria's not only got to get her own life together but also take on a city full of white-collar real estate criminals who are undermining Boston's ethnic minorities. And she's not just a full-figured woman in a society of lean wolfhounds, but also a bleeding heart liberal, a '60s softy, in an age of Reaganomics. It's a pleasure when Piercy lets Daria sit back and just be herself, frustrated, angry or confused." Piercy contends, however, that she does not try to control characters like Daria; the characters write themselves. In an interview with Luzzi, Piercy asserted that her "characters do have their own momentum and I can't force them to do things they won't do. Sometimes in the first draft, they disturb the neat outlines of the previously arranged plot, but mostly I try to understand them well enough before I start to have the plot issue directly out of the characters." And in the eyes of some critics, Piercy succeeded at this task in *Fly Away Home.* As Sweet observed in *Ms.:* "The real plot is in Daria's growing awareness of herself and her social context."

Piercy's 1991 novel, *He, She & It,* again deals with women's roles and participation in society at large. Rather than dealing with contemporary time periods, however, Piercy has events take place in the twenty-first century, also weaving in a myth from the sixteenth century. In the novel, the author creates a Jewish community of the future called Tikva where the scientist Shira has come to stay with her grandmother, Malkah, after losing a custody battle for her son. Malkah has recently helped develop a cyborg named Yod to protect their community from outside warring forces. While working with Yod, Malkah is reminded of an old Yiddish myth about a rabbi who creates a man of clay, a golem, and gives it life and socialization so that it will protect a Jewish enclave from their enemy. The golem saves the city and the Jews, and then is destroyed when he becomes uncontrollable. Like the rabbi, Malkah has given life to Yod and designates Shira the task of socializing him; eventually Shira falls in love with Yod. Yod saves Tikva, assists Shira in rescuing her son, and in the end, destroys himself and the workshop he was produced in so that his prototypes can not be used as weapons against their will. Shira considers recreating a new lover from the remaining data but concludes that, for the importance of free will, all the information should be destroyed.

Piercy's innovative technique in *He, She & It* was hailed by some critics. "Her approach is so lively and imaginative, her people so energetic, her two worlds realized in such stimulating detail that the novel is never a typical sci-fi adventure or a depressing account of disasters," commented Diana O'Hehir in her review for *Belles Lettres.* The distinguishing feature of the novel, according to the London *Times Literary Supplement*'s Anne-Marie Conway, "is the way Marge Piercy combines the story of Shira and Yod with the Yiddish myth of the Golem."

He, She & It received mixed reviews overall. Admiring Piercy's creativity, O'Hehir commented, "I was amazed at the fertility of Piercy's imaginings," but then pointed out that "what is lacking is an examination of the questions about creativity, science, and destruction that Piercy appears to be raising at the beginning of her book." "Marge Piercy confronts large issues in this novel: the social consequences of creating anthropomorphic cyborgs, the dynamics of programming both humans and machines, the ethical question of our control of machines that might feel as well as think," wrote Malcome Bosse in his review for *New York Times Book Review.* He then noted that Piercy's "ambitious new novel is not likely to enhance her reputation." Bosse finds Piercy's futuristic account beyond belief and contends the book "reads more like an extended essay on freedom of conscience than a full-rigged work of fiction." Conway found, however, that once the novel moves past the heavily detailed opening chapters, "Piercy relaxes and begins to enjoy telling her story."

In *The Longings of Women* Piercy returned to contemporary times in offering the stories of three women. Mary, at sixty-one, finds herself homeless following a divorce from her first husband and abandonment by a more recent lover. She stays alive by cleaning houses, typically sleeping at the airport or in churches. One of her clients, Leila, is the novel's second main character. A college professor, Leila is unhappily married to a philandering husband. The third protagonist, Becky, is a twenty-five-year-old woman accused of conspiring to murder her husband. Despite their different circumstances, all three women long for a place of their own—a place in which they can find privacy and from which they can seek love.

Critics once again noted Piercy's strongly feminist stance. Terming the novel "lively, densely textured" and "a feminist cautionary tale," *Chicago Tribune Books* reviewer Judith Wynn remarked that "Piercy is not an elegant writer. Interesting, swift-moving plots and careful social observation are her main strengths." Other critics found it more difficult to overlook Piercy's craft in favor of her message. *Washington Post Book World* contributor Constance Casey, for instance, called Piercy's writing "artless and humorless." And Pauli Carnes in the *Los Angeles Times Book Review* focused on the author's creation of another "sorry lot" of men: "murderous; alcoholic; self-indulgent; irresponsible; immature; emotionally stunted." Still, Casey praised Piercy's "militant sympathy and her eye for concrete detail."

Piercy's 1998 *Storm Tide,* penned with her husband Ira Wood, was described by *Library Journal*'s Andrea Lee Shuey as "a well-written novel, where imperfect people do foolish things with unfortunate results." The novel focuses on David Greene, a former small-town baseball hero who years later returns to Cape Cod and begins an affair with a married lawyer, Judith Silver. David, at the request of both Judith and her husband (who does not mind the affair), decides to run for a position as town selectman. David's opponent is supported by one of the leading men in the town, Johnny Lynch, and David begins an affair with one of Lynch's employees, Crystal Sinclair, all of which contribute to disaster for David. "Sex is played like a weapon in [*Storm Tide*], and David's [the] perfect target," remarked *Los Angeles Times* contributor Thomas Curwen.

A reviewer for *Publishers Weekly* called *Storm Tide* a "clunky, bloodless collaborative effort from two authors who have each produced better solo work," but added that "the novel does succeed on a lesser scale in its perceptive, stinging depiction of a parochial seaside resort." In *Library Journal,* Andrea Lynn Shuey praised the work, explaining that *Storm Tide* contains a "well-constructed plot" with "characters [who] are real."

Three Women, Piercy's 1999 novel, tells the story of independent women covering three generations in a family. The main characters are Beverly Blume, a seventy-two-year-old civil rights activist and feminist who recently suffered a stroke; Beverly's daughter, Suzanne, a forty-nine-year-old attorney and mother of two daughters who is beginning a new relationship; and Suzanne's oldest daughter, Elena, who has returned home after facing several personal troubles, including drug use. The novel, showing the growing bond that develops between the three women, is told from each of the main characters' perspectives, though focusing on Suzanne. Francine Fialkoff in *Library Journal* deemed *Three Women* "a somewhat disappointing effort from an old stalwart [that] may nevertheless be in demand among her fans." A *Publishers Weekly* reviewer observed that "Piercy keeps the plot humming with issues of motherhood, Judaism, generational tensions, sexuality, and independence," doing so in a pacing that is "confident." The same reviewer concluded: "Piercy's insight into her characters' emotional lives is an accurate reflection of intergenerational tensions."

Percy's sixteenth novel, *The Third Child,* is something of an updated variant on the Romeo and Juliet story. The child of the title, Melissa Dickinson, is the third of four children born to a conservative senator from Pennsylvania and his elegant, scheming wife. Melissa despises her parents for neglecting her, and she welcomes the chance to escape the household when she enters Wesleyan University. In a writing class at college she meets, and quickly falls in love with, just the kind of young man that her parents would most object to. He is part African American, Jewish, and adopted, and his adoptive parents are political foes of Melissa's father. He also has a dark secret, which comes to light when he learns more about Melissa's father. Reviews of the novel tended to be unflattering. In *Library Journal,* Beth E. Andersen wrote that Piercy "disappoints with her reliance on stereotypical characters and on modern fiction's literary device du jour—plot resolution at gunpoint." The *Publishers Weekly* reviewer agreed that the novel's resolution "is rather abrupt and over the top," but added that "it affirms that the most treacherous traps are those set by ignorance and innocence." *Kirkus Reviews* found the supporting characters to be little more than "cardboard cutouts" and the heroine "too whiny and self-centered to pity." Some critics dissented from this view, however. Donna Seaman, for example, wrote in *Booklist* that "there is nothing predictable about Piercy's extraordinarily magnetizing characters or this novel's bold and galvanizing story."

In addition to her novels, Piercy has published books of poetry, each of which reflects her political sympathies and feminist point of view. "I am not a poet who writes primarily for the approval or attention of other poets," she explained in her introduction to *Circles on the Water.* "Usually the voice of the poems is mine. Rarely do I speak through a mask or persona," she once told *CA.* "The experiences, however, are not always mine, and although my major impulse to autobiography has played itself out in poems rather than novels, I have never made a distinction in working up my own experience and other people's. I imagine I speak for a constituency, living and dead, and that I give utterance to energy, experience, insight, words flowing from many lives. I have always desired that my poems work for others. 'To Be of Use' is the title of one of my favorite poems and one of my best-known books."

Piercy's poetry recounts not only the injustices of sexism, but also such pleasures of daily life as making love or gardening. "There is always a danger that poems about little occurrences will become poems of little consequence, that poems which deal with current issues and topics will become mere polemic and propaganda, that poems of the everyday will become pedestrian," observed Jean Rosenbaum in *Modern Poetry Studies.* "To a very large extent, however, Marge Piercy avoids these dangers because most of her poetry contributes to and extends a coherent vision of the world as it is now and as it should be." Writing in the *New York Times Book Review,* Margaret Atwood referred to Piercy's perception as "the double vision of the utopian: a view of human possibility—harmony between the sexes, among races and between humankind and nature—that makes the present state of affairs clearly unacceptable by comparison."

In her poems, Piercy's outrage often explodes. "You exiled the Female into blacks and women and colonies," she writes in *To Be of Use,* lashing out at the mechanistic men who rule society. "You became the armed brain and the barbed penis and the club. / You invented agribusiness, leaching the soil to dust, / and pissed mercury in the rivers and shat slag on the plains."

Some critics claim that Piercy at her angriest is Piercy at her best, but the poet does not limit herself to negativism. She also writes of sensuality, humor, playfulness, and the strength that lies buried in all women and the ways it can be tapped. In *Hard Loving,* Piercy describes the energy in women's bodies as it moves through their hands and their fingers to direct the world, while a verse from *The Moon Is Always Female* contains advice about writing.

In addition to social problems, Piercy's poetry focuses "on her own personal problems," Victor Contoski explained in *Modern Poetry Studies,* "so that tension exists not only between 'us' and 'them,' but between 'us' and 'me.'" Her poetry is both personal—that is, addressed from a particular woman to a particular man—and public, meaning that it is concerned with issues that pertain to all of society. "Doing It Differently," published in *To Be of Use,* stresses that the legal system still maintains laws that treat women as property, demonstrates that even private relationships are tinged by social institutions, and questions the equality between men and women.

Available Light and *Mars and Her Children,* Piercy's subsequent books of poetry, cover a diverse range of topics, including nature, eating fruit, kitchen remodeling, love, and death. In an interview with the *Los Angeles Times*'s Jocelyn McClurg, Piercy explained her range and diversity by stating, "I think I'm somebody who believes there are no poetic subjects, that anything you pay attention to, if you truly pay attention, there's a poem in it. Because poetry is a kind of constant response to being alive." *Booklist*'s Donna Seaman viewed *Available Light* overall as expressing the confused feelings of growing older but described *Mars and Her Children* as a "spectrum of moods" dealing with Piercy's love for life.

What Are Big Girls Made Of?, Piercy's 1997 poetry collection, "invokes several public and private issues that have long haunted or angered her," according to John Taylor in *Poetry.* Several issues and subjects are examined in this collection, including marriage, Piercy's deceased older half-brother, dysfunctional families, sex, animals, society and politics, and feminism. Lara Merlin in *World Literature Today* commented of *What Are Big Girls Made Of?:* "The volume as a whole can be seen as Piercy's attempt to come to terms with the damage and waste she feels characterizes gender relations, and perhaps relations in general, in this country and then to begin to change them." Merlin also called the collection "a series of angry, often humorous, sometimes striking poems in an unabashedly feminist vein." Some critics appear to find Piercy's poems of a political nature in this work not as strong as those of other subject matter. For instance, a *Publishers Weekly* reviewer, though commenting that "less fully felt are poems with a social conscience," praised Piercy's use of "more transcendent subject matter." The same reviewer claimed that the collection is "as accessible and as crammed with experience as a novel." Judy Clarence in *Library Journal* stated, "Most of these poems are very effective, and magical moments abound." Clarence called the work a "strong collection" that she "highly recommend[s] for all libraries."

Piercy is also the author of two 1999 poetry collections: *Early Grrrl: The Early Poems of Marge Piercy* and *The Art of Blessing the Day: Poems with a Jewish Theme.* Of the first of these works, Ellen Kaufman in *Library Journal* commented, "This selection may not include her strongest work, but will be important to those who follow her closely." *Early Grrrl* collects various pieces of Piercy's from the mid-1970s and earlier on, including pieces from works currently out of print. *The Art of Blessing the Day* "is in many ways the best [of her poetry collections] yet," according to Judy Clarence in *Library Journal,* who further added that the work "brings together poems written to celebrate Piercy's Jewishness."

In a *Judaism* review, Steven Schneider elaborated on that theme, pointing to one entry, "The Chuppah," concerning the hand-held canopy under which Jewish marriages are performed. In Piercy's view, the chuppah is a metaphor "for all the activity that takes place between Piercy and her third husband. . . . Just as the chuppah creates an open space beneath its canopy, so too does Piercy envision her marriage as an open space, where she and her partner live, eat, sleep, celebrate, and struggle together." These poems, said Schneider, "draw upon traditional Jewish symbols like the chuppah and the mezuzah [a portion of the Talmud, sealed to the front door of a Jewish home], and Piercy will use these as a springboard for lyrics that represent her own distinctive relationship to Judaism. She consciously makes such ritual objects her own by integrating them into her life and poetry."

Piercy's 2003 collection of poetry, *Colors Passing through Us,* also generated much praise. Comparing Piercy's prose with her verse, Ellen Kaufman wrote in *Library Journal* that "Although Piercy has fun exaggerating her 'bad reputation' as a militant feminist . . . her poems can be warm and loving." She added that "Piercy fans, of which there are many, will relish this collection." "Piercy's poems seem so natural and right, as perfectly formed as an egg or a daffodil," wrote Donna Seaman in *Booklist.* Seaman expressed admiration for Piercy's humor and sensuality, and remarked: "Vital, bold, and visionary, Piercy is grateful for every hour of life and every drop of wisdom gleaned therefrom."

In an essay for the *Guardian,* Piercy compared fiction to poetry, finding that each genre can inspire the other. When working on a novel, for instance, she explains that if stuck in a difficult passage, "I may jump ahead to smoother ground, or I may pause and work on poems exclusively for a time. If I lack ideas for one genre, usually I have them simmering for the other." The mind "wraps itself around a poem," Piercy continues. "It is almost sensual, particularly if you work on a computer. You can turn the poem round and about and upside down, dancing with it a kind of bolero of two snakes twisting and coiling, until the poem has found its right and proper shape." Her fiction, she adds, "comes from the same party of my psyche that cannot resist eavesdropping on strangers' conversations. I am a nosy person. I have learned to control that part of myself, but I am still a good interviewer and a good listener because I am madly curious about what people's lives are like."

BIOGRAPHICAL AND CRITICAL SOURCES:

BOOKS

American Women Writers, second edition, St. James Press (Detroit, MI), 2000.

Barr, Marlene, editor, *Future Females: A Critical Anthology,* Bowling Green State University Popular Press (Bowling Green, OH), 1981.

Barr, Marleen S., *Lost in Space: Probing Feminist Science Fiction and Beyond,* University of North Carolina Press (Chapel Hill, NC), 1993.

Bartkowski, Francs, *Feminist Utopias,* University of Nebraska Press (Lincoln, NE), 1989.

Contemporary American Women Writers: Narrative Strategies, edited by Catherine Rainwater and William J. Scheick, University of Kentucky Press (Lexington, KY), 1985.

Contemporary Literary Criticism, Thomson Gale (Detroit, MI), Volume 3, 1975, Volume 6, 1976, Volume 14, 1980, Volume 18, 1981, Volume 27, 1984, Volume 62, 1991.

Contemporary Novelists, 6th edition, St. James Press (Detroit, MI), 1996.

Contemporary Poets, 6th edition, St. James Press (Detroit, MI), 1996.

Contemporary Women Poets, St. James Press (Detroit, MI), 1998.

Delany, Sheila, *Writing Woman: Woman Writers and Women in Literature Medieval to Modern,* Schocken (New York, NY), 1983.

Dictionary of Literary Biography, Thomson Gale (Detroit, MI) Volume 120: *American Poets since World War II, Third Series,* 1992, Volume 227: *American Novelists since World War II, Sixth Series,* 2000.

Ferguson, Mary Anne, *Images of Women in Literature,* Houghton (Boston, MA), 1986.

Freedman, Diane P., *An Alchemy of Genres: Cross-Genre Writing by American Feminist Poet-Critics,* University Press of Virginia (Charlottesville, VA), 1992.

Future Females: A Critical Anthology, edited by Marlene Barr, Bowling Green State University Popular Press (Bowling Green, OH), 1981.

Hicks, Jack, *In the Singer's Temple: Prose Fiction of Barthelme, Gaines, Brautigan, Piercy, Kesey, and Kosinski,* University of North Carolina Press (Chapel Hill, NC), 1981.

Hoegland, Lisa Marie, *Feminism and Its Fiction,* University of Pennsylvania Press (Philadelphia, PA), 1998.

Jackson, Richard, *Acts of Mind: Conversations with Contemporary Poets,* University of Alabama Press (Tuscaloosa, AL), 1983.

Keulen, Margaret, *Radical Imagination: Feminist Conceptions of the Future in Ursula Le Guin, Marge Piercy, and Sally Miller,* Peter Lang (New York, NY), 1991.

Kimball, Gayle, editor, *Women's Culture: The Women's Renaissance of the Seventies,* Scarecrow (Lanham, MD), 1981.

Kremer, Lillian S., *Women's Holocaust Writing,* University of Nebraska Press (Lincoln, NE), 1999.

Michael, Magali Cornier, *Feminism and the Postmodern Impulse: Post-World War II Fiction,* State University of New York Press (Albany, NY), 1996.

Modern American Literature, Volume 3, 5th edition, St. James Press (Detroit, MI), 1999.

Pearlman, Mickey, and Katherine Usher Henderson, *Inter/View: Talks with America's Writing Women,* University Press of Kentucky (Lexington, KY), 1990.

Representations of Motherhood, edited by Donna Bassin, Margaret Honey, and Meryle Mahrer Kaplan, Yale University Press (New Haven, CT), 1994.

Rigney, Barbara Hill, *Lilith's Daughters: Women and Religion in Contemporary Fiction,* University of Wisconsin Press (Madison, WI), 1982.

Rosindky, Natalie, *Feminist Futures: Contemporary Women's Speculative Fiction,* UMI Research (Ann Arbor, MI), 1984.

St. James Guide to Jewish Writers Worldwide, St. James Press (Detroit, MI), 1996.

St. James Guide to Science-Fiction Writers, 4th edition, St. James Press (Detroit, MI), 1996.

Thielman, Pia, *Marge Piercy's Women: Visions Capture and Subdued,* R.G. Fischer (Frankfurt, Germany), 1986.

Walker, Sue, and Eugenie Hamner, editors, *Ways of Knowing: Essays on Marge Piercy,* Negative Capability Press (Mobile, AL), 1991.

PERIODICALS

America, December 29, 1973.

American Book Review, June-July, 1992, Marleen S. Barr, review of *He, She & It.*

Atlantic, August, 1971; September, 1973.

Belles Lettres, spring, 1992, p. 25.

Bloomsbury Review, January, 1999, review of *Storm Tide,* p. 16.

Booklist, March 15, 1992, p. 1332; March 15, 1998, review of *What Are Big Girls Made Of?,* p. 1209; April 15, 1998, review of *Storm Tide,* p. 1357; February 1, 1999, Donna Seaman and Jack Helbig, review of *The Art of Blessing the Day: Poems with a Jewish Theme* and *Early Grrrl: The Early Poems of Marge Piercy,* p. 959; July, 1999, Donna Seaman, review of *Three Women,* p. 1895; September 15, 1999, Ray Olson, review of *Fooling with Words: A Celebration of Poets and Their Craft,* p. 215; February 1, 2000, Donna Seaman, review of *Bearing Life: Women's Writings on Childlessness,* p. 1004; June 1, 2001, David Pitt, review of *So You Want to Write: How to Master the Craft of Fiction and the Personal Narrative,* p. 1825; November 15, 2001, Brad Hooper, review of *Sleeping with Cats: A Memoir,* p. 522; March 1, 2003, Donna Seaman, review of *Colors Passing through It,,* p. 1141; September 1, 2003, Donna Seaman, review of *The Third Child,* p. 7.

Boston Globe, October 17, 1991, Alison Bass, review of *He, She & It.*

Boston Herald, June 14, 1998, Judith Wynn, "Cape Romance *Storm Tide* Ought to Make Waves on the Beach," p. O75.

Chicago Sun Times, March 20, 1994, Wendy Smith, review of *The Longings of Women.*

Chicago Tribune, April 10, 1984; April 7, 1985; March 27, 1988.

Chicago Tribune Book World, January 13, 1980; June 8, 1980; February 14, 1982; April 24, 1983; February 26, 1984.

City Limits, July 2-9, 1992, David V. Barrett, review of *Body of Glass.*

Detroit Free Press, February 28, 1982; May 1, 1994, Susan Hall-Balduf, review of *The Longings of Women.*

Detroit News, February 24, 1980; March 21, 1982; March 4, 1984.

Guardian (Manchester, England), January 6, 2000, Marge Piercy, "Look Both Ways," p. 10.

Houston Chronicle, January 20, 2002, Sharon Gibson, "How Marge Piercy Broke Tough Childhood Mold," p. 21.

Independent, May 19, 1992, Rosemary Bailey, review of *Body of Glass.*

Journal of Cooperative Living, spring, 1994, Lisa Davis, "Marge Piercy on Cooperative Living," pp. 57-58.

Journal of Narrative Technique, spring, 1993, Elaine Orr, "Mothering as Good Fiction: Instances from Marge Piercy's *Women on the Edge of Time,*" pp. 61-79.

Judaism, spring, 2001, Steven Schneider, "Contemporary Jewish-American Women's Poetry," p. 199.

Kenyon Review, spring, 1998, John Rodden, "A Harsh Day's Light: An Interview with Marge Piercy," p. 132.

Kirkus Reviews, April 15, 1998, review of *Storm Tide,* p. 520; August 1, 1999, review of *Three Women,* p. 1160; November 1, 2001, review of *Sleeping with Cats: A Memoir,* p. 1538; September 15, 2003, review of *The Third Child,* p. 1150.

Library Journal, February 15, 1992, p. 171; January, 1994, p. 164; February 1, 1997, Judy Clarence, review of *What Are Big Girls Made Of?,* p. 84; May

15, 1998, Andrea Lee Shuey, review of *Storm Tide,* p. 117; February 1, 1999, Ellen Kaufman, review of *Early Grrrl: The Early Poems of Marge Piercy,* p. 93; June 1, 1999, Judy Clarence, review of *The Art of Blessing the Day: Poems with a Jewish Theme,* p. 120; July, 1999, Francine Fialkoff, review of *Three Women,* p. 135; July, 2001, Lisa Cihlar, review of *So You Want to Write: How to Master the Craft of Fiction and the Personal Narrative,* p. 103; January, 2002, Carolyn Craft, review of *Sleeping with Cats: A Memoir,* p. 104; April 15, 2003, Ellen Kaufman, review of *Colors Passing through It,* p. 90; October 15, 2003, Beth E. Andersen, review of *The Third Child,* p. 99.

Lilith, summer, 1999, Karen Prager Kramer, review of *What Are Big Girls Made Of?*

Los Angeles Times, December 15, 1988; December 26, 1991, Devon Jersild, review of *He, She & It;* October 14, 1996, Michael Harris, review of *City of Darkness, City of Light;* June 24, 1998, Thomas Curwen, review of *Storm Tide.*

Los Angeles Times Book Review, April 3, 1994, p. 5; May 8, 1999, Zachary Karabell, review of *The Art of Blessing the Day: Poems with a Jewish Theme,* p. 2; October 3, 1999, review of *Three Women,* p. 11.

Modern Poetry Studies, number 3, 1977.

Ms. July, 1978; January, 1980; June, 1982; March, 1984; October-November, 1999, Laura Ciolkowski, review of *Three Women,* p. 93.

Nation, December 7, 1970; November 30, 1974; December 4, 1976; March 6, 1982, pp. 280-282.

New Leader, July 13, 1987, Hope Hale Davis, review of *Gone to Soldiers,* p. 19.

New Republic, December 12, 1970; October 27, 1973; February 9, 1980.

New Statesman, May 18, 1979.

Newsweek, January 24, 1994, review of *The Longings of Women.*

New York Daily News, June 17, 1995, Bill Bell, review of *The Longings of Women.*

New Yorker, April 10, 1971; February 13, 1978; February 22, 1982.

New York Times, October 21, 1969; October 23, 1970; January 19, 1978; January 15, 1980; February 6, 1982; February 2, 1984.

New York Times Book Review, November 9, 1969; August 12, 1973; January 22, 1978; November 26, 1978; February 24, 1980; February 7, 1982, pp. 6-7, 30-31; August 8, 1982; February 5, 1984; December 22, 1991, p. 22; March 20, 1994, Patricia Volk, review of *The Longings of Women,* p. 23; August 23, 1998, Ruth Goughlin, review of *Storm Tide,* p. 16; October 31, 1999, Betsy Groban, review of *Three Women,* p. 25; December 26, 1999, review of *Storm Tide,* p. 20.

People Weekly, April 4, 1994, p. 29.

Platte Valley Review, winter, 1990, Elizabeth G. Peck, "More than Ideal: Size and Weight Obsessions in Literary Works by Marge Piercy, Margaret Atwood and André Dubus."

Poetry, March, 1971; April, 1994, p. 39; January, 1998, John Taylor, review of *What Are Big Girls Made Of?,* p. 221.

Prairie Schooner, fall, 1971.

Progressive, January, 2001, Michelle Gerise Godwin, "Marge Piercy" (interview), p. 27.

Publishers Weekly, January 18, 1980; August 23, 1991, review of *He, She & It,* p. 42; March 23, 1992, review of *Mars and Her Children,* p. 65; December 13, 1993, review of *The Longings of Women,* p. 61; January 23, 1995, review of *The Book of Eros: Arts and Letters from Yellow Silk,* p. 62; July 24, 1995, Paul Nathan, "Looking Abroad," p. 15; September 23, 1996, review of *City of Darkness, City of Light,* p. 54; January 27, 1997, review of *What Are Big Girls Made Of?,* p. 94; April 27, 1998, review of *Storm Tide,* p. 42; February 22, 1999, review of *Early Grrrl: The Early Poems of Marge Piercy,* p. 91; August 16, 1999, review of *Three Women,* p. 57; August 6, 2001, "Mysteries of Writing," p. 81; December 10, 2001, review of *Sleeping with Cats: A Memoir,* p. 60; November 10, 2003, review of *The Third Child,* p. 42.

Reference & User Services Quarterly, spring, 1998, review of *What Are Bigs Girls Made Of?,* p. 275.

St. Louis Post, October 13, 1991, Gail Boyer, review of *He, She and It.*

Saturday Review, March 1, 1980; February, 1982.

Tikkun, September, 1999, review of *The Art of Blessing the Day: Poems with a Jewish Theme,* p. 81.

Times Literary Supplement, March 7, 1980; January 23, 1981; July 23, 1982; June 15, 1984; May 29, 1992, p. 21.

Toronto Star, June 25, 1994, Helen Heller, review of *The Longings of Women.*

Tribune Books (Chicago, IL), April 17, 1994, p. 3.

U.S. News & World Report, May 18, 1987, Alvin P. Sanoff, "A Woman Writer Treads on Male Turf," p. 74.

Village Voice, February 18, 1980; March 30, 1982.

Washington Post, December 31, 2001, Colman McCarthy, "A Woman in Touch with Her Felines," p. C03.

Washington Post Book World, January 27, 1980; February 7, 1982; May 30, 1982; February 19, 1984; March 27, 1994, p. 5.

Washington Times, July 19, 1998, Merle Rubin, review of *Storm Tide.*

World Literature Today, autumn, 1997, Lara Merlin, review of *What Are Big Girls Made Of?,* p. 792.

ONLINE

Early Grrrl: The Early Poems of Marge Piercy, http://www.leapfrogpress.com/ (February 28, 2002).

LitLinks, http://www.bedfordstmartins.com/ (August 3, 2004).

Marge Piercy Home Page, http://www.archer-books.com/Piercy/ (August 3, 2004).

* * *

PIERS, Robert
See ANTHONY, Piers

* * *

PINSKY, Robert 1940-

PERSONAL: Born October 20, 1940, in Long Branch, NJ; son of Milford Simon (an optician) and Sylvia (Eisenberg) Pinsky; married Ellen Jane Bailey (a clinical psychologist), December 30, 1961; children: Nicole, Caroline Rose, Elizabeth. *Education:* Rutgers University, B.A., 1962; Stanford University, Ph.D., 1966. *Religion:* Jewish.

ADDRESSES: Office—Department of English, Boston University, 236 Bay State Rd., Boston, MA 02215-1403. *E-mail*—rpinsky@bu.edu.

CAREER: University of Chicago, Chicago, IL, assistant professor of humanities, 1967-68; Wellesley College, Wellesley, MA, associate professor of English, 1968-80; University of California, Berkeley, professor of English, 1980-88; Boston University, Boston, MA, professor of English and creative writing, 1988—. Visiting lecturer, Harvard University, Cambridge, MA, 1979-80; Hurst Professor, Washington University, St. Louis, MO, 1981.

MEMBER: PEN, American Academy of Arts and Letters (appointed, 1999).

AWARDS, HONORS: Woodrow Wilson, Wallace Stegner, and Fulbright fellow, Stanford University; Massachusetts Council on the Arts grant, 1974; Oscar Blumenthal Prize, *Poetry* (Chicago, IL), 1978; American Academy of Arts and Letters Award, 1979; Saxifrage Prize, 1980; Guggenheim fellow, 1980; William Carlos Williams Prize, 1984; *Los Angeles Times Book Review* Award, Howard Morton Landon Prize for translation, both 1995, both for *The Inferno of Dante: A New Verse Translation;* Shelley Memorial Award, Poetry Society of America, 1996; Lenore Marshall Prize, and Pulitzer Prize nomination, both 1996, both for *The Figured Wheel: New and Collected Poems 1966-1996;* named Poet Laureate of the United States, 1997-2000; Harold Washington Literary Award, 1999; PEN/Voelcker Award for "an American poet at the height of his or her powers," 2004.

WRITINGS:

POEMS

Sadness and Happiness, Princeton University Press (Princeton, NJ), 1975.

An Explanation of America, Princeton University Press (Princeton, NJ), 1979.

History of My Heart, Ecco Press (New York, NY), 1984.

The Want Bone, Ecco Press (New York, NY), 1990.

(Translator) *The Inferno of Dante: A New Verse Translation,* illustrations by Michael Mazur, Farrar, Straus (New York, NY), 1994.

The Figured Wheel: New and Collected Poems, 1966-1996, Farrar, Straus (New York, NY), 1996.

Jersey Rain, Farrar, Straus (New York, NY), 2000.

OTHER

Landor's Poetry, University of Chicago Press (Chicago, IL), 1968.

The Situation of Poetry: Contemporary Poetry and Its Traditions, Princeton University Press (Princeton, NJ), 1976.

Robert Pinsky (recording), New Letters (Kansas City, MO), 1983.

(Translator, with Robert Hass) Czeslaw Milosz, *The Separate Notebooks,* Ecco Press (New York, NY), 1984.

Amy Clampitt and Robert Pinsky Reading Their Poems (recording), Archive of Recorded Poetry and Literature (Washington, DC), 1984.

Poetry and the World, Ecco Press (New York, NY), 1988.

Dorothy Barresi and Robert Pinsky Reading Their Poems (recording), Archive of Recorded Poetry and Literature (Washington, DC), 1992.

The Poet and the Poem from the Library of Congress: Robert Pinsky (recording), Archive of Recorded Poetry and Literature (Washington, DC), 1995.

Digital Culture and the Individual Soul (recording), Archive of Recorded Poetry and Literature (Washington, DC), 1997.

The Sounds of Poetry: A Brief Guide, Farrar, Straus (New York, NY), 1998.

(Collector) *The Handbook of Heartbreak: 101 Poems of Lost Love and Sorrow,* Rob Weisbach Books (New York, NY), 1998.

Poet Laureate Consultant in Poetry Robert Pinsky Reading His Poems in the Montpelier Room, Library of Congress, May 7, 1998, Archive of Recorded Poetry and Literature (Washington, DC), 1998.

Poetry and American Memory (recording), Archive of Recorded Poetry and Literature (Washington, DC), 1998.

Sharing the Gifts: Readings by 1997-2000 Poet Laureate Consultant in Poetry Robert Pinsky, 1999-2000 Special Poetry Consultants Rita Dove, Louise Glück, W.S. Merwin, 1999 Witter Bynner Fellows David Gewanter, Campbell McGrath, Heather McHugh (recording), Archive of Recorded Poetry and Literature (Washington, DC), 1999.

Robert Pinsky Reading Selections from the Anthology, "Americans' Favorite Poems, the Favorite Poem Project," and Discussing Them in the Mumford Room, Library of Congress, October 7, 1999 (recording), Archive of Recorded Poetry and Literature (Washington, DC), 1999.

The Poet and the Poem from the Library of Congress—Favorite Poets (recording), Archive of Recorded Poetry and Literature (Washington, DC), 1999.

(Author of introduction) David Noevich Goberman, *Carved Memories: Heritage in Stone from the Russian Jewish Pale,* Rizzoli (New York, NY), 2000.

(Editor, with Maggie Dietz) *Americans' Favorite Poems: The Favorite Poem Project Anthology,* Norton (New York, NY), 2000.

(Selector) Cate Marvin, *World's Tallest Disaster: Poems,* Sarabande Books (Louisville, KY), 2001.

(Editor, with Maggie Dietz) *Poems to Read: A New Favorite Poem Project Anthology,* W.W. Norton (New York, NY), 2002.

Democracy, Culture, and the Voice of Poetry, Princeton University Press (Princeton, NJ), 2002.

A Favorite Poem Reading with Frank Bidart, Louise Glück, and Robert Pinsky (recording), Recorded Sound Reference Center (Washington, DC), 2003.

(Editor) *William Carlos Williams: Selected Poems,* Library of America (New York, NY), 2004.

(Editor, with Maggie Dietz) *An Invitation to Poetry: A New Favorite Poem Project Anthology,* Norton (New York, NY), 2004.

Contributor of articles and poems to *American Review, American Poetry Review,Antaeus, Poetry,Shenandoah,* and *Yale Review.* Poetry editor, *New Republic,* 1978-86, and *Slate.com.*

SIDELIGHTS: Robert Pinsky is a poet and critic whose work reflects his concern for a contemporary poetic diction that nonetheless speaks of a wider experience. Elected Poet Laureate of the United States in 1997, Pinsky took his duties in that post quite seriously. His tenure as poet laureate was marked by ambitious efforts to prove the power of poetry, not just as an intellectual pursuit in the ivory tower, but as a meaningful and integral part of American life. "I think poetry is a vital part of our intelligence, our ability to learn, our ability to remember, the relationship between our bodies and minds," he told the *Christian Science Monitor.* "Poetry's highest purpose is to provide a unique sensation of coordination between the intelligence, emotions and the body. It's one of the most fundamental pleasures a person can experience." In a *New York Times Book Review* essay, Pinsky wrote: "Poetry is, among other things, a technology for remembering. But this fact may touch our lives far more profoundly than jingles for remembering how many days there are in June. The buried conduits among memory and emotion and the physical sounds of language may touch our inner life every day. . . . Poetry, a form of language far older than prose, is under our skins."

Pinsky once commented: "I would like to write a poetry which could contain every kind of thing, while keeping all the excitement of poetry." Pinsky's language, Willard Spiegelman stated in the *Dictionary of Literary Biography Yearbook,* "while obeying the idiomatic rules of [his] own age, is intelligible beyond the fashions of a given time." Calling Pinsky "a successful and assiduous poet laureate," *New York Times Book Review* correspondent Adam Kirsch added: "The tasks of the public poet usually suit him well, because his intelligence seems, at bottom, less lyrical than discursive, even didactic. This poetic mode is much less favored now than in the past, but as Pinsky proves, it is still able to give pleasure."

In his volumes of criticism, including *The Situation of Poetry: Contemporary Poetry in Its Traditions, Poetry and the World,* and *The Sounds of Poetry: A Brief Guide,* Pinsky presents his views on the nature of poetry. In *The Situation of Poetry,* he writes of the poet's need to "find a language for presenting the role of a conscious soul in an unconscious world." This emphasis on the actual leads Pinsky to see contemporary poetry as far more continuous with earlier poetry than many critics would believe. As Denis Donoghue remarked in the *New York Times Book Review,* Pinsky "believes, and is pleased to show, that contemporary poetry exhibits more continuity than change." Writing in the *Georgia Review,* Charles Molesworth commented that "given the pluralistic state of our poetry (and the jumbled social values it builds on), Pinsky's approach remains appropriate." Donoghue concluded that "the mind at work in *The Situation of Poetry* is lively, fresh and critical without being obsessed by the rigor of criticism."

In the essays of *Poetry and the World,* Pinsky expands on his concept of poetry and, in a series of essays, examines the impact words have had on his own life. "In his foreword," wrote John L. Brown in *World Literature Today,* "he claims that these various elements all concern 'the relation of poetry to its great, shadowy social context, the world.' They are also linked by a common tone, a tone of relaxed, unpretentious conversation comprehensible to the common reader." "Pinsky's criticism is far removed from that of his deconstructionist academic colleagues," Brown explained. "He proclaims his respect for literary tradition. . . . He has none of the urge to destroy the past which fired the avant-garde movements of this century." "Even the autobiographical digressions demonstrate a heartening sense of vocation," declared Amy Edith Johnson in the *New York Times Book Review.* "Mr. Pinsky's honorable practice confirms the dignity and creative dimension of . . . the function of criticism at the present time."

The Sounds of Poetry is a slim volume that can serve as a primer on the mechanics of poetry and also as a "treatise on the social functions of poetry," to quote James Longenbach in the *Nation.* The critic added that the work "is not only interesting but suspenseful to read. Without discussing the meaning of poems, Pinsky has created a keenly idiosyncratic account of the place of poetry in our time." *Atlantic Monthly* contributor David Barber noted that *The Sounds of Poetry* "is an achievement for which there is surprisingly little precedent: an authoritative yet accessible introduction to the tools of the poet's trade that can be read with profit by the serious student and the amateur alike." Barber characterized the volume as "less that of a solemn classroom lecture than that of a spirited audio tour, with Pinsky offering up various devices and motifs for inspection and providing a lively running commentary on how to fine-tune the ear to respond to the distinctive verbal energies that make poetry 'poetic.'" Longenbach concluded: "Whatever else it does, *The Sounds of Poetry* suggests why its author, who once wrote a poetry distinguished by subject matter, has become a poet of crotchety, gorgeous sounds. By showing us how to surrender ourselves to this bright confusion, Pinsky gives us the liberty to understand more than ever before."

In his own poetry, Pinsky has followed the principles set out in his criticism. "In Pinsky's poetry and criticism," explained Spiegelman, "there lies an abiding unity, of which the principal ingredients are ethical ambition, sanity, a sense of humor, and something to say." Critics of Pinsky's first collection, *Sadness and Happiness,* compared the work to Ranier Marie Rilke, James Wright, and Robert Lowell. "The feeling that, somehow, American poetry has entered a new era of confidence is borne out by . . . *Sadness and Happiness,*" declared *Yale Review* contributor Louis L. Martz. "Pinsky is the most exhilarating new poet that I have read since A.R. Ammons entered upon the scene. . . . The whole of the modern world is for Pinsky a region where the soul . . . has to face its mysteries; and the outer conditions for him are no worse or no better than they ever were for any generation."

Pinsky's book-length poem, *An Explanation of America,* examines the history of the United States in the same way that poet Robert Lowell had done, but, said Spiegelman, "his characteristic tone is less agonized and tense, more subdued than Lowell's." Although both poets draw on similarities between modern America and the ancient Roman Empire, the critic continued, "where Lowell's Rome is Juvenal's, Pinsky selects the earlier empire, Augustus's and Horace's, for his historical analogy to America." "Not the least remarkable thing about Robert Pinsky's remarkable [book]," stated Michael Hamburger in the *Nation,* "is that it seems to defy not only all the dominant trends in contemporary poetry but all the dominant notions—both American and non-American—of what is to be expected of an American poet." "In its philosophical approach, classical learning, and orderly structure," remarked *Hudson Review* contributor James Finn Cotter, *An Explanation of America* "resembles the work of William Cullen Bryant more than that of Hart Crane, but it is not old-fashioned. It is as American as Bryant's and Crane's long poems, as embedded in the past, and as identified with the woods and prairies."

Pinsky continues his examination of history—sometimes national, sometimes personal—in two later collections of poetry. "*History of My Heart,* which appeared in 1984," observed J.D. McClatchy in the *New Republic,* "was Pinsky's breakthrough, and my guess is that it will come to be seen as one of the best books of the past decade." McClatchy elaborated: "He might still use poetry as (in Emerson's phrase) 'a platform whence we may command a view of our present life, a purchase by which we may move it,' but he took his stand on the contradictions and desires of the self."

The best poems in Pinsky's 1990 collection, *The Want Bone,* according to McClatchy, "are more personal. They do not wrestle with religious angels or intellectual demons, the myths imposed on us by tradition. Instead, they address the self, those autobiographical myths we make out of memories." *Poetry* essayist Paul Breslin wrote: "In *The Want Bone,* Pinsky faces the limits of the pleasure principle that sustains *History of My Heart.* There, the erotic is the basis of the social, the drive that, not so much through sublimation as through cultivation, enables us to delight and sustain each other, and to delight in art. Here, desire is irreducible hunger."

The Figured Wheel: New and Collected Poems, 1966-1996 "will remind readers that here is a poet who, without forming a mini-movement or setting himself loudly at odds with the dominant tendencies of American poetry, has brought into it something new," maintained Katha Pollitt in the *New York Times Book Review.* Breslin felt that *The Figured Wheel* "signals a major turn in Pinsky's stylistic development. . . . [In] its hurling together of the apocalyptic and vast with the mundane and the particular, it fairly bristles with linguistic energy." The critic added: "The keen analytical intelligence of the earlier poetry does not disappear. But it is intellect in service to wonder, more ready to acknowledge the radical strangeness and intractability of the world it must try to comprehend." Pollitt claimed: "What makes Mr. Pinsky such a rewarding and exciting writer is the sense he gives, in the very shape and structure of his poems, of getting at the depths of human experience, in which everything is always repeated but also always new."

Pinsky's interest in a poetry of contemporary speech and wide-ranging subject matter led him in 1994 to publish a new translation of Dante's *Inferno.* He had been asked, with a group of nineteen other poets, to participate in a reading of the poem at the 92nd Street YMCA in New York City in May of 1993. Pinsky became fascinated with the work of the thirteenth-century Italian poet. "It just gripped me, like a child with a new video game," he told *New York Times* contributor Diana Jean Schemo. "I literally couldn't stop working on it." "I'm not fluent in Italian, but I love languages," Pinsky continued in an interview with *New York Times Book Review* contributor Lynn Karpen. "This was like being a child with a new toy. I called the translation a feat of metrical engineering, and I worked obsessively. It's the only writing I have ever done where it's like reading yourself to sleep each night. We have pillowcases stained with ink where my wife took the pen out of my hand at night."

Despite the fact that about fifty English-language translations of the *Inferno* have been published in the twentieth century alone, critics largely celebrated Pinsky's work. "The primary strength of this translation," declared *New Yorker* contributor Edward Hirsch, "is the way it maintains the original's episodic and narrative velocity while mirroring its formal shape and character. It is no small achievement to reproduce Dante's rhyme scheme and at the same time sound fresh and natural in English, and Pinsky succeeds in creating a supple American equivalent for Dante's vernacular music where many others have failed." "His skill and power as a poet inform every line of this splendid translation," stated John Ahern in the *New York Times Book Review.* "He shapes sinewy lines whose edges you can actually hear. This is true verse, not the typographical arrangement of poetic prose." The reviewer concluded: "From the beginning, his translation propels us through a gripping narrative whose drama is always in sharp focus and whose characters speak in distinctive voices. . . . [I]f he does not quite attain Dante's full symphonic range, no one has come closer."

Pinsky was named poet laureate in 1997 and served until 2000. The position carries a modest stipend, but its appeal lies in its visibility to the general public. Formerly a retiring person, Pinsky became a public figure, and he used the notoriety to promote a new project. Under his direction, ordinary Americans were invited to name their favorite poems—and some entrants were asked to read for a permanent audio archive at the Library of Congress. Pinsky set a goal of recording one hundred people, but he was inundated with letters and e-mails from all over the nation, and those participating represented all ages, all walks of life, and all levels of education. "The Favorite Poem Project is partly to demonstrate that there is more circulation of poetry and more life of poetry than there might seem with the stereotype," Pinsky explained in the *Progressive.* "I must say that the Favorite Poem readings, beyond my expectation, are very moving."

With Maggie Dietz, Pinsky edited a representative volume of reader responses called *Americans' Favorite Poems: The Favorite Poem Project Anthology.* A *Publishers Weekly* reviewer stated that "the selections are as diverse as the nation that chose them." *Americans' Favorite Poems* proved so popular that two subsequent collections have appeared: *Poems to Read: A New Favorite Poem Project Anthology* and *An Invitation to Poetry: A New Favorite Poem Project Anthology. Booklist* contributor Donna Seaman called *Poems to Read* "a graceful, sometimes jubilant, sometimes lyrical, sometimes brooding, but always welcoming and stirring collection."

Jersey Rain, published in 2000, was Pinsky's first collection of completely new work since *The Want Bone* appeared a decade earlier. Reviewing the work in *Library Journal,* Christian Graham observed that Pinsky's poems range from the mythic to the confessional. "Occasionally, his differing manners collide strangely," Graham stated, "but Pinsky delivers, as ever, intelligent, pensive poetry of great beauty." A critic in *Publishers Weekly* felt that the work's "lighter pieces will delight fans, but the poems with more profound aspirations lack a penetrating introspection." According to Lee Oser in *World Literature Today,* "the book holds interest both as a marker of poetry's development after modernism, and as the work of a fine and resourceful craftsman."

An *Atlantic Monthly* correspondent recognized Pinsky as "one of the most distinguished poets of his generation," and Breslin commented that Pinsky "has emerged as the finest American poet-critic since Randall Jarrell." For his own part, the last American poet laureate of the twentieth century told the *Progressive:* "I think the rhythms in a lot of my writing are an attempt to create that feeling of a beautiful, gorgeous jazz solo that gives you more emotion and some more and coming around with some more, and it's the same but it's changed, and the rhythm is very powerful, but it is also lyricism. I think I've been trying to create something like that in my writing for a long time."

BIOGRAPHICAL AND CRITICAL SOURCES:

BOOKS

Contemporary Literary Criticism, Thomson Gale (Detroit, MI), Volume 9, 1978, Volume 19, 1981, Volume 38, 1986.

Contemporary Poets, 7th edition, St. James Press (Detroit, MI), 2001.

Dictionary of Literary Biography Yearbook, 1982, Thomson Gale (Detroit, MI), 1983.

Poetry for Students, Volume 18, Thomson Gale (Detroit, MI), 2003.

Spiegelman, Willard, *The Didactic Muse,* Princeton University Press (Princeton, NJ), 1989.

PERIODICALS

American Poetry Review, July-August, 2003, Tony Hoaglund, "Three Tenors: Gluck, Hass, Pinsky, and the Deployment of Talent," pp. 37-42.

American Scholar, spring, 1999, Adam Kirsch, review of *The Sounds of Poetry,* p. 140.

Atlantic Monthly, March, 1999, David Barber, "What Makes Poetry 'Poetic?'," p. 114; October, 1999, p. 6.

Booklist, June 1, 2002, Donna Seaman, review of *Poems to Read: A New Favorite Poems Project Anthology,* p. 1670.

Christian Science Monitor, April 21, 1998, Marjorie Coeyman, "Poet Laureate's Request: Lend Me Your Voices," p. B8.

Georgia Review, spring, 1985.

Hudson Review, spring, 1980, pp. 131-145.

Library Journal, May 1, 2000, Graham Christian, review of *Jersey Rain,* p. 118; July 1, 2002, Daniel L. Guillory, review of *Poems to Read,* p. 85; October 15, 2002, Scott Hightower, review of *Democracy, Culture, and the Voice of Poetry,* p. 73.

Life, October, 1998, Melissa Faye Greene and Jillian Edelstein, "Poetry U.S.A.," p. 114.

Nation, January 26, 1980, pp. 86-87; September 21, 1998, James Longenbach, review of *The Sounds of Poetry,* p. 34.

New Republic, September 24, 1990, pp. 46-48; October 28, 2002, David Bromwich, "The Roughs and Beards," p. 25.

New Yorker, January 23, 1995, pp. 87-90.

New York Times, January 31, 1995, pp. B1, B2.

New York Times Book Review, February 20, 1977, Denis Donoghue, review of *The Situation of Poetry;* July 23, 1989, Amy Edith Johnson, review of *Poetry and the World,* p. 19; September 25, 1994, "A Man Goes Into a Bar, See, and Recites: 'The Quality of Mercy Is Not Strained,'" pp. 15-16; January 1, 1995, Lynn Karpen, "A Fear of Metrical Engineering," and John Ahern, "Vulgar Eloquence," p. 3; August 18, 1996, Katha Pollitt, "World of Wonders"; April 9, 2000, Adam Kirsch, "Vox Populi."

Poetry, October, 1990, pp. 39-41; July, 1997, Paul Breslin, review of *The Figured Wheel: New and Collected Poems 1966-1996,* p. 226; August, 1999, Christian Wiman, review of *The Sounds of Poetry,* p. 286.

Progressive, May, 1999, Anne-Marie Cusac, "Robert Pinsky," p. 35.

Publishers Weekly, October 25, 1999, "Home Grown," p. 77; March 6, 2000, review of *Jersey Rain,* p. 105.

TriQuarterly, winter, 1994, "A Conversation with Robert Pinsky," pp. 21-37.
Utne Reader, September-October, 1999, Anne-Marie Cusac, "Robert Pinsky's Grand Slam," p. 98.
World Literature Today, autumn, 1989, pp. 751-752; autumn, 2000, Lee Oser, review of *Jersey Rain,* p. 820.
Writer, November, 1999, Susan Kelly, "An Interview with Robert Pinsky," p. 18.
Yale Review, autumn, 1976.

ONLINE

Academy of American Poets Web site, http://www.poets.org/ (August 10, 2004), "Robert Pinsky."
Boston University Web site, http://www.bu.edu/ (October 17, 2003).
Favorite Poem Project Web site, http://www.favoritepoem.org/ (November 22, 2000).
Poetry & Literature Center of the Library of Congress Web site, http://www.loc.gov/poetry/poetry.html/ (August 9, 2004).

* * *

PINTA, Harold
See PINTER, Harold

* * *

PINTER, Harold 1930-
(David Baron, Harold Pinta)

PERSONAL: Born October 10, 1930, in Hackney, London, England; son of Hyman (a tailor) and Frances (Mann) Pinter; married Vivien Merchant (an actress), September 14, 1956 (divorced, 1980); married Antonia Fraser (a writer), November, 1980; children: (first marriage) Daniel. *Education:* Attended several drama schools, including Royal Academy of Dramatic Art, 1948.

ADDRESSES: *Agent*—Judy Daish Associates, 2 St. Charles Pl., London W10 6EG, England.

CAREER: Poet and playwright. Worked variously as a "chucker-out" in a dance hall, a waiter, a dishwasher, and a salesman; actor, under stage name David Baron, from 1948-58; performed with Shakespearean repertory company in Ireland, 1950-52, with Donald Wolfit's Bournemouth Repertory Company, and with other repertory companies, 1952-58, and infrequently in other roles, beginning 1960s, including as Mich, in *The Caretaker,* 1961, and as Interrogator, in *One for the Road,* 2001. Director of plays, 1970—; National Theatre, London, England, associate director, 1973—.

MEMBER: League of Dramatists, Modern Language Association (honorary fellow).

AWARDS, HONORS: London *Evening Standard* drama award, 1961, Antoinette Perry ("Tony") Award nomination for Best Play and Newspaper Guild of New York award, both 1962, all for *The Caretaker;* Italia Prize, 1963, for television play *The Lover;* two Screenwriters Guild Awards, for television play and for screenplay, both 1963; New York Film Critics Award, 1964, for *The Servant;* British Academy of Film and Television Artists (BAFTA) Award, 1965 and 1971; Commander, Order of the British Empire, 1966; New York Drama Critics Circle Award, Whitbread Anglo-American Theater Award, and Tony Award, all 1967, all for *The Homecoming;* Shakespeare Prize (Hamburg, West Germany [now Germany]), 1970; Writers Guild Award, 1971; Best New Play award, *Plays & Players,* 1971, and Tony Award nomination, 1972, both for *Old Times;* Austrian State Prize in Literature, 1973; New York Drama Critics Circle Award, 1980; Pirandello prize, 1980; Common Wealth Award, Bank of Delaware, 1981; Elmer Holmes Bobst Award for Arts and Letters, 1985; David Cohen British Literature prize, 1995; Nobel Prize in Literature, Swedish Academy, 2005. Honorary degrees include University of Reading, 1970, University of Birmingham, 1971, University of Glasgow, 1974, University of East Anglia, 1974, University of Stirling, 1979, Brown University, 1982, University of Hull, 1986, University of Sussex, 1990, University of East London, 1994, and University of Sofia (Bulgaria), 1995; honorary fellowship from Queen Mary College, 1987.

WRITINGS:

PLAYS AND SCREENPLAYS

The Room (also see below), first produced in Bristol, England, 1957; produced on Broadway at Booth Theatre, 1967.
The Birthday Party: A Play in Three Acts (first produced in Cambridge, England, 1958; produced in New York, NY at Booth Theatre, 1967; also see below), Encore (London, England), 1959, Samuel French (New York, NY), 1960, 2nd revised edition, Eyre Methuen (London, England), 1981.

The Dumb Waiter (also see below), first produced in German translation by Willy H. Thiem in Frankfurt-am-Main, West Germany, 1959; produced Off-Broadway with *The Collection* at Cherry Lane Theatre, 1962.

A Slight Ache (also see below), produced for BBC-Radio Third Programme, 1959; produced on stage in London, England, 1961.

Trouble in the Works [and] *The Black and White* (also see below), produced as part of *One to Another* (revue), in Hammersmith, England, 1959.

Request Stop, Last to Go, Special Offer, [and] *Getting Acquainted* (also see below), produced on the West End as part of *Pieces of Eight* (revue), 1959.

A Night Out (also see below), produced for BBC-Radio Third Programme, 1960; produced on stage on the West End, 1961.

The Caretaker: A Play in Three Acts (produced in London, England, 1960; produced on Broadway, 1961; also see below), Methuen (London, England), 1960, 2nd edition, 1962, reprinted, 1982.

Night School (television drama; also see below), Associated Rediffusion Television, 1960.

The Dwarfs (also see below; produced BBC-Radio Third Programme, 1960; produced on stage with *The Lover* in London, England, 1963), Grove (New York, NY), 1990.

The Collection (television drama; also see below), Associated Rediffusion Television, 1961; produced on stage on the West End, 1962; produced Off-Broadway with *The Dumb Waiter,* 1962.

The Lover (television drama; also see below), Associated Rediffusion Television, 1963; produced on stage with *The Dwarfs* in London, England, 1963.

The Servant (screenplay), Springbok-Elstree, 1963.

Dialogue for Three (radio drama; BBC-Radio Third Programme, 1964), published in *Stand,* Volume 6, number 3, 1963.

(With Samuel Beckett and Eugene Ionesco) *The Compartment* (unproduced screenplay), published in *Project 1,* Grove (New York, NY), 1963.

That's Your Trouble (radio drama; also see below), BBC-Radio Third Programme, 1964.

That's All (radio drama; also see below), BBC-Radio Third Programme, 1964.

Applicant (radio drama; also see below), BBC-Radio Third Programme, 1964.

Interview (radio drama; also see below), BBC-Radio Third Programme, 1964.

The Guest (screenplay; adapted from *The Caretaker*), Janus (London, England), 1964.

The Pumpkin Eater (screenplay; also see below), Rank, 1964.

The Homecoming: A Play in Two Acts (also see below; produced in Cardiff, Wales, 1965), Samuel French (New York, NY), 1965, revised edition, Karnac (London, England), 1968.

Tea Party (television drama; produced on BBC-Television, 1965; produced Off-Broadway with *The Basement,* 1968; also see below), Methuen (London, England), 1965, Grove (New York, NY), 1966.

The Basement (television drama; also see below), BBC-Television, 1967; produced Off-Broadway with *Tea Party,* 1968.

The Quiller Memorandum (screenplay; also see below), Twentieth Century-Fox, 1967.

Accident (screenplay; also see below), Cinema V, 1967.

Pinter People (television interview and sketches), National Broadcast Service (NBC-TV), 1968.

The Birthday Party (screenplay), Continental, 1968.

Landscape (radio drama; produced for BBC-Radio Third Programme, 1968; also see below), Pendragon Press (London, England), 1968.

Night (also see below), produced on West End as part of *We Who Are about To. . .* (later revised as *Mixed Doubles: An Entertainment on Marriage*), 1969.

Landscape [and] *Silence* (also see below), produced on the West End, 1969.

Sketches, produced in New York, NY, 1969.

Old Times (produced on the West End, 1971), Grove (New York, NY), 1971.

The Go-Between (screenplay; also see below), World Film Services, 1971.

The Homecoming (screenplay), American Film Theatre, 1971.

Monologue (television drama; produced for BBC-Television, 1973, then on stage), Covent Garden Press (London, England), 1973.

No Man's Land (produced on the West End, 1975), Grove (New York, NY), 1975.

The Last Tycoon (screenplay; also see below), Paramount, 1975.

(With Joseph Losey and Barbara Bray) *The Proust Screenplay: À la recherche du temps perdu* (based on the novel by Marcel Proust), Grove (New York, NY), 1978.

Betrayal (produced on the West End, 1978), Eyre Methuen (London, England), 1978, Grove (New York, NY), 1979.

Other Pinter Pauses (revue), produced in New York, NY, 1979.

The Hothouse (produced in London, England, 1980), Grove (New York, NY), 1980.

Family Voices: A Play for Radio (produced for BBC-Radio Third Programme, 1981; produced on stage at the West End, 1981; also see below), Grove (New York, NY), 1981.

(Adaptor) *The French Lieutenant's Woman* (screenplay; based on the novel by John Fowles; also see below), United Artists, 1981, published as *The French Lieutenant's Woman: A Screenplay,* Little, Brown (Boston, MA), 1981.

A Kind of Alaska (produced on West End, 1982; also see below), Samuel French (New York, NY), 1981.

Victoria Station (also see below), Samuel French (New York, NY), 1982.

Other Places (triple bill; includes *Family Voices, A Kind of Alaska,* and *Victoria Station;* produced in London, England, 1982; also see below), Methuen (London, England), 1982, Grove (New York, NY), 1983, revised version replacing *Family Voices* with *One for the Road* produced in New York, NY, 1984.

Betrayal (screenplay), Twentieth Century-Fox/International Classics, 1983.

Precisely (sketch), produced in London, England, as part of *The Big One,* 1983.

One for the Road (produced in Hammersmith, England, 1984), Samuel French (New York, NY), 1984.

Turtle Diary (screenplay), United British Artists/Britannic, 1986.

Mountain Language (produced on the West End, 1988), Faber & Faber (London, England), 1988.

The Handmaid's Tale (screenplay; based on the novel by Margaret Atwood), Cinecom Entertainment, 1990.

The Comfort of Strangers (screenplay; based on the novel by Ian McEwan; also see below), Erre Produzioni/Sovereign Pictures, 1990.

Party Time & The New World Order, Grove/Atlantic (New York, NY), 1993.

Moonlight (play), Grove (New York, NY), 1993.

Also author of *Langrishe, Go Down* (also see below), 1977. Contributor to *Seven Plays of the Modern Theater,* edited by Harold Clarman, Grove (New York, NY), 1962.

COLLECTIONS

The Birthday Party and Other Plays (includes *The Room* and *The Dumb Waiter*), Methuen (London, England), 1960, published as *The Birthday Party and The Room,* Grove (New York, NY), 1961.

A Slight Ache and Other Plays (includes *A Night Out, The Dwarfs, Trouble in the Works, The Black and White, Request Stop, Last to Go,* and *Applicant*), Methuen (London, England), 1961.

The Caretaker and The Dumb Waiter, Grove (New York, NY), 1961.

Three Plays: A Slight Ache, The Collection, The Dwarfs, Grove (New York, NY), 1962.

The Collection and The Lover (includes prose piece "The Examination"), Methuen (London, England), 1963.

The Dwarfs and Eight Review Sketches (includes *Trouble in the Works, The Black and White, Request Stop, Last to Go, Applicant, Interview, That's All,* and *That's Your Trouble*), Dramatists Play Service (New York, NY), 1965.

Tea Party and Other Plays (includes *The Basement* and *Night School*), Methuen (London, England), 1967.

The Lover, Tea Party, The Basement: Two Plays and a Film Script, Grove (New York, NY), 1967.

A Night Out, Night School, Revue Sketches: Early Plays, Grove (New York, NY), 1968.

Landscape and Silence (includes *Night*), Methuen (London, England), 1969, Grove (New York, NY), 1970.

Five Screenplays (includes *Accident, The Caretaker, The Pumpkin Eater, The Quiller Memorandum,* and *The Servant*), Methuen (London, England), 1971, revised version, replacing *The Caretaker* with *The Go-Between,* Karnac (London, England), 1971, Grove (New York, NY), 1973.

Plays, four volumes, Methuen (London, England), 1975–81, published with essay "Writing for the Theatre" as *Complete Works,* four volumes, Grove (New York, NY), 1977–81.

The French Lieutenant's Woman and Other Screenplays (includes *Langrishe, Go Down* and *The Last Tycoon*), Methuen (London, England), 1982.

Other Places: Three Plays (includes *A Kind of Alaska, Victoria Station,* and *Family Voices*), Grove (New York, NY), 1983.

The Comfort of Strangers, and Other Screenplays, Faber & Faber (Boston, MA), 1990.

Celebration; and, The Room, Grove (New York, NY), 1999.

Collected Screenplays, three volumes, Faber & Faber (London, England), 2000.

OTHER

Mac (on Anew McMaster), Pendragon Press (London, England), 1968.

(Editor, with John Fuller and Peter Redgrove) *New Poems 1967: A P.E.N. Anthology,* Hutchinson (London, England), 1968.

Poems, edited by Alan Clodd, Enitharmon (London, England), 1968, 2nd edition, 1971.

Poems and Prose, 1949-1977, Grove (New York, NY), 1978, revised edition published as *Collected Poems and Prose,* Methuen (London, England), 1986, Grove (New York, NY), 1996.

I Know the Place: Poems, Greville Press (Warwick, England), 1979.

(Editor, with Geoffrey Godbert and Anthony Astbury) *A Hundred Poems by a Hundred Poets: An Anthology,* Methuen (London, England), 1986.

The Heat of the Day, Faber & Faber (London, England), 1989.

Ten Early Poems, State Mutual Book & Periodical Service (Bridgehampton, NY), 1990.

(Editor, with Anthony Astbury and Geoffrey Godbert) *Ninety-nine Poems in Translation: An Anthology,* Grove (New York, NY), 1994.

Various Voices: Prose, Poetry, Politics, 1948-1998, Grove (New York, NY), 1998.

Contributor of poems, under pseudonym Harold Pinta, to *Poetry London.*

SIDELIGHTS: In an interview with a *New Yorker* contributor, Harold Pinter, one of the foremost British dramatists of the twentieth century, cryptically explained the geneses of three of his early plays: "I went into a room and saw one person standing up and one person sitting down, and a few weeks later I wrote *The Room.* I went into another room and saw two people sitting down, and a few years later I wrote *The Birthday Party.* I looked through a door into a third room, and saw two people standing up and I wrote *The Caretaker.*" Since *The Room* opened in 1957, Pinter's work has excited, puzzled, and frustrated audiences and academicians alike. While some have praised his work for its originality, others have dismissed it as willfully obscure—responses evoked by the plays' unconventional plots and character development, their inexplicable logic and inconclusive resolutions, and their distinctive dialogue, echoing the inanities of everyday speech as well as its silences. In spite of their disparagers, Pinter's plays are frequently produced—in English and in translation—and continue to attract popular and scholarly attention.

Born October 30, 1930, in Hackney, East London, England, Pinter grew up in a working-class neighborhood, which, despite some dilapidated housing, railway yards, and a dirty canal, he remembers fondly. However, like other English children who grew up in London during the air raids of World War II, he learned first hand about living with imminent and omnipresent terror, a theme that appears in much of his work.

Pinter's theatrical career started early. While attending Hackney Downs Grammar School he won title roles in *Macbeth* and *Romeo and Juliet. Hackney Downs School Magazine* recorded his dramatic debuts. Of young Pinter's Macbeth, the magazine's critic wrote in the summer of 1947: "Word-perfect, full-voiced, Pinter took the tragic hero through all the stages of temptation, hesitation, concentration, damnation. He gave us both Macbeth's conflicts, inner and outer, mental and military, with vigour, insight, and remarkable acting resource." The summer 1948 review of Pinter's Romeo, if somewhat less laudatory, pointed nonetheless to the young actor's flair for the dramatic: "Pinter again bore the heat and burden of the evening with unfailing vitality. . . . Perhaps he excelled where strong action reinforces the words—as where he flung himself on the floor of the Friar's cell in passionate histrionic abandon."

Both these reviews are remarkably prescient: what the young actor apparently learned, in part at least from playing Macbeth and Romeo, Pinter the playwright uses. His characters are at their most compelling when their conflicts are "inner" and "mental," unseeable and therefore frequently unnameable; his plots, despite their surface calm and minimal physical action, nonetheless demonstrate "histrionic abandon," the result of verbal brilliance and stunning visual imagery.

Along with acting, young Pinter displayed a talent for athletics: in 1948 he broke the school record for running 220 yards and equaled the record for running 100 yards. His continued interest in cricket and squash is reflected in his work: the characters in *No Man's Land* are named after famous cricket players, while in *Betrayal* the game of squash is symbolically important to the play's meaning. In Pinter's screenplays, sports and sports imagery are similarly illuminating.

Besides his successes at play—both on field and on stage—*Hackney Downs School Magazine* also recorded those of a literary bent: an essay and two poems which attest to the young artist's sensitivity to language. In his essay, "James Joyce," published in the winter, 1946, issue, Pinter discusses the novelist's poetic use of language: "and slowly the words subside into softness, softly drifting." His juvenile poetry features the alliteration, repetition, and play with language that appears in his adult work, drama and poetry alike.

Pinter's verbal acumen was also rewarded outside the world of belles lettres: it helped the young man ward off East End thugs. As Pinter recalled in a *Paris Review* interview with Lawrence M. Bensky: "I did encounter [violence] in quite an extreme form. . . . If you looked remotely like a Jew you might be in trouble. Also, I went to a Jewish club, by an old railway arch, and there were quite a lot of people often waiting with broken milk bottles in a particular alley we used to walk through. There were one or two ways of getting out of it—one was purely physical, of course, but you couldn't do anything about the milk bottles—*we* didn't have any milk bottles. The best way was to talk to them, you know, sort of 'Are you all right?' 'Yes, I'm all right.' 'Well, that's all right then, isn't it?' and all the time keep walking toward the lights of the main road." Manipulating language in order to shield oneself from physical or emotional harm without conveying rational information is a skill possessed by many of Pinter's dramatic characters.

Pinter left grammar school in 1947 and, although he earned a grant to study acting at the Royal Academy of Dramatic Art (RADA) the following year, he only remained there for a few months. As he explained in his *New Yorker* interview, Pinter spent the next ten years writing—"Not plays. Hundreds of poems . . . and short prose pieces"—and acting: "My experience as an actor has influenced my plays. . . . I think I certainly developed some feeling for construction . . . and for speakable dialogue." As an actor Pinter grew intimately familiar with the dramatic properties of the stage and the spoken word, while as a poet he explored the emotive possibilities of language.

In 1950 *Poetry London* published several of his poems under the pseudonym "Harold Pinta," and the poet began work as a professional radio and television actor. In *Poems and Prose, 1949-1977* Pinter declares that in 1951 he began a two-year stint with Anew McMaster's touring company in Ireland, his "first job proper on the stage;" after returning from Ireland, he acted in repertory companies under the stage name of David Baron. In 1957 Pinta the poet and Baron the actor collaborated on a one-act play, *The Room,* the writing of which took Pinter the playwright "four days, working in the afternoons," he told *New Yorker.*

After *The Room,* Pinter's plays came fast. During 1957 he wrote *The Dumb Waiter,* a one-act play, and *The Birthday Party,* his first full-length play, which ran for only one week and got terrible reviews, with one notable exception—Harold Hobson's appraisal in the London *Sunday Times:* "Now I am well aware that Mr. Pinter's play received extremely bad notices last Thursday morning. At the moment I write these lines it is uncertain even whether the play will still be in the bill when they appear, though it is probable it will soon be seen elsewhere. Deliberately, I am willing to risk whatever reputation I have as a judge of plays by saying that *The Birthday Party* is . . . a First, and that Mr. Pinter, on the evidence of this work, possesses the most original, disturbing and arresting talent in theatrical London."

Despite *The Birthday Party*'s lackluster debut, during 1958 and 1959 Pinter continued to write plays for radio and stage: *A Slight Ache; The Hothouse* (which was not produced until 1980); revue sketches; and *A Night Out.* With his second full-length play, *The Caretaker,* the playwright received critical accolades. Kenneth Tynan commented in the *Observer* that with *The Caretaker* "Pinter has begun to fulfill the promise that I signally failed to see in *The Birthday Party* two years ago. The latter play was a clever fragment grown dropsical with symbolic content. . . . In *The Caretaker* symptoms of paranoia are still detectable . . . but their intensity is considerably abated; and the symbols have mostly retired to the background. What remains is a play about people." *The Caretaker* ran for twelve months in London's West End and in October, 1961, opened on Broadway, again to critical, but not commercial, success. In *New York Times,* Howard Taubman wrote that the play "proclaims its young English author as one of the important playwrights of our day."

Important and prolific, Pinter continued to write plays; short ones, including *Night School* and *The Dwarfs, The Collection* and *The Lover, Tea Party;* and full-length ones, such as *Old Times, No Man's Land, Betrayal,* and *The Homecoming,* the last which established Pinter's reputation as a major dramatist. More recently he has concentrated on short but intriguing theatrical pieces: *Family Voices, Victoria Station, A Kind of Alaska,* and *One for the Road.*

Although they cannot be easily classified according to dramatic schools, Pinter's plays nonetheless reflect movements in the British theatre of the second half of the twentieth century, including realism, epic theatre, and absurdism. Early critics perceived the author of *The Room* and *The Birthday Party* to be a member of the "kitchen sink" school of realism, joining the works of John Osborne, Shelagh Delaney, and other British playwrights who drew characters from the working class and their dialogue from regional speech. Especially in his first few plays, Pinter's lower-class characters with their Cockney idiom and their bleak settings recall the social, psychological, and linguistic verisimilitude found in "kitchen sink" drama. However, his is a surface realism. He is not essentially, as Martin Esslin pointed out in *Pinter the Playwright,* a realistic dramatist: "This is the paradox of his artistic personality. The dialogue and the characters are real, but the over-all effect is one of mystery, of uncertainty, of poetic ambiguity." Nor does Pinter regard himself as belonging to this dramatic school: "I'd say what goes on in my plays is realistic, but what I'm doing is not realism," he declared in *Paris Review* interview.

Epic theater appeared to have the least influence on Pinter. Unlike such contemporaries as John Arden, Arnold Wesher, and Edmund Bond who were greatly influenced by German playwright Bertolt Brecht, Pinter has, for the most part, eschewed such Brechtian conventions as protagonists who represent the working class or themes that are socially and politically timely. However, in *The Hothouse,* a farcical play set in a mental institution, and in *One for the Road,* a disturbing one-act play that takes place in a government retaining home, Pinter touches on social commentary—the insidious inanity of bureaucracies and the mechanistic sadism of totalitarianism—and, epic-like, appeals primarily to his audience's intellect rather than to its emotions.

In its characteristic predilection for examining the private rather than the social sphere, Pinter's work is perhaps most clearly influenced by the absurdists, particularly by Irish playwright and novelist Samuel Beckett. Admittedly, the world of Pinter's *Betrayal* is not that of Beckett's *Endgame;* the disjunction within the former results from marital discord, within the latter from existential fragmentation. Nevertheless, as Esslin noted in *Pinter the Playwright:* "Existential adjustment, coming to terms with one's own being, precedes, and necessarily predetermines, one's attitude to society, politics, and general ideas. Like Beckett and [Franz] Kafka Pinter's attitude . . . is that of an existentialist: the mode of a man's *being* determines his *thinking.* Hence, to come to grips with the true sources of their attitudes, the playwright must catch his characters at the decisive points in their lives, when they are confronted with the crisis of adjustment to themselves." As in much of absurdist drama, the names and behaviors of Pinter's characters, the plays' props and sets, resonate symbolically: "Riley" in *The Room* and *Family Voices,* the matchseller in *A Slight Ache,* the statue of Buddha in *The Caretaker,* vases and olives in *The Collection,* for example. Although Stanley in *The Birthday Party* is not *Endgame*'s Hamm or Clov, he contains elements of both—blindness and entrapment—and his fate is similarly and existentially capricious.

Belonging to no single school, Pinter has drawn from each to create a body of work idiosyncratically and recognizably his own. Those dramatic elements that are identifiably "Pinteresque" include his characters' mysterious pasts, his theme of the intruder, and his use of language—textual and subtextual—and of silence. In *Pinter the Playwright* Esslin quoted a letter received by Pinter shortly after *The Birthday Party* opened: "Dear Sir, I would be obliged if you would kindly explain to me the meaning of your play *The Birthday Party.* These are the points I do not understand: 1. Who are the two men? 2. Where did Stanley come from? 3. Were they all supposed to be normal? You will appreciate that without the answers to my questions I cannot fully understand your play." Pinter is said to have replied: "Dear Madam, I would be obliged if you would kindly explain to me the meaning of your letter. These are the points which I do not understand: 1. Who are you? 2. Where do you come from? 3. Are you supposed to be normal? You will appreciate that without the answers to my questions I cannot fully understand your letter." Both query and response are telling. Traditional dramatic exposition and character development have accustomed theater audiences to expect playwrights to provide enough information about the past to make the characters' present situations and motivations explicable. Like the inquisitive letter writer, playgoers request of dramatic art the logic and order that life outside the theater denies. Pinter, along with many other twentieth-century dramatists, refuses his audience this luxury.

In *The Birthday Party,* for example, Stanley Webber lives as the only boarder in Meg and Petey Boles's boarding house. The play's central mystery, and therefore a large part of its dramatic tension, evolves from the relationship between Stanley and the two men, Goldberg and McCann, who arrive at the boarding house. From the start, questions about the past arise and remain unanswered. Who is Stanley Webber? Why is he vegetating at the Boles's? What is his relationship with Meg? With the promiscuous neighbor, Lulu? Is it, or is it not, his birthday? Is he, or is he not, a pianist? Why do Goldberg and McCann want to find him? Why do they take him, dressed "in a dark well cut suit and white collar," to Monty? Who is Monty? The more information the audience receives the more confused it becomes.

Because the past is unverifiable, all that viewers can know about a Pinter character is what they themselves discern. And this source or caliber of information often does not satisfy audiences familiar primarily with conventional dramatic exposition, especially since Pinter's characters confuse viewers with contradiction. Consequently, audiences remain uncertain of motivations and are unable to verify what little they can surmise, a predicament that coincides with life outside the theater. How can we know, Esslin asked in *Pinter the Playwright,* with "any semblance of certainty, what motivates our own wives, parents, our own children?" We cannot. And Pinter's drama impedes all our attempts to know, despite (or perhaps because of) the anxiety that this raising of unanswerable questions creates.

Equally unsettling both to audiences and the plays' central figures is the theme of the intruder who invariably enters the rooms, basements, flats, and houses of Pinter's characters and in some way disrupts the residents. At times the intruder is a stranger, such as Riley, who enters Rose's haven in *The Room;* the matchseller whom Flora and Edward invite into their home in *A Slight Ache;* Spooner, whom Hirst picks up at a pub in *No Man's Land.* At other times the intruder is a friend or family member; in *The Homecoming,* for example, Teddy returns with his wife to his father's home; in *The Basement,* Stott takes his lover to visit an old friend; and in *Old Times,* Anna visits her former roommate.

In an unsigned insert to the program brochure of a 1960 performance of *The Room* and *The Dumb Waiter* Pinter addresses the theme of the inevitability of an intruder: "Given a man in a room and he will sooner or later receive a visitor. A visitor entering the room will enter with intent. If two people inhabit the room the visitor will not be the same man for both. A man in a room who receives a visit is likely to be illuminated or horrified by it. The visitor himself might as easily be horrified or illuminated. . . . A man in a room and no one entering lives in expectation of a visit." Physical, psychological, or emotional disruption caused by the intruder provides the dramatic tension of most of Pinter's plays. For example, in *Betrayal* Jerry intrudes into Robert and Emma's marriage by initiating an affair with his best friend's wife. In *Family Voices* Voice 1 intrudes as a roomer upon the Withers family, and he, in turn, is intruded upon—although he appears not to realize it—by Voice 2, his mother, who entreats him to return home, and by Voice 3, his dead father, who intrudes upon life. Deborah, the central character in *A Kind of Alaska,* also intrudes upon life by awakening after twenty-nine years: in a sense, she becomes an intrusion to herself—a middle-aged woman imposing herself upon the young girl who was afflicted with sleeping sickness those many years before. In a Pinter play, intrusion inevitably will occur.

The dramatist's uncannily realistic sounding dialogue, replete with the linguistic inanities—pauses, tautologies, nonverbal sounds, disjunctive responses—and the verbal acts—defense, acquiescence, coercion, aggression—of everyday conversation, is also typically "Pinteresque." Yet despite its surface realism, Pinter crafts his dialogue with a poet's tools, including the caesurae, or silences. Although it is often parodied by his detractors and imitated by his admirers, the explicitly assigned "Pinter-pause" is invariably meaningful, reflecting a number of responses including puzzlement—Gus's pondering over the mysterious menu in *The Dumb Waiter* —illumination—Aston's finally realizing that Davies will not allow him to remain as caretaker or boarder in *The Caretaker*—and retrenchment—Ruth and Lenny's engaging in a verbal duel for control in *The Homecoming.* Pinter's pauses comprise lines without words, lines that frequently speak as loudly as, or sometimes louder than, words.

Another silence—a noisy one—exists in Pinter's plays. In a speech delivered at the 1962 National Student Drama Festival in Bristol and published as the introduction to the first volume of the *Complete Works,* the playwright addresses this form of verbal hiatus: "There are two silences. One when no word is spoken. The other when perhaps a torrent of language is being employed. This speech is speaking of a language locked beneath it. That is its continual reference. The speech we hear is an indication of that which we don't hear. It is a necessary avoidance, a violent, sly, anguished or mocking smoke screen which keeps the other in its place. When true silence falls we are still left with echo but are nearer nakedness. One way of looking at speech is to say that it is a constant stratagem to cover nakedness." In order to cover their nakedness, Pinter's characters frequently discuss topics that have little to do with what is really on their minds: for instance, Rose in *The Room* chatters on about the weather and the apartment house in her attempt to reassure herself of the sanctuary of her room; Deeley, in *Old Times,* describes Kate's bathing habits to Anna in order to establish his intimacy with his wife and belittle the relationship between the two friends; and Robert, in *Betrayal,* discusses squash and lunch in a veiled assault on his wife. In instances such as these, language functions primarily on a subtextual level; it is not the meaning of the words that is essential, but how the characters use speech to bring about their different ends: to hide the pain of a relationship gone awry, the desperation of being lonely and homeless, the fear of relinquishing control. Unheard melodies in Pinter's language are often far less sweet than those heard.

Yet melodies heard can indeed be sweet. Lexical associations, double entendre, puns, exotic diction, onomatopoeia, and repetition—all poetic devices—call attention to the playwright's use of language. An early play written originally for radio and therefore dependent upon words alone to convey meaning, *A Slight Ache,* exemplifies Pinter's language at its most brilliant and meaningful. Language becomes this play's central theme: the character who possesses verbal acumen survives unscathed—as did young Pinter en route to his club in London's East End—while those who lose control over language are doomed.

Rich in sensory appeal and dense with imagery, *A Slight Ache* has little action. A married couple, Edward and Flora, spend "the longest day of the year" at their country house. After breakfast, Edward notices a matchseller, who has apparently been there for "weeks," standing by the back gate. This day, however, Edward decides to invite the matchseller in to determine why he persists in remaining by the gate while making no attempt to sell his wares. The matchseller, who remains mute throughout the play, tacitly accepts the invitation, and Edward and Flora take turns playing host and hostess to their silent guest. During the course of the play, Edward grows increasingly weak and finally collapses on the floor; the matchseller, on the other hand, appears progressively rejuvenated. At play's end, Flora passes the tray of wet, useless matches to her prostrate husband and leaves with her new partner, the matchseller.

Of the names of Pinter's characters, Bernard Dukore wrote in *Theatre Journal:* "Namesakes provide important clues that warrant attention, especially of a writer like Pinter, who carefully and precisely measures every aspect of his plays, including varying lengths and pauses. It is unlikely that he would be less sensitive to or painstaking with his character's name." Sometimes the names of Pinter's characters straightforwardly suggest personality traits—Bert Hudd, the monosyllabic, sadistic trucker of *The Room,* for example—but more often they signify allusively, often ironically—Dakore noted the "ruth-less" Ruth of *The Homecoming* returning to her husband's people as does the Old Testament Ruth before her. Flora's name suggests benevolent and fecund nature but her actions point to manipulative emasculation. She orchestrates her husband's demise.

Early in the play Flora establishes her supremacy over Edward by acting the part of an indulgent parent, "calmly" correcting her husband while teaching him the plants' proper names: "Edward—you know that shrub outside the toolshed. . . . That's convolvulus." As though speaking to a small child, Flora also explains to her husband the need for the canopy, "To shade you from the sun." To label elements within one's environment is, in a sense, to control those elements and that environment. By naming the plants in her garden, Flora establishes dominance over her immediate environment. She also "names" Edward: she refers to him by his given name an inordinate number of times—considering they are the only two speakers in the play—and uses the faintly scatological sobriquet, "Weddie. Beddie Weddie." She also christens the matchseller: "I'm going to . . . call you Barnabas."

In contrast to his wife, Edward is unable to name the plants in his garden, a shortcoming Pinter points to in the play's opening dialogue: "You know perfectly well what grows in your garden," Flora states, and Edward replies, "Quite the contrary. It is clear that I don't." Nor can Edward recall the name of the squire's red-headed daughter, with whom he was enamored: "The youngest one was the best of the bunch. Sally. No, no, wait a minute, no, it wasn't Sally, it was . . . Fanny." Moreover, he calls lunch *petit dejeuner* (French for "breakfast") and rants at his guest for consuming "duck," although Flora has invited the matchseller to share a midday goose. Her husband's inability to label and thereby control his environment—garden or dining room—dooms him before his more able wife; he is fated to succumb to Flora and her new ally, the matchseller, who remains nameless to her husband.

As Edward grows weaker he grows even less able to use language effectively. Early in the play he attempts fastidiousness in his choice of words: "It will not bite you! Wasps don't bite. . . . They sting. It's snakes . . . that bite. . . . Horseflies suck." Later he haltingly differentiates between a road and a lane: "It's not a road at all. What is it? It's a lane." Despite his efforts at linguistic precision, Edward loses control when confronted by the matchseller to whom he offers an inappropriately discriminating choice of drinks: "Now look, what will you have to drink? A glass of ale? Curacao Fockink Orange? Ginger beer? Tia Maria? A Wachenheimer Fuchsmantel Reisling Beeren Auslese? Gin and it? Chateauneuf-du-Pape? A little Asti Spumanti? Or what do you say to a straightforward Piesporter Goldtropfschen Feine Auslese (Reichsgraf von Kesselstaff)?" Like the provocatively named plants—honeysuckle, convolvulus, clematis—in Edward and Flora's garden, these drinks amuse in the sexual suggestiveness and continental inclusiveness. Less comically, the list reflects Edward's growing anxiety. The language through which he earlier attempts denotative exactness in reference to wasps and lanes carries him away—from one exotic beverage to another. Toward the play's end, Edward is reduced to nonverbal communication: "Aaaaahhhh." Flora retains control over language. She endures.

In his work since *No Man's Land,* Pinter has relied less on verbal indulgence and more on elements of design to evoke meaning. The poet-playwright seems to be increasingly influenced by the scenarist-playwright, a change resulting perhaps from the requirements and possibilities of cinema. Over the years, four of Pinter's plays have been filmed: *The Caretaker, The Birthday Party, The Homecoming,* and *Betrayal.* He has also written ten screenplays based on other writers' novels: *The Servant, The Pumpkin Eater, The Quiller Memorandum, Accident, The Go-Between, Langrishe, Go Down, The Last Tycoon, The French Lieutenant's Woman, Turtle Diary, The Handmaid's Tale,* and *The Comfort of Strangers.* Although this list appears disparate, it possesses internal logic. The playwright scenarist adapts fiction whose themes and subjects are those of his own dramatic art: adultery; role reversal or role confusion; duplicity; physical, psychological and emotional cruelty; artistic stasis; homosexuality; and perverted birthday celebrations, to mention only a few of these motifs. Furthermore, like his plays, the novels he has adapted for the screen focus predominantly on character rather than on plot. Even in a spy thriller like *The Quiller Memorandum,* assassinations, attempted murders, and scenes of torture fade from memory more rapidly than do the characters. Another denominator common to the stage plays and screenplays is Pinter's exploration of time and memory, topics he has dealt with frequently since writing *Old Times* in 1970. Simple flashback accommodates the characters' memories in the screenplay versions of *The Pumpkin Eater* and *Accident;* but *The Go-Between* and *The French Lieutenant's Woman* require more innovative techniques to deal with their sophisticated examinations of time. A technique Pinter uses in the screenplays—flashbacks interwoven with flashforwards—reappears in his play *Betrayal.* In short, Pinter's work in film expands upon the interests he explores on the stage.

Although Pinter is not essentially a comic writer, he does write very funny dialogue. When characters posture, as when Edward lists the contents of his liquor cabinet for the matchseller's benefit in *A Slight Ache,* Deeley flaunts his familiarity with the past to denigrate his houseguest in *Old Times,* or when Robert recounts his experience at the American Express office where he has just learned of his wife's affair with his best friend in *Betrayal,* their speeches are frequently comic, often extravagantly so. In *Pinter the Playwright,* Esslin reprinted Pinter's 1960 response to an open letter "deploring the gales of laughter about the unhappy plight of the old tramp" in *The Caretaker:* "An element of the absurd is, I think, one of the features of the play, but at the same time I did not intend it to be merely a laughable farce. If there hadn't been other issues at stake the play would not have been written. . . . Where the comic and the tragic (for want of a better word) are closely interwoven, certain members of the audience will always give emphasis to the comic as opposed to the other, for by doing so they rationalize the other out of existence. . . . Where . . . indiscriminate mirth is found, I feel it represents a cheerful patronage of the characters on the part of the merrymakers, and thus participation is avoided. This laughter is in fact a mode of precaution, a smoke-screen, a refusal to accept what is happening as recognizable. . . . From this kind of uneasy jollification I must, of course, disassociate myself. . . . As far as I'm concerned, *The Caretaker* is funny, up to a point. Beyond that point it ceases to be funny, and it was because of that point that I wrote it."

In *The Caretaker,* as in all of Pinter's plays, comic elements illuminate non-comic ones. On one hand, humor serves as a balm, easing audience discomfort at witnessing the characters' pain; on the other, it intensifies the discomfort by forcing pain into contiguity with laughter so that the distinctions between the two disappear, and the audience is left precariously straddling the fine line that separates the comic from the noncomic. In his best work, Pinter leaves his audiences at that moment when the plays cease altogether to be funny—when bright lights "photograph" the silent threesome in the final tableau of *Old Times* or fade as Hirst takes one last drink in *No Man's Land,* when the curtain falls on Max imploring Ruth to kiss him in *The Homecoming* or on Meg blissfully unaware that Stanley has been taken away in *The Birthday Party.* Ultimately, Pinter's plays emphasize that which is not comic, and despite their considerable humor, his vision is not a comic one.

Though best known for his dramatic works, Pinter has also published several volumes of poetry and edited collections of world poetry, including *Ninety-nine Poems in Translation,* a companion volume to *A Hundred Poems by a Hundred Poets: An Anthology. Ninety-nine Poems in Translation* contains diverse selections by Antiphanes, Guillaume Apollinaire, Paul Eluard, Henri Michaux, Pablo Neruda, and Cesar Vallejo, among many others. Considered a rather conservative and idiosyncratic assemblage of poetry, including a large percentage of European men and no representatives from Africa or India, Pinter along with his coeditors attempts to draw attention to the art of translation. While the editors seek to remain faithful to the original, Josephine Balmer noted in an *Observer* review, "the editors were searching more for 'a verifiable accuracy of feeling' than crude linguistic equivalence." A *Publishers Weekly* reviewer concluded that "the cacophony of voices . . . makes this an immensely enjoyable anthology."

Unquestionably, Pinter's work has greatly influenced a number of contemporary dramatists on both sides of the Atlantic; critics and scholars alike consider his full-length works *The Birthday Party, The Caretaker, The Homecoming, Old Times, No Man's Land,* and *Betrayal* to be among the most important plays of the mid-twentieth century. His more recent work has been more sparse, although in it Pinter continues to experiment with the possibilities of theater, to search for the exact verbal and visual image, and to strive for theatrical economy. However, by the late 1990s, he had become, according to *Contemporary Review* contributor Michael Karwowski, an increasingly political playwright. As Karwowski noted, the playwright's continued "celebrity has depended more on his politics than on his plays. The master of the dramatic pause now seems more of a rebel without a pause, taking almost every opportunity to make moral pronouncements on current affairs." Those pronouncements, however, have taken the form of poetry and essays, as collected in his 1998 anthology *Various Voices: Prose, Poetry, Politics, 1948-1998.* While Karwowski disagreed with Pinter's efforts at re-writing the intent underlying his writings, the critic explained that "Pinter has also been prepared to re-interpret his greatest stage plays [*The Birthday Party* and *The Caretaker*] in political terms, as an incipient expression of his moral condemnation of injustice." As the critic concluded: "'Never trust the artist. Trust the tale.'"

Although Pinter's body of work continues to encourage scrutiny and reexamination from not only the author, but from scholars as well, it remains among the most respected work written for the modern stage. In a speech published in the fourth volume of the *Complete Works,* the playwright declared: "The image must be pursued with the greatest vigilance, calmly, and once found, must be sharpened, graded, accurately focused and maintained, and the key word is economy, economy of movement and gesture, of emotion and its expression . . . so there is no wastage and no mess." Whether a woman clutches her eyes (*The Room*), a man drinks to stasis (*No Man's Land*), or a cabby sits silently in his taxi (*Victoria Station*), Pinter's dramatic images and the vision they embody remain in his audience's memories long after the stage lights have faded.

BIOGRAPHICAL AND CRITICAL SOURCES:

BOOKS

Billington, Michael, *The Life and Work of Harold Pinter,* [London, England], 1996.

Contemporary Literary Criticism, Thomson Gale (Detroit, MI), Volume 1, 1973, Volume 3, 1975, Volume 6, 1976, Volume 9, 1978, Volume 11, 1979, Volume 15, 1980, Volume 27, 1984, Volume 58, 1990, Volume 73, 1993.

Contemporary Theatre, Film, and Television, Volume 20, Thomson Gale (Detroit, MI), 1999.

Encyclopedia of World Biography, 2nd edition, Thomson Gale (Detroit, MI), 1998.

Encyclopedia of World Literature in the Twentieth Century, 3rd edition, St. James Press (Detroit, MI), 1999.

Esslin, Martin, *Pinter the Playwright,* Methuen (London, England), 1984.

Gale, Steven H., *Harold Pinter: An Annotated Bibliography,* G.K. Hall (Boston, MA), 1978.

International Dictionary of Films and Filmmakers, Volume 4: *Writers and Production Artists,* 2nd edition, St. James Press (Detroit, MI), 1993.

International Dictionary of Theatre, Volume 2: *Playwrights,* St. James Press (Detroit, MI), 1994.

Kerr, Walter, *Harold Pinter,* Columbia University Press (New York, NY), 1967.

Knowles, Ronald, *Understanding Harold Pinter,* University of South Carolina Press (Columbia, SC), 1995.

Modern British Literature, 2nd edition, St. James Press (Detroit, MI), 2000.

Pinter, Harold, and Mel Gussow, editor, *Conversations with Pinter,* Grove (New York, NY), 1996.

Regal, Martin S., *Harold Pinter: A Question of Timing,* St. Martin's Press (New York, NY), 1995.

PERIODICALS

American Film, October, 1990, p. 16.

American Theatre, October, 2001, Roger Copeland, "A Room of His Own," p. 22.

Chicago Tribune, September 26, 1989.

Connoisseur, January, 1991, p. 34.

Contemporary Review, November, 2003, Michael Karwowski, "Harold Pinter—A Political Playwright?," p. 291.

Ecologist, July, 1999, David Edwards, review of *Various Voices: Prose, Poetry, Politics, 1948-1998,* pp. 283-284.

Economist, September 25, 1999, review of *The Proust Screenplay,* p. 99.

English Review, September, 2003, John Hudson, "Power and Impotence in 'The Homecoming,'" p. 31.

Hackney Downs School Magazine, winter, 1946; summer, 1947.

Library Journal, October 15, 1989; July, 1994, p. 98; February 15, 1999, Rebecca Miller, review of *Various Voices,* p. 150.

Maclean's, April 25, 1994.
Modern Drama, Volume 27, 1984.
Nation, April 2, 1990; January 20, 1992.
New Republic, February 11, 1991; April 29, 1991; December 20, 1993.
New Statesman, March 11, 1994; July 14, 2003, Adam Newey, "A Howl of Disapproval," p. 31.
New Statesman & Society, October 28, 1988; December 7, 1990.
Newsweek, March 26, 1990.
New Yorker, February 25, 1967; September 20, 1993.
New York Review of Books, October 7, 1999, review of *Various Voices* and *The Proust Screenplay,* p. 28.
New York Times, October 5, 1961; October 15, 1961; October 6, 1989; November 9, 1989; July 27, 2001, Ben Brantley, "Festival Review: Pinter's Silences, Richly Eloquent."
New York Times Book Review, May 9, 1999, review of *Various Voices,* p. 27.
New York Times Magazine, December 5, 1971.
Observer (London, England), June 25, 1960; April 10, 1994, p. 22; November 8, 1998, review of *Various Voices,* p. 15; September 5, 1999, review of *Various Voices,* p. 14.
Paris Review, fall, 1966, Lawrence M. Bensky, interview with Pinter.
Progressive, March, 2001, Anne-Marie Cusac, interview with Pinter, p. 32.
Publishers Weekly, June 27, 1994, p. 66; February 15, 1999, review of *Various Voices,* p. 94.
Spectator, October 31, 1998, review of *Various Voices,* p. 50.
Sunday Times (London, England), May 25, 1958, Harold Hobson, review of *The Birthday Party.*
Theatre Journal, 1981, Bernard Dukore.
Time, February 7, 1994.
Time International, July 9, 2001, James Inverne, "Sounds of Silence," p. 52.
Times Educational Supplement, November 27, 1998, review of *Various Voices,* p. 11.
Times Literary Supplement, March 5, 1999, review of *Various Voices,* p. 25; May 4, 2001, David Nokes, "For Sun Read Snow," p. 6.
Variety, February 1, 1993.
World Literature Today, autumn, 1996, p. 965; autumn, 1999, Eric Sterling, review of *Various Voices,* pp. 750-751.

ONLINE

Harold Pinter's Home Page, http://www.haroldpinter.org/ (April 28, 2005).
Pegasos Authors' Calendar, http://www.kirjasto.sci.fi/ (April 28, 2004), "Harold Pinter."

PLIMPTON, George 1927-2003
(George Ames Plimpton)

PERSONAL: Born March 18, 1927, in New York, NY; died September 25, 2003, in New York, NY; son of Francis T.P. (a lawyer and former U.S. deputy representative to the United Nations) and Pauline (Ames) Plimpton; married Freddy Medora Espy (a photography studio assistant), March 28, 1968 (divorced, 1988); married Sarah Whitehead Dudley, 1991; children: (first marriage) Medora Ames, Taylor Ames, (second marriage) Olivia Hartley, Laura Dudley. *Education:* Harvard University, A.B., 1948; King's College, Cambridge, B.A., 1952, M.A., 1954. *Politics:* Democrat.

CAREER: Writer and editor. Editor of Harvard *Lampoon,* c. 1948-50; *Paris Review,* principal editor, beginning 1953, publisher, with Doubleday & Co., of Paris Review Editions (books), beginning 1965. *Horizon,* associate editor, 1959-61; *Sports Illustrated,* contributing editor, beginning 1967; *Harper's,* associate editor, beginning 1972; *Food and Wine,* contributing editor, 1978; *Realities,* member of editorial advisory board, 1978. American Literature Anthology program, director, beginning 1967; National Foundation on the Arts and Humanities, chief editor of annual anthology of work from literary magazines; adviser on John F. Kennedy Oral History Project. Instructor at Barnard College, 1956-58; associate fellow, Trumbull College, Yale, 1967. Occasional actor in films; journalistic participant in sporting and musical events. Honorary commissioner of New York City fireworks, beginning 1973. Trustee, National Art Museum of Sport, beginning 1967, WNET-TV, beginning 1973, Police Athletic League, beginning 1976, African Wildlife Leadership Foundation, beginning 1980, and Guild Hall, East Hampton, beginning 1980. *Military service:* U.S. Army, 1945-48; became second lieutenant.

MEMBER: PEN, Pyrotechnics Guild International, American Pyrotechniques Association, NFL Alumni Association, Mayflower Descendants Society; clubs include Century Association, Racquet and Tennis, Brook, Dutch Treat, Coffee House, Devon Yacht, Travelers (Paris), Explorers.

AWARDS, HONORS: Distinguished achievement award, University of Southern California, 1967; Mark Twain Award, International Platform Association, 1982; inducted into Ordre des Arts et des Lettres (France), 1994; named chevalier, French Legion of Honor, 2002; inducted into American Academy of Arts and Letters,

2002. Recipient of honorary degrees from Franklin Pierce College, 1968, Hobart Smith College, 1978, Stonehill College, 1982, University of Southern California, 1986, and Pine Manor College, 1988.

WRITINGS:

EDITOR

Writers at Work: The Paris Review Interviews, Viking (New York, NY), Volume 1, 1957, Volume 2, 1963, Volume 3, 1967, Volume 4, 1976, Volume 5, 1981, Volume 6, 1984, Volume 7, 1986, Volume 8, 1988, Volume 9, 1992.

(With Peter Ardery) *The American Literary Anthology,* number 1, Farrar, Straus (New York, NY), 1968, number 2, Random House (New York, NY), 1969, number 3, Viking (New York, NY), 1970.

(With Jean Stein) *American Journey: The Times of Robert Kennedy* (interviews), Harcourt (New York, NY), 1970.

Jean Stein, *Edie: An American Biography,* Knopf (New York, NY), 1982, published as *Edie: American Girl,* Grove Press (New York, NY), 1994.

(With Christopher Hemphill) Diana Vreeland, *D.V.,* Random House (New York, NY), 1984.

Fireworks: A History and Celebration, Doubleday (Garden City, NY), 1984.

Poets at Work: The Paris Review Interviews, Viking (New York, NY), 1989.

Women Writers at Work, Viking (New York, NY), 1989.

The Writer's Chapbook: A Compendium of Fact, Opinion, Wit, and Advice from the Twentieth-Century's Preeminent Writers, Viking (New York, NY), 1989.

The Best of Bad Hemingway: Choice Entries from the Harry's Bar & American Grill Imitation Hemingway Competition, Harcourt (San Diego, CA), Volume 1, 1989, Volume 2, 1991.

The Paris Review Anthology, Norton (New York, NY), 1990.

Playwrights at Work, Modern Library (New York, NY), 2000.

Home Run, Harcourt (San Diego, CA), 2001.

As Told at the Explorers Club: More than Fifty Gripping Tales of Adventure, Lyons Press (Guilford, CT), 2003.

Latin American Writers at Work/The Paris Review, introduction by Derek Walcott, Modern Library (New York, NY), 2003.

SPORTS WRITING

Out of My League (baseball anecdotes), Harper (New York, NY), 1961.

Paper Lion (football anecdotes), Harper (New York, NY), 1966.

The Bogey Man (golf anecdotes), Harper (New York, NY), 1968.

(Editor and author of introduction) Pierre Etchebaster, *Pierre's Book: The Game of Court Tennis,* Barre Publishers (Barre, MA), 1971.

(With Alex Karras and John Gordy) *Mad Ducks and Bears: Football Revisited* (football anecdotes), Random House (New York, NY), 1973.

One for the Record: The Inside Story of Hank Aaron's Chase for the Home Run Record, Harper (New York, NY), 1974.

Shadow Box (boxing anecdotes), Putnam (New York, NY), 1977.

One More July: A Football Dialogue with Bill Curry, Harper (New York, NY), 1977.

Sports!, photographs by Neil Leifer, H.N. Abrams (New York, NY), 1978.

A Sports Bestiary (cartoons), illustrated by Arnold Roth, McGraw-Hill (New York, NY), 1982.

Open Net (hockey anecdotes), Norton (New York, NY), 1985.

The Curious Case of Sidd Finch (baseball novel), Macmillan (New York, NY), 1987, reprinted, Four Walls Eight Windows (New York, NY), 2004

The X Factor, Whittle Direct (Knoxville, TN), 1990, revised edition, Norton (New York, NY), 1995.

The Best of Plimpton, Atlantic Monthly Press (New York, NY), 1990.

The Official Olympics Triplecast Viewer's Guide, Barcelona commemorative edition, Pindar, 1992.

The Norton Book of Sports, Norton (New York, NY), 1992.

George Plimpton on Sports, Lyons Press (Guilford, CT), 2003.

OTHER

The Rabbit's Umbrella (juvenile), Viking (New York, NY), 1955.

(With William Kronick) *Plimpton! Shoot-out at Rio Lobo* (script), American Broadcasting Company (ABC-TV), 1970.

Plimpton! The Man on the Flying Trapeze (script), ABC-TV, 1970.

(With William Kronick) *Plimpton! Did You Hear the One About . . . ?* (script), ABC-TV, 1971.

(With William Kronick) *Plimpton! The Great Quarterback Sneak* (script), ABC-TV, 1971.

(With William Kronick) *Plimpton! Adventure in Africa* (script), ABC-TV, 1972.

(Author of introduction) Bill Plympton, *Medium Rare: Cartoons,* Holt (New York, NY), 1978.

(Author of introduction) *Oakes Ames: Jottings of a Harvard Botanist, 1874-1950,* edited by Pauline Ames Plimpton, Harvard University Press (Cambridge, MA), 1980.

(With Jean Kennedy Smith) *Chronicles of Courage: Very Special Artists* (interviews), Random House (New York, NY), 1993.

Truman Capote: In Which Various Friends, Enemies, Acquaintances, and Detractors Recall His Turbulent Career, Doubleday (Garden City, NY), 1997.

Pet Peeves; or, Whatever Happened to Doctor Rawff?, Atlantic Monthly Press (New York, NY), 2000.

A & E Biographies: Ernest Shackleton, DK Publishing (New York, NY), 2003.

The Man in the Flying Lawn Chair: And Other Excursions and Adventures, Random House (New York, NY), 2004.

Contributor to books, including Bernard Oldsey, editor, *Ernest Hemingway: The Papers of a Writer,* Garland (New York, NY), 1981; and *The Great Life: A Man's Guide to Sports, Skills, Fitness, and Serious Fun,* 2000; author of foreword for *The Art of the Bookplate,* by James P. Keenan, Barnes & Noble Books (New York, NY), 2003; contributor of articles to *Time* and other magazines.

ADAPTATIONS: *Paper Lion,* the story of Plimpton's experiences as a short-term member of the Detroit Lions football team, was filmed by United Artists in 1968. Alan Alda portrayed Plimpton, but the author himself also had a role—he played William Ford.

SIDELIGHTS: "Although throughout his long career George Plimpton devoted considerable energy to literary pursuits of the highest caliber, including editing the prestigious *Paris Review,* he became widely known to the public at large for writing about his failed attempts in sports and other endeavors far beyond his capabilities. Among literary journalists George Plimpton is so unusual that he marches not just to a different drummer but more nearly to a different orchestra," declared Sam G. Riley in *Dictionary of Literary Biography.* Authorities called Plimpton a "professional amateur," for, although writing is his primary occupation, he also pitched in a post-season All-Star game in Yankee Stadium; held the position of last-string rookie quarterback for the Detroit Lions in 1963; golfed in several Pro-Am tournaments; briefly appeared in a basketball game for the Boston Celtics; boxed with former light heavyweight champion Archie Moore; and served as a goalie for the Boston Bruins hockey team in 1977 and the Edmonton Oilers in 1985. He also fought in a bullfight staged by Ernest Hemingway in 1954, and worked as a trapeze artist, lion-tamer, and clown for the Clyde Beatty-Cole Brothers Circus.

Among his less-strenuous activities, Plimpton developed a stand-up comedy routine and performed it in Las Vegas. He served as a percussionist with the New York Philharmonic and as a guest conductor of the Cincinnati Symphony. He was in several films, including *Rio Lobo, Beyond the Law, Reds,* and *Good Will Hunting.* On television Plimpton hosted specials and appeared in several commercials.

In his writings, Plimpton lost his "professional amateur" status and worked to high standards as a consummate professional. "Plimpton's career as a literary journalist largely has been founded upon the appeal of contrast," mused Riley. "First, there is the internal element of contrast: on one hand, the serious editor of belles lettres, on the other, the purveyor of entertaining journalistic nonfiction and televised specials. Foremost is the contrast that he himself presents vis-a-vis the people he has competed against in his myriad adventures: the tweedy, genteel literary figure at play on the turf of rougher, more hardbitten types, the bon vivant amid serious athletes, and the amateur generalist head to head with professional specialists." Reviewers consider *Paper Lion,* Plimpton's book about his football adventures with the Detroit Lions, a classic of sports writing. It "is the best book written about pro football—maybe about any sport—because he captured with absolute fidelity how the average fan might feel given the opportunity to try out for a professional football team," explained Hal Higdon in *Saturday Review.* As Plimpton recalled many years later in an interview with *Time,* "the story I got was one I couldn't have, if I had not marched onto the field and tried my best. In my big game, as the quarterback, you will remember that I lost 32 yards in four plays. Very humiliating."

The book attracted sports fans not only through its innovative concept—a writer actually taking the field with a professional team—but also through the author's command over language. "Practically everybody loves George's stuff because George writes with an affection for his fellow man, has a rare eye for the bizarre, and a nice sense of his own ineptitude," declared Trent Frayne in the Toronto *Globe and Mail.* Ernest Hemingway once said, according to Frayne, "'Plimpton is the dark side of the moon of Walter Mitty.'"

Many writers have echoed Hemingway's statement. However, although Plimpton's adventures superficially resemble those of James Thurber's famous fictional character, there are many differences between the two. "In his participatory journalism [Plimpton] has been described wrongly as a Walter Mitty, and he is nothing of the sort. This is no daydreaming nebbish," declared Joe Flaherty in *New York Times Book Review.* Plimpton's adventures are tangible rather than imaginary. Yet, while Mitty in his dreams is a fantastic success at everything he undertakes, Plimpton's efforts almost invariably result in failure and humiliation. "Plimpton has stock in setting himself up as a naif . . . many of us are familiar with his gangling, tweedy demeanor and Oxford accent. He plays the 'fancy pants' to our outhouse Americana," Flaherty asserted. "Plimpton doesn't want to be known as an athlete," explained Cal Reynard in *Arizona Daily Star.* "He figures his role in sports is that of the spectator, but he wants to get closer to the game than the stands."

After more than twenty years of writing nonfiction about sports, Plimpton published his first sports novel, *The Curious Case of Sidd Finch,* in 1987. Plimpton based the story on a *Sports Illustrated* article he had written for the 1985 April Fools Day issue about a former Harvard man-cum-Buddhist-monk, Siddhartha "Sidd" Finch, who can pitch a baseball faster than any other pitcher in the history of the game—about 150 miles per hour. Plimpton, in his article, claimed that Finch was about to sign with the New York Mets and speculated about the impact an unhittable pitcher would have on the game of baseball. *The Curious Case of Sidd Finch* expands on the article, telling how Finch, after much self-doubt, is persuaded to play for the Mets and, on his return to Shea Stadium, pitches what former major league pitcher Jim Brosnan, writing in *Washington Post Book World,* called "THE perfect game;" he strikes out the entire batting lineup of the St. Louis Cardinals in perfect order.

Reviewers have commented on *The Curious Case of Sidd Finch* with mixed feelings. Although Brosnan found the novel "sort of like a shaggy-dog tale that once was a crisp one-liner," he continued, "*The Curious Case of Sidd Finch* is not the rollicking farce I'd hoped for, but it's worth a reading." Lee Green, writing in *Los Angeles Times Book Review,* called the book a "wonderfully wry and whimsical debut novel," while National League president and *New York Times Book Review* contributor A. Bartlett Giamatti stated that "Plimpton's control is masterly," and added that baseball "culture is splendidly rendered with an experienced insider's knowledge, and the whole saga of Finch's brief, astonishing passage through big-league baseball is at once a parody of every player's as-told-to biography, a satire on professional sports, an extended (and intriguing) meditation on our national pastime and a touching variant on the novel of education as Sidd learns of the world."

Although his sports writing remains his best-known work, Plimpton also wrote on a wide range of other subjects. His own upper-class roots provided him with a number of unique social connections, including a close relationship with the Kennedy family. He was a Harvard classmate of Robert Kennedy's, and was walking directly in front of the senator when he was assassinated in 1968. In *American Journey: The Times of Robert F. Kennedy* he edits 347 interviews that form a picture of Robert Kennedy's life and the procession of his funeral train from New York to Washington.

Plimpton's own interest centered on the small literary magazine he edited from 1953 until his death in 2003. As James Warren explained in *Chicago Tribune,* "It's the *Paris Review,* not the chronicles of his own sporting foibles . . . that constitutes the soul—and takes up much of the time—of Plimpton's life." *Paris Review,* unlike many other literary magazines, focuses on creative writing rather than criticism. Many famous American writers—including Jack Kerouac, Philip Roth, Richard Ford, T. Coraghessan Boyle, and V.S. Naipaul—published first efforts or complete works within its pages.

Plimpton's interviews with writers about the craft of writing were a major attraction of the journal. It was the *Paris Review,* explained Nona Balakian in *New York Times,* that first "developed a new kind of extended and articulate interview that combined the Boswellian aim with an exploration of the ideas of major contemporary writers on the art of fiction and poetry." "The thing that makes these interviews different from most interviews," wrote Mark Harris in Chicago's *Tribune Books,* "is that they go on long enough to get somewhere. If they do not arrive at the point I dreamily hoped for—creativity totally clarified with a supplementary manual on How To Write—they supply very good instruction nevertheless." The result, Balakian concluded, is "a heightened awareness of a writer's overall purpose and meaning."

Poets at Work and *Women Writers at Work,* both edited by Plimpton, consist of interviews that originally appeared in *Paris Review. Poets at Work* includes conversations with T.S. Eliot, Marianne Moore, Anne Sexton, Allen Ginsberg, William Carlos Williams, James Dickey, and others. Poet Donald Hall described the interviews in his introduction to the volume as "literary history as gossip." *Women Writers at Work* joins the interviews with Marianne Moore and Anne Sexton with those of Dorothy Parker, Rebecca West, Isak Dinesen, and ten other noted twentieth-century women writers. Summarizing the significance of both volumes, *Listener* contributor Peter Parker wrote that "these interviews are a permanent and invaluable record of the working practices, opinions and observations of those who have reflected our century in their poetry and prose." In 2000, another volume in the series, *Playwrights at Work,* appeared, collecting interviews conducted by Plimpton and others dating back to a 1956 talk with Thornton Wilder. Among the dozen or so other pieces are discussions with August Wilson, Wendy Wasserstein, and two with Arthur Miller. "There's an authentic edginess throughout this instructive and salutary book that makes it a reminder of the variety, the vulnerability, and the awful strictness of the playwright's art," remarked John Stokes in a *Times Literary Supplement* review of the volume.

The Writer's Chapbook belongs to the same series, bringing together additional interviews from *Paris Review* under the editorial supervision of Plimpton. The emphasis here is on subject matter—plot, character, writer's bloc, etc.—rather than an individual author, and the resulting compendium of miscellany offers insight into the writing profession through intimate and often offhanded conversations with established literary figures such as T.S. Eliot, W.H. Auden, and Ezra Pound. According to *New York Times Book Review* contributor David Kirby, "There is little fact and less advice in the 'Chapbook,' its subtitle notwithstanding, but there are plenty of opinions, most of them rather negative: poetry readings are nightmares, politics and writing don't mix, professors and critics (the terms are interchangeable) don't know what they are talking about."

The Paris Review Anthology, also edited by Plimpton, features selections from the journal since its establishment. "The overall tone of *The Paris Review* is high spirited, even mischievous," wrote Kirby. The volume includes the quintessential *Paris Review* story "Night Flight to Stockholm" by Dallas Wiebe, which describes how an aspiring writer eventually wins the Noble Prize in literature by sending dismembered parts of his body along with submissions to major literary journals. Kirby concluded that *The Paris Review Anthology* "is historically important as well, since it reminds readers how a new era in letters began."

Plimpton returned to sports and the competitive spirit with *The X Factor: A Quest for Excellence,* his investigation into the attributes possessed by winners. After narrowly losing a game of horseshoes to President-elect George Bush, Plimpton set out to uncover the universal secret of success through conversations with various sports legends, coaches, and top executives. "Suffice to say that where Mr. Plimpton draws upon his X factor is in his prose style, in his unfailing ability to find the perfectly funny word or phrase," wrote Christopher Lehmann-Haupt in *New York Times.* "What also never lets him down is his capacity to get the most unlikely people to take part in his offbeat fantasies." In the end, Plimpton managed to get a rematch with President Bush.

In 1997 Plimpton assembled a literary memoir, *Truman Capote: In Which Various Friends, Enemies, Acquaintances, and Detractors Recall His Turbulent Career.* American writer Capote, who during his career had earned several well-placed enemies in the world of literature and high society for his barely disguised caricatures of them in a short story titled "The Côte Basque," died in 1984. "I knew him myself," Plimpton once noted to a *Time* interviewer in discussing the controversial writer. "He lived down the street in Sagaponack, Long Island. A good friend for awhile, though he felt toward the end of his life that I had made fun of him in a story I wrote ['The Snows of Studio Fifty-four'] which was a parody of Ernest Hemingway's 'The Snows of Kilimanjaro.'"

With *The Norton Book of Sports* Plimpton provides an eclectic collection of stories by both sport writers and literary figures, including Mark Twain, Thomas Wolfe, James Joyce, and Robert Bly. Chicago *Tribune Books* contributor Robert Olen Butler wrote, "Plimpton has assembled this collection of commentary, fiction, reminiscence, poetry and journalism wonderfully well, filling us with that impression of sports which is always hard to explain, that behind the seeming triviality of these games there resides something profound." A 2000 collection, *Home Run,* brought together Plimpton's choices for an anthology of baseball writing, but one with a more specific focus: the ultimate, but occasional thrill of the home run. He contributes the first essay himself, on the first recorded statistical occurrence of it in baseball history, when Ross Barnes hit one during a Chicago White Stockings game in 1876. Contributors include John Updike, Don DeLillo, and Bernard Malamud. "Plimpton's selection of pieces is very astute," noted *Library Journal* reviewer John Maxymuk.

The Best of Plimpton brings together examples of the author's writings over a period of thirty-five years. "While his contemporaries were off writing about war, sex and assorted other social upheavals, Plimpton was writing humorously and indelibly about taking poet Marianne Moore to the World Series, playing the triangle with the New York Philharmonic, boxing heavyweight Archie Moore," wrote Malcolm Jones Jr. in *Newsweek.* "Plimpton's subject is passion, whether he finds it in the major leagues, in a man who catches grapes in his mouth or in a bespectacled boy playing football."

"Plimpton has enjoyed a career unlike that of any other literary figure—journalist, author, editor, or otherwise," concluded Riley. "His varied accomplishments render his career hard to sum up, but a quotation he himself used in *The Norton Book of Sports* from poet Donald Hall . . . says it fairly well: 'Half my poet friends think I am insane to waste my time writing about sports and to loiter in the company of professional athletes. The other half would murder to be in my place.'" Still, he once commented in his *Time* interview, "all sports are predicated on error," and his experiences as a novice were not as crucial to the outcome of the game than one might believe. His month as a percussionist in the New York Philharmonic, in comparison, was far more traumatic. "In music, you cannot make a mistake. And the fear of doing this, particularly since I can't read music, was frightening to put it mildly. Evening after evening of pure terror in London, Ontario, playing an instrument called the bells. I destroyed Gustav Mahler's 'Fourth Symphony' by mishitting an instrument called the sleigh bells. I dream about that from time to time, and wake up covered with sweat."

Following Plimpton's death in September of 2003, *Paris Review* created the Plimpton Prize in honor of its longtime editor. The prize recognizes the best piece of writing by a newcomer. Plimpton's dedication to *Paris Review* also continued after his death when, as reported by JoAnne Viviano in *America's Intelligence Wire,* he stated in his will, "it is my wish and hope that the space in my apartment . . . which is currently made available rent free to the *Paris Review* shall continue to be made available without charge for so long as reasonably possible." In an obituary in *New Yorker,* David Remnick described Plimpton as "a serious man of serious accomplishments who just happened to have more fun than a van full of jugglers and clowns. He was game for anything and made a comic art of his Walter Mitty dreams and inevitable failures."

BIOGRAPHICAL AND CRITICAL SOURCES:

BOOKS

Anderson, Elliott, and Mary Kinzie, editors, *The Little Magazine in America: A Modern Documentary History,* Pushcart Press (New York, NY), 1978.

Authors in the News, Volume 1, Thomson Gale (Detroit, MI), 1976.

Contemporary Literary Criticism, Volume 36, Thomson Gale (Detroit, MI), 1986.

Dictionary of Literary Biography, Volume 185: *American Literary Journalists, 1945-1995, First Series,* Thomson Gale (Detroit, MI), 1997.

Plimpton, George, *Poets at Work: The Paris Review Interviews,* introduction by Donald Hall, Viking (New York, NY), 1989.

Talese, Gay, *The Overreachers,* Harper (New York, NY), 1965.

PERIODICALS

America's Intelligence Wire, October 21, 2003, JoAnne Viviano "Late Founder of Paris Review Leaves Will Specifying Home for His Literary Journal."

America, February 20, 1993, p. 2.

Antioch Review, winter, 1990, p. 121.

Arizona Daily Star, March 24, 1974, Cal Reynard.

Belles Lettres, summer, 1990, p. 47.

Bloomsbury Review, March-April, 1990, p. 7.

Book, July, 2001, Chris Barsanti, review of *Home Run,* p. 74.

Booklist, September 15, 1989, p. 136; October 1, 1990, p. 248; May 1, 2000, Ray Olson, review of *Playwrights at Work,* p. 1640; November 15, 2003, Gilbert Taylor, review of *As Told at the Explorers Club: More than Fifty Gripping Tales of Adventure,* p. 566.

Book Week, October 23, 1966.

Chicago Tribune, December 22, 1986; June 15-June 16, 1987.

Christian Science Monitor, December 5, 1968.

Commentary, October, 1967.

Commonweal, September 14, 1990, p. 523.

Detroit News, March 16, 1986.

Editor & Publisher, April 20, 1985, pp. 7-8.

Esquire, January, 1976, pp. 115-117, 142, 144, 146; November, 1985, p. 243.

Gentleman's Quarterly, October, 1989, pp. 183, 186.

Globe and Mail (Toronto, Ontario, Canada), July 7, 1984; February 8, 1986; June 14, 1986.

Harper's, June, 2000, "A Writer's Gift," p. 51; December, 2003, Lewis H. Lapham, "Pilgrim's Progress," p. 11.

Harper's Bazaar, November, 1973, pp. 103, 134-135, 142.

Kliatt, September, 1989, p. 25.

Library Journal, November 1, 1989, p. 91; March 1, 1990, p. 94; April 1, 1992, p. 124; March 1, 1995, p. 79; May 15, 2001, John Maxymuk, review of

Home Run, p. 130; March 15, 2003, Anna Youssefi, review of *Latin American Writers at Work: The Paris Review,* p. 85; November 15, 2003, Alison Hopkins, review of *As Told at the Explorers Club: More than Fifty Gripping Tales of Adventure,* p. 88.
Listener, October 26, 1989, Peter Barker, review of *Poets at Work* and *Women Writers at Work,* p. 33.
Los Angeles Times, July 22, 1982; March 20, 1987.
Los Angeles Times Book Review, September 30, 1984; June 21, 1987.
Midwest Quarterly, spring, 1989, pp. 372-386.
Milwaukee Journal, November 12, 1974.
Nation, June 10, 1991, pp. 762-763.
Newsweek, January 14, 1991, Malcom Jones, Jr., review of *The Best of Plimpton,* p. 52.
New Yorker, November 12, 1966; June 27, 1994, p. 44.
New York Herald Tribune, April 23, 1961.
New York Review of Books, February 23, 1967; February 7, 1974.
New York Times, November 12, 1973; July 29, 1977; November 16, 1977; March 28, 1981; June 14, 1984; November 14, 1985; July 30, 1987; March 6, 1995, Christopher Lehmann-Haupt, review of *The X Factor: A Quest for Excellence,* p. B2, C16.
New York Times Book Review, April 23, 1961; November 10, 1968; January 6, 1974; July 31, 1977; November 6, 1977; June 17, 1984; September 23, 1984; November 24, 1985; July 5, 1987; March 4, 1990, David Kirby, review of *The Writer's Chapbook,* p. 11; July 2, 1995, p. 11.
Observer, June 23, 1991.
Playboy, December, 1990, p. 29; April, 1995, p. 34.
Publishers Weekly, October 2, 2000, review of *The Great Life,* p. 79; April 30, 2001, "Baseball's Been Good to Them," p. 67; February 3, 2003, review of *Latin American Writers at Work,* p. 66.
Saturday Review, December 10, 1966, Hal Higdon, review of *Paper Lion;* August 14, 1971.
Spectator, October 14, 1978.
Sports Illustrated, September 13, 1965, p. 4; August 3, 1992, p. 6; December 22, 2003, "A Feast of Classic Plimpton: Brilliant—and Beautiful—Reissues by a Writer Who Couldn't Just Watch," p. 23.
Time, April 7, 1967, p. 40; December 19, 1977; September 10, 1984; December 8, 1986; April 13, 1987, pp. 9-11; June 8, 1987.
Times Literary Supplement, December 1, 1978; January 21, 1983; December 21, 1984; August 2, 1985; September 5, 1986; March 20, 1987; September 29, 2000, John Stokes, "Raffishness Rampant," p. 21.
Tribune Books (Chicago, IL), May 3, 1981; September 2, 1984; October 14, 1984; November 24, 1985; July 5, 1987; June 14, 1992, p. 6; December 6, 1992, p. 13.
Village Voice, June 11, 1991, p. 30.
Wall Street Journal, August 28, 1984.
Washington Post, January 7, 1986.
Washington Post Book World, May 27, 1984; September 2, 1984; June 21, 1987; July 9, 1989; October 21, 1990; March 12, 1995.
Writers Digest, June, 1974, pp. 17-18.

OBITUARIES:

PERIODICALS

Economist (U.S.), October 11, 2003 p. 86.
Nation, October 20, 2003, p. 7.
Newsweek, October 6, 2003, p. 8.
New Yorker, October 6, 2003, p. 46.
New York Times, September 27, 2003, p. A13.
People, October 13, 2003, p. 93.
Sporting News, October 6, 2003, p. 8.
Sports Illustrated, October 6, 2003, p. 40.
Time, October 6, 2003, p. 25.

ONLINE

MSNBC.com, http://www.msnbc.com/ (September 26, 2003).

* * *

PLIMPTON, George Ames
See PLIMPTON, George

* * *

POHL, Frederik 1919-
(Elton V. Andrews, Paul Fleur, S.D. Gottesman, Lee Gregor, Warren F. Howard, Cyril Judd, a joint pseudonym, Paul Dennis Lavond, Scott Mariner, Ernst Mason, Edson McCann, a joint pseudonym, James McCreigh, Jordan Park, a joint pseudonym, Charles Satterfield, Donald Stacy, Dirk Wilson)

PERSONAL: Born November 26, 1919, in New York, NY; son of Fred George (a salesman) and Anna Jane (Mason) Pohl; married Doris Baumgardt, 1940 (divorced, 1944); married Dorothy LesTina, August, 1945 (divorced, 1947); married Judith Merril, 1948 (divorced, 1952); married Carol M. Ulf Stanton, September 15, 1952 (divorced, 1983); married Elizabeth Anne Hull (a professor of English), July, 1984; children: Ann (Mrs. Walter Weary), Karen (Mrs. Robert Dixon), Frederik III (deceased), Frederik IV, Kathy. *Education:* Attended public schools in Brooklyn, NY, "dropped out in senior year." *Politics:* Democrat. *Religion:* Unitarian.

ADDRESSES: Home and office—855 S. Harvard Dr., Palatine, IL 60067.

CAREER: Writer. Popular Publications, New York, NY, editor, 1939-43; Popular Science Publishing Co., New York, NY, editor in book department and assistant circulation manager, 1946-49; literary agent, 1946- 53; freelance writer 1953-60; *Galaxy* magazine, New York, NY, editor, 1961-69; Ace Books, New York, NY, executive editor, 1971-72; Bantam Books, New York, NY, science fiction editor, 1973-79. Staff lecturer, American Management Association, 1966-69; cultural exchange lecturer in science fiction for U.S. Department of State in Yugoslavia, Romania, and the Soviet Union, 1974; also lecturer at more than two hundred colleges in the United States, Canada, and abroad; represented United States at international literary conferences in England, Italy, Brazil, Canada, and Japan. Has appeared on more than four hundred radio and television programs in nine countries. County committeeman, Democratic Party, Monmouth City, NJ, 1956-69; trustee, The Harbour School, Red Bank, NJ, 1972-75, and First Unitarian Church of Monmouth City, 1973-75. *Military service:* U.S. Army Air Forces, 1943-45; received seven battle stars.

MEMBER: Science Fiction Writers of America (president, 1974-76), Authors Guild (Midwest area representative; member of council, 1975—), British Interplanetary Society (fellow), American Astronautical Society, World Science Fiction (president, 1980-82), American Association for the Advancement of Science (fellow), World Future Society, American Civil Liberties Union (trustee, Monmouth County, NJ, 1968-71), New York Academy of Sciences.

AWARDS, HONORS: Edward E. Smith Award, 1966; Hugo Award, World Science Fiction Convention, 1966, 1967, and 1968, for best editor, 1974, for short story, "The Meeting," 1978, for best novel, *Gateway,* and 1986, for story "Fermi and Frost"; H.G. Wells Award, 1975; Nebula Award, Science Fiction Writers of America, 1977, for best novel, *Man Plus,* and 1978, for best novel, *Gateway;* John W. Campbell Award, Center for the Study of Science Fiction, 1978, for *Gateway,* and 1986, for *The Years of the City;* National Book Award, 1980, for *JEM;* Popular Culture Association annual award, 1982; guest of honor at science fiction convention in Katowice, Poland, 1987; Grand Master Award, Science Fiction Writers of America, 1993; Milford award, 1995; Gallun award, 1998; Prix Utopia, 2000; Hubbard Lifetime Achievement, 2000.

WRITINGS:

(Under pseudonym James McCreigh) *Danger Moon,* American Science Fiction (Sydney, Australia), 1953.

(With Lester del Rey, under joint pseudonym Edson McCann) *Preferred Risk,* Simon & Schuster (New York, NY), 1955.

Alternating Currents (short stories), Ballantine (New York, NY), 1956.

(Under pseudonym Donald Stacy) *The God of Channel 1,* Ballantine (New York, NY), 1956.

(With Walter Lasly) *Turn the Tigers Loose,* Ballantine (New York, NY), 1956.

Edge of the City (novel; based on screenplay by Robert Alan Aurthur), Ballantine (New York, NY), 1957.

The Case against Tomorrow, Ballantine (New York, NY), 1957.

Slave Ship, Ballantine (New York, NY), 1957.

Tomorrow Times Seven: Science Fiction Stories, Ballantine (New York, NY), 1959.

The Man Who Ate the World, Ballantine (New York, NY), 1960.

Drunkard's Walk (also see below), Ballantine (New York, NY), 1960.

(Under pseudonym Ernst Mason) *Tiberius* (biography), Ballantine (New York, NY), 1960.

Turn Left at Thursday: Three Novelettes and Three Stories, Ballantine (New York, NY), 1961.

The Expert Dreamers, Doubleday (New York, NY), 1962.

The Abominable Earthman, Ballantine (New York, NY), 1963.

The Case against Tomorrow: Science Fiction Short Stories, Ballantine (New York, NY), 1965.

A Plague of Pythons, Ballantine (New York, NY), 1965.

The Frederik Pohl Omnibus, Gollancz (London, England), 1966, portions published as *Survival Kit,* Panther (London, England), 1979.

Drunkard's Walk, Penguin (Harmondsworth, England), 1966.

Digits and Dastards, Ballantine (New York, NY), 1968.

The Age of the Pussyfoot (also see below), Ballantine (New York, NY), 1969.

Day Million (short stories), Ballantine (New York, NY), 1970.

Practical Politics, 1972 (nonfiction), Ballantine (New York, NY), 1971.

The Gold at the Starbow's End, Ballantine (New York, NY), 1972.

(With wife, Carol Pohl) *Jupiter,* Ballantine (New York, NY), 1973.

The Best of Frederik Pohl, introduction by Lester del Rey, Doubleday (New York, NY), 1975.

The Early Pohl, Doubleday (New York, NY), 1976.

In the Problem Pit, Bantam (New York, NY), 1976.

Man Plus, Random House (New York, NY), 1976.

Gateway, St. Martin's Press (New York, NY), 1977, reprinted, Ballantine (New York, NY), 2004.

The Way the Future Was: A Memoir, Ballantine (New York, NY), 1978.

JEM: The Making of a Utopia, St. Martin's Press (New York, NY), 1979.

Beyond the Blue Event Horizon, Ballantine (New York, NY), 1980.

Syzygy, Bantam (New York, NY), 1981.

The Cool War, Ballantine (New York, NY), 1981.

Planets Three, Berkley (New York, NY), 1982.

Bilpohl, Two Novels: Drunkard's Walk and The Age of the Pussyfoot, Ballantine (New York, NY), 1982.

Starburst, Ballantine (New York, NY), 1982.

Starbow, Ballantine (New York, NY), 1982.

(Author of introduction) *New Visions: A Collection of Modern Science Fiction Art,* Doubleday (New York, NY), 1982.

Midas World, St. Martin's Press (New York, NY), 1983.

Heechee Rendezvous, Ballantine (New York, NY), 1984.

The Years of the City, Simon & Schuster (New York, NY), 1984.

The Merchant's War, St. Martin's Press (New York, NY), 1984.

Pohlstars, Ballantine (New York, NY), 1984.

Black Star Rising, Ballantine (New York, NY), 1985.

The Coming of the Quantum Cats, Bantam (New York, NY), 1986.

Terror, Berkley (New York, NY), 1986.

Chernobyl, Bantam (New York, NY), 1987.

The Annals of the Heechee, Ballantine (New York, NY), 1987.

Narabedla Ltd., Del Rey (New York, NY), 1988.

The Day the Martians Came, St. Martin's Press (New York, NY), 1988.

Homegoing, Del Rey (New York, NY), 1989.

The Gateway Trip: Tales and Vignettes of the Heechee, illustrated by Frank Kelly Freas, Easton Press (Norwalk, CT), 1990.

The World at the End of Time, Ballantine (New York, NY), 1990.

Outnumbering the Dead, illustrated by Steve Crisp, Century, 1990.

(With Isaac Asimov) *Our Angry Earth,* Tor (New York, NY), 1991.

Stopping at Slowyear, illustrated by Rob Alexander, Axolotl Press (Seattle, WA), 1991.

Mining the Oort, Ballantine (New York, NY), 1992.

(With Thomas T. Thomas) *Mars Plus,* Baen (New York, NY), 1994.

The Voices of Heaven, Tor (New York, NY), 1994.

The Other End of Time, Tor (New York, NY), 1996.

The Siege of Eternity, Tor (New York, NY), 1997.

O Pioneer!, Tor (New York, NY), 1998.

The Far Shore of Time, Tor (New York, NY), 1999.

Chasing Science: Science As a Spectator Sport (nonfiction), Tor (New York, NY), 2000.

The Boy Who Would Live Forever: A Novel of Gateway, Tor (New York, NY), 2004.

Platinum Pohl: The Collected Best Stories, Tor (New York, NY), 2005.

Also coauthor, with Marion Zimmer Bradley, of *Elbow Room.* Contributor, sometimes under pseudonyms, to *Galaxy, Worlds of Fantasy, Science Fiction Quarterly, Rogue, Impulse, Astonishing, Imagination, If, Beyond, Playboy, Infinity,* and other magazines.

WITH CYRIL M. KORNBLUTH

(Under joint pseudonym Cyril Judd) *Gunner Cade,* Simon & Schuster, 1952.

(Under joint pseudonym Cyril Judd) *Outpost Mars,* Abelard Press (New York, NY), 1952.

The Space Merchants (also see below), Ballantine (New York, NY), 1953, 2nd edition, 1981.

Search the Sky, Ballantine (New York, NY), 1954.

Gladiator-at-Law, Ballantine (New York, NY), 1955.

A Town Is Drowning, Ballantine (New York, NY), 1955.

Presidential Year, Ballantine (New York, NY), 1956.

(Under joint pseudonym Jordan Park) *Sorority House,* Lion Press (New York, NY), 1956.

(Under joint pseudonym Jordan Park) *The Man of Cold Raaes,* Pyramid Publications (New York, NY), 1958.

Wolfbane, Ballantine (New York, NY), 1959.

The Wonder Effect (short stories), Ballantine (New York, NY), 1962, revised edition published as *Critical Mass,* Bantam (New York, NY), 1977.

Before the Universe and Other Stories: The Best of the Early Work of Science Fiction's Most Famous Team of Collaborators, Bantam (New York, NY), 1980.

Venus, Inc., (includes *The Space Merchants* and *The Merchants' War*), Doubleday (New York, NY), 1985.

Our Best: The Best of Frederik Pohl and C.M. Kornbluth, Baen (New York, NY), 1987.

WITH JACK WILLIAMSON

Undersea Quest (also see below), Gnome Press (New York, NY), 1954.

Undersea Fleet (also see below), Gnome Press (New York, NY), 1956.

Undersea City (also see below), Gnome Press (New York, NY), 1958.

The Reefs of Space (also see below), Ballantine (New York, NY), 1963.

Starchild (also see below), Ballantine (New York, NY), 1965.

Rogue Star (also see below), Ballantine (New York, NY), 1969.

Farthest Star: The Saga of Cuckoo, Ballantine (New York, NY), 1975.

The Starchild Trilogy: The Reefs of Space, Starchild, and Rogue Star, Doubleday, 1977.

Wall around a Star, Ballantine (New York, NY), 1983.

Land's End, St. Martin's Press (New York, NY), 1988.

The Singers of Time, Doubleday (New York, NY), 1991.

The Undersea Trilogy (contains *Undersea Quest, Undersea Fleet,* and *Undersea City*), Baen (New York, NY), 1992.

EDITOR

Beyond the End of Time, Permabooks (Garden City, NY), 1952.

Star Science Fiction Stories, six volumes, Ballantine (New York, NY), 1953–1959.

Shadow of Tomorrow, Permabooks (Garden City, NY), 1953.

Star Short Novels, Ballantine (New York, NY), 1954.

(And author of introduction) *Assignment in Tomorrow: An Anthology,* Hanover House (Garden City, NY), 1954.

Star of Stars, Doubleday (New York, NY), 1960, published as *Star Fourteen,* Whiting & Wheaton (London, England), 1966.

The Expert Dreamer, Doubleday (New York, NY), 1962.

Time Waits for Winthrop and Four Other Short Novels from "Galaxy," Doubleday (New York, NY), 1962.

The Best Science Fiction from "Worlds of If" Magazine, Galaxy Publishing, 1964.

The Seventh Galaxy Reader, Doubleday (New York, NY), 1964.

The Eighth Galaxy Reader, Doubleday (New York, NY), 1965, published as *Final Encounter,* Curtis Books (New York, NY), 1965.

The If Reader of Science Fiction, Doubleday (New York, NY), 1966.

The Ninth Galaxy Reader, Doubleday (New York, NY), 1966.

The Tenth Galaxy Reader, Doubleday (New York, NY), 1967, published as *Door to Anywhere,* Curtis Books (New York, NY), 1967.

The Second If Reader of Science Fiction, Doubleday (New York, NY), 1968.

The Eleventh Galaxy Reader, Doubleday (New York, NY), 1969.

Nightmare Age, Ballantine (New York, NY), 1970.

Best Science Fiction for 1972, Ace Books (New York, NY), 1973.

(With Carol Pohl) *Jupiter,* Ballantine (New York, NY), 1973.

(With Carol Pohl) *Science Fiction: The Great Years,* Ace Books (New York, NY), Volume 1, 1973, Volume 2, 1976.

The Science Fiction Roll of Honor: An Anthology of Fiction and Nonfiction by Guests of Honor at World Science Fiction Conventions, Random House (New York, NY), 1975.

(And author of introduction) *The Best of C.M. Kornbluth,* Doubleday (New York, NY), 1976.

(With Carol Pohl) *Science Fiction Discoveries,* Bantam (New York, NY), 1976.

The Best of C.M. Kornbluth, Doubleday (New York, NY), 1976.

(With Martin H. Greenberg and Joseph D. Olander) *Science Fiction of the Forties,* Avon (New York, NY), 1978.

(With Martin H. Greenberg and Joseph D. Olander) *Galaxy: Thirty Years of Innovative Science Fiction,* Playboy Press (Chicago, IL), 1980.

Nebula Winners Fourteen, Harper (New York, NY), 1980.

(With Martin H. Greenberg and Joseph D. Olander) *The Great Science Fiction Series: Stories from the Best of the Series from 1944 to 1980,* Harper (New York, NY), 1980.

(With son, Frederik Pohl IV) *Science Fiction: Studies in Film,* Ace Books (New York, NY), 1981.

Yesterday's Tomorrows: Favorite Stories from Forty Years As a Science Fiction Editor, Berkley (New York, NY), 1982.

(With wife, Elizabeth Anne Hill) *Tales from the Planet Earth,* St. Martin's Press (New York, NY), 1986.

(With others) *Worlds of If: A Retrospective Anthology,* Bluejay Books, 1986.

Asimov, Isaac, *Our Angry Earth,* Tor (New York, NY), 1991.

The SFWA Grand Masters, Volume 1, Tor (New York, NY), 1999.

The SFWA Grand Masters, Volume 2, Tor (New York, NY), 2000.

The SFWA Grand Masters, Volume 3, Tor (New York, NY), 2001.

SIDELIGHTS: "Like all the other great men in SF," wrote Algis Budrys in the *Magazine of Fantasy and Science Fiction,* "Frederik Pohl is idiosyncratic, essentially self-made, and brilliant. Unlike many of the others, he has an extremely broad range of interests and education." In addition to his obvious affinity for science and writing, Pohl has also shown a lively interest in music and politics. During the course of his long career, which spans more than sixty years, he has made his mark as a writer, editor, literary agent, and enthusiastic promoter of science fiction. He is, Robert Scholes and Eric S. Rabkin asserted in *Science Fiction: History, Science, Vision,* "one of the few men to make a genuine impact on the science fiction field."

Pohl attended school sporadically as a child, and dropped out completely "as soon as it was legal," as he once commented. The library fed his hunger for knowledge, and he read voraciously. "'Catholic' is the word for my tastes," he explained. "There were days when I would take out a book at random and go home to see what I had found. A lot of what I read was so profoundly trashy that I no longer remember it at all, but in among the volumes of trash were precious insights and inspirations. Somewhere in my mid-teens I discovered the Russians—Tolstoi, Gogol, Pushkin, Dostoevski—and the weirder Americans like Thorne Smith and James Branch Cabell. Before I was old enough to vote I came across the French decadents—Proust and Huysmans in particular, as well as Baudelaire and Anatole France." Visits to museums, movies, and bookstores rounded out his education.

During the 1930s he became involved with several groups devoted to the new field of science fiction, where he met many writers who would be his fellow pioneers in the field: C.M. Kornbluth, Isaac Asimov, and James Blish, among others. By the 1950s, he had written a number of influential books with Kornbluth, which "pioneered and excelled in a completely new kind of science fiction," wrote Charles Platt in *Dream Makers: The Uncommon People Who Write Science Fiction.* "They invented and played with 'Sociological SF'—alternate futures here on Earth, exaggerating and satirizing real-life social forces and trends." The best of these collaborations was *The Space Merchants,* a satirical look at a world ruled by advertising; the book was inspired by Pohl's own short stint in an advertising agency. In this world, "exploitation of resources, pollution of environment, and overpopulation are all rampant," Scholes and Rabkin pointed out, "while the advertisers use every device of behavior control including addictive substances in the products. The beauty of [the book] is that it manages to be absurd and at the same time frighteningly close to the way that many people actually think. The lightness of touch and consistency of imagination make it a true classic of science fiction." "This novel is the single work most mentioned when Pohl's fiction is discussed," Stephen H. Goldman of the *Dictionary of Literary Biography* explained. "It is on every critic's list of science fiction classics and has never been out of print since its first appearance. While Pohl and Kornbluth produced other highly readable novels *The Space Merchants* remains their single greatest achievement." The book has been translated into over fifteen languages, including Japanese, Hebrew, Serbo-Croatian, Dutch, and Latvian.

As editor of *Galaxy* and later with Bantam Books, Pohl was a strong supporter of the "new wave" writers in science fiction—writers who borrowed literary techniques from mainstream literature to use in their science fiction, while eliminating what they saw as the genre's clichés. Ironically, Pohl came under fire from some of these writers for being too conservative. "I published the majority of 'new-wave' writers," Pohl told Platt. "It wasn't the stories I objected to, it was the snottiness of the proponents . . . . The thing that the 'new wave' did that I treasure was to shake up old dinosaurs, like Isaac [Asimov], and for that matter me . . . , and show them that you do not really have to construct a story according to the 1930s pulp or Hollywood standards."

Some of the new wave's influence can be seen in Pohl's prize-winning novel *Gateway.* The author has said he considers it his best novel, and many commentators agree with that assessment. *Gateway* is the story of the discovery of an ancient spaceport of the Heechee, a long-dead civilization. Each spaceship found at the port is operable, but so highly advanced that the propulsion system and the destination for which it is programmed are incomprehensible to humans. A few brave adventurers dare to travel in the ships in a kind of lottery system. "Occasionally," wrote Goldman, "one of the Heechee ships lands at a site that is filled with undiscovered artifacts, and the human riders share in the financial rewards these discoveries can bring." At other times, the adventurers never return, or return dead. The story, Mark Rose of the *New Republic* found, "conveys a vivid sense of the pathos and absurdity of human ignorance in attempting to exploit a barely understood universe." Patrick Parrinder of the *Times Literary Supplement* agreed: "The novel is remarkable for its portrayal of human explorers rushing into space in a mood of abject fear and greed, in machines they cannot understand or control."

The story of the spaceport and its hazardous explorations is interspersed with seriocomic scenes involving a guilt-ridden adventurer—an adventurer who made a fortune during a trip on which he was forced to abandon the woman he loves—and his computer psychoanalyst. "Pohl's touch is always light and sure," Rose commented, "and, indeed parts of the novel are extremely funny." Goldman noted that in *Gateway* "Pohl has finally balanced the demands of an imaginative world and the presentation of a highly complex character . . . . This balance has led to his most successful novel thus far." In *Gateway,* Roz Kaveney of *Books and Bookmen* believed, Pohl "successfully combined wit and humanity in a novel of character. [The result is] a highly competent, darkly witty entertainment." Other critics found the computer psychoanalyst a particularly believable character. "What makes this book so intriguing," Peter Ackroyd wrote in the *Spectator,* "is not its occasional satire and consistent good humor, but the fact that Pohl has managed to convey the insistent presence of the non-human, a presence which may indeed haunt our future."

Pohl's next novel, *JEM: The Making of a Utopia,* also won critical praise, including the National Book Award in 1980. Set in the near future when the Earth has been divided into three camps—People, Fuel, and Food—the novel tells the story of three bands of human colonists on another planet. When there is a war and a resulting social breakdown on Earth, the colony is suddenly independent and "must then find a way to reconcile its divisions, both among the colonists and between the colonists and the three excellently depicted native sapient species, if it is to survive," wrote Tom Easton of the *Magazine of Fantasy and Science Fiction.* Gerald Jonas, writing in the *New York Times Book Review,* compared *JEM* to *The Space Merchants* because "*JEM* is also social satire—but without the humor." "It is essentially a political allegory," Alex de Jonge of the *Spectator* observed, "describing the struggle between the world's three blocs . . . each attempting to colonize a planet."

The colonization of Jem repeats some mistakes made on Earth. "With systematic, undeviating logic," wrote Budrys, "Pohl depicts the consequent rape of Jem. As each of the expeditions struggles to do its best, there are moments of hope, and moments of triumph. But they are all no more than peaks on a downhill slope. The ending of it all is so genuinely sad that one realizes abruptly how rarely SF evokes pure sorrow, and how profound Pohl's vision was in conceiving of this story." Russell Lord of the *Christian Science Monitor* found it is Pohl's "basically poetic imagination that elevates this novel to a high position among the author's works."

Pohl's 1982 novel, *Starburst,* was a sequel to one he had written a decade earlier, *The Gold at Starbow's End. Starburst* concerns four American couples, all perfect physical specimens and geniuses to boot. They are tricked into undertaking a space mission to a nonexistent planet by a scientist who wants to give them limitless time to expand their human knowledge. Their transmissions back to Earth eventually overload the planet's computers, bringing about catastrophe for the planet. A *Publishers Weekly* writer commented, "This novel is Pohl at his best, blending science, speculation and satire to fascinate us from first page to last." And a contributor to *Voice of Youth Advocates* called *Starburst* a "creatively cryptic blending of narrative, scientific, and mythological description. Speculation at its best by the master of the genre!"

In *The Voices of Heaven,* published in 1994, Pohl features Barry di Hoa, who is hijacked from his comfortable perch on the Moon and forcibly placed on a ship bound for the planet Pava. Once here, he discovers a society of humans in the grips of a fundamentalist religion, whose leaders are prone to instigating mass suicide. He also meets the Lepsnative Pavan creatures that take the form of giant caterpillars early in their life form before evolving into butterflies. Pohl uses the narrative to expound on familiar questions of religion, state, and human behavior. A contributor to the *Washington Post Book World* remarked that the author created "as chilling an ending as you'll find in modern science fiction" and averred that *The Voices of Heaven* is "perhaps the most perfectly constructed of all Pohl's books."

During the 1990s Pohl made another significant contribution to the science fiction genre with a trio of novels known as the Eschaton Sequence: *The Other End of Time, The Siege of Eternity,* and *The Far Shore of Time.* The story concerns a war over Earth, fought between two alien races: the scarecrow-like Others and the Horch, who are reminiscent of dinosaurs. The Others have implanted transmitters into the brains of many people so that they could monitor key thoughts and senses. The Others promise to protect humans from the Horch, but they also plan to turn them into slaves. "In this war against Ultimate Evil, [human beings] are the hobbits, but without the cuteness, and only the sourest of comic relief," commented Russell Letson in *Locus.* He went on to say that the irony that pervades *The Far Shore of Time* made it "the strongest book of the three and a real keeper." *Kirkus Reviews* contributor Paul M. Lamey rated *The Far Shore of Time* "solidly engrossing and professionally rendered," and a *Publishers Weekly* writer found that "Pohl's fertile imagination and subtle characterizations are as evident as ever. The book's densely packed action and impressive world-building make it a gratifying wrap- up to an entertaining series."

During the early 2000s Pohl continued to publish new work, including the nonfiction volume *Chasing Science: Science As a Spectator Sport* and the fiction volume *The Boy Who Would Live Forever: A Novel of Gateway.* A book of Pohl's writings, *Platinum Pohl: The Collected Best Stories,* was also released. It is interesting to note that *The Boy Who Would Live Forever* is a return to the Heechee and the Gateway Universe after a fourteen-year break from the topic. The story begins when two human boys travel to the Heechee way station. The boys then find themselves embroiled in an effort to save the Heechee from the Kugel, a rival alien species. Critics noted that fans of the Heechee will be glad to read the new release and also noted that the plot of the story leaves room for future installments. In addition, *Library Journal* reviewer Jackie Cassada applauded the story's "gentle humor," while a *Kirkus Reviews* contributor stated that the story is "an astonishing eyeful, rich and absorbing."

Although his work as a science fiction writer has brought him an international reputation, Pohl has also played a large role in science fiction publishing, having served stints as the editor of *Galaxy* magazine, and as editor with the paperback publishing firms of Ballantine, Ace Books, and Bantam. In these positions, he has helped to develop new talent in the genre and publish daring or experimental work by more experienced writers. Among the books Pohl has brought into print are Joanna Russ's *The Female Man,* a controversial feminist novel, and Samuel Delany's *Dhalgren,* a novel that had been seeking a publisher for many years before Pohl took a chance on it. *Dhalgren* went on to sell over one million copies.

For every promising new talent Pohl has nurtured, there have been many instances of frustration, however. In a 1970 interview with Paul Walker for *Speaking of Science Fiction,* Pohl remarked that the economic demands of the sci-fi industry led to a plethora of overwritten manuscripts. Even those submissions he has read that have some good qualities, he said, "are fat, bloated, stretched out, milked. The reason for this is the pressure of the market; there is little market for short stories and novelettes, an insatiable market for novels. So if you are a writer of moderate talent and standing, what do you do with your short story ideas? Why, you do what everybody else does: you pad them out to 60,000 words, whether they can stand it or not."

Joseph McClellan, writing in the *Washington Post Book World,* offered an insight into what has made Pohl's writing among the best in twentieth-century science fiction. "Pohl's work," McClellan wrote, "offers science fiction at its best: basic human problems . . . woven deftly into an intricate plot; pure adventure happening to believable (if not deeply drawn) characters in surroundings almost beyond the borders of imagination; and at the end, when other questions have been laid to rest, the posing of a new question as unfathomable as time and space themselves."

Offering a different view, essayist David N. Samuelson noted in *Bookvoices for the Future* that Pohl's reputation as a master of his craft does not preclude criticism of his work. While the author "is at the top of American SF writers who are 'fan oriented,'" wrote Samuelson, Pohl still "shows significant defects" as an artist. "Even the best of his fiction is sometimes marred by the intrusion of melodrama, sentimentality, unrationalized fantasy, and other features more or less calculated to appeal to an addicted audience. For the most part, his work seems to lack depth, density, an authentic personal voice, and a sense of style as anything more than a serviceable medium." In Samuelson's opinion, Pohl's shortcomings as a writer stem in part from his commercial instincts as an editor. Years of producing marketable fiction has "no doubt limited him at times to what he though his known audience was willing to accept. If it was narrow and provincial, so were his stories prior to 1952. When satire and social criticism were in, he still felt constrained to gild them with snappy patter, melodramatic plots and irrelevant aliens. His Hugos as editor were won for a magazine committed largely to adventure stories and essentially lightweight material."

For his part, Pohl has said that he has schooled himself "to disregard criticism, or at least to discount nine-tenths of it."

Criticism notwithstanding, Pohl remains a "star among stars," according to Robert Wilcox in the *St. James Guide to Science Fiction Writers,* who added that the author has "shaped and seasoned the literature of science fiction as almost no one else has. His kaleidoscopic background has equipped him with skills and values possessed by few if any rivals." In *Locus* Pohl shared his thoughts on what a friend, John Rackham, once termed the 'science fiction method': "The science fiction method is dissection and reconstruction. You look at the world around you, and you take it apart into all its components. Then you take some of those components, throw them away, and plug in different ones, start it up and see what happens."

BIOGRAPHICAL AND CRITICAL SOURCES:

BOOKS

Aldiss, Brian, *Billion Year Spree: The History of Science Fiction,* Doubleday (New York, NY), 1973.

Amis, Kingsley, *New Maps of Hell: A Survey of Science Fiction,* Harcourt (New York, NY), 1960.

Carter, Paul A., *The Creation of Tomorrow: Fifty Years of Magazine Science-Fiction,* Columbia University Press (New York, NY), 1977.

Clareson, Thomas D., and Thomas L. Wymer, editors, *Voices for the Future,* Volume 3, Bowling Green University (Bowling Green, OH), 1984.

Clareson, Thomas D., *Frederik Pohl,* Borgo Press (San Bernardino, CA), 1987.

Contemporary Literary Criticism, Volume 18, Thomson Gale (Detroit, MI) 1981.

Dictionary of Literary Biography, Volume 8: *Twentieth-Century American Science-Fiction Writers,* Thomson Gale (Detroit, MI) 1981.

Platt, Charles, *Dream Makers: The Uncommon People Who Write Science Fiction,* Berkley (New York, NY), 1980.

Pohl, Frederik, *The Way the Future Was: A Memoir,* Ballantine (New York, NY), 1978.

St. James Guide to Science-Fiction Writers, St. James Press (Detroit, MI), 1996.

Scholes, Robert, and Eric S. Rabkin, *Science Fiction: History, Science, Vision,* Oxford University Press (New York, NY), 1977.

Short Story Criticism, Volume 25, Thomson Gale (Detroit, MI) 1997.

Vision, Oxford University Press (New York, NY), 1977.

Walker, Paul, *Speaking of Science Fiction: The Paul Walker Interviews,* Luna Press, 1978.

PERIODICALS

Analog, February, 1977; January, 1979; December, 1979; May, 1980; December, 1999, Tom Easton, review of *The Far Shore of Time,* p. 135.

Booklist, May 1, 1999, Roland Green, review of *The SFWA Grand Masters,* Volume 1, p. 1582; August, 1999, Roberta Johnson review of *The Far Shore of Time,* p. 2038; March 1, 2000, Roland Green, review of *The SFWA Grand Masters,* Volume 2, p. 1200; September 15, 2004, Frieda Murray, review of *The Boy Who Would Live Forever: A Novel of Gateway,* p. 216.

Books and Bookmen, November, 1979.

Christian Science Monitor, June 20, 1979.

Kirkus Reviews, April 1, 1999, Paul M. Lamey, review of *The SFWA Grand Masters,* Volume 1, p. 496; June 15, 1999, Paul M. Lamey, review of *The Far Shore of Time,* p. 928; August 15, 2004, review of *The Boy Who Would Live Forever,* p. 782.

Library Journal, May 15, 1998, review of *O Pioneer!;* April 15, 1999, Devon Thomas, review of *The SFWA Grand Masters,* Volume 1, p. 149; August 1, 1999, Jackie Cassada, review of *The Far Shore of Time,* p. 148; September 15, 2004, Jackie Cassada, review of *The Boy Who Would Live Forever,* p. 52.

Locus, August, 1999, Russell Letson, review of *The Far Shore of Time,* p. 25; October, 2000, "Frederik Pohl: Chasing Science," pp. 6, 71- 72.

Los Angeles Times, December 11, 1986.

Magazine of Fantasy and Science Fiction, March, 1978; September, 1979.

New Republic, November 26, 1977.

New Statesman, April 15, 1977.

New York Times, September 7, 1983.

New York Times Book Review, March 27, 1977; May 20, 1979; November 15, 1987; April 24, 1988; July 2, 1989; July 10, 1994, p. 30.

Publishers Weekly, July 31, 1978; October 19, 1990, review of *The Gateway Trip: Tales and Vignettes of the Heechee;* September 27, 1991, review of *Our Angry Earth;* April 6, 1992, review of *Outnumbering the Dead;* May 23, 1994, p. 82; September 22, 1997, review of *The Siege of Eternity,* May 25, 1998, review of *O Pioneer!;* May 24, 1999, review of *The SFWA Grand Masters,* Volume 1, p. 74; July 26, 1999, review of *The Far Shore of Time,* p. 67; November 27, 2000, review of *Chasing Science,* p. 68; October 17, 2005, review of *Platinum Pohl: The Collected Best Stories,* p. 44.

Rapport, November 2, 1994, p. 26.
Science Fiction Chronicle, August, 1999, Don D'Ammassa, review of *The SFWA Grand Masters,* Volume 1, p. 44.
Spectator, January 28, 1978.
Times (London, England), November 24, 1983; August 8, 1985; January 16, 1988; January 17, 1991.
Times Literary Supiplement, January 14, 1977; January 27, 1978; May 14, 1983.
Tribune Books (Chicago, IL), March 15, 1987; August 16, 1987; August 21, 1988; July 15, 1990; December 30, 1990.
USA Today Magazine, December, 1999, Frederik Pohl, "Goodbye Traffic Jams and Mega-Airports?," p. 5.
Voice of Youth Advocates, April, 1984; December, 1986, p. 240; April, 1987, p. 40; February, 1991, p. 366; April, 1991, pp. 46-47.
Washington Post, October 4, 1987.
Washington Post Book World, March 14, 1980; November 23, 1980; July 25, 1982; February 28, 1988; April 30, 1989; June 26, 1994, p. 2.

* * *

PORTER, Katherine Anne 1890-1980 (M.T.F., a joint pseudonym)

PERSONAL: Born May 15, 1890, in Indian Creek, TX; died of cancer, September 18, 1980, in Silver Spring, MD; daughter of Harrison Boone and Mary Alice (Jones) Porter; married c. 1906 (divorced c. 1909; married Eugene Dove Pressly (employed by American Consulate in Paris), 1933 (divorced, 1938); married Albert Russel Erskine Jr. (a professor of English), 1938 (divorced, 1942). *Education:* Educated in convent and private schools. *Hobbies and other interests:* Outdoor life, old music, medieval history, reading, cookery, and gardening.

CAREER: Professional writer. Lecturer and teacher at writer conferences; speaker at more than 200 universities and colleges in the United States and Europe. Writer-in-residence, or member of English faculties, at Olivet College, 1940, Stanford University, 1948-49, University of Michigan, 1953-54, University of Virginia, 1958, and Washington and Lee University (first female faculty member in school's history), 1959. Ewing Lecturer, University of California, Los Angeles, 1959; first Regents Lecturer, University of California, Riverside, 1961. Member, President Lyndon Johnson's committee on presidential scholars.

MEMBER: National Institute of Arts and Letters (vice president, 1950-52), American Academy of Arts and Letters.

AWARDS, HONORS: Guggenheim fellowships, 1931, 1938; first annual gold medal, Society of the Libraries of New York University, 1940, for *Pale Horse, Pale Rider;* Library of Congress fellow in regional American literature, 1944; chosen one of six representatives of American literature at International Expositions of the Arts in Paris, 1952; Ford Foundation grant, 1959-61; State Department grants for international exchange of persons to Mexico, 1960, 1964; first prize, O. Henry Memorial Award, 1962, for "Holiday"; Emerson-Thoreau Bronze Medal for Literature, American Academy of Arts and Sciences, 1962; Pulitzer Prize, 1966, and National Book Award, 1966, both for *The Collected Stories of Katherine Anne Porter;* gold medal, National Institute of Arts and Letters, 1967; creative arts award, Brandeis University, 1971-72. Honorary degrees include D.Litt. from University of North Carolina, 1949, Smith College, 1958, and Wheaton College; D.H.L. from University of Michigan, 1954, and University of Maryland, 1966; and D.F.A. from LaSalle College.

WRITINGS:

(With Mae T. Franking as M.T.F.) *My Chinese Marriage,* Duffield (New York, NY), 1921.
Outline of Mexican Popular Arts and Crafts, Young & McCallister, 1922.
What Price Marriage, Sears, 1927.
Flowering Judas (story), Harcourt (New York, NY), 1930, 2nd expanded edition published as *Flowering Judas, and Other Stories,* 1935.
(Translator and compiler) *Katherine Anne Porter's French Songbook,* Harrison Co., 1933.
Hacienda: A Story of Mexico, Harrison Co., 1934.
Noon Wine, Schuman's, 1937.
Pale Horse, Pale Rider: Three Short Novels, Harcourt (New York, NY), 1939.
(Translator) Fernandez de Lizardi, *The Itching Parrot,* Doubleday (New York, NY), 1942.
(Author of preface) Flores and Poore, *Fiesta in November,* Houghton (Boston, MA), 1942.
The Leaning Tower, and Other Stories, Harcourt (New York, NY), 1944.
The Days Before: Collected Essays and Occasional Writings, Harcourt (New York, NY), 1952, revised and enlarged edition published as *The Collected Essays and Occasional Writings of Katherine Anne Porter,* Delacorte (New York, NY), 1970.
The Old Order: Stories of the South from Flowering Judas, Pale Horse, and the Leaning Tower, Harcourt (New York, NY), 1955.
Fiction and Criticism of Katherine Anne Porter, University of Pittsburgh Press (Pittsburgh, PA), 1957, revised edition, 1962.

Ship of Fools (novel), Little, Brown (Boston, MA), 1962.

The Collected Stories of Katherine Anne Porter, Harcourt (New York, NY), 1965.

A Christmas Story, illustrations by Ben Shahn, Dial (New York, NY), 1967.

The Never Ending Wrong, Little, Brown (Boston, MA), 1977.

Conversations, University Press of Mississippi (Jackson, MS), 1987.

Letters of Katherine Anne Porter, edited and selected by Isabel Bayley, Atlantic Monthly Press (New York, NY), 1990.

"This Strange, Old World" and Other Book Reviews, edited by Darlene Harbour Unrue, University of Georgia Press (Athens, GA), 1991.

Uncollected Early Prose of Katherine Anne Porter, edited by Ruth M. Alvarez and Thomas F. Walsh, University of Texas Press (Austin, TX), 1993.

Contributor to numerous magazines.

ADAPTATIONS: Ship of Fools was filmed by Columbia in 1965; *Noon Wine* was dramatized and filmed for television's "ABC Stage 67" in 1967; the movie rights to *Pale Horse, Pale Rider* were sold in 1970; Porter's short story "The Jilting of Granny Weatherall," was filmed for television and broadcast March 3, 1979, on Public Broadcasting Service's "American Short Story."

SIDELIGHTS: Although her output was relatively small, Katherine Anne Porter was one of the most recognized and acclaimed American writers of short fiction of the mid-twentieth century. In 1966 she won both the Pulitzer Prize and the National Book Award for *The Collected Stories of Katherine Anne Porter,* many of which were written between 1922 and 1940. Porter also authored one novel, *Ship of Fools,* which took almost thirty years to write and was one of most awaited literary products of its day when published in 1962. Although the novel drew mixed reviews, Porter's reputation still rests firmly on the strength of the twenty-seven stories included in her *Collected Stories,* which are marked by an economy of style and a controlled portrayal of character and emotion. Laurie Johnston noted in the *New York Times* that Porter's "storytelling had a quality of translucence—a smoothly polished, surface objectivity that nevertheless moved the reader to share the underlying turmoil of her characters and their often frightening interrelationships." Robert Penn Warren, writing in the *Washington Post,* went so far as to state that Porter was "certainly unsurpassed in our century or country—perhaps any time or country—as a writer [of] fiction in the short forms of story or novella. . . . Her work remains a monument to a tremendous talent—even genius. It is permanent."

Born on a dirt farm in Texas in 1890, Porter and her three siblings were raised by her grandmother, the author's mother having died when Porter was two years old. A strong-willed woman, Porter's grandmother would provide her granddaughter with the determination to go beyond the confines of a traditional woman's role and attempt to forge a career as a writer later in life. Meanwhile, Porter's upbringing remained chaotic; after the death of her grandmother when she was eleven, Porter was left in the care of her cousins, whose dairy ranch near San Antonio later became the setting for Porter's highly praised novella *Noon Wine,* first published in 1937. The two years of formal education Porter received in Texas provided her with the means to support herself as part-owner of a small school of dramatic arts in Victoria, Texas, which she ran with her sister, Annie Gay, from the time she was fourteen. The need to support herself ended when Porter married at age sixteen; the marriage, which lasted for nine years, was the first of several.

Porter's dreams of becoming an actress, which she attempted to implement after leaving her first husband, were quickly cut short after she contracted tuberculosis. Near death at one point, her brother supported her stay at Carlsbad Sanatorium in San Angelo, Texas, in 1916. Leading a quiet, sheltered existence there for two years allowed Porter time for introspection; she began to reconsider her dreams of becoming an actress and eventually decided to put her creative energies into becoming a writer. With the help of a fellow patient, she left Carlsbad in 1918 and went to work as a journalist. From there, a move to New York City followed, and Porter slowly began to build her expertise as a writer by working as a publicist, composing stories for children's magazines, and ghostwriting Mae T. Franking's *My Chinese Marriage.* Over the next decade she worked to amass experiences and expertise—in 1921 she went to Mexico to study Aztec and Mayan art designs, and her 1923 short story "The Martyr" was inspired by the Mexican muralist Diego Rivera—although her lack of a comprehensive education made Porter self-conscious about her aptitude for her chosen profession until the success of her first published short story, "Maria Concepcion," in 1922. Porter was thirty-two.

Although she considered herself primarily a writer, Porter was often forced to adopt sidelines in order to support an increasingly lavish lifestyle. All the while she continued to write, burning "trunksful" of manuscripts. She once told a *Paris Review* interviewer: "I practiced writing in every possible way that I could. . . . This has been the intact line of my life which directs my actions, determines my point of view, profoundly affects my character and personality, my social beliefs and economic status and the kind of friendships I form. . . . I made no attempt to publish anything until I was thirty, but I have written and destroyed manuscripts quite literally by the trunkful. I spent fifteen years wandering about, weighted horribly with masses of paper and little else. Yet for this vocation I was and am willing to live and die, and I consider very few other things of the slightest importance."

During the remainder of Porter's career, her writing, though limited in quantity, remained high in quality, reflecting the people and experiences she encountered. In fact, much developed from memories of Texas, despite Porter's ambivalent relationship with that area of the United States for much of her adult life. In 1927, encouraged by a group of southern friends that included Caroline Gordon, Allen Tate, and Robert Penn Warren, she went to Salem, Massachusetts, intending to write a biography of Puritan theologian Cotton Mather; although the biography was never finished, the stark New England setting brought back memories of her early childhood, and the short story "The Jilting of Granny Wetherall" was the result. Writing in the *Virginia Quarterly Review,* James William Johnson characterized Porter's themes in this manner: "critical judgment, as accurate and impartial as a carpenter's level, has limited her artistry in several ways. It has not permitted her to universalize but has confined her to being a 'witness to life.' Consequently her fiction has been closely tied to what she herself has experienced firsthand. The fact that Miss Porter's essays parallel her stories in theme—love, marriage, alien cultures—is significant in this light. Her artistic preoccupation with 'truth' has prevented the fictional generalizations often thought of as scope." Indeed, even when a third marriage found Porter living in Paris, France, the fiction she produced there echoed her experiences of growing up in poverty in Texas.

"My whole attempt," Porter once wrote of her work as an author, "has been to discover and understand human motives, human feeling, to make a distillation of what human relations and experiences my mind has been able to absorb. I have never known an uninteresting human being, and I have never known two alike; there are broad classifications and deep similarities, but I am interested in the thumbprint. I am passionately involved with these individuals who populate all these enormous migrations, calamities; these beings without which, one by one, all the 'broad movements of history' could never take place. One by one—as they were born."

These feelings for humanity are reflected throughout Porter's oeuvre, which although including such critically acclaimed short story collections as 1930's *Flowering Judas* and 1939's *Pale Horse, Pale Rider,* brought their author scant public notice compared to that garnered by her long-awaited novel, *Ship of Fools.* "Miss Porter's short stories have been marked by a mastery of technique, mind and society itself, without lapsing into popular cliches," maintained George Hendrick in his biography *Katherine Anne Porter.* "No matter whether she has written about Mexicans, Texans, Irishmen, or Germans, one feels that she knows the people and their backgrounds perfectly; she has lived and relived the experiences and emotions so thoroughly that she has often written her stories and short novels in a matter of hours or days."

"In my view," Warren would write of his friend in the *Saturday Review* shortly after her death in September of 1980, "the final importance of Katherine Anne Porter is not merely that she has written a number of fictions which have enlarged and deepened the nature of the story . . . , but that she has created an *ouevre*—a body of work, including fiction, essays, letters, and journals—that bears the stamp of a personality distinctive, delicately perceptive, keenly aware of the depth and darkness of human experience, delighted by the . . . triumphs of human kindness and warmth, and thoroughly committed to a quest for meaning in the midst of the ironic complexities of man's lot." With the revival of interest in women's writing in the wake of the feminist movement, much of this *oeuvre* was collected or republished in response to the reconsideration of her work by scholars.

Porter's efforts as a journalist were collected in *"This Strange, Old World" and Other Book Reviews,* which includes criticism she penned for publications such as the *New York Herald Tribune, New Republic, Nation,* and the *New York Times* between 1920 and 1958. As editor Darlene Harbour Unrue noted in her preface to the collection, "Porter's book reviews are reflections of her aesthetics, her worldview, and the themes and subjects that fill her fiction. Neither an academician nor a rigid thinker, Porter approached others' works with a freshness and what she might have called a poet's perspective." Cited by *Western American Literature* reviewer Thomas Austenfeld as providing "critics with fresh arguments in the ongoing discussion of Porter's artistic development," *Uncollected Early Prose of*

Katherine Anne Porter includes twenty-four of the short stories she wrote while under the spell of Mexico, dating between 1920 and 1932. *Katherine Anne Porter: Conversations* and *Letters of Katherine Anne Porter,* also published as a result of renewed interest in the writer, further illuminate the life and talent of a woman whose life remained masked by a myth of her own making. Calling Porter's letters "marvels, letter-writing raised to a minor art," Sally Fitzgerald wrote in Chicago's *Tribune Books* that through the author's correspondence "we begin to understand some of the fascination she exercised for so many people in her lifetime. Her generosity and capacity for enthusiastic response to the world, and respect for what she called 'goodness,' are evident, along with her egoism, vanity, fickleness, unreliability, and chronic inability to discipline herself for the best use of her talents."

Commenting on the reasons for the reexamination of Porter's work only after a long period of neglect, Reynolds Price had this to say in the *New York Times Book Review:* "The quality of her mind and of the stories she told is fearless, steely and lethal to the most widely cherished illusions of the species—our poisonous grip on romance and self-regard, our panicked insistence on overinflating the bounds of masculinity, femininity, matrimony and parentage. Porter's stories take an aim as accurate and deadly as Nathaniel Hawthorne's, and her prose is leaner, for dissecting deeper. The results are dazzling." Porter believed strongly that creative individuals had a responsibility to squarely face the turmoil of modern life. "[N]othing is pointless, and nothing is meaningless if the artist will face it," she wrote. "And it's his business to face it. He hasn't got the right to sidestep it like that. Human life itself may be almost pure chaos, but the work of the artist—the only thing he's good for—is to take these handfuls of confusion and disparate things, things that seem to be irreconcilable, and put them together in a frame to give them some kind of shape and meaning."

BIOGRAPHICAL AND CRITICAL SOURCES:

BOOKS

Aldridge, John W., *Time to Murder and Create,* McKay (New York, NY), 1966.

Authors in the News, Volume 2, Thomson Gale (Detroit, MI), 1976.

Chandra, Lakshmi, *Katherine Anne Porter: Fiction as History,* Arnold (New Delhi, India), 1992.

Contemporary Literary Criticism, Thomson Gale (Detroit, MI), Volume 1, 1973, Volume 3, 1975, Volume 7, 1977, Volume 10, 1979, Volume 13, 1980, Volume 15, 1980, Volume 27, 1984, Volume 101, 1997.

Dictionary of Literary Biography, Thomson Gale (Detroit, MI), Volume 4: *American Writers in Paris, 1920-1939,* 1980, Volume 9: *American Novelists, 1910-1945,* 1981, Volume 102: *American Short-Story Writers, 1910-1945,* Second Series, 1991.

Dictionary of Literary Biography Yearbook: 1980, Thomson Gale (Detroit, MI), 1981.

Givner, Joan, *Katherine Anne Porter: A Life,* University of Georgia Press (Athens, GA), 1991.

Hardy, J. E., *Katherine Anne Porter,* Ungar (New York, NY), 1973.

Hartley, L. C., and G. Core, editors, *Katherine Anne Porter,* University of Georgia Press (Athens, GA), 1969.

Hendrick, George, and Willene Hendrick, *Katherine Anne Porter,* revised edition, Twayne (Boston, MA), 1988.

Hilt, Kathryn, and Ruth M. Alvarez, *Katherine Anne Porter: An Annotated Bibliography,* Garland (New York, NY), 1990.

Machann, Clinton, and William Bedford Clark, editors, *Katherine Anne Porter and Texas: An Uneasy Relationship,* Texas A & M University Press, 1990.

Mooney, Harry John, editor, *The Fiction and Criticism of Katherine Anne Porter,* University of Pittsburgh Press (Pittsburgh, PA), 1962.

Nance, William L., *Katherine Anne Porter and the Art of Rejection,* University of North Carolina Press (Durham, NC), 1964.

Stout, Janis P., *Katherine Anne Porter: A Sense of the Times,* University Press of Virginia (Charlottesville, VA), 1995.

Stout, Janis P., *Strategies of Reticence: Silence and Meaning in the Works of Jane Austen, Willa Cather, Katherine Anne Porter, and Joan Didion,* University Press of Virginia (Charlottesville, VA), 1990.

Tanner, James T. F., *The Texas Legacy of Katherine Anne Porter,* University of North Texas Press (Denton, TX), 1991.

Unrue, Darlene Harbour, *Understanding Katherine Anne Porter,* University of South Carolina Press (Columbia, SC), 1988.

Unrue, Darlene Harbour, editor, *"This Strange, Old World" and Other Book Reviews,* University of Georgia Press (Athens, GA), 1991.

Walsh, Thomas F., *Katherine Anne Porter and Mexico: The Illusion of Eden,* University of Texas Press (Austin, TX), 1992.

West, Ray B., Jr., *Katherine Anne Porter* (pamphlet), University of Minnesota Press (Minneapolis, MN), 1963.

Wilson, Edmund, *Classics and Commercials,* Farrar, Straus (New York, NY), 1950.

PERIODICALS

American Literature, September, 1992, pp. 616-617.

Belles Lettres, spring, 1990.

Harper's, September, 1965.

Mississippi Quarterly, winter, 1992, George Cheatham, "'This Strange Old World,' and Other Book Reviews," p. 121.

Modern Fiction Studies, winter, 1988, pp. 642-643.

New Republic, April 19, 1939; December 4, 1965.

New York Times, March 16, 1966.

New York Times Book Review, April 1, 1962; May 27, 1990, pp. 1, 23-24; April 16, 1995, p. 17.

Paris Review, number 29, 1963-64.

Partisan Review, spring, 1966.

Saturday Review, December, 1980, pp. 10-11.

Sewanee Review, spring, 1974.

Studies in Shorter Fiction, fall, 1991, p. 574.

Tribune Books (Chicago, IL), April 29, 1990, pp. 3, 5.

Twentieth Century Literature, April, 1967.

Virginia Quarterly Review, autumn, 1960, pp. 598-613.

Washington Post, May 15, 1970; May 18, 1981.

Washington Star, May 11, 1975.

Western American Literature, November, 1992, pp. 239-240; May, 1995, p. 133.

OBITUARIES:

PERIODICALS

Chicago Tribune, September 20, 1980.

Newsweek, September 29, 1980.

New York Times, September 19, 1980.

Times (London, England), September 20, 1980.

Washington Post, September 19, 1980; September 20, 1980.

* * *

POTOK, Chaim 1929-2002

PERSONAL: Born Herman Harold Potok, February 17, 1929, in New York, NY; died of brain cancer, July 23, 2002, in Merion, PA; changed given name to Chaim, pronounced "*Hah*-yim"; son of Benjamin Max (in business) and Mollie (Friedman) Potok; married Adena Sarah Mosevitzky, June 8, 1958; children: Rena, Naama, Akiva. *Education:* Yeshiva University, B.A. (summa cum laude), 1950; Jewish Theological Seminary, M.H. L., 1954; University of Pennsylvania, Ph.D., 1965. *Hobbies and other interests:* Oil painting, photography.

CAREER: Writer. Ordained rabbi (Conservative). Jewish Theological Seminary, New York, NY, national director, Leaders Training Fellowship, 1954-55; Camp Ramah, Ojai, CA, director, 1957-59; University of Judaism, Los Angeles, CA, instructor, 1957-59; Har Zion Temple, Philadelphia, PA, scholar-in-residence, 1959-63; Jewish Theological Seminary, member of faculty of Teachers' Institute, 1963-64; *Conservative Judaism,* New York, NY, managing editor, 1964-65; Jewish Publication Society, Philadelphia, PA, editor-in-chief, 1965-74, special projects editor, beginning 1974. Visiting professor, University of Pennsylvania, 1983, 1992-98, Bryn Mawr College, 1985, and Johns Hopkins University, 1995-98. *Military service:* Served as U.S. chaplain in Korea, 1956-57.

MEMBER: Authors Guild, Dramatists Guild, Authors League of America, Rabbinical Assembly, PEN, Artists Equity.

AWARDS, HONORS: Edward Lewis Wallant Award, and National Book Award nomination, both for *The Chosen;* Athenaeum Award for *The Promise;* Jewish National Book Award, 1997, for *The Gift of Asher Lev;* National Foundation for Jewish Culture Achievement Award; O. Henry Award, 1999, for "Moon."

WRITINGS:

NOVELS

The Chosen (also see below), Simon & Schuster (New York, NY), 1967, with introduction by Daniel Walden, Ballantine (New York, NY), 2003.

The Promise (sequel to *The Chosen*), Knopf (New York, NY), 1969.

My Name Is Asher Lev, Knopf (New York, NY), 1972.

In the Beginning, Knopf (New York, NY), 1975.

The Book of Lights, Knopf (New York, NY), 1981.

Davita's Harp, Knopf (New York, NY), 1985.

The Gift of Asher Lev (sequel to *My Name Is Asher Lev*), Knopf (New York, NY), 1990.

I Am the Clay, Knopf (New York, NY), 1992.

CHILDREN'S LITERATURE

The Tree of Here, Knopf (New York, NY), 1993.
The Sky of Now, Knopf (New York, NY), 1995.
Zebra and Other Stories, Knopf (New York, NY), 1998.

OTHER

Jewish Ethics (pamphlet series), 14 volumes, Leaders Training Fellowship (New York, NY), 1964–1969.
The Jew Confronts Himself in American Literature, Sacred Heart School of Theology (Hales Corners, WI), 1975.
Wanderings: Chaim Potok's History of the Jews (nonfiction), Knopf (New York, NY), 1978.
Ethical Living for a Modern World, Jewish Theological Seminary of America (New York, NY), 1985.
Theo Tobiasse: Artist in Exile (nonfiction), Rizzoli International (New York, NY), 1986.
The Gates of November: Chronicles of the Slepak Family (nonfiction), Knopf (New York, NY), 1996.
(With Isaac Stern) *My First Seventy-nine Years,* Knopf (New York, NY), 1999.
(Adaptor, with Aaron Posner) *The Chosen* (play; based on Potok's novel), Dramatists Play Service (New York, NY), 2001.
Old Men at Midnight (novellas), Knopf (New York, NY), 2001.

Author of short story "Moon." Also contributor of short stories and articles to *TriQuarterly, Commentary, Reconstructionist, Moment, Esquire, American Judaism, Forward, Saturday Review, New York Times Book Review, Kenyon Review, American Voice, New England Review,* and other periodicals. Selected readings were recorded and released on cassette by National Public Radio, 1995.

ADAPTATIONS: The Chosen, a Landau Productions movie based on Potok's novel of the same name, was distributed by Twentieth Century-Fox, written by Edwin Gordon, and starred Robbie Benson, Maximilian Schell, Rod Steiger, and Barry Miller, 1982; *The Chosen* was also adapted as a musical for the stage and produced in New York, NY, 1987, and as an audiobook, Recorded Books, 2003.

SIDELIGHTS: Chaim Potok is familiar to many readers as the author of best-selling novels like *The Chosen* and *The Promise.* Less well known, though equally important to Potok, was his devotion to Judaism: he was an ordained rabbi and a respected scholar of Judaic texts. Potok's personal attempts to reconcile these disparate commitments enrich his fiction, as many of his works explore the ways in which men and women learn to deal with cultural conflict. As Potok once explained in *Philadelphia Inquirer:* "While this tension is exhausting, . . . it is fuel for me. Without it, I would have nothing to say."

Because of his Jewish heritage, Potok was frequently called an American Jewish writer, although he preferred the label of "American writer writing about a small and particular American world," as he once stated in an essay for *Studies in American Jewish Literature.* His vision, and his novels, attracted readers of many different religious faiths during his lifetime, and his works continued to provide readers with insight and inspiration after his death. According to *New York Times Book Review* contributor Hugh Nissenson, this attraction exists, in part, because of Potok's "talent for evoking the physical details of this world: the tree-lined streets, the apartment filled with books, the cold radiators, the steaming glasses of coffee." Potok, however, attributed the success of his novels to the universality of his subject matter. Quoting James Joyce, he once explained to Millie Ball in *Times-Picayune:* "'In the particular is contained the universal.' When you write about one person or set of people, if you dig deeply enough, you will ultimately uncover basic humanity."

Potok's own life shows a similarity to that of some of his characters. Raised in an Orthodox Jewish family, he was drawn to the less-restrictive doctrine of Conservative Judaism as a young adult and was eventually ordained a Conservative rabbi. Potok's interest in writing and literature, sparked by Evelyn Waugh's *Brideshead Revisited* and James Joyce's *A Portrait of the Artist as a Young Man,* was opposed by both his family and teachers. His mother, for example, when told of her son's aspiration to write, remarked, "'You want to be a writer? Fine. You be a brain surgeon, on the side [you'll write stories],'" as Potok recalled in *Fort Lauderdale News.* His teachers at Jewish parochial school responded similarly, disappointed that the young man would want to take time away from studying the Talmud to read and write fiction. Potok once discussed these reactions in an interview with S. Lillian Kremer in *Studies in American Jewish Literature:* "There was anger. There was rage. I still experience it. . . . [The] Jewish tradition . . . casts a very definite denigrating eye upon the whole enterprise of fiction. . . . Scholarship is what counts in the Jewish tradition, Talmudic scholarship, not the product of the imagination."

This conflict between religious and secular commitments became a recurring theme in Potok's novels. In his first book, *The Chosen,* Potok portrays Danny Saunders, a young man torn between fulfilling the expectations of his rabbi father and satisfying his own need for secular knowledge. The Saunders family belongs to the Jewish sect called Hasidim, whose members are "known for their mystical interpretation of Judaic sources and intense devotion to their spiritual leaders," according to Kremer, writing in *Dictionary of Literary Biography.* When Danny becomes an adult, he is expected to take on his father's role as *tzaddik,* which Nissenson described as "a teacher, spiritual adviser, mediator between his community of followers and God, and living sacrifice who takes the suffering of his people—of all Israel—upon himself." To strengthen Danny's soul and thus prepare him "to assume the burdens of his followers," wrote Kremer, Rabbi Saunders has raised his son according to the unusual Hasidic tradition which dictates that under certain circumstances a father and son should speak only when discussing religious texts.

In direct contrast to the Saunders are the Malters: Reuven, who becomes Danny's close friend, and Reuven's father, who tutors Danny in secular subjects. As Orthodox Jews, the Malters "emphasize a rational, intellectual approach to Judaic law and theology," explained Kremer. Reuven's father recognizes the importance of Judaic scholarship, but he, unlike Rabbi Saunders, encourages his son to study secular subjects as well. Furthermore, Malter has built his relationship with Reuven on mutual love and respect, not suffering. Though Danny's problems with his father are crucial to the narrative, *The Chosen* is more than a story of parental and religious conflict but also about the form in which Judaism will survive, either couched in supersition or in a new form of secularism.

The Chosen received mixed criticism from reviewers. *New York Times* contributor Eliot Fremont-Smith described the book as "a long, earnest, somewhat affecting and sporadically fascinating tale of religious conflict and generational confrontation in which the characters never come fully alive because they are kept subservient to theme: They don't have ideas so much as they represent ideas." While *New Republic* contributor Philip Toynbee observed that Potok's prose has "too many exhausted phrases and dead words," the critic maintained that *The Chosen* "is a fascinating book in its own right. Few Jewish writers have emerged from so deep in the heart of orthodoxy: fewer still have been able to write about their emergence with such an unforced sympathy for both sides and every participant." Concluded Nissenson: "The structural pattern of the novel, the beautifully wrought contrapuntal relationship of the boys, and their fathers, is complete. We rejoice, and we weep a little, at those haunting Hasidic melodies which transfigure their words."

Potok's novel *My Name Is Asher Lev* is a variation "on an almost classic theme: the isolation of the artist from society," according to Thomas Lask in *New York Times.* Despite its conventional theme, the novel has what Lask called "a feeling of freshness, of something brand-new" that he attributed not to "the artist and his driving needs but [to] the society from which he is inexorably isolating himself: the intense, ingrown, passionate, mystical world of Hasidism." The protagonist, Asher Lev, lives in a familial and spiritual environment in which his parents are devout Hasidim and his father is actively involved in rebuilding the postwar Jewish community in Europe. Lev, however, is a gifted artist, and his father neither understands nor respects his son's artistry. While art is not expressly forbidden in the Hasidic tradition, it is considered "blasphemous at worst and mere indulgence of personal vanity at best," according to Kremer in *Dictionary of Literary Biography.* The tenuous relationship between Lev and his father is strained further when Lev, as a part of his studies, learns to draw crucifixions and nudes.

Although Lev does not consciously reject his heritage, he finds it impossible to repress his artistic instinct. Lask observes that while both Lev and the Hasidic community do their "best to retain the old relationship, . . . there seems to be an artistic destiny greater than both of them." Lev's reluctance to abandon his religious tradition is a significant difference between Potok's characters and those of other American Jewish writers, according to Kremer. "They do not share the assimilationist goals of the Jews about whom Saul Bellow and Philip Roth write. . . . In the instances when Potok's characters enter the secular public world, they maintain orthodox private lives." Even after he has left his family and community, Lev identifies himself as an observant Jew. Thus, as John H. Timmerman observed in *Christian Century,* Lev "stands *not* in open rebellion against, but as a troubled seeker of, his place within a tradition."

In 1990 Potok published *The Gift of Asher Lev,* a sequel to *My Name Is Asher Lev.* The novel begins twenty years after the events in the first book: Lev has become a highly acclaimed artist living in southern France, has married, and has a son and a daughter. When he receives news that his uncle Yitzchok has died, Lev returns to Brooklyn for the funeral. Almost as soon as he arrives, he wishes to return to France, but his wife and children become attached to Lev's family and prefer the familial atmosphere of the Hasidic community to the relative isolation they experienced in France. Lev's father and the Rebbe, the spiritual leader of the Hasidim, want his family to stay as well, and it is not long before Lev discovers that their motive is to groom his son for leadership of the Rebbe's international movement. The novel concludes—in a manner reminiscent of the biblical story of Abraham and Isaac—with Lev "sacrificing" his son to God. He leaves his son and family in Brooklyn and returns to France to resume his artistic career, which, he discovers, has been revitalized by the whole experience.

Critical reaction to *The Gift of Asher Lev* was mixed. Chicago *Tribune Books* contributor Andy Solomon believed that "there is much about the book to admire," such as Potok's ability to add detail to his settings and portray the spirit of the Hasidic community. However, the critic also noted flaws in the narrative and complained that Lev is not the compelling character he was in the first book. "As Asher sleepwalks through these pages," wrote Solomon, "so too does the plot wander, despite some resolutions that form toward the end. The world of the Hasidim is intriguing, and Potok has knowledgeable insights to share about art. But Asher Lev casts far less spell in this revisit than he did two decades ago." Nikki Stiller observed in *New York Times Book Review* that Lev becomes a somewhat muted character in the sequel because he "never considers abandoning orthodoxy." Stiller added that Potok "does not wrestle with the angel of autonomy." Brian Morton, however, asserted in *Times Literary Supplement* that when paired with the previous Asher Lev novel, *The Gift of Asher Lev* "covers much the same ground with considerable subtlety." Of Potok's writings, Morton also concluded that the author demonstrates "a marked awareness of the internal tensions of modern Judaism, which are prior to its conflicts and accommodations with the Gentile world. His Judaism has content, not just form; beliefs, not just abstract 'pieties'; an exact mentality that participates in a wider society at the same time as it belongs to a distinct enclave."

Potok's novels *In the Beginning, The Book of Lights, Davita's Harp* continue to elaborate upon the theme of conflict between the religious and secular worlds. In *Davita's Harp,* however, the author tells this story from a female perspective. "That leap takes sensitivity and some daring, and Potok handles it well," stated *Detroit News* contributor Lisa Schwarzbaum, adding that *Davita's Harp* is "a warm, decent, generous and patient exploration of important issues facing Jewish women today." When the novel opens, Davita is eight years old. She is the daughter of a Jewish mother and a Christian father who have abandoned their respective religions and are now devoted communists. Davita experiments with both faiths, but she is entranced by the Jewish rituals practiced by her neighbors and eventually embraces Orthodox Judaism. She soon realizes the limitations of her religion, however, when she is denied a prize as the best student in her parochial school graduating class solely because she is a girl.

A *Time* critic observed that "during the conflict between Davita's reverence for Hebraic tradition and her determination to make a place for herself, the narrative becomes far livelier and suggests possibilities for a worthier sequel." Paul Cowan commented in *New York Times Book Review* that the first quarter of *Davita's Harp,* which concerns the political activities of Davita's parents, contains "some of Mr. Potok's most disappointing pages," but that "as Davita comes to life, so does the book." *Chicago Tribune Book World* contributor George Cohen maintained that the work provides "an engrossing plot—Potok is a master storyteller—but much of the pleasure in reading *Davita's Harp* is the beauty of the language." One of the harsher critical remarks about *Davita's Harp* was voiced by Andrew Weinberger, who commented in *Los Angeles Times Book Review:* "The problem with this novel is that it is too predictable, too familiar. . . . Potok could do better, one feels, than to walk down this old road again."

Set in Korea during the 1950s, *I Am the Clay* portrays the difficult journey of two aged peasants and a young orphaned boy from Seoul to a refugee camp. "Potok focuses in on the struggle for survival as the farmer, his wife and the boy battle hunger, sickness, cold, exhaustion and the land itself," observed Irving Abrahamson in the Chicago *Tribune Books.* The book was deemed "a modern myth" by Barbara Gold Zingman in *New York Times Book Review,* the critic going on to note that *I Am the Clay* explores themes of human connection amid suffering and the confusion and hope associated with mystical and religious belief.

Potok has also written works for children and young adults. In *The Tree of Here* he introduces a young boy named Jason who is troubled by his family's frequent relocations. The "tree" of the title is a dogwood tree that serves as a symbol of rootedness and the sense of being home. *The Sky of Now* depicts a glider flight experienced by ten-year-old Brian, who suffers from a fear of heights. *Zebra and Other Stories* is a collection of coming-of-age tales suitable for both teens and adults. The characters in *Zebra* face the challenges of parental divorce and bullying, blended families and social consciousness as they discover their places in an adult world. *Horn Book* contributor Nancy Vasilakis felt that the stories contain "layers of meaning, and teens will discover that one reading won't be enough." In *Booklist,* Stephanie Zvirin declared *Zebra* to be a "wonderful introduction" to Potok's work, adding that although the stories are written for younger readers, the author "respects his audience enough to allow them to draw from it what they will." A *Kirkus Reviews* critic commented, "Readers sensitive to nuances of language and situation will be totally absorbed by these profound character studies."

Potok's final work of fiction, *Old Men at Midnight,* is a series of three linked novellas that examine war and all it horrors. Ilana David Dinn is the character who appears throughout all three stories as she learns the tales of three different men and their various experiences in the Holocaust, under Communist despot Josef Stalin, and in World War II. A *Publishers Weekly* reviewer found that the character of Illana was reduced "to little more than a cipher." The reviewer added, "But 'The War Doctor,' the grimmest and most nuanced of the stories, alone is worth the price of admission." Chris Barsanti, writing in *Book,* noted, "The stories themselves are masterfully written. This delicately realized book about history and memory is shot through with flashes of humanity." *Booklist* contributor Kristine Huntley called *Old Men at Midnight* "moving and powerful."

In addition to fiction, Potok also wrote the nonfiction book *Wanderings: Chaim Potok's Story of the Jews.* Although factual, *Wanderings* is similar to Potok's novels, Jack Riemer suggested in *America.* "Just as [in *The Chosen* Potok] . . . sought for his self in the guise of a story about a young man wrestling with modernity, so here he searches for his soul in the form of a confrontation with his roots and with his memories." Potok once explained to Robert Dahlin in *Publishers Weekly:* "I went wandering inside my own tradition, its history. . . . And I didn't move on until I understood."

Wanderings, a lavishly illustrated book, was described by *Chicago Tribune Book World* contributor Dan Rottenberg as "a rare phenomenon: a coffee-table book with some real intellectual bite to it." Beginning with the family of Abraham, *Wanderings* traces 4,000 years of Jewish history. Potok portrays the Jews as a people who have cohabited with—and been persecuted by—many different civilizations throughout history, and who, despite their small population, have usually managed to survive their persecutors. According to Rottenberg, "what emerges from Potok's mixture of history, Scriptures, novelistic writing, and personal reminiscences is a portrait of Judaism as very much a living, breathing, kicking organism."

Several reviewers maintain that Potok's training as a novelist served him well in his first foray into nonfiction. Rottenberg, for example, wrote, "The eye of the novelist can enhance our understanding of history, especially when the novelist is someone like Potok, whose fictitious work has always been firmly rooted in cultural and historical scholarship. . . . Potok is able to paint scenes for us, to put flesh on his characters, to speculate about their motives, without abandoning the detachment of the historian." *New York Times Book Review* contributor Alan Mintz described *Wanderings* as "a mixed performance. Mr. Potok can produce a good, strong narrative that also maintains a sense of historical proportion; and his occasional evocations of settings and feelings do contribute to a fuller sense of the past. But often the pursuit of drama gets him into trouble and the writing becomes stylized." Michael J. Bandler, however, suggested in *Christian Science Monitor* that "one cannot resist the temptation to observe without being facetious that as a historian, Potok solidifies his reputation as a fine novelist."

Potok also helped violinist Isaac Stern craft an autobiography titled *My First Seventy-nine Years.* The work details Stern's musical career as well as his role in saving Carnegie Hall from destruction and his devotion to the nation of Israel. Although the book is told from a first-person point of view and is purportedly Stern's voice, "Potok makes it flow beautifully, in a voice that is vital and exciting," according to Ray Olson in *Booklist.* Carol J. Binkowski, writing in *Library Journal,* deemed the book "a sensitive and engrossing history of a man and an era."

In a piece for the Web site *Jvibe,* Elizabeth Silver observed that Potok "remains a revered scholar in not only the Jewish and literary communities, but throughout the world. His philosophy of cultures transcends into all realms of humanity. Chaim Potok has spent the majority of his life silently mapping the territory of his Jewish past through his novels that have captivated people into his fictional worlds because of their universal truths." Silver concluded: "Potok has the ability to write novels that touch so many distinct people and also dive into the core of problems in today's society with such honesty and realism."

In an obituary for Potok, who died in 2002, *Newsweek* contributor Alex Rubin summed up the writer's work this way: "His fictional characters remained bound within the insular world of Hasidic Judaism, but his powerfully human prose transcended religious denomination." Robert Gottlieb, who was Potok's editor for more than three decades, told Carlin Romano in an obituary in *Philadelphia Inquirer,* "Whether we're talking about 10 years from now or 30 years from now, *The Chosen* will be in print, and thousands and thousands of people will discover it and be moved and educated by it."

BIOGRAPHICAL AND CRITICAL SOURCES:

BOOKS

Authors in the News, Thomson Gale (Detroit, MI), Volume 1, 1976, Volume 2, 1976.

Contemporary Literary Criticism, Thomson Gale (Detroit, MI), Volume 2, 1974, Volume 7, 1977, Volume 14, 1980, Volume 26, 1983.

Dictionary of Literary Biography, Thomson Gale (Detroit, MI), Volume 28: *Twentieth-Century American-Jewish Fiction Writers,* 1984, Volume 152: *American Novelists since World War II, Fourth Series,* 1995.

Dictionary of Literary Biography Yearbook: 1984, Thomson Gale (Detroit, MI), 1985.

Walden, Daniel, editor, *Conversations with Chaim Potok,* University Press of Mississippi (Jackson, MS), 2001.

PERIODICALS

America, February 7, 1979, Jack Riemer.

Book, November-December, 2001, Chris Barsanti, review of *Old Men at Midnight,* p. 65.

Booklist, January 1 and 15, 1996, Julie Corsaro, review of *The Sky of Now,* p. 848; July, 1998, Stephanie Zvirin, review of *Zebra and Other Stories,* p. 1878; September 15, 1999, Ray Olson, review of *My First Seventy-nine Years,* p. 96; September 15, 2003, Kristine Huntley, review of *Old Men at Midnight,* p. 195.

Book Week, April 23, 1967.

Chicago Tribune, December 1, 1987.

Chicago Tribune Book World, November 26, 1978, Dan Rottenberg, review of *Wanderings: Chaim Potok's History of the Jews;* October 11, 1981; March 24, 1985, George Cohen.

Christian Century, February 17, 1982; May 16, 1984.

Christian Science Monitor, February 12, 1979, Michael J. Bandler.

CLA Journal, June, 1971.

Commentary, October, 1972; April, 1979; March, 1982.

Detroit News, March 17, 1985, Lisa Schwarzbaum, review of *Davita's Harp.*

Fort Lauderdale News, March 22, 1976.

Horn Book, November, 1998, Nancy Vasilakis, review of *Zebra and Other Stories,* p. 739.

Kirkus Reviews, April 1, 1992, p. 423; July 1, 1998, review of *Zebra and Other Stories.*

Library Journal, November 1, 1999, Carol J. Binkowski, review of *My First Seventy-nine Years,* p. 86.

Los Angeles Times Book Review, November 8, 1981; May 26, 1985, Andrew Weinberger.

New Republic, June 7, 1967, Philip Toynbee, review of *The Chosen.*

New Yorker, November 17, 1975; November 9, 1981.

New York Times, April 24, 1967; September 12, 1969; April 21, 1972; December 3, 1975; November 2, 1986; July 24, 1987; January 3, 1988; January 7, 1988.

New York Times Book Review, May 7, 1967; September 14, 1969; April 16, 1972; October 19, 1975; December 17, 1978, Alan Mintz; October 11, 1981; March 31, 1985, Paul Cowan, review of *Davita's Harp,* p. 12; May 13, 1990, Nikki Stiller, review of *The Gift of Asher Levi,* p. 29; June 28, 1992, Barbara Gold Zingman, review of *I Am the Clay,* p. 18; December 26, 1999, David Mermelstein, review of *My First Seventy-nine Years,* p. 14.

Philadelphia Bulletin, May 16, 1974.

Philadelphia Inquirer, April 27, 1976.

Publishers Weekly, May 22, 1978; December 12, 1986, p. 46; August 30, 1993, p. 96; November 27, 1995, p. 69; November 5, 2001, review of *Old Men at Midnight,* p. 43.

Saturday Review, September 20, 1969; April 15, 1972.

School Library Journal, October, 1993, p. 108; January, 1996, Susan Scheps, review of *The Sky of Now,* p. 93.

Studies in American Jewish Literature, number 4, 1985.

Time, November 3, 1975; October 19, 1981; March 25, 1985.

Times (London, England), December 20, 1990.

Times Literary Supplement, March 5, 1970; October 6, 1972; April 9, 1976; May 28, 1982; November 2, 1990, Brian Morton.

Times-Picayune (New Orleans, LA), February 25, 1973.

Tribune Books (Chicago, IL), May 6, 1990, Andy Solomon; May 17, 1992, Irving Abrahamson, review of *I Am the Clay,* p. 6.

Village Voice Literary Supplement, February, 1995.

Washington Post, November 27, 1981.
Washington Post Book World, December 13, 1978.

ONLINE

Chaim Potok Home Page, http://www.lasierra.edu/˜ballen/potok/ (April 13, 2004).
Jvibe, http://www.jvibe.com/popculture/ (December, 1999), Elizabeth Silver, interview with Potok.

OBITUARIES:

PERIODICALS

Baltimore Sun, July 24, 2002.
Guardian (Manchester, England), July 31, 2002, p. 18.
Los Angeles Times July 24, 2002 p. B11.
Newsweek, August 5, 2002, Alex Rubin, p. 6.
New York Times, July 24, 2002, p. A17.
Philadelphia Daily News, July 24, 2002, p 31.
Times (London, England), July 26, 2002 p. 31.
Washington Post, July 24, 2002, p. B05.

ONLINE

New York Times Online, http://www.nytimes.com/ (July 24, 2002).
Philadelphia Enquirer Online, http://www.philly.com/ (July 24, 2002).
Salon.com, http://www.salon.com/ (July 23, 2002).

* * *

POWELL, Anthony 1905-2000
(Mark Members, Anthony Dymoke Powell)

PERSONAL: Surname rhymes with "Noel"; born December 21, 1905, in London, England; died March 28, 2000, in Somerset, England; son of Philip Lionel William (an army officer) and Maude Mary (Wells-Dymoke) Powell; married Lady Violet Pakenham (daughter of fifth Earl of Longford), December 1, 1934; children: Tristram, John. *Education:* Balliol College, Oxford, B.A., 1926, M.A., 1944.

CAREER: Writer, 1930—. Affiliated with Duckworth Co., Ltd. (publishing house), London, England, 1926-35; Warner Brothers of Great Britain, scriptwriter, 1936. Trustee of National Portrait Gallery, London, England, 1962-76. *Military service:* Welch Regiment, Infantry, 1939-41, Intelligence Corps, 1941-45; served as liaison officer at War Office; became major; received Order of the White Lion (Czechoslovakia), Order of Leopold II (Belgium), Oaken Crown and Croix de Guerre (both Luxembourg).

AWARDS, HONORS: Named Commander of Order of the British Empire, 1956; James Tait Black Memorial Prize, 1958, for *At Lady Molly's;* W.H. Smith Fiction Award, 1974, for *Temporary Kings;* Bennett Award, *Hudson Review,* and T.S. Eliot Award, Ingersoll Foundation, both 1984, both for body of work; named Companion of Honor, 1988. D.Litt., University of Sussex, 1971, University of Leicester and University of Kent, 1976, Oxford University, 1980, and Bristol University, 1982.

WRITINGS:

NOVELS

Afternoon Men, Duckworth (London, England), 1931, Holt (New York, NY), 1932.
Venusberg (also see below), Duckworth (London, England), 1932, Popular Library (New York, NY), 1978.
From a View to a Death, Duckworth (London, England), 1933, published as *Mr. Zouch, Superman: From a View to a Death,* Vanguard (New York, NY), 1934.
Agents and Patients (also see below), Duckworth (London, England), 1936, Popular Library (New York, NY), 1978.
What's Become of Waring?, Cassell (London, England), 1939, Little, Brown (Boston, MA), 1963.
Two Novels: Venusberg [and] *Agents and Patients,* Periscope-Holliday (New York, NY), 1952.
(Under pseudonym Mark Members) *Iron Aspidistra,* Sycamore Press, 1985.
The Fisher King, Norton (New York, NY), 1986.

"A DANCE TO THE MUSIC OF TIME" SERIES; NOVELS

A Question of Upbringing, Scribner (New York, NY), 1951.
A Buyer's Market, Heinemann (London, England), 1952, Scribner (New York, NY), 1953.
The Acceptance World, Heinemann (London, England), 1955, Farrar, Straus (New York, NY), 1956.

At Lady Molly's, Heinemann (London, England), 1957, Little, Brown (Boston, MA), 1958.

Casanova's Chinese Restaurant, Little, Brown (Boston, MA), 1960.

The Kindly Ones, Little, Brown (Boston, MA), 1962.

The Valley of Bones, Little, Brown (Boston, MA), 1964.

The Soldier's Art, Little, Brown (Boston, MA), 1966.

The Military Philosophers, Heinemann (London, England), 1968, Little, Brown (Boston, MA), 1969.

Books Do Furnish a Room, Little, Brown (Boston, MA), 1971.

Temporary Kings, Little, Brown (Boston, MA), 1973.

Hearing Secret Harmonies, Heinemann (London, England), 1975, Little, Brown (Boston, MA), 1976.

"A DANCE TO THE MUSIC OF TIME" OMNIBUS VOLUMES

A Dance to the Music of Time: First Movement (contains *A Question of Upbringing, A Buyer's Market,* and *The Acceptance World*), Little, Brown (Boston, MA), 1963.

A Dance to the Music of Time: Second Movement (contains *At Lady Molly's, Casanova's Chinese Restaurant,* and *The Kindly Ones*), Little, Brown (Boston, MA), 1964.

A Dance to the Music of Time: Third Movement (contains *The Valley of Bones, The Soldier's Art,* and *The Military Philosophers*), Little, Brown (Boston, MA), 1971.

A Dance to the Music of Time: Fourth Movement (contains *Books Do Furnish a Room, Temporary Kings,* and *Hearing Secret Harmonies*), Little, Brown (Boston, MA), 1976.

The Album of Anthony Powell's Dance to the Music of Time, edited by Violet Powell, Thames and Hudson (London, England), 1987.

A Dance to the Music of Time (complete collection), University of Chicago Press (Chicago, IL), 1995.

OTHER

(Editor) *Barnard Letters, 1778-1884,* Duckworth (London, England), 1928.

Caledonia: A Fragment (poems), privately printed, 1934.

(Editor and author of introduction) *Novels of High Society from the Victorian Age,* Pilot Press (London, England), 1947.

John Aubrey and His Friends, Scribner (New York, NY), 1948, revised edition, Barnes and Noble (New York, NY), 1963.

(Editor and author of introduction) John Aubrey, *Brief Lives and Other Selected Writings,* Scribner (New York, NY), 1949.

Two Plays: The Garden God [and] *The Rest I'll Whistle,* Heinemann (London, England), 1971, Little, Brown (Boston, MA), 1972.

To Keep the Ball Rolling: The Memoirs of Anthony Powell, Volume 1: *Infants of the Spring,* Heinemann (London, England), 1976, published as *Infants of the Spring: The Memoirs of Anthony Powell,* Holt (New York, NY), 1977, Volume 2: *Messengers of Day,* Holt (New York, NY), 1978, Volume 3: *Faces in My Time,* Heinemann (London, England), 1980, Holt (New York, NY), 1981, Volume 4: *The Strangers Are All Gone,* Heinemann (London, England), 1982, Holt (New York, NY), 1983, abridged edition of all four volumes published as *To Keep the Ball Rolling,* foreword by Ferdinand Mount, Penguin (Harmondsworth, Sussex, England), 1983, University of Chicago Press (Chicago, IL), 2001.

O, How the Wheel Becomes It! (novella), Holt (New York, NY), 1983.

Miscellaneous Verdicts: Writings on Writers, 1946-1989, Heinemann (London, England), 1990, University of Chicago Press (Chicago, IL), 1992.

Under Review: Further Writings on Writers, 1946-1990, University of Chicago Press (Chicago, IL), 1994.

Journals 1982-1986, Heinemann (London, England), 1995.

Journals 1987-1989, Heinemann (London, England), 1996.

Journals 1990-1992, Heinemann (London, England), 1997.

A Writer's Notebook, Heinemann (London, England), 2000.

Contributor to books, including *Burke's Landed Gentry,* Burke's Peerage Publications, 1965, and *Constant Lambert* by Richard Shead, Simon Publications, 1973. Author of introduction to *Raffles* by E.W. Hornung, Eyre & Spottiswoode, 1950, and *The Orchid Trilogy* by Jocelyn Brooke, Secker & Warburg, 1981. Author of preface to *The Complete Ronald Firbank,* Duckworth, 1961.

ADAPTATIONS: A Dance to the Music of Time was adapted for television by Hugh Whitemore and appeared on Britain's Channel 4, 1997. Several recordings of *A Dance to the Music of Time* have been produced, including a twenty-four audio cassette version read by Simon Callow, Hodder Headline Audiobooks, 1997, and a sixty-five audio cassette version read by David Case, Books on Tape. Simon Russell Beale also read for *Dance to the Music of Time: Question of Upbringing* and *Dance to the Music of Time: Buyer's Market,* both for Cover to Cover Cassettes.

SIDELIGHTS: Novelist Anthony Powell spent more than forty years chronicling the changing fortunes of Great Britain's upper class in the twentieth century. He is best known for his twelve-volume series *A Dance to the Music of Time,* the longest fictional work in the English language. Published in installments over almost twenty-five years, *A Dance to the Music of Time* follows a number of characters from adolescence in 1914 to old age and death in the late 1960s. *New Yorker* critic Naomi Bliven called the series "one of the most important works of fiction since the Second World War," and *New Republic* reviewer C. David Benson described the novels as "the most sophisticated chronicle of modern life we have." In the Toronto *Globe and Mail,* Douglas Hill observed that Powell "has had the good fortune to be in the right place at the right time and among the right people, and to be able to watch all this passing scene and transform the most apparently insignificant moments into the fabric of his fiction."

Newsweek correspondent Gene Lyons found Powell "entirely provincial, yet not at all a snob . . . an aristocratic man of letters in the best British tradition." Lyons continued, "He is a contemporary of that extraordinary group of English writers who were born during the first decade of this century." Indeed, Powell enjoyed close friendships with Evelyn Waugh, Cyril Connolly, and George Orwell, and he knew numerous other important writers, including Dylan Thomas and F. Scott Fitzgerald. Powell grew up in comfortable circumstances—he was descended from nobility—and was educated at Eton and Oxford. As Benson noted, however, the author's entire generation "was marked by having experienced the extinction of the privileged England of their childhoods which was replaced by a completely different post-war world." In his fiction Powell explores the extinction, or rather the metamorphosis, of the British upper class.

Powell graduated from Oxford in 1926 and took a job with Duckworth, a major publishing house in London. While he served as an editor at Duckworth, Powell began to write fiction of his own; eventually, Duckworth published four of his five early novels. *Dictionary of Literary Biography* contributor James Tucker described Powell's first few books as "entertaining, light, but not lightweight." Tucker also observed that in his early works Powell "appears to be interested in societies under threat, either from their own languor and foolishness or from huge political reverses or from calculated infiltration by arrivistes." Powell's first novel, *Afternoon Men,* has become his best-known prewar work. A satire of the upper-middle-class penchant for aimlessness, *Afternoon Men* begins and ends with party invitations. Tucker observed that, in the novel, Powell "expertly depicts the banality of the lives under scrutiny by having characters talk with a remorseless, plodding simplicity, as if half-baked, half-drunk, or half-asleep after too many nights on the town."

Even though Powell's first five novels sold only several thousand copies apiece, by the 1930s the author "had come to be recognized as one of several significant novelists who had emerged in Britain since World War I," Tucker related. Like most Englishmen his age, however, Powell's career was interrupted when World War II began. He enlisted in the Welsh Regiment and then served four years with the Intelligence Corps as liaison to the War Office. When the war ended, Powell still did not return to fiction for some time. Instead, he wrote a comprehensive biography of John Aubrey, a seventeenth-century writer and antiquary of Welsh descent. Only when *John Aubrey and His Friends* was completed did Powell return to fiction—but he did so in a grand way. Tucker reported, "Believing that many authors went on producing what were virtually the same characters in book after book, though with different names and in fresh circumstances, [Powell] wanted to break out from the confines of the 80,000-word novel. The roman-fleuve would allow him to recognize the problem openly and continue with established characters through successive volumes. During the late 1940s, while visiting the Wallace Collection in London, he saw Nicolas Poussin's painting *A Dance to the Music of Time* and felt he had at last found the theme and title of his work."

The Poussin painting depicts the four seasons as buxom young maidens, dancing under a threatening sky to music provided by a wizened, bearded man—Father Time. Powell's work, too, involves "dancers," a coterie of interrelated men and women living in modern Britain, whose lives intersect on the whims of fate. As Tucker noted, "scores of major characters dance their way in and out of one another's lives—and especially one another's beds—often in seemingly random style; yet when the whole sequence is seen together there is some sort of order. To put it more strongly than that would be wrong; but music and dance do imply a system, harmony, pattern."

In an essay for *South Atlantic Quarterly,* Kerry McSweeney remarked that *A Dance to the Music of Time* deals with "a densely populated swath of upper-class, upper-middle-class, artistic, and Bohemian life in England from the twenties to the seventies. The vehicle of presentation is the comedy of manners. Attention is consistently focused on the nuances of social behavior, the idiosyncracies of personal style, and the intricacies of sexual preference. All of the characters in the series . . . are seen strictly from the outside—that is, in terms of how they choose to present themselves to the world." In the early volumes, the characters leave school to establish careers which are often less important than the whirl of social obligations. The middle volumes concern the years of the Second World War, and the later volumes send many of the characters to their deaths. In *The Situation of the Novel,* Bernard Bergonzi called *A Dance to the Music of Time* "a great work of social comedy in a central English tradition" that "also conveys the cumulative sense of a shabby and dispirited society." A *Washington Post Book World* reviewer found the series "an addictive social fantasy, strictly controlled by the author's sense of the ambiguity of human relationships and an indispensable literary style." *Contemporary Novelists* contributor Robert K. Morris described it as "a panoramic sequence of extraordinary scope and complexity. A work that has never relinquished its surface brilliance at portraying the insular, private, self-contained, snobbish world of the British middle and upper classes, has more latterly become a vast canvas of English life between the wars and afterwards, and in the profoundest way no less than a comic epic on time, history, and change."

The action in *A Dance to the Music of Time* is revealed by Nicholas Jenkins, a nonparticipant observer who is happily married, urbane, and loyal to his values. From his vantage point in society, Jenkins describes the ascent of several power-hungry men—chief among them Kenneth Widmerpool—who become consumed by the perfection of their public images. "Widmerpool becomes the perfect foil for Nick Jenkins's emergent decency, dignity, and probity," Morris related. Bliven thought the series "subtly but ever more insistently contrasts the quest for power with the urge to create. The power seekers are killers and lovers of death, and the defenses against them are disinterestedness, playfulness, and, above all, artistic dedication." Tucker saw the tension between Jenkins and Widmerpool as "the difference between a man who is nothing but ambition, a sort of burlesque Faust, and another who represents enduring standards of humaneness, creativity, and artistic appreciation in a shoddy world." *Salon.com* writer John Perry commented, "So many disagreeable qualities converge in the person of Kenneth Widmerpool, lesser hands would have made him a buffoon. But Powell never dismisses him. . . . Powell clearly shows his virtues, his ambition and toughness—admired by his colleagues even when they hate him."

A Dance to the Music of Time does not provide a continuous narrative; rather, it presents a series of minutely observed vignettes, described with an understated prose. "What strikes one first about [the series]," Tucker wrote in *The Novels of Anthony Powell,* "is its elaborate texture and seemingly cast-iron poise, qualities suiting the narrator's wisdom, favoured status, knowledge and assurance. . . . The prose is largely appositional: to borrow the mode, plain statement followed by commentary or modification or conjecture, so that the reader feels himself presented with a very wide choice of possible responses; the uncertainties of real life are caught. . . . This modulated dignity, mandarin with the skids under it, gives Powell's style its distinction." In the *New York Review of Books,* Michael Wood commented that the most "persistent pleasure" to be gained from Powell's masterwork "is that of having your expectations skillfully and elegantly cheated: the musician plays a strange chord, or an old chord you haven't heard for a long time, even a wrong note now and then."

Lyons observed that *A Dance to the Music of Time* provides a remarkable steadfastness of vision—"the novel's closing pages, written 25 years after the opening, make so perfect a fit they might have been the product of a single morning's work." Similarly, Stephen J. Tapscott related in *Texas Quarterly* that "for all its diversity of character, sequence, and history, Powell's Dance is a remarkably integral work." Perry thought Powell's "rare sense of balance and dignity allow him to manipulate a cast of 500 through seven decades, creating a web of shifting relationships impossible in any 'factual' literary form—and a 20th century social history, more rigorous, multilayered and infinitely more entertaining than any academic publication."

Powell's series has found numerous champions in both Great Britain and the United States. Chicago *Tribune Books* reviewer Larry Kart called *A Dance to the Music of Time* the "century's finest English-language work of fiction." In *The Sense of Life in the Modern Novel,* Arthur Mizener wrote that the effect of the work "is a very remarkable one for the mid-twentieth century. It is as if we had come suddenly on an enormously intelligent but completely undogmatic mind with a vision of experience that is deeply penetrating and yet wholly recognizable, beautifully subtle in ordination and yet quite unostentatious in technique, and in every respect undistorted by doctrine." *Commonweal* contributor Arnold Beichman praised Powell's novels for their "great cosmic sadness about our lives," adding: "It is Powell's skill and power in depicting man's helplessness that makes [his] novels so unforgettable, so wonderfully sad." Speaking to the universality of *A Dance to the Music of Time, National Review* correspondent Anthony Lejeune concluded that Powell "makes us see not only his world, but ours, through his eyes. Not only his characters, but our own lives and the lives which are constantly weaving and unweaving themselves around us, become part of the pattern, part of the inexplicable dance."

After completing *A Dance to the Music of Time,* Powell remained active, producing a four-volume memoir, journals and other nonfiction works, a novella titled *O, How the Wheel Becomes It!,* and a novel, *The Fisher King. The Fisher King* involves passengers on an educational cruise around the British Isles, particularly the character Saul Henchman, a renowned photographer and emasculated veteran of World War II who loses the devotion of his beautiful companion, Barberina Rookwood, to another passenger. Powell incorporates significant mythical allusions—Henchman represents the impotent "Fisher King" of Arthurian legend, and the cruise ship is named "Alecto" after one of the Furies from Greek mythology. A departure from his "stylized" and "basically realistic" narrative of *A Dance to the Music of Time, The Fisher King* "gives us a fresh chance to savor Mr. Powell's irony and urbanity, and his dexterous turns of phrase," commented *New York Times* reviewer John Gross. According to John Bayley, writing in the *Los Angeles Times Book Review, "The Fisher King* is a rare work of art for a number of reasons, not least because of the skill and economy with which it makes an absorbing narrative out of the simplest daily materials—gossip, vanity, curiosity, the routine ways in which consciousness works on the situations that intrigue it." *New York Times Book Review* contributor John Espey observed that "Mr. Powell remains the master storyteller, ever quick to catch the conscience of the king, not to mention that of his reader."

Powell also produced several collections of criticism. *Miscellaneous Verdicts: Writings on Writers, 1946-1989* is an assemblage of Powell's literary reviews, divided into four sections that offer appraisal of classic English writers, Marcel Proust, Powell's contemporaries, and American writers. "Powell, like all his literary friends, reviewed constantly," related *Washington Post Book World* reviewer Daniel Max. "And although he does not make any claim to have particularly enjoyed it or having gotten much more on paper than the sort of comments that people find useful in deciding whether to buy a book or not, he has the innate respect for any professional, competent job done without complaint." Though some critics viewed Powell's analysis as uninspired and relatively conservative, Anthony Burgess remarked in an *Observer* review, "This is an urbane book, quietly erudite, very sensible, highly civilized, remarkably useful."

Under Review: Further Writings on Writers, 1946-1990 is another collection of Powell's literary journalism dealing with British, Irish, and Continental writers, passing over their American counterparts altogether. This collection, more biographical than critical, includes portraits of a wide range of authors in four sections titled "The Nineties," "Bloomsbury and Non-Bloomsbury," "Some Novels and Novelists," and "The Europeans"—the latter section featuring Victor Hugo, Leo Tolstoy, and Fyodor Dostoyevsky, among others. According to Chicago *Tribune Books* reviewer Merle Rubin, "Powell also happens to be a model book reviewer: an elegantly understated critic more inclined to err on the side of kindness than of severity. Straightforward, focused, seldom if ever using a review as an excuse to sound off on pet topics, demonstrate his superiority to the book's author or write up a storm of showy prose, he is not only erudite but also genuinely wise—the kind of passionate, informed and discriminating reader that other writers dream of."

In *The Novels of Anthony Powell,* James Tucker suggested that one feels "a plea throughout Powell's books for the natural warmth and vitality of life to be allowed their expression. . . . The distinction of Powell's novels is that they engagingly look at surfaces and, at the same time, suggest that this is by no means enough. They will continually disturb the surface to show us much more. In their quiet way they direct us towards a good, practical, unextreme general philosophy of life." *Voice Literary Supplement* contributor Ann Snitow observed that Powell can be recommended "for his long, honorable battle with language, his unavoidable anxieties, his preference for kindness over gaudier virtues. If he's brittle, it's because he knows things break; he's never complacent in either his playfulness or his hauteur." Snitow concluded, "Powell's a writer who values humility—antique word—a virtue now so necessary, and even more rare and obscure, perhaps, than Powell himself."

BIOGRAPHICAL AND CRITICAL SOURCES:

BOOKS

Allen, Walter, *The Modern Novel,* Dutton (New York, NY), 1965.

Bergonzi, Bernard, *The Situation of the Novel,* University of Pittsburgh Press (Pittsburgh, PA), 1970.

Bergonzi, Bernard, *Anthony Powell,* Longman (London, England), 1971.

Brennan, Neil Francis, *Anthony Powell,* Prentice Hall (New York, NY), 1995.

Contemporary Literary Criticism, Thomson Gale (Detroit, MI), Volume 1, 1973, Volume 3, 1975, Volume 7, 1977, Volume 9, 1978, Volume 10, 1979, Volume 31, 1985.

Contemporary Novelists, sixth edition, St. James Press (Detroit, MI), 1996, pp. 816-819.

Dictionary of Literary Biography, Volume 15: *British Novelists, 1930-1959,* Thomson Gale (Detroit, MI), 1983.

Encyclopedia of World Biography, second edition, Volume 12, Thomson Gale (Detroit, MI), 1998, pp. 422-423.

Encyclopedia of World Literature in the Twentieth Century, third edition, Volume 3, St. James Press (Detroit, MI), 1999, pp. 587-591.

Felber, Lynette, *Gender and Genre in Novels without End,* University Press of Florida (Gainesville, FL), 1996.

Gorra, Michael Edward, *The English Novel at Mid-Century: From the Leaning Tower,* St. Martin's Press (New York, NY), 1990.

Hall, James, *The Tragic Comedians,* Indiana University Press (Bloomington, IN), 1963.

Joyau, Isabelle, *Investigating Powell's "A Dance to the Music of Time,"* St. Martin's Press (New York, NY), 1994.

Karl, Frederick R., *A Reader's Guide to the Contemporary English Novel,* Farrar, Straus (New York, NY), 1962.

Lilley, George P., *Anthony Powell, A Bibliography,* Oak Knoll (New Castle, DE), 1993.

McEwan, Neil, *Anthony Powell,* St. Martin's Press (New York, NY), 1991.

Mizener, Arthur, *The Sense of Life in the Modern Novel,* Houghton (Boston, MA), 1964.

Modern British Literature, second edition, Volume 3, St. James Press (Detroit, MI), 2000, pp. 23-32.

Morris, Robert K., *The Novels of Anthony Powell,* University of Pittsburgh Press (Pittsburgh, PA), 1968.

Ries, Lawrence R., *Wolf Masks: Violence in Contemporary Poetry,* Kennikat (Port Washington, NY), 1977.

Russell, John D., *Anthony Powell, A Quintet, Sextet and War,* Indiana University Press (Bloomington, IN), 1970.

Selig, Robert L., *Time and Anthony Powell: A Critical Study,* Associated University Presses (Cranbury, NJ), 1991.

Shapiro, Charles, *Contemporary British Novelists,* Southern Illinois University Press (Carbondale, IL), 1965.

Spurling, Hilary, *Invitation to the Dance: A Guide to Anthony Powell's "Dance to the Music of Time,"* Little, Brown (Boston, MA), 1978.

Symons, Julian, *Critical Occasions,* Hamish Hamilton (London, England), 1966.

Tucker, James, *The Novels of Anthony Powell,* Columbia University Press (New York, NY), 1976.

PERIODICALS

American Scholar, autumn, 1993, Alan Rutenberg, review of *Miscellaneous Verdicts: Writings on Writers, 1946-1989,* p. 619.

Atlantic Monthly, March, 1962; January, 1996, Barbara Wallraff, review of *A Dance to the Music of Time,* pp. 108-111; June, 2001, Christopher Hitchens, review of *To Keep the Ball Rolling: The Memoirs of Anthony Powell,* pp. 94-99.

Best Sellers, March 15, 1969.

Booklist, May 15, 2000, Bill Ott, review of *A Dance to the Music of Time,* p. 1792.

Books and Bookmen, April, 1971; March, 1976; January, 1977.

Book Week, April 9, 1967.

Chicago Tribune Book World, July 19, 1981, Larry Kart, review of *A Dance to the Music of Time.*

Christian Science Monitor, October 6, 1960; January 25, 1967; March 16, 1967; March 9, 1981, Maggie Lewis, review of *Faces in My Time,* section B, p. 3.

Commonweal, July 31, 1959; May 12, 1967; May 30, 1969; May 5, 2000, Edward T. Wheeler, review of *A Dance to the Music of Time,* p. 31.

Contemporary Literature, spring, 1976.

Critique, spring, 1964.

Economist, February 18, 1995, review of *Journals 1982-1986,* p. 89.

Encounter, February, 1976.

Globe and Mail (Toronto, Ontario, Canada), March 31, 1984, Douglas Hill.

Hudson Review, summer, 1967; spring, 1976; winter, 1981-82; autumn, 1984.

Kenyon Review, winter, 1960.

Listener, October 14, 1968; September 11, 1975; May 11, 1978.

London Magazine, January, 1969.

London Review of Books, May 18, 1983; February 8, 2001, Michael Wood, "Six Scotches More," pp. 14-16.

Los Angeles Times, March 30, 2000, p. A26.

Los Angeles Times Book Review, May 22, 1983, Michael F. Harper, review of *The Strangers Are All Gone,* p. 4; November 6, 1983, Richard Eder, review of *O, How the Wheel Becomes It!,* p. 1; April 17, 1986, John Bayley, review of *The Fisher King,* p. 16.

Nation, May 29, 1967; December 10, 1973; June 19, 1976.

National Review, December 7, 1973; June 11, 1976; January 11, 1985, John R. Coyne, "Kirk and Powell: The Ingersoll Prizes," p. 42.

New Criterion, May, 2001, Ben Downing, review of *To Keep the Ball Rolling,* p. 70.

New Leader, November 26, 1973.

New Republic, September 24, 1962; April 22, 1967; October 27, 1973; June 11, 1977; February 27, 1984, David Heim, review of *O, How the Wheel Becomes It!,* pp. 39-40; August 19, 1996, William H. Pritchard, review of *A Dance to the Music of Time,* pp. 51-55.

New Review, September, 1974.

New Statesman, June 25, 1960; July 6, 1962; May 19, 1980; May 21, 1982, Stephen Brook, review of *The Strangers Are All Gone,* p. 23; January 6, 1984, Alan Brien, review of *A Dance to the Music of Time,* p. 22.

New Statesman and Society, February 3, 1995, Michael Horovitz, review of *Journals 1982-1986,* p. 39.

Newsweek, March 24, 1969; October 29, 1973; April 5, 1976; April 25, 1983, Gene Lyons, review of *The Strangers Are All Gone,* pp. 86-87; September 2, 1985, Gene Lyons, "The Dance of Time: At 79, Epic Novelist Anthony Powell Is Spry as Ever," pp. 66-67.

New Yorker, July 3, 1965; June 3, 1967; May 10, 1976; August 22, 1983, review of *The Strangers Are All Gone,* pp. 94-95; December 18, 1995, Jeremy Treglow, review of *A Dance to the Music of Time,* pp. 106-112.

New York Herald Tribune Books, February 11, 1962.

New York Review of Books, May 18, 1967; November 1, 1973; May 28, 1998, Christopher Hitchens, "Powell's Way," pp. 47-52.

New York Times, March 14, 1968; March 13, 1969; September 8, 1971; February 17, 1972; February 4, 1981, Anatole Broyard, review of *Faces in My Time,* section C, p. 21; November 16, 1984, Edwin McDowell, "An Author Wins Recognition Late," section C, p. 28; September 23, 1986, Jone Gross, review of *The Fisher King,* section C, p. 17.

New York Times Book Review, January 21, 1962; September 30, 1962; March 19, 1967; March 9, 1969; October 14, 1973; November 1, 1973; April 11, 1976; February 8, 1981, Frances Taliaferro, review of *Faces in My Time,* p. 15; June 26, 1983, review of *The Strangers Are All Gone,* pp. 9-11; January 22, 1984, Charles Michener, review of *O, How the Wheel Becomes It!,* p. 25; October 19, 1986, John Espey, review of *The Fisher King,* p. 30; February 21, 1988.

Observer, October 10, 1967; October 13, 1968; February 14, 1971; May 20, 1990, Anthony Burgess, review of *Miscellaneous Verdicts.*

Publishers Weekly, April 5, 1976; December 5, 1980, Genevieve Stuttaford, review of *Faces in My Time,* p. 47; September 16, 1983, Barbara A. Bannon, review of *Oh, How the Wheel Becomes It!,* p. 118; August 1, 1986, Sybil Steinberg, review of *The Fisher King,* p. 66; May 2, 1994, review of *Under Review: Further Writings on Writers, 1946-1990,* p. 298.

Saturday Review, March 18, 1967; March 8, 1969; November 11, 1973; April 17, 1976; August, 1983, William Cole, review of *The Strangers Are All Gone,* pp. 48-49.

Sewanee Review, spring, 1974; summer, 2001, Jay Parini, "Anthony Powell: 1905-2000," pp. 437-438.

South Atlantic Quarterly, winter, 1977, Kerry McSweeney, review of *A Dance to the Music of Time.*

Spectator, June 24, 1960; September 16, 1966; October 18, 1968; September 13, 1975; October 9, 1976; June 5, 1982; February 29, 1992, Stephen Spender, review of *Under Review,* pp. 33-34; January 28, 1995, Andrew Barrow, review of *Journals 1982-1986,* pp. 28-29; April 6, 1996, David Sexton, review of *Journals, 1987-1989,* pp. 27-28; May 17, 1997, Bevis Hillier, review of *Journals 1990-1992,* pp. 37-39; February 3, 2001, D.J. Taylor, review of *A Writer's Notebook,* p. 33.

Texas Quarterly, spring, 1978, Stephen J. Tapscott, review of *A Dance to the Music of Time,* pp. 105-106.

Time, August 11, 1958; March 3, 1967; March 28, 1969; March 9, 1981, Melvin Maddocks, review of *Faces in My Time,* pp. 72-73.

Times (London, England), April 3, 1980; May 13, 1982; June 16, 1983; April 3, 1986.

Times Literary Supplement, October 17, 1968; March 28, 1980; June 24, 1983; September 21, 1984; April 4, 1986; May 18-24, 1990, Philip Nicholas Furbank, review of *Miscellaneous Verdicts,* p. 524; March 20, 1992, David Plante, review of *Under Review,* p. 22.

Tribune Books (Chicago, IL), September 28, 1986; July 12, 1992, p. 1; September 25, 1994, Merle Rubin, review of *Under Review,* p. 6.

Twentieth Century, July, 1961.

Virginia Quarterly Review, summer, 1976; spring, 1978; autumn, 1985; autumn, 2001, review of *To Keep the Ball Rolling,* p. 133.

Voice Literary Supplement, February, 1984.

Washington Post Book World, April 4, 1976; May 30, 1976; October 9, 1977; September 17, 1978; January 18, 1981; October 12, 1986; December 13, 1987; July 26, 1992, Daniel Max, review of *Miscellaneous Verdicts.*

World Literature Today, summer, 1979.

ONLINE

Anthony Powell Society Web Site, http://www.anthonypowell.org.uk/ (February 21, 2002).

Salon.com, http://www.salon.com/ (April 15, 2000), John Perry, "Anthony Powell."

OBITUARIES:

PERIODICALS

Economist, April 8, 2000, p. 95.

Los Angeles Times, March 30, 2000, p. A9.

National Review, May 1, 2000.

Newsweek, April 10, 2000, p. 10.

New York Times, March 30, 2000, p. A26.

U.S. News and World Report, April 10, 2000, p. 54.

* * *

POWELL, Anthony Dymoke
See POWELL, Anthony

* * *

POWERS, Richard 1957-
(Richard S. Powers)

PERSONAL: Born June 18, 1957, in Evanston, IL; father a school principal; married Jane Kuntz (a professor of French), 2001. *Education:* University of Illinois, Urbana-Champaign, B.S., 1979, M.A., 1979. *Hobbies and other interests:* Music.

ADDRESSES: Office—Department of English, University of Illinois, 608 South Wright, Urbana, IL 61801. *E-mail*—rpowers@uiuc.edu.

CAREER: Writer and educator. Worked as a computer programmer and data processor, in Boston, MA, beginning 1980; University of Illinois, Urbana, professor of creative writing, 1992-96, Swanlund Chair in English, 1996—.

MEMBER: American Academy of Arts and Sciences (elected fellow, 1998).

AWARDS, HONORS: Richard and Hilda Rosenthal Foundation Award for best American fiction, American Academy and Institute of Arts and Letters, special citation from PEN/Hemingway Foundation, and nomination for best novel award, National Book Critics Circle, all 1986, all for *Three Farmers on Their Way to a Dance;* MacArthur Foundation grant, 1989; National Book Critics Circle Award nomination for fiction, 1992, for *The Gold Bug Variations;* National Book Award nomination for fiction, 1993, for *Operation Wandering Soul;* Lannon Literary Award, 1999; Vursell Prize, American Academy and Institute of Arts and Letters, and *New York Times* notable book designation, both 2000, both for *Plowing the Dark;* National Book Critics Circle Award nomination, *New York Times* notable book designation, and London *Evening Standard* best books of the year designation, all 2003, and W.H. Smith Literary Award, and Ambassador Book Award, both 2004, all for *The Time of Our Singing;* Corrington Award for Literary Excellence; Dos Passos Prize for Literature.

WRITINGS:

NOVELS

Three Farmers on Their Way to a Dance, Beech Tree Books (New York, NY), 1985.

Prisoner's Dilemma, Beech Tree Books (New York, NY), 1988.

The Gold Bug Variations, Morrow (New York, NY), 1991.

Operation Wandering Soul, Morrow (New York, NY), 1993.

Galatea 2.2, Farrar, Straus & Giroux (New York, NY), 1995.

Gain, Farrar, Straus & Giroux (New York, NY), 1998.

Plowing the Dark, Farrar, Straus & Giroux (New York, NY), 2000.

The Time of Our Singing, Farrar, Straus & Giroux (New York, NY), 2003.

Contributor to periodicals, including *Harper's, New Yorker,* and *Yale Review.*

WORK IN PROGRESS: A novel about brain injury and memory loss.

SIDELIGHTS: American author Richard Powers is the acclaimed writer of a series of ambitious, intellectual, and highly praised novels that include *Prisoner's Dilemma, Gain,* and *The Time of Our Singing.* Within these works, noted Joseph Dewey in his *Understanding Richard Powers,* the author creates protagonists who, when confronted with challenging, tantalizing, or even threatening circumstances, "shift between the impulse to connect and its inevitable crash and burn; between the Emersonian urge to embrace the difficult ad-lib of the world and the Dickinsonesque need to recoil from its evident bruising into the supple sanctuary of the aesthetic enterprise, to withdraw into the secure refuge of a novel, a piece of music, a movie house, a museum, even cyberspace." Writing in *Contemporary Novelists,* Tom LeClair also summarized Powers's work, noting that his novels deal with "historical subjects, including 20th-century wars, and his scientific orientations, including cybernetics and biology"; that they show Powers's "interests in neurology and cognition, media such as photography and film, and the disasters of contemporary American life"; and that they use "autobiography to examine the sources and values of fictions." "What distinguishes Powers's work," contended LeClair, "is his imaginative earnestness, this prodigy's premodern urge to impart his knowledge to readers."

Particularly during his early career Powers gained a reputation as somewhat of a recluse due to his avoidance of the press. One of five children born to an Illinois high-school principal, Powers left the stable, suburban midwestern United States to live first in a Chicago suburb, and then, from ages ten through fifteen, in Thailand, where his father found a job with the International School of Bangkok despite the political unrest then affecting Southeast Asia. Perhaps because of this relocation, as a child Powers immersed himself in musical instruments such as the cello, clarinet, and saxophone, as well as in reading nonfiction. An interest in science prompted him to declare physics as his major when he enrolled at the University of Illinois, but a new interest in European modernist literature surfaced during his science studies, prompting Powers to also earn his M.A. in English in 1979. After college he moved to Boston and worked in the computer programming field, all the while continuing his wide reading and immersing himself in the world of the arts, science, history, and ideas.

Powers began his literary career in the mid-1980s with *Three Farmers on Their Way to a Dance,* in which a nameless narrator becomes obsessed with uncovering information about August Sander's 1914 photograph of three well-dressed men strolling outside Cologne, Germany. The same photograph—which captivated Powers's own interest when he saw it on display in a Boston museum he frequented—is later uncovered by a magazine editor who is, in turn, searching for a woman he saw only briefly at an Armistice Day parade. As the narrator's hunt brings him to a greater understanding of the horrific World War I era, so too does it cause him to cross paths with the questing editor. These respective searches prompt a greater sense of the interconnectedness of all things. George Kearns, writing in the *Hudson Review,* described *Three Farmers on Their Way to a Dance* as "ambitious and dazzling" and deemed the work "a splendid fiction." In addition, Kearns praised Powers as "a learned writer."

Powers's next published work, *Prisoner's Dilemma,* focuses on a peculiar family whose members come to terms with death and, perhaps more importantly, with themselves. The family is dominated by the father, a retired history teacher who seems to have conducted child-rearing as an extended examination. Now fully grown, his four offspring alternately fear and revere their father, and they each find themselves in difficult emotional circumstances when the possibility arises that the patriarch is gravely ill. Each of the characters in Powers's novel contributes narration, and the father provides commentary of a different sort by recording fictive tales of life in an imaginary American town. One of the offspring secretly studies the recordings and thus manages to gain a greater understanding of his quirky parent.

Upon publication in 1988, *Prisoner's Dilemma* confirmed Powers's reputation as a daring, insightful writer. Frederick Busch, in a Chicago *Tribune Books* appraisal, hailed *Prisoner's Dilemma* as "a long, intelligent look at large and small issues" and called it a "fine novel." Maureen Howard proclaimed in *Nation* that *Prisoner's Dilemma* is "magnificent" and "grand fiction," while Tom LeClair affirmed in a *New Republic* review that Powers surpasses his earlier work by producing "a better novel, more mature and assured." LeClair concluded by classifying the writer as "a major American novelist."

Written during an extended stay in the Netherlands, *The Gold Bug Variations,* Powers's third novel, embraces romance, science, and computer technology. The novel's central figure is Stuart Ressler, a biologist involved in DNA research. The narrative shifts back and forth between the 1950s, during which time Ressler is pursuing his scientific endeavors, and the 1980s, when he holds a low-level position at a database operation. In the 1980s narrative, two of Ressler's coworkers determine to uncover why he ceased scientific work. Although the two coworkers eventually become romantically involved, their romantic relationship is quickly threatened by another inquiry. With *The Gold Bug Variations,* Powers won further recognition as a versatile and demanding storyteller. Louis B. Jones, writing in the *New York Times Book Review,* described the novel as "a dense, symmetrical symphony in which no note goes unsounded," and added: "Just seeing so much sheer cleverness packed into 639 pages is a remarkable experience." *Time* contributor Paul Gray, noting that some readers might find the novel's title—a reference to Edgar Allan Poe's seminal mystery as well as J.S. Bach's great keyboard work—"a little too cute," added that "the rest are in for a read of dazzling, sometimes intimidating complexity." *The Gold Bug Variations,* Gray concluded, is a "masterly novel."

Gain presents the long history of Clare Corporation, a fictitious soap manufacturer that resembles Proctor & Gamble, and the life of Laura, a woman who eventually loses her struggle with ovarian cancer. Laura and one of Clare's factories both reside in the same midwestern city. In *Gain,* "Powers lays out parallel narrative lines—one telling the history of American business, the other examining the life of a contemporary homemaker," commented Tom LeClair, going on to note in his *Nation* review: "On a second reading one finds some ingenious connections and subtle analogues between the stories, but the novel essentially relies on old-fashioned suspense." In contrast, Mark Shecner declared in a review for the *New Leader* that "Powers's history of soap [is not] always gripping; it is too much the fever chart in prose—boom, bust, next boom, next bust—populated by characters who only occasionally step out of their textbook personae long enough to become believable." Claiming that "character development is not the strong suit of *Gain,*" Shecner asserted: "The book is, rather, a succession of vivid moments, and Powers is never better than in his sharp exposures of the discrepancy between the cruelty of the young nation and its piety."

Although *Booklist* reviewer Joann Wilkinson called *Gain* both "incredibly moving and incredibly dull," she praised the story for presenting "an ordinary woman's heroic struggle" in "a powerful and poignant" manner. As LeClair described in his *Nation* review, Powers's "close focus on a year of her life is what soap opera used to be—women's daily tragedy. . . . A plucky divorcee with a sulky daughter and virtual-reality son, a spineless lover and bumbling ex-husband, Laura thinks of her house and garden as a 'safe haven' from human conditions and disease." Shecner contended in his *New Leader* review that readers are not compelled to truly know Powers's protagonist; "as she dies of cancer, Laura does not quite exist for us except as the sum of her sufferings, her treatments, her incomprehension of everything that is going on." Shecner, considering Powers's immense literary abilities, expressed surprise that in *Gain* "the corporation, for all its corruption and obtuseness, shines more brightly than the people it destroys." But in his *Nation* review, LeClair noted that he "found the richness of information in *Gain* both emotionally and intellectually compelling." Describing the novel as a "somber book, not to everyone's taste," *Library Journal* contributor Mark Kloszewski added that, as is characteristic of Powers's work in general, *Gain* "has something important to say."

Describing Powers's first six novels—which include *Gain* and *The Gold Bug Variations* as well as the science-fiction work *Galatea 2.2*—as "persuasively angry at the conditions of twentieth-century life and remarkably sympathetic to its victims," LeClair maintained that the novelist's chief purpose is "to save lives. . . . His means have been ingeniously formed stories—novel as meditation on a photograph, as taped fantasy and chromosomal dance, as literary collage and connectionist brainscape." In the *New Leader,* Shecner observed: "The new thing these days is Infofiction, writing that is part storytelling and part textbook, or sometimes one part storytelling and two parts textbook. . . . The novelist is now a researcher . . . and none is more devoted to the info side of Infofiction than Richard Powers."

In *Plowing the Dark,* Powers again produces a highly researched novel in which several story strands intersect around their examination of the purpose and effect of representational art. "Despite the second commandment (and a similar prohibition in the Koran), creative people have been trying to simulate the visible world ever since the dawn of mankind," explained *Washington Post Book World* contributor Steven Moore. Every painting, sketch, movie, diorama, play, or other visual entertainment has as its goal to mimic and often to improve on humanity, and each emanates from the human imagination. With this theological conflict in mind, Powers draws his readers to Seattle, Washington, where a research company called TetraSys is attempting to perfect virtual reality technology by re-creating some of art's great works and making them accessible in three dimensions. In Powers's story, one can not only view a painting, one can now enter it; according to an *Atlantic Monthly* writer, "Virtual reality . . . is not just the next step in technology; it is the ultimate goal of all technology, of all symbolic thought since the cave painting." Powers's main protagonist, disillusioned artist

Adie Klarpol, is hired by the company to help transform the room in which the computer-generated imagery is generated into a replica of the Hagia Sophia. In the process she is won over to the potential of the new technology for transcending and freeing creative humans from an art bound by what actually exists in nature. Ultimately, however, the more sinister motives of TetraSys emerge, causing Klarpol to reconsider her beliefs.

From the U.S. West Coast, Powers shifts his story to Beirut, Lebanon, where a young Iranian-American university ESL teacher named Taimur Martin is held captive—malnourished and chained, blindfolded, to a bed in an isolated cell—by a group of hard-line Islamic fundamentalists. Isolated for over four years, the teacher has mentally abandoned his tortured reality, in effect using his imagination to create a separate "virtual" reality composed of songs, memories, stories, and contemplation as a means of coping. As an *Atlantic Monthly* reviewer noted, what Martin endures in physical torture and discomfort, Klarpol "undergoes emotionally: abandonment, imprisonment, isolation, the struggle to sustain the imagination."

Dubbing Powers "one of our brainier novelists," the *Atlantic Monthly* contributor placed the author at the forefront of the aforementioned Infofiction—or what he called "encyclopedic postmodernism"—writing that, while some discursive literary types get the technology wrong, for Powers "mathematics and physics are not just gaudy abstractions . . . , they are concrete experiences." However, the critic continued, such a wealth of technical detail threatens to smother the "delicate and vigorous" novel genre; Powers's "characters seem to interest him only as vehicles for meditating on Big Ideas and Great Events," while plot and dramatic tension wither. As Michiko Kakutani noted in a *New York Times* review, *Plowing the Dark* becomes "a static if often provocative book that reads like a series of essays with a couple of glittering set pieces tossed in to grab the reader's attention."

As Valerie Sayers noted in her *Commonweal* review of *Plowing the Dark,* the character of Klarpol serves Powers's purpose primarily in the artist's capacity as a "technological illiterate"; her character "functions as the outsider and innocent learning the political and moral implications of a technology that is capable of representing reality in (nearly) all its dimensions." In contrast, Martin's story is far from abstract; "a reader who abides with Martin in his solitary cell will emerge spent and shaken," Sayers asserted, impressed by the "emotional realities" of the prisoner's story. Klarpol and her coworkers in the Cavern "lose touch with the outside world, with their lives, with the motives of the corporation that hired them," explained *Los Angeles Times* reviewer Michael Harris. "Imagination seduces them, even as it proves to be Taimur's salvation in captivity." These two story lines are threaded independently through the book until the end, when, according to Moore, Powers "pulls off one of the most astonishing feats" in literature by causing these two stories to "dovetail in . . . a daring, unpredictable and emotionally powerful way."

In *The Time of Our Singing,* Powers deals with modern American culture and issues surrounding race, particularly as it both divides and brings people together. The central tension of the novel is embodied in its first few pages, as internationally acclaimed African American opera singer Marian Anderson sings on the Mall in Washington, DC, in April of 1939, having been prevented by members of the Daughters of the American Revolution from performing at Constitution Hall. At this concert, a black music student named Delia meets David Strom, a German-Jewish physicist, and the two fall in love. Soon married, they attempt to live without regard to their biracial reality, and raise three children who are each talented musically: Jonah, Joseph—the novel's narrator—and Ruth. As the children grow up and address both their gifts and their cultural and racial heritage, they follow divergent paths through the social turmoil of the second half of the twentieth century; as Emma Brockes noted in the Manchester *Guardian,* the novel centers on music as a social metaphor that encompasses race and class differences. Powers "builds page-long riffs around the performances of Jonah . . . , answering coldness with something that comes closer, at times, to schmaltz. If there is occasionally too much soaring and whooping and lifting of hearts, the metaphor gets nicely at the workings of social hierarchy, how arbitrary and changing it is, a system into race as a single variable is fed." Praising the novel as "an ambitious and wholly believable modern tragedy" that serves as "the crowing glory of an already impressive and underrated body of work," *Spectator* contributor G.E. Armitage added that *The Time of Our Singing* stands as "proof that there are still some writers for whom the telling of necessary, intelligent and engaging tales still matters."

At 631 pages long, *The Time of Our Singing* nonetheless drew readers, as well as critical praise. Noting that "it is hard to think of another novel since Thomas Mann's *Doctor Faustus* that uses music so effectively and with such authority," Chicago *Tribune Books* contributor Steven G. Kellman added that by positioning his characters within a milieu in which they encounter race-based city riots, Powers "has not made a joyful noise. Out of the troubled zeitgeist" of the second half of the twentieth century, the novelist "has fashioned a major cantata in a minor key." In the *Review of Contemporary Fiction,* James Dewey praised *The Time of Our Singing* as "a deeply affective meditation on time, racial identity, and the complex engine of memory, big ideas that are here offered within a narrative of heartbreaking poignancy in which . . . characters confront . . . the landmark moments of midcentury history."

Despite his growing literary reputation, Powers continues to keep a low profile, maintaining that public interest in the artist ultimately slights and is irrelevant to the art itself. "That's what always seems to happen in this culture," he related to John F. Baker in a *Publishers Weekly* profile, "you grab hold of a personality and ignore the work." Still, Powers has admitted that the absurdity of American culture—which he described as "an amazing mess"—also serves as a source of inspiration for his writing. "One of the great things about American fiction today is its outrageousness . . . ," he told Baker. "You've only got to read certain writers to realize the country is wonderfully mad."

On a more serious note, as Powers told Julia Keller of the *Chicago Tribune,* "The purpose of art is to remind us that there are an infinite number of options that we haven't even considered yet." With each new book, Powers also reminds readers that options exist with regard to the author's area of focus as well as to his choice of style and genre. "When you reserve the right to reinvent yourself with each new book," he told Keller, "the downside is that the readership attracted to your previous book is going to be baffled. They're not necessarily going to want to travel with you." While acknowledging that such a shifting focus may limit his chance to ever rank as a best-selling novelist, with each book Powers seeks out and exposes new interconnections in the world around him, playing out what *New Yorker* contributor Sven Birkerts called his "intense private struggle . . . for equilibrium."

BIOGRAPHICAL AND CRITICAL SOURCES:

BOOKS

Contemporary Literary Criticism, Volume 93, Thomson Gale (Detroit, MI), 1996.

Contemporary Novelists, 6th edition, St. James Press (Detroit, MI), 1996.

Dewey, Joseph, *Understanding Richard Powers,* University of South Carolina Press, 2002.

PERIODICALS

Atlantic Monthly, July, 2000, review of *Plowing the Dark,* pp. 95-97; January-February, 2003, review of *The Time of Our Singing,* pp. 190-193.

Booklist, June 1, 1998, Joann Wilkinson, p. 1726.

Christian Science Monitor, October 10, 1995, Ron Fletcher, review of *Galatea 2.2,* p. 13.

Commonweal, September 8, 2000, Valerie Sayers, review of *Plowing the Dark,* p. 35.

Critique, fall, 1996, Tom LeClair, "The Prodigious Fiction of Richard Powers, William Vollman, and David Foster Wallace."

Guardian (Manchester, England), March 14, 2003, Emma Brockes, "Magic Powers" (interview), p. 2.

Hudson Review, spring, 1986, George Kearns, review of *Three Farmers on Their Way to a Dance,* pp. 133-134.

Library Journal, May 1, 1998, Mark Kloszewski, review of *Gain,* p. 140.

Los Angeles Times, July 11, 2000, Michael Harris, review of *Plowing the Dark,* section E, p. 3.

Nation, May 14, 1988, Maureen Howard, review of *Prisoner's Dilemma,* pp. 680-684; July 27, 1998, Tom LeClair, review of *Gain,* p. 33.

New Leader, June 29, 1998, Marc Shecner, review of *Gain,* p. 26.

New Republic, April 25, 1988, Tom LeClair, review of *Prisoner's Dilemma,* pp. 40-42; May 14, 2001, Michael Ravitch, review of *Plowing the Dark,* p. 45.

New Yorker, January 13, 2003, Sven Birkets, review of *The Time of Our Singing,* p. 85.

New York Review of Books, January 11, 2001, John Leonard, "Mind Painting," pp. 42-48.

New York Times, June 27, 1995, Michiko Kakutani, review of *Galatea 2.2,* section C, p. 19; June 20, 2000, Kakutani, review of *Plowing the Dark,* section E, p. 8.

New York Times Book Review, September 1, 1985, Marco Portales, review of *Three Farmers on Their Way to a Dance,* p. 14; September 10, 1989, review of *Prisoner's Dilemma,* p. 42; August 25, 1991, Louis B. Jones, review of *The Gold Bug Variations,* pp. 9-10; July 18, 1993, Meg Wolitzer, review of *Operation Wandering Soul,* p. 19; July 23, 1995, Robert Cohen, review of *Galatea 2.2,* p. 17.

Review of Contemporary Fiction, summer, 2000, Charles B. Harris, review of *Plowing the Dark,* p. 165; spring, 2003, Joseph Dewey, review of *The Time of Our Singing,* p. 133.

Spectator, March 8, 2003, G.E. Armitage, "The Sound of Music," p. 42.

Time, September 2, 1991, Paul Gray, review of *The Gold Bug Variations,* p. 68.

Times Literary Supplement, May 8, 1992, Roy Porter, review of *The Gold Bug Variations,* p. 20.

Tribune Books (Chicago, IL), February 28, 1988, Frederick Busch, review of *Prisoner's Dilemma,* p. 3; January 12, 2003, Steven G. Kellman, review of *The Time of Our Singing,* p. 1.

Wall Street Journal, July 13, 1993, Lee Lescaze, review of *Operation Wandering Soul,* section A, p. 14; July 5, 1995, Merle Rubin, review of *Galatea 2.2,* section A, p. 7.

Washington Post Book World, June 4, 2000, Steven Moore, review of *Plowing the Dark,* p. 6.

ONLINE

Richard Powers Web site, http://www.richardpowers.net/ (October 29, 2004).

Salon.com, http://www.salon.com/ (July, 1998), Laura Miller, interview with Powers.

* * *

POWERS, Richard S.
See POWERS, Richard

* * *

POWERS, Tim 1952-
(William Ashbless, Timothy Thomas Powers)

PERSONAL: Born February 29, 1952; son of Richard (an attorney) and Noel (Zimmerman) Powers; married Serena Batsford (a legal secretary), 1980. *Education:* California State University, Fullerton, B.A., 1976. *Religion:* Roman Catholic.

ADDRESSES: Agent—Russell Galen, Scott Meredith Literary Agency, 845 Third Ave., New York, NY 10022.

CAREER: Writer.

AWARDS, HONORS: Philip K. Dick Memorial Award, 1984, for *The Anubis Gates,* and 1986; Prix Apollo, c. 1984, for *The Anubis Gates;* Philip K. Dick Award, 1985, for *Dinner at Deviant's Palace;* Mythopoeic Fantasy Award, 1990, for *The Stress of Her Regard;* World Fantasy Award for Best Novel, World Fantasy Convention, 1993, for *Last Call,* and 2001, for *Declare;* International Horror Guild best novel award, 2001, for *Declare.*

WRITINGS:

NOVELS

The Skies Discrowned, Laser (Toronto, Ontario, Canada), 1976, revised edition published as *Forsake the Sky,* Tom Doherty Associates, 1986.

An Epitaph in Rust, Laser (Toronto, Ontario, Canada), 1976, revised edition, NESFA Press (Cambridge, MA), 1989.

The Drawing of the Dark, Ballantine Books (New York, NY), 1979.

The Anubis Gates, Ace Books (New York, NY), 1983.

Dinner at Deviant's Palace, Ace Books (New York, NY), 1985.

On Stranger Tides, Ace Books (New York, NY), 1987.

The Stress of Her Regard, Ace Books (New York, NY), 1989.

Last Call, Morrow (New York, NY), 1992.

Expiration Date, TOR (New York, NY), 1996.

Earthquake Weather, TOR (New York, NY), 1997.

Fault Lines, GuildAmerica, 1998.

Declare, William Morrow (New York, NY), 2001.

OTHER

(As William Ashbless) *Twelve Hours of the Night* (poetry), Cheap Street (New Castle, VA), 1985.

Night Moves (short stories), introduction by James P. Blaylock, Axolotl (Seattle, WA), 1986, published as *Night Moves and Other Stories,* Subterranean Press (Burton, MI), 2000.

(With James P. Blaylock) *The Way down the Hill* (short stories), Axolotl (Seattle, WA), 1986.

(As William Ashbless) *A Short Poem* (poetry), Folly Press (Tacoma, WA), 1987.

(With Richard B. Isaacs) *The Seven Steps to Personal Safety: How to Avoid, Deal with, or Survive the Aftermath of a Once-in-a-Lifetime Violent Confrontation* (nonfiction), Center for Personal Defense Studies (New York, NY), 1993.

(With Blaylock) *The William Ashbless Memorial Cookbook,* Subterranean Press (Burton, MI), 2001.

Contributor of science fiction short stories to periodicals, including *Magazine of Fantasy and Science Fiction.*

SIDELIGHTS: Two-time winner of the Philip K. Dick Memorial Award, science fiction and fantasy novelist Tim Powers is recognized for his intricately plotted stories filled with well-rounded and often outlandish characters. In many of his novels, including *The Anubis Gates* and *The Stress of Her Regard,* Powers deals with time travel, and these historical fantasies are often populated by authentic figures. He also favors fantastic episodes featuring supernatural and mythical characters and exhibits a penchant for the horrific, adventurous, and grotesque. "A Tim Powers science fiction novel never fails to titillate and elucidate with the dark and the bizarre," Sue Martin remarked in the *Los Angeles Times Book Review,* "and all with such original, eccentric color and style."

Powers won his first Philip K. Dick Memorial Award for his action-packed science fiction mystery and horror thriller *The Anubis Gates.* The novel details the adventures of Brendan Doyle, a twentieth-century English professor who travels to 1810 London to attend a lecture given by English romantic poet Samuel Taylor Coleridge. When he is kidnapped by gypsies and consequently misses his return trip to 1983, the mild-mannered Doyle is forced to become a street-smart con man, escape artist, and swordsman in order to survive in the dark and treacherous London underworld. He defies bullets, black magic, murderous beggars, freezing waters, imprisonment in mutant-infested dungeons, poisoning, and even a plunge back to 1684. Coleridge himself and poet Lord Byron make appearances in the novel, which also features a poor tinkerer who creates genetic monsters and a werewolf that inhabits others' bodies when his latest becomes too hairy.

The Anubis Gates met with an enthusiastic critical reception. Reviewers commended Powers's inventive and lively storyline and applauded his finesse in managing the twisting and jam-packed plot. In addition, critics praised his characters, especially his roguish beggars, whom they compared to some of the wretched characters of English novelist Charles Dickens. "Plotted with manic fervour, executed with exhilarating dexterity at breakneck speed," lauded Colin Greenland in the *Times Literary Supplement,* "*The Anubis Gates* is a virtuoso performance, a display of marvelous fireworks that illuminates everything in flashes, with scant afterglow."

Powers followed *The Anubis Gates* with *Dinner at Deviant's Palace,* a post-nuclear holocaust fantasy set in Los Angeles. The novel centers on a powerful "psychic vampire"—commandant of the foul nightclub Deviant's Palace—and his followers, who brainwash Los Angeles inhabitants and seize control of the entire city. Gregorio Rivas is a "redeemer," a member of a group out to reclaim the city, who sets out to save his former lover from the cult's sinister grasp. He barely escapes with his life after he encounters its alien, blood-thirsty demon leader. Radioactive wastelands and monstrous creatures, along with dark, underworld characters and spirits, round out the fantastic elements of *Dinner at Deviant's Palace.*

With his imaginative *On Stranger Tides,* Powers returned to historical fantasy. This novel traces the high-sea adventures of an eighteenth-century fortune-seeking young man, John Chandagnac. While traveling to the West Indies on a mission to retrieve his father's stolen inheritance, Chandagnac is shanghaied by the notorious pirate Blackbeard—now plagued with voodoo ghosts—and forced to join his band of zombie pirates. Also captured is a sorcerer with a fixation for matriarchs, and a crazed widower who totes his wife's severed head in a box. With Chandagnac as gourmet chef, this motley crew ventures through the Caribbean and to a treacherous Florida swamp in search of the legendary Fountain of Youth. Their swashbuckling adventures lead them to encounters with ghosts, beach-strolling corpses, dancing dead chickens, animated plants, and finally to a watery reservoir used to resurrect the dead. "Tim Powers has written across the entire range of the literature of the fantastic," declared Orson Scott Card in his *Washington Post Book World* review, "but he is at his best when writing gonzo historical novels . . . like *On Stranger Tides.*"

Powers's 1989 historical fantasy, *The Stress of Her Regard,* also takes place against a backdrop of dark, supernatural, and mythical phenomenon. Set in 1815, the novel revolves around physician Michael Crawford and his relationship with the nephelim, or demonic vampire lovers. Blamed for his bride's violent murder—she was actually mutilated by Crawford's jealous demon lover—and hunted by his wife's schizophrenic twin sister, Crawford flees to London, where he encounters the great romantic poets John Keats, Percy Bysshe Shelley, and Lord Byron, all of whom are engrossed with the supernatural nephelim underworld and creatively inspired by their own demonic muses. Chillingly haunted by his fiendish muse, Crawford endures supernatural battles and schemes. Ultimately, in a high-altitude confrontation with the Egyptian Sphinx, both Byron and Crawford are released from the affections of their evil lovers.

Many critics pronounced *The Stress of Her Regard* a fascinating work conveying a fantastic story behind romanticism. Howard Mittelmark in the *Washington Post Book World* called the novel an "ingenious tale of erotic love and supernatural conspiracies," but conceded that the narrative line falters under Powers's complex mythological web. *The Stress of Her Regard* "is immensely clever stuff. . . . Powers's prose is often vivid and arresting," the critic continued, "but ultimately it is all too much." Although Sue Martin, in the *Los Angeles Times Book Review* found *The Stress of Her Regard* a trifle lengthy, she thought the novel a "shining example" of Powers's strengths—his originality, his action-crammed plots, and his ventures into the mysterious, dark, and supernatural. "All in all," the critic added, "Powers' unique voice in science fiction continues to grow stronger."

Powers's voice was heard again in 1992 with another highly regarded novel, *Last Call.* Against the backdrop of a Las Vegas where humans and spirits commune casually, one-eyed gambler Scott Crane teams up with the ghost of gangster Bugsy Siegel. Siegel, who wields ultimate power in "Sin City," is the target of would-be usurpers, including Georges Leon, who himself is challenged by his long-missing son, Crane. The competition hinges on a card game called Assumption; "with its recurring Tarot-card symbols, fantastic creatures . . . and poetic epigraphs," noted a *Publishers Weekly* contributor, *Last Call* "is not an easy read; it is, however, distinctive and commanding." In a *Library Journal* piece, Denise Dumars listed *Last Call* along with such modern classics as *The Handmaid's Tale* and *Flowers for Algernon* as ideal books with which to introduce readers to science fiction.

A playful spirit also characterizes 1996's *Expiration Date,* which is set among a group of Southern California addicts. The twist is that the addicts are not attracted to drugs or alcohol, but to ghosts. In fact, the spirits of the dead are given new life when inhaled by the living, who get a "rush" from the flood of memories released by the deceased. All this provides a good business for hobo-turned-spirit-pusher Sherman Oaks. When a runaway preteen inhales the ghost of Thomas Alva Edison, "a feeding frenzy begins among West Coast ghost eaters eager to absorb the great inventor's genius," according to a *Publishers Weekly* reviewer, who praised the novel for its "minefield of exploding surprises." To Carl Hays of *Booklist,* Powers's brand of quirky otherworldliness "may baffle fans of more conventional fantasy, but his colorful characters and delightful sense of the absurd should continue to attract new readers."

Powers integrated fantasy with espionage in the 2000 thriller, *Declare.* Set against the Cold War, the book opens in 1963, with agent Andrew Hale summoned by British Intelligence to finish a mission begun in Turkey many years earlier. The mission involves a trip to Mount Ararat, the purported final resting point of Noah's Ark, which Hale believed has become the sanctuary of djinns, bloodthirsty supernatural beings that can take the form of humans. The Soviet Union is being protected by one of those djinns, in the guise of an elderly woman; if this being is allowed to make contact with other djinns, chaos could result. "As in Powers's previous novels," observed *National Review's* Lawrence Person, "fictional events are intertwined with meticulously researched historical fact." A *Publishers Weekly* writer thought that the author's integration of spy fiction and sci-fi "simply do not blend," but also cited *Declare* as "offbeat and daringly imaginative." Person found the novel "a worthy addition to the genre" of Christian fiction, which incorporates spiritual matters into conventional plot. And to *Library Journal* critic Devon Thomas, fans of such spy plotters as John LeCarre "will appreciate the authentic period detail" of *Declare.*

Writing in an entirely different vein, Powers and coauthor James P. Blaylock assumed the identity of a Victorian poet, William Ashbless. This character's verse was collected in two volumes followed by a bizarre cookbook-memoir, *The William Ashbless Memorial Cookbook,* which featured such recipes as the "Can O' Beans Salad" and a protest by the poet that he is not dead. "Goofiness abounds," was the succinct assessment of a *Publishers Weekly* contributor.

In an essay for the *St. James Guide to Science Fiction Writers,* Bernadette Lynn Bosky suggested that "it may be impossible to convey fully the elaborate and coherent weirdness of a novel by Tim Powers. . . . Especially in the later novels, all this is conveyed in an assured prose, with a range of tones both humorous and serious, generally transparent but marked by strong descriptions and striking metaphors. Still not as well known as he should be," Bosky concluded, "Powers gets greater acclaim with each novel, and deservedly so."

BIOGRAPHICAL AND CRITICAL SOURCES:

BOOKS

Joyce, Tom, and Christopher P. Stephens, *A Checklist of Tim Powers,* Ultramarine (Hastings-on-Hudson, NY), 1991.

St. James Guide to Fantasy Writers, St. James Press (Detroit, MI), 1996.
St. James Guide to Science Fiction Writers, St. James Press (Detroit, MI), 1996.

PERIODICALS

Booklist, January 1, 1996, Carl Hays, review of *Expiration Date,* p. 799.
Library Journal, November 15, 2000, Devon Thomas, review of *Declare,* p. 97; August, 2001, Denise Dumars, "Out of This World: SF for Novices," p. 196.
Los Angeles Times Book Review, August 27, 1989, Sue Martin, review of *The Stress of Her Regard,* p. 12.
National Review, September 17, 2001, Lawrence Person, review of *Declare.*
Publishers Weekly, February 24, 1992, review of *Last Call,* p. 47; December 18, 1995 review of *Expiration Date,* p. 44; November 27, 2000, review of *Declare,* p. 51; December 18, 2000, review of *Night Moves and Other Stories,* p. 60; May 28, 2001, review of *Dinner at Deviant's Palace,* p. 56; February 11, 2002, "February Publications," p. 167.
Security Management, October, 1994, Terry Shirokoff, review of *The Seven Steps to Personal Safety: How to Avoid, Deal with, or Survive the Aftermath of a Once-in-a-Lifetime Violent Confrontation,* p. 91.
Times Literary Supplement, July 5, 1987, Colin Greenland, review of *The Anubis Gates,* p. 757.
Washington Post Book World, October 25, 1987, Orson Scott Card, review of *On Stranger Tides,* p. 6; November 26, 1989, Howard Mittelmark, review of *The Stress of Her Regard,* p. 6.

OTHER

Tim Powers Page, http://easyweb.easynet.co.uk/ (January 5, 2002), "The Works of Tim Powers."

* * *

POWERS, Timothy Thomas
See POWERS, Tim

* * *

PRATCHETT, Terry 1948-

PERSONAL: Born April 28, 1948, in Beaconsfield, England; son of David (an engineer) and Eileen (a secretary; maiden name, Kearns) Pratchett; married; wife's name Lyn; children: Rhianna. *Hobbies and other interests:* Growing carnivorous plants.

ADDRESSES: Agent—Colin Smythe, Ltd., P.O. Box 6, Gerrards Cross, Buckinghamshire SL9 8XA, England.

CAREER: Novelist. Journalist in Buckinghamshire, Bristol, and Bath, England, 1965-80; press officer, Central Electricity Board, Western Region, 1980-87.

AWARDS, HONORS: British Science-Fiction Award, 1989, for "Discworld" series, and 1990, for *Good Omens;* Writers Guild of Great Britain best children's book award, 1993, for *Johnny and the Dead;* British Book Award citation, 1993, as Fantasy and Science Fiction Author of the Year; awarded Order of the British Empire, 1998; Carnegie Medal, and *Guardian* Children's Fiction Prize, both 2002, both for *The Amazing Maurice and His Educated Rodents;* Mythopoeic Fantasy Award for children's literature, Mythopoeic Society, 2005, for *A Hat Full of Sky;* honorary doctor of letters, University of Warwick, 1999.

WRITINGS:

"DISCWORLD" FANTASY SERIES

The Colour of Magic (also see below), St. Martin's Press (New York, NY), 1983, published as *The Color of Magic,* 2000.
The Light Fantastic, St. Martin's Press (New York, NY), 1986.
Equal Rites, Gollancz (London, England), 1986, New American Library (New York, NY), 1987.
Mort, New American Library (New York, NY), 1987.
Sourcery, Gollancz (London, England), 1988, New American Library (New York, NY), 1989.
Wyrd Sisters, Gollancz (London, England), 1988, Roc (New York, NY), 1990.
Pyramids, Penguin (New York, NY), 1989.
Eric, Gollancz (London, England), 1989.
Guards! Guards!, Gollancz (London, England), 1989, Roc (New York, NY), 1991.
Moving Pictures, Gollancz (London, England), 1990, Roc (New York, NY), 1992.
Reaper Man, Gollancz (London, England), 1991, Roc (New York, NY), 1992.
Witches Abroad, Gollancz (London, England), 1991, New American Library (New York, NY), 1993.
Small Gods, Gollancz (London, England), 1992, HarperCollins (New York, NY), 1994.
(With Stephen Briggs) *The Streets of Ankh Morpork,* Corgi (London, England), 1993, Bantam (New York, NY), 1994.

Mort: A Discworld Big Comic (graphic novel), illustrated by Graham Higgins, Gollancz (London, England), 1994.

Lords and Ladies, Gollancz (London, England), 1993, HarperCollins (New York, NY), 1995.

(With Stephen Briggs) *The Discworld Companion,* Gollancz (London, England), 1994.

(With Stephen Briggs) *The Discworld Mapp,* Corgi (London, England), 1995.

Men at Arms, Gollancz (London, England), 1993, HarperCollins (New York, NY), 1996.

Terry Pratchett's Discworld Quizbook: The Unseen University Challenge, Vista, 1996.

Interesting Times, HarperPrism (New York, NY), 1994.

Soul Music, HarperPrism (New York, NY), 1995.

Feet of Clay, HarperPrism (New York, NY), 1996.

Maskerade, HarperPrism (New York, NY), 1997.

Hogfather, HarperPrism (New York, NY), 1998.

Jingo, HarperPrism (New York, NY), 1998.

Carpe Jugulum, HarperPrism (New York, NY), 1999.

The Last Continent, HarperPrism (New York, NY), 1999.

(With Ian Stewart and Jack Cohen) *The First Discworld Novels* (contains *The Colour of Magic* and *The Light Fantastic*), Dufour Editions (Chester Springs, PA), 1999.

The Fifth Elephant, HarperCollins (New York, NY), 2000.

The Truth, Corgi (London, England), 2001.

The Last Hero: A Discworld Fable, illustrated by Paul Kidby, HarperCollins (New York, NY), 2001.

Night Watch, HarperCollins (New York, NY), 2003.

The Science of Discworld II: The Globe, Ebury (London, England), 2002.

Monstrous Regiment, HarperCollins (New York, NY), 2003.

The Wee Free Men, HarperCollins (New York, NY), 2003.

A Hat Full of Sky, HarperCollins (New York, NY), 2004.

Going Postal, HarperCollins (New York, NY), 2004.

Thud!, HarperCollins (New York, NY), 2005.

Where's My Cow?, HarperCollins (New York, NY), 2005.

"BROMELIAD" TRILOGY; JUVENILE FANTASY

Truckers (also see below), Doubleday (New York, NY), 1989.

Diggers (also see below), Delacorte (New York, NY), 1990.

Wings (also see below), Doubleday (New York, NY), 1990.

The Bromeliad Trilogy (contains *Truckers, Diggers,* and *Wings*), HarperCollins (New York, NY), 2003.

OTHER

The Carpet People (juvenile fantasy), Smythe, 1971, revised edition, Doubleday (New York, NY), 1992.

The Dark Side of the Sun (science fiction), St. Martin's Press (New York, NY), 1976.

Strata (science fiction), St. Martin's Press (New York, NY), 1981.

The Unadulterated Cat, illustrated by Gray Jolliffe, Gollancz (London, England), 1989.

(With Neil Gaiman) *Good Omens: The Nice and Accurate Predictions of Agnes Nutter, Witch,* Workman (New York, NY), 1990.

Only You Can Save Mankind (for young adults), Doubleday (New York, NY), 1992.

Johnny and the Dead (juvenile), Doubleday (New York, NY), 1993.

Johnny and the Bomb, Acacia, 1997.

Thief of Time, Doubleday (New York, NY), 2001.

The Amazing Maurice and His Educated Rodents, HarperCollins (New York, NY), 2001.

Nancy Ogg's Cookbook, Corgi (New York, NY), 2003.

ADAPTATIONS: *Truckers* was adapted into a television series by Cosgrove Hall, Thames Video, 1992; *Music from the Discworld,* based on Pratchett's series, was composed and performed by Dave Greenslade, Virgin Records, 1994; the video games "Discworld" and "Discworld II: Missing Presumed. . . " were developed by Sony/Psygnosis, 1994, 1996; *Johnny and the Dead* was adapted as a television series, London Weekend Television, 1995, and for the stage by Stephen Briggs, Oxford University Press, 1996; *Wyrd Sisters* was adapted for the stage by Briggs, Corgi (London, England), 1996; *Mort* was adapted for the stage by Briggs, Corgi (London, England), 1996; *Guards! Guards!* was adapted for the stage by Briggs, Corgi (London, England), 1997; *Men at Arms* was adapted for the stage by Briggs, Corgi (London, England), 1997; *Wyrd Sisters* was adapted as a television series, Cosgrove Hall Films, 1997; *Soul Music* was adapted as a television series, Cosgrove Hall Films, 1997; *The Wee Free Men* has been announced for adaptation into a feature film, directed by Sam Raimi, for Sony Pictures Entertainment.

SIDELIGHTS: British author Terry Pratchett is best known for his popular "Discworld" series, a humorous fantasy set in a world that rests upon a giant turtle's back. With more than thirty "Discworld" books to his credit, Pratchett is one of Great Britain's most recognizable and popular authors. "Pratchett's texts are woven from the stuff of fantasy," wrote Nicolas Tredell in *Contemporary Novelists.* "His fiction is both a hilarious parody of the fantasy genre and a genuine contribution to it, in that it creates a rich, imaginative 'multiverse' that absorbs and intrigues the reader. It shares with the strongest fantasy a concern with fundamental issues such as death, and it incorporates aspects of contemporary culture such as fast food and rock music." The "Discworld" novels do not build upon one another, but instead can be read in any order—a fact that has contributed to their popularity. Tredell noted: "Taken together these novels create an imaginative zone that is rich and strange, offering the reader both the pleasures of discovery, as new aspects are revealed, and of recognition, as familiar figures recur." David Langford concluded in the *St. James Guide to Fantasy Writers:* "Pratchett's achievement in the Discworld series is slightly frightening: so many books since 1983, and so consistently funny with scarcely a wobble." "Discworld"—as well as most of Pratchett's other works—offers parodies of the creations of other famous science-fiction and fantasy writers, such as J.R.R. Tolkien and Larry Niven, while it spoofs such modern trends as New Age philosophy and universal concerns like death, religion, and politics. "Nevertheless, buried amongst the slapstick comedy and witty word-play are serious considerations of humanity and its foibles. In a genre assailed by shoddiness, mediocrity, and . . . the endless series," asserted *Locus* reviewer Faren Miller, "Pratchett is never shoddy, and under the laughter there's a far from mediocre mind at work." Indeed, to quote Tredell, "The Discworld is full of stories that bear on our social and metaphysical concerns."

Pratchett wrote his first full-length work of fiction at the age of seventeen and published it as *The Carpet People,* in 1971. Aimed at young readers, the book describes a whole world set in a carpet, populated by creatures called deftmenes, mouls, and wights. The novel's protagonist, Snibril the Munrung, travels with his brother, Glurk, through the many Carpet regions—which are set off by different colors—to do battle against the evil concept of Fray. A *Times Literary Supplement* reviewer recommended *The Carpet People* and further noted that "the Tolkienian echoes may draw in some older readers."

The Dark Side of the Sun and *Strata,* both science-fiction novels by Pratchett, appear to spoof aspects of Larry Niven's "Ringworld," a huge, flat world that completely circles a star, according to Don D'Ammassa in *Twentieth-Century Science Fiction Writers. The Dark Side of the Sun,* in D'Ammassa's words, features "manipulation of the laws of chance"—a subject also prominent in Niven's *Ringworld; Strata* discusses the construction of artificial planets and resembles *Ringworld* "in many superficial ways." Edward Dickey, reviewing *The Dark Side of the Sun* in *Best Sellers,* observed that "it should have strong appeal for science fiction fans" and called the novel "entertaining fiction lightened by occasional touches of whimsy." Allan Jenoff, critiquing *Strata* in *Science Fiction and Fantasy Book Review,* found it "amusing and readable."

Pratchett used the concept of a flat world again when he embarked upon his first "Discworld" novel, *The Colour of Magic.* This time, however, he took an approach more suitable to the fantasy genre than to science fiction. As Philippa Toomey reported in the London *Times:* "A great turtle swims through space. On its back are four giant elephants, on whose shoulders the disc of the world rests. We know this only because the extremely inquisitive inhabitants of the small kingdom of Krull lowered some early astrozoologists over the edge to have a quick look." Pratchett has pointed out that many mythologies across the world espouse the notion that the world is a flat place being carried on the back of a great turtle.

The protagonist of the first "Discworld" novel, *The Colour of Magic,* is a hapless wizard named Rincewind; he teams up with a tourist from a remote portion of the disc for a series of precarious adventures. The resulting tale, according to W.D. Stevens in *Science Fiction and Fantasy Review,* is "one of the funniest, and cleverest, [sword and sorcery] satires to be written." Rincewind returns in Pratchett's second "Discworld" novel, *The Light Fantastic.* This time he must try to prevent Discworld from colliding with a red star that has recently appeared in its sky. The next book in the series, *Equal Rites,* puts the emphasis on the character of Granny Weatherwax, whom Tom Hutchinson in the London *Times* hailed as "one of my favorite fantasy heroines." Granny Weatherwax returns in *Wyrd Sisters,* this time accompanied by two fellow witches, one of whom, Magrat Garlick, likes to indulge in "New Age fripperies," according to Miller in *Locus.* In *Wyrd Sisters* Granny and her companions form a trio of witches reminiscent of those in William Shakespeare's play *Macbeth* and attempt to foil the plot of the evil Lord Felmet and his wife, who have usurped the rightful king. *Wyrd Sisters* led Miller to express his amazement at Pratchett for creating "an open-ended series that just keeps getting better."

Subsequent "Discworld" novels have introduced other compelling characters, including Death and his apprentice, Mort, as well as a bungling set of night watchmen who save the capital city of Ankh-Morpork from an invading dragon. The series does not shrink from addressing controversial topics, exploring issues such as immortality, dogmatic religion, oppressive politics, and the influential power of fairy tales. Langford observed: "Once established, the astrophysics of Discworld receded into the background, fleetingly mentioned in later books as 'series glue.' Discworld is a place where any story can be told, and its geography is fluid. But (and this is a major strength) it is not just another of those realms where anything can happen. Events are governed by a steely commonsense which may only be overruled by the important need to insert another joke or demented footnote. Nevertheless," the critic continued, "the surface hilarity glitters all the more for having such solid, uncompromising bones: in the best of the series the silly footnotes and mirthful throwaway lines are ornaments on a structure of steel."

The "Discworld" novel *The Fifth Elephant* revolves around some valuable natural deposits of minerals and high-quality fat, left behind when a cosmic elephant crashed and burned in the Uberwald region at the beginning of time. Policeman Sam Vimes, traveling to Uberwald to find the valuable Scone of Stone, becomes involved in what a reviewer for *Publishers Weekly* called "an exuberant tale of mystery and invention" in which Pratchett "skewers everything" including political, religious, and economic systems, to achieve a book that is "a heavyweight of lightness." *Booklist* reviewer Roland Green praised the author's humor and also his effective writing style, commenting: "He never lets a proper tone flag; thus, in the midst of all the satire, Vimes' death struggle with the werewolves is as grim as any thriller's climax, and the growing love between Captain Carrot and Corporal Angua the werewolf is handled straight. Pratchett is now inviting comparison with Kurt Vonnegut, but if he ends up with a reputation equivalent only to that of P.G. Wodehouse, the world will be the better for his having written."

In *Night Watch* Vimes has been made a duke and is living the good life with his wife, who is expecting their child. Still, he cannot forget his days on duty, and finds himself going on patrol even when he is not required to do so. A surge of occult power sends him back to the past, but with some differences: He is now in charge of the future and required to remember everything correctly. "Discworld remains a place of punning, entertaining footnotes, and farce, in which Ankh-Morpork is still a great city," commented Regina Schroeder in *Booklist.*

Monstrous Regiment gave eager readers still more tales of Discworld. In this novel Pratchett introduces readers to the region of Borogravia, whose religion forbids chocolate, cats, dwarfs, the color blue, babies, and cheese, among other things. The story concerns Polly Perks, a determined barmaid who disguises herself as a man to more easily search for her brother in the infantry. To Polly's surprise, most of her fellow conscripts are similarly disguised. *New York Times* reviewer Kerry Fried noted that while the story is full of puns and humor, Pratchett's real subject is "the pity of war." Noting that the plot "can move from farce to sadness in seconds," Fried concluded that while *Monstrous Regiment* "is most often spirited and shambolic . . . it has some serious heft."

In 1989 Pratchett published the first of his "Bromeliad" fantasy trilogy for children. *Truckers* introduces young readers to the nomes, four-inch-high people from another planet who have crashed on Earth and who have made a new world for themselves under the floorboards of a department store. Other nomes, however, have also found their way to Earth and live on the outside; the fun begins when one of these, Masklin, meets with the nomes of the store. When they learn that the store is going out of business and will be torn down, together the nomes must cooperate to find a new home and to escape their old one in a human-sized truck. "A wild and hilarious chase sequence follows, with the baffled police doubting their sanity," observed a *Horn Book* reviewer. Elizabeth Ward in the *Washington Post Book World* summed up *Truckers* as "a delightful surprise" and a "benevolent little satire."

Diggers, the second "Bromeliad" installment, takes Masklin and his fellow nomes to their new home in an abandoned quarry. However, problems ensue when humans attempt to reactivate the quarry. "In the book's funniest scene," according to Patrick Jones in *Voice of Youth Advocates,* "a group of nomes 'attacks' one of the humans, ties him to his desk chair, and stuffs a note in his hand proclaiming: 'leave us alone.'" "Satire and allegory abound," a *Horn Book* reviewer concluded of *Diggers,* but the critic also noted that the nomes' "trials and emotions are both moving and amusing." In *Wings* Masklin and his friends attempt to return to their home planet by placing the Thing—a "magic" box which in *Truckers* had warned them of the store's demise—aboard a communications satellite so that it can summon their mother ship, which has been waiting for them throughout their earthly exile. Margaret A. Chang lauded this last book of the series in the *School Library Journal* as a "cheerful, unpretentious tale." A *Junior Bookshelf* correspondent wrote of *Wings:* "Here is a real effort of creativity, and a criticism of society no less forceful for being clothed in the garb of comedy."

Pratchett has also penned books outside his two famed series. With Neil Gaiman, author of the popular "Sandman" comic books and several highly praised graphic novels, Pratchett wrote *Good Omens: The Nice and Accurate Predictions of Agnes Nutter, Witch.* The story, which met with mixed reviews when it was published in 1990, spoofs the Bible's Book of Revelation and concerns the efforts of both an angel and a demon to prevent the end of the world because they have grown fond of mankind and life on Earth. Their tactics include such strategies as deliberately misplacing the Antichrist, who resides in an English suburb. Joe Queenan, critiquing the book in the *New York Times Book Review,* complained of "schoolboy wisecracks about Good, Evil, the Meaning of Life and people who drink Perrier." But Howard Waldrop in the *Washington Post* praised *Good Omens:* "When the book is talking about the big questions, it's a wow. It leaves room in both the plot and the readers' reactions for the characters to move around in and do unexpected but very human things."

In 1992 Pratchett penned the young-adult novel *Only You Can Save Mankind,* which, with its computer-game-playing protagonist, spoofs, among other things, the 1991 Persian Gulf War. Johnny, the book's hero, finds the tables turned upon him when the aliens he is fighting in his computer game suddenly surrender and enlist his aid. This humorous but ultimately serious tale has led to more "Johnny" titles, including *Johnny and the Dead* and *Johnny and the Bomb.* "Pratchett's philosophy is based on a humorous view of life and humanity," stated a reviewer in *Junior Bookshelf,* "and the fact that most of the characters in *Johnny and the Dead* are indeed dead does not mean that they are the less funny. The comedy and the philosophy are inseparable."

Pratchett won Great Britain's top award for children's literature with his book *The Amazing Maurice and His Educated Rodents.* In this tale, a cat named Maurice is behind a money-making scheme that involves rats and a piper named Keith. Trouble arises when the rats consume some magical trash and subsequently begin to develop moral scruples, questioning their way of life. "Pratchett's absorbing, suspenseful adventure is speeded along by the characters' wisecracking patter and deepened . . . by a willingness to tackle the questions of existence," stated Anita L. Burkham in *Horn Book.* Miranda Doyle commented in her *School Library Journal* review that *The Amazing Maurice and His Educated Rodents* is "laugh-out-loud" funny, but also added, "Despite the humorous tone of the novel, there are some genuinely frightening moments."

Pratchett commented: "I've been a journalist of some sort all my working life, and I suppose I tend to think of the books as a kind of journalism—although writing them is as much fun as anyone can have by themselves sitting down with all their clothes on.

"I can't speak for the United States—three thousand miles is a great barrier to casual feedback—but what does gratify me in the United Kingdom is that the 'Discworld' books, which are not intended for children, have a big following among kids who, in the words of one librarian, 'don't normally read.'

"I got my education from books. The official schooling system merely prevented me from reading as many books as I would have liked. So from personal experience I know that getting children to read is *important.* Civilization depends on it."

BIOGRAPHICAL AND CRITICAL SOURCES:

BOOKS

Contemporary Novelists, 6th edition, St. James Press (Detroit, MI), 1996.

St. James Guide to Children's Writers, 5th edition, St. James Press (Detroit, MI), 1999.

St. James Guide to Fantasy Writers, St. James Press (Detroit, MI), 1996.

Twentieth-Century Science Fiction Writers, St. James Press (Chicago, IL), 1991.

PERIODICALS

Analog Science Fiction & Fact, November, 2000, Tom Easton, review of *The Fifth Elephant,* p. 132.

Best Sellers, November, 1976, pp. 249-250.

Book, November-December, 2002, Chris Barsanti, "Terry Pratchett's Flat-out Success," p. 26; March-April, 2003, review of *Night Watch,* p. 39; May-June, 2003, review of *The Wee Free Men,* p. 30.

Booklist, April 15, 1998, Wilma Longstreet, review of *Johnny and the Dead,* p. 1460; June 1, 1998, Roland Green, review of *Jingo,* p. 1736; January 1, 2000, Roland Green, review of *The Fifth Elephant,* p. 834; August, 2000, Ray Olson, review of *The Truth,* p. 2075; September 15, 2001, Ray Olson, review of *The Last Hero,* p. 164; January 1, 2002, Sally Estes, review of *The Amazing Maurice and His Educated Rodents,* p. 842; September 1, 2002, Regina Schroeder, review of *Night Watch,* p. 7;

April 15, 2003, Sally Estes, review of *The Wee Free Men,* p. 1465; August, 2003, Regina Schroeder, review of *Monstrous Regiment,* p. 1927.

Courier-Mail (Brisbane, Australia), July 5, 2003, Jason Nahrung, review of *The Wee Free Men,* p. M8.

Denver Post, May 27, 2001, Candace Horgan, review of *Thief of Time,* p. I6.

Fantasy Review, November, 1986, pp. 31-32.

Financial Times, June 13, 2002, Neil Gaiman, review of *The Amazing Maurice and his Educated Rodents,* p. 4.

Guardian, November 19, 1997, p. T14; November 9, 2002, A.S. Byatt, review of *Night Watch,* p. 27.

Horn Book, March-April, 1990, p. 202; May-June, 1991, p. 332; March-April, 2002, Anita L. Burkam, review of *The Amazing Maurice and His Educated Rodents,* p. 217; May-June, 2003, Anita L. Burkam, review of *The Wee Free Men,* p. 355.

Independent, May 19, 1998, p. 20.

Junior Bookshelf, December, 1990, p. 300; August, 1993, p. 157.

Library Journal, March 15, 2000, Jackie Cassada, review of *The Fifth Elephant,* p. 132; October 1, 2000, Douglas C. Lord, review of *Feet of Clay* and *Guards! Guards! Guards!* (audio versions), p. 165; October 15, 2000, Jackie Cassada, review of *The Truth,* p. 108; March 15, 2001, Douglas C. Lord, reviews of *Hogfather* and *Jingo* (audio versions), p. 126; November 15, 2001, Jackie Cassada, reviews of *The Last Hero,* p. 100, and *Thief of Time,* p. 166; November 15, 2002, Jackie Cassada, review of *Night Watch,* p. 106.

Locus, January, 1989, p. 17; October, 1991, pp. 15, 17; June, 1992, p. 17; September, 1992, p. 66; February, 1993, p. 58.

Magazine of Fantasy and Science Fiction, March, 1998, Michelle West, review of *Maskerade,* p. 31; April, 1999, Michelle West, review of *Hogfather,* p. 36; October, 2000, Michelle West, review of *The Fifth Elephant,* p. 44; March, 2002, review of *The Last Hero,* p. 34.

New Scientist, May 18, 2002, Roger Bridgman, "Narrative Drive: What Makes Us Human?," p. 56; February, 2004, Michelle West, review of *Monstrous Regiment,* p. 35.

New Statesman, August 29, 1986, p. 26; January 29, 1988, p. 30; January 3, 1992, p. 33.

New York Times, September 28, 2003, Kerry Fried, review of *Monstrous Regiment,* p. 21.

New York Times Book Review, October 7, 1990, p. 27; December 15, 2002, Therese Littleton, review of *Night Watch,* p. 28; June 22, 2003, J.D. Biersdorfer, review of *The Wee Free Men,* p. 23; September 28, 2003, Kerry Fried, review of *Monstrous Regiment,* p. 21.

Observer (London, England), August 18, 2002, Rachel Redford, review of *The Amazing Maurice and His Educated Rodents* (audio version), p. 19.

Publishers Weekly, October 26, 1998, review of *Hogfather,* p. 47; September 27, 1999, review of *Carpe Jugulum,* p. 77; March 6, 2000, review of *The Fifth Elephant,* p. 87; October 30, 2000, review of *The Truth,* p. 52; April 9, 2001, review of *Thief of Time,* p. 55; October 15, 2001, review of *The Last Hero,* p. 51; November 5, 2001, review of *The Amazing Maurice and His Educated Rodents,* p. 70; September 30, 2002, review of *Night Watch,* p. 54; May 12, 2003, review of *The Wee Free Men,* p. 68; September 8, 2003, review of *Monstrous Regiment,* p. 61.

School Library Journal, September, 1991, pp. 258-259; August, 1998, Susan Salpini, review of *Jingo,* p. 197; April, 2000, review of *Carpe Jugulum,* p. 162; July, 2000, review of *The Fifth Elephant,* p. 130; August, 2000, Ray Olson, review of *The Truth,* p. 2075; December, 2001, Miranda Doyle, review of *The Amazing Maurice and His Educated Rodents,* p. 142; May, 2003, Sue Giffard, review of *The Wee Free Men,* p. 158.

Science Fiction and Fantasy Book Review, April, 1982, p. 20; March, 1984, p. 35.

Times (London, England), February 12, 1987; August 9, 1990; November 21, 1991, p. 16; December 21, 1997, p. N3; February 4, 1998, p. S6.

Times Literary Supplement, April 28, 1972, p. 475.

Voice of Youth Advocates, February, 1991, p. 366.

Washington Post, December 20, 1990.

Washington Post Book World, February 11, 1990, p. 6; March 27, 1994, p. 11.

ONLINE

Terry Pratchett Books, http://www.terrypratchettbooks.com/ (January 7, 2004).

* * *

PRICE, Edward Reynolds
See PRICE, Reynolds

* * *

PRICE, Reynolds 1933-
(Edward Reynolds Price)

PERSONAL: Born February 1, 1933, in Macon, NC; son of William Solomon and Elizabeth (Rodwell) Price. *Education:* Duke University, A.B. (summa cum laude), 1955; Merton College, Oxford, B. Litt., 1958.

ADDRESSES: Home—813 Duke Station, Box 99014, Durham, NC 27708. *Office*—Department of English, Duke University, 304G Allen Bldg., Durham, NC 27708. *Agent*—Harriet Wasserman Literary Agency, Inc., 137 East 36th St., New York, NY 10016-3528.

CAREER: Duke University, Durham, NC, instructor, 1958-61, assistant professor, 1961-68, associate professor, 1968-72, professor of English, 1972-77, James B. Duke Professor of English, 1977—, acting chair, 1983. Writer-in-residence at University of North Carolina—Chapel Hill, 1965, University of Kansas, 1967, 1969, 1980, and University of North Carolina—Greensboro, 1971; Glasgow Professor, Washington and Lee University, 1971; faculty member, Salzburg Seminar, Salzburg, Austria, 1977. National Endowment for the Arts literature advisory panel, member, 1973-77, chair, 1977.

MEMBER: American Academy and Institute of Arts and Letters, Phi Beta Kappa, Phi Delta Theta.

AWARDS, HONORS: Angier Duke scholar, 1955; Rhodes scholar, 1955-58; William Faulkner Foundation Award for notable first novel, and Sir Walter Raleigh Award, both 1962, both for *A Long and Happy Life;* Guggenheim fellow, 1964-65; National Association of Independent Schools Award, 1964; National Endowment for the Arts fellow, 1967-68; National Institute of Arts and Letters Award, 1971; Bellamann Foundation Award, 1972; Lillian Smith Award, 1976; Sir Walter Raleigh Award, 1976, 1981, 1984, 1986; North Carolina Award, 1977; D. Litt., St. Andrew's Presbyterian College, 1978, Wake Forest University, 1979, Washington and Lee University, 1991, and Davidson College, 1992; National Book Award nomination for translation, 1979, for *A Palpable God;* Roanoke-Chowan Poetry Award, 1982; National Book Critics Circle Award for fiction, 1986, for *Kate Vaiden;* Elmer H. Bobst Award, 1988; Fund for New American Plays grant, 1989, for *New Music;* R. Hunt Parker Award, North Carolina Literary and Historical Society, 1991; finalist for Pulitzer Prize in fiction, 1994, for *The Collected Stories.*

WRITINGS:

NOVELS

A Generous Man, Atheneum (New York, NY), 1966.

A Long and Happy Life, Atheneum (New York, NY), 1987.

Love and Work, Atheneum (New York, NY), 1968.

The Surface of Earth (also see below), Atheneum (New York, NY), 1975.

The Source of Light (also see below), Atheneum (New York, NY), 1981.

Mustian: Two Novels and a Story, Atheneum (New York, NY), 1983.

Kate Vaiden, Atheneum (New York, NY), 1986.

Good Hearts, Atheneum (New York, NY), 1988.

The Tongues of Angels, Atheneum (New York, NY), 1990.

Blue Calhoun, Atheneum (New York, NY), 1992.

Michael Egerton, Creative Education (Mankato, MN), 1993.

The Promise of Rest (also see below), Scribner (New York, NY), 1995.

Roxanna Slade, Scribner (New York, NY), 1998.

A Singular Family, Scribner (New York, NY), 1999.

A Great Circle: The Mayfield Trilogy (contains *The Surface of Earth, The Source of Light,* and *The Promise of Rest*), Scribner (New York, NY), 2001.

Noble Norfleet, Scribner (New York, NY), 2002.

The Good Priest's Son, Scribner (New York, NY), 2005.

SHORT STORIES

The Names and Faces of Heroes, Atheneum (New York, NY), 1963.

Permanent Errors (short stories and novella), Atheneum (New York, NY), 1970.

The Foreseeable Future: Three Long Stories, Atheneum (New York, NY), 1990.

An Early Christmas, North Carolina Wesleyan College Press (Rocky Mount, NC), 1992.

The Collected Stories, Atheneum (New York, NY), 1993.

PLAYS

Early Dark (three-act; adapted from *A Long and Happy Life;* first produced Off-Broadway, 1978), Atheneum (New York, NY), 1977.

Private Contentment, Atheneum (New York, NY), 1984.

New Music (trilogy; contains *August Snow, Night Dance,* and *Better Days;* produced in Cleveland, OH, 1989), Atheneum (New York, NY), 1990.

Night Dance, Dramatists Play Service (New York, NY), 1991.

Better Days, Dramatists Play Service (New York, NY), 1991.

August Snow, Dramatists Play Service (New York, NY), 1991.

Full Moon and Other Plays, Theatre Communications Group (New York, NY), 1993.

POETRY

Late Warnings: Four Poems, Albondocani (New York, NY), 1968.

Lessons Learned: Seven Poems, Albondocani (New York, NY), 1977.

Nine Mysteries: Four Joyful, Four Sorrowful, One Glorious, Palaemon Press (Winston-Salem, NC), 1979.

The Annual Heron, Albondocani (New York, NY), 1980.

Vital Provisions, Atheneum (New York, NY), 1982.

The Laws of Ice, Atheneum (New York, NY), 1986.

House Snake, Lord John (Northridge, CA), 1986.

The Use of Fire, Atheneum (New York, NY), 1990.

The Collected Poems, Scribner (New York, NY), 1997.

OTHER

(Author of introduction) Henry James, *The Wings of the Dove,* C.E. Merrill (Columbus, OH), 1970.

Things Themselves: Essays and Scenes, Atheneum (New York, NY), 1972.

Presence and Absence: Versions from the Bible (originally published as a pamphlet by the Friends of Duke University Library), Bruccoli Clark (Bloomfield Hills, MI), 1973.

The Good News according to Mark, West Coast Print Center (Berkeley, CA), 1976.

Oracles: Six Versions from the Bible, Friends of the Duke University Library (Durham, NC), 1977.

A Palpable God: Thirty Stories Translated from the Bible with an Essay on the Origins and Life of Narrative, Atheneum (New York, NY), 1978.

Christ Child's Song at the End of the Night, R. Price, self-published (Durham, NC), 1978.

A Final Letter, Sylvester and Orphanos, 1980.

Country Mouse, City Mouse (essay), North Carolina Wesleyan College Press (Rocky Mount, NC), 1981.

The Chapel, Duke University, Duke University Press (Durham, NC), 1986.

A Common Room: New and Selected Essays, 1954-1987, Atheneum (New York, NY), 1987.

Real Copies, North Carolina Wesleyan College Press (Rocky Mount, NC), 1988.

Clear Pictures: First Loves, First Guides (memoir), Atheneum (New York, NY), 1989.

Back before Day, North Carolina Wesleyan College Press (Rocky Mount, NC), 1989.

Home Made, North Carolina Wesleyan College Press (Rocky Mount, NC), 1990.

A Whole New Life: An Illness and a Healing (memoir), Atheneum (New York, NY), 1994.

The Honest Account of a Memorable Life: An Apocryphal Gospel, North Carolina Wesleyan College Press (Rocky Mount, NC), 1994.

(Editor and contributor) *The Three Gospels: The Good News according to Mark, the Good News according to John, an Honest Account of a Memorable Life,* Scribner (New York, NY), 1996.

Learning a Trade: A Craftsman's Notebook, 1955-1997, Duke University Press (Raleigh, NC), 1998.

Letter to a Man in the Fire: Does God Exist and Does He Care?, Scribner (New York, NY), 1999.

Feasting the Heart: Fifty-two Commentaries for the Air, Scribner (New York, NY), 2000.

A Perfect Friend (juvenile), Atheneum (New York, NY), 2000.

A Serious Way of Wondering: The Ethics of Jesus Imagined, Scribner (New York, NY), 2003.

Contributor of poetry, reviews, and articles to periodicals, including *Time, Harper's, Saturday Review,* and *Washington Post.* Contributor to books, including *The Arts and the Public,* University of Chicago Press, 1967; and *Symbolism and Modern Literature: Studies in Honor of Wallace Fowlie,* Duke University Press, 1978. Editor, *Archive,* 1954-55; advisory editor, *Shenandoah,* 1964—. Writer, with James Taylor, of song "Copperline."

Price's books have been translated into over sixteen languages, including French, German, and Italian.

ADAPTATIONS: Clear Pictures was the basis for a television program of the same name produced by the Public Broadcasting System (PBS), 1995.

SIDELIGHTS: Reynolds Price wears many hats—novelist, short-story writer, poet, playwright, essayist, teacher—but he is perhaps best known for works that feature the back roads and small towns of his native North Carolina. While Price dislikes the "southern writer" label, he nevertheless acknowledges the influence of venerable southern authors such as Eudora Welty. "One of the things [Welty] showed me as a writer was that the kinds of people I had grown up with were the kind of people one could write marvelous fiction about," he told the *Washington Post.* By concentrating on those aspects of the rural South he is most familiar with, Price has created a body of work noted for both its unique sense of place and offbeat characters. A bout with cancer of the spinal cord left Price paralyzed from the waist down in 1984; while the experience changed the writer's physical world, it also led to one of the most fertile periods of his career, including the publication of his much-acclaimed novel *Kate Vaiden.* Price explained his prolific output to the *Washington Post* by saying: "I don't write with a conscious sense of the hangman at my door, of my own mortality. But I am a tremendously driven person, and I have gotten more so since sitting down. Words just come out of me the way my beard comes out. Who could stop it?"

Price was born in Macon, North Carolina. His father was a traveling salesman who stayed close to home, while his mother was an "eccentric rogue" whose individuality greatly influenced her young son. Early on, Price found he had an aptitude for writing. His skill eventually won him a scholarship to Duke University and, after graduation, a Rhodes scholarship to study at Oxford University. After his return from England, Price accepted a teaching position at Duke University, where his students included Anne Tyler and Josephine Humphries. Price still resides in North Carolina, preferring to remain where he feels most comfortable: near his students in a house filled with memorabilia he affectionately refers to as "a *lotta* stuff."

Price received a great deal of praise for his first novel, *A Long and Happy Life.* Primarily the story of country girl Rosacoke Mustain, *A Long and Happy Life* was especially lauded for its sense of style and strong characterizations. Interestingly, many critics compared the stylistic and thematic concerns of *A Long and Happy Life* to those in Price's highly praised 1986 novel, *Kate Vaiden.* Much of the praise given to both *A Long and Happy Life* and the more recent *Kate Vaiden* relates to Price's strong characterizations of women. According to Elaine Kendall in the *Los Angeles Times Book Review, A Long and Happy Life* "belonged almost entirely to the heroine Rosacoke Mustain, and each of the novels and stories following that stunning debut have been enlightened by unforgettable female protagonists. *Kate Vaiden* is the ultimate extension of Price's thesis, a first-person-singular novel written as the autobiography of a woman coming of age in the South during the Depression and war years." "At once tender and frightening, lyrical and dramatic, this novel is the product of a storyteller working at the height of his artistic powers," Michiko Kakutani commented in the *New York Times.* Price maintained that in focusing on characters like Kate, he was attempting to debunk the idea that "a man cannot 'understand' a woman and vice versa." By giving his female and male characters complex personas and motivations, Price created what he described for Kendall as "a contained look at a human hero," a character who is as much everywoman as everyman.

Carefully drawn characters constitute just one hallmark of Price's work. In novels such as *The Surface of Earth* and *The Source of Light*—which tell the stories of Eva Kendal and Forrest Mayfield and their descendants—he explores the boundaries of narrative, especially those that exist between written and spoken language, and the tension that arises between the individual and the family. "Basically, all my novels and short stories are invented, with little pieces of actual, observed reality and dialogue. The speech of my characters often comes from natives of eastern North Carolina, which is my home country," Price told Herbert Mitgang in the *New York Times.* Price's use of language is also heavily influenced by the Southern oral tradition. This tradition of tale-telling, with its heavy emphasis on history and drama, has offered a wealth of thematic concepts for Price. He told Elizabeth Venant in the *Los Angeles Times Book Review* that, "as long as there remains anything that's recognizably Southern—this strange society with a tremendously powerful black presence in it, its very strong connections with some sort of Christianity, a major heritage as an agrarian society, a slave-owning past, a tragic war fought and lost on the premises—as long as there's any kind of continuing memory of that, then I think literature will continue to rise from it."

Price concludes the story of the Mayfields in *The Promise of Rest.* Set in the 1990s, this novel centers on Hutchins, the grandson of Eva Kendal and Forrest Mayfield, who has become a poet/professor ensconced in his position in the English department at Duke University. He is divorced and his only son has left the family far behind for a life as an architect in New York City. When Hutch discovers that his son is suffering the ravages of AIDS, he travels north to bring the boy home to die. Here, noted John Gregory Brown in the *Los Angeles Times Book Review,* "Price takes on the horror of AIDS, a subject that seems a far departure from the usual bodily tragedies and triumphs of will that run like a swelling stream through the Southern novel." Yet, continued Brown, "this subject is no departure at all, for what is AIDS if not one more of this earth's unspeakable tragedies . . . bringing families together and tearing them apart."

"A book about the death from AIDS of a young man whose only sin was love should be urgent and alarming. It should risk detail," Peter S. Prescott wrote in the

New York Times Book Review. But "Price musters no such feeling, and this is his novel's principal failure." In the opinion of *Washington Post Book World* contributor Bruce Bawer, however, "There is, to be sure, much that is moving and memorable" in *The Promise of Rest.* "Compared to the earlier Mayfield novels, this one is direct, authentic and at times heartbreaking in its urgency; at best, it has a spare spiritual power." Bawer noted Price's depiction of the tension between the goals of the individual and those of the family, but for Bawer, this characteristic weakened the book. "In the end, this book feels at odds with itself," he wrote, "torn between a respect for individual integrity and the notion that family counts above all." Brown conceded that "this novel is less successful than so much of Price's earlier work. But," he continued, "the very sincerity of *The Promise of Rest,* its unflinching gaze, its awful candor, can only leave the reader sad and grateful for such a book."

In *Roxanna Slade* Price presents another strong female protagonist who tells her own story. Once again, the setting is a small North Carolina town. Born in the year 1900, Roxanna recounts her life from her own, feisty, ninety-four-year-old perspective. "Using a first-person narrative plays to Price's strengths," a *Kirkus Reviews* critic noted: "Roxanna's language is frank, seemingly unadorned, but subtly colored both by a tart regional flavor and a nicely idiosyncratic rhythm and pace." Roxanna's life is not an exceptional or distinguished one, but, according to Vanessa V. Friedman in *Entertainment Weekly,* "a life that is quiet—and quietly enthralling." An early tragedy—the drowning death of her first love—causes Roxanna to have a nervous breakdown. After her recovery she eventually marries the older brother of the man she had loved. She has children and grapples with the tasks of being a mother, until she discovers that her husband has engaged in a long-term infidelity. While trying to come to terms with it, she suffers the death of her parents. A *Kirkus Reviews* contributor pointed out that in addition to depicting Roxanna's life, Price "also creates a rich portrait of a community dragged reluctantly out of its venerable agricultural existence into the raucous modern world."

Price drew on his memories of growing up in this "strange society" in order to write the memoir *Clear Pictures: First Loves, First Guides.* Begun during a particularly painful period in the author's convalescence following cancer treatments, *Clear Pictures* covers the first twenty-one years of his life. Price spends a great deal of time discussing the influence of his parents, especially his mother, Elizabeth, who, he admits, was in many ways the model for Kate Vaiden. Price also recreates, in great detail, the small towns that formed the backdrop of his youth: Macon, Asheboro, and Warrenton.

Clear Pictures met with an enthusiastic reception from critics, many of whom were impressed by Price's ability to depict the past in vibrant detail. Jonathan Kirsch in the *Los Angeles Times Book Review* remarked that Price "has returned to the secret world of his own childhood, a place where others have found a threatening and dangerous darkness, but Price discovered only the purest light. To be sure, he found suffering and terror and even death, and he describes them in sometimes heartbreaking detail, but *Clear Pictures* still glows with that bright, healing light." "Remarkable for its Proustian detail," noted Genevieve Stuttaford in *Publishers Weekly,* Price's "lucid biography portrays a mind learning to trust and reach out to the world."

Since his cancer diagnosis, Price has drawn much of his own inspiration from a past made clearer by self-hypnosis. First prescribed as an analgesic for the pain of his illness, self-hypnosis opened a floodgate of memories. "The sensation was so powerful that I felt as if I'd whiffed a potent drug," Price wrote in *Clear Pictures.* "As I began to feel the gathered force of so much past, I turned to write a story I'd planned but never begun." Price also used these memories when writing *The Tongues of Angels,* a novel about a precocious young boy's turbulent stay at summer camp. On one level a very basic look at camp life, *The Tongues of Angels* also contains discussions heavily grounded in philosophic thought. Many of Price's friends were moved by the book, especially those who had attended summer camp themselves. Price expressed his surprise at this development to John Blades of the *Chicago Tribune:* "I hadn't realized what a nerve I was touching. It seems that most of my friends . . . have strong and pleasant memories of their weeks, sometimes years, at summer camp. And they look back with a lot of fondness on the goofy but loveable institution that summer camp was in those days."

Price worked hard to prevent his illness from impeding either his life or his work. A basically happy man who claimed, "I think I am programmed to laugh every five minutes," he declined to discuss his recovery until publishing the memoir *A Whole New Life: An Illness and a Healing.* This book follows Price from the early, unrecognized signs of his cancer through diagnosis, surgery, and other treatments he underwent, to recovery and adaptation to life in a wheelchair. Of Price's account, *Time* contributor William A. Henry III wrote, "Joltingly frank, the dryly written tale ranges from religious visions . . . to matter-of-fact discussions of the mechanics of paraplegic excretion." Geoffrey Wolff commented in the *Washington Post Book World,* "There is about *A Whole New Life* an atmosphere of ferocious sanity and serenity."

A Whole New Life is the story of a man in a battle for his life. As Richard Selzer observed in the *Los Angeles Times Book Review,* "The man who emerges from these pages is feisty, gritty, angry, sometimes snobbish and, notwithstanding, most appealing. He makes no effort to portray himself as a saint or a martyr." Yet, because Price is also a writer, his memoir contains unique insights into a terrible condition. "Rarely if ever has a patient of Price's writerly gifts taken on the story of physical devastation," Henry maintained. "The weight of the subject has somewhat muted and simplified his normally fizzy prose. But the events emerge with awful clarity." Selzer concluded with gratitude that Price was able with time to look back on his experience. "There can be no sweeter use made of adversity than this act of generosity that comes in the form of a book," Selzer wrote.

Noble Norfleet, a novel in the tradition of the Southern gothic, is filled with outlandish happenings. It begins on Easter morning, when the title character, a seventeen-year-old student, awakens. He has lost his virginity the night before in the arms of his Spanish teacher. As the morning unfolds, he finds that his mentally-ill mother—deserted by her husband years before—has murdered his two younger siblings, stabbing them through their hearts with an ice pick. Although Noble's mother is arrested and imprisoned, it is unclear whether she really committed the crimes or if Noble, who is the narrator, is really the guilty party. His story continues, as he is subjected to the homosexual advances of his minister, joins the army and becomes a medic in Viet Nam, and finally returns home. Suzanne Rhodenbaugh, reviewing the novel in the *St. Louis Post-Dispatch,* found the extreme events in *Noble Norfleet* so unbelievable as to render the book "often preposterous." Rhodenbaugh found the characters undeveloped and noted that the narrative "feels cobbled together." In her opinion, "Almost the only parts of this book that read as authentic and earned are the mysterious-crazy comments of the incarcerated, criminally insane mother, and the responses of elderly hospital patients." Linda Richards, a contributor to *January Online,* also felt that *Noble Norfleet* fails to accomplish all its author intended, yet she believed that it is still "a beautiful book. The writing here is superb, the characters finely drawn," Richards continued. "The first two-thirds of the book are nearly perfect. Price spins a beautiful web of tension and dangles many possibilities."

Price has been encouraged by the return of many aspiring young writers to their Southern roots. While some of these authors find inspiration in the fast pace of urban areas like Atlanta, others are rediscovering the storytelling tradition so closely identified with Southern culture. Price has also derived great pleasure and inspiration from his teaching and his students, many of whom maintain contact with the author long after they leave school. When teaching his writing course, he completes the same writing tasks he assigns his students. "I discovered earlier that I couldn't offer only one story for discussion, because the students were afraid of insulting the teacher," Price related to *Publishers Weekly.* "But if I do all the fairly elementary exercises required right from the beginning, that gives the students a truer sense that I'm in the same canoe as they are. They give me a quiet, fresh pair of glasses."

By writing along with his students, Price has also renewed his interest in the short story, a form he put aside for many years. Together with his older stories, stories written during his courses provide the material for *The Collected Stories,* which was nominated for a Pulitzer Prize. Reviewing the collection for the *Washington Post Book World,* Sven Birkerts concluded: "Price is a superb storyteller. His idiom, pitched to the rhythms of natural speech and built up of things seen, touched and tasted, is fresh and compelling, and he homes in unfailingly on the details that matter. This compendium, spanning the work of decades, shows off the full range of his talents."

Price began contributing commentaries to National Public Radio in 1995, and in 2000 many of these were collected in *Feasting the Heart: Fifty-two Commentaries for the Air.* "Recurring themes Price explores with particularly compelling insight include the cultural and emotional blessings of a small-town Southern boyhood, the difficulties—and surprising advantages—of being physically disabled . . . and the richness of his experiences as both a student and a teacher. Price displays an impressive talent for using few words to convey a great deal," reported a *Publishers Weekly* reviewer. A *Booklist* critic was also pleased with the collection, crediting Price with demonstrating "humor, poignancy," and "concision."

Price's *The Collected Poems* appeared in 1997. It brings together three previous volumes—*Vital Provisions,* 1982, *The Laws of Ice,* 1986, and *The Use of Fire,*

1990—along with more than eighty previously uncollected poems written since 1984. John Taylor, writing in *Poetry,* stated: "Here is a thick tome summing up a man's existence." According to Taylor, *The Collected Poems* "traces—especially in the sections written after 1984—a remarkable man's constant efforts to move from 'self-absorption,' as Price phrases it . . . to 'rescue,' by which he means 'a gradual outward look again at the world and other creatures.'" Price's "self-absorption" refers to his paralysis and his daily bouts with pain. Many of the poems have religious content, and Taylor feels that Price's "grappling with Biblical history and Christian eschatology manifests his faith in poetry as a tool not only for apprehending the spiritual but also (and especially) for healing nihilism and despair." Reviewing *The Collected Poems* for *Library Journal,* Graham Christian noted: "Price has always stood apart from contemporary movements in poetry, and although it is true he is not a technical innovator, it would be perilous to ignore him: he has a rare facility for making the strange familiar, and the familiar fresh." Brad Hooper of *Booklist,* who lauded Price as "one of the few true men of letters" in the United States, observed: "Despite his astonishingly wide vocabulary, soaring metaphors, and unhidden intelligence and knowledge, his poems are attractively accessible."

Price's novels, short stories, poems and memoirs often manifest a religious sensibility that reflects not only his upbringing but also his experience as a writer. In *The Three Gospels: The Good New according to Mark, the Good News according to John, an Honest Account of a Memorable Life,* he offers his translation of the gospels of apostles Mark and John as well as his own gospel. The result, according to Larry Woiwode in the *Washington Post Book World,* is a valuable book for anyone desiring a better understanding of these cornerstones of the Christian faith. Price's "prefaces to each are excellent," wrote Woiwode. "In fact, if anyone wanted an introduction to the Gospels, or wondered why they should have one, I would turn them first to Price's book, rather than any contemporary theologian. Price's book is that good, tempering a breadth of scholarly study with his good sense as an intuitive storyteller." The reviewer added that Price's versions make "a wonderfully engrossing book. It moves with a care and lucidity that should offend few . . . and should provide a new perspective for many."

Price's religious interests and concerns can also be found in *Letter to a Man in the Fire: Does God Exist and Does He Care?* In 1997 Price received a letter from a young medical student dying of cancer who asked the author the two questions Price included in the book's title. After speaking with the young man, Price decided that a lecture he was scheduled to deliver should address these questions. This volume expands upon that lecture, exploring the existence of human misery and why a righteous God would allow suffering to exist. To answer the question, Price presents a series of experiences from both his own life and other lives he has witnessed. He also gives examples from the Bible, Buddhist and Hindu scriptures, Dante, T.S. Eliot, and John Milton. Christian, again writing in *Library Journal,* felt that while "Price's ever-engaging prose does not offer new solutions to the problem of evil . . . many readers will gain comfort and insight from his depiction of a noninterfering but deeply loving God." James Wood in the *New Republic* granted that "Price's book is moving, and it is often wise and truthful about the mystery of suffering in a God-directed world." At the same time, Woods continued, *Letter to a Man in the Fire* "descends into circularity and a certain benign simplicity. Price has a weakness for seeing some good in all the defenses of God."

Price turns his storyteller's art to an analysis of the Bible in *A Serious Way of Wondering: The Ethics of Jesus Imagined.* As in his earlier books on religion, he clearly identifies himself as one who believes that Jesus Christ lived, and was a human incarnation of God. Yet he goes on to explore his many disagreements with institutionalized religions. The book had its genesis in lectures about ethics, as demonstrated by Jesus. Covering the gospel stories and filled with digressions on society, ethics, and his own life, the book also includes imagined narratives that illustrate the ways the author believes Christ would have reacted to a homosexual, a suicide, and woman who lives outside of traditional roles. *Booklist* reviewer Donna Chavez called these fictional passages "lucid, intelligent, never self-serving," and stated that "the results of his work are certain to provoke debate." A *Publishers Weekly* writer described the book as "elegant and passionate," and remarked that the stories within "compel us to imagine creatively our engagements with Jesus' teachings and the impact of those teachings on our lives." In an interview with Henry Carrigan for *Publishers Weekly,* Price commented: "I would hope that lots of different kinds of Christians would be able to read these stories and think about particular ethical dilemmas. I would hope that churches might encourage people to invent stories for a variety of ethical situations as a way of helping people to engage deeply the questions raised by those situations. Orthodox and Protestant Christianity has missed the boat on particular ethical issues such as homosexuality, but inventing stories offers us a way to imagine anew what Jesus might have done when confronted with a particular ethical dilemma."

Shortly after graduating from Duke University in 1955 Price began keeping a notebook "to set down in a single place anything . . . that seemed of possible use to the writer I meant to be." *Learning a Trade: A Craftsman's Notebook, 1955-1997* presents more than forty years of such entries. Hooper, again writing in *Booklist,* stated: "The entries are hardly what could be called scribbling or jottings, because Price's famous eloquence (his penchant for luxurious metaphors and mixing down-home conversational style with 'big-wordism') is manifest in every perfectly executed sentence." A reviewer for *Publishers Weekly* felt that the lack of annotation "makes individual sections nearly incomprehensible if one has not read the titles in question," but also noted that the "dynamics of Price's creative process—complete with stops and restarts, repetitions and second thoughts—are illustrated in impressive detail." Reviewing *Leaning a Trade* for *Library Journal,* Henry L. Carrigan, Jr. commented: "The sketches for stories and novels, from *A Long and Happy Life* to . . . *Roxanna Slade,* as well as reflections on his teachers, family, and friends, give us a rare glimpse of the development of one of our master craftsmen. . . . To read these notebooks is to glimpse into the growth of a writer from apprentice to master."

BIOGRAPHICAL AND CRITICAL SOURCES:

BOOKS

Contemporary Literary Criticism, Thomson Gale (Detroit, MI), Volume 3, 1975, Volume 6, 1976, Volume 13, 1980, Volume 43, 1987, Volume 50, 1988, Volume 63, 1991.

Contemporary Novelists, 7th edition, St. James Press (Detroit, MI), 2001.

Contemporary Southern Writers, St. James Press (Detroit, MI), 1999.

Dictionary of Literary Biography, Thomson Gale (Detroit, MI), Volume 2: *American Novelists since World War II,* 1978, Volume 218: *American Short-Story Writers since World War II, Second Series,* 1999; Volume 278: *American Novelists since World War II, Seventh Series,* 2003.

Humphries, Jefferson, editor, *Conversations with Reynolds Price,* University Press of Mississippi (Jackson, MS), 1991.

Kimball, Sue Leslie, and Lynn Veach Sadler, editors, *Reynolds Price: From "A Long and Happy Life" to "Good Hearts,"* Methodist College Press (Fayetteville, NC), 1989.

Ray, William, *Conversations: Reynolds Price and William Ray,* Memphis State University (Memphis, TN), 1976.

Schiff, James A., *Understanding Reynolds Price,* University of South Carolina Press (Columbia, SC), 1996.

Schiff, James A., editor, *Critical Essays on Reynolds Price,* G.K. Hall, 1998.

PERIODICALS

America, October 15, 1988, p. 259; July 28, 1990, p. 67; August 31, 1991, p. 121; March 16, 1996, p. 18.

Atlanta Journal and Constitution, May 10, 1992, p. N8; June 14, 1992, p. N10; May 29, 1994, p. N8; August 14, 1994, p. M1; May 28, 1995, p. K10; May 31, 1995, p. C2; September 28, 2002, Phil Kloer, "Overachieving Visit for Prolific Price," p. C2.

Booklist, January 1, 1999, review of *Roxanna Slade,* p. 779; March 1, 1999, Brad Hooper, review of *Letter to a Man in the Fire: Does God Exist and Does He Care?,* p. 1131; August, 1999, review of *The Promise of Rest,* p. 2024, review of *Roxanna Slade,* p. 2025; October 15, 2000, Brad Hooper, review of *Feasting the Heart: Fifty-two Commentaries for the Air,* p. 410; November 15, 2000, Gillian Engberg, review of *A Perfect Friend,* p. 642; June 1, 2001, Joanne Wilkinson, review of *Blue Calhoun,* p. 1838; May 1, 1997, p. 1475; February 15, 1998, p. 948; November 15, 1998, p. 561; January 1, 1999, p. 779; March 1, 1999, p. 1131; June 1, 2003, Donna Chavez, review of *A Serious Way of Wondering: The Ethics of Jesus Imagined,* p. 1713.

Boston Globe, June 2, 1992, p. 55; June 6, 1993, p. B41; May 21, 1995, p. 77.

Chicago Tribune, May 11, 1990; May 26, 1994, section 5, p. 2; February 11, 1996, section 15, p. 1.

Christian Century, July 10, 1991, p. 678; November 23, 1994, p. 1108; November 22, 1995, p. 1128; June 5, 1996, p. 633; August 9, 2003, review of *A Serious Way of Wondering,* p. 32.

Christian Science Monitor, June 25, 1986, p. 21; June 8, 1992, p. 14.

Commonweal, August 12, 1988, p. 438; December 1, 1989, p. 678; May 22, 1992, p. 17; December 3, 1993, p. 22; June 17, 1994, p. 24; December 2, 1994, pp. 24, 29; September 11, 1998, p. 41.

Detroit News, July 17, 1989.

Entertainment Weekly, June 5, 1998, p. 77.

Globe and Mail (Toronto, Ontario, Canada), July 2, 1988.

Horn Book, September, 2000, review of *A Perfect Friend,* p. 580.

Interpretation, January, 2000, Dwight N. Peterson, review of *Letter to a Man in the Fire,* p. 104.

Kirkus Reviews, April 1, 1998, review of *Roxanna Slade,* p. 304.

Library Journal, April 1, 1997, p. 98; April 15, 1998, p. 116; February 1, 1999, p. 88; May 1, 1999, Graham Christian, review of *Letter to a Man in the Fire,* p. 86; June 15, 2003, review of *A Serious Way of Wondering,* p. 78.

London Review of Books, April 23, 1987, p. 18.

Los Angeles Times, July 12, 1993, p. E3.

Los Angeles Times Book Review, July 10, 1986; May 17, 1987, p. 13; January 3, 1988, p. 10; May 22, 1988, p. 3; August 3, 1989; May 27, 1990, p. 3; July 22, 1990, p. 14; June 16, 1991, p. 7; June 21, 1992, p. 12; May 22, 1994, pp. 1, 8; May 7, 1995, p. 1; July 16, 1995, pp. 4, 15.

Nation, July 30, 1990, p. 139; March 13, 1995, p. 58; March 20, 1995, pp. 391-394; June 15, 1998, p. 30.

National Review, June 7, 1993, p. 68; October 24, 1994, p. 73.

New England Journal of Medicine, June 23, 1994, p. 1834.

New Republic, September 29, 1986, p. 40; July 4, 1988, p. 34; February 1, 1999, p. 42.

Newsweek, June 23, 1986, p. 78; July 17, 1989, p. 54.

New Yorker, September 22, 1986, p. 116; August 14, 1989, p. 91.

New York Review of Books, September 25, 1986, p. 55.

New York Times, June 24, 1986; January 4, 1987; June 26, 1989; August 26, 1989; November 4, 1989; May 8, 1992, p. C28; May 18, 1996, p. 7.

New York Times Book Review, June 29, 1986, p. 1; February 14, 1988, p. 21; May 8, 1988, p. 10; June 4, 1989, p. 10; May 13, 1990, p. 13; July 7, 1991, p. 5; May 24, 1992, p. 10; February 28, 1993, p. 1; July 4, 1993, p. 8; July 10, 1994, p. 9; May 14, 1995, p. 9; May 19, 1996, p. 12; January 24, 1999, Renee Tursi, review of *Learning a Trade: A Craftsman's Notebooks, 1955-1997,* p. 18; May 3, 1999, p. 25; May 23, 1999, Edward Hirsch, review of *Letter to a Man in the Fire,* p. 25; July 12, 1998; January 24, 1999; May 23, 1999; June 23, 2002, Tony Earley, review of *Noble Norfleet,* p. 7.

Observer (London, England), February 22, 1987, p. 29.

Palm Beach Post, March 25, 2001, Scott Eyman, review of *Feasting the Heart,* p. 6J.

People, May 11, 1999, p. 48.

Poetry, August, 1991, pp. 282-284; January, 1998, p. 227.

Publishers Weekly, March 13, 1987; April 21, 1989; December 15, 1989; January 24, 1991; March 14, 1994, p. 55; May 9, 1994, p. 51; January 8, 1996, p. 25; April 8, 1996, p. 60; May 26, 1997, p. 81; February 2, 1998, p. 78; November 16, 1998, p. 64; February 22, 1999, p. 81; November 1, 1999, review of *Letter to a Man in the Fire,* p. 51; August 14, 2000, review of *A Perfect Friend,* p. 355; October 2, 2000, review of *Feasting the Heart,* p. 70; May 27, 2002, review of *Noble Norfleet,* p. 33; May 12, 2003, review of *A Serious Way of Wondering,* p. 61, Henry Carrigan, interview with Price, p. 62.

St. Louis Post-Dispatch, June 9, 2002, Suzanne Rhodenbaugh, review of *Noble Norfleet,* p. F10.

San Francisco Review of Books, July, 1995, pp. 25-27.

School Library Journal, February, 2001, Helen Foster James, review of *A Perfect Friend,* p. 122.

Seattle Times, June 23, 2002, Robert Allen Papinchak, review of *Noble Norfleet,* p. K10.

Southern Living, September, 1990, p. 126; September, 1992, p. 38; May, 1994, p. 142.

Southern Review, autumn, 1980, p. 853; spring, 1986, p. 329; summer, 1988, p. 686; spring, 1992, pp. 371-89; winter, 1993, p. 16; spring, 2000, James Schiff, review of *Learning a Trade,* p. 429.

Studies in the Literary Imagination, spring, 2002, Victor Strandberg, "The Religious/Erotic Poetry of Reynolds Price," p. 61.

Tennessean, August 24, 2003, Ray Waddle, review of *A Serious Way of Wondering,* p. D16.

Time, July 10, 1989, p. 62; May 14, 1990, p. 89; May 23, 1994, pp. 66-67; May 22, 1995, p. 73.

Times (London, England), February 5, 1987.

Times Literary Supplement, May 22, 1987, p. 558.

Tribune Books (Chicago, IL), January 25, 1987, p. 6; December 13, 1987, p. 3; April 17, 1988, p. 6; June 26, 1988, p. 1; June 11, 1989, p. 6; May 6, 1990, p. 3; June 2, 1991, p. 6; May 16, 1993, p. 1; September 25, 1994, p. 5; June 11, 1995, p. 3.

USA Today, June 27, 1986, p. D4; May 13, 1992, p. D4; June 18, 1993, p. D4; February 11, 1994, p. D7.

U.S. Catholic, September, 1999, Patrick McCormick, review of *Letter to a Man in the Fire,* p. 46.

Variety, March 21, 1994, p. 66.

Voice Literary Supplement, June, 1988, p. 13.

Wall Street Journal, June 26, 1992, p. A9.

Washington Post, September 7, 1986; January 13, 1987.

Washington Post Book World, July 6, 1986, p. 1; February 14, 1988, p. 6; April 10, 1988, p. 5; June 18, 1989, p. 3; May 6, 1990, p. 3; June 2, 1991, p. 1; May 10, 1992, p. 5; May 30, 1993, pp. 1, 7; June 12, 1994, pp. 1, 10; July 16, 1995, p. 4; May 5, 1996, pp. 4-5.

World Literature Today, spring, 1994, pp. 370-371; summer, 2000, Marvin J. LaHood, review of *Letter to a Man in the Fire,* p. 607.

ONLINE

January Magazine, http://www.januarymagazine.com/ (June, 2002), Linda Richards, review of *Noble Norfleet.*

MetroActive, http://www.metroactive.com/ (November 10, 2003), David Templeton, "The Vision Thing."

* * *

PROSE, Francine 1947-

PERSONAL: Born April 1, 1947, in Brooklyn, NY; daughter of Philip (a physician) and Jessie (a physician; maiden name, Rubin) Prose; married Howard Michels (a sculptor), September 24, 1976; children: Bruno, Leon. *Education:* Radcliffe College, B.A., 1968; Harvard University, M.A., 1969. *Religion:* Jewish.

ADDRESSES: *Home*—New York, NY. *Agent*—Georges Borchardt, Georges Borchardt, Inc., 136 East 57th St., New York, NY 10022.

CAREER: Writer and book reviewer. Harvard University, Cambridge, MA, teacher of creative writing, 1971-72; University of Arizona, Tucson, visiting lecturer in fiction, 1982-84; Warren Wilson College, Swannanoa, NC, member of faculty in master of fine arts program, beginning 1984. Instructor at Bread Loaf Writers Conference, summer, 1984; has also taught at the Iowa Writers' Workshop, the Sewanee Writers' Conference, and Johns Hopkins University.

MEMBER: PEN, Associated Writing Programs.

AWARDS, HONORS: Jewish Book Council Award, 1973, for *Judah the Pious;* MLLE Award, *Mademoiselle,* 1975; Edgar Lewis Wallant Memorial Award, Hartford Jewish Community Center, 1984, for *Hungry Hearts;* finalist, National Book Award, 2000, for *Blue Angel.*

WRITINGS:

FICTION, EXCEPT AS NOTED

Judah the Pious, Atheneum (New York, NY), 1973.

The Glorious Ones, Atheneum (New York, NY), 1974.

Marie Laveau, Berkley Publishing (New York, NY), 1977.

Animal Magnetism, Putnam (New York, NY), 1978.

Household Saints, St. Martin's Press (New York, NY), 1981.

Hungry Hearts, Pantheon (New York, NY), 1983.

Bigfoot Dreams, Pantheon (New York, NY), 1986.

Women and Children First (short stories), Pantheon (New York, NY), 1988.

Primitive People, Farrar, Straus & Giroux (New York, NY), 1992.

The Peaceable Kingdom (short stories), Farrar, Straus & Giroux (New York, NY), 1993.

Hunters and Gatherers, Farrar, Straus & Giroux (New York, NY), 1995.

Guided Tours of Hell (novellas), Holt (New York, NY), 1997.

Blue Angel, HarperCollins (New York, NY), 2000.

Household Saints, HarperCollins (New York, NY), 2003.

NONFICTION

(With others) *On Writing Short Stories,* edited by Tom Bailey, Oxford University Press (New York, NY), 2000.

The Lives of the Muses: Nine Women and the Artists They Inspired, HarperCollins (New York, NY), 2002.

Sicilian Odyssey, National Geographic Society (Washington, DC), 2003.

Gluttony: The Seven Deadly Sins, New York Public Library (New York, NY), 2003.

(Editor) *The Mrs. Dalloway Reader,* Harcourt (Orlando, FL), 2003.

YOUNG ADULT FICTION

After (young adult novel), HarperCollins (New York, NY), 2003.

A Changed Man (novel), HarperCollins (New York, NY), 2005.

CHILDREN'S FICTION

Stories from Our Living Past (Jewish tales; includes teacher's guide), illustrated by Erika Weihs, Behrman (New York, NY), 1974.

Dybbuk: A Story Made in Heaven, illustrated by Mark Podwal, Greenwillow (New York, NY), 1996.

(Reteller) *The Angel's Mistake: Stories of Chelm* (folklore), illustrated by Mark Podwal, Greenwillow (New York, NY), 1997.

You Never Know: A Legend of the Lamed-Vavniks (folklore), illustrated by Mark Podwal, Greenwillow (New York, NY), 1998.

The Demon's Mistake: A Story from Chelm (folklore), illustrated by Mark Podwal, Greenwillow (New York, NY), 2000.

Leopold, the Liar of Leipzig, illustrated by Einav Aviram, Joanna Cotler Books (New York, NY), in press.

TRANSLATOR

(With Madeline Levine) Ida Fink, *A Scrap of Time: And Other Stories,* Pantheon (New York, NY), 1987.

(With Joanna Weschler) Ida Fink, *The Journey,* Farrar, Straus & Giroux (New York, NY), 1992.

Carter Wilson, *A Green Tree and a Dry Tree* (fiction), University of New Mexico Press (Albuquerque, NM), 1995.

(With Philip Boehm) Ida Fink, *Traces: Short Stories,* Metropolitan Books (New York, NY), 1997.

Contributor of fiction and articles to periodicals, including *Mademoiselle, Redbook, Harper's Bazaar, Glamour, New York Times Magazine, Atlantic, Village Voice, Elle, O, Redbook, Real Simple, Victoria,* and *Commentary.* Contributor of essay to *Elizabeth Murray: Paintings, 1999-2003: March 7-April 19, 2003,* PaceWildenstein (New York, NY), 2003.

SIDELIGHTS: Francine Prose has enjoyed a long and accomplished career as an author of unique novels and short stories for adults and also for children, works of fiction that blend elements of the real with the fantastic. She published her first novel, *Judah the Pious,* when she was in her twenties, and many critics praised it as a work beyond its author's years. The story is about an eighteenth-century rabbi who teaches the King of Poland that there are some things in the world that defy ordinary reason. In this book, Prose first demonstrates techniques, themes, and writing styles that appear throughout her body of work. Her deceptively simple style and fanciful subject matter lend themselves well to her later children's stories.

Prose has added elements of the fanciful, allegorical, or magical to nearly every book she has written, whether it is the voodoo conjured by title character Marie Laveau in the novel set in nineteenth-century New Orleans, the strange belief in a "universal fluid" that connects all creatures and can do almost anything in *Animal Magnetism,* or the confusion between appearances and reality and elements of spirituality in *Hungry Hearts.* Some of these books, such as *Hungry Hearts* and *Judah the Pious,* have Jewish characters, but most of Prose's adult titles cover a diverse range of people, including seventeenth-century Italian actors in *The Glorious Ones,* the half-Black title character in *Marie Laveau,* or the modern-day tabloid journalist in *Bigfoot Dreams.*

While Prose's adult works have touched on various subjects, her fiction for children, which she began writing in earnest in the mid-1990s, all has a basis in Jewish folklore. Her first children's book, *Stories from Our Living Past,* is a collection of Jewish tales published only a year after her debut novel. With her second work for a younger audience, however, Prose took liberties with tradition for the sake of the story.

In *Dybbuk: A Story Made in Heaven,* the author combines the Jewish legend, about how angels in heaven match lovers before they are born, with the folklore story of the supernatural dybbuk. Leah and Chonon are two youngsters from nearby shtetls who fall in love, but Leah's parents want her to marry Benya, an old, mean man who is rich. Just when she is about to be forced to marry Benya, Leah begins to talk and sneeze the same way that Chonon does. The rabbi declares that she is possessed by Chonon's dybbuk, and nothing can be done to help her until the two lovers are allowed to wed. Reviewers such as Hazel Rochman of *Booklist* found the story "wonderfully theatrical; there's no way to read this without acting the parts and laughing out loud." *Bulletin of the Center for Children's Books* commentator Betsy Hearne wrote: "It's fun and it's funny—one of those picture books which, by staying true to an ethnic tradition, reaches beyond it as well."

In the role of reteller in *The Angel's Mistake: Stories of Chelm,* Prose presents the Jewish legend of a town inhabited entirely by foolish people. The founders of Chelm, the legend goes, arrived on Earth when two angels accidentally dropped a bag of foolish souls and they all ended up in one spot instead of scattered through the world as intended. The townspeople do such ridiculous things as wear their hats upside down to keep them dry and carry a huge rock up a mountain to let it roll down because that is supposedly easier than carrying it to its original destination. The villagers burn the town down after lighting a fire that goes out of control when the firemen try to smother it with wooden logs, and the fools finally scatter across the countryside as the angels had first planned. Hanna B. Zeiger, writing in *Horn Book,* called Prose's retelling "a pleasant addition to the many stories of Chelm." The author's matter-of-fact tone, which is characteristic of her adult fiction, makes the Chelmites' exploits all the more funny. As one *Kirkus Reviews* critic noted, Prose has created an "understated, humorous narrative. Families will find this a savory treat for sharing."

Prose continues to alternate between adult fiction and books on Jewish folklore for children, including the more recent *You Never Know: A Legend of the Lamed-Vavniks.* This story is about a simple cobbler, Poor Stupid Schmuel. Because of his habit of fixing shoes for free, he is thought by the town to be a fool. But when his successful prayers end both a drought and a flood, they realize that he is instead a Lamed-Vavnik, one of the thirty-six righteous men born in every generation. *You Never Know* was praised as "fresh and memorable" by a *Publishers Weekly* critic and as "an excellent read-aloud" by *School Library Journal* contributor Susan Scheps.

Prose branched out into the YA genre with *After,* a story about the lingering effects of a school shooting. After the shooting at Pleasant Valley High, nearby Central High is taken over by purported grief counselor Dr. Willner. But instead of providing counseling, Willner instead turns Central into a virtual prison. Protagonist Tom's friends are caught up in Willner's web of control, and some are sent away and never heard from again. Eventually, Tom learns that the repression at his school is only a small part of a wider plan: students all across the country are being sent away to gulag-style camps as part of the so-called "Operation Turnaround." As Tom gains more knowledge of these events, he and his friend Becca fight against the evil administration and their brainwashed parents, risking their lives in the process. "Because the narrative is kept faithfully inside [Tom's] mind, readers are skillfully left just as unsettled, frightened, and confused as he is himself," commented a *Kirkus Reviews* critic.

After "raises all-too-relevant questions about the fine line between safety as a means of protection versus encroachment on individual rights and free will," noted a *Publishers Weekly* contributor. This was the point, as Prose explained in an interview for *Publishers Weekly:* "I'd been doing a lot of thinking about the new security measures . . . taken in schools since the Columbine shootings. I'd even heard that a hotline had been formed for students to report any kids acting 'weird' at their school. I mean really, don't all kids act weird in adolescence? The issue of security and the loss of civil liberties are suddenly so much in our culture, but no one's asking kids how they feel about it."

BIOGRAPHICAL AND CRITICAL SOURCES:

BOOKS

Contemporary Literary Criticism, Volume 45, Thomson Gale (Detroit, MI), 1987.

Dictionary of Literary Biography, Volume 234: *American Short-Story Writers since World War II,* Thomson Gale (Detroit, MI), 2001.

PERIODICALS

Booklist, April 15, 1996, Hazel Rochman, review of *Dybbuk: A Story Made in Heaven,* p. 1444; June 1, 1998, Hazel Rochman, review of *You Never Know: A Legend of the Lamed-Vavniks,* p. 1774; August, 2000, Hazel Rochman, review of *The Demons' Mistake: A Story from Chelm,* p. 2144; June 1, 2003, Bill Ott, review of *After,* p. 1762.

Bulletin of the Center for Children's Books, April, 1996, Betsy Hearne, review of *Dybbuk,* p. 276; July-August, 1997, p. 408.

Horn Book, July-August, 1997, Hanna B. Zeiger, review of *The Angel's Mistake: Stories of Chelm,* p. 468; July-August, 1998, Hanna B. Zeiger, review of *You Never Know,* p. 504; May-June, 2003, Roger Sutton, review of *After,* p. 357.

Kirkus Reviews, March 1, 1996, p. 379; April 15, 1997, review of *The Angel's Mistake,* p. 648; March 15, 2003, review of *After,* p. 476.

Knight Ridder/Tribune News Services, April 11, 2001, Marta Salij, interview with Prose, p. 4830.

Los Angeles Times, October 14, 2002, Susan Salter Reynolds, interview with Prose, p. E-11.

Nation, June 16, 2003, review of *After,* p. 41.

New York Times Book Review, October 18, 1998, Robin Tzannes, review of *You Never Know,* p. 31.

Publishers Weekly, February 12, 1996, review of *Dybbuk,* p. 71; April 28, 1997, review of *The Angel's Mistake,* p. 76; May 18, 1998, review of *You Never Know,* p. 79; August 28, 2000, review of *The Demons' Mistake,* p. 83; February 24, 2003, interview with Prose, p. 72, and review of *After,* p. 73.

School Library Journal, April, 1996, Marcia W. Posner, review of *Dybbuk,* pp. 127-128; August, 1998, Susan Scheps, review of *You Never Know,* p. 154; October, 2000, Teri Markson, review of *The Demons' Mistake,* p. 152; May, 2003, Vicki Reutter, review of *After,* p. 160.

ONLINE

Atlantic Unbound, http://www.theatlantic.com/ (March 11, 1998), Katie Bolick, "As the World Thrums: A Conversation with Prose."

Barnes & Noble.com, http://www.barnesandnoble.com/ (November 6, 2003), Jamie Brenner, interview with Prose.

Bookreporter.com, http://www.bookreporter.com/ (July 28, 2000), interview with Prose.

* * *

PROULX, Annie
See PROULX, E. Annie

* * *

PROULX, E. Annie 1935-
(Annie Proulx, Edna Annie Proulx)

PERSONAL: Surname is pronounced "Pru"; born August 22, 1935, in Norwich, CT; daughter of George Napolean and Lois Nelly (Gill) Proulx; married and divorced three times, including James Hamilton Lang, 1969 (divorced 1990), children: Jon Lang, Gillis Lang, Morgan Lang, Muffy Clarkson. *Education:* Attended Colby College; University of Vermont, Burlington, B.A. (cum laude), 1969; Sir George Williams University (now Concordia University), M.A., 1973, enrolled in Ph.D. program until 1975. *Hobbies and other interests:* Fishing, canoeing, skiing, bicycling, reading.

ADDRESSES: Home—Wyoming. *Office*—c/o Scribner Publishing Co., 866 3rd Ave. Fl. 7, New York, NY 10022. *Agent*—Liz Darhansoff, Darhansoff, Verrill, Felman Literary Agents, 236 W. 26th St., New York, NY 10001.

CAREER: Writer of articles, book reviews, and fiction and nonfiction books, 1975—. Founder and editor of rural Vermont newspaper *Behind the Times,* 1984-86.

MEMBER: PEN, Phi Beta Kappa, Phi Alpha Theta.

AWARDS, HONORS: Kress fellow, Harvard University, 1974; Gardens Writers of America Award, 1986; Vermont Council on the Arts fellowship, 1989; National Endowment for the Arts grant, 1991; Guggenheim fellow, 1992; PEN/Faulkner Award for Fiction, 1993, for *Postcards;* National Book Critics Circle Award nomination for best fiction, National Book Award for fiction, *Chicago Tribune* Heartland Prize for Fiction, and *Irish Times* International Fiction Prize, all 1993, and Pulitzer Prize for fiction, 1994, all for *The Shipping News;* honorary D.H.L., University of Maine, 1994; Dos Passos Prize for Literature, 1996, for *Accordion Crimes;* National Magazine award, 1998, and O. Henry Prize, both for *Brokeback Mountain;* award for fiction, *New Yorker,* 2000, for *Close Range: Wyoming Stories;* Best Foreign Language Novels of 2002/Best American Novel Award, Chinese Publishing Association and Peoples' Literature Publishing House, 2002, for *That Old Ace in the Hole.*

WRITINGS:

Heart Songs and Other Stories, Scribner (New York, NY), 1988.

Postcards (novel), Scribner (New York, NY), 1992.

The Shipping News (novel), Scribner (New York, NY), 1993.

Accordion Crimes (novel), Scribner (New York, NY), 1996.

(Under name Annie Proulx) *Brokeback Mountain* (short story; also see below), Fourth Estate (London, England), 1998, Scribner (New York, NY), 2005.

(Under name Annie Proulx) *Close Range: Wyoming Stories,* watercolors by William Matthews, Scribner (New York, NY), 1999.

(Under name Annie Proulx) *That Old Ace in the Hole* (novel), Scribner (New York, NY), 2002.

(Under name Annie Proulx) *Bad Dirt: Wyoming Stories 2,* Scribner (New York, NY), 2004.

(Under name Annie Proulx; with Larry McMurtry and Diana Ossana) *Brokeback Mountain: Story to Screenplay,* Scribner (New York, NY), 2006.

OTHER

(With Lew Nichols) *Sweet and Hard Cider: Making It, Using It, and Enjoying It,* Garden Way (Charlotte, VT), 1980, third edition, under name Annie Proulx, published as *Cider: Making, Using, and Enjoying Sweet and Hard Cider,* Storey Publications (North Adams, MA), 2003.

"What'll You Take for It?": Back to Barter, Garden Way (Charlotte, VT), 1981.

(With Lew Nichols) *The Complete Dairy Foods Cookbook: How to Make Everything from Cheese to Custard in Your Kitchen,* Rodale Press (Emmaus, PA), 1982.

The Gardener's Journal and Record Book, Rodale Press (Emmaus, PA), 1983.

Plan and Make Your Own Fences and Gates, Walkways, Walls, and Drives, Rodale Press (Emmaus, PA), 1983.

The Fine Art of Salad Gardening, Rodale Press (Emmaus, PA), 1985.

The Gourmet Gardener: Growing Choice Fruits and Vegetables with Spectacular Results, illustrated by Robert Byrd, Fawcett Columbine (New York, NY), 1987.

Contributor of stories to anthologies, including *Fiction, Flyfishing, and the Search for Innocence,* Birch Brook Press, 1994; contributor of essay to Andrea Modica, *Treadwell: Photographs,* Chronicle Books (San Francisco, CA), 1996. Contributor of articles to periodicals, including *African Arts, Equinox, New York Times, National Wildlife, Yankee, Down East, Country Journal, Outside, Chicago Tribune, Walking,* and *Horticulture;* contributor of short stories to *Ploughshares, Gray's Sporting Journal, Seventeen, Esquire,* and *Harrowsmith.*

ADAPTATIONS: *The Shipping News* was adapted for film in 2001 and released by Miramax. Larry McMurtry and Dianna Ossana adapted *Brokeback Mountain* for a film directed by Ang Lee, released 2005.

SIDELIGHTS: In both short fiction and novels that show how human resilience is shaped and honed in harsh, rusticated, sometimes merciless, yet ultimately beautiful geographic outposts, E. Annie Proulx captures a unique facet of the mythic American character. It is a facet that she has embodied in her own life as a writer, going against the odds by raising three sons, supporting her family by working as a freelance journalist, and slowly establishing herself as a unique literary stylist and a consumate storyteller. In the late 1980s Proulx's writing career finally blossomed, earning her much critical and public acclaim for her fiction. Her 1992 novel, *Postcards,* won the PEN/Faulkner Award for Fiction, while *The Shipping News,* published a year later, received numerous honors, including the National Book Award and a Pulitzer Prize. Proulx is also the author of the short story *Brokeback Mountain.* Originally published in London, England, in 1998, the story, which is about two homosexual cowboys in 1960s Wyoming, was adapted and released in 2005 as a widely publicized and controversial American film.

Born in Connecticut, Proulx attended Colby College, and then studied history at the University of Vermont and Sir George Williams University (now renamed Concordia University), where she earned her M.A. in 1973. She then worked as a freelance writer, "a classic example of shifting from the frying pan to the fire," as she once explained. Living in northern Vermont "in brutally poor circumstances," she wrote articles on "weather, apples, canoeing, mountain lions, mice, cuisine, libraries, African beadwork, cider and lettuces" for magazines. In between, she penned short stories, at the rate, as she recalled, of "about two a year."

Proulx related her experiences moving from writing nonfiction to producing the nine tales collected in *Heart Songs and Other Stories,* telling John Blades of the *Chicago Tribune:* "After 19 years of writing tedious nonfiction, all these stories were just bottled up inside me, waiting to get out. Now writing fiction is sheer play." Assessing the volume, Elaine Kendall of the *Los Angeles Times* described *Heart Songs* as "hard stories set in a bleak climate; a closed, narrow world hostile to strangers and rough on its own." Set in northern New England, the stories in *Heart Songs* feature characters that Kenneth Rosen, writing in the *New York Times Book Review,* called "shy, battered, depleted." As they would with her subsequent fiction, some critics remarked upon the strange names of Proulx's characters and what reviewer Kendall called "a terse quirky humor" displayed in several stories. Of Proulx's tales, Rosen concluded: "Their sometimes enigmatic, often lyrical images seem to complement New England's lavish but barren beauty."

Each chapter of Proulx's first novel, *Postcards,* begins with a postcard connected in some way to the character Loyal Blood or to the parents and siblings Blood left behind after the ambiguous death of his girlfriend. The Blood family has worked their farm in New England for generations, but with Loyal's departure a decline begins, and through descriptions of his aimless wanderings over the next thirty years, *Postcards* documents the slow death of the small American family farm.

Reviewers praised *Postcards* for its commentary on the American condition, but reserved their most lavish accolades for Proulx's abilities as a storyteller. Frederick Busch of the *Chicago Tribune Book World* stated: "What makes this rich, dark and brilliant feast of a book is its furious action, its searing contemplations, its language born of the fury and the searching and the author's powerful sense of the gothic soul of New England." David Bradley, writing in the *New York Times*

Book Review, concluded: "Story makes this novel compelling; technique makes it beautiful. What makes *Postcards* significant is that Ms. Proulx uses both story and technique to make real the history of post-World War II America."

The thread that connects Proulx's second novel, *The Shipping News*, to her earlier fiction is its setting in a hostile climate. Newfoundland, a remote Canadian province known for its sudden storms and icy seas, provides the harsh backdrop to the story of Quoyle, a huge, hapless journalist living in upstate New York. His unfaithful wife dies in a car wreck, leaving him with their two daughters and an overwhelming grief. When Quoyle's aunt arrives she easily convinces him to pack up his family and travel to Newfoundland to reclaim the family land and start over. According to a reviewer for the *Atlantic:* "Proulx blends Newfoundland argot, savage history, impressively diverse characters, fine descriptions of weather and scenery, and comic horseplay without ever lessening the reader's interest in Quoyle's progress."

The Shipping News received an outpouring of critical acclaim upon its release. Howard Norman in the *New York Times Book Review* acknowledged "Proulx's surreal humor and her zest for the strange foibles of humanity." Emphasizing the effect of the watery setting of *The Shipping News* on the reader, Stephen Jones of the *Chicago Tribune Book World* asserted: "In spite of Proulx's invitations to dream in the coves, her plot rushes out of a confluence between the force of the characters and their environment to buoy you on. The result is that rare creation, a lyric page turner."

Proulx told Nicci Gerrard of the London *Observer:* "Eight years ago, I was looking for canoeing waters and I unfolded an old map of Newfoundland. Each place-name had a story—Dead Man's Cove, Seldom Come Bay and Bay of Despair, Exploits River, Plunder Beach. I knew I had to go there, and within 10 minutes of arriving, I'd fallen in love. I am pulled by the harshness of the weather, the strength of the landscape which is dark and stormy and rough, . . . the sense of a land holding its own against people."

Following on the commercial and critical success of *The Shipping News*, Proulx produced *Accordion Crimes*. A novel in the picaresque tradition, this work follows an accordion as it moves from owner to owner during the span of a century. Proulx uses this technique as a forum in which to discuss the immigrant experience in America, with the novel's nine sections each set among a different ethnic group: a German settlement in Iowa; a Louisiana Cajun family; and a Mexican immigrant in Texas, among others. The accordion's change-of-ownership is initiated in each instance by a disaster of some sort; many of these, in typical Proulx fashion, take the form of grisly deaths related in parentheses by the author. "Instead of the river of time, you get a lawn sprinkler effect, a kind of jittery, jammed, off-balance feeling," Proulx told Sybil Steinberg in a interview for *Publishers Weekly*.

While not greeted with the kind of uniform praise as its immediate predecessor, *Accordion Crimes* nonetheless elicited many warm reviews from critics. Chicago *Tribune Books* reviewer Bharati Mukherjee remarked, "With Proulx as biographer, the accordion's life story becomes more than an occasion for dazzling displays of writing . . . . Proulx proves her thesis with bleak persistence: America hates its non-Anglo immigrants." Writing in the *Bloomsbury Review*, Steven C. Ballinger praised Proulx's storytelling skill: "She can pick the telling characteristic the way a watercolorist's stroke sets the scene. When she sets a dialect in motion through a character, it is absolute and sure." Some reviewers felt that Proulx's technique results in less-than-fully developed characters. *New York Times* critic Christopher Lehmann-Haupt, for instance, noted that "the moment you begin to identify with any of the novel's characters, the narrative pushes you away by conveying in various ways that they aren't worth bothering with." And *Newsweek* reviewer Malcolm Jones, Jr., called *Accordion Crimes* "a book with no unifying narrative drive. The chapters are meant to work as separate stories, but that's all they are, a collection of stories." Still, explained Lehmann-Haupt, "Such is the energy of Ms. Proulx's prose, the authenticity of her dialogue and the brilliance of her invention that you can't help being caught up by some of her set pieces." Commenting on her use of creative devices in this book, Proulx told Steinberg: "Everything that happens to characters comes welling out of the place. Even their definition of themselves, and a lot of this book is about the definition of self."

After writing her first three novels, Proulx turned her focus once again to short stories, finally returning to the novel form in 2003 with a paean to Texas titled *That Old Ace in the Hole*. In an interview with Katie Bolick for *Atlantic Unbound*, Proulx discussed the shift from writing novels to penning short fiction as "intensely pleasurable—a break in the set of mind for a novel, which is a long, hard piece of work. At least you can see the end of a short story in a fairly short period; a month or six weeks for each one. There's a pleasing rhythm in the writing of short stories, and the challenge is greater; I find them harder than novels to write, not only because of the conciseness and the fact that every single word, every piece of punctuation, has to drive the story forward, but also because writing stories with both depth and surface is a considerable challenge."

Her fiction collection *Close Range: Wyoming Stories* contains eleven tales that, as Dean Bakopoulos noted in the *Progressive,* focus on "the mythic legends of drunken cowboys, rodeo heroes, betrayed lovers, and aging ranchers, while exploring all the loneliness, blood, and dirt of the Western landscape." Bakopoulos also commented that, as a whole, *Close Range* "is powerful fiction, and somehow Proulx manages to give each story the plot, depth of character, sense of setting, and thematic weight of an entire novel." As Charlotte L. Glover, noted in the *Library Journal,* "Proving that the Pulitzer Prize for *The Shipping News* was no fluke, Proulx once again demonstrates her creative mastery of the English language." Particularly of note, Glover added, is *Brokeback Mountain,* which received a *New Yorker* award for fiction and focuses on two ranch hands who have an erotic relationship, go on to have traditional family lives, and then come together once again. A *Publishers Weekly* reviewer, noting that the stories in *Close Range* run the gamut from "bleakly humorous" to "poignant," commented that Proulx's "ability to merge the matter-of-fact and the macabre, and her summary of life's pain in a terse closing sentence, will elicit gasps of pain and understanding. In the close range of a distinctive landscape, Proulx encapsulates the wide range of human experience: loss, longing and the Spartan determination to go on from day to day."

Proulx's follow-up collection of short stories, *Bad Dirt: Wyoming Stories 2,* is predominantly set in fictional Elk Tooth, Wyoming (where eighty people live in a three-bar town). The characters that populate these stories have strange names and stranger quirks. Proulx seems to indicate that it takes a character to live with the isolation and poverty characteristically found in the country. While reviewers did find fault with the collection, most concluded that it was still a worthy addition to Proulx's oeuvre. "The collection trips up, though, with the inclusion of a handful of stories that veer into magical realism," *New Statesman* contributor William Skidelsky stated. However, Skidelsky also commented that Proulx's "trademark skills are on display in these tales; they include a talent for metaphor, a wry sense of humour and an ability to sum up a whole life in a sentence." Interestingly, an *Economist* critic echoed this sentiment, noting Proulx's "masterful ability to condense a character's life into punchy sentences that underpin vivid images."

Of her writing career, Proulx told Gerrard: "I came to writing late, and I'm racing against the clock to get everything down. My head is jammed with stories; they are pushing to get out." After living for many years in Vermont, Proulx now lives in Wyoming where, as she told Steinberg in *Publishers Weekly,* there is "room to walk. There's something about being able to shoot your eyes very far ahead. In northern New England, the trees got in the way."

BIOGRAPHICAL AND CRITICAL SOURCES:

BOOKS

Contemporary Literary Criticism, Gale (Detroit, MI), Volume 81, 1994.

PERIODICALS

Atlantic, April, 1993, pp. 131-132.

Booklist, March 15, 1999, Donna Seaman, review of *Close Range: Wyoming Stories,* p. 1261.

Bloomsbury Review, September-October, 1996, p. 18.

Chicago Tribune, March 29, 1993, sec. 5, p. 3.

Commonweal, December 1, 1995, p. 24.

Critique, spring, 1999, p. 239.

Economist, January 8, 2005, review of *Bad Dirt: Wyoming Stories 2,* p. 76.

English Journal, January, 1996, p. 94.

Entertainment Weekly, January 3, 2003, review of *That Old Ace in the Hole,* p. 68.

Library Journal, May 1, 1999, Charlotte L. Glover, review of *Close Range: Wyoming Stories,* p. 115.

Los Angeles Times, December 30, 1988; January 20, 1992, p. E2.

Nation, June 24, 1996, p. 29.

New Republic, May 30, 1994, p. 35.

New Statesman, January 10, 2005, William Skidelsky, review of *Bad Dirt,* p. 56.

New Statesman and Society, December 3, 1993, p. 39.

Newsweek, June 10, 1996, p. 88.

New York Times, April 21, 1993, p. C15; June 17, 1996, p. C14.

New York Times Book Review, January 29, 1989, p. 30; March 22, 1992, p. 7; April 4, 1993, p. 13; June 23, 1996, p. 12.

Observer (London, England), November 14, 1993, p. 18.

Progressive, September, 1999, Dean Bakopoulos, review of *Close Range: Wyoming Stories,* p. 43.

Publishers Weekly, August 15, 1980, p. 53; March 18, 1983, pp. 68-69; April 18, 1994, p. 10; April 15, 1996, p. 48; June 3, 1996, Sybil Steinberg, "E. Annie Proulx: An American Odyssey," p. 57; March 29, 1999, review of *Close Range: Wyoming Stories,* p. 91.

Spectator, December 18, 2004, Digby Durrant, review of *Bad Dirt,* p. 92.

Studies in Canadian Literature (annual), 1998, pp. 49-70.

Time, June 24, 1996, p. 82; May 17, 1999, John Skow, review of *Close Range: Wyoming Stories,* p. 88.

Times Literary Supplement, Ocotber 23, 1998, Lucy Atkins, review of *Brokeback Mountain,* p. 24.

Tribune Books (Chicago, IL), January 12, 1992, pp. 1, 4; March 21, 1993, pp. 1, 9; June 9, 1996, p. 1.

Voice Literary Supplement, April, 1993, p. 29.

Wall Street Journal, June 14, 1996, p. A12.

Washington Post, April 21, 1993, p. B1; May 17, 1993, pp. B1, B4.

Women's Review of Books, September, 1996, p. 11.

Yale Review, October, 1993, pp. 133-135.

ONLINE

Atlantic Unbound, http://www.theatlantic.com/unbound/ (November 12, 1997), Katie Bolick, "Imagination Is Everything: A Conversation with E. Annie Proulx."

* * *

PROULX, Edna Annie
See PROULX, E. Annie

* * *

PUIG, Manuel 1932-1990

PERSONAL: Born December 28, 1932, in General Villegas, Argentina; died July 22, 1990, in Cuernavaca, Mexico; son of Baldomero (a businessperson) and Maria Elena (a chemist; maiden name, Delledonne) Puig. *Education:* Attended University of Buenos Aires, beginning 1950, and Centro Sperimentale di Cinematografia, beginning 1955; studied languages and literature at private institutes.

CAREER: Translator and Spanish and Italian teacher in London, England, and Rome, Italy, 1956-57; assistant film director in Rome and Paris, France, 1957-58; worked as a dishwasher in London and in Stockholm, Sweden, 1958-59; assistant film director in Buenos Aires, Argentina, 1960; translator of film subtitles in Rome, 1961-62; Air France, New York, NY, clerk, 1963-67; writer, 1967-90. *Military service:* Argentina Air Force, 1953; served as translator.

AWARDS, HONORS: La traicion de Rita Hayworth named one of the best foreign novels of 1968-69 by *Le Monde* (France); San Sebastian Festival best script award, 1974, for *Boquitas pintadas,* and jury prize, 1978, for *El lugar sin limites;* American Library Association notable book designation, 1979, for *The Kiss of the Spider Woman; Plays & Players* Award for most promising playwright, 1985, for *Kiss of the Spider Woman.*

WRITINGS:

La traicion de Rita Hayworth, Sudamericana (Buenos Aires, Argentina), 1968, reprinted, Casa de las Americas, 1983, translation by Suzanne Jill Levine published as *Betrayed by Rita Hayworth,* Dutton (New York, NY), 1971, reprinted, 1987.

Boquitas pintadas, folletin (also see below), Sudamericana, 1969, translation by Jill Levine published as *Heartbreak Tango: A Serial,* Dutton (New York, NY), 1973.

The Buenos Aires Affair: Novela policial, Sudamericana, 1973, translation by Jill Levine published as *The Buenos Aires Affair: A Detective Novel,* Dutton (New York, NY), 1976.

El beso de la mujer arana (also see below), Seix-Barral (Barcelona, Spain), 1976, translation by Thomas Colchie published as *The Kiss of the Spider Woman,* Knopf (New York, NY), 1979, published as *The Kiss of the Spider Woman and Two Other Plays,* Norton (New York, NY), 1994.

Pubis angelical (also see below), Seix-Barral (Barcelona, Spain), 1979, translation by Elena Brunet published under same title, Vintage (New York, NY), 1986.

El beso de la mujer arana (play; adapted from his novel; also see below), first produced in Spain, 1981, translation by Allan Baker titled *Kiss of the Spider Woman,* first produced in London, England, at the Bush Theatre, 1985, produced in Los Angeles, CA, at the Cast Theatre, 1987.

Eternal Curse on the Reader of These Pages, Random House (New York, NY), 1982, Spanish translation by the author published as *Maldicion eterna a quien lea estas paginas,* Seix Barral (Barcelona, Spain), 1982.

Sangre de amor correspondido, Seix Barral (Barcelona, Spain), 1982, translation by Jan L. Grayson published as *Blood of Requited Love,* Vintage (New York, NY), 1984.

Bajo un manto de estrellas: Pieza en dos actos [and] *El beso de la mujer arana: Adaptacion escenica realizada por el autor* (plays; also see below), Seix Barral (Barcelona, Spain), 1983, 12th edition, French & European Publications, 1992.

Under a Mantle of Stars: A Play in Two Acts (produced in the original Spanish as *Bajo un manto de estrellas*), translation by Ronald Christ, Lumen Books (New York, NY), 1985, revised edition, 1993.

La cara del villano; Recuerdo de Tijuana (play; title means "Face of the Scoundrel; Memory of Tijuana"), Seix Barral (Barcelona, Spain), 1985.

Mystery of the Rose Bouquet (play; produced at the Bush Theatre, 1987; produced in the original Spanish as *Misterio del ramo de rosas*), translation by Allan Baker, Faber (London, England), 1988.

Cae la noche tropical, Seix Barral (Barcelona, Spain), 1988, translation by Jill Levine published as *Tropical Night Falling,* Simon & Schuster (New York, NY), 1991.

Materiales inciales para la traicion de Rita Hayworth, Universidad Nacional de la Plata, Facultad de Humanidades y Ciencias de la Educacion, Centro de Estudioes de Teoria y Critica Literaria (La Plata, Buenos Aires, Argentina), 1996.

Triste Golondrina Macho; Amor del Bueno; Muy Senor Mio, Beatriz Viterbo Editora (Roasario, Argentina), 1998.

Also author of screenplays for *Boquitas Pintadas,* adapted from his novel, 1974, *El lugar sin limites,* adapted from José Donoso's novel, 1978, and *Pubis angelical,* adapted from his 1979 novel. Plays anthologized in G.W. Woodyard and Marion P. Holt, editors, *Drama Contemporary: Latin America,* PAJ Publications, 1986. Contributor to various periodicals, including *Omni.*

ADAPTATIONS: *The Kiss of the Spider Woman* was made into a film by Brazilian director Hector Babenco in 1985 and starred Raul Julia, William Hurt (in an Oscar-winning performance), and Sonia Braga. It was also adapted as a Broadway musical by John Kander, Fred Ebb, and Terrence McNally, 1994.

SIDELIGHTS: As a boy growing up in rural Argentina, novelist Manuel Puig spent countless hours in the local movie house viewing screen classics from the United States and Europe. His enchantment with films led him to spend several years pursuing a career as a director and screenwriter until he discovered that what he wanted to write was better suited to fiction; nevertheless, Puig's work is saturated with references to films and other popular phenomena. However, "if Puig's novels are 'pop,'" observed Jonathan Tittler in his *Narrative Irony in the Contemporary Spanish-American Novel,* it is because "he incorporates into his fiction elements of mass culture—radionovelas, comic books, glamour magazines, and in *Betrayed by Rita Hayworth,* commercial movies—in order to unveil their delightfully insidious role in shaping contemporary life." Puig echoed the design of these media, "us[ing] those forms as molds to cast his corny, bathetic material in a form displaying a witty, ironic attitude toward that material," noted Ronald Christ in *Commonweal.* Ronald Schwartz concurred with this assessment; writing in his study *Nomads, Exiles, and Emigres: The Rebirth of the Latin American Narrative, 1960-80,* the critic contended that Puig employed "the techniques of pop art to communicate a complex vision of his own world. It is [the] cinematic influence that makes *Betrayed by Rita Hayworth* and Puig's subsequent novels some of the most original contemporary Latin American narratives."

In *Betrayed by Rita Hayworth* "the idea of the novel is simple: the drama and pathos of moviegoing as a way of life in the provinces, where often people get to respond to life itself with gestures and mock programs taken over from film," explained *New York Times Book Review* contributor Alexander Coleman. The story is narrated primarily through the eyes of Toto, a young boy born in the Argentinian pampas, and recounts the everyday life of his family and friends. "The novel's charm," claimed *Newsweek* writer Walter Clemons, "is in the tender gravity with which Puig records the chatter of Toto's family and neighbors. Kitchen conversations, awkwardly written letters and flowery schoolgirl diary entries . . . combine to evoke lives of humblest possibility and uncomplaining disappointment." While this description may sound gloomy, stated Coleman, nevertheless *Betrayed by Rita Hayworth* "is a screamingly funny book, with scenes of such utter bathos that only a student of final reels such as Puig could possibly have verbally re-created [it] for us." "Above all, Puig has captured the language of his characters," D.P. Gallagher reported in his *Modern Latin American Literature,* and explained: "There is no distance separating him from the voices he records, moreover, for they are the voices that he was brought up with himself, and he is able to reproduce them with perfect naturalness, and without distortion or parodic exaggeration. That is not to say that his novels are not very polished and very professional," the critic continued. "Like all the best

Latin American novels . . . , they are structured deliberately as fictions. But the authenticity with which they reflect a very real environment cannot be questioned."

Puig's next novel, *Heartbreak Tango,* "in addition to doing everything that *Rita Hayworth* did (and doing it better, too) actually proclaims Puig not only a major writer but a major stylist whose medium brings you both the heartbreak *and* the tango," Christ declared in *Review 73.* Bringing together letters, diaries, newspapers, conversations, and other literary artifices, *Heartbreak Tango,* as *New York Times* reviewer Christopher Lehmann-Haupt related, "reconstructs the lives of several Argentine women, most of whom have in common the experience of having once passionately loved a handsome, ne'er-do-well and doomed young man who died of tuberculosis." Mark Jay Mirsky commented in the *Washington Post Book World* that at first "I missed the bustle, noise and grotesque power of *Betrayed by Rita Hayworth.* The narrative of *Heartbreak Tango* seemed much thinner, picking out the objects and voices of its hero [and] heroines with too obvious a precision." Nevertheless, the critic admitted, "as we are caught up in the story, this taut line begins to spin us around." Michael Wood, however, believed that it is this "precision" which makes *Heartbreak Tango* the better novel. As he detailed in a *New York Review of Books* article, *Heartbreak Tango* "seems to me even better than Puig's earlier *Betrayed by Rita Hayworth* because its characters' moments are clearer, and because the general implication of the montage of cliche and cheap romance and gossip is firmer." The critic added that "the balance of the new book," between irony and sentimentalism, "is virtually perfect." Gallagher presented a similar opinion in the *New York Times Book Review,* noting that "it has been said that [*Heartbreak Tango*] is a parody, but that underestimates the balance between distance and compassion that Puig achieves. His characters are camp, but they are not camped up, and their fundamental humanity cannot be denied." Despite this serious aspect, the critic remarked that *Heartbreak Tango* "is a more accessible book than its predecessor without being less significant. It is compelling, moving, instructive and very funny." "At the same time," concluded David William Foster in *Latin American Literary Review,* "no matter how 'popular' or 'proletarian' the novel may appear to be on the surface, the essential and significant inner complexity of [*Heartbreak Tango*], like that of *Betrayed by Rita Hayworth,* bespeaks the true artistic dimensions of Puig's novel."

"The appearance of Manuel Puig's new novel, *The Buenos Aires Affair,* is especial cause for celebration," Ronald De Feo asserted in the *National Review,* "not only because the book makes for fascinating reading, but also because it demonstrates that its already highly accomplished author continues to take chances and to grow as an artist." Subtitled *A Detective Novel,* the story takes place in the city and investigates a kidnapping involving two sexually deviant people. "It is not devoid of the lucid and witty observation of absurd behaviour that characterized" *Heartbreak Tango,* maintained a *Times Literary Supplement* reviewer, "but it is altogether more anguished." As Toby Moore elaborated in another *Times Literary Supplement* review, "Puig's subject is the tangle made up of love and sexual desire. . . . In *The Buenos Aires Affair* the anxieties and inhibitions of the two characters are so great that they never get to a point of love; all they have is the dream of sex which obsesses and torments them." The author sets this psychological drama within the framework of a traditional thriller; "what makes Puig so fascinating," wrote *New York Times Book Review* contributor Robert Alter, is "the extraordinary inventiveness he exhibits in devising new ways to render familiar material." De Feo, however, faulted the author for being "a shade too inventive, [for] we are not always convinced that [these methods] are necessary. But," the critic added, "the book is more intense, serious, and disturbing than the other novels, and it is a welcome departure for this searching, gifted writer." And a *Times Literary Supplement* writer claimed that *The Buenos Aires Affair* "is technically even more accomplished than the previous novels, and Sr Puig is able to handle a wide variety of narrative devices in it without ever making them seem gratuitous."

Shortly after the publication of *The Buenos Aires Affair* in 1973, Puig found it more difficult to remain in Argentina; the book had been banned, presumably because of its sexual content, and the political situation was becoming more restrictive. This increasingly antagonistic climate led Puig into a self-imposed exile, and is reflected in what is probably his best-known work, *The Kiss of the Spider Woman.* Set almost entirely in an Argentinian jail cell, the novel focuses on Valentin, a radical student imprisoned for political reasons, and Molina, a gay window-dresser being held on a "morals" charge, who recounts his favorite 1930s and 1940s movies as a means of passing time. "In telling the story of two cellmates, Puig strips down the narrative to a nearly filmic level—dialogue unbroken even to identify the speakers, assuming we can project them onto our own interior screens," related Carol Anshaw in the *Voice Literary Supplement.* "If this insistent use of unedited dialogue tends to make the book read a bit like a radio script, however," observed *New York Times Book Review* contributor Robert Coover, "it is Mr. Puig's fascination with old movies that largely provides [the novel's] substance and ultimately defines its plot, its shape. What we hear," the critic continued, "are the voices of two suffering men, alone and often in the dark, but what we see . . . [is] all the iconographic imagery, magic and romance of the movies." The contrast between the two men, who gradually build a friendship "makes this Argentinian odd couple both funny and affecting," Larry Rohter stated in the *Washington Post Book World.* But when Molina is released in hopes that he will lead officials to Valentin's confederates, "the plot turns from comedy to farce and Puig's wit turns mordant."

In addition to the continuous dialogue of the jail cell and surveillance report after Molina's release, *The Kiss of the Spider Woman* contains several footnotes on homosexuality whose "clumsy academic style serves to emphasize by contrast that the two prisoners' dialogue is a highly contrived storytelling device, and not the simulation of reality you may take it to be at first," commented Lehmann-Haupt. Because of this, the critic explained, the book becomes "a little too tricky, like a well-made, 19th-century play." Other reviewers, however, found *The Kiss of the Spider Woman* "far and away [Puig's] most impressive book," as Anshaw said. "It is not easy to write a book which says something hopeful about human nature and yet remains precise and unsentimental," Maggie Gee remarked in the *Times Literary Supplement.* "Puig succeeds, partly because his bleak vision of the outside world throws into relief the small private moments of hope and dignifies them, partly through his deft manipulation of form." Schwartz similarly concluded that *The Kiss of the Spider Woman* "is not the usual jumble of truncated structures from which a plot emerges but, rather, a beautifully controlled narrative that skillfully conveys basic human values, a vivid demonstration of the continuing of the genre itself." Inspired by a stay in New York, *Eternal Curse on the Reader of These Pages* was written directly in English and, similar to *The Kiss of the Spider Woman,* is mainly comprised of an extended dialogue. Juan José Ramirez is an elderly Argentinian living in exile in New York and Lawrence John is the irritable, taciturn American who works part-time caring for him. But as their dialogues progress, Lehmann-Haupt notes, "it becomes increasingly difficult to tell how much is real and how much the two characters have become objects of each other's fantasy life." *Los Angeles Times Book Review* critic Charles Champlin, although he believed these dialogues constitute a technical "tour de force," questioned "whether a technical exercise, however clever, [is] the best way to get at this study of conflicting cultures and the ambiguities in the relationship." Gilbert Sorrentino similarly felt that *Eternal Curse* is "a structural failure, . . . for the conclusion, disastrously, comments on and 'explains' an otherwise richly ambivalent and mysterious text." The critic continued in the *Washington Post Book World:* "It's too bad, because Puig *has* something, most obviously a sense that the essential elements of life, life's serious 'things,' are precisely the elements of soap opera, sit-coms, and B-movies." But Lehmann-Haupt thought *Eternal Curse* is "more austere and intellectually brittle than any of [Puig's] previous books, [and] less playful and dependent on the artifacts of American pop culture," and called the novel a "fascinating tour de force." "Puig is an artist, . . . and his portrait of two men grappling with their suffering is exceedingly moving and brilliantly done," declared William Herrick in the *New Leader.* "Strangely, the more space I put between the book and myself, the more tragic I find it. It sticks to the mind. Like one cursed, I cannot find peace, cannot escape from its pain."

Echoing themes of Puig's previous work, maintained *Nation* contributor Jean Franco, "politics and sexuality are inseparable in *Pubis Angelical.*" Alternating the story of Ana, an Argentinian exile dying of cancer in Mexico, with her fantasies of a 1930s movie star and a futuristic "sexual soldier," *Pubis Angelical* speaks "of the political nightmares of exile, disappearance, torture and persecution," described Franco, "though as always in Puig's novels, the horror is tempered by the humor of his crazy plots and kitsch stage props." "Puig is both ruthless and touching in his presentation of Ana's muddled but sincere life," stated Jason Wilson in the *Times Literary Supplement;* "and if he is sometimes too camp, he can also be very funny." The critic elaborated: "His humour works because he refuses to settle for any single definition of woman; Ana is all feeling and intuition . . . although she is also calculating, and unfeeling about her daughter."

While Ana's advancing cancer and the problems of her dream counterparts are severe, "however seriously Puig is questioning gender assumptions and behavior his voice is never a solemn one," Nick Caistor claimed in the *New Statesman.* "The work as a whole fairly bristles with ingenuity and energy," Robert Towers wrote in the *New York Review of Books;* "the thematic parallels between the three texts seem almost inexhaustible, and one finishes the novel with a sense of having grasped only a portion of them." Nevertheless, the critic faulted *Pubis Angelical* for being "an impressive artifact rather than a fully engrossing work of fictional art." Steve Erickson likewise criticized the novel, commenting in the *New York Times Book Review* that "what's amazing about 'Pubis Angelical' is how utterly in love it is with its own artificiality." The critic added that "the novel fails most devastatingly" in the portrayals of Ana's fantasies: "There's nothing about their lives to suggest that . . . they have a reality for her." While Jay Cantor similarly believed that "it isn't till the last quarter of the book that the fantasies have sufficient, involving interest," he acknowledged in the *Los Angeles Times Book Review* that "there is an audacity to Puig's method, and an intellectual fire to Puig's marshaling of motifs that did then engage me." "In any case, whatever the whole [of the novel] amounts to, each individual part of 'Pubis Angelical' develops its own irresistible drama," countered Lehmann-Haupt. "Though it takes an exercise of the intellect to add them together, they finally contribute to what is the most richly textured and extravagant fiction [Puig] has produced so far."

In *Blood of Requited Love* Puig recounts a failed romance between a construction worker, Josemar, and the young daughter of a successful businessman in rural Brazil. The story is based largely on Puig's interviews with a real-life carpenter. As in other novels, Puig employs extended dialogue incorporating multiple voices to juxtapose reality and fantasy, and to illustrate entrapment caused by despair. Dean Flower called the novel "another dazzling *tour de force*," in the *Hudson Review*, "both a book-length dramatic monologue and a kind of philosophical inquiry into the dialectics of narrative self-invention." According to Norman Lavers in *American Book Review*, "It is the way that the novel is narrated that marks it as Puig's. For almost the first time in Puig there is a narrator, and the narrator seems almost like that chatty nineteenth-century omniscient author, except he is so unreliable—perhaps exaggerating the subjectivity of the standard authorial voice—that only the most careful reading can ferret out when he is telling the truth. However, the narrator turns out to be Josemar himself, telling his own story in the third person." Stephen Dobyns concluded in a *Times Literary Supplement* review that *Blood of Requited Love* "is a sad book and a very impressive one. We move from seeing Josemar as a selfish brute, to feeling sympathy and compassion; he is completely responsible for his life and he is trapped."

Tropical Night Falling, originally published two years before Puig's death in 1990, also involves the effective use of dialogue, interspersed with letters, to portray both internal and external conflict. The novel follows the conversations and correspondence of two elderly sisters in Rio who debate and attempt to disentangle the emotional lives of their family, neighbors, and the function of romance in the contemporary world. *Times Literary Supplement* contributor John Butt praised the novel, noting that "the ending is a masterpiece of graceful bathos that is characteristic of Puig at his funniest." Peter Matthews wrote in an *Observer* review, "This spare, elegant chamber piece was Puig's last novel . . . and it must be his saddest." Butt similarly concluded that *Tropical Night Falling* "shows that this unusual and attractive voice among modern novelists was strong to the last." "Less interested in depicting things as they might be, and concerned with things as they are, Puig does not resort to make-believe," Alfred J. MacAdam added in *Modern Latin American Narratives: The Dreams of Reason*. "His characters are all too plausible" and their lives "simply unfold over days and years until they run their meaningless course."

It is this ordinary, commonplace quality of life, however, that the author preferred to investigate; as he once told *Washington Post* interviewer Desson Howe: "I find literature the ideal medium to tell certain stories that are of special interest to me. Everyday stories with no heroics, the everyday life of the gray people." And films play such a large role in his work because of the contrast they provided to this mundane world: "I think I can understand the reality of the 1930s by means of the unreality of their films," Puig also remarked in a *Los Angeles Times* interview with Ann Marie Cunningham. "The films reflect exactly what people dreamed life could be. The relationships between people in these films are like the negative of a photograph of real life." "I can only understand realism," the author further explained to *New York Times* writer Samuel G. Freedman. "I can only approach my writing with an analytical sense. . . . I can write dreams, but I use them as part of the accumulation of detail, as counterpoint."

Because of his realistic yet inventive portrayals, contended Schwartz, Puig was respected as "a novelist moving in the direction of political commitment in his depiction of the provincial and urban middle class of Argentina, something that has never before been attempted so successfully in Latin American letters." The critic concluded: "Clearly, Puig, thriving self-exiled from his native country, [was] . . . an eclectic stylist, a consummate artist."

BIOGRAPHICAL AND CRITICAL SOURCES:

BOOKS

Amicola, José, editor, *Homenaje a Manuel Puig*, Universidad Nacional de La Plata, 1993.

Barcarisse, Pamela, *Impossible Choices: The Implications of the Cultural References in the Novels of Manuel Puig,* University of Calgary (Calgary, Alberta, Canada), 1993.

Contemporary Literary Criticism, Thomson Gale (Detroit, MI), Volume 3, 1975, Volume 5, 1976, Volume 10, 1979, Volume 28, 1984, Volume 65, 1990.

Dictionary of Literary Biography, Volume 113: *Modern Latin-American Fiction Writers, First Series,* Thomson Gale (Detroit, MI), 1992.

Duran, Victor M., *A Marxist Reading of Fuentes, Vargas Llosa, and Puig,* University Press of America (Lanham, MD), 1994.

Fabry, Genevieéve, *Personaje y lectura en cinco novelas de Manuel Puig,* Frankfurt am Main: Vervuet (Madrid, Spain), 1998.

Gallagher, D. P., *Modern Latin American Literature,* Oxford University Press (New York, NY), 1973.

Giordano, Alberto, *Manuel Puig: la conversación infinita,* B. Viterbo Editora (Rosario, Argentina), 2001.

Lorenzano, Sandra, editor, *La literatura es una pelicula: revisiones sobre Puig,* Universidad Nacional Autónoma de México, 1997.

MacAdam, Alfred J., *Modern Latin American Narratives: The Dreams of Reason,* University of Chicago Press (Chicago, IL), 1977.

Minelli, María Alejandra, *Manuel Puig, por una sutil diferencia,* Ediciones Florida Blanca (Buenos Aires, Argentina), 1995.

Páez, Roxana, *Manuel Puig: del pop a la extrañeza,* Editorial Almagesto (Buenos Aires, Argentina), 1995.

Schwartz, Ronald, *Nomads, Exiles, and Emigres: The Rebirth of the Latin American Narrative, 1960-80,* Scarecrow Press (Metuchen, NJ), 1980.

Tittler, Jonathan, *Narrative Irony in the Contemporary Spanish-American Novel,* Cornell University Press (Ithaca, NY), 1984.

Tittler, Jonathan, *Manuel Puig,* Twayne Publishers (New York, NY), 1993.

PERIODICALS

American Book Review, May, 1985, p. 9.

Americas, September-October 1990, pp. 62-62; March-April, 1992, p. 60.

Commonweal, June 24, 1977.

Critique, fall, 1997, pp. 65-80.

Hudson Review, summer, 1985, p. 307.

Journal of Evolutionary Psychology, August, 2001, pp. 146-151.

Journal of Men's Studies, spring, 2000, p. 323.

Latin American Literary Review, fall, 1972.

Los Angeles Times, January 30, 1987; February 3, 1987.

Los Angeles Times Book Review, June 20, 1982; December 28, 1986.

Michigan Acamedician, September, 2002, p. 105.

Nation, April 18, 1987.

National Review, October 29, 1976.

New Leader, June 28, 1982.

New Statesman, October 2, 1987.

Newsweek, October 25, 1971; June 28, 1982.

New York Review of Books, December 13, 1973; January 24, 1980; December 18, 1986.

New York Times, November 28, 1973; April 23, 1979; June 4, 1982; September 25, 1984; August 5, 1985; December 22, 1986; October 25, 1988.

New York Times Book Review, September 26, 1971; December 16, 1973; September 5, 1976; April 22, 1979; July 4, 1982; September 23, 1984; December 28, 1986.

Observer, July 5, 1992, p. 63.

Publishers Weekly, August 23, 1991, p. 47.

Review 73, fall, 1973.

Romanic Review, May, 1996, pp. 419-430.

Times (London, England), August 23, 1985.

Times Literary Supplement, November 6, 1970; August 31, 1973; September 21, 1984; October 16, 1987; August 11-17, 1989, p. 877; July 3, 1992, p. 27.

Tribune Books (Chicago, IL), April 15, 1979.

Voice Literary Supplement, April, 1987; April, 1989.

Washington Post, November 16, 1985.

Washington Post Book World, November 25, 1973; April 22, 1979; August 1, 1982.

World Literature Today, winter, 1981.

ONLINE

Center for Book Culture Web site, http://www.centerforbookculture.org/ (August 13, 2004), Jorgelina Corbatta and Ivan Stevan, "Brief Encounters: An Interview with Puig."

New York Times Online, http://partners.nytimes.com/ (August 13, 2004), "Featured Author: Manuel Puig."

Otro Campo Web site, http://www.otrocampo.com/ (August 13, 2004), Carla Marcantonio, "Manuel Puig and the Queering of Film Melodrama."

* * *

PULLMAN, Philip 1946-
(Philip Nicholas Pullman)

PERSONAL: Born October 19, 1946, in Norwich, England; son of Alfred Outram (an airman) and Audrey (homemaker; maiden name, Merrifield) Pullman; married Judith Speller (a teacher), August 15, 1970; children: James, Thomas. *Education:* Oxford University, B.A., 1968; Weymouth College of Education, earned teaching degree. *Politics:* Liberal. *Hobbies and other interests:* Drawing, music.

ADDRESSES: Agent—A.P. Watt, 20 John St., London WC1N 2DR, England; Ellen Levine, 432 Park Ave. S, Ste. 1205, New York, NY 10016.

CAREER: Author, playwright, scriptwriter, and educator. Teacher at Ivanhoe, Bishop Kirk, and Marston middle schools, Oxford, England, 1970-86; writer, 1986—. Lecturer at Westminster College, North Hinksey, Oxford, 1988-95.

MEMBER: Society of Authors (chairman, 2001-03).

AWARDS, HONORS: Lancashire County Libraries/National and Provincial Children's Book Award and Best Books for Young Adults listing, *School Library Journal,* both 1987, Children's Book Award, International Reading Association, Preis der Leseratten, ZDF Television (Germany), and Best Books for Young Adults listing, American Library Association (ALA), all 1988, all for *The Ruby in the Smoke;* Best Books for Young Adults listing, ALA, 1988, and Edgar Allan Poe Award nomination, Mystery Writers of America, 1989, both for *Shadow in the North;* Carnegie Medal, British Library Association, and *Guardian* Children's Fiction Award, both 1996, both for *Northern Lights;* Top of the List in youth fiction, *Booklist,* 1996, for *The Golden Compass* (U.S. edition of *Northern Lights*); Smarties Award, Rowntree Mackintosh Co., 1996, for *The Firework-Maker's Daughter;* Whitbread Book of the Year Award and Whitbread Children's Book Award, both 2001, both for *The Amber Spyglass;* Securicor Omega Express Author of the Year and Whitaker/BA Author of the Year, both 2002; Carnegie Medal nomination, 2005, for *The Scarecrow and His Servant.*

WRITINGS:

"SALLY LOCKHART" SERIES; YOUNG ADULT HISTORICAL FICTION

The Ruby in the Smoke, Alfred A. Knopf (New York, NY), 1985.

The Shadow in the Plate, Oxford University Press (Oxford, England), 1987, published as *Shadow in the North,* Alfred A. Knopf (New York, NY), 1988.

The Tiger in the Well, Alfred A. Knopf (New York, NY), 1990.

The Tin Princess, Alfred A. Knopf (New York, NY), 1994.

Sally Lockhart Slipcase (omnibus; contains *The Tin Princess, The Tiger in the Well, Shadow in the North,* and *The Ruby in the Smoke*), Scholastic, 2004.

"HIS DARK MATERIALS" YOUNG ADULT FANTASY NOVELS

Northern Lights, Scholastic (England), 1995, published as *The Golden Compass,* Alfred A. Knopf (New York, NY), 1996.

The Subtle Knife, Alfred A. Knopf (New York, NY), 1997.

The Amber Spyglass, Alfred A. Knopf (New York, NY), 2000.

Lyra's Oxford, illustrated by John Lawrence, Alfred A. Knopf (New York, NY), 2003.

OTHER YOUNG ADULT FICTION

How to Be Cool (humorous fiction), Heinemann (London, England), 1987.

The Broken Bridge, Macmillan (London, England), 1990, Alfred A. Knopf (New York, NY), 1992.

The White Mercedes (realistic fiction), Macmillan (London, England), 1992, Alfred A. Knopf (New York, NY), 1993.

(Editor) *Detective Stories: Chosen by Philip Pullman,* illustrated by Nick Hardcastle, Kingfisher (New York, NY), 1998.

FOR CHILDREN; FICTION

Count Karlstein, or The Ride of the Demon Huntsman (picture book), Chatto & Windus (London, England), 1982, new edition, illustrated by Patrice Aggs, Doubleday (London, England), 1991, new edition, illustrated by Diana Bryan, Alfred A. Knopf (New York, NY), 1998.

Spring-Heeled Jack: A Story of Bravery and Evil (graphic novel), illustrated by David Mostyn, Doubleday (London, England), 1989, Alfred A. Knopf (New York, NY), 1991.

The Wonderful Story of Aladdin and the Enchanted Lamp (retelling), illustrated by David Wyatt, Picture Hippo, 1995 reprinted as *Aladdin and the Enchanted Lamp,* illustrated by Sophy Williams, Arthur A. Levine Books (New York, NY), 2005.

The Firework-Maker's Daughter (fantasy), Corgi, 1996, illustrated by S. Saelig Gallagher, Arthur A. Levine Books (New York, NY), 1999.

Clockwork, or All Wound Up, illustrated by Peter Bailey, Doubleday (London, England), 1996, new edition, illustrated by Leonid Gore, Scholastic/ Arthur A. Levine Books (New York, NY), 1998.

I Was a Rat!, illustrated by Kevin Hawkes, Alfred A. Knopf (New York, NY), 2000.

Puss in Boots: The Adventures of That Most Enterprising Feline, illustrated by Ian Beck, Alfred A. Knopf (New York, NY), 2000.

The Scarecrow and His Servant, illustrated by Peter Bailey, Alfred A. Knopf (New York, NY), 2005.

"THE NEW CUT GANG" SERIES

Thunderbolt's Waxworks, illustrated by Mark Thomas, Viking (New York, NY), 1994.

The Gas-Fitter's Ball, illustrated by Mark Thomas, Viking (New York, NY), 1995.

OTHER

Ancient Civilizations (nonfiction), illustrated by G. Long, Wheaton (Exeter, England), 1978.

Galatea (fantasy; for adults), Gollancz (London, England), 1978, Dutton (New York, NY), 1979.

Pullman is also the author of scripts for television. Author of introduction, John and Mary Gribbin, *The Science of "His Dark Materials,"* Hodder & Stoughton (London, England), in press.

PLAYS

Sherlock Holmes and the Adventure of the Sumatran Devil (produced at Polka Children's Theatre, Wimbledon, 1984), published as *Sherlock Holmes and the Adventure of the Limehouse Horror,* Thomas Nelson (London, England), 1993.

The Three Musketeers (adapted from Alexandre Dumas's novel), produced at Polka Children's Theatre, Wimbledon, England, 1985.

Frankenstein (adapted from Mary Shelley's novel), produced at Polka Children's Theatre, Wimbledon, England, 1987), Oxford University Press (Oxford, England), 1990.

Puss in Boots, produced at Polka Children's Theater, Wimbledon, England, 1997.

ADAPTATIONS: *How to Be Cool* was televised by Granada-TV in the United Kingdom, 1988. *The Golden Compass* and *The Amber Spyglass* were made into sound recordings. The first three books in the "His Dark Materials" series have been optioned by New Line Cinema for production as motion pictures. Two plays based on "His Dark Materials," adapted by Nicholas Wright, were produced at the National Theatre, London, 2003-04.

WORK IN PROGRESS: A novel, *The Book of Dust,* in the "His Dark Materials" series.

SIDELIGHTS: The English bestow two prestigious literary prizes every year: the Whitbread Award and the Booker Prize. In 2001, Philip Pullman won the Whitbread Book of the Year Award for *The Amber Spyglass,* an unprecedented accolade for someone who is seen primarily as a writer for younger readers. Never before had the Whitbread Book of the Year been awarded to a young adult novel, or any children's book for that matter—in fact, the Whitbread has a category for children's literature, and *The Amber Spyglass* won *that* award too. Most critics agree that the award comes as recognition for Pullman's unique and imaginative "His Dark Materials" trilogy, comprising *The Golden Compass, The Subtle Knife,* and *The Amber Spyglass.* Drawing its energy from myth, science fiction, classical literature, the Bible, and speculative philosophy, Pullman's trilogy succeeds for children as a ripping good-versus-evil adventure, and for teens and adults as a thoughtful venture into alternative realities.

Considered a writer of great range, depth, and imagination, Pullman is recognized as one of the most talented creators of children's literature to have entered the field in the last quarter century. The author of fiction, nonfiction, and picture books as well as a playwright and reteller, he is best known for writing fantasy and historical fiction for young adults, and historical fiction and fantasy for primary and middle graders. Pullman is lauded as a gifted storyteller who adds a distinctive, original touch to such literary forms as the mystery, the thriller, the horror story, and the problem novel. As a writer of historical fiction, he usually sets his books in Victorian England, a period that he is credited for recreating with accuracy. His works are often praised for their meticulous research, and he uses prior eras or fantasy worlds to treat themes with strong parallels to contemporary society such as feminism, prejudice, and adjustment to new technology. Pullman is known as the creator of four books about Sally Lockhart, a brave and independent young woman who solves mysteries in nineteenth-century London. Filled with underworld atmosphere, larger-than-life characters, and cliff-hanging suspense as well as thoughtful, provocative themes, these works have inspired Pullman's comparison to classic novelists such as Charles Dickens and Wilkie Collins.

The author is far more famous, however, as the creator of the "His Dark Materials" series, the best-selling epic tales set in an Arctic-like region that revolve around the concept of daemons, animal familiars that contain the souls of their human counterparts, and the quest of Lyra Belacqua, a feisty, shrewd teenager, to find the origin of Dust, a mysterious substance integral to the composition of the universe. Called "science fantasies" by their author in an interview in *Publishers Weekly,* these novels are regarded as extraordinary works that combine exciting adventures with thought-provoking philosophical content. Although many of Pullman's books are considered sophisticated and demanding, most reviewers note their accessibility while acknowledging the author's ability to explore moral and ethical issues in riveting stories. Chris Routh of *School Librarian* commented that Pullman "has already confirmed his status as one of today's top storytellers," while Anne E. Deifendeifer, writing in *Children's Books and Their Creators,* noted, "At their best, Pullman's novels, daring and inventive, are page turners that immediately hook readers into the story and often introduce them to the Victorian age." In his entry in *Twentieth-Century Young Adult Writers,* Keith Barker claimed, "Pullman plays with the rules of fiction as few young-adult writers attempt to do." The critic concluded that the author's "unpredictability of plot and character coupled with the sheer readability of his novels earn them the right to be widely read."

Born in Norwich, England, to Alfred Pullman, an airman for the Royal Air Force, and his wife, Audrey, a homemaker and amateur dramatist who also worked for the British Broadcasting Corporation (BBC), Pullman spent much of his early life traveling. At the age of six, he went to live in Southern Rhodesia, now Zimbabwe, where his father was sent on assignment. "Africa," Pullman wrote in his essay in *Something about the Author Autobiography Series (SAAS),* "was full of strange things," including some wonderful smells such as roasting mealies (corn on the cob). He remembered, "I loved that smell so much that when years and years later I happened to smell it unexpectedly in a street market in London, where someone was roasting mealies to sell, I found tears springing to my eyes." When his father's tour of duty ended, Pullman returned to England, where he spent happy times with his grandfather and grandmother in Drayton, a small village in Norfolk. His grandfather, a clergyman in the Church of England, was rector of the church there. His grandfather, Pullman noted in *SAAS,* was "the centre of the world. There was no one stronger than he was, or wiser, or kinder. . . . When I was young he was the sun at the centre of my life." In addition to his other attributes, Pullman's grandfather was an accomplished storyteller; his grandson remembered, "He took the simplest little event and made a story out of it."

After his father was killed on a mission in Africa, Pullman and his younger brother went to live in Norfolk while their mother went to London to look for work. Shortly thereafter, Pullman's mother received a letter saying that her husband was to receive the Distinguished Flying Cross, an award that was presented to the family by Queen Elizabeth at Buckingham Palace. Later, Pullman discovered that his father, who had incurred gambling debts and was involved in extramarital affairs, was suspected of committing suicide by crashing his plane. Pullman wrote, "Sometimes I think he's really alive somewhere, in hiding, with a different name. I'd love to meet him."

When Pullman was nine, his mother married an airman friend of her late husband's. When his stepfather was sent to Australia on assignment, the family went with him. Pullman made a spectacular discovery in Australia—comic books. He wrote in *SAAS,* "When one day my stepfather brought me a Superman comic, it changed my life. I'd been a reader for a long time, but a reader of books; I'd never known comics. When I got this one, I devoured it and demanded more. I adored them." Most of all, the author remembered, "I adored Batman. Those poorly printed stories on their cheap yellowing newsprint intoxicated me, enthralled me, made me dizzy with passion." In evaluating what he loved about the Batman comics, Pullman noted, "What I wanted was to *brood* over the world of Batman and dream actively. It was the first stirring of the storytelling impulse. I couldn't have put it like this, but what I wanted was to take characters, a setting, words, and pictures and weave a pattern out of them; not *be* Batman, but write about him." He added, "I knew instinctively at once, that the telling of stories was delicious, and it all belonged to me."

In Australia, Pullman began telling ghost stories to his school friends and to his brother in their bedroom at night. The author recalled, "I don't know whether he enjoyed it, or whether he even listened, but it wasn't for his benefit; it was for mine. I remember vividly the sense of diving into the dark as I began the story, with no idea at all what was going to happen or whether the story would 'come out' as I called it, by which I meant make sense or come to a neat end. I remember the exhilaration of the risk: Would I find something to say? Would I dry up? And I remember the thrill, the bliss, when, a minute ahead of getting there, I saw a twist I could give to the end, a clever way of bringing back that character who'd come into it earlier and vanished inconclusively, a neat phrase to tie it all up with. Many other things happened in Australia, but my discovery of storytelling was by far the most important."

After moving back to the United Kingdom, Pullman settled in Llanbedr, a village on the north coast of Wales where he would spend the next decade. "[Of] all the things I remember from those years," he wrote in *SAAS,* "the most exciting came when I discovered art." When Pullman was fifteen, he became interested in the history of painting. A book called *A History of Art* was "more precious to me than any Bible," Pullman wrote. He also began drawing. Pullman learned the Welsh landscape by sketching it, and, he noted, "came to care for it with a lover's devotion." In his young adult novel *The Broken Bridge,* a work that the author called "a love letter to a landscape" in *SAAS,* he describes a young woman who makes the same discoveries. As a teenager, Pullman also became enthralled by poetry. One of his English teachers, Enid Jones, was instrumental in developing his interest; he wrote in *SAAS,* "I owe her a great debt." Jones introduced Pullman to Milton, Wordsworth, and the English metaphysical poets and, he remembered, "took me to places I never dreamed of." In addition to learning reams of poetry by heart, Pullman began writing poems in literary forms such as the sonnet, the rondeau, and the ballad; in the process, he recalled, "I developed a great respect for craftsmanship."

After winning a scholarship to Oxford to study English, Pullman became the first person in his family to attend university. However, he wrote in *SAAS,* "it wasn't long before I found out that I didn't enjoy English as much as I thought I would, anyway. I was doing it because I wanted to learn how to write, but that wasn't what they were interested in teaching." While at Oxford, Pullman realized that he was destined to be a storyteller, not a poet. After graduation, he began to write a novel. Shortly thereafter, he moved to London and worked at a men's clothing store and in a library while writing three pages a day—a regime to which he still adheres—in his spare time. In 1970, Pullman married Judith Speller, a teacher; the couple has two sons. His wife influenced Pullman's next career move; he wrote in *SAAS,* "I liked what she told me about [teaching]." After attending Weymouth College of Education, Pullman got his degree and began teaching middle school in Oxford.

For twelve years, Pullman taught Greek mythology to his students by telling them stories of the gods and heroes, including oral versions of *The Iliad* and *The Odyssey.* Writing in *SAAS,* the author confirmed that the "real beneficiary of all that storytelling wasn't so much the audience as the storyteller. I'd chosen—for what I thought, and think still, were good educational reasons—to do something that, by a lucky chance, was the best possible training for me as a writer. To tell great stories over and over again, testing and refining the language and observing the reaction of the listeners and gradually improving the timing and the rhythm and the pace, was to undergo an apprenticeship that probably wasn't very different, essentially, from the one that Homer himself underwent three thousand years ago."

In 1978, Pullman published his first novel, *Galatea,* a book for adults that outlines how flautist Martin Browning, searching for his missing wife, embarks on a series of surreal adventures. Now considered a cult classic among aficionados of science fiction and fantasy literature, the novel is described by its author in *SAAS* as "a book I can't categorize." He added, "I'm still proud of it." After completing *Galatea,* Pullman began writing and producing plays for his students; he wrote in *SAAS,* "I enjoyed doing school plays so much that I've written for children ever since." Pullman's first book for young people is *Ancient Civilizations,* a nonfiction title about the cultures of several Mediterranean, Eastern, Middle Eastern, and South American countries that R. Baines of *Junior Bookshelf* called "a lively and informative work."

Pullman's next book, *Count Karlstein,* is an adaptation of a story that the author had originally written as a play. The book was also published as a graphic novel. Taking his inspiration from Victorian pulp fiction and from such tales of derring-do as Anthony Hope's *The Prisoner of Zenda,* Pullman created a gothic farce set in a Swiss castle that describes how a fourteen-year-old servant girl and her English tutor foil a plot by the evil Count Karlstein to sacrifice his two young nieces to Zamiel, the Demon Huntsman, in exchange for riches. Writing in the *New Statesman,* Charles Fox noted, "To compare this book with T.H. White's *Mistress Masham's Repose* is to risk hyperbole, yet it shares a similar concern with making the improbable seem remarkably precise." Pullman has also adapted *The Three Musketeers, Frankenstein,* and a story featuring Sherlock Holmes into plays, and has turned the latter two into books of his own. In his review of *Frankenstein* in *School Librarian,* Derek Paget claimed, "Pullman's is a good adaptation, keeping a firm grip on the perennial fascination of the story." Noting the adapter's inclusion of a section on genetic engineering as well as his suggestions for lesson plans in English and drama, Paget concluded that *Frankenstein* is "certainly a book for the library, and would be worth a production by youth or school drama groups."

In 1986, Pullman published *The Ruby in the Smoke,* a historical novel for young adults that became the first of his series of books about Sally Lockhart. A thriller set in Victorian London that was inspired by the English melodramas of the period, *Ruby* concerns the whereabouts of a priceless stone that mysteriously disappeared during the Indian mutiny. Sixteen-year-old Sally, a recently orphaned girl who is savvy about such subjects as business management, military strategy, and firearms, becomes involved in the opium trade when she receives a cryptic note written in a strange hand soon after hearing word of her father's drowning off Singapore. Like its successors, *The Ruby in the Smoke* includes abundant—often violent—action, murky atmosphere, and an examination of Victorian values from a modern perspective. Writing in *British Book News Children's Books,* Peter Hollindale claimed, "This is a splendid book. . . . It is a first-rate adventure story." David Churchill commented in the *School Librarian:* "There are not many books that offer such promise of satisfaction to so many children, of both sexes, of secondary age." Brooke L. Dillon in *Voice of Youth Advocates* noted the "beautifully crafted writing" and "the fact that Pullman respects his teenaged audience enough to treat them to a complex, interwoven plot." Writing in *SAAS,* Pullman claimed, "With *The Ruby in the Smoke* I think I first found my voice as a children's author."

The next volume in the series, *The Shadow in the Plate,* was published in the United Kingdom in 1987, and as *Shadow in the North* in the United States the next year. In this novel, Sally, now a financial consultant, and Frederick Garland, a photographer turned detective who was introduced in the previous story, solve a mystery with connections to the aristocracy, the Spiritualism movement, and a conspiracy that involves the production of an ultimate weapon. Pullman introduces readers to such issues as the moral implications of the Industrial Revolution while profiling Sally's growing love for Frederick. At the end of the novel, Frederick is killed, and Sally announces that she is pregnant with his child. Writing in *School Librarian,* Dennis Hamley called *The Shadow in the Plate* a "super read and a story to mull over afterwards for a significance which belies its outward form," while Michael Cart in *School Library Journal* noted that Pullman "once again demonstrates his mastery of atmosphere and style." Peter Hollindale claimed in *British Book News Children's Books* that the work "could mystify and disturb young children who may have liked the earlier one" and noted that it "is part of a children's trilogy, not *Bleak House.*" However, *Junior Bookshelf* contributor Marcus Crouch concluded that *Shadow* "is the kind of tale in which the reader willingly suspends critical judgement in favour of a wholehearted 'good read.'"

In the third volume of the "Sally Lockhart" series, *The Tiger in the Well,* Sally is a successful tycoon as well as a single mother with a two-year-old daughter, Harriet. When Sally receives a court summons informing her that she is being sued for divorce by a man she does not know, the heroine is faced with the prospect of losing her daughter and her property. After her court date, Sally—who has lost custody of Harriet as well as her home and her job—disappears into the Jewish ghetto of London's East End in order to find out who is behind the ruse. Pullman outlines Sally's developing social conscience through her experiences, which expose her to an anti-Semitic campaign, while drawing parallels between her treatment and that of the ghetto residents. Writing in *Voice of Youth Advocates,* Joanne Johnson noted that, as in his previous books in the series, Pullman "has recreated nineteenth-century London in good detail. His portrayal of the chauvinism rampant in British law during that time is a lesson to all." Marcus Crouch commented in *Junior Bookshelf:* "Not for the first time in the sequence, but with greater relevance, the name of Dickens comes to mind." The critic concluded that, like its predecessors, *The Tiger in the Well* "is compulsively readable. Unlike them the strong action runs parallel with sound social observations." Writing in *Books for Keeps,* Geoff Fox commented that the book "tastes delicious like the Penny Dreadfuls beloved of one of the novel's characters. . . . At another level, the book is a social document with the detail of Mayhew and the compassion of Dickens."

The final volume of the "Sally Lockhart" series, *The Tin Princess,* takes place in Central Europe rather than in Victorian London. A swashbuckling adventure set in the tiny kingdom of Razkavia, which lies between Germany and Austria, the novel introduces two new protagonists, Cockney Adelaide, a former prostitute featured in *The Ruby in the Smoke* who is now queen of Razkavia, and her friend and translator, Becky Winter. During the course of the story, Adelaide and Becky become caught up in political intrigue and romance, and Sally Lockhart makes a cameo appearance. Writing in

Booklist, Ilene Cooper noted that the author's passion for details "gets in the way" and that "too many names and places and plot twists" confuse the readers; however, the critic concluded, fans of Pullman's writing "should find much to enjoy here." Roger Sutton in the *Bulletin of the Center for Children's Books* commented in a similar vein, noting that the plot "is far too complicated for its own good" but concluded that while Pullman "appreciates the excesses of Victorian melodrama he is never seduced by them."

With the popular and critical reaction to "His Dark Materials," a series named for a phrase from John Milton's *Paradise Lost,* Pullman became an international phenomenon. Originally envisioned as a trilogy, the "His Dark Materials" series has expanded to more volumes and has been optioned for film. It is one of those rare publishing successes that finds as many readers among adults as it does among children and is particularly popular with college students—and their professors, who sometimes use it in classes on how to write children's literature. "The books can obviously be read at more than one level," observed John Rowe Townsend in *Horn Book.* "To younger readers they offer narratives of nonstop excitement with attractive young central characters. Adolescents and adults, putting more experience into their reading, should be able to draw more out. There are features of 'His Dark Materials' that will give older readers a great deal to think about." The chief elements that Pullman asks his older readers to ponder are no less than the nature of God, Satan, and the power that organized religion exerts on the independent mind. Townsend concluded: "This [work] has weight and richness, much that is absorbing and perceptive, and ample food for serious thought. It has flaws; but a large, ambitious work with flaws can be more rewarding than a cabined and confined perfection and 'saying something truthful and realistic about human nature' is surely what all fiction, including fantasy, should be trying to do."

In the first volume, which was published in the United Kingdom in 1995 as *Northern Lights* and in the United States in 1996 as *The Golden Compass,* Pullman describes an alternate world—parallel to our own but featuring technology from a hundred years ago as well as inventions from the future and the recent past—in which humans and daemons in animal form are tied with emotional bonds that if broken cause considerable damage, even death. Lyra, a young orphan girl with the skills of a natural leader, lives with her daemon Pantalaimon at Oxford. After children around the country begin disappearing and her uncle Lord Asriel is imprisoned during an expedition to the Arctic, Lyra embarks on a journey North with an alethiometer, a soothsaying instrument that looks like a golden compass. There she discovers that the youngsters are being held in a scientific experimental station where they are subjected to operations to separate them from their daemons. As the story progresses, Pullman discloses that Lyra, the key figure in an ancient prophecy, is destined to save her world and to move into another universe. Writing in the *Times Educational Supplement* about *Northern Lights,* Jan Mark noted: "Never did anything so boldly flout the usual protective mimicry of the teen read. This novel really does discuss the uniqueness of humanity—the fact of the soul." Julia Eccleshare commented in *Books for Keeps:* "The weaving together of story and morality is what makes *Northern Lights* such an exceptional book. Never for a moment does the story lose ground in the message it carries." Writing in *Horn Book* about the U.S. edition, Ann A. Flowers called *The Golden Compass* an "extraordinary, compelling fantasy. . . . Touching, exciting, and mysterious by turns, this is a splendid work." Although Jane Langton claimed in the *New York Times Book Review* that the novel does not achieve the stature of *The Lord of the Rings, A Wizard of Earthsea,* or *The Mouse and His Child,* the critic concluded that "it is still very grand indeed. There is scene after scene of power and beauty."

While writing *Northern Lights/The Golden Compass,* Pullman knew that he was creating a significant work. He told Julie C. Boehning of *Library Journal,* "I felt as if everything I'd read, written, and done in my whole life had been in preparation for this book." In 1996, *Northern Lights* was awarded the Carnegie Medal, Great Britain's highest literary award specifically for children's literature.

In the next novel in the series, *The Subtle Knife,* Lyra meets Will Parry, a boy from Oxford who escapes into an alternative city after killing a man. Like Lyra, Will is destined to help save the universe from destruction; in addition, he possesses a counterpart to her golden compass, a knife that can cut through anything—even the borders between worlds. While Lyra and Will search for Dust and for Will's explorer father, it becomes evident that Lord Asriel, Lyra's guardian from the first book, is preparing to re-stage the revolt of the angels against God and that Lyra has been chosen to be the new Eve. *Horn Book* critic Ann A. Flowers commented that Pullman "offered an exceptional romantic fantasy in *The Golden Compass,* but *The Subtle Knife* adds a mythic dimension that inevitably demands even greater things from the finale." Sally Estes in *Booklist* noted, "Often the middle book in a trilogy is the weakest; such is not the case here." Estes called *The Subtle Knife* a "resoundingly successful sequel." Writing in *Voice of Youth Advocates* about both *The Subtle Knife* and its predecessor, Jennifer Fakolt commented that these volumes "are, simply, magnificent. Pullman has the power of a master fantasist. He imbues an age-old classical struggle with a new mythic vision, the depth and realization of which are staggering." Fakolt concluded that the "two titles stand in equal company with the works of J.R.R. Tolkien and C.S. Lewis."

In an interview with Julia Eccleshare in *Books for Keeps,* Pullman discussed the background of "His Dark Materials": "What I really wanted to do was *Paradise Lost* in 1,200 pages. From the beginning I knew the shape of the story. It's the story of The Fall which is the story of how what some would call sin, but I would call consciousness, comes to us. The more I thought about it the clearer it became. It fell naturally into three parts. Though it's long, I've never been in danger of getting lost because the central strand is so simple." Pullman's central thrust is to reveal the Biblical God as an elderly, powerless figurehead, manipulated by a head angel named Metatron, who is power-hungry and autocratic in the extreme. Lord Asriel and his wife, Mrs. Coulter—both ambiguous figures capable of both good and evil—oppose Metatron and the powers of Heaven. It is Lyra and Will, and their various fantastic helpers, who finally bring about, in Volume Three, *The Amber Spyglass,* literally the death of God.

Published to much anticipation in 2000, *The Amber Spyglass* is perhaps the most successful of the first three "His Dark Materials" novels. It won the Whitbread Award over the shortlisted adult novels, biographies, and nonfiction published in Great Britain in 2000 and prompted an author tour of the United States as well. The novel culminates with Will and Lyra descending into the realm of death and returning to life again, reversing the loss of Dust from the universe, and—by expressing their love for one another—putting an end to the iron autocracy led by Metatron and the demented deity. "The witches and wizards in the 'Harry Potter' books will seem like cartoon characters compared with those in Pullman's religious pantheon," declared Ilene Cooper in *Booklist.* "The first two books in the series exposed the Church as corrupt, bigoted, and evil. Now Pullman takes on Heaven itself. . . . 'His Dark Materials' has taken readers on a wild, magnificent ride that, in its totality, represents an astounding achievement." Eva Mitnick in *School Library Journal* found the message in *The Amber Spyglass* "clear and exhilarating," adding that the book offers "a subtle and complex treatment of the eternal battle between good and evil."

In interviews, Pullman has maintained that he used the vehicle of fantasy in "His Dark Materials" to make starkly realistic points about human nature. He told *School Library Journal:* "When I found myself writing this book, what I wanted to do was to use the apparatus of fantasy in order to do what writers of realism are more typically interested in doing, namely, to explore this business about being a human being—what it feels like and what it's like, what it means for us to grow up, to pass away from our childhood, to suffer, to learn, to grow, to develop, to die, and so on. And that's what I mean by saying that it's not really a work of fantasy. It's as realistic as I could make it."

Pullman has also had success with his stand-alone titles for readers of various ages. For example, *How to Be Cool,* a humorous satire published in 1987 in which a group of teens expose a government agency that decides which fashions will be hip, was called "a perfect gift for iconoclastic teenagers" by Peter Hollindale of *British Book News Children's Supplement; How to Be Cool* was made into a television program by Granada-TV in 1988. *The Broken Bridge,* a young adult novel published in 1990, is considered a major departure for its author. The story features Ginny Howard, a sixteen-year-old Haitian/English girl living with her single father in a small Welsh town. Anxious to begin her career as a painter, Ginny learns that she is illegitimate, that she has a half-brother, and that her mother, whom she assumed was dead, is actually alive. Ginny meets this parent—who tells her that she is a painter, not a mother—and learns about her father's abused childhood, while evaluating her own heritage, character, and direction. Writing in the *New York Times Book Review,* Michael Dorris said, "It's a credit to the storytelling skill of Philip Pullman that this contemporary novel succeeds as well as it does. As the plot tumbles forward, . . . the writing remains fresh, the settings original and the central characters compelling." Nancy Vasilakis in *Horn Book* praised Pullman for "skillfully manipulating the conventions of the mystery and the problem novel," while a critic in *Publishers Weekly* saw "the emotional truths that Pullman reveals" as being "so heartfelt and raw that they hardly read like fiction."

Pullman returned to nineteenth-century London for the setting of his "New Cut Gang" series, comic mysteries for middle graders that feature a gang of urchins in the 1890s. In a review of the first book in the series, *Thunderbolt's Waxworks,* D. A Young in *Junior Bookshelf* commented that Pullman "creates a convincing picture of his chosen time and place with the lightest of touches," while Jan Mark, reviewing the same title in *Carousel,* noted that the narrative introduces "an extraordinary vocabulary of scientific terms and nineteenth-century slang. You get very educated without noticing it." Pullman has also written works that reflect his fascination with folktale and myth. In *The Firework-Maker's Daughter,* a book that won the Smarties Award in 1996, the author describes how Lila, the daughter of a fireworks maker who is in the final stages of apprenticeship, goes on a quest with Hamlet, a talking white elephant that belongs to the king of her country, and Chulak, the elephant's keeper. Their journey takes them to the lair of the Fire-fiend, a figure who holds the key to firework making. In the process, Lila discovers herself. A critic in *Reading Time* said, "This is the stuff of myths. . . . It is an exciting story, not only for its own sake but for the other layer of meaning which lurks beneath the surface." Writing in *Magpies,* Rayma Turton commented, "Lila is all a feminist could ask for," and concluded that *The Firework-Maker's Daughter* is "the work of a master storyteller."

Clockwork, or All Wound Up, a short novel with echoes of *Faust* and the ballet *Coppelia,* is noted for weaving an examination of the process of storytelling with a spine-tingling tale. The book describes how Fritz, a talented tale-spinner, and Karl, a clockmaker's apprentice who has failed to complete his latest assignment, a clockwork child, are joined with the subject of one of Fritz's stories, Dr. Kalmerius, a clockmaker thought to have connections with the Devil. Writing in *School Librarian,* Chris Routh called *Clockwork* "a fantastic and spine-chilling tale," adding that it "begs to be read in one sitting (who could bear to put it down?)." The critic concluded by asking, "Who said the art of storytelling is dead?" George Hunt of *Books for Keeps* described the book as a "fascinating meditation on the intricate machinations of narrative," and simultaneously "a funny, frightening, and moving story." Writing in *Carousel,* Adèle Geras concluded, "This story could not be more modern, yet it has the weight and poetry of the best folktales. Not to be missed on any account."

In *I Was a Rat!,* a scruffy little boy tries to convince people that he actually is a rat. By some trick of magic he was turned into a boy in order to accompany a woman to a ball—and then, at the stroke of midnight, he was playing when he should have been transformed back into a rat. Now he seeks help wherever he can find it—from the tabloid press, from his adoptive parents, and from the new princess herself, who he remembers as his old friend Mary Jane. The story turns the *Cinderella* fairy tale on its head in a humorous way but also manages to make points about modern society and the way people respond to unconventional requests. A *Horn Book* reviewer described *I Was a Rat!* as a "playful spoofing of sensational news stories, mob mentality, and the royal family." In a starred review of the work, *School Library Journal* correspondent Connie Tyrrell Burns noted that, while Pullman is having fun here, he still "leaves readers with some thought-provoking ideas."

Pullman once explained in *SAAS:* "I am first and foremost a storyteller. In whatever form I write—whether it's the novel, or the screenplay, or the stage play, or even if I tell stories (as I sometimes do)—I am always the servant of the story that has chosen me to tell it and I have to discover the best way of doing that. I believe there's a pure line that goes through every story and the more closely the telling approaches that pure line, the better the story will be. . . . The story must tell me." When asked by Kit Alderdice in *Publishers Weekly* what he finds most satisfying about his career, Pullman responded, "The fundamental thing that I do find important and gratifying is that I simply have the time—never as much time as I would like—but I simply have the time to sit here and enjoy the company of my stories and my characters. That's an enormous pleasure, and a great privilege." He added in *SAAS,* "Sometimes I can hardly believe my luck."

BIOGRAPHICAL AND CRITICAL SOURCES:

BOOKS

Children's Literature Review, Volume 20, Thomson Gale, 1990, pp. 185-188.

Gallo, Donald, editor, *Speaking for Ourselves, Too,* National Council of Teachers of English, 1993.

Silvey, Anita, editor, *Children's Books and Their Creators,* Houghton Mifflin (Boston, MA), 1995, p. 544.

Something about the Author Autobiography Series, Volume 17, Thomson Gale (Detroit, MI), pp. 297-312.

Squires, Claire, *Philip Pullman's "His Dark Materials" Trilogy: A Reader's Guide,* Continuum (New York, NY), 2003.

Twentieth-Century Young Adult Writers, St. James Press (Detroit, MI), 1994, pp. 543-544.

PERIODICALS

Book, September, 2000, Jennifer D'Anastasio and Kathleen Odean, "Built to Last," p. 88; November-December, 2002, Anna Weinberg, "Are You There, God? It's Me, Philip Pullman," p. 11.

Booklist, February 15, 1994, Ilene Cooper, review of *The Tin Princess,* p. 1075; July, 1997, Sally Estes, review of *The Subtle Knife,* p. 1818; October 1, 2000, Ilene Cooper, "Darkness Visible—Philip Pullman's Amber Spyglass," p. 354.

Bookseller, June 29, 2001, Caroline Sylge, "Performing Books," p. 8.

Books for Keeps, May, 1992, Geoff Fox, "Philip Pullman," p. 25; September, 1996, Julia Eccleshare, "Northern Lights and Christmas Miracles," p. 15; March, 1997, George Hunt, review of *Clockwork, or All Wound Up,* p. 25.

British Book News Children's Books, March, 1986, Peter Hollindale, review of *The Ruby in the Smoke,* pp. 33-34; December, 1986, Peter Hollindale, review of *The Shadow in the Plate,* pp. 30-31; March, 1988, Peter Hollindale, review of *How to Be Cool,* p. 30.

Bulletin of the Center for Children's Books, February, 1994, Roger Sutton, review of *The Tin Princess,* pp. 199-200.

Carousel, spring, 1997, Adèle Geras, review of *Clockwork, or All Wound Up,* p. 19; spring, 1997, Jan Mark, review of *Thunderbolt's Waxworks,* p. 19.

Commonweal, November 17, 2000, Daria Donnelly, "Big Questions for Small Readers," p. 23.

Horn Book, March-April, 1992, Nancy Vasilakis, review of *The Broken Bridge,* p. 211; July-August, 1996, Ann A. Flowers, review of *The Golden Compass,* pp. 464-465; September-October, 1997, Ann A. Flowers, review of *The Subtle Knife,* pp. 578-579; January, 2000, review of *I Was a Rat!,* p. 82; July-August, 2002, John Rowe Townsend, "Paradise Reshaped," p. 415.

Junior Bookshelf, April, 1982, R. Baines, review of *Ancient Civilizations,* p. 75; December, 1986, Marcus Crouch, review of *The Shadow in the Plate,* pp. 229-230; June, 1991, Marcus Crouch, review of *The Tiger in the Well,* p. 127; December, 1994, D.A. Young, review of *Thunderbolt's Waxworks,* pp. 231-232; November, 2000, Gregory Maguire, review of *The Amber Spyglass,* p. 735.

Library Journal, February 15, 1996, Julie C. Boehning, "Philip Pullman's Paradise," p. 175.

Magpies, May, 1997, Rayma Turton, review of *The Firework-Maker's Daughter,* p. 35.

National Review, March 25, 2002, Andrew Stuttaford, "Sunday School for Atheists," p. 56.

New Statesman, December 3, 1982, Charles Fox, "Once and Future Image," pp. 21-22; October 30, 2000, Amanda Craig, "Burning Dazzle," p. 53.

Newsweek, October 30, 2000, "Pullman's Progress," p. 80.

New York Times Book Review, May 17, 1992, Michael Dorris, "Galloping Adolescence," p. 24; May 19, 1996, Jane Langton, "What Is Dust?," p. 34.

Publishers Weekly, January 1, 1992, review of *The Broken Bridge,* p. 56; May 30, 1994, Kit Alderdice, "In the Studio with Philip Pullman," pp. 24-25; September 25, 2000, review of *The Amber Spyglass,* p. 119; September 25, 2000, Kit Alderdice, "PW Talks with Philip Pullman," p. 119; December 18, 2000, Shannon Maughan, "Whose Dark Materials?," p. 25.

Reading Time, May, 1997, review of *The Firework-Maker's Daughter,* p. 30.

School Librarian, June, 1986, David Churchill, review of *The Ruby in the Smoke,* p. 174; December, 1986, Dennis Hamley, review of *The Shadow in the Plate,* p. 368; November, 1990, Derek Paget, review of *Frankenstein,* p. 157; May, 1997, Chris Routh, review of *Clockwork, or All Wound Up,* p. 90.

School Library Journal, May, 1988, Michael Cart, review of *Shadow in the North,* p. 112; March, 2000, Connie Tyrrell Burns, review of *I Was a Rat!,* p. 241; October, 2000, Eva Mitnick, review of *The Amber Spyglass,* p. 170.

Times Educational Supplement, July 21, 1995, Jan Mark, review of *Northern Lights,* p. 23.

Voice of Youth Advocates, October, 1987, Brooke L. Dillon, review of *The Ruby in the Smoke,* p. 206; December, 1990, Joanne Johnson, review of *The Tiger in the Well,* p. 288; June, 1998, Jennifer Fakolt, review of *The Golden Compass* and *The Subtle Knife,* p. 133.

* * *

PULLMAN, Philip Nicholas
See PULLMAN, Philip

* * *

PYGGE, Edward
See BARNES, Julian

* * *

PYNCHON, Thomas, Jr. 1937-
(Thomas Ruggles Pynchon, Jr.)

PERSONAL: Born May 8, 1937, Glen Cove, Long Island, NY; son of Thomas Ruggles (an industrial surveyor) and Katherine Frances Bennett Pynchon. *Education:* Cornell University, B.A., 1958.

ADDRESSES: Agent—c/o Author Mail, Plume, Penguin USA, 375 Hudson St., New York, NY 10014.

CAREER: Writer. Boeing Aircraft, Seattle, WA, writer for in-house organ. *Military service:* U.S. Navy, two years, c. 1950s.

AWARDS, HONORS: William Faulkner novel award, 1963, for *V.;* Rosenthal Foundation Award, National Institute of Arts and Letters, 1967, for *The Crying of Lot 49;* National Book Award, 1974, for *Gravity's Rainbow* (refused); Howells Medal, National Institute and American Academy of Arts and Letters, 1975, for body of work.

WRITINGS:

V. (novel; portions of Chapter 3 first published as the short story "Under the Rose," in *Noble Savage,* number 3; other portions first published in *New World Writing*), Lippincott (Philadelphia, PA), 1963.

The Crying of Lot 49 (novel; selection first published as "The World [This One], the Flesh [Mrs. Oedipa Maas], and the Testament of Pierce Inverarity," in *Esquire,* December, 1965; other portions published in *Cavalier*), Lippincott (Philadelphia, PA), 1966.

Gravity's Rainbow (novel), Viking (New York, NY), 1973, reprinted, Plume (New York, NY), 2003.

(Author of introduction) Richard Farina, *Been Down So Long It Looks Like Up to Me,* Penguin Books (New York, NY), 1983.

Slow Learner (short story collection; contains "The Secret Integration," "The Small Rain," "Low-lands," "Entropy," and "Under the Rose"), Little, Brown (Boston, MA), 1984.

Vineland (novel), Little, Brown (Boston, MA), 1990.

(Author of introduction) Donald Barthelme, *The Teachings of Don B.: Satires, Parodies, Fables, Illustrated Stories, and Plays,* Random House (New York, NY), 1992.

(With others) *Deadly Sins* (essays; originally published in *New York Times Book Review*), illustrated by Etienne Delessert, Morrow (New York, NY), 1993.

Mason and Dixon, Henry Holt (New York, NY), 1997.

(Author of foreword) George Orwell, *1984,* afterword by Erich Fromm, Plume (New York, NY), 2003.

Also author of short stories published by Aloes Books, including *Mortality and Mercy in Vienna,* 1976, and *Low-Lands,* 1978. Contributor of short stories and essays to periodicals, including *New York Times Magazine, New York Times Book Review,Cornell Writer, Holiday,Cornell Alumni News, Saturday Evening Post,* and *Kenyon Review.*

SIDELIGHTS: According to *Time* contributor Joel Stein, American author Thomas Pynchon "created epic modernism" by unfettering "the detail-saturated realism of James Joyce and Virginia Woolf . . . from the confining world of marriage problems and parental blame and everything else that has made novels so small" to tranform the form into "a lens" for epic tales. Despite such a lofty accomplishment, Pynchon, somewhat ironically, is perhaps better known for *not* being known. The most significant biographical fact about the author of *Gravity's Rainbow* and *The Crying of Lot 49* is his anonymity: Pynchon has remained so wary of publicity that the only known facts about him consist of slim facts relating to his birth and education. For a time it was commonplace to compare Pynchon with J.D. Salinger, another famous American novelist noted for evading public scrutiny, but that comparison proved inadequate: Salinger, at least, could be located. Evidence and conjecture suggests that, while a daring and iconoclastic writer, Pynchon is in his personal life intensely private and intensely shy.

Pynchon's work strikes many readers as intensely difficult. This difficulty needs emphasizing inasmuch as it is not an extrinsic characteristic—one that a more careful author could have avoided, or one that the reader can circumvent with a good plot summary. Indeed, much of the difficulty arises precisely because Pynchon's plots resist summarization, just as his narrators resist reduction to a single identifiable voice and his range of reference seems virtually endless. The radical disruptions in his works that led the Pulitzer Prize editorial board to refuse to grant him the fiction award for *Gravity's Rainbow* also inspired Edward Mendelson to write in the *Yale Review* that "Pynchon is, quite simply, the best living novelist in English," and rank *Gravity's Rainbow* with James Joyce's *Ulysses* and Thomas Mann's *The Magic Mountain* as one of the greatest novels of the twentieth century. It is clear that difficulty may provoke reflection as well as reaction. Pynchon still has vocal detractors, but as Khachig Tololyan wrote in the *New Orleans Review,* "It is no longer possible to be seriously interested in contemporary American literature and yet to claim jauntily that one 'just can't get through' Thomas Pynchon's books."

The structural difficulty central to Pynchon's texts early became a theme, so that to a degree all Pynchon's novels are about difficulties in reading—and about "reading" as a metaphor for all the ways in which people try to make sense of the world in which they find themselves. In Pynchon's work, the act of reading parallels the act of deciphering a world problematically constructed of codes. Treating *The Crying of Lot 49,* Frank

Kermode observed in an essay collected in Seymour Chatman's *Approaches to Poetics,* "What Oedipa is doing is very like reading a book," and the statement applies as well to Herbert Stencil in *V.* and to any number of questing heroes in *Gravity's Rainbow.* The notion of "reading" experience as a way of discerning meanings occurs as early as the 1960 short story "Entropy," in which, as Joseph Tabbi observed in a *Pynchon Notes* article, the undergraduate Pynchon was already working to "create an imaginative order in art that would engage randomness and indeterminacy in modern life and in the changing physical world." In *V.,* published in 1963, apparent randomness and indeterminacy are qualities of the fictional universe that confronts the reader as well as the characters, and the central action of the quest is disconcertingly similar to the reader's own act of interpretation.

In a wider sense, "reading" is the process by which people make a story out of experience and call it history. As Tony Tanner remarked in his article "V. and V-2," collected in Mendelson's *Pynchon: A Collection of Critical Essays, V.* is very much aligned with the short story "Entropy" in its concern for the possible running-down of history, for a gradual decline, which the narrator terms decadence. But while Pynchon's work "is certainly about a world succumbing to entropy, it is also about the subtler human phenomena, the need to see patterns which may easily turn into the tendency to suspect plots." Tanner's synopsis plays on a double meaning inherent in the word "plot." In one sense a plot is a story line, the bare outline of "what happens" in a work of fiction. In another sense, however, a plot is a conspiracy, an underlying story of secret manipulation that reveals "what really happened." Insofar as history is "plotted" it may entail both of these meanings: if it tells a story it may do so precisely because someone has created that story, arranged things to produce certain results. A conspirator and an author clearly have something in common if the pun is taken seriously. Perhaps history itself has authors. Perhaps crucial events take place because somebody planned things that way.

V. is "about" plotting in this disturbing sense inasmuch as it raises questions about history within its own structure. The chapters taking place in the narrative present, in the years 1956 and 1957, are punctuated by chapters set at various times in the previous three-quarters of a century. The jumps between "past" and "present" are violent and to some extent unexplained. In some cases the reader can be reasonably sure that one of the protagonists, Herbert Stencil, is narrating the "historical" story, but in other cases it is radically unclear where the story is coming from or why it occurs at this point in the "present" action. The problem of connections thus becomes a major concern of the reader, who in making sense of Pynchon's novel is suddenly immersed in the same enterprise as Stencil himself.

Stencil's activity, a form of quest, involves looking through segments of recent history for manifestations of a woman known to him only as V. In the process Stencil serves as a persona of the reader, for as Melvyn New noted in the *Georgia Review,* "While Herbert Stencil searches for clues to the meaning of the woman, V., accumulating his notecards, his sources, his linkages, we, as readers, parallel his activity, making our own accumulations, driven by the same urge to fit the pieces together, to arrive at the meaning of the novel *V.*" The central dilemma of this quest depends on the double meaning of "plot." If the connections that Stencil discerns between the events of history are real, they seem to be evidence of a conspiracy bringing the twentieth century to a state of apocalyptic decadence, a situation analogous to the entropic run-down posited by thermodynamic theory as the terminus of the physical universe. If these connections are not real, but only projected out of a need to find order in the events of history, historical events become meaningless: uncaused and unmotivated, and causing and motivating nothing in the present.

The Crying of Lot 49 has only one protagonist, another quester with the quest-hero's resonant name of Oedipa, and only one line of action, which remains resolutely chronological. Readers are thus largely spared the task of making connections within the story and left to observe the spectacle of the hero making her own connections which is to say either discerning them in or projecting them onto a satirically envisioned landscape of Southern California at mid-century. The parodic quality of *V.* is if anything intensified in *The Crying of Lot 49,* where Oedipa Maas (the surname means "more" in Spanish and is close to "measure" in German) is joined by Manny DiPresso, Stanley Koteks, Genghis Cohen, and a rock group called the Paranoids. Manfred Puetz suggested in his study *The Story of Identity: American Fiction of the Sixties* that Pynchon's characters tend to be stereotypical and "curiously one-dimensional" precisely because of the interpretive dilemmas in which they find themselves: "they remain caught in their situations" and "act out the same obsessions in compulsive repetitiveness." Certainly the metaphors of entrapment that confine Oedipa also define her. She is most memorably a princess in a tower weaving a tapestry that comes to constitute the world.

Like *V., The Crying of Lot 49* is concerned with the "plot" of history, embodied in the force that might be behind a spectral underground association called the Tristero. The novel is also more explicit than *V.* in its assertion of decoding activities as characteristic of scientific thinking and to this end uses the concept of entropy as an aspect of both physics and information theory. As Ann Mangel noted in an essay in *Mindful Pleasures: Essays on Thomas Pynchon,* "By building his fiction on the concept of entropy, or disorder, and by flaunting the irrelevance, redundancy, disorganization, and waste involved in language, Pynchon radically separates himself from earlier twentieth-century writers, like [William Butler] Yeats, [T. S.] Eliot, and Joyce." But this antimodernism becomes productive, a critique of the modernist rage for order and in the process an exemplary postmodernism, inasmuch as it sees in the order of closed artistic systems an analogue of the conditions for entropic rundown. Mangel continued, "The complex, symbolic structures [that the modernists] created to encircle chaotic experience often resulted in the kinds of static, closed systems Pynchon is so wary of."

The publication of *Gravity's Rainbow* in 1973 secured Pynchon's reputation. The controversy over the Pulitzer was widely publicized and criticized, with many readers regarding the editorial board's decision as comparable to acts of the repressive power structure that the novel painstakingly documents. In addition, *Gravity's Rainbow* won the National Book Award (Pynchon refused it, sending "Professor" Irwin Corey, a self-proclaimed master of double-talk, to the awards ceremony as his surrogate) and the William Dean Howells Award of the American Academy of Arts and Letters for the best novel of the decade. Both the acclaim and the hostility that this book engendered testify to its innovations. As Tololyan observed in the *New Orleans Review,* it surpasses many traditional definitions "of what can be considered literary," upsetting "narrow generic and modal categories" of criticism and refusing "to fulfill a set of expectations nurtured by reading the great novels of the nineteenth century, or the slighter fictions of our time."

One index of the scope of *Gravity's Rainbow* is the fact that it was reviewed in *Scientific American* and discussed at length in *Technology and Culture.* In the latter journal Joseph Slade hailed Pynchon as "the first American novelist to accept the duty of which [Aldous] Huxley speaks," the duty "to seek powerful means of expressing the nature of technology and the crises it has generated." In *Readings from the New Book of Nature: Physics and Metaphysics in the Modern Novel,* Robert Nadeau identified these crises with the collapse of "the Newtonian world view, which features along with the Western mind itself either-or categorical thinking, simple causality, immutable law, determinism, and discrete immutable substances;" but Alan Friedman, writing in Charles Clerc's collection *Approaches to "Gravity's Rainbow,"* found more recent scientific world views equally unsatisfactory: "Unfortunately, the visions from science do not provide more hopeful guides away from the horrors *Gravity's Rainbow* reveals in life and death. Doctrinaire acceptance of any of these visions proves as sterile as the nonscience-related images that obsess characters." Richard Poirier, in the *Saturday Review of the Arts,* suggested that, on the contrary, scientific data permeate the book not to provide solutions to conceptual difficulties but to compound these difficulties by offering yet another tradition to which the language can allude. The central symbol of the novel, the V-2 rocket, is thus even more overdetermined than central symbols tend to be; it is "Moby Dick and the Pequod all in one, both the Virgin and the Dynamo of Pynchon's magnificent book."

Poirier went on to comment, "More than any living writer, including Norman Mailer, [Pynchon] has caught the inward movements of our time in outward manifestations of art and technology so that in being historical he must also be marvelously exorbitant," and the "exorbitant" quality of *Gravity's Rainbow* may constitute its greatest threat to traditional ideas of the "literary." In *Technology and Culture,* Slade pointed to Pynchon's "faith in the unity of Creation"; but a number of other critics see in *Gravity's Rainbow* a work constituted in opposition to existing notions of unity, and especially in opposition to the unity of the artistic work celebrated by the earlier masters of literary modernism. For example, Brian McHale, writing in *Poetics Today,* called *Gravity's Rainbow* a "postmodern text" that subverts the emphasis on coherence of the "modernist reading" it seems to elicit. Charles Russell concurred that the novel pushes at conventional boundaries and noted in *Approaches to "Gravity's Rainbow,"* "Indeed, *Gravity's Rainbow* is but one manifestation of a widespread literary fascination with the nature and limits of aesthetic and social language during the past two decades." And John Muste, writing in *Boundary 2,* found in the circular image of the mandala (a preoccupation of the southwest African Herero characters prominent in the novel) an emblem of the reader's situation. "Confronted with a text which contains a veritable cornucopia of clues," Muste observed that "we search diligently and sometimes desperately for ways of arranging these clues in a meaningful pattern. *Gravity's Rainbow* invites, even demands, such efforts, and steadfastly rebuffs them. It gives nothing away. At the center of the mandala rests that infuriating empty circle, that refusal to impose meaning or to confirm either our fondest wishes or our direst fears."

The publication of *Gravity's Rainbow* marked the beginning of a seventeen-year silence on Pynchon's part, interrupted only by the 1984 release of *Slow Learner,* a collection of five previously published short stories. In 1990, however, Pynchon reentered the literary mainstream with *Vineland,* a novel taking its title from the fictional northern California county in which it takes place. Focusing on a group of 1960s beatniks after they lived through the disillusionment of the following decade into the television-dominated culture of the 1980s, *Vineland* features a pot-growing handyman, landscaper, and former rock singer named Zoyd Wheeler, his teenaged daughter Prairie, and Frenesi Gates, his ex-wife. The book's complex plot begins with Zoyd's being forced into hiding when a prosecutor from Washington, DC—and Frenesi's jealous former lover—tries to kidnap Prairie in an attempt to resume his relationship with Frenesi, who has disappeared. Unlike Pynchon's previous novels, *Vineland* contains numerous references to popular culture and alludes to many fewer scholarly, literary, or historical ideas. Critics can still trace, however, Pynchon's trademark themes of entropy and paranoia, and many have commented on the wit, humor, and extraordinary facility with language that Pynchon demonstrates in the novel.

While finding much about *Vineland* to praise, reviewers generally agree that Pynchon's much-anticipated novel does not surpass either *Gravity's Rainbow* or *The Crying of Lot 49* as his best work. *Vineland* "won't inspire the same sort of fanatic loyalty and enthusiasm that *Gravity's Rainbow* did," asserted David Strietfeld in *Fame,* adding: "The new novel has got a much more mainstream flavor. . . . Call it Pynchon Lite." Expressing severe criticism was *Listener* contributor John Dugdale, who maintained that *Vineland*'s grounding in contemporary American life detracts from the importance of Pynchon's themes: *Vineland* "is an unsatisfactory, stripped-down novel lacking the internal tension which sustained its predecessors: the interplay between abstract concepts and human stories, past art and modern lives, the scholarly and the streetwise. By misguidedly choosing to quit the literature of ideas, Pynchon robs his writing of both its vitality and its distinctiveness." But Paul Gray, writing in *Time,* was more appreciative of *Vineland* and its portrait of betrayal, conformity, materialism, and shallowness: "It is, admittedly, disquieting to find a major author drawing cultural sustenance from *The Brady Bunch* and *I Love Lucy* instead of *The Odyssey* and the Bible," Gray admitted. "But to condemn Pynchon for this strategy is to confuse the author with his characters. He is a gifted man with anti-elitist sympathies. Like some fairly big names in innovative fiction, including Flaubert, Joyce and Faulkner, Pynchon writes about people who would not be able to read the books in which they appear. As a contemporary bonus, Pynchon's folks would not even be interested in trying. That is part of the sadness and the hilarity of this exhilarating novel."

In *Mason & Dixon,* Pynchon weaves together fact with a kind of logical fantasy derived in various measures from fact, probability, and imagination to create what amounts to an allegory of national progress in the formative years of the United States. Narrated in authentic-sounding period prose by the Rev. Wicks Cherrycoke, the novel follows the journey of the surveyors who divided the country into North and South, from their first meeting until the drawing of the famous line which bears their name. Like the rest of Pynchon's work, *Mason & Dixon* is long, dense, and difficult. Even a sympathetic reviewer like Michiko Kakutani in the *New York Times* admitted that the novel "could have used some judicious editing" to prevent its being "daunting to many readers." Most critics, Kakutani included, are fascinated by Pynchon's complex narrative tapestry. T. Coraghessan Boyle, in the *New York Times Book Review,* stated: "The method is sublime. It allows for the surveyors' story to become an investigation into the order of the universe, clockwork deity and all, and yet at the same time to reflect the inadequacy of reason alone to explain the mystery that surrounds us. The haunted world, the suprareal, the ghostly and the impossible have the same valence as the facts of history as we receive them. If the traditional historical novel attempts to replicate a way of life, speech and costume, [this] post-modernist version seeks only to be just that, a version." In the *Nation,* John Leonard noted that "from the depths of a jaunty disenchantment, [Pynchon] calls into brilliant question the very ways we measure, map and misconstrue history, landscape, time, space, stars and self."

BIOGRAPHICAL AND CRITICAL SOURCES:

BOOKS

Arlett, Robert, *Epic Voices: Inner and Global Impulse in the Contemporary American and British Novel,* Susquehanna University Press, 1996.

Chambers, Judith, *Thomas Pynchon,* Twayne (New York, NY), 1992.

Chatman, Seymour, editor, *Approaches to Poetics,* Columbia University Press (New York, NY), 1973.

Clerc, Charles, editor, *Approaches to "Gravity's Rainbow,"* Ohio State University Press, 1983.

Contemporary Literary Criticism, Thomson Gale (Detroit, MI), Volume 2, 1974, Volume 3, 1975, Volume 6, 1976, Volume 9, 1978, Volume 11, 1979, Volume 18, 1981, Volume 33, 1985, Volume 62, 1991, Volume 72, 1992.

Cooper, Peter L., *Signs and Symptoms: Thomas Pynchon and the Contemporary World,* University of California Press (Berkeley, CA), 1983.

Cowart, David, *Thomas Pynchon: The Art of Allusion,* Southern Illinois University Press (Carbondale, IL), 1980.

Dictionary of Literary Biography, Thomson Gale (Detroit, MI), Volume 2: *American Novelists since World War II,* 1978, Volume 173: *American Novelists since World War II, Fifth Series,* 1996.

Dugdale, John, *Thomas Pynchon: Allusive Parables of Power,* Macmillan (New York, NY), 1990.

Grant, J. Kerry, *A Companion to "The Crying of Lot 49,"* University of Georgia Press, 1994.

Green, Geoffrey, *The Vineland Papers: Critical Takes on Pynchon's Novel,* Dalkey Archive Press, 1994.

Hite, Molly, *Ideas of Order in the Novels of Thomas Pynchon,* Ohio State University Press, 1983.

Hurm, Gerd, *Fragmented Urban Images: The American City in Modern Fiction from Stephen Crane to Thomas Pynchon,* P. Lang (New York, NY), 1991.

Madsen, Deborah L., *The Postmodernist Allegories of Thomas Pynchon,* St. Martin's Press (New York, NY), 1991.

Mendelson, Edward, editor, *Pynchon: A Collection of Critical Essays,* Prentice-Hall (Englewood Cliffs, NJ), 1978.

Nadeau, Robert, *Readings from the New Book on Nature: Physics and Metaphysics in the Modern Novel,* University of Massachusetts Press (Amherst, MA), 1981.

Newman, Robert D., *Understanding Thomas Pynchon,* University of South Carolina Press, 1986.

Plater, William M., *The Grim Phoenix: Reconstructing Thomas Pynchon,* University of Indiana Press, 1978.

Puetz, Manfred, *The Story of Identity: American Fiction of the Sixties,* Metzlersche Verlagsbuchhandlung, 1979.

Sakrajda, Mira, *Postmodern Discourses of Love: Pynchon, Barth, Coover, Gass, and Barthelme,* Peter Lang (New York, NY), 1997.

Schaub, Thomas H., *Pynchon: The Voice of Ambiguity,* University of Illinois Press, 1981.

Scotto, Robert M., *Three Contemporary Novelists: An Annotated Bibliography of Works by and about John Hawkes, Joseph Heller, and Thomas Pynchon,* G.K. Hall (New York, NY), 1977.

Short Story Criticism, Volume 14, Thomson Gale (Detroit, MI), 1994.

Siegel, Mark R., *Pynchon: Creative Paranoia in "Gravity's Rainbow,"* Kennikat Press, 1978.

PERIODICALS

Boundary 2, Volume 3, 1975; Volume 5, number 1, 1976; Volume 8, 1980; Volume 9, number 2, 1981.

Chicago Tribune Book World, April 8, 1984.

College Literature, spring, 2001, Patrick McHugh, "Cultural Politics, Postmodernism, and White Guys: Affect in *Gravity's Rainbow,*" p. 1.

Commentary, September, 1963; September, 1973.

Commonweal, July 8, 1966; August 15, 1997, p. 20.

Contemporary Literature, summer, 1974; autumn, 1977; autumn, 1979; spring, 1980.

Critique, summer, 2003, John K. Young, "Pynchon in Popular Magazines," p. 389.

English Journal, July, 2000, Michael Santa Maria, "In Praise of Thomas Pynchon," p. 136.

Explicator, fall, 2000, Steven Carver, review of *The Crying of Lot 49,* p. 50; summer, 2001, p. 216.

Extrapolation, spring, 2002, Randy Shroeder, "Inheriting Chaos," p. 89.

Fame, winter, 1990, David Strietfeld, review of *Vineland.*

Georgia Review, Volume 33, number 1, 1979.

Globe and Mail (Toronto, Ontario, Canada), June 30, 1984; January 20, 1990.

Listener, February 1, 1990, John Dugdale, review of *Vineland.*

Literature/Film Quarterly, Volume 6, 1978.

Los Angeles Times, December 10, 1989.

Los Angeles Times Book Review, May 6, 1984; December 31, 1989.

Modern Fiction Studies, Volume 23, 1977.

Nation, September 25, 1967; July 16, 1973; February 26, 1990; May 12, 1997.

New Leader, May 23, 1966.

New Orleans Review, Volume 5, 1977, article by Khachig Tololyan.

Newsweek, April 1, 1963; May 2, 1966; May 20, 1974; April 9, 1984; January 8, 1990.

New York Review of Books, June 23, 1966; March 22, 1973.

New York Times, March 29, 1984; December 26, 1989; April 29, 1997, p. C11.

New York Times Book Review, April 21, 1963; April 28, 1963; May 1, 1966; July 17, 1966; March 11, 1973; April 15, 1984; October 28, 1984; January 14, 1990; May 18, 1997, p. 9.

Partisan Review, Volume 30, 1963; Volume 33, 1966; Volume 36, 1969; Volume 15, 1973; Volume 17, 1975.

Playboy, March 7, 1977.

Poetics Today, Volume 1, numbers 1-2, 1979, article by Brian McHale.

Punch, April 26, 1967.
Pynchon Notes, February, 1984; fall, 1984.
Saturday Night, August, 1966.
Saturday Review, April 30, 1966.
Saturday Review of the Arts, Volume 1, number 3, 1973, Richard Poirier, review of *Gravity's Rainbow.*
Southern Humanities Review, Volume 18, number 4, 1984.
Technology and Culture, Volume 23, 1982.
Time, April 23, 1984; January 15, 1990; May 5, 1997, p. 98; July 9, 2001, Joel Stein, "The Case for Thomas Pynchon," p. 50.
Times (London, England), January 10, 1985; February 3, 1990.
Times Literary Supplement, October 11, 1963; January 11, 1985; February 2, 1990.
Tribune Books (Chicago, IL), January 14, 1990.
Tri-Quarterly, winter, 1967.
Twentieth Century Literature, Volume 21, number 2, 1975; Volume 25, number 1, 1979; fall, 2002, Sammy Cahn, "Mason & Dixon & the Ampersand," p. 264.
Virginia Quarterly Review, summer, 1963; autumn, 1970.
Washington Post, December 6, 1989.
Washington Post Book World, April 22, 1984; January 7, 1990.
Yale Review, Volume 62, 1973; Volume 67, 1975.

* * *

PYNCHON, Thomas Ruggles, Jr.
See PYNCHON, Thomas, Jr.

* * *

QUINDLEN, Anna 1953-

PERSONAL: Born July 8, 1953, Philadelphia, PA; daughter of Robert V. (a management consultant) and Prudence Quindlen; married Gerald Krovatin (a lawyer), 1978; children: Quin, Christopher, Maria. *Education:* Barnard College, B.A., 1974. *Religion:* Roman Catholic.

ADDRESSES: Home—New York, NY; Hoboken, NJ; Cherry Valley, PA. *Office*—c/o New York Times, 229 W. 43rd St., New York, NY 10036. *Agent*—Amanda Urban, International Creative Management, 40 W. 57th St., New York, NY 10019.

CAREER: New York Post, New York, NY, reporter, 1974-77; *New York Times,* New York, NY, general assignment and city hall reporter, 1977-81, author of biweekly column "About New York," 1981-83, deputy metropolitan editor, 1983-85, author of weekly column, "Life in the 30s" (syndicated), 1986-88, author of biweekly column "Public & Private" (syndicated), 1990-95; *Newsweek,* author of biweekly column "Last Word," 1999—. Member, Barnard College Board of Trustees, Board of St. Luke's School, Planned Parenthood Federation of America board of advocates, and NARAL Foundation board.

MEMBER: Author's Guild (member of council).

AWARDS, HONORS: Mike Berger Award for distinguished reporting, 1983, for best writing about New York City; named woman of the year, *Glamour,* 1991; Pulitzer Prize for Commentary, Columbia University Graduate School of Journalism, 1992, for "Public & Private" columns; fellow of Academy of Arts and Sciences, 1996; honors from Women in Communications, Associated Press, and Society of Silurians; Poynter journalism fellow, Yale University; Victoria fellow in contemporary issues, Rutgers University; University Medal of Excellence, Columbia University; honorary doctorates from Dartmouth College, Denison University, Moravian College, Mount Holyoke College, Smith College, and Stevens Institute of Technology.

WRITINGS:

Living Out Loud (columns), Random House (New York, NY), 1988.
Object Lessons (novel), Random House (New York, NY), 1991.
The Tree That Came to Stay (children's book), illustrated by Nancy Carpenter, Crown (New York, NY), 1992.
Thinking Out Loud: On the Personal, the Political, the Public, and the Private (columns), Fawcett (New York, NY), 1994.
Poems for Life: Famous People Select Their Favorite Poem and Say Why It Inspires Them, Arcade (New York, NY), 1995.
One True Thing (novel), Dell (New York, NY), 1995.
(With Nick Kelsh) *Naked Babies,* Penguin (New York, NY), 1996.
Happily Ever After (children's book), Viking (New York, NY), 1997.
(With Nick Kelsh) *Siblings* (sequel to *Naked Babies*), Penguin (New York, NY), 1998.
Black and Blue (novel), Random House (New York, NY), 1998.

A Short Guide to a Happy Life, Random House (New York, NY), 2000.

Blessings, Random House (New York, NY), 2002.

Loud and Clear, Random House (New York, NY), 2004.

Imagined London: A Tour of the World's Greatest Fictional City, National Geographic (Washington, DC), 2004.

Also author of *How Reading Changed My Life,* Ballantine (New York, NY), 1998; and *Being Perfect,* Random House (New York, NY), 2005.

ADAPTATIONS: One True Thing was adapted as a film starring Rene Zellweger and Meryl Streep, Universal, 1998.

SIDELIGHTS: Anna Quindlen, author of best-selling novels *Object Lessons, Black and Blue,* and *A Short Guide to a Happy Life* and the recipient of the 1992 Pulitzer Prize for Commentary, gained national attention and a loyal following as a syndicated newspaper columnist at the *New York Times* and as a contributor to *Newsweek* magazine's "Last Word" column. Marked by their unaffected style, Quindlen's essays are rooted at a domestic level, but address universal concerns. Toronto *Globe and Mail* contributor John Allemang noted that Quindlen "is the unofficial voice that news most obviously lacks, the personal columnist who finds her truths in the little things." Sybil Steinberg, writing in *Publishers Weekly,* further lauded Quindlen's style, remarking that in her work the author "tackles the basic questions of life with trenchant and sensitive insight; she has a gift for turning the quotidian into the existential, the mundane into the meaningful."

Another distinguishing characteristic of Quindlen's prose is her proud and outspoken expression of her feminist leanings. In the *New Republic,* Karen Lehrman observed that in her columns "Quindlen seem[s] at times to be trying to shock *New York Times* readers with her 'femaleness,' her daring intimacy." The author defended her approach in an interview with *Commonweal* writer Alexander M. Santora: "I write for me . . . . I tend to write about what we have come, unfortunately, to call women's issues. Those are issues that directly affect my life and those are issues that are historically underreported."

Although fiction was her first love, Quindlen pursued a journalism career as the most viable, stable outlet for her writing activity. She landed a job as a reporter before college graduation and, three years later, was offered a position at one of the nation's most venerable newspapers, the *New York Times.* Quindlen worked as a general-assignment reporter, periodically reminding her superiors of her interest in writing the paper's "About New York" column, a coveted post which she was eventually granted. In an interview with Chris Lamb of *Editor & Publisher,* the author explained how this assignment improved her writing skills: "I developed a voice of my own without using the first person and I developed the ability to come up with column ideas." In her next career step, Quindlen advanced in the editorial ranks, becoming deputy metropolitan editor. When her first child was born, however, she left the hectic newsroom to care for him and write a novel. During this time she agreed to write a freelance column targeted at female readers that would run in the *Times*'s "Home" section. She held no lofty expectations for this venture. As Quindlen told Steinberg, "I thought of the column as a way to make a little bit of money while writing my novel. I was just trying hard not to disgrace myself."

Quindlen's weekly columns proved so successful, though, that other newspapers approached her with job offers. Executive editor Abe Rosenthal kept Quindlen at the *New York Times* with a permanent slot as the author of a weekly column called "Life in the 30s." In "Life in the 30s" Quindlen wrote about her own life during the mid- to late-1980s, earning praise for her honesty and accessible writing style, while drawing readers with astute observations of family life. She also became an unintended voice for the baby-boom generation. *Newsweek* contributor Melinda Beck observed that the author "occasionally tackles news issues, but she is more at home in the rocky emotional terrain of marriage, parenthood, secret desires and self-doubts." Her candor generated substantial mail from readers eager to share their own stories. Beck quoted Quindlen's editor as saying, "It's as if, by revealing so much of herself, she gives readers permission to explore their innermost selves."

While Quindlen was writing biweekly opinion pieces, her novel *Object Lessons* was published in 1991. Explaining the work's focal point, she told Steinberg, "I can't think of anything to write about except families. They are a metaphor for every other part of society." *Object Lessons* serves as both a coming-of-age account and the story of a family growing apart but eventually reconciling during the course of a summer in the mid-1960s. Told through the eyes of twelve-year-old Maggie Scanlan, the work follows the events of a large Irish-Catholic family living in suburban New York. Brash and domineering patriarch John Scanlan runs a construction company, controlling his sons with his financial power. Only Maggie's father, Tommy, has rebelled against this manipulation by marrying Connie, a lower-class Italian girl, and refusing to work directly for his father.

During this summer, however, the family's well-being is threatened by a housing development behind Tommy's house. Built by a rival construction company, the project signals the Scanlan construction company's waning influence. Connie's daily interactions with the foreman, an old friend, strain her relationship with Tommy. Other family ties are tested after John suffers a stroke and exerts more pressure on Tommy to run the business and buys him a new house. As Maggie observes her parents trying to cope with their problems, her own world unravels when her best friend rejects her, her mean-spirited cousin Monica gets pregnant, and local boys begin noticing her on a romantic level. Noting the author's successful rendering of adolescent confusion, *Time* contributor Martha Duffy noted, "Quindlen is at her best writing about the dislocations of growing up, the blows a child does not see coming." In her appraisal of *Object Lessons* for the *New York Times Book Review,* Anne Tyler deemed the novel "intelligent, highly entertaining, and laced with acute perceptions about the nature of day-to-day family life."

While *Object Lessons* sat atop the bestseller lists, Quindlen continued writing her "Public & Private" columns. Her contributions to journalism were recognized in 1992 when she received the Pulitzer Prize for Commentary. Expressing her appreciation for the honor, she remarked in the *New York Times,* "I think of a column as having a conversation with a person that it just so happens I can't see . . . . It's nice to know that my end of the conversation was heard." Her second collection of *New York Times* columns, *Thinking Out Loud: On the Personal, the Political, the Public, and the Private,* covers topics as diverse as the Persian Gulf War, absentee fathers, and abortion. A *Kirkus Reviews* writer complimented Quindlen for writing with greater maturity and depth than in her previous collection. The book, Quindlen later explained, was her attempt to comment on world events from an "underrepresented and valuable female viewpoint."

Quindlen's second novel, *One True Thing,* deals with a person's right to die. The narrator, a twenty-four-year-old woman jailed for killing her dying mother, describes her story. Ellen had been asked by her father to return home after her college graduation to help nurse her dying mother. Always a "daddy's girl" and having previously dismissed her mother as an anachronism, Ellen was unprepared for the world she entered. A *Booklist* reviewer described the book as not an "easy read about how cancer ravages Ellen's once radiant and ever-nurturing mother, but it is eminently satisfying to witness Ellen's transformation from an often glib, emotionally suppressed overachiever into a woman who begins to fathom the meaning of love." A *Kirkus Reviews* writer described the novel as "wrenching, albeit flawed." In explaining Quindlen's handling of reestablishing the relationship between mother and daughter, the writer went on to say that "Quindlen shines, capturing perfectly the casual intimacy that mothers and daughters share, as well as the friction between women of two very different generations." The story has a mystery-like ending, which the *Kirkus Reviews* writer applauded, saying that when Quindlen "gets it right—which is often—she places herself in the league of Mary Gordon and Sue Miller."

Quindlen's third novel, *Black and Blue,* tells a story of spousal abuse. Frannie Benedetto, an abused woman, takes herself and her nine-year-old son Robert away from their violent home to start anew in a distant state, but things go awry. *Literary Guild* reviewer Miranda de Ray wrote, "Just when things seem like they're going well, they go terribly wrong. The pages leading up to that heart-stopping climax are turned with lightning-quick speed." Maggie Paley, writing in the *New York Times Book Review,* believed that Quindlen's attempt to "dramatize the gravity of domestic violence . . . is nowhere near as convincing as the news reports all of us have seen," but concedes that the book is a page-turner. Jill Smolowe in *People* complimented Quindlen for "demonstrating the same winning qualities that inform her journalism: close observation, well-reasoned argument and appealing economy of language." A *Time* magazine reviewer took this sentiment a step further, adding that Quindlen "has caught the evil essence," and described *Black and Blue* as being "to domestic violence what *Uncle Tom's Cabin* was to slavery—a morally crystallizing act of propaganda that works because it has the ring of truth."

In 1999, after a break from column-writing to write her first few novels, Quindlen assumed the role of biweekly columnist for *Newsweek*'s "Last Word," succeeding the late Meg Greenfield and alternating with George F. Will. *Newsweek* chairman and editor-in- chief Richard M. Smith praised Quindlen in a press release posted on the *Writenews* Web site, saying "Anna's wonderfully creative mind, her no-nonsense thinking and her unerring sense of justice and injustice have made her one of the most powerful voices of her generation."

The year following her *Newsweek* appointment Quindlen published the bestselling *A Short Guide to a Happy Life,* a brief but poignant compilation of Quindlen's advice on enjoying life. The book offers pointers, such as: "Don't ever confuse the two, your life and your work"; and "think of life as a terminal illness, because if you do, you will live it with joy and passion, as it ought to be lived." Writing for *Spirituality and Health Online,* reviewers Frederic and Mary Ann Brusset described the book as "a brief but snappy treasure trove of advice that sounds like it was given as a commencement address for college students." Many of Quindlen's inspirations stem from her grief over the death of her mother when Quindlen was nineteen. The tragedy caused Quindlen to appreciate life and view it in a different way. "So much of her writing deals with her life before and after her mother's death; she speaks honestly about how much her life changed as a result of that loss. I admire her writing style, and her ability to tell it like it is—as she does in this little book, a reminder to all to appreciate the wonder," praised Maria Shriver in *O: The Oprah Magazine.*

The stately house in *Blessings,* which bears the novel's name, is modeled after the Quindlen's family home in Pennsylvania. When the story begins, the novel's main character, Lydia, is eighty years old and haunted by memories. When a baby is left on the doorstep of the house a young, lovable, ex-con caretaker discovers it and tries to persuade Lydia to help him keep the young infant. While the initial setting of the novel is intriguing, reviewer Nancy Pate concluded in the *Orlando Sentinel* that "what eventually hooks readers is the story of Lydia Blessings and her secret history." Nothing in Lydia's life has been the way it appeared: Lydia's husband was really in love with her late brother, Sunny, and Lydia became pregnant, but the child was not her husband's. Lydia's mother proclaimed to be Episcopalian, but was really Jewish. As Lydia reminiscences, shocking revelations unfold. "Quindlen drops clues to the past throughout the book," Pate added. "Some are like pebbles barely rippling the surface . . . . But others are like rocks—the flaming red of a child's hair, of ashes scattered across a pond—that plop into the narrative so loudly that subsequent revelations become anticlimatic." Critics praised the characterization in the book—including the characterization of the house itself. "The grand old house in *Blessings* is a force of safety, home and family," remarked Susannah Meadows in a review for *Newsweek International.* "There is a reassuring, steady feel to the writing and an intriguing spikeness to the characters," contended *Miami Herald* reviewer Amy Driscoll. A *Kirkus Reviews* contributor enjoyed the book's message about life and marriage, but concluded that *Blessings* does not measure up to Quindlen's prior works. The reviewer ultimately described the book as "comfortable, not Quindlen's best."

Quindlen's *Imagined London: A Tour of the World's Greatest Fictional City* is a an exploration of London as it is and as it has been described in literary classics by writers such as Charles Dickens, George Eliot, and Virginia Woolf. Although the book received positive reviews, it was the collection of columns *Loud and Clear* (published earlier that same year), which earned true acclaim. Taken from her *New York Times* and *Newsweek* columns, the essays in the collection cover Quindlen's usual topics: observations about the world at large and observations of the world at home. With her famous humor and insight, Quindlen discusses everything from September 11 to women's issues to the war in Iraq to Harry Potter. A *Publishers Weekly* contributor praised the book's range and stated that "these razor-sharp musings " are Quindlen "at the top of her game." Donna Seaman, writing in *Booklist,* was equally impressed. She concluded: "A valiant writer who addresses every aspect of our lives with both gravitas and humor, Quindlen is a tonic for mind and soul."

BIOGRAPHICAL AND CRITICAL SOURCES:

PERIODICALS

Booklist, August 18, 1994; November 1, 1996; June 1, 1999, review of *Black and Blue,* p. 1797; September 15, 2002, Donna Seaman, review of *Blessings,* p. 180; February 1, 2004, Donna Seaman, review of *Loud and Clear,* p. 930; September 15, 2004, Donna Seaman, review of *Imagined London: A Tour of the World's Greatest Fictional City,* p. 201.

Chicago Tribune, October 17, 1988.

Christian Science Monitor, December 5, 1996, p. B1; February 11, 1998.

Commonweal, February 14, 1992, pp. 9-13.

Editor & Publisher, November 30, 1991, pp. 32-34.

Entertainment Weekly, March 12, 1999, review of *Black and Blue,* p. 63.

Globe and Mail (Toronto, Ontario, Canada), June 1, 1991; June 12, 1999, review of *Black and Blue,* p. D4.

Journal of Adolescent and Adult Literacy, March, 1999, review of *How Reading Changed My Life,* p. 504.

Kirkus Reviews, March 1, 1993; July 15, 1994; October 1, 1996; September 1, 2002, review of *Blessings;* July 1, 2004, review of *Imagined London,* p. 622.

Library Journal, February 15, 1999, review of *Black and Blue,* p. 126; October 15, 2002, Nancy Pearl, review of *Blessings.*

Literary Guild, March, 1998, p. 15.

Miami Herald, September 18, 2001, Amy Driscoll, review of *Blessings.*

Ms., September, 1988, p. 88; January-February, 1998, p. 83.

New Republic, June 10, 1991, pp. 38-41.

Newsweek, April 4, 1988, p. 65.

Newsweek International, October 14, 2002, Susannah Meadows, review of *Blessings.*

New York, December 24, 1990, p. 100.

New York Times, December 1, 1988; April 18, 1991; April 8, 1992; May 11, 1997, p. 35; June 22, 1997, p. 6; February 6, 1998, p. E43.

New York Times Book Review, April 14, 1991, pp. 7, 9; December 29, 1996, p. 15; October 19, 1997, p. 7; November 16, 1997, p. 52; February 8, 1998; March 21, 1999, review of *Black and Blue,* p. 32.

O: The Oprah Magazine, December, 2001, Maria Shriver, review of *A Short Guide to a Happy Life,* p. 132.

Off Our Backs, December, 2001, review of *Black and Blue,* p. 34.

Orlando Sentinel, September 18, 2001, Nancy Pate, review of *Blessings.*

People, June 3, 1991, pp. 26-27; October 17, 1994.

Publishers Weekly, March 15, 1991, pp. 40-41; July 1, 1996; December 2, 2002, review of *Blessings,* p. 21; February 23, 2004, review of *Loud and Clear,* p. 61.

School Library Journal, May, 1999, review of *Siblings,* p. 162; June, 2005, Susan H. Woodcock, review of *Being Perfect,* p. 191.

Time, April 8, 1991, p. 76; February 23, 1998, Lance Morrow, review of *Black and Blue* p. 84.

USA Today, November 14, 1996.

ONLINE

Book Reporter, http://www.bookreporter.com/ (March 19, 2003), "Anna Quindlen, Bio."

Houston Chronicle Online, http://chron.com/ (September 20, 2002), Sharan Gibson, review of *Blessings.*

Royce Carlton Incorporated Web site, http://www.roycecarlton.com/ (November 24, 2003), "Anna Quindlen."

Spirituality and Health Online, http://www.spiritualityhealth.com/ (March 19, 2003), Frederic and Mary Ann Brusset, review of *A Short Guide to a Happy Life.*

Writenews, http://www.writenews.com/ (June 16, 1999), *Newsweek* press release.

* * *

QUINN, Simon

See SMITH, Martin Cruz

R

RADCLYFFE-HALL, Marguerite
See HALL, Radclyffe

* * *

RAMPLING, Anne
See RICE, Anne

* * *

RAND, Ayn 1905-1982
(Alice Rosenbaum)

PERSONAL: First name rhymes with "pine"; born Alice Rosenbaum, February 2, 1905, in St. Petersburg, Russia; came to United States, 1926, naturalized, 1931; died March 6, 1982, in New York, NY; daughter of Fronz (a chemist) and Anna Rosenbaum; married Charles Francis "Frank" O'Connor (an artist), April 15, 1929. *Education:* University of Petrograd (now University of St. Petersburg), graduated with highest honors in history, 1924. *Politics:* Radical for capitalism. *Religion:* Atheist.

CAREER: Worked as tour guide at Peter and Paul Fortress; Cecil B. DeMille Studio, Hollywood, CA, movie extra and junior screenwriter, 1926-32, began as filing clerk, became office head in wardrobe department; worked as screenwriter for Universal Pictures, Paramount Pictures, and Metro-Goldwyn-Mayer, 1932-34; freelance script reader for RKO Pictures, then Metro-Goldwyn-Mayer, both New York, NY, 1934-35; typist for Eli Jacques Kahn (architect), New York, NY, doing research work for *The Fountainhead,* 1937; Paramount Pictures, New York, NY, script reader, 1941-43; Hal Wallis Productions, Hollywood, CA, screenwriter, 1944-49; full-time writer and lecturer, 1951-82. Visiting lecturer at Yale University, 1960, Princeton University, 1960, Columbia University, 1960 and 1962, University of Wisconsin, 1961, Johns Hopkins University, 1961, Harvard University, 1962, Massachusetts Institute of Technology, 1962. Presenter of annual Ford Hall Forum, Boston, MA, beginning 1963.

AWARDS, HONORS: Doctor of Humane Letters, Lewis and Clark College, 1963.

WRITINGS:

NOVELS

We the Living (also see below), Macmillan (New York, NY), 1936, 60th anniversary edition, Dutton (New York, NY), 1995.

Anthem, Cassell (New York, NY), 1938, revised edition, Pamphleteers, Inc., 1946, 50th anniversary edition, with new introduction by Leonard Peikoff, Dutton (New York, NY), 1995.

The Fountainhead (also see below), Bobbs-Merrill, 1943 (New York, NY), with special introduction by Rand, 1968, reprinted, Plume (New York, NY), 1994.

Atlas Shrugged, Random House (New York, NY), 1957.

NONFICTION

For the New Intellectual: The Philosophy of Ayn Rand, Random House (New York, NY), 1961.

(With Nathaniel Branden) *The Virtue of Selfishness: A New Concept of Egoism,* New American Library (New York, NY), 1964.

(With Nathaniel Branden and others) *Capitalism: The Unknown Ideal,* New American Library (New York, NY), 1966.

Introduction to Objectivist Epistemology, Objectivist, 1967.

The Romantic Manifesto: A Philosophy of Literature, World Publishing (Cleveland, OH), 1969.

Philosophy: Who Needs It, introduction by Leonard Peikoff, Bobbs-Merrill (New York, NY), 1982.

The New Left: The Anti-Industrial Revolution, New American Library (New York, NY), 1982.

The Ayn Rand Lexicon: Objectivism from A to Z, introduction and notes by Leonard Peikoff, New American Library (New York, NY), 1984.

The Voice of Reason: Essays in Objectivist Thought, edited by Leonard Peikoff, New American Library (New York, NY), 1989.

The Ayn Rand Column, Second Renaissance Books, 1990.

The Ayn Rand Letters: 1971-1976, Second Renaissance Books, 1990.

The Ayn Rand Reader, edited by Gary Hull and Leonard Peikoff, Plume (New York, NY), 1999.

Return of the Primitive: The Anti-industrial Revolution, Meridian (New York, NY), 1999.

Russian Writings on Hollywood, Ayn Rand Institute (Marina del Ray, CA), 1999.

Why Businessmen Need Philosophy, Ayn Rand Institute (Marina del Ray, CA), 1999.

The Art of Fiction: A Guide for Writers and Readers, edited by Tore Böckman, Plume (New York, NY), 2000.

The Art of Nonfiction: A Guide for Writers and Readers, edited by Peter Schwartz, Plume (New York, NY), 2001.

PLAYS

Night of January 16th (produced as *Woman on Trial* at Hollywood Playhouse, October, 1934, first produced on Broadway as *Night of January 16th,* at Ambassador Theater, September 16, 1935; produced as *Penthouse Legend,* 1973), Longmans, Green, 1936, New American Library (New York, NY), 1971.

The Unconquered (adaptation of *We the Living*), first produced on Broadway, February 14, 1940.

OTHER

Love Letters (screenplay; adapted from the novel by Chris Massie), Paramount, 1945.

You Came Along (screenplay), Paramount, 1945.

The Fountainhead (filmscript; adaptation her novel), Warner Bros., 1949.

The Early Ayn Rand: A Selection from Her Unpublished Fiction, with introduction and notes by Norman Peikoff, New American Library (New York, NY), 1984.

Letters of Ayn Rand, edited by Michael S. Berliner, Dutton (New York, NY), 1995.

Ayn Rand's Marginalia: Her Critical Comments on the Writings of over Twenty Authors, edited by Robert Mayhew, Second Renaissance Books, 1996.

Journals of Ayn Rand, edited by David Harriman, Dutton (New York, NY), 1997.

Co-editor and contributor, *The Objectivist Newsletter,* 1962-65, and its successor, *The Objectivist* (monthly journal), 1966-71; writer and publisher, *The Ayn Rand Letter,* 1971-76. Columnist for *Los Angeles Times.*

ADAPTATIONS: *Night of January 16th* was filmed by Paramount and released in 1941. A year later, *We the Living* was filmed in Italy; a revised and abridged version of the Italian film was released in the United States in 1988. Film rights to *Atlas Shrugged* were purchased by Crusader Entertainment, 2003. Books by Rand adapted as audiobooks include *The Virtue of Selfishness* and *Capitalism: The Unknown Ideal,* Blackstone Audio, 2001.

SIDELIGHTS: "Ayn Rand is dead. So, incidentally, is the philosophy she sought to launch dead; it was in fact stillborn." William F. Buckley's derogatory obituary in the *National Review* sounded a note of wishful thinking on the part of Ayn Rand's persistent critics. Rather than quelling interest in her or her philosophy, Rand's death, in March of 1982, initiated a new era of academic interest and fueled the continued promotion of her philosophies by her adherents. Also fuelling Rand scholarship, *Philosophy: Who Needs It,* a volume of essays Rand planned but did not complete, came out the year of her death; and *The Early Ayn Rand: A Selection from Her Unpublished Fiction,* was issued in 1984.

Rand—born Alice Rosenbaum in St. Petersburg, Russia, in 1905—occupies a unique position in the history of American literature. In many ways she was a paradox: a writer of popular romances whose ideas were taken seriously, a fierce individualist who collected many followers. Politically and aesthetically, she defied the cultural currents of her times. Her lifelong enmity to collectivist political systems was engendered by her personal experiences growing up in Russia and living through the Bolshevik revolution and the beginnings of the Soviet system. She was an American patriot in the manner that only one who has emigrated from a totalitarian regime can be.

Capitalism was the system Rand championed; one of her best-known novels, *Atlas Shrugged,* is described as, among other things, a theodicy of capitalism. A rugged individualist and a believer in rational self-interest, Rand was a proponent of laissez-faire capitalism, a system she defined as the only social system based on the recognition of individual rights, the only system that bans force from social relationship, and the only system that fundamentally opposes war. Rand's defense of capitalism on moral grounds is unique. She based this defense on her view that only capitalism is consonant with man's rational nature, protective of his survival as man, and fundamentally just.

Rand's championing of individual rights and minimal government is part of her appeal to the Libertarian political movement, although she herself denounced Libertarians, calling them hippies of the right and advocates of anarchism. Neither, however, would she ally herself with most conservatives because of what she called their mysticism, their staunch support of religion. Among Rand's most persistent concerns about America was her belief that capitalism was being sold out by the very people who should be its strongest advocates. Rand felt that rather than supporting capitalism for the morality of its central vision, most capitalists defended it only on practical bases.

In her essay "Global Balkanization" Rand pointed out the following paradoxes: "Capitalism has been called a system of greed—yet it is the system that raised the standard of living of its poorest citizens to heights no collectivist system has ever begun to equal, and no tribal gang can conceive of. Capitalism has been called nationalistic—yet it is the only system that banished ethnicity, and made it possible, in the United States, for men of various, formerly antagonistic nationalities to live together in peace. Capitalism has been called cruel—yet it brought such hope, progress and general good will that the young people of today, who have not seen it, find it hard to believe. As to pride, dignity, self-confidence, self-esteem—these are characteristics that mark a man for martyrdom in a tribal society and under any social system except capitalism."

Tibor Machan explained in the *Occasional Review* that "for Rand, as for Aristotle, the question How should a human community be organized? can only be answered after the question How should I, a human being, live my life? has been answered. Rand follows the Greek tradition of regarding politics as a subfield of ethics."

Rand's firsthand experience of Communism determined her politics for life. Her family lived through the privations of World War I and then struggled to adapt themselves to the new Communist regime. For her, life in Russia at that time was dreary, and the future held little hope, particularly for one who rejected the system in power. Rand wanted to write about a world as it could be, to show life as she felt it was meant to be lived. As a young girl, she had decided to become a writer. Still, she chose to major in history at the University of Petrograd—now the University of St. Petersburg. She dismissed literature and philosophy, the fields in which she would later make her mark, because she had rejected the majority of what the academic world valued in both of those fields. Aristotle is the only philosopher to whom she acknowledges any intellectual debt; early in her life, she had been attracted to the theories of Friedrich Wilhelm Nietzsche, but she discarded his writing when she encountered his *The Birth of Tragedy* with its antirational stance. Barbara Branden noted in *The Passion of Ayn Rand* that Nietzsche, according to Rand, "said that reason is an inferior faculty, that drunken-orgy emotions were superior. That finished him as a spiritual ally." Her favorite novelists were Victor Hugo and Fyodor Dostoevsky, her favorite playwrights Friedrich Schiller and Edmond Rostand.

After graduating with highest honors from the university, Rand found work as a tour guide in the Peter and Paul Fortress. Dreadfully unhappy in Soviet Russia, she was rescued from her dead-end job by a letter from relatives in America. An invitation from the Portnoy family to visit them in Chicago was her passage to freedom. She left Russia in 1926 and never saw members of her immediate family again, except for a sister with whom she was reunited briefly in the early 1970s.

In the United States Alice Rosenbaum became Ayn Rand. Her unique personality and insistent individuality are reflected in her name choice. Her first name, which should be pronounced to sound like the German number one, "ein," rhymes with "pine." The last name she adopted from the Remington-Rand typewriter she used to write her first movie scenarios in America.

Despite her raw language skills, Rand left Chicago after a brief stay and headed for Hollywood where she hoped to make her living writing for the movies. On her second day in town she was befriended by her favorite American director, Cecil B. DeMille, who took her to watch the shooting of *The King of Kings* and then gave Rand work first as an extra and then as a junior writer. Rand's April 15, 1929, marriage to Charles Francis "Frank" O'Connor, also an extra in *The King of Kings,* insured that she would be allowed to stay in America.

Shortly after her marriage, Rand got a job in the wardrobe department of RKO. She hated the work, but it provided sustenance while she improved her English and perfected her craft. Her progress was remarkable, and she was one of a very few writers—like Joseph Conrad and Vladimir Nabokov—to attain artistic success in a language nonnative to them. It is possible that one of Rand's few childhood friends was Nabokov's sister. Barbara Branden tells of the relationship, based on common intellectual interests, in her biography of Rand.

Rand's first novel was written in response to a promise she had made to a friend of her family at a farewell party given for her before she left Russia. Her friend had implored her to tell Americans that Russia was a huge cemetery and that its citizens were slowly dying; in *We the Living* Rand details the deterioration of spirit and body under the Communist system. In particular, she wanted to show that Communism wreaks havoc not only on average people but particularly on the best and the brightest. All three of the major characters are destroyed. The heroine loses her life; the anti-Communist hero loses his spirit; and the Communist hero's faith and life are so undermined by the excesses he sees in the system that he takes his own life. By making one of her major characters a hero of the revolution, one who had believed fervently in the Communist cause, Rand was able to communicate basic flaws in the system.

In her foreword to the 1959 edition of *We the Living* Rand warns readers not to dismiss the story of Russia of the 1920s as inapplicable to the Russia of their own day: "*We the Living* is not a story about Soviet Russia in 1925. It is a story about Dictatorship, any dictatorship, anywhere, at any time, whether it be Soviet Russia, Nazi Germany, or—which this novel might do its share in helping to prevent—a socialist America." Rand continually emphasized that her opposition to Communism was based on the evil of its essential principle, that Man should exist for the sake of the state. She warned Americans against accepting the myth that the Communist ideal was noble, although its methods might be evil.

The publishing world was not taken with Rand's accomplishments in *We the Living,* which was rejected by many publishing houses as either too intellectual or too anti-Soviet. It was not until after Rand had achieved some success as a playwright that *We the Living* finally appeared in 1936. Macmillan, the publisher, had so little faith in the novel that they did little promotion and issued only one edition of three thousand copies. The reviews were not enthusiastic. Although Lee E. Cannon in the *Christian Century* called it "vigorous" and emotionally intense, Ben Belitt in the *Nation* questioned the accuracy of Rand's depiction of the USSR, claiming that the author was out "to puncture a bubble—with a bludgeon." Rand was often subsequently accused of overkill.

Though neither her publisher nor her reviewers expected much from the book, *We the Living* earned word-of-mouth recommendation and sold more copies in its second year than just after publication. However, Macmillan had destroyed the type and *We the Living* was not published again in the United States until it was reissued by Random House in 1959. It has since sold more than two million copies.

Rand's primary reputation is as a novelist, but her first professional success was as a playwright. In all, she wrote four plays, two of which were produced on Broadway. She originally called her first play "Penthouse Legend," but its title was changed twice. Under the title *Woman on Trial* it opened in October, 1934, at the Hollywood Playhouse under the direction of E.E. Clive. Al Woods then purchased the rights, and under the title *Night of January 16th* it began a seven-month run on Broadway in September of 1935. A 1973 revival bearing Rand's original title *Penthouse Legend* was not so successful.

Night of January 16th is significant for dramatic ingenuity as well as for historical sidelights. Rand developed the innovative theatrical device of using audience members at each performance to serve as the jury in this courtroom drama. (A number of celebrities acted as jurors for the play: Jack Dempsey served on the opening night jury; Helen Keller was foreman for an all-blind jury.) Rand wrote alternative endings for the cast to use in response to either the guilty or the not guilty verdict. Moreover, the Broadway production provided actor Walter Pidgeon in the role of "Guts" Regan with a vehicle to revive his flagging career. The play also inspired Gertrude M. Moffat, chair of the New York League of Women Voters, to write to the *New York Times* to complain of the all-male juries who were initially selected to judge Karen Andre, the defendant in the play. Moffat used the play to question a New York law that specified "male" jurors; women should be judged by their peers, which include women, she argued. The New York law was subsequently changed.

Anthem, a novella first published in England in 1938, is Rand's shortest work. A parable-like dystopian tale, it portrays a totally collectivized world after some great war or holocaust. Originally titled *Ego,* the work illustrates the negative effects on society of the suppression of individual ego and talent for the supposed good of all: When, in the name of all, no individual is allowed to stand above the others, then all stand in darkness. In the *New York Times Book Review* Gerald Raftery called the work "a surprising favorite among high-school tastemakers." Larry M. Arnoldson reported in the *Journal of Reading* that his reading of *Anthem* to his high school class created a log jam for the school librarian who had only one copy of each of Rand's novels and over fifty students on a waiting list for the books.

The Fountainhead might not have been published at all were it not for the faith of Archibald G. Ogden, then a new young editor for Bobbs-Merrill. He wired the head of the company, who had told him to reject it, "If this is not the book for you, then I am not the editor for you." At that point it had already been refused by some dozen other publishers.

Rand had done extensive research before she began writing *The Fountainhead,* which was originally titled "Secondhand Lives." Although she worked for some time in the office of Eli Jacques Kahn, a famous New York architect, Rand's main purpose was not to extol the profession of architecture. The central theme in this novel, as in the ones before it, is individualism versus collectivism, the difference being that in *The Fountainhead* the focus is not on the political system, as it was in *We the Living,* but on what Rand called collectivism in the soul. *The Fountainhead* is a defense of egoism, a positive rational egoism. Protagonist Howard Roark explains to Dominique Francon at one point in the book, "To say 'I love you' one must know first how to say the 'I.'" The egoism Rand defined in this novel is an integral part of the individualism she championed, just as the selfishness she described is a virtue as opposed to the selflessness she abhorred.

In *The Fountainhead* Rand moved closer to her goal of creating the ideal man. Because of the resemblance in their professions and architectural styles, it was generally assumed that Howard Roark was modeled after Frank Lloyd Wright. Barbara Branden asserted in *Who Is Ayn Rand?: An Analysis of the Novels of Ayn Rand,* however, that Rand insisted, "The only resemblance is in their basic architectural principles and in the fact that Wright was an innovator fighting for modern architecture against tradition. There is no similarity in their respective characters, nor in their philosophical convictions, nor in the events in their lives." Rand had tried unsuccessfully to interview Wright while she was writing her novel. It was only after the success of *The Fountainhead* that they established an amicable relationship. Eventually he designed a home for her; it was never built.

Asked about the models for her other main characters, Rand remarked that Wynand could have been William Randolph Hearst or Henry Luce or Joseph Pulitzer. Harold Laski, the British socialist, was the main model for Ellsworth Toohey. Other lesser sources for Toohey were Heywood Broun, Lewis Mumford, and Clifton Fadiman, although when Rand met Fadiman some years later, they liked each other. A young woman Rand had met in Hollywood, whose main goal was not to have things because she wanted them but only so that she would have more than her neighbors, was the inspiration for Peter Keating. Rand characterized the book's heroine, Dominique Francon, as herself in a bad mood.

In *The Fountainhead* Rand declares that Roark's success progresses "as if an underground stream flowed through the country and broke out in sudden springs that shot to the surface at random, in unpredictable places." She might have been discussing the publishing history of her novel. Although D.L. Chambers, the head of Bobbs-Merrill, had ultimately supported Ogden's dedication to the book, he did not give *The Fountainhead* his wholehearted support once it was published. Rather than print significant numbers of new editions as the book gained popularity, he kept issuing small editions that quickly went out of print. When Bobbs-Merrill decided to produce a twenty-fifth anniversary deluxe edition in 1968, Nora Ephron, not an admirer of Rand's theories or writing abilities, noted in the *New York Times Book Review* that *The Fountainhead* was "one of the most astonishing phenomena in publishing history." At that date it had sold over two and one-half million copies. By the 1980s the number of copies sold was closer to four and one-half million.

Positive reviewers appreciated the powerful writing, intensity, and dramatic plot of *The Fountainhead.* Rand's favorite review was by Lorine Pruette in the *New York Times Book Review.* Pruette correctly identified *The Fountainhead* as a novel of ideas, pointing out that a novel of ideas by an American woman was a rarity. She lauded the quality of Rand's intellect, calling her "a writer of great power" with "a subtle and ingenious mind and the capacity of writing brilliantly, beautifully, bitterly."

The success of *The Fountainhead* brought Rand to the attention of her kind of reader: individuals who shared her perception of life. It also precipitated a lucrative movie sale, which necessitated a move back to Hollywood from New York, where Rand and her husband had moved for the Broadway production of "Night of January 16th." In California they bought a house of steel and glass in very modern design, a house that might have been designed by Roark. There Rand wrote the screenplay for *The Fountainhead* and major parts of *Atlas Shrugged.*

In 1950 Nathaniel Branden wrote a fan letter to Rand which so impressed her that she did something quite uncharacteristic: she answered his letter. Their meeting set in motion a series of events that would profoundly affect many lives. By the time Rand's next book was published, Branden had joined Frank O'Connor on the dedication page. Her afterword describes Branden as her "ideal reader" and "intellectual heir." Branden and his wife, Barbara Weidman Branden, became more than fans and students; they became close friends and intellectual allies. The Brandens' move to New York was followed shortly by a similar move by Rand and Frank O'Connor.

The Brandens introduced many of their friends and relatives to Rand and these people formed a close group called by Rand "the class of '43" because of their shared interest in *The Fountainhead,* which had been published in that year. She also called them "the children," by which she meant that they were the children of her brain. Members of this group included Alan Greenspan, who became head of the Federal Reserve System and economic advisor to several presidents; Leonard Peikoff, Barbara Branden's cousin and Rand's literary executor; Nathaniel Branden's sister, Elayne Kalberman, circulation manager for *The Objectivist Newsletter;* Kalberman's husband, Harry Kalberman; Allan Blumenthal; Edith Efron; Mary Ann Rukavina; and Robert and Beatrice Hessen. They were privy to a prepublication reading of *Atlas Shrugged,* and from their ranks the philosophical movement Rand called Objectivism was born.

Atlas Shrugged was to be Rand's last novel, but it initiated her career as a well-known philosopher and public figure. She became a popular campus speaker in the 1960s, a regular at the Ford Hall Forum, and a columnist for the *Los Angeles Times.* She was interviewed by Johnny Carson, Tom Snyder, Phil Donahue, and *Playboy.* Branden began teaching her basic philosophical principles through a twenty-lecture course of study offered by Nathaniel Branden Lectures and eventually the Nathaniel Branden Institute. A publication branch of the Institute printed essays and monographs; a book service sold approved books. The first issue of *The Objectivist Newsletter,* which was published from 1962-65, contained articles by Rand, both Brandens, and Greenspan. *The Objectivist Newsletter* was replaced in 1966 by *The Objectivist.* In 1971 the format was changed to a simple typewritten letter called *The Ayn Rand Letter.* Rand continued issuing numbers of this letter until February of 1976.

In *Atlas Shrugged* Rand accomplished her goal of creating the ideal man. His name is John Galt, and he and a number of like-minded followers succeed in stopping the motor of the world by removing themselves and their productive capacities from exploitation by those forces they regard as looters and leeches. All of Rand's novels dramatize the primacy of the individual. The unique and precious individual human life is the standard by which good is judged. If something nourishes and sustains life, it is good; if it negates or impoverishes the individual's pursuit of happiness, then it is evil. The secondary themes in Rand's fiction unfold as the logical consequence of her major theme, but it was not until *Atlas Shrugged,* the fullest explication in fiction of her philosophy, that Rand worked out all the political, economic, and metaphysical implications of that theme.

Critical calumny greeted the publication of *Atlas Shrugged,* especially from the battlements of the conservative establishment. Whittaker Chambers in the *National Review* called it "remarkably silly," "bumptious," and "preposterous." He remarked, "Out of a lifetime of reading, I can recall no other book in which a tone of overriding arrogance was so implacably sustained. Its shrillness is without reprieve. Its dogmatism is without appeal." *Catholic World*'s Riley Hughes called it a "shrill diatribe against 'non-productive' people." Hughes further claimed that though Rand decried mysticism, her book is full of parallels to Christianity: "Her John Galt is offered as a secular savior (Dagny is his Magdalene); and his disciples find him at his place of torture." In the *Saturday Review,* Helen Beal Woodward, who conceded that "Rand is a writer of dazzling virtuosity," reacted negatively to the "stylized vice-and-virtue characters" and "prolixity." Woodward found *Atlas Shrugged* a book "shot through with hatred."

Such critical attacks had no effect on the reading public, who made *Atlas Shrugged* a multi-million dollar selling phenomenon. *Atlas Shrugged,* like *Uncle Tom's Cabin,* is a book that fueled a movement. Its publication established Rand as a thinker whose influence extended to such diverse locales as Parliament (former Prime Minister Margaret Thatcher was an admirer); tennis courts (Billie Jean King acknowledged Rand's effect on her); the Federal Reserve System (Greenspan called her instrumental in forming his thinking); and the Alaskan legislature, which issued a citation in memoriam of Rand at the request of Dick Randolph, a Libertarian legislator.

The publication of *For the New Intellectual: The Philosophy of Ayn Rand* in 1961 began a series of nonfiction books that anthologized her essays on such diverse subjects as the American public school system, Romanticism, and racism. In her nonfiction writings as well as in her fiction, she characterizes the main areas of conflict in the field of human rights: (1) individualism versus collectivism, (2) egoism versus altruism, (3) reason versus mysticism. In Rand's philosophy all of these areas are interconnected. Reason is the tool by which the individual discerns that which is life-sustaining and ego-nourishing. Collectivism, altruism, and mysticism work against individual freedom, a healthy ego, and rationality.

Rand's career as the leader of an intellectual movement had two phases. Until 1968 Branden was her chief spokesperson and teacher of her philosophies. In that year Rand broke with both Brandens, who had separated by then. The rupture, with its public response, established divisions between friends and relatives that never healed. It also established divisions among her other admirers: some remained purists, continuing to call themselves Objectivists and publishing only that which was sanctioned by Rand or which did not deviate from her dictums; others acknowledged influence, but moved from the letter of Rand's philosophy to other interpretations and permutations. Leonard Peikoff became Rand's associate editor for *The Objectivist.* Peikoff also edited posthumous volumes of Rand's writings, including *The Voice of Reason: Essays in Objectivist Thought.* A *Kirkus Reviews* contributor called this collection of Rand's thoughts on art, politics, literature, philosophy, and economics "prickly, well-articulated polemic, at times persuasive, at times infuriating: prime Rand." Also commenting on the collection, which includes diatribes against modern art and the Catholic Church, and a eulogy for Marilyn Monroe, a *Booklist* reviewer wrote that the essays "are entirely characteristic of [Rand]—surprisingly emotional and dogmatic for a professed rationalist."

To the end of her life, Rand continued to create controversy and inordinate audience response. She possessed great charisma and an intense intellectuality that affected both admirers and detractors. Her last years were clouded by ill health—she lost a lung to cancer—and grief—her husband, who she called her greatest value, died in 1979. Yet she made an appearance on a Phil Donahue show in 1979, affirming her love of life and her belief that there is no hereafter. If she believed in a hereafter, she explained, her desire to be with her husband would necessitate her committing suicide so as to join him. Some four months before her death, she delivered a speech at the conference of the National Committee for Monetary Reform. Thus until her death alone in her apartment on March 6, 1982, Rand's unquenchable spirit continued to assert itself.

The publication of Rand's private correspondence more than a decade after her death confirmed her superior intellect and revealed the tenacity with which she held her lifelong political and philosophical convictions. Commenting on *Letters of Ayn Rand* in the *New York Times Book Review,* Christopher Cox remarked that the writer "was constitutionally opposed to others' paraphrases of her ideas. Fortunately, her own private letters provide the most concisely written explanation upon them so far." According to *Washington Post Book World* contributor Jeffrey A. Frank, "Rand's outlook and spirit were more or less intact from the time she disembarked to her dying day. She wouldn't—or couldn't—change." Cox added, "the brutal honesty of her letters provides not only a wealth of serious thought but also some of the most entertaining passages in a remarkable volume that easily rises to the level of literature." Rand proclaimed in a 1934 letter to H.L. Mencken, quoted by Frank, "I believe that man will always be an individualist, whether he knows it or not, and I want to make it my duty to make him know it."

BIOGRAPHICAL AND CRITICAL SOURCES:

BOOKS

Baker, James T., *Ayn Rand,* Twayne (Boston, MA), 1987.

Barnes, Hazel Estella, *An Existential Ethics,* Knopf (New York, NY), 1967.

Branden, Barbara, *The Passion of Ayn Rand,* Doubleday (New York, NY), 1986.

Branden, Nathaniel, *My Years with Ayn Rand,* Jossey-Bass, 1998.

Branden, Nathaniel, *Who Is Ayn Rand?: An Analysis of the Novels of Ayn Rand,* with biographical essay by Barbara Branden, Random House (New York, NY), 1977.

Cerf, Bennett, *At Random,* Random House (New York, NY), 1977.

Contemporary Literary Criticism, Thomson Gale (Detroit, MI), Volume 3, 1975, Volume 30, 1984, Volume 44, 1987, Volume 79, 1993.

Den Uyl, Douglas, and Douglas Rasmussen, editors, *The Philosophical Thought of Ayn Rand,* University of Illinois Press (Champaign, IL), 1984.

Ellis, Albert, *Is Objectivism a Religion?,* Lyle Stuart, 1968.

Erickson, Peter F., *The Stance of Atlas: An Examination of the Philosophy of Ayn Rand,* Herakles Press (Portland, OR), 1997.

Gladstein, Mimi Reisel, *The Ayn Rand Companion,* Greenwood Press (Westport, CT), 1984.

Haydn, Hiram, *Words and Faces,* Harcourt (New York, NY), 1974.

O'Neill, William, *With Charity Toward None: An Analysis of Ayn Rand's Philosophy,* Philosophical Library, 1971.

Paxton, Michael, *Ayn Rand: A Sense of Life; The Companion Book,* Gibbs Smith, 1998.

Peary, Gerald, and Roget Shatzkin, editors, *The Modern American Novel and the Movies,* Unger (New York, NY), 1978.

Rand, Ayn, *The Fountainhead,* Bobbs-Merrill (New York, NY), 1968.

Rand, Ayn, *We the Living,* Random House (New York, NY), 1959.

Schwartz, Peter, editor, *The Battle for Laissez-Faire Capitalism,* Intellectual Activist, 1983.

Sciabarra, Chris Matthew, *Ayn Rand: The Russian Radical,* Pennsylvania State University Press, 1995.

Slusser, George E., Eric S. Rabkin, and Robert Scholes, editors, *Coordinates: Placing Science Fiction and Fantasy, Alternative Series,* Southern Illinois University Press (Carbondale, IL), 1984.

Tuccille, Jerome, *It Usually Begins with Ayn Rand,* Stein & Day (New York, NY), 1972.

PERIODICALS

Atlantic, November, 1957, review of *Atlas Shrugged;* May, 2003, Edward Sorel, "Ayn Rand," p. 90.

Booklist, December 15, 1988, p. 667; February 15, 2001, Donna Seaman, review of *The Art of Nonfiction: A Guide for Writers and Readers,* p. 1110.

Boston Review, December, 1984.

Catholic World, January, 1958.

Chicago Sunday Tribune, October 13, 1957.

Christian Century, July 1, 1936; December 13, 1961.

Christianity Today, July 18, 1982.

Christian Science Monitor, October 10, 1957.

College English, February, 1978.

Commonweal, November 8, 1957, review of *Atlas Shrugged.*

English Journal, February, 1983.

House and Garden, August, 1949.

Journal of Reading, March, 1982.

Journal of Thought, January, 1969.

Kirkus Reviews, December 1, 1988, p. 1724.

Library Journal, February 15, 2001, Susan M. Colowick, review of *The Art of Nonfiction,* p. 178.

Life, April 7, 1967.

Los Angeles Times, November 12, 1988.

Los Angeles Times Book Review, September 2, 1984.

Ms., September, 1978.

Nation, April 22, 1936.

National Review, December 28, 1957, review of *Atlas Shrugged;* October 3, 1967; October 9, 1995, p. 61.

New Republic, April 24, 1961; December 10, 1966; February 21, 1970.

New Statesman, March 11, 1966.

Newsweek, March 27, 1961.

New Yorker, October 26, 1957, review of *Atlas Shrugged;* June 26, 1995, p. 66; July 24, 1995, p. 70.

New York Herald Tribune Book Review, October 6, 1957.

New York Herald Tribune Books, April 19, 1936.

New York Times, April 19, 1936; October 13, 1957, review of *Atlas Shrugged;* March 9, 1966; March 10, 1982; September 13, 1987.

New York Times Book Review, May 16, 1943, Lorine Pruette, review of *The Fountainhead;* April 9, 1961; February 27, 1966, Gerald Raftery, review of *Anthem;* December 22, 1967; May 5, 1968; August 6, 1995, p. 9.

Objectivist Forum, June, 1982; August, 1982; October, 1982; December, 1982.

Occasional Review, winter, 1976.

Personalist, spring, 1971.

Playboy, March, 1964.

Publishers Weekly, November 18, 1988, p. 58; May 8, 1995, p. 278.

Rampart Journal of Individualist Thought, spring, 1968.

Reason, November, 1973; May, 1978; December, 1982.

Religious Humanism, winter, 1970.

San Francisco Chronicle, April 9, 1961.

Saturday Evening Post, November 11, 1961.

Saturday Review, October 12, 1957.

Saturday Review of Literature, April 18, 1936.

Time, October 14, 1957; September 30, 1974.

Washington Post Book World, December 12, 1982; July 9, 1995.
West Coast Review of Books, November, 1984.

OTHER

"Donahue," WGN-TV, Chicago, Illinois, April 29, 1979.

* * *

RANDALL, Robert
See SILVERBERG, Robert

* * *

RANKIN, Ian 1960-
(Jack Harvey, Ian James Rankin)

PERSONAL: Born April 28, 1960, in Cardenden, Fife, Scotland; married; two sons. *Education:* University of Edinburgh, M.A. (with honors), 1982.

ADDRESSES: *Agent*—Dominick Abel, 146 W. 82nd St., No. 1B, New York, NY 10024.

CAREER: Novelist and short-story and nonfiction writer. Worked variously as a swineherd, a taxman, viticulturist, hi-fi journalist, and folktale collector.

MEMBER: Crime Writers' Association (United Kingdom), International Association of Crime Writers.

AWARDS, HONORS: Elected a Hawthornden fellow in 1987; Chandler-Fulbright fellowship in detective fiction, 1991-92; Dagger Award for best short story, Crime Writers' Association, 1994; Edgar Allan Poe Award, 2004, for *Resurrection Men;* various short story prizes.

WRITINGS:

NOVELS

The Flood, Polygon (Edinburgh, Scotland), 1986.
Watchman, Bodley Head (London, England), 1988, Doubleday (New York, NY), 1991.
Westwind, Barrie & Jenkins (London, England), 1990.
Set in Darkness, Orion (London, England), 2000.
The Falls, Orion (London, England), 2001.

"INSPECTOR REBUS" SERIES; DETECTIVE NOVELS

Knots and Crosses, Doubleday (Garden City, NY), 1987.
Hide and Seek: A John Rebus Mystery, Barrie & Jenkins, 1991, Penzler Books (New York, NY), 1994.
Strip Jack, Orion (London, England), 1992, St. Martin's Press (New York, NY), 1994.
Wolfman, Century (London, England), 1992.
The Black Book: An Inspector Rebus Novel, Orion (London, England), 1993, Penzler Books (New York, NY), 1994.
Mortal Causes, Orion (London, England), 1994, Simon & Schuster (New York, NY), 1995.
Let it Bleed, Orion (London, England), 1995, Simon & Schuster (New York, NY), 1996.
Black and Blue, St. Martin's Press (New York, NY), 1997.
The Hanging Garden, St. Martin's Press (New York, NY), 1998.
Dead Souls, St. Martin's Minotaur (New York, NY), 1999.
Death Is Not the End, St. Martin's Minotaur (New York, NY), 2000.
Set in Darkness, Orion (London, England), 2000.
Resurrection Men, Little, Brown (Boston, MA), 2004.
A Question of Blood, Little, Brown (Boston, MA), 2004.
Fleshmarket Close, Orion (London, England), 2004.
Fleshmarket Alley, Little, Brown (Boston, MA), 2005.

NOVELS; AS JACK HARVEY

Witch Hunt, Headline (London, England), 1993.
Bleeding Hearts, Headline (London, England), 1994.
Blood Hunt, Headline (London, England), 1995.

OTHER

A Good Hanging and Other Stories (short stories), Little, Brown (Boston, MA), 1992.

Contributor of short stories to periodicals, including *Ellery Queen Mystery Magazine;* contributor of articles to periodicals.

SIDELIGHTS: Ian Rankin has "established himself as one of the most talented young British crime novelists," in the opinion of *Twentieth-Century Crime and Mystery Writers* essayist Ian A. Bell. Rankin is best known for his series of crime novels featuring Detective Inspector John Rebus. In these works, which are often referred to as "police procedurals" for their focus on solving a crime, Rankin combines the dialect and setting of his native Scotland with poetic prose and gritty realism.

The "Rebus" stories are set in Edinburgh, and Bell noted that they "often exploit the stark contrast between that city's genteel facade and some of its squalid realities." Rebus himself is a complex, well-drawn character, in the opinion of numerous reviewers. He is sensitive, brooding, and somewhat insecure, but he is also tough and relentless. He is aware that even when he solves a case, the triumph of justice is fleeting; there will always be more evil and corruption. *Booklist* contributor Emily Melton noted that "Rankin is a genius at finding the perfect blend of curmudgeonly guile, stubborn gruffness, and unsuspecting vulnerability for Rebus, who . . . is a refreshing if lonely champion of truth and justice." Melton also praised Rankin for delivering "sparkling wit, superb plotting, and a host of surprising twists."

Rankin introduced readers to Rebus with his second novel, *Knots and Crosses.* In this work, the detective attempts to find the murderer of several young girls with the help of his policewoman girlfriend and Jim Stevens, a reporter. A critic for *Books* dubbed *Knots and Crosses* a "well constructed, exciting" story, and a *Kirkus Reviews* contributor praised Rankin's "solidly drawn characters, [and] keen psychological insights." Reporter Stevens makes a brief appearance in Rankin's next effort, *Watchman,* in which British Secret Service agent Miles Flint struggles with IRA terrorists. Although a contributor for *Kirkus Reviews* found this work "slightly disappointing" in comparison with *Knots and Crosses,* the reviewer also highlighted the book's "tense, convincing finale."

In *Wolfman,* Rebus is temporarily reassigned to the London office to help in the investigation of a serial killer whose signature mark is the bite he takes out of his victims. A reviewer for *Books* remarked that "Rebus is a character drawn in the round, and realism is the hallmark of the book." In *Strip Jack,* Rankin's next mystery to feature Rebus, a popular member of the British Parliament is found in a brothel during a police raid, shortly after which his wife is beaten to death. Critical response was generally positive to what *New York Times Book Review* critic Marilyn Stasio dubbed an "intricately knotted murder plot"; in the *Chicago Tribune,* Dick Adler singled out Rankin's "crisp, refreshing prose," and a *Kirkus Reviews* contributor highlighted Rankin's "offbeat characters and . . . eccentric but appealing narrative style."

In *Hide and Seek,* Rebus investigates a modern-day Dr. Jekyll and Mr. Hyde case. Male prostitutes are the victims, and their killer appears to be a devil worshiper. "For all its modern grit, this multilayered story is as deeply moralistic as Stevenson's classic horror tale about the divided passions of the human soul," mused Marilyn Stasio in the *New York Times Book Review.* "In Mr. Rankin's subtle treatment of the theme, every character seems to have two faces—or a Cain-like brother—to reflect his corrupt dark side." *Black and Blue* finds Rebus looking into another serial killer case—this one involving a "copycat killer" who imitates the grisly crimes of another murderer Rebus was involved with thirty years earlier. A *Kirkus Reviews* writer called *Black and Blue* Rebus's "biggest and most grueling" case and added, "Rankin's dexterity in juggling plots and threats and motives lights up the darkness with a poet's grace. Reading him is like watching somebody juggle a dozen bottles of single malt without spilling a drop."

Rebus's adult daughter, Sammy, is depicted throughout the series as one of the few bright points in his personal life. In *The Hanging Garden,* Sammy is almost killed in a suspicious hit-and-run accident. Rebus believes the incident is related to some of his recent work. With his daughter threatened, Rebus's "ferocity is ratcheted up a notch," according to Bill Ott in *Booklist.* As Ott continued: "Nobody does grit like Rankin. The Rebus novels live on texture; the taste of cold coffee and the grinding edges of frayed nerves take on a visceral reality as the cops slog toward answers that only bring more questions. Against the unremitting grayness of this world, Rebus's beleaguered humanity shines in bold relief."

In *Fleshmarket Close,* the crusty policeman discovers that he has sympathy for the collectively oppressed. Senay Boztas wrote in the London *Sunday Times,* "The case forces [Rebus] . . . to confront the plight of refugees and the conditions in which they are held at a detention camp, based on the notorious Dungavel centre in Lanarkshire," and described *Fleshmarket Close* as Rankin's "most overtly political novel to date."

As Bell observed, although there is often extreme violence in the "Rebus" books, Rankin's "cool and laconic tone prevents the narratives from sensationalising the events they include, and perhaps the most impressive feature of his writing is the way it seems to meditate on the complexities of human motivation. . . . Earlier Rebus novels struggled to articulate these complex issues, but more recent efforts have been extremely successful."

Rankin once noted of his series: "My Inspector Rebus books are Scottish novels first, and mysteries second. I want to write about contemporary Scotland, and particularly contemporary Edinburgh, showing how the past infuses (and infects) the present. A novel like *The Black Book* depends more on the writings of Robert Louis Stevenson and James Hogg than it does on any whodunit forebear. Edinburgh is schizophrenic; it exhibits a definite dual personality. A look into history told me that this was nothing new, and hinted that in writing about my nation's twisted present, I might be saying something about its past psychoses too. A critic with an eye for an oxymoron once stated that I'd invented 'Tartan *Noir.*' Maybe that's not so far from the truth."

BIOGRAPHICAL AND CRITICAL SOURCES:

BOOKS

St. James Guide to Crime and Mystery Writers, 6th edition, St. James Press (Detroit, MI), 1996.

Spy Fiction: A Connoisseur's Guide, Facts on File (New York, NY), 1990.

PERIODICALS

Booklist, December 1, 1996, p. 643; October 1, 1997, p. 309; August 19, 1998.

Books, April, 1987, review of *Knots and Crosses,* p. 32; March, 1992, p. 12.

Chicago Tribune, March 6, 1994.

Entertainment Weekly, January 30, 1998, p. 61.

Kirkus Reviews, August 1, 1987, p. 1117; May 1, 1991, p. 568; January 1, 1994, p. 22; September 1, 1994, p. 1171; October 1, 1996, p. 1430; October 1, 1997, review of *Black and Blue.*

Library Journal, December, 1996, p. 151; August, 1997, p. 168.

Los Angeles Times Book Review, July 10, 1994, p. 8.

New Statesman and Society, November 13, 1992, p. 36.

New York Times Book Review, April 17, 1994, p. 19; July 3, 1994, p. 17; October 9, 1994, p. 34; January 21, 1996, p. 31; January 5, 1997, p. 20; December 14, 1997, p. 30.

Publishers Weekly, January 17, 1994, p. 410; September 12, 1994, p. 85; October 7, 1996, p. 64; August 25, 1997, review of *Black and Blue,* p. 48.

Sunday Times (London, England), March 28, 2004, Senay Boztas, "It's PC Rebus As Detective Finds His Conscience," p. 14.

Times Literary Supplement, May 2, 1986; September 23, 1994, review of *Mortal Causes,* p. 22; February 28, 1997, p. 22.

Tribune Books (Chicago, IL), March 6, 1994, p. 6; January 5, 1997, p. 4.

Wilson Library Bulletin, April, 1994, p. 98.

ONLINE

Ian Rankin Home Page, http://www.ianrankin.net/ (August 15, 2004).

* * *

RANKIN, Ian James
See RANKIN, Ian

* * *

RAO, Raja 1909(?)-

PERSONAL: Born November 21, 1909 (one source says November 8, 1908), in Hassan, Mysore, India; son of H.V. (a professor) and Srimathi (Gauramma) Krishnaswamy; married Camille Mouly (an academic), 1931 (divorced, c. 1939); married Katherine Jones (an actress), November, 1965; children: Christopher. *Education:* Madras University, graduated; attended the University of Montpellier and the Sorbonne; attended Hunter College of the City University of New York.

ADDRESSES: Home—1808 Pearl, Austin, TX 78701. *Office*—Department of Philosophy, College of Humanities at Austin, University of Texas, Austin, TX 78712.

CAREER: Editor of the literary journal *Tomorrow,* c. 1940s; University of Texas, began as lecturer in Indian philosophy, 1965, became professor of philosophy, 1980-83.

AWARDS, HONORS: Neustadt International Prize for Literature, 1988.

WRITINGS:

FICTION

Kanthapura, George Allen & Unwin (London, England), 1938, New Directions (New York, NY), 1963, Greenwood Press (Westport, CT), 1977.

The Cow of the Barricades and Other Stories, Oxford University Press (London, England), 1947.

The Serpent and the Rope, Murray (London, England), 1960, Pantheon (New York, NY), 1963, Ind-U.S. Incorporated, 1968, Overlook Press (Woodstock, NY), 1986.

The Cat and Shakespeare: A Tale of India, Macmillan (New York, NY), 1965.

Comrade Kirillov (originally published in French), Ind-U.S. Incorporated, 1976.

The Policeman and the Rose: Stories, Oxford University Press (Delhi, India), 1978.

On the Ganga Ghat, Vision Books (New Delhi, India), 1989.

The Best of Raja Rao, selected and edited by Makarand Paranjape, Katha Classics (New Delhi, India), 1998.

The Great Indian Way: A Life of Mahatma Gandhi, Vision Books (New Delhi, India), 1998.

OTHER

(Editor, with Iqbal Singh) *Changing India,* George Allen & Unwin (London, England), 1939.

(Editor, with Iqbal Singh) *Whither India?,* Padmaja Publications (Baroda, India), 1948.

(Editor) Jawaharlal Nehur, *Soviet Russia: Some Random Sketches and Impressions,* Chetana, 1949.

The Chessmaster and His Moves, Vision Books (New Delhi, India), 1988.

The Meaning of India, Vision Books (New Delhi, India), 1996.

Contributor of articles to journals, including *Jaya Karnataka.*

SIDELIGHTS: A leading English-language Indian author, Raja Rao is best known for novels in which he examines metaphysical themes by involving characters with diverse ideas, outlooks, and backgrounds. As these individuals establish relationships, they are prompted to compare and reexamine their personal, political, spiritual, and cultural values, and through them Rao frequently contrasts Indian philosophy and spiritualism with Western society's emphasis on dualism and rationalism. While often entangled in irreconcilable conflicts with those they love, Rao's protagonists gain insights into the nature of identity, existence, illusion, and reality. In 1988, Rao became the tenth author awarded the Neustadt International Prize for Literature, a biennial honor bestowed upon a living writer who has made significant contributions in poetry, fiction, or drama.

To authentically recreate the local color of Indian life and speech patterns, Rao often experiments with English language, syntax, and fictional forms. This interest is particularly evident in his first novel, *Kanthapura,* where he combines an anecdotal, stream-of-consciousness style with slight use of punctuation to capture the dialect and upbeat lifestyle of an Indian village. In this work, which is narrated by a grandmother, a young man returns to his native village after having left to study at a university and promotes the ideals and values of Mohandas Gandhi. The man is mocked by several residents and violently apprehended by authorities for his nonviolent defiance of traditional social norms. While relating these incidents in colloquial language replete with colorful aphorisms, the grandmother embellishes her tale with numerous references to local customs, daily activities, superstitions, rituals, and legends.

In his next novel, *The Serpent and the Rope,* Rao examines themes relating to illusion and reality. In this work, a young Brahmin named Rama gains greater understanding of identity and truth from experiences with his extended family in India, his encounters and studies in France, and his visits to England. Rama attempts to assimilate into a Western lifestyle after marrying a French woman, but a visit to India reawakens ties to his heritage. While vividly detailing daily life in France and India, this deeply symbolic metaphysical novel contrasts Western rationality and Hindu mysticism, explores ideals pertaining to Catholicism, Marxism, Freudianism, and fascism, and develops numerous parallels between myths, legends, and histories of different cultures.

Rao's third novel, *The Cat and Shakespeare: A Tale of India,* is a comic fable narrated by an Indian bureaucrat who is implicated in adultery, murder, and thievery. This novel features such symbolic events as droughts and illnesses, sudden appearances by a cat during portentous misunderstandings, and the actions and pronouncements of a mystical man who frequently transcends a metaphorical wall between appearance and reality.

The Chessmaster and His Moves, first of a projected trilogy of novels, is narrated by a man named Sivarama, who pursues absolute truths through mathematics and relationships with women. Employing Hindu myths to shape and order the narrative, Rao introduces characters from various cultures who are defined by their ideas and opinions on such matters as politics, history, love, art, and religion. Through their encounters, these individuals reassess their ideals, discover self-perpetuated myths, and come to a greater understanding of their individual identities.

Most of the pieces collected in *The Cow of the Barricades and Other Stories* and *The Policeman and the Rose* are fictional vignettes of village life in India. The tales focus upon traditions, social unrest, and various other representative concerns. *The Policeman and the Rose* is a symbolic story that illuminates differences between India and the West. In *Comrade Kirillov,* Rao examines the influence of history on the individual and develops an extended comparison between Vedantism and Marxism. The title character of this novella is the namesake of an individual in Fedor Dostoevsky's novel *The Possessed.* Both protagonists represent their author's suspicions about individuals who promote political reform by drawing upon ideas and models from outside their native lands. Rao's character, for example, champions change through means that are antithetical to the principles of Gandhi.

BIOGRAPHICAL AND CRITICAL SOURCES:

BOOKS

Bhattacharya, P. C., *Indo-Anglian Literature and the Works of Raja Rao,* Atma Ram (Delhi, India), 1983.

Contemporary Literary Criticism, Thomson Gale (Detroit, MI), Volume 25, 1983, Volume 56, 1989.

Naik, M. K., *Raja Rao,* Twayne (New York, NY), 1972, revised edition, 1982.

Narasimhaiah, C. D., *Raja Rao,* Arnold-Heinemann (New Delhi, India), 1973.

Sharma, K. K., editor, *Perspectives on Raja Rao: An Anthology of Critical Essays,* Vimal Prakashan (Ghaziabad, India), 1980.

Sharrad, Paul, *Raja Rao and Critical Tradition,* Sterling, 1988.

Smith, Larry E., editor, *Discourse across Culture: Strategies in World Englishes,* Prentice-Hall (New York, NY), 1987.

PERIODICALS

America, February 29, 1964.

Ariel, October, 1992, Senath W. Perera, "Towards a Limited Emancipation: Women in Raja Rao's *Kanthapura,*" pp. 99-110.

Books, April 7, 1963.

Books Abroad, autumn, 1966.

Book Week—The Sunday Herald Tribune, January 31, 1965.

Christian Science Monitor, January 16, 1964.

Commonweal, January 25, 1963; May 15, 1964.

International Fiction Review, summer, 1980.

Journal of Commonwealth Literature, August, 1991, K.C. Belliappa, "The Question of Form in Raja Rao's *The Serpent and the Rope,*" pp. 158-168; winter, 1995, Chitra Sankaran, "Misogyny in Raja Rao's *The Chessmaster and His Moves,*" pp. 87-96; spring, 1998, Tabish Khair, "Raja Rao and Alien Universality," pp. 75-84; spring, 1999, Anshuman Mondal, "The Ideology of Space in Raja Rao's *Kanthapura,*" p. 103.

Literary Criterion, summer, 1965.

Modern Fiction Studies, spring, 1993, Alpana Sharma Knippling, "R.K. Narayan, Raja Rao and Modern English Discourse in Colonial India," pp. 169-186.

Nation, March 16, 1963.

New Leader, June 21, 1965.

New York Times, January 20, 1965.

New York Times Book Review, April 14, 1963; January 5, 1964; January 17, 1965.

Publishers Weekly, February 14, 1986, Sybil Steinberg, review of *The Serpent and the Rope,* p. 66.

Saturday Review, January 16, 1965.

Time, February 22, 1963.

Virginia Quarterly Review, winter, 1980.

World Literature Today, autumn, 1988.

World Literature Written in English, November, 1973; November, 1975.

ONLINE

Pegasos Web Site, http://www.kirjasto.sci.fi/ (September 8, 2004), "Raja Rao."

* * *

RAVENNA, Michael
See WELTY, Eudora

* * *

REED, Ishmael 1938-
(Emmett Coleman)

PERSONAL: Born February 22, 1938, in Chattanooga, TN; son of Henry Lenoir (a fundraiser for YMCA) and Thelma Coleman (a homemaker and salesperson); stepfather, Bennie Stephen Reed (an auto worker); married Priscilla Rose Thompson, September, 1960 (divorced, 1970); married Carla Blank (a modern dancer), 1970; children: (first marriage) Timothy, Brett (daughter); (second marriage) Tennessee Maria (daughter). *Education:* Attended State University of New York at Buffalo, 1956-60. *Politics:* Independent.

ADDRESSES: Office—c/o Author Mail, Avon Books, 1790 Broadway, New York, NY 10019.

CAREER: Writer. *Empire Star Weekly,* staff writer, 1960-62; freelance writer, New York, NY, 1962-67. *East Village Other,* New York, NY, cofounder, 1965; *Advance,* Newark, NJ, cofounder, 1965. Yardbird Publishing Co., Berkeley, CA, cofounder, 1971, editorial director, 1971-75; Reed, Cannon & Johnson Communications Co. (publisher and producer of videocassettes), Berkeley, cofounder, 1973—; Before Columbus Foundation (producer and distributor of work of unknown ethnic writers), Berkeley, cofounder, 1976—; Ishmael Reed and Al Young's *Quilt* (magazine), Berkeley, cofounder, 1980—. Teacher at St. Mark's in the Bowery prose workshop, 1966; guest lecturer, University of California, Berkeley, 1968—, University of Washington, 1969-70, State University of New York at Buffalo, summer, 1975, and fall, 1979, Yale University, fall, 1979, Dartmouth College, summers, 1980-81, Sitka Community Association, summer, 1982, University of Arkansas at Fayetteville, 1982, Columbia University, 1983, Harvard University, 1987, and Regents lecturer, University of California, Santa Barbara, 1988. Judge of National Poetry Competition, 1980, King's County Literary Award, 1980, and University of Michigan Hopwood Award, 1981. Chair of Berkeley Arts Commission, 1980 and 1981. Coordinating Council of Literary Magazines, chair of board of directors, 1975-79, advisory board chair, 1977-79. Executive producer of pilot episode of soap opera *Personal Problems* and copublisher of *The Steve Cannon Show: A Quarterly Audio-Cassette Radio Show Magazine.*

MEMBER: Authors Guild, Authors League of America, PEN, Celtic Foundation.

AWARDS, HONORS: Certificate of Merit, California Association of English Teachers, 1972, for *19 Necromancers from Now;* nominations for National Book Award in fiction and poetry, 1973, for *Mumbo Jumbo* and *Conjure: Selected Poems, 1963-1970;* nomination for Pulitzer Prize in poetry, 1973, for *Conjure;* Richard and Hinda Rosenthal Foundation Award, National Institute of Arts and Letters, 1975, for *The Last Days of Louisiana Red;* John Simon Guggenheim Memorial Foundation award for fiction, 1974; Guggenheim fellowship, 1975; American Academy award, 1975; National Institute of Arts and Letters honor, 1975; Poetry in Public Places winner (New York City), 1976, for poem "From the Files of Agent 22," and for a bicentennial mystery play, *The Lost State of Franklin,* written in collaboration with Carla Blank and Suzushi Hanayagi; Lewis Michaux Award, 1978; American Civil Liberties Award, 1978; Pushcart Prize for essay "American Poetry: Is There a Center?," 1979; Wisconsin Arts Board fellowship, 1982; associate fellow of Calhoun College, Yale University, 1982; American Civil Liberties Union publishing fellowship; three New York State publishing grants for merit; three National Endowment for the Arts publishing grants for merit; California Arts Council grant; associate fellow, Harvard Signet Society, 1987—; Langston Hughes Medal for Lifetime Achievement, 1994; Honorary doctorate, State University of New York at Buffalo, 1995; MacArthur fellowship, 1998.

WRITINGS:

FICTION

The Free-Lance Pallbearers, Doubleday (Garden City, NY), 1967.

Yellow Back Radio Broke-Down, Doubleday (Garden City, NY), 1969.

Mumbo Jumbo, Doubleday (Garden City, NY), 1972.

The Last Days of Louisiana Red, Random House (New York, NY), 1974.

Flight to Canada, Random House (New York, NY), 1976.

The Terrible Twos, St. Martin's Press (New York, NY), 1982.

Reckless Eyeballing, St. Martin's Press (New York, NY), 1986.

The Terrible Threes, Atheneum (New York, NY), 1989.

Japanese by Spring, Atheneum (New York, NY), 1993.

NONFICTION

Shrovetide in Old New Orleans (essays), Doubleday (Garden City, NY), 1978.

God Made Alaska for the Indians: Selected Essays, Garland (New York, NY), 1982.

Writin' Is Fightin': Thirty-seven Years of Boxing on Paper, Atheneum (New York, NY), 1988, revised and expanded edition published as *Writing Is Fighting: Forty-three Years of Boxing on Paper,* Addison-Wesley (Reading, MA), 1998.

Airing Dirty Laundry, Addison-Wesley (Reading, MA), 1993.
The Reed Reader, Basic Books (New York, NY), 2000.
Another Day at the Front: Dispatches from the Race War, Basic Books (New York, NY), 2002.
Blues City: A Walk in Oakland, Crown (New York, NY), 2003.

Contributor to numerous volumes, including *Amistad I: Writings on Black History and Culture,* Vintage Books (New York, NY), 1970; *The Black Aesthetic,* Doubleday (Garden City, NY), 1971; *Nommo: An Anthology of Modern Black African and Black American Literature,* Macmillan (New York, NY), 1972; *Cutting Edges: Young American Fiction for the '70s,* Holt (New York, NY), 1973; *Superfiction; or, The American Story Transformed: An Anthology,* Vintage Books (New York, NY), 1975; and *American Poets in 1976,* Bobbs-Merrill (New York, NY), 1976.

PLAYS

Hell Hath No Fury . . . , produced by the Playwrights and Directors Project of the Actors Studio in New York, NY, June, 1980.
Savage Wilds, produced at the Julia Morgan Theater, Berkeley, CA, January, 1988.
Hubba City, produced at the Black Repertory Theatre, 1988.
The Preacher and the Rapper, produced in New York, NY, 1994.

Also author of *The Lost State of Franklin* with Carla Blank and Suzushi Hanayagi, 1976.

EDITOR

(As Emmett Coleman) *The Rise, Fall, and . . . ? of Adam Clayton Powell,* Beeline (Albany, NY), 1967.
(Also author of introduction, and contributor) *19 Necromancers from Now,* Doubleday (Garden City, NY), 1970.
(With Al Young) *Yardbird Lives!,* Grove (New York, NY), 1978.
(And contributor) *Calafia: The California Poetry,* Yardbird Books (Berkeley, CA), 1979.
(With Kathryn Trueblood and Shawn Wong) *The Before Columbus Foundation Fiction Anthology: Selections from the American Book Awards, 1980-1990,* Norton (New York, NY), 1992.
MultiAmerica: Essays on Cultural Wars and Cultural Peace, Viking (New York, NY), 1997.
From Totems to Hip-Hop (collected poetry), Thunder Mouth Press (New York, NY), 2003.

POETRY

Catechism of d Neoamerican Hoodoo Church, Paul Breman (London, England), 1970, Broadside Press (Highland Park, MI), 1971.
Conjure: Selected Poems, 1963-1970, University of Massachusetts Press (Amherst, MA), 1972.
Chattanooga: Poems, Random House (New York, NY), 1973.
A Secretary to the Spirits, illustrations by Betye Saar, NOK Publishers (New York, NY), 1977.
New and Collected Poems, Atheneum (New York, NY), 1988.

Poetry also represented in anthologies, including *Where Is Vietnam? American Poets Respond: An Anthology of Contemporary Poems,* Doubleday, 1967; *The New Black Poetry,* International Publishers (New York, NY), 1969; *The Norton Anthology of Poetry,* Norton (New York, NY), 1970; *The Poetry of the Negro, 1746-1970,* Doubleday (Garden City, NY), 1970; *Afro-American Literature: An Introduction,* Harcourt (San Diego, CA), 1971; *The Writing on the Wall: 108 American Poems of Protest,* Doubleday (Garden City, NY), 1971; *Major Black Writers,* Scholastic (New York, NY), 1971; *The Black Poets,* Bantam (New York, NY), 1971; *The Poetry of Black America: Anthology of the 20th Century,* Harper (New York, NY), 1972; and *Giant Talk: An Anthology of Third World Writings,* Random House (New York, NY), 1975.

OTHER

Ishmael Reed Reading His Poetry (cassette), Temple of Zeus, Cornell University Press (Ithaca, NY), 1976.
Ishmael Reed and Michael Harper Reading in the UCSD New Poetry Series (reel), University of California, San Diego (San Diego, CA), 1977.
(With Al Young) *Personal Problems* (video script), 1980.
(Author of introduction) Elizabeth A. Settle and Thomas A. Settle, *Ishmael Reed: A Primary and Secondary Bibliography,* G.K. Hall (Boston, MA), 1982.
Cab Calloway Stands in for the Moon, Bamberger (Flint, MI), 1986.

(With Richard Nagler) *Oakland Rhapsody: The Secret Soul of an American Downtown,* North Atlantic Books (Berkeley, CA), 1995.

Conversations with Ishmael Reed, edited by Bruce Dick and Amritjit Singh, University Press of Mississippi (Jackson, MS), 1995.

The Poet and the Poem from the Library of Congress, Ishmael Reed (cassette), Library of Congress (Washington, DC), 1996.

Ishmael Reed and Garrett Hongo Reading Their Poems in the Mumfoud Room (cassette), Library of Congress (Washington, DC), 1996.

Also author, with wife, Carla Blank, and Suzushi Hanayagi, of a bicentennial mystery play, *The Lost State of Franklin.*

Author of foreword, *Dark Eros,* edited by Reginald Martin, St. Martin's Press (New York, NY), 1997. Contributor of fiction to such periodicals as *Fiction, Iowa Review, Nimrod, Players, Ramparts, Seattle Review,* and *Spokane Natural;* contributor of articles and reviews to numerous periodicals, including *Black World, Confrontation, Essence, Le Monde, Los Angeles Times, New York Times, Playgirl, Rolling Stone, Village Voice, Washington Post,* and *Yale Review;* and contributor of poetry to periodicals, including *American Poetry Review, Black Scholar, Black World, Essence, Liberator, Negro Digest, Noose, San Francisco Examiner, Oakland Tribune, Life, Connoisseur,* and *Umbra.* Cofounder of periodicals *East Village Other* and *Advance* (Newark community newspaper), both 1965. Editor of *Yardbird Reader,* 1972-76; editor-in-chief, *Y'Bird* magazine, 1978-80; and coeditor of *Quilt* magazine, 1981.

ADAPTATIONS: Some of Reed's poetry has been scored and recorded on *New Jazz Poets;* a dramatic episode from *The Last Days of Louisiana Red* appears on *The Steve Cannon Show: A Quarterly Audio-Cassette Radio Show Magazine,* produced by Reed, Cannon & Johnson Communications.

SIDELIGHTS: The novels of writer Ishmael Reed "are meant to provoke," wrote *New York Times* contributor Darryl Pinckney. "Though variously described as a writer in whose work the black picaresque tradition has been extended, as a misogynist or an heir to both [Zora Neale] Hurston's folk lyricism and [Ralph] Ellison's irony, he is, perhaps because of this, one of the most underrated writers in America. Certainly no other contemporary black writer, male or female, has used the language and beliefs of folk culture so imaginatively, and few have been so stinging about the absurdity of American racism." Yet this novelist, poet, and essayist is not simply a voice of black protest against racial and social injustices but instead a confronter of universal evils, a purveyor of universal truths.

Reed's first novel, *The Free-Lance Pallbearers,* introduces several thematic and stylistic devices that reappear throughout his canon. In the novel, Reed's first satirical jab is at the oppressive, stress-filled, Western/European/Christian tradition. But in *The Free-Lance Pallbearers,* the oppressor/oppressed, evil/good dichotomy does not absolve blacks. While Reed blames whites, called HARRY SAM in the novel, for present world conditions, he also attacks culpable individuals from different strata in the black community and satirizes various kinds of black leaders in the twentieth century. Among the black characters whom Reed describes negatively are Elijah Raven, the Muslim/Black Nationalist whose ideas of cultural and racial separation in the United States are exposed as lies; Eclair Pockchop, the minister fronting as an advocate of the people's causes, later discovered performing an unspeakable sex act on SAM; the black cop who protects white people from the blacks in the projects and idiotically allows a cow-bell to be put around his neck for "meritorious service"; Doopeyduk's neighbors, who are too stupid to remember their own names; and finally Doopeyduk himself, whose pretensions of being a black intellectual render all his statements and actions absurd. Reed reserves his most scathing satire for the black leaders who cater to SAM in his palace.

The rhetoric of popular black literature in the 1960s is also satirized in *The Free-Lance Pallbearers.* The polemics of the time, characterized by colloquial diction, emotionalism, direct threats, automatic writing, and blueprints for a better society, are portrayed as representing the negative kind of literature required of blacks by the reading public. Reed suggests that while literature by blacks might have been saying that blacks would no longer subscribe to white dictates, in fact the converse was true, manifested in the very literature that the publishing houses generally were printing at the time.

In his novel, *Yellow Back Radio Broke-Down,* Reed begins to use at length Hoodoo (or Voodoo) methods and folklore as a basis for his work. Underlying all of the components of Hoodoo, according to scholars, are two precepts: 1) the idea of syncretism, or the combination of beliefs and practices with divergent cultural origins, and 2) the concept of time. Even before the exportation of slaves to the Caribbean, Hoodoo was a syncretic religion, absorbing all that it considered useful from other West African religious practices. As a religion formed to combat degrading social conditions by dignifying and connecting man with helpful supernatural forces, Hoodoo is said to thrive because of its syncretic flexibility, its ability to combine different influences and transfigure them into that which helps the "horse," or the one possessed by the attributes of a Hoodoo god. Hoodoo is bound by certain dogma or rites, but such rules are easily changed when they become oppressive, myopic, or no longer useful.

Reed turns this concept of syncretism into a literary method that combines aspects of "standard" English, including dialect, slang, argot, neologisms, or rhyme, with less "standard" language, taken from the streets, popular music, and television. By mixing language from different sources, Reed employs expressions that can both evoke interest and humor through seeming incongruities and create the illusion of real speech. In the *Black American Literature Forum,* Michel Fabre drew a connection between Reed's use of language and his vision of the world, suggesting that "his so-called nonsense words raise disturbing questions . . . about the very nature of language." Often, "the semantic implications are disturbing because opposite meanings coexist." Thus Reed emphasizes "the dangerous interchangeability of words and of the questionable identity of things and people" and "poses anguishing questions about self-identity, about the mechanism of meaning and about the nature of language and communication."

Syncretism and synchronicity, along with other facets of Hoodoo as literary method, are central to *Yellow Back Radio Broke-Down.* The title is street-talk for the elucidation of a problem, in this case the racial and oligarchical difficulties of an Old West town, Yellow Back Radio; these difficulties are explained, or "broke down," for the reader. The novel opens with a description of the Hoodoo fetish, or mythical cult figure, Loop Garoo. Loop embodies diverse ethnic backgrounds and a history and power derived from several religions.

Reed's first major volume of poetry, called *Conjure: Selected Poems, 1963-1970,* was followed by *Chattanooga: Poems,* and *A Secretary to the Spirits.* Reed draws most of the symbols in his poetry from Afro-American and Anglo-American historical and popular traditions—two distinct but intertwined sources for the Afro-American aesthetic. "Black Power Poem" succinctly states the Hoodoo stance in the West: "may the best church win. / shake hands now and come out conjuring"; "Neo-Hoodoo Manifesto," defines all that Hoodoo is and thus sheds light on the ways Reed uses its principles in writing.

The theme of Reed's *Mumbo Jumbo* is the origin and composition of the "true Afro-American aesthetic." Testifying to the novel's success in fulfilling this theme, Houston Baker in *Black World* said *Mumbo Jumbo* "gives one a sense of the broader vision and the careful, painful, and laborious 'fundamental brainwork' that are needed if we are to define the eternal dilemma of the Black Arts and work fruitfully toward its melioration. . . . [The novel's] overall effect is that of amazing talent and flourishing genius." *Mumbo Jumbo*'s first chapter is crucial in that it presents the details of the highly complex plot in synopsis or news-flash form. Reed has a Hoodoo detective named Papa LaBas (representing the Hoodoo god Legba) search out and reconstruct a black aesthetic from remnants of literary and cultural history. Lending the narrative authenticity, Reed inserts facts from nonfictional, published works, photographs, historical drawings, and a bibliography.

At the opening of *Mumbo Jumbo,* set in New Orleans in the 1920s, white municipal officials are trying to respond to "Jes Grew," an outbreak of behavior outside of socially conditioned roles; white people are "acting black" by dancing half-dressed in the streets to an intoxicating new loa (the spiritual essence of a fetish) called jazz. Speaking in tongues, people abandon racist and other oppressive endeavors because it is more fun to "shake that thing." One of the doctors assigned to treat the pandemic of Jes Grew comments, "There are no isolated cases in this thing. It knows no class no race no consciousness." No one knows where the germ has come from; it "jes grew." In the synoptic first chapter, the omniscient narrator says Jes Grew is actually "an anti-plague. Some plagues caused the body to waste away. Jes Grew enlivened the host."

Hoodoo time resurfaces in *Mumbo Jumbo.* Certain chapters detailing past events in the past tense are immediately followed by chapters set in the present, mirroring Hoodoo/oral culture. The juxtaposition links all of the actions within a single narrative time frame. Commenting on his use both of time and of fiction-filled newsflashes, Reed said in *Shrovetide in Old New Orleans* that in writing *Mumbo Jumbo,* he "wanted to write about a time like the present or to use the past to prophesy about the future."

The close of *Mumbo Jumbo* finds Jes Grew withering with the burning of its text, the Book of Thoth, which lists the sacred spells and dances of the Egyptian god Osiris. LaBas says Jes Grew will reappear some day to make its own text: "A future generation of young artists will accomplish this," says LaBas, referring to the writers, painters, politicians, and musicians of the 1960s.

In the course of the narrative, Reed constructs his history of the true Afro-American aesthetic and parallels the uniting of Afro-American oral tradition, folklore, art, and history with a written code, a text, a literate recapitulation of history and practice. By calling for a unification of text and tradition, Reed equates the Text (the Afro-American aesthetic) with all other "Holy" codifications of faith. *Mumbo Jumbo,* which itself becomes the Text, appears as a direct, written response to the assertion that there is no "black" aesthetic, that black contributions to the world culture have been insignificant at best.

The Last Days of Louisiana Red consists of three major story lines that coalesce toward the close of the novel to form its theme. The book begins with the tale of Ed Yellings, an industrious, middle-class black involved in the propagation of Hoodoo. Through experimentation in his business, Solid Gumbo Works, Yellings discovers a cure for cancer and is hard at work to refine and market this remedy and other remedies for the various aspects of Louisiana Red, the Hoodoo name for all evil. When he is mysteriously murdered, Hoodoo detective Papa LaBas appears to investigate. The action of the novel involves participants in the second and third story lines, the tale of the Chorus and the recounting of the mythical Antigone's decision to oppose the dictates of the state. The Chorus symbolizes black Americans who will not disappear. Even though they are relegated by more powerful forces to minor roles, they work for the right to succeed or fail depending upon their merits. Therein lies Reed's theme in *The Last Days of Louisiana Red.*

In *The Terrible Twos,* Reed maintains the implicit notions of Hoodoo while using his main story line to resurrect another apocryphal tale: the legend of Santa Claus and his assistant/boss, Black Peter. The time frame of the novel is roughly Christmas 1980 to Christmases of the 1990s. The evil of *The Terrible Twos* is selfishness fed by an exclusive monetary system, such as capitalism. Reed does not endorse any other sort of government now in existence but criticizes any person or system that ignores what is humanly right, in favor of what is economically profitable. Santa Claus (an out-of-work television personality) exemplifies the way Hoodoo fights this selfish evil: by bringing those who were prosperous to the level of those who have nothing and are abandoned. Santa characterizes American capitalists, those with material advantages, as infantile, selfish and exclusionary because their class station does not allow them to empathize with those who are different. The story continues in *The Terrible Threes,* set in the late 1990s and featuring many of the same characters. In the sequel, John O'Brien revealed in *Washington Post Book World,* "the country is in a state of chaos, having chased its president into a sanatorium after he revealed on national television a White House conspiracy to purge America of its poor and homeless, as well as to destroy Nigeria." "Reed's eerie, weird, implausible world has a way of sounding all too real, too much like what we hear on the evening news," O'Brien concluded. "And Reed has an unnerving sense of what will show up next on our televisions. He is without doubt our finest satirist since Twain."

Several critics warned that readers will find *Threes* nearly incomprehensible without first reading *Twos.* Further, *New York Times Book Review* critic Gerald Early observed, "The major problem with *The Terrible Threes* is that it seems to vaporize even as you read it; the very telling artifices that held together Mr. Reed's novelistic art in previous works, that cunning combination of boundless energy and shrewdly husbanded ingenuity, are missing here." *Los Angeles Times Book Review* contributor Jacob Epstein found that "Reed's vision of the future (and our present and past) is original and subversive. Subversion is out of style these days, but unfashionable or not, Reed is an always interesting writer and this book deserves to be read."

Reckless Eyeballing is a satiric allegory. Ian Ball, a black male writer, responds to the poor reception of his earlier play, *Suzanna,* by writing *Reckless Eyeballing,* a play sure to please those in power with its vicious attacks against black men. ("Reckless eyeballing" was one of the accusations against Emmett Till, the young Chicago black man who was murdered in Mississippi in 1953 for "looking and whistling at a white woman.") Tremonisha Smarts, a black female writer whose first name is drawn from a Scott Joplin opera of that title, is alternately popular and unpopular with the white women who are promoting her books. The battle for whose vision will dominate in the literary market and popular culture is fierce.

Reed followed his publication of *The Reed Reader,* a sampling of his writings including plays, fiction, essays, and poems, with *Another Day at the Front: Dispatches from the Race War.* According to Clifford Thompson in *Black Issues Book Review, Another Day at the Front* is "based on the central, guiding belief that African Americans are under attack in a war fought through propaganda." *Booklist*'s Vernon Ford said the book "offers a remarkable work of race in America," focusing on everything from "historical context to contemporary realities."

In *Blues City: A Walk in Oakland,* "Reed tours historic districts and homes, and attends parades, festivals and performances, to discover the many worlds within Oakland," wrote a *Publishers Weekly* reviewer. While the book "doesn't live up to the 'husky and brawling' swagger of the city Reed describes," continued the reviewer, it is "filled with facts, dates, and a variety of cultural events." *Booklist*'s Vanessa Bush called *Blues City* "an eclectic look at the multicultural city that thrives in the shadows of the better known and celebrated San Francisco."

Reed's *From Totems to Hip-Hop* is a survey of American poetry, including such legendary poets as Robert Frost and T.S. Eliot, to rapper Tupac Shakur. "The result is a significant publication that will create a new generation of readers as well as a much-needed cultural consensus," noted Daniel Guillory in *Library Journal. Booklist*'s Donna Seaman agreed, calling *From Totems to Hip-Hop* "a dynamic and original anthology, an unprecedented amalgam of poets representing many facets of American culture and society."

In addition to his novels and poetry, Reed has also written numerous essays and nonfiction pieces about contemporary American society and politics. Thirty-five of these essays, were collected and published as *Airing Dirty Laundry.* Among Reed's subjects are the misrepresentation of blacks by the mass media, the misguided attacks on multicultural education in schools, and contemporary black intellectuals who have had a significant impact on white America, even though most whites have not heard of them. Jill Nelson, writing in the *New York Times Book Review,* observed: "Always provocative, sometimes infuriating, this collection reminds us that the purpose of art is not to confirm and coddle but to provoke and confront."

BIOGRAPHICAL AND CRITICAL SOURCES:

BOOKS

African American Writers, Scribner (New York, NY), 1991.

Boyer, Jay, *Ishmael Reed,* Boise State University Press (Boise, ID), 1993.

Contemporary African American Novelists: A Bio-Bibliographical Critical Sourcebook, Greewood Press (Westport, CT), 1999.

Contemporary Literary Criticism, Thomson Gale (Detroit, MI), Volume 2, 1974, Volume 3, 1975, Volume 5, 1976, Volume 6, 1976, Volume 8, 1980, Volume 32, 1985.

Contemporary Novelists, 7th edition, St. James Press (Detroit, MI), 2001.

Contemporary Poets, 7th edition, St. James Press (Detroit, MI), 2001.

Contemporary Southern Writers, St. James Press (Detroit, MI), 1999.

Dictionary of Literary Biography, Thomson Gale (Detroit, MI), Volume 2: *American Novelists since World War II,* 1978, Volume 5: *American Poets since World War II,* 1980, Volume 33: *Afro-American Fiction Writers after 1955,* 1984, Volume 227: *American Novelists since World War II, Sixth Series,* 2000.

Encyclopedia of World Biography, Volume 23, Thomson Gale (Detroit, MI), 2003.

Encyclopedia of World Literature in the Twentieth Century, St. James Press (Detroit, MI), 1999.

Joyce, Joyce Ann, *Warriors, Conjurers, and Priests: Defining African-Centered Literary Criticism,* Third World Press (Chicago, IL), 1994.

Klinkowitz, Jerome, *Literary Subversions: New American Fiction and the Practice of Criticism,* Southern Illinois University Press (Carbondale, IL), 1985.

Ludwig, Sami, *Concrete Language: Intercultural Communication in Maxine Hong Kingston's "The Woman Warrior" and Ishmael Reed's "Mumbo Jumbo,"* [New York], 1996.

Martin, Reginald, *Ishmael Reed and the New Black Aesthetic Critics,* Macmillan (London, England), 1987.

Modern American Literature, St. James Press (Detroit, MI), 1999.

O'Donnell, Patrick, and Robert Con Davis, editors, *Intertextuality and Contemporary American Fiction,* Johns Hopkins University Press (Baltimore, MD), 1989.

Ostendorf, Berndt, *Black Literature in White America,* Noble (Totowa, NJ), 1982.

St. James Encyclopedia of Popular Culture, St. James Press (Detroit, MI), 2000.

Settle, Elizabeth A., and Thomas A. Settle, *Ishmael Reed: A Primary and Secondary Bibliography,* G.K. Hall (Boston, MA), 1982.

PERIODICALS

Amerasia Journal, February, 1999, review of *Multi-America: Essays on Cultural Wars and Cultural Peace,* p. 181.

American Book Review, May-June, 1983; October-November, 1994, p. 17.

American Poetry Review, May-June, 1976; January-February, 1978.

Arizona Quarterly, autumn, 1979.
Black American Literature Forum, Volume 12, 1978; spring, 1979; spring, 1980; fall, 1984.
Black Enterprise, January, 1973; December, 1982; April, 1983; October, 1994, p. 169.
Black Issues Book Review, March, 2002, review of *Mumbo Jumbo,* review of *The Free-Lance Pallbearers,* review of *Flight to Canada,* p. 26; January-February, 2003, Clifford Thompson, "Call Him Ishmael: The Controversial (Some Say Reckless) Cultural Critic Ishmael Reed Returns a New Collection of Essays Appropriately Titled *Another Day at the Front,*" p. 40, review of *Another Day at the Front: Dispatches from the Race War,* p. 52.
Black World, October, 1971; December, 1972; January, 1974; June, 1974; June, 1975; July, 1975.
Booklist, June 1, 2000, Vanessa Bush, review of *The Reed Reader,* p. 1838; December 15, 2002, Vernon Ford, review of *Another Day at the Front,* p. 713; February 15, 2003, review of *From Totems to Hip-Hop,* p. 1038; September 15, 2003, review of *Blues City: A Walk in Oakland,* p. 198.
Chicago Review, fall, 1976.
Chicago Tribune Book World, April 27, 1986.
Critical Inquiry, June, 1983.
Dalhousie Review, spring, 2000, review of *The Reed Reader,* p. 137.
Essence, July, 1986; July, 1994, p. 38.
Harper's, December, 1969.
Iowa Review, spring, 1982, pp. 117-131.
Kirkus Reviews, November 1, 2002, review of *Another Day at the Front,* p. 1598; June 15, 2003, review of *Blues City: A Walk in Oakland,* p. 850.
Library Journal, April 1, 2003, Daniel L. Guillory, review of *From Totems to Hip-Hop,* p. 104.
Los Angeles Times, April 29, 1975.
Los Angeles Times Book Review, April 20, 1986; June 4, 1989; April 14, 1991, p. 10.
MELUS, spring, 1984.
Mississippi Quarterly, winter, 1984-85, pp. 21-32.
Mississippi Review, Volume 20, numbers 1-2, 1991.
Modern Fiction Studies, summer, 1976; spring, 1988, pp. 97-123.
Modern Poetry Studies, autumn, 1973; autumn, 1974.
Nation, September 18, 1976; May 22, 1982
Negro American Literature Forum, winter, 1967; winter, 1972.
Negro Digest, February, 1969; December, 1969.
New Republic, November 23, 1974.
New Yorker, October 11, 1969.
New York Review of Books, October 5, 1972; December 12, 1974; August 12, 1982; January 29, 1987; October 12, 1989, p. 20.
New York Times, August 1, 1969; August 9, 1972; June 17, 1982; April 5, 1986; September 28, 1995, p. A1; February 7, 1996, p. C12; May 13, 1997, p. C14.
New York Times Book Review, August 6, 1972; November 10, 1974; September 19, 1976; July 18, 1982; March 23, 1986; May 7, 1989; April 7, 1991, p. 32; February 13, 1994, p. 28.
Obsidian, spring-summer, 1979; spring-summer, 1986, pp. 113-127.
Partisan Review, spring, 1975.
People, December 16, 1974.
Phylon, December, 1968; June, 1975.
Publishers Weekly, June 23, 2003, review of *Blues City,* p. 53.
Review of Contemporary Fiction, summer, 1984; spring, 1987; summer, 1994, p. 227.
San Francisco Review of Books, November, 1975; January-February, 1983.
Saturday Review, October 14, 1972; November 11, 1978.
Times Literary Supplement, May 18, 1990, p. 534; July 15, 1994, p. 22.
Tribune Books (Chicago, IL), April 11, 1993, p. 3; December 12, 1993, p. 4.
Twentieth Century Literature, April, 1974.
Village Voice, January 22, 1979.
Virginia Quarterly Review, winter, 1973.
Washington Post Book World, March 16, 1986; June 25, 1989, pp. 4, 6; November 12, 1989, p. 16; April 14, 1991, p. 12; January 26, 1992, p. 12; March 21, 1993, p. 6.
Western American Literature, winter, 2002, review of *Yellow Back Radio Broke-Down,* p. 325.
World Literature Today, autumn, 1978.

ONLINE

Center for Book Culture, http://www.centerforbookculture.org/ (February 11, 2003), review of *The Free-Lance Pallbearers.*
Publishers Group West, http://www.pgw.com/ (February 11, 2003), description of *From Totems to Hip-Hop.*
State University of New York at Buffalo, http://www.math.buffalo.edu/ (November 25, 2003), Mathematics Department, Professor Scott W. Williams, "Ishmael Reed."

* * *

REID, Desmond
See MOORCOCK, Michael

RENDELL, Ruth 1930-
(Ruth Barbara Rendell, Barbara Vine)

PERSONAL: Born February 17, 1930, London, England; daughter of Arthur Grasemann (a teacher) and Ebba (a teacher) Kruse; married Donald Rendell, 1950 (divorced, 1975; remarried, 1977); children: Simon. *Education:* Educated in Essex, England. *Hobbies and other interests:* Reading, walking, opera.

ADDRESSES: *Home*—26 Cornwall Terrace Mews, London NW1 5LL, England. *Agent*—Sterling Lord Agency, 660 Madison Ave., New York, NY 10021.

CAREER: Writer. Express and Independent Newspapers, West Essex, England, reporter and subeditor for the Chigwell *Times,* 1948-52.

AWARDS, HONORS: Edgar Allan Poe Award, Mystery Writers of America, 1974, for story "The Fallen Curtain," 1976, for collection *The Fallen Curtain and Other Stories,* 1984, for story "The New Girlfriend," and 1986, for novel *A Dark-Adapted Eye;* Gold Dagger Award, Crime Writers Association, 1977, for *A Demon in My View,* 1986, for *Live Flesh,* and 1987, for *A Fatal Inversion;* British Arts Council bursary, 1981; British National Book Award, 1981, for *The Lake of Darkness;* Popular Culture Association Award, 1983; Silver Dagger Award, Crime Writers Association, 1984, for *The Tree of Hands; Sunday Times* award for Literary Excellence, 1990.

WRITINGS:

MYSTERY NOVELS

From Doon with Death (also see below), John Long (London, England), 1964, Doubleday (Garden City, NY), 1965.

To Fear a Painted Devil, Doubleday (Garden City, NY), 1965.

Vanity Dies Hard, John Long (London, England), 1966, published as *In Sickness and in Health,* Doubleday (New York, NY), 1966.

A New Lease of Death (also see below), Doubleday (Garden City, NY), 1967, published as *Sins of the Fathers,* Ballantine (New York, NY), 1970.

Wolf to the Slaughter, John Long (London, England), 1967, Doubleday (Garden City, NY), 1968.

The Secret House of Death, John Long (London, England), 1968, Doubleday (Garden City, NY), 1969.

The Best Man to Die (also see below), John Long (London, England), 1969, Doubleday (Garden City, NY), 1970.

A Guilty Thing Surprised, Doubleday (Garden City, NY), 1970.

No More Dying Then, Hutchinson (London, England), 1971, Doubleday (Garden City, NY), 1972.

One Across, Two Down, Doubleday (Garden City, NY), 1971.

Murder Being Once Done, Doubleday (Garden City, NY), 1972.

Some Lie and Some Die, Doubleday (Garden City, NY), 1973.

The Face of Trespass, Doubleday (Garden City, NY), 1974.

Shake Hands Forever, Doubleday (Garden City, NY), 1975.

A Demon in My View, Doubleday (Garden City, NY), 1977.

A Judgment in Stone, Hutchinson (London, England), 1977, Doubleday (Garden City, NY), 1978.

A Sleeping Life, Doubleday (Garden City, NY), 1978.

Make Death Love Me, Doubleday (Garden City, NY), 1979.

The Lake of Darkness, Doubleday (Garden City, NY), 1980.

Put On by Cunning, Hutchinson (London, England), 1981, published as *Death Notes,* Pantheon (New York, NY), 1981.

Master of the Moor, Pantheon (New York, NY), 1982.

The Speaker of Mandarin, Pantheon (New York, NY), 1983.

The Killing Doll, Pantheon (New York, NY), 1984.

The Tree of Hands, Pantheon (New York, NY), 1984.

An Unkindness of Ravens, Pantheon (New York, NY), 1985.

Live Flesh, Pantheon (New York, NY), 1986.

Heartstones, Harper (New York, NY), 1987.

Talking to Strangers, Hutchinson (London, England), 1987, published as *Talking to Strange Men,* Pantheon (New York, NY), 1987.

The Veiled One, Pantheon (New York, NY), 1988.

The Bridesmaid, Mysterious Press (New York, NY), 1989.

Going Wrong, Mysterious Press (New York, NY), 1990.

Kissing the Gunner's Daughter, Mysterious Press (New York, NY), 1992.

The Crocodile Bird, Crown (New York, NY), 1993.

Simisola, Random House (New York, NY), 1995.

Ginger and the Kingsmarkham Chalk Circle, Phoenix (London, England), 1996.

The Keys to the Street, Random House (New York, NY), 1996.
Road Rage, Crown (New York, NY), 1997.
Bloodlines, Wheeler (Rockland, MA), 1997.
Whydunit (Perfectly Criminal 2), Severn House (London, England), 1997.
Thornapple, Travelman (London, England), 1998.
A Sight for Sore Eyes: A Novel, Crown (New York, NY), 1999.
Harm Done: An Inspector Wexford Mystery, Crown (New York, NY), 1999.
Adam and Eve and Pinch Me, Crown (New York, NY), 2001.
The Babes in the Wood, Crown (New York, NY), 2002.
The Rottweiler, Crown (New York, NY), 2004.

STORY COLLECTIONS

The Fallen Curtain and Other Stories, Hutchinson (London, England), 1976, published as *The Fallen Curtain: Eleven Mystery Stories by an Edgar Award-Winning Writer,* Doubleday (Garden City, NY), 1976.
Means of Evil and Other Stories, Hutchinson (London, England), 1979, published as *Five Mystery Stories by an Edgar Award-Winning Writer,* Doubleday (Garden City, NY), 1980.
The Fever Tree and Other Stories, Hutchinson (London, England), 1982, Pantheon (New York, NY), 1983, published as *The Fever Tree and Other Stories of Suspense,* Ballantine (New York, NY), 1984.
The New Girlfriend and Other Stories, Hutchinson (London, England), 1985, published as *The New Girlfriend and Other Stories of Suspense,* Pantheon (New York, NY), 1986.
(Editor) *A Warning to the Curious: The Ghost Stories of M.R. James,* Hutchinson (London, England), 1986.
Collected Short Stories, Hutchinson (London, England), 1987, published as *Collected Stories,* Pantheon (New York, NY), 1988.
Wexford: An Omnibus (contains *From Doon with Death, A New Lease of Death,* and *The Best Man to Die*), Hutchinson (London, England), 1988.
(With Colin Ward) *Undermining the Central Line,* Chatto & Windus (London, England), 1989.
The Copper Peacock and Other Stories, Mysterious Press (New York, NY), 1991.
The Fifth Wexford Omnibus (contains *Means of Evil, An Unkindness of Ravens,* and *The Veiled One*), Hutchinson (London, England), 1991.
(With photographs by Paul Bowden) *Ruth Rendell's Suffolk,* Hutchinson (London, England), 1992.
Blood Lines: Long and Short Stories, Crown (New York, NY), 1996.
(Editor) *The Reason Why: An Anthology of the Murderous Mind,* Crown (New York, NY), 1996.
Piranha to Scurfy and Other Stories, Vintage (New York, NY), 2002.

Contributor of short stories to *Ellery Queen's Mystery Magazine.*

UNDER PSEUDONYM BARBARA VINE

A Dark-Adapted Eye, Viking (New York, NY), 1985.
A Fatal Inversion, Bantam (New York, NY), 1987.
(With others) *Yes, Prime Minister: The Diaries of the Right Honorable James Hacker,* Salem House Publishers, 1988.
The House of Stairs, Harmony Books (New York, NY), 1989.
Gallowglass, Harmony Books (New York, NY), 1990.
King Solomon's Carpet, Harmony Books (New York, NY), 1992.
Anna's Book, Harmony Books (New York, NY), 1993.
No Night Is Too Long, Harmony Books (New York, NY), 1994.
The Brimstone Wedding, Harmony Books (New York, NY), 1996.
The Chimney Sweeper's Boy: A Novel, Harmony Books (New York, NY), 1998.
Grasshopper, Harmony Books (New York, NY), 2000.
The Blood Doctor, Shaye Areheart Books (New York, NY), 2002.

ADAPTATIONS: *A Judgment in Stone* was filmed as *The Housekeeper,* Rawfilm/Schulz Productions, 1987; several of Rendell's Wexford mysteries have been adapted for British television and subsequently aired on the Arts and Entertainment network's "Masters of Mystery" series.

SIDELIGHTS: Ruth Rendell is a prolific author who, writing under her own name and the pseudonym Barbara Vine, has enthralled both the general public and literary critics with her skillfully written mysteries and suspenseful stories. She has the ability, according to *Dictionary of Literary Biography* contributor Patricia A. Gabilondo, to render tales that could be considered formulaic, into something "always suspenseful and viscerally compelling." In her first novel, the author introduced Chief Inspector Reginald Wexford, a proper Englishman whose town of Kingsmarkham, Sussex, is plagued by many murders. Wexford has been the subject of numerous sequels and has won much praise for his creator for the deft characterizations, clever plots, and surprising endings that mark these books. While the Wexford books are straightforward police procedural novels, the books Rendell publishes under the Vine pseudonym are more gothic, often involving twisted psychology to produce edgy thrillers. Writing in the *Times Literary Supplement,* Francis Wyndham praised the author for her "masterly grasp of plot construction [and] highly developed faculty for social observation." David Lehman of *Newsweek* commented that "few detective writers are as good at pulling such last-second rabbits out of their top hats—the last page making us see everything before it in a strange, new glare."

Rendell's Wexford character is middle-aged, happily married, and the father of two grown daughters. His extensive reading allows him to quote from a wide range of literature during his murder investigations, but despite his erudition, Wexford is not cynical, eccentric, or misanthropic as are many literary detectives. His well-adjusted manner serves as contrast to the many strange mysteries he investigates. Social differences are frequently illuminated in these mysteries, and Rendell has been singled out as particularly skillful at portraying England's social stratification, even in the details of her descriptions of architectural details. Gabilondo mused, "Her meticulous description of setting serves to create atmosphere and, more important, to communicate the intimate relation between the physical and the psychological, especially in terms of the way that landscapes, whether urban or rural, take on the imprints of sociological change and personal conflict."

Wexford is also notable for his philosophical turn of mind and his keen empathy for his fellow man, in whatever the circumstances. His sensitivity makes him quite desirable to the women he encounters, yet Wexford remains determinedly devoted to his wife. Wexford's greatest disdain is for the "inanities of modernity," wrote Gabilondo. "Through Wexford's often ironic eye, Rendell paints a remarkably specific portrait of the changes that have occurred in English life—the encroachment of suburban sprawl, the banal homogenization of consumer culture, the dispossessed youth, the problems with unemployment, and the growing complexities of civil bureaucracies. Able to see both sides of any issue, as well as to grasp the essential poignancy of the human condition, Wexford finds himself often at odds with his official role, for his reliance on intuition and the imagination usually runs counter to the official line, offering a rich resource of dramatic tension," concluded Gabilondo. Wexford's open-mindedness is contrasted with the more narrow vision and rigid morality of his partner, Inspector Michael Burden. Unlike many series characters, Wexford and Burden age and go through many significant changes as the series progresses.

Rendell's early Wexford mysteries dealt frequently with desire and taboo, while in her later books she takes on social issues in a more direct manner. Feminism, ecoterrorism, and other modern concerns are examined, not always in a flattering light. In *A Sleeping Life,* gender-identity conflicts figure prominently in the murder case, while Wexford's daughter becomes involved in a radical feminist group. Rendell actually drew the ire of real-life feminist groups after the publication of *An Unkindness of Ravens,* which features a man-hating group called Action for the Radical Reform of Intersexual Attitudes (ARRIA). Members of the group vow to carry weapons and refrain from marriage; it even seems that some members advocate the murder of a man as an initiation rite. The author also ruffled feathers with *Kissing the Gunner's Daughter,* which challenges the popular notion that class stratification is much less meaningful in Britain than it has been in the past. Racism is addressed in *Simisola,* another Wexford novel; the problems of urban and suburban sprawl are considered in *Road Rage;* and the subject of wife-beating is approached in *Harm Done.*

Various types of psychological torment are central in Rendell's other books. *A Judgment in Stone* portrays an illiterate woman whose inability to read has led to a life of shame, isolation, and regression. *The Killing Doll* features Dolly Yearman, a schizophrenic whose delusions eventually lead her to murder. *Live Flesh* is told from the point of view of a convicted murderer and rapist, who lives in a strange symbiotic relationship with the police officer he crippled with a gunshot wound. In *The Bridesmaid,* the Pygmalion myth is turned inside out as a beautiful girl is shown to be marred by her mental instability. Despite her flaws, she becomes the object of sexual obsession for Philip; eventually, she brings him to the brink of murder. One of the author's most ambitious novels is *The Keys to the Street,* which uses the concentric circles and paths of London's Regent Park to follow the interconnected threads of human lives, particularly that of a well-to-do man who lives on the streets in the wake of a family tragedy and a young woman struggling to assert her independence. Although it may be the author's "most compassionate and most complex treatment of the human condition," according to Gabilondo, it left "most reviewers disappointed in her failure to bring all the strands together. The effectiveness of the structure, however, lies in this intentional failure to make everything connect. In Rendell's psychological thrillers, those avenues of emotional connection, like the misaligned arcs of Regent's Park, often do not meet, frustrating the hopes and dreams of her characters' lives." A very positive assessment of the book was offered by Emily Melton in *Booklist,* however; she wrote that it is "at once tragic, shocking, satisfying, and hopeful," and added, "Without a doubt, Rendell ranks with today's finest writers, and this book is one of her best. . . . Superbly written and beautifully constructed, the story is unique, powerful, and provocative."

Adam and Eve and Pinch Me is a "gem from the British master," wrote a *Publishers Weekly* reviewer, filled with characters "so vivid they live beyond the frame of the novel." At the center of the plot is Minty Knox, a woman in her thirties who works in a dry-cleaners and is obsessed with germs and cleanliness. Her hygiene phobias, as well as the ghosts she imagines she sees, figure prominently in a plot that is "intricate but brisk," according to the writer, "a literary page-turner, both elegant and accessible." *Booklist* reviewer Connie Fletcher called the book "madly absorbing," and advised, "Rendell's characters are fully drawn, and we become completely caught up in their struggles." Discussing her writing with a *Publishers Weekly* interviewer, Rendell commented, "I do write about obsession, but I don't think I have an obsession for writing. I'm not a compulsive writer. I like to watch obsession in other people, watch the way it makes them behave."

Gabilondo concluded: "Rendell's greatest contribution, in addition to her gifts as a storyteller, has been to track the social and the psychological circulation of that vast system—political, familial, cultural, and genetic—in which people are forced to play out their lives, through a body of work that takes readers not into the cozy drawing rooms of traditional English mystery but into the lives and psyches of men and women in a vividly contemporary Britain."

BIOGRAPHICAL AND CRITICAL SOURCES:

BOOKS

Contemporary Literary Criticism, Thomson Gale (Detroit, MI), Volume 28, 1984, Volume 48, 1988, Volume 50, 1988.

Dictionary of Literary Biography, Thomson Gale (Detroit, MI), Volume 87: *British Mystery and Thriller Writers since 1940,* 1989, Volume 276: *British Mystery and Thriller Writers since 1960,* 2003.

Mystery and Suspense Writers: The Literature of Crime, Detection, and Espionage, Scribner (New York, NY), 1998.

PERIODICALS

Advertiser (Adelaide, Australia), July 27, 2002, Katharine England, review of *The Blood Doctor,* p. W13.

Antioch Review, winter, 1997, review of *The Keys to the Street,* p. 122.

Belles Lettres, summer, 1993, p. 50; spring, 1994, p. 13.

Booklist, August, 1996, Emily Melton, review of *The Keys to the Street,* p. 1856; August, 1997, Emily Melton, review of *Road Rage,* p. 1848; December 1, 1998, Emily Melton, review of *A Sight for Sore Eyes,* p. 620; April 15, 1999, review of *Kissing the Gunner's Daughter,* p. 1458; August, 1999, review of *A Judgement in Stone,* p. 2025; September 1, 1999, Stephanie Zvirin, review of *Harm Done,* p. 8; November 1, 1999, Karen Harris, review of *A Sight for Sore Eyes,* p. 551; June 1, 2000, Mary McCay, review of *Harm Done,* p. 1922; November 1, 2000, Connie Fletcher, review of *Piranha to Scurfy and Other Stories,* p. 493; November 15, 2001, Connie Fletcher, review of *Adam and Eve and Pinch Me,* p. 524; September 1, 2003, Stephanie Zvirin, review of *The Babes in the Wood,* p. 7.

Chicago Tribune, August 29, 1989; October 31, 1993.

Chicago Tribune Book World, December 19, 1982.

Christian Science Monitor, July 6, 1992, p. 13.

Detroit News, August 12, 1979.

Entertainment Weekly, March 15, 2002, review of *Adam and Eve and Pinch Me,* p. 72.

Europe Intelligence Wire, October 20, 2002, Katie Owen, review of *The Babes in the Wood*; November 2, 2002, Rachel Simhon, review of *The Babes in the Wood.*

Globe and Mail (Toronto, Ontario, Canada), May 31, 1986; September 16, 1989.

Independent (London, England), August 18, 2001, Jane Jakeman, review of *Adam and Eve and Pinch Me,* p. 9; June 15, 2002, Jane Jakeman, "Where Does Ruth Rendell End and 'Barbara Vine' Begin?," p. 30.

Kirkus Reviews, July 15, 2003, review of *The Babes in the Wood,* p. 942.

Library Journal, February 1, 1999, Caroline Mann, review of *A Sight for Sore Eyes,* p. 122; August, 1999, Michael Rogers, review of *Some Lie and Some Die,* p. 149; September 1, 1999, Michael Rogers, review of *Murder Being Once Done,*

p. 238; October 1, 1991, p. 144; October 15, 1995; January, 1996, p. 149; September 1, 1999, Francine Fialkoff, review of *Harm Done,* p. 237; October 1, 1999, Sandy Glover, review of *A Sight for Sore Eyes,* p. 150; May 15, 2000, Danna Bell-Russel, review of *Harm Done,* p. 142; June 15, 2000, Michael Rogers, review of *A Judgement in Stone,* p. 122; December, 2000, Jane la Plante, review of *Piranha to Scurfy and Other Stories,* p. 194; December, 2001, Caroline Mann, review of *Adam and Eve and Pinch Me,* p. 175; October 1, 2003, Caroline Mann, review of *The Babes in the Wood,* p. 122.

Los Angeles Times, June 3, 1992, p. E1.

Los Angeles Times Book Review, August 3, 1980; May 8, 1983; November 21, 1993, p. 12.

Maclean's, May 19, 1986; April 10, 1995, p. 58.

Mademoiselle, February, 1996, p. 94.

New Statesman, September 6, 1996, Carol Birch, review of *The Keys to the Street,* p. 47; October 30, 1998, Francis Gilbert, review of *A Sight for Sore Eyes.*

Newsweek, September 21, 1987.

New York Times, September 9, 1988; February 4, 1990; June 12, 1992, p. C12; April 10, 1995, p. C9.

New York Times Book Review, June 25, 1967; June 23, 1968; August 24, 1969; February 26, 1974; June 2, 1974; December 1, 1974; April 27, 1975; November 23, 1975; February 27, 1977; October 13, 1996, Marilyn Stasio, review of *The Keys to the Street,* p. 29; September 7, 1997, Marilyn Stasio, review of *Road Rage,* p. 34; January 23, 1979; October 14, 1979; February 24, 1980; April 4, 1999, Marilyn Stasio, review of *A Sight for Sore Eyes,* p. 20; November 21, 1999, Marilyn Stasio, review of *Harm Done,* p. 80; March 3, 2002, Marilyn Stasio, review of *Adam and Eve and Pinch Me,* p. 21; August 4, 2002, Marilyn Stasio, review of *The Blood Doctor,* p. 19.

Publishers Weekly, August 16, 1991, p. 49; October 23, 1995; April 22, 1996, p. 61; July 29, 1996, review of *Keys to the Street,* p. 73; July 7, 1997, review of *Road Rage,* p. 53; February 8, 1999, review of *A Sight for Sore Eyes,* p. 197; October 18, 1999, review of *Harm Done,* p.73; November 13, 2000, review of *Piranha to Scurfy and Other Stories,* p. 89; January 28, 2002, review of *Adam and Eve and Pinch Me,* p. 274, interview with Ruth Rendell, p. 275; September 29, 2003, review of *The Babes in the Wood,* p. 46.

Saturday Review, January 30, 1971.

School Library Journal, March, 1997, Judy McAloon, review of *The Keys to the Street,* p. 216.

Seattle Times, February 10, 2002, Adam Woog, review of *Adam and Eve and Pinch Me,* p. J11.

Spectator, November 19, 1994, p. 47; October 4, 2003, Antonia Fraser, "And Now for My Next Trick. . . ," review of *The Rottweiler,* p. 55.

Times (London, England), December 11, 1987; October 5, 1995.

Times Literary Supplement, February 23, 1967; December 21, 1967; April 23, 1970; October 1, 1976; June 5, 1981; July 23, 1982; October 7, 1994, p. 30.

Virginian Pilot, July 22, 2001, review of *Grasshopper,* p. E3.

Washington Post, May 19, 1992, p. B2.

Washington Post Book World, September 20, 1981; October 31, 1993.

* * *

RENDELL, Ruth Barbara
See RENDELL, Ruth

* * *

RENSIE, Willis
See EISNER, Will

* * *

REXROTH, Kenneth 1905-1982

PERSONAL: Born December 22, 1905, in South Bend, IN; moved to Chicago, IL, at the age of twelve; died June 6, 1982, in Montecito, CA, of a heart ailment; son of Charles Marion (a wholesale druggist) and Delia (Reed) Rexroth; married Andree Deutcher, 1927 (died, 1940); married Marie Kass, 1940 (divorced, 1948); married Marthe Larsen, 1949 (divorced, 1961); married Carol Tinker (a poet), 1974; children: (by third marriage) Mary, Katharine. *Education:* Attended the Chicago Art Institute and the Art Students League, New York City; largely self-educated.

CAREER: Poet, translator, playwright, essayist, and painter. Worked as mucker, harvest hand, packer, fruit picker, forest patrolman, factory hand, and attendant in a mental institution. Held one-man art shows in Los Angeles, Santa Monica, New York, Chicago, Paris, and San Francisco. *The Nation,* San Francisco correspondent, beginning 1953-82. Co-founder of the San Francisco Poetry Center. Columnist for the *San Francisco Examiner,* 1958-68; *San Francisco Magazine,* 1968-82; *San Francisco Bay Guardian,* 1968-82. Taught at various universities, including San Francisco State College, 1964; University of Wisconsin, Madison; and University of California, Santa Barbara, part-time lecturer, 1968-82. Lectured and gave poetry readings throughout the world.

MEMBER: National Institute of Arts and Letters.

AWARDS, HONORS: California Literature Silver Medal Award for poetry, 1941, for *In What Hour,* 1945, for *The Phoenix and the Tortoise,* and 1980, for *The Morning Star;* Guggenheim fellowship in poetry, 1948 and 1949; Eunice Teitjens Award, 1957; Shelley Memorial Award, 1958; Amy Lowell fellowship, 1958; Longview Award; Chapelbrook Award; National Institute of Arts and Letters grant, 1964; American Academy grant, 1964; Rockefeller grant, 1967; Akademische Austausdienfp, 1967; Fulbright fellowship, 1974; Academy of American Poets' Copernicus Award, 1975; National Endowment for the Arts grant, 1977.

WRITINGS:

In What Hour (poetry), Macmillan (New York, NY), 1940.

The Phoenix and the Tortoise (poetry), New Directions (New York, NY), 1944.

The Art of Worldly Wisdom (poetry), Decker Press (Prairie City, IL), 1949.

The Signature of All Things: Poems, Songs, Elegies, Translations, and Epigrams, New Directions (New York, NY), 1950.

Beyond the Mountains (verse plays; produced in New York, NY, at Cherry Lane Theatre, 1951), New Directions (New York, NY), 1951, reprinted, 1974.

The Dragon and the Unicorn (poetry; originally published in part in *New Directions Annual,* 1950-51), New Directions (New York, NY), 1952.

Thou Shalt Not Kill (poetry), Goad Press (Sunnyvale, CA), 1955.

In Defense of the Earth (poetry), New Directions (New York, NY), 1956.

The Homestead Called Damascus (poem), New Directions (New York, NY), 1963.

Natural Numbers: New and Selected Poems, New Directions (New York, NY), 1963.

An Autobiographical Novel, Doubleday (New York, NY), 1966, revised and expanded edition, New Directions (New York, NY), 1991.

The Collected Shorter Poems of Kenneth Rexroth, New Directions (New York, NY), 1967.

The Heart's Garden, the Garden's Heart (poems and calligraphic designs), Pym-Randall Press (Cambridge, MA), 1967.

Collected Longer Poems of Kenneth Rexroth, New Directions (New York, NY), 1968.

The Spark in the Tender of Knowing (poetry), Pym-Randall Press (Cambridge, MA), 1968.

Sky Sea Birds Tree Earth House Beasts Flowers, Unicorn Press (Santa Barbara, CA), 1971.

American Poetry in the Twentieth Century (essays), Herder & Herder (New York, NY), 1971.

The Rexroth Reader, edited and with a foreword by Eric Mottram, Cape (London, England), 1972.

New Poems, New Directions (New York, NY), 1974.

The Silver Swan: Poems Written in Kyoto, 1974-75 (also see below), Copper Canyon Press (Port Townsend, WA), 1976.

On Flower Wreath Hill (poem; also see below), Blackfish Press (Burnaby, British Columbia, Canada), 1976.

The Morning Star (includes *The Silver Swan, On Flower Wreath Hill,* and *The Love Songs of Marichiko*), New Directions (New York, NY), 1979.

Saucy Limericks and Christmas Cheer, Morrow (Santa Barbara, CA), 1980.

Selected Poems, New Directions (New York, NY), 1984.

Flower Wreath Hill: Later Poems, (combines *New Poems* and *The Morning Star*), New Directions (New York, NY), 1991.

Kenneth Rexroth and James Laughlin: Selected Letters, edited by Lee Bartlett, Norton (New York, NY), 1991.

Sacramental Acts: The Love Poems of Kenneth Rexroth, edited and with an introduction by Sam Hamill and Elaine Laura Kleiner, Copper Canyon Press (Port Townsend, WA), 1997.

The Complete Poems of Kenneth Roxroth, Copper Canyon Press (Port Townsend, WA), 2003.

Also author of shorter works of poetry, including broadsides and "Lament for Dylan Thomas," 1955, and "As the Full Moon Rises," published by Old Marble Press; author of *Original Sin,* a ballet, which was performed by the San Francisco Ballet in 1961; author of autobiographical work *Excerpts from a Short Life,* 1981. Contributor of poetry, translations, essays, and criticism to numerous popular and academic periodicals.

ESSAYS

Bird in the Bush: Obvious Essays, New Directions (New York, NY), 1959.

Assays, New Directions (New York, NY), 1962.

Classics Revisited, Quadrangle Books (Chicago, IL), 1968, New Directions (New York, NY), 1986.
The Alternative Society: Essays from the Other World, Herder & Herder (New York, NY), 1970.
With Eye and Ear, Herder & Herder (New York, NY), 1970.
The Elastic Retort: Essays in Literature and Ideas, Seabury (New York, NY), 1973.
Communalism: From Its Origin to the Twentieth Century, Seabury (New York, NY), 1974.
World Outside the Window: The Selected Essays of Kenneth Rexroth, edited by Bradford Morrow, New Directions (New York, NY), 1987.
More Classics Revisited, edited by Bradford Morrow, New Directions (New York, NY), 1989.

EDITOR

(And author of introduction) D.H. Lawrence, *Selected Poems,* New Directions (New York, NY), 1948.
New British Poets: An Anthology, New Directions (New York, NY), 1949.
Fourteen Poems of O.V. de Lubicz-Milosz, Peregrine Press (San Francisco, CA), 1952, Copper Canyon Press (Port Townsend, WA), 1984.
(And translator) *One Hundred Poems from the Japanese,* New Directions (New York, NY), 1955.
(And translator with Ling O. Chung) *The Orchid Boat: Women Poets of China,* Herder & Herder (New York, NY), 1972.
Czeslav Milosz, *The Selected Poems of Czeslav Milosz,* Seabury (New York, NY), 1973.
David Meltzer, *Tens: Selected Poems, 1961-71,* McGraw (New York, NY), 1973.
(And author of introduction) Jessica Tarahata Hagedorn and others, *Four Young Women: Poems,* McGraw (New York, NY), 1973.
The Buddhist Writings of Lafcadio Hearn, Ross-Erikson, 1977.
(And translator with Ikuko Atsumi) *The Burning Heart: The Women Poets of Japan,* Seabury (New York, NY), 1977.
(And author of introduction and translator with Atsumi) Kazuko Shiraishi, *Seasons of Sacred Lust—Selected Poems,* New Directions (New York, NY), 1978.

TRANSLATOR

One Hundred Poems from the French, Jargon (Highland, NC), 1955, reprinted, Pym-Randall Press (Cambridge, MA), 1970.
One Hundred Poems from the Chinese, New Directions (New York, NY), 1956.
Thirty Spanish Poems of Love and Exile, City Lights (San Francisco, CA), 1956.
(And author of introduction) *Poems from the Greek Anthology,* University of Michigan Press (Ann Arbor, MI), 1962.
Pierre Reverdy, *Selected Poems,* New Directions (New York, NY), 1969.
Love and the Turning Year: One Hundred More Chinese Poems, New Directions (New York, NY), 1970.
One Hundred More Poems from the Japanese, New Directions (New York, NY), 1976.
(With Chung) *Li Ch'ing Chao: The Complete Poems,* New Directions (New York, NY), 1979.
Women Poets of Japan, New Directions (New York, NY), 1982.
The Noble Traveller: The Life & Selected Writings of Oscar V. de Lubicz Milosz, Lindisfarne Press (West Stockbridge, MA), 1985.
Tu Fu, *Tu Fu, Kenneth Rexroth, Brice Marden,* Blumarts, 1987.
Love Poems from the Japanese, Shambhala (Boston, MA), 1994.

SIDELIGHTS: In a reminiscence written for the *Los Angeles Times Book Review,* Kenneth Rexroth's friend and former student Thomas Sanchez portrayed the author as a "longtime iconoclast, onetime radical, Roman Catholic, Communist fellow traveler, jazz scholar, I.W.W. anarchist, translator, philosopher, playwright, librettist, orientalist, critical essayist, radio personality, newspaper columnist, painter, poet and longtime Buddhist." While Rexroth played all these roles, he is best recognized for his contributions to modern American poetry. The length and breadth of his career resulted in a body of work that not only chronicles his personal search for visionary transcendence but also reflects the artistic, cultural, and political vicissitudes of more than half a century. Commented John Unterecker in a 1967 *New York Times Book Review:* "Reading through all of Kenneth Rexroth's shorter poems is a little like immersing oneself in the literary history of the last forty years; for Rexroth experimented with almost all of the poetic techniques of the time, dealt, at least in passing, with all of its favorite themes."

A prolific painter and poet by age seventeen, Rexroth traveled through a succession of avant-garde and modernist artistic movements, gaining a reputation as a radical by associating with labor groups and anarchist political communities. He experimented amid Chicago's "second renaissance" in the early 1920s, explored modernist techniques derived from the European-born "revolution of the word," played an integral part in the anarchist-pacifist politics and poetic mysticism that pervaded San Francisco's Bay Area in the 1940s, and affiliated himself with the "Beat Generation" in the mid-1950s. Intellectually as well as artistically eclectic, Rexroth scorned institutionalized education and criticism, calling American academics "corn belt Metaphysicals and country gentlemen," as M.L. Rosenthal noted in *The Modern Poets.* After quitting school in his early teens, the poet pursued a curriculum of self-education that included not only literature from diverse cultures and times but encompassed science, philosophy, theology, anthropology, Oriental thought and culture, and half a dozen languages. William R. McKaye of the *Washington Post* emphasized: "In an era in which American colleges crank out graduates who seemingly have never read anything, Rexroth . . . [appeared] well on the way to having read everything. And 'everything' is not just the standard European classics in translation: it is the Latins and Greeks in the original; it is the Japanese and Chinese; it is poetry of all kinds; finally, as a sort of spicy sauce over all, it is such . . . curiosities as the literature of alchemy, the writings of 18th and 19th century Anglican divines and the 'Religio Medici' of Sir Thomas Browne."

James Laughlin, founder of the New Directions Publishing Corporation which published and kept in print most of Rexroth's books, agreed that the poet found his mature style in *The Phoenix and the Tortoise* and *The Signature of All Things.* "When he hit his true vein, a poetry of nature mixed with contemplation and philosophy, it was magnificent," Laughlin claimed in a tribute written for the *Dictionary of Literary Biography Yearbook: 1982.* Published in 1944, *The Phoenix and the Tortoise* was called by Morgan Gibson in his book *Kenneth Rexroth,* "much more coherent in style and theme" than Rexroth's earlier work while focusing less on experimentation and politics. Instead, the book initiated a study of "the 'integral person' who, through love, discovers his responsibility for all in a world of war, cold war, and nuclear terror." The true achievement of *The Phoenix and the Tortoise* and Rexroth's next book, *The Signature of All Things,* was the emergence of "poems that affirm more convincingly than ever the transcendent power of personal love," Gibson stated. "Read *The Signature of All Things,*" Laughlin urged. "It, how shall I put it, pulls everything in human life together. It is all there, all the things we cherish, all our aspirations, and over it all a kind of Buddhist calm." Reviewing *The Signature of All Things* in the *New York Times,* Richard Eberhart outlined both Rexroth's intent and his accomplishment: "Mr. Rexroth's purpose is to make a particular kind of poem which will be classical in its restraint, but without severity; personal, revealing, and confessional, without being sentimental; and it must, according to his bent, eschew symbolism and any kind of ambiguous imagery for a narrative or statement strength based on noun and verb, but not weakened by adjectives."

The form Rexroth adopted in his mature work, which he called "natural numbers," was unrhymed and syllabic rather than metrically regular. Generally varying from seven to nine syllables per line, the structure allowed him to emphasize the "natural cadences of speech," which Gibson pointed out had been important to the poet from the days of his earliest Cubist experiments. Looking back to the 1950s, Karl Malkoff remarked in a 1970 *Southern Review:* "Rexroth . . . never stopped experimenting with rhythms, which not surprisingly are crucial to the success of his poems. Here his work is most vulnerable; here his successes, when they come, are most striking. When . . . Rexroth hit upon the seven syllable line as a temporary resolution, he was accused of writing prose broken up into lines. . . . Actually, on rereading, Rexroth's ear proves reasonably reliable." When he published his first collection of selected work in 1963, the poet entitled it *Natural Numbers: New and Selected Poems,* thus reaffirming the importance of an element critics had dismissed earlier as ineffective or unimportant.

Rexroth's tetralogy of verse plays in "natural numbers," *Beyond the Mountains,* proves not only his devotion to the natural patterns of speech but indicates his knowledge of classical Greek and Oriental literature. Gibson claimed in his study that the author's "poetic, philosophical, and visionary powers [reached] their epitome" in the four dramas "Phaedra," "Iphigenia at Aulis," "Hermaios," and "Berenike." While the characters were based in Greek tragedy, Rexroth's style reflected Japanese *Noh* drama. As Gibson related, an "important quality of *Noh* found in Rexroth's plays is *yugen,* a term derived from Zen Buddhism and defined by Arthur Waley as 'what lies beneath the surface'; the subtle, as opposed to the obvious; the hint, as opposed to the statement." Although several commentators felt *Beyond the Mountains* suffered from obscurity or was more complex than necessary—including R.W. Flint, who wrote in *Poetry* that the "plotting has been just a shade too ambitious for [Rexroth's] poetic gift"—the renowned poet William Carlos Williams applauded both the work's language and its form. "Rexroth is one of the leading craftsmen of the day," proclaimed Williams in the *New York Times.* "There is in him no compromise with the decayed line of past experience. His work is cleanly straightforward. The reek of polluted Shakespeare just isn't in it, or him. I don't know any Greek, but I can imagine that a Greek, if he knew our language as we ought to but don't, would like the athletic freshness of the words."

A common concern for poetry as straightforward, spoken language was only one of the links between Rexroth and the Beat Generation. Quoting Jack Kerouac in *Dictionary of Literary Biography,* Ann Charters and Brown Miller defined the term Beat Generation as "'members of the generation that came of age after World War II who, supposedly as a result of disillusionment stemming from the Cold War, [espoused] mystical detachment and relaxation of social and sexual tension.' Emerging at a time of great postwar change, the Beat Generation was more than a literary movement, but at its heart was its literature." Charters and Miller explained how Rexroth came to be connected with the movement: "By the mid-1950s many of the poets who were to become famous as Beat writers—Lawrence Ferlinghetti, Allen Ginsberg, Jack Kerouac, Michael McClure, Gary Snyder, Philip Whalen—had moved to San Francisco, attracted by the climate of radical poetry and politics, and they were soon part of Rexroth's circle. . . . Considering the diverse aspects of Rexroth's interests in avant-garde art, radical politics, and Eastern philosophy, one can understand why he seemed the perfect mentor for the Beats."

Rexroth occupied a central position in the Bay Area's literary community at the time. Characterized as "anarchopacifist in politics, mystical-personalist in religions, and experimental in esthetic theory and practice" by Gibson, the community revolved around the Pacifica Foundation, with its public arts radio station, and the Poetry Center at San Francisco State College, both of which Rexroth helped establish. As a contributor to *Nation,* the *San Francisco Chronicle,* and the *New York Times,* he also wielded a certain critical power across the country. Rexroth used these forums to champion the younger poets' work in articles like his February, 1957, *Nation* review entitled "San Francisco's Mature Bohemians." Most instrumental in linking Rexroth with the Beats, however, may have been the frequent poetry readings—often to jazz accompaniment—that Rexroth attended or helped organize from 1955 to 1957.

Rexroth considered the readings essential to foment "poetry as voice, not as printing," as he told readers in his *American Poetry in the Twentieth Century.* Supporting the Beats morally with reviews and with his presence at their events, including his series of readings at the Cellar jazz club, Rexroth earned the title "Godfather of the Beats." "Kenneth Rexroth seemed to appear everywhere at their side like the shade of Virgil guiding Dante through the underworld," Alfred Kazin wrote in *Contemporaries.* "Rexroth . . . suddenly became a public figure."

Undoubtedly influencing the Beats more than they influenced him, the poet nonetheless was considered part of the school he instructed by many conservative or academic critics. As such, he often was dismissed or opposed as being part of a nonconformist craze. Some reviewers looked beyond the image, however, to assess the poet's work itself. "Rexroth's *In Defense of the Earth* [1956] showed him the strongest of West Coast anarchist poets because he is a good deal more than a West Coast anarchist poet," emphasized Rosenthal. "He is a man of wide cultivation and, when not too busy shocking the bourgeois reader (who would like nothing better), a genuine poet." Added Gibson: "Rexroth's book of the Beat period, *In Defense of the Earth,*. . . is no period piece. . . . These poems of love and protest, of meditation and remembrance, stand out as some of his most deeply felt poems."

Despite the vehement support Rexroth expressed for the birth of the Beat Generation, he became disillusioned when he saw the movement's more prominent members become "hipsters." Miller and Charters state that the poet "seemed to have become jealous of [the Beats'] success and widespread attention from the national press. He had fought for many years for his own recognition as a Poet," they pointed out, "and as [the Beats'] popularity increased, his growing hostility toward [them] was expressed in a series of articles over the next several years." Nevertheless, Rexroth remained supportive of certain aspects of some Beat writers' works while condemning the movement as a whole. Several critics now note this point, attributing both Rexroth's animosities and his preferences to an individual integrity not influenced by blind allegiance—or enmity—to any literary collective.

Rexroth's position as a central yet independent figure in American literature was further strengthened by a personal account of his youth, entitled *An Autobiographical Novel.* According to Dean Stewart, writing in the *Los Angeles Times Book Review,* the 1966 work "did most to enhance [Rexroth's] image as a living historical personality; his essays in book form and spreading reputation as a keen social critic and insightful philosopher also helped." Yet, while his role as the "outsider's insider" in the literary world became widely acknowledged, serious attention to his own poetry seemed to receive secondary consideration. Commented Stewart: "For a poet who has constantly said he 'only writes prose for money,' Rexroth rivals H.L. Mencken as a terse and cogent critic. But like Mencken, the largely forgotten lexicographer, little-read essayist and much remembered personality, Rexroth may share a similar descending fame from poet to translator to essayist to personality."

Gibson emphasized that in order to appreciate the importance of what Rexroth presents in *An Autobiographical Novel* the reader must understand Rexroth's world view as it evolves through all his works. Integral to the development of the poet's vision were his translation of foreign verse (both contemporary and ancient) and his study of Oriental thought. Rexroth felt an artistic kinship with the Greeks and Romans of classical times and with Japanese and Chinese writers. As Peter Clothier pointed out in a *Los Angeles Times* review of Rexroth's last Japanese translations: "The sharpness of focus and the directly experiential quality of . . . [Oriental] poets are close to Rexroth's own aesthetic. . . . Rexroth has long championed this directness and simplicity of diction in poetry, a clarity of image and emotion clearly compatible with the Japanese aesthetic." Although, as Gibson commented, literary critics have yet to explore the relationships between Rexroth's translations and his own poetry, it has been generally recognized that his later poems are characterized by a serenity and quiet intensity that reflect Oriental art and philosophy.

The Heart's Garden, the Garden's Heart, New Poems, and *The Morning Star*—Rexroth's major poetry collections published after his autobiography—illustrate both his involvement with Oriental culture and his final resolutions of philosophical and technical concerns. Rexroth was, stated Victor Howes in the *Christian Science Monitor,* looking "for a sort of day-to-day mysticism." It was "a poetry of direct statement and simple clear ideas," the critic continued. "A poetry free of superfluous rhetoric. One might call it a poetry of moments." Agreed Richard Eberhart in *Nation,* "Rexroth . . . settled down to the universal validity of stating simple and deep truths in a natural way." "Though he [had] always been a visionary, he spent more than three decades searching for a philosophical rationale for his experience, for history, and for nature. In the 1960s he seems to have abandoned that kind of quest in favor of pure visionary experience," Gibson summarized. "[*The Heart's Garden, the Garden's Heart*], an extended Buddhist-Taoist meditation written in Japan, shows the depths of his resignation and enlightenment."

Written as Rexroth celebrated his sixtieth birthday, *The Heart's Garden, the Garden's Heart* did not "aim at giving answers to final questions that have none," explained Luis Ellicott Yglesias in the *New Boston Review.* "Instead it is a meditation on a handful of central images that have been treasured for centuries because they have the virtue of clarifying experience to the points of making it possible to relinquish life with the facility of a ripe apple dropping from its branch." A critic in *New Leader,* who recognized in Rexroth's earlier works a dialogue between the poet's "conceptualizing mind" and his "experiencing sensibility," felt the two were reconciled in the volume. Out of the fusion "there appears a unique contemplative intensity," the critic stated in *New Leader.* "What has been forged is a supercharged imagism in which every physical object, every scene, every picture the poet creates, is loaded with burdens of meaning that cannot otherwise be expressed." This reconciliation of the immediate and the enduring continued in *New Poems,* which Herbert Leibowitz said were composed "of a flash or revelatory image and silent metamorphoses." Describing what he saw as Rexroth's achievement, Leibowitz continued in the *New York Times Book Review:* "Syntax is cleared of the clutter of subordinate clauses, that contingent grammar of a mind hesitating, debating with itself, raging against death and old age. The dynamics of his poems are marked *piano*—even storms are luminous rather than noisy." The quietness, as well as a vital eroticism, carried over to Rexroth's volume of verse *The Morning Star.* Containing three previously published collections, including the sequence that Rexroth pretended was translated from the Japanese (*The Love Songs of Marichiko*), the book offers a "directness and clarity" not usually associated with Western art, according to David Kirby in the *Times Literary Supplement.* "How different this is from the Rexroth of *The Phoenix and the Tortoise,* who sounds like Lawrence and Pound and Whitman, or the one who wrote [*Thou Shalt Not Kill*] in *In Defense of the Earth.* . . . Now he appears to belong, or to want to belong, at least as much as a publishing writer can, to the Buddhist bodhisattvas [or other Eastern religions]."

Kenneth Rexroth and James Laughlin: Selected Letters offers letters exchanged between 1937 and 1982 between Rexroth and James Laughlin, the founder of the New Directions publishing house. The letters reveal the friendship between the men as well as their ongoing professional relationship; Laughlin published most of Rexroth's important poetry collections, while Rexroth in turn led a number of influential writers to Laughlin and New Directions. "Rexroth is often preoccupied with his own financial need in his letters to Laughlin. Most often his tone is accusatory," noted John Tritica in *Western American Literature.* Indeed, Rexroth often castigated Laughlin for not supporting him sufficiently or for not publishing authors that he thought deserved to be published. "More than anything, the letters testify to the forbearance and patience of James Laughlin as a friend," remarked Gerald Nicosia in the *Los Angeles Times Book Review.*

"Revolutionary and conservative, worldly and spiritual, Asian and western ideas from traditions that may seem irreconcilable were uniquely harmonized in Rexroth's world view as expressed [throughout] his philosophical poetry and essays," Gibson wrote in his study *Kenneth Rexroth.* Concluded Douglas Dunn in *Listener:* "Insufficient credit has been granted to Rexroth's identity as an old-fashioned, honest-to-God man of letters of downright independence of mind. . . . His temper [was] too independent, too scholarly, for cut-and-dried allegiances. He [turned] his back on Eliot and Pound. He [had] the irritating habit—for the mediocre, that is, the literary side-takers—of liking some but not all of certain poets or movements. Like all good examples in modern poetry, he has been seen as a figure instead of as a creator; as a representative rather than as a participant. That he is all four of these persons at once comes as a sweet discovery from a reading of his work instead of from side-glances at other people's estimates of his reputation."

BIOGRAPHICAL AND CRITICAL SOURCES:

BOOKS

Concise Dictionary of American Literary Biography: The New Consciousness, 1941-1968, Thomson Gale (Detroit, MI), 1987.

Contemporary Literary Criticism, Thomson Gale (Detroit, MI), Volume 1, 1973; Volume 2, 1974; Volume 6, 1976; Volume 11, 1976; Volume 22, 1982; Volume 49, 1988.

Dictionary of Literary Biography, Thomson Gale (Detroit, MI), Volume 16: *The Beats: Literary Bohemians in Postwar America,* 1983, Volume 48: *American Poets, 1880-1945, Second Series,* 1986, Volume 165: *American Poets since World War II: Fourth Series,* 1996, Volume 212: *Twentieth-Century American Western Writers, Second Series,* 1999.

Dictionary of Literary Biography Yearbook: 1982, Thomson Gale (Detroit, MI), 1983.

Gardner, Geoffrey, editor, *For Rexroth,* Ark (New York, NY), 1980.

Gibson, Morgan, *Kenneth Rexroth,* Twayne (Boston, MA), 1972.

Gibson, Morgan, *Revolutionary Rexroth: Poet of East-West Wisdom,* Archon (Hamden, CT), 1986.

Gutierrez, Donald, *The Holiness of the Real: The Short Verse of Kenneth Rexroth,* Fairleigh Dickinson University Press (Madison, NJ), 1996.

Hamalian, Linda, *A Life of Kenneth Rexroth,* Norton (New York, NY), 1991.

Kazin, Alfred, *Contemporaries,* Little, Brown (Boston, MA), 1962.

Kerouac, Jack, *The Dharma Bums,* Signet Books (New York, NY), 1958.

Knabb, Ken, *The Relevance of Rexroth,* Bureau of Public Secrets (Berkeley, CA), 1990.

Lipton, Lawrence, *The Holy Barbarians,* Messner (New York, NY), 1959.

Meltzer, David, editor, *The San Francisco Poets,* Ballantine (New York, NY), 1971.

Parkinson, Thomas, *A Casebook on the Beat,* Crowell (New York, NY), 1961.

Rosenthal, M. L., *The Modern Poets: A Critical Introduction,* Oxford University Press (New York, NY), 1960.

PERIODICALS

America, August 4, 1973, December 20, 1975.

American Association of Political and Social Science Annals, September, 1975.

American Literature, March, 1972.

American Poetry Review, November, 1978.

Antioch Review, number 3, 1971.

Best Sellers, August 1, 1971; February, 1980.

Bloomsbury Review, June, 1991, p. 7.

Booklist, March 1, 1949; April 1, 1969; November 1, 1973; February 1, 1975; February 15, 1975; October 15, 1976; July 1, 1978; October 1, 1979.

Book Review, March, 1971.

Books, December 22, 1940.

Book Week, December 24, 1944.

Choice, November, 1969; October, 1971; October, 1972; January, 1974; April, 1974; March, 1975; June, 1975; May, 1977; March, 1978; July-August, 1978.

Christian Century, September 4, 1940; July 1, 1970; May 19, 1971.

Christian Science Monitor, August 31, 1940; July 11, 1967; January 9, 1969; September 14, 1970; February 6, 1980.

Commentary, December, 1957.

Commonweal, December 6, 1974.
Comparative Literature, Volume 10, 1958.
Contemporary Literature, summer, 1969.
Harper's, August, 1967.
Hudson Review, spring, 1960; summer, 1967; summer, 1968; autumn, 1968; summer, 1971; autumn, 1974.
Journal of Asian Studies, November, 1973; May, 1978.
Kirkus Reviews, February 1, 1949; April 1, 1970; May 15, 1971; November 1, 1972; February 1, 1973; September 1, 1974; November 1, 1974; November 1, 1979.
Kyoto Review, Volume 15, fall, 1982.
Library Journal, June 15, 1949; July, 1970; August, 1971; July, 1972; September 15, 1972; December 15, 1972; October 15, 1974; January 15, 1975; September 1, 1976; September 15, 1977; October 15, 1979; November 15, 1979; May 15, 1987; May 1, 1991.
Library Review, autumn, 1977.
Life, September 9, 1957.
Listener, June 16, 1977.
London Magazine, April/May, 1974.
Los Angeles Free Press, January 10, 1969.
Los Angeles Times, October 3, 1978; February 5, 1980.
Los Angeles Times Book Review, August 3, 1980; June 20, 1982; May 5, 1991, p. 1; June 26, 1994, p. 8.
Minnesota Review, spring, 1962; fall, 1962.
Nation, February 12, 1949; June 10, 1950; September 28, 1957; June 6, 1966; March 18, 1968; April 22, 1968; March 24, 1969; December 31, 1973.
National Observer, December 9, 1968.
New Boston Review, Volume 3, number 3, December, 1977.
New Leader, April 24, 1967; February 17, 1969; October 27, 1969; September 21, 1970.
New Republic, August 12, 1940; August 8, 1949; February 9, 1953; February 18, 1957; September 16, 1957.
New Statesman, January 2, 1976.
New Yorker, December 30, 1944; March 26, 1949; May 20, 1950; February 4, 1956; May 3, 1958; August 10, 1987, p. 80.
New York Herald Tribune, May 7, 1950; February 1, 1953.
New York Herald Tribune [Weekly] Book Review, June 12, 1949; October 2, 1949; May 7, 1950; February 19, 1956.
New York Times, December 19, 1948; August 6, 1950, January 28, 1951; February 15, 1953; January 1, 1956; November 22, 1964; July 23, 1967; August 17, 1968; July 10, 1970.
New York Times Book Review, July 23, 1967; November 16, 1969; February 15, 1970; October 4, 1970; March 23, 1975; November 23, 1980.
Ohio Review, winter, 1976.
Parnassus, spring, 1981.
Poetry, November, 1940; June, 1950; May, 1956; June, 1957; July, 1963; December, 1967; April, 1969.
Prairie Schooner, winter, 1971-72.
Progressive, June, 1975.
Psychology Today, July, 1975.
Publishers Weekly, September 1, 1969; April 13, 1970; September 28, 1970; January 1, 1973; October 8, 1979; April 3, 1987; February 1, 1991.
Quarterly Review of Literature, Volume 9, number 2, 1957.
Reporter, April 3, 1958; March 3, 1960; May 19, 1966.
Rolling Stone, February 4, 1993.
sagetrieb, Volume 2, number 3, winter, 1983.
San Francisco Chronicle, May 29, 1949; March 12, 1950; January 29, 1956; February 10, 1957.
Saturday Review, June 16, 1956; November 9, 1957; February 12, 1966; March 15, 1969.
Saturday Review of Literature, June 4, 1949; September 17, 1949; May 20, 1950.
Southern Review, spring, 1970.
Spectator, March 13, 1959.
Sydney Southerly (Sydney, Australia), Volume 28, 1968.
Time, December 2, 1957; February 25, 1966.
Times Literary Supplement, April 30, 1971; June 16, 1972; March 25, 1977; May 30, 1980.
U.S. Quarterly Booklist, June, 1950.
Virginia Quarterly Review, summer, 1973; spring, 1975.
Voice Literary Supplement, December, 1984.
Washington Post, August 29, 1968; February 1, 1971.
Washington Post Book World, January 6, 1974; June 29, 1975; March 12, 1978; April 14, 1991, p. 4.
Weekly Book Review, January 14, 1945.
Western American Literature, summer, 1992, p. 121; fall, 1992, p. 280.
World Literature Today, winter, 1978; spring, 1978; autumn, 1978; winter, 1981.

* * *

RICE, Anne 1941-
(Anne Rampling, A.N. Roquelaure)

PERSONAL: Born Howard Allen O'Brien, October 4, 1941, in New Orleans, LA; name changed, c. 1947; daughter of Howard (a postal worker, novelist, and sculptor) and Katherine (Allen) O'Brien; married Stan Rice (a poet and painter), October 14, 1961 (died, December, 2002); children: Michele (deceased), Christopher. *Education:* Attended Texas Woman's University, 1959-60; San Francisco State College (now University), B.A., 1964, M.A., 1971; graduate study at

University of California at Berkeley, 1969-70. *Hobbies and other interests:* Traveling, ancient Greek history, archaeology, social history since the beginning of recorded time, old movies on television, attending boxing matches.

ADDRESSES: Agent—Jacklyn Nesbit Associates, 598 Madison Ave., New York, NY 10022.

CAREER: Writer. worked variously as a waitress, cook, theater usherette, and insurance claims examiner. Appeared on television series *Ellen,* 1996.

MEMBER: Authors Guild, Authors League of America.

AWARDS, HONORS: Joseph Henry Jackson Award honorable mention, 1970.

WRITINGS:

NOVELS

The Feast of All Saints, Simon & Schuster (New York, NY), 1980.
Cry to Heaven, Knopf (New York, NY), 1982.
The Mummy: or, Ramses the Damned, Ballantine (New York, NY), 1989.
Servant of the Bones, Knopf (New York, NY), 1996.
Violin, Knopf (New York, NY), 1997.
Christ the Lord: Out of Egypt, Knopf (New York, NY), 2005.

"VAMPIRE CHRONICLES" SERIES

Interview with the Vampire (also see below), Knopf (New York, NY), 1976.
The Vampire Lestat (also see below), Ballantine (New York, NY), 1985.
The Queen of the Damned (also see below), Knopf (New York, NY), 1988.
Vampire Chronicles (contains *Interview with the Vampire, The Vampire Lestat,* and *The Queen of the Damned*), Ballantine (New York, NY), 1989.
The Tale of the Body Thief, Knopf (New York, NY), 1992.
Memnoch the Devil, Knopf (New York, NY), 1995.
The Vampire Armand, Knopf (New York, NY), 1998.
Pandora: New Tales of the Vampires, Random House (New York, NY), 1998.
Vittorio the Vampire, Knopf (New York, NY), 1999.
Merrick, Knopf (New York, NY), 2000.
Blood and Gold, Knopf (New York, NY), 2001.
Blackwood Farm, Knopf (New York, NY), 2002.
Blood Canticle, Knopf (New York, NY), 2003.

"WITCHING HOUR" TRILOGY

The Witching Hour, Knopf (New York, NY), 1990.
Lasher, Knopf (New York, NY), 1993.
Taltos, Knopf (New York, NY), 1994.

EROTIC NOVELS; UNDER PSEUDONYM A.N. ROQUELAURE

The Claiming of Sleeping Beauty, Dutton (New York, NY), 1983.
Beauty's Punishment, Dutton (New York, NY), 1984.
Beauty's Release: The Continued Erotic Adventures of Sleeping Beauty, Dutton (New York, NY), 1985.
The Sleeping Beauty Novels (contains *The Claiming of Sleeping Beauty, Beauty's Punishment,* and *Beauty's Release: The Continued Erotic Adventures of Sleeping Beauty*), New American Library (New York, NY), 1991.

NOVELS; UNDER PSEUDONYM ANNE RAMPLING

Exit to Eden, Arbor House (New York, NY), 1985.
Belinda, Arbor House (New York, NY), 1986.

OTHER

Interview with the Vampire (screenplay; adapted from the novel of the same title), Geffen Pictures, 1994.
(Author of introduction) Alice Borchardt, *Devoted,* Dutton (New York, NY), 1995.
(Author of foreword) Franz Kafka, *The Metamorphosis, In the Penal Colony, and Other Stories,* Schocken (New York, NY), 1995.
(Author of introduction) Kelly Klein, *Underworld,* Knopf (New York, NY), 1995.
(Author of introduction) Alice Borchardt, *Beguiled,* Dutton (New York, NY), 1997.
The Anne Rice Reader, edited by Katherine Ramsland, Ballantine (New York, NY), 1997.

ADAPTATIONS: Exit to Eden was adapted for film by Deborah Amelon and Bob Brunner, directed by Garry Marshall, starring Dana Delaney and Dan Ackroyd,

1994; and *Queen of the Damned* was adapted for film by Scott Abbott and Michael Petroni, directed by Michael Rymer, starring Stuart Townsend, 2001. *The Vampire Lestat* was adapted as a graphic novel by Faye Perozich, Ballantine, 1991; and *The Tale of the Body Thief* was adapted as a graphic novel. *Feast of All Saints* was adapted as a television miniseries, Showtime/ABC, 2001. Elton John and Bernie Taupin adapted Rice's "Vampire Chronicles" novels as the stage musical *The Vampire Lestat,* to be produced on Broadway, 2005. Rice's novels have been adapted as audiobooks.

SIDELIGHTS: Considered one of the leading practitioners of Gothic writing in the twentieth century, popular novelist Anne Rice has built her career, according to *New York Times Book Review* critic Daniel Mendelsohn, by sticking to "the Big Themes: good versus evil, mortality and immortality." Indeed, these themes have provided Rice with such prolific material that, as Bob Summer observed in *Publishers Weekly,* "She needs two pseudonyms—Anne Rampling and A.N. Roquelaure—to distinguish the disparate voices in her books, [which have] won both critical acclaim and a readership of cult proportions." Under her own name, Rice crafts novels about the bizarre and the supernatural; under the Rampling pseudonym, she writes contemporary and mainstream fiction; and under the Roquelaure *nom de plume* she spins sadomasochistic fantasies. Rice has pointed out that each name represents a part of her divided self. As she told *New York Times* interviewer Stewart Kellerman, she is "a divided person with different voices, like an actor playing different roles." Discussing this subject with Sarah Booth Conroy in a *Washington Post* interview, Rice said, "I think sometimes that if I had had perhaps a few more genes, or whatever, I would have been truly mad, a multiple personality whose selves didn't recognize each other."

Rice has characterized her early childhood as happy but unconventional. However, at the age of fourteen Rice lost her mother to alcoholism, and soon afterwards the family relocated to Texas. She married her high school sweetheart, poet Stan Rice, at age twenty; "I fell completely in love with Stan, and I'm still completely in love with him," declared Rice in a *New York Times* interview; tragically, after over four decades of marriage, Rice died of cancer in 2002. A year after they were married the Rices moved from Texas to San Francisco, where Rice gave birth to daughter Michele. It was there that she had a prophetic dream: "I dreamed my daughter, Michele, was dying—that there was something wrong with her blood," she recalled in her *People* interview. Several months later, Michele was diagnosed with a rare form of leukemia and died shortly before her sixth birthday. "Two years later, her image was reincarnated as the child vampire Claudia in [*Interview with the Vampire*], Anne's first published work," wrote Gerri Hirshey in *Rolling Stone. Interview with the Vampire* "was written out of grief, the author says, in five weeks of 'white-hot, access-the-subconscious' sessions between 10:00 p.m. and dawn," added Hirshey.

As its title indicates, *Interview with the Vampire* recounts the events of one evening in which Louis, the vampire of the title, tells a young reporter his life story. The novel, which Rice actually began in the late 1960s as a short story, developed into something much larger. "I got to the point where the vampire began describing his brother's death, and the whole thing just exploded! Suddenly, in the guise of Louis, a fantasy figure, I was able to touch the reality that was mine," explained Rice in a *Publishers Weekly* interview. "Through Louis' eyes, everything became accessible."

It is Rice's unusual and sympathetic treatment of vampires, according to critics, that gives her "Vampire Chronicles" their particular appeal. "Rice brings a fresh and powerful imagination to the staples of vampire lore; she makes well-worn coffins and crucifixes tell new tales that compose a chillingly original myth," observed Nina Auerbach in *New York Times Book Review.* "Because Rice identifies with the vampire instead of the victim (reversing the usual focus), the horror for the reader springs from the realization of the monster within the self," wrote Ferraro. "Moreover, Rice's vampires are loquacious philosophers who spend much of eternity debating the nature of good and evil. Trapped in immortality, they suffer human regret. They are lonely, prisoners of circumstance, compulsive sinners, full of self-loathing and doubt." All that separates the vampires from humans and makes them outsiders is their hunt for human blood and their indestructible bodies. With flawless, alabaster skin, colorful glinting eyes, and hair that shimmers and seems to take on a life of its own, they were described by H.J. Kirchhoff in a Toronto *Globe and Mail* review as "romantic figures, super-humanly strong and fast, brilliant and subtle of thought and flamboyant of manner."

The status of vampire as outsider, Mendelsohn argued, allows Rice to explore deep human themes like the meaning of suffering and death from the unique viewpoint of "alien characters in . . . exotic milieus" who nevertheless exhibit an "underlying troubled humanity." *Interview with the Vampire,* wrote Mendelsohn, is a success precisely because its main character is aesthetically refined and sensitive, "a nice Byronic departure from your garden-variety Nosferatu with his unkempt nails and bad table manners."

Walter Kendrick praised the scope of *Interview with the Vampire* in *Voice Literary Supplement,* writing that "it would have been a notable tour de force even if its characters had been human." Kendrick also suggested, however, that "Rice's most effective accomplishment . . . was to link up sex and fear again." Several critics made much the same point. Conroy maintained that "not since Mary Shelley's *Frankenstein* and Louisa May Alcott's penny dreadful novelettes has a woman written so strongly about death and sex." Similarly, in a *New York Times Book Review* article, Leo Braudy observed that "Rice exploits all the sexual elements in [vampire myths] with a firm self-consciousness of their meaning." The sensuous description of Louis's first kill is an example: "I knelt beside the bent, struggling man and, clamping both my hands on his shoulders, I went into his neck. My teeth had only just begun to change, and I had to tear his flesh, not puncture it; but once the wound was made, the blood flowed . . . . The sucking mesmerized me, the warm struggling of the man was soothing to the tension of my hands; and there came the beating of the drum again, which was the drumbeat of his heart."

Rice frankly acknowledges her novel's erotic content. "No matter what I write," she told *Lambda Book Report* writer Melinda L. Shelton, "my characters always turn out to be bisexual. It just happens, and I'm very happy with it—I think it's what I see as an ideal." Noting that *The Tale of the Body,* which centers on a homoerotic relationship between Lestat and David Talbot, topped bestseller lists for weeks, Rice observed, "when you talk about desire, and you talk about liberation, you're basically talking about universal things."

Despite the critical and popular success of *Interview with the Vampire,* Rice did not immediately produce a sequel, instead turning her attention to writing mainstream fiction and erotica. When *The Vampire Lestat* appeared nearly ten years later, both fans and critics welcomed Rice's return to her vampire characters. In this second novel of the "Vampire Chronicles," Lestat, creator of Louis in *Interview with the Vampire,* awakens from a sleep of many years to find himself in the 1980s. A rock band practicing in a house nearby rouses him, and a few days later, he is dressed in leather and roaring around on a big black Harley Davidson motorcycle.

The Vampire Lestat is structured as an autobiography written as part of the marketing campaign to launch Lestat's new rock and roll career. It takes the reader through "a history of vampirism, from its beginnings in ancient Egypt, through its manifestations in Roman Gaul, Renaissance Italy, pre-Revolutionary Paris and *belle epoque* New Orleans, and a further discussion of the philosophical, ethical and theological implications of vampirism," wrote Kirchhoff, adding that "Rice is a beautiful writer. Her prose glitters and every character in Lestat's dark odyssey is unique." Although *New York Times* contributor Michiko Kakutani maintained that Rice recounts her history "in lugubrious, cliche-ridden sentences that repeat every idea and sentiment a couple or more times," Auerbach found *The Vampire Lestat* to be "ornate and pungently witty," and deemed that "in the classic tradition of Gothic fiction, it teases and tantalizes us into accepting its kaleidoscopic world. Even when they annoy us or tell us more than we want to know, its undead characters are utterly alive."

The Queen of the Damned, which also contains background details about vampire history and lore, drew more muted critical response. Kendrick found the novel "verbose, sluggish, and boring," and written as if "Rice didn't believe her fantasies anymore." However, Kakutani appreciated its "well-developed sense of fun," and Laurence Coven, in a *Los Angeles Times Book Review* article, deemed the book "an exhilarating blend of philosophic questing and pure, wondrous adventure."

The Tale of the Body Thief continues the "Vampire Chronicles," and find Lestat so weary of his immortality that he attempts suicide. He fails, but is soon approached by a mortal who offers to exchange bodies for a few days. Eager for even a taste of mortality, Lestat agrees, only to have his partner in this transaction vanish with his immortal body. Sarah Smith, in *Washington Post Book World,* lauded the book's "whiplash speed," "page-turner plot," "beautifully realized atmosphere," and "real storytelling intelligence." The passages in which Lestat, confined to the night for two centuries, once again experiences daylight are "Rice at her best, looking through the outsider's eyes with all the outsider's alienated power," Smith added. Writing in *Chicago Tribune,* Dan Greenberg termed Rice's description of the body exchange "brilliant," and went on to say that "Lestat's reactions to pulling on a mortal body like a suit of ill-fitting clothes and suddenly having to re-learn vulgar, unvampirelike bodily functions—urinating, eating, defecating, making love—are downright dazzling."

In 1995's *Memnoch the Devil* Lestat, accustomed to being the hunter, finds he is now the prey, his pursuer none other than Satan, who tries to enlist Lestat to become his assistant. Lestat refuses, but accepts the Devil's offer for a tour of heaven, hell, and purgatory. After seeing all this, his guide tells him that he will have another chance to accept the job offer. "With the stage thus set, the book transmogrifies into a modern *Paradise Lost,* The Universe according to Rice," explained Kevin Allman in a review of *Memnoch the Devil* for *Washington Post Book World.* "Many, many pages . . . are devoted to her personal cosmology and angelology," Allman added, "to her versions of creation, evolution and the Crucifixion. It's a tour that's interesting at times and poky at others."

Several reviewers complained that *Memnoch the Devil* contains too much talk, and that Rice perhaps took on more than she could handle with this novel. A *Publishers Weekly* reviewer found that Rice's attempts to answer meaning-of-life questions overshadows her narrative, and felt that "God and the Devil . . . too often end up sounding like arguing philosophy majors." For Michael McLeod in *Chicago Tribune, Memnoch the Devil* proves a disappointing conclusion to the "Vampire Chronicles." He noted that while the book deals with the mysteries of life, death, and eternity more "dramatically and directly" than any other installment in Rice's series, "the proportions of the author's writing are so epic that her dark hero gets lost among them." "If Rice really is retiring her flagship vampire," McLeod added, "it's puzzling she made him play out his last scene as Satan's sidekick." Allman concluded with a more positive assessment of *Memnoch the Devil,* stating that "Rice has penned an ambitious close to this long-running series, as well as a classy exit for a classic horror character."

The Vampire Armand, the sixth installment in her "Vampire Chronicles," returns to a character first introduced in *Interview with the Vampire.* Armand, a boy in sixteenth-century Italy, is kidnapped and sold as a slave, ending up in the Venetian palace of Marius, a vampire who teaches the boy history and art. Once Marius makes Armand into a vampire, the pair concentrate on hunting down "evil" people, which draws the anger of a Satanic vampire cult intent on making Armand its own. Though some reviewers suggested that *The Vampire Armand* is less powerful than the earlier books in the series, others welcomed the novel warmly. Michael Porter, in *New York Times Book Review,* found it an "absorbing account of another all-too-human ghoul" who is struggling to be a Christian, while a contributor to *Publishers Weekly* praised the novel's "exquisite details of erotic romps and political intrigues" as well as its "lavishly poetic" treatment of Armand's religious crisis.

The "Vampire Chronicles" continue with *Merrick,* a biracial female vampire who has voodoo powers. The action moves from New Orleans to the Central American rainforest, and Rice reunites readers with Lestat and several other characters from past novels. More so than other novels in the series, *Merrick* features strong female characters. "As time passes, I am writing more and more with women characters," Rice noted to Julia Kamysz Lane in *Book.* "It's becoming easier to write about my femininity. But anytime I write a book with a strong woman protagonist, I run a risk because people simply treat women protagonists differently than men. They tend to insult and trivialize female characters in fiction . . . . If *Interview with the Vampire* had been about a male and a female, and Louis had really been a woman, people would have dismissed it out of hand as a cheap romance."

Merrick drew a mixed response from critics. Janet Maslin in *New York Times Book Review* suggested that Rice's powers "have served her mightily, so mightily that the stories now grow weary," but acknowledged that carelessly written passages or recycled plot elements would not bother Rice's legion of fans at all. *Library Journal* reviewer Ann Kim commented that *Merrick* "lacks the resonance and vivid passion of [Rice's] earlier writings," and *Booklist* reviewer Ray Olson expressed a similar opinion. A contributor to *Publishers Weekly,* however, found that Rice's "imaginative talents for atmosphere and suspense" enhance the novel with "riveting" detail.

Although the "Vampire Chronicles" earned increasingly lackluster reviews from critics, the series retained its fan following, and Rice continued to produce further installments. In *Blood and Gold* she profiles Marius, the creature who gave Lestat immortality and also loved the vampire Pandora, herself the subject of another installment in the series. Called "intriguing yet rushed" by a *Publishers Weekly* contributor, *Blood and Gold* follows Marius from his birth in imperial Rome and his transformation into a vampire at the hands of Druids. Readers follow Marius through the millennium, as he acts as the protector of Those Who Must Be Kept. *Blood Canticle* once again finds Lestat center stage, as narrator of his reaction to meeting the devil and his search for redemption. In *Publishers Weekly* a reviewer noted that in *Blood Canticle,* "Writing as if her blood-inked quill were afire, Rice seems truly possessed by her Brat Prince of darkness as she races through the story," and added that *Blood Canticle* might well serve as a closing novel of the series.

The erotic overtones featured in the "Vampire Chronicles" are given full range in books Rice has published under the pseudonym A.N. Roquelaure. *The*

Claiming of Sleeping Beauty, Beauty's Punishment, and *Beauty's Release: The Continued Erotic Adventures of Sleeping Beauty* are loosely based on the story of Sleeping Beauty and are described as sadomasochistic pornography by some critics. "A.N. Roquelaure is an S&M pornographer with a shocking penchant for leather collars . . . . and other kinky bijoux," stated Hirshey. Conroy asserted, however, that "despite the content, all is presented with something of the breathless, innocent, gingham-ruffled voice of fairy tales." Rice addresses the critical assessment of these works as pornographic in a *People* interview: "I wrote about the fantasy that interested me personally and that I couldn't find in bookstores. I wanted to create a Disneyland of S&M. Most porno is written by hacks. I meant it to be erotic and nothing else—to turn people on. Sex is good. Nothing about sex is evil or to be ashamed of." Moreover, in a *Lear's* interview, Rice maintained, "They're of high quality . . . . and I'm very proud that I wrote them."

Writing under the pseudonym Anne Rampling, Rice has written two conventional novels, *Exit to Eden* and *Belinda,* which combine erotica and romance. Carolyn See contended in *Los Angeles Times* that "Rampling attempts a fascinating middle ground" between the "straight erotica" of Roquelaure, and the "semi-serious literature" of Rice. *Exit to Eden* tells the story of Lisa Kelly, a gorgeous young woman in skimpy lace and high leather boots who exudes sexuality. Raised by an Irish-Catholic family that abhors the idea of sex, Kelly discovers at an early age that she is obsessed by sadomasochism. This obsession, combined with her executive skills, leads her to an island on the Caribbean where she opens the Club—a resort "which is something between a luxury hotel and an S-M brothel," said See. The second half of the novel relates Kelly's exit with friend Elliott from a lifestyle they once perceived as Edenic. They settle in New Orleans and start dating, proving that "one man and one woman can make a happy life together and be transformed by love, the most seductive fantasy of all," wrote See, adding that Rice "makes a lovely case here. Let's take what we've learned of sex and bring it back into the real world, she suggests. It's time, isn't it?"

Belinda is divided into three parts, the first describing the life of Jeremy Walker, a famous author and illustrator of children's books, who lives alone in an old house. Not only is he desperately lonely, but he is also cut off from his sexuality until Belinda comes along. She is a fifteen-year-old runaway who smokes, drinks, and is willing to partake in every erotic fantasy Jeremy concocts. Although Belinda urges him not to search for clues to her past, he does, so she runs away. The second part of the novel describes Belinda's childhood and her relationship with her mother. The final part of the book follows Jeremy's search for Belinda and includes several happy endings—"True love triumphs," claimed See in her *Los Angeles Times* review of *Belinda.* "Sex is as nice as champagne and friendship, Rampling earnestly instructs us. Value it! Don't be puritanical morons *all* your life."

Rice uses her large antebellum mansion in New Orleans as the setting for her "Witching Hour" trilogy opener, *The Witching Hour.* The mansion in the novel belongs to the Mayfair family and its generations of witches. Rowan, the thirteenth witch, has extrasensory powers and must defend herself from Lasher, the personification of evil. Leading Ferraro through a tour of her home, Rice described the scenes that took place in each of the rooms: "'There's the fireplace where Rowan and Lasher sat on Christmas morning,' she says matter-of-factly, a smile tugging at her lips . . . . Up a flight of stairs, to Rice's office, where she ignores the messy desk and points dramatically to an ornate bed—'where Deirdre died,' she says, of another of the book's characters."

"What is unnerving about all this is not that Rice switches back and forth between her fictional and factual worlds, but that they seem to coexist, with equal intensity. It is as if she has somehow brought about the haunting of her own house," wrote Ferraro. Patrick McGrath, indicated in *New York Times Book Review* that "despite its tireless narrative energy, despite its relentless inventiveness, the book is bloated, grown to elephantine proportions because more is included than is needed." But Susan Isaacs, in a *Washington Post Book World* review, opined that "Rice offers more than just a story; she creates myth. In *The Witching Hour,* she presents a rich, complicated universe that operates by both natural and supernatural law, and she does so with . . . consummate skill."

The "Witching Hour" trilogy also includes the novels *Lasher* and *Taltos;* Rice would later meld the series with her popular "Vampire Chronicles" in the novels *Merrick, Blackwood Farm* and *Blood Canticle.* In *Lasher* the title character, whose presence in spirit was key to *The Witching Hour,* assumes human form as the son of Rowan Mayfair and seeks a woman with whom he can reproduce. *Taltos* centers on a kindly immortal giant named Ashlar who becomes involved with the Mayfair clan.

Numerous reviewers of both books viewed that the large cast of characters and baroque plotlines are weaknesses, and found the series as a whole to be less compelling than the "Vampire Chronicles." "You might . . . need a scorecard to keep all the Mayfair witches separate," wrote Dick Adler in his Chicago *Tribune Books* review of *Lasher.* While Paul West, critiquing *Lasher* for *New York Times Book Review,* wrote that Rice narrates her story "in plodding prose, but she does tell it as if it interested her," Elizabeth Hand in *Washington Post Book World* found much to praise in Rice's "Witching Hour" series. With *Lasher,* Hand explained, Rice "concocts a heady and potent salmagundi of contemporary witchcraft, Caribbean voodoo, aristocratic decadence and good old-fashioned Celtic paganism, and makes what should be an unpalatable mess as wickedly irresistible as a Halloween stash of Baby Ruths." Even though its characters are supernatural, *Lasher* is actually "an old-fashioned family saga," Hand added. "Rice's Mayfairs are as gorgeous and doomed and steeped in the South as Scarlett O'Hara."

During the early 1980s Rice published two historical novels that Conroy considered "of great depth, research and enchantment." In *The Feast of All Saints* she writes about free people of color, those mulattoes who numbered about 18,000 and lived in nineteenth-century Louisiana. The novel centers around the Ferronaire family, focusing on golden-colored Marcel and his sister Marie, who could pass for white. Living in the midst of the antebellum South, they are never really a part of it, and the novel examines this discrimination and the choices each character must make because of it. Penelope Mesic, in a *Chicago Tribune Book World* review, considered *The Feast of All Saints* "an honest book, a gifted book, the substantial execution of a known design," and *Los Angeles Times Book Review* contributor Valerie Miner suggested that "this new book is rare, combining a 'real story,' a profound theme and exquisite literary grace."

Cry to Heaven, another historical novel, enters the world of the Italian castrati, famous male sopranos who were castrated as boys so their voices would remain high. Tonio Treschi, the hero, is a Venetian heir whose brother has him abducted, castrated, and exiled from his home. The rest of the novel relates the pursuit of the goals that obsess him—to become one of the best singers in Europe, and to take his revenge on his brother. Alice Hoffman described *Cry to Heaven* in *New York Times Book Review* as "bold and erotic, laced with luxury, sexual tension, [and] music," and added that "here passion is all, desires are overwhelming, gender is blurred." Hoffman concluded that *Cry to Heaven* "is a novel dazzling in its darkness, and there are times when Rice seems like nothing less than a magician: It is a pure and uncanny talent that can give a voice to monsters and angels both."

Rice returned to historical fiction with *Servant of the Bones,* which Mendelsohn dubbed a "supernatural melodrama," and *Violin,* a gothic romance involving a Stradivarius violin. As in *Memnoch the Devil,* Rice packs much information and philosophizing into *Servant of the Bones.* The book centers on the dark angel Azriel, whose history stretches back to ancient Babylon and later brings him into contact with two powerful teachers during the Middle Ages. After sleeping for six centuries, Azriel awakens in the late twentieth century to become embroiled in a plot to stop billionaire Gregory Bilkin from destroying the Third World with a powerful virus. Mendelsohn, admitting that the novel attempts to say interesting things about complex themes, complained that "Rice's reach has seriously exceeded her grasp." The critic argued that, in contrast to her approach in earlier books, Rice presents metaphysical conflicts too literally here; the reviewer missed the richness of atmosphere and detail, the "writing" that he believed made her earlier books so notable. Though similar criticism greeted *Violin,* which *New York Times Book Review* contributor Bill Hayes found "tedious," Rice's popularity remained as high as ever—especially when she turned her attention once again to the subject of vampires.

Christ the Lord: Out of Egypt is a historical novel that is religious in nature. Similar in a sense to *Memnoch the Devil, Christ the Lord* is based on biblical events. The latter, however, is much less apocryphal (or fantastical) and tells of the seven-year-old Jesus, his daily life, and his struggle to come to terms with his strange abilities in the face of his ignorance as to who he truly is. The plot, then, revolves around Jesus' eventual discovery of his divine origins. The story takes place roughly 2,000 years ago and reviewers praised Rice's historical accuracy. According to various critics, her portrayal of daily life in first-century Judaea is detailed and well researched. Reviewers also spoke highly of Rice's handling of the story of Jesus' childhood. The novel is "both a work of devotion and a work of fiction," commented Lev Grossman in *Time.* Grossman also stated that Rice's "intensely literal, historical, reverent treatment" is "written in simple, sedate language." Indeed, critics seemed to agree that the book's minimalist language is integral to its success. A *Publisher's Weekly* contributor noted the "the riches of the sparse prose Rice adopts," and *Library Journal* critic Tamara Butler concluded that "Rice's superb storytelling skills enable her to succeed where many other writers have failed."

Rice's "Vampire Chronicles" series created a legion of devoted fans who snapped up each new book and thronged The Anne Rice Collection, the author's New

Orleans retail shop that sold everything from clothing and fragrances to dolls based on her fictional characters. Citing her admiration for another bestselling author, Charles Dickens, Rice explained to Lane: "I've discovered that, over time, it is not an insult to be called a popular writer. It's a wonderful compliment, really. If people only read my books for entertainment, if they only read them to take their minds off their troubles, that's fine." While Rice's popularity has showed no sign of waning, following the death of her husband in 2002 the author announced that she was done with vampires. As she explained in *Book,* even before her husband passed away "I had made the decision that I wanted to move away from the witches and vampires altogether. I wanted to write something completely different. I no longer really wanted to write about people who were damned or who were condemned . . . . and I think [*Blood Canticle*] is about that—being the end of the road, the last of the chronicles."

BIOGRAPHICAL AND CRITICAL SOURCES:

BOOKS

Badley, Linda, *Writing Horror and the Body: The Fiction of Stephen King, Clive Barker, and Anne Rice,* Greenwood Press (Westport, CT), 1996.

Beahm, George, editor, *The Unauthorized Anne Rice Companion,* Andrews and McMeel (New York, NY), 1996.

Charlton, James, editor, *Fighting Words: Writers Lambast Other Writers—From Aristotle to Anne Rice,* Algonquin Books of Chapel Hill (Chapel Hill, NC), 1994.

Contemporary Literary Criticism, Volume 41, Gale (Detroit, MI), 1987.

Dickinson, Joy, *Haunted City: An Unauthorized Guide to the Magical, Magnificent New Orleans of Anne Rice,* Carol Publishing Group (Secaucus, NJ), 1995.

Hoppenstand, Gary, and Ray B. Browne, editors, *The Gothic World of Anne Rice,* Bowling Green Popular Press, 1996.

Marcus, Jana, *In the Shadow of the Vampire: Reflections from the World of Anne Rice,* Thunder's Mouth Press (New York, NY), 1997.

Ramsland, Katherine M., *Prism of the Night: A Biography of Anne Rice,* Dutton (New York, NY), 1991.

Ramsland, Katherine M., *The Vampire Companion: The Official Guide to Anne Rice's The Vampire Chronicles,* Ballantine (New York, NY), 1993.

Ramsland, Katherine M., *The Witches' Companion: The Official Guide to Anne Rice's Lives of the Mayfair Witches,* Ballantine (New York, NY), 1994.

Ramsland, Katherine M., *The Anne Rice Trivia Book,* Ballantine (New York, NY), 1994.

Ramsland, Katherine M., *The Roquelaure Reader: A Companion to Anne Rice's Erotica,* Plume (New York, NY), 1996.

Ramsland, Katherine M., editor, *The Anne Rice Reader: Writers Explore the Universe of Anne Rice,* Ballantine (New York, NY), 1997.

Rice, Anne, *Interview with the Vampire,* Knopf (New York, NY), 1976.

Riley, Michael, *Conversations with Anne Rice,* Ballantine (New York, NY), 1996.

Roberts, Bette B., *Anne Rice,* Twayne (New York, NY), 1994.

Smith, Jennifer, *Anne Rice: A Critical Companion,* Greenwood Press (New York, NY), 1996.

PERIODICALS

Atlanta Constitution, November 11, 1994, p. P5; July 31, 1995, p. B1.

Atlanta Journal and Constitution, October 4, 1992, p. N8; January 27, 1993, p. A3; June 27, 1993, p. A3; October 3, 1993, p. N10.

Book, September, 2000, p. 32; November-December, 2002, Chris Barsanti, review of *Blackwood Farm,* p. 84; November-December, 2003, Steve Wilson, review of *Blood Canticle,* p. 76, and interview, p. 13.

Booklist, May 15, 1996, p. 1547; July, 2000, p. 1975; August, 2001, Kristine Huntley, review of *Blood and Gold,* p. 2051; August, 2002, Kristine Huntley, review of *Blackwood Farm,* p. 1887; September 1, 2003, Kristine Huntley, review of *Blood Canticle,* p. 7.

Boston Globe, September 30, 1994, p. 64.

Chicago Tribune, October 15, 1993, section 1, p. 22; October 26, 1993, section 5, pp. 1, 2; March 5, 1995, section 12, p. 1; August 31, 1995, section 5, p. 2.

Chicago Tribune Book World, January 27, 1980; February 10, 1980.

Christian Science Monitor, November 14, 1994, p. 13.

Entertainment Weekly, March 19, 1999, p. 98; October 31, 2003, Alynda Wheat, review of *Blood Canticle,* p. 77.

Globe and Mail (Toronto, Ontario, Canada), March 15, 1986; November 5, 1988.

Kirkus Reviews, August 15, 1990; August 1, 2003, review of *Blood Canticle,* p. 989.

Lambda Book Report, October, 2000, Melinda L. Shelton, interview with Rice, p. 6.

Lear's, October, 1989, interview with Rice.

Library Journal, September 1, 1999, p. 254; September 1, 2000, p. 252; October 1, 2001, Patricia Altner, review of *Blood and Gold,* p. 143; September 1, 2003, Patricia Altner, review of *Blood Canticle,* p. 210; October 15, 2003, Kristen L. Smith, review of *Blackwood Farm,* p. 113; November 1, 2005, Tamara Butler, review of *Christ the Lord: Out of Egypt,* p. 70.

Locus, September, 1992, pp. 17, 19; October, 1993, p. 25.

Los Angeles Times, August 18, 1988; August 15, 1993; September 21, 1994, p. F1; November 28, 1994, p. B7.

Los Angeles Times Book Review, February 3, 1980; December 19, 1982; July 1, 1985; October 27, 1986; November 6, 1988; October 25, 1992, pp. 1, 9; August 15, 1993, p. 10; October 31, 1993, p. 3.

MacLean's, November 16, 1992, p. 68.

National Review, September 3, 1976.

New Republic, May 8, 1976, pp. 29-30.

Newsweek, November 5, 1990.

New York Times, September 8, 1982; September 9, 1982, p. C25; October 19, 1985, p. 16; October 15, 1988; November 7, 1988; October 28, 1993, pp. C15, C20; November 11, 1994, p. A51.

New York Times Book Review, March 2, 1976; May 2, 1976, pp. 7, 14; February 17, 1980, p. 17; October 10, 1980; October 10, 1982, p. 14; October 27, 1985, p. 15; November 27, 1988; June 11, 1989; November 4, 1990; October 24, 1993, p. 38; December 4, 1994, p. 82; July 23, 1995, p.14; August 11, 1996; October 19, 1997; April 19, 1998; December 20. 1998; March 28, 1999, p. 18; October 26, 2000

New York Times Magazine, October 14, 1990.

People, December 5, 1988; November 16, 1998, p. 47; January 11, 1999, p. 113; April 5, 1999, p. 51; December 22, 2003, p. 101.

Publishers Weekly, October 28, 1988; February 10, 1989; November 3, 1989; June 5, 1995, p. 51; August 24, 1998, p. 45; October 26, 1998, p. 19; January 11, 1999, p. 53; August 13, 2000, p. 324; October 2, 2000, p. 45; September 24, 2001, review of *Blood and Gold,* p. 74; September 2, 2002, review of *Blackwood Farm,* p. 52; October 6, 2003, review of *Blood Canticle,* p. 66; October 10, 2005, review of *Christ the Lord,* p. 38.

Rolling Stone, November 20, 1986; July 13, 1995, p. 92.

Saturday Review, February 2, 1980, p. 37.

Spectator, December 3, 1994, pp. 56-57.

Success, October 2000, p. 96.

Time, September 9, 1989; October 31, 2005, Lev Grossman, review of *Christ the Lord,* p. 86.

Tribune Books (Chicago, IL), October 27, 1988; May 28, 1989; November 11, 1990; October 18, 1992, p. 3; October 17, 1993, p. 3; October 9, 1994, p. 5.

Variety, August 21, 2000, p. 33.

Voice Literary Supplement, June, 1982; November, 1987; November, 1988.

Wall Street Journal, June 17, 1976, p. 14.

Washington Post, November 6, 1988; October 30, 1992, p. B1.

Washington Post Book World, January 27, 1980, p. 6; October 3, 1982, pp. 7, 9; December 1, 1985, pp. 1, 7; October 26, 1986; November 6, 1988; June 18, 1989; February 11, 1990; October 28, 1990; October 30, 1992, p. 1; October 4, 1993, pp. 4-5; October 10, 1993, p. 4; October 9, 1994, p. 4; January 15, 1995, p. 4; August 6, 1995, p. 2.

ONLINE

Official Anne Rice Home Page, http://www.annerice.com/ (April 23, 2004).

* * *

RICH, Adrienne 1929-
(Adrienne Cecile Rich)

PERSONAL: Born May 16, 1929, Baltimore, MD; daughter of Arnold Rice (a physician) and Helen Elizabeth (a musician; maiden name, Jones) Rich; married Alfred Haskell Conrad (an economist), June 26, 1953 (died, 1970); partner of Michelle Cliff (a writer and editor), beginning 1976; children: David, Paul, Jacob. *Education:* Radcliffe College, A.B. (cum laude), 1951.

ADDRESSES: *Home*—Northern CA. *Agent*—c/o W.W. Norton Co., 500 5th Ave., New York, NY 10110.

CAREER: Poet and writer. Conductor of workshop, YM-YWHA Poetry Center, New York, NY, 1966-67; visiting lecturer, Swarthmore College, Swarthmore, PA, 1967-69; adjunct professor in writing division, Columbia University, Graduate School of the Arts, New York, NY, 1967-69; City College of the City University of New York, New York, NY, lecturer in SEEK English program, 1968-70, instructor in creative writing program, 1970-71, assistant professor of English, 1971-72, and 1974-75; Fannie Hurst Visiting Professor of Creative Literature, Brandeis University, Waltham, MA, 1972-73; Lucy Martin Donnelly fellow, Bryn Mawr College, Bryn Mawr, PA, 1975; professor of English,

Douglass College, Rutgers University, New Brunswick, NJ, 1976-78; A. D. White Professor-at-Large, Cornell University, Ithaca, NY, 1982-85; Clark Lecturer and distinguished visiting professor, Scripps College, Claremont, CA, 1983, 1984; visiting professor, San Jose State University, San Jose, CA, 1984-96; Burgess Lecturer, Pacific Oaks College, Pasadena, CA, 1986; professor of English and feminist studies, Stanford University, Stanford, CA, 1986-92; Marjorie Kovler visiting fellow, University of Chicago, Chicago, IL, 1989; National Director, The National Writers' Voice Project, 1992—. Member of advisory board, Boston Woman's Fund, National Writers Union, Sisterhood in Support of Sisters in South Africa and New Jewish Agenda.

MEMBER: PEN, Modern Language Association (honorary fellow, 1985—), National Writers Union, Poetry Society of America, American Academy of Arts and Letters, American Academy of Arts and Sciences, Phi Beta Kappa.

AWARDS, HONORS: Yale Series of Younger Poets award for *A Change of World,* 1951; Guggenheim fellowships, 1952 and 1961; Ridgely Torrence Memorial Award, Poetry Society of America, 1955; Grace Thayer Bradley Award, Friends of Literature (Chicago) for *The Diamond Cutters and Other Poems,* 1956; Phi Beta Kappa Poet, College of William and Mary, 1960, Swarthmore College, 1965, and Harvard University, 1966; National Institute of Arts and Letters award for poetry, 1961; Amy Lowell traveling fellowship, 1962; Bollingen Foundation translation grant, 1962; Bess Hokin Prize, *Poetry* magazine, 1963; Litt.D., Wheaton College, 1967; National Translation Center grant, 1968; Eunice Tietjens Memorial Prize, *Poetry* magazine, 1968; National Endowment for the Arts grant, 1970, for poems in *American Literary Anthology: 3;* Shelley Memorial Award, Poetry Society of America, 1971; Ingram Merrill Foundation grant, 1973- 74; National Book Award, 1974, for *Diving into the Wreck: Poems, 1971-1972;* Litt.D., Wheaton College, 1967; National Medal of the Arts (declined), 1977; National Book Critics Circle Award in Poetry nomination, 1978, for *The Dream of a Common Language: Poems, 1974- 1977;* Litt.D., Smith College, 1979; Fund for Human Dignity Award, National Gay Task Force, 1981; *Los Angeles Times* Book Prize nomination, 1982, for *A Wild Patience Has Taken Me This Far: Poems, 1978- 1981;* Ruth Lilly Poetry Prize, Modern Poetry Association and American Council for the Arts, 1986; Brandeis University Creative Arts Medal in Poetry, 1987; Litt.D., College of Wooster, Ohio, 1988; National Poetry Association Award, 1989, for distinguished service to the art of poetry; Elmer Holmes Bobst Award in Arts and Letters, New York University Library, 1989; Bay Area Book Reviewers Award in Poetry, 1990, 1996; Litt.D., Harvard University, 1990; The Common Wealth Award in Literature, 1991; Robert Frost Silver Medal for Lifetime Achievement in Poetry, Poetry Society of America, 1992; Litt.D., Swarthmore College, 1992; William Whitehead Award of the Gay and Lesbian Publishing Triangle for Lifetime Achievement in Letters, 1992; Lambda Book Award in Lesbian Poetry, 1992, for *An Atlas of the Difficult World: Poems, 1988- 1991,* 1996, for *Dark Fields of the Republic, 1991- 1995,* and 2002, for *Fox;* Lenore Marshall/*Nation* Poetry Prize and *Los Angeles Times* Book Award, 1992, and Poets' Prize, 1993, all for *An Atlas of the Difficult World: Poems, 1988- 1991,* MacArthur Foundation fellowship, 1994; Tanning Prize of the Academy of American Poets, 1996; Wallace Stevens Award for proven mastery in the art of poetry, 1997; Lannan Foundation Lifetime Achievement Award, 1999; Lammy Award for lesbian poetry, Lambda Literary Foundation, 2002, for *Fox: Poems, 1998-2000;* National Book Critics Circle Award for poetry, 2004, for *The School among the Ruins: Poems, 2000-2004.*

WRITINGS:

POETRY

A Change of World, with foreword by W.H. Auden, Yale University Press (New Haven, CT), 1951.

Poems, Oxford University Poetry Society (New York, NY), 1952.

The Diamond Cutters and Other Poems, Harper (New York, NY), 1955.

Snapshots of a Daughter-in-Law: Poems, 1954-1962, Harper (New York, NY), 1963, revised edition, Norton (New York, NY), 1967.

Necessities of Life, Norton (New York, NY), 1966.

Selected Poems, Chatto & Windus (London, England), 1967.

Leaflets: Poems, 1965- 1968, Norton (New York, NY), 1969.

The Will to Change: Poems, 1968- 1970, Norton (New York, NY), 1971.

Diving into the Wreck: Poems, 1971- 1972, Norton (New York, NY), 1973.

Poems: Selected and New, 1950- 1974, Norton (New York, NY), 1974.

Twenty-one Love Poems, Effie's Press (Emeryville, CA), 1977.

The Dream of a Common Language: Poems, 1974-1977, Norton (New York, NY), 1978.

A Wild Patience Has Taken Me This Far: Poems, 1978-1981, Norton (New York, NY), 1981.

Sources, Heyeck Press (Woodside, CA), 1983.
The Fact of a Doorframe: Poems Selected and New, 1950-1984, Norton (New York, NY), 1984.
Your Native Land, Your Life, Norton (New York, NY), 1986.
Time's Power: Poems, 1985- 1988, Norton (New York, NY), 1988.
An Atlas of the Difficult World: Poems, 1988-1991, Norton (New York, NY), 1991.
Collected Early Poems, 1950- 1970, Norton (New York, NY), 1993.
Dark Fields of the Republic, 1991- 1995, Norton (New York, NY), 1995.
Selected Poems, 1950- 1995, Salmon Publishers (Knockeven, Ireland), 1996.
Midnight Salvage: Poems, 1995- 1998, Norton (New York, NY), 1999.
Fox: Poems, 1998-2000, Norton (New York, NY), 2001.
The School among the Ruins: Poems, 2000-2004, Norton (New York, NY), 2004.

Also guest editor for *Best American Poetry of 1996,* Scribner (New York, NY), 1996.

PROSE

Of Woman Born: Motherhood As Experience and Institution, Norton (New York, NY), 1976, 10th anniversary edition with a revised introduction, 1986.
Women and Honor: Some Notes on Lying (pamphlet), Motheroot Publishing/ Pittsburgh Women Writers (Pittsburgh, PA), 1977.
On Lies, Secrets, and Silence: Selected Prose, 1966-1978, Norton (New York, NY), 1979.
Compulsory Heterosexuality and Lesbian Existence (pamphlet), Antelope Publications (Denver, CO), 1980.
Blood, Bread and Poetry: Selected Prose, 1979-1986, Norton (New York, NY), 1986.
(With Susan Morland) *Birth of the Age of Women,* Wild Caret (Hereford, England), 1991.
What Is Found There: Notebooks on Poetry and Politics, Norton (New York, NY), 1993.
Arts of the Possible: Essays and Conversations, Norton (New York, NY), 2001.

TRANSLATOR

(And editor, with Aijaz Ahmad and William Stafford) *Poems by Ghalib,* Hudson Review (New York, NY), 1969.
Mark Insingel, *Reflections,* Red Dust (New York, NY), 1973.

Also contributor of translations to *Poets on Street Corners: Portraits of Fifteen Russian Poets,* edited by Olga Carlisle, Random House (New York, NY), 1968; *A Treasury of Yiddish Poetry,* edited by Irving Howe and Eliezer Greenberg, Holt (New York, NY), 1969; and *Selected Poems of Mirza Ghalib,* edited by Aijaz Ahmad, Columbia University Press (New York, NY), 1971, World Treasury of Poetry, 1996.

OTHER

Ariadne: A Play in Three Acts and Poems (drama), J.H. Furst (Baltimore, MD), 1939.
Not I, but Death: A Play in One Act (drama), J.H. Furst (Baltimore, MD), 1941.

Columnist, *American Poetry Review,* 1972-73. Coeditor, *Sinister Wisdom,* 1981-84; contributing editor, *Chrysalis: A Magazine of Women's Culture;* founding coeditor, *Bridges: A Journal of Jewish Feminists and Our Friends,* 1989-92.

SIDELIGHTS: "Adrienne Rich is not just one of America's best feminist poets," wrote Margaret Atwood in *Second Words: Selected Critical Prose,* "or one of America's best woman poets, she is one of America's best poets." Rich's poetry has not always been described as "feminist." She "began as [a] poet-ingenue," according to Carol Muske in the *New York Times Book Review,* "polite copyist of Yeats and Auden, wife and mother. She has progressed in life (and in her poems . . .) from young widow and disenchanted formalist, to spiritual and rhetorical convalescent, to feminist leader . . . and *doyenne* of a newly-defined female literature." In *Poet and Critic* David Zuger described a similar metamorphosis in Rich's work: "The twenty-year-old author of painstaking, decorous poems that are eager to 'maturely' accept the world they are given becomes a . . . poet of prophetic intensity and 'visionary anger' bitterly unable to feel at home in a world 'that gives no room / to be what we dreamt of being.'"

Albert Gelpi observed that Rich's stance in her early poems is far from feminist. In *American Poetry since 1960: Some Critical Perspectives,* Gelpi noted that in W.H. Auden's foreword to *A Change of World,* Rich's introductory book of poetry, Auden said her poems "are neatly and modestly dressed, speak quietly but do not mumble, respect their elders but are not cowed by them, and do not tell fibs." "In other words," Gelpi explained, the poems reflect "the stereotype—prim, fussy and schoolmarmish—that has corseted and strait-laced women-poets into 'poetesses' whom men could deprecate with admiration." In *Writing Like a Woman,* Alicia Ostriker stated, "Rich at this point [was] a cautious good poet in the sense of being a good girl, a quality noted with approval by her early reviewers."

Many critics found in Rich's book *Snapshots of a Daughter-in-Law: Poems, 1954-1962* the first indication of both the end of Rich's imitative efforts and the beginning of her concern with feminist issues. In *Southwest Review,* Willard Spiegelman called *Snapshots* "the liminal volume, attempting a journey from one self, world, poetic form, to another." Spiegelman noted that the poem "Roof-walker" articulates Rich's precarious position as a poet balancing between two modes of writing: "exposed, larger than life, / and due to break my neck." Ostriker also commented on the change in Rich's poetry evident in *Snapshots.* Calling the collection "Rich's break-through volume," Ostriker noted that the book's title poem "consists of fragmentary and odd-shaped sections instead of stanzas, and has the immediacy and force which Rich did not attempt earlier."

Snapshots offers the reader a change in the form of Rich's poetry, as Ostriker observed. This change, according to Anne Newman in the *Dictionary of Literary Biography,* includes "dropping the initial capital letter in each line, increasing enjambment, using speech cadences in place of formal meters, limiting the use of rhyme, and varying stanza length." The content of Rich's poetry changes also. Her work begins to reflect her personal confrontation with what it means to be female in a male-dominated society. In Rich's 1971 essay, "When We Dead Awaken: Writing As Re-vision," quoted by Newman, the poet comments: "In the late fifties I was able to write, for the first time, directly about experiencing myself as a woman—Until then I had tried very hard *not* to identify myself as a female poet. Over two years I wrote . . . 'Snapshots of a Daughter-in-Law' (1958-60), in a longer, looser mode than I'd ever trusted myself with before. It was an extraordinary relief to write that poem."

Rich has been criticized for the harsh depictions of males in her poetry. This is especially true in reviews of *Diving into the Wreck: Poems, 1971-1972* and *A Wild Patience Has Taken Me This Far: Poems, 1978- 1981.* Ostriker commented on what she calls Rich's "partisanship" and observed, "Men in [*Diving into the Wreck*] are depicted universally and exclusively as parisitic on women, emotionally threatened by them, brutal . . . and undeserving of pity." In *Parnassus* Helen Vendler noted that the poem "Rape" from *Diving into the Wreck,* seems to bestow on all men the image of the sadistic rapist portrayed in the work. "This poem," she wrote, "like some others [in the volume], is a deliberate refusal of the modulations of intelligence in favor of . . . propaganda." Similarly, in the *Voice Literary Supplement,* Kathryn Kilgore called *A Wild Patience* "a ritual of man-hatred" while in the *Times Literary Supplement* Jay Parini stated that in some of the poems in the volume Rich "wilfully misrepresents men, committing the same act of distortions that she complains about elsewhere."

On the other hand, *Diving into the Wreck* was granted the prestigious National Book Award (Rich, along with Audre Lorde and Alice Walker, declined the award as an individual but accepted it on behalf of women whose voices have been silenced, and donated the cash award to the Sisterhood of Black Single Mothers). The book was praised by many critics. For example, *Michigan Quarterly Review* contributor Laurence Goldstein contended that it is "Rich's finest single volume," and observed that the title poem is "a modern classic." In *Harvard* magazine Ruth Whitman called the same piece "one of the great poems of our time." In her *Ms.* review of the book, Erica Jong noted that Rich handles political issues well in her poetry. "Rich is one of the few poets," she stated, "who can deal with political issues in her poems without letting them degenerate into social realism." Focusing on the title poem, Jong also denies that Rich is anti-male. A portion of the poem reads: "And I am here, the mermaid whose dark hair / streams black, the merman in his armored body. / We circle silently / about the wreck. / We dive into the hold. / I am she: I am he." Jong commented, "This stranger-poet-survivor carries 'a book of myths' in which her/his 'names do not appear.' These are the old myths . . . that perpetuate the battle between the sexes. Implicit in Rich's image of the androgyne is the idea that we must write new myths, create new definitions of humanity which will not glorify this angry chasm but heal it." *A Wild Patience* received similar if not as abundant praise. For instance, Sara Mandlebaum noted in *Ms.* that in the volume "the radicalism of [Rich's] vision . . . remains strong and invigorating: the writing as lyrical . . . and moving as ever—and even more honest."

Rich's prose has caused as much controversy as her poetry. Newman discussed the reception of *Of Woman Born: Motherhood As Experience and Institution,* Rich's study of the concept of motherhood. "Some critical reactions to the book," Newman observed, "are almost vehement, claiming Rich's perspective has been clouded by a rage that has led her into biased statements and a strident style. Others, who have read it with more sympathy, call it scholarly and well researched and insist that it should not be read . . . for polemics." In her *New York Times Book Review* critique of the volume, for example, Francine du Plessix Gray wrote, "It is vexing to see such a dedicated feminist playing the dangerous game of using the oppressor's tactics. Going from mythologization of history to remythologization of male and female character traits, Rich indulges in stereotypes throughout the book." Speaking of the same book, but representative of the other half of the critics, Laura E. Casari commented in *Prairie Schooner:* In *Of Woman Born* Rich "thoroughly documents the powerlessness of women in a patriarchal culture and vividly depicts its results."

Rich's second prose work, *On Lies, Secrets, and Silence: Selected Prose, 1966-1978,* furthers her feminist aesthetic. This volume contains one of Rich's most-noted essays, "When We Dead Awaken: Writing as Re-Vision," in which Rich clarifies the need for female self-definition. It was during this time, in 1976, that Rich also came out as a lesbian. In *Blood, Bread and Poetry: Selected Prose, 1979-1986,* Rich continues to explore issues of lesbianism while addressing such topics as racial identity and racism. Rich's fourth book of prose, *What Is Found There: Notebooks on Poetry and Politics,* contains meditations on politics, poetry, and poets. Focusing on such writers as Muriel Rukeyser, Audre Lorde, Wallace Stevens, and June Jordan, Rich emphasizes her belief that poetry is inevitably political and that "poetry can break open locked chambers of possibility, restore numbed zones to feeling, recharge desire." Rich, according to *Nation* writer Jan Montefiore, goes on to "address the social, ecological, and political dilemmas and contradictions of the United States, defining and identifying herself with a specifically American stream of radical poetry."

In the verse collections *Your Native Land, Your Life, Time's Power: Poems, 1985-1988,* and *An Atlas of the Difficult World: Poems, 1988-1991,* Rich addresses new issues while continuing to develop feminist themes. The long sequence titled "Sources" in *Your Native Land, Your Life* is Rich's first major attempt to confront her Jewish heritage and the effects of the Holocaust on her life and work. In "Living Memory," a long poem in *Time's Power,* Rich faces the consequences of time and aging and also meditates on her bond to the American landscape. Marilyn Hacker pointed out in the *Nation* that this volume ranges "backward through personal and international history, geographically from southern California to Vermont to the Golan Heights. These texts present a variety of dramatis personae, and do not flinch at the knottiest moral conundrums." *An Atlas of the Difficult World* focuses on such issues as poverty, the Persian Gulf War, and the exploitation of minorities and women. Rich's use of personal experience, first-person narratives, and language prompted critics to compare this collection to the works of Emily Dickinson and Walt Whitman. *Hudson Review* critic Dick Allen observed, "Rich's book is truly a small atlas; but it is also the mature poetry of a writer who knows her own power, who speaks in the passionate, ambitious blending of the personal and the universal forever present in major work. She will be read and studied for centuries to come."

In 1997 at the age of seventy, Rich refused the National Medal for the Arts, and brought the debate over government funding for the arts to national attention. In her letter to Jane Alexander of the National Endowment for the Arts, Rich explained her refusal of the award, "There is no simple formula for the relationship of art to justice. But I do know that art—in my own case the art of poetry—means nothing it if simply decorates the dinner table of power which holds it hostage." Rich's actions showed that time had not quelled her passion. Noted reviewer Traci Hukill in *Metro Active,* Rich's "criticism of a cynical administration that has blessed a swiftly widening gap in wealth and power is assurance that time has not mellowed her craving for justice."

However, upon publication of *Midnight Salvage, Poems, 1995-1998,* at least one critic saw a "more somberly reflective" Rich. As Adam Newey noted in the *New Statesman,* "The tide of anger so evident in earlier work has abated here." But according to Dana Gioia in the *San Francisco Magazine,* Rich remained driven by her quest for justice. "She is a human acetylene torch," Gioia wrote, "intent on searing through oppression and convention." Though he seems to find her perhaps too serious ("Rich is too busy denouncing human folly ever to stop and enjoy it."), he asserted that "No other living poet . . . has made such a profound impression on American intellectual life." *Midnight Salvage* is a collection of poems "with the spiritual pull of overcoming," noted Ace Boggess in the *Adirondack Review.* He explained that he received the book on the day before the September 11, 2001, terrorist attacks on the United States. While the poems preceded the events of that day, Boggess saw a connection between the attacks and the poems. "I soon realized it was because the poems in this book contain something universal," he contended, "a common reality revealed in the finite experiences of the one." According to reviewer Rafael Campo in the *Progressive,* "Central to Rich's latest book, *Midnight Salvage,* is the quest for personal happiness—and the problem of defining 'happiness'—in an American society that continues to exploit its most defenseless citizens, and in the face of a larger world where contempt for human rights leads to nightmare. Her solution has as much to do with empathy as it does with revolution."

Rich continued to focus on social injustice and introspection in *Fox: Poems, 1998-2000,* a short volume of just twenty-five poems. Critic Ruthann Robson felt that the collection was too short, writing in the *Lambda Book Report* that "the cumulative effect of this volume may be blunted by its brevity." Robson also asserted that the poems lacked Rich's usual wit and spark. But Boggess was impressed more with the collection's complexity than its brevity. "Seeing the beautiful structure of 'Architecture' or grasping the prophetic feel of 'Ends of the Earth,' one gets drawn deeply into the poems in *Fox* the same way one gets drawn into the relationship crises of friends," Boggess wrote. "It can be a struggle at times and a pleasure at others, but one always learns something along the way and hopes to live long enough to see a conclusion."

In *Arts of the Possible,* a return to prose, Rich once again examines her role as a feminist, Jewish, lesbian poet- activist and encourages similar introspection in her readers. The book is a collection of eleven essays, four of which were previously published and included to give a sense of the progression of Rich's thoughts. According to B.A. St. Andrews in *World Literature Today,* the book "externalizes various debates within the passionate mind of Adrienne Rich." The same reviewer described Rich's writing in the book as "unflinching not because she redefines the Truth but because she serves it, not because she answers questions but because she raises them at all." Wendy Mnookin in the *Radcliffe Quarterly* summarized that "Rich explores the role of the artist and, indeed, anyone 'trying to live conscientiously.'" St. Andrews also noted that "Rich requires of us an ancient, humble, salubrious act: a rigorous examination of conscience with the aim of self- governance and self-improvement."

Rich won the National Book Critics Circle Award for her collection *The School among the Ruins: Poems, 2000-2004.* The book of poems attempts to capture the myriad world events that have defined the beginning of the twenty-first century. Throughout her career, Rich has been exceedingly drawn away from formal verse, and the predominantly short prose poems in the volume are free verse meditations on "the displacement of exiles, the encroachment of modernity on human dignity, and the effects of America's war against terror on the stateside psyche," noted Meghan O'Rourke in *Artforum.* Although O'Rourke felt the collection veered too much into "rhetoric," *Library Journal* Diane Scharper felt that Rich's "poetry [is] achieved by juxtaposition and contrast." Donna Seaman, writing in *Booklist* noted the snippets of cell-phone and television-news dialogue, concluding that Rich "get[s] the fractured timbre of the times just right."

Through over fifty years of public introspection and examination of society and self, Adrienne Rich has chronicled her journey in poetry and prose. "I began as an American optimist," she commented in *Credo of a Passionate Skeptic,* "albeit a critical one, formed by our racial legacy and by the Vietnam War . . . I became an American Skeptic, not as to the long search for justice and dignity, which is part of all human history, but in the light of my nation's leading role in demoralizing and destabilizing that search, here at home and around the world. Perhaps just such a passionate skepticism, neither cynical nor nihilistic, is the ground for continuing."

BIOGRAPHICAL AND CRITICAL SOURCES:

BOOKS

Atwood, Margaret,*Second Words: Selected Critical Prose,* Beacon Press (Boston, MA), 1984.

Dickie, Margaret, *Stein, Bishop & Rich: Lyrics of Love, War & Place,* University of North Carolina Press (Chapel Hill, NC), 1997.

Dictionary of Literary Biography, Volume 5: *American Poets since World War II, First Series,* Gale (Detroit, MI), 1980.

Ostriker, Alicia, *Writing Like a Woman,* University of Michigan Press (Ann Arbor, MI), 1983.

Oxford Companion to Women's Writing in the United States, Oxford University Press (New York, NY), 1995.

Shaw, Robert B., editor, *American Poetry since 1960: Some Critical Perspectives,* Dufour Editions (Chester Springs, PA), 1974.

Sielke, Sabine, *Fashioning the Female Subject: The Intertextual Networking of Dickinson, Moore, and Rich,* University of Michigan Press (Ann Arbor, MI), 1997.

Templeton, Alice, *The Dream and the Dialogue: Adrienne Rich's Feminist Poetics,* University of Tennessee Press (Knoxville, TN), 1994.

Werner, Craig Hansen, *Adrienne Rich: The Poet and Her Critics,* American Library Association (Chicago, IL), 1988.

PERIODICALS

Adirondack Review, September 13, 2001, Ace Boggess, review of *Fox: Poems, 1998- 2000.*

Advocate, June 22, 1999, review of *Midnight Salvage,* p. 7; June 19, 2001, review of *Arts of the Possible,* p. 97.

American Book Review, August, 1994, p. 16; November, 2001, review of *Arts of the Possible,* p. 5.

American Poetry Review, September- October, 1973; March-April, 1975; July-August, 1979; July-August, 1992, pp. 35-38.

Artforum, October-November, 2004, Meghan O'Rourke, review of *The School among the Ruins: Poems, 2000-2004,* p. 54.

Atlantic, June, 1978.

Belles Lettres, fall, 1994, p. 37.

Bloomsbury Review, March, 1999, review of *Midnight Salvage,* p. 7.

Booklist, January 1, 1999, review of *Midnight Salvage,* p. 821; March 15, 1999, review of *Midnight Salvage,* p. 1276; October 1, 2001, Donna Seaman, review of *Fox,* p. 295; August, 2004, Donna Seaman, review of *The School among the Ruins,* p. 1982.

Bookwatch, June, 1999, review of *Midnight Salvage,* p. 2.

Choice, October, 2001, review of *Arts of the Possible,* p. 4.

Christian Science Monitor, August 18, 1966; July 24, 1969; January 26, 1977.

Contemporary Literature, winter, 1975; winter, 1992, pp. 645-664; spring, 1993, pp. 61-87.

Economist, March 13, 1999, review of *Midnight Salvage,* p. 14.

Harper's, December, 1973; November, 1978.

Harvard Magazine, July-August, 1975; January-February, 1977.

Hudson Review, autumn, 1971; autumn, 1975; summer, 1992, pp. 319-330; winter, 2002, review of *Fox,* p. 687.

Kirkus Reviews, January 15, 1999, review of *Midnight Salvage,* p. 104; March 1, 2001, review of *Arts of the Possible,* p. 1527.

Lambda Book Report, October 2001, Ruthann Robson, review of *Fox,* p. 25.

Library Journal, April 1, 1999, review of *Midnight Salvage,* p. 57; September 15, 2001, review of *Fox,* p. 85; April 15, 2002, review of *Fox,* p. 90; August, 2004, Diane Scharper, review of *The School among the Ruins,* p. 86.

Los Angeles Times, April 23, 1986; June 7, 1986.

Los Angeles Times Book Review, October 17, 1982; March 25, 1984; April 1, 2001, review of *Arts of the Possible,* p. 11.

Los Angeles Times Book Section, August 3, 1997, Adrienne Rich, "Why I Refused the National Medal for the Arts."

Massachusetts Review, autumn, 1983.

Michigan Quarterly Review, summer, 1976; winter, 1983; fall, 1996, pp. 586- 607.

Modern Poetry Studies, autumn, 1977.

Monthly Review, June 2001, Adrienne Rich, "Credo of a Passionate Skeptic."

Ms., July, 1973; December, 1981; August 2001, review of *Arts of the Possible,* p. 80.

Nation, July 28, 1951; October 8, 1973; July 1, 1978; December 23, 1978; June 7, 1986, pp. 797- 798; October 23, 1989; November 30, 1992, pp. 673-674.

New Leader, May 26, 1975.

New Republic, November 6, 1976; December 9, 1978; June 2, 1979; January 7-14, 1985.

New Statesman, March 26, 1999, Adam Newey, review of *Midnight Salvage,* p. 57.

Newsweek, October 18, 1976.

New Yorker, November 3, 1951; April 25, 1994, p. 111.

New York Review of Books, May 7, 1970; October 4, 1973; September 30, 1976; December 17, 1981; November 21, 1991, pp. 50-56.

New York Times, May 13, 1951; August 25, 1973.

New York Times Book Review, July 17, 1966; May 23, 1971; December 30, 1973; April 27, 1975; October 10, 1976; June 11, 1978; April 22, 1979; December 9, 1981; December 20, 1981; January 7, 1985; January 20, 1985; December 8, 1991, p. 7; November 7, 1993, p. 7; April 21, 1996, pp. 32-33.

Off Our Backs, January, 2002, review of *Arts of the Possible,* p. 51.

Parnassus, fall- winter, 1973; spring-summer, 1979.

Partisan Review, winter, 1978.

Poet and Critic, Volume 9, number 2, 1976; Volume 10, number 2, 1978.

Poetry, February, 1955; July, 1963; March, 1970; February, 1976; August, 1992, pp. 284-304; April 1999, "The Best American Poetry, 1996."

Prairie Schooner, summer, 1978.

Progressive, January, 1994, Matthew Rothschild, "Adrienne Rich: 'I Happen to Think Poetry Makes a Huge Difference'"; July, 1999, Rafael Campo, review of *Midnight Salvage,* p. 43; January, 2002, review of *Fox,* p. 40.

Publishers Weekly, March 26, 2001, review of *Arts of the Possible,* p. 83; August 6, 2001, review of *Fox,* p. 86; November 1, 1999, review of *Midnight Salvage,* p. 55.

Radcliffe Quarterly, summer, 2001, Wendy Mnookin, review of *Arts of the Possible.*

Salmagundi, spring- summer, 1973; spring-summer, 1979.
San Francisco Magazine, January, 1999, Dana Gioia, review of *Midnight Salvage.*
Saturday Review, December 18, 1971; November 13, 1976.
Southern Review, April, 1969; summer, 1999, review of *Southern Midnight,* p. 621.
Southwest Review, autumn, 1975.
Times Literary Supplement, November 23, 1967; June 9, 1972; April 20, 1973; November 12, 1982; July 20, 1984; July 8, 1994, p. 9.
Village Voice, November 8, 1976.
Voice Literary Supplement, December, 1981.
Washington Post Book World, December 23, 1973; November 14, 1976; December 5, 1976; December 3, 1978; May 6, 1979; May 20, 1982; November 11, 2001, review of *Fox,* p. 295.
Women's Review of Books, December, 1983; April, 1987, pp. 5-6; March, 1990, pp. 12- 13.
World Literature Today, winter, 1979; autumn, 2000, Sandra Cookson, review of *Midnight Salvage,* p. 821; summer-autumn, 2002, B.A. St. Andrews, review of *Arts of the Possible,* p73.
Yale Review, autumn, 1956; autumn, 1978; April, 1999, review of *Midnight Salvage,* p. 175.

ONLINE

American Poems, http://www.americanpoems.com/ (June 2, 2003), "Adrienne Rich."
Dana Gioia Online, http://www.danagioia.com/ (January, 1999), review of *Midnight Salvage.*
Metro Active, http://www.metroactive.com/ (June 6, 2003), Traci Hukill, "Adrienne Rich Explores Horror and Hope in *Midnight Salvage.* "
Norton Poets Online, http://www.nortonpoets.com/ (June 2, 2003).
St. Martin's Press, http://www.bedfordstmartins.com/ (June 2, 2003).

* * *

RICH, Adrienne Cecile
See RICH, Adrienne

* * *

RICH, Barbara
See GRAVES, Robert

RICHLER, Mordecai 1931-2001

PERSONAL: Born January 27, 1931, in Montreal, Quebec, Canada; died of cancer, July 3, 2001, in Montreal, Quebec, Canada; son of Moses Isaac and Lily (Rosenberg) Richler; married Florence Wood, July 27, 1960; children: Daniel, Noah, Emma, Martha, Jacob. *Education:* Attended Sir George Williams University, 1949-51. *Religion:* "Jewish atheist."

CAREER: Writer. Freelance writer in Paris, France, 1952-53, London, England, 1954-72, and Montreal, Quebec, Canada, 1972-2001. Sir George Williams University, writer-in-residence, 1968-69; Carleton University, visiting professor of English, 1972-74. Member of editorial board, Book-of-the-Month Club, beginning 1972.

MEMBER: Montreal Press Club.

AWARDS, HONORS: President's medal for nonfiction, University of Western Ontario, 1959; Canadian Council junior art fellowships, 1959 and 1960, senior arts fellowship, 1967; Guggenheim Foundation creative writing fellowship, 1961; *Paris Review* humor prize, 1967, for section from *Cocksure* and *Hunting Tigers under Glass;* Governor-General's Literary Award, Canada Council, 1968, for *Cocksure* and *Hunting Tigers under Glass,* and 1971, for *St. Urbain's Horseman; London Jewish Chronicle* literature award, 1972, for *St. Urbain's Horseman;* Berlin Film Festival Golden Bear, Academy Award nomination, and Screenwriters Guild of America award, all 1974, all for screenplay *The Apprenticeship of Duddy Kravitz;* ACTRA Award for best television writer—drama, Academy of Canadian Cinema and Television, 1975; Book of the Year for Children Award, Canadian Library Association, and Ruth Schwartz Children's Book Award, Ontario Arts Council, both 1976, for *Jacob Two-Two Meets the Hooded Fang; London Jewish Chronicle* H.H. Wingate award for fiction, 1981, for *Joshua Then and Now;* named a Literary Lion, New York Public Library, 1989; Commonwealth Writers Prize, Book Trust, 1990, for *Solomon Gursky Was Here;* Giller Prize, 1997, for *Barney's Version;* Richler typeface commissioned in memory of the author by Giller Prize committee and Random House of Canada, 2001.

WRITINGS:

NOVELS

The Acrobats, Putnam (New York, NY), 1954, published as *Wicked We Love,* Popular Library (New York, NY), 1955.

Son of a Smaller Hero, Collins (Toronto, Ontario, Canada), 1955, Paperback Library (New York, NY), 1965, new edition, with an introduction by George Woodcock, McClelland & Stewart (Toronto, Ontario, Canada), 1966.

A Choice of Enemies, Collins (Toronto, Ontario, Canada), 1957, reprinted, McClelland & Stewart (Toronto, Ontario, Canada), 1977.

The Apprenticeship of Duddy Kravitz, Little, Brown (Boston, MA), 1959.

The Incompatible Atuk, McClelland & Stewart (Toronto, Ontario, Canada), published as *Stick Your Neck Out,* Simon & Schuster (New York, NY), 1963.

Cocksure, Simon & Schuster (New York, NY), 1968.

St. Urbain's Horseman, Knopf (New York, NY), 1971.

Joshua Then and Now, Knopf (New York, NY), 1980.

Solomon Gursky Was Here, Viking (New York, NY), 1989.

Barney's Version, Knopf (New York, NY), 1997.

FOR CHILDREN

Jacob Two-Two Meets the Hooded Fang, Knopf (New York, NY), 1975, reprinted, Bullseye Books (New York, NY), 1994.

Jacob Two-Two and the Dinosaur, Knopf (New York, NY), 1987.

Jacob Two-Two's First Spy Case, Farrar, Straus (New York, NY), 1995.

SCREENPLAYS

(Adapter) *Insomnia Is Good for You* (based on a story by Lewis Greifer), Associated British Pictures, 1957.

(With Nicholas Phipps) *No Love for Johnnie,* Embassy, 1962.

(With Geoffrey Cotterell and Ivan Foxwell) *Tiara Tahiti,* Rank, 1962.

(With Nicholas Phipps) *The Wild and the Willing,* Rank, 1962, released as *Young and Willing,* Universal, 1965.

Life at the Top, Royal International, 1965.

The Apprenticeship of Duddy Kravitz (adapted from his novel of the same title), Paramount, 1974.

(With David Giler and Jerry Belson) *Fun with Dick and Jane,* Bart/Palevsky, 1977.

Joshua Then and Now (adapted from his novel of the same title), Twentieth Century-Fox, 1985.

TELEVISION AND RADIO PLAYS

The Acrobats (based on his novel of the same title), Canadian Broadcasting Company (CBC)-Radio, 1956, CBC-TV, 1957.

Friend of the People, CBC-TV, 1957.

Paid in Full, ATV (England), 1958.

Benny, the War in Europe, and Myerson's Daughter Bella, CBC-Radio, 1958.

The Trouble with Benny (based on a short story), ABC (England), 1959.

The Apprenticeship of Duddy Kravitz (based on his novel of the same title), CBC-TV, 1960.

The Spare Room, CBC-Radio, 1961.

Q for Quest (excerpts from his fiction), CBC-Radio, 1963.

The Fall of Mendel Krick, British Broadcasting Corp. (BBC-TV), 1963.

It's Harder to Be Anybody, CBC-Radio, 1965.

Such Was St. Urbain Street, CBC-Radio, 1966.

The Wordsmith (based on a short story), CBC-Radio, 1979.

OTHER

Hunting Tigers under Glass: Essays and Reports, McClelland & Stewart (Toronto, Ontario, Canada), 1969.

The Street: Stories, McClelland & Stewart (Toronto, Ontario, Canada), 1969, New Republic, 1975.

(Editor) *Canadian Writing Today* (anthology), Peter Smith (Magnolia, MA), 1970.

Shoveling Trouble (essays), McClelland & Stewart (Toronto, Ontario, Canada), 1972.

Notes on an Endangered Species and Others (essays), Knopf (New York, NY), 1974.

The Suit (animated filmstrip), National Film Board of Canada, 1976.

Images of Spain, photographs by Peter Christopher, Norton (New York, NY), 1977.

The Great Comic Book Heroes and Other Essays, McClelland & Stewart (Toronto, Ontario, Canada), 1978.

(Editor) *The Best of Modern Humor,* Knopf (New York, NY), 1984.

Home Sweet Home: My Canadian Album (essays), Knopf (New York, NY), 1984, published as *Home Sweet Home,* Penguin (New York, NY), 1985.

(Author of book) *Duddy* (play; based on his novel *The Apprenticeship of Duddy Kravitz,*) first produced in Edmonton, Alberta, 1984.

Broadsides: Reviews and Opinions, Viking (New York, NY), 1990.
(Editor) *Writers on World War II: An Anthology,* Knopf (New York, NY), 1991.
Oh Canada! Oh Quebec! Requiem for a Divided Country, Knopf (New York, NY), 1992.
The Language of Signs, McKay (New York, NY), 1992.
This Year in Jerusalem, Knopf (New York, NY), 1994.
Belling the Cat: Essays, Reports, and Opinions, Knopf (New York, NY), 1998.
On Snooker, Lyons Press (Guilford, CT), 2001.
Dispatches from the Sporting Life, Lyons Press (Guilford, CT), 2001.

Also author, with André Fortier and Rollo May, of *Creativity and the University* (1972 Frank Gerstein Lectures), York University, 1975. Contributor to Canadian, U.S., and British periodicals.

Richler's papers are collected at the University of Calgary Library in Alberta.

ADAPTATIONS: Richler's children's book *Jacob Two-Two Meets the Hooded Fang* was filmed by Cinema Shares International and recorded by Christopher Plummer for Caedmon Records, both 1977; film rights were sold for both *Stick Your Neck Out* and *Cocksure.*

SIDELIGHTS: "To be a Canadian and a Jew," as Mordecai Richler wrote in his book *Hunting Tigers under Glass: Essays and Reports,* "is to emerge from the ghetto twice." Richler referred to the double pressures of being in both a religious minority and the cultural enigma that was twentieth-century Canada. Yet in his decades as a novelist, screenwriter, and essayist, Richler established himself as one of the few representatives of Canadian Jewry known outside his native country. In fact, upon his unexpected death in 2001 at the age of seventy, his obituary ran on the first page of *New York Times*—making him the first Canadian to have that honor in nearly twenty years.

Richler's status as a double outsider gave him a unique perspective from which to satirize what Mark Steyn, in *New Criterion,* described as Canada's "grubby world of feeble evasions and genteel absurdities." Richler, as Steyn noted, delighted in poking fun at "the faintheartedness of a liberalism so defensive that, as he wrote in 1959, it couldn't bear to contemplate 'a Negro whoremonger, a contended adulterer, or a Jew who cheats on his income tax, buys a Jag with his ill-gotten gains, and is all the happier for it.'" What is particularly impressive, in Steyn's view, is how accurately Richler foresaw the "political correctness" that came to engulf North American society—and how gleefully the writer risked offending his various targets, whether they be Jews, Anglo-Canadians, or Quebec separatists.

That many of his fictional works feature Jewish-Canadian protagonists in general—most notably in his best-known book, *The Apprenticeship of Duddy Kravitz*—and natives of Montreal in particular, attests to the author's strong attachment to his early years. Richler was born in the Jewish ghetto of Montreal to a religious family of Russian emigres. It was a neighborhood where, according to *Chicago Tribune* writer Ron Grossman, "Grinding poverty and lofty dreams sat side by side, as did unemployed Talmudic scholars and delicatessen philosophers. The local card players' hangout was owned by a communist freethinker who doubled as a bookie and vociferously rejected the biblical account of Creation." Finding himself at odds with his parents' religious focus, Richler abandoned Orthodox customs by his teens, "gradually becoming more interested both in a wider world and in writing," as R.H. Ramsey observed in *Dictionary of Literary Biography.* After a stint at Sir George Williams University, Richler cashed in an insurance policy and used the money to sail to Liverpool, England. Eventually he found his way to Paris, where he spent some years emulating such expatriate authors as Ernest Hemingway and Henry Miller, then moved on to London, where he worked as a news correspondent.

During those early years Richler produced his first novel, *The Acrobats,* a book he later characterized as "more political than anything I've done since, and humorless," as he told Walter Goodman in a *New York Times* interview, adding that the volume, published when he was age twenty-three, "was just a very young man's novel. Hopelessly derivative. Like some unfortunate collision of [Jean-Paul] Sartre and Hemingway and [Louis-Ferdinand] Celine, all unabsorbed and undigested. I wasn't writing in my own voice at all. I was imitating people." But Richler found his voice soon after, with novels like *Son of a Smaller Hero, A Choice of Enemies,* and *The Incomparable Atuk.* Ramsey found that from these efforts on, "two tendencies dominate Richler's fiction: realism and satire. [Many of the early stories are] realistic, their plots basically traditional in form, their settings accurately detailed, their characters motivated in psychologically familiar ways." At the other extreme, Ramsey continued, there is "pure satiric fantasy, [with] concessions to realism slight. In [such works] Richler indulges the strong comic vein in his writing as he attacks Canadian provincialism and the spurious gratifications of the entertainment medium."

Richler gained further notice with three of his best-known titles, *The Apprenticeship of Duddy Kravitz, St. Urbain's Horseman,* and *Joshua Then and Now.* These books share a common theme—that of a Jewish-Canadian protagonist at odds with society—and all three novels revolve around the idea of the way greed can taint success. *The Apprenticeship of Duddy Kravitz* presents its eponymous hero as a ghetto-reared youth on a never-ending quest to make a name for himself in business. It is also "the first of Richler's novels to exhibit fully his considerable comic talents, a strain that includes much black humor and a racy, colloquial, ironic idiom that becomes a characteristic feature of Richler's subsequent style," according to Ramsey.

Comparing *The Apprenticeship of Duddy Kravitz* to other such modern coming-of-age stories, such as James Joyce's *Portrait of the Artist as a Young Man* and D.H. Lawrence's *Sons and Lovers,* A.R. Bevan, in a new introduction to Richler's novel, found that the book, "in spite of its superficial affinity with the two novels mentioned above, ends with [none of their] affirmation." The character of Duddy, "who has never weighted the consequences of his actions in any but material terms, is less alone in the physical sense than the earlier young men, but he is also much less of a man. . . . He is a modern 'anti-hero' (something like the protagonist in Anthony Burgess's *A Clockwork Orange*) who lives in a largely deterministic world, a world where decisions are not decisions and where choice is not really choice." In *Modern Fiction Studies,* John Ower saw *The Apprenticeship of Duddy Kravitz* as "a 'Jewish' novel [with] both a pungent ethnic flavor and the convincingness that arises when a writer deals with a milieu with which he is completely familiar." For Richler, Ower continued, "the destructive psychological effects of the ghetto mentality are equalled and to some extent paralleled by those of the Jewish family. Like the society from which it springs, this tends to be close and exclusive, clinging together in spite of its intense quarrels. The best aspect of such clannishness, the feeling of kinship which transcends all personal differences, is exemplified by Duddy. Although he is in varying degrees put down and rejected by all of his relatives except his grandfather, Duddy sticks up for them and protects them."

For all its success, *The Apprenticeship of Duddy Kravitz* was still categorized by most scholars as among Richler's early works. By the time *St. Urbain's Horseman* was published in 1971, the author had all but sealed his reputation as a sharp cultural critic. In this work, a character named Jacob Hersh, a Canadian writer living in London, questions "not only how he rose to prominence but also the very nature and quality of success and why, having made it, [he] is dissatisfied," as Ramsey put it. Hersh's success as a writer "brings with it a guilt, a sense of responsibility, and an overwhelming paranoia, a belief that his good fortune is largely undeserved and that sooner or later he will be called to account," Ramsey added. In his guilt-based fantasies, Hersh dreams that he is a figure of vengeance protecting the downtrodden, a character based on the Horseman, a shadowy figure from Hersh's past. "Richler prefaces *St. Urbain's Horseman* with a quotation from [British poet W. H.] Auden which suggests that he does not wish to be read as a mere entertainer, a fanciful farceur," noted David Myers in *Ariel.* "What is there in *Horseman* that would justify us as regarding it as such a[n affirming] flame? Certainly the despair that we find there is serious enough; the world around Jake Hersh is sordid and vile." The author accords sympathy "to only two characters in his novel, Jake and his wife Nancy," Myers said. "They are shown to feel a very deep love for one another and the loyalty of this love under duress provides the ethical counterbalance to the sordidness, instability, lack of integrity, injustice, and grasping materialism that Richler is satirizing in this book."

In the opinion of Kerry McSweeney, writing in *Studies in Canadian Literature,* the novel "gives evidence everywhere of technical maturity and full stylistic control, and combines the subjects, themes and modes of Richler's earlier novels in ways that suggest—as does the high seriousness of its epigraph—that Richler was attempting a cumulative fictional statement of his view on the mores and values of contemporary man. But while *St. Urbain's Horseman* is a solid success on the level of superior fictional entertainment, on the level of serious fiction it must be reckoned a considerable disappointment. It doesn't deliver the goods and simply does not merit the kind of detailed exegesis it has been given by some Canadian critics." Elaborating on this thesis, McSweeney added that everything in the novel "depends on the presentation of Jake, especially of his mental life and the deeper reaches of his character, and on the intensity of the reader's sympathetic involvement with him. Unfortunately, Jake is characterized rather too superficially. One is told, for example, but never shown, that he is charged with contradictions concerning his professional life; and for all the time devoted to what is going on in his head he doesn't really seem to have much of a mental life. Despite the big issues he is said to be struggling with, *St. Urbain's Horseman* can hardly claim serious attention as a novel of ideas."

Robert Fulford offered a different view. In his *Saturday Night* article, Fulford lauded *St. Urbain's Horseman* as "the triumphant and miraculous bringing-together of all those varied Mordecai Richlers who have so densely populated our literary landscape for so many years. From this perspective it becomes clear that all those Richlers have a clear purpose in mind—they've all been waiting out there, working separately, honing their talents, waiting for the moment when they could arrive at the same place and join up in the creation of a magnificent *tour de force,* the best Canadian book in a long time."

The third of Richler's later novels, *Joshua Then and Now,* again explores a Jewish-Canadian's moral crises. Joshua Shapiro, a prominent author married to a gentile daughter of a senator, veers between religious and social classes and withstands family conflicts, especially as they concern his father Reuben. It is also a novel full of mysteries. Why, asked *Village Voice* critic Barry Yourgrau, "does the book open in the present with this 47-year-old Joshua a rumple of fractures in a hospital bed, his name unfairly linked to a scandalous faggotry, his wife doped groggy in a nuthouse and he himself being watched over by his two elderly fathers?" The reason, Yourgrau continued, "is Time. The cruelest of fathers is committing physical violence on Joshua's dearest friends (and crucial enemies)."

Joshua—sometimes shown in flashback as the son of the ever-on-the-make Reuben and his somewhat exhibitionist mother (she performed a striptease at Joshua's bar mitzvah)—"is another one of Richler's Jewish *arrivistes,* like Duddy Kravitz [and] Jacob Hersh," said *New Republic* critic Mark Shechner. After noting Joshua's unrepentant bragging, Shechner called the character "a fairly unpleasant fellow, and indeed, though his exploits are unfailingly vivid and engaging—even fun—they rarely elicit from us much enthusiasm for Joshua himself. He is as callow as he is clever, and, one suspects, Richler means him to be an anti-type, to stand against the more common brands of self-congratulation that are endemic to Jewish fiction. From Sholom Aleichem and his Tevye to [Saul] Bellow and [Bernard] Malamud, . . . Jewish fiction has repeatedly thrown up figures of wisdom and endurance, observance and rectitude. . . . Richler, by contrast, adheres to a tradition of dissent that runs from Isaac Babel's Odessa stories through Daniel Fuchs's *Williamsburg Trilogy* and Budd Schulberg's *What Makes Sammy Run?,* which finds more color, more life, and more fidelity to the facts of Jewish existence in the demimonde of hustlers, heavies, strong-arm types and men on the make than in the heroes of *menschlichkeit,*" which is Yiddish slang for the quality of goodness.

Whatever message *Joshua Then and Now* might deliver, the lasting appeal of the novel, to John Lahr, is that "Richler writes funny. Laughter, not chicken soup, is the real Jewish penicillin. . . . Richler's characters enter as philosophers and exit as stand-up comics, firing zingers as they go," as Lahr explained in a *New York* article. On the other hand, *New York Times Book Review* writer Thomas R. Edwards, while acknowledging the novel's humor, found it "dangerously similar in theme, situation and personnel to a number of Mordecai Richler's other novels—*'Son of a Smaller Hero,' 'The Apprenticeship of Duddy Kravitz,' 'Cocksure'* and *'St. Urbain's Horseman.'* It's as if a rich and unusual body of fictional material had become a kind of prison for a writer who is condemned to repeat himself ever more vehemently and inflexibly." Mark Harris, in *Washington Post Book World,* expressed similar criticism, finding the novel "resplendent with every imaginable failure of characterization, relevance, style or grammar." An *Atlantic* critic, on the other hand, saw the book as "good enough to last, perhaps Richler's best novel to date."

Nine years would pass before Richler published another novel. When he broke the silence in 1989 with *Solomon Gursky Was Here,* several reviewers welcomed the novel as worth the wait, and England's Book Trust honored it with a Commonwealth Writers Prize. The story focuses on Moses Berger, an alcoholic Jewish writer whose life's obsession is to write a biography of the legendary Solomon Gursky. Gursky, of a prominent Jewish-Canadian family of liquor distillers, may have died years ago in a plane crash, but Berger finds numerous clues that suggest he lived on in various guises, a trickster and meddler in international affairs. Jumping forward and backward in time, from events in the Gursky past to its present, Richler "manages to suggest a thousand-page family chronicle in not much more than 400 pages," observed Bruce Cook in Chicago's *Tribune Books.* The critic lauded the novel's humor and rich texture, concluding, "Page for page, there has not been a serious novel for years that can give as much pure pleasure as this one." Acknowledging the inventiveness of Richler's narrative, Francine Prose in *New York Times Book Review* nonetheless found the book somewhat marred by predictable or flat characters. Other critics suggested that there was too much going on in the novel, and for some its humor seemed a bit too black. *Village Voice* writer Joel Yanofsky affirmed the book despite its weaknesses: "If the structure of Richler's story is too elaborate at times, if the narrative loose ends aren't all pulled together, it's a small price to pay for a book this beguiling and rude, this serious, this fat and funny." Jonathan Kirsch, in *Los Angeles Times Book Review,* called it "a worthy addition" to Richler's canon, the work "of a storyteller at the height of his powers."

Richler returned to familiar themes in his final novel, *Barney's Version.* "Once again, we are introduced to a

Jewish Montrealer who leaves behind his hardscrabble roots to achieve fortune and (a modicum of) fame," as Michiko Kakutani described it in *New York Times.* The reader learns about Barney's three marriages, his television company (Totally Useless Productions), and his best friend's mysterious death, which Barney may or may not have caused. "*Barney's Version* is crammed with larger-than-life characters," observed *Times Literary Supplement* contributor D.J. Enright. "There are no relaxed interstices in the narrative: every rift is loaded with ore, not always precious: a case, one may feel, of over-egged cake, or over-gefilte fish." Yet this energy, Enright added, is a significant merit in a novel about a character who is "hard to take." James Shapiro in *New York Times Book Review* found that "What saves this novel from being merely a recycling of Richler's stock material is its fascination with the unreliability of narrative and memory." Barney admits up front that he is prone to embellish a bit to improve the story, and partway through the book we learn that Barney is developing Alzheimer's, which makes it even harder for him to remember how things really happened. "This question of memory's reliability is an unexpected move on Richler's part," Shapiro continued, "in large part because the satiric drift of his fiction ultimately rests on the conviction that it's possible to know what really happened, who was right and who was wrong."

In addition to his adult fiction, Richler also penned a series of popular books for younger readers. *Jacob Two-Two Meets the Hooded Fang* has become something of a children's classic in the author's native Canada, and after a space of ten years Richler produced two sequels: *Jacob Two-Two and the Dinosaur* and *Jacob Two-Two's First Spy Case.* In *Jacob Two-Two and the Dinosaur,* eight-year-old Jacob, who is constantly battling his sibling's barrage of teasing remarks, has moved with his family from England to Montreal. When his parents return from a safari in Kenya, they give Jacob a small green lizard, which they discovered near an ancient block of ice recently dislodged by an earthquake. He dubs his new pet Dippy, and Dippy becomes his best friend. Dippy also becomes larger, having a voracious appetite for food that Jacob can hardly satisfy. It soon becomes clear that Dippy is in fact a diplodocus, one of the larger varieties of vegetarian dinosaurs that inhabited the Earth during the Jurassic period. Jacob and Dippy's adventures truly begin when the Canadian government authorities realize that there is a dinosaur in their midst and attempt to combat it through the usual channels. "The range and bite of this novel's hilarity will come as no surprise to fans of Mordecai Richler's adult fiction," noted *New York Times Book Review* critic Francine Prose, adding that the novel is as entertaining to adults as it is to children. That conclusion was also made by Howard Engel, reviewing Richler's third children's book, *Jacob Two-Two's First Spy Case,* for *Books in Canada.* Engel dubbed Jacob's attempt to outsmart local bully Loathsome Leo Louise and give his private school principal and nasty geography teacher their comeuppance a "wonderfully funny and cunning tale." "It is the trick of the clever writer of children's stories to engage both parent-reader and child-listener in his lines," Engel added. "The humour and the passion of the adventure are snapped up by the one, while the other catches the sly social comment and satire."

Among his nonfiction works, Richler's *Home Sweet Home: My Canadian Album, Oh Canada! Oh Quebec! Requiem for a Divided Country, This Year in Jerusalem,* and *Broadsides: Reviews and Opinions* all drew attention. While these works focus on Richler's native country and his identity as a Canadian, they have distinctly different styles and purposes. *Home Sweet Home,* for example, focuses on Canadian culture, addressing subjects from nationalism to hockey, while in *Oh Canada! Oh Quebec!* Richler turns his considerable intellect and wit to the problem of Quebec separatism, and *This Year in Jerusalem* focuses more personally on Richler's identity as a Canadian Jew—a theme also present in *Oh Canada! Oh Quebec! Broadsides* focuses on both the writing life and modern literature. Richler's interest in early twentieth-century literature, in particular, resulted in his editorship of *Writers on World War II,* a compendium of war writing by some of North America and Europe's most eminent authors.

A Toronto *Globe and Mail* writer called *Home Sweet Home* "a different sort of book, but no less direct and pungent in its observations about what makes a society tick," and in another *Globe and Mail* article, Joy Fielding saw the book as "a cross-country tour like no other, penetrating the Eastern soul, the Western angst, and the French-Canadian spirit." *Home Sweet Home* drew admiring glances from American as well as Canadian critics. Peter Ross, of *Detroit News,* wrote, "Wit and warmth are constants and though Richler can temper his fondness with bursts of uncompromising acerbity, no reader can fail to perceive the depth of his feelings as well as the complexities of Canada." And *Time*'s Stefan Kanfer observed that "even as he celebrates [Canada's] beauties, the author never loses sight of his country's insularity: when Playboy Films wanted to produce adult erotica in Toronto, he reports, officials wanted to know how much Canadian content there would be in the features. But Richler also knows that the very tugs and pulls of opposing cultures give the country its alternately appealing and discordant character."

It is precisely these tugs and pulls of opposing cultures that Richler exposes in *Oh Canada! Oh Quebec!,* a book that set off such a furor among Canadian politicians and press that one Canadian Member of Parliament even called for a banning of the book—to no avail. Anthony Wilson-Smith summed up the controversy in *Maclean's:* "The objection in each case: that Richler's view of Quebec and its nationalist movement is overly harsh and unfair—particularly his assertion that the province's history reflects a deep strain of anti-Semitism." While Richler's earlier works abound with wit and humour, in *Oh Canada! Oh Quebec!,* "his mood . . . hovers much closer to exasperation," wrote Wilson-Smith. Robin W. Winks, writing in *New York Times Book Review,* stated more bluntly: "He is, for the most part, simply angry."

Winks declared that in the book Richler is "concerned, above all, with the Condition of Canada," and called the book "an unsystematic but powerful examination of what Mr. Richler regards as the idiocy of the day"—the legislation and organizations that enforce and oversee the exclusive use of the French language on all public signage in the province of Quebec. But even more compelling is Richler's claim that many of Quebec's leading politicians and intellectuals have been anti-Semitic, and, as Winks reported, that this anti-Semitism is linked to the Quebec separatist movement through the figure of Abbe Lionel-Adolphe Groulx. As Wilson-Smith reported, Richler makes the damaging claim that Groulx's paper, *Le Devoir,* "'more closely resembled *Der Sturmer* [a German Nazi newspaper of the same period] than any other newspaper I can think of.'"

Still, as Wilson-Smith reported, Richler does evince affection for his native province: "'There is nowhere else in the country as interesting, or alive.'" And it is this sentiment—love for his native land and all of the contradictory impulses that make for a Canadian Jew—that haunts *This Year in Jerusalem.* Louis Simpson quotes Richler's account of his hybrid identity in his review of the volume for *New York Times Book Review:* Richler described himself as "'a Canadian, born and bred, brought up not only on Hillel, Rabbi Akiba and Rashi, but also on blizzards, Andrew Allan's CBC Radio "Stage" series, a crazed Maurice Richard skating in over the blue line . . . the Dieppe raid.'"

This Year in Jerusalem is a nonfiction account of a year Richler spent in Israel and is, according to *Maclean's* writer Morton Ritts, "less a study of the character of politics than the politics of character." What makes this a book not just about Israel, but about Canada and Richler as well, is that Richler connects his journey to Israel with his personal heritage as a young Zionist in Canada with a grandfather who was both a rabbi and a "celebrated Hasidic scholar," according to Louis Simpson in *New York Times Book Review: "This Year in Jerusalem* is history made personal."

By telling the tale of the spiritual journey whereby Richler became, in Ritts's words, "more rebel than rebbe (spiritual leader)," by giving his real-life young Zionist companions pseudonyms and tracing their stories over several decades, by talking to Israelis and Palestinians from all walks of life, and by examining, as Ritts also put it, the "trouble between Jew and gentile, French and English, the Orthodox and secular, Arab and Israeli, hawk and dove, Israeli Jew and North American Jew," Richler infuses the book with his novelist's craft. Simpson called *This Year in Jerusalem* "lively reporting" and "interesting," while Ritts claimed that the work showed Richler "at the top of his own game."

Richler's *On Snooker: The Game and the Characters Who Play It,* completed shortly before his death in 2001, is a wide-ranging collection of essays on the game also known as pocket billiards. *Books in Canada* reviewer L.M. Morra appreciated the book's scope and humor, noting that Richler not only chronicles his own youthful exploits in the pool halls of Montreal's shadier neighborhoods, but adds "arch, broad vignettes" about various snooker "characters" and insightful and ironic observations about the game as "an analogy for the act of writing, for the artistry and monumental effort involved in any literary undertaking." Donald Trelford, in the London *Observer,* pointed out that several serious writers, including John Updike and Norman Mailer, have written with similar enthusiasm for sports, and added that the strength of Richler's book is the author's "rich exuberance." A final collection of essays, *Dispatches from the Sporting Life,* contains pieces on a wide range of sports from fishing and ice hockey to bodybuilding and wrestling, and includes descriptions of Richler's encounters with such athletes as Wayne Gretzky, Pete Rose, and Gordie Howe.

"Throughout his career Richler . . . spanned an intriguing gulf," concluded Ramsey in his *Dictionary of Literary Biography* piece. "While ridiculing popular tastes and never catering to popular appeal, he has nevertheless maintained a wide general audience. Though drawing constantly on his own experience, he rejects the writer as personality, wishing instead to find acceptance not because of some personal characteristic or because of the familiarity of his subject matter to a Canadian reading public but because he has something fresh to say about humanity and says it in a well-crafted form, which even with its comic exuberance, stands firmly in the tradition of moral and intellectual fiction."

BIOGRAPHICAL AND CRITICAL SOURCES:

BOOKS

Authors in the News, Volume 1, Thomson Gale (Detroit, MI), 1976.

Children's Literature Review, Volume 17, Thomson Gale (Detroit, MI), 1989.

Contemporary Literary Criticism, Thomson Gale (Detroit, MI), Volume 3, 1975, Volume 5, 1976, Volume 9, 1978, Volume 13, 1980, Volume 18, 1981, Volume 46, 1988, Volume 70, 1992.

Dictionary of Literary Biography, Volume 53: *Canadian Writers since 1960, First Series,* Thomson Gale (Detroit, MI), 1986.

Encyclopedia of World Literature in the Twentieth Century, third edition, St. James Press (Detroit, MI), 1999.

Klinck, Carl F., and others, editors, *Literary History of Canada: Canadian Literature in English,* University of Toronto Press (Toronto, Ontario, Canada), 1965.

New, W. H., *Articulating West,* New Press, 1972.

Northey, Margot, *The Haunted Wilderness: The Gothic and Grotesque in Canadian Fiction,* University of Toronto Press (Toronto, Ontario, Canada), 1976.

Peck, David, editor, *Identities and Issues in Literature,* Salem Press (Pasadena, CA), 1997.

Ramraj, Victor J., *Mordecai Richler,* Twayne (Boston, MA), 1983.

Richler, Mordecai, *The Apprenticeship of Duddy Kravitz,* introduction by A.R. Bevan, McClelland & Stewart (Toronto, Ontario, Canada), 1969.

Richler, Mordecai, *Hunting Tigers under Glass: Essays and Reports,* McClelland & Stewart (Toronto, Ontario, Canada), 1969.

Richler, Mordecai, *Broadsides: Reviews and Opinions,* Viking (New York, NY), 1990.

St. James Guide to Children's Writers, fifth edition, St. James Press (Detroit, MI), 1999.

Sheps, G. David, editor, *Mordecai Richler,* McGraw-Hill/Ryerson, 1971.

Woodcock, George, *Mordecai Richler,* McClelland & Stewart (Toronto, Ontario, Canada), 1970.

PERIODICALS

Antioch Review, winter, 1999, review of *Barney's Version,* p. 104.

Ariel, January, 1973.

Atlantic, July, 1980; May, 1990, p. 132.

Books in Canada, August-September, 1984; August-September, 1987, pp. 35-36; November, 1990, pp. 35-56; January-February, 1991, pp. 18-20; December, 1995, p. 34; September-October, 2001, L.M. Morra, "On Snooker and Writing," pp. 13-14.

Canadian Book Review Annual, 1998, review of *Belling the Cat,* p. 275.

Canadian Children's Literature, Volume 49, 1988, pp. 43-44.

Canadian Forum, January, 1998, review of *Barney's Version,* p. 42.

Canadian Literature, spring, 1973; summer, 1973; winter, 1998, review of *Barney's Version,* p. 188.

Commentary, October, 1980; June, 1990.

Detroit News, July 29, 1984, Peter Ross, review of *Home Sweet Home.*

Entertainment Weekly, January 16, 1998, review of *Barney's Version,* p. 65.

Esquire, August, 1982.

Essays on Canadian Writing, fall, 1998, review of *Barney's Version,* p. 187.

Globe and Mail (Toronto, Ontario, Canada), May 5, 1984; June 24, 1985; June 13, 1987.

Insight on the News, June 25, 1990, pp. 62-63.

Knight-Ridder/Tribune News Service, July 25, 2001, Ron Grossman, "The Us-and-Them Universe of Writer Mordecai Richler," p. K5493.

Los Angeles Times Book Review, August 19, 1984; June 17, 1990, p. 4; January 25, 1998, review of *Barney's Version,* p. 6.

Maclean's, May 7, 1984; November 13, 1989, pp. 64-67; November 26, 1990, pp. 78-79; December 31, 1990, pp. 18-19; December 30, 1991, p. 26; March 30, 1992, pp. 66-67; April 13, 1992, pp. 28-30; September 12, 1994, p. 66.

Modern Fiction Studies, autumn, 1976, John Ower.

Nation, July 5, 1980; June 4, 1990, pp. 785-86, 788-91.

National Review, December 19, 1994, p. 56.

New Criterion, September 2001, volume 20, p. 123.

New Republic, May 18, 1974; June 14, 1980; December 5, 1983; May 7, 1990, pp. 42-44.

Newsweek, June 16, 1980; February 3, 1986.

New York, June 16, 1980; April 16, 1990, pp. 95-96.

New Yorker, January 19, 1998, review of *Barney's Version,* p. 81.

New York Review of Books, July 17, 1980; March 5, 1998, review of *Barney's Version,* p. 40.

New York Times, June 22, 1980; December 16, 1997, Michiko Kakutani, "Incorrigible Rogue Returns with a Wisp of Regret," p. 10.

New York Times Book Review, May 4, 1975; October 5, 1975; June 22, 1980; September 11, 1983; February

5, 1984; June 3, 1984; October 18, 1987; April 8, 1990, p. 7; April 27, 1990, p. 7; May 24, 1992; November 13, 1994, p. 64; May 18, 1997, Jim Gladstone, "Magical Mysteries," p. 29; December 21, 1997, James Shapiro, "The Way He Was—or Was He?," p. 4; May 31, 1998, review of *Barney's Version,* p. 22; December 6, 1998, review of *Barney's Version,* p. 66; March 21, 1999, review of *Barney's Version* and *The Apprenticeship of Duddy Kravitz,* p. 32.

Observer (London, England), November 8, 1998, review of *Barney's Version,* p. 16; October 14, 2001, Donald Trelford, "A Breaking Story."

Publishers Weekly, April 27, 1990, pp. 45-46; August 15, 1994, p. 83.

Queen's Quarterly, summer, 1990, pp. 325-327.

Quill and Quire, September, 1990, p. 62; November, 1995, p. 45; February, 1998, review of *Barney's Version,* p. 41; July, 1998, review of *Belling the Cat,* p. 30; June, 1999, review of *The Apprenticeship of Duddy Kravitz* (audio version), p. 61.

Rapport, April, 1998, review of *Barney's Version,* p. 21.

Saturday Night June, 1971; March, 1974.

Spectator, August 25, 1981; July 25, 1992, pp. 33-34.

Studies in Canadian Literature, summer, 1979, Kerry McSweeney.

Time, June 16, 1980; November 7, 1983; April 30, 1984; May 14, 1990, p. 91.

Times Literary Supplement, April 2, 1976; September 26, 1980; August 3, 1984; December 21, 1984; June 15-21, 1990, p. 653; April 10, 1992, p. 5; September 5, 1997, D.J. Enright, "Larger than Life;" November 30, 2001, Julian Barnes, review of *On Snooker: The Game and the Characters Who Play It,* p. 8.

Tribune Books (Chicago, IL), April 8, 1990, p. 6.

Village Voice, June 2, 1980; May 1, 1984; May 1, 1990, p. 86.

Washington Post, November 9, 1983.

Washington Post Book World, June 29, 1980; May 10, 1987.

World Literature Today, autumn, 1990, pp. 639-40; winter, 1999, review of *Barney's Version,* p. 149.

ONLINE

Canoe, http://www.canoe.ca/ (August 26, 2001), Jerry Gladman, review of *On Snooker.*

National Post Online, http://www.nationalpost.com/ (July 5, 2001), Mark Steyn, "In the Shadow of His Balls."

Random House of Canada Web site, http://www.randomhouse.ca/ (January 6, 2002), "Mordecai Richler."

RÍOS, Alberto 1952-
(Alberto Alvaro Ríos)

PERSONAL: Born September 18, 1952, in Nogales, AZ; son of Alberto Alvaro (a justice of the peace) and Agnes (a nurse; maiden name, Fogg) Ríos; married Maria Guadalupe Barron (a librarian), September 8, 1979; children: Joaquin. *Education:* University of Arizona, B.A. (English literature and creative writing), 1974, B.A. (psychology), 1975, M.F.A., 1979; attended law school at the University of Arizona, 1975-76. *Politics:* "Liberal/Democrat." *Religion:* "Cultural Catholic."

ADDRESSES: Home—3038 N. Pennington Dr., Chandler, AZ 85224. *Office*—Department of English, Arizona State University, Tempe, AZ 85287. *E-mail*—aarios@asu.edu.

CAREER: Arizona Commission on the Arts, Phoenix, artist in Artists-in-Education Program, 1978-83, consultant, 1983—; Arizona State University, Tempe, assistant professor, 1982-85, associate professor, 1985-89, professor, 1989-94, Regents' Professor of English, 1994—, cochair of Hispanic Research and Development Committee, 1983—, director, Creative Writing Program, 1986-89. Counselor and instructor in English and algebra in Med-Start Program at University of Arizona, summers, 1977-80. Writer-in-residence at Central Arizona College, Coolidge, 1980-82. Board of directors, Associated Writing Programs, 1988—, secretary, 1989—; board of directors, Arizona Center for the Book, 1988—, vice chairman, 1989—. Member of National Advisory Committee to the National Artists-in-Education Program, 1980; member of grants review panel, Arizona Commission on the Arts, 1983; member, National Endowment for the Arts Poetry Panel. Judge of New York City High School Poetry Contest. Gives poetry readings, lectures, and workshops.

AWARDS, HONORS: First place in Academy of American Arts poetry contest, 1977, for "A Man Then Suddenly Stops Moving"; writer's fellowship in poetry from the Arizona Commission on the Arts, 1979; fellowship grant in creative writing from National Endowment for the Arts, 1980; Walt Whitman Award from the National Academy of American Poets, 1981, for *Whispering to Fool the Wind;* second place in *New York Times* annual fiction award competition, 1983, for "The Way Spaghetti Feels"; Western States Book Award (fiction), 1984, for *The Iguana Killer;* New Times Fiction Award, 1983; Pushcart Prize for fiction, 1986, and poetry, 1988, 1989; Chicanos Por La Causa Community

Appreciation Award, 1988; National Book Award nominee in poetry category, 2002, for *The Smallest Muscle in the Human Body;* Distinguished Achievement Award, Western Literature Association, 2002.

WRITINGS:

Elk Heads on the Wall (poetry chapbook), Mango Press (San Jose, CA), 1979.
Sleeping on Fists (poetry chapbook), Dooryard Press (Story, WY), 1981.
Whispering to Fool the Wind (poetry), Sheep Meadow (New York, NY), 1982.
The Iguana Killer: Twelve Stories of the Heart, Blue Moon/Confluence (Lewiston, ID), 1984.
Five Indiscretions (poetry), Sheep Meadow (New York, NY), 1985.
The Lime Orchard Woman: Poems, Sheep Meadow (New York, NY), 1988.
The Warrington Poems, Pyracantha Press (Tempe, AZ), 1989.
Teodoro Luna's Two Kisses, Norton (New York, NY), 1990.
Pig Cookies and Other Stories, Chronicle Books (San Francisco, CA), 1995.
The Curtain of Trees: Stories, University of New Mexico Press (Albuquerque, NM), 1999.
Capirotada: A Nogales Memoir, University of New Mexico Press (Albuquerque, NM), 1999.
The Smallest Muscle in the Human Body (poetry), Copper Canyon Press (Port Townsend, WA), 2002.

Contributor of poetry, fiction, and drama to anthologies, including *Southwest: A Contemporary Anthology,* edited by Karl Kopp and Jane Kopp, Red Earth Press, 1977; *Hispanics in the United States: An Anthology of Creative Literature,* edited by Gary D. Keller and Francisco Jimenez, Bilingual Review Press, 1980; *The Norton Anthology of Modern Poetry,* edited by Richard Ellmann, Robert O' Clair, and John Benedict, Norton, 1988; and *American Literature,* Prentice-Hall, 1990. Contributor to periodicals, including *American Poetry Review, Little Magazine, Bloomsbury Review,* and *Paris Review.* Also contributor of translations to *New Kauri* and *Poetry Pilot.* Corresponding editor, *Manoa,* 1989—; editorial board, *New Chicano Writing,* 1990—.

ADAPTATIONS: Ríos's poetry has been set to music in "Toto's Say," by James DeMars, and "Away from Home," EMI.

WORK IN PROGRESS: A novel "about a married couple who move to Arizona from Mexico."

SIDELIGHTS: Alberto Ríos has won acclaim as a writer who uses language in lyrical and unexpected ways in both his poems and short stories, which reflect his Chicano heritage and contain elements of magical realism. "Ríos's poetry is a kind of magical storytelling, and his stories are a kind of magical poetry," commented Jose David Saldivar in the *Dictionary of Literary Biography.* Ríos grew up in a Spanish-speaking family but was forced to speak English in school, leading him to develop a third language, "one that was all our own," as he described it. Ríos once commented, "I have been around other languages all my life, particularly Spanish, and have too often thought of the act of translation as simply giving something two names. But it is not so, not at all. Rather than filling out, a second name for something pushes it forward, forward and backward, and gives it another life."

Saldivar wrote of Ríos, "Many of his important early poems dramatize the essence of this uncanny third language." There are examples of these in the prize-winning collection *Whispering to Fool the Wind,* which contains poems that Mary Logue, writing in the *Voice Literary Supplement,* called "written miracles" that "carry the feel of another world." These poems, she noted, are informed by his upbringing in the border town of Nogales, Arizona, "where one is neither in this country nor the other."

Saldivar explained that Ríos tells stories in verse, something that many writers have been unable to do successfully. Ríos, however, is able to bring to life characters such as a man who dies of anger when a seamstress refuses to give him pins with which to display his butterfly collection. "Throughout *Whispering to Fool the Wind* magical-realist events are related with the greatest of accuracy without being forced on the reader," Saldivar wrote. "It is left up to readers to interpret things for themselves in a way that is most familiar to them."

Saldivar deemed "Nani," about Ríos's grandmother, the best poem in the collection "and one of the most remarkable poems in Chicano literature." It "captures the reality of the invented third language," he said, with lines such as "'To speak, now-foreign words I used to speak, too, dribble down her mouth. . . . By the stove she does something with words and looks at me only with her back.'" Logue also praised the poet's unusual use of language, observing that "Ríos's tongue is both foreign and familiar, but always enchanting."

In *Five Indiscretions,* "most of the poems achieve a level of excellence not far below the peak moments of [Ríos's] earlier poetry," Saldivar asserted. Almost all of these poems deal with romantic and sexual relationships between men and women, with the poet taking both male and female viewpoints. This collection has "regrettably . . . not received the acclaim and attention it deserves," Saldivar opined. "The few book reviews, however, praised his ability to represent gender issues and his use of the American language."

Ríos's award-winning book of short stories, *The Iguana Killer: Twelve Stories of the Heart,* contains tales "explor[ing] the luminous world of his childhood and border culture," Saldivar related. The title story centers on a young Mexican boy who uses a baseball bat to become his country's leading iguana killer. "The Birthday of Mrs. Pineda" is about an oppressed wife who finally gets a chance to speak for herself. This and "The Way Spaghetti Feels" are, in Saldivar's estimate, "the best stories in the book"; he commented that they "border on the metafictional and magical-realist impulse in postmodern fiction."

These characteristics also are evident in the 1995 work *Pig Cookies and Other Stories,* set in a small Mexican town where cookies exhibit supernatural powers and life takes other surprising twists and turns. "The tales in this collection glisten with a magical sheen, at once other-worldly and real," remarked Greg Sanchez in *World Literature Today.* "Ríos takes us from the realm of imagination to the concrete and back again with surprising fluidity." Ríos also creates winning characters, wrote a *Publishers Weekly* reviewer: "These poignant, funny tales of the rich, unsuspected lives of regular folks transcend time and place." In 1999 Ríos published a collection titled *The Curtain of Trees: Stories,* which focuses on residents of small towns along the border of Arizona and Mexico. A *Publishers Weekly* critic stated that the "characters are from another era (circa the 1950s), roaming the unpaved streets of small villages, their lives made vividly real through the author's powerful sensitivity and sharp eye for detail."

Capirotada: A Nogales Memoir, "a monologue that is funny, intimate, and as sweet as a candy placed in your palm by a friend," according to *Booklist* critic GraceAnne A. DeCandido, appeared in 1999. In *Capirotada,* Ríos describes his experiences growing up in Nogales, Arizona, which shared a border with its sister city of Nogales, Mexico. A *Publishers Weekly* reviewer called the work "an extremely personal family history filled with small anecdotes and finely drawn landscapes." In *Library Journal,* Gwen Gregory remarked, "This well-balanced narrative recalls the universal experiences of childhood and unique personal reminiscences of the author."

The Smallest Muscle in the Human Body, a 2002 collection of poems, "focuses squarely on childhood experiences and memories," noted a *Publishers Weekly* reviewer. Poems like "My Chili" and "Chinese Food in the Fifties" celebrate local dining customs, and "Gray Dogs" is one of several poems that contain animal imagery. According to Robert Murray Davis in *World Literature Today,* Ríos "is most successful . . . when, on the one hand, he does not strive too hard for paradox and, on the other, when he does not take refuge in mere nostalgia." The book's title, taken from the poem "Some Extensions on the Sovereignty of Science," refers to the stapedius muscle in the ear, which prevents humans from hearing their own heartbeat. "The muscle does important work I think, but at the same time, it keeps us from something that belongs to us," Ríos told Leslie A. Wootten in *World Literature Today.* "We are protected from particular sounds for our own good. There are many things in life we are protected from hearing, seeing, smelling, tasting, touching, and feeling. In large measure, the poems in this book—and all my books—struggle to bring into view what we've been protected from experiencing. But by this, I mean the small things as well as the large."

Indeed, while Ríos's Chicano heritage informs his writing and while he is one of that culture's important voices, his work "is anything but narrow and exclusive," contended Robert McDowell in an essay for *Contemporary Poets.* Ríos, McDowell said, is dedicated "to finding, declaring, and celebrating the diversity and power of community in the experience of those around him. Thus, his vision is more outward directed, less private than might at first glance be apparent." Saldivar added that "Ríos is surely one of the major vernacular voices in the postmodern age."

BIOGRAPHICAL AND CRITICAL SOURCES:

BOOKS

Contemporary Poets, 7th edition, St. James Press (Detroit, MI), 2001.

Dictionary of Literary Biography, Volume 122: *Chicano Writers, Second Series,* Thomson Gale (Detroit, MI), 1992.

Poetry for Students, Volume 11, Thomson Gale (Detroit, MI), 2001.

PERIODICALS

American Book Review, October, 1993, John Jacob, "Androgyny's Whisper."

Americas Review, fall-winter, 1996, William Barillas, "Words Like the Wind: An Interview with Alberto Ríos," pp. 116-129.

Bloombury Review, January-February, 1996, Leslie A. Wootten, "Writing on the Edge: An Interview with Alberto Alvaro Ríos."

Booklist, October 15, 1999, GraceAnne A. DeCandido, review of *Capirotada: A Nogales Memoir,* p. 411.

Confluencia, fall, 1990, Lupe Cárdenas and Justo Alarcón, "Entrevista: An Interview with Alberto Ríos," p. 119.

Glimmer Train, spring, 1998, Susan McInnis, "Interview with Alberto Ríos," pp. 105-121.

Hayden's Ferry Review, fall-winter, 1992, Deneen Jenks, "The Breathless Patience of Alberto Rios," pp. 115-123.

Library Journal, October 1, 1999, Gwen Gregory, review of *Capirotada,* p. 120.

New York Times Book Review, February 9, 1986; September 17, 1995, p. 25.

Publishers Weekly, March 20, 1995, review of *Pig Cookies and Other Stories,* p. 54; April 26, 1999, review of *The Curtain of Trees,* p. 55; August 30, 1999, review of *Capirotada,* p. 62; April 29, 2002, review of *The Smallest Muscle in the Human Body,* pp. 65-66.

Research, spring-summer, 1997, Sheilah Britton, "Discovering the Alphabet of Life: An Interview with Alberto Ríos," pp. 38-41.

South Carolina Review, fall, 2001, Timothy S. Sedore, "An American Borderer: An Interview with Alberto Ríos," pp. 7-17.

Voice Literary Supplement, October, 1982.

World Literature Today, spring, 1996, Greg Sanchez, review of *Pig Cookies and Other Stories,* p. 415; July-September, 2003, Leslie A. Wootten, "The Edge in the Middle: An Interview with Alberto Ríos," pp. 57-60, and Robert Murray Davis, review of *The Smallest Muscle in the Human Body,* p. 105.

ONLINE

Academy of American Poets Web site, http://www.poets.org/poets/ (July 9, 2004), "Alberto Ríos."

Arizona State University Web Site, http://www.public.asu.edu/˜aarios/ (August 10, 2004), "Alberto Ríos."

* * *

RÍOS, Alberto Alvaro
See RÍOS, Alberto

RIVERS, Elfrida
See BRADLEY, Marion Zimmer

* * *

RIVERSIDE, John
See HEINLEIN, Robert A.

* * *

ROBB, J.D.
See ROBERTS, Nora

* * *

ROBBE-GRILLET, Alain 1922-

PERSONAL: Born August 18, 1922, in Brest, France; son of Gaston (a manufacturer) and Yvonne (Canu) Robbe-Grillet; married Catherine Rstakian, October 23, 1957. *Education:* Institut National Agronomique, ingenieur agronome.

ADDRESSES: Home—18 Boulevard Maillot, 92200 Neuilly-sur-Seine, France. *Office*—Editions de Minuit, 7 rue Bernard-Palissy, 75006 Paris, France. *Agent*—Georges Borchardt, 136 East 57th St., New York, NY 10022.

CAREER: Institut National des Statistiques, Paris, France, charge de mission, 1945-50; engineer with Institut des Fruits et Agrumes Coloniaux, Morocco, French Guinea, Martinique, and Guadeloupe, 1949-51; Editions de Minuit, Paris, France, literary advisor, beginning 1954. Has traveled and lectured in Europe, Asia, and North and South America. Visiting professor, New York University and University of California, Los Angeles. Writer and director of films.

MEMBER: Legion d'Honneur (Officier du Merite, Officier des Arts et Lettres; France).

AWARDS, HONORS: Prix Feneon, 1954, for *Les Gommes;* Prix des Critiques, 1955, for *Le Voyeur;* Prix Louis Delluc, 1963, for *L'Immortelle;* best screenplay, Berlin Festival, 1969, for *L'Homme qui ment;* Premio Internazionale Mondello, 1982, for *Djinn;* elected to Academie Française, 2004.

WRITINGS:

Les Gommes (novel), Editions de Minuit (Paris, France), 1953, translation by Richard Howard published as *The Erasers,* Grove (New York, NY), 1964, new edition edited by J.S. Wood, Prentice-Hall (Englewood Cliffs, NJ), 1970.

Le Voyeur (novel), Editions de Minuit (Paris, France), 1955, translation by Richard Howard published as *The Voyeur,* Grove (New York, NY), 1958, published under original French title, edited and with an introduction by Oreste F. Pucciani, Ginn-Blaisdell (Waltham, MA), 1970.

La Jalousie (novel), Editions de Minuit (Paris, France), 1957, translation by Richard Howard published as *Jealousy* (also see below), Grove (New York, NY), 1959, published as *Jealousy: Rhythmic Themest* (limited edition), pen and ink drawings by Michele Forgeois, Allen Press, 1971, published under original French title, edited by Germaine Bree and Eric Schoenfeld, Macmillan (New York, NY), 1963.

Dans le labyrinthe (novel), Editions de Minuit (Paris, France), 1959, translation by Richard Howard published as *In the Labyrinth* (also see below), Grove (New York, NY), 1960, published as *Dans le labyrinthe* [and] *Dans les couloirs du Metropolitain* [and] *Le Chambre secrete,* with an essay by Gerard Genette, Union Generale d'Editions (Paris, France), 1964.

L'Année dernière à Marienbad: Cine-roman (screenplay), Editions de Minuit (Paris, France), 1961, translation by Richard Howard published as *Last Year at Marienbad,* Grove (New York, NY), 1962, published as *Last Year at Marienbad: A Cine-Novel,* J. Calder (London, England), 1962.

Instantanés (short stories; also see below), Editions de Minuit (Paris, France), 1962, translation by Bruce Morrisette published as *Snapshots,* Grove (New York, NY), 1968, new edition, 1972.

Pour un nouveau roman (essays), Editions de Minuit (Paris, France), 1963, translation by Barbara Wright published as *Snapshots* [and] *Toward a New Novel,* Calder & Boyars (London, England), 1965, translation by Richard Howard published as *For a New Novel: Essays on Fiction,* Grove (New York, NY), 1966.

La Maison de rendez-vous (novel), Editions de Minuit (Paris, France), 1965, translation by Richard Howard published by Grove (New York, NY), 1966, translation by Sheridan Smith published as *The House of Assignation: A Novel,* Calder & Boyars (London, England), 1970.

Two Novels by Robbe-Grillet (contains *Jealousy* and *In the Labyrinth*), introductory essays by Bruce Morrisette and Roland Barthes), translated by Richard Howard, Grove (New York, NY), 1965.

Projet pour le révolution à New York (novel), Editions de Minuit (Paris, France), 1970, translation by Richard Howard published as *Project for a Revolution in New York,* Grove (New York, NY), 1972.

Rêves de jeunes filles, photographs by David Hamilton, Laffont (Paris, France), 1971, translation by Elizabeth Walter published as *Dreams of a Young Girl,* Morrow (New York, NY), 1971, translation by Elizabeth Walter published as *Dreams of Young Girls,* Collins (London, England), 1971.

Les Demoiselles d'Hamilton, photographs by David Hamilton, Laffont (Paris, France), 1972.

Glissements progressifs du plaisir (screenplay; also see below), Editions de Minuit (Paris, France), 1974.

Construction d'un temple en ruines a la déesse Vanadé, etchings by Paul Delvaux, Bateau-Lavoir (Paris, France), 1975.

La Belle captive (novel; also see below), illustrations by René Magritte, Bibliothèque des Arts (Lausanne, France), 1975, reprinted, University of California Press (Berkeley, CA), 1995.

Topologie d'une cité fantôme (novel), Editions de Minuit (Paris, France), 1976, translation by J.A. Underwood published as *Topology of a Phantom City,* Grove (New York, NY), 1976.

Temple aux miroirs, photographs by Irina Ionesco, Seghers (Paris, France), 1977.

Un Régicide (novel), Editions de Minuit (Paris, France), 1978.

Souvenirs du triangle d'or (novel), Editions de Minuit (Paris, France), 1978, translation by J.A. Underwood published as *Recollections of the Golden Triangle,* Calder (London, England), 1984, Grove (New York, NY), 1986.

Djinn: Un trou rouge entre les paves disjoints (novel; also see below), Editions de Minuit (Paris, France), 1981, translation by Yvone Lenard and Walter Wells published as *Djinn,* Grove (New York, NY), 1982.

Generative Literature and Generative Art: New Essays, York Press, 1983.

Le Miroir qui revient (memoir), Editions de Minuit (Paris, France), 1985, translation by Jo Levy published as *Ghosts in the Mirror,* Calder & Boyars (London, England), 1988, Grove (New York, NY), 1989.

Angélique; ou, L'Enchantement, Editions de Minuit (Paris, France), 1988.

Les Derniers jours de Corinthe, Editions de Minuit (Paris, France), 1994.

La Reprise (novel), Editions de Minuit (Paris, France), 2001.

C'est Gradia qui vous appelle (novel), Editions de Minuit (Paris, France), 2002.

SCREENPLAYS

L'Année dernière à Marienbad, Cocinor, 1961.

(And director) *L'Immortelle* (produced by Cocinor, 1963), Editions de Minuit (Paris, France), 1963, translation by A.M. Sheridan Smith published as *The Immortal One,* Calder & Boyars (London, England), 1971.

(And director) *Trans-Europ-Express,* Lux-C.C.F., 1966.

(And director) *L'Homme qui ment,* Lux-C.C.F., 1968.

L'Eden et après, Plan Films, 1970, adapted for French television and produced as *N'a pris les des,* Channel 3, 1975.

(And director) *Glissements progressifs du plaisir,* Fox, 1974.

(And director) *Le Jeu avec le feu,* U.G.C., 1975.

(And director) *La Belle captive,* Argos Films, 1983.

(With others) *Tax andria,* Iblis, 1996.

OTHER

The Erotic Dream Machine (interview with Alain Robbe-Gillet on his films), Southern Illinois University Press (Carbondale, IL), 2003.

Also author of *Traces suspectes en surfaces,* lithographs by Robert Rauschenberg. Contributor to books, including *Le Rendez-vous* (textbook; includes *Djinn*), Holt (New York, NY), 1981; *George Segal: Invasion Blanche,* Galerie Beaubourg, 1990; and *Mark Tansey,* Los Angeles County Museum of Art, Chronicle Books, 1993. Contributor to periodicals, including *L'Express, Evergreen Review, New Statesman, Nouvelle Revue Française, Critique* (Paris, France), and *Revue de Paris.*

SIDELIGHTS: The name Alain Robbe-Grillet is tied to the French avant-garde literary form known as the *nouveau roman,* or the New Novel, which he helped propagate. This is a mode characterized by the deconstruction of narrative authority, metafictional techniques, and *chosisme,* the last a literary technique by which objects or actions are described to meticulous length. As the acknowledged leader and spokesman of the New Novelists in France, Robbe-Grillet has denounced those who talk of the novelist's social responsibility; for him the novel is not a tool and probably has little effect on society. "For us," he once wrote, "literature is not a means of expression, but a search. And it does not even know for what it searches. . . . [But] we prefer our searches, our doubts, our contradictions, our joy of having yet invented something." The New Novelists under Robbe-Grillet's leadership introduced new, experimental concepts into the French novel. Occasionally described as "the school of sight" or "the pen camera," the form of writing Robbe-Grillet expounds concentrates on vision and gives minute descriptions of matter-of-fact objects.

For Robbe-Grillet and his school, phenomenology replaced traditional psychology; personality was rendered indefinable and fluid; and objective description became the primary goal. Moral judgments are avoided: "The world is neither significant nor absurd," said Robbe-Grillet. "It simply is." Furthermore, "our concept of the world around us is now only fragmentary, temporary, contradictory even, and always disputable. How can a work of art presume to illustrate a preordained concept, whatever it might be?" Robbe-Grillet's preoccupation with inanimate objects has led critics, notably François Mauriac, to suggest that the author dehumanizes literature. Moreover, confusion for many readers results from the lack of distinction between a seen object and one that is imagined; reality for Robbe-Grillet is always flowing from one state to another. Descriptions are repeated with slight variations, leading to charges of obscurity and tedium.

At university Robbe-Grillet studied agriculture, focusing his energy on studying the diseases of banana trees in the tropics. He brought this same sense of scientific detachment to his first widely read novel, the thriller homage *Les Gommes.* The book, according to an essay by H.A. Wylie in the *Bucknell Review,* "studies one man's attempt to penetrate misleading appearances and circumstances in order to arrive at a true understanding of a relatively simple situation." Indeed, the third-person narrator of *Les Gommes* and the author's other early novels suggests "a unified source of information," which "becomes the theoretical basis for an image of the world; the voice seems to speak in absolutes," as George H. Szanto wrote in *Narrative Consciousness: Structure and Perception in the Fiction of Kafka, Beckett, and Robbe-Grillet.* The story opens in a provincial café, where the proprietor "is preparing mechanically for the day and ruminating on the murder the previous evening of a neighbor, Daniel Dupont" as John Fletcher described it in the *Dictionary of Literary Biography.* Meanwhile, a customer named Garinati asks about Wallas, a lodger of the café owner; as it turns out, Garinati is an assassin who killed Dupont. Or did he? Garinati "fired one shot at Dupont," Fletcher noted, "but missed, wounding his victim only slightly. But he does not know that Dupont has survived: the morning papers carry the news that Dupont died from several shots" to mislead the shooter and track him down. Wallas's place in the story becomes clearer when a revolver of his is discovered at the crime scene. In Fletcher's view, *Les Gommes* is "shaped like an ancient tragedy, with a prologue, five chapters like acts in a play, and an epilogue."

Le Voyeur, Robbe-Grillet's follow-up novel, is set in the Breton coastal region of France, where the author had spent part of his childhood. The book centers on Mathias, a traveling watch salesman who finds himself unaccountably attracted to a teenage girl of questionable moral behavior. The girl, Jacqueline, reminds Mathias of his youthful infatuation for a girl named Violette—significant, said Fletcher, because the French word for rape is *viol.* Jacqueline disappears; her battered body washes ashore the next day. "The reader quickly notices that something in the story has been left out," Fletcher commented. "Mathias's schedule has a gap in it, a period of time . . . which is not accounted for in the otherwise detailed exposition of his activities." Mathias is nearly clinically removed from awareness of his own actions; as Szanto described it, the character has an "inability to differentiate between 'real' and 'imaginary' events." Indeed, "the time during which Mathias kills Jacqueline is a blank both in the book and in Mathias's mind," Szanto wrote. "The latter position must be assumed by the reader for him to realize the existence of this empty space."

Of the early Robbe-Grillet novels, *La Jalousie* is regarded by many critics as one of the writer's more important efforts. Set on a tropical banana plantation—hearkening to the author's early vocation—the book involves an untrusting husband who spies on his wife, referred to as A, in an effort to confirm his suspicion that she is having an affair with a neighboring man. The French word "jalousie" means both jealousy and slatted shutters, a double reference that alludes to the blinds through with the husband peers. Again the characters remain connected to, yet distant from, their actions. In the tradition of *chosisme, La Jalousie,* noted Ben Stoltzfus in a *Symposium* essay, "confines itself for the most part to situating, describing and defining objects and events in space." Fletcher pointed to a scene in which the obsessed husband watches his wife and her lover, Franck, together; Franck is killing a centipede as A watches, "herself scrutinized for her reactions by the jealous narrator, is paralleled later in a passage in which the solitary husband imagines Franck killing another insect in a hotel room he has rented with A. The analogy between the episodes—the one described and the one imagined—is assisted by another double meaning in French: the word *serviette* can mean both table napkin and hand towel." Franck has used a napkin to crush the centipede; the insect's bloody residue on the wall drives the husband to ponder sexual relations between his wife and her lover. The husband's descent in perversity, added Fletcher, is what makes *La Jalousie* "a tour de force as a psychological novel."

The 1959 novel *Dans le labyrinthe* completes the quartet of early Robbe-Grillet novels that helped define the author's style. Again a detached narrative voice calls the action in this story of a "fever-wracked solider . . . who wanders hopelessly in search of somebody's father," as Szanto described it in *Narrative Consciousness.* The unfortunate protagonist becomes "trapped in the labyrinth of history, war, mythology, language." Szanto added, "He becomes lost in a maze of familiar things which he expects to mean something, but which in fact are disorienting, as the author-protagonist explores one street after another, one dead-end after the next, opens doors that lead nowhere, ascends, descends staircases that, as in a Kafka novel, will never lead him to the place where he is supposed to meet the father."

In an entry for the book *Novel and Film: Essays in Two Genres,* Bruce Morrisette saw an element of game-playing in Robbe-Grillet's early novels. Beginning with *Les Gommes,* he suggested, the author "employs myth as hidden structure and establishes ingenious correspondences between myth and the semioccult 'game' of tarot cards." And "while there are no outright or hidden references to games" in *Le Voyeur* and *La Jalousie,* Morrisette noted, "both novels show serial patternings with analogies to the general conception of game structure." But it is with *Dans le labyrinthe* that Robbe-Grillet "offers, for the first but not the last time. . . , outright analogies with those board games that depend for their effect on multiple attempts, with advances and retreats, with side excursions into dead ends, with repeated efforts to find the 'right' path to the center and win the game." In Morrisette's view, even the novel's title "invites the comparison, and the paragraphs of the text often give the effect of a throw of the dice permitting no movement . . . or of frantic turnings from right to left."

La Belle captive, according to Albert Mobilio in the *Voice Literary Supplement,* is "a great place to sample [Robbe-Grillet's] clinical lyricism." The surreal novel, with seventy-seven reproductions of paintings by René Magritte interspersed, involves a dream narrative with disjointed unconscious imagery inspired by Magritte."*La Belle captive* offers a deviant eroticism," wrote Lynne Diamond-Nigh in *American Book Review.* "The heretofore dominant mode of novelistic presentation, realism, also gives way to a proliferating, intermeshing, and digressive narrative that owes more to its Other, the romance, than to the novel." "There's a good deal of voyeuristic, not to mention fetishistic back-and-forth involved," Chicago *Tribune Books* contributor Nicholas Delbanco observed. "Stones and roses, mirrors and mermaids recur. . . . What we have are dream sequences, cross-cuts and riddles, the stuff of fantasy, not fictive fact."

Recollections of the Golden Triangle, set in a South American city, describes a sex cult whose male adherents rape and sacrifice adolescent girls. The novel, characterized by "misogyny, paranoia, hallucination and vampirism" according to a *Publishers Weekly* reviewer, is alternately narrated in first and third person, including the voice of a deranged medical doctor who participates in the sadistic killings. The non-linear plot juxtaposes events in the labyrinthine corridors of an opera house, jail, and private club, while various minutely described objects related to the murders allude to the geometric shape of the triangle. "All of this is in the most literal sense a pretext for one of Mr. Robbe-Grillet's most brilliant and hypnotic textual games," said *New York Times Book Review* contributor William W. Stowe.

In *Ghosts in the Mirror,* the first volume of a projected three volume autobiographic series, Robbe-Grillet recounts childhood experiences in Paris and Brest, including affectionate portrayals of his parents, and offers insight into his artistic sensibilities. Michael Wood stated in *New Statesman & Society,* Robbe-Grillet "does collect details, miniatures, miscellaneous objects, does long for the order which will result from their classification. . . . He wants us to see the monsters and the ghosts which lurk in the ascetic landscape of his novels and films." Commenting on Roland Barthes, Albert Camus, and Jean-Paul Sartre, Robbe-Grillet defends his art while eschewing ideology and Truth. "Truth," he wrote, "in the final analysis, has only ever served oppression." Paul West concluded in the *New York Times Book Review* that "Robbe-Grillet reminds us that language, that uniquely human thing, is subjective to begin with and can never with authority reveal the nature of anything."

In 2001 Robbe-Grillet, at age eighty, published *La Reprise,* his first novel since 1981's *Djinn.* Set in postwar Berlin, the book follows "the increasingly disorienting report of an [aging]spy," as *New Statesman* reviewer Gerry Feehily put it. The main character, Henri, is assigned to investigate mysterious happenings in the Soviet-controlled sector of Berlin. He witnesses a murder and finds incriminating evidence against a former Third Reich officer on the body, but the corpse vanishes before Henri can file his report. His search of Berlin takes Henri on a voyage of memory to his youth. "As the title suggests," Feehily added, *Le Reprise* "is a return of sorts, not only of the addled spy to his lost origins, but also of Robbe-Grillet to the themes and motifs of his early masterpiece."

Robbe-Grillet's style has been to a great extent borrowed from the cinema; indeed, his book-turned-film *Last Year at Marienbad* is considered a classic. According to critic Peter Cortland this style "concentrates on distorted visual images because it is representing mental life, which is of necessity different from the physical 'life,' or arrangement, of things in the material world." John Weightman believed Robbe-Grillet wants his books to have "the solidity and independent existence of a statue or a picture, which resists any anecdotal or intellectual summary." As Robbe-Grillet once noted: "It seems that the conventions of photography (its two-dimensional character, black and white coloring, the limitations of the frame, the differences in scale according to the type of shot) help to free us from our own conventions."

In a retrospective essay published in *Three Decades of the French New Novel,* Robbe-Grillet pointed out of his favored literary form that in its maturity the word "nouveau" is "somewhat comical. It is comical, however, in a way which, all in all, suits me rather well and, aside from the fact that the New Novel has continually renewed itself . . . , it may be said that its novelty remains intact since the revolution which it started in the 1950s never really materialized. Contrary to what I naively hoped as a young man, all of literature was not really turned upside down by the Nouveau Roman and, here again, I am interested in knowing why." Even in his later years, said Fletcher in the *Dictionary of Literary Biography* entry, Robbe-Grillet remains a literary figurehead, "in spite of the fact that he has become . . . something of a globe-trotting guru, a frequent presence at conferences and colloquia where his work and that of the other New Novelists is discussed. In his early career, he had virtually the whole of the French literary establishment against him; now, . . . he has become a prominent member of that establishment. He is thus no longer the revitalizing force in contemporary French writing that he was in the 1950s. The time is perhaps ripe for a new Robbe-Grillet to appear on the French literary scene: one who will oppose his hegemony with all the zestful vigor which Robbe-Grillet himself deployed against the cultural leaders of his own generation."

BIOGRAPHICAL AND CRITICAL SOURCES:

BOOKS

Contemporary Literary Criticism, Thomson Gale (Detroit, MI), Volume 1, 1973, Volume 2, 1974, Volume 4, 1975, Volume 6, 1976, Volume 8, 1978, Volume 10, 1979, Volume 14, 1980, Volume 43, 1987, Volume 128, 2000.

Cruickshank, John, editor, *The Novelist As Philosopher,* Oxford University Press (New York, NY), 1962.

Dictionary of Literary Biography, Volume 83: *French Novelists since 1960,* Thomson Gale (Detroit, MI), 1989.

Fragola, Anthony N., *The Erotic Dream Machine, Interviews with Alain Robbe-Grillet on His Films,* Southern Illinois University Press (Carbondale, IL), 1992.

Le Sage, Laurent, *The French New Novel,* Pennsylvania State University Press, 1962.

Mauriac, Claude, *The New Literature,* Braziller (New York, NY), 1959.

Milman, Yoseph, *Opacity in the Writings of Robbe-Grillet, Pinter, and Zach: A Study in the Poetics of Absurd Literature,* E. Mellen Press (Lewiston, NY), 1991.

Moore, Henry T., *French Literature since World War II,* Southern Illinois University Press (Carbondale, IL), 1966.

Morrisette, Bruce, *Novel and Film: Essays in Two Genres,* University of Chicago Press (Chicago, IL), 1985.

Nelson, Roy Jay, *Causality and Narrative in French Fiction from Zola to Robbe-Grillet,* Ohio State University Press (Columbus, OH), 1990.

Oppenheim, Lois, editor, *Three Decades of the French New Novel,* University of Illinois Press (Champaign, IL), 1986.

Peyre, Henri, *French Novelists of Today,* Oxford University Press (New York, NY), 1967.

Ramsay, Raylene L., *Robbe-Grillet and Modernity: Science, Sexuality, and Subversion,* University Press of Florida, 1992.

Ramsay, Raylene L., *The French New Autobiographies: Sarraute, Duras, and Robbe-Grillet,* University Press of Florida, 1996.

Robbe-Grillet, Alain, *Ghosts in the Mirror,* Grove (New York, NY), 1989.

Roland, Lillian D., *Women in Robbe-Grillet: A Study in Thematics and Diegetics,* P. Lang (New York, NY), 1993.

Stoltzfus, Ben Frank, *Alain Robbe-Grillet and the New French Novel,* Southern Illinois University Press (Carbondale, IL), 1961.

Sturrock, I., *The French New Novel,* Oxford University Press (New York, NY), 1969.

Szanto, George H., *Narrative Consciousness: Structure and Perception in the Fiction of Kafka, Beckett, and Robbe-Grillet,* University of Texas Press (Austin, TX), 1972.

Troiano, Maureen DiLonardo, *New Physics and the Modern French Novel: An Investigation of Interdisciplinary Discourse,* P. Lang (New York, NY), 1995.

Twentieth-Century Crime and Mystery Writers, third edition, St. James Press (Detroit, MI), 1991.

Twentieth-Century Culture: French Culture, 1900-1975, Thomson Gale (Detroit, MI), 1995.

PERIODICALS

American Book Review, May, 1996, Lynne Diamond-Nigh, review of *La Belle captive,* p. 13.

Bucknell Review, Volume 15, number 2, 1967, H.A. Wylie, "Alain Robbe-Grillet: Scientific Humanist," pp. 1-9.

Burlington, May, 1998, review of *La Belle captive,* p. 343.

Critique (Paris, France), August, 1954; September-October, 1955; July, 1959.

Critique, winter, 1963-64.

Evergreen Review, Volume 2, number 5, 1956; Volume 3, number 10, 1959.

Film Quarterly, fall, 1963.

French Review, February, 1998, review of *La Belle captive,* p. 488; March, 1999, review of *La Belle captive,* p. 709.

Hudson Review, winter, 1972-73.

Library Journal, October 1, 1986, p. 111.

Listener, February 15, 1968.

Modern Language Notes, May, 1962; May, 1963.

Modern Language Quarterly, September, 1962.

Nation, April 25, 1959.

New Statesman, January 21, 2002, Gerry Feehily, "Oedipus Wrecks," p. 43.

New Statesman & Society, February 17, 1961.

New York Review of Books, June 1, 1972.

New York Times Book Review, November 22, 1959; May 28, 1972; September 28, 1986, William W. Stowe, review of *Recollections of the Golden Triangle,* p. 26; January 27, 1991, p. 24.

Nouvelle Revue Française, November, 1960.

PMLA, September, 1962.

Publishers Weekly, August 29, 1986, review of *Recollections of the Golden Triangle,* p. 390; January 4, 1991, p. 66; February 6, 1995, p. 78.

Review of Contemporary Fiction, fall, 1999, Juan Goytisolo, "Literature Pursued by Politics," p. 38.

Spectator, December 16, 1960.

Symposium, winter, 1976, Ben Stoltzfus, "Alain Robbe-Grillet: The Reflexive Novel as Process and Poetry," pp. 343-357.

Temps Modernes, June, 1957; July, 1960.

Time, July 20, 1962.

Times Literary Supplement, March 12, 1999, review of *Jealousy,* p. 33.

Tribune Books (Chicago, IL), June 4, 1995, Nicholas Delbanco, review of *La Belle captive,* p. 6.
Vogue, January 1, 1963.
Voice Literary Supplement, April, 1995, Albert Mobilio, review of *La Belle captive.*
Wisconsin Studies in Contemporary Literature, Volume 1, number 3, 1960.
World Literature Today, spring, 2002, Betsy Gwyn, review of *Le Reprise,* p. 178.
Yale French Studies, summer, 1959.

* * *

ROBBINS, Thomas Eugene
See ROBBINS, Tom

* * *

ROBBINS, Tom 1936-
(Thomas Eugene Robbins)

PERSONAL: Born 1936, in Blowing Rock, NC; son of George T. and Katherine (Robinson) Robbins; married third wife, Alexa D'Avalon; children: (from previous relationships) Rip and Fleetwood Starr (sons). *Education:* Attended Washington and Lee University, 1950-52, Richmond Professional Institute (now Virginia Commonwealth University), and University of Washington.

ADDRESSES: *Home*—Box 338, LaConner, WA 98257. *Agent*—Phoebe Larmore, 228 Main St., Venice, CA 90291.

CAREER: Writer. *Richmond Times-Dispatch,* Richmond, VA, copy editor, 1960-62; *Seattle Times* and *Seattle Post-Intelligencer,* Seattle, WA, copy editor, 1962-63; *Seattle Magazine,* Seattle, reviewer and art critic, 1964-68. Conducted research in New York City's East Village for an unwritten book on Jackson Pollock. *Military service:* U.S. Air Force; served in Korea.

WRITINGS:

Guy Anderson (biography), Gear Works Press, 1965.
Another Roadside Attraction (novel), Doubleday (New York, NY), 1971.
Even Cowgirls Get the Blues (novel), Houghton Mifflin (Boston, MA), 1976.
Still Life with Woodpecker (novel), Bantam (New York, NY), 1980.
Jitterbug Perfume (novel), Bantam (New York, NY), 1984.
Skinny Legs and All (novel), Bantam (New York, NY), 1990.
Half Asleep in Frog Pajamas (novel), Bantam (New York, NY), 1994.
Fierce Invalids Home from Hot Climates (novel), Bantam (New York, NY), 2000.
Villa Incognito, Bantam (New York, NY), 2003.

Contributed liner notes to *Tower of Song: The Songs of Leonard Cohen* (CD), 1995.

ADAPTATIONS: *Even Cowgirls Get the Blues* was adapted for film by Gus Van Sant and released by Fine Line Features, 1994.

SIDELIGHTS: For all his influence on the West Coast literary scene, Tom Robbins told the *New York Times* in 1993 that his relatively small output of novels (seven in a span of approximately thirty years) is based on the fact that "I try never to leave a sentence until it's as perfect as I can make it. So there isn't a word in any of my books that hasn't been gone over 40 times." Indeed, this attention to verbal effect has earned Robbins significant acclaim, even among critics who find fault with the off-beat humor, plotting, and philosophizing that have made his novels best-sellers.

Robbins began his career as a journalist, writing music and art reviews for newspapers in Richmond, Virginia, and Seattle. He moved to the Pacific Northwest to escape the cultural conservatism of the South and a family he described, in a *BookPage* interview, as "kind of a Southern Baptist version of The Simpsons." He wholeheartedly embraced the 1960s-era experimentation he found on the West Coast, and allegedly was inspired to try his hand at fiction after using LSD, which he once told a reporter for *Rolling Stone* was the most rewarding experience of his life. His first novel, *Another Roadside Attraction,* appeared in 1971, but sold poorly until it was issued in paperback; when college students discovered this novel about the mummified corpse of Jesus stolen from the Vatican and displayed in an American roadside zoo, they were hooked. Robbins became "the biggest thing to hit the 'youth market' in years," according to *New York Times Magazine* reporter Mitchell S. Ross. Robbins' popularity among young readers, most critics agree, can be attributed to the fact that his novels encompass the counter-cultural "California" or

"West Coast" school of writing, whose practitioners also include the likes of Ken Kesey and Richard Brautigan. In the words of R.H. Miller, writing in the *Dictionary of Literary Biography Yearbook,* the West Coast school emphasizes "the themes of personal freedom, the pursuit of higher states of being through Eastern mysticism, the escape from the confining life of urban California to the openness of the pastoral Pacific Northwest. Like the writings of his mentors, Robbins' own novels exhibit an elaborate style, a delight in words for their own sake, and an open, at times anarchical, attitude toward strict narrative form."

All of these qualities are evident in the author's first novel, *Another Roadside Attraction.* In this story, a collection of eccentrics with names like Plucky Purcell and Marx Marvelous become involved with the mummified body of Jesus Christ, which somehow ends up at the Capt. Kendrick Memorial Hot Dog Wildlife Preserve, formerly Mom's Little Dixie Diner. As Ross saw it, the novel's plot "is secondary to the characters and tertiary to the style. [These characters] are nothing like your next-door neighbors, even if you lived in Haight-Ashbury in the middle '60s." Jerome Klinkowitz, digging deeper into the novel's meaning, declared in his book, *The Practice of Fiction in America: Writers from Hawthorne to the Present,* that in *Another Roadside Attraction,* Robbins "feels that the excessive rationalization of Western culture since [seventeenth-century philosopher Rene] Descartes has severed man from his roots in nature. Organized religion has in like manner become more of a tool of logic and control than of spirit. Robbins' heroine, Amanda, would reconnect mankind with the benign chaos of the natural world, substituting magic for logic, style for substance, and poetry for the analytical measure of authority." Klinkowitz also found that the author is "a master of plain American speech . . . and his greatest trick is to use its flat style to defuse the most sacred objects."

Robbins followed *Another Roadside Attraction* with what would become, perhaps, his best-known novel. In *Even Cowgirls Get the Blues,* the author "shows the same zest of his earlier book, but the plot is focused and disciplined, mostly because Robbins had learned by this time to use the structure of the journey as a major organizing principle in the narrative," according to Miller. This tale concerns one Sissy Hankshaw, an extraordinary hitchhiker due mainly to the fact that she was born with oversized thumbs. One of her rides takes her to the Rubber Rose Ranch, run by Bonanza Jellybean and her cowgirls, "whom Sissy joins in an attempt to find freedom from herself, as she participates in their communal search for that same freedom," Miller related. "They yearn for an open, sexual, unchauvinistic world, much like that of the Chink, a wizened hermit who lives near the ranch and who has absorbed his philosophy of living from the Clock people, a tribe of Indians, and from Eastern philosophy."

Again, plot takes a backseat to the intellectual forces that drive the characters. To *Nation* critic Ann Cameron, *Even Cowgirls Get the Blues* showed "a brilliant affirmation of private visions and private wishes and the power to transform life and death. A tall tale and a parable of essential humanness, it is a work of extraordinary playfulness, style and wit." In his study, *Tom Robbins,* author Mark Siegel saw two "major paradoxes in [the author's ideas]. One is the emphasis he places on individual fulfillment while he simultaneously castigates egotism. The second is his apparent devotion to Eastern philosophies in *Another Roadside Attraction.* . . . Actually the two issues are closely related, both stemming from Robbins's notion that any truly fulfilling way of life must evolve from the individual's recognition of his true, personal relationship to the world."

"Robbins has an old trunk of a mind," said Thomas LeClair in a *New York Times Book Review* piece on *Cowgirls.* "[He] knows the atmosphere on Venus, cow diseases, hitchhiking manuals, herbs, the brain's circuitry, whooping cranes, circles, parades, Nisei internment," adding that these visions "add up to a primitivism just pragmatic enough to be attractive and fanciful enough to measure the straight society." In Ross's opinion, the author's style "generates its own head of steam and dances past the plot, characters and clockwork philosophy."

Paradoxical elements have become one of Robbins' literary trademarks. As he put it in a *January Magazine* interview in 2000, "Reality is contradictory. And it's paradoxical. . . . If you had to pick one word to describe the nature of the universe—I think that word would be paradox. That's true at the subatomic level, right through sociological, psychological, philosophical levels on up to cosmic levels." Such a view, Robbins pointed out, prompts a comic approach to life—though not one that suggests that life "is trivial or frivolous. Quite the contrary. There's nothing the least bit frivolous about the playful nature of the universe. Playfulness at a fully conscious level is extremely profound. . . . Wit and playfulness are a desperately serious transcendence of evil."

While many critics acknowledged the exhilarating effects of Robbins' literary playfulness, some objected to its overuse. As Ross put it in his review of *Cowgirls,* "a piling on of wisecracks is made to substitute for description." This penchant for wisecracking represented a sore point for some critics in Robbins' next novel, *Still Life with Woodpecker. Saturday Review* writer Julie B. Peters stated that in this tale of a princess's romance with an outlaw, the prose "is marbled with limping puns heavily splattered with recurrent motifs and a boyish zeal for the scatological." Taking a similar tack, *Commonweal* critic Frank McConnell pointed out that "a large part of the problem in reading Robbins [is that] he's so *cute:* his books are full of cute lines populated by unrelentingly cute people, even teeming with cute animals—frogs, chipmunks and chihuahuas in *Still Life with Woodpecker.* No one ever gets hurt very badly. . . . And although the world is threatened by the same dark, soulless business cartels that threaten the worlds of [Thomas] Pynchon, [Norman] Mailer, and our century, in Robbins it doesn't seem, finally, to matter. Love or something like it really does conquer all in his parables, with a mixture of stoned gaiety, positive thinking, and Sunday Supplement Taoism."

In telling the story of the unusual relationship between Princess Leigh-Cheri, heiress of the Pacific island of Mu, and good-hearted terrorist Bernard Micky Wrangle, alias Woodpecker, the author frames the tale by a monologue "having to do with his [Robbins'] efforts to type out his narrative on a Remington SL-3 typewriter, which at the end fails him, and he has to complete the novel in longhand," wrote Miller. The reviewer also found that the moral of *Still Life with Woodpecker* "is not as strong as that of the earlier two [novels], and while the plot seems more intricately interlaced, it has the complexity and exoticism of grand opera but little of its brilliance."

The generally disappointed reaction of critics to *Still Life with Woodpecker* left some of them wondering whether Robbins, with his free-form style, was keeping in touch with the needs of fiction readers in the upwardly mobile 1980s. The author addressed his critics' reservations with *Jitterbug Perfume,* published in 1984. In this novel, Seattle waitress Priscilla devotes her life to inventing the ultimate perfume. The challenge is taken up in locales as varied as New Orleans and Paris, while back in Seattle, Wiggs Dannyboy, described by *Washington Post Book World* reviewer Rudy Rucker as "a Timothy Leary work-alike who's given up acid for immortality research," enters the scene to provide insights on the 1960s.

Comparing *Jitterbug Perfume* to the author's other works, Rucker noted that the first two novels were sixties creations—"filled with mushrooms and visions, radicals and police. *Still Life with Woodpecker* is about the '70s viewed as the aftermath of the '60s." And in *Jitterbug Perfume,* "Robbins is still very much his old Pan-worshiping self, yet his new book is lovingly plotted, with every conceivable loose end nailed down tight. Although the ideas are the same as ever, the form is contemporary, new-realistic craftsmanship. Robbins toys with the 1980s' peculiar love/hate for the 60s through his invention of the character Wiggs Dannyboy." To John House, the work "is not so much a novel as an inspirational fable, full of Hallmark sweetness, good examples and hope springing eternal." House, in a *New York Times Book Review* article, went on to say that he found Robbins' style "unmistakable—oblique, florid, willing to sacrifice everything for an old joke or corny pun." While *Jitterbug Perfume* "is still less exuberant than 'Cowgirls,'" according to Don Strachan in the *Los Angeles Times Book Review,* the former is still "less diminished than honed. The author may still occasionally stick his foot in the door of his mouth, as he would say in one of those metaphors he loves to mix with wordplay salads, but then he'll unfurl a phrase that will bring your critical mind to its knees."

Robbins greeted a new decade with a new novel. *Skinny Legs and All* takes on the 1990s big issues with the author's sixties verve. Critic Joe Queenan commented in the *New York Times Book Review* that the novel "makes you want to dust off all those old Firesign Theater records and don those frayed, tie-dyed bell bottoms one last time." The story centers on Ellen Cherry Charles, waitress and would-be artist. She moves to New York City with her downscale husband, Boomer, hoping to break into the art world. It is Boomer, however, with his primitive trailer-art and homegrown wisdom ("If God didn't prefer for us to drink at night, he wouldn't have made neon"), who becomes the intelligentsia's darling. Along the way the reader meets overly enthusiastic evangelist Buddy Winkler, the Arab-and-Jewish restaurant partners Abu and Spike, the world's most erotic belly-dancer, and a set of inanimate objects (spoon, sock, can of baked beans) that, thanks to reincarnation, suddenly become very animated.

Queenan found all this funny—up to a point. Robbins is at his best, Queenan opined, "when he is being snide, witty or downright juvenile. . . . But when [he] gets on his high horse, the results are pure bunkum." Charles Dickinson offered a similar opinion. "Robbins is fed up with a lot of the things about this world and the people in it," noted the *Chicago Tribune* critic. "In fact, there are times when it seems the only reason Robbins wrote this novel was to provide a framework for the delineation of his complaints; and that is the sole—but not unimportant—weakness in this book."

"I'm asking you to consider that hyper intelligent entities—agents of the overmind; aliens, if you will—could be abducting our frogs as part of a benign scheme to free us from the tyranny of the historical continuum and reunite our souls with the other-dimensional." That's just one of the propositions Robbins puts forth in his 1994 novel, *Half Asleep in Frog Pajamas.* The story, written in the second-person, ostensibly covers four days in the life of Seattle stockbroker Gwen Mati—but as usual in a Robbins book, the plot serves only as a framework to parade such characters as Gwen's friend Q-Jo, a 300-lb. psychic; lecherous businessman Larry Diamond, just back from a sabbatical in Timbuktu (and author of the aliens/frogs theory); straight man/foil Belford Dunn; and Andre, Belford's born-again monkey. ("It seems that Belford helped Andre find religion after the simian was caught helping a famous French heir rob the rich of their jewels," explained *Chicago Tribune* reviewer Chris Petrakos.)

In assessing *Half Asleep,* critics generally stayed true to their view of Robbins: funny, but given to preachiness. To Petrakos, "the frequently hilarious mingling of characters and sensibilities in the early half of the book bogs down in later pages. The whole idea of a born-again monkey seems undeveloped, as is the character of the psychic. While there are great weird bits and lyrical observations, as there are in all Robbins' novels, there's not the kind of wild exhilaration that one might expect."

"My theory on Tom Robbins," asserted Karen Karbo, writing in the *New York Times Book Review,* "is that unless his work was imprinted on you when you were 19 and stoned, you'll find him forever unreadable." *Half Asleep,* she claimed, "is vintage Robbins, a recommendation for those of you who can stand it." *Washington Post*'s Rudy Rucker was more accommodating in his evaluation: while he tired of the ceaseless ramblings of the Larry Diamond character, he advised like-minded readers "to indulge [the author] a little, as Robbins can still write phrases of mind-boggling beauty. On a foggy, rainy day in Seattle: 'Your building is surrounded by the soft, the gray, and the moist, as if it is being digested by an oyster.'"

True to form, Robbins presents another bizarre conflation of characters, events, and ideas in *Fierce Invalids Home from Hot Climates,* published in 2000 and his longest novel to date. The book was inspired in part by a journal entry by travel writer Bruce Chatwin. "That brief entry," Robbins told an interviewer for *Amazon.com,* "struck the flint of my imaginative Zippo, causing me to ask myself the most essential question of the creative process: 'What if . . . ?'" The book involves the adventures of CIA operative Switters as he careens through assignments from the Peruvian jungle to the Syrian desert, encountering a mad shaman, a convent of lapsed nuns, and the third prophecy of Fatima, kept well-guarded by the Vatican. As is typical of Robbins' work, the novel is filled with wordplay, offbeat humor, and extreme plot devices. "*Fierce Invalids* is a sort of gonzo *Celestine Prophecy,*" observed *New York Times Book Review* contributor James Poniewozik. "Anyone familiar with Robbins will recognize Switters as a lightly camouflaged, if heavily armed, author surrogate, a trickster god bearing the Robbinsian theme that we bring evil on ourselves by taking things too seriously." Though he appreciated the book's humor, Poniewozik identified an "irritating" quality in the novel. "Robbins's satisfaction with his outre protagonist borders on smugness," he complained. Objecting to the book's oversimplified preachiness, the critic wrote that "Robbins manages, in the same breath, both to pander and to condescend to his backpack-slinging audience."

Robbins did not stray from his eccentric path in 2003's *Villa Incognito,* a novel which includes drug-smuggling MIA Americans who decided to stay missing, a mythic, animal-like Japanese creature who has a child with a human, along with a host of political and social issues. A reviewer in *Book* gave a good summation of how critics saw this novel, "Robbins devotees will lap this up; the rest of us may remain unconvinced."

Robbins, who was named one of "The 100 Best Writers of the Twentieth Century" by *Writer's Digest,* received the Golden Umbrella Award—his first literary prize—in 1997. Yet he continues to see his work in a playful light. Admitting to *January Magazine* that he writes to entertain, Robbins distinguished himself from authors who write *merely* to entertain: "What I try to do," he explained, "is to mix fantasy and spirituality, sexuality, humor and poetry in combinations that have never quite been seen before in literature. And I guess when a reader finishes one of my books . . . I would like for him or her to be in the state that they would be in after a Fellini film or a Grateful Dead concert. Which is to say that they've encountered the life force in a large, irrepressible and unpredictable way and . . . their sense of wonder has been awakened and all of their possibilities have been expanded."

BIOGRAPHICAL AND CRITICAL SOURCES:

BOOKS

Contemporary Literary Criticism, Thomson Gale (Detroit, MI), Volume 9, 1978, Volume 32, 1985, Volume 64, 1991.

Dictionary of Literary Biography Yearbook: 1980, Thomson Gale (Detroit, MI), 1981.
Hoyser, Catherine Elizabeth, *Tom Robbins: A Critical Companion,* Greenwood Press, 1997.
Klinkowitz, Jerome, *The Practice of Fiction in America: Writers from Hawthorne to the Present,* Iowa State University Press (Ames, IA), 1980.
Nadeau, Robert, *Readings from the New Book on Nature: Physics and Metaphysics in the Modern Novel,* University of Massachusetts Press (Amherst, MA), 1981.
Robbins, Tom, *Skinny Legs and All,* Bantam (New York, NY), 1990.
Robbins, Tom, *Half Asleep in Frog Pajamas,* Bantam (New York, NY), 1994.
Siegel, Mark, *Tom Robbins,* Boise State University Press, 1980.

PERIODICALS

Book, May-June, 2003, pp. 79-80.
Booklist, March 15, 2000, p. 1293; February 15, 2003, p. 1019.
Chicago Review, autumn, 1980.
Chicago Tribune, April 1, 1990, p. 3; November 17, 1994, p. 2.
Commonweal, March 13, 1981.
Detroit News, October 5, 1980; January 6, 1985.
Entertainment Weekly, May 12, 2000, p. 72; May 2, 2003, p. 74.
Kirkus Reviews, February 15, 2003, p. 265.
Library Journal, March 1, 2000, p. 53; March 15, 2003, p. 116.
Literature and Psychology, fall, 2001, pp. 59-60.
Los Angeles Times Book Review, December 16, 1984; April 15, 1990; September 25, 1994, p. 3.
Nation, August 28, 1976; October 25, 1980.
New Boston Review, December, 1977.
New Republic, June 26, 1971.
New Statesman, August 12, 1977.
Newsweek, September 29, 1980.
New York Times, December 30, 1993.
New York Times Book Review, May 23, 1976; September 28, 1980; December 9, 1984; April 15, 1990, p. 12; October 30, 1994, p. 27; May 21, 2000.
New York Times Magazine, February 12, 1978.
People Weekly, June 12, 2000, p. 51.
Playboy, June, 2000, p. 45.
Publishers Weekly, March 20, 2000, p. 68.
Saturday Review, September, 1980.
Seattle Weekly, May 4, 2000.
Times Literary Supplement, October 31, 1980.
Toronto Star, June 20, 2000.
Washington Post, December 18, 1994, p. 5.
Washington Post Book World, October 25, 1980.

ONLINE

Amazon.com, http://www.amazon.com/ (May 31, 2005), interview with Tom Robbins.
BookPage, http://www.bookpage.com/ (August 18, 2004), Michael Sims, "Tom Robbins: An Outrageous Writer in a Politically Correct Era."
January Magazine, http://www.januarymagazine.com/ (June, 2000), Linda Richards, "Tom Robbins Interview."
Salon.com, http://www.salon.com/ Tracy Johnson, "Tom Robbins."
Seattle Weekly Web Site, http://www.seattleweekly.com/ (August 18, 2004), Michael Downey, "Tom Robbins: My Life and Work."

* * *

ROBERTS, Nora 1950-
(J.D. Robb)

PERSONAL: Born October 10, 1950, in Washington, DC; daughter of Bernard Edward (a company president) and Eleanor (a company vice president; maiden name, Harris) Robertson; married Ronald Aufdem-Brinke, August 17, 1968 (divorced, January, 1985); married Bruce Wilder (a carpenter), July 6, 1985; children: (first marriage) Daniel, Jason. *Education:* Attended public schools in Silver Spring, MD. *Politics:* Democrat. *Religion:* Roman Catholic.

ADDRESSES: *Home*—Keedysville, MD. *Agent*—Amy Berkower, Writers House, Inc., 21 West 26th St., New York, NY 10010. *E-mail*—write2nora@msn.com.

CAREER: Novelist, 1979—. Wheeler & Korpeck, Silver Spring, MD, legal secretary, 1968-70; The Hecht Co., Silver Spring, clerk, 1970-72; R. & R. Lighting, Silver Spring, secretary, 1972-75.

MEMBER: Romance Writers of America, Washington Romance Writers.

AWARDS, HONORS: Golden Medallion, Romance Writers of America, 1982, for *The Heart's Victory,* 1983, for *This Magic Moment* and *Untamed,* 1984, for *Opposites Attract* and *A Matter of Choice,* and 1986, for *One Summer;* named best contemporary author by *Romantic Times,* 1984; Reviewer's Choice Award, *Romantic Times,* 1984, for *Reflections,* 1985, for *Partners,* and 1986, for *One Summer;* MacGregor series named best series by *Romantic Times,* 1985; Silver Certificate, *Affaire du Coeur,* 1985, for the MacGregor series; Waldenbooks Award, 1985, for *One Man's Art,* 1986, for *A Will and a Way,* 1988, for *The Last Honest Woman,* 1993, for *Gabriel's Angel* and for *For the Love of Lilah;* Maggie Award, Georgia Romance Writers of America, 1985, for *Partners;* first author inducted into Romance Writers of America Hall of Fame, 1986; RITA Award, Romance Writers of America, 1990, for *Public Secrets,* 1991, for *Night Shift,* and 1992, for *Divine Evil;* B. Dalton Award for *Public Secrets, A Man for Amanda,* and *Suzannah's Surrender;* Rita Award for best romantic suspense novel for *Three Fates,* Romance Writers of America, 2003.

WRITINGS:

ROMANCE NOVELS

Blithe Images, Silhouette (New York, NY), 1982.
Song of the West, Silhouette (New York, NY), 1982.
Search for Love, Silhouette (New York, NY), 1982.
Island of Flowers, Silhouette (New York, NY), 1982.
The Heart's Victory, Silhouette (New York, NY), 1982.
From This Day, Silhouette (New York, NY), 1983.
Her Mother's Keeper, Silhouette (New York, NY), 1983.
Once More with Feeling, Silhouette (New York, NY), 1983.
Untamed, Silhouette (New York, NY), 1983.
Reflections, Silhouette (New York, NY), 1983.
Dance of Dreams, Silhouette (New York, NY), 1983, reprinted, Hall (Thorndike, ME), 2000.
Tonight and Always, Silhouette (New York, NY), 1983, reprinted, 1990.
This Magic Moment, Silhouette (New York, NY), 1983.
Endings and Beginnings, Silhouette (New York, NY), 1984.
Storm Warning, Silhouette (New York, NY), 1984.
Sullivan's Woman, Silhouette (New York, NY), 1984.
Rules of the Game, Silhouette (New York, NY), 1984.
Less of a Stranger, Silhouette (New York, NY), 1984.
A Matter of Choice, Silhouette (New York, NY), 1984.
The Law Is a Lady, Silhouette (New York, NY), 1984.
First Impressions, Silhouette (New York, NY), 1984.
Opposites Attract, Silhouette (New York, NY), 1984.
Promise Me Tomorrow, Silhouette (New York, NY), 1984.
Partners, Silhouette (New York, NY), 1985.
The Right Path, Silhouette (New York, NY), 1985.
Boundary Lines, Silhouette (New York, NY), 1985.
Dual Image, Silhouette (New York, NY), 1985.
Night Moves, Harlequin (Toronto, Canada), 1985.
Summer Desserts, Silhouette (New York, NY), 1985.
Lessons Learned, Silhouette (New York, NY), 1986.
The Art of Deception, Silhouette (New York, NY), 1986.
One Summer, Silhouette (New York, NY), 1986.
Second Nature, Silhouette (New York, NY), 1986.
Treasures Lost, Treasures Found, Silhouette (New York, NY), 1986.
Risky Business, Silhouette (New York, NY), 1986.
A Will and a Way, Silhouette (New York, NY), 1986.
Home for Christmas, Silhouette (New York, NY), 1986.
Mind over Matter, Silhouette (New York, NY), 1987.
Temptation, Silhouette (New York, NY), 1987.
Hot Ice, Bantam (New York, NY), 1987, reprinted, 2002.
Sacred Sins, Bantam (New York, NY), 1987.
Brazen Virtue, Bantam (New York, NY), 1988.
Local Hero, Silhouette (New York, NY), 1988.
The Name of the Game, Silhouette (New York, NY), 1988.
Rebellion, Harlequin (Toronto, Canada), 1988.
Sweet Revenge, Bantam (New York, NY), 1989.
Loving Jack, Silhouette (New York, NY), 1989.
Best Laid Plans, Silhouette (New York, NY), 1989.
Lawless, Harlequin (Toronto, Canada), 1989.
Gabriel's Angel, Harlequin (Toronto, Canada), 1989.
The Welcoming, Silhouette (New York, NY), 1989.
Public Secrets, Bantam (New York, NY), 1990.
Genuine Lies, Bantam (New York, NY), 1991.
With This Ring, Harlequin (Toronto, Canada), 1991.
Carnal Innocence, Bantam (New York, NY), 1992.
Unfinished Business, Harlequin (Toronto, Canada), 1992.
The Welcoming, Chivers North America (Hampton, NH), 1992.
Honest Illusions, Putnam (New York, NY), 1992.
Divine Evil, Bantam (New York, NY), 1992.
Second Nature, Harlequin (Toronto, Canada), 1993.
Private Scandals, Putnam (New York, NY), 1993.
Boundary Lines, Harlequin (Toronto, Canada), 1994.
Hidden Riches, Putnam (New York, NY), 1994.
(With others) *Birds, Bees and Babies: The Best Mistake,* Silhouette (New York, NY), 1994.
Silhouette Christmas: All I Want for Christmas, Silhouette (New York, NY), 1994.
True Betrayals, Putnam (New York, NY), 1995.
Montana Sky, Putnam (New York, NY), 1996.
From the Heart, Thorndike Press (Thorndike, ME), 1997.

Sanctuary, Putnam (New York, NY), 1997.
The Reef, Putnam (New York, NY), 1998.
Homeport, Putnam (New York, NY), 1998.
Genuine Lies, Bantam (New York, NY), 1998.
River's End, Putnam (New York, NY), 1999.
Irish Rebel, Silhouette (New York, NY), 2000.
Carolina Moon, Berkley (New York, NY), 2001.
The Villa, Putnam (New York, NY), 2001.
Midnight Bayou, Putnam (New York, NY), 2001.
Three Fates, Putnam (New York, NY), 2002.
Chesapeake Blue, Putnam (New York, NY), 2002.
A Little Magic, Berkley (New York, NY), 2002.
Cordina's Crown Jewel, Silhouette (New York, NY), 2002.
Cordina's Royal Family, Silhouette (New York, NY), 2002.
Birthright, Putnam (New York, NY), 2003.
Engaging the Enemy, Silhouette (New York, NY), 2003.
Northern Lights, Putnam (New York, NY), 2004.
Red Lily, Jove (New York, NY), 2005.

"MACGREGOR" SERIES

Playing the Odds, Silhouette (New York, NY), 1985.
Tempting Fate, Silhouette (New York, NY), 1985.
All the Possibilities, Silhouette (New York, NY), 1985.
One Man's Art, Silhouette (New York, NY), 1985.
For Now, Forever, Silhouette (New York, NY), 1987.
Rebellion, Harlequin (Toronto, Canada), 1988.
In from the Cold, Harlequin (Toronto, Canada), 1990.
The MacGregor Brides, Silhouette (New York, NY), 1997.
The Winning Hand, Silhouette (New York, NY), 1998.
The MacGregor Grooms, Silhouette (New York, NY), 1998.
The MacGregors: Serena-Caine, Silhouette (New York, NY), 1998.
The MacGregors: Daniel-Ian, Harlequin (Toronto, Canada), 1999.
The MacGregors: Alan-Grant, Silhouette (New York, NY), 1999.
The Perfect Neighbor, Harlequin (Toronto, Canada), 1999.

"IRISH" SERIES

Irish Thoroughbred, Silhouette (New York, NY), 1981.
Irish Rose, Silhouette (New York, NY), 1988.
Irish Rebel, Silhouette (New York, NY), 2000.

"CORDINA" SERIES

Affaire Royale, Silhouette (New York, NY), 1986.
Command Performance, Silhouette (New York, NY), 1987.
The Playboy Prince, Silhouette (New York, NY), 1987.

"O'HURLEY" SERIES

The Last Honest Woman, Silhouette (New York, NY), 1988.
Dance to the Piper, Silhouette (New York, NY), 1988.
Skin Deep, Silhouette (New York, NY), 1988.
Without a Trace, Silhouette (New York, NY), 1991.

"THOSE WILD UKRAINIANS" SERIES

Taming Natasha, Silhouette (New York, NY), 1990.
Luring a Lady, Silhouette (New York, NY), 1991.
Falling for Rachel, Silhouette (New York, NY), 1993.
Convincing Alex, Silhouette (New York, NY), 1994.
Waiting for Nick, Silhouette (New York, NY), 1997.
Considering Kate, Silhouette (New York, NY), 2001.

"NIGHT" SERIES

Night Shift, Silhouette (New York, NY), 1991.
Night Shadow, Silhouette (New York, NY), 1991.
Nightshade, Silhouette (New York, NY), 1993.
Night Smoke, Silhouette (New York, NY), 1994.
*Night Shield,*Silhouette (New York, NY), 2000.

"CALHOUN WOMEN" SERIES

Courting Catherine, Silhouette (New York, NY), 1991.
A Man for Amanda, Silhouette (New York, NY), 1991.
For the Love of Lilah, Silhouette (New York, NY), 1991.
Suzannah's Surrender, Silhouette (New York, NY), 1991.
Megan's Mate, Silhouette (New York, NY), 1996.

"HORNBLOWER" SERIES

Time Was, Silhouette (New York, NY), 1993.
Times Change, Silhouette (New York, NY), 1993.

"BORN IN. . . " SERIES

Born in Fire, Jove (New York, NY), 1994.
Born in Ice, Jove (New York, NY), 1995.
Born in Shame, Jove (New York, NY), 1996.

"MACKADE" SERIES

The Return of Rafe MacKade, Silhouette (New York, NY), 1995.
The Pride of Jared MacKade, Silhouette (New York, NY), 1995.
The Heart of Devin MacKade, Silhouette (New York, NY), 1996.
The Fall of Shane MacKade, Silhouette (New York, NY), 1996.

"STAR" SERIES

Hidden Star, Silhouette (New York, NY), 1997.
Captive Star, Silhouette (New York, NY), 1997.
Secret Star, Silhouette (New York, NY), 1998.

"DONOVAN LEGACY" SERIES

Captivated, Silhouette (New York, NY), 1992.
Entranced, Silhouette (New York, NY), 1992.
Charmed, Silhouette (New York, NY), 1992.
Enchanted, Silhouette (New York, NY), 1999.
Donovan Legacy, Harlequin (Toronto, Canada), 1999.

"QUINN BROTHERS" TRILOGY AND SEQUEL

Sea Swept, Thorndike Press (Thorndike, ME), 1998.
Rising Tides, Jove (New York, NY), 1998.
Inner Harbor, Thorndike Press (Thorndike, ME), 1999.

"DREAM" TRILOGY

Holding the Dream, Thorndike Press (Thorndike, ME), 1997.
Daring to Dream, Thorndike Press (Thorndike, ME), 1997.
Finding the Dream, Thorndike Press (Thorndike, ME), 1997.
Three Complete Novels by Nora Roberts (includes *Daring to Dream, Holding the Dream,* and *Finding the Dream*), Putnam (New York, NY), 1999.

"THREE SISTERS ISLAND" TRILOGY

Dance upon the Air, Jove (New York, NY), 2001.
Heaven and Earth, Jove (New York, NY), 2001.
Face the Fire, Jove (New York, NY), 2002.

"IRELAND" TRILOGY

Jewels of the Sun, Jove (New York, NY), 1999.
Tears of the Moon, Jove (New York, NY), 2000.
Heart of the Sea, Jove (New York, NY), 2000.

"ONCE UPON A. . . " SERIES; WITH OTHERS

Once upon a Castle, Jove (New York, NY), 1998.
Once upon a Star, Jove (New York, NY), 1999.
Once upon a Rose, Jove (New York, NY), 2001.
Once upon a Kiss, Berkley (New York, NY), 2002.
Once upon a Midnight, Jove (New York, NY), 2003.

"KEY" SERIES

Key of Light, Jove (New York, NY), 2003.
Key of Knowledge, Jove (New York, NY), 2003.
Key of Valor, Jove (New York, NY), 2004.

UNDER PSEUDONYM J.D. ROBB; EXCEPT AS NOTED

(With Susan Plunkett, Dee Holmes, and Claire Cross) *Silent Night,* Putnam (New York, NY), 1998.
(As J.D. Robb and Nora Roberts) *Remember When,* Putnam (New York, NY), 2003.

"IN DEATH" SERIES; UNDER PSEUDONYM J.D. ROBB

Naked in Death, Berkley (New York, NY), 1995.
Glory in Death, Berkley (New York, NY), 1995.
Rapture in Death, Berkley (New York, NY), 1996.
Ceremony in Death, Berkley (New York, NY), 1997.
Vengeance in Death, Berkley (New York, NY), 1997.
Holiday in Death, Berkley (New York, NY), 1998.
Immortal in Death, Berkley (New York, NY), 1998.

Midnight in Death: Anthology, Berkley (New York, NY), 1998.
Loyalty in Death, Berkley (New York, NY), 1999.
Conspiracy in Death, Berkley (New York, NY), 1999.
Witness in Death, Berkley (New York, NY), 2000.
Judgment in Death, Berkley (New York, NY), 2000.
Betrayal in Death, Berkley (New York, NY), 2001.
Seduction in Death, Berkley (New York, NY), 2001.
(With Laurell K. Hamilton, Susan Krinard, and Maggie Shayne) *Out of this World,* Jove (New York, NY), 2001.
Reunion in Death, Berkley (New York, NY), 2002.
Purity in Death, Berkley (New York, NY), 2002.
Portrait in Death, Berkley (New York, NY), 2003.
Imitation in Death, Berkley (New York, NY), 2003.
Divided in Death, Berkley (New York, NY), 2004.
Visions in Death, Putnam (New York, NY), 2004.
Memory in Death, Putnam (New York, NY), 2006.

ADAPTATIONS: Film rights to six of Roberts's books, *Blue Smoke, Carolina Moon, The Villa, Montana Sky, Brazen Virtue,* and *River's End,* were bought by Mandalay Television.

SIDELIGHTS: With over 150 books to her credit, and frequently publishing more than half a dozen titles per year, Nora Roberts has established herself convincingly not only as a prolific author but an award-winning author of romance novels. According to Barbara E. Kemp in *Twentieth-Century Romance and Historical Writers,* Roberts's prodigious output has done little to diminish its quality. "Roberts's well deserved reputation and following," Kemp observed, "are based on her skill as a writer." She went on to add that readers have learned that they can depend upon Roberts to "provide an interesting, often adventure-filled plot, colorful, well-researched settings, well-defined, believable characters, and a satisfying love story." According to Roberts's Web site, in 2001 an average of thirty-four Nora Roberts novels were sold every minute.

In addition to the ever-present element of romance, Roberts's novels often blend elements from other genres, including those of mystery, science fiction, and fantasy. In *Sacred Sins* the heroine, psychiatrist Tess Court, comes to the aid of homicide detectives who are tracking down a serial killer. *Time Was* and *Time Changes* detail the exploits and love affairs of time-traveling brothers from the twenty-third century. The supernatural, including witches and psychic healers, features prominently in Roberts's "Donovan Legacy" series, which revolves around three cousins who possess extrasensory powers. The "Donovan Legacy" books can also be numbered among Roberts's popular family-series novels. Other series that center on the exploits of particular families include "Those Wild Ukrainians," the award-winning "MacGregor" novels, and the "Cordina" series, which deals with the royal family of an imaginary Mediterranean country that bears more than a passing resemblance to Monaco. Kemp credited the success of Roberts's family series with the fact that she "develops [the families] . . . with such skill that there is a real sense of belonging and continuity, much as there is in a real family." Roberts likes to publish connecting books in paperback so as readers finish one book in a series, they can reach for the next.

Like a number of other established romance writers, Roberts has begun to broaden the base of her readership by branching out into mainstream novels. About Roberts's first mainstream novel, *Honest Illusions,* Joyce Slater noted in Chicago's *Tribune Books* that the author "has a warm feel for her characters and an eye for the evocative detail." A reviewer in *Authors and Artists for Young Adults* considered Roberts's *Montana Sky* "her real breakthrough to mainstream." In the novel, Jack Mercy leaves his Montana Ranch to his three daughters, half-sisters who don't know one another at all. Jack requires that the women live together for a year, or the ranch will be sold. The women must learn to live with one another, while dealing with a series of crimes on the ranch.

Roberts has authored a number of books under the pseudonym J.D. Robb. Her "In Death" series, set more than fifty years in the future, focuses on New York City police lieutenant Eve Dallas. Like many of Roberts's characters, Eve Dallas is a strong, determined and intelligent woman, something that appeals to Roberts's female readers. Making her debut in *Naked in Death,* the character of Dallas continues to solve crimes in the subsequent novels. "Intensely female yet unfeminine in any traditional sense, Dallas has a complex edge that transcends genre stereotypes," wrote a *Publishers Weekly* reviewer about *Portrait in Death.*

Roberts published *Remember When* using both her own name and her pseudonym, J.D. Robb. The novel is broken into two parts, tied together by a diamond heist. Laine Tavish, the daughter of an infamous thief, owns an antique store. As the novel progresses, she becomes the target of a killer out to recover her father's share of the take. She also falls in love with Max Gannon, an insurance investigator in search of the missing diamonds. Fast-forward fifty years into the future, when Laine's granddaughter, Samantha, writes a book about the still missing diamonds. When another murder occurs, Lt. Eve Dallas is on scene to investigate. A *Publishers Weekly* reviewer noted, "A true master of her craft, Roberts has penned an exceptional tale that burns with all the brilliance and fire of a finely cut diamond." *Booklist* reviewer John Charles concluded, *Remember When* "is another addictive blend of scintillating prose and sharply etched characters that will dazzle and delight her devoted readers."

Roberts's success as an author may be credited to the fact that she spends eight hours per day writing. Roberts's name has consistently remained on the *New York Times* Best-sellers List. A *Publishers Weekly* reviewer summarized Roberts's abilities as a writer, calling her "a storyteller of immeasurable diversity and talent." *Library Journal*'s Michael Rogers remarked, "Roberts is always a crowd pleaser." Debbie Ann Weiner's review of *The Villa* on *BookReporter* noted Roberts's "remarkable ability to write one engrossing best-seller after another."

"Relationships are Roberts's stock in trade," noted Jeanny V. House in a review of *River's End* published on *BookReporter,* "not just the romances, which Roberts presents with skill and passion, but also the relationships between family and friends." Roberts once told *CA:* "I write relationship books, most often about ongoing romantic involvements. Writing stories about people and their emotions is my primary motivation. Entertainment is always the primary focus."

BIOGRAPHICAL AND CRITICAL SOURCES:

BOOKS

Authors and Artists for Young Adults, Volume 35, Thomson Gale (Detroit, MI), 2000.

Little, Denise, and Laura Hayden, editors, *The Official Nora Roberts Companion,* introduction by Roberts, Berkley (New York, NY), 2002.

Twentieth-Century Romance and Historical Writers, 3rd edition, St. James Press (Detroit, MI), 1994.

PERIODICALS

Booklist, July, 1992, review of *Honest Illusions,* p. 1920; January 1, 1997, review of *Sanctuary,* p. 780; May 15, 1994, p. 1665; March 15, 1998, p. 1203; September 15, 1998, p. 707; January 1, 1999, Melanie Duncan, review of *River's End,* p. 793; November 15, 1999, Patty Engelmann, review of *Jewels of the Sun,* p. 608; September 15, 2000, Nina Davis, review of *Pride of Jared MacKade,* p. 225, and Donna Seaman, review of *Jewels of the Sun,* p. 226; December 1, 2000, review of *Tears of the Moon,* p. 743, and review of *Sacred Sins,* p. 743; April 15, 2001, review of *Dance upon the Air,* p. 1508; July, 2001, review of *Out of this World,* p. 1991; August, 2001, Whitney Scott, review of *The Villa,* p. 2143; September 1, 2001, review of *Midnight Bayou,* p. 4; September 15, 2001, review of *Considering Kate,* p. 212; October 1, 2001, review of *Once upon a Rose,* p. 304; December 15, 2001, audio book review of *Brazen Virtue,* p. 745; March 1, 2002, review of *Reunion in Death,* p. 1098; May 15, 2002, Diana Tixier Herald, review of *Face the Fire,* p. 1582; August, 2003, John Charles, review of *Remember When,* p. 1927.

BookPage, June, 2001, review of *Dance upon the Air,* p. 24; October, 2001, review of *Once upon a Rose,* p. 30; April, 2002, review of *Three Fates,* p. 8.

Bookseller, June 20, 2003, "So Good They Named Her Twice: Having Had Considerable Success with Romance Veteran Nora Roberts, Piatkus Is Now Relaunching the Writer's Alter Ego, J.D. Robb," p. 28.

Bookwatch, February, 1999, audio book review of *Inner Harbor,* p. 10.

Detroit Free Press, August 5, 2001, review of *Dance upon the Air,* p. 4E.

Drood Review of Mystery, January, 2001, review of *Carolina Moon,* p. 22.,

Kirkus Reviews, January 1, 1999, review of *River's End,* p. 15; February 1, 2001, review of *The Villa,* p. 129; September 1, 2001, review of *Midnight Bayou,* p. 1241; January 1, 2003, review of *Birthright,* p. 21; July 15, 2003, review of *Remember When,* p. 933.

Kliatt, January, 1999, audio book review of *Sanctuary,* p. 47; July, 1999, audio book review of *A Man for Amanda,* p. 44.

Library Journal, June 15, 1992, p. 103; June 1, 1994, review of *Hidden Riches,* p. 162; August, 1995, review of *Born in Ice,* p. 64; February 1, 1996, p. 139; November 1, 1998, p. 138; February 1, 1999, Jodie L. Israel, review of *River's End,* p. 123, and review of *The Reef,* p. 137; February 15, 1999, Michael Rogers, review of *Holding the Dream,* p. 189; April 15, 1999, audio book review of *Inner Harbor,* p. 164; June 1, 1999, audio book review of *River's End,* p. 206; February 15, 2000, Margaret Ann Hanes, review of *Carolina Moon,* p. 198; March 1, 2000, Jodi L. Israel, review of *Jewels of the Sun,* p. 142; February 15, 2001, review of *The Villa,* p. 155; March 1, 2001, audio book review of *Glory in Death,* p. 152; May 15, 2001, Kristin Ramsdell, review of *Dance upon the Air,* p. 107; June 15, 2001, Barbara Perkins, review of *The Villa,* p. 122; January, 2002, review of *Dance upon the Air,* p. 51; February 15, 2002, review of *Three Fates,* p. 131; March 15, 2002, review of *Betrayal in Death,* p. 126; August, 2002, Shelley Mosley, review of *Chesapeake Blue,* p. 146; September 1, 2003, Margaret Hanes, review of *Remember When,* p. 210; October 1, 2003, Jodi L. Israel, audio book review of *Birthright,* p. 132.

Locus, May, 2001, review of *Betrayal in Death,* p. 29.

Los Angeles Times Book Review, July 15, 1990, p. 14; July 24, 1994, p. 10.

New York Times, March 26, 2001, review of *The Villa,* p. E7.

New York Times Book Review, February 17, 1985; February 14, 1993, p. 23.

Off Our Backs, December, 2001, Mary E. Atkins, review of *Dance upon the Air,* p. 35.

People, July 1, 1996, Kristin McMurran, "Page Churner," p. 31; March 31, 1997, p. 41; May 4, 1998, p. 97; March 26, 2001, review of *The Villa,* p. 48.

Publishers Weekly, November 15, 1991, p. 69; May 18, 1992, review of *Honest Illusions,* p. 57; May 9, 1994, review of *Hidden Riches,* p. 62; December 4, 1995, review of *Born in Shame,* p. 58; January 22, 1996, review of *Montana Sky,* p. 59; February 3, 1997, p. 95; February 23, 1998, Judy Quinn, "Nora Roberts: A Celebration of Emotions," p. 46; July 6, 1998, pp. 29, 57; September 29, 1998, pp. 73, 99; January 11, 1999, review of *River's End,* p. 52; March 22, 1999, review of *Conspiracy in Death,* p. 89; April 12, 1999, Alec Foege, "Close to Home," p. 139; October 11, 1999, review of *Jewels of the Sun,* p. 73; November 1, 1999, p. 24; December 6, 1999, p. 24; January 31, 2000, review of *Carolina Moon,* p. 79; June 19, 2000, review of *Tears of the Moon,* p. 64; October 30, 2000, review of *Once upon a Dream,* p. 53; February 19, 2001, review of *Betrayal in Death,* p. 75; May 14, 2001, review of *Dance upon the Air,* p. 59; July 9, 2001, review of *Out of This World,* p. 53; August 6, 2001, review of *Seduction in Death,* p. 66; September 3, 2001, review of *Midnight Bayou,* p. 55; September 10, 2001, review of *Once upon a Rose,* p. 68; November 26, 2001, review of *Heaven and Earth,* p. 45; February 18, 2002, review of *Reunion in Death,* p. 81; April 1, 2002, audio book review of *Three Fates,* p. 30, and review of *Three Fates,* p. 52; May 6, 2002, review of *Face the Fire,* p. 41; February 24, 2003, review of *Portrait in Death,* p. 58; March 24, 2003, review of *Birthright,* p. 59; August 25, 2003, review of *Remember When,* p. 39, and review of *Imitation in Death,* p. 45; September 8, 2003, Dick Donahue, "Roberts Rules Redux," p. 18; September 29, 2003, review of *Once upon a Midnight,* p. 49.

School Library Journal, June, 1995, review of *Born in Fire,* p. 146; March, 1996, pp. 234-235; September, 1999, review of *River's End,* p. 244.

Science Fiction Chronicle, June, 2001, review of *Betrayal in Death,* p. 40; March, 2002, audio book review of *Rapture in Death,* p. 39.

Times (London, England), August 11, 1997, p. 84.

Tribune Books (Chicago, IL), June 28, 1992, p. 6; March 24, 1996, p. 4; May 11, 1997, p. 11.

Voice of Youth Advocates, February, 1999, review of *Sea Swept,* p. 418.

Wall Street Journal, February 17, 1984.

Washington Post Book World, February 7, 1999, review of *River's End,* p. 7.

Writer, September, 2003, "What Makes Readers Love Nora Roberts's Romances?," p. 10.

ONLINE

All about Romance, http://www.likesbooks.com/ (June 2, 2003), Blythe Barnhill, review of *The Perfect Neighbor* and *Carnal Innocence;* Jennifer L. Schendel, review of *Once upon a Kiss;* Marianne Stillings, review of *Once upon a Rose* and *Carolina Moon;* Colleen McMahon, review of *Carolina Moon;* Candy Tan, review of *Once upon a Star;* Jane Jorgenson, review of *Brazen Virtue;* Linda Mowery, review of "MacGregor" series; interview with Roberts; Andrea Pool, review of *Dance upon the Air.*

Best Reviews, http://thebestreviews.com/ (June 2, 2003), Harriet Klausner, review of *Birthright* and *Heaven and Earth;* review of *Once upon a Star;* Janice Bennett, review of *Heaven and Earth;* Kelly Hartsell, review of *Heart of the Sea.*

BookReporter, http://www.bookreporter.com/ (June 2, 2003), Sonia Chopra, review of *Three Fates;* Debbie Ann Weiner, review of *The Villa;* Jeanny V. House, review of *River's End.*

Books I Loved, http://booksiloved.com/ (June 2, 2003), Jennifer Santiago, review of *Midnight Bayou.*

Crescent Blues, http://www.crescentblues.com/ (June 2, 2003), "Nora Roberts: The Joy of Make Believer."

MyShelf, http://www.myshelf.com/ (June 2, 2003), Brenda Weeaks, review of *Once upon a Star.*

MysteryReader, http://www.mysteryreader.com/ (April 24, 2001), review of *The Villa.*

Nora Roberts Web site, http://www.noraroberts.com/ (November 20, 2003).
Paranormal Romance Reviews, http://pnr.thebestreviews.com/ (June 2, 2003), Harriet Klausner, review of *Chesapeake Blue, Three Fates, Once upon a Kiss, Once upon a Rose, Dance upon the Air,* and *Heart of the Sea;* Leslie Tramposch, review of *Dance upon the Air* and *Enchanted;* Marilyn Heyman, review of *Once upon a Rose.*
Readers Read, http://www.readersread.com/ (June 2, 2003), review of *Midnight Bayou.*
Road to Romance, http://www.roadtoromance.ca/ (June 2, 2003), Traci Bell, review of *Dance upon the Air.*
RomanceReader, http://www.romancereader.com/ (January 19, 1998) review of *The MacGregors: Alan-Grant;* (February 3, 1999) review of *The Perfect Neighbor;* (February 22, 1999) review of *River's End;* (March 23, 1999) review of *Conspiracy in Death;* (October 13, 1999) review of *Jewels of the Sun;* (October 15, 1999) review of *Enchanted;* (October 25, 1999) review of *Loyalty in Death;* (March 7, 2001) review of *The Villa;* (March 26, 2001) review of *Betrayal in Death;* (August 3, 2001) review of *Seduction in Death* and *Out of This World;* (November 27, 2001) review of *Midnight Bayou;* (January 14, 2002) review of *Dance upon the Air;* (February 19, 2002) review of *Cordina's Crown Jewel;* (March 15, 2002) review of *Reunion in Death;* (March 26, 2002) review of *Three Fates;* Jean Mason, review of *Carolina Moon,* review of *Irish Rebel;* Susan Scribner, review of *Inner Harbor;* Cathy Sova, review of *The MacGregor Brides;* Diane Grayson, review of *The Perfect Neighbor.*
RomanceReview, http://www.aromancereview.com/ (June 2, 2003), review of *Carnal Innocence.*

* * *

ROBERTSON, Ellis
See ELLISON, Harlan

* * *

ROBERTSON, Ellis
See SILVERBERG, Robert

* * *

ROBINSON, Kim Stanley 1952-

PERSONAL: Born March 23, 1952, in Waukegan, IL; married Lisa Howland Nowell, 1982. *Education:* University of California—San Diego, B.A., 1974, Ph.D., 1982; Boston University, M.A., 1975.

ADDRESSES: Home—17811 Romelle Ave., Santa Ana, CA 92705. *Agent*—Patrick Delahunt, John Schaffner Associates Inc., 114 East 28th St., New York, NY 10016.

CAREER: Novelist. Visiting lecturer at University of California—San Diego, 1982 and 1985, and University of California—Davis, 1982-84 and 1985.

AWARDS, HONORS: Nebula Award nomination, Science Fiction and Fantasy Writers of America, 1981, for "Venice Drowned"; Hugo Award, World Science Fiction Society, 1982, for "To Leave a Mark"; World Fantasy Award for best novella, World Fantasy Convention, 1983, and Nebula Award, both for "Black Air"; *Locus* Award for best first novel, 1985, for *The Wild Shore:* Nebula Award for best novella, 1987, for *The Blind Geometer;* Nebula Award for best novel, 1993, for *Red Mars;* Hugo Award for best novel, World Science Fiction Society, 1994, for *Green Mars,* and 1997, for *Blue Mars;* National Science Foundation grant, 1995; Hugo Award nomination in best novel category, World Science Fiction Society, and Arthur C. Clarke Award shortlist, both 2003, both for *The Years of Rice and Salt.*

WRITINGS:

The Wild Shore, Ace (New York, NY), 1984.
Icehenge, Ace (New York, NY), 1984.
The Novels of Philip K. Dick (criticism), UMI Research Press (Ann Arbor, MI), 1984.
The Memory of Whiteness: A Scientific Romance, Tor (New York, NY), 1985.
The Blind Geometer, illustrations by Judy King-Rieniets, Cheap Street (New Castle, VA), 1986.
The Planet on the Table (science fiction short stories; includes "Venice Drowned," "Mercurial," "Ridge Running," "The Disguise," "The Lucky Strike," and "Black Air"), Tor (New York, NY), 1986.
The Gold Coast, Tor (New York, NY), 1988.
Escape from Kathmandu, T. Doherty (New York, NY), 1989, Orb (New York, NY), 1994.
Pacific Edge, Tor (New York, NY), 1990.
A Short, Sharp Shock, illustrations by Arnie Fenner, M.V. Ziesing (Shingletown, CA), 1990.
Pulphouse Science-Fiction Short Stories, Black Air, Pulphouse (Eugene, OR), 1991.
Red Mars, Bantam (New York, NY), 1993.
(Editor) *Future Primitive: The New Ecotopias,* Tor (New York, NY), 1994.
Remaking History and Other Stories, Orb (New York, NY), 1994.

Green Mars, Bantam (New York, NY), 1994.
Pacific Edge, Orb (New York, NY), 1995.
Blue Mars, Bantam (New York, NY), 1996.
Antarctica, Bantam (New York, NY), 1998.
The Martians, Bantam (New York, NY), 1999.
The Years of Rice and Salt, Bantam (New York, NY), 2002.
Forty Signs of Rain, Bantam (New York, NY), 2004.

Stories represented in anthologies, including *Orbit 18* and *Orbit 19,* both edited by Damon Knight, Harper (New York, NY), 1975 and 1977; *Clarion SF,* edited by Kate Wilhelm, Berkley (New York, NY), 1977; *Universe 11, Universe 12, Universe 13, Universe 14,* and *Universe 15,* all edited by Terry Carr, Doubleday (New York, NY), 1981-85; and *The Year's Best Science Fiction 1,* edited by Gardner Dozois and Jim Frenkel, Bluejay Books, 1984. Contributor to periodicals, including *Isaac Asimov's Science Fiction Magazine.*

SIDELIGHTS: Science-fiction novelist Kim Stanley Robinson has written prolifically, but he is probably best known for *Red Mars, Green Mars,* and *Blue Mars,* his epic trilogy about the twenty-first-century colonization of that planet. The trilogy, according to Edward James in the *Times Literary Supplement,* has established Robinson "as the pre-eminent contemporary practitioner of science fiction. He has earned that position by taking the central tenet of science fiction—the extrapolation of current history—to greater lengths than any of his predecessors, and the Mars books are likely to be the touchstone of what is possible in the genre for a long time to come."

Despite the rigorous scientific detail that characterizes his best-known work, Robinson is not a scientist. Instead, his credentials are decidedly literary. Born in Waukegan, Illinois, in 1952, Robinson grew up in Orange County, California, and graduated from the University of California—San Diego in 1974 with a degree in literature. He went on to earn a master's degree in English from Boston University the following year, and then returned to the University of California to earn a doctorate in literature in 1982. He wrote his dissertation on the novels of Philip K. Dick, who is best known for *Do Androids Dream of Electric Sheep?*

Robinson's first novel, *The Wild Shore,* was the eagerly awaited vanguard of a new line of science fiction books from Ace Books. With a reputation for discovering excellent and little-known authors, the Ace Specials were first published in the 1960s, eventually discontinued, and then resurrected by their former editor, Terry Carr, beginning with Robinson's novel in 1984. *The Wild Shore* depicts the United States in the aftermath of a nuclear holocaust of mysterious origin as a country reduced to primitive technology and quarantined by an unknown outside force. Assessed Algis Budrys in the *Magazine of Fantasy and Science Fiction,* "what [Robinson] has here is a Class A science fiction idea . . . a future which is both clearly possible and yet has not hitherto been notably proposed."

Throughout the novel Robinson concentrates on his protagonists, residents of a southern California town who generally know little and care even less about their history and about the world beyond them. According to Budrys, the regional flavor and strong characterization of Robinson's book recall the writings of John Steinbeck and Mark Twain; "Robinson has brought an American culture to life as surely as was ever done by anyone who had a real American culture to research," judged the critic. Writing in the *Washington Post Book World,* Stephen P. Brown praised the "vivid depth" of characterization "rarely encountered in science fiction."

In *The Memory of Whiteness,* published the following year, music is the universal language of a space-faring civilization. With access to free energy, humanity has colonized all the sun's planets and developed a "rich mixture of cultures, based on divergent notions of political order, but unified by an appreciation of music," noted Gerald Jonas in the *New York Times Book Review.* A genius, Johannes Wright, attempts to use the language of music to express universal truths in his compositions for a computer-enhanced instrument known as the Orchestra, but enemies seek to destroy him and the Orchestra. Jonas expressed disappointment in being unable to identify with Wright, whose genius places him beyond the reader, but appreciated Robinson's variations on the theme of music's power. The critic judged the end, in which Wright lands on Mercury after performing on various other planets, "most spectacular."

A number of Robinson's short stories, originally published in the late 1970s and early 1980s, appear in his 1986 collection *The Planet on the Table.* Exploring future societies or alternate histories, Robinson "invests his flights of imagination with a palpable sense of place," asserted Jonas in another *New York Times Book Review* article. The stories earned praise for their merits as straight fiction as well as for their science fiction content and prompted Jonas's commendation of Robinson's "powerful and consistent science fiction voice."

Depicting another future society is Robinson's 1988 novel *The Gold Coast,* the second in his trilogy of "Orange County" books. (The first was *The Wild Shore.*) Set in twenty-first-century California, the book portrays a populace inundated by freeways, shopping malls, and apartment complexes, where the "people are as frantic as the landscape is dense, and there's a deadness in the soul of most," noted T. Jefferson Parker in the *Los Angeles Times Book Review.* The protagonist of the story, twenty-seven-year-old poet Jim McPherson, joins a terrorist group that sabotages national defense plants. Jim's father works for such a defense contractor, leaving Jim caught between his own idealist views condemning military buildup and his father's values. Parker commended *The Gold Coast* for the ideas that Robinson addresses, noting that the author has "extrapolated a future . . . that feels accurate, arresting and frightening. . . . Who among us, watching a wasteful defense industry that helps to drain an already overspent economy . . . doesn't share Jim's outrage and disgust?" In what the reviewer deemed an "ambitious, angry, eccentric" book, Robinson exhibits "breathless, headlong prose" and some "beautifully written rhapsodies." More important, concluded Parker, "Robinson has succeeded at a novelist's toughest challenge: He's made us look at the world around us. This isn't escapist stuff—it sends you straight into a confrontation with yourself."

In the trilogy's concluding book, *Pacific Edge,* Robinson creates his version of utopia. This novel's El Modena, California, is part of a new society brought about by peaceful revolution, where multinational corporations no longer rule and technology serves people's simpler, eco-friendly lifestyles. Newly elected town council member Kevin finds himself in the midst of a conflict when water-rights issues and the potential commercial development of a pristine hillside threaten to split the community. The political troubles are further complicated by personal relationships between allies and opponents. *New York Times Book Review* contributor Jonas maintained that "Through a blend of dirt-under-the-fingernails naturalism and lyrical magical realism, [Robinson] invites us to share his characters' intensely personal, intensely local attachment to what they have. The result is a bittersweet utopia that may shame you into entertaining new hope for the future."

Robinson is an avid mountain trekker who loves wilderness landscapes, and much in his fiction seeks to shed light on the disconnection he sees between urban life and nature. "I spend about as much time as I can in the wilderness," he told Sebastian Cooke in an *Eidolon* interview. "It's got me thinking about the environmental catastrophe we're sitting on the edge of and solutions to that. It doesn't make any sense just to throw up your hands in despair and say, 'The world is doomed!'" Robinson does not see environmental movements like those suggested in *Pacific Edge* as utopian. "There will always be competing interests that will be viciously fought over . . . to pretend otherwise is what makes people uninterested," Robinson told Cooke.

Just such conflicting human interests drive Robinson's award-winning and best-selling "Mars" trilogy. Totaling some 1,600 pages and taking six years to write, *Red Mars, Green Mars,* and *Blue Mars* chronicle human efforts over a period of several hundred years to colonize and "terraform" Mars. The colors in the books' titles represent the stages of Martian transformation: red for its original state, green for the successful introduction of plant life there, and blue for the eventual creation of oceans and an oxygen-enriched atmosphere. In *Red Mars,* the first one hundred colonists—carefully selected scientists with diverse views about the political and ethical aspects of their mission—journey to a lifeless Mars to begin the terraforming process. "The science of *Red Mars* is impeccably researched, convincing, and often thrilling in its moments of peril and grand implications," Faren Miller wrote in *Locus.* Liaisons and clashes soon emerge between strong personalities like those of team leaders Frank Chalmers and Maya Toitova, early Mars pioneer John Boone, political renegade Arkady Bogdanov, and subversive ecologist Hiroko Ao, among others.

Perhaps the most fierce and divisive is the argument that persists throughout the trilogy: whether Mars should be terraformed as quickly and fully as possible—a position advocated by the "Green" character Sax Russell and strongly supported by Earth governments—or whether its natural environment and evolution should be studied and preserved—a less-popular position held by geologist Ann Clayborne and her "Red" followers. By the end, initial visions for Mars's future are nearly subsumed by the multicultural complexities and mixed motives of an influx of new settlers, which lead to acts of sabotage and ultimately, a violent revolt. "In the debate over terraforming and its consequences, Mr. Robinson has all the makings of a philosophical novel of suspense. The stakes are high, the sides are shrewdly drawn, the players on both sides range from politically naive idealists to ambitious manipulators without discernable scruples," wrote Jonas.

Robinson's own views on the terraforming issue "are almost perfectly split down the middle, which I think is one of the driving emotional forces in me for writing" the "Mars" trilogy, he told Cooke in *Eidolon*. "There's a part of me that thinks that terraforming is a beautiful spiritual, almost religious project and that to be able to walk around on Mars in the open air . . . is absolutely one of the greatest human projects and ought to be done." He added, however, that he also thought this was a desecration of a unique, beautiful landscape. The different views give energy to the characters and the argument.

Red Mars begins with a murder in an established Martian settlement, then backtracks to the beginning of the colonization story so that readers may trace the motive, a plot device some critics found faulty. Many noted, however, that the plot is less important to Robinson than point of view: each chapter is told from the perspective of a different character, allowing Robinson to put forth a society of views that is in keeping with the scale of the terraforming effort. "His point is the reshaping of a world; people are hardly more than footnotes, and if their motives ultimately seem a little thin and their actions futile, never mind," concluded Tom Easton in *Analog*.

The colonists are eventually upstaged, many conclude, by Mars itself, through Robinson's descriptive landscaping and the science and technology he uses to bring Mars to life. "On one level, the planet itself becomes a major character," observed Jonas in the *New York Times Book Review*. The reader feels the changes in the atmosphere and the "beauty of this fundamentally inhuman setting and its effects on its all-too-human inhabitants," Jonas concluded.

Green Mars, which begins about twenty years later, chronicles the next forty years of life on Mars. Due to anti-aging treatments, many of the first one hundred colonists are still around, though driven underground by the failed rebellion which concluded *Red Mars*. Focusing on the coming-of-age in a southern colony established by rebel Hiroko Ao, the plot recalls some of the pioneering spirit of *Red Mars*. For the most part, however, *Green Mars* is devoted to the process of creating a central Martian government out of its numerous colonies. It concludes with revolutionary war and an environmental disaster on Earth.

Some critics thought that *Green Mars* suffers from "the middle book problem," struggling to keep up the established pace while at the same time trying to be more than just a bridge between the first and final books. "There are just enough kidnappings, murders, rescues, disasters, and acts of sabotage to keep it all exciting, but the tale is driven by the problems of gaining independence from both earthly governments and the giant corporations who continually seek ways of exploiting the Martian colony. This leads to long passages of political and economic debate that slow down Robinson's momentum," remarked Gary K. Wolfe in *Locus*. Another *Locus* contributor, Russell Letson, asserted: "The breadth of Robinson's interests makes for a dense and intellectually ambitious book: psychology, political-economic theory, history, the planetary sciences and ecology, and the interactions of all these. Robinson often shows a reluctance to depend on plot as the driving force of the narrative." With most of the action taking place off stage, Letson noted that "it's as if Robinson were avoiding as much of the vulgarity of the action as he could and still have a narrative in which crucial events occur. What we get instead is a book tied together by thematics and character."

Having successfully gained independence from Earth, Martian society's biggest threat in *Blue Mars* is the ongoing battling between the Reds, who want to sever ties with earth and protect what is left of untouched Mars, and the Greens who want to continue altering the planet for human use. At the risk of setting an ice age in motion, Green leader Sax Russell attempts to make peace with Red leader Ann Clayborne by removing from orbit the mirrors that create the atmospheric heat necessary for terraforming. As a result, the rival factions must together begin hammering out an appropriate government for themselves. Meanwhile, Earth faces a population crisis and impending planetary flooding, as its polar ice cap melts and ocean levels rise due to global warming. The crisis puts pressure on Mars to allow for the immigration of Terran refugees and leads to further Martian conflict.

"Robinson is as meticulous with his details as ever," noted *Science Fiction Weekly* contributor Clinton Lawrence, "whether he's describing the mechanisms of memory, the political and economic theories behind the new Martian constitution, or his characters' internal emotional and mental struggles." Lawrence added: "In *Blue Mars* it becomes clear that Robinson is writing about humanity's next great cultural leap as much as he is writing about the colonization of Mars."

Since completing the "Mars" trilogy, Robinson has moved some of his fiction back to Earth. In 1995 he won a National Science Foundation grant—the first science fiction writer to do to so—and spent six weeks in Antarctica accompanying a glacier research team on field work and visiting the McMurdo American base camp there to research his book, *Antarctica.* With Antarctica's oil riches at stake, the potential environmental, political, and territorial conflicts of the twenty-first century set the stage for this novel, which depicts a time in the near future when overpopulation, global warming, and deforestation have escalated to life-threatening proportions. "Robinson brings to this novel a passionate concern for landscape, ecology, and the effects of the 'Gotterdammerung capitalism' that he sees as the most serious threat to the survival of our species," explained a *Publishers Weekly* critic. The reviewer continued: "Moving back and forth between breathtaking descriptions of the alien, out-of-scale beauty of Antarctica, gripping tales of adventure on the ice and astute analyses of the ecopolitics of the southernmost continent, Robinson has created another superb addition to what is rapidly becoming one of the most impressive bodies of work in [science fiction]."

Robinson is also the author of *The Years of Rice and Salt,* an alternative history for Earth that imagines that the Black Death which swept Europe in the fourteenth century completely extinguished the European way of life. Into this vacuum move Chinese and Islamic culture. Robinson proceeds to tell a tale that bears recognizable parallels to actual history, but a history as it might have happened if Western culture had not been the driving force in the world. "The book may challenge readers less historically versed, particularly in non-Western cultures, than its author," observed *Booklist* contributor Roland Green about *The Years of Rice and Salt,* which he nevertheless termed "vast" and "magisterial." *Library Journal* reviewer Jackie Cassada was similarly positive, praising Robinson's "superb storytelling and imaginative historic speculation" in this "standout novel."

In *Forty Signs of Rain,* the first novel of a promised global warming trilogy, Robinson tells the story of a climate catastrophe threatening the world and the struggles of sedulous scientists to convince a myopic government of the imminent disaster. Wrote Clay Evans of the *Scripps Howard News Service:* "Robinson is a smart, careful author and researcher. But the book is not very much fun." Evans thought the problem lies in Robinson's veering away from the natural drama of the story to focus on domestic tedium in the protagonist's life. On the other hand, *Tampa Tribune* contributor Amy Smith Linton said that Robinson "combines fiercely intelligent speculative science and a keen grasp of global economics, along with memorable characters. The result is convincing fiction that's spooky and thought-provoking." *New York Times Book Review* critic Gerald Jonas observed that Robinson provides "an unforgettable demonstration of what can go wrong when an ecological balance is upset," and while he does not quite succeed in making bureaucratic apathy exciting, "he comes close to making mathematics the stuff of drama," he concluded.

BIOGRAPHICAL AND CRITICAL SOURCES:

BOOKS

Contemporary Literary Criticism, Volume 34, Thomson Gale (Detroit, MI), 1985.

Contemporary Novelists, 6th edition, St. James Press (Detroit, MI), 1996.

St. James Guide to Science-Fiction Writers, 4th edition, St. James Press (Detroit, MI), 1995.

Science-Fiction Writers, 2nd edition, Scribner's (Detroit, MI), 1999.

PERIODICALS

Analog Science Fiction and Fact, April, 1990, review of *Escape from Kathmandu,* p. 178; August, 1990, review of *A Short, Sharp Shock,* p. 143; September, 1991, review of *Pacific Edge,* p. 161; April, 1992, review of *Remaking History,* p. 164; July, 1993, review of *Red Mars,* p. 248; August, 1993, review of *Red Mars,* p. 249.

Booklist, October 15, 1989, review of *Escape from Kathmandu,* p. 430; November 1, 1990, review of *Pacific Edge,* p. 504; October 15, 1991, review of *Remaking History,* p. 416; January 1, 1993, review of *Red Mars,* pp. 795, 800; January 15, 1994, review of *Red Mars,* p. 866; February 1, 1994, review of *Green Mars,* p. 979; July, 1994, review of *Future Primitive,* pp. 1916, 1929; May 1, 1996, review of *Blue Mars,* p. 1469; April 1, 1999, review of *Antarctica,* p. 1401; July, 1999, review of *The Martians,* p. 1896; January 1, 2002, Roland Green, review of *The Years of Rice and Salt,* p. 777.

Book Report, November, 1990, review of *Escape from Kathmandu,* p. 66.

Books, July, 1989, review of *The Gold Coast,* p. 12; June, 1997, review of *Blue Mars,* p. 20.

Books and Culture, November, 1998, review of *Antarctica,* p. 47.

Bookwatch, March, 1992, review of *Remaking History,* p. 9; May, 1994, review of *Green Mars,* p. 8; July, 1995, review of *The Gold Coast,* p. 9.

Columbus Dispatch, August 17, 2004, review of *Forty Signs of Rain,* p. 4E.

Davis Enterprise, November 2, 1997, Elisabeth Sherwin, "Next Stop for Mars Junkies? How about 'Antarctica.'"

Economist, June 15, 1996, p. S13.

Eidolon, July, 1993, Sebastian Cooke, "An Earth-Man with a Mission."

Entertainment Weekly, June 11, 2004, review of *Forty Signs of Rain,* p. 129.

Extrapolation, spring, 1997, review of *Red Mars,* p. 57.

Independent, January 19, 2004, review of *Forty Signs of Rain,* p. 14.

Kirkus Reviews, October 15, 1989, review of *Escape from Kathmandu,* p. 1506; October 15, 1991, review of *Pacific Edge,* p. 1431; December 1, 1992, review of *Red Mars,* p. 1472; February 1, 1994, review of *Green Mars,* p. 104; May 1, 1996, review of *Blue Mars,* p. 650; May 15, 1998, review of *Antarctica,* p. 685.

Kliatt, September, 1990, review of *Escape from Kathmandu,* p. 24; March, 1993, review of *Red Mars,* p. 20; July, 1994, review of *Green Mars,* p. 18; September, 1995, review of *Green Mars,* p. 24; July, 1996, review of *A Short, Sharp Shock,* p. 22; September, 1997, review of *Future Primitive,* p. 23.

Library Journal, December, 1989, review of *Escape from Kathmandu,* p. 177; November 15, 1991, review of *Remaking History,* p. 111; November 15, 1992, review of *Red Mars,* p. 103; March 15, 1994, review of *Green Mars,* p. 104; July, 1996, review of *Blue Mars,* p. 170; January, 1997, review of *Blue Mars,* p. 51; July, 1998, review of *Antarctica,* p. 141; August 19, 1999, review of *The Martians,* p. 147; February 15, 2002, Jackie Cassada, review of *The Years of Rice and Salt,* pp. 180-181.

Locus, October, 1989, review of *Escape from Kathmandu,* p. 15; November, 1989, review of *The Blind Geometer,* p. 58; January, 1990, review of *Escape from Kathmandu,* p. 52; April, 1990, review of *Escape from Kathmandu,* p. 38; August, 1990, review of *A Short, Sharp Shock,* pp. 15, 31; October, 1990, review of *Icehenge,* p. 53; December, 1990, review of *Pacific Edge,* p. 55; January, 1991, review of *Pacific Edge,* p. 15, and review of *A Short, Sharp Shock,* p. 54; February, 1991, review of *Pacific Edge,* pp. 17, 36, 58; July, 1991, review of *Pacific Edge,* p. 48; November, 1991, review of *Remaking History,* p. 15; December, 1991, review of *Remaking History,* p. 17; January, 1992, review of *Remaking History,* p. 59; July, 1992, review of *Red Mars,* p. 23; October, 1992, Faren Miller, review of *Red Mars,* pp. 19, 21; February, 1993, review of *Red Mars,* p. 25; April, 1993, review of *Red Mars,* p. 49; May, 1993, review of *Red Mars,* p. 52; October, 1993, review of *Green Mars,* p. 23; November, 1993, review of *Green Mars,* pp. 17, 27; February, 1994, review of *Green Mars,* pp. 36-37, 74; April, 1994, review of *Escape from Kathmandu,* p. 50; May, 1994, review of *Green Mars,* p. 50; July, 1994, review of *Green Mars,* p. 60; September, 1994, review of *Future Primitive,* pp. 23, 64; November, 1994, review of *Remaking History and Other Stories,* p. 68; April, 1999, review of *The Martians,* p. 19; October, 1999, review of *The Martians,* p. 23.

Los Angeles Times Book Review, March 13, 1988; February 3, 1991, review of *Pacific Edge,* p. 11; January 5, 1992, review of *Remaking History,* p. 4.

Magazine of Fantasy and Science Fiction, May, 1984.

New Scientist, January 30, 1993, review of *Red Mars,* p. 50; March 13, 1993, review of *Red Mars,* p. 47; May 24, 1997, review of *Blue Mars,* p. 47; October 25, 1997, review of *Antarctica,* p. 49; July 31, 1999, review of *Pacific Edge,* p. 61.

New Statesman, December 5, 1997, review of *Antarctica,* p. 67.

New York Times Book Review, October 20, 1985; September 21, 1986; December 9, 1990, review of *Pacific Edge,* p. 32; June 2, 1991, review of *Pacific Edge,* p. 34; January 31, 1993, Gerald Jonas, review of *Red Mars,* p. 25; May 8, 1994, review of *Green Mars,* p. 25; June 5, 1994, review of *Green Mars,* p. 36; December 4, 1994, review of *Green Mars,* p. 81; June 30, 1996, Gerald Jonas, review of *Blue Mars,* p. 28; September 26, 1996, review of *The Martians,* p. 26; July 12, 1998, review of *Antarctica,* p. 1357; December 6, 1998, review of *Antarctica,* p. 95; December 5, 1999, review of *The Martians,* p. 101; April 28, 2002, Gerald Jonas, review of *The Years of Rice and Salt,* p. 20; June 20, 2004, review of *Forty Signs of Rain,* p. 17.

Publishers Weekly, October 20, 1989, review of *Escape from Kathmandu,* p. 44; October 12, 1990, review of *Pacific Edge,* p. 49; October 4, 1991, review of *Remaking History,* p. 82; December 14, 1992, review of *Red Mars,* p. 54; February 21, 1994, review of *Green Mars,* p. 249; June 20, 1994, review of *Future Primitive,* p. 98; November, 1994, review of *Green Mars,* p. 41; May 1, 1995, review of *The Wild Shore, Pacific Edge,* and *The Gold Coast,* p. 53; May 13, 1996, review of *Blue Mars,* p. 60; November 4, 1996, review of *Blue Mars;* May 11, 1998, review of *Antarctica,* p. 54; November 2, 1998, review of *Antarctica,* p. 44; July 26, 1999, review of *The Martians,* p. 67.

Reason, December, 1996, review of *Blue Mars,* p. 37.

School Library Journal, May, 1994, review of *Red Mars,* p. 144; December, 1994, review of *Red*

Mars, p. 39; February, 1995, review of *Green Mars,* p. 139.

Science Fiction Chronicle, January, 1990, review of *Escape from Kathmandu,* p. 34; June, 1991, review of *Pacific Edge,* p. 35; February, 1992, review of *Remaking History,* p. 33; February, 1993, review of *Red Mars,* p. 32; August, 1994, review of *Future Primitive,* p. 38; October, 1994, review of *Future Primitive,* p. 47; February, 1995, review of *Green Mars,* p. 7; July, 1995, review of *The Wild Shore,* p. 37; August, 1995, review of *The Wild Shore, The Gold Coast,* and *Pacific Edge,* p. 48; December, 1998, review of *Antarctica,* p. 50.

Science-Fiction Studies, March, 1994, review of *Red Mars,* p. 51.

Science Fiction Weekly, June 17, 1996, Clinton Lawrence, interview with Robinson and review of *Blue Mars.*

Scripps Howard News Service, June 30, 2004, Clay Evans, review of *Forty Signs of Rain.*

Small Press Review, April, 1991, review of *A Short, Sharp Shock,* p. 10.

Tampa Tribune, August 8, 2004, Amy Smith Linton, review of *Forty Signs of Rain.*

Times Literary Supplement, December 8, 1989, review of *The Gold Coast,* p. 1368; October 2, 1992, review of *Red Mars,* p. 20; May 3, 1996, Edward James, "The Landscape of Mars," p. 23; June 18, 1999, review of *The Martians,* p. 24.

Village Voice, January 17, 1989, review of *The Gold Coast,* p. 58.

Voice of Youth Advocates, February, 1991, review of *Icehenge,* p. 389; June, 1991, review of *Pacific Edge,* p. 113; October, 1991, review of *Pacific Edge,* p. 280; June, 1992, review of *Remaking History,* p. 114; April, 1993, review of *Remaking History,* p. 16, and review of *Red Mars,* p. 23; October, 1994, review of *Green Mars,* p. 226; February, 1995, review of *Future Primitive,* p. 347; April, 1997, review of *Blue Mars,* p. 9; February, 1999, review of *Antarctica,* p. 447; April, 1999, review of *Antarctica,* p. 15.

Washington Post Book World, April 22, 1984; August 25, 1985; November 26, 1989, review of *Escape from Kathmandu,* p. 6; November 25, 1990, review of *Pacific Edge,* p. 8; July 28, 1991, review of *A Sensitive Dependence on Initial Conditions,* p. 11; January 26, 1992, review of *Remaking History,* p. 6; February 27, 1994, review of *Green Mars,* p. 11; June 26, 1994, review of *Future Primitive,* p. 11; December 4, 1994, review of *Green Mars,* p. 16; December 7, 1997, review of *Antarctica,* p. 10; October 31, 1999, review of *The Martians,* p. 8.

West Coast Review of Books, Volume 16, number 1, 1991, review of *Pacific Edge,* p. 32.

Wilson Library Bulletin, February, 1993, review of *Red Mars,* p. 90; April, 1994, review of *Green Mars,* pp. 102-103; February, 1995, review of *Future Primitive,* p. 75.

World and I, April, 1994, review of *Red Mars* and *Green Mars,* p. 324.

* * *

ROBINSON, Lloyd
See SILVERBERG, Robert

* * *

ROBINSON, Marilynne 1944-

PERSONAL: Born in Sandpoint, ID, in 1944 (one source says 1943; another, 1947); married; children: two sons. *Education:* Brown University, B.A.; University of Washington, M.A., Ph.D.

ADDRESSES: *Home*—Massachusetts. *Office*—c/o Farrar, Straus, and Giroux, 19 Union Square W., New York, NY 10003.

CAREER: Writer.

AWARDS, HONORS: Ernest Hemingway Foundation award for best first novel from PEN American Center, Richard and Hinda Rosenthal Award from the American Academy and Institute of Arts and Letters, PEN/Faulkner fiction award nomination, and Pulitzer Prize nomination, all 1982, all for *Housekeeping; Los Angeles Times* Book Award nomination, 2004, National Book Critics Circle Award for fiction, 2004, PEN/Faulkner Award nomination, 2005, and Pulitzer Prize for fiction, 2005, all for *Gilead.*

WRITINGS:

Housekeeping (novel), Farrar, Straus (New York, NY), 1981.

Mother Country: Britain, the Nuclear State, and Nuclear Pollution, Farrar, Straus (New York, NY), 1989.

The Death of Adam: Essays on Modern Thought, Houghton (Boston, MA), 1998.

Puritans and Prigs, Holt (New York, NY), 1999.
Gilead, Farrar, Straus & Giroux (New York, NY), 2004.

Contributor of stories and articles to periodicals, including the *New York Times Book Review* and *Harper's;* a chapter from *Housekeeping* was published under the title "Loss" as a poem in *Quarto* magazine.

ADAPTATIONS: Housekeeping was adapted by Bill Forsyth into a film and released by Columbia in 1987.

SIDELIGHTS: Marilynne Robinson's novel *Housekeeping* earned its author the 1982 Ernest Hemingway Foundation award for best first novel, a 1982 Richard and Hinda Rosenthal Award, and a nomination for the Pulitzer Prize. It has garnered praise from numerous literary critics, such as Marc Granetz, who in *New Republic* deemed *Housekeeping* "a beautiful and unusual novel about transience and durability [that] revolves around familiar objects, details of everyday life. . . . Every sentence of *Housekeeping* is well written. And, as if that isn't remarkable enough, this is Marilynne Robinson's first novel." Paul Gray of *Time* remarked of *Housekeeping* that "this first novel does much more than show promise; it brilliantly portrays the impermanence of all things, especially beauty and happiness, and the struggle to keep what can never be owned." And, in Anatole Broyard's assessment in the *New York Times, Housekeeping* is "a first novel that sounds as if the author has been treasuring it up all her life, waiting for it to form itself. . . . You can feel in the book a gathering voluptuous release of confidence, a delighted surprise at the unexpected capacities of language, a close, careful fondness for people that we thought only saints felt. . . . Miss Robinson works with light, dark, water, heat, cold, textures, sounds and smells. . . . Though her ambition is tall, she remains down to earth, where the best novels happen."

In *Housekeeping* Robinson follows the lives of two adolescent girls through several guardianship changes. The story begins as a woman named Helen returns to her childhood home in Fingerbone, a small community isolated in the mountains of Idaho. With her, she brings her two daughters, Ruth and Lucille, and she leaves them on the porch of their grandmother's home. Helen then drives a car into the nearby lake, where her father drowned when she was a child. After Helen's suicidal drowning, Ruth and Lucille fall under the care of their grandmother, who attempts to restore normalcy to their lives through daily routine. After Ruth and Lucille's grandmother dies, the girls are cared for by two maiden great-aunts who also try to use unchanging daily routine to provide reassurance and stability in life. But the aunts, set in their habits, cannot adapt to the changing needs of children and so, leaving the girls, return to their former residence and the orderly lifestyle that they prefer.

The girls' next guardian is their mother's sister Sylvie, an eccentric drifter whose idea of housekeeping is "a merging of love and squalor," explained Julie Kavanagh in her *Times Literary Supplement* review of *Housekeeping.* Characteristic of this merging are Sylvie's collection of scraps, newspapers, and emptied food containers and her willingness to allow the outside to come inside the house in the form of animals and dead leaves. According to Kavanagh, Sylvie's housekeeping habits signify the novel's main theme—"an acceptance of transience, an acceptance which Sylvie embodies."

This acceptance of transience is tied to the idea that "memory and loss can paradoxically be a reminder of an eternal reunion to come," Kavanagh commented. And *Housekeeping* shows one of the girls, Ruth, discovering and adopting Sylvie's way of viewing life and death. Suzanne O'Malley reaffirmed this interpretation of Sylvie's perspective in *Ms.* magazine, stating that "Sylvie's peculiar brand of housekeeping included letting leaves gather in the corners. Ruth speculates that Sylvie actually took care not to disturb the leaves. . . . The point is not that Sylvie and her nieces lived in squalor—though that may be true enough—but that those who expect the past to leap to life at any minute consider 'accumulation to be the essence of housekeeping.'"

While Ruth accompanies Sylvie in her nighttime boat excursions on the lake where Sylvie's sister and father drowned and watches her strange aunt meditate in the dark on the past and come to terms with change, the other girl, Lucille, becomes increasingly alienated from her sister and aunt. Lucille dislikes being different from other adolescents, wants to fit in, be a part of Fingerbone society, and live a normal life. So she leaves her sister with Sylvie and moves in with one of her school teachers. From this point on, noted Art Seidenbaum in the *Los Angeles Times,* Sylvie and Ruth become "more like each other . . . less like their immediate neighbors [and] less like any people who must do rather than drift."

Eventually the residents of Fingerbone decide that Ruth's living with Sylvie is detrimental to the girl, and that they must take Ruth away from Sylvie. To prevent this, Ruth and Sylvie burn down their house, leave Fingerbone via the railway bridge over the lake, and take up a life of drifting. The novel's narrative begins to reflect this drifting, mingling the thoughts, dreams, and perceptions of Ruth, the narrator of *Housekeeping.* And, according to Le Anne Schreiber in the *New York Times Book Review,* "these distinctions break down utterly" as Ruth feels the pressure from the town to conform or split from Sylvie and realizes that they must leave Fingerbone. "The controlled lyricism of Ruth's language, which had been anchored in sensuous detail, becomes unmoored." The novel, like Ruth, then becomes "fevered and hallucinatory," concluded Schreiber. Kavanagh similarly noted the change in *Housekeeping*'s style once Ruth and Sylvie decide to leave home: "The previously realistic narrative now begins to mirror the drifters' new freedom and to take the form of arcane, meandering reflections. That the pair have symbolically transcended the mundane by crossing the bridge is reiterated by a free . . . prose-style." Anne Morddel, a contributor to *Contemporary Novelists,* observed that "Robinson's style itself is evocative of drifting and drifters' tales, with long, often poetic descriptions that suddenly snap back to the original point or deflect to a new, unrelated one."

Several critics considered *Housekeeping* to be a sort of long prose poem. According to Schreiber, *Housekeeping* "reads as slowly as poetry—and for the same reason: The language is so precise, so distilled, so beautiful that one doesn't want to miss any pleasure it might yield up to patience." Kavanagh likewise remarked, "It is a complex work, and as such should be read slowly and carefully." But, Kavanagh concluded, "this is not to say that it is impenetrable or over-intense. The author's control of plot, her eye for eccentricity, her clarity, quiet humour and delicate touch, invest the book with a lightness that successfully counterbalances the density of thought." Morddel saw some faults in the novel, such as some angry outbursts from Ruth that seem out of character. However, she emphasized that "these are small flaws in a book that is so rich with thought and feeling that it compels the reader to slow down and truly read."

After *Housekeeping* Robinson published a couple of nonfiction works, *Mother Country: Britain, the Nuclear State, and Nuclear Pollution,* and *The Death of Adam: Essays on Modern Thought.* The former is a passionate denunciation of the British government's management of the Sellafield nuclear processing plant. "The documentation behind the essay is exhaustive; the selective bibliography takes up twenty-two pages," noted Thomas Schaub in a *Contemporary Literature* profile of Robinson. "Throughout, Robinson's analysis of Sellafield is driven by a twin outrage: not only at the tons of nuclear waste being dumped into the sea each day, but also at the fact that a government which makes claims for the moralism of its acts is superintending this degradation of the earth." Robinson told Schaub the Sellafield situation represented "a profound abuse of the environment in an enormously, densely populated part of the world. And unless everything they've told us about radioactive contamination was some kind of a malicious fairy tale, there can only be very grievous consequences, and nothing was done to make us aware of this at all." She did not spare environmental organizations from her criticism; in her interview with Schaub, she asserted that they have "an enormous amount of information . . . that is never, ever communicated to people in this country." *New York Times Book Review* contributor Len Ackland, however, found a shortage of useful information in Robinson's book. Her "clear and justified passion unfortunately exceeds the evidence she brings to bear," he wrote, saying "the reader will search in vain for facts" that back up her arguments. He also thought she spent too much time on other subjects before dealing with Sellafield; he wished for "a rigorous short essay instead of this lengthy polemic."

Numerous essays on a plethora of topics are collected in *The Death of Adam.* Subjects include theologian John Calvin, the relationship of the McGuffey reader to nineteenth-century American social reform movements, and Charles Darwin's theory of evolution. In a review for *Christian Century,* Kathleen Norris described the collection as "rigorous but invigorating. . . a bracing book of truly contrarian essays." Norris observed, "With a novelist's sharp eye, Robinson exposes our bland acceptance of capitalist brutalities, our addiction to anxiety, our idolization of success, and our attendant loss of the ability to comprehend the significance of events. . . . While Robinson sometimes rants, as a contrarian is wont to do, her book is large in spirit." Norris particularly praised Robinson's handling of religion: "A rigorous thinker, blessedly conscious of history, Robinson makes a frontal assault on the easy, dismissive stereotypes of religion that abound in our culture." Similarly, Roger Kimball commented in the *New York Times Book Review,* "One would have to search far and wide to find another contemporary novelist writing articulate essays defending the theology of John Calvin or the moral and social lives of the Puritans. We all know that Puritans were dour, sex-hating, joy-abominating folk—except that, as Robinson shows, this widely embraced caricature is a calumny." A *Publishers Weekly* reviewer noted the large role Robinson's essays give to morality and reported that "for the most part her moral integrity is accompanied by an equally rigorous intellectual integrity." Kimball perceived a "current of high moral seriousness" in the book and averred that "one of Robinson's great merits as an essayist is her refusal to take her opinions secondhand. Her book is a goad to renewed curiosity." Norris concluded, "Ideologues of all stripes are likely to be enraged by this book—which seems like poetic justice to me. But if readers are willing to engage a book that may chip away at their ignorance and challenge their most dearly held assumptions and stereotypes, then Robinson's book will do its work."

In 2004, Robinson published *Gilead,* her first novel since *Housekeeping.* Writing for the *New York Times Book Review,* James Woods introduced his review of the novel by commenting, "To bloom only every twenty years would make, you would think, for anxious or vainglorious flowerings. But Marilynne Robinson. . . seems to have the kind of sensibility that is sanguine about intermittence." Woods went on to observe that Robinson' apparent draught in producing a second novel was not at all due to suffering from writer's block, rather the author was simply "moving at her own speed." By doing so, the critic felt *Gilead* had turned out a "fiercely calm. . . beautiful work." Many reviewers of the work focused on Robinson's lack of hurry in producing a follow-up novel to her successful *Housekeeping.* In his review of the book, Thomas Meaney, writing for *Commentary,* stated: "Robinson is not ambitious in the ordinary sense. She has written one highly regarded novel. . . but no more fiction until now. . . . she also achieves moments of near-Melvillean grandeur and dazzling lucidity, where her meandering syntax reaches for metaphors that are not only vessels of her religious faith but also an invitation to engage it."

The novel is religious in its topic in that, told from the point of view of a preacher reflecting on the meaning of life, it deals with humanity's inability to fully grasp God and the many questions that are raised in the attempt to attain godliness. However, while the religious looms over the book, it is personalized in the narrative, which takes shape around a father attempting to pass his life's knowledge to his son. Simon Baker summarized the book for *Spectator* by saying, "Set in 1956, it takes the form of a long letter from John Ames, a seventy-six-year-old Iowa preacher who is dying of heart disease, to his only son, who is six. The letter is Ames's attempt to bequeath to his son a distillation of a lifetime's quiet reflection and, in doing so, present a picture of his family's history." Baker regarded the novel as a success and stated that Robinson "has ended a quarter-century's silence with a masterly study of the dying of the light." In addition, Malcolm Jones, reviewing the novel for *Newsweek* concluded, "Good novels about spiritual life are rare. This is one of the best." Indeed, acclaim for Robinson's work was widespread, as *Gilead* earned both the National Book Critics Circle Award and the Pulitzer Prize for fiction.

BIOGRAPHICAL AND CRITICAL SOURCES:

BOOKS

Contemporary Literary Criticism, Volume 25, Thomson Gale, 1983.

Contemporary Novelists, St. James, 1996.

PERIODICALS

Atlantic Monthly, December, 2004, Mona Simpson, "The Minister's Tale: Marilynne Ronbinson's Long-Awaited Second Novel Is an Almost Otherworldly Book—and Reveals Robinson as a Somewhat Otherworldly Figure Herself," review of *Gilead,* p. 135.

Christian Century, November 18, 1998, Kathleen Norris, review of *The Death of Adam: Essays on Modern Thought,* p. 1101.

Commentary, August 16, 2005, Thomas Meaney, "In God's Creation," review of *Gilead,* p. 81.

Contemporary Literature, summer, 1994, Thomas Schaub, interview and review of *Mother Country: Britain, the Nuclear State, and Nuclear Pollution,* p. VI.

Los Angeles Times, January 14, 1981, Art Seidenbaum, review of *Housekeeping.*

Ms., April, 1981, Suzanne O'Malley, review of *Housekeeping.*

New Republic, February 21, 1981, Marc Granetz, review of *Housekeeping.*

Newsweek, December 6, 2004, Malcolm Jones, "Wrestling with Angels; 'Housekeeping' Author Returns with a Keeper," review of *Gilead,* p.87.

New York Times, January 7, 1981, Anatole Broyard, review of *Housekeeping.*

New York Times Book Review, February 8, 1981, Le Anne Schreiber, review of *Housekeeping;* July 16, 1989, Len Ackland, review of *Mother Country,* p. 7; February 7, 1999, Roger Kimball, review of *The Death of Adam;* November 28, 2004, James Wood, "Acts of Devotion," review of *Gilead,* p. 1.

Publishers Weekly, July 27, 1998, review of *The Death of Adam,* p. 60.

Spectator, April 16, 2005, Simon Baker, "Looking Back Without Anger," review of *Gilead,* p. 47.

Time, February 2, 1981, Paul Gray, review of *Housekeeping.*

Times Literary Supplement, April 3, 1981, Julie Kavanagh, review of *Housekeeping.*

* * *

RODMAN, Eric
See SILVERBERG, Robert

* * *

RODRÍGUEZ, Luis J. 1954-

PERSONAL: Born July 9, 1954, in El Paso, TX; son of Alfonso (a laboratory technician) and Maria Estela (a seamstress and homemaker; maiden name, Jimenez) Rodríguez; married Camila Martinez, August 10, 1974 (divorced November, 1979); married Paulette Theresa Donalson, November, 1982 (divorced February, 1984); married Maria Trinidad Cardenas (an editor and interpreter), March 28, 1988; children: (first marriage) Ramiro Daniel, Andrea Victoria; (third marriage) Ruben Joaquin, Luis Jacinto. *Education:* Attended California State University, 1972-73, Rio Hondo Community College, California Trade-Technical Institute, Watts Skills Center, Mexican-American Skills Center, East Los Angeles College, 1978-79, University of California at Berkeley, 1980, and University of California at Los Angeles. *Politics:* "Revolutionary." *Religion:* "Catholic/Indigenous Spirituality."

ADDRESSES: *Home*—Pacoima, CA. *Office*—Tia Chucha Café Cultural, 12737 Glenoaks Blvd., Sylmar, CA 91342.

CAREER: Worked variously as a school bus driver, lamp factory worker, truck driver, paper mill utility worker, millwright apprentice, steel mill worker, foundry worker, carpenter, and chemical refinery worker, 1972-79; Eastern Group Publications, Los Angeles, CA, photographer and reporter for seven East Los Angeles weekly newspapers, 1980; reporter for newspapers, including *San Bernadino Sun* (CA), 1980-85; *People's Tribune,* Chicago, IL, editor, 1985-88; computer typesetter for various firms in the Chicago area, including the Archdiocese of Chicago, 1987-89; writer, lecturer, and critic, 1988—; part-time news writer for WMAQ-AM in Chicago, 1989-92. Director of mural project for the Bienvenidos Community Center, 1972; public affairs associate for American Federation of State, County, and Municipal Employees (AFL-CIO), 1982-85; publisher and editor of *Chismearte,* 1982-85; facilitator of Barrio Writers Workshops, Los Angeles, 1982-85; board member of KPFK-FM, Pacifica Station in Los Angeles, 1983-85; founder and director of Tia Chucha Press, 1989—; writer-in-residence, Shakespeare and Company, Paris, France, 1991; writer-in-residence, North Carolina's "Word Wide," 2000; founder of organizations, including Rock a Mole (rhymes with guacamole) Productions, League of Revolutionaries for a New America, the Guild Complex, Youth Struggling for Survival, and Tia Chucha's Café Cultural. Mosaic Multicultural Foundation, Washon, WA, elder and teacher, 1993—; Increase the Peace, Chicago, IL, participant, 1995—. Conductor of talks, readings, and workshops in prisons, juvenile facilities, public and private schools, migrant camps, churches, universities, community centers, and homeless shelters throughout the United States, Canada, Mexico, Puerto Rico, Central America, and Europe, 1980—.

MEMBER: PEN USA West, Poets and Writers, American Poetry Society, National Writers Union, Academy of American Poets, Association of American Cultures, Los Angeles Latino Writers Association (director/publisher, 1982-85).

AWARDS, HONORS: Best of the *Los Angeles Weekly,* 1985; Poetry Center Book Award, San Francisco State University, for *Poems across the Pavement,* 1989; Illinois Arts Council poetry fellowships, 1992, 2000; Lannan fellowship in poetry, 1992; Dorothea Lange/Paul Taylor Prize, Center for Documentary Studies, Duke University, 1993; Carl Sandburg Literary Award for nonfiction, and *New York Times Book Review* Notable Book, both 1993, and *Chicago-Sun Times* Book Award for nonfiction, 1994, all for *Always Running: La Vida Loca—Gang Days in L.A.;* Hispanic Heritage Award for literature, 1998; Lila Wallace-*Reader's Digest* Writers' Award, 1996; National Association for Poetry Therapy Public Service Award, 1997; Paterson Prize for Books for Young Adults, 1999; *Skipping Stones* magazine honor awards, 1999 and 2000; Silver Book Award, *Foreword* magazine, 1999; Parents' Choice Books for Children Award, 1999; Illinois Author of the Year Award, 2000; Americas Award for Children's and Young Adult Literature Commended Title, 2000; Premio Fronterizo Border Book Festival, Las Cruces, New Mexico, 2001; Unsung Heroes of Compassion award, 2001; PEN West/Josephine Miles Award for Literary Excellence, for *The Concrete River.*

WRITINGS:

Poems across the Pavement, Tia Chucha Press (Chicago, IL), 1989.
The Concrete River (poems), Curbstone Press (Willimantic, CT), 1991.
Always Running: La Vida Loca—Gang Days in L.A. (memoir), Curbstone Press (Willimantic, CT), 1993.
América Is Her Name (for children), illustrated by Carlos Vazquez, Curbstone Press (Willimantic, CT), 1998.
Trochemoche: New Poems, Curbstone Press (Willimantic, CT), 1998.
It Doesn't Have to Be This Way: A Barrio Story (for children), illustrated by Daniel Galvez, Children's Book Press (San Francisco, CA), 1999.
Hearts and Hands: Creating Community in Violent Times, Seven Stories Press (New York, NY), 2001.
The Republic of East L.A.: Stories, Rayo (New York, NY), 2002.
My Nature Is Hunger: New and Selected Poems, Curbstone Press (Willimantic, CT), 2005.
Music of the Mill: A Novel, Rayo (New York, NY), 2005.

Contributor of articles, reviews, and poems to periodicals, including *Los Angeles Times, Nation, U.S. News & World Report, Utne Reader, Philadelphia Inquirer Magazine, Chicago Reporter, Poets and Writers, Chicago Tribune, American Poetry Review, TriQuarterly, Bloomsbury Review, Rattle,* and *Latina.* Also contributor to anthologies, including *The Outlaw Bible of American Poetry, Letters of a Nation: A Collection of Extraordinary American Letters, Las Christmas: Favorite Latino Authors Share Their Holiday Memories, Inside the L.A. Riots: What Happened and Why It Will Happen Again, Mirrors beneath the Earth: Short Fiction by Chicano Writers, After Aztlan: Latino Writers in the '90s, Fifty Ways to Fight Censorship, With the Wind at My Back and Ink in My Blood: A Collection of Poems by Chicago's Homeless, Unsettling America: An Anthology of Contemporary Multicultural Poetry, Power Lines: A Decade of Poetry at Chicago's Guild Complex,* and *Voices: Readings from El Grito.*

Rodríguez's work has been translated into German, French, Arabic, and Spanish.

WORK IN PROGRESS: My Nature Is Hunger: New and Selected Poems, to be published by Curbstone Press; "Nations," an original treatment for a possible TV pilot and series for Shore Media Productions, registered with the Writers Guild.

SIDELIGHTS: In his 1993 memoir, poet-author-journalist Luis J. Rodríguez encapsulates the trapped feeling of the Latino in East Los Angeles: "It never stopped this running. We were constant prey, and the hunters soon became big blurs: The police, the gangs, the junkies, the dudes on Garvey Boulevard who took our money, all smudge into one." But the enemy was not always on the street for young Mexican Americans like Rodríguez: "Sometimes they were teachers who jumped on us Mexicans as if we were born with a hideous stain. We were always afraid, always running." It was this feeling of persecution, of being the target of others, that led young men like Rodríguez into gang membership.

Always Running: La Vida Loca—Gang Days in L.A. is Rodríguez's personal statement, his mea culpa, both a cautionary tale and gut-wrenching personal document. Written two decades after his own gang activity, the book was partly inspired by his own son, Ramiro, who was himself becoming involved in gangs at the time Rodríguez was writing his book. The memoir was not enough of a palliative, however, to keep Ramiro out of trouble: Rodríguez's son was sent to prison in 1998 for attempted murder. Despite school bans on the book and a mini-controversy over its content, Rodríguez still believes it should be essential reading for many. "I actually hope my book will lose its validity some day," he told Patrick Sullivan in an interview for the *Sonoma County Independent,* "that there isn't a need for a book like *Always Running*. . . . But right now that's not the case. The book is very relevant, and as long as that's the case, then we should make sure that people can get access to it."

Rodríguez has written three books of poetry and two children's books in addition to this partly fictionalized memoir. He has also chronicled the Mexican-American experience and spoken out articulately for social justice and equity in the country through journalistic articles to national publications such as the *Los Angeles Times, Nation,* and *U.S. News & World Report,* but he continues to view himself primarily as a poet. As he told Aaron Cohen in an interview for *Poets and Writers,* "Poetry is the foundation of everything I do. It's poetry with a sense of social engagement. The written, powerful expressive language of poetry is the springboard for everything I want to write."

Rodríguez is no stranger to the mean streets he depicts in his work. Born in El Paso, Texas, on July 9, 1954, he spent two years in Ciudad Juarez, Mexico, before his family immigrated to the United States in 1956. His father, Alfonso Rodríguez, a school principal in Mexico, brought his family north because the pay was so poor in his native country that he could not support his children. Once settled in the Watts community of south central Los Angeles, Alfonso and his family were presented with the cruel reality of low-status work and constant racism. His father held a number of jobs, ultimately working as a laboratory custodian, while Rodríguez's mother, Maria Estela Jimenez, worked as a seamstress. Rodríguez grew up with three siblings and three nieces, the daughters of his half-sister, and in 1962 the family moved to the East Los Angeles community of South San Gabriel. Rodríguez's teenage years were spent in the barrio there.

These were turbulent years for the young Rodríguez, who felt like he was always on the outside, harassed by both Anglo children and the police. To find a sense of solidarity and belonging, he joined a gang in East Los Angeles. Dropping out of school at fifteen, he led a life during the 1960s and 1970s characterized by ever-escalating violence and mayhem. Jailed for attempted murder, he was released only to take part in a fire bombing of a home and in store robberies. Sex and drugs formed a continual base line to his life. "Everything lost its value for me," Rodríguez wrote in *Always Running,* describing the nihilism of those days. "Death seemed the only door worth opening, the only road toward a future."

But Rodríguez was one of the fortunate ones. From his early youth he had tried to find a safe haven in books, in an interior life. Even as a very young child, as he told Cohen, "I found refuge in books because I was a shy, broken-down little kid. They were fairytale books, Walt Disney books, whatever. I would go inside and hide myself in books and not have to worry about the yelling and screaming and bullets flying." Even as a gang member, he was composing verses based on his experiences on the streets. This propensity for self-reflection came in handy when, at the height of the Chicano Movement, Rodríguez was pulled from the gangs by the lure of education and political activism. A recreational leader at a local youth center introduced Rodríguez to Mexican history and a new way of looking at himself, while a counselor at school, when he returned to graduate in 1970, also helped to make the young man into a student leader instead of a gang dupe, taking pride in his culture, in his race, in his heritage. Slowly Rodríguez turned away from violence to the world of words.

Graduating from high school in 1970, Rodríguez won his first literary award two years later, the Quinto Sol Literary Award, which earned him 250 dollars and a trip to Berkeley. Throughout the 1970s Rodríguez continued writing while holding down blue collar jobs. He also married for the first time and became the father of two children. Then in 1980 he became a full-time writer, working as a journalist and photographer for several Los Angeles newspapers.

Rodríguez became heavily involved in the East Los Angeles political and literary scene, serving as director of the Los Angeles Latino Writers Association and publishing the literary magazine *Chismearte,* in whose pages some of the bright and rising stars of Latino literature were first introduced to a wider public. By the mid 1980s, divorced, remarried, and divorced again, Rodríguez had resettled in Chicago, where he worked as an editor on the *People's Tribune,* a weekly leftist journal. He also became deeply involved in not only literary matters, giving poetry workshops and crafting his journalism, but also in social issues, working with gang members, the homeless, convicts, and migrants. During this time he established Tia Chucha Press, the publishing house of the Guild Complex, an arts center in Chicago focusing on multicultural issues. In 1988, he married for a third time and has two children by this marriage.

In 1989 his Tia Chucha Press published his first collection of poetry, *Poems across the Pavement,* verses that focus on "life in America," according to Dina G. Castillo, writing in *Dictionary of Literary Biography,* "but his America is one that relatively few people want to acknowledge." Castillo described the America Rodríguez portrays as "an environment fraught with economic oppression, racism, cultural alienation, class battles, industrial displacement, strained human relations, and street turmoil in Los Angeles and Chicago." Rodríguez depicts this situation in poems in the collection such as "'Race' Politics," "No Work Today," "Tombstone Poets," and "Alabama," which take the reader on "an emotional roller coaster," according to Castillo. Some of the poems were written when Rodríguez was still a teenager, and all display the influence of his own favorite writers, poets from Walt Whitman to Pablo Neruda, and Latino and African American authors such as Claude Brown and Piri Thomas, whose work portrayed the hard lives of society's outcasts and downtrodden.

A second collection, *The Concrete River,* appeared in 1991, confirming Rodríguez's early promise and delving more deeply into the themes of urban violence, race relations, gender conflicts, and drug addiction that he explored in his first volume of poetry. An interesting development in *The Concrete River* is the use of both poetry and prose in longer pieces, ones that tie together to provide a witnessing of his own past, from Mexico to Watts to East Los Angeles to Chicago. In the first of five sections, with the poem "Prelude to a Heartbeat," Rodríguez talks of his youth in Watts, "Where fear is a deep river. / Where hate is an overgrown weed." His dangerous gang years are dealt with in the second section, while his failed first marriage comes to center stage in the third, "Always Running": "When all was gone, / the concrete river / was always there / and me, always running." Other sections deal with his life as a blue-collar worker and with his new life in Chicago, away from the city that molded him and nearly destroyed him.

Castillo noted that Rodríguez uses the "motifs of concrete and pavement to represent all that has limited him in the past but that nevertheless became the source of his literary creativity." For Rodríguez there is some value, some resiliency to be gained from such a hard life. "He views poetry as the water that runs through the concrete river," Castillo observed, "cleansing and restoring life." A reviewer for *Publishers Weekly* concluded, "This poetry is of the barrio yet stubbornly refuses to be confined in it—Rodríguez's perceptive gaze and storyteller's gift transport his world across neighborhood boundaries." Audrey Rodríguez, writing in *Bilingual Review,* noted that *The Concrete River* "involves a return to and recovery of the past . . . and a recognition of chaos, death, and the reality of a place that locks in or jeopardizes the thinking-feeling self." The critic concluded that the poet "is one of Chicano literature's most gifted and committed artists today. . . . His is a refreshing voice—of rebellion and beauty—in an increasingly narrow age of literature's disengagement from the ground of great art and true history." *The Concrete River* won the Paterson Poetry Prize and the PEN West/Josephine Miles Award for Literary Excellence. In 1992 Rodríguez received both an Illinois Arts Council poetry fellowship and a Lannan fellowship in poetry.

For his next work, Rodríguez moved away from poetry, but not from the lyrical inspiration, to tell in prose form the story of his own years in a Los Angeles gang. He dedicated his book to the twenty-five of his childhood friends who died victims of gang violence before the author reached the age of eighteen. In *Always Running: La Vida Loca—Gang Days in L.A.*Rodríguez also explains the needs out of which the Hispanic gang culture springs. As Dale Eastman reported in *New City* magazine, "Socially ostracized and economically segregated from their white counterparts, the young children of mostly migrant workers who had come north to earn a living, first formed clicas, or clubs, to create some sense of belonging." These Mexican youths were denied, for the most part, membership in other organizations, be it the Boy Scouts or even athletic teams. These alternate, ad hoc youth clubs slowly evolved into the gangs of today, many of them simply another way to hang out with friends. Eastman further noted, "As increasing numbers of Mexicans moved into the barrio areas, the clubs adopted a more dangerous profile, offering much-needed protection from rival groups and a sense of power in an increasingly powerless world."

As Rodríguez grew older, he became increasingly involved in drugs and gang violence. Gary Soto, critiquing *Always Running* in the *New York Times Book Review,* noted that "the body count rises page by page. The incidents become increasingly bizarre and perversely engaging. Mr. Rodríguez is jailed for attempted murder, then let go. He participates in the firebombing of a home. He robs stores. He experiments with heroin. He wounds a biker with a shotgun blast, is arrested, then let go. When police officers beat him to the ground, his 'foot inadvertently came up and brushed one of them in the chest,' and he is booked for assault and eventually tried and jailed." But Rodríguez also tells how he escaped the gang life, and he brings *Always Running* up to date by discussing the role of gangs in the 1992 riots in Los Angeles, and his own son's gang involvement in Chicago. Soto concluded that *Always Running* "is a chilling portrait of gang life during the 1960s, a gang life that haunts us even now. . . . The book is fierce and fearless."

Castillo noted that while some critics call the book "a memoir, others have qualified it as a novel of redemption because of its fictional/poetic qualities." As Rodríguez noted to Cohen, the book is a little of both, for he "synthesized events and reorganized the material so that it would work as literature [fiction] but still maintain the truth and reality of the situation." Castillo further observed, "Often poetic, the narration is nevertheless a straight presentation of life as it was for Rodríguez. Readers witness a childhood and adult behavior that is surprising for its violence." Ultimately, Rodríguez was saved from the violence by two mentors who showed him a different path; such a path was not open to Chava, a former gang leader whom Rodríguez meets at the end of the book outside a party. Battered and wounded—Chava carries a colostomy bag as a result of a stabbing—this once feared enemy is "a fragment of the race, drunk, agonized, crushed, and I can't hate him anymore; I can't see him as the manifestation of craziness and power he once possessed; he's a caricature, an apparition, but also more like me, capable of so much ache beneath the exterior of so much strength."

Other reviewers lauded Rodríguez's gritty tale, while a storm of controversy began to brew over its use in the schools. Suzanne Ruta called the book "beautifully written and politically astute" in an *Entertainment Weekly* review, while Floyd Salas, writing in the *Los Angeles Times,* felt it was "a pilgrim's progress, a classic tale of the new immigrant in the land of the melting pot." Salas went on to describe *Always Running* as "a tome of the torturous, faltering, sometimes progressing, sometimes repressing journey of a gifted migrant. With this memorable, often tragic story, Rodríguez has fulfilled that journey by achieving the American dream of success in art and life." Fred Whitehead, reviewing the book in *National Catholic Reporter,* concluded, "By expressing the pain of those most destroyed, Rodríguez never lets us forget where we need to go together. He thinks it is possible for us all to deal with these problems, not by way of patching here and there, but through fundamental change." Echoing these sentiments, a reviewer for the *Progressive* wrote that this "beautifully written insider's account of what it's like to live in the desolation of America's urban ghettoes" tells "how our society leaves minorities and the poor no viable alternatives. . . . The problem, Rodríguez makes clear, is not with the gangs but with the society that creates gangs."

In artistic content, Rodríguez was perhaps too successful in his reproduction of the climate of violence in which he grew up. Several school boards around the country banned the book from their library shelves, criticizing it for promoting violence. But Rodríguez is steadfast. The book neither glorifies nor demonizes gang involvement, Rodríguez asserts. He told Sullivan, "both views distort reality." The book contains, according to its many supporters, a message that will reach kids in gangs, that touches their lives directly and that may lead them—as a similar approach did for Rodríguez himself—out of the violence and into the light. *Nation* contributor Ilan Stavans echoed this very desire: "Although gang life may be impossible to eradicate fully, one hopes that *Always Running* (a fortunate title) will be read where it most counts, and widely, and have an impact." Rodríguez has maintained a busy schedule of writing and speaking in schools since the publication of *Always Running,* becoming a spokesman for Latino causes, as well as for youth and the dispossessed. Deeply involved in social causes, he has also continued to publish distinguished and innovative verse and prose. In 1998 he added to his poetry publications with *Trochemoche: New Poems*—"helter-skelter" in Spanish. These verses are once again highly autobiographical in nature and explore the phases of Rodríguez's life from gang member to "his more sedate role as a Chicago publisher," as Lawrence Olszewski noted in a *Library Journal* review of the collection. In the poem "Notes of a Bad Cricket," Rodríguez assays his inner worlds: "There is a mixology of brews within me; I've tasted them all, still fermenting / as grass-high anxieties. I am rebel's pen, rebel's son, father of revolution in verse." Olszewski went on to observe the "head-on, no-holds barred style" that "smacks more of newspaper accounts than lyricism without succumbing to sensationalism." Susan Smith Nash described the collection as "raw, honest, hard-hitting" in *World Literature Today,* with voices that "are dissident, angry, raised in protest." Nash further commented that these voices "are truly unforgettable."

Additionally, Rodríguez has branched out into new territory with his children's books, *América Is Her Name* and *It Doesn't Have to Be This Way.* Castillo called the former book "a sensitive story for young children" in *Dictionary of Literary Biography.* The story of nine-year-old América Soliz, an illegal Mexican immigrant living in a Chicago barrio, the book takes young readers inside the head and heart of this young girl whose greatest wish is simply to return to her native Oaxaca. But when a Puerto Rican poet visits her English-as-a-second-language (ESL) class one day, she is inspired to become a citizen of the world through poetry.

Writing in *School Library Journal,* Denise E. Agosto felt that the "story is generally well told, and its message is an important one." Agosto concluded that *América Is Her Name* is a "solid choice for bilingual and ESL collections." Though a reviewer for *Publishers Weekly* thought the book "ponderous" and "wordy," *Skipping Stones* critic Beth Erfurth called the book a "story about hopes, memories, and dreams amid a reality of discrimination and despair," and found it to be an "inspiration to readers of all ages."

In a second picture book, *It Doesn't Have to Be This Way,* Rodríguez tells another cautionary tale about gangs. Ten-year-old Monchi relates his own near miss with joining a gang—saved by the shooting of his older cousin, a girl who has advised him to avoid the gangs. Dreamer, the older cousin, is left in a wheelchair as a result of the shooting, but Monchi refuses to be drawn into the cycle of retribution that others demand. "The message is spelled out," wrote Hazel Rochman in a *Booklist* review, "but Rodríguez's personal experience, as a teenage gang member and now as an adult counselor, gives the story immediacy." *School Library Journal* writer Reina Huerta felt the book could be "a springboard for discussion."

Rodríguez returned to adult prose with *Hearts and Hands: Creating Community in Violent Times* and *The Republic of East L.A.: Stories.* In the former book, Rodríguez "takes a long, hard look at the endemic violence and the 'cultural malaise of isolation and meaningless' that he sees as defining swaths of U.S. culture," as a *Publishers Weekly* contributor described it. Rodríguez mixes stories of his own life, including his current work with young people at risk of joining gangs, with sociological and political analyses of the pathologies of urban life. In the latter book, Rodríguez tackles many of the same topics, but this time through fiction: "twelve gritty, hard-hitting snapshots," as a *Publishers Weekly* contributor described the short stories of *The Republic of East L.A.* Although acknowledging that the author "is skillful at rendering the aura of East L.A.," a *Kirkus Reviews* critic thought that in this, his first foray into fiction, Rodríguez "too often shoots for a kind of scope that he has yet to master." On the other hand, the *Publishers Weekly* reviewer wrote that "the collection as a whole attains a spirited, resilient rhythm."

In June 2000, Rodríguez left Chicago and returned to the Los Angeles area. Eighteen months later, his new project, Tia Chucha's Café Cultural, opened its doors. Named after his eccentric but independent aunt, the cafe/bookstore/art gallery/computer center/performance center seeks to empower the local Latino community through art. As Rodríguez and his wife told *Los Angeles Times* reporter Maria Elena Fernandez, Sylmar (where the cafe is located) and the surrounding towns of San Fernando, Arleta, Sun Valley, and Pacoima (where the Rodríguez family lives), with a combined population of 400,000, are eighty percent Latino and, before the opening of Tia Chucha's, had not one bookstore or community art center.

Rodríguez once commented, "Despite great odds, today I'm a poet and writer of note, driven by the great social upheavals of our day. I say to any young person—especially one linked to a great cause such as the fundamental progress of humanity—never give up. We all have the capabilities of great art and poetry. It's a matter of tapping into that creative reservoir we contain as human beings. Once tapped, this reservoir is inexhaustible. Skills and technique can always be learned. Opening up to our innate powers as communicators and artists is a strong foundation for obtaining such skills."

The poet also once noted in his *Contemporary Authors Autobiography Series* essay that after a life lived through cultural and economic hardships, his "resolve has only strengthened" and his "vision has only sharpened." Sober, reconciled with family members and the world at large, Rodríguez faces the future with optimism. He concluded, "There are difficult roads ahead; if anything, I'm more prepared for them than I have ever been. According to the ancient Mexican people, we are living under the Fifth Sun. *Nahui Ollin.* A time of change. Of movement. From the heart of a person to the heart of the universe."

BIOGRAPHICAL AND CRITICAL SOURCES:

BOOKS

Contemporary Authors Autobiography Series, Volume 29, Thomson Gale (Detroit, MI), 1998.

Dictionary of Literary Biography, Volume 209: *Chicano Writers, Third Series,* Thomson Gale (Detroit, MI), 1999.

Rodríguez, Luis J., *Always Running: La Vida Loca—Gang Days in L.A.,* Curbstone Press (Willimantic, CT), 1993.

Rodríguez, Luis J., *The Concrete River,* Curbstone Press (Willimantic, CT), 1991.

Rodríguez, Luis J., *Trochemoche: New Poems,* Curbstone Press (Wilimantic, CT), 1998.

Schwartz, Michael, *Luis J. Rodríguez,* Raintree/Steck-Vaughn, 1997.

PERIODICALS

Bilingual Review, September-December, 1996, Audrey Rodríguez, "Contemporary Chicano Poetry," pp. 203-207.

Booklist, August, 1999, Hazel Rochman, review of *It Doesn't Have to Be This Way,* p. 2059; April 15, 2002, Carlos Orellana, review of *The Republic of East L.A.: Stories,* p. 1383.

Chicago Tribune, February 25, 1993.

Entertainment Weekly, February 12, 1993, Suzanne Ruta, review of *Always Running,* p. 51.

Hartford Courant, March 5, 1993, pp. C1, C8.

Hispanic, June, 1993, p. 72.

Hungry Mind Review, summer, 1993.

Kirkus Reviews, March 1, 2002, review of *The Republic of East L.A.: Stories,* p. 285.

Library Journal, June 15, 1998, Lawrence Olszewski, review of *Trochemoche,* p. 82; April 1, 2004, Nancy Pearl, "California, here I come." p. 144.

Los Angeles Magazine, May 2002, Ariel Swartley, "It's East L.A., Jake; Luis J. Rodríguez, in and out of time," p. 99.

Los Angeles Times, July 25, 1996, Mark Cromer, "After Swearing off Alcohol, 'Always Running' Author Luis Rodríguez Is Still on the Move," p. 5; December 18, 2001, Maria Elena Fernandez, "Poet of the Streets," p. E1; December 23, 2001, Jonathan Kirsch, "West Words: When Rage Becomes Poetry," p. R2.

Los Angeles Weekly, March 7, 1993, Floyd Salas, "Leaving the Gang Behind," p. 2.

Nation, April 12, 1993, Ilan Stavans, review of *Always Running,* pp. 494-498.

National Catholic Reporter, January 8, 1993, Fred Whitehead, review of *Always Running,* p. 61.

NEA Today, February, 1996, Anita Merina, "Peacemaker," p. 7.

New City, February 8, 1993, Dale Eastman, review of *Always Running,* pp. 10, 12.

New York Times Book Review, February 14, 1993, Gary Soto, "The Body Count in the Barrio," p. 26.

Poets and Writers, January-February, 1995, Aaron Cohen, "An Interview with Luis J. Rodríguez," pp. 50-55.

Progressive, September, 1993, review of *Always Running,* p. 43.

Publishers Weekly, May 17, 1991, review of *The Concrete River,* p. 58; February 1, 1993, p. 86; September 23, 1996, p. 12; April 13, 1998, review of *América Is Her Name,* p. 75; August 16, 1999, review of *It Doesn't Have to Be This Way,* p. 85; November 5, 2001, review of *Hearts and Hands,* p. 58; March 18, 2002, review of *The Republic of East L.A.,* p. 76.

Rattle Magazine, winter, 1999, interview with Luis Rodríguez.

School Library Journal, September, 1998, Denise E. Agosto, review of *América Is Her Name,* p. 180; October, 1999, Reina Huerta, review of *It Doesn't Have to Be This Way,* p. 124; April, 2002, Brianna Yamashita, "Latino Author Plants Cultural Roots," p. S7.

Skipping Stones, May-August, 1999, Beth Erfurth, review of *América Is Her Name,* p. 6.

Sojourners, March, 1999, p. 57.

Sonoma County Independent, February 4, 1999, Patrick Sullivan, "Class War: Luis J. Rodríguez Casts a Skeptical Eye on Attempts to Ban His Autobiography," pp. 21-22.

Sun Magazine, April, 2000, Derrick Jensen, interview with Luis Rodríguez.

World Literature Today, winter, 1999, Susan Smith Nash, review of *Trochemoche,* p. 156.

ONLINE

Academy of American Poets Web site, http://www.poets.org/ (August 5, 2004), biography of Luis J. Rodríguez.

Harper Collins Web site, http://www.harpercollins.com/ (August 5, 2004).

League of Revolutionaries for a New America Web site, http://www.lrna.net (August 5, 2004), biography of Luis J. Rodríguez.

Luis J. Rodríguez Home Page, http://www.luisjrodriguez.com/ (August 5, 2004).

Steven Barclay Agency, http://www.barclayagency.com/ (May 23, 2002).

Word Sculptors, http://www.wordsculptors.com/ (May 23, 2002), Luis Rodríguez's home page.

OTHER

The Choice of a Lifetime: Returning from the Brink of Suicide (video), New Day Films, 1996.

In Their Own Voices: A Century of Recorded Poetry (audio cassette), Ehino/Word Beat Records, 1996.

La Vida Loca: El testimonio de un pandillero en Los Angeles (audio cassette), AudioLibros del Mundo, 1998.

Luis Rodríguez (video), Lannan Foundation, 1992.

Making Peace: Youth Struggling for Survival (video), Moira Productions, 1997.

A Snake in the Heart: Poems and Music by Chicago's Spoken Word Performers (audio cassette), Tia Chucha Press, 1994.

* * *

RODRIGUEZ, Richard 1944-

PERSONAL: Born July 31, 1944, in San Francisco, CA; son of Leopoldo (a dental technician) and Victoria (a clerk-typist; maiden name, Moran) Rodriguez. *Education:* Stanford University, B.A., 1967; Columbia University, M.A., 1969; graduate study at University of California, Berkeley, 1969-72, 1974-75, and Warburg Institute, London, 1972-73. *Religion:* Roman Catholic.

ADDRESSES: *Home*—San Francisco, CA. *Agent*—Georges Borchardt, Inc., 136 East 57th St., New York, NY 10022.

CAREER: Journalist. Held a variety of jobs, including janitorial work and freelance writing, 1977-81; writer, 1981—; University of Chicago, Perlman lecturer, 1984; journalist and essayist for PBS series *MacNeil-Lehrer NewsHour;* Pacific News Service, editor.

AWARDS, HONORS: Fulbright fellowship, 1972-73; National Endowment for the Humanities fellowship, 1976-77, and Frankel Medal; Commonwealth Club gold medal, 1982; Christopher Award, 1982, for *Hunger of Memory: The Education of Richard Rodriguez;* Anisfield-Wolf Award for Race Relations, 1982; George Foster Peabody Award, 1997, for work on the *MacNeil-Lehrer NewsHour;* International Journalism Award from World Affairs Council of California.

WRITINGS:

Hunger of Memory: The Education of Richard Rodriguez (autobiography), David R. Godine (Boston, MA), 1982.

Days of Obligation: An Argument with My Mexican Father (autobiography), Viking Penguin (New York, NY), 1992.

(Author of foreword) Franz Schurmann, *American Soul,* Mercury House (San Francisco, CA), 1995.

(Contributor) *King's Highway,* 1999.

Brown: The Last Discovery of America, Viking (New York, NY), 2002.

Writings have also appeared in *American Scholar,New Republic, Wall Street Journal, Los Angeles Times, Harper's,* and *Washington Post.*

SIDELIGHTS: In the opinion of *New York Times* critic Le Anne Schreiber, *Hunger of Memory: The Education of Richard Rodriquez* is an "honest and intelligent account of how education can alter a life." Richard Rodriguez's autobiographical account also offers a negative view of bilingual education and affirmative action policies that some readers have applauded and others have decried.

Hunger of Memory details Rodriguez's journey through the U.S. public education system and his resultant loss of ethnicity. The son of Mexican-American immigrants, unable to speak English when he entered a Sacramento, California, elementary school, Rodriguez went on to earn a master's degree and was a Fulbright scholar studying English renaissance literature in London when he abruptly decided to leave academic life. The choice was prompted by the feeling that he was "the beneficiary of truly disadvantaged Mexican-Americans." "I benefited on their backs," he told *Publishers Weekly* interviewer Patricia Holt.

The alienation from his culture began early in Rodriguez's life; as soon, in fact, as he learned the "public" language that would separate him from his family. Catholic nuns who taught Rodriguez asked that his parents speak English to him at home. When they complied, related the author in a *Newsweek* article by Jean Strouse, the sound of his "private" language, Spanish, and its "pleasing, soothing, consoling reminder of being at home" were gone. Paul Zweig observed in the *New York Times Book Review* that "son and parents alike knew that an unnamable distance had come between them." Rodriguez's parents were eventually "intimidated by what they had worked so diligently to bring about: the integration of their son into the larger world of gringo life so that he, unlike they themselves, could go far, become, one day, powerful, educated," noted the reviewer.

While Rodriguez reached the goals his parents had sought for him, he eventually began to fight the very policies that helped him to attain those goals. In ten years of college and postgraduate education, Rodriguez received assistance grounded in merit but based in part on his minority status. He left London and tried to reestablish the long-since-severed connection with his parents. He failed to recover his lost ethnicity, remaining "an academic . . . a kind of anthropologist in the family kitchen." Rodriguez's revolt against affirmative action began when he turned down several university-level teaching jobs. As Schreiber explained, "He wrote letters to all the chairmen of English departments who thought they had found the perfect answer to affirmative action in Richard Rodriguez. He declined their offers of jobs, because he could not withstand the irony of being counted a 'minority' when in fact the irreversibly successful effort of his life had been to become a fully assimilated member of the majority." Rodriguez spent the next six years writing *Hunger of Memory,* parts of which appeared in magazines before being brought together in book form.

Rodriguez's arguments against affirmative action stem from his belief, as he told *Detroit Free Press* reporter Suzanne Dolezal, that "the program has primarily benefited people who are no longer disadvantaged, . . . as I no longer was when I was at Stanford, [by] ignoring the educational problems of people who are genuinely disadvantaged, people who cannot read or write." His opposition to bilingual education is just as vocal. "To me," he told the *Publishers Weekly* interviewer, "public educators in a public schoolroom have an obligation to teach a public language. Public language isn't just English or Spanish or any other formal language. It is the language of public society, the language that people outside that public sector resist. For Mexican-Americans it is the language of *los gringos.* For Appalachian children who speak a fractured English or Black children in a ghetto, the problem is the same it seems to me. . . . My argument has always been that the imperative is to get children away from those languages that increase their sense of alienation from the public society."

Hunger of Memory was praised by several critics, especially for its discussion of the impact of language on life. Le Anne Schreiber found that "what matters most about this intensely thoughtful book is that Richard Rodriguez has given us the fruit of his long meditation upon language—his intimate understanding of how we use language to create private and public selves, his painful awareness of what we gain and lose when we gain and lose languages." Paul Zweig judged that "the chapters Mr. Rodriguez devotes to his early experiences of language are uncannily sensitive to the nuances of language learning, the childhood drama of voices, intonations." A *New Yorker* review commended Rodriguez as "a writer of unusual grace and clarity, . . . eloquent in all his reflections."

Rodgriquez's 1992 book, *Days of Obligation: An Argument with My Mexican Father,* is a collection of previously published autobiographical essays. In this collection, Rodriguez returns to many of the issues he probed in *Hunger of Memory:* language, history, and the immigrant history. He also explores in detail his feelings about his Mexican and Amerindian heritages as well as his personal experiences in AIDS-ravaged San Francisco. Reviewing the book in Chicago's *Tribune Books,* Rockwell Gray commented, "In these revisionary essays, Rodriguez ranges widely over issues of personal allegiance, homeland, ethnic identity, the future of Roman Catholicism and the shibboleth of 'diversity' invoked to gloss over the rifts in an increasingly fragmented American society."

Several critics remarked that *Days of Obligation* lacks the intuitive, coherent structure of *Hunger of Memory* but averred that the book once again displays the author's skill in producing powerful autobiographical writing. For instance, *Washington Post Book World* critic Jonathan Yardley noted, "though the earnestness of Rodriguez's self-examination remains affecting and convincing, *Days of Obligation* . . . never states in sufficiently clear terms either the nature of the argument or the author's own line of reasoning." Though admitting that the book can be "maddeningly presumptuous and determinedly obscure," *New York Times Book Review* contributor David L. Kirp exclaimed that "In its most powerful passages, 'Days of Obligation' reveals the writer as a tightrope walker who balances pessimism and the defeat of predictable expectations against the discovery of the profoundly unanticipated." Concluded Gray, "The wrestling with his elusive and insistent past makes these sinuous ruminations worthy of inclusion in the long American tradition of spiritual autobiography." With his 2002 volume *Brown: The Last Discovery of America,* Rodriguez "completes his trilogy, published in 10-year installments, that attempts to redescribe the American predicament through his own carefully examined experience," according to Anthony Walton in the *New York Times Book Review.* The color denoted in the book's title represents not only Rodriguez's own racial makeup but what he feels the nation is becoming as it grows more openly accepting of its mix of many cultures. As Bill Ott explained in a *Booklist* review, as Rodriguez "sets out to contemplate the meaning of brown in America, and his own brownness, he once again confronts the split between his different selves. But this time," Ott concluded, "instead of bouncing from one self to another, he seeks and finds reconciliation in the very impurity of being brown, the 'ability of bodies to experience two or several things at once.'" Ott summed up *Brown* as a "challenging, eloquent, witty, searingly beautiful book."

Rodriguez once noted: "I see myself straddling two worlds of writing: journalism and literature. There is Richard Rodriguez, the journalist—every day I spend more time reading newspapers and magazines than I do reading novels and poetry. I wander away from my desk for hours, for weeks. I want to ask questions of the stranger on the bus. I want to consider the political and social issues of the day. Then there is Richard Rodriguez, the writer. It takes me a very long time to write. What I try to do when I write is break down the line separating the prosaic world from the poetic word. I try to write about everyday concerns—an educational issue, say, or the problems of the unemployed—but to write about them as powerfully, as richly, as well as I can."

"My model in this marriage of journalism and literature is, of course, George Orwell. Orwell is the great modern example. He embarrasses other journalists by being more. He never let the urgency of the moment overwhelm his concern for literary art. But, in like measure, he embarrasses other writers because he had the courage to attend to voices outside the window, he was not afraid to look up from his papers. I hope I can be as brave in my life."

BIOGRAPHICAL AND CRITICAL SOURCES:

PERIODICALS

America, May 22, 1982, pp. 403-404; September 23, 1995, p. 8.

American Review, fall-winter, 1988, pp. 75-90.
American Scholar, spring, 1983, pp. 278-285, winter, 1994, p. 145.
Booklist, March 1, 2002, Bill Ott, review of *Brown: The Last Discovery of America,* p. 1184, January 1, 2003, review of *Brown: The Last Discovery of America,* p. 791.
Christian Science Monitor Monthly, March 12, 1982, pp. B1, B3.
Commentary, July, 1982, pp. 82-84, July-August, 2002, Dan Seligman, review of *Hispanics All,* p. 76.
Diacritics, fall, 1985, pp. 25-34.
Melus, spring, 1987, pp. 3-15; summer, 2003, Hector A. Tores, p. 164.
Nation, June 17, 2002, Ilan Stavans, review of *Brown: The Last Discovery of America,* p. 30.
New York Times Book Review, November 22, 1992, p. 42; April 7, 2002, Anthony Walton, "Greater than All the Parts," p. 7.
Reason, August-September, 1994, p. 35.
Time, January 25, 1993, p. 70.
Tribune Books (Chicago, IL), December 13, 1992, p. 1.
Washington Post Book World, November 15, 1992, p. 3.

* * *

ROGERS, Samuel Shepard, VII
See SHEPARD, Sam

* * *

ROQUELAURE, A.N.
See RICE, Anne

* * *

ROSENBAUM, Alice
See RAND, Ayn

* * *

ROTH, Henry 1906-1995

PERSONAL: Born February 8, 1906, in Tysmenica, Galicia, Austria-Hungary (now part of the Ukraine); died October 13, 1995; son of Herman (a waiter) and Leah (Farb) Roth; married Muriel Parker (a musician, composer, and elementary school principal; deceased); children: Jeremy, Hugh. *Education:* College of the City of New York (now City College of the City University of New York), B.S., 1928. *Religion:* Jewish.

CAREER: Writer. Worked "in writing and idleness," New York City, 1929-38; with Works Progress Administration (WPA), 1939; substitute high school teacher, Bronx, NY, 1939-41; precision metal grinder, New York City, 1941-45, Providence, RI, and Boston, MA, 1945-46; taught in a one-room school in Maine, 1947-48; Augusta State Hospital, Augusta, ME, attendant,1949-53; waterfowl farmer, 1953-63; tutor in math and Latin, 1956-65.

AWARDS, HONORS: Grant from National Institute of Arts and Letters, 1965; Townsend Harris Medal, City College of the City University New York, 1965; D.H. Lawrence fellowship, University of NewMexico, 1968; Litt.D., University of New Mexico, and Hebrew Union College of Cincinnati, both 1994; National Book Critics Circle Awards finalist for fiction, 1997, for *From Bondage.*

WRITINGS:

Call It Sleep (novel), Ballou, 1934, 2nd edition with a history by Harold U. Ribalow, a critical introduction by Maxwell Geismar, and a personal appreciation by Meyer Levin, Pageant, 1960, published with a foreword by Walter Allen, M. Joseph (London), 1963.
(Contributor) *The Best American Short Stories, 1967,* Houghton (Boston), 1967.
Nature's First Green (memoir), Targ, 1979.
Shifting Landscape: A Composite, 1925-1987, Jewish Publication Society, 1987, published as *Shifting Landscape,* with foreword by Alfred Kazin, Farrar, Straus (New York, NY), 1991.
Mercy of a Rude Stream, St. Martin's (New York, NY), Volume 1: *A Star Shines over Mt. Morris Park,* 1994, Volume 2: *A Diving Rock on the Hudson,* 1995, Volume 3: *From Bondage,* 1996, Volume 4: *Requiem for Harlem,* 1998.

Contributor to periodicals, including *Atlantic Monthly, Commentary, Midstream, New Yorker, Signatures: Work in Lavender,* and *Studies in American Jewish Literature.*

Roth's manuscripts are housed at Boston University and the New York Public Library.

SIDELIGHTS: "The death of Henry Roth . . . at the age of eighty-nine brought to an end one of the most unusual careers in modern letters," stated Morris Dickstein in the *Times Literary Supplement.* Roth, whose first novel, 1934's *Call It Sleep,* was followed by over six decades of literary silence, rallied with the monumental *Mercy of a Rude Stream.* Published between 1994 and 1996, the first three volumes of this highly-autobiographical six-volume work were described by Dickstein in the *Washington Post Book World* as "a diagnostic work, a case study cast as personal fiction." But, as the critic added, "that the book exists at all is a miracle, an almost posthumous gift. By returning to literature and resuming his story in old age, Roth has wrestled an unlikely trophy from the clutches of unhappiness, depression and inner turmoil."

Roth's first and best-known novel, *Call It Sleep* received laudatory reviews upon publication. Alfred Hayes termed it "as brilliant as [James] Joyce's *Portrait of the Artist,* but with a wider scope, a richer emotion, a deeper realism." The book went into two printings—four thousand copies—and then disappeared, leading an underground existence until its republication in 1960. In 1956 the *American Scholar* had asked certain notable critics to list the most neglected books of the past twenty-five years. Alfred Kazin and Leslie Fiedlerboth chose *Call It Sleep,* making it the only book named twice. On October 25, 1961, Irving Howe's front-page review of *Call Sleep* in the *New York Times Book Review* marked the first time such space was devoted to a paperback reprint. Howe described the book as "one of the few genuinely distinguished novels written by a 20th-century American, [one which] achieves an obbligato of lyricism such as few American novels can match. . . . Intensely Jewish in tone and setting, *Call It Sleep* rises above all the dangers that beset the usual ghetto novel: it does not deliquesce into nostalgia, nor sentimentalize poverty and parochialism. The Jewish immigrant milieu happens to be its locale, quite as Dublin is Joyce's and Mississippi [William] Faulkner's."

Roth's popular novel concerns the life of a young Jewish boy growing up on New York's Lower East Side in the years prior to World War I. Many critics disagree about the central theme or purpose of *Call It Sleep;* James Ferguson felt that it "is essentially the story of the development of a religious sensibility. Its implications are far more profoundly theological, even metaphysical, than they are social." In *Proletarian Writers of the Thirties,* Gerald Green wrote that Roth had social motivation in writing the novel: "Unlike the fashionable terrorists, Roth never loses hope, even if salvation speaks to us through cracked lips." And Walter Allen saw the book as "the most powerful evocation of the terrors of childhood ever written. We are spared nothing of the rawness of cosmopolitan slum life." *Call It Sleep* has also been cited for its political undertones—Roth was a member of the Communist Party at the time he wrote the novel but would later repudiate it—its depiction of Jewish domestic life, and its autobiographical aspects.

Howe believed that *Call It Sleep* is ultimately successful due to its presentation of the mind of the young boy. "Yet the book is not at all the kind of precious or narrowing study of a child's sensibility that such a description might suggest. We are locked into the experience of a child, but are limited to his grasp of it," the critic noted. Roth acknowledged the autobiographical qualities of the novel but emphasized the methods he used in manipulating events remembered from his childhood. "I was working with characters, situations and events that had in part been taken from life, but which I molded to give expression to what was oppressing me. To a considerable extent I was drawing on the unconscious to give shape to remembered reality. Things which I could not fully understand but which filled me with apprehension played a critical role in determining the form of the novel."

In his middle years, Roth distanced himself from his first novel, saying that "the man who wrote that book at the age of 27 is dead. I am a totally different man. Almost." Although he made some attempts at starting another novel, he became dissatisfied and destroyed the manuscript. Instead, Roth took on a variety of other jobs, satisfying his need to write by composing short stories. Many of these pieces of short fiction are collected in *Shifting Landscape.* Spanning the period from 1925 to 1987 and edited by longtime friend Mario Materassi, the volume includes not only fiction but also essays, journals, and excerpts from both interviews and correspondence. "Roth's imagination had always been ruminative, sensuous and introspective," explained Dickstein. "He was endlessly absorbed by the mystery of himself. . . . In the interstitial prose of *Shifting Landscape,* which is the real fabric of the book, . . . Roth examines himself as a case and weaves explanations around his deep sense of failure. Yet these autobiographical tales signify his dogged persistence as a writer, even when he was not writing."

It was Israel's Six-Day War in 1967 that finally prompted Roth to begin to attempt another novel-length work of fiction. The war gave the writer back his Jewishness, "a place in the world andan origin," as he told David Bronsen in *Partisan Review.* "Having started to write, it seemed natural to go on from there, and I have been writing long hours every day since then. I am not yet sure what it is leading to, but it is necessary and is growing out of a new allegiance, an adhesion that comes from belonging."

What his writing was leading to was the proposed six-volume autobiographical novel entitled *Mercy of a Rude Stream.* The first part, published in 1994 as *A Star Shines over Mt. Morris Park,* recounts the boyhood years of Ira Stigman. Shy, bookish, and feeling like an outsider, the boy attempts to repudiate his Jewishness and withdraws into a world of literature. "One irony this first volume explores at leisure," comments Lorna Sage in the *Observer,* is that [Roth's] vocation appeared to him under a false guise, as a romantic vision of exile—Art as the only homeland—whereas his subject and his inspiration lay in the very family and race that he struggled to extricate himself from."

Mercy of a Rude Stream continues with *Diving Rockon Diving Rock,* finds Roth's protagonist expelled from his Bronx high school, confused about what course his life willtake, and mired in the conflicting emotions of adolescence before emerging with the resolve to become a writer. In *From Bondage* Stigman has reached college, only to come under the sway of a circle of avidly pro-Joyce intellectuals and find himself entangled in a sexual relationship with of one of his female professors—who is also the lover of his best friend. This sexual liaison is made all the more complicated by reviving Stigman's guilt over an incestuous relationship he once had with his sister. In reading each of the novels comprising *Mercy in a Rude Stream,* comparisons with Roth's classic first novel continue to arise, according to Mary Gordon in the *New York Times Book Review.* "And so, how do we read these new works, trailing behind them both a history and a work of literature?," Gordon wondered before concluding: "We read them on their own clearly articulated terms and, having agreed to do that, we are wholly taken up by the touching and fascinating record of a marred life that insists on pressing on us its pulsing, painfully relentless vitality."

Despite his increased commitment to writing fiction during his final years, Roth's domestic life remained of primary importance. "I find my greatest pleasure in matrimony, mathematics and puttering about the premises, in that order," he once said, adding that "I am daily compelled to admiration at the miracle of my wife."

BIOGRAPHICAL AND CRITICAL SOURCES:

BOOKS

Allen, Walter, *The Modern Novel,* Dutton, 1965.

Contemporary Literary Criticism, Thomson Gale, Volume 2, 1974, Volume 6, 1976, Volume 11, 1979.

Dictionary of Literary Biography, Volume 28: *Twentieth-Century American-Jewish Fiction Writers,* Thomson Gale, 1984.

Howe, Irving, *World of Our Fathers,* Harcourt, 1976.

Kellman, Steven G., *Redemption: The Life of Henry Roth,* W.W. Norton, 2005.

Lyons, Bonnie, *Henry Roth: The Man and His Work,* Cooper Square, 1977.

Madden, Daniel, editor, *Proletarian Writers of the Thirties,* Southern Illinois University Press, 1968.

PERIODICALS

Centennial Review, spring, 1974.

Commentary, August, 1960; August, 1977; September, 1984; May, 1994, p. 44.

Economist, February 12, 1994, p. 91.

Jewish Social Studies, July, 1966.

Life, January 8, 1965.

Los Angeles Times, December 8, 1987; December 11, 1987.

Los Angeles Times Book Review, January 10, 1988; 9, 1995, p. 10.

Modern Fiction Studies, winter, 1966.

New Leader, December 27, 1993, p. 27.

Newsweek, January 31, 1994, p. 59.

New Yorker, March 25, 1996, p. 33.

New York Review of Books, March 3, 1994, p. 24.

New York Times, April 15, 1971.

New York Times Book Review, October 25, 1964; August 15, 1993, p. 3; January 16, 1994, pp. 3-4; February 26, 1995,pp. 5-6; December 10, 1995, p. 47.

Observer, February 27, 1994.

Partisan Review, Volume 36, number 2, 1969.

Publishers Weekly, November 27, 1987; April 22, 1996, p. 59.

Saturday Review, November 21, 1964.

Shenandoah, fall, 1973.

Studies in American Jewish Literature, spring, 1979.

Studies in the Novel, winter, 1975.

Time, January 31, 1994, p. 111; February 4, 1994, p. 14; February 25, 1994, p. 20; January 5, 1996, p. 7.

Twentieth Century Literature, October, 1966; January, 1969.

Washington Post, October 25, 1987.

Washington Post Book World, October 3, 1982; February 20, 1994, p. 6.

* * *

ROTH, Philip 1933-
(Philip Milton Roth)

PERSONAL: Born March 19, 1933, in Newark, NJ; son of Herman (an insurance manager) and Bess (Finkel) Roth; married Margaret Martinson, February 22, 1959 (died, 1968); married Claire Bloom, April 29, 1990 (divorced, June, 1994). *Education:* Attended Rutgers University, Newark, 1950-51; Bucknell University, A.B., 1954; University of Chicago, M.A., 1955, additional study, 1956-57.

ADDRESSES: *Agent*—c/o Jeffrey Posternak, The Wylie Agency, 250 W. 57th St., Ste. 2114, New York, NY 10107.

CAREER: Writer. University of Chicago, Chicago, IL, instructor, 1956-58; visiting lecturer, University of Iowa, Iowa City, 1960- 62, and State University of New York at Stony Brook, 1967-68; Hunter College, City University of New York, distinguished professor, 1989-92. Writer-in- residence, Princeton University, 1962-64, and University of Pennsylvania, 1965-80. *Military service:* U.S. Army, 1955-56.

MEMBER: American Academy of Arts and Letters, Phi Beta Kappa.

AWARDS, HONORS: Aga Khan Award, *Paris Review,* 1958; Houghton Mifflin literary fellowship, 1959; National Institute of Arts and Letters grant, 1959; National Book Award for fiction, 1960, and Daroff Award, Jewish Book Council of America, both 1960, both for *Goodbye, Columbus, and Five Short Stories;* Guggenheim fellowship, 1960; O. Henry second prize award, 1960; Ford Foundation grant in playwriting, 1965; American Book Award nomination, 1980, for *The Ghost Writer;* National Book Critics Circle nomination, 1983, and American Book Award nomination, 1984, both for *The Anatomy Lesson;* National Book Critics Circle Award, 1987, and National Jewish Book Award for Fiction, Jewish Book Council, 1988, both for *The Counterlife;* National Arts Club Medal of Honor, 1991; National Book Critics Circle Award, 1992, for *Patrimony;* PEN/Faulkner Award for Fiction, 1993, for *Operation Shylock;* Karl Capek Prize (Czech Republic), 1994; National Book Award for fiction, 1995, for *Sabbath's Theater;* Pulitzer Prize for fiction, 1998, for *American Pastoral;* Ambassador Book Award, English-Speaking Union, 1998, for *I Married a Communist;* W.H. Smith Literary Award, 2000, National Jewish Book Award for Fiction, Jewish Book Council, 2000, and PEN/Faulkner Award for Fiction, 2001, all for *The Human Stain;* Gold Medal for Fiction, American Academy of Arts and Letters, 2001; Medal for Distinguished Contribution to American Letters, National Book Foundation, 2002; National Book Critics Circle Award nomination, 2004, and Sidewise Award for Alternate History, 2005, both for *The Plot against America.*

WRITINGS:

Goodbye, Columbus, and Five Short Stories, Houghton Mifflin (Boston, MA), 1959, published as *Goodbye, Columbus,* 1989, reprinted under original title, New Modern Library (New York, NY), 1995.

Letting Go (novel), Random House (New York, NY), 1962.

When She Was Good (novel), Random House (New York, NY), 1967.

Portnoy's Complaint (novel), Random House (New York, NY), 1969, reprinted, 2002.

Our Gang (novel), Random House (New York, NY), 1971, published with a new preface and revised notes by the author, Bantam (New York, NY), 1973, reprinted as *Our Gang: Starring Tricky and His Friends,* Vintage (New York, NY), 2002.

The Breast (novel), Holt (New York, NY), 1972, revised edition, Farrar, Straus (New York, NY), 1982.

The Great American Novel, Holt (New York, NY), 1973.

My Life As a Man (novel), Holt (New York, NY), 1974.

Reading Myself and Others (nonfiction), Farrar, Straus (New York, NY), 1975, reprinted, Vintage (New York, NY), 2001.

The Professor of Desire (novel), Farrar, Straus (New York, NY), 1977.

The Ghost Writer (novel; also see below), Farrar, Straus (New York, NY), 1979.

A Philip Roth Reader, Farrar, Straus (New York, NY), 1980.

Zuckerman Unbound (novel; also see below), Farrar, Straus (New York, NY), 1981.

The Anatomy Lesson (novel; also see below), Farrar, Straus (New York, NY), 1983.

(Adaptor, with Tristram Powell) *The Ghost Writer* (television play; based on Roth's novel), Public Broadcasting System, 1984.

Zuckerman Bound: A Trilogy and Epilogue (includes *The Ghost Writer, Zuckerman Unbound,* and *The Anatomy Lesson* with epilogue "The Prague Orgy"), Farrar, Straus (New York, NY), 1985, published as *The Prague Orgy,* J. Cape (London, England), 1985.

The Counterlife (novel), Farrar, Straus (New York, NY), 1986.

The Facts: A Novelist's Autobiography, Farrar, Straus (New York, NY), 1988.

Deception (novel), Simon & Schuster (New York, NY), 1990.

Patrimony: A True Story, Simon & Schuster (New York, NY), 1991.

Operation Shylock: A Confession, Simon & Schuster (New York, NY), 1993.

Sabbath's Theater (novel), Houghton Mifflin (Boston, MA), 1995.

American Pastoral (novel), Houghton Mifflin (Boston, MA), 1997.

I Married a Communist (novel), Houghton Mifflin (Boston, MA), 1998.

The Human Stain (novel), Houghton Mifflin (Boston, MA), 2000.

The Dying Animal (novel), Houghton Mifflin (Boston, MA), 2001.

Shop Talk: A Writer and His Colleagues and Their Work, Houghton Mifflin (Boston, MA), 2001.

The Plot against America Houghton Mifflin (Boston, MA), 2004.

Novels & Stories, 1959-1962 (contains *Goodbye, Columbus, and Five Short Stories* and *Letting Go*), edited by Ross Miller, Library of America (New York, NY), 2005.

Novels, 1967-1972 (contains *When She Was Good, Portnoy's Complaint, Our Gang,* and *The Breast*), edited by Ross Miller, Library of America (New York, NY), 2005.

Everyman (novel), Houghton Mifflin (Boston, MA), 2006.

Founding editor of Penguin book series "Writers from the Other Europe." Contributor of short stories to anthologies and articles to periodicals, including *Esquire, Harper's, New Yorker, Commentary,* and *Paris Review.*

ADAPTATIONS: Goodbye, Columbus was adapted for film by Arnold Schulman, directed by Larry Peerce, Paramount, 1969; *Portnoy's Complaint* was adapted for film by director Ernest Lehman, Warner Bros., 1972; *The Human Stain* was adapted for film, directed by Robert Benton, Mirimax, 2003. Three of Roth's short stories were adapted for the theater by Larry Arrick and produced as *Unlikely Heroes.*

SIDELIGHTS: Philip Roth established himself among leading twentieth-century American authors through his careful scrutiny and biting satire directed at post-World War II America. As *Washington Post Book World* contributor David Lehman noted, "At the top of his game, Philip Roth is our Kafka: a Jewish comic genius able to spin a metaphysical joke to a far point of ingenuity—the point at which artistic paradox becomes moral or religious parable." In these parables—from *Goodbye, Columbus, and Five Short Stories,* through *Portnoy's Complaint* and the Nathan Zuckerman novels, to *Sabbath's Theater*—Roth has continued to explore Jewish family life in the city and the conflicted characters that it creates. Neil Klugman, Alexander Portnoy, Zuckerman, Mickey Sabbath, and even Philip Roth are among the memorable characters Roth has created to pursue his themes.

In addition to the acclaim he has received for his writing, Roth has gained a measure of notoriety for his blurring of fact and fiction. The author draws much of his literary material from his personal experiences, but then alters the facts to fit the story he wants to tell. Because of their close ties with their author's life, Roth's books have invited much speculation about what is truth and what is invention. As David Lehman stated in the *Washington Post Book World:* "A master illusionist, Roth is adept at fooling the public into thinking that the outlandish fantasies in his fiction must reflect autobiographical fact." But, Tobias Wolff explained in the *Los Angeles Times Book Review,* this is just what Roth wants: "Roth's purpose in all this is not merely playful or cantankerous; what he means to do, and does, is make the strongest possible case for fiction's autonomy by suggesting and then repudiating its connection with 'the facts.' It's a nervy, sometimes hilarious, now and then exasperating performance; his road of excess doesn't always lead to the palace of wisdom. But it often does."

The importance of Roth's childhood memories growing in Depression-era Newark, New Jersey, and in a first-generation Jewish community become evident in *Goodbye, Columbus, and Five Short Stories.* The title piece, a novella, gained the most acclaim for the then-twenty-six-year-old author. The story examines the relationship between Neil Klugman, a lower-middle-class Newark native, and Brenda Patimkin, a product of the burgeoning postwar Jewish nouveau riche. The depiction of the Patimkin family as boorish creatures of leisure infuriated some critics and impressed others with its candor. *Goodbye, Columbus* was in fact the first of many Roth books to be castigated from synagogue pulpits. "To be sure, Roth was hardly the first American-Jewish writer to cross verbal swords with the 'official' Jewish community," pointed out Sanford Pinsker in the *Dictionary of Literary Biography.* "But Roth's book brought the antagonisms to a rapid boil. Granted, no social critic has an easy task. The 'glad tidings' he or she brings us about ourselves are never welcome, and, quite understandably, offended readers go to great lengths to prove that such writers are morbidly misanthropic, clearly immoral, merely insane—or, as in Roth's case, all of the above." The flood of criticism aimed at *Goodbye, Columbus* didn't stem the book's popularity, though. Several critics praised the new voice in American fiction, and the collection went on to win the National Book Award in 1960.

The two novels that followed *Goodbye, Columbus*—*Letting Go* and *When She Was Good* —did not receive the same attention afforded Roth's debut. Yet any doubts about Roth's ability to both attract and shock his audience were quelled with the publication of *Portnoy's Complaint.* Variously described as "the work of a virtuoso" by Robert Fulford in *Saturday Night* and as "a desperately dirty novel" by Saul Maloff in *Commonweal,* the novel thoroughly divided readers and remains the work most closely associated with its author. Conflict and repression punctuate the book's story about a young Jewish man's infatuation with Gentile girls and his constant state of war with his overbearing mother.

The theme and plot of *Portnoy's Complaint* are sometimes seen as taking a back seat to the book's sharply drawn characters, particularly the iconographic Jewish mother Sophie Portnoy—who, with a long bread knife in her hands, seems a castrating vision—and Sophie's son, Alex. In another *Dictionary of Literary Biography* essay, Jeffrey Helterman compared protagonist Alex Portnoy with the hero of James Joyce's *Portrait of the Artist As a Young Man:* "Like Stephen Dedalus, Alexander Portnoy yearns for freedom from the repressive laws of his youth—and like Dedalus, Portnoy feels love as well as revulsion for that youth. In Portnoy's case, the laws are those of Jewish domesticity imposed by a mother whose domineering exterior hides a mass of guilt and fear. Her rules— . . . beware of polio, don't fool around with shiksas [Yiddish for Gentile women], don't feel innocent when you can feel guilty—are the manifestation of a classic superego."

Portnoy's frustration with his situation is manifested in his constant masturbation, described in graphic detail by Roth. The depiction of what some critics dubbed "onanism" became a major point of contention and helped earn the novel charges of pornography. Furthermore, the author's continuing satiric examination of Jewish-American life sparked further debate within that ethnic and religious community. As Pinsker described it, "The anti-Roth crusade that the rabbis began with *Goodbye, Columbus* turned into a full-scale suburban war" with *Portnoy's Complaint.*

Some of the criticism aimed at *Portnoy's Complaint* centers on the book's tone. As Fulford wrote: "In one crucial way [the work] is a disappointment. On first reading I was caught up in Roth's brilliance and audacity. [But on further readings,] I discovered that the jokes were funny only once, that the situations quickly lost their freshness." "Though the satire in *Portnoy's Complaint* is generally first-rate, the book hardly ever rises to irony," noted Anatole Broyard in *The Critic As Artist: Essays on Books, 1920-1970.* "Irony requires dimension, the possibility of grandeur, and what we have here is a series of caricatures. Father, mother, sister, mistresses—even Portnoy himself—each has one act, one *shtik.*"

To Pinsker, *Portnoy's Complaint* "is simultaneously a confessional act and an attempt to exorcize lingering guilts. His is a complaint in the legalistic sense of an indictment handed down against those cultural forces that have wounded him; it is a complaint in the old-fashioned sense [of] an illness . . . and, finally it is a complaint in the more ordinary, existential sense of the word." As such a confession, Barry Wallenstein, writing in the *Catholic World,* noted that the novel "strikes deeper, pleases on more levels and . . . seems truer than all of Roth's previous books." Irving H. Buchen, writing in *Studies in the Twentieth Century,* called *Portnoy's Complaint* "a great book, not because of its passing off a strain of Judaism as all of Judaism, and certainly not because of its unsympathetic and unfair attack on parents; but rather because it is a passionate, honest and comprehensive portrait of a man and generation in anguish." Patricia Meyer Spacks in the *Yale Review* also found that Portnoy's complaint is not confined to the Jewish-American experience. "Portnoy sees his own problems as products of his Jewishness, but readers are not obliged to share his view." Instead, she noted that readers "are invited to understand the suffering and the comedy of modern man, who seeks and finds explanations for his plight but is unable to resolve it, whose understanding is as limited as his sense of possibility, who is forced to the analyst to make sense of his experience."

The next few years brought a trio of Roth novels that ranged from the acerbic to the slapstick to the experimental. *Our Gang,* a biting indictment of the Nixon administration, features a president called Trick E. Dixon and a cabinet that is remarkable for its ability to use language to confound the citizens it is supposed to be serving. Next came *The Breast,* a novel influenced by Franz Kafka's *The Metamorphosis,* the story of a man who turns into a cockroach. In Roth's experimental version, however, a professor is turned into a six-foot female breast. More satire followed with *The Great American Novel* about a long-ago baseball league, the Patriot, and its assembly of motley teams.

In *The Dying Animal* Roth continues with the story of David Kepesh, the protagonist in both *The Breast* and *The Professor of Desire.* Now age seventy, Kepesh is a lecturer at New York College who long ago abandoned his wife and child and is notorious for sleeping with his students. In *The Dying Animal* Kepesh recounts his affair eight years earlier with a former Cuban student named Consuela. Kepesh also takes time to reminisce about his earlier life and family and to comment on American culture, the sexual revolution, and the relationship among love, pleasure, and freedom. Although Kepesh supposedly "loves" women, Lisa Allardice, writing in the *New Statesman,* pointed out that "there is little room for love in Roth's nihilistic vision. It is only when Consuela, cruelly punished for the youth and beauty that so tormented the ageing Kepesh, has been brutally desexualised by breast cancer that he can finally see her as a human being, not just a great pair of tits."

Knight Ridder/Tribune contributor Christopher Kelly noted that, at times, *The Dying Animal* seems like "a dirty book with pretensions," but went on to add that "in the last thirty pages of this slim volume, Roth offers up a brilliantly written examination of coming to terms with one's own mortality." *Booklist* contributor Donna Seaman commented that "Kepesh may be selfish and manipulative, but Roth has imbued him with profound integrity and blazing intelligence—his riffs on sexual politics and the inanity of mass culture are not to be missed." Noting that the novel is not among Roth's best, *Nation* contributor Keith Gessen nonetheless praised *The Dying Animal* as "remarkable for its fealty to the ground Roth has always worked. It cedes nothing, apologizes for nothing; it deepens, thereby, the seriousness of all his previous books."

Besides *Portnoy's Complaint,* Roth is most often noted for his series of novels featuring protagonist Nathan Zuckerman. While the novelist has denied that the Zuckerman stories are autobiographical, "it may be fairly added that though *The Ghost Writer* is not in any literal sense a roman à clef, certain personal traits are unmistakably caught—not in full portrait, of course, but in broad strokes, a gesture here, a tone of voice there, a turn of mind everywhere," noted *Commonweal* critic Saul Maloff. Certainly some details about Zuckerman parallel Roth's life. Zuckerman is in his mid- twenties when the book opens in the 1950s, as Roth was; he is a struggling writer from Newark, as Roth was. *The Ghost Writer* finds Zuckerman seeking an audience with the venerable, reclusive novelist E.I. Lonoff (who "strongly suggests Bernard Malamud," says Maloff). He has strong personal reasons for wanting to see Lonoff, as Helterman explained in the *Dictionary of Literary Biography Yearbook:* "Zuckerman seeks a surrogate father because his own father, a well-meaning, loving podiatrist, has refused to see the aesthetic virtues in Zuckerman's story 'Higher Education,' which uses an old family quarrel to show grasping, greedy Jews." Given the rare privilege of an invitation to Lonoff's Berkshire farmhouse, Zuckerman also meets Lonoff's neglected wife and another house guest, the mysterious Amy Bellette, with whom Zuckerman falls in love. Parts of the novel involve Zuckerman's fantasies about visiting his estranged father and presenting Amy as his bride.

In a *Village Voice* article, Eliot Fremont- Smith praised *The Ghost Writer* as Roth's "most controlled and elegant work. It is serious, intelligent, dramatic, acutely vivid, slyly and wickedly funny, almost formal in its respect for theme, almost daredevil in ambition, and almost wrenching so close it hurts." Writing in *Commentary* critic Pearl K. Bell found the book unsatisfying and noted that by the end of the story, the book "seems rather thin, . . . because it promises an intellectual and moral range which it does not wholly attain. Roth seems reluctant to engage himself fully with the demanding question he asks in many different ways throughout the novel: must life be sacrificed to art, in the uncompromising manner of a Lonoff?" Still other reviewers found the novel to be a work rich in meaning and value. The novel, said *Washington Post Book World* contributor Jonathan Penner, "provides further evidence that [the author] can do practically anything with fiction. His narrative power—the ability to delight the reader simultaneously with the telling and the tale, employing economy that looks like abundance, ornament that turns out to be structure—is superb. He is so good in this book that even when he's bad, he's good."

A "comedy about fame and its discontents," as James Wolcott described it in *Esquire, Zuckerman Unbound* finds Roth continuing the Zuckerman saga several years later. At this point Zuckerman has become famous—

and infamous—for his "dirty" opus *Carnovsky,* a book that bears a resemblance to Roth's own *Portnoy's Complaint.* "Not that the novel is at all straightforward autobiography," noted *Nation* reviewer Richard Gilman. "Roth is too much the artist for that. But there is something disingenuous about his attempt wholly to dissociate himself from his protagonist." *Zuckerman Unbound* "is in part an account of Nathan's struggle to accept the consequences of his eclat, to feel justified in having become so flashingly eminent," Gilman continues. "He's totally misunderstood, feels himself unreal. Strangers address him as Carnovsky, his book's protagonist."

Zuckerman faces more dilemmas in this sequel: Alvin Pepler, a fellow Newark native, has latched himself onto Zuckerman and makes his life miserable by constantly lamenting the loss of his brief fame on a game show because he did not fit the all-American image. Zuckerman sees a parallel between Pepler's bitterness and his own. As Isa Kapp pointed out in the *New Republic,* "While their speech is different, victim [Zuckerman] and victimizer [Pepler] are psychological birds of a feather, preening their egos and brooding over their good name." *Zuckerman Unbound* offers many other turns for Zuckerman. His marriage is in a shambles and his resentful father dies. The father's last word to his rebellious son is a mystery: "Vaster? Better? Faster? Could it have been bastard?," recounted *Los Angeles Times Book Review* critic Elaine Kendall.

"Zuckerman is almost a latter-day Emma Bovary, his life disrupted not by reading about desire, but by desiring to write," explained Edward Rothstein in the *New York Review of Books.* "He is a victim, bound by fictive yearnings. He could ask, 'Did fiction do this to me?' just as David Kepesh did after he turned into a giant breast in Roth's Kafkaesque fable. Does Zuckerman, only slightly less constricted by his desires, know how bound he is? How is Zuckerman unbound?" *Chicago Tribune Book World* reviewer Bernard Rodgers noted that *Zuckerman Unbound* "offers its readers the all too infrequent joy of watching a master storyteller at the height of his powers practice his craft."

"When *Zuckerman Unbound* appeared, . . . it was widely assumed to be Nathan's farewell to his past and [Roth's] farewell to his alter ego Nathan. But Roth had [more] in mind," reported Gary Giddins in the *Village Voice.* The third installment of the Zuckerman saga soon appeared, titled *The Anatomy Lesson.* Now in the early 1970s, the forty-year-old Zuckerman suffers from untreatable back pains and decides to give up the literary life to become a doctor. He enrolls in the University of Chicago medical school, but "the decision restores his creative urges in an unfortunate way," according to *Time* writer R.Z. Sheppard. "He buttonholes strangers with wildly obscene monologues describing himself as Milton Appel, a no-holds-barred pornographer. Appel is the name of Zuckerman's nemesis, a leading literary critic who once branded *Carnovsky* and its author vulgar and demeaning." (Those readers following the roman à clef elements in the "Zuckerman" books will note that Irving Howe wrote a 1972 *Commentary* essay sharply critical of Roth's writings.)

Again the consequences of art on the artist's life is a theme of Roth's novel *The Anatomy Lesson.* The novel "isn't necessarily dependent on the earlier novels for plot elements; it can be read—if not fully savored—on its own," Giddens wrote. "Yet the trilogy gains irony and gravity from the manifold ways in which the three volumes interlock. In *Zuckerman Unbound* Roth succumbed to Walter Brennan Syndrome and gave the best and funniest part to a supporting character, . . . Alvin Pepler; Nathan's plight paled by comparison. *The Anatomy Lesson* redeems its predecessor, putting the middle volume and Nathan in perspective, and highlighting themes only sketched the first and second times around. It clarifies Roth's ambivalence about Nathan."

In *The Ghost Writer, Zuckerman Unbound,* and *The Anatomy Lesson,* Roth has created his "most complex and structurally satisfying work," concluded Sheppard. The novel trilogy "is a disciplined string ensemble compared with *Portnoy's Complaint,* which had the primal power of a high school band. Yet Zuckerman and Portnoy have close ties. Both star in comedies of the unconscious, burlesques of psychoanalytic processes whose irreverence and shocking explicitness challenge the pieties that protect hidden feelings." In 1984 the novels were published together as *Zuckerman Bound: A Trilogy and Epilogue.* Here, Roth adds an epilogue, "The Prague Orgy," in which Zuckerman is bound for Czechoslovakia. This episode finds the novelist in the birthplace of Franz Kafka, where he tries to obtain a rare Yiddish manuscript. What he finds is such a degree of artistic and personal repression that he begins to reevaluate his own priorities in life.

Roth's next Zuckerman book, *The Counterlife,* follows the critical self-examination of his hero, this time contrasted to those of his brother, Henry Zuckerman (also known as Sherman Zuckerman in a previous incarnation). Henry, a solidly middle-class dentist, husband, and father, who has never forgiven Nathan for the sins of *Carnovsky,* faces the choice of heart-disease-related impotence or a life-threatening operation to cure the defect. In the first section of the novel, "Basel," Henry undergoes the operation, but does not survive it. However, in the second part of *The Counterlife,* "Judea," Henry has survived, left his family, and joined up with a fanatical Zionist. Writing in the *New Yorker,* John Updike commented: "In the fourth chapter, it is Nathan who has the heart problem, the impotence, and the mistress called Maria. In pursuing these variations, the virtuoso imaginer rarely falters; satisfying details of place and costume, beautifully heard and knitted dialogues, astonishing diatribes unfold in chapters impeccably shaped, packed, and smoothed. No other writer combines such a surface of colloquial relaxation and even dishevelment with such a dense load of intelligence."

A bit more skeptical about *The Counterlife* was Christopher Lehmann-Haupt, who, in his *New York Times* review, noted that in the knockabout nature of the work and the shifting characters among the Zuckerman clan, "it's as if the novelist were saying, since I can make you believe in anything, the ultimate challenge is to make you believe in nothing. So we learn to count on nothing. Yet the novel pays a price for sabotaging its own reality. We become so aware of the narrative's duplicity that all that is left to us is the burden of the author's self-consciousness as an artist and a Jew." But to Richard Stern in Chicago's *Tribune Books,* the plot twists in *The Counterlife* constitute an enjoyable look at a fiction writer at work: "an equivalent of action painting. Then there is the delight of liberation . . . . The claustrophobia which oppresses so many self-reflexive novels—novels about themselves—isn't here because Roth's worldly intelligence, satiric power, gift for portraiture, milieu, scene and action, are too strong to be mesmerized by technical discovery. If the writer has a measure of Tolstoyan worldliness in him, he will not have to pay the price of being caged by the techniques of exhibition." The critic concluded that the author "has made another remarkable advance in his illustrious career."

As with *The Counterlife,* Roth's best-selling novel *Deception* is also somewhat experimental. This time, the author explores the relationship between fiction and reality by writing an ambiguous tale about a struggling Jewish writer's diary. The journal recounts the protagonist's conversations with his lover, but when his wife discovers the diary and confronts him with it he tells her it is only a writing exercise. The problem of the novel then becomes a question of what is truth and what is falsehood, a subject that allows Roth to address the more general issue of the relationship between all authors and their work. *Esquire* contributor Lee Eisenberg praised *Deception* as still another successful effort by a talented author: "A good case, I think, can be made that Philip Roth will be one of those whose books will live well into the next century . . . . Some of [*Deception*] is funny, some of it is angry, some of it is wise. As always with Roth, the writing has perfect pitch."

In *Sabbath's Theater* Roth returns to the issues he confronted in *Portnoy's Complaint,* only this time the protagonist is not a young man but an old man whose failures set him on a quest toward suicide. Writing in the *Los Angeles Times Book Review,* Richard Eder described Mickey Sabbath as a literary descendent of Portnoy. "Here, full-fledged, repellent, fascinating, and fearfully long-winded, is the offspring: Mickey Sabbath, a former puppeteer, an obsessive white- bearded seducer and a reverse alchemist who consistently turns the gold of human possibility into the lead of a mono-maniacal ego." Sabbath has lost his first and second wives, his lover, and his jobs, but in the end he does not choose suicide. Eder concluded, "Roth, who cannot make his protagonist immortal and probably does not intend to, has made him interminable."

Kakutani, writing in the *New York Times,* noted that a "plodding pursuit of defiance lends *Sabbath's Theater* a static and claustrophobic air, resulting in a novel that's sour instead of manic, nasty instead of funny, lugubrious instead of liberating." Kakutani also faulted the book for not going beyond the egocentricism of its main character: "The novel fails to open out into a larger comment on society or our shared experience of mortality: Sabbath remains such a willfully selfish character that his adventures become a kind of black hole, absorbing rather than emitting light." Doron Weber of the *Boston Review* conceded that the novel's theme of old age and growing impotency is not new. "But," added Weber, "this theme is handled with more lyrical energy, greater sexual frankness, and, simultaneously, sharper comedy and deeper seriousness than usual." William H. Pritchard observed in the *New York Times Book Review* that "Roth's genius for juxtaposing impressions, feelings and names that usually don't belong together continually enlivens the narrative. His extraordinarily active style revels in the play of words." Weber's final evaluation of *Sabbath's Theater* was that it is "a striking and original work which shows a major American novelist renewing himself with a darkly complex, comic masterpiece."

Roth continues his winning ways with *American Pastoral,* the story of a Newark Jew who realizes considerable success and contentment only to see his life undone by his imbalanced daughter. According to *Commentary* essayist Norman Podhoretz—who credits himself with having "'discovered'[Roth] as a writer of fiction"— *American Pastoral* serves as evidence that Roth's "entire outlook on the world had been inverted." For Podhoretz, that inversion involves Roth's attitude towards both middle-class Jews, who had often served Roth as a ready target for ridicule, and those fellow members of the Jewish intelligentsia who mocked the Jewish middle classes. But in *American Pastoral,* Podhoretz asserted, "it was the ordinary Jews . . . who were celebrated—for their decency, their sense of responsibility, their seriousness about their work, their patriotism—and here, for once, those who rejected and despised such virtues were shown to be either pathologically nihilistic or smug, self-righteous, and unimaginative." Podhoretz was not entirely impressed with the novel, however, finding it "repetitious" and, thus, "overly insistent and sometimes tiresome."

I Married a Communist may have been prompted by the critical depiction of Roth in *Leaving a Doll's House,* a memoir by his ex-wife, renowned actress Claire Bloom. The story concerns a radio actor whose life is undone by his own ex-wife's caustic memoir. The hero of *I Married a Communist* is Ira Ringold, whose decline is recalled by his brother, Murray, and related to Roth regular Nathan Zuckerman. Murray tells how Ira clashed with his wife's daughter and how he suffered from blacklisting after his vengeful former spouse exposed him as a dutiful communist. Murray adds that Ira plotted his own violent revenge until his weapons were taken from him. The novel ends with what *New Leader* reviewer Marck Schechner called a "starry coda" that finds Zuckerman gazing into the heavens and contemplating a world free of betrayals and deceptions.

Schechner deemed the novel "striking" and affirmed that it "contains some gems of character analysis and a high-amp prose that pulls us in no matter what indecencies Roth happens to commit." Paul Gray, meanwhile, wrote in *Time* that Roth's handling of his material "is constantly mesmerizing." Somewhat less impressed was John Derbyshire, who wrote in the *National Review* that *I Married a Communist* is "not a bad novel, as novels go nowadays," then decried the novel's nostalgia for 1950s leftism. "The book's problem is one of attitude: the assumption that we all share the sentiments of the Old Left," Derbyshire contended. "Not a fondness for Communism . . . but a gnawing, unsleeping, undiminished, everlasting hatred of anti- Communism." *Nation* reviewer John Leonard characterized the novel as "a rant," while *New Republic* critic James Wood regarded the book as "only an essay about politics, and a rather conventional one."

A more generous assessment of the novel came from *New Statesman* reviewer Stuart Barrows, who called *I Married a Communist* an "uneven work" but conceded that the novel's concluding pages are "as moving as anything [Roth] has written." Podhoretz, who deemed the novel "one of Roth's less successful books," concluded his *Commentary* essay by speculating that "perhaps the best is yet to come from Philip Roth." Podhoretz contended that Roth "will only be able to mine the full lode of riches . . . within him if he can finally summon the courage to 'let go' altogether of the youthful habits of mind and spirit . . . [that] keep him from digging into the depths that are . . . so full of potential reward for him and for the literature of this country."

The Human Stain is the third novel of the trilogy composed of *American Pastoral* and *I Married a Communist.* The novel relates the story of Coleman Silk, a married professor living in a New England college town. Forced from his job by accusations that he made racist comments, Silk falls into an affair with the college's janitor. As attention falls on Silk's deeds, none know that he holds an even greater secret. A contributor for *Publishers Weekly* described the ending as "exquisitely imagined" and Roth as "at the peak of his imaginative skills."

In *The Facts: A Novelist's Autobiography* and *Patrimony: A True Story,* Roth makes a startling change in course from the semiautobiographical to the autobiographical. In a *New York Times* interview with Mervyn Rothstein, Roth explained how his depression following surgery led to his writing *The Facts:* "I began to write these memoirs as a way of facing something other than my difficulties . . . . And I wrote myself out of a serious depression." But many reviewers of *The Facts,* which covers Roth's life from childhood to the late 1960s, question the verity of its contents because of Roth's use of a complicating literary device. He begins the book with a letter to Nathan Zuckerman asking for advice about the manuscript, and at the end of *The Facts* Zuckerman replies in a letter that, in essence, tells Roth to stick to fiction.

Lehmann-Haupt in the *New York Times* asserted that, given "the author's acute awareness of confessional narrative's manipulativeness and unreliability, Roth has no purpose other than irony in calling this highly ambiguous portrait of his youth *The Facts.*" But Roth contradicts this notion when he tells Rothstein that he used the Zuckerman letter only to pose the question of whether life's problems are more poignantly addressed through fiction or nonfiction: "My impulse is to problematize material. I don't like when it sits flat on the page. I like when it's opposed by something else, by another point of view." Some critics, like Joseph Coates of Chicago's *Tribune Books,* recognized that what "Roth says here is undoubtedly true, but the nonaggressive thrust of his argument [with Zuckerman] rings false." *Washington Post Book World* contributor D.M. Thomas believed that the author's portrayals of the people in his life "lack dramatic vitality in their presentation."

In contrast, many critics consider *Patrimony: A True Story* to be, as Wolff asserted, "one of Roth's very best" books. A recounting of the final months of Roth's father's life, *Patrimony* does not so much as mention any of his alter-ego characters, "neither is there any slight of hand blurring the line between literature and life," stated a reviewer in *Publishers Weekly.* Robert Pinsky also commented in the *New York Times Book Review* that "the self-portrait in this book is more rounded and less self-conscious than in" *The Facts.* Chronicling his father Herman's physical decline caused by a brain tumor, the book counterpoints this illness "at almost every turn by startled self-realization on the part of his son," wrote Sven Birkerts in Chicago's *Tribune Books.* The gap that had been created between Roth and his father when Roth came of age is bridged during these last months of Herman Roth's life, and the book becomes, according to *Washington Post Book World* critic Jonathan Yardley, not "a dirge for the departed but . . . a celebration of living."

Critics widely praised *Patrimony* for its frank and unsentimental portrayal of a parent's gradual death. Yardley asserted that the author "deserves both praise and gratitude for meeting death head-on." "Roth," Birkerts similarly wrote, "has looked past all comfort and condolence to find the truth—about himself and his father; about death and the fear of it; and about the absolute vulnerability to which love condemns us all." Roth's tribute to Herman Roth, related Michiko Kakutani in the *New York Times,* is "a way of preventing his father 'from becoming ethereally attenuated as the years went by,' a way of turning yet another chapter in his life into a book."

In his two autobiographical books and the novel *Deception,* Roth oscillates between his real and imagined worlds. However, in *Operation Shylock: A Confession,* he offers up his most convoluted examination of the blurred line between fact and fiction, creator and created. He represents *Operation Shylock* as a true story, just as its subtitle suggests. Instead of denying that the book is thinly veiled autobiography, he embraced its origins as such in interviews and book signings. The book tells the story of writer Philip Roth who, after recovering from the side-effects of some medication, discovers that a man in Israel is posing as Philip Roth, the writer. Roth—the real Roth—goes to Israel where he encounters the impostor, various figures involved in the Arab-Israeli conflict, and the trial of John Demjanjuk, the retired Cleveland auto worker who was charged with having been "Ivan the Terrible," a notorious S.S. guard at the Treblinka concentration camp during World War II. Roth is enlisted by Israeli intelligence to complete a spy operation known as "Shylock." Along this twisting and turning journey, Roth touches upon many current issues. The book "blends the idea of the double (from ego psychology and gothic literature) with the idea of codependency (from contemporary psychobabble)," observed David Lehman in the *Washington Post Book World.* And, as Harold Bloom explained in the *New York Review of Books,* "The hypocracies and brutalities of Israeli policy toward the Palestinians emerge with frightening vividness in *Operation Shylock,* which nevertheless balances the hypocrisies and brutalities with a sense of the Israelis' desperation for survival. What emerges from Roth's novel is the terrible paradox that Israel is no escape from the burdens of the Diaspora."

Despite Roth's assurances and the book's connection to the events of the day, critics argued that *Operation Shylock* is not a confession, and is not autobiographical. Roth himself gives weight to this when he concludes the book with the liar's paradox, writing, "This confession is false." As a *Publishers Weekly* reviewer observed, "The plot is like a house of mirrors; the narrator and his fraudulent twin impersonate each other with dizzying speed, which allows Roth to present the reverse side of every argument his characters make. He deliberately courts shock value: the events he depicts are both comical and horrible, often simultaneously." Roth's story outside his story, most critics concluded, was yet another look at imagination and reality. Bloom maintained, "What fascinates about *Operation Shylock* is the degree of the author's experimentation in shifting the boundaries between his life and his work." Jenny Turner commented in the *London Review of Books,* "Much of the material Roth has gathered into the *Shylock* bundle . . . is nothing short of stunning: fiction fulfilling one of its most honourable roles as a series of thought- experiments, giving voice to tangled, emotionally overdetermined ideas and theories that somebody somewhere is bound to be thinking anyway, and which are safer tried out in a novel than unleashed in their inchoate form on the world outside." Bloom commented,

"A superb prose stylist, particularly skilled in dialogue, he now has developed the ability to absorb recalcitrant public materials into what earlier seemed personal obsessions."

In *Shop Talk: A Writer and His Colleagues and Their Work,* Roth presents readers with previously published material, primarily conversations between Roth and some of the greats of European literature, including Primo Levi, Milan Kundera, and Isaac Bashevis Singer. The book also includes a piece about Roth's friend the painter Philip Guston and homages to Bernard Malamud and Saul Bellow. Although *Review of Contemporary Fiction* contributor David W. Madden found the title somewhat misleading because the book does not focus on the craft of writing, he noted that "Roth discusses Kafka, Bruno Schulz, and Judaism, as well as politics and the media, as banes and inspirations for creativity." Paul Evans, writing in *Book,* commented, "Throughout this slim but provocative volume, Roth himself is consistently engaging, whether he's meditating on the work of two interesting Czech writers, Aaron Appelfeld and Ivan Klima, or reminiscing about his mentors, Bernard Malamud and Saul Bellow."

During his career Roth has expanded his fact-fiction mix beyond the parameters of his own life to the political consciousness of his generation in *I Married a Communist.* He continues to expand it still further in *The Plot against America,* an historical fiction that takes place in the World War II era. In Roth's novel famed pilot Charles Lindbergh defeats Franklin D. Roosevelt in the 1940 presidential election. Instead of urging America's participation in the war, President Lindbergh pacifies German chancellor Adolph Hitler and, as a result, has American Jews fearing for their lives. As pointed out by *Book* contributor Andrew Hearst, Roth continues to be "as prodigious as ever." "Three and a half decades later," the critic added, "Roth still has a lot of nerve and courage."

Two volumes of Roth's collected works and the novel *Everyman* were published following the release of *The Plot against America.* The title of *Everyman* is taken from a fifteenth-century morality play of the same title, and, not surprisingly, Roth never names his character. The protagonist, an old man in his seventies, dies at the beginning of the story, and the remainder of the novel is a look back at his life. Pervasive ill health, three failed marriages, two estranged sons, one daughter, and a healthy older brother are the mainstays of the protagonist's life. Much more inward-looking than its predecessor, *Everyman* was well received by critics. Although a *Kirkus Reviews* critic felt that the story is "marred by redundancy," the critic also stated that it is "energized by vivid writing, palpable emotional intensity and several wrenching scenes." A *Publishers Weekly* contributor concluded by stating that the book "is an artful yet surprisingly readable treatise on . . . being human and struggling and aging at the beginning of the new century."

BIOGRAPHICAL AND CRITICAL SOURCES:

BOOKS

Appelfeld, Aron, *Beyond Despair: Three Lectures and a Conversation with Philip Roth,* translated by Jeffrey M. Green, Fromm International (New York, NY), 1994.

Berman, Jeffrey, *The Talking Cure: Literary Representations of Psychoanalysis,* New York University Press (New York, NY), 1985.

Bestsellers 90, Issue 3, Gale (Detroit, MI), 1990.

Cohen, Sarah Blacher, editor, *Comic Relief: Humor in Contemporary American Literature,* University of Illinois Press (Carbondale, IL), 1978.

Contemporary Literary Criticism, Gale (Detroit, MI), Volume 1, 1973, Volume 2, 1974, Volume 3, 1975, Volume 4, 1975, Volume 6, 1976, Volume 9, 1978, Volume 15, 1980, Volume 22, 1982, Volume 31, 1985, Volume 47, 1988, Volume 66, 1991, Volume 86, 1995.

Cooper, Alan, *Philip Roth and the Jews,* State University of New York Press (Albany, NY), 1996.

Danziger, Marie A., *Text/ Countertext: Fear, Guilt, and Retaliation in the Postmodern Novel,* P. Lang (New York, NY), 1996.

Dictionary of Literary Biography, Gale (Detroit, MI), Volume 2: *American Novelists since World War II,* 1978, Volume 28: *Twentieth-Century American-Jewish Fiction Writers,* 1984, Volume 173: *American Novelists since World War II, Fifth Series,* 1996.

Dictionary of Literary Biography Yearbook: 1982, Gale (Detroit, MI), 1983.

Gindin, James, *Harvest of a Quiet Eye: The Novel of Compassion,* Indiana University Press (Bloomington, IN), 1971.

Guttman, Allen, *The Jewish Writer in America: Assimilation and the Crisis of Identity,* Oxford University Press (New York, NY), 1971.

Harrison, Gilbert A., editor, *The Critic As Artist: Essays on Books, 1920-1970,* Liveright (New York, NY), 1972.

Hoffman, Frederick J., *The Modern Novel in America,* revised edition, Regnery (Washington, DC), 1963.

Howe, Irving, *The Critical Point,* Horizon (New York, NY), 1973.

Hyman, Stanley Edgar,*The Critic's Credentials: Essays and Reviews by Stanley Edgar Hyman,* edited by Phoebe Pettingell, Atheneum (New York, NY), 1978.

Kazin, Alfred, *Contemporaries,* Little, Brown (Boston, MA), 1962.

Malin, Irving, *Jews and Americans,* Southern Illinois University Press (Carbondale, IL), 1965.

McDaniel, John, *The Fiction of Philip Roth,* Haddonfield House (Haddonfield, NJ), 1974.

Milbauer, Asher Z., and Donald G. Watson, editors, *Reading Philip Roth,* Macmillan (London, England), 1988.

Pinsher, Sanford, *The Comedy That "Hoits": An Essay on the Fiction of Philip Roth,* University of Missouri Press (Columbia, MO), 1975.

Podhoretz, Norman, *Doings and Undoings,* Farrar, Straus (New York, NY), 1964.

Pughe, Thomas, *Comic Sense: Reading Robert Coover, Stanley Elkin, and Philip Roth,* Birkhauser (Basel, Switzerland), 1994.

Rogers, Bernard F., Jr., *Philip Roth: A Bibliography,* Scarecrow Press (Metuchen, NJ), 1974.

Rogers, Bernard F., Jr., *Philip Roth,* Twayne (Boston, MA), 1978.

Roth, Philip, *Patrimony: A True Story,* Simon & Schuster (New York, NY), 1991.

Short Story Criticism, Volume 26, Gale (Detroit, MI), 1997.

Solotaroff, Theodore, *The Red Hot Vacuum and Other Pieces on the Writings of the Sixties,* Atheneum (New York, NY), 1970.

Walden, Daniel, editor, *The Changing Mosaic: From Cahan to Malamud, Roth, and Ozick,* State University of New York Press (New York, NY), 1993.

Weinberg, Helen, *The New Novel in America: The Kafkan Mode in Contemporary Fiction,* Cornell University Press (Ithaca, NY), 1970.

Wisse, Ruth, *The Schlemiel As Modern Hero,* University of Chicago Press (Chicago, IL), 1971.

World Literature Criticism: 1500 to the Present, Gale (New York, NY), Volume 5, 1992.

PERIODICALS

Atlantic, July, 1962; April, 1969, p. 64; December, 1971; November, 1977; May, 1993, p. 129; May, 2001, Jason Cowley, review of *The Dying Animal,* p. 118.

Book, September, 2001, Paul Evans, review of *Shop Talk: A Writer and His Colleagues and Their Work,* p. 78; September-October, 2003, "Dirty Works," p. 36.

Booklist, July, 1995, p. 1836; May 15, 2001, Donna Seaman, review of *The Dying Animal,* p. 1708; September 15, 2001, Donna Seaman, review of *Shop Talk,* p. 181.

Boston Globe, March 7, 1993, p. B43.

Boston Review, October-November, 1995, p. 37.

Catholic World, Volume 209, June, 1969, p. 129.

Chicago Tribune, March 22, 1993, section 5, p. 1.

Chicago Tribune Book World, May 31, 1981; November 6, 1983; June 23, 1985.

Christian Science Monitor, April 29, 1993, p. 11.

Commentary, December, 1972; September, 1974; December, 1979; September, 1981; January, 1984; February, 1994, p. 43; December, 1995, p. 61; October, 1998.

Commonweal, March 21, 1969; November 9, 1979; January 15, 1999.

Critique, Volume 14, number 3, p. 16.

Detroit Free Press, April 1, 1990; January 13, 1991.

Detroit News, April 4, 1990.

English Studies, December, 1984, p. 495.

Esquire, May, 1970; June, 1981; September, 1981, p. 92; February, 1990.

Harper's, July, 1974.

Hudson Review, summer, 1969, p. 320.

International Fiction Review, January, 1975.

Journal of Popular Culture, fall, 1972, p. 374.

Kirkus Reviews, February 15, 2006, review of *Everyman,* p. 156.

Knight Ridder/Tribune News Service, June 13, 2001, Christopher Kelly, review of *The Dying Animal,* p. K5276.

Library Journal, August, 2001, Gene Shaw, review of *Shop Talk,* p. 108.

Literature and Psychology, Volume 19, number 3, p. 57.

London Review of Books, May 13, 1993, p. 20; October 19, 1995, p. 10.

Los Angeles Times, April 15, 1990.

Los Angeles Times Book Review, June 7, 1981; November 13, 1983; May 26, 1985; January 11, 1987; September 11, 1988; March 25, 1990; January 6, 1991; March 7, 1993, p. 3; August 27, 1995, p. 3.

Midstream, June-July, 1969, p. 3.

Nation, March 10, 1969, p. 311; December 27, 1975; September 15, 1979; June 13, 1981; June 7, 1993, p. 778; November 16, 1998, John Leonard, review of *I Married a Communist,* p. 26; June 11, 2001, Keith Gessen, review of *The Dying Animal,* p. 42.

National Review, July 19, 1974; October 16, 1981; March 29, 1993, p. 68; September 28, 1998.

New Leader, November 2, 1998, p. 16.
New Republic, June 8, 1974; June 7, 1975; October 6, 1979; May 23, 1981; December 19, 1983; November 21, 1988; April 30, 1990; April 5, 1993, p. 31; October 23, 1995, p. 33; October 12, 1998, James Wood, review of *I Married a Communist,* p. 38.
New Statesman, September 21, 1973; November 9, 1978; April 9, 1993, p. 57; October 20, 1995, p. 40; October 16, 1998; February 25, 2002, Lisa Allardice, review of *The Dying Animal,* p. 56.
Newsweek, February 24, 1969; November 8, 1971; June 3, 1974; December 30, 1974; September 10, 1979; June 8, 1981; November 7, 1983; January 12, 1987; March 26, 1990; January 14, 1991; March 8, 1993, p. 55; March 22, 1993, p. 71; August 21, 1995, p. 53.
New York, June 3, 1974; March 8, 1993, p. 83; September 4, 1995, p. 48.
New Yorker, March 2, 1987; March 15, 1993, p. 109.
New York Review of Books, November 16, 1972; May 31, 1973; June 13, 1974; October 27, 1977; June 25, 1981; April 11, 1985; April 22, 1993, p. 45; November 16, 1995, p. 20.
New York Times, May 9, 1981; May 11, 1981; October 19, 1983; May 15, 1985; August 1, 1985; December 17, 1986; December 29, 1986; September 6, 1988; September 15, 1988; March 5, 1990; January 1, 1991; March 4, 1993, p. C17; March 9, 1993, p. C13; August 22, 1995, p. B2; August 7, 1996.
New York Times Book Review, May 17, 1959; June 17, 1962; February 23, 1969; November 7, 1971; September 27, 1972; May 6, 1973; June 2, 1974; May 25, 1975; September 18, 1977; September 2, 1979; May 24, 1981; October 30, 1983; January 1, 1984; May 19, 1985; January 4, 1987; September 25, 1988; March 11, 1990; January 6, 1991; March 7, 1993, p. 1; March 20, 1994, p. 28; December 4, 1994, p. 89; August 27, 1995, p. 7.
Observer (London, England), March 14, 1993, p. 58.
Paris Review, fall, 1984, p. 215.
Partisan Review, summer, 1973.
People, April 12, 1993, p. 27.
Playboy, December, 1969, p. 151; June, 1993, p. 38.
Publishers Weekly, August 26, 1988; January 4, 1990; February 15, 1993, p. 197; December 12, 1994, p. 11; June 12, 1995, p. 44; March 27, 2000, review of *The Human Stain,* p. 51; July 2, 2001, review of *Shop Talk,* p. 60; February 20, 2006, review of *Everyman,* p. 132.
Ramparts, May, 1969, p. 29.
Review of Contemporary Fiction, David W. Madden, review of *Shop Talk,* p. 151.
Saturday Night, April, 1969.
Saturday Review, April 11, 1959; June 16, 1962; November 6, 1971; December, 1979; June, 1981.
Saul Bellow Journal, summer, 1989.
Southern Review, January, 1972, p. 41; autumn, 1993, pp. 764, 767.
Studies in American Jewish Literature, fall, 1989, p. 154.
Studies in the Twentieth Century, number 6, 1970, p. 97.
Tikkun, January- February, 2002, Ronald Bush, review of *The Dying Animal,* p. 77; May, 2002, Ken Gordon, review of *Shop Talk,* p. 73.
Time, May 11, 1959; June 15, 1962; May 17, 1968, p. 102; June 10, 1974; September 3, 1979; May 25, 1981; November 7, 1983; January 19, 1987, Paul Gray, "The Varnished Truths of Philip Roth," p. 78; September 19, 1988; March 8, 1993, p. 68; January 3, 1994, p. 79; September 11, 1995, p. 82; October 12, 1998, p. 114.
Times (London, England), March 5, 1987.
Times Literary Supplement, April 17, 1969, p. 405; October 18, 1975; December 7, 1979; August 28, 1981; February 24, 1984; March 13, 1987; March 26, 1993, p. 19.
Tribune Books (Chicago, IL), January 11, 1987; September 4, 1988; March 11, 1990; January 6, 1991; March 7, 1993, p. 1; June 26, 1994, p. 8.
Twentieth Century Literature, July, 1973, p. 203.
USA Today, March 5, 1993, p. D3.
Village Voice, June 20, 1974; October 8, 1979; November 1, 1983; January 27, 1987.
Virginia Quarterly Review, summer, 1969.
Wall Street Journal, March 19, 1993, p. A8.
Washington Post, October 30, 1983; January 6, 1987; May 10, 1993, p. B1; March 15, 1993, p. D2; April 20, 1994, p. D1.
Washington Post Book World, November 7, 1971; September 17, 1972; May 3, 1973; September 2, 1979; May 31, 1981; October 30, 1983; June 16, 1985; January 4, 1987; August 28, 1988; April 1, 1990; January 6, 1991; March 14, 1993, p. 1.
World, May 8, 1983.
Yale Review, June, 1969, p. 623; spring, 1972.

* * *

ROTH, Philip Milton
See ROTH, Philip

* * *

ROWLING, J.K. 1965-
(Kennilworthy Whisp, Newt Scamander, Joanne Kathleen Rowling)

PERSONAL: Born July 31, 1965, Chipping Sodbury, England; married a journalist (divorced); married Neil

Murray (an anesthesiologist), December 26, 2001; children: (first marriage) Jessica Rowling, (second marriage) David Gordon Rowling Murray, Mackenzie Jean Rowling Murray. *Education:* Graduated from Exeter University, 1987.

ADDRESSES: Home—Perthshire, Scotland. *Agent*—c/o Author Mail, Scholastic, Inc., 555 Broadway, New York, NY 10012.

CAREER: Author of books for children, 1987—. Former teacher in Scotland and Portugal.

AWARDS, HONORS: British Book Award, Children's Book of the Year, and Nestlé Smarties Gold Award, both 1997, both for *Harry Potter and the Philosopher's Stone; Publishers Weekly* Best Book, *Booklist* Editor's Choice, ALA Notable Book, New York Public Library Best Book of the Year, *Parenting* Book of the Year Award, all 1998, and Rebecca Caudill Young Readers' Book Award, 2001, all for *Harry Potter and the Sorcerer's Stone;* Children's Book of the Year shortlist citation, Nestlé Smarties Gold Award, both 1998, and *Booklist* Editor's Choice, ALA Best Book for Young Adults, *School Library Journal* Best Book of the Year, all 1999, all for *Harry Potter and the Chamber of Secrets;* Whitbread Prize for Children's Literature, Nestlé Smarties Gold Award, *Booklist* Editor's Choice, *Los Angles Times* Best Book, and ALA Notable Book, all 1999, all for *Harry Potter and the Prisoner of Azkaban;* W.H. Smith Children's Book of the Year Award, 2000, and Hugo Award for Best Novel, Scottish Arts Council Book Award, and Whitaker's Platinum Book Award, all 2001, all for *Harry Potter and the Goblet of Fire;* Prince of Asturias Concord Prize, 2003; *Harry Potter and the Goblet of Fire* was voted Britain's fifth-best-loved novel by the British public as part of the BBC's The Big Read (the first three in the series also reached the top 100), 2003; Bram Stoker Award in work for young readers category, 2003, and W.H. Smith Book Award in fiction category, 2004, both for *Harry Potter and the Order of the Phoenix;* recipient of Doctor honoris causa degree, Edinburgh University, 2004.

WRITINGS:

Harry Potter and the Philosopher's Stone, Bloomsbury (London, England), 1997, published as *Harry Potter and the Sorcerer's Stone,* Scholastic/Arthur A. Levine Books (New York, NY), 1998.

Harry Potter and the Chamber of Secrets, Bloomsbury (London, England), 1998, Scholastic (New York, NY), 1999.

Harry Potter and the Prisoner of Azkaban, Scholastic (New York, NY), 1999.

Harry Potter and the Goblet of Fire, Scholastic (New York, NY), 2000.

(Under name Newt Scamander) *Fantastic Beasts and Where to Find Them,* special edition with a foreword by "Albus Dumbledore," Arthur A. Levine Books (New York, NY), 2001.

(Under name Kennilworthy Whisp) *Quidditch through the Ages,* Arthur A. Levine Books (New York, NY), 2001.

Harry Potter and the Order of the Phoenix, Scholastic (New York, NY), 2003.

Harry Potter and the Half-Blood Prince, Scholastic (New York, NY), 2005.

ADAPTATIONS: Five of the Harry Potter books have been adapted or optioned for film by Warner Bros., starring Daniel Radcliffe, Rupert Grint, and Emma Watson: *Harry Potter and the Sorcerer's Stone,* directed by Chris Columbus, 2001; *Harry Potter and the Chamber of Secrets, directed by Chris Columbus,* 2002; *Harry Potter and the Prisoner of Azkaban,* directed by Alfonso Cuarón, 2004; *Harry Potter and the Goblet of Fire,* directed by Mike Newell, 2005; and *Harry Potter and the Order of the Phoenix,* directed by David Yates. All six Harry Potter books have been adapted for audio cassette and CD-Rom, read by Jim Dale, by Listening Library.

WORK IN PROGRESS: The seventh—and final—novel in the Harry Potter series.

SIDELIGHTS: J.K. Rowling, author of the Harry Potter series, is one of the most popular writers of all time. As of mid-2005, worldwide sales of her books surpassed 280 million copies. The Harry Potter titles are available in more than 200 countries and have been translated into sixty-two languages. Such success initially caught Rowling off guard: In *January Magazine,* Linda Richards observed, "When J.K. Rowling began writing the novel that would become *Harry Potter and the Philosopher's Stone* in the early 1990s, she didn't see the fame in her own crystal ball. 'I thought I'd written something that a handful of people might quite like.'" With each new installment, however, the popularity of the Harry Potter series grows. Releases of the volumes have become media events, and millions of people have become familiar with terms such as muggles (non-magical folk) and quidditch (the most popular wizard sport). In short, Harry Potter is a publishing phenomena, and as *Time* reviewer Lev Grossman stated, "The Hogwarts Express is here, and you can either lie down on the tracks or get on board."

Readers in England were first introduced to Harry Potter in 1997 in *Harry Potter and the Philosopher's Stone,* while U.S. readers had to wait another year until the book was published in America under the title *Harry Potter and the Sorcerer's Stone.* Harry is an orphaned boy living with his aunt Petunia, uncle Vernon, and cousin Dudley Dursley at number four, Privet Drive in England. Harry is unloved, bullied, and underfed, and he believes there is nothing special about himself, other than the lightning-shaped scar on his forehead. Just before Harry's eleventh birthday, though, he receives a mysterious letter—his first correspondence ever—that is confiscated by his uncle, along with hundreds of subsequent letters from the same sender. Despite Mr. Dursley's attempts to take the family into hiding to avoid the mail, the letters continue coming. Finally one is delivered in person by Rubeus Hagrid, a representative of Hogwarts School of Witchcraft and Wizardry, where Harry has been accepted. Harry soon learns the truth about his family, a topic about which the Dursleys have always refused to speak. Harry was the lone survivor of an attack on the Potter family by the Lord Voldemort, a dark wizard so feared that he is most often referred to only as "You Know Who." Before he could walk, Harry was famous in the wizarding world as "The Boy Who Lived." Moreover, Voldemort's spell rebounded on him and he was wounded and has not been seen for ten years.

The news of his ancestry and talents opens up a new world for Harry. Hagrid accompanies Harry on his first foray into the wizarding community: Diagon Alley in London, where Harry shops for school supplies, such as a wand, cauldron, robes, quills, and spell books. The following month, Harry arrives at King's Cross train station, platform nine and three-quarters, to take the Hogwarts Express to the castle that will be his school and home. Before setting off, Harry auspiciously meets the nine-member Weasley family, whose youngest son, Ron, will become Harry's best friend—as does muggle-born Hermione Granger. The first major event at school is the sorting ceremony, during which incoming students are assigned to one of four school houses named after Hogwarts' founding wizards: Gryffindor, Hufflepuff, Ravenclaw, or Slytherin. Harry, Ron, and Hermione all get sorted into Gryffindor, a particular relief for Harry, who was strongly considered for Slytherin, a house known for producing dark wizards.

Hogwarts, overseen by headmaster Albus Dumbledore—who is the only wizard Lord Voldemort ever feared—is a place where Harry is accepted, well-fed, and has friends for the first time in his life. He takes classes such as Transfiguration, Charms, Care of Magical Creatures, Herbology, and Defense against the Dark Arts. Not all is well, however. Harry despises his Potions class due to the teacher, Professor Snape, who loathes and harasses Harry. And, as the year progresses, Harry and his friends uncover a plot to steal a valuable item hidden at Hogwarts. The Sorcerer's Stone is used to create the Elixir of Life, which makes the drinker immortal. Harry eventually secures the stone, discovering that a weakened Lord Voldemort has been seeking it to help him recover his strength and return to power. Thus, for the second time Harry defeats Voldemort.

Critical reception of the Harry Potter novels has been almost universally approving. *New Statesman* contributor Amanda Craig "loved" *Harry Potter and the Sorcerer's Stone* and hailed Rowling's tale as full of "zest and brio." A *Horn Book,* reviewer deemed the work "a charming and readable romp . . . filled with delightful magic details" Writing in the *New Republic,* Lee Siegel believed that the book was so appealing because of Rowling's "wholehearted absorption in her universe." Siegel also praised Rowling's characterization, noting, "Harry and his friends Hermione and Ron Weasley are good kids, but they are not innocent, Wordsworthian kids. They usually do the right thing, and they always feel bad when they do the wrong thing." *New York Times* reviewer Michiko Kakutani explained that "the achievement of the Potter books is . . . the creation of a richly imagined and utterly singular world, as detailed, as improbable and as mortal as our own." Bill Ott of *Booklist* concluded: "New generations will be reading Harry Potter because it has been so important a part of this generation. Twenty years from now grown-up Harry fans will want to share these books with their own children."

Book two of the series, *Harry Potter and the Chamber of Secrets,* opens with a lonely and miserable Harry who believes his new friends have forgotten him, since they have not contacted him all summer. Soon, however, an unexpected magical visitor breaks up the monotony at Privet Drive. A house elf named Dobby arrives to warn Harry against returning to school, implying that a plot exists to kill him. Harry refuses to stay away, and as Dobby tries to protect the young wizard, a series of fiascoes ensue, which result in Harry being locked up by the Dursleys and nearly expelled before the school term even starts. Dobby proves correct about danger existing at the school: soon several Hogwarts inhabitants are mysteriously attacked and petrified. According to legend, there is a secret chamber within Hogwarts that houses a terrible beast who attacks individuals who are not pure-blood wizards. Furthermore, this chamber can only be opened by the true heir of Salazar Slytherin. When Harry is revealed to the entire school as a Parselmouth, or a person who can speak to snakes, other students suspect and fear that he is Slytherin's heir and is responsible for opening the chamber. The staff also worries that if the attacks do not cease, Hogwarts will be forced to close.

By chance Harry discovers a diary and, through it, travels back in time fifty years, when similar assaults occurred and a girl was killed. Hagrid, a student at the time, was suspected of opening the chamber and was expelled. Meanwhile, the boy who accused Hagrid, Tom Riddle, was given an award for special services to the school after the attacks stopped. Harry, Ron, and Hermione can't believe that their friend and teacher Hagrid could be capable of such an act, so they attempt to discern the real culprit. During the investigation, Hermione is attacked and petrified, but she still manages to pass along clues about the creature's identity. After Ginny Weasley, Ron's younger sister, is kidnapped and taken into the chamber, Harry, Ron, and teacher Gilderoy Lockhart discover an entrance to the secret room and set off on a rescue mission. When the party is divided, however, Harry must go on alone. He finds Ginny and a young man in the chamber. The man reveals himself as Tom Marvolo Riddle, whose name forms the anagram "I am Lord Voldemort." This Voldemort is a shadow of his former self, revealed through the diary he owned as a teenager. Harry kills the basilisk responsible for the attacks, vanishes Riddle/Voldemort, saves Ginny, and in the process reveals himself as a true Gryffindor.

Harry Potter and the Chamber of Secrets was also well received, ending up on numerous "best book of the year" lists. A *Publishers Weekly* critic announced, "Rowling might be a Hogwart's graduate herself, for her ability to create such an engaging, imaginative, funny, and, above all, heart- pounding suspenseful yarn is nothing short of magical." *Booklist* reviewer Sally Estes also praised *Chamber of Secrets,* saying, "The mystery, zany humor, sense of a traditional British school (albeit with its share of ghosts, including Moaning Myrtle who haunts the girls' bathroom), student rivalry, and eccentric faculty, all surrounded by the magical foundation so necessary in good fantasy, are as expertly crafted here as in the first book."

Starting with book three of the series, the U.S. and British editions were published concurrently. *Harry Potter and the Prisoner of Azkaban* begins with news that a murderer named Siruis Black has escaped from the wizard prison Azkaban. Harry discovers that Black—who had been his parents' friend, best man at their wedding, and is Harry's godfather—is suspected of being the informant who enabled Voldemort to find and kill James and Lily Potter. The wizarding community also fears that the fugitive will attempt to kill Harry. As a result, security is tightened at Hogwarts, and the school's perimeter is patrolled by dementors, who are also Azkaban prison guards. Dementors are ghastly robed and hooded creatures who can drain all happiness from humans and can even rob them of their souls. They have an especially strong affect on Harry, who faints and hears terrified pleading and screaming in his head when they draw near.

Hogwarts' new Defense against the Dark Arts teacher, Remus Lupin, (who was also a friend of the Potters) teaches Harry an advanced spell that repels dementors. Harry also takes a new subject, Divination, but is skeptical and irritated by Professor Trelawney's repeated predictions of his untimely death. However one day, she seems to make a real prophecy when she intones that the Dark Lord's "servant will break out . . . to rejoin his master." Later that evening, a large black dog attacks Ron on the school grounds and drags him away. Harry and Hermione follow, ending up in a house in the village of Hogsmeade. There they find out that the dog is Sirius Black in magical disguise; Professor Remus Lupin is a werewolf; and Ron's pet rat, Scabbers, is a wizard named Peter Pettigrew, who was actually responsible for the betrayal and murders for which Sirius Black was accused. Because Pettigrew escapes, there are no credible adult witnesses to corroborate the story, and Sirius is to be taken back to prison. Harry uses the Patronus spell to save his godfather from the soul-extracting kiss of the dementors, and, later, Harry and Hermione free Sirius from custody and procure transportation for him so he can go into hiding.

Harry Potter and the Prisoner of Azkaban again earned Rowling critical praise, and the volume won Britain's prestigious Whitbread Prize for Children's Literature. *New Statesman* contributor Amanda Craig pointed out that "the third book is basically the same as the first two, but that doesn't matter . . . There is comfort in formulas as good as this one and the inventiveness, the jokes, the characterization, and suspense are as enthralling as ever." In *Horn Book,* Martha V. Parravano assessed that the new characters introduced in this volume "are particularly interesting." And a *Publishers Weekly* reviewer remarked that in *Harry Potter and the Prisoner of Azkaban*'s "finale . . . is utterly thrilling."

The fourth installment of the series, *Harry Potter and the Goblet of Fire,* features Harry and his friends' attendance at the Quidditch World Cup, a worldwide championship for the wizard sport. The school year also has an international flair as Hogwarts hosts the Triwizard Tournament and guests from the schools of Durmstrang and Beauxbatons. Only students who are at least seventeen can enter the competition, so the entire school is stunned when Harry is selected as a participant. Harry fares well in the first two tasks, which include facing dragons and merpeople, and is tied for the lead in the competition with the other Hogwarts' champion, Cedric Diggory. In the final task, which involves navigating through a maze filled with enchantments and dangerous creatures, Harry and Cedric reach the finish line at the same time. Deciding they will share the prize, they grab the Triwizard Cup simultaneously, realizing too late that it is a portkey—a device that can transport wizards. The two are taken to a cemetery, where Lord Voldemort and his assistant, Peter Pettigrew, are waiting. Voldemort immediately kills Cedric, but he temporarily spares Harry, since he needs some of the teenager's blood to create a potion that will return him to human form. When that proves successful, Voldemort calls back his followers, or Death Eaters, and in their presence plans to torture and murder Harry. With unexpected help, Harry escapes and returns to Hogwarts with Cedric's body. It turns out that entering Harry in the competition was a plot by another of Voldemort's followers, who has been impersonating a Hogwarts teacher all school year. A devastated Harry can barely appreciated that he has escaped Voldemort again and been able to alert the wizarding community about his return.

Entertainment Weekly reviewer Kristen Baldwin observed that *Harry Potter and the Goblet of Fire* "lulls the reader for so long with its lovely, meandering tale that when Rowling finally gets to the Harry/Voldemort showdown, the effect—a huge shift in tone for the series—is shocking." A *Newsweek* contributor stated, "For pure narrative power, this is the best Potter book yet." *School Library Journal* reviewer Eva Mitnick praised the "hefty volume,"saying that it "is brimming with all of the imagination, humor, and suspense that characterized the first books. So many characters, both new and familiar, are so busily scheming, spying, studying, worrying, fulminating, and suffering from unrequited first love that it is a wonder that Rowling can keep track, much less control, of all of the plot lines. She does, though, balancing humor, malevolence, school-day tedium, and shocking revelations with the aplomb of a circus performer." Writing in *New Statesman* Craig concluded, "This one of those rare books that more than live up to the hype."

Fans had to wait three years for the publication of the next Harry Potter book. In the interim, Rowling published *Quidditch through the Ages,* a supplement to the Harry Potter series, under the pseudonym Kennilworthy Whisp. The slim paperback was made to look like a real text from Hogwarts and was paired with a second Rowling book, *Fantastic Beasts and Where to Find Them,* published under the name Newt Scamander. "Harry Potter Fans who pride themselves on knowing every minute bit of Hogwart's trivia will devour both books," noted Mitnick. "In her 'Kennilworthy Whisp' persona, Rowling displays an entertainingly dry wit, apparently describing the most preposterous events with a straight face," added a *MouthShut* reviewer.

At the start of *Harry Potter and the Order of the Phoenix,* Harry is troubled at nighttime by dreams of the cemetery and an unknown corridor, and in the daytime by a lack of news about Voldemort's activities. He learns that the Ministry of Magic has denied Voldemort's return and that the wizard newspaper *The Daily Prophet* is attempting to discredit both Harry and Professor Dumbledore for insisting otherwise. Meanwhile the Order of the Phoenix, a group of wizards led by Dumbledore who have previously fought against Voldemort, convene at a London house owned by Sirius Black to plan their battle strategy. Harry, who has grown into a petulant teenager, is incensed that he is not allowed any news from the Order or his friends and that Dumbledore insists he stay at Privet Drive. He soon finds his own surroundings exciting enough, as he and his cousin Dudley are attacked by dementors. Harry's use of magic to repel them gets him in trouble with the Ministry, and they charge him with misuse of magic and unsuccessfully try to expel him from Hogwarts.

Back at school, Harry's strange dreams continue, and near Christmas time he dreams he is a snake and that he bites Mr. Weasley. He awakens with the horrible knowledge that he witnessed an actual event. Luckily he alerts Dumbledore so that Mr. Weasley is found, taken to the hospital, and saved. The frightening incident confirms that Harry has been accessing Voldemort's thoughts and actions. It works both ways, though, and this leads to tragedy. Voldemort is able to make Harry dream of his godfather being kidnapped and tortured at the Ministry of Magic, so Harry and five other students set off from Hogwarts to save Sirius. There they discover it is a setup by Voldemort and his Death Eaters, who have lured them to the Ministry to retrieve a prophecy concerning Harry and the Dark Lord. The students hold off the Death Eaters until reinforcements from the Order of the Phoenix arrive. In the ensuing battle, Sirius is killed and the prophecy is destroyed. Dumbledore, though, is able to recount it for Harry: it explains that Harry has been marked as Voldemort's equal, and that—in the end—one must die at the hands of the other.

Writing in *Time,* Lev Grossman commented, "Just when we might have expected J.K. Rowling's considerable imaginative energies to flag . . . she has hit peak form and is gaining speed." *School Library Journal* reviewer Eva Mitnick maintained that "the power of this book comes from the young magician's struggles with his emotions and identity." *Kliatt* contributor Paula Rohrlick deemed *Harry Potter and the Order of the Phoenix* "engrossing and satisfying." Arthur A. Levine commented on Harry's anger in an online review of the book for the University of Wisconsin Cooperative Children's School of Education: "It is one of the ways J.K. Rowling is addressing the transition of her main character from courageous, open-hearted boy to a young man weighed down by all that he has seen. Harry is also struggling, like many adolescents, to adjust to changes that he doesn't always understand in his relationships with friends and mentors." In a review for *January Magazine,* Sue Bursztynski also noted that unlike earlier novels in the series, "this novel is no longer children's literature." Bursztynski theorized that "Rowling has written on several levels for a wide variety of readers. It is a richly realized universe that becomes more complex with each book."

Voldemort and his followers are operating openly by the start of *Harry Potter and the Half-Blood Prince,* which *New York Times* reviewer Michiko Kakutani deemed "the darkest and most unsettling installment yet." The Minister of Magic has to explain to the muggle Prime Minister that recent murders, as well as an apparent hurricane and bridge collapse, are the work of dark wizards. Harry's classmate and nemesis, Draco Malfoy, is also now in the service of Voldemort, and he is plotting against someone at Hogwarts. Professor Snape, who has Dumbledore's full trust, has promised to help Draco achieve his goal or else carry out the plot for him. At school Harry voices suspicion about Malfoy's activities and possible motives, but neither his friends nor teachers believe him.

The wizarding world now accepts that Harry is the "chosen one" who can save them from the Dark Lord's reign of terror. Yet Harry continues on at Hogwarts, taking a full class load and serving as Quidditch team captain. He comes into possession of a book, formerly owned by someone calling himself the Half-Blood Prince, that helps him achieve top grades in his Potions class. He also takes private lessons with Dumbledore, which consist of the two using a pensieve to examine Voldemort's life via different peoples' memories. The hope is that the more Harry learns about Voldemort, the better chance he has of finding a way to defeat him. Harry and Dumbledore determine that Voldemort has placed pieces of his soul into six random objects or horcruxes, and that these must be destroyed before there can be any hope of killing the dark wizard. In their quest to attain one particular horcrux, Dumbledore is gravely injured. When he and Harry return to the castle, they find the Death Eaters have attacked and there is a battle taking place. Dumbledore puts a spell on Harry—who is wearing his invisibility cloak—so he can't take part in the fight. Malfoy's target is finally revealed, and it is Dumbledore. When Draco cannot bring himself to complete his mission, Professor Snape steps in and kills Dumbledore with the *Avada Kedavra* curse. At book's end, Harry realizes the extent of his isolation and understands the path he must now take.

National Review contributor David J. Montgomery remarked, "Once again [Rowling] has spun an immensely enjoyable journey through the magical world of Harry Potter, a near breathless story of heroism, intrigue, and cowardly villainy." The *New York Times*'s Michiko Kakutani noted that the novel "pulls together dozens of plot stands from previous volumes, underscoring how cleverly and carefully J.K. Rowling has assembled this giant jigsaw puzzle of an epic." Sue Corbett, writing in the *Miami Herald,* judged that the author's "writing and storytelling have matured just as much as Harry has." Commenting on the death of the beloved headmaster, Toronto *Globe and Mail* critic Sandra Martin simply stated, "Call out the grief counsellers." Associated Press reviewer Deepti Hajela remarked that *Harry Potter and the Half-Blood Prince* shares "the charm, intelligence and hilarity" of the previous five volumes, but that it "also has a poignancy, complexity and sadness we probably couldn't have imagined when we started reading the first one." And Meghan Cox Gurdon wrote in the *Wall Street Journal* that "what leaps out from the intricate storyline and wonderfully fresh prose . . . of *Harry Potter and the Half- Blood Prince* is the jaw-dropping scope of J.K. Rowling's achievement even before she publishes the last in the series."

BIOGRAPHICAL AND CRITICAL SOURCES:

BOOKS

Baggett, David, and Shawn E. Klein, editors, *Harry Potter and Philosophy: If Aristotle Ran Hogwarts,* Open Court (Chicago, IL), 2004.

Beahm, George, *Muggles and Magic: J.K. Rowling and the Harry Potter Phenomenon,* Hampton Roads Publishing (Charlottesville, VA), 2004.

Chippendale, Lisa A., *Triumph of the Imagination: The Story of Writer J.K. Rowling,* Chelsea House (Philadelphia, PA), 2002.

Heilman, Elizabeth, editor, *Harry Potter's World: Multidisciplinary Critical Perspectives,* Routledge-Falmer (New York, NY), 2003.

Kirk., Connie Ann, *J.K. Rowling: A Biography,* Greenwood Press (Westport, CT), 2003.

Moore, Sharon, editor, *Harry Potter, You're the Best!: A Tribute from Fans the World Over,* St. Martin's Griffin (New York, NY), 2001.

Wiener, Gary, editor, *Readings on J.K. Rowling,* Greenhaven Press (San Diego, CA), 2004.

PERIODICALS

Book, September, 2000, Robert Allen Papinchak, review of *Harry Potter and the Goblet of Fire,* p. 74; September-October, 2003, Steve Wilson, review of *Harry Potter and the Order of the Phoenix,* p. 88.

Booklist, May 15, 1999, Sally Estes, review of *Harry Potter and the Chamber of Secrets,* p. 1690; January 1, 2000, review of *Harry Potter and the Chamber of Secrets,* p. 822, review of *Harry Potter and the Prisoner of Azkaban,* p. 822, Bill Ott, review of *Harry Potter and the Sorcerer's Stone,* p. 988; March 15, 2000, review of *Harry Potter and the Chamber of Secrets,* p. 1360, review of *Harry Potter and the Prisoner of Azkaban,* p. 1360; April 15, 2000, Sally Estes, review of *Harry Potter and the Chamber of Secrets,* p. 1546, review of *Harry Potter and the Prisoner of Azkaban,* p. 1546; December 1, 2000, Stephanie Zvirin, review of *Harry Potter and the Goblet of Fire,* p. 693; April 15, 2001, Sally Estes, review of *Harry Potter and the Goblet of Fire,* p. 1561; May 1, 2001, Stephanie Zvirin, review of *Harry Potter and the Sorcerer's Stone,* p. 1611, Ilene Cooper, review of *Fantastic Beasts: And Where to Find Them,* p. 1683, review of *Quidditch through the Ages,* p. 1683.

Books for Keeps, September, 1997, p. 27.

Christianity Today, Michael G. Maudlin, review of *Harry Potter and the Goblet of Fire,* p. 117.

Detroit News, July 15, 2005, Michael H. Hodges, "Wizard Wraps Nation in His Powerful Spell."

Entertainment Weekly, July 21, 2000, Kristen Baldwin, review of *Harry Potter and the Goblet of Fire,* p. 72; August 4, 2000, "Rowling Thunder," p. 44; August 11, 2000, "Hocus Focus," p. 28.

Globe and Mail (Toronto, Ontario, Canada), July 16, 2005, Sandra Martin, review of *Harry Potter and the Half-Blood Prince.*

Guardian, February 16, 1999, p. EG4.

Horn Book, November, 1999, audio review of *Harry Potter and the Sorcerer's Stone,* p. 764; January, 1999, review of *Harry Potter and the Sorcerer's Stone,* p. 71; November, 1999, Martha V. Parravano, review of *Harry Potter and the Prisoner of Azkaban;*November, 2000, Martha V. Parravano, review of *Harry Potter and the Goblet of Fire,* p. 762; September-October, 2003, Martha V. Parravano, review of *Harry Potter and the Order of the Phoenix,* p. 619.

Kliatt, September, 2003, Paula Rohrlick, review of *Harry Potter and the Order of the Phoenix,* p.12.

Library Journal, June 1, 2001, review of *Harry Potter and the Prisoner of Azkaban,* p. S53.

Miami Herald, July 17, 2005, Sue Corbett, review of *Harry Potter and the Half-Blood Prince.*

National Review, October 11, 1999, "It's Witchcraft," p. 60; July 18, 2005, David J. Montgomery, review of *Harry Potter and the Half-Blood Prince.*

New Republic, November 22, 1999, Lee Siegel, "Harry Potter and the Spirit of Age: Fear of Not Flying," p. 40.

New Statesman, December 5, 1997, p. 64; July 12, 1999, Amanda Craig, review of *Harry Potter and the Prisoner of Azkaban,* pp. 47- 49; July 17, 2000, Amanda Craig, review of *Harry Potter and the Goblet of Fire,* p. 54.

Newsweek, July 17, 2000, "Why Harry's Hot," p. 52.

New York Times, July 8, 2000, Alan Cowell, "All Aboard the Potter Express," pp. 1330-1332; July 16, 2005, Michiko Kakutani, "Harry Potter Works His Magic Again in a Far Darker Tale."

People, December 2, 2002, Samantha Miller, "Where's Harry? J.K. Rowling Has a Baby on the Way. Fine, but What about the Next Potter?," p. 211.

Publishers Weekly, December 21, 1998, p. 28; January 4, 1999, p. 30; January 11, 1999, p. 24; May 31, 1999, review of *Harry Potter and the Chamber of Secrets,* p. 94; July 19, 1999, review of *Harry Potter and the Prisoner of Azkaban,*; July 19, 1999, Shannon Maughan, "The Harry Potter Halo," pp. 92-94; October 11, 1999, audio review of *Harry Potter and the Sorcerer's Stone,* p. 30; February 15, 1999, p. 33; July 24, 2000, "All Eyes on Harry," p. 31; June 30, 2003, review of *Harry Potter and the Order of the Phoenix,* p. 79.

Reading Teacher, October, 1999, review of *Harry Potter and the Sorcerer's Stone,* p. 183.

Mercury News (San Jose, CA), July 16, 2005, John Orr, review of *Harry Potter and the Half-Blood Prince.*

School Librarian, August, 1997, p. 147.

School Library Journal, August, 2000, Eva Mitnick, review of *Harry Potter and the Goblet of Fire,* p. 188; September, 2000, Eva Mitnick, review of

Harry Potter and the Goblet of Fire, p. 82; June, 2001, Eva Mitnick, review of *Quidditch through the Ages,* p. 155; August, 2003, Eva Mitnick, review of *Harry Potter and the Order of the Phoenix,* p. 165.

Science Fiction Chronicle, December, 1999, review of *Harry Potter and the Sorcerer's Stone,* p. 42.

Teacher Librarian, December, 1999, review of *Harry Potter and the Sorcerer's Stone,* p. 48.

Time, April 12, 1999, p. 86; July 17, 2000, review of *Harry and the Goblet of Fire,* p. 70; June 30, 2003, Lev Grossman, review of *Harry Potter and the Order of the Phoenix,* p. 60; July 25, 2005, Lev Grossman, "J.K. Rowling Hogwarts and All," p. 60.

USA Today, October, 1998.

Wall Street Journal, July 19, 2005, Meghan Cox Gurdon, "Magical Prose."

ONLINE

January Magazine, http://www.januarymagazine.com/ (October, 2000) Linda Richards, "J.K. Rowling"; (February 11, 2003) Linda Richards, "Harry's Real Magic"; (July, 2003) Sue Bursztynski, "Growing Up with Harry."

J.K. Rowling Official Site, http://www.jkrowling.com/ (July 1, 2005).

Manchester Online, http://www.manchesteronline.co.uk/ (July 18, 2005), Cathy Winston, review of *Harry Potter and the Half-Blood Prince.*

Mercury News, http://www.mercurynews.com/ (July 16, 2005), Deepti Hajela, Associated Press review of *Harry Potter and the Half-Blood Prince.*

MouthShut, http://www.mouthshut.com/ (November 21, 2001), "Everything You Wanted to Know about Quidditch."

MuggleNet.com—The Ultimate Harry Potter Site, http://www.mugglenet.com/ (July 1, 2005).

Salon.com, http://www.salon.com/ (March 31, 1999), "Of Magic and Single Motherhood."

Scholastic, http://www.scholastic.com/ (February 11, 2003), "Meet J.K. Rowling."

University of Wisconsin Cooperative Children's School of Education, http:// www.soemadison.wisc.edu/ccbc/ (November 25, 2003), "Harry Potter Reviews and Distinctions."

USA Today Online, http://www.usatoday.com/ (September 10, 2003), Jacqueline Blais, "Not Everyone's Wild about Harry Potter."

* * *

ROWLING, Joanne Kathleen
See ROWLING, J.K.

ROY, Arundhati 1960(?)-

PERSONAL: Born c. 1960, in Kerala, India; daughter of Rajib (a tea plantation manager) and Mary (a teacher) Roy; married Pradip Krishen (a filmmaker), c. 1993. *Education:* Attended architectural school.

ADDRESSES: *Home*—New Delhi, India. *Agent*—c/o Author Mail, Random House, 201 E. 50th St., New York, NY 10022.

CAREER: Actor, screenwriter, and novelist. Worked as an architect; sold cakes on a beach in Goa, India.

AWARDS, HONORS: Booker Prize, 1997, for *The God of Small Things;* Grand Prize of the World Academy of Culture (Paris, France), 2002; Lannan Award for Cultural Freedom; Sydney Peace Prize, 2004; Sahitya Akademi Award (India), 2006 (author refused award).

WRITINGS:

The God of Small Things (novel), Random House (New York, NY), 1997.

The End of Imagination (essay; also see below), D.C. Books (Kottayam, India), 1998.

The Greater Common Good (essay; also see below), India Book Distributor (Bombay, India), 1999.

The Cost of Living (contains *The End of Imagination* and *The Greater Common Good*), Modern Library (New York, NY), 1999.

Power Politics (essays), South End Press (Cambridge, MA), 2001, also published as *Power Politics: The Reincarnation of Rumpelstiltskin,* D.C. Books (Kottayam, India), 2001.

The Algebra of Infinite Justice (essays), Flamingo (London, England), 2002.

In Which Annie Gives it Those Ones: The Original Screenplay, Penguin Books (New York, NY), 2003.

War Talk (essays), South End Press (Cambridge, MA), 2003.

(With David Barsamian) *The Checkbook and the Cruise Missile: Conversations with Arundhati Roy,* South End Press (Cambridge, MA), 2004.

Public Power in the Age of Empire (essays), Seven Stories Press (New York, NY), 2004.

An Ordinary Person's Guide to Empire (essays), South End Press (Cambridge, MA), 2004.

Also author of screenplays; author of television series about India's nationalist movement.

WORK IN PROGRESS: A novel about nuclear power.

SIDELIGHTS: Arundhati Roy created an international sensation with her debut novel, *The God of Small Things,* which first earned its author a million-dollar publishing advance. The novel garnered Roy Britain's most prestigious literary award, the Booker Prize; she was the first citizen of India to win that award. Following the success of her first novel, Roy remained in the public eye due to her social activism, as well to as her outspoken criticism of globalization and the negative influence exerted by the United States on global culture. She has even been imprisoned for her activities and opinions, which she has expressed in many essays, including those collected in *The Cost of Living* and *Power Politics.*

Roy grew up in Kerala, India, a child of Syrian Christian and Hindu parents. When her parents divorced, Roy's mother fought for and won an inheritance, despite the bias of Indian laws favoring male heirs. The victory was perhaps more significant ethically than financially, for Roy still found it necessary to live in a slum area in order to save enough money to attend school in New Delhi. She began by studying architecture, but eventually drifted from that and took up an acting career. This led to success as a screenwriter, which put the writer in a good position to negotiate the contract for her first book. After first appearing in 1997, *The God of Small Things* has been translated into more than forty languages and has sold several million copies internationally.

The God of Small Things focuses on themes of history and the individual, as experienced by twin siblings. The novel's title, according to Meenakshi Ganguly in *Time* magazine, refers to the deity that rules over "social propriety." The novel tells the story of Ammu, a divorced mother of twin children. Rahel, Ammu's daughter, eventually ends up in the United States, while her son, Estha, becomes mute, but despite their physical separation the twins retain an empathic bond. The novel also explores Ammu's forbidden love with the carpenter Velutha who belongs to the class of untouchables, and portrays family relatives who have come back to visit their homeland from Great Britain. One of the visitors ends up dead, and Ammu's affair comes to a tragic end.

Ganguly noted that *The God of Small Things* is "infused with endless, cinematic fast-forwards that telegraph the tragedy ahead." The critic cautioned that "Indian readers may be put off by the incessantly brutal depiction of their country . . . . Buildings are in near-rot and roads are graced with squashed animals." Michiko Kakutani of the *New York Times* praised the novel, hailing it as "dazzling" and "a richly layered story of familial betrayal and thwarted romantic passion." Kakutani compared Roy to British Victorian novelist Charles Dickens and twentieth-century American novelist William Faulkner for her handling of issues pertaining to race, class, society, and character, and reported that critics in the author's native India have compared her to South American novelist Gabriel García Márquez. The critic also asserted that "Roy does a marvelous job of conjuring the anomalous world of childhood, its sense of privilege and frustration, its fragility, innocence and unsentimental wisdom."

Roy used her newfound fame and money to further her work as an activist, and also attracted additional attention with her essay *The Greater Common Good,* which has been published in book form. In this essay she denounces the multimillion dollar Sardar Sarovar Dam project on the Narmada river in western India. Although promoters have touted the dam as a solution to India's power and water shortages, opponents of the project believe that it will cause widespread social and environmental chaos, as it would submerge 245 villages and displace some forty million people. In another essay, *The End of Imagination,* Roy decries the nuclear bomb tests conducted by India in May of 1998. Why, she asks, did India spend the massive amounts of money it took to build and test the bomb when the country has 400 million citizens living in complete poverty and illiteracy? Both essays have been reprinted in the volume *The Cost of Living.* While a *Publishers Weekly* writer stated that "Roy surely has meaningful things to say about India," the critic added that "she is not yet nearly as accomplished a political critic as she is a novelist." *The Cost of Living* is, in the reviewer's opinion, "marred by general attacks on 'the system' and personal digressions that distract a reader from the substantive issues at hand." In *Library Journal,* Ravi Shenoy allowed that Roy's "polemical tract" is "not a dispassionate inquiry," but added that nonetheless it "raises some important questions about the real price of 'development,' whether in the form of big dams or bombs."

Power Politics presents more of Roy's essays, as she criticizes the political elite of India and that group's participation in globalization despite enormous social and environmental costs. The essays are "pithy and elegant," according to a writer in the *New Internationalist.* James Gerein urged in his *World Literature Today* review that readers of this book should "set aside prejudgments, follow her arguments, and try to empathize with what it would be like to lose one's land, village, job, income, way of life, and perhaps life itself to the imperatives of globalization. Her thesis is not some bleedingheart fantasy but a largely unreported consequence of big business pounding the voiceless down to compost level."

War Talk likewise presents Roy's views and her passion for them, as she explores the connections between violence, poverty, and globalization. Judy Coode reported in *Sojourners,* "Roy is an incisive, infuriated citizen of the world, and she is determined not to allow the powers that thrive on imbalance and inequity to silence her. The essays are fairly easy to read, though at times their subject matter is difficult to stomach. Roy barely restrains herself from screaming in frustration at humans and their inability to recognize the connection between inequality and the lack of peace. She exposes herself fully, writing with such emotion and articulation that the reader can almost see her expression of righteous fury and hear her . . . strong voice choked with tears." Despite the seemingly unrelieved seriousness of Roy's writing, Donna Seaman noted in a *Booklist* review of *War Talk* that, "So fluent is her prose, so keen her understanding of global politics, and so resonant her objections to nuclear weapons, assaults against the environment, and the endless suffering of the poor that her essays are as uplifting as they are galvanizing."

An Ordinary Person's Guide to Empire, another collection of Roy's essays and lectures, was released in 2004. The collection discusses topics familiar to her readers: the occupation of Iraq, biased or ignorant reporting, and corporations that profit from restrictions that governments place upon their citizens, among other things. Unlike many other leftist essayists, however, Roy does not only inform and dissent, she also seeks to resolve. Indeed, *Colorlines* magazine contributor C.S. Soong stated that Roy's "eye is always on the prize: How can those on the side of justice and equality actually win? What's the quickest, most efficient way to overthrow the structures and policies we've come to despise?" Critics, of course, praised the collection. While *Reviewer's Bookwatch* writer Willis M. Buhle commented that the book "spares nothing in its effort to show the raw, real, and often vicious truth," Soong concluded that "Roy's best weapons are her words, and to read her . . . is to understand the power and importance of words and ideas to the evolving global justice movement."

Roy has spoken of her unconventional, independent mother as an influence she is very thankful for. She told David Barsamian in an interview for *Progressive:* "I thank God that I had none of the conditioning that a normal, middle-class Indian girl would have. I had no father, no presence of this man telling us that he would look after us and beat us occasionally in exchange. I didn't have a caste, and I didn't have a class, and I had no religion, no traditional blinkers, no traditional lenses on my spectacles, which are very hard to shrug off." She further commented to Barsamian: "I don't see a great difference between *The God of Small Things* and my works of nonfiction. As I keep saying, fiction is truth. I think fiction is the truest thing there ever was. My whole effort now is to remove that distinction. The writer is the midwife of understanding."

BIOGRAPHICAL AND CRITICAL SOURCES:

BOOKS

Contemporary Literary Criticism, Volume 109, Gale (Detroit, MI), 1998.

Contemporary Novelists, 7th edition, St. James Press (Detroit, MI), 2001.

The Critical Studies of Arundhati Roy's "The God of Small Things," Atlantic Publishers & Distributors (New Delhi, India), 1999.

Dictionary of Literary Biography Yearbook: 1997, Gale (Detroit, MI), 1998.

PERIODICALS

Booklist, May 1, 1997, Donna Seaman, review of *The God of Small Things,* p. 1480; April 15, 2003, Donna Seaman, review of *War Talk,* p. 1433.

Christian Science Monitor, November 24, 1997, Merle Rubin, review of *The God of Small Things,* p. 11.

Colorlines, Winter, 2004, C.S. Soong, review of *An Ordinary Person's Guide to Empire,* p. 53.

Ecologist, September, 2000, "I Wish I Had the Guts to Shut Up," p. 29.

Entertainment Weekly, May 16, 1997, Suzanne Ruta, review of *The God of Small Things,* p. 109.

Guardian, September 29, 2001, review of *The Algebra of Infinite Justice,* p. 1; November 30, 2002, Natasha Walter, review of *The Algebra of Infinite Justice,* p. 11.

Harper's Bazaar, May, 1997, p. 117.

Herizons, spring, 2001, Subbalakshmi Subramanian, review of *The Cost of Living,* p. 33.

Journal of Contemporary Asia, May, 2003, Zaheer Baber, review of *The Cost of Living,* p. 284.

Kirkus Reviews, review of *The God of Small Things,* p. 412.

Library Journal, April 15, 1997, Barbara Hoffert, review of *The God of Small Things,* p. 120; July, 1997, Eric Bryant, review of *The God of Small Things,* p. 102; October 15, 1999, Ravi Shenoy, review of *The Cost of Living,* p. 90.

Los Angeles Times Book Review, June 1, 1997, Richard Eder, "As the World Turns," p. 2.

Maclean's, October 27, 1997, "A Literary Queen," p. 64.

Mother Jones, January- February, 2002, Arlie Russell Hochschild, interview with Roy, p. 74.

Nation, September 29, 1997, Amitava Kumar, "Rushdie's Children," pp. 36- 38.

National Review, February 7, 2000, Kanchan Limaye, review of *The Cost of Living,* p. 50.

New Internationalist, October, 2002, review of *Power Politics,* p. 31.

New Republic, December 29, 1997, James Wood, review of *The God of Small Things,* p. 32; April 29, 2002, Ian Buruma, review of *Power Politics,* p. 25.

New Statesman, June 27, 1997, Amanda Craig, "But What about This Year's Barbados Novel?," p. 49; April 30, 2001, Salil Tripathi, "The Goddess against Big Things," p. 22.

Newsweek, May 26, 1997, Laura Shapiro, "Disaster in a Lush Land," p. 76.

Newsweek International, March 18, 2002, interview with Roy, p. 94.

New Yorker, June 23, 1997, John Updike, "Mother Tongues," pp. 156-159.

New York Review of Books, August 14, 1997, Rosemary Dinnage, review of *The God of Small Things,* p. 16.

New York Times, June 3, 1997, Michiko Kakutani, review of *The God of Small Things,* p. B4; July 29, 1997, Elisabeth Bumiller, "A Novelist Begins with a Splash," p. B1; October 15, 1997, Sarah Lyall, "Indian's First Novel Wins Booker Prize in Britain," p. A4; January 12, 2000, Celia W. Dugger, "Author Seized," p. A6; August 7, 2001, Salman Rushdie, "A Foolish Dam and a Writer's Freedom," p. A19; November 3, 2001, Celia W. Dugger, "An Indian Novelist Turns Her Wrath on the U.S.," p. A3; March 7, 2002, "India Jails Novelist for Criticizing a Court Ruling," p. A4.

New York Times Book Review, May 25, 1997, Alice Truax, "A Silver Thimble in Her Fist," p. 5; November 25, 2001, Alex Abramovich, review of *Power Politics,* p. 28.

Observer (London, England), November 17, 2002, review of *The Algebra of Infinite Justice,* p. 20.

People, July 14, 1997, Francine Prose, review of *The God of Small Things,* p. 30; November 3, 1997, Thomas Fields-Meyer, "No Small Thing: A Stunning Debut Novel Earns Arundhati Roy the Fruits of Stardom," p. 107; May 11, 1998, p. 161.

Progressive, April, 2001, David Barsamian, interview with Roy.

Publishers Weekly, March 3, 1997, review of *The God of Small Things,* p. 62; September 20, 1999, review of *The Cost of Living,* p. 61; May 14, 2001, John F. Baker, "Roy's Indian Wars," p. 20; July 30, 2001, review of *Power Politics,* p. 72.

Reviewer's Bookwatch, March, 2005, Willis M. Buhle, review of *An Ordinary Person's Guide to Empire.*

Sojourners, July- August, 2003, Judy Coode, review of *War Talk,* p. 57.

Time, April 14, 1997.

Vogue, October, 2002, Daphne Beal, "Portrait of a Renegade," p. 244.

Washington Post, October 20, 1997, Kenneth J. Cooper, "For India, No Small Thing: Native Daughter Arundhati Roy Wins Coveted Booker Prize," p. C1.

Whole Earth, winter, 2001, "India Will Not Behave," p. 78, Paul Hawken, review of *Power Politics,* p. 81.

World Literature Today, winter, 1998, Ramlal Agarwal, review of *The God of Small Things,* p. 208; summer, 2002, James Gerein, review of *Power Politics,* p. 79.

World Press Review, January, 1997, John Zubrzycki, review of *The God of Small Things,* p. 39.

World Watch, May, 2002, Curtis Runyan, review of *Power Politics,* p. 17.

Writer, November, 1998, Lewis Burke Frumkes, "A Conversation with Arundhati Roy," p. 23.

ONLINE

Salon.com, http://www.salon.com/ (September 30, 1997), Reena Jana, interview with Roy.

* * *

RULE, Ann 1935-
(Andy Stack)

PERSONAL: Born October 22, 1935, in Lowell, MI; daughter of Chester R. (an athletics coach) and Sophie (a teacher) Stackhouse; married Bill Rule (a teacher and technical writer; divorced, 1972); children: Laura, Leslie, Andy, Mike, Bruce. *Education:* University of Washington, B.A., 1954; graduate study at University of Washington; received degree in police science. *Hobbies and other interests:* Gardening, walking, pets, collecting "way too many things."

ADDRESSES: Home—Box 98846, Seattle, WA 98198. *Agent*—The Foley Agency, 34 East 38th St., New York, NY 10016. *E-mail*—annier37@aol.com.

CAREER: Writer. Has worked as a police officer in Seattle, WA, and as a caseworker for the Washington State Department of Public Assistance.

AWARDS, HONORS: Achievement Award, Pacific Northwest Writers Conference, 1991; two Anthony Awards, from Bouchercon; Peabody Award for miniseries *Small Sacrifices;* Readers' Choice Awards, *Reader's Digest,* 2003.

WRITINGS:

NONFICTION

Beautiful Seattle, Beautiful America (Woodburn, OR), 1979, published as *Beautiful America's Seattle,* Beautiful America (Woodburn, OR), 1989.
The Stranger beside Me, Norton (New York, NY), 1980, revised twentieth anniversary edition, Norton (New York, NY), 2000.
Small Sacrifices: A True Story of Passion and Murder, New American Library (New York, NY), 1987.
If You Really Loved Me: A True Story of Desire and Murder, Simon & Schuster (New York, NY), 1991.
Everything She Ever Wanted: A True Story of Obsessive Love, Murder, and Betrayal, Simon & Schuster (New York, NY), 1992.
Dead by Sunset: Perfect Husband, Perfect Killer?, Simon & Schuster (New York, NY), 1995.
Bitter Harvest: A Woman's Fury, a Mother's Sacrifice, Simon & Schuster (New York, NY), 1997.
. . . And Never Let Her Go: Thomas Capano, the Deadly Seducer, Simon & Schuster (New York, NY), 1999.
Every Breath You Take: A True Story of Obsessive Revenge and Murder, Free Press (New York, NY), 2001.
Heart Full of Lies: A True Story of Desire and Death, Free Press (New York, NY), 2003.
Without Pity: Ann Rule's Most Dangerous Killers, Pocket Books (New York, NY), 2003.
Green River, Running Red: The Real Story of the Green River Killer, America's Deadliest Serial Murderer, Free Press (New York, NY), 2004.

"ANN RULE'S CRIME FILES" SERIES

A Rose for Her Grave and Other True Cases (also see below), Pocket Books (New York, NY), 1993.
You Belong to Me and Other True Cases, Pocket Books (New York, NY), 1994.
A Fever in the Heart and Other True Cases, Pocket Books (New York, NY), 1996.
In the Name of Love and Other True Cases, Pocket Books (New York, NY), 1998.
The End of the Dream: The Golden Boy Who Never Grew Up and Other True Cases, Pocket Books (New York, NY), 1999.
A Rage to Kill and Other True Cases, Pocket Books (New York, NY), 1999.
Empty Promises and Other True Cases, Pocket Books (New York, NY), 2001.
Last Dance, Last Chance and Other True Cases, Pocket Books (New York, NY), 2003.
Kiss Me, Kill Me, and Other True Cases, Pocket Books (New York, NY), 2004.

Also author of *Ann Rule's Omnibus* (contains *A Rose for Her Grave, You Belong to Me,* and *A Fever in the Heart*).

"TRUE CRIME ANNALS" SERIES; UNDER PSEUDONYM ANDY STACK

Lust Killer, New American Library (New York, NY), 1983.
Want-Ad Killer, New American Library (New York, NY), 1983.
The I-Five Killer, New American Library (New York, NY), 1984.

OTHER

Possession (novel), Norton (New York, NY), 1983.

Contributor to various periodicals, including *Cosmopolitan, Good Housekeeping, Ladies' Home Journal, Seattle Times, True Confessions,* and *True Detective.*

ADAPTATIONS: An adaptation of *Small Sacrifices: A True Story of Passion and Murder* was broadcast on ABC-TV, 1989; *Dead by Sunset, . . . And Never Let Her Go,* and *Small Sacrifices* have been produced as television miniseries; *Ann Rule Presents: The Stranger beside Me,* a docudrama produced by the USA Network and based on Rule's book *The Stranger beside Me,* aired on March 21, 2003.

SIDELIGHTS: Ann Rule's writing has earned her a reputation as an expert on criminal behavior. She is the author of such best-selling books as *The Stranger beside Me, Small Sacrifices: A True Story of Passion and Murder,* and numerous other books which discuss the lives of notorious killers. In addition to lecturing on the subject of crime, she has provided testimony in court cases and has lent her expertise in order to help police agencies understand the behavior of psychopathic murderers. Although she has earned respect for the books published under her own name, some of her early work was done under the pseudonym Andy Stack. In the *New York Times,* Rule stated that publishers at the time "thought nobody would want to read a crime story written by a female."

Rule's interest in crime developed from a very early age. As a child, she spent time with her grandfather, a sheriff in Stanton, Michigan. "It fascinated me how grandpa could take a broken button or a blood drop and figure out who done it," she remarked in an interview with *People.* Rule attended the University of Washington, where she studied creative writing and criminology, and later became a police officer in Seattle. She lost her position on the force, however, when people found out about her extreme nearsightedness.

After her husband suspended his professional career to resume his education, Rule decided to provide for her family by writing stories about actual crimes. Through researching her pieces, Rule spent time with arson and homicide divisions of the police department, attended specialty classes in police science, and built a network of contacts with people involved in law enforcement throughout the Northwest.

In the early 1970s Rule worked on a suicide hot-line at the Seattle Crisis Center with a student intern named Ted Bundy. Of Bundy, Rule told *People,* "I used to think that if I were younger or my daughters were older, this would be the perfect man." Bundy was convicted of murder in 1978 and was ultimately implicated in the slaying of more than thirty-five women. Before Bundy's arrest and conviction, Rule was commissioned to write a book on a string of murders committed in the Northwest. The work was eventually published as *The Stranger beside Me,* an account of Bundy that earned critical acclaim due in part to Rule's association with the killer. In the *New York Times Book Review* Thomas Thompson remarked that the author "does have an extraordinary angle that makes *The Stranger beside Me* dramatic and, occasionally, as chilling as a bedroom window shattering at midnight."

During the initial investigation into the Seattle-area murders, as information about the killer became known, Rule became increasingly suspicious about Bundy's possible involvement and provided investigators with a tip that her associate might be the killer, but was relieved when the police did not follow up on her lead. Rule felt in some way duped by Bundy, however, when his guilt was confirmed; Bundy did not share the negative character traits associated with such notorious serial killers as Charles Manson, Richard Speck, and John Gacy. He was a handsome, educated, and charismatic individual with political aspirations. In *The Stranger beside Me,* Rule reports how Bundy moved to Salt Lake City, where he became a Mormon and studied to become a lawyer, then to Colorado and Florida. In each state, law enforcement officials were faced with investigations into gruesome murders that Bundy allegedly committed.

After Bundy was arrested for the murder of two members of the Chi Omega sorority at Florida State University, he chose to act as his own lawyer. Although he was given the opportunity to accept a seventy-five-year term of imprisonment, he chose to defend himself in a trial and was subsequently given the death penalty. Throughout *The Stranger beside Me,* Rule reports on how she and others were fooled by Bundy because he was successful at displaying the positive aspects of his character while hiding his negative traits. Of the time that she spent with Bundy at the crisis center, she wrote, as quoted by Thompson, "If, as many people believe today, Ted Bundy took lives, he also saved lives. I know he did, because I was there when he did it."

In *Small Sacrifices,* published in 1987, Rule relates the story of Diane Downs, a mother of three who claimed that she stopped her car on the highway to assist a "bushy-haired stranger" who had flagged her down. According to Downs, the stranger then proceeded to shoot her and her children. One of her children died, one was paralyzed, and one survived after having a stroke. In her book, Rule shows how police were wary about

Downs's story from the time they first heard it. In the emergency room, Downs seemed more concerned about whether there were holes in her new car than she was about the condition of her children. Also, when one police officer heard that Downs had been shot, he predicted the location of her wound—in an area that would not cause fatal injury, indicating that the injury was self-inflicted. Rule also notes that authorities are usually suspicious when they hear victims speak of a bushy-haired stranger, identified by the police as a "BHS." Rule writes, as quoted by Carolyn Banks in the *Washington Post:* "The BHS is the guy who isn't there, the man the defendant claims is *really* responsible. . . . Of course, the BHS can never be produced in court." Downs was eventually tried and convicted of the crimes committed against her children.

Rule delves into Downs's past in *Small Sacrifices,* noting how Downs was the victim of considerable sexual abuse as a child. As a teenager, she slit her wrists in a failed suicide attempt. Rule relates that Downs entered into a destructive marital relationship in order to extricate herself from her difficult family situation and achieved happiness only after giving birth to a child. Downs later gave birth to a second infant, but then had an abortion to terminate a third pregnancy. Feeling guilty about the abortion, Downs decided to atone for her action by conceiving a fourth child. Instead of choosing her husband to father the child, though, she selected a coworker. "I picked somebody that was attractive . . . healthy . . . not abusive of drugs and alcohol, strong—bone structure—you know, the whole bit: a *good specimen.* It was really clinical," Downs said, as recorded in *Small Sacrifices.*

After watching a television show that focused on surrogate parenting, Downs convinced herself that she could make a living by providing other couples with babies. According to Rule, Downs had plans to begin a surrogate-parenting clinic of her own. Later, she entered into an affair with Lew Lewiston, a married man who was averse to the idea of fathering children. The prosecution charged that after Lewiston ended his relationship with Downs, she tried to kill her offspring to appease her former lover. Downs was convicted of the crime and sentenced to life plus fifty years of imprisonment. She escaped from jail in the early 1990s and was found ten days later at the home of Wayne Seifer, a psychiatric assistant and the spouse of one of Downs's fellow convicts. At the time of the breakout, Rule predicted that, based on her subject's pattern of behavior, Downs would seek out a suitable mate with the intention of getting pregnant during her time away from prison. At the time of the escape, Rule knew that Downs had read *Small Sacrifices* and was not pleased with the way the author had portrayed her. In an interview with *Publishers Weekly* the author stated, "I'm not paranoid about my safety, but there are some people I won't write about: drug dealers, cults, motorcycle gangs and organized crime. I don't want someone I don't even know coming back at me." In *People* she revealed that she supports the death penalty in cases that involve serial killers, because too many of them are released from prison and end up repeating their pattern of crime.

Upon its release, *Small Sacrifices* was praised by several reviewers. Banks, for instance, noted that "Ann Rule is able to relate Diane Downs's crimes—as she did Ted Bundy's in her earlier *The Stranger beside Me*—with high tension. Rule has an instinct for suspense, knowing just what information to leak to the reader and when." And Eileen Ogintz of the *Chicago Tribune* acknowledged that "the book is superbly researched. It succeeds because Rule knew what details, eyewitness accounts and evidence to include—and what not to."

As she began to earn a living through her crime writing, Rule started to feel guilty about deriving an income from reporting on the misfortunes of others. A psychologist, however, convinced her that "what matters is how you feel about people," as recounted in her *Publishers Weekly* interview. His advice contributed to Rule's approach toward reporting on crime. "I get to know the victim so well that I can see and feel the pain that these people go through: the victim, the victim's family and the family of the perpetrator. Out of consideration for them, I often leave out as much as I include." In the *New York Times,* Rule also remarked to Robert Lindsey on how she has assisted authorities at the United States Justice Department in implementing a plan for tracking seemingly unrelated murders. Such work, she noted, "is kind of my vindication for profiting from other people's tragedies. I'd like to put myself out of the business of being a crime writer and go on to other things. Sadly, the serial murder keeps going on."

In the early 1990s Rule released *If You Really Loved Me,* which tells about the murder of Linda Brown, the fifth wife of David Arnold Brown, a man who amassed considerable wealth in the field of data retrieval. The Browns lived in Orange County, California, with their infant daughter, Krystal, Linda's seventeen-year-old sister, Patricia Bailey, and David's fourteen-year-old daughter from a previous marriage, Cinnamon. At the beginning of her book, Rule describes the homicide as it was originally interpreted by the police. According to Patricia Bailey, Cinnamon shot Linda and then fled from the house. Investigating officer Fred McLean discovered Cinnamon in a doghouse in the backyard, wearing a vomit-and urine-stained sweat suit—an indication that she had tried to commit suicide by swallowing pills. She also had a note: "Dear God, please forgive me. I didn't mean to hurt her," as quoted in the *New York Times Book Review* by critic Maggie Paley.

Cinnamon confessed to the murder but later admitted that she did not remember committing the crime. She was sentenced to a minimum of twenty-seven years of imprisonment, beginning in a juvenile detention facility. In the second section of the book, Rule presents facts concerning the investigation of the case. Authorities discovered that before the murder, David Brown continually manipulated family members by pretending to be gravely ill and seeking medical attention for bouts of depression. In order to win the devotion of his wife, daughters, and sister-in-law, he fed them promises, threatened them, and provided them with gifts. On a number of occasions, he also coerced the women who lived with him into having sexual relations with him.

Authorities became concerned upon discovering that Brown received more than $800,000 in insurance settlements after his wife's death. Additionally, he continued to share a residence with his sister-in-law, whom he married in 1986. Rule noted that as time passed, Brown visited Cinnamon less frequently. Cinnamon, meanwhile, was refused the opportunity to be paroled because she continued to attest that she had no memory of committing the murder. After hearing a secretly taped session between Brown and his daughter, as well as Cinnamon's own testimony as to what occurred on the day that her stepmother was murdered, authorities brought David Brown to trial, convicted him of the crime, and sentenced him to life in prison.

Robert Campbell of the *Los Angeles Times Book Review* felt that *If You Really Loved Me* could have been structured in order to provide readers with a greater sense of suspense. He did, however, praise Rule for her handling of the second half of her four-part book. Campbell felt that "Part Three, 'The Arrest and the Death List,' presents as gripping a plot and as complicated an investigation of a complex character as any imagined in fiction, and Part Four, 'The Trial,' wraps up the whole affair with a great deal of energy and skill." And Paley, although she wanted Rule to provide more insight into David Brown, remarked that Rule "writes of detectives, their procedures and temperaments in a flat, just-the-facts style that has quiet authority. She spins a narrative with the skill of these detectives, who must hold in their minds contradictory statements, observations and assessments and make sense—and a good case—out of them all." In the Toronto *Globe and Mail* Margaret Cannon called *If You Really Loved Me* "a harrowing story of how [investigators] were able to sift through the lies and fears of two teen-aged girls to bring a vicious killer to justice. Rule has a clear prose style that seldom slips into wordiness. . . . and she has a deft sense of humor."

Rule probes the case of another murderous husband in *Dead by Sunset: Perfect Husband, Perfect Killer?* Brad Cunningham was handsome, charismatic, successful, and violent with women. After the birth of three sons, Cunningham's fourth wife, Cheryl Keeton, a lawyer, left the abusive marriage and would not allow Cunningham to see the boys. Although Cunningham was the prime suspect in Keeton's murder when her badly beaten body was found in 1986, police could not connect him with the crime. Eventually Keeton's law firm hired an attorney so her estate could bring a wrongful death lawsuit against Cunningham. By the time the civil case began, Cunningham was married to his fifth wife. The jury returned a guilty verdict and assessed a huge judgment. The verdict in the civil case compelled the district attorney's office to indict Cunningham two years later—seven years after Keeton's murder; he was convicted in 1994 and sentenced to a minimum of twenty-two years in prison.

In *Bitter Harvest: A Woman's Fury, a Mother's Sacrifice,* Rule probed the case of Dr. Debora Green, a brilliant, well-to-do woman who was apparently devoted to her three children. When her husband left her for another woman, however, Green took her revenge in an unspeakable fashion: she set fire to their home, starting a blaze that resulted in the deaths of two of their three children. Arson investigators even believed that she had deliberately planned the blaze in such a way that would block the children's escape routes. Rule chronicles the unhappy marriage and the other failures that lurked beneath Green's apparent successes. Despite her formidable intellect, she had failed at her medical practice and become addicted to alcohol and drugs, as well as struggling with a serious weight problem. Before murdering her children, she had attempted to poison her husband. *Bitter Harvest* is an "outstanding chronicle of a crime investigation," according to Christine A. Moesch in *Library Journal,* and it is also a "riveting profile of a brilliant mind and empty soul." The reviewer for *Publishers Weekly* stated that *Bitter Harvest* is "another tension-filled, page-turning chronology and analysis of a psychopath in action."

Another apparently successful, respectable person who committed foul crimes is exposed in . . . *And Never Let Her Go: Thomas Capano, the Deadly Seducer.* Thomas Capano was an attorney with prestigious connections. He came from a respected family in Delaware, was married, and appeared to be leading an enviable life. In reality, he had numerous mistresses. One of them was Anne Marie Fahey, a secretary to the state's governor and a woman seventeen years his junior. This troubled, anorexic woman with a history of being abused became one of Capano's obsessions. Eventually she tried to end their relationship, but soon after that she was reported missing. In the investigation that followed, it was shown that Capano had murdered her and, with the help of his brothers, stuffed her body into a large cooler which he dumped into the Atlantic. He later tried to pin the blame for his crime on one of his other mistresses. . . . *And Never Let Her Go* is a "compassionate portrayal of the victim and a chilling portrayal of her killer," according to a *Booklist* reviewer, who went on to call the book a "true page-turner, a compelling rendering of a crime committed by a deeply troubled, egotistical sociopath." The disturbing story is, "in Rule's capable hands, the raw material for a modern-day tragedy," remarked a *Publishers Weekly* contributor.

Every Breath You Take: A True Story of Obsessive Revenge and Murder concerns the murder of Sheila Bellush, a wife and mother of six children. As a young woman, Bellush met and married Allen Blackthorne, a charming yet violent sociopath, but she left the marriage after enduring years of abuse. Though Blackthorne and Bellush both remarried, Blackthorne developed an obsessive need to punish his ex-wife for divorcing him. Having told her sister that she feared for her life, Bellush was later found murdered, surrounded by her young children. Police quickly arrested the killers-for-hire, and Blackthorne was prosecuted for the murder. "Rule presents the facts of a murder case with all the intrigue, suspense and characterization of an accomplished novelist," according to a *Publishers Weekly* critic. In *Booklist* Brad Hooper stated, "Rule excels at painting psychologically perceptive portraits of all the characters in this stranger-than-fiction but nevertheless real-life drama."

In *Heart Full of Lies: A True Story of Desire and Death,* Rule "meticulously documents the case of a woman who used domestic abuse as an excuse to kill her husband," wrote *New York Times Book Review* critic John D. Thomas. Rule examines the murder of Chris Northon, whose wife, Liysa Northon, claimed that she shot at and accidentally killed her abusive husband to protect herself from attack. Police investigating the crime found Norton's body wrapped up in a sleeping bag, with a well-placed bullet wound to the head. In *Heart Full of Lies* the author informs readers "about Northon and her desire to control the lives of those around her and about Chris, who worked desperately to keep his marriage afloat," observed *Library Journal* critic Danna Bell-Russel. "You can still see the cop in Rule: she interrogates witnesses, tracks down inconsistencies in stories, slogs through victims' letters and e-mails, analyzes forensic evidence, attends trials," wrote *Booklist* contributor Connie Fletcher.

In her interview with *Publishers Weekly,* Rule explained the appeal of her work to many readers. "Whenever I'm signing books, invariably someone comes up to me, usually a young mother trailing a small child or a grandmotherly looking woman, and says, 'Why do I love the books you write? What's wrong with me?' I always ask them what they would do if they found a spider in the bathtub. Nine times out of ten they tell me that they would remove the spider with a tissue and put it outside. I believe that the gentlest among us are the most fascinated by the cruelest. We simply cannot believe that anyone would hurt someone else."

BIOGRAPHICAL AND CRITICAL SOURCES:

BOOKS

Bestsellers 90, Volume 2, Thomson Gale (Detroit, MI), 1990.

Contemporary Popular Writers, St. James Press (Detroit, MI), 1997.

Rule, Ann, *Small Sacrifices: A True Story of Passion and Murder,* New American Library (New York, NY), 1987.

Rule, Ann, *The Stranger beside Me,* Norton (New York, NY), 1980.

PERIODICALS

Booklist, September 1, 1995, Sue-Ellen Beauregard, review of *Dead by Sunset: Perfect Husband, Perfect Killer?,* p. 4; Sue-Ellen Beauregard, review of *Bitter Harvest: A Woman's Fury, a Mother's Sacrifice,* p. 666; October 1, 1999, review of . . . *And Never Let Her Go: Thomas Capano, the Deadly Seducer,* p. 307; December 15, 2000, David Pitt, review of *Empty Promises and Other True Cases,* p. 766; September 15, 2001, Brad Hooper, review of *Every Breath You Take: A True Story of Obses-*

sion, Revenge and Murder, p. 163; October 1, 2003, Connie Fletcher, review of *Heart Full of Lies: A True Story of Desire and Death,* p. 274.

Chicago Tribune, May 11, 1987.

Globe and Mail (Toronto, Ontario, Canada), May 25, 1991, p. C7.

Good Housekeeping, September, 1991, p. 42.

Houston Chronicle, March 31, 2001, Ann Hodges, review of . . . *And Never Let Her Go* (mini-series), p. 9.

Kirkus Reviews, August 15, 1995, p. 1172; January 1, 1998, review of *Bitter Harvest,* p. 41.

Kliatt, November, 1993, p. 36; November, 1994, p. 38; September, 1998, review of *Bitter Harvest* (audio version), p. 67.

Law Institute Journal, July, 1996, Morgana Keast, review of *A Rose for Her Grave and Other True Cases,* p. 78.

Library Journal, October 1, 1995, Christine A. Moesch, review of *Dead by Sunset,* p. 101; November 1, 1996, Sandra K. Lindheimer, review of *A Fever in the Heart and Other True Cases,* p. 91; February 1, 1998, Christine A. Moesch, review of *Bitter Harvest,* p. 100; March 15, 1998, Denise A. Garofalo, review of *Bitter Harvest* (audio version), p. 109; April 1, 2000, Gordon Blackwell, review of . . . *And Never Let Her Go,* p. 149; October 1, 2000, Michael Rogers, review of *The Stranger beside Me,* p. 153; February 1, 2004, Danna Bell-Russel, review of *Heart Full of Lies* (audiobook), p. 140.

Los Angeles Times, May 7, 1987.

Los Angeles Times Book Review, May 8, 1983; October 30, 1983; April 29, 1984; August 18, 1991, p. 9.

New Law Journal, May 31, 1996, review of *Dead by Sunset,* p. 811.

New Republic, March 28, 1981.

New York Times, February 21, 1984; July 11, 2001, Maureen Dowd, "The Lost Girls," p. A21.

New York Times Book Review, August 24, 1980; June 14, 1987; May 26, 1991, p. 12; January 3, 1993, p. 5; October 22, 1995, Walter Walker, review of *Dead by Sunset,* p. 38; March 15, 1998, Carolyn T. Hughes, review of *Bitter Harvest,* p. 26; December 21, 2003, John D. Thomas, "Books in Brief: Nonfiction," p. 20.

People, September 14, 1987; November 20, 1995, David Hiltbrand, review of *Dead by Sunset* (television miniseries), p. 17; January 26, 1998, J.D. Reed, review of *Bitter Harvest,* p. 35; January 1, 2000, review of . . . *And Never Let Her Go,* p. 41.

Publishers Weekly, May 3, 1991; October 25, 1993, p. 59; August 8, 1994, p. 418; September 4, 1995, review of *Dead by Sunset,* p. 56; December 22, 1997, review of *Bitter Harvest,* p. 49; August 9, 1999; September 20, 1999, review of . . . *And Never Let Her Go,* p. 66; April 1, 2002, review of *Every Breath You Take* (audiobook review), p. 31.

Saturday Review, August, 1980.

Savvy, August, 1987, p. 13.

Time, June 28, 2004, Andrea Sachs, "The Rule of Law," p. A10.

Virginian Pilot-Ledger Star, March 3, 1998, Charlene Cason, review of *Bitter Harvest,* p. E5.

Washington Post, May 13, 1987; March 12, 1998, Carolyn Banks, review of *Bitter Harvest,* p. C2; November 1, 1999, Jonathan Groner, "In Delaware, a Murder under the Microscope," p. C4.

Washington Post Book World, August 17, 1980; January 24, 1999, review of *The End of the Dream: The Golden Boy Who Never Grew Up and Other True Cases,* p. 12; September 5, 1999, review of . . . *And Never Let Her Go,* p. 5; October 17, 1999, Marie Arana, "Ann Rule: A Career in True Crime," p. 8, Ann Rule, "The Writing Life," p. 8; November 1, 1999, Jonathan Groner, review of . . . *And Never Let Her Go,* p. C4.

Women's Review of Books, June, 1998, Jeffrey Ann Goudie, review of *Bitter Harvest,* p. 26.

Writer, December, 2001, p. 66.

Writer's Digest, December, 1992, p. 27.

ONLINE

Ann Rule's Official Home Page, http://www.annrules.com/ (August 10, 2004).

Celebrity Café, http://www.thecelebritycafe.com/ (October 1, 2001), Dominick A. Miserandino, interview with Ann Rule.

Writers Review, http://www.writersreview.com/ (October 1, 2001), interview with Ann Rule.

* * *

RUSHDIE, Ahmed Salman
See RUSHDIE, Salman

* * *

RUSHDIE, Salman 1947-
(Ahmed Salman Rushdie)

PERSONAL: Born June 19, 1947, in Bombay, Maharashtra, India; son of Anis Ahmed (in business) and Negin (Butt) Rushdie; married Clarissa Luard (in publishing), May 22, 1976 (divorced, 1987); married Marianne

Wiggins (an author), 1988 (divorced, 1990); married Elizabeth West, 1997 (divorced, 2004); married Padma Lakshmi, 2004. children: (first marriage) Zafar (son); (second marriage) Milan (daughter). *Education:* King's College, Cambridge, M.A. (history; with honors), 1968.

ADDRESSES: Office—c/o Deborah Rogers Ltd., 49 Blenheim Crescent, London W11, England. *Agent*—Wylie Agency Ltd., 36 Parkside, London SW1X 7JR, England.

CAREER: Writer. Fringe Theatre, London, England, actor, 1968- 69; freelance advertising copywriter, 1970-73, 1976-80; writer, 1975—. Executive member of Camden Committee for Community Relations, 1976-83; member of advisory board, Institute of Contemporary Arts, beginning 1985; member of British Film Institute Production Board, beginning 1986. Honorary visiting professor of humanities, Massachusetts Institute of Technology, 1993.

MEMBER: International PEN, Royal Society of Literature (fellow; president, 2004—), Society of Authors, National Book League (member of executive committee), International Parliament of Writers (chair).

AWARDS, HONORS: Booker McConnell Prize for fiction, and English- speaking Union Literary Award, both 1981, and James Tait Black Memorial Prize, 1982, all for *Midnight's Children;* British Arts Council bursary award, 1981; Prix du Meilleur Livre Etranger, 1984, for *Shame;* Whitbread Prize, and Booker McConnell Prize shortlist, 1988, for *The Satanic Verses;* Mythopoeic Fantasy Award for children's literature, 1992, for *Haroun and the Sea of Stories;* British Book Award for author of the year, *Publishing News,* Booker McConnell Prize shortlist, and Whitbread Novel Award, all 1995, all for *The Moor's Last Sigh;* Aristeion Literary Prize, 1996; Mantova Literary Prize (Italy), 1997; Budapest Grand Prize for Literature (Hungary), 1998; Commandeur de l'Ordre des Arts et des Lettres (France), 1999; Freedom of the City, Mexico City (Mexico), 1999; Whitbread Novel Award shortlist, 2005, for *Shalimar The Clown.*

WRITINGS:

NOVELS

Grimus, Gollancz (London, England), 1975, Modern Library (New York, NY), 2003.

Midnight's Children, Knopf (New York, NY), 1981, reprinted, Random House (New York, NY), 2006.

Shame, Knopf (New York, NY), 1983.

The Satanic Verses, Viking (New York, NY), 1988.

The Moor's Last Sigh, J. Cape (London, England), 1995, Knopf (New York, NY), 1996.

The Ground beneath Her Feet, Holt (New York, NY), 1999.

Fury, Random House (New York, NY) 2001.

Shalimar the Clown, Random House (New York, NY) 2005.

OTHER

The Jaguar Smile: A Nicaraguan Journey, Viking (New York, NY), 1987.

Haroun and the Sea of Stories (juvenile), Granta Books (London, England), 1990.

Imaginary Homelands: The Collected Essays, Viking (London, England), 1991, published as *Imaginary Homelands: Essays and Criticism, 1981-1991,* Viking (New York, NY), 1992.

The Wizard of Oz: BFI Film Classics, Indiana University Press (Bloomington, IN), 1992.

Soldiers Three & In Black & White, Viking Penguin (London, England), 1993.

The Rushdie Letters: Freedom to Speak, Freedom to Write, edited by Steve MacDonogh, University of Nebraska Press (Lincoln, NE), 1993.

East, West (short stories), Pantheon Books (New York, NY), 1994.

(Editor, with Elizabeth West) *Mirrorwork: Fifty Years of Indian Writing, 1947- 1997,* Holt (New York, NY), 1997.

Conversations with Salman Rushdie, edited by Michael Reder, University Press of Mississippi (Jackson, MS), 2000.

(Adapter, with Simon Reade and Tim Supple) *Salman Rushdie's Midnight's Children* (play; produced in London, England, 2004), Modern Library (New York, NY), 2003.

Step across This Line: Collected Nonfiction 1992-2002, Random House (New York, NY), 2003.

Also author of television screenplays *The Painter and the Pest,* 1985, and *The Riddle of Midnight,* 1988; author of screen adaptation of "The Firebird's Nest." Contributor to *Granta Thirty-nine: The Body,* Viking Penguin, 1992; contributor to magazines and newspapers, including *Atlantic, Granta,* London *Times, London Review of Books, New Statesman,* and *New York Times.*

ADAPTATIONS: The Ground beneath Her Feet was adapted for film by Gemini Films; *Haroun and the Sea of Stories* was adapted as an opera by Charles Wuorinen.

SIDELIGHTS: While Indian-born British author Salman Rushdie began his writing career quietly, he has become one of the twentieth century's most well-known writers, not only for the ire he attracted from Islamic fundamentalists after publication of his *Satanic Verses,* but also for his thought-provoking examinations of a changing sociopolitical world landscape. Rushdie's first published novel, *Grimus,* which tells of a Native American who receives the gift of immortality and begins an odyssey to find life's meaning, initially attracted attention among science-fiction readers. Discovering the novel, Mel Tilden called the book "engrossing and often wonderful" in a *Times Literary Supplement* review. Tilden determined the book to be "science of the word," recognizing at the same time that it "is one of those novels some people will say is too good to be science fiction, even though it contains other universes, dimensional doorways, alien creatures and more than one madman." Though critics variously called the work a fable, fantasy, political satire, or magical realism, most agreed with David Wilson's assessment in *Times Literary Supplement* that *Grimus* is "an ambitious, strikingly confident first novel" and that Rushdie was an author to watch. Rushdie's subsequent career has proven Wilson correct.

Rushdie turns to India, his birthplace, for the subject of his second book. An allegory, *Midnight's Children* chronicles the history of modern India throughout the lives of 1,001 children born within the country's first hour of independence from Great Britain on August 15, 1947. Saleem Sinai, the novel's protagonist and narrator, is one of two males born at the precise moment of India's independence—the stroke of midnight—in a Bombay nursing home. Moonfaced, stained with birthmarks, and possessed of a "huge cucumber of a nose," Sinai becomes by a twist of fate "the chosen child of midnight." He later explains to the reader that a nurse, in "her own revolutionary act," switched the newborn infants. The illegitimate son of a Hindu street singer's wife and a departing British colonist was given to a prosperous Muslim couple and raised as Saleem Sinai. His midnight twin, called Shiva, was given to the impoverished Hindu street singer who, first cuckolded and then widowed by childbirth, was left to raise a son on the streets of Bombay. Thus, in accordance with class privilege unrightfully bestowed, Sinai's birth was heralded by fireworks and celebrated in newspapers; a congratulatory letter from Jawaharlal Nehru portended his future. "You are the newest bearer of the ancient face of India which is also eternally young," wrote the prime minister. "We shall be watching over your life with the closest attention; it will be, in a sense, the mirror of our own."

Midnight's Children begins more than thirty years after the simultaneous births of Sinai and independent India. Awaiting death in the corner of a Bombay pickle factory where he is employed, Sinai—prematurely aged, impotent, and mutilated by a personal history that parallels that of his country—tells his life story to Padma, an illiterate working girl who loves and tends him. All of midnight's children, Sinai discloses, possess magical gifts, including prophecy and wizardy.

Sinai and the rest of midnight's children "incorporate the stupendous Indian past, with its pantheon, its epics, and its wealth of folklore," summarized *New York Times* critic Robert Towers, "while at the same time playing a role in the tumultuous Indian present." "The plot of this novel is complicated enough, and flexible enough, to smuggle Saleem into every major event in the subcontinent's past thirty years," wrote Clark Blaise in *New York Times Book Review.* "It is . . . a novel of India's growing up; from its special, gifted infancy to its very ordinary, drained adulthood. It is a record of betrayal and corruption, the loss of ideals, culminating with 'the Widow's' Emergency rule." Although *Midnight's Children* "spans the recent history, both told and untold, of both India and Pakistan as well as the birth of Bangladesh," commented Anita Desai in *Washington Post Book World,* "one hesitates to call the novel 'historical' for Rushdie believes . . . that while individual history does not make sense unless seen against its national background, neither does national history make sense unless seen in the form of individual lives and histories."

Midnight's Children was almost unanimously well received and won England's most exalted literary award, the Booker McConnell Prize for fiction, in 1981. The novel also elicited favorable comparisons to Laurence Sterne's *Tristram Shandy,* Gabriel García Marquéz's *One Hundred Years of Solitude,* Günter Grass's *The Tin Drum,* Saul Bellow's *The Adventures of Augie March,* Louis-Ferdinand Celine's *Death on the Installment Plan,* and V.S. Naipaul's *India: A Wounded Civilization.* And yet, opined Blaise, "It would be a disservice to Salman Rushdie's very original genius to dwell on literary analogues and ancestors. This is a book to accept on its own terms, and an author to welcome into world company."

In 2003 Rushdie collaborated with Simon Reade and Tim Supple to adapt *Midnight's Children* for the New York and London stage. Writing in *Back Stage,* Simi Horwitz describes the three-plus hours play as "a frenetic work punctuated by video projections—including fantasy sequences and historical film clips-and brightly flashing lights." In a review of the London staging of the play, Matt Wolf of *Variety* commented, "Within minutes a narrative is set in motion that weds the personal to the political, the past to the present, and some surprisingly crude stagecraft to a use of video and film that after a while makes one wonder whether Rushdie's source novel wouldn't have been better off as the BBC miniseries he has long wanted it to be."

Like *Midnight's Children,* Rushdie's third book, *Shame,* blends history, myth, politics, and fantasy in a novel that is both serious and comic. *Shame* explores such issues as the uses and abuses of power and the relationship between shame and violence. The idea for the novel, reported interviewer Ronald Hayman in *Books and Bookmen,* grew out of Rushdie's interest in the Pakistani concept of *sharam.* An Urdu word, *sharam* conveys a hybrid of sentiments, including embarrassment, modesty, and the sense of having an ordained place in the world. It speaks to a long tradition of honor that permits, and at times even insists upon, seemingly unconscionable acts. In developing this concept, Rushdie told Hayman, he began "seeing shame in places where I hadn't originally seen it." He explained: "I'd be thinking about Pakistani politics; and I'd find there were elements there that I could use. I had a feeling of stumbling on something quite central to the codes by which we live." Rushdie elaborated in a *New York Times Book Review* interview with Michael T. Kaufman: "There are two axes—honor and shame, which is the conventional axis, the one along which the culture moves, and this other axis of shame and shamelessness, which deals with morality and the lack of morality. *Shame* is at the hub of both axes."

Rushdie develops his theme of shame and violence in a plot so complex and densely populated with characters that, as Towers commented in *New York Times,* "it is probably easier to play croquet (as in 'Alice in Wonderland') with flamingos as mallets and hedgehogs as balls than to give a coherent plot summary of *Shame.*" The novel's story line spans three generations and centers on the families of two men—Raza Hyder, a celebrated general, and Iskander Harappa, a millionaire playboy. Their life-and-death struggle, played out against the political backdrop of their country, is based on late twentieth-century Pakistani history. The two characters themselves are based on real-life Pakistani President Zia ul-Haq and former Prime Minister Zulfikar Ali Bhutto, who was deposed by Zia in 1977 and later executed.

Sufiya Zinobia, the novel's heroine, is the embodiment of both shame and violence. Her shame is born with her and is evidenced by her crimson blush. Later, as she absorbs the unfelt shame of others, Sufiya's blushes take on such intensity that they boil her bath water and burn the lips of those who kiss her. Eventually the heat of her shame incubates violence, turning Sufiya into a monster capable of wrenching the heads off of grown men. As the incarnation of an entire nation's shame, wrote Una Chaudhuri, "Sufiya Zinobia is the utterly convincing and terrifying product of a culture lost in falsehood and corruption."

The novel's marginal hero is Sufiya Zinobia's husband, Omar Khayyam Shakil. Introduced at length at the beginning of the book, he disappears for long periods of time thereafter. "I am a peripheral man," he admits shamelessly; "other people have been the principal actors in my life story." The son of an unknown father and one of three sisters, all claiming to be his mother, Shakil was "scorned by the townspeople for his shameful origins," observed Margo Jefferson in *Voice Literary Supplement,* and "he developed a defensive shamelessness." Omar Khayyam Shakil feels himself "a fellow who is not even the hero of his own life; a man born and raised in the condition of being out of things."

Rushdie's choice of a "not-quite hero" for a "not-quite country" addresses an issue that Chaudhuri felt to be central to the book's theme. "Peripherality," she postulated, "is the essence of this land's deepest psychology and the novel's true hero: Shame. It is the doom of those who cannot exist except as reflections of other's perceptions, of those who are unable to credit the notion of individual moral autonomy." *New York Times* critic Christopher Lehmann-Haupt concluded that "the tragedy of *Shame* lies both in the evasion of historical destiny and in embracing that destiny too violently."

Following *Shame* and the publication of *The Jaguar Smile: A Nicaraguan Journey,* a nonfiction account of the political and social conditions Rushdie observed during his 1986 trip to Nicaragua, the author published the novel that made his name known even to non-readers. *The Satanic Verses* outraged Muslims around the world who were infuriated by what they believed to be insults to their religion. The book was banned in a dozen countries and caused demonstrations and riots in India,

Pakistan, and South Africa, during which a number of people were killed or injured. Charging Rushdie with blasphemy, Iranian leader Ayatollah Ruhollah Khomeini proclaimed that the author and his publisher should be executed; multi-million dollar bounties were offered to anyone who could carry out this decree. This *fatwa,* or death sentence, was reaffirmed by the Iranian government as late as 1993; three people involved with the book's publication were subsequently attacked and one, Rushdie's Japanese translator, was fatally injured.

Religious objections to *The Satanic Verses* stems from sections of the book that concern a religion resembling Islam and whose prophet is named Mahound—a derisive epithet for Mohammed. Offense was taken to scenes in which a scribe named Salman alters the prophet's dictation, thus bringing into question the validity of the Koran, the holy book of Islam. In addition, many Muslims claim that Rushdie repeatedly makes irreverent use of sacred names throughout the book. London *Observer* contributor Blake Morrison explained that to many Muslims Rushdie "has transgressed by treating the Holy Word as myth . . . not truth; by treating the Prophet as a fallible human rather than as a deity; and above all by bringing a skeptical, playful, punning intelligence to bear on a religion which, in these fundamentalist times, is not prepared to entertain doubts or jokes about itself."

For his part, Rushdie has argued that *The Satanic Verses* are not meant to be an attack on the Islamic religion, but that it has been interpreted as such by what he called in *Observer* "the contemporary Thought Police" of Islam who have erected taboos in which one "may not discuss Muhammed as if he were human, with human virtues and weaknesses. One may not discuss the growth of Islam as a historical phenomenon, as an ideology born out of its time." Rushdie explained that in Islam Muhammed, unlike Jesus in the Christian religion, "is not granted divine status, but the text is." A number of critics pointed out that the whole controversy could have been avoided if Rushdie's detractors took into consideration that all of the objectionable scenes take place in the character Gibreel Farishta's dreams, and are part of his insanity-inspired delusions. "It must be added," remarked *Time* critic Paul Gray, "that few of those outraged by *The Satanic Verses* have ever seen it, much less opened it."

The Satanic Verses is a complex narrative that tells several stories within a story in a manner that has been compared to *A Thousand and One Nights.* The central story concerns two men who miraculously survive a terrorist attack on an Air India flight. Gibreel Farishta, a famous Indian actor, acquires a halo; Saladin Chamcha, whose occupation involves providing voices for radio and television programs, metamorphoses into a satyr-like creature. Gibreel becomes deluded into thinking he is the archangel Gabriel, and much of the novel is preoccupied with a number of his dreams, which take on the form of "enigmatic and engrossing" parables, according to *Times Literary Supplement* contributor Robert Irwin. Each story, including the controversial tale concerning Mahound, comments on "the theme of religion and its inexorable, unwelcome and dubious demands." The novel concludes with a confrontation between Gibreel and Saladin, but at this point the distinction between which character is good and which evil has been blurred beyond distinction. Michael Wood remarked in *New Republic* that *The Satanic Verses* gives the reader the feeling that the writer is "trying to fill out a Big Book. But the pervading intelligence of the novel is so acute, the distress it explores so thoroughly understood, that the dullness doesn't settle, can't keep away the urgent questions and images that beset it. This is Rushdie's most bewildered book, but it is also his most thoughtful."

After being forced into hiding to escape the ire of Islamic fundamentalists, Rushdie penned a fairy tale for children that appeared in the United States early in 1991. *Haroun and the Sea of Stories,* conceived by the author as a bedtime story for his son, is a fanciful tale with an important underlying message for adults. A talented storyteller, Rashid receives his gift from the Sea of Stories located on a moon called Kahina. When a water genie's error disconnects Rashid's invisible water faucet, the storyteller loses his abilities. His son Haroun, however, resolves to help his father and journeys to Kahina to meet Walrus, ruler of Gup and controller of the Sea of Stories. Haroun arrives to find the people of Gup at war with Chub and its wicked ruler, Khattam-Shud. Khattam-Shud is poisoning the sea with his factory-ship in an effort to destroy all stories because within each story is a world that he cannot control. After many adventures, Haroun and his allies from Gup destroy Khattam-Shud, saving the Sea of Stories and restoring Rashid's storytelling powers.

Underlying the fantastical plot of *Haroun and the Sea of Stories* is a clear message against the stifling of artistic freedom by figures like Khomeini, whom several reviewers pointed out to be represented by Khattam-Shud. But the Khomeinis of the world are not the only problem; Rushdie's book also tells how the Walrus hordes sunlight for the Sea of Stories by stopping the moon's rotation, thus unwittingly giving Khattam-Shud his power because the evil ruler thrives on darkness. "If a Khomeini can come to power," explained Richard Eder in *Los Angeles Times Book Review,* "it is in part because the West has arrogated sunlight to itself, and left much of the globe bereft of it. Rushdie defies the Ayatollah's curse. It is he, not his persecutor, who is the true defender of the Third World."

In 1995, six years after Khomeini initially ordered Rushdie's death, the writer published a collection of short fiction titled *East, West.* Composed of nine short stories divided into three sections—"East," set in India; "West," set in Europe; and "East-West," set in England—the book's central theme is what the author described to *Newsweek* interviewer Sarah Crichton as "cultural movement and mongrelization and hybridity," a reflection, in fact, of Rushdie's own background. Rushdie's "heritage was derived from the polyglot tumult of multi- ethnic, post-colonial India," Shashi Tharoor explained in *Washington Post Book World.* "His style combined a formal English education with the cadences of the Indian oral story-telling tradition . . . . He brought a larger world—a teeming, myth-infused, gaudy, exuberant, many-hued and restless world—past the immigration inspectors of English literature. And he enriched this new homeland with breathtaking, risk-ridden, imaginative prose of rare beauty and originality." Each story contains characters embodying diverse cultures who interact on a variety of social and emotional planes. Most of them are "a pleasure to read," wrote John Bemrose in *Maclean's.* "Like his great master, Charles Dickens, Rushdie goes in for encyclopedic comedy, with rich people and beggars rubbing shoulders across his pages. His language has something of Dickens's energetic verbosity, while his characters like to wear, for the most part, the gaudy clothes of caricature." Bemrose noted that while most of Rushdie's novels are long, sprawling works, "the stories in *East, West* have the careful precision of ivory miniatures. And all of them, beneath their infectiously playful surfaces, ponder the imponderables of human fate."

Rushdie's name was back on bestseller lists in 1995 with *The Moor's Last Sigh.* A novel that offers a satirical view of the politics of India; its publication seemed almost to mirror that of *The Satanic Verses.* Containing an undisguised parody of powerful Hindu fundamentalist leader Bal Thackeray and making gentle fun of India's first prime minister, Nehru—a stuffed dog bears the leader's first name, Jawaharlal— *The Moor's Last Sigh* was quickly yanked from bookstore shelves in India's capital city and subjected to an embargo by the Indian government.

Narrated by Moraes "the Moor" Zogoiby, *The Moor's Last Sigh* is framed by a dilemma reminiscent of that of the storyteller Scheherazade. The Moor's deranged captor, who was an acquaintance of Moraes's late, famous mother, demands to know the woman's family history. The Moor extends his life by cushioning his tale with a thousand incidental facts—some true, some imagined—and follows the thread of narrative from ancestor and Portuguese explorer Vasco da Gama through the rise and fall of a Portuguese trade dynasty, the meeting of his parents in the 1950s, childhood memories of his flamboyant artist mother, Aurora, and his own exile from India. As a *Publishers Weekly* reviewer noted, the novel hints at a dark fate for India: "The society Rushdie portrays so powerfully is rife with corruption; pluralism is dying and a dangerous separatism is on the rise, encouraging hatred and despair."

Although many critics have interpreted everything Rushdie wrote following the imposition of the fatwa as a cloaked reference to the author's unfortunate personal dilemma, Paul Gray maintained in *Time* that *The Moor's Last Sigh* "is much too teeming and turbulent, too crammed with history and dreams, to fit into any imaginable category, except that of the magically comic and sad . . . . The true subject of *The Moor's Last Sigh* is language in all its uninhibited and unpredictable power to go reality one better and rescue humans from the fate of suffering in silence." Rushdie remained ambivalent on the place of the novel within his own body of work, telling Maya Jaggi in *New Statesman* that *The Moor's Last Sigh* is a "completion of what I began in *Midnight's Children, Shame,* and *The Satanic Verses*—the story of myself, where I came from, a story of origins and memory. But it's also a public project that forms an arc, my response to an age in history that began in 1947 [when India formed a democratic socialist state]. That cycle of novels is now complete."

Rushdie's novel *The Ground beneath Her Feet* is a modern-day retelling of the Orpheus myth, with the hero and heroine cast as rock stars. Ormus Cama, a pop star reminiscent of Elvis Presley and John Lennon, seeks to bring back to life the divine Vina Apsara, a celebrity icon on par with Madonna and Princess Diana, who is swallowed up by an earthquake on Valentine's Day, 1989. Their tragic love story is narrated by the power couple's close friend, the photographer Rai Merchant, who has long been obsessed with Vina himself. Ormus' grief leads him to seek out Vina's slavish fans who painstakingly emulate the star. He latches on to one—Mira Celano—who accompanies him on his "Into the Underworld" tour in search of Vina. Many of the themes prominent in Rushdie's earlier novels appear in *The Ground beneath Her Feet* as well. The book "addresses the themes of exile, metamorphosis and flux," wrote Michiko Kakutani in *New York Times,* "and like those earlier books it examines such issues through the prism of multiple dichotomies: between home and rootlessness, love and death, East and West, reason and the irrational."

Complicated and many-layered, the book brought criticism from some reviewers, including Michael Gorra in *Times Literary Supplement.* "There is too much toomuchness" Gorra noted, with "so many characters, so many incidents—and in all that prosy batter something gets lost." Specifically, wrote James Gardner in *National Review,* the novel's main characters are not "compelling." "He makes the fatal mistake of being too impressed by their rock-star glamour," he continued, "and despite the arbitrary complexities that he attributes to them, he never succeeds in animating them with the emotional vitality that has so memorably enlivened his characters in the past." Other critics appreciated Rushdie's intended message. The author's theme, said a reviewer in *Economist,* "is that the ground beneath our feet is always shifting. Modern culture is in a permanent state of fragmentation . . . . Reality exists on many planes." Sven Birkerts, writing in *Esquire,* compared Rushdie's storytelling abilities to those of Ovid and Scheherazade. "Rushdie roves the world like one in mad pursuit of tale and theme," Birkerts wrote, and *The Ground beneath Her Feet* "tells a grand story—a kind of ur-story—of the age of rock 'n' roll, but in the process spins around it half a hundred veils of myth and hidden meaning." Troy Patterson praised the novel in *Entertainment Weekly* as being "about the power of song itself," noting that "the Ulysses-like namedropping also evokes memories of dreams dreamt and heroes adored."

Fury at first appears to be more straightforward than many of Rushdie's previous novels. The book follows Malik Solanka, the Indian-born, Cambridge-educated philosopher and creator of the pop-culture phenomenon of the "Little Brain," a philosophically minded doll who becomes the star of a successful television show. Malik succumbs to a serious midlife crisis, hastily leaves his wife and child in London, and attempts to begin anew as an academic at a Manhattan university. Malik is uncomfortable with modern society and is subject to fits of rage, which increasingly come to dominate his life. In Malik's quest for renewal he becomes involved with two women, the second of which, the beautiful Neela, forces Malik into an epiphany of sorts as the narrative veers into the magic realism for which Rushdie has come to be known. Complicating matters is Malik's resemblance to a Panama hat-wearing serial killer, who is murdering young women from the city's society elite.

Some critics took issue with Rushdie's portrayal of American society in *Fury.* By date-stamping the book with names like Monica Lewinsky, Tommy Hilfiger, and Courtney Love, " *Fury* is immediately obsolete," maintained James Wood in *New Republic.* A reviewer for *Economist* said that "Rushdie is usually too effervescent a writer to be pompous, but here he is drawn into making overwrought and grandiose pronouncements on the state of America." Michiko Kakutani in *New York Times* claimed that Rushdie's portrayal of New York "fails not only because it's based on a false observation—the city in 2000 was reeling more from a surfeit of greed and complacency than from free-floating anxiety and anger—but also because Solanka never seems intimately connected to the events he is witnessing in America." Other critics commended Rushdie's scathing view of American society. As Malik attempts to conquer his fury, his story becomes "a fantastic, humorous, and gravely serious tale about the torments of love," wrote Brad Hooper in *Booklist,* "but, even more than that, the abrasions on the soul inflicted by today's cellphone society." Barbara Hoffert of *Library Journal* likewise commended the novel for its evocation of a frantic, skin-deep society: *Fury* "veers precariously through our obsessive times, capturing every nuance exactly."

Other critics focused on different aspects of the novel. Paul Evans, reviewing *Fury* in *Book,* praised Rushdie's fiction as "a metaphysical thriller and a sci-fi-tinged fantasy, a treatise on gender politics and a farce about academia." Evans further concentrated on the idea that to transcend his anger, "Malik must endure the demise of his old self in order to live anew." A reviewer for *Publishers Weekly* wrote that Rushdie "catches roiling undercurrents of incivility and inchoate anger" in "prose crackling with irony." In regards to the book's language, which other critics have compared to that of Vladimir Nabokov, *Publishers Weekly* reviewer said that "his relatively narrow focus results in a crisper narrative; there are fewer puns and a deeper emotional involvement with his characters."

In *Shalimar The Clown* Rushdie focuses not on the state of America, but on the state of the world. The characters in the novel traverse the globe, from Germany to France to Kashmir to Los Angeles, California. The story opens as Max Ophuls, named after the famous director, is killed in Los Angeles. The plot then moves backward in time, and across several continents, to portray the events that led up to the murder. Reviews of the book were mixed, and critics could not even agree on the book's overarching theme. While *Nation* critic Lee Siegel quoted a passage from the novel, "'our lives, our stories, flowed into one another's, were no longer our own, individual, discrete,'" as an illustration of the theme, a *Publishers Weekly* contributor simply stated that "the focus of the novel is extremism." The latter statement refers to the Holocaust, territorial disputes over Kashmir, and Islamic terrorism, all of which figure significantly into the story's plot. Yet another reviewer had an entirely different impression of the novel's meaning. Writing in the *Atlantic Monthly,* Christopher Hitchens stated that the book illustrates "gone is the time when anywhere was exotic or magical or mythical, or even remote." However, it seems that the *Publishers Weekly* contributor best summed up these very different readings by concluding that "*Shalimar the Clown* is a powerful parable about the willing and unwilling subversion of multiculturalism."

In addition to fiction, Rushdie has published several essay collections. *Imaginary Homelands: Essays and Criticism, 1981- 1991* is a selection of essays and other short journalistic pieces. Some of the essays, such as "One Thousand Days in a Balloon," which Rushdie presented at an unannounced appearance at Columbia University in 1991, and "Why I Have Embraced Islam," an explanation of his commitment to the religion whose popular leaders violently reject and continue to persecute him, were written after he was forced into hiding. Others, dating from before the *fatwa,* picture a writer gradually forming his own concepts of what constitutes truth and beauty in literature. These works, *Commonweal* contributor Paul Elie elaborated, "serve as a reminder that once upon a time"—before the wrath of fundamentalist Islam fell upon on the author's head—"he was just another middling British writer, holding forth on this and that with more intelligence and enthusiasm than was required of him."

In 2003 a new collection of Rushdie's nonfiction writings was published as *Step across This Line: Collected Nonfiction, 1992- 2002.* Donald Morrison, writing in *Time International,* commented that in this book Rushdie shows himself to be a "thoughtful and feisty essayist." *Booklist* contributor Donna Seaman praised the works included, noting that the author "has written stirring and significant essays about his harrowing, often surreal life."

In September of 1998, the fatwa against Rushdie was lifted by the Iranian government, though certain fundamentalist Muslim groups, claiming that a fatwa cannot be lifted, increased the reward for killing him to $2.8 million. In addition, in 2004 an Iranian extremist Islamic group calling itself the General Staff for the Glorification of Martyrs of the Islamic World offered another 100,000 dollar reward for Rushdie. As a result, the author has continued to keep security tight, although he frequently travels between his homes in London, New York, and India, gives interviews and makes public appearances. In 1999 he even joined the rock group U2 on stage to perform the song "The Ground beneath Her Feet," which was inspired by Rushdie's book. A short time later, Rushdie was finally granted a visa to return to India; he was quoted in *Time* as saying that lifting of this restriction "feels like another step back into the light."

Journalist Christopher Hitchens hypothesized in *Progressive* that "if it were not for the threat of murder, and the fact that this murder has been solicited by a religious leadership, I believe that Salman Rushdie might now be the Nobel Laureate in literature. . . . He has raised a body of fiction that explores the world of the post-colonial multi-ethnic and the multi-identity exile or emigrant. He has done so, moreover . . . by making experiments in language that recall those of [James] Joyce." "All of his works," continued Hitchens, "are designed to show that there is no mastery of language unless it is conceded that language is master."

BIOGRAPHICAL AND CRITICAL SOURCES:

BOOKS

Goonetilleke, D.C.R.A.,*Salman Rushdie,* St. Martin's Press (New York, NY), 1998.

Gorra, Michael Edward, *After Empire: Scott, Naipaul, Rushdie,* University of Chicago Press (Chicago, IL), 1997.

Kuortti, Joel, *Place of the Sacred: The Rhetoric of the Satanic Verses Affair,* P. Lang (New York, NY), 1997.

Kuortti, Joel, *The Salman Rushdie Bibliography: A Bibliography of Salman Rushdie's Work and Rushdie Criticism,* P. Lang (New York, NY), 1997.

Kuortti, Joel, *Fictions to Live in: Narration as an Argument for Fiction in Salman Rushdie's Novels,* P. Lang (New York, NY), 1998.

Rushdie, Salman, *Midnight's Children,* Knopf (New York, NY), 1981.

Rushdie, Salman, *Shame,* Knopf (New York, NY), 1983.

PERIODICALS

Atlanta Journal Constitution, January 21, 1996, Alan Ryan, review of *The Moor's Last Sigh,* p. L11.

Atlantic Monthly, February, 1996, Phoebe-Lou Adams, review of *The Moor's Last Sigh,* p. 114; September, 2005, Christopher Hitchens, review of *Shalimar the Clown,* p. 123.

Back Stage, April 4, 2003, Simi Horwitz, review of *Midnight's Children* (play), p. 3.

Biography, summer, 2003, Ruchir Joshi, review of *Step across This Line: Collected Nonfiction, 1992-2002,* p. 554.

Book, September, 2001, Paul Evans, review of *Fury,* p. 67.

Booklist, November 1, 1995, Brad Hooper, review of *The Moor's Last Sigh,* p. 435; June 1, 2001, Brad Hooper, review of *Fury,* p. 1798; September 15, 2002, Donna Seaman, review of of *Step across This Line,* p. 194.

Books and Bookmen, September, 1983, Ronald Hayman.

Boston Globe, January 14, 1996, Gail Caldwell, "For Love of Mother," p. B43.

Chicago Tribune, February 17, 1989; September 24, 1990.

Chicago Tribune Book World, March 15, 1981; April 26, 1981; January 22, 1984; January 22, 1995, p. 3; January 14, 1996, Beverly Fields, "Salman Rushdie Returns," pp. 1, 4; January 28, 1996, John Blades, "An Interview with Salman Rushdie," p. 3.

Christian Century, October 14, 1998, "Rushdie Hails End of 'Terrorist Threat,'" p. 931.

Christian Science Monitor, March 2, 1989; January 26, 1995, p. B1, B4; February 7, 1996, Merle Rubin, "Extravagant, Madcap Vision of an Indian Clan," p. 13.

Commonweal, September 25, 1981; December 4, 1981; November 4, 1983, Una Chaudhuri, review of *Shame,* p. 590; December 4, 1992; February 9, 1996, Sara Maitland, "The Author Is Too Much with Us," pp. 22- 23.

Economist, October 3, 1998, "The Lifting of an Unliftable Fatwa: Iran," p. 49; May 15, 1999, "Boys' Toys," p. 12; August 25, 2001, "Signifying Nothing."

Encounter, February, 1982.

Entertainment Weekly, April 16, 1999, Troy Patterson, "What a Rushdie! The Majestic New Novel from the Author of *The Satanic Verses,* Salman Rushdie, Takes on Sex, Drugs, and Rock & Roll. And Don't Be Surprised if You Hear Some of the Lyrics in a U2 Song," p. 52.

Esquire, May 1, 1999, Sven Birkerts, "Sex, Drugs, and That Other Thing," p. 60.

Harper's, February, 1998, "The Pen Is Crueler than the Sword," p. 18.

Illustrated London News, October, 1988.

India Today, September 15, 1988; October 31, 1988; March 15, 1989.

Interview, May, 1999, Deborah Treisman, "Salman Rushdie's Rock 'n' Roll," p. 122.

Library Journal, August, 2001, Barbara Hoffert, review of *Fury,* p. 166; October 15, 2002, Shelly Cox, review of *Step across This Line,* p. 73.

London Review of Books, September 29, 1988; July 9, 1992, p. 17; September 7, 1995, Michael Wood, "Shenanigans," pp. 3, 5.

Los Angeles Times Book Review, August 26, 1979; December 25, 1983; November 11, 1990; January 7, 1996, Richard Eder, "English as a Wicked Weapon," pp. 3, 13.

Maclean's, March 6, 1995, p. 86; October 9, 1995, John Bemrose, "Tower of Babble," p. 85; May 24, 1999, Anthony Wilson-Smith, "The Revival of Salman Rushdie: While Still Wary, the Author Is Gradually Emerging from the Shadow of a Death Sentence," p. 54.

Mother Jones, April- May, 1990.

Nation, January 1, 1996, Jessica Hagedorn, "They Came for the Hot Stuff," pp. 25-27; December 22, 1997, Christopher Hitchens, "Satanic Curses," p. 8; October 3, 2005, Lee Siegel, review of *Shalimar the Clown,* p. 28.

National Review, December 31, 1995, James Bowman, "Absolutely Fabulist," pp. 46-7; May 17, 1999, James Gardner, "Rock and Rushdie," p. 61.

New Republic, May 23, 1981; March 6, 1989; March 13, 1989; December 10, 1990; March 18, 1996, James Wood, "Salaam Bombay," pp. 38-41; April 26, 1999, James Wood, "Lost in the Punhouse," p. 94; September 24, 2001, James Wood, "The Nobu Novel," p. 32.

New Statesman, May 1, 1981; September 23, 1994, p. 40; September 8, 1995, Maya Jaggi, "The Last Laugh," pp. 20-21; September 8, 1995, Aamer Hussein, "City of Mongrel Joy," pp. 39-40.

New Statesman & Society, September 30, 1988; March 29, 1991; May 29, 1992, pp. 39- 40.

Newsweek, April 20, 1981; February 12, 1990, December 9, 1991, p. 79; February 6, 1995, Sarah Crichton, review of *East, West,* pp. 59-60; January 8, 1996, "The Prisoner in the Tower," p. 70.

New Yorker, July 27, 1981; January 9, 1984.

New York Review of Books, September 24, 1981; March 2, 1989; March 21, 1996, J.M. Coetzee, "Palimpsest Regained," pp. 13-16.

New York Times, April 23, 1981, Robert Towers, review of *Midnight's Children*; November 2, 1983; January 27, 1989; February 13, 1989; February 15, 1989; February 16, 1989; February 17, 1989; February 18, 1989; February 20, 1989; February 21,

1989; February 22, 1989; February 23, 1989; February 24, 1989; February 25, 1989; March 1, 1989; March 28, 1991, p. 26; December 2, 1995, John F. Burns, "Another Rushdie Novel, Another Bitter Epilogue;" December 28, 1995, Michiko Kakutani, "Rushdie on India: Serious, Crammed yet Light," pp. C13, C20; January 14, 1996, Norman Rush, "Doomed in Bombay," p. 7; January 17, 1996, Nina Barnton, "Sentenced to Death but Recalled to Life," pp. C1-2; April 13, 1999, Michiko Kakutani, "Turning Rock-and-Roll into Quakes;" August 31, 2001, Michiko Kakutani, "A Dollmaker and His Demons in the Big City."

New York Times Book Review, April 19, 1981, Clark Blaise, review of *Midnight's Children,* p. 1; March 28, 1982; November 13, 1983, Michael T. Kaufman, "Author from Three Countries" (interview), p. 3; January 29, 1989; November 11, 1990; June 2, 1991, p. 15; January 15, 1995, pp. 1, 16-17; January 14, 1996, p. 7; April 18, 1999, Charles McGrath, "Rushdie Unplugged."

Observer (London, England), February 9, 1975; July 19, 1981; September 25, 1988; January 22, 1989; February 19, 1989; November 11, 1990, p. 1.

Progressive, October, 1997, Christopher Hitchens, "Salman Rushdie: 'Even This Colossal Threat Did Not Work. Life Goes On,'" p. 34.

Publishers Weekly, November 11, 1983; January 30, 1995, Sybil Steinberg, "A Talk with Salman Rushdie: Six Years into the Fatwa," pp. 80-82; October 2, 1995, review of *The Moor's Last Sigh,* p. 52; July 16, 2001, a review of *Fury,* p. 166; July 25, 2005, review of *Shalimar the Clown,* p. 39.

Quill and Quire, April, 1996, Nancy Wigston, review of *The Moor's Last Sigh,* p. 25.

Saturday Review, March, 1981.

Spectator, June 13, 1981.

Time, February 13, 1989; February 27, 1989; September 11, 1995; January 15, 1996, Paul Gray, "Rushdie: Caught on the Fly," p. 70, "Writing to Save His Life," pp. 70-71; February 22, 1999, Maseeh Rahman, "Homecoming to What? Rushdie's Planned Return to India Is of Symbolic Value to Him but an Opportunity for Vengeance to Many," p. 241; April 26, 1999, Paul Gray, "Ganja Growing in the Tin: Salman Rushdie Reimagines Orpheus as a Modern Rock Star, and Almost Brings It Off," p. 99.

Time International, December 23, 2002, Donal Morrison, review of *Step across This Line,* p. 63.

Times (London, England), October 5, 1995.

Times Literary Supplement, February 21, 1975; May 15, 1981; September 9, 1983; September 30, 1988; September 28, 1990; April 9, 1999, Michael Gorra, "It's Only Rock and Roll but I Like It," p. 25.

Variety, February 10, 2003, Matt Wolf, review of *Midnight's Children* (play), p. 43.

Vogue, November, 1983.

Voice Literary Supplement, November, 1983, Margo Jefferson, review of *Shame.*

Washington Post, January 18, 1989; February 15, 1989; February 17, 1989; February 18, 1989; January 20, 1996, Linton Weeks, "Salman Rushdie, out and About," p. C1.

Washington Post Book World, March 15, 1981; November 20, 1983; January 29, 1989; January 8, 1995, pp. 1, 11; January 7, 1996, Michael Dirda, "Where the Wonders Never Cease," pp. 1-2.

World Literature Today, winter, 1982.

ONLINE

BBC Web site, http://www.bbc.co.uk/ (March 12, 2002).

* * *

RUSSO, Richard 1949-

PERSONAL: Born July 15, 1949, in Johnstown, NY; son of James W. Russo and Jean Findlay (LeVarn) Russo; married; wife's name Barbara Marie; children: Emily, Kate. *Education:* Received B.A.; University of Arizona, Ph.D., 1980, M.F.A., 1981.

ADDRESSES: *Home*—Maine. *Agent*—c/o Author Mail, Knopf Publishing, 299 Park Ave., Fourth Floor, New York, NY 10171.

CAREER: Novelist. Southern Illinois University at Carbondale, former fiction instructor; Colby College, Waterville, ME, former professor.

MEMBER: Associated Writing Programs.

AWARDS, HONORS: Pennsylvania Council of Arts fellow, 1983; annual award for fiction from Society of Midland Authors, c. 1989, for *The Risk Pool;* Best Books of 2001, *Library Journal,* and Pulitzer Prize in fiction, 2002, for *Empire Falls.*

WRITINGS:

Mohawk (novel), Random House (New York, NY), 1986.

The Risk Pool (novel), Random House (New York, NY), 1988.

Nobody's Fool (novel), Random House (New York, NY), 1993.

Straight Man (novel), Random House (New York, NY), 1997.

(With Robert Benton) *Twilight* (screenplay), Paramount, 1998.

(Author of introduction) *The Collected Stories of Richard Yates,* Holt (New York, NY), 2001.

Empire Falls (novel), Knopf (New York, NY), 2001.

The Whore's Child and Other Stories, Knopf (New York, NY), 2002.

Contributor of short fiction to periodicals, including *Prairie Schooner, Mid-American Review,* and *Sonora Review.* Contributing editor of *Puerto del Sol.*

ADAPTATIONS: Nobody's Fool was adapted as a screenplay by Robert Benton, produced by Paramount in 1994, starring Paul Newman; *Empire Falls* was adapted as a 3-hour mini-series by Russo for HBO, directed by Fred Schepisi and starring Paul Newman. The series aired in May, 2005.

SIDELIGHTS: Dubbed the "Stendahl of blue-collar America" by Tom Bissell in *Esquire,* Pulitzer Prize-winning author Richard Russo is noted for his novels depicting life in the declining small towns of America. In his first two highly acclaimed books, *Mohawk* and *The Risk Pool,* he focuses on the estrangement and melancholy felt by many of the residents of Mohawk, a fictional locale in upstate New York. *Nobody's Fool* is set in a similar town called North Bath, while his fourth book, *Straight Man,* takes place at a third-rate university in an isolated Pennsylvania town, presenting an academic satire. In his fifth novel, *Empire Falls,* which earned the writer the 2002 Pulitzer, Russo returns to the blue collar milieu of his earlier novels, but also blends comedic touches found in *Straight Man.* Russo is also the author of a collection of short stories, *The Whore's Child and Other Stories,* as well as screenplays, and has been compared to such renowned American writers as Sherwood Anderson and Sinclair Lewis. According to Hilma Wolitzer in *Tribune Books,* he "brilliantly evokes the economic and emotional depression of a failing town, a place where even the weather is debilitating and the inhabitants seem to struggle merely to stay in place."

Russo's first novel, *Mohawk,* opens in 1967. A leather-tannery town that falls victim to increasing unemployment as well as chemical dumping in its water supply, Mohawk is home to such working-class characters as Dan Wood, who is bound to a wheel chair due to an automobile accident; Anne, an intelligent woman in love with Dan, though he married her cousin; Mather Grouse, Anne's father, who, while a proud and decent character, is guilt-ridden over incidents in his past; and Rory Gaffney, an unsavory man with a propensity toward violence. "Nearly every one of these people . . . has suffered some sort of terrible loss," related Michiko Kakutani in the *New York Times.* For this reason, decided the reviewer, the work "has a tendency to swerve toward contrived melodrama." Kakutani concluded, though, that *Mohawk* "remains an immensely readable and sympathetic novel, a novel that attests to its author's considerable ambition and talent. Mr. Russo has an instinctive gift for capturing the rhythms of small-town life." Likewise, David Montrose declared in the *Times Literary Supplement* that *Mohawk* is "an accomplished piece of fictional architecture."

Russo followed *Mohawk* with *The Risk Pool,* "a far more ambitious work, with a Dickensian sprawl and charm," according to Wolitzer. Narrated by Mohawk resident Ned Hall, the work spans thirty years of Ned's life as he is caught between feuding parents. Ned's father, Sam, a carousing gambler and petty thief, abandons the family for the first several years of Ned's childhood. After Ned's mother, Jenny, suffers a mental breakdown, Sam claims his son for a time, toting him to local pool-halls and bars. As the story progresses, Ned—shuttled between both parents before leaving for college—tries to both understand and earn the love of his unpredictable father.

The Risk Pool elicited widespread praise. Calling it a "superbly original, maliciously funny book," Jack Sullivan asserted in the *New York Times Book Review,* "It is Mr. Russo's brilliant, deadpan writing that gives their wasted lives and miserable little town such haunting power and insidious charm." Similarly, Kakutani declared *The Risk Pool* "fine, closely observed" and "full-bodied," maintaining that Russo writes with "genuine passion" and a "straightforward and newly authoritative narrative approach." The reviewer continued, "What's more, with Ned and Sam, Mr. Russo has succeeded in creating characters with the emotional weight of people we've known in real life. They embed themselves in our imaginations, and their personal losses—of love, of hope and of ambition—become an elegy for the town of Mohawk itself, for a time and place on the verge of vanishing from the American scene."

In his next novel, *Nobody's Fool,* Russo moved to a different town in the same region of upstate New York. Unlike Mohawk, the fictional town of North Bath has a glamorous past from a time when mineral springs brought fortunes to the area. Those springs suddenly, mysteriously dried up in 1868, however, and the town has never recovered. North Bath is a dark reflection of its prosperous neighbor, Schuyler Springs—which is Russo's fictionalized rendering of Saratoga Springs, a wealthy resort town.

"I needed a different kind of environment," Russo explained in a *Publishers Weekly* interview with Sybil Steinberg. "There wasn't any sense in Mohawk of a greater day, a kind of mythical past which the inhabitants harked back to as a Golden Age. Also, I needed a rich relative right down the road in order to make comparisons and address the book's central issues of luck and free will and fate. Demographically, Mohawk wouldn't work." *Nobody's Fool* has a large cast of eccentric characters, vividly brought to life by Russo. Novelist E. Annie Proulx, reviewing the novel for *Tribune Books,* called it a "rude, comic, harsh, galloping story of four generations of small-town losers, the best literary portrait of the backwater burg since 'Main Street.' Here is a masterly use of the wisecrack, the minor inflection, the between-the-lines meaning. Heavy messages hang under small-talk like keels under boats. Russo's pointillist technique makes his characters astonishingly real, and gradually the tiny events and details coalesce, build up in meaning and awaken in the reader a desire to climb into the page and ask for a beer."

With his fourth novel, *Straight Man,* Russo moved from New York to Pennsylvania for a tale of petty politics at an insignificant state college. The book is "hilarious," in the opinion of *New York Times Book Review* writer Tom De Haven. The critic went on to say that despite the abundant humor, the author is certainly "interested in more than generating laughter," and called *Straight Man* "the funniest serious novel I have read since . . . *Portnoy's Complaint.*" The central figure is Hank Devereaux, the chairman of the bitter, paranoid English department. Devereaux reacts to possible cuts in the department's budget by putting on a Groucho Marx-style fake nose and glasses and appearing on the local evening news, holding a live duck by the neck and threatening to kill a duck a day until the money is assured. "As in Russo's earlier novels, there is a lot of ambling and driving around, and frequent stops along the way," reported De Haven. "Plot is a minor consideration. . . . The novel's greatest pleasures derive not from any blazing impatience to see what happens next, but from pitch-perfect dialogue, persuasive characterization and a rich progression of scenes, most of them crackling with an impudent, screwball energy reminiscent of Howard Hawks's movies."

Ron Charles, a reviewer for the *Christian Science Monitor,* described *Straight Man* as a "fully written novel" that is "neither sad nor overwrought for he evinces plenty of elegance and flawless timing. He demonstrates that it's possible to laugh at, and with, someone simultaneously." Charles also commented on the complexity found in the author's work: "Russo writes repartee that crackles with wit but never slides into artifice. Though his characters are often struggling against deep-seated sadness, the force of his wit is enough to convince us that such pain and sadness are not inevitable or final." Proulx affirmed that enthusiasm for Russo's skill, declaring, "If ever time travel is invented, let Richard Russo be first through the machine to bring back a true account. No one writing today catches the detail of life with such stunning accuracy."

Empire Falls, Russo's fifth novel, reprises the blue-collar world of his earlier books, this time set in a dying mill town in Maine rather than upstate New York. The title comes from the name of the town in the novel, but also resonates with the larger theme of dissolution. The river that flows through Empire Falls is central to the book's imagery. The patriarch of the powerful Whiting clan, owners of the now defunct textile mill that was the town's primary industry, tried in vain to change the course of that river, just as the protagonist of the novel, Miles Roby, tries to change the course of his own life. Years earlier, Miles left behind a college education and possible career as a professor to return home to care for his ailing mother. Taking a perpetual lease on the Empire Grill from Mrs. Whiting, last of that family, he remained in the town, married a woman he did not love, and became stuck in a numbing life, yet he has never lost his essential decency.

Miles's one hope is that his teenage daughter, Tick, will escape Empire Falls, as he was intended to. The book is also told from Tick's point of view in present-tense chapters that chronicle her growing frustration at the adult world and "it's essential dishonesty," as Russo writes. Tick's only close friend is a silent loner at school who is full of a rage that is ready to boil over. Miles's wife has meanwhile run off with the local fitness center owner and become an aerobics instructor; his father—always cadging beer money—is attempting to get the local priest to fund a trip to Key West. Mrs. Whiting, too, tries to control Miles, and there is a secret at the heart of her manipulations that bespeaks some deep connection between the Robys and Whitings. The rest of the community—a rich gathering of malcontents and regular folks—gathers daily at the Grill, sipping weak coffee and hoping things will get better before they get worse.

Critical reception to Russo's *Empire Falls* was overwhelmingly positive. "Russo is brave enough to conceive a large ambition but too smart to overreach," wrote A.O. Scott in the *New York Times Book Review.* "His sympathy for weakness and self-deception . . . does not rule out stern satiric judgment." Scott further praised Russo's "unerring" command of his story, calling him "one of the best novelists around." Janet Maslin, reviewing the novel in the *New York Times,* felt it was a "rich, humorous, elegantly constructed novel" and Russo's "most seductive book thus far." For Joanne Wilkinson, writing in *Booklist, Empire Falls* is a "warmhearted novel of sweeping scope," and one that balances "irreverent, mocking humor with unending empathy for . . . characters and their foibles." Similarly, a contributor for *Publishers Weekly* called it Russo's "biggest, boldest novel yet." The same reviewer concluded, "When it comes to evoking the cherished hopes and dreams of ordinary people, Russo is unsurpassed." "*Empire Falls* is dense in the best sense of the word," declared Bruce Fretts in *Entertainment Weekly,* further noting that with this "deeply ambitious book, Richard Russo has found new life as a writer."

In his 2002 publication, *The Whore's Child and Other Stories,* Russo presents his first foray into short fiction, seven tales that are in the main, according to *Booklist* writer Wilkinson, "considerably harder-edged and bleaker than his novels." Of these stories, three feature literature professors, as Russo himself was until he retired from teaching to write full time in the late 1990s. Only two deal with the same blue-collar world that his novels explore. The title story deals with a Belgian nun who takes a creative writing class, bares her soul in a steamy memoir, and then is discomfited when her work is reinterpreted by the class. "Joy Ride" tells the story of a mother fleeing from her husband with her teenage son in tow; "Poison" is about the reunion of a pair of fifty-something writers; "The Farther You Go" presents an oddly sympathetic abusive husband; and a cinematographer confronts the painter who was his late wife's lover in "Monhegan Light." As Rand Richards Cooper noted in the *New York Times Book Review,* the collection "abjures Russo's typical working-class settings and protagonists in favor of professors and writers caught in the drift of middle age, worried about illness and physical decline and experiencing deep ambivalence about marriage."

Critical praise met this new turn in Russo's writing career. Wilkinson felt that, despite the "darkness of his themes, all of the stories are told with great authority and near flawless technique." Maslin, writing in the *New York Times,* noted that the title story presents an "astonishing examination of the writing process," and that in all of the tales, Russo proves himself to be "the architect of stories you can't put down." A contributor for *Kirkus Reviews* found "Joy Ride" to be a "wonderful distillation of Russo's gifts for crystal-clear narration, subtle character portrayal, and irrepressible humor, and is capped by a tonally perfect bittersweet conclusion." Francine Prose called Russo's stories "well-crafted and deftly plotted" in *People.* Summing up the impact of this debut short story collection, *Book*'s James Schiff asserted that the book "provides a wealth of delights and rewards from an author who's surely hitting full stride," while a reviewer for *Publishers Weekly* concluded that the book "is a winner."

"It's no secret that in my books I'm trying to make the comic and the serious rub up against each other just as closely and uncomfortably as I can," Russo told Alden Mudge in a *Book Page* online interview. "My books are elegiac in the sense that they're odes to a nation that even I sometimes think may not exist anymore except in my memory and my imagination. I find that by ignoring a lot of American culture you can write more interesting stories. . . . I just pray for continued good health, because I've got other stories to tell."

BIOGRAPHICAL AND CRITICAL SOURCES:

BOOKS

Russo, Richard, *Empire Falls,* Knopf (New York, NY), 2001.

PERIODICALS

American Spectator, December, 1993, p. 30.

Antioch Review, winter, 1994, p. 173.

Atlanta Journal-Constitution, August 24, 1997, p. L12.

Atlantic Monthly, June, 2001, James Marcus, review of *Empire Falls,* p. 104.

Book, July, 2001, Don McLeese, review of *Empire Falls,* p. 63; July-August, 2002, James Schiff, review of *The Whore's Child and Other Stories,* p. 76.

Booklist, September 15, 1986, p. 103; May 15, 1993, p. 1676; March 15, 1994, p. 1350; May 15, 1997, p. 1541; January 1, 1998, p. 835; April 1, 2001, Joanne Wilkinson, review of *Empire Falls,* p. 1429; May 1, 2002, Joanne Wilkinson, review of *The Whore's Child and Other Stories,* p. 1444.

Books, July, 1993, James Schiff, review of *The Whore's Child and Other Stories,* p. 17.
Boston Globe, June 27, 1993, p. 94; January 26, 1995, p. 49.
Chicago Tribune, February 19, 1995, Section 5, p. 1.
Christian Century, March 8, 1995, p. 259.
Christian Science Monitor, October 6, 1997, Ron Charles, review of *Straight Man,* p. 14.
Chronicle of Higher Education, August 8, 1997, p. B8.
Commonweal, February 24, 1995, p. 54.
Economist, May 26, 2001, review of *Empire Falls,* p. 8.
Entertainment Weekly, June 25, 1993, p. 99; June 24, 1994, p. 99; July 18, 1997, p. 79; May 18, 2001, Bruce Fretts, "Maine Attraction," p. 72.
Esquire, June, 2001, Tom Bissell, review of *Empire Falls,* p. 42.
Hollywood Reporter, November 5, 2001, Zorianna Kit, "Benton to Helm Russo's 'Falls' at Stone Village," p. 3.
Kirkus Reviews, July 15, 1986, p. 1059; September 1, 1988, p. 1271; April 1, 1993, p. 404; May 15, 2002, review of *The Whore's Child and Other Stories,* p. 695.
Library Journal, November 15, 1988, p. 86; April 15, 1993, p. 128; April 15, 1994, p. 140; June 15, 1997, p. 99; October 1, 1997, p. 147; July, 2001, David W. Henderson, review of *Empire Falls,* p. 126.
Listener, March 30, 1989, p. 27.
National Catholic Reporter, November 19, 1993, p. 31; January 20, 1995, p. 30; September 26, 1997, p. 33.
National Review, December 31, 1994, p. 62; April 6, 1998, p. 58.
New Republic, March 30, 1998, p. 26.
New Statesman, July 30, 1993, p. 39.
New York, November 21, 1988, p. 132; May 31, 1993, p. 60; January 16, 1995, p. 56.
New Yorker, February 6, 1989, p. 106; July 19, 1993, p. 87; August 18, 1997, p. 71.
New York Times, October 15, 1986, Michiko Kakutani, review of *Mohawk,* p. 23; November 2, 1988, Michiko Kakutani, review of *The Risk Pool;* May 10, 2001, Janet Maslin, review of *Empire Falls,* p. E9; July 8, 2002, Janet Maslin, review of *The Whore's Child and Other Stories,* p. E8.
New York Times Book Review, October 12, 1986, p. 28; December 18, 1988, Jack Sullivan, review of *The Risk Pool,* p. 14; November 26, 1989, p. 34; June 20, 1993, p. 13; May 8, 1994, p. 24; July 6, 1997, Tom De Haven, review of *Straight Man,* p. 10; June 24, 2001, A.O. Scott, "Townies," p. 8; July 14, 2002, Rand Richards Cooper, review of *The Whore's Child and Other Stories,* p. 10.
Observer, March 12, 1989, p. 45.
People, August 11, 1997, p. 40; May 21, 2001, Erica Sanders, review of *Empire Falls,* p. 51; July 22, 2002, Francine Prose, review of *The Whore's Child and Other Stories,* p. 35.
Publishers Weekly, August 8, 1986, p. 66; September 16, 1988, p. 62; January 6, 1989, p. 50; October 6, 1989, p. 96; March 29, 1993, p. 34; June 7, 1993, Sybil Steinberg, interview with Richard Russo, pp. 43-44; November 1, 1993, p. 47; April 11, 1994, p. 62; September 5, 1994, p. 33; May 12, 1997, p. 56; July 7, 1997, p. 32; April 9, 2001, review of *Empire Falls,* p. 48; April 29, 2002, "A Pulitzer Prize Windfall," p. 20; May 20, 2002, review of *The Whore's Child and Other Stories,* p. 44.
Rolling Stone, March, 1997, p. 74.
Time, May 31, 1993, p. 66; July 14, 1997, p. 84.
Times Educational Supplement, September 3, 1993, p. 22.
Times Literary Supplement, March 6, 1987, David Montrose, review of *Mohawk,* p. 246; June 9, 1989, p. 634; July 2, 1993, p. 23.
Tribune Books (Chicago), October 12, 1986, p. 5; October 30, 1988, Hilma Wolitzer, review of *The Risk Pool,* p. 1; May 30, 1993, p. 1; December 5, 1993, p. 1; July 31, 1994, p. 2; August 3, 1997, p. 3.
USA Today, February 2, 1995, p. D4; July 3, 1997, p. D6.
Washington Post Book World, November 27, 1988, p. 7; December 24, 1989, p. 12; June 6, 1993, p. 8; July 17, 1994, p. 12; July 20, 1997, p. 3.
World and I, October, 2001, Edward Hower, "Small-Town Dreams," p. 243.

OTHER

Book Page, http://www.bookpage.com/ (May, 2001), Alden Mudge, "Richard Russo Renders Timely Portrait of American Life."
Identity Theory, http://www.identitytheory.com/ (August 13, 2002), Robert Birnbaum, "Interview: Richard Russo."
New York State Writers Institute, http://www.albany.edu/ (August 13, 2002), "Richard Russo."
Powell's.com Interviews, http://www.powells.com/ (June 6, 2001), Dave Weich, "Richard Russo's Working Arrangements."

* * *

RYBCZYNSKI, Witold 1943-
(Witold Marian Rybczynski)

PERSONAL: Born March 1, 1943, in Edinburgh, Scotland; son of Witold K. (an engineer) and Anna (a lawyer; maiden name, Hoffman) Rybczynski; married Shirley Hallam, 1974. *Education:* McGill University, B.Arch., 1966, M.Arch., 1973.

ADDRESSES: Home—7801 Lincoln Dr., Philadelphia, PA 19118. *Agent*—Andrew Wylie, 250 West 57 St., New York, NY 10107.

CAREER: Worked as architect and planner for Moshe Safdie on Habitat 67 and as planner of housing and new towns in northern Canada, 1966-71; in practice as registered architect, 1970-82; McGill University, Montreal, research associate, 1972-74, assistant professor, 1975-78, became associate professor, 1978, professor of architecture until 1993; University of Pennsylvania, Philadelphia, Meyerson Professor of Urbanism, 1993—. Consultant to World Bank, United Nations, International Research Center, and Banco de Mexico in Nigeria, India, the Philippines, and Mexico, 1976—.

AWARDS, HONORS: Honorary fellow, American Institute of Architects, 1993; Alfred Jurzykowski Foundation Award, 1993; honorary M.A., University of Pennsylvania, 1994; Athanaeum of Philadelphia Literary Award, 1997 and 2001; Christopher Award, 2000; Anthony J. Lukas Prize, 2000, for *A Clearing in the Distance.*

WRITINGS:

(With Alexander Morse) *Patent Survey, 1859-1974: The Use of Elemental Sulphur in Building,* McGill University/Minimal Cost Housing Group, School of Architecture, McGill University (Montreal, Canada), 1974.

(Editor) *Use It Again, Sam,* McGill University/Minimal Cost Housing Group, School of Architecture, McGill University (Montreal, Canada), 1977.

Paper Heroes: A Review of Appropriate Technology, Doubleday (Garden City, NJ), 1980.

Taming the Tiger: The Struggle to Control Technology, Viking (New York, NY), 1983.

Home: A Short History of an Idea, Viking (New York, NY), 1986.

The Most Beautiful House in the World, Viking (New York, NY), 1989.

Waiting for the Weekend, Viking (New York, NY), 1991.

Looking Around: A Journey through Architecture, Viking (New York, NY), 1993.

A Place for Art: The Architecture of the National Gallery of Canada, National Gallery of Canada (Ottawa, Canada), 1993.

City Life: Urban Expectations in a New World, Scribner (New York, NY), 1995.

A Clearing in the Distance: Frederick Law Olmsted and America in the Nineteenth Century, Scribner (New York, NY), 1999.

One Good Turn: A Natural History of the Screwdriver and the Screw, Scribner (New York, NY), 2000.

The Look of Architecture, Oxford University Press (New York, NY), 2001.

The Perfect House: A Journey with the Renaissance Master Andrea Palladio, Scribner (New York, NY), 2002.

Member of the advisory board, *Encyclopedia Americana,* 1993—, the editorial board, *Open House International,* 1993—, and *Urban Design International,* 1995—; coeditor of *Wharton Real Estate Review,* 1996—.

SIDELIGHTS: In general, reviewers of *Home: A Short History of an Idea* conclude that architect Witold Rybczynski had two basic aims in mind: the first, to provide a survey of the gradual establishment of ease and comfort in the home over the centuries, and the second, to fault modernism with ignoring these past achievements and turning to aesthetics instead. With regard to Rybczynski's first aim, Jonathan Yardley noted in his *Washington Post Book World* article that "the idea of 'home' . . . may seem as old as the hills, but as . . . Rybczynski demonstrates in this exceptionally interesting and provocative book, it is a relatively modern notion that did not really begin until after the Middle Ages." As history would have it, living conditions in medieval times were sober, indeed; family members, as well as servants and visitors, had all of their activities confined to one room. According to Rybczynski, with the advent of both the separation of the workplace from the home in the seventeenth century and technological advances that were to flourish from that time on, a house started to take on the richness of a home. Privacy, intimacy, and comfort became increasingly possible and meaningful.

Rybczynski moves through the centuries recording the domestic changes that characterize this progression from public house to private home, and includes such highlights as the popularization of the extremely comfortable furniture of the Rococo movement in France in the eighteenth century and the Georgian tradition of the same time in England which consisted of a decor that was practical yet refined. In the opinion of Brina Caplan in the *Nation,* "as a historical survey, *Home* traces the technological and psychological changes that produced our modern sense of domestic ease. But while Rybczynski is explaining how we achieved comfort, he is also arguing that we are well on the way to losing it. He has a case to make against the 'fundamental poverty of modern architectural ideas.'" According to Wendy Smith in the *Village Voice,* Rybczynski felt the "fundamental poverty" of modern architecture is due to the failure of architects to learn from history; "unlike [Tom Wolfe's] *From Bauhaus to Our House,* however, *Home* is no hysterical polemic against modernism. Rybczynski's concern isn't with shouting condemnation from the rooftops a là Tom Wolfe, but with understanding how contemporary architects came to ignore 300 years of experience in arranging comfortable, convenient homes. . . . It's not the appearance of older buildings he misses . . . it's the attitude they reflected: an attention to human needs in the creation of spaces that were practical as well as pleasing to the eye. His closing chapter calls for a return to the idea of comfort in the home, an acknowledgement that houses are places for people to live, not forums for architects' aesthetic manifestos." Rybczynski, for example, criticizes the domestic deco of French architect and theorist Le Corbusier, describing it as cubelike, austere, and conducive to mass production, noted Christopher Lehmann-Haupt in the *New York Times.* Lehmann-Haupt further maintained that "Rybczynski knows the way out of the dilemma that he believes Modernism has led us into. It is, simply enough, to rediscover what is *comfortable,* and to do so not just by recapturing bourgeois styles of the past, but instead by re-examining bourgeois traditions."

When *Home* was published in 1986, Rybczynski "became an overnight authority on the subject of comfort," wrote *Globe & Mail* contributor Adele Freedman. As was the case with several other critics, William H. Gass for the *New York Times Book Review* felt that Rybczynski "tells the story of the development of the private dwelling from house to home . . . in a sensitive and balanced way." Additionally, remarks Gass, "Rybczynski's call for a reexamination of the bourgeois tradition is one that should be heeded, and when he remarks, for example, that the seventeenth-century Dutch interior can teach us a good deal about living in small spaces he is surely right." When it comes to Rybczynski's criticism of modern architecture, however, some critics disagree with his stance. As Gass saw it, "what remains a problem is [Rybczynski's] basic opposition of art and comfort and the question whether an artist can really come to any kind of decent terms with the values of the middle class—because if living well remains a good revenge, living beautifully is yet better, indeed, best." Freedman likewise commented that "it was in the cards, but nonetheless wearisome, that a champion of intimacy, privacy, coziness, convenience and pragmatism would blame 'modernity' for banishing comfort in the name of esthetics." Yardley, however, viewed *Home* as "highly persuasive," and Lehmann-Haupt considered it a "delightful, intelligent book." Moreover, *New Yorker* contributor John Lukacs deemed it "exquisitely readable . . . a triumph of intelligence."

Rybczynski became Meyerson Professor of Urbanism at the University of Pennsylvania in the 1990s, and also published *City Life: Urban Expectations in a New World* mid-decade. The work was inspired by a friend's visit to Paris and her query upon her return as to why North American cities have failed to achieve the spectacular elegance of their European counterparts. In *City Life,* Rybczynski chronicles the history of urban development in North America from the first planned colonial towns like Philadelphia and Williamsburg to later metropolises noted for their daunting sprawl, like Los Angeles. Though he was examining a subject that had been well-dissected by other scholars of American and urban history, Rybczynski won praise for adding some fresh perspectives. "Threaded throughout the usual stories," wrote Brenda Scheer in her review of the tome for the *Journal of the American Planning Association,* "are lively descriptions of the attitudes that American city builders brought to their new world."

Rybczynski explains that American planners sought space, an obvious reaction to centuries of overcrowded conditions in European cities, and such desires were also blessed by an availability of land. *City Life* also shows how many cities that achieved greatness in the nineteenth century were built on the grid plan—among them New York and Chicago—which allowed for flexibility and quick expansion. He also reflects upon the importance of commerce to American cities. "Rybczynski points out that we have always viewed the city as a convenience, rather than as a timeless or monumental artifact," Scheer noted, and asserted in conclusion that the author "has offered not only a look at our past but an explanation for our current state of affairs." Paul Elie, reviewing the book for *Commonweal,* faulted *City Life* for lacking a more critical approach, but termed the author "an uncommonly curious and nimble cultural critic. . . . Like many of the best cultural critics, Rybczynski doesn't state his case so much as give form to the virtues he espouses. Thus his book has the qualities that he most admires in urban life. It is orderly but not too planned. . . . Past and present are always jostling against each other."

For his next book, Rybczynski approached one of the giants of American urban history, a man whose genius was only truly appreciated well after his 1903 death. *A*

Clearing in the Distance: Frederick Law Olmsted and America in the Nineteenth Century charts the life of America's greatest landscape architect. Olmsted was the designer of New York's Central Park, Prospect Park in Brooklyn, an estate in North Carolina for the Vanderbilt dynasty, and several other enduring marvels of what he considered "the three grand elements of pastoral landscape": meadows, forest, and water. Rybczynski writes about Olmsted's rather accidental path toward greatness: the son of a Connecticut dry-goods merchant, he found it difficult to settle on a profession for many years. He tried farming, became a sailor, and wrote about slavery for the *New York Times.* In 1857, a failed publishing venture spurred him to take a job as the superintendent for what New York City authorities had deemed "the Central Park." This was acreage set aside to serve as a public area, but it was not yet designed, and an architect by the name of Calvert Vaux suggested that Olmsted submit something. His plan won the competition, and Olmsted found that the gift for landscape architecture came naturally to him.

A Clearing in the Distance charts Olmsted's rise to eminence, but Rybczynski also chronicles the almost farcical struggles with local bureaucrats that plagued Olmsted's career. He was hired as the city planner of Buffalo, New York, and completed the design in less than a day's work, but for a park planned in the center, a local politician nearly won out in his bid to build a house in the middle of it. Rybczynski stresses that Olmsted was driven by personal conviction that public greenery was essential to the quality of life for all urban dwellers. Its restorative powers, he argued, should not be available just to the upper classes.

Rybczynski's biography reveals that Olmsted suffered from bouts of depression nearly all of his adult life and began to evidence signs of Alzheimer's disease in his early seventies. He handed over his business to his stepson and was confined in his last years to a sanitarium whose grounds he had designed but likely no longer recognized as his own handiwork. The biography won accolades for its author. "Like all fine biographers, Rybczynski has such a profound feeling for his subject that he is often at his best when the least is known and he is forced to impose his informed speculations upon the silent places in the life," remarked Robert Wilson in a review for *American Scholar. New York Times Book Review* critic Suzanna Lessard also praised *A Clearing in the Distance.* "The author has written a transparent book, in which he is a largely retiring but very pleasant guide," opined Lessard. "Every so often, he steps forward in a delightful, casual way"—in moments, as the critic noted, when the biographer recounts his own obstacles in researching Olmsted's life. Lessard described it as "a straightforward work, thorough and respectful, yet easeful in a way that is reminiscent of Olmsted himself."

In 1999, Rybczynski was invited by the *New York Times* to become a panelist for its "tool of the millennium" feature. The experience prompted him to write a short book on the history of his favorite tool. *One Good Turn: A Natural History of the Screwdriver and the Screw* was published in 2000, and discusses the screw and its companion at various points in history. It was crucial to some Renaissance weaponry, he finds, but advances in technology brought innovations and more widespread usage. "Siege engines . . . the precision lathe, door hinges and the great minds of ancient Greek geometry also figure among the threads of Rybczynski's tightly wound exposition," noted a *Publishers Weekly* reviewer.

The Look of Architecture, a short but succinct survey of style in architecture, came about as a result of a three-lecture series the author gave in the New York Public Library in 1999. In it, he discusses the ongoing relationship between architecture and style. He believes that, as does style, architecture mirrors the culture in which it exists and often imitates contemporary fashion. According to Michael Spinella of *Booklist,* he praises architects who build "with style and flair but also with firm foundations, grace, and the public interest at heart." A *Publishers Weekly* reviewer commented on Rybczynski's "ability to puncture [the architectural profession] pretensions without mean-spiritedness" and felt that, in this book, "the intimate, conversational tone he adopts manages to convey a lot of information in a very agreeable way."

BIOGRAPHICAL AND CRITICAL SOURCES:

BOOKS

Rybczynski, Witold, *Home: A Short History of an Idea,* Viking (New York, NY), 1986.

PERIODICALS

American Scholar, summer, 1999, Robert Wilson, review of *A Clearing in the Distance: Frederick Law Olmsted and America in the Nineteenth Century,* p. 142.

Atlantic, July 14, 1999.

Booklist, May 15, 1999, Donna Seaman, review of *A Clearing in the Distance,* p. 1659; June 1, 2001, Michael Spinella, review of *The Look of Architecture,* p. 1820.

Business Week, August 2, 1999, "The Man Who Brought Nature to the City," p. 12.

Chicago Tribune, July 28, 1986.

Commonweal, February 23, 1996, Paul Elie, review of *City Life,* p. 19.

Economist, July 17, 1999, "American City Parks," p. 7.

Fortune, June 21, 1999, Andrew Ferguson, "The Man Who Gave Us a Place to Relax," p. 48.

Globe & Mail (Toronto, Ontario, Canada), November 7, 1987.

Journal of the American Planning Association, fall, 1996, Brenda Scheer, review of *City Life,* p. 535.

Knight Ridder/Tribune News Service, October 23, 2002, Inga Saffron, review of *The Perfect House: A Journey with the Renaissance Architect Andrea Palladio,* p. K0125.

Library Journal, May 15, 1999, Grant A. Fredericksen, review of *A Clearing in the Distance,* p. 104; August, 2001, Paul Glassman, review of *The Look of Architecture,* p. 101.

Los Angeles Times Book Review, July 13, 1986.

Nation, December 20, 1986, Brina Caplan, review of *Home: A Short History of an Idea.*

Newsweek, August 18, 1986.

New Yorker, September 1, 1986.

New York Review of Books, December 4, 1986.

New York Times, July 14, 1986, Christopher Lehmann-Haupt, review of *Home.*

New York Times Book Review, November 6, 1983, August 3, 1986; June 13, 1999, Suzanna Lessard, "Scape Artist."

Planning, March, 1996, Harold Henderson, review of *City Life,* p. 33.

Public Interest, winter, 2000, David Brooks, "Designing the Cityscape," p. 99.

Publishers Weekly, May 31, 1999, review of *A Clearing in the Distance,* p. 76; June 12, 2000, review of *One Good Turn: A Natural History of the Screwdriver and the Screw,* p. 59; June 18, 2001, review of *The Look of Architecture,* p. 73.

Time, August 4, 1986.

Times Literary Supplement, May 6, 1988.

Village Voice, August 12, 1986, Wendy Smith, review of *Home.*

Washington Post, June 17, 1980, Jonathan Yardley, review of *Home.*

Washington Post Book World, September 25, 1983, July 6, 1986; December 5, 1999, p. X10.

Whole Earth, fall, 1999, Marianne Cramer, review of *A Clearing in the Distance,* p. 86.

* * *

RYBCZYNSKI, Witold Marian
See RYBCZYNSKI, Witold

* * *

RYDER, Jonathan
See LUDLUM, Robert

S

SÁBATO, Ernesto 1911-
(Ernesto R. Sábato)

PERSONAL: Born June 24, 1911, in Rojas, Argentina; son of Francisco Sabato (a mill owner) and Juana Ferrari; married Matilde Kusminsky-Richter, 1936; children: Jorge Federico, Mario. *Education:* National University of La Plata, Ph.D., 1937; additional study at Joliot-Curie Laboratory (Paris, France), 1938, and Massachusetts Institute of Technology, 1939.

ADDRESSES: Home—1676 Santos Lugares, Buenos Aires, Argentina. *Office*—Langeri 3135, Santos Lugares, Argentina.

CAREER: National University of La Plata, La Plata, Argentina, professor of theoretical physics, 1940-43; novelist and essayist, 1943—. Guest lecturer at universities throughout the United States and Europe. Chairman of National Commission on the Disappearance of Persons (Argentina), 1983.

AWARDS, HONORS: Argentine Association for the Progress of Science fellowship in Paris, 1937; sash of honor from Argentine Writers Society and Municipal Prose prize from the City of Buenos Aires, both 1945, both for *Uno y el universo;* prize from the Institute of Foreign Relations (West Germany; now Germany), 1973; Grand Prize of Honor from the Argentine Writers Society, from Premio Consagracion Nacional (Argentina), and from Chevalier des Arts et des Lettres (France), all 1974; Prix au Meilleur Livre Etranger (Paris), 1977, for *Abaddon, el Exterminador;* Gran Cruz al Merito Civil (Spain) and Chevalier de la Legion D'Honneur (France), both 1979; Gabriela Mistral Prize from Organization of American States, 1984; Miguel de Cervantes Prize from the Spanish Ministry of Culture, 1985; Commandeur de la Legion d'Honneur (France), 1987; Jerusalem Literary Prize, Wolf Foundation, 1989, medal of honor, 2002.

WRITINGS:

NOVELS

El tunel, Sur, 1948, translation by Harriet de Onis published as *The Outsider,* Knopf, 1950, translation by Margaret Sayers Peden published as *The Tunnel,* Ballantine, 1988.

Sobre heroes y tumbas, Fabril, 1961, reprinted, Seix Barral, 1981, excerpt published as *Un dios desconocido: Romance de la muerte de Juan Lavalle (de "Sobre heroes y tumbas"),* A.S. Dabini, 1980, translation by Stuart M. Gross of another excerpt published as Report on the Blind in *TriQuarterly,* Fall-Winter, 1968–69, translation by Helen Lane of entire novel published as *On Heroes and Tombs,* David Godine, 1981.

Abaddon, el Exterminador (title means "Abaddon, The Exterminator"), Sudamericana, 1974, revised edition, Seix Barral, 1978, translation by Andrew Hurley published as *The Angel of Darkness,* Ballantine (New York, NY), 1991.

(With Leon Benaros) *Eduardo Falu,* Ediciones Jucar, 1974.

ESSAYS

Uno y el universo (title means "One and the Universe"), Sudamericana, 1945.

Hombres y engranajes (title means "Men and Gears"), Emece, 1951, reprinted, 1985.

Heterodoxia (title means "Heterodoxy"), Emece, 1953.

El otro rostro del peronismo: Carta abierta a Mario Amadeo (title means "The Other Face of Peronism: Open Letter to Mario Amadeo"), Lopez, 1956.

El caso Sabato: Torturas y libertad de prensa—Carta abierta al Gral. Aramburu (title means "Sabato's Case: Torture and Freedom of the Press—Open Letter to General Aramburu"), privately printed, 1956.

Tango: Discusion y clave (title means "Tango: Discussion and Key"), Losada, 1963.

El escritor y sus fantasmas (title means "The Writer and His Ghosts"), Aguilar, 1963, revised edition, Seix Barral, 1979.

(Coeditor with Ernesto Schoo) Antonio Berni, *Ramona Montiel,* Editorial "El Mate," 1966.

Tres aproximaciones a la literatura de nuestro tiempo: Robbe-Grillet, Borges, Sartre (title means "Approaches to the Literature of Our Time. . . "; essays), Universitaria (Chile), 1968, German translation as *Sartre gegen Sartre: 3 Essays,* translated by Wolfgang A. Luchting, Limes-Verlag, 1974.

La convulsion politica y social de nuestro tiempo (title means "The Political and Social Upheaval of Our Time"), Edicom, 1969.

Ernesto Sabato: Claves politicas (title means "Ernesto Sabato: Political Clues"), Alonso, 1971.

La cultura en la encrucijada nacional (title means "Culture in the National Crossroads"), Ediciones de Crisis, 1973.

(With Jorge Luis Borges) *Dialogos* (title means "Dialogues"), Emece, 1976.

El Escritor y la crisis contemporánea, Edit. Casa de la Cultura Ecuatoriana, 1976, English translation as *The Writer in the Catastrophe of Our Time,* translated by Asa Zatz, Council Oak Books/Hecate, University of Oklahoma, 1990.

Apologias y rechazos (title means "Apologies and Rejections"), Seix Barral, 1979.

(Editor) Francisco Uzal, *Nacion, sionismo y masoneria* Corregidor, 1980.

La robotizacion del hombre y otras paginas de ficcion y reflexion (title means "The Robotization of Man and Other Pages of Fiction and Reflection"), Centro Editorial del America Latina, 1981.

Sabato oral, edited by Mario Paoletti, Ediciones Cultura Hispanica del Instituto de Cooperacion Iberoamericana, 1984.

Entre la letra y la sangre: converaciones con Carlos Catania, Seix Barral, 1988.

La Mejor de Ernesto Sabato, Seix Barral, 1989.

El Pintor Ernesto Sabato, Agencia Espanola de Cooperacion Internacional, 1991.

The Writer in the Catastrophe of Our Time, Council Oak Books, 1990.

Informe Sobre Ciegos, Anaya & M. Muchnik, 1994.

(With others) *Liber Fridman: pinturas,* Ediciones de Arte Gaglianone, 1995.

(With others) *Libros, personas, vida: Daniel Divinsky/ Kuki Miler y Ediciones de la Flor, Buenos Aires, 1967-1997,* Universidad de Guadalajaro, 1997.

Antes del fin, Seix Barral, 1998.

(Compiler with Elvira Gonzalez Fraga) *Cuentos que me apasionaron,* (two volumes), Planeta, 1999–2000.

Medio siglo con Sabato: entrevistas, edited by Julia Constenla, J. Vergara Editor, 2000.

La Resistencia, Seix Barral, 2000.

COLLECTIONS

Obras de ficcion (title means "Works of Fiction"; contains *El tunel* and *Sobre heroes y tumbas*), Losada, 1966.

Itinerario (title means "Itinerary"; selections from Sabato's novels and essays), Sur, 1969.

Obras: Ensayos (title means "Works: Essays"), Losada, 1970.

Paginas vivas (title means "Living Pages"), Kapelusz, 1974.

Antologia (title means "Anthology"), Libreria del Colegio, 1975.

Narrativa completa (title means "Complete Narrative"), Seix Barral, 1982.

Paginas de Ernesto Sabato (title means "Pages from Ernesto Sabato"), Celtia (Buenos Aires, Argentina), 1983.

OTHER

(Translator with Margarita Heiberg de Bose) Kurt Lipfert, *La Television: una breve exposicion del estado actual de la tecnica de la television = Das Fernschen,* Espasa-Calpe Argentina, 1940.

Nacimiento y muerte del sol: evolucion estelar y energia intraatomica = Birth and Death of the Sun, Espasa-Calpe Argentina, 1942.

(Translator) Bertrand Russell, *El A.B.C. de le relatividad = The ABC of Relativity,* Ediciones Iman, 1943.

(Editor) *Mitomagia: Los temas del misterio* (title means "Mitomagia: Themes of the Mysterious"), Ediciones Latinoamericanas, 1969.

(Author of introduction) *Testimonios: Chile, septiembre, 1973* (title means "Eyewitness Accounts: Chile, September, 1973"), Jus, 1973.

(With Antonio Berni) *Cuatro hombres de pueblo,* Libreria de la Ciudad, 1979.

(Editor with Anneliese von der Lipper) *Viaje a los mundos imaginarios,* Legasa, 1983.

Creación y tragedia: la esperanza ante la crísis: conferencia, Fundaci6n José Manuel Lara (Seville, Spain), 2002.

España en los diarios de mi vejez, Seix Barral (Buenos Aires, Argentina), 2004.

Contributor to *Sur* and other periodicals.

SIDELIGHTS: When one considers that Argentine novelist and essayist Ernesto Sábato published only three novels, the impact he had on Hispanic literature is remarkable: His first novel, *The Tunnel,* was a best-seller in his native land; his second work of fiction, *On Heroes and Tombs,* according to Emir Rodriguez Monegal in the *Borzoi Anthology of Latin American Literature,* "became one of the most popular contemporary novels in Latin America." *Abaddon, el Exterminador* ("Abbadon, The Exterminator"), Sábato's third novel, was similarly acclaimed and was granted France's highest literary award—the Prix au Meilleur Livre Etranger. Sabato's importance was officially recognized in 1985 when he received the first Miguel de Cervantes Prize (considered the equivalent of the Nobel in the Hispanic world) from Spain's King Juan Carlos. Harley Dean Oberhelman, in his study of the author titled *Ernest Sábato,* called Sabato "Argentina's most discussed contemporary novelist." His appeal rests largely in his portrayals of Argentine society under the domination of military strongmen such as Juan Peron and others, with his recurrent themes of incest, blindness, insanity, and abnormal psychology reflecting the distress of the Argentine people.

Born into a large, prosperous family of Italian origin, at age thirteen Sábato left the rural community where he had grown up to attend school in the city of La Plata. The transition from familial life to life alone in an unfamiliar urban area was a disturbing one for the future writer, and Sábato found order in his otherwise turbulent world in the study of mathematics. His academic studies were briefly interrupted for a five-year period, however, when he became involved in the Argentine communist movement. Soon, upon learning of Stalinist atrocities, he lost faith in the communist cause and decided to retreat again to his academic work.

Sábato's success as a student earned him a research fellowship for study in Paris, and, while there his interest in writing was born. Deeply impressed by the surrealist movement, he secretly began writing a novel. Although his writing started to play an increasingly important role in his life, Sábato continued his scientific research and accepted a teaching position upon his return to Argentina. Nonetheless, his literary efforts continued and he became a regular contributor to the popular Argentine magazine *Sur.* Teaching was to remain his livelihood until 1943 when a conflict with the Juan Peron government resulted in his dismissal from his posts.

Commenting on his departure from the scientific world, Sábato wrote in an autobiographical essay appearing in English translation in *Salmagundi,* "The open, public transition from physics to literature was not an easy one for me; on the contrary, it was painfully complicated. I wrestled with my demons a long time before I came to a decision in 1943—when I resolved to sequester myself, with wife and son, in a cabin in the sierras of Cordoba, far from the civilized world. It was not a rational decision. . . . But in crucial moments of my existence I have always trusted more in instinct than in ideas and have constantly been tempted to venture where reasonable people fear to tread."

While living in the cabin for a year Sábato wrote an award-winning book of essays, *Uno y el universo,* in which he condemned the moral neutrality of science. Three years later his first novel, *The Tunnel,* appeared. Profoundly influenced by psychological thought and existential in tone, the work evoked comparison to the writings of French authors Albert Camus and Jean-Paul Sartre. It is the story of an Argentine painter who recounts the events leading up to his murder of his mistress. As an exercise in self-analysis for the lonely painter, unable to communicate his thoughts and feelings, *The Tunnel* contains many of the themes found in Sabato's later work. "The almost total isolation of a man in a world dominated by science and reason," notes Oberhelman, "is the most important of these themes, but at the same time the reader sees the inability of man to communicate with others, an almost pathological obsession with blindness, and a great concern for Oedipal involvement as important secondary themes."

The landmark of Sábato's work is his 1961 novel, *On Heroes and Tombs,* which appeared in an English edition in 1981. It tells the story of Martin del Castillo and his love for Alejandra Vidal Olmos. Alejandra's father, Fernando Vidal Olmos, apparently involved in an incestuous relationship with his daughter, is another important figure in the book, along with Bruno Bassan, a childhood friend of Fernando. The work is lengthy and complex and has spawned numerous critical interpretations. "When it first appeared . . . ," wrote *Newsweek* contributor Jim Miller, "Ernesto Sábato's Argentine epic was widely praised. This belated translation finally lets Americans see why. Bewitched, baroque, monumental, his novel is a stunning symphony of dissonant themes—a Gothic dirge, a hymn to hope, a tango in hell." Commenting on the novel's intricacy, John Butt observed in the *Times Literary Supplement,* "This monster novel . . . works on so many levels, leads down so many strange paths to worlds of madness, surrealistic self-analysis and self-repudiation, and overloads language so magnificently and outrageously, that the reader comes out of it with his critical nerve shot, tempted to judge it as 'great' without knowing why." Also noting the novel's multifaceted contents, Ronald Christ in his *Commonweal* review refers to it as "wild, hypnotizing, and disturbing."

On Heroes and Tombs is divided into four parts, the third being a novel-within-a-novel called "Report on the Blind." *Review* contributor William Kennedy characterized this portion of the novel—a first-person exploration of Fernando's theories about a conspiracy of blind people who rule the world—as "a tour de force, a document which is brilliant in its excesses, a surreal journey into the depths of Fernando's personal, Boschian hells, which in their ultimate landscapes are the provinces of a 'terrible nocturnal divinity, a demoniacal specter that surely held supreme power over life and death.'" In his *Washington Post Book World* review Salman Rushdie calls this section "the book's magnificent high point and its metaphysical heart." In Sabato's hands Fernando's paranoidal ravings fuse with the rest of the novel making the work at once a cultural, philosophical, theological, and sociological study of man and his struggle with the dark side of his being. According to Oberhelman, *On Heroes and Tombs* "without a doubt is the most representative national novel of Argentina written in the twentieth century." Kennedy described the impact of the work when he concludes: "We read Sábato and we shudder, we are endlessly surprised, we exult, we are bewildered, fearful, mesmerized. He is a writer of great talent and imagination."

Sábato's third novel, *Abbadon, el Exterminador,* was published in Spanish in 1974 and in English translation as *The Angel of Darkness* in 1991. The novel's structure is circular, with the beginning of the novel corresponding to the end of the story in chronological terms. The original Spanish title refers to a character in the Book of Revelation, and the story revolves around a writer named Ernesto Sábato who becomes a four-foot-tall bat and who may or may not be the "angel of darkness" of the title. The plot is filled with nightmarish events, political intrigue, and "a huge cast of eccentric characters from every walk of Argentine life," noted Allen Josephs in the *New York Times Book Review.* Critics note that readers unfamiliar with Sábato's previous novels will have difficulty understanding the plot, since many of the characters from the two earlier novels reappear here. Writing in the *Times Literary Supplement,* John Butt remarked that *The Angel of Darkness* is "a magnificent, haunting, often horrifying novel whose every page confronts us with some paradox central to our condition." Butt also averred that the novel is "easily as impressive" as Sabato's earlier masterpiece, *On Heroes and Tombs.* While *Spectator* reviewer Cressida Connolly feels that "Sabato's failings are all flaws of excess" and that "the vast surfeit of story strands makes the plot unmanageably bulky," she also reserves high praise for the novel by comparing it to a painting by Francis Bacon: "You may recoil at the image, but you could not fail to be awed by the technique, and you recognise at once that its true subject is the human condition." Josephs explains that "Not everyone will want to wrestle with this intransigent angel of a book, but the undaunted will encounter a truly hellish match." And Butt concluded that *The Angel of Darkness* is "a masterpiece of bitter and sophisticated irony."

In addition to his award-winning novels, Sabato has also produced numerous essay collections. Although most of these have not been translated into English, one that has is *The Writer in the Catastrophe of Our Time.* The forty essays in this collection focus on art, writing, and philosophy, revealing Sabato's continual preoccupation with the meaning and impact of artistic pursuits.

BIOGRAPHICAL AND CRITICAL SOURCES:

BOOKS

Contemporary Literary Criticism, Thomson Gale (Detroit, MI), Volume 10, 1979, Volume 23, 1983.
Dictionary of Literary Biography, Volume 145: *Modern Latin-American Fiction Writers, Second Series,* Thomson Gale (Detroit, MI), 1994.
Hispanic Writers, Thomson Gale (Detroit, MI), 1991.
Oberhelman, Harley Dean, *Ernesto Sábato,* Twayne, 1970.
Rodriguez Monegal, Emir, *The Borzoi Anthology of Latin American Literature,* Knopf, 1986.

PERIODICALS

Americas, January-February 1991, pp. 14-19.
Commonweal, June 18, 1982.

Hispanofila, September, 1991.
Library Journal, July, 1990, p. 97.
London Review of Books, January 27, 1994, p. 23.
Modern Fiction Studies, autumn, 1986.
Newsweek, September 21, 1981.
New York Times Book Review, August 28, 1988; December 29, 1991, p. 13.
Publishers Weekly, June 15, 1990, p. 64; August 9, 1991.
Review, May-August, 1981.
Review of Contemporary Fiction, fall, 1990, p. 226.
Salmagundi, spring-summer, 1989.
Spectator, August 1990, pp. 4-9.
Times Literary Supplement, August 13, 1982; May 29, 1992, p. 22.
UNESCO Courier, June 18, 1982.
Washington Post Book World, August 16, 1981.

ONLINE

Easy Buenos Aires City Web site, http://www.easybuenosairescity.com/ (August 10, 2004), biography of Ernesto Sábato.
Literatura.org Web site, http://www.literatura.org/ (August 10, 2004), biography of Ernesto Sabato.
Modern World Web site, http://www.themodernworld.com/ (August 10, 2004), Milan M. Cirkovic "Borges: Influences and References."
ZNet Web site, http://www.zmag.org/ (August 10, 2004), "Manu Chao, Jose Saramago, Ernesto Sábato on Indigenous Counter-Reform."

* * *

SABATO, Ernesto R.
See SABATO, Ernesto

* * *

SACCO, Joe 1960-

PERSONAL: Born 1960, in Malta; immigrated to United States. *Education:* University of Oregon, B.A., 1981.

ADDRESSES: *Home*—Queens, NY. *Agent*—Author Mail, c/o Fantagraphics Books, 7563 Lake City Way NE, Seattle, WA 98115.

CAREER: Artist and writer. Artwork exhibited in galleries, including University of Buffalo Art Gallery. Comics coeditor, *Portland Permanent Press,* 1985-86.

AWARDS, HONORS: Harvey Award, Small Publishers Expo, and American Book Award, both 1996, both for *Palestine;* nominations for two Ignatz Awards, Small Publishers Expo, 1998.

WRITINGS:

NONFICTION COMIC BOOKS

Yahoo, Fantagraphics (Seattle, WA), 1994.
War Junkie, Fantagraphics (Seattle, WA), 1995.
Palestine, (originally published as a nine-issue comics series, 1993-1996), Volume 1: *A Nation Occupied,* Volume 2: *In the Gaza Strip,* Fantagraphics (Seattle, WA), 1996.
(Contributing illustrator) Harvey Pekar, *American Splendor on the Job,* Dark Horse (Portland, OR), 1997.
Safe Area Gorazde: The War in Eastern Bosnia, 1992-1995, introduction by Christopher Hitchens, Fantagraphics (Seattle, WA), 2000.
The Fixer: A Story from Sarajevo, Drawn and Quarterly (San Francisco, CA), 2003.
Notes from a Defeatist, Fantagraphics (Seattle, WA), 2003.

OTHER

(Illustrator) Priscilla Murolo, *From the Folks Who Brought You the Weekend: A Short, Illustrated History of Labor in the United States,* New Press (New York, NY), 2001.
(Author of introduction) Eric Drooker, *Blood Song: A Silent Ballad,* Harcourt (San Diego, CA), 2002.

Also wrote *Centrifugal Bumble Puppy* and *Spotlight on the Genius That Is Joe Sacco.*

Artist and author of comic strip "Painfully Portland," *Willamette Week.* Contributor to periodicals, including *Buzzard, Comics Journal, Drawn and Quarterly, Prime Cuts,* and *Real Stuff.* Work represented in anthologies, including *Zero Zero,* Fantagraphics, 1997.

SIDELIGHTS: Joe Sacco is an artist and writer who describes himself in *Time* as "a really good cartoonist who does journalism." Sacco was born in Malta in 1960, and he spent much of his childhood in Australia before arriving in the United States. He studied journalism at the University of Oregon, and after graduating in 1981 held editorial positions in Los Angeles and Portland and worked on a comic book titled *Centrifugal Bumble Puppy.* In the late 1980s he accompanied a rock band on a tour of Europe, and after the tour ended he settled in Germany. Around this time, he began producing *Yahoo,* a comic book described by Richard Gehr in a *Voice Literary Supplement* article as "refreshingly weird." Sacco's work in *Yahoo* includes "In the Company of Long Hair," an account of his rock tour of Europe, and "When Good Bombs Happen to Bad People," a tale of air strikes. "In a cold, cruel world," wrote Gehr, "Sacco's brain turns out to be one of the most frightened and frustrated places around." *War Junkie,* another of Sacco's early books, won him recognition in *Publishers Weekly* as an artist and writer whose "graphic inventiveness and storytelling ability are always vivid and hilariously candid."

Sacco eventually returned briefly to the United States, then headed back to Germany before traveling to the Middle East, where he studied the plight of Palestinians living in the Gaza Strip. "I went there specifically to write comic books about it," he told Kathleen E. Bennett in an article in *Drizzle.* "I went there specifically to do interviews and just do this whole journalistic thing."

Palestine is a two-volume account of Sacco's experiences in the West Bank and the Gaza Strip. Assessing the first volume, *A Nation Occupied,* Heidi Olmack wrote in the *Utne Reader,* "Sacco uses the comic book format to its fullest extent." She called the book "a frantic scrapbook of snapshots, newspaper stories, history briefings, and high-action drama." Another reviewer, Tom Crippen, wrote in the *Voice Literary Supplement* that Sacco's work possesses the "immediacy and visual energy of a movie," and added that "he's excellent at composition and layout." Dick Doughty, assessing both *A Nation Occupied* and *In the Gaza Strip,* declared in the *Journal of Palestine Studies* that "Sacco has penned a vivid and substantial pair of books." Gordon Flagg in *Booklist* praised the creator of *In the Gaza Strip* as "a top-rank talent who has staked out a unique place for himself in the comics world." Ty Burr, meanwhile, wrote in *Entertainment Weekly* that "Sacco's realistic cartooning style fits the story," and a *Publishers Weekly* critic affirmed that Sacco "has produced a fascinating . . . account as impressive for its idiosyncratic personal tone as for its scrupulous documentation."

After working in the Middle East, Sacco traveled to Bosnia, the center of a multi-faction conflict involving Serbs, Croats, and Muslims. "I spent a lot of time sitting in cafes and bars talking," he recalled for Chris Hedges in the *New York Times.* "It's not high-powered. If people talk about rock music, I talk about rock music. I am interested in what people care about, what they think about, and this gives me an ability to enter the world they live in."

Sacco's experiences in Bosnia inspired *Safe Area Gorazde: The War in Eastern Bosnia, 1992-1995,* which includes recollections of genocidal atrocities committed by Serb nationalists. Joel Stein, reviewing the book in *Time,* said that "though Sacco hasn't made the logistics of the conflict much easier to comprehend, his detailed, personal reporting does show how nationalism can lead once friendly neighbors to burn one another's houses." A *Publishers Weekly* critic proclaimed the book "an extraordinary work of both journalism and comics nonfiction," and added that it is "almost overwhelming." Another critic, Gordon Flagg, wrote in *Booklist* of the work's "undeniable power," and Claude Lalumière wrote in *January* that the book "delivers . . . a perspective and texture no other journalistic form could have captured." Lalumière added, "Sacco's powerful book is a moving plea for us all to stop behaving like psychopathic idiots."

The Fixer: A Story from Sarajevo, published in 2003, revisits the Balkan theme. The story's "fixer" is Neven, "one who, for cash, leads foreign journalists through the fragmented postwar landscape and sniffs out the grittiest 'underground' news stories for them," noted Emily Lloyd in *School Library Journal.* In an interview with Calvin Reid for *Publishers Weekly* Sacco explained that "using [Neven] allowed me to tell the story of how journalists often have to rely on totally uncreditable people who have their own agendas." "In his way he took me under his wing, and I appreciated that because he was a tough guy and I was a little afraid when I was there. It was good to be around this guy because it felt like his street credibility was rubbing off on me on some level. It wasn't until later that I learned he didn't have street credibility with everyone," Sacco added in an interview with Kristine McKenna in *LA Weekly.* "His art combines detailed, realistic background with somewhat more cartoony figures," Steve Raiteri observed in *Library Journal.* Gordon Flagg, in *Booklist,* found that "Sacco's mastery of the comics medium allows him to present a story as detailed as any print journalism and more expressive than the most adept film documentary."

Sacco's work has been exhibited in various galleries and institutions, including the University of Buffalo. Patricia Donovan, in the *University of Buffalo Reporter,* acknowledged that Sacco "is considered one of the absolute cream of the crop of alternative and underground cartoonists," and a writer for the *University of Buffalo Art Gallery* noted that Sacco's works "address the complexities of life . . . and record voices from the margins as an act of present-tense history-making."

"I take lots of photos for reference; otherwise I do what any reporter does," said Sacco describing his technique for Flagg of *Booklist.* "I do lots of interviews; I keep a journal and look for stories. When I return home I index my notes, write the story and begin to draw. I don't draw much in the field, maybe some sketches. In the field it's about getting to know people." In *LA Weekly* Kristine McKenna asked Sacco about his influences. He said: "Robert Crumb and Brueghel the Elder—he's a big influence on me. I love the solidity of the people in his paintings, and his work provides a window into daily life in Flanders during the 16th century in a way the Italian Renaissance simply doesn't. When I first got to Gorazde, it looked like the Middle Ages because there were hardly any cars running and the electricity was mostly off, and I thought, 'Wow! I can draw just like Brueghel!' I really got into drawing people doing things like chopping wood."

BIOGRAPHICAL AND CRITICAL SOURCES:

PERIODICALS

Booklist, January 1, 1996, Gordon Flagg, review of *Palestine,* Volume 2: *In the Gaza Strip,* p. 775; June 1, 2000, Gordon Flagg, review of *Safe Area Gorazde: The War in Eastern Bosnia, 1992-1995;* February 1, 2003, Gordon Flagg, review of *Notes from a Defeatist,* p. 969; December 15, 2003, Gordon Flagg, review of *The Fixer: A Story from Sarajevo,* p. 735

Entertainment Weekly, October 7, 1994, Ty Burr, review of *Palestine,* Volume 1: *A Nation Occupied,* p. 71.

Journal of Palestine Studies, winter, 1998, Dick Doughty, reviews of *Palestine,* Volumes 1 and 2.

LA Weekly, January 2-8, 2004, "Brueghel in Bosnia, Kristine McKenna Talks with Graphic Journalist Joe Sacco."

Library Journal, March 1, 2004, Steve Raiteri, review of *The Fixer: A Story from Sarajevo.*

New York Times, June 1, 1997, Chris Hedges, "A Cartoonist Sketches the Outline of Bosnia's Path," p. 4.

Publishers Weekly, August 29, 1994, review of *Palestine,* Volume 1, p. 71; June 12, 1995, review of *War Junkie,* p. 58; June 12, 2000, review of *Safe Area Gorazde,* p. 60; November 24, "*PW* Talks with Joe Sacco," interview with Calvin Reid, p. 56.

School Library Journal, May, 2004, Emily Lloyd, review of *The Fixer: A Story from Sarajevo,* p. 178.

Time, May 1, 2000, Joel Stein, "What's Going On?"

Utne Reader, March-April, 1995, Heidi Olmack, review of *Palestine,* Volume 1, p. 111.

Voice Literary Supplement, Richard Gehr, "But Enough about You . . . ," pp. 28-29; October, 1995, Tom Crippen, review of *Palestine,* Volume 1, p. 12.

ONLINE

Drizzle, http://www.drizzle.com/ (December 1, 2001), Kathleen E. Bennett, "Joe Sacco's Palestine: Where Comics Meets Journalism."

January, http:/ www.januarymagazine.com/ (September, 2000), Claude Lalumière, "The Not-So-Comic Question of Ethnic Nationalism."

Lambiek, http://www.lambiek.net/ (December 3, 2001).

University of Buffalo Art Gallery, http://ubartgalleries.buffalo.edu/ (August 28, 2004).

University of Buffalo Reporter, http://www.buffalo.edu/reporter/ (January 28, 1999), Patricia Donovan, "Into the 'Comix' Netherworld."

* * *

SACKS, Oliver 1933-
(Oliver Wolf Sacks)

PERSONAL: Born July 9, 1933, in London, England; immigrated to the United States, 1960; British citizen; son of Samuel (a physician) and Muriel Elsie (a physician; maiden name, Landau) Sacks. *Education:* Queen's College, Oxford, B.A., 1954, M.A., B.M., and B.Ch., all 1958; residencies at University of California, San Francisco and University of California, Los Angeles, 1961-65. *Hobbies and other interests:* Swimming, scuba diving, cycling, mountaineering.

ADDRESSES: Office—2 Horatio Street, Apt. 3G, New York, NY 10014-1638. *Agent*—The Wylie Agency, 250 West 57th St., New York, NY 10107.

CAREER: Middlesex Hospital, London, England, intern in medicine, surgery, and neurology, 1958-60; Mt. Zion Hospital, San Francisco, CA, rotating intern, 1961-62; University of California, Los Angeles, resident in neurology, 1962-65; Yeshiva University, Albert Einstein College of Medicine, Bronx, NY, fellow in neurochemistry and neuropathology, 1965-66, instructor, 1966-75, assistant professor, 1975-78, associate professor, 1978-

85, clinical professor of neurology, 1985; Beth Abraham Hospital, Bronx, staff neurologist, 1966—. University of California, Santa Cruz, Cowell College, visiting professor, 1987. Consultant neurologist at Bronx Psychiatric Center, 1966-1991, and at Little Sisters of the Poor, New York City; adjunct Professor of Psychiatry, New York University Medical Center, 1992—.

MEMBER: American Academy of Neurology (fellow), American Neurological Association, American Academy of Arts and Letters, New York State Medical Society, New York Institute for the Humanities, Alpha Omega Alpha, British Pteridological Society.

AWARDS, HONORS: Hawthornden Prize, 1974, for *Awakenings;* Oskar Pfister Award, American Psychiatric Association, 1988; Guggenheim fellowship, 1989; Harold D. Vursell Memorial Award, American Academy and Institute of Arts and Letters, 1989; Guggenheim fellowship, 1989; Odd Fellows book award, 1991; D.H. L., Georgetown University, 1990, and College of Staten Island, City University of New York, 1991; honorary D.S., Tufts University and New York Medical College, both 1991; Scriptor Award, University of Southern California, 1991; Professional Support Award, National Headache Foundation, 1991; presidential citation, American Academy of Neurology, 1991; presidential award, American Neurological Association, 1991; Prix Psyche, 1991; honorary D.M.S., Medical College of Pennsylvania, 1992; honorary D.S., Bard College, 1992; George S. Polk Award for magazine reporting, 1994; *Esquire*/Apple/Waterstone's Book of the Year Award, 1995; Mainichi Publishing Culture Award, 1996.

WRITINGS:

Migraine, University of California Press (Berkeley, CA), 1970, revised and enlarged edition, Vintage (New York, NY), 1992.

Awakenings, Duckworth (London, England), 1973, Doubleday (New York, NY), 1974, published with a new foreword by the author, Summit Books (New York, NY), 1987.

A Leg to Stand On, Summit Books (New York, NY), 1984, revised edition, Touchstone (New York, NY), 1992.

The Man Who Mistook His Wife for a Hat, and Other Clinical Tales, Duckworth (London, England), 1985, Summit Books (New York, NY), 1986.

Seeing Voices: A Journey into the World of the Deaf, University of California Press (Berkeley, CA), 1989, new revised edition, Picador (London, England), 1991.

An Anthropologist on Mars: Seven Paradoxical Tales, Knopf (New York, NY), 1995.

The Island of the Colorblind; and Cycad Island, Knopf (New York, NY), 1997.

Uncle Tungsten: Memories of a Chemical Boyhood, Knopf (New York, NY), 2001.

Vintage Sacks, Vintage (New York, NY), 2001.

Oaxaca Journal, National Geographic (Washington, DC), 2002.

Contributor to books, including *Hidden Histories of Science,* edited by Robert B. Silvers, New York Review of Books, 1996; and Wim Kayzer, *A Glorious Accident: Understanding Our Place in the Cosmic Puzzle,* W.H. Freeman (New York, NY), 1997. Contributor to *New York Review of Books, New Yorker, Discover, New York Times,* and other periodicals and various journals.

ADAPTATIONS: Harold Pinter's play *A Kind of Alaska* is based on one of the case histories from *Awakenings; Awakenings* was adapted into a movie with the same title, starring Robin Williams and Robert De Niro, and directed by Penny Marshall, 1990; the title case study from *The Man Who Mistook His Wife for a Hat, and Other Clinical Tales* was adapted into an opera with the same title by Michael Nyman and into the play *The Man Who. . .* by Peter Brook; a case history from *An Anthropologist on Mars: Seven Paradoxical Tales* served as inspiration for the play *Molly Sweeney* by Brian Friel, and the 1999 movie *At First Sight.*

SIDELIGHTS: Oliver Sacks, among the best-known and most highly respected neurologists working in the United States, made a name for himself among his peers in the field of neurology with his work with post-encephalitic patients in a hospitals in the Bronx, New York, during the late 1960s. He gained a wider audience with the publication of *The Man Who Mistook his Wife for a Hat* in 1985. Sacks' autobiography, *Uncle Tungsten: Memories of a Chemical Boyhood,* reveals a great deal about the family traditions that formed the physician/author's passion for science in its many forms. As John Gross wrote in the *Spectator,* "There were broader scientific traditions in the family" and "as his own interest in science flowered he could rely on the encouragement of a formidable family support system." Sack's Uncle Dave, the most important of these inventors, ran a firm that made light bulbs with filaments of tungsten wire. "Sacks has consistently offered us fascinating, intense, thoughtful chronicles of the uncanny worlds of his neurological patients—a kind of *Ripley's Believe It or Not* for the intellectual and artistic set," as Wendy Lesser observed in the *New York*

Times Book Review. "In books like *Awakenings, An Anthropologist on Mars,* and *The Man Who Mistook His Wife for a Hat* he has explored the terrain where physical and mental ailments blur into spiritual quandaries, moral inquiries and exemplary tales about the infinite variety and adaptability of the human organism. Oliver Sacks has become our modern master of the case study, an artistic form whose antecedents lie in the scientific work of practitioners like A.R. Luria and Sigmund Freud." Sacks's work has also reached other audiences through adaptations for the stage and screen. Three of his case histories have been made into plays, one into an opera, and *Awakenings* was the subject of a major motion picture starring Robin Williams and Robert De Niro.

In his book *Migraine,* first published in 1970 and later updated and enlarged for publication in 1985 and 1992, Sacks examines a condition known to mankind for thousands of years. As Sacks points out, though it is a common affliction, the migraine is little understood, its symptoms varying widely from one person to the next. Headache is but one of many symptoms that may include convulsions, vomiting, depression, and visual hallucinations. Drawing upon his observation of numerous patients, Sacks focuses not on cures but on an explanation of the function migraine serves for its human sufferers and an insistence on treating an illness in the contest of an individual's whole life.

Migraine attracted a varied readership. Writing in the *New York Times,* Michiko Kakutani found that Sacks' "commentary is so erudite, so gracefully written, that even those people fortunate enough to never have had a migraine in their lives should find it equally compelling." Israel Rosenfield maintained in the *New York Times Review of Books* that the work "should be read as much for its brilliant insights into the nature of our mental functioning as for its discussion of migraine."

Upon his arrival at Beth Abraham Hospital in the late 1960s, Sacks discovered a group of patients suffering from a range of debilitating symptoms, the worst of which was a "sleep" so deep the sufferer was beyond arousal. The patients, he learned, were survivors of a sleeping sickness epidemic that had occurred between 1916 and 1927. In his second book, *Awakenings,* Sacks tells of his attempts to help this group. Recognizing the similarities between the symptoms exhibited by his patients and those of sufferers of Parkinson's disease, Sacks decided to begin administering L-dopa, a drug proven effective in treating Parkinson's disease. L-dopa initially produced dramatic results; patients out of touch with the world for over four decades suddenly emerged from their sleep. Sacks discovered, however, that the drug was not a miracle cure. Side-effects and the shock of waking an unchanged person in a changed world proved too much for some in the group. Some others withdrew into trance-like states; others succeeded, but only by achieving a balance between the illness and the cure, the past and the present.

Sacks's portrayal of the complexities of this episode earned him considerable praise from readers of *Awakenings.* "Well versed in poetry and metaphysics, [Sacks] writes from the great tradition of Sir Thomas Browne," noted *Newsweek* reviewer Peter S. Prescott, "probing through medicine and his own observations of fear, suffering and total disability toward an investigation of what it means not only to be, but to become a person." "Some would attribute this achievement to narrative skill, others to clinical insight," commented Gerald Weissman in the *Washington Post;* "I would rather call this feat of empathy a work of art."

A Leg to Stand On is a doctor's memoir of his own experience as a patient. As Jerome Bruner explained in the *New York Review of Books,* Sacks's book "is about a horribly injured leg, his own, what he thought and learned while living through the terrors and raptures of recovering its function." In 1976 while mountaineering in Scandinavia, Sacks fell and twisted his left knee. Although surgery repaired the physical damage—torn ligaments and tendons—the leg remained immobile. Sacks found he had lost his inner sense of the leg; it seemed to him detached and alien, not his own. His inability to recover disturbed him, and the surgeon's dismissal of his concerns only heightened his anxiety.

In his bestselling collection of case histories titled *The Man Who Mistook His Wife for a Hat,* "Sacks tells some two dozen stories about people who are also patients, and who manifest strange and striking peculiarities of perception, emotion, language, thought, memory or action," observed John C. Marshall in the *New York Times Book Review.* "And he recounts these histories with the lucidity and power of a short-story writer." One of the case histories Sacks presents is that of an instructor of music who suffers from a visual disorder. While able to see the component parts of objects, he is unable to perceive the whole they compose. Leaving Sacks's office after a visit, this patient turns to grab his hat and instead grabs his wife's face. Another history features two autistic twins unable to add or subtract but capable of determining the day of the week for any date past or present and of calculating twenty-digit prime numbers.

"Blessed with deep reserves of compassion and a metaphysical turn of mind," commented Kakutani, "Sacks writes of these patients not as scientific curiosities but as individuals, whose dilemmas—moral and spiritual, as well as psychological—are made as completely real as those of characters in a novel."

As it demonstrates the variety of abnormal conditions that can arise from damage to the brain, *The Man Who Mistook His Wife for a Hat* also touches larger themes. *Nation* contributor Brina Caplan was impressed by the book's portrayal of "men and women [who] struggle individually with a common problem: how to reconcile being both a faulty mechanism and a thematic, complex and enduring self." As Walter Clemmons suggested in *Newsweek,* "Sacks's humane essays on these strange cases are deeply stirring, because each of them touches on our own fragile 'normal' identities and taken-for-granted abilities of memory, attention, and concentration."

Seeing Voices: A Journey into the World of the Deaf is a departure from Sacks's case studies of neurological disorders. Yet, as in his other works, in this exploration of deafness and the deaf Sacks continues to challenge readers' assumptions of what is normal. As Simon J. Carmel explained in *Natural History,* "When Sacks started to read books on the deaf, he was so enraptured that he began a journey into their silent world." The result is a book in three parts. In the first part, Sacks outlines the history of the deaf. As he points out, prior to the mid-1700s, those who were born deaf were generally considered uneducable and were neglected. Then the French Abbe Charles-Michel de l'Epée shattered these assumptions. He learned the sign language of some of the deaf in Paris and adapted it to teach the deaf to read. His school for the deaf, which opened in 1755, trained teachers who spread deaf education throughout Europe and America. During the years since, two approaches to deaf education have persisted. The focus of education in oralist schools is on teaching deaf students to speak, lip read, and to use signed English. The focus of Sign schools—those using American Sign Language, or ASL—is on helping deaf students to learn Sign as a native language and use it to learn other things. The remaining two parts of the book, noted Prescott, are "an examination (and celebration) of the complexity and richness of Sign, the true language of the deaf; and an account of [the March 1988] uprising at Gallaudet University, which for the first time placed a deaf president in charge."

Even with such reservations like those expressed by Paul West that Sacks overuses footnotes, *Seeing Voices* challenges the assumptions of the hearing. As West puts it in the *New York Times Book Review,* "Sacks, whose heart is in the right place, wants the deaf to have all they need, but most of all, their own natural and private language. He brings afresh to our attention a problem that is never easily going to be solved." Carmel concluded, "Above all, I must admit that Sacks's book is most informative and stimulating, and I must praise his intense research and crystal-clear understanding of the deaf world. So I strongly recommend that his book be read by those individuals who want a better understanding of the cultural, educational, historical, linguistic, psychological, and sociological discipline of deafness."

Sacks returns to his examination of how people cope with neurological disorders in *An Anthropologist on Mars: Seven Paradoxical Tales.* In these seven case histories Sacks again probes what it means to be normal through the lives of people who seem anything but normal. He includes the story of a painter who has lost the ability to see anything but black and white, a surgeon with Tourette's syndrome, an autistic boy who has an uncanny gift for drawing, an autistic Ph.D. who is the world's greatest authority on cattle behavior, and a man who has regained his eyesight after decades of blindness. With each, Sacks shows the balance of science and humanity that characterizes all of his writing. Ethan Canin observed this quality in the *Washington Post Book World:* "Sacks possesses the physician's love for classification and logical dissection, but once again we see that he is also blessed with the humanist's wonder at character and grace, at the ineffable sadness and wondrous joy of art." In Lesser's opinion, *An Anthropologist on Mars* is "Sacks's best book to date because it very self-consciously explores both the physician's and the patients' peculiar ways of thinking."

In *The Island of the Colorblind and Cycad Island,* Sacks continues his skillful blend of clinical expertise and storytelling, and explores the inner realm of people on Pingelap, a remote Micronesian island, where one in every twelve people is born with total hereditary colorblindness. At first, Sacks noted, "I had vision, only half fantastic, of an entire achromatopic culture with its own singular tastes, arts, cooking, and clothing. . . . Would they, perhaps, lacking any sense of something missing, have a world no less dense and vibrant than our own?"

Traveling with Dr. Knut Nordby, a colorblind Norwegian scientist, Sacks finds that the islanders' culture is not as affected by colorblindness as he had believed, perhaps because most islanders have normal vision. However, the affected islanders become fascinated by Dr. Nordby, who reassures them that they are not alone in the world. As D.M. Thomas suggested in the *New York Times Book Review,* the book is "an ordinary—if well-written—travel essay," but he also noted that one of Sacks's gifts as a writer is "the ability to show how patients who are truly isolated and insulated by a disease can still retain their humanity, their dignity."

"Cycad Island," the second essay in the book, is an exploration of a mysterious disease on Guam, a progressive paralysis with a mysterious cause that has not affected islanders born after the 1950s. One suspect was the cycad tree; in the past, the islanders used its seeds, which are toxic, for food. The book becomes a meditation on the palmlike tree, which has fascinated Sacks since his childhood, when it represented a distant realm of peace and the Eden of his dreams. Guam, however, is no Eden, but an ecological disaster, ruined by nuclear testing, deforestation, and other predations from the outside world. Christopher Lehmann-Haupt, in the *New York Times Book Review,* commented that Sacks's "human inquisitiveness lends a philosophical perspective to every threatening change. . . . And the way his subjects accept their fate redeems his story from gloom, even lending it a certain gaiety."

In addition to being compelling reading, Sacks's writing also serves a larger purpose. "What he's arguing for is a set of neglected values: empathetic, emotional, individual, storylike," noted Caplan. "To ignore those values, he suggests, means constructing a science of cold, rigid design." As Paul Baumann in *Commonweal* summed it up, "Sacks's larger ambition is to develop what he calls an 'existential neurology' or 'romantic science' that will shed the rigid computational paradigms of traditional neurology and open itself up to the dynamic 'powers' of the mind."

BIOGRAPHICAL AND CRITICAL SOURCES:

BOOKS

Contemporary Literary Criticism, Volume 67, Thomson Gale (Detroit, MI), 1992, pp. 284-309.

PERIODICALS

Boston Globe, December 29, 1985, p. A13; March 24, 1986, p. 23; August 27, 1989, p. 87; November 12, 1989, p. M8; January 25, 1991, p. 29.

Chicago Tribune, August 20, 1989, sec. 14, p. 5; November 3, 1989, sec. 5, p. 1.

Commonweal, March 28, 1986; February 9, 1990, p. 88.

Globe and Mail (Toronto, Ontario, Canada), February 21, 1987.

Interview, October, 1989, p. 24.

Journal of the American Medical Association, July 8, 1988, p. 273; February 9, 1994, p. 478.

Library Journal, March 1, 1996, p. 48; January, 1997, p. 140; February 15, 1997, p. 176.

Los Angeles Times, March 18, 1986, p. 6; September 24, 1989, p. B7.

Los Angeles Times Book Review, March 23, 1986; September 6, 1987, p. 14; February 23, 1997, p. 4.

Nation, February 22, 1986, Brina Caplan review of *The Man Who Mistook His Wife for a Hat.*

Natural History, November, 1989, pp. 88-92, 94-95.

Newsweek, July 15, 1974; August 20, 1984; December 30, 1985; March 2, 1986; March 13, 1986; March 27, 1986; October 2, 1989, p. 72.

New York Review of Books, September 27, 1984; March 2, 1986; March 13, 1986; March 27, 1986; January 29, 1987, p. 39; March 28, 1991, p. 65; March 6, 1997, p. 15.

New York Times, May 24, 1984; June 19, 1985; January 25, 1986; September 30, 1989, p. A14; February 7, 1995, pp. C13, C18; February 14, 1995, p. C19; January 9, 1997, p. C18.

New York Times Book Review, July 7, 1985, Michiko Kakutani, review of *Migraine;* March 2, 1986, John C. Marshall review of *The Man Who Mistook His Wife for a Hat;* October 8, 1989, pp. 17-18; February 19, 1995, p. 1; December 3, 1995, p. 80; January 19, 1997, p. 7.

People, March 17, 1986; February 11, 1991, p. 91.

Publishers Weekly, January 1, 1996, p. 69; November 25, 1996, p. 63; December 2, 1996, p. 31.

Spectator, December 24, 2001, p. 30.

Time, March 20, 1995, pp. 68-70.

Times Literary Supplement, December 14, 1973; June 22, 1984; February 7, 1986.

Wall Street Journal, June 17, 1986, p. 26.

Washington Post, October 30, 1987; January 13, 1991, pp. F1, F6.

Washington Post Book World, August 26, 1984; February 16, 1986; September 10, 1989, p. 1; March 5, 1995, p. 2.

Yale Review, winter, 1988, p. 172.

* * *

SACKS, Oliver Wolf

See SACKS, Oliver

SAGAN, Carl 1934-1996
(Carl Edward Sagan)

PERSONAL: Born November 9, 1934, New York, NY; died of pneumonia, a complication of myelodysplasia (a bone marrow disease), December 19, 1996, in Seattle, WA; son of Samuel (a cloth cutter and, later, a factory manager) and Rachel (Gruber) Sagan; married Lynn Alexander (a scientist), June 16, 1957 (divorced, 1963); married Linda Salzman (a painter), April 6, 1968 (divorced); married Ann Druyan (a writer); children: (first marriage) Dorion Solomon, Jeremy Ethan; (second marriage) Nicholas; (third marriage) Alexandra, Rachel, Samuel Democritus. *Education:* University of Chicago, A.B. (with general and special honors), 1954, B.S., 1955, M.A., 1956, Ph.D., 1960.

CAREER: Scientist, author. University of California, Berkeley, Miller research fellow in astronomy, 1960-62; Harvard University, Cambridge, MA, 1962-68, assistant professor of astronomy; Smithsonian Institution, Astrophysical Observatory, Cambridge, MA, astrophysicist, 1962-68; Cornell University, Ithaca, NY, associate professor, 1968-70, professor of astronomy and space sciences, 1970-96, David Duncan Professor of Astronomy and Space Sciences, 1976-96, director of Laboratory for Planetary Studies, 1968-96, associate director of Center for Radiophysics and Space Research, 1972-81; visiting professor at many universities throughout the United States. President, Carl Sagan Productions, Inc. (television programming), 1981-96. President, Planetary Society, 1979-96. Fellow, Robotics Institute, Carnegie-Mellon University, 1982-96; Distinguished Visiting Scientist, Jet Propulsion Laboratory, California Institute of Technology, 1986-96. Member of Committee to Review Project Blue Book (U.S. Air Force), 1956-66. Experimenter, Mariner 2 mission to Venus, 1962, Mariner 9 and Viking missions to Mars, Voyager mission to the outer solar system, Galileo mission to Jupiter; designer of Pioneer 10 and 11 and Voyager 1 and 2 interstellar messages. Member of council, Smithsonian Institution, 1975-85; member, board of directors, Council for the Advancement of Science Writing, 1972-77; member, Usage Panel, American Heritage Dictionary of the English Language, 1976-96; member, Fellowship Panel, John S. Guggenheim Memorial Foundation, 1976-81; chair, Study Group on Machine Intelligence and Robotics, NASA, 1977-79; member, board of directors, Council for a Livable World Education Fund, 1980-96; member, board of advisors, Children's Health Fund, 1988-96; co-chair, Science, Global Forum of Spiritual and Parliamentary Leaders on Human Survival, 1988-96; member, International Board of Advisors, *Asahi Shimbun,* Tokyo, 1991-96; member, Advisory Council, National Institutes for the Environment, 1991-96; member, American Committee on U.S.-Soviet Relations, 1983-96. Judge, National Book Awards, 1975. Member of various advisory groups of National Aeronautics and Space Administration; consultant to National Academy of Science; member of advisory panel, Civil Space Station Study, Office of Technology Assessment, U.S. Congress, 1982-96.

MEMBER: American Academy of Arts and Sciences (fellow), Council on Foreign Relations, International Astronomical Union (member of organizing committee, Commission of Physical Study of Planets), International Council of Scientific Unions (vice chair, working group on moon and planets, committee on space research), International Academy of Astronautics, International Society for the Study of the Origin of Life (member of council, 1980-96), PEN International, American Astronomical Society (councillor; chair, division of planetary sciences, 1975-76), American Physical Society (fellow), American Geophysical Union (fellow; president, planetology section, 1980-82), American Association for the Advancement of Science (fellow; chair, astronomy section, 1975), American Institute of Aeronautics and Astronautics (fellow), American Astronautical Society (fellow; member of council, 1976-81), Federation of American Scientists (member of council, 1977-81, 1984-88; sponsor), Society for the Study of Evolution, British Interplanetary Society (fellow), Astronomical Society of the Pacific, Genetics Society of America, Authors Guild, Authors League of America, Writers Guild of America, American Federation of Television and Radio Artists (fellow), Phi Beta Kappa, Sigma Xi, Explorers Club.

AWARDS, HONORS: Alfred P. Sloan Foundation research fellowship at Harvard University, 1963-67; A. Calvert Smith Prize, Harvard University, 1964; National Aeronautics and Space Administration, Apollo Achievement Award, 1970; Prix Galabert (international astronautics prize), 1973; John W. Campbell Memorial Award, World Science Fiction Convention, 1974, for *The Cosmic Connection: An Extraterrestrial Perspective;* Pulitzer Prize for literature, 1978, for *The Dragons of Eden: Speculations on the Evolution of Human Intelligence; Cosmos* named among best books for young adults, American Library Association, 1980; Academy of Family Films and Family Television Award for Best Television Series of 1980, American Council for Better Broadcasts Citation for Highest Quality Television Programming of 1980-81, Silver Plaque from Chicago Film Festival, President's Special Award from Western Educational Society for Telecommunication, 1981,

George Foster Peabody Award for Excellence in Television Programming, University of Georgia, 1981, and Ohio State University annual award for television excellence, 1982, all for *Cosmos* television series; American Book Award nominations for *Cosmos* (hardcover) and *Broca's Brain: Reflections on the Romance of Science* (paperback), both 1981; Humanist of the Year Award, American Humanist Association, 1981; Hugo Award, World Science Fiction Convention, 1982, for the book *Cosmos;* John F. Kennedy Astronautics Award, American Astronautical Society, 1983; Locus Award, 1986, for *Contact;* Arthur C. Clarke Award for Exploration and Development of Space, 1984; Peter Lavan Award for Humanitarian Service, Bard College, 1984; New Priorities Award, Fund for New Priorities in America, 1984; Sidney Hillman Foundation Prize Award, for "outstanding contributions to world peace," 1984; SANE National Peace Award, 1984; Olive Branch Award, New York University, 1984, 1986, and 1989; Physicians for Social Responsibility Annual Award for Public Service, 1985; Leo Szilard Award for Physics in the Public Interest, with Richard P. Turco and others, for "the discovery of nuclear winter," American Physical Society, 1985; Nahum Goldmann Medal, "in recognition of distinguished service to the cause of peace and many accomplishments in science and public affairs," Word Jewish Congress, 1986; Brit HaDorot Award, Shalom Center, 1986; Annual Award of Merit, American Consulting Engineers Council, 1986; Maurice Eisendrath Award for Social Justice, Central Conference of American Rabbis and the Union of American Hebrew Congregations, 1987; Konstantin Tsiolkovsky Medal, Soviet Cosmonautics Federation, 1987; George F. Kennan Peace Award, SANE/Freeze, 1988; Helen Caldicott Peace Leadership Award, with Ann Druyan, Women's Action for Nuclear Disarmament, 1988; UCLA Medal, University of California at Los Angeles, 1991; Distinguished Leadership award, Nuclear Age Peace Foundation, 1993; First Carl Sagan Understanding of Science award, 1994; *Los Angeles Times* Award for Science and Technology, 1996, for *The Demon-Haunted World: Science as a Candle in the Dark.* Honorary degrees from many U.S. universities.

WRITINGS:

(With W.W. Kellogg) *The Atmospheres of Mars and Venus,* National Academy of Sciences (Washington, DC), 1961.

Organic Matter and the Moon, National Academy of Sciences (Washington, DC), 1961.

(With I.S. Shklovskii) *Intelligent Life in the Universe,* Holden-Day (San Francisco, CA), 1963.

(With Jonathan Norton Leonard) *Planets,* Time-Life Science Library (New York, NY), 1966.

Planetary Exploration: The Condon Lectures, University of Oregon Press (Eugene, OR), 1970.

(Editor, with Tobias C. Owen and Harlan J. Smith) *Planetary Atmospheres,* D. Reidel (New York, NY), 1971.

(Editor, with K.Y. Kondratyev and M. Rycroft) *Space Research XI,* two volumes, Akademie Verlag, 1971.

(With R. Littauer and others) *The Air War in Indochina,* Center for International Studies, Cornell University (Ithaca, NY), 1971.

(Editor, with Thorton Page) *UFOs: A Scientific Debate,* Cornell University Press (Ithaca, NY), 1972.

(Editor) *Soviet-American Conference on the Problems of Communication with Extraterrestrial Intelligence,* MIT Press (Cambridge, MA), 1973.

(Editor) *Communication with Extraterrestrial Intelligence,* MIT Press (Cambridge, MA), 1973.

(With Ray Bradbury, Arthur Clarke, Bruce Murray, and Walter Sullivan) *Mars and the Mind of Man,* Harper (New York, NY), 1973.

(With R. Berendzen, A. Montagu, P. Morrison, K. Stendhal, and G. Wald) *Life beyond Earth and the Mind of Man,* U.S. Government Printing Office (Washington, DC), 1973.

The Cosmic Connection: An Extraterrestrial Perspective (selection of several book clubs, including Library of Science Book Club and Natural History Book Club), Doubleday (New York, NY), 1973, new edition published as *Carl Sagan's Cosmic Connection: An Extraterrestrial Perspective,* with essays by Freeman Dyson, Ann Druyan, and David Morrison, Cambridge University Press (New York, NY), 2000.

Other Worlds, Bantam (New York, NY), 1975.

The Dragons of Eden: Speculations on the Evolution of Human Intelligence, Random House (New York, NY), 1977.

(With others) *Murmurs of Earth: The Voyager Interstellar Record,* Random House (New York, NY), 1978, commemorative edition with CD-ROM, Warner New Media, 1992.

Broca's Brain: Reflections on the Romance of Science, Random House (New York, NY), 1979.

Cosmos (also see below), Random House (New York, NY), 1980, new edition, 2002.

(With R. Garwin and others) *The Fallacy of Star Wars,* Vintage Books (New York, NY), 1984.

(With Paul R. Ehrlich, Donald Kennedy, and Walter Orr Roberts) *The Cold and the Dark,* Norton (New York, NY), 1984.

(With Ann Druyan) *Comet,* Random House (New York, NY), 1985, Ballantine Books (New York, NY), 1997.

Contact (novel), Random House (New York, NY), 1985.

(With Richard Turco) *A Path Where No Man Thought: Nuclear Winter and the End of the Arms Race,* Random House (New York, NY), 1989.

(With Ann Druyan) *Shadows of Forgotten Ancestors: A Search for Who We Are,* Random House (New York, NY), 1992.

Pale Blue Dot: A Vision of the Human Future in Space, Random House (New York, NY), 1994.

The Demon-Haunted World: Science as a Candle in the Dark, Random House (New York, NY), 1995.

Billions and Billions: Thoughts on Life and Death at the Brink of the Millennium, Random House (New York, NY), 1997.

Also author of *The Quest for Life Beyond the Earth.* Author of radio and television scripts, including (with Ann Druyan and Steven Soter) *Cosmos* series, Public Broadcasting System, 1980, and scripts for Voice of America, American Chemical Society radio series, and British Broadcasting Corp. Contributor to *Encyclopedia Americana, Encyclopaedia Britannica,* and *Whole Earth Catalog,* 1971. Contributor of more than 600 papers to scientific journals, and of articles to periodicals, including *National Geographic, Saturday Review, Discovery, Washington Post, Natural History, Scientific American,* and *New York Times. Icarus: International Journal of Solar System Studies,* associate editor, 1962-68, editor-in-chief, 1968-79; member of editorial board, *Origins of Life,* 1974-96, *Climatic Change,* 1976-96, and *Science,* 1979-96.

ADAPTATIONS: Planets has been adapted as a film. *Contact* was adapted as a film in 1997 starring Jodie Foster.

SIDELIGHTS: As one of the most widely known and outspoken scientists in America, Carl Sagan made both his living and a considerable reputation in astronomy, biology, physics, and the emerging science of exobiology, the study of extraterrestrial life. In his best-selling books, such as *The Dragons of Eden: Speculations on the Evolution of Human Intelligence* and *Broca's Brain: Reflections on the Romance of Science,* and in the extremely popular television series *Cosmos* (itself adapted into book form), Sagan, according to Frederic Golden of *Time,* "sends out an exuberant message: science is not only vital for humanity's future well-being, but it is rousing good fun as well."

The Cornell University-based scientist, who published his first research article ("Radiation and the Origin of the Gene") at age twenty-two, grew up in Brooklyn, New York, the son of an American-born mother and a Russian-immigrant father. Sagan described himself as a science-fiction addict from an early age who became hooked on astronomy after learning that each star in the evening sky represented a distant sun. He told Golden: "This just blew my mind. Until then the universe had been my neighborhood. Now I tried to imagine how far away I'd have to move the sun to make it as faint as a star. I got my first sense of the immensity of the universe." In a *New Yorker* interview, Sagan told Henry S.F. Cooper, Jr.: "I didn't make a decision to pursue astronomy; rather, it just grabbed me and I had no thought of escaping. But I didn't know that you could get paid for it. . . . Then, in my sophomore year in high school, my biology teacher . . . told me he was pretty sure Harvard paid [noted astronomer] Harold Shapley a salary. That was a splendid day—when I began to suspect that if I tried hard I could do astronomy full time, not just part time." At sixteen, Sagan entered the University of Chicago on a scholarship. As early as his undergraduate days, the student began earning a reputation as a maverick; according to Golden, Sagan organized a popular campus lecture series and included himself as one of the speakers. At the same time, he shunned traditional courses of study in favor of his own intellectual pursuits.

On leaving the University of Chicago with a Ph.D. in astronomy and astrophysics in 1960, Sagan began research at Harvard University where, with colleague James Pollack, he challenged standard scientific views on the periodic lightening and darkening surface of Mars. Sagan's theory—that the alternating shades of surface light were caused by wind storms—was confirmed several years later from the Mariner 9 Mars orbiter. Sagan's proposals regarding the Venus greenhouse effect, the organic haze on Titan, and other matters, while initially debated by scientists, have come to be accepted by the scientific community at large. Speculations of that type cemented Sagan's image as an iconoclast.

Sagan's writing career evolved along with his scientific career. In 1963 he became interested in a Russian book called *Intelligent Life in the Universe* and was given permission to work on its English translation. In the process Sagan added ten new chapters (more than doubling the original length of the book), thus becoming, according to Stuart Bauer in *New York,* "more than 60 per cent responsible for the first comprehensive treatment of the entire panorama of natural evolution, covering the origin of the universe, the evolution of the stars and planets, and the beginning of life on earth." (Bauer credits Sagan's expansion of the Russian original for the fact that *Intelligent Life in the Universe* has since gone into fourteen printings.) The scientist further distinguished himself as an expert in these fields in 1971, when, according to Bauer, "the *Encyclopaedia Britannica* invited [Sagan] to write its definitive 25,000-word essay on 'Life'; in 1973, in a manner of speaking, he took out a patent on it—U.S. Patent 3,756,934 for the production of amino acids from gaseous mixtures."

The Dragons of Eden, Sagan's first popular book to delve outside the study of astronomy, was published in 1977. Thereafter, it won the Pulitzer Prize for nonfiction in 1978. The book explored the history and evolution of human intelligence, explaining the current state of research in the field and speculating on what future researchers might discover. Robert Manning of *Atlantic Monthly* thought *The Dragons of Eden* to be "rational, elegant and witty" but warned that reading parts of it is "akin to climbing the Matterhorn without crampons or ice ax. One must pay attention to every crack and cranny." R.J. Herrnstein wrote in *Commentary* that although the author is "asking his readers to change their minds about almost nothing," he does so with "grace, humor and style." John Updike, on the other hand, found fault with the author's choice of subject matter. "Versatile though he is," Updike remarked in the *New Yorker,* "[Sagan] is simply not enough saturated in his subject to speculate; what he can do is summarize and, to a limited degree, correlate the results of scattered and tentative modern research on the human brain. . . . [His] speculations, where they are not cheerfully wild, seem tacked on and trivial."

The inspiration for Sagan's next work, *Broca's Brain,* came during a tour of the Musee de l'Homme in Paris, where he came upon a collection of jars containing human brains. Examining one of the jars, he found he was holding the brain of Paul Broca, a distinguished nineteenth-century anatomist. The idea for a book "flashed through his mind," according to Judy Klemsrud of the *New York Times Book Review. Broca's Brain,* a compilation of essays ranging in topic from ancient astronauts to mathematically-gifted horses, became another bestseller, prompting Sagan to tell Klemsrud that he believed "the public is a lot brighter and more interested in science than they're given credit for. . . . They're not numbskulls. Thinking scientifically is as natural as breathing."

Most critics praised Sagan's scientific expertise as exhibited in *Broca's Brain,* but some, including Maureen Bodo of *National Review,* thought that "Sagan is on less firm ground when speculating on semi-philosophical topics." This view was shared by *New York Times Book Review* critic Robert Jastrow. Although Jastrow wrote that "the skeptical chapters on pseudoscience . . . are delightful" and that Sagan was "capable of first-class reasoning when disciplined," he added that the scientist "soars all too often on flights of meaningless fancy." Ultimately, though, Jastrow found *Broca's Brain* worth reading, as did *Science* magazine's Richard Berendzen. "For the nonspecialist," Berendzen wrote, "the book will be frustrating reading, with uneven technical detail, loose connections, and an overabundance of polysyllabic jargon. But if the reader can make it through, this curious volume can answer old questions, raise new ones, open vistas, become unforgettable. In short, Sagan has done it again. The book's title might be *Broca's Brain,* but its subject is Sagan's."

Television played an important part in Carl Sagan's career. In the early 1970s he appeared on *The Tonight Show* and, as *New York*'s Bauer puts it, "launched into a cosmological crash course for adults. It was one of the great reckless solos of late-night television." After the scientist finished his long monologue on the evolution of the earth, Bauer wrote, "one was willing to bet that if a million teenagers had been watching, at least a hundred thousand vowed on the spot to become full-time astronomers like him." Late in 1980, Sagan's involvement with the medium led to the television series *Cosmos,* an eight million-dollar Public Broadcasting System production that eventually reached a worldwide audience of 400 million viewers—or, as Sagan preferred to think of it, three percent of the earth's population. Filmed over a period of three years on forty locations in twelve countries, *Cosmos,* introduced and narrated by Sagan, and written by Sagan, Ann Druyan, and Steven Soter, used elaborate sets and special effects to explain the wide spectrum of the universe, from the expanse of a solar black hole to the intricacies of a living cell.

Cosmos is "dazzling" in its theme and presentation, observed Harry F. Waters in *Newsweek;* yet the reviewer felt that "Sagan undermines the show's scientific credibility by lapsing into fanciful speculation. . . . Equally unsettling is Sagan's perpetual expression of awestruck reverence as he beholds the heavens." John S. DeMott, who likewise found Sagan's presentation "unabashedly awestruck," wrote in *Time* that "each segment [of *Cosmos*] has flair, excellent special effects and a dash of good ethical showmanship" and called Sagan "a man clearly in love with his subject."

As *Cosmos* became public television's most highly-rated series (surpassed only in 1990 by *The Civil War*), Sagan's book adaptation, *Cosmos,* proved equally popular, topping the bestseller lists for seventy weeks. In a *Christian Science Monitor* review, Robert C. Cowen found the book to be "as magnificent, challenging, and idiosyncratic . . . as the TV series." James A. Michener, writing in the *New York Times Book Review,* called *Cosmos* "a cleverly written, imaginatively illustrated summary . . . about our universe." Sagan's style, according to Michener, was "iridescent, with lights flashing upon unexpected juxtapositions of thought." The reviewer summed up, "*Cosmos* is an inviting smorgasbord of nutritious ideas well worth sampling." Citing the author's "personal voice," *Washington Post Book World* critic Eliot Marshall felt that Sagan "lends his work a resonance and coherence it would otherwise lack." Marshall concluded that *Cosmos* is "a little overbearing, but still informative and entertaining."

Sagan followed the success of *Cosmos* with other works, including his first novel, *Contact.* This science-fiction thriller centers on the character of Eleanor Arroway, an astronomer who, as Sagan did, leads the search for life on other planets. In *Contact,* however, Earth receives a message from an alien civilization on the star Vega (making the inhabitants "Vegans"), which tosses Eleanor into a chaotic mix of media and politics. Sagan's background injects the tale with pertinent and realistic details and provides support for the contemplation of loftier issues of science, intellectualism, and politics. (The book was later adapted as an award-winning film, starring Jodie Foster as Eleanor.)

Many reviewers noted that Sagan's enthusiasm for his subject permeated the novel. In the *Voice Literary Supplement,* Eliot Fremont-Smith commented, "what I thought would be the biggest fault . . . [Sagan's] cloying sincerity, becomes the greatest strength. *Contact* is an enthusiast's book and those benzels really spin." Or as Peter Nicholls, writing for the *Washington Post Book World* remarked, "Sagan is certainly a better scientist than a novelist. As a novel the book is slow; as a portrait of the way scientists think, it is quite interesting, in what it gives away as well as in what it consciously tells us." Gregory Benford in the *New York Times Book Review* noted, "The authorial voice has clearly done its homework, piling on detail. One gets the feel of a senior writing a term paper with the teacher looking over his shoulder; the sentences smother momentum, only occasionally . . . sparkling with the Sagan wit." He concluded, "*Contact* fulfills no high literary promise, but it does deal with issues seldom discussed, and worth pondering."

Sagan devoted much of his time to writing and lecturing about the long-term effects of nuclear warfare, including coauthoring (with Richard Turco) *A Path Where No Man Thought: Nuclear Winter and the End of the Arms Race.* The scientist's vision of the total devastation and widespread death brought on by radiation poisoning made him a leading spokesman in the nuclear disarmament movement. Representing this cause, Sagan appeared in a panel debate with such figures as William F. Buckley, Jr., Elie Wiesel, and Henry Kissinger, following a broadcast of the highly publicized television film *The Day After,* which dramatized the aftermath of a nuclear attack on Lawrence, Kansas.

Sagan next ventured into scientific study focusing on human origins with *Shadows of Forgotten Ancestors: A Search for Who We Are.* Coauthored with his wife, Ann Druyan, the book is a Darwinian search for evidence of human origins in the behavior and physiology of other life forms, especially monkeys and apes. The book begins with a focus on the beginnings of the solar system and resulting DNA, with later chapters devoted to explaining human origins based on behavioral and anatomical similarities between humans and other creatures. According to several reviewers, *Shadows of Forgotten Ancestors* showcases Sagan's ability to relate complex scientific theories to the layman. Marvin Harris in the *Washington Post Book World* found the work to be "a fine [example] of readable, exciting and provocative big sky popular science," while a *Kirkus Reviews* contributor called it "crack science-writing for the masses."

Sagan's 1994 book, *Pale Blue Dot: A Vision of the Human Future in Space,* returned to the subject of the universe. In *Pale Blue Dot,* Sagan takes his easy-to-understand concepts of the universe one step further, attempting to foretell the future of humans in space in the event of the destruction of Earth and the rest of the solar system. He reviews the history of space flight, including the discoveries of the Voyager spacecraft, and looks forward to humans "terraforming" other worlds to make them livable in order to preserve the species. The title itself refers to the image of the earth from the Voyager's perspective in space, supposedly Sagan's idea, which reduces earthly, human issues to mere dust.

Critics were fairly consistent in their praise of this work. Sagan continued to be commended for his ability to "impart a healthy dose of science (to readers), making it palatable to the lay reader by using jargon-free English buoyed by emotion and humor," as Leon Jaroff noted in *Time.* This seems to be the expectation of readers of his work, commented Charles Sheffield in the *Washington Post Book World,* "We assume that Sagan will be lucid and erudite, with an easy grasp of science, philosophy and history. This book does not disappoint us."

A year before his death, Sagan issued *The Demon-Haunted World: Science as a Candle in the Dark.* The 1995 publication picked up where *Pale Blue Dot* left off in working to debunk not just religious beliefs but New Age philosophies, UFO sightings, and other "irrational beliefs." Sagan "rallies the forces of reason and scientific literacy," commented a *Kirkus Reviews* contributor, against an onslaught of superstition and religious fundamentalism. As a leading astronomer and "true" believer in life beyond Earth, he especially takes issue with UFO sightings, but he also covers a wide spectrum of beliefs based in scientific ignorance. Sagan even includes checklists for evaluating scientific evidence.

Reviewers continued to appreciate Sagan's passion tinged with humor for his subject. Martin Gardner, writing for the *Washington Post Book World,* commented on Sagan's wit in relaying various scientific swindles and hoaxes. He added, however, that "such ersatz wonders . . . pale beside those of authentic science—wonders that glow throughout all of Sagan's marvelous, wonder-saturated books." While Lynn Phillips took issue with Sagan's purely scientific view of human issues, commenting in the *Nation* that he "begins to resemble the popular caricature of the scientist as a half-man: all brain and no heart," Phillips found him to "make his case for rational thinking attractive and imperative."

BIOGRAPHICAL AND CRITICAL SOURCES:

BOOKS

Cohen, Daniel, *Carl Sagan: Superstar Scientist,* Dodd, Mead (New York, NY), 1987.

Contemporary Issues Criticism, Volume 2, Thomson Gale (Detroit, MI), 1984.

Contemporary Literary Criticism, Volume 30, Thomson Gale (Detroit, MI), 1984.

Ginenthal, Charles, *Carl Sagan and Immanuel Velikovsky,* Ivy Press Books (Forest Hills, NY), 1990, New Falcon Publications (Tempe, AZ), 1995.

Swift, David W., *SETI Pioneers: Scientists Talk about Their Search for Extraterrestrial Intelligence,* University of Arizona Press (Tuscon, AZ), 1990.

Terzian, Yervant, and Elizabeth Bilson, *Carl Sagan's Universe,* Cambridge University Press (New York, NY), 1997.

PERIODICALS

America, February 7, 1981, William J. O'Malley, "Carl Sagan's Gospel of Scientism," pp. 95-98.

Atlantic Monthly, August, 1977, Robert Manning, review of *The Dragons of Eden: Speculations on the Evolution of Human Intelligence.*

Christian Science Monitor, November 19, 1980, Robert C. Cowen, review of *Cosmos,* p. 17.

Commentary, August, 1977, R.J. Herrnstein, review of *The Dragons of Eden;* May, 1981.

Detroit News, May 27, 1977.

Humanist, July-August, 1981, William J. Harnack, "Carl Sagan: Cosmic Evolution vs. the Creationist Myth," pp. 5-11; March-April, 1993, Edd Doerr, review of *Shadows of Forgotten Ancestors: A Search for Who We Are,* p. 39.

Los Angeles Times Book Review, November 22, 1992, p. 11.

Nation, May 20, 1996, Lynn Phillips, review of *The Demon-Haunted World: Science as a Candle in the Dark,* pp. 25-28.

National Review, August 3, 1979, Maureen Bodo, review of *Broca's Brain;* April 22, 1996, Phillip E. Johnson, review of *The Demon-Haunted World,* p. 57.

New Statesman, April 4, 1980, Peter Wilsher, review of *Broca's Brain,* pp. 515-516.

Newsweek, June 27, 1977; August 15, 1977; October 6, 1980, Harry F. Waters, review of *Cosmos,* p. 75; November 23, 1981, "Anti-nukes, U.S. Style," pp. 44-45.

New York, September 1, 1975, Stuart Bauer, review of *Intelligent Life in the Universe.*

New Yorker, June 21, 1976; June 28, 1976; August 2, 1977, John Updike, review of *The Dragons of Eden.*

New York Review of Books, June 9, 1977.

New York Times, May 17, 1977.

New York Times Book Review, May 29, 1977; June 10, 1979; July 19, 1979; January 25, 1981, James A. Michener, review of *Cosmos,* pp. 7-8; November 3, 1985, p. 12; January 6, 1991, Len Ackland, review of *A Path Where No Man Thought: Nuclear Winter and the End of the Arms Race,* p. 7; January 15, 1995, Rudy Abramson, review of *Pale Blue Dot: A Vision of the Human Future in Space,* p. 12; April 7, 1996, James Gorman, review of *The Demon-Haunted World,* p. 10.

New York Times Magazine, May 28, 1978.

Omni, June, 1983, Ben Bova, "Planetary Blues," pp. 24-25.

People, December 15, 1980, Kristin McMurran, "His *Cosmos* a Huge Success, Carl Sagan Turns Back to Science and Saturn's Rings," pp. 42-45.

Psychology Today, January-February, 1996, "A Slayer of Demons" (interview with Sagan), pp. 30-36.

Rolling Stone, December 25, 1980, Jonathan Cott, review of *Cosmos,* pp. 43-49.

School Library Journal, December, 1992, David Schwam-Baird, review of *Shadows of Forgotten Ancestors,* p. 28.

Science, July 6, 1979, Richard Berendzen, review of *Broca's Brain.*

Science Digest, March, 1982, Isaac Asimov, review of *Intelligent Life in the Universe,* p. 36.

Scientific American, May, 1995, Philip Morrison, review of *Pale Blue Dot,* p. 106; June, 1996, Joe Nickell, review of *The Demon-Haunted World,* p. 106.

Time, January 24, 1974; September 29, 1980, John S. DeMott, review of *Cosmos,* p. 83; October 20, 1980, Frederic Golden, "The Cosmic Explainer" (profile of Sagan), pp. 62-67; December 14, 1981, "Big Bank Bust," p. 68; January 9, 1995, Leon Jaroff, review of *Pale Blue Dot,* p. 71, 73; March 27, 1995, "Ailing, Carl Sagan," p. 25.

Voice Literary Supplement, November, 1985, Eliot Fremont-Smith, review of *Contact.*

Wall Street Journal, April 26, 1996, Jim Holt, review of *The Demon-Haunted World,* section A, pp. 10, 13.

Washington Post Book World, May 27, 1977; November 17, 1980, Eliot Marshall, review of *Cosmos;* October 13, 1985, Peter Nicholls, review of *Contact,* p. 6; September 27, 1992; December 11, 1994, Charles Sheffield, review of *Pale Blue Dot;* March 17, 1996, Martin Gardner, review of *The Demon-Haunted World,* pp. 1, 10.

* * *

SAGAN, Carl Edward
See SAGAN, Carl

* * *

SALINGER, J.D. 1919-
(Jerome David Salinger)

PERSONAL: Born January 1, 1919, in New York, New York; son of Sol (an importer) and Miriam (Jillich) Salinger; allegedly married September, 1945; wife's name Sylvia (a physician; divorced, 1947); married Claire Douglas, February 17, 1955 (divorced, October, 1967); children: (second marriage) Margaret Ann, Matthew. *Education:* Graduated from Valley Forge Military Academy, 1936; attended New York University, Ursinus College, and Columbia University.

ADDRESSES: Home—Cornish, NH. *Agent*—Harold Ober Associates, Inc., 425 Madison Ave., New York, NY 10017.

CAREER: Writer. Worked as an entertainer on Swedish liner M.S. *Kungsholm* in the Caribbean, 1941. *Military service:* U.S. Army, 1942-46; served in Europe; became staff sergeant; received five battle stars.

WRITINGS:

The Catcher in the Rye (novel), Little, Brown (Boston, MA), 1951.

Nine Stories, Little, Brown (Boston, MA), 1953, published as *For Esme—With Love and Squalor, and Other Stories,* Hamish Hamilton (London, England), 1953.

Franny and Zooey (two stories; "Franny" first published in *New Yorker,* January 29, 1955, and "Zooey," *New Yorker,* May 4, 1957), Little, Brown (Boston, MA), 1961.

Raise High the Roof Beam, Carpenters; and Seymour: An Introduction ("Raise High the Roof Beam, Carpenters" first published in *New Yorker,* November 19, 1955, and "Seymour," *New Yorker,* June 6, 1959), Little, Brown (Boston, MA), 1963.

The Complete Uncollected Short Stories of J.D. Salinger, two volumes, [California], 1974.

Hapworth 16, 1924 (novella), Orchises (Washington, DC), 1997.

Contributor to periodicals, including *Harper's, Story, Collier's, Saturday Evening Post, Cosmopolitan,* and *Esquire.*

Collections of Salinger's correspondence are housed at the Harry Ransom Humanities Research Center, University of Texas at Austin, and at the Firestone Library, Princeton University.

ADAPTATIONS: The story "Uncle Wiggily in Connecticut" was adapted as the motion picture *My Foolish Heart,* 1950. The story "Raise High the Roofbeam, Carpenters" was adapted as a dance performance by the Silver-Brown Dance Company. It premiered June 12, 2005, at the 92nd St. Y in New York.

SIDELIGHTS: J.D. Salinger first rose to prominence with the publication of *The Catcher in the Rye* in 1951. Prior to this, Salinger had written only a handful of short stories published in popular magazines. While Salinger's novel is more complex than many first-time readers perceive, its appeal to both adolescents and adults remains strong, conferring upon it the status of a classic novel. Salinger's work following the phenomenal success of *The Catcher in the Rye* has been modest considering the promise demonstrated by that first book. Salinger collected a number of short pieces in *Nine Stories,* each of which demonstrate his command of middle-class American colloquial speech, mastery of eccentric characterization, and deft irony.

Salinger's *Franny and Zooey* consists of two long short stories, previously published in the *New Yorker,* and featuring the fictional Glass family. Salinger later published another Glass family story sequence, *Raise High the Roof Beam, Carpenters;* and *Seymour: An Introduction,* again from two previously published *New Yorker* pieces. Another part of the Glass family chronicle, *Hapworth 16, 1924,* a novella-length story told in the form of a letter, originally published in the *New Yorker* in 1965, has since been published.

Salinger has been criticized by reviewers for focusing so much of his attention on the Glass family. He has also annoyed critics with his outright refusal to participate in a debate of his works. While Salinger's fictional characters have been endlessly analyzed and discussed, the author himself has remained a mystery. Since the publication of *The Catcher in the Rye,* he has avoided all contact with the public. Because of this, the record of his life remains incomplete.

Salinger published his first short story, "The Young Folks," in 1940 in *Story* magazine, founded and edited by one of Salinger's former teachers. Encouraged by the story's success, Salinger continued to write even while serving in the army during World War II. Back home many of his stories were being published in magazines including *Collier's,* the *Saturday Evening Post, Esquire,* and *Cosmopolitan.*

After the war Salinger continued to write stories for magazine publication. His story "Slight Rebellion off Madison," was published in the *New Yorker* in December, 1946. It was at this time that Salinger began his career as a writer of serious fiction. Between 1946 and 1951 he published seven stories in the *New Yorker.*

Among the stories Salinger published during the late 1940s was "A Perfect Day for Bananafish," the first story featuring the mysterious, brooding, and tragic Seymour Glass, a character who haunts much of Salinger's later work. Initiating the long, complex saga of the Glass family, the story examines Seymour's life, spiritual quest, and unhappy end around which all of the Glass stories are organized. It also contains themes and concerns central to Salinger's work: the conflict between the spiritual questor and the crass materialist, the loss of childhood innocence in a perverse world, and the search for genuine love amidst often adulterated human relationships.

Although this story ends with the shocking scene of Seymour committing suicide, it does not depend on sensationalism to achieve its impact. Rather, the ending builds naturally from the ambivalence created in the reader's mind toward the troubled character of Seymour, who seems simultaneously innocent and threatening, spiritual and vaguely perverse. This depth of characterization is a trademark of Salinger's fiction. In *J.D. Salinger, Revisited,* Warren French, considered "A Perfect Day for Bananafish" among the "best-known" stories written since the end of World War II and declared that its complexities and significance make it more than simply a "springboard" to the later Glass cycle.

Most of the stories Salinger wrote and collected in *Nine Stories* demonstrate the seemingly insoluble dilemmas people face in their lives. In many of these stories, frequent victims of the sinister nature of the modern world are children groping with the mysterious problems of the adult world. Such is the case in the stories "Teddy," "Down at the Dinghy," and "The Laughing Man." Other stories focus upon the problems of adults, portraying them as hapless figures unable to deal with the complex emotional entanglements of their lives or as active exploiters of other people. In the story "Pretty Mouth and Green My Eyes," a man tries to comfort a late-night caller who suspects his absent wife of infidelity. While the man calmly and rationally explains away the caller's fears, he is lying in bed next to his friend's wife. Such lapses in personal morality are also a common feature of Salinger's work, making this story typical of what French called "the pit of the modern urban hell," and one of the writer's most "bitter, cynical stories."

Salinger demonstrates in his fiction what Dan Wakefield described in an article in *Salinger: A Critical and Personal Portrait* as the search for love. Wakefield argued that the search for unadulterated emotional contact is central to Salinger's work, which, he concluded, can be seen as "the history of human trouble and the poetry of love." The power of unqualified love as a restorative agent against the evils of life is perhaps best illustrated in "For Esme—With Love and Squalor." Some critics consider this story Salinger's finest piece of short fiction.

In the story a young English girl, Esme, redeems an American soldier suffering from combat fatigue. Struck by her innocent beauty, precocity, and native charm, the narrator promises to write a story for Esme about "squalor." Almost a year later while the soldier is recovering from a nervous reaction to combat, he receives a battered package from Esme in which he finds, enclosed with a letter, the gift of her dead father's watch. In the letter she reminds him of his promise to write a story for her about "squalor," wishes him well, and remarks that she hopes he comes through the war with all of his "faculties intact." Reading her letter and contemplating its unselfish expression of affection, the narrator finds himself able to sleep (a restorative agent in Salinger's fiction). His recovery allows him to write this story and fulfill his promise six years later, which he does after receiving an invitation to Esme's wedding.

This gesture of Esme's—what Ihab Hassan, in *Salinger: A Critical and Personal Portrait,* called "The Rare Quixotic Gesture"—represents Salinger's most eloquent answer to the dilemma of modern life. It also lies close to the center, as Hassan noted, of *The Catcher in the Rye.* While *Catcher's* Holden Caulfield rebels against his society, he does not attempt to overturn the established values system. Holden instead insists that those values be restored from the perversion they have suffered under the world of "phonies."

As the novel stands today, it represents perhaps the most sensitive portrait of coming-of-age in America in the years following World War II. Few other books have had as great an impact on a generation—so much so that Holden Caulfield has entered the popular mythology of American culture alongside such figures Jay Gatsby and Huck Finn. As Edgar Branch pointed out in *Salinger: A Critical and Personal Portrait,*the pattern of similarity between Huck and Holden is striking, making *The Catcher in the Rye* "a kind of *Huckleberry Finn* in modern dress."

Holden, like Huck, flees from the world of conventionality. Holden's flight from Pencey Prep a few days before the beginning of Christmas vacation is partly a reaction to his inability to cope with his schoolmates, but also a vain attempt to forestall his flunking out of school. During the course of the story readers learn that this is his third failure at school and part of a pattern of neurotic behavior, much of which, one suspects, is Holden's reaction to the death of a younger brother. Although Holden is well aware of his own limitations, he fails to identify or understand his inability to come to terms with the conditions of the adult world; he instead directs his complaints against the world of "phoniness," which includes most adults.

Taking flight from this world, Holden plans to head west, but begins his journey by traveling to New York to say goodbye to his sister. On the way he participates in a series of humorous adventures. Such confusion in direction is characteristic of Holden, who often behaves impulsively. In fact, one of Salinger's more subtle devices is to undercut his main character by placing him in situations wherein his own phoniness is exposed, and yet making his character all the more engaging through what readers perceive as his sensitivity and intelligence. Throughout the story Holden adopts many roles to deceive other people. His motivation, however, is not to exploit others, but rather to establish contact with them. In this respect, much of Holden's sympathetic appeal lies in his loneliness and difficulty in trying to sort out the confusing impulses of the adult world.

Another source of the novel's success lies in its elaborate structure that on the surface seems rambling and inconclusive. However, as Carl F. Strauch demonstrated in *Wisconsin Studies in Contemporary Literature,* a close scrutiny of the novel reveals "complex patterns" of "symbolic structure of language, motif, episode, and character," all of which contribute to its affirmative quality. Strauch took issue with critics who discounted the novel's significance, calling it instead a "masterpiece that moves effortlessly on the colloquial surface and at the same time uncovers, with hypnotic compulsion, a psychological drama of unrelenting terror and final beauty."

Despite his confusion and ignorance, Holden is able to communicate and even express his experience in metaphoric terms. In the most crucial scene in the novel Holden, misquoting a line from Robert Burns, describes his mission in life as a "catcher in the rye," a figure who wishes to keep all of the children in the world from falling off "some crazy cliff." This, then, is Holden's "quixotic gesture," his reaching out to others in an act of selfless love, even from the depths of his own confusion and grief. The ultimate irony is that Holden's gesture is doomed to failure. He cannot prevent his own fall into the adulterated world of experience, much less the fall of others. This irony does not diminish the quality of Holden's gesture, making it instead all the more profound.

It is little wonder that *The Catcher in the Rye* became a favorite among young people. It skillfully validates adolescent experience with its spirit of rebellion. However, it was not until after the publication of *Nine Stories* that Salinger began to attract serious critical attention. Through the later 1950s his notoriety was further enhanced by the gradual unfolding of the Glass saga in the pages of the *New Yorker.*

Perhaps the best way to grasp the long and complex story of the Glass family is to consider its separately published parts as a complete unit. The Glass saga consists of six short stories that have been published as "A Perfect Day for Bananafish" (in *Nine Stories*), *Franny and Zooey, Raise High the Roof Beam, Carpenters; and Seymour: An Introduction,* and *Hapworth 16, 1924.* Eberhard Alsen, in his study *Salinger's Glass Stories As a Composite Novel,* identified three major themes in the Glass cycle: the concern for the lack of spiritual values in contemporary America, the development of Buddy as a writer, and Seymour's quest for enlightenment.

Although Seymour Glass is at the core of the Glass cycle, he actually appears only in "A Perfect Day for Bananafish," in which he commits suicide. Whether or not Seymour's final act confirms his role as a true visionary or a "failed guru" is the subject of considerable critical debate; however, the issue is moot since Seymour's success or failure in resolving his own spiritual conflicts is far less important than the effect his teaching has in helping to resolve the conflicts of his younger siblings. It is the latter influence that makes Seymour the crucial figure in the series.

In "Franny," the youngest of the Glass daughters suffers physical and nervous collapse as she tries to reconcile her desire for a pure spiritual experience with her involvement in a sexual relationship with her crude, insensitive boyfriend. Franny's crisis continues into the companion story, "Zooey," in which her elder brother, a successful television actor, is able to mediate her concerns by reminding her of the example of Seymour, who once helped Zooey understand the importance of accepting the worldly nature of religious experience.

In "Raise High the Roof Beam, Carpenters," Buddy Glass retrospectively narrates his attendance at Seymour's wedding in 1942, an event the groom chose not to attend, eloping instead with his fiancee Muriel. Again, in this story Seymour is physically absent, but his peculiar character generates discussion about him by the indignant wedding guests. Buddy overhears and records their negative comments, which reinforce his own understanding of his brother's special sensibility. Buddy recognizes that Seymour will not allow what he actually is to be compromised by the world's perceptions of him.

In another case, the problem of accurately perceiving his brother prompts Buddy years later to write "Seymour: An Introduction," which he intends to serve as a guide for the "general reader" to the saintly nature of his dead brother. In the narrative, Buddy often reveals more about himself and his own opinions of life and literature than he does about Seymour. In this respect the "Introduction" is never quite complete; Seymour remains a mysterious presence not fully comprehensible to the reader. Buddy's "Introduction" is described by French as a fascinating, "even if not a convincing work."

The final segment of the Glass cycle, "Hapworth 16, 1924," consists of a long letter written by Seymour, aged seven, to his family describing his and five-year-old Buddy's experiences at summer camp. The masterful prose and flashy displays of erudition seem entirely implausible for a young child, even one with Seymour's special gifts; however, as French suggested, the disparity between what is plausible and what appears on the page only underscores the "heart-rending evocations of an exquisitely sensitive young person trapped in a situation for which he can find no physical or metaphysical justification."

While Salinger is generally applauded for *The Catcher in the Rye,* his subsequent work raised questions as to the degree of his overall talent. Norman Mailer remarked in his *Advertisements for Myself* that Salinger was "the greatest mind to ever stay in prep school." Mailer complained that Salinger avoids the discomforting subjects demanded of serious writers. These comments were reinforced by Alfred Kazin who, in a review of *Franny and Zooey* collected in *Salinger: A Critical and Personal Portrait,* accused Salinger of appealing to a "vast public" of readers "released by our society to think of themselves as endlessly sensitive, spiritually alone, gifted, and whose suffering lies in the narrowing of their consciousness to themselves."

Despite the generally negative reaction to *Franny and Zooey,* the novel became a popular success, and for a time through the 1960s Salinger's fiction attracted considerable attention. However, interest in his later work evaporated after the appearance of the final Glass stories. *The Catcher in the Rye* remains a widely read, critical success. There is little doubt that with this novel alone Salinger has made an enduring contribution.

BIOGRAPHICAL AND CRITICAL SOURCES:

BOOKS

Alsen, Eberhard, *Salinger's Glass Stories As a Composite Novel,*Whitson (Troy, NY), 1983.

Authors and Artists for Young Adults, Volume 2, Thomson Gale (Detroit, MI), 1989, pp. 201-210, Volume 36, 2000.

Belcher, W. F., and J.W. Lee, editors, *J.D. Salinger and the Critics,*Wadsworth (Belmont, CA), 1962.

Bloom Harold, *The Catcher in the Rye,* Chelsea House (New York, NY), 1995.

Bloom, Harold, editor, *J.D. Salinger: Modern Critical Views,* Chelsea House (New York, NY), 1987.

Cambridge Dictionary of American Biography, Cambridge University Press (New York, NY), 1995.

Carpenter, Humphrey, *Secret Gardens: A Study of the Golden Age of Children's Literature,* Houghton Mifflin (Boston, MA), 1985.

Children's Literature Review, Volume 18, Thomson Gale (Detroit, MI), 1989, pp. 171-194.

Concise Dictionary of American Literary Biography: The New Consciousness, 1941-1968, Thomson Gale (Detroit, MI), 1987, pp. 448-458.

Contemporary Literary Criticism, Thomson Gale (Detroit, MI), Volume 1, 1973, Volume 3, 1975, Volume 8, 1978, Volume 12, 1980, Volume 55, 1989, Volume 56, 1989.

Contemporary Novelists, 7th edition, St. James Press (Detroit, MI), 2001.

Contemporary Popular Writers, St. James Press (Detroit, MI), 1997.

Dictionary of Literary Biography, Thomson Gale (Detroit, MI), Volume 2: *American Novelists since World War II,* 1978, pp. 434-444, Volume 102: *American Short-Story Writers, 1910-1945,* 1991, pp. 258-265.

Donelson, Kenneth L., and Alleen Pace Nilsen, *Literature for Today's Young Adults,* Scott, Foresman (Glenview, IL), 1980.

Encyclopedia of American Biography, HarperCollins (New York, NY), 1996.

Encyclopedia of World Biography, 2nd edition, Thomson Gale (Detroit, MI), 1998.

Engel, Steven, *Readings on The Catcher in the Rye,* Greenhaven Press (San Diego, CA), 1998.

Filler, Louis, editor, *Seasoned "Authors" for a New Season: The Search for Standards in Popular Writing,* Bowling Green University Popular Press (Bowling Green, OH), 1980.

French, Warren, editor, *The Fifties: Fiction, Poetry, Drama,* Everett/Edwards (De Land, FL), 1970, pp. 1-39.

French, Warren, *J.D. Salinger,* Twayne (New York, NY), 1963, revised edition, G.K. Hall (Boston, MA), 1976.

French, Warren, *J.D. Salinger, Revisited,* Twayne (New York, NY), 1988.

Geismar, Maxwell, *American Moderns: From Rebellion to Conformity,* Hill & Wang (New York, NY), 1958.

Grunwald, Anatole, editor, *Salinger: A Critical and Personal Portrait,* Harper (New York, NY), 1962.

Gwynn, Frederick L., and Joseph L. Blotner, *The Fiction of J.D. Salinger,* Pittsburgh University Press (Pittsburgh, PA), 1958.

Hamilton, Ian, *In Search of J.D. Salinger,* Random House (New York, NY), 1988.

Hamilton, Kenneth, *J.D. Salinger: A Critical Essay,* Eerdmans (Grand Rapids, MI), 1967.

Hassan, Ihab, *Radical Innocence: Studies in the Contemporary American Novel,* Princeton University Press (Princeton, NJ), 1961.

Holzman, Robert S., and Gary L. Perkins, *J.D. Salinger's "The Catcher in the Rye,"* Research & Education Association (Piscataway, NJ), 1995.

Kazin, Alfred, *Contemporaries,* Atlantic Monthly Press (Boston, MA), 1962.

Kotzen, Kip, editor, *With Love and Squalor: Fourteen Writers Respond to the Work of J.D. Salinger,* Broadway Books (New York, NY), 2001.

Laser, Marvin, and Norman Fruman, editors, *Studies in J.D. Salinger,* Odyssey (New York, NY), 1963.

Lundquist, James, *J.D. Salinger,* Ungar (New York, NY), 1979.

Madinaveitia, Catherine, *Brodie's Notes on J.D. Salinger's "The Catcher in the Rye,"* Pan (London, England), 1987.

Mailer, Norman, *Advertisements for Myself,* Putnam (New York, NY), 1959, pp. 467-468.

Marsden, Malcolm M., editor, *"If You Really Want to Know": A Catcher Casebook,* Scott, Foresman (Glenview, IL), 1963.

Maynard, Joyce, *At Home in the World: A Memoir,* Picador USA (New York, NY), 1998.

Miller, James E., Jr., *J.D. Salinger,* Minnesota University Press (Minneapolis, MN), 1965.

Pinsker, Sanford, *The Catcher in the Rye: Innocence under Pressure,* Twayne (New York, NY), 1993.

Rosen, Gerald, *Zen in the Art of J.D. Salinger,* Creative Arts (Berkeley, CA), 1977.

St. James Guide to Young Adult Writers, 2nd edition, St. James Press (Detroit, MI), 1999.

Salinger, Margaret A., *Dream Catcher: A Memoir,* Washington Square Press (New York, NY), 2000.

Salzberg, Joel, editor, *Critical Essays on Salinger's "The Catcher in the Rye,"* Hall (Boston, MA), 1990.

Salzman, Jack, editor, *New Essays on "The Catcher in the Rye,"* Cambridge University Press (New York, NY), 1992.

Schulz, Max F., *Radical Sophistication: Studies in Contemporary Jewish-American Novelists,* Ohio University Press (Athens, OH), 1969, pp. 198-217.

Short Story Criticism, Thomson Gale (Detroit, MI), Volume 2, 1989.

Simonson, Harold P., and E.P. Hager, editors, *"Catcher in the Rye": Clamor vs. Criticism,* Heath (Boston, MA), 1963.

Sublette, Jack R.,*J.D. Salinger: An Annotated Bibliography, 1938-1981,* Garland (New York, NY), 1984.

Weinberg, Helen, *The New Novel in America: The Kafkan Mode in Contemporary American Fiction,* Cornell University Press (Ithaca, NY), 1970.

Wenke, John, *J.D. Salinger: A Study of the Short Fiction,* Twayne (Boston, MA), 1991.

PERIODICALS

America, January 26, 1963.

American Imago, spring-summer, 1965, pp. 57-76; summer, 1968, pp. 140-162.

American Literature, November, 1968, pp. 352-369.

American Quarterly, winter, 1977, pp. 547-562.

American Scholar, summer, 1999, review of *Franny and Zooey,* p. 128.

American Speech, October, 1959, pp. 172-181.

Atlantic, August, 1961, pp. 27-31.

Booklist, February 15, 1992, review of *The Catcher in the Rye,* p. 1101; June 1, 1995, review of *The Catcher in the Rye,* p. 1761; November 15, 1999, review of *Catcher in the Rye,* p. 601.

Book Week, September 26, 1965.

Chicago Review, winter, 1958, pp. 3-19.

Chicago Tribune, June 17, 1987.

College English, March, 1954, pp. 315-325; November, 1956, pp. 76-80; January, 1961, pp. 262-264; December, 1961, pp. 226-229; December, 1965, pp. 248-251.

College Language Association Journal, March, 1963, pp. 170-183.

Commentary, September, 1987, pp. 61-64.

Commonweal, February 23, 1973, pp. 465-469.

Comparative Literature Studies, March, 1997, review of *The Catcher in the Rye,* p. 260.

Crawdaddy, March, 1975.

Critical Inquiry, autumn, 1976, pp. 15-38.

Criticism, summer, 1967, pp. 275-288.

Critique, spring-summer, 1965.

Daily Eagle (Claremont, NH), November 13, 1953, p. 1.

Dalhousie Review, autumn, 1967, pp. 394-399.

English Journal, March, 1964; April, 1992, review of *The Catcher in the Rye,* p. 87; April, 1993, review of *The Catcher in the Rye,* p. 88.

Entertainment Weekly, July 15, 1994, review of *The Catcher in the Rye,* p. 80.

Globe and Mail, December 1, 2001, review of *The Catcher in the Rye,* p. D34.

Guardian Weekly, September 11, 1994, review of *The Catcher in the Rye,* p. 28.

Harper's, February, 1959, pp. 83-90; October, 1962, pp. 46-48; December, 1962.

Horizon, May, 1962.

Hungry Mind Review, fall, 1995, review of *Nine Stories,* p. 54; summer, 1999, review of *Nine Stories,* p. 45.

Life, November 3, 1961, pp. 129-130, 132, 135, 137-138, 141-142, 144.

London Review, winter, 1969-1970, pp. 34-54.

Los Angeles Times, November 7, 1986.

Mademoiselle, August, 1961.

Mainstream, February, 1959, pp. 2-13.

Modern Fiction Studies, autumn, 1966.

Modern Language Quarterly, December, 1964, pp. 461-472.

Mosaic, fall, 1968, pp. 3-17.

Nation, November 14, 1959, pp. 360-363.

New England Quarterly, December, 1997, review of *The Catcher in the Rye,* p. 567.

New Republic, October 19, 1959, pp. 19-22; April 28, 1973, pp. 30-32.

Newsweek, May 30, 1961; January 28, 1963; July 30, 1979.

New York Herald Tribune Book Review, July 15, 1951.

New York Post Weekend Magazine, April 30, 1961, p. 5.

New York Times, November 3, 1974, pp. 1, 69; April 12, 1977, section 1, p. 3; November 8, 1986; August 4, 1987; October 6, 1987; September 3, 1989; February 20, 1997, review of *Hapworth 16, 1924,* p. C15; September 13, 1998.

New York Times Book Review, September 17, 1961; June 3, 1979.

Observer (London), July 31, 1994, review of *The Catcher in the Rye,* p. 21, review of *The Catcher in*

the Rye, p. 2; August 28, 1994, review of *For Esme—With Love and Squalor,* p. 21.
Partisan Review, fall, 1962, pp. 594-598.
People, October 31, 1983.
Publications of the Modern Language Association of America (PMLA), October, 1974, pp. 1065-1074.
Raleigh News and Observer, January 1, 2000, p. A2.
Ramparts, May, 1962, pp. 47-66.
Renascence, summer, 1970, pp. 171-182; spring, 1971, pp. 115-128; spring, 1972, pp. 159-167.
San Francisco Review, May, 1996, review of *Raise High the Roof Beams, Carpenters; and, Seymour: An Introduction,* p. 48.
Saturday Review, September 16, 1961; November 4, 1961.
Studies in Short Fiction, spring, 1967, pp. 217-224; spring, 1970, pp. 248-256; winter, 1973, pp. 27-33; summer, 1981, pp. 251-259; winter, 1981, pp. 1-15.
Time, September 15, 1961, pp. 84-90.
Times Educational Supplement, September 30, 1994, review of *The Catcher in the Rye,* p. 18.
Tricycle, summer, 1996, review of *Franny and Zooey,* p. 107.
Twentieth Century Literature, October, 1958, pp. 92-99.
University Review, autumn, 1966, pp. 19-24.
Village Voice, August 22, 1974.
Washington Post, November 6, 1986; November 8, 1986; November 19, 1986; December 4, 1986; December 12, 1986; January 30, 1987; February 4, 1987; February 9, 1987; February 13, 1987; May 5, 1987; October 7, 1987; December 6, 1989.
Washington Post Book World, December 10, 1995, review of *The Catcher in the Rye,* p. 4; February 7, 1999, review of *For Esme—With Love and Squalor,* p. 4.
Western Humanities Review, spring, 1956, pp. 129-137; summer, 1963, pp. 271-277.
Western Review, summer, 1957, pp. 261-280.
Wisconsin Studies in Contemporary Literature, winter, 1961, pp. 5-30; winter, 1963, pp. 109-149.

ONLINE

Art and Culture Network, http://www.artandculture.com/ (June 2, 2003), biography of J.D. Salinger.
Canoe Web site, http://cgi.canoe.ca/ (November 18, 2003).
Salinger Web site, http://www.salinger.org/ (November 18, 2003).
Today in Literature, http://www.todayinliterature.com/ (June 2, 2003), "J.D. Salinger."

SALINGER, Jerome David
See SALINGER, J.D.

* * *

SALZMAN, Mark 1959-
(Mark Joseph Salzman)

PERSONAL: Born December 3, 1959, in Greenwich, CT; son of Joseph (an artist) and Martha (a musician; maiden name, Zepp) Salzman; married Jessica Yu (a documentary filmmaker). *Education:* Yale University, B.A. (summa cum laude), 1982. *Hobbies and other interests:* Playing the cello, martial arts.

ADDRESSES: *Agent*—Neil Olsen, Donadio and Olson, Inc., 121 W. 27th St. No. 704, New York, NY 10001.

CAREER: Hunan Medical College, Changsha, China, teacher of English, 1982-84; writer and actor. Once worked as a dishwasher in a Chinese restaurant.

MEMBER: Phi Beta Kappa.

AWARDS, HONORS: Literary Lions Award, New York Public Library, Christopher Award, and Pulitzer Prize nomination for nonfiction, all 1987, all for *Iron and Silk;* Alex Award, Young Adult Library Services Association, 2004, for *True Notebooks.*

WRITINGS:

Iron and Silk: A Young American Encounters Swordsmen, Bureaucrats, and Other Citizens of Contemporary China (memoir), Random House (New York, NY), 1987.
The Laughing Sutra (novel), Random House (New York, NY), 1991.
(With Shirley Sun) *Iron and Silk* (screenplay; adapted from Salzman's book), Prestige, 1991.
The Soloist (novel), Random House (New York, NY), 1994.
Lost in Place: Growing Up Absurd in Suburbia (memoir), Random House (New York, NY), 1995.
Lying Awake (novel), Knopf (New York, NY), 2000.
True Notebooks (nonfiction), Knopf (New York, NY), 2003.

SIDELIGHTS: Mark Salzman is a scholar of Chinese language and literature who has distinguished himself as an author of nonfiction and fiction books; he is also a screenwriter and actor. He is well known for his *Iron and Silk: A Young American Encounters Swordsmen, Bureaucrats, and Other Citizens of Contemporary China,* his memoir about his experiences in China. Salzman learned Chinese while working as a dishwasher in a Chinese restaurant and became interested in martial arts after watching action films. In 1982, after graduating with honors from Yale University, he went to China and began working at Hunan Medical College, where he taught English to doctors and medical students. He stayed in China for two years, and in that time he studied martial arts and calligraphy and practiced to maintain his skills as a cellist. More importantly, he managed to befriend a range of people and thus obtain keen, personal insights into Chinese life.

Iron and Silk is essentially a series of sketches and vignettes, some of which are particularly amusing. In one notable episode, Salzman attends a lecture and notes its dullness to a just-awakened audience member, who relates that one's appreciation of such a speech is directly related to one's ability to sleep through it. On another occasion, Salzman assigns his students the task of relating their happiest moments, whereupon one student fondly recalls eating duck in Beijing, then confesses that his wife had actually dined in Beijing, not him, and that she had related the tale on so many occasions that he felt as if he too had enjoyed it.

Salzman also writes in *Iron and Silk* of his efforts to master *wushu,* China's traditional martial art. Notable in these sketches is the portrait of his teacher, Pan Qinfu, one of the art's most accomplished exponents. Pan is a fearsome instructor who intimidates with his spellbinding gaze as well as with his actual physical prowess. Indeed, Salzman discovers that concentrated staring is actually an integral aspect of *wushu.* He also learns that mastery—whether of *wushu* or calligraphy—can be perceived as the easily realized result of focused attention and diligence. "All you have to do is be kind and work hard," his calligraphy instructor tells him in the book, as quoted by Jean Fritz in the *Washington Post Book World.* The instructor adds that the mastery of eating and sleeping are more difficult because they are less easy to actually control.

Upon publication in 1987, *Iron and Silk* received substantial praise. *New York Times* critic John Gross found Salzman's book "altogether admirable," and Carolyn Wakeman, writing in the *Los Angeles Times Book Review,* deemed the memoir "remarkable" and "utterly compelling." Another reviewer, J.D. Brown, wrote in Chicago's *Tribune Books* that with *Iron and Silk* Salzman had fashioned "a rich series of anecdotes." Richard Selzer, in his appraisal for the *New York Times Book Review,* found the book compelling and appealing. "If there were a prize for most winning writer," Selzer affirmed, "Mark Salzman would [win] it."

Iron and Silk intrigued filmmakers as a work of considerable potential for adaptation. Salzman, however, was determined to write the adaptation himself. In addition, he planned to play the lead role. Nicholas D. Kristof, in a *New York Times* article, reported that moguls "laughed" when Salzman revealed his film ambitions. But in 1989 he collaborated with filmmaker Shirley Sun on an adaptation, and by the end of that year they had actually completed filming. Much of the film is derived from the book's episodes. There are even martial-arts sequences, complete with Pan Qinfu playing himself. But in fashioning the film, Salzman and Sun, who directed the adaptation, also developed a romance story line in which Salzman—named Mark Franklin in the film—falls in love with a Chinese woman whose parents are aghast at her attraction to the foreigner. The love story does not end in a conventionally happy manner.

Iron and Silk was well received upon its release in 1991. *Los Angeles Times* reviewer Kevin Thomas found the film "unsophisticated and bittersweet," and noted Salzman's "impressive martial arts skills" and "pleasant screen presence." Likewise, Janet Maslin reported in the *New York Times* that the film "has an essential guilelessness." She also observed that it "includes a lot of interesting observations about Chinese life," and she described Salzman's perspective as that of "an affectionate and sharp-eyed observer."

In 1991 Salzman also published a novel, *The Laughing Sutra,* about a Chinese man, Hsun-ching, who travels to the United States in search of a legendary Buddhist text. Accompanying Hsun-ching on his adventure is Colonel Sun, a two-thousand-year-old warrior of penetrating gaze. Together, the adventurers conduct an essentially comic journey. In San Francisco, for instance, they witness a dwarf-tossing exhibition, attend an art exhibit full of buffoonish patrons, and encounter profiteering Buddhists.

Writing about *The Laughing Sutra* in the *Chicago Tribune,* William H. Banks, Jr. deemed it a "fish-out-of-water adventure story." Among the novel's enthusiasts was Allan Appel, who declared in the *Washington Post Book World* that Salzman produced "a wonderful book." He concluded that "the fortunate reader will find himself entranced, entertained and very definitely enlightened."

For his next work, Salzman drew upon another passion in his life—the cello, which he began playing at the age of seven—to create a novel about thwarted artistic ambitions. He dedicated *The Soloist,* his 1994 novel, to his mother, who abandoned her career as harpsichordist to raise her family. Its hero is thirty-four-year-old Reinhart (Renne) Sundheimer, who was once a child virtuoso on the instrument, but who now teaches at a university. "I wanted to create a character who had a hard time with his dreams," the author told Suzanne Mantell in *Publishers Weekly.* Once a feted teenager, Renne became obsessed with the notion of perfect pitch at eighteen and felt his hearing was failing him. Now, he cannot bear to hear his own music and survives by teaching music at a Los Angeles university, though he fantasizes about returning to the concert stage.

Renne's life begins to change when he agrees to teach a nine-year-old Korean girl, an apparent prodigy herself. Then Renne is called for jury duty, and he is selected to decide the outcome of a trial for a gruesome urban slaying. A disturbed young man went on a Zen retreat, and his teacher gave him a koan, or spiritual riddle, to solve; the student's solution was to beat the master to death. "Just as you begin to suspect that the novel will end inconclusively, Salzman winds the story down subtly," stated a *Publishers Weekly* reviewer. Renne is the lone jury holdout on the case, and he solves the koan himself. He also awakens from a long period of romantic inactivity when he falls for another juror. The author, wrote Diane Cole in the *New York Times Book Review,* "finds engaging points of comparison between the disciplines of meditation and music."

The heroine of Salzman's 2000 novel *Lying Awake* is a Roman Catholic nun, Sister John of the Cross, whose all-night prayer vigils have brought her visions and even spiritual ecstasies. She then writes about them in verse form, and her published works have earned her and her Carmelite order a degree of international fame. But Sister John's visions begin to coincide with painful migraine headaches, and after she collapses from one, she consents to an appointment with a specialist. The doctor tells her that it is a form of epilepsy that is triggering the visions and it is treatable; in fact, it may endanger her life if she lets it go untreated. The news triggers a crisis of faith for the sister. A *Publishers Weekly* reviewer remarked that expressing such abstract concepts as spiritual ecstasy in fiction is difficult, but "what Salzman conveys with perfect clarity is that momentary, extraordinary mental state in which physical pain becomes pure, lucid grace poised between corporeal reality and eternity." *Entertainment Weekly* reviewer George Hodgman observed that *Lying Awake* "should be shortlisted for all the literary prizes, but it has the kind of grace that doesn't demand them."

In 1995 Salzman published a memoir of his eccentric but pleasant childhood under the title *Lost in Place: Growing Up Absurd in Suburbia.* Here he recounts his early years in Connecticut, living in an artistically gifted household; his father painted in the evenings as a salve against a day job he hated, while his mother gave music lessons. Salzman recounts his discovery of martial arts at the age of thirteen, and his interest in Buddhism, the Chinese language, and martial arts, which he studied until his early teens. Salzman's obsession then turned to the cello, and he studied music at Yale University until he burned out after a year and underwent an existential crisis for which his father provided pragmatic advice. In a review of *Lost in Place* by Sara Nelson for *People,* the critic praised Salzman as "a charming, self-effacing writer" who is still familiar "with the peculiar combination of arrogance and terror that comprises teenage angst." Blake Morrison, in a *New York Times Book Review* assessment, described the book as a "Bildungsroman," or coming-of-age story and added that several of the book's adult characters, including Salzman's parents, "are beautifully observed."

In his 2003 work *True Notebooks,* Salzman focuses on the lives and thoughts of a teen culture far different from that of his own past. The book was inspired by his experience teaching creative writing to a group of teenagers incarcerated in the Los Angeles Juvenile Hall. Most of these "high-risk" offenders had committed serious crimes and were destined to continue through the prison system, some of them for life. Salzman presents their writings, and "documents his insecurities, his frustrations, and his occasional inability to coax much work or interest . . . from the class," noted a *Kirkus Reviews* contributor. Salzman does not dwell on the negative, however, but instead finds humor, poignancy, and talent in these teens' writings. As a reviewer noted in *Publishers Weekly,* Salzman's book's "power comes from keeping its focus squarely on these boys, their writing, and their coming-to-terms with the mess their lives had become."

BIOGRAPHICAL AND CRITICAL SOURCES:

PERIODICALS

America, March 19, 2001, John B. Breslin, "Mad for God," p. 34.

Booklist, September 1, 1995, Joanne Wilkinson, review of *Lost in Place: Growing Up Absurd in Suburbia,* p. 37; September 15, 2000, Michael Spinella, review of *Lying Awake,* p. 219.
Chicago Tribune, February 18, 1991, section 2, p. 3, William H. Banks, Jr., review of *The Laughing Sutra.*
Christian Century, November 22, 2000, Gordon Houser, review of *Lying Awake,* p. 1227.
Detroit Free Press, January 6, 1991.
Entertainment Weekly, August 18, 1995, D.A. Ball, review of *Lost in Place,* p. 51; October 6, 2000, George Hodgman, review of *Lying Awake,* p. 80.
Globe and Mail (Toronto, Ontario, Canada), February 16, 1991, p. C8.
Kirkus Reviews, July 3, 2003, review of *True Notebooks,* p. 900.
Library Journal, October 15, 2000, Starr Smith, review of *Lying Awake,* p. 104.
Los Angeles Times, March 8, 1991, Kevin Thomas, review of film *Iron and Silk,* p. F8.
Los Angeles Times Book Review, May 24, 1987, Carolyn Wakeman, review of *Iron and Silk,* p. 2.
National Catholic Reporter, March 23, 2001, Judith Bromberg, review of *Lying Awake,* p. 12.
National Review, September 25, 1987, Katherine Dalton, review of *Iron and Silk,* p. 62.
New York Times, January 9, 1987, John Gross, review of *Iron and Silk;* January 22, 1989; February 15, 1991, Janet Maslin, review of film *Iron and Silk,* p. C12.
New York Times Book Review, February 1, 1987, Richard Selzer, review of *Iron and Silk,* p. 9; February 6, 1994, Diane Cole, review of *The Soloist,* p. 22; August 13, 1995, Blake Morrison, "Growing Up Somehow," p. 11.
People, October 2, 1995, Sara Nelson, review of *Lost in Place,* p. 30.
Publishers Weekly, October 12, 1990, Sybil Steinberg, review of *Laughing Sutra,* p. 47; October 11, 1993, review of *The Soloist,* p. 68; January 17, 1994, Suzanne Mantell, "Mark Salzman: He Uses Fiction to Question What Happens when Dreams Don't Come True," p. 357; June 26, 1995, review of *Lost in Place,* p. 101; July 17, 2000, review of *Lying Awake,* p. 171; June 16, 2003, review of *True Notebooks,* p. 57.
Smithsonian, July, 1987, William Dieter, review of *Iron and Silk,* p. 142.
Time, March 2, 1987, p. 76.
Tribune Books (Chicago, IL), January 25, 1987, J.D. Brown, review of *Iron and Silk,* p. 6.
Washington Post Book World, January 25, 1987, p. 8; March 3, 1991, Allan Appel, review of *The Laughing Sutra,* p. 9.

SALZMAN, Mark Joseph
See SALZMAN, Mark

* * *

SANCHEZ, Sonia 1934-

PERSONAL: Original name Wilsonia Benita Driver; born September 9, 1934, in Birmingham, AL; daughter of Wilson L. (a schoolteacher) and Lena (Jones) Driver; married Albert Sanchez (divorced); children: Anita, Morani Neusi, Mungu Neusi. *Education:* Hunter College (now Hunter College of the City University of New York), B.A., 1955; New York University, post graduate study; Wilberforce University, Ph.D., 1972. *Politics:* "Peace, freedom, and justice."

ADDRESSES: *Home*—407 W. Chelten Ave., Philadelphia, PA 19144. *Office*—Department of English/ Women's Studies, Temple University, 10th Floor Anderson Hall, 1114 W. Berks St., Philadelphia, PA 19122.

CAREER: Staff member, Downtown Community School, San Francisco, CA, 1965-67, and Mission Rebels in Action, 1968-69; San Francisco State College (now University), San Francisco, CA, instructor, 1966-68; University of Pittsburgh, Pittsburgh, PA, assistant professor, 1969-70; Rutgers University, New Brunswick, NJ, assistant professor, 1970-71; Manhattan Community College of the City University of New York, New York, NY, assistant professor of literature and creative writing, 1971-73; City College of the City University of New York, teacher of creative writing, 1972; Amherst College, Amherst, MA, associate professor, 1972-75; University of Pennsylvania, Philadelphia, PA, 1976-77; Temple University, Philadelphia, PA, associate professor, 1977, professor, 1979—, faculty fellow in provost's office, 1986-87, presidential fellow, 1987-88. Distinguished Minority Fellow, University of Delaware; Distinguished Poet-in-Residence, Spelman College; and Zale Writer-in-Residence at Sophie Newcomb College, Tulane University.

MEMBER: Literature Panel of the Pennsylvania Council on the Arts.

AWARDS, HONORS: PEN writing award, 1969; National Institute of Arts and Letters grant, 1970; National Endowment for the Arts award, 1978-79; Honorary Citizen of Atlanta, 1982; Tribute to Black Women

Award, Black Students of Smith College, 1982; Lucretia Mott Award, 1984; American Book Award, Before Columbus Foundation, 1985, for *homegirls and handgrenades;* Pennsylvania Governor's Award in the humanities, 1989, for bringing great distinction to herself and her discipline through remarkable accomplishment; Welcome Award, Museum of Afro-American History (Boston, MA), 1990; Oni Award, International Black Women's Congress, 1992; Women Pioneers Hall of Fame Citation, Young Women's Christian Association, 1992; Roots Award, Pan-African Studies Community Program, 1993; PEN fellowship in the arts, 1993-94; Legacy Award, Jomandi Productions, 1995; American Book Award, 1995; honorary Doctor of Human Letters from Temple University, 1998; Lindback Award for Distinguished Teaching, 1999; Robert Frost medal in poetry, 2001; honorary degree from Haverford College, 2004.

WRITINGS:

FOR ADULTS

Homecoming (poetry), Broadside Press (Detroit, MI), 1969.

We a BaddDDD People (poetry), with foreword by Dudley Randall, Broadside Press (Detroit, MI), 1970.

(Editor) *Three Hundred and Sixty Degrees of Blackness Comin' at You* (poetry), 5X Publishing Co., 1971.

Ima Talken Bout the Nation of Islam, TruthDel, 1972.

Love Poems, Third Press (New York, NY), 1973.

A Blues Book for Blue Black Magical Women (poetry), Broadside Press (Detroit, MI), 1973.

(Editor and contributor) *We Be Word Sorcerers: 25 Stories by Black Americans,* Bantam (New York, NY), 1973.

I've Been a Woman: New and Selected Poems, Black Scholar Press (Sausalito, CA), 1978.

Crisis in Culture—Two Speeches by Sonia Sanchez, Black Liberation Press, 1983.

homegirls and handgrenades (poetry), Thunder's Mouth Press (New York, NY), 1984.

(Contributor) Mari Evans, editor, *Black Women Writers (1950-1980): A Critical Evaluation,* introduced by Stephen Henderson, Doubleday-Anchor (Garden City, NY), 1984.

Under a Soprano Sky, Africa World (Trenton, NJ), 1987.

(Compiler and author of introduction) Allison Funk, *Living at the Epicenter: The 1995 Morse Poetry Prize,* Northeastern University Press (Boston, MA), 1995.

Wounded in the House of a Friend (poems), Beacon Press (Boston, MA), 1995.

Does Your House Have Lions? (poems), Beacon Press (Boston, MA), 1997.

Like the Singing Coming off the Drums: Love Poems, Beacon Press (Boston, MA), 1998.

Shake Loose My Skin: New and Selected Poems, Beacon Press (Boston, MA), 1999.

FOR CHILDREN

It's a New Day: Poems for Young Brothas and Sistuhs, Broadside Press (Detroit, MI), 1971.

The Adventures of Fathead, Smallhead, and Squarehead, illustrated by Taiwo DuVall, Third Press (New York, NY), 1973.

A Sound Investment and Other Stories, Third World Press, 1979.

PLAYS

The Bronx Is Next, first produced in New York, NY, at Theatre Black, October 3, 1970 (included in *Cavalcade: Negro American Writing from 1760 to the Present,* edited by Arthur Davis and Saunders Redding, Houghton [Boston, MA], 1971).

Sister Son/ji, first produced with *Cop and Blow and Players Inn* by Neil Harris and *Gettin' It Together* by Richard Wesley as *Black Visions,* Off-Broadway at New York Shakespeare Festival Public Theatre, 1972 (included in *New Plays From the Black Theatre,* edited by Ed Bullins, Bantam [New York, NY], 1969).

Uh Huh; But How Do It Free Us?, first produced in Chicago, IL, at Northwestern University Theater, 1975 (included in *The New Lafayette Theatre Presents: Plays with Aesthetic Comments by Six Black Playwrights, Ed Bullins, J.E. Gaines, Clay Gross, Oyamo, Sonia Sanchez, Richard Wesley,* edited by Bullins, Anchor Press [Garden City, NY], 1974).

Malcolm Man/Don't Live Here No More, first produced in Philadelphia, PA, at ASCOM Community Center, 1979.

I'm Black When I'm Singing, I'm Blue When I Ain't, first produced in Atlanta, GA, at OIC Theatre, April 23, 1982.

Also author of *Dirty Hearts,* 1972.

CONTRIBUTOR TO ANTHOLOGIES

Robert Giammanco, editor, *Poetro Negro* (title means "Black Power"), Giu, Laterza & Figli, 1968.

Le Roi Jones and Ray Neal, editors, *Black Fire: An Anthology of Afro-American Writing,* Morrow (New York, NY), 1968.

Dudley Randall and Margaret G. Burroughs, editors, *For Malcolm: Poems on the Life and Death of Malcolm X,* Broadside Press (Detroit, MI), 1968.

Walter Lowenfels, editor, *The Writing on the Wall: One Hundred Eight American Poems of Protest,* Doubleday (Garden City, NY), 1969.

Arnold Adoff, editor, *Black Out Loud: An Anthology of Modern Poems by Black Americans,* Macmillan (New York, NY), 1970.

Walter Lowenfels, editor, *In a Time of Revolution: Poems from Our Third World,* Random House (New York, NY), 1970.

June M. Jordan, editor, *Soulscript,* Doubleday (Garden City, NY), 1970.

Gwendolyn Brooks, editor, *A Broadside Treasury,* Broadside Press (Detroit, MI), 1971.

Dudley Randall, editor, *Black Poets,* Bantam (New York, NY), 1971.

Orde Coombs, editor, *We Speak as Liberators: Young Black Poets,* Dodd (New York, NY), 1971.

Bernard W. Bell, editor, *Modern and Contemporary Afro-American Poetry,* Allyn & Bacon (Boston, MA), 1972.

Arnold Adoff, editor, *The Poetry of Black America: An Anthology of the 20th Century,* Harper (New York, NY), 1973.

JoAn and William M. Chace, *Making It New,* Canfield Press (San Francisco, CA), 1973.

Donald B. Gibson, editor, *Modern Black Poets,* Prentice-Hall (Englewood Cliffs, NJ), 1973.

Stephen Henderson, editor, *Understanding the New Black Poetry: Black Speech and Black Music as Poetic References,* Morrow (New York, NY), 1973.

J. Paul Hunter, editor, *Norton Introduction to Literature: Poetry,* Norton (New York, NY), 1973.

James Schevill, editor, *Breakout: In Search of New Theatrical Environments,* Swallow Press, 1973.

Lucille Iverson and Kathryn Ruby, editors, *We Become New: Poems by Contemporary Women,* Bantam (New York, NY), 1975.

Quincy Troupe and Rainer Schulte, editors, *Giant Talk: An Anthology of Third World Writings,* Random House (New York, NY), 1975.

Henry B. Chapin, editor, *Sports in Literature,* McKay (New York, NY), 1976.

Cleanth Brooks and Robert Penn Warren, editors, *Understanding Poetry,* Holt (New York, NY), 1976.

Ann Reit, editor, *Alone amid All the Noise,* Four Winds/ Scholastic (New York, NY), 1976.

Erlene Stetson, editor, *Black Sister: Poetry by Black American Women, 1746-1980,* Indiana University Press (Bloomington, IN), 1981.

Amiri Baraka and Amina Baraka, editors, *Confirmation: An Anthology of African-American Women,* Morrow (New York, NY), 1983.

Burney Hollis, editor, *Swords upon This Hill,* Morgan State University Press (Baltimore, MD), 1984.

Jerome Rothenberg, editor, *Technicians of the Sacred: A Range of Poetries from Africa, America, Asia, Europe and Oceania,* University of California Press (Berkeley, CA), 1985.

Marge Piercy, editor, *Early Ripening: American Women's Poetry Now,* Pandora (New York, NY), 1987.

Poems also included in *Night Comes Softly, Black Arts, To Gwen with Love, New Black Voices, Blackspirits, The New Black Poetry, A Rock against the Wind, America: A Prophecy, Nommo, Black Culture,* and *Natural Process.*

OTHER

Author of column for *American Poetry Review,* 1977-78, and for *Philadelphia Daily News,* 1982-83. Contributor of poems to *Minnesota Review, Black World,* and other periodicals. Contributor of plays to *Scripts, Black Theatre, Drama Review,* and other theater journals. Contributor of articles to several journals, including *Journal of African Civilizations.*

Co-author with Bruce Graham and Michael Holliger of "Philiadephia Diary: AnInteractive Script," a companion to a PBS film that documents 24 hours in three different Philadelphia neighborhoods.

SIDELIGHTS: In addition to being an important activist, poet, playwright, professor, and a leader of the black studies movement, Sonia Sanchez has also written books for children. She introduced young people to the poetry of black English in her 1971 work *It's a New Day: Poems for Young Brothas and Sistuhs,* created a moral fable for younger children in 1973's *The Adventures of Fathead, Smallhead, and Squarehead,* and produced a collection of short tales for children in 1979's *A Sound Investment and Other Stories.* As William Pitt Root noted in *Poetry* magazine: "One concern [Sanchez] always comes back to is the real education of Black children."

Sanchez was born Wilsonia Benita Driver on September 9, 1934, in Birmingham, Alabama. Her mother died when she was very young, and she was raised by her grandmother until she too died when the author was six years old. Her father was a schoolteacher, and as a result she and her siblings spoke standard English instead of a southern or black dialect. It was not until she and her brother rejoined her father in Harlem, New York, when she was nine years old, that Sanchez learned the speech of the streets that would become so important to her poetry. Sanchez also stuttered as a child; this led her to writing, which she has done since she was very young.

Sanchez also learned about racism at a very young age. She recalled in an interview with Claudia Tate for Tate's *Black Women Writers at Work:* "I also remember an aunt who spat in a bus driver's face—that was the subject of one of my first poems—because he wanted her to get off as the bus was filling up with white people. . . . Well, my aunt would not get off the bus, so she spat, and was arrested. That was the first visual instance I can remember of encountering racism." She did not leave racism behind when her family moved north, however. She told Tate that "coming north to Harlem for 'freedom' when I was nine presented me with a whole new racial landscape." Sanchez continued, "Here was the realization of the cornerstore, where I watched white men pinch black women on their behinds. And I made a vow that nobody would ever do that to me unless I wanted him to. I continued to live in the neighborhood, went to that store as a nine-year-old child, and continued to go there as a student at Hunter College. When I was sixteen to eighteen they attempted to pinch my behind. I turned around and said, 'Oh no you don't.' They knew I was serious." She has been fighting racism and sexism ever since.

After graduating from Hunter College in 1955, Sanchez did postgraduate study at New York University. During the early 1960s she was an integrationist, supporting the ideas of the Congress of Racial Equality. But after listening to the ideas of Black Muslim leader Malcolm X, who believed blacks would never be truly accepted by whites in the United States, she focused more on her black heritage as something separate from white Americans. She began teaching in the San Francisco area in 1965, first on the staff of the Downtown Community School and later at San Francisco State College (now University). There she was a pioneer in developing black studies courses, including a class in black English.

In 1969, Sanchez published her first book of poetry for adults, *Homecoming.* She followed that up with 1970's *We a BaddDDD People,* which especially focused on black dialect as a poetic medium. At about the same time her first plays, *Sister Son/ji* and *The Bronx Is Next,* were being produced or published. In 1971, she published her first work for children, *It's A New Day: Poems for Young Brothas and Sistuhs.* Shortly afterwards, she joined the Nation of Islam, also referred to as the Black Muslims. Sanchez enjoyed the spirituality and discipline of the religion, but she always had problems with its repression of women. She explained to Tate: "It was not easy being in the Nation. I was/am a writer. I was also speaking on campuses. In the Nation at that time women were supposed to be in the background. My contribution to the Nation has been that I refused to let them tell me where my place was. I would be reading my poetry some place, and men would get up to leave, and I'd say, 'Look, my words are equally important.' So I got into trouble." Sanchez stated: "One dude said to me once that the solution for Sonia Sanchez was for her to have some babies. . . . I already had two children. . . . I fought against the stereotype of me as a black woman in the movement relegated to three steps behind. It especially was important for the women in the Nation to see that. I told them that in order to pull this 'mother' out from what it's under we gonna need men, women, children, but most important, we need minds." She added: "I had to fight. I had to fight a lot of people in and outside of the Nation due to so-called sexism. I spoke up. I think it was important that there were women there to do that. I left the Nation during the 1975-76 academic year."

While she was a Black Muslim, however, Sanchez produced her second children's book, *The Adventures of Fathead, Smallhead, and Squarehead.* A moral fable about a pilgrimage to Mecca, the tale began as a story for her own children. In an interview with *African American Review* contributor Susan Kelly, Sanchez remembered, "my children had asked me to make up a story one night in New York City before we moved to Amherst. They would always say, 'Read, read, read!' So I would read to them. And one night, they said, 'Don't read; make up a story.'" The resulting tale became *The Adventures of Fathead, Smallhead, and Squarehead.*

A Sanchez book of interest to a teenaged audience is *Shake Loose My Skin: New and Selected Poems.* Featuring verse from her older publications, as well as four new entries, *Shake Loose My Skin* offers a sampling of Sanchez's work spanning over thirty years. In her poems, she tackles topics ranging from bigotry to poverty to drug abuse. "This collection should draw wide attention to the consistency of Sanchez's achievement," believed a *Publishers Weekly* contributor. *Library Journal* critic Ann K. van Buren found that this book "leaves one in awe of the stretches of language Sanchez has helped to legitimize."

Because of the political nature of most of her writings and her involvement in black power causes, Sanchez feels that her academic career has suffered from persecution by government authorities. She told Tate: "While I helped to organize the black studies program at San Francisco State, the FBI came to my landlord and said put her out. She's one of those radicals." Sanchez continued: "Then I taught at Manhattan Community College in New York City, and I stayed there until my record was picked up. You know how you have your record on file, and you can go down and look at it. Well, I went down to look at it, because we had had a strike there, and I had been arrested with my students. I went to the dean to ask for my record, and he told me that I could not have my record because it was sent downtown." Sanchez said: "That's when I began to realize just how much the government was involved with teachers in the university. I then tried to get another job in New York City—no job. I had been white-balled. The word was out, I was too political. . . . That's how I ended up at Amherst College, because I couldn't get a job in my home state. That's what they do to you. If they can't control what you write, they make alternatives for you and send you to places where you have no constituency."

After leaving Amherst, Sanchez eventually became a professor at Temple University in Philadelphia, Pennsylvania, where she has since taught for many years. Temple has recognized Sanchez as a distinguished teacher and awarded her an honorary doctorate in 1998. Sanchez has also edited several books, and contributed poetry and articles on black culture to anthologies and periodicals. Summing up the importance of Sanchez's work, Kalamu ya Salaam concluded in *Dictionary of Literary Biography:* "Sanchez is one of the few creative artists who have significantly influenced the course of black American literature and culture."

In her interview with Kelly, Sanchez concluded, "It is that love of language that has propelled me, that love of language that came from listening to my grandmother speak black English. . . . It is that love of language that says, simply, to the ancestors who have done this before you, 'I am keeping the love of life alive, the love of language alive. I am keeping words that are spinning on my tongue and getting them transferred on paper. I'm keeping this great tradition of American poetry alive.'"

BIOGRAPHICAL AND CRITICAL SOURCES:

BOOKS

Children's Literature Review, Volume 18, Thomson Gale (Detroit, MI), 1989.

Dictionary of Literary Biography, Volume 41: *Afro-American Poets since 1955,* Thomson Gale (Detroit, MI), 1985, pp. 295-306.

Dictionary of Literary Biography, Documentary Series, Volume 8, Thomson Gale (Detroit, MI), 1991.

Joyce, Joyce A. *Ijala: Sonia Sanchez and the African poetic tradition,* Third World Press (Chicago, IL), 1996.

Tate, Claudia, editor, *Black Women Writers at Work,* Continuum, 1983, pp. 132-148.

PERIODICALS

African American Review, spring, 2000, Yoshinobu Hakutani, review of *Like the Singing Coming off the Drums,* p. 180; winter, 2000, Susan Kelly, "Discipline and Craft: An Interview with Sonia Sanchez," p. 679.

American Visions, October, 1999, Denolyn Carroll, review of *Shake Loose My Skin: New and Selected Poems,* p. 35.

Black Issues Book Review, July-August, 2004, TaRessa Stovall, "Black Arts to the Tenth Power: Living Legend Sonia Sanchez Is the Literary Headliner in the 10th Season of the 10-day National Black Arts Festival in Atlanta," pp. 24-25.

Booklist, February 15, 1999, Donna Seaman, review of *Shake Loose My Skin,* p. 1028.

Library Journal, February 1, 1999, Ann K. van Buren, review of *Shake Loose My Skin,* p. 93.

Poetry, October, 1973, William Pitt Root, pp. 44-48.

Publishers Weekly, December 21, 1998, review of *Shake Loose My Skin,* p. 63.

ONLINE

African-American Literature Book Club, http://www.authors.aalbc.com/ (August 9, 2004), biography of Sonia Sanchez.

PBS Web site http://www.pbs.org/ (August 9, 2004), biography of Sonia Sanchez.

Rutgers University Web site, http://www.scils.rutgers.edu (August 9, 2004), biography of Sonia Sanchez.

Sonia Sanchez—The Academy of American Poets, http://www.poets.org/ (December 15, 2001).

Temple University Web site, http://www.temple.edu/ (August 9, 2004), biography of Sonia Sanchez.

* * *

SANDERS, Noah
See BLOUNT, Roy, Jr.

* * *

SANDERS, Winston P.
See ANDERSON, Poul

* * *

SANDFORD, John
See CAMP, John

* * *

SAROYAN, William 1908-1981
(Sirak Goryan)

PERSONAL: Born August 31, 1908, in Fresno, CA; died of cancer, May 18, 1981, in Fresno, CA; son of Armenak (a Presbyterian preacher and writer) and Takoohi Saroyan; married Carol Marcus, February, 1943 (divorced, November, 1949; remarried, 1951; divorced, 1952); children: Aram, Lucy. *Education:* Left high school at age fifteen.

CAREER: Short story writer, playwright, and novelist. Began selling newspapers at the age of eight for the *Fresno Evening Herald;* worked in his uncle's law office, then held numerous odd jobs, including that of grocery clerk, vineyard worker, postal employee, and office manager of San Francisco Postal Telegraph Co. Co-founder of Conference Press, 1936. Organized and directed Saroyan Theatre, August, 1942 (closed after one week). Writer-in-residence, Purdue University, 1961. *Military service:* U.S. Army, 1942-45.

AWARDS, HONORS: O. Henry Award, 1934, for "The Daring Young Man on the Flying Trapeze"; Drama Critics Circle Award, and Pulitzer Prize for drama (declined), both 1940, both for *The Time of Your Life;* Academy Award for best screenplay, 1943, for *The Human Comedy;* California Literature Gold Medal, 1952, for *Tracy's Tiger;* American Book Award nomination, 1980, for *Obituaries;* William Saroyan International Prize for Writing established by Stanford University Libraries/ William Saroyan Foundation, 2002.

WRITINGS:

SHORT STORIES

The Daring Young Man on the Flying Trapeze and Other Stories (also see below), Random House (New York, NY), 1934, reprinted, Yolla Bolly, 1984.

Inhale and Exhale (includes International Harvester; also see below), Random House (New York, NY), 1936, Books for Libraries Press, 1972.

Three Times Three (also see below), Conference Press, 1936.

Little Children, Harcourt (New York, NY), 1937.

A Gay and Melancholy Flux (compiled from *Inhale and Exhale* and *Three Times Three*), Faber (London, England), 1937.

Love, Here Is My Hat, and Other Short Romances, Modern Age Books, 1938.

The Trouble with Tigers, Harcourt (New York, NY), 1938.

A Native American, George Fields, 1938.

Peace, It's Wonderful, Modern Age Books, 1939.

3 Fragments and a Story, Little Man, 1939.

My Name Is Aram, Harcourt (New York, NY), 1940, revised edition, 1966.

Saroyan's Fables, Harcourt (New York, NY), 1941.

The Insurance Salesman and Other Stories, Faber (London, England), 1941.

48 Saroyan Stories, Avon (New York, NY), 1942.

Thirty-One Selected Stories, Avon (New York, NY), 1943.

Someday I'll Be a Millionaire Myself, Avon (New York, NY), 1944.

Dear Baby, Harcourt (New York, NY), 1944.

The Saroyan Special: Selected Short Stories, Harcourt (New York, NY), 1948, reprinted, Books for Libraries Press, 1970.

The Fiscal Hoboes, Press of Valenti Angelo, 1949.

The Assyrian, and Other Stories, Harcourt (New York, NY), 1950.

The Whole Voyald and Other Stories, Atlantic-Little, Brown (Boston, MA), 1956.

After Thirty Years: The Daring Young Man on the Flying Trapeze (includes essays), Harcourt (New York, NY), 1964.

Best Stories of William Saroyan, Faber (London, England), 1964.

Deleted Beginning and End of a Short Story, Lowell-Adams House Printers (Cambridge, MA), 1965.

My Kind of Crazy and Wonderful People, Harcourt (New York, NY), 1966.

Man with the Heart in the Highlands, and Other Stories, Dell (New York, NY), 1968.

My Name Is Saroyan (autobiography), edited by James H. Tashjian, Coward-McCann (New York, NY), 1983.

Madness in the Family, edited by Leo Hamalian, New Directions (New York, NY), 1988.

The Man with the Heart in the Highlands and Other Stories, New Directions (New York, NY), 1993.

Fresno Stories, New Directions (New York, NY), 1994.

NOVELS

The Human Comedy (also see below), Harcourt (New York, NY), 1943, revised edition, 1966.

The Adventures of Wesley Jackson (also see below), Harcourt (New York, NY), 1946.

The Twin Adventures: The Adventures of William Saroyan, a Diary; The Adventures of Wesley Jackson, A Novel, Harcourt (New York, NY), 1950.

Rock Wagram, Doubleday (New York, NY), 1951.

Tracy's Tiger (fantasy), Doubleday (New York, NY), 1951, revised edition, Ballantine (New York, NY), 1967.

The Laughing Matter, Doubleday (New York, NY), 1953.

Mama I Love You, (originally named "The Bouncing Ball"), Atlantic-Little, Brown (Boston, MA), 1956, reprinted, Dell, 1986 (New York, NY).

Papa You're Crazy, Atlantic-Little, Brown (Boston, MA), 1957.

Boys and Girls Together, Harcourt (New York, NY), 1963, reprinted, Barricade, 1995.

One Day in the Afternoon of the World, Harcourt, 1964.

PLAYS

The Hungerers: A Short Play, S. French (New York, NY), 1939.

My Heart's in the Highlands (produced on Broadway at Guild Theatre, April 13, 1939; first published in *One-Act Play Magazine,* December, 1937; also see below), Harcourt (New York, NY), 1939.

The Time of Your Life (produced on Broadway at Booth Theatre, October 25, 1939; produced in London, England, by Royal Shakespeare Company, 1982; also see below), Harcourt (New York, NY), 1939, acting edition, S. French (New York, NY), 1969, Methuen (London, England), 1983.

A Theme in the Life of the Great American Goof (ballet-play; also see below), produced in New York City at Center Theatre, January, 1940.

Subway Circus, S. French (New York, NY), 1940.

The Ping-Pong Game (produced in New York, 1945), S. French (New York, NY), 1940.

A Special Announcement, House of Books, 1940.

The Beautiful People (produced under the author's direction on Broadway at Lyceum Theatre, April 21, 1940), Harcourt (New York, NY), 1941.

Three Plays: My Heart's in the Highlands, The Time of Your Life, Love's Old Sweet Song, Harcourt (New York, NY), 1940.

Love's Old Sweet Song (first produced on Broadway at Plymouth Theatre, May 2, 1940; also see below), S. French (New York, NY), 1941.

Radio Play, CBS-Radio, 1940.

The People with Light Coming out of Them (radio play; first broadcast, 1941), Free Company (New York, NY)/CBS-Radio, 1941.

Three Plays: The Beautiful People, Sweeney in the Trees, Across the Board on Tomorrow Morning, Harcourt (New York, NY), 1941.

Jim Dandy, A Play, Little Man Press (Cincinnati, OH), 1941, published as *Jim Dandy: Fat Man in a Famine,* Harcourt (New York, NY), 1947.

Across the Board on Tomorrow Morning, first produced in Pasadena, CA, February, 1941, produced under the author's direction on Broadway at Belasco Theatre, on the same bill with *Talking to You,* August, 1942.

Hello out There (first produced in Santa Barbara, CA, at Lobeto Theatre, September, 1941, produced on Broadway at Belasco Theatre, September, 1942), S. French (New York, NY), 1949.

Razzle-Dazzle (short plays; includes *A Theme in the Life of the Great American Goof*), Harcourt (New York, NY), 1942.

Talking to You, produced in New York, 1942.

The Good Job (screenplay based on his story "A Number of the Poor"), Loew, 1942.

The Human Comedy (screenplay scenario based on his novel), Metro-Goldwyn-Mayer, 1943.

Get away Old Man (produced on Broadway at Cort Theatre, November, 1943), Harcourt (New York, NY), 1944.

Sam Ego's House (produced in Hollywood, 1947), S. French (New York, NY), 1949.

Don't Go away Mad, produced in New York, 1949.

Don't Go away Mad, and Two Other Plays: Sam Ego's House; A Decent Birth, A Happy Funeral, Harcourt (New York, NY), 1949.

The Son, produced in Los Angeles, CA, 1950.
Once around the Block (produced in New York, 1950), S. French (New York, NY), 1959.
A Lost Child's Fireflies, produced in Dallas, TX, 1954.
Opera, Opera, produced in New York, 1955.
Ever Been in Love with a Midget?, produced in Berlin, Germany, 1957.
The Cave Dwellers (produced on Broadway in New York City, October 19, 1957), Putnam (New York, NY), 1958.
Cat, Mouse, Man, Woman, 1958.
The Slaughter of the Innocents (produced in The Hague, Netherlands, 1957), S. French (New York, NY), 1958.
Dentist and Patient and Husband and Wife, 1968.
The Paris Comedy; or, The Secret of Lily (produced in Vienna, Austria, 1960), published as *The Paris Comedy; or, The Dogs, Chris Sick, and 21 Other Plays,* also published as *The Dogs; or, The Paris Comedy, and Two Other Plays: Chris Sick; or, Happy New Year Anyway, Making Money, and Nineteen Other Very Short Plays,* Phaedra (London, England), 1969.
Sam, the Highest Jumper of Them All; or, The London Comedy (produced in London under the author's direction, 1960), Faber (London, England), 1961.
(With Henry Cecil) *Settled out of Court,* produced in London, 1960.
High Time along the Wabash, produced in West Lafayette, IN, at Purdue University, 1961.
Ah, Man, music by Peter Fricker, produced in Adelburgh, Suffolk, England, 1962.
Four Plays: The Playwright and the Public, The Handshakers, The Doctor and the Patient, This I Believe, 1963.
The New Play, 1970.
Bad Men in the West, produced in Stanford, CA, 1971.
Armenians, produced 1974.
(With others) *People's Lives,* produced in New York, NY, 1974.
The Rebirth Celebration of the Human Race at Artie Zabala's Off-Broadway Theater, produced in New York, NY, July 10, 1975.
Two Short Paris Summertime Plays of 1974: Assassinations and Jim, Sam and Anna, Santa Susana Press, 1979.
Play Things, produced 1980.
The Armenian Trilogy, California State University Press, 1986.
Warsaw Visitor and Tales from the Vienna Streets, Southern Illinois University Press (Carbondale, IL), 1990.

Also author of plays *Something about a Soldier, Hero of the World,* and *Sweeney in the Trees,* produced c. 1940. Author of radio plays and *There's Something I Got to Tell You.* Author of teleplays *The Oyster and the Pearl,* televised, 1953. Plays represented in anthologies, including *Famous American Plays of the 1930s,* edited by Harold Clurman, and *One Act: Eleven Short Plays of the Modern Theatre,* edited by Samuel Moon.

OTHER

A Christmas Psalm (poetry), Gelber, Lilienthal, 1935.
Those Who Write Them and Those Who Collect Them, Black Archer Press, 1936.
The Time of Your Life (miscellany), Harcourt (New York, NY), 1939.
Christmas, 1939 (poetry), Quercus Press, 1939.
Harlem as Seen by Hirschfield, Hyperion Press (New York, NY), 1941.
Hilltop Russians in San Francisco, James Ladd Delkin, 1941.
Fragment, Albert M. Bender, 1943.
(With Henry Miller and Hilaire Hiler) *Why Abstract?,* New Directions (New York, NY), 1945, reprinted, Haskell House, 1974.
(Author of introduction) Khatchik Minasian, *The Simple Songs of Khatchik Minasian,* Colt Press, 1950.
The Bicycle Rider in Beverly Hills (autobiography), Scribner (New York, NY), 1952, reprinted, Ballantine (New York, NY), 1971.
The William Saroyan Reader, Braziller (New York, NY), 1958, reprinted, Barricade (New York, NY), 1994.
Here Comes, There Goes, You Know Who (autobiography), Trident, 1962, reprinted, Barricade (New York, NY), 1995.
My Lousy Adventures with Money, New Strand (London, England), 1962.
A Note on Hilaire Hiler, Wittenborn, 1962.
Me (juvenile), Crowell-Collier, 1963.
Not Dying: An Autobiographical Interlude (autobiography), Harcourt (New York, NY), 1963.
Short Drive, Sweet Chariot (reminiscences), Phaedra (London, England), 1966.
(Author of introduction) *The Arabian Nights,* Platt & Munk (New York, NY), 1966.
Look at Us; Let's See; Here We Are; Look Hard, Speak Soft; I See, You See, We All See; Stop, Look, Listen; Beholder's Eye; Don't Look Now But Isn't That You? (Us? U.S.?), Cowles, 1967.
I Used to Believe I Had Forever, Now I'm Not So Sure, Cowles, 1968.
(Author of foreword) Barbara Holden and Mary Jane Woebcke, *A Child's Guide to San Francisco,* Diablo Press, 1968.

Horsey Gorsey and the Frog (juvenile), illustrated by Grace Davidian, R. Hale, 1968.

Letters from 74 rue Taitbout, or Don't Go, but If You Must, Say Hello to Everybody, World (Cleveland, OH), 1968, published as *Don't Go, but If You Must, Say Hello to Everybody,* Cassell (London, England), 1970.

Days of Life and Death and Escape to the Moon, Dial (New York, NY), 1970.

(Editor and author of introduction) *Hairenik, 1934-1939: An Anthology of Short Stories and Poems* (collection of Armenian-American literature), Books for Libraries Press, 1971.

Places Where I've Done Time, Praeger (New York, NY), 1972.

The Tooth and My Father, Doubleday (New York, NY), 1974.

An Act or Two of Foolish Kindness, Penmaen Press & Design, 1976.

Sons Come and Go, Mothers Hang In Forever, Franklin Library, 1976.

Morris Hirschfield, Rizzoli International, 1976.

Chance Meetings, Norton (New York, NY), 1978.

(Compiler) *Patmuatsk'ner / Uiliem Saroyean; hayat-s'uts' Hovhannes Sheohmelean* (selected Armenian stories), Sewan, 1978.

Obituaries, Creative Arts, 1979, second edition, 1979.

Births, introduction by David Kherdian, Creative Arts, 1983.

The New Saroyan Reader: A Connoisseur's Anthology of the Writings of William Saroyan, edited by Brian Derwent, Creative Arts, 1984.

The Circus (juvenile), Creative Education (Mankato, MN), 1986.

The Pheasant Hunter: About Fathers and Sons, Redpath Press, 1986.

The Parsley Garden (juvenile), Creative Education (Mankato, MN), 1989.

Also author of *Famous Faces and Other Friends,* 1976. Writer of song lyrics, including "Come on-a My House" with Ross Bagdasarian, in 1951. Contributor to *Overland Monthly, Hairenik* (Armenian-American magazine), *Story, Saturday Evening Post, Atlantic, Look, McCall's,* and other periodicals.

The Human Comedy and *The Adventures of Wesley Jackson* have been translated into Russian; *Mama I Love You* and *Papa You're Crazy* have been translated into French.

ADAPTATIONS: A film version of *The Human Comedy* starring Mickey Rooney was released in 1943; United Artists made a film based on *The Time of Your Life* starring Jimmy Cagney in 1948; an opera version of *Hello, out There* prepared by composer Jack Beeson was widely performed in 1953; a television adaptation of *The Time of Your Life* was produced on *Playhouse 90,* 1958; "Ah, Sweet Mystery of Mrs. Murphy" was produced by NBC-TV, 1959; "The Unstoppable Gray Fox" was produced by CBS-TV, 1962; *My Heart's in the Highlands* was adapted for opera by Beeson and broadcast on television March 18, 1970; selections from *Making Money and Nineteen Other Very Short Plays* were presented on television by NET Playhouse, December 8, 1970; a musical version of *The Human Comedy* was produced on Broadway by Joseph Papp in 1986.

SIDELIGHTS: William Saroyan's career began in 1934 with the publication of *The Daring Young Man on the Flying Trapeze and Other Stories.* From that time on, he wrote prolifically, producing a steady stream of short stories, plays, novels, memoirs, and essays. His career can be divided into five phases. From 1934 to 1939 he wrote short stories; from 1939 to 1943 his energies were directed toward playwriting; the years 1943-1951 saw the appearance of his first two novels—*The Human Comedy* and *The Adventures of Wesley Jackson*—as well as plays and short fiction; between 1951 and 1964 Saroyan published a series of novels dealing with marriage and the family; and finally, from 1964 until his death in 1981, Saroyan devoted himself primarily to the exploration of his past through autobiographical writings.

It is through the short-story genre that Saroyan made his initial impact as a writer. During this first creative period, he published eight volumes; in the preface to *The Assyrian, and Other Stories,* he estimated that during these years he wrote "five hundred short stories, or a mean average of one hundred per annum." These early collections project a wide variety of thematic concerns, yet they are united in their portrayal of America between the two world wars. Saroyan's first books reflect the painful realities of the economic depression of the 1930s. The young writer without a job in his first famous story "The Daring Young Man on the Flying Trapeze" goes to be interviewed for a position and finds that "already there were two dozen young men in the place." The story "International Harvester" from the 1936 collection *Inhale and Exhale* also gives a bleak vision of complete economic collapse: "Shamefully to the depths fallen: America. In Wall Street they talk as if the end of this country is within sight."

Readers clearly saw their troubled lives vividly portrayed in Saroyan's stories; though they depicted the agony of the times, the stories also conveyed great hope and vigorously defiant good spirits. However, as Maxwell Geismar remarked in *Writers in Crisis: The American Novel, 1925-1940,* "the depression of the 1930s, apparently so destructive and so despairing," was actually a time of "regeneration" for the major writers of the period. Furthermore, "the American writer had gained moral stature, a sense of his own cultural connection, a series of new meanings and new values for his work." The crisis these writers were experiencing was, of course, more than merely economic. A deep cultural schism had rocked Europe since Friedrich Nietzsche's nineteenth-century apocalyptic prophecies and affected such American writers as Henry Miller, whose *Tropic of Cancer* appeared in the same year as Saroyan's first collection of short fiction.

Collections of Saroyan's short stories continued to appear regularly until 1956; after that point, his stories mostly appeared only in periodicals such as the *New Yorker* and *Atlantic Monthly.* A collection of seventeen Saroyan stories written during this later period were collected and published as *Madness in the Family* in 1988. The stories cover typical Saroyan terrain: eccentric characters, minor plot development, and a focus on the Armenian immigrant community near Fresno, California. Reviewing the collection in the Chicago *Tribune Books,* John Blade remarked on "the buoyant, daredevil quality of so many of the stories" in the book.

Between 1939 and 1943, Saroyan published and produced his most famous plays. Works such as *My Heart's in the Highlands, The Beautiful People,* and *Across the Board on Tomorrow Morning* were well received by some critics and audiences; *The Time of Your Life* won the Pulitzer Prize as the best play of the 1939-1940 season, but Saroyan refused the award on the grounds that businessmen should not judge art. Although championed by critics like George Jean Nathan, Saroyan had a strained relationship with the theatrical world. From the time his first play appeared on Broadway, critics called his work surrealistic, sentimental, or difficult to understand. His creation of a fragile, fluid, dramatic universe full of strange, lonely, confused, and gentle people startled theatergoers accustomed to conventional plots and characterization. His instinctive and highly innovative sense of dramatic form was lost on many audiences. These plays were a wonderful amalgam of vaudeville, absurdism, sentiment, spontaneity, reverie, humor, despair, philosophical speculation, and whimsy. His plays introduced a kind of rambunctious energy into staid American drama. His "absurdity" bore a direct relationship to his sorrow at observing the waste of the true, vital impulses of life in the contemporary world. His artist figures—Joe, Jonah Webster, Ben Alexander—all feel within themselves the dying of the old order and the painful struggle to give birth to a new consciousness.

In 1941, after two active years on Broadway, Saroyan traveled to Hollywood to work on the film version of *The Human Comedy* for Metro-Goldwyn-Mayer. When the scenario was completed, it was made into a successful motion picture. From the beginning of his career, Saroyan had committed himself to celebrating the brotherhood of man, and in *The Human Comedy* he preached a familiar sermon: love one another, or you shall perish. This portrayal of love's power in small-town America offered consolation to millions ravaged by the suffering and death brought on by World War II.

Saroyan went on to publish four novels between 1951 and 1964: *Rock Wagram, The Laughing Matter, Boys and Girls Together,* and *One Day in the Afternoon of the World.* Each novel explores in fictional form the troubled years of Saroyan's own marriage to Carol Marcus and that marriage's aftermath. These thinly disguised transcriptions of Saroyan's own life might be termed the "fatherhood novels," for they are linked thematically through the author's concern with founding a family. Each Armenian-American protagonist in these novels is searching for—or has already found—a wife and children, his emblems of human community. Edward Krickel, in a *Georgia Review* article, correctly pointed out that sex and love in Saroyan's novels are not ends in themselves, but rather "lead to family and the honorable roles of parent and grandparent, in short the traditional view. Children are the glory of the relationship." In the novels, as in the plays and short stories, the family symbolizes the family of humanity in microcosm and localizes the desire for universal brotherhood that had always marked Saroyan's vision. The Webster family in *The Beautiful People,* the Macauleys in *The Human Comedy,* the Alexanders in *My Heart's in the Highlands,* and the Garoghlanians in *My Name Is Aram* all were his imaginary families before he sought to become a father himself and realize his dreams.

During the 1930s and 1940s Saroyan reached the peak of his fame; by the mid-1950s his reputation had declined substantially. Many critics have dismissed him for not being what they wanted him to be, rather than considering the writer's virtues and faults on his own terms. Saroyan was aware early in his career that he was being neglected, as is apparent from his reaction in *Razzle-Dazzle* to the critical reception of the plays: "As it happened first with my short stories, my plays appeared so suddenly and continued to come so swiftly that no one was quite prepared to fully meet and appreciate them, so that so far neither the short stories nor the plays have found critical understanding worthy of them. If the critics have failed, I have not. I have both written and criticized my plays, and so far the importance I have given them, as they have appeared, has been supported by theatrical history. If the critics have not yet agreed with me on the value of my work, it is still to be proved that I am not the writer I say I am. I shall some day startle those who now regard me as nothing more than a show-off, but I shall not startle myself." What he said of his short stories and plays proved to be true of the novels and autobiographical writings as well.

Peter Collier, writing in the *New York Times Book Review,* attributed the critical devaluation of Saroyan's work to the fact that "the generation of academic critics had now come to power who were overseeing the development of the kind of dense, cerebral literature which justified their profession." Saroyan's often flippant and antiacademic tone was not calculated to endear him to the professors. Another complaint commonly voiced by critics was Saroyan's tendency toward "escapism." Philip Rahv found Saroyan's role as lover of mankind irritating; in the *American Mercury* Rahv wrote that in *The Human Comedy* Saroyan insisted "evil is unreal," although the world was obviously mired in pain and tragedy. Linked to this charge of escapism was Saroyan's nonpolitical stance; he supported no 'ism' and was therefore accused of lacking a social conscience. This attitude put him out of favor with the proletarian writers of the 1930s who were eager to enlist him in their cause. Although Saroyan always affirmed the brotherhood of man, he recognized no authorities, no leaders, no programs to save the world.

Among the negative comments about Saroyan's works is the charge that he was a simple-minded, sentimental romantic whose naive optimism did not reflect the terrible realities of the age. However, the angst of the twentieth century pervades his work; his brooding depression appears not only in the later books but also in an early play, *The Time of Your Life.* Saroyan's lonely and pathetic characters sense the oncoming fury of World War II, and the knowledge that life is poised at the rim of disaster haunts their dialogue. Commentators have almost completely ignored this darker, despairing existential side of Saroyan's work.

Though the alienation and melancholy that characterize much of Saroyan's work are typical of twentieth-century literature, the feeling of rootlessness that pervades his imagination finds an important source in his Armenian heritage. In 1896, twelve years before Saroyan's birth, 200,000 Armenians were massacred by the Turks. In 1915, the Turks deported the Armenian population of 2,500,000 to Syria and Mesopotamia; more than a million and a half Armenians were killed during this process. The Armenian migration began in earnest; of those who escaped deportation, many fled to Russia and the United States. Armenak and Takoohi Saroyan were among the thousands who came to America during the first wave of the massacres. William, the only one of their four children to be born in America, was born in Fresno, California.

In California's San Joaquin Valley, Saroyan's parents found a region similar to their native land. Although Armenians would establish communities in other parts of America, California attracted the greatest number because it was the ideal region for a predominantly agricultural people. Although California seemed idyllic, the racial conflicts that had driven the Armenians to their newfound land continued. In the autobiographical *Here Comes, There Goes, You Know Who,* Saroyan remarked: "The Armenians were considered inferior, they were pushed around, they were hated, and I was an Armenian. I refused to forget it then, and I refuse to forget it now, but not because being an Armenian had, or has, any particular significance." Because the Armenians were not really absorbed into American life, isolated within their own communities, it is no accident that Saroyan's work conveys a powerful sense of not being at home in the world.

If the Armenian people were symbolically homeless in their American exile, Saroyan himself, after the age of three, was literally homeless. The death of his father in 1911 surely contributed to his lifelong obsession with death and estrangement. Saroyan's mother was forced to place him in an orphanage, and it is evident from his autobiographical writings that his childhood was often profoundly unhappy. Midway through his career, Saroyan wondered, as he says in *Here Comes, There Goes, You Know Who:* "Well, first of all, just where was my home? Was it in Fresno, where I was born? Was it in San Jose, where my father died? Was it in Oakland, where I spent four very important years? . . . Home was in myself, and I wasn't there, that's all . . . I was far from home." The poverty of his early life drove him to literature, and to the quest for meaning: "I took to writing at an early age to escape from meaninglessness, uselessness, unimportance, insignificance, poverty, enslavement, ill health, despair, madness, and all manner of other unattractive, natural, and inevitable things. I have managed to conceal my madness fairly effectively," he wrote in *Here Comes, There Goes, You Know Who.*

Saroyan returned obsessively throughout his career to the theme of "madness," to a consideration of the possible reasons for his sorrow and psychic dislocation. He revealed a kind of "race-melancholy" underlying the Armenian temperament. In the late story "The Assyrian," he explored the dark side of his sensibility under the guise of an Assyrian hero, Paul Scott: "The longer he'd lived, the more he'd become acquainted with the Assyrian side, the old side, the tired side, the impatient and wise side, the side he had never suspected existed in himself until he was thirteen and had begun to be a man." Another foreign alter ego, the Arab in *The Time of Your Life,* repeats to himself: "No foundation. All the way down the line"—at once expressing the pain of the exile and Saroyan's own sense of disorder and spiritual emptiness.

Saroyan also identified this madness with illness, which was, he declared in *The Bicycle Rider in Beverly Hills,* "an event of the soul more than of the body." He asserted in the same volume, "I have been more or less ill all my life," a statement remarkable for both its extremism and its honesty. In *Days of Life and Death and Escape to the Moon,* a late memoir, he drew together various aspects of his own self-analysis in reexamining the past: "Most of the time illnesses of one sort or another came to me regularly, all the year round. I can't believe it is all from the sorrow in my nature, in my family, in my race, but I know some of it is." Saroyan was thus aware that his psychology derived from his Armenian heritage, the effects of his family life, and some quality inherent in his own personality.

If Saroyan was not at home in the world as it was, he was very much at home in his own imaginative recreation of it in his work. There may not be "real" homes and families like the one depicted in Saroyan's play *The Beautiful People,* but that is beside the point. As Wallace Stevens pointed out, the artist must *create* nobility, must press back against the world's chaos to create a livable sphere of existence. For Saroyan, art was a way toward health, toward reconciliation, toward psychic regeneration. He observed in the preface to *Don't Go away Mad, and Two Other Plays* that he needed to write "because I hate to believe I'm sick or half-dead; because I want to get better; because writing is my therapy."

Deeply aware of the fragmentation and spiritual anarchy of life in the modern world, Saroyan exhibited a driving impulse toward joy, self-realization, and psychic integration. In the introduction to *Three Plays* he remarked that "the imperative requirement of our time is to restore faith to the mass and integrity to the individual. The integration of man is still far from realized. In a single age this integration can be immeasurably improved, but it is impossible and useless to seek to imagine its full achievement. Integration will begin to occur when the individual is uninhibited, impersonal, simultaneously natural and cultured, without hate, without fear, and rich in spiritual grace." Saroyan's work, then, records the attempt to integrate the divided self.

Following the final dissolution of his marriage in 1952 Saroyan turned increasingly to the exploration of his past through a series of autobiographies, memoirs, and journals. Although he continued to publish plays and fiction, autobiography became his main form of self-expression. This impulse reflected a shift in emphasis from art to life, from "doing" to "being," from the creation of works to the creation of self. Saroyan sought in memory a key to his identity, a meaningful pattern underlying the chaos of experience. In *The Bicycle Rider in Beverly Hills,* he wrote: "I want to think about the things I may have forgotten. I want to have a go at them because I have an idea they will help make known how I became who I am." Like Whitman, Thomas Wolfe, and Henry Miller, Saroyan obsessively focused on his own responses, emotions, and experiences in search of the psychological matrices of his behavior and personality. The writings of his final phase, however, are not only an important source of biographical insights—they also represent some of his best prose.

There is in these last writings a vibrant joy, a deep pleasure taken in small details of daily living. Saroyan buys cheap second-hand books in a Paris shop, brings home basil plants to his apartment, delights in solitude and reading. He writes of casual long walks, visits to libraries, meetings with dear friends. Musing over the strange disjunctions of a long life, he remembers many people: family, writers, former teachers, childhood comrades.

Saroyan's search in these last years was the search of his youth. His continuing antipathy toward authority, repression, and the fettering of the human spirit made him an influence on writers of the Beat Generation, who responded to his innovative, hip, casual, jazzy voice. Beginning his career in San Francisco, meeting ground of the spiritual East and expansive West, Saroyan wrote of beautiful people and preached love not war; he had been a flower-child of the 1930s. It is thus no accident that he was a literary godfather to such writers as Jack Kerouac and J.D. Salinger.

In his last work published during his lifetime, *Obituaries,* Saroyan wrote: "My work is writing, but my real work is being." Essentially a collection of monologues, *Obituaries* consists of writings produced at the same time every day for a period of one month. A companion volume, *Births,* published posthumously in 1983, likewise contains Saroyan's musings on the subject of births, musings that he produced in half-hour sessions every day for a month.

In Rahv's conception, Saroyan was a literary "redskin." As Stephen Gould Axelrod explained in *Robert Lowell: Life and Art,* Rahv believed that "American literature composes itself into a debate between 'palefaces' and 'redskins.' The 'palefaces' (Henry James, T.S. Eliot, and Allen Tate would belong to this part) produce a patrician art which is intellectual, symbolic, cosmopolitan, disciplined, cultured. The 'redskins' (Walt Whitman and William Carlos Williams would tend to belong here) produce a plebian art which is emotional, naturalistic, nativist, energetic, in some sense *un*cultured. . . . All such formulations attest to a basic bifurcation [or, rift] in American literature between writers who experience primarily with the head and those who experience primarily with the blood." Saroyan wanted to feel the world directly, intuitively—like D.H. Lawrence, "with the blood." Saroyan's work is thus a great deal more complex than many commentators have acknowledged. His writing is a blend of the affirmative, mystical, and rambunctious qualities of the American romantic sensibility and of the profound sadness that finds its source in the tragic history of the Armenian people. On the one hand, Saroyan was thoroughly American in his persistent expansiveness, verve and spontaneity. Yet he was also the Armenian grieving for his lost homeland, speaking for those lost in an alien culture.

Precisely this sense of man's essential aloneness links Saroyan's work directly to the main currents of modern philosophical thought and to the major modernist writers; he has acknowledged his deep love for the work of both Samuel Beckett and Eugene Ionesco. One of the few observers to have discerned this important aspect of Saroyan's work was Edward Hoagland, who, in the *Chicago Tribune Book World* essay, called Saroyan "brother at once to Thomas Mann and to [Samuel Beckett.]" The existential strain was noted by Thelma Shinn, who remarked in *Modern Drama* that his work may be seen as the record of the search for meaning within the self. The difficulty of this quest for true meaning was also emphasized by William Fisher, who argued in *College English* that in mid-career Saroyan's "novels and plays became strange battlegrounds where belief struggled with skepticism." These articles are among the few devoted to a serious consideration of Saroyan's place in modern literature.

BIOGRAPHICAL AND CRITICAL SOURCES:

BOOKS

Aaron, Daniel, *Writers on the Left,* Oxford University Press (New York, NY), 1977.

Agee, James, *Agee on Film,* McDowell, Obolensky, 1958.

Axelrod, Stephen Gould, *Robert Lowell: Life and Art,* Princeton University Press (Princeton, NJ), 1978.

Balakian, Nona, *The Armenian-American Writer,* AGBU, 1958.

Balakian, Nona, *Critical Encounters,* Bobbs-Merrill (New York, NY), 1978.

Balakian, Nona, *The World of William Saroyan: A Literary Interpretation,* Bucknell University Press (Lewisburg, PA), 1997.

Calonne, David Stephen, *William Saroyan: My Real Work Is Being,* University of North Carolina Press (Durham, NC), 1983.

Contemporary Literary Criticism, Thomson Gale (Detroit, MI), Volume 1, 1973, Volume 8, 1978, Volume 10, 1979, Volume 29, 1984, Volume 34, 1985, Volume 56, 1989.

Dictionary of Literary Biography, Thomson Gale (Detroit, MI), Volume 7: *Twentieth-Century American Dramatists,* 1981, Volume 9: *American Novelists, 1910-1945,* 1981, Volume 86: *American Short Story Writers 1910-1945,* 1989.

Dictionary of Literary Biography Yearbook: 1981, Thomson Gale (Detroit, MI), 1982.

Esslin, Martin, *The Theatre of the Absurd,* Doubleday (New York, NY), 1961.

Floan, Howard, *William Saroyan,* Twayne (Boston, MA), 1966.

French, Warren, editor, *The Thirties: Fiction, Poetry, Drama,* Everett/Edwards, 1967, pp. 211-219.

Geismar, Maxwell, *Writers in Crisis: The American Novel, 1925-1940,* Hill and Wang (New York, NY), 1966.

Gifford, Barry, and Lawrence Lee, *Saroyan: A Biography,* Harper (New York, NY), 1984.

Gold, Herbert, *A Walk on the West Side: California on the Brink,* Arbor House, 1981.

Kazin, Alfred, *Starting out in the Thirties,* Vintage (New York, NY), 1980.

Keyishian, Harry, *Critical Essays on William Saroyan,* Prentice Hall (Englewood Cliffs, NJ), 1995.

Kherdian, David, *A Bibliography of William Saroyan: 1934-1964,* Howell, 1965.

Krutch, Joseph Wood, *The American Drama since 1918,* Braziller (New York, NY), 1957.

Lee, Lawrence, and Barry Gifford, *Saroyan: A Biography,* University of California Press (Berkeley, CA), 1998.
Leggett, John, *A Daring Young Man: A Biography of William Saroyan,* Knopf (New York, NY), 2002.
Lipton, Lawrence, *The Holy Barbarians,* Messner, 1959.
Martin, Jay, *Always Merry and Bright: The Life of Henry Miller,* Penguin (New York, NY), 1980.
McCarthy, Mary, *Sights and Spectacles,* Farrar (New York, NY), 1956.
Rosa, Alfred, editor, *The Old Century and the New: Essays in Honor of Charles Angoff,* Fairleigh Dickinson University Press (Rutherford, NJ), 1978, pp. 192-206.
Saroyan, Aram, *Last Rites: The Death of William Saroyan,* Harcourt (New York, NY), 1983.
Saroyan, Aram, *William Saroyan,* Harcourt (New York, NY), 1983.
Saroyan, William, *The Time of Your Life,* Harcourt (New York, NY), 1939.
Saroyan, William, *Three Plays,* Harcourt (New York, NY), 1940.
Saroyan, William, *Razzle-Dazzle,* Harcourt (New York, NY), 1942.
Saroyan, William, *Don't Go away Mad, and Two Other Plays,* Harcourt (New York, NY), 1949.
Saroyan, William, *The Assyrian, and Other Stories,* Harcourt (New York, NY), 1950.
Saroyan, William, *The Bicycle Rider in Beverly Hills,* Scribner (New York, NY), 1952.
Saroyan, William, *Here Comes, There Goes, You Know Who,* Trident, 1962.
Saroyan, William, *Days of Life and Death and Escape to the Moon,* Dial (New York, NY), 1970.
Saroyan, William, *Not Dying,* Barricade Books (New York, NY), 1997.
Stevens, Wallace, *The Necessary Angel: Essays on Reality and the Imagination,* Knopf (New York, NY), 1951.
Straumann, Heinrich, *American Literature in the Twentieth Century,* Harper (New York, NY), 1965.
Trilling, Diana, *Reviewing the Forties,* Harcourt (New York, NY), 1978.
Weales, Gerald C., *American Drama since World War II,* Harcourt (New York, NY), 1962.
Wilson, Edmund, *The Boys in the Back Room: Notes on California Novelists,* Colt Press, 1941.
Wilson, Edmund, *Classics and Commercials,* Farrar, Straus (New York, NY), 1950, pp. 26-31, 327-330.

PERIODICALS

American Mercury, September, 1943, Philip Rahv, review of *The American Comedy.*
Chicago Tribune Book World, July 5, 1970.
College English, March, 1955, pp. 336-340, 385.
Commonweal, November 4, 1942.
Detroit Free Press, May 22, 1981.
Esquire, October, 1960, pp. 85-91.
Georgia Review, fall, 1970, pp. 281-296.
Los Angeles Times, May 19, 1981; June 7, 1981.
Los Angeles Times Book Review, April 10, 1988, p. 11.
Modern Drama, September, 1972, pp. 185-194.
New Republic, March 1, 1943; March 9, 1953.
New York Times Book Review, April 2, 1972; August 15, 1976; May 20, 1979, pp. 7, 49-51; August 21, 1983.
Pacific Spectator, winter, 1947.
Punch, January 31, 1973.
Quarterly Journal of Speech, February, 1944.
Saturday Review of Literature, December 28, 1940.
Soviet Literature, number 12, 1977, pp. 159-166.
Studies in Short Fiction, spring, 1993, Gerald Locklin, review of *The Man with the Heart in the Highlands and Other Stories,* p. 199.
Theatre Arts, December, 1958.
Times Literary Supplement, June 22, 1973.
Tribune Books (Chicago, IL), May 1, 1988, John Blade, review of *Madness in the Family,* p. 3.
Virginia Quarterly Review, summer, 1944.
Western American Literature, winter, 1986, p. 369; fall, 1988, p. 283.
World Literature Today, winter, 1985, p. 100.

* * *

SARTON, Eleanor May
See SARTON, May

* * *

SARTON, May 1912-1995
(Eleanor May Sarton)

PERSONAL: Born Eleanore Marie Sarton, May 3, 1912, in Wondelgem, Belgium; died of breast cancer, July 16, 1995; brought to United States, 1916; naturalized U.S. citizen, 1924; daughter of George Alfred Leon (a historian of science) and Eleanor Mabel (an artist and designer; maiden name, Elwes) Sarton; partner of Judy Matlack (an English professor), c. 1945-58. *Politics:* Democrat. *Religion:* Unitarian Universalist.

CAREER: Poet and novelist. Eva Le Gallienne's Civic Repertory Theatre, New York, NY, apprentice, 1929-33; Associated Actors Theatre, New York, NY, founder and director, 1933-35; Stuart School, Boston, MA, instructor in creative writing, 1937-42; Harvard University, Cambridge, MA, Briggs-Copeland Instructor in English Composition, 1949-52; Bread Loaf Writer's Conference, Middlebury, VT, lecturer, 1950, 1951, 1953; Boulder Writers' Conference, Boulder, CO, lecturer, 1955; Wellesley College, Wellesley, MA, lecturer in creative writing, 1960-64; Lindenwood College, St. Charles, MO, poet-in-residence, 1965. Danforth visiting lecturer, Arts Program, 1959; Phi Beta Kappa visiting scholar, 1960; visiting lecturer, Agnes Scott College, 1972. Gave poetry readings and lectured extensively at colleges and universities throughout the United States. *Wartime service:* Wrote documentary scripts for the United States War Information Office with the East and West Society, New York, during World War II.

MEMBER: Poetry Society of America, New England Poetry Society, American Academy of Arts and Sciences (fellow).

AWARDS, HONORS: Golden Rose Award, New England Poetry Society, 1945; Bland Memorial Prize, *Poetry,* 1945; Reynolds Lyric Award, Poetry Society of America, 1952; Lucy Martin Donnelly fellowship, Bryn Mawr College, 1953-54; Guggenheim fellow in poetry, 1954-55; Johns Hopkins University Poetry Festival award, 1961; Emily Clark Balch Prize, 1966; National Endowment for the Arts grant, 1967; Sarah Josepha Hale Award, 1972; Alexandrine Medal, College of St. Catherine, 1975; Ministry to Women Award, Unitarian Universalist Women's Federation, 1982; Avon/COCOA Pioneer Woman Award, 1983; Fund for Human Dignity Award, 1985; Human Rights Award, 1985; American Book Award, Before Columbus Foundation, 1985, for *At Seventy: A Journal;* Maryann Hartman Award, University of Maine, 1986; lifetime achievement award, Women's Building/West Hollywood Connexxus Women's Center, 1987; Northeast Author Award, Northeast Booksellers Association, 1990. Honorary doctorate from Russell Sage College, 1959, New England College, 1971, Clark University, 1975, Bates College, 1976, Colby College, 1976, University of New Hampshire, 1976, Thomas Starr King School of Religious Leadership, 1976, Nasson College, 1980, University of Maine, 1981, Bowdoin College, 1983, Union College, 1984, Bucknell University, 1985, Providence College, 1989, and Centenary College, 1990.

WRITINGS:

POETRY

Encounter in April, Houghton (Boston, MA), 1937.
Inner Landscape, Houghton (Boston, MA), 1939.
The Lion and the Rose, Rinehart (Boulder, CO), 1948.
The Land of Silence, Rinehart (Boulder, CO), 1953.
In Time like Air, Rinehart (Boulder, CO), 1958.
Cloud, Stone, Suit, Vine, Norton (New York, NY), 1961.
A Private Mythology, Norton (New York, NY), 1966.
As Does New Hampshire, Richard R. Smith, 1967.
A Grain of Mustard Seed, Norton (New York, NY), 1971.
A Durable Fire, Norton (New York, NY), 1972.
Collected Poems: 1930-1973, Norton (New York, NY), 1974.
Selected Poems, Norton (New York, NY), 1978.
Halfway to Silence, Norton (New York, NY), 1980.
Letters from Maine: New Poems, Norton (New York, NY), 1984.
Honey in the Hive: Judith Matlack, 1898-1982, Warren (Boston, MA), 1988.
The Silence Now: New and Uncollected Earlier Poems, Norton (New York, NY), 1988.
Collected Poems: 1930-1993, Norton (New York, NY), 1993.
Coming into Eighty, Norton (New York, NY), 1994.

FICTION

The Single Hound, Houghton (Boston, MA), 1938.
The Bridge of Years, Doubleday (New York, NY), 1946.
Underground River (play), Play Club, 1947.
Shadow of a Man, Rinehart (Boulder, CO), 1950.
A Shower of Summer Days, Rinehart (Boulder, CO), 1952.
Faithful Are the Wounds, Rinehart (Boulder, CO), 1955.
The Fur Person: The Story of a Cat, Rinehart (Boulder, CO), 1957.
The Birth of a Grandfather, Rinehart (Boulder, CO), 1957.
The Small Room, Norton (New York, NY), 1961.
Joanna and Ulysses (young adult), Norton (New York, NY), 1963.
Mrs. Stevens Hears the Mermaids Singing, Norton (New York, NY), 1965, revised edition, 1974.
Miss Pickthorn and Mr. Hare (fable), Norton (New York, NY), 1966.
The Poet and the Donkey, Norton (New York, NY), 1969.
Kinds of Love, Norton (New York, NY), 1970.
As We Are Now, Norton (New York, NY), 1973.
Punch's Secret (juvenile), Harper (New York, NY), 1974.
Crucial Conversations, Norton (New York, NY), 1975.

A Walk through the Woods (juvenile), Harper (New York, NY), 1976.

A Reckoning, Norton (New York, NY), 1978.

Anger, Norton (New York, NY), 1982.

The Magnificent Spinster, Norton (New York, NY), 1985.

The Education of Harriet Hatfield, Norton (New York, NY), 1989.

NONFICTION

I Knew a Phoenix: Sketches for an Autobiography, Rinehart (Boulder, CO), 1959.

Plant Dreaming Deep (memoir), Norton (New York, NY), 1968.

Journal of a Solitude, Norton (New York, NY), 1973.

A World of Light: Portraits and Celebrations, Norton (New York, NY), 1976.

The House by the Sea, Norton (New York, NY), 1977.

Writings on Writing, Puckerbrush Press (Orono, ME), 1980.

Recovering: A Journal 1978-1979, Norton (New York, NY), 1980.

At Seventy: A Journal, Norton (New York, NY), 1984.

May Sarton: A Self-Portrait, edited by Marita Simpson and Martha Wheelock, Norton (New York, NY), 1986.

(Editor) Eleanor Mabel Sarton, *Letters to May,* Puckerbrush Press (Orono, ME), 1986.

After the Stroke: A Journal, Norton (New York, NY), 1988.

Endgame: A Journal of the Seventy-Ninth Year, Norton (New York, NY), 1992.

Sarton Selected: An Anthology of the Journals, Novels, and Poems of May Sarton, edited and with an introduction and notes by Bradley Dudley Daziel, Norton (New York, NY), 1992.

Encore: A Journal of the Eightieth Year, Norton (New York, NY), 1993.

May Sarton: Among the Usual Days: A Portrait: Unpublished Poems, Letters, Journals, and Photographs, selected and edited by Susan Sherman, Norton (New York, NY), 1993.

From May Sarton's Well: Writings of May Sarton, selected and with photographs by Edith Royce Schade, Papier-Mache Press (Watsonville, CA), 1994.

At Eighty-Two: A Journal, Norton (New York, NY), 1996.

May Sarton: Selected Letters, two volumes, edited and introduction by Susan Sherman, Norton (New York, NY), *1916-1954,* 1997, *1955-1995,* 2002.

Dear Juliette: Letters of May Sarton to Juliette Huxley, edited by Susan Sherman, Norton (New York, NY), 1999.

Also author of screenplays *Toscanini: The Hymn of Nations,* 1944, *Valley of the Tennessee,* 1944, and *A Better Tomorrow: Progressive Education in New York City.* Contributor to *The Movement of Poetry,* Johns Hopkins Press, 1962. Contributor of poetry, short stories, and essays to periodicals; first published poems appeared in *Poetry* magazine, December, 1930. Sarton's papers are archived in the Berg Collection of the New York Public Library and the Maine Women Writers Collection of the University of New England.

ADAPTATIONS: *A World of Light: Portraits and Celebrations* was adapted for a film featuring Sarton. Film rights to *A Reckoning, Mrs. Stevens Hears the Mermaids Singing, Kinds of Love,* and *As We Are Now* were optioned.

SIDELIGHTS: May Sarton was a prolific author who was long considered by her very loyal readers to be a gifted and sensitive writer of poetry, novels, and journals. Although at first overlooked by literary critics, in the later part of her career reviewers and feminist academics began to discover Sarton's work, lauding her as an important contemporary American author.

Critics have found Sarton's poetry, fiction, and autobiographical writings to be inspirational, touching, honest, and thought-provoking. She examines such universally appealing themes as love, friendship, relationships, and the search for self-knowledge, personal fulfillment, and inner peace. In her many books, Sarton also explores many social and political concerns, including issues of feminism and sexuality. As Penelope Moffet wrote in the *Los Angeles Times,* Sarton's "fiction, nonfiction, and poetry have a broad range and audience, encompassing the personal impacts of political events, the nature of marriages and friendships, the experiences of aging and illness, and the deaths of friends."

"Not only is she a poet, not only does she write novels and journals, but she holds herself up for all to see, large, clear," wrote George Bailin of the writer in *May Sarton: Woman and Poet.* "She examines her thinking in the open, so that one can see what a writer is, what is being accomplished, why, how. This artist reveals herself fully, and outlines the spirit of the times as well." Linda Barrett Osborne noted in the *Washington Post Book World* that "in whatever May Sarton writes one can hear the human heart pulsing just below the surface."

"Examined as a whole," Lenora P. Blouin wrote in *May Sarton: A Bibliography,* "the body of May Sarton's writing is almost overwhelming. It reveals an artist who has not remained stagnant or afraid of change. 'Truth,' especially the truth within herself, has been her life-long quest." "It is clear that May Sarton's best work," suggested Sheila Ballantyne in the *New York Times Book Review,* "whatever its form, will endure well beyond the influence of particular reviews or current tastes. For in it she is an example: a seeker after truth with a kind of awesome energy for renewal, an ardent explorer of life's important questions. Her great strength is that when she achieves insight, one believes—because one has witnessed the struggle that preceded the knowledge; her discoveries do not come cheap."

Critics have termed Sarton's poetry calm, cultured, and urbane. A reviewer for *Poetry* described it as "fluent, fluid, humble with a humility not entirely false, cultivated rather than worldly, tasteful, civilized, and accomplished." In *Babel to Byzantium,* James Dickey commented that Sarton "attains a delicate simplicity as quickeningly direct as it is deeply given, and does so with the courteous serenity, the clear, caring, intelligent and human calm of the queen of a small, well-ordered country." "In her most perfect poems," a reviewer for *Choice* wrote, ". . . the fusion of passion and discipline is marvelously realized." Reviewing *Collected Poems: 1930-1973,* Elizabeth Knies described the volume as "intelligently conceived and finely wrought" and called it "the consummation of a distinguished career and a major achievement in its own right."

Several reviewers have hailed Sarton's ability to connect with the essence of humanity. In an appraisal of *Collected Poems: 1930-1993, Belles Lettres* critic Andrea Lockett praised Sarton's skillful use of images and added that "the content of the poems goes straight to the marrow of human experience." In a *Poetry* review of *Collected Poems: 1930-1973,* James Martin remarked that "Sarton's poems enter and illuminate every natural corner of our lives. . . . Sarton has, for more than forty years, made patient, enduring testament. . . . Sarton's poems are so strong in their faith and in their positive response to the human condition that they will outlast much of the fashionable, cynical poetry of our era."

Sarton's poetic labors continued far into her old age. After recovering from a 1986 stroke, she told *Los Angeles Times* interviewer Penelope Moffet that the most difficult aspect of her recuperation period was the temporary inability to write poetry. When she returned to writing, many of her poems explored growing older. Her final poetry book, *Coming into Eighty,* deals bluntly with the realities of aging and the difficulties of performing everyday tasks. "In form the poems are very restrained, but not in emotion," a *Publishers Weekly* reviewer observed.

In addition to her poems, Sarton also wrote many novels and frequently received acclaim for these works. Critics cited such qualities as her strong narrative technique, her sensitive and revealing character portrayals, and her simple, unadorned prose style. Jane S. Bakerman explained in *Critique* that Sarton's novels generally deal with two overarching themes: first, "the driving need of each individual to 'create' himself, to come to a deep and positive kind of self-understanding which will both liberate and discipline him so that he can live in the deepest and highest reaches." Bakerman continued: "In the process of achieving that understanding, the individual must, also, come to understand others and his relations with them."

Sarton's first novel, *The Single Hound,* was hailed as "beautiful and distinguished" by Jane Spence Southron in the *New York Times Book Review.* In this tale of two poets, Sarton endows her characters with "rich, bountiful life . . . deeply rooted in that humanity which is ageless," Southron wrote. A few years later Sarton's *The Bridge of Years,* a story of a Belgian family resisting fascism, won praise; it is a "delicately lovely novel," enthused Florence Haxton Bullock in the *New York Herald Tribune Weekly Book Review.* "Its style is limpid, unpretentious, beautifully expressive, and its content is beyond all things warmly and humanly emotional."

Faithful Are the Wounds, released in 1955, deals with a liberal U.S. academic who is driven to suicide by the political repressiveness of the times. It is "by all odds [Sarton's] . . . best" novel, according to Edward Weeks in the *Atlantic Monthly,* although *Yale Review* contributor Paul Pickrel found the characters and their motivations excessively ambiguous. *Mrs. Stevens Hears the Mermaids Singing,* published in 1965, is considered by many to be a groundbreaking work and Sarton's most important novel. The book explores the inspirations of a poet who also happens to be a lesbian—making it one of the first novels written for a general audience to feature a lesbian central character portrayed in a positive fashion.

As Sarton's body of work grew, she began to address sexuality, feminism, and other social concerns in her fiction. "Although Sarton's books could hardly be called political novels (with the exception of *Faithful Are the Wounds*), most of them are set in the framework of an acute social conscience," commented Valerie Miner in a review of *The Magnificent Spinster* for the *Women's Review of Books.* This novel, a story of a lifelong friendship between two distinguished women, shows its protagonists fighting sexism, racism, and other forces of oppression. It also, Miner noted, deals with "lesbian attraction . . . without the throat-clearing fanfare of more didactic lesbian novels."

Sarton resisted being pegged as strictly a lesbian or feminist writer: "The vision of life in my work is not limited to one segment of humanity . . . and has little to do with sexual proclivity," Sarton wrote in *Recovering: A Journal 1978-1979. New York Times Book Review* critic Sheila Ballantyne, though, found this professed universality contradicted by the characterizations in Sarton's novel *Anger.* Ballantyne believed that in this book, Sarton used gender stereotypes in portraying the marriage of an emotional, artistic woman and a cold, distant man. In the *Washington Post Book World,* however, Linda Barrett Osborne commented that "the ideas developed in *Anger* reach beyond the conflict of men and women and consider the deeper questions of personal, emotional, and artistic growth"—these deeper questions being frequent themes of Sarton's. "To see it as part of the body of Sarton's work amplifies and enhances the book, and gives it a resonance it might not otherwise have," Osborne concluded.

In addition to poetry and novels, Sarton published many journals, beginning with 1973's *Journal of a Solitude.* She had written memoirs previously, but turned to journal writing in a quest for "a more immediate, less controlled record," as Rockwell Gray put it in a Chicago *Tribune Books* review of *Encore: A Journal of the Eightieth Year.* Suzanne Owens, describing *Journal of a Solitude* as "a brooding work," pointed out the difference between memoirs and journals in an essay for *May Sarton: Woman and Poet:* "the daily and scrupulous recording of life through journal writing may be a much darker work than the memoir softened by memory." Sarton's journals found a wide audience; she became "perhaps best known for the journals that have chronicled her life of solitude on the coast and in the interior of New England, her passionate love of other women and her wrestle with the demons of creativity," remarked Sue Halpern in a review of *Endgame: A Journal of the Seventy-ninth Year* for the *New York Times Book Review.* Halpern termed Sarton's journals "reflective, honest, engaged and circumspect." While readers could tire of *Endgame*'s detailing of Sarton's physical ills, Halpern wrote, this is part of a truthful recounting of this period of Sarton's life, and the book has numerous uplifting moments as well.

Encore likewise devotes some space to the infirmities of Sarton's old age, while also dealing with her interactions with friends and observations of current events. *New York Times* contributor Herbert Mitgang found *Encore* "consistently charming," and *Bloomsbury Review* writer Nancy Schwartzkopff deemed it "a celebration of life." Rockwell Gray, however, thought it marred by "narcissistic vanity and self-regard that surface unbecomingly in so many of her entries." The work would benefit, Gray went on, from "greater stringency and self-criticism." *Women's Review of Books* contributor Edith Milton had a similar complaint: "What fails [Sarton] . . . is her imagination. Nowhere does she push her observation beyond herself."

Many of Sarton's previously unpublished poems, letters, journals, and photographs are collected in *May Sarton: Among the Usual Days: A Portrait.* Selected and edited by Susan Sherman, a close friend of Sarton's, the material provides "a complex but seamless portrait," commented Phyllis F. Mannocchi in the *NWSA Journal.* There was more to come from Sarton, however; *At Eighty-Two: A Journal* was published the year of the writer's death, serving as a "poignantly intimate" look at the writer, according to a *Publishers Weekly* reviewer.

Sarton died of breast cancer on July 16, 1995, after what Mel Gussow, in an obituary for the *New York Times,* termed a "remarkably prolific career." Sarton had expressed a wish for readers to see the interrelationships of her numerous writings: "It is my hope," she once wrote, "that all [my work] may come to be seen as a whole, the communication of a vision of life that is unsentimental, humorous, passionate, and, in the end, timeless." Since her death, Sarton's friend Sherman has edited and collected much of her previously unpublished correspondence. Sarton's "passion for words and relationships emerged in the scores of letters she wrote to her friends, family, and critics," Henry L. Carrigan, Jr., wrote in a review of one such collection, *May Sarton: Selected Letters, 1955-1995,* for *Library Journal.*

Dear Juliette: Letters of May Sarton to Juliette Huxley contains letters between Sarton and Juliette Huxley, the wife of biologist Julian Huxley, with whom she had a lesbian affair after abandoning Huxley himself, who had first been her lover. "Evidently, Sarton had a certain capacity for self-deception," *Library Journal* reviewer David Kirby commented about her perception of the relationship between herself and the Huxleys, but in the letters "she is never less than totally captivating." *Booklist* reviewer Brad Hooper concluded that the letters provide the reader with a sense of "Sarton's passion—passion not only toward Juliette but also toward her calling in life, which was poetry writing."

BIOGRAPHICAL AND CRITICAL SOURCES:

BOOKS

Blotner, Joseph, *The Modern American Political Novel: 1900-1960,* University of Texas Press (Austin, TX), 1966.

Blouin, Lenora, *May Sarton: A Bibliography,* Scarecrow Press (Metuchen, NJ), 1978.

Contemporary Literary Criticism, Thomson Gale (Detroit, MI), Volume 4, 1975, Volume 14, 1980, Volume 49, 1988.

Dickey, James, *Babel to Byzantium,* Farrar, Straus (New York, NY), 1968.

Dictionary of Literary Biography, Volume 48: *American Poets, 1880-1945, Second Series,* Thomson Gale (Detroit, MI), 1986.

Dictionary of Literary Biography Yearbook: 1981, Thomson Gale (Detroit, MI), 1982.

Hunting, Constance, editor, *May Sarton: Woman and Poet,* National Poetry Foundation (Orono, ME), 1982.

Peters, Margot, *May Sarton: A Biography,* Knopf (New York, NY), 1997.

Rule, Jane, *Lesbian Images,* Doubleday (New York, NY), 1975.

Sarton, May, *Recovering: A Journal 1978-1979,* Norton (New York, NY), 1980.

Silbey, Agnes, *May Sarton,* Twayne (New York, NY), 1972.

PERIODICALS

Arizona Quarterly, winter, 1962.

Atlantic Monthly, January, 1953; May, 1955, Edward Weeks, review of *Faithful Are the Wounds,* pp. 74, 76; June, 1975.

Belles Lettres, spring, 1994, Jeanne Braham, review of *Encore: A Journal of the Eightieth Year* and *May Sarton: Among the Usual Days, a Portrait,* pp. 35-37, Andrea Lockett, review of *Collected Poems: 1930-1993,* p. 37.

Bloomsbury Review, September/October, 1993, Nancy Schwartzkopff, review of *Encore,* p. 22.

Booklist, June 1, 1999, Brad Hooper, review of *Dear Juliette: Letters of May Sarton to Juliette Huxley,* p. 1785.

Book Week, December 29, 1963.

Boston Globe, May 14, 1950; May 15, 1992, p. 94; December 10, 1992, p. 67.

Chicago Tribune, May 7, 1950.

Choice, January, 1979.

Christian Science Monitor, April 8, 1939; June 10, 1950; November 13, 1978.

Commonweal, July 4, 1975.

Critique, Volume 20, number 2, 1978, Jane S. Bakerman.

English Journal, April, 1989, Louise J. Weiner, review of *Journal of a Solitude, The House by the Sea,* and *After the Stroke,* p. 91.

Georgia Review, winter, 1994, Fred Chappell, review of *Collected Poems,* pp. 784-799.

Hudson Review, summer, 1967.

Library Journal, July, 1999, David Kirby, review of *Dear Juliette,* p. 90; April 15, 2002, Henry L. Carrigan, Jr., review of *May Sarton: Selected Letters, 1955-1995,* p. 86.

Los Angeles Times, March 16, 1957; December 24, 1980; October 8, 1982; April 2, 1984, Elaine Kendall, review of *At Seventy,* p. 10; April 29, 1987, Penelope Moffet, interview with Sarton.

Massachusetts Review, summer, 1967.

New Leader, March 28, 1955.

New Republic, June 8, 1974.

New Yorker, February 27, 1954, p. 115.

New York Herald Tribune Weekly Book Review, April 21, 1946, Florence Haxton Bullock, review of *The Single Hound,* p. 5.

New York Times, November 20, 1983, Enid Nemy, "May Sarton: Creative Solitude at 71," p. 74; August 18, 1993, Herbert Mitgang, review of *Encore,* section C, p. 17.

New York Times Book Review, March 20, 1938, p. 6; March 5, 1939, p. 5; September 8, 1957, p. 4; November 24, 1963; October 24, 1965; November 12, 1978; October 17, 1982, Sheila Ballantyne, review of *Anger,* pp. 14, 37-38; March 27, 1988, Nancy Mairs, review of *After the Stroke,* p. 30; July 2, 1989, Alfred Corn, review of *The Education of Harriet Hatfield,* p. 5; July 21, 1989; June 21, 1992, Sue Halpern, review of *Endgame: A Journal of the Seventy-Ninth Year,* p. 18; January 7, 1996, Terry Teachout, review of *At Eighty-two: A Journal,* p. 12.

NWSA Journal, spring, 1995, Phyllis F. Mannocchi, review of *May Sarton: Among the Usual Days,* pp. 131-137.

Poetry, July, 1937, pp. 229-231; April, 1968; May, 1975, August, 1992, pp. 284-304.

Publishers Weekly, June 24, 1974; October 31, 1994, reviews of *Coming Into Eighty* and *From May Sarton's Well: Writings of May Sarton,* pp. 55-56; October 16, 1995, review of *At Eighty-Two,* pp. 48-49; May 31, 1999, review of *Dear Juliette,* p. 77.

Punch, April 11, 1962.

Sewanee Review, spring, 1958.

Southern Review, spring, 1967.

Time, March 21, 1938; October 1, 1965.

Tribune Books (Chicago, IL), August 15, 1993, Rockwell Gray, review of *Encore,* p. 14.

Village Voice, June 13, 1974.

Virginia Quarterly Review, spring, 1962.

Washington Post, October 10, 1980; December 23, 1985.

Washington Post Book World, December 12, 1982, Linda Barrett Osborne, review of *Anger,* p. 11.

Western Humanities Review, autumn, 1971.

Women's Review of Books, December, 1985, pp. 7-8; December, 1993, Edith Milton, review of *Encore,* pp. 8-9.

Yale Review, June, 1955, Paul Pickrel, review of *Faithful Are the Wounds,* pp. 634-640.

ONLINE

Academy of American Poets, http://www.poets.org/ (September 9, 2004), "May Sarton."

Literary Traveler Web Site, http://www.literarytraveler.com/ (September 9, 2004), Deborah Straw, "Permanence and May Sarton."

Penn Library Web Site, http://digital.library.upenn.edu/ (September 9, 2004), Lenora P. Blouin, "May Sarton: A Poet's Life."

Unitarian Universalist Association Web Site, http://www.uua.org/ (September 9, 2004), Lenora P. Blouin, "May Sarton."

* * *

SARTRE, Jean-Paul 1905-1980 (Jacques Guillemin)

PERSONAL: Born June 21, 1905, in Paris, France; died of a lung ailment, April 15, 1980, in Paris, France; son of Jean-Baptiste (a naval officer) and Anne-Marie (Schweitzer) Sartre; children: Arlette el Kaim-Sartre (adopted). *Education:* Attended Lycée Louis-le-Grand; École Normale Superieure, agrege de philosophie, 1930; further study in Egypt, Italy, Greece, and in Germany under Edmund Husserl and Martin Heidegger. *Politics:* Communist, but not party member. *Religion:* Atheist.

CAREER: Philosopher and author of novels, plays, screenplays, biographies, and literary and political criticism. Professor of philosophy at Lycée le Havre, 1931-32 and 1934-36, Institut Français, Berlin, Germany, 1933-34, Lycée de Laon, 1936-37, Lycée Pasteur, 1937-39, and Lycée Condorcet, 1941-44. *Les Temps modernes,* 1944, founder and editor, beginning 1945. Lecturer at various institutions in United States, including Harvard, Columbia, Yale, and Princeton universities, and in Europe, the USSR, and China. *Military service:* Meteorological Corps, 1929-31; French Army, 1939-40; prisoner of war in Germany for nine months, 1940-41. Served in resistance movement, 1941-44, wrote for its underground newspapers, *Combat* and *Les Lettres Françaises.* Cofounder, French Rally of Revolutionary Democrats.

MEMBER: American Academy of Arts and Sciences, Modern Language Association of America (honorary fellow).

AWARDS, HONORS: Roman populiste prize, 1940, for *Le mur;* French Legion d'honneur, 1945 (refused); New York Drama Critics Award for best foreign play of the season, 1947, for *No Exit;* French Grand Novel Prize, 1950, for *La Nausée;* Omegna prize (Italy), 1960, for total body of work; Nobel Prize for Literature, 1964 (refused); honorary doctorate from Hebrew University, 1976.

WRITINGS:

PHILOSOPHY

L'imagination, Librairie Felix Alcan, 1936, French and European Publications, 1970, translation by Forrest Williams published as *Imagination: A Psychological Critique,* University of Michigan Press (Ann Arbor, MI), 1962.

Esquisse d'une theorie des emotions, Hermann, 1939, translation by Bernard Frechtman published as *The Emotions: Outline of a Theory,* Philosophical Library, 1948, translation by Philip Mairet published as *Sketch for a Theory of the Emotions,* Methuen (London, England), 1962.

L'imaginaire: psychologie phenomenologique de l'imagination, Gallimard (Paris, France), 1940, translation published as *The Psychology of Imagination,* Philosophical Library, 1948, translated by Jonathan Webber as *The Imaginary: A Phenomenological Psychology of the Imagination,* Routledge (New York, NY), 2003.

L'etre et le néant: essai d'ontologie phenomenologique, Gallimard (Paris, France), 1943, translation by Hazel E. Barnes published as *Being and Nothingness: An Essay on Phenomenological Ontology,* Philosophical Library, 1956, reprinted, Regnery (Washington, DC), 1996, abridged edition, Citadel, 1964, portions published as *The Wisdom of Jean-Paul Sartre,* Philosophical Library, 1968.

L'existentialisme est un humanisme, Nagel, 1946, translation by Bernard Frechtman published as *Existentialism* (also see below), Philosophical Library, 1947, translation by Philip Mairet published as *Existentialism and Humanism,* Methuen (London, England), 1948.

Existentialism and Human Emotions (selections from *Existentialism* and *Being and Nothingness: An Essay on Phenomenological Ontology*), Philosophical Library, 1957.

Transcendence of the Ego: An Existentialist Theory of Consciousness, translation by Forrest Williams and Robert Kirkpatrick, Noonday, 1957, original French edition published as *La transcendance de l'ego: Esquisse d'une description phenomenologique,* J. Vrin, 1965.

Critique de la raison dialectique: precede de question de methode, Gallimard (Paris, France), 1960, translation by Alan Sheridan-Smith published as *Critique of Dialectical Reason: Theory of Practical Ensembles,* Humanities, 1976.

(With others) *Marxisme et existentialisme,* Plon (Paris, France), 1962, translation by John Matthews published as *Between Existentialism and Marxism,* NLB, 1974.

Choix de textes, edited by J. Sebille, Nathan, 1962, 2nd edition, 1966.

Essays in Aesthetics, selected and translated by Wade Baskin, Philosophical Library, 1963.

Search for a Method, translation by Hazel Barnes, Knopf (New York, NY), 1963, published as *The Problem of Method,* Methuen (London, England), 1964, original French edition published as *Question de methode,* Gallimard (Paris, France), 1967.

The Philosophy of Existentialism, edited by Wade Baskin, Philosophical Library, 1965.

The Philosophy of Jean-Paul Sartre (translated excerpts), edited by Robert Denoon Cummings, Random House (New York, NY), 1965.

Of Human Freedom, edited by Wade Baskin, Philosophical Library, 1967.

Essays in Existentialism, selected and edited with a foreword by Wade Baskin, Citadel, 1967.

Textes choisis, edited by Marc Beigbeder and Gerard Deledalle, Bordes, 1968.

Verite et existence, edited by Arlette el Kaim-Sartre, Gallimard (Paris, France), 1990.

FICTION

La nausée, Gallimard (Paris, France), 1938, translation by Lloyd Alexander published as *Nausea,* New Directions (New York, NY), 1949, published as *The Diary of Antoine Requentin,* J. Lehmann, 1949, new edition with illustrations by Walter Spitzer, Lidis, 1964, new translation by Robert Baldick, Penguin, 1965.

Le mur, Gallimard (Paris, France), 1939, with an introduction and notes by Walter Redferm, Bristol Classics Press (London, England), 1997, translation published as *The Wall, and Other Stories,* preface by Jean-Louis Curtis, New Directions (New York, NY), 1948.

Les chemins de la liberte, Volume 1: *L'age de raison,* Gallimard (Paris, France), 1945, new edition with illustrations by Walter Spitzer, Lidis, 1965, Volume 2: *Le Sursis,* Gallimard, 1945, Volume 3: *La mort dans l'ame,* Gallimard, 1949, French and European Publications, 1972, translation published as *The Roads of Freedom,* Volume 1: *The Age of Reason,* translation by Eric Sutton, Knopf (New York, NY), 1947, new edition with introduction by Henri Peyre, Bantam (New York, NY), 1968, Volume 2: *The Reprieve,* translation by Eric Sutton, Knopf, 1947, Volume 3: *Iron in the Soul,* translation by Gerard Hopkins, Hamish Hamilton (London, England), 1950, translation by Hopkins published as *Troubled Sleep,* Knopf, 1951.

Intimacy, and Other Stories, translation by Lloyd Alexander, Berkley Publishing, 1956.

PLAYS

Les mouches (also see below; produced in Paris, France, 1942; translation by Stuart Gilbert produced as *The Flies* in New York, NY, 1947), Gallimard (Paris, France), 1943, new edition edited by F.C. St. Aubyn and Robert G. Marshall, Harper (New York, NY), 1963.

Huis-clos (also see below; produced in Paris, France, 1944; translation by Marjorie Gabain and Joan Swinstead produced as *The Vicious Circle* in London, England, 1946; translation by Paul Bowles produced as *No Exit* on Broadway, 1946), Gallimard (Paris, France), 1945, new edition edited by Jacques Hardre and George B. Daniel, Appleton (New York, NY), 1962.

The Flies (also see below) [and] *In Camera,* translation by Gilbert, Hamish Hamilton (London, England), 1946, published with *No Exit,* Knopf (New York, NY), 1947, original French edition published as *Huis-clos* [and] *Les mouches,* Gallimard (Paris, France), 1964.

Morts sans sepulture (also see below; produced with *La putain respectueuse* in Sweden, 1946; produced in Paris, France, 1946; translation produced as *Men without Shadows* on London's West End, 1947; translation produced as *The Victors* in New York, NY, 1948), Marguerat, 1946.

La putain respectueuse (also see below; produced with *Morts sans sepulture* in Sweden, 1946; produced in Paris, France, 1946), Nagel, 1946, translation published as *The Respectful Prostitute* (also see below; produced in London, England, 1948; produced on Broadway, 1948), Twice a Year Press, 1948.

Theatre I (contains *Les mouches, Huis-clos, Morts sans sepulture,* and *La putain respectueuse*), Gallimard (Paris, France), 1947.

Les jeux sont faits (screenplay; produced by Gibe-Pathe Films, 1947), Nagel, 1947, new edition edited by Mary Elizabeth Storer, Appleton (New York, NY), 1952, translation by Louise Varese published as *The Chips Are Down,* Lear, 1948.

Les mains sales (also see below; produced in Paris, France, 1948; translation by Kitty Black produced as *Crime Passionnel* on London's West End, 1948, and adapted by Daniel Taradash and produced as *The Red Gloves* in New York, NY, 1948), Gallimard (Paris, France), 1948, published as *Les mains sales: Piece en sept tableaux,* edited by Geoffrey Brereton, Methuen (London, England), 1963, new edition with analysis and notes by Gaston Meyer, Bordas, 1971.

L'engrenage (screenplay), Nagel, 1948, translation by Mervyn Savill published as *In the Mesh,* A. Dakers, 1954.

Three Plays (contains *The Victors, Dirty Hands* [translation of *Les mains sales*], and *The Respectable Prostitute*), translation by Lionel Abel, Knopf (New York, NY), 1949.

Three Plays: Crime Passionnel, Men without Shadows, [and] *The Respectable Prostitute,* translation by Kitty Black, Hamish Hamilton (London, England), 1949.

Le diable et le bon dieu (produced in Paris, France, 1951), Gallimard (Paris, France), 1951, translation by Kitty Black published as *Lucifer and the Lord* (also see below), Hamish Hamilton (London, England), 1953, published as *The Devil and the Good Lord, and Two Other Plays,* Knopf (New York, NY), 1960.

(Adapter) Alexandre Dumas, *Kean* (also see below; produced in Paris, France, 1953), Gallimard (Paris, France), 1954, translation by Kitty Black published as *Kean, or Disorder and Genius,* Hamish Hamilton (London, England), 1954, Vintage (New York, NY), 1960.

No Exit, and Three Other Plays (contains *No Exit, The Flies, Dirty Hands,* and *The Respectful Prostitute*), Random House (New York, NY), 1955.

Nekrassov (also see below; produced in Paris, France, 1955), Gallimard (Paris, France), 1956, translation by Sylvia and George Leeson published as *Nekrassov* (produced in London, England, 1957), Hamish Hamilton (London, England), 1956, French and European Publications, 1973.

Les sequestres d'Altona (also see below; produced in Paris, France, 1959), Gallimard (Paris, France), 1960, new edition edited and with an introduction by Philip Thody, University of London Press (London, England), 1965, translation by S. Leeson and G. Leeson published as *Loser Wins,* Hamish Hamilton (London, England), 1960, published as *The Condemned of Altona* (also see below; produced on Broadway, 1966), Knopf (New York, NY), 1961.

Crime Passionnel: A Play, translation by Kitty Black, Methuen (London, England), 1961.

Theatre (contains *Les mouches, Huis-clos, Morts sans sepulture, La putain respectueuse, Les mains sales, Le diable et le bon dieu, Kean, Nekrassov,* and *Les sequestres d'Altona*), Gallimard (Paris, France), 1962.

Bariona, Anjou-Copies, 1962, 2nd edition, E. Marescot, 1967.

The Condemned of Altona, Men without Shadows, [and] *The Flies,* Penguin, 1962.

Orphee noir (first published in *Anthologie de la nouvelle poesie negre et malgache de langue françeaise,* Presses Universitaires de France, 1948), translation by S.W. Allen published as *Black Orpheus,* University Place Book Shop, c. 1963.

La putain respectueuse, piece en un acte et deux tableaux: suivi de Morts sans sepulture, piece en deux actes et quatre tableax, Gallimard (Paris, France), 1963.

The Respectable Prostitute [and] *Lucifer and the Lord,* translation by Kitty Black, Penguin, 1965.

(Adapter) Euripides, *Les troyennes* (produced in Paris, France, 1965), Gallimard (Paris, France), 1966, translation by Ronald Duncan published as *The Trojan Women* (also see below), Knopf (New York, NY), 1967.

Three Plays (contains *Kean, or Disorder and Genius, Nekrassov,* and *The Trojan Women*), Penguin, 1969.

Five Plays (contains *No Exit, The Flies, Dirty Hands, The Respectful Prostitute,* and *The Condemned of Altona*), Franklin Library, 1978.

Also author of screenplays *Typhus,* 1944, and *Les sorcieres de Salem* (adapted from Arthur Miller's *The Crucible*); author of unpublished play *All the Treasures of the Earth.*

ESSAYS

Réflexions sur la question juive, P. Morihien, 1946, translation by George J. Becker published as *Anti-Semite and Jew,* Schocken (New York, NY), 1948, reprinted, 1995, translation by Erik de Mauney published as *Portrait of the Anti-Semite,* Secker & Warburg (London, England), 1948.

Baudelaire, Gallimard (Paris, France), 1947, translation by Martin Turnell published as *Baudelaire,* Horizon (London, England), 1949, New Directions (New York, NY), 1950.

Situations I, Gallimard (Paris, France), 1947, published as *Critiques litteraires,* 1975.

Situations II, Gallimard (Paris, France), 1948.

Qu'est-ce que le litterature? (first published in *Situations II*), Gallimard (Paris, France), 1949, translation by Bernard Frechtman published as *What Is Literature?,* Philosophical Library, 1949, published as *Literature and Existentialism,* Citadel, 1962.

Situations III, Gallimard (Paris, France), 1949.

(With David Rousset and Gerard Rosenthal) *Entretiens sur la politique,* Gallimard (Paris, France), 1949.

Saint Genet, comedien et martyr, Gallimard (Paris, France), 1952, translation by Bernard Frechtman published as *Saint Genet: Actor and Martyr,* Braziller (New York, NY), 1963.

Literary and Philosophical Essays (excerpts from *Situations I* and *III*), translation by Annette Michelson, Criterion, 1955.

Literary Essays (excerpts from *Situations I* and *III*), translation by Michelson, Philosophical Library, 1957.

Sartre on Cuba, Ballantine (New York, NY), 1961.

Situations IV: Portraits, Gallimard (Paris, France), 1964, translation by Benita Eisler published as *Situations,* Braziller (New York, NY), 1965.

Situations V: Colonialisme et neo-colonialisme, Gallimard (Paris, France), 1964, translation published as *Colonialism and Neocolonialism,* Routledge (New York, NY), 2001.

Les communistes et la paix (first published in *Situations VI*), Gallimard (Paris, France), 1964, translation by Martha H.Fletcher and John R. Kleinschmidt (bound with "A Reply to Claude Lefort" translated by Philip R. Berk) published as *The Communists and Peace,* Braziller (New York, NY), 1968.

Situations VI: Problemes du Marxisme, Part I, Gallimard, (Paris, France) 1966.

(Contributor) Aimé Cesaire, *Das politische Denken Lumumbas,* Klaus Wagenbach, 1966.

Situations VII: Problemes du Marxisme, Part II, Gallimard (Paris, France), 1967.

On Genocide, with commentary on the International War Crimes Tribunal by Sartre's adopted daughter, Arlette el Kaim-Sartre, Beacon Press (Boston, MA), 1968.

The Ghost of Stalin, translation by Martha H. Fletcher and John R. Kleinschmidt, Braziller (New York, NY), 1968, translation by Irene Clephane published as *The Spectre of Stalin,* Hamish Hamilton (London, England), 1969.

Les communistes ont peur de la revolution, J. Didier (Paris, France), 1969.

(With Vladimir Dedijer) *War Crimes in Vietnam,* Bertrand Russell Peace Foundation, 1971.

L'idiot de la famille, Gallimard (Paris, France), 1971, translation by Carol Cosman published as *The Family Idiot: Gustave Flaubert, 1821-1857,* three volumes, University of Chicago Press, 1981–89.

Situations VIII: autour de 1968, French and European Publications, 1972.

Situations IX: melanges, French and European Publications, 1972.

Situations X: politique et autobiographie, French and European Publications, 1976, translation by Paul Auster and Lydia Davis published as *Life/Situations: Essays Written and Spoken,* Pantheon (New York, NY), 1977.

OTHER

Sartre par lui-meme, edited by Francis Jeanson, Seuil (Paris, France), 1959, translation by Richard Seaver published as *Sartre by Himself,* Outback Press, 1978.

(Author of text) Andre Masson, *Vingt-deux dessins sur le theme du desir,* F. Mourtot, 1961.

Les mots (autobiography), Gallimard (Paris, France), 1963, translation by Bernard Frechtman published as *The Words,* Braziller (New York, NY), 1964, translation by Clephane published as *Words,* Hamish Hamilton (London, England), 1964.

(Editor with Bertrand Russell) *Das Vietnam Tribunal,* Rowohlt, 1970.

Gott ohne Gott (contains *Bariona* and a dialogue with Sartre), edited by Gotthold Hasenhuttl, Graz (Austria), 1972.

Un theatre de situations, compiled and edited by Michel Contat and Michel Rybalka, Gallimard (Paris, France), 1973, translation by Frank Jellinck published as *Sartre on Theater,* Pantheon (New York, NY), 1976.

Oeuvres romanesques, edited by Contat and Rybalka, Gallimard (Paris, France), 1981.

Cahiers pour une morale, Gallimard (Paris, France), 1983.

Carnets de la drole de guerre, Gallimard (Paris, France), 1983, new edition, 1995.

(With Simone de Beauvoir) *Lettres au Castor et a quelques autres,* Volume 1: *1926-1939,* translated by Lee Fahnestock and Norman MacAfee as *Witness to My Life: The Letters of Jean-Paul Sartre to Simone de Beauvoir, 1926-1939,* Scribner (New York, NY), 1992, Volume 2: *1940-1963,* translated by Fahnestock and MacAfee as *Quiet Moments in a War: The Letters of Jean-Paul Sartre to Simone de Beauvoir, 1940-1963,* Macmillan (New York, NY), 1993.

Le scenario Freud, Gallimard (Paris, France), 1984, translation by Quintin Hoare published as *The Freud Scenario,* University of Chicago Press (Chicago, IL), 1985.

The War Diaries of Jean-Paul Sartre, Random House (New York, NY), 1985.

Notes from a Phony War, Gallimard (Paris, France), 1995.

(With Benny Levy) *Hope Now: The 1980 Interviews,* translated by Adrian van den Hoven, University of Chicago Press (Chicago, IL), 1996.

Existential Psychoanalysis, Regnery (Washington, DC), 1997.

Jean-Paul Sartre: Basic Writings, Routledge (New York, NY), 2000.

Sartre and Camus: A Historic Confrontation, edited by David A. Sprintzen and Adrian van den Hoven, Humanity Books (Amherst, NY), 2004.

Contributor to numerous books, including *L'Affaire Henri Martin* (title means "The Henry Martin Affair"), Gallimard (Paris, France), 1953; and to anthologies and periodicals. Editor of *La Cause du peuple,* beginning 1970, *Tout!,* beginning 1970, and *Revolution!,* beginning 1971.

ADAPTATIONS: The Chips Are Down, a film based on Sartre's screenplay *Le jeux sont faits,* was produced by Lopert, 1949; *Les mains sales,* a film based on Sartre's play of the same title, was produced by Rivers Films, 1951 and later released in the United States as *Dirty Hands; La putain respectueuse,* a film based on Sartre's play of the same title, was produced by Agiman Films and Artes Films, 1952; *The Respectable Prostitute,* a film based on Sartre's play *La putain respectueuse,* was produced by Gala, 1955; *Les orgueilleux,* a film based on Sartre's original screenplay *Typhus,* was produced by Jean Productions, 1953, and was released in the United States as *The Proud and the Beautiful* by Kingsley, 1956; *Huis-clos,* a film based on Sartre's play of the same title, was produced by Jacqueline Audry, 1954; *Kean, Genio e Sregolatezza,* a film based on an Alexandré Dumas play adapted by Sartre, was produced by Lux Films, 1957; *Les sequestres d'Altona,* a film based on Sartre's play of the same title, was produced by Titanus Films, 1963 and released in the United States as *The Condemned of Altona* by Twentieth Century-Fox, 1963; a television production based on *Huis-clos* was broadcast on O.R.T.F. (French Radio-Television) in 1965; *Le mur,* a film based on Sartre's short story of the same title, was produced by Niepce Films, 1967; *The Roads to Freedom,* a thirteen-week television serial based on Sartre's novels, *The Age of Reason, The Reprieve,* and *Troubled Sleep* was produced by the British Broadcasting Corp., 1970.

SIDELIGHTS: Jean-Paul Sartre was one of the major intellectual figures of the twentieth century, doubtless the greatest of his immediate generation in France. In the words of Sartrean scholars Michel Contat and Michel Rybalka in *The Writings of Jean-Paul Sartre,* he was "uncontestably the most outstanding philosopher and writer" of his age. Henri Peyre, in his preface to *The Condemned of Altona,* called Sartre "the most powerful intellect at work . . . in the literature of Western Europe," the "Picasso of literature." Since his death in 1980, Sartre's reputation has not waned, and with perspective it is clear that he represented his age much as, in different ways, Voltaire (1694-1778), Victor Hugo (1802-1885), and André Gide (1869-1951) represented theirs. "To understand Jean-Paul Sartre," wrote Iris Murdoch in *Sartre: Romantic Rationalist,* "is to understand something important about the present time."

Sartre was the chief proponent of French existentialism, a philosophic school—influenced by Sören Kierkegaard and German philosophers—that developed around the close of the World War II. Existentialism stresses the primacy of the thinking person and of concrete individual experience as the source of knowledge; this philosophy also emphasized the anguish and solitude inherent in the making of choices.

Sartre's literary and philosophic careers are inextricably bound together, and are best understood in relation to one another and to their biographic context. An only child, Sartre decided at an early age to be a writer. According to *The Words,* the autobiography of his youth, this decision was made in conscious opposition to the wishes of his grandfather, Charles Schweitzer (who, after the death of Sartre's father, raised the boy with the help of Sartre's grandmother). Schweitzer, a domineering Protestant who was nevertheless very fond of his grandson and extremely indulgent with him, appeared to young Sartre as insincere, a consummate charlatan. Schweitzer preached the serious values of the bourgeoisie and tried to denigrate a career in letters as precarious, unsuitable for stable middle-class people. In reaction, Sartre proposed to make writing *serious,* to adopt it as the center of his life and values. He also chose it as a kind of self-justification in a world where a child was not taken seriously. "By writing I was existing. I was escaping from the grown-ups," he wrote in *The Words.*

When his mother remarried, Sartre moved from Paris to La Rochelle with her and his stepfather, a solemn professional man with whom he felt little in common. All the same, young Sartre followed the path of a professional, finishing his lycée studies in Paris and completing university work at the École Normale Superieure. There he met feminist intellectual Simone de Beauvoir, who was to be a lifelong companion, though by no means his only love interest.

As a student Sartre became interested in philosophy, pursuing it through the agregation—the highest French degree preparing for a teaching career. Sartre was steeped in the Cartesian rationalist tradition whereby the subject's existence is proven by his thought, although eventually he largely departed from this philosophy. The topic of his thesis, the imagination, shows how his philosophic concerns supported his early interest in creative writing. Other of his treatises of the 1930s concern the emotions and what Sartre called the transcendence of the ego—or the nature of the self—which, he argued, is created by the individual instead of being a given. At the same time that he was pursuing these investigations on the imagination, Sartre became acquainted with phenomenology, a branch of philosophy associated with such German scholars as Edmund Husserl, with whom Sartre studied for a year in Berlin.

Throughout the 1930s Sartre's philosophic and literary pursuits supported each other and developed along parallel lines. At the beginning of the decade he began work on a fictional piece first called "A Pamphlet on Contingency"—contingency being lack of foundation—which developed into his first novel, *Nausea.* It illustrates what de Beauvoir dubbed his "opposition aesthetics"—his desire to use literature as a critical tool. The novel's title indicates the hero's reaction toward existence: when he discovers that life is absurd, he feels repulsed. Nothing, it would seem, can save him, except the discovery that he might be able to write a novel that would have internal necessity and be a rival to life; he proposes to save himself through an act of aesthetic creation. Sartre said in *The Words:* "At the age of thirty, I executed the masterstroke of writing in *Nausea*—quite sincerely, believe me—about the bitter unjustified existence of my fellow men and of exonerating my own."

Nausea was received with praise and had considerable success. In *Esprit,* reviewer Armand Robin called *Nausea* "undoubtedly one of the distinctive works of our time." Later, in *Sartre: A Philosophic Study,* Anthony Richards Manser called it "that rare thing: a genuinely philosophic novel."

Sartre revealed himself to be a master psychologist in his next fictional work, the short story collection *The Wall.* Particularly impressive is the title story, which recounts an episode from the Spanish Civil War, and the final one, "The Childhood of a Leader," which, while autobiographical to a considerable degree, has as its main plot thread the making of a Fascist. These stories reveal the author's command of dialogue and metaphor and illustrate exceptionally interesting ideas about human relationships, sexuality, insanity, childhood development, and the meaning of action.

By the late 1930s Sartre was known as a promising writer but he was not yet considered an important philosopher. This assessment changed in 1943 when he produced *Being and Nothingness: An Essay on Phenomenological Ontology,* the major philosophical work of the first half of his career. While closely related to his treatises on imagination and to the views of experience he had expressed in his fiction, *Being and Nothingness* is not confined to these subjects. Rather, in defining being, or what *is,* as what *appears,* it explores all phenomena. The essay examines man, the being who questions being, and concludes that he is both his body occupying a place in the world—that is, an object among objects—and a subject or a consciousness reflecting on objects. Sartre contends that all consciousness is consciousness of *something.* Since it is basically a negating—or distinguishing—function (saying that this chair, for instance, is *not* this table), consciousness produces the concept of nothingness; man is the being by whom negation is introduced into an otherwise complete world. Though its influence penetrated slowly, *Being and Nothingness* helped assure its author's fame after 1945.

Sartre attempted to expand upon *Being and Nothingness* with *Truth and Existence,* which, although completed in 1948, did not see print until 1989. In the essay the philosopher explores the connections between ethics, truth, and ignorance, and the panorama of history, and portrays bad faith among men and women as the intentional choice to remain ignorant by abrogating hard work in favor of a reliance upon fate and destiny.

In *Being and Nothingness,* Sartre wrote that one of the most important characteristics of consciousness is its freedom. He soon drew explicitly the corollary that ontological freedom, in which man is "condemned to be free," as he wrote in *Being and Nothingness,* must entail political freedom also. That is, freedom is a goal as well as a given and must be embodied in praxis, or practical action. The very popular *The Flies,* which retells the Greek story of the murder of Clytemnestra by her children Orestes and Electra, emphasizes man's fundamental freedom, against which even the gods are powerless. *No Exit,* often anthologized and perhaps the best known of all of Sartre's works, deals with the absence of freedom when one allows oneself to exist through and for others, rather than living authentically. Sartre stated in *L'Express* that its famous conclusion, "Hell is other people," did not describe what *had to be* true concerning human relationships, but what *was* true when relationships with others became corrupt or twisted.

The theme of freedom may be even more elaborately treated in less-famous Sartre plays of the 1940s. *Morts sans sepulture* (*The Victors*), which shocked the sensibilities of many theatergoers because it deals with torture during the German Occupation, indicates how extreme the Sartrean view of freedom could be. The play offers the view that even under torture and threat of death, one is free to choose; that this choice cannot be evaded, nor can it be made other than in utter loneliness; and that one is responsible for all its consequences. *Les mains sales* (*Dirty Hands*) treats the difficulty of political choice, the necessity of political compromise, and the refusal to let one's freedom be alienated or appropriated by others.

Between 1945 and 1950 Sartre also published three more novels—*The Age of Reason, The Reprieve,* and *Troubled Sleep*—collectively called *Roads to Freedom.* These works deal with an ineffectual hero in a morally and politically indifferent France before World War II. The series illustrates what Sartre described in "What Is Literature?" as a literature of praxis: "action in history and on history . . . a synthesis of historical relativity and moral and metaphysical absolute." In *The Reprieve* Sartre carries further than any other French writer of his period the techniques of jumping from one plot thread to another, without transition, and of pursuing simultaneous plots. While making for very difficult reading, these techniques suggest collective action and thus support his portrait of what it was like to be in Europe at the time of the Munich Crisis of 1938.

After the war Sartre published many articles on literature and politics, notably the important essay "What Is Literature?" in *Situations II.* Here he states that all prose literature is necessarily committed to making a political and social statement and is directed to one's own contemporaries; the practice of literature, he insists, is built on freedom—the writer's and the reader's. As he put it in *Situations II,* literature is "the subjectivity of a society in permanent revolution."

After the war, though considerably lionized and taken by many youthful readers to be the preeminent spokesman for their generation, Sartre continued to develop intellectually and undergo changes that were to have far-reaching effects on his work. In the prewar years, he had been generally uninterested in politics. While despising fascist parties and the bourgeoisie from which they—and he—came, Sartre had not participated in political action, nor even bothered to vote, considering his fiction and philosophic texts sufficient expressions of his unfavorable views of society. Now he became thoroughly politicized, speaking out on such issues as the French presence in Indochina, which he opposed, and even participating in a leftist, but non-Communist, postwar political movement.

By the close of the 1940s, with the advent of the cold war, Sartre accepted that a non-communist leftist party was a contradiction. He returned to Karl Marx's writings, with which he had previously been only roughly familiar, and began steeping himself in Marxism to rework his positions and think *against* what he had previously held. Throughout the rest of his career Sartre denounced many of his previous attitudes and practiced systematic self-debate. Although he became a resolute neo-Marxist, he was never a member of the French Communist Party, but was instead often its critic and that of the former Soviet Union. However, he was always staunchly opposed to Western capitalism, NATO, and the United States.

The radicalization of his thinking seemed essential to Sartre because the fame that had overtaken him during the 1940s had the effect, or so he thought, of making him a public being; he felt that he was being appropriated by others. This threat increased his sense of alienation. He also resented what he felt would be his inevitable acceptance by the bourgeoisie; he was becoming respectable, read by the middle classes. This attitude explains why, in 1964, he refused the Nobel Prize for Literature; to nim, it was a middle-class recognition that would have the effect of making him appear inoffensive.

In a 1964 *Le Monde* interview with Jacqueline Piatier, Sartre summarized his political changes: "I discovered abruptly that alienation, exploitation of man by man, undernourishment, relegated to the background metaphysical evil, which is a luxury." This discovery led to profound transformations in Sartre as a writer. Although he continued to regard his earlier works as well written, he also now viewed them as inauthentic because they resulted from a bourgeois decision to write, a decision based on personal rebellion and on the idolatry of words. Moreover, he came to believe that fiction could no longer serve his purpose. He even abandoned drama, although he had argued earlier that theater is an ideal means of showing characters in situations where they must commit themselves wholly to their actions and thereby create values.

While Sartre's career as a semipopular writer came to a close in 1950, several works published after that date are among his greatest. The *Critique of Dialectical Reason,* his second major philosophic work, is essential to the understanding of all he wrote after his radicalization and is so closely connected to certain of his other texts that whole sections were transferred from one to another. It is far from a popular work; even more than in *Being and Nothingness,* the vocabulary and concepts of its 750-plus pages are difficult, and the analysis is so abstruse and sometimes meandering that even professional philosophers have found some of it incomprehensible.

Intended as a synthesis of existentialist philosophy and Marxism, the *Critique* calls on and belongs to disciplines as various as anthropology, history, psychology, economics, and philosophy. Its aim is to give a philosophical basis to Marxism and, on that basis, to investigate further the dialectic of history and its intelligibility. Dialectical reasoning, which is opposed to the analytic method, involves the Hegelian synthesis of contraries. Sartre's thesis is that, whereas analytical reason has been the tool of the oppressive classes, dialectical reason, which offers a different understanding of history and its possibilities, is the "practical awareness of an oppressed class fighting against its oppressor," "the objective spirit of the working class," as he put it in the *Critique.* While still insisting on the possibility of human freedom, the treatise shows how this freedom is conditioned, alienated, made powerless by historical and social developments.

In the field of biography, Sartre published in 1947 a short volume on poet Charles Baudelaire. Using what in *Being and Nothingness* he called existential psychoanalysis, Sartre explains Baudelaire's character and career as an original conscious choice—the choice to remain infantile, narcissistic, dependent on his mother, a failure. In opposition to Freud, Sartre shows that the poet's choice reveals psychological freedom, not psychological determinism. The next biography, *Saint Genet: Actor and Martyr,* is a masterly analysis of writer Jean Genet, a convicted thief and multiple offender known for his shocking plays and novels concerned with homosexuality, anarchy, and rebellion against authority. The biography ascribes Genet's career as a thief to a conscious decision made in childhood to be what others accused him of being. To Sartre, Genet is a splendid example of a man who *made himself* as he wanted to be by inverting other people's values.

Some twelve years later, Sartre published his autobiography, a self-accusatory work. The title, *The Words,* refers to the idolatry of literature he had practiced up to about 1950. The autobiography was judged by Francis Jeanson in *Sartre dans sa vie* as "the most accessible, and doubtless the most successful, of all the nonphilosophical works of Sartre." It demolishes "the myth of a Messiah-writer of a dechristianized bourgeoisie," according to *Revue des Sciences Humaines* contributor Marc Bensimon. As a study in characters (his mother, his grandfather, the Alsatian bourgeoisie from which they sprang, his father's family), it is superb. As self-analysis, it is even more outstanding. Few writers have portrayed so searchingly their early childhood and their choice of a vocation or have judged so severely the adult who grew from the child. The book was, Sartre says within its pages, the fruit of an awakening from "a long, bitter, and sweet delusion." *The Words* reads almost like fiction; it is brief and its style is witty, aphoristic, penetrating—classical, in a word, although its method is dialectical.

At the opposite extreme is Sartre's final biographic work, *The Family Idiot,* a 2,800-page analysis of Gustave Flaubert. Flaubert had long interested Sartre, both attracting him and repulsing him. Sartre wanted to explore chiefly the particular circumstances and the dialectical relationships that made Flaubert into a bourgeois who hated the bourgeoisie, a passive man incapable of pursuing an ordinary career, and, generally, a misfit and a neurotic, as well as a great writer. The investigation ranges far afield, from Flaubert's antecedents and family, to his infancy (reconstructed with the help of Sartre's dialectical method, here called progressive-regressive) and youth, to all aspects of the social and economic situation in which he matured. Sartre wished to show, he said in an interview given to *Le Monde,* that "everything can be communicated . . . that every human being is perfectly capable of being understood if the appropriate methods are used."

After 1950 Sartre published and saw into production two theatrical adaptations and three original plays, two of which are surely among his greatest. *The Devil and the Good Lord,* his personal favorite, is, like the volume on Genet, concerned with values, absolutely and pragmatically. An uncompromising statement of atheism, the play explores in a historical context—sixteenth-century Reformation Germany—the interdependency of good and evil and illustrates the necessity of adopting means that suit the ends. A second major play of the 1950s is the lengthy *The Condemned of Altona,* which concerns a German World War II veteran who has barricaded himself in his room for years. Tended only by his sister, the veteran has persuaded himself that Germany won the war. Although concerned explicitly with that conflict and its aftermath, the play was intended to refer also to the Algerian War, then in progress. The play impugns Nazi Germany and the type of men it produced—not just SS soldiers but also members of the upper bourgeoisie who found Nazism useful because it served their economic interests. More generally, it condemns capitalist Europe, whose conflicts over markets and expansion had caused two world wars.

Declaring to John Gerassi—in a 1971 *New York Times Magazine* interview—that "commitment is an *act,* not a word," Sartre expressed his political beliefs by participating in demonstrations, marches, and campaigns, although he was not well (he suffered from failing eyesight and circulatory troubles, among other ailments). Sartre took stands on literally dozens of political and social issues around the world. Such topics as decent housing in France, conscientious objection in Israel, the Vietnamese War, repression in the Congo, Basque separatism, the troubles in Northern Ireland, torture in Argentina, and the Russian invasion of Afghanistan show the range of his concerns. Denouncing as ossified the French Communist Party and all other parties intellectually dependent upon the Soviet Union, Sartre supported Maoist attempts at a new radicalization of Marxist theory and action. This political activity both increased interest in his writings and made him notorious throughout Europe.

From the beginning of his career, Sartre wanted to make people think, feel, see, and ultimately act differently. Like his earlier views, summarized in *Existentialism Is a Humanism,* Sartre's later morality is both a difficult and a hopeful one. People *can* change, he proclaimed, but they would prefer to remain in their errors (to practice injustice, for instance) or to cling to what he had called bad faith. Because of the acceleration of violence and international competition, they *must* change, he insisted. Since the oppressive and privileged classes will not willingly give up their privileges, these must be wrested from them by violence and revolution; then new relationships between human beings, based on reciprocity and openness instead of rivalry and secrecy, will be possible, Sartre declared.

As his health deteriorated, Sartre wrote less but gave lengthy interviews that are a sort of intellectual autobiography. He remained fascinated with himself and his career, perhaps more so than other great writers, but more surprisingly so, since he had wished to move away from the cult of the individual to the idea of the *general* man, "anyone at all," as he put it in *The Words.* He was, as Josette Pacaly declared in *Sartre au miroir,* "a Narcissus who does not like himself."

Twelve years after Sartre's death in 1980, his daughter authorized the publication of several collections of letters that illuminate the private life and thoughts of the philosopher. *Witness to My Life: The Letters of Jean-Paul Sartre to Simone de Beauvoir, 1926-1939* relates to the early years of the unconventional Sartre-de Beauvoir love relationship, the period during which he wrote his first fictional and philosophical works and during which Sartre served as a professor of philosophy at several universities. Many ideas that the novelist-philosopher included in such novels as *The Age of Reason* and *Being and Nothingness* "were first formulated in letters written at the beginning of [World War II], when, exiled from the distractions of Paris, he profited from the enforced leisure of camp life," according to Ronald Hayman in *New York Times Book Review.* "Though the publication of these letters brings rather too many private parts into public view, and though they illuminate only the comparatively brief periods when Sartre and Beauvoir were separated, they enable us to see the whole partnership in a new perspective," the critic added.

The philosopher's experiences of serving as an officer attached to a French meteorological unit and, later, as a prisoner of war, are recounted through letters collected as *Quiet Moments in a War: The Letters of Jean-Paul Sartre to Simone de Beauvoir, 1940-1963.* "In these letters, we have in effect an intimate portrait of the precocious philosopher emerging into a kind of intellectual and spiritual maturity," explained Peter T. Connor in *America.* Many of the letters written to his lover from his uneventful wartime post show Sartre engaged in "deep and searching ruminations," added Connor, "staking out his philosophical position vis-a-vis Husserl and Heidegger, overcoming his 'inferiority complex vis-a-vis the far Left' and reflecting on the inner meaning that his philosophy holds for him." Enthralled by the collection, Penelope Mesic added in Chicago's *Tribune Books:* "It is irresistible, when reading the life of a philosopher, to compare the writer's conduct with his theories. But the foremost philosopher of freedom, in prison, comes across rather well. . . . In these letters we almost casually discover an exemplary life."

Seen as a whole, Sartre's career reveals numerous contradictions. A bourgeois, he hated the middle classes and wanted to chastise them; "I became a traitor and remained one," he wrote in *The Words.* Yet he was not a true proletarian writer. An individualist in many ways and completely opposed to regimentation, he nevertheless attacked the individualistic tradition and insisted on the importance of the collectivity; he moved from the extremely solitary position of an existentialist to concern for society above all. A writer possessed of an outstanding ear for language and other literary skills, he came to suspect literature as inauthentic and wrote a superb autobiography to denounce writing. An atheist, he often spoke with the fervor of an evangelist and repeated that man was responsible for his own errors and must mend his ways. A reformer and moralist, he led an existence that would seem to many decidedly immoral. Of such contradictions, he was of course, aware.

BIOGRAPHICAL AND CRITICAL SOURCES:

BOOKS

Aron, Raymond, *History and the Dialectic of Violence: Analysis of Sartre's "Critique de la raison dialectique,"* Harper (New York, NY), 1975.

Aronson, Ronald, *Jean-Paul Sartre,* Schocken (New York, NY), 1980.

Aronson, Ronald, *Camus and Satre: The Story of a Friendship and the Quarrel That Ended It,* University of Chicago Press (Chicago, IL), 2004.

Astruc, Alexandre and Michel Contat, *Sartre by Himself,* Urizen Books, 1978.

Barnes, Hazel, *Sartre,* Lippincott (Philadelphia, PA), 1973.

Bauer, George H., *Sartre and the Artist,* University of Chicago Press (Chicago, IL), 1969.

Beauvoir, Simone de, *Adieux: A Farewell to Sartre,* Pantheon (New York, NY), 1984.

Beauvoir, Simone de, *All Said and Done,* Putnam (New York, NY), 1974.

Beauvoir, Simone de, *Memoirs of a Dutiful Daughter,* World Publishing (New York, NY), 1959.

Beauvoir, Simone de, *The Force of Circumstance,* Putnam (New York, NY), 1965.

Beauvoir, Simone de, *The Prime of Life,* World Publishing (New York, NY), 1962.

Bertholet, Denis, *Sartre,* Plon (Paris, France), 2000.

Bree, Germaine, *Camus and Sartre: Crisis and Commitment,* Delacorte (New York, NY), 1972.

Catalano, Joseph S., *A Commentary on Jean-Paul Sartre's "Being and Nothingness,"* Harper (New York, NY), 1974.

Catalano, Joseph S., *Good Faith and Other Essays: Perspectives on a Sartrean Ethics,* Rowman & Littlefield (New York, NY), 1995.

Caws, Peter, *Sartre,* Routledge & Kegan Paul (New York, NY), 1979.

Champigny, Robert, *Stages on Sartre's Way,* Indiana University Press, 1959.

Champigny, Robert, *Humanism and Human Racism: A Critical Study of Essays by Sartre and Camus,* Mouton and Co., 1972.

Champigny, Robert, *Sartre and Drama,* French Literature Publications, 1982.

Chiodi, Pietro, *Sartre and Marxism,* Harvester (New York, NY), 1976.

Cohen-Salal, Annie, *Sartre: A Life,* Pantheon (New York, NY), 1987.

Collins, Douglas, *Sartre as Biographer,* Harvard University Press (Cambridge, MA), 1980.

Contat, Michel and Michel Rybalka, compilers, *The Writings of Jean-Paul Sartre,* Northwestern University Press, 1974.

Contemporary Literary Criticism, Thomson Gale (Detroit, MI), Volume 1, 1973, Volume 4, 1975, Volume 7, 1977, Volume 9, 1978, Volume 13, 1980, Volume 18, 1981, Volume 24, 1983, Volume 44, 1987, Volume 50, 1988, Volume 52, 1989.

Cranston, Maurice, *Sartre,* Oliver & Boyd, 1962.

Cranston, Maurice, *The Quintessence of Sartrism,* Harper (New York, NY), 1971.

Cumming, Robert D., *The Philosophy of Jean-Paul Sartre,* Random House (New York, NY), 1965.

Danto, Arthur, *Jean-Paul Sartre,* Viking (New York, NY), 1975.

Dempsey, Peter J. R., *The Psychology of Sartre,* Cork University Press (Cork, Ireland), 1950.

Deutscher, Max, *Genre and Void: Looking Back at Sartre and Beauvoir,* Ashgate (Burlington, VT), 2003.

Dictionary of Literary Biography, Volume 72: *French Novelists, 1930-1960,* Thomson Gale (Detroit, MI), 1988.

Farr, Anthony, *Sartre's Radicalism and Oakeshott's Conservatism: The Duplicity of Freedom,* St. Martin's Press (New York, NY), 1998.

Fell, Joseph P. III, *Emotion in the Thought of Sartre,* Columbia University Press (New York, NY), 1965.

Flynn, Thomas, *Sartre, Foucault, and Historical Reason: Toward an Existentialist Theory of History,* University of Chicago Press (Chicago, IL), 1997, published as *Sartre, Foucault, and Reason in History: Toward an Existentialist Theory,* 1997.

Fourny, Jean-François, and Charles D. Minahen, editors, *Situating Sartre in Twentieth-Century Thought and Culture,* St. Martin's Press (New York, NY), 1997.

Fox, Nik Farrell, *The New Sartre: Explorations in Postmodernism,* Continuum (New York, NY), 2003.

Grene, Marjorie, *Sartre,* New Viewpoints, 1973.

Guerlac, Suzanne, *Literary Polemics: Bataille, Sartre, Valery, Breton,* Stanford University Press (Stanford, CA), 1997.

Halpern, Joseph, *Critical Fictions: The Literary Criticism of Jean-Paul Sartre,* Yale University Press (New Haven, CT), 1976.

Hayim, Gila J., *The Existential Sociology of Jean-Paul Sartre,* University of Massachusetts Press (Amherst, MA), 1980.

Hayim, Gila J., *Existentialism and Sociology: The Contribution of Jean-Paul Sartre,* Transaction (New York, NY), 1996.

Hayman, Ronald, *Sartre: A Life,* Simon & Schuster (New York, NY), 1987.

Howells, Christina, *Sartre's Theory of Literature,* Modern Humanities Research Association, 1979.

Howells, Christina, *Sartre,* Longman (London, England), 1995.

Jackson, Tommie Lee, *The Existential Fiction of Ayi Kewi Armah, Albert Camus, and Jean-Paul Sartre,* University Press of America, 1996.

Jeanson, Francis, *Sartre and the Problem of Morality,* Indiana University Press, 1950.

Jeanson, Francis, *Sartre dans sa vie,* Seuil, 1974.

Kaelin, Eugene Francis, *An Existentialist Ethic: The Theories of Sartre and Merleau-Ponty,* University of Wisconsin Press (Madison, WI), 1962.

Kamber, Richard, *On Sartre,* Thomson Learning (Wadsworth, CA), 2000.

King, Thomas M., *Sartre and the Sacred,* University of Chicago Press (Chicago, IL), 1974.

Kirsher, Douglas, *The Schizoid World of Jean-Paul Sartre and R.D. Laing,* Humanities, 1976.

La Capra, Dominick, *A Preface to Sartre,* Cornell University Press, 1978.

Laing, R.D. and D.G. Cooper, *Reason and Violence: A Decade of Sartre's Philosophy, 1950-1960,* Tavistock, 1964.

Lamblin, Bianca, *A Disgraceful Affair: Simone de Beauvoir, Jean-Paul Sartre, and Bianca Lamblin,* Northeastern University Press (Boston, MA), 1996.

Lapointe, François, and Claire Lapointe, *Jean-Paul Sartre and His Critics,* Philosophy Documentation Center, Bowling Green State University, 1980.

Lévy, Bernard Henri, *Sartre: The Philosopher of the Twentieth Century,* translated by Andrew Brown, Polity Press (Cambridge, England), 2003.

Levy, Neil, *Being Up-to-Date: Foucault, Sartre, and Postmodernity,* Peter Lang (New York, NY), 2001.

Manser, Anthony Richards, *Sartre: A Philosophic Study,* Athlone Press, 1966.

Martin, Thomas, *Oppression and the Human Condition: An Introduction to Sartrean Existentialism,* Rowman & Littlefield (Lanham, MD), 2002.

McCall, Dorothy, *The Theatre of Jean-Paul Sartre,* Columbia University Press (New York, NY), 1969.

McMahon, Joseph H., *Human Being: The World of Jean-Paul Sartre,* University of Chicago Press (Chicago, IL), 1971.

Molnar, Thomas S., *Sartre: Ideologue of Our Time,* Funk (New York, NY), 1968.

Morris, Phyllis S., *Sartre's Concept of a Person: An Analytic Approach,* University of Massachusetts Press (Amherst, MA), 1976.

Murdoch, Iris, *Sartre: Romantic Rationalist,* Yale University Press (New Haven, CT), 1953.

Peyre, Henri, *Jean-Paul Sartre,* Columbia University Press (New York, NY), 1968.

Plank, William, *Sartre and Surrealism,* UMI Research Press (Ann Arbor, MI), 1981.

Rajan, Tilottama, *Deconstruction and the Remainders of Phenomenology: Sartre, Derrida, Foucault, Braudrillard,* Stanford University Press (Stanford, CA), 2002.

Ranwez, Alain D., *Jean-Paul Sartre's "Les Temps Modernes": A Literary History, 1945-1952,* Whitson, 1981.

Salvan, Jacques, *To Be or Not to Be: An Analysis of Jean-Paul Sartre's Ontology,* Wayne State University Press (Detroit, MI), 1962.

Salvan, Jacques, *The Scandalous Ghost: Sartre's Existentialism,* Wayne State University Press (Detroit, MI), 1967.

Santoni, Ronald E., *Bad Faith, Good Faith, and Authenticity in Sartre's Early Philosophy,* Temple University Press, 1995.

Sartre, Jean-Paul, *Situations II,* Gallimard (Paris, France), 1948.

Sartre, Jean-Paul, *Sartre par lui-meme,* edited by Francis Jeanson, Seuil (Paris, France), 1959, translation by Richard Seaver published as *Sartre by Himself,* Outback Press, 1978.

Sartre, Jean-Paul, *Les mots,* Gallimard (Paris, France), 1963, translation by Bernard Frechtman published as *The Words,* Braziller (New York, NY), 1964.

Sartre, Jean-Paul, *Hope Now: The 1980 Interviews,* edited by Benny Levy, University of Chicago Press (Chicago, IL), 1996.

Schilpp, Paul, editor, *The Philosophy of Jean-Paul Sartre,* Open Court, 1981.

Scriven, Michael, *Sartre's Existential Biographies,* Macmillan (New York, NY), 1984.

Sheridan, James F., *Sartre: The Radical Conversion,* Ohio University Press, 1969.

Stack, George, *Sartre's Philosophy of Social Existence,* Warren Green, 1977.

Stern, Alfred, *Sartre: His Philosophy on an Existential Psychoanalysis,* Liberal Arts Press, 1953, revised edition, Delacorte (New York, NY), 1967.

Stewart, John, editor, *The Debate between Sarte and Merleau-Ponty,* Northwestern University Press, 1998.

Streller, Justus, *Jean-Paul Sartre: To Freedom Condemned,* Philosophical Library, 1960.

Thody, Philip, *Jean-Paul Sartre: A Literary and Political Study,* Hamish Hamilton (London, England), 1960.

Warnock, Mary, *The Philosophy of Sartre,* Hutchinson Library Service (London, England), 1965.

Warnock, Mary, *Sartre: A Collection of Critical Essays,* Doubleday (New York, NY), 1971.

Wider, Kathleen, *The Bodily Nature of Consciousness: Sartre and Contemporary Philosophy,* 1997.

Wilcocks, Robert, *Jean-Paul Sartre: A Bibliography of International Criticism,* University of Alberta Press, 1975.

Wilson, Colin, *Anti-Sartre,* Borgo Press (San Bernardino, CA), 1981.

Wilson, Colin, *Below the Iceberg: Anti-Sarte and Other Essays,* Borgo Press (San Bernardino, CA), 1996.

PERIODICALS

America, September 10, 1994, Peter T. Connor, review of *Quiet Moments in a War: The Letters of Jean-Paul Sartre to Simone de Beauvoir, 1940-1963,* pp. 25, 26.

Choice, July-August 1993, p. 1786.

Chronicle of Higher Education, November 21, 2003, Scott McLemee, "Sartre Redux: A New Generation of Scholars Explores the Philosophy and Politics of the Founder of Existentialism," pp. 10-13.

Critical Inquiry, winter, 2004, p. 379.

Esprit, number 38, 1938, Armand Robin, review of *Nausea.*

Express, October 11, 1965.

Figaro, June 26, 1951.

French Studies, April, 2002, p. 269.

Georgia Review, fall, 1994, pp. 610-15.

Journal of European Studies, June, 2003, p. 177.

Journal of Philosophical Research (annual), 2002, Kenneth L. Anderson, "Transformations of Subjectivity in Sartre's Critique of Dialectical Reason," p. 267.

Library Journal, May 1, 1996, p. 97.

London Review of Books, December 3, 1992, pp. 15-16.

Los Angeles Times, May 24, 1992, pp. 2, 9.

New Republic, June 1, 1968; August 30, 1975.

Newsweek, October 5, 1964.

New York Review of Books, August 7, 1975.

New York Times, October 23, 1964; September 1, 1971.

New York Times Book Review, October 11, 1964; December 27, 1981; August 9, 1987; July 19, 1992, pp. 13-14; January 9, 1994, p. 18.

New York Times Magazine, October 17, 1971, John Gerassi, interview with Sartre.

Monde, April 18, 1964.

Modern Language Review, October, 2002, pp. 835-849.

Philosophy Today, December 31, 2001, Jennifer Anna Gosetti, "Phenomenological Literature," p. 18.

Quadrant, January-February, 2004, p. 5.

Sartre Studies International, ongoing.

Times (London, England), November 22, 1984; November 28, 1985; July 11, 1986.

Times Literary Supplement, April 2, 1964; June 25, 1976; January 29, 1982; May 11, 1984; July 11, 1986.

Tribune Books (Chicago, IL), January 2, 1994, pp. 1, 9.

* * *

SATTERFIELD, Charles
See POHL, Frederik

* * *

SAUNDERS, Caleb
See HEINLEIN, Robert A.